**THE BANTAM NEW COLLEGE SPANISH & ENGLISH DICTIONARY**

---

COMPREHENSIVE: More than 70,000 words and phrases in education, business, travel, science, history, literature, art and music, social sciences, law, medicine, diplomacy, international affairs, matters of everyday life . . . American and British usage. Hundreds of neologisms.

AUTHORITATIVE: Based on reliable spoken and written sources and organized to achieve the utmost clarity, precision, and convenience.

EASY TO USE: All words are found in one single alphabet for each language, including proper names and abbreviations.

---

A NEW LANDMARK
IN SPANISH-ENGLISH DICTIONARIES
FOR THE MODERN USER OF WORDS!

## THE BANTAM NEW COLLEGE DICTIONARY SERIES

### Edwin B. Williams, General Editor

---

Edwin B. Williams, A.B., A.M., Ph.D., Doct. d'Univ., LL.D, L.H.D. was chairman of the Department of Romance Languages, dean of the Graduate School, and provost of the University of Pennsylvania. He was a member of the American Philosophical Society and the Hispanic Society of America and the author of *The Bantam New College Spanish & English Dictionary* and the Scribner's (formerly the Holt) *Spanish and English Dictionary* and many other works on the Spanish, Portuguese and French languages.

THE BANTAM NEW COLLEGE

# SPANISH & ENGLISH DICTIONARY

# DICCIONARIO INGLÉS y ESPAÑOL

BY EDWIN B. WILLIAMS
Professor of Romance Languages
University of Pennsylvania

BANTAM BOOKS
TORONTO · NEW YORK · LONDON · SYDNEY

THE BANTAM NEW COLLEGE
SPANISH & ENGLISH DICTIONARY

*A Bantam Book / November 1968*
*34 printings through March 1981*

*Library of Congress Catalog Card Number: 68-29099*



ISBN 0–553–20085–2

*Published simultaneously in the United States and Canada*

---



---

PRINTED IN THE UNITED STATES OF AMERICA

43 42 41 40 39 38 37 36 35

# CONTENTS

# PREFACE

This book is based on primary spoken and written sources. It is designed for speakers of either language who wish to find words or the meanings of words in the foreign language. Its purpose is, therefore, fourfold. It gives to the English-speaking user (1) the Spanish words he needs to express his thoughts in Spanish and (2) the English meanings of Spanish words he needs to understand Spanish, and to the Spanish-speaking user (3) the English words he needs to express his thoughts in English and (4) the Spanish meanings of English words he needs to understand English.

In order to accomplish the purpose of (1) and (3), discriminations are provided in the source language except that, because of the special facility with which the subject of the verb can be shown in Spanish and because of the convenience of showing the object with personal **a**, discriminations in the form of subject and/or object are given in Spanish on the English-Spanish side as well as on the Spanish-English side. For the purpose of (2) and (4) discriminations are not needed and are not given because the user will always have the context of what he hears or reads to guide him. However, some glosses whose purpose is not to show discrimination but rather to elaborate on the meaning of what may be judged to be an unfamiliar or obscure word or expression in the user's native language are provided in that language.

All words are treated in a fixed order according to the parts of speech and the functions of verbs; and meanings with subject, usage, and regional labels come after more general meanings.

In order to facilitate the finding of the meaning and use sought for, changes within a vocabulary entry in part of speech and function of verb, in irregular inflection, in the gender of Spanish nouns, and in the pronunciation of English words are marked with parallels instead of the usual semicolons.

Periods are omitted after labels and grammatical abbreviations and at the end of vocabulary entries.

The feminine form of a Spanish adjective used as a noun (or a Spanish feminine noun having identical spelling with the feminine form of an adjective) which falls alphabetically in a separate position from the adjective is treated in that position and is listed again as a cross reference under the adjective.

# PRÓLOGO

Hemos basado este libro en fuentes originales del lenguaje hablado y escrito. Está destinado a los hablantes de uno u otro idioma que buscan palabras o significados de palabras en el idioma extranjero. Tiene, por lo tanto, los cuatro siguientes propósitos: al usuario de habla inglesa le suministra (1) las palabras españolas que necesita para expresar su pensamiento en español y (2) los significados ingleses de las palabras españolas que necesita para comprender el español; y al usuario de habla española le suministra (3) las palabras inglesas que necesita para expresar su pensamiento en inglés y (4) los significados españoles de las palabras inglesas que necesita para comprender el inglés.

Para lograr los propósitos indicados bajo los números (1) y (3), se suministran diferenciaciones (es decir, distinciones entre dos o más significados de una palabra) en la lengua-fuente; pero, dada la facilidad con que el sujeto del verbo puede indicarse en español y dada la conveniencia de destacar el objeto del verbo con la preposición **a**, las diferenciaciones consistentes en el sujeto o el objeto, o ambos, se dan en español tanto en la parte de inglés-español como en la parte de español-inglés. Para los propósitos indicados bajo los números (2) y (4) no se necesitan diferenciaciones y no se dan, porque el usuario siempre tendrá como guía el contexto de lo que oye o lee. Con todo, algunas glosas que no tienen por objeto indicar diferenciaciones sino más bien dilucidar el sentido de lo que parece ser una palabra o expresión raras u obscuras en la lengua nativa del usuario, se indican en esta lengua.

Los vocablos se tratan consecutivamente de acuerdo con las partes de la oración y las funciones verbales; y los significados marcados con calificativos de tema, uso y país van después de los significados más generales.

Para facilitar la búsqueda del significado y el uso deseados, los cambios en la parte de la oración y función verbal, en la flexión, en el género de los nombres españoles y en la pronunciación de las palabras inglesas van señalados con doble raya vertical, en vez del punto y coma de costumbre.

Se han omitido los puntos después de los calificativos y abreviaturas gramaticales y al fin de los artículos.

La forma femenina de un adjetivo español usado como sustan-

The gender of Spanish nouns is shown on both sides of the Dictionary except that the gender of masculine nouns ending in **-o**, feminine nouns ending in **-a, -dad, -tad, -tud, -ión,** and **-umbre,** masculine nouns modified by an adjective ending in **-o,** and feminine nouns modified by an adjective ending in **-a** is not shown on the English-Spanish side.

Numbers referring to the model conjugations of Spanish verbs are placed before the abbreviations indicating the part of speech. The complete list of model verbs includes models of all verbs that show a combination of two types of irregularity, e.g., **esforzar, seguir, teñir.**

Proper nouns and abbreviations are listed in their alphabetical position in the main body of the Dictionary. Thus **España** and **español** do not have to be looked up in two different parts of the book. And all subentries are listed in strictly alphabetical order.

The centered period is used in vocabulary entries of irregularly inflected words to mark off the final syllable that has to be detached before the syllable showing the inflection is added, e.g., **lá·piz** *m* (*pl* **-pices**) and **falsi·fy** [ˈfɔlsɪ ˌfaɪ] *v* (*pret & pp* **-fied**).

There are three kinds of compound words in English: (1) solid, e.g., **steamboat,** (2) hyphenated, e.g., **long-range,** and (3) spaced, e.g., **high school.** In this Dictionary the pronunciation of all English simple words is shown in a new adaptation of the symbols of the International Phonetic Alphabet and in brackets. The pronunciation of English compound words is not shown provided the pronunciation of the components is shown where they appear as independent vocabulary entries, except that the accentuation of solid and hyphenated compounds is indicated in the vocabulary entry itself, e.g., **fall'out',** the IPA pronunciation of **fall** and **out** being shown where these words appear as independent vocabulary entries.

Since vocabulary entries are not determined on the basis of etymology, homographs are included in a single entry. When the pronunciation of an English homograph changes, this is shown in the proper place after parallels.

E.B.W.

The author wishes to express his gratitude to many persons who have worked with him in lexicographical research and development and who helped him directly in the compilation of this book and particularly to the following: Paul Aguilar, William Beigel, Henry H. Carter, Eugenio Chang-Rodríguez, R. Thomas Douglass, David Louis Gold, Allison Gronberg, James E. Iannucci, Christopher Stavrou, Roger J. Steiner, John C. Traupman, and José Vidal.

tivo (o de un sustantivo femenino que se escribe lo mismo que la forma femenina de un adjetivo), que cae alfabéticamente en lugar apartado del adjetivo, se trata en este lugar y se consigna otra vez bajo el adjetivo con una referencia a la palabra traducida anteriormente.

El género de los nombres españoles aparece en ambas partes del Diccionario; pero no aparece en la parte de inglés-español el género de los nombres masculinos que terminan en **-o,** los nombres femeninos que terminan en **-a, -dad, -tad, -tud, -ión** y **-umbre,** los nombres masculinos modificados por un adjetivo que termina en **-o** ni los nombres femeninos modificados por un adjetivo que termina en **-a.**

Los números que se refieren a los modelos de conjugación de los verbos españoles van antes de las abreviaturas que indican la parte de la oración. La lista completa de los modelos de conjugación incluye muchos que muestran una combinación de dos irregularidades, p.ej., **esforzar, seguir, teñir.**

Los nombres propios y las abreviaturas se consignan en su propio lugar alfabético en el texto del Diccionario. No hay, pues, que buscar **España** y **español** en dos partes distintas del libro. Y todos los artículos secundarios van colocados en riguroso orden alfabético.

Se usa el punto divisorio en los artículos de palabras de flexión irregular para señalar la sílaba final que debe separarse antes de agregar la sílaba que denota la flexión, p.ej., **lá·piz** (*pl* **-pices**) y **falsi·fy** [ˈfɔlsɪˌfaɪ] *v* (*pret & pp* **-fied**).

Hay tres clases de palabras compuestas en inglés: (1) las sólidas, p.ej., **steamboat,** (2) las escritas con guión, p.ej., **long-range** y (3) las separadas en dos o más elementos, p.ej., **high school.** En este Diccionario se muestra la pronunciación de todas las palabras inglesas simples por medio de una nueva adaptación de los símbolos del Alfabeto fonético internacional y entre corchetes. No se muestra la pronunciación de las palabras inglesas compuestas cuando la pronunciación de los componentes consta en los lugares donde aparecen como artículos independientes, si bien la acentuación de las palabras compuestas sólidas y las escritas con guión se indica en la voz alfabetizada misma, p.ej., **fall′out′,** pues la pronunciación de **fall** y **out** va indicada según el Alfabeto fonético internacional en los lugares donde estas palabras aparecen como artículos independientes.

Como la constitución de los artículos no se ha determinado a base de su etimología, se incluyen bajo un mismo artículo todos los homógrafos de una palabra. Cuando varía la pronunciación de un homógrafo inglés, se indica en su propio lugar después de la doble raya vertical.

E.B.W.

# Labels and Grammatical Abbreviations
# Calificativos y abreviaturas gramaticales

*abbr* abbreviation—abreviatura
(acronym) acrónimo—a word formed from the initial letters or syllables of a series of words—palabra formada de las letras o sílabas iniciales de una serie de palabras
*adj* adjective—adjetivo
*adv* adverb—adverbio
(aer) aeronautics—aeronáutica
(agr) agriculture—agricultura
(alg) algebra—álgebra
(Am) Spanish American—hispanoamericano
(anat) anatomy—anatomía
(archaic) arcaico
(archeol) archeology—arqueología
(archit) architecture—arquitectura
(Arg) Argentine—argentino
(arith) arithmetic—aritmética
*art* article—artículo
(arti) artillery—artillería
(astr) astronomy—astronomía
(aut) automobiles—automóviles
(bact) bacteriology—bacteriología
(bb) bookbinding—encuadernación
(Bib) Biblical—bíblico
(billiards) billar
(biochem) biochemistry—bioquímica
(biol) biology—biología
(Bol) Bolivian—boliviano
(bowling) bolos
(bot) botany—botánica
(box) boxing—boxeo
(Brit) British—británico
(CAm) Central American—centroamericano
(cards) naipes
(carp) carpentry—carpintería
(chem) chemistry—química
(chess) ajedrez
(Chile) Chilean—chileno
(Col) Colombian—colombiano
(coll) colloquial—familiar
(com) commercial—comercial
*comp* comparative—comparativo
*cond* conditional—condicional
*conj* conjunction—conjunción
(C-R) Costa Rican—costarriqueño
(Cuba) Cuban—cubano
(culin) cooking—cocina
*def* definite—definido
*dem* demonstrative—demostrativo
(dent) dentistry—odontología
(dial) dialectal—dialectal
(eccl) ecclesiastical—eclesiástico
(econ) economics—economía
(Ecuad) Ecuadorian—ecuatoriano
(educ) education—educación
(elec) electricity—electricidad
(electron) electronics—electrónica
(El Salv) El Salvador
(ent) entomology—entomología
*f* feminine noun—nombre femenino
(fa) fine arts—bellas artes
*fem* feminine—femenino
(fencing) esgrima
(feud) feudalism—feudalismo
(fig) figurative—figurado
*fpl* feminine noun plural—nombre femenino plural
*fsg* feminine noun singular—nombre femenino singular
*fut* future—futuro
(geog) geography—geografía
(geol) geology—geología
(geom) geometry—geometría
*ger* gerund—gerundio
(gram) grammar—gramática
(Guat) Guatemalan—guatemalteco
(heral) heraldry—heráldica
(hist) history—historia
(Hond) Honduran—hondureño
(hort) horticulture—horticultura
(hum) humorous—jocoso
(hunt) hunting—caza
(ichth) ichthyology—ictiología
*imperf* imperfect—imperfecto
*impers* impersonal—impersonal
*impv* imperative—imperativo
*ind* indicative—indicativo
*indecl* indeclinable—indeclinable
*indef* indefinite—indefinido
*inf* infinitive—infinitivo
(ins) insurance—seguros
*interj* interjection—interjección
*interr* interrogative—interrogativo
*intr* intransitive verb—verbo intransitivo
*invar* invariable—invariable
(iron) ironical—irónico
(Lat) Latin—latín
(law) derecho
(letterword) a word in the form of an abbreviation which is pronounced by sounding the names of its letters in succession and which functions as a part of speech—palabra en forma de abreviatura la cual se pronuncia haciendo sonar el nombre de cada letra consecutivamente y que funciona como parte del discurso
(log) logic—lógica
*m* masculine noun—nombre masculino
(mach) machinery—maquinaria
(mas) masonry—albañilería
*masc* masculine—masculino
(math) mathematics—matemática
(mech) mechanics—mecánica
(med) medicine—medicina
(metal) metallurgy—metalurgia
(meteor) meteorology—meteorología
(Mex) Mexican—mejicano
*mf* masculine or feminine noun according to sex—nombre masculino o nombre femenino según el sexo
(mil) military—militar
(min) mining—minería
(mineral) mineralogy—mineralogía
(mountaineering) alpinismo
(mov) moving pictures—cine
*mpl* masculine noun plural—nombre masculino plural
*msg* masculine noun singular—nombre masculino singular
(mus) music—música
(myth) mythology—mitología

*m & f* masculine and feminine noun without regard to sex—nombre masculino y femenino sin tener en cuenta el sexo
(naut) nautical—náutico
(nav) naval—naval militar
*neut* neuter—neutro
(obs) obsolete—desusado
(obstet) obstetrics—obstetricia
(opt) optics—óptica
(orn) ornithology—ornitología
(paint) painting—pintura
(Pan) Panamanian—panameño
(Para) Paraguayan—paraguayo
(pathol) pathology—patología
*pers* personal—personal
(Peru) Peruvian—peruano
(pharm) pharmacy—farmacia
(philol) philology—filología
(philos) philosophy—filosofía
(phonet) phonetics—fonética
(phot) photography—fotografía
(phys) physics—física
(physiol) physiology—fisiología
*pl* plural—plural
(poet) poetical—poético
(pol) politics—política
*poss* possessive—posesivo
*pp* past participle—participio pasado
(P-R) Puerto Rican—puertorriqueño
*prep* preposition—preposición
*pres* present—presente
*pret* preterit—pretérito
*pron* pronoun—pronombre
(psychol) psychology—sicología
(rad) radio—radio
*ref* reflexive verb—verbo reflexivo
*reflex* reflexive—reflexivo
*rel* relative—relativo
(rhet) rhetoric—retórica
(rr) railway—ferrocarril
*s* substantive—substantivo
(SAm) South American—sudamericano
(scornful) despreciativo
(sculp) sculpture—escultura
(S-D) Santo Domingo—República Dominicana
(sew) sewing—costura
*sg* singular—singular
(slang) jerga
*spl* substantive plural—substantivo plural
*ssg* substantive singular—substantivo singular
*subj* subjunctive—subjuntivo
*super* superlative—superlativo
(surg) surgery—cirugía
(surv) surveying—agrimensura
(taur) bullfighting—tauromaquia
(telg) telegraphy—telegrafía
(telp) telephony—telefonía
(telv) television—televisión
(tennis) tenis
(theat) theater—teatro
(theol) theology—teología
*tr* transitive verb—verbo transitivo
(typ) printing—imprenta
(Urug) Uruguayan—uruguayo
*v* verb—verbo
var variant—variante
*v aux* auxiliary verb—verbo auxiliar
(Ven) Venezuelan—venezolano
(vet) veterinary medicine—veterinaria
(vulg) vulgar—grosero
(W-I) West Indian—antillano
(zool) zoology—zoología

PART ONE

# Spanish-English

## Spanish Pronunciation

The Spanish alphabet has twenty-eight letters. Note that **ch, ll,** and **ñ** are considered to be separate single letters and are so treated in the alphabetization of Spanish words. While **rr** is considered to be a distinct sign for a particular sound, it is not included in the alphabet and, except in syllabification—notably for the division of words at the end of a line—, is not treated as a separate letter, perhaps because words never begin with it.

These twenty-eight letters plus the sign **rr** are listed below with their names and a description of their sounds.

| LETTER | NAME | SOUND |
|---|---|---|
| **a** | a | Like **a** in English **father,** e.g., **casa, fácil.** |
| **b** | be | When initial or preceded by **m,** like **b** in English **book,** e.g., **boca, combate.** When standing between two vowels and when preceded by a vowel and followed by **l** or **r,** like **v** in English **voodoo** except that it is formed with both lips, e.g., **saber, hablar, sobre.** It is generally silent before **s** plus a consonant and often dropped in spelling, e.g., **oscuro** for **obscuro.** |
| **c** | ce | When followed by **e** or **i,** like **th** in English **think** in Castilian and like **c** in English **cent** in American Spanish, e.g., **acento, cinco.** When followed by **a, o, u,** or a consonant, like **c** in English **come,** e.g., **cantar, como, cubo, acto, creer.** |
| **ch** | che | Like **ch** in English **much,** e.g., **escuchar.** |
| **d** | de | Generally, like **d** in **dog,** e.g., **diente, rendir.** When standing between two vowels, when preceded by a vowel and followed by **r,** and when final, like **th** in English **this,** e.g., **miedo, piedra, libertad.** |
| **e** | e | At the end of a syllable, like **a** in English **fate,** but without the glide the English sound sometimes has, e.g., **beso, menos.** When followed by a consonant in the same syllable, like **e** in English **met,** e.g., **perla, selva.** |
| **f** | efe | Like **f** in English **five,** e.g., **flor, efecto.** |
| **g** | ge | When followed by **e** or **i,** like **h** in English **home,** e.g., **gente, giro.** When followed by **a, o, u,** or a consonant, like **g** in English **go,** e.g., **gato, gota, agudo, grande.** |
| **h** | hache | Always silent, e.g., **hombre, alcohol.** |
| **i** | i | Like **i** in English **machine,** e.g., **camino, ida.** When preceded or followed by another vowel, it has the sound of English **y,** e.g., **tierra, reina.** |
| **j** | jota | Like **h** in English **home,** e.g., **jardín, junto.** |
| **k** | ka | Like English **k,** e.g., **kilociclo.** |
| **l** | ele | Like **l** in English **laugh,** e.g., **lado, ala.** |
| **ll** | elle | Somewhat like **lli** in **William** in Castilian and like **y** in English **yes** in American Spanish, e.g., **silla, llamar.** |
| **m** | eme | Like **m** in English **man,** e.g., **mesa, amar.** |
| **n** | ene | Generally, like **n** in English **name,** e.g., **andar, nube.** Before **v,** like **m** in English **man,** e.g., **invierno, enviar.** Before **c** [k] and **g** [g], like **n** in English **drink,** e.g., **finca, manga.** |

| LETTER | NAME | SOUND |
|---|---|---|
| **ñ** | eñe | Somewhat like **ni** in English **onion,** e.g., **año, enseñar.** |
| **o** | o | At the end of a syllable, like **o** in English **note,** but without the glide the English sound sometimes has, e.g., **boca, como.** When followed by a consonant in the same syllable, like **o** in English **organ,** e.g., **poste, norte.** |
| **p** | pe | Like **p** in English **pen,** e.g., **poco, aplicar.** It is often silent in **septiembre** and **séptimo.** |
| **q** | cu | Like **c** in English **come.** It is always followed by **ue** or **ui,** in which the **u** is silent, e.g., **querer, quitar.** The sound of English **qu** is represented in Spanish by **cu,** e.g., **frecuente.** |
| **r** | ere | Strongly trilled, when initial and when preceded by **l, n,** or **s,** e.g., **rico, alrededor, honra, israelí.** Pronounced with a single tap of the tongue in all other positions, e.g., **caro, grande, amar.** |
| **rr** | erre | Strongly trilled, e.g., **carro, tierra.** |
| **s** | ese | Generally, like **s** in English **say,** e.g., **servir, casa, este.** Before a voiced consonant (**b, d, g** [g], **l, r, m, n**), like **z** in English **zero,** e.g., **esbelto, desde, rasgar, eslabón, mismo, asno.** |
| **t** | te | Like **t** in English **stamp,** e.g., **tiempo, matar.** |
| **u** | u | Like **u** in English **rude,** e.g., **mudo, puño.** It is silent in **gue, gui, que,** and **qui,** but not in **güe** and **güi,** e.g., **guerra, guisa, querer, quitar,** but **agüero, lingüístico.** When preceded or followed by another vowel, it has the sound of English **w,** e.g., **fuego, deuda.** |
| **v** | ve or uve | Like Spanish **b** in all positions, e.g., **vengo, invierno, uva, huevo.** |
| **x** | equis | When followed by a consonant, like **s** in English **say,** e.g., **expresar, sexto.** Between two vowels, like **gs,** e.g., **examen, existencia, exótico;** and in some words, like **s** in **say,** e.g., **auxilio, exacto.** In **México** (for **Méjico**), like Spanish **j.** |
| **y** | ye or i griega | In the conjunction **y,** like **i** in English **machine.** When standing next to a vowel or between two vowels, like **y** in English **yes,** e.g., **yo, hoy, vaya.** |
| **z** | zeda or zeta | Like **th** in English **think** in Castilian and like **c** in English **cent** in American Spanish, e.g., **zapato, zona.** |

# SPANISH–ENGLISH

## A

**A, a** (a) *f* first letter of the Spanish alphabet
**a** *prep* at; for, to; on, upon; in, into; by; from; **a decir verdad** to tell the truth; **a la española** in the Spanish manner; **a lo que parece** as it seems; **a no ser por** if it weren't for; **a saberlo yo** if I had known it; **oler a** to smell of
**abacería** *f* grocery store
**abace•ro -ra** *mf* grocer
**abad** *m* abbot
**abadejo** *m* codfish; (orn) kinglet; (ent) Spanish fly
**abadesa** *f* abbess
**abadía** *f* abbacy; abbey
**abaje•ño -ña** *adj* (Mex) coastal, lowland || *mf* (Mex) lowlander
**abaje•ro -ra** *adj* (Arg) lower, under || *f* (Arg) bellyband, bellystrap; (Arg) saddlecloth
**abaji•no -na** *adj* (Col, Chile) northern || *mf* (Col, Chile) northerner
**abajo** *adv* down, underneath; downwards; downstairs; **abajo de** down; **más abajo** lower down; **río abajo** downstream || *interj* down with . . .!
**abalanzar** §60 *tr* to hurl || *ref* to rush; to venture; (*un caballo*) to rear
**abalizar** §60 *tr* to mark with buoys || *ref* (naut) to take bearings
**abalorio** *m* glass bead
**abaluartar** *tr* to bulwark
**abanderado** *m* colorbearer
**abanderar** *tr* (*un buque*) to register
**abanderizar** §60 *tr* to organize into bands || *ref* to band together; (Chile, Peru) to join up
**abandonar** *tr* to abandon, to forsake || *intr* to give up || *ref* to abandon oneself; to give up
**abandonismo** *m* defeatism
**abandonista** *adj* & *mf* defeatist
**abandono** *m* abandon, abandonment; neglect; forlornness; yielding, giving up
**abanicar** §73 *tr* to fan
**abanico** *m* fan; fanlight; (coll) sword; **abanico de chimenea** fire screen
**abaniquear** *tr* to fan
**abaniqueo** *m* fanning; gesticulations
**abanto** *adj* skittish (*bull*)
**abaratar** *tr* to cheapen; (*precios*) to lower || *intr* & *ref* to get cheap
**abarca** *f* sandal
**abarcar** §73 *tr* to embrace; to encompass; to surround; (Am) to corner, monopolize
**abarloar** *tr* (naut) to bring alongside || *ref* to snuggle up
**abarquillar** *tr* & *ref* to curl up
**abarrotar** *tr* to bar; to bind, to fasten; to jam, to pack, to stuff; to overstock || *ref* (Am) to become a glut on the market
**abarrote** *m* (naut) packing; **abarrotes** (Am) groceries; (Am) hardware
**abarrotería** *f* (Guat) grocery store; (CAm) hardware store
**abarrote•ro -ra** *mf* (Am) grocer
**abastecer** §22 *tr* to supply, to provide
**abastecimiento** *m* supplying; supplies, provisions
**abasto** *m* supply; abundance; **dar abasto** to be sufficient
**abatanar** *tr* to full
**abatí** *m* (Arg, Para) corn; (Arg, Para) corn whiskey
**abati•do -da** *adj* downcast; abject, contemptible || *f* abatis
**abatir** *tr* to lower; to knock down; to shoot down; to take apart; to humble; to discourage || *intr* (aer) to drift; (naut) to have leeway || *ref* to be discouraged; to be humbled; to drop, fall; to swoop down
**abdicar** §73 *tr* & *intr* to abdicate
**abdomen** *m* abdomen
**abecé** *m* A B C
**abecedario** *m* A B C's
**abedul** *m* birch
**abeja** *f* bee; **abeja maestra** or **abeja reina** queen bee
**abejar** *m* apiary, beehive
**abejarrón** *m* bumblebee
**abeje•ro -ra** *mf* beekeeper
**abejorro** *m* bumblebee
**abertura** *f* aperture; opening; crack, slit; cove; openness, frankness
**abeto** *m* fir tree; hemlock; **abeto del Norte, abeto falso** spruce tree
**abier•to -ta** *adj* open; frank
**abigarra•do -da** *adj* motley, variegated
**abigeo** *m* horse thief, cattle thief
**abijar** *tr* (Col) to sic
**abiselar** *tr* to bevel
**abismar** *tr* to cast down; to humble; to spoil, ruin || *ref* to sink; to cave in; to be humbled; to give in; to lose oneself; (Am) to be surprised
**abismo** *m* abyss, chasm
**ablandabre•vas** *m* (*pl* **-vas**) or **ablandahi•gos** *m* (*pl* **-gos**) good-for-nothing
**ablandar** *tr* to soften; to soften up; to soothe; to loosen || *intr* (*el tiempo*) to moderate || *ref* to soften; to relent; (*el tiempo*) to moderate
**ablativo** *m* ablative
**aboba•do -da** *adj* stupid, stupid-looking
**abobar** *tr* to make stupid || *ref* to grow stupid

**aboca•do -da** *adj* (*vino*) mild, smooth; vulnerable; **abocado a** verging on
**abocar** §73 *tr* to bite; to pour; to bring near || *intr* to enter || *ref* to approach; to have an interview
**abocinar** *tr* to give a flare to || *intr* to fall on the face || *ref* to flare
**abochornar** *tr* to overheat; to make blush || *ref* to blush; to wilt
**abofetear** *tr* to slap in the face
**abogacía** *f* law, legal profession
**abogaderas** *fpl* (CAm) specious arguments
**abogado** *m* lawyer; **abogado de secano** quack lawyer; **abogado firmón** lawyer who will sign anything; **abogado trampista** shyster
**abogar** §44 *intr* to plead; **abogar por** to advocate, to back
**abolengo** *m* ancestry, descent; inheritance
**abolir** §1 *tr* to revoke, to repeal
**abolladura** *f* dent; bump, bruise; embossing
**abollar** *tr* to bump, to bruise; to dent; to stun; to emboss || *ref* to get bumped, get bruised; to dent, be dented
**abollonar** *tr* to emboss
**abombar** *tr* to make convex; (coll) to stun, confound || *ref* to rot, to decompose
**abominación** *f* abomination
**abominar** *tr* to detest, abominate || *intr* — **abominar de** to abominate
**abona•do -da** *adj* trustworthy; apt, likely || *mf* subscriber; (*al gas, electricidad, etc.*) consumer; (*a una localidad en el teatro*) season-ticket holder; (*al ferrocarril*) commuter
**abonanzar** §60 *intr* (*el tiempo*) to clear up; (*el viento*) to abate
**abonar** *tr* to vouch for; to certify; to improve; to fertilize; **abonar en cuenta a** to credit to the account of || *intr* (*el tiempo*) to clear up || *ref* to subscribe
**abonaré** *m* promissory note
**abono** *m* subscription; credit; installment; voucher; fertilizer, manure
**abordar** *tr* to approach; to accost; to undertake, to plan; (naut) to board; (naut) to run afoul of; (naut) to dock || *intr* to run afoul; (naut) to put into port
**aborígenes** *mpl* aborigines
**aborrascar** §73 *ref* to get stormy
**aborrecer** §22 *tr* to abhor, detest, hate; to bore || *ref* to get bored
**aborrecible** *adj* abhorrent, hateful
**aborrega•do -da** *adj* (*nubes*) fleecy; (*cielo*) mackerel
**abortar** *tr & intr* to abort
**aborto** *m* abortion
**abotagar** §44 *ref* to become bloated, to swell up
**abotonador** *m* buttonhook
**abotonar** *tr* to button || *intr* to bud
**abovedar** *tr* to arch, to vault
**abozalar** *tr* to muzzle
**abra** *f* cove; vale; fissure; (Mex) clearing
**abrasar** *tr* to set fire to, to burn; to parch; to nip; to squander; to shame || *intr* to burn || *ref* to burn; to become parched; (fig) to be burning up
**abrasi•vo -va** *adj & m* abrasive
**abrazadera** *f* clasp, clip, clamp; (typ) bracket
**abrazar** §60 *tr* to embrace, to clasp; to include; to take in || *ref* (*dos personas*) to embrace
**abrazo** *m* embrace, hug
**abrebo•cas** *m* (*pl* **-cas**) mouth prop, mouth gag
**abrebote•llas** *m* (*pl* **-llas**) bottle opener
**abrecar•tas** *m* (*pl* **-tas**) knife, letter opener
**abreco•ches** *m* (*pl* **-ches**) doorman
**abrela•tas** *m* (*pl* **-tas**) can opener
**abreos•tras** *m* (*pl* **-tras**) oyster knife
**abrevadero** *m* watering place, drinking trough
**abrevar** *tr* to water; to wet, soak; to irrigate; to size || *ref* to drink
**abreviación** *f* abridgment, abbreviation, shortening; hastening
**abreviar** *tr* to abridge; to abbreviate; to shorten; to hasten || *intr* to be quick; **abreviar con** to make short work of
**abreviatura** *f* abbreviation; **en abreviatura** (coll) in a hurry
**abridor** *m* opener; grafting knife; **abridor de guantes** glove stretcher
**abrigadero** *m* windbreak
**abrigar** §44 *tr* to shelter; to protect; (*esperanzas, sospechas*) to harbor || *ref* to take shelter; to wrap oneself up
**abrigo** *m* shelter; aid, support; cover, wrap; overcoat; (naut) harbor; **abrigo antiaéreo** air-raid shelter; **abrigo de entretiempo** topcoat, spring-and-fall coat; **al abrigo de** sheltered from, protected from; sheltered by, protected by; (*ropa*) **de mucho abrigo** heavy
**abril** *m* April
**abrir** *m* opening; **en un abrir y cerrar de ojos** (coll) in the twinkling of an eye || §83 *tr* to open; to unlock, unfasten; (*el apetito*) to whet; (*el bosque*) (Am) to clear || *intr* to open || *ref* to open; **abrirse a** or **con** to unbosom oneself to
**abrochador** *m* buttonhook
**abrochar** *tr* to button, to hook, to fasten
**abrojo** *m* thistle, thorn; **abrojos** reef, hidden rocks
**abrótano** *m* southernwood
**abruma•dor -dora** *adj* crushing, oppressing; overwhelming
**abrumar** *tr* to crush, oppress; to overwhelm; to annoy || *ref* to become foggy
**abrup•to -ta** *adj* abrupt, steep; rough, rugged
**absceso** *m* abscess
**absenta** *f* absinth
**ábsida** *f* or **ábside** *m* apse
**absoluta** *f* dogmatic statement; (mil) discharge

**absolutamente** *adv* absolutely; (Am) by no means
**absolu•to -ta** *adj* absolute; (coll) arbitrary || *m* absolute; **en absoluto** absolutely not || *f* see **absoluta**
**absolvederas** *fpl* — **tener buenas absolvederas** (coll) to be an indulgent confessor
**absolver** §47 & §83 *tr* to absolve; to solve, to answer
**absorbente** *adj* absorbent; (*interesante*) absorbing
**absorber** *tr* to absorb; to use up; to attract
**absor•to -ta** *adj* absorbed; entranced
**abste•mio -mia** *adj* abstemious
**abstener** §71 *ref* to abstain
**abstinente** *adj* abstinent
**abstracción** *f* abstraction; absorption, deep thought; **hacer abstracción de** to leave out, to disregard
**abstrac•to -ta** *adj* abstract
**abstraer** §75 *tr* to abstract || *intr* — **abstraer de** to do without, leave aside || *ref* to be abstracted or absorbed; **abstraerse de** to do without, leave aside
**abstraí•do -da** *adj* absorbed in thought; withdrawn
**abstru•so -sa** *adj* abstruse
**absurdidad** *f* absurdity
**absur•do -da** *adj* absurd || *m* absurdity
**abuchear** *tr & intr* to boo, to hoot
**abuela** *f* grandmother; **cuénteselo a su abuela** (coll) tell that to the marines
**abuelo** *m* grandparent; grandfather; **abuelos** grandparents; ancestors
**abulta•do -da** *adj* bulky, massive
**abultar** *tr* to enlarge; to exaggerate || *intr* to be bulky
**abundamiento** *m* abundance; **a mayor abundamiento** with greater reason
**abundante** *adj* abundant
**abundar** *intr* to abound
**abur** *interj* (coll) good-bye!, so long!
**aburri•do -da** *adj* bored; tiresome
**aburrir** *tr* to bore, tire || *ref* to become bored
**abusar** *intr* to go too far; **abusar de** to abuse; to impose on; to overindulge in
**abusión** *f* superstition
**abusi•vo -va** *adj* abusive
**abuso** *m* abuse; imposition
**abyec•to -ta** *adj* abject
**A.C.** *abbr* **año de Cristo**
**acá** *adv* here, around here; **acá y allá** here and there; **de ayer acá** since yesterday; **¿de cuándo acá?** since when?; **desde entonces acá** since then; **más acá** here closer; **muy acá** right here
**acaba•do -da** *adj* complete, perfect; worn-out, exhausted || *m* finish
**acabar** *tr* to end, finish, complete || *intr* to end; to die; **acabar con** to put an end to; to end in; **acabar de** to finish; to have just, e.g., **acaba de salir** he has just left; **acababa de salir** he had just left; **acabar por** to end in; to end by; **no acabar de decidirse** to be unable to make up one's mind || *ref* to end; to be exhausted; to be all over; to run out of, e.g., **se me acabó el café** I have run out of coffee
**acabóse** *m* (coll) limit, last straw
**acacia** *f* acacia; **acacia falsa** locust tree
**academia** *f* academy
**académi•co -ca** *adj* academic || *mf* academician
**acaecer** §22 *intr* to happen, to occur
**acaecimiento** *m* happening, occurrence
**acalora•do -da** *adj* heated; warm; fiery, excited
**acalorar** *tr* to heat, to warm; to incite, to encourage; to stir up || *ref* to become heated; to warm up
**acallar** *tr* to quiet, to silence; to pacify
**acampada** *f* camp
**acamar** *tr* (*las mieses la lluvia o el viento*) to beat down, to blow over
**acampamento** *m* camp, encampment
**acampana•do -da** *adj* bell-shaped
**acampar** *tr, intr & ref* to encamp
**acanalar** *tr* to groove; to flute; to channel; to corrugate
**acantila•do -da** *adj* rocky; steep, precipitous || *m* cliff, bluff
**acantonamiento** *m* cantonment
**acantonar** *tr* to canton, to quarter || *ref* to be quartered; **acantonarse en** to limit one's activities to
**acaparar** *tr* to corner; to monopolize; to hoard
**acaramela•do -da** *adj* candied; (coll) smooth, honey-tongued
**acarar** *tr* to bring face to face
**acarear** *tr* to bring face to face; to face, to brave
**acariciar** *tr* to caress; (*una ilusión*) to cherish
**acarraladura** *f* (Chile, Peru) run (*in stockings*)
**acarreadi•zo -za** *adj* transportable
**acarrear** *tr* to cart, transport, carry along; to cause, occasion || *ref* to incur, to bring upon oneself
**acarreo** *m* cartage, drayage; conveyance
**acartonar** *ref* (coll) to shrivel up, become wizened
**acasera•do -da** *adj* (Chile, Peru) home-loving; (*parroquiano*) (Chile, Peru) regular || *mf* (Chile, Peru) stay-at-home, homebody; (Chile, Peru) regular customer
**acaso** *m* chance, accident; **al acaso** at random || *adv* maybe, perhaps; **por si acaso** in case of need, just in case
**acatar** *tr* to respect, to hold in awe; to observe
**acatarrar** *tr* to chill, give a cold to; (Chile, Mex) to bother, annoy || *ref* to catch cold; (Am) to get tipsy
**acaudala•do -da** *adj* rich, well-to-do
**acaudalar** *tr* to acquire, to accumulate
**acaudillar** *tr* to lead, to command; to direct
**acceder** *intr* to accede; to agree
**accesible** *adj* accesible
**accesión** *f* accession; acquiescence; access, entry
**accésit** *m* second prize, honorable mention

**acceso** *m* access, approach; attack, fit, spell; **acceso prohibido** no admittance
**acceso·rio -ria** *adj* accessory || *m* accessory, fixture, attachment; **accesorios** (theat) properties
**accidenta·do -da** *adj* agitated; restless; rough, uneven || *mf* victim, casualty
**accidental** *adj* accidental; acting, pro-tempore, temporary
**accidentar** *tr* to injure, hurt || *ref* to faint
**accidente** *m* accident; (*del terreno*) roughness, unevenness; fainting spell
**acción** *f* action; gesture; (*parte del capital de una sociedad*) share; stock certificate; **acción crecedera** growth stock; **acción de gracias** thanksgiving; **acción liberada** stock dividend
**accionar** *tr* to drive || *intr* to gesticulate
**accionista** *mf* shareholder, stockholder
**acebo** *m* holly tree
**acebuche** *m* wild olive
**acecinar** *tr* to dry-cure, to dry-salt; (*el salmón o el arenque*) to kipper || *intr* to shrivel up
**acechar** *tr* to watch, to spy on
**acecho** *m* watching, spying; **al acecho** or **en acecho** on the watch, spying
**acedar** *tr* to turn sour; to embitter || *ref* to turn sour; to wither
**acedía** *f* sourness; crabbedness; heartburn
**ace·do -da** *adj* sour, tart; crabbed
**aceitar** *tr* to oil; to grease
**aceite** *m* oil; olive oil; **aceite de hígado de bacalao** cod-liver oil; **aceite de linaza** linseed oil; **aceite de pie de buey** neat's-foot oil; **aceite de ricino** castor oil; **aceite mineral** coal oil
**aceite·ro -ra** *adj* oil || *mf* oiler; oil dealer || *f* oilcan; oil cup; **aceiteras** cruet stand
**aceito·so -sa** *adj* oily, greasy
**aceituna** *f* olive
**aceituno** *m* olive tree
**acelerador** *m* accelerator
**acelerar** *tr & ref* to accelerate; to hasten, hurry
**acelga** *f* Swiss chard
**acémila** *f* beast of burden, pack animal; (coll) dolt; (coll) drudge
**acendra·do -da** *adj* refined; stainless, spotless
**acendrar** *tr* to refine; to purify, make stainless
**acento** *m* accent; **acento de altura** pitch accent; **acento ortográfico** written accent, accent mark; **acento prosódico** stress accent, tonic accent
**acentuar** §21 *tr* to accent; to accentuate, emphasize
**aceña** *f* water-driven flour mill
**acepción** *f* meaning
**acepillar** *tr* to plane; to brush; to smooth
**aceptable** *adj* acceptable
**aceptación** *f* acceptance
**aceptar** *tr* to accept; to agree
**acequia** *f* irrigation ditch; (Bol, Col, Peru) stream, rivulet
**acera** *f* sidewalk
**acera·do -da** *adj* steel, steely; (fig) cutting, biting, sharp
**acerar** *tr* to steel, to harden; to line with a sidewalk || *ref* to harden; to steel oneself
**acer·bo -ba** *adj* sour, bitter; harsh
**acerca** *adv* — **acerca de** about, with regard to
**acercamiento** *m* approach, rapprochement
**acercar** §73 *tr* to bring near or nearer || *ref* to approach, to come near or nearer
**acería** *f* steel mill
**acerico** *m* small cushion; pincushion
**acero** *m* steel; sword; courage, spirit
**acérri·mo -ma** *adj* all-out; (*enemigo*) bitter
**acerrojar** *tr* to bolt
**acerta·do -da** *adj* fit, right; skillful, sure; well-aimed
**acertante** *mf* winner
**acertar** §2 *tr* to hit; to hit upon; to figure out correctly; to find; to do right || *intr* to be right; to succeed; to guess right; **acertar a** to happen to; to succeed in; **acertar con** to come upon; to find
**acertijo** *m* conundrum, riddle
**acervo** *m* heap; assets, estate; shoal; store, fund, hoard
**acetato** *m* acetate
**acéti·co -ca** *adj* acetic
**acetificar** §73 *tr & ref* to acetify
**acetileno** *m* acetylene
**acetona** *f* acetone
**acia·go -ga** *adj* unlucky, ill-fated, evil
**acíbar** *m* aloes; bitterness, sorrow
**acicalar** *tr* to polish, to burnish; to dress, to dress up || *ref* to get all dressed up
**acicate** *m* long-pointed spur; incentive, stimulus
**acidez** *f* acidity
**acidificar** §73 *tr & ref* to acidify
**áci·do -da** *adj* acid, tart, sour || *m* acid
**acierto** *m* lucky hit, good shot; good guess; tact, prudence; ability, skill; accuracy; success
**aci·mut** *m* (*pl* **-muts**) azimut
**aclamación** *f* acclaim, applause
**aclamar** *tr & intr* to acclaim, to hail, to cheer
**aclarar** *tr* to brighten, to clear; to rinse; to explain || *intr* to get bright; to clear up; to dawn
**aclarato·rio -ria** *adj* explanatory
**aclimatar** *tr & ref* to acclimate
**acobardar** *tr* to cow, intimidate || *ref* to be frightened
**acocear** *tr* to kick; to trample upon, to ill-treat
**acocil** *m* Mexican crayfish; **estar como un acocil** (Mex) to blush, to be abashed
**acoda·do -da** *adj* elbow-shaped
**acodar** *tr* (*el brazo*) to lean; to prop; (hort) to layer || *ref* to lean
**acodillar** *tr* to bend at an angle || *ref* to double up; to bend, to crumple
**acoger** §17 *tr* to receive, to welcome;

to accept || *ref* to take refuge; to resort
**acogida** *f* reception, welcome; meeting place, confluence; refuge, shelter; **dar acogida a** (com) to honor
**acolada** *f* accolade
**acolchar** *tr* to quilt, to pad
**acolchí** *m* (Mex) red-winged blackbird
**acólito** *m* acolyte; altar boy
**acollador** *m* (naut) lanyard
**acomedi•do -da** *adj* (Am) obliging
**acometer** *tr* to attack; to undertake; (*el sueño, la enfermedad, el deseo a una persona*) to overcome
**acometida** *f* attack; (*p.ej., de una línea eléctrica*) house connection
**acomodación** *f* accommodation
**acomodadi•zo -za** *adj* accommodating, obliging
**acomoda•do -da** *adj* convenient, suitable; comfort-loving; well-to-do
**acomoda•dor -dora** *adj* accommodating, obliging || *mf* usher
**acomodar** *tr* to accommodate; to usher; to reconcile; to suit; to furnish, to supply || *intr* to be suitable, be convenient || *ref* to comply; to come to terms; to hire out; to make oneself comfortable
**acomodo** *m* arrangement, adjustment; lodgings; job, position; (Chile) neatness, tidiness
**acompañamiento** *m* accompaniment; escort, retinue; (theat) extras, supernumeraries
**acompañanta** *f* female companion or escort; accompanist
**acompañante** *m* companion; accompanist
**acompañar** *tr* to accompany; to escort; to enclose; to sympathize with
**acompasa•do -da** *adj* rhythmic; slow; easy-going; cautious
**aconchar** *tr* to push to safety; (naut) to beach, run aground || *ref* to take shelter; (naut) to run aground; (Chile) to form a deposit
**acondiciona•do -da** *adj* conditioned; **bien acondicionado** well-disposed; in good condition; **mal acondicionado** ill-disposed; in bad condition
**acondicionador** *m* conditioner; **acondicionador de aire** air conditioner
**acondicionamiento** *m* conditioning; **acondicionamiento del aire** air conditioning
**acondicionar** *tr* to condition; to put in condition; to repair; to season || *ref* to qualify; to find a job
**acongojar** *tr* to grieve, to afflict || *ref* to grieve
**aconsejable** *adj* advisable
**aconsejar** *tr* to advise, to counsel, to warn || *ref* to seek advice, to get advice
**acontecer** §22 *intr* to happen, to occur
**acontecimiento** *m* happening, event
**acopiar** *tr* to gather together
**acopio** *m* gathering; stock; abundance
**acoplado** *m* (Arg, Chile, Urug) trailer trolley car
**acoplamiento** *m* coupling; joint; connection
**acoplar** *tr* to couple; to join; to connect; to hitch; to reconcile || *ref* to be reconciled; to mate; to be intimate
**acoquinar** *tr* to intimidate
**acoraza•do -da** *adj* armored, armorplated; (coll) contrary || *m* battleship
**acorazar** §60 *tr* to armor-plate
**acorchar** *tr* to line with cork; to turn into cork || *ref* to get spongy; to wither, shrivel; to become corky or pithy; to get numb
**acorchetar** *tr* to bracket
**acordar** §61 *tr* to agree upon; to authorize; to reconcile; to make level or flush; to remind of; to tune || *intr* to agree; to blend || *ref* to be agreed, come to an agreement; to remember; **acordarse de** to remember
**acorde** *adj* agreed, in accord; in tune || *m* accord; (mus) chord
**acordeón** *m* accordion
**acordonar** *tr* to cord, to lace; (*monedas*) to knurl, to mill; to rope off
**acornar** §61 *tr* gore; to butt
**acornear** *tr* to gore; to butt
**acorralar** *tr* to corral, to corner; to intimidate
**acortar** *tr* to shorten; to reduce; to slow down; to check, to stop || *ref* to become shorter; to hold back; to be timid; to slow down; to shrink
**acosar** *tr* to harass; to pester
**acostar** §61 *tr* to lay down; to put to bed; (naut) to bring alongside || *ref* to lie down; to go to bed
**acostumbra•do -da** *adj* accustomed; customary, usual
**acostumbrar** *tr* to accustom || *intr* to be accustomed || *ref* to accustom oneself; to become accustomed
**acotación** *f* boundary mark; marginal note; elevation mark
**acotamiento** *m* boundary mark; marginal note; elevation mark; stage direction
**acotar** *tr* to mark off, to map; to annotate; to admit, to accept; to check; to vouch for; to select; to mark elevations on
**acotillo** *m* sledge hammer
**acre** *adj* acrid; austere; biting, mordant
**acrecentamiento** *m* increase, growth; promotion
**acrecentar** §2 *tr* to increase; to promote || *ref* to increase; to bud, to blossom
**acreditar** *tr* to accredit; to credit; to get a reputation for || *ref* to get a reputation, to prove oneself
**acree•dor -dora** *adj* accrediting; deserving || *mf* creditor; **acreedor hipotecario** mortgagee
**acribar** *tr* to sift; to riddle
**acribillar** *tr* to riddle; (coll) to harass, to plague, to pester
**acriminar** *tr* to incriminate; to exaggerate
**acrimonio•so -sa** *adj* acrid; acrimonious

**acriollar** *ref* (Am) to acquire Spanish American ways
**acrisolar** *tr* to purify, to refine; to reveal, to bring out
**acrobacia** *f* acrobatics
**acróbata** *mf* acrobat
**acrobatismo** *m* acrobatics
**acrónimo** *m* acronym
**acrópo•lis** *f* (*pl* **-lis**) acropolis
**acróstico** *m* acrostic
**acta** *f* minutes; certificate; **acta notarial** affidavit; **actas** proceedings, transactions; **levantar acta** to write up the minutes
**actitud** *f* attitude; **en actitud de** getting ready to
**activar** *tr* to activate; to hasten, to expedite
**actividad** *f* activity
**acti•vo -va** *adj* active ‖ *m* (com) assets; (com) credit side
**acto** *m* act; ceremony, function; commencement; thesis; **acto continuo** right afterward; **acto seguido** right afterward; **acto seguido de** right after; **hacer acto de presencia** to honor with one's presence
**actor** *m* actor; agent; **primer actor** leading man
**ac•triz** *f* (*pl* **-trices**) actress; **primera actriz** leading lady
**actuación** *f* acting, performance; action; operation; behavior
**actual** *adj* present, present-day; up-to-date ‖ *m* current month
**actualidad** *f* present time; timeliness; **actualidades** current events; newsreel; **actualidad escénica** theater news; **actualidad gráfica** news in pictures
**actualizar** §60 *tr* to bring up to date
**actualmente** *adv* at present, at the present time
**actuante** *mf* participant
**actuar** §21 *tr* to actuate ‖ *intr* to act; to perform
**actua•rio -ria** *mf* actuary
**acuaplano** *m* aquaplane
**acuarela** *f* water color
**acuario** *m* aquarium
**acuartelar** *tr* to billet, to quarter
**acuáti•co -ca** *adj* aquatic
**acuatizaje** *m* (aer) alighting on water; (*de nave espacial*) splashdown
**acuatizar** §60 *intr* (aer) to alight on water
**acucia** *f* zeal, diligence; yearning
**acuciar** *tr* to goad, to prod; to harass; to yearn for
**acuclillar** *ref* to squat, to crouch
**acuchilla•do -da** *adj* knife-shaped; schooled by experienced; (*vestido*) slashed
**acuchillar** *tr* to stab; to stab to death; to slash
**acudir** *intr* to come up, to respond; to apply; to hang around; to come to the rescue
**acueducto** *m* aqueduct
**acuerdo** *m* accord; agreement; memory; **de acuerdo con** in accord with; **de común acuerdo** with one accord; **estar en su acuerdo** to be in one's right mind; **ponerse de acuerdo** to come to an agreement; **recobrar su acuerdo** to come to; **tomar un acuerdo** to make a decision; **volver en su acuerdo** to come to; to change one's mind
**acuitar** *tr & intr* to grieve
**acullá** *adv* yonder, over there
**acumulador** *m* storage battery
**acumular** *tr* to accumulate, to gather; to store up ‖ *intr & ref* to accumulate, to gather
**acunar** *tr* to rock; to cradle
**acuñación** *f* coining, minting; wedging
**acuñar** *tr* to coin, to mint; to wedge; to key, to lock; (typ) to quoin
**acuo•so -sa** *adj* watery; juicy
**acurrucar** §73 *ref* to squat, to crouch; to huddle
**acusación** *f* accusation
**acusa•do -da** marked ‖ *mf* accused
**acusar** *tr* to accuse; to show; (*recibo de una carta*) to acknowledge ‖ *ref* to confess
**acusati•vo -va** *adj & m* accusative
**acuse** *m* acknowledgment
**acústi•co -ca** *adj* acoustic ‖ *f* acoustics
**achacar** §73 *tr* to impute, to attribute
**achaco•so -sa** *adj* ailing, sickly
**achaparra•do -da** *adj* stocky; stubby; chubby
**achaparrar** *ref* to become stunted
**achaque** *m* sickliness, indisposition; excuse, pretext; matter, subject; weakness; (coll) monthlies
**achatar** *tr* to flatten
**achica•do -da** *adj* childish; abashed, disconcerted
**achicador** *m* scoop
**achicar** §73 *tr* to make smaller; to humble; to bail, to bail out
**achicoria** *f* chicory
**achicharrar** *tr* to scorch; to bedevil ‖ *ref* to get scorched
**achispa•do -da** *adj* tipsy
**achispar** *tr* to make tipsy ‖ *ref* to get tipsy
**achuchar** *tr* to incite; to crumple, crush; to jostle ‖ *ref* (Arg, Urug) to shiver, have a chill
**adagio** *m* adage
**adalid** *m* chief; guide, leader; champion
**adama•do -da** *adj* womanish; chic, stylish
**adamar** *ref* to become effeminate
**adán** *m* (coll) dirty, ragged fellow, lazy, careless fellow ‖ **Adán** *m* Adam
**adaptación** *f* adaptation
**adaptar** *tr* to adapt
**adarga** *f* oval or heart-shaped leather shield
**adarvar** *tr* to bewilder, to stun
**A. de C.** *abbr* **año de Cristo**
**adecentar** *tr* to clean up, to tidy up ‖ *ref* (coll) to put on a clean shirt, to dress up
**adecua•do -da** *adj* fitting, suitable
**adecuar** *tr* to fit, to adapt
**adefesio** *m* (coll) nonsense; (coll) outlandish outfit; (coll) queer-looking fellow

**adehala** *f* gratuity, extra
**adehesar** *tr* to convert into pasture
**adelanta•do -da** *adj* precocious; bold, forward; (*reloj*) fast; **por adelantado** in advance || *m* provincial governor
**adelantamiento** *m* anticipation; advancement, promotion, progress
**adelantar** *tr* to move forward; to outstrip, get ahead of; to advance; to promote; to improve || *intr* to advance; to improve; to be fast || *ref* to move forward; to gain, be fast
**adelante** *adv* ahead; forward; **más adelante** farther on; later || *interj* go ahead!; come in!
**adelanto** *m* advance, progress, improvement; advancement; payment in advance
**adelfa** *f* oleander
**adelgazar** §60 *tr* to make thin; to taper; to purify; to argue subtly about; to weaken, lessen || *intr & ref* to get thin; to taper
**ademán** *m* attitude; gesture; **ademanes** manners; **en ademán de** getting ready to; **hacer ademán de** to make a move to
**además** *adv* moreover, besides; **además de** in addition to, besides
**adentellar** *tr* to sink one's teeth into
**adentrar** *intr & ref* to go in; **adentrarse en el mar** to go farther out to sea
**adentro** *adv* inside; **mar adentro** out at sea; **ser muy de adentro** to be like a member of the family; **tierra adentro** inland || **adentros** *mpl* inmost being, inmost thoughts; **en** or **para sus adentros** to oneself, to himself, etc.
**adep•to -ta** *adj* initiated || *mf* follower
**aderezar** §60 *tr* to dress, adorn; to cook; (*una tela*) to starch; to season; to repair; to lead; (*bebidas*) to mix; (*vinos*) to blend || *ref* to dress, get ready
**aderezo** *m* dressing; seasoning, condiment; starch; finery; equipment; set of jewelry
**adestrar** §2 *tr & ref* var of **adiestrar**
**adeuda•do -da** *adj* indebted, in debt
**adeudar** *tr* to owe; to be liable for; to charge || *intr* to become related by marriage || *ref* to run into debt
**adeudo** *m* debt, indebtedness; customs duty; charge, debit
**adherencia** *f* adhesion; **tener adherencias** to have connections
**adherente** *adj* adherent || *m* adherent; **adherentes** accessories
**adherir** §68 *intr & ref* to adhere; to stick
**adhesión** *f* adherence, adhesion
**adhesi•vo -va** *adj* adhesive
**adición** *f* addition; (*en un café o restaurante*) check
**adicionar** *tr* to add; to add to
**adic•to -ta** *adj* devoted; supporting || *mf* supporter, follower
**adiestrar** *tr* to train; to teach; to lead, to guide || *ref* to train, to practice
**adietar** *tr* to put on a diet
**adinera•do -da** *adj* wealthy, well-to-do
**adiós** *m* adieu, good-bye || *interj* adieu!, good-bye!
**aditamento** *m* addition; accessory
**aditi•vo -va** *adj & m* additive
**adivinación** *f* prophecy; guessing, divination; **adivinación del pensamiento** mind reading
**adivina•dor -dora** *mf* guesser; good guesser; **adivinador del pensamiento** mind reader
**adivinaja** *f* (coll) riddle, puzzle
**adivinanza** *f* riddle; guess
**adivinar** *tr* to prophesy; to guess, to divine; (*un enigma*) to solve; (*el pensamiento ajeno*) to read
**adivi•no -na** *mf* fortuneteller; guesser
**adjetivo** *m* adjective
**adjudicar** §73 *tr* to adjudge, to award || *ref* to appropriate
**adjuntar** *tr* to join, connect; to add; to enclose
**adjun•to -ta** *adj* added, attached; enclosed || *mf* associate || *m* adjunct; adjective
**adminículo** *m* aid, auxiliary; gadget; meddler; **adminículos** emergency equipment
**administración** *f* administration, management; headquarters
**administra•dor -dora** *mf* administrator, manager; **administrador de correos** postmaster
**administrar** *tr* to administer, to manage
**admiración** *f* admiration; wonder; exclamation mark
**admira•dor -dora** *mf* admirer
**admirar** *tr* to admire; to surprise || *ref* to wonder; **admirarse de** to wonder at
**admisible** *adj* admissible
**admisión** *f* admission; (mach) intake
**admitir** *tr* to admit; to allow; to accept, recognize; to agree to
**adobar** *tr* to repair, restore; to dress, prepare; to cook, stew; (*carne, pescado*) to pickle; (*pieles*) to tan
**adobe** *m* adobe
**adobo** *m* repairing; dressing; cooking; pickling; tanning; pickled meat or fish
**adocena•do -da** common, ordinary
**adoctrinar** *tr* to indoctrinate, to teach, to instruct
**adolecer** §22 *intr* to fall sick; **adolecer de** to suffer from || *ref* — **adolecerse de** (archaic) to sympathize with, feel sorry for
**adolescencia** *f* adolescence
**adolescente** *adj & mf* adolescent
**adonde** *conj* where, whither
**adónde** *adv* where, whither
**adopción** *f* adoption
**adoptar** *tr* to adopt
**adoquín** *m* paving stone, paving block; (coll) blockhead
**adoquina•do -da** *adj* paved with cobblestones || *m* cobblestone paving
**adorable** *adj* adorable
**adoración** *f* adoration, worship; **Adoración de los Reyes** Epiphany

**adora•dor -dora** *mf* adorer, worshiper || *m* suitor
**adorar** *tr & intr* to adore, to worship
**adormecer** §22 *tr* to put to sleep || *ref* to go to sleep; to get sleepy
**adormeci•do -da** *adj* sleepy, drowsy; numb; calm
**adormilar** *ref* to doze, to drowse
**adornar** *tr* to adorn; (*un cuento*) to embroider
**adornista** *mf* decorator
**adorno** *m* adornment, decoration; **adorno de escaparate** window dressing
**adosar** *tr* to lean; to push close
**adquirir** §40 *tr* to acquire; **adquirir en propiedad** to buy, to purchase
**adquisición** *f* acquisition
**adrede** *adv* on purpose
**Adriáti•co -ca** *adj & m* Adriatic
**adscribir** §83 *tr* to attribute; to assign
**adscripción** *f* attribution; assignment
**aduana** *f* customhouse; **aduana seca** inland customhouse
**aduane•ro -ra** *adj* customhouse; customs || *m* customhouse officer, customs inspector
**aduar** *m* Arab settlement; gipsy camp; Indian ranch
**adueñar** *ref* to take possession
**adujar** *tr* (naut) to coil || *ref* (naut) to curl up
**adular** *tr* to flatter, to fawn on
**adu•lón -lona** *adj* (coll) fawning, groveling || *mf* (coll) fawner
**adúltera** *f* adulteress
**adulterar** *tr* to adulterate || *intr* to commit adultery || *ref* to become adulterated, to spoil
**adulterio** *m* adultery
**adúlte•ro -ra** *adj* adulterous || *m* adulterer || *f* see **adúltera**
**adul•to -ta** *adj & mf* adult
**adulzar** §60 *tr* to sweeten; (*metales*) to soften
**adunar** *tr* to join, bring together
**adus•to -ta** *adj* grim, stern, gloomy; scorching hot
**advenedi•zo -za** *adj* strange; foreign || *mf* stranger; foreigner; outsider; parvenu, upstart; nouveau riche
**advenimiento** *m* advent, coming; accession; **esperar el santo advenimiento** (coll) to wait in vain
**advenir** §79 *intr* to come, arrive; to happen
**adverbio** *m* adverb
**adversa•rio -ria** *mf* adversary
**adversidad** *f* adversity
**advertencia** *f* observation; notice, remark; warning; preface
**adverti•do -da** *adj* capable, clever, wide-awake
**advertir** §68 *tr* to notice, observe; to notify, warn; to point out || *ref* to become aware
**Adviento** *m* (eccl) Advent
**adyacente** *adj* adjacent
**aeración** *f* aeration; ventilation; air conditioning
**aére•o -a** *adj* air, aerial; overhead, elevated; airy, light, fanciful
**aéroatómi•co -ca** *adj* air-atomic
**aerodinámi•co -ca** *adj* aerodynamic || *f* aerodynamics
**aeródromo** *m* aerodrome, airdrome; **aeródromo de urgencia** emergency-landing field
**aeroespacial** *adj* aerospace
**aerofumigación** *f* crop dusting
**aeromedicina** *f* aviation medicine
**aeromodelismo** *m* model-airplane building
**aeromodelista** *mf* model-airplane builder
**aeromodelo** *m* model airplane
**aeromotor** *m* windmill; airplane motor
**aeromoza** *f* air hostess, stewardess
**aeronauta** *mf* aeronaut
**aeronáuti•co -ca** *adj* aeronautic || *f* aeronautics
**aeronave** *f* airship; **aeronave cohete** rocket ship
**aeropista** *f* landing strip
**aeroplano** *m* aeroplane
**aeroposta** *f* air mail
**aeropostal** *adj* air-mail
**aeropropulsor** *m* airplane engine; **aeropropulsor por reacción** jet engine
**aeropuerto** *m* airport
**aeroscala** *f* transit point
**aerosol** *m* aerosol
**aeroste•ro -ra** *adj* aviation || *m* flyer; airman
**aeroterrestre** *adj* air-ground
**aerovía** *f* airway
**afable** *adj* affable, friendly, agreeable
**afama•do -da** *adj* noted, famous
**afamar** *tr* to make famous || *ref* to become famous
**afán** *m* hard work; eagerness, zeal; task; worry
**afanar** *tr* to press, hurry || *intr* to strive, toil || *ref* to strive, toil; to busy oneself
**afano•so -sa** *adj* hard, laborious; hard-working
**afarolar** *ref* (Am) to make a fuss, to get excited
**afear** *tr* to deface, to disfigure; to blame
**afeblecer** §22 *intr* to grow feeble, to get thin
**afección** *f* affection, fondness; (med) affection
**afectación** *f* affectation
**afecta•do -da** *adj* affected; **estar afectado de** (*p.ej., los riñones*) to have (*e.g., kidney*) trouble
**afectar** *tr* to affect; (Am) to hurt, to injure || *ref* to be moved, be stirred
**afecti•vo -va** *adj* emotional
**afec•to -ta** *adj* fond; kind; affected; **afecto a** fond of; (*un empleo, un servicio, etc.*) attached to; **afecto de** suffering from || *m* affection, fondness; emotion
**afectuo•so -sa** *adj* affectionate; kind
**afeitado** *m* shave; **afeitado a ras** close shave
**afeitar** *tr* to shave; to adorn; (*la cara*) to paint || *ref* to shave; to paint
**afeite** *m* cosmetics, rouge, make-up
**afeminación** *f* effeminacy
**afemina•do -da** *adj* effeminate

**afeminar** *tr* to effeminate ‖ *ref* to become effeminate
**aferra·do -da** *adj* stubborn, obstinate
**aferrar** *tr* to seize; to catch; to hook; (naut) to moor; (naut) to furl ‖ *ref* to interlock, hook together; to cling; to insist
**Afganistán, el** Afghanistan
**afga·no -na** *adj & mf* Afghan
**afianzar** **§60** *tr* to guarantee, vouch for; to bail; to fasten; to prop up; to grasp; to support ‖ *ref* to hold fast, to steady oneself
**afición** *f* fondness, liking, taste; ardor, zeal; fans, public
**aficiona·do -da** *adj* fond; amateur; **aficionado a** fond of ‖ *mf* amateur; fan, follower
**aficionar** *tr* to win, to win the attachment of ‖ *ref* — **aficionarse a** or **de** to become fond of; to become a follower of, become a fan of
**afiebra·do -da** *adj* feverish
**afi·jo -ja** *adj* affixed ‖ *m* affix
**afila·do -da** *adj* sharp; tapering; pointed; peaked
**afilador** *m* grinder, sharpener; razor strop
**afilalápi·ces** *m* (*pl* **-ces**) pencil sharpener
**afilar** *tr* to grind, to sharpen; (*una navaja de afeitar*) to strop; (Arg & Urug) to flirt with ‖ *ref* to sharpen, get sharp; to taper, get thin
**afiliar** **§77 & regular** *tr* to affiliate, take in ‖ *ref* — **afiliarse a** to join
**afiligranar** *tr* to filigree; to adorn, embellish
**afilón** *m* knife sharpener; razor strop
**afín** *adj* near, bordering; like, similar; related ‖ *mf* relative by marriage
**afinador** *m* tuner; tuning hammer, tuning key
**afinar** *tr* to purify, refine, perfect; to trim; to tune
**afincar** **§73** *intr & ref* to buy up real estate
**afinidad** *f* affinity; **por afinidad** by marriage
**afirmar** *tr* to strengthen, secure, fasten; to assert ‖ *ref* to hold fast; to steady oneself
**afirmati·vo -va** *adj & f* affirmative
**aflicción** *f* affliction; sorrow, grief
**afligir** **§27** *tr* to afflict, to grieve ‖ *ref* to grieve
**aflojar** *tr* to slacken, to let go; to loosen ‖ *intr* to slacken, to slow up; to abate, lessen ‖ *ref* to come loose; to slacken
**aflora·do -da** *adj* flour; fine, elegant
**aflorar** *tr* to sift ‖ *intr* to crop out
**afluencia** *f* flowing; affluence, abundance; crowd, jam, rush; fluency
**afluente** *adj* flowing; abundant; fluent ‖ *m* tributary
**afluir** **§20** *intr* to flow; to pour, to flock
**afmo.** *abbr* **afectísimo**
**afofar** *tr* to make fluffy, make spongy
**afonizar** **§60** *tr & ref* to unvoice
**aforar** *tr* to gauge, to measure; to appraise
**aforismo** *m* aphorism
**afortuna·do -da** *adj* fortunate; happy
**afrancesa·do -da** *adj & mf* Francophile
**afrecho** *m* bran
**afrenta** *f* affront
**afrentar** *tr* to affront ‖ *ref* to be ashamed
**África** *f* Africa
**africa·no -na** *adj & mf* African
**afrodisía·co -ca** *adj & m* aphrodisiac
**afrontar** *tr* to bring face to face; to defy ‖ *ref* — **afrontarse con** to confront, to meet face to face
**afuera** *adv* outside ‖ *interj* clear the way!, look out! ‖ **afueras** *fpl* outskirts, environs
**agachadiza** *f* snipe; **hacer la agachadiza** (coll) to duck
**agachar** *tr* to lower, bend down ‖ *ref* to crouch, to squat; to cower; (SAm) to give in, yield
**agalla** *f* gallnut; (*de pez*) gill; (*de ave*) ear lobe; **agallas** (coll) courage, guts
**ágape** *m* banquet, love feast
**agarrada** *f* (coll) brawl, fight, scrap
**agarra·do -da** *adj* (coll) stingy, tight ‖ *f* see **agarrada**
**agarrar** *tr* to grab, to grasp; to take hold of; (coll) to get, obtain ‖ *intr* to take hold; to take root; to stick ‖ *ref* to grapple; to have a good hold; to worry; **agarrarse a** to take hold of, to cling to
**agarrochar** *tr* to jab with a goad
**agarrotar** *tr* to garrote; to bind, to tie up ‖ *ref* to become numb
**agasajar** *tr* to regale, to lionize, to make a fuss over
**agasajo** *m* kindness, attention; lionization; favor, gift; treat; party
**agavillar** *tr* to bind or tie in sheaves ‖ *ref* to band together
**agazapar** *tr* (coll) to grab, to nab ‖ *ref* (coll) to crouch; (coll) to hide
**agencia** *f* agency; bureau; (Chile) pawn shop; **agencia de noticias** news agency
**agenciar** *tr* to manage to bring about; to promote ‖ *ref* to manage
**agenda** *f* notebook
**agente** *m* agent; policeman; **agente de policía** policeman; **agente viajero** traveling salesman, commercial traveler
**agigantar** *tr* to make huge ‖ *ref* to become huge
**ágil** *adj* agile; flexible, light
**agilitar** *tr & ref* to limber up
**agita·do -da** *adj* agitated, excited; (*mar*) rough; exalted
**agitar** *tr* to agitate; to shake; to wave; to stir ‖ *intr* to agitate ‖ *ref* to be agitated; to shake; to wave; to get excited; (*el mar*) to get rough
**aglomeración** *f* agglomeration; crowd; built-up area
**aglomerado** *m* briquet, coal briquet
**aglutinar** *tr* to stick together ‖ *ref* to cake
**agnósti·co -ca** *adj & mf* agnostic
**agobiar** *tr* to overburden; to exhaust, oppress

**agolpar** *ref* to flock, to throng
**agonía** *f* agony, throes of death; agony, anguish; yearning; craving
**agonizar** §60 *tr* (*al moribundo*) to assist, to attend; (coll) to harass || *intr* to be in the throes of death
**agorar** §3 *tr* to augur, foretell
**agore•ro -ra** *adj* fortunetelling; ill-omened; superstitious || *mf* fortuneteller
**agostar** *tr* to burn up, to parch || *ref* to dry up; (*la esperanza, la felicidad*) to fade away
**agostero** *m* harvest helper
**agosto** *m* August; harvest; harvest time; **hacer su agosto** to make hay while the sun shines
**agota•do -da** *adj* exhausted; sold out; out of print
**agotar** *tr* to exhaust, to wear out, to use up || *ref* to become exhausted, to be used up; to go out of print; to run out
**agracia•do -da** *adj* charming, graceful; nice, pretty || *mf* winner
**agradable** *adj* agreeable
**agradar** *tr* to please || *intr* to be pleasing || *ref* to be pleased
**agradecer** §22 *tr* to thank; **agradecerle a uno una cosa** to thank someone for something
**agradeci•do -da** *adj* thankful, grateful; rewarding
**agradecimiento** *m* thanks, gratitude
**agrado** *m* agreeableness, graciousness; pleasure, liking
**agrandar** *tr* to enlarge || *ref* to grow larger
**agranelar** *tr* (*cuero*) to grain, to pebble
**agrapar** *tr* to clamp
**agrariense** *adj* & *mf* agrarian
**agra•rio -ria** *adj* agrarian
**agravar** *tr* to weigh down; to aggravate; to exaggerate; to oppress || *ref* to get worse
**agraviar** *tr* to wrong, offend || *ref* to take offense
**agravio** *m* wrong, offense; **agravios de hecho** assault and battery
**agravio•so -sa** *adj* offensive, insulting
**agraz** *m* (*pl* **agraces**) sour grape; sour-grape juice; (coll) bitterness, displeasure; **en agraz** prematurely
**agredir** §1 *tr* to attack, assault
**agregado** *m* aggregate; concrete block; attaché; (Arg) tenant farmer
**agregar** §44 *tr* to add; to attach; to appoint || *ref* to join
**agremiado** *m* union member
**agremiar** *tr* to unionize
**agresión** *f* aggression
**agresi•vo -va** *adj* aggressive
**agre•sor -sora** *adj* aggressive || *mf* aggressor
**agreste** *adj* country, rustic; wild, rough; uncouth
**agriar** §77 & **regular** *tr* to make sour; to exasperate || *ref* to turn sour; to become exasperated
**agrícola** *adj* agricultural || *mf* farmer
**agricultura** *f* agriculture
**agridulce** *adj* bittersweet
**agriera** *f* (Chile) heartburn; **agrieras** (Col) cruet stand
**agrietar** *tr* & *ref* to crack
**agrimensor** *m* surveyor
**agrimensura** *f* surveying
**agringar** §44 *ref* (Am) to act like a gringo
**a•grio -gria** *adj* sour, acrid; uneven, rough; brittle || **agrios** *mpl* citrus fruit
**agronomía** *f* agronomy
**agropecua•rio -ria** *adj* land-and-cattle, farm
**agrumar** *tr* & *ref* to curd, to clot
**agrupar** *tr* & *ref* to group, to cluster
**agrura** *f* sourness; unpleasantness; **agruras** citrus fruit
**agua** *f* water; (*de un tejado*) slope; **agua abajo** downstream; **agua arriba** upstream; **agua bendita** holy water; **agua corriente** running water; **agua de Colonia** eau de Cologne; **agua de marea** tidewater; **agua gaseosa** carbonated water; **agua oxigenada** hydrogen peroxide; **aguas** mineral springs; (*de sedas; de piedras preciosas*) water, sparkle; **aguas mayores** equinoctial tide; feces; **aguas menores** ordinary tide; urination; **cubrir aguas** to have under roof; **entre dos aguas** under water, under the surface of the water; (coll) undecided
**aguacate** *m* avocado, alligator pear
**aguacero** *m* shower
**aguada** *f* source of water; water color; watering station
**aguade•ro -ra** *adj* water || *m* watering place
**agua•do -da** *adj* watery; thin, watered; (Am) weak, washed out, limp; (Am) dull, insipid || *f* see **aguada**
**agua•dor -dora** *mf* water carrier || *m* paddle, bucket
**aguafies•tas** *mf* (*pl* **-tas**) kill-joy, wet blanket, crapehanger
**aguafortista** *mf* etcher
**aguafuerte** *f* etching; **grabar al aguafuerte** to etch
**aguaje** *m* watering place; tidal wave; strong current; (*de buque*) wake
**aguamala** *f* jellyfish
**aguamanil** *m* ewer, wash pitcher; washstand
**aguama•nos** *m* (*pl* **-nos**) water for washing hands; washstand
**aguamarina** *f* aquamarine
**aguanie•ves** *f* (*pl* **-ves**) wagtail
**aguano•so -sa** *adj* watery, soaked
**aguantar** *tr* to hold up, sustain; to bear, endure, tolerate; to hold back, control || *intr* to last, to hold out || *ref* to restrain oneself; to keep quiet; **aguantarse las lágrimas** to swallow one's tears
**aguante** *m* patience, endurance; strength, vigor
**aguar** §10 *tr* to water; to spoil, to mar || *ref* to become watery; to fill up with water; to be spoiled
**aguardar** *tr* to await, to wait for; to grant time to || *intr* to wait; **aguardar a que** to wait until

**aguardentera** *f* liquor bottle, brandy flask
**aguardentería** *f* liquor store
**aguardento·so -sa** *adj* brandy; (*voz*) whiskey
**aguardiente** *m* brandy; spirituous liquor; **aguardiente de caña** rum; **aguardiente de manzana** applejack
**aguardo** *m* hunter's blind
**aguasar** *ref* (Arg & Chile) to become countrified
**aguazal** *m* swamp, pool
**agudeza** *f* acuteness, acuity; sharpness; witticism; **agudeza visual** visual acuity
**agu·do -da** *adj* acute; sharp; keen; witty
**agüero** *m* augury; omen; forecast
**aguerri·do -da** *adj* inured, hardened
**aguijada** *f* goad, spur; prod
**aguijar** *tr* to goad, spur, prod ‖ *intr* to hurry along
**aguijón** *m* goad, spur; sting; thorn; stimulus; **dar coces contra el aguijón** to kick against the pricks
**aguijonear** *tr* to goad, incite; to sting
**águila** *f* eagle; **ser un águila** to be wide-awake, be a wizard
**aguile·ño -ña** *adj* aquiline; sharp-featured
**aguilón** *m* (*de grúa*) boom, jib; (*del tejado*) gable
**aguinaldo** *m* Christmas gift, Epiphany gift; Christmas carol
**aguja** *f* needle; hatpin; steeple, spire; (*del reloj*) hand; **aguja de gancho** crochet needle; **aguja de hacer media** knitting needle; **aguja de zurcir** darning needle; **agujas** (rr) switch; **buscar una aguja en un pajar** to look for a needle in a haystack
**agujerear** *tr* to make a hole in, to pierce, to perforate
**agujero** *m* hole; pincushion
**agujeta** *f* (*de la jeringa*) needle; shoestring; **agujetas** stitches, twinges
**agusanar** *ref* to get wormy; to become worm-eaten
**aguzanie·ves** *f* (*pl* **-ves**) wagtail
**aguzar** **§60** *tr* to sharpen; to incite, stir up; to stare at; (*las orejas*) to prick up
**ah-chís** *interj* kerchoo!
**aherrojar** *tr* to fetter, to shackle; to oppress
**aherrumbrar** *tr & ref* to rust
**ahí** *adv* there; **de ahí que** hence; **por ahí** that way
**ahija·do -da** *mf* godchild; protégé ‖ *m* godson ‖ *f* goddaughter
**ahilar** *ref* to faint from hunger; to waste away; to grow poorly; to turn sour
**ahincar** **§73** *tr* to urge, press; to importune ‖ *ref* to hasten
**ahinco** *m* earnestness, zeal, eagerness
**ahitar** *tr* to cloy, to surfeit, to stuff
**ahi·to -ta** *adj* surfeited, stuffed; fed up, disgusted ‖ *m* surfeit; indigestion
**ahoga·do -da** *adj* drowned; smothered; sunk; close, unventilated; **mate ahogado** stalemate; **perecer ahogado** to drown; **verse ahogado** (coll) to be swamped
**ahogar** **§44** *tr* to drown; to suffocate, smother; (*cal*) to slake; (*plantas*) to soak; to oppress; to extinguish; to stalemate ‖ *ref* to drown; to suffocate; to drown oneself
**ahogo** *m* shortness of breath; great sorrow; stringency
**ahondar** *tr* to make deeper; to go deep into ‖ *intr* to go deep, go deeper
**ahora** *adv* now; presently; **ahora bien** now then, so then; **ahora mismo** right now; **por ahora** for the present
**ahorcajar** *ref* to sit astride
**ahorcar** **§73** *tr* to hang ‖ *ref* to hang, be hanged; to hang oneself
**ahorra·do -da** *adj* saving, thrifty
**ahorrar** *tr* to save; to spare ‖ *ref* to save or spare oneself
**ahorrati·vo -va** *adj* saving, thrifty; stingy ‖ *f* economy
**ahorro** *m* economy; **ahorros** savings
**ahuchar** *tr* to hoard
**ahuecar** **§73** *tr* to hollow, hollow out; to loosen, fluff up; **ahuecar la voz** to speak in deep and solemn tones ‖ *ref* to be puffed up
**ahumar** *tr* to smoke ‖ *intr* to be smoky ‖ *ref* to get smoked up; to look or taste smoky; (coll) to get drunk
**ahusar** *tr & ref* to taper
**ahuyentar** *tr* to put to flight; to scare away ‖ *ref* to flee, run away
**aira·do -da** *adj* angry; wild; depraved
**airar** **§4** *tr* to anger ‖ *ref* to get angry
**aire** *m* air; **al aire libre** in the open air; **darse aires** to put on airs
**airear** *tr* to air, aerate, ventilate ‖ *ref* to get aired; to catch cold
**airón** *m* aigrette, panache; gray heron
**airo·so -sa** *adj* airy; drafty; graceful, light; resplendent; successful
**aislación** *f* insulation
**aislacionista** *adj & mf* isolationist
**aislador** *m* insulator
**aislamiento** *m* isolation; (elec) insulation
**aislar** **§4** *tr* to isolate; to detach, separate; (elec) to insulate ‖ *ref* to live in seclusion
**ajar** *m* garlic field ‖ *tr* to crumple, to muss; (*marchitar*) to wither; to tamper with; to abuse, ill-treat ‖ *ref* to get mussed; to wither
**ajedrea** *f* (bot) savory
**ajedrecista** *mf* chess player
**ajedrez** *m* chess; chess set
**ajenjo** *m* (*Artemisia*) wormwood; (*licor*) absinthe; (*sinsabores y penas*) (fig) wormwood, bitterness; **ajenjo del campo** or **ajenjo mayor** (*Artemisia absinthium*) wormwood
**aje·no -na** *adj* another's; extraneous, foreign; different; contrary; free; insane; uninformed; **lo ajeno** what belongs to someone else
**ajetrear** *tr* to drive, harass ‖ *ref* to bustle about; to fidget
**ajetreo** *m* bustle, fuss
**ají** *m* (*pl* **ajíes**) chili; chili sauce; po-

**nerse como un ají** (Chile) to turn red as a tomato
**aji•mez** *m* (*pl* **-meces**) mullioned window
**ajo** *m* garlic; garlic clove; garlic sauce
**ajorca** *f* bracelet, anklet
**ajornalar** *tr* to hire by the day || *ref* to hire out by the day
**ajuar** *m* housefurnishings; trousseau
**ajuiciar** *tr* to bring to one's senses || *ref* to come to one's senses
**ajusta•do -da** *adj* just, right; tight, close-fitting
**ajustar** *tr* to adapt, to fit, to adjust; to hire; to arrange; to reconcile; to fasten; to settle || *intr* to fit || *ref* to fit; to hire out; to be hired; to come to an agreement
**ajuste** *m* fit; fitting, adjustment; hiring; arrangement; reconciliation; settlement; agreement
**ajusticiar** *tr* to execute, to put to death
**ala** *f* wing; (*del sombrero*) brim; (*de puerta, mesa, etc.*) leaf; (*de pez*) fin; (*de hélice*) blade; (football) end; **ahuecar el ala** (coll) to beat it; **ala en flecha** (aer) sweptback wing; **alas** boldness, courage; **volar con sus propias alas** to stand on one's own feet
**Alá** *m* Allah
**alabanza** *f* praise
**alabar** *tr* to praise || *ref* to boast
**alabarda** *f* halberd
**alabardero** *m* halberdier; hired applauder, claqueur
**alabastro** *m* alabaster
**álabe** *m* drooping branch; bucket, paddle; cog
**alabear** *tr & ref* to warp
**alacena** *f* cupboard, wall closet; (naut) locker; (Mex) booth, stall
**alacrán** *m* scorpion
**ala•do -da** *adj* winged
**alamar** *m* frog (*button and loop on a garment*)
**alambica•do -da** *adj* precious, oversubtle, fine-spun; begrudged
**alambicar** §73 *tr* to distill; to refine to excess
**alambique** *m* still, alembic; (*de laboratorio*) retort; **por alambique** sparingly
**alambrada** *f* chicken wire; wire mesh; (mil) barbed wire; (elec) wiring
**alambrado** *m* chicken wire; wire mesh; wire fence; (elec) wiring; (mil) wire entanglement
**alambraje** *m* (elec) wiring
**alambrar** *tr* to fence with wire; to string with wire; to wire
**alambre** *m* wire; **alambre cargado** live wire; **alambre de púas** barbed wire; **alambre sin aislar** bare wire
**alambrera** *f* wire screen; wire cover
**alameda** *f* poplar grove; mall, shaded walk
**álamo** *m* poplar; **álamo de Italia** Lombardy poplar; **álamo negro** black poplar; **álamo temblón** aspen
**alampar** *ref* to have a craving
**alancear** *tr* to lance, to spear
**alano** *m* mastiff, great Dane
**alarde** *m* display, ostentation; (mil) review; **hacer alarde de** to make a show of; to boast of
**alardear** *intr* to boast, brag, show off
**alardo•so -sa** *adj* showy, ostentatious
**alargar** §44 *tr* to extend, lengthen, stretch; to hand; to increase; to let out || *ref* to go away, withdraw; to grow longer; to be long-winded
**alarido** *m* howl, shout, yell, whoop
**alarma** *f* alarm; (aer) alert; **alarma aérea** air-raid warning; **alarma de incendios** fire alarm; **alarma de ladrones** burglar alarm
**alarmar** *tr* to alarm; to alert || *ref* to become alarmed
**alarmista** *mf* alarmist
**alastrar** *tr* (*las orejas*) to throw back; (naut) to ballast || *ref* to lie flat, to cower
**ala•zán -zana** *adj* sorrel, reddish-brown || *mf* sorrel horse
**alba** *f* dawn, daybreak
**albacea** *m* executor || *f* executrix
**albahaquero** *m* flowerpot
**alba•nés -nesa** *adj & mf* Albanian
**albañal** *m* sewer, drain
**albañil** *m* mason, bricklayer
**albañilería** *f* masonry
**albarán** *m* rent sign; bulletin; (com) check list
**albarca** *f* sandal
**albarda** *f* packsaddle
**albardilla** *f* (*tejadillo sobre los muros*) coping; shoulder pad
**albaricoque** *m* apricot
**albaricoquero** *m* apricot tree
**alba•tros** *m* (*pl* **-tros**) albatross
**albayalde** *m* white lead
**albear** *intr* to turn white; (Arg) to get up at dawn
**albedrío** *m* free will; fancy, caprice, pleasure; **libre albedrío** free will
**albéitar** *m* veterinarian
**alberca** *f* pond, pool; tank, reservoir; **en alberca** roofless
**albérchigo** *m* clingstone peach
**albergar** §44 *tr* to shelter, to harbor; to house || *intr & ref* to take shelter; to take lodgings
**albergue** *m* shelter, refuge; lodging; den, lair
**albero** *m* dishcloth, dishrag; white earth
**al•bo -ba** *adj* (poet) white || *f* see **alba**
**albóndiga** *f* meat ball, fish ball
**albor** *m* whiteness; dawn
**alborada** *f* dawn; morning serenade; reveille
**alborear** *intr* to dawn
**albor•noz** *m* (*pl* **-noces**) terry cloth; burnoose; cardigan; beach robe
**alborota•do -da** *adj* hasty, rash; noisy; rough
**alborota•dor -dora** *mf* agitator, rioter
**alborotapue•blos** *mf* (*pl* **-blos**) (coll) rabble rouser; (coll) gay noisy person
**alborotar** *tr* to agitate, arouse, stir up || *intr* to make a racket || *ref* to get excited; to riot; (*la mar*) to get rough
**alboroto** *m* agitation, disturbance;

noise, riot; **alborotos** (CAm) candied popcorn; **armar un alboroto** to raise a racket
**alborozar** §60 *tr* to gladden, to cheer, to overjoy, to elate
**alborozo** *m* joy, merriment, elation
**albricias** *fpl* reward for good news; reward given on the occasion of some happy event; **en albricias de** as a token of || *interj* good news!, congratulations!
**albufera** *f* saltwater lagoon
**ál·bum** *m* (*pl* **-bumes**) album; **álbum de recortes** scrapbook
**albumen** *m* albumen
**albúmina** *f* albumin
**albuminar** *tr* (phot) to emulsify
**albur** *m* risk, chance
**alcachofa** *f* artichoke
**alcahue·te -ta** *mf* bawd, procurer, go-between; screen, fence; (coll) schemer; (coll) gossip
**alcahuetear** *tr* to procure; to harbor || *intr* to pander
**alcaide** *m* governor, warden, jailer
**alcalde** *m* mayor, chief burgess; **alcalde de monterilla** small-town mayor; **tener el padre alcalde** to have a friend at court
**alcaldesa** *f* mayoress
**álcali** *m* alkali
**alcali·no -na** *adj* alkaline
**alcallería** *f* pottery
**alcana** *f* henna
**alcance** *m* reach, scope, extent; range; pursuit; capacity; late news; import; coverage; brains, intelligence; **al alcance de** within reach of, within range of; **alcance de la vista** eyesight, eyeshot; **alcance del oído** earshot; **dar alcance a** to catch up with
**alcancía** *f* child's bank; bin, hopper
**alcanfor** *m* camphor
**alcantarilla** *f* sewer; culvert
**alcantarillar** *tr* to sewer
**alcanza·do -da** *adj* needy, hard up
**alcanzar** §60 *tr* to reach; to overtake, catch up to; to grasp; to obtain; to understand; to live through || *intr* to succeed; (*un arma de fuego*) to carry; to manage; to suffice
**alcaravea** *f* caraway
**alcázar** *m* fortress; castle, royal palace; quarterdeck
**alce** *m* elk, moose
**alcista** *adj* bullish || *mf* (fig) bull
**alcoba** *f* bedroom; **alcoba de respeto** master bedroom
**alcohol** *m* alcohol
**alcohóli·co -ca** *adj & mf* alcoholic
**alcor** *m* hill, elevation, eminence
**alcornoque** *m* cork oak; (coll) blockhead
**alcorque** *m* cork-soled shoe; trench for water around a tree
**alcorza** *f* sugar paste, sugar icing; **ser una alcorza** (Arg) to be highly emotional
**alcurnia** *f* ancestry, lineage
**alcuza** *f* olive-oil can
**aldaba** *f* knocker, door knocker; bolt, crossbar; latch; hitching ring; **aldaba dormida** deadlatch; **tener buenas aldabas** to have pull
**aldabonazo** *m* knock on the door
**aldea** *f* village, hamlet
**aldea·no -na** *adj* village; rustic || *mf* villager
**aleación** *f* alloy
**alear** *tr* to alloy || *intr* to flap the wings; to flap one's arms; to convalesce
**aleccionar** *tr* to teach, instruct; to train, to coach
**aleda·ño -ña** *adj* bordering || *m* border, boundary
**alegar** §44 *tr* to allege; to declare, assert || *intr* (Col, Hond) to quarrel
**alegoría** *f* allegory
**alegóri·co -ca** *adj* allegoric(al)
**alegrar** *tr* to cheer, gladden; (*un fuego*) to stir || *ref* to be glad, to rejoice; (coll) to get tipsy
**alegre** *adj* glad; bright, gay; cheerful, light-hearted; careless; fast, spicy; **alegre de cascos** scatterbrained
**alegría** *f* cheer, joy, gladness; brightness, gaiety
**aleja·do -da** *adj* distant, remote
**alejandri·no -na** *adj & mf* Alexandrine
**alejar** *tr & ref* to move aside, to move away
**alelar** *tr* to make stupid || *ref* to grow stupid
**aleluya** *m & f* hallelujah || *m* Easter time || *f* doggerel; daub; **aleluya navideña** Christmas card || *interj* hallelujah!
**ale·mán -mana** *adj & mf* German
**Alemania** *f* Germany
**alenta·do -da** *adj* brave, spirited; proud, haughty; (Am) well, healthy || *f* deep breath
**alentar** §2 *tr* to encourage, to cheer up || *intr* to breathe || *ref* to take heart; to get well, to recover
**alerce** *m* larch
**alergia** *f* allergy
**alero** *m* eaves
**alerón** *m* aileron
**alerta** *adv* on the alert || *interj* watch out!, look out! || *m* (mil) alert; (mil) watchword
**alertar** *tr* to alert
**aler·to -ta** *adj* alert, watchful, vigilant
**alesaje** *m* bore
**alesna** *f* awl
**aleta** *f* small wing; (*de pez*) fin; (*de hélice*) blade
**aletargar** §44 *tr* to benumb; to put to sleep || *ref* to get drowsy, fall asleep
**aletear** *intr* to flap the wings; to flap, flip, flutter
**aleve** *adj* treacherous, perfidious
**alevosía** *f* treachery, perfidy
**alevo·so -sa** *adj* treacherous, perfidious
**alfabetizar** §60 *tr* to alphabetize; to teach reading and writing to
**alfabeto** *m* alphabet
**alfaneque** *m* buzzard
**alfanje** *m* cutlass
**alfarería** *f* pottery
**alfarero** *m* potter

**alféizar** *m* splay; embrasure
**alfeñicar** §73 *tr* to candy, to ice ‖ *ref* (coll) to grow thin; (coll) to be affected, to be finical
**alfeñique** *m* almond-flavored sugar paste; (coll) affectation, prudery; (coll) thin, delicate person, weakling
**alfé·rez** *m* (*pl* **-reces**) (mil) second lieutenant; (mil) subaltern (Brit); **alférez de fragata** (nav) ensign; **alférez de navío** (nav) lieutenant (j.g.)
**alfil** *m* bishop
**alfiler** *m* pin; **alfiler de corbata** stickpin, scarfpin; **alfiler de madera** clothespin; **alfiler de seguridad** safety pin; **alfileres** pin money
**alfilerar** *tr* to pin, to pin up
**alfiletero** *m* pincase, needlecase
**alfombra** *f* carpet; rug
**alfombrar** *tr* to carpet
**alforfón** *m* buckwheat
**alforja** *f* shoulder bag; traveling supplies; **pasarse a la otra alforja** (coll) to go too far, take too much liberty
**alforza** *f* pleat, tuck
**al·foz** *m* (*pl* **-foces**) outskirts; dependence; mountain pass
**alga** *f* alga; **alga marina** seaweed; **algas** algae
**algaida** *f* brush, thicket; sandbank
**algalia** *f* civet; catheter
**algarabía** *f* Arabic; (coll) gibberish, jabber; (coll) hubbub, uproar
**algarada** *f* outcry; uproar
**algarroba** *f* carob bean
**algarrobo** *m* carob
**algazara** *f* Moorish battle cry; din, uproar
**álgebra** *f* algebra
**algebrai·co -ca** *adj* algebraic
**álgi·do -da** *adj* cold, icy, frigid
**algo** *pron indef* something; anything; **algo por el estilo** something of the sort ‖ *adv* somewhat, a little, rather
**algodón** *m* cotton; **algodón pólvora** guncotton; **estar criado entre algodones** to be brought up in comfort
**algodoncillo** *m* milkweed
**algodono·so -sa** *adj* cottony
**alguacil** *m* bailiff; mounted police officer at the head of the processional entrance of the bullfighters
**alguien** *pron indef* somebody, someone
**algún** *adj indef* apocopated form of **alguno,** used only before masculine singular nouns and adjectives
**algu·no -na** *adj indef* some, any; not any; **alguna vez** sometimes; ever ‖ *pron indef* someone; **algunos** some
**alhaja** *f* jewel, gem; **buena alhaja** a bad egg, a sly fellow
**alharaca** *f* fuss, ado, ballyhoo; **hacer alharacas** to make a fuss
**alharaquien·to -ta** *adj* fussy, noisy
**alhe·lí** *m* (*pl* **-líes**) gillyflower (*Matthiola incana*); wallflower (*Cheiranthus*)
**alheña** *f* henna; blight, mildew
**alheñar** *tr* to henna; to blight, mildew ‖ *ref* (*el pelo*) to henna
**alhucema** *f* lavender
**alhumajo** *m* pine needles
**alia·do -da** *adj* allied ‖ *mf* ally
**aliaga** *f* furze, gorse
**alianza** *f* alliance; wedding ring; (Bib) covenant
**aliar** §77 *tr* to ally ‖ *ref* to ally, become allied; to form an alliance
**alias** *adv* & *m* alias
**alicaí·do -da** *adj* failing, weak; (coll) crestfallen, discouraged
**alicates** *mpl* pliers
**aliciente** *m* inducement, incentive
**alienar** *tr* to alienate; to enrapture
**aliento** *m* breath, breathing; courage, spirit; **dar aliento a** to encourage; **de mucho aliento** arduous, difficult, endless; **nuevo aliento** second wind; **sin aliento** out of breath
**alifafe** *m* (coll) complaint, indisposition
**aligerar** *tr* to lighten; to alleviate, to ease; to hasten; to shorten
**aligustre** *m* privet
**alijador** *m* lighter; lighterman; sander
**alijar** *tr* to unload, to lighten; to sandpaper
**alimaña** *f* varmint, small predacious animal
**alimentar** *tr* to feed, nourish; (*p.ej., esperanzas*) to cherish, foster ‖ *ref* to feed, to nourish oneself
**alimenti·cio -cia** *adj* alimentary, nourishing
**alimento** *m* food, nourishment; encouragement; **alimentos** foodstuffs; allowance; alimony
**alindar** *tr* to mark off; to embellish, to prettify ‖ *intr* to border, be contiguous
**alinear** *tr* & *ref* to align, to line up
**aliñar** *tr* to dress, to season
**aliño** *m* dressing, seasoning
**aliquebra·do -da** *adj* (coll) crestfallen
**alisar** *tr* to smooth; to polish, to sleek; to iron lightly
**aliso** *m* alder tree
**alistar** *tr* to list; to enlist, to enroll; to stripe ‖ *ref* to enlist, to enroll; to get ready
**aliteración** *f* alliteration
**aliviar** *tr* to alleviate, to relieve, to soothe; to remedy; to lighten; to hasten ‖ *ref* to get better, to recover
**alivio** *m* alleviation, relief; remedy
**aljaba** *f* quiver
**aljama** *f* mosque; synagogue; Moorish quarter; ghetto
**aljamía** *f* Spanish of Moors and Jews; Spanish written in Arabic characters
**aljez** *m* gypsum
**aljibe** *m* water tender, tank barge; oil tanker; cistern
**aljófar** *m* imperfect pearl; (fig) dewdrops
**aljofifa** *f* floor mop
**aljofifar** *tr* to mop
**alma** *f* soul, heart, spirit; (*persona*) living soul; crux, heart; sweetheart; (*de carril*) web; (*de cañón*) bore; (*de escalera*) newel; **dar el alma,**

**entregar el alma, rendir el alma** to give up the ghost
**almacén** *m* warehouse; store, department store; storehouse; (phot) magazine
**almacenaje** *m* storage
**almacenar** *tr* to store; to store up, to hoard
**almacenista** *mf* storekeeper || *m* warehouseman
**almáciga** *f* seedbed, tree nursery
**almádana** *f* spalling hammer
**almagre** *m* red ocher
**almajara** *f* (hort) hotbed
**almanaque** *m* almanac; calendar
**almeja** *f* clam
**almena** *f* merlon
**almenaje** *m* battlement
**almendra** *f* almond; (*de cualquier fruto drupáceo*) kernel; **almendra amarga** bitter almond; **almendra de Málaga** Jordan almond; **almendra tostada** burnt almond
**almendrado** *m* macaroon
**almendro** *m* almond tree
**almiar** *m* haystack, hayrick
**almíbar** *m* simple syrup; fruit juice; **estar hecho un almíbar** (coll) to be as sweet as pie
**almibarar** *tr* to preserve in syrup; (*sus palabras*) to honey || *intr* to candy
**almidón** *m* starch; (Am) paste; **almidón de maíz** cornstarch
**almidona•do -da** *adj* starched; (coll) spruce, dapper; (coll) stiff, prim
**almidonar** *tr* to starch
**alminar** *m* minaret
**almiranta** *f* admiral's wife; flagship
**almirante** *m* admiral
**almi•rez** *m* (*pl* **-reces**) brass mortar
**almizcle** *m* musk
**almizclera** *f* muskrat
**almizclero** *m* musk deer
**almohada** *f* pillow; **consultar con la almohada** to sleep it over
**almohadilla** *f* cushion; pad; (Chile) pincushion
**almohaza** *f* currycomb
**almohazar** **§60** *tr* to currycomb
**almoneda** *f* auction; clearance sale
**almonedar** *tr* to auction
**almorranas** *fpl* piles, hemorrhoids
**almorta** *f* grass pea
**almorzar** **§35** *tr* to lunch on || *intr* to lunch, have lunch
**almuecín** *m* or **almuédano** *m* muezzin
**almuerzo** *m* lunch
**alna•do -da** *mf* stepchild
**aloca•do -da** *adj* mad, wild, reckless || *mf* madcap
**alocar** **§73** *tr* to drive crazy
**alocución** *f* address, speech
**áloe** *m* or **aloe** *m* aloe; aloes
**alojar** *tr* to lodge; to quarter, billet || *intr & ref* to lodge; to be quartered or billeted
**alondra** *f* lark
**aloquecer** **§22** *ref* to go crazy, to lose one's mind
**alosa** *f* shad
**alpargata** *f* hemp sandal, espadrille
**alpende** *m* tool shed; lean-to, penthouse
**Alpes** *mpl* Alps
**alpestre** *adj* alpine
**alpinismo** *m* mountain climbing
**alpi•no -na** *adj* alpine
**alpiste** *m* canary seed, birdseed; **quedarse alpiste** (coll) to be disappointed
**alquería** *f* farmhouse
**alquibla** *f* kiblah
**alquiladi•zo -za** *adj & mf* hireling
**alquilar** *tr* to rent, to let, to hire || *ref* to hire out; to be for rent
**alquiler** *m* rent, rental, hire; **alquiler de coches** car-rental service; **alquiler sin chófer** drive-yourself service; **de alquiler** for rent, for hire
**alquilona** *f* cleaning woman, charwoman
**alquimia** *f* alchemy
**alquitarar** *tr* to distill
**alquitrán** *m* tar; **alquitrán de hulla** coal tar
**alquitranado** *m* tarpaulin
**alquitranar** *tr* to tar
**alrededor** *adv* around; **alrededor de** around; about, approximately || **alrededores** *mpl* environs, surroundings, outskirts
**Alsacia** *f* Alsace
**alsacia•no -na** *adj & mf* Alsatian
**alta** *f* discharge from hospital; (mil) certificate of induction into active service; **dar de alta** to discharge from the hospital; **darse de alta** to join, be admitted; (mil) to report for duty
**altane•ro -ra** *adj* towering; arrogant, haughty
**altar** *m* altar; **altar mayor** high altar; **conducir al altar** to lead to the altar
**alta•voz** *m* (*pl* **-voces**) loudspeaker
**altea** *f* (bot) marsh mallow
**alteración** *f* alteration; disturbance; uneven pulse; altercation, quarrel
**alterar** *tr* to alter; to disturb; to agitate, upset; to falsify; to lessen || *ref* to alter; to be disturbed; to be agitated; to lessen; (*el pulso*) to flutter
**altercación** *f* or **altercado** *m* argument, wrangle, bickering
**altercar** **§73** *intr* to argue, bicker, wrangle
**alternar** *tr & intr* to alternate; **alternar con** to go around with
**alternativa** *f* choice, option; admission as a matador; **no tener alternativa** to have no choice
**alter•no -na** *adj* alternate
**alteza** *f* sublimity || **Alteza** *f* (*tratamiento*) Highness
**altibajo** *m* downward thrust; **altibajos** uneven ground; ups and downs
**altillo** *m* hillock; (*oficina en una tienda o taller*) balcony; (Arg, Ecuad) attic, garret
**altimetría** *f* altimetry
**altiplanicie** *f* tableland
**altitud** *f* altitude; height
**altivez** *f* or **altiveza** *f* arrogance, haughtiness, pride
**alti•vo -va** *adj* haughty, proud; high, lofty
**al•to -ta** *adj* high; upper; top; loud;

(*horas*) late; **ponerse tan alto** to take offense, to be hoity-toity || *m* height, altitude; story, floor; stop, halt; **de alto a bajo** from top to bottom; **hacer alto** to stop; **pasar por alto** to overlook, disregard || *f* see **alta** || **alto** *adv* high up; loud; aloud || **alto** *interj* halt!

**altoparlante** *m* loudspeaker

**altozanero** *m* (Col) public errand boy

**altozano** *m* hill, knoll; upper part of town; (CAm, Col, Ven) parvis

**altruísta** *adj* altruistic || *mf* altruist

**altura** *f* height, altitude; high seas; juncture, point, stage; (mus) pitch; (naut) latitude; **a estas alturas** at this juncture; **a la altura de** (naut) off; **estar a la altura de** to be up to, to be equal to; to be abreast of; **por estas alturas** (coll) around here

**alucinación** *f* hallucination

**alud** *m* avalanche

**aludi•do -da** *adj* above-mentioned

**aludir** *intr* to allude

**alumbra•do -da** *adj* lighted; enlightened; (coll) tipsy || *m* lighting; lighting system

**alumbramiento** *m* lighting; childbirth, accouchement

**alumbrar** *tr* to light, illuminate; (*a los ciegos*) to give sight to; to enlighten; (*aguas subterráneas*) to discover and bring to the surface || *intr* to have a child || *ref* (coll) to get tipsy

**alumbre** *m* alum

**aluminio** *m* aluminum

**alumnado** *m* student body

**alum•no -na** *mf* (*niño criado como si fuera hijo*) foster child; (*discípulo*) pupil, student; **alumno mimado** teacher's pet

**alunizaje** *m* lunar landing

**alunizar** **§60** *intr* to land on the moon

**alusión** *f* allusion

**álveo** *m* bed of a stream, river bed

**alvéolo** *m* alveolus; (*de diente*) socket; (*de rueda de agua*) bucket

**alza** *f* rise, advance, increase; **jugar al alza** to bull the market

**alzada** *f* height (*e.g., of a horse*)

**alzado** *m* lump sum, cash settlement; front elevation; (bb) quire, gathering

**alzapaño** *m* curtain holder; tieback

**alzapié** *m* snare, trap

**alzaprima** *f* crowbar, lever; (*de instrumento de arco*) (mus) bridge

**alzaprimar** *tr* to pry, pry up; to arouse, stir up

**alzapuer•tas** *m* (*pl* **-tas**) (archaic) dumb player, supernumerary

**alzar** **§60** *tr* to raise, lift, hoist; to pick up; (*la hostia*) to elevate; to hide, lock up; (*naipes*) to cut; (bb) to gather || *ref* to rise, to get up; to revolt; **alzarse con** to abscond with

**alzaválvu•las** *m* (*pl* **-las**) tappet

**allá** *adv* there, over there; back there; **allá en** over in; back in; **el más allá** the beyond; **más allá** farther on, farther away; **más allá de** beyond; **por allá** thereabouts; that way

**allanar** *tr* to level, smooth, flatten; (*una dificultad*) to iron out, to overcome, to get around; (*una casa*) to break into; the subdue || *intr* to level off || *ref* to tumble down; to yield, to submit; to humble oneself

**allega•do -da** *adj* near, close; related; partisan || *mf* relative; partisan

**allegar** **§44** *tr* to collect, gather; to reap || *intr* to approach || *ref* to approach; to be attached, be a follower, agree

**allende** *adv* beyond; **allende de** besides, in addition to || *prep* beyond

**allí** *adv* there; **allí dentro** in there; **por allí** that way; around there

**ama** *f* housekeeper; housewife, lady of the house; landlady, proprietress; **ama de casa** housewife; **ama de cría** or **de leche** wet nurse; **ama de llaves** housekeeper; **ama seca** dry nurse

**amable** *adj* amiable, kind, obliging; (*digno de ser amado*) lovable

**ama•do -da** *adj & mf* beloved

**ama•dor -dora** *adj* fond, loving || *mf* lover

**amadrigar** **§44** *tr* to welcome, receive with open arms || *ref* to burrow; to go into seclusion

**amaestrar** *tr* to teach, to coach; (*a los animales*) to train

**amagar** **§44** *tr* to show signs of, to threaten; to feint || *intr* to look threatening

**amago** *m* threat, menace; sign, indication; feint

**amainar** *tr* to lessen; (naut) to lower, shorten || *intr* to subside, die down; to lessen; to yield || *ref* to lessen; to yield

**amalgama** *f* amalgam

**amalgamar** *tr & ref* to amalgamate

**amamantar** *tr* to nurse, to suckle

**amancebamiento** *m* cohabitation, concubinage, liaison

**amancebar** *ref* to cohabit, to live in concubinage

**amancillar** *tr* to stain, spot; to sully, to tarnish

**amanecer** *m* dawn, daybreak || *v* **§22** *intr* to dawn, to begin to get light; to begin to appear; to get awake, to start the day

**amanecida** *f* dawn, daybreak

**amanera•do -da** *adj* mannered, affected

**amansar** *tr* (*a un animal*) to tame; (*a un caballo*) to break; to soothe, to appease

**amante** *adj* fond, loving || *mf* lover

**amaño** *m* skill, cleverness, dexterity; trick; **amaños** tools, implements

**amapola** *f* poppy

**amar** *tr* to love

**amaraje** *m* alighting on water

**amarar** *intr* to alight on water

**amargar** **§44** *tr* to make bitter; to embitter; (*una tertulia, una velada*) to spoil || *intr & ref* to become bitter; to become embittered

**amar•go -ga** *adj* bitter; sour; distressing || **amargos** *mpl* bitters

**amargura** *f* bitterness; sorrow, grief

**amarillear** *intr* to turn yellow, to show yellow

**amarillecer** §22 *intr* to become yellow
**amarillen•to -ta** *adj* yellowish
**amarillez** *f* yellowness
**amari•llo -lla** *adj & m* yellow
**amarra** *f* mooring cable; **amarras** support, protection; **soltar las amarras** (naut) to cast off
**amarrar** *tr* to moor; to lash, to tie up; (*las cartas*) to stack
**amartelar** *tr* to make love to; to make jealous || *ref* to fall in love; to become jealous
**amartillar** *tr* to hammer; (*un arma de fuego*) to cock
**amasar** *tr* to knead; to mix; to massage; (*dinero*) to amass; to concoct
**amatista** *f* amethyst
**Amazonas** *m* Amazon
**ambages** *mpl* ambiguity, quibbling; **sin ambages** straight to the point
**ámbar** *m* amber
**Amberes** *f* Antwerp
**ambición** *f* ambition
**ambicionar** *tr* to strive for, to be eager for
**ambicio•so -sa** *adj* ambitious; eager; **ambicioso de figurar** social climber
**ambiente** *m* atmosphere
**ambi•gú** *m* (*pl* **-gúes**) buffet supper; bar, refreshment bar
**ambigüedad** *f* ambiguity
**ambi•guo -gua** *adj* ambiguous; (*género*) (gram) common
**ámbito** *m* boundary, limit; compass, scope
**ambladura** *f* amble
**amblar** *intr* to amble
**am•bos -bas** *adj & pron indef* both; **ambos a dos** both, both together
**ambrosía** *f* ragweed
**ambulancia** *f* ambulance; **ambulancia de correos** mail car, railway post office
**ambulante** *adj* itinerant, traveling || *m* railway mail clerk
**amedrentar** *tr* to frighten, to scare
**amelona•do -da** *adj* melon-shaped; (coll) mentally retarded; (coll) lovesick
**amén** *interj* amen! || *m* amen || *adv* — **amén de** (coll) aside from; (coll) in addition to
**amenaza** *f* threat, menace
**amenazar** §60 *tr* to threaten, menace
**amenguar** §10 *tr* to lessen, to diminish; to belittle; to dishonor
**amenidad** *f* amenity
**amenizar** §60 *tr* to make pleasant, to brighten, to cheer
**ame•no -na** *adj* agreeable, pleasant
**amento** *m* catkin
**América** *f* America; **la América Central** Central America; **la América del Norte** North America; **la América del Sur** South America; **la América Latina** Latin America
**americana** *f* sack coat, jacket
**americanizar** §60 *tr* to Americanize
**america•no -na** *adj & mf* American; Spanish American || *f* see **americana**
**amerizar** §60 *intr* to alight on water
**ametralladora** *f* machine gun
**ametrallar** *tr* to machine-gun
**amiba** *f* amoeba
**amiga** *f* friend; mistress; schoolmistress; girls' school
**amigable** *adj* amicable, friendly
**amigacho** *m* (coll) chum, crony, pal
**amígdala** *f* tonsil
**amigdalitis** *f* tonsillitis
**ami•go -ga** *adj* friendly; fond || *mf* friend; sweetheart; **amigo del alma** bosom friend || *f* see **amiga**
**amigote** *m* (coll) chum, crony, pal
**amilanar** *tr* to terrify, intimidate
**aminorar** *tr* to lessen, to diminish
**amistad** *f* friendship; liaison; **hacer las amistades** (coll) to make up; **romper las amistades** (coll) to fall out, become enemies
**amistar** *tr* to bring together || *ref* to become friends
**amisto•so -sa** *adj* friendly
**amnistía** *f* amnesty
**amnistiar** §77 *tr* to amnesty, to grant amnesty to
**amo** *m* head of family; landlord, proprietor; boss; **ser el amo del cotarro** (coll) to rule the roost
**amoblar** §61 *tr* to furnish
**amodorrar** *ref* to get drowsy; to fall asleep; to grow numb
**amohinar** *tr* to annoy, irritate, vex
**amojonar** *tr* to mark off with landmarks
**amoladera** *f* grindstone, whetstone
**amolar** §61 *tr* to grind, sharpen; (coll) to bore, to annoy
**amoldar** *tr* to mold; to model, to pattern, to fashion; to adjust, adapt
**amonestación** *f* admonition; marriage banns
**amonestar** *tr* to admonish, to warn; to publish the banns of
**amoníaco** *m* ammonia
**amontonar** *tr* to heap, pile; to accumulate; to hoard || *ref* to collect, to gather; to crowd; (coll) to get angry; (Mex) to gang up
**amor** *m* love; **al amor del agua** with the current; obligingly; **al amor de la lumbre** by the fire, in the warmth of the fire; **amores** love affair; **amor propio** amour-propre; conceit; **por amor de** for the sake of
**amorata•do -da** *adj* livid, black-and-blue
**amordazar** §60 *tr* to muzzle; to gag
**amorío** *m* (coll) love-making; (coll) love affair
**amoro•so -sa** *adj* loving, affectionate, amorous
**amortajar** *tr* to shroud; (carp) to mortise
**amortecer** §22 *tr* to deaden, to muffle || *ref* to die away, become faint
**amortiguador** *m* shock absorber; door check; (*de automóvil*) bumper; **amortiguador de luz** dimmer; **amortiguador de ruido** muffler
**amortiguar** §10 *tr* to deaden, to muffle; to soften, tone down; to dim; to damp; (*un golpe*) to cushion; (*ondas electromagnéticas*) to damp

**amortizar** §60 *tr* to amortize; (*una deuda*) to pay off
**amoscar** §73 *ref* (coll) to get peeved; (Mex) to blush, be embarrassed
**amotina•do -da** *adj* mutinous, rebellious || *mf* mutineer, rebel, rioter
**amotinar** *tr* to stir up; to incite to mutiny || *ref* to rise up, mutiny, rebel
**amover** §47 *tr* to discharge, dismiss
**amovible** *adj* removable, detachable
**amparar** *tr* to shelter, protect || *ref* to seek shelter; to protect oneself
**amparo** *m* shelter, protection, refuge; stall; aid, favor
**amperio** *m* ampere
**amperio-hora** *m* (*pl* **amperios-hora**) ampere-hour
**ampliación** *f* amplification; (phot) enlargement
**ampliar** §77 *tr* to amplify, enlarge; to widen; (phot) to enlarge
**amplificador** *m* amplifier
**amplificar** §73 *tr* to amplify; to expand, enlarge; to magnify
**am•plio -plia** *adj* ample; spacious, roomy
**amplitud** *f* amplitude; roominess
**ampo** *m* dazzling white; snowflake
**ampolla** *f* blister; bubble; cruet; bulb, light bulb
**ampollar** *tr* & *ref* to blister
**ampolleta** *f* vial; sandglass, hourglass; bulb, light bulb; cruet
**ampulosidad** *f* bombast, pomposity
**ampulo•so -sa** *adj* bombastic, pompous
**amputar** *tr* to amputate
**amueblar** *tr* to furnish
**amujera•do -da** *adj* effeminate
**amuleto** *m* amulet, charm
**amurallar** *tr* to wall, to wall in
**amurcar** §73 *tr* to gore
**amusgar** §44 *tr* (*las orejas el toro, el caballo*) to throw back
**anacardo** *m* cashew; cashew nut
**anacronismo** *m* anachronism
**ánade** *mf* duck
**anadear** *intr* to waddle
**anadeo** *m* waddle, waddling
**anales** *mpl* annals
**analfabetismo** *m* illiteracy
**analfabe•to -ta** *adj* & *mf* illiterate
**análi•sis** *m* & *f* (*pl* **-sis**) analysis; **análisis gramatical** parsing; **análisis ocupacional** job analysis
**analista** *mf* analyst; annalist
**analíti•co -ca** *adj* analytic(al)
**analizar** §60 *tr* to analyze; **analizar gramaticalmente** to parse
**analogía** *f* analogy; similarity
**análo•go -ga** *adj* analogous; similar
**ana•ná** *m* (*pl* **-naes**) pineapple
**ananás** *m* pineapple
**anaquel** *m* shelf
**anaranja•do -da** *adj* & *m* (*color*) orange
**anarquía** *f* anarchy
**anárqui•co -ca** *adj* anarchic(al)
**anarquista** *mf* anarch, anarchist
**anatema** *m* & *f* anathema; curse
**anatomía** *f* anatomy
**anatómi•co -ca** *adj* anatomic(al) || *mf* anatomist
**anatomista** *mf* anatomist
**anca** *f* croup, haunch; buttock, rump; **a ancas** or **a las ancas** mounted behind another person
**ancianidad** *f* old age
**ancia•no -na** *adj* old, aged || *m* old man; (eccl) elder || *f* old woman
**ancla** *f* anchor; **echar anclas** to cast anchor; **levar anclas** to weigh anchor
**anclar** *intr* to anchor
**anclote** *m* kedge, kedge anchor
**ancón** *m* bay, cove
**áncora** *f* anchor
**ancorar** *intr* to anchor
**an•cho -cha** *adj* wide, broad; full, ample; loose, loose-fitting || *m* width, breadth
**anchoa** *f* anchovy
**anchura** *f* width, breadth; fullness, ampleness; looseness; comfort, ease
**anchuro•so -sa** *adj* wide, broad; spacious, roomy
**andada** *f* thin, hard-baked cracker; **andadas** (*de conejos y otros animales*) tracks; **volver a los andadas** to revert to one's old tricks
**andaderas** *fpl* gocart, walker
**anda•do -da** *adj* gone by, elapsed; frequented, trodden; worn, used; ordinary || *m* (Am) gait || *f* see **andada**
**andadores** *mpl* leading strings
**andadura** *f* pace, gait; amble; (Mex) mount
**Andalucía** *f* Andalusia
**anda•luz -luza** *adj* & *mf* Andalusian
**andaluzada** *f* (coll) tall story, exaggeration, fish story
**andamiaje** *m* scaffolding
**andamio** *m* scaffold; platform
**andanada** *f* (naut) broadside; (taur) covered upper section; (coll) scolding; (fig) fusillade
**andante** *adj* walking; errant, wandering
**andanza** *f* wandering, rambling; fate, fortune
**andar** *m* gait, pace, walk || §5 *tr* (*p.ej., dos millas*) to go; (*un camino*) to go down or up || *intr* to go, to walk; to run; to travel; to act, to behave; (*p.ej., un reloj*) to go, to run, to work; to be, to feel; to go by, to pass, to elapse; to go (*to bear up, to last*), e.g., **anduve diez horas sin comer** I went ten hours without eating || *ref* to go by, to pass, to elapse; to go away; **andarse sin** to go without
**andarie•go -ga** *adj* wandering, roving; swift, fleet
**andas** *fpl* litter; stretcher; bier
**andén** *m* railway platform; quay; footpath
**Andes** *mpl* Andes
**andi•no -na** *adj* Andean
**andraje•ro -ra** *mf* ragpicker
**andrajo** *m* rag, tatter; ragamuffin, scalawag
**andrajo•so -sa** *adj* ragged, raggedy, in tatters

**andurriales** *mpl* byways, out-of-the-way place
**anea** *f* cattail, bulrush
**aneblar** §2 *tr* to cloud; to becloud ‖ *ref* to become clouded; to get dark
**anécdota** *f* anecdote
**anegar** §44 *tr* to flood; to drown ‖ *ref* to become flooded; to drown
**ane•jo -ja** *adj* annexed; accessory ‖ *m* annex; dependency; supplement
**anemia** *f* anaemia
**anémi•co -ca** *adj* anaemic
**anestesia** *f* anaesthesia
**anestesiar** *tr* anaesthetize
**anestési•co -ca** *adj & m* anaesthetic
**aneurisma** *m & f* aneurysm
**anexar** *tr* to annex
**ane•xo -xa** *adj* annexed; accessory ‖ *m* annex; dependency
**anfi•bio -bia** *adj* amphibious
**anfiteatro** *m* amphitheater
**anfitrión** *m* (coll) host
**anfitriona** *f* (coll) hostess
**ánfora** *f* (Am) voting urn, ballot box
**anfractuo•so -sa** *adj* winding, tortuous
**angarillas** *fpl* handbarrow; panniers; cruet stand
**ángel** *m* angel; **ángel custodio** or **de la guarda** guardian angel; **ángel patudo** (coll) wolf in sheep's clothing; **tener ángel** to have great charm
**angelical** or **angéli•co -ca** *adj* angelic(al)
**angina** *f* angina; **angina de pecho** angina pectoris
**angloparlante** *adj* English-speaking ‖ *mf* speaker of English
**anglosa•jón -jona** *adj & mf* Anglo-Saxon
**angos•to -ta** *adj* narrow
**anguila** *f* eel; **anguilas** (*para botar un barco al agua*) ways; **escurrirse como una anguila** to be as slippery as an eel
**angular** *adj* angular
**ángulo** *m* angle; corner
**angulo•so -sa** *adj* (*facciones*) angular
**angustia** *f* anguish, distress, grief
**angustia•do -da** *adj* distressed, grieved
**angustiar** *tr* to distress, afflict, grieve
**angustio•so -sa** *adj* distressed, grieved; worrisome
**anhelar** *tr* to crave, to want badly ‖ *intr* to pant; to yearn; **anhelar por** to long for
**anhélito** *m* hard breathing
**anhelo** *m* craving; yearning, longing
**anhelo•so -sa** *adj* eager, yearning; breathless, panting
**anhi•dro -dra** *adj* anhydrous
**Aníbal** *m* Hannibal
**anidar** *tr* to harbor, to shelter ‖ *intr & ref* to nestle, make a nest; to live
**anilina** *f* aniline
**anilla** *f* curtain ring; (*en la gimnasia*) ring; hoop
**anillo** *m* ring; cigar band; **anillo de compromiso** or **de pedida** engagement ring; **anillo sigilar** signet ring
**ánima** *f* soul; (*de arma de fuego*) bore
**animación** *f* animation; liveliness; bustle, movement
**anima•do -da** *adj* animated, lively
**animador** *m* (*de un café-cantante*) master of ceremonies
**animal** *adj & m* animal
**animar** *tr* to enliven; to encourage; to strengthen; to drive ‖ *ref* to take heart, feel encouraged
**ánimo** *m* mind, spirit; courage, valor, energy; attention, thought
**animosidad** *f* animosity, ill will
**animo•so -sa** *adj* brave, courageous; spirited; ready, disposed
**aniña•do -da** *adj* babyish, childish
**anión** *m* anion
**aniquilar** *tr* to annihilate, destroy ‖ *ref* to be annihilated; to decline, waste away; to be humbled
**anís** *m* anise; anise-flavored brandy
**aniversa•rio -ria** *adj & m* anniversary
**anoche** *adv* last night
**anochecer** *m* nightfall, dusk ‖ *v* §22 *intr* to grow dark; to arrive or happen at nightfall; to end the day; to go to sleep ‖ *ref* to get dark; to get cloudy; (coll) to slip away
**anochecida** *f* nightfall, dusk
**anodi•no -na** *adj* innocuous, ineffective, harmless
**ánodo** *m* anode
**anomalía** *f* anomaly
**anóma•lo -la** *adj* anomalous
**anonadar** *tr* to annihilate, destroy; to overwhelm; to humble
**anóni•mo -ma** *adj* anonymous ‖ *m* anonymity; **guardar** or **conservar el anónimo** to preserve one's anonymity
**anormal** *adj* abnormal
**anotar** *tr* to annotate; **to note, jot** down; to point out
**anquilosa•do -da** *adj* stiff-jointed; old-fashioned
**ánsar** *m* goose; wild goose
**ansia** *f* anxiety, anguish; eagerness; **ansias** (Ven) nausea
**ansiar** §77 & **regular** *tr* to long for, yearn for ‖ *intr* to be madly in love
**ansiedad** *f* anxiety, worry; pain
**ansio•so -sa** *adj* anxious; anguished; longing; covetous
**ant.** *abbr* **anticuado**
**anta** *f* elk
**antagonismo** *m* antagonism
**antaño** *adv* last year; of yore, long ago
**antárti•co -ca** *adj* antarctic
**ante** *prep* before, in the presence of; in front of; at, with ‖ *m* elk; buff
**antea•do -da** *adj* buff; (Mex) damaged, shopworn
**anteanoche** *adv* the night before last
**anteayer** *adv* the day before yesterday
**antebrazo** *m* forearm
**antecámara** *f* antechamber, anteroom
**antecedente** *adj* antecedent ‖ *m* antecedent; **antecedentes** antecedents
**anteceder** *tr* to precede, to go before
**antece•sor -sora** *mf* predecessor; ancestor
**antedatar** *tr* to antedate
**antedi•cho -cha** *adj* aforesaid, above-mentioned
**antelación** *f* previousness, anticipation
**antemano** — **de antemano** in advance, beforehand

**antena** *f* (ent) antenna; (rad) antenna, aerial; **en antena** on the air; **llevar a las antenas** to put on the air
**antenombre** *m* title, honorific
**anteojera** *f* spectacle case; blinker, blinder
**anteojo** *m* eyeglass; spyglass; **anteojos** eyeglasses, spectacles; binoculars; blinkers
**antepasa•do -da** *adj* before last ‖ **antepasados** *mpl* ancestors
**antepecho** *m* railing, guardrail; parapet; window sill
**antepenúltima** *f* antepenult
**anteponer** §54 *tr* to place in front; to prefer
**anteportada** *f* half title, bastard title
**anteportal** *m* porch, vestibule
**antepuerta** *f* portière
**antepuerto** *m* entrance to a mountain pass; (naut) outer harbor
**anterior** *adj* front; previous; earlier
**antes** *adv* before; sooner, soonest; rather; previously; **antes bien** rather; on the contrary; **antes de** before; **antes (de) que** before; **cuanto antes** as soon as possible
**antesala** *f* antechamber; (*p.ej., de médico*) waiting room; **hacer antesala** to dance attendance
**antiaére•o -a** *adj* anti-aircraft
**antiartísti•co -ca** *adj* inartistic
**antibéli•co -ca** *adj* antiwar
**anticartel** *adj* antitrust
**anticientífi•co -ca** *adj* unscientific
**anticipación** *f* preparation, anticipation; **con anticipación** in advance
**anticipa•do -da** *adj* future; advance; **por anticipado** in advance
**anticipar** *tr* to anticipate, hasten; to move ahead ‖ *ref* to happen early; **anticiparse a** to anticipate, to get ahead of
**anticipo** *m* anticipation; advance payment, down payment; retaining fee
**anticoncepti•vo -va** *adj & m* contraceptive
**anticongelante** *m* antifreeze
**anticonstitucional** *adj* unconstitutional
**anticua•do -da** *adj* antiquated; old-fashioned; obsolete
**anticua•rio -ria** *adj* antiquarian ‖ *mf* antiquarian, antiquary; antique dealer
**anticuerpo** *m* antibody
**antideporti•vo -va** *adj* unsportsmanlike
**antiderrapante** *adj* nonskid
**antideslizante** *adj* nonskid
**antideslumbrante** *adj* antiglare
**antidetonante** *adj & m* antiknock
**antídoto** *m* antidote
**antieconómi•co -ca** *adj* uneconomic(al)
**antier** *adv* (coll) the day before yesterday
**antiesclavista** *adj* antislavery ‖ *mf* abolitionist
**anti•faz** *m* (*pl* **-faces**) veil, mask
**antífona** *f* anthem
**antigás** *adj invar* gas (*e.g., mask, shelter*)
**antigramatical** *adj* ungrammatical
**antigualla** *f* antique; (coll) relic, antique; (coll) has-been
**antiguar** §10 *intr & ref* to attain seniority
**antigüedad** *f* antiquity; seniority; (*mueble u otro objeto de arte antiguos*) antique; **antigüedades** antiquities; antiques
**anti•guo -gua** *adj* old; ancient; antique; former ‖ *mf* veteran; senior
**antihigiéni•co -ca** *adj* unsanitary
**antílope** *m* antelope
**antilla•no -na** *adj & mf* West Indian
**Antillas** *fpl* Antilles
**antimonio** *m* antimony
**antiobre•ro -ra** *adj* antilabor
**antiparras** *spl* (coll) spectacles
**antipatía** *f* dislike, antipathy
**antipáti•co -ca** *adj* disagreeable, uncongenial
**antipatrióti•co -ca** *adj* unpatriotic
**antiproyectil** *adj* antimissile
**antirresbaladi•zo -za** *adj* nonskid
**antisemíti•co -ca** *adj* anti-Semitic
**antisépti•co -ca** *adj & m* antiseptic
**antisono•ro -ra** *adj* soundproof
**antisoviéti•co -ca** *adj* anti-Soviet
**antitanque** *adj* antitank
**antíte•sis** *f* (*pl* **-sis**) antithesis
**antitoxina** *f* antitoxin
**antojadi•zo -za** *adj* capricious, whimsical
**antojar** *ref* to seem; to fancy; to seem likely; to have a notion to + *inf;* to take a fancy to + *inf*
**antojo** *m* caprice, fancy, whim; snap judgment; birthmark; **antojos** moles, warts; **a su antojo** as one pleases
**antología** *f* anthology
**antónimo** *m* antonym
**antorcha** *f* torch; **antorcha a soplete** blowtorch
**antracita** *f* anthracite
**ántrax** *m* anthrax
**antro** *m* cave, cavern; (fig) den
**antropología** *f* anthropology
**antruejo** *m* carnival
**anual** *adj* annual
**anualidad** *f* annuity; year's pay; annual occurrence
**anuario** *m* yearbook; directory; bulletin, catalogue; **anuario telefónico** telephone directory
**anublar** *tr* to cloud; to dim, darken; to blight, to wither ‖ *ref* to become cloudy; to be withered; (*las esperanzas de uno*) to fade away
**anudar** *tr* to tie, fasten, knot; to unite; to resume ‖ *ref* to get knotted; to be united; to fade away, to wilt, to fail
**anuente** *adj* consenting
**anular** *tr* to annul; to nullify; to remove, to discharge ‖ *ref* to be passed over
**anunciar** *tr* to announce; to advertise ‖ *intr* to advertise
**anunciante** *mf* advertiser
**anuncio** *m* announcement; advertisement
**anverso** *m* obverse
**anzuelo** *m* fishhook; **picar en el anzuelo** or **tragar el anzuelo** to swallow the bait, swallow the hook

**añadi•do -da** *adj* additional || *m* false hair, switch
**añadidura** *f* addition; extra weight, extra measure; **de añadidura** extra, in the bargain; **por añadidura** besides
**añadir** *tr* to add; to increase
**añafil** *m* straight Moorish trumpet
**añagaza** *f* bird call; decoy, lure; trap, trick
**añe•jo -ja** *adj* aged; stale; musty, rancid
**añicos** *mpl* bits, pieces; **hacer añicos** to tear to pieces, to break to pieces; **hacerse añicos** (coll) to wear oneself out
**añil** *m* indigo; bluing
**añilar** *tr* to dye with indigo; (*la ropa blanca*) to blue
**año** *m* year; **año bisiesto** leap year; **año económico** fiscal year; **año lectivo** school year; **año luz** (*pl* **años luz**) light-year; **años** birthday; **cumplir . . . años** to be . . . years old
**añoranza** *f* longing, sorrow
**añorar** *tr* to long for, to sorrow for; to grieve over || *intr* to yearn; to sorrow, to grieve
**año•so -sa** *adj* aged, old
**aojada** *f* (Col) skylight; (Col) transom
**aojar** *tr* to cast the evil eye on, to jinx
**aojo** *m* evil eye, jinx
**aovar** *intr* to lay eggs
**ap.** *abbr* **aparte, apóstol**
**apabilar** *tr* to trim
**apabullar** *tr* (coll) to mash, crush; (coll) to squelch
**apacentar §2** *tr & ref* to pasture, to graze; to feed
**apacible** *adj* gentle, mild; calm
**apaciguamiento** *m* pacification, appeasement
**apaciguar §10** *tr* to pacify, to appease || *ref* to calm down
**apachurrar** *tr* to crush, squash, mash
**apadrinar** *tr* to sponsor; to act as godfather for; to back, support; to second
**apagabron•cas** *m* (*pl* **-cas**) bouncer
**apagador** *m* extinguisher; (*de piano*) damper
**apagaincen•dios** *m* (*pl* **-dios**) fire extinguisher
**apagar §44** *tr* to extinguish, to put out; (*la luz, la radio*) to turn off; (*la cal*) to slake; (*el sonido*) to damp, to muffle; (*el fuego del enemigo*) to silence; (*la sed*) to quench; (*el dolor*) to deaden || *ref* to go out; to subside, calm down, fade away
**apagón** *m* blackout
**apalabrar** *tr* to bespeak; to consider || *ref* to agree
**apalancar §73** *tr* to raise with a lever or crowbar
**apalear** *tr* to shovel; to beat; to pile up
**apandar** *tr* (coll) to steal
**apantallar** *tr* (elec) to shield, to screen; (Am) to dazzle, amaze
**apañar** *tr* to grasp; to pick up; to steal; to repair, to mend; (coll) to wrap up || *ref* (coll) to be handy
**apañuscar §73** *tr* (coll) to crumple, to rumple; (coll) to steal; (CAm, Col, Ven) to jam, to crowd
**aparador** *m* sideboard, buffet; showcase; workshop
**aparar** *tr* to prepare; to adorn; to block; (*las manos, la falda, el pañuelo, la capa*) to hold out
**aparato** *m* apparatus; ostentation, show; exaggeration; radio set; television set; telephone; airplane; camera; bandage, application; (theat) scenery, properties; **aparato auditivo** hearing aid; **aparato de relojería** clockwork; **aparatos sanitarios** bathroom fixtures; **ponerse al aparato** to go or to come to the phone
**aparato•so -sa** *adj* showy, pompous, ostentatious
**aparcamiento** *m* parking; parking space
**aparcar §44** *tr & intr* to park
**aparcería** *f* partnership, sharecropping
**aparce•ro -ra** *mf* partner, sharecropper; (Arg) customer
**aparear** *tr* to pair, to match; to mate || *ref* to pair; to mate
**aparecer §22** *intr & ref* to appear; to show up
**aparecido** *m* ghost, specter
**aparejador** *m* builder
**aparejar** *tr* to prepare; to prime, to size; to harness
**aparejo** *m* preparation; harness; set, kit; priming, sizing; (mas) bond; **aparejos** tools, implements, equipment
**aparentar** *tr* to feign, pretend; to look, to look to be
**aparente** *adj* apparent, seeming; evident; right, proper
**aparición** *f* apparition
**apariencia** *f* appearance, aspect; sign, indication; **salvar las apariencias** to save face
**aparqueamiento** *m* parking
**aparquear** *tr & intr* to park
**aparqueo** *m* parking
**aparragar §44** *ref* (Am) to crouch, to squat; (CAm) to loll, to sprawl
**apartadero** *m* siding, side track; turnout
**aparta•do -da** *adj* distant, remote; aloof; (*camino*) side, back; different || *m* side room; post-office box; vocabulary entry; section
**apartamento** *m* apartment, apartment house
**apartar** *tr* to take aside; to separate; to push away; to shunt; (*el ganado*) to sort || *ref* to separate; to move away, keep away, stand aside; to withdraw; to get divorced; to give up
**aparte** *adv* apart, aside; **aparte de** apart from || *prep* apart from || *m* (theat) aside
**apasiona•do -da** *adj* passionate; devoted, tender, loving; sore
**apasionar** *tr* to impassion, appeal deeply to; to afflict || *ref* to become impassioned; to be stirred up; to fall madly in love
**apatía** *f* apathy

**apáti•co -ca** *adj* apathetic
**apatusco** *m* (coll) ornament, finery
**apdo.** *abbr* **apartado**
**apeadero** *m* horse block; flag stop, wayside station; platform; temporary quarters
**apear** *tr* to help dismount, to help down; to bring down; to remove; to overcome; to prop up || *ref* to dismount, get off; to back down; to stop, to put up
**apechugar** §44 *intr* to push with the chest; **apechugar con** (coll) to make the best of
**apedazar** §60 *tr* to mend, to patch; to cut or tear to pieces
**apedrear** *tr* to stone; to stone to death; to pit; to speckle || *intr* to hail || *ref* to be damaged by hail; to be pitted
**apegar** §44 *ref* to become attached, grow fond
**apego** *m* attachment, fondness
**apelación** *f* (coll) medical consultation; (coll) remedy, help; (law) appeal
**apelar** *intr* to appeal, make an appeal; to have recourse; to refer
**apeldar** *tr* — **apeldarlas** (coll) to flee, run away
**apelmazar** §60 *tr* to squeeze, compress || *ref* to cake
**apelotonar** *tr* to form into a ball || *ref* to form a ball; to curl up
**apellidar** *tr* to call, to name; to proclaim
**apellido** *m* name; surname, last name, family name; **apellido de soltera** maiden name
**apenar** *tr & ref* to grieve
**apenas** *adv* hardly, scarcely; **apenas si** hardly, scarcely || *conj* no sooner, as soon as
**apéndice** *m* appendage; (anat) appendix
**apendicitis** *f* appendicitis
**apercancar** §73 *ref* (Chile) to get moldy, to mildew
**apercibir** *tr* to prepare; to provide; to warn; to perceive; (coll) to collect || *ref* to get ready; to be provided; **apercibirse de** to notice
**apergaminar** *ref* (coll) to dry up, to become yellow and wrinkled
**aperitivo** *m* appetizer
**aperla•do -da** *adj* pearly
**apero** *m* tools, equipment, outfit; (Am) riding gear
**aperrear** *tr* to set the dogs on; to harass, plague, pester
**apersogar** §44 *tr* to tether
**apersona•do -da** *adj* — **bien apersonado** presentable; **mal apersonado** unpresentable
**apersonar** *ref* to appear in person; to have an interview
**apertura** *f* opening
**apesadumbrar** or **apesarar** *tr & ref* to grieve
**apestar** *tr* to infect with the plague; to corrupt; (coll) to sicken, to nauseate; to infest || *intr* to stink || *ref* to be infected with the plague
**apesto•so -sa** *adj* stinking, foul-smelling; pestilent; sickening
**apetecer** §22 *tr* to hunger for, to thirst for, to crave
**apetecible** *adj* desirable, tempting
**apetencia** *f* hunger, appetite, craving
**apetito** *m* appetite
**apetito•so -sa** *adj* tasty; tempting; gourmand
**ápex** *m* apex
**apiadar** *tr* to move to pity; to take pity on || *ref* to have pity
**ápice** *m* apex; bit, whit; crux; **estar en los ápices de** (coll) to be up in
**apilar** *tr & ref* to pile, to pile up
**apimpollar** *ref* to sprout, to put forth shoots
**apiñar** *tr & ref* to crowd, to jam
**apio** *m* celery
**apisonadora** *f* road roller
**apisonar** *tr* to tamp; to roll
**aplacar** §73 *tr* to placate, appease, pacify; (*la sed*) to quench
**aplanar** *tr* to smooth, make even; (coll) to astonish || *ref* to collapse; to become discouraged
**aplanchar** *tr* to iron
**aplanetizar** §60 *intr* to land on another planet
**aplastar** *tr* to flatten, crush, smash; (coll) to dumbfound
**aplaudir** *tr & intr* to applaud
**aplauso** *m* applause; **aplausos** applause
**aplazar** §60 *tr* to postpone; to convene; to summon
**aplicación** *f* appliance, application; diligence
**aplica•do -da** *adj* industrious, studious; applied
**aplicar** §73 *tr* to apply; to attribute || *ref* to apply; to apply oneself
**aplomar** *tr* to plumb; to make straight or vertical || *intr* to be vertical || *ref* to collapse; (Chile) to be embarrassed; (Mex) to be slow, be backward
**aplomo** *m* aplomb, poise, self-possession; gravity
**apoca•do -da** *adj* diffident, timid, irresolute; humble, lowly
**apocar** §73 *tr* to cramp, contract; to narrow; to humble, belittle
**apodar** *tr* to nickname; to make fun of
**apodera•do -da** *adj* empowered, authorized || *m* proxy; attorney
**apoderar** *tr* to empower, to authorize || *ref* — **apoderarse de** to seize, grasp; to take possession of
**apodo** *m* nickname
**apofonía** *f* ablaut
**apogeo** *m* apogee; (fig) height, apogee
**apolilla•do -da** *adj* moth-eaten, mothy
**apolilladura** *f* moth hole
**apolillar** *tr* (*la polilla, p.ej., las ropas*) to eat || *ref* to become moth-eaten
**apología** *f* eulogy
**apoltronar** *ref* to loaf around; to loll, to sprawl
**apontizaje** *m* deck-landing
**apontizar** §60 *intr* to deck-land
**apoplejía** *f* apoplexy
**apopléti•co -ca** *adj & mf* apoplectic
**aporcar** §73 *tr* (*las hortalizas*) to hill

**aporrear** *tr* to beat, to club, to cudgel; to annoy || *ref* to drudge, to slave
**aportación** *f* contribution; dowry
**aportar** *tr* to contribute; to bring; to lead; (*como dote*) to bring || *intr* to show up; to reach port
**aporte** *m* contribution
**aposentar** *tr* to put up, to lodge || *ref* to take lodging
**aposento** *m* lodging; room; inn
**apostadero** *m* stand, post; naval station
**apostar** *tr* to post, to station || **§61** *tr* to bet, to wager || *intr* to bet; to compete
**apostilla** *f* note, comment
**apóstol** *m* apostle
**apóstrofe** *m & f* apostrophe (*words addressed to absent person*)
**apóstrofo** *m* apostrophe (*written sign*)
**apostura** *f* neatness, spruceness; bearing, carriage
**apoyabra•zos** *m* (*pl* **-zos**) armrest
**apoyali•bros** *m* (*pl* **-bros**) book end
**apoyar** *tr* to support, hold up; to lean, rest; to abet, back || *intr & ref* to lean, rest, be supported
**apoyatura** *f* (mus) grace note
**apoyo** *m* support, prop; backing, approval
**apreciable** *adj* appreciable; estimable
**apreciación** *f* appraisal
**apreciar** *tr* to appreciate; to appraise; to esteem
**aprecio** *m* appreciation, esteem
**aprehender** *tr* to apprehend, catch; to think, conceive
**aprehensión** *f* apprehension
**aprehensi•vo -va** *adj* apprehensive
**aprehensor** *m* captor
**apremiar** *tr* to press, urge; to compel, force; to hurry; to harass; (*a un deudor*) to dun || *intr* to be urgent
**apremio** *m* pressure; urgency; compulsion; oppression; surtax for late payment; (*demanda de pago*) dun
**aprender** *tr & intr* to learn
**apren•diz -diza** *mf* apprentice; **aprendiz de imprenta** printer's devil
**aprendizaje** *m* apprenticeship; **pagar el aprendizaje** (coll) to pay for one's inexperience
**aprensar** *tr* to press; to oppress
**aprensión** *f* apprehension; misgiving, prejudice
**aprensi•vo -va** *adj* apprehensive
**apresar** *tr* to grasp, to seize; to capture
**aprestador** *m* primer
**aprestar** *tr* to prepare; (*tejidos*) to process; to prime; to size || *ref* to get ready
**apresto** *m* preparation; equipment; priming; sizing
**apresurar** *tr & ref* to hurry, to hasten
**apretadera** *f* strap, rope; **apretaderas** (coll) pressure
**apreta•do -da** *adj* compact, tight; close, intimate; dense, thick; difficult, dangerous; (coll) mean, stingy; **estar muy apretado** (coll) to be in a bad way
**apretar §2** *tr* to tighten; to squeeze; to pinch; to hug; to harass, to importune; to afflict, to beset; (*un botón*) to press; (*los puños*) to clench; (*los dientes*) to grit; (*la mano*) to shake || *intr* to pinch; to insist; to get worse; to push hard, press forward; **apretar a correr** to start running; **apretar con** (coll) to close in on || *ref* to grieve, be distressed; to crowd
**apretón** *m* pressure, squeeze; struggle; dash, run; **apretón de manos** handshake
**apretura** *f* crush, jam; tightness; fix, trouble; need, want
**aprietarropa** *m* clothespin
**aprieto** *m* crush, jam; fix
**aprisa** *adv* fast, quickly
**aprisco** *m* sheepfold
**aprisionar** *tr* to imprison; to bind, tie; to shackle
**aprobación** *f* approbation, approval; pass, passing grade
**aproba•do -da** *adj* excellent || *m* pass
**aprobar §61** *tr & intr* to approve; to pass
**aprontar** *tr* to hand over without delay; to expedite
**apropia•do -da** *adj* appropriate, fitting, proper
**apropiar** *tr* to hand over; to fit, adapt || *ref* to appropriate; to preëmpt
**aprovechable** *adj* available, usable
**aprovecha•do -da** *adj* thrifty; stingy; diligent; well-spent || *mf* opportunist
**aprovechar** *tr* to make good use of, take advantage of; (*una caída de agua*) to harness || *intr* to be useful; to progress, improve || *ref* — **aprovecharse de** to avail oneself of, to take advantage of
**aprovisionar** *tr* to provision, supply, furnish
**aproxima•do -da** *adj* approximate, rough
**aproximar** *tr* to bring near; to approximate || *ref* to come near; to approximate
**aptitud** *f* aptitude; suitability
**ap•to -ta** *adj* apt; suitable
**apuesta** *f* bet, wager
**apues•to -ta** *adj* neat, spruce, elegant || *f* see **apuesta**
**apulgarar** *ref* to become mildewed
**apuntador** *m* (theat) prompter
**apuntalar** *tr* to prop up, underpin
**apuntar** *tr* to point; to point at; to aim; to aim at; to take note of; to sharpen; to stitch, to darn, to patch; to correct; to prompt; to stake, to put up; (theat) to prompt || *intr* to begin to appear; to dawn || *ref* (*el vino*) to begin to turn sour; to register; (coll) to get tipsy
**apunte** *m* note; rough sketch; stake; (coll) rogue, rascal; (theat) cue
**apuñalar** *tr & intr* to stab
**apuñear** *tr* to punch
**apura•do -da** *adj* needy, hard up; difficult, dangerous; (coll) hurried, rushed
**apurar** *tr* to purify, refine; to clear up, verify; to finish; to drain, use up,

exhaust; to hurry, press; to annoy || *ref* to worry, grieve; to exert oneself, to strive
**apuro** *m* need, want; grief, sorrow; (Am) haste, urgency; **apuros** financial embarrassment
**aquejar** *tr* to grieve, afflict
**aquel, aquella** *adj dem* (*pl* **aquellos, aquellas**) that, that . . . yonder
**aquél, aquélla** *pron dem* (*pl* **aquéllos, aquéllas**) that; that one, that one yonder; the one; the former || *m* (coll) charm, appeal
**aquelarre** *m* witches' Sabbath
**aquello** *pron dem* that; that thing, that matter
**aquende** *adv* on this side || *prep* on this side of
**aquerenciar** *ref* to become fond or attached
**aquí** *adv* here; **aquí dentro** in here; **de aquí en adelante** from now on; **por aquí** this way
**aquiescencia** *f* acquiescence
**aquietar** *tr* to quiet, to calm
**aquilatar** *tr* to assay; to check; to refine
**Aquiles** *m* Achilles
**aquilón** *m* north wind
**ara** *f* altar; altar slab; **en aras de** for the sake of
**árabe** *adj* Arab, Arabian; (archit) Moresque || *mf* Arab, Arabian || *m* (*idioma*) Arabic
**Arabia, la** Arabia
**arábi•go -ga** *adj* Arabian, Arabic || *m* (*idioma*) Arabic; **estar en arábigo** (coll) to be Greek
**aracanga** *f* macaw
**arado** *m* plow
**Aragón** *m* Aragon
**arago•nés -nesa** *adj & mf* Aragonese
**arancel** *m* tariff
**arancela•rio -ria** *adj* tariff, customs
**arándano** *m* whortleberry; **arándano agrio** cranberry
**arandela** *f* bobèche; (mach) washer
**araña** *f* spider; chandelier
**arañar** *tr* to scratch; to scrape; (coll) to scrape together
**arañazo** *m* scratch
**araño** *m* scratching
**aráquida** *f* peanut
**arar** *tr* to plow
**arbitraje** *m* arbitration
**arbitrar** *tr & intr* to arbitrate; to referee; to umpire
**arbitra•rio -ria** *adj* arbitrary
**arbitrio** *m* free will; means, ways; **arbitrios** excise taxes
**arbitrista** *mf* wild-eyed dreamer
**árbi•tro -tra** *mf* arbiter; referee || *m* umpire
**árbol** *m* tree; axle, shaft; **árbol del caucho** rubber plant; **árbol de levas** camshaft; **árbol de mando** drive shaft; **árbol de Navidad** Christmas tree; **árbol motor** drive shaft
**arbola•do -da** *adj* wooded; (*mar*) high || *m* woodland
**arboleda** *f* grove
**arbollón** *m* sewer, drain
**arbotante** *m* flying buttress
**arbusto** *m* shrub
**arca** *f* chest, coffer; tank; ark; **arca de agua** water tower; **arca de la alianza** ark of the covenant; **arca de Noé** ark, Noah's ark
**arcada** *f* arcade; archway; stroke of bow; **arcadas** retching
**arcai•co -ca** *adj* archaic
**arcaísmo** *m* archaism
**arcaizante** *adj* obsolescent
**arcángel** *m* archangel
**arca•no -na** *adj & m* secret
**arcar** §73 *tr* to arch
**arce** *m* maple tree
**arcilla** *f* clay; **arcilla figulina** potter's clay
**arco** *m* arch; (*de cuna o mecedor*) rocker; (elec, geom) arc; (mus) bow; **arco iris** rainbow; **arco triunfal** triumphal arch; memorial arch
**arcón** *m* large chest; bin, bunker
**archiduque** *m* archduke
**archienemigo** *m* archenemy
**archipiélago** *m* archipelago; (coll) mass, entanglement || **Archipiélago** *m* Aegean Sea
**archiva•dor -dora** *mf* file clerk || *m* filing cabinet; letter file
**archivar** *tr* to file; to file away; (coll) to hide away
**archivero** *m* city clerk
**archivo** *m* archives; files; filing; (Col) office
**ardentía** *f* heartburn; (*en las olas de la mar*) phosphorescence
**arder** *tr* to burn || *intr* to burn; to blaze; **estar que arde** to be coming to a head || *ref* to burn up
**ardid** *m* artifice, trick, wile
**ardi•do -da** *adj* burnt-up; bold, intrepid; (Am) angry
**ardiendo** *adj invar* burning
**ardiente** *adj* ardent; fiery, passionate; burning, hot
**ardilla** *f* squirrel; **ardilla de tierra** gopher; **ardilla ladradora** prairie dog; **ardilla listada** chipmunk
**ardillón** *m* gopher
**ardite** *m* old Spanish coin of little value; **no me importa un ardite** (coll) I don't care a hang; **no valer un ardite** (coll) to be not worth a straw
**ardor** *m* ardor; eagerness, fervor, zeal; vehemence; courage, dash
**ardoro•so -sa** *adj* fiery, enthusiastic; balky, restive
**ar•duo -dua** *adj* arduous, difficult
**área** *f* area; small plot
**arena** *f* sand; grit; arena; **arena movediza** quicksand; **arenas** arena; (pathol) stones
**arenal** *m* sandy place; quicksand
**arenga** *f* harangue
**arengar** *tr & intr* to harangue
**arenis•co -ca** *adj* sandy, gritty; sand || *f* sandstone
**areno•so -sa** *adj* sandy
**arenque** *m* herring
**areómetro** *m* hydrometer
**arepa** *f* (Am) corn griddle cake
**arete** *m* eardrop, earring
**arfada** *f* (naut) pitching
**arfar** *intr* (naut) to pitch

**argadijo** or **argadillo** *m* bobbin, reel; (coll) restless fellow
**argado** *m* prank, trick, artifice
**argamasa** *f* mortar
**argamasar** *tr* to mortar, to plaster; (*los materiales de construcción*) to mix
**árgana** *f* (mach) crane; **árganas** panniers
**Argel** *f* Algiers
**Argelia** *f* Algeria
**argeli•no -na** *adj & mf* Algerian
**argentar** *tr* to silver
**argenti•no -na** *adj & mf* Argentine, Argentinean || **la Argentina** Argentina, the Argentine
**argolla** *f* large iron ring; (*que se pone en la nariz a un animal*) ring; (Am) engagement ring
**argonauta** *m* Argonaut
**argucia** *f* subtlety; trick
**argüir** §6 *tr* to argue, argue for; to prove; to accuse || *ref* to argue, to dispute
**argumenta•dor -dora** *adj* argumentative || *mf* arguer
**argumentar** *tr* to argue for; to prove || *intr & ref* to argue, dispute
**argumento** *m* argument
**aria** *f* (mus) aria
**aridez** *f* aridity, dryness
**ári•do -da** *adj* arid; (*aburrido, falto de interés*) dry
**ariete** *m* battering ram; **ariete hidráulico** hydraulic ram
**arimez** *m* projection
**a•rio -ria** *adj & mf* Aryan || *f* see **aria**
**aris•co -ca** *adj* churlish, surly, evasive; (*caballo*) vicious
**arista** *f* edge; (*intersección de dos planos*) ridge; (*del grano de trigo*) beard; **arista de encuentro** (archit) groin
**aristocracia** *f* aristocracy
**aristócrata** *mf* aristocrat
**aristocráti•co -ca** *adj* aristocratic
**Aristóteles** *m* Aristotle
**aristotéli•co -ca** *adj & mf* Aristotelian
**aritméti•co -ca** *adj* arithmetical || *mf* arithmetician || *f* arithmetic
**arlequín** *m* harlequin
**arma** *f* arm, weapon; **alzarse en armas** to rise up, rebel; **arma blanca** steel blade; **arma corta** pistol; **arma de fuego** firearm; **jugar a las armas** to fence; **sobre las armas** under arms
**armada** *f* fleet, armada; navy
**armadía** *f* raft, float
**armadijo** *m* trap, snare
**arma•do -da** *adj* armed; (*hormigón*) reinforced || *f* see **armada**
**arma•dor -dora** *mf* assembler || *m* recruiter of fishermen and whalers
**armadura** *f* armor; framework; skeleton; (elec) armature; (*de imán*) keeper
**armamento** *m* armament
**armar** *tr* to arm; (*un arma*) to load; (*una bayoneta*) to fix; to mount, assemble; to build; to equip; (*el hormigón*) to reinforce; (*una nave*) to fit out; (*caballero*) to dub; (coll) to start, stir up; **armarla** (coll) to start a row || *ref* to arm oneself; to get ready; (Am) to balk
**armario** *m* closet, wardrobe; **armario botiquín** medicine cabinet; **armario de luna** wardrobe with mirror; **armario frigorífico** refrigerator
**armatoste** *m* hulk
**armazón** *f* frame; assemblage; skeleton
**armella** *f* screw eye, eyebolt
**arme•nio -nia** *adj & mf* Armenian || **Armenia** *f* Armenia
**armería** *f* arms shop; arms museum; arms
**armero** *m* gunsmith; (*para las armas*) rack
**armiño** *m* ermine
**armisticio** *m* armistice
**armonía** *f* harmony
**armóni•co -ca** *adj & m* harmonic || *f* harmonica; **armónica de boca** mouth organ
**armonio•so -sa** *adj* harmonious
**armonizar** §60 *tr & intr* to harmonize
**arnés** *m* armor, coat of mail; harness; **arneses** harness, trappings; outfit, equipment; accessories
**aro** *m* hoop; rim; **aro de émbolo** piston ring
**aroma** *m* aroma, fragrance
**aromáti•co -ca** *adj* aromatic
**arpa** *f* harp
**arpar** *tr* to claw, scratch; to tear, rend
**arpegio** *m* arpeggio
**arpeo** *m* grappling iron
**arpía** *f* harpy; (coll) shrew, jade
**arpillera** *f* burlap, sackcloth
**arpista** *mf* harpist
**arpón** *m* harpoon
**arponear** *tr & intr* to harpoon
**arqueada** *f* (mus) bow
**arquear** *tr* to arch; (*la lana*) to beat; (*una nave*) to gauge; to audit || *intr* to retch || *ref* to bow
**arqueología** *f* archeology
**arquería** *f* arcade
**arquero** *m* archer, bowman
**arquitecto** *m* architect
**arquitectóni•co -ca** *adj* architectural
**arquitectura** *f* architecture
**arrabal** *m* suburb; **arrabales** outskirts
**arracada** *f* earring with pendant
**arracimar** *ref* to cluster, to bunch
**arraiga•do -da** *adj* deep-rooted; property-owning, landed
**arraigar** §44 *tr* to establish, to strengthen || *intr* to take root || *ref* to take root; to become settled
**arraigo** *m* taking root; stability; property, real estate
**arramblar** *tr* to cover with sand or gravel; to sweep away
**arrancadero** *m* starting point
**arrancar** §73 *tr* to root up, pull out, pull up; to snatch, to wrest; (*lágrimas*) to draw forth || *intr* to start; to set sail; (coll) to leave; to originate
**arranque** *m* pull; fit, impulse; jerk, sudden start; sally, outburst; (aut) start, starter; **arranque a mano** (aut) hand cranking; **arranque automático** (aut) self-starter

**arrapiezo** *m* rag, tatter; (coll) whippersnapper
**arras** *fpl* earnest money, pledge; dowry
**arrasar** *tr* to level; to wreck, to demolish; to fill to the brim || *intr* to clear up || *ref* to clear up; to fill up
**arrastra•do -da** *adj* (coll) mean, crooked || *mf* (coll) wretch, crook
**arrastrar** *tr* to drag, drag along; to drag down; to impel || *intr* to drag, to trail; to crawl, creep || *ref* to drag, to trail; to crawl, creep; to drag on; to cringe
**arrastre** *m* drag; crawl; washout; influence; haulage; (*influencia política y social*) (Cuba, Mex) drag
**arrayán** *m* myrtle
**arre** *interj* gee!, get up!
**arreador** *m* muleteer; (SAm) whip
**arrear** *tr* to drive || *intr* (coll) to hurry || *ref* to lose all one's money
**arrebata•do -da** *adj* rash, reckless; (*color del rostro*) flushed, ruddy
**arrebatar** *tr* to snatch; to carry away; to attract; to move, to stir || *ref* to be carried away, to be overcome
**arrebatiña** *f* scuffle, scramble; **andar a la arrebatiña** (coll) to scramble
**arrebato** *m* rage, fury; ecstasy, rapture
**arrebol** *m* (*de las nubes*) red; (*de las mejillas*) rosiness; (*afeite*) rouge; **arreboles** red clouds
**arrebozar** §60 *tr* to muffle || *ref* to muffle one's face
**arrebujar** *tr* to jumble together; to wrap || *ref* to wrap oneself up
**arreciar** *intr* & *ref* to grow worse; to become more violent; to grow stronger
**arrecife** *m* stone-paved road; dike; reef; **arrecife de coral** coral reef
**arredrar** *tr* to drive back; to frighten || *ref* to draw back; to shrink; to be frightened
**arregazar** §60 *tr* to tuck up
**arreglar** *tr* to adjust, regulate, settle; to arrange; to fix, repair || *ref* to adjust, settle; to arrange; to conform; **arreglárselas** (coll) to manage, to make out
**arreglo** *m* adjustment, regulation; settlement; arrangement; order, rule; agreement; **con arreglo a** in accordance with
**arregostar** *ref* (coll) to take a liking
**arregosto** *m* (coll) liking, taste
**arrellanar** *ref* to loll, to sprawl; to like one's work
**arremangar** *tr* (*las mangas*) to turn up; (*la ropa*) to tuck up || *ref* to turn up one's sleeves; to tuck up one's dress; (coll) to take a firm stand
**arremeter** *tr* to attack, assail; (*un caballo*) to spur || *intr* to attack; to be offensive to look at; **arremeter contra** to light into, sail into
**arremetida** *f* attack; (*de un caballo*) sudden start; push; short, wild run
**arremolinar** *ref* to crowd, mill around; to whirl
**arrendajo** *m* (orn) jay; (coll) mimic
**arrendar** §2 *tr* to rent; (*una caballería*) to tie || *ref* to rent, be rented
**arreo** *m* adornment; (SAm) drove; **arreos** harness, trappings
**arrepenti•do -da** *adj* repentant || *mf* penitent
**arrepentimiento** *m* repentance
**arrepentir** §68 *ref* to repent, be repentant; **arrepentirse de** (*p.ej., un pecado*) to repent
**arrequives** *mpl* finery; (coll) attendant circumstances
**arresta•do -da** *adj* bold, daring
**arrestar** *tr* to arrest || *ref* to rush boldly
**arresto** *m* arrest; boldness, daring; **bajo arresto** under arrest
**arrezagar** §44 *tr* to tuck up
**arriada** *f* flood
**arriar** §77 *tr* to flood; (naut) to lower, to strike; (naut) to slacken || *ref* to be flooded
**arriba** *adv* up, upward; above; upstairs; uptown; on top; **arriba de** up; **de arriba abajo** from top to bottom; from beginning to end; superciliously; **más arriba** farther up; **río arriba** upstream || *interj* up with . . .!
**arribada** *f* arrival (*by sea*); **de arribada** (naut) emergency
**arribar** *intr* to put into port; to arrive; (naut) to fall off to leeward; to recover, make a comeback
**arribista** *adj* & *mf* parvenu, upstart
**arribo** *m* arrival
**aricete** *m* shoal, bar
**arriendo** *m* rent, rental; lease
**arriero** *m* muleteer
**arriesga•do -da** *adj* dangerous, risky; bold, daring
**arriesgar** §44 *tr* to risk, jeopardize || *ref* to take a risk
**arrimadillo** *m* wainscot
**arrimar** *tr* to bring close, move up; (*un golpe*) to give; to abandon, neglect; to give up; to get rid of || *ref* to come close, move up; to snuggle up; to lean; to depend
**arrinconar** *tr* to corner; to put aside; to abandon, neglect; to get rid of || *ref* to live in seclusion
**arrisca•do -da** *adj* enterprising; brisk, spirited; craggy
**arriscar** §73 *tr* to risk || *ref* to take a risk; (*las reses*) to plunge over a cliff
**arrisco** *m* risk
**arrivista** *adj* & *mf* parvenu, upstart
**arrizar** §60 *tr* to reef
**arroba** *f* Spanish weight of about 25 pounds
**arrobar** *tr* to entrance, to enrapture || *ref* to be enraptured
**arrobo** *m* ecstasy, rapture
**arroce•ro -ra** *adj* rice || *mf* rice grower; rice merchant
**arrocinar** *tr* to bestialize || *ref* to become bestialized; to fall madly in love
**arrodajar** *ref* (CAm) to squat down with one's legs crossed
**arrodillar** *ref* to kneel, to kneel down
**arrogancia** *f* arrogance

**arrogante** *adj* arrogant
**arrogar** §44 *tr* to adopt ‖ *ref* to arrogate to oneself
**arrojadi•zo -za** *adj* for throwing, projectile
**arroja•do -da** *adj* bold, fearless, rash
**arrojalla•mas** *m* (*pl* **-mas**) flame thrower
**arrojar** *tr* to throw, to hurl; to emit; to bring forth; to yield ‖ *ref* to rush, rush forward
**arrojo** *m* boldness, fearlessness, rashness
**arrollado** *m* (elec) coil
**arrolla•dor -dora** *adj* sweeping, devastating
**arrollamiento** *m* winding
**arrollar** *tr* to roll; to roll up; to wind, to coil; (*al enemigo*) to rout; to dumbfound; (coll) to knock down, to run over
**arropar** *tr* to wrap, to wrap up ‖ *ref* to bundle up
**arrope** *m* grape syrup; honey syrup
**arropía** *f* taffy
**arrostrar** *tr* to face; to like ‖ *intr* — **arrostrar con** or **por** to face, to resist ‖ *ref* to rush into the fight
**arroyada** *f* gully; flood, freshet
**arroyo** *m* stream, brook; gutter; street; (*de lágrimas, sangre, etc.*) stream
**arroz** *m* rice
**arrufar** *tr* to sic, to incite
**arruga** *f* wrinkle; crease, rumple
**arrugar** §44 *tr* to wrinkle; to crease, rumple; (*la frente*) to knit ‖ *ref* to wrinkle; to crease, rumple; to shrink, shrivel
**arruinar** *tr* to ruin ‖ *ref* to go to ruin
**arrullar** *tr* to sing to sleep, to lull to sleep; (coll) to court, to woo ‖ *intr* to coo ‖ *ref* to coo; (*las palomas*) to bill
**arrullo** *m* billing and cooing; lullaby
**arrumaje** *m* stowage; ballast
**arrumar** *tr* to stow ‖ *ref* to become overcast
**arrumbar** *tr* to cast aside, to neglect; to silence; (*una costa*) to determine the lay of ‖ *intr* (*naut*) to take bearings ‖ *ref* to get seasick; (naut) to take bearings
**arsenal** *m* arsenal, armory; dockyard, shipyard
**arsénico** *m* arsenic
**art.** *abbr* **artículo**
**arte** *m* & *f* art; trick; knack; fishing gear; **artes y oficios** arts and crafts; **bellas artes** fine arts; **no tener arte ni parte en** to have nothing to do with
**artefacto** *m* artifact; appliance, device, contrivance; **artefactos de alumbrado** lighting fixtures; **artefactos sanitarios** bathroom fixtures
**artemisa** *f* sagebrush
**arteria** *f* artery
**artería** *f* craftiness, cunning
**arte•ro -ra** *adj* crafty, cunning, sly
**artesa** *f* trough; Indian canoe
**artesanía** *f* craftsmanship
**artesa•no -na** *mf* artisan, craftsman ‖ *f* craftswoman
**artesón** *m* kitchen tub; coffer, caisson (*in ceiling*)
**árti•co -ca** *adj* arctic
**articulación** *f* articulation; (*de huesos*) joint; **articulación universal** universal joint
**articular** *tr* to articulate
**articulista** *mf* feature writer
**artículo** *m* article; item; joint; (*en un diccionario*) entry; **artículo de fondo** leader, editorial; **artículos de consumo** consumers' goods; **artículos de deporte** sporting goods; **artículos de primera necesidad** basic commodities; **artículos para caballeros** men's furnishings
**artífice** *mf* artificer; craftsman
**artificial** *adj* artificial
**artificio** *m* artifice; workmanship; appliance, device; cunning; trick, ruse
**artificio•so -sa** *adj* ingenious, skillful; cunning, scheming, deceptive
**artilugio** *m* (coll) contraption, jigger
**artillería** *f* artillery
**artillero** *m* artilleryman, gunner
**artimaña** *f* trap; (coll) trick, cunning
**artista** *mf* artist
**artísti•co -ca** *adj* artistic
**artolas** *fpl* mule chair, cacolet
**artríti•co -ca** *adj* & *mf* arthritic
**artritis** *f* arthritis
**arúspice** *m* diviner, soothsayer
**arveja** *f* vetch, tare; (Chile) pea
**arzobispo** *m* archbishop
**arzón** *m* saddletree; **arzón delantero** saddlebow; **arzón trasero** cantle
**as** *m* ace; **as de fútbol** football star; **as de la pantalla** movie star; **as del volante** speed king
**asa** *f* handle; juice; **en asas** with arms akimbo
**asa•do -da** *adj* roasted; **bien asado** well done; **poco asado** rare ‖ *m* roast
**asador** *m* spit
**asadura** *f* entrails
**asalaria•do -da** *mf* wage earner
**asaltar** *tr* to assail, to assault, to storm; to overtake, overcome
**asalto** *m* assault, attack; (box) round; (mil) storm; **tomar por asalto** to take by storm
**asamblea** *f* assembly
**asar** *tr* to roast ‖ *ref* to be burning up
**asbesto** *m* asbestos
**ascendencia** *f* ancestry
**ascendente** *adj* ascending; up
**ascender** §51 *tr* to promote ‖ *intr* to ascend, go up; to be promoted; **ascender a** to amount to
**ascendiente** *adj* ascending; up ‖ *mf* ancestor ‖ *m* ascendancy, upper hand
**ascensión** *f* ascension, ascent
**ascenso** *m* ascent; promotion
**ascensor** *m* elevator; freight elevator
**ascensorista** *mf* elevator operator
**asceta** *mf* ascetic
**ascéti•co -ca** *adj* ascetic
**asco** *m* disgust, nausea, loathing; **dar asco** (coll) to turn the stomach; **estar hecho un asco** (coll) to be filthy; **hacer ascos de** (coll) to turn one's nose

up at; **ser un asco** (coll) to be contemptible; (coll) to be worthless
**ascua** *f* ember, live coal; **estar sobre ascuas** (coll) to be on needles and pins || **ascuas** *interj* (coll) ouch!
**asea·do -da** *adj* clean, neat, tidy
**asear** *tr & ref* to clean up, tidy up
**asechamiento** *m* or **asechanza** *f* snare, trap
**asechar** *tr* to set a trap for
**asediar** *tr* to besiege; to harass
**asedio** *m* siege
**asegundar** *tr* to repeat right away
**aseguración** *f* insurance policy
**asegura·dor -dora** *mf* insurer, underwriter
**asegurar** *tr* to fasten, secure; to assure; to assert; to seize; to imprison; (*garantizar por un precio contra determinado accidente o pérdida*) to insure || *ref* to make sure; to take out insurance
**asemejar** *tr* to make like; to compare; to resemble || *ref* to be similar
**asenso** *m* assent; **dar asenso a** to believe
**asentada** *f* sitting; **de una asentada** at one sitting
**asentaderas** *fpl* (coll) buttocks
**asentadillas — a asentadillas** sidesaddle
**asenta·do -da** *adj* sedate; stable || *f* see **asentada**
**asentador** *m* strap, razor strap
**asentar** §2 *tr* to seat; to place; to establish; to tamp down, to level; to hone, sharpen; to note down; (*un golpe*) to impart; (*en la mente de uno*) to impress; to affirm; to suppose || *intr* to be becoming || *ref* to sit down; to be established, to establish oneself; to settle
**asentimiento** *m* assent
**asentir** §68 *intr* to assent
**aseo** *m* cleanliness, neatness, tidiness; care; toilet
**asépti·co -ca** *adj* aseptic
**aseptizar** §60 *tr* to purify, make aseptic
**asequible** *adj* accessible, obtainable
**aserción** *f* assertion
**aserradero** *m* sawmill
**aserra·dor -dora** *mf* sawyer; (coll) fiddler || *f* power saw
**aserraduras** *fpl* sawdust
**aserrar** §2 *tr* to saw
**aserrín** *m* sawdust
**aserto** *m* assertion
**asesinar** *tr* to assassinate, to murder
**asesinato** *m* assassination, murder
**asesi·no -na** *adj* murderous || *mf* assassin, murderer
**asesorar** *tr* to advise || *ref* to seek advice; to get advice
**asestar** *tr* to aim; to shoot; (*un golpe*) to deal
**aseveración** *f* assertion, declaration
**aseverar** *tr* to assert, to declare
**asfaltar** *tr* to asphalt
**asfalto** *m* asphalt
**asfixia** *f* asphyxiation
**asfixiar** *tr* to asphyxiate
**así** *adv* so, thus; **así . . . como** both . . . and; **así como** as soon as; as well as; **así que** as soon as; with the result that; **así y todo** even so, anyhow; **por decirlo así** so to speak; **y así sucesivamente** and so on
**Asia** *f* Asia; **el Asia Menor** Asia Minor
**asiáti·co -ca** *adj & mf* Asian, Asiatic
**asidero** *m* handle; occasion, pretext
**asi·duo -dua** *adj* assiduous; frequent, persistent
**asiento** *m* seat; site; (*de un edificio*) settling; (*de una botella, una silla, etc.*) bottom; sediment; list, roll; wisdom, maturity; **asiento de rejilla** cane seat; **asiento lanzable** (aer) ejection seat; **asientos** buttocks; **planchar el asiento** (Am) to be a wallflower; **tome Vd. asiento** have a seat
**asignación** *f* assignment; salary; allowance
**asignar** *tr* to assign
**asignatura** *f* course, subject
**asila·do -da** *mf* inmate
**asilar** *tr* to shelter; to place in an asylum; to silo || *ref* to take refuge; to be placed in an asylum
**asilo** *m* asylum; shelter, refuge; (*para menesterosos*) home; **asilo de huérfanos** orphan asylum; **asilo de locos** insane asylum; **asilo de pobres** poorhouse
**asilla** *f* fastener; collarbone; **asillas** shoulder pole
**asimetría** *f* asymmetry
**asimilar** *tr* to compare; to take in || *intr* to be alike || *ref* to assimilate; **asimilarse a** to resemble
**asimismo** *adv* also, likewise
**asir** §7 *tr* to grasp, seize || *intr* to take root || *ref* to take hold; to fight, to grapple; **asirse a** or **de** to cling to
**Asiria** *f* Assyria
**asi·rio -ria** *adj & mf* Assyrian
**asistencia** *f* attendance; assistence; reward; audience, persons present; welfare, social work; (Mex) sitting room, parlor; **asistencias** allowance, support
**asistenta** *f* charwoman, cleaning woman
**asistente** *adj* attendant; present || *m* assistant, helper; bystander, spectator, person present; (mil) orderly
**asistir** *tr* to assist, help; to attend; to serve, wait on || *intr* to be present; **asistir a** to be present at, to attend
**asma** *f* asthma
**asna** *f* she-ass, jenny ass; **asnas** rafters
**asnal** *adj* donkey; (coll) brutish
**asno** *m* ass, donkey, jackass
**asociación** *f* association
**asocia·do -da** *adj* associated; associate || *mf* associate, partner
**asociar** *tr* to associate; to take as partner || *ref* to become associated; to become a partner; to become partners
**asolamiento** *m* razing, destruction
**asolar** *tr* to parch, burn || *ref* to become parched || §61 *tr* to raze, destroy
**asolear** *tr* to sun || *ref* to bask; to get sunburned

**asomar** *tr* (*p.ej., la cabeza*) to show, to stick out || *intr* to begin to show or appear; to show || *ref* to show, to appear; to stick out; to get tipsy
**asombradi•zo -za** *adj* timid, shy
**asombrar** *tr* to shade; (*un color*) to darken; to frighten; to astonish, amaze || *ref* to be frightened; to be astonished, be amazed
**asombro** *m* fright; astonishment
**asombro•so -sa** *adj* astonishing, amazing
**asomo** *m* mark, token, sign; appearance; **ni por asomo** nothing of the kind, not by a long shot
**asordar** *tr* to deafen
**aspa** *f* X-shaped figure; reel; (*de molino de viento*) wheel, vane; propeller blade
**aspar** *tr* to reel; to crucify; to annoy, harass || *ref* to writhe; to take great pains
**aspaviento** *m* fuss, excitement
**aspecto** *m* aspect
**aspereza** *f* harshness; roughness; bitterness, sourness; gruffness
**asperjar** *tr* to sprinkle; to sprinkle with holy water
**áspe•ro -ra** *adj* harsh; rough; bitter; gruff
**áspid** *m* asp
**aspirador** *m* vacuum cleaner; **aspirador de gasolina** (aut) vacuum tank
**aspirante** *m* applicant, candidate; **aspirante a cabo** private first class; **aspirante de marina** midshipman
**aspirar** *tr* to suck in, draw in; to inhale || *intr* to aspire; to inhale, to breathe in
**aspirina** *f* aspirin
**asquear** *tr* to loathe || *ref* to be nauseated
**asquero•so -sa** *adj* disgusting, loathsome; nauseating; squeamish
**asta** *f* spear; shaft; flagpole, staff, mast; antler; (*de toro*) horn; **a media asta** at half-mast; **dejar en las astas del toro** (coll) to leave high and dry
**asta•do -da** *adj* horned || *m* bull
**ástato** *m* astatine
**aster** *m* aster
**asterisco** *m* asterisk
**astil** *m* handle; shaft
**astilla** *f* chip, splinter
**astillar** *tr & ref* to chip, splinter
**Astillejos** *mpl* (astr) Castor and Pollux
**astillero** *m* dockyard, shipyard
**astro** *m* star, heavenly body; (fig) star, leading light
**astrología** *f* astrology
**astronauta** *m* astronaut
**astronáuti•co -ca** *adj* astronautic || *f* astronautics
**astronave** *f* spaceship; **astronave tripulada** manned spaceship
**astronomía** *f* astronomy
**astronómi•co -ca** *adj* astronomic(al)
**astróno•mo -ma** *mf* astronomer
**astro•so -sa** *adj* ill-fated; vile, contemptible; (coll) ragged, shabby
**astucia** *f* cunning, craftiness; trick
**asturia•no -na** *adj & mf* Asturian
**astu•to -ta** *adj* astute, cunning; tricky
**asueto** *m* day off; (coll) leisure
**asumir** *tr* to assume, take on
**asunción** *f* assumption
**asunto** *m* subject, matter; affair, business; theme; **asuntos internacionales** world affairs
**asurar** *tr* to burn; to parch; to harass, worry
**asurcar** §73 *tr* to furrow, to plow
**asustadi•zo -za** *adj* scary, skittish
**asustar** *tr* to scare, frighten
**atabal** *m* kettledrum; timbrel
**ataca•do -da** *adj* irresolute, undecided; mean, stingy
**atacar** §73 *tr* to attack; to attach, fasten; to pack, jam; (*un barreno*) to tamp; to corner, to contradict || *intr* to attack
**ata•do -da** *adj* timid, shy; weak, irresolute; insignificant; cramped || *m* pack, bundle, roll
**ataguía** *f* cofferdam
**atajar** *tr* to stop, intercept, interrupt; to partition off || *intr* to take a short cut || *ref* to be abashed
**atajo** *m* short cut; (*en un escrito*) cut
**atalaya** *m* guard, lookout || *f* watchtower; elevation
**atalayar** *tr* to watch from a watchtower; to spy on
**atanquía** *f* depilatory ointment
**atañer** §70 *tr* to concern
**ataque** *m* attack
**atar** *tr* to tie, fasten
**ataracea** *f* marquetry, inlaid work
**atarantar** *tr* to stun, daze
**atardecer** *m* late afternoon || *v* §22 *intr* to draw toward evening; to happen in the late afternoon
**atarea•do -da** *adj* busy
**atarear** *tr* to give an assignment to; to overload with work || *ref* to toil, to work hard, to keep busy
**atarjea** *f* sewer
**atarugar** §44 *tr* to peg, to wedge; to plug; to stuff, to fill; (coll) to silence, shut up || *ref* (coll) to become confused
**atasajar** *tr* to slash, hack; (*carne*) to jerk
**atascadero** *m* mudhole; (fig) pitfall
**atascar** §73 *tr* to stop, to stop up, clog, obstruct || *ref* to get stuck; to stuff oneself; to clog, get clogged
**atasco** *m* sticking, clogging; obstruction
**ataúd** *m* casket, coffin
**ataujía** *f* damascene work
**ataujiar** §77 *tr* to damascene
**ataviar** §77 *tr* to dress, adorn, deck out
**atavío** *m* dress, adornment; **atavíos** finery, frippery, chiffons
**atediar** *tr* to tire, bore
**ateísmo** *m* atheism
**ateísta** *mf* atheist
**atelaje** *m* harness
**atemorizar** §60 *tr* to frighten
**atemperar** *tr* to soften, moderate, temper; to adjust, adapt
**Atenas** *f* Athens
**atención** *f* attention; **en atención a** in view of

**atender** §51 *tr* to attend to; to heed, pay attention to; to take care of; (*a los parroquianos*) to wait on
**atener** §71 *ref* — **atenerse a** to abide by, to rely on
**ateniense** *adj & mf* Athenian
**atenta•do -da** *adj* moderate, prudent; cautious || *m* attempt, assault
**atentar** *tr* to attempt, to try to commit || *intr* — **atentar a** or **contra** (*p.ej., la vida de una persona*) to attempt || §2 *ref* to grope
**aten•to -ta** *adj* attentive; courteous, polite || *f* favor (*letter*)
**atenuar** §21 *tr* to extenuate
**ate•o -a** *adj & mf* atheist
**aterciopela•do -da** *adj* velvety
**ateri•do -da** *adj* stiff, numb with cold
**aterrada** *f* landfall
**aterrajar** *tr* to thread, to tap
**aterraje** *m* landing
**aterrar** *tr* to terrify || §2 *tr* to destroy, demolish; to cover with earth || *intr* to land || *ref* to stand inshore
**aterrizaje** *m* landing; **aterrizaje a ciegas** blind landing; **aterrizaje aplastado** or **en desplome** pancake landing; **aterrizaje forzoso** emergency landing
**aterrizar** §60 *intr* to land
**aterronar** *tr* to make lumpy || *ref* to cake, to lump
**aterrorizar** §60 *tr* to terrify
**atesorar** *tr* to treasure; to hoard; (*virtudes, perfecciones*) to possess
**atesta•do -da** *adj* stuffed, jammed; obstinate, stubborn || *m* certificate
**atestar** *tr* (law) to attest || §2 & **regular** *tr* to jam, pack, stuff, cram; (coll) to stuff
**atestiguar** §10 *tr* to attest, testify, depose
**atezar** §60 *tr* to tan; to blacken || *ref* to become tanned, become sunburned
**atiborrar** *tr* to stuff || *ref* (coll) to stuff, stuff oneself
**atiesar** *tr* to stiffen; to tighten || *ref* to become stiff; to become tight
**atildar** *tr* to mark with a tilde, dash, or accent mark; to point out; to find fault with; to tidy up, to trim, to adorn
**atina•do -da** *adj* careful, keen, wise
**atinar** *tr* to find, come upon || *intr* to guess, guess right; to be right; to manage
**atisbadero** *m* peephole
**atisbar** *tr* to watch, spy on
**atisbo** *m* glimpse, look, peek
**atizar** §60 *tr* to stir, to poke; to snuff; to rouse; (*p.ej., un puntapié*) to let go
**Atlánti•co -ca** *adj & m* Atlantic
**at•las** *m* (*pl* **-las**) atlas
**atleta** *mf* athlete
**atleticismo** *m* athletics
**atléti•co -ca** *adj* athletic || *f* athletics
**atmósfera** *f* atmosphere
**atmosféri•co -ca** *adj* atmospheric
**atoar** *tr* (naut) to tow
**atocinar** *tr* (*un cerdo*) to cut up; to make into bacon; (coll) to murder || *ref* to get angry; to fall madly in love
**atocha** *f* esparto
**atolondra•do -da** *adj* confused; scatterbrained
**atolondrar** *tr* to confuse, bewilder
**atolladero** *m* mudhole; obstacle, difficulty
**atollar** *intr & ref* to get stuck, to get stuck in the mud
**atómi•co -ca** *adj* atomic
**átomo** *m* atom
**atóni•to -ta** *adj* astounded, aghast
**atontar** *tr* to stun; to confuse, bewilder
**atorar** *tr* to clog, obstruct || *intr & ref* to stick, get stuck; to choke
**atormentar** *tr* to torment; to torture
**atornillar** *tr* to screw, screw on
**atortolar** *tr* to rattle, scare, intimidate
**atosigar** §44 *tr* to poison; to harass || *ref* to be in a hurry
**atrabanca•do -da** *adj* overworked; (Mex) hasty, rash; (Ven) deep in debt
**atrabancar** §73 *tr & intr* to rush through
**atrabilia•rio -ria** *adj* irascible, grouchy
**atracador** *m* hold-up man
**atracar** §73 *tr* to hold up; to bring up; (naut) to bring alongside, to dock; (coll) to stuff || *intr* (naut) to come alongside, to dock || *ref* (coll) to stuff; (Am) to quarrel
**atracción** *f* attraction; amusement
**atraco** *m* holdup
**atracón** *m* (coll) stuffing, gluttony; (Am) fight; (Am) push, shove
**atracti•vo -ca** *adj* attractive || *m* attraction; attractiveness
**atraer** §75 *tr* to attract
**atragantar** *tr* to choke down || *ref* to choke; **atragantarse con** to choke on
**atraillar** §4 *tr* to leash; to master, subdue
**atrampar** *ref* to fall into a trap; to be stopped up; to stick; to get stuck
**atrancar** §73 *tr* to bar; to obstruct || *intr* (coll) to stride; (coll) to read falteringly || *ref* to get stuck; (*una ventana*) to stick; (Mex) to stick to one's opinion
**atrapamos•cas** *m* (*pl* **-cas**) flytrap; (bot) Venus's-flytrap
**atrapar** *tr* (coll) to trap, to catch; to get, to land, to net
**atrás** *adv* back, backward; behind; before; previously; **atrás de** back of, behind; **hacerse atrás** to back up, move back; **hacia atrás** backwards; the other way
**atrasa•do -da** *adj* late; (*reloj*) slow; needy; back; retarded; in arrears; **atrasado de medios** short of funds; **atrasado de noticias** behind the times
**atrasar** *tr* to slow down; to retard; to set back, to turn back; to delay; to leave behind; to postdate || *intr* to be slow || *ref* to be slow; to lose time; to lag, to stay behind; to be late; to be in debt
**atraso** *m* delay, slowness; backwardness; lag; **atrasos** arrears, delinquency

**atravesar** §2 *tr* to cross, to go across; to pierce; to pass through, go through; to put crosswise; to stake, wager || *ref* to butt in; to fight, wrangle; to get stuck
**atrayente** *adj* attractive
**atreguar** §10 *tr* to give a truce to; to grant an extension to || *ref* to agree to a truce
**atrever** *ref* to dare; **atreverse con** or **contra** to be impudent toward
**atrevi·do -da** *adj* bold, daring; impudent
**atrevimiento** *m* boldness, daring; impudence
**atribuir** §20 *tr* to attribute, ascribe || *ref* to assume
**atribular** *tr & ref* to grieve
**atributo** *m* attribute
**atril** *m* lectern; music stand
**atrincherar** *tr* to entrench || *ref* to dig in
**atrio** *m* hall, vestibule; court, courtyard; parvis
**atri·to - ta** *adj* contrite
**atrocidad** *f* atrocity; (coll) enormity
**atrofia** *f* atrophy
**atrofiar** *tr & ref* to atrophy
**atrojar** *tr* (*granos*) to garner; (Mex) to befuddle
**atrona·do -da** *adj* reckless, thoughtless
**atronar** §61 *tr* to deafen; to stun || *intr* to thunder
**atropella·do -da** *adj* brusk, violent; hasty; tumultuous
**atropellar** *tr* to trample; to knock down; to run over; to disregard; to do hurriedly || *intr & ref* to act hastily or recklessly
**atropello** *m* trampling; knocking down; running over; abuse, insult; outrage
**a·troz** *adj* (*pl* **-troces**) atrocious; (coll) huge, enormous
**atto.** *abbr* **atento**
**atufar** *tr* to anger, irritate || *ref* to get angry; (*el vino*) to turn sour
**atún** *m* tuna
**aturdi·do -da** *adj* reckless, harebrained
**aturdir** *tr* to stun; to perplex, bewilder
**atusar** *tr* to trim; to smooth || *ref* to dress fancily; (*el bigote*) to twist
**audacia** *f* audacity
**au·daz** *adj* (*pl* **-daces**) audacious
**audición** *f* audition; hearing; concert; listening
**audiencia** *f* audience, hearing; audience chamber; royal tribunal; provincial high court
**audífono** *m* hearing aid; earphone
**audiofrecuencia** *f* audio frequency
**audiómetro** *m* audiometer
**auditor** *m* judge advocate; **auditor de guerra** judge advocate (*in army*); **auditor de marina** judge advocate (*in navy*)
**auditorio** *m* (*concurso de oyentes*) audience; (*local*) auditorium
**auge** *m* height, acme; boom; vogue; **estar en auge** to be booming
**augur** *m* augur
**augurar** *tr* to augur; (Am) to wish || *intr* to augur
**augurio** *m* augury; (Am) wish
**augus·to -ta** *adj* august
**aula** *f* classroom, lecture room; **aula magna** assembly hall
**aulaga** *f* gorse, furze
**aullar** §8 *intr* to howl
**aullido** *m* howl, howling
**aúllo** *m* howl
**aumentar** *tr* to augment, increase, enlarge; to promote; (coll) to exaggerate || *intr & ref* to augment, increase
**aumento** *m* augmentation, increase, enlargement; promotion; **ir en aumento** to be on the increase
**aun** *adv* even; **aun cuando** although
**aún** *adv* still, yet
**aunar** §8 *tr & ref* to join, unite; to combine, mix
**aunque** *conj* although, though
**aúpa** *interj* up!; **de aúpa** (coll) swanky; **los de aúpa** (taur) the picadors
**aupar** §8 *tr* (coll) to help up; (coll) to extol
**aura** *f* gentle breeze; breath; popularity; turkey vulture
**áure·o -a** *adj* gold, golden
**aureola** *f* halo, aureole
**auricular** *m* earpiece, receiver; **auricular de casco** headpiece
**auriga** *m* (poet) coachman, charioteer
**aurora** *f* aurora, dawn; roseate hue
**ausencia** *f* absence
**ausentar** *tr* to send away || *ref* to absent oneself
**ausente** *adj* absent; absent-minded || *mf* absentee
**auspiciar** *tr* (Am) to sponsor, foster, back
**auspicio** *m* auspice; **bajo los auspicios de** under the auspices of
**auste·ro -ra** *adj* austere; harsh; honest; penitent
**Australia** *f* Australia
**australia·no -na** *adj & mf* Australian
**Austria** *f* Austria
**austría·co -ca** *adj & mf* Austrian
**austro** *m* south wind
**auténtica** *f* certificate; certification
**autenticar** §73 *tr* to authenticate
**auténti·co -ca** *adj* authentic; real || *f* see **auténtica**
**autillo** *m* tawny owl
**auto** *m* edict; short Biblical play; miracle play; auto; **auto de prisión** commitment, warrant for arrest; **auto sacramental** play in honor of the Sacrament
**autoamortizable** *adj* self-liquidating
**autobanco** *m* drive-in bank
**autobiografía** *f* autobiography
**autobombo** *m* self-glorification
**autobús** *m* autobus, bus
**autocamión** *m* motor truck
**autocráti·co -ca** *adj* autocratic(al)
**autócto·no -na** *adj* native, indigenous
**autodefensa** *f* self-defense
**autodeterminación** *f* self-determination
**autodidac·to -ta** *adj* self-taught
**autodisciplina** *f* self-discipline
**autódromo** *m* automobile race track
**auto-escuela** *f* driving school
**autógena** *f* welding
**autogobierno** *m* self-government

**autografiar** §77 *tr* to autograph
**autógra•fo -fa** *adj* & *m* autograph
**autoguia•do -da** *adj* self-guided, homing
**automación** *f* automation
**autómata** *m* automaton
**automáti•co -ca** *adj* automatic
**automatización** *f* automation
**automóvil** *m* automobile
**automovilista** *mf* motorist
**autonomía** *f* autonomy; cruising radius
**autóno•mo -ma** *adj* autonomous, independent
**autopiano** *m* player piano
**autopista** *f* turnpike, automobile road
**autopsia** *f* autopsy
**au•tor -tora** *mf* author; (*de un crimen*) perpetrator || *f* authoress
**autoridad** *f* authority; pomp, display
**autorita•rio -ria** *adj* & *mf* authoritarian
**autoriza•do -da** *adj* authoritative
**autorizar** §60 *tr* to authorize; to legalize; to exalt
**autorretrato** *m* self-portrait
**autoservicio** *m* self-service
**autostop** *m* hitchhiking; **viajar en autostop** to hitchhike
**autostopista** *mf* hitchhiker
**auto-teatro** *m* drive-in movie theater
**autovía** *m* railway motor coach || *f* turnpike, automobile road
**auxiliar** *adj* auxiliary || *mf* auxiliary; aid, helper; substitute teacher || *v* §77 & **regular** *tr* to aid, help, assist; (*a un moribundo*) to attend
**auxilio** *m* aid, help, assistance; **acudir en auxilio a** or **de** to come to the aid of; **auxilio en carretera** road service; **primeros auxilios** first aid
**avahar** *tr* to steam; to breathe warmth on || *intr* to steam, give off vapor || *ref* to steam, give off vapor; to warm one's hands with one's breath
**aval** *m* indorsement; countersignature
**avalancha** *f* avalanche
**avalorar** *tr* to estimate; to encourage
**avaluación** *f* appraisal, valuation
**avaluar** §21 *tr* to appraise, to estimate
**avalúo** *m* appraisal, valuation
**avance** *m* advance; advance payment; (com) balance; (com) estimate; (mov) preview
**avante** *adv* (naut) fore
**avanza•do -da** *adj* advanced; **avanzado de edad** advanced in years || *f* outpost, advance guard
**avanzar** §60 *tr* to advance, extend; to propose || *intr* & *ref* to advance; to approach
**avanzo** *m* balance sheet; estimate
**avaricia** *f* avarice
**avaricio•so -sa** *adj* avaricious
**avarien•to -ta** *adj* avaricious || *mf* miser
**ava•ro -ra** *adj* miserly || *mf* miser
**avasallar** *tr* to subject, subjugate, enslave || *ref* to submit
**ave** *f* bird; fowl; **ave canora** songbird: **ave de corral** barnyard fowl; **ave de mal agüero** Jonah, jinx; **ave de paso** bird of passage; **ave de rapiña** bird of prey; **ave fría** lapwing; **ave zancuda** wading bird
**avecinar** *tr* to bring near || *ref* to approach; to take up residence
**avecindar** *tr* to domicile || *ref* to become a resident
**avejentar** *tr* & *ref* to age prematurely
**avejigar** §44 *tr, intr* & *ref* to blister
**avellana** *f* hazelnut
**avellanar** *tr* to countersink || *ref* to shrivel, shrivel up
**avellano** *m* hazel, hazel tree
**avemaría** *f* Hail Mary, Ave Maria; **al avemaría** at sunset; **en un avemaría** (coll) in a jiffy; **saber como el avemaría** (coll) to have a thorough knowledge of
**avena** *f* oats
**avenar** *tr* to drain
**avenate** *m* gruel, oatmeal gruel
**avenencia** *f* agreement; deal, bargain
**avenida** *f* avenue; allée; flood, freshet; gathering, assemblage
**aveni•do -da** *adj* — **bien avenido** in agreement; **mal avenido** in disagreement || *f* see **avenida**
**avenimiento** *m* agreement; reconciliation
**avenir** §79 *tr* to reconcile, bring together || *ref* to be reconciled, to agree; to compromise; to correspond
**aventa•dor -dora** *mf* winnower || *m* fan
**aventaja•do -da** *adj* excellent, outstanding; advantageous
**aventajar** *tr* to advance; to put ahead; to excel || *ref* to advance, win an advantage; to excel
**aventar** §2 *tr* to fan; to winnow; to scatter to the winds; to blow; (coll) to drive away || *ref* to swell up; (coll) to flee, run away
**aventón** *m* (Guat, Mex, Peru) push, shove; (*llevada gratuita*) (Mex) free ride; **pedir aventón** (Mex) to hitchhike
**aventura** *f* adventure; danger, risk
**aventura•do -da** *adj* hazardous, venturesome
**aventurar** *tr* to adventure, to venture, to hazard || *ref* to adventure, to take a risk; to venture, to risk
**aventure•ro -ra** *adj* adventuresome, adventurous || *m* adventurer, soldier of fortune || *f* adventuress
**avergonzar** §9 *tr* to shame; to embarrass || *ref* to be ashamed; to be embarrassed
**avería** *f* aviary; breakdown, failure; (com) damage; (naut) average
**averiar** §77 *tr* to damage || *ref* to suffer damage; to break down
**averiguable** *adj* ascertainable
**averiguar** §10 *tr* to ascertain, to find out
**aversión** *f* aversion, dislike; **cobrar aversión a** to take a dislike for
**aves•truz** *m* (*pl* **-truces**) ostrich
**avezar** §60 *tr* to accustom || *ref* to become accustomed
**aviación** *f* aviation
**avia•dor -dora** *mf* aviator, flyer || *m* aviator, airman; (mil) airman; **aviador postal** air-mail pilot || *f* aviatrix, airwoman
**aviar** §77 *tr* to make ready, prepare;

(coll) to equip, provide; **estar, encontrarse** or **quedar aviado** (coll) to be in a mess, be in a jam || *ref* to hurry; (aer) to take off
**avia·triz** (*pl* **-trices**) aviatrix
**avidez** *f* avidity, greediness
**ávi·do -da** *adj* avid, greedy, eager
**aviejar** *tr & ref* to age prematurely
**aviento** *m* winnowing fork, pitchfork
**avie·so -sa** *adj* crooked, distorted; evil-minded, perverse
**avilantar** *ref* to be insolent
**avilantez** *f* insolence; meanness
**avillana·do -da** *adj* rustic, boorish
**avillanar** *tr* to debase, make boorish || *ref* to become boorish
**avinagra·do -da** *adj* (coll) vinegarish, sour, crabbed
**avinagrar** *tr* to sour || *ref* to become sour; to turn into vinegar
**avío** *m* provision; arrangement; (Am) load; **¡al avío!** let's go!; **avíos** equipment, tools, outfit; **avíos de pescar** fishing tackle
**avión** *m* airplane; (orn) martin; **avión birreactor** twin-jet plane; **avión de caza** pursuit plane; **avión a chorro, avión de propulsión a chorro** or **a reacción** jet plane
**avión-correo** *m* mailplane
**avioneta** *f* small plane; **avioneta de alquiler** taxiplane
**avisaco·ches** *m* (*pl* **-ches**) car caller
**avisa·do -da** *adj* prudent, wise; **mal avisado** rash, thoughtless
**avisa·dor -dora** *adj* warning || *mf* informer; adviser || *m* electric bell; **avisador de incendio** fire alarm
**avisar** *tr* to advise, inform; to warn; to report on
**aviso** *m* advice, information; warning; care, prudence; dispatch boat; (Am) advertisement; **sobre aviso** on the lookout
**avispa** *f* wasp
**avispa·do -da** *adj* (coll) brisk, wide-awake
**avispar** *tr* to spur; (coll) to stir up || *ref* to fret, worry
**avispón** *m* hornet
**avistar** *tr* to descry || *ref* to meet, have an interview
**avituallar** *tr* to supply, provision || *ref* to take in supplies
**avivar** *tr* to brighten, enlive, revive || *intr & ref* to brighten, revive
**avizor** *adj* watchful, alert || *m* watcher; **avizores** (slang) eyes
**avizorar** *tr* to watch, spy on || *ref* to hide and watch, to spy
**ax** *interj* ouch!, ow!
**axioma** *m* axiom
**axiomáti·co -ca** *adj* axiomatic
**ay** *interj* ay!, alas! **¡ay de mí!** woe is me! || *m* sigh
**aya** *f* nurse, governess
**ayer** *adj & m* yesterday
**ayo** *m* tutor
**ayuda** *m* valet; **ayuda de cámara** valet de chambre || *f* help, aid; enema
**ayudanta** *f* assistant; **ayudanta de cocina** kitchenmaid
**ayudante** *m* aid, assistant; adjutant; **ayudante de campo** aide-de-camp
**ayudar** *tr* to aid, help, assist
**ayunar** *intr* to fast
**ayu·no -na** *adj* fasting; uninformed; **en ayunas** or **en ayuno** fasting; before breakfast; uninformed; missing the point || *m* fast, fasting
**ayuntamiento** *m* town or city council; town or city hall; sexual intercourse
**azabacha·do -da** *adj* jet, jet-black
**azabache** *m* jet; **azabaches** jet trinkets
**aza·cán -cana** *adj* menial || *mf* drudge || *m* water carrier
**azada** *f* hoe
**azadón** *m* hoe; grub hoe; **azadón de peto** or **de pico** mattock
**azadonar** *tr* to hoe
**azafata** *f* air hostess, stewardess; lady of the queen's wardrobe
**azafate** *m* wicker tray
**azafrán** *m* saffron
**azafrana·do -da** *adj* saffron
**azafranar** *tr* to saffron
**azahar** *m* orange or lemon blossom
**azar** *m* chance, hazard; accident, misfortune; fate, destiny; losing card; losing throw; (*persona o cosa que traen mala suerte*) Jonah
**azarar** *ref* to go awry; to get rattled
**azaro·so -sa** *adj* hazardous, risky; unlucky
**ázi·mo -ma** *adj* unleavened
**azófar** *m* brass
**azoga·do -da** *adj* fidgety, restless || *m* quicksilver foil; **temblar como un azogado** (coll) to shake like a leaf
**azogar** §44 *tr* (*un espejo*) to silver || *ref* to have mercury poisoning; (coll) to shake, become agitated
**azogue** *m* quicksilver; market place; (coll) mirror
**azor** *m* goshawk
**azorar** *tr* to abash; to excite, stir up
**Azores** *fpl* Azores
**azotar** *tr* to whip, to scourge; to beat; to flail; to beat down upon
**azote** *m* whip; lash; (fig) scourge; **azotes y galeras** (coll) tiresome fare
**azotea** *f* flat roof, roof terrace
**azteca** *adj & mf* Aztec
**azúcar** *m* sugar; **azúcar de caña** cane sugar; **azúcar de remolacha** beet sugar
**azucarar** *tr* to sugar, to sugarcoat; (coll) to sugar over
**azucare·ro -ra** *adj* sugar || *m* sugar bowl
**azucena** *f* Madonna lily, white lily
**azufrar** *tr* to sulphur
**azufre** *m* sulfur; brimstone
**azul** *adj & m* blue; **azul marino** navy blue
**azular** *tr* to color blue, to dye blue
**azulear** *intr* to turn blue
**azulejar** *tr* to tile, to cover with tiles
**azulejo** *m* glazed colored tile; (orn) roller; (orn) indigo bunting; (orn) bee eater
**azuzar** §60 *tr* to sic; (coll) to tease, incite

## B

**B, b** (be) *f* second letter of the Spanish alphabet
**B.** *abbr* **Beato, Bueno**
**baba** *f* drivel, spittle, slobber; (*de culebras, peces, etc.*) slime
**babear** *intr* to slobber, to drivel; to froth, foam
**babel** *m & f* (coll) bedlam, confusion; **estar en babel** (coll) to be daydreaming
**babero** *m* bib
**Babia** *f* — **estar en Babia** (coll) to be daydreaming
**babieca** *adj* (coll) silly, simple ‖ *mf* (coll) simpleton
**Babilonia** *f* (*imperio*) Babylonia; (*ciudad*) Babylon
**babilóni•co -ca** *adj* Babylonian
**babilo•nio -nia** *adj & mf* Babylonian ‖ *f* see **Babilonia**
**bable** *m* Asturian dialect; patois
**babor** *m* (naut) port
**babosa** *f* slug
**babosear** *tr* to slobber over ‖ *intr* to slobber
**babo•so -sa** *adj* slobbery; (*con las damas*) (coll) mushy ‖ *m* (CAm) scoundrel ‖ *f* see **babosa**
**babucha** *f* slipper, mule
**babuino** *m* baboon
**bacalao** or **bacallao** *m* codfish
**baceta** *f* (cards) widow
**bacía** *f* basin, vessel; shaving dish
**bacilo** *m* bacillus
**bacín** *m* chamber pot
**Baco** *m* Bacchus
**bacteria** *f* bacterium
**bacteria•no -na** *adj* bacterial
**bacteriología** *f* bacteriology
**bacteriólo•go -ga** *mf* bacteriologist
**báculo** *m* staff; crook; (fig) staff, comfort; **báculo pastoral** crozier
**bache** *m* hole, rut; blip; **bache aéreo** air pocket
**bachi•ller -llera** *adj* garrulous ‖ *mf* garrulous person ‖ **bachiller** *mf* bachelor
**bachillerar** *tr* to confer the bachelor's degree on ‖ *ref* to receive the bachelor's degree
**bachillerato** *m* baccalaureate, bachelor's degree
**bachillerear** *intr* (coll) to babble, prattle
**bachillería** *f* (coll) babble, prattle; (coll) gossip
**badajo** *m* clapper
**badana** *f* (dressed) sheepskin; **zurrarle a uno la badana** (coll) to tan someone's hide
**badén** *m* gully, gutter
**badil** *m* fire shovel
**badulaque** *m* (coll) nincompoop
**bagaje** *m* beast of burden; (mil) baggage
**bagatela** *f* trinket; triviality; (Chile, Peru) pinball
**bagazo** *m* waste pulp, bagasse
**bagre** *adj* (Bol, Col) showy, gaudy; (CAm) sly, slick; (SAm) coarse, ill-bred; (Mex) stupid ‖ *m* catfish
**bahía** *f* bay
**bahorrina** *f* (coll) slop; (coll) riffraff
**bailable** *adj* for dancing ‖ *m* ballet
**bailadero** *m* dance floor, dance hall
**baila•dor -dora** *mf* dancer
**bailar** *tr* (*p.ej., un vals*) to dance; (*un trompo*) to spin ‖ *intr* to dance; to spin; to wobble
**baila•rín -rina** *mf* dancer ‖ *f* ballerina; **bailarina ombliguista** (coll) belly dancer
**baile** *m* dance; ball; ballet; **baile de etiqueta** dress ball, formal dance; **baile de los globos** bubble dance; **baile de máscaras** masked ball, masquerade ball; **baile de San Vito** (pathol) Saint Vitus's dance; **baile de trajes** costume ball, fancy-dress ball
**baja** *f* (*de los precios*) fall, drop; (*en la guerra*) casualty; **dar baja** to go down, decline; **dar de baja** to drop; (mil) to mark absent; **darse de baja** to drop out; **jugar a la baja** to bear the market
**bajaca** *f* (Ecuad) hair ribbon
**bajada** *f* descent; slope; downspout; (rad) lead-in wire
**bajagua** *f* (Mex) cheap tobacco
**bajamar** *f* low tide
**bajar** *tr* to lower, take down; to bring down; (*la escalera*) to go down, descend; to humble ‖ *intr* to come down, to go down; to get off ‖ *ref* to bend down; to get off; to humble oneself
**bajel** *m* ship, vessel
**bajeza** *f* humbleness, lowliness; meanness, baseness
**bajío** *m* shoal, sandbank; pitfall; (Am) lowland
**bajista** *adj* bearish ‖ *mf* (fig) bear
**ba•jo -ja** *adj* low, under, lower; short; mean, base; lowly, humble; (mus) bass ‖ *m* shoal, sandbank; (mus) bass ‖ *f* see **baja** ‖ **bajo** *adv* down; low, in a low voice ‖ **bajo** *prep* under
**bajón** *m* bassoon; (*en el caudal, la salud, etc.*) (coll) decline, loss
**bajonista** *mf* bassoon player
**bajorrelieve** *m* bas-relief
**bala** *f* bullet; bale; **bala fría** spent bullet; **bala perdida** stray bullet
**balaca** *f* (Am) boasting, show
**balada** *f* ballad; (mus) ballade
**bala•dí** *adj* (*pl* **-díes**) trivial, paltry
**baladro** *m* scream, shout, outcry
**baladronada** *f* boast, boasting
**baladronear** *intr* to boast, to brag
**bálago** *m* chaff
**balance** *m* balance, balance sheet; rocking, swinging; hesitation, doubt; (*de una nave*) rolling
**balancear** *tr* to balance ‖ *intr & ref* to rock, to swing; to hesitate, to waver; (*la nave*) to roll
**balancín** *m* balance beam; singletree; rocker arm; seesaw

**balandra** *f* sloop
**balandrán** *m* cassock
**balanza** *f* scales, balance; comparison, judgment; **balanza de pagos** balance of payments
**balar** *intr* to bleat; (coll) to pine
**balastar** *tr* to ballast
**balasto** *m* ballast
**balaustre** *m* baluster, banister
**balay** *m* (Am) wicker basket
**balazo** *m* shot; bullet wound
**balbucear** *tr* to stammer || *intr* to stammer, stutter; to babble, to prattle
**balbucir** §1 *tr & intr* var of **balbucear**
**Balcanes, los** the Balkans
**balcarrotas** *fpl* (SAm) sideburns; (Mex) locks falling over sides of face
**balcón** *m* balcony
**baldar** *tr* to cripple; to incapacitate; to inconvenience; to trump
**balde** *m* bucket, pail; **de balde** free, gratis; over, in excess; **en balde** in vain
**baldear** *tr* to wash with pails of water; (*una excavación*) to bail out
**baldí•o -a** *adj* uncultivated; idle, lazy; careless; useless, vain; unfounded || *m* untilled land
**baldón** *m* insult; blot, disgrace
**baldonar** *tr* to insult; to stain, disgrace
**baldosa** *f* floor tile, paving tile; flagstone
**baldra•gas** *m* (*pl* **-gas**) (coll) jellyfish
**balduque** *s* red tape, wrapping tape
**balear** *adj* Balearic || *tr* to shoot at, to shoot, to shoot to death
**balido** *m* bleat, bleating
**balísti•co -ca** *adj* ballistic
**baliza** *f* buoy, beacon; danger signal
**balizaje** *m* (aer) airway lighting; (naut) buoys
**balizar** §60 *tr* to mark with buoys; to mark off
**balnea•rio -ria** *adj* bathing || *m* watering place, spa
**balompié** *m* football, soccer
**balón** *m* football; bale; balloon
**baloncesto** *m* basketball
**balota** *f* ballot
**balotar** *intr* to ballot
**balsa** *f* pool, puddle; raft; float; corkwood; **balsa salvavidas** life float
**bálsamo** *m* balsam, balm
**balsear** *tr* to cross by raft; to ferry across
**balsero** *m* ferryman
**bálti•co -ca** *adj* Baltic
**baluarte** *m* bulwark
**ballena** *f* whale; whalebone; (*de corsé*) stay
**ballesta** *f* crossbow; spring, auto spring
**ba•llet** *m* (*pl* **-llets**) ballet
**bambalinas** *fpl* (theat) flies, borders
**bambolear** *intr* to sway, reel, wobble
**bambolla** *f* (coll) hulk; (coll) show, sham; (coll) show-off
**bam•bú** *m* (*pl* **-búes**) bamboo
**banana** *f* banana; (rad) plug
**banane•ro -ra** *adj* banana || *m* banana tree
**banano** *m* banana tree
**banas** *fpl* (Mex) banns
**banasta** *f* hamper, large basket
**banca** *f* bench; banking; stand, fruit stand; (*en el juego*) bank; **banca de hielo** iceberg; **hacer saltar la banca** to break the bank
**banca•rio -ria** *adj* banking, bank
**bancarrota** *f* bankruptcy; **hacer bancarrota** to go bankrupt
**bancarrote•ro -ra** *adj & mf* bankrupt
**banco** *m* bench; bank; (*de peces*) school; **banco de ahorros** savings bank; **banco de hielo** iceberg; **banco de liquidación** clearing house
**banda** *f* band; ribbon; faction, party; flock; border, edge; bank, shore; (*de la mesa de billar*) cushion; **banda de rodamiento** (aut) tread; **banda de tambores** drum corps; **irse a la banda** (naut) to list
**bandada** *f* flock, covey; (*de gente*) (coll) flock
**bandaje** *m* tire
**bandazo** *m* swerving; (naut) lurch
**bandear** *tr* (Am) to go through, to pierce; (Am) to pursue; (Am) to make love to || *ref* to manage
**bandeja** *f* tray; (Am) dish, platter
**bandera** *f* flag, banner; **con banderas desplegadas** with flying colors
**banderilla** *f* (taur) banderilla; **poner una banderilla a** (coll) to taunt; (coll) to hit for a loan
**banderín** *m* (mil) color corporal; recruiting post
**banderola** *f* streamer, pennant; (Am) transom
**bandido** *m* bandit
**bando** *m* proclamation; faction, side
**bandolera** *f* bandoleer; female bandit; **en bandolera** across the shoulders
**bandolero** *m* highwayman, brigand
**bandurria** *f* Spanish lute
**banquero** *m* banker
**banqueta** stool, footstool; (Guat, Mex) sidewalk
**banquete** *m* banquet
**banquetear** *tr, intr & ref* to banquet
**banquisa** *f* floe, iceberg
**bañadera** *f* (Am) bathtub
**bañado** *m* chamber pot; (Am) marshland
**baña•dor -dora** *adj* bathing || *mf* bather || *m* bathing suit
**bañar** *tr* to bathe; to dip; to coat by dipping || *ref* to bathe
**bañera** *f* bathtub
**bañista** *mf* bather; frequenter of a spa or seaside resort
**baño** *m* bath; bathing; bathroom; bathtub; **baño de asiento** sitz bath; **baño de ducha** shower bath; **baños** bathing place; spa
**bao** *m* (naut) beam
**baptista** *adj & mf* Baptist
**baptisterio** *m* baptistery
**baque** *m* thud, thump; bump, bruise
**baquelita** *f* bakelite
**ba•quet** *m* (*pl* **-quets**) bucket seat
**baqueta** *f* ramrod; drumstick; **correr baquetas** or **pasar por baquetas** to run the gauntlet
**baquía** *f* (Am) knowledge of the road, paths, rivers, etc. of a region; (Am) manual skill

**baquia•no -na** *adj* (Am) skillful, expert || *mf* (Am) scout, pathfinder, guide
**báqui•co -ca** *adj* Bacchic
**bar** *m* bar; cocktail bar
**barahunda** *f* uproar, tumult
**baraja** *f* (*de naipes*) deck, pack; gang, mob; confusion, mix-up
**barajadura** *f* shuffling; dispute, quarrel
**barajar** *tr* (*naipes*) to shuffle; to jumble, to mix || *intr* to shuffle; to fight, quarrel || *ref* to get jumbled or mixed
**baranda** *f* railing; (*de la mesa de billar*) cushion
**barandilla** *f* balustrade, railing
**barata** *f* cheapness; barter; (Mex) bargain sale; (Chile, Peru) cockroach
**baratija** *f* trinket
**baratillo** *m* second-hand goods; second-hand shop; bargain counter
**bara•to -ta** *adj* cheap || *m* bargain sale; **dar de barato** (coll) to admit for the sake of argument; **de barato** gratis, free || *f* see **barata** || **barato** *adv* cheap
**báratro** *m* (poet) hell
**baratura** *f* cheapness
**baraúnda** *f* uproar, tumult
**barba** *f* (*parte de la cara*) chin; (*pelo en ella*) beard; (*del papel*) deckle edge; (*de ave*) gill, wattle; **barba española** Spanish moss; **barbas** whiskers; **hacer la barba a** to shave; to bore, annoy; (Mex) to fawn on; **llevar por la barba** to lead by the nose; **mentir por la barba** (coll) to tell fish stories || *m* (theat) old man
**barbacoa** *f* barbecue; (Col) kitchen cupboard; (Peru) attic
**barbada** *f* lower jaw of horse; bridle curb || **la Barbada** Barbados
**barbar** *intr* to grow a beard; to strike root
**barbaridad** *f* barbarism; outrage; piece of folly; (coll) large amount; **¡qué barbaridad!** how awful!, what nonsense!
**barbarie** *f* barbarity, barbarism
**barbarismo** *m* illiteracy; outrage; (gram) barbarism
**bárba•ro -ra** *adj* barbaric; barbarous || *mf* barbarian
**barbear** *tr* to reach with the chin; to be as high as || *intr* to reach the same height; **barbear con** to be as high as
**barbechar** *tr* to plow for seeding; to fallow
**barbecho** *m* fallow; **firmar como en un barbecho** (coll) to sign with one's eyes closed
**barbería** *f* barber shop
**barberil** *adj* barber
**barbe•ro -ra** *mf* barber; (Mex) flatterer
**barbilampi•ño -ña** *adj* smooth-faced, beardless; beginning, green
**barbilla** *f* tip of chin; (*de pluma*) barb; (*de pez*) wattle
**bar•bón -bona** *adj* bearded || *m* greybeard; solemn old fellow; billy goat
**barboquejo** *m* chin strap
**barbotar** *tr* & *intr* to mutter, to mumble
**barbu•do -da** *adj* bearded, long-bearded, heavy-bearded || *m* shoot, sucker
**barbullar** *tr* & *intr* to blabber
**barca** *f* small boat; bark
**barcia** *f* chaff
**barco** *m* boat, ship; **barco de carga** cargo boat; **barco náufrago** shipwreck
**barchi•lón -lona** *mf* (Ecuad, Peru) nurse, orderly; (Arg, Bol, Peru) quack
**barda** *f* thatch; bard, horse armor
**bardana** *f* burdock
**bardar** *tr* to thatch; (*un caballo*) to bard
**bardo** *m* bard
**bargueño** *m* carved inlaid secretary
**bario** *m* barium
**barjuleta** *f* haversack
**barloventear** *intr* to wander around; to turn to windward
**barlovento** *m* windward
**bar•niz** *m* (*pl* **-nices**) varnish; (*de la loza, la porcelana, etc.*) glaze; gloss, polish; (*conocimientos superficiales*) smattering; (aer) dope
**barnizar** §60 *tr* to varnish
**barómetro** *m* barometer; **barómetro aneroide** aneroid barometer
**barón** *m* baron
**baronesa** *f* baroness
**barquero** *m* boatman
**barquilla** *f* (naut) log; (naut) log chip; (aer) nacelle
**barquillero** *m* waffle iron; harbor boatman
**barquillo** *m* cone; waffle
**barquín** *m* bellows
**barra** *f* bar; (*de dinamita*) stick; (*en el tribunal*) bar, railing; **barra colectora** (elec) bus bar; **barra de labios** or **para los labios** lipstick; **barra imantada** bar magnet; **barras paralelas** (sport) parallel bars
**barrabasada** *f* (coll) fiendish prank, mean trick
**barraca** *f* cabin, hut; cottage; (Am) storage shed
**barracón** *m* barracks; fair booth
**barragana** *f* concubine
**barranca** *f* gorge, ravine, gully
**barranco** *m* gorge, ravine, gully; difficulty, obstruction; (Am) cliff, precipice
**barrar** *tr* to daub, to smear
**barrear** *tr* to barricade; to bar shut
**barredera** *f* street sweeper
**barre•dor -dora** *mf* sweeper; **barredora de alfombras** carpet sweeper; **barredora de nieve** snowplow
**barredura** *f* sweeping; **barreduras** sweepings
**barremi•nas** *m* (*pl* **-nas**) mine sweeper
**barrena** *f* auger, drill, gimlet; (*espiga para taladrar*) bit; (aer) spin; **barrena picada** (aer) tail spin; **entrar en barrena** (aer) to go into a spin
**barrenar** *tr* to drill; (*un buque*) to scuttle; to blast; to upset, to frustrate; to violate
**barrende•ro -ra** *mf* sweeper
**barreno** *m* large drill; drill hole; blast

hole; pride, vanity; (Chile) mania, pet idea; **dar barreno a** (*un buque*) to scuttle
**barreño** *m* earthen dishpan
**barrer** *tr* to sweep, to sweep away; to graze || *intr* to sweep; **barrer hacia dentro** to look out for oneself
**barrera** *f* barrier; barricade; (mil) barrage; crockery cupboard; tollgate; (rr) crossing gate; (taur) fence around inside of ring; (taur) first row of seats; **barrera de arrecifes** barrier reef; **barrera de paso a nivel** (rr) crossing gate
**barriada** *f* district, quarter
**barrica** *f* cask, barrel
**barriga** *f* belly; (*de una vasija, una pared, etc.*) bulge
**barri•gón -gona** or **barrigu•do -da** *adj* big-bellied
**barril** *m* barrel
**barrilero** *m* cooper, barrel maker
**barrio** *m* ward, quarter; suburb; **barrio bajo** slums; **barrio comercial** shopping district, business district; **el otro barrio** the other world; **estar vestido de barrio** (coll) to be dressed in house clothes
**barro** *m* mud; clay; earthenware; pimple; (coll) money; (Arg, Urug) blunder
**barro•co -ca** *adj & m* baroque
**barro•so -sa** *adj* muddy; pimply
**barrote** *m* heavy bar; bolt; cross brace
**barruntar** *tr* to guess; to sense
**barrunto** *m* guess, conjecture; sign, token, foreboding
**bartola** *f* (coll) belly; **a la bartola** (coll) lazily
**bartolina** *f* (CAm, W-I) jail, dungeon
**bártulos** *mpl* household tools; **liar los bártulos** (coll) to pack up one's belongings
**barullo** *m* confusion, tumult
**basar** *tr* to base; to build || *ref* — **basarse en** to base one's judgment on, to rely on
**basca** *f* nausea, squeamishness; (coll) fit of temper, tantrum
**basco•so -sa** *adj* nauseated, squeamish
**báscula** *f* scales; platform scale
**base** *f* base; basis; **a base de** on the basis of
**bási•co -ca** *adj* basic
**Basilea** *f* Basle, Basel
**basílica** *f* basilica
**basilisco** *m* basilisk; **estar hecho un basilisco** (coll) to be in a rage
**basquear** *intr* to be nauseated
**bastante** *adj* enough || *adv* enough; fairly, rather || *m* enough
**bastar** *intr* to be enough, to suffice; to abound, be more than enough || *ref* to be self-sufficient
**bastardilla** *f* italics
**bastar•do -da** *adj & mf* bastard
**bastidor** *m* frame; stretcher; (theat) wing; **entre bastidores** behind the scenes
**bastilla** *f* hem
**bastillar** *tr* to hem
**bas•to -ta** *adj* coarse, rough; uncouth || *m* packsaddle; (*naipe*) club; **el basto** the ace of clubs
**bastón** *m* stick, staff; cane, walking stick; baton; **bastón de esquiar** ski pole or stick
**bastoncillo** *m* small stick; (*de la retina*) rod
**bastonear** *tr* to cane, to beat
**basura** *f* sweepings; rubbish, litter, refuse; horse manure
**basurero** *m* trash can; rubbish dump; rubbish collector
**bata** *f* smock; dressing gown, wrapper; **bata de baño** bathrobe
**batacazo** *m* thud, bump
**bataclán** *m* (Cuba) burlesque show
**bataclana** *f* (Cuba) showgirl, stripteaser
**batahola** *f* (coll) racket, hubbub
**batalla** *f* battle; (*de un vehículo*) wheel base; (*de la silla de montar*) seat; (paint) battle piece; **batalla campal** pitched battle; **librar batalla** to do battle
**batallar** *intr* to battle, to fight; to hesitate, to waver
**bata•llón -llona** *adj* (*cuestión*) controversial, moot || *m* battalion
**batata** *f* sweet potato; (Arg) timidity
**bate** *m* baseball bat
**batea** *f* tray; flat-bottomed boat; (rr) flatcar
**bateador** *m* batter
**batear** *tr & intr* to bat
**batel** *m* small boat
**batelero** *m* boatman
**batería** *f* battery; footlights; **batería de cocina** kitchen utensils
**bati•do -da** *adj* (*camino*) beaten; (*tejido*) moiré || *m* batter; milk shake; (rad) beat || *f* battue; combing, search
**batidor** *m* beater; scout, ranger; **batidor de huevos** egg beater; **batidor de oro** goldbeater
**batidora** *f* beater, mixer
**batiente** *m* jamb; (*hoja de puerta*) leaf, door; (*de piano*) damper; wash, place where surf breaks
**batihoja** *m* goldbeater; sheet-metal worker
**batimiento** *m* beating; (phys) beat
**batín** *m* smoking jacket
**batintín** *m* Chinese gong
**batir** *tr* to beat; to batter, beat down; (*las alas*) to flap; (*manos*) to clap; (*las olas*) to ply; **batir tiendas** (mil) to strike camp
**bato** *m* simpleton, rustic
**batuque** *m* (Arg) uproar, rumpus, jamboree; **armar un batuque** (Arg) to raise a rumpus
**baturrillo** *m* hodgepodge
**batuta** *f* (mus) baton; **llevar la batuta** (coll) to boss the show
**baúl** *m* trunk; **baúl mundo** large trunk; **baúl ropero** wardrobe trunk
**bauprés** *m* bowsprit
**bautismo** *m* baptism; **bautismo de aire** first flight
**bautista** *adj* Baptist || *mf* Baptist; baptizer; **el Bautista** John the Baptist
**bautisterio** *m* baptistery

**bautizar** §60 *tr* to baptize; (*el vino*) (coll) to water
**bautizo** *m* baptism; christening party
**báva•ro -ra** *adj & mf* Bavarian
**Baviera** *f* Bavaria
**baya** *f* berry
**bayeta** *f* baize
**ba•yo -ya** *adj* bay || *m* bay horse || *f* see **baya**
**bayoneta** *f* bayonet
**bayonetear** *tr* (Am) to bayonet
**baza** *f* trick; **meter baza en** (coll) to butt into
**bazar** *m* bazaar
**ba•zo -za** *adj* yellowish-brown || *m* yellowish brown; spleen || *f* see **baza**
**bazofia** *f* refuse, offal, garbage
**bazuca** *f* bazooka
**bazucar** §73 *tr* to stir, to shake; to tamper with
**be** *m* baa
**beata** *f* lay sister
**beatería** *f* cant, hypocrisy
**beatificar** §73 *tr* to beatify
**beatísi•mo -ma** *adj* most holy
**bea•to -ta** *adj* blessed; pious, devout; bigoted, prudish || *mf* beatified person; devout person; bigot; (coll) churchgoer || *f* see **beata**
**bebé** *m* baby; doll
**bebede•ro -ra** *adj* (archaic) drinkable || *m* watering place; (Col, Ecuad, Mex) watering trough
**bebedi•zo -za** *adj* drinkable || *m* potion, philter
**bebe•dor -dora** *adj* drinking || *mf* drinker; hard drinker
**beber** *m* drink, drinking || *tr & intr* to drink; **beber de** or **en** to drink out of || *ref* to drink, drink up; (*p.ej., un libro*) to drink in
**bebestible** *adj* drinkable || *m* drink
**bebezón** *f* (Col) drunk, spree
**bebible** *adj* drinkable
**bebi•do -da** *adj* tipsy, unsteady || *f* drink
**bebistrajo** *m* (coll) dose, mixture
**beborrotear** *intr* (coll) to tipple
**beca** *f* scholarship, fellowship; (*de los colegiales*) sash
**becacín** *m* snipe, whole snipe
**becacina** *f* snipe, great snipe
**becada** *f* woodcock
**beca•rio -ria** *mf* scholar, fellow
**becerra** *f* snapdragon
**becerrillo** *m* calfskin
**bece•rro -rra** *mf* yearling calf || *m* calfskin || *f* see **becerra**
**becuadro** *m* (mus) natural sign
**bedel** *m* beadle
**befa** *f* jeer, flout, scoff
**befar** *tr* to jeer at, to scoff at || *intr* (*un caballo*) to move the lips
**be•fo -fa** *adj* blobber-lipped; knock-kneed || *m* (*de animal*) lip || *f* see **befa**
**béisbol** *m* baseball
**bejuco** *m* cane, liana
**beldad** *f* beauty
**beldar** §2 *tr* to winnow
**belén** *m* crèche; (coll) bedlam, confusion; (coll) madhouse; (coll) gossip || **Belén** Bethlehem
**bel•fo -fa** *adj* (*labio*) blobber; blobber-lipped || *m* (*de animal*) lip; blobber lip
**belga** *adj & mf* Belgian
**Bélgica** *f* Belgium
**bélgi•co -ca** *adj* Belgian || *f* see **Bélgica**
**belicista** *mf* warmonger
**béli•co -ca** *adj* warlike
**belico•so -sa** *adj* bellicose
**beligerante** *adj & mf* belligerent
**belitre** *adj* low, mean || *m* scoundrel
**bella•co -ca** *adj* cunning, sly; wicked || *mf* scoundrel
**bellaquear** *intr* to cheat, be crooked; (SAm) to be stubborn; (SAm) to rear
**bellaquería** *f* cunning, slyness; wickedness
**belleza** *f* beauty; **belleza exótica** glamour girl
**be•llo -lla** *adj* beautiful, fair
**bellota** *f* acorn; carnation bud
**bem•bo -ba** *adj* (Am) thick-lipped; (Mex) simple, silly || *mf* (*persona*) (Am) thicklips
**bemol** *adj & m* (mus) flat; **tener bemoles** (coll) to be a tough job
**bencina** *f* benzine
**bendecir** §11 *tr* to bless; to consecrate; **bendecir la mesa** to say grace
**bendición** *f* benediction, blessing; godsend; (*en la mesa*) grace; **bendiciones** wedding ceremony; **echar la bendición a** (coll) to have nothing more to do with
**bendi•to -ta** *adj* blessed, saintly; simple, silly; happy; (*agua*) holy; **como el pan bendito** (coll) as easy as pie || *m* simple-minded soul
**benedícite** *m* grace; **rezar el benedícite** to say grace
**benedicti•no -na** *adj & mf* Benedictine || *m* benedictine
**beneficencia** *f* beneficence; charity, welfare; social service
**beneficia•do -da** *mf* person or charity receiving the proceeds of a benefit performance
**beneficiar** *tr* to benefit; (*la tierra*) to cultivate; (*una mina*) to work, to exploit; (*minerales*) to process, to reduce; (*una región del país*) to serve; to season; (Am) to slaughter || *ref* — **beneficiarse de** to take advantage of
**beneficia•rio -ria** *mf* beneficiary
**beneficio** *m* benefit; profit, gain, yield; (*de una mina*) exploitation; smelting, ore reduction; benefit performance; **a beneficio de** for the benefit of; on the strength of
**beneficio•so -sa** *adj* beneficial, profitable
**benéfi•co -ca** *adj* charitable, benevolent
**beneméri•to -ta** *adj & mf* worthy; **benemérito de la patria** national hero
**beneplácito** *m* approval, consent
**benevolencia** *f* benevolence
**benévo•lo -la** *adj* benevolent, kind-hearted
**bengala** *f* Bengal light; (aer) flare

**benignidad** *f* benignity, mildness, kindness; (*del tiempo*) mildness
**benig•no -na** *adj* benign, mild, kind; (*tiempo*) clement, mild
**benjamín** *m* baby (*the youngest child*)
**beodez** *f* drunkenness
**beo•do -da** *adj & mf* drunk
**berbi•quí** *m* (*pl* **-quíes**) brace; **berbiquí y barrena** brace and bit
**berenjena** *f* eggplant
**berenjenal** *m* eggplant patch; (coll) predicament, jam, fix
**bergante** *m* scoundrel, rascal
**bergantín** *m* (naut) brig; **bergantín goleta** (naut) brigantine
**berilio** *m* beryllium
**berkelio** *m* berkelium
**berli•nés -nesa** *adj* Berlin ‖ *mf* Berliner
**bermejear** *intr* to turn bright red; to look bright red
**berme•jo -ja** *adj* vermilion, bright-red
**berme•jón -jona** *adj* red, reddish
**bermellón** *m* vermilion
**berrear** *intr* to bellow, to low; to bawl, yowl
**berrenchín** *m* (coll) rage, tantrum
**berrido** *m* bellow; scream, yowl
**berrín** *m* (coll) touchy person, cross child
**berrinche** *m* (coll) tantrum, conniption
**berro** *m* water cress
**berza** *f* cabbage
**berzal** *m* cabbage patch
**besalamano** *m* announcement, written in the third person and marked B.L.M. (*kisses your hand*)
**besamanos** *m* levee, reception at court; throwing kisses
**besar** *tr* to kiss; (coll) to graze ‖ *ref* (coll) to bump heads together
**beso** *m* kiss; **beso sonado** buss
**bestia** *adj* stupid ‖ *mf* dunce ‖ *f* beast; **bestia de carga** beast of burden
**bestial** *adj* beastly; (coll) terrific
**besucar** **§73** *tr & intr* (coll) to keep on kissing
**besu•cón -cona** *adj* (coll) kissing ‖ *mf* (coll) kisser
**besuquear** *tr & intr* (coll) to keep on kissing
**betabel** *m* (Mex) beet
**betún** *m* bitumen, pitch; shoe polish
**bezo** *m* blubber lip; proud flesh
**bezu•do -da** *adj* thick-lipped
**biberón** *m* nursing bottle
**Biblia** *f* Bible
**bíbli•co -ca** *adj* Biblical
**bibliófi•lo -la** *mf* bibliophile
**bibliografía** *f* bibliography
**bibliógra•fo -fa** *mf* bibliographer
**biblioteca** *f* library; **biblioteca de consulta** reference library; **biblioteca de préstamo** lending library
**biblioteca•rio -ria** *mf* librarian
**bibliotecnia** *f* bookmaking
**bicameral** *adj* bicameral
**bicarbonato** *m* bicarbonate
**bicicleta** *f* bicycle
**bichero** *m* boat hook
**bicho** *m* bug, insect; vermin; animal; fighting bull; simpleton; brat; **bicho viviente** (coll) living soul; **mal bicho** scoundrel; ferocious bull
**bidón** *m* (*bote, lata*) can; (*tonel de metal*) drum
**biela** *f* connecting rod
**bielda** *f* winnowing rack; winnowing
**bieldar** *tr* to winnow
**bieldo** *m* winnowing pitch rake
**bien** *adv* well; readily; very; indeed; **ahora bien** now then; **bien como** just as; **bien que** although; **más bien** rather; somewhat; **no bien** as soon as; scarcely ‖ *s* welfare; property; darling; **bienes** wealth, riches, possessions; **bienes de fortuna** worldly possessions; **bienes dotales** dower; **bienes inmuebles** real estate; **bienes muebles** personal property; **bienes raíces** real estate; **bienes relictos** estate; **bienes semovientes** livestock; **bien público** commonweal; **en bien de** for the sake of
**bienal** *adj* biennial
**bienama•do -da** *adj* dearly beloved
**bienandanza** *f* happiness, prosperity
**bienaventura•do -da** *adj* happy, blissful; blessed; simple
**bienaventuranza** *f* happiness, bliss; blessedness
**bienestar** *m* well-being, welfare
**bienhabla•do -da** *adj* well-spoken
**bienhada•do -da** *adj* fortunate, lucky
**bienhe•chor -chora** *adj* beneficent ‖ *m* benefactor ‖ *f* benefactress
**bienintenciona•do -da** *adj* well-meaning
**bienio** *m* biennium
**bienquerencia** *f* affection, fondness
**bienquistar** *tr* to bring together, reconcile
**bienvenida** *f* safe arrival; welcome; **dar la bienvenida a** to welcome
**bienveni•do -da** *adj* welcome ‖ *f* see **bienvenida**
**bienvivir** *intr* to live in comfort; to live decently, properly
**bif•tec** *m* (*pl* **-tecs**) beefsteak
**bifurcar** **§73** *ref* to branch, to fork
**bigamia** *f* bigamy
**bíga•mo -ma** *adj* bigamous ‖ *mf* bigamist
**bigornia** *f* two-horn anvil
**bigote** *m* mustache; **bigotes** (*del gato*) whiskers; **tener bigotes** (coll) to have a mind of one's own
**bilingüe** *adj* bilingual
**bilis** *f* bile; **descargar la bilis** to vent one's spleen
**billar** *m* billiards; billiard table; billiard room; **billar romano** pinball
**billete** *m* ticket; note, bill; **billete de abono** season ticket; commutation ticket; **billete de banco** bank note; **billete de ida y vuelta** round-trip ticket; **billete kilométrico** mileage ticket; **medio billete** half fare
**billetero** *m* billfold; ticket agent
**billón** *m* (U.S.A.) trillion; (Brit) billion
**bimotor** *adj* twin-motor ‖ *m* twin-motor plane
**biofísi•co -ca** *adj* biophysical ‖ *f* biophysics

**biografía** *f* biography
**biógra•fo -fa** *mf* biographer
**biología** *f* biology
**biólo•go -ga** *mf* biologist
**biombo** *m* folding screen
**bióxido** *m* dioxide
**bioquími•co -ca** *adj* biochemical || *mf* biochemist || *f* biochemistry
**bipartición** *f* fission, splitting
**biplano** *m* biplane
**biplaza** *m* (aer) two-seater
**birimbao** *m* jews'-harp
**birlar** *tr* to knock down, to shoot down; (coll) to outwit; **birlar algo a alguien** (coll) to snitch something from someone
**birlocha** *f* kite
**Birmania** *f* Burma
**birma•no -na** *adj* & *mf* Burmese
**birreta** *f* biretta, red biretta
**birrete** *m* mortarboard, academic cap
**bis** *interj* encore! || *m* encore
**bisabue•lo -la** *mf* great-grandparent || *m* great-grandfather || *f* great-grandmother
**bisagra** *f* hinge
**bisar** *tr* to repeat
**bisbisar** *tr* (coll) to mutter, mumble
**bisecar** §73 *tr* to bisect
**bisel** *m* bevel edge
**biselar** *tr* to bevel
**bisies•to -ta** *adj* leap
**bismuto** *m* bismuth
**bisnie•to -ta** *mf* great-grandchild || *m* great-grandson || *f* great-granddaughter
**biso•jo -ja** *adj* squint-eyed, cross-eyed
**bisonte** *m* bison; buffalo
**biso•ño -ña** *adj* green, inexperienced || *mf* greenhorn, rookie
**bisté** *m* or **bistec** *m* beefsteak
**bisun•to -ta** *adj* dirty, greasy
**bisutería** *f* costume jewelry
**bitácora** *f* binnacle
**bitoque** *m* bung; (CAm) sewer; (Mex) spigot
**Bizancio** Byzantium
**bizanti•no -na** *adj* & *mf* Byzantine
**bizarría** *f* gallantry, bravery; magnanimity
**biza•rro -rra** *adj* gallant, brave; magnanimous
**bizcar** §73 *tr* to wink || *intr* to squint
**biz•co -ca** *adj* squint-eyed, cross-eyed
**bizcocho** *m* biscuit; cake, sponge cake; hardtack; bisque
**bizma** *f* poultice
**bizmar** *tr* to poultice
**biznie•to -ta** *mf* var of **bisnieto**
**bizquear** *intr* to squint
**bizquera** *f* squint
**blanca** *f* steel blade; **sin blanca** (coll) penniless
**blanca•zo -za** *adj* (coll) whitish
**blan•co -ca** *adj* white; (*tez*) fair; (*fuerza*) water; (*arma*) steel; (*cobarde*) (coll) yellow; blank || *mf* (*persona*) white; (coll) coward || *m* (*color*) white; blank; target; aim, object; interval; white heat; blank form; **dar en el blanco** to hit the mark; **en blanco** (*hoja*) blank; **hacer blanco** to hit the mark; **quedarse en blanco** to not get the point; to be disappointed || *f* see **blanca**
**blancor** *m* whiteness
**blancura** *f* whiteness; purity
**blancuz•co -ca** *adj* whitish; dirty-white
**blandear** *tr* to persuade; to brandish || *intr* & *ref* to yield, give in
**blandengue** *adj* (coll) soft, colorless
**blandir** §1 *tr*, *intr* & *ref* to brandish
**blan•do -da** *adj* bland, soft; indulgent; flabby; sensual; (coll) cowardly; (*ojos*) (coll) tender
**blandón** *m* wax candle; candlestick
**blandura** *f* blandness, softness; tolerance; flabbiness; sensuality; flattery; mild weather; (coll) cowardice
**blanquear** *tr* to whiten, bleach; to blanch; to whitewash; to tin || *intr* to turn white
**blanqueci•no -na** *adj* whitish
**blanqui•llo -lla** *adj* white, whitish || *m* (Guat, Mex) egg; (Chile, Peru) white peach
**blanqueci•no -na** *adj* whitish
**blasfemar** *intr* to blaspheme, to curse
**blasfemia** *f* blasphemy
**blasfe•mo -ma** *adj* blasphemous || *mf* blasphemer
**blasón** *m* (*ciencia de los escudos de armas; escudo de armas*) heraldry; (heral) charge; (fig) glory, honor
**blasonar** *tr* to emblazon; (fig) to emblazon, to extol || *intr* to boast; **blasonar de** to boast of being
**bledo** *m* straw; **no me importa un bledo** or **no se me da un bledo de ello** that doesn't matter a rap to me
**blindaje** *m* armor; (elec) shield
**blindar** *tr* to armor, armor-plate; (elec) to shield
**b.l.m.** *abbr* **besa la mano**
**bloc** *m* (*pl* **bloques**) pad
**blon•do -da** *adj* blond, fair, flaxen, light; (Arg) curly || *f* blond lace
**bloque** *m* block; (*de papel*) pad; **bloque de hormigón** concrete block
**bloquear** *tr* to blockade; (*un coche, un tren*) to brake; (*créditos*) to freeze
**bloqueo** *m* blockade; (*de crédito*) freezing; **bloqueo vertical** (telv) vertical hold
**b.l.p.** *abbr* **besa los pies**
**blusa** *f* blouse, smock; (*de mujer*) shirtwaist; (Col) jacket
**boardilla** *f* dormer window; garret
**boato** *m* show, pomp
**bobada** *f* folly, piece of folly
**bobalías** *mf* (coll) simpleton, dunce
**bobali•cón -cona** *adj* simple, silly || *mf* simpleton, nitwit
**bobear** *intr* to talk nonsense; to dawdle, loiter around
**bobería** *f* folly, nonsense
**bóbilis: de bóbilis** (coll) free, for nothing; (coll) without effort
**bobina** *f* bobbin; (elec) coil; **bobina de chispas** spark coil; **bobina de encendido** ignition coil, spark coil; **bobina de sintonía** tuning coil
**bobinar** *tr* to wind
**bo•bo -ba** *adj* simple, foolish, stupid || *mf* simpleton, fool || *m* (archaic) clown, jester

**boca** *f* mouth; speech; taste, flavor; (*del estómago*) pit; **a boca de jarro** immoderately; at close range; **boca de agua** hydrant; **boca de dragón** (bot) snapdragon; **boca de riego** hydrant; **buscarle a uno la boca** to draw someone out; **decir con la boca chica** (coll) to offer as a mere formality; **no decir esta boca es mía** (coll) to not say a word
**bocacalle** *f* street entrance
**boca•caz** *m* (*pl* **-caces**) spillway
**bocadillo** *m* tape, ribbon; snack, bite; farmer's snack in the field; sandwich
**bocadito** *m* little bit; (Cuba) cigarillo (*cigaret wrapped in tobacco*)
**bocado** *m* bite, morsel; bit; **bocado de Adán** Adam's apple; **no tener para un bocado** (coll) to not have a cent
**bocal** *m* narrow-mouthed pitcher; (*de un puerto*) narrows
**bocallave** *f* keyhole
**bocamanga** *f* cuff, wristband
**bocanada** *f* (*de líquido*) swallow; (*de humo*) puff; (*de viento*) gust; boasting
**bocartear** *tr* to crush, to stamp
**bocera** *f* smear on lips
**boceto** *m* sketch, outline; wax model, clay model
**bocina** *f* horn, trumpet; auto horn; phonograph horn; (Am) ear trumpet
**bocio** *m* goiter
**bocoy** *m* large barrel
**bocha** *f* bowling ball
**boche** *m* small hole in ground for boys' game; (Ven) slight, snub
**bochinche** *m* uproar, tumult, row
**bochorno** *m* sultry weather; blush, embarrassment, shame
**bochorno•so -sa** *adj* sultry, stuffy; embarrassing, shameful
**boda** *f* marriage, wedding; **bodas de Camacho** banquet, lavish feast
**bodega** *f* wine cellar; dock warehouse; granary; (*de nave*) hold; (coll) cellar; (*hombre que bebe mucho*) (coll) tank; (Am) grocery store
**bodegón** *m* hash house, beanery; saloon; still life
**bodegue•ro -ra** *mf* cellarer; (Am) grocer
**bodijo** *m* (coll) unequal match; (coll) simple wedding
**bodoque** *m* lump; (coll) dunce, dolt; (Mex) bump, lump
**bodoquera** *f* peashooter
**bóer** *mf* Boer
**bofe** *m* (coll) lung; (P-R) cinch, snap; **echar el bofe** or **los bofes** (coll) to drudge, to grind; **bofes** lights (*of sheep, etc.*)
**bofetada** *f* slap in the face
**boga** *mf* rower || *f* vogue, fashion; rowing
**bogar** §44 *intr* to row
**bogavante** *m* lobster
**bohardilla** *f* dormer window; garret
**bohe•mio -mia** *adj & mf* Bohemian
**bohío** *m* (Am) hut, shack
**boicotear** *tr* to boycott
**boicoteo** *m* boycott, boycotting
**boina** *f* beret
**boj** *m* boxwood
**boja** *f* southernwood
**bojar** *tr* to measure the perimeter of; (*el cuero*) to scrape clean || *intr* to measure
**bola** *f* ball; marble; bowling; shoe polish; shoeshine; (cards) slam; lie, deceit; (Mex) brawl, riot; **bola de alcanfor** moth ball; **bola de cristal** crystal ball; **bola de nieve** snowball; **bola rompedora** wrecking ball; **bolas** Gaucho lasso tipped with balls; **dejar que ruede la bola** to let things take their course; **raspar la bola** (Chile) to clear out, beat it
**bolada** *f* (*de una bola*) throw; (Am) luck, opportunity; (Arg) billiard stroke; (Chile) dainty, tidbit; (Guat, Mex) lie, fib
**bolazo** *m* hit with a ball; **de bolazo** (coll) hurriedly, right away; (Mex) at random
**bolchevique** *adj & mf* Bolshevik
**bolchevismo** *m* Bolshevism
**boleada** *f* (Arg) hunting with bolas; (Mex) shoeshine; (Peru) flunking
**bolear** *tr* (coll) to throw; (Arg) to catch with bolas; (*zapatos*) (Mex) to shine; (SAm) to kick out, to flunk || *intr* to play for fun; to lie; to boast || *ref* (Arg, Urug) to rear and fall backwards; (Arg, Urug) to upset; (Arg, Urug) to blush
**bole•ro -ra** *mf* bolero dancer || *m* bolero (*dance; music; jacket*); (Mex) bootblack || *f* bowling alley; **bolera encespada** bowling green
**boleta** *f* pass, permit, admission ticket; (mil) billet; (Am) ballot
**boletería** *f* (Am) ticket office
**boletín** *m* bulletin; ticket; form; press release
**boleto** *m* (Am) ticket
**boliche** *m* bowling; bowling alley; (SAm) hash house
**bólido** *m* fireball, bolide
**bolígrafo** *m* ball-point pen
**bolillo** *m* bobbin for making lace; frame for stiffening lace cuffs
**Bolivia** *f* Bolivia
**bolivia•no -na** *adj & mf* Bolivian
**bolo** *m* ninepin, tenpin; dunce, blockhead; (*de escalera*) newel; (cards) slam; **bolos** bowling, ninepins, tenpins; **jugar a los bolos** to bowl
**Bolonia** *f* Bologna
**bolsa** *f* purse, pocketbook; pouch; stock exchange, stock market; (*en el vestido*) bag, pucker; grant, award; **bolsa de agua caliente** hot-water bottle; **bolsa de hielo** ice bag; **bolsa de trabajo** employment bureau; **hacer bolsa** (*un vestido*) to bag; **jugar a la bolsa** to play the market
**bolsear** *tr* (Arg, Bol, Urug) to jilt; (Am) to pick the pocket of; (Chile) to sponge on
**bolsillo** *m* pocket; purse, pocketbook
**bolsista** *m* broker, stockbroker; (CAm, Mex) pickpocket

**bolso** *m* purse, pocketbook; **bolso de mano** handbag
**bollo** *m* bun, roll; bump, lump; dent; (*en un vestido*) puff; (*en adorno de tapicería*) tuft; **bollo de crema** cream puff
**bomba** *f* pump; bomb; fire engine; lamp globe; high hat; firecracker; soap bubble; bombshell; **a prueba de bombas** bombproof; **bomba atómica** atomic bomb; **bomba cohete** rocket bomb; **bomba de hidrógeno** hydrogen bomb; **bomba de incendios** fire engine; **bomba de profundidad** depth bomb; **bomba de sentina** bilge pump; **bomba rompedora** blockbuster; **bomba volante** buzz bomb; **caer como una bomba** (coll) to fall like a bombshell; (coll) to burst in unexpectedly
**bombachas** *fpl* loose-fitting baggy trousers
**bombardear** *tr & intr* to bomb; to bombard; **bombardear en picado** to dive-bomb
**bombardeo** *m* bombing; bombarding; **bombardeo en picado** dive bombing
**bombardero** *m* bomber; bombardier
**bomba-reloj** *f* time bomb
**bombazo** *m* bomb explosion; bomb hit; bomb damage
**bombear** *tr* to bomb; to ballyhoo, to puff up; (Am) to pump; (SAm) to reconnoiter; (Col) to fire, dismiss || *ref* to camber, bulge
**bombero** *m* fireman; pumpman
**bombilla** *f* bulb, light bulb; lamp chimney; (Am) tube for sucking up maté; **bombilla de destello** flash bulb
**bombillo** *m* trap, stench trap; (naut) pump
**bombista** *m* lamp maker; (*el que da bombos*) (coll) booster
**bom•bo -ba** *adj* (coll) astounded, stunned; (W-I) lukewarm || *m* bass drum; ballyhoo; (naut) barge, lighter; **dar bombo a** (coll) to ballyhoo, puff up; **irse al bombo** (Arg) to fail || *f* see **bomba**
**bombón** *m* bonbon, candy
**bombona** *f* carboy
**bombonera** *f* candy box
**bona•chón -chona** *adj* (coll) good-natured, kind, simple
**bonancible** *adj* (*tiempo*) fair; (*mar*) calm; (*viento*) moderate
**bonanza** *f* fair weather, calm seas; prosperity, boom; rich ore pocket
**bona•zo -za** *adj* (coll) kind-hearted
**bondad** *f* kindness; favor; **tener la bondad de** to have the kindness to
**bondado•so -sa** *adj* kind, generous
**bonete** *m* cap, hat; candy bowl
**boniato** *m* sweet potato
**bonificar** §73 *tr* to improve; to give a discount on
**boni•to -ta** *adj* pretty, nice; pretty good
**bono** *m* bond; food voucher
**boñiga** *f* manure, cow dung
**boqueada** *f* gasp of death
**boquear** *tr* to pronounce, utter || *intr* to gasp
**boquerel** *m* nozzle
**boquete** *m* gap, breach, opening
**boquiabier•to -ta** *adj* open-mouthed
**boquian•cho -cha** *adj* wide-mouthed
**boquiangos•to -ta** *adj* narrow-mouthed
**boquihundi•do -da** *adj* hollow-mouthed
**boquilla** *f* (*de instrumento de viento*) mouthpiece; (*de pipa*) stem; (*de cigarro*) tip; (*de aparato de alumbrado*) burner; cigar holder, cigarette holder; (*de manguera*) nozzle; opening in irrigation canal; opening at bottom of trouser leg
**boquirro•to -ta** *adj* (coll) garrulous
**boquiverde** *adj* (coll) obscene, smutty
**bórax** *m* borax
**borbollar** or **borbollear** *intr* to bubble up
**borbollón** *m* bubbling; **a borbollones** impetuously
**borborigmos** *mpl* rumbling of the bowels
**borbotar** *intr* to bubble up, bubble over
**borce•guí** *m* (*pl* **-guíes**) high shoe
**borda** *f* hut; (naut) gunwale; **arrojar, echar** or **tirar por la borda** to throw overboard
**bordada** *f* (naut) tack; **dar bordadas** (naut) to tack; to pace to and fro
**bordado** *m* embroidery
**bordadura** *f* embroidery
**bordar** *tr* to embroider
**borde** *m* border, edge; fringe; rim; **borde de la acera** curb; **borde del mar** seaside
**bordear** *tr* to border || *intr* to go on the edge; (naut) to tack
**bordo** *m* (naut) board; (naut) side; (naut) tack; (Guat, Mex) dam, dike; **a bordo** (naut) on board; **al bordo** (naut) alongside; **de alto bordo** seagoing; distinguished, important
**bordón** *m* (*de tambor*) snare; pilgrim's staff; pet word; burden, refrain
**bordonear** *intr* to grope along with a stick; to go around begging
**borgoña** *m* Burgundy (*wine*) || **la Borgoña** Burgundy
**borgo•ñón -ñona** *adj & mf* Burgundian
**boricua** or **borinque•ño -ña** *adj & mf* Puerto Rican
**borla** *f* tassel; powder puff; **tomar la borla** to take a higher degree, to take the doctor's degree
**borne** *m* binding post; (*de la lanza*) tip
**bornear** *tr* to bend, to twist; (*sillares pesados*) to set in place || *intr* to swing at anchor || *ref* to warp
**borra** *f* fuzz, nap, lint
**borrachera** *f* drunkenness; spree, binge; great exaltation; (coll) piece of folly; **pegarse una borrachera** to go on a binge
**borrachín** *m* drunkard
**borra•cho -cha** *adj* drunk; (*habitualmente*) drinking || *mf* drunkard
**borrador** *m* blotter, day book; rough draft; (Am) eraser
**borradura** *f* striking out, scratching out
**borraj** *m* borax

**borrajear** *tr & intr* to scribble; to doodle
**borrar** *tr* to scratch out, cross out; to erase, rub out; to darken, obscure; to blot, to smear
**borrasca** *f* storm, tempest; upset, setback
**borrasco•so -sa** *adj* stormy
**borregos** *mpl* (coll) fleecy clouds
**borrica** *f* she-ass; (coll) stupid woman
**borrico** *m* ass, donkey; sawhorse; (coll) stupid fellow, ass
**borricón** *m* or **borricote** *m* (coll) drudge
**borrón** *m* blot; rough draft; blemish; (fig) blot, stain
**borronear** *tr* to scribble
**borro•so -sa** *adj* blurred, smudgy, fuzzy; muddy, thick
**boruca** *f* noise, clamor, uproar
**borujo** *m* lump, clump
**boscaje** *m* woodland; (paint) woodland scene
**bosque** *m* forest, woodland; **bosque maderable** timberland
**bosquejar** *tr* to sketch, to outline; to make a rough model of
**bosquejo** *m* sketch, outline; rough model
**bostezar §60** *intr* to yawn, gape
**bostezo** *m* yawn, yawning
**bota** *f* shoe, boot; leather wine bag; liquid measure (*125 gallons or 516 liters*); **bota de agua** gum boot; **bota de montar** riding boot; **ponerse las botas** (coll) to hit the jack pot, come out on top
**botador** *m* boat pole; punch, nailset
**botadura** *f* launching
**botafuego** *m* (coll) hothead, firebrand
**botalón** *m* (naut) boom; **botalón de foque** (naut) jib boom
**botáni•co -ca** *adj* botanical || *mf* botanist || *f* botany
**botanista** *mf* botanist
**botar** *tr* to throw, hurl; to throw away, throw out; (*un buque*) to launch; (*el timón*) to shift; (Am) to fire, dismiss; (Am) to squander || *intr* to jump; to bounce || *ref* (*un caballo*) to buck
**botarate** *m* madcap, wild man; (Am) spendthrift
**bote** *m* boat, small boat; can, jar, pot; bounce; blow, thrust; (Mex) jug, jail; **bote de paso** ferryboat; **bote de porcelana** apothecary's jar; **bote de remos** rowboat; **bote de salvamento** or **bote salvavidas** lifeboat; **de bote en bote** (coll) crowded, jammed; **de bote y voleo** (coll) thoughtlessly
**botella** *f* bottle
**botica** *f* drug store; medicine
**botica•rio -ria** *mf* druggist, apothecary
**botija** *f* earthenware jug with short narrow neck; (CAm, Ven) hidden treasure; **decirle a uno botija verde** (Cuba) to let someone have it, to tell someone off; **estar hecho una botija** (*un niño*) (coll) to be cross and scream; (*una persona*) (coll) to be fat, be pudgy
**botijo** *m* earthenware jar with spout and handle
**botín** *m* booty, plunder, spoils; spat, legging; (Chile) sock
**botina** *f* shoe, high shoe
**botiquín** *m* medicine kit, first-aid kit; medicine chest; first-aid station; (Ven) saloon
**bo•to -ta** *adj* (*sin filo o punta*) blunt, dull; (fig) dull, slow || *m* leather bag || *f* see **bota**
**botón** *m* button; (*de mueble o puerta*) knob; (*de reloj de bolsillo*) stem; (bot) bud; (elec) push button; **botón de oro** buttercup; **botón de puerta** doorknob; **botones** *msg* bellboy, bellhop
**bou** *m* fishing with a dragnet between two boats
**bóveda** *f* dome, vault; crypt; (aut) cowl; **bóveda celeste** canopy of heaven
**boxeador** *m* boxer; (Mex) brass knuckles
**boxear** *intr* to box
**boxeo** *m* boxing
**bóxer** *m* brass knuckles
**boxibalón** *m* punching bag
**boya** *f* buoy; **boya salvavidas** life buoy
**boyante** *adj* buoyant; lucky, successful; (*que no cala lo que debe calar*) (naut) light
**boyera** or **boyeriza** *f* ox stable
**boyerizo** or **boyero** *m* ox driver
**bozal** *adj* simple, stupid; (*negro*) just brought in || *m* muzzle; head-harness bells; (Am) headstall
**bozo** *m* down on upper lip; lips, mouth; headstall
**B.p.** *abbr* **Bendición papal**
**Br.** *abbr* **bachiller**
**bracear** *intr* to swing the arms; to swim with overhead strokes; to struggle
**brace•ro -ra** *adj* arm, hand; thrown with the hand || *m* man who offers his arm to a lady; day laborer; **de bracero** arm in arm
**bra•co -ca** *adj* pug-nosed
**braga** *f* diaper, clout; hoisting rope; **bragas** panties, step-ins; breeches; **calzarse las bragas** (coll) to wear the pants
**bragadura** *f* crotch
**braga•zas** *m* (*pl* **-zas**) (coll) easy mark, henpecked fellow
**braguero** *m* (*para hernias*) truss; (*entrepiernas*) crotch
**bragueta** *f* fly
**bragui•llas** *m* (*pl* **-llas**) (coll) brat
**brama** *f* rut, mating, mating time
**bramante** *adj* bellowing, roaring || *m* packthread, twine
**bramar** *intr* to bellow, roar; (*el viento*) to howl; to rage, storm
**bramido** *m* bellow, roar; howling; raging
**brasa** *f* live coal, red-hot coal
**brasero** *m* brazier; (Col) bonfire; (Mex) hearth, fireplace
**Brasil, el** Brazil
**brasile•ño -ña** *adj & mf* Brazilian
**bravata** *f* bravado, bragging; **echar bravatas** to talk big

**bravear** *intr* to talk big, to four-flush
**braveza** *f* bravery; ferocity; (*de los elementos*) fury, violence
**braví·o -a** *adj* ferocious; wild, untamed, uncultivated; crude, unpolished; (*mar*) rough, wild; (*terreno*) rough, rugged
**bra·vo -va** *adj* (*valiente*) brave; fine, excellent; fierce, savage, wild; (*mar*) rough; magnificent; angry, mad; (*perro*) vicious; (*toro*) game; (coll) boasting; (*chili*) (coll) strong || *interj* bravo!
**bravu·cón -cona** *adj* (coll) four-flushing || *mf* (coll) fourflusher
**bravura** *f* bravery; fierceness; gameness; bravado, boasting
**braza** *f* fathom
**brazada** *f* stroke, pull (*with the arm*); **brazada de pecho** breast stroke
**brazado** *m* armful, armload
**brazal** *m* arm band; **brazal de luto** mourning band
**brazalete** *m* bracelet
**brazo** *m* arm; (*de animal*) foreleg; **a brazo partido** hand to hand (*i.e., without weapons*); **asidos del brazo** arm in arm; **brazo derecho** right-hand man; **brazos** hands, workmen; backers; **hecho un brazo de mar** dressed to kill
**brea** *f* tar, wood tar; calking substance; packing canvas; **brea seca** rosin
**brear** *tr* to annoy, mistreat, beat; to tar
**brebaje** *m* beverage, drink
**brécol** *m* or **brécoles** *mpl* broccoli
**brecha** *f* opening; (*en un muro*) breach; breakthrough
**brega** *f* fight, struggle, quarrel; trickery; drudgery
**bregar** §44 *intr* to strive, struggle, toil
**breña** *f*, **breñal** *m* or **breñar** *m* rocky thicket
**bresca** *f* honeycomb
**Bretaña** *f* Brittany; **la Gran Bretaña** Great Britain
**brete** *m* fetters, shackles; tight squeeze, fix
**bretones** *mpl* Brussels sprouts
**breva** *f* early fig; cinch, snap
**breval** *m* early-fig tree
**breve** *adj* brief, short; **en breve** shortly, soon
**brevedad** *f* brevity, shortness; **a la mayor brevedad** as soon as possible
**brevete** *m* note, mark
**brezal** *m* heath, moor
**brezo** *m* heath, heather
**briba** *f* loafing; **andar a la briba** to loaf around
**bri·bón -bona** *adj* loafing, crooked || *mf* loafer, crook
**bribonada** *f* loafing, crookedness
**bribonear** *intr* to loaf around, to be crooked
**brida** *f* bridle
**brigada** *f* brigade; gang, squad; warrant officer
**brillante** *adj* bright, brilliant, shining || *m* diamond, gem
**brillantez** *f* brilliance
**brillar** *intr* to shine; to sparkle
**brillazón** *f* (Arg, Bol, Urug) pampa mirage
**brillo** *m* brightness, brilliance; sparkle; **sacar brillo a** to shine
**brillo·so -sa** *adj* (*que brilla por el mucho uso*) shiny; (Am) shining, brilliant
**brin** *m* canvas
**brincar** §73 *tr* to bounce up and down; to skip, skip over || *intr* to jump, to leap; (coll) to be touchy, get angry easily
**brinco** *m* bounce; jump, leap; **en dos brincos** or **en un brinco** in an instant
**brindador** *m* toaster
**brindar** *tr* to invite; to offer; **brindar a uno con una cosa** to offer someone something || *intr* — **brindar a** or **por** to drink to, to toast || *ref* — **brindarse a** to offer to
**brin·dis** *m* (*pl* **-dis**) invitation, treat; toast
**brío** *m* spirit, enterprise; elegance; **cortar los bríos a** to cut the wings of
**brío·so -sa** *adj* spirited, lively, enterprising; elegant
**brisa** *f* breeze; residue of pressed grapes
**brisera** *f* or **brisero** *m* (Am) glass lamp shade (*for candles*)
**británi·co -ca** *adj* British, Britannic
**brita·no -na** *adj* British || *mf* Briton, Britisher
**brizna** *f* chip, particle; (Ven) drizzle
**bri.** *abbr* **barril**
**broca** *f* reel, spindle; drill, bit
**brocado** *m* brocade
**brocal** *m* (*de pozo*) curbstone; (*de bota*) mouthpiece; (*de banqueta*) (Mex) curb
**brocamantón** *m* diamond brooch
**bróculi** *m* broccoli
**brocha** *f* brush; loaded dice; **de brocha gorda** house (*painter*); (coll) crude, heavy-handed
**brochada** *f* stroke with a brush; rough sketch
**brochazo** *m* stroke with a brush
**broche** *m* clasp, clip, fastener; (*conjunto de dos piezas*) hook and eye; (Chile) paper clip; **broche de oro** punch line; **broche de presión** snap, catch; **broches** (Ecuad) cuff buttons
**brocheta** *f* skewer
**broma** *f* joke, jest; fun; shipworm; **bromas aparte** joking aside; **en broma** in fun, jokingly; **gastar una broma a** to play a joke on
**bromear** *intr & ref* to joke, jest; to have a good time
**bromhídri·co -ca** *adj* hydrobromic
**bromista** *adj* joking || *mf* joker
**bromo** *m* bromine
**bromuro** *m* bromide
**bronca** *f* (coll) row, quarrel; (coll) rough joke, poor joke; **armar una bronca** (coll) to start a row
**bronce** *m* bronze; **bronce de cañón** gun metal
**broncea·do -da** *adj* bronze; tanned, sunburned || *m* bronzing; bronze finish; tan, sunburn

**broncear** *tr, intr & ref* to bronze; to tan, sunburn
**bron•co -ca** *adj* coarse, rough; gruff, crude; (*voz*) harsh, hoarse ‖ *f* see **bronca**
**bronquitis** *f* bronchitis
**broquel** *m* buckler, shield; (fig) shield
**broqueta** *f* skewer
**brota** *f* bud, shoot
**brotadura** *f* budding, sprouting; gushing; (*de la piel*) eruption, rash
**brotar** *tr* to bring forth, to produce ‖ *intr* to bud, sprout; to gush; (*la piel*) to break out
**brote** *m* bud, shoot; outbreak; (*de petróleo*) gush, spurt
**broza** *f* (*maleza*) underbrush; (*hojas, ramas, cortezas*) brushwood; (*desperdicio*) trash, rubbish; printer's brush
**bruces** — **dar** or **caer de bruces** to fall on one's face
**bruja** *f* witch, sorceress; barn owl; (*mujer fea*) hag; (*mujer de mala vida*) prostitute; (W-I) spook
**brujear** *tr* (*bestias salvajes*) (Ven) to hunt ‖ *intr* to practice witchcraft
**brujería** *f* witchcraft, sorcery, magic
**brujo** *m* sorcerer, wizard
**brújula** *f* (*flechilla*) magnetic needle; (*instrumento*) compass; (*agujero para la puntería*) sight; **perder la brújula** to lose one's touch
**brujulear** *tr* (*las cartas*) to uncover gradually; (coll) to suspect
**brulote** *m* fire ship; (Arg, Chile, Bol) vulgarity, insult
**bruma** *f* fog, mist
**brumo•so -sa** *adj* foggy, misty
**bruñido** *m* burnish, polish; burnishing
**bruñir** §12 *tr* to burnish, to polish; to put rouge on; (CAm) to annoy
**brus•co -ca** *adj* brusque, gruff; sudden; (*curva*) sharp
**bruselas** *fpl* tweezers ‖ **Bruselas** Brussels
**brusquedad** *f* brusqueness, gruffness; suddenness; (*de una curva*) sharpness
**brutal** *adj* brutal; sudden; (coll) huge, terrific; (coll) stunning
**brutalidad** *f* brutality; stupidity; (coll) tremendous amount
**bruteza** *f* brutality; (archaic) roughness
**bru•to -ta** *adj* brute; rough, coarse; stupid; gross ‖ *mf* (*persona*) brute; blockhead ‖ *m* (*animal*) brute
**bu** *m* (*pl* **búes**) (coll) bugaboo; **hacer el bu a** (*coll*) to scare, frighten
**bucear** *intr* to dive, be a diver; to delve, search
**buceo** *m* diving
**bucle** *m* curl, lock
**buche** *m* (*de ave*) craw, crop, maw; (*de líquido*) mouthful; (*del vestido*) bag, pucker; (*para secretos*) bosom; (coll) belly; (Ecuad) high hat; (Guat, Mex) goiter; **sacar el buche a** (coll) to make (*someone*) open up
**budín** *m* pudding
**buen** *adj* var of **bueno**, used before masculine singular nouns
**buenamente** *adv* with ease; gladly, willingly; conveniently
**buenaventura** *f* fortune, good luck; (*adivinación*) fortune; **decirle a uno la buenaventura** to tell someone his fortune
**bue•no -na** *adj* good; kind; (*sano*) well; (*tiempo*) good, fine; **a buenas** willingly; **¡buena es ésa** (or **ésta**)! (coll) that's a good one; **de buenas a primeras** all of a sudden; from the start; **¿de dónde bueno?** (coll) where have you been?, what's new?
**buey** *m* ox, bullock, steer
**búfa•lo -la** *mf* buffalo
**bufanda** *f* muffler, scarf
**bufar** *intr* to snort
**bufete** *m* writing desk; law office; (*de un abogado*) clients; law practice; (Am) refreshment; (Col) bedpan; **abrir bufete** to open a law office
**bufido** *m* snort
**bu•fo -fa** *adj* comic; (Ven) spongy ‖ *mf* buffoon
**bu•fón -fona** *adj* clownish ‖ *m* clown, buffoon; jester; peddler
**bufonada** *f* buffoonery; sarcasm
**bufonería** *f* buffoonery; peddling
**bufones•co -ca** *adj* clownish; coarse, crude
**bugui-bugui** *m* boogie-woogie
**buharda** *f* dormer; dormer window; garret
**buhardilla** *f* dormer window; garret
**buho** *m* eagle owl; (coll) shy fellow
**buhonería** *f* peddler's kit; peddler's wares
**buhonero** *m* peddler, hawker
**buitre** *m* vulture
**buje** *m* axle box, bushing
**bujería** *f* gewgaw, trinket
**bujía** *f* candle; candlestick; candle power; (*de motor de explosión*) spark plug
**bulbo** *m* bulb
**bulevar** *m* boulevard
**bulevardero** *m* boulevardier, man about town
**Bulgaria** *f* Bulgaria
**búlga•ro -ra** *adj & mf* Bulgarian
**bulto** *m* bulk, volume; bust, statue; parcel, piece of baggage; bump, swelling; pillowcase; form, mass; **a bulto** broadly, by guess; **buscar el bulto a** (coll) to keep after; **de bulto** evident; **escurrir** or **huir el bulto** (coll) to duck
**bulla** *f* noise; crowd; loud argument
**bullaje** *m* crush, mob (*of people*)
**bullanga** *f* racket, disturbance
**bullebulle** *mf* (coll) busybody, bustler
**bullicio** *m* brawl, riot, uprising; (*rumor que hace mucha gente*) rumble
**bullicio•so -sa** *adj* brawling, riotous; rumbling ‖ *mf* rioter
**bullir** §13 *tr* to move ‖ *intr* to boil; to abound; to bustle, to hustle; to swarm; to move, to stir; (coll) to be restless ‖ *ref* to move, to stir
**buniato** *m* sweet potato
**buñuelo** *m* cruller, fritter, bun; (coll) botch, bungle
**buque** *m* ship, vessel; (*de una nave*)

hull; (*de cualquier cosa*) capacity; (C-R) doorframe; **buque almirante** admiral; **buque cisterna** tanker; **buque de guerra** warship; **buque de vapor** steamer, steamship; **buque de vela** sailboat; **buque escucha** vedette; **buque escuela** training ship; **buque fanal** or **buque faro** lightship; **buque mercante** merchantman, merchant vessel; **buque portaminas** mine layer; **buque tanque** tanker; **buque velero** sailing vessel
**burbuja** *f* bubble
**burbujear** *intr* to bubble
**burdégano** *m* hinny
**burdel** *m* brothel, disorderly house
**Burdeos** Bordeaux
**bur•do -da** *adj* coarse, rough
**burear** *tr* (Col) to fool || *intr* to have fun
**burga** *f* hot springs
**bur•gués -guesa** *adj* middle-class, bourgeois; (*antiartístico*) bourgeois || *m* middle-class man || *f* middle-class woman
**burguesía** *f* middle class, bourgeoisie; **alta burguesía** upper middle class; **pequeña burguesía** lower middle class
**burla** *f* hoax, trick; joke; ridicule; **burlas aparte** joking aside; **de burlas** in fun, for fun
**burladero** *m* safety island, safety zone; (*en las plazas de toros*) covert; (*en los túneles*) safety niche; hiding place
**burla•dor -dora** *adj* joking; deceptive || *mf* wag, prankster, practical joker || *m* seducer, libertine
**burlar** *tr* to make fun of; to deceive; to disappoint; to outwit, frustrate; (*a una mujer*) to seduce || *intr* to scoff || *ref* to joke; **burlarse de** to make fun of
**burlería** *f* derision, mockery; deception, trick; scorn, derision; fish story
**burles•co -ca** *adj* (coll) funny, comic, burlesque
**burlete** *m* weather stripping
**bur•lón -lona** *adj* joking || *mf* joker || *m* mockingbird
**bu•ró** *m* (*pl* **-rós**) writing desk; (Mex) night table
**burócrata** *mf* jobholder, bureaucrat
**burra** *f* she-ass; stupid woman; drudge (*woman*)
**burrajear** *tr & intr* to scribble; to doodle
**burra•jo -ja** *adj* (Mex) coarse, stupid || *m* dung (*used as fuel*)
**bu•rro -rra** *adj* (coll) stupid, asinine || *m* donkey, jackass; sawbuck, sawhorse; (Mex) stepladder; **burro cargado de letras** (coll) learned jackass; **burro de carga** (coll) drudge || *f* see **burra**
**bursátil** *adj* stock-market
**busca** *f* search; **en busca de** in search of
**buscani•guas** *m* (*pl* **-guas**) (Col) snake
**buscapié** *m* (*para dar a entender algo*) hint; (*para averiguar algo*) feeler || **busca•piés** *m* (*pl* **-piés**) snake
**buscaplei•tos** *mf* (*pl* **-tos**) (Am) troublemaker
**buscar** §73 *tr* to seek, to hunt, to look for; (Mex) to provoke; **buscar tres pies al gato** to be looking for trouble || *ref* to take care of oneself; **buscársela** (coll) to manage to get along; (coll) to ask for it
**buscareta** *f* wren
**buscarrui•dos** *mf* (*pl* **-dos**) (coll) troublemaker
**buscavi•das** *mf* (*pl* **-das**) (coll) snoop, busybody; (coll) go-getter
**bus•cón -cona** *adj* searching; cheating || *mf* seeker; thief, cheat; (min) prospector || *f* loose woman
**busi•lis** *m* (*pl* **-lis**) (coll) trouble; **ahí está el busilis** (coll) that's the trouble; **dar en el busilis** (coll) to hit the nail on the head
**búsqueda** *f* search, hunt
**busto** *m* bust
**butaca** *f* armchair, easy chair; orchestra seat
**butifarra** *f* Catalonian sausage; (coll) loose sock, loose stocking; (Peru) ham and salad sandwich
**bution•do -da** *adj* lewd, lustful
**buz** *m* (*pl* **buces**) kiss of gratitude and reverence; lip; **hacer el buz** (archaic) to bow and scrape
**buzo** *m* diver
**buzón** *m* plug, stopper; mailbox, letter box; (*agujero para echar las cartas*) slot, letter drop; **buzón de alcance** special-delivery box; late-collection slot

## C

**C, c** (ce) *f* third letter of the Spanish alphabet
**c.** *abbr* **capítulo, compañía, corriente, cuenta**
**c** *abbr* **caja, cargo, contra, corriente**
**cabal** *adj* exact; full, complete, perfect; **no estar en sus cabales** to be not in one's right mind || *adv* exactly; completely || *interj* right!
**cábala** *f* intrigue; divination
**cabalgada** *f* raid on horseback; gathering of riders
**cabalgador** *m* rider, horseman
**cabalgadura** *f* mount, horse; beast of burden
**cabalgar** §44 *intr* to go horseback riding
**cabalgata** *f* cavalcade

**caballa** *f* mackerel
**caballada** *f* drove of horses; (Am) nonsense, stupidity
**caballaje** *m* stud service
**caballazo** *m* (Am) collision of two horses, trampling by a horse; (Chile, Peru) bitter attack
**caballerango** *m* (Mex) stableman
**caballeres•co -ca** *adj* chivalric, knightly; gentlemanly
**caballerete** *m* (coll) dude
**caballería** *f* mount, horse, mule; cavalry; chivalry, knighthood; **andarse en caballerías** (coll) to fall all over oneself in compliments; **caballería andante** knight-errantry; **caballería mayor** horse, mule; **caballería menor** ass, donkey
**caballeriza** *f* stable; stable hands
**caballerizo** *m* groom, stableman
**caballe•ro -ra** *adj* riding, mounted; stubborn || *m* knight, nobleman; gentleman; mister; horseman, cavalier, rider; **armar caballero** to knight; **caballero andante** knight errant; **caballero de industria** crook, adventurer, sharper; **Caballero de la triste figura** Knight of the Rueful Countenance (*Don Quijote*); **ir caballero en** to ride
**caballerosidad** *f* chivalry, gentlemanliness
**caballerote** *m* boorish fellow, cad
**caballete** *m* (*bastidor para sostener un cuadro o pizarra*) easel; (*de tejado*) ridge, hip; (*lomo de tierra*) ridge; (*artificio usado como soporte*) trestle, sawbuck, horse; (*de la nariz*) bridge; chimney cap; (*del ave*) breastbone; little horse
**caballista** *m* horseman; mounted smuggler || *f* horsewoman
**caballito** *m* little horse; merry-go-round; **caballito del diablo** dragonfly
**caballo** *m* horse; (*en ajedrez*) knight; playing card (*figure on horseback equivalent to queen*); **a caballo** on horseback; **a caballo de** astride; **a caballo regalado no se le mira el diente** never look a gift horse in the mouth; **caballo blanco** (*persona que da dinero para una empresa dudosa*) angel; **caballo de batalla** battle horse; (*de una controversia*) gist, main point; (*aquello en que uno sobresale*) forte, strong point; **caballo de carreras** race horse; **caballo de fuerza** French horsepower, metric horsepower; **caballo de tiro** draft horse; **caballo de Troya** Trojan horse; **caballo de vapor** French horsepower, metric horsepower; **caballo de vapor inglés** horsepower; **caballo mecedor** rocking horse, hobbyhorse; **caballo padre** stallion; **caballo semental** stallion
**caballu•no -na** *adj* horse, horselike
**cabaña** *f* cabin, hut; drove, flock; livestock; pastoral scene; (Arg) cattle-breeding ranch
**cabañuelas** *fpl* (Arg, Bol) first summer rains; (Mex) winter rains
**caba•ret** *m* (*pl* **-rets**) cabaret
**cabecear** *tr* (*un libro*) to put a headband on; (*el vino*) to head; (*una media*) to put a new foot on || *intr* to nod; to bob the head; (*en señal de negación*) to shake the head; (*los caballos*) to toss the head; (*la caja de un carruaje*) to lurch; (*un buque*) to pitch
**cabeceo** *m* (*de la cabeza*) nod, bob, shake; (*de la caja del carruaje*) lurching; (*del buque*) pitch, pitching
**cabecera** *f* (*de cama, mesa, etc.*) head; bedside; headboard; headwaters; (*de una casa, un campo*) end; (*del capítulo de un libro*) heading; (*de periódico*) headline; capital, county seat; bolster, pillow; (typ) headpiece, vignette; **cabecera de cartel** top billing; **cabecera de puente** (mil) bridgehead
**cabecilla** *mf* (coll) scalawag || *m* ringleader || *f* **cabecilla de alfiler** pinhead
**cabellar** *intr* to grow hair; to put on false hair || *ref* to put on false hair
**cabellera** *f* head of hair; foliage; (*del cometa*) coma; (bot) mistletoe
**cabello** *m* hair; **cabello de Venus** maidenhair; **cabellos de ángel** cotton candy; **en cabello** with the hair down; **en cabellos** bareheaded; **traído por los cabellos** far-fetched
**cabellu•do -da** *adj* hairy
**caber §14** *intr* to fit, to go; to have enough room; to be possible; to happen, to befall; **no cabe duda** there is no doubt; **no cabe más** that's the limit; **no caber de** to be bursting with; **no caber en sí** to be beside oneself; to be puffed up with pride; **todo cabe en** anything can be expected of
**cabestrar** *tr* to put a halter on
**cabestrillo** *m* sling
**cabestro** *m* halter; **llevar** or **traer del cabestro** (coll) to lead by the halter; (fig) to lead by the nose
**cabeza** *f* head; chief city, capital; **cabeza de chorlito** (coll) scatterbrains; (Arg) forgetful person; **cabeza de motín** ringleader; **cabeza de playa** beachhead; **cabeza de puente** bridgehead; **cabeza de turco** butt, scapegoat; **cabeza mayor** head of cattle; **cabeza menor** head of sheep, goats, etc.; **de cabeza** headfirst; on end; on one's own; by heart; **ir cabeza abajo** (coll) to go downhill; **irse de la cabeza** to go out of one's mind; **mala cabeza** headstrong person; **por su cabeza** on one's own; **romperse la cabeza** (coll) to rack one's brains
**cabezada** *f* butt with the head; blow on the head; (*de buque*) pitch, pitching; (*de bota*) instep; (*de libro*) headband; **dar cabezadas** to nod; (*un buque*) to pitch
**cabezal** *m* pillow, cushion; bolster
**cabezo** *m* hillock; summit, peak; reef
**cabe•zón -zona** *adj* big-headed; stubborn; (*licor*) (Chile) strong || *m* (*en la ropa*) hole for the head; tax register
**cabezonada** *f* (coll) stubbornness

**cabezu·do -da** *adj* big-headed; (coll) headstrong; (*vino*) heady
**cabezuela** *f* little head; (*harina gruesa del trigo*) middling; cornflower
**cabida** *f* room, space, capacity; influence, pull; **tener cabida en** to be included in
**cabildear** *intr* to lobby
**cabildeo** *m* lobbying
**cabildero** *m* lobbyist
**cabildo** *m* chapter (*of a cathedral*); chapter meeting; town hall
**cabina** *f* cabin; (*locutorio del teléfono*) booth; bathhouse, dressing room
**cabio** *m* rafter; joist
**cabizba·jo -ja** *adj* crestfallen, downcast
**cable** *m* cable; rope, hawser; **cable de remolque** towline; **cable de retén** guy wire
**cablegrafiar** §77 *tr & intr* to cable
**cablegráfi·co -ca** *adj* cable
**cablegrama** *m* cablegram
**cabo** *m* end, tip; (*punta de tierra que penetra en el mar*) cape; (*mango*) handle; small bundle; small piece; boss, foreman; cord, rope, cable; (mil) corporal; **al cabo** finally, at last; **al cabo de** at the end of; **atar cabos** (coll) to put two and two together; **Cabo de Buena Esperanza** Cape of Good Hope; **Cabo de Hornos** Cape Horn; **cabos** (*de caballo*) paws, nose, and mane; eyes, eyebrows, and hair; clothing; **cabo suelto** (coll) loose end; **estar al cabo de** (coll) to be well informed about; **llevar a cabo** to carry out, to accomplish
**cabotaje** *m* coasting trade
**cabra** *f* goat; nanny goat; (Chile) light two-wheel carriage; (Chile) sawbuck; (Col, Cuba, Ven) trick, gyp, loaded dice; **cabras** light clouds
**cabrahigo** wild fig
**cabrería** *f* goat stable; goat-milk dairy
**cabre·ro -ra** *mf* goatherd
**cabrestante** *m* capstan
**cabrilla** *f* sawbuck, sawhorse; (ichth) grouper; **cabrillas** skipping stones; (*olas blancas en el mar*) whitecaps
**cabrillear** *intr* (*el mar*) to be covered with whitecaps; to shimmer
**cabrio** *m* rafter; joist
**cabrí·o -a** *adj* goat; goatish || *m* herd of goats
**cabriola** *f* caper; somersault; **dar cabriolas** to cut capers
**cabriolear** *intr* to caper, frisk, prance
**cabritilla** *f* kid, kidskin
**cabrito** *m* kid; **cabritos** (Chile) popcorn
**cabrón** *m* buck, billy goat; (coll) complaisant cuckold; (Chile) pimp
**cabronada** *f* (coll) shamelessness; (coll) shameless forbearance
**cabru·no -na** *adj* goat
**cacahuate** *adj* (Mex) pocked || *m* peanut
**cacahuete** *m* peanut
**cacahuete·ro -ra** *mf* peanut vendor
**cacalote** *m* (Mex) raven; (CAm, Mex) candied popcorn; (Cuba) break, blunder
**cacao** *m* chocolate tree; cocoa, chocolate; **pedir cacao** (Am) to call quits; **tener mucho cacao** (Guat) to have a lot of pep
**cacaraña** *f* pit, pock
**cacarear** *tr* (coll) to crow over, boast of || *intr* (*la gallina*) to cackle; (*el gallo*) to crow
**cacareo** *m* (*de la gallina*) cackling; (*del gallo*) crowing; (*de una persona*) (coll) crowing, boasting
**cacatúa** *f* cockatoo
**cacea** *f* trolling; **pescar a la cacea** to troll
**cacear** *tr* to stir with a dipper or ladle || *intr* to troll
**cacería** *f* hunting; hunting party; (*animales cobrados en la caza*) bag; hunting scene
**cacerola** *f* casserole, saucepan
**cacique** *m* Indian chief; bossy fellow; (*en asuntos políticos*) (coll) boss; (Chile) lazy lummox; **cacique veranero** Baltimore oriole, hangbird
**caciquismo** *m* bossism
**caco** *m* thief, pickpocket; (coll) coward
**cacto** *m* cactus
**cacumen** *m* summit; acumen, keen insight
**cacha·co -ca** *adj* (SAm) sporty || *m* (SAm) sport, dude
**cachada** *f* (Am) thrust or wound made with the horns
**cachalote** *m* sperm whale
**cachar** *tr* to break to pieces; (*la madera*) to slit, split; (Arg, Ecuad, Urug) to make fun of; (Am) to butt with the horns; (Chile) to grasp, understand
**cacharpari** *m* (Arg, Bol, Peru) send-off party
**cacharro** *m* crock, earthen pot; piece of crockery; piece of junk; (CAm, W-I) jail; (Col) trinket
**cachaza** *f* (coll) sloth, phlegm; rum; (Am) first froth on cane juice when boiled
**cachazu·do -da** *adj* (coll) slothful, phlegmatic || *mf* (coll) sluggard
**cachear** *tr* to frisk
**cacheo** *m* frisking
**cachete** *m* slap in the face; cheek, swollen cheek; dagger
**cachetero** *m* dagger; dagger man
**cachetina** *f* (coll) brawl, fistfight
**cachicuer·no -na** *adj* horn-handled
**cachillada** *f* brood, litter
**cachimba** *f* (*para fumar*) (Am) pipe; (Arg, Urug) well, spring; (Chile) revolver
**cachimbo** *m* (*para fumar*) (Am) pipe; (Cuba) sugar mill; **chupar cachimbo** (Ven) to smoke a pipe; (*un niño*) (Ven) to suck its finger
**cachiporra** *f* billy, bludgeon
**cachivache** *m* good-for-nothing; **cachivaches** broken pottery; pots and pans; junk, trash
**cacho** *m* slice, piece; (*mercadería que no se vende*) (Chile) drug on the market

**cachón** *m* (*ola de agua*) breaker; splash of water; **cachones** surf
**cachon•do -da** *adj* (*perra*) in rut; sexy
**cacho•rro -rra** *mf* cub, whelp, pup ‖ *m* little pistol
**cachucha** *f* rowboat; cap; Andalusian dance
**cachuela** *f* gizzard; fricassee of pork
**cachu•pín -pina** *mf* (CAm, Mex) Spanish settler in Latin America
**cada** *adj* each; every; **cada vez más** more and more; **cada vez que** whenever
**cadalso** *m* stand, platform; (*para la ejecución de un reo*) scaffold
**cadarzo** *m* floss, floss silk
**cadáver** *m* corpse, cadaver
**cadavéri•co -ca** *adj* cadaverous
**cadena** *f* chain; **cadena de presidiarios** chain gang; **cadena perpetua** life imprisonment
**cadencia** *f* cadence, rhythm
**cadencio•co -sa** *adj* rhythmical
**cadenero** *m* (surv) lineman
**cadera** *f* hip
**cadete** *m* (mil) cadet; (Arg, Bol) apprentice (*without pay*), errand boy
**cadillo** *m* burdock
**cadmio** *m* cadmium
**caducar** §73 *intr* to be in one's dotage; to be worn out; to lapse, expire
**caedi•zo -za** *adj* tottery, ready to fall over ‖ *m* (Am) lean-to
**caer** §15 *intr* to fall; to droop; to fall due; to be, be found; to fade; (*el sol, el día, el viento*) to decline; to happen; **caer a** to face, overlook; **caer bien** to fit; to be becoming; (coll) to make a hit; **caer de plano** to fall flat; **caer en** (*cierto día*) to come on, fall on, happen on; (*cierta página*) to be found on; **caer en cama** to fall ill; **caer en favor** to be in favor; **caer en la cuenta** to catch on, get the point; **caer en que** to realize that; **caer mal** to fit badly; to be unbecoming; (coll) to fall flat; **no caigo** (coll) I don't get it ‖ *ref* to fall, fall down; to be, be found; **caerse de su peso, caerse de suyo** to be self-evident; **caerse muerto de** (*p.ej., alegría, miedo, risa*) to be overcome with
**café** *adj* (Am) tan ‖ *m* coffee; coffee tree; coffee house; café; (Arg) reprimand; (Mex) tantrum; **café cantante** night club; **café de maquinilla** drip coffee; **café solo** black coffee
**cafetal** *m* coffee plantation
**cafetera** *f* coffee pot; (Arg) jalopy; **cafetera eléctrica** electric percolator
**cafetería** *f* cafeteria
**cafete•ro -ra** *adj* coffee ‖ *mf* coffee dealer; coffee-bean picker ‖ *f* see **cafetera**
**cafeto** *m* coffee tree
**cagar** §44 *tr* (coll) to spot, stain, spoil ‖ *intr* to defecate ‖ *ref* to defecate; to be scared
**cagatin•ta** *m* or **cagatin•tas** *m* (*pl* **-tas**) office drudge, penpusher
**ca•gón -gona** *adj* (coll) cowardly ‖ *mf* (coll) coward
**caída** *f* fall; spill, tumble; drop; failure; blunder, slip; (*de una cortina*) hang; **a la caída de la noche** at nightfall; **a la caída del sol** at sunset; **caída de agua** waterfall; **caída radiactiva** fallout; **caídas** coarse wool; (coll) witticisms
**caí•do -da** *adj* fallen; (*cuello*) turndown; (*párpado, hombro*) drooping; dejected, crestfallen; **caído en desuso** obsolete ‖ **caídos** *mpl* interest due; **los caídos** (*en la guerra*) the fallen ‖ *f* see **caída**
**caimán** *m* alligator; (coll) schemer
**Caín** *m* Cain; **pasar las de Caín** (coll) to have a frightful time
**Cairo, El** Cairo
**caja** *f* box; case, chest, coffer; (*de caudales*) safe, strongbox; (*para dinero contante*) cashbox; (*dinero contante*) cash; (*ataúd*) casket, coffin; (*de reloj de bolsillo*) case; (*donde se pagan las cuentas en los hoteles*) desk; cashier's desk; (*del aparato de radio o televisión*) cabinet; (*de coche*) body; (*tambor*) drum; (*de fusil*) stock; (*de ascensor, de escalera*) shaft, well; (mach) housing; (typ) case; **caja alta** upper case; **caja baja** lower case; **caja clara** snare drum; **caja de ahorros** savings bank; **caja de cambio de marchas** transmission-gear box; **caja de caudales** safe; **caja de cigüeñal** crankcase; **caja de colores** paintbox; **caja de embalaje** packing box or case; **caja de enchufe** (elec) outlet; **caja de engranajes** gear case; **caja de fuego** firebox; **caja de fusibles** fuse box; **caja de ingletes** miter box; **caja de menores** petty cash; **caja de registro** manhole; **caja de reloj** watchcase; **caja de seguridad** safe; safe-deposit box; **caja de sorpresa** jack-in-the-box; **caja de velocidades** transmission-gear box; **caja fuerte** safe, bank vault; **caja postal de ahorros** postal savings bank; **caja registradora** cash register; **despedir** or **echar con cajas destempladas** (coll) to send packing, to give the gate
**caje•ro -ra** *mf* boxmaker; (*en un banco*) cashier, teller; (*en un hotel*) desk clerk
**cajeta** *f* little box; tobacco box; **de cajeta** (CAm, Mex) fine
**cajetilla** *f* pack (*of cigarettes*)
**cajetín** *m* rubber stamp; (typ) box
**cajista** *mf* compositor
**cajón** *m* large box, bin; (*caja movible de un mueble*) drawer; (*que se cierra con llave*) locker; (*que sirve de tienda*) booth, stall; (Chile) long gully; (Mex) dry-goods store; (SAm) coffin; **cajón de aire comprimido** caisson; **cajón de sastre** (coll) odds and ends; (coll) muddlehead; **ser de cajón** (coll) to be in vogue, be the thing
**cal** *f* lime; **cal apagada** slaked lime; **cal viva** quicklime; **de cal y canto** (coll) strong, tough
**cala** *f* calla lily; cove, inlet; (*de fruta*)

sample slice; (*de buque*) hold; suppository
**calabacear** *tr* (*a un alumno*) (coll) to flunk; (*una mujer a un pretendiente*) (coll) to jilt
**calabacera** *f* calabash, pumpkin, squash
**calabaza** *f* calabash, gourd, pumpkin, squash; (coll) dolt; **dar calabaza a** (*un alumno*) (coll) to flunk; (*un pretendiente*) (coll) to jilt
**calabo•bos** *m* (*pl* **-bos**) (coll) steady drizzle
**calabocero** *m* jailer, warden
**calabozo** *m* dungeon; cell, prison cell
**calada** *f* soaking; (*del ave de rapiña*) swoop; (coll) scolding
**calado** *m* openwork, drawn work; fretwork; (*del agua*) depth; (naut) draught
**calafatear** *tr* to calk
**calafateo** *m* calking
**calamar** *m* squid
**calambre** *m* cramp
**calamidad** *f* calamity
**calamita** *f* magnetic needle
**calamito•so -sa** *adj* calamitous
**cálamo** *m* reed, stalk; (poet) pen; (poet) flute, reed
**calamoca•no -na** *adj* (*algo embriagado*) (coll) tipsy; (*chocho*) (coll) doddering
**calaña** *f* nature, kind; pattern; fan
**calar** *tr* to pierce; to soak; to wedge; to cut open work in; (*un melón*) to cut a plug in; (*la bayoneta*) to fix; (*un puente levadizo*) to lower; (*las redes de pesca*) to lower in the water; (*un buque cierta profundidad*) to draw; (*a una persona o las intenciones de una persona*) to size up, to see through; (Arg) to stare at || *ref* to get soaked, get drenched; (*introducirse*) to slip in; (*el ave de rapiña*) to swoop down; to miss fire; (*el sombrero*) to pull down tight; (*las gafas*) to stick on; **calarse hasta los huesos** to get soaked to the skin
**cala•to -ta** *adj* (Peru) naked; (Peru) penniless
**calavera** *m* daredevil; libertine || *f* skull; (*imitación de la calavera*) death's-head; (Mex) tail light
**calaverada** *f* recklessness, daredeviltry; (Am) escapade
**calaverear** *tr* to spoil, make ugly || *intr* (coll) to act recklessly; (Am) to go on a spree
**calcado** *m* tracing
**calcañal** *m* or **calcañar** *m* heel
**calcar** §73 *tr* to trace; to copy, imitate; to tread on
**calce** *m* wedge; iron tire; iron tip; (*de un documento*) (CAm, Mex, P-R) bottom, foot
**calceta** *f* stocking; fetter, shackle; **hacer calceta** to knit
**calcetería** *f* hosiery; hosiery shop
**calcete•ro -ra** *mf* hosier; stocking mender
**calcetín** *m* sock
**calcificar** §73 *tr & ref* to calcify
**calcio** *m* calcium
**calco** *m* tracing; copy, imitation
**calcula•dor -dora** *adj* calculating; (*egoísta, interesado*) (fig) calculating || *mf* calculator || *f* calculating machine
**calcular** *tr & intr* to calculate; (*suponer*) (fig) to calculate
**cálculo** *m* calculation; (math, pathol) calculus; **cálculo biliar** gallstone; **cálculo renal** kidney stone
**calchona** *f* (Chile) goblin, bogey; (Chile) witch, old hag
**calda** *f* heating, warming; **caldas** hot springs
**caldeamiento** *m* heating
**caldear** *tr* to heat; to weld || *ref* to get hot; to get overheated
**caldeo** *m* heating; welding
**caldera** *f* boiler; pot, kettle; (Arg) coffee pot, teapot
**calderero** *m* boilermaker
**calderilla** *f* holy-water vessel; copper coin; small change; mountain currant
**caldero** *m* kettle, pot; (*reloj de bolsillo*) (Arg) turnip
**calderón** *m* caldron; (*signo*) (mus) pause, hold
**caldo** *m* broth; sauce, gravy, dressing; salad dressing; (Mex) syrup; (Mex) sugar-cane juice; **caldo de la reina** eggnog; **caldos** wet goods
**calefacción** *f* heating; **calefacción por agua caliente** hot-water heat; **calefacción por aire caliente** hot-air heat
**calefactor** *m* heater man; (electron) heater, heater element
**calefón** *m* (Arg) hot-water heater
**calendar** *tr* to date
**calendario** *m* calendar; **hacer calendarios** (coll) to meditate; (coll) to make wild predictions
**calenta•dor -dora** *adj* heating || *m* heater; warming pan; (*reloj de bolsillo*) (coll) turnip; **calentador a gas** gas heater; **calentador de agua** water heater
**calentamiento** *m* heating
**calentar** §2 *tr* to heat; to warm; to beat; (Chile) to bore, annoy; **calentar la silla** (*detenerse demasiado*) to warm a chair || *ref* to heat up, run hot; to warm oneself; to warm up; (*estar en celo las bestias*) to be in heat; (Chile, Ven) to become annoyed, get angry
**calentón** *m* (coll) warm-up; **darse un calentón** (coll) to stop and warm up
**calentura** *f* fever, temperature
**calenturien•to -ta** *adj* feverish; exalted; (Chile) consumptive
**calenturón** *m* high fever
**calenturo•co -sa** *adj* feverish
**calera** *f* limekiln; limestone quarry
**calesa** *f* chaise
**caleta** *f* cove, inlet
**caletre** *m* (coll) judgment, acumen
**calibrador** *m* calipers; **calibrador de alambre** wire gauge
**calibrar** *tr* to calibrate; to gauge
**calibre** *m* caliber; gauge; bore, diameter
**calicanto** *m* rubble masonry

**cali·có** *m* (*pl* **-cós**) calico
**calidad** *f* quality; condition, term; rank, nobility; importance; **a calidad de que** provided that; **en calidad de** in the capacity of
**cáli·do -da** *adj* warm, hot
**calidoscopio** *m* kaleidoscope
**calientaca·mas** *m* (*pl* **-mas**) bed warmer
**calienta·piés** *m* (*pl* **-piés**) foot warmer
**caliente** *adj* hot; fiery, vehement; (*en celo*) hot; **caliente de cascos** hotheaded; **en caliente** while hot; at once
**califa** *m* caliph
**califato** *m* caliphate
**calificación** *f* qualification; (*nota en un examen*) grade, mark; rating, standing
**calificar** §73 *tr* to qualify; to certify; to ennoble; (*un examen*) to mark; (*en los registros electorales*) (Chile) to register || *ref* (archaic) to prove one's noble birth; (*en los registros electorales*) (Chile) to register
**calificati·vo -va** *adj* qualifying || *m* (*nota en la escuela*) grade, mark; (*en un diccionario*) usage label
**California** *f* California; **la Baja California** Lower California
**caligrafía** *f* penmanship
**calina** *f* haze
**calino·so -sa** *adj* hazy
**Calíope** *f* Calliope
**calipso** *m* calypso || **Calipso** *f* Calypso
**calistenia** *f* calisthenics
**calisténi·co -ca** *adj* calisthenic
**cá·liz** *m* (*pl* **-lices**) chalice; **cáliz de dolor** cup of sorrow
**cali·zo -za** *adj* lime, limestone || *f* limestone
**calma** *f* calm; calm weather; quiet, tranquillity; slowness; (*cesación*) letup, suspension; **calma chicha** dead calm; **calmas ecuatoriales** doldrums; **en calma** in suspension; (*mercado*) steady; (*mar*) calm, smooth
**calmante** *adj* soothing; pain-relieving || *m* sedative
**calmar** *tr* to calm, sooth || *intr* to grow calm; to abate || *ref* to calm down
**calmazo** *m* dead calm
**cal·mo -ma** *adj* barren, treeless; fallow, uncultivated || *f* see **calma**
**calmo·so -sa** *adj* calm; (coll) slow, lazy
**calmu·do -da** *adj* calm; (*viento*) (naut) light; (*tiempo*) (naut) mild
**caló** *m* gypsy slang, underworld slang
**calofriar** §77 *ref* to become chilled
**calofrío** *m* chill
**calor** *m* heat; warmth; (fig) warmth, enthusiasm; **hace calor** it is hot, it is warm; **tener calor** (*una persona*) to be hot, be warm
**calorífe·ro -ra** *adj* heat || *m* heater, furnace; heating system; foot warmer
**calorífu·go -ga** *adj* heatproof; fireproof
**caloro·so -sa** *adj* warm, hot; (fig) warm, enthusiastic, hearty
**calotear** *tr* (Arg) to gyp, cheat
**calpul** *m* (Guat) gathering, meeting; (Hond) Indian mound
**caluma** *f* (Peru) gorge in the Andes; (Peru) Indian hamlet
**calumnia** *f* calumny, slander
**calumniar** *tr* to slander
**calumnio·so -sa** *adj* slanderous
**caluro·so -sa** *adj* warm, hot; (fig) warm, enthusiastic, hearty
**calva** *f* bald spot; bare spot, clearing; (*en un tejido*) worn spot
**calvario** *m* (*sufrimiento moral*) cross; (coll) series of misfortunes; (coll) string of debts || **Calvario** *m* Calvary; Stations of the Cross
**calvero** *m* clearing; clay pit
**calvez** *f* or **calvicie** *f* baldness
**cal·vo -va** *adj* bald; barren, bare || *f* see **calva**
**calza** *f* wedge; (coll) stocking; **calzas** hose, breeches, tights; **en calzas prietas** (coll) in a tight fix
**calzada** *f* highway, causeway; (S-D) sidewalk
**calzado** *m* footwear, shoes
**calzador** *m* shoehorn
**calzar** §60 *tr* to shoe, put shoes on; to provide with shoes; (*cierto tamaño de zapatos, guantes, etc.*) to wear, to take; (*un zapato a una persona*) to fit; to wedge; (*una rueda*) to block, scotch; (*la pata de una mesa*) to block up; to tip or trim with iron; (*plantas*) (hort) to hill || *intr* (Arg) to get the place sought; **calzar bien** to wear good footwear; **calzar mal** to wear poor footwear || *ref* to get; (*zapatos, guantes*) to put on, to wear; to put one's shoes on; (*a una persona*) (coll) to dominate, to manage
**calzo** *m* wedge; chock, skid
**calzón** *m* trousers, pants; **calzones** trousers, breeches; **calzarse los calzones** to wear the pants
**calzonarias** *fpl* (Col) suspenders
**calzona·zos** *m* (*pl* **-zos**) (coll) jellyfish; (coll) henpecked husband
**calzoncillos** *mpl* underdrawers
**callada** *f* (naut) abatement, lull; **a las calladas** or **de callada** (coll) on the quiet; **dar la callada por respuesta** to give no answer
**calla·do -da** *adj* silent; mysterious, secret || *f* see **callada**
**callampa** *f* (Chile) felt hat; (Chile) large ear; (Chile) mushroom
**callana** *f* (SAm) Indian baking bowl; (*reloj de bolsillo*) (Chile) turnip; (Chile) behind; (Chile, Peru) flowerpot
**callao** *m* pebble
**callar** *tr* to silence; to not mention; (*un secreto*) to keep; to calm, quiet || *intr & ref* to become silent, keep silent; to keep quiet, keep still; **callarse la boca** (coll) to shut up, to clam up
**calle** *f* street; **calle de travesía** cross street; **calle mayor** main street; **dejar en la calle** (coll) to deprive of one's livelihood
**calleja** *f* side street, alley; (coll) subterfuge, pretext
**callejear** *intr* to walk around the streets, to ramble around
**calleje·ro -ra** *adj* street; gadabout || *m*

street guide; list of addresses of newspaper subscribers
**callejón** *m* alley, lane; **callejón sin salida** blind alley
**callejuela** *f* side street, alley; (coll) subterfuge, pretext
**callicida** *m* corn cure
**callo** *m* callus; (*en el pie*) corn; **callos** tripe
**callo·so -sa** *adj* callous
**cama** *f* bed; (*para las bestias*) bedding, litter; **cama imperial** four-poster; **cama turca** day bed; **guardar cama** to be sick in bed
**camachuelo** *m* (orn) bullfinch
**camada** *f* brood, litter; layer, stratum; (*de ladrones*) den
**camafeo** *m* cameo
**camaleón** *m* chameleon
**cámara** *f* chamber; hall; (*cuerpo legislador*) house, chamber; (*aparato fotográfico*) camera; (*tubo de goma del neumático*) inner tube; (*del arma de fuego*) chamber, breech; (*para cartuchos*) magazine; board, council; (*mueble donde se conservan los alimentos*) icebox; (*evacuación*) bowels; (aer) cockpit; **cámara agrícola** grange; **cámara ardiente** funeral chamber; **cámara de compensación** clearing house; **cámara de fuelle** folding camera; **cámara de las máquinas** (naut) engine room; **Cámara de los Comunes** House of Commons; **Cámara de los Lores** House of Lords; **cámara de oxígeno** oxygen tent; **Cámara de Representantes** House of Representatives; **cámara frigorífica** cold-storage room; **cámara indiscreta** candid camera; **cámaras** loose bowels
**camarada** *m* comrade
**camarera** *f* waitress; chambermaid, maid; (*en los barcos*) stewardess; (*que sirve a una reina o princesa*) lady in waiting
**camarero** *m* waiter; valet; (*en un barco o avión*) steward
**camarilla** *f* clique, coterie, cabal; palace coterie
**camarín** *m* boudoir; (theat) dressing room
**cámaro** *m* var of **camarón**
**camarógrafo** *m* cameraman
**camarón** *m* shrimp, prawn; (CAm, Col) tip, gratuity; (Ven) nap; **ponerse como un camarón** (Am) to blush
**camarote** *m* stateroom, cabin
**camasquin·ce** *mf* (*pl* **-ce**) (coll) meddlesome person, kibitzer
**cambalachar** *tr & intr* var of **cambalachear**
**cambalache** *m* exchange, swap; (Arg) second-hand shop
**cambalachear** *tr* to swap, exchange, trade off || *intr* to swap, exchange
**cambiadis·cos** *m* (*pl* **-cos**) record changer
**cambiante** *adj* changing; fickle; iridescent || **cambiantes** *mpl* iridescence
**cambiar** *tr* to change; to exchange || *intr* to change; **cambiar de** (*p.ej.*, *sombreros, ropa, trenes*) to change; **cambiar de marcha** to shift gears || *ref* to change
**cambiavía** *m* (Am) switch; (Am) switchman
**cambio** *m* change; exchange; rate of exchange; (aut) shift; (rr) switch; **cambio de marchas, cambio de velocidades** gearshift; **en cambio** on the other hand
**cambista** *mf* moneychanger; banker || *m* (Arg) switchman
**cambullón** *m* (Mex, Col, Ven) barter, exchange; (Chile) subversion; (Peru) scheming, trickery
**camelar** *tr* (coll) to flirt with; (coll) to cajole, to tease
**camelo** *m* (coll) flirtation; (coll) joke; (coll) false rumor
**camellero** *m* camel driver
**camello** *m* camel
**camellón** *m* drinking trough; flower bed
**came·ro -ra** *adj* bed || *mf* maker of bedding || *m* (Col) highway
**camilla** *f* stretcher; couch; round table with heater underneath; (Mex) clothing store
**camillero** *m* stretcher-bearer
**caminante** *mf* walker; traveler on foot || *m* groom attending his master's horse
**caminar** *tr* (*cierta distancia*) to walk || *intr* to walk; to go; to travel, to journey; to behave
**caminata** *f* (coll) long walk, hike; (coll) outing, jaunt
**camine·ro -ra** *adj* road, highway
**camino** *m* road, way; (*viaje*) journey; (*tira larga que se pone en mesas o pisos*) (SAm) runner; **a medio camino (entre)** halfway (between); **camino de** on the way to; **camino de herradura** bridle path; **camino de hierro** railway; **camino de ruedas** wagon road; **Camino de Santiago** Way of St. James (*Milky Way*); **camino de sirga** towpath; **camino de tierra** dirt road; **camino real** highroad; **camino trillado** beaten path; **echar camino adelante** to strike out
**camión** *m* truck, motor truck; (Mex) bus; **camión volquete** dump truck
**camionaje** *m* trucking
**camione·ro -ra** *adj* truck || *m* trucker, teamster
**camioneta** *f* light truck
**camión-grúa** *m* tow truck
**camionista** *m* trucker, teamster
**camisa** *f* (*de hombre*) shirt; (*de mujer*) chemise; (*de la culebra*) slough; (*de un libro*) jacket; (*para papeles*) folder; (*de una pieza mecánica*) jacket, casing; (*de un horno de fundición*) lining; **camisa de agua** water jacket; **camisa de dormir** nightshirt; **camisa de fuerza** strait jacket; **cambiarse la camisa** to become a turncoat
**camisería** *f* haberdashery; shirt factory
**camise·ro -ra** *mf* haberdasher; shirt maker

**camiseta** *f* undershirt; (*de traje de baño*) top
**camisola** *f* stiff shirt
**camisolín** *m* dickey, shirt front
**camón** *m* bay window; **camón de vidrios** glass partition
**camorra** *f* (coll) quarrel, row; **armar camorra** (coll) to raise Cain, to raise a row; **buscar camorra** (coll) to be looking for trouble
**camorrista** *adj* (coll) quarrelsome ‖ *mf* (coll) quarrelsome person
**camote** *m* (Mex) sweet potato; (Am) onion; (Chile) lie, fib; (Chile, Peru) sweetheart; (Arg, Ecuad) blockhead; (Mex) churl; (El Salv) black-and-blue mark; **tomar un camote** (Am) to become infatuated
**camotear** *tr* (Arg) to filch, to snitch; (Guat) to bother ‖ *intr* (Mex) to wander around aimlessly
**campal** *adj* pitched (*battle*)
**campamento** *m* camp; encampment
**campana** *f* bell; (*para la protección de plantas*) bell glass, bell jar; (*de las guarniciones de alumbrado eléctrico*) canopy; **campana de buzo** diving bell; **por campana de vacante** (Mex) rarely, seldom
**campanada** *f* stroke of a bell, ring of a bell; scandal
**campanario** *m* belfry, steeple
**campanear** *tr* (*las campanas*) to ring ‖ *intr* to ring the bells ‖ *ref* (coll) to strut
**campanero** *m* bell ringer; bell founder
**campanil** *adj* bell ‖ *m* belfry, bell tower
**campanilla** *f* hand bell; door bell; bubble; (anat) uvula; **de (muchas) campanillas** (coll) of great importance
**campano** *m* cowbell
**campante** *adj* (coll) proud, satisfied; (coll) outstanding
**campanu•do -da** *adj* bell-shaped; pompous, high-sounding
**campaña** *f* campaign; cruise; countryside
**campar** *intr* to camp; to excel, stand out
**campear** *intr* to go to pasture; (*las sementeras*) to turn green; to stand out, excel; to reconnoiter; (Am) to ride through the fields to check the cattle
**campecha•no -na** *adj* (coll) frank, good-natured, cheerful ‖ *f* (Mex) mixed drink; (Ven) hammock
**campeche** *m* logwood
**campeón** *m* champion; **campeón de venta** best seller
**campeona** *f* championess
**campeonato** *m* championship
**campe•ro -ra** *adj* unsheltered, in the open
**campesi•no -na** *adj* country, rural, peasant ‖ *mf* peasant, farmer ‖ *m* countryman ‖ *f* countrywoman
**campestre** *adj* country, rural
**campiña** *f* countryside, open country
**campo** *m* (*terreno sembradío; sitio o foco de varias actividades*) field; (*en oposición a la ciudad*) country; ground, background; (*campamento*) (mil) camp; **a campo traviesa** across country; **campo de batalla** battlefield; **campo de juego** playground; **campo de tiro** range, shooting range; **campo santo** cemetery; **levantar el campo** (mil) to break camp; **quedar en el campo** to fall in battle
**camposanto** *m* cemetery
**camuesa** *f* pippin (*apple*)
**camueso** *m* pippin (*tree*)
**camuflaje** *m* camouflage
**camuflar** *tr* to camouflage
**can** *m* dog; (*de arma de fuego*) trigger
**cana** *f* grey hair; **echar una cana al aire** (coll) to cut loose, to step out; **peinar canas** (coll) to be getting old
**Canadá, el** Canada
**canadiense** *adj* & *mf* Canadian
**canal** *m* (*cauce artificial*) canal; (*estrecho en el mar*) channel; (anat) duct, canal; (telv) channel; **Canal de la Mancha** English Channel; **Canal de Panamá** Panama Canal; **Canal de Suez** Suez Canal; **canal alimenticio** alimentary canal ‖ *f* channel; (*conducto del tejado*) gutter; (*estría*) flute, groove; pipe; (*de un libro*) fore edge
**canalización** *f* (*de agua o gas*) mains, pipes; ductwork; (elec) wiring; **canalización de consumo** (elec) house current
**canalizar** §60 to channel; to pipe; (elec) to wire
**canalizo** *m* (naut) waterway, fairway
**canalón** *m* rain-water spout; shovel hat; **canalones** ravioli
**canalla** *m* (coll) churl, scoundrel ‖ *f* (coll) riffraff, canaille
**canallada** *f* (coll) dirty trick, meanness
**canana** *f* cartridge belt
**canapé** *m* sofa, couch
**Canarias** *fpl* Canaries
**cana•rio -ria** *adj* & *mf* Canarian ‖ *m* canary, canary bird ‖ *fpl* see **Canarias**
**canasta** *f* basket, hamper
**canastilla** *f* basket; (*ropa para el niño que ha de nacer*) layette; (*equipo de novia*) (dial) trousseau
**canastillo** *m* basket-weave tray
**canasto** *m* hamper ‖ **canastos** *interj* confound it!
**cáncamo** *m* eyebolt; **cáncamo de argolla** ringbolt
**cancanear** *intr* (coll) to loaf around; (Am) to stammer
**cancel** *m* storm door; (Am) folding screen
**cancela** *f* door of ironwork
**cancelar** *tr* to cancel; (*una deuda*) to pay off
**cáncer** *m* cancer
**cancero•so -sa** *adj* cancerous
**cancilla** *f* lattice gate
**canciller** *m* chancellor
**cancillería** *f* chancellery
**canción** *f* song; poem, lyric poem; **canción de amor** love song; **canción de cuna** cradlesong, lullaby; **canción típica** folk song; **volver a la misma canción** to sing the same old song
**cancionero** *m* songbook; anthology

**cancionista** *mf* popular singer
**canco** *m* (Chile) flowerpot; (Chile) earthen jug; (Chile) chamber pot; (Bol) buttock; **cancos** (Chile) woman's broad hips
**cancón** *m* (coll) bugaboo; **hacer un cancón a** (Mex) to try to bluff
**cancha** *f* field, ground; race track; golf links; tennis court; cockpit; (Urug) path, way; **estar en su cancha** (Arg, Chile, Urug) to be in one's element; **tener cancha** (Arg) to have pull || *interj* gangway!
**canche** *adj* (Col) tasteless, poorly seasoned; (CAm) blond
**candado** *m* padlock
**candar** *tr* to lock, to padlock
**candela** *f* candle; candlestick; fire, light; **con la candela en la mano** at death's door
**candelabro** *m* candelabrum
**candelecho** *m* elevated hut for watching the vineyard
**candelero** *m* candlestick; brass olive-oil lamp; fishing torch
**candelilla** *f* catkin; (Arg, Chile) will-o'-the-wisp; (Am) glowworm
**candida•to -ta** *mf* candidate
**candidatura** *f* candidacy; list of candidates; voting paper
**candidez** *f* whiteness; innocence
**cándi•do -da** white; simple, innocent
**candil** *m* open olive-oil lamp
**candilejas** *fpl* footlights
**candon•go -ga** *adj* fawning, slick; loafing, shirking || *mf* fawner, flatterer; loafer, shirker || *f* fawning; teasing
**candonguear** *tr* (coll) to kid, tease || *intr* (coll) to scheme to get out of work
**candor** *m* innocence, ingenuousness
**caneca** *f* glazed earthen bottle
**cane•co -ca** *adj* (Arg, Bol) tipsy || *f* see **caneca**
**canela** *f* cinnamon; (*cosa fina*) (coll) peach
**canela•do -da** *adj* cinnamon-colored
**cane•lo -la** *adj* cinnamon || *m* (*árbol*) cinnamon || *f* see **canela**
**canelón** *m* rain-water spout; large icicle; cinnamon candy
**cane•sú** *m* (*pl* **-súes**) (*prenda*) guimpe; (*pieza de una prenda*) yoke
**cangilón** *m* jug, jar, bucket; (*de draga*) bucket, scoop; (Am) rut, track
**cangrejo** *m* crab
**cangrena** *f* gangrene
**cangrenar** *ref* to have gangrene
**canguro** *m* kangaroo
**caníbal** *adj* & *mf* cannibal
**canica** *f* (*bolita*) marble; (*juego*) marbles
**canicie** *f* whiteness (*of hair*)
**canícula** *f* dog days || **Canícula** *f* Dog Star
**caniculares** *mpl* dog days
**cani•jo -ja** *adj* (coll) weak, sickly || *mf* (coll) weakling
**canilla** *f* shank (*of leg*); (*espita, grifo*) tap; bobbin, spool; (Mex) strength
**cani•no -na** *adj* canine || *m* canine, canine tooth || *f* excrement of dogs
**canje** *m* exchange
**canjear** *tr* to exchange
**ca•no -na** *adj* gray; gray-haired; hoary, old || *f* see **cana**
**canoa** *f* canoe; launch
**canoe•ro -ra** *mf* canoeist
**canon** *m* canon
**canóni•co -ca** *adj* canonical || *f* rules of canonical life
**canóniga** *f* (coll) nap before eating; (coll) drunk
**canónigo** *m* canon
**canonizar** **§60** *tr* to canonize; to approve
**canonjía** *f* (coll) sinecure
**cano•ro -ra** *adj* (*voz*) melodious; (*ave*) song, sweet-singing
**cano•so -sa** *adj* gray-haired
**canotié** *m* straw hat, skimmer
**cansa•do -da** *adj* tired, weary; exhausted, worn-out; tiresome
**cansancio** *m* tiredness, fatigue
**cansar** *tr* to tire, weary; to bore || *intr* be tiresome || *ref* to tire, get tired
**cantable** *adj* tuneful, singable || *m* (*del libreto de una zarzuela*) lyric; (*de una zarzuela*) musical passage
**canta•dor -dora** *mf* singer of popular songs
**cantaletear** *tr* (Am) to say over and over again; (Am) to make fun of
**cantalupo** *m* cantaloupe
**cantante** *adj* singing || *mf* singer
**cantar** *m* song, singing; chant; **Cantar de los Cantares** Song of Songs || *tr* to sing; to chant; to sing of; **cantarlas claras** (coll) to speak out|| *intr* to sing; to chant; (coll) to creak, squeak; (coll) to squeal, to peach; **cantar de plano** (coll) to make a full confession
**cántara** *f* jug, pitcher
**cantárida** *f* Spanish fly
**canta•rín -rina** *adj* (*voz*) melodious; (coll) fond of singing || *mf* singer || *m* professional singer
**cántaro** *m* jug, pitcher; jugful; ballot box; **llover a cántaros** to rain pitchforks
**canta•triz** *f* (*pl* **-trices**) singer
**cantera** *f* quarry; talent, genius
**cántico** *m* canticle
**cantidad** *f* quantity; amount; sum; **cantidad de movimiento** (mech) momentum
**cantiga** *f* poem of the troubadours
**cantilena** *f* ballad, song; **salir con la misma cantilena** (coll) to sing the same old song
**cantimplora** *f* siphon; carafe, decanter; (*frasco para llevar bebida*) canteen; (Col) powder flask; (Guat) mumps
**cantina** *f* cantine; lunchroom, station restaurant; (Am) barroom
**cantinera** *f* camp follower
**cantinero** *m* bartender
**canto** *m* song; singing; (*división del poema épico*) canto; (*de notas iguales y uniformes*) chant; (*extremidad*) edge; (*esquina*) corner; (*de cuchillo*) back; (*de pan*) crust; stone, pebble; **canto de corte** cutting edge; **canto del cisne** swan song
**cantonera** *f* corner reinforcement; corner table, corner shelf; streetwalker

**cantonero** *m* corner loafer
**can·tor -tora** *adj* singing; (*pájaro*) song || *mf* singer || *m* chanter; minstrel; poet, bard
**canto·so -sa** *adj* rocky, stony
**canturrear** *tr & intr* to hum
**canturreo** *m* hum, humming
**canzonetista** *mf* popular singer
**caña** *f* cane; reed; stalk, stem; (*del brazo o la pierna*) long bone; (*de bota o media*) leg; wineglass; **caña de azúcar** sugar cane; **caña de pescar** fishing rod
**cañada** *f* glen, ravine, gully; cattle path; (Am) brook
**cañamazo** *m* canvas, burlap; embroidered canvas
**cañamiel** *f* sugar cane
**cáñamo** *m* hemp
**cañamones** *mpl* birdseed
**cañaveral** *m* canebrake; sugar-cane plantation
**cañería** *f* pipe; pipe line; piping; **cañería maestra** gas main, water main
**cañero** *m* pipe fitter, plumber; (Am) sugar-cane dealer; (SAm) cheat; (SAm) bluffer
**cañista** *m* pipe fitter, plumber
**caño** *m* pipe, tube; gutter, sewer; ditch; (*chorro*) spurt, jet; (*canal angosto*) channel; organ pipe; (*río pequeño*) (Col) stream
**cañón** *m* (*pieza de artillería*) cannon; (*valle estrecho*) canyon; (*de arma de fuego; de pluma*) barrel; (*pluma de ave*) quill; (*de escalera*) well; (*de columna; de ascensor*) shaft; organ pipe; (Col) trunk of tree; **cañón de campaña** fieldpiece; **cañón de chimenea** flue, chimney flue; **cañón obús** howitzer
**cañonear** *tr* to cannonade, to shell
**cañutazo** *m* (coll) gossip
**caoba** *f* mahogany
**caos** *m* chaos
**caóti·co -ca** *adj* chaotic
**cap.** *abbr* **capitán, capítulo**
**capa** *f* cloak, cape, mantle; (*de pintura*) coat; (*lo que cubre*) bed, layer; (*apariencia, pretexto*) (fig) cloak, mask; **capa del cielo** canopy of heaven; **andar de capa caída** to be on the decline, be in a bad way; (*comedia*) **de capa y espada** cloak-and-sword; (*intriga, espionaje*) **de capa y espada** cloak-and-dagger; **so capa de** under the guise of
**capacidad** *f* capacity
**capacitar** *tr* to enable, qualify; to empower || *ref* to become qualified
**capacha** *f* fruit basket; (SAm) jail
**capacho** *m* fruit basket; hamper; (*de albañil*) hod
**capar** *tr* to geld, castrate; to curtail
**caparazón** *m* caparison; horse blanket; nose bag; (*de crustáceo*) shell
**caparrosa** *f* vitriol
**capa·taz** *m* (*pl* **-taces**) overseer, foreman, boss
**ca·paz** *adj* (*pl* **-paces**) (*grande*) capacious, spacious; (*que tiene cierta aptitud; diestro, instruido*) capable; **capaz de** capable of; with a capacity of; **capaz para** competent in; qualified for; with room for
**capcio·so -sa** *adj* crafty, deceptive
**capea** *f* amateur free-for-all bullfight
**capear** *tr* (*al toro*) to challenge; (*el mal tiempo*) to weather; (coll) to deceive, take in || *intr* (naut) to lay to; (Guat) to play hooky
**capellán** *m* chaplain
**capeo** *m* capework (*of bullfighter*)
**caperucita** *f* little pointed hood; **Caperucita Roja** Little Red Ridinghood
**caperuza** *f* pointed hood; chimney cap
**capilla** *f* (*parte de una iglesia con altar*) chapel; (*de los reos de muerte*) death house; (*pliego suelto*) proof sheet; cowl, hood, cape; **estar en capilla** to be in the death house; (coll) to be on pins and needles; **estar expuesto en capilla ardiente** to be on view, to lie in state
**capiller** *m* churchwarden, sexton
**capillo** *m* baby cap; baptismal cap; hood; cocoon; (*del cigarro*) filler
**capirotazo** *m* fillip
**capirote** *m* hood; doctor's cap and hood; cardboard or paper cone (*worn on head*); fillip
**capitación** *f* poll tax
**capital** *adj* capital; main, principal; paramount; (*enemigo*) mortal || *m* (*dinero que produce renta*) capital; (*dinero que se presta para producir renta*) principal || *f* capital
**capitalismo** *m* capitalism
**capitalista** *adj* capitalistic || *mf* capitalist; shareholder, investor
**capitalizar** §60 *tr* to capitalize; (*los intereses devengados*) to compound
**capitán** *m* captain; leader; **capitán de bandera** flag captain; **capitán de corbeta** (nav) lieutenant commander; **capitán del puerto** harbor master
**capitana** *f* flagship
**capitanear** *tr* to captain; to lead, to command
**capitanía** *f* captaincy; (mil) company
**capitel** *m* (*de una iglesia*) spire; (*de una columna*) capital
**capitolio** *m* capitol
**capítula** *f* chapter (*of Scriptures*)
**capitular** *tr* to accuse; to agree on || *intr* to capitulate
**capitulear** *intr* (Arg, Chile, Peru) to lobby
**capituleo** *m* (Arg, Chile, Peru) lobbying
**capitulero** *m* (Arg, Chile, Peru) political henchman, lobbyist
**capítulo** *m* chapter; chapter house; subject, matter; errand; main point; **ganar capítulo** (coll) to win one's point; **llamar a capítulo** to take to task, call to account; **perder capítulo** (coll) to lose one's point
**ca·pó** *m* (*pl* **-pós**) hood (*of auto*)
**capolar** *tr* to cut to pieces, chop up
**ca·pón -pona** *adj* castrated || *m* eunuch; (*pollo*) capon; bundle of firewood; (*golpe*) (coll) fillip || *f* shoulder strap
**caponera** *f* coop for fattening capons; place of welcome; (*cárcel*) (coll) coop, jail

**caporal** *m* chief, leader; (Am) foreman (*on cattle ranch*)
**capota** *f* bonnet; (aer) cowling; (aut) top
**capotaje** *m* (aer) nosing over
**capotar** *intr* to upset; (aer) to nose over
**capote** *m* cape, cloak; (coll) frown, scowl; (Chile, Mex) beating; **capote de monte** poncho; **de capote** (Mex) on the sly; **dar capote a** (coll) to flabbergast; (*un rezagado*) (coll) to leave hungry; **decir para su capote** to say to oneself; **echar un capote** (coll) to turn the conversation
**capotear** *tr* (*al toro*) to challenge; (*dificultades*) to evade, duck; (coll) to beguile, take in; (*una obra teatral*) to cut, make cuts in
**Capricornio** *m* Capricorn
**capricho** *m* caprice, whim, fancy
**capricho•so -sa** *adj* capricious, whimsical; willful
**caprichu•do -da** *adj* (coll) capricious, whimsical
**cápsula** *f* capsule; (*de botella*) cap
**capsular** *tr* to cap
**captación** *f* capture; (*de las aguas de un río*) harnessing; (rad) tuning in, picking up
**captar** *tr* to catch; (*la confianza de una persona*) to win; (*las aguas de un río*) to harness; (*las ondas radiofónicas*) to tune in, to pick up; (*lo que uno dice*) to get, grasp || *ref* to attract, win
**captura** *f* capture, catch
**capturar** *tr* to capture, catch
**capucha** *f* cowl, hood; circumflex accent
**capuchina** *f* garden nasturtium, Indian cress; Capuchin nun; confection of egg yolks
**capucho** *m* cowl, hood
**capuchón** *m* lady's cloak and hood; (*de una plumafuente*) cap; (aut) valve cap
**capullo** *m* cocoon; coarse spun silk; bud; **capullo de rosa** rosebud
**capuzar** §60 *tr* to throw in headfirst; (*un buque*) to overload at the bow
**caqui** *adj* khaki || *m* khaki; Japanese persimmon
**caquinos** *mpl* (Mex) guffaw, outburst of laughter
**cara** *f* face; look, countenance; façade, front; (*de disco de fonógrafo*) side; **a cara descubierta** openly; **a cara o cruz** heads or tails; **cara a** facing; **cara al público** with an audience; **cara de acelga** (coll) sallow face; **cara de ajo** (coll) vinegar face; **cara de hereje** (*persona de feo aspecto*) (coll) fright, baboon; **cara de vinagre** (coll) vinegar face; **dar la cara** to take the consequences; **de cara** in the face; facing; **echar a cara o cruz** to flip a coin; **hacer cara a** to stand up to; **tener buena cara** to look well, to look good; **tener mala cara** to look ill, to look bad
**cárabe** *m* amber
**carabina** *f* carbine; (coll) chaperon
**caracol** *m* snail; snail shell; (*de pelo*) curl; (*trazado en espiral*) spiral; (*del oído*) cochlea
**carácter** *m* (*pl* **caracteres**) character; (*marca que se pone a las reses*) brand
**característi•co -ca** *adj* characteristic || *m* (theat) old man || *f* characteristic; (theat) old woman
**caracteriza•do -da** *adj* distinguished
**caracterizar** §60 *tr* to characterize; to confer a distinction on; (*un personaje en la escena*) to interpret || *ref* to dress and make up for a role
**caramba** *interj* confound it!; upon my word!
**carámbano** *m* icicle
**carambola** *f* carom; (coll) double shot; (coll) trick, cheating
**carambolear** *intr* to carom || *ref* (coll) to get tipsy
**caramelo** *m* caramel; drop, lozenge
**carantamaula** *f* (coll) ugly false face; (*persona*) (coll) ugly mug
**carantoña** *f* (coll) ugly false face; **carantoñas** (coll) adulation, fawning
**carátula** *f* mask; (*profesión de actor*) stage, theater; (Am) title page; (*de reloj*) (Mex, Guat) face
**caravana** *f* caravan; (*casa rodante*) trailer
**caravanera** *f* caravansary
**caray** *m* var of **carey**
**carbohielo** *m* dry ice
**carbóli•co -ca** *adj* carbolic
**carbón** *m* (*de leña*) charcoal; (*de piedra*) coal; (*electrodo de carbono de la lámpara de arco o la pila*) carbon; black crayon; (*honguillo parásito*) smut; **carbón de bujía** cannel coal, jet coal; **carbón tal como sale** run-of-mine coal
**carboncillo** *m* charcoal, charcoal pencil
**carbonera** *f* bunker, coal bunker; coalbin; (Col) coal mine
**carbonería** *f* coalyard
**carbone•ro -ra** *adj* coal, charcoal; coaling || *mf* coaldealer; charcoal burner || *f* see **carbonera**
**carbonilla** *f* fine coal; (*en los cilindros*) carbon
**carbonizar** §60 *tr* to char
**carbono** *m* carbon
**carbunclo** *m* (*piedra*) carbuncle; (pathol) carbuncle
**carbunco** *m* (pathol) carbuncle
**carbúnculo** *m* (*piedra*) carbuncle
**carburador** *m* carburetor
**carburo** *m* carbide
**carcacha** *f* (Mex) jalopy
**carcaj** *m* quiver
**carcajada** *f* outburst of laughter
**cárcel** *f* jail, prison; (*para oprimir dos piezas de madera encoladas*) clamp
**carcele•ro -ra** *adj* jail || *m* jailer, warden
**carcoma** *f* woodworm, borer; anxiety, worry; spendthrift
**carcomer** *tr* to bore, gnaw away at; to undermine, to harass || *ref* to become worm-eaten
**cardán** *m* universal joint
**cardenal** *m* cardinal; cardinal bird; black-and-blue mark

**cardenillo** *m* verdigris
**cárde•no -na** *adj* purple; dapple-gray; (*agua*) opaline
**cardía•co -ca** *adj* cardiac || *mf* (*persona que padece del corazón*) cardiac || *m* (*remedio*) cardiac
**cardinal** *adj* cardinal
**cardo** *m* thistle
**cardume** *m* school (*of fish*)
**carear** *tr* to bring face to face; to compare || *intr* — **carear a** to overlook || *ref* to meet face to face
**carecer** §22 *intr* — **carecer de** to lack, need, be in want of
**carecimiento** *m* lack, need, want
**carencia** *f* lack, need, want
**carente** *adj* — **carente de** lacking
**careo** *m* meeting; confrontation
**care•ro -ra** *adj* (coll) dear, expensive
**carestía** *f* scarcity, want, dearth; high prices; **carestía de la vida** high cost of living
**careta** *f* mask; **careta antigás** gas mask
**carey** *m* hawksbill turtle; tortoise shell
**carga** *f* load, loading; (*mercancías que se transportan*) freight, cargo; (*peso u obligación que pesan sobre una persona*) burden; (*de substancia explosiva, de electricidad, de soldados contra el enemigo*) charge; charge, responsibility, obligation; **carga de familia** dependent; **carga de punta** (elec) peak load; **carga útil** pay load; **echar la carga a** to put the blame on; **volver a la carga** to keep at it
**cargaderas** *fpl* (Col) suspenders
**cargadero** *m* loading platform; freight station
**carga•do -da** *adj* loaded; (*cielo*) overcast, cloudy; (*atmósfera, tiempo*) close, sultry; (*alambre eléctrico*) hot, charged; (*café, té*) strong; (*rato, hora*) busy; **cargado de años** along in years; **cargado de espaldas** round-shouldered, stoop-shouldered
**cargador** *m* loader, stevedore; carrier, porter; (*de acumulador*) charger
**cargamento** *m* load; (naut) loading; (naut) cargo, shipment
**cargante** *adj* (coll) boring, annoying, tiresome
**cargar** §44 *tr* (*un peso, mercancías; un carro, un mulo, un barco; un horno; un arma de fuego; a una persona*) to load; (*a una persona con un peso u obligación*) to burden; (*un acumulador; al enemigo*) to charge; (*a una persona*) to charge with; to entrust with; (coll) to annoy, bore, weary; **cargar en cuenta a** (*una persona*) to charge to the account of; **cargar** (*a una persona*) **de** to charge with; to burden with || *intr* to load; (*el viento*) to turn; to crowd; to incline, tip; (*el acento*) to fall; (coll) to eat too much, drink too much; **cargar con** to pick up; to walk away with; (*un fusil*) to shoulder; to take on; **cargar sobre** to rest on; to bother, pester; to devolve on || *ref* (*el cielo*) to become overcast; (*el viento*) to turn; (coll) to become annoyed, be bored; **cargarse de** to have a lot of; (*lágrimas*) to be bathed in
**cargaréme** *m* receipt, voucher
**cargazón** *f* loading; (*en el estómago, la cabeza, etc.*) heaviness; mass of heavy clouds; (Arg) clumsy job; (Chile) good crop
**cargo** *m* job, position; duty, responsibility; burden, weight; management; (*falta que se atribuye a uno; cantidad que uno debe y la acción de anotarla*) charge; **a cargo de** in charge of; **cargo de conciencia** sense of guilt; **girar a cargo de** to draw on; **hacerse cargo de** to take charge of; to realize, become aware of; to look into; **librar a cargo de** to draw on; **vestir el cargo** to look the part
**cargosear** *tr* (Arg, Chile) to pester
**cargo•so -sa** *adj* annoying, bothersome; onerous, costly
**carguero** *m* (naut) freighter; (Arg, Urug) beast of burden
**cariaconteci•do -da** *adj* (coll) downcast, woebegone
**cariar** §77 *tr & intr* to decay
**cariátide** *f* caryatid
**Caribdis** *f* Charybdis
**caribe** *adj* Caribbean || *m* savage, brute
**caricatura** *f* (*descripción o figura grotescas; retrato festivo*) caricature; (*retrato festivo*) cartoon
**caricaturista** *mf* caricaturist; cartoonist
**caricaturizar** §60 *tr* to caricature; to cartoon
**caricia** *f* caress; endearment
**caridad** *f* charity; **la caridad bien ordenada empieza por uno mismo** charity begins at home
**caries** *f* decay, tooth decay; caries
**carilla** *f* (*de colmenero*) mask; (*de libro*) page
**carille•no -na** *adj* full-faced
**carillón** *m* carillon
**carine•gro -gra** *adj* swarthy
**cariño** *m* love, affection; loved one; (Chile) gift, present; **cariños** caresses, endearments; (Arg) greetings
**cariño•so -sa** *adj* loving, affectionate
**caripare•jo -ja** *adj* (coll) stone-faced, impassive
**carirraí•do -da** *adj* brazen-faced, shameless
**carita** *f* little face; **dar** or **hacer carita** (*una mujer coqueta*) (Mex) to smile back
**caritati•vo -va** *adj* charitable
**cariz** *m* (*de la atmósfera, el tiempo*) appearance, look; (*de un asunto*) (coll) look, outlook; (*de la cara de uno*) (coll) look; **mal cariz** black look, scowl
**carlinga** *f* (aer) cockpit
**Carlomagno** *m* Charlemagne
**Carlos** *m* Charles
**carlota** *f* pudding; **carlota rusa** charlotte russe || **Carlota** *f* Charlotte
**carmen** *m* song, poem; house and garden (*in Granada*)
**carmesí** (*pl* **-síes**) *adj & m* crimson
**carnada** *f* bait; (coll) bait, trap
**carnal** *adj* carnal; (*hermano*) full; (*primo*) first

**carne** *f* (*parte blanda del cuerpo humano y del animal*) flesh; (*la comestible del animal*) meat; **carne de cañón** cannon fodder; **carne de cerdo asada** roast pork; **carne de cordero** lamb; **carne de gallina** goose flesh; **carne de horca** gallows bird; **carne de res** beef; **carne de ternera** veal; **carne de vaca asada** roast of beef; **carne de venado** venison; **carne fiambre** cold meat; **carne sin hueso** (coll) cinch, snap; **carne y sangre** flesh and blood; **cobrar carnes** (coll) to put on flesh; **en carnes** naked; **en vivas carnes** stark-naked

**carnear** *tr* (Arg, Chile, Urug) to butcher, slaughter; (Arg, Urug) to stab; (Chile) to take in, swindle

**carnero** *m* sheep; (*carne de este animal*) mutton; (*osario*) charnel house; family vault; (*persona que no tiene voluntad propia*) (Arg, Chile) sheep; **cantar para el carnero** (Arg, Bol, Urug) to die; **no hay tales carneros** there's no truth to it

**car•net** *m* (*pl* **-nets**) notebook; membership card; (Arg) dance card; **carnet de chófer** driver's license; **carnet de identidad** identification card

**carnicería** *f* butcher shop, meat market; (fig) carnage, massacre

**carnice•ro -ra** *adj* carnivorous; bloodthirsty || *mf* butcher

**carnosidad** *f* fleshiness, corpulence; (*excrecencia carnosa anormal*) proud flesh

**carno•so -sa** *adj* fleshy; meaty, fat

**ca•ro -ra** *adj* (*de subido precio; amado, querido*) dear || *f* see **cara** || **caro** *adv* dear

**carpa** *f* carp; (Am) awning, tent; (Am) stand at a fair; **carpa dorada** goldfish

**carpanta** *f* (coll) raging hunger

**carpeta** *f* (*cubierta para mesas*) table cover; (*par de cubiertas para documentos*) letter file, portfolio; (*factura*) invoice; (Col) accounting department; (Peru) writing desk

**carpintería** *f* carpentry; carpenter shop; **carpintería de taller** millwork

**carpintero** *m* carpenter; woodpecker; **carpintero de carreta** wheelwright

**carra•co -ca** *adj* (coll) old, decrepit || *f* (*barco viejo*) tub, hulk; (*instrumento de madera para producir un ruido desapacible*) rattle; (*berbiquí*) ratchet drill || **la Carraca** Cádiz navy yard

**carraspear** *intr* to be hoarse

**carraspera** *f* hoarseness

**carrera** *f* (*paso del que corre*) run; (*lucha de velocidad*) race; (*sitio para correr*) race track; (*espacio recorrido corriendo*) course, stretch; (*curso de la vida, profesión*) career; (*calle*) avenue, boulevard; (*raya, crencha*) part (*in hair*); (*en las medias*) run; (*hilera*) row, line; (*viga*) rafter, girder; (*movimiento del émbolo del motor*) stroke; **a carrera abierta** at full speed; **carrera a pie** foot race; **carrera ascendente** upstroke; **carrera de baquetas** gantlet; **carrera de caballos** horse race; **carrera de campanario** steeplechase; **carrera de obstáculos** obstacle race; steeplechase; **carrera de relevos** relay race; **carrera descendente** downstroke; **carrera de vallas** hurdle race; **carreras** horse racing, turf

**carrerista** *adj* horsy || *mf* racegoer; auto racer; bicycle racer || *m* outrider || *f* (slang) streetwalker

**carreta** *f* cart; **carreta de bueyes** oxcart

**carrete** *m* reel, spool; fishing reel; (elec) coil

**carretear** *tr* to cart, haul; (*un carro, una carreta*) to drive; (aer) to taxi || *intr* (aer) to taxi

**carretera** *f* highway, road; **carretera de peaje** turnpike; **carretera de vía libre** expressway, limited-access highway

**carretería** *f* carts; wagon work; carting business; wagon shop

**carrete•ro -ra** *adj* wagon, carriage || *m* wheelwright; teamster; charioteer; **jurar como un carretero** (coll) to swear like a trooper || *f* see **carretera**

**carretilla** *f* wheelbarrow; baggage truck; (*para enseñar a los niños a andar*) gocart; (*buscapiés*) snake, serpent; (Arg, Chile, Urug) jaw; **carretilla de mano** handcart; **carretilla elevadora** lift truck; **de carretilla** (coll) offhand

**carretón** *m* cart, wagon, dray; gocart; (rr) truck; (Am) covered wagon

**carricoche** *m* covered wagon

**carricuba** *f* street sprinkler

**carril** *m* (*barra de acero en el ferrocarril*) rail, track; (*huella*) track, rut; (*hecho por el arado*) furrow; lane, path; (Chile) train; (Chile, P-R) railroad; **carril de toma** third rail

**carrilera** *f* track, rut

**carrilero** *m* (Peru) railroader

**carrillera** *f* jaw; chin strap

**carrillo** *m* cheek, jowl; pulley; **comer a dos carrillos** (coll) to eat like a glutton; (coll) to have two sources of income; (coll) to play both sides

**carrizo** *m* ditch reed

**carro** *m* cart, wagon; (mach) carriage; (Am) car, auto; **carro alegórico** float; **carro blindado** armored car; **carro correo** mail car; **carro de asalto** tank; **carro de combate** combat car, tank; **carro de equipajes** baggage car; **carro de mudanza** moving van; **carro de riego** street sprinkler; **carro frigorífico** refrigerator car; **carro fúnebre** hearse; **Carro mayor** Big Dipper; **Carro menor** Little Dipper; **carro romano** chariot; **pare Vd. el carro** hold your horses

**ca•rró** *m* (*pl* **-rrós**) diamond

**carrocería** *f* (*de automóvil*) body

**carrocha** *f* eggs (*of insect*)

**carromato** *m* covered wagon

**carro•ño -ña** *adj* & *f* carrion

**carroza** *f* coach, carriage; **carroza alegórica** float; **carroza fúnebre** hearse

**carruaje** *m* carriage

**carta** *f* (*comunicación escrita*) letter; (*constitución escrita de un país*) charter; (*naipe*) card, playing card; map; **carta aérea** air-mail letter; **carta blanca** carte blanche; **carta certificada** registered letter; **carta de marear** (naut) chart; **carta de naturaleza** naturalization papers; **carta general** form letter; **carta por avión** air-mail letter; **poner las cartas boca arriba** to put one's cards on the table
**cartabón** *m* carpenter's square
**cartagi•nés -nesa** *adj & mf* Carthaginian
**Cartago** *f* Carthage
**cartapacio** *m* notebook; schoolboy's satchel; writing book; (*papeles contenidos en una carpeta*) file, dossier
**cartear** *intr* to play low cards (*in order to see how the game stands*) || *ref* to write to each other
**cartel** *m* show bill, poster, placard; cartel, trust; (*pasquín*) lampoon; (*de toreros*) bill, line-up; (*del torero*) fame, reputation; **cartel de teatro** bill, show bill; **dar cartel a** (coll) to headline; **se prohibe fijar carteles** post no bills; **tener cartel** (coll) to be the rage
**cartela** *f* card; bracket
**cartelera** *f* billboard; (*en los periódicos*) amusement page, theater section
**cartelero** *m* billposter
**cartelón** *m* show bill
**carteo** *m* finessing; exchange of letters
**cárter** *m* (mach) housing; **cárter de engranajes** gearcase; **cárter del cigüeñal** crankcase
**cartera** *f* portfolio; pocket flap; **cartera de bolsillo** billfold, wallet
**cartería** *f* sorting room
**carterista** *m* pickpocket, purse snatcher
**cartero** *m* letter carrier, postman
**cartilagino•so -sa** *adj* gristly
**cartílago** *m* gristle
**cartilla** *f* primer, speller, reader; notebook; (*de la caja de ahorros*) deposit book; **cartilla de racionamiento** ration book
**cartivana** *f* (bb) hinge, joint
**cartón** *m* cardboard, pasteboard; cardboard box; **cartón de yeso y fieltro** plasterboard; **cartón picado** stencil; **cartón tabla** wallboard
**cartoné** — **en cartoné** (bb) in boards, bound in boards
**cartucho** *m* cartridge
**cartulina** *f* fine cardboard
**casa** *f* (*edificio para habitar*) house; (*hogar, domicilio*) home; (*establecimiento comercial o industrial*) firm, concern; (*familia*) household; (*escaque*) square; **a casa** home, homeward; **casa consistorial** town hall, city hall; **casa de azotea** penthouse; **casa de campo** country house; **casa de caridad** poorhouse; **casa de citas** house of assignation; **casa de correos** post office; **casa de empeños** pawnshop; **casa de expósitos** foundling home; **casa de fieras** menagerie; **casa de huéspedes** boarding house; **casa de juego** gambling house; **casa de locos** madhouse; **casa de modas** dress shop; **casa de moneda** mint; **casa de préstamos** pawnshop; **casa de salud** private hospital; **casa de socorro** first-aid station; **casa de vecindad** or **de vecinos** apartment house, tenement house; **casa editorial** publishing house; **casa matriz** main office; **casa pública** brothel; **casa real** royal palace; royal family; **casas baratas** low-cost housing; **casa solar** or **solariega** ancestral mansion, manor house; **casa y comida** board and lodging; **¡convida la casa!** the drinks are on the house!; **en casa** home, at home; **ir a buscar casa** to go house hunting; **poner casa** to set up housekeeping
**casaca** *f* dress coat; (coll) marriage contract; (Guat, Hond) lively whispered conversation; **volver la casaca** (coll) to become a turncoat
**casade•ro -ra** *adj* marriageable
**casa•do -da** *adj* married || *mf* married person
**casal** *m* country place; (Arg) pair, couple
**casamente•ro -ra** *adj* matchmaking || *mf* matchmaker
**casamiento** *m* marriage; wedding
**casapuerta** *f* entrance hall, vestibule
**casaquilla** *f* jacket
**casar** *tr* to marry; to marry off; to match; to harmonize; (law) to annul, repeal || *intr* to marry, get married || *ref* to marry, get married; **no casarse con nadie** (coll) to get tied up with nobody
**casatienda** *f* store and home combined
**cascabel** *m* sleigh bell, jingle bell; rattlesnake; **ponerle cascabel al gato** (coll) to bell the cat
**cascabelear** *intr* to jingle; (coll) to act tactlessly
**cascabeleo** *m* jingle
**cascabele•ro -ra** *adj* (coll) tactless, thoughtless || *mf* (coll) featherbrain || *m* baby's rattle
**cascabillo** *m* jingle bell; chaff, husk; cup of acorn
**cascada** *f* cascade, waterfall
**cascajo** *m* pebble; gravel, rubble; (coll) broken jar; (coll) piece of junk; **estar hecho un cascajo** (coll) to be old and worn-out, to be a wreck
**cascanue•ces** *m* (*pl* **-ces**) nutcracker
**cascar** §73 *tr* to crack, break, split; (coll) to beat, strike, hit || *ref* to crack, break, split
**cáscara** *f* hull, peel, rind, shell; bark, crust; **cáscara rueda** (Arg) ring-around-a-rosy; **ser de la cáscara amarga** (coll) to be wild and flighty; (coll) to hold advanced views; (Mex) to be determined
**cascarón** *m* eggshell
**cascarra•bias** *mf* (*pl* **-bias**) (coll) crab, grouch
**casco** *m* (*pieza que sirve para proteger la cabeza del soldado, el bombero, etc.*) helmet; (*uña de las caba-*

*llerías*) hoof; (*pedazo de vasija rota*) potsherd; (*capa de la cebolla*) coat, shell; (*del sombrero*) crown; (*cuerpo de la nave*) hull; (*de un barco inservible*) hulk; (*barril, pipa*) barrel, tank, cask, vat; (*pieza del teléfono*) headset, headpiece; bottle; (mach) shell, casing; (*gajo de la naranja*) (Arg, Col, Chile) slice; (Peru) chest, breast; **casco de población** or **casco urbano** city limits; **romperse los cascos** (coll) to rack one's brain
**casera** *f* landlady; housekeeper
**casería** *f* country place; (Am) customers
**caserío** *m* country house; small settlement, hamlet
**case•ro -ra** *adj* homemade; homeloving; (*remedio*) household; house, home; (*sencillo*) homely || *mf* owner, proprietor; renter; caretaker; janitor; (Am) huckster; (Am) vendor || *m* landlord || *f* see **casera**
**caseta** *f* (*casa sin piso alto*) cottage; (*de una feria*) stall, booth; bathhouse
**casi** *adv* almost, nearly; **casi nada** next to nothing; **casi nunca** hardly ever
**casilla** *f* hut, shack, shed; cabin, lodge; stall, booth; (*escaque*) square; (*compartimiento en un mueble*) pigeonhole; (*división del papel rayado*) column, square; (*taquilla*) ticket office; (*de locomotora o camión*) cab; (Bol, Chile, Peru, Urug) post-office box; (Ecuad) water closet; (Cuba) bird trap; **sacarle a uno de sus casillas** (coll) to jolt someone out of his old habits; (coll) to drive someone crazy
**casille•ro -ra** *mf* (rr) crossing guard || *m* filing cabinet, set of pigeonholes
**casino** *m* casino; club; clubhouse
**caso** *m* case; chance; event; **caso de conformidad** in case you agree; **caso que** in case; **de caso pensado** deliberately, on purpose; **en todo caso** at all events; **hacer al caso** (coll) to be to the purpose; **hacer caso de** (coll) to take into account, pay attention to; **hacer caso omiso de** to pass over in silence, not mention; **no venir al caso** to be beside the point; **poner por caso** to take as an example; **venir al caso** to be just the thing
**casorio** *m* (coll) hasty marriage, unwise marriage
**caspa** *f* dandruff, scurf
**cáspita** *interj* well, well!, upon my word!
**caspo•so -sa** *adj* full of dandruff
**casquete** *m* (*cubierta que se ajusta al casco de la cabeza*) skullcap; skull, cranium; (*pieza de la armadura que cubre el casco de la cabeza*) helmet; (*pieza del teléfono*) headset
**casquillo** *m* butt, cap, tip; bushing, sleeve; ferrule; (Am) horseshoe
**casquiva•no -na** *adj* (coll) scatterbrained
**casta** *f* caste; kind, quality; breed, race
**castaña** *f* chestnut; (*moño*) knot, chignon; demijohn; **castaña de Indias** horse chestnut; **castaña de Pará** Brazil nut
**castañeta** *f* castanet; snapping of the fingers
**castañetear** *tr* (*los dedos*) to snap, to click; (*p.ej., una seguidilla*) to click off with the castanets || *intr* to click; (*los dientes*) to chatter
**casta•ño -ña** *adj* chestnut, chestnut-colored; (*p.ej., pelo*) brown; (*p.ej., ojos*) hazel || *m* chestnut tree; **castaño de Indias** horse chestnut || *f* see **castaña**
**castañuela** *f* castanet; **estar como unas castañuelas** (coll) to be bubbling over with joy
**castella•no -na** *adj & mf* Castilian || *m* Castilian, Spanish (*language*) || *f* chatelaine
**casticidad** *f* purity, correctness (*in language*)
**casticismo** *m* purism
**castidad** *f* chastity
**castiga•dor -dora** *mf* punisher || *m* (coll) seducer, Don Juan
**castigar** §44 *tr* to punish, chastise; (*la carne*) to mortify; (*los gastos*) to cut down, curtail; (*obras, escritos*) to correct, emend; (*un tornillo*) (Mex) to tighten
**castigo** *m* punishment, chastisement
**Castilla** *f* Castile; **Castilla la Nueva** New Castile; **Castilla la Vieja** Old Castile
**castillo** *m* castle; (*montura sobre un elefante*) howdah; **castillo en el aire** castle in Spain, castle in the air; **castillo de naipes** house of cards; **castillo de proa** forecastle
**casti•zo -za** *adj* chaste, pure, correct; pure-blooded; real, regular
**cas•to -ta** *adj* chaste, pure || *f* see **casta**
**castor** *m* beaver
**castrar** *tr* to castrate; (*una planta*) to prune, cut back; to weaken
**casual** *adj* casual, accidental, chance
**casualidad** *f* accident, chance; chance event; **por casualidad** by chance
**casuca** or **casucha** *f* shack, shanty
**casulla** *f* chasuble
**cata** *f* tasting; taste, sample
**catacal•dos** *mf* (*pl* **-dos**) (coll) rolling stone; (coll) busybody
**catacumba** *f* catacomb
**cata•lán -lana** *adj & mf* Catalan, Catalonian
**catalejo** *m* spyglass
**catalogar** §44 *tr* to catalogue
**catálogo** *m* catalogue
**Cataluña** *f* Catalonia
**cataplasma** *f* poultice; **cataplasma de mostaza** mustard plaster
**catapulta** *f* catapult
**catapultar** *tr* to catapult
**catar** *tr* to taste, sample; to check, examine; to be on the look out for
**catarata** *f* cataract, waterfall; (pathol) cataract
**catarro** *m* (*inflamación de las membranas mucosas*) catarrh; (*resfriado*) head cold
**catástrofe** *f* catastrophe

**catavino** *m* cup for tasting wine
**catavi•nos** *m* (*pl* **-nos**) winetaster; (*borracho*) (coll) rounder
**catear** *tr* to hunt, look for; (*a un alumno*) to flunk; (Am) to explore; (*una casa*) (Am) to search
**catecismo** *m* catechism
**cátedra** *f* chair, professorship; academic subject; teacher's desk; classroom; **poner cátedra** to hold forth
**catedral** *f* cathedral
**catedrático** *m* university professor
**categoría** *f* category; status, standing; class, kind; condition, quality; **de categoría** prominent
**caterva** *f* throng, crowd
**catéter** *m* catheter
**cateterizar §60** *tr* to catheterize
**cátodo** *m* cathode
**católi•co -ca** *adj* catholic; Catholic; **no estar muy católico** (coll) to be under the weather || *mf* Catholic; **católico romano** Roman Catholic
**catorce** *adj & pron* fourteen || *m* fourteen; (*en las fechas*) fourteenth
**catorcea•vo -va** *adj & m* fourteenth
**catorza•vo -va** *adj & m* fourteenth
**catre** *m* cot; **catre de tijera** folding cot
**catrecillo** *m* campstool, folding canvas chair
**ca•trín -trina** *adj* (CAm, Mex) sporty, swell || *mf* (CAm, Mex) sport, dude
**caucasia•no -na** or **caucási•co -ca** *adj & mf* Caucasian
**Cáucaso** *m* Caucasus
**cauce** *m* river bed; channel, ditch, trench
**caución** *f* precaution; (law) bail, security
**caucionar** *tr* to guard against; (law) to give bail for
**cauchal** *m* rubber plantation
**caucho** *m* rubber; rubber plant; (Col) rubber raincoat; **caucho esponjoso** foam rubber; **cauchos** (*chanclos*) (Am) rubbers
**caudal** *adj* of great volume || *m* (*de agua*) volume; abundance; wealth
**caudalo•so -sa** *adj* of great volume; abundant; rich, wealthy
**caudillo** *m* chief, leader; military leader; caudillo, head of state
**causa** *f* cause; (law) suit, trial; (Chile) bite, snack; (Peru) potato salad; **a** or **por causa de** on account of, because of
**causa•dor -dora** *adj* causing || *mf* (*persona*) cause
**causante** *mf* (*persona*) cause; (law) principal, constituent; (Mex) taxpayer
**causar** *tr* to cause
**causear** *tr* (Chile) to get the best of || *intr* (Chile) to have a bite
**causeo** *m* (Chile) bite, snack
**cáusti•co -ca** *adj* caustic
**cautela** *f* caution
**cautelo•so -sa** *adj* cautious, guarded
**cauterizar §60** *tr* to cauterize
**cautín** *m* soldering iron
**cautivar** *tr* to take prisoner; to attract, win over; (*encantar*) to captivate
**cautiverio** *m* or **cautividad** *f* captivity
**cauti•vo -va** *adj & mf* captive
**cau•to -ta** *adj* cautious
**cavar** *tr* to dig, dig up || *intr* (*una herida*) to go deep; (*el caballo*) to paw; **cavar en** to study thoroughly, to delve into
**caverna** *f* cavern, cave
**cavidad** *f* cavity
**cavilar** *tr* to brood over || *intr* to worry, fret
**cavilo•so -sa** *adj* suspicious, mistrustful; (CAm) gossipy; (Col) touchy
**cayado** *m* (*de pastor*) crook; (*de obispo*) crozier
**cayo** *m* key, reef; **Cayo Hueso** Key West; **Cayos de la Florida** Florida Keys
**caz** *m* (*pl* **caces**) flume, millrace
**caza** *m* pursuit plane, fighter; **caza de reacción** jet fighter || *f* chase, hunt; hunting; (*animales que se cazan*) game; **a caza de** on the hunt for; **caza al hombre** man hunt; **caza de grillos** fool's errand, wild-goose chase; **ir de caza** to go hunting
**cazaautógra•fos** *mf* (*pl* **-fos**) autograph seeker
**caza•dor -dora** *adj* hunting || *m* hunter; huntsman; **cazador de alforja** trapper; **cazador de cabezas** head-hunter; **cazador de dotes** fortune hunter; **cazador furtivo** poacher || *f* huntress; hunting jacket; jacket
**cazanoti•cias** (*pl* **-cias**) *m* newshawk || *f* newshen
**cazar §60** *tr* to chase; to hunt; to catch; (*en un descuido o error*) (coll) to catch up; (*un descuido o error*) (coll) to catch; (*adquirir con maña*) (coll) to wangle; (*con halagos o engaños*) to take in || *intr* to hunt
**cazarreactor** *m* jet fighter
**cazcalear** *intr* (coll) to buzz around
**cazo** *m* dipper, ladle; glue pot; (*de cuchillo*) back
**cazuela** *f* earthen casserole; stew; (archaic) gallery for women; (SAm) chicken stew
**cazu•rro -rra** *adj* (coll) sullen, surly
**cazuz** *m* ivy
**C. de J.** *abbr* **Compañía de Jesús**
**cebada** *f* barley
**cebadera** *f* nose bag
**cebador** *m* (mach) primer
**cebar** *tr* (*a un animal*) to fatten; (*un horno*) to feed; (*un arma de fuego, una bomba, un carburador*) to prime; (*una pasión, la esperanza*) to nourish; (*atraer*) to lure; (*un clavo, un tornillo*) to make catch, make take hold; (*un anzuelo*) to bait || *intr* (*un clavo, un tornillo*) to catch, take hold || *ref* (*una enfermedad, una epidemia*) to rage; **cebarse en** to be absorbed in; to vent one's fury on
**cebo** *m* fattening; feed; bait; lure; (*carga de un arma de fuego*) primer; priming
**cebolla** *f* onion; bulb; (*del velón*) oil receptacle
**cebra** *f* zebra
**ce•bú** *m* (*pl* **-búes**) zebu

**ceca** *f* mint; **de Ceca en Meca** or **de la Ceca a la Meca** hither and thither, from pillar to post
**cecear** *intr* to lisp
**ceceo** *m* lisp, lisping
**cecina** *f* dried beef
**cedazo** *m* sieve
**ceder** *tr* to yield, cede, give up ‖ *intr* to yield, give way, give in; to slacken, relax; to go down, decline
**cedro** *m* cedar; **cedro de Virginia** juniper, red cedar
**cédula** *f* (*de papel*) slip; form, blank; rent sign; certificate, document; **cédula de vecindad** or **cédula personal** identification papers
**cedulón** *m* proclamation, public notice; (*pasquín*) lampoon
**céfiro** *m* zephyr
**cegar** §66 *tr* to blind; (*un agujero*) to plug, stop up; (*una puerta, una ventana*) to wall up ‖ *intr* to go blind; to be blinded ‖ *ref* to be blinded
**cega•to -ta** *adj* (coll) dim-sighted, weak-eyed
**ceguedad** *f* blindness
**ceguera** *f* blindness
**Ceilán** Ceylon
**ceila•nés -nesa** *adj & mf* Ceylonese
**ceja** *f* (*pelo sobre la cuenca del ojo*) eyebrow; edge, rim; cloud cap; (Am) clearing for a road; **arquear las cejas** to raise one's eyebrows; **fruncir las cejas** to knit one's brow; **quemarse las cejas** to burn the midnight oil
**cejar** *intr* to back up; to turn back; to slacken
**cejijun•to -ta** or **ceju•do -da** *adj* beetle-browed; (coll) scowling
**celada** *f* ambush; trap, trick
**celador** *m* guard (*e.g., in a museum*); (elec) lineman; (Urug) policeman
**celaje** *m* cloud effect; skylight, transom; (Am) ghost
**celar** *tr* to see to; to watch over, to keep an eye on; to hide; to carve
**celda** *f* cell; **celda de castigo** solitary confinement
**celdilla** *f* cell; niche
**celebración** *f* celebration; applause; (*de una reunión*) holding
**celebrante** *m* (*sacerdote*) celebrant
**celebrar** *tr* to celebrate; (*una reunión*) to hold; (*aprobar*) to welcome; (*un matrimonio*) to perform; (*misa*) to say ‖ *intr* (*decir misa*) to celebrate; to be glad ‖ *ref* to take place, be held; to be celebrated
**célebre** *adj* celebrated, famous; (coll) funny, witty; (Am) pretty
**celebridad** *f* (*fama; persona*) celebrity
**celeridad** *f* speed, swiftness
**celeste** *adj* celestial; sky-blue
**celestial** *adj* celestial, heavenly; (coll) stupid, silly
**celestina** *f* procuress, bawd
**celestinaje** *m* procuring, pandering
**celibato** *m* celibacy; (coll) bachelor
**célibe** *adj* celibate, single, unmarried ‖ *mf* celibate, single person ‖ *m* bachelor ‖ *f* spinster
**celinda** *f* mock orange
**celo** *m* zeal; envy; (*impulso reproductivo en las bestias*) heat, rut; **celos** jealousy
**celofán** *m* or **celofana** *f* cellophane
**celosía** *f* (*celotipia*) jealousy; (*enrejado de listoncillos*) lattice window, jalousie
**celo•so -sa** *adj* (*que tiene celo*) zealous; (*que tiene celos*) jealous; fearful, distrustful; (naut) unsteady
**celotipia** *f* jealousy
**celta** *adj* Celtic ‖ *mf* Celt ‖ *m* (*idioma*) Celtic
**célti•co -ca** *adj* Celtic
**célula** *f* cell
**celuloide** *m* celluloid; **llevar al celuloide** to put on the screen
**cellisca** *f* sleet, sleet storm
**cellisquear** *intr* to sleet
**cementerio** *m* cemetery
**cemento** *m* cement; concrete; **cemento armado** reinforced concrete
**cena** *f* supper; dinner ‖ **la Cena** the Last Supper
**cena•dor -dora** *mf* diner-out ‖ *m* arbor, bower, summerhouse
**cenaduría** *f* (Mex) supper club
**cenagal** *m* quagmire
**cenago•so -sa** *adj* muddy, miry
**cenaoscu•ras** *mf* (*pl* **-ras**) (coll) recluse; (coll) skinflint
**cenar** *tr* to have for supper, have for dinner ‖ *intr* to have supper, have dinner
**cencerrada** *f* tin-pan serenade
**cencerrear** *intr* to keep jingling; to rattle, jangle; (coll) to play out of tune
**cencerro** *m* cowbell; **a cencerros tapados** (coll) cautiously
**cendal** *m* gauze, sendal
**cenefa** *f* edging, trimming, border
**cenicero** *m* ash tray
**cenicien•to -ta** *adj* ashen, ash-gray ‖ **la Cenicienta** Cinderella
**cenit** *m* zenith
**ceniza** *f* ash; ashes; **cenizas** ashes; **huir de las cenizas y caer en las brasas** to jump from the frying pan into the fire
**ceni•zo -za** *adj* ashen, ash-gray ‖ *f* see **ceniza**
**cenojil** *m* garter
**cenote** *m* (Mex) deep underground water reservoir
**censo** *m* census; **levantar el censo** to take the census
**censor** *m* censor; **censor jurado de cuentas** certified public accountant
**censura** *f* censure; censoring; gossip; **censura de cuentas** auditing
**censurar** *tr* (*criticar, reprobar*) to censure; (*formar juicio de*) to censor
**centauro** *m* centaur
**centa•vo -va** *adj* hundredth ‖ *m* hundredth; cent
**centella** *f* flash of lightning; flash of light; spark; (*de ingenio, de ira*) (fig) spark, flash
**centellar** or **centellear** *intr* to flash, to spark; to glimmer, gleam, twinkle
**centenar** *m* hundred; **a centenares** by the hundreds

**centena·rio -ria** *adj* centennial || *mf* centenarian || *m* centennial
**cente·no -na** *adj* hundredth || *m* rye
**centési·mo -ma** *adj & m* hundredth
**centígra·do -da** *adj* centigrade
**centímetro** *m* centimeter
**cénti·mo -ma** *adj* hundredth || *m* hundredth; centime
**centinela** *mf* (*persona*) watch, guard || *m & f* (*soldado*) sentinel, sentry; **hacer de centinela** to stand sentinel
**centípedo** *m* centipede
**central** *adj* central || *m* sugar mill, sugar refinery || *f* headquarters, main office; powerhouse; (telp) exchange, central; **central de correos** main post office; **central de teléfonos** telephone exchange
**centralizar §60** *tr & ref* to centralize
**centrar** *tr* to center
**céntri·co -ca** *adj* center, central; (*próximo al centro de la ciudad*) downtown
**centro** *m* center; middle; business district, downtown; club; object, goal, purpose; **centro de mesa** centerpiece; **centro docente** educational institution; **pegar centro** (CAm) to hit the bull's-eye
**Centro América** *f* Central America
**centroamerica·no -na** *adj & mf* Central American
**cénts.** *abbr* **céntimos**
**ceñi·do -da** *adj* tight, tight-fitting; lithe, svelte; thrifty
**ceñidor** *m* belt, girdle, sash
**ceñir §72** *tr* to gird; to girdle; to fasten around the waist; to fasten, to tie; to abridge, shorten; to surround; (*la espada*) to gird on; (mil) to besiege || *ref* (*reducirse en los gastos*) to tighten one's belt; (*a pocas palabras*) to restrict oneself; to adapt oneself; **ceñirse a** (*p.ej., un muro*) to hug, keep close to
**ceño** *m* frown; (*del cielo, las nubes, el mar*) threatening look; (*cerco, aro*) hoop, ring, band; **arrugar el ceño** to knit one's brow; **mirar con ceño** to frown at
**ceño·so -sa** or **ceñu·do -da** *adj* beetle-browed; frowning, grim, gruff
**cepa** *f* (*de árbol*) stump; (*de la cola del animal*) stub; (*de la vid*) vinestalk; (*de una famila o linaje*) strain; **de buena cepa** of well-known quality
**cepillar** *tr* to plane; to brush; to smooth
**cepillo** *m* (*instrumento para alisar la madera*) plane; (*utensilio para limpieza*) brush; (*cepo para limosnas*) charity box, poor box; (CAm, Mex) flatterer; **cepillo de cabeza** hairbrush; **cepillo de dientes** toothbrush; **cepillo de ropa** clothesbrush; **cepillo de uñas** nail brush
**cepo** *m* (*de limosnas*) poor box; (*rama de árbol*) bough, branch; (*trampa*) snare, trap; (*del yunque*) stock; (*para devanar la seda*) reel; clamp, vise; (*para asegurar a un reo*) stocks, pillory; **¡cepos quedos!** (coll) quiet!, stop it!
**cera** *f* wax; **cera de abejas** beeswax; **cera de los oídos** earwax; **cera de lustrar** polishing wax; **cera de pisos** floor wax; **ceras** honeycomb; **ser como una cera** to be wax in one's hands
**cerámi·co -ca** *adj* ceramic
**cerbatana** *f* peashooter; ear trumpet; (coll) spokesman, go-between
**cerca** *m* (coll) close-up; **tener buen cerca** (coll) to look good at close quarters || *f* fence, wall; **cerca viva** hedge || *adv* near; **cerca de** near, close to; about; to, at the court of; **de cerca** closely; at close range
**cercado** *m* fence, wall; walled-in garden or field
**cercanía** *f* nearness, proximity; **cercanías** neighborhood, vicinity
**cerca·no -na** *adj* close, near; adjoining, neighboring; (*que debe acontecer en breve*) early
**cercar §73** *tr* to fence in, wall in; to encircle, surround; to crowd around; (mil) to besiege
**cercenar** *tr* to clip, trim; to curtail; to cut out
**cerciorar** *tr* to inform, assure || *ref* to find out; **cerciorarse de** to ascertain, find out about
**cerco** *m* (*aro, anillo*) hoop, ring; (*marco de puerta o ventana*) casing, frame; (*círculo que aparece alrededor del sol o la luna*) halo; (*reunión de personas*) circle, group; fence, wall; (mil) siege; **poner cerco a** (mil) to lay siege to
**cerda** *f* bristle, horsehair; (*hembra del cerdo*) sow
**cerdear** *intr* to be weak in the forelegs; (*las cuerdas de un instrumento*) to rasp, to grate; (coll) to hold back, look for excuses
**Cerdeña** *f* Sardinia
**cerdo** *m* hog; (*persona sucia*) (coll) pig, swine; (*hombre sin cortesía*) (coll) cad, ill-bred fellow; **cerdo de muerte** pig to be slaughtered; **cerdo de vida** pig not old enough to be slaughtered; **cerdo marino** porpoise
**cerdo·so -sa** *adj* bristly
**cereal** *adj & m* cereal
**cerebro** *m* brain; (*seso, inteligencia*) brain, brains
**ceremonia** *f* ceremony; formality; **de ceremonia** formal; **hacer ceremonias** to stand on ceremony; **por ceremonia** as a matter of form
**ceremonio·so -sa** *adj* ceremonious, punctilious; (*que gusta de ceremonias*) formal
**cereza** *f* cherry
**cerezo** *m* cherry tree
**cerilla** *f* wax taper; wax match
**cerillera** *f* or **cerillero** *m* match box
**cerneja** *f* fetlock
**cerner §51** *tr* to sift; (*el horizonte*) to scan || *intr* to bud, blossom; to drizzle || *ref* to waddle; (*el ave*) to soar, to hover; (*un mal*) to threaten; **cernerse sobre** (*amenazar*) to hang over
**cernícalo** *m* (orn) sparrow hawk; (coll) ignoramus; (coll) jag, drunk

**cernir** §28 *tr* to sift
**cero** *m* zero; **ser un cero a la izquierda** (coll) to not count, to be a nobody
**cerote** *m* shoemaker's wax; (coll) fear
**cerotear** *tr* (*el hilo*) to wax || *intr* (Chile) to drip
**cerra•do -da** *adj* closed; close; incomprehensible; (*cielo*) cloudy, overcast; (*barba*) thick; (*curva*) sharp; (coll) quiet, reserved, secretive; (coll) dense, stupid
**cerradura** *f* lock; closing, locking; **cerradura embutida** mortise lock
**cerrajería** *f* locksmith business; hardware; hardware store
**cerrajero** *m* locksmith; hardware dealer; (*el que trabaja el hierro frío*) ironworker
**cerrar** §2 *tr* to close, shut; to lock; to bolt; (*el puño*) to clench; to enclose; (*la radio*) to turn off; **cerrar con llave** to lock || *intr* to close, to shut; (*la noche*) to fall; **cerrar con** (*el enemigo*) to close in on; **cerrar en falso** (*una puerta, cerradura, etc.*) to not catch || *ref* to close, to shut; to lock; **cerrarse en falso** to not heal right
**cerrazón** *f* gathering storm clouds; (Arg) heavy fog
**cerre•ro -ra** *adj* free, loose; untamed; haughty; (Mex) rough, unpolished; (*café*) (Ven) bitter
**cerril** *adj* rough, uneven; wild, untamed; (coll) boorish, rough
**cerrillar** *tr* to knurl, to mill
**cerro** *m* hill, hillock; (*entre dos surcos*) ridge; (*espinazo*) backbone; (*del animal*) neck; **en cerro** bareback; **echar por los cerros de Úbeda** (coll) to talk nonsense; **por los cerros de Úbeda** (coll) off the beaten path
**cerrojo** *m* bolt; **cerrojo dormido** dead bolt
**certamen** *m* literary competition; contest, match
**certe•ro -ra** *adj* certain, sure, accurate; well-informed; (*tiro*) well-aimed; (*tirador*) good, crack
**certeza** *f* certainty
**certidumbre** *f* certainty; sureness
**certificación** *f* certification; certificate
**certifica•do -da** *adj* registered || *m* registered letter, registered package; certificate; **certificado de estudios** transcript
**certificar** §73 *tr* to certify; (*una carta*) to register
**certitud** *f* certainty
**cerval** *adj* deer; (*miedo*) intense
**cervato** *m* fawn
**cervecería** *f* brewery; beer saloon
**cervece•ro -ra** *adj* beer || *mf* brewer
**cerveza** *f* beer; **cerveza a presión** draught beer; **cerveza de marzo** bock beer
**cer•viz** *f* (*pl* **-vices**) cervix; nape of the neck; **bajar** or **doblar la cerviz** to humble oneself; **levantar la cerviz** to raise one's head, become proud; **ser de dura cerviz** to be ungovernable
**cesación** *f* cessation, suspension
**cesante** *adj* retired, out of office || *mf* pensioner
**cesantía** *f* retirement; dismissal (*of a public official*)
**cesar** *intr* to stop, cease
**César** *m* Caesar
**cese** *m* ceasing; notice of retirement; **cese de alarma** all-clear; **cese de fuego** ceasefire
**césped** *m* lawn, sward; sod, turf
**cesta** *f* basket; (*para jugar a la pelota*) wicker scoop; **cesta de costura** sewing basket; **cesta para compras** market basket
**cesto** *m* basket; washbasket; **cesto de la colada** clothesbasket, washbasket; **estar hecho un cesto** (coll) to be overcome with sleep; **ser un cesto** (coll) to be crude and ignorant
**cetrería** *f* falconry
**cetrero** *m* falconer
**cetri•no -na** *adj* (*tez*) sallow; jaundiced, melancholy
**cetro** *m* scepter; (*para aves*) perch, roost; (eccl) verge; **cetro de bufón** bauble; **cetro de locura** fool's scepter; **empuñar el cetro** to ascend the throne
**cf.** *abbr* **confesor**
**cg.** *abbr* **centigramo**
**C.I.** *abbr* **cociente intelectual**
**cía.** *abbr* **compañía**
**cía** *f* hipbone
**cianamida** *f* cyanamide
**cianuro** *m* cyanide
**ciar** §77 *intr* to back up; to back water; to ease up
**ciborio** *m* ciborium
**cicatear** *intr* (coll) to be stingy
**cicate•ro -ra** *adj* (coll) stingy || *mf* (coll) miser, niggard
**cica•triz** *f* (*pl* **-trices**) scar
**cicatrizar** §60 *tr* to heal; (*una impresión dolorosa*) (Arg) to heal || *ref* to heal; to scar
**Cicerón** *m* Cicero
**ciclamor** *m* Judas tree; **ciclamor del Canadá** redbud
**cícli•co -ca** *adj* cyclic(al)
**ciclismo** *m* bicycle racing
**ciclista** *mf* bicyclist; bicycle racer
**ciclo** *m* cycle; series (of lectures); (*en las escuelas*) (Arg, Urug) term
**ciclón** *m* cyclone
**cicuta** *f* hemlock
**cidra** *f* citron (*fruit*)
**cidrada** *f* citron (*candied rind*)
**cidro** *m* citron (*tree or shrub*)
**cie•go -ga** *adj* blind; blocked, stopped up; **más ciego que un topo** blind as a bat || *mf* blind person || *m* blind man || *f* blind woman; **a ciegas** blindly; thoughtlessly; without looking
**cielo** *m* sky, heavens; (*clima, tiempo*) skies, climate, weather; (*de una cama*) canopy; (*mansión de los bienaventurados*) Heaven; **a cielo abierto** in the open air, outdoors; **a cielo descubierto** openly; **a cielo raso** in the open air, outdoors; in the country; **cielo de la boca** roof of the mouth; **cielo máximo** (aer) ceiling;

**cielo raso** ceiling; **llovido del cielo** heaven-sent, manna from heaven
**cielorraso** *m* ceiling
**ciem•piés** *m* (*pl* **-piés**) centipede
**cien** *adj* hundred, a hundred, one hundred
**ciénaga** *f* swamp, marsh, mudhole
**ciencia** *f* science; knowledge; learning; **a ciencia cierta** with certainty
**cieno** *m* mud, mire, silt
**cieno•so -sa** *adj* muddy, miry, silty
**ciento** *adj & m* hundred, a hundred, one hundred; **por ciento** per cent
**cierne** *m* budding, blossoming; **en cierne** in blossom; only beginning
**cierrarrenglón** *m* marginal stop
**cierre** *m* closing; shutting; snap, clasp, fastener; latch, lock; (*de una tienda, de la Bolsa*) close; (*paro de trabajo*) shutdown; **cierre cremallera** zipper; **cierre de portada** metal shutter (*of store front*); **cierre de puerta** door check; **cierre hermético** weather stripping; **cierre relámpago** zipper
**cierro** *m* closing; shutting; (Chile) fence, wall; (Chile) envelope
**cier•to -ta** *adj* certain; a certain; (*acertado, verdadero*) true; (*seguro*) sure; **por cierto** for sure || **cierto** *adv* surely, certainly
**cierva** *f* hind
**ciervo** *m* deer, stag, hart
**cierzo** *m* cold north wind
**cifra** *f* (*número*) cipher; (*escritura secreta*) code; (*enlace de dos o más letras empleado en sellos*) device, monogram, emblem; abbreviation; amount, sum; **en cifra** in code; in brief; mysteriously
**cifrar** *tr* to cipher, to code; to abridge; to calculate; **cifrar la dicha en** to base one's happiness in; **cifrar la esperanza en** to place one's hope in || *ref* to be abridged; **cifrarse en** to be based on
**cifrario** *m* (com) code
**cigarra** *f* harvest fly, locust
**cigarrera** *f* cigar case; cigar girl
**cigarrería** *f* cigar store, tobacco store
**cigarre•ro -ra** *mf* cigar maker; cigar dealer || *f* see **cigarrera**
**cigarrillo** *m* cigarette; **cigarrillo con filtro** filter cigarette
**cigarro** *m* cigar; **cigarro de papel** cigarette; **cigarro puro** cigar
**cigoñal** *m* well sweep; (*del motor de explosión*) crankshaft
**cigüeña** *f* stork; crank, winch
**cigüeñal** *m* var of **cigoñal**
**cilicio** *m* haircloth, hair shirt
**cilindrada** *f* piston displacement
**cilindrar** *tr* to roll
**cilíndri•co -ca** *adj* cylindrical
**cilindro** *m* cylinder; roll, roller; (Mex) barrel organ, hand organ
**cima** *f* (*de árbol*) top; (*de montaña*) top, summit; **dar cima a** to complete, to carry out; **por cima** (coll) at the very top
**cimarra** *f* — **hacer cimarra** (Arg, Chile) to play hooky
**cima•rrón -rrona** *adj* (*animal*) (Am) wild, untamed; (*planta*) (Am) wild; (*esclavo*) (Am) fugitive; (*marinero*) (Am) lazy; (*mate*) (Arg, Urug) black, bitter
**cimarronear** *intr* (Arg, Urug) to drink black maté || *ref* (*el esclavo*) (Am) to flee, run away
**címbalo** *m* cymbal
**cimbel** *m* decoy pigeon, stool pigeon
**cimborio** or **cimborrio** *m* dome
**cimbrar** or **cimbrear** *tr* to brandish; to swing, sway; to bend; (coll) to thrash, beat || *ref* to swing, sway; to shake
**cimbre•ño -ña** *adj* flexible, pliant; lithe, willowy
**cimentar** §2 *tr* to found, establish; to lay the foundations of
**cime•ro -ra** *adj* top, uppermost
**cimiento** *m* foundation, groundwork; basis, source
**cimitarra** *f* scimitar
**cinabrio** *m* cinnabar
**cinanquia** *f* quinsy
**cinc** *m* (*pl* **cinces**) zinc
**cincel** *m* chisel, graver
**cincelar** *tr* to chisel, engrave
**cinco** *adj & pron* five; **las cinco** five o'clock || *m* five; (*en las fechas*) fifth; **¡choque Vd. esos cinco!** or **¡vengan esos cinco!** put it here!, shake!; **decirle a uno cuántas son cinco** (coll) to tell someone what's what
**cincograbado** *m* zinc etching
**cincuenta** *adj, pron & m* fifty
**cincuenta•vo -va** *adj & m* fiftieth
**cincha** *f* cinch; **a revienta cinchas** at breakneck speed; (Am) reluctantly
**cinchar** *tr* to cinch; to band, to hoop
**cincho** *m* girdle, sash; iron hoop; iron tire
**cine** *m* movie; **cine en colores** color movies; **cine hablado** talkie; **cine mudo** silent movie; **cine parlante** talkie; **cine sonoro** sound movie
**cineasta** *mf* motion-picture producer; movie fan || *m* movie actor || *f* movie actress
**cinedrama** *m* screenplay
**cinelandia** *f* (coll) movieland
**cinema** *m* var of **cine**
**cinematografiar** §77 *tr & intr* to cinematograph, to film
**cinematógrafo** *m* cinematograph; motion picture; motion-picture projector; motion-picture theater
**cinematurgo** *m* scriptwriter
**cinescopio** (telv) *m* kinescope
**cineteatro** *m* movie house
**cinéti•co -ca** *adj* kinetic || *f* kinetics
**cínga•ro -ra** *adj & mf* gypsy
**cíni•co -ca** *adj* cynical; impudent; slovenly, untidy || *mf* cynic || *m* Cynic
**cinismo** *m* cynicism; impudence
**cinta** *f* ribbon; (*tira de papel, celuloide, etc.*) tape; film; measuring tape; (*borde de la acera*) curb; fillet, scroll; **cinta aislante** electric tape, friction tape; **cinta de medir** tape measure; **cinta de teleimpresor** ticker tape; **cinta grabada de televisión** video tape; **cinta perforada** punched tape

**cintillo** *m* hatband; fancy hat cord; ring set with a gem; (*borde de la acera*) (P-R) curb; (Am) hair ribbon
**cinto** *m* belt, girdle; waist
**cintura** *f* (*parte estrecha del cuerpo humano sobre las caderas*) waist; waistline; (*de una chimenea*) throat; **meter en cintura** (coll) to bring to reason
**cinturón** *m* belt, sash; sword belt; **cinturón de asiento** seat belt; **cinturón salvavidas** (naut) safety belt
**cipo** *m* milestone; signpost; memorial pillar
**cipote** *adj* (Col, Ven) stupid; (Guat) chubby ‖ *mf* (Hond, El Salv, Ven) brat
**ciprés** *m* cypress
**circo** *m* circus
**circón** *m* zircon
**circonio** *m* zirconium
**circuito** *m* circuit; (*de carreteras, ferrocarriles, etc.*) network; race track; **corto circuito** (elec) short circuit
**circulación** *f* circulation; traffic; **circulación rodada** vehicular traffic
**circular** *adj* circular ‖ *f* circular, circular letter ‖ *tr & intr* to circulate
**círculo** *m* circle; club; clubhouse
**circuncidar** *tr* to circumcise; to clip, curtail
**circundante** *adj* surrounding
**circundar** *tr* to surround, go around
**circunferencia** *f* circumference
**circunfle•jo -ja** *adj* circumflex
**circunlocución** *f* or **circunloquio** *m* circumlocution
**circunnavegación** *f* circumnavigation
**circunnavegar §44** *tr* to circumnavigate
**circunscribir §83** *tr* to circumscribe ‖ *ref* to hold oneself down; to be held down
**circunscripción** *f* circumscription; district, subdivision
**circunspec•to -ta** *adj* circumspect
**circunstancia** *f* circumstance
**circunstancia•do -da** *adj* circumstantial, detailed
**circunstancial** *adj* circumstantial
**circunstanciar** *tr* to circumstantiate, to describe in detail
**circunstante** *adj* surrounding; present ‖ *mf* bystander, onlooker
**circunveci•no -na** *adj* neighboring
**circunvolar §61** *tr* to fly around
**cirial** *m* (eccl) processional candlestick
**ciriga•llo -lla** *mf* gadabout
**ciríli•co -ca** *adj* Cyrillic
**cirio** *m* wax candle
**Ciro** *m* Cyrus
**ciruela** *f* plum; **ciruela claudia** greengage; **ciruela pasa** prune
**ciruelo** *m* plum, plum tree; (coll) stupid fellow
**cirugía** *f* surgery; **cirugía cosmética, decorativa** or **estética** face lifting
**ciruja•no -na** *mf* surgeon
**ciscar §73** *tr* (coll) to soil, dirty ‖ *ref* (coll) to soil one's clothes, to have an accident
**cisco** *m* culm; (coll) row, disturbance
**cisma** *m* schism; discord, disagreement; (Arg) worry, concern; (Col) gossip; (Col) fastidiousness
**cismáti•co -ca** *adj* schismatic; dissident; (Col) gossipy; (Col) fastidious ‖ *mf* schismatic; dissident
**cisne** *m* swan; (Arg) powder puff
**cisterna** *f* cistern; reservoir
**cita** *f* date, appointment, engagement; (*mención, pasaje textual*) citation, quotation; **cita a ciegas** blind date; **cita previa** by appointment; **darse cita** to make a date
**citación** *f* citation, quotation; (*ante un juez*) citation, summons
**citar** *tr* to make a date with, have an appointment with; to cite, to quote; (*ante un juez*) to cite, to summon; (*al toro*) to incite, provoke ‖ *ref* to make a date, have an appointment
**cítara** *f* (mus) zither
**ciudad** *f* city; city council; **la ciudad Condal** Barcelona; **la ciudad del Apóstol** Santiago de Compostela; **la ciudad del Betis** Seville; **la ciudad del Cabo** Capetown or Cape Town; **la ciudad de los Califas** Cordova; **la ciudad de los Reyes** Lima, Peru; **la ciudad de María Santísima** Seville; **la ciudad Imperial** or **Imperial ciudad** Toledo
**ciudadanía** *f* citizenship
**ciudada•no -na** *adj* city; citizen; civic ‖ *mf* citizen; urbanite
**ciudadela** *f* citadel; (Cuba) tenement house
**cívi•co -ca** *adj* civic; city; domestic; public-spirited
**civil** *adj* civil; civilian ‖ *mf* civilian ‖ *m* guard, policeman
**civilidad** *f* civility
**civilista** *adj* civil-law ‖ *mf* authority on civil law; (Chile) antimilitarist
**civilización** *f* civilization
**civilizar §60** *tr* to civilize
**civismo** *m* good citizenship
**cizalla** *f* shears; metal shaving, metal clipping; **cizalla de guillotina** gate shears, guillotine shears; **cizallas** shears
**cizallar** *tr* to shear
**cizaña** *f* darnel; contamination, corruption; discord; **sembrar cizaña** to sow discord
**clac** *m* (*pl* **claques**) opera hat, claque, crush hat; (*sombrero de tres picos*) cocked hat
**clamar** *tr* to cry out for ‖ *intr* to cry out; **clamar contra** to cry out against; **clamar por** to cry out for
**clamor** *m* clamor, outcry; (*toque de difuntos*) knell, toll; fame
**clamorear** *tr* to clamor for ‖ *intr* to clamor; (*tocar a muerto*) to toll
**clamoreo** *m* clamoring; tolling
**clamoro•so -sa** *adj* clamorous; loud, noisy
**clan** *m* clan
**clandestinista** *mf* (Guat) bootlegger
**clandesti•no -na** *adj* clandestine
**claque** *f* claque, hired clappers
**clara** *f* white of egg; bald spot; (*de un trozo de tela*) thin spot; (*en el tiempo lluvioso*) break, let-up

**claraboya** *f* (*ventana en el techo*) skylight; (*en la parte alta de la pared*) transom; (*esp. en las iglesias la parte superior de la nave que tiene una serie de ventanas*) clerestory
**clarear** *tr* to brighten, light up || *intr* (*empezar a amanecer*) to get light, to dawn; (*el mal tiempo*) to clear up || *ref* (*una tela*) to show through; (coll) to show one's hand
**clarecer** §22 *ref* to dawn
**clarete** *m* claret
**claridad** *f* clarity; clearness; brightness; fame, glory; blunt remark; **claridades** plain language
**clarido·so -sa** *adj* (CAm, Mex) blunt, rude, plain-spoken
**clarificar** §73 *tr* to clarify; to brighten, light up; (*lo que estaba turbio*) to clear
**clarín** *m* clarion; fine cambric; (Chile) sweet pea
**clarinada** *f* clarion call; (coll) uncalled-for remark
**clarinete** *m* clarinet
**clarión** *m* chalk
**clarividencia** *f* clairvoyance; clearsightedness
**clarividente** *adj* clairvoyant; clear-sighted || *mf* clairvoyant
**cla·ro -ra** *adj* clear; (*de color*) light; (*pelo*) thin, sparse; (*té*) weak; famous, illustrious; (*cerveza*) light; **a las claras** publicly, openly, frankly || *m* gap; (*en el bosque*) glade, clearing; space, interval; (*ventana u otra abertura*) light; (*claraboya*) skylight; (*en las nubes*) break; **claro de luna** brief moonlight; **de claro en claro** evidently; from one end to the other; **pasar la noche de claro en claro** to not sleep all night; **poner** or **sacar en claro** to explain, clear up; (*un borrador*) to copy || *f* see **clara** || **claro** *adv* clearly || **claro** *interj* sure!, of course!; **¡claro está!, ¡claro que sí!** sure!, of course!
**claror** *m* brightness; **claror de luna** moonlight, moonglow
**claru·cho -cha** *adj* (coll) watery, thin
**clase** *f* class; classroom; **clase alta** upper class; **clase baja** lower class; **clase media** middle class; **clase obrera** working class; **clases** non-commissioned officers, warrant officers; **clases pasivas** pensioners
**clasicista** *mf* classicist
**clási·co -ca** *adj* classical || *mf* classicist || *m* classic
**clasificador** *m* filing cabinet
**clasificar** §73 *tr* to classify; to class; to sort; to file || *ref* to class
**clasismo** *m* segregation
**clasista** *mf* segregationist
**claudicar** §73 *intr* (*cojear*) to limp; (*obrar defectuosamente*) to bungle; (coll) to back down
**claustral** *adj* cloistral
**claustro** *m* cloister; (*junta de la universidad*) faculty
**cláusula** *f* (*de un contrato u otro documento*) clause; (gram) sentence
**clausula·do -da** *adj* (*estilo*) choppy || *m* series of clauses
**clausular** *tr* to close, finish, conclude
**clausura** *f* confinement; seclusion; enclosure; adjournment
**clausurar** *tr* (*una asamblea, un tribunal, etc.*) to close, to adjourn; (*un comercio por orden gubernativa*) to suspend, to close up
**clava** *f* club
**clavadista** *mf* (Mex) diver
**clava·do -da** *adj* studded with nails; exact, precise; (*reloj*) stopped; sharp, e.g., **a las siete clavadas** at seven o'clock sharp || *m* (Mex) dive
**clavar** *tr* to nail; (*un clavo*) to drive; (*una daga, un punzón*) to stick; (*una piedra preciosa*) to set; (*los ojos, la atención*) to fix; (*a un caballo al herrarlo*) to prick; (coll) to cheat || *ref* to prick oneself; (coll) to get cheated; (Mex) to dive; **clavárselas** (CAm) to get drunk
**clave** *m* harpsichord || *f* (*de un enigma, código, etc.*) key; (*piedra con que se cierra el arco*) (archit) keystone; (mus) clef
**clavel** *m* carnation, pink; **clavel de ramillete** sweet william; **clavel reventón** double-flowered carnation
**clavelón** *m* marigold
**clavellina** *f* carnation, pink
**clave·ro -ra** *mf* keeper of the keys || *m* clove tree || *f* nail hole
**claveta** *f* peg, wooden peg
**clavetear** *tr* to stud; to tip, put a tip on; to wind up, settle
**clavicordio** *m* clavichord
**clavícula** *f* clavicle, collarbone
**clavija** *f* pin, peg, dowel; (elec) plug; (mus) peg; **apretarle a uno las clavijas** (coll) to put the screws on someone
**clavillo** or **clavito** *m* brad, tack; (*que sujeta las hojas de unas tijeras*) pin, rivet; clove
**clavo** *m* nail; (*capullo seco de la flor del clavero*) clove; migraine; keen sorrow; (*artículo que no se vende*) (Arg, Bol, Chile) drug on the market; (Col) bad deal; (Hond, Mex) rich vein of ore; (Ven) heartburn; **clavo de alambre** wire nail; **clavo de especia** (*flor*) clove; **clavo de herrar** horseshoe nail; **dar en el clavo** (coll) to hit the nail on the head
**clemátide** *f* clematis
**clemencia** *f* clemency
**clemente** *adj* clement, merciful
**cleptóma·no -na** *mf* kleptomaniac
**clerecía** *f* clergy
**clerical** *adj* & *m* clerical
**clericato** *m* or **clericatura** *f* priesthood
**clerigalla** *f* (contemptuous) priests
**clérigo** *m* cleric, priest; **clérigo de misa y olla** (coll) priestlet
**clerizonte** *m* shabby-looking priest; fake priest
**clero** *m* clergy
**clerófo·bo -ba** *adj* priest-hating || *mf* priest hater
**cliché** *m* (*lugar común*) cliché
**cliente** *mf* (*parroquiano de una tienda*)

customer; (*de un abogado*) client; (*de un médico*) patient; (*de un hotel*) guest
**clientela** *f* customers; clientele; patronage, protection; practice
**clima** *m* climate; country, region; **clima artificial** air conditioning
**climatizar** §60 *tr* to air-condition
**clíni·co -ca** *adj* clinical || *mf* clinician || *f* clinic; private hospital; **clínica de reposo** nursing home, convalescent home
**cliqueteo** *m* clicking
**clisar** *tr* (typ) to plate
**clisé** *m* (*plancha clisada*) cliché, plate; (phot) plate; (*lugar común*) cliché
**clo** *m* cluck; **decir clo** (Chile) to kick the bucket; **hacer clo clo** (*la gallina clueca*) to cluck
**cloaca** *f* sewer
**clocar** §81 *intr* to cluck
**cloquear** *intr* to cluck
**cloqueo** *m* cluck, clucking
**clorhídri·co -ca** *adj* hydrochloric
**cloro** *m* chlorine
**clorofila** *f* chlorophyll
**cloroformizar** §60 *tr* to chloroform
**cloroformo** *m* chloroform
**cloruro** *m* chloride
**club** *m* (*pl* **clubs**) club; **club náutico** yacht club
**clubista** *mf* club member
**clue·co -ca** *adj* broody; (coll) decrepit
**c.m.b., C.M.B.** *abbr* **cuyas manos beso**
**coa** *f* (Mex) hoe; (Chile) thieves' jargon
**coacción** *f* coercion, compulsion
**coaccionar** *tr* to coerce, compel
**coacervar** *tr* to pile up
**coactar** *tr* to coerce, compel
**coadunar** *tr & ref* to mix together
**coadyuvar** *tr & intr* to help, aid, assist
**coagular** *tr & ref* (*la sangre*) to coagulate; (*la leche*) to curdle
**coágulo** *m* clot
**coalición** *f* coalition
**coalla** *f* woodcock
**coartada** *f* alibi
**coartar** *tr* to limit, restrict
**coba** *f* (coll) hoax; (coll) flattery
**cobalto** *m* cobalt
**cobarde** *adj* cowardly; timid; (*vista*) dim, weak || *mf* coward
**cobardear** *intr* to act cowardly; to be timid
**cobardía** *f* cowardice; timidity
**cobayo** *m* guinea pig
**cobertera** *f* lid; bawd, procuress
**cobertizo** *m* shed; (*tejado saledizo*) covered balcony, penthouse
**cobertor** *m* bedcover, bedspread; lid
**cobertura** *f* cover; covering; (*garantía metálica*) coverage
**cobija** *f* curved tile; top, lid; short mantilla; (W-I) guano roof; **cobijas** (Am) bedclothes
**cobijar** *tr* to cover; to shelter, protect
**cobijo** *m* covering; shelter, protection; (*hospedaje sin manutención*) lodging
**cobra** *f* team of mares used in threshing; (hunt) retrieval
**cobra·dor -dora** *adj* (*perro*) retrieving || *mf* collector; trolley conductor
**cobranza** *f* collecting; (hunt) retrieval
**cobrar** *tr* (*lo perdido*) to recover; (*lo que otro le debe*) to collect; (*un cheque*) to cash; (*cierto precio*) to charge; to acquire, get; (*una cuerda*) to pull in; (hunt) to retrieve; (*pedir, reclamar*) (Am) to dun; **cobrar afición a** to take a liking for; **cobrar al número llamado** (telp) to reverse the charges; **cobrar ánimo** to take courage; **cobrar carnes** to put on flesh; **cobrar fuerzas** to gain strength || *intr* to get hit || *ref* to recover, to come to
**cobre** *m* copper; copper or brass kitchen utensils; **batir el cobre** (coll) to hustle, to work with a will; **cobres** (mus) brasses
**cobre·ño -ña** *adj* copper
**cobrero** *m* coppersmith
**cobri·zo -za** *adj* coppery
**cobro** *m* collection; recovery; **cobro contra entrega** collect on delivery; **en cobro** in a safe place
**coca** *f* (*en una cuerda*) kink; (coll) head; **de coca** (Mex) free; (Mex) in vain
**cocaína** *f* cocaine
**cocción** *f* cooking, baking; (*de objetos cerámicos*) baking, burning
**cocear** *intr* to kick; (*resistir*) (coll) to balk, rebel
**cocer** §16 *tr* to cook; to boil; (*pan; ladrillos*) to bake; to digest || *intr* to cook; to boil; to ferment || *ref* to suffer a long time
**coci·do -da** *adj* cooked || *m* Spanish stew
**cociente** *m* quotient; **cociente intelectual** intelligence quotient
**cocina** *f* (*pieza*) kitchen; (*arte*) cooking, cuisine; (*aparato*) stove; **cocina de presión** pressure cooker; **cocina económica** kitchen range
**cocinar** *tr* to cook || *intr* to meddle
**cocine·ro -ra** *mf* cook
**cocinilla** *m* (coll) meddler || *f* kitchenette; chafing dish; **cocinilla sin fuego** fireless cooker
**coco** *m* cocoanut; (*moño*) topknot, chignon; (*duende*) (coll) bogeyman; (*gesto, mueca*) (coll) face, grimace; (*sombrero hongo*) (Col, Ecuad) derby hat; **hacer cocos** (coll) to make a face; (*los enamorados*) (coll) to make eyes
**cocodrilo** *m* crocodile
**cócora** *adj* (coll) boring, tiresome || *mf* (coll) bore, pest
**coco·so -sa** *adj* worm-eaten
**cocotero** *m* cocoanut palm or tree
**coctel** *m* or **cóctel** *m* cocktail; cocktail party
**coctelera** *f* cocktail shaker
**cocuma** *f* (Peru) roast corn on the cob
**cochambre** *m* (coll) dirty, stinking thing, pigsty
**cochambro·so -sa** *adj* (coll) dirty, stinking
**coche** *m* carriage; coach; car; taxi; (*puerco*) hog; **caminar en el coche de San Francisco** to go or to ride on shank's mare; **coche bar** (rr) club

car; **coche bomba** fire engine; **coche celular** Black Maria, prison van; **coche de alquiler** cab, hack; **coche de carreras** racing car; **coche de correos** mail car; **coche de plaza** or **de punto** cab, hack; **coche de serie** (aut) stock car; **coche fúnebre** hearse

**coche-cama** *m* (*pl* **coches-camas**) sleeping car

**cochecillo** *m* baby carriage; **cochecillo para inválidos** wheelchair; **cochecillo para niños** baby carriage

**coche-comedor** *m* (*pl* **coches-comedores**) (rr) diner, dining car

**coche-correo** *m* (*pl* **coches-correo**) (rr) mail car

**coche-fumador** *m* (*pl* **coches-fumadores**) (rr) smoker, smoking car

**coche-habitación** *m* (*pl* **coches-habitación**) trailer

**cochera** *f* coach house; livery stable; carbarn; garage

**cochería** *f* (Arg, Chile) livery stable

**coche•ro -ra** *adj* easy to cook || *m* coachman, driver; **cochero de punto** cabby, hackman || *f* see **cochera**

**cocherón** *m* coach house; (*depósito de locomotoras*) roundhouse

**coche-salón** *m* (*pl* **coches-salón**) (rr) parlor car

**cochevira** *f* lard

**cochina** *f* sow; (*mujer sucia y desaliñada*) trollop

**cochinada** *f* (coll) piggishness, filthiness; (coll) dirty trick

**cochinillo** *m* sucking pig

**cochi•no -na** *adj* (coll) piggish, filthy; (*tacaño*) (coll) stingy; (Ven) cowardly || *mf* hog; (*persona muy sucia*) (coll) pig, dirty person || *f* see **cochina**

**cochite hervite** *adj, adv & m* (coll) helter-skelter

**cochitril** *m* pigsty; (coll) den, hovel

**cochura** *f* batch of dough

**codadura** *f* (hort) layer

**codal** *adj* elbow || *m* prop, shoring

**codazo** *m* poke, nudge; **dar codazo a** (Mex) to tip off

**codear** *tr* (SAm) to sponge on || *intr* to elbow, elbow one's way || *ref* to hobnob, to rub elbows

**codelincuencia** *f* complicity

**codelincuente** *mf* accomplice

**codera** *f* elbow patch; elbow itch

**códice** *m* codex

**codicia** *f* covetousness, greed, cupidity

**codiciar** *tr* to covet

**codicilo** *m* codicil

**codicio•so -sa** *adj* covetous, greedy; (*laborioso*) hard-working

**codificar** §73 *tr* to codify

**código** *m* code; **código penal** criminal code

**codillo** *m* (*de animal*) knee; (*estribo*) stirrup; (*de un tubo*) elbow; (*de la rama cortada*) stump

**codo** *m* elbow; **dar de codo a** to nudge; (coll) to spurn; **empinar el codo** (coll) to crook the elbow; **hablar por los codos** (coll) to talk too much

**codor•niz** *f* (*pl* **-nices**) quail

**coeducación** *f* coeducation

**coeficiente** *adj & m* coefficient

**coetáne•o -a** *adj & mf* contemporary

**coexistencia** *f* coexistence

**coexistir** *intr* to coexist

**cofa** *f* (naut) top; **cofa de vigía** (naut) crow's-nest

**cofrade** *mf* member, fellow member || *m* brother || *f* sister

**cofradía** *f* brotherhood, sisterhood; association, fraternity

**cofre** *m* coffer, chest, trunk

**cogedor** *m* dustpan; coal shovel, ash shovel

**coger** §17 *tr* to catch, seize, take hold of: to collect, gather, pick; to overtake; to surprise; to hold || *intr* to be, be located; to fit || *ref* to get caught; to cling; to get involved

**cogida** *f* (coll) collecting, gathering, picking; (taur) hook

**cogollo** *m* (*de la lechuga*) heart; (*de la berza*) head; (*de una planta*) shoot; (*del árbol*) top; (*lo mejor*) cream, pick

**cogote** *m* back of the neck

**cogotera** *f* havelock

**cogotu•do -da** *adj* thick-necked; (coll) proud, stiff-necked; (SAm) moneyed

**cogulla** *f* cowl, frock; **cogulla de fraile** (bot) monkshood

**cohabitar** *intr* to live together; (*el hombre y la mujer*) to cohabit

**cohechar** *tr* to bribe; to plow just before sowing || *intr* to take a bribe

**cohecho** *m* bribe

**coherede•ro -ra** *mf* coheir || *f* coheiress

**coherente** *adj* coherent

**cohesión** *f* cohesion

**cohete** *m* (*fuego artificial*) rocket, skyrocket; (*motor a reacción*) rocket; (coll) fidgety person; **cohete de señales** (aer) flare; **cohete lanzador** booster rocket

**cohibente** *adj* (elec) nonconducting

**cohibi•do -da** *adj* timid, self-conscious

**cohibir** *tr* to check, restrain, inhibit; (Mex) to oblige

**cohombro** *m* cucumber

**cohonestar** *tr* to gloss over, to rationalize

**coima** *f* rake-off paid to operator of a gambling table; concubine; (SAm) bribe

**coincidencia** *f* coincidence

**coincidir** *intr* to coincide; to happen at the same time; to be at the same time (*at a given place*); to agree

**coito** *m* coition, coitus

**coja** *f* lame woman; (coll) lewd woman

**cojear** *intr* to limp; (*una mesa, una silla*) to wobble; (*adolecer de algún vicio*) to slip, lapse, have a weakness

**cojera** *f* (*anormalidad del que cojea*) lameness; (*movimiento del que cojea*) limp

**cojijo** *m* bug, insect; (coll) peeve

**cojijo•so -sa** *adj* peevish

**cojín** *m* cushion

**cojincillo** *m* pad

**cojinete** *m* cushion; sewing cushion; (mach) bearing; **cojinete de bolas** ball bearing; **cojinete de rodillos** roller bearing

**co•jo -ja** *adj* lame, crippled; (*mesa, silla*) wobbly; (*pierna*) game || *mf* lame person, cripple || *f* see **coja**
**cojón** *m* testicle
**cok** *m* var of **coque**
**col.** *abbr* **colonia, columna**
**col** *f* cabbage; **col de Bruselas** Brussels sprouts
**cola** *f* (*de animal, de ave, de cometa*) tail; (*de un vestido*) train, trail; (*de personas que esperan turno*) queue; (*extremidad posterior*) tail end, rear end; (*de una clase de alumnos*) bottom; (*pasta fuerte*) glue; **cola del pan** bread line; **cola de milano** or **de pato** dovetail; **cola de pescado** isinglass; **cola de retazo** size, sizing; **hacer cola** to queue, to stand in line
**colaboración** *f* collaboration; (*en un periódico, coloquio, etc.*) contribution
**colaboracionista** *mf* collaborationist
**colabora•dor -dora** *adj* collaborating || *mf* collaborator; contributor
**colaborar** *intr* to collaborate; (*en un periódico, coloquio, etc.*) to contribute
**colación** *f* (*cotejo; refacción ligera*) collation; (*de un grado de universidad*) conferring; parish land; **sacar a colación** to mention, bring up; **traer a colación** to bring up; to adduce as proof; to bring up irrelevantly
**colacionar** *tr* to collate; to compare; (*un beneficio*) to confer
**colactánea** *f* foster sister
**colactáneo** *m* foster brother
**colada** *f* washing powder; wash; (*garganta entre montañas*) gulch; cattle run; **todo saldrá en la colada** (coll) it will all come out in the wash; (coll) the day of reckoning will come
**coladera** *f* strainer; (Mex) sewer
**coladero** *m* strainer; cattle run; narrow pass
**colador** *m* strainer, colander
**colapez** *f* or **colapiscis** *f* isinglass
**colapso** *m* breakdown, collapse; **colapso nervioso** nervous breakdown
**colar** *tr* (*un grado universitario*) to confer || §61 *tr* (*un líquido*) to strain; to bleach in hot lye, to buck; (*metales*) to cast; (*una moneda falsa*) (coll) to pass off; **colar el hueso por** (coll) to squeeze through || *intr* to run, to ooze; to squeeze through; to come in, slip in; (coll) to drink wine; **colar a fondo** to sink; **no colar** (*una cosa*) (coll) to not be believed || *ref* to seep, seep through; to slip in, slip through; to make a slip; to lie; **colarse de gorra** (coll) to crash the gate
**colateral** *adj* collateral || *mf* (*pariente*) collateral || *m* (com) collateral
**colcrén** *m* cold cream
**colcha** *f* quilt, counterpane, bedspread
**colchón** *m* mattress; **colchón de aire** air mattress; **colchón de muelles** bedspring, spring mattress; **colchón de plumas** feather bed
**coleada** *f* wag (*of the tail*); (Mex, Ven) throwing the bull by twisting its tail
**colear** *tr* (taur) to grab by the tail; (*la res*) (Mex, Ven) to throw by twisting the tail; (Col, Ven) to nag, harass; (Guat) to trail after; (*reprobar en un examen*) (Chile) to flunk || *intr* to wag the tail; (aer) to fishtail; (coll) to stay alive, to keep going; (*los últimos vagones de un tren*) (Am) to sway; **colear en** (*cierta edad*) (CAm, W-I) to border on, be close to; **todavía colea** (coll) it's not over yet
**colección** *f* collection
**coleccionar** *tr* to collect
**coleccionista** *mf* collector
**colecta** *f* collection for charity; (eccl) collect
**colectar** *tr* to collect; (*obras antes sueltas*) to collect in one volume
**colecti•cio -cia** *adj* new, untrained, green; (*tomo*) omnibus
**colecti•vo -va** *adj* collective
**colector** *m* collector; catch basin; (elec) commutator; (aut) manifold
**colega** *mf* colleague || *m* confrere
**colegial** *m* schoolboy
**colegiala** *f* schoolgirl
**colegiatura** *f* scholarship; (Mex) tuition
**colegio** *m* school, academy; (*sociedad de hombres de una misma profesión*) college (*e.g., of cardinals, electors*)
**colegir** §57 *tr* to gather, collect; to conclude, infer
**cólera** *m* cholera || *f* anger, wrath; (*bilis*) bile; **montar en cólera** to fly into a rage
**colérico -ca** *adj* choleric, irascible
**colesterol** *m* cholesterol
**coleta** *f* pigtail; (*del torero*) cue, queue; (coll) postscript; **cortarse la coleta** to quit the bull ring; to quit, retire; **tener** or **traer coleta** to have serious consequences
**coletero** *m* wren
**coleto** *m* buff jacket; (coll) body, one's body, oneself; **decir para su coleto** (coll) to say to oneself; **echarse al coleto** (coll) to eat up, drink up; (coll) to read from cover to cover
**colgadero** *m* hanger, hook; clothes rack
**colgadizo** *m* lean-to, penthouse; projection over a door, canopy
**colga•do -da** *adj* pending, unsettled; **dejar colgado** (coll) to disappoint, frustrate; **quedarse colgado** (coll) to be disappointed, frustrated
**colgador** *m* clothes hanger, coat hanger
**colgajo** *m* rag, tatter
**colgante** *adj* hanging, dangling; (*puente*) suspension || *m* drop, pendant; (archit) festoon; (P-R) watch fob
**colgar** §63 *tr* to hang; to impute, attribute; (*a un alumno*) to flunk; (*a un reo*) (coll) to hang || *intr* to hang, hang down, dangle; to droop; (telp) to hang up; **colgar de** to hang from, hang on; to depend on
**coli•brí** *m* (*pl* **-bríes**) humming bird
**cóli•co -ca** *adj* & *m* colic || *f* upset stomach
**coliche** *m* (coll) at-home, open house
**coliflor** *f* cauliflower

**coligar** §44 *ref* to join forces, make common cause
**colilla** *f* butt, stump, stub
**co•lín -lina** *adj* (*caballo o yegua*) bobtailed ‖ *m* bobwhite; **colín de Virginia** bobwhite ‖ *f* see **colina**
**colina** *f* hill, knoll
**colindante** *adj* adjacent, contiguous
**colindar** *intr* to be adjacent
**colino•so -sa** *adj* hilly
**colirio** *m* eyewash
**coliseo** *m* coliseum
**colisión** *f* collision; bruise, bump
**colista** *mf* (coll) person standing in line
**colma•do -da** *adj* abundant, plentiful ‖ *m* food store, grocery store; seafood restaurant
**colmar** *tr* to fill up; (*las esperanzas de uno*) to fulfill; to overwhelm; **colmar de** to shower with, overwhelm with
**colmena** *f* beehive
**colmenar** *m* apiary
**colmene•ro -ra** *mf* beekeeper
**colmillo** *m* eyetooth, canine tooth; (*del elefante*) tusk; **tener el colmillo retorcido** (coll) to cut one's eyeteeth
**col•mo -ma** *adj* brimful, overflowing ‖ *m* overflow; thatch, thatch roof; (*de un sorbete*) topping; **eso es el colmo** (coll) that's the limit; **para colmo de** to top off
**colocación** *f* (*acción de poner una persona o cosa en un lugar*) location; (*disposición de una cosa respecto del lugar que ocupa*) placement; (*inversión de dinero*) investment; (*empleo*) position, employment, job
**colocar** §73 *tr* to place, put; (*una trampa*) to set ‖ *ref* to get placed, find a job; (*venderse*) to sell
**colodra** *f* milk bucket; drinking horn; (*bebedor de vino*) (coll) toper
**colofón** *m* colophon
**colofonia** *f* rosin
**coloide** *adj* & *m* coloid
**colon** *m* colon; (gram) main clause
**Colón** *m* Columbus
**colonia** *f* colony; cologne; silk ribbon; housing development; (W-I) sugar plantation ‖ **Colonia** *f* Cologne; **la Colonia del Cabo** Cape Colony
**colonial** *adj* colonial; overseas ‖ **coloniales** *mpl* imported foods
**colonizar** §60 *tr* & *intr* to colonize
**colono** *m* colonist, settler; tenant farmer; (W-I) owner of sugar plantation
**coloquial** *adj* colloquial
**coloquialismo** *m* colloquialism
**coloquio** *m* colloquy, talk, conference
**color** *m* color; (*substancia para pintar*) paint; (*para pintarse el rostro*) rouge; **colores** (*bandera*) colors; (*persona*) **de color** colored; (*zapatos*) tan; **sacar los colores a** to make blush; **so color de** under color of, under pretext of; **verlo todo de color de rosa** to see everything through rose-colored glasses
**colora•do -da** *adj* red, reddish; (*libre, obsceno*) off-color; (*aparentemente justo y razonable*) specious; **ponerse colorado** to blush
**colorado•te -ta** *adj* (coll) ruddy, sanguine
**colorante** *adj* & *m* coloring
**colorar** *tr* to color; to dye; to stain
**colorear** *tr* to color; (fig) to color, excuse, palliate ‖ *ref* (*la cereza, el tomate, etc.*) to redden, turn red
**colorete** *m* rouge; **ponerse colorete** to put on rouge
**colorir** §1 *tr* to color; (fig) to color, to palliate ‖ *intr* to take on color
**colosal** *adj* colossal
**coloso** *m* colossus
**columbrar** *tr* to discern, descry, glimpse; to guess
**columna** *f* column; **quinta columna** fifth column
**columnata** *f* colonnade
**columnista** *mf* columnist
**columpiar** *tr* to swing ‖ *ref* to swing; to seesaw; (coll) to swing, swagger
**columpio** *m* swing; **columpio de tabla** seesaw
**colusión** *f* collusion
**collada** *f* mountain pass; (naut) steady blow
**collado** *m* hill, height
**collar** *m* necklace; dog collar, horse collar; (*aro de hierro asegurado al cuello del malhechor*) collar, band; (*plumas del cuello de ciertas aves*) frill, ring; (*cadena que rodea el cuello como insignia*) cord, chain; (mach) collar
**collera** *f* horse collar; chain gang; **colleras** (Arg, Chile) cuff links
**co•llón -llona** *adj* (coll) cowardly ‖ *mf* (coll) coward
**coma** *m* (pathol) coma ‖ *f* comma; (*en inglés se emplea el punto en aritmética para separar los enteros de las fracciones decimales*) decimal point
**comadre** *f* mother or godmother (*with respect to each other*); gossip (*woman*); friend, neighbor (*woman*)
**comadrear** *intr* (coll) to gossip, go around gossiping
**comadreja** *f* weasel
**comadrería** *f* (coll) gossip, idle gossip
**comadre•ro -ra** *adj* (coll) gossipy ‖ *mf* (coll) gossip
**comadrón** *m* accoucheur
**comadrona** *f* midwife
**comandancia** *f* command; commander's headquarters; (mil) majority
**comandante** *m* commander, commandant; (mil) major
**comandar** *tr* (mil, nav) to command
**comando** *m* (mil) command; **comando a distancia** remote control
**comarca** *f* district, region, country
**comarcar** §73 *tr* to plant in a line at regular intervals ‖ *intr* to border, be contiguous
**comato•so -sa** *adj* comatose
**comba** *f* bend, curve; warp, bulge; skipping rope; **saltar a la comba** to jump rope, to skip rope
**combar** *tr* to bend, curve ‖ *ref* to bend, curve; to warp, bulge; to sag
**combate** *m* combat, fight; **combate revancha** (box) return bout; **fuera de**

combate hors de combat; (box) knockout
**combatiente** *adj & m* combatant
**combatir** *tr* to combat, fight; to beat, beat upon || *intr & ref* to combat, fight, struggle
**combinación** *f* combination; (*de trenes*) connection
**combinar** *tr & ref* to combine
**com•bo -ba** *adj* bent, curved, crooked; warped || *m* trunk or rock to stand wine casks on || *f* see **comba**
**combustible** *adj* combustible || *m* (*substancia que arde con facilidad*) combustible; (*substancia que sirve para calentar, cocinar, etc.*) fuel
**combustión** *f* combustion
**comede•ro -ra** *adj* eatable || *m* manger, feed trough; (Mex) haunt, hangout; **limpiarle a uno el comedero** (coll) to deprive someone of his bread and butter
**comedia** *f* drama, play; theater; comedy; (fig) farce; **comedia cómica** (*drama de desenlace festivo*) comedy; **hacer la comedia** (coll) to pretend, make believe
**comedian•te -ta** *mf* (coll) hypocrite || *m* actor, comedian || *f* actress, comedienne
**comedi•do -da** *adj* courteous, polite; moderate; (Am) obliging, accommodating
**comedimiento** *m* courtesy, politeness; moderation
**comediógra•fo -fa** *mf* playwright
**comedir** §50 *ref* to be courteous; to restrain oneself, be moderate; (Am) to be obliging; **comedirse a** (Am) to offer to, to volunteer to
**comedón** *m* blackhead
**come•dor -dora** *adj* heavy-eating || *m* dining room; restaurant, eating place; dining-room suite; **comedor de beneficencia** soup kitchen
**comején** *m* termite
**comendador** *m* prelate, prior; knight commander; (*de una orden militar*) commander
**comensal** *mf* dependent, servant; table companion
**comentar** *tr* to comment on || *intr* to comment; (coll) to gossip
**comentario** *m* comment, commentary; **commentarios** (coll) talk, gossip
**comentarista** *mf* commentator
**comento** *m* comment, commentary; deceit, falsehood
**comenzar** §18 *tr & intr* to commence, begin, start
**comer** *m* eating, food || *tr* to eat; to feed on; to gnaw away; to consume; (*alguna renta*) to enjoy; to itch; (*una pieza en el juego de damas*) to take; **comer vivo** (coll) to have it in for; **sin comerlo ni beberlo** (coll) without having anything to do with it; **tener qué comer** (coll) to have enough to live on || *intr* to eat; to dine, to have dinner; to itch || *ref* to eat up; (*las uñas*) to bite; (*el dinero*) (coll) to consume, eat up; (*omitir*) to skip, skip over; **comerse unos a otros** (coll) to be at loggerheads
**comerciable** *adj* marketable; sociable
**comercial** *adj* commercial, business
**comerciante** *mf* merchant, trader, dealer; **comerciante al por mayor** wholesaler; **comerciante al por menor** retailer
**comerciar** *intr* to trade, to deal
**comercio** *m* commerce, trade, business; store, shop; business center; commerce, intercourse; **comercio de artículos de regalo** gift shop; **comercio exterior** foreign trade
**comestible** *adj* eatable || *m* food, foodstuff
**cometa** *m* comet || *f* kite
**cometer** *tr* (*un crimen, una falta*) to commit; (*un negocio a una persona*) to commit, to entrust; (*figuras retóricas*) to employ
**cometido** *m* assignment, duty; commitment
**comezón** *f* itch
**comicastro** *m* ham, ham actor
**comicios** *mpl* polls; **acudir a los comicios** to go to the polls
**cómi•co -ca** *adj* comic, comical; dramatic || *mf* actor; comedian; **cómico de la legua** strolling player, barnstormer || *f* actress; comedienne
**comida** *f* (*alimento*) food; (*el que se toma a horas señaladas*) meal; (*el principal de cada día*) dinner; **comida corrida** (Mex) table d'hôte
**comidilla** *f* (coll) hobby; **la comidilla del pueblo** (coll) the talk of the town
**comienzo** *m* beginning, start; **a comienzos de** around the beginning of
**comilitona** *f* (coll) spread, feast
**comi•lón -lona** *adj* (coll) heavy-eating || *mf* (coll) hearty eater || *f* (coll) hearty meal, spread
**comillas** *fpl* quotation marks
**cominear** *intr* (*el hombre*) (coll) to fuss around like a woman
**comiquear** *intr* to put on amateur plays
**comiquillo** *m* ham, ham actor
**comisar** *tr* to seize, confiscate
**comisario** *m* commissary; commissioner; **comisario de a bordo** purser
**comisión** *f* commission; committee; (*recado*) errand
**comisiona•do -da** *mf* commissioner || *m* committeeman
**comisionar** *tr* to commission
**comiso** *m* seizure, confiscation; confiscated goods
**comisura** *f* corner (*e.g., of lips*)
**comité** *m* committee
**comitente** *mf* constituent
**comitiva** *f* retinue, suite; procession
**como** *adv* as, like; so to speak, as it were || *conj* as; when; if; so that; as soon as; as long as; inasmuch as; **así como** as soon as; **como no** unless; **como que** because, inasmuch as; **como quien dice** so to speak; **tan luego como** as soon as
**cómo** *adv* how; why; what; **¿a cómo es . . .?** how much is . . .?; **¿cómo no?** why not?
**cómoda** *f* bureau, commode, chest

**comodidad** *f* comfort; convenience; advantage, interest
**comodín** *m* joker, wild card; gadget, jigger; excuse, alibi
**cómo·do -da** *adj* handy, convenient; comfortable ‖ *f* see **cómoda**
**como·dón -dona** *adj* (coll) comfort-loving, self-indulgent, easy-going
**compac·to -ta** *adj* compact
**compadecer** §22 *tr* to pity, feel sorry for ‖ *ref* to harmonize; **compadecerse con** to harmonize with; **compadecerse de** to pity, feel sorry for
**compadraje** *m* clique, cabal
**compadrar** *intr* to become a godfather; to become friends
**compadre** *m* father or godfather (*with respect to each other*); friend, companion
**compadrear** *intr* (coll) to be close friends; (Arg, Urug) to brag, show off
**compadrería** *f* close companionship
**compadrito** *m* (Arg) bully
**compaginar** *tr* to arrange, put in order ‖ *ref* to fit, agree; to blend
**companage** *m* snacks, cold cuts
**compañerismo** *m* companionship
**compañe·ro -ra** *mf* companion; partner; mate; **compañero de cama** bedfellow; **compañero de cuarto** roommate; **compañero de juego** playmate; **compañero de viaje** fellow traveler ‖ *f* (*esposa*) helpmeet
**compañía** *f* company; society; **compañía de desembarco** (nav) landing force; **hacerle compañía a una persona** to keep someone company
**compañón** *m* testicle; **compañón de perro** orchid
**comparación** *f* comparison
**comparar** *tr* to compare
**comparati·vo -va** *adj* comparative
**comparecencia** *f* (law) appearance
**comparecer** §22 *intr* (law) to appear
**comparendo** *m* (law) summons
**comparsa** *mf* (theat) supernummerary, extra ‖ *f* supernummeraries, extras
**compartimiento** *m* distribution, division; compartment
**compartir** *tr* to distribute, divide; to share
**compás** *m* (*brújula*) compass; (*instrumento para trazar curvas*) compass or compasses; rule, measure; (mus) time, measure; (mus) bar, measure; (mus) beat; **a compás** (mus) in time; **compás de calibres** calipers; **compás de división** dividers; **llevar el compás** (mus) to keep time
**compasible** *adj* compassionate; pitiful
**compasión** *f* compassion; **¡por compasión!** for pity's sake!
**compasi·vo -va** *adj* compassionate
**compatri·cio -cia** or **compatriota** *mf* fellow countryman, compatriot
**compeler** *tr* to compel
**compendiar** *tr* to condense, to summarize
**compendio** *m* compendium; **en compendio** in a word
**compendio·so -sa** *adj* compendious
**compensación** *f* compensation; (com) clearing, clearance
**compensar** *tr* to compensate; to compensate for ‖ *intr* to compensate ‖ *ref* to be compensated for
**competencia** *f* (*aptitud*) competence; (*rivalidad*) competition; dispute; area, field; **de la competencia de** in the domain of; **sin competencia** unmatched (*prices*)
**competente** *adj* competent; reliable
**competer** *intr* to be incumbent
**competición** *f* competition
**competi·dor -dora** *adj* competing ‖ *mf* competitor
**competir** §50 *intr* to compete
**compilación** *f* compilation
**compilar** *tr* to compile
**compinche** *mf* (coll) chum, crony, pal
**complacencia** *f* complacency
**complacer** §22 *tr* to please, to humor ‖ *ref* to be pleased, take pleasure
**complaciente** *adj* obliging; indulgent
**comple·jo -ja** *adj & m* complex; **complejo de inferioridad** inferiority complex
**complementar** *tr* to complement
**complemento** *m* complement; completion; perfection; accessory; **complemento directo** (gram) direct object
**completar** *tr* to complete; to perfect
**comple·to -ta** *adj* complete; (*autobús, tranvía*) full
**complexión** *f* constitution
**complexiona·do -da** *adj* — **bien complexionado** strong, robust; **mal complexionado** weak, frail
**comple·xo -xa** *adj* complex
**complica·do -da** *adj* complicated, complex
**complicar** §73 *tr* to complicate; to involve ‖ *ref* to become complicated; to become involved
**cómplice** *mf* accomplice, accessory
**complicidad** *f* complicity
**com·plot** *m* (*pl* **-plots**) plot, intrigue
**compone·dor -dora** *mf* composer, compositor; typesetter; arbitrator; repairer ‖ *m* stick, composing stick; **amigable componedor** mediator, umpire
**componenda** *f* compromise, settlement, reconciliation
**componente** *adj* component, constituent ‖ *m* component, constituent; member ‖ *f* (mech) component
**componer** §54 *tr* to compose; to compound; to mend, repair; to pacify, reconcile; to arrange, put in order; (coll) to restore, strengthen; (*huesos dislocados*) (Am) to set; (Col) to bewitch ‖ *ref* to compose oneself; to get dressed; to make up, become friends again; (*pintarse el rostro*) to make up; **componérselas** (coll) to make out, to manage
**comportable** *adj* bearable, tolerable
**comportamiento** *m* behavior, conduct
**comportar** *tr* to support; (Am) to bring about, entail ‖ *ref* to act, behave
**comporte** *m* behavior; carriage, bearing
**composición** *f* composition; agreement; (*circunspección*) composure, restraint; **hacer una composición de lugar** to carefully lay one's plans

**compositi•vo -va** *adj* (gram) combining
**composi•tor -tora** *mf* composer || *m* (Arg, Urug) horse trainer, trainer of fighting cocks
**compostura** *f* composition; agreement; (*circunspección*) composure, restraint; repair, repairing, mending; (*aseo*) neatness; adulteration; (Arg, Urug) training
**compota** *f* compote, preserves; **compota de frutas** stewed fruit; **compota de manzanas** applesauce
**compotera** *f* (*vasija*) compote
**compra** *f* purchase, buy; shopping; **compra al contado** cash purchase; **compra a plazos** installment buying; **hacer compras, ir de compras** to go shopping
**compra•dor -dora** *mf* purchaser, buyer; shopper
**comprar** *tr* to purchase, to buy; (*sobornar*) to buy off || *intr* to shop
**compraventa** *f* dealing, business, bargain, trading; resale
**comprender** *tr* (*entender*) to understand; (*entender; abrazar*) to comprehend; (*contener, incluir*) to comprise
**comprensible** *adj* comprehensible, understandable
**comprensión** *f* understanding, comprehension; inclusion
**comprensi•vo -va** *adj* understanding; comprehensive; **comprensivo de** inclusive of
**compresa** *f* (med) compress; **compresa higiénica** sanitary napkin
**compresión** *f* compression
**comprimido** *m* tablet
**comprimir** *tr* to compress; to restrain, repress; to flatten
**comprobación** *f* checking, verification; proof
**comprobante** *adj* proving || *m* certificate, voucher, warrant; proof; claim check
**comprobar** §61 *tr* to check, verify; to prove
**comprometer** *tr* to compromise, endanger, jeopardize; to force, to oblige; (*un negocio a un tercero*) to entrust || *ref* to promise; to commit oneself; to become engaged
**comprometi•do -da** *adj* awkward, embarrassing; engaged to be married
**comprometimiento** *m* commitment, promise; predicament, awkward situation; compromise
**compromiso** *m* commitment, promise; appointment, engagement; predicament, awkward situation; betrothal
**compuerta** *f* hatch, half door; floodgate, sluice
**compues•to -ta** *adj* & *m* composite, compound
**compulsar** *tr* to collate; to make an authentic copy of
**compungi•do -da** *adj* remorseful
**compungir** §27 *tr* to make remorseful || *ref* to feel remorse
**compurgar** §44 *tr* (*el reo la pena*) (Mex) to finish serving
**computador** *m* computer
**computar** *tr* & *intr* to compute
**cómputo** *m* computation, calculation
**comulgante** *mf* (eccl) communicant
**comulgar** §44 *tr* to administer communion to || *intr* to take communion
**comulgatorio** *m* communion rail, altar rail
**común** *adj* common || *m* community; water closet; toilet; **el común de las gentes** the general run of people; **por lo común** commonly
**comunal** *adj* common; community || *m* community
**comune•ro -ra** *adj* popular || *m* shareholder
**comunicación** *f* communication; connection
**comunicado** *m* communiqué; letter to the editor; official announcement
**comunica•dor -dora** *adj* communicating
**comunicante** *mf* communicant, informant
**comunicar** §73 *tr* to communicate; to notify, inform; to connect, put into communication || *intr* to communicate || *ref* to communicate; to communicate with each other
**comunicati•vo -va** *adj* communicative
**comunidad** *f* community
**comunión** *f* communion; political party; sect
**comunismo** *m* communism
**comunista** *mf* communist
**comunistizar** §60 *tr* to convert to communism || *ref* to become communistic
**comunizar** §60 *tr* to communize
**con** *prep* with; to, towards; in spite of; **con que** and so; whereupon; **con tal (de) que** provided that; **con todo** however, nevertheless
**conato** *m* effort, endeavor; (*delito que no llegó a consumarse*) attempt
**cónca•vo -va** *adj* concave
**concebible** *adj* conceivable
**concebir** §50 *tr* & *intr* to conceive
**conceder** *tr* to concede, admit; to grant
**concejal** *m* alderman, councilman; **concejales** city fathers
**concejo** *m* town council; town hall; council meeting; (*expósito*) foundling
**concentrar** *tr* & *ref* to concentrate
**concéntri•co -ca** *adj* concentric
**concepción** *f* conception
**concepto** *m* concept; opinion, judgment; (*dicho ingenioso*) conceit, witticism; point of view; **en concepto de** under the head of; **tener buen concepto de** or **tener en buen concepto** to have a high opinion of, to hold in high esteem
**conceptuar** §21 *tr* to deem, to judge, to regard
**conceptuo•so -sa** *adj* witty, epigrammatic
**concerniente** *adj* relative
**concernir** §28 *tr* to concern
**concertar** §2 *tr* to concert; to mend, repair; (*un casamiento; la paz*) to arrange; (*huesos dislocados*) to set; (*poner de acuerdo*) to reconcile; (*un pacto*) to conclude; to harmonize || *intr* to concert; to agree || *ref* to

come to terms, become reconciled; to agree
**concertino** *m* concertmaster
**concertista** *mf* (mus) manager; (mus) performer, soloist
**concesión** *f* concession, admission; grant
**concesionario** *m* licensee; (*comerciante*) dealer
**concesi•vo -va** *adj* concessive
**conciencia** *f* (*conocimiento que uno tiene de su propia existencia*) consciousness; (*sentimiento del bien y del mal*) conscience; (*conocimiento*) awareness; **cobrar conciencia de** to become aware of; **en conciencia** in all conscience
**concienzu•do -da** *adj* conscientious; thorough
**concierto** *m* concert, harmony; (*función de música*) concert; (*composición de música*) concerto
**concilia•dor -dora** *adj* conciliatory
**conciliar** *tr* to conciliate, to reconcile ‖ *ref* (*el respeto, la estima, etc.*) to conciliate, to win
**concilio** *m* (eccl) council
**conci•so -sa** *adj* concise
**concitar** *tr* to stir up, incite, agitate
**conciudadano -na** *mf* fellow citizen
**concluir** §20 *tr* to conclude; to convince ‖ *intr & ref* to conclude, to end
**conclusión** *f* conclusion
**concluyente** *adj* conclusive, convincing
**concomitar** *tr* to accompany, go with
**concordancia** *f* concordance; (gram, mus) concord
**concordar** §61 *tr* to harmonize; to reconcile; to make agree ‖ *intr* to agree
**concordia** *f* concord; **de concordia** by common consent
**concre•to -ta** *adj* concrete
**concubina** *f* concubine
**concubio** *m* (archaic) bedtime
**concuñada** *f* sister-in-law
**concuñado** *m* brother-in-law
**concurrencia** *f* (*acaecimiento de varios sucesos en un mismo tiempo*) concurrence; (*competencia comercial*) competition; (*ayuda*) assistance; crowd, gathering, attendance
**concurrente** *adj* concurrent; competing ‖ *mf* competitor, contender, entrant
**concurri•do -da** *adj* crowded, full of people; well-attended
**concurrir** *intr* to concur; to gather, meet, come together; to compete, contend; to coincide; **concurrir con** (*p.ej., dinero*) to contribute
**concursante** *mf* contender
**concursar** *tr* to declare insolvent ‖ *intr* to contend, to compete
**concurso** *m* contest, competition; (*de gente*) concourse, crowd, throng; backing, coöperation; show, exhibition; **concurso de acreedores** meeting of creditors; **concurso de belleza** beauty contest; **concurso hípico** horse show
**concusión** *f* concussion; extortion, shakedown
**concha** *f* (*de molusco o crustáceo*) shell; (*cada una de las dos partes del caparazón de los moluscos bivalvos*) half shell; (*en que se sirve el pescado*) scallop; (*carey*) tortoise shell; oyster; shellfish; horseshoe bay; (theat) prompter's box; **concha de peregrino** scallop shell; (zool) scallop; (*ostras*) **en su concha** on the half shell; **tener muchas conchas** (coll) to be sly, cunning
**conchabanza** *f* comfort; (coll) collusion, cabal
**conchabar** *tr* to join, unite; (Am) to hire ‖ *ref* (coll) to gang up; (Am) to hire out
**conchabero** *m* (Col) pieceworker
**condado** *m* county; earldom
**conde** *m* count, earl; gypsy chief
**condecoración** *f* decoration
**condecorar** *tr* to decorate
**condena** *f* sentence; penalty, jail term; **condena judicial** conviction
**condenación** *f* condemnation; (*la eterna*) damnation
**condena•do -da** *adj* condemned; damned; (Chile) shrewd, clever ‖ *mf* sentenced person; **los condenados** the damned
**condenar** *tr* to condemn; to convict; (*a la pena eterna*) to damn; (*p.ej., una ventana*) to shut off, to block up; (*una habitación*) to padlock ‖ *ref* to condemn oneself, confess one's guilt; (*a la pena eterna*) to be damned
**condensar** *tr* to condense ‖ *ref* to condense, be condensed
**condesa** *f* countess
**condescendencia** *f* acquiescence, compliance
**condescender** §51 *intr* to acquiesce, comply; **condescender a** to accede to
**condescendiente** *adj* acquiescent, obliging
**condición** *f* condition, state; position, situation; standing; nature, character, temperament; **a condición (de) que** on condition that; **en buenas condiciones** in good condition, in good shape; **tener condición** to have a bad temper
**condicional** *adj* conditional
**condimentar** *tr* to season
**condimento** *m* condiment, seasoning
**condiscípulo** *m* fellow student
**condolencia** *f* condolence
**condoler** §47 *ref* to condole; **condolerse de** to sympathize with, feel sorry for, commiserate with
**condonar** *tr* to condone, overlook
**conducción** *f* conveyance, transportation; guiding, leading; (aut) drive, driving; **conducción a la derecha** right-hand drive; **conducción a la izquierda** left-hand drive; **conducción interior** closed car
**conducente** *adj* conducive
**conducir** §19 *tr* to conduct; to manage, direct; to guide, lead; to convey, transport; to drive; to employ, hire ‖ *intr* to lead; to conduce ‖ *ref* to conduct oneself, behave
**conducta** *f* conduct; management, direction; guidance; conveyance; conduct, behavior

**conducto** *m* pipe; conduit; (anat) duct, canal; agency, intermediary, channel; **por conducto de** through
**conduc•tor -tora** *adj* conducting || *mf* driver, motorist; (*cobrador en un vehículo público*) (Am) conductor || *m & f* (elec & phys) conductor; **buen conductor, buena conductora** good conductor; **mal conductor, mala conductora** bad or poor conductor || *m* (rr) engineman, engine driver
**conectar** *tr* to connect
**conejera** *f* burrow, warren; (coll) joint, dive
**conejillo** *m* young rabbit; **conejillo de Indias** guinea pig
**conejo** *m* rabbit
**conexión** *f* connection
**conexionar** *tr* to connect; to put in touch || *ref* to connect; to make contacts
**confabulación** *f* collusion, connivance
**confabular** *ref* to connive, scheme, plot
**confección** *f* making, preparation, confection; tailoring; ready-made suit; **confección a medida** suit made to order; **de confección** ready-made
**confeccionar** *tr* (*ropa*) to make; (*una receta*) to make up, concoct
**confeccionista** *mf* ready-made clothier
**confederación** *f* confederacy; alliance
**confedera•do -da** *adj & mf* confederate
**confederar** *tr & ref* to confederate
**conferencia** *f* (*reunión para tratar asuntos internacionales, etc.*) conference; (*plática para tratar de algún negocio*) interview; (*disertación en público o en la universidad*) lecture; **conferencia telefónica** (telp) long-distance call
**conferenciante** *mf* conferee; lecturer
**conferenciar** *intr* to confer, hold an interview
**conferencista** *mf* (Arg) lecturer
**conferir** §68 *tr* to confer, award, bestow; to discuss; to compare || *intr* to confer
**confesante** *mf* confessor
**confesar** §2 *tr, intr & ref* to confess
**confesión** *f* confession; denomination, faith, religion
**confe•so -sa** *adj* confessed; (*judío*) converted || *mf* converted Jew || *m* lay brother
**confesonario** *m* confessional
**confesor** *m* confessor
**confiable** *adj* reliable, dependable
**confia•do -da** *adj* unsuspecting; haughty, self-confident
**confianza** *f* confidence; self-confidence, self-assurance; familiarity; secret deal; **de confianza** reliable
**confianzu•do -da** *adj* (coll) overconfident; (Am) overfamiliar
**confiar** §77 *tr* to confide, entrust; to strengthen the confidence of || *intr & ref* to confide, trust; **confiar** or **confiarse de** or **en** to confide in, trust in; to rely on
**confidencia** *f* confidence; secret
**confidencial** *adj* confidential
**confiden•te -ta** *adj* trustworthy, faithful || *mf* confident || *m* spy; informer; secret agent; love seat
**configurar** *tr* to shape, form
**confín** *m* confine, border, boundary; **los confines** the confines
**confina•do -da** *adj* exiled || *m* prisoner
**confinamiento** *m* confinement; abutment
**confinar** *tr* to exile; to confine || *intr* to border
**confirmar** *tr* to confirm
**confiscar** §73 *tr* to confiscate
**confita•do -da** *adj* hopeful, confident; (*bañado de azúcar*) candied
**confitar** *tr* (*frutas*) to candy; (*en almíbar*) to preserve; (*endulzar*) to sweeten
**confite** *m* candy, bonbon, confection; **confites** confectionery
**confitera** *f* candy box; candy jar
**confitería** *f* confectionery; confectionery store
**confite•ro -ra** *mf* confectioner || *f* see **confitera**
**confitura** *f* preserves, confiture; **confituras** confectionery
**conflagración** *f* conflagration
**conflagrar** *tr* to set fire to
**conflicto** *m* conflict; (*apuro*) fix, jam
**confluencia** *f* confluence
**confluir** §20 *intr* to flow together; to crowd, gather
**conformador** *m* hat block
**conformar** *tr* to shape; (*un sombrero*) to block || *intr & ref* to conform, to comply, to yield, to agree
**conforme** *adj* in agreement || *adv* depending on circumstances; fine, O.K.; **conforme a** according to || *conj* as, in proportion as; as soon as || *m* approval
**conformidad** *f* conformance, conformity; resignation
**confort** *m* comfort
**confortable** *adj* comfortable; comforting
**confortante** *adj* comforting; tonic || *mf* comforter || *m* tonic
**confr.** *abbr* **confesor**
**confricar** *tr* to rub
**confrontar** *tr* (*poner en presencia; cotejar*) to confront || *intr* to border; to agree || *ref* to get along, to agree; **confrontarse con** (*hacer frente a*) to confront
**confundir** *tr* to confuse; (*turbar, dejar desarmado*) to confound || *ref* to become confused; (*en la muchedumbre*) to get lost
**confusión** *f* confusion
**confutar** *tr* to confute
**congelador** *m* freezer
**congelar** *tr* to congeal, freeze; (*créditos*) (fig) to freeze || *ref* to congeal, freeze
**congenial** *adj* congenial (*having the same nature*)
**congeniar** *intr* to be congenial, to get along well
**congéni•to -ta** *adj* congenital
**congestión** *f* congestion
**congestionar** *tr* to congest || *ref* to congest, become congested

**conglobar** *tr* to lump together
**congoja** *f* anguish, grief
**congojo·so -sa** *adj* distressing; distressed
**congosto** *m* narrow mountain pass
**congraciar** *tr* to win over || *ref* to ingratiate oneself; **congraciarse con** to get into the good graces of
**congratulación** *f* congratulation
**congratular** *tr* to congratulate || *ref* to congratulate oneself, to rejoice
**congregación** *f* congregation; **la Congregación de los fieles** the Roman Catholic Church
**congregar** §44 *tr* to bring together || *ref* to congregate, to come together
**congresal** *m* (Arg, Chile) congressman
**congresista** *mf* delegate; member of congress || *m* congressman
**congreso** *m* (*asamblea legislativa*) congress; (*reunión para deliberar sobre intereses comunes*) meeting, convention
**congrio** *m* conger eel
**cóni·co -ca** *adj* conical
**conjetura** *f* conjecture, guess
**conjeturar** *tr* & *intr* to conjecture, guess
**conjugación** *f* conjugation
**conjugar** §44 *tr* to conjugate; to combine
**conjunción** *f* conjunction; combination
**conjuntamente** *adv* together
**conjuntista** *m* chorus man || *f* chorus girl
**conjunti·vo -va** *adj* conjunctive; subjunctive
**conjun·to -ta** *adj* joined, combined, united || *m* whole, entirety, ensemble; unit; group; (theat) chorus; **de conjunto** general; **en conjunto** as a whole; **en su conjunto** in its entirety
**conjura** or **conjuración** *f* conspiracy, plot
**conjuramentar** *tr* to swear in || *ref* to take an oath
**conjurar** *tr* to swear in; to conjure, entreat; to conjure away, to exorcise || *intr* to conspire, plot || *ref* to conspire, join in a conspiracy
**conjuro** *m* (*invocación supersticiosa*) conjuration; adjuration, entreaty
**conllevar** *tr* (*los trabajos*) to share in bearing; (*a una persona*) to tolerate, stand for; (*las adversidades*) to suffer
**conmemorar** *tr* to commemorate, memorialize
**conmigo** *pron* with me, with myself
**conmilitón** *m* fellow soldier
**conminar** *tr* to threaten
**conmoción** *f* commotion; concussion, shock
**conmove·dor -dora** *adj* touching, moving, stirring
**conmover** §47 *tr* to touch, move, affect; to stir, stir up; to shake, upset || *ref* to be touched, be moved
**conmutación** *f* commutation
**conmutador** *m* (elec) change-over switch
**conmutar** *tr* to commute
**connivencia** *f* connivance; **estar en connivencia** to connive
**cono** *m* cone; **cono de proa** nose cone; **cono de viento** (aer) wind cone, wind sock
**conoce·dor -dora** *adj* knowledgeable || *mf* expert, connoisseur
**conocer** §22 *tr* to know; to meet, get to know; to tell, to distinguish; (law) to try || *intr* to know; **conocer de** or **en** to know, have knowledge of || *ref* to know oneself; to know each other; to meet, meet each other
**conoci·do -da** *adj* known, well-known, familiar; distinguished, prominent || *mf* acquaintance
**conocimiento** *m* knowledge; understanding; acquaintance; consciousness; (com) bill of lading; **con conocimiento de causa** knowingly, with full knowledge; **conocimiento de embarque** (com) bill of lading; **conocimientos** knowledge; **hablar con pleno conocimiento de causa** to know what one is talking about; **perder el conocimiento** to lose consciousness; **por su real conocimiento** (Arg) for real money; **recobrar el conocimiento** to regain consciousness; **venir en conocimiento de** to come to know
**conque** *adv* and so || *m* (coll) condition, terms
**conquista** *f* conquest
**conquista·dor -dora** *adj* conquering || *m* conqueror; (*ladrón de corazones*) lady-killer
**conquistar** *tr* to conquer; (*ganar la voluntad de*) to win over
**consabi·do -da** *adj* well-known; above-mentioned
**consagrar** *tr* to consecrate; to devote; to dedicate; (*una nueva palabra*) to authorize || *ref* to devote oneself; to make a name for oneself
**consciente** *adj* conscious
**conscripción** *f* conscription
**conscripto** *m* conscript, draftee
**consecución** *f* obtaining, getting
**consecuencia** *f* (*correspondencia lógica entre sus elementos*) consistency; (*acontecimiento que resulta necesariamente de otro*) consequence; **en consecuencia** accordingly; **guardar consecuencia** to remain consistent; **traer a consecuencia** to bring in
**consecuente** *adj* (*que tiene proporción consigo mismo*) consistent; (*que sigue en orden a otra cosa*) consecutive
**consecuti·vo -va** *adj* consecutive
**conseguir** §67 *tr* to get, obtain; **conseguir** + *inf* to succeed in + *ger*
**conseja** *f* story, fairy tale; cabal
**conseje·ro -ra** *adj* advisory || *mf* advisor, counselor; councilor
**consejo** *m* advice, counsel; board; council; **consejos** advice; **un consejo** a piece of advice
**consenso** *m* consensus
**consenti·do -da** *adj* spoiled, pampered; (*marido*) indulgent
**consenti·dor -dora** *adj* acquiescent; pampering || *mf* acquiescent person; (*de niños*) pamperer || *m* cuckold

**consentimiento** *m* consent
**consentir** §68 *tr* to allow; to admit; to pamper, to spoil || *intr* to consent; to come loose; **consentir** + *inf* to think that + *ind;* **consentir con** to be indulgent toward; **consentir en** to consent to || *ref* to begin to crack up; (Arg) to be proud
**conserje** *m* janitor, concierge
**conserva** *f* preserves; preserved food; pickles; (naut) convoy; **conservas alimenticias** canned goods; **llevar en su conserva** (naut) to convoy; **navegar en (la) conserva** (naut) to sail in a convoy
**conservación** *f* conservation; preservation; self-preservation; maintenance, upkeep
**conserva•dor -dora** *adj* preservative; (pol) conservative || *mf* conservative || *m* curator
**conservar** *tr* to conserve, keep, maintain; to preserve || *ref* to take good care of oneself; to keep
**conservati•vo -va** *adj* conservative, preservative
**conservatorio** *m* (*p.ej., de música*) conservatory; (Arg) private school; (Chile) hothouse, greenhouse
**conservera** *f* cannery; (Mex) preserve dish
**conservería** *f* canning
**conserve•ro -ra** *adj* canning || *mf* canner || *f* see **conservera**
**considerable** *adj* considerable; large, great, important
**consideración** *f* consideration; **ser de consideración** to be of importance, be of concern; **someter a consideración** to take under advisement
**considera•do -da** *adj* (*que guarda consideración a los demás*) considerate; (*digno de respeto*) respected, esteemed; (*que obra con reflexión*) cautious, prudent
**considerando** *conj & m* whereas
**considerar** *tr* to consider; to treat with consideration
**consigna** *f* slogan; watchword; (mil) orders; (rr) checkroom
**consignación** *f* consignment
**consignar** *tr* to consign; to assign; to state in writing, to set forth
**consignatario** *m* consignee
**consigo** *pron* with him, with her, with them, with you; with himself, with herself, with themselves, with yourself or yourselves
**consiguiente** *adj* consequential; **ir** or **proceder consiguiente** to act consistently || *m* consequence; **por consiguiente** consequently, therefore
**consilia•ro -ria** *mf* advisor, counselor
**consistencia** *f* consistence, consistency
**consistente** *adj* consistent
**consistir** *intr* to consist; **consistir en** (*estar compuesto de*) to consist of; (*residir en*) to consist in
**consistorio** *m* consistory; town council; town hall
**conso•cio -cia** *mf* copartner; companion, fellow member
**consola** *f* console, console table; bracket
**consolación** *f* consolation
**consolar** §61 *tr* to console
**consolidar** *tr* to fund, refund; to strengthen; to repair
**consommé** *m* consommé
**consonancia** *f* consonance; rhyme
**consonante** *adj* consonantal; rhyming || *m* rhyme || *f* consonant
**consonar** §61 *intr* to be in harmony; to rhyme
**cónsone** *adj* harmonious || *m* (mus) chord
**consorcio** *m* consortium; partnership; fellowship
**consorte** *mf* consort, mate, spouse; partner, companion; **consortes** (law) colitigants; (law) accomplices
**conspi•cuo -cua** *adj* outstanding, prominent
**conspiración** *f* conspiracy
**conspirar** *intr* to conspire
**constancia** *f* constancy; certainty, proof
**constante** *adj* constant; steady, regular; sure, certain || *f* constant
**constar** *intr* to be clear, be certain; to be on record; to have the right rhythm; **constar de** to consist of; **hacer constar** to state, make known; **y para que conste** in witness whereof
**constatación** *f* proof
**constatar** *tr* to prove, establish, show
**constelación** *f* constellation; climate, weather; epidemic
**consternar** *tr* to depress, dismay
**constipación** *f* or **constipado** *m* cold, cold in the head
**constipar** *tr* (*los poros*) to stop up || *ref* to catch cold
**constitución** *f* constitution
**constituir** §20 *tr* to constitute; to establish, found; **constituir en** to force into || *ref* — **constituirse en** to set oneself up as
**constituti•vo -va** *adj & m* constituent
**constituyente** *adj* (*para dictar o reformar la constitución*) constituent
**constreñir** §72 *tr* to constrain, force, compel; to constrict, compress
**construcción** *f* construction; building, structure; **construcción de buques** shipbuilding
**construc•tor -tora** *adj* construction || *mf* builder, constructor; **constructor de buques** shipbuilder
**construir** §20 *tr* to build, to construct
**consuegro** *m* fellow father-in-law (*with respect to the father of one's son-in-law or daughter-in-law*), father-in-law of one's child
**consuelda** *f* comfrey; **consuelda real** field larkspur; **consuelda sarracena** goldenrod
**consuelo** *m* consolation; joy, delight; **sin consuelo** inconsolably; (coll) to excess
**consueta** *m* (theat) prompter
**consuetudina•rio -ria** *adj* customary, usual
**cónsul** *m* consul
**consulado** *m* consulate, consulship; (*casa u oficina*) consulate

**consular** *adj* consular
**consulta** *f* consultation; opinion; reference
**consultación** *f* consultation
**consultar** *tr* to consult; to take up, discuss; to advise || *intr* to consult, confer
**consulti•vo -va** *adj* advisory
**consul•tor -tora** *mf* consultant
**consultorio** *m* doctor's office
**consuma•do -da** *adj* consummate || *m* consommé
**consumar** *tr* to consummate; to fulfill, carry out
**consumición** *f* consumption; drink (*in bar or restaurant*)
**consumi•do -da** *adj* (coll) thin, weak, emaciated; (coll) fretful
**consumi•dor -dora** *mf* consumer; customer (*in bar or restaurant*)
**consumir** *tr* to consume; to exhaust; (coll) to harass, wear down || *ref* to consume, waste away; to long, yearn
**consumo** *m* consumption; drink (*in bar or restaurant*); customers; **consumos** octroi
**consunción** *f* consumption; (pathol) consumption
**consuno** *adv* — **de consuno** together, in accord
**consunti•vo -va** *adj* consumptive; (*crédito*) consumer
**contabilidad** *f* accounting, bookkeeping
**contabilista** *mf* accountant, bookkeeper
**contabilizadora** *f* computer
**contabilizar** §60 *tr* to enter in the ledger
**contable** *adj* countable || *mf* accountant, bookkeeper
**contactar** *intr* to contact, be in contact
**contacto** *m* contact; **ponerse en contacto con** to get in touch with
**conta•do -da** *adj* scarce, rare; **al contado** cash, for cash; **contados** a few; **de contado** right away; **por de contado** of course
**contador** *m* counter; accountant; (*que mide el agua, gas, electricidad*) meter; (law) receiver; **contador de abonado** house meter; **contador kilométrico** speedometer; **contador público titulado** certified public accountant
**contaduría** *f* accountancy; accountant's office; box office for advanced sales
**contagiar** *tr* to infect; to corrupt
**contagio** *m* contagion
**contagio•so -sa** *adj* contagious
**contaminación** *f* contamination
**contaminar** *tr* to contaminate; (*un texto*) to corrupt; (*la ley de Dios*) to break
**contante** *adj* (*dinero*) ready
**contar** §61 *tr* to count; to regard, consider; to tell, relate; **contar . . . años** to be . . . years old; **dejarse contar diez** (box) to take the count; **tiene sus horas contadas** his days are numbered || *intr* to count; **a contar desde** beginning with; **contar con** to count on, rely on; to reckon with; to expect to
**contemplación** *f* contemplation; leniency, condescension
**contemplar** *tr* to contemplate; to be lenient to || *intr* to contemplate
**contemporáne•o -a** *adj* contemporaneous, contemporary || *mf* contemporary
**contemporizar** §60 *intr* to temporize
**contención** *f* containment; contention, strife; (law) suit, litigation
**contencio•so -sa** *adj* contentious
**contender** §51 *intr* to contend
**contendiente** *mf* contender, contestant
**contener** §71 *tr* to contain || *ref* to contain oneself
**conteni•do -da** *adj* moderate, restrained || *m* content, contents
**contenta** *f* gift or treat; indorsement; (mil) certificate of good conduct; (law) release
**contentadi•zo -za** *adj* easy to please
**contentamiento** *m* contentment
**contentar** *tr* to content; (com) to indorse; (Am) to reconcile
**conten•to -ta** *adj* content, contented, glad || *m* content, contentment; **a contento** to one's satisfaction; **no caber de contento** (coll) to be beside oneself with joy || *f* see **contenta**
**contera** *f* tip, metal tip
**contesta** *f* (Am) answer; (Mex) chat
**contestación** *f* answer; argument, debate; **mala contestación** (coll) back talk
**contestar** *tr* to answer || *intr* to answer; to agree
**contexto** *m* interweaving; context
**conticinio** *m* dead of night
**contienda** *f* contest, dispute, fight
**contigo** *pron* with thee, with you
**conti•guo -gua** *adj* contiguous, adjoining
**continencia** *f* continence
**continental** *adj* continental
**continente** *adj* continent || *m* (*cosa que contiene en sí a otra*) container; (*aire del semblante, compostura del cuerpo*) mien, bearing; (*gran extensión de tierra rodeada por los océanos*) continent
**contingencia** *f* contingency
**contingente** *adj* contingent || *m* contingent; share, quota
**continuar** §21 *tr & intr* to continue; **continuará** to be continued
**continuidad** *f* continuity
**conti•nuo -nua** *adj* continuous, continual; (mach) endless || **continuo** *adv* continuously
**contonear** *ref* to strut, swagger
**contoneo** *m* strut, swagger
**contorcer** §74 *ref* to writhe
**contorno** *m* contour, outline; **contornos** environs, neighborhood
**contorsión** *f* contorsion
**contra** *prep* against; toward, facing || *m* (*concepto opuesto*) con || *f* trouble, inconvenience; (*al comprador*) (Cuba) gift, extra; (Chile) antidote; **llevar la contra a** (coll) to disagree with
**contraalmirante** *m* rear admiral
**contraatacar** §73 *tr & intr* to counterattack
**contraataque** *m* counterattack

**contrabajo** *m* contrabass, double bass
**contrabajón** *m* double bassoon
**contrabalancear** *tr* to counterbalance
**contrabalanza** *f* counterbalance
**contrabandear** *intr* to smuggle
**contrabandista** *adj* smuggling; contraband || *mf* smuggler, contrabandist
**contrabando** *m* smuggling, contraband; **meter de contrabando** to smuggle, smuggle in
**contrabarrera** *f* second row of seats (*in bull ring*)
**contracalle** *f* parallel side street
**contracarril** *m* (rr) guardrail
**contracción** *f* contraction; (*reducción del ritmo normal de los negocios*) recession; (*al estudio*) (Chile, Peru) concentration
**contracepti•vo -va** *adj & m* contraceptive
**contracorriente** *f* countercurrent, crosscurrent; (*entre aguas*) undertow
**contrachapado** *m* plywood
**contradecir** §24 *tr* to contradict
**contradicción** *f* contradiction
**contradic•tor -tora** *adj* contradictory || *mf* contradicter
**contradicto•rio -ria** *adj* contradictory
**contraer** §75 *tr* to contract; (*deudas*) to incur; (*el discurso o idea*) to condense || *ref* to contract; to shrink; (Chile, Peru) to concentrate, apply oneself
**contraescalón** *m* riser (*of stairway*)
**contraespía** *mf* counterspy
**contraespionaje** *m* counterespionage
**contrafallar** *tr & intr* to overtrump
**contrafallo** *m* overtrump
**contrafigura** *f* counterpart
**contrafuero** *m* infringement, violation
**contrafuerte** *m* abutment, buttress
**contragolpe** *m* counterstroke; kickback; (box) counter
**contrahace•dor -dora** *adj* counterfeiting; fake || *mf* counterfeiter; fake; impersonator
**contrahacer** §39 *tr* to counterfeit, copy, imitate; to fake; to impersonate; (*un libro*) to pirate || *ref* to pretend to be
**contra•haz** *f* (*pl* **-haces**) wrong side
**contrahe•cho -cha** *adj* counterfeit, fake; deformed
**contrahechura** *f* counterfeit, fake
**contrahuella** *f* riser (*of stairway*)
**contralor** *m* comptroller
**contralto** *mf* contralto (*person*) || *m* contralto (*voice*)
**contraluz** *f* view against the light; **a contraluz** against the light
**contramaestre** *m* foreman; (naut) boatswain; **segundo contramaestre** boatswain's mate
**contramandar** *tr* to countermand
**contramandato** *m* countermand
**contramano** *adv* — **a contramano** in the wrong direction, the wrong way
**contramarcha** *f* countermarch; reverse
**contramarchar** *intr* to countermarch; to go in reverse
**contraofensiva** *f* counteroffensive
**contraorden** *f* cancellation
**contraparte** *f* counterpart
**contrapasar** *intr* to go over to the other side
**contrapelo** *adv* — **a contrapelo** against the hair, against the grain; the wrong way; **a contrapelo de** against, counter to
**contrapesar** *tr* to offset, counterbalance
**contrapeso** *m* counterweight; counterbalance; (*para completar el peso de carne, etc.*) makeweight
**contraponer** §54 *tr* to set opposite; to oppose; to compare
**contraproducente** *adj* self-defeating, unproductive
**contraprueba** *f* second proof
**contrapuerta** *f* storm door; vestibule door
**contrapuntear** *tr* to sing in counterpoint; to taunt, be sarcastic to || *ref* to taunt each other
**contrapunto** *m* counterpoint
**contrapunzón** *m* nailset, punch
**contrariar** §77 *tr* to counteract, to oppose; to annoy, provoke
**contrariedad** *f* opposition; interference; annoyance, bother
**contra•rio -ria** *adj* opposite, contrary; harmful || *mf* enemy, opponent, rival || *m* opposite, contrary; **al contrario** on the contrary; **de lo contrario** otherwise
**contrarreferencia** *f* cross reference
**Contrarreforma** *f* Counter Reformation
**contrarregistro** *m* (*para comprobar si algún género ha pasado por la frontera*) double check; (*de una experiencia científica*) control
**contrarréplica** *f* (law) rejoinder
**contrarrestar** *tr* to resist, counteract; (*la pelota*) to return
**contrarrevolución** *f* counterrevolution
**contrasentido** *m* misinterpretation; mistranslation; nonsense
**contraseña** *f* countersign; baggage check; **contraseña de salida** (mov, theat) check
**contrastar** *tr* to resist; (*las pesas y medidas*) to check || *intr* to resist; to contrast
**contraste** *m* resistance; contrast; assayer; assayer's office; (naut) sudden shift in the wind
**contratar** *tr* to contract for; to hire, engage
**contratiempo** *m* misfortune, disappointment, setback
**contratista** *mf* contractor
**contrato** *m* contract
**contratreta** *f* counterplot
**contratuerca** *f* lock nut, jam nut
**contraveneno** *m* counterpoison, antidote
**contravenir** §79 *intr* to act contrary; **contravenir a** to contravene, act counter to
**contraventana** *f* window shutter
**contravidriera** *f* storm sash
**contrayente** *mf* contracting party (*to a marriage*)
**contribución** *f* contribution; tax; **contribución de sangre** military service;

**contribución industrial** excise tax; **contribución territorial** land tax
**contribui•dor -dora** *mf* contributor; taxpayer
**contribuir** §20 *tr & intr* to contribute
**contribuyente** *mf* contributor; taxpayer
**contrición** *f* contrition
**contrincante** *m* competitor, rival; fellow candidate
**contristar** *tr* to sadden
**contri•to -ta** *adj* contrite
**control** *m* control, check
**controlar** *tr* to control, check
**controversia** *f* controversy
**controvertible** *adj* controversial, controvertible
**controvertir** §68 *tr* to controvert
**contubernio** *m* cohabitation; evil alliance
**contumacia** *f* contumacy; (law) contempt
**contu•maz** *adj* (*pl* **-maces**) contumacious; germ-bearing; (law) guilty of contempt of court
**contumelia** *f* contumely
**contundente** *adj* bruising; impressive, convincing
**contundir** *tr* to bruise
**conturbar** *tr* to trouble, worry, upset
**contusión** *f* contusion
**contusionar** *tr* (Chile) to bruise
**convalecencia** *f* convalescence
**convalecer** §22 *intr* to convalesce, recover
**convaleciente** *adj & mf* convalescent
**convalidar** *tr* to confirm
**conveci•no -na** *adj* neighboring || *mf* neighbor
**convencer** §78 *tr* to convince
**convencimiento** *m* conviction
**convención** *f* (*acuerdo; conformidad; asamblea*) convention; (Am) political convention
**convencional** *adj* conventional
**convenible** *adj* docile, compliant; (*precio*) fair, reasonable
**conveniencia** *f* (*comodidad*) convenience; (*acuerdo, convenio*) agreement; fitness, suitability; (*formas sociales*) propriety; domestic employment; **conveniencias** income, property
**conveniencie•ro -ra** *adj* (coll) comfort-loving
**conveniente** *adj* (*cómodo*) convenient; fit, suitable; advantageous; proper
**convenio** *m* pact, covenant, treaty
**convenir** §79 *intr* to agree; (*concurrir, juntarse*) to convene; to be suitable, be becoming; to be important, to be necessary; **conviene a saber** to wit, namely || *ref* to agree, come to an agreement
**conventillo** *m* (SAm) tenement house
**convento** *m* convent, monastery; **convento de religiosas** convent
**converger** §17 or **convergir** §27 *intr* to converge; to concur
**conversa** *f* (coll) chat, conversation
**conversación** *f* conversation
**conversacional** *adj* conversational
**conversar** *intr* to converse; to live, dwell
**conversión** *f* conversion
**conver•so -sa** *adj* converted || *mf* convert || *m* lay brother || *f* see **conversa**
**convertible** *adj* convertible || *m* (aut) convertible
**convertir** §68 *tr* to convert; to turn || *ref* to convert; to be converted; **convertirse en** to turn into, become
**conve•xo -xa** *adj* convex
**convic•to -ta** *adj* convicted, found guilty
**convida•do -da** *mf* guest || *f* (coll) treat
**convidar** *tr* to invite; to treat; to move, incite; **convidarle a uno con alguna cosa** to treat someone to something || *ref* to offer one's services
**convincente** *adj* convincing
**convite** *m* invitation; treat, banquet, party; **convite a escote** Dutch treat
**convivir** *intr* to live together
**convocar** §73 *tr* to convoke, call together; (*p.ej., una huelga*) to call; to acclaim
**convoy** *m* convoy; escort; cruet stand; (rr) train
**convoyar** *tr* to convoy
**convulsionar** *tr* to convulse
**conyugal** *adj* conjugal
**cónyuge** *mf* spouse, consort || **cónyuges** *mpl* couple, husband and wife
**co•ñac** *m* (*pl* **-ñacs** or **-ñaques**) cognac
**cooperación** *f* coöperation
**cooperar** *intr* to coöperate
**cooperati•vo -va** *adj* coöperative
**coordena•do -da** *adj* coördinate || *f* (math) coördinate
**coordinante** *adj* (gram) coördinating
**coordinar** *tr & intr* to coördinate
**copa** *f* goblet, wineglass; (*del sombrero*) crown; brazier; vase; drink; sundae; playing card, representing a bowl, equivalent to heart; (*del dolor*) (fig) cup; (sport) cup
**copar** *tr* (*la puesta equivalente a todo el dinero de la banca*) to cover; (*todos los puestos en una elección*) to sweep; (mil) to cut off and capture
**copartícipe** *mf* copartner, joint partner
**copear** *intr* to sell wine or liquor by the glass; (coll) to tipple
**copero** *m* cabinet for wineglasses
**copete** *m* (*cabello levantado sobre la frente*) pompadour; (*de plumas; de una montaña*) crest; (*de un caballo*) forelock; (*de lana, cabello, plumas, etc.*) tuft; (*de un mueble*) top, finial; (*de un sorbete*) topping; **de alto copete** aristocratic, important; **tener mucho copete** to be high-hat
**copetu•do -da** *adj* tufted; high, lofty; (coll) high-hat
**copia** *f* plenty, abundance; copy; **copia al carbón** carbon copy; **copia fiel** true copy
**copiador** *m* copier, copying machine
**copiante** *mf* copier, copyist
**copiar** *tr* to copy, copy down
**copiloto** *m* copilot
**copio•so -sa** *adj* copious, abundant

**copista** *mf* copier, copyist
**copla** *f* couplet; ballad, popular song; **coplas** (coll) verse, poetry; **coplas de ciego** (coll) doggerel
**cople•ro -ra** *mf* vendor of ballads; poetaster
**coplista** *mf* poetaster
**copo** *m* bundle of cotton, flax, hemp, etc. to be spun; **copo de nieve** snowflake; **copos de jabón** soap flakes
**copón** *m* ciborium, pyx
**copo•so -sa** *adj* bushy; flaky, woolly
**copu•do -da** *adj* bushy, thick
**copular** *ref* to copulate
**coque** *m* coke
**coqueluche** *f* whooping cough
**coqueta** *adj* coquettish || *f* coquette, flirt; (W-I) dressing table
**coquetear** *intr* to coquette, to flirt; to try to please everybody
**coquetería** *f* coquetry, flirting; affectation
**coque•tón -tona** *adj* (coll) coquettish, kittenish || *m* (coll) flirt, lady-killer
**coracha** *f* leather bag
**coraje** *m* anger; mettle, spirit
**coraju•do -da** *adj* (coll) ill-tempered; (Arg) brave, courageous
**coral** *adj* (mus) choral || *m* (mus) chorale; (*zoófito; esqueleto calizo del zoófito; color*) coral; **corales** coral beads
**corambre** *f* hides, skins
**Corán** *m* Koran
**coranvo•bis** *m* (*pl* **-bis**) (coll) fat solemn look
**coraza** *f* armor; cuirass; (sport) guard
**corazón** *m* heart; (*centro de una cosa*) core; **de corazón** heartily; **hacer de tripas corazón** to pluck up courage
**corazonada** *f* impulsiveness; hunch, presentiment; (coll) entrails
**corbata** *f* necktie, cravat; scarf; **corbata de mariposa, corbata de lazo** bow tie; **corbata de nudo corredizo** four-in-hand tie
**corbatín** *m* bow tie
**corbeta** *f* corvette
**Córcega** *f* Corsica
**corcel** *m* steed, charger
**corcova** *f* hump, hunch
**corcova•do -da** *adj* humpbacked, hunchbacked || *mf* humpback, hunchback
**corcovar** *tr* to bend
**corcovear** *intr* to buck; (Am) to grumble; (Mex) to be afraid
**corcha** *f* cork bark; cork bucket (*for cooling wine*)
**corchea** *f* (mus) quaver, eighth note
**corche•ro -ra** *adj* cork || *f* cork bucket (*for cooling wine*)
**corcheta** *f* eye (*of hook and eye*)
**corchete** *m* snap; hook and eye; hook (*of hook and eye*); (*signo*) bracket; **corchete de presión** snap fastener
**corcho** *m* cork; cork, cork stopper; cork wine cooler; cork box; cork mat; **corcho bornizo, corcho virgen** virgin cork
**cordada** *f* (mountaineering) party of two or three men roped together
**cordaje** *m* cordage; (naut) rigging
**cordal** *adj* wisdom (*tooth*) || *m* (mus) tailpiece
**cordel** *m* cord, string; (distance of) five steps; cattle run; **a cordel** in a straight line
**cordelejo** *m* string; **dar cordelejo a** to make fun of; (Mex) to keep putting off
**cordera** *f* ewe lamb; (*mujer dócil y humilde*) (fig) lamb
**cordería** *f* cordage
**corderillo** *m* lambskin
**corderi•no -na** *adj* lamb || *f* lambskin
**cordero** *m* lamb; lambskin; (*hombre dócil y humilde*) (fig) lamb
**corderuna** *f* lambskin
**cordial** *adj* cordial; (*dedo*) middle || *m* cordial
**cordialidad** *f* cordiality
**cordillera** *f* chain of mountains
**cordobana** *f* — **andar a la cordobana** (coll) to go naked
**cordón** *m* lace; (*de cuerda o alambre*) strand; cordon; milled edge of coin; (*de monje*) rope belt; **cordón umbilical** umbilical cord
**cordoncillo** *m* rib, ridge; braid; (*de monedas*) milling
**cordura** *f* prudence, wisdom
**Corea** *f* Korea; **la Corea del Norte** North Korea; **la Corea del Sur** South Korea
**corea•no -na** *adj* & *mf* Korean
**corear** *tr* to compose for a chorus; to accompany with a chorus; to join in singing; to agree obsequiously with
**coreografía** *f* choreography
**coriáce•o -a** *adj* leathery
**Corinto** *f* Corinth
**corista** *m* choir priest; (theat) chorus man || *f* chorus girl, chorine
**cori•to -ta** *adj* naked; bashful, timid
**cormorán** *m* cormorant
**cor•nac** *m* (*pl* **-nacs**) or **cornaca** *m* mahout
**cornada** *f* hook with horns; goring; (*en la esgrima*) upward thrust
**cornadura** or **cornamenta** *f* (*del toro, la vaca, etc.*) horns; (*del ciervo*) antlers
**cornamusa** *f* bagpipe
**córnea** *f* cornea
**cornear** *tr* to butt; to gore
**corneja** *f* daw, crow
**cornejo** *m* dogwood
**córne•o -a** *adj* horn, horny || *f* see **córnea**
**corneta** *f* bugle; swineherd's horn; **corneta acústica** ear trumpet; **corneta de llaves** cornet, cornet-à-pistons; **corneta de monte** hunting-horn
**cornisa** *f* cornice
**cornisamento** *m* (archit) entablature
**corno** *m* horn; dogwood; **corno inglés** (mus) English horn
**Cornualles** Cornwall
**cornucopia** *f* cornucopia; sconce with mirror
**cornu•do -da** *adj* horned, antlered; cuckold || *m* cuckold
**coro** *m* chorus; choir; choir loft; **a**

**coros** alternately; **de coro** by heart; **hacer coro a** to echo

**corolario** *m* corollary

**corona** *f* (*cerco de metal; moneda; dignidad real; parte visible de una muela*) crown; (*cerco de flores*) garland, wreath; (*aureola*) halo; (*de eclesiástico*) tonsure; (*la que corresponde a un título nobiliario*) coronet; **corona nupcial** bridal wreath

**coronación** *f* coronation

**coronamento** or **coronamiento** *m* coronation; completion, termination; (archit) coping; (naut) taffrail

**coronar** *tr* to crown; to complete, finish; to top, surmount; (checkers) to crown

**coronel** *m* colonel

**coronelía** *f* colonelcy

**coronilla** *f* (*de la cabeza*) crown; **andar** or **bailar de coronilla** (coll) to be hard at it; **estar hasta la coronilla** (coll) to be fed up

**corpiño** *m* bodice, waist; (Arg) brassière

**corporación** *f* corporation

**corporal** *adj* corporal, bodily

**corpu•do -da** *adj* corpulent

**corpulen•to -ta** *adj* corpulent

**corpúsculo** *m* corpuscle; particle

**corral** *m* corral, stockyard; barnyard; fishpound; theater; **corral de madera** lumberyard; **corral de vacas** (coll) pigpen; **hacer corrales** (coll) to play hooky

**correa** *f* strap, thong; (aer, mach) belt; **besar la correa** (coll) to eat humble pie; **correa de seguridad** (aer, aut) safety belt

**corrección** *f* (*acción de corregir; reprensión*) correction; (*calidad de correcto*) correctness

**correcti•vo -va** *adj* & *m* corrective

**correc•to -ta** *adj* correct

**correc•tor -tora** *mf* corrector; **corrector de pruebas** proofreader

**corredera** *f* track, slide; slide valve; (*del trombón*) slide; (naut) log; (naut) log line; (*puerta*) **de corredera** sliding

**corredi•zo -za** *adj* slide; sliding; (*nudo*) slip

**corre•dor -dora** *adj* running || *mf* runner || *m* corridor; porch, gallery; (*el que interviene en compras y ventas de efectos comerciales, etc.*) broker; (mil) scout; **corredor de apuestas** bookmaker

**corregidor** *m* Spanish magistrate; chief magistrate of Spanish town

**corregir** §57 *tr* to correct; to temper, moderate || *intr* (W-I) to have a bowel movement || *ref* to mend one's ways

**correlación** *f* correlation

**correlacionar** *tr* & *intr* to correlate

**correlati•vo -va** *adj* & *m* correlative

**correncia** *f* bashfulness; (coll) looseness of the bowels

**correntí•o -a** *adj* running; (coll) free, easy || *f* (coll) looseness of the bowels

**corren•tón -tona** *adj* jolly, full of fun

**correnton•so -sa** *adj* (Am) swift, rapid

**correo** *m* mail; post office; mail train; postman; courier; **correo aéreo** air mail; **correo urgente** special delivery; **echar al correo** to mail, to post

**correo•so -sa** *adj* leathery, tough

**correr** *tr* (*un caballo*) to run, to race; (*un riesgo*) to run; to travel over; to overrun; (*una cortina*) to draw; (*un toro*) to fight; to chase, pursue; to auction; to confuse; (Am) to throw out; **correrla** (coll) to run around all night || *intr* to run; to race; to pass, elapse; to circulate, be common talk; to be current; **a todo correr** at full speed; **correr a** to sell for; **correr a cargo de** or **por cuenta de** to be the business of; **correr con** to be on good terms with; to be in charge of; (*mes*) **que corre** current || *ref* (*a derecha o a izquierda*) to turn; to be confused; to be embarrassed, be ashamed; to slide, glide; (*una bujía, un color*) to run; to go too far

**correría** *f* short trip, excursion; foray, raid

**correspondencia** *f* correspondence; contact, communication; agreement, harmony; (*en el metro*) connection; (*en una carretera*) interchange

**corresponder** *intr* to correspond; (*dos habitaciones*) to communicate; **corresponder a** (*un beneficio, el afecto de una persona*) to return, reciprocate; to concern; to be up to || *ref* (*comunicarse por escrito*) to correspond; (*dos cosas*) to correspond with each other; to be in agreement; to be attached to each other

**correspondiente** *adj* corresponding; correspondent; respective || *mf* correspondent

**corresponsal** *mf* correspondent

**corretaje** *m* brokerage

**corretear** *tr* (Am) to harass, pursue; (CAm) to drive away; (Chile) to speed up || *intr* (coll) to race around

**correveidi•le** *mf* (*pl* **-le**) (coll) gossip; (coll) go-between

**corrida** *f* run; bullfight; (*carrera de entrenamiento de un caballo*) (Am) trial run; **corrida de banco** (Am) run on the bank; **corrida de toros** bullfight

**corri•do -da** *adj* (*peso, medida*) in excess; (*letra*) cursive; continued, unbroken; abashed, ashamed; (coll) worldly-wise, sophisticated || *m* overhang; (Am) street ballad || *f* see **corrida**

**corriente** *adj* (*agua*) running; (*actual*) current; common, ordinary; regular; well-known; fluent || *adv* all right, O.K. || *m* current month; **al corriente** on time; informed, aware, posted || *f* current, stream; (elec) current; **corriente de aire** draft; **Corriente del Golfo** Gulf Stream; **ir contra la corriente** to go against the tide

**corrillo** *m* circle, clique

**corrimiento** *m* running; sliding; watery

discharge; embarrassment, shyness; landslide; (Am) rheumatism
**corro** *m* (*cerco de gente; espacio circular*) ring; (*juego de niñas*) ring-around-a-rosy; **corro de brujas** fairy ring; **hacer corro** to make room
**corroborar** *tr* to corroborate; to strengthen
**corroer** §62 *tr & ref* to corrode
**corromper** *tr* to corrupt; to spoil; to rot; to seduce; to bribe; (coll) to annoy || *intr* to smell bad || *ref* to become corrupted; to spoil; to rot
**corrosión** *f* corrosion
**corrosi•vo -va** *adj & m* corrosive
**corrugar** §44 *tr* to shrink; to wrinkle
**corrupción** *f* corruption; seduction; bribery; stench
**corruptela** *f* corruption
**corruptible** *adj* corruptible; (*p.ej., frutas*) perishable
**corrusco** *m* (coll) crust of bread
**corsa** *f* (naut) day's run
**corsario** *m* corsair
**corsé** *m* corset
**cor•so -sa** *adj & mf* Corsican || *m* (naut) privateering; (SAm) drive, promenade || *f* see **corsa**
**corta** *f* clearing, cutting, felling
**cortaalam•bres** *m* (*pl* **-bres**) wire cutter
**cortabol•sas** *m* (*pl* **-sas**) (coll) pickpocket
**cortacésped** *m* lawn mower
**cortaciga•rros** *m* (*pl* **-rros**) cigar cutter
**cortacircui•tos** *m* (*pl* **-tos**) (elec) fuse
**cortacorriente** *m* (elec) change-over switch
**cortada** *f* (Am) cut, cutting
**cortadillo** *m* drinking cup
**corta•do -da** *adj* (*estilo*) choppy; (SAm) hard up || *f* see **cortada**
**corta•dor -dora** *adj* cutting || *mf* cutter || *m* butcher || *f* cutting machine
**cortafrío** *m* cold chisel
**cortafuego** *s* fire wall
**cortahie•los** *m* (*pl* **-los**) icebreaker
**cortalápi•ces** *m* (*pl* **-ces**) pencil sharpener
**cortante** *adj* cutting, sharp || *m* butcher; butcher knife
**cortapape•les** *m* (*pl* **-les**) paper cutter
**cortapi•cos** *m* (*pl* **-cos**) (ent) earwig; **cortapicos y callares** (coll) little children should be seen and not heard
**cortaplu•mas** *m* (*pl* **-mas**) penknife
**cortapu•ros** *m* (*pl* **-ros**) cigar cutter
**cortar** *tr* to cut; to trim; to chop; to cut off; to cut out, omit; to cut short; to cut up; to carve; (*la corriente; la ignición*) to cut off || *intr* to cut; (*el viento, el frío*) to be cutting; **cortar de vestir** to cut cloth; (coll) to gossip || *ref* to become speechless; (*la leche*) to curdle, turn sour; (*la piel*) to chap, to crack
**cortarrenglón** *m* marginal stop
**cortaú•ñas** *m* (*pl* **-ñas**) nail clipper
**cortavi•drios** *m* (*pl* **-drios**) glass cutter
**cortaviento** *m* windshield
**corte** *m* cut; cutting; (*filo de un arma, cuchillo, etc.; borde de un libro*) edge; cross section; (*de un vestido*) cut, fit; piece of material; **corte de pelo** haircut; **corte de pelo a cepillo** crew cut; **corte de traje** suiting || *f* (*de un rey*) court; (*corral*) yard; stable, fold; (*tribunal de justicia*) (Am) court; **Cortes** Parliament; **darse cortes** (SAm) to put on airs; **hacer la corte a** to pay court to; **la Corte** the Capital (*Madrid*)
**cortedad** *f* shortness; smallness; lack; bashfulness
**cortejar** *tr* to escort, attend, court; to court, to woo
**cortejo** *m* courting; courtship; (*séquito*) cortege; gift, treat; (coll) beau
**cortera** *f* (Chile) streetwalker
**cortero** *m* (Chile) day laborer
**cortés** *adj* courteous, polite, courtly
**cortesana** *f* courtesan
**cortesana•zo -za** *adj* overpolite, obsequious
**cortesanía** *f* courtliness
**cortesa•no -na** *adj* courtly, courteous || *m* courtier || *f* see **cortesana**
**cortesía** *f* courtesy, politeness, courtliness; gift, favor; (*inclinación de la cabeza o el cuerpo en señal de respeto*) curtsy; (*de una carta*) conclusion; **hacer una cortesía** to make a bow; to curtsy
**corteza** *f* bark; peel, rind, skin; (*de pan*) crust; coarseness; (*envoltura exterior de un órgano*) cortex; **corteza cerebral** cortex
**cortijo** *m* farm, farmhouse
**cortil** *m* barnyard
**cortina** *f* curtain; **correr la cortina** to pull the curtain aside; **cortina de hierro** iron curtain; **cortina de humo** smoke screen
**cortinal** *m* fenced-in field
**cortinilla** *f* shade, window shade
**cortisona** *f* cortisone
**cor•to -ta** *adj* short; dull; bashful, shy; speechless; **a la corta o a la larga** sooner or later; **desde muy corta edad** from earliest childhood || *f* see **corta**
**cortocircuitar** *tr & ref* (elec) to short-circuit
**cortocircuito** *m* (elec) short circuit
**cortometraje** *m* (mov) short
**corva** *f* ham, back of knee; (vet) curb
**corvejón** *m* gambrel, hock; (orn) cormorant
**cor•vo -va** *adj* arched, bent, curved || *m* hook || *f* see **corva**
**cor•zo -za** *mf* roe deer
**cosa** *f* thing; **cosa de** a matter of; **cosa de cajón** a matter of course; **cosa de mieles** (coll) something fine; **cosa de nunca acabar** endless bore; **cosa de oír** something worth hearing; **cosa de risa** something to laugh at; **cosa de ver** something worth seeing; **cosa nunca vista** (coll) something unheard-of; **cosa que** (Am coll) so that; **cosa rara** strange to say; **como si tal cosa** (coll) as if nothing had happened; **en cosa de** in a matter of; **no . . . gran cosa** not much; **no haber**

**tal cosa** to be not so; **otra cosa** something else; **¿qué cosa?** what's new?
**cosa•co -ca** *adj & mf* Cossack || *m* Cossack (*horseman*)
**coscolina** *f* (Mex) loose woman
**cos•cón -cona** *adj* sly, crafty
**cosecha** *f* crop, harvest; harvest time; **cosecha de vino** vintage; **de su cosecha** (coll) out of one's own head
**cosechar** *tr* to harvest, reap || *intr* to harvest
**coseche•ro -ra** *mf* harvester, reaper; vintner
**cose-pape•les** *m* (*pl* **-les**) stapler
**coser** *tr* to sew; to join, unite closely; **coser a preguntas** to riddle with questions; **coser a puñaladas** to cut to pieces || *intr* to sew; **ser coser y cantar** (coll) to be a cinch || *ref* — **coserse con** or **contra** to be closely attached to
**cosméti•co -ca** *adj & m* cosmetic
**cósmi•co -ca** *adj* cosmic
**cosmonauta** *mf* cosmonaut
**cosmopolita** *adj & mf* cosmopolitan
**cosmos** *m* cosmos; (bot) cosmos
**coso** *m* enclosure for bullfighting
**cosquillas** *fpl* tickling, ticklishness; **buscarle a uno las cosquillas** (coll) to try to irritate a person; **no sufrir cosquillas** or **tener malas cosquillas** (coll) to be touchy
**cosquillear** *tr* to tickle; to tease, taunt; to stir up the curiosity of; to scare || *intr* to tickle || *ref* to be curious; to enjoy oneself
**cosquilleo** *m* tickling, tickling sensation
**cosquillo•so -sa** *adj* ticklish; (*que se ofende fácilmente*) touchy
**costa** *f* coast, shore; cost, price; **a toda costa** at all costs; **Costa Brava** Mediterranean coast in province of Gerona, Spain; **Costa Firme** Spanish Main; **costa marítima** seacoast; **costas** (law) costs
**costado** *m* side; (*del ejército*) flank; (Mex) station platform; **costados** ancestors, stock
**costal** *m* bag, sack; **costal de los pecados** human body (*full of sin*); **estar hecho un costal de huesos** (coll) to be nothing but skin and bones
**costanera** *f* slope; **costaneras** rafters
**costane•ro -ra** *adj* sloping; coastal || *f* see **costanera**
**costanilla** *f* short steep street
**costar §61** *intr* to cost; **cueste lo que cueste** cost what it may
**costarricense** or **costarrique•ño -ña** *adj & mf* Costa Rican
**coste** *m* cost; **a coste y costas** at cost
**costear** *tr* to pay for, to defray the cost of; to sail along the coast of || *intr* to sail along the coast || *ref* to pay; to pay one's way
**coste•ño -ña** *adj* sloping; coastal
**coste•ro -ra** *adj* coastal
**costilla** *f* rib; (coll) **wealth; costillas** back, shoulders
**costillu•do -da** *adj* heavy-set, broad-shouldered
**costo** *m* cost; **costo de la vida** cost of living; **costo, seguro y flete** cost, insurance, and freight
**costo•so -sa** *adj* costly, expensive; grievous
**costra** *f* scab, scale; (*moco de una vela*) snuff
**costro•so -sa** *adj* scabby, scaly
**costumbre** *f* custom, habit; **de costumbre** usual; usually; **tener por costumbre** to be in the habit of
**costumbrista** *mf* critic of manners and customs
**costura** *f* sewing, needlework; dressmaking; (*unión de dos piezas cosidas*) seam; **alta costura** fashion designing, haute couture
**costurera** *f* seamstress, dressmaker
**costurero** *m* sewing table
**cota** *f* coat of arms; coat of mail
**cotarrera** *f* (coll) gossipy woman
**cotarro** *m* night shelter (*for beggars and tramps*); **alborotar el cotarro** (coll) to raise a row
**cotejar** *tr* to compare, collate
**cotejo** *m* comparison, collation
**cotidia•no -na** *adj* daily, everyday
**cotilla** *f* (coll) gossip, tattletale
**cotín** *m* (sport) backstroke
**cotización** *f* quotation; dues
**cotizante** *adj* dues-paying
**cotizar §60** *tr* to quote; to prorate || *intr* to collect dues; to pay dues
**coto** *m* price; fixed price; term, limit
**cotón** *m* printed cotton
**cotona** *f* (Am) work shirt
**cotonía** *f* dimity
**cotorra** *f* parrot; parakeet; magpie; (coll) chatterbox; (Mex) night shelter
**cotorrear** *intr* (coll) to gossip, gabble
**cotufa** *f* Jerusalem artichoke; delicacy, tidbit; **hacer cotufas** (Bol) to be fastidious; **pedir cotufas en el golfo** (coll) to ask for the moon
**coturno** *m* buskin
**covacha** *f* cave; (Am) cubbyhole; (Am) shanty; (Am) doghouse
**covachuelista** *m* (coll) clerk, government clerk
**coxcojita** *f* hopscotch; **a coxcojita** hippety-hop
**coy** *m* (naut) hammock
**coyunda** *f* strap for yoking oxen; sandal string; marriage; tyranny
**coyuntura** *f* joint, articulation; (*sazón, oportunidad*) juncture
**coz** *f* (*pl* **coces**) kick; big end; ebb; (coll) insult; **dar coces contra el aguijón** to kick against the pricks
**c.p.b., C.P.B.** *abbr* **cuyos pies beso**
**cps.** *abbr* **compañeros**
**crabrón** *m* hornet
**crac** *m* (*ruido seco*) crack; crash; **hacer crac** to crash, to fail
**cráneo** *m* cranium, skull
**crápula** *f* drunkenness, debauchery; riffraff
**crapulo•so -sa** *adj* drunken; vicious, evil
**crascitar** *intr* to crow, croak

**cra•so -sa** *adj* fat, greasy, thick; (*ignorancia*) crass, gross
**cráter** *m* crater
**creación** *f* creation
**crea•dor -dora** *adj* creative || *mf* creator
**crear** *tr* to create; to appoint; to found || *ref* to make for oneself, to build up; to trump up
**creati•vo -va** *adj* creative
**crecede•ro -ra** *adj* growth; large enough to allow for growth
**crecepelo** *m* hair restorer
**crecer §22** *intr* to grow; to increase; (*el río*) to rise, swell; (*la luna*) to wax || *ref* to grow; to take on more authority; to get bolder
**creces** *fpl* growth, increase; excess, extra; **con creces** amply, in abundance
**crecida** *f* freshet, flood
**creciente** *adj* growing, increasing || *f* — **creciente de la luna** waxing of the moon, crescent; **creciente del mar** high tide, flood tide
**crecimiento** *m* growth, increase
**credenciales** *fpl* credentials
**crédito** *m* credit
**credo** *m* creed; credo; **con el credo en la boca** (coll) with one's heart in one's mouth; **en un credo** (coll) in a trice
**crédu•lo -la** *adj* credulous
**creederas** *fpl* — **tener buenas creederas** (coll) to be gullible
**creencia** *f* belief; (*crédito que se presta a un hecho*) credence; (*secta*) creed
**creer §43** *tr & intr* to believe; **¡ya lo creo!** (coll) I should say so! || *ref* to believe; to believe oneself to be
**creíble** *adj* believable, credible
**crema** *f* cream; cold cream; shoe polish; (gram) diaeresis; **crema de menta** crème de menthe; **crema desvanecedora** vanishing cream
**cremación** *f* cremation
**cremallera** *f* rack; zipper
**cremato•rio -ria** *adj & m* crematory
**crémor** *m* cream of tartar
**cremo•so -sa** *adj* creamy
**crencha** *f* part (*in hair*); hair on each side of part
**crepitar** *intr* to crackle
**crepuscular** *adj* twilight
**crepúsculo** *m* twilight
**cresa** *f* maggot
**crespar** *tr & ref* to curl
**cres•po -pa** *adj* curly; curled; angry, irritated; stylish, conceited; (*estilo*) turgid || *m* (Am) curl
**crespón** *m* crape; **crespón fúnebre** crape; mourning band
**cresta** *f* crest; **cresta de gallo** cockscomb; (bot) cockscomb
**creta** *f* chalk || **Creta** *f* Crete
**cretense** *adj & mf* Cretan
**cretona** *f* cretonne
**creyente** *adj* believing || *mf* believer
**creyón** *m* crayon
**cría** *f* brood, litter; breeding; raising, rearing; nursing
**criada** *f* female servant, maid; **criada de casa, criada de servir** housemaid
**criadero** *m* nursery, tree nursery; fish hatchery; oyster bed
**criadilla** *f* testicle; potato
**cria•do -da** *adj* — **bien criado** well-bred; **mal criado** ill-bred || *mf* servant || *f* see **criada**
**cria•dor -dora** *mf* breeder || *f* wet nurse
**criamiento** *m* care, upkeep
**crianza** *f* raising, rearing; nursing; (*urbanidad*) breeding, manners; **buena crianza** good breeding; **mala crianza** bad breeding
**criar §77** *tr* to raise, rear, bring up; to breed; to grow; to nurse, nourish; to fatten; to create; to foster
**criatura** *f* (*toda cosa creada; persona que debe su cargo o situación a otra*) creature; little child, little creature
**criba** *f* screen, sieve
**cribar** *tr* to screen, sieve
**cribo** *m* screen, sieve
**cric** *m* (*pl* **crics**) jack
**crimen** *m* crime; **crimen de lesa majestad** lese majesty
**criminal** *adj & mf* criminal
**criminar** *tr* to accuse, incriminate
**crimino•so -sa** *adj & mf* criminal
**crines** *fpl* mane
**crío** *m* (coll) baby, infant
**crio•llo -lla** *adj & mf* Creole
**cripta** *f* crypt
**crisálida** *f* chrysalis
**crisantemo** *m* chrysanthemum
**cri•sis** *f* (*pl* **-sis**) crisis; (*pánico económico*) depression, slump; mature judgment; **crisis del servicio doméstico** servant problem; **crisis de llanto** crying fit; **crisis de vivienda** housing shortage; **crisis ministerial** cabinet crisis; **crisis nerviosa** fit of nerves
**crisma** *f* (coll) head, bean
**crisol** *m* crucible
**crispar** *tr* to cause to twitch || *ref* to twitch
**crispatura** *f* twitch, twitching
**crispir** *tr* to grain, to marble
**cristal** *m* crystal; glass; pane of glass; mirror, looking glass; **cristal cilindrado** plate glass; **cristal de reloj** watch crystal; **cristal de roca** rock crystal; **cristal hilado** glass wool, spun glass; **cristal tallado** cut glass
**cristalera** *f* China closet; sideboard; glass door
**cristalería** *f* glassworks, glass store; glassware; glass cabinet
**cristali•no -na** *adj* crystalline || *m* lens, crystalline lens
**cristalizer §60** *tr & ref* to crystallize
**cristianar** *tr* (coll) to baptize, christen
**cristiandad** *f* Christendom
**cristianismo** *m* Christianity
**cristianizar §60** *tr* to Christianize
**cristia•no -na** *adj & mf* Christian || *m* soul, person; Spanish; (coll) watered wine
**Cristo** *m* Christ; crucifix; **donde Cristo dió las tres voces** (coll) in the middle of nowhere
**Cristóbal** *m* Christopher
**criterio** *m* criterion
**crítica** *f* (*jucio sobre una obra literaria, etc.; censura de la conducta de al-*

*guno*) criticism; (*arte de juzgar una obra literaria, etc.*) critique; gossip
**criticar** §73 *tr & intr* to criticize
**críti•co -ca** *adj* critical; (*criticón*) (Am) critical (*faultfinding*) || *mf* critic || *f* see **crítica**
**criti•cón -cona** *adj* (coll) critical, faultfinding || *mf* (coll) critic, faultfinder
**critiquizar** §60 *tr* to overcriticize
**crizneja** *f* braid of hair
**croar** *intr* to croak
**croata** *adj & mf* Croatian
**crocante** *m* almond brittle, peanut brittle
**crocitar** *intr* to crow, croak
**croco** *m* crocus
**croché** *m* crochet
**crochet** *m* (box) hook
**croma•do -da** *adj* chrome || *m* chromium plating
**cromar** *tr* to chrome
**cromo** *m* chromium
**cromosoma** *m* chromosome
**crónica** *f* chronicle; news chronicle, feature story
**cróni•co -ca** *adj* chronic; longstanding; (*vicio*) inveterate || *f* see **crónica**
**cronista** *mf* chronicler; reporter, feature writer; **cronista de radio** newscaster
**cronología** *f* chronology
**cronometra•dor -dora** *mf* (sport) timekeeper
**cronometraje** *m* (sport) clocking, timing
**cronómetro** *m* chronometer; stop watch
**croqueta** *f* croquette
**cro•quis** *m* (*pl* **-quis**) sketch
**croscitar** *intr* to crow, croak
**crótalo** *m* rattlesnake; castanet
**cruce** *m* crossing; crossroads, intersection; exchange (*e.g., of letters*); (*avería*) (elec) crossed wires, short circuit; **cruce a nivel** grade crossing; **cruce en trébol** cloverleaf intersection
**crucero** *m* crossroads; railroad crossing; (archit) transept; (aer, naut) cruise, cruising; (nav) cruiser; **crucero a nivel** grade crossing
**crucial** *adj* crucial
**crucificar** §73 *tr* to crucify
**crucifijo** *m* crucifix
**crucifixión** *f* crucifixion
**crucigrama** *m* crossword puzzle
**cruda** *f* (Mex) hangover
**crudeza** *f* crudeness, rawness; (*del agua*) hardness; harshness, roughness; (coll) blustering; **crudezas** undigested food
**cru•do -da** *adj* crude, raw; (*agua*) hard; harsh, rough; (*tiempo*) raw; (*lienzo*) unbleached; **estar crudo** (P-R) to be rusty; (Mex) to have a hangover || *f* see **cruda**
**cruel** *adj* cruel
**crueldad** *f* cruelty
**cruen•to -ta** *adj* bloody
**crujía** *f* corridor, hall; hospital ward; block of houses; (naut) midship gangway; **crujía de piezas** suite of rooms; **sufrir una crujía** (coll) to have a hard time of it
**crujido** *m* creak; crackle; clatter; chatter; rustle
**crujir** *intr* to creak; to crackle; to clatter; to chatter; to rustle; to crunch
**crup** *m* croup
**crustáce•o -a** *adj* crustaceous || *m* crustacean
**cruz** *f* (*pl* **cruces**) cross; (*de una moneda*) tails; (typ) dagger; **Cruz del Sur** Southern Cross; **¡cruz y raya!** (coll) that's enough!; **de la cruz a la fecha** from beginning to end
**cruzada** *f* (*expedición contra los infieles; propaganda contra un vicio*) crusade; crossroads, intersection
**cruza•do -da** *adj* crossed; (*de raza mixta*) cross; double-breasted || *m* (*el que toma parte en una cruzada*) crusader; (*caballero de una orden militar*) knight; twill || *f* see **cruzada**
**cruzar** §60 *tr* to cross; (*la tela*) to twill; (*cartas*) to exchange; to crossbreed; (naut) to cruise, cruise over || *intr* to cross; to cruise || *ref* to cross each other, to cross one's another's path; (*alistarse para una cruzada*) to take the cross; **cruzarse con** (*otro automóvil*) to pass; **cruzarse de brazos** (*estar ocioso*) to cross one's arms
**cs.** *abbr* **céntimos, cuartos**
**cte.** *abbr* **corriente**
**c/u** *abbr* **cada uno**
**cuad.** *abbr* **cuadrado**
**cuaderna** *f* (naut) frame
**cuaderno** *m* notebook; folder; **cuaderno de bitácora** (naut) logbook; **cuaderno de hojas cambiables** or **sueltas** loose-leaf notebook
**cuadra** *f* hall, large room; stable; dormitory, ward; croup, rump; (Am) block
**cuadra•do -da** *adj* square; square-shouldered; perfect || *m* square; (*regla*) ruler; (*en las medias*) clock; **de cuadrado** perfectly; (*que se mira frente a frente*) full-faced
**cuadragési•mo -ma** *adj & m* fortieth
**cuadrangular** *adj* quadrangular || *m* home run
**cuadrángu•lo -la** *adj* quadrangular || *m* quadrangle
**cuadrante** *m* quadrant; (*de reloj*) face, dial; **cuadrante solar** sundial
**cuadrar** *tr* to square; to please; (*al toro*) (taur) to square off, to line up || *ref* to square; to stand at attention; (coll) to take on a serious air
**cuadrilla** *f* group, party; crew, gang
**cuadrillazo** *m* (SAm) surprise attack
**cuadrillo** *m* (*saeta*) bolt (*arrow*)
**cuadrimotor** *m* four-motor plane
**cua•dro -dra** *adj* square || *m* square; (*lienzo, pintura*) painting, picture; (*marco de pintura, ventana, etc.*) frame; (*de jardín*) patch, flower bed; staff, personnel; (mil) cadre; (sport) team; (theat) scene; (coll) sight, mess; **a cuadros** checked; **cuadro de costumbres** sketch of manners and customs; **cuadro de distribución** switchboard; **cuadro indicador** score

board; **cuadro vivo** tableau; **en cuadro** square, e.g., **ocho pulgadas en cuadro** eight inches square; (coll) topsy-turvy; **quedarse en cuadro** to be all alone in the world; (mil) to be skeletonized || *f* see **cuadra**
**cuadrúpe•do -da** *adj & m* quadruped
**cuádruple** *adj & m* quadruple
**cuadruplicar** §73 *tr & ref* to quadruple
**cuajada** *f* curd
**cuajado** *m* mincemeat
**cuajar** *tr* to curd, curdle, thicken, jelly; (coll) to please, to suit || *intr* (coll) to take hold, catch on, jell, take shape; (Mex) to chatter, prattle || *ref* to curd, curdle, thicken, jelly; to sleep sound; (coll) to become crowded
**cuajo** *m* curd; (Mex) chatter, prattle; (*en la escuela*) (Mex) recess
**cual** *adj rel & pron rel* such as; **el cual** which; who; **lo cual** which; **por lo cual** for which reason || *adv* as || *prep* like
**cuál** *adj interr & pron interr* which, what; which one
**cualidad** *f* quality, characteristic, trait
**cualquier** *adj indef* (*pl* **cualesquier**) apocopated form of **cualquiera,** used only before masculine nouns and adjectives
**cualquiera** (*pl* **cualesquiera**) *pron indef* anyone; **cualquiera que** whichever; whoever || *adj indef* any || *adj rel* whichever || *m* (*persona poco importante*) nobody
**cuan** *adv* as
**cuán** *adv* how, how much
**cuando** *conj* when; although; in case; since; **aun cuando** even if, even though; **cuando más** at most; **cuando menos** at least; **cuando mucho** at most; **cuando quiera** whenever; **de cuando en cuando** from time to time || *prep* (coll) at the time of
**cuándo** *adv* when; **cuándo . . . cuándo** sometimes . . . sometimes; **¿de cuándo acá?** since when?; how come?
**cuantía** *f* quantity; importance; **delito de mayor cuantía** felony; **delito de menor cuantía** misdemeanor; **de mayor cuantía** first-rate; **de menor cuantía** second-rate, of little importance
**cuantiar** §77 *tr* to estimate, appraise
**cuánti•co -ca** *adj* quantum
**cuantio•so -sa** *adj* large, substantial
**cuan•to -ta** *adj rel & pron rel* as much as, whatever, all that which; **cuantos** as many as, all those who, everybody who; **unos cuantos** some few || **cuanto** *adv* as soon as; as long as; **cuanto antes** as soon as possible; **cuanto más . . . tanto más** the more . . . the more; **cuanto más que** all the more because; **en cuanto** as soon as; while; insofar as; **en cuanto a** as to, as for; **por cuanto** inasmuch as; **por cuanto . . . por tanto** inasmuch as . . . therefore || **cuan•to** *m* (*pl* **-ta**) quantum
**cuán•to -ta** *adj interr & pron interr* how much; **cuántos** how many || **cuánto** *adv* how, how much; how long; how long ago; **cada cuánto** how often
**cuáque•ro -ra** *adj & mf* Quaker
**cuarenta** *adj, pron & m* forty
**cuarenta•vo -va** *adj & m* fortieth
**cuarentena** *f* forty; quarantine; forty days, forty months, forty years; **poner en cuarentena** to quarantine; to withhold one's credence in
**cuaresma** *f* Lent
**cuaresmal** *adj* Lenten
**cuarta** *f* fourth, fourth part; (*de la mano*) span; (CAm, W-I) horse whip
**cuartago** *m* nag, pony
**cuartear** *tr* to divide in four parts; to divide; (*la aguja*) (naut) to box; (CAm, W-I) to whip || *ref* to crack, split; (taur) to step aside, dodge
**cuartel** *m* quarter; (*de una ciudad*) section, ward; (*terreno*) lot; flower bed; (mil) barracks; (*buen trato*) (mil) quarter; (*armazón de tablas para cerrar la escotilla*) (naut) hatch; (coll) house, home; **cuartel de bomberos** engine house, firehouse; **cuarteles** (mil) quarters; **cuartel general** (mil) headquarters
**cuartelada** *f* mutiny, military uprising
**cuarte•rón -rona** *mf* quadroon || *m* quarter; (*de puerta*) panel; (*de ventana*) shutter
**cuarteto** *m* quartet
**cuartilla** *f* sheet of paper
**cuar•to -ta** *adj* fourth; quarter || *m* fourth; quarter; room, bedroom; quarter-hour; **cuarto creciente** (*de la luna*) first quarter; **cuarto de aseo** lavatory; **cuarto de baño** bathroom; **cuarto de dormir** bedroom; **cuarto de estar** living room; **cuarto delantero** (*de la res*) forequarter; **cuarto de los niños** nursery; **cuarto de luna** quarter; **cuarto menguante** (*de la luna*) last quarter; **cuarto obscuro** (phot) darkroom; **cuartos** (coll) money, cash; **cuarto trasero** (*p.ej., de vaca*) rump || *f* see **cuarta**
**cuarzo** *m* quartz
**cuate** *adj* (Mex) twin; (Mex) like || *mf* (Mex) twin; (Mex) pal
**cuatrilli•zo -za** *mf* quadruplet
**cuatrinca** *f* foursome
**cuatro** *adj & pron* four; **las cuatro** four o'clock || *m* four; (*en las fechas*) fourth; (*de voces*) quartet; **más de cuatro** (coll) quite a number
**cuatrocien•tos -tas** *adj & pron* four hundred || **cuatrocientos** *m* four hundred
**cuba** *f* cask, barrel; tub, vat; (*persona de mucho vientre*) (coll) tub; (*persona que bebe mucho*) (coll) toper; **cuba de riego** street sprinkler
**cuba•no -na** *adj & mf* Cuban
**cubeta** *f* keg, cask; pail; bowl, toilet bowl; (*del termómetro*) cup; (chem, phot) tray; (Mex) high hat
**cubicaje** *m* piston displacement, cylinder capacity
**cubicar** *tr* (*elevar al cubo*) to cube; to measure the volume of; to have a piston displacement of

**cúbi•co -ca** *adj* cubic; (*raíz*) cube
**cubierta** *f* cover; envelope; roof; (*de un libro*) paper cover; (*de un neumático*) casing, shoe; (*del motor de un coche*) hood; (naut) deck; **bajo cubierta separada** under separate cover; **cubierta de aterrizaje** (nav) flight deck; **cubierta de cama** bedcover; **cubierta de mesa** table cover; **cubierta de paseo** (naut) promenade deck; **cubierta de vuelo** (nav) flight deck; **cubierta principal** (naut) main deck; **entre cubiertas** (naut) between decks
**cubiertamente** *adv* secretly
**cubier•to -ta** *adj* covered; (*cielo*) overcast || *m* cover, roof, shelter; (*servicio de mesa para una persona*) cover; knife, fork, and spoon; table d'hôte, prix fixe; **a cubierto de** under cover of; protected from; **bajo cubierto** under cover, indoors || *f* see **cubierta**
**cubil** *m* (*de fieras*) lair, den; (*de arroyo*) bed
**cubilete** *m* (*de cocinero*) copper mold; dicebox; mince pie; (Am) high hat; (SAm) scheming, wirepulling
**cubo** *m* bucket; (*de rueda*) hub; (*de un candelero; de una llave de caja*) socket; cube; (mach) barrel, drum; (math) cube; (Arg) finger bowl
**cubreasiento** *m* seat cover
**cubrecama** *f* counterpane, bedcover
**cubrecorsé** *m* corset cover
**cubrefuego** *m* curfew
**cubrelibro** *m* jacket
**cubrenuca** *f* havelock
**cubrerrueda** *f* mudguard
**cubresexo** *m* G-string
**cubretablero** *m* (aut) cowl
**cubretetera** *f* cozy, tea cozy
**cubrir §83** *tr* to cover, cover over, cover up || *ref* to cover oneself; to be covered; to put one's hat on; (*el cielo*) to become overcast; (*satisfacer una deuda*) to cover
**cucaña** *f* greased pole to be climbed as a game; (coll) cinch
**cucañe•ro -ra** *mf* (coll) loafer, parasite
**cucar §73** *tr* to wink; to make fun of; (*la caza*) to sight; (Am) to incite, stir up || *intr* (*el ganado*) to go off on a run (*when bitten by flies*)
**cucaracha** *f* roach, cockroach
**cucarache•ro -ra** *adj* (W-I) sly, tricky; (W-I) amorous, lecherous
**cucarda** *f* cockade
**cuclillas** — **en cuclillas** squatting, crouching
**cuclillo** *m* cuckoo; (coll) cuckold
**cu•co -ca** *adj* sly, tricky; (coll) cute || *mf* (coll) sly person || *m* bogeyman; cuckoo
**cu•cú** *m* (*pl* **-cúes**) cuckoo (*call*)
**cuculla** *f* cowl, hood
**cucurucho** *m* paper cone, ice-cream cone; **hacer cucurucho a** (Chile) to deceive, take in
**cuchara** *f* spoon; (*cazo*) dipper, ladle; (*para áridos; para achicar el agua en los botes*) scoop; (*de albañil*) trowel; (Mex) pickpocket; **cuchara de sopa** tablespoon; **media cuchara** (coll) ordinary fellow; (Am) fellow with heavy accent; (Mex) mason's helper; **meter su cuchara** to butt in
**cucharada** *f* spoonful; ladleful; scoop
**cucharear** *tr* to spoon, ladle out
**cucharetear** *intr* (coll) to stir the pot, stir with a spoon; (coll) to meddle
**cucharilla** *f* teaspoon; (*de soldador*) ladle
**cucharón** *m* large spoon; soup ladle, dipper; scoop; **despacharse con el cucharón** (coll) to look out for number one
**cuchichear** *intr* to whisper
**cuchilla** *f* knife; (*hoja de arma blanca de corte*) blade; (*de patín de hielo*) runner; (*cerro escarpado*) hogback; (*de interruptor*) (elec) blade; (poet) sword; **cuchilla de carnicero** butcher knife, cleaver
**cuchillada** *f* slash, gash, hack; **cuchilladas** fight, quarrel; **dar cuchillada** (*un actor o un teatro*) (coll) to be the hit of the town
**cuchillería** *f* cutlery; cutler's shop
**cuchillero** *m* cutler
**cuchillo** *m* knife; (*en un vestido*) gore; (naut) triangular sail; **cuchillo de trinchar** carving knife; **cuchillo de vidriero** putty knife; **pasar a cuchillo** to put to the sword
**cuchitril** *m* hovel, den
**cuchufleta** *f* (coll) joke, fun, wisecrack
**cuchufletear** *intr* (coll) to joke, make fun, wisecrack
**cuelga** *f* fruit hung up for keeping; (coll) birthday present
**cuelgaca•pas** *m* (*pl* **-pas**) cloak hanger
**cuello** *m* (*del cuerpo*) neck; (*de una prenda*) collar; shirt collar; **cuello almidonado** stiff collar; **cuello de camisa** shirtband; **cuello de cisne** gooseneck; **cuello de pajarita** or **doblado** wing collar; **levantar el cuello** (coll) to get back on one's feet again
**cuenca** *f* wooden bowl; (*del ojo*) socket; basin, river basin; **cuenca de polvo** dust bowl
**cuenco** *m* earthen bowl; hollow
**cuenta** *f* count, calculation; account; (*factura*) bill; (*en un restaurante*) check; (*del rosario*) bead; **abonar en cuenta a** to credit to the account of; **a cuenta** or **a buena cuenta** on account; **adeudar en cuenta a** to charge to the account of; **a fin de cuentas** after all; **caer en la cuenta** (coll) to get the point; **cargar en cuenta a** to charge to the account of; **correr por cuenta de** to be the responsibility of, to be under the administration of; **cuenta corriente** current account; **cuenta de gastos** expense account; **cuenta de la vieja** (coll) counting on one's fingers; **cuentas del gran capitán** overdrawn account; **cuentas galanas** (coll) illusions; **darse cuenta de** to realize, become aware of; **de cuenta** of importance; **más de la cuenta** too long; too much; **pedir cuentas a** to bring to account; **por la cuenta** apparently;

por mi cuenta to my way of thinking; tomar por su cuenta to take upon oneself; vamos a cuentas (coll) let's settle this
**cuentacorrentista** *mf* depositor
**cuentago•tas** *m* (*pl* -tas) dropper, medicine dropper
**cuentakilóme•tros** *m* (*pl* -tros) odometer
**cuente•ro -ra** *adj* (coll) gossipy ‖ *mf* (coll) gossip
**cuentista** *adj* (coll) gossipy ‖ *mf* story teller; short-story writer; (coll) gossip
**cuento** *m* story, tale; short story; prop, support; tip, point; (*cómputo*) count; (coll) gossip, evil talk; (coll) disagreement; **cuento de hadas** fairy tale; **cuento del tío** (SAm) gyp, swindle; **cuento de nunca acabar** (coll) endless affair; **cuento de penas** (coll) hard-luck story; **cuento de viejas** old wives' tale; **Cuentos de Calleja** collection of nursery stories; **dejarse de cuentos** (coll) to come to the point; **estar en el cuento** to be well-informed; **¡puro cuento!** pure fiction!; **sin cuento** countless; **traer a cuento** to bring up; **venir a cuento** (coll) to be opportune; **vivir del cuento** to live by one's wits
**cuerda** *f* cord, rope; watch spring; winding a watch or clock; (*acción de ahorcar*) hanging; fishing line; (aer, anat, geom) chord; (mus) string; **acabarse la cuerda** to run down, e.g., **se acabó la cuerda** the watch ran down; **bajo cuerda** secretly, underhandedly; **cuerda de presos** chain gang; **cuerda de remolcar** tow rope; **cuerda de tripa** (mus) catgut; **cuerda tirante** tight rope; **dar cuerda a** to give free rein to; (*un reloj*) to wind; **sin cuerda** unwound, run-down
**cuer•do -da** *adj* wise, prudent; sane ‖ *f* see **cuerda**
**cuerna** *f* antler; horns
**cuerno** *m* horn; (mus) horn; **cuerno de caza** huntinghorn; **cuerno inglés** (mus) English horn
**cuero** *m* (*pellejo de buey*) hide; (*después de curtido*) leather; wineskin; **cuero cabelludo** scalp; **cuero en verde** rawhide; **en cueros** stark-naked
**cuerpear** *intr* (Arg) to duck, dodge
**cuerpo** *m* body; (*parte del vestido hasta la cintura*) waist; (*talle, aspecto*) build; (*de escritos, leyes, etc.*) corpus; corps, staff; (mil) corps; **cuerpo a cuerpo** hand to hand; **cuerpo celeste** heavenly body; **cuerpo compuesto** (chem) compound; **cuerpo de aviación** air corps; **cuerpo de baile** corps de ballet; **cuerpo de bomberos** fire brigade, fire company; **cuerpo de ejército** army corps; **cuerpo de redacción** editorial staff; **cuerpo simple** (chem) simple substance; **dar con el cuerpo en tierra** (coll) to fall flat on the ground; **de cuerpo entero** full-length; **de medio cuerpo** half-length; **descubrir el cuerpo** to drop one's guard; **en cuerpo** or **en cuerpo de camisa** in shirt sleeves; **estar de cuerpo presente** to be on view, to lie in state; **hacer del cuerpo** (coll) to have a movement of the bowels
**cueru•do -da** *adj* (Am) thick-skinned; (Am) annoying, boring; (Am) bold, shameless
**cuervo** *m* raven; **cuervo marino** cormorant; **cuervo merendero** rook
**cuesco** *m* (*de la fruta*) stone; (*del molino de aceite*) millstone; (coll) windiness
**cuesta** *f* hill, slope, grade; charity drive; **cuesta abajo** downhill; **cuesta arriba** uphill; **llevar a cuestas** (coll) to be burdened with
**cuestión** *f* question; dispute, quarrel; matter; **cuestión batallona** much-debated question; **cuestión palpitante** burning question; **en cuestión de** in a matter of
**cuestionable** *adj* questionable
**cuestionar** *tr* to question ‖ *intr* (Arg) to argue
**cuestionario** *m* questionnaire
**cuestua•rio -ria** or **cuestuo•so -sa** *adj* profitable, lucrative
**cuetear** *ref* (Col) to blow up, explode; (Col) to die, kick the bucket; (Mex) to get drunk
**cueva** *f* cave; cellar; (*de ladrones, fieras, etc.*) den
**cufi•fo -fa** *adj* (Chile) tipsy
**cugulla** *f* cowl
**cui•co -ca** *adj* (Am) foreign, outside ‖ *m* (Mex) cop, policeman
**cuidado** *m* care, concern, worry; **¡cuidado con . . .!** beware of . . .!, look out for!; **de cuidado** dangerously; **estar de cuidado** (coll) to be dangerously ill; **pierda Vd. cuidado** don't worry; **salir de su cuidado** (*una mujer*) to be delivered; **tener cuidado** to beware, be careful
**cuidadora** *f* (Mex) governess, chaperon
**cuidado•so -sa** *adj* careful, concerned, worried; watchful
**cuidar** *tr* to take care of, to watch over ‖ *intr* — **cuidar de** to take care of, to care for; to care to ‖ *ref* to take care of oneself; **cuidarse de** to care about; to be careful to
**cuita** *f* trouble, worry; longing, yearning
**cuja** *f* bedstead
**culata** *f* buttock, haunch; (*de la escopeta*) butt; (*de imán*) keeper, yoke; **culata de cilindro** cylinder head
**culatazo** *m* kick, recoil
**culebra** *f* snake; (*del alambique*) coil; **culebra de anteojos** cobra; **culebra de cascabel** rattlesnake; **saber más que las culebras** (coll) to be foxy
**culebrear** *intr* to wriggle; to wind, meander; to zigzag
**culebrón** *m* (coll) foxy fellow; (Mex) poor farce
**cule•co -ca** *adj* (Am) self-satisfied; (Am) madly in love
**cu•lí** *m* (*pl* -líes) coolie

**culina•rio -ria** *adj* culinary
**culipandear** *intr & ref* (CAm, W-I) to welsh, be evasive
**culminar** *intr* to culminate
**culo** *m* seat, behind, backside; (*de animal*) buttocks; (*de un vaso*) bottom; **culo de mal asiento** (coll) fidgety person; **volver el culo** (coll) to run away
**culote** *m* base
**culpa** *f* blame, guilt, fault; **echar la culpa a** to put the blame on; **tener la culpa** to be wrong, to be to blame
**culpable** *adj* blamable, guilty, culpable
**culpa•do -da** *adj* guilty ‖ *mf* culprit
**culpar** *tr* to blame, censure, accuse ‖ *ref* to take the blame
**cultedad** *f* fustian, affectation
**culteranismo** *m* euphuism, Gongorism
**cultiparlar** *intr* to speak in a euphuistic manner
**cultismo** *m* learned word; cultism, Gongorism
**cultivar** *tr* to cultivate; to till
**cultivo** *m* cultivation; **cultivo de secano** dry farming
**cul•to -ta** *adj* cultivated, cultured; (*vocablo*) learned ‖ *m* worship; cult; **culto a la personalidad** personality cult
**cultura** *f* culture, cultivation
**culturar** *tr* to cultivate, to till
**cumbre** *adj* top, greatest ‖ *f* summit; acme, pinnacle
**cúmel** *m* kümmel
**cumiche** *m* (CAm) baby (*youngest member of family*)
**cúmplase** *m* approval, O.K.
**cumplea•ños** *m* (*pl* **-ños**) birthday
**cumpli•do -da** *adj* full; perfect; (*en muestras de urbanidad*) correct ‖ *m* correctness; courtesy; present
**cumplimentar** *tr* to compliment; to pay a complimentary visit to; to carry out, execute; (*un cuestionario*) to fill out
**cumplimente•ro -ra** *adj* (coll) effusive, obsequious
**cumplimiento** *m* (*muestra de urbanidad*) compliment; (*conducta decorosa*) correctness; fulfillment; perfection; **por cumplimiento** as a matter of pure formality
**cumplir** *tr* to fulfill, perform, execute; **cumplir años** to have a birthday; **cumplir . . . años** to be . . . years old ‖ *intr* to fall due; to expire; to keep one's promise; to finish one's service in the army; **cumplir con** to fulfill; to fulfill one's obligation to; **cumplir por** to act on behalf of; to pay the respects of ‖ *ref* to be fulfilled, to come true; to fall due; **cúmplase** approved
**cumquibus** *m* (coll) wherewithal
**cúmulo** *m* heap, pile, lot
**cuna** *f* cradle
**cundido** *m* olive, vinegar, and salt for shepherds; olive oil, cheese. and honey to make children eat
**cundir** *intr* to spread; to swell, puff up; to increase
**cunear** *tr* to cradle, rock in a cradle ‖ *intr* (coll) to rock, swing, sway
**cune•co -ca** *mf* (Ven) baby (*youngest member of family*)
**cuneta** *f* gutter, ditch
**cuña** *f* wedge; (typ) quoin; **ser buena cuña** (coll) to take up a lot of room
**cuñada** *f* sister-in-law
**cuñado** *m* brother-in-law
**cuñete** *m* keg
**cuño** *m* die; stamp; mark
**cuota** *f* quota, share; fee, dues; tuition fee
**cupé** *m* coupé
**cupo** *m* quota, share; (Mex) capacity
**cupón** *m* coupon
**cúpula** *f* cupola; dome
**cuquillo** *m* cuckoo
**cura** *m* curate; (coll) priest; **este cura** (*yo*) (coll) yours truly (*I*) ‖ *f* cure; care, treatment; **cura de aguas** water cure; **cura de almas** care of souls; **cura de hambre** starvation diet; **cura de reposo** rest cure; **cura de urgencia** first aid; **no tener cura** (coll) to be hopeless, be incorrigible
**curaca** *m* (SAm) boss, chief ‖ *f* (Bol, Peru) priest's housekeeper
**curación** *f* cure, treatment
**curade•ro -ra** *mf* caretaker ‖ *m* (law) guardian
**curande•ro -ra** *mf* quack, healer
**curar** *tr* (*a un enfermo*) to treat; (*sanar*) to cure, to heal; (*curtir*) to cure; (*la madera*) to season; (*una herida*) to dress ‖ *intr* to cure; to recover; **curar de** to take care of; to recover from; to mind, pay attention to ‖ *ref* to cure; to cure oneself; to get well, to recover; (Am) to get drunk; **curarse de** to recover from, get over; **curarse en salud** to be forewarned
**curati•vo -va** *adj & f* curative
**curda** *f* (coll) jag, drunk
**cureña** *f* gun carriage
**curia** *f* (hist) curia; (*de rey*) court; (*conjunto de abogados*) bar
**curiales•co -ca** *adj* hairsplitting, legalistic
**curiosear** *tr* (coll) to pry into ‖ *intr* (coll) to snoop; (coll) to browse around
**curiosidad** *f* curiosity; (*objeto de arte raro y curioso*) curio; neatness, tidiness; care, carefulness
**curio•so -sa** *adj* curious; neat, tidy; careful ‖ *mf* busybody ‖ *m* (Ven) healer, medical man
**currinche** *m* (coll) cub reporter; (coll) hit playwright
**cu•rro -rra** *adj* (coll) flashy, sporty ‖ *m* (coll) sport, dandy
**curruca** *f* (orn) whitethroat; **curruca de cabeza negra** blackcap, warbler
**curruta•co -ca** *adj* (coll) dudish, sporty; (Am) chubby ‖ *m* (coll) dude, sport ‖ *f* (coll) chic dame
**cursa•do -da** *adj* skilled, experienced; (*asignatura*) taken
**cursante** *mf* student
**cursar** *tr* (*una materia, estudios*) to take, to study; (*conferencias*) to attend; (*una carta*) to forward; (*un*

*paraje*) to frequent, to haunt || *intr* to study; to be current
**cursería** *f* cheapness, flashiness, vulgarity; flashy lot of people
**cursi** *adj* cheap, flashy, vulgar, loud || *m* sporty guy || *f* flashy dame
**cursien•to -ta** *adj* (Am) diarrheic
**cursilería** *f* cheapness, flashiness, vulgarity; flashy lot of people
**cursillo** *m* refresher course; short course of lectures
**cursi•vo -va** *adj* cursive; italic || *f* cursive; italics
**curso** *m* course; academic year, school year; price, quotation, current rate; **curso académico** academic year; **curso legal** legal tender; **cursos** loose bowels; **dar curso a** to give way to; to forward
**cursor** *m* slide; sliding contact; **cursor de procesiones** marshal
**curtiduría** *f* tannery
**curtiembre** *f* (Am) tannery
**curtir** *tr* (*las pieles*) to tan; (*el cutis de una persona*) to tan, sunburn; to harden, to inure; **estar curtido en** to be skilled in, be expert in || *ref* to become tanned, sunburned; to become hardened; to be weather-beaten
**curva** *f* curve; bend
**curvadura** *f* painful exhaustion
**cur•vo -va** *adj* curved, bent || *f* see **curva**
**cusca** *f* (Col) jag, drunk; (Mex) prostitute, slut
**cúspide** *f* (*de montaña*) peak; (*de diente*) cusp; apex, tip, top
**custodia** *f* custody, care; (*de un preso*) guard; (eccl) monstrance
**custodiar** *tr* to guard, watch over
**custodio** *m* custodian; guard
**cususa** *f* (CAm) rum
**cu•tí** *m* (*pl* **-tíes**) bedtick, ticking
**cutícula** *f* cuticle
**cutio** *m* work, labor
**cu•tis** *m* (*& f*) (*pl* **-tis**) skin, complexion; **cutis anserina** goose flesh
**cu•yo -ya** *adj rel* whose
**c/v** *abbr* **cuenta de venta**

## Ch

**Ch, ch** (che) *f* fourth letter of the Spanish alphabet
**chabacanada** or **chabacanería** *f* crudeness, coarseness, vulgarity
**chabaca•no -na** *adj* crude, coarse, vulgar || *m* (Mex) apricot tree
**chabola** *f* shack, shanty; (mil) foxhole
**chacal** *m* jackal
**chacanear** *tr* (Chile) to spur, goad on; (Chile) to annoy, bother
**chacare•ro -ra** *mf* (SAm) farm laborer, field worker; (Col) quack doctor; (Urug) gossip
**chacarrachaca** *f* (coll) row, racket
**chacolotear** *intr* to clatter
**chacota** *f* laughter, racket; **hacer chacota de** (coll) to make fun of
**chacotear** *intr* to laugh and make a racket
**chacra** *f* (Am) farm house; (Am) small farm; (Am) sown field
**chacua•co -ca** *adj* (Am) ugly, crude, boorish || *m* (CAm) cigar butt; (CAm) cheap cigar
**cháchara** *f* (coll) chatter, idle talk; **cháchara**s (coll) trinkets, junk
**chacharear** *intr* (coll) to chatter
**chafallar** *tr* (coll) to botch
**chafandín** *m* conceited ass
**chafar** *tr* to rumple, muss; to flatten; (coll) to cut short; (Chile) to dismiss, send off
**chafarrinar** *tr* to blot, stain
**chafarrinón** *m* blot, stain; **echar un chafarrinón a** (coll) to insult, throw mud at
**chaflán** *m* chamfer
**chaflanar** *tr* to chamfer
**chal** *m* shawl
**cha•lán -lana** *adj* horse-dealing || *mf* horse dealer; horse trader || *m* (Am) broncobuster, horsebreaker || *f* scow, flatboat
**chalanear** *tr* (*un negocio*) to pull off shrewdly; (*un caballo*) (Am) to break; (Arg) to take advantage of || *intr* to horse-trade
**chalanería** *f* horse trading
**chalanes•co -ca** *adj* horse-trading
**chaleco** *m* vest, waistcoat
**chalupa** *f* small two-master; launch, lifeboat; (Mex) corncake
**chama•co -ca** *mf* (Mex) youngster, urchin
**chamago•so -sa** *adj* (Mex) dirty, filthy; (Mex) botched
**chamarasca** *f* brushwood; brush fire
**chamarille•ro -ra** *mf* junk dealer, second-hand dealer || *m* gambler
**chamari•llón -llona** *mf* poor card player
**chamarra** *f* sheepskin jacket
**chamarreta** *f* loose jacket; (Am) square poncho
**chamba** *f* fluke, scratch
**chambelán** *m* chamberlain; (Mex) atomizer, spray
**chambergo** *m* (orn) bobolink; (Arg) soft hat
**chambe•rí** *adj* (*pl* **-ríes**) (Peru) showy, flashy
**cham•bón -bona** *adj* (coll) awkward, clumsy; (coll) lucky
**chambonada** *f* (coll) awkwardness, clumsiness; (coll) stroke of luck
**chambonear** *intr* to foozle
**chambra** *f* blouse; (Ven) din, uproar
**chambrana** *f* trim (*around a door*)
**chamburgo** *m* (Col) stagnant water, puddle

**chamico** *m* jimson weed; **dar chamico a** (SAm) to bewitch
**chamorrar** *tr* (coll) to shear
**champán** *m* sampan; (coll) champagne
**champaña** *m* champagne
**cham•pú** *m* (*pl* **-púes**) shampoo
**chamuscar** §73 *tr* to singe, scorch; (Mex) to undersell
**chamusco** *m* singe, scorch
**chamusquina** *f* singeing; (coll) fight, row, quarrel; **oler a chamusquina** (coll) to look like a fight; (coll) to smack of heresy
**chancar** §73 *tr* (Am) to crush; (Am) to beat, beat up; (Am) to botch
**chancear** *intr & ref* to joke, jest
**chance•ro -ra** *adj* joking, jesting
**canciller** *m* chancellor
**chancla** *f* old shoe; house slipper
**chancleta** *mf* (coll) good-for-nothing || *f* slipper; (Ven) accelerator
**chanclo** *m* overshoe, rubber
**chancha** *f* cheat, lie; (Chile) slut; **hacer la chancha** (Bol, Col, Chile) to play hooky
**chanche•ro -ra** *mf* (Arg, Chile) pork butcher
**chan•cho -cha** *adj* (Am) dirty, filthy || *m* (Am) pig || *f* see **chancha**
**chanchulle•ro -ra** *mf* (coll) crook
**changador** *m* (SAm) errand boy
**changarro** *m* (Mex) small shop
**chan•go -ga** *adj* (Chile) dull, stupid; (Mex) sly, crafty || *mf* (Mex) monkey || *m* (Arg) house boy
**chan•guí** *m* (*pl* **-guíes**) (coll) trick, deception
**chantaje** *m* blackmail
**chantajista** *mf* blackmailer
**chantar** *tr* to put on; (SAm) to throw hard; (Urug) to keep waiting || *ref* (*p.ej., el sombrero*) to clap on
**chantre** *m* cantor, precentor
**chanza** *f* joke, jest
**chapa** *f* sheet, plate; (*hoja fina de madera*) veneer; (*en las mejillas*) flush; (coll) good sense, judgment; (Chile) lock, bolt; **chapa de circulación** (aut) license plate; **chapas** flipping coins
**chapa•do -da** *adj* plated; veneered; **chapado a la antigua** old-fashioned
**chapalear** *intr* (*el agua; las manos y los pies en el agua*) to splash; (*la herradura floja*) to clatter
**chapar** *tr* to cover or line with sheets of metal; to veneer
**chaparrear** *intr* to pour
**chapa•rro -rra** *mf* (Mex) child, little one; (Mex) runt || *m* scrub oak
**chaparrón** *m* downpour
**chapea•do -da** *adj* lined with sheets of metal; veneered || *m* plywood; veneer
**chapear** *tr* to cover or line with sheets of metal; to veneer
**chapista** *m* tinsmith, tinman
**chapitel** *m* (*remate de torre*) spire; (*capitel de columna*) capital
**chapodar** *tr* to trim, clear of branches; to curtail
**chapotear** *tr* to sponge, moisten || *intr* to splash
**chapucear** *tr & intr* to botch, bungle
**chapuce•ro -ra** *adj* crude, rough; clumsy, bungling || *mf* bungler; amateur || *m* blacksmith; junk dealer
**chapurrar** *tr & intr* to jabber
**chapurreo** *m* jabber
**cha•puz** *m* (*pl* **-puces**) duck, ducking
**chapuzar** §60 *tr, intr & ref* to duck
**chaqué** *m* cutaway coat, morning coat
**chaqueta** *f* jacket
**chaquetilla** *f* short jacket; (Ecuad) lady's vest
**chaquetón** *m* reefer, pea jacket
**charamusca** *f* (Am) brushwood, firewood; (Mex) candy twist
**charanga** *f* (mil) brass band
**charangue•ro -ra** *adj* crude, rough; bungling, clumsy || *mf* bungler
**charca** *f* pool
**charco** *m* puddle
**charla** *f* (coll) talk, chat; (coll) talk, lecture; (coll) chatter, prattle
**charla•dor -dora** *adj* (coll) garrulous; (coll) gossipy || *mf* (coll) chatterbox; (coll) gossip
**charlar** *intr* (coll) to talk, chat; (coll) to chatter, prattle
**charla•tán -tana** *adj* garrulous; gossipy || *mf* chatterbox; gossip; charlatan
**charlatanería** *f* garrulity, loquacity
**charlatanismo** *m* charlatanism; garrulity, loquacity
**charnela** *f* (*de puerta; de molusco*) hinge; (mach) knuckle
**charol** *m* varnish; patent leather; (Am) lacquered tray; **calzarse las de charol** (Arg, Urug) to hit the jackpot; **darse charol** (coll) to blow one's own horn
**charola•do -da** *adj* shiny
**charolar** *tr* to varnish, to lacquer
**charpa** *f* pistol belt; (*cabestrillo*) sling
**charquear** *tr* (*carne de vaca*) (Am) to jerk; (Am) to slash, cut to pieces
**charqui** *m* (Am) jerked beef
**charrada** *f* country dance; boorishness; (coll) tawdry ornamentation
**charretera** *f* epaulet; garter; (*del aguador*) (coll) shoulder pad
**charriada** *f* (Mex) rodeo
**cha•rro -rra** *adj* coarse, ill-bred; flashy, loud, showy; Salamanca || *mf* peasant; Salamanca peasant || *m* broad-brimmed hat; Mexican cowboy
**chasca** *f* brushwood
**chascar** §73 *tr* (*la lengua*) to click; (*algún manjar*) to crunch; (*engullir*) to swallow || *intr* to crack, crackle
**chascarrillo** *m* (coll) funny story
**chas•co -ca** *adj* (Arg, Bol) crinkly, crinkly-haired || *m* joke, trick; disappointment; **dar un chasco a** to play a trick on; **llevar** or **llevarse (un) chasco** to be disappointed
**chas•cón -cona** *adj* (Bol, Chile) disheveled; (Bol, Chile) bushy-haired; (Bol, Chile) clumsy, unskilled
**cha•sis** *m* (*pl* **-sis**) chassis
**chasquear** *tr* (*un látigo*) to crack; to play a trick on; to disappoint || *intr* to crack || *ref* to be disappointed
**chasqui** *m* (SAm) messenger, courier
**chasquido** *m* crack; crackle
**chata** *f* barge, scow; flatcar; bedpan
**chatarra** *f* iron slag; junk, scrap iron

**chatarrería** *f* junk yard
**chatarre•ro -ra** *mf* junk dealer, scrap-iron dealer
**cha•to -ta** *adj* flat; flat-nosed; blunt; (Am) commonplace; (Am) disappointed || *m* (coll) wineglass || *f* see **chata**
**chatre** *adj* (Chile, Ecuad) all dressed up
**cha•val -vala** *adj* (coll) young || *m* (coll) lad || *f* (coll) lass
**chaveta** *f* cotter pin; **perder la chaveta** (coll) to go out of one's head
**chayote** *m* (Am) chayote, vegetable pear; (Am) dunce, fool
**chazar** §60 *tr* (*la pelota*) to stop; (*el sitio donde paró la pelota*) to mark
**che** *interj* (SAm) say!, hey!
**che•co -ca** *adj & mf* Czech
**checoeslova•co -ca** *adj & mf* Czecho-Slovak
**Checoeslovaquia** *f* Czecho-Slovakia
**checoslova•co -ca** *adj & mf* Czecho-Slovak
**Checoslovaquia** *f* Czecho-Slovakia
**chechén** *m* (Mex) poison ivy
**chécheres** *mpl* (Am) trinkets, junk
**chelín** *m* shilling
**cheque** *m* check; **cheque de viajeros** traveler's check
**chica** *f* lass, little girl; girl; (coll) my dear; **chica de cita** call girl; **chica de la vida alegre** party girl
**chicalote** *m* Mexican poppy
**chicle** *m* (Am) chewing gum
**chiclear** *intr* (Mex) to chew gum
**chi•co -ca** *adj* small, little; young || *mf* child, youngster || *m* lad, little boy; (coll) young fellow; (coll) old man; (Am) hand, turn || *f* see **chica**
**chicolear** *intr* to pay compliments, to flirt || *ref* (Arg, Peru) to enjoy oneself
**chico•te -ta** *mf* husky youngster || *m* (coll) cigar; (Am) cigar stub; (Am) whip
**chicue•lo -la** *adj* small, little || *m* little boy || *f* little girl
**chicha** *f* corn liquor; **no ser ni chicha ni limonada** (coll) to be good for nothing
**chícharo** *m* (Am) pea; (Col) poor cigar; (Mex) apprentice
**chicharra** *f* harvest fly; (coll) chatterbox; **cantar la chicharra** (coll) to be hot and sultry
**chicharrón** *m* residue of hog's fat; burnt meat; (coll) sunburned person; (Am) wrinkled person
**chichear** *tr & intr* to hiss
**chi•chón -chona** *adj* (CAm) easy; (SAm) joking; (Guat) large-breasted || *m* lump, bump on the head
**chifla** *f* hissing, whistling; paring knife; **estar de chifla** (Mex) to be in a bad humor
**chifla•do -da** *adj* (coll) daffy, nutty || *mf* (coll) crackbrain, nut
**chifladura** *f* (coll) daffiness, nuttiness; (coll) whim, wild idea
**chiflar** *tr* (*a un actor*) to hiss; (*vino o licor*) to gulp down; (*el cuero*) to pare || *intr* to whistle; (*las aves*) (Guat, Mex) to sing || *ref* to go crazy
**chifle** *m* whistle; (*para cazar aves*) bird call; powder flask
**chiflido** *m* whistle, hiss
**chiflón** *m* (SAm) cold blast of air; (Am) rapids; (Am) slide of loose stone
**chilaba** *f* jelab, jellaba
**Chile** *m* Chile
**chile•no -na** *adj & mf* Chilean
**chilla** *f* fox call, hare call; clapboard; (Chile) small fox; (Mex) top gallery
**chillar** *intr* to shriek; to squeak; to hiss, sizzle; (*los colores*) to scream || *ref* (Am) to take offense
**chillido** *m* shriek, scream
**chi•llón -llona** *adj* shrill, high-pitched; (coll) screaming; (*color*) loud
**chimenea** *f* chimney, smokestack; fireplace, hearth; stovepipe hat; (naut) funnel
**chimpancé** *m* chimpanzee
**china** *f* Chinese woman; china, porcelain; pebble; (Am) nursemaid; (Col) spinning top || **China** *f* China
**chinche** *mf* (coll) bore, tiresome person || *m* (*clavito de cabeza chata*) thumbtack || *f* (*insecto*) bedbug; **caer** or **morir como chinches** to die like flies
**chinchorre•ro -ra** *adj* (coll) gossipy, mischievous
**chincho•so -sa** *adj* (coll) boring, tiresome
**chinero** *m* china closet
**chines•co -ca** *adj* Chinese || **chinescos** *mpl* (mus) bell tree
**chingar** §44 *tr* (coll) to tipple; (CAm) to bob, dock; (CAm, Mex) to bother, annoy || *ref* (coll) to tipple; (Am) to fail
**chin•go -ga** *adj* (CAm) short; (CAm) dull, blunt; (CAm) naked
**chinguirito** *m* (Am) cheap rum; (Am) swig of liquor
**chi•no -na** *adj & mf* Chinese || *m* (*idioma*) Chinese; (Col) boy, newsboy; (Mex) curl || *f* see **china**
**chipichipi** *m* (Am) drizzle, mist
**Chipre** *f* Cyprus
**chiquero** *m* pigsty; bull pen
**chiquillada** *f* childish prank
**chiqui•to -ta** *adj* small, little || *mf* little one || *m* (*de vino*) snifter; (Arg) moment, instant || *f* five cents; **no andarse con** or **en chiquitas** (coll) to talk right off the shoulder
**chiribita** *f* spark; daisy; **chiribitas** (coll) spots before the eyes
**chiribitil** *m* garret; cubbyhole
**chirimbolos** *mpl* (coll) utensils, vessels
**chirimía** *f* hornpipe
**chiripa** *f* (billiards) fluke, scratch; (coll) stroke of luck
**chirivía** *f* parsnip
**chirle** *adj* (coll) insipid, tasteless
**chirlo** *m* slash or scar on the face
**chirlota** *f* (Mex) meadow lark
**chirona** *f* (coll) jail, jug
**chirriar** §77 *intr* to creak, squeak; to shriek; to hiss, sizzle; to sing or play out of tune || *ref* (Col) to go on a spree; (Col) to shiver

**chirrido** *m* creak, squeak; shriek; hiss, sizzle
**chis** *interj* sh-sh!; **¡chis, chis!** pst!
**chischás** *m* clash of swords
**chisguete** *m* (coll) swig of wine; (coll) squirt
**chisme** *m* piece of gossip; (coll) trinket; **chisme de vecindad** (coll) idle talker; **chismes** gossip; articles; **chismes de aseo** toilet articles
**chismear** *intr* to gossip
**chismo•so -sa** *adj* gossipy, catty || *mf* gossip
**chispa** *f* spark; (*pequeña cantidad*) drop; lightning; (fig) sparkle, wit; (coll) drunk, spree; (Col) rumor; **coger una chispa** (coll) to go on a drunk; **chispa de entrehierro** (elec) jump spark; **chispas** sprinkle (*of rain*); **dar chispa** (Guat, Mex) to work, to click; **echar chispas** (coll) to blow up, hit the ceiling
**chispeante** *adj* sparkling
**chispear** *intr* to spark; to sparkle; to drizzle, to sprinkle
**chis•po -pa** *adj* (coll) tipsy || *m* (coll) swallow, drink || *f* see **chispa**
**chisporrotear** *intr* (coll) to spark, to sputter
**chispo•so -sa** *adj* sputtering, sparking
**chisquero** *m* pocket lighter
**chistar** *intr* to speak, say something; **no chistar** to not say a word
**chiste** *m* joke; witticism; **caer en el chiste** (coll) to get the point; **dar en el chiste** (coll) to hit the nail on the head
**chistera** *f* fish basket; (coll) top hat
**chisto•so -sa** *adj* funny; witty || *mf* funny person; wit
**chita** *f* anklebone; quoits; **a la chita callando** (coll) quietly, secretly; **dar en la chita** (coll) to hit the nail on the head
**chiticalla** *mf* (*persona que no revela lo que sabe*) (coll) clam || *f* (coll) secret
**chito** *interj* hush!, sh-sh!
**chivato** *m* kid, young goat; (*soplón*) (coll) squealer; (Bol) apprentice, helper; (Chile) cheap rum
**chi•vo -va** *mf* kid || *m* billy goat || *f* nanny goat
**chocante** *adj* shocking; coarse, crude; (Col) annoying; (Mex) disagreeable
**chocar §73** *tr* to shock, annoy, irritate; to surprise; (*vasos*) to clink; (coll) to please; **¡choque Vd. esos cinco!** (coll) shake! || *intr* to shock; to collide; to clash, fight
**chocarre•ro -ra** *adj* coarse, crude || *mf* crude joker
**choclo** *m* wooden overshoe; (Mex) low shoe; (SAm) tender ear of corn
**chocolate** *m* chocolate
**chocha** *f* woodcock
**chochear** *intr* to be in one's dotage; (coll) to dote, be infatuated
**chochera** *f* dotage; (Arg, Peru) favorite
**cho•chez** *f* (*pl* **-checes**) dotage; doting act or remark
**cho•cho -cha** *adj* doting; doddering || *m* stick of cinnamon candy; **chochos** candy to quiet a child || *f* see **chocha**
**chófer** *m* chauffeur
**chofeta** *f* fire pan (*for lighting cigars*)
**cho•lo -la** *adj* (Am) half-breed (*Indian and white*); (Am) half-civilized (*Indian*) || *mf* (Am) Indian; (Am) half-breed; (Am) half-civilized Indian; (Chile) coward; (SAm) darling
**cholla** *f* (coll) noodle, head; (coll) ability, brains
**chomite** *m* (Mex) coarse wool; (Mex) woolen skirt
**chopo** *m* black poplar; (coll) gun, rifle; **chopo de Italia** Lombardy poplar; **chopo del Canadá** or **de Virginia** cottonwood; **chopo lombardo** Lombardy poplar
**choque** *m* shock; collision, impact; clash, conflict, skirmish; (elec) choke, choke coil
**choricería** *f* sausage shop
**chorizo** *m* smoked pork sausage
**chorlito** *m* plover, golden plover; (coll) scatterbrains
**chorrear** *intr* to gush, spurt, spout; to drip; to trickle
**chorrera** *f* spout, channel; cut, gulley; rapids; lace front, jabot; (Arg) string, stream
**chorrillo** *m* constant stream; **irse por el chorrillo** (coll) to follow the current; **tomar el chorrillo de** (coll) to get the habit of
**chorro** *m* jet, spurt; stream, flow; **a chorros** in abundance; **chorro de arena** sandblast
**chotaca•bras** *m* (*pl* **-bras**) goatsucker
**chotear** *tr* (Am) to make fun of; (Guat) to keep an eye on
**choteo** *m* (Am) jeering, mocking
**choza** *f* hut, cabin, lodge
**chubasco** *m* squall, shower; (fig) temporary setback; **chubasco de agua** rainstorm; **chubasco de nieve** blizzard
**chubasco•so -sa** *adj* stormy, threatening
**chucruta** *f* sauerkraut
**chucha** *f* (coll) female dog, bitch; (coll) drunk, jag; (Col) opossum; (Col) body odor
**chuchaque** *m* (Ecuad) hangover
**chuchear** *tr* (*caza menor*) to trap || *intr* to whisper
**chuchería** *f* knickknack, trinket; delicacy, tidbit
**chu•cho -cha** *adj* (CAm) mean, stingy; (*fruto*) (Col) watery; (Col) wrinkled || *m* (coll) dog || *f* see **chucha**
**chue•co -ca** *adj* (Mex) twisted, bent; (SAm) bow-legged; (Mex) crippled || *m* (Mex) dealing in stolen goods || *f* stump; hockey; hockey ball
**chufa** *f* groundnut
**chufletear** *intr* (coll) to joke, jest
**chula** *f* flashy dame (*in lower classes of Madrid*)
**chulada** *f* light-hearted remark; vulgarity
**chul•co -ca** *mf* (Bol) baby (*youngest child*)
**chulear** *tr* to tease; (Mex) to flirt with
**chuleta** *f* chop, cutlet; (coll) slap, smack; (*de los estudiantes*) (coll) crib, pony; **chuleta de cerdo** pork

chop; **chuleta de ternera** veal chop; **chuletas** sideburns, side whiskers
**chu·lo -la** *adj* flashy, sporty; foxy, slick; (Guat, Mex) pretty, cute ‖ *m* sporty fellow (*in lower classes of Madrid*); pimp, procurer; gigolo; butcher's helper; (taur) attendant on foot ‖ *f* see **chula**
**chumbera** *f* prickly pear
**chunga** *f* (coll) jest, fun
**chunguear** *ref* (coll) to jest, joke
**chupa** *f* frock, coat; (Arg) drunk, jag; (Arg) tobacco pouch
**chupa·do -da** *adj* (coll) thin, skinny; (Am) drunk; (*falda*) (Am) tight ‖ *f* suck; pull (*on a cigar*)
**chupador** *m* teething ring, pacifier
**chupaflor** *m* (Mex, Ven) hummingbird
**chupamirto** *m* (Mex) hummingbird
**chupar** *tr* to suck; (*la hacienda ajena*) to milk, sap; (coll) to absorb ‖ *intr* to suck ‖ *ref* to get thin, lose strength; (*los labios*) to smack
**chupatin·tas** *mf* (*pl* **-tas**) (coll) office drudge
**chupete** *m* (*para un niño*) pacifier; (Am) lollipop; **de chupete** (coll) fine, splendid
**chu·pón -pona** *mf* (coll) swindler ‖ *m* (bot) sucker, shoot; (mach) plunger
**chupópte·ro -ra** *mf* (coll) sponger
**chuquisa** *f* (Chile, Peru) prostitute
**churrasco** *m* (Am) barbecue
**churrasquear** *tr* (Am) to barbecue
**churre** *m* (coll) filth, dirt, grease
**churrete** *m* dirty spot (*on hands or face*)
**churrigueres·co -ca** *adj* churrigueresque; loud, flashy, tawdry
**chu·rro -rra** *adj* (*lana*) coarse; (*carnero*) coarse-wooled ‖ *m* coarse-wooled sheep; fritter; (coll) botch
**churrulle·ro -ra** *adj* gossipy, loquacious ‖ *mf* gossip, chatterbox
**churrusco** *m* burnt piece of bread
**churumbela** *f* hornpipe, flageolet; (Am) maté cup; (Col) worry, anxiety; (Col, Ecuad) pipe
**churumo** *m* (coll) substance (*money, brains, etc.*)
**chus** *interj* here! (*to call a dog*); **no decir chus ni mus** (coll) to not say boo
**chus·co -ca** *adj* droll, funny; (Peru) ill-mannered; (*perro*) (Peru) mongrel
**chusma** *f* galley slaves; mob, rabble
**chuza** *f* (Mex) strike (*in bowling*)

# D

**D, d** (de) *f* fifth letter of the Spanish alphabet
**D.** *abbr* **don**
**D.ª** *abbr* **doña**
**daca** give me, hand over; **andar al daca y toma** (coll) to be at cross purposes
**dactilógra·fo -fa** *mf* typist, typewriter ‖ *m* typewriter
**dactilograma** *m* fingerprint
**dádiva** *f* gift, present
**dadivo·so -sa** *adj* liberal, generous
**da·do -da** *adj* given; **dado que** provided, as long as ‖ *m* die; **cargar los dados** to load the dice; **dados** dice; **el dado está tirado** the die is cast
**daga** *f* dagger
**dalia** *f* dahlia
**dama** *f* lady, dame; maid-in-waiting; (*en el juego de damas*) king; (*en el ajedrez y los naipes*) queen; (theat) leading lady; concubine, mistress; **dama joven** (theat) young lead; **damas** checkers; **señalar dama** (*en el juego de damas*) to crown a man
**damajuana** *f* demijohn
**damasquina·do -da** *adj & m* damascene
**damasquinar** *tr* to damascene
**damasqui·no -na** *adj* damascene
**damero** *m* checkerboard
**damisela** *f* young lady; courtesan
**damnación** *f* damnation
**damnificar** §73 *tr* to damage, hurt
**da·nés -nesa** *adj* Danish ‖ *mf* Dane ‖ *m* (*idioma*) Danish
**dáni·co -ca** *adj* Danish
**Danubio** *m* Danube
**danza** *f* dance; dancing; dance team; **danza de cintas** Maypole dance; **danza de figuras** square dance; **meter en la danza** (coll) to drag in, involve
**danza·dor -dora** *mf* dancer
**danzar** §60 *tr* to dance ‖ *intr* to dance; (coll) to butt in
**danza·rín -rina** *mf* dancer; (coll) meddler, scatterbrain
**dañable** *adj* harmful; reprehensible
**daña·do -da** *adj* bad, wicked; spoiled
**dañar** *tr* to hurt, damage, injure; to spoil ‖ *ref* to be damaged; to spoil
**dañi·no -na** *adj* harmful, destructive, noxious; wicked
**daño** *m* damage, harm; (Arg) witchcraft; **a daño de** on the responsibility of; **daños y perjuicios** (law) damages; **en daño de** to the detriment of; **hacer daño** to be harmful; **hacer daño a** to hurt; **hacerse daño** to hurt oneself; to get hurt
**daño·so -sa** *adj* harmful, injurious
**dar** §23 *tr* to give; to cause; to hit, strike; (*el reloj la hora*) to strike; (*cartas*) to deal; (*un paseo*) to take; (*los buenos días*) to wish; (*un film*) to show; (*una capa de pintura*) to put on, apply; **dar a conocer** to make known; **dar a luz** to bring out, publish; **dar cuerda a** (*un reloj*) to wind; **dar curso a** to circulate; **dar de beber a** to give something to drink to; **dar de comer a** to give

something to eat to; **dar la razón a** to admit that (*someone*) is right; **dar prestado** to lend; **dar palmadas** to clap the hands; **dar por** to consider as; **dar que hablar** to cause talk; to stir up criticism; **dar que hacer** to cause annoyance or trouble; **dar que pensar** to give food for thought; to give rise to suspicion || *intr* to take place; to hit, strike; (*el reloj; dos, tres, etc. horas*) to strike; to tell, intimate; **dar a** to overlook; **dar con** to run into; **dar contra** to run against, strike against; **dar de sí** to stretch, to give; **dar en** to overlook; to hit; to run into; to fall into; to be bent on; (*un chiste*) to catch on to; **dar sobre** to overlook; **dar tras** to pursue hotly || *ref* to give oneself up; to give in, yield; to occur, be found; **darse a** to devote oneself to; **darse a conocer** to make a name for oneself, make oneself known; to get to know each other; **darse cuenta de** to realize, become aware of; **darse la mano** to shake hands; **dárselas de** to pose as; **darse por aludido** to take the hint; **darse por entendido** to show an understanding; to show appreciation; **darse por ofendido** to take offense; **darse por vencido** to give up, to acknowledge defeat

**dardo** *m* dart; cutting remark

**dares y tomares** *mpl* (coll) quarrels, disputes

**dársena** *f* basin, dock, inner harbor

**data** *f* date; (*en una cuenta*) item; **de larga data** of long standing; **estar de mala data** (coll) to be in a bad humor

**datar** *tr & intr* to date; **datar de** to date from

**dátil** *m* date

**datilera** *f* date, date palm

**dati•vo -va** *adj & m* dative

**dato** *m* datum; basis, foundation

**de** *prep* of; from; about; **acompañado de** accompanied by; **cubierto de** covered with; **de noche** in the nighttime; **de no llegar nosotros a la hora** if we do not arrive on time; **más de** more than; **tratar de** to try to

**deán** *m* (eccl) dean

**debajo** *adv* below, underneath; **debajo de** below, under

**debate** *m* debate; altercation, argument

**debatir** *tr & intr* to debate; to fight, argue || *ref* to struggle

**debe** *m* debit

**debelar** *tr* to conquer, vanquish

**deber** *m* duty; (*deuda*) debt; homework, school work; **últimos deberes** last rites || *tr* to owe || *v aux* to have to, ought to, must, should; **deber de** must, most likely || *ref* to be committed; **deberse a** to be due to

**debidamente** *adv* duly

**debi•do -da** *adj* due, owed; proper, right; **debido a** due to

**débil** *adj* weak

**debilidad** *f* weakness, debility

**debilitar** *tr & ref* to weaken

**débito** *m* debt, debit; responsibility

**debutar** *intr* to make one's start, appear for the first time

**decadencia** *f* decadence

**decadente** *adj & mf* decadent

**decaer** §15 *intr* to decay, decline, fail, weaken; (naut) to drift from the course

**decampar** *intr* (mil) to decamp

**decanato** *m* deanship

**decano** *m* dean

**decanta•do -da** *adj* puffed-up, overrated

**decapitar** *tr* to decapitate

**decelerar** *tr, intr, & ref* to decelerate

**decencia** *f* decency

**decenio** *m* decade

**dece•no -na** *adj & m* tenth

**decentar** §2 *tr* to cut the first slice of; to begin to damage || *ref* to get bedsores

**decente** *adj* decent, proper; decent-looking

**decepción** *f* disappointment

**decepcionar** *tr* to disappoint

**decidi•do -da** *adj* decided, determined

**decidir** *tr* to decide; to persuade || *intr & ref* to decide

**deci•dor -dora** *adj* facile, fluent, witty

**decimal** *adj & m* decimal

**déci•mo -ma** *adj & m* tenth

**decimocta•vo -va** *adj* eighteenth

**decimocuar•to -ta** *adj* fourteenth

**decimono•no -na** *adj* nineteenth

**decimonove•no -na** *adj* nineteenth

**decimoquin•to -ta** *adj* fifteenth

**decimosépti•mo -ma** *adj* seventeenth

**decimosex•to -ta** *adj* sixteenth

**decimoterce•ro -ra** *adj* thirteenth

**decimoter•cio -cia** *adj* thirteenth

**decir** *m* say-so; **al decir de** according to || §24 *tr* to say; to tell; (*disparates*) to talk; **como si dijéramos** so to speak, in a manner of speaking; **decir entre sí** to say to oneself; **decirle a uno cuántas son cinco** (coll) to tell a person what's what; **decir para sí** to say to oneself; **decir por decir** to talk for talk's sake; **decir que no** to say no; **decir que sí** to say yes; **decírselo a una persona deletreado** (coll) to spell it out to a person; **es decir** that is to say; **mejor dicho** rather; **¡por algo te lo dije!** I told you so!; **por decirlo así** so to speak || *intr* to suit, fit; **¡diga!** (*al contestar el teléfono*) hello! || *ref* to be said; to be called; **se dice** it is said, they say

**decisión** *f* decision

**decisi•vo -va** *adj* decisive

**declamar** *tr & intr* to declaim

**declaración** *f* declaration; (*en bridge*) bid

**declarante** *mf* declarant, deponent; (*en el juego de bridge*) bidder

**declarar** *tr* to declare; (*en bridge*) to bid; (law) to depose || *ref* to declare oneself; to break out, take place

**declarati•vo -va** *adj* declarative

**declinación** *f* declination; fall, drop; decline; (gram) declension

**declinar** *tr & intr* to decline

**declive** *m* descent, declivity, slope

**declividad** *f* declivity
**decollaje** *m* (aer) take-off
**decollar** *intr* (aer) to take off
**decomisar** *tr* to seize, confiscate
**decomiso** *m* seizure, confiscation
**decoración** *f* decoration; memorizing; (theat) set, scenery; **decoraciones** (theat) scenery; **decoración interior** interior decoration
**decorado** *m* decoration; (theat) décor, scenery; memorizing
**decora•dor -dora** *mf* decorator
**decorar** *tr* to decorate; to memorize
**decoro** *m* decorum; honor, respect; decency, propriety
**decoro•so -sa** *adj* decorous; respectful; decent
**decrecer** §22 *intr* to decrease, grow smaller, grow shorter
**decrepitar** *intr* to crackle
**decrépi•to -ta** *adj* decrepit
**decretar** *tr* to decree
**decreto** *m* decree
**decurso** *m* course; **en el decurso de** in the course of
**dechado** *m* sample, model, example; (*labor de las niñas*) sampler
**dedada** *f* touch, spot; **dar una dedada de miel a** (coll) to feed the hopes of
**dedal** *m* thimble
**dedalera** *f* foxglove
**dedeo** *m* (mus) finger dexterity
**dedicación** *f* dedication
**dedicar** §73 *tr* to dedicate; to devote; to autograph || *ref* to devote oneself
**dedicatoria** *f* dedication
**dedil** *m* fingerstall
**dedillo** *m* little finger; **saber** or **tener al dedillo** (coll) to have at one's finger tips, to have a thorough knowledge of
**dedo** *m* finger; toe; (coll) bit; **alzar el dedo** (*en señal de dar palabra*) (coll) to raise one's hand; **cogerse los dedos** (coll) to burn one's fingers; **dedo auricular** little finger; **dedo cordial, de en medio,** or **del corazón** middle finger; **dedo gordo** thumb; big toe; **dedo índice** index finger, forefinger; **dedo meñique** little finger; **dedo mostrador** forefinger; **dedo pulgar** thumb; big toe; **estar a dos dedos de** (coll) to be within an ace of; **irse de entre los dedos** (coll) to slip between the fingers; **tener en la punta de los dedos** (coll) to have at one's finger tips
**deducción** *f* deduction; drawing off
**deducir** §19 *tr* (*concluir*) to deduce; (*rebajar*) to deduct; (law) to allege
**defecar** §73 *intr* to defecate
**defección** *f* defection
**defeccionar** *intr & ref* (Chile) to defect
**defecti•vo -va** *adj* defective
**defecto** *m* defect; shortage, lack; **en defecto de** for lack of
**defectuo•so -sa** *adj* defective; lacking
**defender** §51 *tr* to defend; to protect; to delay, interfere with
**defensa** *f* defense; fender, guard; (*del toro*) horn; (*del elefante*) tusk; (*del automóvil*) (Am) bumper; **defensa marítima** (Arg) sea wall; **defensa propia** self-defense
**defensi•vo -va** *adj & f* defensive
**defen•sor -sora** *adj* defending || *mf* defender; (law) counsel for the defense
**deferencia** *f* deference
**deferente** *adj* deferential
**deferir** §68 *tr to* delegate || *intr* to defer
**deficiencia** *f* deficiency
**deficiente** *adj* deficient
**défi•cit** *m* (*pl* **-cits**) deficit
**deficita•rio -ria** *adj* deficit
**definición** *f* definition; decision, verdict
**defini•do -da** *adj* definite; sharp, defined
**definir** *tr* to define; to settle, determine
**definiti•vo -va** *adj* definitive; **en definitiva** after all, in short
**deflación** *f* deflation
**deflector** *m* baffle
**deformación** *f* deformation; (rad) distortion
**deformar** *tr* to deform; to disfigure; to distort
**deforme** *adj* deformed
**deformidad** *f* deformity; gross error
**defraudar** *tr* to defraud, to cheat; (*las esperanzas de una persona*) to defeat; (*la claridad del día*) to cut off
**defuera** *adv* outside; **por defuera** on the outside
**defunción** *f* decease, demise
**degeneración** *f* (*acción y efecto de degenerar*) degeneration; (*estado de degenerado; depravación*) degeneracy
**degenera•do -da** *adj & mf* degenerate
**degenerar** *intr* to degenerate
**deglutir** *tr & intr* to swallow
**degollar** §3 *tr* to cut the throat of; to kill, massacre; (*un vestido*) to cut low in the neck; (*el actor una obra dramática*) to butcher, to murder; (coll) to become obnoxious to
**degradante** *adj* degrading
**degradar** *tr* to degrade; (mil) to break
**degüello** *m* throat-cutting; massacre; (*de un arma*) neck; **tirar a degüello** (coll) to try to harm
**degustar** *tr* (*probar*) to taste; (*percibir con deleite el sabor de*) to savor
**dehesa** *f* pasture land, meadow; (taur) range
**deidad** *f* deity
**deificar** §73 *tr* to deify
**dejación** *f* abandonment; (CAm, Chile, Col) negligence
**dejadez** *f* laziness; negligence; slovenliness; low spirits
**deja•do -da** *adj* lazy; negligent; slovenly; dejected
**dejamiento** *m* laziness; negligence; indolence, languor, indifference
**dejar** *tr* to leave; to abandon; to let, allow, permit; **dejar caer** to drop, let fall; **dejar feo** (coll) to slight; **dejar fresco** (coll) to leave in the lurch; **dejar por** + *inf* or **que** + *inf* to leave (*something*) to be + *pp*, e.g., **hemos dejado dos manuscritos por corregir** or **que corregir** we left two manuscripts to be corrected || *intr* to stop; **dejar de** to stop, to cease; to fail to || *ref* to be slovenly, to neglect oneself; (*una barba*) to grow; **dejarse de**

(*disparates*) to cut out; (*preguntas*) to stop asking; (*dudas*) to put aside; **dejarse ver** to show up; to be evident
**dejillo** *m* (*gusto que deja alguna comida*) aftertaste; (*acento regional*) local accent
**dejo** *m* (*gusto que deja alguna comida*) aftertaste; abandonment; slovenliness, neglect; local accent; (*placer o disgusto que queda después de hecha una cosa*) (fig) aftertaste
**delación** *f* accusation, denunciation
**delantal** *m* apron
**delante** *adv* before, ahead, in front; **delante de** before, ahead of, in front of
**delantera** *f* front; front row; advantage, lead; cowcatcher; **coger** or **tomar la delantera a** to get ahead of; to get a start on; **delanteras** overalls
**delante·ro -ra** *adj* front, foremost, first || *f* see **delantera**
**delatar** *tr* to accuse, denounce
**delega·do -da** *mf* delegate
**delegar** **§44** *tr* to delegate
**deleitable** *adj* delectable, enjoyable
**deleitar** *tr & ref* to delight
**deleite** *m* delight
**deleito·so -sa** *adj* delightful
**deletrear** *tr & intr* to spell; to decipher
**deletreo** *m* spelling
**deleznable** *adj* (*poco durable*) perishable; (*que se rompe fácilmente*) crumbly, fragile; (*que se desliza con facilidad*) slippery
**delfín** *m* (*primogénito del rey de Francia*) dauphin; (*mamífero cetáceo*) dolphin
**delgadez** *f* thinness, leanness; delicateness, lightness; perspicacity
**delga·do -da** *adj* thin, lean; delicate, light; sharp, perspicacious; (*terreno*) poor, exhausted || *adv* — **hilar delgado** (coll) to hew close to the line; (coll) to split hairs
**deliberar** *tr & intr* to deliberate
**delicadeza** *f* delicacy, delicateness; scrupulousness
**delica·do -da** *adj* delicate; scrupulous
**delicia** *f* delight
**delicio·so -sa** *adj* delicious, delightful
**delincuencia** *f* guilt, criminality
**delincuente** *adj* guilty, criminal || *mf* criminal
**delineante** *mf* designer || *m* draughtsman
**delinquir** **§25** *intr* to transgress, be guilty
**deliquio** *m* faint, swoon; weakening
**delirante** *adj* delirious
**delirar** *intr* to be delirious, rant, rave; to talk nonsense
**delirio** *m* delirium; nonsense
**delito** *m* crime; **delito de incendio** arson; **delito de lesa majestad** lese majesty; **delito de mayor cuantía** (law) felony; **delito de menor cuantía** (law) misdemeanor
**deludir** *tr* to delude
**demacra·do -da** *adj* emaciated, wasted, thin
**demago·go -ga** *mf* demagogue
**demanda** *f* demand, petition; charity box; lawsuit; undertaking; (*del Santo Grial*) quest; **en demanda de** in search of; **tener demanda** to be in demand
**demanda·do -da** *mf* (law) defendant
**demandante** *mf* (law) complainant, plaintiff
**demandar** *tr* to ask for, request; (law) to sue || *intr* (law) to sue, bring suit
**demarcar** **§73** *tr* to demarcate
**demás** *adj* — **el demás . . .** the other . . . , the rest of the . . .; **estar demás** to be useless, to be in the way; **lo demás** the rest; **por lo demás** furthermore, besides || *pron* others; **los demás** the others, the rest || *adv* besides; **por demás** in vain; too, too much
**demasía** *f* excess, surplus; daring, boldness; evil, guilt, wrong; insolence; **en demasía** excessively, too much
**demasia·do -da** *adj & pron* too much; **demasia·dos -das** too many || **demasiado** *adv* too, too much, too hard
**demasiar** **§77** *intr* (coll) to go too far
**demediar** *tr* to divide in half; to use up half of; to reach the middle of || *intr* to be divided in half
**demente** *adj* insane || *mf* lunatic
**democracia** *f* democracy
**demócrata** *mf* democrat
**democráti·co -ca** *adj* democratic
**demoler** **§47** *tr* to demolish
**demolición** *f* demolition
**demonía·co -ca** *adj* demoniacal
**demonio** *m* demon, devil; **estudiar con el demonio** (coll) to be full of devilishness
**demora** *f* delay
**demorar** *tr & ref* to delay
**demostración** *f* demonstration
**demostra·dor -dora** *mf* demonstrator || *m* hand (*of clock*)
**demostrar** **§61** *tr* to demonstrate
**demostrati·vo -va** *adj* demonstrative
**demudar** *tr* to change, alter; to disguise, cloak || *ref* to change countenance, to color
**denegación** *f* denial, refusal
**denegar** **§66** *tr* to deny, to refuse
**denegrecer** **§22** *tr* to blacken || *ref* to turn black
**dengo·so -sa** *adj* affected, finicky, overnice; (Col) strutting
**dengue** *m* affectation, finickiness, overniceness; (Col) strut, swagger
**denguear** *ref* (Col) to strut, swagger
**denigrar** *tr* to defame, revile; to insult
**denominación** *f* denomination
**denoda·do -da** *adj* bold, daring
**denostar** **§61** *tr* to abuse, insult, mistreat
**denotar** *tr* to denote
**densidad** *f* density; darkness, confusion
**den·so -sa** *adj* dense; dark, confused; crowded, thick, close
**denta·do -da** *adj* toothed; (*sello de correo*) perforated || *m* gear; teeth
**dentadura** *f* set of teeth; **dentadura artificial** or **postiza** denture
**dental** *adj & f* dental
**dentellada** *f* bite; tooth mark
**dentellar** *intr* (*los dientes*) to chatter
**dentellear** *tr* to nibble, nibble at
**dentera** *f* (coll) envy; (coll) eagerness;

**dar dentera** to set the teeth on edge; to make the mouth water
**dentición** *f* teething
**dentífri•co -ca** *adj* (*pasta, polvos*) tooth || *m* dentifrice
**dentista** *mf* dentist
**dentistería** *f* dentistry
**dentística** *f* (Chile) dentistry
**dentro** *adv* inside, within; **dentro de** inside, within; **dentro de poco** shortly; **por dentro** on the inside
**denuedo** *m* bravery, courage, daring
**denuesto** *m* abuse, insult, mistreatment
**denuncia** *f* denunciation; report; proclamation
**denunciar** *tr* to denounce; to report; (*la guerra*) to proclaim
**deparar** *tr* to furnish, provide; to offer, present
**departamento** *m* department; (rr) compartment; (*piso*) (Am) apartment; naval district (*in Spain*)
**departir** *intr* to chat, converse
**depauperación** *f* impoverishment; exhaustion, weakening
**depauperar** *tr* to impoverish; to exhaust, weaken
**dependencia** *f* dependence, dependency; branch, branch office; relationship, friendship; accessory; personnel
**depender** *intr* to depend; **depender de** to depend on; to be attached to, to belong to
**dependienta** *f* female employee, clerk
**dependiente** *adj* dependent; branch || *mf* employee, clerk
**deplorable** *adj* deplorable
**deplorar** *tr* to deplore
**deponer** §54 *tr* to depose; to set aside, remove; (*las armas*) to lay down || *intr* to depose; (*evacuar el vientre*) to have a movement; (CAm, Mex) to vomit
**deportación** *f* deportation
**deporta•do -da** *mf* deportee
**deportar** *tr* to deport
**deporte** *m* sport; outdoor recreation
**deportista** *mf* sport fan || *m* sportsman || *f* sportswoman
**deporti•vo -va** *adj* sport, sports
**depositante** *mf* depositor
**depositar** *tr* to deposit; (*la esperanza, la confianza*) to put, place; (*el equipaje*) to check; (*a una persona en seguro*) to commit; to store || *ref* to deposit, settle
**deposita•rio -ria** *mf* trustee; (*de un secreto*) repository || *m* public treasurer
**depósito** *m* deposit; depot, warehouse; tank, reservoir; (*de libros en una biblioteca*) stack; (mil) depot; **depósito comercial** bonded warehouse; **depósito de agua** reservoir; **depósito de cadáveres** morgue; **depósito de cereales** grain elevator; **depósito de equipajes** (rr) checkroom; **depósito de gasolina** (aut) gas tank; **depósito de locomotoras** roundhouse; **depósito de municiones** munition dump
**depravación** *f* depravity, depravation
**deprava•do -da** *adj* depraved
**depravar** *tr* to deprave || *ref* to become depraved
**deprecar** §73 *tr* to entreat, implore
**depreciación** *f* depreciation
**depreciar** *tr & ref* to depreciate
**depresión** *f* depression; drop, dip; (*en un muro*) recess
**deprimir** *tr* to depress; to press down; to push in; to belittle; to humiliate || *ref* to be depressed; (*la frente de una persona*) to recede
**depurar** *tr* to purify, cleanse; to purge
**derecha** *f* right hand; right-hand side; (pol) right; **a la derecha** on the right, to the right
**derechamente** *adv* rightly; straight, direct; properly; wisely
**derechazo** *m* blow with the right; (box) right
**dereche•ro -ra** *adj* right, just
**derechista** *adj* rightist || *mf* rightist, right-winger
**dere•cho -cha** *adj* right; right-hand; right-handed; straight; upright, standing || *m* right; law; exemption, privilege; road, path; (*de tela, papel, tabla*) right side; **derecho consuetudinario** common law; **derecho de gentes** law of nations, international law; **derecho de subscripción** (*a una nueva emisión de acciones*) (com) right; **derecho de tránsito** or **paso** right of way; **derecho internacional** international law; **derecho penal** criminal law; **derechos** dues, fees, taxes; (*de aduana*) duties; **derechos de almacenaje** storage, cost of storage; **derechos de autor** royalty; **derechos del hombre** rights of man; **derechos de propiedad literaria** or **derechos reservados** copyright; **según derecho** by right, by rights || *f* see **derecha** || **derecho** *adv* straight, direct; rightly
**deriva** (aer, naut) drift; **ir a la deriva** (naut) to drift, to be adrift
**derivado** *m* by-product
**derivar** *tr* to derive || *intr & ref* to derive, be derived; (aer, naut) to drift
**derogar** §44 *tr* to abolish, destroy, repeal
**derrabar** *tr* to dock, cut off the tail of
**derrama•do -da** *adj* extravagant, lavish
**derramamiento** *m* pouring, spilling; shedding; spreading; lavishing, wasting
**derramar** *tr* to pour, to spill; (*sangre*) to shed; to spread, publish abroad; (*dinero*) to lavish, waste || *ref* to run over, overflow; to spread, scatter; (*una corriente, un río*) to open, empty; (*la plumafuente*) to leak
**derrame** *m* pouring, spilling; (*de sangre*) shed, shedding; spread, scattering; lavishing, wasting; overflow; leakage; slope; chamfering; (pathol) discharge, effusion
**derredor** *m* circumference; **al** or **en derredor** around, round about
**derrelicto** *m* (naut) derelict
**derrelinquir** §25 *tr* to abandon, forsake
**derrenga•do -da** *adj* crooked, out of shape; crippled, lame
**derrengar** §44 or §66 *tr* to bend, make crooked; to cripple

**derreniego** *m* (coll) curse
**derreti•do -da** *adj* madly in love; (*mantequilla*) drawn || *m* concrete
**derretimiento** *m* thawing, melting; intense love, passion
**derretir** §50 *tr* to thaw, melt; (*la mantequilla*) to draw; (*la hacienda*) to squander || *ref* to thaw, melt; to fall madly in love; to be quite susceptible; (coll) to be worried, be impatient
**derribar** *tr* to destroy, tear down, knock down; to wreck; (*un árbol*) to fell; to bring down, shoot down; to overthrow; to humiliate || *ref* to fall down, tumble down; to throw oneself on the ground
**derribo** *m* demolition, wrecking; (*de un árbol*) felling; overthrow; (*de un avión enemigo*) bringing down; **derribos** debris, rubble
**derrocadero** *m* rocky precipice
**derrocar** §73 or §81 *tr* to throw or hurl from a height; to ruin, wreck, tear down; to bring down, humble, overthrow
**derrocha•dor -dora** *mf* wastrel, squanderer
**derrochar** *tr* to waste, squander
**derroche** *m* wasting, squandering, extravagance
**derrota** *f* defeat, rout; road, route, way; (*de embarcación*) course
**derrotadamente** *adv* shabbily, poorly
**derrotar** *tr* to rout, put to flight; to wear out; to ruin || *ref* (naut) to drift from the course
**derrotero** *m* course, route; ship's course
**derrotismo** *m* defeatism
**derrotista** *adj* & *mf* defeatist
**derrubiar** *tr* & *ref* to wash away, wear away
**derrubio** *m* washout
**derruir** §20 *tr* to tear down, demolish
**derrumbadero** *m* crag, precipice; hazard, risky business
**derrumbamiento** *m* headlong plunge; cave-in, collapse; **derrumbamiento de tierra** landslide
**derrumbar** *tr* to throw headlong || *ref* to plunge headlong; to collapse, cave in, crumble
**derrumbe** *m* precipice; landslide; cave-in
**derviche** *m* dervish
**desabonar** *ref* to drop one's subscription
**desabono** *m* cancellation of subscription; discredit, disparagement
**desabor** *m* insipidity, tastelessness
**desabotonar** *tr* to unbutton || *intr* to blossom, bloom
**desabri•do -da** *adj* insipid, tasteless; gruff, surly; (*tiempo*) unsettled
**desabrigar** §44 *tr* to uncover, bare || *ref* to bare oneself; to undress
**desabrir** *tr* to give a bad taste to; to displease, to embitter
**desabrochar** *tr* to unclasp, unbutton, unfasten || *ref* (coll) to unbosom oneself
**desacalorar** *ref* to cool off
**desacatamiento** *m* incivility, disrespect
**desacatar** *tr* to treat disrespectfully
**desacato** *m* incivility, disrespect, contempt; (*para con las cosas sagradas*) profanation
**desacelerar** *tr* & *ref* to decelerate
**desacerta•do -da** *adj* mistaken, wrong
**desacertar** §2 *intr* to be mistaken, be wrong
**desacierto** *m* error, mistake, blunder
**desacomoda•do -da** *adj* inconvenient; out of work; in straightened circumstances
**desacomodar** *tr* to inconvenience; to discharge, dismiss
**desacomodo** *m* discharge, dismissal
**desaconseja•do -da** *adj* ill-advised
**desaconsejar** *tr* to dissuade
**desacordar** §61 *tr* to put out of tune || *ref* to get out of tune; to become forgetful
**desacorde** *adj* out of tune; incongruous
**desacostumbra•do -da** *adj* unusual
**desacostumbrar** *tr* to break of a habit
**desacreditar** *tr* to discredit; to disparage
**desacuerdo** *m* discord, disagreement; error, mistake; unconsciousness; forgetfulness
**desadaptación** *f* maladjustment
**desadeudar** *tr* to free of debt || *ref* to get out of debt
**desadormecer** §22 *tr* to awaken; to free of numbness || *ref* to get awake; to shake off the numbness
**desadorna•do -da** *adj* unadorned, plain; bare, uncovered
**desadverti•do -da** *adj* unnoticed; inattentive
**desadvertimiento** *m* inadvertence
**desafección** *f* dislike
**desafec•to -ta** *adj* adverse, hostile; opposed || *m* dislike
**desaferrar** *tr* to unfasten, loosen; to make (*a person*) change his mind; (*las áncoras*) to weigh
**desafiar** §77 *tr* to challenge, defy, dare; to rival, compete with
**desafición** *f* dislike
**desaficionar** *tr* to cause to dislike
**desafilar** *tr* to make dull || *ref* to become dull
**desafina•do -da** *adj* flat, out of tune
**desafío** *m* challenge, dare; rivalry, competition
**desafora•do -da** *adj* colossal, huge; disorderly, outrageous
**desafortuna•do -da** *adj* unfortunate
**desafuero** *m* excess, outrage
**desagracia•do -da** *adj* ungraceful, graceless
**desagradable** *adj* disagreeable
**desagradar** *tr* & *intr* to displease || *ref* to be displeased
**desagradeci•do -da** *adj* ungrateful
**desagradecimiento** *m* ungratefulness
**desagrado** *m* displeasure
**desagraviar** *tr* to make amends to, to indemnify
**desagravio** *m* amends, indemnification
**desagregación** *f* disintegration
**desagregar** §44 *ref* to disintegrate
**desaguadero** *m* drain, outlet; (*ocasión de continuo gasto*) (fig) drain
**desaguar** §10 *tr* to drain, empty; to

squander, waste || *intr* to flow, empty || *ref* to drain, be drained
**desagüe** *m* drainage, sewerage; drain, outlet
**desaguisa•do -da** *adj* illegal || *m* offense, outrage, wrong
**desahijar** *tr* (*las crías del ganado*) to wean || *ref* (*las abejas*) to swarm
**desahogadamente** *adv* freely; comfortably, easily; impudently
**desahoga•do -da** *adj* brazen, forward; roomy; in comfortable circumstances
**desahogar** §44 *tr* to relieve, comfort; (*deseos, pasiones*) to give free rein to || *ref* to take it easy, get comfortable; to unbosom oneself, open up one's heart; to get out of debt; **desahogarse en** (*denuestos*) to burst forth in
**desahogo** *m* brazenness; ample room; comfort; outlet, relief; comfortable circumstances
**desahuciar** *tr* to deprive of hope; to evict, oust, dispossess || *ref* to lose all hope
**desahucio** *m* eviction, ousting, dispossession
**desaira•do -da** *adj* unattractive, unprepossessing; unsuccessful
**desairar** *tr* to slight, snub, disregard
**desaire** *m* slight, snub, disregard; unattractiveness, lack of charm
**desajustar** *tr* to put out of order || *ref* to get out of order; to disagree
**desalabanza** *f* belittling, disparagement
**desalabar** *tr* to belittle, disparage
**desala•do -da** *adj* eager, in a hurry
**desalar** *tr* to desalt; to clip the wings of || *ref* to hasten, rush; **desalarse por** to be eager to
**desalentar** §2 *tr* to put out of breath; to discourage || *ref* to become discouraged
**desalforjar** *ref* to loosen one's clothing
**desaliento** *m* discouragement
**desalinización** *f* desalinization
**desaliña•do -da** *adj* slovenly, untidy; careless, slipshod
**desaliño** *m* slovenliness, untidiness; carelessness, neglect
**desalma•do -da** *adj* cruel, inhuman
**desalojar** *tr* to oust, evict; (*al enemigo*) to dislodge; (*el camino*) to clear || *intr* to leave, move away, move out
**desalquila•do -da** *adj* vacant, unrented
**desalterar** *tr* to calm, quiet
**desalumbra•do -da** *adj* dazzled, blinded; confused, unsure of oneself
**desamable** *adj* unlikeable, unlovable
**desamar** *tr* to dislike, hate, detest
**desamarrar** *tr* to untie, unfasten; (naut) to unmoor
**desamistar** *ref* to fall out, become estranged
**desamor** *m* dislike, coldness; hatred
**desamorrar** *tr* to make (*a person*) talk
**desamparar** *tr* to abandon, forsake; to give up
**desamparo** *m* abandonment, desertion; helplessness
**desamuebla•do -da** *adj* unfurnished
**desandar** §5 *tr* to retrace, go back over
**desandraja•do -da** *adj* ragged, in tatters
**desangrar** *tr* to bleed; to drain; (fig) to bleed, impoverish || *ref* to lose a lot of blood
**desanimación** *f* discouragement, downheartedness
**desanima•do -da** *adj* discouraged, downhearted; (*reunión*) lifeless, dull
**desanimar** *tr* to discourage, dishearten || *ref* to become discouraged
**desánimo** *m* discouragement
**desanublar** *tr & ref* to clear up, brighten up
**desanudar** *tr* to untie; to disentangle
**desapacible** *adj* unpleasant, disagreeable
**desapadrinar** *tr* to disavow; to disapprove
**desaparecer** §22 *intr & ref* to disappear
**desapareci•do -da** *adj* missing; extinct || **desaparecidos** *mpl* missing persons
**desaparecimiento** *m* disappearance
**desaparejar** *tr* to unharness, unhitch; (naut) to unrig
**desaparición** *f* disappearance; (Ven) death
**desapasiona•do -da** *adj* dispassionate, impartial
**desapego** *m* dislike, coolness, indifference
**desapercibi•do -da** *adj* unprepared; wanting; unnoticed
**desapiada•do -da** *adj* merciless, pitiless
**desaplica•do -da** *adj* idle, lazy
**desapodera•do -da** *adj* headlong, impetuous; violent, wild; excessive
**desapoderar** *tr* to dispossess; to deprive of power || *ref* — **desapoderarse de** to lose possession of, give up possession of
**desapolillar** *tr* to free of moths || *ref* (coll) to expose oneself to the weather
**desapreciar** *tr* to depreciate
**desaprecio** *m* depreciation
**desaprender** *tr* to unlearn
**desaprensión** *f* composure, nonchalance
**desapretar** §2 *tr* to slacken, loosen; (typ) to unlock
**desaprobación** *f* disapproval
**desaprobar** §61 *tr & intr* to disapprove
**desapropiar** *tr* to divest || *ref* — **desapropiarse de** to divest oneself of
**desaprovecha•do -da** *adj* unproductive; indifferent, lackadaisical
**desaprovechar** *tr* to not take advantage of || *intr* to slip back
**desarmable** *adj* dismountable
**desarmador** *m* hammer (*of gun*); (Mex) screwdriver
**desarmar** *tr* to disarm; to dismount, dismantle, take apart; (*la cólera*) to temper, calm || *intr & ref* to disarm
**desarme** *m* disarmament; dismantling, dismounting
**desarraigar** §44 *tr* to uproot, dig up; to expel, drive out
**desarregla•do -da** *adj* out of order; slovenly, disorderly; intemperate
**desarrollar** *tr & intr* to develop; to unroll, unfold || *ref* to develop; to unroll, unfold; to take place
**desarrollo** *m* development; unrolling, unfolding
**desarropar** *tr & ref* to undress
**desarrugar** §44 *tr & ref* to unwrinkle

**desarzonar** *tr* to unsaddle, unhorse
**desasea·do -da** *adj* dirty, unclean, slovenly
**desasentar** §2 *tr* to remove; to displease || *ref* to stand up
**desaseo** *m* dirtiness, uncleanliness, slovenliness
**desasir** §7 *tr* to let go, let go of || *ref* to come loose; to let go; **desasirse de** to let go of; to give up, get free of
**desasosegar** §66 *tr* to disquiet, worry, disturb
**desasosiego** *m* disquiet, worry
**desastra·do -da** *adj* disastrous; unfortunate, wretched; ragged, shabby
**desastre** *m* disaster; **ir al desastre** to go to rack and ruin
**desastro·so -sa** *adj* disastrous
**desatacar** §73 *tr* to unbuckle, untie
**desatar** *tr* to untie, undo, unfasten; to solve, unravel || *ref* to come loose; to free oneself; (*la tempestad*) to break loose; to forget oneself, go too far; **desatarse en** (*denuestos*) to burst forth in
**desatascar** §73 *tr* to pull out of the mud; (*un conducto obstruído*) to unclog; (*a una persona de un apuro*) to extricate
**desataviar** §77 *tr* to disarray, undress
**desatavío** *m* disarray, undress, slovenliness
**desate** *m* (*de palabras*) flood; **desate del vientre** loose bowels
**desatención** *f* inattention; discourtesy, disrespect
**desatender** §51 *tr* to slight, disregard, pay no attention to
**desatenta·do -da** *adj* wild, disorderly, extreme
**desaten·to -ta** *adj* inattentive; discourteous, disrespectful
**desatina·do -da** *adj* wild, disorderly; foolish, nonsensical || *mf* fool
**desatinar** *tr* to bewilder, confuse || *intr* to talk nonsense, to act foolishly; to lose one's bearings
**desatino** *m* folly, nonsense; awkwardness, loss of touch
**desatolondrar** *tr* to bring to || *ref* to come to one's senses
**desatollar** *tr* to pull out of the mud
**desatornillar** *tr* to unscrew
**desatraillar** §4 *tr* to unleash
**desatrampar** *tr* to unclog
**desatrancar** §73 *tr* to unbar, unbolt; to unclog
**desatufar** *ref* to get out of the close air; to cool off, quiet down
**desautoriza·do -da** *adj* unauthorized
**desavenencia** *f* disagreement, discord
**desavenir** §79 *tr* to cause disagreement among || *ref* to disagree; **desavenirse con** to differ with, disagree with
**desaventura** *f* misfortune
**desaviar** §77 *tr* to mislead, lead astray
**desayuna·do -da** *adj* — **estar desayunado** to have had breakfast
**desayunar** *intr* to breakfast || *ref* to breakfast; **desayunarse con** to have breakfast on; **desayunarse de** to get the first news of
**desayuno** *m* breakfast
**desazón** *f* insipidity, tastelessness; annoyance, displeasure; discomfort
**desazonar** *tr* to make tasteless; to annoy, displease || *ref* to feel ill
**desbancar** §73 *tr* to win the bank from; to cut out, to supplant
**desbandada** *f* — **a la desbandada** helter-skelter, in confusion
**desbandar** *ref* to run away; to disband; to desert
**desbarajustar** *tr* to put out of order || *ref* to get out of order, break down
**desbarata·do -da** *adj* (coll) debauched, corrupt || *mf* (coll) libertine
**desbaratar** *tr* to destroy, spoil, ruin; to squander, waste; (mil) to rout, throw into confusion || *intr* to talk nonsense || *ref* to be unbalanced
**desbarrancadero** *m* (Am) precipice
**desbastar** *tr* to smooth off; to waste, weaken; (*a una persona inculta*) to polish || *ref* to become polished
**desbautizar** §60 *ref* (coll) to lose one's temper
**desbeber** *intr* (coll) to urinate
**desbloquear** *tr* to relieve the blockade of; (*crédito*) to unfreeze
**desboca·do -da** *adj* (*pieza de artillería*) wide-mouthed; (*herramienta*) nicked; (*caballo*) runaway; (*persona*) (coll) foul-mouthed
**desbocar** §73 *tr* to break the mouth of, break the spout of || *intr* (*un río*) to empty; (*una calle*) to run, open, end || *ref* (*un caballo*) to run away, to break loose; to curse, swear
**desbordamiento** *m* overflow
**desbordar** *tr* to overwhelm || *intr & ref* to overflow
**desbozalar** *tr* to unmuzzle
**desbravar** *tr* to tame, break in || *intr & ref* to abate, moderate; to cool off, calm down
**desbrozar** §60 *tr* to clear of underbrush, to clear of rubbish
**desbulla** *f* oyster shell
**desbulla·dor -dora** *mf* oyster opener || *m* oyster fork
**desbullar** *tr* (*la ostra*) to open
**descabal** *adj* incomplete, imperfect
**descabalgar** §44 *intr* to dismount, alight from a horse
**descabella·do -da** *adj* disheveled; rash, wild
**descabellar** *tr* to muss, dishevel
**descabeza·do -da** *adj* crazy, rash, wild
**descabezar** §60 *tr* to behead; (*un árbol*) to top; (*una dificultad*) (coll) to get the best off; **descabezar el sueño** to doze, snooze || *intr* to border || *ref* to rack one's brains
**descabullir** §13 *ref* to sneak out, slip away; to refuse to face the facts
**descacharra·do -da** *adj* (CAm) dirty, slovenly, ragged
**descaecer** §22 *intr* to decline, lose ground
**descaecimiento** *m* weakness; depression, despondency
**descalabazar** §60 *ref* (coll) to rack one's brain
**descalabra·do -da** *adj* banged on the

head; **salir descalabrado** to come out the loser, to be worsted
**descalabrar** *tr* to bang on the head; to knock down || *ref* to bang one's head
**descalabro** *m* misfortune, setback, loss
**descalificar** §73 *tr* to disqualify
**descalzar** §60 *tr* (*las botas, los guantes*) to take off; (*a una persona*) to take the shoes or stockings off; to undermine || *ref* to take one's shoes or stockings off; to take one's gloves off; (*las botas, los guantes*)to take off; (*el caballo*) to lose a shoe
**descal•zo -za** *adj* barefooted; seedy, down at the heel
**descamar** *ref* to scale, scale off
**descaminadamente** *adv* off the road, on the wrong track
**descaminar** *tr* to mislead, lead astray || *ref* to get lost; to run off the road
**descamino** *m* going astray; leading astray; nonsense; contraband, smuggled goods
**descamisa•do -da** *adj* shirtless, ragged || *m* wretch, ragamuffin
**descampa•do -da** *adj* free, open || *m* open country
**descansadero** *m* resting place, stopping place
**descansa•do -da** *adj* rested, refreshed; calm, restful
**descansar** *tr* to rest, relieve; (*la cabeza, el brazo*) to rest, lean || *intr* to rest; to lean; to not worry; (*yacer en el sepulcro*) to rest; **descansar en** to trust in
**descanso** *m* rest; peace, quiet; (*de la escalera*) landing; (theat) intermission; (Chile) toilet
**descantillar** *tr* to chip off; to deduct
**descañonar** *tr* to pluck; to shave against the grain; (coll) to gyp
**descapiruzar** §60 *tr* (Col) to muss, rumple, crumple
**descapotable** *adj* & *m* (aut) convertible
**descara•do -da** *adj* barefaced, brazen, saucy
**descarar** *ref* to be impudent; **descararse a** to have the nerve to
**descarga** *f* unloading; (*de un arma de fuego*) discharge; (com) discount; (elec) discharge; **descarga de aduana** customhouse clearance
**descargar** §44 *tr* to unload; (*de una deuda u obligación*) to free; (*un arma de fuego*) to discharge; (*un golpe*) to strike, to deal; (elec) to discharge || *intr* to unload; (*un río*) to empty; (*una calle, paseo*) to open; (*una nube en lluvia*) to burst || *ref* to unburden oneself; to resign; **descargarse con** or **en uno de algo** to unload something on someone; **descargarse de** to get rid of; to resign from; (*una imputación, un cargo*) to clear oneself of
**descargo** *m* unloading; (*de una obligación*) discharge; (*del cargo que se hace a uno*) release, acquittal; receipt
**descargue** *m* unloading
**descariño** *m* coolness, indifference
**descarnadamente** *adv* right off the shoulder, bluntly
**descarnar** *tr* to remove the flesh from; to chip; to wear away; to detach from earthly matters || *ref* to lose flesh
**descaro** *m* brazenness, effrontery
**descarriar** §77 *tr* to mislead, to lead astray || *ref* to go wrong, to go astray
**descarrilamiento** *m* derailment
**descarrilar** *intr* to jump the track; (coll) to wander from the point || *ref* to jump the track
**descartable** *adj* disposable
**descartar** *tr* to cast aside, reject; to discard || *ref* to shirk, evade; **descartarse de** (*un compromiso*) to shirk, evade
**descarte** *m* casting aside, rejection; discarding; (*cartas desechadas*) discard; shirking, evasion
**descasar** *tr* to divorce; to disturb, disarrange
**descascar** §73 *tr* to husk, shell, peel || *ref* to break to pieces; to jabber, talk too much
**descascarar** *tr* to shell, peel || *ref* to shell off, peel off
**descascarillar** *tr* & *ref* to shell, peel
**descasta•do -da** *adj* ungrateful, ungrateful to one's family
**descaudala•do -da** *adj* ruined, penniless
**descendencia** *f* descent
**descendente** *adj* descendent, descending; (*tren*) down
**descender** §51 *tr* to bring down, lower; (*la escalera*) to descend, to go down || *intr* to descend, go down; to flow, run; to decline
**descendiente** *mf* descendant
**descenso** *m* descent; (*de temperatura*) drop; decline
**descentralizar** §60 *tr* to decentralize
**desceñi•do -da** *adj* loose-fitting, loose
**descepar** *tr* to pull up by the roots; to extirpate, exterminate
**descerebrar** *tr* to brain
**descerraja•do -da** *adj* (coll) corrupt, evil, wicked
**descifrar** *tr* to decipher, to decode, to figure out
**desclasificar** §73 *tr* to disqualify
**descocer** §16 *tr* to digest
**descoco** *m* (coll) impudence, insolence
**descocholla•do -da** *adj* (Chile) ragged
**descolar** *tr* to dock, crop; (*a un empleado*) (CAm) to discharge, fire; (Mex) to slight, snub
**descolgar** §63 *tr* to unhook; to take down, lower; (*el auricular*) to pick up || *ref* to come down, come off; to show up suddenly; **descolgarse con** (coll) to blurt out
**descolón** *m* (Mex) slight, snub
**descolorar** *tr* & *ref* to discolor, to fade
**descolori•do -da** *adj* faded, off color
**descollante** *adj* prominent, outstanding; chief, main
**descollar** §61 *intr* to tower, stand out; (fig) to excel, stand out
**descomedi•do -da** *adj* immoderate, excessive; rude, discourteous
**descomedir** §50 *ref* to be rude, be discourteous
**descomer** *intr* to have a bowel movement

**descómo•do -da** *adj* inconvenient
**descompasa•do -da** *adj* extreme, excessive
**descompletar** *tr* to break (*a set or series*)
**descomponer** §54 *tr* to decompose; to disturb, disorganize; to put out of order; to set at odds || *ref* to decompose; (*una persona, la salud de una persona*) to fall to pieces; (*el tiempo*) to change for the worse; (*el rostro*) to become distorted; (*un aparato*) to get out of order; to lose one's temper; **descomponerse con** to get angry with
**descomposición** *f* decomposition; disorder, disorganization; discord
**descompostura** *f* decomposition; disorder, untidiness; brazenness
**descompresión** *f* decompression
**descompues•to -ta** *adj* out of order; brazen, discourteous; irritated; (Am) drunk
**descomulgar** §44 *tr* to excommunicate
**descomunal** *adj* huge, colossal, enormous, extraordinary
**desconcerta•do -da** *adj* out of order; disconcerted, baffled, bewildered; slovenly; unbridled
**desconcertar** §2 *tr* to put out of order; to disturb, upset; (*un hueso*) to dislocate; to disconcert, bewilder
**desconcierto** *m* disrepair; disorder; mismanagement; confusion; discomfiture; disagreement; lack of restraint; loose bowels
**desconchabar** *tr* (Am) to dislocate || *ref* (Am) to become dislocated; (Am) to disagree, fall out
**desconchado** *m* scaly part of wall; (*en la porcelana*) chip
**desconchar** *tr & ref* to chip, chip off; to scale off
**desconectar** *tr* to detach; to disconnect
**desconfia•do -da** *adj* distrustful, suspicious
**desconfianza** *f* distrust
**desconfiar** §77 *intr* to lose confidence; **desconfiar de** to lose confidence in, to distrust
**desconformar** *intr* to dissent, disagree || *ref* to not go well together
**descongelar** *tr* to melt; to defrost; (com) to unfreeze
**desconocer** §22 *tr* to not know; to disavow, disown; to not recognize; to slight, ignore; to not see || *ref* to be unknown; to be quite changed, be unrecognizable
**desconocidamente** *adv* unknowingly
**desconoci•do -da** *adj* unknown; strange, unfamiliar; ungrateful || *mf* unknown, unknown person
**desconsentir** §68 *tr* to not consent to
**desconsidera•do -da** *adj* ill-considered; inconsiderate
**desconsola•do -da** *adj* disconsolate, downhearted; (*estómago*) weak
**desconsuelo** *m* disconsolateness, grief; upset stomach
**descontaminación** *f* decontamination
**descontar** §61 *tr* to discount; to deduct; to take for granted; **dar por descontado que** to take for granted that
**descontentadi•zo -za** *adj* hard to please
**desconten•to -ta** *adj & m* discontent
**descontinuar** §21 *tr* to discontinue
**desconvenir** §79 *intr* to disagree; to not go together, to not match; to not be suitable || *ref* to disagree
**desconvidar** *tr* to cancel an invitation to; (*lo prometido*) to take back
**descopar** *tr* to top (*a tree*)
**descorazonar** *tr* to discourage
**descorchar** *tr* to remove the bark from; (*una botella*) to uncork; to break into
**descornar** §61 *tr* to dehorn || *ref* (coll) to rack one's brains
**descorrer** *tr* to run back over; (*una cortina, un cerrojo*) to draw || *intr & ref* to flow, run off
**descortés** *adj* discourteous, impolite
**descortesía** *f* discourtesy, impoliteness
**descortezar** §60 *tr* to strip the bark from; to take the crust off; (coll) to polish || *ref* (coll) to become polished
**descoser** *tr* to unstitch, to rip || *ref* to loose one's tongue; (coll) to break wind
**descosi•do -da** *adj* disorderly, wild; indiscreet; desultory || *m* wild man; rip, open seam
**descote** *m* low neck
**descoyuntar** *tr* to dislocate; to bore, annoy || *ref* (*p.ej., el brazo*) to throw out of joint
**descrédito** *m* discredit
**descreer** §43 *tr* to disbelieve; to discredit || *intr* to disbelieve
**descreí•do -da** *adj* disbelieving, unbelieving || *mf* disbeliever, unbeliever
**descriar** §77 *ref* to spoil; to waste away
**describir** §83 *tr* to describe
**descripción** *f* description
**descripti•vo -va** *adj* descriptive
**descto.** *abbr* **descuento**
**descuadrar** *intr* to disagree; **descuadrar con** (Mex) to displease
**descuajar** *tr* to liquefy, dissolve; to uproot; to discourage || *ref* to liquefy; to drudge
**descuartizar** §60 *tr* to tear to pieces; to quarter
**descubierta** *f* open pie; inspection; reconnoitering; (naut) scanning the horizon; **a la descubierta** openly; in the open; reconnoitering
**descubiertamente** *adv* clearly, openly
**descubier•to -ta** *adj* bareheaded; (*campo*) bare, barren; (*expuesto a reconvenciones*) under fire || *m* deficiency, shortage; exposition of the Holy Sacrament; **al descubierto** in the open; unprotected; (*sin tener disponibles las acciones que se venden*) short, e.g., **vender al descubierto** to sell short || *f* see **descubierta**
**descubri•dor -dora** *mf* discoverer || *m* (mil) scout
**descubrimiento** *m* discovery
**descubrir** §83 *tr* to discover; to uncover, lay open, reveal; to invent; (*p.ej., una estatua*) to unveil || *ref* to take off one's hat, uncover; to be discovered; to open one's heart

**descuello** *m* excellence, superiority; great height; haughtiness
**descuento** *m* discount; deduction, rebate
**descuerar** *tr* (Chile) to skin, flay; (Chile) to discredit, flay
**descuerno** *m* (coll) slight, snub
**descuida•do -da** *adj* careless, negligent; slovenly, dirty; off guard
**descuidar** *tr* to overlook, neglect; to divert, distract, relieve || *ref* to be careless, not bother; to be diverted
**descuide•ro -ra** *mf* sneak thief
**descuido** *m* carelessness, negligence, neglect; slip, mistake, blunder; oversight; **al descuido** with studied carelessness; **en un descuido** (Am) when least expected
**descuita•do -da** *adj* carefree
**desde** *prep* since, from; after; **desde ahora** from now on; **desde entonces** since then, ever since; **desde hace** for, e.g., **estoy aquí desde hace cinco días** I've been here for five days; **desde luego** at once; of course; **desde que** since
**desdecir** §24 *intr* to slip back; to be out of harmony || *ref* — **desdecirse de** to take back, retract
**desdén** *m* scorn, disdain; **al desdén** with studied neglect
**desdenta•do -da** *adj* toothless
**desdeñar** *tr* to scorn, disdain || *ref* to be disdainful; **desdeñarse de** to loathe, despise; to not deign to
**desdeño•so -sa** *adj* scornful, disdainful
**desdicha** *f* misfortune; indigence
**desdicha•do -da** *adj* unfortunate, unlucky; poor, wretched; (coll) backward, timid
**desdinerar** *tr* to impoverish
**desdoblar** *tr & intr* to unfold, spread open; to split, divide
**desdorar** *tr* to remove the gold or gilt from; to tarnish, sully; to disparage
**desdoro** *m* tarnish, blemish, blot; disparagement
**deseable** *adj* desirable
**desear** *tr* to desire, wish
**desecar** §73 *tr & ref* to dry; to drain
**desechable** *adj* disposable
**desechar** *tr* to discard, to throw out, to cast aside; to underrate; to blame, censure; (*la llave de una puerta*) to turn
**desecho** *m* remainder; offal, rubbish; castoff; scorn, contempt; (Am) short cut; **desecho de hierro** scrap iron
**desegregación** *f* desegregation
**desellar** *tr* to unseal
**desembalaje** *m* unpacking
**desembalar** *tr* to unpack
**desembarazar** §60 *tr* to free, clear, empty, open || *ref* to free oneself; to be cleared, be emptied; **desembarazarse de** to get rid of
**desembarazo** *m* naturalness, lack of restraint; (Am) delivery, childbirth; **con desembarazo** naturally, readily
**desembarcadero** *m* wharf, pier, landing
**desembarcar** §73 *tr* to unload, debark, disembark || *intr* to land, debark, disembark; (*de un carruaje*) to get out, alight; (*la escalera al plano bajo*) to end || *ref* to land, debark, disembark
**desembarco** *m* landing, debarkation, disembarkation; (*de la escalera*) landing
**desembarque** *m* unloading, debarkation, disembarkation
**desembocadura** *f* (*de una calle*) opening, outlet; (*de un río*) mouth
**desembocar** §73 *intr* (*una calle*) open, to end; (*un río*) to flow, empty
**desembolsar** *tr* to disburse, pay out
**desembolso** *m* disbursement, payment
**desembragar** §44 *tr* (*el motor*) to disengage || *intr* to throw the clutch out
**desembrague** *m* disengagement, clutch release
**desembravecer** §22 *tr* to tame; to calm, quiet, pacify
**desembriagar** §44 *tr & ref* to sober up
**desembrollar** *tr* to untangle, unravel
**desemejante** *adj* — **desemejante de** dissimilar from or to, unlike; **desemejantes** dissimilar, unlike
**desemejar** *tr* to change, disfigure || *intr* to be different, not look alike
**desempacar** §73 *tr* to unpack, unwrap || *ref* to cool off, calm down
**desempalagar** §44 *tr* to rid of nausea || *ref* to get rid of nausea
**desempañar** *tr* (*el vidrio*) to wipe the steam or smear from; to take the diaper off
**desempapelar** *tr* to unwrap; (*una pared, una habitación*) to scrape the wallpaper from
**desempaquetar** *tr* to unpack; to unwrap
**desempatar** *tr* to break the tie between; (*los votos*) to break the tie in
**desempate** *m* breaking a tie
**desempedrar** §2 *tr* to remove the paving stones from; (*un sitio empedrado*) (coll) to pound; **ir desempedrando la calle** (coll) to dash down the street
**desempeñar** *tr* (*un papel*) to play (*a rôle*); (*un cargo*) to fill, perform; (*a uno de un empeño*) to disengage; (*un deber*) to discharge; to free of debt; to take out of hock || *ref* to get out of a jam; to get out of debt
**desempeño** *m* acting, performance; disengagement; (*de un deber*) discharge; payment of a debt; taking out of hock
**desempernar** *tr* to unbolt
**desemplea•do -da** *adj & mf* unemployed
**desempleo** *m* unemployment
**desempolvar** *tr* to dust; to renew, take up again || *ref* to brush up
**desempolvorar** *tr* to dust, dust off
**desencadenar** *tr* to unchain, unleash || *ref* to break loose
**desencajar** *tr* to dislocate; to disconnect || *ref* to get out of joint; (*el rostro*) to be contorted
**desencaminar** *tr* to lead astray, mislead
**desencantamiento** *m* disenchantment, disillusion
**desencantar** *tr* to disenchant, disillusion
**desencantarar** *tr* (*nombres o números*) to draw; (*un nombre o nombres*) to exclude from balloting

**desencanto** *m* disenchantment, disillusion
**desencarecer** §22 *tr* to lower the price of || *intr & ref* to come down in price
**desencerrar** §2 *tr* to release, set free; to disclose, reveal
**desencoger** §17 *tr* to unfold, spread out || *ref* to relax, shake off one's timidity
**desencolar** *tr* to unglue || *ref* to become unglued
**desenconar** *tr* to take the soreness out of; to calm down
**desenchufar** *tr* to unplug, to disconnect
**desendiosar** *tr* to bring down a peg
**desenfadaderas** *fpl* — **tener buenas desenfadaderas** (coll) to be resourceful
**desenfada•do -da** *adj* free, easy, unconstrained
**desenfado** *m* ease, naturalness; relaxation, calmness
**desenfoca•do -da** *adj* out of focus
**desenfrena•do -da** *adj* unbridled, wanton, licentious
**desenfrenar** *tr* to unbridle || *ref* to yield to temptation; to fly into a passion; (*la tempestad, el viento*) to break loose
**desenfreno** *m* unruliness, wantonness, licentiousness
**desenfundar** *tr* to take out of its sheath, bag, pillowcase, etc.
**desenganchar** *tr* to unhook, uncouple, unfasten, disengage; to unhitch
**desenganche** *m* unhooking, disengaging; unhitching
**desengañar** *tr* to disabuse, undeceive; to disillusion; to disappoint
**desengaño** *m* disabusing; disillusionment; disappointment; plain fact, plain truth
**desengrana•do -da** *adj* out of gear
**desengranar** *tr* to unmesh; to disengage, throw out of gear
**desengraso** *m* (Chile) dessert
**desenlace** *m* outcome, result; (*de un drama, novela, etc.*) dénouement
**desenlazar** §60 *tr* to untie; to solve; (*el nudo de un drama*) to unravel
**desenmarañar** *tr* to disentangle; (*una cosa obscura*) to unravel
**desenmascarar** *tr* to unmask || *ref* to take one's mask off
**desenojar** *tr* to appease, to free of anger || *ref* to calm down; to be amused
**desenredar** *tr* to disentangle; to clear up || *ref* to extricate oneself
**desenredo** *m* disentanglement; (*de un drama, novela, etc.*) dénouement
**desenrollar** *tr* to unroll, unwind, unreel
**desensartar** *tr* to unstring, unthread
**desensillar** *tr* to unsaddle (*a horse*)
**desentablar** *tr* to disrupt; to break off (*a bargain, friendship, etc.*)
**desentender** §51 *ref* — **desentenderse de** to take no part in, to not participate in; to affect ignorance of, pretend to be unaware of
**desenterrar** §2 *tr* to dig up; to disinter; (fig) to unearth, dig up; (fig) to recall to mind
**desentona•do -da** *adj* out of tune, flat
**desentonar** *tr* to humble, bring down a peg || *intr* to be out of tune; to be out of harmony || *ref* to talk loud and disrespectfully
**desentono** *m* dissonance, false note; loud tone of voice
**desentornillar** *tr* to unscrew
**desentrampar** *ref* (coll) to get out of debt
**desentrañar** *tr* to disembowel; to figure out, unravel || *ref* to give away all that one has
**desentrena•do -da** *adj* out of training
**desentronizar** §60 *tr* to dethrone; to strip of influence
**desentumecer** §22 *tr* to relieve of numbness || *ref* to be relieved of numbness
**desenvainar** *tr* to unsheathe; (*las uñas el animal*) to show, stretch out; (coll) to bare, uncover, show
**desenvoltura** *f* naturalness, ease of manner, offhandedness; fluency; lewdness, boldness (*chiefly in women*)
**desenvolver** §47 & §83 *tr* to unfold, unroll, unwrap; to unwind; to unravel, clear up; to develop || *ref* to unroll; to unwind; to develop, evolve; to extricate oneself; to be forward
**desenvuel•to -ta** *adj* free and easy, offhand; fluent; brazen, bold, lewd
**deseo** *m* desire, wish
**deseo•so -sa** *adj* desirous, anxious
**desequilibra•do -da** *adj* unbalanced
**desequilibrar** *tr* to unbalance || *ref* to become unbalanced
**desequilibrio** *m* disequilibrium, imbalance; derangement, mental instability
**deserción** *f* desertion
**desertar** *tr & intr* to desert
**desertor** *m* deserter
**deservicio** *m* disservice
**desesperación** *f* despair; **ser una desesperación** to be unbearable
**desespera•do -da** *adj* despairing, desperate || *mf* desperate person
**desesperanza** *f* hopelessness
**desesperanza•do -da** *adj* hopeless
**desesperanzar** §60 *tr* to discourage || *ref* to lose hope
**desesperar** *tr* to drive to despair; (coll) to exasperate || *intr* to lose hope; (coll) to be exasperated || *ref* to be desperate, lose all hope
**desestancar** §73 *tr* to open up, to unclog; to make free of duty; to open the market to
**desestimar** *tr* to hold in low regard; to refuse, reject
**deséxito** *m* failure
**desfachata•do -da** *adj* (coll) brazen, impudent
**desfachatez** *f* (coll) brazenness, impudence
**desfalcar** §73 *tr & intr* to embezzle
**desfalco** *m* embezzlement
**desfallecer** §22 *tr* to weaken || *intr* to grow weak; to faint, faint away; to lose courage
**desfalleci•do -da** *adj* weak; faint
**desfallecimiento** *m* weakness; fainting; discouragement
**desfavorable** *adj* unfavorable
**desfigurar** *tr* to disfigure; to distort,

misrepresent; to disguise; to change, alter || *ref* to look different
**desfiladero** *m* defile, pass
**desfilar** *intr* to defile, parade, file by
**desfile** *m* review, parade
**desflorar** *tr* to deflower; to mention in passing
**desfogar** §44 *tr* (*un horno*) to vent; (*la cal*) to slake; (*una pasión*) to give free rein to || *intr* (*una tempestad*) to break into rain and wind || *ref* to give vent to one's anger
**desfondar** *tr* to stave in; (*una nave*) to bilge; (agr) to trench-plow
**desforestar** *tr* to deforest
**desgaire** *m* slovenliness; disdain, scorn; **al desgaire** scornfully; carelessly, with affected carelessness
**desgajar** *tr* to tear off; to split off || *ref* to come off, to come loose; to arise, originate; to separate, break away
**desgana** *f* lack of appetite; indifference; boredom; **a desgana** unwillingly, reluctantly
**desgarba•do -da** *adj* ungainly, uncouth
**desgarrar** *tr* to tear, rend; (*la flema*) to cough up || *ref* to tear oneself away
**desgarro** *m* tear, rent; brazenness, effrontery; boasting, bragging; (Chile, Col) phlegm, mucus
**desgastar** *tr* to wear away, wear down; to weaken, spoil || *ref* to wear away; to grow weak, decline
**desgaste** *m* wear, wearing away
**desgoberna•do -da** *adj* ungovernable, uncontrollable
**desgobernar** §2 *tr* to misgovern; (*un hueso*) to dislocate || *intr* (naut) to steer poorly || *ref* to twist and turn in dancing
**desgobierno** *m* misgovernment; dislocation
**desgonzar** §60 *tr* to unhinge; to disconnect
**desgracia** *f* misfortune; (*acontecimiento adverso*) mishap; (*pérdida de favor*) disfavor, disgrace; (*aspereza en el trato*) gruffness; (*falta de gracia*) lack of charm; **correr con desgracia** to have no luck; **por desgracia** unfortunately
**desgracia•do -da** *adj* unfortunate; unattractive, unpleasant; disagreeable || *mf* wretch, unfortunate
**desgraciar** *tr* to displease; to spoil || *ref* to spoil; to fail; to fall out, to disagree
**desgranar** *tr* (*el maíz*) to shell; (*un racimo*) to pick the grapes from || *ref* (*piezas ensartadas*) to come loose
**desgreñar** *tr* to dishevel || *ref* to get disheveled; to pull each other's hair
**deshabita•do -da** *adj* unoccupied
**deshabituar** §21 *tr* to break of a habit
**deshacer** §39 *tr* to undo; to untie; to take apart; to wear away, consume, destroy; to melt; to put to flight, to rout; (*un tratado o negocio*) to violate || *ref* to get out of order; to vanish, disappear; **deshacerse de** to get rid of; **deshacerse en** (*cumplidos*) to lavish; (*lágrimas*) to burst into; **deshacerse por** to strive hard to
**desharrapa•do -da** *adj* ragged, in rags
**deshebillar** *tr* to unbuckle
**deshebrar** *tr* to unravel, unthread
**deshecha** *f* sham, pretense; dismissal; **hacer la deshecha** to feign, pretend; (Mex) to pretend lack of interest
**deshelar** §2 *tr* to thaw, melt; to defrost; (aer) to deice || *intr* to thaw, melt
**deshereda•do -da** *adj* disinherited; underprivileged
**desheredar** *tr* to disinherit || *ref* to be a disgrace to one's family
**desherrar** §2 *tr* to unchain, unshackle; (*a una caballería*) to unshoe
**desherrumbrar** *tr* to remove the rust from
**deshidratar** *tr* to dehydrate
**deshielo** *m* thaw, melting; defrosting
**deshilachar** *ref* to fray
**deshila•do -da** *adj* in a file; **a la deshilada** in single file; secretly || *m* openwork, drawn work
**deshilar** *tr* to unweave; (*reducir a hilos*) to shred || *ref* to fray; to get thin
**deshilvana•do -da** *adj* disconnected, desultory
**deshincar** §73 *tr* to pull up, to pull out
**deshinchar** *tr* to deflate; (*la cólera*) to give vent to || *ref* (*un tumor*) to go down; (*una persona orgullosa*) (coll) to become deflated
**deshojar** *tr* to strip of leaves; to tear the pages out of || *ref* to lose the leaves
**deshollejar** *tr* (*la uva*) to peel, skin; (*las habichuelas*) to shell
**deshollina•dor -dora** *mf* chimney sweep; (coll) curious observer || *m* long-handled brush or broom
**deshones•to -ta** *adj* immodest, indecent; improper
**deshonor** *m* dishonor; disgrace
**deshonorar** *tr* to dishonor; to degrade; to disfigure
**deshonra** *f* dishonor; disrespect; **tener a deshonra** to consider improper
**deshonrabue•nos** *mf* (*pl* **-nos**) (coll) slanderer; (coll) black sheep
**deshonrar** *tr* to disgrace; (*a una mujer*) to seduce; to insult
**deshonro•so -sa** *adj* disgraceful, improper, discreditable
**deshora** *f* wrong time; **a deshora** at the wrong time, inopportunely; suddenly, unexpectedly
**deshuesar** *tr* (*la carne de un animal*) to bone; (*la fruta*) to stone, to take the pits out of
**deshumedecer** §22 *tr* to dehumidify
**desidia** *f* laziness, indolence
**desidio•so -sa** *adj* lazy, indolent || *mf* lazy person
**desier•to -ta** *adj* desert; deserted || *m* desert; wilderness
**designar** *tr* to designate; (*un trabajo*) to plan
**designio** *m* design, plan, scheme
**desigual** *adj* unequal; unlike; rough, uneven; difficult; inconstant
**desigualar** *tr* to make unequal || *ref* to become unequal; (*aventajarse*) to get ahead

**desigualdad** *f* inequality; roughness, unevenness
**desilusión** *f* disillusionment; disappointment
**desilusionar** *tr* to disillusion; to disappoint || *ref* to become disillusioned; to be disappointed
**desimanar** or **desimantar** *tr* to demagnetize
**desimpresionar** *tr* to undeceive
**desinclina•do -da** *adj* disinclined
**desinencia** *f* (gram) termination, ending
**desinfectante** *adj & m* disinfectant
**desinfectar** or **desinficionar** *tr* to disinfect
**desinflación** *f* deflation
**desinflamar** *tr* to take the soreness out of
**desinflar** *tr* to deflate; to let the air out of; (*a una persona*) (coll) to deflate
**desintegración** *f* disintegration
**desintegrar** *tr & ref* to disintegrate
**desinterés** *m* disinterestedness
**desinteresa•do -da** *adj* (*imparcial*) disinterested; (*poco interesado*) uninterested
**desinteresar** *ref* to lose interest
**desintonizar §60** *tr* (rad) to tune out; (rad) to put out of tune
**desistir** *intr* to desist
**desjarretar** *tr* to hamstring; (coll) to bleed to excess
**desjuicia•do -da** *adj* lacking judgment, senseless
**desjuntar** *tr* to disjoin, separate
**deslabonar** *tr* to unlink; to disconnect || *ref* to come loose; to withdraw
**deslastrar** *tr* to unballast
**deslava•do -da** *adj* faded, colorless; barefaced || *mf* barefaced person
**deslavar** *tr* to wash superficially; to fade, to take the life out of
**desleal** *adj* disloyal; unfair
**deslealtad** *f* disloyalty
**deslechar** *tr* (Col) to milk
**desleír §58** *tr* to dissolve; to dilute; (*los colores, la pintura*) to thin; (*sus pensamientos*) to express too diffusely || *ref* to dissolve; to become diluted
**deslengua•do -da** *adj* foul-mouthed, shameless
**desliar §77** *tr* to untie, undo; to unravel || *ref* to come untied
**desligar §44** *tr* to untie, unbind; to disentangle; to excuse || *ref* to come untied, come loose
**deslindar** *tr* to mark the boundaries of; to distinguish; to define, explain
**des•liz** *m* (*pl* **-lices**) sliding; (*superficie lisa*) slide; slip, blunder; peccadillo, indiscretion
**deslizade•ro -ra** *adj* slippery || *m* slippery place; launching way
**deslizadi•zo -za** *adj* slippery
**deslizador** *m* (aer) glider
**deslizar §60** *tr* to slide; (*decir por descuido*) to let slip || *intr* to slide; to slip; to glide || *ref* to slide; to slip; to glide; to slip away, sneak away; (*un reparo*) to slip out; (*caer en una flaqueza*) to slide back, to backslide
**deslomar** *tr* to break or strain the back of || *ref* to break or strain one's back; **no deslomarse** (coll) to not strain oneself
**deslucí•do -da** *adj* quiet, lackluster; dull, undistinguished
**deslucir §45** *tr* to tarnish; to deprive of charm, deprive of distinction; to discredit
**deslumbramiento** *m* dazzle, glare; bewilderment, confusion
**deslumbrante** *adj* dazzling; bewildering, confusing
**deslumbrar** *tr* to dazzle; to bewilder, confuse
**deslustra•do -da** *adj* dull, flat, dingy; (*vidrio*) ground, frosted
**deslustrar** *tr* to tarnish; to dull, dim; (*el vidrio*) to frost; to discredit || *ref* to tarnish
**deslustre** *m* tarnishing; dulling, dimming; discredit; (*del vidrio*) frosting
**deslustro•so -sa** *adj* ugly, unbecoming
**desmadejar** *tr* to enervate, weaken
**desmagnetizar §60** *tr* to demagnetize
**desmán** *m* excess, misconduct; misfortune, mishap
**desmanchar** *tr* (Chile) to clean of spots
**desmanda•do -da** *adj* disobedient, unruly
**desmandar** *tr* to cancel, countermand || *ref* to misbehave; to go away, keep apart; to get out of control
**desmanear** *tr* to unfetter, unshackle
**desmantela•do -da** *adj* dilapidated
**desmantelar** *tr* to dismantle; (naut) to unmast; (naut) to unrig
**desmaña** *f* awkwardness, clumsiness
**desmaña•do -da** *adj* awkward, clumsy
**desmaya•do -da** *adj* faint, languid, weak; unconscious; (*color*) dull
**desmayar** *tr* to depress, discourage || *intr* to lose heart, be discouraged; to falter || *ref* to faint
**desmayo** *m* depression, discouragement; faint, fainting fit; weeping willow
**desmedi•do -da** *adj* excessive; boundless, limitless
**desmedir §50** *ref* to go too far, be impudent
**desmedra•do -da** *adj* weak, run-down
**desmedrar** *tr* to impair || *intr & ref* to decline, deteriorate
**desmejorar** *tr* to impair, spoil || *intr & ref* to decline, go into a decline
**desmelenar** *tr* to muss, dishevel, rumple
**desmembrar §2** *tr* to dismember
**desmemoria** *f* forgetfulness
**desmemoria•do -da** *adj* forgetful
**desmemoriar** *ref* to become forgetful
**desmentida** *f* contradiction; **dar una desmentida a** to give the lie to
**desmentir §68** *tr* to belie, give the lie to; to conceal || *intr* to be out of line || *ref* to contradict oneself
**desmenudear** *tr & intr* (Col) to sell at retail
**desmenuzar §60** *tr* to crumble; to chop up; to examine in detail; to criticize harshly || *ref* to crumb, crumble
**desmerece•dor -dora** *adj* unworthy
**desmerecer §22** *tr* to be unworthy of || *intr* to decline in value; **desmerecer de** to compare unfavorably with
**desmesura** *f* excess, lack of restraint

**desmesura·do -da** *adj* excessive, disproportionate; insolent || *mf* insolent person
**desmigajar** *tr & ref* to crumble, break up
**desmigar** §44 *tr & ref* to crumble, crumb
**desmilitarizar** §60 *tr* to demilitarize
**desmirria·do -da** *adj* (coll) exhausted, emaciated, run-down
**desmochar** *tr* (*un árbol*) to top; (*al toro*) to dehorn; (*una obra artística*) to cut
**desmodular** *tr* to demodulate
**desmola·do -da** *adj* toothless
**desmontable** *adj* demountable
**desmontar** *tr* (*un terreno*) to level; (*un bosque*) to clear; to dismantle, dismount, take apart, knock down; (*las piezas de artillería del enemigo*) to knock out; (*al jinete el caballo*) to unhorse, to throw; (*un arma de fuego*) to uncock || *ref* to dismount, alight
**desmoralizar** §60 *tr* to demoralize
**desmoronadi·zo -za** *adj* crumbly
**desmoronar** *tr* to wear away || *ref* to wear away; to crumble, decline
**desmotadera** *f* burler; **desmotadera de algodón** cotton gin
**desmotar** *tr* (*la lana*) to burl; (*el algodón*) to gin
**desmovilizar** §60 *tr* to demobilize
**desmurador** *m* mouser
**desnatadora** *f* cream separator
**desnatar** *tr* to skim; to remove the slag from; to take the choicest part of
**desnaturalizar** §60 *tr* to denaturalize; (*el alcohol*) to denature; to alter, pervert
**desnivel** *m* unevenness; difference of level
**desnivelar** *tr* to make uneven || *ref* to become uneven
**desnudar** *tr* to undress; to strip, lay bare; (*la espada*) to draw || *ref* to undress, get undressed; to become evident; **desnudarse de** to get rid of
**desnudez** *f* nakedness; bareness
**desnu·do -da** *adj* naked, nude; bare; destitute, penniless || **el desnudo** the nude
**desnutrición** *f* undernourishment, malnutrition
**desnutri·do -da** *adj* undernourished
**desobedecer** *tr & intr* to disobey
**desobediencia** *f* disobedience
**desobediente** *adj* disobedient
**desocupación** *f* unemployment; idleness, leisure
**desocupa·do -da** *adj* unemployed; idle; free, unoccupied, vacant, empty || *mf* unemployed person
**desocupar** *tr* to empty, vacate || *intr* (*una mujer*) (coll) to be delivered || *ref* to become empty, vacated; to become unemployed, become idle
**desodorante** *adj & m* deodorant
**desodorizar** §60 *tr* to deodorize
**desoír** §48 *tr* to not hear, to pretend not to hear
**desolación** *f* desolation
**desola·do -da** *adj* desolate, disconsolate
**desolar** §61 *tr* to desolate, lay waste || *ref* to be desolate, be disconsolate
**desoldar** §61 *tr* to unsolder || *ref* to come unsoldered
**desolla·do -da** *adj* (coll) brazen, impudent
**desollar** §61 *tr* to skin, flay; to harm, hurt; **desollar vivo** (*hacer pagar mucho más de lo justo*) (coll) to fleece, to skin alive; (*murmurar acerbamente de*) (coll) to flay
**desopilar** *ref* to roar with laughter
**desopinar** *tr* to defame, discredit
**desorbita·do -da** *adj* (Am) popeyed; (Am) crazy
**desorbitar** *ref* to pop wide-open
**desorden** *m* disorder
**desordena·do -da** *adj* disorderly, unruly
**desordenar** *tr* to put out of order || *ref* to get out of order; to be unruly; to go too far
**desoreja·do -da** *adj* (coll) infamous, degraded; (*que canta mal*) (Peru) off tune; (Cuba) shameless; (Cuba) spendthrift, prodigal; (Guat) stupid; (Chile) without handles
**desorganizar** §60 *tr* to disorganize
**desorientar** *tr* to lead astray; to confuse
**desovar** *intr* to spawn
**desove** *m* spawning; spawning season
**desovillar** *tr* to unravel, disentangle; to encourage
**desoxidar** *tr* to deoxidize; to clean of rust
**despabiladeras** *fpl* snuffers
**despabila·do -da** *adj* wide-awake
**despabilar** *tr* (*una candela*) to snuff, to trim; (*la hacienda*) to dissipate; (*una comida*) to dispatch; (*robar*) to snitch; (*matar*) to dispatch || *ref* to brighten up; to wake up; (Am) to leave, disappear
**despacio** *adv* slow, slowly; at leisure; (Arg, Chile) in a low voice
**despacio·so -sa** *adj* slow, easy-going
**despachaderas** *fpl* (coll) surly reply; (coll) resourcefulness
**despacha·do -da** *adj* (coll) brazen, impudent; (coll) quick, resourceful
**despachante** *m* (Arg) clerk; **despachante de aduana** (Arg) customhouse broker
**despachar** *tr* to send, to ship; to dispatch, expedite; to discharge, dismiss; to decide, settle; to sell; (*a los parroquianos*) to wait on; (*la correspondencia*) to attend to; to hurry; (*matar*) (coll) to dispatch, to kill || *intr* to hurry; to make up one's mind; to work, be employed || *ref* to hurry; (*una mujer*) to be delivered; to speak out
**despacho** *m* shipping; dispatch, expedition; discharge, dismissal; (*tienda*) store, shop; (*aposento para el estudio*) study; (*aposento para los negocios*) office; (*comunicación por telégrafo o teléfono*) dispatch; (Chile) attic; **despacho de billetes** ticket office; **despacho de localidades** box office; **estar al despacho** to be pending; **tener buen despacho** to be expeditious

**despachurrar** *tr* to crush, smash, squash; (*dejar sin tener que replicar*) (coll) to squelch; (*lo que uno trata de decir*) (coll) to butcher, murder
**despampanante** *adj* (coll) stunning, terrific
**despampanar** *tr* (*las vides*) to prune, to trim; (coll) to astound || *intr* (coll) to give vent to one's feelings || *ref* to fall and hurt oneself
**despancar** **§73** *tr* to husk (*corn*)
**desparejar** *tr* (*dos cosas que forman pareja*) to break, separate (*a pair*)
**desparpajar** *tr* to tear apart || *intr* (coll) to rant, rave || *ref* (coll) to rant, rave; (CAm, Mex, W-I) to wake up
**desparramar** *tr* to scatter, spread; (*el agua*) to spill; (*la hacienda*) to squander || *ref* to scatter, spread; to make merry
**despartir** *tr* to divide, part, separate; to reconcile
**despatarrada** *f* (coll) split (*in dancing*); **hacer la despatarrada** (coll) to stretch out on the floor pretending to be ill or injured
**despatarrar** *tr* to dumbfound || *ref* (coll) to open one's legs wide, to fall down with legs outspread; (coll) to lie motionless; to be dumbfounded
**despavori•do -da** *adj* terrified
**despea•do -da** *adj* footsore
**despear** *ref* to get sore feet
**despecti•vo -va** *adj* contemptuous; (gram) pejorative
**despecha•do -da** *adj* spiteful, enraged
**despechar** *tr* to spite, enrage; (*destetar*) (coll) to wean || *ref* to be enraged; to despair, lose hope
**despecho** *m* spite; despair; (Am) weaning; **a despecho de** despite, in spite of; **por despecho** out of spite
**despechugar** **§44** *tr* to carve the breast of || *ref* (coll) to go with bare breast, to bare one's breast
**despedazar** **§60** *tr* to break to pieces; (*la honra de uno*) to ruin; (*el alma de una persona*) to break || *ref* to break to pieces; **despedazarse de risa** (coll) to split one's sides laughing
**despedida** *f* farewell, leave-taking; (*de una carta*) close, conclusion; (*copla final*) envoi
**despedir** **§50** *tr* to throw; to emit, send forth; to discharge, dismiss; (*al que sale de la casa*) to see off; (*un mal pensamiento*) to banish; **despedir en la puerta** to see to the door || *ref* to take leave, say good-by; to give up one's job; **despedirse a la francesa** to take French leave; **despedirse de** to take leave of, say good-by to
**despega•do -da** *adj* (coll) gruff, surly
**despegar** **§44** *tr* to loosen, unglue, unseal; to open; to separate, detach || *intr* (aer) to take off || *ref* to come off; **despegarse con** to be unbecoming to
**despego** *m* dislike, indifference
**despegue** *m* (aer) take-off
**despeina•do -da** *adj* unkempt
**despeja•do -da** *adj* (*frente*) wide; (*día, cielo*) clear, cloudless; bright, sprightly; (*en el trato*) unconstrained
**despejar** *tr* to clarify, explain; to free; (*una incógnita*) (math) to find || *ref* to brighten up, cheer up; (*el cielo, el tiempo; una situación dificultosa*) to clear up; (*un borracho*) to sober up
**despejo** *m* ease, naturalness; talent, intelligence, understanding
**despeluzar** **§60** *tr* to muss the hair of; to make the hair of (*a person*) stand on end || *ref* (*el pelo*) to stand on end
**despeluznante** *adj* hair-raising, horrifying
**despellejar** *tr* to skin, flay; (coll) to slander, malign
**despenar** *tr* to console; (coll) to kill; (Chile) to deprive of hope
**despender** *tr* to spend, squander; (*el tiempo*) to waste
**despensa** *f* pantry; food supplies; day's marketing; stewardship; (naut) storeroom
**despensero** *m* butler, steward; (naut) storekeeper
**despeñade•ro -ra** *adj* precipitous || *m* precipice; danger, risk
**despeñadi•zo -za** *adj* precipitous
**despeñar** *tr* to hurl, throw, push || *ref* to hurl oneself, jump; to fall headlong; (*en vicios, pecados, pasiones*) to plunge downward
**despeño** *m* plunge; headlong fall; ruin, failure, collapse; (coll) loose bowels
**despepitar** *tr* to seed, remove the seeds from || *ref* to rush around madly, to go around screaming; **despepitarse por** (coll) to be mad about
**desperdicia•do -da** *adj* wasteful, prodigal || *mf* spendthrift, prodigal
**desperdiciar** *tr* to waste, squander; (*la ocasión de aprovechar una cosa*) to miss, to lose
**desperdicio** *m* waste, squandering; **desperdicios** waste; waste products; by-products; rubbish; **no tener desperdicio** (coll) to be excellent, be useful
**desperdigar** **§44** *tr* to separate, scatter
**desperecer** **§22** *ref* to long eagerly
**desperezar** **§60** *ref* to stretch, to stretch one's arms and legs
**desperfecto** *m* blemish, flaw, imperfection
**desperna•do -da** *adj* footsore, weary
**desperta•dor -dora** *mf* awakener || *m* alarm clock; warning
**despertar** **§2** *tr* to awaken; to arouse, stir || *intr & ref* to awaken, wake up
**despestañar** *tr* to pluck the eyelashes of || *ref* to look hard, strain one's eyes
**despiada•do -da** *adj* cruel, pitiless
**despichar** *tr* to squeeze dry; (Col, Chile) to crush, flatten || *intr* (coll) to croak, die
**despidiente** *m* stick placed between a hanging scaffold and wall; **despidiente de agua** flashing
**despido** *m* layoff, discharge
**despier•to -ta** *adj* wide-awake, alert; **soñar despierto** to daydream
**despilfarra•do -da** *adj* wasteful; ragged || *mf* prodigal; raggedy person

**despilfarrar** *tr* to squander, waste || *ref* (coll) to spend recklessly
**despilfarro** *m* squandering, waste, extravagance; slovenliness
**despintar** *tr* to remove the paint from; to disfigure, distort, spoil; **no despintarle a uno los ojos** to not take one's eyes from a person || *intr* to decline, slip back; **despintar de** to be unworthy of || *ref* to fade, wash off; **no despintársele a uno** (coll) to not fade from one's memory
**despiojar** *tr* to delouse; (coll) to free from poverty
**despique** *m* revenge
**despistar** *tr* to outwit, to throw off the track || *ref* to run off the track, run off the road
**desplacer** *m* displeasure || §22 *tr* to displease
**desplantar** *tr* to uproot; to throw out of plumb || *ref* to get out of plumb; to lose one's upright posture
**desplaya•do -da** *adj* broad, open, wide || *m* (Arg) wide sandy beach
**desplayar** *tr* to widen, spread out || *ref* (*el mar*) to recede from the beach
**desplaza•do -da** *adj* displaced || *mf* displaced person
**desplazar** §60 *tr* (*cierto peso de agua*) to displace; to move, to transport || *ref* to move
**desplegar** §66 *tr* to unfold, spread; to display; to explain; (mil) to deploy || *ref* to unfold, spread out; (mil) to deploy
**despliegue** *m* unfolding, spreading out; display; (mil) deployment
**desplomar** *tr* to throw out of plumb || *ref* to get out of plumb; to collapse, tumble; to fall down in a faint; (*un trono*) to crumble; (aer) to pancake
**desplome** *m* leaning; collapse, tumbling; falling in a faint; downfall; (aer) pancaking
**desplumar** *tr* to pluck; (*dejar sin dinero*) (coll) to fleece || *ref* to molt
**despoblado** *m* wilderness, deserted spot
**despoblar** §61 *tr* to depopulate; to lay waste; to clear, lay bare
**despojar** *tr* to strip, despoil, divest; to dispossess || *ref* to undress; **despojarse de** to divest oneself of; (*ropa*) to take off
**despojo** *m* dispoilment; dispossession; booty, plunder, spoils; prey, victim; **despojos** scraps, leavings; mortal remains; second-hand building materials
**despolarizar** §60 *tr* to depolarize
**despolvar** *tr* to dust
**despolvorear** *tr* to dust, dust off; to scatter
**desportillar** *tr* to chip, nick || *ref* to chip, chip off
**desposa•do -da** *adj* handcuffed; newly married || *mf* newlywed
**desposar** *tr* to marry || *ref* to be betrothed, get engaged; to get married
**desposeer** §43 *tr* to dispossess || *ref* — **desposeerse de** to divest oneself of
**desposorios** *mpl* betrothal, engagement; marriage, nuptials
**déspota** *m* despot
**despóti•co -ca** *adj* despotic
**despotismo** *m* despotism
**despotricar** §73 *intr* & *ref* to rave, rant
**despreciable** *adj* contemptible, despicable
**despreciar** *tr* to scorn, despise; to slight, snub; to overlook, forgive; to reject || *ref* — **despreciarse de** to not deign to
**despreciati•vo -va** *adj* contemptuous, scornful
**desprecio** *m* scorn, contempt; slight, snub
**desprender** *tr* to loosen, unfasten, detach; to emit, give off; (chem) to liberate || *ref* to come loose, to come off; to issue, come forth; **desprenderse de** to give up, part with; to be deduced from
**desprendi•do -da** *adj* generous, disinterested
**desprendimiento** *m* loosening, detachment; emission, liberation; generosity, disinterestedness; landslide; (chem) liberation
**despreocupación** *f* relaxation; impartiality
**despreocupa•do -da** *adj* relaxed, unconcerned; impartial; indifferent
**despreocupante** *adj* relaxing
**despreocupar** *ref* to relax; **despreocuparse de** to forget about, be unconcerned about
**desprestigiar** *tr* to disparage, run down || *ref* to lose caste, lose one's standing, to lose face
**desprestigio** *m* disparagement; loss of standing, discredit
**despreveni•do -da** *adj* off one's guard; **coger a uno desprevenido** to catch someone unawares
**desproporciona•do -da** *adj* disproportionate
**despropósito** *m* absurdity, nonsense
**desproveer** §43 & §83 *tr* to deprive
**desprovis•to -ta** *adj* destitute; **desprovisto de** lacking, devoid of
**después** *adv* after, afterwards; **después de** after; **después (de) que** after
**despuli•do -da** *adj* ground (*glass*)
**despumar** *tr* to skim
**despuntar** *tr* to dull, blunt; (*un cabo o punta*) (naut) to double, round || *intr* to begin to sprout; (*empezar a amanecer*) to dawn; to stand out || *ref* to get dull
**desquiciar** *tr* to unhinge; to shake loose, upset; to unsettle, perturb; to overthrow, undermine
**desquitar** *tr* to recover, retrieve; to compensate || *ref* to retrieve a loss; to get revenge, get even
**desquite** *m* recovery, retrieval; retaliation, revenge; (sport) return match
**desrazonable** *adj* unreasonable
**desrielar** *intr* (Am) to jump the track
**destaca•do -da** *adj* outstanding, distinguished
**destacamiento** *m* (mil) detachment; (mil) detail
**destacar** §73 *tr* to highlight, point up; to emphasize; to make stand out;

(mil) to detach; (mil) to detail || *intr* to stand out, be conspicuous || *ref* to stand out, to project; (fig) to stand out
**destajar** *tr* to arrange for, establish the terms for; (*la baraja*) to cut; (Am) to carve up
**destaje•ro -ra** or **destajista** *mf* pieceworker, jobber; free lance
**destajo** *m* piecework; job, contract; **a destajo** by the piece, by the job; freelancing; **hablar a destajo** (coll) to talk too much
**destapar** *tr* to open, uncover, take the lid off; to uncock, unplug; to reveal || *ref* to get uncovered; to throw off the covers; to unbosom oneself
**destaponar** *tr* to uncock, unplug; (*una botella; las fosas nasales*) to unstop
**destartala•do -da** *adj* tumble-down, ramshackle
**destazar §60** *tr* to carve up
**destechar** *tr* to unroof
**destejar** *tr* to remove the tiles from; to leave unprotected
**destejer** *tr* to unbraid, unknit, unweave; to upset, disturb
**destellar** *tr & intr* to flash
**destello** *m* flash, beam, sparkle
**destempla•do -da** *adj* disagreeable, unpleasant; inharmonious, out of tune; indisposed; (*clima; pulso*) irregular
**destemplanza** *f* unpleasantness; discord; indisposition; (*del pulso*) irregularity; (*del tiempo*) inclemency; excess
**destemple** *m* dissonance; indisposition; disorder, disturbance
**desteñir §72** *tr* to discolor || *intr & ref* to fade
**desternillante** *adj* sidesplitting
**desternillar** *ref* — **desternillarse de risa** to split one's sides with laughter
**desterra•do -da** *adj* exiled || *mf* exile
**desterrar §2** *tr* to exile, to banish; (fig) to banish
**destetar** *tr* to wean || *ref* — **destetarse con** to have known since childhood
**destete** *m* weaning
**destiempo** *m* — **a destiempo** untimely
**destiento** *m* surprise, shock
**destierro** *m* exile; backwoods
**destilación** *f* distillation
**destiladera** *f* still; scheme, stratagem
**destilar** *tr* to distill; to filter; to exude || *intr* to drip
**destilatorio** *m* distillery; (*alambique*) still
**destilería** *f* distillery
**destinación** *f* destination
**destinar** *tr* to destine; to assign, designate
**destinata•rio -ria** *mf* addressee; consignee; (*de homenaje, aplausos*) recipient
**destino** *m* (*lugar a donde va una persona o una remesa*) destination; (*suerte, encadenamiento fatal de los sucesos*) fate, destiny; employment; place of employment; **con destino a** bound for
**destituir §20** *tr* to deprive; to dismiss, discharge
**destorcer §74** *tr* to untwist, straighten || *ref* to become untwisted; (naut) to drift
**destornilla•do -da** *adj* rash, reckless, out of one's head
**destornillador** *m* screwdriver
**destornillar** *tr* to unscrew || *ref* to lose one's head, go berserk
**destoser** *ref* to cough (*artificially, to attract attention*)
**destrabar** *tr* to loosen, untie, detach
**destraillar §4** *tr* to unleash
**destral** *m* hatchet
**destreza** *f* skill, dexterity
**destripacuen•tos** *m* (*pl* **-tos**) (coll) butter-in
**destripar** *tr* to disembowel, to gut; to crush, mangle; (coll) to spoil (*a story by telling its outcome*)
**destripaterro•nes** *m* (*pl* **-nes**) (coll) clodhopper
**destriunfar** *tr* to force to play trump
**destrocar §81** *tr* to swap back again
**destronar** *tr* to dethrone; to overthrow
**destroncar §73** *tr* to chop down; to chop off; to ruin; to exhaust, wear out
**destrozar §60** *tr* to shatter, break to pieces; to destroy; to squander; (*al ejército enemigo*) to wipe out
**destrozo** *m* havoc, destruction; rout, annihilation, defeat
**destrucción** *f* destruction
**destructi•vo -va** *adj* destructive
**destructor** *m* (nav) destroyer
**destruir §20** *tr* to destroy || *ref* (alg) to cancel each other
**desuellaca•ras** *m* (*pl* **-ras**) (coll) sloppy barber; (coll) scoundrel
**desuello** *m* skinning, flaying; shamelessness; (*precio excesivo*) (coll) highway robbery
**desuncir §36** *tr* to unyoke
**desunir** *tr* to disunite; to take apart || *ref* to disunite; to come apart
**desusa•do -da** *adj* obsolete, out of use; uncommon, unusual; **estar desusado** (*perder la práctica*) to be rusty
**desuso** *m* disuse; **caído en desuso** obsolete
**desvaí•do -da** *adj* lank, ungainly; (*color*) dull
**desvainar** *tr* to shell
**desvali•do -da** *adj* helpless, destitute
**desvalijar** *tr* (*una valija, baúl, etc.*) to rifle; to rob, wipe out
**desvalorar** *tr* to devalue
**desvalorizar §60** *tr* to devalue
**desván** *m* garret, loft
**desvanecedor** *m* (phot) mask
**desvanecer §22** *tr* to dispel, dissipate; (*una conspiración*) to break up; (*la sospecha*) to banish; (phot) to mask || *ref* to disappear, vanish, evanesce; to evaporate; to faint, faint away, swoon; (rad) to fade
**desvanecimiento** *m* disappearance, evanescence; dissipation; pride, vanity; faintness, fainting spell; (phot) masking; (rad) fading, fadeout
**desvaria•do -da** *adj* delirious, raving
**desvariar §77** *intr* to be delirious, to rave, to rant
**desvarío** *m* delirium, raving; absurdity,

nonsense, extravagance; whim, caprice; inconstancy
**desvela•do -da** *adj* wakeful, sleepless; watchful, vigilant; anxious, worried
**desvelar** *tr* to keep awake, not let sleep || *ref* to keep awake, go without sleep; to be watchful, be vigilant; **desvelarse por** to be anxious about, be worried about
**desvelo** *m* wakefulness, sleeplessness; watchfulness, vigilance; anxiety, worry, concern
**desvenar** *tr* to strip (*tobacco*)
**desvencija•do -da** *adj* rickety, ramshackle
**desvencijar** *tr* to break, tear apart || *ref* to go to rack and ruin
**desvendar** *tr* to unbandage, to undress
**desventaja** *f* disadvantage
**desventajo•so -sa** *adj* disadvantageous
**desventura** *f* misfortune
**desventura•do -da** *adj* unfortunate; faint-hearted; stingy
**desvergonza•do -da** *adj* shameless, impudent
**desvergüenza** *f* shamelessness, impudence
**desvestir §50** *tr & ref* to undress
**desviación** *f* deviation, deflection; detour; (rad, telv) drift
**desviacionismo** *m* deviationism
**desviacionista** *mf* deviationist
**desviadero** *m* (rr) siding, turnout
**desvia•do -da** *adj* devious
**desviar §77** *tr* to deviate, deflect; to turn aside; to dissuade; to parry, ward off; (rr) to switch || *ref* to deviate, deflect; to turn aside; to branch off; to be dissuaded
**desvío** *m* deviation, deflection; coldness, indifference; detour; (rr) siding, sidetrack
**desvirgar §44** *tr* to deflower, ravish
**desvirtuar §21** *tr* to weaken, spoil, impair
**desvivir** *ref* — **desvivirse por** to be crazy about; **desvivirse por** + *inf* to be eager to + *inf*, to do one's best to + *inf*
**desvolvedor** *m* wrench
**desvolver §47 & §83** *tr* to alter, change; (*la tierra*) to turn up; (*una tuerca o tornillo*) to loosen, unscrew
**detall** *m* — **al detall** at retail
**detalladamente** *adv* in detail
**detallar** *tr* to detail, tell in detail; to retail, sell at retail
**detalle** *m* detail; (Am) retail; **ahí está el detalle** that's the point
**detallista** *mf* retailer; person fond of details
**detección** *f* detection
**detectar** *tr* to detect
**detective** *m* detective
**detector** *m* detector; **detector de mentiras** lie detector
**detención** *f* detention, detainment; delay; care, thoroughness
**detener §71** *tr* to detain; to stop; to arrest; to keep, retain; (*el aliento*) to hold || *ref* to stop; to linger, tarry
**detenidamente** *adv* carefully, thoroughly
**deteni•do -da** *adj* careful, thorough; hesitant, timid; stingy, mean || *mf* person held in custody
**detenimiento** *m* var of **detención**
**detergente** *adj & m* detergent
**deteriorar** *tr & ref* to deteriorate
**deterioro** *m* deterioration
**determinación** *f* determination; decision
**determina•do -da** *adj* determined, resolute; (*artículo*) (gram) definite
**determinar** *tr* to determine; to cause, to bring about || *ref* to decide
**detestar** *tr* to detest; to curse; **detestar** + *inf* to hate to + *inf*
**detonar** *intr* to detonate
**detraer §75** *tr* to withdraw, take away, detract; to defame, vilify
**detrás** *adv* behind; **detrás de** behind, back of; **por detrás** behind; behind one's back; **por detrás de** behind the back of
**detrimento** *m* harm, detriment
**deuda** *f* debt; indebtedness
**deu•do -da** *mf* relative || *m* kinship || *f* see **deuda**
**deu•dor -dora** *adj* indebted || *mf* debtor; **deudor hipotecario** mortgagor; **deudor moroso** delinquent (*in payment*)
**devalar** *intr* (naut) to drift from the course
**devaluación** *f* devaluation
**devanar** *tr* to wind, to roll; (*un cuento*) to unfold || *ref* (CAm, Mex, W-I) to roll with laughter; (CAm, Mex, W-I) to writhe in pain
**devanear** *intr* to talk nonsense; to loaf around
**devaneo** *m* nonsense; loafing; flirtation
**devastación** *f* devastation
**devastar** *tr* to devastate
**develar** *tr* to reveal; (*p.ej., una estatua*) to unveil
**devengar §44** *tr* (*salarios*) to earn; (*intereses*) to draw, to earn
**devoción** *f* devotion
**devolución** *f* return, restitution
**devolver §47 & §83** *tr* to return, give back, send back; to pay back; (coll) to vomit || *ref* (Am) to return, come back
**devorar** *tr* to devour
**devo•to -ta** *adj* devout; devoted; devotional || *mf* devotee; devout person || *m* object of worship
**D.F.** *abbr* **Distrito Federal**
**d/f** *abbr* **días fecha**
**dho.** *abbr* **dicho**
**día** *m* day; daytime; daylight; **al día** per day; up to date; **al otro día** on the following day; **buenos días** good morning; **dar los días a** to wish (*someone*) many happy returns of the day; **de día** in the daytime, in the daylight; **día de años** birthday; **día de ayuno** fast day; **día de carne** meat day; **día de engañabobos** December 28th, day when practical jokes are played on unsuspecting people; **día de inauguración** (fa) private view; **día de la raza** Columbus Day; **día del juicio** judgment day; **día de los caídos** Memorial Day; **día de los difuntos**

All Souls' Day; **día de ramos** Palm Sunday; **día de Reyes** Epiphany; **día de todos los santos** All Saints' Day; **día de trabajo** workday; weekday; **día de vigilia** fast day; **día festivo** holiday; **día laborable** workday, weekday; **día lectivo** school day; **día puente** day off between two holidays; **el día de Año Nuevo** New Year's Day; **el día menos pensado** (coll) when least expected; **el mejor día** some fine day; **en cuatro días** in a few days; **en pleno día** in broad daylight; **en su día** in due time; **ocho días** a week; **poner al día** to bring up to date; **quince días** two weeks, a fortnight; **tener sus días** to be up in years; **un día sí y otro no** every other day; **vivir al día** to live from hand to mouth

**diabetes** *f* diabetes

**diabéti•co -ca** *adj & mf* diabetic

**diablillo** *m* imp

**diablo** *m* devil; (Chile) ox-drawn log drag; **ahí será el diablo** (coll) there will be the devil to pay; **diablo cojuelo** tricky devil; **diablos azules** (Am) delirium tremens

**diablura** *f* devilment, deviltry, mischief

**diabóli•co -ca** *adj* devilish, diabolical

**diaconisa** *f* deaconess

**diácono** *m* deacon

**diacríti•co -ca** *adj* diacritical

**diadema** *f* diadem; (*adorno femenino*) tiara

**diáfa•no -na** *adj* diaphanous

**diafragma** *m* diaphragm

**diagno•sis** *f* (*pl* **-sis**) diagnosis

**diagnosticar** §73 *tr* to diagnose

**diagonal** *adj* diagonal || *f* diagonal, bias

**diagrama** *m* diagram

**dialecto** *m* dialect

**diálogo** *m* dialogue

**diamante** *m* diamond

**diametral** or **diamétri•co -ca** *adj* diametrical

**diámetro** *m* diameter

**diana** *f* bull's-eye; (mil) reveille; **hacer diana** to hit the bull's-eye

**diantre** *m* (coll) devil || *interj* (coll) the devil!, the deuce!

**diapasón** *m* tuning fork; pitch pipe; (*p.ej., del violín*) finger board; **bajar el diapasón** (coll) to lower one's voice, to change one's tune

**diapositiva** *f* slide, lantern slide

**dia•rio -ria** *adj* daily || *m* diary; daily, daily paper; **diario hablado** newscast

**diarismo** *m* (Am) journalism

**diarrea** *f* diarrhea

**diástole** *f* diastole

**diatermia** *f* diathermy

**dibujante** *mf* sketcher, illustrator || *m* draftsman

**dibujar** *tr* to draw, sketch, design; to outline || *ref* to be outlined; to appear, show

**dibujo** *m* drawing, sketch, design; outline; **dibujo al carbón** charcoal drawing; **dibujo animado** animated cartoon; **no meterse en dibujos** (coll) to attend to one's business

**di•caz** *adj* (*pl* **-caces**) sarcastic, witty

**dicción** *f* diction; word

**diccionario** *m* dictionary

**diciembre** *m* December

**dicloruro** *m* dichloride

**dicotomía** *f* dichotomy; (*entre médicos*) split fee

**dictado** *m* dictation; **escribir al dictado** to take dictation; (*lo que otro dicta*) to take down

**dictador** *m* dictator

**dictadura** *f* dictatorship

**dictáfono** *m* dictaphone

**dictamen** *m* dictum, judgment, opinion

**dictar** *tr* to dictate; (*una ley*) to promulgate; to inspire, suggest; (*una conferencia*) (Am) to give, deliver (*a lecture*)

**dicterio** *m* taunt, insult

**dicha** *f* happiness; luck; **por dicha** by chance

**dicharache•ro -ra** *adj* (coll) obscene, vulgar

**dicharacho** *m* (coll) obscenity, vulgarity; (coll) wisecrack

**di•cho -cha** *adj* said; **dicho y hecho** no sooner said than done; **mejor dicho** rather; **tener por dicho** to consider settled || *m* saying; promise of marriage, one's word; witticism; (coll) insult; **dicho de las gentes** (coll) talk, hearsay, gossip || *f* see **dicha**

**dicho•so -sa** *adj* happy; lucky, fortunate; annoying, tiresome

**didácti•co -ca** *adj* didactic

**diecinueve** *adj & pron* nineteen || *m* nineteen; (*en las fechas*) nineteenth

**diecinuevea•vo -va** *adj & m* nineteenth

**dieciocha•vo -va** *adj & m* eighteenth

**dieciocho** *adj & pron* eighteen || *m* eighteen; (*en las fechas*) eighteenth

**dieciséis** *adj & pron* sixteen || *m* sixteen; (*en las fechas*) sixteenth

**dieciseisa•vo -va** *adj & m* sixteenth

**diecisiete** *adj & pron* seventeen || *m* seventeen; (*en las fechas*) seventeenth

**diecisietea•vo -va** *adj & m* seventeenth

**diente** *m* tooth; (*de elefante y otros animales*) tusk, fang; (*de peine, sierra, rastrillo*) tooth; (*de rueda dentada*) cog; **dar diente con diente** (coll) to shake all over; **decir entre dientes** (coll) to mutter, to mumble; **diente canino** eyetooth, canine tooth; **diente de león** dandelion; **estar a diente** (coll) to be famished; **tener buen diente** (coll) to be a hearty eater; **traer entre dientes** (coll) to have a grudge against; (coll) to talk about

**diére•sis** *f* (*pl* **-sis**) diaeresis; (*señal que indica la metafonía*) umlaut

**dies•tro -tra** *adj* right; handy, skillful; shrewd, sly; favorable; **a diestro y siniestro** wildly, right and left || *m* expert fencer; bullfighter on foot; matador; halter, bridle || *f* right hand; **juntar diestra con diestra** to join forces

**dieta** *f* diet; **dietas** per diem; **estar a dieta** to diet, be on a diet

**dietario** *m* family budget

**dietista** *mf* dietitian

**diez** *adj & pron* ten; **las diez** ten o'clock || *m* ten; (*en las fechas*) tenth
**diezmar** *tr* (*causar gran mortandad en*) to decimate; (*pagar el diezmo de*) to tithe
**diezmo** *m* tithe
**difamación** *f* defamation, vilification
**difamar** *tr* to defame, to vilify
**diferencia** *f* difference; **a diferencia de** unlike; **partir la diferencia** to split the difference
**diferenciar** *tr* to differentiate || *intr* (*discordar*) to differ, dissent || *ref* (*distinguirse una cosa de otra*) to differ, be different
**diferente** *adj* different
**diferir** §68 *tr* to defer, postpone, put off || *intr* to differ, be different
**difícil** *adj* difficult, hard; hard to please
**difícilmente** *adv* with difficulty
**dificultad** *f* difficulty; (*reparo que se opone a una opinión*) objection
**dificultar** *tr* to make difficult; to consider difficult || *intr* to raise objections || *ref* to become difficult
**dificulto·so -sa** *adj* difficult, troublesome; objecting; (coll) ugly, homely
**difidencia** *f* distrust
**difidente** *adj* distrustful
**difteria** *f* diphtheria
**difundir** *tr* to diffuse; to spread, disseminate; to divulge, publish; to broadcast || *ref* to diffuse; to spread
**difun·to -ta** *adj & mf* deceased; **difunto de taberna** dead-drunk || *m* corpse
**difu·so -sa** *adj* diffuse; extended; wordy
**digerible** *adj* digestible
**digerir** §68 *tr* to digest; **no digerir** to not bear, to not stand || *intr* to digest
**digestible** *adj* digestible
**digestión** *f* digestion
**digesti·vo -va** *adj & m* digestive
**digesto** *m* (law) digest
**dígito** *m* digit
**dignación** *f* condescension
**dignar** *ref* to deign, to condescend
**dignatario** *m* dignitary, official
**dignidad** *f* dignity; bishop, archbishop
**dignificar** §73 *tr* to dignify
**dig·no -na** *adj* worthy; fitting, suitable; (*grave, decoroso*) dignified
**digresión** *f* digression
**dije** *m* amulet, charm, trinket; (*persona de excelentes cualidades*) (coll) jewel; (coll) person all dressed-up; (coll) handy person
**dilacerar** *tr* to tear to pieces; (*la honra, el orgullo*) to damage
**dilación** *f* delay
**dilapidar** *tr* to squander
**dilatación** *f* expansion; serenity
**dilatar** *tr* to dilate, expand; to defer, postpone; (*p.ej., la fama*) to spread || *ref* to dilate, expand; to spread; to be wordy; (Am) to delay
**dilección** *f* true love
**dilec·to -ta** *adj* dearly beloved
**dilema** *m* dilemma
**diletante** *adj & mf* dilettante
**diligencia** *f* diligence; step, démarche; errand; dispatch, speed; stagecoach; **hacer una diligencia** to do an errand; (coll) to have a bowel movement
**diligente** *adj* diligent; quick, ready
**dilucidar** *tr* to elucidate, explain
**dilución** *f* dilution
**dilui·do -da** *adj* dilute
**diluir** §20 *tr* to dilute; to thin || *ref* to dilute; to melt; to dissolve
**diluviar** *intr* to rain hard, to pour
**diluvio** *m* deluge
**dimanar** *intr* to spring up; **dimanar de** to spring from, originate in
**dimensión** *f* dimension
**dimes** *mpl* — **andar en dimes y diretes con** (coll) to bicker with
**diminuti·vo -va** *adj & m* (gram) diminutive
**diminu·to -ta** *adj* tiny, diminutive; defective
**dimisión** *f* resignation
**dimisorias** *fpl* — **dar dimisorias a** (coll) to discharge, to fire
**dimitir** *tr* to resign, resign from || *intr* to resign
**din** *m* (coll) dough, money
**Dinamarca** *f* Denmark
**dinamar·qués -quesa** *adj* Danish || *mf* Dane || *m* Danish (*language*)
**dinámi·co -ca** *adj* dynamic
**dinamita** *f* dynamite
**dinamitar** *tr* to dynamite
**dínamo** *f* dynamo
**dinasta** *m* dynast
**dinastía** *f* dynasty
**dindán** *m* ding-dong
**dinerada** *f* or **dineral** *m* large sum of money
**dinero** *m* money; currency; wealth; **dinero contante** cash; **dinero contante y sonante** ready cash, spot cash; **dinero de bolsillo** pocket money
**dinero·so -sa** *adj* moneyed, wealthy
**dintel** *m* lintel, doorhead
**dióce·si** *f* or **dióce·sis** *f* (*pl* **-sis**) diocese
**diodo** *m* diode
**dios** *m* god; **Dios mediante** God willing; **¡por Dios!** goodness!, for heaven's sake; **¡válgame Dios!** bless me!; **¡vaya con Dios!** off with you!
**diosa** *f* goddess
**diploma** *m* diploma
**diplomacia** *f* diplomacy
**diploma·do -da** *adj & mf* graduate
**diplomar** *tr & ref* (Am) to graduate
**diplomáti·co -ca** *adj* diplomatic || *mf* diplomat
**diptongar** §44 *tr & ref* to diphthongize
**diptongo** *m* diphthong
**diputación** *f* congress; commission
**diputa·do -da** *mf* deputy, representative
**diputar** *tr* to commission, delegate; to designate
**dique** *m* dike, jetty; dry dock; check, stop; **dique seco** dry dock
**dirección** *f* direction; (*señas en una carta*) address; administration, management; directorship; (aut) steering; **de dirección única** one-way; **dirección a la derecha** right-hand drive; **dirección a la izquierda** left-hand drive; **perder la dirección** to lose control of the car
**directi·vo -va** *adj* managing || *mf* director, manager || *f* management
**direc·to -ta** *adj* direct; straight

**direc•tor -tora** *adj* directing, guiding; managing, governing || *mf* director, manager; (*de un periódico*) editor; (*de una escuela*) principal; (*de una orquesta*) conductor; **director de escena** stage manager; **director de funeraria** funeral director; **director gerente** managing director
**directorio** *m* directorship; directory
**dirigente** *mf* leader, head, executive
**dirigible** *adj & m* dirigible
**dirigir §27** *tr* to direct; to manage; (*un automóvil*) to steer; (*una carta; la palabra*) to address; (*una obra*) to dedicate || *ref* to go, to betake oneself; to turn; **dirigirse a** to address; to apply to
**dirimir** *tr* to dissolve, annul; (*una dificultad*) to solve; (*una controversia*) to settle, mediate
**discar §73** *tr & intr* to dial
**disceptar** *intr* to discuss, debate
**discerniente** *adj* discerning
**discernir §28** *tr* to discern; to distinguish
**disciplina** *f* discipline; **disciplinas** scourge, whip
**disciplina•do -da** *adj* disciplined; (*flores*) many-colored
**disciplinar** *tr* to discipline; to teach; to scourge, whip
**disciplinazo** *m* lash
**discípu•lo -la** *mf* disciple; pupil
**disco** *m* disk; (*del gramófono*) record, disk; (sport) discus; **disco de cola** (rr) taillight; **disco de goma** (*para un grifo*) washer (*for a spigot*); **disco de identificación** identification tag; **disco de larga duración** long-playing record; **disco de señales** (rr) semaphore; **disco selector** (telp) dial; **siempre el mismo disco** (coll) the same old song
**discóbolo** *m* discus thrower
**discófi•lo -la** *mf* record lover, discophile
**dísco•lo -la** *adj* ungovernable, wayward
**disconforme** *adj* disagreeing
**discontinuar §21** *tr* to discontinue
**discordancia** *f* discordance
**discordar §61** *intr* to be out of tune; to disagree
**discorde** *adj* discordant, disagreeing; (mus) discordant, out of tune
**discordia** *f* discord
**discoteca** *f* record cabinet; record library
**discreción** *f* discretion; wit; witticism; **a discreción** at discretion; (mil) unconditionally
**discrepancia** *f* discrepancy; dissent
**discrepar** *intr* to differ, to disagree
**discretear** *intr* to try to be clever, to try to sparkle
**discre•to -ta** *adj* (*juicioso*) discreet; (*discontinuo*) discrete; witty
**discrimen** *m* risk, hazard; difference
**discriminación** *f* discrimination
**discriminar** *tr* to discriminate against || *intr* to discriminate
**discriminato•rio -ria** *adj* discriminatory
**disculpa** *f* excuse, apology
**disculpar** *tr* to excuse; (coll) to pardon, overlook || *ref* to apologize; **disculparse con** to apologize to; **disculparse de** to apologize for
**discurrir** *tr* to contrive, invent; to guess, conjecture || *intr* to ramble, roam; to occur, take place; to discourse; to reason; to pass, elapse
**discursi•vo -va** *adj* meditative
**discurso** *m* discourse, speech; (*paso del tiempo*) course; **discurso de sobremesa** after-dinner speech
**discusión** *f* discussion
**discutible** *adj* debatable
**discutir** *tr* to discuss || *intr* to discuss; to argue
**disecar §73** *tr* to dissect; (*un animal muerto*) to stuff; (*una planta*) to mount
**diseminar** *tr* to disseminate; to scatter || *ref* to scatter
**disensión** *f* (*oposición*) dissent; (*contienda*) dissension
**disentería** *f* dysentery
**disentir §68** *intr* to dissent
**diseñar** *tr* to draw, sketch; to design, outline
**diseño** *m* drawing, sketch; design, outline
**disertar** *intr* to discourse, discuss
**diser•to -ta** *adj* fluent, eloquent
**disfavor** *m* disfavor
**disforme** *adj* formless; monstrous, ugly
**disforzar §35** *ref* (Peru) to be prudish, be finical
**dis•fraz** *m* (*pl* **-fraces**) disguise; (*traje de máscara*) costume, fancy dress
**disfrazar §60** *tr* to disguise || *ref* to disguise oneself; to wear fancy dress, to masquerade, to dress in costume
**disfrutar** *tr* to enjoy, to use || *intr* — **disfrutar de** to enjoy, to use; **disfrutar con** to enjoy, take enjoyment in
**disfrute** *m* enjoyment, use
**disgregar §44** *tr & intr* to disintegrate, break up
**disgusta•do -da** *adj* tasteless, insipid; sad, sorrowful; disagreeable; (Mex) hard to please
**disgustar** *tr* to displease || *ref* to be displeased; to fall out, become estranged
**disgusto** *m* displeasure; annoyance, unpleasantness; grief, sorrow; difference, quarrel; **a disgusto** against one's will
**disidencia** *f* dissidence; (*de una doctrina*) dissent
**disidente** *adj* dissident || *mf* dissident, dissenter
**disidir** *intr* to dissent
**disíla•bo -ba** *adj* dissyllabic || *m* dissyllable
**disímil** *adj* dissimilar
**disimilar** *tr & ref* to dissimilate
**disimula•do -da** *adj* sly, underhanded; **a lo disimulado** or **a la disimulada** underhandedly; **hacer la disimulada** (coll) to feign ignorance
**disimular** *tr* to dissemble, dissimulate, hide, conceal; to overlook, pardon || *intr* to dissemble, dissimulate
**disimulo** *m* dissembling, dissimulation; indulgence

**disipación** *f* dissipation
**disipa·do -da** *adj* dissipated; spendthrift || *mf* debauchee; spendthrift
**disipar** *tr* to dissipate || *ref* to be dissipated; to disappear, evanesce
**dislate** *m* nonsense
**dislocar** §73 *tr* to dislocate || *ref* to dislocate; to be dislocated
**disloque** *m* (coll) tops, top notch
**disminuir** §20 *tr, intr & ref* to diminish
**disociar** *tr* to dissociate
**disolución** *f* dissolution; disbandment; (*relajación de costumbres*) dissoluteness, dissipation
**disolu·to -ta** *adj* dissolute || *mf* debauchee
**disolver** §47 & §83 *tr* to dissolve; to disband; to destroy, ruin || *intr & ref* to dissolve
**disonancia** *f* dissonance
**disonar** §61 *intr* to be dissonant, lack harmony, disagree; to cause surprise; to sound bad
**dispar** *adj* unlike, different; (*que no hace juego*) odd
**disparada** *f* (Am) sudden flight; **a la disparada** (Am) like a shot, in mad haste; **de una disparada** (Arg) right away; **tomar la disparada** (Arg) to take to one's heels
**disparadero** *m* trigger
**disparador** *m* trigger; (*de reloj*) escapement; **poner en el disparador** (coll) to drive mad
**disparar** *tr* to throw, hurl; to shoot, to fire || *intr* to rant, talk nonsense || *ref* to dash away, rush away; (*un caballo*) to run away; (*una escopeta*) to go off; to be beside oneself
**disparata·do -da** *adj* absurd, nonsensical; frightful
**disparatar** *intr* to talk nonsense; to act foolishly
**disparate** *m* folly, nonsense; blunder, mistake; (coll) outrage
**dispare·jo -ja** *adj* unequal, different, uneven, disparate; rough, broken
**disparidad** *f* disparity
**disparo** *m* shot, discharge; nonsense; (mach) release, trip; **cambiar disparos** to exchange shots
**dispendio** *m* waste, extravagance
**dispendio·so -sa** *adj* expensive
**dispensar** *tr* to excuse, to pardon; to exempt; to dispense; to dispense with
**dispensario** *m* dispensary; **dispensario de alimentos** soup kitchen
**dispepsia** *f* dyspepsia
**dispersar** *tr & ref* to disperse
**displicente** *adj* disagreeable; cross, fretful, peevish
**disponer** §54 *tr* to dispose, arrange; to direct, order || *intr* to dispose; **disponer de** to dispose of, have at one's disposal || *ref* to prepare, get ready; to get ready to die, make one's will
**disponible** *adj* available, disposable
**disposición** *f* disposition, arrangement, layout; inclination; preparation; disposal; predisposition; state of health; elegance; **estar a la disposición de** to be at the disposal of, be at the service of; **última disposición** last will and testament
**dispositivo** *m* appliance, device
**dispues·to -ta** *adj* ready, prepared; comely, graceful; clever, skillful; **bien dispuesto** well-disposed; well, in good health; **mal dispuesto** ill-disposed, unfavorable; ill, indisposed
**disputa** *f* dispute; fight, struggle; **sin disputa** beyond dispute
**disputar** *tr* to dispute, to question; to argue over; to fight for || *intr* to dispute; to debate, to argue; to fight
**disque·ro -ra** *mf* record dealer
**distancia** *f* distance; **a distancia** at a distance; **a larga distancia** long-distance; **tomar distancia** to stand aside, to stand off
**distante** *adj* distant
**distar** *intr* to be distant, be far; to be different
**distender** §51 *tr* to distend; (*p.ej., las piernas*) to stretch || *ref* to distend; to relax; (*un reloj*) to run down
**distensión** *f* distension; relaxation of tension
**distinción** *f* (*honor, prerrogativa*) distinction; (*diferencia*) distinctness; **a distinción de** unlike
**distingui·do -da** *adj* distinguished; refined, urbane, smooth
**distinguir** §29 *tr* to distinguish; to give distinction to; to make out
**distinti·vo -va** *adj* distinctive || *m* badge, insignia; distinction; distinctive mark
**distin·to -ta** *adj* distinct; different; **distintos** various, several
**distorsión** *f* distortion
**distracción** *f* distraction; (*licencia en las costumbres*) dissipation; (*substracción de fondos*) embezzlement
**distraer** §75 *tr* to distract; to amuse, divert, entertain; to seduce; to embezzle
**distraí·do -da** *adj* absent-minded, distracted; licentious, dissolute; (Chile, Mex) untidy, careless
**distribución** *f* distribution; electric supply system; timing gears, valve gears
**distribui·dor -dora** *adj* distributing || *mf* distributor || *m* (aut) distributor; slide valve; **distribuidor automático** vending machine
**distribuir** §20 *tr* to distribute
**distrito** *m* district; (rr) section; **distrito electoral** precinct; **distrito postal** zone, postal zone
**disturbar** *tr* to disturb
**disturbio** *m* disturbance
**disuadir** *tr* to dissuade
**disyunti·vo -va** *adj* disjunctive || *f* dilemma
**disyuntor** *m* circuit breaker
**dita** *f* bond, surety
**diuca** *m* (Arg, Chile) teacher's pet || *f* (Arg, Chile) finch (*Fringilla diuca*)
**diur·no -na** *adj* day, daytime
**diva** *f* goddess; (mus) diva
**divagación** *f* digression; wandering
**divagar** §44 *intr* to digress; to ramble, wander
**diván** *m* divan

**divergir** §27 *intr* to diverge
**diversidad** *f* diversity; abundance
**diversificación** *f* diversification
**diversificar** §73 *tr* & *ref* to diversify
**diversión** *f* diversion
**diver•so -sa** *adj* diverse, different; **diversos** several, various, divers
**diverti•do -da** *adj* amusing, funny; (Am) tipsy
**divertimiento** *m* diversion, amusement
**divertir** §68 *tr* to divert; to amuse ‖ *ref* to enjoy oneself, have a good time
**dividendo** *m* dividend
**dividir** *tr* to divide ‖ *ref* to divide, be divided; to separate
**divieso** *m* boil
**divinidad** *f* divinity; (*persona dotada de gran belleza*) beauty
**divinizar** §60 *tr* to deify; to exalt, extol
**divi•no -na** *adj* divine
**divisa** *f* badge; emblem; motto; goal, ideal; currency, foreign exchange
**divisar** *tr* to descry, espy
**división** *f* division
**divisor** *m* (math) divisor; **máximo común divisor** greatest common divisor; **divisor de voltaje** (rad) voltage divider
**divisoria** *f* dividing line; (geog) divide
**di•vo -va** *adj* godlike, divine ‖ *m* god; (mus) opera star ‖ *f* see **diva**
**divorciar** *tr* to divorce ‖ *ref* to divorce, get divorced
**divorcio** *m* divorce; divergency (*in opinion*); (Col) jail for women
**divulgación** *f* divulging, disclosure; popularization
**divulgar** §44 *tr* to divulge, disclose; to popularize
**D.ⁿ** *abbr* **don**
**dobladillar** *tr* to hem
**dobladillo** *m* hem
**dobla•do -da** *adj* rough, uneven; stocky, thickset; double-dealing ‖ *m* (mov) dubbing
**doblaje** *m* (mov) dubbing
**doblar** *tr* to double; to fold, to crease; to bend; (*una esquina*) to turn, to round; (*un promontorio*) to double; (*una película, generalmente en otro idioma*) to dub; (bridge) to double; (Mex) to shoot down ‖ *intr* to turn; (*tocar a muerto*) to toll; (mov, theat) to double, stand in; (bridge) to double ‖ *ref* to double; to fold, to crease; to bend; to bow, to stoop; to give in, yield
**doble** *adj* double; heavy, thick; stocky, thickset; deceitful, two-faced ‖ *adv* double, doubly ‖ *mf* (mov, theat) double, stand-in ‖ *m* double; fold, crease; (*toque de difuntos*) toll, knell; (*suma que se paga por la prórroga de una operación a plazos en la bolsa*) margin; **al doble** doubly
**doblegar** §44 *tr* to fold; to bend; (*una espada*) to brandish, flourish; to sway, dominate ‖ *ref* to fold; to bend; to give in, to yield
**doblete** *adj* medium ‖ *m* (*piedra falsa; cada una de dos palabras que poseen un mismo origen*) doublet; (bridge) doubleton
**do•blez** *m* (*pl* **-bleces**) fold, crease; (*del pantalón*) cuff; duplicity, double-dealing
**doce** *adj* & *pron* twelve; **las doce** twelve o'clock ‖ *m* twelve; (*en las fechas*) twelfth
**docea•vo -va** *adj* & *m* twelfth
**docena** *f* dozen; **docena del fraile** baker's dozen
**docencia** *f* (Arg) teaching; (Arg) teaching staff
**docente** *adj* educational, teaching
**dócil** *adj* docile; soft, ductile
**doc•to -ta** *adj* learned ‖ *mf* scholar
**doc•tor -tora** *mf* doctor ‖ *f* (coll) bluestocking
**doctorado** *m* doctorate
**doctoran•do -da** *mf* candidate for the doctor's degree
**doctorar** *tr* to grant the doctor's degree to ‖ *ref* to get the doctor's degree
**doctrina** *f* doctrine; teaching, instruction; learning; catechism; preaching the Gospel
**doctrinar** *tr* to teach, instruct
**doctrino** *m* orphan (*in orphanage*); **parecer un doctrino** (coll) to look scared
**documentación** *f* documentation; **documentación del buque** ship's papers
**documental** *adj* documentary ‖ *m* (mov) documentary
**documentar** *tr* to document
**documento** *m* document; **documento de prueba** (law) exhibit
**dogal** *m* (*para atar las caballerías*) halter; (*para ahorcar a un reo*) noose, halter, hangman's rope; **estar con el dogal a la garganta** or **al cuello** (coll) to be in a tight spot
**dogmáti•co -ca** *adj* dogmatic
**do•go -ga** *mf* bulldog
**dolamas** *fpl* or **dolames** *mpl* hidden defects of a horse; (Am) complaints, aches and pains
**dolar** §61 *tr* to hew
**dólar** *m* dollar
**dolencia** *f* ailment, complaint
**doler** §47 *tr* to ache, to pain; to grieve, distress; **dolerle a uno el dinero** (coll) to hate to spend money ‖ *intr* to ache, to hurt, to pain ‖ *ref* to complain; to feel sorry; to repent
**doliente** *adj* sick, ill; aching, suffering; sad, sorrowful ‖ *mf* sufferer, patient ‖ *m* mourner
**dolo** *m* deceit, fraud, guile
**dolor** *m* ache, pain; grief, sorrow; regret, repentance; **dolor de cabeza** headache; **dolor de muelas** toothache; **dolor de oído** earache; **dolor de yegua** (CAm) lumbago; **estar con dolores** to be in labor
**dolori•do -da** *adj* sore, painful; grieving, disconsolate
**doloro•so -sa** *adj* painful; sorrowful, sad
**dolo•so -sa** *adj* deceitful, guileful
**domador** *m* horsebreaker; animal tamer
**domar** *tr* to tame, to break; to master
**domeñar** *tr* to master, subdue
**domesticar** §73 *tr* to domesticate; to tame

**domésti•co -ca** *adj* domestic, household || *mf* domestic, servant
**domiciliar** *tr* to domicile, settle; (*una carta*) (Mex) to address || *ref* to be domiciled, to take up one's residence
**domicilio** *m* domicile, home; dwelling, house; **domicilio social** home office, company office
**dominación** *f* domination; (mil) eminence, high ground
**dominante** *adj* dominant; (*mandón*) domineering || *f* (mus) dominant
**dominar** *tr* to dominate; to check, restrain, subdue; (*una ciencia, un idioma*) to master || *intr* to dominate; (*mandar imperiosamente*) to domineer || *ref* to restrain oneself
**dómine** *m* (coll) schoolmaster, Latin teacher; (coll) pedant
**domingo** *m* Sunday; **domingo de ramos** Palm Sunday; **domingo de resurrección** Easter Sunday; **guardar el domingo** to keep the Sabbath
**dominguillo** *m* tumbler
**dominica•no -na** *adj & mf* Dominican
**dominio** *m* dominion; domain; (*de una ciencia, de un idioma*) mastery; (*del aire*) supremacy
**domi•nó** *m* (*pl* **-nós**) (*traje*) domino; (*juego*) dominoes; (*fichas*) set of dominoes
**dom.º** *abbr* **domingo**
**domo** *m* dome
**dompedro** *m* four-o'clock
**don** *m* gift, present; talent, natural gift; Don (*Spanish title used before masculine Christian names*); **don de acierto** knack for doing the right thing; **don de errar** knack for doing the wrong thing; **don de gentes** charm, social grace; **don de lenguas** linguistic facility; **don de mando** ability to lead, generalship
**dona** *f* gift, present; **donas** wedding presents from the bridegroom to the bride
**donación** *f* gift, bequest; endowment
**donada** *f* lay sister
**donado** *m* lay brother
**dona•dor -dora** *mf* donor
**donaire** *m* charm, grace; witticism; cleverness
**donairo•so -sa** *adj* charming, graceful; witty; clever
**donar** *tr* to donate, to give
**doncel** *adj* mild, mellow || *m* (*joven noble aun no armado caballero*) bachelor; (*hombre virgen*) virgin
**doncella** *f* maiden, virgin; housemaid; lady's maid; maid of honor; (Col, Ven) felon, whitlow
**doncellez** *f* maidenhood, virginity
**doncellona** or **doncellueca** *f* spinster, maiden lady
**donde** *conj* where; wherever; in which; **donde no** otherwise; **por donde quiera** anywhere, everywhere || *prep* (Am) at or to the house, office, or store of
**dónde** *adv* where; **a dónde** where, whither; **de dónde** from where, whence; **por dónde** which way; for what cause, for what reason
**dondequiera** *adv* anywhere; **dondequiera que** wherever
**dondiego** *m* four-o'clock; **dondiego de día** morning-glory; **dondiego de noche** four-o'clock
**donillero** *m* sharper, smoothy
**donjuán** *m* four-o'clock
**donosidad** *f* charm, grace, wit
**dono•so -sa** *adj* charming, graceful, witty
**donostiarra** *adj* San Sebastian || *mf* native or inhabitant of San Sebastian
**donosura** *f* charm, grace, wit
**doña** *f* Doña (*Spanish title used before feminine Christian names*)
**doñear** *intr* (coll) to hang around women
**doquier** or **doquiera** *conj* wherever; **por doquier** everywhere
**dorada** *f* (ichth) gilthead
**doradillo** *m* fine brass wire
**dora•do -da** *adj* golden; gilt || *m* gilt, gilding; **dorados** bronze trimmings (*on furniture*) || *f* see **dorada**
**dorar** *tr* to gold-plate; to gild; (*tostar ligeramente*) to brown; (*paliar*) to sugar-coat || *ref* to turn golden; to turn brown
**dormi•lón -lona** *adj* (coll) sleepy || *mf* (coll) sleepyhead || *f* reclining armchair; (Mex) headrest; (Ven) sleeping gown; (Am) mimosa; **dormilonas** pearl earrings
**dormir** **§30** *tr* to put to sleep; (*p.ej., una borrachera*) to sleep off || *intr* to sleep; to spend the night || *ref* to sleep; to fall asleep; (*entorpecerse, p.ej., el pie*) to go to sleep
**dormirlas** *m* hide-and-seek
**dormitar** *intr* to doze, nap
**dormitorio** *m* bedroom; (*muebles propios de esta habitación*) bedroom suit
**dorsal** *m* (sport) number (*worn on shirt*)
**dorso** *m* back
**dos** *adj & pron* two; **las dos** two o'clock || *m* two; (*en las fechas*) second
**dosal•bo -ba** *adj* (*horse*) with two white feet
**doscien•tos -tas** *adj & pron* two hundred || **doscientos** *m* two hundred
**dosel** *m* canopy, dais
**doselera** *f* valance, drapery
**dosificación** *f* dosage
**dosificar** **§73** *tr* (*un medicamento*) to dose, to give in doses
**do•sis** *f* (*pl* **-sis**) dose
**dos-pie•zas** *m* (*pl* **-zas**) two-piece bathing suit
**dotación** *f* (*de una mujer; de una fundación*) endowment; (nav) complement; (aer) crew; (*de remeros*) (sport) crew; staff, personnel
**dotar** *tr* to give a dowry to; to endow; (*un buque*) to man; (*una oficina*) to staff; to equip; to fix the wages for
**dote** *m & f* dowry, marriage portion || *m* (*en el juego de naipes*) stack of chips || *f* endowment, talent, gift; **dotes de mando** leadership
**dovela** *f* voussoir
**doza•vo -va** *adj & m* twelfth
**d/p** *abbr* **días plazo**

**dracma** *f* (*moneda griega*) drachma; (*peso farmacéutico*) dram
**draga** *f* dredge; (*barco*) dredger
**dragado** *m* dredging
**dragami·nas** *m* (*pl* **-nas**) mine sweeper
**dragar** §44 *tr* to dredge
**dragón** *m* dragon; (*planta*) snapdragon; (*soldado*) dragoon
**dragonear** *intr* (Am) to flirt; (Am) to boast; **dragonear de** (Am) to boast of being; (Am) to pretend to be, to pass oneself off as
**drama** *m* drama
**dramáti·co -ca** *adj* dramatic || *mf* (*autor*) dramatist; actor || *f* (*arte y género*) drama
**dramatizar** §60 *tr* to dramatize
**dramaturgo** *m* dramatist
**drásti·co -ca** *adj* drastic
**dren** *m* drain
**drenaje** *m* drainage
**drenar** *tr* to drain
**driblar** *tr & intr* to dribble
**dril** *m* drill; duck; **dril de algodón** denim
**driza** *f* (naut) halyard
**dro.** *abbr* **derecho**
**droga** *f* drug; annoyance, bother; deceit, trick; (Chile, Mex, Peru) bad debt; (Cuba) drug on the market; **drogas milagrosas** wonder drugs
**drogado** *m* doping
**drogar** §44 *tr* to dope
**droguería** *f* drug store; drug business; (*comercio de substancias usadas en química, industria, medicina, bellas artes*) drysaltery (Brit)
**drogue·ro -ra** *mf* druggist; drysalter (Brit)
**droguista** *mf* druggist; (coll) crook, cheat; (Arg) toper, drunk
**drolàti·co -ca** *adj* droll, snappy
**dromedario** *m* dromedary; big heavy animal; (coll) brute (*person*)
**druida** *m* druid
**dúa** *f* (min) gang of workmen
**dual** *adj & m* dual
**dualidad** *f* duality; (Chile) tie vote
**ducado** *m* duchy, dukedom; (*moneda antigua*) ducat; **gran ducado** grand duchy
**dúctil** *adj* ductile; easy to handle
**ducha** *f* (*chorro de agua en una cavidad del cuerpo*) douche; (*chorro de agua sobre el cuerpo entero*) shower bath; (*lista en los tejidos*) stripe; **ducha en alfileres** needle bath
**duchar** *tr* to douche; to give a shower bath to || *ref* to douche; to take a shower bath
**du·cho -cha** *adj* experienced, expert, skillful || *f* see **ducha**
**duda** *f* doubt; **sin duda** doubtless, no doubt, without doubt
**dudable** *adj* doubtful
**dudar** *tr* to doubt; to question || *intr* to hesitate; **dudar de** to doubt
**dudo·so -sa** *adj* doubtful; dubious
**duela** *f* stave (*of barrel*)
**duelista** *m* duelist
**duelo** *m* (*combate entre dos*) duel; grief, sorrow; bereavement, mourning; (*los que asisten a los funerales*) mourners; **batirse en duelo** to duel, to fight a duel; **duelos** hardships; **sin duelo** in abundance
**duende** *m* elf, goblin; gold cloth, silver cloth; (coll) restless daemon; **tener duende** (coll) to be burning within
**due·ño -ña** *mf* owner, proprietor; **dueño de sí mismo** one's own master; **ser dueño de** to be master of; to be at liberty to, be free to || *m* master, landlord || *f* mistress, landlady, housekeeper; duenna; matron; **dueña de casa** housewife
**duermevela** *f* (coll) doze, light sleep; (*sueño fatigoso e interrumpido*) fitful sleep
**dula** *f* common pasture land; land irrigated from common ditch
**dulce** *adj* sweet; (*agua*) fresh; (*metal*) soft, ductile; gentle, mild, pleasant; (*manjar*) tasteless, insipid || *m* candy; piece of candy; preserves; **dulce de almíbar** preserved fruit; **dulces** candy
**dulcera** *f* candy dish, preserve dish
**dulcería** *f* candy store, confectionery store
**dulce·ro -ra** *adj* (coll) sweet-toothed || *mf* confectioner || *f* see **dulcera**
**dulcificar** §73 *tr* to sweeten; to appease, mollify || *ref* to sweeten, turn sweet
**dulcinea** *f* (coll) sweetheart; (coll) ideal
**dulzaina** *f* flageolet
**dulza·rrón -rrona** *adj* (coll) cloying, sickening
**dulzura** *f* sweetness; pleasantness, kindliness; (*del clima*) mildness; endearment, sweet word
**duna** *f* dune
**dun·do -da** *adj* (CAm, Col) simple, stupid || *mf* (CAm, Col) simpleton
**dúo** *m* duet, duo
**duodéci·mo -ma** *adj & m* twelfth
**duodeno** *m* duodenum
**duplica·do -da** *adj & m* duplicate; **por duplicado** in duplicate
**duplicar** §73 *tr* to duplicate; to double; to repeat
**duplicata** *f* duplicate
**duplicidad** *f* (*falsedad*) duplicity; (*calidad de doble*) doubleness
**du·plo -pla** *adj & m* double
**duque** *m* duke; **gran duque** grand duke
**duquesa** *f* duchess; **gran duquesa** grand duchess
**dura** *f* (coll) durability; **de dura** or **de mucha dura** (coll) strong, durable
**durable** *adj* durable, lasting
**duración** *f* duration, endurance; (*espacio de tiempo del uso de una cosa*) life
**durade·ro -ra** *adj* durable, lasting
**durante** *prep* during, for
**durar** *intr* to last; to remain; (*la ropa*) to last, to wear, to wear well
**durazno** *m* peach; peach tree
**dureza** *f* hardness; harshness, roughness; **dureza de corazón** hardheartedness; **dureza de oído** hardness of hearing; **dureza de vientre** constipation
**durmiente** *adj* sleeping || *mf* sleeper || *m* girder, sleeper, stringer; (Am) tie, railroad tie; (Ven) steel bar

**du•ro -ra** *adj* hard; (*huevo*) hard-boiled; harsh, rough; cruel; stubborn, obstinate; unbearable; strong, tough; stingy; (*tiempo*) stormy; **duro de corazón** hard-hearted; **duro de oído** hard of hearing; **estar muy duro con** to be hard on; **ser duro de pelar** (coll) to be hard to put across; (coll) to be hard to deal with || *m* dollar (*Spanish coin worth five pesetas*) || *f* see **dura** || **duro** *adv* hard
**dux** *m* (*pl* **dux**) doge
**d/v** *abbr* **días vista**

## E

**E, e** (e) *f* sixth letter of the Spanish alphabet
**e** *conj* (used before words beginning with *i* or *hi* not followed by a vowel) and
**ea** *interj* hey!
**ebanista** *m* cabinetmaker, woodworker
**ebanistería** *f* cabinetmaking, woodwork; cabinetmaker's shop
**ébano** *m* ebony
**ebriedad** *f* drunkenness
**e•brio -bria** *adj* drunk; (*p.ej., de ira*) blind || *mf* drunk
**ebrio•so -sa** *adj* drinking || *mf* drinker
**ebullición** *f* boiling
**eccema** *m* & *f* eczema
**ecléctico -ca** *adj* & *mf* eclectic
**eclesiásti•co -ca** *adj* & *m* ecclesiastic
**eclipsar** *tr* to eclipse; (fig) to outshine || *ref* to be in eclipse; (fig) to disappear
**eclipse** *m* eclipse
**eclip•sis** *f* (*pl* **-sis**) var of **elipsis**
**eclisa** *f* (rr) fishplate
**eco** *m* echo; (*del tambor*) rumbling; **hacer eco** to echo; to attract attention; **tener eco** to be well received, to catch on
**economato** *m* stewardship; commissary, company store, coöperative store
**economía** *f* economy; want, poverty; **economía política** economics; **economías** savings
**económi•co -ca** *adj* economic; (*que gasta poco; poco costoso*) economical; cheap; miserly, niggardly
**economista** *mf* economist
**economizar** **§60** *tr* to economize, to save; to avoid || *intr* to economize, save; to skimp
**ecónomo** *m* steward, trustee; supply priest
**ecuación** *f* equation
**ecuador** *m* equator || **el Ecuador** Ecuador
**ecuánime** *adj* calm, composed; impartial
**ecuanimidad** *f* equanimity; impartiality
**ecuatoria•no -na** *adj* & *mf* Ecuadoran, Ecuadorian
**ecuestre** *adj* equestrian
**ecuméni•co -ca** *adj* ecumenic(al)
**eczema** *m* & *f* eczema
**echacan•tos** *m* (*pl* **-tos**) (coll) good-for-nothing
**echacuer•vos** *m* (*pl* **-vos**) (coll) pimp, procurer; (coll) cheat
**echada** *f* cast, throw; **man's** length; (Arg, Mex) boast, hoax
**echadero** *m* place to stretch out
**echadi•zo -za** *adj* discarded, waste; spying || *mf* foundling || *m* spy
**echa•do -da** *adj* stretched out; (C-R) lazy, indolent || *f* see **echada**
**echar** *tr* to throw, throw away, throw out; to issue, emit; to publish; to discharge, dismiss; to swallow; (*p.ej., agua*) to pour; (*p.ej., un cigarrillo*) to smoke; (*la baraja*) to deal; (*una partida de cartas*) to play; (*una llave*) to turn; (*un discurso*) to deliver; (*un drama*) to put on; (*maldiciones*) to utter; (*pelo, dientes, renuevos*) to grow, put forth; (*impuestos*) to impose, to levy; (*la buenaventura*) to tell; (*precio, distancia, edad, etc.*) to ascribe, attribute; (*una mirada*) to cast; (*sangre*) to shed; (*la culpa*) to lay; (*una mano*) to lend; **echar abajo** to demolish, destroy; to overthrow; **echar a pasear** (coll) to dismiss unceremoniously; **echar a perder** to spoil, to ruin; **echar a pique** to sink; **echar de menos** to miss; **echarla de** (coll) to claim to be, boast of being; **echarlo todo a rodar** (coll) to upset everything; (coll) to hit the ceiling || *intr* — **echar a** to begin to; to burst out (*e.g., crying*); **echar a perder** to spoil, to ruin; **echar de ver** to notice, to happen to see; **echar por** (*un empleo, un oficio*) to go into, take up; (*la derecha, la izquierda*) to turn toward; (*un camino*) to go down || *ref* to throw oneself; to lie down, stretch out; (*el viento*) to fall; (*un abrigo*) to throw on; (*una gallina*) to set; **echarse a** to begin to; **echarse a morir** (coll) to give up in despair; **echarse a perder** to spoil, to be ruined; **echarse atrás** to back out; **echarse de ver** to be easy to see; **echárselas de** to claim to be, to boast of being; **echarse sobre** to rush at, fall upon
**echazón** *f* jettison, jetsam
**echiquier** *m* Exchequer
**edad** *f* age; **edad crítica** change of life; **edad de quintas** draft age; **edad escolar** school age; **Edad Media** Middle Ages; **edad viril** prime of life; **mayor edad** majority; **menor edad** minority
**edecán** *m* aide-de-camp
**edición** *f* edition; publication; **la segun-**

**da edición de** (coll) the spit and image of
**edicto** *m* edict
**edificación** *f* construction, building; buildings; (*inspiración con el buen ejemplo*) edification, uplift
**edificante** *adj* edifying
**edificar** §73 *tr* to construct, build; (*dar buen ejemplo a*) to edify, to uplift
**edificio** *m* edifice, building
**editar** *tr* to publish
**edi•tor -tora** *adj* publishing || *mf* publisher
**editorial** *adj* publishing; editorial || *m* editorial || *f* publishing house
**editorialista** *mf* (Am) editorial writer
**editorializar** §60 *intr* (Urug) to editorialize
**edredón** *m* eider down
**educación** *f* education
**educacional** *adj* educational
**educa•dor -dora** *mf* educator
**educan•do -da** *mf* pupil, student
**educar** §73 *tr* to educate; (*los sentidos*) to train; (*al niño o el adolescente*) to rear, to bring up
**educati•vo -va** *adj* educational
**EE.UU.** *abbr* **Estados Unidos**
**efectismo** *m* sensationalism
**efectista** *adj* sensational, theatrical || *mf* sensationalist
**efectivamente** *adv* actually, really; as a matter of fact
**efecti•vo -va** *adj* actual, real; (*empleo, cargo*) regular, permanent; (*vigente*) effective; **hacer efectivo** to carry out; (*un cheque*) to cash; **hacerse efectivo** to become effective || *m* cash; **efectivo en caja** cash on hand
**efecto** *m* effect; end, purpose; article; (*en el juego de billar*) English; **a ese efecto** for that purpose; **al efecto** for the purpose; **con efecto** or **en efecto** indeed, as a matter of fact; **efecto útil** efficiency, output; **llevar a efecto** or **poner en efecto** to put into effect, to carry out; **surtir efecto** to work, to have the desired effect
**efectuar** §21 *tr* to carry out, to effect, to effectuate || *ref* to take place
**efervescencia** *f* effervescence
**efervescente** *adj* effervescent
**eficacia** *f* efficacy
**efi•caz** *adj* (*pl* **-caces**) efficacious, effectual; efficient
**eficiencia** *f* efficiency
**eficiente** *adj* efficient
**efigie** *f* effigy
**efíme•ro -ra** *adj* ephemeral
**efugio** *m* evasion, subterfuge
**efusión** *f* effusion; (*manifestación de afectos muy viva*) warmth, effusiveness; **efusión de sangre** bloodshed
**efusi•vo -va** *adj* effusive
**égida** *f* aegis
**egip•cio -cia** *adj* & *mf* Egyptian
**Egipto** *m* Egypt
**eglantina** *f* sweetbriar
**eglefino** *m* haddock
**égloga** *f* eclogue
**egoísmo** *m* egoism
**egoísta** *adj* egoistic || *mf* egoist
**egotismo** *m* egotism
**egotista** *adj* egotistic(al) || *mf* egotist
**egre•gio -gia** *adj* distinguished, eminent
**egresar** *intr* (Am) to graduate
**egreso** *m* departure; (Am) graduation
**eje** *m* (*pieza alrededor de la cual gira un cuerpo*) axle, shaft; (*línea que divide en dos mitades; línea recta alrededor de la cual se supone que gira un cuerpo*) axis; (fig) core, crux; **eje de balancín** rocker, rockershaft; **eje de carretón** axletree; **eje motor** drive shaft
**ejecución** *f* execution
**ejecutante** *mf* performer
**ejecutar** *tr* to execute; to perform
**ejecutivamente** *adv* expeditiously
**ejecuti•vo -va** *adj* urgent, pressing; insistent; executive || *m* (Am) executive
**ejecu•tor -tora** *adj* executive || *mf* executor; **ejecutor de la justicia** executioner; **ejecutor testamentario** executor (*of a will*) || *f* — **ejecutora testamentaria** executrix
**ejemplar** *adj* exemplary || *m* pattern, model; (*de una obra impresa*) copy; precedent; (*caso que sirve de escarmiento*) example; **ejemplar de cortesía** complimentary copy; **ejemplar muestra** sample copy; **sin ejemplar** unprecedented; as a special case
**ejemplarizar** §60 *tr* (Am) to set an example to; (Am) to exemplify
**ejemplificar** §73 *tr* to exemplify
**ejemplo** *m* example, instance; **por ejemplo** for example, for instance; **sin ejemplo** unexampled
**ejercer** §78 *tr* (*la medicina*) to practice; (*la caridad*) to show, exercise; (*una fuerza*) to exert || *intr* to practice; **ejercer de** to practice as, to work as
**ejercicio** *m* exercise; drill, practice; (*de un cargo u oficio*) tenure; (*uso constante*) exertion; (*año económico*) fiscal year; **hacer ejercicio** to take exercise; (mil) to drill
**ejercitar** *tr* to exercise; to practice; to drill, to train || *ref* to exercise; to practice
**ejército** *m* army; **ejército permanente** standing army; **los tres ejércitos** the three arms of the service
**ejido** *m* commons
**ejote** *m* (CAm, Mex) string bean
**el, la** (*pl* **los, las**) *art def* the || *pron dem* that, the one; **el que** who, which, that; he who, the one that
**él** *pron pers masc* he, it; him, it
**elabora•do -da** *adj* elaborate; finished
**elaborar** *tr* to elaborate; (*una teoría*) to work out; (*el metal, la madera*) to fashion, to work
**elación** *f* magnanimity, nobility; (*de estilo y lenguaje*) pomposity
**elástica** *f* knit undershirt; **elásticas** (Ven) suspenders
**elasticidad** *f* elasticity
**elásti•co -ca** *adj* elastic || *m* elastic; (Am) bedspring || *f* see **elástica**
**eléboro** *m* hellebore
**elección** *f* election; choice
**electi•vo -va** *adj* elective
**elec•to -ta** *adj* elect
**electorado** *m* electorate

**electorero** *m* henchman, heeler
**electricidad** *f* electricity
**electricista** *mf* electrician
**eléctrico -ca** *adj* electric(al)
**electrificar** **§73** *tr* to electrify
**electrizar** **§60** *tr* to electrify
**electro** *m* electromagnet
**electroafeitadora** *f* electric shaver
**electrocutar** *tr* to electrocute
**electrodo** *m* electrode
**electrodoméstico -ca** *adj* electric-household
**electróge·no -na** *adj* generating electricity || *m* electric generator
**electroimán** *m* electromagnet
**electrólisis** *f* electrolysis
**electrólito** *m* electrolyte
**electromagnéti·co -ca** *adj* electromagnetic
**electromo·tor -tora** or **-triz** *adj* (*pl* **-tores -toras -trices**) electromotive
**electrón** *m* electron
**electróni·co -ca** *adj* electronic || *f* electronics
**electrostáti·co -ca** *adj* electrostatic
**electrotecnia** *f* electrical engineering
**electrotipar** *tr* to electrotype
**electrotipo** *m* electrotype
**elefante** *m* elephant; **elefante blanco** (fig) (SAm) white elephant
**elegancia** *f* elegance; style, stylishness
**elegante** *adj* elegant; stylish || *mf* fashion plate
**elegía** *f* elegy
**elegía·co -ca** *adj* elegiac
**elegible** *adj* eligible
**elegir** **§57** *tr* to elect; to choose, select
**elemental** *adj* (*primordial; simple, no compuesto*) elemental; (*que se refiere a los principios de una ciencia o arte; de fácil comprensión*) elementary
**elemento** *m* element; (*de una pila o batería*) cell; **elemento de compuestos** (gram) combining form; **estar en su elemento** to be in one's element
**elenco** *m* catalogue, list, table; (theat) (Am) cast
**elevación** *f* elevation; **elevación a potencias** (math) involution
**eleva·do -da** *adj* elevated, high; lofty, sublime
**elevador** *m* (Am) elevator; **elevador de granos** (Am) grain elevator
**elevar** *tr* to elevate, to lift; (math) to raise || *ref* to ascend, rise; to be exalted; to become conceited
**elfo** *m* elf
**elidir** *tr* to eliminate; (*una vocal*) to elide
**eliminar** *tr* to eliminate; to strike out
**elipse** *f* (geom) ellipse
**elip·sis** *f* (*pl* **-sis**) (gram) ellipsis
**elípti·co -ca** *adj* (geom & gram) elliptic(al)
**elisión** *f* elision
**elocución** *f* public speaking, elocution
**elocuencia** *f* eloquence
**elocuente** *adj* eloquent
**elogiable** *adj* praiseworthy
**elogiar** *tr* to praise, eulogize
**elogio** *m* praise, eulogy
**elogio·so -sa** *adj* (Am) laudatory, glowing
**elote** *m* (Mex, Guat) ear of corn; **coger asando elotes** (CAm) to catch in the act; **pagar los elotes** (CAm) to be the goat
**elucidar** *tr* to elucidate
**eludir** *tr* to elude, evade, avoid
**ella** *pron pers fem* she, it; her, it; (coll) the trouble
**ello** *pron pers neut* it; (coll) the trouble; **ello es que** the fact is that || *m* (psychoanalysis) id
**E.M.** *abbr* **Estado Mayor**
**emancipar** *tr* to emancipate
**embadurnamiento** *m* daub, daubing
**embadurnar** *tr* to daub
**embaír** **§1** *tr* to deceive, take in, hoax
**embajada** *f* embassy; ambassadorship; (iron) fine proposition
**embajador** *m* ambassador; **embajadores** ambassador and wife
**embajadora** *f* ambassadress
**embalaje** *m* packing; package; (sport) sprint
**embalar** *tr* to pack || *intr* (sport) to sprint || *ref* (*el motor*) to race; (sport) to sprint
**embaldosado** *m* tile paving
**embaldosar** *tr* to pave with tile
**embalsamar** *tr* to embalm; to perfume
**embalsar** *tr* to dam, to dam up
**embalse** *m* dam; damming; backwater
**embanastar** *tr* to put in a basket; to pack, jam, overcrowd
**embanquetar** *tr* (Mex) to line with sidewalks
**embarazada** *adj fem* pregnant || *f* pregnant woman
**embarazar** **§60** *tr* (*estorbar*) to embarrass; to obstruct; to make pregnant || *ref* to be embarrassed, be encumbered; to become pregnant
**embarazo** *m* embarrassment; obstruction; awkwardness; pregnancy
**embarazo·so -sa** *adj* embarrassing, troublesome
**embarbillar** *tr* to rabbet
**embarcación** *f* boat, ship; embarkation (*of passengers*)
**embarcadero** *m* pier, wharf; (rr) (Am) platform; **embarcadero de ganado** (Arg) loading chute; **embarcadero flotante** landing stage
**embarcador** *m* shipper
**embarcar** **§73** *tr* to ship || *intr* to entrain || *ref* to embark, to ship; to get involved
**embarco** *m* embarkation (*of passengers*)
**embargar** **§44** *tr* to embargo; to paralyze; (law) to seize, attach
**embargo** *m* embargo; indigestion; (law) seizure, attachment; **sin embargo** however, nevertheless
**embarnizar** **§60** *tr* to varnish
**embarque** *m* shipment, embarkation (*of freight*)
**embarrada** *f* (Am) blunder
**embarrancar** **§73** *tr, intr & ref* to run into a ditch; (*una nave*) to run aground
**embarrar** *tr* to splash with mud; to

smear, stain; (CAm, Mex) to involve in a shady deal; **embarrarla** (Arg) to spoil the whole thing
**embarrilar** *tr* to barrel, put in barrels
**embarullar** *tr* (coll) to muddle, make a mess of; (coll) to bungle, botch
**embastar** *tr* to baste, to stitch
**embate** *m* blow, attack; (*del mar*) beating, dashing; (*de viento*) gust; **embates de la fortuna** hard knocks
**embaucar** §73 *tr* to trick, bamboozle, swindle
**embaula·do -da** *adj* crowded, packed, jammed
**embaular** §8 *tr* to put in a trunk; (coll) to jam, pack in
**embayar** *ref* (Ecuad) to fly into a rage
**embazar** §60 *tr* to dye brown; to hinder, obstruct; to astound, dumbfound || *ref* to get bored; to be upset, get sick at the stomach
**embebecer** §22 *tr* to entertain, amuse, fascinate, enchant
**embeber** *tr* to absorb, soak up; to soak; to contain, include; to embed; to contract, shrink || *intr* to contract, shrink || *ref* to be enchanted, be enraptured; to become absorbed or immersed; to become well versed
**embebi·do -da** *adj* (*vocal*) elided; (*columna*) engaged
**embelecar** §73 *tr* to cheat, dupe, bamboozle
**embeleco** *m* cheating, fraud; (coll) bore; **embelecos** cuteness
**embeleñar** *tr* to dope, stupefy; to enchant, bewitch
**embelesar** *tr* to charm, enrapture, fascinate
**embeleso** *m* charm, fascination, delight
**embellece·dor -dora** *adj* embellishing, beautifying || *m* (aut) hubcap || *f* beautician
**embellecer** §22 *tr* to embellish, beautify
**embellecimiento** *m* embellishment, beautification
**embermejecer** §22 *tr* to dye red; to make blush || *ref* to blush
**emberrinchar** *ref* (coll) to fly into a rage
**embestida** *f* attack, assault; (*detención intempestiva*) (coll) buttonholing
**embesti·dor -dora** *mf* (coll) beat, sponger
**embestir** §50 *tr* to attack, assail; to strike; (coll) to buttonhole, waylay || *intr* to attack, to charge, to rush
**embetunar** *tr* to blacken; to cover with tar
**embicar** §73 *tr* (Mex) to turn upside down, to tilt || *intr* (Arg, Chile) to run aground
**emblandecer** §22 *tr* to soften; to placate, mollify || *ref* to soften, to yield
**emblanquecer** §22 *tr* to whiten; to bleach || *ref* to turn white
**emblema** *m* emblem
**emblemáti·co -ca** *adj* emblematic(al)
**embobar** *tr* to amaze, fascinate || *ref* to stand gaping
**embocadero** *m* mouth, outlet
**embocadura** *f* nozzle; (*de río*) mouth; (*del freno; de instrumento de viento*) mouthpiece; (*de cigarrillo*) tip; (*del vino*) taste; stage entrance
**embocar** §73 *tr* to catch in the mouth; to put in the mouth; to take on, undertake; (coll) to gulp down; (coll) to try to put over || *intr & ref* to enter, pass
**embolada** *f* stroke
**embolado** *m* bull with wooden balls on horns; (theat) minor role; (coll) trick, hoax
**embolar** *tr* (*los cuernos del toro*) to put wooden balls on; (*el calzado*) to shine
**embolia** *f* embolism
**émbolo** *m* (mach) piston; **émbolo buzo** (mach) plunger
**embolsar** *tr* to pocket, take in
**embonar** *tr* (Am) to fertilize; (Am) to suit, be becoming to
**emboquillar** *tr* (*los cigarrillos*) to put tips on; (*una galería o túnel*) to cut an entrance in; (*las junturas entre los ladrillos*) (Chile) to point, to chink
**emborrachar** *tr* to intoxicate || *ref* to get drunk; (*los colores de una tela*) to run
**emborrar** *tr* to stuff, pad, wad; (coll) to gulp down
**emborrascar** §73 *tr* to stir up, irritate || *ref* to get stormy; (*un negocio*) to fail; (*la veta de una mina*) (Arg, CAm, Mex) to peter out
**emborronar** *tr* to blot; to scribble
**emboscada** *f* ambush, ambuscade
**emboscado** *m* draft dodger
**emboscar** §73 *tr* (*tropas para sorprender al enemigo*) to ambush || *ref* to ambush, lie in ambush; to shirk, take an easy way out
**embota·do -da** *adj* blunt, dull; (Chile) black-pawed
**embotadura** *f* bluntness, dullness
**embotar** *tr* to blunt, to dull; to dull, weaken; (*el tabaco*) to put in a jar
**embotella·do -da** *adj* (*discurso*) prepared || *m* bottling; (*del tráfico*) bottleneck
**embotellamiento** *m* bottling; traffic jam
**embotellar** *tr* to bottle; (*un negocio*) to tie up; (nav) to bottle up
**embotijar** *tr* (*un suelo*) to underlay with jugs || *ref* (coll) to swell up with anger
**embovedar** *tr* to vault, vault over; to put in a vault
**emboza·do -da** *adj* muffled up || *mf* person muffled up to eyes
**embozar** §60 *tr* to muffle up to the eyes; (*p.ej., a un perro*) to muzzle; to disguise || *ref* to muffle oneself up to the eyes
**embozo** *m* muffler, cloak held over the face; fold back (*of bed sheet*); cunning, dissimulation; **quitarse el embozo** (coll) to drop one's mask
**embragar** §44 *tr* (*el motor*) to engage || *intr* to throw the clutch in
**embrague** *m* clutch; engagement
**embravecer** §22 *tr* to enrage, make angry || *ref* to get angry; (*el mar*) to get rough

**embraveci•do -da** *adj* angry; rough, wild
**embrear** *tr* to tar, cover with tar; to calk with tar
**embregar** §44 *ref* to wrangle
**embriagar** §44 *tr* to intoxicate, make drunk; to enrapture || *ref* to get drunk
**embriaguez** *f* drunkenness; rapture
**embridar** *tr* to bridle; to check, restrain
**embriología** *f* embriology
**embrión** *m* embryo
**embroca** *f* poultice
**embrocar** §73 *tr* to empty; (*el toro al torero*) to catch between the horns || *ref* (C-R) to fall on one's face; (Mex) to put on over the head
**embrollar** *tr* to tangle, muddle, embroil
**embrollo** *m* entanglement, muddle, embroilment; deception, trick
**embromar** *tr* to joke with, play jokes on; (Am) to bore, annoy || *ref* (Am) to be bored, be annoyed
**embrujar** *tr* to bewitch
**embrutecer** §22 *tr* to brutify, stupefy
**embuchado** *m* pork sausage; subterfuge; (*de la urna electoral*) stuffing (of ballot box)
**embudar** *tr* to put a funnel in; to trick, trap
**embudista** *adj* tricky, scheming || *mf* schemer
**embudo** *m* funnel; trick; (mil) shell hole; **embudo de bomba** (mil) bomb crater
**embullar** *tr* to stir up, excite, key up || *ref* to become excited, keyed up
**emburujar** *tr* to jumble, pile up || *ref* (Am) to wrap oneself up
**embuste** *m* lie, falsehood, trick; **embustes** baubles, trinkets; (*del niño*) cuteness
**embuste•ro -ra** *adj* lying, false, tricky || *mf* liar, cheat
**embuti•do -da** *adj* inlaid, flush || *m* inlay, marquetry; pork sausage; (Am) lace insertion
**embutir** *tr* to stuff, pack tight; to insert; to inlay; to set flush; (*una hoja de metal*) to fashion, to hammer into shape || *ref* to squeeze in; (coll) to stuff oneself
**emergencia** *f* emergence; incident
**emerger** §17 *intr* to emerge; (*un submarino*) to surface
**emersión** *f* emersion; (*de un submarino*) surfacing
**eméti•co -ca** *adj & m* emetic
**emigración** *f* emigration; migration
**emigra•do -da** *mf* émigré
**emigrante** *adj & mf* emigrant
**emigrar** *intr* to emigrate; to migrate
**eminencia** *f* eminence
**eminente** *adj* eminent
**emisa•rio -ria** *mf* emissary || *m* outlet
**emisión** *f* (*acción de exhalar; acción de lanzar ondas luminosas, etc.*) emission; (*títulos creados de una vez*) (com) issue; (*acción de emitir títulos nuevos*) (com) issuance; (rad) broadcast; **emisión seriada** (rad) serial
**emi•sor -sora** *adj* emitting; broadcasting || *m* (rad) transmitter || *f* broadcasting station
**emitir** *tr* to emit, send forth; to issue, give out; (*p.ej., opiniones*) to utter, express; (com) to issue; (rad) to broadcast
**emoción** *f* emotion
**emocional** *adj* emotional
**emocionante** *adj* moving, touching; thrilling, exciting
**emocionar** *tr* to move, stir; to thrill
**emoti•vo -va** *adj* emotional
**empacadi•zo -za** *adj* (Arg) touchy
**empaca•do -da** *adj* (Arg) gruff, grim
**empacar** §73 *tr* to pack, to crate || *ref* to be stubborn; (*un animal*) (Am) to balk, get balky
**empa•cón -cona** *adj* (Am) stubborn; (Am) balky
**empacha•do -da** *adj* backward, fumbling
**empachar** *tr* to hinder, embarrass; to disguise; to surfeit, upset the stomach of || *ref* to blush, be embarrassed; to be upset, have indigestion
**empacho** *m* hindrance; embarrassment, bashfulness; indigestion
**empacho•so -sa** *adj* sickening; shameful
**empadronar** *tr* to register, to take the census of || *ref* to register, be registered in the census
**empalagar** §44 *tr* to cloy, pall, surfeit; to bore, to weary
**empalago•so -sa** *adj* cloying, sickening, mawkish; boring, annoying; fawning
**empalar** *tr* impale
**empalizada** *f* palisade, stockade, fence
**empalizar** §60 *tr* to fence in
**empalmar** *tr* to splice, connect, join, couple; to combine || *intr* to connect, make connections; **empalmar con** to connect with; to follow, succeed
**empalme** *m* splice, connection, joint, coupling; combination; (elec) joint; (rr) connection, junction
**empanada** *f* pie; fraud
**empanadilla** *f* pie
**empana•do -da** *adj* unlighted, unventilated || *f* see **empanada**
**empanar** *tr* to crumb, to bread; (*las tierras*) to sow with wheat
**empantanar** *tr* to flood; to obstruct
**empaña•do -da** *adj* dim, misty; blurred, fogged; (*voz*) flat
**empañar** *tr* (*a las criaturas*) to swaddle; to blur, fog, dim, dull; to tarnish, sully || *ref* to blur, fog, dim, dull
**empañetar** *tr* (Am) to plaster
**empapar** *tr* to soak; to soak up, absorb; to drench || *ref* to soak; to be soaked; to become imbued; (coll) to be surfeited
**empapelado** *m* papering, paper hanging; wallpaper; paper lining
**empapela•dor -dora** *mf* paper hanger
**empapelar** *tr* to wrap in paper; to paper, line with paper; to wallpaper; (coll) to bring a criminal charge against
**empaque** *m* packing; (coll) look, appearance, mien; stiffness, stuffiness; (Am) brazenness
**empaquetadura** *f* gasket

**empaquetar** *tr* to pack; to jam, stuff || *ref* to pack; to pack in; (coll) to dress up
**empareda·do -da** *mf* recluse || *m* sandwich
**emparedar** *tr* to wall in, to confine
**emparejar** *tr* to pair, to match; to smooth, make level; to even, make even; (*una puerta*) to close flush || *intr* to come up, come abreast; **emparejar con** to catch up with || *ref* to pair, to match
**emparentar** §2 *intr* to become related by marriage; **emparentar con** (*buena gente*) to marry into the family of; (*una familia rica*) to marry into
**emparrado** *m* arbor, bower
**emparrillar** *tr* to grill
**empasta·dor -dora** *mf* (Am) bookbinder
**empastadura** *f* (Am) binding
**empastar** *tr* (*un diente*) to fill; (*un libro*) to bind with stiff covers; (Am) to convert into pasture land || *ref* (Chile) to be overgrown with weeds
**empaste** *m* (*de diente*) filling; stiff binding
**empastelar** *tr* (typ) to pie
**empatar** *tr* (*en la votación y los juegos*) to tie; (Am) to join, connect; (Am) to tie, fasten || *intr* to tie || *ref* to tie; **empatársela a una persona** to be a match for someone; **empatárselo a una persona** (Guat, Hond) to put it over on someone
**empate** *m* tie, draw; (Col) penholder; (Ven) waste of time
**empavar** *tr* (Ecuad) to annoy; (Peru) to kid, to razz
**empavesado** *m* (naut) dressing, bunting
**empavesar** *tr* to bedeck with flags and bunting; (*un buque*) to dress; (*un monumento*) to veil || *ref* to become overcast
**empavonar** *tr* to blue; (Am) to grease, spread grease over || *ref* (CAm) to dress up
**empecina·do -da** *adj* (Am) stubborn
**empederni·do -da** *adj* hardened, inveterate; hard-hearted
**empedra·do -da** *adj* cloud-flecked; pock-marked; (*caballo*) dark-spotted || *m* stone paving
**empedrar** §2 *tr* to pave with stones; to bespatter
**empegado** *m* tarpaulin
**empegar** §44 *tr* to coat with pitch, to dip in pitch; (*el ganado lanar*) to mark with pitch
**empeine** *m* instep; (*de la bota*) vamp; (*enfermedad cutánea*) tetter; (*región central del hipogastrio*) pubes
**empelotar** *ref* (coll) to get all tangled up; (coll) to get into a row; (Am) to take all one's clothes off; (Mex, W-I) to fall madly in love
**empella** *f* vamp
**empellar** *tr* to push, shove
**empeller** §31 *tr* to push, shove
**empellón** *m* push, shove; **a empellones** pushing, roughly
**empenachar** *tr* to adorn with plumes
**empeña·do -da** *adj* (*disputa*) bitter, heated; **no empeñado** noncommitted
**empeñar** *tr* (*dar en prenda*) to pawn; (*una lucha*) to launch, begin; (*prendar, hipotecar*) to pledge; (*la palabra*) to pledge; to force, compel || *ref* to commit oneself, bind oneself; to go into debt; (*una lucha, una disputa*) to begin, to start; **empeñarse en** to engage in; to persist in, insist on
**empeñe·ro -ra** *mf* (Mex) pawnbroker
**empeño** *m* pledge, engagement, commitment; (*prenda*) pawn; pawnshop; persistence, insistence; eagerness, perseverance; effort, endeavor; pledge, backer, patron; favor, protection; **con empeño** eagerly
**empeño·so -sa** *adj* (Am) eager, persistent
**empeorar** *tr* to impair, make worse || *intr & ref* to get worse, deteriorate
**empequeñecer** §22 *tr* (*hacer más pequeño*) to make smaller, to dwarf; (*amenguar la importancia de*) to belittle || *ref* to get smaller, to dwarf
**emperador** *m* emperor; **los emperadores** the emperor and empress
**empera·triz** *f* (*pl* **-trices**) empress
**emperchar** *tr* to hang on a clothes rack
**emperejilar** *tr & ref* (coll) to dress up, to spruce up
**emperezar** §60 *tr* to delay, put off || *intr & ref* to get lazy
**empericar** §73 *ref* (Col, Ecuad) to get drunk; (Mex) to blush
**emperifollar** *tr & ref* to dress up gaudily
**empernar** *tr* to bolt
**empero** *conj* but, however, yet
**emperrar** *ref* (coll) to get stubborn
**empezar** §18 *tr & intr* to begin
**empicar** §73 *ref* to become infatuated
**empicotar** *tr* to pillory
**empiema** *m* empyema
**empina·do -da** *adj* high, lofty; steep; stiff, stuck-up || *f* (aer) zoom, zooming; **irse a la empinada** (*un caballo*) to rear
**empinar** *tr* to raise, lift; to tip over; (aer) to zoom; (*el codo*) (coll) to crook || *intr* to be a toper || *ref* to stand on tiptoe; (*un caballo*) to rear; to tower, rise high; (aer) to zoom
**empingorota·do -da** *adj* influential; (coll) proud, haughty
**empingorotar** *tr* (coll) to put on top || *ref* (coll) to climb up, get up; (coll) to be stuck-up
**empíre·o -a** *adj & m* empyrean
**empíri·co -ca** *adj* empiric(al) || *mf* empiricist
**empizarrado** *m* slate roof
**empizarrar** *tr* to roof with slate
**emplastar** *tr* to put a plaster on; to put make-up on; (*un negocio*) to tie up, obstruct || *ref* to put make-up on; to smear oneself up
**emplásti·co -ca** *adj* sticky
**emplasto** *m* plaster, poultice
**emplazamiento** *m* emplacement, location; (law) summons
**emplazar** §60 *tr* to place, locate; to summon, to summons
**emplea·do -da** *mf* employee; (*de ofi-*

*cina, de tienda*) clerk; **empleado público** civil servant
**emplear** *tr* to employ; to use; (*el dinero*) to invest; **estarle a uno bien empleado** (coll) to serve someone right || *ref* to be employed; to busy oneself; **empleárselo mal** (coll) to act up, to misbehave
**empleo** *m* employ, employment; use; job, position, occupation
**empleomanía** *f* (coll) eagerness to hold public office
**empleóma•no -na** *mf* (Am) public officeholder, bureaucrat
**emplomar** *tr* to lead; to line with lead; (*un techo*) to cover with lead; to put a lead seal on; (*un diente*) (Arg) to fill
**emplumar** *tr* to put a feather on; to adorn with feathers; to tar and feather; (Hond) to thrash; **emplumarlas** (Col) to beat it || *intr* to fledge, grow feathers
**emplumecer** §22 *intr* to fledge, grow feathers
**empobrecer** §22 *tr* to impoverish || *intr* & *ref* to become poor
**empodrecer** §22 *intr* & *ref* to rot
**empolva•do -da** *adj* (Mex) rusty
**empolvar** *tr* to cover with dust; (*el rostro*) to powder || *ref* to get dusty; (*el rostro*) to powder; (Mex) to get rusty
**empolla•do -da** *adj* primed for an examination
**empollar** *tr* (*huevos*) to brood, hatch; (*estudiar con mucha detención*) (coll) to bone up on || *intr* (coll) to grind, be a grind; **empollar sobre** (coll) to bone up on || *ref* to hatch; to bone up on
**empo•llón -llona** *mf* (coll) grind
**emponcha•do -da** *adj* (SAm) poncho-wearing; (SAm) crafty, hypocritical; (SAm) suspicious-looking
**emponzoñar** *tr* to poison; to corrupt
**emporcar** §81 *tr* to soil, to dirty
**empotra•do -da** *adj* built-in; recessed
**empotrar** *tr* to embed, recess, fasten in a wall || *intr* & *ref* to fit, interlock
**emprende•dor -dora** *adj* enterprising
**emprender** *tr* to undertake; **emprenderla con** (coll) to squabble with, have it out with; **emprenderla para** (coll) to set out for
**empreñar** *tr* to make pregnant || *ref* to become pregnant
**empresa** *f* enterprise, undertaking; company, concern, firm; device, motto; (*la parte patronal*) management; **empresa anunciadora** advertising agency; **empresa de tranvías** traction company; **pequeña empresa** small business
**empresarial** *adj* managerial
**empresa•rio -ria** *mf* contractor; business leader, industrialist; manager; promoter; theatrical manager; **empresario de circo** showman; **empresario de pompas fúnebres** undertaker; **empresario de publicidad** advertising man; **empresario de teatro** impresario, theater manager
**emprestar** *tr* to borrow
**empréstito** *m* loan, government loan
**empujar** *tr* to push, to shove; to replace || *intr* to push, to shove
**empujatierra** *f* bulldozer
**empuje** *m* push; (*fuerza o presión ejercidas por una cosa sobre otra*) thrust; (*espíritu emprendedor*) enterprise, push
**empujón** *m* hard push, shove; **tratar a empujones** (coll) to push around
**empuñadura** *f* (*de la espada*) hilt; (coll) first words of a story; (*de bastón o paraguas*) (Am) handle
**empuñar** *tr* to seize, grasp, clutch; (*un empleo o puesto*) to obtain; (*la mano*) (Chile) to clench; (Bol) to punch; **empuñar el bastón** (fig) to seize the reins
**emular** *tr* & *intr* to emulate; **emular con** to emulate, vie with
**ému•lo -la** *adj* emulous || *mf* rival
**emulsión** *f* emulsion
**emulsionar** *tr* to emulsify
**en** *prep* at; in; into; by; on; of, e.g., **pensar en** to think of
**enaceitar** *tr* to oil || *ref* to get oily, get rancid
**enagua** *f* petticoat; (Am) skirt; **enaguas** petticoat
**enagüillas** *fpl* kilt, short skirt
**enajenación** *f* alienation; estrangement; rapture; (*distracción*) absent-mindedness; **enajenación mental** mental derangement
**enajenar** *tr* (*la propiedad, el dominio; a un amigo*) to alienate, estrange; to enrapture, to transport || *ref* to be enraptured, be transported; **enajenarse de** to dispossess oneself of; (*un amigo*) to become alienated from
**enaltecer** §22 *tr* to exalt, extol
**enamoradi•zo -za** *adj* susceptible
**enamora•do -da** *adj* lovesick; (*propenso a enamorarse*) susceptible || *mf* sweetheart || *m* lover
**enamorar** *tr* to make love to; to enamor, captivate || *ref* to fall in love
**enamoricar** §73 *ref* (coll) to trifle in love
**enangostar** *tr* & *ref* to narrow
**ena•no -na** *adj* dwarfish || *mf* dwarf
**enarbolar** *tr* to hoist, hang out; (*una espada*) to brandish || *ref* to get angry; (*el caballo*) to rear
**enarcar** §73 *tr* to arch; (*los toneles*) to hoop || *ref* to become confused, be bashful; (*el caballo*) (Mex) to rear
**enardecer** §22 *tr* to inflame, excite || *ref* to get excited; (*una parte del cuerpo*) to become inflamed, get sore
**enarenar** *tr* to throw sand on || *ref* (naut) to run aground
**enastar** *tr* (*una herramienta*) to put a handle on; (*una bandera*) to put a shaft on
**encabalgamiento** *m* gun carriage; trestlework; (*en el verso*) enjambment
**encabalgar** §44 *tr* to provide with horses || *intr* to lean, to rest
**encaballar** *tr* to overlap; (typ) to pie
**encabezamiento** *m* heading; (*fórmula con que comienza un documento*)

opening words; tax list; tax rate; **encabezamiento de factura** billhead
**encabezar §60** *tr* (*un escrito*) to put a heading or title on; to head; to register; (*vinos*) to fortify
**encabritar** *ref* (*un caballo*) to rear; (*un buque*) to shoot up, pitch up; (*un avión*) to nose up
**encadenar** *tr* to chain, put in chains; to brace, buttress; to bind, tie together; to tie down
**encajar** *tr* to fit, fit in, make fit; to insert, put in; (*un golpe*) to give, let go; (*dinero*) to put away; (*un chiste*) to tell at the wrong time; to palm off; to throw, hurl; **encajar una cosa a uno** to foist something on someone, to palm something off on someone || *intr* to fit; (*una puerta*) to close right || *ref* to squeeze one's way; (*una prenda de vestir*) to put on; (coll) to butt in, to intrude
**encaje** *m* (*tejido de mallas*) lace; (*labor de taracea*) inlay, mosaic; recess, groove; fitting, matching; insertion; appearance, look
**encaje•ro -ra** *mf* lacemaker; lace dealer
**encajonado** *m* cofferdam
**encajonar** *tr* to box, crate, case; to squeeze in || *ref* (*un río*) to narrow, narrow down; to squeeze in, squeeze through
**encalambrar** *ref* (Am) to get cramps
**encalar** *tr* (*espolvorear con cal*) to lime, sprinkle with lime; (*blanquear con cal*) to whitewash
**encalma•do -da** *adj* (*mercado de valores*) dull, quiet; (*mar, viento*) becalmed
**encalvecer §22** *intr* to get bald
**encalladero** *m* sand bank, shoal
**encallar** *intr* to run aground; to fail, get stuck
**encallecer §22** *intr* (*la piel*) to become callous || *ref* to become callous; (fig) to become callous, become hardened
**encamar** *tr* to spread out on the ground || *ref* (coll) to take to bed; (*el grano*) to droop, bend over
**encaminar** *tr* to direct, show the way to; (*sus esfuerzos, su atención*) to direct || *ref* to set out
**encanalar** *tr* to channel, to pipe
**encandecer §22** *tr* to make white-hot
**encandila•do -da** *adj* (*sombrero*) cocked; (coll) stiff, erect
**encandilar** *tr* to daze, befuddle; (*un fuego*) to stir || *ref* (*los ojos*) to flash
**encanecer §22** *intr & ref* to turn gray; to get old; to become moldy
**encanta•do -da** *adj* (coll) absent-minded, distracted; (*casa*) (coll) rambling
**encanta•dor -dora** *adj* charming, enchanting || *mf* charmer || *f* enchantress
**encantamiento** *m* charm, enchantment
**encantar** *tr* to charm, enchant, bewitch
**encante** *m* auction sale; auction house
**encanto** *m* charm, enchantment, spell
**encantusar** *tr* (coll) to coax, wheedle
**encañada** *f* gorge, ravine
**encañar** *tr* (*el agua*) to pipe; (*las tierras*) to drain; (*las plantas*) to prop up; to wind on a spool
**encañizada** *f* reed fence; weir
**encañonar** *tr* to pipe; to wind on a spool; (*un pliego*) (typ) to tip in
**encaperuzar §60** *tr* to put a hood on || *ref* to put on one's hood
**encapotar** *tr* to cloak || *ref* to frown; to cloud over, become overcast
**encaprichar** *ref* to insist on getting one's way; to become infatuated
**encaracolado** *m* spiral ornament, spiral work
**encara•do -da** *adj* — **bien encarado** well-featured; **mal encarado** ill-featured
**encaramar** *tr* to raise up, lift up; to praise, extol; (coll) to elevate, exalt || *ref* to climb, get on top; to rise, to tower; (Am) to blush
**encarar** *tr* to aim, point; (*una dificultad*) to face || *intr & ref* to come face to face
**encarcelar** *tr* to incarcerate, imprison, jail; (*piezas de madera recién encoladas*) to clamp; to plaster in || *ref* to stay indoors
**encarecer §22** *tr* (*el precio*) to raise; to raise the price of; to extol; to urge; to overrate || *intr & ref* to rise, to rise in price
**encarecidamente** *adv* earnestly, insistently, eagerly
**encarga•do -da** *mf* agent, representative; **encargado de negocios** chargé d'affaires
**encargar §44** *tr* (*mercancías*) to order; (*confiar*) to entrust; to urge, to warn || *ref* to take charge, be in charge
**encargo** *m* assignment, job, charge; (*pedido*) order; warning; **como de encargo** or **ni de encargo** (coll) just the thing, as if made to order
**encariñar** *tr* to awaken love in || *ref* — **encariñarse con** to become fond of, become attached to
**encarnación** *f* incarnation, embodiment
**encarna•do -da** *adj* red; flesh-colored; (*de forma humana*) incarnate
**encarnar** *tr* to incarnate, to embody; (*el anzuelo*) to bait || *intr* to become incarnate; (*una herida*) to heal over
**encarnecer §22** *intr* to put on flesh
**encarniza•do -da** *adj* bloodshot; bloody, fierce, bitter, hard-fought
**encarnizar §60** *tr* to anger, provoke || *ref* to get angry; to become fierce; **encarnizarse con** or **en** to be merciless to
**encaro** *m* aim; stare; blunderbuss
**encarrilar** *tr* to put back on the rails; to set right, to put on the right track; to guide, direct
**encarruja•do -da** *adj* wrinkled; (*pelo*) kinky; (*terreno*) (Mex) rough
**encartar** *tr* to enroll, register; to outlaw; (*un naipe*) to slip in || *ref* to be unable to discard
**encartonar** *tr* to cover with cardboard; (*libros*) to bind in boards
**encasar** *tr* (*un hueso dislocado*) to set (*a broken bone*)
**encasillado** *m* set of pigeonholes; (*lista*

*de candidatos apoyados por el gobierno*) government slate; (SAm) checkerwork
**encasillar** *tr* to pigeonhole; to sort out, classify; (*el gobierno a un candidato*) to slate
**encasquetar** *tr* (*un sombrero*) to stick on the head; (*una idea*) to drive in; to force on
**encasquillar** *tr* to put a tip on; (*un caballo*) (Am) to shoe || *ref* to stick, get stuck
**encastilla•do -da** *adj* haughty, proud
**encastillar** *tr* to fortify with castles; to pile up || *ref* to stick, get stuck; to take to the hills; to stick to one's opinion
**encastrar** *tr* to engage, to mesh
**encastre** *m* engaging, meshing; groove, socket; insert
**encauchar** *tr* to cover with rubber, line with rubber
**encausar** *tr* to prosecute, to sue, to bring to trial
**encausticar §73** *tr* to wax
**encáustico** *m* floor wax, furniture polish
**encauzar §60** *tr* (*una corriente*) to channel; to guide, direct
**encavar** *ref* to hide, burrow
**encebollado** *m* beef stew with onions
**encelar** *tr* to make jealous || *ref* to get jealous; to be in rut
**encella** *f* cheese mold
**encenagar §44** *ref* to get covered with mud; to wallow in vice
**encencerrar** *tr* (*al ganado*) to put a bell on
**encendada** *f* kindling, brush
**encendedor** *m* lighter; **encendedor de bolsillo** pocket lighter
**encender §51** *tr* to light, kindle; to ignite, set fire to; (*la luz, la radio*) to turn on; (*la lengua*) to burn; to stir up, excite || *ref* to catch fire, to ignite; to become excited; to blush
**encendi•do -da** *adj* bright, high-colored; red, flushed; keen, enthusiastic || *m* ignition
**encenizar §60** *tr* to cover with ashes || *ref* to get covered with ashes
**encepar** *tr* to put in the stocks || *intr & ref* to take deep root
**encera•do -da** *adj* wax, wax-colored; (*huevo*) boiled || *m* oilcloth; tarpaulin; (*pizarra*) blackboard
**encerar** *tr* to wax || *intr & ref* (*el grano*) to ripen, turn yellow
**encerotar** *tr* (*el hilo*) to wax
**encerradero** *m* sheepfold; (taur) bull pen
**encerrar §2** *tr* to shut in; to lock in, lock up; to contain, include; to encircle; to imply || *ref* to lock oneself in; to go into seclusion; **encerrarse con** to be closeted with
**encespedar** *tr* to sod
**encía** *f* gum
**encíclica** *f* encyclical
**enciclopedia** *f* encyclopedia
**enciclopédi•co -ca** *adj* encyclopedic
**encierro** *m* locking up, confinement; inclusion: encirclement; lockup, prison; solitary confinement; retirement, retreat; (taur) bull pen
**encima** *adv* above, overhead, on top; at hand, here now; besides, in addition; **de encima** (Chile) in the bargain; **echarse encima** to take upon oneself; **encima de** on, upon; above, over; **por encima** hastily, superficially; **por encima de** above, over; in spite of; **quitarse de encima** to get rid of, to shake off
**encina** *f* holm oak, evergreen oak
**encinta** *adj* pregnant
**encintado** *m* curb
**encintar** *tr* to trim with ribbons; to provide with curbs
**enclaustrar** *tr* to cloister; to hide away
**enclavar** *tr* to nail; to pierce, transfix; (*el pie del caballo*) to prick; (coll) to cheat
**enclave** *m* enclave
**enclavijar** *tr* to dowel; (*un instrumento*) to peg
**enclenque** *adj* sickly, feeble
**enclíti•co -ca** *adj & m* enclitic
**enclocar §81** *intr & ref* to brood
**encofrado** *m* planking, timbering; (*para el hormigón*) form
**encoger §17** *tr* to shrink, shrivel; to discourage; to draw in || *intr* to shrink, shrivel || *ref* to shrink, shrivel; to be discouraged; to be bashful; (*humillarse*) to cringe; (*en la cama*) to curl up; **encogerse de hombros** to shrug one's shoulders
**encogi•do -da** *adj* bashful, timid
**encogimiento** *m* shrinkage; crouch; bashfulness, timidity; **encogimiento de hombros** shrug
**encojar** *tr* to cripple, to lame || *ref* to become lame; (coll) to feign illness
**encolar** *tr* to glue; (*la superficie que ha de pintarse*) to size; (*el vino*) to clarify; (*p.ej., una pelota*) to throw out of reach
**encolerizar §60** *tr* to anger || *ref* to get angry
**encomendar §2** *tr* to commend, entrust, commit; to knight || *ref* to commend oneself; to send regards
**encomiar** *tr* to praise, extol
**encomienda** *f* charge, commission; commendation, praise; favor, protection; knight's cross; royal land grant (*with Indian inhabitants*); (Am) parcel post; (Mex) fruit stand
**encomio** *m* encomium
**enconamiento** *m* soreness; rancor, ill will
**enconar** *tr* to make sore, inflame; to aggravate, irritate || *ref* to get sore, become inflamed; (*una herida; el ánimo de uno*) to rankle, to fester
**enconchar** *ref* (Am) to draw back into one's shell, keep aloof
**encono** *m* rancor, ill will; (Col, Chile, Mex, W-I) soreness
**encono•so -sa** *adj* sore, sensitive; harmful; rancorous
**encontra•do -da** *adj* opposite, facing; contrary; hostile; **estar encontrados** to be at odds
**encontrar** *tr* to encounter, to meet; (*ha-*

*llar*) to find || *intr* to meet; to collide || *ref* to meet, meet each other; to be, be situated; to find oneself; **encontrarse con** to meet, run into
**encontrón** *m* bump, jolt, collision
**encopeta·do -da** *adj* aristocratic, of noble descent; conceited, boastful
**encorajar** *tr* to encourage || *ref* to fly into a rage
**encorajinar** *ref* (coll) to fly into a rage; (Chile) to break up, go to ruin
**encorchar** *tr* (*botellas*) to cork; (*abejas*) to hive
**encordar §61** *tr* (*un violín, una raqueta*) to string; to wrap, wind up with rope
**encordelar** *tr* to string; to tie with strings
**encornudar** *tr* to cuckold, make a cuckold of || *intr* to grow horns
**encorralar** *tr* to corral
**encortinar** *tr* to curtain
**encorvada** *f* stoop, bending over; **hacer la encorvada** (coll) to malinger
**encorvar** *tr* to bend over || *ref* to stoop, bend over; to be partial, be biased
**encovar §61** *tr & ref* to hide away
**encrespar** *tr* to curl; (*el pelo*) to make stand on end; (*plumas*) to ruffle; (*las olas*) to stir up; to irritate, anger || *ref* to curl; to bristle, stand on end; (*el mar, las olas*) to get rough; to get involved; to bristle, get angry
**encresta·do -da** *adj* proud, haughty
**encrucijada** *f* crossroads, street intersection; ambush, snare, trap
**encrudecer §22** *tr* to make raw; to aggravate
**encuadernación** *f* bookbinding; (*taller*) bindery; **encuadernación a la holandesa** half binding
**encuaderna·dor -dora** *mf* bookbinder
**encuadernar** *tr* to bind; **sin encuadernar** unbound
**encuadrar** *tr* (*encerrar en un marco o cuadro*) to frame; (*incluir dentro de sí*) to encompass; (*encajar*) to insert, fit in; (Arg) to summarize
**encuadre** *m* film adaptation; (mov & telv) frame
**encubar** *tr* to put in a cask or vat; (min) to shore up
**encubierta** *f* fraud, deception
**encubrimiento** *m* concealment; (law) complicity
**encubrir §83** *tr* to hide, conceal || *ref* to hide; to disguise oneself
**encuentro** *m* encounter, meeting; clash, collision; (*hallazgo*) find; (sport) game, match; **encuentro fronterizo** border clash; **llevarse de encuentro** (CAm, Mex, W-I) to knock down, run over; (CAm, Mex, W-I) to drag down to ruin; **mal encuentro** foul play; **salir al encuentro a** to go to meet; to get ahead of; to take a stand against
**encuerar** *tr* (Am) to strip of clothes; (Am) to fleece || *ref* (Am) to strip, get undressed
**encuesta** *f* inquiry; (*cuestionario para conocer la opinión pública*) poll, survey
**encuitar** *ref* to grieve
**encumbra·do -da** *adj* high, lofty; sublime; influential
**encumbramiento** *m* height, elevation; exaltation
**encumbrar** *tr* to raise, elevate; to exalt || *ref* to rise; to be exalted; to be proud; to be flowery, use flowery speech; (*subir una cosa a mucha altura*) to tower
**encunar** *tr* to cradle; to catch between the horns
**encurtido** *m* pickle
**encurtir** *tr* to pickle
**enchapado** *m* veneer
**enchapar** *tr* to veneer
**encharcar §73** *tr* to make a puddle of; (*el estómago*) to upset || *ref* to turn into a puddle; to wallow in vice
**enchavetar** *tr* to key
**enchilada** *f* (Guat, Mex) corn cake with tomato sauce seasoned with chili
**enchilado** *m* (Cuba, Mex) shellfish stew with chili sauce
**enchinar** *tr* to pave with pebbles; (Mex) to curl || *ref* (Mex) to get goose flesh
**enchispar** *tr* (Am) to make drunk || *ref* (Am) to get drunk
**enchivar** *ref* (Col, Ecuad, CAm) to fly into a rage
**enchufar** *tr* (*un tubo o caño*) to fit; (*dos tubos o caños*) to connect, connect together; (*dos negocios*) to merge; (elec) to connect, plug in || *intr* to fit || *ref* to merge
**enchufe** *m* fitting; (*de tubo o caño*) male end; (*de dos tubos*) joint; (elec) connector; (elec) plug; (elec) receptacle; (coll) sinecure, easy job; **tener enchufe** (coll) to have pull, to have a drag
**enchufismo** *m* (coll) spoils system
**enchufista** *m* (coll) spoilsman
**ende** *adv* — **por ende** therefore
**endeble** *adj* feeble, weak; worthless
**endecha** *f* dirge
**endechadera** *f* hired mourner
**endemia** *f* endemic
**endémi·co -ca** *adj* endemic
**endemonia·do -da** *adj* possessed of the devil; furious, wild; (coll) devilish
**endentar §2** *tr & intr* to mesh
**endentecer §22** *intr* to teethe
**enderezar §60** *tr* to stand up; to straighten; to direct; to put in order; to regulate || *intr* to go straight || *ref* to stand up, straighten up; to head, make one's way; to go straight; (aer) to flatten out, to level off
**endeuda·do -da** *adj* indebted
**endeudar** *ref* to run into debt; to acknowledge one's indebtedness
**endevota·do -da** *adj* pious, devout; fond, devoted
**endiabla·do -da** *adj* devilish; deformed, ugly; mean, wicked; (Arg) difficult, complicated
**endilgar §44** *tr* (coll) to send, direct; (coll) to spring, unload
**endiosar** *tr* to deify || *ref* to get stuck-up; to get absorbed
**endominga·do -da** *adj* Sunday; all dressed up

**endomingar** §44 *ref* to get dressed in one's Sunday best
**endosante** *mf* endorser
**endosar** *tr* (*un documento de crédito*) to endorse; (*una cosa poco grata*) to unload
**endosata•rio -ria** *mf* endorsee
**endoso** *m* endorsement
**endriago** *m* fabulous monster
**endri•no -na** *adj* sloe-colored || *m* (*arbusto*) sloe, blackthorn || *f* (*fruto*) sloe
**endrogar** §44 *ref* (Am) to run into debt
**endulzar** §60 *tr* to sweeten; to make bearable
**endura•dor -dora** *adj* saving, stingy
**endurar** *tr* to harden; to delay, put off; (*tolerar*) to endure; to save, spare || *ref* to get hard
**endurecer** §22 *tr* to harden; (*robustecer, acostumbrar*) to inure
**endureci•do -da** *adj* hard, strong; inured; hard-hearted; tenacious, obstinate
**enebrina** *f* juniper berry
**enebro** *m* juniper
**enecha•do -da** *adj & mf* foundling
**eneldo** *m* dill
**enema** *f* enema
**enemiga** *f* enmity, hatred
**enemi•go -ga** *adj* enemy; hostile || *mf* enemy, foe; **el enemigo malo** the Evil One || *f* see **enemiga**
**enemistad** *f* enmity
**enemistar** *tr* to make an enemy of; to make enemies of || *ref* to become enemies
**energía** *f* energy; power
**enérgi•co -ca** *adj* energetic
**energúme•no -na** *adj* fiendish || *mf* crazy person, wild person
**enero** *m* January
**enervar** *tr* to enervate; to weaken
**enési•mo -ma** *adj* nth
**enfadadi•zo -za** *adj* peevish, irritable
**enfadar** *tr* to annoy, bother; to anger
**enfado** *m* annoyance, bother; anger
**enfado•so -sa** *adj* annoying, disagreeable
**enfaldar** *ref* to tuck up one's skirt
**enfardar** *tr* to bale, to pack
**énfa•sis** *m* (*pl* **-sis**) emphasis; bombast, affected speech
**enfasizar** §60 *tr* to emphasize
**enfáti•co -ca** *adj* emphatic; affected
**enfermar** *tr* to make sick || *intr* to get sick
**enfermedad** *f* sickness, illness, disease
**enfermera** *f* nurse; **enfermera ambulante** visiting nurse
**enfermería** *f* infirmary
**enfermero** *m* male nurse
**enfermi•zo -za** *adj* sickly; (*clima*) unhealthy
**enfer•mo -ma** *adj* sick, ill; (*enfermizo*) sickly; **enfermo de amor** lovesick || *mf* patient
**enfermo•so -sa** *adj* (Am) sickly
**enfiestar** *ref* (Am) to have a good time
**enfilar** *tr* to line up; (*p.ej., perlas*) to string; to aim; to go down, to go up; (mil) to enfilade || *intr* to bear
**enfisema** *m* emphysema
**enflaquecer** §22 *tr* to make thin; to weaken || *intr* to get thin; to flag, slacken || *ref* to get thin, lose weight
**enflauta•do -da** adj (coll) pompous, inflated
**enflautar** *tr* to blow up, inflate; (coll) to cheat
**enfocar** §73 *tr* to focus; (fig) to size up
**enfoque** *m* focus, focusing; (fig) approach (*to a problem*)
**enfoscar** §73 *tr* to trim with mortar; to patch with mortar; to darken, make dark || *ref* to become sullen, become grouchy; to become absorbed in business; to become overcast
**enfrailar** *tr* to make a friar or monk of || *ref* to become a friar or monk
**enfranque** *m* shank
**enfrascar** §73 *tr* to bottle || *ref* to become involved, intangled; to be sunk in work; to have a good time
**enfrenar** *tr* (*un caballo*) to bridle; (*un tren*) to brake; to check
**enfrentar** *tr* to put face to face; (*p.ej., al enemigo*) to face || *intr* to be facing || *ref* to meet face to face; **enfrentarse con** to stand up to; to cope with
**enfrente** *adv* opposite, in front; **enfrente de** opposite, in front of; opposed to
**enfriadera** *f* bottle cooler, ice pail
**enfriar** §77 *tr* to cool, to chill; (Am) to kill || *intr & ref* to cool off
**enfundar** *tr* to sheathe, to put in a case; to stuff; (*un tambor*) to muffle
**enfurecer** §22 *tr* to infuriate, anger || *ref* to rage
**enfurruñar** *ref* (coll) to sulk
**engalanar** *tr* to adorn, deck out, dress
**engalla•do -da** *adj* straight, erect; haughty
**engallador** *m* checkrein
**enganchar** *tr* to hook; (*un caballo*) to hitch; (*un coche de ferrocarril*) to couple; to recruit; to inveigle || *intr* to get caught || *ref* to get caught; (mil) to enlist
**enganche** *m* hook; hooking; hitching; coupling; inveigling; recruiting; enlisting; (rr) coupler
**engañabo•bos** *mf* (*pl* **-bos**) (coll) bamboozler
**engaña•dor -dora** *adj* deceptive; (*simpático*) winsome
**engañar** *tr* to deceive, cheat, fool; (*el tiempo*) to while away; (*el sueño, el hambre*) to ward off; to wheedle || *ref* to be mistaken
**engañifa** *f* (coll) deception, trick
**engaño** *m* deception, deceit, fraud; mistake; falsehood; **llamarse a engaño** to back out because of fraud
**engaño•so -sa** *adj* deceptive
**engargantar** *tr* (*un ave*) to stuff the throat of || *intr & ref* to mesh, to engage
**engarzar** §60 *tr* to link, string, wire; to curl; to enchase; (Col) to hook
**engastar** *tr* to enchase, mount, set
**engaste** *m* enchasing, mounting, setting
**engatusar** *tr* (coll) to coax, wheedle; to inveigle

**engendrar** *tr* to beget, engender; (geom) to generate
**engendro** *m* foetus; botch, bungle; (*criatura informe*) runt, stunt; **mal engendro** (coll) young tough
**engolfar** *intr* to go far out in the ocean || *ref* to go far out in the ocean; to become deeply involved; to be lost in thought
**engoma•do -da** *adj* (Chile) all dressed up || *m* (CAm) hangover
**engomar** *tr* to gum || *ref* (Am) to have a hangover
**engorda** *f* (Am) fattening; (Am) animals being fattened
**engordar** *tr* to fatten || *intr* to get fat; (coll) to get fat, get rich
**engorro** *m* bother, nuisance, obstacle
**engorro•so -sa** *adj* annoying
**engoznar** *tr* to hinge, to hang on a hinge
**engranaje** *m* gear, gears, teeth; (fig) link, connection; **engranaje de distribución** (aut) timing gears; **engranaje de tornillo sin fin** worm gear
**engranar** *tr* to gear, to mesh; to throw into gear || *intr* to gear, to mesh
**engrandecer** **§22** *tr* to amplify, enlarge, magnify; to exalt, extol; to enhance
**engrane** *m* gear; mesh
**engranerar** *tr* (*el grano*) to store
**engrapar** *tr* to clamp, to cramp
**engrasador** *m* grease cup; **engrasador de pistón** grease gun
**engrasar** *tr* to grease; to smear with grease
**engrase** *m* greasing; grease
**engravar** *tr* to spread gravel over
**engredar** *tr* to chalk, to clay
**engreí•do -da** *adj* conceited, vain
**engreimiento** *m* conceit, vanity
**engreír** **§58** *tr* to make conceited; (Am) to spoil, pamper || *ref* to become conceited
**engreña•do -da** *adj* disheveled
**engrescar** **§73** *tr* to incite to fight; to incite to merriment || *ref* to pick a fight; to join in the fun
**engrifar** *tr* to curl, to crisp || *ref* to curl up; to stand on end; (*un caballo*) to rear
**engrillar** *tr* to shackle, fetter || *ref* (*las patatas*) to sprout
**engringar** **§44** *ref* to act like a foreigner
**engrosar** **§61** *tr* to broaden; to enlarge || *intr* to get fat || *ref* to broaden; to swell, get bigger
**engrudar** *tr* to paste
**engrudo** *m* paste
**engualdrapar** *tr* to caparison
**enguapear** *ref* (Mex) to get drunk
**enguirnaldar** *tr* to garland, to wreathe; to trim, bedeck
**engullir** **§13** *tr* to gulp down
**engurrio** *m* sadness, melancholy
**enhebrar** *tr* (*una aguja*) to thread; (*perlas*) to string; (*mentiras*) (coll) to rattle off
**enhestar** **§2** *tr* to stand upright, to erect; to hoist, lift up
**enhies•to -ta** *adj* upright, straight, erect
**enhilar** *tr* to thread; to direct; to line up; (*ideas*) to marshal || *intr* to set out
**enhorabuena** *adv* safely, luckily; **enhorabuena que** thank heavens that || *f* congratulations; **dar la enhorabuena a** to congratulate
**enhoramala** *adv* unluckily, under an unlucky star; **nacer enhoramala** to be born under an unlucky star; **vete enhoramala** go to the devil
**enhornar** *tr* to put into the oven
**enigma** *m* enigma, riddle, puzzle
**enigmáti•co -ca** *adj* enigmatic(al)
**enjabonar** *tr* to soap, to lather; (*adular*) (coll) to soft-soap; (*reprender*) (coll) to upbraid
**enjaezar** **§60** *tr* to harness, put trappings on
**enjalbegado** *m* whitewashing
**enjalbegar** **§44** *tr* to whitewash; (*el rostro*) to paint || *ref* to paint the face
**enjambrar** *intr* (*las abejas*) to swarm; to multiply in great numbers
**enjambre** *m* swarm
**enjaretado** *m* grating, lattice work
**enjarrar** *ref* (C-R, Mex) to stand with arms akimbo
**enjaular** *tr* to cage; (coll) to jail, lock up
**enjergar** **§44** *tr* (coll) to launch, get started, to start on a shoestring
**enjoyar** *tr* to adorn with jewels; to set with precious stones; to adorn
**enjuagadien•tes** *m* (*pl* **-tes**) mouthwash
**enjuagar** **§44** *tr* to rinse, rinse out
**enjuague** *m* rinse; rinsing water; mouthwash; rinsing cup; (coll) plot
**enjugador** *m* drier; clotheshorse
**enjugama•nos** *m* (*pl* **-nos**) towel, hand towel
**enjugaparabri•sas** *m* (*pl* **-sas**) windshield wiper
**enjugar** **§44** *tr* (*secar*) to dry; (*el sudor*) to wipe, wipe off; (*lágrimas*) to wipe away; (*deudas, un déficit*) to wipe out || *ref* to lose weight
**enjuiciamiento** *m* procedure; prosecution, suit; trial; judgment, sentence
**enjuiciar** *tr* to prosecute, to sue; to try; to judge
**enjundio•so -sa** *adj* fatty, greasy; solid, substantial
**enju•to -ta** *adj* (*tiempo, clima; ojos*) dry; lean, skinny; quiet, stolid || **enjutos** *mpl* brushwood; (*para excitar la gana de beber*) tidbits
**enlabiar** *tr* to entice, take in; to press one's lips against
**enlace** *m* connection, linking; relationship; betrothal, engagement; marriage; (mil, phonet) liaison; (rr) connection, junction
**enlaciar** *tr, intr & ref* to wither, wilt, shrivel; to rumple
**enladrillado** *m* brickwork; bricklaying; brick paving
**enladrillar** *tr* to pave with bricks
**enlajado** *m* (Ven) flagstone
**enlajar** *tr* (Ven) to pave with flagstones
**enlardar** *tr* to baste
**enlatado** *m* canning
**enlatar** *tr* to can; (Am) to roof with tin, to line with tin
**enlazar** **§60** *tr* to connect, to link; to lace; (*un animal con el lazo*) to lasso

|| *intr* (*p.ej., dos trenes*) to connect || *ref* to be connected, to be linked; to connect; to get married; to become related by marriage

**enlechar** *tr* to grout

**enlistonado** *m* lathing, lath

**enlistonar** *tr* to lath

**enlodar** *tr* to muddy, smear with mud; to plaster with mud; to seal with mud; (fig) to sling mud at

**enloquecer** §22 *tr* to drive crazy || *intr* to go crazy

**enloquecimiento** *m* insanity, madness

**enlosado** *m* flagstone paving

**enlosar** *tr* to pave with flagstone

**enlozar** §60 *tr* (Am) to enamel

**enlozado** *m* (Am) enamelware

**enlucido** *m* plaster, coat (*of plaster*)

**enlucir** §45 *tr* (*una pared*) to plaster; (*la plata*) to polish

**enlutar** *tr* to put in mourning, to hang with crape; to darken, sadden || *ref* to dress in mourning

**enmaderar** *tr* to cover with boards; to build the framework for

**enmagrecer** §22 *tr* to make thin || *intr & ref* to get thin

**enmalecer** §22 *tr* to spoil || *ref* to get full of weeds, to be overgrown with weeds

**enmarañar** *tr* to entangle; to confuse || *ref* to become entangled; to become overcast, get cloudy

**enmarcar** §73 *tr* to frame

**enmarchitar** *tr & ref* to wither

**enmaridar** *intr & ref* to take a husband

**enmarillecer** §22 *ref* to turn yellow, to turn pale

**enmasar** *tr* (*tropas*) to mass

**enmascarar** *tr* to mask; to camouflage || *ref* to put on a mask; to masquerade

**enmasillar** *tr* to putty

**enmendación** *f* emendation

**enmendar** §2 *tr* (*corregir*) to emend; (*reformar*) to amend; (*resarcir*) to make amends for || *ref* to amend, to mend one's ways, to go straight

**enmienda** *f* (*corrección*) emendation; (*propuesta de variante*) amendment; (*satisfacción del daño hecho*) amends

**enmohecer** §22 *tr* to make moldy; to rust; to neglect || *ref* to get moldy; to rust; (*la memoria*) to get rusty; to fade away

**enmontar** *ref* (CAm, Mex, Col, Ven) to become overgrown with brush

**enmudecer** §22 *tr* to hush, to silence || *intr* to hush up, keep quiet; to become dumb, lose one's voice

**enmuescar** §73 *tr* to notch; (carp) to mortise

**ennegrecer** §22 *tr* to blacken, dye black || *ref* to turn black; (*el porvenir*) to be black

**ennoblecer** §22 *tr* to ennoble; to glorify, enhance

**ennoblecimiento** *m* ennoblement; glory, splendor; (*grandeza de alma*) nobility

**enodio** *m* fawn, young deer

**enojada** *f* (Mex) fit of anger

**enojadi•zo -za** *adj* irritable, ill-tempered

**enojar** *tr* to anger; to annoy, vex || *ref* to get angry; **enojarse con** or **contra** to get angry with (*a person*); **enojarse de** to get angry at (*a thing*)

**enojo** *m* anger; annoyance, bother

**eno•jón -jona** *adj* (Chile, Ecuad, Mex) irritable, ill-tempered

**enojo•so -sa** *adj* annoying, bothersome

**enorgullecer** §22 *tr* to fill with pride, make proud || *ref* to be proud; **enorgullecerse de** to pride oneself on

**enorme** *adj* enormous, huge

**enquiciar** *tr* (*una puerta, una ventana*) to hang; to fasten, make firm

**enrabiar** *tr* to enrage || *intr* to have rabies || *ref* to become enraged

**enramar** *tr* (*ramos*) to intertwine; to adorn with branches || *intr* to sprout branches || *ref* to hide in the branches

**enranciar** *tr* to make rancid || *ref* to get rancid

**enrarecer** §22 *tr* to rarefy; to make scarce || *intr* to become scarce || *ref* to rarefy; to become scarce

**enrarecimiento** *m* (*p.ej., del aire*) thinness; scarceness, scarcity

**enrasar** *tr* to make flush; to grade, to level || *intr* to be flush

**enratonar** *ref* (coll) to get sick from eating mice; (Ven) to have a hangover

**enredadera** *adj* (*planta*) climbing || *f* climbing plant, vine

**enreda•dor -dora** *mf* (coll) gossip, busybody

**enredar** *tr* to catch in a net; (*redes, una trampa*) to set; to tangle up; to involve, to entangle; (*una pelea*) to start; to intertwine, interweave; to endanger, compromise || *intr* to romp around, be frisky || *ref* to get tangled up; to get involved, become entangled; (coll) to have an affair

**enredijo** *m* entanglement

**enredo** *m* tangle; involvement, entanglement, complication; restlessness; friskiness; mischievous lie; (*de una novela, un drama*) plot; (*trato ilícito de hombre y mujer*) liaison

**enre•dón -dona** *adj* scheming || *mf* schemer

**enredo•so -sa** *adj* entangled, complicated, difficult

**enrejado** *m* grating, trellis, latticework; iron railing; grill; openwork embroidery

**enrejar** *tr* to grate, lattice; (*una ventana*) to put a grate on; to fence with an iron grating; (*ladrillos, tablas*) to pile alternately crosswise; (Mex) to darn

**enrielar** *tr* to make into ingots; (Am) to lay rails on; (Am) to put on the tracks; (Am) to put on the right track

**enriquecer** §22 *tr* to enrich || *intr & ref* to get rich

**enrisca•do -da** *adj* craggy, full of cliffs

**enrizar** §60 *tr & ref* to curl

**enrocar** §73 *tr & intr* (chess) to castle

**enrodrigar** §44 *tr* to prop, prop up

**enrojar** *tr* to redden, make red; (*el*

*horno*) to heat up || *ref* to redden, turn red
**enrojecer** §22 *tr* to make red; to make red-hot; to make blush || *intr* to blush || *ref* to turn red; to get red-hot; to flush; to get sore, get inflamed
**enromar** *tr* to make dull, make blunt
**enronquecer** §22 *tr* to make hoarse || *intr & ref* to get hoarse
**enronquecimiento** *m* hoarseness
**enroque** *m* (chess) castling
**enroscar** §73 *tr* to coil, twist; to screw in || *ref* to coil, twist
**enrubiar** *tr* to bleach, make blond || *ref* to turn blond
**enrubio** *m* bleaching; bleaching lotion
**enrular** *tr & ref* (Arg) to curl
**ensacar** §73 *tr* to bag, put in a bag
**ensaimada** *f* twisted coffee cake
**ensalada** *f* salad; hodgepodge; fiasco, flop
**ensaladera** *f* salad bowl
**ensalmar** *tr* (*un hueso*) to set; to treat or heal by incantation
**ensalmo** *m* incantation, spell; **como por ensalmo** as if by magic
**ensalzar** §60 *tr* to exalt, elevate, extol
**ensamblar** *tr* to assemble, join, fit together; **ensamblar a cola de milano** or **a cola de pato** to dovetail
**ensanchador** *m* glove stretcher
**ensanchar** *tr* to widen, to enlarge; (*una prenda ajustada*) to ease, let out; (*el corazón*) to unburden || *intr & ref* to be proud and haughty
**ensanche** *m* widening, extension; (*de una calle*) extension; suburban development; allowance (*for enlargement of garment*)
**ensandecer** §22 *intr* to go crazy
**ensangrenta•do -da** *adj* bloody, gory
**ensangrentar** §2 *tr* to bathe in blood; to stain with blood || *ref* to rage, to go wild; (*p.ej., las manos*) to bloody, make bloody
**ensañar** *tr* to anger, enrage || *ref* to be cruel, be merciless; (*una enfermedad*) to rage
**ensartar** *tr* (*una aguja*) to thread; (*cuentas*) to string; to stick; (coll) to rattle off || *ref* to squeeze in
**ensayar** *tr* to try, try on, try out; (*un espectáculo*) to rehearse; (*minerales*) to assay; to teach, train; to test || *ref* to practice
**ensaye** *m* assay
**ensayista** *mf* essayist; (Chile) assayer
**ensayo** *m* trying, trial; testing, test; (*género literario*) essay; (*de minerales*) assay; exercise, practice; (theat) rehearsal; **ensayo general** dress rehearsal
**ensenada** *f* inlet, cove
**enseña** *f* standard, ensign
**enseña•do -da** *adj* trained, informed; (*perro de caza*) trained
**enseñanza** *f* teaching; education, instruction; (*ejemplo que sirve de experiencia*) lesson; **enseñanza superior** higher education
**enseñar** *tr* to teach; to train; to show, point out || *intr* to teach
**enseñorear** *ref* to control oneself; **enseñorearse de** to take possession of
**enseres** *mpl* utensils, equipment, household goods
**enseriar** *ref* (Am) to become serious
**ensillar** *tr* to saddle
**ensimismamiento** *m* absorption in thought, deep thought
**ensimismar** *ref* to become absorbed in thought; (Chile, Ecuad, Peru) to be proud, be boastful
**ensoberbecer** §22 *tr* to make proud || *ref* to become proud; (*el mar, las olas*) to swell, get rough
**ensoberbecimiento** *m* haughtiness
**ensombrecer** §22 *tr* to darken || *ref* to get dark; to become sad and gloomy
**ensoña•dor -dora** *adj* dreamy || *mf* dreamer
**ensopar** *tr* to dip, to dunk; (Am) to soak, to drench
**ensordece•dor -dora** *adj* deafening
**ensordecer** §22 *tr* to deafen; (*una consonante sonora*) to unvoice || *intr* to become deaf; to play deaf, to not answer || *ref* to unvoice
**ensortijar** *tr* to curl, make curly; (*la nariz de un animal*) to ring, put a ring in || *ref* to curl
**ensuciar** *tr* to dirty, soil; to stain, smear; to defile, sully || *ref* to soil oneself; to take bribes
**ensueño** *m* dream; daydream
**entablado** *m* flooring; wooden framework
**entablar** *tr* to board, board up; (*un hueso roto*) to splint; (*una conversación*) to start; (*p.ej., una batalla*) to launch; (*un pleito*) to bring; (*las piezas del ajedrez y de las damas*) to set up || *ref* (*el viento*) to settle
**entable** *m* boarding; (*en los juegos de ajedrez y damas*) position of men; (Col) business, undertaking
**entablillar** *tr* (*un hueso roto*) to splint
**enta•blón -blona** *adj* (Peru) blustering, bragging || *mf* (Peru) bully
**entalegar** §44 *tr* to bag, put in a bag; (*dinero*) to hoard
**entalladura** *f* carving, sculpture; engraving; slot, groove, mortise; cut, incision (*in a tree*)
**entallar** *tr* to carve, to sculpture; to engrave; to notch; to groove, mortise; (*un traje*) to fit, to tailor || *intr* to take shape; (*el vestido*) to fit; (coll) to go well, be fitting
**entallecer** §22 *intr & ref* to shoot, to sprout
**entapizar** §60 *tr* to tapestry, to hang with tapestry; to cover with a fabric; to overgrow, to spread over
**entarimado** *m* parquet, inlaid floor, hardwood floor
**entarimar** *tr* to parquet, to put an inlaid floor on || *ref* (coll) to put on airs
**entarugar** §44 *tr* to pave with wooden blocks || *ref* (*el sombrero*) (Ven) to stick on
**ente** *m* being; (coll) guy, queer duck
**enteca•do -da** or **ente•co -ca** *adj* sickly, frail

**enteleri•do -da** *adj* shaking with cold, shaking with fright; (Am) sickly, frail
**entena** *f* lateen yard
**entenado -da** *mf* stepchild || *m* stepson || *f* stepdaughter
**entendederas** *fpl* (coll) brains; **tener malas entendederas** (coll) to have no brains
**entende•dor -dora** *adj* understanding, intelligent || *mf* understanding person; **al buen entendedor, pocas palabras** a word to the wise is enough
**entender** *m* understanding, opinion || §51 *tr* to understand; to intend, mean || *intr* — **entender de** to be a judge of; to be experienced as; **entender de razón** to listen to reason; **entender en** to be familiar with, to deal with || *ref* to be understood; to be meant; to have a secret understanding; **entenderse con** to get along with; to concern; (*una mujer*) to have an affair with
**entendi•do -da** *adj* expert, skilled; informed; **no darse por entendido** to take no notice, to pretend not to understand; **los entendidos** informed sources; **un entendido en** a well-informed person in
**entendimiento** *m* understanding
**entenebrecer** §22 *tr* to darken; to confuse || *ref* to get dark; to become confused
**entera•do -da** *adj* informed, posted; (Chile) conceited; (Chile) intrusive, meddlesome || *mf* insider
**enterar** *tr* to inform, acquaint; (Am) to pay; (Arg, Chile) to complete || *intr* (Chile) to get better; (Chile) to drift along || *ref* to find out; (Am) to recover; **enterarse de** to find out about, to become aware of
**entereza** *f* entirety, completeness; wholeness; perfection; fairness; constancy, fortitude; strictness
**enteri•zo -za** *adj* in one piece
**enternece•dor -dora** *adj* moving, touching
**enternecer** §22 *tr* to move, to touch || *ref* to be moved to pity
**enternecimiento** *m* pity, compassion
**ente•ro -ra** *adj* entire, whole, complete; honest, upright; firm, energetic; sound, vigorous; (*tela*) strong, heavy || *m* (arith) integer; (Am) payment; (Chile) balance; **por entero** entirely, wholly, completely
**enterrador** *m* gravedigger
**enterramiento** *m* burial, interment; (*hoyo*) grave; (*monumento*) tomb
**enterrar** §2 *tr* to bury, inter; to outlive, survive || *ref* to hide away
**entesar** §2 *tr* to stretch, make taut
**entibar** *tr* to prop up, shore up || *intr* to rest, lean
**entibiar** *tr* to cool off; to temper, moderate || *ref* to cool off, cool down
**entidad** *f* entity; importance, consequence, moment; body, organization
**entierro** *m* burial, interment; (*hoyo*) grave; (*monumento*) tomb; funeral; funeral cortege; buried treasure
**entintar** *tr* to ink; to ink in; to stain with ink; to dye
**entoldar** *tr* to cover with awnings; to adorn with hangings || *ref* to get cloudy, become overcast; to swell with pride
**entomología** *f* entomology
**entonación** *f* intonation; blowing of bellows
**entona•do -da** *adj* arrogant; haughty; harmonious, in tune
**entonar** *tr* to intone; to sing in tune; (*el órgano*) to blow; (*colores*) to harmonize; to tone, tone up; (*alabanzas*) to sound || *intr* to sing in tune || *ref* to be puffed up with pride
**entonces** *adv* then || *m* — **por aquel entonces** at that time
**entonelar** *tr* to put in barrels, put in casks
**entongar** §44 *tr* (Mex, W-I) to pile up, pile in rows; (Col) to drive crazy
**entono** *m* intoning; arrogance, haughtiness
**entontecer** §22 *tr* to make foolish, make stupid || *intr & ref* to become foolish, become stupid
**entorchado** *m* bullion; **ganar los entorchados** to win one's stripes
**entorna•do -da** *adj* ajar, half-closed
**entornar** *tr* to half-close; (*los ojos*) to squint; (*una puerta*) to leave ajar; (*volcar*) to upset || *ref* to upset
**entornillar** *tr* to twist, to screw up
**entorpecer** §22 *tr* to stupefy; to obstruct, delay; to benumb; (*una cerradura, una ventana*) to make stick || *ref* to stick, get stuck
**entortar** §61 *tr* to bend, make crooked; to knock out the eye of || *ref* to bend, get crooked
**entrada** *f* entrance, entry; admission; arrival; income, receipts; admission ticket; entrance hall; (*número de personas que asisten a un espectáculo*) house; (*producto de cada función*) gate; (*amistad en alguna casa*) entree; (*naipes que guarda un jugador*) hand; (*de una comida*) entree; (*visita breve*) (coll) short call; (Col) down payment; (Mex) attack, onslaught; (elec) input; **dar entrada a** to admit; to give an opening to; (*un buque*) to give the right of entry to; **entrada de taquilla** gate; **entrada general** top gallery; **entrada llena** full house; **mucha entrada** good house, good turnout; **se prohibe la entrada** no admittance
**entra•do -da** *adj* (Chile) officious, self-assertive; **entrado en años** advanced in years || *f* see **entrada**
**entra•dor -dora** *adj* (Mex) lively, energetic; (*enamoradizo*) (Am) susceptible; (Chile) officious, self-assertive
**entrama•do -da** *adj* half-timbered || *m* timber framework
**entram•bos -bas** *adj & pron indef* both; **entrambos a dos** both
**entrampar** *tr* to ensnare, trap; to trick, deceive; (coll) to overload with debt || *ref* to get trapped; to be tricked; (coll) to run into debt

**entrante** *adj* entering; (*p.ej., tren*) inbound, incoming; (*próximo, que viene*) next ‖ *mf* entrant; **entrantes y salientes** (coll) hangers-on
**entraña** *f* internal organ; (fig) heart, center; **entrañas** entrails; (fig) heart, feeling; (fig) disposition, temper
**entrañable** *adj* close, intimate
**entrañar** *tr* to put away deep, bury deep; to involve; (*malos pensamientos*) to harbor ‖ *ref* to go deep into; to be buried deep; to be close, be intimate
**entrapajar** *tr* to wrap up, to bandage
**entrar** *tr* to bring in; to overrun, invade; to influence ‖ *intr* to enter, go in, come in; (*un río*) to empty; (*el viento, la marea*) to rise; to attack; to begin; **entrar a matar** (taur) to go in for the kill; **entrar en** to enter, enter into, go into; to fit into; to adopt, take up; **que entra** next
**entre** *prep* (*en medio de*) between; (*en el número de*) among; (*en el intervalo de*) in the course of; **entre manos** at hand; **entre mí** to myself; **entre que** while; **entre tanto** meanwhile; **entre Vd. y yo** between you and me
**entreabier·to -ta** *adj* half-open; (*puerta*) ajar
**entreabrir** §83 *tr* to half-open; to leave ajar
**entreacto** *m* entr'acte
**entreca·no -na** *adj* graying, grayish
**entrecarril** *m* (Ven) gauge
**entrecejo** *m* space between the eyebrows; frown; **fruncir el entrecejo** to frown; **mirar con entrecejo** to frown at
**entrecoger** §17 *tr* to catch, seize; to press hard, to hold down
**entrecoro** *m* chancel
**entrecorta·do -da** *adj* broken, intermittent
**entrecortar** *tr* to break in on, keep interrupting
**entre·cruz** *m* (*pl* **-cruces**) interweaving
**entrecruzar** §60 *tr & ref* to intercross; to interweave, interlace; to interbreed
**entrecubiertas** *fpl* between-decks
**entrechocar** §73 *ref* to collide, to clash
**entredicho** *m* interdiction, prohibition; (law) injunction; (Bol) alarm bell; **poner en entredicho** to cast doubt upon
**entredós** *m* (*tira de encaje*) insertion; (typ) long primer
**entrefilete** *m* short feature, special item
**entrefi·no -na** *adj* medium
**entrega** *f* delivery; (*p.ej., de una plaza fuerte*) surrender; (*cuaderno de un libro que se vende suelto*) fascicle; (*de una revista*) issue, number; **por entregas** in instalments
**entregar** §44 *tr* to deliver; to hand over, surrender; to fit in, insert; **entregarla** (coll) to die ‖ *ref* to give in, surrender; to abandon oneself; to devote oneself; **entregarse de** to take possession of, take charge of
**entrehierro** *m* (elec) spark gap; (phys) air gap
**entrelazar** §60 *tr* to interlace, interweave
**entremediar** *tr* to put between
**entremedias** *adv* in between; in the meantime; **entremedias de** between; among
**entremés** *m* hors d'œuvre, side dish; short farce (*inserted in an auto or performed between two acts of a comedia*)
**entremesear** *tr* (*una conversación*) to enliven
**entremeter** *tr* to put in, to insert ‖ *ref* to meddle, intrude, butt in
**entremeti·do -da** *adj* meddling, meddlesome ‖ *mf* meddler, intruder, busybody
**entremezclar** *tr & ref* to intermingle, intermix
**entremorir** §30 & §83 *intr* to flicker, die out
**entrenador** *m* (sport) coach, trainer, handler
**entrenamiento** *m* (sport) coaching, training
**entrenar** *tr & ref* (sport) to coach, to train
**entrepaño** *m* (*de una puerta*) panel; (*espacio entre dos columnas, etc.*) pier; shelf
**entreparecer** §60 *ref* to show through
**entrepiernas** *fpl* crotch; patches in the crotch of trousers; (Chile) bathing trunks
**entrepuentes** *mpl* between-decks; (naut) steerage
**entrerrenglonar** *tr* to write between the lines
**entrerriel** *m* gauge
**entrerrisa** *f* giggle
**entrerrosca** *f* (mach) nipple
**entresacar** §73 *tr* to pick, pick out, select; to cull, sift; (*árboles; el pelo*) to thin out
**entresijo** *m* secret; mystery; **tener muchos entresijos** to be mysterious, to be hard to figure out
**entresuelo** *m* mezzanine, entresol
**entretallar** *tr* to carve, to engrave; to carve in bas-relief; to do openwork in; to intercept
**entretanto** *adv* meantime, meanwhile ‖ *m* meanwhile; **en el entretanto** in the meantime
**entretecho** *m* (Arg, Chile, Urug) attic, garret
**entretejer** *tr* to interweave
**entretela** *f* interlining
**entretelar** *tr* to interline
**entretención** *f* (Am) amusement, entertainment
**entretener** §71 *tr* to amuse, entertain; (*el tiempo*) to while away; to maintain, keep up; to put off, delay; (*el dolor*) to allay; (*el hambre*) to stave off (*by taking a bite before mealtime*); to try to get one's mind off ‖ *ref* to amuse oneself, to be amused
**entreteni·do -da** *adj* amusing, entertaining; (rad) continuous, undamped ‖ *f* kept woman; **dar la entretenida a** or **dar con la entretenida a** to stall off by constant talk

**entretenimiento** *m* amusement, entertainment; upkeep, maintenance
**entretiempo** *m* in-between season; **de entretiempo** spring-and-fall (*coat*)
**entreventana** *f* pier
**entrever** §80 *tr* to glimpse, descry, catch a glimpse of; to guess, suspect
**entreverar** *tr* to mix ‖ *ref* (Arg) to get all mixed together; (*dos grupos de caballería*) (Arg) to clash in hand-to-hand combat
**entrevía** *f* gauge
**entrevista** *f* interview
**entrevistar** *ref* to have an interview
**entristecer** §22 *tr* to sadden, make sad ‖ *ref* to sadden, become sad
**entrojar** *tr* to store in a granary
**entrometer** *tr & ref* var of **entremeter**
**entrometi·do -da** *adj & mf* var of **entremetido**
**entronar** *tr* to enthrone
**entroncamiento** *m* connection, relationship; (*de caminos, ferrocarriles*) (Am) junction
**entroncar** §73 *tr* to prove relationship between ‖ *intr* to be related; (*dos caminos, ferrocarriles, etc.*) (Am) to connect
**entronerar** *tr* (*una bola de billar*) to pocket
**entronizar** §60 *tr* to enthrone; to exalt; to popularize ‖ *ref* to be puffed up with pride
**entronque** *m* connection, relationship; (*de caminos, ferrocarriles*) (Am) junction
**entruchar** *tr* (coll) to decoy, to trick
**entru·chón -chona** *adj* (coll) tricky ‖ *mf* (coll) trickster
**entuerto** *m* wrong, harm, injustice
**entumecer** §22 *tr* to make numb ‖ *ref* (*un miembro*) to get numb, go to sleep; (*el mar*) to swell, get rough
**entupir** *tr* to stop up, clog; to pack tight ‖ *ref* to get stopped up, get clogged
**enturbiar** *tr* to stir up, make muddy; to confuse, upset
**entusiasmar** *tr* to enthuse, make enthusiastic ‖ *ref* to enthuse, become enthusiastic
**entusiasmo** *m* enthusiasm; inspiration
**entusiasta** *adj* enthusiastic ‖ *mf* enthusiast
**entusiásti·co -ca** *adj* enthusiastic
**enumerar** *tr* to enumerate
**enunciar** *tr* to enunciate, to enounce
**enunciati·vo -va** *adj* (gram) declarative
**envainar** *tr* to sheathe
**envalentonar** *tr* to embolden, make bold ‖ *ref* to pluck up, take courage
**envanecer** §22 *tr* to make vain ‖ *ref* to become vain, get conceited
**envanecimiento** *m* vanity, conceit
**envarar** *tr* to make numb, to stiffen
**envasar** *tr* (*p.ej., trigo*) to pack, to sack; (*p.ej., vino*) to bottle; (*p.ej., pescado*) to can; (*una espada*) to thrust, poke; (*mucho vino*) to put away ‖ *intr* to tipple
**envase** *m* container; bottle, jar; can; packing; bottling; canning; **envase de hojalata** tin can
**envedijar** *ref* to get tangled; (coll) to come to blows
**envejecer** §22 *tr* to age, make old ‖ *intr & ref* to age, grow old; to get out of date
**envejeci·do -da** *adj* old, aged; experienced, tried
**envenenar** *tr* to poison; (*llenar de amargura*) to envenom, embitter; (*las palabras o conducta de una persona*) to put an evil interpretation on ‖ *ref* to take poison
**enverdecer** §22 *intr* to turn green
**envergadura** *f* (*de las alas abiertas del ave*) spread; (*ancho de una vela*) breadth; (aer) span, wingspread; (fig) compass, spread, reach
**envés** *m* wrong side; (*del cuerpo humano*) back
**enviado** *m* envoy
**enviar** §77 *tr* to send; (*mercancías*) to ship; **enviar a buscar** to send for; **enviar a paseo** (coll) to send on his way, to dismiss without ceremony; **enviar por** to send for
**enviciar** *tr* to corrupt, vitiate; (*mimar*) to spoil ‖ *intr* to have many leaves and little fruit ‖ *ref* to become addicted; **enviciarse con** or **en** to addict oneself to, become addicted to
**envidar** *tr* to bid against, to bet against ‖ *intr* to bid, to bet
**envidia** *f* envy; desire
**envidiable** *adj* enviable
**envidiar** *tr* to envy, to begrudge; to desire, want
**envidio·so -sa** *adj* envious; greedy, covetous ‖ *mf* envious person
**envilecer** §22 *tr* to debase, vilify, revile ‖ *ref* to degrade oneself
**envío** *m* sending; (*de mercancías*) shipment; (*de dinero*) remittance; (*en una obra*) autograph, inscription
**envirota·do -da** *adj* stiff, stuck-up
**envite** *m* bet; bid, offer, invitation; push, shove; (*apuesta adicional a un lance o suerte*) side bet; **al primer envite** right off, at the start
**enviudar** *intr* (*una mujer*) to become a widow; (*un hombre*) to become a widower
**envoltorio** *m* bundle; (*defecto en el paño*) knot
**envoltura** *f* cover, wrapper, envelope; swaddling clothes
**envolver** §47 & §83 *tr* to wrap, wrap up; (*hilo, cinta*) to wind, roll up; (*al niño*) to swaddle; to imply, mean; to involve; to envelop; (*dejar cortado y sin salida en la disputa*) to floor; (mil) to encircle ‖ *ref* to become involved; to have an affair
**enyerbar** *tr* (Col, Chile, Mex) to bewitch ‖ *ref* (Am) to be covered with grass; (Mex) to fall madly in love; (Mex) to take poison
**enyesar** *tr* to plaster; to put in a plaster cast; (*la tierra, el vino*) to gypsum
**enyugar** §44 *tr* to yoke
**enzima** *f* enzyme
**enzolvar** *tr* (Mex) to clog, stop up
**epazote** *m* (CAm, Mex) Mexican tea
**E.P.D.** *abbr* **en paz descanse**

**epénte·sis** *f* (*pl* **-sis**) epenthesis
**eperlano** *m* smelt
**épica** *f* epic poetry
**epice·no -na** *adj* (gram) epicene, common
**épi·co -ca** *adj* epic || *m* epic poet || *f* see **épica**
**epicúre·o -a** *adj* epicurean || *mf* epicurean, epicure
**epidemia** *f* epidemic
**epidémi·co -ca** *adj* epidemic
**epidemiología** *f* epidemiology
**epidermis** *f* epidermis; **tener la epidermis fina** or **sensible** (coll) to be touchy
**Epifanía** *f* Epiphany, Twelfth-day
**epígrafe** *m* epigraph; inscription; headline, title; device, motto
**epigrama** *m* epigram
**epilepsia** *f* epilepsy
**epilépti·co -ca** *adj & mf* epileptic
**epilogar** §44 *tr* to sum up, summarize
**episcopalista** *adj & mf* Episcopalian
**episodio** *m* episode
**epistemología** *f* epistemology
**epístola** *f* epistle
**epitafio** *m* epitaph
**epíteto** *m* epithet
**epitomar** *tr* to epitomize
**epítome** *m* epitome
**E.P.M.** *abbr* **en propia mano**
**época** *f* epoch; **hacer época** to be epoch-making
**epopeya** *f* epic, epic poem
**equidad** *f* equity; (*templanza habitual*) equableness; (*moderación en el precio*) reasonableness
**equiláte·ro -ra** *adj* equilateral
**equilibrar** *tr* to balance, equilibrate; (*el presupuesto*) to balance || *ref* to balance, equilibrate
**equilibrio** *m* equilibrium, balance, equipoise; (*del presupuesto*) balancing; **equilibrio político** balance of power
**equilibrista** *mf* balancer, ropedancer
**equinoccial** *adj* equinoctial
**equinoccio** *m* equinox
**equipaje** *m* baggage; piece of baggage; equipment; (naut) crew; **equipaje de mano** hand baggage
**equipar** *tr* to equip
**equiparar** *tr* to compare
**equi·pier** *m* (*pl* **-piers**) teammate
**equipo** *m* equipment, outfit; crew, gang; (sport) team; **equipo de novia** trousseau; **equipo de urgencia** first-aid kit
**equitación** *f* horsemanship, riding
**equitati·vo -va** *adj* fair, equitable; (*tranquilo*) equable
**equivalente** *adj & m* equivalent
**equivaler** §76 *intr* to be equal, be equivalent
**equivocación** *f* mistake; mistakenness
**equivoca·do -da** *adj* mistaken, wrong
**equivocar** §73 *tr* (*una cosa por otra*) to mistake, to mix || *ref* to be mistaken, to make a mistake; to be wrong; **equivocarse con** to be mistaken for; **equivocarse de** to be wrong in, take the wrong . . .
**equívo·co -ca** *adj* equivocal, ambiguous || *m* equivocation, ambiguity; pun
**equivoquista** *mf* equivocator; punster
**era** *f* era, age; threshing floor; vegetable patch, garden bed
**eral** *m* two-year-old bull
**erario** *m* state treasury
**erección** *f* erection; foundation, establishment
**eremita** *m* hermit
**ergástulo** *m* dungeon, slave prison
**ergio** *m* erg
**erguir** §33 *tr* to raise; to straighten up || *ref* to straighten up; to swell with pride
**erial** *adj* unplowed, uncultivated || *m* unplowed land, uncultivated land
**erigir** §27 *tr* to erect, build; to found, establish; (*a nueva condición*) to elevate || *ref* — **erigirse en** to be elevated to; to set oneself up as
**eriza·do -da** *adj* bristling, bristly, spiny
**erizar** §60 *tr* to make stand on end, cause to bristle || *ref* to stand on end, to bristle
**erizo** *m* (*mamífero*) hedgehog; (*zurrón espinoso de la castaña*) bur, thistle; (*púas de hierro que coronan lo alto de una muralla*) cheval-de-frise; (*persona de carácter áspero*) (coll) curmudgeon; **erizo de mar** (zool) sea urchin
**ermita** *f* hermitage
**ermita·ño -ña** *mf* hermit
**erogación** *f* (*de bienes o caudales*) distribution; (Am) expenditure; (Peru, Ven) gift, charity; (Mex) outlay
**erogar** §44 *tr* to distribute; (Ecuad) to contribute; (Mex) to cause
**erosión** *f* erosion
**erosionar** *tr & ref* to erode
**erradicar** §73 *tr* to eradicate
**erra·do -da** *adj* mistaken, wrong
**errar** §34 *tr* to miss || *intr* to err, to be mistaken, to be wrong; to wander || *ref* to be mistaken, to be wrong
**errata** *f* erratum; printer's error
**erróne·o -a** *adj* erroneous
**error** *m* error, mistake; **error de pluma** clerical error; **salvo error u omisión** barring error or omission
**eructar** *intr* to belch; (coll) to brag
**eructo** *m* belch, belching
**erudición** *f* erudition, learning
**erudi·to -ta** *adj* erudite, learned || *mf* scholar, savant; **erudito a la violeta** egghead, highbrow
**erugino·so -sa** *adj* rusty
**erumpir** *intr* (*un volcán*) to erupt
**erupción** *f* eruption
**esbel·to -ta** *adj* slender, lithe, willowy
**esbirro** *m* bailiff, constable; (*el que ejecuta órdenes injustas*) myrmidon, henchman
**esbozar** §60 *tr* to sketch, outline
**esbozo** *m* sketch, outline
**escabechar** *tr* to pickle; (*el pelo, la barba*) to dye; (*reprobar en un examen*) (coll) to flunk; (coll) to stab to death || *ref* to dye one's hair; (*el pelo, la barba*) to dye
**escabeche** *m* pickle; pickled fish; hair dye

**escabel** *m* stool; footstool; (*para medrar*) stepping stone
**escabio·so -sa** *adj* mangy
**escabro·so -sa** *adj* scabrous, risqué; scabrous, uneven, rough, harsh
**escabuche** *m* weeding hoe
**escabullir** §13 *ref* to slip away, sneak away; to slip out, wiggle out
**escafandra** *f* diving suit; **escafandra espacial** space suit
**escafandrista** *mf* diver
**escala** *f* (*escalera de mano*) ladder, stepladder; (*línea graduada de instrumento*) scale; (*de buque*) call; (*de avión*) stop; (*puerto donde toca una embarcación*) port of call; (*serie de las notas musicales*) scale; **en escala de** on a scale of; **en grande escala** on a large scale; **escala móvil** (*de salarios*) sliding scale; **hacer escala** (naut) to call
**escalada** *f* scaling, climbing; breaking in; escalation
**escalador** *m* climber; (*ladrón*) burglar, housebreaker
**escalación** *f* escalation
**escalafón** *m* roster, roll, register
**escalar** *tr* (*subir, trepar*) to scale; to break in, to burglarize; (*la compuerta de la acequia*) to open || *intr* to climb; (naut) to call || *ref* to escalate
**escalato·rres** *m* (*pl* **-rres**) steeplejack, human fly
**escalda·do -da** *adj* (coll) cautious, scared, wary; (*mujer*) (coll) lewd, loose
**escaldar** *tr* to scald; to make red hot || *ref* to get scalded; to chafe
**escalera** *f* stairs, stairway; (*la portátil*) ladder; (*de naipes*) sequence; (*en el póker*) straight; **de escalera abajo** from below stairs, from the servants; **escalera de caracol** winding stairway; **escalera de escape** fire escape; **escalera de husillo** winding stairway; **escalera de incendios** fire escape; **escalera de mano** ladder; **escalera de salvamento** fire escape; **escalera de tijera** or **escalera doble** ladder; **escalera excusada** or **falsa** private stairs; **escalera extensible** extension ladder; **escalera hurtada** secret stairway; **escalera mecánica, móvil** or **rodante** escalator, moving stairway
**escalerilla** *f* low step; car step; (*en las medias*) runner; (*de naipes*) sequence; thumb index
**escalfar** *tr* (*huevos*) to poach; (*el pan*) to bake brown
**escalinata** *f* stone steps, front steps
**escalo** *m* burglary, breaking in
**escalofria·do -da** *adj* chilly
**escalofrío** *m* chill
**escalón** *m* step, rung; (*grada de la escalera*) tread; (fig) step, echelon, grade; (*paso con que uno adelanta sus pretensiones*) (fig) stepping stone; (mil) echelon; (rad) stage
**escalonar** *tr* to space out, spread out; (*las horas de trabajo*) to stagger; (mil) to echelon
**escalope** *m* (*loncha delgada de carne*) scallop (*thin slice of meat*)
**escalpar** *tr* to scalp
**escalpelo** *m* scalpel
**escama** *f* scale; fear, suspicion
**escamar** *tr* (*los peces*) to scale; (coll) to frighten || *ref* to be frightened
**escamondar** *tr* to trim, to prune
**escamo·so -sa** *adj* scaly
**escamotea·dor -dora** *mf* prestidigitator; swindler
**escamotear** *tr* to whisk out of sight, cause to vanish; (*una carta*) to palm; to swipe, to snitch
**escampada** *f* (coll) clear spell, break in rain
**escampar** *tr* to clear out || *intr* to stop raining; to ease up; **¡ya escampa!** (coll) there you go again! || *ref* — **escamparse del agua** (Am) to get in out of the rain
**escampavía** *f* (naut) cutter, revenue cutter
**escamujar** *tr* (*un árbol, esp. un olivo*) to prune; (*ramas*) to clear out
**escanciar** *tr* (*vino*) to pour, to serve, to drink || *intr* to drink wine
**escandalizar** §60 *tr* to scandalize || *ref* to be scandalized; to be outraged, be exasperated
**escándalo** *m* scandal; **causar escándalo** to make a scene
**escandalo·so -sa** *adj* scandalous; noisy, riotous; (Am) loud, flashy
**escandallo** *m* (naut) sounding lead; (*del contenido de varios envases*) testing, sampling; cost accounting
**escandina·vo -va** *adj* & *mf* Scandinavian
**escandir** *tr* (*versos*) to scan
**escansión** *f* scansion; (telv) scanning
**escaño** *m* settle, bench with a back; (*en las Cortes*) seat; (Am) park bench; (Guat) nag
**escañuelo** *m* footstool
**escapada** *f* escape, flight; short trip, quick trip
**escapar** *tr* to free, to save; (*un caballo*) to drive hard || *intr* to escape; to flee, run away; **escapar en una tabla** to have a narrow escape || *ref* to escape; to flee, run away; (*el gas, el agua*) to leak; **escapársele a uno** to let slip; to not notice
**escaparate** *m* show window; (*armario con cristales*) cabinet; (Am) wardrobe, clothes closet
**escaparatista** *mf* window dresser
**escapatoria** *f* escape, getaway; (*de atenciones, deberes, etc.*) (fig) escape; (*efugio, pretexto*) (coll) evasion, subterfuge
**escape** *m* escape; flight; (*de gas, agua*) leak; (*de reloj*) escapement; (aut) exhaust valve; (aut) exhaust, exhaust pipe; **a escape** at full speed, on the run; **escape de rejilla** (rad) grid leak; **escape libre** (aut) cutout
**escápula** *f* shoulder blade, scapula
**escaque** *m* square; **escaques** chess
**escarabajear** *tr* (coll) to bother, worry, harass || *intr* to swarm, crawl; to scrawl, scribble
**escarabajo** *m* black beetle; (*imperfec-*

*ción en los tejidos*) flaw; (*persona pequeña*) (coll) runt
**escaramuza** *f* skirmish
**escaramuzar** §60 *intr* to skirmish
**escarapela** *f* (*divisa en forma de lazo*) cockade; dispute ending in hair pulling
**escarapelar** *intr & ref* to quarrel, to wrangle
**escarbadien•tes** *m* (*pl* **-tes**) toothpick
**escarbar** *tr* (*el suelo*) to scratch, scratch up; (*la lumbre*) to poke; (*los dientes, los oídos*) to pick; to pry into
**escarcha** *f* frost, hoarfrost
**escarchar** *tr* (*confituras*) to frost, put frosting on; (*la tierra del alfarero*) to dilute with water; to spangle ‖ *intr* — **escarcha** there is frost
**escardar** or **escardillar** *tr* to weed, weed out
**escardillo** *m* weeding hoe
**escariar** *tr* to ream
**escarlata** *adj* scarlet ‖ *f* scarlet fever
**escarlatina** *f* scarlet fever
**escarmentar** §2 *tr* to make an example of ‖ *intr* to learn one's lesson
**escarmiento** *m* example, lesson, warning; caution, wisdom; punishment
**escarnecer** §22 *tr* to scoff at, make fun of
**escarnio** *m* scoff, scoffing
**escarola** *f* endive
**escarpa** *f* scarp, escarpment; (Mex) sidewalk
**escarpa•do -da** *adj* steep; abrupt, craggy
**escarpia** *f* hooked spike
**escarpín** *m* pump
**escasear** *tr* to give sparingly; to cut down on, to avoid; to bevel ‖ *intr* to be scarce
**escase•ro -ra** *adj* sparing; saving, frugal; stingy ‖ *mf* skinflint
**escasez** *f* (*falta de una cosa*) scarcity; (*pobreza*) need, want; (*mezquindad*) stinginess
**esca•so -sa** *adj* (*poco abundante*) scarce; (*no cabal*) scant; (*muy económico*) parsimonious, frugal; (*tacaño*) stingy; (*oportunidad*) dim, slim, slight; **estar escaso de** to be short of
**escatimar** *tr & intr* to scrimp
**escena** *f* (*parte del teatro donde se representan las obras*) stage; (*subdivisión de un acto*) scene; incident, episode; **poner en escena** to stage
**escenario** *m* stage; (*disposición de la representación*) setting; (*guión de un cine*) scenario; (*antecedentes de una persona o cosa*) background
**escenarista** *mf* scenarist
**escéni•co -ca** *adj* scenic
**escenificar** §73 *tr* to adapt for the stage
**escépti•co -ca** *adj* sceptic(al) ‖ *mf* sceptic
**Escila** *f* Scylla; **entre Escila y Caribdis** between Scylla and Charybdis
**Escipión** *m* Scipio
**escisión** *f* (biol) fission; (surg) excision
**esclarecer** §22 *tr* to light up, brighten; to explain, elucidate; to ennoble ‖ *intr* to dawn
**esclareci•do -da** *adj* noble, illustrious
**esclavitud** *f* slavery
**esclavización** *f* enslavement
**esclavizar** §60 *tr* to enslave
**escla•vo -va** *adj & mf* slave
**escla•vón -vona** *adj & mf* Slav
**esclusa** *f* lock; floodgate; **esclusa de aire** caisson
**esclusero** *m* lock tender
**escoba** *f* broom
**escobada** *f* sweep; sweeping
**escobar** *tr* to sweep with a broom
**escobazar** §60 *tr* to sprinkle with a wet broom
**escobén** *m* (naut) hawse
**escobilla** *f* brush, whisk; gold and silver sweepings; (elec) brush
**escocer** §16 *intr* to smart, sting ‖ *ref* to hurt; to chafe, become chafed
**esco•cés -cesa** *adj* Scotch, Scottish ‖ *mf* Scot ‖ *m* Scotchman; (*whisky; dialecto*) Scotch; **los escoceces** the Scotch, the Scottish
**Escocia** *f* Scotland; **la Nueva Escocia** Nova Scotia
**escofina** *f* rasp
**escofinar** *tr* to rasp
**escoger** §17 *tr* to choose, pick out
**escogi•do -da** *adj* choice, select
**escolar** *adj* school ‖ *m* pupil
**escolaridad** *f* schooling, school attendance; curriculum
**escolimo•so -sa** *adj* (coll) impatient, gruff, restless
**escolta** *f* escort
**escoltar** *tr* to escort
**escollar** *intr* (Arg) to run aground on a reef; (Arg, Chile) to fail
**escollera** *f* jetty, breakwater
**escollo** *m* (*peñasco a flor de agua*) reef, rock; (*peligro*) pitfall; (*obstáculo*) stumbling block
**escombrar** *tr* to clear out
**escombro** *m* (*pez*) mackerel; **escombros** debris, rubble, rubbish
**esconder** *tr* to hide, conceal; to harbor, contain ‖ *ref* to hide; to lurk
**escondi•do -da** *adj* hidden; **a escondidas** secretly; **a escondidas de** without the knowledge of
**escondite** *m* hiding place; (*juego de muchachos*) hide-and-seek; **jugar al escondite** to play hide-and-seek
**escondrijo** *m* hiding place
**escopeta** *f* shotgun; **escopeta blanca** gentleman hunter; **escopeta de caza** fowling piece; **escopeta de viento** air rifle; **escopeta negra** professional hunter
**escopetazo** *m* gunshot; gunshot wound; bad news, blow
**escoplear** *tr* to chisel
**escoplo** *m* chisel
**escorbuto** *m* scurvy
**escoria** *f* dross, scoria, slag; (fig) dross, dregs
**escorial** *m* cinder bank, slag dump
**escorpión** *m* scorpion
**escorzar** §60 *tr* to foreshorten
**escorzo** *m* foreshortening
**escota** *f* (naut) sheet
**escota•do -da** *adj* low-neck ‖ *m* low neck
**escotadura** *f* low neck, low cut in neck
**escotar** *tr* to cut to fit; to draw water

from, to drain; to cut low in the neck || *intr* to go Dutch
**escote** *m* low neck; (*encajes en el cuello de una vestidura*) tucker; **ir a escote** or **pagar a escote** to go Dutch
**escotilla** *f* (naut) hatchway, scuttle
**escotillón** *m* hatch, trap door, scuttle; (theat) trap door
**escozor** *m* burning, smarting, stinging; grief, sorrow
**escriba** *m* scribe
**escribanía** *f* court clerkship; desk; writing materials
**escribano** *m* court clerk; lawyer's clerk
**escribiente** *mf* clerk, office clerk; **escribiente a máquina** typist
**escribir** §83 *tr & intr* to write || *ref* to enroll, enlist; to write to each other; **no escribirse** to be impossible to describe
**escriño** *m* casket, jewel case; straw basket
**escri•to -ta** *adj* streaked || *m* writing; (law) brief, writ; **poner por escrito** to write down, put in writing
**escri•tor -tora** *mf* writer
**escritorio** *m* writing desk; office; **escritorio ministro** kneehole desk, office desk; **escritorio norteamericano** rolltop desk
**escritura** *f* writing; script, handwriting, longhand; (law) deed, indenture; (law) sworn statement; **escritura al tacto** touch typewriting || **Escritura** *f* Scripture; **Sagrada Escritura** Holy Scripture, Holy Writ
**escriturar** *tr* to notarize; (*p.ej., a un actor*) to book || *ref* (taur) to sign up for a fight
**escrnía.** *abbr* **escribanía**
**escrno.** *abbr* **escribano**
**escrófula** *f* scrofula
**escrúpulo** *m* scruple
**escrupulo•so -sa** *adj* scrupulous; exact
**escrutar** *tr* to scrutinize; (*los votos*) to count
**escrutinio** *m* scrutiny; counting of votes
**escuadra** *f* (*pequeño número de personas o de soldados*) squad; (*pieza de metal para asegurar las ensambladuras*) angle iron; (*de carpintero*) square; (*de dibujante*) triangle; (nav) squadron
**escuadrar** *tr* (carp) to square
**escuadrilla** *f* (aer) squadron
**escuadrón** *m* (mil) squadron
**escualidez** *f* squalor
**escuáli•do -da** *adj* squalid
**escualor** *m* squalor
**escucha** *mf* listener || *m* (mil) scout, vedette || *f* listening; (*en un convento*) chaperon; **estar de escucha** (coll) to eavesdrop
**escuchar** *tr* to listen to; (*atender a*) to heed; (*radiotransmisiones*) to monitor || *intr* to listen || *ref* to like the sound of one's own voice
**escudar** *tr* to shield
**escudero** *m* esquire; nobleman; lady's page
**escudete** *m* escutcheon; (*refuerzo en la ropa*) gusset; (*planchuela delante de la cerradura*) escutcheon, escutcheon plate
**escudilla** *f* bowl
**escudo** *m* shield; buckler; (*delante de la cerradura*) escutcheon plate; **escudo de armas** coat of arms; **escudo térmico** (*de una cápsula espacial*) heat shield
**escudriñar** *tr* to scrutinize
**escuela** *f* school; **escuela de artes y oficios** trade school; **escuela de párvulos** kindergarten; **escuela de verano** summer school; **escuela dominical** Sunday school; **Escuela Naval Militar** Naval Academy; **hacer escuela** to be the leader of a school (*of thought*)
**escuelante** *mf* (Mex) schoolteacher || *m* (Mex) schoolboy || *f* (Mex) schoolgirl
**escuerzo** *m* toad
**escue•to -ta** *adj* free, unencumbered; bare, unadorned
**escuintle** *adj* (Mex) sickly || *m* (*perro*) (Mex) mutt; (Mex) brat
**esculcar** §73 *tr* (dial & Am) to frisk
**esculpir** *tr & intr* to sculpture, to carve; to engrave
**escultismo** *m* outdoor activities
**escultista** *m* outdoorsman
**escultor** *m* sculptor
**escultora** *f* sculptress
**escultura** *f* sculpture
**escultural** *adj* sculptural; statuesque
**escupidera** *f* cuspidor; (Am) chamber pot
**escupidura** *f* spit; fever blister
**escupir** *tr & intr* to spit
**escurrepla•tos** *m* (*pl* **-tos**) dish rack
**escurridero** *m* drainpipe; drainboard; slippery spot
**escurridi•zo -za** *adj* slippery
**escurri•do -da** *adj* narrow-hipped; (Am) abashed, confused
**escurridor** *m* colander
**escurriduras** *fpl* dregs, lees
**escurrir** *tr* (*una vasija; un líquido; la vajilla*) to drain; to wring, wring out; **escurrir el bulto** (coll) to duck || *intr* to drip, ooze, trickle; to slide, to slip || *ref* to drip, ooze, trickle; to slide, to slip; to slip away; (*un reparo*) to slip out
**esdrúju•lo -la** *adj* accented on the antepenult || *m* word or verse accented on the antepenult
**ese, esa** *adj dem* (*pl* **esos, esas**) that (*near you*) || **ese** *f* sound hole (*of violin*); **hacer eses** to reel, stagger
**ése, ésa** *pron dem* (*pl* **ésos, ésas**) that (*near you*); **ésa** your city
**esencia** *f* essence; **esencia de pera** banana oil; **quinta esencia** quintessence
**esencial** *adj & m* essential
**esfera** *f* sphere; (*del reloj*) dial
**esféri•co -ca** *adj* spherical || *m* football
**esfinge** *f* sphinx; spiteful woman
**esforza•do -da** *adj* brave, vigorous, enterprising
**esforzar** §35 *tr* to strengthen, to invigorate; to encourage || *ref* to exert oneself; to strive
**esfuerzo** *m* effort, exertion, endeavor; courage, vigor, spirit

**esfumar** *tr* to stump || *ref* to disappear, fade away
**esgarrar** *tr* (*la flema*) to try to cough up || *intr* to clear the throat
**esgrima** *f* fencing
**esgrimidura** *f* fencing
**esgrimir** *tr* to wield, to brandish; (*un argumento*) to swing || *intr* to fence
**esgrimista** *mf* (Arg, Chile, Peru) fencer; (Chile) swindler, panhandler
**esguazar** §60 *tr* to ford
**esguazo** *m* fording; ford
**esguince** *m* dodge, duck; (*gesto de disgusto*) frown; twist, sprain, wrench
**eslabón** *m* (*de cadena*) link; (*hierro acerado para sacar fuego de un pedernal; cilindro de acero para afilar cuchillos*) steel
**eslabonar** *tr* to link; to link together, to string together || *intr* to link
**eslálom** *m* slalom
**esla•vo -va** *adj* Slav, Slavic || *mf* Slav || *m* (*idioma*) Slavic
**esla•vón -vona** *adj & mf* Slav
**eslogan** *m* (*consigna usada en fórmulas publicitarias*) slogan
**eslora** *f* (naut) length
**eslova•co -ca** *adj & mf* Slovak
**esmaltar** *tr* to enamel; to embellish
**esmalte** *m* enamel; **esmalte para las uñas** nail polish
**esmera•do -da** *adj* careful, painstaking
**esmeralda** *f* emerald
**esmerar** *tr* to polish, to shine; to examine, to check || *ref* to take pains, to do one's best
**esmeril** *s* emery
**esmeriladora** *f* emery wheel
**esmerilar** *tr* to grind or polish with emery
**esmero** *m* care, neatness
**esmoladera** *f* grindstone
**esmoquin** *m* tuxedo, dinner coat
**esnob** *adj* snobbish || *mf* (*pl* **esnobs**) snob
**esnobismo** *m* snobbery, snobbishness
**esnobista** *adj* snobbish
**eso** *pron dem* that; **a eso de** about; **eso es** that's it; that is; **por eso** for that reason; therefore
**esófago** *m* esophagus
**espaciador** *m* space bar
**espacial** *adj* space, spatial
**espaciar** §77 (Arg, Chile) & **regular** *tr* to space; to spread, scatter || *ref* to expatiate; to amuse oneself, to relax
**espacio** *m* space; **espacio de chispa** spark gap; **espacio exterior** outer space; **espacio libre** (*entre dos cosas*) clearance; **espacio muerto** (*en el cilindro de un motor*) clearance; **por espacio de** in the space of
**espacio•so -sa** *adj* spacious, roomy; slow, deliberate
**espada** *m* swordsman; (taur) matador || *f* sword; playing card (*representing a sword*) equivalent to spade; **entre la espada y la pared** between the devil and the deep blue sea
**espadachín** *m* swordsman; (*amigo de pendencias*) bully
**espadaña** *f* cattail, bulrush, reed mace; (*campanario*) bell gable
**espadilla** *f* (*remo que se usa como timón*) scull; (*aguja para sujetar el pelo*) bodkin; red insignia of Order of Santiago
**espadín** *m* rapier
**espadón** *m* (coll) brass hat
**espalar** *tr* to shovel
**espalda** *f* back; **a espaldas de uno** behind one's back; **de espaldas a** with one's back to; **tener buenas espaldas** to have broad shoulders; **volver las espaldas a** to turn a cold shoulder to
**espaldar** *m* (*de silla*) back; (*enrejado para plantas*) trellis, espalier
**espaldarazo** *m* slap on the back; (*ceremonia para armar caballero*) accolade; **dar el espaldarazo a** to accept, approve
**espalera** *f* trellis, espalier
**espantada** *f* (*de un animal*) sudden flight; (*desistimiento ocasionado por el miedo*) cold feet
**espantadi•zo -za** *adj* shy, skittish, scary
**espantajo** *m* scarecrow; (*persona fea*) fright
**espantamos•cas** *m* (*pl* **-cas**) (*para poner a los caballos*) fly net; (*aparato para asustar y alejar las moscas*) fly chaser
**espantapája•ros** *m* (*pl* **-ros**) scarecrow
**espantar** *tr* to scare, frighten; to scare away || *ref* to get scared; to be surprised, to marvel
**espanto** *m* fright, terror; (*amenaza*) threat; (Am) ghost
**espanto•so -sa** *adj* frightening, terrifying
**España** *f* Spain; **la Nueva España** New Spain (*Mexico in the early days*)
**espa•ñol -ñola** *adj* Spanish; **a la española** in the Spanish manner || *mf* Spaniard || *m* (*idioma*) Spanish; **los españoles** the Spanish || *f* Spanish woman
**españolizar** §60 *tr* to make Spanish, to Hispanicize; to translate into Spanish || *ref* to become Spanish
**esparadrapo** *m* sticking plaster
**esparaván** *m* spavin
**esparavel** *m* mortarboard
**esparcimiento** *m* spreading, scattering, dissemination; diversion, relaxation; frankness, openness
**esparcir** §36 *tr* to spread, scatter; to divert, relax || *ref* to spread, scatter; to disperse; to take it easy, to relax
**espárrago** *m* asparagus; (*perno*) stud bolt; awning pole
**esparrancar** §73 *ref* to spread one's legs wide apart
**esparta•no -na** *adj & mf* Spartan
**esparto** *m* esparto grass
**espasmo** *m* spasm
**espasmódi•co -ca** *adj* spasmodic
**espásti•co -ca** *adj* spastic
**espato** *m* spar; **espato flúor** fluor spar
**espátula** *f* spatula; putty knife
**especia** *f* spice
**especia•do -da** *adj* spicy
**especial** *adj* especial, special
**especialidad** *f* speciality; (*ramo a que se consagra una persona o negocio*) specialty
**especialista** *mf* specialist

**especializar** §60 *tr, intr & ref* to specialize
**especiar** *tr* to spice
**especie** *f* (*categoría de la clasificación biológica*) species; (*clase, género*) sort, kind; (*caso, asunto*) matter; (*chisme, cuento*) news, rumor; appearance, pretext, show; remark; **en especie** in kind; **soltar una especie** to try to draw someone out
**especie•ro -ra** *mf* spice dealer || *m* spice box
**especificar** §73 *tr* to specify; to itemize
**específi•co -ca** *adj* specific || *m* specific; patent medicine
**espécimen** *m* (*pl* **especímenes**) specimen
**especio•so -sa** *adj* (*engañoso*) specious; nice, neat, perfect
**especiota** *f* (coll) hoax, wild idea
**espectáculo** *m* spectacle; **dar un espectáculo** to make a scene; **espectáculo de atracciones** side show
**especta•dor -dora** *mf* witness; spectator
**espectral** *adj* ghostly
**espectro** *m* specter, phantom, ghost; (phys) spectrum
**especular** *tr* to check, examine; to contemplate || *intr* to speculate
**espejear** *intr* to sparkle
**espejismo** *m* mirage
**espejo** *m* mirror, looking glass; model; **espejo de cuerpo entero** full-length mirror, pier glass; **espejo de retrovisión** rear-view mirror; **espejo de vestir** full-length mirror, pier glass; **espejo retrovisor** rear-view mirror
**espelunca** *f* cave, cavern
**espeluznante** *adj* hair-raising
**espera** *f* wait, waiting; (*puesto para cazar*) blind, hunter's blind; composure, patience, respite; delay; (law) stay; **no tener espera** to be of the greatest urgency
**esperanza** *f* hope; **tener puesta su esperanza en** to pin one's faith on
**esperanza•do -da** *adj* hopeful (*having hope*)
**esperanza•dor -dora** hopeful (*giving hope*)
**esperanzar** §60 *tr* to give hope to
**esperanzo•so -sa** *adj* hopeful, full of hope
**esperar** *tr* (*aguardar*) to wait for, to await; (*tener esperanza de conseguir*) to expect, to hope for; **ir a esperar** to go to meet || *intr* to wait; to hope; **esperar** + *inf* to hope to + *inf;* **esperar a que** to wait until; **esperar desesperando** to hope against hope; **esperar en** to put one's hope in; **esperar que** to hope that; **esperar sentado** to have a good wait
**esperinque** *m* smelt
**esperma** *f* sperm
**espesar** *m* depth, thickness (*of woods*) || *tr* to thicken; (*un tejido*) to weave tighter || *ref* to thicken, to get thick or thicker
**espe•so -sa** *adj* thick; dirty, greasy
**espesor** *m* thickness; (*de un flúido, gas, masa*) density
**espesura** *f* thickness; (*matorral*) thicket; (*cabellera muy espesa*) shock of hair; dirtiness, greasiness
**espetar** *tr* to skewer; to pierce, pierce through; **espetar algo a** to spring something on || *ref* to be solemn, be pompous; (coll) to settle down
**espetón** *m* (*hurgón*) poker; (*asador*) skewer, spit; jab, poke
**espía** *mf* spy; (coll) squealer || *f* (naut) warping; (*cuerda*) (naut) warp
**espiar** §77 *tr* to spy on || *intr* to spy; (naut) to warp
**espichar** *tr* to prick; (*dinero*) (Chile) to cough up; (Chile, Peru) to tap || *intr* (coll) to die || *ref* (Mex, W-I) to get thin
**espiche** *m* (*arma o instrumento puntiagudo*) prick; (naut) peg, bung
**espichón** *m* stab, prick
**espiga** *f* (bot) ear, spike; peg, pin, tenon; (*clavo sin cabeza*) brad; (*badajo*) clapper; (*de una llave*) stem
**espigar** §44 *tr* to glean; to tenon, to dowel || *intr* (*los cereales*) to form ears || *ref* to grow tall, to shoot up
**espigón** *m* sharp point, spur; (*mazorca*) ear of corn; (*cerro puntiagudo*) peak; breakwater
**espina** *f* thorn, spine; (*de los peces*) fishbone; doubt, uncertainty; sorrow; (anat) spine; **dar mala espina a** (coll) to worry; **espina de pescado** herringbone; **espina de pez** fishbone; **espina dorsal** spinal column; **estar en espinas** (coll) to be on pins and needles
**espinaca** *f* spinach; **espinacas** spinach
**espinal** *adj* spinal
**espinapez** *m* herringbone; thorny matter, difficulty
**espinar** *m* thorny spot; (fig) thorny matter || *tr* to prick; (*árboles*) to protect with thornbushes; to hurt, offend
**espinazo** *m* backbone; (*de un arco*) keystone
**espinel** *m* trawl, trawl line
**espineta** *f* spinet
**espinilla** *f* (*de la pierna*) shin, shinbone; (*granillo en la piel*) blackhead
**espino** *m* hawthorn; **espino artificial** barbed wire; **espino negro** blackthorn
**espinochar** *tr* (*el maíz*) to husk
**espino•so -sa** *adj* thorny; (*pez*) bony; (*difícil*) (fig) thorny, knotty
**espiocha** *f* pickaxe
**espión** *m* spy
**espionaje** *m* spying, espionage
**espira** *f* turn
**espiración** *f* breathing; exhalation
**espiral** *adj* spiral || *f* (*línea curva que da vueltas alrededor de un punto*) spiral; (*del reloj*) hairspring; (*de humo*) curl, wreath
**espirar** *tr* to breath; to encourage || *intr* to breathe; to exhale, expire; (*el viento*) (poet) to blow gently
**espiritismo** *m* espiritualism
**espirito•so -sa** *adj* spirited, lively; (*licor*) spirituous
**espíritu** *m* spirit; (*mente*) mind; (*aparecido, fantasma*) ghost, spirit; **espíritu de equipo** teamwork; **Espíritu Santo** Holy Ghost, Holy Spirit; **dar, despe-**

**dir, exhalar** or **rendir el espíritu** to give up the ghost
**espiritual** *adj* spiritual; sharp, witty
**espiritualismo** *m* spiritualism
**espita** *f* tap, cock; (coll) tippler
**espitar** *tr* to tap
**esplendidez** *f* splendor, magnificence
**espléndi•do -da** *adj* splendid, magnificent; generous, open-handed; (poet) brilliant, radiant
**esplendor** *m* splendor
**esplendoro•so -sa** *adj* resplendent
**espliego** *m* lavender
**esplín** *m* melancholy
**espolada** *f* prick with spur; **espolada de vino** (coll) shot of wine
**espolear** *tr* to spur, to spur on
**espoleta** *f* fuse; (*hueso*) wishbone
**espolón** *m* (*del gallo, una montaña, un buque de guerra*) spur; dike, jetty, mole, cutwater; (*prominencia córnea de las caballerías*) fetlock; (*sabañón*) chilblain
**espolvorear** *tr* (*quitar el polvo de; esparcir el polvo sobre*) to dust; (*el azúcar*) to sprinkle
**esponja** *f* sponge; (*sablista*) (coll) sponge, sponger; **beber como una esponja** (coll) to drink like a fish; **tirar la esponja** (coll) to throw in (or up) the sponge
**esponja•do -da** *adj* proud, puffed-up; (coll) fresh, healthy
**esponjar** *tr* to puff up, make fluffy || *ref* to puff up, become fluffy; (coll) to be puffed up, be conceited; (coll) to look fresh and healthy
**esponjo•so -sa** *adj* spongy
**esponsales** *mpl* betrothal, engagement
**espontanear** *ref* to make a clean breast of it; to open one's heart
**espontáne•o -a** *adj* spontaneous || *m* (taur) spectator who jumps into the ring to take on the bull
**espora** *f* spore
**esporádi•co -ca** *adj* sporadic
**esposa** *f* wife; **esposas** handcuffs, manacles
**esposar** *tr* to handcuff, to manacle
**espo•so -sa** *mf* spouse || *m* husband || *f* see **esposa**
**espuela** *f* spur; **echar la espuela** (coll) to take a nightcap; **espuela de caballero** delphinium, rocket larkspur; **espuela de galán** nasturtium
**espuerta** *f* two-handled esparto basket
**espulgar** §44 *tr* to delouse; to scrutinize
**espuma** *f* foam; (*en un vaso de cerveza; saliva parecida a la espuma*) froth; (*película de impurezas en la superficie de un líquido*) scum; **crecer como espuma** (coll) to grow like weeds; (coll) to have a meteoric rise; **espuma de caucho** foam rubber; **espuma de jabón** lather; **espuma de mar** meerschaum
**espumadera** *f* skimmer
**espumajear** *intr* to froth at the mouth
**espumajo•so -sa** *adj* foamy, frothy
**espumante** *adj* foaming; (*vino*) sparkling
**espumar** *tr* to skim || *intr* to foam, to froth; (*el jabón*) to lather; (*el vino*) to sparkle; to increase rapidly
**espumarajo** *m* froth, frothing at the mouth
**espumilla** *f* voile; (CAm, Ecuad) meringue
**espumo•so -sa** *adj* foamy, frothy; (*cubierto de una película*) scummy; (*jabonoso*) lathery; (*vino*) sparkling
**espu•rio -ria** *adj* spurious
**espurrear** or **espurriar** *tr* to squirt with water from the mouth
**esputar** *tr & intr* to spit
**esputo** *m* spit, saliva
**esq.** *abbr* **esquina**
**esqueje** *m* cutting, slip
**esquela** *f* note; announcement; death notice; **esquela amorosa** billet-doux
**esqueléti•co -ca** *adj* skeleton; skeletal, thin, wasted
**esqueleto** *m* skeleton; (CAm, Mex) blank form; (Chile) sketch, outline
**esquema** *m* scheme, diagram
**es•quí** *m* (*pl* **-quís**) ski; skiing; **esquí acuático** water ski; water skiing; **esquí remolcado** skijoring
**esquia•dor -dora** *adj* ski || *mf* skier
**esquiar** §77 *intr* to ski
**esquiciar** *tr* to sketch
**esquicio** *m* sketch
**esquifar** *tr* (naut) to fit out, to man
**esquife** *m* skiff
**esquiismo** *m* skiing
**esquila** *f* sheepshearing; hand bell
**esquilar** *tr* to shear, to fleece
**esquilimo•so -sa** *adj* (coll) fastidious, squeamish
**esquilmar** *tr* to harvest; (*las plantas el jugo de la tierra*) to drain, exhaust; (*una fuente de riqueza*) to drain, squander, use up; to carry away, steal
**esquilmo** *m* harvest, farm produce; (Mex) farm scrapings
**esquilmo•so -sa** *adj* (coll) fastidious
**esquimal** *adj & mf* Eskimo
**esquina** *f* corner; (SAm) corner store; **a la vuelta de la esquina** around the corner; **doblar la esquina** to turn the corner; **hacer esquina** (*un edificio*) to be on the corner; **las cuatro esquinas** puss in the corner
**esquina•do -da** *adj* sharp-cornered; difficult, unsociable
**esquinar** *tr* to be on the corner of; to put in the corner; to alienate || *intr* — **esquinar con** to be on the corner of || *ref* — **esquinarse con** to fall out with
**esquinazo** *m* (coll) corner; (Arg, Chile) serenade; **dar esquinazo a** (coll) to give the slip to, to shake off
**esquinencia** *f* quinsy
**esquinera** *f* (Am) corner piece (*of furniture*)
**esquirla** *f* splinter
**esquirol** *m* scab, strikebreaker
**esquisto** *m* schist
**esquite** *m* (CAm, Mex) popcorn
**esquivar** *tr* to avoid, evade, shun; to dodge || *ref* to withdraw; to dodge
**esquivez** *f* aloofness, gruffness
**esqui•vo -va** *adj* aloof, gruff

**estable** *adj* stable, permanent; full-time || *mf* regular guest, permanent guest
**establecer** §22 *tr* to establish, to institute || *ref* to settle, take up residence; to start a business, to open an office
**establecimiento** *m* establishment; place of business; decree, ordinance, statute
**establo** *m* stable
**estaca** *f* stake, picket, pale; cudgel, club; (*clavo largo*) spike; (hort) cutting
**estacada** *f* stockade, palisade; dueling ground; **dejar en la estacada** to leave in the lurch; **quedarse en la estacada** to succumb on the field of battle, to fall in a duel; to fail; to lose out
**estacar** §73 *tr* to stake, to stake off; to tie to a stake || *ref* to stand stiff
**estación** *f* (*cada una de las cuatro divisiones del año*) season; (*sitio en que paran los trenes; radioemisora*) station; (*lugar en que se hace alto en un paseo, etc.*) stop; **estación balnearia** bathing resort; **estación de cabeza** (rr) terminal; **estación de carga** freight station; **estación de empalme** junction; **estación de gasolina** gas station, filling station; **estación de la seca** dry season; **estación de paso** (rr) way station; **estación de radiodifusión** broadcasting station; **estación de seguimiento** tracking station; **estación de servicio** service station; **estación difusora** or **emisora** broadcasting station; **estación gasolinera** gas station, filling station; **estación telefónica** telephone exchange
**estacional** *adj* seasonal
**estacionamiento** *m* stationing; parking; parking lot
**estacionar** *tr* to station; to stand, to park || *intr* to stand, to park || *ref* to station oneself; to be stationary; to stand, to park; **se prohibe estacionarse** no standing, no parking
**estaciona·rio -ria** *adj* stationary
**estada** *f* stay, stop
**estadía** *f* (*ante un pintor*) sitting; (com) demurrage; (Am) stop, stay
**estadio** *m* stadium; phase, stage; (*longitud*) furlong
**estadista** *mf* (*perito en estadística*) statistician || *m* statesman
**estadística** *f* statistics
**estadísti·co -ca** *adj* statistical || *m* (Am) statistician || *f* see **estadística**
**estadiunense** *adj* American, United States || *mf* American
**estadi·zo -za** *adj* (*aire*) heavy, stifling; (*agua*) stagnant
**estado** *m* state; state, condition, status; statement, report; **en estado de buena esperanza** or **en estado interesante** in the family way; **estado civil** marital status; **estado de ánimo** state of mind; **estado de cuentas** (com) statement; **estado libre asociado** commonwealth; **estado llano** commons, common people; **estado mayor** (mil) staff; **estado mayor conjunto** joint chiefs of staff; **estado mayor general** general staff; **Estados Unidos** *msg* the United States; **estado tapón** buffer state; **estar en estado de guerra** to be under martial law; **los Estados Unidos** *mpl* the United States; **tomar estado** to take a wife; to go into the church
**estado-policía** *m* (*pl* **estados-policías**) police state
**estadounidense** or **estadunidense** *adj* American, United States || *mf* American
**estafa** *f* swindle, trick; (*estribo*) stirrup
**estafar** *tr* to swindle, trick; to overcharge
**estafeta** *f* post, courier; post office; diplomatic mail
**estallar** *intr* to burst; to explode; (*un incendio, una revolución; la guerra*) to break out; (*la ira*) to break forth
**estallido** *m* report, crash, explosion; crack; (*p.ej., de la guerra*) outbreak; **dar un estallido** to crash, explode
**estambre** *m* (*hebras de lana e hilo formado de ellas*) worsted; (bot) stamen; **estambre de la vida** course or thread of life
**estampa** *f* stamp, print, engraving; press, printing; footstep, track; aspect, appearance; **dar a la estampa** to publish, bring out; **parecer la estampa de la herejía** (coll) to be a sight, be a mess; **la propia estampa de** the very image of
**estampado** *m* printing, stamping; printed fabric, cotton print
**estampar** *tr* to stamp, to print, to engrave; (*en el ánimo*) to fix, engrave; (*p.ej., el pie*) to leave a mark of; (bb) to tool; (*arrojar con fuerza*) (coll) to dash, to slam
**estampida** *f* report, crash, explosion; (Am) stampede
**estampido** *m* report, crash, explosion; **estampido sónico** (aer) sonic boom
**estampilla** *f* (*sello con letrero para estampar*) stamp; (*sello con una firma en facsímile*) rubber stamp; (*sello de correos o fiscal*) (Am) stamp
**estampillar** *tr* to stamp; to rubber-stamp
**estanca·do -da** *adj* stagnant; (fig) stagnant, dead
**estancar** §73 *tr* to stanch; to stem, check; (*un negocio*) to suspend, hold up; to corner; to monopolize || *ref* to become stagnant, to become choked up
**estancia** *f* stay, sojourn; (*aposento*) living room; day in hospital; cost of day in hospital; (*estrofa*) stanza; (mil) bivouac; (Arg, Urug, Chile) cattle ranch; (Col) small country place; (Ven) truck farm
**estanciero** *m* (Am) rancher, cattle raiser
**estan·co -ca** *adj* stanch, watertight || *m* government monopoly; cigar store, government store (*for sale of tobacco, matches, postage stamps, etc.*); archives; (Ecuad) liquor store
**estándar** *m* standard
**estandardizar** §60 or **estandarizar** §60 *tr* to standardize
**estandarte** *m* banner, standard

**estandartizar** §60 *tr* to standardize
**estanque** *m* basin, reservoir; pond, pool
**estanque•ro -ra** *mf* storekeeper, tobacconist; (Ecuad) saloonkeeper || *m* reservoir tender
**estanquillo** *m* cigar store, government store (*for sale of tobacco, matches, postage stamps, etc.*); (Col, Ecuad) bar, saloon; (Mex) booth, stand
**estante** *adj* located, being; settled, permanent || *m* shelf; shelving; bookcase, open bookcase
**estantería** *f* shelves, shelving; book stack
**estañar** *tr* to tin; to tin-plate; to solder; (Ven) to hurt, injure; (Ven) to fire
**estaño** *m* tin
**estaquilla** *f* peg, dowel, pin; (*clavo pequeño sin cabeza*) brad; (*clavo largo*) spike
**estaquillar** *tr* to peg, dowel; to nail
**estar** §37 *v aux* (*to form progressive form*) to be, e.g., **están aprendiendo el español** they are learning Spanish || *intr* to be; to be in, be home; to be ready; **¿a cuántos estamos?** what day of the month is it?; **¡está bien!** O.K.!, all right!; **estar a** to cost, sell at; **estar bien** to be well; **estar bien con** to be on good terms with; **estar de** to be (*on a temporary basis*); **estar de más** (coll) to be in the way; (coll) to be unnecessary; (coll) to be idle; **estar de viaje** to be on a trip; **estar mal** to be sick, be ill; **estar mal con** to be on bad terms with; **estar para** to be about to; **estar por** to be for, be in favor of; to be about to; to have a mind to; to remain to be + *pp;* **estar sobre sí** to be wary, be on one's guard || *ref* (*p.ej., en casa*) to stay; (*p.ej., quieto*) to keep
**estarcido** *m* stencil
**estarcir** §36 *tr* to stencil
**estatal** *adj* state
**estáti•co -ca** *adj* static; dumbfounded, speechless
**estatificar** §73 *tr* to nationalize
**estatizar** §60 *tr* (Am) to nationalize
**estatua** *f* statue; **quedarse hecho una estatua** (coll) to stand aghast
**estatuir** §20 *tr* to order, decree; to establish, prove
**estatura** *f* stature
**estatuta•rio -ria** *adj* statutory
**estatuto** *m* statute
**estay** *m* (naut) stay; **estay mayor** (naut) mainstay
**este, esta** *adj dem* (*pl* **estos, estas**) this || *m* east; east wind
**éste, ésta** *pron dem* (*pl* **éstos, éstas**) this one, this one here; the latter; **ésta** this city
**estela** *f* (*de un buque*) wake; (*de cohete, humo, cuerpo celeste, etc.*) trail
**estepa** *f* steppe
**estera** *f* mat; matting; **cargado de esteras** (coll) out of patience
**esterar** *tr* to cover with matting || *intr* (coll) to bundle up for the cold
**estercolar** *m* dunghill || §61 *tr* to dung, to manure
**estercolero** *m* manure pile, dunghill; manure collector
**estereofóni•co -ca** *adj* stereophonic, stereo
**estereoscópi•co -ca** *adj* stereoscopic, stereo
**estereotipa•do -da** *adj* stereotyped
**estéril** *adj* (*que no produce nada*) sterile; (*inútil, vano*) futile
**esterilizar** §60 *tr* to sterilize || *ref* to become sterile
**esterlina** *adj fem* (*libra*) sterling (*pound*)
**esternón** *m* breastbone
**estero** *m* tideland; estuary; (Arg) swamp, marsh; (Chile) stream; (Col, Ven) pool, puddle
**esterto** *m* death rattle; (*ruido en ciertas enfermedades, perceptible por la auscultación*) stertor, râle; **estertor agónico** death rattle
**esteta** *mf* aesthete || *f* beautician
**estéti•co -ca** *adj* aesthetic || *f* aesthetics
**estetoscopio** *m* stethoscope
**estiaje** *m* low water
**estiba** *f* (naut) stowage
**estibador** *m* stevedore, longshoreman
**estibar** *tr* to pack, to stuff; (naut) to stow
**estiércol** *m* dung, manure
**esti•gio -gia** *adj* Stygian || **Estigia** *f* Styx
**estigma** *m* stigma
**estigmatizar** §60 *tr* to stigmatize
**estilar** *tr* (*una escritura*) to draw up in proper form; to be given to || *intr & ref* to be in fashion
**estilete** *m* (*puñal*) stiletto
**estilo** *m* style; **por el estilo** like that, of the kind; **por el estilo de** like; **estilo directo** (gram) direct discourse; **estilo indirecto** (gram) indirect discourse
**estilográfica** *f* fountain pen
**estima** *f* esteem; (naut) dead reckoning
**estimable** *adj* estimable; considerable; appreciable, computable; esteemed
**estimación** *f* esteem, estimation; estimate, evaluation
**estimar** *tr* (*tener en buen concepto*) to esteem; (*apreciar, valuar*) to estimate; to think, believe; to appreciate, thank; to be fond of, to like; **estimar en poco** to hold in low esteem
**estimativa** *f* judgment; instinct
**estimulante** *adj & m* stimulant
**estimular** *tr* to stimulate
**estímulo** *m* stimulus
**estío** *m* summer
**estipendio** *m* stipend; wages
**estípti•co -ca** *adj* styptic; constipated; mean, stingy
**estipular** *tr* to stipulate
**estiradamente** *adv* scarcely, hardly; violently
**estira•do -da** *adj* conceited, stuck-up; prim, neat; tight, closefisted
**estirar** *tr* to stretch; (*alambre, metal*) to draw; (*planchar ligeramente*) to iron lightly; (*un escrito, discurso, cargo, etc.*) (fig) to stretch out; (*el dinero*) (fig) to stretch || *ref* to stretch; to put on airs

**estirón** *m* jerk, tug; **dar un estirón** (coll) to grow up in no time
**estirpe** *f* race, stock, lineage; (*linaje*) strain, pedigree
**estival** *adj* summer
**esto** *pron dem* that; **en esto** at this point; **por esto** for this reason
**estocada** *f* thrust, stab, lunge; (*herida*) stab, stab wound; (*cosa que ocasiona dolor*) blow
**Estocolmo** *f* Stockholm
**estofa** *f* brocade; quality, kind
**estofado** *m* stew
**estoi•co -ca** *adj & mf* stoic
**estóli•do -da** *adj* stupid, imbecile
**estómago** *m* stomach; **estómago de avestruz** iron digestion; **tener buen estómago** or **mucho estómago** (coll) to be thick-skinned; (coll) to have an easy conscience
**estopa** *f* (*de lino o cáñamo*) tow; (*de calafatear*) (naut) oakum; **estopa de acero** steel wool; **estopa de algodón** cotton waste
**estopilla** *f* (*tela muy sutil*) lawn; (*tela ordinaria de algodón*) cheesecloth
**estoque** *m* rapier; sword lily, gladiola
**estoquear** *tr* to stab with a rapier
**estor** *m* blind, shade, window shade
**estorbar** *tr* to hinder, obstruct; to inconvenience, bother, annoy || *intr* (coll) to be in the way
**estorbo** *m* hindrance, obstruction; inconvenience, bother, annoyance
**estorbo•so -sa** *adj* hindering; bothersome, annoying
**estornino** *m* starling; **estornino de los pastores** grackle, myna
**estornudar** *intr* to sneeze
**estornudo** *m* sneeze, sneezing
**estrado** *m* (*tarima del trono*) dais; lecture platform; (archaic) lady's drawing room; **estrados** courtrooms, law courts; **citar para estrados** to subpoena
**estrafala•rio -ria** *adj* (coll) queer, eccentric, odd; (coll) sloppy, sloppily dressed || *mf* (coll) screwball
**estragar** §44 *tr* to spoil, damage, vitiate
**estrago** *m* damage, ruin, havoc
**estrambote** *m* tail (*of sonnet*)
**estrambóti•co -ca** *adj* (coll) odd, queer
**estrangul** *m* (mus) reed, mouthpiece
**estrangular** *tr & ref* to strangle, to choke
**estraperlear** *intr* to deal in the black market
**estraperlista** *adj* black-market || *mf* black-market dealer
**estraperlo** *m* black market
**estrapontín** *m* folding seat, jump seat
**estratagema** *f* stratagem; craftiness
**estratega** *m* strategist
**estrategia** *f* strategy; **alta estrategia** grand strategy
**estratégi•co -ca** *adj* strategic(al) || *m* strategist
**estratificar** §73 *tr & ref* to stratify
**estrato** *m* stratum, layer
**estratosfera** *f* stratosphere
**estraza** *f* rag; brown paper
**estrechar** *tr* (*reducir a menor ancho*) to narrow; (*apretar*) to tighten; to press, pursue; to force, compel; to hug, embrace; to squeeze; **estrechar la mano a** to shake hands with || *ref* to narrow down; to contract; to hug, embrace; (*reducir los gastos*) to retrench; **estrecharse en** to squeeze in; **estrecharse la mano** (*dos personas*) to shake hands
**estrechez** *f* narrowness; rightness; (*amistad íntima*) closeness, intimacy; austerity, strictness; poverty, want, need; trouble, jam; **estrechez de miras** narrow outlook, narrow-mindedness; **hallarse en gran estrechez** to be in dire straits
**estre•cho -cha** *adj* narrow; tight; close, intimate; austere, strict; stingy, tight; poor, needy; mean || *m* (*paso angosto en el mar*) strait; fix, predicament
**estrechura** *f* narrowness; tightness; closeness, intimacy; austerity, strictness; trouble, predicament
**estregar** §66 *tr* to rub hard; to scour
**estregón** *m* hard rub
**estrella** *f* star; (typ) asterisk, star; (mov & theat) star; (*hado, destino*) (fig) star; **estrella de los Alpes** edelweiss; **estrella de mar** starfish; **estrella de rabo** comet; **estrella filante** or **fugaz** shooting star; **estrella fulgurante** (astr) flare star; **estrella polar** polestar; **estrella vespertina** evening star; **ver las estrellas** (coll) to see stars
**estrella•do -da** *adj* (*cielo*) starry; star-spangled; star-shaped; (*huevos*) fried
**estrellamar** *m* starfish
**estrellar** *adj* star || *tr* to star, to spangle with stars; (*huevos*) to fry; to shatter, dash to pieces || *ref* to be spangled with stars; to crash; **estrellarse con** to clash with
**estrellón** *m* large star; (*fuego artificial*) star; (Am) smash-up
**estremecer** §22 *tr* to shake; (*el aire*) to rend; (fig) to shake, upset || *ref* to shake, tremble, shiver, shudder
**estrena** *f* (*regalo que se da en señal de agradecimiento*) handsel; first use
**estrenar** *tr* to use for the first time, to wear for the first time; (*un drama*) to perform for the first time; (*un cine*) to show for the first time; to try out for the first time || *ref* to make the day's first transaction; to appear for the first time; (*un drama, un cine*) to open
**estrenista** *mf* first-nighter
**estreno** *m* beginning, debut; première, first performance; first use
**estre•nuo -nua** *adj* strenuous, vigorous, enterprising
**estreñimiento** *m* constipation
**estreñir** §72 *tr* to constipate
**estrépito** *m* racket, crash; fuss, show
**estrepito•so -sa** *adj* loud, noisy, boisterous; notorious; shocking
**estría** *f* flute, groove
**estriar** §77 *tr* to flute, groove
**estribar** *intr* to lean, rest; to be based, to depend
**estriberón** *m* stepping stone
**estribillo** *m* (*de un poema*) burden, refrain; pet word, pet phrase

**estribo** *m* (*de coche*) step; (*de automóvil*) running board; (*apoyo para el pie*) footboard; (*para el pie del jinete*) stirrup; abutment, buttress; (fig) foundation, support; **perder los estribos** to fly off the handle, to lose one's head
**estribor** *m* starboard
**estricnina** *f* strychnine
**estricote** *m* (Ven) riotous living; **al estricote** hither and thither
**estric•to -ta** *adj* strict, severe, rigorous; proper, punctual; (*sentido de una palabra*) narrow
**estrictura** *f* (pathol) stricture
**estrige** *f* barn owl; (*Athene noctua*) little owl
**estro** *m* poetic inspiration; (*de animal*) rut, heat
**estrofa** *f* strophe
**estroncio** *m* strontium
**estropajo** *m* mop; dishcloth; **servir de estropajo** (coll) to be forced to do the dirty work; (coll) to be treated with indifference
**estropajo•so -sa** *adj* (coll) raggedy, slovenly; (*carne*) (coll) tough, leathery; (coll) spluttering
**estropear** *tr* to spoil, ruin, damage; to abuse, mistreat; to cripple, maim || *ref* to spoil, go to ruin; to fail
**estropicio** *m* (coll) breakage; (coll) havoc, ruin; (coll) fracas, rumpus
**estructura** *f* structure
**estruendo** *m* noise, crash, boom; confusion, uproar; pomp, show; fame
**estruendo•so -sa** *adj* noisy, booming
**estrujar** *tr* to squeeze; to press, crush, mash; to bruise; to rumple; (coll) to drain, exhaust
**estuante** *adj* hot, burning
**estuario** *m* estuary; tideland
**estucar** §73 *tr* to stucco
**estuco** *m* stucco; **estuco de París** plaster of Paris
**estuche** *m* case, box; (*caja y utensilios que se guardan en ella*) kit; casket, jewel case; (*para tijeras*) sheath; **estuche de afeites** compact, vanity case; **ser un estuche** (coll) to be a handy fellow
**estudia•do -da** *adj* affected, studied
**estudiantado** *m* student body
**estudiante** *mf* student
**estudiantil** *adj* student
**estudiar** *tr* to study; (*la lección a una persona*) to hear (*someone's lesson*) || *intr* to study; **estudiar para . . .** to study to become . . .
**estudio** *m* study; (*aposento*) studio; (mus) étude; **altos estudios** advanced studies
**estudio•so -sa** *adj* studious || *m* student, scholar
**estufa** *f* stove; steam cabinet, steam room; foot stove; (*invernáculo*) hothouse
**estul•to -ta** *adj* stupid, silly, foolish
**estupefac•to -ta** *adj* stupefied, dumbfounded
**estupen•do -da** *adj* stupendous; (coll) famous, distinguished
**estúpi•do -da** *adj* stupid || *mf* dolt
**estupor** *m* stupor; surprise, amazement
**estuprar** *tr* to rape, violate
**estupro** *m* rape, violation
**estuque** *m* stucco
**esturión** *m* sturgeon
**etapa** *f* stage; **a etapas pequeñas** by easy stages
**éter** *m* ether
**etére•o -a** *adj* ethereal
**eternidad** *f* eternity
**eternizar** §60 *tr* to prolong endlessly || *ref* to be endless, be interminable
**eter•no -na** *adj* eternal
**éti•co -ca** *adj* ethical || *f* ethics
**etileno** *m* ethylene
**etilo** *m* ethyl
**étimo** *m* etymon
**etimología** *f* etymology
**etíope** *adj* & *mf* Ethiopian
**etiópi•co -ca** *adj* & *m* Ethiopic
**etiqueta** *f* (*marbete*) tag, label; (*ceremonial que se debe observar*) etiquette; (*ceremonia en la manera de tratarse*) formality; **de etiqueta** formal, full-dress; **de etiqueta menor** semiformal; **estar de etiqueta** to have become cool toward each other
**etiquetar** *tr* to tag, to label
**etiquete•ro -ra** *adj* formal, ceremonious; full of compliments
**etiquez** *f* (pathol) consumption
**étni•co -ca** *adj* ethnic(al); (gram) gentilic
**etnografía** *f* ethnography
**etnología** *f* ethnology
**E.U.A** *abbr* **Estados Unidos de América**
**eucalipto** *m* eucalyptus
**Eucaristía** *f* Eucharist
**eufemismo** *m* euphemism
**eufemísti•co -ca** *adj* euphemistic
**eufonía** *f* euphony
**eufóni•co -ca** *adj* euphonic, euphonious
**euforia** *f* euphoria; endurance, fortitude
**eufuísmo** *m* euphuism
**eufuísti•co -ca** *adj* euphuistic
**eugenesia** *f* eugenics
**eunuco** *m* eunuch
**euritmia** *f* regular pulse
**euro** *m* east wind
**Europa** *f* Europe
**europe•o -a** *adj* & *mf* European
**eutanasia** *f* euthanasia
**eutrapelia** *f* moderation; lightheartedness; simple pastime
**evacuación** *f* evacuation; **evacuación de basuras** garbage disposal
**evacuar** §21 & **regular** *tr* to evacuate; (*un trámite*) to transact; (*una visita*) to pay; (*un encargo, un asunto*) to do, carry out; **evacuar el vientre** to have a movement of the bowels || *intr* to evacuate; to have a movement of the bowels
**evadi•do -da** *adj* escaped || *mf* escapee
**evadir** *tr* to avoid, evade, elude || *ref* to evade; to escape, to flee
**evaluar** §21 *tr* to evaluate; to value
**evangéli•co -ca** *adj* evangelic(al)
**evangelio** *m* (coll) gospel, gospel truth || **Evangelio** *m* Gospel, Evangel
**evangelista** *m* Gospel singer or chanter;

(Mex) public writer, penman || **Evangelista** *m* Evangelist
**evaporar** *tr & ref* to evaporate
**evaporizar** §60 *tr, intr & ref* to vaporize
**evasión** *f* (*efugio, evasiva*) evasion; (*fuga*) escape
**evasi•vo -va** *adj* evasive || *f* loophole, pretext, excuse
**evento** *m* chance, happening, contingency; (Col) sports event; **a todo evento** in any event
**eventual** *adj* contingent; (*emolumentos; gastos*) incidental
**eventualidad** *f* eventuality, contingency; uncertainty
**evidencia** *f* evidence, obviousness; (*prueba judicial*) (Am) evidence; **evidencia moral** moral certainty
**evidenciar** *tr* to show, make evident
**evidente** *adj* evident, obvious
**evitable** *adj* avoidable
**evitación** *f* avoidance; prevention
**evitar** *tr* to avoid, shun; (*p.ej., el polvo*) to keep off; to prevent; **evitar** + *inf* to avoid + *ger;* to save from + *ger,* e.g., **la luz de la luna nos evitó tener que encender los faroles** the light of the moon saved us from having to light the lights
**evo** *m* (poet) age, aeon; (theol) eternity
**evocar** §73 *tr* to evoke; (*p.ej., los demonios*) to invoke
**evolución** *f* evolution; change, development (*of one's point of view, plans, conduct, etc.*)
**evolucionar** *intr* to evolve; to change, develop; (mil & nav) to maneuver
**ex** *adj* ex- (*former*), e.g., **el ex presidente** the ex-president
**ex abrupto** *adv* brashly || *m* brash remark
**exacción** *f* (*de impuestos, deudas, multas, etc.*) exaction, levy; (*cobro injusto*) extortion
**exacerbar** *tr* to exacerbate, aggravate
**exactitud** *f* exactness; punctuality
**exac•to -ta** *adj* exact; punctual, faithful || **exacto** *interj* right!
**exactor** *m* tax collector
**exagerar** *tr* to exaggerate
**exalta•do -da** *adj* exalted; extreme, hotheaded; wrought-up; radical
**exaltar** *tr* to exalt; to extol || *ref* to be wrought-up, get excited
**examen** *m* examination; **examen de ingreso** entrance examination; **sufrir un examen** to take an examination
**examinar** *tr* to examine; to inspect || *ref* to take an examination; **examinarse de ingreso** to take entrance examinations
**exangüe** *adj* bloodless; (coll) weak, exhausted; (coll) dead
**exánime** *adj* (*sin vida*) lifeless; (*desmayado*) faint, in a faint, lifeless
**exasperar** *tr* to exasperate
**Exc.ª** *abbr* **Excelencia**
**excandecer** §22 *tr* to incense, enrage
**excarcelación** *f* release
**excarcelar** *tr* (*a un preso*) to release
**excavadora** *f* power shovel
**excavar** *tr* to excavate; to loosen soil around
**excedente** *adj* excess; excessive; on leave || *m* excess, surplus
**exceder** *tr* (*ser mayor que*) to exceed; (*aventajar*) to excel || *ref* to go too far, go to extremes; **excederse a sí mismo** to outdo oneself
**excelencia** *f* excellence, excellency; **por excelencia** par excellence; **Su Excelencia** Your Excellency
**excelente** *adj* excellent
**excel•so -sa** *adj* lofty, sublime || **el Excelso** the Most High
**excéntrica** *f* eccentric
**excentricidad** *f* eccentricity
**excéntri•co -ca** *adj* eccentric; (*barrio*) outlying || *mf* eccentric || *f* see **excéntrica**
**excepción** *f* exception; **a excepción de** with the exception of
**excepcional** *adj* exceptional
**excepto** *prep* except
**exceptuar** §21 *tr* to except; (*eximir*) to exempt
**excerpta** or **excerta** *f* excerpt
**excesi•vo -va** *adj* excessive; excess
**exceso** *m* excess; **exceso de equipaje** excess baggage; **exceso de peso** excess weight; **exceso de velocidad** speeding
**excitable** *adj* excitable
**excitación** *f* excitement; excitation
**excitante** *adj & m* stimulant
**excitar** *tr* to excite, stir up, stimulate || *ref* to become excited
**exclamación** *f* exclamation
**exclamar** *tr & intr* to exclaim
**exclaustrar** *tr* (*a un religioso*) to secularize
**excluir** §20 *tr* to exclude
**exclusión** *f* exclusion; **con exclusión de** to the exclusion of
**exclusiva** *f* rejection, turndown; sole right, monopoly; (*anticipación de una noticia por un periódico*) news beat
**exclusive** *adv* exclusively || *prep* exclusive of, not counting
**exclusivista** *adj* exclusive, clannish || *mf* snob
**exclusi•vo -va** *adj* exclusive || *f* see **exclusiva**
**Exc.ᵐᵒ** *abbr* **Excelentísimo**
**ex combatiente** *m* ex-serviceman
**excomulgar** §44 *tr* to excommunicate; (coll) to ostracize, banish
**excomunión** *f* excommunication
**excoriar** *tr* to skin || *ref* to skin oneself; (*p.ej., el codo*) to skin
**excrementar** *intr* to have a bowel movement
**excremento** *m* excrement
**exculpar** *tr* to exculpate, exonerate
**excursión** *f* excursion, outing
**excursionista** *mf* excursionist, tourist
**excusa** *f* excuse; **a excusa** secretly; **excusa es decir** it is unnecessary to say
**excusabaraja** *f* basket with lid
**excusable** *adj* excusable; avoidable
**excusadamente** *adv* unnecessarily
**excusa•do -da** *adj* exempt; unnecessary; private, set apart; (*puerta*) side || *m* toilet
**excusa•lí** *m* (*pl* **-líes**) small apron

**excusar** *tr* to excuse; to exempt; to avoid; to prevent; to make unnecessary; **excusar** + *inf* to not have to + *inf* || *ref* to excuse oneself; to apologize; **excusarse de** + *inf* to decline to + *inf*
**exención** *f* exemption
**exencionar** *tr* to exempt
**exentamente** *adv* freely; frankly, simply
**exentar** *tr* to exempt
**exen•to -ta** *adj* exempt; open, unobstructed; free, disengaged
**exequias** *fpl* obsequies
**exfolia•dor -dora** *adj* (Am) tear-off
**exhalación** *f* exhalation; flash of lightning; shooting star; fume, vapor; **como una exhalación** (coll) like a flash of lightning
**exhalar** *tr* to exhale, emit; (*suspiros, quejas*) to breathe forth; **exhalar el último suspiro** to breathe one's last || *ref* to exhale; (*con el ejercicio violento del cuerpo*) to breathe hard; to hurry; to crave
**exhausti•vo -va** *adj* exhaustive
**exhaus•to -ta** *adj* exhausted; (coll) wasted away
**exheredar** *tr* to disinherit
**exhibición** *f* exhibition; exhibit
**exhibir** *tr* to exhibit; (Mex) to pay || *ref* (coll) to make oneself evident
**exhilarante** *adj* exhilarating; (*gas*) laughing
**exhortar** *tr* to exhort
**exhumar** *tr* to exhume
**exigencia** *f* exigency, requirement
**exigente** *adj* exigent, demanding
**exigir §27** *tr* to exact, require, demand
**exi•guo -gua** *adj* meager, scanty
**exila•do -da** *adj & mf* (Am) exile
**exi•mio -mia** *adj* choice, select, superior; distinguished
**eximir** *tr* to exempt
**existencia** *f* existence; **en existencia** in stock; **existencias** (com) stock
**existente** *adj* existing, extant; in stock
**existir** *intr* to exist
**exitazo** *m* smash hit
**exitista** *adj* (Arg) me-too || *mf* (Arg) me-tooer
**éxito** *m* (*resultado feliz*) success; (*canción, cine, etc. que ha tenido mucho éxito*) hit; (*resultado de un negocio*) outcome, result; **éxito de librería** best seller; **éxito de taquilla** box-office hit, good box office; **éxito de venta** best seller; **éxito rotundo** smash hit
**exito•so -sa** *adj* (Arg) successful
**ex li•bris** *m* (*pl* **-bris**) bookplate
**éxodo** *m* exodus; **éxodo de técnicos** brain drain
**exonerar** *tr* to exonerate, to relieve; to discharge, dismiss; **exonerar el vientre** to have a movement of the bowels
**exorar** *tr* to beg, entreat
**exorbitante** *adj* exorbitant
**exorcizar §60** *tr* to exorcise
**exornar** *tr* to adorn, embellish
**exóti•co -ca** *adj* exotic; striking, stunning, glamorous
**expandir** *tr & ref* (Arg, Chile) to expand, extend, spread
**expansión** *f* expansion; (*manifestación efusiva*) expansiveness; (*difusión de una opinión*) spread; rest, recreation
**expansionar** *ref* to expand; to open one's heart; to relax, take it easy
**expansi•vo -va** *adj* expansive
**expatria•do -da** *adj & mf* expatriate
**expectación** *f* expectancy
**expectativa** *f* expectation; **estar en la expectativa de** to be expecting, to be on the lookout for
**expectorar** *tr & intr* to expectorate
**expedición** *f* (*excursión para realizar una empresa*) expedition; (*remesa*) shipment; (*de un certificado, títulos, etc.*) issuance; (*agilidad, facilidad*) expedition
**expedi•dor -dora** *mf* sender, shipper
**expediente** *m* expedient; makeshift, apology; (*agilidad, facilidad*) expedition; (*todos los papeles correspondientes a un asunto*) dossier; (law) action, proceedings; **expediente académico** (educ) record
**expedienteo** *m* red tape
**expedir §50** *tr* to send, ship, remit; (*títulos*) to issue; (*despachar, cursar*) to expedite
**expeditar** *tr* (Am) to expedite
**expediti•vo -va** *adj* expeditious
**expedi•to -ta** *adj* ready; clear, open, unencumbered
**expeler** *tr* to expel, eject
**expende•dor -dora** *mf* dealer, retailer; ticket agent; **expendedor de moneda falsa** distributor of counterfeit money
**expendeduría** *f* cigar store (*for sale of state-monopolized articles*)
**expender** *tr* to spend; to dispense; to sell at retail; (*moneda falsa*) to circulate
**expendio** *m* (Am) shop, store; (Am) retail; (Mex) cigar store
**expensar** *tr* (Chile, Guat, Mex) to pay the cost of
**expensas** *fpl* expenses
**experiencia** *f* (*enseñanza que se adquiere con la práctica o con el vivir; suceso en que uno ha participado, cosa que uno ha experimentado*) experience; (*ensayo, experimento*) experiment
**experimenta•do -da** *adj* experienced
**experimentar** *tr* to experience, undergo, feel; to test, try, try out || *intr* to experiment
**experimento** *m* experiment
**exper•to -ta** *adj & m* expert
**expiación** *f* expiation, atonement; purification
**expiar §77** *tr* to expiate, atone for; to purify
**expirar** *intr* to expire
**explanación** *f* grading, leveling; explanation
**explanada** *f* esplanade
**explanar** *tr* to grade, to level; to explain
**explayar** *tr* to enlarge, extend || *ref* to spread out, extend; to go for an outing; to expatiate, talk at length; **explayarse con** to unbosom oneself to
**explicación** *f* explanation

**explicar** §73 *tr* to explain; (*exponer*) to expound; (*exculpar*) to explain away; (*una clase*) to teach || *intr* to explain || *ref* to explain oneself; to understand, make out
**explicati•vo -va** *adj* explanatory
**explíci•to -ta** *adj* explicit
**exploración** *f* exploration; (mil) scouting; (telv) scanning
**explora•dor -dora** *mf* explorer || *m* boy scout; (mil) scout
**explorar** *tr* to explore; (mil) to scout; (telv) to scan
**explosión** *f* explosion; (*de gases en un motor*) combustion
**explosi•vo -va** *adj & m* explosive || *f* (phonet) explosive
**explotación** *f* operation, running; exploitation
**explotar** *tr* to operate, to run; (*una mina*) to work; to exploit || *intr* to explode
**exponente** *m* exponent
**exponer** §54 *tr* to expose; (*explicar*) to expound; (*a un niño recién nacido*) to abandon || *intr* to display, show, exhibit; (eccl) to expose the Host || *ref* to expose oneself; to be on view
**exportación** *f* exportation, export; (*mercaderías que se exportan*) exports
**exporta•dor -dora** *mf* exporter
**exportar** *tr & intr* to export
**exposición** *f* exposition; (*a un peligro; con relación a los puntos cardinales*) exposure; (phot) exposure; (rhet) exposition; **exposición universal** world's fair
**exposímetro** *m* light meter
**expósi•to -ta** *mf* foundling
**exposi•tor -tora** *mf* exhibitor
**exprés** *m* express train; (Mex) express company
**expresa•do -da** *adj* above-mentioned
**expresamente** *adv* express, expressly
**expresar** *tr* to express || *ref* to express oneself
**expresión** *f* expression; (*acción de exprimir*) squeezing; (*zumo exprimido*) juice; **expresiones** regards
**expresi•vo -va** *adj* expressive; kind, affectionate
**expre•so -sa** *adj* express || *m* (*tren muy rápido; correo extraordinario*) express; (Am) express company
**exprimidera** *f* squeezer; **exprimidera de naranjas** orange squeezer
**exprimi•do -da** *adj* lean, skinny; stiff, stuck-up; affected, prim, prudish
**exprimidor** *m* wringer; squeezer; **exprimidor de ropa** clothes wringer
**exprimir** *tr* to squeeze, press; (*p.ej., la ropa blanca*) to wring, wring out; (*extraer apretando*) to express
**ex profeso** *adv* on purpose
**expropiar** *tr* to expropriate
**expues•to -ta** *adj* dangerous, hazardous
**expugnar** *tr* to take by storm
**expulsanie•ves** *m* (*pl* **-ves**) snowplow
**expulsar** *tr* to expel
**expulsión** *f* expulsion
**expurgar** §44 *tr* to expurgate
**exquisi•to -ta** *adj* exquisite
**extasiar** §77 & **regular** *ref* to go into ecstasy
**éxta•sis** *m* (*pl* **-sis**) ecstasy
**extáti•co -ca** *adj* ecstatic
**extemporal** *adj* unseasonable
**extemporáne•o -a** *adj* unseasonable; untimely, inopportune
**extender** §51 *tr* to extend, to stretch out, to spread out; to spread; (*un documento*) to draw up || *ref* to extend, to stretch out; to spread; **extenderse a** or **hasta** to amount to
**extendidamente** *adv* at length, in detail
**extensión** *f* extension; (*vasta superficie, p.ej., del océano*) expanse; (*alcance, importancia*) extent; extending
**extensi•vo -va** *adj* extensive; **hacer extensivos a** to extend (*e.g., good wishes*) to
**exten•so -sa** *adj* extensive, extended, vast; **por extenso** at length, in detail
**extenuar** §21 *tr* to weaken, emaciate
**exterior** *adj* exterior, outer, outside; foreign || *m* exterior, outside; appearance, bearing; **al exterior** or **a lo exterior** on the outside; outwardly; **del exterior** from abroad; **en el exterior** on the outside; abroad; **en exteriores** (mov) on location
**exterioridad** *f* externals, outward appearance; **exterioridades** pomp, show
**exteriorista** *adj* outgoing, outgiving || *mf* extrovert
**exteriorizar** §60 *tr* to reveal || *ref* to unbosom one's heart
**exterminar** *tr* to exterminate
**exterminio** *m* extermination
**exter•no -na** *adj* external || *mf* day pupil
**extinción** *f* extinction; cancellation, elimination
**extinguir** §29 *tr* to extinguish, put out; to wipe out, put an end to; to fulfil, carry out; (*un plazo, un tiempo*) to spend, to serve || *ref* to be extinguished, go out; to come to an end
**extin•to -ta** *adj* (*volcán*) extinct; (Am) deceased || *mf* (Am) deceased
**extintor** *m* fire extinguisher; **extintor de espuma** foam extinguisher; **extintor de granada** fire grenade
**extirpar** *tr* to extirpate, to eradicate
**extorno** *m* premium adjustment (*based on change in policy*)
**extorsión** *f* extortion; harm, damage
**extorsionar** *tr* to harm, damage; (Am) to extort
**extra** *adj* extra; **extra de** (coll) in addition to, besides || *mf* (theat) extra || *m* (*de un periódico*) extra; (coll) extra, bonus
**extracción** *f* extraction; (*en la lotería*) drawing numbers; **extracción de raíces** (math) evolution
**extractar** *tr* (*un escrito*) to abstract
**extracto** *m* (*de un escrito*) abstract; (pharm) extract
**extracurricular** *adj* extracurricular
**extradición** *f* extradition
**extraer** §75 *tr* to extract; to pull; (*la raíz*) (math) to extract
**extrafuerte** *adj* heavy-duty
**extralimitar** *ref* to go too far
**extramural** *adj* extramural

**extranjerismo** *m* borrowing
**extranje•ro -ra** *adj* foreign, alien || *mf* foreigner, alien; **extranjero enemigo** enemy alien || *m* foreign country; **al extranjero** abroad; **del extranjero** from abroad; **en el extranjero** abroad
**extrañar** *tr* to banish, expatriate; to surprise; to find strange; (Am) to miss || *ref* to be surprised; to refuse
**extrañeza** *f* strangeness, peculiarity; (*desavenencia*) estrangement; wonder, surprise
**extra•ño -ña** *adj* foreign; (*raro, singular*) strange; extraneous; **extraño a** unconnected with || *mf* foreigner
**extraoficial** *adj* unofficial
**extraordina•rio -ria** *adj* extraordinary; extra, special || *m* extra dish; special mail; (*de un periódico*) extra
**extrapla•no -na** *adj* extra-flat
**extrapolar** *tr & intr* to extrapolate
**extrarradio** *m* outer edge of town
**extrasensorial** *adj* extrasensory
**extravagancia** *f* (*singularidad, ridiculez*) extravagance, wildness, folly
**extravagante** *adj* (*singular, ridículo*) extravagant, wild, foolish; (*correspondencia en la casa de correos*) in transit
**extravia•do -da** *adj* lost, misplaced; astray, gone astray; (*lugar*) out-of-the-way
**extraviar** §77 *tr* to lead astray, mislead; to mislay, misplace || *ref* to get lost, go astray; to go wrong; to get out of line
**extravío** *m* going astray; loss; misleading; misconduct; misplacement
**extrema** *f* (*escasez grande*) (coll) extremity; (*de la vida*) (coll) end, last moment
**extremar** *tr* to carry far, carry to the limit || *ref* to strive hard
**extremaunción** *f* extreme unction
**extreme•ño -ña** *adj* frontier
**extremidad** *f* extremity; end, tip; **extremidades** (*pies y manos*) extremities; **la última extremidad** one's last moment
**extremista** *mf* extremist
**extre•mo -ma** *adj* extreme; utmost; critical, desperate || *m* extremity; (*de la calle*) end; (*del dedo*) tip; (*punto último*) extreme; great care; (*de una conversación, una carta*) point; winter pasture; **al extremo de** to the point of; **de extremo a extremo** from one end to the other; **hacer extremos** to be demonstrative, to gush || *f* see **extrema**
**extremo•so -sa** *adj* extreme, forthright; effusive, gushy, demonstrative
**extrínse•co -ca** *adj* extrinsic
**extroverti•do -da** *mf* extrovert
**exuberante** *adj* exuberant; luxuriant
**exudar** *tr & intr* to exude
**exultante** *adj* exultant
**exultar** *intr* to exult
**exvoto** *m* votive offering
**eyacular** *tr & intr* to ejaculate

# F

**F, f** (efe) *f* seventh letter of the Spanish alphabet
**f.a.b.** *abbr* **franco a bordo**
**fabada** *f* pork-and-bean stew (*in Asturias*)
**fábrica** *f* factory, plant; building, masonry; (eccl) vestry
**fabricación** *f* manufacture; **fabricación en serie** mass production
**fabricante** *mf* manufacturer
**fabricar** §73 *tr* to manufacture; to devise, invent; to fabricate
**fabril** *adj* factory
**fabriquero** *m* manufacturer; charcoal burner; churchwarden
**fábula** *f* fable; (*p.ej., de un drama*) plot, story; rumor, gossip; (*mentira*) story, lie; (*objeto de murmuración*) talk of the town
**fabulario** *m* book of fables
**fabulo•so -sa** *adj* fabulous
**facción** *f* faction; feature; battle; **estar de facción** (mil) to be on duty; **facciones** features
**facciona•rio -ria** *adj* factional
**faceta** *f* facet
**facetada** *f* (Mex) flat joke
**face•to -ta** *adj* (Mex) affected; (Mex) finicky || *f* see **faceta**
**facial** *adj* facial
**fácil** *adj* easy; pliant, yielding; likely; loose, wanton
**facilidad** *f* facility, ease, easiness; **facilidades de pago** easy payments
**facilitar** *tr* to facilitate, to expedite; to furnish, supply
**facili•tón -tona** *adj* (coll) bumbling, brash || *mf* (coll) bumbler
**facinero•so -sa** *adj* wicked || *mf* villain
**facistol** *m* choir desk
**facón** *m* (Arg, Urug) gaucho knife
**facsímile** *m* facsimile
**factible** *adj* feasible
**factor** *m* factor; commission merchant; baggageman; freight agent
**factoría** *f* trading post; (Ecuad, Peru) foundry; (Mex) factory
**factura** *f* invoice, bill; workmanship; **factura simulada** pro forma invoice; **según factura** as per invoice
**facturación** *f* invoicing, billing; (*del equipaje*) checking
**facturar** *tr* to invoice, to bill; (*el equipaje*) to check
**facultad** *f* faculty; (*de la universidad*) school; knowledge, skill; power; **facultad de altos estudios** graduate school

**facultar** *tr* to empower, to authorize
**facultati•vo -va** *adj* faculty; optional || *m* doctor, physician
**facundia** *f* eloquence, fluency
**facun•do -da** *adj* eloquent, fluent
**facha** *mf* (*adefesio*) (coll) sight || *f* look, appearance; **facha a facha** face to face
**fachada** *f* façade; (*de un libro*) title page; (coll) look, build, bearing; **hacer fachada con** to overlook, to look out on
**facha•do -da** *adj* — **bien fachado** good-looking || *f* see **fachada**
**fachenda** *m* (coll) boaster, show-off || *f* (coll) boasting
**fachendear** *intr* (coll) to boast, to show off
**fachendista, fachen•dón -dona, fachendo•so -sa** *adj* (coll) boastful || *mf* (coll) boaster, show-off
**fachinal** *m* (Arg) marshland
**fada** *f* fairy, witch
**faena** *f* work; toil; chore, task, job; (taur) windup; (taur) stunt, trick; (mil) fatigue, fatigue duty; (Guat, Mex, W-I) extra work, overtime; (Ecuad) morning work in the field; (Chile) gang of farm hands
**faenero** *m* (Chile) farm hand
**Faetón** *m* Phaëthon
**fagot** *m* bassoon
**faisán** *m* pheasant
**faja** *f* sash, girdle; bandage; band, strip; newspaper wrapper; (*de carretera*) lane; (*de tierra*) strip; **faja central** or **divisoria** median strip; **faja medical** supporter
**fajar** *tr* to wrap; to bandage; to swaddle; (*un periódico o revista*) to put a wrapper on; (Am) to beat, thrash; (Am) to attack || *ref* to put on a sash
**fajardo** *m* meat pie
**fajín** *m* sash
**fajina** *f* fagot; fire wood; (mil) call to quarters
**fajo** *m* bundle; (*de papel moneda*) roll; (Am) swig; (Mex) blow; (Mex) leather belt; **fajos** swaddling clothes
**falacia** *f* deception; deceitfulness
**falange** *f* phalanx
**falangia** *f* daddy-longlegs
**fa•laz** *adj* (*pl* **-laces**) deceitful; deceptive
**falba•lá** *m* (*pl* **-laes**) gore; flounce, ruffle
**falce** *m* sickle; falchion
**falda** *f* skirt, dress; (*regazo*) lap; flap, fold; (*del sombrero*) brim; foothill; (*mujer*) (coll) skirt; **cosido a las faldas de** tied to the apron strings of
**falde•ro -ra** *adj* skirt; (*perro*) lap; lady-loving || *m* lap dog
**faldillas** *fpl* skirts, coattails
**faldón** *m* coattail; shirttail; saddle flap
**falible** *adj* fallible
**falsada** *f* swoop (*of bird of prey*)
**falsa•rio -ria** *adj* lying || *mf* falsifier, crook; liar
**falsear** *tr* to falsify; to counterfeit; to forge; (*la verdad*) to distort; (*una cerradura*) to pick; to bevel || *intr* to sag, to buckle; to give, give way
**falsedad** *f* falsity; (*mentira*) falsehood
**falsete** *m* falsetto; plug, tap; door (*between rooms*)
**falsetista** *f* falsetto
**falsía** *f* falsity, treachery; unsteadiness
**falsificación** *f* falsification; fake; counterfeit; forgery
**falsificar** **§73** *tr* to falsify; to fake; to counterfeit; to forge
**falsilla** *f* guide lines
**fal•so -sa** *adj* false; counterfeit; (*caballo*) vicious || *m* patch; **coger en falso** (Mex) to catch in a lie; **envidar en falso** to bluff
**falta** *f* fault; lack, want; misdeed; absence; (*ausencia de la clase*) cut; (sport) fault; **a falta de** for want of; **echar en falta** to miss; **falta de ortografía** misspelling; **hacer falta** to be needed; to be lacking; **hacerle falta a uno** to need, e.g., **le hacen falta a Juan estos libros** John needs these books; to miss, e.g., **Vd. me hace mucha falta** I miss you very much; **sin falta** without fail
**faltar** *intr* to be missing, be lacking, be wanting; to fall short; to run out; to be absent; to fail; to die; to lack, to need, e.g., **me falta dinero** I lack money, I need money; **faltar a la clase** to cut class; **faltar a la verdad** to fail to tell the truth; **faltar a una cita** to fail to keep an appointment; **faltar . . . para** to be . . . to, e.g., **faltan cinco minutos para las dos** it is five minutes to two; **faltar poco para** to come near; **faltar por** to remain to be, e.g., **faltan por escribir dos cartas** two letters remain to be written
**fal•to -ta** *adj* short, lacking; (*peso o medida*) short; (Arg) dull, stupid; (Col) proud, vain; **falto de** short of || *f* see **falta**
**fal•tón -tona** *adj* (coll) dilatory, remiss; (Arg) simple-minded
**falto•so -sa** *adj* (coll) addlebrained; (Col) quarrelsome; (CAm, Mex) disrespectful
**faltriquera** *f* pocket; handbag; **faltriquera de reloj** watch fob; **rascarse la faltriquera** (coll) to cough up
**falúa** *f* barge, tender
**falucho** *m* felucca
**falla** *f* failure, breakdown; defect; (geol) fault; (Mex) baby's bonnet
**fallar** *tr* to trump; to judge, pass judgment on || *intr* to fail, to miss; to misfire; to sag, weaken; to break down; to judge, pass judgment
**falleba** *f* espagnolette
**fallecer** **§22** *intr* to die; to fail, expire
**falleci•do -da** *adj* deceased, late
**falli•do -da** *adj* unsuccessful; bankrupt; (*deuda*) uncollectible
**fallir** **§13** *intr* to fail; (Ven) to go bankrupt
**fa•llo -lla** *adj* (Chile) silly, simple; **estar fallo a** to be out of (*cards of a suit*) || *m* short suit; decision; judgment, verdict; **tener fallo a** or **de** to be out of || *f* see **falla**
**fama** *f* fame; reputation; rumor; (Chile) bull's-eye; **correr fama** to be ru-

mored; **es fama** it is said, it is rumored
**faméli•co -ca** *adj* famished, starving
**familia** *f* family
**familiar** *adj* familiar; family; (*sin ceremonia*) informal; (*lenguaje, estilo*) colloquial || *m* member of the family; member of the household; acquaintance; **familiar dependiente** dependent
**familiaridad** *f* familiarity
**familiarizar** §60 *tr* to familiarize || *ref* to become familiar; to become too familiar; to familiarize oneself
**famo•so -sa** *adj* famous; (*excelente*) (coll) famous; (*formidable*) (coll) some, e.g., **famoso sujeto** some guy
**fámu•lo -la** *mf* (coll) servant
**fanal** *m* beacon, lighthouse; lantern; bell glass, bell jar; lamp shade
**fanáti•co -ca** *adj* fanatic(al) || *mf* fanatic; (sport) fan
**fanatismo** *m* fanaticism
**fanega** *f* 1.58 bu.; **fanega de tierra** 1.59 acres
**fanfarria** *f* fanfare; (coll) blustering
**fanfa•rrón -rrona** *adj* (coll) blustering, bragging; (coll) flashy || *mf* (coll) blusterer, braggart
**fanfarronada** *f* (coll) bluster, bravado
**fanfarronear** *intr* (coll) to bluster, to brag
**fanfarronería** *f* (coll) blustering, bragging, sword rattling
**fanfurriña** *f* (coll) pet, peeve
**fango** *m* mud, mire; **llenar de fango** (fig) to sling mud at
**fango•so -sa** *adj* muddy; sticky, gooey
**fantasear** *tr* to dream of || *intr* to fancy, to daydream; **fantasear de** to boast of being
**fantasía** *f* fantasy; fancy; conceit, vanity; imagery; **con fantasía** (Arg) hard; **de fantasía** fancy, imitation; **tocar por fantasía** (Ven) to play by ear
**fantasio•so -sa** *adj* (coll) vain, conceited
**fantasma** *m* phantom, ghost; stuffed shirt; (telv) ghost; **fantasma magnético** magnetic curves || *f* scarecrow, hobgoblin
**fantas•món -mona** *adj* (coll) conceited || *mf* (coll) conceited person || *m* (coll) stuffed shirt; (coll) scarecrow
**fantásti•co -ca** *adj* fantastic; fancy; conceited
**fantoche** *m* puppet, marionette; (coll) nincompoop, whippersnapper
**faquín** *m* street porter, errand boy
**fara•lá** *m* (*pl* **-laes**) ruffle, flounce; (coll) frill
**faramalla** *mf* (coll) cheat, swindler || *f* (coll) jabber, claptrap; (coll) bluff, fake; (Chile) bragging
**faramalle•ro -ra** or **farama•llón -llona** *adj* (coll) scheming, swindling || *mf* (coll) schemer, swindler
**farándula** *f* (*baile*) farandole; (coll) gossip, scheming; (coll) theater people; (*de gente*) (Arg) crush, milling
**farandulear** *intr* (coll) to boast, to show off
**Faraón** *m* Pharaoh
**faraute** *m* herald, messenger; interpreter; (*actor*) prologue; (coll) busybody
**fardel** *m* bag, bundle; (coll) sloppy person
**fardo** *m* bundle, package
**farfa•lá** *m* (*pl* **-laes**) ruffle, flounce
**farfullar** *tr* (*p.ej., una lección*) (coll) to sputter through; (*p.ej., una tarea*) (coll) to stumble through || *intr* (coll) to sputter
**faringe** *f* pharynx
**fariseo** *m* pharisee; Pharisee; (coll) lanky good-for-nothing
**farmacéuti•co -ca** *adj* pharmaceutical || *mf* pharmacist
**farmacia** *f* pharmacy, drug store; **farmacia de guardia** drug store open all night
**fármaco** *m* drug, medicine
**faro** *m* lighthouse, beacon; floodlight; (aut) headlight; (fig) beacon; **faro piloto** (aut) spotlight; **faros de carretera** (aut) bright lights; **faros de cruce** (aut) dimmers; **faros de población** or **de situación** (aut) parking lights
**farol** *m* lamp, light; lantern; street light; (rr) headlight; (coll) conceited fellow; (Bol) bay window; **farol de tope** (naut) headlight
**farola** *f* lighthouse; street lamp, lamppost
**farolear** *intr* (coll) to boast, brag
**farole•ro -ra** *adj* (coll) boasting || *mf* (coll) boaster || *m* lamplighter
**farolillo** *m* heartseed; Canterbury bell; **farolillo veneciano** Chinese lantern, Japanese lantern
**farota** *f* (coll) minx, vixen
**farotear** *intr* (Col) to romp around, make a racket
**faro•tón -tona** *adj* (coll) brazen, cheeky || *mf* (coll) cheeky person
**farra** *f* salmon trout; (SAm) revelry
**fárrago** *m* hodgepodge
**farro** *m* grits
**farru•co -ca** *adj* (coll) bold, fearless; (coll) ill-humored || *mf* (coll) Galician abroad, Asturian abroad
**farru•to -ta** *adj* (Arg, Bol, Chile) sickly
**farsa** *f* farce; humbug
**farsante** *adj & mf* (coll) fake, fraud, humbug
**fas** — **por fas o por nefas** rightly or wrongly, in any event
**fascinante** *adj* fascinating
**fascinar** *tr* to fascinate, to bewitch; to cast a spell on, cast the evil eye on
**fascismo** *m* fascism
**fascista** *adj & mf* fascist
**fase** *f* phase
**fastidiar** *tr* to bore, annoy; to cloy, sicken; to disappoint || *ref* to get bored; to suffer, be a victim
**fastidio** *m* boredom, annoyance; distaste, nausea
**fastidio•so -sa** *adj* boring, annoying; cloying, sickening; annoyed, displeased
**fas•to -ta** *adj* happy, blessed || *m* pomp, show

**fastuo•so -sa** *adj* vain, pompous; magnificent
**fatal** *adj* fatal; bad, evil; (law) unextendible
**fatalidad** *f* fatality; misfortune
**fatalismo** *m* fatalism
**fatalista** *mf* fatalist
**fatalmente** *adv* fatally; inevitably; unfortunately; badly, poorly
**fatídi•co -ca** *adj* ominous, fateful
**fatiga** *f* fatigue; hard breathing; **fatigas** hardship
**fatigar** §44 *tr* to fatigue, tire, weary; to annoy, bother || *ref* to get tired
**fatigo•so -sa** *adj* fatiguing, tiring; (coll) trying, tedious
**fa•tuo -tua** *adj* fatuous; conceited || *mf* simpleton
**fauces** *fpl* (anat) fauces; (fig) jaws, mouth
**fauna** *f* fauna
**fauno** *m* faun
**faus•to -ta** *adj* happy, fortunate || *m* pomp, magnificence
**fausto•so -sa** *adj* magnificent
**fau•tor -tora** *mf* abettor; accomplice
**favor** *m* favor; **a favor de** under cover of; by means of; in favor of; **hágame Vd. el favor de** do me the favor to; **por favor** please; **vender favores** to peddle influence
**favorable** *adj* favorable
**favorecer** §22 *tr* to favor; to flatter
**favoritismo** *m* favoritism
**favori•to -ta** *adj & mf* favorite
**fayanca** *f* unstable posture
**faz** *f* (*pl* **faces**) face; aspect, look; (*de monedas o medallas*) obverse; **faces** cheeks; **faz a faz** face to face
**F.C.** *abbr* **ferrocarril**
**fe** *f* faith; testimony, witness; certificate; **¡a fe mía!** upon my faith!; **dar fe de** to certify; **en fe de lo cual** in witness whereof; **fe de erratas** list of errata; **hacer fe** to be valid; **la fe del carbonero** simple faith
**fealdad** *f* ugliness
**Febe** *f* Phoebe
**feble** *adj* weak, sickly; (*moneda, aleación*) lacking in weight or fineness
**Febo** *m* Phoebus
**febrero** *m* February
**febril** *adj* feverish
**fécula** *f* starch
**feculen•to -ta** *adj* starchy; fecal
**fecundar** *tr* to fecundate, to fertilize
**fecun•do -da** *adj* fecund, fertile
**fecha** *f* date; **con fecha de** under date of; **de larga fecha** of long standing; **hasta la fecha** to date
**fechador** *m* (Chile, Mex) canceler, postmark
**fechar** *tr* to date
**fechoría** *f* misdeed, villainy
**federación** *f* federation
**federal** *adj & mf* federal
**federar** *tr & ref* to federate
**Federico** *m* Frederick
**feéri•co -ca** *adj* fairy
**fehaciente** *adj* authentic
**feldespato** *m* feldspar
**felicidad** *f* felicity, happiness; luck
**felicitar** *tr* to felicitate, congratulat wish happiness to
**feli•grés -gresa** *mf* parishioner, chur member
**feligresía** *f* parish; congregation
**Felipe** *m* Philip
**fe•liz** *adj* (*pl* **-lices**) happy; luck (*oportuno*) felicitous
**fe•lón -lona** *adj* perfidious, treachero || *mf* wicked person
**felonía** *f* perfidy, treachery
**felpa** *f* plush; (coll) drubbing; (co severe reprimand
**felpu•do -da** *adj* plushy, downy || mat, door mat
**femenil** *adj* feminine, womanly
**femeni•no -na** *adj* feminine; (*sexo*) f male || *m* feminine
**fementi•do -da** *adj* false, treacherous
**feminismo** *m* feminism
**fenecer** §22 *tr* to finish, to close || *in* to come to an end; to die
**Fenicia** *f* Phoenicia
**feni•cio -cia** *adj & mf* Phoenician || see **Fenicia**
**fé•nix** *m* (*pl* **-nix** or **-nices**) phoenix
**fenobarbital** *m* phenobarbital
**fenomenal** *adj* phenomenal
**fenómeno** *m* phenomenon; (coll) mo ster, freak
**fe•o -a** *adj* ugly || *m* (coll) slight; **hac un feo a** (coll) to slight || **feo** *ad* (Arg, Col, Mex) bad, e.g., **oler f** to smell bad
**feo•te -ta** *adj* ugly, hideous
**feral** *adj* cruel, bloody
**fe•raz** *adj* (*pl* **-races**) fertile
**féretro** *m* bier
**feria** *f* weekday; market; fair; day of (Mex) change; (CAm) extra; **revolv la feria** (coll) to upset the applecart
**ferial** *adj* week (*day*); market (*day*) *m* market; fair
**feriante** *adj* fair-going || *mf* fairgoer
**feriar** *tr* to buy, to sell; to give, presen (Mex) to give change for
**feri•no -na** *adj* wild, savage; (*to* whooping (*cough*)
**fermentación** *f* ferment; fermentation
**fermentar** *tr & intr* to ferment
**fermento** *m* ferment
**ferocidad** *f* ferocity, fierceness
**ferósti•co -ca** *adj* (coll) irritable; (col hideous
**fe•roz** *adj* (*pl* **-roces**) ferocious, fierce
**férre•o -a** *adj* iron
**ferrería** *f* ironworks, foundry
**ferretear** *tr* to trim with iron; to wor in iron
**ferretería** *f* ironworks; hardware; har ware store
**ferrete•ro -ra** *mf* hardware dealer
**ferrocarril** *m* railroad, railway; **ferr carril de cremallera** rack railway mountain railroad
**ferrocarrile•ro -ra** *adj* (Am) railroa rail || *m* (Am) railroader
**ferrotipo** *m* tintype
**ferrovia•rio -ria** *adj* railroad, rail || railroader
**fértil** *adj* fertile
**fertilizar** §60 *tr* to fertilize

**férula** *f* flexible splint; ferule; **estar bajo la férula de** to be under the thumb of
**férvi·do -da** *adj* fervid; (*fiebre; sed*) burning
**ferviente** *adj* fervent
**fervor** *m* fervor, zeal
**fervoro·so -sa** *adj* ardent, zealous
**festejar** *tr* to fete, honor, entertain; to celebrate; to court, to woo; (Mex) to beat, thrash
**festejo** *m* feast, entertainment; celebration; courting, wooing; (Peru) revelry; **festejos** public festivities
**festín** *m* feast, banquet
**festinar** *tr* (Am) to hurry through; (CAm) to entertain
**festival** *m* festival, music festival
**festividad** *f* festivity; feast day; witticism
**festi·vo -va** *adj* festive, gay; witty; (*digno de celebrarse*) solemn
**festón** *m* festoon
**festonear** *tr* to festoon
**fetiche** *m* fetish
**féti·do -da** *adj* fetid, foul
**feto** *m* fetus
**feú·co -ca** or **feú·cho -cha** *adj* hideous, repulsive
**feudal** *adj* feudal
**feudalismo** *m* feudalism
**feudo** *m* fief; **feudo franco** freehold
**fiable** *adj* trustworthy
**fiado** *m* — **al fiado** on credit; **en fiado** on bail
**fia·dor -dora** *mf* bail; **salir fiador por** to go bail for || *m* fastener; catch, pawl; (Chile, Ecuad) chin strap
**fiambre** *adj* cold, cold-served; (*noticias*) old, stale || *m* cold lunch, cold food; stale news; (Arg) dull party; **fiambres** cold cuts
**fiambrera** *f* dinner pail, lunch basket
**fiambrería** *f* (Arg) delicatessen store
**fianza** *f* guarantee, surety; bond; bail; **fianza carcelera** bail
**fiar §77** *tr* to entrust, confide; to guarantee; to give credit to; to sell on credit || *intr & ref* to trust
**fiasco** *m* fiasco
**fibra** *f* fiber; (fig) fiber, strength, vigor; **fibras del corazón** heartstrings
**fibro·so -sa** *adj* fibrous
**ficción** *f* fiction
**ficciona·rio -ria** *adj* fictional
**fice** *m* (ichth) hake
**ficti·cio -cia** *adj* fictitious
**ficha** *f* chip; counter; domino; filing card; police record; (elec) plug; **ficha catalográfica** index card; **llevar ficha** to have a police record; **ser una buena ficha** (Am) to be a sly fox
**ficha·dor -dora** *mf* file clerk
**fichar** *tr* to file; to play, to move; (coll) to black-list; (Cuba) to cheat || *intr* (Col) to die
**fichero** *m* card index, filing cabinet
**fidedig·no -na** *adj* reliable, trustworthy
**fideicomisa·rio -ria** *mf* trustee
**fideicomiso** *m* trusteeship
**fidelería** *f* (Arg, Ecuad, Peru) vermicelli factory, noodle factory
**fidelidad** *f* fidelity; punctiliousness; **alta fidelidad** (rad) high fidelity
**fideo** *m* (coll) skinny person; (Arg) joke; (Arg) confusion, disorder; **fideos** vermicelli
**Fidias** *m* Phidias
**fiducia·rio -ria** *adj & mf* fiduciary
**fiebre** *f* fever; **fiebre del heno** hay fever; **fibre tifoidea** typhoid fever
**fiel** *adj* faithful; exact; punctilious; honest, trustworthy || *m* inspector of weights and measures; (*en las balanzas*) pointer; (*de las tijeras*) pin; **fiel de romana** inspector of weights in a slaughterhouse; **los fieles** the faithful
**fielato** *m* inspector's office; octroi
**fieltro** *m* felt; felt hat; felt rug
**fiera** *f* wild animal; (*persona*) fiend; (taur) bull; **ser una fiera para** (coll) to be a fiend for
**fierabrás** *m* (coll) spitfire, little terror
**fierecilla** *f* shrew
**fiereza** *f* fierceness; cruelty; deformity
**fie·ro -ra** *adj* fierce, wild; cruel; deformed, ugly; huge, tremendous; **echar** or **hacer fieros** to bluster || *f* see **fiera**
**fiesta** *f* feast, holy day; holiday; celebration, festivity; **estar de fiesta** (coll) to be in a holiday mood; **fiesta de la hispanidad** or **fiesta de la raza** Columbus Day; **fiesta de todos los santos** All Saints' Day; **fiesta onomástica** saint's day, birthday; **fiestas** holiday, vacation; **hacer fiesta** to take off (*from work*); **hacer fiestas a** to act up to, to fawn on; **la fiesta brava** bullfighting; **no estar para fiestas** (coll) to be in no mood for joking; **por fin de fiestas** to top it off; **se acabó la fiesta** (coll) let's drop it
**fieste·ro -ra** *adj* merry, gay || *mf* merrymaker, party-goer
**figón** *m* cheap restaurant
**figura** *f* figure; face, countenance; (*naipe*) face card; (mus) note; (theat) character; **figura retórica** figure of speech; **hacer figura** to cut a figure
**figuración** *f* representation; (Arg) status, social standing
**figura·do -da** *adj* figurative
**figurar** *tr* to depict, trace, represent; to feign || *intr* to figure, to be in the limelight || *ref* to figure, to imagine
**figurati·vo -va** *adj* figurative, representative
**figurería** *f* face, grimace
**figurilla** *mf* (coll) silly little runt || *f* figurine
**figurín** *m* dummy, model; fashion plate
**figurina** *f* figurine
**figurita** *mf* (coll) silly little runt
**figurón** *m* (coll) stuffed shirt; **figurón de proa** (naut) figurehead
**fija** *f* hinge; trowel; (*caballo*) (Peru) sure bet; **la fija** (coll) sure thing
**fijacarte·les** *m* (*pl* **-les**) billposter
**fijación** *f* fixing, fastening; posting; **fijación de precios** price fixing
**fijado** *m* (phot) fixing
**fija·dor -dora** *adj* fixing || *m* carpenter who installs doors and windows; fixing bath; sprayer; (mas) pointer; hair set, hair spray
**fijamárge·nes** *m* (*pl* **-nes**) margin stop

**fijapeina•dos** *m* (*pl* **-dos**) hair set, hair spray
**fijar** *tr* to fix; to fasten; (*carteles*) to post; (*una fecha; los cabellos; una imagen fotográfica; los precios; la atención; una hora, una cita*) to fix; (*residencia*) to establish; to paste, glue || *ref* to settle; to notice; **fijarse en** to notice; to pay attention to; to be intent on
**fijeza** *f* firmness, stability; steadfastness; **mirar con fijeza** to stare at
**fi•jo -ja** *adj* fixed; firm, solid, secure, fast; sure, determined; **de fijo** surely || *f* see **fija**
**fil** *m* — **estar en fil** or **en un fil** to be alike; **fil derecho** leapfrog
**fila** *f* row, line; file; (*línea que los soldados forman de frente*) rank; (coll) dislike, hatred; **cerrar las filas** (mil) to close ranks; **en fila** in single file; **en filas** (mil) in active service; **fila india** single file, Indian file; **llamar a filas** (mil) to call to the colors; **pasarse a las filas de** to go over to; **romper filas** (mil) to break ranks
**filamento** *m* filament
**filantropía** *f* philanthropy
**filántro•po -pa** *mf* philanthropist
**filar** *tr* (naut) to pay out slowly
**filarmóni•co -ca** *adj* philharmonic
**filatelia** *f* philately
**filatelista** *mf* philatelist
**filatería** *f* fast talking; wordiness
**filate•ro -ra** *adj* fast-talking; wordy || *mf* fast talker; great talker
**file•no -na** *adj* (coll) cute, tiny
**filete** *m* (*de carne o pescado*) filet or fillet; (*asador*) spit; edge, rim; narrow hem; (*de tornillo*) thread; snaffle bit; (archit, bb) fillet; (typ) rule, fancy rule
**filetear** *tr* to fillet; (*un tornillo*) to thread; (bb) to tool
**filiación** *f* filiation; description, characteristics; (mil) regimental register
**filial** *adj* filial || *f* affiliate, branch
**filiar** §77 *tr* to register || *ref* to enroll
**filibustero** *m* filibuster, buccaneer
**filigrana** *f* filigree; (*en el papel*) watermark
**filipi•no -na** *adj* Filipine, Filipino || *mf* Filipino || **Filipinas** *fpl* Philippines
**Filipo** *m* Philip (*of Macedonia*)
**Filis** *f* Phyllis
**filiste•o -a** *adj & mf* Philistine || *m* tall, fat fellow
**film** *m* (*pl* **films** or **filmes**) film
**filmar** *tr* to film
**filo** *m* edge; ridge; dividing line; (CAm, Mex) hunger; **al filo de** at, at about; **dar filo a** to sharpen; **filo del viento** direction of the wind; **pasar al filo de la espada** to put to the sword; **por filo** exactly
**filobús** *m* trolley bus, trackless trolley
**filocomunista** *adj & mf* procommunist
**filología** *f* philology
**filólo•go -ga** *mf* philologist
**filón** *m* seam, vein; (fig) gold mine
**filo•so -sa** *adj* (Am) sharp
**filosofía** *f* philosophy
**filosófi•co -ca** *adj* philosophic(al)
**filóso•fo -fa** *mf* philosopher
**filote** *m* (Col) corn silk; (Col) ear of green corn
**filtración** *f* filtering; leak; (fig) leak, loss
**filtrado** *m* filtrate
**filtrar** *tr* to filter || *intr* to leak; to ooze || *ref* to filter; (*el dinero*) to leak away, to disappear
**filtro** *m* filter; (*brebaje para conciliar el amor*) philter, love potion
**filu•do -da** *adj* (SAm) sharp-edged
**filván** *m* featheredge
**fimo** *m* dung, manure
**fin** *m* end; aim, purpose, end; **a fin de** to, in order to; **a fin de que** in order that, so that; **a fines de** toward the end of, late in; **al fin** finally; **al fin del mundo** far, far away; **al fin y a la postre** or **al fin y al cabo** after all, in the end; **dar fin a** to put an end to; **fin de semana** weekend; **por fin** finally, in short; **sin fin** endless; endlessly; **un sin fin de** no end of
**fina•do -da** *adj* deceased, late || *mf* deceased
**final** *adj* final || *m* end; (mus) finale; **por final** finally || *f* (sport) finals; **final de partido** windup
**finalidad** *f* end, purpose
**finalista** *mf* finalist
**finalizar** §60 *tr* to end, terminate; (*una escritura*) (law) to execute || *intr* to end, terminate
**financiación** *f* financing
**financiar** *tr* to finance
**financie•ro -ra** *adj* financial || *mf* financier
**finanzas** *fpl* finances
**finar** *intr* to die || *ref* to yearn
**finca** *f* property, piece of real estate; farm, ranch; **buena finca** (coll) sly fellow
**fincar** §73 *tr* (P-R) to cultivate, to farm || *intr* to buy up real estate; (Col) to reside, rest, be based || *ref* to buy up real estate
**fincha•do -da** *adj* (coll) vain, conceited
**fi•nés -nesa** *adj* Finnic; Finnish || *mf* Finn || *m* (*idioma uraliano*) Finnic; (*idioma de Finlandia*) Finnish
**fineza** *f* fineness; kindness, courtesy; token of affection, favor
**fingi•do -da** *adj* fake, sham; false, deceitful
**fingir** §27 *tr & intr* to feign, pretend, fake || *ref* to pretend to be
**finiquitar** *tr* (*una cuenta*) to settle, to close; (coll) to finish, wind up
**finiquito** *m* settlement, closing; **dar finiquito a** to settle, close; (coll) to finish, wind up
**finíti•mo -ma** *adj* bordering, neighboring
**fini•to -ta** *adj* finite
**finlan•dés -desa** *adj* Finnish || *mf* Finn, Finlander || *m* Finnish
**Finlandia** *f* Finland
**fi•no -na** *adj* fine; (*ligero, casi transparente*) sheer; (*esbelto*) thin, slender; (*paño, papel, etc.*) thin; (*agua*)

pure; polite, courteous; shrewd, cunning
**finta** *f* feint
**finura** *f* fineness, excellence; politeness, courtesy
**finústi•co -ca** *adj* (coll) overobsequious
**firma** *f* signature; signing; firm; firm name; mail to be signed; **con mi firma** under my hand; **firma en blanco** blank check
**firmamento** *m* firmament
**firmante** *adj* signatory ‖ *mf* signer, signatory
**firmar** *tr & intr* to sign
**firme** *adj* firm, steady; solid, hard; staunch, unswerving ‖ *adv* firmly, steadily ‖ *m* roadbed; **de firme** hard, e.g., **llover de firme** to rain hard
**firmeza** *f* firmness; constancy, fortitude
**firmón** *m* shyster who signs anything
**fiscal** *adj* fiscal, treasury ‖ *m* treasurer; district attorney; busybody
**fiscalizar** **§60** *tr* to control, inspect; to prosecute; to pry into
**fisco** *m* state treasury, exchequer
**fisga** *f* fish spear; prying, snooping; banter, raillery
**fisgar** **§44** *tr* to harpoon, fish with a spear; to pry into ‖ *intr* to pry, to snoop; to mock, to jeer ‖ *ref* to mock, to jeer
**fis•gón -gona** *mf* (coll) mocker, jester; (coll) snooper, busybody
**físi•co -ca** *adj* physical; (Mex, W-I) finicky, prudish ‖ *mf* physicist ‖ *m* physique ‖ *f* physics
**fisiología** *f* physiology
**fisiológi•co -ca** *adj* physiological
**fisión** *f* fission
**fisionable** *adj* fissionable
**fisonomía** *f* physiognomy
**fistol** *m* sly fellow; (Mex) necktie pin
**fisura** *f* (anat, min) fissure; **fisura del paladar** cleft palate
**fla•co -ca** *adj* thin, skinny; feeble, weak, frail; insecure, unstable ‖ *m* weak spot
**flacu•cho -cha** *adj* (coll) skinny
**flagrante** *adj* occurring, actual; **en flagrante** in the act
**flamante** *adj* bright, flaming; brand-new, spick-and-span
**flameante** *adj* flamboyant
**flamear** *intr* to flame; to flare up (*with anger*); to flutter, to wave
**flamen•co -ca** *adj* Flemish; buxom; Andalusian gypsy; (coll) flashy, snappy, gypsyish ‖ *mf* Fleming ‖ *m* (*idioma*) Flemish; Andalusian gypsy dance, song, or music; (orn) flamingo
**fláme•o -a** *adj* flamelike
**flamíge•ro -ra** *adj* (poet) flaming; (archit) flamboyant
**flan** *m* custard
**flanco** *m* side, flank; **coger por el flanco** to catch off guard
**Flandes** *f* Flanders
**flanquear** *tr* to flank
**flaquear** *intr* to weaken, flag; to become faint; to become discouraged
**flaqueza** *f* thinness, skinniness; weakness; instability
**flato** *m* gas; (Am) gloominess, melancholy
**flato•so -sa** *adj* flatulent, windy; (Am) gloomy, melancholy
**flauta** *f* flute
**flautín** *m* piccolo
**flautista** *mf* flautist, flutist
**flebitis** *f* phlebitis
**fleco** *m* fringe; ragged edge; **flecos** bangs
**flecha** *f* arrow; (aer) sweepback
**flechar** *tr* (*el arco*) to draw; (*a una persona*) to wound with an arrow, to kill with an arrow; (coll) to infatuate
**flechero** *m* archer, bowman
**fleje** *m* iron strap, iron hoop
**flema** *f* phlegm
**flemáti•co -ca** *adj* phlegmatic(al)
**flemón** *m* gumboil
**flequillo** *m* bangs
**Flesinga** *f* Flushing
**fletante** *m* shipowner; (Arg, Chile, Ecuad) conveyancer
**fletar** *tr* (*una nave*) to charter; (*ganado*) to load; (*bestias de carga, carros, etc.*) (Arg, Chile, Ecuad, Mex) to hire ‖ *ref* (Arg) to sneak in, slip in; (Cuba, Mex) to beat it, clear out
**flete** *m* (naut) freight, cargo; (Arg, Bol, Col, Urug) race horse; **salir sin flete** (Col, Ven) to beat it
**flexible** *adj* flexible; (*sombrero*) soft ‖ *m* soft hat; (elec) flexible cord
**flexo** *m* gooseneck lamp
**flinflanear** *intr* to tinkle
**flirt** *m* flirting
**flirtear** *intr* to flirt
**flojear** *intr* to ease up, to idle; to flag, weaken
**flojedad** *f* slackness, looseness; limpness; laziness; weakness
**flojel** *m* fluff, nap; down, soft feathers
**flo•jo -ja** *adj* slack, loose; limp; languid, lazy; weak; (*precios*) sagging; (*viento*) light; lax, careless
**flor** *f* flower; (*de árbol frutal*) blossom; (*del cuero*) grain; (fig) compliment, bouquet; **a flor de** even with, flush with; **a flor de agua** at water level; **decir flores a** to flatter; to flirt with; **flor de la edad** bloom of youth; **flor de la vida** prime of life; **flor del campo** wild flower; **flor de lis** (*escudo de armas de Francia*) lily, fleur-de-lis; **flor de mano** paper flower, artificial flower; **la flor de la canela** the tops; **la flor y nata de** the cream of
**flora** *f* flora
**floral** *adj* floral
**florcita** *f* (Am) little flower; **andar de florcita** (Arg, Bol, Chile, Urug) to stroll around with a flower in one's buttonhole, to take it easy
**florear** *tr* to flower, decorate with flowers; (*los naipes*) to stack; (*harina*) to bolt ‖ *intr* (*la punta de la espada*) to quiver; to twang away on a guitar; (coll) to throw bouquets
**florecer** **§22** *intr* to flower, to blossom, to bloom; (*prosperar*) to flourish ‖ *ref* to become moldy
**floreciente** *adj* flowering, florescent; flourishing

**florenti•no -na** *adj & mf* Florentine
**floreo** *m* idle talk; bright remark; (*de la punta de la espada*) quivering; (*de la guitarra*) twanging; (mus) flourish; **andarse con floreos** (coll) to beat about the bush
**florera** *f* flower girl
**florería** *f* (Am) flower shop
**flore•ro -ra** *adj* flattering, jesting || *mf* flatterer, jester; florist || *m* (*vaso para flores*) vase; (*maceta con flores*) flowerpot; flower stand, jardiniere; (*cuadro, pintura*) flower piece || *f* see **florera**
**florescencia** *f* florescence
**floresta** *f* woods, woodland; grove; rural setting; anthology
**florete** *m* (*esgrima*) fencing; (*espadín*) foil
**floretear** *tr* to decorate with flowers || *intr* to fence
**flori•do -da** *adj* flowery, full of flowers; choice, select
**florilegio** *m* anthology
**floripondio** *m* (SAm) angel's-trumpet
**florista** *mf* florist
**floristería** *f* flower shop
**florón** *m* large flower; finial; rosette; (typ) tailpiece, vignette
**flota** *f* fleet
**flotación** *f* buoyancy
**flotador** *m* float
**flotaje** *m* log driving
**flotante** *adj* floating; (*barba*) flowing || *m* (Col) braggart
**flotar** *intr* to float; (*una bandera*) to wave
**flote** *m* floating; **a flote** afloat
**fluctuar** §21 *intr* to fluctuate; to bob up and down; to wave; to waver; to be in danger
**fluente** *adj* fluent, flowing; (*hemorroides*) bleeding
**fluidez** *f* fluidity
**flúi•do -da** *adj* fluid; (*estilo, lenguaje*) fluent || *m* fluid
**fluir** §20 *intr* to flow
**flujo** *m* flow, flux; (*acceso de la marea*) floodtide; **flujo de risa** fit of noisy laughter; **flujo de vientre** loose bowels; **flujo y reflujo** ebb and flow
**flúor** *m* fluorine
**fluorescencia** *f* fluorescence
**fluorescente** *adj* fluorescent
**fluorhídri•co -ca** *adj* hydrofluoric
**fluorización** *f* fluoridation
**fluorizar** §60 *tr* to fluoridate
**fluoroscopio** *m* fluoroscope
**fluoruro** *m* fluoride
**flux** *m* (*en el póker*) flush; (Am) suit of clothes; **estar en flux** (Am) to be penniless; **hacer flux** (coll) to blow in everything without settling accounts; **tener flux** (Am) to be lucky
**fluxión** *f* (*acumulación morbosa de humores*) congestion; (*enrojecimiento de la cara y el cuello*) flush; (*constipado de narices*) cold in the head; **fluxión de muelas** swollen cheek; **fluxión de pecho** pneumonia
**foca** *f* seal
**focal** *adj* focal
**foco** *m* focus; (*de vicios*) center; (*de un absceso*) core; electric light
**fodo•lí** *adj* (*pl* **-líes**) meddlesome
**fodon•go -ga** *adj* (Mex) dirty, slovenly
**fo•fo -fa** *adj* soft, fluffy, spongy
**fogaje** *m* (*contribución*) hearth money; (Arg) fire, blaze; (Arg, Mex) rash, eruption; (Am) blush, flush
**fogata** *f* blaze, bonfire
**fogón** *m* cooking stove; (*de máquina de vapor*) firebox
**fogonazo** *m* powder flash
**fogonero** *m* fireman, stoker
**fogosidad** *f* fire, spirit, dash
**fogo•so -sa** *adj* fiery, spirited
**fol.** *abbr* **folio**
**folgo** *m* foot muff
**foliar** *tr* to folio
**folio** *m* folio; **al primer folio** right off; **de a folio** (coll) enormous; **en folio** folio
**folklore** *m* folklore
**follaje** *m* foliage; gaudy ornament; (*palabrería*) fustian
**follar** *tr* to shape like a leaf || §61 *tr* to blow with bellows
**folletín** *m* newspaper serial (*printed at bottom of page*); pamphlet
**folleto** *m* brochure, pamphlet, tract
**fo•llón -llona** *adj* careless, indolent, lazy; arrogant, cowardly || *mf* lazy loafer, knave || *m* noiseless rocket
**fomentar** *tr* to foment; to foster, encourage, promote; to warm
**fonda** *f* inn, restaurant; (Chile) refreshment stand
**fondeadero** *m* anchorage
**fondea•do -da** *adj* (Am) well-heeled
**fondear** *tr* (*un buque*) to search; to scrutinize, examine closely || *intr* to cast anchor || *ref* (Am) to save up for a rainy day
**fondillos** *mpl* seat (*of trousers*)
**fondista** *mf* innkeeper
**fondo** *m* bottom; (*de un cuarto, una tienda*) back, rear; (*del mar, de una piscina, etc.*) floor; (*de un cilindro, barril, etc.*) head; background; (*de una casa*) depth; (*de un paño*) ground; (*caudal*) fund; (*lo esencial*) bottom; **a fondo** thoroughly; **bajos fondos sociales** underworld, scum of the earth; **colar a fondo** to sink; **dar fondo** to cast anchor; **echar a fondo** to sink; **en el fondo** at bottom; **estar en fondos** to have funds available; **fondo de amortización** sinking fund; **fondos** (*caudales, dinero*) funds; **irse a fondo** to go to the bottom; (*un negocio*) to fail; **tener buen fondo** to be good-natured
**fonducho** *m* cheap eating house
**fonéti•co -ca** *adj* phonetic
**fono** *m* (Chile) earphone
**fonocaptor** *s* pickup
**fonógrafo** *m* phonograph
**fonología** *f* phonology
**fontanería** *f* plumbing; water-supply system
**fontane•ro -ra** *adj* fountain || *m* plumber, tinsmith
**foque** *m* (naut) jib; (coll) piccadilly collar

**foraji•do -da** *adj* fugitive || *mf* fugitive, outlaw, bandit

**foráne•o -a** *adj* foreign, strange; offshore

**foraste•ro -ra** *adj* outside, strange; foreign || *mf* outsider, stranger

**forbante** *m* freebooter

**forcejar** or **forcejear** *intr* to struggle, resist, contend

**forceju•do -da** *adj* strong, husky, robust

**fór•ceps** *m* (*pl* **-ceps**) forceps

**forestal** *adj* forest

**forja** *f* forge; forging; silversmith's forge; foundry, ironworks; mortar

**forjar** *tr* to forge; to build with stone and mortar; to roughcast; (*mentiras*) to forge || *ref* to forge; to hatch, think up

**forma** *f* form, shape; way; (*de un libro*) format; **de forma que** so that, with the result that; **tener buenas formas** to have a good figure

**formación** *f* formation; **formación de palabras** word formation

**formal** *adj* formal, ceremonious; express, definite; reliable; sedate; serious

**formalidad** *f* formality; reliability; seriousness

**formar** *tr* to form; to shape, to fashion; to train, educate || *intr* to form; to form a line, to stand in line || *ref* to form; to form a line, to stand in line; to take form, to grow, to develop

**formato** *m* format

**formidable** *adj* formidable

**formidolo•so -sa** *adj* scared, frightened; frightful, horrible

**fórmula** *f* formula; prescription; **por fórmula** as a matter of form

**formular** *tr* to formulate

**formulario** *m* form, blank; **formulario de pedido** order blank

**forni•do -da** *adj* husky, sturdy, robust

**foro** *m* forum; (*abogacía*) bar; (*del escenario*) back, rear

**forraje** *m* forage, fodder

**forrajear** *tr & intr* to forage

**forrar** *tr* to line; (*un vestido*) to face; (*un libro, un paraguas*) to cover; (*un lienzo*) to stretch || *ref* (Guat, Mex) to stuff oneself

**forro** *m* lining; cover, covering; (naut) sheathing, planking; **forro de freno** brake lining; **ni por el forro** (coll) not by a long shot

**fortalecer** §22 *tr* to fortify, strengthen

**fortaleza** *f* fortitude; strength, vigor; fortress, stronghold

**fortificación** *f* fortification

**fortificante** *m* tonic

**fortificar** §73 *tr* to fortify

**fortín** *m* small fort; bunker

**fortui•to -ta** *adj* fortuitous

**fortuna** *f* fortune; **correr fortuna** (naut) to ride the storm; **de fortuna** makeshift; **por fortuna** fortunately; **probar fortuna** to try one's luck

**fortunón** *m* (coll) windfall

**forza•do -da** *adj* forced; (*p.ej., entrada*) forcible; (*sonrisa*) (fig) forced; (*trabajos*) hard || *m* galley slave

**forzar** §35 *tr* to force

**forzo•so -sa** *adj* unavoidable; strong, husky; (*trabajos*) hard; (*aterrizaje; marcha*) forced || *f* — **hacer la forzosa a** (coll) to put the squeeze on

**forzu•do -da** *adj* strong, husky, robust

**fosa** *f* grave; (aut) pit; **fosa de los leones** (Bib) lions' den

**fosar** *tr* to dig a ditch around

**fos•co -ca** *adj* dark; cross, sullen; (*tiempo*) threatening

**fosfato** *m* phosphate

**fosforera** *f* matchbox

**fosforescente** *adj* phosphorescent

**fósforo** *m* (*cuerpo simple*) phosphorus; match; **fósforo de seguridad** safety match

**fósil** *adj & m* fossil

**foso** *m* hole, pit; (*que rodea un castillo o fortaleza*) moat; (theat & aut) pit

**fotingo** *m* (Am) jalopy, jitney

**foto** *f* (coll) photo; **foto fija** (phot) still

**fotodrama** *m* photoplay

**fotofija** *m* photo-finish camera

**fotogéni•co -ca** *adj* photogenic

**fotograbado** *m* photoengraving

**fotografía** *f* (*arte*) photography; (*imagen, retrato*) photograph; photograph gallery

**fotografiar** §77 *tr & intr* to photograph

**fotógra•fo -fa** *mf* photographer

**fotómetro** *m* light meter

**fotoperiodismo** *m* photojournalism

**fotopila** *f* solar battery

**fotostatar** *tr & intr* to photostat

**fotóstato** *m* photostat

**fototubo** *m* phototube

**fra.** *abbr* **factura**

**frac** *m* (*pl* **fraques**) full-dress coat, tails, swallow-tailed coat

**fracasar** *intr* to fail; to break to pieces

**fracaso** *m* failure; breakdown, crash

**fracción** *f* fraction

**fraccionar** *tr* to divide up; to break up

**fracciona•rio -ria** *adj* fractional

**fractura** *f* fracture; breaking open, breaking in

**fracturar** *tr* to fracture; to break open, break in || *ref* (*p.ej., un brazo*) to fracture

**fragancia** *f* fragrance; good reputation

**fragante** *adj* fragrant; **en fragante** (archaic) in the act

**fragata** *f* frigate; **fragata ligera** corvette

**frágil** *adj* fragile; (*quebradizo; que cae fácilmente en el pecado*) frail; (Mex) poor, needy

**fragmento** *m* fragment

**fragor** *m* crash, roar, thunder

**fragoro•so -sa** *adj* noisy, thundering

**fragosidad** *f* roughness, unevenness; (*de un bosque*) thickness, denseness; rough road

**frago•so -sa** *adj* rough, uneven; thick, dense; noisy, thundering

**fragua** *f* forge

**fraguar** §10 *tr* to forge; to hatch, scheme; (*mentiras*) to forge || *intr* to forge; (*la cal, el cemento*) to set

**fraile** *m* friar, monk; **fraile de misa y olla** (coll) friarling; **fraile rezador** praying mantis

**frambesia** *f* (pathol) yaws

**frambuesa** *f* raspberry
**frambueso** *m* raspberry bush
**francachela** *f* (coll) feast, spread; (coll) carousal, high time; (Arg) excessive familiarity
**francalete** *m* strap with buckle
**fran•cés -cesa** *adj* French; **despedirse a la francesa** (coll) to take French leave ‖ *m* Frenchman; (*idioma*) French ‖ *f* Frenchwoman
**francesada** *f* French remark; French invasion of Spain in 1808
**francesilla** *f* French roll; (bot) turban buttercup
**Francia** *f* France
**Francisca** *f* Frances
**francisca•no -na** *adj & mf* Franciscan
**Francisco** *m* Francis
**francmasón** *m* Freemason
**francmasonería** *f* Freemasonry
**fran•co -ca** *adj* generous, liberal; outspoken, candid, frank; (*camino*) free, open; (*suelo*) loamy; free, gratis; Frankish; **franco a bordo** free on board; **franco de porte** postpaid ‖ *mf* Frank ‖ *m* franc; (*idioma*) Frankish
**francolín** *m* black partridge
**franco•te -ta** *adj* (coll) frank, whole-hearted
**francotirador** *m* sniper
**franela** *f* flannel
**frangente** *m* accident, mishap
**frangir** §27 *tr* to break up, break to pieces
**frangollar** *tr* (coll) to bungle, to botch
**frangollo** *m* porridge; mash for cattle; (coll) bungle, botch
**franja** *f* fringe; strip, band; (opt) fringe
**franjar** *tr* to fringe
**franquear** *tr* to exempt; to cross, go over; to grant; to free, enfranchise; (*un camino*) to open, to clear; (*una carta*) to frank, pay the postage for; **a franquear en destino** postage will be paid by addressee ‖ *ref* to yield; **franquearse con** to open one's heart to
**franqueo** *m* freeing, liberation; postage; **franqueo concertado** postage permit
**franqueza** *f* generosity; candidness, frankness; freedom
**franquía** *f* (naut) sea room; **en franquía** (naut & fig) in the open
**franquicia** *f* franchise; exemption, tax exemption; **franquicia postal** franking privilege
**franquista** *mf* Francoist
**frasca** *f* leaves, twigs, brush; (Guat, Mex) high jinks
**frasco** *m* flask; (*p.ej., de aceitunas*) jar
**frase** *f* phrase; (*oración cabal*) sentence; idiom; **frase hecha** saying, proverb; cliché; **gastar frases** (coll) to talk all around the subject
**frasear** *tr* to phrase ‖ *intr* (coll) to talk all around the subject
**frasquera** *f* bottle frame, liquor case
**fratás** *m* plastering trowel
**fraternal** *adj* brotherly, fraternal
**fraternidad** *f* fraternity, brotherhood
**fraternizar** §60 *intr* to fraternize
**frater•no -na** *adj* brotherly, fraternal
**fraude** *m* fraud
**fraudulen•to -ta** *adj* fraudulent
**fray** *m* Fra
**frecuencia** *f* frequency; **alta frecuencia** high frequency; **baja frecuencia** low frequency; **con frecuencia** frequently
**frecuentar** *tr* (*ir con frecuencia a*) to frequent; to keep up, repeat
**frecuente** *adj* frequent; (*usual*) common
**fregadero** *m* sink, kitchen sink
**frega•do -da** *adj* (Am) annoying, bothersome; (SAm) stubborn; (Am) cunning; (P-R) brazen ‖ *m* scrubbing; mopping; (coll) mess
**frega•dor -dora** *mf* dishwasher
**fregar** §66 *tr* (*restregar*) to rub; (*restregar para limpiar*) to scrub, to scour; (*el pavimento*) to mop; (*los platos*) to wash; (Am) to annoy, bother
**fregasue•los** *m* (*pl* **-los**) mop, floor mop
**frega•triz** *f* (*pl* **-trices**) var of **fregona**
**fre•gón -gona** *adj* (Am) annoying, bothersome; (Am) brazen ‖ *f* (*criada que friega el pavimento*) scrub woman; (*criada que lava la vajilla*) dishwasher, scullery maid
**freiduría** *f* fried-fish shop
**freír** §58 & §83 *tr* to fry; (coll) to bore to death ‖ *intr* to fry; **dejarle a uno freír en su aceite** (coll) to let someone stew in his own juice ‖ *ref* to fry; (coll) to be bored to death; **freírsele a** to try to fool, to scheme to deceive
**fréjol** *m* kidney bean
**frenar** *tr* to bridle, to check, hold back; (*un automóvil, tren*) to brake
**frene•sí** *m* (*pl* **-síes**) frenzy
**frenéti•co -ca** *adj* frantic; mad, furious; wild
**frenillo** *m* muzzle; **no tener frenillo en la lengua** (coll) to not mince one's words
**freno** *m* (*parte de la brida*) bit; (*aparato para parar el movimiento de los vehículos*) brake; (fig) brake, check, curb; **freno de contrapedal** coaster brake; **morder el freno** to champ the bit
**frenología** *f* phrenology
**frentazo** *m* (Mex) rebuff
**frente** *m & f* (*de un edificio*) front ‖ *m* (mil) front, front line; **al frente de** at the head of, in charge of ‖ *f* brow, forehead; face, front; head; **a frente** straight ahead; **arrugar la frente** to knit the brow; **de frente** straight ahead; abreast; **en frente de** in front of; against, opposed to; **frente a** in front of; compared with
**freo** *m* channel, strait
**fresa** *f* strawberry; (*de fresadora*) cutter
**fresado** *m* milling, millwork
**fresadora** *f* milling machine
**fresal** *m* strawberry patch
**fresar** *tr* to mill
**fresca** *f* fresh air; cool part of the day; (coll) blunt remark, piece of one's mind
**fresca•chón -chona** *adj* bouncing, buxom; (*viento*) brisk
**fresca•les** *mf* (*pl* **-les**) (coll) forward sort of person

**frescamente** *adv* recently; cheekily, brazenly
**fres•co -ca** *adj* (*acabado de hacer o suceder*) fresh; (*moderadamente frío*) cool; (*pintura*) fresh, wet; (*tela, vestido*) light; calm, unruffled; buxom, ruddy; (coll) cheeky, fresh; **estar fresco** (coll) to be in a fine pinch; **quedarse tan fresco** (coll) to show no offense, to be indifferent or unconcerned || *m* coolness; fresh air; fresh bacon; (fa) fresco; (Am) cool drink; **al fresco** in the open air; in the night air; **hace fresco** it is cool; **tomar el fresco** to go out for some fresh air || *f* see **fresca**
**frescor** *m* freshness; cool, coolness
**fresco•te -ta** *adj* (coll) plump and rosy
**frescura** *f* freshness; cool, coolness; unconcern, offhand manner; sharp reply; (coll) cheek, impudence
**fresno** *m* ash tree; (*madera*) ash
**fresquera** *f* meat closet, food cabinet, icebox
**fresquería** *f* (Am) ice-cream parlor, soft-drink store
**fresque•ro -ra** *mf* fish dealer; (Peru) soft-drink vendor || *f* see **fresquera**
**freudismo** *m* Freudianism
**freza** *f* dung; spawning; hole made by game
**frialdad** *f* coldness; carelessness, laxity; stupidity; (pathol) frigidity; (pathol) impotence; (fig) coolness, coldness
**friáti•co -ca** *adj* chilly; awkward, stupid; (*ropa*) cold
**fricar §73** *tr* to rub
**fricasé** *m* fricassee
**fricción** *f* rubbing; massage; (pharm) rubbing liniment; (phys) friction
**friccionar** *tr* to rub; to massage
**friega** *f* rubbing, massage; (Am) annoyance, bother; (Am) flogging, whipping
**frigidez** *f* frigidity; coldness
**frígi•do -da** *adj* frigid; cold
**frigorífero** *m* freezing chamber
**frigorífi•co -ca** *adj* refrigerating; cold-storage || *m* refrigerator; (Arg, Urug) packing house, cold-storage plant
**fríjol** *m* bean, kidney bean; **fríjol de media luna** Lima bean; **¡fríjoles!** (W-I) absolutely no!
**frijolear** *tr* (Guat) to annoy, molest
**frijolizar §60** *tr* (Peru) to bewitch
**frí•o -a** *adj* cold; dull, weak, colorless; (fig) cold, cool || *m* cold; **fríos** (Am) chills and fever; **coger frío** to catch cold; **hace frío** it is cold; **tener frío** (*una persona*) to be cold; **tomar frío** to catch cold
**friole•ro -ra** *adj* chilly || *f* trifle, trinket; snack, bite
**frisar** *tr* to rub; to fit, fasten; (naut) to calk || *intr* to agree, get along; **frisar con** or **en** to border on
**friso** *m* dado, wainscot; (archit) frieze
**fri•són -sona** *adj & mf* Frisian
**fritada** *f* fry
**fri•to -ta** *adj* fried; (coll) bored to death || *m* fry; (Ven) daily bread
**fritura** *f* fry
**frívo•lo -la** *adj* frivolous; trifling
**fronda** *f* leaf; (*del helecho*) frond; sling-shaped bandage; **frondas** frondage, foliage
**frondo•so -sa** *adj* leafy; woodsy
**frontalera** *f* yoke pad
**frontera** *f* frontier, border; front, façade
**fronteri•zo -za** *adj* frontier, border; facing, opposite
**fronte•ro -ra** *adj* frontier, border; facing, opposite; front || *f* see **frontera**
**frontín** *m* (Mex) flip, fillip
**fron•tis** *m* (*pl* **-tis**) front, façade
**frontispicio** *m* frontispiece; (coll) face
**frontón** *m* (*encima de puertas o ventanas*) gable, pediment; pelota court; pelota wall; handball court
**frotamiento** *m* rubbing; (phys) friction
**frotar** *tr* to rub; to chafe || *ref* to rub
**fro•tis** *m* (*pl* **-tis**) (bact) smear
**fructuo•so -sa** *adj* fruitful
**frugal** *adj* (*en comer y beber*) temperate; (*no muy abundante*) frugal
**fruición** *f* enjoyment, satisfaction; (*del mal ajeno*) evil satisfaction
**fruiti•vo -va** *adj* enjoyable
**frunce** *m* shirr, shirring, gathering
**frunci•do -da** *adj* grim, gruff, stern; (Chile) temperate; (Chile) sad, gloomy || *m* shirr, shirring, gathering
**fruncir §36** *tr* to wrinkle, pucker, pleat; (*la frente*) to knit; (*los labios*) to curl, to purse; (*la verdad*) to twist, disguise; to shirr, to gather || *ref* to affect modesty, to be shocked
**fruslería** *f* trifle, trinket; (coll) futility, triviality
**frusle•ro -ra** *adj* futile, trivial, trifling || *m* rolling pin
**frustrar** *tr* to frustrate, to thwart
**fruta** *f* fruit; **fruta del tiempo** fruit in season; **fruta de sartén** fritter, pancake; **frutas** fruit; **frutas agrias** citrus fruit
**frutal** *adj* fruit || *m* fruit tree
**frutería** *f* fruit store
**frute•ro -ra** *adj* fruit || *mf* fruit dealer || *m* fruit dish; tray of imitation fruit
**frutilla** *f* (*del rosario*) bead; Chilean strawberry; gumdrop
**fruto** *m* (bot & fig) fruit; **fruto de bendición** legitimate offspring; **frutos** produce; **sacar fruto de** to derive benefit from
**fu** *interj* faugh!, fie!; (*del gato*) spit!; **ni fu ni fa** (coll) neither this nor that
**fucilazo** *m* heat lightning, sheet lightning
**fuego** *m* fire; (*para encender un cigarrillo*) light; (*de arma de fuego*) firing; lighthouse, beacon; hearth, home; rash, eruption; sore, fever blister; **abrir fuego** to open fire; **echar fuego** (coll) to blow up, hit the ceiling; **¡fuego!** fire!; **fuego fatuo** will-o'-the-wisp; **fuego graneado** or **nutrido** drumfire; **fuegos artificiales** fireworks; **hacer fuego** to fire, to shoot; **marcar a fuego** to brand; **pegar fuego a** to set fire to, to set on fire; **poner a fuego y sangre** to lay waste; **prenderse fuego** to catch on fire; **romper fuego** to open fire; to

stir up a row; **tocar a fuego** to sound the fire alarm

**fuelle** *m* fold, pucker, wrinkle; (*instrumento para soplar*) bellows; (*cubierta de coche*) folding carriage top; wind clouds; (*persona soplona*) (coll) gossip, talebearer

**fuente** *f* fountain, spring; public hydrant; font, baptismal font; platter, tray; (fig) source; **beber en buenas fuentes** (coll) to have good sources of information; **fuente de gasolina** gasoline pump; **fuente de sodas** soda fountain; **fuente para beber** drinking fountain; **fuentes termales** hot springs

**fuer** *m* — **a fuer de** as a, by way of

**fuera** *adv* out, outside; away, out of town; **desde fuera** from the outside; **fuera de** outside of; away from; out of; aside from; in addition to; **fuera de que** aside from the fact that; **fuera de sí** beside oneself; **por fuera** on the outside

**fuere•ño -ña** *mf* (Mex) hick, stranger

**fuero** *m* law, statute; code of laws; jurisdiction; exemption, privilege; **fuero interior** conscience, inmost heart; **fueros** (coll) pride, arrogance

**fuerte** *adj* strong; hard; loud; heavy; **hacerse fuerte** to stick to one's guns; (mil) to hole up, to dig in || *adv* hard; loud || *m* fort, fortress; forte, strong point

**fuerza** *f* force, strength, power; (*de un ejército*) main body; literal meaning; (phys) force; **a fuerza de** by dint of, by force of; **a la fuerza** forcibly, by force; **a viva fuerza** by main strength; **fuerza aérea** air force; **fuerza de agua** water power; **fuerza de sangre** animal power; **fuerza mayor** (law) force majeure, act of God; **fuerza motriz** motive power; **fuerza pública** police; **fuerza viva** kinetic energy; **hacer fuerza** to strain, struggle; to carry weight; **por fuerza** perforce, necessarily; **ser fuerza** + *inf* to be necessary to + *inf*

**fuete** *m* (Am) whip

**fufar** *intr* (*el gato*) to spit

**fuga** *f* flight; (*salida de un gas o líquido*) leak; ardor, vigor; (mus) fugue; **darse a la fuga** to take flight, to run away; **poner en fuga** to put to flight

**fugar** §44 *ref* to flee, escape, run away

**fu•gaz** *adj* (*pl* **-gaces**) fleeting, passing; (*estrella*) shooting

**fugiti•vo -va** *adj* & *mf* fugitive

**fugui•llas** *m* (*pl* **-llas**) (coll) hustler

**fula•no -na** *mf* so-and-so

**fulcro** *m* fulcrum

**fulgor** *m* brilliance, radiance

**fulgurar** *intr* to flash

**fulmicotón** *m* guncotton

**fulminar** *tr* to strike with lightning; to strike dead; (*censuras, amenazas, etc.*) to thunder; (*balas o bombas*) to hurl

**fullería** *f* trickery, cheating

**fulle•ro -ra** *adj* crooked, cheating || *mf* crook, cheat; **fullero de naipes** cardsharp

**fumada** *f* puff, whiff

**fumadero** *m* smoking room; **fumadero de opio** opium den

**fuma•dor -dora** *adj* smoking || *mf* smoker

**fumar** *tr* to smoke || *intr* to smoke; **fumar en pipa** to smoke a pipe; **se prohibe fumar** no smoking || *ref* (coll) to squander; (coll) to stay away from; (*la clase*) (coll) to cut

**fumarada** *f* (*de humo*) puff; (*de tabaco*) pipeful

**fumigación** *f* fumigation; **fumigación aérea** crop dusting

**fumigar** §44 *tr* to fumigate

**fumista** *m* stove or heater repairman; stove or heater dealer

**fumistería** *f* stove or heater shop

**fumo•so -sa** *adj* smoky

**funámbu•lo -la** *mf* ropewalker

**función** *f* function; duty, office, function; (*espectáculo teatral*) show, performance; **entrar en funciones** to take office, take up one's duties; **función benéfica** charitable performance; **función de aficionados** amateur performance; **función de títeres** puppet show; **función secundaria** side show

**funcional** *adj* functional

**funcionario** *m* functionary, public official, civil servant

**funcione•ro -ra** *adj* (coll) officious, fussy

**fund.** *abbr* **fundador**

**funda** *f* case, sheath, envelope, slip; (*para una espada*) scabbard; (*para proteger los muebles*) slip cover; **funda de almohada** pillowcase; **funda de asientos** seat cover; **funda de gafas** spectacle case

**fundación** *f* foundation

**fundadamente** *adv* with good reason; on good authority

**funda•dor -dora** *adj* founding || *mf* founder

**fundamental** *adj* fundamental

**fundamentar** *tr* to lay the foundations of

**fundamento** *m* foundation; (*razón, motivo*) grounds, reason; basis; reliability, sense; (Col) skirt

**fundar** *tr* to found, to base || *ref* — **fundarse en** to be based on; to base one's opinion on

**fundente** *adj* molten || *m* flux

**fundería** *f* foundry

**fundible** *adj* fusible

**fundición** *f* (*acción de fundir*) founding; (*fábrica*) foundry; (*herrería*) forge; (*hierro colado*) cast iron; (typ) font

**fundidor** *m* founder, foundryman

**fundir** *tr* (*p.ej., metales*) to found; (*campanas, estatuas*) to cast; (*derretir para purificar*) to smelt; (*colores*) to mix; (*un filamento eléctrico*) to burn out || *intr* to smelt || *ref* to melt; to fuse; (*un filamento eléctrico*) to burn out; (fig) to fuse, merge; (Am) to fail, founder

**fúnebre** *adj* (*marcha, procesión*) funeral; (*triste*) funereal

**funeral** *adj* funeral; (*triste, lúgubre*)

funereal || *m* funeral; **funerales** funeral
**funerala — a la funerala** (mil) with arms inverted (*as a token of mourning*)
**funera•rio -ria** *adj* funeral || *m* mortician, funeral director || *f* (*empresa*) undertaking establishment; (*local*) funeral home, funeral parlor
**funes•to -ta** *adj* ill-fated; sad, sorrowful; (*p.ej., influencia*) baneful
**fungir** §27 *intr* (CAm, Mex) to act, function
**fungo** *m* (pathol) fungus
**fungo•so -sa** *adj* fungous
**funicular** *adj* & *m* funicular
**fuñique** *adj* awkward; dull, tiresome
**furgón** *m* wagon, truck; (rr) freight car, boxcar; (rr) caboose
**furgoneta** *f* light truck, delivery truck
**furia** *f* fury
**furibun•do -da** *adj* furious, frenzied
**furio•so -sa** *adj* furious; (*muy grande*) terrific, tremendous
**furor** *m* rage, furor; **hacer furor** to be all the rage
**furti•vo -va** *adj* furtive; sneaky; poaching
**furúnculo** *m* boil
**fusa** *f* (mus) demisemiquaver
**fus•co -ca** *adj* dark
**fusela•do -da** *adj* streamlined
**fuselaje** *m* fuselage
**fusible** *adj* fusible || *m* (elec) fuse
**fusil** *m* gun, rifle
**fusilar** *tr* to shoot, execute; (coll) to plagiarize
**fusilazo** *m* (*tiro de fusil*) gunshot, rifle shot; (*relámpago sin ruido*) heat lightning, sheet lightning
**fusilería** *f* rifle corps; rifles, guns; (*descarga*) fusillade
**fusión** *f* fusion; melting; **fusión de empresas** (com) merger
**fusionar** *tr* & *ref* to fuse, to merge
**fusta** *f* brushwood, twigs; teamster's whip
**fustán** *m* fustian; (Am) cotton petticoat; (Ven) skirt
**fuste** *m* wood, timber; shaft, stem; (fig) importance, substance
**fustigar** §44 *tr* to whip, lash; to rebuke harshly
**fútbol** *m* football; soccer; **fútbol asociación** soccer
**fútil** *adj* futile, trifling, inconsequential
**futilidad** *f* futility
**futre** *m* (SAm) dandy, dude
**futu•ro -ra** *adj* future || *m* future; (gram) future; (coll) fiancé; **futuros** (com) futures || *f* fiancée

# G

**G, g** (ge) *f* eighth letter of the Spanish alphabet
**G.** *abbr* **gracia**
**gaba•cho -cha** *adj* & *mf* Pyrenean; (coll) Frenchy || *m* (coll) Frenchified Spanish (*language*)
**gabán** *m* overcoat
**gabardina** *f* gabardine; raincoat with belt
**gabarra** *f* barge, lighter
**gabarro** *m* (*en una piedra*) nodule; (*en un tejido*) flaw, defect; mistake
**gabinete** *m* cabinet; (*de médico, abogado, etc.*) office; studio, study; laboratory; (Col) glassed-in balcony; **de gabinete** armchair, theoretical; **gabinete de aseo** washroom; **gabinete de lectura** reading room
**gablete** *m* gable
**gacela** *f* gazelle
**gaceta** *f* government journal; (Am) newspaper; **mentir más que la gaceta** to lie like a trooper
**gacetilla** *f* town talk, gossip column; short item
**gacetillero** *m* gossip columnist
**gacetista** *mf* newspaper reader; newsmonger
**gacha** *f* watery mass; (Col, Ven) earthenware bowl; **gachas** mush, pap; porridge; (coll) mud; **gachas de avena** oatmeal; **hacerse unas gachas** to be mushy
**ga•cho -cha** *adj* turned down; flopping; (*sombrero*) slouch; **a gachas** on all fours || *f* see **gacha**
**gachumbo** *m* (SAm) hard fruit shell
**gachu•pín -pina** *mf* (CAm, Mex) Spanish settler in Latin America
**gaéli•co -ca** *adj* Gaelic || *mf* Gael || *m* Gaelic (*language*)
**gafa** *f* clamp; (*enganche de los anteojos*) temple; **gafas** glasses; **gafas de sol** or **gafas para sol** sunglasses
**gafe** *m* (coll) jinx, hoodoo
**ga•fo -fa** *adj* claw-handed; (Am) footsore || *f* see **gafa**
**gaguear** *intr* (Am) to stutter
**gaita** *f* hornpipe; hurdy-gurdy; (coll) chore, hard task; (coll) neck; **gaita gallega** bagpipe
**gaite•ro -ra** *adj* (coll) flashy, gaudy || *m* piper, bagpipe player
**gajes** *mpl* wages, salary; **gajes del oficio** cares of office, occupational annoyances
**gajo** *m* broken branch; (*de un racimo de uvas*) small stem; (*división interior de ciertas frutas*) slice; (*de horca*) tine, prong; (*ramal de montes*) spur; (Am) curl
**gala** *f* fine clothes; (*lo más selecto*) choice, cream; (Am) tip, fee; **de gala** full-dress; **hacer gala de** to glory in; **llevarse la gala** to win approval
**galafate** *m* slick thief
**galai•co -ca** *adj* Galician
**galán** *m* good-looking fellow; lover,

gallant, ladies' man; (*el que sirve de escolta a una dama*) escort, cavalier; (theat) leading man; **galán joven** (theat) juvenile; **primer galán** (theat) leading man
**galancete** *m* (theat) juvenile
**gala·no -na** *adj* elegant, graceful; spruce, smartly dressed; rich, tasteful
**galante** *adj* (*con las damas*) gallant; (*con los caballeros*) flirtatious; (*mujer*) wanton, loose
**galantear** *tr* to court, woo, make love to; to sue, entreat
**galantería** *f* gallantry; charm, elegance; generosity
**galanura** *f* charm, elegance
**galápago** *m* pond tortoise; (*del arado*) moldboard; light saddle; ingot
**galardón** *m* reward, recompense
**galardonar** *tr* to reward, recompense
**galaxia** *f* galaxy
**galeón** *m* (naut) galleon
**galeote** *m* galley slave
**galera** *f* covered wagon; women's jail; (*de hospital*) ward; (naut & typ) galley
**galerada** *f* wagonload; (typ) galley; (typ) galley proof
**galería** *f* gallery; **galería de tiro** shooting gallery; **galerías** department store; **hablar para la galería** (coll) to play to the gallery
**galerna** *f* stormy wind from the northwest (*on the northern coast of Spain*)
**Gales** *f* Wales; **el país de Gales** Wales; **la Nueva Gales del Sur** New South Wales
**ga·lés -lesa** *adj* Welsh || *m* Welshman; Welsh (*language*) || *f* Welsh woman
**gal·go -ga** *adj* (Col) sweet-toothed || *m* greyhound || *f* greyhound bitch; rolling stone; mange, rash
**Galia, la** Gaul
**gálibo** *m* template, pattern; (rr) gabarit
**galicismo** *m* Gallicism
**gáli·co -ca** *adj* Gallic || *m* syphilis; syphilitic
**galillo** *m* uvula; (coll) gullet
**galimatí·as** *m* (*pl* **-as**) (coll) gibberish, nonsense; (coll) confusion
**galiparla** *f* Frenchified Spanish
**ga·lo -la** *adj* Gaulish || *mf* Gaul || *m* Gaulish (*language*)
**galocha** *f* clog, wooden shoe
**galón** *m* braid, galloon; (*medida para líquidos*) gallon; (mil) chevron, stripe
**galopar** *intr* to gallop
**galope** *m* gallop; **a galope** at a gallop; in great haste; **a galope tendido** on the run
**galopea·do -da** *adj* (coll) hasty, sketchy || *m* (coll) beating, punching
**galopear** *intr* to gallop
**galopillo** *m* scullion, kitchen boy
**galopín** *m* ragamuffin; (*hombre taimado*) wise guy; (naut) cabin boy
**galpón** *m* (SAm) iron shed; (Col) tile works
**galvanizar** §60 *tr* to electroplate; to galvanize
**galvanoplastia** *f* electroplating
**galladura** *f* tread (*of egg*)
**gallardete** *m* streamer, pennant
**gallardía** *f* gallantry; elegance; nobility; generosity
**gallar·do -da** *adj* gallant; elegant; noble; generous; (*temporal*) fierce
**gallear** *intr* to stand out, excel; (coll) to shout, yell, threaten
**galle·go -ga** *adj & mf* Galician
**gallera** *f* cockpit
**galleta** *f* hardtack, ship biscuit; cracker; little pitcher; (coll) slap
**gallina** *adj* chicken-hearted || *mf* chicken-hearted person || *f* hen; **estar como gallina en corral ajeno** (coll) to be like a fish out of water; **gallina ciega** blindman's buff; **gallina de Guinea** guinea fowl
**gallinería** *f* poultry shop; cowardice
**galline·ro -ra** *mf* poultry dealer || *m* hencoop, henhouse; poultry basket; top gallery; babel, madhouse
**gallipavo** *m* turkey; (coll) sour note
**gallito** *m* (*el que figura sobre los demás*) somebody; **gallito del lugar** cock of the walk
**gallo** *m* cock, rooster; (coll) false note, sour note; (coll) boss; frog in the throat; **gallo de bosque** wood grouse; **gallo de pelea** gamecock; **tener mucho gallo** (coll) to be cocky
**gallofa** *f* vegetables; French roll; talk, gossip
**gallofear** *intr* to beg, bum, loaf around
**gallofe·ro -ra** *adj* begging, loafing || *mf* beggar, loafer
**gama** *f* doe, female fallow deer; (mus & fig) gamut
**gamberrismo** *m* gangsterism, rowdyism
**gambe·rro -rra** *adj & mf* libertine || *m* hoodlum, tough, rowdy
**gambeta** *f* crosscaper; caper, prance
**gambito** *m* gambit
**gamo** *m* buck, male fallow deer
**gamón** *m* asphodel
**gamonal** *m* field of asphodel; (Am) boss
**gamuza** *f* chamois
**gana** *f* desire; will; **darle a uno la gana de** to feel like, e.g., **le da la gana de trabajar** he feels like working; **de buena gana** willingly; **de gana** in earnest; willingly; **de mala gana** unwillingly; **tener ganas de** to feel like, to have a mind to
**ganadería** *f* cattle, livestock; brand, stock; cattle raising; cattle ranch
**ganade·ro -ra** *adj* cattle, livestock || *mf* cattle breeder; cattle dealer || *m* cattleman
**ganado** *m* cattle, livestock; **ganado caballar** horses; **ganado cabrío** goats; **ganado lanar** sheep; **ganado mayor** large farm animals (*cows, bulls, horses, and mules*); **ganado menor** small farm animals (*sheep, goats, pigs*); **ganado menudo** young cattle; **ganado moreno** swine; **ganado ovejuno** sheep; **ganado porcino** swine; **ganado vacuno** cattle
**gana·dor -dora** *adj* winning; earning; (coll) hard-working || *mf* winner; earner
**ganancia** *f* gain, profit; (Guat, Mex)

extra, bonus; **ganancias y pérdidas** profit and loss
**ganancial** *adj* profit
**gananci·so -sa** *adj* gainful, profitable; earning ‖ *mf* earner
**ganapán** *m* errand boy; (coll) boor
**ganapierde** *m & f* giveaway
**ganar** *tr* (*dinero trabajando*) to earn; (*la victoria luchando*) to win; (*beneficios en los negocios*) to gain; (*a una persona en una contienda*) to beat, defeat; (*aventajar*) to excel; (*la voluntad de una persona*) to win over; (*alcanzar*) to reach; **ganar algo a alguien** to win something from someone; **ganar de comer** to earn a living ‖ *intr* to earn; (*mejorar*) to improve ‖ *ref* to win over; **ganarse la vida** to earn a livelihood
**ganchero** *m* log driver; (Chile) oddjobber; (Ecuad) gentle mount
**ganchillo** *m* crochet needle; crochet, crochet work; **hacer ganchillo** to crochet
**gancho** *m* hook; shepherd's crook; coaxer; procurer, pimp; (Am) hairpin; (Col, Ecuad) lady's saddle; **gancho de botalones** (naut) gooseneck; **echar el gancho a** (coll) to hook in, to land; **tener gancho** (*una mujer*) (coll) to have a way with the men
**gandaya** *f* (coll) bumming, loafing
**gandujar** *tr* to pleat, shirr
**gan·dul -dula** *adj* (coll) loafing, idling ‖ *mf* (coll) loafer, idler
**gandulear** *intr* (coll) to loaf, idle
**ganfo·rro -rra** *mf* (coll) scoundrel
**ganga** *f* bargain
**ganglio** *m* ganglion
**gangocho** *m* (Am) burlap
**gango·so -sa** *adj* snuffling, nasal
**gangrena** *f* gangrene
**gangrenar** *tr & ref* to gangrene
**ganguear** *intr* to snuffle, talk through the nose
**gangue·ro -ra** *adj* (coll) bargain-hunting; (coll) self-seeking ‖ *mf* (coll) bargain hunter
**gano·so -sa** *adj* desirous; (*caballo*) (Chile) spirited, fiery
**gan·so -sa** *mf* (coll) dope, dullard ‖ *m* goose; gander; **ganso bravo** wild goose ‖ *f* female goose
**Gante** Ghent
**ganzúa** *f* (*garfio*) picklock, lock pick; (*persona*) picklock; (coll) pumper (*of secrets*)
**gañán** *m* farm hand; rough, husky fellow
**gañido** *m* yelp; croak
**gañir** §12 *intr* (*el perro*) to yelp; (*p.ej., el cuervo*) to croak
**garabatear** *tr* to scribble ‖ *intr* to hook; to beat about the bush; to scribble
**garabato** *m* hook; pothook; scribbling; weeding hoe; (*bozal*) muzzle; (*de una mujer*) (coll) winsomeness; **garabato de carnicero** meathook; **garabatos** wiggling of hands and fingers
**garabato·so -sa** *adj* full of scrawls; (coll) winsome
**garage** *m* or **garaje** *m* garage
**garagista** *m* garage man
**garambaina** *f* gaudy trimming; **garambainas** simpering, smirking; (coll) scribble
**garante** *adj* responsible ‖ *mf* **guarantor,** voucher
**garantía** *f* guarantee, guaranty
**garantir** §1 *tr* to guarantee
**garantizar** §60 *tr* to guarantee
**garañón** *m* stud jackass; stud camel; (Am) stallion
**garapiña** *f* icing, sugar-coating; (Am) iced pineapple drink
**garapiñar** *tr* to ice, to sugar-coat; to candy
**garapiñera** *f* ice-cream freezer
**garbanzo** *m* chickpea; **garbanzo negro** (fig) black sheep
**garbillar** *tr* to sieve, screen, riddle
**garbillo** *s* sieve, screen; riddled ore
**garbo** *m* jauntiness, grace, fine bearing; generosity
**garbo·so -sa** *adj* jaunty, graceful, spruce, sprightly; generous
**gardu·ño -ña** *mf* (archaic) sneak thief ‖ *f* stone marten, beech marten
**garete** *m* — **al garete** (naut) adrift
**garfa** *f* claw
**garfio** *m* hook, gaff
**gargajear** *intr* to cough up phlegm, to hawk
**gargajo** *m* phlegm
**garganta** *f* throat; (*de un río, una vasija, etc.*) neck, throat; (*del pie*) instep; (*entre montañas*) ravine, gorge; (*del arado*) sheath; (*de una polea*) groove; (archit) shaft; **tener buena garganta** to have a good voice
**gargantear** *intr* to warble
**gargantilla** *f* necklace
**gárgara** *f* gargling; **gárgaras** (*líquido*) (Am) gargle; **hacer gárgaras** to gargle
**gargarear** *intr* (Am) to gargle
**gargarismo** *m* gargling; (*líquido*) gargle
**gargarizar** §60 *intr* to gargle
**gárgola** *f* gargoyle
**garguero** *m* gullet; (*caña del pulmón*) windpipe
**garita** *f* sentry box; porter's lodge; (*de una fortificación*) watchtower; railroad-crossing box; privy (*with one seat*); **garita de centinela** sentry box; **garita de señales** (rr) signal tower
**garito** *m* gambling den
**garlito** *m* fish trap; (coll) trap, snare
**garlopa** *f* jack plane, trying plane
**garra** *f* claw, talon; catch, hook; **caer en las garras de** (coll) to fall into the clutches of
**garrafa** *f* carafe, decanter; **garrafa corchera** demijohn
**garrafal** *adj* awful, terrible
**garrafiñar** *tr* (coll) to snatch
**garrafón** *m* carboy, demijohn
**garramar** *tr* (coll) to snitch
**garranchuelo** *m* crab grass
**garrapata** *f* cattle tick, sheep tick; (mil) disabled horse; (Chile) little runt; (Mex) slut
**garrapatear** *intr* to scrawl, scribble
**garrapato** *m* pothook, scrawl; **garrapatos** scrawl
**garri·do -da** *adj* handsome, elegant
**garroba** *f* carob bean

**garrocha** *f* goad; (sport) pole
**garrotazo** *m* blow with a club
**garrote** *m* club, cudgel; garrote (*method of execution; iron collar used for such execution*); (Mex) brake; **dar garrote a** to garrote
**garrote•ro -ra** *adj* (Chile) stingy || *m* (Mex) brakeman
**garrotillo** *m* croup
**garrucha** *f* pulley, sheave
**gárru•lo -la** *adj* chirping; (*hablador*) garrulous; (*arroyo*) babbling; (*viento*) rustling
**garúa** *f* (Am) drizzle
**garuar** §21 *intr* (Am) to drizzle
**garulla** *f* (coll) mob, rabble
**garza** *f* heron; **garza real** gray heron
**gar•zo -za** *adj* blue || *f* see **garza**
**garzón** *m* boy, youth; suitor; woman chaser
**gas** *m* gas; **gas de alumbrado** illuminating gas; **gas exhilarante** or **hilarante** laughing gas; **gas lacrimógeno** tear gas
**gasa** *f* gauze, chiffon; (*tira de gasa negra con que se rodea el sombrero en señal de luto*) hatband
**Gascuña** *f* Gascony
**gasear** *tr* to gas
**gaseo•so -sa** *adj* gaseous || *f* soda water, carbonated water
**gasificar** §73 *tr* to gasify; to exalt, elate || *ref* to gasify
**gasista** *m* gas fitter; (Chile) gasworker
**gasoducto** *m* gas pipe line
**gasógeno** *m* gas generator, gas producer; mixture of benzine and alcohol used for lighting and cleaning
**gas-oil** *m* diesel oil
**gasolina** *f* gasoline
**gasolinera** *f* motor boat; gas station, filling station
**gasómetro** *m* gasholder, gas tank
**gastadero** *m* waste
**gasta•do -da** *adj* worn-out; used up; spent; (*chiste*) (coll) crummy, corny
**gasta•dor -dora** *adj & mf* spendthrift || *m* convict; (mil) sapper, pioneer
**gastadura** *f* worn spot
**gastar** *tr* (*dinero, tiempo*) to spend; (*en cosas inútiles*) to waste; (*echar a perder con el uso*) to wear out; (*consumir*) to use up; (*p.ej., una barba*) to wear; (*un coche*) to keep; **gastarlas** (coll) to act, behave || *intr* to spend || *ref* to wear; to wear out; to become used up; to waste away
**gasto** *m* cost, expense; wear; **gastos de conservación** or **de entretenimiento** upkeep; **gastos de explotación** operating expenses; **gastos menudos** petty expenses; **hacer el gasto** (coll) to do most of the talking; (coll) to be the subject of conversation; **hacer frente a los gastos** to meet expenses; **meterse en gastos con** to go to the expense of
**gasto•so -sa** *adj* wasteful, extravagant
**gástri•co -ca** *adj* gastric
**gastronomía** *f* gastronomy
**gastróno•mo -ma** *mf* gourmet
**gata** *f* she-cat; low-hanging cloud; (coll) Madrid woman; (Mex) maid, servant girl; **a gatas** on all fours, on hands and knees
**gatada** *f* catty act
**gatatumba** *f* (coll) faked attention, fake emotion, faked pain
**gatazo** *m* (coll) gyp
**gatea•do -da** *adj* catlike; grained, striped || *m* crawling, climbing; (coll) scratching, clawing
**gatear** *tr* (coll) to scratch, claw; (coll) to snitch || *intr* to crawl, to climb
**gatera** *f* cathole; (naut) hawsehole
**gatería** *f* (coll) cats; (coll) gang of toughs; (coll) fake humility
**gate•ro -ra** *adj* full of cats || *mf* cat lover || *f* see **gatera**
**gates•co -ca** *adj* (coll) catlike, feline
**gatillo** *m* (*de arma de fuego*) trigger; (coll) little pickpocket
**gato** *m* cat; tomcat; (*instrumento para levantar pesos*) jack, lifting jack; (coll) sly fellow; (coll) sneak thief; (coll) native of Madrid; **gato montés** wildcat; **gato rodante** dolly; **vender gato por liebre** (coll) to gyp, cheat
**gauchada** *f* (SAm) sly trick; (SAm) good turn
**gauchaje** *m* (SAm) gathering of Gauchos
**gauches•co -ca** *adj* Gaucho
**gau•cho -cha** *adj* (SAm) Gaucho; (Arg, Chile) sly, crafty || *m* (SAm) Gaucho; (SAm) good horseman || *f* (Arg) mannish woman; (Arg) loose woman
**gaulteria** *f* wintergreen
**gaveta** *f* drawer, till
**gavia** *f* ditch, drain; (*ave*) gull; (min) gang of basket passers; (naut) topsail
**gavilán** *m* sparrow hawk; (*de la pluma*) nib; (*en la escritura*) hair stroke; (Am) ingrowing nail
**gavilla** *f* sheaf, bundle; gang
**gaviota** *f* sea gull
**gavota** *f* gavotte
**gaya** *f* colored stripe; (*ave*) magpie
**gayar** *tr* to trim with colored stripes
**ga•yo -ya** *adj* gay, bright, showy || *m* (orn) jay || *f* see **gaya**
**gayola** *f* cage; (coll) jail
**gayomba** *f* Spanish broom
**gazapa** *f* (coll) lie
**gazapatón** *m* (coll) blunder, slip
**gazapera** *f* rabbit warren; (coll) gang, gang of thugs; (coll) brawl, row
**gazapo** *m* young rabbit; sly fellow; slip, boner, blunder; (*de actor*) fluff
**gazmiar** *tr* (*oliendo*) to sniff; (*comiendo*) to nibble || *ref* (coll) to complain
**gazmoñada** or **gazmoñería** *f* prudishness, priggishness
**gazmoñe•ro -ra** or **gazmo•ño -ña** *adj* prudish, priggish, strait-laced, demure || *mf* prude, prig
**gaznápiro** *m* gawk, boob, bumpkin
**gaznate** *m* gullet; (Mex) fritter
**gazpacho** *m* cold vegetable soup; (Hond) leftovers
**gazuza** *f* (coll) hunger
**Gedeón** *m* Gideon
**gehena** *m* Gehenna
**géiser** *m* geyser
**gel** *m* gel

**gelatina** *f* gelatine
**gema** *f* gem; (bot) bud
**geme•lo -la** *adj & mf* twin; **gemelos** twins; binoculars; cuff links; **gemelos de campo** field glasses; **gemelos de teatro** opera glasses || **Gemelos** *mpl* (astr) Gemini
**gemido** *m* moan, groan; wail, whine; howl, roar
**Géminis** *m* (astr) Gemini
**gemiquear** *intr* (Chile) to whine
**gemir** §50 *intr* to moan, groan; to wail, whine; to howl, roar
**gen** *m* gene
**genciana** *f* gentian
**gendarme** *m* (Am) policeman
**genealogía** *f* genealogy
**generación** *f* generation
**genera•dor -dora** *adj* generating || *m* generator
**general** *adj* general; common, usual; **en general** or **por lo general** in general || *m* general; **general de brigada** brigadier, brigadier general; **general de división** major general || **generales** *fpl* general information, personal data
**generala** *f* general's wife; call to arms
**generalato** *m* generalship
**generalidad** *f* generality; majority; **la generalidad de** the general run of
**generalísimo** *m* generalissimo
**generalizar** §60 *tr & intr* to generalize || *ref* to become generalized
**generar** *tr* to generate
**genéri•co -ca** *adj* generic; (*artículo*) indefinite; (*nombre*) common; showing gender
**género** *m* kind, sort; way, manner; cloth, material; (biol, log) genus; (gram) gender; **de género** genre; **género chico** one-act play, one-act operetta; **género de punto** knit goods, knitwear; **género humano** humankind; **género ínfimo** light vaudeville; **género novelístico** fiction; **género picaresco** burlesque; **géneros** goods, merchandise, material; **géneros de pieza** yard goods; **géneros para vestidos** dress goods
**genero•so -sa** *adj* generous; highborn; noble, magnanimous; (*vino*) rich, full
**géne•sis** *f* (*pl* **-sis**) genesis || **el Génesis** (Bib) Genesis
**genéti•co -ca** *adj* genetic || *f* genetics
**genial** *adj* inspired, genius-like; pleasant, agreeable; temperamental
**genlazo** *m* (coll) fiery temper
**genio** *m* (*índole, carácter*) temperament, disposition; (*don altísimo de invención; persona que lo posee; espíritu tutelar, deidad pagana*) genius; fire, spirit
**genital** *adj* genital || **genitales** *mpl* genitals
**geniti•vo -va** *adj & m* genitive
**genocida** *adj* genocidal || *mf* genocide
**genocidio** *m* genocide
**Génova** *f* Genoa
**geno•vés -vesa** *adj & mf* Genoese
**gente** *f* people; (*parentela, familia*) folks; race, nation; troops; **gente baja** lower classes, rabble; **gente bien** nice people; **gente de bien** decent people; **gente de capa parda** country people; **gente de coleta** (coll) bullfighters; **gente de color** colored people; **gente de la cuchilla** (coll) butchers; **gente de la vida airada** bullies; underworld; **gente del bronce** bright, lively people; **gente del rey** convicts; **gente de mal vivir** toughs, underworld; **gente de mar** seafaring people; **gente de paz** (*palabras con las cuales se contesta al que pregunta ¿quién?*) friend; **gente de pluma** (coll) clerks; **gente de su majestad** convicts; **gente de trato** tradespeople; **gente forzada** convicts; **gente menuda** (coll) small fry; (coll) common people
**gentecilla** *f* (coll) mob, rabble
**gentil** *adj* heathen, gentile; elegant, genteel; noble || *mf* heathen, pagan
**gentileza** *f* elegance, gentility, courtesy; gallantry; show, splendor; (*hidalguía*) nobility
**gentilhombre** *m* (*pl* **gentileshombres**) gentleman; messenger to the king; my good man; **gentilhombre de cámara** gentleman in waiting
**gentili•cio -cia** *adj* national; family; (gram) gentile
**gentilidad** *f* heathendom
**gentío** *m* crowd, mob
**gentualla** or **gentuza** *f* (coll) rabble, riffraff
**genui•no -na** *adj* genuine
**geofísi•co -ca** *adj* geophysical || *mf* geophysicist || *f* geophysics
**geografía** *f* geography
**geográfi•co -ca** *adj* geographic(al)
**geógra•fo -fa** *mf* geographer
**geología** *f* geology
**geológi•co -ca** *adj* geologic(al)
**geólo•go -ga** *mf* geologist
**geómetra** *mf* geometrician
**geometría** *f* geometry; **geometría del espacio** solid geometry
**geométri•co -ca** *adj* geometric(al)
**geopolíti•co -ca** *adj* geopolitical || *f* geopolitics
**geranio** *m* geranium
**gerencia** *f* management; manager's office
**gerente** *m* manager, director; **gerente de publicidad** advertising manager; **gerente de ventas** sales manager
**geriatría** *f* geriatry
**geriatra** *adj* geriatrical || *mf* geriatrician
**geriátri•co -ca** *adj* geriatrical
**germanía** *f* gypsy slang, cant of thieves
**germanizar** §60 *tr* to Germanize
**germen** *m* germ; **germen plasma** germ plasm
**germicida** *adj* germicidal || *m* germicide
**germinal** *adj* germ; germinal
**germinar** *intr* to germinate
**gerontología** *f* gerontology
**gerundio** *m* gerund; present participle; bombastic writer or speaker
**gestación** *f* gestation
**gestear** *intr* to make faces
**gesticular** *intr* to make a face, to make faces; (*hacer ademanes*) to gesticulate

**gestión** *f* step, measure; management; action, proceeding, negotiation
**gestionar** *tr* to promote, pursue; to manage; to negotiate
**gesto** *m* face; wry face, grimace; look, appearance; (*movimiento, ademán*) gesture
**ges•tor -tora** *adj* managing ‖ *m* manager
**gestu•do -da** *adj* (coll) cross-looking
**ghetto** *m* ghetto
**giba** *f* hump; (coll) annoyance
**giga** *f* jig
**giganta** *f* giantess
**gigante** *adj* giant ‖ *m* giant; (*en las procesiones*) giant figure
**gigantes•co -ca** *adj* gigantic
**gigantez** *f* giant size
**gigantilla** *f* large-headed masked figure; little fat woman
**gigan•tón -tona** *mf* huge giant ‖ *m* giant figure
**gigote** *m* chopped-meat stew; **hacer gigote** (coll) to chop up
**gimnasia** *f* gymnastics; **gimnasia sueca** Swedish movements, setting-up exercises
**gimnasio** *m* gymnasium; secondary school, academy
**gimnasta** *mf* gymnast
**gimnásti•co -ca** *adj* gymnastic ‖ *f* gymnastics
**gimotear** *intr* (coll) to whine
**gimoteo** *m* (coll) whining
**ginebra** *f* gin; (*de voces*) buzz, din; confusion, disorder ‖ **Ginebra** *f* Geneva
**ginebri•no -na** *adj & mf* Genevan
**ginecología** *f* gynecology
**ginecólo•go -ga** *mf* gynecologist
**ginesta** *f* Spanish broom
**gira** *f* var of **jira**
**gira•do -da** *mf* drawee
**gira•dor -dora** *mf* drawer
**giralda** *f* weathercock (*in the form of person or animal*)
**girándula** *f* girandole
**girar** *tr* (*una visita*) to pay; (com) to draw ‖ *intr* to turn; to rotate, gyrate; to trade; (com) to draw
**girasol** *m* sunflower; sycophant
**girato•rio -ria** *adj* revolving ‖ *f* revolving bookcase
**gi•ro -ra** *adj* (Guat) drunk; (Mex) cocky ‖ *m* turn; rotation; revolution; course, trend, turn; turn of phrase; boast, threat; gash, slash; line of business; trade; (com) draft; **giro a la vista** sight draft; **giro postal** money order ‖ *f* see **gira**
**girofle** *m* clove
**giroscopio** *m* gyroscope
**gis** *m* (Col) slate pencil
**gitana** *f* gypsy woman, gypsy girl
**gitanada** *f* gypsy trick; fawning, flattery
**gitanería** *f* band of gypsies; gypsy life; fawning, flattery
**gitanes•co -ca** *adj* gypsyish
**gita•no -na** *adj* gypsy; flattering; sly, tricky ‖ *mf* gypsy ‖ *m* Gypsy (*language*) ‖ *f* see **gitana**
**glacial** *adj* glacial; (*zona*) frigid; (fig) cold, indifferent
**glaciar** *m* glacier
**glándula** *f* gland; **glándula cerrada** ductless gland
**glasé** *m* glacé silk
**glasea•do -da** *adj* glossy, shiny
**glicerina** *f* glycerin
**global** *adj* total; global, world-wide
**globo** *m* globe; (*aparato que, lleno de un gas, se eleva en el aire*) balloon; (*bomba de lámpara*) globe, lamp shade; **globo del ojo** eyeball; **globo sonda** trial balloon; **lanzar un globo sonda** (fig) to send up a trial balloon
**glóbulo** *m* globule; (physiol) corpuscle; **glóbulo rojo** red cell
**gloria** *f* glory; **ganar la gloria** to go to glory; **oler a gloria** (coll) to smell heavenly; **saber a gloria** (coll) to taste heavenly
**gloriar** §77 *tr* to glorify ‖ *intr* to recite the rosary ‖ *ref* to glory
**glorieta** *f* arbor, bower, summerhouse; public square; traffic circle
**glorificar** §73 *tr* to glorify ‖ *ref* to glory
**glorio•so -sa** *adj* glorious; boastful
**glosa** *f* gloss
**glosa•dor -dora** *adj* commenting ‖ *mf* commentator
**glosar** *tr* to gloss; to audit; (Col) to scold ‖ *intr* to find fault
**glosario** *m* glossary
**glóti•co -ca** *adj* glottal
**glo•tón -tona** *adj* gluttonous ‖ *mf* glutton
**glotonería** *f* gluttony
**glucosa** *f* glucose
**gluglú** *m* (*del agua*) gurgle, glug; (*del pavo*) gobble; **hacer gluglú** to gurgle, to glug
**gluglutear** *intr* to gobble
**gnomo** *m* gnome
**gob.** *abbr* **gobierno**
**gobernación** *f* governing; government; department of the interior; (Arg) territory
**goberna•dor -dora** *adj* governing ‖ *m* governor
**gobernalle** *m* rudder, helm
**gobernante** *adj* governing ‖ *mf* ruler ‖ *m* (coll) self-appointed head
**gobernar** §2 *tr* to govern; to guide, direct; to control, rule; (*un buque*) to steer ‖ *intr* to govern; to steer
**goberno•so -sa** *adj* (coll) orderly
**gobierno** *m* government; governor's office, governorship; management; control, rule; guidance; (*de un buque*) navigability; **de buen gobierno** (*buque*) navigable; **gobierno de monigotes** puppet government; **gobierno doméstico** housekeeping; **gobierno exilado** government in exile; **para su gobierno** for your guidance; **servir de gobierno** (coll) to serve as a guide
**goce** *m* enjoyment
**go•do -da** *adj* Gothic ‖ *mf* Goth; Spanish noble; (Arg, Chile) Spaniard
**gofio** *m* (Am) roasted corn meal
**gol** *m* goal
**gola** *f* gullet
**goldre** *m* quiver
**goleta** *f* schooner
**golf** *m* golf

**golfán** *m* white water lily
**golfista** *mf* golfer
**gol•fo -fa** *mf* ragamuffin || *m* gulf; open sea; **golfo de Méjico** Gulf of Mexico; **golfo de Vizcaya** Bay of Biscay
**Gólgota, el** (Bib) Golgotha
**golilla** *f* gorget, ruff; magistrate's collar; pipe flange; (*de los caños de barro*) collar, sleeve; (*del gallo*) (Am) erectile bristles
**golondrina** *f* swallow
**golosina** *f* delicacy, tidbit; eagerness, appetite; trifle
**golosinear** *intr* to go around eating candy
**golo•so -sa** *adj* sweet-toothed; (*glotón*) gluttonous; (*apetitoso*) tasty
**golpe** *m* blow, stroke, hit; bump, bruise; heartbeat; crowd, throng, flock; (*del bolsillo*) flap; (*pestillo*) bolt, latch; (*de licor*) shot; surprise, wonder; (*infortunio*) blow; witticism; **dar golpe** to make a hit; **de golpe** all at once, suddenly; **de golpe y porrazo** slambang; **de un golpe** at one stroke; **golpe de ariete** water hammer; **golpe de estado** coup d'état; **golpe de fortuna** stroke of fortune; **golpe de gracia** coup de grâce; **golpe de mano** surprise attack; **golpe de mar** surge; **golpe de ojo** glance; **golpe de teatro** dramatic turn of events; **golpe de tos** fit of coughing; **golpe de vista,** glance, look; view; **golpe en vago** miss, flop; **golpe mortal** deathblow; **no dar golpe** to not raise a hand, not do a stroke of work
**golpear** *tr* to strike, hit, beat; to bump, bruise || *intr* to beat, strike; (*el reloj*) to tick; (*el motor de combustión interna*) to knock
**golpete** *m* door catch, window catch
**golpetear** *tr & intr* to beat; to rattle
**golpismo** *m* government by coup d'état
**gollería** *f* delicacy, dainty; **pedir gollerías** (coll) to ask for too much
**gollete** *m* throat, neck; (*de botella*) neck
**goma** *f* gum, rubber; (*tira de goma elástica*) rubber band; (*neumático*) tire; **goma arábiga** gum arabic; **goma de borrar** eraser, rubber; **goma de mascar** chewing gum; **goma espumosa** foam rubber; **goma laca** shellac
**gomecillo** *m* (coll) blind man's guide
**gomia** *f* bugaboo; (coll) waster; (coll) glutton
**gomo•so -sa** *adj* gum; gummy || *m* dude, dandy
**góndola** *f* gondola
**gondolero** *m* gondolier
**gongo** *m* gong
**gonorrea** *f* gonorrhea
**gordal** *adj* large-size
**gordia•no -na** *adj* Gordian
**gordi•flón -flona** or **gordin•flón -flona** *adj* (coll) chubby, pudgy, fatty || *mf* (coll) fatty
**gor•do -da** *adj* fat, plump; fatty, greasy; coarse; big, large; whopping big; (*agua*) hard || *m* fat, suet; (coll) first prize (*in lottery*) || **gordo** *adv* — **hablar gordo** (coll) to talk big
**gordura** *f* fatness, plumpness, stoutness, corpulence; fat, grease
**gorgojo** *m* grub, weevil; (coll) dwarf, runt; **gorgojo del algodón** boll weevil
**gorgojo•so -sa** *adj* grubby
**gorgón** *m* (Col) concrete
**gorgonear** *intr* (*el pavo*) to gobble
**gorgoritear** *intr* (coll) to trill
**gorgorito** *m* (coll) trill
**gorgotear** *intr* to burble, gurgle
**gorgotero** *m* peddler, hawker
**gorigori** *m* (coll) lugubrious funeral chant
**gorila** *f* gorilla
**gorjear** *intr* to warble, trill || *ref* (*el niño*) to gurgle
**gorra** *f* cap; bumming, sponging; **andar de gorra** to sponge; **colarse de gorra** (coll) to crash the gate; **gorra de visera** cap; **vivir de gorra** to live on other people
**gorrada** *f* tipping the hat
**gorrear** *intr* (Ecuad) to sponge
**gorretada** *f* tipping the hat
**gorrión** *m* sparrow; **gorrión triguero** bunting
**gorrista** *adj* sponging || *mf* sponger
**gorro** *m* cap, bonnet; baby's bonnet; **gorro de dormir** nightcap
**go•rrón -rrona** *adj* sponging || *mf* sponger || *m* pivot; journal, gudgeon
**gota** *f* drop; (pathol) gout; **gotas** touch of rum or brandy in coffee; **sudar la gota gorda** (coll) to work one's head off
**gotear** *intr* to drip, dribble; (*llover a gotas espaciadas*) to sprinkle
**gotera** *f* drip, dripping; mark left by dripping; (*en el techo*) leak; (*adorno de una cama*) valance; **estar lleno de goteras** (coll) to be full of aches and pains; **es una gotera** (coll) it's a constant drain; **goteras** (coll) aches, pains; (Col) environs, outskirts
**góti•co -ca** *adj* Gothic; noble, illustrious || *m* Gothic
**goto•so -sa** *adj* gouty || *mf* gout sufferer
**gozar** §60 *tr* (*poseer*) to enjoy || *intr* to enjoy oneself; **gozar de** (*poseer*) to enjoy || *ref* to enjoy oneself; to rejoice
**gozne** *m* hinge
**gozo** *m* joy, enjoyment; **no caber en sí de gozo** (coll) to be beside oneself with joy; **saltar de gozo** to leap with joy
**gozo•so -sa** *adj* joyful; **gozoso con** or **de** joyful over
**gozque** *m* or **gozquejo** *m* little yapping dog
**grabación** *f* (*de disco*) recording; **grabación sobre cinta** tape recording
**grabado** *m* engraving; print, cut, picture; (*de disco*) recording; **grabado en madera** wood engraving, woodcut; **grabado fuera de texto** inset, insert
**graba•dor -dora** *adj* recording || *mf* engraver || *f* recorder; **grabadora de cinta** tape recorder
**grabadura** *f* engraving
**grabar** *tr* to engrave; (*un sonido, una canción, un disco, etc.*) to record;

**grabar en** or **sobre cinta** to tape-record || *ref* to become engraved
**gracejada** *f* (CAm, Mex) cheap comedy, clownishness
**gracejar** *intr* to be engaging, be witty; to joke
**gracejo** *m* lightness, winsome manner, charm; (CAm, Mex) clown
**gracia** *f* witticism, witty remark, joke; grace; gracefulness; favor; pardon; (*de un chiste*) point; (coll) name; **caer en gracia a** to be pleasing to; **de gracia** gratis; **decir dos gracias a** (coll) to tell someone a thing or two; **en gracia a** because of; **gracia de Dios** daily bread; air and sunshine; **gracias** thanks; **¡gracias!** thanks!; **gracias a** thanks to; **¡gracias a Dios!** thank heavens!; **hacer gracia** to be pleasing; **hacer gracia de algo a uno** to exempt or free someone from something; **hacerle a uno gracia** to strike someone as funny; **¡linda gracia!** nonsense!; **tener gracia** to be funny, be surprising
**graciable** *adj* kind, gracious; easy to grant
**grácil** *adj* thin, small, slender
**gracio•so -sa** *adj* (*que tiene donaire, gracia*) graceful; (*afable, fino*) gracious; (*agudo, chistoso*) funny, witty; (*que se da de balde*) free, gratis || *mf* comic || *m* gracioso (*gay, comic character in Spanish comedy*)
**grada** *f* step, stair; row of seats; grandstand; altar step; (agr) harrow; (*plano inclinado sobre el cual se construyen los barcos*) slip; **gradas** stone steps; (Chile, Peru) atrium; **gradas al aire libre** bleachers
**gradar** *tr* (agr) to harrow
**gradería** *f* stone steps; row of seats; bleachers; **gradería cubierta** grandstand
**gradiente** *m* (phys) gradient || *f* (Am) slope, gradient
**grado** *m* step; grade; degree; (*título que se da en las universidades*) degree; (*sección en las escuelas*) grade, form, class; (mil) rank; **de buen grado** willingly; **de grado en grado** by degrees; **de grado o por fuerza** willy-nilly; **de mal grado** unwillingly; **en sumo grado** to a great extent; **mal de mi grado** unwillingly, against my wishes
**graduación** *f* graduation; (*de las bebidas espirituosas*) strength; (mil) rank
**gradual** *adj* gradual
**graduan•do -da** *mf* (*persona próxima a graduarse en la universidad*) graduate (*candidate for a degree*)
**graduar** **§21** *tr* to graduate, to grade; (*un grifo, una válvula, etc.*) to regulate; to appraise, estimate || *ref* to graduate
**grafía** *f* graph
**gráfi•co -ca** *adj* graphic(al); printing; illustrated; picture, camera || *m* diagram || *f* graph
**grafito** *m* graphite
**grafospasmo** *m* writer's cramp
**gragea** *f* colored candy; sugar-coated pill
**grajear** *intr* (*los cuervos*) to caw; (*los niños*) to gurgle
**grajien•to -ta** *adj* (Am) foul-smelling
**gra•jo -ja** *mf* rook, crow; (coll) chatterbox || *m* (Am) body odor
**gral.** *abbr* **general**
**gramática** *f* grammar; **gramática parda** (coll) shrewdness, mother wit
**gramatical** *adj* grammatical
**gramáti•co -ca** *adj* grammatical || *mf* grammarian || *f* see **gramática**
**gramil** *m* marking gauge, gauge
**gramo** *m* gram
**gramófono** *m* gramophone
**gramola** *f* console phonograph; portable phonograph
**gran** *adj* apocopated form of **grande,** used only before nouns of both genders in the singular
**grana** *f* seed; seeding; seeding time; red; **dar en grana** to go to seed
**granada** *f* pomegranate; (*proyectil explosivo*) grenade; **granada de mano** hand grenade; **granada de metralla** shrapnel; **granada extintora** fire extinguisher, fire grenade
**granadero** *m* grenadier
**granadilla** *f* passionflower
**granadina** *f* grenadine
**grana•do -da** *adj* choice, select; mature, expert || *m* pomegranate; **granado blanco** rose of Sharon || *f* see **granada**
**granalla** *f* filings
**granangular** *adj* wide-angle
**granate** *m adj invar & m* garnet
**Gran Bretaña, la** Great Britain
**grande** *adj* big, large; great || *m* grandee
**grandeza** *f* bigness, largeness; greatness; (*tamaño*) size; (*magnificencia*) grandeur; grandees; grandeeship
**grandi•llón -llona** *adj* (coll) oversize, overgrown
**grandio•so -sa** *adj* grandiose, grand
**grandor** *m* size
**granea•do -da** *adj* spattered; (*fuego*) heavy and continuous
**granear** *tr* to sow; (*la pólvora; una piedra litográfica*) to grain; to stipple
**granel** — **a granel** in bulk, loose; at random; lavishly
**granelar** *tr* (*el cuero*) to grain
**granero** *m* granary
**granete** *m* center punch
**granífu•go -ga** *adj* hail-dispersing
**granito** *m* granite
**granizada** *f* hailstorm; (Arg, Chile) iced drink
**granizar** **§60** *tr* (*p.ej., golpes*) to hail; to sprinkle || *intr* to hail
**granizo** *m* hail
**granja** *f* farm, grange; dairy; country place
**granjear** *tr* to earn, gain; to win, win over || *ref* to win, win over
**granjería** *f* husbandry; gain, profit
**granje•ro -ra** *mf* farmer; merchant, trader
**grano** *m* grain; (*baya*) berry; (*baya de la uva*) grape; (*tumorcillo en la piel*)

pimple; (*peso*) grain; **grano de belleza** beauty spot; **grano de café** coffee bean; **granos** (*fruto de los cereales*) grain; **ir al grano** (coll) to come to the point
**granuja** *m* scoundrel; (*muchacho vagabundo*) (coll) waif || *f* loose grape; grapeseed
**granujo** *m* (coll) pimple
**granular** *adj* granular; pimply || *tr & ref* to granulate
**gránulo** *m* granule
**grapa** *f* clamp, clip, staple
**grasa** *f* fat, grease; (*polvo*) pounce; (Mex) shoe polish; **grasa de ballena** blubber; **grasas** slag
**grasien•to -ta** *adj* greasy
**grasilla** *f* pounce
**gra•so -sa** *adj* fatty, greasy || *m* fattiness, greasiness || *f* see **grasa**
**grasones** *mpl* wheat porridge
**graso•so -sa** *adj* greasy; (pathol) fatty
**grata** *f* wire brush; (*carta*) favor
**gratificar** §73 *tr* to gratify; to reward, recompense; to tip, to fee
**gratín** *m* — **al gratín** au gratin
**gratis** *adv* gratis
**gratisda•to -ta** *adj* free, gratis
**gratitud** *f* gratitude
**gra•to -ta** *adj* pleasing; free; (Bol, Chile) grateful || *f* see **grata**
**gratui•to -ta** *adj* gratuitous; free, gratis
**grava** *f* gravel; crushed stone
**gravamen** *m* burden, obligation; encumbrance, lien; assessment
**gravar** *tr* to burden, encumber; to assess
**grave** *adj* grave, serious, solemn; hard, difficult; (*que pesa*) heavy; (*sonido*) grave, deep, low; (*música*) majestic, noble; (*negocio*) important; (*enfermedad*) serious; (*acento*) grave; paroxytone
**gravedad** *f* gravity; seriousness; **de gravedad** seriously; gravely; **gravedad nula** weightlessness, zero gravity
**gravedo•so -sa** *adj* heavy, pompous
**gravidez** *f* pregnancy
**grávi•do -da** *adj* pregnant
**gravitación** *f* gravitation
**gravitar** *intr* to gravitate; **gravitar sobre** to weigh down on
**gravo•so -sa** *adj* burdensome, onerous, costly; boring, tiresome
**graznar** *intr* to caw, to croak; to cackle; (*al cantar*) (fig) to cackle
**graznido** *m* caw, croak; cackle; (*canto que disuena mucho*) (fig) cackle
**Grecia** *f* Greece
**grecia•no -na** *adj* Grecian
**gre•co -ca** *adj & mf* Greek
**greda** *f* clay, fuller's earth
**grega•rio -ria** *adj* (*que vive confundido con otros*) gregarious; slavish, servile
**gregoria•no -na** *adj* Gregorian
**gremial** *adj* guild; trade-union, union || *m* guildsman; union member
**gremio** *m* guild, corporation; trade union, union; association, society
**greña** *f* confusion, entanglement; (*de cabello*) shock, tangled mop; **andar a la greña** (coll) to get into a hot argument; (*dos mujeres*) (coll) to pull each other's hair
**greñu•do -da** *adj* bushy-headed, shock-headed
**gres** *m* sandstone; stoneware
**gresca** *f* tumult, uproar; row, quarrel
**grey** *f* (*de ganado menor*) flock; group, party; nation, people; (*de fieles*) flock, congregation
**grie•go -ga** *adj* Greek || *mf* Greek || *m* (*idioma*) Greek; **hablar en griego** (coll) to not make sense
**grieta** *f* crack, crevice, chink; (*en la piel*) chap
**grieta•do -da** *adj* crackled || *m* crackleware
**grietar** *ref* to crack, split; (*la piel*) to become chapped
**gri•fo -fa** *adj* (*pelo*) kinky, tangled; (*letra*) script; (W-I) colored; (Mex) drunk; (Col) conceited || *mf* (W-I) colored person; (Mex) drunk || *m* faucet, spigot, tap, cock; (myth) griffin; (Peru) gas station
**grilla** *f* female cricket; (rad) grid; (Col) fight, quarrel; (SAm) annoyance, bother; **¡ésa es grilla!** (coll) you expect me to believe that!
**grillar** *intr* (*el grillo*) to chirp || *ref* (*las semillas, bulbos, etc.*) to sprout
**grillete** *m* fetter, shackle
**grillo** *m* (*insecto*) cricket; (*brote tierno*) sprout, shoot; **grillos** fetters, shackles
**grima** *f* fright, horror; **dar grima** to grate on the nerves
**grin•go -ga** *mf* (disparaging) foreigner; (*anglosajón*) (Am) gringo || *m* (coll) gibberish
**griñón** *m* (*toca de monja*) wimple; (*melocotón*) nectarine
**gripe** *f* grippe
**gris** *adj* gray; dull, gloomy || *m* gray; **hacer gris** (*el tiempo*) (coll) to be sharp, be brisk
**grisáce•o -a** *adj* grayish
**gri•sú** *m* (*pl* **-súes**) firedamp
**grita** *f* shouting; hubbub, uproar; **dar grita a** (coll) to hoot at
**gritar** *intr* to shout, cry out
**gritería** *f* shouting, outcry, uproar
**grito** *m* cry, shout; scream, shriek; **el último grito** (coll) the latest thing, all the rage; **poner el grito en el cielo** (coll) to raise the roof, to scream wildly
**gro.** *abbr* **género**
**Groenlandia** *f* Greenland
**grosella** *f* currant; **grosella silvestre** gooseberry
**grosellero** *m* currant bush; **grosellero silvestre** gooseberry bush
**grosería** *f* grossness, coarseness; churlishness, rudeness; stupidity; vulgarity
**grose•ro -ra** *adj* gross, coarse; churlish, rude; stupid; vulgar || *mf* churl, boor
**grosor** *m* thickness, bulk
**grosura** *f* fat, suet, tallow; meat diet; coarseness, vulgarity
**grotes•co -ca** *adj* grotesque
**grúa** *f* crane, derrick; **grúa de bote** (naut) davit; **grúa de auxilio** wrecking crane; **grúa de caballete** gantry crane

**grúa-remolque** *m* tow truck
**grue•so -sa** *adj* big, thick, bulky, heavy; coarse, ordinary; stout, fat; (*mar*) rough, heavy; **en grueso** in gross, in bulk || *f* (*doce docenas*) gross
**grulla** *f* (orn) crane
**grumete** *m* ship's boy, cabin boy
**grumo** *m* clot, curd; bunch, cluster
**grumo•so -sa** *adj* clotty, curdly
**gruñido** *m* (*de cerdo*) grunt; (*de perro cuando amenaza*) growl; (*de persona*) grumble; (*de puerta*) creak; (coll) grumble, scolding
**gruñir §12** *intr* (*el cerdo*) to grunt; (*el perro*) to growl; (*una persona*) to grumble; (*una puerta*) to creak
**gru•ñón -ñona** *adj* (coll) grumpy, grumbly || *mf* (coll) crosspatch
**grupa** *f* croup, rump
**grupada** *f* squall
**grupal** *adj* group
**grupo** *m* group; (mach & elec) unit
**gruta** *f* grotto
**grutes•co -ca** *adj & m* (fa) grotesque
**Gruyère** *m* Swiss cheese
**gte.** *abbr* **gerente**
**guaca** *f* (Bol, Peru) Indian tomb; (Am) hidden treasure
**guacal** *m* (Am) crate
**guacama•yo -ya** *adj* (P-R) flashy, sporty || *m* (Am) macaw
**guachapear** *tr* to splash with the feet; to bungle, botch || *intr* to clank, clatter
**guachinan•go -ga** *adj* (Am) flattering, sly || *mf* (disparaging term used by Cubans) Mexican
**gua•cho -cha** *adj* (SAm) homeless, orphan; (SAm) odd, unmatched
**guadal** *m* (Am) bog, swamp; (Am) sand hill, dune
**Guadalupe** *f* Guadeloupe
**guadama•cí** *m* (*pl* **-cíes**) embossed leather
**guadaña** *f* scythe
**guadañadora** *f* mowing machine
**guadañar** *tr* to cut with a scythe
**guadarnés** *m* harness room; harness man
**guagua** *f* trifle; (SAm) baby; (W-I) bus; (Col) paca
**guajada** *f* (Mex) nonsense, folly
**guaje** *adj* (Hond, Mex) foolish, stupid || *m* (Hond, Mex) calabash, gourd; (CAm) piece of junk
**guaji•ro -ra** *mf* (W-I) peasant, yokel
**guajolote** *m* (Am) turkey; (Mex) simpleton
**gualda** *f* (bot) weld, dyer's rocket
**gual•do -da** *adj* yellow || *f* see **gualda**
**gualdrapa** *f* housing, trappings; (coll) dirty rag hanging from clothes
**gualdrapear** *tr* to line up head to tail || *intr* (*las velas*) to flap
**Gualterio** *m* Walter
**guanaco** *m* (SAm) dope, simpleton; (SAm) tall lanky fellow; (zool) guanaco
**guanajo** *m* (W-I) boob, dunce; (Am) turkey
**guano** *m* (Am) palm tree; (Am) bird manure
**guante** *m* glove; **arrojar el guante** to throw down the gauntlet; **echar un guante** to pass the hat; **guantes** tip, fee; **recoger el guante** to take up the gauntlet; **salvo el guante** (coll) excuse my glove
**guantelete** *m* gauntlet
**guantería** *f* glove shop
**guapear** *intr* (coll) to bluster, to swagger; (coll) to dress to kill
**guape•tón -tona** *adj* (coll) handsome; (coll) flashy, sporty; (coll) bold, fearless || *m* (coll) bully, tough
**guapeza** *f* (coll) good looks; (coll) flashiness, sportiness; (coll) boldness, daring; (coll) bravado
**gua•po -pa** *adj* (coll) handsome, good-looking; (coll) flashy, sporty; (coll) bold, daring || *m* (*hombre pendenciero*) bully; gallant, lady's man
**guapura** *f* (coll) good looks
**guarache** *m* (Mex) leather sandal; (Mex) tire patch
**guarapo** *m* sugar-cane juice; (Am) fermented juice of sugar cane
**guarda** *mf* guard, custodian || *m* (Arg) trolley-car conductor; **guarda de la aduana** customhouse officer; **guarda forestal** forest ranger || *f* guard, custody; (*de la ley*) observance; (*de la espada*) guard; (*de la cerradura*) ward; (bb) flyleaf
**guardabarrera** *mf* (rr) gatekeeper
**guardaba•rros** *m* (*pl* **-rros**) fender, mudguard, dashboard
**guardabosque** *m* gamekeeper; forest ranger; (Am) shortstop
**guardabrisa** *m* windshield; (naut) glass candle shade
**guardacantón** *m* spur stone
**guardacarril** *m* (rr) railguard
**guardacar•tas** *m* (*pl* **-tas**) letter file
**guardaco•ches** *m* (*pl* **-ches**) car watcher
**guardacos•tas** *m* (*pl* **-tas**) revenue cutter, coast guard cutter; **guardacostas** *mpl* (*servicio*) coast guard
**guarda•dor -dora** *adj* guarding, protecting; mindful, observant; stingy || *m* guardian, keeper; observer
**guardaespal•das** *m* (*pl* **-das**) bodyguard
**guardafango** *m* fender, mudguard
**guardafre•nos** *m* (*pl* **-nos**) (rr) brakeman, flagman
**guardafuego** *m* fender, fireguard
**guardagu•jas** *m* (*pl* **-jas**) (rr) switchman
**guardajo•yas** *m* (*pl* **-yas**) jewel case
**guardalado** *m* railing, parapet
**guardalmacén** *m* warehouseman; (Cuba) country station master
**guardamalleta** *f* valance
**guardameta** *m* goalkeeper
**guardamue•bles** *m* (*pl* **-bles**) warehouse, furniture warehouse
**guardanieve** *m* snowshed
**guardapelo** *m* locket
**guardapolvo** *m* (*sobretodo ligero*) duster; (*resguardo para preservar del polvo*) cover, cloth; (*del reloj*) inner lid; (*sobre una puerta o ventana*) hood
**guardapuerta** *f* storm door
**guardar** *tr* to guard; to watch over; to protect; to put away; to show, observe; to save, e.g., **¡Dios guarde a**

**la Reina** God save the Queen || *intr* to keep, to save; **¡guarda!** look out!, watch out! || *ref* to be on one's guard; **guardarse de** to look out for, watch out for, guard against
**guardarraya** *f* (CAm, W-I) boundary line, property line
**guardarropa** *mf* keeper of the wardrobe || *m* (*armario donde se guarda la ropa*) wardrobe; (*local destinado a la custodia de ropa en establecimientos públicos*) checkroom, cloakroom; check boy || *f* check girl, hat girl
**guardarropía** *f* (theat) wardrobe
**guardasilla** *f* chair rail
**guardaventana** *f* storm window
**guardavía** *m* (rr) trackwalker, lineman
**guardavida** *m* lifeguard
**guardavien•tos** *m* (*pl* **-tos**) (*abrigo contra los vientos*) windbreak; (*mitra de chimenea*) chimney pot
**guardavivo** *m* bead, corner bead
**guardería** *f* guard, guardship; **guardería infantil** day nursery
**guardesa** *f* woman guard
**guardia** *m* guard, guardsman; **guardia civil** rural policeman; **guardia marina** midshipman, middy; **guardia urbano** policeman || *f* (*cuerpo de hombres armados; manera de defenderse en la esgrima*) guard; (naut) watch; **de guardia** on duty; on guard; **guardia civil** rural police; **guardia de asalto** shock troops; **guardia de corps** (mil) bodyguard; **guardia de cuartillo** (naut) dogwatch; **guardia suiza** Swiss Guards
**guar•dián -diana** *mf* guardian || *m* watchman
**guardilla** *f* attic; attic room
**guardo•so -sa** *adj* careful, neat, tidy; (*que ahorra mucho*) thrifty; (*mezquino*) stingy
**guarecer** §22 *tr* to take in, give shelter to; to keep, preserve; (*a un enfermo*) to treat || *ref* to take refuge, take shelter
**guarida** *f* den, lair; shelter; haunt, hangout, hide-out
**guarismo** *m* cipher, figure
**guarnecer** §22 *tr* to trim, adorn; to equip, provide; to bind, to edge; (*joyas*) to set; to stucco, to plaster; (*frenos*) to line; (*un cojinete*) to bush; (*una plaza fuerte*) to man, garrison; (culin) to garnish
**guarnición** *f* trimming; equipping; binding, edging; (*de joyas*) setting; stuccoing, plastering; (*de la espada*) guard; (*de frenos*) lining; (*del émbolo*) packing; (*tropa que guarnece un lugar*) garrison; (culin) garnish; **guarniciones** fixtures, fittings; (*de la caballería*) harness
**guarnicionar** *tr* to garrison
**guarnicionero** *m* harness maker
**gua•rro -rra** *mf* hog
**guasa** *f* (coll) heaviness, churlishness; (coll) joking, kidding
**guasca** *f* (Am) rawhide; (Am) whip; **dar guasca a** (Am) to whip, thrash
**guasería** *f* (SAm) coarseness, crudity; (Chile) timidity
**gua•so -sa** *adj* (SAm) coarse, crude, uncouth || *mf* (Chile) peasant || *f* see **guasa**
**gua•són -sona** *adj* (coll) heavy, churlish; (coll) funny, comical || *mf* (coll) dullard, churl; (coll) joker, kidder
**guata** *f* wadding, padding; (Arg, Chile, Peru) belly, paunch; (*de una pared*) (Chile) bulging, warping; (Ecuad) boon companion; **echar guata** (Chile) to prosper
**guatemalte•co -ca** *adj* & *mf* Guatemalan
**guáter** *m* (coll) toilet, water closet
**guau** *m* (*ladrido del perro*) bowwow; (bot) woodbine, Virginia creeper; **guau guau** (*perro*) bowwow || *interj* bowwow!
**guay** *interj* — **¡guay de mí!** (poet) woe is me!
**guayaba** *f* guava, guava apple
**guayabo** *m* guava tree; (Am) lie, trick
**guayaco** *m* lignum vitae
**Guayana** *f* Guiana
**gubernamental** *adj* governmental; (*defensor*) strong-government
**gubernati•vo -va** *adj* governmental
**gubia** *f* gouge
**guedeja** *f* shock of hair; lion's mane
**guerra** *f* war, warfare; billiards; **Gran guerra** Great War; **guerra a muerte** war to the death; **guerra bacteriana** germ warfare; **guerra de guerrillas** guerrilla warfare; **guerra de las dos Rosas** War of the Roses; **guerra de los Cien Años** Hundred Years' War; **guerra del Transvaal** Boer War; **guerra de ondas** radio jamming; **guerra de Troya** Trojan War; **guerra fría** cold war; **Guerra Mundial** World War; **guerra relámpago** blitzkrieg; **hacer la guerra** to wage war
**guerrea•dor -dora** *adj* warring || *mf* warrior
**guerrear** *intr* to war, wage war, fight; to struggle, resist
**guerre•ro -ra** *adj* war, warlike; warring; (coll) mischievous || *mf* fighter || *m* warrior, soldier, fighting man || *f* tight-fitting military jacket
**guerrilla** *f* band of skirmishers; guerrilla band; guerrilla warfare
**guerrillear** *intr* to skirmish; to wage guerrilla warfare
**guerrillero** *m* guerrilla
**guía** *mf* guide, leader; adviser || *m* (mil) guide || *f* guide; guidance; directory; (*del viajero*) guidebook; (*caballo*) leader; (*de la bicicleta*) handle bar; (*del bigote*) turned-up end; (*de la sierra*) fence; marker; shoot, sprout; (mach) guide; (rr) timetable; **guías** reins; **guía sonora** sound track; **guía telefónica** telephone directory
**guiadera** *f* (mach) guide
**guiar** §77 *tr* to guide, to lead; (*un automóvil*) to steer, to drive; to pilot; (*una planta, una vid*) to train || *intr* to shoot, to sprout || *ref* — **guiarse por** to be guided by, to go by
**guija** *f* pebble; grass pea
**guijarro** *m* cobble, cobblestone
**guije•ño -ña** *adj* pebbly; hard-hearted

**guijo** *m* gravel
**guijo·so -sa** *adj* gravelly; pebbly
**guillame** *m* rabbet plane
**Guillermo** *m* William
**guillotina** *f* guillotine; paper cutter
**guillotinar** *tr* to guillotine
**guimbalete** *m* pump handle
**guinda** *f* sour cherry
**guindal** *m* sour cherry tree
**guindaleza** *f* (naut) hawser
**guindar** *tr* to hoist, raise; (coll) to win; (*ahorcar*) (coll) to hang, to string up
**guindilla** *m* (coll) policeman, cop; Guinea pepper
**guindo** *m* sour cherry tree
**guindola** *f* (naut) boatswain's chair; (naut) life buoy
**guinea** *f* (*moneda*) guinea
**guineo** *m* small banana
**guinga** *f* gingham
**guiña** *f* (Col, Ven) bad luck
**guiñada** *f* wink; (naut) yaw
**guiñapo** *m* rag, tatter; ragamuffin
**guiñar** *tr* (*el ojo*) to wink || *intr* to wink; (naut) to yaw || *ref* to wink at each other
**guiño** *m* wink; **hacer guiños a** to make eyes at; **hacerse guiños** to make faces at each other
**guión** *m* banner, standard; cross (*carried before prelate in procession*); (*signo ortográfico*) hyphen; (*signo ortográfico largo*) dash; (mil) guidon; (mov & theat) scenario; (rad & telv) script; (mus) repeat sign; **guión de montaje** (mov) cutter's script; **guión de rodaje** (mov) shooting script
**guionista** *mf* (mov) scenarist; (mov) scriptwriter; (mov) subtitle writer
**guirigay** *m* (coll) gibberish; (coll) confusion, hubbub
**guirindola** *f* frill, jabot
**guirlache** *m* almond brittle, peanut brittle
**guirnalda** *f* garland, wreath
**guisa** *f* way, manner, wise; **a guisa de** in the manner of, like
**guisado** *m* stew, meat stew
**guisante** *m* pea; **guisante de olor** sweet pea
**guisar** *tr* to cook; to stew; to arrange, prepare || *intr* to cook
**guiso** *m* dish
**guisote** *m* hash
**guita** *f* twine; (coll) dough, money
**guitarra** *f* guitar
**guitarrista** *mf* guitarist
**gui·tón -tona** *mf* tramp, bum
**gula** *f* gluttony; gorging, guzzling
**gulo·so -sa** *adj* gluttonous; guzzling
**gumía** *f* Moorish poniard
**gurrumi·no -na** *adj* weak, puny || *m* henpecked husband || *f* uxoriousness
**gusanear** *intr* to swarm
**gusanera** *f* nest of worms; (coll) ruling passion
**gusanien·to -ta** *adj* wormy, grubby
**gusanillo** *m* small worm; twist stitch; (*de la barrena*) spur; **matar el gusanillo** (coll) to take a shot of liquor before breakfast
**gusano** *m* worm; **gusano de luz** glowworm; **gusano de seda** silk worm; **gusano de tierra** earthworm
**gusano·so -sa** *adj* wormy, grubby
**gusarapo** *m* waterworm, vinegar worm
**gustación** *f* tasting; taste
**gustar** *tr* to taste; to try, sample; to please, be pleasing to; to like, e.g., **me gustan estas peras** I like these pears || *intr* to like, e.g., **como Vd. guste** as you like; **gustar de** to like; to like to
**gustillo** *m* slight taste, touch
**gusto** *m* taste; flavor; liking; caprice, whim; pleasure; **a gusto** as you like it; **con mucho gusto** with pleasure, gladly; **encontrarse a gusto** or **estar a gusto** to like it (*e.g., in the country*); **tanto gusto** so glad to meet you
**gusto·so -sa** *adj* tasty; agreeable, pleasant; ready, willing, glad
**gutapercha** *f* gutta-percha
**gutural** *adj* guttural

## H

**H, h** (hache) *f* ninth letter of the Spanish alphabet
**haba** *f* bean, broad bean; (*simiente del café y el cacao*) bean; **ser habas contadas** (coll) to be a sure thing
**Habana, La** Havana
**haber** *m* salary, wages; credit, credit side; **haberes** property, wealth || *v* §38 *tr* to have; to get, get hold of || *v aux* to have, e.g., **lo he visto a menudo** I have seen it often; **haber de** + *inf* to be to + *inf*, e.g., **ha de llegar a mediodía** he is to arrive at noon || *v impers* there to be, e.g., **ha habido tres personas allí** there were three people there; **haber que** + *inf* to be necessary to + *inf*; **no hay de qué** you're welcome, don't mention it || *ref* to behave oneself; **habérselas con** to deal with; to have it out with
**habichuela** *f* kidney bean; **habichuela verde** string bean
**hábil** *adj* skillful, capable; (*día*) work
**habilidad** *f* skill, ability, capability; (*lo que se ejecuta con gracia*) feat; (*enredo, embuste*) scheme, trick
**habilido·so -sa** *adj* skillful
**habilitación** *f* qualification; backing, financing; equipping, outfitting; **habilitaciones** fixtures
**habilitar** *tr* to qualify; to back, finance; to equip, fit out; (*en un examen*) to pass
**habitable** *adj* inhabitable

**habitación** *f* habitation; (*edificio donde se habita*) house, home, dwelling; (*aposento de la casa o el hotel*) room; (*donde vive una especie vegetal o animal*) habitat
**habitante** *mf* (*de una casa*) dweller, occupant; (*de una población*) inhabitant
**habitar** *tr* to inhabit, live in; (*una casa, un piso*) to occupy || *intr* to live
**hábito** *m* garment, dress; habit, custom; **ahorcar los hábitos** (coll) to doff the cassock, to leave the priesthood; (coll) to change jobs; **el hábito no hace al monje** clothes don't make the man
**habitua•do -da** *mf* habitué
**habitual** *adj* habitual; regular, usual
**habituar** §21 *tr* to accustom || *ref* to become accustomed
**habitud** *f* relationship, connection; custom, habit
**habla** *f* speech; **al habla** speaking
**habla•dor -dora** *adj* talkative; gossipy || *mf* talker, chatterbox; gossip
**habladuría** *f* cut, sarcasm; **andar con habladurías** to go around gossiping
**hablante** *adj* speaking || *mf* speaker
**hablar** *tr* (*una lengua*) to speak, to talk; (*disparates*) to talk || *intr* to speak, to talk; **es hablar por demás** it's wasted talk; **estar hablando** (*una pintura, una estatua*) to be almost alive; **hablar claro** to talk straight from the shoulder
**hablilla** *f* story, piece of gossip
**hablista** *mf* speaker, good speaker
**hacede•ro -ra** *adj* feasible, practicable
**hacenda•do -da** *adj* landed, property-owning || *mf* landholder, property owner; (Am) cattle rancher; (Am) plantation owner
**hacendar** §2 *tr* (*el dominio de bienes raíces*) to pass on || *ref* to buy property in order to settle down
**hacende•ro -ra** *adj* thrifty
**hacendista** *m* economist, fiscal expert; man of independent means
**hacendo•so -sa** *adj* hard-working, thrifty
**hacer** §39 *tr* (*crear, producir, formar*) to make; (*ejecutar, llevar a cabo*) to do; (*un baúl*) to pack; (*un papel*) to play; (*un mandato*) to give; (*un drama*) to act, perform; to pretend to be; (*una pregunta*) to ask; **hace** ago, e.g., **hace un mes** a month ago; **hacer** + *inf* to have + *inf*, e.g., **le hice tomar un libro en la biblioteca** I had him get a book at the library; to make + *inf*, e.g., **el médico me hizo guardar cama** the doctor made me stay in bed; to have + *pp*, e.g., **hará construir una casa** he will have a house built; **hacer . . . que** to be . . . since, e.g., **hace un año que yo estuve aquí** it is a year since I was here; to be for . . ., e.g., **hace un año que estoy aquí** I have been here for a year; for expressions like **hacer frío** to be cold, see the noun || *intr* to act; **hacer a** to fit; **hacer al caso** (coll) to be to the purpose; **hacer como que** + *ind* to pretend to + *inf;* **hacer de** to act as, to work as; **hacer por** to try to || *ref* to become, get to be, grow; **hacerse a** to become accustomed to; **hacerse a un lado** to step aside; **hacerse con** to make off with; **hacerse chiquito** (coll) to sing small; **hacérsele a uno difícil** to strike one as difficult; **hacerse viejo** to grow old; (coll) to kill time
**hacia** *prep* toward; (*cierta hora o época*) about, near; **hacia abajo** downward; **hacia adelante** forward; **hacia arriba** upward; **hacia atrás** backward; (coll) the wrong way; **hacia dentro** inward; **hacia fuera** outward
**hacienda** *f* farmstead, landed estate, country property; property, possessions; (Arg) cattle, livestock; (Am) ranch; **hacienda pública** public finance, federal income; **haciendas** household chores
**hacina** *f* pile, heap; shock, stack
**hacinar** *tr* to pile, heap, stack
**hacha** *f* axe; (*hacha pequeña*) hatchet; torch, firebrand; four-wick wax candle; **hacha de armas** battleaxe
**hachazo** *m* blow with an axe
**hachear** *tr & intr* to hew, hack, or chop with an axe
**hachero** *m* torchbearer; (*candelero*) torch stand; (*leñador*) woodcutter
**hachich** *m* or **hachís** *m* hashish
**hacho** *m* torch; (*sitio elevado cerca de la costa*) beacon, beacon hill
**hada** *f* fairy; (*mujer que encanta por su belleza, gracia, etc.*) charmer; **hada madrina** fairy godmother
**hadar** *tr* (*determinar el hado*) to predestine, foreordain; (*pronosticar*) to foretell; (*encantar*) to charm, cast a spell on
**hado** *m* fate, destiny
**haiga** *m* (slang) flashy auto; (slang) sport
**halagar** §44 *tr* (*lisonjear*) to flatter; (*demostrar cariño a*) to cajole, fawn on; (*agradar*) to gratify, please
**halago** *m* flattery; cajolery; gratification; **halagos** flattery, blandishments
**halagüe•ño -ña** *adj* flattering; fawning; gratifying, pleasing; bright, rosy, promising
**halar** *tr* (naut) to haul, to pull
**halcón** *m* falcon
**halconear** *intr* (*la mujer*) to chase after men
**halconería** *f* falconry
**halconero** *m* falconer
**halda** *f* skirt; **poner haldas en cinta** (coll) to pull up one's skirts to run; (coll) to roll up one's sleeves
**halieto** *m* fish hawk, osprey
**hálito** *m* breath; vapor; (poet) gentle breeze
**halitosis** *f* halitosis
**halo** *m* halo
**halógeno** *m* halogen
**halterio** *m* dumbbell
**haluro** *m* halide
**hallar** *tr* to find; (*averiguar*) to find out, discover || *ref* to find oneself; to be; **hallarse bien con** to be satisfied with; **hallárselo todo hecho** to never

have to turn a hand; **no hallarse** to feel uncomfortable, to not like it

**hallazgo** *m* (*cosa hallada*) find; (*acción de hallar*) finding, discovery; (*premio al que ha hallado una cosa perdida*) reward, finder's reward, e.g., **diez dólares de hallazgo** ten dollars reward

**hallulla** *f* bread baked on embers or hot stones; (Chile) fine bread

**hamaca** *f* hammock

**hamamelina** *f* witch hazel

**hambre** *f* hunger; (*escasez general de comestibles*) famine; **matar de hambre** to starve to death; **morir de hambre** to starve to death, die of starvation; **pasar hambre** to go hungry; **tener hambre** to be hungry

**hambrear** *tr & intr* to starve, to famish

**hambrien•to -ta** *adj* hungry, starving

**hambruna** *f* (SAm) mad hunger; (Ecuad) starvation

**hamburguesa** *f* hamburger sandwich

**hamo** *m* fishhook

**hampa** *f* underworld life; denizens of the underworld

**hampes•co -ca** *adj* underworld

**hampón** *m* bully, tough

**hangar** *m* (aer) hangar

**hara•gán -gana** *adj* idling, loafing, lazy || *mf* idler, loafer

**haraganear** *intr* to idle, to loaf, to hang around

**harapien•to -ta** *adj* ragged, tattered

**harapo** *m* rag, tatter; **andar** or **estar hecho un harapo** (coll) to go around in rags

**harapo•so -sa** *adj* ragged, tattered

**harén** *m* harem

**harina** *f* (*especialmente del trigo*) flour; (*de cualquier grano*) meal; **estar metido en harina** (coll) to be deeply absorbed; (coll) to be fat and heavy; **harina de avena** oatmeal; **harina de maíz** corn meal; **ser harina de otro costal** (coll) to be a horse of another color

**harine•ro -ra** *adj* flour || *m* flour dealer; flour bin

**harino•so -sa** *adj* floury, mealy

**harnear** *tr* (Col, Chile) to sift

**harnero** *m* sieve

**ha•rón -rona** *adj* lazy || *mf* lazy loafer

**harpillera** *f* burlap, sackcloth

**hartar** *tr* to stuff, to cram; to satisfy, to satiate; to tire, to bore; to overwhelm, deluge || *intr* to have one's fill || *ref* to stuff; to be satiated; to tire, be bored

**hartazgo** or **hartazón** *m* fill, bellyful; **darse un hartazgo** (coll) to eat one's fill; **darse un hartazgo de** (coll) to have or to get one's fill of

**har•to -ta** *adj* full, fed up; very much; **harto de** full of, fed up with, sick of || **harto** *adv* enough; very, quite

**hartura** *f* fill, satiety; full satisfaction; abundance

**hasta** *adv* even || *prep* until, till; to, as far as; down to, up to; as much as; **hasta ahora** up till now; **hasta aquí** so far; **hasta después** (coll) so long, good-by; **hasta la vista** or **hasta luego** so long, good-by; **hasta mañana** see you tomorrow; **hasta más no poder** to the utmost; **hasta no más** to the utmost; **hasta que** until, till

**hastial** *m* gable end; (*hombrón rústico*) bumpkin

**hastiar** §77 *tr* to surfeit, sicken, cloy; (*fastidiar*) to bother, annoy, bore

**hastío** *m* surfeit, loathing, disgust; bother, annoyance, boredom

**hataca** *f* large wooden ladle; (*cilindro para extender la masa*) rolling pin

**hatajo** *m* small herd, small flock; (*p.ej., de disparates*) (coll) lot, flock

**hato** *m* (*de ganado vacuno*) herd; (*de ovejas*) flock; (*de ropa*) pack, bundle; (*de gente*) clique, ring; (*de gente malvada*) gang; everyday outfit; (*de disparates*) flock, lot; (Am) cattle ranch; **liar el hato** (coll) to pack up, pack one's baggage; **revolver el hato** (coll) to stir up trouble

**haya** *f* beech tree; (*madera*) beech || **La Haya** The Hague

**hayaca** *f* (Ven) mince pie

**hayo** *m* (Col) coca; (Col) coca leaves (*mixed for chewing*)

**hayuco** *m* beechnut, mast

**haz** *m* (*pl* **haces**) bunch, bundle; (*de leña*) fagot; (*de mieses*) sheaf; (*de rayos*) beam, pencil; (*de soldados*) file || *f* (*pl* **haces**) face; (*de la tierra*) surface; (*de paño o tela*) right side; (*de un edificio*) façade, front; **a sobre haz** on the surface; **ser de dos haces** to be two-faced

**hazaña** *f* feat, exploit, deed

**hazañería** *f* fuss

**hazañe•ro -ra** *adj* fussy

**hazaño•so -sa** *adj* gallant, courageous

**hazmerreír** *m* (coll) laughingstock, butt

**he** *adv* behold, lo and behold; **he aquí** here is, here are; **he allí** there is, there are

**hebilla** *f* buckle

**hebra** *f* thread; fiber; (*en la madera*) grain; (*del discurso*) (fig) thread; **de una hebra** (Chile) all at once; **pegar la hebra** (coll) to strike up a conversation; (coll) to keep on talking

**hebre•o -a** *adj & mf* Hebrew || *m* (*idioma*) Hebrew; (coll) usurer

**hebro•so -sa** *adj* fibrous, stringy

**hecatombe** *f* hecatomb

**hechicera** *f* witch, sorceress; (*mujer que por su belleza cautiva*) enchantress

**hechicería** *f* witchcraft, sorcery, wizardry; (fig) fascination, charm

**hechice•ro -ra** *adj* bewitching, charming, enchanting; magic || *mf* sorcerer, magician; charmer, enchanter || *m* wizard, sorcerer || *f* see **hechicera**

**hechizar** §60 *tr* to bewitch, cast a spell on; (fig) to bewitch, charm, enchant || *intr* to practice sorcery; (fig) to be charming, to enchant

**hechi•zo -za** *adj* fake, artificial; (*de quita y pon*) detachable; made, manufactured; (*producto*) (Am) local, home || *m* spell, charm; magic, sorcery; (fig) magic, sorcery, glamour; (fig) charmer; **hechizos** (*de una mujer*) charms

**he•cho -cha** *adj* accustomed; finished; turned into; (*traje*) ready-made; (*llegado a la edad adulta*) full-grown ‖ *m* act, deed; fact; event; (*hazaña*) feat; **de hecho** in fact; **en hecho de verdad** as a matter of fact; **estar en el hecho de** to catch on to; **hecho consumado** fait accompli ‖ **hecho** *interj* all right!, OK!
**hechura** *f* form, shape, cut, build; creation, creature; workmanship; (Chile) drink, treat; **hechuras** cost of making; **no tener hechura** to be impracticable
**heder** §51 *tr* to bore, annoy, tire ‖ *intr* to stink, to reek
**hediondez** *f* stench, stink
**hedion•do -da** *adj* stinking, smelly; annoying, boring; obscene, filthy, dirty ‖ *m* bean trefoil; skunk
**hedor** *m* stench, stink
**helada** *f* freezing; (*escarcha*) frost; **helada blanca** hoarfrost
**heladera** *f* refrigerator; (Chile) ice-cream tray
**heladería** *f* (Am) ice-cream parlor
**hela•do -da** *adj* cold, icy; (*pasmado por el miedo, la sorpresa, etc.*) frozen; (*esquivo, indiferente*) cold, chilly; (*cubierto de azúcar*) (Ven) iced ‖ *m* cold drink; (*manjar*) water ice; (*sorbete*) ice cream; **helado al corte** brick ice cream ‖ *f* see **helada**
**hela•dor -dora** *adj* freezing ‖ *f* ice-cream freezer
**helar** §2 *tr* to freeze; to harden, congeal; to dumbfound; to discourage ‖ *intr* to freeze ‖ *ref* to freeze; to harden, congeal, set; (*cubrirse de hielo*) to ice
**helecho** *m* fern
**helénl•co -ca** *adj* Hellenic
**hele•no -na** *adj* Hellenic ‖ *mf* Hellene
**helero** *m* glacier
**hélice** *f* helix; (*de un buque*) screw, propeller; (*de un avión*) propeller
**helicóptero** *m* helicopter
**helio** *m* helium
**heliotropo** *m* heliotrope
**helipuerto** *m* heliport
**hematíe** *m* red cell
**hembra** *adj invar* (*animal, planta, herramienta*) female; weak, thin, delicate ‖ *f* female; (*del corchete*) eye; (*tuerca*) nut; **hembra de terraja** (mach) die
**hembraje** *m* (SAm) females of a flock or herd
**hembrilla** *f* (mach) female part or piece; (*armella*) eyebolt
**hemeroteca** *f* periodical library
**hemiciclo** *m* (*semicírculo*) hemicycle; (*gradería semicircular*) amphitheater; (*espacio central del salón de sesiones de las Cortes*) floor
**hemisferio** *m* hemisphere
**hemistiquio** *m* hemistich
**hemofilia** *f* hemophilia
**hemoglobina** *f* hemoglobin
**hemorragia** *f* hemorrhage
**hemorroides** *fpl* hemorrhoids
**hemóstato** *m* hemostat
**henal** *m* hayloft
**henar** *m* hayfield
**henchir** §50 *tr* to fill; (*un colchón*) to stuff; (*a una persona, p.ej., de favores*) to heap, to shower ‖ *ref* to be filled; to stuff, to stuff oneself
**hendedura** *f* crack, split, cleft
**hender** §51 *tr* to crack, split, cleave; (*el aire, las ondas*) to cleave; to make one's way through ‖ *ref* to crack, to split
**hendidura** *f* crack, split, cleft
**henil** *m* hayloft, haymow
**henna** *f* henna
**heno** *m* hay
**heñir** §72 *tr* to knead; **hay mucho que heñir** (coll) there's still a lot of work to do
**heraldía** *f* heraldry
**heráldi•co -ca** *adj* heraldic ‖ *f* heraldry
**heraldo** *m* herald
**herbáce•o -a** *adj* herbaceous
**herbajar** *tr & intr* to graze
**herbaje** *m* herbage
**herba•rio -ria** *adj* herbal ‖ *m* (*libro*) herbal; (*colección*) herbarium
**herbicida** *m* weed killer
**herbo•so -sa** *adj* grassy
**hercúle•o -a** *adj* herculean
**heredad** *f* country estate
**heredar** *tr & intr* to inherit; **heredar a** to inherit from
**herede•ro -ra** *mf* heir, inheritor; owner of an estate; **heredero forzoso** heir apparent ‖ *m* heir ‖ *f* heiress
**heredita•rio -ria** *adj* hereditary
**hereje** *mf* heretic
**herejía** *f* heresy; insult, outrage; (coll) outrageous price
**herencia** *f* heritage, inheritance; (*transmisión de caracteres biológicos*) heredity; (*patrimonio de un difunto*) estate
**heréti•co -ca** *adj* heretic(al)
**herida** *f* injury, wound; insult, outrage; **renovar la herida** to open an old sore; **tocar en la herida** to sting to the quick
**heri•do -da** *adj* hurt, wounded; (*ofendido*) hurt ‖ *mf* injured person, wounded person; **los heridos** the injured, the wounded ‖ *f* see **herida**
**herir** §68 *tr* to injure, hurt, wound; (*ofender*) (fig) to hurt; (*golpear*) to strike; (*el sol sobre*) to beat down upon; (*un instrumento de cuerda*) to play; (*la cuerda de un instrumento*) to pluck; to touch, to move
**hermana** *f* sister; **hermana de leche** foster sister; **hermana política** sister-in-law; **media hermana** half sister
**hermanar** *tr* to match, to mate; to combine, join; to harmonize ‖ *ref* to match; to become attached as brothers or sisters or brother and sister
**hermanastra** *f* stepsister
**hermanastro** *m* stepbrother
**hermandad** *f* brotherhood; sisterhood; close friendship; close relationship
**herma•no -na** *adj* (*p.ej., idioma*) sister ‖ *mf* companion, mate ‖ *m* brother; **hermano de leche** foster brother; **hermano político** brother-in-law; **hermanos** brother and sister; brothers

and sisters; **hermanos siameses** Siamese twins; **medio hermano** half brother; **primo hermano** first cousin || *f* see **hermana**
**herméti•co -ca** *adj* hermetic(al); airtight; impenetrable; tight-lipped
**hermosear** *tr* to beautify, to embellish
**hermo•so -sa** *adj* beautiful; (*caballero*) handsome
**hermosura** *f* beauty; (*mujer hermosa*) belle, beauty
**hernia** *f* hernia
**héroe** *m* hero
**heroi•co -ca** *adj* heroic; (*remedio*) desperate
**heroína** *f* heroine; (pharm) heroin
**heroísmo** *m* heroism
**herrada** *f* wooden bucket
**herrador** *m* horseshoer
**herradura** *f* horseshoe; **mostrar las herraduras** (*un caballo*) to kick, be vicious; (coll) to show one's heels
**herraje** *m* hardware, ironwork
**herramental** *adj* tool || *m* toolbox, tool bag
**herramienta** *f* tool; set of tools; (coll) teeth; (coll) horns
**herrar** §2 *tr* (*guarnecer con hierro*) to fit with hardware; (*un caballo*) to shoe; (*marcar con hierro candente*) to brand; (*un barril*) to hoop
**herrería** *f* forge, blacksmith shop; blacksmithing; ironworks; rumpus
**herrero** *m* blacksmith; **herrero de grueso** ironworker; **herrero de obra** steelworker
**herrete** *m* tip, metal tip
**herretear** *tr* to tip, put a metal tip on
**herrín** *m* rust
**herrón** *m* (*tejo de hierro horadado*) quoit; (*arandela*) washer
**herrumbre** *f* rust; (*honguillo parásito*) rust, plant rot
**herrumbro•so -sa** *adj* rusty
**herventar** §2 *tr* to boil
**hervidero** *m* boiling; bubbling spring; (*en el pecho*) rattle; (*de gente*) swarm
**hervidor** *m* boiler, cooker
**hervir** §68 *intr* to boil; (*el mar; una persona encolerizada*) to boil, to seethe; to swarm, to teem
**hervor** *m* boil, boiling; (*de la juventud*) fire, restlessness; **alzar el hervor** to begin to boil
**hervoro•so -sa** *adj* ardent, fiery, impetuous
**heterócli•to -ta** *adj* irregular; unconventional
**heterodinar** *tr* to heterodyne
**heterodi•no -na** *adj* heterodyne
**heterodo•xo -xa** *adj* heterodox
**heterogeneidad** *f* heterogeneity
**heterogéne•o -a** *adj* heterogeneous
**hexámetro** *m* hexameter
**hez** *f* (*pl* **heces**) (fig) scum, dregs; **heces** lees, dregs; feces, excrement
**hiato** *m* hiatus
**hibisco** *m* hibiscus
**hibridación** *f* hybridization
**hibridar** *tr & intr* to hybridize
**híbri•do -da** *adj & m* hybrid
**hidal•go -ga** *adj* noble, illustrious || *m* nobleman || *f* noblewoman
**hidalguez** *f* or **hidalguía** *f* nobility
**hidra** *f* hydra
**hidratar** *tr & ref* to hydrate
**hidrato** *m* hydrate
**hidráuli•co -ca** *adj* hydraulic || *f* hydraulics
**hidroala** *m* (*vehículo mixto de buque y avión*) hydrofoil
**hidroaleta** *f* (*miembro alar del hidroala*) hydrofoil
**hidroavión** *m* hydroplane
**hidrocarburo** *m* hydrocarbon
**hidroeléctri•co -ca** *adj* hydroelectric
**hidrófi•lo -la** *adj* (*algodón*) absorbent (*cotton*)
**hidrofobia** *f* hydrophobia
**hidrófu•go -ga** *adj* waterproof
**hidrógeno** *m* hydrogen
**hidropesía** *f* dropsy
**hidróxido** *m* hydroxide
**hiedra** *f* ivy
**hiel** *f* bile, gall; (fig) gall, bitterness, sorrow; **echar la hiel** (coll) to strain, to overwork
**hielo** *m* ice; (fig) coldness, coolness; **hielo flotante** drift ice, ice pack; **hielo seco** dry ice; **romper el hielo** (*quebrantar la reserva*) to break the ice
**hiena** *f* hyena
**hienda** *f* dung
**hierba** *f* grass; (*especialmente la que tiene propiedades medicinales*) herb; **hierba de la plata** honesty; **hierba del asno** evening primrose; **hierba de París** truelove; **hierba gatera** catnip; **hierba pastel** woad; **hierbas** grass, pasture; herb poison; (coll) years of age (*said of animals*); **mala hierba** weed; (coll) wayward young fellow
**hierbabuena** *f* mint
**hierro** *m* iron; (*marca candente que se pone a los ganados*) brand; **hierro colado** cast iron; **hierro colado en barras** pig iron; **hierro de desecho** scrap iron; **hierro de marcar** branding iron; **hierro dulce** wrought iron; **hierro fundido** cast iron; **hierro galvanizado** galvanized iron; **hierro ondulado** corrugated iron; **hierros** irons, fetters; **llevar hierro a Vizcaya** to carry coals to Newcastle
**higa** *f* baby's fist-shaped amulet; (coll) scorn, contempt; **dar higa** to miss fire; **no dar dos higas por** (coll) to not give a rap for
**hígado** *m* liver; **echar los hígados** (coll) to strain, to overwork; **hígados** (coll) guts, courage; **malos hígados** (coll) hatred, grudge
**higiene** *f* hygiene
**higiéni•co -ca** *adj* hygienic
**higo** *m* fig; **higo chumbo** prickly pear; **higo paso** dried fig; **no valer un higo** (coll) to be not worth a continental
**higuera** *f* fig tree; **higuera chumba** prickly pear
**hija** *f* daughter; **hija política** daughter-in-law
**hijas•tro -tra** *mf* stepchild || *m* stepson || *f* stepdaughter
**hi•jo -ja** *mf* child; (*de un animal*) young; **hijo de bendición** legitimate child; good child; **hijo de la cuna**

foundling; **hijo del amor** love child; **hijo de leche** foster child || *m* son; **cada hijo de vecino** (coll) every man Jack, every mother's son; **hijo del agua** good sailor; good swimmer; **hijo de su padre** (coll) chip off the old block; **hijo de sus propias obras** self-made man; **hijo político** son-in-law; **hijos** children; descendants || *f* see **hija**

**hijodalgo** *m* (*pl* **hijosdalgo**) nobleman

**hijuela** *f* little girl, little daughter; (*tira de tela*) gore; branch drain; side path

**hijuelero** *m* rural postman

**hijuelo** *m* shoot, sucker

**hila** *f* row, line; (*acción de hilar*) spinning; **a la hila** in single file; **hilas** (*hebras para curar heridas*) lint

**hilacha** *f* shred, fraying; **hilacha de acero** steel wool; **hilacha de algodón** cotton waste; **hilacha de vidrio** spun glass; **hilachas** lint; **mostrar la hilacha** (Arg) to show one's worst side

**hilachos** *mpl* (Mex) rags, tatters

**hilacho•so -sa** *adj* frayed, raggedy

**hilada** *f* row, line; (mas) course

**hilado** *m* spinning; (*hilo*) yarn, thread

**hila•dor -dora** *adj* spinning || *mf* spinner || *f* spinning machine

**hilandería** *f* spinning; spinning mill

**hilande•ro -ra** *adj* spinning || *m* spinning mill

**hilar** *tr & intr* to spin; **hilar delgado** to hew close to the line; **hilar largo** to drag on

**hilarante** *adj* laughable; (*gas*) laughing

**hilaza** *f* yarn, thread; lint; **descubrir la hilaza** (coll) to show one's true nature

**hilera** *f* row, line; fine thread, fine yarn; (*parhilera*) ridgepole; (mil) file

**hilo** *m* thread; (*hebras retorcidas*) yarn; (*alambre*) wire; (*de perlas*) string; (*de agua*) thin stream; (*de luz*) beam; linen, linen fabric; (*de un discurso, de la vida*) (fig) thread; **hilo bramante** twine; **hilo de la muerte** end of life; **hilo de masa** (aut) ground wire; **hilo de medianoche** midnight sharp; **hilo dental** dental floss; **hilo de tierra** (elec) ground wire; **irse al hilo** or **tras el hilo de la gente** to follow the crowd; **manejar los hilos** to pull strings; **perder el hilo de** to lose the thread of

**hilván** *m* basting, tacking; basting stitch; (Chile) basting thread; (Ven) hem; **hablar de hilván** (coll) to jabber along

**hilvanar** *tr* to baste, to tack; to sketch, outline; (*hacer con precipitación*) (coll) to hurry; (Ven) to hem || *intr* to baste, to tack

**himnario** *m* hymnal, hymn book

**himno** *m* hymn; **himno nacional** national anthem

**hin** *m* neigh, whinny

**hincadura** *f* driving, thrusting, sticking

**hincapié** *m* stamping the foot; **hacer hincapié en** (coll) to lay great stress on, to emphasize

**hincar** §73 *tr* to drive, thrust, stick, sink; (*la rodilla*) to go down on, to fall on || *ref* to kneel, kneel down; **hincarse de rodillas** to go down on one's knees

**hincha** *mf* (sport) fan, rooter || *f* (coll) grudge, ill will

**hinchable** *adj* inflatable; (*goma de mascar*) bubble

**hincha•do -da** *adj* swollen; swollen with pride; (*estilo, lenguaje*) pompous, high-flown || *m* (*de un neumático*) inflation || *f* (sport) fans, rooters

**hinchar** *tr* to swell; to inflate; (*un neumático*) to pump up; to exaggerate, embroider || *ref* to swell; to swell up, become puffed up (*with pride*)

**hinchazón** *f* swelling; vanity, conceit; (*del estilo, lenguaje*) bombast

**hinchismo** *m* (sport) fans, rooters

**hin•dú -dúa** (*pl* **-dúes -dúas**) *adj & mf* Hindoo, Hindu

**hiniesta** *f* Spanish broom

**hinojo** *m* fennel; **de hinojos** on one's knees

**hipar** *intr* to hiccup; (*los perros cuando siguen la caza*) to pant, to snuffle; (*gimotear*) to wimper; to be worn out; **hipar por** to long for; to long to

**hiperacidez** *f* hyperacidity

**hipérbola** *f* (geom) hyperbola

**hipérbole** *f* (rhet) hyperbole

**hiperbóli•co -ca** *adj* (geom & rhet) hyperbolic

**hipersensible** *adj* (*alérgico*) hypersensitive

**hipertensión** *f* hypertension, high blood pressure

**hípi•co -ca** *adj* horse, equine

**hipnosis** *f* hypnosis

**hipnóti•co -ca** *adj* hypnotic || *mf* hypnotic || *m* (*medicamento que provoca el sueño*) hypnotic

**hipnotismo** *m* hypnotism

**hipnotista** *mf* hypnotist

**hipnotizar** §60 *tr* to hypnotize

**hipo** *m* hiccup; longing, desire; **tener hipo contra** to have a grudge against; **tener hipo por** to desire eagerly

**hipocondría•co -ca** *adj & mf* hypochondriac

**hipocresía** *f* hypocrisy

**hipócrita** *adj* hypocritical || *mf* hypocrite

**hipodérmi•co -ca** *adj* hypodermic

**hipódromo** *m* hippodrome, race track

**hipopótamo** *m* hippopotamus

**hiposulfito** *m* hyposulfite

**hipoteca** *f* mortgage; **¡buena hipoteca!** (coll) you may believe it, if you want to!

**hipotecar** §73 *tr* to mortgage

**hipoteca•rio -ria** *adj* mortgage

**hipotenusa** *f* hypotenuse

**hipóte•sis** *f* (*pl* **-sis**) hypothesis

**hipotéti•co -ca** *adj* hypothetic(al)

**hiriente** *adj* cutting, stinging

**hirsu•to -ta** *adj* hairy, bristly; (fig) brusque, gruff

**hirviente** *adj* boiling

**hisopear** *tr* to sprinkle with holy water

**hisopo** *m* (bot) hyssop; aspergillum, sprinkler of holy water; (Am) paint brush, shaving brush

**hispalense** *adj & mf* Sevillian

**hispáni•co -ca** *adj* Hispanic
**hispanista** *mf* Hispanist
**hispa•no -na** *adj* Spanish; Spanish American || *mf* Spaniard; Spanish American
**hispanohablante** *adj* Spanish-speaking || *mf* speaker of Spanish
**híspi•do -da** *adj* bristly, spiny
**histéri•co -ca** *adj* hysteric(al)
**histerismo** *m* hysteria
**histología** *f* histology
**historia** *f* history; story, tale; **de historia** (coll) notorious, infamous; **dejarse de historias** (coll) to come to the point; **historia de lagrimitas** (coll) sob story; **historias** (coll) gossip, meddling; **pasar a la historia** to become a thing of the past; **picar en historia** to turn out to be serious
**historia•do -da** *adj* richly adorned; overadorned; (*cuadro, dibujo*) storied
**historial** *adj* historical || *m* record, dossier
**historiar** §77 & **regular** *tr* to tell the history of; to tell the story of; (*un suceso histórico*) (fa) to depict
**históri•co -ca** *adj* historic(al)
**historieta** *f* anecdote, brief story; **historieta gráfica** comic strip
**histrión** *m* actor; juggler, buffoon
**histrióni•co -ca** *adj* histrionic
**hita** *f* brad; landmark, milestone
**hi•to -ta** *adj* fixed, firm; (*casa, calle*) next; (*caballo*) black || *m* (*clavo fijado en la tierra*) peg, hob; (*juego*) quoits; (*blanco*) target; (*mojón*) landmark, milestone; **dar en el hito** to hit the nail on the head; **mirar de hito en hito** to eye up and down || *f* see **hita**
**Hno.** *abbr* **Hermano**
**hoba•chón -chona** *adj* (coll) lumpish
**hocicar** §73 *tr* to nuzzle, to root; (coll) to keep on kissing || *intr* to nuzzle, to root; to run into a snag; (*la proa*) (naut) to dip
**hocico** *m* snout; (*de una persona*) (coll) snout; sour face; **caer de hocicos** (coll) to fall on one's face; **meter el hocico en todo** (coll) to poke one's nose into everything; **poner hocico** (coll) to make a face
**hogaño** *adv* (coll) this year; (coll) at the present time
**hogar** *m* fireplace, hearth; furnace; home; family life; (*hoguera*) bonfire
**hogare•ño -ña** *adj* home-loving || *mf* homebody, stay-at-home
**hogaza** *f* large loaf of bread
**hoguera** *f* bonfire
**hoja** *f* (*de planta, libro, mesa, muelle, puerta plegadiza, etc.; pétalo de flor*) leaf; (*de planta acuática*) pad; (*de papel*) sheet; blank sheet; (*de cuchillo, sierra, espada, etc.*) blade; (*hojuela de metal*) foil; (*de persiana*) slat; (*del patín*) runner; **doblar la hoja** (coll) to change the subject; **hoja clínica** clinical chart; **hoja de afeitar** razor blade; **hoja de embalaje** packing slip; **hoja de encuadernador** (bb) end paper; **hoja de estaño** tin foil; **hoja de estudios** transcript; **hoja de guarda** (bb) flyleaf; **hoja del anunciante** tear sheet; **hoja de lata** tin, tin plate; **hoja de nenúfar** lily pad; **hoja de paga** pay roll; **hoja de parra** fig leaf; **hoja de pedidos** order blank; **hoja de rodaje** (mov) shooting record; **hoja de ruta** waybill; **hoja de servicios** service record; **hoja de trébol** cloverleaf (*intersection*); **hoja maestra** master blade (*of spring*); **hojas del autor** (typ) advance sheets; **hoja suelta** leaflet, handbill; (bb) flyleaf; **hoja volante** leaflet, handbill
**hojalata** *f* tin, tin plate
**hojalatería** *f* tinsmith's shop; tinwork
**hojalatero** *m* tinsmith, tinner
**hojaldre** *m & f* puff paste
**hojarasca** *f* dead leaves; trash, rubbish; bluff, vain show
**hojear** *tr* to leaf through || *intr* to scale off; (*las hojas de los árboles*) to flutter
**hojita** *f* leaflet; **hojita de afeitar** razor blade
**hojo•so -sa** *adj* leafy
**hojuela** *f* (*hoja de otra compuesta*) leaflet; (*fruta de sartén*) pancake; (*hoja muy delgada de metal*) foil; **hojuela de estaño** tin foil
**hola** *interj* hey!, hello!
**Holanda** *f* Holland
**holan•dés -desa** *adj* Dutch; **a la holandesa** (*bb*) half-bound || *mf* Hollander || *m* Dutchman; (*idioma*) Dutch || *f* Dutch woman
**holga•chón -chona** *adj* (coll) lazy, idle || *mf* (coll) loafer, idler
**holgadero** *m* hangout
**holga•do -da** *adj* idle, unoccupied; (*vestido*) loose, full, roomy; (*que vive con bienestar*) fairly well-off
**holganza** *f* idleness, leisure; pleasure, enjoyment
**holgar** §63 *intr* to idle, be idle; to take it easy, to rest up; to not fit, be too loose; to be unnecessary, be of no use; to be glad || *ref* to be glad; to be amused
**holga•zán -zana** *adj* idle, lazy || *mf* idler, loafer
**holgazanear** *intr* to idle, loaf, bum around
**hol•gón -gona** *adj* pleasure-loving || *mf* loafer, lizard
**holgorio** *m* (coll) fun, merriment
**holgura** *f* looseness, fulness; enjoyment, merriment; comfort, easy circumstances; (mach) play
**holocausto** *m* holocaust
**hollar** §61 *tr* to tread on, to trample on
**hollejo** *m* hull, peel, skin
**hollín** *m* soot
**hollinar** *tr* (Chile) to cover with soot
**hollinien•to -ta** *adj* sooty
**hombracho** *m* big husky fellow
**hombrada** *f* manly act
**hombradía** *f* manliness, courage
**hombre** *m* man; (coll) husband, man; (coll) my boy, old chap; **buen hombre** good-natured fellow; **¡hombre al agua!** or **¡hombre a la mar!** man overboard!; **hombre bueno** arbiter,

referee; **hombre de bien** honorable man; **hombre de buenas prendas** man of parts; **hombre de dinero** man of means; **hombre de estado** statesman; **hombre de letras** man of letters; **hombre de mundo** man of the world; **hombre de suposición** man of straw; **hombre hecho** grown man || *interj* man alive!, upon my word!
**hombre-anuncio** *m* sandwich man
**hombrear** *tr* (Arg) to carry on the shoulders; (Mex) to aid, back || *intr* to try to be somebody; (*una mujer*) to be mannish; **hombrear con** to try to equal
**hombrecillo** *m* little man; (*lúpulo*) hop
**hombrera** *f* (*del vestido*) shoulder; shoulder pad; epaulet
**hombre-rana** *m* (*pl* **hombres-ranas**) frogman
**hombría** *f* manliness; **hombría de bien** honor, probity
**hombrillo** *m* (*de la camisa*) yoke; shoulder piece
**hombro** *m* shoulder; **arrimar el hombro** to lend a hand, put one's shoulder to the wheel; **encoger los hombros** to let one's shoulders droop; **encogerse de hombros** to shrug one's shoulders; to crouch, to shrink with fear; to not answer; **mirar por encima del hombro** to look down upon; **salir en hombros** to be carried off on the shoulders of the crowd
**hombru·no -na** *adj* (coll) mannish
**homenaje** *m* homage; (feud) homage; (Chile) gift, favor; **homenaje de boca** lip service; **rendir homenaje a** to swear allegiance to
**homeópata** *mf* homeopath
**homeopatía** *f* homeopathy
**homicida** *adj* homicidal || *mf* homicide
**homicidio** *m* homicide
**homilía** *f* homily
**homogeneidad** *f* homogeniety
**homogeneizar §60** *tr* to homogenize
**homogéne·o -a** *adj* homogeneous
**homologación** *f* confirmation, ratification; (sport) validation
**homologar §44** *tr* to confirm, ratify; (*un récord*) (sport) to validate
**homóni·mo -ma** *adj* homonymous; of the same name || *mf* namesake || *m* homonym
**homosexual** *adj & mf* homosexual
**homúnculo** *m* (coll) guy, little runt
**honda** *f* sling
**hondazo** *m* blow with a sling
**hondear** *tr* (naut) to sound
**hondillos** *mpl* patches in the crotch of pants
**hon·do -da** *adj* deep; (*terreno*) low || *m* bottom || *f* see **honda** || **hondo** *adv* deep
**hondón** *m* (*de la aguja*) eye; (*de un vaso*) bottom; lowland
**hondonada** *f* lowland, ravine
**hondura** *f* depth, profundity; **meterse en honduras** (coll) to go beyond one's depth
**hondure·ño -ña** *adj & mf* Honduran
**honestidad** *f* decency; chastity; modesty; honesty, probity; fairness, reasonableness
**hones·to -ta** *adj* decent; chaste, pure; modest; honest, upright; (*precio*) fair, reasonable
**hongo** *m* fungus, mushroom; (*sombrero*) bowler, derby
**honor** *m* honor; **en honor a la verdad** as a matter of fact, to tell the truth; **hacer honor a** to do honor to; (*la firma*) to honor
**honorable** *adj* honorable
**honora·rio -ria** *adj* honorary || *s* fee, honorarium
**honorífi·co -ca** *adj* honorific
**honra** *f* honor; **tener a mucha honra** to be proud of
**honradez** *f* honesty, integrity
**honra·do -da** *adj* honorable
**honrar** *tr* to honor || *ref* to feel honored
**honrilla** *f* — **por la negra honrilla** out of concern for what people will say
**honro·so -sa** *adj* honorable
**hopo** *m* tuft, shock (*of hair*); bushy tail; **seguir el hopo a** (coll) to keep right after
**hora** *f* hour; (*momento determinado para algo*) time; **a la hora** on time; **a la hora de ahora** right now; **a la hora en punto** on the hour; **a las pocas horas** within a few hours; **dar hora** to fix a time; **dar la hora** (*el reloj*) to strike; **de última hora** up-to-date; most up-to-date; (*noticias*) late; **en buen hora** or **en hora buena** safely, luckily; all right; **en mal hora** or **en hora mala** unluckily, in an evil hour; **fuera de horas** after hours; **hasta altas horas** until late into the night; **hora de acostarse** bedtime; **hora de aglomeración** rush hour; **hora de comer** mealtime; **hora deshorada** fatal hour; **hora de verano** daylight-saving time; **hora de verdad** (taur) kill; **hora legal** or **oficial** standard time; **hora punta** peak hour; rush hour; **horas de consulta** office hours (*of a doctor*); **horas de ocio** leisure hours; **horas de punta** rush hour; **horas extraordinarias de trabajo** overtime
**horadar** *tr* to drill, bore, pierce
**hora·rio -ria** *adj* hour || *m* hour hand; clock; (*de ferrocarriles*) timetable; **horario escolar** roster
**horca** *f* (*para levantar la paja*) pitchfork; (*para ahorcar a un condenado*) gallows, gibbet; (*de ajos, cebollas, etc.*) string
**horcajadas** — **a horcajadas** astride, astraddle
**horcajadillas** — **a horcajadillas** astride, astraddle
**horcajadura** *f* crotch
**horcajo** *m* (*confluencia de dos ríos*) fork; (*para mulas*) yoke
**horcón** *m* pitchfork; forked prop (*for fruit trees*); (Am) upright, prop
**horchata** *f* orgeat
**horda** *f* horde
**horizontal** *adj & f* horizontal
**horizonte** *m* horizon

**horma** *f* form, mold; shoe tree; hat block; **hallar la horma de su zapato** (coll) to meet one's match
**hormiga** *f* ant; (*enfermedad que causa comezón*) itch
**hormigón** *m* concrete; **hormigón armado** reinforced concrete
**hormigonera** *f* concrete mixer
**hormigo•so -sa** *adj* ant; full of ants; ant-eaten; (*picante*) itchy
**hormiguear** *intr* (*ponerse en movimiento gente o animales*) to swarm; (*experimentar una sensación de hormigas corriendo por el cuerpo*) to crawl, to creep; to abound, to teem
**hormiguero** *m* anthill; (*de gente*) swarm, mob
**hormillón** *m* hat block
**hormón** *m* or **hormona** *f* hormone
**hornacina** *f* niche
**hornada** *f* (*cantidad que se cuece de una vez en un horno*) batch, bake; (*conjunto de individuos de una misma promoción*) crop
**hornazo** *m* Easter cake filled with hard-boiled eggs; Easter gift to Lenten preacher
**horne•ro -ra** *mf* baker
**hornilla** *f* kitchen grate; pigeonhole
**hornillo** *m* kitchen stove; hot plate; (*de la pipa de fumar*) bowl
**horno** *m* oven, furnace; (*para cocer ladrillos*) kiln; **alto horno** blast furnace; **horno de cal** limekiln; **horno de fundición** smelting furnace; **horno de ladrillero** brickkiln
**horóscopo** *m* horoscope; **sacar un horóscopo** to cast a horoscope
**horqueta** *f* pitchfork; fork, prop; (*ángulo agudo en un río*) (Arg) bend
**horquilla** *f* pitchfork; (*de bicicleta*) fork; (*de microteléfono*) cradle; (*alfiler para sujetar el pelo*) hairpin
**hórreo** *m* granary; (in Asturias and Galicia) crib or granary raised on pillars (*to protect grain from mice and dampness*)
**horrible** *adj* horrible
**horripilante** *adj* hair-raising, blood-curdling
**horror** *m* horror; **tener horror a** to have a horror of
**horrorizar** §60 *tr* to horrify
**horroro•so -sa** *adj* horrid; (coll) hideous, ugly
**hortaliza** *f* vegetable
**hortela•no -na** *adj* garden ‖ *mf* gardener
**hortera** *m* (coll) clerk, helper ‖ *f* wooden bowl
**hortícola** *adj* horticultural
**horticul•tor -tora** *mf* horticulturist
**horticultura** *f* horticulture
**hos•co -ca** *adj* dark, dark-skinned; sullen, grim, gloomy
**hospedaje** *m* lodging
**hospedar** *tr* to lodge ‖ *ref* to lodge, stop, put up
**hospedería** *f* hospice; inn, hostelry
**hospede•ro -ra** *mf* innkeeper
**hospicio** *m* hospice; poorhouse; orphan asylum
**hospital** *m* hospital; **estar hecho un hospital** (*una persona*) (coll) to be full of aches and pains; (*una casa*) (coll) to be turned into a hospital; **hospital de la sangre** poor relations; **hospital de primera sangre** (mil) field hospital; **hospital robado** (coll) bare house
**hospitala•rio -ria** *adj* hospitable
**hospitalidad** *f* hospitality; (*estancia del enfermo en el hospital*) hospitalization
**hospitalizar** §60 *tr* to hospitalize
**hosquedad** *f* darkness; sullenness, grimness, gloominess
**hostería** *f* inn, hostelry
**hostia** *f* sacrificial victim; wafer; (eccl) wafer, Host
**hostigar** §44 *tr* to scourge; to harass; to pester; (Am) to cloy, surfeit
**hostigo•so -sa** *adj* (Am) cloying, sickening
**hostil** *adj* hostile
**hostilidad** *f* hostility
**hostilizar** §60 *tr* to antagonize; (*al enemigo*) to harry, harass
**hotel** *m* (*establecimiento donde se da comida y alojamiento por dinero*) hotel; (*casa particular lujosa*) mansion
**hotele•ro -ra** *adj* hotel ‖ *mf* hotelkeeper
**hoy** *adv & s* today; **de hoy a mañana** any time now; **de hoy en adelante** from now on; **hoy día** nowadays
**hoya** *f* hole, pit, ditch; (*sepultura*) grave; valley; (*almáciga*) seedbed; (Am) river basin
**hoyanca** *f* potter's field
**hoyo** *m* hole; grave; pockmark
**hoyo•so -sa** *adj* full of holes
**hoyuelo** *m* dimple; (*juego de muchachos*) pitching pennies
**hoz** *f* (*pl* **hoces**) sickle; narrow pass, defile; **de hoz y de coz** (coll) headlong, recklessly
**hozar** §60 *tr & intr* to nuzzle, to root
**hta.** *abbr* **hasta**
**huacal** *m* var of **guacal**
**huachinango** *m* (Mex) red snapper
**hucha** *f* workingman's chest; (*alcancía*) toy bank; (*dinero ahorrado*) savings, nest egg
**huchear** *intr* to cry, shout
**hue•co -ca** *adj* hollow; (*mullido*) soft, fluffy, spongy; (*voz*) deep, resounding; vain, conceited; (*estilo, lenguaje*) affected, pompous ‖ *m* hollow; interval; (*en un muro, una hilera de coches, etc.*) opening; (*empleo sin proveer*) (coll) opening; **hueco de la axila** armpit; **hueco de escalera** stair well
**huélfago** *m* (vet) heaves
**huelga** *f* (*ocio*) rest, leisure, idleness; recreation; pleasant spot; (*cesación del trabajo en señal de protesta*) strike; (mach) play; **huelga de brazos caídos** sit-down strike; **huelga de hambre** hunger strike; **huelga patronal** lockout; **huelga sentada** sit-down strike; **ir a la huelga** or **ponerse en huelga** to go on strike
**huelguista** *mf* striker
**huella** *f* track, footprint; trace, mark; rut; (*acción de hollar*) tread, tread-

ing; (*peldaño en que se asienta el pie*) tread; **huella dactilar** or **digital** fingerprint; **huella de sonido** sound track; **seguir las huellas de** to follow in the footsteps of
**huérfa•no -na** *adj* orphan; orphaned; alone, deserted || *mf* orphan; (Chile, Peru) foundling
**hue•ro -ra** *adj* rotten; (fig) empty, hollow; (Guat, Mex) blond; **salir huero** (coll) to flop, to turn out bad || *mf* (Guat, Mex) blond
**huerta** *f* vegetable garden; fruit garden; irrigated region
**huerte•ro -ra** *mf* (Arg, Peru) gardener
**huerto** *m* (*de árboles frutales*) orchard; (*de verduras*) kitchen garden
**huesa** *f* grave
**huesillo** *m* (Chile, Peru) sun-dried peach
**hueso** *m* bone; (*de ciertas frutas*) stone, pit; drudgery; **a otro perro con ese hueso** (coll) tell that to the marines; **calarse hasta los huesos** to get soaked to the skin; **hueso de la alegría** crazy bone, funny bone; **hueso de la suerte** wishbone; **hueso duro de roer** (coll) a hard nut to crack; **la sin hueso** (coll) the tongue; **no dejarle a uno un hueso sano** (coll) to beat someone up; (coll) to pick someone to pieces; **no poder con sus huesos** (coll) to be all in; **soltar la sin hueso** (coll) to talk too much; (coll) to pour forth insults; **tener los huesos molidos** (coll) to be all fagged out
**hueso•so -sa** *adj* bony
**hués•ped -peda** *mf* (*persona alojada en casa ajena*) guest; (*persona que hospeda a otra en su casa*) host; (*mesonero*) innkeeper, host
**hueste** *f* followers; (*ejército*) army, host
**huesu•do -da** *adj* bony, big-boned
**hueva** *f* roe, fish roe
**hueve•ro -ra** *mf* egg dealer || *f* eggcup; oviduct
**huevo** *m* egg; **huevo a la plancha** fried egg; **huevo al plato** shirred egg; **huevo del té** tea ball; **huevo de zurcir** darning egg or gourd; **huevo duro** hard-boiled egg; **huevo escalfado** poached egg; **huevo estrellado** or **frito** fried egg; **huevo pasado por agua** soft-boiled egg; **huevos revueltos** scrambled eggs
**huída** *f* flight; (*de un líquido*) leak; (*ensanche en un agujero*) flare, splay; (*de caballo*) shying
**huidi•zo -za** *adj* fugitive; evasive
**huincha** *f* (SAm) tape; (SAm) tape measure
**huipil** *m* (Mex) colorful poncho worn by Indian women
**huir §20** *tr* to flee, avoid, shun; (*el cuerpo*) to duck || *intr* to flee; (*el tiempo*) to fly; (*de la memoria*) to slip || *ref* to flee
**hule** *m* (*tela impermeable*) oilcloth; rubber; (taur) blood, goring
**hulear** *intr* (CAm) to gather rubber
**hulla** *f* coal; **hulla azul** tide power; wind power; **hulla blanca** white power, water power
**hullera** *f* colliery, coal mine
**humanidad** *f* humanity; (coll) fatness
**humanista** *adj & mf* humanist
**humanita•rio -ria** *adj & mf* humanitarian
**huma•no -na** *adj* (*perteneciente al hombre*) human; (*compasivo, misericordioso; civilizador*) humane
**humareda** *f* cloud of smoke
**humeante** *adj* smoking, smoky; steamy, reeking
**humear** *tr* (SAm) to fumigate || *intr* to smoke; to steam, to reek; to put on airs; (*reliquias de un alboroto, enemistad, etc.*) to last, persist
**humectador** *m* humidifier
**humedad** *f* humidity, dampness, moisture
**humedecer §22** *tr* to humidify, dampen, moisten, wet
**húme•do -da** *adj* humid, damp, moist
**humero** *m* smokestack, chimney
**húmero** *m* humerus
**humildad** *f* humility
**humilde** *adj* humble
**humilladero** *m* calvary, road shrine; prie-dieu
**humillante** *adj* humiliating
**humillar** *tr* (*abatir el orgullo de*) to humble; (*avergonzar*) to humiliate; (*la cabeza*) to bow; (*el cuerpo, las rodillas*) to bend || *ref* to humble oneself; to cringe, grovel
**humo** *m* smoke; steam, fume; **a humo de pajas** (coll) lightly, thoughtlessly; **bajar los humos a** (coll) to humble, take down a peg; **echar más humo que una chimenea** to smoke like a chimney; **humos** airs, conceit; hearths, homes; **irse todo en humo** to go up in smoke; **tragar el humo** to inhale; **vender humos** to peddle influence
**humor** *m* humor; **de mal humor** out of humor; **estar de humor para** to be in the humor for; **seguir el humor a** to humor
**humorismo** *m* humor, humorousness
**humorista** *mf* humorist
**humorísti•co -ca** *adj* humorous
**humo•so -sa** *adj* smoky
**hundible** *adj* sinkable
**hundir** *tr* to sink; to plunge; (*abrumar*) to overwhelm; to confound, confute; to destroy, ruin || *ref* to sink; to collapse; to settle, cave in; to come to ruin; (coll) to disappear, vanish
**húnga•ro -ra** *adj & mf* Hungarian || *m* (*idioma*) Hungarian
**Hungría** *f* Hungary
**hupe** *m* punk
**huracán** *m* hurricane
**hurañía** *f* shyness, unsociability
**hura•ño -ña** *adj* shy, unsociable
**hurgar §44** *tr* to poke; (fig) to stir up, incite; **peor es hurgallo** (i.e., **hurgarlo**) better keep hands off || *intr* to poke || *ref* (*la nariz*) to pick
**hurgón** *m* poker; (coll) thrust, stab
**hurgonazo** *m* (*con hurgón*) poke; (coll) jab, stab, thrust

**hurgonear** *tr* to poke; (coll) to jab, to stab at
**hurgonero** *m* poker
**hu•rón -rona** *adj* (coll) shy, diffident || *mf* (coll) prier, snooper; (coll) shy person, diffident person || *m* ferret
**huronear** *tr* to ferret, hunt with a ferret; (coll) to ferret out
**huronera** *f* ferret hole; (coll) lair, hiding place
**hurtadillas** — **a hurtadillas** by stealth, on the sly; **a hurtadillas de** unbeknown to
**hurtar** *tr* to steal; (*en pesos y medidas*) to cheat; (*el suelo*) to wear away; to plagiarize; **hurtar el cuerpo** to dodge, to duck || *ref* to withdraw, to hide
**hurto** *m* thieving; theft; **a hurto** stealthily, on the sly; **coger con el hurto en las manos** to catch with the goods
**husma** *f* snooping; **andar a la husma** to go around snooping
**husmear** *tr* to scent, to smell out; (coll) to pry into || *intr* (*la carne*) to smell bad, to become gamy
**husmo** *m* gaminess, high odor; **estar al husmo** (coll) to wait for a chance
**huso** *m* (*para hilar*) spindle; (*para devanar*) bobbin; (*cilindro del torno*) drum; **huso horario** time zone; **ser más derecho que un huso** (coll) to be as straight as a ramrod
**huta** *f* hunter's blind
**huy** *interj* ouch!
**huyente** *adj* (*frente*) receding; (*ojeada*) shifty

# I

**I, i** (i) *f* tenth letter of the Spanish alphabet
**ib.** *abbr* **ibídem**
**ibéri•co -ca** *adj* Iberian
**ibe•ro -ra** *adj & mf* Iberian
**íbice** *m* ibex
**ice•berg** *m* (*pl* **-bergs**) iceberg
**iconoclasia** *f* or **iconoclasmo** *m* iconoclasm
**iconoclasta** *mf* iconoclast
**iconoscopio** *m* (telv) iconoscope
**ictericia** *f* jaundice
**ictericia•do -da** *adj* jaundiced
**ictiología** *f* ichthyology
**ida** *f* going; departure; rashness; sally; trail; **de ida y vuelta** round-trip; **idas y venidas** comings and goings
**idea** *f* idea; **mudar de idea** to change one's mind
**ideal** *adj & m* ideal
**idealista** *adj & mf* idealist
**idealizar** §60 *tr* to idealize
**idear** *tr* to think up, to devise
**idemista** *adj* yes-saying || *mf* yes sayer
**idénti•co -ca** *adj* identic(al); (*muy parecido*) very similar
**identidad** *f* identity, sameness
**identificación** *f* identification
**identificar** §73 *tr* to identify
**ideología** *f* ideology
**idíli•co -ca** *adj* idyllic
**idilio** *m* idyll
**idioma** *m* language; (*modo particular de hablar*) idiom, speech
**idiomáti•co -ca** *adj* idiomatic; language, linguistic
**idiosincrasia** *f* idiosyncrasy
**idiota** *adj* idiotic || *mf* idiot
**idiotez** *f* idiocy
**idiotismo** *m* ignorance; (*idiotez*) idiocy; (gram) idiom
**i•do -da** *adj* wild, scatterbrained; (Am) drunk || **los idos** the dead || *f* see **ida**
**idolatrar** *tr* to idolize
**idolatría** *f* idolotry; (*amor excesivo a una persona*) idolization
**ídolo** *m* idol
**idoneidad** *f* fitness, suitability
**idóne•o -a** fit, suitable
**idus** *mpl* ides
**iglesia** *f* church; **entrar en la iglesia** to go into the church; **llevar a la iglesia** to lead to the altar
**iglesie•ro -ra** *adj* (Arg) church-going || *mf* (Arg) church goer
**igna•ro -ra** *adj* ignorant
**ignominio•so -sa** *adj* ignominious
**ignorancia** *f* ignorance
**ignorante** *adj* ignorant || *mf* ignoramus
**ignorar** *tr* to not know, be ignorant of
**igno•to -ta** *adj* unknown
**igual** *adj* equal; (*liso, llano*) smooth, even, level; (*no variable*) firm, constant, equable; indifferent; **me es igual** it makes no difference to me || *m* equal; equal sign; **al igual de** like, after the fashion of; **al igual que** as; while, whereas; **en igual de** instead of
**iguala** *f* equalization; agreement
**igualización** *f* equalization; agreement
**igualar** *tr* to equal; (*alisar, allanar*) to smooth, to even, to level; to make equal, to match; to deem equal || *intr & ref* to be equal
**igualdad** *f* equality; smoothness, evenness; **igualdad de ánimo** equanimity
**igualmente** *adv* likewise; **igualmente que** the same as
**ijada** *f* (*de animal*) flank; (*del cuerpo humano*) loin; (*dolor en estas partes*) stitch; **tener su ijada** to have its weak side or point
**ijadear** *intr* to pant
**ijar** *m* flank; loin
**ilegal** *adj* illegal
**ilegible** *adj* illegible
**ilegíti•mo -ma** *adj* illegitimate
**ile•so -sa** *adj* unscathed, unharmed
**iletra•do -da** *adj* unlettered, uncultured
**ilíci•to -ta** *adj* illicit, unlawful
**ilimita•do -da** *adj* limitless
**ilitera•to -ta** *adj* illiterate
**ilógi•co -ca** *adj* illogical
**iludir** *tr* to elude, evade

**iluminación** *f* illumination
**iluminar** *tr* to illuminate, light, light up || *ref* to light up, brighten
**ilusión** *f* illusion; (*esperanza infundada*) delusion; enthusiasm, zeal; dream; **forjarse** or **hacerse ilusiones** to kid oneself, to indulge in wishful thinking
**ilusionar** *tr* to delude || *ref* to have illusions, to indulge in wishful thinking; to be enraptured, be beguiled
**ilusionista** *mf* prestidigitator, magician
**ilusi•vo -va** *adj* illusive
**ilu•so -sa** *adj* deluded, misguided; (*propenso a ilusionarse*) visionary
**iluso-rio -ria** *adj* illusory
**ilustración** *f* illustration; enlightenment; illustrated magazine
**ilustra•do -da** *adj* illustrated; learned, informed; enlightened
**ilustrar** *tr* (*adornar con grabados alusivos al texto*) to illustrate; to make illustrious, make famous; to explain, elucidate; to enlighten || *ref* to become famous; to be enlightened
**ilustre** *adj* illustrious
**imagen** *f* image; picture
**imaginación** *f* imagination
**imaginar** *tr, intr & ref* to imagine
**imagina•rio -ria** *adj* imaginary
**imaginati•vo -va** *adj* imaginative || *f* imagination; understanding
**imaginería** *f* fancy colored embroidery; carving or painting of religious images
**imán** *m* magnet; (fig) loadstone; **imán de herradura** horseshoe magnet; **imán inductor** (elec) field magnet
**imanar** or **imantar** *tr* to magnetize
**imbatible** *adj* unbeatable
**imbécil** *adj & mf* imbecile
**imbecilidad** *f* imbecility
**imberbe** *adj* beardless
**imbornal** *m* drain hole
**imborrable** *adj* indelible; ineffaceable; unforgettable
**imbuir** §20 *tr* to imbue
**imitación** *adj invar* imitation || *f* imitation; **a imitación de** in imitation of; **de imitación** imitation, fake
**imita•do -da** *adj* imitated; mock, sham; imitation
**imitar** *tr* to imitate
**impaciencia** *f* impatience
**impacientar** *tr* to make impatient || *ref* to get impatient
**impaciente** *adj* impatient
**impacto** *m* impact, hit; (*señal que deja el proyectil*) mark; **impacto directo** direct hit
**impar** *adj* odd, uneven; (*que no tiene igual*) unmatched || *m* odd number
**imparcial** *adj* impartial; (*que no entra en ningún partido*) nonpartisan
**impartir** *tr* to distribute, impart
**impás** *m* finesse
**impasible** *adj* impassible, impassive
**impávi•do -da** *adj* dauntless, fearless, intrepid
**impecable** *adj* impeccable
**impedancia** *f* impedance
**impedi•do -da** *adj* disabled, crippled, paralytic
**impedimento** *m* impediment, obstacle, hindrance
**impedir** §50 *tr* to hinder, prevent
**impeler** *tr* to impel; to spur, incite
**impenetrable** *adj* impenetrable
**impenitente** *adj & mf* impenitent
**impensable** *adj* unthinkable
**impensa•do -da** *adj* unexpected
**imperar** *intr* to rule, reign, command
**imperati•vo -va** *adj & m* imperative
**imperceptible** *adj* imperceptible
**imperdible** *m* safety pin
**imperdonable** *adj* unpardonable, unforgivable
**imperecede•ro -ra** *adj* imperishable, undying
**imperfección** *f* imperfection
**imperfec•to -ta** *adj & m* imperfect
**imperial** *adj* imperial || *f* imperial, roof (*of a coach or bus*)
**imperialista** *adj & mf* imperialist
**impericia** *f* unskillfulness, inexpertness
**imperio** *m* empire; dominion, sway
**imperio•so -sa** *adj* (*que manda con imperio*) imperious; (*indispensable*) imperative
**imperi•to -ta** *adj* unskilled, inexpert
**impermeable** *adj* impermeable; waterproof || *m* raincoat
**impersonal** *adj* impersonal
**impertérri•to -ta** *adj* dauntless, intrepid
**impertinencia** *f* impertinence; irrelevance; fussiness
**impertinente** *adj* impertinent; (*que no viene al caso*) irrelevant; (*nimiamente susceptible*) fussy || **impertinentes** *mpl* lorgnette
**impetrar** *tr* to beg, beg for; to obtain by entreaty
**ímpetu** *m* impetus; force; haste
**impetuo•so -sa** *adj* impetuous
**impiedad** *f* (*falta de religión*) impiety; (*falta de compasión*) pitilessness
**impí•o -a** *adj* (*irreligioso*) impious; (*falto de compasión*) pitiless
**impla** *f* wimple
**implacable** *adj* relentless
**implantar** *tr* to implant; to introduce
**implicar** §73 *tr* (*envolver*) to implicate; (*incluir en esencia*) to imply || *intr* to stand in the way
**implíci•to -ta** *adj* implicit, implied
**implorar** *tr* to implore
**implume** *adj* featherless
**imponente** *adj* imposing || *mf* depositor, investor
**imponer** §54 *tr* (*la voluntad de uno, silencio, tributos*) to impose; (*dinero a rédito*) to invest; (*dinero en depósito*) to deposit; to instruct; to impute falsely || *intr* to dominate, command respect || *ref* (*responsabilidades*) to assume; to command attention, command respect; **imponerse a** to dominate, command the respect of; **imponerse de** to learn, to find out
**imponible** *adj* taxable
**impopular** *adj* unpopular
**impopularidad** *f* unpopularity
**importación** *f* importation; import; imports
**importa•dor -dora** *mf* importer
**importancia** *f* importance; (*extensión,*

*tamaño*) size; **ser de la importancia de** to be the concern of
**importante** *adj* important; large
**importar** *tr* (*introducir en un país*) to import; to amount to; to involve, imply; to concern || *intr* to import; to be important; to matter
**importe** *m* amount
**importunar** *tr* to importune
**importu•no -na** *adj* (*molesto*) importunate; (*fuera de sazón*) inopportune
**imposibilita•do -da** *adj* paralyzed, disabled
**imposibilitar** *tr* to make impossible || *ref* to become paralyzed, become disabled
**imposible** *adj* impossible
**imposición** *f* (*de la voluntad de uno*) imposition; burden; imposture; (*de dinero*) deposit; (typ) make-up
**impos•tor -tora** *mf* impostor; slanderer
**impostura** *f* imposture
**impotable** *adj* undrinkable
**impotencia** *f* impotence
**impotente** *adj* impotent
**impracticable** *adj* impracticable, impassable; impractical
**impregnar** *tr* to impregnate, to saturate
**impremedita•do -da** *adj* unpremeditated
**imprenta** *f* printing; printing shop; (*lo que se publica impreso*) printed matter; (*máquina para imprimir o prensar; conjunto de periódicos o periodistas*) press
**imprentar** *tr* (*la ropa*) (Chile) to press, to iron; (Ecuad) to mark
**imprescindible** *adj* indispensable, essential
**impresentable** *adj* unpresentable
**impresión** *f* (*efecto producido en el ánimo; señal que una cosa deja en otra por presión*) impression; (*acción de imprimir*) printing; (*los ejemplares de una edición*) edition, issue; (phot) print; **impresión dactilar** or **digital** fingerprint
**impresionable** *adj* impressionable
**impresionante** *adj* impressive
**impresionar** *tr* to impress; (*un disco fonográfico*) to record; (phot) to expose || *intr* to make an impression || *ref* to be impressed
**impreso** *m* printed paper or book; **impresos** printed matter
**impre•sor -sora** *mf* printer
**imprevisible** *adj* unforeseeable
**imprevisión** *f* improvidence, lack of foresight
**imprevi•sor -sora** *adj* improvident
**imprevis•to -ta** *adj* unforeseen, unexpected || **imprevistos** *mpl* emergencies, unforeseen expenses
**imprimar** *tr* to prime
**imprimir** *tr* (*respeto, miedo; movimiento*) to impart || §83 *tr* to stamp, imprint, impress; (*un disco fonográfico*) to press; (typ) to print
**improbable** *adj* improbable
**improbar** §61 *tr* to disapprove
**improbidad** *f* dishonesty; hardness, arduousness
**impro•bo -ba** *adj* dishonest; (*trabajo*) arduous
**improcedente** *adj* wrong; unfit, untimely
**improducti•vo -va** *adj* unproductive; unemployed
**impronunciable** *adj* unpronounceable
**improperar** *tr* to insult, revile
**improperio** *m* insult, affront
**impropi•cio -cia** *adj* unpropitious
**impro•pio -pia** *adj* improper; (*ajeno*) foreign
**impróspe•ro -ra** *adj* unsuccessful
**impróvi•do -da** *adj* unprepared
**improvisación** *f* improvisation; meteoric rise; (mus) impromptu
**improvisadamente** *adv* suddenly, unexpectedly; extempore
**improvisar** *tr & intr* to improvise
**improvi•so -sa** *adj* unforeseen, unexpected
**imprudencia** *f* imprudence; **imprudencia temeraria** criminal negligence
**imprudente** *adj* imprudent
**impudicia** *f* immodesty
**impúdi•co -ca** *adj* immodest
**impues•to -ta** *adj* informed || *m* tax; **impuesto sobre la renta** income tax
**impugnar** *tr* to impugn, to contest
**impulsar** *tr* to impel; to drive
**impulsión** *f* impulse, drive
**impulsi•vo -va** *adj* impulsive
**impulso** *m* impulse
**impune** *adj* unpunished
**impunidad** *f* impunity
**impureza** *f* impurity
**impu•ro -ra** *adj* impure
**imputar** *tr* to impute; to credit on account
**inabordable** *adj* unapproachable
**inacabable** *adj* endless, interminable
**inaccesible** *adj* inaccessible
**inacción** *f* inaction
**inacentua•do -da** *adj* unaccented
**inactividad** *f* inactivity
**inacti•vo -va** *adj* inactive
**inadecua•do -da** *adj* inadequate; unsuited
**inadvertencia** *f* inadvertence, oversight
**inadverti•do -da** *adj* inadvertent, unwitting; careless, thoughtless; unseen, unnoticed
**inagotable** *adj* inexhaustible
**inaguantable** *adj* unbearable
**inalámbri•co -ca** *adj* wireless
**inalcanzable** *adj* unattainable
**inamisto•so -sa** *adj* unfriendly
**inamovible** *adj* irremovable; undetachable; (*incorporado*) built-in
**inamovilidad** *f* irremovability; tenure, permanent tenure
**inane** *adj* inane
**inanición** *f* starvation
**inanima•do -da** *adj* inanimate, lifeless
**inapelable** *adj* unappealable; unavoidable
**inapetencia** *f* loss of appetite
**inapreciable** *adj* inappreciable; imperceptible
**inarmóni•co -ca** *adj* unharmonious
**inarrugable** *adj* wrinkle-free
**inarticula•do -da** *adj* inarticulate
**inartísti•co -ca** *adj* inartistic
**inasequible** *adj* unattainable; unobtainable

**inastillable** *adj* nonshatterable, shatterproof
**inatacable** *adj* unattackable; **inatacable por** resistant to
**inaudi•to -ta** *adj* unheard-of; outrageous
**inauguración** *f* inauguration; (*de una estatua*) unveiling
**inaugural** *adj* inaugural
**inaugurar** *tr* to inaugurate; (*p.ej., una estatua*) to unveil
**inaveriguable** *adj* unascertainable
**inca** *mf* Inca
**incai•co -ca** *adj* Inca, Incan
**incalificable** *adj* unqualifiable; (*infame, atroz*) unspeakable
**incambiable** *adj* unchangeable
**incandescent** *adj* incandescent
**incansable** *adj* untiring, indefatigable
**incapacitar** *tr* to incapacitate; (law) to declare incompetent
**inca•paz** *adj* (*pl* **-paces**) incapable, unable; not large enough; stupid; (law) incompetent; (coll) frightful, unbearable
**incasable** *adj* unmarriageable; opposed to marriage; (*por su fealdad*) unable to find a husband
**incautar** *ref* — **incautarse de** to hold until claimed; (law) to seize, to attach
**incau•to -ta** *adj* unwary, heedless
**incendajas** *fpl* kindling
**incendiar** *tr* to set on fire || *ref* to catch fire
**incendia•rio -ria** *adj* incendiary || *mf* incendiary, firebug
**incendio** *m* fire; (fig) fire, passion
**incensar** §2 *tr* to incense, to burn incense before; (fig) to flatter
**incensario** *m* censer, incense burner
**incenti•vo -va** *adj & m* incentive
**inceremonio•so -sa** *adj* unceremonious
**incertidumbre** *f* uncertainty, incertitude
**incesante** *adj* unceasing
**incesto** *m* incest
**incestuo•so -sa** *adj* incestuous
**incidencia** *f* incidence; **por incidencia** by chance
**incidente** *adj* incident; incidental || *m* incident
**incidir** *tr* to make an incision in || *intr* — **incidir en culpa** to fall into guilt; **incidir en** or **sobre** to strike, to impinge on
**incienso** *m* incense; (*olíbano*) frankincense
**incier•to -ta** *adj* uncertain
**incineración** *f* incineration; (*de cadáveres*) cremation
**incinerar** *tr* to incinerate; (*cadáveres*) to cremate
**incipiente** *adj* incipient
**incisión** *f* incision; (*mordacidad en el lenguaje*) incisiveness, sarcasm
**incisi•vo -va** *adj* incisive; biting, sarcastic
**inci•so -sa** *adj* (*estilo del escritor*) choppy || *m* comma; clause; sentence
**incitar** *tr* to incite
**incivil** *adj* rude, impolite
**inciviliza•do -da** *adj* uncivilized
**inclemencia** *f* inclemency; **a la inclemencia** in the open, without shelter
**inclemente** *adj* inclement
**inclinación** *f* inclination; bent, leaning, propensity; nod, bow
**inclinar** *tr, intr & ref* to incline; to bend, to bow
**ínclí•to -ta** *adj* illustrious, renowned
**incluir** §20 *tr* to include; (*en una carta*) to inclose
**inclusa** *f* foundling home
**incluse•ro -ra** *mf* (coll) foundling
**inclusión** *f* inclusion; friendship
**inclusive** *adv* inclusive, inclusively || *prep* including
**inclusi•vo -va** *adj* inclusive
**inclu•so -sa** *adj* inclosed || *f* see **inclusa** || **incluso** *adv* inclusively; (*hasta, aun*) even || **incluso** *prep* including
**incobrable** *adj* uncollectible; irrecoverable
**incógni•to -ta** *adj* (*no conocido*) unknown; (*que no se da a conocer*) incognito || *mf* (*persona*) incognito || *m* (*condición de no ser conocido*) incognito; **de incógnito** (*sin ser conocido*) incognito || *f* (math & fig) unknown quantity
**incoherente** *adj* incoherent
**íncola** *m* inhabitant
**incolo•ro -ra** *adj* colorless
**incólume** *adj* unharmed, safe
**incombustible** *adj* incombustible, fireproof; cold, indifferent
**incomerciable** *adj* unmarketable
**incomible** *adj* uneatable, inedible
**incomodar** *tr* to inconvenience, to disturb
**incomodidad** *f* inconvenience; annoyance, discomfort
**incómo•do -da** *adj* inconvenient; annoying, uncomfortable || *m* inconvenience; discomfort
**incomparable** *adj* incomparable
**incompartible** *adj* unsharable
**incompasi•vo -va** *adj* pitiless, unsympathetic
**incompatible** *adj* incompatible; (*acontecimientos, citas, horas de clase, etc.*) conflicting
**incompetente** *adj* incompetent
**incompetible** *adj* unmatchable
**incomple•to -ta** *adj* incomplete
**incomponible** *adj* unmendable, beyond repair
**incomprable** *adj* unpurchasable
**incomprensible** *adj* incomprehensible
**incomunicación** *f* isolation, solitary confinement
**inconcebible** *adj* inconceivable
**inconclu•so -sa** *adj* unfinished
**inconcluyente** *adj* inconclusive
**inconcu•so -sa** *adj* undeniable
**incondicional** *adj* unconditional
**incone•xo -xa** *adj* unconnected; (*inaplicable*) irrelevant
**inconfidente** *adj* distrustful
**inconfundible** *adj* unmistakable
**incon•gruo -grua** *adj* incongruous
**inconocible** *adj* unknowable
**inconquistable** *adj* unconquerable; (*que no se deja vencer con ruegos y dádivas*) unbending, unyielding
**inconsciencia** *f* unconsciousness; unawareness

**inconsciente** *adj* unconscious; unaware; **lo inconsciente** the unconscious
**inconsecuencia** *f* (*falta de consecuencia o correspondencia en dichos y hechos*) inconsistency
**inconsecuente** *adj* inconsistent; (*que no se deduce de otra cosa*) inconsequential
**inconsidera•do -da** *adj* inconsiderate
**inconsiguiente** *adj* inconsequential, illogical
**inconsistencia** *f* (*falta de cohesión*) inconsistency
**inconsistente** *adj* inconsistent
**inconsolable** *adj* inconsolable
**inconstante** *adj* inconstant
**inconstitucional** *adj* unconstitutional
**inconsútil** *adj* seamless
**incontable** *adj* countless, innumerable
**incontenible** *adj* irrepressible
**incontestable** *adj* incontestable
**incontinente** *adj* incontinent || *adv* at once, instantly
**incontrastable** *adj* invincible; inconvincible; (*argumento*) unanswerable
**incontrovertible** *adj* incontrovertible
**inconveniencia** *f* inconvenience; unsuitability; impoliteness; impropriety
**inconveniente** *adj* inconvenient; unsuitable; impolite; improper || *m* drawback, disadvantage; objection
**incordio** *m* (coll) bore, nuisance
**incorporación** *f* incorporation, embodiment
**incorpora•do -da** *adj* (*el que estaba echado*) sitting up; (*montado en la construcción*) built-in
**incorporar** *tr* to incorporate, embody || *ref* to incorporate; (*el que estaba echado*) to sit up; **incorporarse a** to join
**incorrec•to -ta** *adj* incorrect
**incrédu•lo -la** *adj* incredulous || *mf* disbeliever, doubter
**increíble** *adj* incredible
**incremento** *m* increment, increase
**increpar** *tr* to chide, to rebuke
**incriminar** *tr* to incriminate; (*un delito, falta, defecto*) to exaggerate the gravity of
**incruen•to -ta** *adj* bloodless
**incrustar** *tr* to incrust; (*embutir por adorno*) to inlay
**incubadora** *f* incubator
**incubar** *tr & intr* to incubate || *ref* (fig) to be brewing
**incuestionable** *adj* unquestionable
**inculcar** §73 *tr* to inculcate || *ref* to become obstinate
**inculpable** *adj* blameless, guiltless
**inculpar** *tr* to accuse, to blame
**incultivable** *adj* untillable
**incul•to -ta** *adj* uncultivated, untilled; uncultured; (*estilo*) coarse, sloppy
**incumbencia** *f* incumbency, duty, obligation, province
**incumbir** *intr* — **incumbir a** to be incumbent on
**incumplimiento** *m* nonfulfillment
**incunable** *m* incunabulum
**incurable** *adj & mf* incurable
**incuria** *f* carelessness, negligence
**incurio•so -sa** *adj* careless, negligent
**incurrir** *intr* — **incurrir en** to incur
**incursión** *f* incursion, inroad, raid
**indagación** *f* investigation, research
**indagar** §44 *tr* to investigate
**indebidamente** *adv* unduly
**indebi•do -da** *adj* undue; wrong
**indecencia** *f* indecency
**indecente** *adj* indecent
**indecible** *adj* unspeakable, unutterable
**indeci•so -sa** *adj* undecided, indecisive; (*contorno, forma*) vague, obscure
**indeclinable** *adj* unavoidable; (gram) indeclinable
**indecoro•so -sa** *adj* improper
**indefectible** *adj* unfailing
**indefendible** *adj* indefensible
**indefen•so -sa** *adj* defenceless, undefended
**indefinible** *adj* indefinable
**indefini•do -da** *adj* indefinite; limitless; vague
**indeleble** *adj* indelible
**indelibera•do -da** *adj* unpremeditated
**indelica•do -da** *adj* indelicate
**indemne** *adj* unharmed, undamaged
**indemnidad** *f* (*seguridad contra un daño*) indemnity
**indemnización** *f* (*compensación*) indemnity, indemnification; **indemnización por despido** severance pay
**indemnizar** §60 *tr* to indemnify
**independencia** *f* independence
**independiente** *adj & mf* independent
**independizar** §60 *tr* to free, to emancipate || *ref* to become independent
**indescriptible** *adj* indescribable
**indeseable** *adj & mf* undesirable
**indesea•do -da** *adj* unwanted
**indesmallable** *adj* runproof
**indestructible** *adj* indestructible
**indetermina•do -da** *adj* indeterminate; (gram) indefinite
**indevo•to -ta** *adj* impious; not fond, not devoted
**india** *f* wealth, riches; **Indias Occidentales** West Indies; **la India** India
**indiana** *f* printed calico
**india•no -na** *adj & mf* Spanish American; East Indian; West Indian || *m* man back from America with great wealth; **indiano de hilo negro** (coll) skinflint || *f* see **indiana**
**indicación** *f* indication; **por indicación de** at the direction of
**indica•do -da** *adj* appropriate, advisable; **muy indicado** just the thing, just the person
**indica•dor -dora** *adj* indicating, pointing || *m* indicator; gauge; (*de tránsito*) traffic signal
**indicar** §73 *tr* to indicate
**indicati•vo -va** *adj & m* indicative
**índice** *m* index; **índice de libros prohibidos** (eccl) Index; **índice de materias** table of contents; **índice en el corte** thumb index
**indiciar** *tr* to betoken, indicate; to surmise, suspect
**indicio** *m* sign, token, indication; **indicios vehementes** circumstantial evidence
**indiferente** *adj* indifferent; (*que no importa*) immaterial

**indígena** *adj* indigenous || *mf* native
**indigente** *adj* indigent
**indigestar** *ref* to be indigestible; (coll) to be disliked, to be unbearable
**indigestible** *adj* indigestible
**indigestión** *f* indigestion
**indignación** *f* indignation
**indigna•do -da** *adj* indignant
**indignar** *tr* to anger, to provoke || *ref* to become indignant
**indignidad** *f* (*falta de mérito*) unworthiness; (*acción reprobable*) indignity
**indig•no -na** *adj* unworthy
**índigo** *m* indigo
**in•dio -dia** *adj & mf* Indian || *f* see **india**
**indirec•to -ta** *adj* indirect || *f* hint, innuendo; **indirecta del padre Cobos** broad hint
**indiscernible** *adj* indiscernible
**indiscre•to -ta** *adj* indiscreet
**indisculpable** *adj* inexcusable
**indiscutible** *adj* undeniable
**indisoluble** *adj* indissoluble
**indispensable** *adj* unpardonable; indispensable
**indisponer** §54 *tr* (*alterar la salud de*) to indispose, upset; to disturb, to upset; **indisponer a uno con** to set someone against, to prejudice someone against || *ref* to become indisposed; **indisponerse con** to fall out with
**indisponible** *adj* unavailable
**indispues•to -ta** *adj* indisposed
**indistintamente** *adv* indistinctly; indiscriminately, without distinction
**indistin•to -ta** *adj* indistinct
**individual** *adj* individual; (*habitación en un hotel; partido de tenis*) single
**individualidad** *f* individuality
**indivi•duo -dua** *adj* individual; indivisible || *mf* (*persona indeterminada*) (coll) individual || *m* (*cada persona*) individual; (*miembro de una corporación*) member, fellow
**indócil** *adj* unteachable; headstrong, unruly
**indocumenta•do -da** *adj* unidentified; unqualified || *mf* nobody (*person of no account*)
**indochi•no -na** *adj & mf* Indo-Chinese || **la Indochina** Indochina
**indoeurope•o -a** *adj & m* Indo-European
**índole** *f* kind, class; nature, disposition, temper
**indolente** *adj* stolid, impassive; (*perezoso*) indolent
**indolo•ro -ra** *adj* painless
**indoma•do -da** *adj* untamed
**indone•sio -sia** *adj & mf* Indonesian || **la Indonesia** Indonesia
**inducción** *f* induction
**inducido** *m* (*de dínamo o motor*) (elec) armature
**inducir** §19 *tr* to induce
**inductor** *m* (*de dínamo o motor*) (elec) field
**indudable** *adj* doubtless
**indulgente** *adj* indulgent
**indultar** *tr* to pardon; to free, exempt
**indulto** *m* pardon; exemption
**indumentaria** *f* clothing, dress; historical study of clothing
**indumento** *m* clothing, dress
**industria** *f* industry; **de industria** on purpose
**industrial** *adj* industrial || *m* industrialist
**industrializar** §60 *tr* to industrialize
**industriar** *tr* to teach, instruct, train || *ref* to get along, to manage
**industrio•so -sa** *adj* industrious
**inédi•to -ta** *adj* unpublished; new, novel, unknown
**inefable** *adj* ineffable
**ineficacia** *f* inefficacy
**inefi•caz** *adj* (*pl* **-caces**) inefficacious, ineffectual
**inelegible** *adj* ineligible
**ineludible** *adj* inescapable
**inenarrable** *adj* indescribable
**inencogible** *adj* unshrinkable
**inencontrable** *adj* unobtainable
**inequidad** *f* inequity
**inequívo•co -ca** *adj* unmistakable
**inercia** *f* inertia
**inerme** *adj* unarmed
**inerte** *adj* inert; slow, sluggish
**inescrupulo•so -sa** *adj* unscrupulous
**inescrutable** or **inescudriñable** *adj* inscrutable
**inespera•do -da** *adj* unexpected, unforeseen; unhoped-for
**inestable** *adj* unstable
**inevitable** *adj* unavoidable, inevitable
**inexactitud** *f* inaccuracy, inexactness
**inexac•to -ta** *adj* inaccurate, inexact
**inexcusable** *adj* inexcusable, unpardonable; unavoidable; indispensable
**inexorable** *adj* inexorable
**inexperiencia** *f* inexperience
**inexplicable** *adj* inexplicable, unexplainable
**inexplica•do -da** *adj* unexplained, unaccounted-for
**inexplora•do -da** *adj* unexplored; (*mar*) uncharted
**inexpresable** *adj* inexpressible
**inexpues•to -ta** *adj* (phot) unexposed
**inexpugnable** *adj* impregnable; firm, unshakable
**inextinguible** *adj* unextinguishable; perpetual, lasting; (*sed*) unquenchable; (*risa*) uncontrollable
**inextirpable** *adj* ineradicable
**infalible** *adj* infallible
**infamación** *f* defamation
**infamar** *tr* to defame, discredit
**infame** *adj* infamous; (coll) vile, frightful || *mf* scoundrel
**infamia** *f* infamy
**infancia** *f* infancy
**infan•do -da** *adj* odious, unmentionable
**infanta** *f* female child; infanta (*any daughter of a king of Spain; wife of an infante*)
**infante** *m* male child; infante (*any son of a king of Spain who is not heir to the throne*); (mil) infantryman; **infante de coro** choirboy
**infantería** *f* infantry; **infantería de marina** marines, marine corps
**infantil** *adj* infant, infantile, childlike; innocent

**infatigable** *adj* indefatigable
**infatuar** §21 *tr* to make vain || *ref* to become vain
**infaus•to -ta** *adj* fatal, unlucky
**infección** *f* infection
**infeccionar** *tr* to infect
**infeccio•so -sa** *adj* infectious
**infectar** *tr* to infect
**infec•to -ta** *adj* foul, corrupt; infected; fetid
**infecun•do -da** *adj* sterile, barren
**infe•liz** (*pl* **-lices**) *adj* unhappy; (coll) simple, good-hearted || *m* wretch, poor soul
**inferior** *adj* inferior; lower; **inferior a** inferior to; lower than; less than; smaller than || *m* inferior
**inferioridad** *f* inferiority
**inferir** §68 *tr* to infer; to lead to, to entail; (*una herida*) to inflict; (*una ofensa*) to cause, offer
**infernáculo** *m* hopscotch
**infernal** *adj* infernal
**infernar** §2 *tr* to damn; to irritate, annoy
**infernillo** *m* chafing dish
**infestar** *tr* infest || *ref* to become infested
**inficionar** *tr* to infect || *ref* to become infected
**infidelidad** *f* infidelity; (*conjunto de infieles*) unbelievers
**infidente** *adj* faithless, disloyal
**infiel** *adj* (*falto de fidelidad*) unfaithful; (*no exacto*) inaccurate, inexact; (*no cristiano*) infidel || *mf* infidel
**infierno** *m* hell; **en el quinto infierno** or **en los quintos infiernos** (coll) far, far away
**infijo** *m* (gram) infix
**infiltrar** *tr & ref* to infiltrate
**ínfi•mo -ma** *adj* lowest; humblest, most abject; meanest, vilest
**infinidad** *f* infinity
**infiniti•vo -va** *adj & m* infinitive
**infini•to -ta** *adj* infinite || *m* infinite; (math) infinity || **infinito** *adv* greatly, very much
**infirme** *adj* infirm
**inflación** *f* inflation; (*vanidad*) conceit
**inflado** *m* inflation (*of a tire*)
**inflamable** *adj* inflammable, flammable
**inflamación** *f* ignition, inflammation; ardor, enthusiasm; (pathol) inflammation
**inflamar** *tr* to set on fire; to inflame || *ref* to catch fire; to become inflamed
**inflar** *tr* to inflate; to exaggerate; to puff up with pride || *ref* to inflate; to be puffed up with pride
**inflexible** *adj* inflexible; unyielding, unbending
**inflexión** *f* inflection; **inflexión vocálica** (*metafonía*) umlaut
**inflexionar** *tr* to umlaut
**infligir** §27 *tr* to inflict
**influencia** *f* influence
**influenciar** *tr* to influence
**influenza** *f* influenza
**influir** §20 *intr* to have influence; to have great weight; **influir en** or **sobre** to influence
**influjo** *m* influence; rising tide
**influyente** *adj* influential
**información** *f* information; (law) judicial inquiry, investigation; **informaciones** testimonial
**informal** *adj* (*que no se ajusta a las reglas debidas*) informal; unreliable
**informar** *tr & intr* to inform || *ref* to inquire, find out
**informati•vo -va** *adj* informational; (*sección de un periódico*) news
**informe** *adj* shapeless, formless; misshapen || *m* piece of information; report; **informes** information; **informes confidenciales** inside information
**infortuna•do -da** *adj* unfortunate, unlucky
**infortunio** *m* misfortune; (*acaecimiento desgraciado*) mishap
**infracción** *f* infraction, infringement
**infraconsumo** *m* underconsumption
**infrac•to -ta** *adj* unperturbable
**infraestructura** *f* substructure; (rr) roadbed
**inframundo** *m* underworld
**infrarro•jo -ja** *adj & m* infrared
**infrascri•to -ta** *adj* undersigned; hereinafter mentioned
**infrecuente** *adj* infrequent
**infringir** §27 *tr* to infringe, to break, to violate
**infructuo•so -sa** *adj* fruitless, unfruitful
**ínfulas** *fpl* conceit, airs; **darse ínfulas** to put on airs
**infunda•do -da** *adj* unfounded, groundless, baseless
**infundio** *m* (coll) lie, fib
**infundir** *tr* to infuse, to instill
**infusión** *f* infusion; (*acción de echar agua sobre el que se bautiza*) sprinkling; **estar en infusión para** (coll) to be all set for
**ingeniar** *tr* to think up || *ref* to manage; **ingeniarse a** or **para** to manage to; **ingeniarse para ir viviendo** to manage to get along
**ingeniería** *f* engineering
**ingeniero** *m* engineer; **ingeniero de caminos, canales y puertos** government civil engineer
**ingenio** *m* talent, creative faculty; talented person; cleverness, skill, wit; (*artificio mecánico*) apparatus, device; (*del encuadernador*) paper cutter; engine of war; **afilar** or **aguzar el ingenio** to sharpen one's wits; **ingenio de azúcar** sugar refinery
**ingeniosidad** *f* ingenuity; wittiness
**ingenio•so -sa** *adj* (*dotado de ingenio; hecho con ingenio*) ingenious; (*agudo, sutil*) witty
**ingéni•to -ta** *adj* innate, inborn
**ingente** *adj* huge, enormous
**ingenuidad** *f* ingenuousness
**inge•nuo -nua** *adj* ingenuous
**ingerir** §68 *tr & ref* var of **injerir**
**Inglaterra** *f* England; **la Nueva Inglaterra** New England
**ingle** *f* groin
**in•glés -glesa** *adj* English; **a la inglesa** in the English manner || *m* Englishman; (*idioma*) English; **el inglés medio** Middle English; **los ingleses** the English || *f* Englishwoman

**ingramatical** *adj* ungrammatical
**ingratitud** *f* ingratitude, ungratefulness
**ingra•to -ta** *adj* (*desagradecido*) ungrateful; (*desagradecido; desagradable, áspero; improductivo*) thankless || *mf* ingrate
**ingravidez** *f* lightness, tenuousness; (*gravedad nula*) weightlessness
**ingrávi•do -da** *adj* light, tenuous; weightless
**ingrediente** *m* ingredient
**ingresa•do -da** *mf* new student
**ingresar** *tr* to deposit || *intr* to enter, become a member; (*beneficios*) to come in || *ref* (Mex) to enlist
**ingreso** *m* entrance; admission; **ingresos** income, revenue
**ingri•mo -ma** *adj* (Am) solitary, alone
**inhábil** *adj* unable; unskillful; unfit, unqualified
**inhabilidad** *f* inability; unskillfulness; unfitness
**inhabilitar** *tr* to disable, to disqualify, to incapacitate
**inhabita•do -da** *adj* uninhabited
**inhabitua•do -da** *adj* unaccustomed
**inherente** *adj* inherent
**inhibir** *tr* to inhibit
**inhospitala•rio -ria** *adj* inhospitable
**inhóspi•to -ta** *adj* inhospitable
**inhumanidad** *f* inhumanity
**inhuma•no -na** *adj* inhuman, inhumane; (Chile) filthy
**iniciación** *f* initiation
**inicial** *adj* & *f* initial
**iniciar** *tr* to initiate || *ref* to be initiated
**iniciativa** *f* initiative
**ini•cuo -cua** *adj* wicked, iniquitous
**iniguala•do -da** *adj* unequaled
**ininteligente** *adj* unintelligent
**ininteligible** *adj* unintelligible
**ininterrumpi•do -da** *adj* uninterrupted
**iniquidad** *f* iniquity
**injerencia** *f* interference, meddling
**injerir §68** *tr* to insert, introduce; (hort) to graft; (*alimentos*) (Am) to take in || *ref* to interfere, meddle, intrude
**injertar** *tr* (hort & surg) to graft
**injerto** *m* (hort & surg) graft
**injuria** *f* offense, insult; abuse, wrong; damage, harm
**injuriar** *tr* to offend, insult; to abuse, to wrong; to harm, damage
**injurio•so -sa** *adj* offensive, insulting; abusive; harmful; (*lenguaje*) profane
**injusticia** *f* injustice
**injustifica•do -da** *adj* unjustified
**injus•to -ta** *adj* unjust
**inmacula•do -da** *adj* immaculate
**inmanejable** *adj* unmanageable; unhandy
**inmarcesible** *adj* unfading
**inmaterial** *adj* immaterial
**inmaturo -ra** *adj* immature
**inmediación** *f* immediacy; proximity, nearness; **inmediaciones** neighborhood, outskirts
**inmediatamente** *adv* immediately; **inmediatamente que** as soon as
**inmedia•to -ta** *adj* immediate; close, adjoining, next; next above; next below; (*pago*) prompt; **venir a las inmediatas** (coll) to get into the thick of the fight
**inmejorable** *adj* superb, unsurpassable
**inmemorial** *adj* immemorial
**inmen•so -sa** *adj* immense
**inmensurable** *adj* immesurable
**inmereci•do -da** *adj* undeserved
**inmergir §27** *tr* to immerse
**inmersión** *f* immersion
**inmigración** *f* immigration
**inmigrante** *mf* immigrant
**inmigrar** *intr* to immigrate
**inminente** *adj* imminent
**inmiscuir §20 & regular** *tr* to mix || *ref* to meddle, to interfere
**inmobila•rio -ria** *adj* real-estate
**inmoble** *adj* motionless; firm, constant
**inmodera•do -da** *adj* immoderate
**inmodes•to -ta** *adj* immodest
**inmódi•co -ca** *adj* excessive
**inmoral** *adj* immoral
**inmortal** *adj* immortal, deathless || *mf* immortal
**inmortalizar §60** *tr* to immortalize
**inmovilizar §60** *tr* to immobilize; (*un caudal*) to tie up
**inmueble** *m* property, piece of real estate; **inmuebles** real estate
**inmun•do -da** *adj* dirty, filthy
**inmune** *adj* immune
**inmunizar §60** *tr* to immunize
**inmutar** *tr* to change, alter; to disturb, upset || *ref* to change, alter; to change countenance; **sin inmutarse** without batting an eye
**inna•to -ta** *adj* innate, inborn; natural
**innatural** *adj* unnatural
**innavegable** *adj* (*río*) unnavigable; (*embarcación*) unseaworthy
**innecesa•rio -ria** *adj* unnecessary
**innegable** *adj* undeniable
**innoble** *adj* ignoble
**inno•cuo -cua** *adj* harmless
**innovación** *f* innovation
**innovar** *tr* to innovate
**innumerable** *adj* innumerable
**inocencia** *f* innocence
**inocentada** *f* (coll) simpleness; (coll) blunder; (Ecuad) April Fools' joke
**inocente** *adj* & *mf* innocent; **coger por inocente** to make an April fool of
**inocen•tón -tona** *adj* (coll) simple, gullible || *mf* (coll) gull, dupe
**inoculación** *f* inoculation
**inocular** *tr* to inoculate; to contaminate, to pervert
**inodo•ro -ra** *adj* odorless || *m* deodorizer; (*excusado que funciona con agua corriente*) toilet
**inofensi•vo -va** *adj* inoffensive
**inolvidable** *adj* unforgettable
**inope** *adj* impecunious
**inopia** *f* indigence
**inoportu•no -na** *adj* inopportune, untimely
**inorgáni•co -ca** *adj* inorganic
**inortodo•xo -xa** *adj* unorthodox
**inoxidable** *adj* (*acero*) stainless; inoxidizable
**inquietante** *adj* disquieting, upsetting
**inquietar** *tr* to disquiet, to worry; to stir up, excite
**inquie•to -ta** *adj* anxious, worried

**inquietud** *f* disquiet, worry, concern
**inquili•no -na** *mf* tenant, renter
**inquina** *f* aversion, dislike, ill will
**inquirir** §40 *tr* to inquire, inquire into
**inquisición** *f* inquiry; inquisition
**insabible** *adj* unknowable
**insaciable** *adj* insatiable
**insania** *f* insanity
**insa•no -na** *adj* insane; imprudent
**insatisfe•cho -cha** *adj* unsatisfied
**inscribir** §83 *tr* to inscribe; (law) to record || *ref* to enroll, register
**inscripción** *f* inscription; enrollment, registration
**insecticida** *adj* & *m* insecticide
**insecto** *m* insect
**insegu•ro -ra** *adj* insecure, unsafe; uncertain
**insensa•to -ta** *adj* foolish, stupid
**insensible** *adj* callous, hard-hearted, unfeeling; imperceptible
**inseparable** *adj* inseparable; undetachable || *mf* inseparable || *m* lovebird
**insepul•to -ta** *adj* unburied
**inserción** *f* insertion
**inserir** §68 *tr* to insert; (*injertar*) to graft, engraft
**insertar** *tr* to insert
**inservible** *adj* useless
**insidia** *f* snare, ambush; plotting
**insidiar** *tr* to ambush, to waylay; to trap, to trick
**insidio•so -sa** *adj* insidious
**insigne** *adj* noted, famous, renowned
**insignia** *f* badge, decoration, insignia; banner, standard
**insignificante** *adj* insignificant
**insince•ro -ra** *adj* insincere
**insinuación** *f* insinuation, hint
**insinuante** *adj* engaging, slick, crafty
**insinuar** §21 *tr* to insinuate; to suggest, to hint at || *ref* to creep in, to slip in; to ingratiate oneself; to flow, to run; **insinuarse en** to work one's way in
**insípi•do -da** *adj* insipid, vapid
**insistir** *intr* to insist
**ínsi•to -ta** *adj* inbred, innate
**insociable** *adj* unsociable
**insolencia** *f* insolence
**insolentar** *tr* to make insolent || *ref* to become insolent
**insolente** *adj* insolent
**insóli•to -ta** *adj* unusual
**insoluble** *adj* insoluble
**insolvencia** *f* insolvency
**insomne** *adj* sleepless
**insomnio** *m* insomnia
**insondable** *adj* fathomless; inscrutable
**insonorizar** §60 *tr* to soundproof
**insono•ro -ra** *adj* soundproof
**insospecha•do -da** *adj* unsuspected
**insostenible** *adj* untenable
**inspección** *f* inspection; inspectorship
**inspeccionar** *tr* to inspect
**inspiración** *f* inspiration; inhalation
**inspirante** *adj* inspiring
**inspirar** *tr* & *intr* to inspire; (*atraer a los pulmones*) to inhale, to breathe in || *ref* to be inspired
**instalación** *f* plant, factory; outfit, equipment; arrangements, fittings; installment; **instalación sanitaria** plumbing
**instalar** *tr* to install || *ref* to settle
**instantáne•o -a** *adj* instantaneous || *f* snapshot
**instante** *m* instant, moment; **al instante** right away, immediately; **por instantes** uninterruptedly; any time
**instantemente** *adv* insistently, urgently
**instar** *tr* to press, to urge || *intr* to be pressing, to be urgent
**instaurar** *tr* to restore; to reëstablish
**instigar** §44 *tr* to instigate
**instilar** *tr* to instill
**instinti•vo -va** *adj* instinctive
**instinto** *m* instinct
**institución** *f* institution; **instituciones** (*de un Estado*) constitution; (*de una ciencia, arte, etc.*) principles
**instituir** §20 *tr* to institute, found
**instituto** *m* institute; (*de una orden religiosa*) rule, constitution; **instituto de segunda enseñanza** or **de enseñanza media** high school
**institu•triz** *f* (*pl* **-trices**) governess
**instrucción** *f* instruction; education
**instructi•vo -va** *adj* instructive
**instruc•tor -tora** *mf* teacher, instructor || *m* (mil) drillmaster || *f* instructress
**instruí•do -da** *adj* well-educated; well-posted
**instruir** §20 *tr* to instruct; (*un proceso o expediente*) to draw up
**instrumentar** *tr* to instrument
**instrumentista** *mf* instrumentalist
**instrumento** *m* instrument; (*persona que se emplea para alcanzar un resultado*) tool; **instrumento de cuerda** (mus) stringed instrument; **instrumento de viento** (mus) wind instrument
**insubordina•do -da** *adj* insubordinate
**insubstituíble** *adj* irreplaceable
**insudar** *intr* to drudge
**insuficiente** *adj* insufficient
**insufrible** *adj* insufferable
**ínsula** *f* island; one-horse town
**insular** *adj* insular || *mf* islander
**insulina** *f* insulin
**insulsez** *f* tastelessness; dullness, heaviness
**insul•so -sa** *adj* tasteless; dull, heavy
**insultar** *tr* to insult || *ref* to faint, swoon
**insulto** *m* insult; fainting spell
**insume** *adj* expensive
**insumergible** *adj* unsinkable
**insuperable** *adj* insurmountable
**insurgente** *adj* & *mf* insurgent
**insurrección** *f* insurrection
**intac•to -ta** *adj* intact, untouched
**intachable** *adj* blameless, irreproachable
**integración** *f* integration
**integridad** *f* integrity; virginity
**ínte•gro -gra** *adj* integral, whole; honest
**intelecto** *m* intellect
**intelectual** *adj* & *mf* intellectual
**intelectualidad** *f* intellectuality; (*conjunto de los intelectuales de un país o región*) intelligentsia
**inteligencia** *f* intelligence; **estar en inteligencia con** to be in collusion with
**inteligente** *adj* intelligent; trained, skilled
**inteligible** *adj* intelligible

**intemperancia** *f* intemperance
**intemperante** *adj* intemperate
**intemperie** *f* inclement weather; **a la intemperie** in the open, unsheltered
**intempesti•vo -va** *adj* unseasonable, inopportune, untimely
**intención** *f* intention; (*cautelosa advertencia*) caution; (*instinto dañino de un animal*) viciousness; **con intención** deliberately, knowingly; **de intención** on purpose
**intendencia** *f* intendance; (SAm) mayoralty
**intendente** *m* intendant; quartermaster general; (SAm) mayor
**intensar** *tr & ref* to intensify
**intensidad** *f* intensity
**intensificar** §73 *tr & ref* to intensify
**intensión** *f* intensity
**intensi•vo -va** *adj* intensive
**inten•so -sa** *adj* intense
**intentar** *tr* to try, to attempt; to intend; to try out
**intento** *m* intent, purpose; **de intento** on purpose
**intentona** *f* (coll) rash attempt (*e.g., to rob, escape, etc.*)
**interacción** *f* interaction
**interamerica•no -na** *adj* inter-American
**intercalar** *tr* to intercalate, to insert
**intercambiar** *tr & ref* to interchange
**intercambio** *m* interchange, exchange
**interceder** *intr* to intercede
**interceptar** *tr* to intercept
**intercep•tor -tora** *mf* interceptor || *m* trap; separator; (aer) interceptor
**interdecir** §24 *tr* to interdict, forbid
**interés** *m* interest; **intereses creados** vested interests; **poner a interés** to put out at interest
**interesa•do -da** *adj* interested || *mf* interested party
**interesante** *adj* interesting
**interesar** *tr* to interest; to involve || *intr* to be interesting || *ref* — **interesarse en** or **por** to be interested in, take an interest in
**interescolar** *adj* interscholastic, intercollegiate
**interfec•to -ta** *adj* murdered || *mf* victim of murder
**interferencia** *f* interference
**interferir** §68 *tr* to interfere with || *intr* to interfere
**interfono** *m* intercom
**ínterin** *adv* meanwhile || *conj* (coll) while, as long as || *s* (*pl* **intérines**) temporary incumbency
**interinar** *tr* to fill temporarily, to fill in an acting capacity
**interi•no -na** *adj* temporary, acting, interim
**interior** *adj* interior, inner, inside; home, domestic || *m* interior, inside; mind, soul; **interiores** entrails, insides
**interioridad** *f* inside; **interioridades** inside story, private matters
**interjección** *f* interjection
**interlinear** *tr* to interline; (typ) to space, to lead
**interlocu•tor -tora** *mf* speaker, party; interviewer
**intermedia•rio -ria** *adj & mf* intermediary || *m* (com) middleman
**interme•dio -dia** *adj* intermediate || *m* interval, interim; (mus) intermezzo; (theat) intermission, entr'acte
**intermitente** *adj* intermittent
**internacional** *adj* international
**internacionalizar** §60 *tr* to internationalize
**interna•do -da** *mf* (mil) internee || *m* boarding school
**internamiento** *m* internment
**internar** *tr* to send inland; to intern || *intr* to move inland || *ref* to move inland; to take refuge, to hide; to insinuate oneself; **internarse en** to go deeply into
**internista** *mf* internist
**inter•no -na** *adj* internal; inside || *mf* boarding-school student; **interno de hospital** intern
**interpelar** *tr* to seek the protection or aid of; to interrogate; to interpellate
**interpolar** *tr* to interpolate; to interpose; to interrupt briefly
**interponer** §54 *tr* to interpose; to appoint as mediator || *ref* to intervene, intercede
**interprender** *tr* to take by surprise
**interpresa** *f* surprise action; surprise seizure
**interpretar** *tr* to interpret
**intérprete** *mf* interpreter
**interrogación** *f* interrogation; question mark
**interrogar** §44 *tr & intr* to question, interrogate
**interrumpir** *tr* to interrupt
**interruptor** *m* (elec) switch; **interruptor automático** (elec) circuit breaker; **interruptor del encendido** (aut) ignition switch; **interruptor de resorte** (elec) snap switch
**intersección** *f* (geom) intersection
**intersticio** *m* interstice; interval
**intervalo** *m* interval
**intervención** *f* intervention; inspection; (*de cuentas*) audit, auditing; (surg) operation; **intervención de los precios** price control; **no intervención** nonintervention
**intervenir** §79 *tr* to take up, work on; to inspect, supervise; (*cuentas*) to audit; (*un teléfono*) to tap; (surg) to operate on || *intr* to mediate, intervene, intercede; to participate; to happen
**interventor** *m* election supervisor; (com) auditor
**inter•viev** *m* (*pl* **-vievs**) interview
**intervievar** *tr* to interview
**intesta•do -da** *adj & mf* intestate
**intesti•no -na** *adj* internal; domestic || *m* intestine; **intestino delgado** small intestine; **intestino grueso** large intestine
**intimación** *f* announcement, notification
**intimar** *tr* to announce || *intr & ref* to become well-acquainted, to become intimate
**intimidad** *f* intimacy; (*parte íntima o personal*) privacy
**intimidar** *tr* intimidate

**ínti•mo -ma** *adj* intimate; (*más interno*) innermost
**intitular** *tr* to entitle || *ref* to use a title; to be called
**intocable** *mf* untouchable
**intolerante** *adj & mf* intolerant
**inton•so -sa** *adj* unshorn; ignorant; (*libro o revista*) uncut || *mf* ignoramus
**intoxicar** **§73** *tr* to poison, intoxicate
**intracruzamiento** *m* inbreeding
**intraquilidad** *f* uneasiness, worry
**intraquilizar** **§60** *tr* to make uneasy, worry
**intranqui•lo -la** *adj* uneasy, worried
**intransigente** *adj & mf* intransigent, diehard
**intransiti•vo -va** *adj* intransitive
**intratable** *adj* unmanageable; impassable; unsociable
**intrepidez** *f* intrepidity
**intrépi•do -da** *adj* intrepid
**intriga** *f* intrigue
**intrigar** **§44** *tr* (*excitar la curiosidad de*) to intrigue || *intr* to intrigue || *ref* to be intrigued
**intrinca•do -da** *adj* intricate
**intrincar** **§73** *tr* to complicate; to confuse, bewilder
**intríngu•lis** *m* (*pl* **-lis**) (coll) hidden motive, mystery
**intrínse•co -ca** *adj* intrinsic(al)
**introducción** *f* introduction
**introducir** **§19** *tr* to introduce; to insert, put in || *ref* to gain access; to meddle, interfere, intrude
**introito** *m* (*de un escrito o una oración*) introduction; (*de un poema dramático*) prologue; (eccl) introit
**introspecti•vo -va** *adj* introspective
**introverti•do -da** *mf* introvert
**intruso -sa** *adj* intrusive || *mf* intruder, interloper
**intuición** *f* intuition
**intuir** **§20** *tr* to guess, to sense
**intuito** *m* view, glance, look; **por intuito de** in view of
**inundación** *f* flood, inundation
**inundar** *tr* to flood, to inundate
**inurba•no -na** *adj* discourteous, unmannerly
**inusita•do -da** *adj* (*no ordinario*) unusual; obsolete, out of use
**inusual** *adj* unusual
**inútil** *adj* useless
**invadir** *tr* to invade
**invalidar** *tr* to invalidate
**invalidez** *f* invalidity
**inváli•do -da** *adj & mf* invalid
**invariable** *adj* invariable
**invasión** *f* invasion
**inva•sor -sora** *mf* invader
**invectiva** *f* invective
**invectivar** *tr* to inveigh against
**invencible** *adj* invincible
**invención** *f* invention; finding, discovery; deception
**invendible** *adj* unsalable
**inventar** *tr* to invent
**inventariar** **§77 & regular** *tr* to inventory
**inventario** *m* inventory
**inventi•vo -va** *adj* inventive || *f* inventiveness
**invento** *m* invention
**inven•tor -tora** *adj* inventive || *mf* inventor
**inverecun•do -da** *adj* shameless, brazen
**inverisímil** *adj* improbable, unlikely
**invernáculo** *m* greenhouse, hothouse, conservatory
**invernada** *f* wintertime; (SAm) pasture land; (Ven) torrential rain
**invernadero** *m* greenhouse, hothouse; winter resort; winter pasture
**invernal** *adj* winter || *m* cattle shed (*in winter-pasture land*)
**invernar** **§2** *intr* to winter; to be winter
**inverni•zo -za** *adj* winter; wintery
**inverosímil** *adj* improbable, unlikely
**inversión** *f* inversion; (*de dinero*) investment; (gram) inverted order
**inversionista** *adj* investment || *mf* investor
**inver•so -sa** *adj* inverse, opposite; **a** or **por la inversa** on the contrary
**invertebra•do -da** *adj & m* invertebrate
**inverti•do -da** *adj* inverted || *mf* invert
**invertir** **§68** *tr* to invert; (*dinero*) to invest; (*tiempo*) to spend; to reverse
**investidura** *f* investment, investiture; station, standing
**investigación** *f* investigation, research
**investigar** **§44** *tr* to investigate || *intr* to research
**investir** **§50** *tr* — **investir con** or **de** (*poner en posesión de*) to invest with
**invetera•do -da** *adj* inveterate, confirmed
**invic•to -ta** *adj* unconquered
**invidencia** *f* blindness
**invidente** *adj* blind || *mf* blind person
**invierno** *m* winter; (Am) rainy season
**invisible** *adj* invisible || *m* (Mex) hair net; **en un invisible** in an instant
**invitación** *f* invitation
**invita•do -da** *mf* guest
**invitar** *tr* to invite
**invocar** **§73** *tr* to invoke
**involunta•rio -ra** *adj* involuntary
**invulnerable** *adj* invulnerable
**inyección** *f* injection
**inyecta•do -da** *adj* bloodshot, inflamed
**inyectar** *tr* to inject || *ref* to become congested; to become inflamed
**ionizar** **§60** *tr* to ionize || *ref* to be ionized
**ir** **§41** *intr* to go; to be becoming, to fit, to suit; to be at stake; **ir a** + *inf* to be going to + *inf* (*to express futurity*); **ir a buscar** to go get, to go for; **ir a parar en** to end up in; **ir con cuidado** to be careful; **ir con miedo** to be afraid; **ir con tiento** to watch one's step; **ir de caza** to go hunting; **ir de pesca** to go fishing; **lo que va de** so far (as); **¡qué va!** of course not!; **¡vaya!** the deuce!; what a . . .! || *ref* to go away; to leak; to wear away; to get old; to break to pieces
**ira** *f* anger, wrath, ire
**iracun•do -da** *adj* angry, wrathful, irate
**Irak, el** Irak or Iraq
**Irán, el** Iran

**ira•nés -nesa** or **ira•nio -nia** *adj & mf* Iranian
**ira•qués -quesa** or **iraquiano -na** *adj & mf* Iraqui
**iris** *m* (*pl* **iris**) (*del ojo*) iris; rainbow
**Irlanda** *f* Ireland
**irlan•dés -desa** *adj* Irish || *m* Irishman; (*idioma*) Irish; **los irlandeses** the Irish || *f* Irishwoman
**ironía** *f* irony
**iróni•co -ca** *adj* ironic(al)
**ironizar** §60 *tr* to ridicule
**irracional** *adj* irrational
**irradiar** *tr* to radiate, to irradiate; (*difundir*) to broadcast || *intr* to radiate
**irrazonable** *adj* unreasonable
**irreal** *adj* unreal
**irrealidad** *f* unreality
**irrebatible** *adj* irrefutable
**irreconocible** *adj* unrecognizable
**irrecuperable** *adj* irretrievable
**irrecusable** *adj* unimpeachable
**irredimible** *adj* irredeemable
**irreemplazable** *adj* irreplaceable
**irreflexión** *f* rashness, thoughtlessness
**irreflexi•vo -va** *adj* rash, thoughtless
**irregular** *adj* irregular || *m* (mil) irregular
**irregularidad** *f* irregularity; embezzlement
**irreligio•so -sa** *adj* irreligious
**irrellenable** *adj* nonrefillable
**irremediable** *adj* irremediable
**irremisible** *adj* unpardonable
**irreparable** *adj* irreparable
**irreprimible** *adj* irrepressible
**irreprochable** *adj* irreproachable
**irresistible** *adj* irresistible
**irresoluble** *adj* unworkable, unsolvable
**irrespetuo•so -sa** *adj* disrespectful
**irresponsable** *adj* irresponsible
**irresuel•to -ta** *adj* hesitant, wavering
**irreverente** *adj* irreverent
**irrigación** *f* irrigation
**irrigar** §44 *tr* to irrigate
**irrisible** *adj* laughable, absurd
**irrisión** *f* derision, ridicule; (coll) laughingstock
**irritante** *adj & m* irritant
**irritar** *tr* to irritate || *ref* to become exasperated
**irrompible** *adj* unbreakable
**irrumpir** *intr* to burst in; **irrumpir en** to burst into
**irrupción** *f* sudden attack; invasion
**isi•dro -dra** *mf* (coll) hick, jake, yokel
**isla** *f* island; (*manzana de casas*) block; **isla de seguridad** safety island, safety zone; **islas Baleares** Balearic Islands; **islas Canarias** Canary Islands; **islas de Barlovento** Windward Islands; **islas de Sotavento** Leeward Islands; **Islas Filipinas** Philippine Islands
**Islam, el** Islam
**islan•dés -desa** *adj* Icelandic || *mf* Icelander || *m* (*idioma*) Icelandic
**Islandia** *f* Iceland
**isle•ño -ña** *adj* island || *mf* islander; (Cuba) Canarian
**isleta** *f* isle
**isósce•les** *adj* (*pl* **-les**) isosceles
**isótopo** *m* isotope
**israe•lí** (*pl* **-líes**) *adj & mf* Israeli
**israelita** *adj & mf* Israelite
**istmo** *m* isthmus
**Italia** *f* Italy
**italia•no -na** *adj & mf* Italian
**itáli•co -ca** *adj* Italic; (typ) italic || *f* (typ) italics
**itinera•rio -ria** *adj & m* itinerary
**izar** §60 *tr* (naut) to hoist, to haul up
**izquierda** *f* left hand; left-hand side; (pol) left; **a la izquierda** left, on the left, to the left
**izquierdear** *intr* to go wild, to go astray, to go awry
**izquierdista** *adj* leftist || *mf* leftist, left-winger
**izquierdizante** *adj* leftish
**izquier•do -da** *adj* left; left-hand; left-handed; crooked; **levantarse del izquierdo** to get out of bed on the wrong side || *f* see **izquierda**

## J

**J, j** (jota) *f* eleventh letter of the Spanish alphabet
**jabalcón** *m* strut, brace
**jaba•lí** *m* (*pl* **-líes**) wild boar
**jabalina** *f* javelin; wild sow
**jabardillo** *m* (*de insectos*) noisy swarm; (coll) noisy throng
**jabeque** *m* (naut) xebec; (coll) gash in the face
**jabón** *m* soap; cake of soap; **dar jabón a** (coll) to softsoap; **dar un jabón a** (coll) to upbraid, to reprimand; **jabón de afeitar** shaving soap; **jabón de Castilla** Castile soap; **jabón de tocador** or **de olor** toilet soap; **jabón de sastre** soapstone, French chalk; **jabón en polvo** soap powder
**jabonado** *m* soaping; (*ropa lavada o por lavar*) wash
**jabonadura** *f* soaping; **dar una jabonadura a** (coll) to lambaste, to upbraid; **jabonaduras** soapy water; soapsuds
**jabonar** *tr* to soap; (coll) to reprimand
**jaboncillo** *m* cake of toilet soap; **jaboncillo de sastre** soapstone, French chalk
**jabone•ro -ra** *adj* soap; (*toro*) yellowish, dirty-white || *mf* soapmaker; soap dealer || *f* soap dish
**jabonete** *m* cake of toilet soap
**jabono•so -sa** *adj* soapy, lathery
**jaca** *f* pony, jennet
**jacal** *m* (Guat, Mex, Ven) hut, shack
**jácara** *f* merry ballad; gay song and

dance; night revelers; (coll) story, argument; (coll) fake, hoax, lie; (coll) annoyance, bother

**jacarear** *intr* (coll) to go serenading, to go singing in the street; (coll) to be disagreeable

**jáca•ro -ra** *adj & m* braggart || *f* see **jácara**

**jacinto** *m* hyacinth

**jaco** *m* nag, jade; gray parrot

**jactancia** *f* boasting, bragging

**jactancio•so -sa** *adj* boastful, bragging

**jactar** *ref* to boast, to brag; **jactarse de** to boast of

**jade** *m* jade

**jadeante** *adj* panting

**jadear** *intr* to pant

**jadeo** *m* panting

**ja•ez** *m* (*pl* **-eces**) harness, piece of harness; ilk, stripe, kind; **jaeces** trappings

**jaguar** *m* jaguar

**jagüel** *m* (Arg) reservoir

**jaharrar** *tr* to plaster

**jalar** *tr* (coll) to pull; (Am) to flirt with || *intr* (Am) to get out, to beat it || *ref* (Am) to get drunk

**jalbegar** §44 *tr* to whitewash; (*el rostro*) to paint || *ref* to paint the face

**jalbegue** *m* whitewash; whitewashing; paint, make-up

**jalda•do -da** *adj* bright-yellow

**jalea** *f* jelly; **hacerse una jalea** (coll) to be madly in love

**jalear** *tr* (*a los que bailan y cantan*) to animate with clapping and shouting; (*a los perros*) to incite, urge on; (*Chile*) to tease, pester || *intr* to dance the jaleo || *ref* to have a noisy time; to swing and sway

**jaleo** *m* cheering, shouting; jamboree; jaleo (*vivacious Spanish solo dance*)

**jalis•co -ca** *adj* (Guat, Mex) drunk || *m* (Mex) straw hat

**jalma** *f* small packsaddle

**jalón** *m* surveying rod, range pole; (Guat, Mex) swig of liquor; (CAm) beau; **jalón de mira** leveling rod

**jalonar** *tr* to stake out, mark out

**jalonear** *tr* (Mex) to pull, to jerk

**jalonero** *m* (surv) rodman

**jamaica** *m* Jamaica rum || *f* (Mex) charity fair

**jamaica•no -na** *adj & mf* Jamaican

**jamaiqui•no -na** *adj & mf* (Am) Jamaican

**jamar** *tr* (coll) to eat

**jamás** *adv* never; ever

**jamba** *f* jamb

**jambaje** *m* doorframe, window frame

**jamelgo** *m* (coll) jade, nag

**jamete** *m* samite

**jamón** *m* ham

**jamona** *f* (coll) fat middle-aged woman

**jamugas** *fpl* mule chair

**jánda•lo -la** *adj & mf* Andalusian

**Jantipa** or **Jantipe** *f* Xanthippe

**Japón, el** Japan

**japo•nés -nesa** *adj & mf* Japanese || *m* (*idioma*) Japanese

**jaque** *m* (*lance del ajedrez*) check; (coll) bully; **dar jaque a** to check; **dar jaque mate a** to checkmate; **en jaque** in check; **estar muy jaque** (coll) to be full of pep; **jaque mate** checkmate; **tener en jaque** to hold a threat over the head of || *interj* check!

**jaquear** *tr* to check; (*al enemigo*) to harass

**jaqueca** *f* sick headache; **dar una jaqueca a** (coll) to bore to death

**jaqueco•so -sa** *adj* boring, tiresome

**jaquemar** *m* jack (*figure which strikes a clock bell*)

**jarabe** *m* syrup; sweet drink; **jarabe de pico** (coll) lip service, idle promise

**jarana** *f* (coll) merrymaking; (coll) rumpus; (coll) carousal, spree; (coll) trick, deceit; (Am) jest, joke; (Am) small guitar; **ir de jarana** (coll) to go on a spree

**jaranear** *tr* (CAm, Col) to swindle, cheat || *intr* (coll) to go on a spree; (coll) to raise a rumpus; (Am) to joke

**jarane•ro -ra** *adj* merrymaking; gay, merry || *mf* merrymaker, reveler

**jarano** *m* sombrero

**jarcia** *f* fishing tackle; (coll) jumble, mess; **jarcias** tackle, rigging; **jarcia trozada** junk (*old cable*)

**jardín** *m* garden, flower garden; (baseball) field, outfield; (naut) privy, latrine; **jardín central** (baseball) center field; **jardín de la infancia** kindergarten; **jardín derecho** (baseball) right field; **jardín izquierdo** (baseball) left field

**jardinera** *f* jardiniere, flower stand; basket carriage; summer trolley car, open trolley car

**jardinería** *f* gardening

**jardine•ro -ra** *mf* gardener; **jardinero adornista** landscape gardener || *m* (baseball) fielder, outfielder || *f* see **jardinera**

**jardinista** *mf* landscape gardener

**jarea** *f* (Mex) hunger

**jarear** *intr* (Bol) to stop for a rest || *ref* (Mex) to flee, run away; (Mex) to swing, to sway; (Mex) to die of starvation

**jareta** *f* (sew) casing

**jari•fo -fa** *adj* showy, spruce, natty

**jaro•cho -cha** *adj* brusk, bluff || *m* insulting fellow; Veracruz peasant

**jarope** *m* syrup; (coll) nasty potion

**jarra** *f* jug, jar, water pitcher; **de jarras** or **en jarras** with arms akimbo

**jarrete** *m* hock, gambrel

**jarretera** *f* garter

**jarro** *m* pitcher; **echar un jarro de agua (fría) a** to pour cold water on

**jarrón** *m* (*vaso para adornar chimeneas, consolas, etc.*) vase; (*sobre un pedestal*) urn

**jaspe** *m* jasper

**jaspea•do -da** *adj* marbled, speckled || *m* marbling, speckling

**jaspear** *tr* to marble, speckle

**jateo** *m* foxhound

**ja•to -ta** *mf* calf

**Jauja** *f* Cockaigne; **¿estamos aquí o en Jauja?** (coll) where do you think you are?; **vivir en Jauja** (coll) to live in the lap of luxury

**jaula** *f* cage; (*embalaje de listones de madera*) crate; (Mex) open freight car; (Cuba, P-R) police wagon; **jaula de locos** insane asylum, madhouse
**jauría** *f* pack (*of hounds*)
**java•nés -nesa** *adj & mf* Javanese || *m* (*idioma*) Javanese
**Javier** *m* Xavier
**jazmín** *m* jasmine; **jazmín de la India** gardenia
**jazz** *m* jazz
**J.C.** *abbr* **Jesucristo**
**jebe** *m* alum; (SAm) rubber
**jedive** *m* khedive
**jefa** *f* female head or leader; **jefa de ruta** hostess (*on a bus*)
**jefatura** *f* headship, leadership; (*de policía*) headquarters
**jefe** *m* chief, head, leader; (*de una tribu*) chieftain; **jefe de cocina** chef; **jefe de coro** choirmaster; **jefe de equipajes** (rr) baggage master; **jefe de estación** stationmaster; **jefe del estado** chief of state; **jefe del gobierno** chief executive; **jefe de redacción** editor in chief; **jefe de ruta** guide; **jefe de tren** (rr) conductor; **quedar jefe** (Chile) to gamble away everything
**jején** *m* gnat, sandfly
**jenabe** *m* or **jenable** *m* mustard
**jengibre** *m* ginger
**Jenofonte** *m* Xenophon
**jeque** *m* sheik
**jerarca** *m* hierarch, head
**jerarquía** *f* hierarchy; **de jerarquía** important
**jeremiada** *f* jeremiad
**jerez** *m* sherry
**jerga** *f* coarse cloth; straw mattress; (*lenguaje especial de ciertos oficios; lenguaje difícil de entender*) jargon
**jergón** *m* straw mattress; (coll) ill-fitting clothes; (*persona torpe y estúpida*) (coll) lummox
**Jericó** Jericho
**jerife** *m* shereef
**jerigonza** *f* (*lenguaje especial de ciertos oficios; lenguaje difícil de entender*) jargon; (*lenguaje vulgar, caló*) slang; (coll) piece of folly
**jeringa** *f* syringe; (*para inyectar materias blandas en una máquina*) gun; (coll) annoyance, plague; **jeringa de engrase** or **grasa** grease gun
**jeringar** §44 *tr* to syringe; to inject; to give an enema to; (coll) to plague
**jeringazo** *m* injection, shot; squirt
**jeringuilla** *f* (*jeringa pequeña*) syringe; (bot) mock orange
**Jerjes** *m* Xerxes
**jeroglífi•co -ca** *adj & m* hieroglyphic
**Jerónimo** *m* Jerome
**jer•sey** *m* (*pl* **-seis**) jersey, sweater
**Jerusalén** Jerusalem
**Jesucristo** *m* Jesus Christ
**jesuíta** *adj & m* Jesuit
**jesuíti•co -ca** *adj* Jesuitic(al)
**Jesús** *m* Jesus; (*imagen del niño Jesús*) bambino; **en un decir Jesús** in an instant; **¡Jesús, María y José!** my gracious!
**jeta** *f* hog's snout, pig face; (*rostro de una persona*) (coll) phiz, mug; **estar con tanta jeta** (coll) to make a long face; **poner jeta** (coll) to pucker one's lips
**jetu•do -da** *adj* thick-lipped; (coll) grim, gruff
**Jhs.** *abbr* **Jesús**
**jíba•ro -ra** *mf* (W-I) white peasant
**jibia** *f* cuttlefish
**jícara** *f* chocolate cup; (CAm, Mex, W-I) calabash cup
**jifia** *f* swordfish
**jilguero** *m* linnet, goldfinch
**jineta** *f* (zool) genet
**jinete** *m* rider, horseman
**jinetear** *tr* (*caballos cerriles*) (Am) to break in || *intr* to show off one's horsemanship
**jinglar** *intr* to swing, to rock
**jingoísmo** *m* jingoism
**jingoísta** *adj & mf* jingo
**jipa•to -ta** *adj* (Am) pale, wan; (Am) insipid, tasteless; (Guat) drunk
**jipijapa** *m* Panama hat || *f* jipijapa; strip of jipijapa straw
**jira** *f* strip of cloth; outing, picnic; trip, tour; swing, political trip
**jirón** *m* rag, tatter, shred; (*de una falda*) facing; pennant; bit, drop, shred; **hacer jirones** to tear to shreds
**jitomate** *m* (Mex) tomato
**joco•so -sa** *adj* jocose, jocular
**jocotal** *m* (CAm, Mex) Spanish plum (*tree*)
**jocote** *m* (CAm, Mex) Spanish plum (*fruit*)
**jocoyote** *m* (Mex) baby (*youngest child*)
**jofaina** *f* washbowl, basin
**jolgorio** *m* (coll) fun, merriment
**jonrón** *m* (baseball) home run
**Jordán** *m* Jordan (*river*); **ir al Jordán** (coll) to be born again
**Jordania** *f* Jordan (*country*)
**jorda•no -na** *adj & mf* Jordanian
**jorguín** *m* sorcerer, wizard
**jorguina** *f* sorceress, witch
**jorguinería** *f* sorcery, witchcraft
**jornada** *f* journey, trip, stage; day's journey; (*horas del trabajo diario del obrero*) workday; (*tiempo que dura la vida de un hombre*) lifetime; battle; (*muerte*) passing; summer residence of diplomat or diplomatic corps; event, occasion; undertaking; (mil) expedition; (*de un drama*) (archaic) act; **a grandes** or **largas jornadas** by forced marches; **al fin de la jornada** in the end; **caminar por sus jornadas** to proceed with circumspection; **hacer mala jornada** to get nowhere; **jornada ordinaria** full time
**jornal** *m* day's work; day's pay; **a jornal** by the day; **jornal mínimo** minimum wage
**jornalero** *m* day laborer
**joroba** *f* hump; (coll) annoyance, bother
**joroba•do -da** *adj* humpbacked, hunchbacked; (coll) annoyed, bothered || *mf* humpback, hunchback
**jorobar** *tr* (coll) to annoy, pester
**jorongo** *m* (Mex) poncho; (Mex) woolen blanket

**jota** *f* (*letra del alfabeto*) J; jota (*Spanish folk dance and music*); jot, iota, tittle; vegetable soup; **sin faltar una jota** (coll) with not a whit left out

**joven** *adj* young; **ser joven de esperanzas** (coll) to have a bright future || *mf* youth, young person; **de joven** as a youth, as a young man, as a young woman

**jovial** *adj* jovial

**joya** *f* jewel; (*brocamantón*) diamond brooch; (*agasajo*) gift, present; (*persona o cosa de mucha valía*) (fig) jewel, gem; **joya de familia** heirloom; **joyas** jewelry; trousseau; **joyas de fantasía** costume jewelry

**joyante** *adj* glossy

**joyelero** *m* jewel case, casket

**joyería** *f* (*conjunto de joyas*) jewelry; jewelry shop; jewelry trade

**joye·ro -ra** *mf* jeweler || *m* jewel case, casket

**Juan** *m* John; **Buen Juan** (coll) sap, easy mark; **Juan Español** the Spanish people, the typical Spaniard; **San Juan Bautista** John the Baptist

**Juana** *f* Jane, Jean, Joan; **Juana de Arco** Joan of Arc, Jeanne d'Arc; **juanas** glove stretcher

**juanete** *m* bunion; high cheekbone

**jubilación** *f* retirement; (*renta de la persona jubilada*) pension, retirement annuity

**jubila·do -da** *adj* retired || *mf* retired person, pensioner

**jubilar** *tr* to retire, to pension; (coll) to throw out || *intr* to rejoice; to retire, be pensioned || *ref* to rejoice; to retire, be pensioned; (Col) to decline, go to pieces; (CAm, Ven) to play hooky; (Cuba, Mex) to become a past master

**jubileo** *m* (coll) much coming and going, great doings; (eccl) jubilee; **por jubileo** (coll) once in a long time

**júbilo** *m* jubilation

**jubilo·so -sa** *adj* jubilant, joyful

**jubón** *m* jerkin

**judaísmo** *m* Judaism

**judería** *f* (*raza judaica*) Jewry; (*barrio de los judíos*) ghetto

**judía** *f* Jewess; kidney bean, string bean; **judía de careta** black-eyed bean; **judía de la peladilla** Lima bean

**judicatura** *f* judicature; (*cargo de juez*) judgeship

**judicial** *adj* judicial, judiciary

**judí·o -a** *adj* Jewish || *mf* Jew || *f* see **judía**

**juego** *m* (*acción de jugar*) play, playing; (*ejercicio recreativo en el cual se gana o se pierde*) game; (*vicio de jugar*) gambling; (*lugar donde se ejecutan ciertos juegos*): (bowling) alley; (tennis) court; (baseball) field; (*tantos necesarios para ganar la partida*) game; (*de muebles*) suit, suite; (*de café*) service; (*de vajilla*) set; (*de luces, colores, aguas*) play; (mach) play; (*p.ej., de diplomacia*) (fig) game; **a juego** to match, e.g., **una silla a juego** a chair to match; **conocer el juego de** to see through, to have the number of; **en juego** at hand; **hacer juego** to match; **hacer juego con** to match, to go with; **juego de alcoba** bedroom suit; **juego de azar** game of chance; **juego de bolas** (mach) ball bearing; **juego de campanas** chimes; **juego de comedor** dining-room suit; **juego de envite** gambling game, game played for money; **juego de escritorio** desk set; **juego de la cuna** cat's cradle; **juego de la pulga** tiddlywinks; **juego del corro** ring-around-a-rosy; **juego del salto** leapfrog; **juego del tres en raya** tick-tack-toe played with movable counters or pebbles; **juego de manos** legerdemain, sleight of hand; (coll) roughhousing; **juego de niños** (*cosa muy fácil*) child's play; **juego de palabras** play on words, pun; **juego de pelota**; ball game; pelota; **juego de piernas** footwork; **juego de por ver** (Chile) game played for fun; **juego de prendas** game of forfeits, forfeits; **juego de suerte** game of chance; **juego de tejo** shuffleboard; **juego de timbres** glockenspiel; **juego de vocablos** or **voces** play on words, pun; **juego limpio** fair play; **juego público** gambling house; **juegos de sociedad** parlor games; **juegos malabares** juggling; flimflam; **juego sucio** foul play; **no ser cosa de juego** to be no laughing matter; **por juego** in fun, for fun; **verle a uno el juego** to be on to someone

**juerga** *f* (coll) carousal, spree; **juerga de borrachera** (coll) drinking bout, binge; **ir de juerga** (coll) to go on a spree

**juerguista** *mf* (coll) carouser, reveler

**jue·ves** *m* (*pl* **-ves**) Thursday; **Jueves Santo** Maundy Thursday

**juez** *m* (*pl* **jueces**) judge; **juez de guardia** coroner; **juez de instrucción** examining magistrate; **juez de paz** justice of the peace; **juez de salida** (sport) starter; **juez de tiempo** (sport) timekeeper

**jugada** *f* (*lance*) play, throw, stroke, move; **mala jugada** dirty trick

**juga·dor -dora** *mf* player; gambler; **jugador de manos** prestidigitator; **jugador de ventaja** sharper

**jugar** §42 *tr* (*p.ej., un naipe, una partida de juego*) to play; (*una espada*) to wield; (*arriesgar*) to stake, to risk; (*las manos, los dedos*) to move; **jugarle a uno las bebidas** to match someone for the drinks || *intr* to play; to gamble; (*hacer juego dos cosas*) to match; (*intervenir*) to figure, participate; **jugar a** (*p.ej., los naipes, el tenis*) to play; **jugar con** (*un contrario*) to play; (*una persona; los sentimientos de una persona*) to toy with; to match; **jugar en** to have a hand in || *ref* (*p.ej., la vida*) to risk; to be at stake; **jugarse el todo por el todo** to stake all, to shoot the works

**jugarreta** *f* (coll) bad play, poor play; (coll) mean trick, dirty trick

**juglar** *m* minstrel, jongleur; (*bufón*) (archaic) juggler
**juglaría** *f* minstrelsy
**jugo** *m* (*p.ej., de la naranja*) juice; (*de la carne*) gravy; (*líquido orgánico*) juice; (fig) gist, essence, substance; **en su jugo** (culin) au jus; **jugo de muñeca** (coll) elbow grease
**jugo•so -sa** *adj* juicy; substantial, important
**juguete** *m* toy, plaything; (*burla*) joke, jest; (theat) skit; **de juguete** toy, e.g., **soldado de juguete** toy soldier; **juguete de movimiento** mechanical toy; **por juguete** for fun, in fun
**juguetear** *intr* to frolic, romp, sport
**juguete•ro -ra** *adj* toy || *mf* toy dealer || *m* whatnot, étagère
**juguete-sorpresa** *m* (*pl* **juguetes-sorpresa**) jack-in-the-box
**jugue•tón -tona** *adj* playful, frolicsome, frisky
**juicio** *m* judgment; (law) trial; **estar en su cabal juicio** to be in one's right mind; **estar fuera de juicio** to be out of one's mind; **juicio de Dios** (hist) ordeal; **pedir en juicio** (law) to sue
**juicio•so -sa** *adj* judicious, wise
**julepe** *m* julep; (coll) scolding; (Am) scare, fright
**julepear** *tr* (coll) to scold; (coll) to whip; (SAm) to scare, frighten; (Mex) to weary, tire out
**julio** *m* July
**julo** *m* lead cow, lead mule
**jumen•to -ta** *mf* ass, donkey
**juncal** *adj* willowy, rushy; (fig) willowy, lissome
**juncia** *f* sedge; **vender juncia** (coll) to boast, brag
**junco** *m* (*embarcación china*) junk; (bot) rush, bulrush; **junco de Indias** (bot) rattan; **junco de laguna** (bot) rush, bulrush
**junco•so -sa** *adj* rushy, full of rushes
**jungla** *f* jungle
**junio** *m* June
**junípero** *m* juniper
**junquera** *f* rush, bulrush
**junquillo** *m* jonquil
**junta** *f* meeting, conference; board, council; junction, union; joint, seam; (*empaquetadura*) gasket; (*arandela*) washer; **junta de comercio** board of trade; **junta de charnela** (mach) knuckle; **junta de sanidad** board of health; **junta universal** (mach) universal joint
**juntamente** *adv* together; at the same time
**juntar** *tr* to join, unite; to gather, gather together; (*una puerta*) to half-close || *ref* to gather together; to go along; to copulate
**jun•to -ta** *adj* joined, united; **jun•tos -tas** together || *f* see **junta** || **junto** *adv* together; at the same time; **junto a** near, close to; **junto con** along with, together with; **todo junto** at the same time, all at once
**juntura** *f* junction; (*p.ej., de una cañería; de un hueso*) joint; connection, coupling
**jura** *f* oath
**jura•do -da** *adj* (*enemigo*) sworn || *m* (*conjunto de ciudadanos encargados de determinar la culpabilidad del acusado; conjunto de examinadores de un certamen*) jury; (*cada uno de los expresados individuos*) juror, juryman
**juramentar** *tr* to swear in || *ref* to take an oath, to be sworn in
**juramento** *m* oath; (*voto, reniego*) curse, swearword; **prestar juramento a** to swear to; **tomar juramento a** to swear in
**jurar** *tr* to swear; (*la verdad de una cosa*) to swear to; to swear allegiance to || *intr* (*pronunciar un juramento*) to swear, take an oath; (*echar votos o reniegos*) to swear, to curse; **jurar** + *inf* to swear to + *inf* || *ref* to swear; **jurársela** or **jurárselas a uno** (coll) to have it in for someone, to swear to get even with someone
**jure•ro -ra** *mf* (SAm) false witness
**jurídi•co -ca** *adj* juridical
**jurisconsulto** *m* (*el que escribe sobre el derecho*) jurist; (*jurisperito*) legal expert
**jurisdicción** *f* jurisdiction
**jurisperito** *m* jurist, legal expert
**jurisprudencia** *f* jurisprudence
**jurista** *mf* jurist
**juro** *m* right of perpetual ownership; **de juro** inevitably, for sure
**justa** *f* joust, tournament
**justamente** *adv* just, just at that time; justly; (*ajustadamente*) tightly
**justar** *intr* to joust, to tilt
**justicia** *f* justice; (*castigo de muerte*) execution; **de justicia** justly, deservedly; **hacer justicia a** to do justice to; **ir por justicia** to go to court, to bring suit
**justicie•ro -ra** *adj* just, fair; stern, righteous
**justificable** *adj* justifiable
**justifica•do -da** *adj* (*hecho*) just, right; (*persona*) just, upright
**justificante** *m* voucher, proof
**justificar** §73 *tr* to justify; (typ) to justify
**justillo** *m* jerkin, waist
**justipreciar** *tr* to estimate, appraise
**jus•to -ta** *adj* just; right, exact; (*apretado*) tight || *mf* just person || *f* see **justa** || **justo** *adv* just; right, in tune; tight; (*con estrechez*) in straitened circumstances
**Jutlandia** *f* Jutland
**ju•to -ta** *mf* Jute
**juvenil** *adj* juvenile, youthful
**juventud** *f* youth; young people
**juzgado** *m* court of law; courtroom; court of one judge
**juzgar** §44 *tr & intr* to judge; **a juzgar por** judging by; **juzgar de** to judge, pass judgment on

## K

**K, k** (ka) *f* twelfth letter of the Spanish alphabet
**kermesse** *f* var of **quermés**
**keroseno** *m* kerosene, coal oil
**kg.** *abbr* **kilogramo**
**kilate** *m* var of **quilate**
**kilo** *m* kilo, kilogram
**kilociclo** *m* kilocycle
**kilogramo** *m* kilogram
**kilometraje** *m* kilometrage, distance in kilometers
**kilométri•co -ca** *adj* kilometric; (coll) interminable, long-drawn-out
**kilómetro** *m* kilometer
**kilovatio** *m* kilowatt
**kilovatio-hora** *m* (*pl* **kilovatios-hora**) kilowatt-hour
**kimono** *m* var of **quimono**
**kinescopio** *m* (telv) kinescope
**kiosco** *m* var of **quiosco**
**kirieleisón** *m* (coll) dirge; **cantar el kirieleisón** (coll) to beg mercy
**km.** *abbr* **kilómetro**
**kph.** *abbr* **kilómetros por hora**
**kv.** *abbr* **kilovatio**
**kv-h** *abbr* **kilovatio-hora**

## L

**L, l** (ele) *f* thirteenth letter of the Spanish alphabet
**la** *art def fem* of **el** || *pron pers fem* her, it; you || *pron dem* that, the one; **la que** who, which, that; she who, the one that
**laberinto** *m* labyrinth, maze
**labia** *f* (coll) fluency, smoothness
**labial** *adj & f* labial
**labio** *m* lip; (fig) edge, lip; **chuparse los labios** to smack one's lips; **labio leporino** harelip; **leer en los labios** to lip-read
**labiolectura** *f* lip reading
**labio•so -sa** *adj* (Am) fluent, smooth
**labor** *f* labor, work; (*cultivo de los campos*) farming, tilling; (*obra de coser, bordar, etc.*) needlework, fancywork, embroidery; **hacer labor** to match; **labor blanca** linen work, linen embroidery; **labor de ganchillo** crocheting
**laborable** *adj* workable; arable, tillable; (*día*) work
**laborante** *m* journeyman; political henchman
**laborar** *tr* to work || *intr* to scheme
**laboratorio** *m* laboratory
**laborio•so -sa** *adj* (*trabajador*) laborious, industrious; (*trabajoso*) laborious, arduous
**laborismo** *m* British Labour Party
**laborista** *adj* Labour || *mf* Labourite
**labra** *f* carving
**labrada** *f* fallow ground (*to be sown the following year*)
**labrade•ro -ra** *adj* arable, tillable
**labra•do -da** *adj* wrought, fashioned; carved; figured, embroidered || *m* carving; **labrado de madera** wood carving || *f* see **labrada**
**labra•dor -dora** *adj* work; farm || *mf* farmer; (*campesino*) peasant || *m* plowman; **el Labrador** Labrador
**labrantí•o -a** *adj* farm || *m* farmland
**labranza** *f* farming; farm, farmland
**labrar** *tr* to work, to fashion; (*la piedra, la madera*) to carve; (*arar*) to plow; (*construir o mandar construir*) to build; to till, to cultivate; to cause, bring about || *intr* to make a lasting impression
**labrie•go -ga** *mf* peasant
**laca** *f* lacquer; shellac; **laca de uñas** nail polish; **lacas** lacquer ware
**lacayo** *m* lackey, footman
**lacear** *tr* to tie with a bow; to adorn with bows; (*la caza*) to drive within shot; (*la caza menor*) to trap, to snare
**laceria** *f* poverty, want; trouble, bother; leprosy
**lacerio•so -sa** *adj* poor, needy
**lacero** *m* lassoer; poacher; dogcatcher
**la•cio -cia** *adj* faded, withered; languid; (*cabello*) lank, straight
**lacóni•co -ca** *adj* laconic
**lacra** *f* fault, defect; (*señal dejada por una enfermedad*) mark, remains; (Am) sore; (Am) scab
**lacrimóge•no -na** *adj* tear, tear-producing
**lacrimo•so -sa** *adj* lachrymose, tearful
**lactar** *tr* to suckle
**lácte•o -a** *adj* milky
**lacustre** *adj* lake
**ladear** *tr* to tip, to tilt; to bend, to lean; (*un avión*) to bank || *intr* to tip, to tilt; to bend, to lean; to turn away, turn off; (*la aguja de brújula*) to deviate || *ref* to tip, to tilt; to bend, to lean; to be equal, be even; (Chile) to fall in love; **ladearse a** (*un dictamen, un partido*) to lean to or toward
**ladeo** *m* tipping, tilting; bending, leaning; inclination, bent
**lade•ro -ra** *adj* side, lateral || *f* hillside
**ladilla** *f* crab louse; **pegarse como ladilla** (coll) to stick like a leech
**ladi•no -na** *adj* crafty, sly, cunning; polyglot
**lado** *m* side; direction; (*del hilo telefónico*) end; **al lado** nearby; **dejar a un lado** to leave aside; **de lado** square, e.g., **diez centímetros de lado** ten centimeters square; **de otro lado**

on the other hand; **de un lado** on the one hand; **echar a un lado** to cast aside; to finish up; **hacer lado** to make room; **hacerse a un lado** to step aside; **lados** backers, advisers; **mirar de lado** or **de medio lado** to look askance at; to sneak a look at; **ponerse al lado de** to take sides with; **por el lado de** in the direction of; **tirar por su lado** to pull for oneself

**ladrar** *tr* (*p.ej., injurias*) to bark || *intr* to bark

**ladrido** *m* bark, barking; (coll) slander, blame

**ladrillador** *m* bricklayer

**ladrillal** *m* brickyard

**ladrillo** *m* brick; (*azulejo*) tile; (*p.ej., de chocolate*) cake; **ladrillo de fuego** or **ladrillo refractario** firebrick

**la•drón -drona** *adj* thievish, thieving || *mf* thief || *m* sluice gate; **ladrón de corazones** heartbreaker, lady-killer

**ladronera** *f* den of thieves; thievery; (*alcancía*) child's bank

**ladronerío** *m* (Arg) gang of thieves; (Arg) wave of thieving

**ladronzue•lo -la** *mf* petty thief

**lagaña** *f* var of **legaña**

**lagar** *m* wine press; olive press; (*establecimiento*) winery

**lagarta** *f* female lizard; (ent) gypsy moth; (coll) sly woman

**lagartija** *f* green lizard; wall lizard

**lagarto** *m* lizard; (coll) sly fellow; **lagarto de Indias** alligator

**lago** *m* lake

**lagotear** *tr & intr* to flatter, to wheedle

**lágrima** *f* tear; (*de cualquier licor*) drop; **beberse las lágrimas** (coll) to hold back one's tears; **deshacerse en lágrimas** to weep one's eyes out; **lágrimas de cocodrilo** crocodile tears; **llorar a lágrima viva** to shed bitter tears

**lagrimear** *intr* to weep easily, to be tearful; (*los ojos*) to fill

**lagrimo•so -sa** *adj* tearful; (*ojos*) watery

**laguna** *f* (*lago pequeño*) lagoon; (*hueco, omisión*) lacuna, gap

**laical** *adj* lay

**laicismo** *m* secularism

**laja** *f* slab, flagstone

**lama** *f* mud, ooze, slime; pond scum

**lambrija** *f* earthworm; (coll) skinny person

**lamedero** *m* salt lick

**lame•dor -dora** *adj* licking || *mf* licker || *m* syrup; **dar lamedor** (coll) to lose at first in order to take in one's opponent

**lamedura** *f* lick, licking

**lamentable** *adj* lamentable

**lamentación** *f* lamentation

**lamentar** *tr, intr & ref* to lament, to mourn

**lamento** *m* lament

**lamento•so -sa** *adj* lamentable; plaintive

**lamer** *tr* to lick; to lap, lap against; (*las llamas un tejado*) to lick || *ref* (*p.ej., los dedos*) to lick

**lame•rón -rona** *adj* (coll) sweet-toothed

**lametada** *f* lap, lick

**lámina** *f* sheet, plate, strip; (*plancha grabada*) engraving; (*pintura en cobre*) copper plate; (*figura estampada*) cut, picture, illustration

**laminador** *m* rolling mill

**laminar** *tr* to laminate; (*el hierro, el acero*) to roll

**lampadario** *m* floor lamp

**lámpara** *f* lamp, light; (*mancha en la ropa*) grease spot, oil spot; (rad) vacuum tube; **atizar la lámpara** (coll) to fill up the glasses again; **lámpara de alcohol** spirit lamp; **lámpara de arco** arc lamp, arc light; **lámpara de bolsillo** flashlight; **lámpara de carretera** (aut) bright light; **lámpara de cruce** (aut) dimmer; **lámpara de pie** floor lamp; **lámpara de sobremesa** table lamp; **lámpara de socorro** trouble light; **lámpara de soldar** blowtorch; **lámpara de techo** ceiling light; (aut) dome light; **lámpara inundante** floodlight; **lámpara testigo** pilot light

**lamparilla** *f* rushlight; aspen

**lampi•ño -ña** *adj* beardless; hairless

**lampista** *mf* lamplighter || *m* tinsmith, plumber, glazier, electrician

**lana** *f* wool; **lana de acero** steel wool; **lana de ceiba** kapoc; **lana de escorias** mineral wool, rock wool; **lana de vidrio** glass wool

**lance** *m* cast, throw; (*en la red*) catch, haul; (*accidente en el juego*) play, move, stroke; (*ocasión crítica*) chance, pass, juncture; incident, event; (*riña*) row, quarrel; (taur) capework; **de lance** cheap; secondhand; **echar buen lance** (coll) to have a break; **lance de honor** affair of honor, duel; **tener pocos lances** (coll) to be dull and uninteresting

**lancero** *m* lancer, spearman, pikeman

**lanceta** *f* (surg) lancet

**lancinante** *adj* piercing

**lancha** *f* barge, lighter; flagstone, slab; (naut) longboat; (nav) launch; (Ecuad) mist, fog; (Ecuad) frost; **lancha automóvil** launch, motor launch; **lancha de auxilio** lifeboat (*stationed on shore*); **lancha de carreras** speedboat; **lancha de desembarco** (nav) landing craft; **lancha salvavidas** lifeboat (*on shipboard*)

**lanchar** *intr* (Ecuad) to get foggy; (Ecuad) to freeze

**lan•dó** *m* (*pl* **-dós**) landau

**landre** *f* swollen gland; hidden pocket

**lanería** *f* wool shop; **lanerías** woolens, woolen goods

**langosta** *f* (*insecto*) locust; (*crustáceo*) lobster, spiny lobster

**langostera** *f* lobster pot

**langostín** *m* or **langostino** *m* prawn (*Peneus*)

**langostón** *m* green grasshopper

**languidecer** §22 *intr* to languish

**languidez** *f* languor

**lángui•do -da** *adj* languid, languorous

**lano•so -sa** *adj* woolly

**lanu•do -da** *adj* woolly; (Ecuad, Ven) coarse, ill-bred

**lanza** *f* lance, pike; (*de la manguera*) nozzle; (*palo de coche*) wagon pole

**lanzabom•bas** *m* (*pl* **-bas**) (aer) bomb release; (mil) trench mortar
**lanzacohe•tes** *m* (*pl* **-tes**) rocket launcher
**lanzadera** *f* shuttle; **parecer una lanzadera** (coll) to buzz around
**lanza•do -da** *adj* sloping; (*salida de una carrera*) (sport) running (*start*)
**lanza•dor -dora** *mf* thrower; **lanzador de lodo** (fig) mudslinger || *m* launcher; (aer) jettison gear; (baseball) pitcher
**lanzaespu•mas** *m* (*pl* **-mas**) foam extinguisher
**lanzalla•mas** *m* (*pl* **-mas**) flame thrower
**lanzamiento** *m* throw, hurl, fling, launch; (*de un buque*) launching; (*de un cohete*) shot, launch; (*p.ej., de víveres*) (aer) airdrop; (*de bombas*) (aer) release; (*de paracaidistas*) (aer) jump; (law) dispossession; (naut) steeve
**lanzami•nas** *m* (*pl* **-nas**) (nav) mine layer
**lanzapla•tos** *m* (*pl* **-tos**) trap
**lanzar** §60 *tr* to throw, hurl, fling; (*un proyecto, un cohete, maldiciones, una ofensiva, un producto nuevo, un buque*) to launch; (*una mirada*) to cast; to vomit, to throw up; (*flores, hojas una planta*) to put forth; (*una advertencia*) to toss, toss out; (aer) to airdrop; (*bombas*) (aer) to release; (law) to dispossess || *ref* to launch, launch forth; to throw oneself; to dash, to rush; (aer) to jump; (sport) to sprint
**lanzatorpe•dos** *m* (*pl* **-dos**) (nav) torpedo tube
**laña** *f* clamp; rivet
**lañar** *tr* to clamp; (*objetos de porcelana*) to rivet
**lapicero** *m* pencil holder; mechanical pencil
**lápida** *f* tablet, stone; **lápida sepulcral** gravestone
**lapidar** *tr* to stone to death
**lá•piz** *m* (*pl* **-pices**) (*grafito*) black lead; (*barrita que sirve para escribir*) pencil, lead pencil; **lápiz de labios** lipstick; **lápiz de pizarra** slate pencil; **lápiz de plomo** graphite; **lápiz estíptico** styptic pencil; **lápiz labial** lipstick
**lapizar** §60 *tr* to mark or line with a pencil
**la•pón -pona** *adj* Lapp || *mf* Lapp, Laplander || *m* (*idioma*) Lapp
**Laponia** *f* Lapland
**lapso** *m* lapse
**laquear** *tr* to lacquer
**lardo•so -sa** *adj* greasy, fatty
**larga** *f* long billiard cue; **dar largas a** to postpone, to put off
**largamente** *adv* at length, extensively; in comfort; generously; long, for a long time
**largar** §44 *tr* to get go, release; to ease, slack; (naut) to unfurl; (coll) to utter; (*un golpe*) (coll) to deal, strike, give; (Col) to give || *ref* to move away; to get away, sneak away, beat it; to take to sea; (*el ancla*) to come loose
**lar•go -ga** *adj* long; abundant; liberal, generous; quick, ready; (coll) shrewd, cunning; (naut) loose, slack; **a la larga** in the long run, in the end; **a lo largo** lengthwise; at great length; far away; **a lo largo de** along; along with; throughout; in the course of; (*el mar*) far out in; **a lo más largo** at most; **hacerse a lo largo** to get out in the open sea; **largo de lengua** loose-tongued; **largo de uñas** light-fingered; **pasar de largo** to pass without stopping; to take a quick look; to miss; **ponerse de largo** to come out, make one's debut; **vestir de largo** to wear long clothes || *m* length || *f* see **larga** || **largo** *adv* at length, at great length; abundantly || **largo** *interj* get out of here!
**largometraje** *m* full-featured film, full-length movie
**largor** *m* length
**larguero** *m* (*palo, madero*) stringer; (*almohada larga*) bolster; (aer) longeron
**largueza** *f* length; liberality, generosity
**larguiru•cho -cha** *adj* (coll) gangling, lanky
**largura** *f* length
**lárice** *m* larch tree
**laringe** *f* larynx
**laringe•o -a** *adj* laryngeal
**laringitis** *f* laryngitis
**laringoscopio** *m* laryngoscope
**larva** *f* larva; mask; (*duende*) hobgoblin
**lascar** §73 *tr* (naut) to pay out, to slacken; (Mex) to scratch, to bruise; (*un objeto de porcelana*) (Mex) to chip
**lascivia** *f* lasciviousness
**lasci•vo -va** *adj* lascivious; playful
**la•so -sa** *adj* tired, exhausted; weak, wan
**lástima** *f* pity; (*quejido*) complaint; **contar lástimas** to tell a hard-luck story; **dar lástima** to be pitiful; **es lástima (que)** it is a pity (that); **estar hecho una lástima** to be a sorry sight; **hacer lástima** to be pitiful; **llorar lástimas** (coll) to put on a show of tears; **poner lástima** to be pitiful; **¡qué lástima!** what a pity!, what a shame!; **¡qué lástima de saliva!** (coll) what a waste of breath!
**lastimar** *tr* to hurt, injure; to hurt, offend; to bruise || *ref* to hurt oneself; to bruise oneself; to complain
**lastime•ro -ra** *adj* hurtful, injurious; pitiful, sad, doleful
**lastimo•so -sa** *adj* pitiful
**lastra** *f* slab, flagstone
**lastrar** *tr* (aer & naut) to ballast
**lastre** *m* (aer & naut) ballast; (fig) wisdom, maturity; (coll) food; (rr) (Chile) ballast
**lat.** *abbr* **latín, latitud**
**lata** *f* (*hojalata*) tin, tin plate; (*envase*) tin, tin can; (*madero sin pulir*) log; (*tabla delgada*) lath; (coll) annoyance, bore; **dar la lata a** (coll) to pester; **estar en la lata** (Col) to be penniless
**latebra** *f* hiding place

**latebro•so -sa** *adj* furtive, secretive
**latente** *adj* latent
**lateral** *adj* lateral
**latido** *m* (*del perro*) yelp; (*del corazón*) beat, throb; (*dolor*) pang, twinge
**latifundio** *m* large neglected landed estate
**latigazo** *m* lash; crack of whip; (*reprensión áspera*) lashing
**látigo** *m* whip, horsewhip; cinch strap
**latiguear** *tr* (Am) to lash, to whip || *intr* to crack a whip
**latiguillo** *m* small whip; (*del actor u orador*) claptrap
**latín** *m* Latin; **latín de cocina** dog Latin, hog Latin; **latín rústico** or **vulgar** Vulgar Latin; **saber latín** or **mucho latín** (coll) to be very shrewd
**latinajo** *m* (coll) dog Latin, hog Latin; (coll) Latin word or phrase (*slipped into the vernacular*)
**latinar** or **latinear** *intr* to use Latin
**lati•no -na** *adj* Latin; (naut) lateen || *mf* Latin
**Latinoamérica** *f* Latin America
**latinoamerica•no -na** *adj* Latin-American || *mf* Latin American
**latir** *tr* (Ven) to annoy, bore, molest || *intr* (*el perro*) to bark, yelp; (*el corazón*) to beat, throb; **me late que** (Mex) I have a hunch that
**latitud** *f* latitude
**la•to -ta** *adj* broad || *f* see **lata**
**latón** *m* brass; (Cuba) garbage pail
**lato•so -sa** *adj* annoying, boring || *mf* bore
**latrocinio** *m* thievery; thievishness
**laucha** *f* (Arg, Chile) mouse
**laúd** *m* (mus) lute; (zool) leatherback turtle
**laudable** *adj* laudable
**láudano** *m* laudanum
**laudato•rio -ria** *adj* laudatory
**laudo** *m* (law) finding, decision
**láurea** *f* laurel wreath
**laurea•do -da** *adj & mf* laureate
**laurean•do -da** *mf* graduate, candidate for a degree
**laurear** *tr* to trim or adorn with laurel; to crown with laurel; to decorate, honor, reward
**laurel** *m* laurel; (*de la victoria*) laurels; **dormirse sobre sus laureles** to rest or sleep on one's laurels
**láure•o -a** *adj* laurel || *f* see **láurea**
**lauréola** *f* crown of laurel, laurel wreath; (*aureola*) halo
**lava** *f* lava; (min) washing
**lavable** *adj* washable
**lavabo** *m* washstand; washroom, lavatory
**lavaca•ras** *mf* (*pl* **-ras**) (coll) fawner, flatterer, bootlicker
**lavaco•ches** *m* (*pl* **-ches**) car washer
**lavade•dos** *m* (*pl* **-dos**) finger bowl
**lavadero** *m* laundry; (*tabla de lavar*) washboard; (*a orillas de un río*) washing place; (Guat, Mex, SAm) placer
**lava•do -da** *adj* (coll) brazen, fresh, impudent || *m* wash, washing; **lavado a seco** dry cleaning; **lavado cerebral** or **de cerebro** brain-washing; **lavado químico** dry cleaning
**lava•dor -dora** *mf* washer || *m* (phot) washer || *f* washing machine; **lavadora de platos** or **de vajilla** dishwasher
**lavadura** *f* washing; (*agua sucia; rozadura de una cuerda*) washings
**lavafru•tas** *m* (*pl* **-tas**) fruit bowl, finger bowl
**lavama•nos** *m* (*pl* **-nos**) (*pila con caño y llave*) washstand; (*jofaina*) washbowl
**lavanda** *f* lavender
**lavandera** *f* laundress, laundrywoman, washerwoman; (orn) sandpiper
**lavandero** *m* launderer, laundryman
**lavándula** *f* lavender
**lavao•jos** *m* (*pl* **-jos**) eyecup
**lavaparabri•sas** *m* (*pl* **-sas**) windshield washer
**lavapla•tos** (*pl* **-tos**) *mf* (*persona*) dishwasher || *m* (*aparato*) dishwasher; (Chile) kitchen sink
**lavar** *tr & ref* to wash
**lavativa** *f* enema; (coll) annoyance, bore
**lavatorio** *m* washing; washstand; toilet; (*ceremonia de lavar los pies*) maundy; (med) wash, lotion; (Am) washroom
**lavazas** *fpl* dirty water, wash water
**laxante** *adj & m* laxative
**laxar** *tr* to ease, to slack; (*el vientre*) to loosen
**la•xo -xa** *adj* lax, slack; (fig) lax, loose
**laya** *f* spade; kind, quality
**layar** *tr* to spade, dig with a spade
**lazada** *f* bowknot
**lazar** **§60** *tr* to lasso
**lazarillo** *m* blind man's guide
**lazari•no -na** *adj* leprous || *mf* leper
**lázaro** *m* raggedy beggar; **estar hecho un lázaro** to be full of sores
**lazo** *m* bow, knot, tie; lasso, lariat; snare, trap; bond, tie; **armar lazo a** (coll) to set a trap for; **caer en el lazo** (coll) to fall into the trap; **lazo de amor** truelove knot; **lazo de unión** (fig) tie, bond
**Ldo.** *abbr* **Licenciado**
**le** *pron pers* to him, to her, to it; to you; him; you
**leal** *adj* loyal, faithful; reliable, trustworthy || *m* loyalist
**lealtad** *f* loyalty; reliability, trustworthiness
**le•brel -brela** *mf* whippet, small greyhound
**lebrillo** *m* earthen washtub
**lebrón** *m* large hare; (coll) coward; (Mex) slicker
**lección** *f* lesson; (*interpretación de un pasaje*) reading; **dar la lección** to recite one's lesson; **echar** or **señalar lección** to assign the lesson; **tomar una lección a** to hear the lesson of
**leccionista** *mf* private tutor
**lecti•vo -va** *adj* school (*e.g., day*)
**lec•tor -tora** *adj* reading || *mf* reader || *m* foreign-language teacher; (*empleado que anota el consumo registrado por el contador de agua, gas o*

*electricidad*) meter reader; **lector mental** mind reader
**lectura** *f* reading; broad culture; public lecture; college subject; (*interpretación de un pasaje*) reading; (elec) playback; (typ) pica; **lectura de la mente** mind reading
**lechada** *f* grout; whitewash; (*para hacer papel*) pulp; (CAm, Mex, W-I) whitewash
**lechar** *tr* (Am) to milk; (CAm, Mex, W-I) to whitewash
**leche** *f* milk; **estar con la leche en los labios** to lack experience, to be young and inexperienced; **leche de manteca** buttermilk; **leche desnatada** skim milk; **leche en polvo** milk powder
**lechecillas** *fpl* sweetbread
**lechera** *f* milkmaid, dairymaid; (*vasija para guardar la leche*) milk can; (*vasija para servir la leche*) milk pitcher
**lechería** *f* dairy, creamery
**leche•ro -ra** *adj* (*que da leche*) milch; (*perteneciente a la leche*) milk; (*cicatero*) (coll) stingy || *m* milkman, dairyman || *f* see **lechera**
**lecho** *m* bed; (*especie de sofá*) couch; (*cauce de río*) bed; layer, stratum; **abandonar el lecho** to get up (*from illness*); **lecho de plumas** (fig) feather bed
**le•chón -chona** *adj* (coll) filthy, sloppy || *mf* suckling pig; (*persona sucia, desaseada*) (coll) pig || *m* pig || *f* sow
**lecho•so -sa** *adj* milky || *m* papaya (*tree*) || *f* papaya (*fruit*)
**lechuga** *f* lettuce; head of lettuce; (*fuelle formado en la tela*) frill; **lechuga romana** romaine lettuce
**lechugui•no -na** *adj* stylish, sporty || *m* dandy || *f* stylish young lady
**lechuza** *f* barn owl, screech owl; (coll) owllike woman
**lechu•zo -za** *adj* owlish; (*muleto*) yearling || *m* bill collector; summons server; (coll) owllike fellow || *f* see **lechuza**
**leer** §43 *tr* to read || *intr* to read; to lecture; **leer en** to read (*someone's thoughts*) || *ref* to read, e.g., **este libro se lee con facilidad** this book reads easily
**leg.** *abbr* **legal, legislatura**
**lega** *f* lay sister
**legación** *f* legation
**legado** *m* (*don que se hace por testamento*) legacy; (*enviado diplomático*) legate
**legajo** *m* file, docket, dossier
**legal** *adj* legal; faithful, prompt, right
**legalidad** *f* legality; faithfulness, promptness
**legalizar** §60 *tr* to legalize; to authenticate
**légamo** *m* slime, ooze
**legamo•so -sa** *adj* slimy, oozy
**legaña** *f* gum (*on edge of eyelids*)
**legaño•so -sa** *adj* gummy
**legar** §44 *tr* to bequeath, to will
**legata•rio -ria** *mf* legatee
**legenda•rio -ria** *adj* legendary
**legible** *adj* legible
**legión** *f* legion
**legislación** *f* legislation
**legisla•dor -dora** *adj* legislating || *mf* legislator
**legislar** *intr* to legislate
**legislati•vo -va** *adj* legislative
**legislatura** *f* session of a legislature; (Am) legislature
**legista** *m* law professor; law student
**legitimar** *tr* to legitimate; to legitimize
**legitimidad** *f* legitimacy
**legíti•mo -ma** *adj* legitimate
**le•go -ga** *adj* lay; uninformed || *m* layman; lay brother || *f* see **lega**
**legua** *f* league; **a leguas** far, far away
**leguleyo** *m* pettifogger
**legumbre** *f* (*hortaliza*) vegetable; (bot) legume; (Chile) vegetable stew
**leíble** *adj* legible, readable
**leída** *f* reading
**leí•do -da** *adj* well-read; **leído y escribido** (coll) posing as learned || *f* see **leída**
**lejanía** *f* distance, remoteness
**leja•no -na** *adj* distant, remote; (*pariente*) distant
**lejía** *f* lye; wash water; (coll) severe rebuke
**lejiadora** *f* washing machine
**lejos** *adv* far; **a lo lejos** in the distance; **de lejos** or **desde lejos** from a distance || *m* glimpse; look from afar; **tener buen lejos** to look good at a distance
**le•lo -la** *adj* stupid, inane
**lema** *m* motto, slogan; theme
**len** *adj* soft, flossy
**lena** *f* spirit, vigor; breathing
**lencería** *f* linen goods, dry goods; linen closet; dry-goods store
**lence•ro -ra** *mf* linen dealer, dry-goods dealer
**lendrera** *f* fine-toothed comb
**lendro•so -sa** *adj* nitty, lousy
**lene** *adj* (*suave al tacto*) soft; (*ligero*) light; kind, agreeable
**lengua** *f* (anat) tongue; (*idioma*) language, tongue; (*de tierra, de fuego, de zapato; badajo de campana; lengua de un animal usada como alimento*) tongue; **buscar la lengua a** (coll) to pick a fight with; **dar la lengua** (coll) to chew the rag; **hacerse lenguas de** (coll) to rave about; **írsele a** (*uno*) **la lengua** (coll) to blab; **lengua madre** or **matriz** mother tongue (*language from which another is derived*); **lengua materna** mother tongue (*language acquired by reason of nationality*); **morderse la lengua** to hold one's tongue; **tener en la lengua** (coll) to have on the tip of one's tongue; **tener la lengua gorda** (coll) to talk thick; (coll) to be drunk; **tener mala lengua** (coll) to be blasphemous; (coll) to have an evil tongue; **tener mucha lengua** (coll) to be a great talker; **tirar de la lengua a** (coll) to draw out; **tomar en lenguas** (coll) to gossip about; **tomar lengua** or **lenguas** to pick up news
**lenguado** *m* sole
**lenguaje** *m* language

**lengua•raz** (*pl* **-races**) *adj* foul-mouthed, scurrilous; polyglot || *mf* linguist
**len•guaz** *adj* (*pl* **-guaces**) garrulous
**lengüeta** *f* (*de la balanza*) pointer, needle; (*del zapato*) tongue; (anat) epiglottis; (carp) tongue; (*de un instrumento de viento*) (mus) reed; (Chile) paper cutter; (Mex) petticoat fringe; (SAm) chatterbox
**lengüetada** *f* licking, lapping
**lengüetear** *intr* to stick the tongue out; to flicker, to flutter; (Am) to jabber, to rant
**lengüilar•go -ga** *adj* (coll) foul-mouthed, scurrilous
**lengüisu•cio -cia** *adj* (Mex, P-R) foul-mouthed, scurrilous
**lenidad** *f* lenience
**lenocinio** *m* pandering, procuring
**lente** *m & f* lens; **lente de aumento** magnifying glass; **lente de contacto** or **lente invisible** contact lens; **lentes** *mpl* nose glasses; **lentes de nariz** or **de pinzas** pince-nez
**lenteja** *f* lentil; (*del reloj*) bob, pendulum bob
**lentejuela** *f* sequin, spangle
**lentitud** *f* slowness
**len•to -ta** *adj* slow; sticky; (*fuego*) low
**leña** *f* firewood, kindling wood; **cargar de leña** (coll) to give a drubbing to; **llevar leña al monte** to carry coals to Newcastle
**leña•dor -dora** *mf* woodcutter || *m* woodsman
**leñame** *m* lumber, timber; stock of firewood
**leñero** *m* wood merchant; wood purchaser; (*sitio donde se guarda la leña*) woodshed
**leño** *m* (*madera*) wood; (*tronco de árbol, limpio de ramas*) log; (coll) sap, blockhead; (poet) ship, vessel; **dormir como un leño** to sleep like a log
**leño•so -sa** *adj* woody
**león** *m* lion
**leona** *f* lioness
**leona•do -da** *adj* tawny, fulvous
**leonera** *f* lion cage, den of lions; (coll) dive, gambling joint; (coll) junk room, lumber room
**leonero** *m* lion keeper; (coll) keeper of a gambling joint
**leontina** *f* watch chain
**leopardo** *m* leopard
**leopoldina** *f* watch fob; (mil) Spanish shako
**leotardo** *m* leotard
**lepe** *m* (Ven) flip in the ear; **saber más que Lepe** to be wide-awake
**leperada** *f* (CAm, Mex) coarseness, vulgarity
**lepisma** *f* (ent) silver fish, fish moth
**lepori•no -na** *adj* hare, harelike
**lepra** *f* leprosy
**leprosería** *f* leper house
**lepro•so -sa** *adj* leprous || *mf* leper
**ler•do -da** *adj* slow, dull; coarse, crude
**lesbianismo** *m* lesbianism
**les•bio -bia** *adj & mf* Lesbian || *f* (*mujer homosexual*) Lesbian, lesbian
**lesión** *f* harm, hurt; (pathol) lesion
**lesionar** *tr* to harm, hurt, injure
**lesi•vo -va** *adj* harmful, injurious
**lesna** *f* awl
**le•so -sa** *adj* hurt, harmed, injured; wounded; offended; perverted; (SAm) simple, foolish
**leste** *m* (naut) east
**letal** *adj* lethal, deadly
**letame** *m* manure
**letanía** *f* litany; (*enumeración seguida*) (coll) litany
**letárgi•co -ca** *adj* lethargic
**letargo** *m* lethargy
**letargo•so -sa** *adj* lethargic
**le•tón -tona** *adj* Lettish || *mf* Lett || *m* (*idioma*) Lettish, Lett
**Letonia** *f* Latvia
**letra** *f* (*del alfabeto*) letter; (*modo de escribir propio de una persona*) hand, handwriting; (*de una canción*) words, lyric; (com) draft; (typ) type; (*sentido material*) (fig) letter; **a la letra** (*al pie de la letra*) to the letter; **a letra vista** (com) at sight; **bellas letras** belles lettres; **cuatro letras** or **dos letras** (*esquela, cartita*) a line; **en letras de molde** in print; **escribir en letra de molde** to print; **las letras y las armas** the pen and the sword; **letra a la vista** (com) sight draft; **letra de cambio** (com) bill of exchange; **letra de imprenta** (typ) type; **letra de mano** handwriting; **letra de molde** printed letter; **letra menuda** fine print; (fig) cunning; **letra muerta** dead letter; **letra negrilla** (typ) boldface; **letra redonda** or **redondilla** (typ) roman; **letras** (*literatura*) letters; (coll) a few words, a line; **primeras letras** elementary education, three R's
**letra•do -da** *adj* learned, lettered; (coll) pedantic || *m* lawyer
**letrero** *m* sign, notice; (*p.ej., en una botella*) label
**letrina** *f* privy, latrine; (*cloaca*) sewer; (*cosa sucia*) (fig) cesspool
**letrista** *mf* lyricist, writer of lyrics (*for songs*); calligrapher, engrosser
**leucemia** *f* leukemia
**leucorrea** *f* leucorrhea
**leudar** *tr* to leaven, to ferment with yeast || *ref* (*la masa con la levadura*) to rise
**leu•do -da** *adj* leavened, fermented
**leva** *f* weighing anchor; (mach) cam; (mil) levy
**levada** *f* (*de la espada, el florete, etc.*) flourish; (*de los astros*) rise; (*del émbolo*) stroke
**levadi•zo -za** *adj* (*puente*) lift
**levadura** *f* leaven; leavening; yeast; (*tabla*) board; **levadura comprimida** yeast cake; **levadura de cerveza** brewer's yeast; **levadura en polvo** baking powder
**levantaco•ches** *m* (*pl* **-ches**) auto jack
**levantada** *f* rising, getting up (*from bed or from sickbed*)
**levantamiento** *m* rise, elevation; insurrection, revolt, uprising; **levantamiento del cadáver** inquest; **levantamiento del censo** census taking; **le-**

vantamiento de planos surveying
**levantar** *tr* to raise, to lift, to elevate; to agitate, rouse, stir up; (*una sesión*) to adjourn; (*la mesa*) to clear; (*la voz*) to raise; (*el campo*) to break; (*gente para el ejército; un sitio; fondos*) to raise; (*el ancla*) to weigh; to straighten up; to build, construct, erect; to establish, found; **levantar casa** to break up housekeeping; **levantar planos** to make a survey || *ref* to rise; (*de la cama*) to get up; (*de una silla*) to stand up; to straighten up; (*sublevarse*) to rise up, rebel
**levantaválvu•las** *m* (*pl* **-las**) valve lifter
**levantaventana** *m* sash lift
**levante** *m* east; (*viento*) levanter || **Levante** *m* (*países de la parte oriental del Mediterráneo*) Levant; northeastern Mediterranean shores of Spain, especially around Valencia, Alicante, and Murcia
**levanti•no -na** *adj* Levantine; of the northeastern Mediterranean shores of Spain || *mf* Levantine; native or inhabitant of the northeastern Mediterranean shores of Spain
**levar** *tr* (*el ancla*) to weigh || *ref* to set sail
**leve** *adj* (*de poco peso*) light; slight, trivial, trifling
**levedad** *f* lightness; trivialness
**leviatán** *m* (Bib & fig) leviathan
**levita** *m* deacon || *f* coat, frock coat
**levitón** *m* heavy frock coat
**léxi•co -ca** *adj* lexical || *m* lexicon; (*caudal de voces de un autor*) vocabulary; (*conjunto de vocablos de una lengua o dialecto*) wordstock
**lexicografía** *f* lexicography
**lexicográfi•co -ca** *adj* lexicographic(al)
**lexicógra•fo -fa** *mf* lexicographer
**lexicología** *f* lexicology
**lexicón** *m* lexicon
**ley** *f* law; loyalty, devotion; norm, standard; (*de un metal*) fineness; **a ley de caballero** on the word of a gentleman; **de buena ley** sterling, genuine; **ley de la selva** law of the jungle; **ley del menor esfuerzo** line of least resistance; **ley marcial** martial law; **ley seca** dry law; **tener** or **tomar ley a** to become devoted to; **venir contra una ley** to break a law
**leyenda** *f* legend
**leyente** *adj* reading || *mf* reader
**lezna** *f* awl
**lía** *f* plaited esparto rope; **lías** lees, dregs
**lianza** *f* (Chile) account, credit (*in a store*)
**liar** §77 *tr* to tie, bind; to tie up, wrap up; (*un cigarrillo*) to roll; (coll) to embroil, to involve; **liarlas** (coll) to beat it; (coll) to kick the bucket || *ref* to join together, to be associated; to have a liaison; (coll) to become embroiled, become involved; **liárselos** (coll) to roll one's own (*i.e., cigarettes*)
**libación** *f* libation; (*acción de beber vino u otro licor*) libation
**liba•nés -nesa** *adj & mf* Lebanese
**Líbano, el** Lebanon
**libar** *tr* to suck; to taste, to sip || *intr* to pour out a libation; to imbibe
**libelo** *m* lampoon, libel; (law) petition
**libélula** *f* dragonfly
**liberación** *f* liberation; (*cancelación de la carga que grava un inmueble*) redemption; (*de una cuenta*) settlement, closing; quittance
**liberal** *adj* liberal; (*expedito*) quick, ready; (pol) liberal; (*de amplias miras*) (Arg) liberal-minded || *mf* (pol) liberal
**liberalidad** *f* liberality
**liberar** *tr* to free
**libertad** *f* liberty, freedom; **libertad de cátedra** academic freedom; **libertad de cultos** freedom of worship; **libertad de empresa** free enterprise; **libertad de enseñanza** academic freedom; **libertad de imprenta** freedom of the press; **libertad de los mares** freedom of the seas; **libertad de palabra** freedom of speech, free speech; **libertad de reunión** freedom of assembly; **libertad vigilada** probation; **plena libertad** free hand; **tomarse la libertad de** to take the liberty to
**liberta•do -da** *adj* bold, daring; free, brash, unrestrained
**liberta•dor -dora** *mf* liberator
**libertar** *tr* to liberate, to set free; (*de un peligro, la muerte, etc.*) to save
**liberta•rio -ria** *adj* anarchistic
**libertinaje** *m* licentiousness, profligacy; impiety, ungodliness
**liberti•no -na** *adj & mf* libertine
**liber•to -ta** *mf* (law) probationer || *m* freedman || *m* freedwoman
**libídine** *f* lewdness, lust; (*impulso a las actividades sexuales*) libido
**libidino•so -sa** *adj* libidinous
**libido** *f* libido
**libra** *f* pound; **libra esterlina** pound sterling
**libraco** or **libracho** *m* (coll) trashy book
**libra•do -da** *mf* (com) drawee
**libra•dor -dora** *mf* (com) drawer
**libranza** *f* (com) draft; **libranza postal** money order
**librar** *tr* to free; to save, to spare; (*la esperanza*) to place; (*batalla*) to give, to join; (com) to draw || *intr* to be delivered, to give birth; (*una religiosa*) to receive a visitor in the locutory; (com) to draw; **librar bien** to come off well, to succeed; **librar mal** to come off badly, to fail || *ref* to free oneself; to escape
**libre** *adj* free; free, brash, outspoken; free, unmarried; free, loose, licentious; innocent, guiltless; **libre de porte** postage prepaid
**librea** *f* livery
**librecambio** *m* free trade
**librecambista** *mf* freetrader
**librepensa•dor -dora** *adj* freethinking || *mf* freethinker
**librería** *f* bookstore, bookshop; book business; (*mueble*) bookshelf; **librería de viejo** second-hand bookshop
**librerii** *adj* book

**librero** *m* bookseller; (*encuadernador*) bookbinder; (Cuba, Mex) bookshelf
**libres•co -ca** *adj* bookish
**libreta** *f* notebook; **libreta de banco** bankbook
**libreto** *m* (mus) libretto
**librillo** *m* earthen washtub; (*de papel de fumar, de sellos, etc.*) book
**libro** *m* book; **ahorcar los libros** (coll) to become a dropout; **a libro abierto** at sight; **hacer libro nuevo** (coll) to turn over a new leaf; **libro a la rústica** paperbound book; **libro de caballerías** romance of chivalry; **libro de cocina** cookbook; **libro de cheques** checkbook; **libro de chistes** joke book; **libro de lance** second-hand book; **libro de mayor venta** best seller; **libro de memoria** memo book; **libro de oro** guest book; **libro de recuerdos** scrapbook; **libro de teléfonos** telephone book; **libro de texto** textbook; **libro diario** day book; **libro en rústica** paperbound book; **libro mayor** (com) ledger; **libro talonario** checkbook, stub book
**libro-registro** *m* (com) book
**licencia** *f* license; leave of absence; (mil) furlough; **licencia absoluta** (mil) discharge; **licencia por enfermedad** sick leave
**licencia•do -da** *adj* pedantic || *mf* licenciate || *m* lawyer; (mil) discharged soldier; (coll) university student (*wearing the long student gown*)
**licenciar** *tr* to license; to allow, permit; to confer the degree of licenciate or master on; (mil) to discharge || *ref* to receive the degree of licenciate or master; to become dissolute; (mil) to be discharged
**licenciatura** *f* licenciate, master's degree; graduation with a licenciate or master's degree; work leading to a licenciate or master's degree
**licencio•so -sa** *adj* licentious
**liceo** *m* (*sociedad literaria, establecimiento de enseñanza popular*) lyceum; (*instituto de segunda enseñanza*) (Chile) lycée; (Mex) primary school
**licitación** *f* bidding
**licita•dor -dora** *mf* bidder
**licitar** *tr* to bid on; (Arg) to buy at auction, to sell at auction || *intr* to bid
**líci•to -ta** *adj* fair, just; licit, legal
**licor** *m* (*bebida espiritosa; cuerpo líquido*) liquor; (*bebida espiritosa preparada por mezcla de azúcar y substancias aromáticas*) liqueur
**licorera** *f* cellaret
**licorista** *mf* distiller; liquor dealer
**licoro•so -sa** *adj* spirituous, alcoholic; (*vino*) rich, generous
**licuar §21 & regular** *tr* to liquefy
**lid** *f* fight, combat; dispute, argument; **en buena lid** by fair means
**líder** *m* leader
**lidia** *f* fight; bullfight
**lidiadera** *f* (Ecuad) quarreling, bickering
**lidia•dor -dora** *mf* fighter || *m* bullfighter
**lidiar** *tr* (*un toro*) to fight || *intr* to fight; **lidiar con** to fight with; to have to put up with
**liebre** *f* hare; (*hombre cobarde*) (coll) coward
**liendre** *f* nit
**lien•to -ta** *adj* damp, dank
**lienza** *f* strip of cloth
**lienzo** *m* linen, linen cloth; linen handkerchief; (*de edificio o pared*) face, front; (*pintura sobre lienzo*) canvas; **lienzo de la Verónica** veronica (*representing face of Christ*)
**liga** *f* (*cinta elástica para asegurar las medias*) garter; (*aleación*) alloy; (*materia pegajosa para cazar pájaros*) birdlime; (*confederación, alianza*) league; (*muérdago*) mistletoe; band; **liga de goma** rubber band
**ligado** *m* (mus & typ) ligature
**ligadura** *f* tie, bond; (mus) ligature, glide; (surg) ligature
**ligamento** *m* ligament
**ligar §44** *tr* to tie, bind; to join, combine; to alloy; (*bebidas*) to mix; (surg) to ligate || *ref* to league together; to be committed; to be bound or attached (*e.g., in friendship*)
**ligereza** *f* lightness; speed, rapidity; fickleness, inconstancy; tactlessness
**lige•ro -ra** *adj* light; (*té*) weak; (*tejido*) light, thin; quick; slight; **a la ligera** lightly; quickly; unceremoniously; **de ligero** thoughtlessly, rashly; **ligero de cascos** light-headed, scatterbrained; **ligero de lengua** loose-tongued; **ligero de pies** light-footed; **ligero de ropa** scantily clad || **ligero** *adv* (Am) fast, rapidly
**lignito** *m* lignite
**ligustro** *m* privet
**lija** *f* (*pez*) dogfish; (*papel que sirve para pulir*) sandpaper; **darse lija** (W-I) to boast, brag, pat oneself on the back
**lijar** *tr* to sand, to sandpaper
**lila** *adj* (coll) silly, simple || *m* lilac (*color*) || *f* lilac (*plant and flower*)
**li•lac** *f* (*pl* **-laques**) lilac
**liliputiense** *adj & mf* Lilliputian
**lima** *f* (*herramienta*) file; sweet lime; sweet-lime tree; (*del tejado*) hip; hip rafter; correcting, polishing; **lima de uñas** nail file; **lima hoya** valley (*of roof*)
**limadura** *f* filing; (*partecillas*) filings
**limalla** *f* filings
**limar** *tr* to file; to file down; to polish, touch up; to smooth, smooth over; (*cercenar*) to curtail
**limaza** *f* (*babosa*) slug; (Ven) large file
**limazo** *m* slime, sliminess
**limbo** *m* (*borde*) edge; (theol) limbo; **estar en el limbo** (coll) to be quite distraught
**limen** *m* (physiol, psychol & fig) threshold
**limenso** *m* (Chile) honeydew melon
**lime•ño -ña** *adj & mf* Limean
**limero** *m* sweet-lime tree
**limita•do -da** *adj* limited; dull-witted

**limitador** *m* — **limitador de corriente** clock meter; slot meter
**limitar** *tr* to limit; to cut down, reduce || *intr* — **limitar con** to border on
**límite** *m* limit; boundary, border
**limítrofe** *adj* bordering
**limo** *m* slime, mud
**limón** *m* lemon; lemon tree; (*de un coche o carro*) shaft
**limonada** *f* lemonade
**limoncillo** *m* citronella
**limonera** *f* shaft
**limonero** *m* lemon tree
**limosna** *f* alms
**limosnear** *intr* to beg
**limosne•ro -ra** *adj* almsgiving, charitable || *mf* almsgiver; (Am) beggar || *m* alms box
**limo•so -sa** *adj* slimy, muddy
**limpia** *f* cleaning
**limpiaba•rros** *m* (*pl* **-rros**) scraper, foot scraper
**limpiabo•tas** *m* (*pl* **-tas**) bootblack
**limpiacrista•les** *m* (*pl* **-les**) windshield washer
**limpiachimene•as** *m* (*pl* **-as**) chimney sweep
**limpiadien•tes** *m* (*pl* **-tes**) toothpick
**limpia•dor -dora** *adj* cleaning || *mf* cleaner
**limpiadura** *f* cleaning; **limpiaduras** cleanings, dirt
**limpiama•nos** *m* (*pl* **-nos**) (Guat, Hond) towel
**limpiamente** *adv* in a clean manner; with ease, skillfully; simply, sincerely; unselfishly
**limpiameta•les** *m* (*pl* **-les**) metal polish
**limpianieve** *m* snowplow
**limpiaparabri•sas** *m* (*pl* **-sas**) windshield wiper
**limpia•piés** *m* (*pl* **-piés**) (Mex) door mat
**limpiapi•pas** *m* (*pl* **-pas**) pipe cleaner
**limpiaplu•mas** *m* (*pl* **-mas**) penwiper
**limpiar** *tr* to clean; (*purificar*) to cleanse; (*de culpas*) to exonerate; (*un árbol*) to clean out, to prune; (*zapatos*) to shine; (*hurtar*) (coll) to snitch; (*a una persona en el juego*) (coll) to clean out; (*dinero en el juego*) (coll) to clean up; (mil) to mop up; **limpiarle a uno de** to clean someone out of || *ref* to clean, to clean oneself
**limpiaú•ñas** *m* (*pl* **-ñas**) nail cleaner, orange stick
**limpiaví•as** *m* (*pl* **-as**) track cleaner
**limpieza** *f* (*acción de limpiar*) cleaning; (*calidad de limpio*) cleanness; (*hábito del aseo*) cleanliness; neatness, tidiness; honesty; chastity; ease, skill; (*observancia de las reglas en los juegos*) fair play; **limpieza de bolsa** (coll) emptiness of the pocketbook; **limpieza de la casa** house cleaning; **limpieza en seco** dry cleaning
**lim•pio -pia** *adj* clean; (*que tiene el hábito del aseo*) cleanly; neat, tidy; honest; chaste; clear, free; **dejar limpio** (coll) to clean out; **en limpio** (com) net; **limpio de polvo y paja** (coll) free, for nothing; (coll) net, after deducting expenses; **poner en limpio** to make a clear or fair copy of; **quedar limpio** (coll) to be cleaned out; **sacar en limpio** to make a clear or clean copy of; to deduce, to understand || *f* see **limpia** || **limpio** *adv* fair; cleanly; **jugar limpio** to play fair
**limpión** *m* (*limpiadura ligera*) lick; (coll) cleaner; (Col) scolding; (Col, Ven) dustcloth; (Ecuad) dishcloth
**limusina** *f* limousine
**lín.** *abbr* **línea**
**lina** *f* (Chile) coarse wool
**linaje** *m* lineage; class, description; **linaje humano** mankind
**linaju•do -da** *adj* highborn || *mf* highborn person
**linaza** *f* flaxseed, linseed
**lince** *adj* keen, shrewd, discerning; (*ojos*) keen || *m* lynx; (fig) keen person
**lincear** *tr* (coll) to see into
**linchamiento** *m* lynching
**linchar** *tr* to lynch
**lindante** *adj* bordering, adjoining
**lindar** *intr* to border, be contiguous; **lindar con** to border on
**linde** *m & f* limit, boundary
**linde•ro -ra** *adj* bordering, adjoining || *m* edge; (Am) boundary stone, landmark || *f* limit, boundary; (bot) spicebush
**lindeza** *f* prettiness, niceness; elegance; witticism, funny remark; (coll) flirting; **lindezas** (coll) insults
**lin•do -da** *adj* pretty, nice; fine, perfect; **de lo lindo** (coll) a lot, a great deal; wonderfully || *m* (coll) dude, sissy
**lindura** *f* prettiness, niceness
**línea** *f* line; (*contorno de una figura, un vestido*) lines; figure, waistline; **conservar la línea** to keep one's figure; **leer entre líneas** to read between the lines; **línea de agua** water line; **línea de batalla** line of battle; **línea de empalme** (rr) branch line; **línea de flotación** water line; **línea de fuego** firing line; **línea de fuerza** (elec) power line; (phys) line of force; **línea del partido** party line; **línea de mira** line of sight; **línea de montaje** assembly line; **línea de puntos** dotted line; **línea de tiro** (mil) line of fire; **línea férrea** railway; **línea internacional de cambio de fecha** international date line; **línea suplementaria** (mus) added line, ledger line
**lineal** *adj* linear
**lineamentos** *mpl* lineaments
**linfa** *f* lymph; (poet) water
**linfáti•co -ca** *adj* lymphatic
**lingote** *m* ingot, slug; (naut) ballast bar
**lingual** *adj & f* lingual
**lingüista** *mf* linguist
**lingüísti•co -ca** *adj* linguistic || *f* linguistics
**linimento** *m* liniment
**lino** *m* flax; (*tela*) linen; (poet) sail
**linóleo** *m* linoleum
**linón** *m* lawn
**linotipia** *f* linotype

**linotípi•co -ca** *adj* linotype
**linotipista** *mf* linotype operator
**linotipo** *m* linotype
**linterna** *f* lantern; **linterna eléctrica** flashlight
**lío** *m* bundle; (*de papeles*) batch; (coll) muddle, mess; (coll) liaison, affair; **armar un lío** (coll) to raise a row; **hacerse un lío** (coll) to get into a jam
**lionesa — a la lionesa** (culin) lyonnaise
**liorna** *f* (coll) hubbub, uproar || **Liorna** *f* Leghorn
**lio•so -sa** *adj* (coll) trouble-making; (coll) knotty, troublesome
**liq.ⁿ** *abbr* **liquidación**
**líq.º** *abbr* **líquido**
**liquen** *m* lichen
**liquidar** *tr* to liquefy; (com) to liquidate || *intr* (com) to liquidate || *ref* to liquefy
**liquidez** *f* liquidity
**líqui•do -da** *adj* & *m* liquid; (com) net || *f* (phonet) liquid
**lira** *f* (mus) lyre; (*numen de un poeta*) inspiration; poems, poetry
**lírica** *f* lyric poetry
**líri•co -ca** *adj* lyric(al); (*músico, operístico*) lyric; (Am) fantastic, utopian || *m* lyric poet; (Arg, Ven) visionary || *f* see **lírica**
**lirio** *m* (bot) iris; **lirio blanco** (*azucena*) Madonna lily; **lirio de agua** (bot) calla, calla lily; **lirio de los valles** (bot) lily of the valley
**lirismo** *m* lyricism; spellbinding; (Am) fancy, illusion
**lirón** *m* (bot) water plantain; (zool) dormouse; (coll) sleepyhead
**lis** *m* (bot) lily || *f* (bot) iris; (heral) fleur-de-lis
**Lisboa** *f* Lisbon
**lisia•do -da** *adj* hurt, injured; crippled; (*muy deseoso*) eager || *mf* cripple
**lisiar** *tr* to hurt, injure; to cripple || *ref* to become crippled
**lisimaquia** *f* loosestrife
**li•so -sa** *adj* even, smooth; (*vestido*) plain, unadorned; (*franco, sincero*) simple, plain-dealing; (Am) brash, insolent; **liso y llano** (coll) simple, easy
**lisonja** *f* flattery
**lisonjear** *tr* to flatter; to please || *intr* to flatter
**lisonje•ro -ra** *adj* flattering; pleasing || *mf* flatterer
**lista** *f* list; (*tira*) strip; (*en un tejido*) colored stripe; (*recuento en alta voz de las personas que deben estar en un lugar*) roll call; **lista de bajas** casualty list; **lista de comidas** bill of fare; **lista de correos** general delivery; **lista de espera** waiting list; **lista de frecuencia** frequency list; **lista de pagos** pay roll; **pasar lista** to call the roll
**listar** *tr* to list
**listero** *m* roll keeper, timekeeper
**lis•to -ta** *adj* ready; quick, prompt; alert, wide-awake; **estar listo** to be ready; to be finished; **listo de manos** (coll) light-fingered; **pasarse de listo** to be shrewd, to be clever || *f* see **lista**
**listón** *m* (*cinta*) ribbon, tape; (*pedazo de tabla angosta*) lath, strip of wood
**listonado** *m* lath, lathing
**lisura** *f* evenness, smoothness; plainness; simpleness, candor; (Am) brashness, insolence
**lit.** *abbr* **literalmente**
**lite** *f* lawsuit
**litera** *f* (*vehículo llevado por hombres o por animales*) litter; (*cama fija en los camarotes*) berth; **litera alta** upper berth; **litera baja** lower berth
**literal** *adj* literal
**litera•rio -ria** *adj* literary
**litera•to -ta** *adj* literary || *mf* literary person; **literatos** literati
**literatura** *f* literature; **literatura de escape** or **de evasión** escape literature
**litigación** *s* litigation
**litigante** *adj* & *mf* litigant
**litigar** §44 *tr* & *intr* to litigate
**litigio** *m* litigation, lawsuit; argument, dispute
**litigio•so -sa** *adj* litigious
**litina** *s* (chem) lithia
**litio** *m* (chem) lithium
**litisexpensas** *fpl* (law) costs
**litografía** *f* (*arte de grabar en piedra para la reproducción en estampa*) lithography; (*estampa*) lithograph
**litografiar** §77 *tr* to lithograph
**litógra•fo -fa** *mf* lithographer
**litoral** *adj* coastal, littoral || *m* coast, shore
**litro** *m* liter
**liturgia** *f* liturgy
**litúrgi•co -ca** *adj* liturgic(al)
**liviandad** *f* lightness; inconstancy, fickleness; lewdness
**livia•no -na** *adj* light; inconstant, fickle; lewd || *m* leading donkey; **livianos** lights, lungs
**lívi•do -da** *adj* livid
**liza** *f* combat, fight; (*campo para lidiar*) lists; **entrar en liza** to enter the lists
**lo** *art def neut* (used with *masc sg* form of *adj*) the, e.g., **lo bueno** the good; what is, e.g., **lo útil** what is useful; **lo mío** what is mine; (used with *adv* or inflected *adj*) the + noun, e.g., **lo aprisa que habla** the speed with which he speaks; **lo tacaños que son** the stinginess of them; how, e.g., **Vd., no sabe lo felices que son** you do not know how happy they are; **lo más** as . . . as, e.g., **lo más temprano posible** as early as possible || *pron pers masc* him, it; you; (with **estar, ser, parecer,** and the like, it stands for an adjective or noun understood and is either not translated or is translated by 'so'), e.g., **Vd. está preparado pero ella no lo está** you are ready but she is not || *pron dem* that; **de lo que** + *verb* than + *verb*, e.g., **ese libro ha costado más dinero de lo que vale** that book cost more money than it is worth; **lo de** the matter of, the question of, e.g., **lo de sus deudas** the matter of your debts; **lo de que** the fact that, the statement that; **lo de siempre** the same old story; **lo que** what, that which; **todo lo que** all

(that), e.g., **me dió todo lo que tenía** he gave me all he had
**loa** *f* praise; (*del teatro antiguo*) prologue; short dramatic poem
**loable** *adj* laudable, praiseworthy
**loar** *tr* to praise
**loba** *f* she-wolf; ridge
**lobagante** *m* lobster (*Homarus*)
**lobanillo** *m* wen, cyst
**lobato** *m* wolf cub
**lo•bo -ba** *adj & mf* (Mex) half-breed || *m* wolf; **coger** or **pillar un lobo** (coll) to go on a jag; **desollar** or **dormir un lobo** (coll) to sleep off a drunk; **lobo de mar** (ichth) sea wolf; (coll) old salt, sea dog; **lobo solitario** (fig) lone wolf || *f* see **loba**
**lóbre•go -ga** *adj* dark, dismal; gloomy
**lobreguez** *f* darkness; gloominess
**lobu•no -na** *adj* wolf, wolfish
**locación** *f* lease
**local** *adj* local || *m* quarters, place
**localidad** *f* (*lugar, sitio*) location, locality; (*plaza en un tren*) accommodations; (theat) seat
**localización** *f* localization; location; **localización de averías** trouble shooting
**localizar** §60 *tr* (*limitar a un punto determinado*) to localize; (*determinar el lugar de*) to locate
**locería** *f* (Am) pottery
**loción** *f* wash; (pharm) lotion
**lo•co -ca** *adj* crazy, insane, mad; terrific, wonderful; **estar loco por** (coll) to be crazy about, to be mad about; **loco de amor** madly in love; **loco de atar** (coll) raving mad; **loco perenne** insane, demented; (coll) full of fun; **loco rematado** (coll) stark-mad; **volver loco** to drive crazy || *mf* crazy person, lunatic || *m* (*bufón*) fool
**locomotora** *f* engine, locomotive; **locomotora de maniobras** shifting engine
**locro** *m* (SAm) meat and vegetable stew
**lo•cuaz** *adj* (*pl* **-cuaces**) loquacious
**locución** *f* expression, locution; idiomatic phrase, idiom
**locuela** *f* speech, way of speaking
**locue•lo -la** *adj* (coll) wild, frisky || *f* see **locuela**
**locura** *f* insanity, madness; folly, madness
**locu•tor -tora** *mf* announcer, commentator
**locutorio** *m* (*en un convento de monjas*) parlor, locutory; telephone booth
**lodazal** *m* mudhole
**lodo** *m* mud, mire; (*substancia que sirve para cerrar junturas, tapar grietas, etc.*) (chem) lute
**lodo•so -sa** *adj* muddy
**logaritmo** *m* logarithm
**logia** *f* (*p.ej., de francmasones*) lodge; (archit) loggia
**lógi•co -ca** *adj* logical || *mf* logician || *f* logic
**logísti•co -ca** *adj* logistic(al) || *f* logistics
**logrado -da** *adj* successful
**lograr** *tr* to get, to obtain; to achieve, attain; **lograr** + *inf* to succeed in + *ger* || *ref* to be successful
**logrear** *intr* to be a moneylender; to profiteer
**logre•ro -ra** *adj* moneylending; profiteering || *mf* moneylender; profiteer; (Chile) sponger
**logro** *m* attainment, success; gain, profit; usury; **dar** or **prestar a logro** to lend at usurious rates
**loma** *f* low hill, elevation
**Lombardía** *f* Lombardy
**lombar•do -da** *adj & mf* Lombard
**lombriguera** *f* wormhole in the ground; (bot) tansy
**lom•briz** *f* (*pl* **-brices**) worm, earthworm; (pathol) worm; (*persona muy alta y delgada*) (coll) beanpole; **lombriz de tierra** earthworm; **lombriz solitaria** tapeworm
**lomera** *f* (*de la guarnición*) backstrap; (*del tejado*) ridgepole; (bb) backing
**lominhies•to -ta** *adj* high-backed; (coll) conceited
**lomo** *m* (*de animal, libro, cuchillo*) back; (*tierra que levanta el arado*) ridge; (*carne de lomo del animal*) loin; (*pliegue del tejido*) crease; (bb) spine; **lomos** ribs
**lona** *f* canvas; sailcloth; (Mex) burlap
**loncha** *f* slab, flagstone; slice, strip
**londinense** *adj* London || *mf* Londoner
**Londres** *m* London; **el Gran Londres** Greater London
**longáni•mo -ma** *adj* long-suffering
**longaniza** *f* pork sausage
**longevidad** *f* longevity
**longe•vo -va** *adj* long-lived
**longitud** *f* length; (astr & geog) longitud
**lonja** *f* exchange, commodity exchange; grocery store; wool warehouse; (*de carne*) slice; (*de cuero*) strip; (*a la entrada de un edificio*) elevated parvis; (Arg) rawhide
**lonjeta** *f* bower, summerhouse
**lonjista** *mf* grocer
**lontananza** *f* (*de una pintura*) background; **en lontananza** in the distance, on the horizon
**loor** *m* praise
**loquear** *intr* to talk nonsense, to play the fool; to carry on, to have a high time
**loquería** *f* (Chile) madhouse, insane asylum
**loque•ro -ra** *mf* guard in a mental hospital || *m* (Arg) confusion, pandemonium; (Arg) insane asylum
**loques•co -ca** *adj* crazy; funny, jolly
**lord** *m* (*pl* **-lores**) lord
**lo•ro -ra** *adj* dark-brown || *m* parrot; cherry laurel; (Chile) spy; (Chile) glass bedpan; (Chile) third degree
**losa** *f* slab, flagstone; tomb
**losange** *m* lozenge; (baseball) diamond
**lote** *m* lot, share, portion; lottery prize; (Cuba, Mex) remnant; (Arg) dunce, simpleton; (Col) swallow, swig; (*de terreno*) (Cuba, Mex) lot
**lotear** *tr* (Chile) to divide up, divide into lots
**lotería** *f* lottery; (*juego casero*) lotto; (*cosa insegura, riesgo*) gamble
**lote•ro -ra** *mf* vendor of lottery tickets
**lotizar** §60 *tr* (Peru) to divide into lots

**loto** *m* lotus
**loza** *f* (*barro cocido y barnizado*) porcelain; crockery, earthenware; **loza fina** china, chinaware
**lozanear** *intr* to be luxuriant; to be full of life || *ref* (*deleitarse*) to luxuriate
**lozanía** *f* luxuriance, verdure; exuberance, vigor; pride, haughtiness
**loza•no -na** *adj* luxuriant, verdant; exuberant, vigorous; proud, haughty
**lubricante** *adj & m* lubricant
**lubricar** §73 *tr* to lubricate
**lúbri•co -ca** *adj* (*resbaladizo; lascivo*) lubricous (*slippery; lewd*)
**lubrificar** §73 *tr* to lubricate
**lucera** *f* skylight
**lucerna** *f* large chandelier; (*abertura, tronera*) loophole
**lucero** *m* bright star; (*planeta*) Venus; (*ventanillo en un muro*) light; **lucero del alba** or **de la mañana** morning star; **lucero de la tarde** evening star; **luceros** (poet) eyes
**luci•do -da** *adj* generous, magnificent; brilliant, successful; sumptuous; (Arg) striking, dashing
**lúci•do -da** *adj* lucid
**luciente** *adj* bright, shining
**luciérnaga** *f* glowworm, firefly
**lucifer** *m* overbearing fellow || **Lucifer** *m* Lucifer
**lucífe•ro -ra** *adj* (poet) bright, dazzling || *m* morning star; (Col) match
**lucimiento** *m* brilliance, luster; show, dash; success; **quedar** or **salir con lucimiento** to come off with flying colors
**lu•cio -cia** *adj* shiny || *m* salt pool; (*pez*) pike, luce
**lucir** §45 *tr* to light, light up; to show, display; (*p.ej., un traje nuevo*) to sport; to help; to plaster || *intr* to shine || *ref* to dress up; to come off with great success; (*sobresalir, distinguirse*) to shine; (coll) to flop, e.g., **lucido me quedé** I was a flop
**lucrar** *tr* to get, obtain || *intr & ref* to profit, make money
**lucrati•vo -va** *adj* lucrative
**lucro** *m* gain, profit; **lucros y daños** profit and loss
**lucro•so -sa** *adj* lucrative
**luctuo•so -sa** *adj* sad, mournful, gloomy
**lucha** *f* fight; (*disputa*) quarrel; (*actividad forzada*) struggle; (*combate cuerpo a cuerpo*) wrestling; **lucha de la cuerda** (sport) tug of war; **lucha por la vida** struggle for existence
**lucha•dor -dora** *mf* fighter; wrestler
**luchar** *intr* (*combatir*) to fight; (*disputar*) to quarrel; (*esforzarse*) to struggle; (*pelear cuerpo a cuerpo*) to wrestle
**ludibrio** *m* derision, mockery, scorn
**ludir** *tr, intr & ref* to rub, rub together
**luego** *adv* next, then; therefore; soon; **desde luego** right away; of course; **hasta luego** good-bye, so long; **luego como** as soon as; **luego de** after, right after; **luego que** as soon as
**luen•go -ga** *adj* long
**lúes** *f* pestilence; **lúes canina** distemper; **lúes venérea** syphilis
**lugano** *m* (orn) siskin
**lugar** *m* place; site, spot; job, position; (*espacio*) room, space; (*asiento*) seat; village, hamlet; (geom) locus; **dar lugar** to make room; **dar lugar a** to give cause for; to give rise to; **en lugar de** instead of, in place of; **hacer lugar** to make room; **lugar común** (*expresión trivial*) commonplace; (*retrete*) toilet, water closet; **lugar de cita** tryst; **lugares estrechos** close quarters; **lugar geométrico** locus; **lugar religioso** place of burial
**lugarejo** *m* hamlet
**lugare•ño -ña** *adj* village || *mf* villager
**lugarteniente** *m* lieutenant
**luge** *m* sled
**lúgubre** *adj* dismal, gloomy, lugubrious
**luir** §20 *tr* (naut) to gall, to wear; (Chile) to muss, to rumple; (*vasijas de barro*) (Chile) to polish || *ref* (Chile) to rub, wear away
**luisa** *f* (bot) lemon verbena
**lujo** *m* luxury; **de lujo** de luxe; **gastar mucho lujo** to live in high style; **lujo de** abundance of, excess of
**lujo•so -sa** *adj* luxurious
**lujuria** *f* lust, lechery
**lujuriante** *adj* (*lozano*) luxuriant, lush; (*libidinoso*) lustful
**lujuriar** *intr* to lust, be lustful; (*los animales*) to copulate
**lujurio•so -sa** *adj* lustful, lecherous || *mf* lecher
**lu•lo -la** *adj* (Chile) lank, slender || *m* (Chile) bundle
**lu•lú** *m* (*pl* **-lúes**) spitz dog
**lumbago** *m* lumbago
**lumbre** *f* light; fire; (*para encender el cigarrillo*) light; (*hueco en un muro por donde entra la luz*) light; brightness, brilliance; knowledge, learning; **echar lumbre** (coll) to blow one's top; **lumbre del agua** surface of the water; **lumbres** tinderbox; **ni por lumbre** (coll) not for love or money; **ser la lumbre de los ojos de** to be the light of the eyes of
**lumbrera** *f* light, source of light; light, lamp; (*abertura por donde entran el aire y la luz*) louver; sky light; dormer window; air duct, ventilating shaft; (*persona insigne*) light, luminary; (mach) port; **lumbreras** eyes
**luminar** *m* luminary
**luminiscente** *adj* luminescent
**lumino•so -sa** *adj* luminous; (*idea*) bright
**luminotecnia** *f* lighting engineering
**lun.** *abbr* **lunes**
**luna** *f* moon; moonlight; (*tabla de cristal*) plate glass; (*espejo*) mirror; (*de los anteojos*) lens, glass; (coll) caprice, whim; **estar de buena luna** to be in a good mood; **estar de mala luna** to be in a bad mood; **luna de miel** honeymoon; **luna llena** full moon; **luna menguante** waning moon; **luna nueva** new moon; **media luna** half moon; (*figura de cuarto de luna creciente o menguante*) crescent; **quedarse a la luna de Valencia** (coll) to be disappointed

**lunar** *adj* lunar || *m* (*mancha de la piel*) mole; (*punto en un diseño de puntos*) polka dot; (fig) stain, blot, stigma; **lunar postizo** beauty spot

**lunáti•co -ca** *adj & mf* lunatic

**lu•nes** *m* (*pl* **-nes**) Monday; **hacer San Lunes** (Am) to knock off on Monday

**luneta** *f* (*de los anteojos*) lens, glass; orchestra seat; (aut) rear window

**lunfardo** *m* (Arg) thief; (Am) underworld slang

**lupa** *m* magnifying glass

**lupanar** *m* brothel, bawdyhouse

**lupia** *mf* (Hond) quack, healer || *f* wen, cyst; **lupias** (Col) small amount of money, small change

**lúpulo** *m* (*vid*) hop; (*flores desecadas de la vid*) hops

**luquete** *m* slice of orange or lemon used to flavor wine; (Chile) bald spot; (*en la ropa*) (Chile) spot, hole

**lu•rio -ria** *adj* (Mex) mad, crazy

**lusitanismo** *m* Lusitanism

**lusitano -na** *adj & mf* Lusitanian, Portuguese

**lustrabo•tas** *m* (*pl* **-tas**) (Am) bootblack

**lustrar** *tr* to shine, to polish || *intr* to wander, roam

**lustre** *m* shine, polish; luster, gloss; (*fama, gloria*) (fig) luster

**lustrina** *f* (Chile) shoe polish

**lustro** *m* five years; chandelier

**lustro•so -sa** *adj* shining, bright, lustrous

**lutera•no -na** *adj & mf* Lutheran

**luto** *m* (*señal exterior de duelo*) mourning; (*duelo, aflicción*) sorrow, bereavement; **estar de luto** to be in mourning; **lutos** crape; **luto riguroso** deep mourning

**lutocar** *m* (Chile) trash cart

**luz** *f* (*pl* **luces**) light; window, light; guiding light; (*dinero*) (coll) money, cash; **a primera luz** at dawn; **a toda luz** or **a todas luces** everywhere; by all means; **dar a luz** to have a child; to give birth to; to bring out, to publish; **entre dos luces** at twilight; (coll) half-seas over; **luces de carretera** (aut) bright lights; **luces de cruce** (aut) dimmers; **luz de balizaje** (aer) marker light; **luz de magnesio** magnesium light; (phot) flash bulb, flashlight; **luz de matrícula** license-plate light; **luz de parada** stop light; **luz trasera** tail light; **sacar a luz** to bring to light; **salir a luz** to come to light; to come out, be published; to take place; **ver la luz** to see the light, see the light of day

**Luzbel** *m* Lucifer

## Ll

**Ll, ll** (elle) *f* fourteenth letter of the Spanish alphabet

**llaga** *f* sore, ulcer; sorrow, grief; (*entre dos ladrillos*) (mas) seam, joint; (fig) ulcer

**llagar §44** *tr* to make sore; to hurt

**llama** *f* flame, blaze; marsh, swamp; (zool) llama; (fig) fire, passion; **saltar de las llamas y caer en las brasas** to jump out of the frying pan into the fire

**llamada** *f* call; (*movimiento con que se llama la atención de uno*) sign, signal; knock, ring; reference, reference mark; (mil) call, call to arms; **batir** or **tocar a llamada** (mil) to sound the call to arms; **llamada a filas** (mil) call to the colors; **llamada a quintas** draft call

**llamadera** *f* goad

**llama•do -da** *adj* so-called || *f* see **llamada**

**llama•dor -dora** *mf* caller || *m* messenger; door knocker; push button

**llamamiento** *m* call; calling, vocation

**llamar** *tr* to call; (*dar nombre a*) to name, to call; to summon; to invoke, call upon; (*la atención*) to attract || *intr* to call; (*golpear en la puerta*) to knock; (*hacer sonar la campanilla*) to ring; (*el viento*) (naut) to veer || *ref* to be called, to be named; **se llama Juan** his name is John

**llamarada** *f* blaze, flare-up; (*encendimiento repentino del rostro*) flush; (fig) flare-up, outburst

**llamarón** *m* (Am) flare-up

**llamati•vo -va** *adj* showy, loud, flashy, gaudy; (*manjar*) thirst-raising

**llamazar** *m* swamp, marsh

**llame** *m* (Chile) bird net, bird trap

**llamear** *intr* to blaze, flame, flash

**llampo** *m* (Chile) ore

**llana** *f* trowel, float; plain; **dar de llana** to smooth with the trowel

**llanada** *f* plain

**llanero** *m* (Am) ranger, plainsman

**llaneza** *f* plainness, simplicity; familiarity; sincerity

**lla•no -na** *adj* even, level, smooth; (*parecido a un plano geométrico*) plane; (*sencillo*) plain, simple; clear, evident; (*palabras*) frank; accented on the next to last syllable || *m* plain; (*de la escalera*) landing || *f* see **llana**

**llanque** *m* (Peru) rawhide sandal

**llanta** *f* (*cerco exterior de la rueda*) tire (*of iron or rubber*); (*borde exterior de la rueda*) rim; (*pieza de hierro más ancha que gruesa*) iron flat; **llanta de goma** rubber tire; **llanta de oruga** (*de un tractor de oruga*) track

**llanto** *m* weeping, crying; **en llanto** in tears

**llanura** *f* evenness, level, smoothness; (*terreno extenso y llano*) plain

**llapan•go -ga** *adj* (Ecuad) barefooted

**llares** *m* pothanger

**llave** *adj* key || *f* (*pieza para abrir y cerrar las cerraduras*) key; (*herramienta*) wrench; (*grifo*) faucet, spigot, cock; (*de arma de fuego*) cock; (elec) switch; (*de un instrumento de viento*) (mus) key; (*de un enigma, secreto, traducción, cifra; lugar estratégico más propicio*) key; **bajo llave** under lock and key; **echar la llave a** to lock; **llave de caja** socket wrench; **llave de caño** pipe wrench; **llave de cubo** socket wrench; **llave de chispa** flintlock; **llave de estufa** damper; **llave de mandíbulas dentadas** alligator wrench; **llave de paso** stopcock; passkey; **llave de purga** drain cock; **llave espacial** space key; **llave inglesa** monkey wrench; **llave maestra** master key, skeleton key; **llave para tubos** pipe wrench
**llave•ro -ra** *mf* keeper of the keys; (*carcelero*) turnkey || *m* key ring
**llavín** *m* latchkey
**llegada** *f* arrival
**llegar §44** *tr* to bring up, bring close || *intr* to arrive; to happen; **llegar a** to arrive at; to reach; to amount to; to be equal to; **llegar a** + *inf* to come to + *inf;* to succeed in + *ger;* **llegar a ser** to become || *ref* to come close
**llena** *f* flood
**llenado** *m* filling
**llena•dor -dora** *adj* (*alimento*) (Chile) filling
**llenar** *tr* to fill; (*un formulario*) to fill out; (*ciertas condiciones*) to fulfill; to satisfy; (*colmar*) to overwhelm || *intr* (*la luna*) to be full || *ref* to fill, fill up; (coll) to stuff oneself; **llenarse a rebosar** to be filled to overflowing
**llene** *m* filling; full tank
**lle•no -na** *adj* full; **lleno a rebosar** full to overflowing; **lleno de goteras** (coll) full of aches and pains || *m* fill, plenty; fulness, full enjoyment; completeness; full moon; (*en el teatro*) full house || *f* see **llena**
**lleva** or **llevada** *f* carrying, conveying; ride; **lleva gratuita** free ride
**llevade•ro -ra** *adj* bearable, tolerable
**llevar** *tr* (*transportar*) to carry; (*traer consigo*) to take; (*conducir*) to lead; to carry away, to take away; (*cuentas, libros; la anotación en los naipes*) to keep; (*la correspondencia con una persona*) to carry on; (*un drama a la pantalla*) to put on; (*buena o mala vida*) to lead; (*aguantar*) to bear, to stand for; (*castigo*) to suffer; to get, obtain; to win; (*cierto precio*) to charge; (*traje, vestido*) to wear; (*armas*) to bear; (*cierto tiempo*) to have been, e.g., **llevo ocho días en cama** I have been in bed for a week; (*ropa*) **a todo llevar** for all kinds of wear; **llevar** (*cierto tiempo*) **a** (*uno*) to be older than (*someone*) by (*a certain age*); (*cierta distancia*) **a** (*uno*) to be ahead of (*someone*) by (*a certain distance*); (*cierto peso*) **a** (*uno*) to be heavier than (*someone*) by (*a certain weight*); **llevarla hecha** (coll) to have it all figured out; **llevar puesto** to wear, to have on; **llevar** + *pp* to have + *pp,* e.g., **lleva conseguidas muchas victorias** he has won many victories || *ref* to carry away; to take, take away; to carry off; to win; to get along; **llevarse algo a alguien** to take something away from someone
**lloradue•los** *mf* (*pl* **-los**) crybaby, sniveler
**lloralásti•mas** *mf* (*pl* **-mas**) (coll) poverty-crying skinflint
**llorar** *tr* to weep over; to mourn, lament || *intr* to weep, to cry; (*los ojos*) to water, to run
**lloriquear** *intr* to whine, to whimper
**lloriqueo** *m* whining, whimpering
**lloro** *m* weeping, crying; tears
**llo•rón -rona** *adj* weeping, crying || *mf* weeper, crybaby || *m* weeping willow; pendulous plume || *f* hired mourner
**lloro•so -sa** *adj* weepy; sad, tearful
**llovedi•zo -za** *adj* (*agua*) rain; (*techo*) leaky
**llover §47** *tr* (*enviar como lluvia*) to rain || *intr* to rain; **como llovido** unexpectedly; **llueva o no** rain or shine; **llueve** it is raining || *ref* (*el techo*) to leak
**llovido** *m* stowaway
**llovizna** *f* drizzle
**lloviznar** *intr* to drizzle
**llovizno•so -sa** *adj* moist, damp (*from drizzle*); (Am) drizzly
**lluvia** *f* rain; rain water; (*copia, muchedumbre*) (fig) shower, downpour; **lluvia radiactiva** fallout, radioactive fallout
**lluvio•so -sa** *adj* rainy

## M

**M, m** (eme) *f* fifteenth letter of the Spanish alphabet
**m.** *abbr* **mañana, masculino, meridiano, metro, minuto, muerto**
**maca** *f* flaw, blemish; bruise (*on fruit*); spot, stain; hammock
**maca•co -ca** *adj* (Am) ugly, misshapen || *m* — **macaco de la India** rhesus
**macadamizar §60** *tr* to macadamize
**macadán** *m* macadam
**macana** *f* cudgel, club; drug on the market; (Am) nonsense; (Arg) botch; (Arg) lie, trick
**macanu•do -da** *adj* terrific, swell, grand; (Col, Ecuad) strong, husky
**macarrón** *m* macaroon; **macarrones** macaroni
**macear** *tr* to mace, hammer || *intr* to pester, to bore
**macelo** *m* slaughterhouse

**macero** *m* macebearer
**maceta** *f* stone hammer; flowerpot; flower vase; (*de herramienta*) handle; (*de cantero*) hammer; (Mex) head
**macfarlán** *m* inverness cape
**macilen•to -ta** *adj* pale, wan, gaunt
**macillo** *m* hammer (*of piano*)
**macis** *m* mace (*spice*)
**macizar** §60 *tr* to fill in, fill up
**maci•zo -za** *adj* solid; massive || *m* solid; flower bed; bulk, mass; massif; wall space
**macu•co -ca** *adj* (Chile) sly, cunning; (Arg, Chile, Ven) important, notable; (Ecuad) old, worthless; (Arg, Chile, Peru) strong, husky || *m* (Arg, Bol, Col) overgrown boy
**mácula** *f* spot; stain; blemish; (coll) trick, deception
**macha** *f* (Bol) drunkenness; (Arg) joke; (Bol) mannish woman
**machaca** *mf* (coll) pest, bore || *f* crusher
**machacar** §73 *tr* to crush, mash, pound || *intr* to pester, bore
**macha•cón -cona** *adj* boring, tiresome, importunate || *mf* bore
**machada** *f* flock of billy goats; (coll) stupidity
**machado** *m* hatchet
**machamartillo** — **a machamartillo** (coll) solidly, firmly, lastingly
**machaque•ro -ra** *adj* (coll) tiresome, boring || *mf* (coll) bore
**machar** *tr* to crush, grind, pound || *ref* (Bol, Ecuad) to get drunk
**machete** *m* machete, cane knife
**machi** *mf* (Chile) quack, healer
**machihembrar** *tr* (*ensamblar a ranura y lengüeta*) to feather; (*ensamblar a caja y espiga*) to mortise
**machina** *f* derrick, crane; pile driver; (P-R) merry-go-round
**macho** *adj invar* (*animal, planta, herramienta*) male; strong, robust; dull, stupid || *m* sledge hammer; abutment, pillar; male; he-mule; dullard; (*del corchete*) hook; (mach) male piece; (coll) he-man; (C-R) blond foreigner; **macho cabrío** he-goat, billy goat; **macho de aterrajar** or **macho de terraja** (mach) tap, screw tap
**machona** *f* (Arg, Bol, Ecuad, Guat) mannish woman
**macho•rro -rra** *adj* barren, sterile || *f* barren woman; (Mex) mannish woman
**machucar** §73 *tr* to beat, pound, bruise
**machu•cho -cha** *adj* sedate, judicious; elderly
**madamita** *m* (coll) sissy
**madeja** *f* hank, skein; tangle of hair; (*hombre flojo*) (coll) jellyfish; **madeja sin cuenda** (coll) hopeless tangle
**madera** *m* Madeira wine || *f* wood; piece of wood; (coll) knack, flair; (coll) makings; **madera aserradiza** lumber; **madera contrachapada** plywood; **madera de sierra** lumber; **madera laminada** plywood
**maderada** *f* raft, float
**maderaje** *m* or **maderamen** *m* woodwork
**maderería** *f* lumberyard
**madere•ro -ra** *adj* lumber || *m* lumberman; carpenter; log driver
**madero** *m* log, beam; ship, vessel; (coll) blockhead
**madrastra** *f* stepmother; bother
**madraza** *f* (coll) doting mother
**madre** *adj* mother || *f* mother; matron; womb; main sewer; river bed; dregs, sediment; **madre adoptiva** foster mother; **madre de leche** wet nurse; **madre patria** mother country, old country; **madre política** mother-in-law; stepmother; **sacar de madre** (coll) to annoy, to upset
**madreperla** *f* (*molusco*) pearl oyster; (*nácar*) mother-of-pearl
**madreselva** *f* honeysuckle
**madriga•do -da** *adj* twice-married; (*toro*) that has sired; (coll) worldly-wise
**madriguera** *f* burrow, lair, den
**madrile•ño -ña** *adj* Madrid || *mf* native or inhabitant of Madrid
**madrina** *f* godmother; patroness, protectress; prop, shore, brace; joke; leading mare; **madrina de boda** bridesmaid; **madrina de guerra** war mother
**madrugada** *f* early morning, dawn; early rising
**madruga•dor -dora** *adj* early-rising || *mf* early riser
**madrugar** §44 *intr* to get up early; to be out in front
**madurar** *tr* to ripen; to mature; to think out || *intr* to ripen; to mature
**madurez** *f* ripeness; maturity
**madu•ro -ra** ripe; mature
**maestra** *f* teacher; elementary girls' school; **maestra de escuela** schoolmistress
**maestranza** *f* arsenal, armory; navy yard; order of equestrian knights
**maestría** *f* mastery; mastership
**maes•tro -tra** *adj* master; masterly; chief, main; (*perro*) trained || *m* master; teacher; (*en la música y la pintura*) maestro; **maestro de capilla** choirmaster; **maestro de ceremonias** master of ceremonies; **maestro de equitación** riding master; **maestro de escuela** elementary schoolteacher; **maestro de esgrima** fencing master; **maestro de obras** master builder || *f* see **maestra**
**Magallanes** *m* Magellan
**magancear** *intr* (Col, Chile) to loaf around
**magan•to -ta** *adj* dull, spiritless
**magia** *f* magic
**magiar** *adj* & *mf* Magyar
**mági•co -ca** *adj* magic || *mf* magician, wizard || *f* magic
**magín** *m* (coll) fancy, imagination
**magisterio** *m* teaching; teachers
**magistrado** *m* magistrate
**magistral** *adj* masterly
**magnáni•mo -ma** *adj* magnanimous
**magnesio** *m* magnesium; (phot) flashlight
**magnetismo** *m* magnetism
**magnetizar** §60 *tr* magnetize
**magneto** *m* & *f* magneto

**magnetofón** *m* or **magnetófono** *m* tape recorder, wire recorder
**magnificar** §73 *tr* to magnify; to exalt
**magnífi•co -ca** *adj* magnificent
**magnitud** *f* magnitude
**mag•no -na** *adj* great, e.g., **Alejandro Magno** Alexander the Great
**mago** *m* magician; soothsayer; (fig) wizard, expert; **Magos de Oriente** Wise Men of the East
**ma•gro -gra** *adj* lean, thin || *m* (coll) loin of pork || *f* slice of ham
**maguar** §10 *ref* (Ven, W-I) to be disappointed
**magüeta** *f* heifer
**magüeto** *m* young bull
**maguey** *m* century plant
**magullar** *tr* to bruise || *ref* to get bruised
**mahometa•no -na** *adj & mf* Mohammedan
**mahometismo** *m* Mohammedanism
**mahonesa** *f* mayonnaise
**maído** *m* meow
**maitines** *mpl* matins
**maíz** *m* maize, Indian corn; **maíz en la mazorca** corn on the cob
**maizal** *m* cornfield
**maja** *f* flashy dame
**majada** *f* sheepfold; dung, manure
**majadería** *f* piece of folly, nonsensical remark
**majade•ro -ra** *adj* pestiferous, stupid || *mf* bore, dunce || *m* pestle
**majar** *tr* to crush, mash, grind, pound; (coll) to annoy, bother
**majestad** *f* majesty
**majestuo•so -sa** *adj* majestic
**ma•jo -ja** *adj* sporty; handsome, dashing; pretty, nice; (coll) all dressed up || *mf* sport || *m* bully || *f* see **maja**
**mal** *adj* apocopated form of **malo,** used only before nouns in masculine singular || *adv* badly, poorly; wrong; hardly, scarcely; **mal de** short of; **mal que le pese** in spite of him || *m* evil; damage, harm; wrong; sickness; misfortune; **mal de altura** mountain sickness; **mal de la tierra** homesickness; **mal de mar** seasickness; **mal de piedra** (pathol) stone; **mal de rayos** radiation sickness; **mal de vuelo** airsickness; **por mal de mis pecados** to my sorrow; **tener a mal** to object to; **¡mal haya . . .!** curses on . . .!
**mala** *f* mail; mailbag; mailboat
**malabarista** *mf* juggler; (Am) sneak thief
**malacate** *m* whim; (*hoisting machine*) (Mex, Hond) spindle
**malaconseja•do -da** *adj* ill-advised
**malagradeci•do -da** *adj* (Am) ungrateful
**malandante** *adj* unlucky, unfortunate
**malandanza** *f* bad luck, misfortune
**malan•drín -drina** *adj* evil, wicked || *mf* scoundrel, rascal
**malaria** *f* malaria
**malaventura** *f* misfortune
**mala•yo -ya** *adj & mf* Malay
**malbaratar** *tr* to undersell; to squander
**malcasa•do -da** *adj* mismated; undutiful
**malcasar** *tr* to mismate || *intr & ref* to be mismated
**malcaso** *m* treachery
**malconten•to -ta** *adj & mf* malcontent
**malcria•do -da** *adj* ill-bred
**malcriar** §77 *tr* to spoil, pamper
**maldad** *f* evil, wickedness
**maldecir** §11 *tr* to curse || *intr* to curse, to damn; **maldecir de** to slander, to vilify
**maldición** *f* malediction, curse; (coll) oath, curse
**maldispues•to -ta** *adj* ill, indisposed; unwilling, ill-disposed
**maldi•to -ta** *adj* damned, accursed; wicked; (Mex) coarse, crude, indecent; **no saber maldita la cosa de** (coll) to not know a single thing about || **el Maldito** the Evil One || *f* (coll) tongue; **soltar la maldita** (coll) to talk too much
**maleante** *adj* wicked, evil || *mf* crook, hoodlum, rowdy
**malear** *tr* to spoil; to corrupt || *ref* to spoil, get spoiled; to be corrupted
**malecón** *m* levee, dike, mole, jetty
**maledicencia** *f* calumny, slander
**maleficiar** *tr* to damage, harm; to curse, bewitch, cast a spell on
**maleficio** *m* curse, spell; witchcraft
**malentender** §51 *tr* to misunderstand
**malentendido** *m* misunderstanding, misapprehension
**malestar** *m* malaise, indisposition
**maleta** *m* (coll) bungler; (coll) ham bullfighter || *f* valise; **hacer la maleta** to pack up
**maletín** *m* satchel
**malevolencia** *f* malice, malevolence
**malévo•lo -la** *adj* malevolent
**maleza** *f* thicket, underbrush; weeds
**malgasta•do -da** *adj* ill-spent
**malgastar** *tr* to waste, squander
**malgenio•so -sa** *adj* (Am) ill-tempered, irritable
**malhabla•do -da** *adj* foul-mouthed
**malhada•do -da** *adj* ill-starred
**malhe•cho -cha** *adj* deformed || *m* misdeed
**malhe•chor -chora** *mf* malefactor || *f* malefactress
**malherir** §68 *tr* to injure badly
**malhumora•do -da** *adj* ill-humored
**malicia** *f* (*maldad*) evil; (*bellaquería, malevolencia*) malice; insidiousness, trickiness; (coll) suspicion
**malicio•so -sa** *adj* evil; malicious; insidious, tricky
**malignar** *tr* to corrupt, vitiate; to spoil
**malignidad** *f* malignity
**malig•no -na** *adj* (*malévolo; pernicioso*) malign; (*malicioso; perjudicial*) malignant; (pathol) malignant
**malintenciona•do -da** *adj* ill-disposed, evil-minded
**malmaridada** *f* (coll) faithless wife
**malmeter** *tr* to lead astray, misguide; to alienate, estrange
**ma•lo -la** *adj* bad, poor, evil; (*travieso*) naughty, mischievous; (*enfermo*) sick, ill; (*que no es como debiera ser*) wrong; (*inflamado, dolorido*) sore; **estar de malas** to be out of luck; **lo malo es que** the trouble is that; **malo con** or **para con** mean to; **por malas o por buenas** willingly or unwillingly;

ser **malo de engañar** to be hard to trick || **el Malo** the Evil One || *f* see **mala**
**malogra·do -da** *adj* late, ill-fated
**malograr** *tr* to miss || *ref* to fail; to come to an untimely end
**malogro** *m* failure; disappointment
**maloliente** *adj* malodorous, foul-smelling
**malón** *m* mean trick; (SAm) Indian incursion; (Chile) surprise party
**malpara·do -da** *adj* hurt; **salir malparado (de)** to fail (in), to come out worsted (in)
**malparar** *tr* to mistreat
**malparir** *intr* to miscarry, have a miscarriage
**malparto** *m* miscarriage
**malquerencia** *f* dislike
**malquerer** §55 *tr* to dislike
**malquistar** *tr* to alienate, estrange || *ref* to become alienated
**malquis·to -ta** *adj* disliked, unpopular
**malrotar** *tr* to squander
**malsa·no -na** *adj* unhealthy
**malsín** *m* mischief-maker
**malsonante** *adj* obnoxious, odious
**malsufri·do -da** *adj* impatient
**malta** *m* malt || *f* asphalt, tar; (Am) dark beer; (Chile) premium beer
**maltraer** §75 *tr* to abuse, ill-treat; to call down, scold
**maltratar** *tr* to abuse, ill-treat, maltreat; to damage, spoil
**maltre·cho -cha** *adj* battered, damaged
**malu·co -ca** or **malu·cho -cha** *adj* (coll) sickish, upset
**malva** *f* mallow; **malva arbórea** hollyhock, rose mallow; **ser como una malva** (coll) to be meek and mild
**malvado -da** *adj* evil, wicked || *mf* evildoer
**malvarrosa** *f* hollyhock, rose mallow
**malvavisco** *m* marsh mallow
**malvender** *tr* to sell at a loss
**malversación** *f* graft, embezzlement, misappropriation
**malversar** *tr & intr* to graft, embezzle
**malvezar** §60 *tr* to give bad habits to || *ref* to acquire bad habits
**malla** *f* mesh, meshing; (*de la armadura*) mail; (*traje*) tights; bathing suit
**mallete** *m* mallet
**Mallorca** *f* Majorca
**mallor·quín -quina** *adj & mf* Majorcan
**mama** *f* mamma
**ma·má** *f* (*pl* **-más**) mamma
**mamada** *f* suck; sucking; (Am) cinch
**mama·lón -lona** *adj* (Ven, W-I) loafing || *mf* (Cuba) sponger
**mamama** *f* (Hond) granny
**mamamama** *f* (Peru) granny
**mamar** *tr* to suck; to learn as a child; (coll) to swallow; (coll) to wangle; **mamóla** (coll) he was taken in || *intr* to suck || *ref* (coll) to swallow; (*obtener sin mérito*) (coll) to wangle; (SAm) to get drunk; **mamarse a uno** (coll) to get the best of someone; (coll) to take someone in; (Col, Chile, Peru) to do away with someone
**mamarracho** *m* (coll) mess, sight; (*hombre ridículo*) milksop
**mamelón** *m* knoll, mound
**mamífe·ro -ra** *adj* mammalian || *m* mammal, mammalian
**mamola** *f* chuck (*under the chin*); **hacer la mamola a** to chuck under the chin; (coll) to take in, make a fool of
**ma·món -mona** *adj* sucking; fond of sucking || *mf* suckling || *m* shoot, sucker; (Guat, Hond) club; (Mex) soft cake || *f* chuck (*under chin*)
**mamonear** *tr* (Guat, Hond) to beat, cudgel; (S-D) to put off, delay; (*el tiempo*) (S-D) to waste
**mamotreto** *m* memo book; (coll) batch of papers; (coll) hulk, bulk
**mampara** *f* screen; folding screen; (Peru) glass door
**mamparo** *m* bulkhead
**mampostería** *f* rubble, rubblework; masonry, stone masonry
**ma·mut** *m* (*pl* **-muts**) mammoth
**manada** *f* (*de ganado vacuno*) herd, drove; (*de ganado lanar*) flock; (*de lobos*) pack; (*de gente*) gang, troop; (*de hierba, trigo, etc.*) handful
**manade·ro -ra** *adj* flowing || *m* spring, source; shepherd
**manantial** *adj* flowing, running || *m* spring, source; (fig) source
**manar** *tr* to run with || *intr* to pour forth, to run; to abound
**manaza** *f* big hand
**mancar** §73 *tr* to maim, cripple || *intr* (*el viento*) (naut) to abate, subside
**manca·rrón -rrona** *adj* (*caballería*) skinny, worn-out; (Chile) tired out, exhausted || *m* old nag; (Chile, Peru) dam, dike
**manceba** *f* mistress, concubine
**mancebía** *f* bawdyhouse, brothel; wild oats; youth
**mance·bo -ba** *adj* youthful || *m* youngster; youth, young man; (*en una farmacia, barbería, etc.*) helper || *f* see **manceba**
**mancerina** *f* saucer with hook to hold chocolate cup
**mancilla** *f* spot, blemish
**mancillar** *tr* to spot, blemish
**man·co -ca** *adj* armless, one-armed; one-handed; defective, faulty || *mf* cripple || *m* (Chile) old nag
**mancomún** — **de mancomún** jointly, in common
**mancomunar** *tr* to unite, combine; (*fuerzas, caudales, etc.*) to pool || *ref* to unite, combine
**mancomunidad** *f* association, union; (*asociación de provincias*) commonwealth
**mancornar** §61 *tr* (*un novillo*) to throw and hold on the ground; (*una res vacuna*) to tie a horn and front leg of; (*dos reses*) to tie together by the horns; (coll) to join, bring together
**mancuernas** *fpl* (Mex) cuff links
**mancuernillas** *fpl* (Guat, Hond) cuff links
**mancha** *f* spot, stain; (*de vegetación*) patch; speckle; (fig) stain, blot; **mancha solar** sunspot
**manchar** *tr* to spot, stain; to speckle;

(fig) to stain, disgrace || *intr* to spot; **¡mancha!** wet paint!
**manda** *f* gift, offer; bequest, legacy
**mandade·ro -ra** *mf* messenger || *m* errand boy
**mandado** *m* order, command; errand; **hacer un mandado** to run an errand
**manda·más** *m* (*pl* **-mases**) (slang) big shot; (*jefe político*) (slang) boss
**mandamiento** *m* order, command; (Bib) commandment; (law) writ; **los cinco mandamientos** (coll) the five fingers of the hand
**mandar** *tr* to order, command; (*legar*) to bequeath; (*enviar*) to send; **mandar** + *inf* to have + *inf*, e.g., **la mandé leer en voz alta** I had her read aloud || *intr* to be in command, be the boss; **mandar llamar** to send for; **mandar por** to send for; **mande Vd.** I beg your pardon || *ref* (*un enfermo*) to manage to get around; (*dos piezas*) to be communicating; **mandarse con** (*otra pieza*) to communicate with; (Am) to be rude to
**mandarina** *f* tangerine
**mandatario** *m* agent, proxy; (Am) chief executive
**mandato** *m* mandate; (Am) term (*of office*)
**mandíbula** *f* jaw, jawbone; **reír a mandíbula batiente** (coll) to roar with laughter
**mandil** *m* apron
**mando** *m* command; control, drive; **alto mando** (mil) high command; **mando a distancia** remote control; **mando a punta de dedo** finger-tip control; **mando de las válvulas** timing gears; **mando por botón** push-button control; **tener el mando y el palo** (coll) to be the boss, rule the roost
**mandolina** *f* mandolin
**man·dón -dona** *adj* bossy || *mf* domineering person || *m* (*en las minas*) (Am) boss, foreman; (*en las carreras de caballos*) (Chile) starter
**mandrágora** *f* mandrake
**mandril** *m* (mach) chuck
**mandrilar** *tr* to bore
**manea** *f* hobble
**manear** *tr* to hobble
**manecilla** *f* (*de reloj*) hand; clasp, book clasp; (bot) tendril; (typ) fist, index
**manejable** *adj* manageable
**manejar** *tr* to manage; to handle, wield; (*un automóvil*) (Am) to drive || *ref* to behave; to get around, move about
**manejo** *m* management; handling; intrigue, scheming; horsemanship; (Am) driving; **manejo a distancia** remote control; **manejo doméstico** housekeeping
**manera** *f* manner, way; **a la manera de** in the manner of; like; **de manera que** so that; **en gran manera** to a great extent; extremely; **sobre manera** exceedingly
**manga** *f* (*parte del vestido*) sleeve; (*tubo de caucho*) hose; waterspout; (bridge) game; **en mangas de camisa** in shirt sleeves; **ir de manga** (coll) to be in cahoots; **manga de agua** waterspout; cloudburst; **manga de camisa** shirt sleeve; **manga de riego** watering hose; **manga de viento** whirlwind; **manga marina** waterspout; **mangas** extras, profits
**mangana** *f* lasso
**manganear** *tr* to lasso; (Peru) to annoy, bother
**manganeso** *m* manganese
**mango** *m* handle; **mango de escoba** broomstick; (aer) stick, control stick
**mangonear** *tr* (Am) to plunder || *intr* (coll) to loaf around; (coll) to meddle; (coll) to dabble
**mangosta** *f* mongoose
**mangote** *m* sleeve protector
**manguera** *f* hose; (*tubo de ventilación*) funnel
**mangueta** *f* fountain syringe; door jamb
**manguitero** *m* furrier
**manguito** *m* muff; sleeve guard; coffee cake; (mach) sleeve
**ma·ní** *m* (*pl* **-níes** or **-nises**) peanut
**manía** *f* mania; craze, whim; (coll) grudge; **tener manía a** (coll) to dislike
**maniabier·to -ta** *adj* open-handed
**manía·co -ca** *adj* maniac(al) || *mf* maniac
**maniatar** *tr* to tie the hands of
**maniáti·co -ca** *adj* stubborn; queer, eccentric; (*entusiasta*) crazy || *mf* crank, eccentric
**manicomio** *m* madhouse, insane asylum
**manicor·to -ta** *adj* closefisted, tight
**manicu·ro -ra** *mf* manicure, manicurist || *f* manicure, manicuring
**mani·do -da** *adj* shabby, worn; hackneyed; (culin) high || *f* haunt, hangout
**manifestación** *f* manifestation; (*reunión pública para dar a conocer un sentimiento u opinión*) demonstration
**manifestante** *mf* demonstrator
**manifestar** §2 *tr* to manifest; (*el Santísimo Sacramento*) to expose || *intr* to demonstrate || *ref* to become manifest
**manifies·to -ta** *adj* manifest || *m* manifesto; (eccl) exposition of the Host; (naut) manifest
**manigua** *f* (Mex, W-I) thicket, jungle; **irse a la manigua** (W-I) to revolt
**manija** *f* handle; clamp; crank
**manilar·go -ga** *adj* ready-fisted; generous
**manilla** *f* bracelet; handcuff, manacle
**manillar** *m* handle bar
**maniobra** *f* handling; lever; maneuver; (naut) gear, tackle
**maniobrar** *intr* to work with the hands; to maneuver; (rr) to shift
**maniota** *f* hobble
**manipula·dor -dora** *mf* manipulator || *m* (telg) key
**manipular** *tr* to manipulate
**mani·quí** (*pl* **-quíes**) *m* manikin, mannequin; (*para exponer prendas de ropa*) dress form; (*de pintores y escultores*) lay figure; (fig) puppet; **ir hecho un maniquí** to be a fashion plate || *f* (*mujer joven que luce los trajes de última moda*) mannequin, model
**manirro·to -ta** *adj* lavish, prodigal

**manivací·o -a** *adj* empty-handed
**manivela** *f* crank; **manivela de arranque** starting crank
**manjar** *m* dish, food, tidbit, delicacy; lift, recreation
**mano** *m* first to play, e.g., **soy mano** I'm first || *f* hand; (*de cuadrúpedo*) forefoot; (*de pintura*) coat; (*de papel*) quire; (*saetilla de reloj u otro instrumento*) hand; (*lance en un juego*) round, hand; (*del elefante*) trunk; pestle, masher; **a la mano** at hand, on hand; within reach; understandable; **a mano airada** violently; **asidos de la mano** hand in hand; **bajo mano** underhandedly; **caer en manos de** to fall into the hands of; **¡dame esa mano!** put it here!; **dar la mano** to lend a hand; **darse las manos** to join hands; to shake hands; **de las manos** hand in hand; **de primera mano** at first hand; first-hand; **de segunda mano** second-hand; **echar mano de** to resort to; **echar una mano** to lend a hand; to play a game; **en buena mano está** (coll) after you, you drink first; **escribir a la mano** to take dictation; **escribir a manos de** to write in care of; **estrecharse la mano** to shake hands; **ganarle a uno por la mano** to steal a march on someone; **lavarse las manos de** to wash one's hands of; **llegar a las manos** to come to blows; **malas manos** awkwardness; **mano de gato** cat's-paw; master hand, master touch; **mano de obra** labor; **mano derecha** right-hand man; **mano de santo** (coll) sure cure; **¡manos a la obra!** let's get to work!; **manos libres** outside work; **manos limpias** extras, perquisites; (coll) clean hands; **manos puercas** (coll) graft; **probar la mano** to try one's hand; **tener mano con** to have a pull with; **tener mano izquierda** (coll) to be on one's toes; **untar la mano a** (coll) to grease the palm of; **venir a las manos** to come to blows; **vivir de la mano a la boca** to live from hand to mouth
**manojo** *m* bunch, bundle, handful; **a manojos** in abundance
**manopla** *f* gauntlet; postilion's whip; (Chile) knuckles, brass knuckles
**manosear** *tr* to finger, to paw; to muss, to rumple; to fiddle with; (Am) to pet || *ref* (Am) to spoon, to neck
**manotada** *f* slap
**manotear** *tr* to slap, to smack || *intr* to gesticulate
**manquedad** *f* lack of one or both hands or arms; disability; deficiency
**mansalva** — **a mansalva** without risk; without warning; **a mansalva de** safe from
**mansarda** *f* mansard, mansard roof
**mansedumbre** *f* gentleness, mildness, meekness; tameness
**mansión** *f* stay, sojourn; abode, dwelling; **hacer mansión** to stop, stay
**man·so -sa** *adj* gentle, mild, meek; tame || *m* bellwether; farm
**manta** *f* blanket; heavy shawl; (coll) beating, thrashing; (Chile, Ecuad) poncho; (Col, Mex, Ven) coarse cotton cloth; **a manta de Dios** copiously; **dar una manta a** to toss in a blanket; **manta de coche** lap robe; **manta de viaje** steamer rug; **tirar de la manta** (coll) to let the cat out of the bag
**mantear** *tr* to toss in a blanket; (Am) to abuse, mistreat
**manteca** *f* (*grasa de los animales, esp. la del cerdo*) lard; butter; pomade; (*dinero*) (slang) dough; **como manteca** smooth as butter; **manteca de puerco** lard; **manteca de vaca** butter
**mantecado** *m* custard ice cream, French ice cream
**mantecón** *m* (coll) mollycoddle, milksop
**mantel** *m* tablecloth; altar cloth
**mantelería** *f* table linen
**mantelillo** *m* embroidered centerpiece
**mantelito** *m* lunch cloth
**mantener** §71 *tr* to maintain; to keep; to keep up; to sustain, defend || *ref* to keep, remain, continue
**mantenida** *f* (Am) kept woman
**mantenido** *m* (*hombre que vive a expensas de su mujer*) (Guat, Mex, W-I) gigolo; (Guat, Mex, W-I) sponger
**mantenimiento** *m* maintenance; food, support, living
**manteo** *m* mantle, cloak
**mantequera** *f* churn, butter churn; butter dish
**mantequería** *f* creamery; delicatessen
**mantequilla** *f* butter; **mantequilla azucarada** hard sauce; **mantequilla derretida** drawn butter
**mantilla** *f* mantilla (*silk or lace head scarf*); **mantillas** swaddling clothes
**mantillo** *m* humus, mold
**manto** *m* mantle, cloak; (*de chimenea*) mantel; (*ropa talar de algunos religiosos, catedráticos, alumnos*) robe, gown; (fig) cloak
**mantón** *m* shawl, kerchief
**manuable** *adj* handy
**manual** *adj* (*que se hace con las manos*) hand; (*fácil de manejar*) handy; easy; easy to understand; easy-going; manual || *m* manual, handbook; notebook
**manubrio** *m* handle; crank, winch
**manuela** *f* open hack (*in Madrid*)
**manufactura** *f* (*fábrica*) factory; (*obra fabricada*) manufacture
**manufacturar** *tr* to manufacture
**manuscribir** §83 *tr* to write by hand
**manuscri·to -ta** *adj & m* manuscript
**manutención** *f* maintenance; care, upkeep; shelter, protection
**manutener** §71 *tr* (law) to maintain, support
**manzana** *f* apple; (*conjunto aislado de varias casas contiguas*) block, city block; (*remate en un mueble*) knob, finial; **manzana de Adán** (Chile) Adam's apple
**manzanar** *m* apple orchard
**manzanilla** *f* camomile; (*aceituna pequeña; vino blanco*) manzanilla (*small olive; white wine*); (*remate en un mueble*) knob, finial

**manzano** *m* apple tree
**maña** *f* skill, dexterity; cunning, craftiness; bad habit, vice; (*de lino, cáñamo, etc.*) bunch; (Am) sister; **darse maña** to manage, contrive; **hacer maña** (Col) to fool around
**mañana** *adv* tomorrow; **¡hasta mañana!** see you tomorrow!; **pasado mañana** the day after tomorrow || *m* tomorrow; (*tiempo venidero*) morrow || *f* morning; **de mañana** in the morning; **muy de mañana** very early in the morning; **por la mañana** in the morning; **tomar la mañana** to get up early; (coll) to have a shot of liquor before breakfast
**mañanear** *intr* to be in the habit of getting up early
**mañane•ro -ra** *adj* morning; early-rising
**mañanica** *f* early morning, break of day
**mañanita** *f* woman's bed jacket
**mañear** *tr* to manage craftily || *intr* to act with cunning
**mañerear** *intr* (Arg) to dawdle, dilly-dally
**mañería** *f* sterility
**mañe•ro -ra** *adj* clever, shrewd; simple, easy; (Am) skittish
**ma•ño -ña** *mf* (coll) Aragonese || *m* (Am) brother || *f* see **maña**
**maño•so -sa** *adj* skillful, clever; crafty, tricky; vicious
**mañuela** *f* craftiness, trickiness
**mañue•las** *mf* (*pl* **-las**) (coll) tricky person
**mapa** *m* map; **mapa itinerario** road map || *f* — **llevarse la mapa** (coll) to take the prize
**mapache** *m* coon, raccoon
**mapamundi** *m* map of the world; (coll) buttocks, behind
**mapurite** *m* (CAm) skunk
**maque** *m* lacquer
**maquear** *tr* to lacquer; (Mex) to varnish
**maqueta** *f* (*en tamaño reducido*) maquette; (*en tamaño natural*) mock-up; (*de un libro*) dummy
**maquillador** *m* (theat) make-up man
**maquillaje** *m* (theat) make-up
**maquillar** *tr & ref* to make up
**máquina** *f* machine; (*motor*) engine; locomotive; plan, project; (fig) machinery; (coll) heap, pile, lot; (Cuba) auto; (Chile) ganging up; **escribir a máquina** to typewrite; **máquina de afeitar** safety razor; **máquina de apostar** gambling machine; **máquina de componer** typesetter; **máquina de coser** sewing machine; **máquina de escribir** typewriter; **máquina de lavar** washing machine; **máquina de sumar** adding machine; **máquina de volar** flying machine; **máquina fotográfica** camera; **máquina parlante** talking machine; **máquina sacaperras** slot machine
**maquinación** *f* machination, scheming
**máquina-herramienta** *f* (*pl* **máquinas-herramientas**) machine tool
**maquinal** *adj* mechanical
**maquinar** *tr* to plot, to scheme
**maquinaria** *f* machinery; applied mechanics
**maquinilla** *f* windlass, winch; clippers; **maquinilla cortapelos** clippers, hair clippers; **maquinilla de afeitar** safety razor; **maquinilla de rizar** curling iron
**maquinista** *mf* (*persona que fabrica máquinas*) machinist; (*persona que dirige una máquina o locomotora*) engineer; **segundo maquinista** (naut) machinist
**mar** *m & f* sea; tide, flood; **alta mar** high seas; **a mares** abundantly, copiously; **arrojarse a la mar** to plunge, take great risks; **baja mar** low tide; **correr los mares** to follow the sea; **hablar de la mar** (coll) to talk wildly, to talk on and on; **hacerse a la mar** to put to sea; **la mar de** (fig) oceans of, large numbers of; **mar alta** rough sea; **mar ancha** high seas; **mar bonanza** calm sea; **mar Caribe** Caribbean Sea, Caribbean; **mar de las Antillas** Caribbean Sea; **mar de las Indias** Indian Ocean; **mar de nubes** cloud bank; **mar Latino** Mediterranean Sea; **mar llena** high tide; **meter la mar en un pozo** to attempt the impossible; **meterse mar adentro** (fig) to go beyond one's depth
**maraña** *f* undergrowth, thicket; silk waste; (*de hilo, pelo, etc.*) tangle; trick, scheme; puzzle
**marañón** *m* cashew
**maraño•so -sa** *adj* scheming || *mf* schemer
**maravilla** *f* wonder, marvel; (bot) marigold, calendula; **a las maravillas** or **a las mil maravillas** magnificently; **a maravilla** wonderfully well; **por maravilla** rarely, occasionally
**maravillar** *tr* to astonish || *ref* to wonder, to marvel; **maravillarse con** or **de** to marvel at, to wonder at
**maravillo•so -sa** *adj* wonderful, marvelous
**marbete** *m* label, tag; baggage check; edge, border; **marbete engomado** sticker
**marca** *f* mark; (*tipo de producto*) make, brand; (*de tamaño*) standard; score; record; height-measuring device; **de marca** outstanding; **marca de agua** watermark; **marca de fábrica** trademark; **marca de reconocimiento** (naut) landmark, seamark; **marca de taquilla** box-office record; **marca registrada** registered trademark
**marca•do -da** *adj* marked, pronounced
**marcaje** *m* (sport) scoring; (sport) interfering; (telp) dialing
**marcapaso** *m* pacemaker
**marcar** §73 *tr* to mark; to brand; to embroider; (*p.ej., un pañuelo*) to initial; (*la hora un reloj*) to show; (*un tanto*) to make, to score; (*el número telefónico*) to dial || *ref* (*un buque*) to take bearings
**marcear** *tr* to shear || *ref* to be March-like
**marcial** *adj* martial; gallant, noble

**marco** *m* frame; framework; (*de pesas y medidas*) standard
**marcha** *f* march; (*funcionamiento*) running, operation; (*p.ej., de los astros*) course, path; (*desenvolvimiento de un asunto*) course, march, progress; (*grado de velocidad*) rate of speed; (*de los engranajes*) (aut) speed; **cambiar de marcha** to shift gears; **en marcha** on the march; underway; in motion; **marcha atrás** reverse; **marcha del hambre** hunger march; **marcha directa** high gear; **marcha forzada** (mil) forced march
**marchamo** *m* customhouse mark; (Arg, Bol) tax on slaughtered cattle
**marchante** *adj* commercial || *m* dealer, merchant; (Am) customer
**marchapié** *m* running board
**marchar** *intr* to march; to run, work, go; to leave, go away; to come along, proceed; **marchar en vacío** to idle || *ref* to leave, go away
**marchitar** *tr* to wilt, wither || *ref* to wilt, wither; to languish
**marchi•to -ta** *adj* withered, faded; (fig) languid
**marea** *f* tide; tideland; gentle sea breeze; dew; drizzle; **marea alta** high tide; **marea baja** low tide; **marea creciente** or **entrante** flood tide; **marea menguante** ebb tide; **marea muerta** neap tide; **marea viva** spring tide; **rendir la marea** to stem the tide
**marea•do -da** *adj* nauseated, sick, lightheaded; seasick
**mareaje** *m* navigation, seamanship; (*de un buque*) course
**marear** *tr* to sail; (coll) to annoy, pester || *intr* (coll) to be annoying || *ref* to get sick, to get giddy; to get seasick; to be damaged at sea; (Am) to fade
**marejada** *f* heavy sea; (*de desorden*) stirring, undercurrent; **marejada de fondo** ground swell
**maremagno** or **maremágnum** *m* (coll) big mess
**mareo** *m* nausea, dizziness, sickness; seasickness; (coll) annoyance
**marfil** *m* ivory
**marfile•ño -ña** *adj* ivory
**mar•fuz -fuza** *adj* (*pl* **-fuces -fuzas**) cast aside, rejected; deceptive
**marga** *f* marl
**margar** §44 *tr* to marl
**margarita** *f* pearl; (bot) daisy; **margarita de los prados** English daisy
**margen** *m* & *f* margin; border, edge; marginal note; **al margen de** aloof from; outside of; independent of; aside from; **dar margen para** to give occasion for; **dejar al margen** to leave out; **quedar al margen de** to be left out of
**marginal** *adj* marginal
**mariache** *m* Mexican band and singers
**marica** *m* (coll) sissy, milksop || *f* magpie
**maricón** *m* (coll) sissy
**maridable** *adj* marital
**maridaje** *m* married life; (fig) union
**maridar** *tr* to combine, unite || *intr* to get married; to live as man and wife
**marido** *m* husband
**mariguana** *f* marihuana
**mariguanza** *f* (Chile) hocus-pocus; (Chile) pirouette; **mariguanzas** (Chile) clowning; (Chile) powwowing
**marimacho** *m* (coll) mannish woman
**marimandona** *f* (coll) queen bee, bossy woman
**marimarica** *m* (coll) sissy
**marimorena** *f* (coll) fight, row
**marina** *f* navy; (*conjunto de buques*) marine, fleet; (*cuadro o pintura*) seascape; shore, seaside; sailing, navigation; **marina de guerra** navy; **marina mercante** merchant marine
**marinar** *tr* to marinate, to salt; (*un buque*) to man || *intr* to be a sailor
**marinera** *f* sailor blouse; (*blusa de niño*) middy, middy blouse
**marinería** *f* sailoring; sailors
**marine•ro -ra** *adj* sea, marine; seaworthy; seafaring || *m* mariner, seaman, sailor; **marinero de agua dulce** (*el que ha navegado poco*) landlubber (*person unacquainted with the sea*); **marinero matalote** (*hombre de mar, rudo y torpe*) landlubber (*awkward and unskilled seaman*) || *f* see **marinera**
**marines•co -ca** *adj* sailor; sailorly
**mari•no -na** *adj* marine, sea || *m* mariner, seaman, sailor || *f* see **marina**
**marioneta** *f* marionette
**mariposa** *f* butterfly; butterfly valve; wing nut; rushlight; (Col) blindman's buff; **mariposa nocturna** moth
**mariposear** *intr* to flit about; to be fickle
**mariposón** *m* (Cuba, Guat, Mex) fickle flirt
**mariquita** *m* (coll) sissy, milksop, popinjay || *f* (ent) ladybird
**marisabidilla** *f* (coll) bluestocking
**mariscal** *m* blacksmith; (mil) marshal; **mariscal de campo** (mil) field marshal
**marisco** *m* shellfish; **mariscos** seafood
**marisma** *f* swamp, marsh, salt marsh
**marisquería** *f* seafood store, seafood restaurant
**maríti•mo -ma** *adj* maritime; marine, sea
**maritor•nes** *f* (*pl* **-nes**) (coll) mannish maidservant, wench
**marmita** *f* pot, boiler, kettle
**marmitón** *m* kitchen scullion
**mármol** *m* marble
**marmóre•o -a** *adj* marble
**marmosete** *m* vignette
**marmota** *f* marmot; sleepyhead; worsted cap; **marmota de Alemania** hamster; **marmota de América** ground hog, woodchuck
**maroma** *f* hemp rope, esparto rope; (Am) acrobatic stunt
**maromear** *intr* (Am) to perform acrobatic stunts, to walk the tight rope; (Am) to wobble, to sway from side to side (*e.g., in politics*); (Am) to hesitate
**marome•ro -ra** *mf* (Am) acrobat, tightrope walker; (Am) weaseler

**marqués** *m* marquis; **los marqueses** the marquis and marchioness
**marquesa** *f* marchioness, marquise; (*sobre la puerta de un hotel*) marquee
**marquesina** *f* cover over field tent; (*sobre la puerta de un hotel*) marquee; locomotive cab
**marquetería** *f* cabinetwork, woodwork; (*taracea*) marquetry
**marra•jo -ja** *adj* sly, tricky; (*toro*) vicious
**marrana** *f* sow; (coll) slattern, slut
**marranada** *f* (coll) piggishness, filth
**marranalla** *f* (coll) rabble, riffraff
**marra•no -na** *adj* base, vile; (coll) dirty, sloppy || *mf* hog || *m* male hog, boar; filthy person, hog; cad, cur || *f* see **marrana**
**marrar** *intr* to miss, fail; to go astray
**marras** *adv* (coll) long ago; **hacer marras que** (Bol, Ecuad) to be a long time since
**marro** *m* game resembling quoits and played with a stone; (*juego de muchachos*) tag; (*ladeo*) dodge, duck; slip, miss
**marrón** *adj invar* maroon (*dark-red*); tan (*shoes*) || *m* maroon; candied chestnut; stone (*used as a sort of quoit*)
**marro•quí** (*pl* **-quíes**) *adj & mf* Moroccan || *m* morocco, morocco leather
**marro•quín -quina** *adj & mf* var of **marroquí**
**marrubio** *m* horehound
**marrue•co -ca** *adj & mf* Moroccan
**Marruecos** *m* Morocco
**marrulle•ro -ra** *adj* cajoling, wheedling || *mf* cajoler, wheedler
**Marsella** *f* Marseille
**marsopa** or **marsopla** *f* porpoise
**mart.** *abbr* **martes**
**marta** *f* pine marten; **marta cebellina** sable, Siberian sable; **marta del Canadá** fisher
**Marte** *m* Mars
**mar•tes** *m* (*pl* **-tes**) Tuesday; **martes de carnaval** or **carnestolendas** Shrove Tuesday
**martillar** *tr* to hammer; to pester, worry || *intr* to hammer
**martillazo** *m* blow with a hammer
**martillear** *tr & intr* var of **martillar**
**martillero** *m* (Chile) auctioneer
**martillo** *m* hammer; auction house; (*persona*) scourge; (mus) tuning hammer; (*de arma de fuego*) cock
**martín** *m* — **martín pescador** (*pl* **martín pescadores**) kingfisher
**martinete** *m* drop hammer; pile driver; (*del piano*) hammer
**martinico** *m* (coll) ghost, goblin
**mártir** *mf* martyr
**martirio** *m* martyrdom
**márts.** *abbr* **mártires**
**marullo** *m* surge, swell
**marxista** *adj & mf* Marxist or Marxian
**marzo** *m* March
**mas** *conj* but
**más** *adv* more; most; **a lo más** at most, at the most; **a más de** besides, in addition to; **como el que más** as the next one, as well as anybody; **cuando más** at the most; **de más** extra; too much, too many; **estar de más** to be in the way; to be unnecessary; to be superfluous; **los más de** most of, the majority of; **más bien** rather; **más de** + *número* more than; **más de lo que** + *verbo* more than; **más que** more than; better than; **no . . . más** no longer; **no . . . más nada** nothing more; **no . . . más que** only || *prep* plus || *m* more; (*signo de adición*) plus
**masa** *f* mass; (*pasta que se forma con agua y harina*) dough; (*masa aplastada*) mash; nature, disposition; (Chile, Ecuad) puff paste; (*p.ej., de un automóvil*) (elec) ground; **las masas** the masses
**masada** *f* farm
**masadero** *m* farmer
**masaje** *m* massage; **masaje facial** facial
**masajear** *tr* to massage
**masajista** *m* masseur || *f* masseuse
**masar** *tr* to knead; to massage
**mascar** §73 *tr* to chew; (coll) to mumble, mutter || *ref* (*un cabo*) (naut) to gall
**máscara** *mf* (*persona*) mask, mummer || *f* mask; (*traje, disfraz*) masquerade; **máscara antigás** gas mask
**mascarada** *f* masquerade
**mascarilla** *f* half mask; false face; death mask
**mascarón** *m* false face; (*persona fea*) fright; (archit) mask; **mascarón de proa** (naut) figurehead
**mascota** *f* mascot
**mascujar** *tr & intr* (coll) to chew with difficulty; (coll) to mumble
**masculi•no -na** *adj* masculine; (*sexo*) male; (*traje*) men's || *m* masculine
**mascullar** *tr & intr* (coll) to mumble, mutter; (coll) to chew with difficulty
**masera** *f* kneading trough
**masilla** *f* putty
**masita** *f* (mil) money withheld for clothing; (Arg, Bol) cake
**masón** *m* Mason
**masonería** *f* Masonry
**mastelero** *m* (naut) topmast
**masticar** §73 *tr* to chew, masticate; to meditate on; to mumble
**mástil** *m* (*de una embarcación*) mast; (*de un violín o guitarra*) neck; stalk; (*de pluma*) shaft, stem; upright
**mas•tín -tina** *mf* mastiff; **mastín danés** Great Dane
**mastodonte** *m* mastodon
**mastuerzo** *m* (bot) cress; (coll) dolt
**masturbar** *ref* to masturbate
**mat.** *abbr* **matématica**
**mata** *f* bush, shrub; blade, sprig; brush, underbrush; **mata de pelo** crop of hair, head of hair; **mata parda** chaparro (*oak*); **saltar de la mata** (coll) to come out of hiding
**mataca•bras** *m* (*pl* **-bras**) cold blast from the north
**matacán** *m* dog poison
**matacande•las** *m* (*pl* **-las**) candle snuffer
**matadero** *m* abattoir, slaughterhouse; (coll) drudgery

**mata·dor -dora** *mf* killer || *m* matador; **matador de mujeres** lady-killer
**matadura** *f* sore, gall
**matafue·gos** *m* (*pl* **-gos**) fire extinguisher; (*oficial*) fireman
**matalo·bos** *m* (*pl* **-bos**) wolf's-bane
**mata·lón -lona** *mf* (coll) skinny old nag
**matalotaje** *m* (naut) ship stores; (coll) mess, hodgepodge
**matamale·zas** *m* (*pl* **-zas**) weed killer
**matamari·dos** *f* (*pl* **-dos**) (coll) many times a widow
**matamo·ros** *m* (*pl* **-ros**) (coll) bully
**matamos·cas** *m* (*pl* **-cas**) fly swatter; flypaper
**matanza** *f* slaughter, massacre; butchering; pork products; (CAm) butcher shop; (Ven) slaughterhouse
**matape·rros** *m* (*pl* **-rros**) (coll) harum-scarum, street urchin
**matar** *tr* to kill; to butcher; (*el fuego, la luz*) to put out; (*la cal*) to slack; (*el metal*) to mat; (*un color*) to tone down; (*un naipe*) to spot; to play a card higher than; (*a un caballo*) to gall; to bore to death; (*el tiempo, el hambre, etc.*) (fig) to kill || *intr* to kill || *ref* to kill oneself; to drudge, overwork; to be disappointed; **matarse con** to quarrel with; **matarse por** to struggle for; to struggle to
**matarratas** *m* rat poison; (*aguardiente de mala calidad*) (coll) rotgut
**matarro·tos** *m* (*pl* **-tos**) (Chile) pawnshop
**matasa·nos** *m* (*pl* **-nos**) quack doctor
**matasellar** *tr* to cancel, to postmark
**matase·llos** *m* (*pl* **-llos**) postmark
**matasie·te** *m* (*pl* **-te**) (coll) bully, swashbuckler
**matatí·as** *m* (*pl* **-as**) (coll) moneylender, pawnbroker
**matazar·zas** *m* (*pl* **-zas**) weed killer
**mate** *adj* dull, flat || *m* checkmate; (SAm) maté; (SAm) maté gourd; **dar mate a** to checkmate; to make fun of; **dar mate ahogado a** to stalemate; **mate ahogado** stalemate
**matear** *tr* to plant at regular intervals; to make dull; (Chile) to checkmate || *ref* (*el trigo*) to sprout; (*un perro de caza*) to hunt through the bushes
**matemáti·co -ca** *adj* mathematical || *mf* mathematician || *f* mathematics; **matemáticas** mathematics
**materia** *f* matter; material, stuff; **materia colorante** dyestuff; **materia prima** or **primera materia** raw material
**material** *adj* material; (*grosero*) crude || *m* material; (*conjunto de objetos necesario para un servicio*) matériel; (typ) matter, copy; **material de guerra** matériel; **material fijo** (rr) permanent way; **material móvil** or **rodante** (rr) rolling stock; **ser material** (coll) to be immaterial
**materialismo** *m* materialism
**materializar** §60 *tr* (*beneficios*) to realize
**maternal** *adj* maternal, mother; (*afectos, cuidados, etc.*) motherly
**maternidad** *f* maternity; motherhood
**mater·no -na** *adj* maternal, mother
**matinal** *adj* morning
**matinée** *f* matinée; dressing gown, wrapper
**ma·tiz** *m* (*pl* **-tices**) shade, hue, nuance
**matizar** §60 *tr* (*diversos colores*) to blend; (*un color, un sonido*) to shade; (*en cuanto al color*) to match
**matón** *m* (coll) bully, browbeater
**matorral** *m* thicket, underbrush
**matraca** *f* rattle, noisemaker; taunting, bantering; bore, pest; **dar matraca a** (coll) to taunt, to tease
**matraquear** *intr* (coll) to make a racket; (coll) to taunt, to tease
**ma·traz** *m* (*pl* **-traces**) flask
**matre·ro -ra** *adj* cunning, shrewd || *m* (SAm) cheat, swindler
**matriarca** *f* matriarch
**matricida** *adj* matricidal || *mf* matricide
**matricidio** *m* matricide
**matrícula** *f* register, roster, roll; licence; registry
**matricular** *tr & ref* to matriculate
**matrimonialmente** *adv* as husband and wife
**matrimoniar** *intr* to marry, get married
**matrimonio** *m* marriage, matrimony; (*marido y mujer*) (coll) married couple; **matrimonio consensual** common-law marriage
**ma·triz** (*pl* **-trices**) *adj* main, first, mother || *f* matrix; (*del libro talonario*) stub; screw nut; first draft
**matrona** *f* matron; (coll) matronly lady
**matronal** *adj* matronly
**matun·go -ga** *adj* (Am) skinny, full of sores || *m* (Am) old nag
**maturran·go -ga** *adj* (SAm) poor, clumsy || *m* (SAm) stranger; (SAm) old nag || *f* (coll) trickery
**Matusalén** *m* Methuselah; **vivir más años que Matusalén** to be as old as Methuselah
**matute** *m* smuggling; smuggled goods; gambling den
**matutear** *intr* to smuggle
**matute·ro -ra** *mf* smuggler
**matutinal** or **matuti·no -na** *adj* morning
**maula** *mf* (coll) lazy loafer; (coll) poor pay; (coll) tricky person, cheat || *f* junk, trash; remnant; trickery
**maulería** *f* remnant shop; trickiness
**maullar** §8 *intr* to meow
**maullido** or **maúllo** *m* meow
**mausoleo** *m* mausoleum
**máxima** *f* maxim; principle
**máxime** *adv* chiefly, mainly, especially
**máxi·mo -ma** *adj* maximum; top; superlative || *m* maximum || *f* see **máxima**
**may.** *abbr* **mayúscula**
**maya** *f* May queen; English daisy
**mayal** *m* flail
**mayear** *intr* to be Maylike
**mayestáti·co -ca** *adj* royal
**mayido** *m* meow
**mayo** *m* May; Maypole
**mayonesa** *f* mayonnaise
**mayor** *adj* greater; larger; older, elder; greatest; largest; oldest, eldest; major; elderly; (*calle*) main; (*altar; misa*) high; **hacerse mayor de edad**

to come of age; **ser mayor de edad** to be of age || *m* chief, head, superior; **al por mayor** wholesale; **mayor de edad** (*persona de edad legal*) major; **mayores** elders; ancestors, forefathers; **mayor general** staff officer
**mayoral** *m* boss, foreman; head shepherd; stagecoach driver; (Arg) streetcar conductor
**mayorazgo** *m* primogeniture; entailed estate descending by primogeniture; first-born son
**mayordoma** *f* stewardess, housekeeper
**mayordomo** *m* steward, butler, majordomo
**mayoreo** *m* (Am) wholesale
**mayoría** *f* (*mayor edad; el mayor número, la mayor parte*) majority; superiority; **alcanzar su mayoría de edad** to come of age; **mayoría de edad** majority
**mayoridad** *f* majority
**mayorista** *adj* (Arg, Chile) wholesale || *mf* (Arg, Chile) wholesaler
**mayorita•rio -ria** *adj* majority
**mayormente** *adv* chiefly, mainly, mostly
**mayúscu•lo -la** *adj* (*letra*) capital; (coll) awful, tremendous || *f* capital, capital letter
**maza** *f* mace; heavy drumstick; (coll) bore, pedant; **la maza y la mona** constant companions; **maza de gimnasia** Indian club
**mazacote** *m* barilla; concrete, cement; botched job; (coll) tough, doughy food; (coll) bore
**mazar** §60 *tr* to churn
**mazmorra** *f* dungeon
**mazo** *m* mallet, maul; bunch; (*de la campana*) clapper; (*hombre fastidioso*) bore, pest
**mazonería** *f* stone masonry; (*obra de relieve*) relief; gold or silver embroidery
**mazorca** *f* ear of corn; cocoa bean; (*husada*) spindleful; (*de un balustre*) spindle; **comer maíz de** or **en la mazorca** to eat corn on the cob
**mazorral** *adj* coarse, crude
**m/c** *abbr* **mi cargo, mi cuenta, moneda corriente**
**m/cta** *abbr* **mi cuenta**
**m/cte** *abbr* **moneda corriente**
**me** (used as object of verb) *pron pers* me, to me || *pron reflex* myself, to myself
**meada** *f* urination, water; urine stain
**meadero** *m* urinal
**meados** *mpl* urine
**meaja** *f* crumb; **meaja de huevo** tread
**meandro** *m* meander; wandering speech, wandering writing
**mear** *tr* to urinate on || *intr & ref* to urinate
**Meca, La Meca**
**mecáni•co -ca** *adj* mechanical; (coll) low, mean || *m* (*obrero perito en el arreglo de las máquinas*) mechanic; (*obrero que fabrica y compone máquinas*) machinist; workman, repairman; driver, chauffeur || *f* mechanics; (*aparato que da movimiento a un artefacto*) machinery, works; (coll) meanness; **mecánicas** (coll) household chores
**mecanismo** *m* mechanism, machinery
**mecanizar** §60 *tr* to mechanize; to motorize
**mecanografía** *f* typewriting; **mecanografía al tacto** touch typewriting
**mecanografiar** §77 *tr & intr* to typewrite
**mecanógra•fo -fa** *mf* typist, typewriter
**mecapale•ro -ra** *m* (Mex) messenger, porter
**mece•dor -dora** *adj* swinging, rocking || *m* stirrer; (*columpio*) swing || *f* rocker, rocking chair
**mecer** §46 *tr* (*un líquido*) to stir; (*la cuna*) to rock || *ref* to rock, swing
**mecha** *f* (*de vela o bujía*) wick; (*tubo de pólvora*) fuse; lock of hair; (*para mechar carne*) slice of bacon; bundle of thread; (Col, Ecuad, Ven) joke
**mechar** *tr* (*la carne*) to lard, interlard
**mechera** *f* (coll) shoplifter
**mechero** *m* (*p.ej., de cigarrillos*) lighter, pocket lighter; (*de aparato de alumbrado*) burner; (*de candelero*) socket; **mechero encendedor** pilot, pilot light
**mechón** *m* cowlick; (Guat) torch
**medalla** *f* medal; medallion
**medallón** *m* medallion; (*joya en que se colocan retratos, etc.*) locket
**médano** *m* dune, sandbank
**media** *f* stocking; (math) mean; **media corta** (Arg) sock; **media media** (Arg, Ecuad, Ven) sock; **y media** half past, e.g., **las dos y media** half past two
**mediación** *f* mediation
**media•do -da** *adj* half over; half-full; **a mediados de** about the middle of; **mediada la tarde** in the middle of the afternoon
**media•dor -dora** *mf* mediator
**mediana** *f* long billiard cue
**medianería** *f* party wall; party fence
**mediane•ro -ra** *adj* middle; mediating || *mf* mediator; partner; owner of a row house
**medianía** *f* average; (*persona que carece de dotes relevantes*) mediocrity
**media•no -na** *adj* middling, medium; average, fair; (coll) mediocre || *f* see **mediana**
**medianoche** *f* midnight; small meat pie
**mediante** *adj* interceding || *prep* by means of, by virtue of
**mediar** *intr* to be half over; to be in the middle; to intercede, mediate; to elapse; to take place
**mediatinta** *f* half-tone
**medible** *adj* measurable
**medical** *adj* medical
**medicamento** *m* medicine
**medicamento•so -sa** *adj* medicinal
**medicastro** *m* quack
**medicina** *f* medicine
**medicinar** *tr* to treat || *ref* to take medicine
**medición** *f* measurement; metering
**médi•co -ca** *adj* medical || *mf* doctor, physician; **médico de cabecera** family physician
**medida** *f* measurement; measure; caution, moderation; **a medida de** in pro-

portion to; according to; **a medida que** in proportion as; **en la medida que** to the extent that; **hecho a la medida** custom-made; **medida para áridos** dry measure; **medida para líquidos** liquid measure; **tomarle a uno las medidas** to take someone's measure, to size up someone
**medidamente** *adv* with moderation
**medidor** *m* measurer; (Mex, SAm) meter
**medie•ro -ra** *mf* hosier; partner
**medieval** *adj* medieval
**medievalista** *mf* medievalist
**medievo** *m* Middle Ages
**me•dio -dia** *adj* middle; medium; medieval; half; a half, e.g., **media libra** a half pound; half a, e.g., **media naranja** half an orange; average, mean; mid, in the middle of, e.g., **a media tarde** in mid afternoon, in the middle of the afternoon; **a medias** half; half-and-half; **ir a medias (con)** to go halves (with), to go fifty-fifty (with) || *m* middle; medium, environment; step, measure; means; (*en el espiritismo*) medium; (baseball) shortstop; (arith) half; (*del ruedo*) (taur) center; **a medio** half; **en medio de** in the middle of; in the midst of; **justo medio** happy medium, golden mean; **por medio de** by means of; **quitarse de en medio** (coll) to get out of the way || *f* see **media** || **medio** *adv* half
**mediocre** *adj* mediocre
**mediocridad** *f* mediocrity
**mediodía** *m* noon, midday; south; **en pleno mediodía** at high noon; **hacer mediodía** to stop for the noon meal
**mediquillo** *m* quack
**medir** §50 *tr* to measure || *intr* to measure || *ref* to act with moderation
**meditabun•do -da** *adj* meditative
**meditar** *tr* to meditate; to plan, contemplate || *intr* to meditate
**mediterráne•o -na** *adj* inland || **Mediterráne•o -na** *adj & m* Mediterranean
**mé•dium** *m* (*pl* **-dium** or **-diums**) medium
**medra** *f* growth, prosperity
**medrana** *f* fear
**medrar** *intr* to thrive, prosper, improve
**medro** *m* growth, prosperity; **medros** progress
**medro•so -sa** *adj* fearful, scared; frightful, terrible
**médula** or **medula** *f* marrow, medulla; (bot) pith; (fig) pith, gist, essence; **médula espinal** spinal cord
**medular** *adj* pithy
**medusa** *f* jellyfish
**mefistoféli•co -ca** *adj* Mephistophelian
**megaciclo** *m* megacycle
**megáfono** *m* megaphone
**me•go -ga** *adj* meek, gentle, mild
**megohmio** *m* megohm
**Méj.** *abbr* **Méjico**
**mejica•no -na** *adj & mf* Mexican
**Méjico** *m* Mexico; **Nuevo Méjico** New Mexico
**meji•do -da** *adj* beaten with sugar and milk
**mejilla** *f* cheek
**mejor** *adj* better; best; (*licitador*) highest; **a lo mejor** (coll) unexpectedly; (coll) worse luck; (coll) perhaps, maybe; **el mejor día** some fine day || *adv* better; best; **mejor dicho** rather
**mejora** *f* growth, improvement; higher bid; alteration
**mejoramiento** *m* improvement
**mejorana** *f* sweet marjoram
**mejorar** *tr* to improve; (*los licitadores el precio de una cosa*) to raise; **mejorando lo presente** present company excepted || *intr & ref* to improve, get better, recover; to make progress; (*el tiempo*) to clear up
**mejoría** *f* improvement; (*en una enfermedad*) betterment, recovery
**mejunje** *m* brew, potion, mixture
**mela•do -da** *adj* honey-colored || *m* (Am) thick cane syrup
**melancolía** *f* (*tristeza vaga*) melancholy; (*depresión moral*) melancholia
**melancóli•co -ca** *adj* melancholy
**melaza** *f* molasses
**melcocha** *f* taffy, molasses candy
**melchor** *m* German silver
**melena** *f* hair falling over the eyes; long hair, loose hair; (*del león*) mane; (*del caballo*) forelock; **andar a la melena** (coll) to pull each other's hair; (coll) to get into a fight; **estar en melena** (coll) to have one's hair down
**melga** *f* (Am) ridge made by plow; (Col, Chile) plot of ground to be sown; (Hond) small piece of work to be finished
**melindre** *m* honey fritter; (*dulce de pasta de mazapán*) ladyfinger; narrow ribbon; prudery, finickiness
**melindrear** *intr* to be prudish, be finicky
**melindro•so -sa** *adj* prudish, finicky
**melocotón** *m* peach tree; peach
**melocotonero** *m* peach tree
**melodía** *f* melody
**melodio•so -sa** *adj* melodious
**melodramáti•co -ca** *adj* melodramatic
**melón** *m* melon; (*Cucumis melo*) muskmelon; (coll) blockhead; (coll) bald head; **melón de agua** watermelon
**melo•so -sa** *adj* sweet, honeyed; gentle, mild, mellow
**mella** *f* dent, nick, notch; gap, hollow; harm, injury; **hacer mella a** to have an effect on; **hacer mella en** to harm
**mellar** *tr* to dent, nick, notch; to harm
**melli•zo -za** *adj & mf* twin
**membrana** *f* membrane; (*del teléfono, micrófono*) diaphragm
**membrete** *m* note, memo; letterhead; heading; written invitation
**membrillero** *m* quince tree
**membrillo** *m* quince; quince tree
**membru•do -da** *adj* brawny, burly
**memeches — a memeches** (CAm) on horseback
**memela** *f* (CAm, Mex) cornmeal pancake
**me•mo -ma** *adj* foolish, simple || *mf* fool, simpleton
**memorán•dum** *m* (*pl* **-dum**) memorandum book, notebook; (*sección en los

*periódicos*) professional services; (*papel con membrete*) letterhead
**memorar** *tr & ref* to remember
**memoria** *f* memory; (*exposición de ciertos hechos*) memoir; account, record; **de memoria** by heart; **encomendar a la memoria** to commit to memory; **hablar de memoria** (coll) to say the first thing that comes to one's mind; **hacer memoria de** to bring up; **memorias** memoirs; regards
**memorial** *m* memorandum book; memorial, petition; (law) brief
**memorizar** **§60** *tr* to memorize
**mena** *f* ore
**menaje** *m* household furniture; school supplies
**mención** *f* mention
**mencionar** *tr* to mention
**men•daz** (*pl* **-daces**) *adj* mendacious ‖ *mf* liar
**mendicante** *adj & mf* mendicant
**mendigante** *adj* begging, mendicant ‖ *mf* beggar, mendicant
**mendigar** **§44** *tr* to beg for ‖ *intr* to beg, go begging
**mendi•go -ga** *mf* beggar
**mendiguez** *f* begging
**mendo•so -sa** *adj* false, wrong
**mendrugo** *m* crumb, crust
**menear** *tr* to stir, to shake; to wiggle; (*la cola*) to wag; (*un negocio*) to manage; **peor es meneallo** (i.e., **menearlo**) better keep hands off ‖ *ref* to shake; to wiggle; to wag; (coll) to hustle, bestir oneself
**meneo** *m* stirring, shaking; wagging; hustling; (coll) drubbing, thrashing
**menester** *m* need; want, lack; job, occupation; **haber menester** to be necessary, to be need for; **menesteres** bodily needs; property; (coll) implements, tools; **ser menester** to be necessary
**menestero•so -sa** *adj* needy ‖ *mf* needy person
**menestra** *f* vegetable soup
**menes•tral -trala** *mf* mechanic
**meng.** *abbr* **menguante**
**mengua** *f* want, lack; poverty; decline; decrease, diminution; **en mengua de** to the discredit of
**mengua•do -da** *adj* timid, cowardly; simple, silly; mean, stingy; wretched, miserable; poor, needy; fatal
**menguante** *adj* decreasing; declining; waning ‖ *f* decrease; decline; low water; ebb tide; **menguante de la luna** wane, waning of the moon
**menguar** **§10** *tr* to diminish, lessen; to discredit ‖ *intr* to diminish, lessen; to decline; to decrease; (*la luna*) to wane; (*la marea*) to fall
**mengue** *m* (coll) devil
**menina** *f* young lady in waiting
**menino** *m* noble page of the royal family
**menor** *adj* less, lesser; smaller; younger; least; smallest; youngest; slightest; minor ‖ *m* minor; **al por menor** retail; **menor de edad** minor; **por menor** retail; in detail, minutely ‖ *f* minor premise
**Menorca** *f* Minorca
**menoría** *f* inferiority, subordination; (*tiempo de menor edad*) minority
**menorista** *adj* (Arg, Chile) retail ‖ *mf* (Arg, Chile) retailer
**menor•quín -quina** *adj & mf* Minorcan
**menos** *adv* less; fewer; least; fewest; **al menos** at least; **a lo menos** at least; **a menos que** unless; **echar de menos** to miss; **¡menos mal!** lucky break!; **menos mal que** it is a good thing that; **no poder menos de** + *inf* to not be able to help + *ger;* **por lo menos** at least; **tener en menos** to think little of; **venir a menos** to decline; to become poor ‖ *prep* less, minus; (*al decir la hora*) of, to, e.g., **las tres menos diez** ten minutes of (or to) three ‖ *m* less; (*signo de resta o sustracción*) minus, minus sign
**menoscabar** *tr* to lessen, diminish, reduce; to damage; to discredit
**menoscabo** *m* lessening, reduction; damage; discredit; **con menoscabo de** to the detriment of
**menoscuenta** *f* part payment
**menospreciable** *adj* despicable, contemptible
**menospreciar** *tr* to underestimate, underrate; to scorn, despise
**menosprecio** *m* underestimation; scorn
**mensaje** *m* message
**mensajería** *f* public conveyance; **mensajerías** transportation company; shipping line
**mensaje•ro -ra** *mf* messenger ‖ *m* harbinger
**men•so -sa** *adj* (Mex) foolish, stupid
**menstruar** **§21** *intr* to menstruate
**menstruo** *m* menses
**mensual** *adj* monthly
**mensualidad** *f* monthly pay, monthly instalment
**ménsula** *f* bracket; elbow rest
**mensurar** *tr* to measure
**menta** *f* mint; **menta piperita** peppermint; **menta romana** or **verde** spearmint
**menta•do -da** *adj* famous, renowned
**mentar** **§2** *tr* to mention
**mente** *f* mind
**mentecatería** or **mentecatez** *f* simpleness, folly
**menteca•to -ta** *adj* simple, foolish ‖ *mf* simpleton, fool
**mentidero** *m* (coll) hangout; (coll) gossip column
**mentir** **§68** *tr* to disappoint ‖ *intr* to lie; to be misleading; (*un color*) to clash; **¡miento!** my mistake!
**mentira** *f* lie; error, mistake; **mentira inocente** or **oficiosa** white lie; **parece mentira** it's hard to believe
**mentirilla** *f* fib, white lie; **de mentirillas** for fun
**mentirón** *m* whopper
**mentiro•so -sa** *adj* lying; false, deceptive; full of errors ‖ *mf* liar
**men•tís** *m* (*pl* **-tís**) insulting contradiction; **dar un mentís a** to give the lie to
**mentón** *m* chin
**me•nú** *m* (*pl* **-nús**) menu

**menudamente** *adv* in detail; at retail
**menudear** *tr* to make frequently; to tell in detail; (Col) to sell at retail || *intr* to happen frequently, to be frequent; to go into detail; (Arg) to grow, increase
**menudencia** *f* smallness; trifle; meticulousness; **menudencias** pork products; (Col, Mex) giblets
**menudeo** *m* constant repetition; detailed accounting; **al menudeo** at retail
**menudillos** *mpl* giblets
**menu•do -da** *adj* small, slight, minute; futile, worthless; meticulous; common, vulgar; petty || *m* innards (*of fowl and other animals*); rice coal; **al menudo** at retail; **a menudo** often; **menudos** small change; **por menudo** in detail; at retail
**meñique** *adj* little, tiny; (*dedo*) little || *m* little finger
**meollo** *m* marrow; pith; (*seso*) brain; brains, intelligence; gist, marrow, essence
**me•ón -ona** *adj* (*niño*) piddling; (*niebla*) dripping
**mequetrefe** *m* (coll) whippersnapper, jackanapes
**mercachifle** *m* peddler; small dealer
**mercadear** *intr* to deal, to trade
**merca•der -dera** *mf* merchant; **mercader de grueso** wholesale merchant
**mercadería** *f* merchandise, commodity; **mercaderías** goods, merchandise
**mercado** *m* market; **lanzar al mercado** to put on the market; **mercado de valores** stock market; **mercado negro** black market
**mercaduría** *f* commodity
**mercancía** *f* trade, commerce; merchandise; piece of merchandise; **mercancías** goods, merchandise || **mercancías** *msg* (*pl* **-as**) freight train
**mercante** *adj & m* merchant
**mercantil** *adj* mercantile
**mercar** §73 *tr* to buy || *intr* to trade, deal
**merced** *f* pay, wages; favor, grace; **a merced de** at the mercy of; **merced a** thanks to; **merced de agua** distribution of irrigating water; **vuestra merced** your grace
**mercena•rio -ria** *adj* mercenary || *m* mercenary; day laborer, hireling
**mercería** *f* haberdashery, notions store; (Am) dry-goods store; (Chile) hardware store
**mercología** *f* marketing
**mercurio** *m* mercury
**merecer** §22 *tr* to deserve, merit; (*lo que se desea*) to attain; (*alabanza*) to win; (*cierta suma*) to be worth; **merecer la pena** to be worth while || *intr* to be deserving; **merecer bien de** to deserve the gratitude of
**mereci•do -da** *adj* deserved || *m* just deserts; **llevar su merecido** to get what's coming to one
**mereciente** *adj* deserving
**merecimiento** *m* desert, merit
**merendar** §2 *tr* to lunch on, have for lunch; to keep an eye on, to peep at || *intr* to lunch || *ref* to manage to get; (*en el juego*) (Chile) to clean out
**merendero** *m* lunchroom; picnic grounds
**merendona** *f* fine spread
**merengar** §44 *tr* to whip (*cream*)
**merengue** *m* meringue
**mere•triz** *f* (*pl* **-trices**) harlot
**meridiana** *f* lounge, couch; afternoon nap; meridian line; **a la meridiana** at noon
**meridia•no -na** *adj* meridian; bright, dazzling || *m* meridian || *f* see **meridiana**
**meridional** *adj* southern || *mf* southerner
**merienda** *f* lunch, snack; (coll) hunchback
**meri•no -na** *adj* merino; (*cabello*) thick and curly || *mf* merino || *m* merino shepherd; merino wool
**mérito** *m* merit, desert; value, worth; **hacer mérito de** to make mention of; **hacer méritos** to try to please, to put one's best foot forward
**merito•rio -ria** *adj* meritorious || *m* volunteer worker; unpaid learner, apprentice
**merluza** *f* (*pez*) hake; (coll) drunk, spree
**merma** *f* decrease, reduction; leakage, shrinkage
**mermar** *tr* to decrease, reduce || *intr* to decrease, shrink, dwindle
**mermelada** *f* marmalade
**me•ro -ra** *adj* mere, pure; (Col, Ven) alone || *m* grouper, jewfish || **mero** *adv* (CAm) almost, soon
**merodea•dor -dora** *adj* marauding || *m* marauder
**merodear** *intr* to maraud
**mes** *m* month; monthly pay; menses; **caer en el mes del obispo** (coll) to come at the right time
**mesa** *f* table; (*mostrador*) counter; (*escritorio*) desk; (*de arma blanca o herramienta*) flat side; (*de escalera*) landing; (*comida*) fare, food; (*conjunto de dirigentes*) board; **alzar la mesa** to clear the table; **hacer mesa limpia** to clean up (*in gambling*); **levantar la mesa** to clear the table; **mesa de batalla** sorting table; **mesa de extensión** extension table; **mesa de juego** gambling table; **mesa de milanos** (coll) scanty fare; **mesa de trucos** pool table; **mesa perezosa** drop table; **poner la mesa** to set or lay the table; **tener a mesa y mantel** to feed, to support; **tener mesa** to keep open house
**mesana** *f* (naut) mizzen
**mesar** *tr* (*los cabellos*) to tear, pull out || *ref* — **mesarse los cabellos** to pull out one's hair; to pull out each other's hair
**mescolanza** *f* (coll) jumble, hodgepodge, medley
**meseguería** *f* harvest watch
**mesera** *f* (Am) waitress
**mesero** *m* journeyman on monthly pay; (Am) waiter
**meseta** *f* plateau, tableland; (*de escalera*) landing

**Mesías** *m* Messiah
**mesilla** *f* mantel, mantelpiece; (*de escalera*) landing; window sill
**mesita** *f* stand, small table; **mesita portateléfono** telephone table
**mesnada** *f* armed retinue; band, company
**mesón** *m* inn, tavern; (Chile) bar; (Chile) counter
**mesone•ro -ra** *adj* inn, tavern ‖ *mf* innkeeper, tavern keeper
**mester** *m* (archaic) craft, trade; (archaic) literary genre; **mester de clerecía** clerical verse of the Middle Ages; **mester de juglaría** popular minstrelsy of the Middle Ages
**mesti•zo -za** *adj & mf* half-breed; (*perro*) mongrel
**mesura** *f* dignity, gravity; calm, restraint; courtesy, civility
**mesura•do -da** *adj* dignified, sedate; calm, restrained; polite; moderate, temperate
**mesurar** *tr* to temper, moderate ‖ *ref* to act with restraint
**meta** *f* goal
**metafonía** *f* umlaut
**metáfora** *f* metaphore
**metafóri•co -ca** *adj* metaphorical
**metal** *m* metal; money; (*de la voz*) timbre; condition, quality; (mus) brass; **el vil metal** (coll) filthy lucre; **metal blanco** nickel silver; **metal de imprenta** type metal
**metale•ro -ra** *adj* (Bol, Chile, Peru) metal ‖ *m* (Bol, Chile, Peru) metalworker
**metáli•co -ca** *adj* metallic ‖ *m* metalworker; cash, coin
**metalistería** *f* metalwork
**metalizar** §60 *tr* to make metallic; to put a metal coating on; to turn into cash ‖ *ref* to become mercenary
**metaloide** *m* nonmetal
**metalurgia** *f* metallurgy
**metamorfo•sis** *f* (*pl* **-sis**) metamorphosis
**metano** *m* methane
**metate** *m* (CAm, Mex) flat stone on which corn is ground
**metáte•sis** *f* (*pl* **-sis**) metathesis
**mete•dor -dora** *mf* smuggler
**metedurία** *f* smuggling
**metemuer•tos** *m* (*pl* **-tos**) stagehand; busybody, meddler
**meteo** *f* weather bureau, weather report
**meteóri•co -ca** *adj* meteoric
**meteoro** or **metéoro** *m* meteor; atmospheric phenomenon
**meteorología** *f* meteorology
**meter** *tr* to put, to place; to insert; (*un ruido*) to make; (*miedo*) to cause; (*mentiras*) to tell; (*chismes, enredos*) to start; (*dinero en el juego*) to stake; to smuggle; (*un golpe*) (Am) to strike ‖ *ref* to project; to meddle, butt in; **meterse a** to set oneself up as; to take it upon oneself to; **meterse con** to pick a quarrel with; **meterse en** to get into; to plunge into; to empty into
**meticulo•so -sa** *adj* meticulous; shy, timid
**meti•do -da** *adj* close, tight; rich, abundant; (Am) meddlesome; **muy metido con** on close terms with; **muy metido en** deeply involved in ‖ *m* push; punch; strong lye; loose leaf; (*tela sobrante en las costuras de una prenda*) seam
**metódi•co -ca** *adj* methodic(al)
**metodista** *adj & mf* Methodist
**método** *m* method
**metraje** *m* distance or length in meters; (*cine*) **de corto metraje** short; (*cine*) **de largo metraje** full-length
**metralla** *f* scrap iron; grapeshot; shrapnel
**métri•co -ca** *adj* metric(al) ‖ *f* prosody
**metro** *m* meter; ruler; tape measure; subway; **metro plegadizo** folding rule
**metrónomo** *m* metronome
**metrópoli** *f* metropolis; mother country
**metropolita•no -na** *adj* metropolitan ‖ *m* subway; (eccl) metropolitan
**Méx.** *abbr* **México**
**mexica•no -na** *adj & mf* (Am) Mexican
**México** *m* (Am) Mexico; **Nuevo México** New Mexico
**mezcla** *f* mixture; (*argamasa*) mortar; (*tejido*) tweed
**mezclar** *tr* to mix; to blend ‖ *ref* to mix; (*introducirse uno entre otros*) to mingle; to intermarry; to meddle
**mezclilla** *f* light tweed
**mezcolanza** *f* jumble, hodgepodge, medley
**mezquinar** *tr* (Am) to be stingy with ‖ *intr* (Am) to be stingy
**mezquindad** *f* meanness, stinginess; need, poverty; smallness, tininess; wretchedness
**mezqui•no -na** *adj* mean, stingy; needy, poor; small, tiny; wretched
**mezquita** *f* mosque
**mi** *adj poss* my
**mí** (used as object of a preposition) *pron pers* me ‖ *pron reflex* myself
**miar** §77 *intr* to meow
**miau** *m* meow
**mica** *f* mica; (Guat) flirt; **ponerse una mica** (CAm) to go on a jag
**mico** *m* long-tailed monkey; libertine; (coll) hoodlum; **dar mico** (coll) to not keep a date
**microbio** *m* microbe
**microbiología** *f* microbiology
**microbús** *m* (Chile) jitney
**microfaradio** *m* microfarad
**microficha** *f* microcard
**micro•film** *m* (*pl* **-films** o **-filmes**) microfilm
**microfilmar** *tr* to microfilm
**micrófono** *m* microphone
**microonda** *f* microwave
**micropelícula** *f* microfilm
**microscópi•co -ca** *adj* microscopic
**microscopio** *m* microscope
**microsurco** *adj invar* microgroove ‖ *m* microgroove
**microteléfono** *m* handset, French telephone
**mi•cho -cha** *mf* (coll) pussy cat
**miedo** *m* fear, dread; **miedo cerval**

great fear; **por miedo de** for fear of; **por miedo (de) que** for fear that; **tener miedo (a)** to be afraid (of); **tener miedo de** to be in fear of, be afraid of; to be afraid to
**miedo•so -sa** *adj* (coll) fearful, afraid
**miel** *f* honey; (*jarabe saturado*) molasses; **dejar con la miel en los labios** to spoil the fun for; **hacerse de miel** to be peaches and cream
**mielga** *f* lucerne
**miembro** *m* member; (*extremidad del hombre y los animales*) member, limb
**mientes** *fpl* mind, thought; wish, desire; **caer en las mientes** or **en mientes** to come to mind; **parar** or **poner mientes en** to reflect on; **venírsele a uno a las mientes** to come to one's mind
**mientras** *conj* while; whereas; **mientras que** while; whereas; **mientras tanto** meanwhile
**miérco•les** *m* (*pl* **-les**) Wednesday; **miércoles de ceniza** Ash Wednesday
**mies** *f* cereal, grain; harvest time; **mieses** grain fields
**miga** *f* (*porción pequeña*) bit; (*parte más blanda del pan*) crumb; (fig) substance; **hacer buenas migas con** to get along well with; **migas** fried crumbs
**migaja** *f* bit, piece; (*de inteligencia*) smattering; **migajas** crumbs; leavings
**migajón** *m* crumb; (coll) substance
**migar** **§44** *tr* (*el pan*) to crumb; (*p.ej., la leche*) to put crumbs in
**migrato•rio -ria** *adj* migratory
**miguelear** *tr* (CAm) to make love to
**miguele•ño -ña** *adj* (Hond) impolite, discourteous
**mijo** *m* millet
**mil** *adj & m* thousand, a thousand, one thousand; **a las mil quinientas** (coll) at an unearthly hour
**milagre•ro -ra** *adj* superstitious; miracle-working
**milagro** *m* (*hecho sobrenatural*) miracle; (*cosa rara*) wonder; votive offering; **colgar el milagro a** (coll) to put the blame on; **vivir de milagro** to have a hard time getting along; to have had a narrow escape
**milagrón** *m* (coll) fuss, excitement
**milagro•so -sa** *adj* miraculous; marvelous, wonderful
**milano** *m* burr, down; (orn) kite
**mil•deu** *m* (*pl* **-deues**) mildew
**milena•rio -ria** *adj* millennial || *m* millennium
**milenio** *m* millennium
**milenrama** *f* yarrow
**milési•mo -ma** *adj & m* thousandth
**miliamperio** *m* milliampere
**milicia** *f* militia; soldiery; warfare; military service
**milicia•no -na** *adj* military || *m* militiaman
**miligramo** *m* milligram
**milímetro** *m* millimeter
**militante** *adj* militant
**militar** *adj* military; army || *m* soldier, military man || *intr* to fight, go to war; to struggle; to serve in the army; (*surtir efecto*) to militate
**militarismo** *m* militarism
**militarista** *adj & mf* militarist
**militarizar** **§60** *tr* to militarize
**mílite** *m* soldier
**milpa** *f* (CAm, Mex) cornfield
**milla** *f* mile
**millar** *m* thousand
**millarada** *f* about a thousand; **echar millaradas** to boast about one's wealth
**millo** *m* millet
**millón** *m* million
**millona•rio -ria** *adj* of a million or more inhabitants || *mf* millionaire
**mimar** *tr* to fondle, to pet; to pamper, indulge, spoil
**mimbre** *m & f* (bot) osier; osier, wicker, withe
**mimbrear** *intr & ref* to sway
**mimbre•ño -ña** *adj* willowy
**mimbrera** *f* (bot) osier, osier willow
**mimbro•so -sa** *adj* osier; (*hecho de mimbre*) wicker
**mimeografiar** **§77** *tr* to mimeograph
**mimeógrafo** *m* mimeograph
**mímica** *f* mimicry; sign language
**mimo** *m* (*entre los griegos y romanos*) mime; fondling, petting; pampering
**mimo•so -sa** *adj* delicate, tender; finicky, fussy
**mina** *f* mine; (*de lápiz*) lead; (fig) mine, gold mine, storehouse; underground passage; (SAm) moll; **beneficiar una mina** to work a mine; **mina de carbón** or **mina hullera** coal mine; **voló la mina** the truth is out
**minado** *m* mine work; (nav) mining
**mina•dor -dora** *adj* (nav) mine-laying || *m* (mil) miner; (nav) mine layer
**minar** *tr* to mine; to undermine; to consume; to plug away at || *intr* to mine
**minarete** *m* minaret
**mineraje** *m* mining; **mineraje a tajo abierto** strip mining
**mineral** *adj & m* mineral
**mineralogía** *f* mineralogy
**minería** *f* mining; mine operators
**mine•ro -ra** *adj* mining || *m* miner; mine operator; (fig) source, origin
**mingitorio** *m* street urinal
**min•gón -gona** *adj* (Ven) spoiled, pampered
**miniar** *tr* to paint in miniature; (*un manuscrito*) to illuminate
**miniatura** *f* miniature
**miniaturización** *f* miniaturization
**míni•mo -ma** *adj* minimum; tiny, small, minute; least, smallest || *m* minimum || *f* tiny bit
**mini•no -na** *mf* (coll) kitty, pussy
**ministerial** *adj* ministerial
**ministerio** *m* ministry, cabinet, government; **formar ministerio** to form a government; **ministerio de Hacienda** Treasury Department (U.S.A.); Treasury (Brit); **ministerio de la Gobernación** Department of the Interior (U.S.A.); Home Office (Brit); **ministerio del Ejército** Department of the Army (U.S.A.); War Office (Brit); **ministerio de Marina** Department of

the Navy (U.S.A.); Board of Admiralty (Brit)
**ministrar** *tr* to administer; to furnish
**ministro** *m* minister; bailiff, constable; **ministro de asuntos exteriores** foreign minister; **ministro de Gobernación** Home Secretary (Brit); **ministro de Hacienda** Secretary of the Treasury (U.S.A.); Chancellor of the Exchequer (Brit); **ministro de Justicia** Attorney General (U.S.A.); **primer ministro** prime minister, premier
**minorar** *tr* to diminish, reduce; to weaken
**minorati•vo -va** *adj & m* laxative
**minoría** *f* minority
**minoridad** *f* minority
**minorita•rio -ria** *adj* minority
**minucia** *f* trifle; **minucias** minutiae
**minucio•so -sa** *adj* minute, meticulous
**minué** *m* or **minuete** *m* minuet
**minúscu•lo -la** *adj* (*letra*) small; (coll) small, tiny || *f* small letter
**minuta** *f* first draft, rough draft; memorandum; menu, bill of fare; roll, list
**minutero** *m* minute hand
**minu•to -ta** *adj* minute || *m* minute || *f* see **minuta**
**mí•o -a** *adj poss* mine; of mine, e.g., **un amigo mío** a friend of mine || *pron poss* mine
**miope** *adj* near-sighted || *mf* near-sighted person
**miopía** *f* near-sightedness
**mira** *f* (*de arma de fuego, telescopio, etc.*) sight; aim, object, purpose; target; watchtower; **estar a la mira** to be on the lookout; **poner la mira en** to have designs on
**mirada** *f* glance, look; **apuñalar con la mirada** to look daggers at; **mirada de soslayo** side glance
**miradero** *m* (*lugar desde donde se mira*) lookout; (*persona o cosa que es objeto de la atención pública*) cynosure
**mira•do -da** *adj* cautious, circumspect; **bien mirado** highly regarded || *f* see **mirada**
**mirador** *m* belvedere; bay window, oriel
**miramiento** *m* considerateness, courtesy, regard; look; **miramientos** (coll) fuss, bother
**miranda** *f* eminence, vantage point
**mirar** *tr* to look at, to watch; to consider, contemplate; **mirar bien** to look with favor on; **mirar por encima** to glance at || *intr* to look, to glance; **¡mira!** look out!; **mirar a** to look at, glance at; to face, overlook; to aim at; to aim to; **mirar por** to look after || *ref* to look at oneself; to look at each other; **mirarse en ello** to watch one's step; **mirarse en una persona** to be all wrapped up in a person
**mirasol** *m* sunflower
**miríada** *f* myriad
**mirilla** *f* peephole; (*para dirigir visuales*) target; (phot) finder
**miriñaque** *m* hoop skirt, crinoline; bauble, trinket; (Arg) cowcatcher
**mirística** *f* nutmeg tree
**mirlar** *ref* (coll) to try to look important
**mirlo** *m* blackbird; (coll) solemn look; **mirlo blanco** (coll) rare bird; **soltar el mirlo** (coll) to start to jabber
**mirmidón** *m* tiny fellow, nincompoop
**mi•rón -rona** *adj* onlooking; nosy || *mf* onlooker; (*de una partida de juego*) kibitzer; busybody
**mirra** *f* myrrh
**mirto** *m* myrtle
**misa** *f* mass; **cantar misa** to say mass; **como en misa** in dead silence; **misa cantada** High Mass; **misa de prima** early mass; **misa mayor** High Mass; **misa rezada** Low Mass
**misal** *m* missal
**misantropía** *f* misanthropy
**misántropo** *m* misanthrope
**misar** *intr* (coll) to say mass; (coll) to hear mass
**misario** *m* acolyte
**misceláne•o -na** *adj* miscellaneous || *f* miscellany
**miserable** *adj* miserable, wretched; mean, stingy; despicable, vile || *mf* cur, cad; wretch; miser
**miseran•do -da** *adj* pitiful
**miserear** *intr* (coll) to be stingy
**miseria** *f* misery, wretchedness; poverty; stinginess; (coll) trifle, pittance; **comerse de miseria** (coll) to live in great poverty
**misericordia** *f* compassion, mercy, pity
**misericordio•so -sa** *adj* merciful
**míse•ro -ra** *adj* miserable, wretched || *mf* wretch
**misión** *f* mission; ration for harvesters; **ir a misiones** to go away as a missionary
**misional** *adj* missionary
**misionario** *m* missionary; envoy, messenger
**misionero** *m* missionary
**misi•vo -va** *adj & f* missive
**mismísi•mo -ma** *adj* very same, self-same
**mis•mo -ma** *adj & pron indef* same; own, very; -self, e.g., **ella misma** herself; myself, e.g., **yo mismo** I myself; yourself, himself, herself, itself; **así mismo** likewise, also; **casi lo mismo** much the same; **lo mismo** just the same; **lo mismo me da** (coll) it's all the same to me; **mismo . . . que** same . . . as; **por lo mismo** for that very reason || **mismo** *adv* right, e.g., **ahora mismo** right now; **aquí mismo** right here
**mistela** *f* flavored brandy; needled must, spiked must
**misterio** *m* mystery; **hablar de misterio** to talk mysteriously
**misterio•so -sa** *adj* mysterious
**misticismo** *m* mysticism
**místi•co -ca** *adj* mystic(al) || *mf* mystic
**mistificación** *f* hoax, mystification
**mistificar** §73 *tr* to hoax, to mystify
**mistifori** *m* (coll) hodgepodge
**misturera** *f* (Peru) flower girl
**mita** *f* mite, cheese mite; (SAm) Indian slave labor; (*turno en el trabajo*) (Arg, Chile) shift, turn

**mitad** *f* half; middle; **a (la) mitad de** halfway through; **cara mitad** (coll) better half; **en la mitad de** in the middle of; **la mitad de** half the; **mitad y mitad** half-and-half; **por la mitad** in half, in the middle
**míti•co -ca** *adj* mythical
**mitigar §44** *tr* to mitigate, appease, allay
**mitin** *m* (*pl* **mitins** or **mítines**) meeting, rally
**mito** *m* myth
**mitología** *f* mythology
**mitológi•co -ca** *adj* mythological
**mitón** *m* mitten
**mitra** *f* chimney pot; (eccl) miter
**mixtificación** *f* hoax, mystification
**mixtificar §73** *tr* to hoax, to mystify
**mixtifori** *m* (coll) hodgepodge
**mixtión** *f* mixture
**mix•to -ta** *adj* mixed || *m* compound number; sulphur match; explosive compound
**mixtura** *f* mixture
**mixturar** *tr* to mix
**mixturera** *f* (Peru) flower girl
**miz** *interj* here, pussy!, here, kitty!
**mízcalo** *m* edible milk mushroom
**m/l** *abbr* **mi letra**
**m/n** *abbr* **moneda nacional**
**mobilia•rio -ria** *adj* personal (*property*) || *m* furniture, suit of furniture
**moblaje** *m* furniture, suit of furniture
**moblar §61** *tr* to furnish
**moca** *m* Mocha coffee || *f* (Ecuad) mudhole; (Mex) wineglass
**mocador** *m* handkerchief
**mocar §73** *tr* to blow the nose of || *ref* to blow one's nose
**mocarro** *m* (coll) snot
**mocasín** *m* moccasin
**mocear** *intr* to act young; to sow one's wild oats
**mocedad** *f* youth; wild oats
**mocerío** *m* young people
**mocero** *adj masc* woman-crazy
**mocetón** *m* strapping young fellow
**mocetona** *f* buxom young woman
**mocil** *adj* youthful
**moción** *f* motion, movement; (*en junta deliberante*) motion; **hacer** or **presentar una moción** to make a motion
**mocionante** *mf* (Am) mover
**mocionar** *tr & intr* (Am) to move
**moci•to -ta** *adj* young || *mf* youngster
**moco** *m* (*humor segregado por una membrana mucosa*) mucus; (*mocarro*) snot; (*extremo del pabilo de una vela*) snuff; **a moco de candil** by candle light; **llorar a moco tendido** (coll) to cry like a baby; **moco de pavo** crest of a turkey; (bot) cockscomb; (col) trifle
**moco•so -sa** *adj* snotty, snively; rude, ill-bred; flip, saucy; mean, worthless || *mf* brat
**mochar** *tr* to butt; (Arg) to rob; (Am) to chop off; (Col) to fire
**mochil** *m* errand boy for farmers in the field
**mochila** *f* knapsack, haversack; tool bag; (mil) ration
**mochín** *m* (slang) executioner
**mo•cho -cha** *adj* blunt, stub, flat; (*árbol*) topped; stub-horned || *m* butt end
**mochuelo** *m* (orn) little owl; (*de una o más palabras*) omission; **cargar con el mochuelo** or **tocarle a** (*uno*) **el mochuelo** (coll) to get the worst of a deal
**moda** *f* fashion, mode, style; **a la moda de** after the fashion of, in the style of; **alta moda** haute couture; **de moda** in fashion; **fuera de moda** out of fashion; **pasar de moda** to go out of fashion
**modales** *mpl* manners
**modalidad** *f* manner, way, nature, kind
**modelar** *tr* to model; to form, shape; to mold || *ref* to model; **modelarse sobre** to pattern oneself after
**modelo** *adj invar* model, e.g., **ciudad modelo** model city || *mf* model, mannequin, fashion model || *m* model, pattern; form, blank; equal, peer; style
**modera•do -da** *adj* moderate
**moderador** *m* regulator; (*para retardar el efecto de los neutrones*) moderator
**moderar** *tr* to moderate, control, restrain || *ref* to moderate, control oneself, restrain oneself
**modernizar §60** *tr* to modernize
**moder•no -na** *adj* modern
**modestia** *f* modesty
**modes•to -ta** *adj* modest
**modicidad** *f* moderateness, reasonableness
**módi•co -ca** *adj* moderate, reasonable
**modificante** *adj* modifying || *m* (gram) modifier
**modificar §73** *tr* to modify
**modismo** *m* idiom
**modista** *f* dressmaker; **modista de sombreros** milliner
**modistería** *f* dressmaking; (Am) ladies' dress shop
**modistilla** *f* (coll) dressmaker's helper; (coll) unskilled dressmaker
**modisto** *m* ladies' tailor
**modo** *m* manner, mode, way; (gram) mood, mode; **al** or **a modo de** like, on the order of; **de buen modo** politely; **de ese modo** at that rate; **de tal modo que** with the result that; **de modo que** so that; and so; **de ningún modo** by no means; **de todos modos** anyhow, at any rate; **en cierto modo** after a fashion; **modo de ser** nature, disposition; **por modo de** as, by way of; **sobre modo** extremely; **uno a modo de** a sort of, a kind of
**modorra** *f* drowsiness, heaviness
**modorrar** *tr* to make drowsy || *ref* to get drowsy, fall asleep; (*la fruta*) to get squashy
**modo•rro -rra** *adj* drowsy, heavy; dull, stupid; (*fruta*) squashy || *f* see **modorra**
**modo•so -sa** *adj* quiet, well-behaved
**modrego** *m* (coll) boor, awkward fellow
**modulación** *f* modulation; **modulación de altura** or **de amplitud** amplitude

modulation; **modulación de frecuencia** frequency modulation
**modular** *tr & intr* to modulate
**modulo•so -sa** *adj* harmonious
**mofa** *f* jeering, scoffing, mockery
**mofeta** *f* skunk; (*gas pernicioso que se desprende de las minas*) blackdamp, firedamp
**mofiete** *m* (coll) fat cheek, jowl
**mofietu•do -da** *adj* fat-cheeked
**mo•gol -gola** *adj & mf* Mongol, Mongolian
**mogollón** *m* — **comer de mogollón** (coll) to sponge
**mo•gón -gona** *adj* one-horned, broken-horned
**mogote** *m* knoll, hillock; stack of sheaves; budding antler
**mohatra** *f* fake sale; cheating
**mohien•to -ta** *adj* moldy, musty; (*hierro*) rusty
**mohín** *m* face, grimace
**mohina** *f* annoyance, displeasure
**mohi•no -na** *adj* sad, melancholy, moody; (*caballo, buey, vaca*) black, black-nosed || *mf* hinny || *m* blue magpie || *f* see **mohina**
**moho** *m* mold, must; (*del hierro*) rust; sloth, laziness; **no dejar criar moho** (coll) to keep in constant use, to use up quickly
**moho•so -sa** *adj* moldy, musty; (*hierro*) rusty; (*chiste*) stale
**Moisés** *m* Moses
**moja•do -da** *adj* wet; (*p.ej., por la lluvia*) drenched, soaked; (*húmedo*) moist; (phonet) liquid || *m* (Mex) wetback
**mojar** *tr* to wet; (*la lluvia a una persona*) to drench, soak; (*humedecer*) to dampen, to moisten; (*ensopar*) to dunk; (coll) to stab || *intr* — **mojar en** to get mixed up in || *ref* to get wet; to get drenched, get soaked
**mojarrilla** *mf* (coll) jolly person
**moje** *m* sauce, gravy
**mojicón** *m* muffin, bun; (coll) slap in the face
**mojiganga** *f* masquerade, mummery; clowning
**mojigatería** or **mojigatez** *f* hypocrisy; prudery, sanctimoniousness
**mojiga•to -ta** *adj* hypocritical; prudish, sanctimonious || *mf* hypocrite; prude, sanctimonious person
**mojinete** *m* (*de un muro*) coping; (*de un tejado*) ridge; (Arg) gable; (Chile) gable end
**mojón** *m* boundary stone, landmark; (*montón sin orden*) pile, heap; (*guía en desplobado*) road mark; (*porción de excremento humano*) turd
**moldar** *tr* to mold; to put molding on
**molde** *m* mold; pattern; cast, stamp, matrix; (*persona*) model, ideal; (*letra*) **de molde** printed; **venir de molde** to be just right
**moldear** *tr* to mold; (*vaciar*) to cast; to put molding on
**moldura** *f* molding
**moldurar** *tr* to put molding on
**mole** *adj* soft || *m* (Mex) stew seasoned with chili sauce || *f* bulk, mass
**molécula** *f* molecule
**molende•ro -ra** *mf* miller, grinder || *m* chocolate grinder; (CAm) grinding table
**moler** §47 *tr* (*granos*) to grind, to mill; to annoy, harass, weary; to tire out, fatigue; (coll) to chew; **moler a palos** (coll) to beat up
**molesquina** *f* moleskin
**molestar** *tr* to disturb, molest; to bother, annoy; to tire, weary || *ref* to bother; to be annoyed; **molestarse en** to take the trouble to
**molestia** *f* disturbance, discomfort; annoyance, bother, nuisance
**moles•to -ta** *adj* bothersome, troublesome; boring, tedious; bored, tired
**molesto•so -sa** *adj* (Am) bothersome
**moleteado** *m* knurl
**moletear** *tr* to knurl
**molibdeno** *m* molybdenum
**molicie** *f* softness; effeminacy, voluptuous living
**moli•do -da** *adj* exhausted, worn out
**molienda** *f* grinding, milling; (*cantidad que se muele de una vez*) grist; (*molino*) mill; (coll) bore, annoyance; (coll) fatigue, weariness
**molimiento** *m* grinding; weariness
**moline•ro -ra** *adj* mill || *m* miller || *f* miller's wife
**molinete** *m* little mill; ventilating fan; (*juguete de papel*) windmill; (*movimiento que se hace con el bastón*) twirl; (*con la espada*) flourish; (naut) windlass; (*rueda de cohetes*) (Mex) pinwheel
**molinillo** *m* hand mill; **molinillo de café** coffee grinder
**molino** *m* mill; **luchar con los molinos de viento** to tilt at windmills; **molino de sangre** animal-driven mill; **molino de viento** windmill; **molino harinero** gristmill, flour mill
**moloc** *m* (Ecuad) mashed potatoes
**molondrón** *m* (coll) lazy bum; (Ven) large inheritance, large amount of money
**molusco** *m* mollusk
**mollar** *adj* soft, tender; mushy, squashy; (*carne*) lean; profitable; (coll) gullible, easily taken in
**mollear** *intr* to give, to yield; to bend
**molleja** *f* gizzard; **criar molleja** (coll) to get lazy; **mollejas** sweetbread
**mollejón** *m* grindstone; (coll) big fat loafer; (coll) good-natured fellow
**mollera** *f* crown (*of the head*); (coll) brains, sense; **cerrado de mollera** (coll) stupid; **duro de mollera** (coll) stubborn
**mollete** *m* muffin
**molli•no -na** *adj* drizzly || *f* drizzle
**mollizna** *f* drizzle
**momentáne•o -a** *adj* momentary
**momento** *m* moment; **al momento** at once; **de un momento a otro** at any moment
**momería** *f* clowning
**mome•ro -ra** *adj* clowning || *mf* clown
**momia** *f* mummy
**momificar** §73 *tr* to mummify

**mo•mio -mia** *adj* lean, skinny ‖ *m* extra; (*ganga*) bargain; sinecure ‖ *f* see **momia**
**momo** *m* face, grimace; (coll) caress
**mona** *f* female monkey; Barbary ape; (coll) ape, copycat; (coll) drunkenness; (*persona*) (coll) drunk; (taur) guard for right leg; **dormir la mona** (coll) to sleep off a drunk; **pillar una mona** (coll) to go on a jag; **pintar la mona** (coll) to put on airs
**monacal** *adj* monachal
**monacato** *m* monkhood
**monacillo** *m* altar boy, acolyte
**monada** *f* monkeyshine; (*gesto*) face, grimace, monkey face; darling; cuteness; flattery; folly, childishness
**monaguillo** *m* altar boy, acolyte
**monaquismo** *m* monasticism
**monarca** *m* monarch
**monarquía** *f* monarchy
**monárqui•co -ca** *adj* monarchic(al) ‖ *mf* monarchist
**monasterio** *m* monastery
**monásti•co -ca** *adj* monastic
**monda** *f* pruning, trimming; parings, peelings; (Am) beating, whipping
**mondadien•tes** *m* (*pl* **-tes**) toothpick
**mondadura** *f* pruning, trimming; **mondaduras** peelings
**mondar** *tr* to clean; to prune, to trim; to peel, pare, hull, husk; (*quitar con engaño los bienes a*) to fleece; (Am) to beat, whip
**mon•do -da** *adj* clean; pure; **mondo y lirondo** (coll) pure, unadulterated ‖ *f* see **monda**
**mondonga** *f* (coll) kitchen wench
**mondongo** *m* intestines, insides; (*del hombre*) (coll) guts
**monear** *intr* (coll) to act like a monkey; (Am) to boast ‖ *ref* (Hond) to plug away; (Hond) to punch each other
**moneda** *f* coin; (coll) money; **la Moneda** the government of Chile; **moneda corriente** currency; (coll) common knowledge; **moneda falsa** counterfeit; **moneda menuda** change; **moneda metálica** or **sonante** specie; **moneda suelta** change; **pagar en la misma moneda** to pay back in one's own coin
**monedar** *tr* to coin, to mint
**monedero** *m* moneybag; **monedero falso** counterfeiter
**monería** *f* monkeyshine; cuteness; childishness
**mones•co -ca** *adj* (coll) apish
**moneta•rio -ria** *adj* monetary
**mon•gol -gola** *adj & mf* Mongol, Mongolian
**monigote** *m* lay brother; rag figure, stuffed form; botched painting, botched statue; (coll) sap, boob
**monipodio** *m* (coll) collusion, deal, plot
**monís** *m* trinket; **monises** (coll) money, dough
**mónita** *f* (coll) cunning, smoothness, slickness
**monitor** *m* monitor
**monja** *f* nun; **monjas** lingering sparks in burning paper
**monje** *m* monk
**monjía** *f* monkhood
**monjil** *adj* nunnish ‖ *m* nun's dress
**mono -na** *adj* (coll) cute, nice; (Am) blond; (*cabello*) (Am) red ‖ *m* monkey, ape; (*traje de faena*) coveralls; whippersnapper, squirt; (taur) attendant of picador; (Chile) pyramid of fruit or vegetables; **estar de monos** (coll) to be on the outs; **mono de Gibraltar** Barbary ape ‖ *f* **see mona**
**monóculo** *m* monocle
**monogamia** *f* monogamy
**monografía** *f* monograph
**monograma** *m* monogram
**monolíti•co -ca** *adj* monolithic
**monologar §44** *intr* to soliloquize
**monólogo** *m* monologue
**monomanía** *f* monomania
**monomio** *m* monomial
**mono•no -na** *adj* (coll) cute, sweet
**monopatín** *m* scooter
**monoplano** *m* monoplane
**monopolio** *m* monopoly
**monopolizar §60** *tr* to monopolize
**monorriel** *m* monorail
**monosabio** *m* (taur) attendant of picador
**monosílabo** *m* monosyllable
**monoteísta** *adj* monotheistic ‖ *mf* monotheist
**monotipia** *f* monotype
**monotipista** *mf* monotype operator
**monotipo** *m* monotype
**monotonía** *f* monotony
**monóto•no -na** *adj* monotonous
**monóxido** *m* monoxide
**monseñor** *m* monseigneur; (eccl) monsignor
**monserga** *f* (coll) gibberish
**monstruo** *m* monster
**monstruosidad** *f* monstrosity
**monstruo•so -sa** *adj* monstruous
**monta** *f* sum, total; **de poca monta** of little account
**montacar•gas** *m* (*pl* **-gas**) hoist, freight elevator
**montadero** *m* horse block
**montadura** *f* mounting; (*de una caballería de silla*) harness; (*engaste*) setting, mount
**montaje** *m* montage; setting up; (mach) assembly; (rad) hookup
**montanero** *m* forest ranger
**montante** *m* post, upright; (*suma*) amount; (*hueco cuadrilongo sobre una puerta*) transom; (*espadón*) broadsword ‖ *f* flood tide
**montaña** *f* mountain; mountain country; **la Montaña** the Province of Santander, Spain; **montaña de hielo** iceberg; **montaña rusa** roller coaster
**monta•ñés -ñesa** *adj* mountain ‖ *mf* mountaineer, highlander
**montaño•so -sa** *adj* mountainous
**montapla•tos** *m* (*pl* **-tos**) dumbwaiter
**montar** *tr* to mount, to get on; (*un caballo, una bicicleta, los hombros de una persona*) to ride; (*un servicio*) to set up, establish; (*un fusil*) to cock; (*una piedra preciosa*) to set, to mount; (*el caballo a la yegua*) to cover; (*un reloj*) to wind; (elec) to hook up; (mach) to assemble, to

mount; (*la guardia*) (mil) to mount; (*un cabo*) (naut) to round; (*un buque*) (naut) to command; (*importar*) to amount to || *intr* to mount; to get on top; to weigh, to be important; **tanto monta** it's all the same || *ref* to mount; to get on top; **montarse en cólera** to fly into a rage

**monta•raz** (*pl* **-races**) *adj* backwoods; wild, untamed || *m* forester, warden

**monte** *m* mountain, mount; woods, woodland; obstruction, interference; backwoods, wilds; bank, kitty; (coll) dirty head of hair; **andar al monte** (coll) to take to the woods; **monte alto** forest; **monte bajo** thicket, brushwood; **monte de piedad** pawnshop; **monte pío** pension fund for widows and orphans; mutual benefit society; **monte tallar** tree farm

**montear** *tr* to hunt, to track down; to make a working drawing of; to arch, to vault

**montecillo** *m* mound, hillock

**montepío** *m* pension fund for widows and orphans; mutual benefit society

**montera** *f* cloth cap; glass roof; wife of hunter; bullfighter's black bicorne; (Hond) drunk, jag

**montería** *f* hunting, big-game hunting; hunting party; (Bol, Ecuad) canoe to shoot the rapids; (Mex) lumbermen's camp

**monterilla** *f* (naut) moonsail

**montero** *m* hunter, huntsman

**montés** or **montesi•no -na** *adj* wild (*e.g., goat*)

**montículo** *m* mound, hillock

**montilla** *f* montilla (*a pale dry sherry*)

**monto** *m* sum, total

**montón** *m* pile, heap; (*de gente*) crowd; (coll) lot, great deal, great many; **a, de,** or **en montón** (coll) taken together; **a montones** (coll) in abundance; **ser del montón** (coll) to be quite ordinary

**montonera** *f* (Am) heap, pile; (Am) band of mounted rebels

**montu•no -na** *adj* wooded; (Am) wild, untamed, rustic

**montuo•so -sa** *adj* wooded, woody; rugged, hilly

**montura** *f* (*cabalgadura*) mount; (*de una cabalgadura*) harness; seat, saddle; (*de una piedra preciosa, de un instrumento astronómico*) mounting; (*de gafas*) frame

**monumento** *m* monument

**monzón** *m* monsoon

**moña** *f* doll; mannequin; ribbon, hair ribbon; (coll) drunk, jag

**moño** *m* topknot; crest, top; (Col) caprice, whim; (*de caballo*) (Chile) forelock; **moños** frippery

**moquear** *intr* to snivel

**moqueo** *m* snivel, sniveling

**moquero** *m* handkerchief

**moquete** *m* punch in the nose

**moquillo** *m* runny nose; (vet) distemper

**moquita** *f* mucus, snivel

**mor** *m* — **por mor de** for love of; because of

**mora** *f* black mulberry; blackberry, brambleberry; white mulberry

**morada** *f* dwelling; stay, sojourn

**mora•do -da** *adj* purple, mulberry || *f* see **morada**

**moral** *adj* moral || *m* black mulberry tree || *f* (*ciencia de la conducta; conducta*) morals; (*espíritu, confianza*) morale; (*p.ej., de una fábula*) (coll) moral

**moraleja** *f* moral

**moralidad** *f* morality; (*de una fábula*) moral

**morar** *intr* to live, dwell

**moratoria** *f* moratorium

**mórbi•do -da** *adj* (*perteneciente a la enfermedad*) morbid; soft, delicate, mellow

**morbo** *m* sickness, illness; **morbo gálico** syphilis; **morbo regio** jaundice

**morbo•so -sa** *adj* morbid, diseased

**morcilla** *f* blood pudding, black pudding; (*añadidura que mete un actor en su papel*) gag

**mor•daz** *adj* (*pl* **-daces**) mordant, mordacious, sharp, caustic

**mordaza** *f* (*pañuelo o instrumento que se pone en la boca para impedir el hablar*) gag; (*aparato que sirve para apretar*) clamp, jaw; pipe vise; **poner la mordaza a** to gag

**mordedura** *f* bite

**morder** §47 *tr* to bite; to nibble at; to wear away; to gossip about, ridicule; (Mex, Ven, W-I) to cheat || *intr* to bite; to take hold

**mordicar** §73 *tr & intr* to bite, sting

**mordida** *f* (Am) bite; (*para eludir una multa*) (Mex) payoff

**mordiente** *m* mordant

**mordiscar** §73 *tr* to nibble at || *intr* to nibble, gnaw away; to champ

**mordisco** *m* nibble, bite; champ

**more•no -na** *adj* brown, dark-brown; dark, dark-complexioned; (*de la raza negra*) (coll) colored; (Am) mulato || *mf* (coll) colored person; (Am) mulato || *m* brunet || *f* brunette; loaf of brown bread; rick of new-mown hay

**morería** *f* Moorish quarter; Moorish land

**moretón** *m* (coll) black-and-blue mark

**morfina** *f* morphine

**morfinomanía** *f* morphine habit, drug habit

**morfinóma•no -na** *adj* addicted to morphine, addicted to drugs || *mf* morphine addict, drug addict

**morfología** *f* morphology

**moribun•do -da** *adj* moribund, dying || *mf* dying person

**morillo** *m* andiron, firedog

**morir** §30 & §83 *intr* to die; (*el fuego, la luz, etc.*) to die away; **morir ahogado** to drown; **morir de risa** to die laughing; **morir de viejo** to die of old age; **morir helado** to freeze to death; **morir quemado** to burn to death; **morir vestido** (coll) to die a violent death || *ref* to die; to be dying; to die away, die out; (*una pierna, un brazo*) to go to sleep; **morirse por** to be crazy about; to be dying to

**moris·co -ca** *adj* Morisco, Moorish ‖ *mf* Moor converted to Christianity (*after the Reconquest*); (*descendiente de mulato y española o de mulata y español*) (Mex) Morisco

**mo·ro -ra** *adj* Moorish; (*vino*) (coll) unwatered ‖ *mf* Moor; **hay moros en la costa** (coll) there's trouble brewing; **moro de paz** man of peace ‖ *f* see **mora**

**moro·cho -cha** *adj* (Am) strong, robust; (SAm) dark

**morón** *m* mound, knoll; moron

**moron·do -da** *adj* bare, stripped

**moro·so -sa** *adj* slow, tardy; (*retrasado en el pago de deudas*) delinquent

**morra** *f* (*de la cabeza*) top, crown; (*de gato*) purr; **andar a la morra** to come to blows

**morrada** *f* slap, punch; (*golpe dado con la cabeza*) butt

**morral** *m* nose bag; (*saco de cazador*) game bag; (*de soldado, viandante, etc.*) knapsack; (coll) boor, lout

**morralla** *f* small fish; (*gente de escaso valor*) rabble, trash; (*mezcla de cosas inútiles*) junk, trash; (Mex) change, small change

**morriña** *f* (coll) blues, melancholy; **morriña de la tierra** (coll) homesickness

**morriño·so -sa** *adj* sickly; (coll) blue, melancholy

**morrión** *m* helmet; (mil) bearskin

**morro** *m* (*cosa redonda*) knob; (*monte redondo*) knoll; (*guijarro*) pebble; (*saliente que forman los labios*) snout; **beber a morro** (slang) to drink out of the bottle; **estar de morro** or **de morros** (coll) to be on the outs; **poner morro** to make a snout

**morrocotu·do -da** *adj* (coll) strong, thick, heavy; (*asunto, negocio*) (coll) weighty; (Am) big, enormous; (Col) rich, wealthy; (Chile) graceless, monotonous

**morsa** *f* walrus

**mortaja** *f* shroud, winding sheet; (carp) mortise; (Am) cigarette paper

**mortal** *adj* mortal; deadly; mortally ill; deathly pale; sure, conclusive ‖ *m* mortal

**mortalidad** *f* mortality; death rate

**mortandad** *f* massacre, mortality, butchery

**morteci·no -na** *adj* dead; dying; failing, weak; **hacer la mortecina** (coll) to play dead, to play possum

**mortero** *m* (*vaso que sirve para machacar; argamasa*) mortar; (*en los molinos de aceite*) nether stone; (arti) mortar

**mortífe·ro -ra** *adj* deadly

**mortificar** §73 *tr* to vex, annoy, bother; to mortify ‖ *ref* (Mex) to be mortified, be embarrassed

**mortuo·rio -ria** *adj* mortuary, funeral; (*casa*) of the deceased ‖ *m* (archaic) funeral

**morueco** *m* ram

**moru·no -na** *adj* Moorish

**mosai·co -ca** *adj* Mosaic ‖ *m* tile, paving tile; mosaic; **mosaico de madera** marquetry

**mosca** *f* fly; (*barba*) imperial; (coll) cash, dough; (coll) disappointment; (coll) bore, nuisance; **aflojar la mosca** (coll) to shell out, to fork out; **mosca borriquera** horsefly; **mosca de las frutas** fruit fly; **mosca del vinagre** fruit fly; **mosca muerta** (coll) hypocrite; **moscas** sparks; **moscas volantes** spots before the eyes; **papar moscas** (coll) to gape, gawk

**moscareta** *f* (orn) flycatcher

**moscona** *f* hussy, brazen woman

**Moscú** Moscow

**mosquear** *tr* (*moscas*) to shoo; to beat, to whip; to answer sharply ‖ *intr* (Mex) to sneak a ride ‖ *ref* to shake off annoyances; to take offense

**mosquero** *m* flytrap; fly swatter

**mosquete** *m* musket

**mosquetear** *intr* (Arg, Bol) to snoop

**mosquete·ro -ra** *adj* idle ‖ *mf* (Arg, Bol) bystander, snooper ‖ *m* musketeer ‖ *f* wallflower

**mosquetón** *m* snap hook

**mosquitera** *f* or **mosquitero** *m* mosquito net; fly net

**mosquito** *m* (*Culex pungens*) mosquito; (*insecto parecido al anterior*) gnat; (coll) tippler

**mostacera** *f* mustard jar

**mostacho** *m* mustache; (coll) spot on the face

**mostachón** *m* macaroon

**mostaza** *f* mustard; (*semilla; munición*) mustard seed; **subírsele a** (*uno*) **la mostaza a las narices** (coll) to fly into a rage

**mosto** *m* must; **mosto de cerveza** wort

**mostrador** *m* (*en las tiendas*) counter; (*en las tabernas*) bar; (*de reloj*) dial

**mostrar** §61 *tr* to show ‖ *ref* to show; to show oneself to be

**mostrear** *tr* to spot, to splash

**mostren·co -ca** *adj* ownerless, unclaimed; (*que no tiene casa ni hogar*) (coll) homeless; (*animal*) (coll) stray; (coll) slow, dull; (coll) fat, heavy ‖ *mf* (coll) dolt, dullard

**mota** *f* mote, speck; (*en el paño*) burl, knot; hill, rise; defect, fault; (Mex, W-I) powder puff

**mote** *m* device, emblem, riddle; (*apodo*) nickname; (Chile) mistake; (SAm) stewed corn

**motear** *tr* to speck, speckle; to dapple, mottle ‖ *intr* (Peru) to eat stewed corn

**motejar** *tr* to call names; to scoff at, make fun of; **motejar de** to brand as

**motín** *m* mutiny, riot

**motinista** *mf* (Peru) rioter

**motivar** *tr* to explain, account for; to rationalize

**moti·vo -va** *adj* motive ‖ *m* motive, reason; (mus) motif; **con motivo de** because of; on the occasion of; **de su motivo propio** on his own accord; **motivo conductor** (mus) leitmotif; **motivos** grounds, reasons; (Chile) finickiness, prudery

**moto** *m* guidepost, landmark || *f* (coll) motorcycle
**motobomba** *f* fire truck, fire engine
**motocarro** *m* three-wheel delivery truck
**motocicleta** *f* motorcycle
**motogrúa** *f* truck crane
**motoli•to -ta** *adj* simple, stupid; **vivir de motolito** to be a sponger, to live on other people || *f* (orn) wagtail; (Ven) decent woman
**motón** *m* (naut) block, pulley
**motonáuti•co -ca** *adj* motorboat || *f* motorboating
**motonautismo** *m* (sport) motorboating
**motonave** *f* motor launch; motor ship
**motoneta** *f* motor scooter; light three-wheel delivery truck
**mo•tor -tora** *adj* motor, motive || *m* motor, engine; **motor a chorro** jet engine; **motor de arranque** (aut) starter, starting motor; **motor de cuatro tiempos** four-cycle engine; **motor de dos tiempos** two-cycle engine; **motor de explosión** internal-combustion engine; **motor fuera de borda** outboard motor; **motor térmico** heat engine || *f* small motor boat
**motorista** *mf* motorist; motorcyclist; motorcycle racer || *m* motorcycle policeman; (Am) motorman
**motorizar** §60 *tr* to motorize
**motosegadora** *f* power mower
**motovelero** *m* (naut) motor sailer
**motriz** *adj fem* (*fuerza*) motive
**movedi•zo -za** *adj* shaky, unsteady; fickle, inconstant; (*arena*) quick, shifting
**mover** §47 *tr* to move; (*la cola el perro*) to wag; (*discordia*) to stir up || *intr* to move; to abort, miscarry; to bud, sprout || *ref* to move; to be moved
**movible** *adj* movable; fickle, inconstant, changeable
**móvil** *adj* movable, mobile; fickle, changeable; moving || *m* moving body; cause, motive
**movilizar** §60 *tr* to mobilize
**movimiento** *m* movement, motion
**moza** *f* girl, lass; mistress, concubine; maid, kitchen maid; (*en algunos juegos de naipes*) last hand; wash bat; **buena moza** or **real moza** good-looking girl or woman; **moza de fortuna** or **del partido** prostitute; **moza de taberna** barmaid
**mozalbete** *m* lad, young fellow
**mozárabe** *adj* Mozarabic || *mf* Mozarab
**mo•zo -za** *adj* young, youthful; single, unmarried || *m* youth, lad; (*camarero*) waiter; (*criado*) servant; porter; (*cuelgacapas*) cloak hanger; **buen mozo** or **real mozo** handsome fellow; **mozo de caballerías** hostler, stable boy; **mozo de café** waiter; **mozo de cámara** (naut) cabin boy; **mozo de ciego** blind man's guide; **mozo de cordel** street porter, public errand boy; **mozo de cuadra** stable boy; **mozo de cuerda** public errand boy; **mozo de espuelas** groom who walks in front of master's horse; **mozo de esquina** street porter, public errand boy; **mozo de estación** station porter; **mozo de estoques** (taur) sword handler; **mozo de hotel** bellboy, bellhop; **mozo de paja y cebada** hostler (*at an inn*); **mozo de restaurante** waiter || *f* see **moza**
**mozue•lo -la** *mf* youngster || *m* lad, young fellow || *f* lass, young girl
**m/p** *abbr* **mi pagaré**
**m/r** *abbr* **mi remesa**
**Mro.** *abbr* **Maestro**
**M.S.** *abbr* **manuscrito**
**mtd.** *abbr* **mitad**
**mu** *m* moo || *f* bye-bye; **ir a la mu** to go bye-bye
**muaré** *adj invar & m* moiré
**muca•mo -ma** *mf* (Arg, Urug) house servant || *f* (Arg, Chile, Urug) servant girl
**muceta** *f* (*de los doctores en los actos universitarios*) hood; (eccl) mozzetta
**muco•so -sa** *adj* mucous || *f* mucous membrane
**múcura** *f* (Bol, Col, Ven, W-I) water pitcher; (Col) thickhead
**muchacha** *f* girl; maid, servant girl
**muchachada** *f* youthful prank
**muchachez** *f* boyishness, girlishness
**mucha•cho -cha** *adj* young, youthful || *mf* youth, young person; servant || *m* boy || *f* see **muchacha**
**muchedumbre** *f* crowd, multitude, flock
**mu•cho -cha** *adj* much, a lot of, a great deal of; (*tiempo*) a long || *pron* much, a lot, a great deal || **mu•chos -chas** *adj & pron* many || **mucho** *adv* much; (*más de lo regular*) hard; often; a long time; **con mucho** by far; **ni con mucho** or **ni mucho menos** not by a long shot; **por mucho que** however much; **sentir mucho** to be very sorry; **tener mucho de** to take after
**muda** *f* change; change of voice; change of clothes; (*cambio de plumas o de piel*) molt, molting; molting season; **estar de muda** to be changing one's voice; **estar en muda** (coll) to keep too quiet; **hacer la muda** to molt; **muda de ropa** change of clothing
**mudable** *adj* fickle, inconstant
**mudada** *f* (Am) change of clothing; (Am) move, change of residence
**mudadi•zo -za** *adj* fickle, inconstant
**mudanza** *f* change; (*cambio de domicilio*) moving; fickleness, inconstancy; (*en el baile*) figure
**mudar** *tr* to change || *intr* to change; **mudar de** to change || *ref* to change; to change clothing; to move; to move away; to have a movement of the bowels; **mudarse de** to change
**mudez** *f* muteness, dumbness; continued silence
**mu•do -da** *adj* dumb, mute; (phonet) voiceless, surd || *mf* mute || *f* see **muda**
**mueblaje** *m* furniture, suit of furniture
**mueble** *adj* movable || *m* piece of furniture; (*p.ej., de un aparato de radio*) cabinet; **muebles** furniture
**mueblería** *f* furniture shop
**mueblista** *mf* furniture dealer
**mueca** *f* face, grimace

**muela** *f* grindstone; knoll, mound; back tooth, grinder; **muela cordal** wisdom tooth; **muela de esmeril** emery wheel; **muela del juicio** wisdom tooth; **muela de molino** millstone
**muellaje** *m* dockage, wharfage
**muelle** *adj* soft; voluptuous || *m* (*pieza elástica de metal*) spring; (*obra en la orilla del mar o de un río*) dock, wharf, pier; (rr) freight platform; **muelle real** mainspring
**muérdago** *m* mistletoe
**muérgano** *m* (Col, Ven) piece of junk, drug on the market; (Col, Ecuad, Ven) boor, nobody
**muermo** *m* (vet) glanders
**muerte** *f* death; **cada muerte de obispo** once in a blue moon; **dar la muerte a** to put to death; **de mala muerte** (coll) crummy, not much of a; **estar a la muerte** to be at death's door; **muerte chiquita** (coll) nervous shudder
**muer•to -ta** *adj* dead; (*apagado, marchito*) flat, dull; (*cal, yeso*) slaked; **muerto de** dying of; **muerto por** crazy about || *mf* corpse, dead person || *m* (*en los naipes*) dummy; **hacerse el muerto** to play possum; to play deaf; **tocar a muerto** to toll
**muesca** *f* nick, notch; (carp) mortise
**muestra** *f* (*porción de un producto que sirve para conocer su calidad*) sample; model, specimen; (*rótulo sobre una tienda u hotel*) sign; show, exhibition, indication; (*esfera de reloj*) dial, face; (*parada del perro para levantar la caza*) set; (*ademán, porte*) bearing; **dar muestras de** to show signs of
**mugido** *m* moo, low; bellow, roar
**mugir** §27 *intr* (*la res vacuna*) to moo, to low; (*con ira*) to bellow; (*el viento, el mar*) to roar
**mugre** *f* dirt, filth, grime
**mugrien•to -ta** *adj* dirty, filthy, grimy
**muguete** *m* lily of the valley
**mujer** *f* woman; (*esposa*) wife; **mujer de gobierno** housekeeper; **mujer de su casa** good manager; **mujer fatal** vamp; **ser mujer** to be a grown woman
**mujeren•go -ga** *adj* (Arg, Urug, CAm) effeminate
**mujerie•go -ga** *adj* feminine, womanly; effeminate, womanish; fond of women; **a mujeriegas** sidesaddle || *m* flock of women
**mujeril** *adj* womanly; womanish
**mújol** *m* mullet, striped mullet
**mula** *f* mule, she-mule; junk, trash; (Arg) ingrate, traitor; (Arg) hoax; (C-R) jag, drunk; (Guat, Hond) anger, rage; (Mex) drug on the market; (Ven) flask; **devolver la mula** (CAm) to pay back in one's own coin; **echar la mula a** (Mex) to rake over the coals; **en mula de San Francisco** on shank's mare
**mulada** *f* drove of mules
**muladar** *m* dungheap, dunghill; dump, trash heap; filth
**mula•to -ta** *adj* & *mf* mulatto
**muleta** *f* (*palo para apoyarse al andar*) crutch; muleta (*cloth attached to a stick, used by matador*); support, prop; snack
**muletilla** *f* cross-handle cane; pet word, pet phrase; (taur) muleta
**mulo** *m* mule
**multa** *f* fine
**multar** *tr* to fine
**multicopista** *m* duplicating machine, copying machine
**multigrafiar** §77 *tr* to multigraph
**multígrafo** *m* multigraph
**multilateral** *adj* multilateral
**multiláte•ro -ra** *adj* multilateral
**múltiple** *adj* multiple, manifold || *m* manifold; **múltiple de admisión** intake manifold; **múltiple de escape** exhaust manifold
**multiplicar** §73 *tr, intr,* & *ref* to multiply
**multiplicidad** *f* multiplicity
**múlti•plo -pla** *adj* multiple, manifold || *m* (math) multiple
**multitud** *f* multitude
**mulli•do -da** *adj* soft, fluffy || *m* stuffing (*for cushions, pillows, etc.*) || *f* bedding, litter (*for animals*)
**mullir** §13 *tr* to soften, fluff up; (*la cama*) to beat up, shake up; (*la tierra*) to loosen around a stalk || *ref* to get fluffy
**munda•no -na** *adj* mundane, worldly; (*mujer*) loose
**mundial** *adj* world-wide, world
**mundillo** *m* arched clotheshorse; cushion for making lace; warming pan; guelder-rose, cranberry tree; world (*of artists, scholars, etc.*)
**mundo** *m* world; **así va el mundo** so it goes; **desde que el mundo es mundo** (coll) since the world began; **echar al mundo** to bring into the world; to bring forth; **el otro mundo** the other world; **gran mundo** high society; **medio mundo** (*mucha gente*) (coll) half the world; **tener mucho mundo** (coll) to know one's way around; **todo el mundo** everybody; **ver mundo** to see the world, to travel
**mundonuevo** *m* peep show
**munición** *f* munition, ammunition; **de munición** (mil) government issue; (coll) done hurriedly
**municionar** *tr* to supply with munition
**municipal** *adj* municipal || *m* policeman
**munícipe** *m* citizen
**municipio** *m* municipality; town council
**munidad** *f* susceptibility to infection
**munífi•co -ca** *adj* munificent
**muñeca** *f* (*figurilla infantil con que juegan las niñas*) doll; (*parte del cuerpo humano en donde se articula la mano con el brazo*) wrist; manikin, dress form; tea bag; (*mujer linda; mozuela frívola*) (coll) doll; **muñeca de trapo** rag doll, rag baby; **muñeca parlante** talking doll
**muñeco** *m* doll (*representing a male child or animal*); dummy, manikin; fop, effeminate fellow; (fig) puppet; (coll) lad, little fellow

**muñequera** *f* strap for wrist watch
**muñequilla** *f* (mach) chuck; (Arg, Chile) young ear of corn
**muñidor** *m* heeler, henchman
**muñir** §12 *tr* to convoke, summon; (pol) to fix, to rig
**muñón** *m* (*p.ej., de un brazo cortado*) stump; (mach) journal, gudgeon; **muñón de cola** dock
**mural** *adj* mural
**muralla** *f* wall, rampart
**murar** *tr* to surround with a wall
**murciélago** *m* bat
**murga** *f* (coll) tin-pan band
**muriente** *adj* dying, faint
**murmujear** *tr & intr* (coll) to mumble
**murmullar** *intr* to murmur
**murmullo** *m* murmur; whisper; (*de aguas corrientes*) ripple; (*del viento*) rustle
**murmurar** *tr* to murmur, to mutter; to murmur at || *intr* to murmur, to mutter; to whisper; (*las aguas corrientes*) to ripple, to purl; (*el viento*) to rustle; (coll) to gossip
**muro** *m* wall
**murria** *f* (coll) blues, dejection
**musa** *f* muse; **las Musas** the Muses; **soplarle a uno la musa** (coll) to be inspired to write poetry; (coll) to be lucky at games of chance
**musaraña** *f* shrew, shrewmouse; bug, worm; **mirar a las musarañas** (coll) to stare vacantly
**músculo** *m* muscle
**musculo•so -sa** *adj* muscular
**muselina** *f* muslin
**museo** *m* museum; **museo de cera** waxworks
**muserola** *f* noseband
**mus•go -ga** *adj* dark-brown || *m* moss
**musgo•so -sa** *adj* mossy, moss-covered
**música** *f* music; (*músicos que tocan juntos*) band; (coll) noise, racket; **con la música a otra parte** (coll) don't bother me, get out; **música celestial** (coll) nonsense, piffle; **música de fondo** background music; **poner en música** to set to music
**musical** *adj* musical
**musicalidad** *f* musicianship
**music-hall** *s* vaudeville theater, burlesque show
**músi•co -ca** *adj* musical || *mf* musician; **músico mayor** bandmaster || *f* see **música**
**musicología** *f* musicology
**musicólo•go -ga** *mf* musicologist
**musiquero** *m* music cabinet
**musitar** *tr & intr* to mutter, mumble
**muslime** *adj & mf* Moslem
**muslo** *m* thigh; (*de ave cocida*) (coll) leg, drumstick
**mustiar** *ref* to wither
**mus•tio -tia** *adj* sad, gloomy; (*marchito*) withered; (Mex) hypocritical; (Mex) stand-offish
**musul•mán -mana** *adj & mf* Mussulman
**mutación** *f* mutation; unsettled weather, change of weather; (biol) mutation, sport; (theat) change of scene
**mutila•do -da** *adj* crippled || *mf* cripple
**mutilar** *tr* to mutilate; to cripple
**múti•lo -la** *adj* mutilated; crippled
**mutis** *m* (theat) exit; **hacer mutis** (theat) to exit; to keep quiet
**mutual** *adj* mutual
**mutualidad** *f* mutuality; mutual benefit; mutual benefit association
**mutualista** *mf* member of a mutual benefit association
**mu•tuo -tua** *adj* mutual, reciprocal
**muy** *adv* very; very much; too, e.g., **es muy tarde para dar un paseo tan largo** it is too late to take such a long walk; **muy de noche** late at night; **Muy señor mío** Dear Sir

## N

**N, n** (ene) *f* sixteenth letter of the Spanish alphabet
**n/** *abbr* **nuestro**
**N.** *abbr* **Norte**
**nabo** *m* turnip; (naut) mast
**Nabucodonosor** *m* Nebuchadnezzar
**nácar** *m* mother-of-pearl
**nacara•do -da** *adj* mother-of-pearl
**nacatamal** *m* (CAm, Mex) meat-filled tamale
**nacela** *f* nacelle
**nacencia** *f* birth; growth, tumor
**nacer** §22 *intr* to be born; to bud, take rise, originate, appear; to dawn || *ref* to bud, to shoot, to sprout; (*abrirse la ropa por las costuras*) to split
**naci•do -da** *adj* natural, innate; apt, proper, fit; **nacida** née or nee || *m* human being; growth, boil
**naciente** *adj* incipient; resurgent; (*sol*) rising || *m* east
**nacimiento** *m* birth; origin, beginning, fountainhead; descent, lineage; (*de agua*) spring, fountainhead; crèche
**nación** *f* nation
**nacional** *adj* national; domestic || *mf* national || *m* militiaman
**nacionalidad** *f* nationality
**nacionalismo** *m* nationalism
**nacionalista** *adj & mf* nationalist
**nacionalizar** §60 *tr* to nationalize || *ref* to be naturalized; to become a citizen
**nacista** *adj & mf* Nazi
**naco** *m* (Arg, Bol, Urug) black rolled leaf of chewing tobacco; (Arg) fear, scare; (Col) stewed corn; (Col) mashed potatoes
**nada** *pron indef* nothing, not . . . anything; **de nada** don't mention it, you're welcome || *adv* not at all
**nadaderas** *fpl* water wings
**nada•dor -dora** *adj* swimming, floating

|| *mf* swimmer || *m* (Chile) fishnet float
**nadar** *intr* to swim; to float; to fit loosely or too loosely; **nadar en** (*riqueza*) to be rolling in; (*suspiros*) to be full of; (*sangre*) to be bathed in
**nadear** *tr* to destroy, wipe out
**nadería** *f* trifle
**nadie** *pron indef* nobody, not . . . anybody; **nadie más** nobody else; **nadie más que** nobody but || *m* nobody; **un don nadie** a nonentity
**nado — a nado** swimming, floating; **echarse a nado** to dive in; **pasar a nado** to swim across
**nafta** *f* naphtha
**nagual** *m* (Guat, Hond) (*dícese de un animal*) inseparable companion; (Mex) sorcerer, wizard; (Mex) lie
**nagualear** *intr* (Mex) to lie; (Mex) to be out looking for trouble all night
**naguas** *fpl* petticoat
**naipe** *m* playing card; deck of cards; **naipe de figura** face card; **tener buen naipe** to be lucky
**naire** *m* mahout
**nalgada** *f* shoulder, ham; blow on or with the buttocks
**nalgas** *fpl* buttocks, rump
**nana** *f* grandma; lullaby, cradlesong; (CAm, Mex, W-I) child's nurse; (Arg, Chile, Urug) child's complaint
**nao** *f* ship, vessel
**napoleóni•co -ca** *adj* Napoleonic
**Napoles** *f* Naples
**napolita•no -na** *adj & mf* Neapolitan
**naranja** *f* orange; **media naranja** (coll) sidekick, better half; **naranja cajel** Seville orange, sour orange; **¡naranjas!** nonsense!
**naranjada** *f* orangeade; orange juice; orange marmalade
**naranjal** *m* orange grove
**naranjo** *m* orange tree; (coll) boob, simpleton
**narciso** *m* narcissus; fop, dandy; **narciso trompón** daffodil || **Narciso** *m* Narcissus
**narcóti•co -ca** *adj & m* narcotic
**narcotizar** **§60** *tr* to dope, to drug
**narguile** *m* hookah
**narigada** *f* (SAm) pinch of snuff
**nari•gón -gona** *adj* big-nosed || *m* big nose
**narigu•do -da** *adj* big-nosed; nose-shaped
**nariguera** *f* nose ring
**na•riz** (*pl* **-rices**) *f* nose; nostril; sense of smell; (*del vino*) bouquet; **nariz de pico de loro** hooknose; **sonarse las narices** to blow one's nose; **tabicarse las narices** to hold one's nose; **tener agarrado por las narices** to lead by the nose
**narración** *f* narration
**narra•dor -dora** *adj* narrating || *mf* narrator
**narrar** *tr* to narrate
**narrati•vo -va** *adj* narrative || *f* (*relato; habilidad en narrar*) narrative
**narria** *f* sled, sledge, drag
**nasal** *adj & f* nasal
**nasalizar** **§60** *tr* to nasalize

**nata** *f* cream; whipped cream; élite, choice; skim, scum
**natación** *f* swimming
**natal** *adj* natal; native || *m* birth; birthday
**natali•cio -cia** *adj* birth || *m* birthday
**natalidad** *f* birth rate
**naterón** *m* cottage cheese
**natillas** *fpl* custard
**natividad** *f* birth; Christmas; (*día; festividad; pintura*) Nativity
**nati•vo -va** *adj* native; natural; natural-born; innate
**na•to -ta** *adj* born, e.g., **criminal nato** born criminal || *f* see **nata**
**natural** *adj* natural; native; (mus) natural || *mf* native || *m* temper, disposition, nature; **al natural** au naturel; rough, unfinished; live; **del natural** from life, from nature
**naturaleza** *f* nature; disposition, temperament; nationality; **naturaleza muerta** still life
**naturalidad** *f* naturalness; nationality
**naturalismo** *m* naturalism
**naturalista** *mf* naturalist
**naturalización** *f* naturalization
**naturalizar** **§60** *tr* to naturalize; to acclimatize || *ref* to become naturalized; to go native
**naturalmente** *adv* naturally; easily, readily
**naufragar** **§44** *intr* to be shipwrecked; to fail
**naufragio** *m* shipwreck; failure, ruin
**náufra•go -ga** *adj* shipwrecked || *mf* shipwrecked person || *m* shark
**náusea** *f* nausea; **dar náuseas a** to nauseate; to sicken, disgust; **tener náuseas** to be nauseated, to be sick at one's stomach
**nauseabun•do -da** *adj* nauseating, nauseous, loathsome, sickening
**nauta** *m* mariner, sailor
**náuti•co -ca** *adj* nautical || *f* sailing, navigation
**nava** *f* hollow plain between mountains
**navaja** *f* folding knife; razor; penknife; tusk of wild boar; razor clam; (coll) evil tongue; **navaja barbera** straight razor
**navajada** *f* or **navajazo** *m* slash, gash
**navajero** *m* razor case; razor cloth
**naval** *adj* naval; nautical; **naval militar** naval
**nava•rro -rra** *adj & mf* Navarrese || **Navarra** *f* Navarre
**navazo** *m* garden in sandy marshland
**nave** *f* ship, vessel; (*de un taller, fábrica, tienda, iglesia, etc.*) aisle; commercial ground floor; hall, shed, bay, building; **nave central** or **principal** (archit) nave; **nave lateral** (archit) aisle
**navegable** *adj* navigable
**navegación** *f* navigation; sailing; sea voyage; **navegación a vela** sailing
**navega•dor -dora** or **navegante** *adj* navigating || *mf* navigator
**navegar** **§44** *tr* to sail || *intr* to navigate, to sail; to move around
**navel** *f* (*pl* **-vels**) navel orange
**Navidad** *f* Christmas; Christmas time;

**¡Felices Navidades!** Merry Christmas!; **contar** or **tener muchas Navidades** to be pretty old
**navidal** *m* Christmas card
**navide·ño -ña** *adj* Christmas
**navie·ro -ra** *adj* ship, shipping || *m* shipowner; outfitter
**navío** *m* ship, vessel; **navío de guerra** warship
**náyade** *f* naiad
**nazare·no -na** *adj & mf* Nazarene || *m* penitent in Passion Week procession || **nazarenas** *fpl* (SAm) large gaucho spurs
**nazi** *adj & mf* Nazi
**N.B.** *abbr* **nota bene (Lat) note well**
**nébeda** *f* catnip
**neblina** *f* fog, mist
**neblino·so -sa** *adj* foggy, misty
**nebulo·so -sa** *adj* nebulous, cloudy, misty, hazy, vague; gloomy, sullen || *f* nebula
**necedad** *f* foolishness, stupidity, nonsense
**necesa·rio -ria** *adj* necessary || *f* water closet, privy
**neceser** *m* toilet case; sewing kit; **neceser de belleza** vanity case; **neceser de costura** workbasket
**necesidad** *f* necessity; need, want; starvation; **de necesidad** from weakness; of necessity; **necesidad mayor** bowel movement; **necesidad menor** urination
**necesita·do -da** *adj* necessitous, poor, needy; **estar necesitado de** to be in need of || *mf* needy person
**necesitar** *tr* to necessitate; to need; **necesitar** + *inf* to have to, to need to + *inf* || *intr* to be in need; **necesitar de** to be in need of, to need || *ref* to be needed, to be necessary
**ne·cio -cia** *adj* foolish, stupid; imprudent; stubborn; (Am) touchy || *mf* fool
**necrología** *f* necrology
**necromancia** *f* necromancy
**néctar** *m* nectar
**neerlan·dés -desa** *adj* Netherlandish, Dutch || *mf* Netherlander || *m* Dutchman; (*idioma*) Netherlandish or Dutch || *f* Dutchwoman
**nefalista** *mf* teetotaler
**nefan·do -da** *adj* base, infamous
**nefas·to -ta** *adj* ominous, fatal, tragic
**negable** *adj* deniable
**negación** *f* negation; denial; refusal
**nega·do -da** *adj* unfit, incompetent; dull, indifferent
**negar §66** *tr* to deny; to refuse; to prohibit; to disown; to conceal || *intr* to deny || *ref* to avoid; to refuse; to deny oneself to callers; **negarse a** to refuse; **negarse a** + *inf* to refuse to + *inf*
**negati·vo -va** *adj* negative || *f* negative; denial; refusal
**negligencia** *f* negligence
**negligente** *adj* negligent
**negociable** *adj* negotiable
**negociación** *f* negotiation; deal, matter
**negociado** *m* department, bureau; affair, business; (SAm) illegal dealing; (Chile) store
**negociante** *m* dealer, trader
**negociar** *tr* to negotiate || *intr* to negotiate; to deal, to trade
**negocio** *m* business; affair, deal, transaction; profit; (SAm) store
**negocio·so -sa** *adj* businesslike
**negrear** *intr* to turn black; to look black
**negre·ro -ra** *adj* slave-trading; (fig) slave-driving || *mf* slave trader; (fig) slave driver
**negrilla** *f* (typ) boldface
**ne·gro -gra** *adj* black; dark; gloomy, dismal; fatal, evil, wicked; Negro; (coll) broke || *mf* Negro; (Am) dear, darling || *m* black; **negro de humo** lampblack
**negror** *m* or **negrura** *f* blackness
**negruz·co -ca** *adj* blackish
**néme·sis** *f* (*pl* **-sis**) (*justo castigo; castigador*) nemesis || **Némesis** *f* Nemesis
**nemoro·so -sa** *adj* (poet) woody, sylvan
**ne·ne -na** *mf* baby; dear, darling || *m* rascal, villain
**nenúfar** *m* white water lily
**neo** *m* neon
**neocelan·dés -desa** *adj* New Zealand || *mf* New Zealander
**neoesco·cés -cesa** *adj & mf* Nova Scotian
**neófi·to -ta** *mf* neophyte
**neologismo** *m* neologism
**neomejica·no -na** *adj & mf* New Mexican
**neomicina** *f* neomycin
**neón** *m* neon
**neoyorki·no -na** *adj* New York || *mf* New Yorker
**Nepal, el** Nepal
**nepa·lés -lesa** *adj & mf* Nepalese
**nepente** *m* nepenthe
**nepote** *m* relative and favorite of the Pope || **Nepote** *m* Nepos
**neptunio** *m* neptunium
**Neptuno** *m* Neptune
**nereida** *f* Nereid
**Nerón** *m* Nero
**nervio** *m* nerve; (*del ala del insecto*) rib; strength, vigor
**nerviosidad** *f* nervousness
**nervio·so -sa** *adj* nervous; energetic, vigorous, sinewy; (*célula; centro; tónico*) nerve; (*sistema; enfermedad; postración, colapso*) nervous
**nervosidad** *f* nervosity; ductility, flexibility; (*de un argumento*) force, cogency
**nervo·so -sa** *adj* var of **nervioso**
**nervu·do -da** *adj* vigorous, sinewy
**nervura** *f* backbone (*of book*)
**nesga** *f* gore
**nesgar §44** *tr* to gore
**ne·to -ta** *adj* net
**neumáti·co -ca** *adj* pneumatic; air || *m* tire
**neumonía** *f* pneumonia
**neuralgia** *f* neuralgia
**neurología** *f* neurology
**neuro·sis** *f* (*pl* **-sis**) neurosis; **neurosis de guerra** shell shock
**neuróti·co -ca** *adj & mf* neurotic
**neutral** *adj & mf* neutral
**neutralidad** *f* neutrality
**neutralismo** *m* neutralism

**neutralista** *adj & mf* neutralist
**neutralizar** §60 *tr* to neutralize
**neu•tro -tra** *adj* neuter; (*que no es de un color ni de otro*) neutral; (bot, chem, elec, phonet, zool) neutral; (*verbo*) intransitive
**neutrón** *m* neutron
**neva•do -da** *adj* snow-covered; snow-white || *f* snowfall
**nevar** §2 *tr* to make snow-white || *intr* to snow
**nevasca** *f* snowfall; snowstorm, blizzard
**nevazón** *f* (SAm) snowfall
**nevera** *f* icebox, refrigerator; icehouse; (P-R) jail
**nevería** *f* ice-cream parlor
**neve•ro -ra** *mf* ice-cream dealer || *m* place of perpetual snow; perpetual snow || *f* see **nevera**
**nevisca** *f* snow flurry
**neviscar** §73 *intr* to snow lightly
**nevo** *m* mole; **nevo materno** birth mark
**nevo•so -sa** *adj* snowy
**ni** *conj* neither, nor; **ni . . . ni** neither . . . nor; **ni . . . siquiera** not even
**niacina** *f* niacin
**nicaragüense** or **nicaragüe•ño -ña** *adj & mf* Nicaraguan
**Nicolás** *m* Nicholas
**nicotina** *f* nicotine
**nicho** *m* niche
**nidada** *f* (*huevos en el nido*) nestful of eggs; (*pajarillos en el nido*) nest, brood, hatch
**nidal** *m* (*donde la gallina pone sus huevos*) nest; nest egg; haunt; source; basis, foundation
**nido** *m* nest; haunt; home; source; (*de ladrones*) nest, den
**niebla** *f* fog, mist, haze; mildew; fog, confusion; **hay niebla** it is foggy; **niebla artificial** smoke screen
**nie•to -ta** *mf* grandchild || *m* grandson; **nietos** grandchildren || *f* granddaughter
**nieve** *f* snow; (Am) water ice
**nigromancia** *f* necromancy
**nihilismo** *m* nihilism
**nihilista** *mf* nihilist
**Nilo** *m* Nile; **Nilo Azul** Blue Nile
**nilón** *m* nylon
**nimbo** *m* nimbus; halo
**nimiedad** *f* excess; fussiness, fastidiousness; (coll) timidity
**ni•mio -mia** *adj* excessive; fussy, fastidious; (Am) tiny
**ninfa** *f* nymph; **ninfa marina** mermaid
**ninfea** *f* white water lily
**ningún** *adj indef* apocopated form of **ninguno**, used only before masculine singular nouns and adjectives
**ningu•no -na** *adj indef* no, not any || *pron indef* none, not any; neither, neither one; **ninguno de los dos** neither one || **ninguno** *pron indef* nobody, no one
**niña** *f* child, girl; (*del ojo*) pupil; **niña del ojo** (coll) apple of one's eye; **niña exploradora** girl scout
**niñada** *f* childishness
**niñera** *f* nursemaid
**niñería** *f* childishness; trifle
**niñero -ra** *adj* fond of children || *f* see **niñera**
**niñez** *f* childhood; childishness; (fig) infancy
**ni•ño -ña** *adj* childlike, childish; young, inexperienced || *mf* child; (*persona joven e inexperta*) babe; **desde niño** from childhood; **niño expósito** foundling; **niño travieso** imp || *m* child, boy; **niño bonito** playboy; **niño de coro** choirboy; **niño de la bola** child Jesus; (coll) lucky fellow; **niño explorador** boy scout; **niño gótico** playboy || *f* see **niña**
**ni•pón -pona** *adj & mf* Nipponese
**níquel** *m* nickel
**niquelar** *tr* to nickel-plate
**nirvana, el** nirvana
**níspero** *m* medlar (*tree and fruit*)
**níspola** *f* medlar (*fruit*)
**nitidez** *f* brightness, clearness; sharpness
**níti•do -da** *adj* bright, clear; sharp
**nitrato** *m* nitrate
**nítri•co -ca** *adj* nitric
**nitro** *m* niter; **nitro de Chile** saltpeter
**nitrógeno** *m* nitrogen
**nitro•so -sa** *adj* nitrous
**nitruro** *m* nitride
**nivel** *m* level; **nivel de burbuja** spirit level; **nivel de vida** standard of living
**nivelar** *tr* to level; to even, make even; to grade; to survey
**no** *adv* not; no; **¿cómo no?** why not?; of course, certainly; **creer que no** to think not, to believe not; **¿no?** is it not so?; **no bien** no sooner; **no más que** not more than; only; **no sea que** lest; **no . . . sino** only; **ya no** no longer
**nobabia** *f* (aer) dope
**noble** *adj* noble || *m* noble, nobleman
**nobleza** *f* nobility
**noción** *f* notion, idea; rudiment
**noci•vo -va** *adj* noxious, harmful
**noctur•no -na** *adj* nocturnal; lonely, sad, melancholy; night, nighttime
**noche** *f* night, nighttime; darkness; **buenas noches** good evening; good night; **de la noche a la mañana** overnight; unexpectedly, suddenly; **de noche** at night, in the nighttime; **esta noche** tonight; **hacer noche en** to spend the night in; **hacerse de noche** to grow dark; **muy de noche** late at night; **por la noche** at night, in the nighttime; **noche buena** Christmas Eve; **noche de estreno** (theat) first night; **noche de uvas** New Year's Eve; **noche vieja** New Year's Eve; watch night
**nochebuena** *f* Christmas Eve
**nochebueno** *m* Christmas cake; Yule log
**nodo** *m* (astr, med, phys) node
**No-Do** *m* (acronym for **Noticiario y Documentales**) newsreel; newsreel theater
**nodriza** *f* wet nurse; vacuum tank
**Noé** *m* Noah
**nogal** *m* walnut; **nogal de la brujería** witch hazel
**nómada** or **nómade** *adj & mf* nomad

**nómadi•co -ca** *adj* nomadic
**nombradía** *f* fame, renown, reputation
**nombra•do -da** *adj* famous
**nombramiento** *m* naming; appointment
**nombrar** *tr* to name; to appoint
**nombre** *m* name; fame, reputation; nickname; watchword; noun; **del mismo nombre** (elec) like; **de nombres contrarios** (elec) unlike; **nombre comercial** firm name; **nombre de lugar** place name; **nombre de pila** first name, Christian name; **nombre de soltera** maiden name; **nombre substantivo** noun; **nombre supuesto** alias
**nomeolvi•des** *f* (*pl* **-des**) forget-me-not; German madwort
**nómina** *f* list, roll; pay roll
**nominal** *adj* nominal; noun
**nominar** *tr* to name; to appoint
**nominati•vo -va** *adj* & *m* nominative
**non** *adj* odd, uneven || *m* odd number
**nonada** *f* trifle, nothing
**no•na -na** *adj* & *m* ninth
**nopal** *m* prickly pear
**norcorea•no -na** *adj* & *mf* North Korean
**nordestada** *f* or **nordeste** *m* (*viento*) northeaster (*wind*)
**noria** *f* chain pump; (*pozo*) draw well; Ferris wheel; (coll) treadmill, drudgery
**norma** *f* norm, standard; rule, method; (carp) square
**normal** *adj* normal; standard; perpendicular
**Normandía** *f* Normandy
**norman•do -da** *adj* & *mf* Norman || *m* Norseman
**norte** *m* north; north wind; (*guía*) (fig) polestar, lodestar
**Norteamérica** *f* North America; America, the United States
**norteamerica•no -na** *adj* & *mf* North American; (*estadunidense*) American
**norte•ño -ña** *adj* northern
**norue•go -ga** *adj* & *mf* Norwegian || **Noruega** *f* Norway
**nos** (used as object of verb) *pron pers* us; to us || *pron reflex* ourselves, to ourselves; each other, to each other
**noso•tros -tras** *pron pers* we; us; ourselves
**nostalgia** *f* nostalgia
**nota** *f* note; (*en la escuela*) mark, grade; (*en el restaurante*) check; (mus) note; **nota de adorno** grace note; **nota tónica** keynote
**notar** *tr* to note; to dictate; to annotate; to criticize; to discredit
**notario** *m* notary, notary public
**noticia** *f* news; notice, information; notion, rudiment; knowledge; **noticias de actualidad** news of the day; **noticias de última hora** late news; **una noticia** a piece of news, a news item
**noticiar** *tr* to notify; to give notice of
**noticia•rio -ria** *adj* news || *m* up-to-the-minute news; newsreel; newscast; **noticiario gráfico** picture page; **noticiario teatral** theater page
**noticie•ro -ra** *adj* news || *m* newsman, reporter; late news
**noticio•so -sa** *adj* informed; learned; well-informed; (Am) newsy || *m* (Am) news item
**notificar** §73 *tr* to notify; to report on
**no•to -ta** *adj* known, well-known || *m* south wind || *f* see **nota**
**notoriedad** *f* general knowledge; fame
**noto•rio -ria** *adj* manifest, well-known
**nov.** *abbr* **noviembre**
**novatada** *f* hazing; beginner's blunder
**nova•to -ta** *adj* beginning || *mf* beginner; freshman
**novecien•tos -tas** *adj* & *pron* nine hundred || **novecientos** *m* nine hundred
**novedad** *f* newness, novelty; news; fashion; happening; change; failing health; **sin novedad** as usual; safe; well; without anything happening
**novel** *adj* new, inexperienced, beginning || *m* beginner
**novela** *f* novel; story, lie; **novela caballista** novel of western life; **novela policíaca** or **policial** detective story; **novela por entregas** serial
**novele•ro -ra** *adj* fond of novelty; fond of fiction; gossipy; fickle
**noveles•co -ca** *adj* novelistic, fictional; romantic, fantastic
**novelista** *mf* novelist
**novelísti•co -ca** *adj* fictional || *f* fiction
**novelizar** §60 *tr* to fictionalize
**nove•no -na** *adj* & *m* ninth
**noventa** *adj*, *pron* & *m* ninety
**noventa•vo -va** *adj* & *m* ninetieth
**novia** *f* fiancée; bride; **novia de guerra** war bride
**noviazgo** *m* engagement, courtship
**novi•cio -cia** *adj* & *mf* novice
**noviembre** *m* November
**novilunio** *m* new moon
**novilla** *f* heifer
**novillada** *f* drove of young bulls; (taur) fight with young bulls by aspiring bullfighters
**novillero** *m* herdsman of young cattle; (taur) aspiring fighter, untrained fighter; (coll) truant
**novillo** *m* young bull; (coll) cuckold; **hacer novillos** (coll) to play truant
**novio** *m* suitor; fiancé; bridegroom; **novios** engaged couple; **bride and** groom, newlyweds
**novocaína** *f* novocaine
**nro.** *abbr* **nuestro**
**N.S.** *abbr* **Nuestro Señor**
**ntro.** *abbr* **nuestro**
**nubada** *f* local shower; abundance
**nubarrón** *m* storm cloud
**nube** *f* cloud; **andar** (*los precios*) **por las nubes** to be sky-high; **bajar de las nubes** to come back to or down to earth; **poner en** or **sobre las nubes** to praise to the skies
**nube-hongo** *f* mushroom cloud
**nubla•do -da** *adj* cloudy || *m* storm cloud; impending danger; abundance; **aguantar el nublado** to suffer resignedly
**nublar** *tr* to cloud, cloud over || *ref* to become cloudy
**nu•blo -bla** *adj* cloudy || *m* storm cloud
**nublo•so -sa** *adj* cloudy; adverse, unfortunate

**nubo•so -sa** *adj* cloudy
**nuca** *f* nape
**nuclear** *adj* nuclear
**núcleo** *m* nucleus; core; (*de nuez*) kernel; (*de la fruta*) stone; (*de un electroimán*) core
**nudillo** *m* **knuckle; stocking stitch; plug** (*in wall*)
**nudo** *m* **knot; bond, tie, union; crux;** tangle, plot; difficulty; (*en el drama*) crisis; center, juncture; (bot) node; (naut) knot; **cortar el nudo gordiano** to cut the Gordian knot; **hacérsele a** (*uno*) **un nudo en la garganta** to get a lump in one's throat
**nudo•so -sa** *adj* knotted, knotty
**nuera** *f* daughter-in-law
**nues•tro -tra** *adj poss* **our** ‖ *pron poss* ours
**nueva** *f* news; piece of news; **nuevas** *fpl* news
**Nueva York** *m & f* New York; **el Gran Nueva York** Greater New York
**Nueva Zelanda** New Zealand
**nueve** *adj & pron* nine; **las nueve** nine o'clock ‖ *m* nine; (*en las fechas*) ninth
**nue•vo -va** *adj* **new; de nuevo** again, anew; **nuevo flamante** brand-new; **¿qué hay de nuevo?** what's new? ‖ *mf* novice; freshman ‖ *f* see **nueva**
**nuevomejica•no -na** *adj & mf* New Mexican
**Nuevo Méjico** *m* New Mexico
**nuez** *f* (*pl* **nueces**) **nut; walnut; Adam's** apple; **nuez dura** (*árbol*) hickory; hickory nut; **nuez moscada** nutmeg
**nulidad** *f* **nullity; incapacity;** (coll) nobody
**nu•lo -la** *adj* **null, void, worthless**
**núm.** *abbr* número
**numen** *m* deity; inspiration
**numeral** *adj* numeral
**numerar** *tr* to number; **to count; to** numerate
**numerario** *m* cash, coin, specie
**numéri•co -ca** *adj* numerical
**número** *m* number; (*de un periódico*) copy, issue; (*de zapatos*) size; lottery ticket; **cargar** or **cobrar al número llamado** (telp) to reverse the charges; **de número** (*dícese de los individuos de una sociedad*) regular; **mirar por el número uno** to look out for number one; **número de serie** series number; **número equivocado** (telp) wrong number
**numero•so -sa** *adj* numerous
**nunca** *adv* never; **no . . . nunca** not . . . ever, never **nunca jamás** never more
**nupcial** *adj* nuptial
**nupcialidad** *f* marriage rate
**nupcias** *fpl* nuptials, marriage; **casarse en segundas nupcias** to marry the second time
**nutria** *f* otter
**nutrición** *f* nutrition
**nutri•do -da** *adj* great, intense, robust, vigorous, steady; full, abounding, rich, heavy; (*carácter, letra*) thick; (*cañoneo*) heavy, sustained
**nutrimento** or **nutrimiento** *m* nourishment, nutriment
**nutrir** *tr* to nourish, to feed; to supply, to stock; to support, back up; to fill to overflowing
**nu•triz** *f* (*pl* **-trices**) **wet nurse**

## Ñ

**Ñ, ñ** (eñe) *f* **seventeenth letter of the** Spanish alphabet
**ñadi** *m* (Chile) broad, shallow swamp
**ñajú** *m* (Am) okra, gumbo
**ñámbar** *m* Jamaica rosewood
**ñame** *m* yam; (W-I) blockhead, dunce
**ñan•dú** *m* (*pl* **-dúes**) nandu, American ostrich
**ña•ño -ña** *adj* (Am) close, intimate; (Am) spoiled, overindulged ‖ *m* (Am) elder brother ‖ *f* (Am) elder sister; (Am) nursemaid; (Am) dear
**ñapa** *f* (Am) something thrown in; **de ñapa** (Am) in the bargain
**ñaque** *m* junk, pile of junk
**ña•to -ta** *adj* (Am) pug-nosed; (Arg) ugly, deformed
**ñeque** *adj* (Am) strong, vigorous; (*dícese de los ojos*) (Am) drooping ‖ *m* (Am) slap, blow; (Am) pep
**ñiqueñaque** *m* (coll) trash
**ñisca** *f* (Am) bit, fragment; (Am) excrement
**ñoclo** *m* macaroon
**ñolombre** *m* (Am) old peasant; **¡viene ñolombre!** (Am) here comes the bogeyman
**ñon•go -ga** *adj* (Am) slow, lazy; (Am) foolish, stupid; (Am) tricky; (Am) suspicious
**ñoñería** or **ñoñez** *f* timidity; inanity; dotage
**ño•ño -ña** *adj* timid; inane; doting

## O

**O, o** (o) *f* eighteenth letter of the Spanish alphabet
**o** *conj* or; **o . . . o** either . . . or
**oa•sis** *m* (*pl* **-sis**) oasis
**ob.** *abbr* obispo
**obduración** *f* obduracy
**obedecer** §22 *tr* (with personal **a**) to obey ‖ *intr* to obey; **obedecer a** to yield to, be due to, be in keeping with, arise from

**obediencia** *f* obedience
**obediente** *adj* obedient
**obelisco** *m* obelisk; (typ) dagger
**obertura** *f* (mus) overture
**obesidad** *f* obesity
**obe•so -sa** *adj* obese
**obispo** *m* bishop
**óbito** *m* decease, demise
**obituario** *m* (Am) obituary
**objeción** *f* objection
**objetable** *adj* objectionable (*open to objection*)
**objetar** *tr* to object; (*dudas*) to raise; (*una razón contraria*) to set up, offer, present; to object to
**objeti•vo -va** *adj & m* objective
**objeto** *m* object; subject matter; **objetos de cotillón** favors
**oblea** *f* wafer; pill, tablet; **hecho una oblea** (coll) nothing but skin and bones
**obli•cuo -cua** *adj* oblique
**obligación** *f* obligation, duty; bond, debenture; **obligaciones** *fpl* family responsibilities
**obligacionista** *mf* bondholder
**obliga•do -da** *adj* obliged, grateful; submissive; (mus) obbligato ‖ *m* (mus) obbligato
**obligar** §44 *tr* to obligate; to oblige
**obliterar** *tr* to cancel
**oblon•go -ga** *adj* oblong
**oboe** *m* oboe; oboist
**oboísta** *mf* oboist
**óbolo** *m* mite
**obra** *f* work; **obra de** a matter of; **obra de consulta** reference work; **obra maestra** masterpiece; **obra pía** charity; (coll) useful effort; **obra prima** shoemaking; **obras** construction, repairs, alterations; **obra segunda** shoe repairing; **poner por obra** to undertake, set to work on
**obra•dor -dora** *mf* worker ‖ *m* workman; shop, workshop ‖ *f* workingwoman
**obrajero** *m* foreman; (Arg) lumberman; (Bol) artisan
**obrar** *tr* to build; to perform; to work ‖ *intr* to work; to act, operate, proceed; to have a movement of the bowels; **obra en mi poder** I have at hand, I have in my possession
**obrera** *f* workingwoman
**obrerismo** *m* labor; labor movement
**obre•ro -ra** *adj* working; labor ‖ *m* workman; **los obreros** labor ‖ *f* see **obrera**
**obrero-patronal** *adj* labor-management
**obscenidad** *f* obscenity
**obsce•no -na** *adj* obscene
**obscurecer** §22 *tr* to darken; to dim; to discredit; to cloud, confuse ‖ *intr* to grow dark ‖ *ref* to cloud over; to become dimmed; (coll) to fade away
**obscuridad** *f* obscurity; darkness
**obscu•ro -ra** *adj* obscure; dark; gloomy; uncertain, dangerous; **a obscuras** in the dark ‖ *m* dark; (paint) shading
**obsequia•do -da** *mf* recipient; guest of honor
**obsequiar** *tr* to fawn over, flatter; to present, to give; to court, to woo
**obsequio** *m* flattery; gift; attention, courtesy; **en obsequio de** in honor of
**obsequio•so -sa** *adj* obsequious; obliging, courteous
**observación** *f* observation
**observa•dor -dora** *adj* observant ‖ *mf* observer
**observancia** *f* observance; deference, respectfulness
**observar** *tr* to observe
**observatorio** *m* observatory
**obsesión** *f* obsession
**obsesionar** *tr* to obsess
**obstaculizar** §60 *tr* to prevent; to obstruct
**obstáculo** *m* obstacle
**obstante** *adj* standing in the way; **no obstante** however, nevertheless; in spite of
**obstar** *intr* to stand in the way; **obstar a** or **para** to hinder, check, oppose
**obstetricia** *f* obstetrics
**obstétri•co -ca** *adj* obstetrical ‖ *mf* obstetrician
**obstinación** *f* obstinacy
**obstina•do -da** *adj* obstinate
**obstinar** *ref* to be obstinate
**obstrucción** *f* obstruction
**obstruir** §20 *tr* to obstruct; to block; to stop up
**obtención** *f* obtaining
**obtener** §71 *tr* to obtain; to keep
**obtenible** *adj* obtainable
**obturador** *m* stopper, plug; (aut) choke; (aut) throttle; (phot) shutter; **obturador de guillotina** drop shutter
**obtu•so -sa** *adj* obtuse
**obús** *m* howitzer; shell; (*de válvula de neumático*) plunger
**obvención** *f* extra, bonus, incidental
**obvencional** *adj* incidental
**obviar** §77 & **regular** *tr* to obviate, prevent ‖ *intr* to stand in the way
**ob•vio -via** *adj* obvious; unnecessary
**oca** *f* goose
**ocasión** *f* occasion; opportunity, chance; danger, risk; **aprovechar la ocasión** to improve the occasion; **aprovechar la ocasión de** to avail oneself of the opportunity to; **asir la ocasión por la melena** to take time by the forelock; **de ocasión** secondhand
**ocasiona•do -da** *adj* dangerous, risky; exposed, subject, liable; annoying
**ocasionar** *tr* to occasion, to cause; to stir up; to endanger
**ocasional** *adj* occasional; causal; causing; (*causa*) responsible; accidental
**ocaso** *m* west; (*de un cuerpo celeste*) setting; sunset; decline; end, death
**occidental** *adj* western; occidental
**occidente** *m* occident
**oceáni•co -ca** *adj* oceanic
**océano** *m* ocean
**ocio** *m* idleness, leisure; distraction, pastime; spare time
**ocio•so -sa** *adj* idle; useless, needless
**oclusión** *f* occlusion
**oclusi•vo -va** *adj & f* occlusive
**ocote** *m* (Mex) torch pine
**octava** *f* octave
**octavilla** *f* handbill; eight-syllable verse

**octavín** *m* piccolo
**octa·vo -va** *adj* eighth || *mf* octoroon || *m* eighth || *f* see **octava**
**oct.ᵉ** *abbr* **octubre**
**octogési·mo -ma** *adj & m* eightieth
**octubre** *m* October
**ocular** *adj* ocular, eye || *m* eyepiece, eyeglass, ocular
**oculista** *mf* oculist; (Am) fawner, flatterer
**ocultar** *tr & ref* to hide
**ocul·to -ta** *adj* hidden, concealed; (*misterioso, sobrenatural*) occult
**ocupación** *f* occupation; occupancy; employment
**ocupa·do -da** *adj* busy; occupied; **ocupada** pregnant
**ocupante** *adj* occupying || *mf* occupant || **ocupantes** *mpl* occupying forces
**ocupar** *tr* to occupy; to busy, keep busy; to employ; to bother, annoy; to attract the attention of || *ref* to be occupied; to be busy; to be preoccupied; to bother
**ocurrencia** *f* occurrence; witticism; bright idea
**ocurrente** *adj* witty
**ocurrir** *intr* to occur, happen; to come; (*venir a la mente*) to occur
**ocha·vo -va** *adj* eighth; octagonal || *m* eighth; octagon
**ochenta** *adj, pron & m* eighty
**ochenta·vo -va** *adj & m* eightieth
**ocho** *adj & pron* eight; **las ocho** eight o'clock || *m* eight; (*en las fechas*) eighth
**ochocien·tos -tas** *adj & pron* eight hundred || **ochocientos** *m* eight hundred
**oda** *f* ode
**odiar** *tr* to hate
**odio** *m* hate, hatred
**odio·so -sa** *adj* odious, hateful
**Odisea** *f* Odyssey
**Odiseo** *m* Odysseus
**odontología** *f* odontology, dentistry
**odontólo·go -ga** *mf* odontologist, dentist
**odre** *m* goatskin wine bag; (coll) toper
**OEA** *f* OAS
**oeste** *m* west; west wind
**ofender** *tr & intr* to offend || *ref* to take offense
**ofensa** *f* offense
**ofensi·vo -va** *adj & f* offensive
**ofen·sor -sora** *adj* offending || *mf* offender
**oferta** *f* offer; gift, present; **oferta y demanda** supply and demand
**oficial** *adj* official || *m* official, officer; skilled workman; clerk, office worker; journeyman; commissioned officer; **oficial de derrota** navigator
**oficiar** *tr* to announce officially in writing; (*la misa*) to celebrate; to officiate at || *intr* to officiate; **oficiar de** (coll) to act as
**oficina** *f* office; shop; pharmacist's laboratory; **oficina de objetos perdidos** lost-and-found department
**oficines·co -ca** *adj* office, clerical; bureaucratic
**oficinista** *mf* clerk, office worker
**oficio** *m* office, occupation; function, rôle; craft, trade; memo, official note; (eccl) office, service; **de oficio** officially; professionally; **hacer oficios de** to function as; **tomar por oficio** (coll) to take to, to keep at
**oficio·so -sa** *adj* diligent; obliging; officious, meddlesome; profitable; unofficial
**ofrecer** *tr & intr* to offer; (*una recepción*) to give || *ref* to offer; to offer oneself; to happen
**ofrecimiento** *m* offer, offering; **ofrecimiento de presentación** introductory offer
**ofrenda** *f* offering; gift
**ofrendar** *tr* to make offerings of; to contribute
**oftalmología** *f* ophthalmology
**oftalmólo·go -ga** *mf* ophthalmologist
**ofuscar** §73 *tr* to obfuscate; to dazzle
**ogro** *m* ogre
**Oh** *interj* O!, Oh!
**ohmio** *m* ohm
**oíble** *adj* audible
**oída** *f* hearing; **de** or **por oídas** by hearsay
**oído** *m* hearing; ear; **abrir tanto oído** to be all ears; **al oído** by listening; confidentially; **decir al oído** to whisper; **hacer** or **tener oídos de mercader** to turn a deaf ear
**oír** §48 *tr* to hear; to listen to; (*una conferencia*) to attend; **oír** + *inf* to hear + *inf*, e.g., **oí entrar a mi hermano** I heard my brother come in; to hear + *ger*, e.g., **oí cantar a la muchacha** I heard the girl singing; to hear + *pp*, e.g., **oí tocar la campana** I heard the bell rung; **oír decir que** to hear that; **oír hablar de** to hear about || *intr* to hear; to listen; **¡oiga!** say!, listen!; the idea!, the very idea!
**ojada** *f* (Col) skylight
**ojal** *m* buttonhole; eyelet; grommet
**ojalá** *interj* God grant . . . !, would to God . . . !; **¡ojalá que . . . !** would that . . . !, I hope that . . . !
**ojeada** *f* glimpse, glance; **buena ojeada** eyeful
**ojear** *tr* to eye, stare at; to hoodoo, to cast the evil eye on; (*la caza*) to start, to rouse; to frighten, to startle
**ojera** *f* eyecup, eyeglass; **ojeras** (*bajo los párpados inferiores*) rings, circles
**ojeriza** *f* grudge, ill will
**ojero·so -sa** *adj* with rings or circles under the eyes
**ojete** *m* eyelet, eyehole
**ojienju·to -ta** *adj* dry-eyed, tearless
**ojituer·to -ta** *adj* cross-eyed
**ojiva** *f* ogive, pointed arch
**ojo** *m* eye; (*de la escalera*) opening, well; (*del puente*) bay, span; (*de agua*) spring; **a ojos vistas** visibly, openly; **costar un ojo de la cara** to cost a mint, to cost a fortune; **dar los ojos de la cara por** to give one's eyeteeth for; **hasta los ojos** up to one's ears; **mirar con ojos de carnero degollado** to make sheep's eyes at; **no pegar el ojo** to not sleep a wink; **ojo de buey** (archit, meteor, naut) bull's-eye; (bot) oxeye; **ojo de la cerradura**

keyhole; **poner los ojos en blanco** to roll one's eyes; **saltar a los ojos** to be self-evident; **valer un ojo de la cara** to be worth a mint || *interj* beware!; look out!; attention!; **¡mucho ojo!** be careful!, watch out!; **¡ojo con . . . !** look out for . . . !; **¡ojo, mancha!** fresh paint!
**ojota** *f* (SAm) sandal; (SAm) tanned llama hide
**ola** *f* wave; (*de gente apiñada*) surge
**ole** *m* or **olé** *m* bravo || *interj* bravo!
**oleada** *f* big wave; (*de gente apiñada*) surge, swell
**oleaje** *m* surge, rush of waves
**óleo** *m* oil; holy oil; oil painting; **los santos óleos** extreme unction
**oleoducto** *m* pipe line
**oler §49** *tr* to smell; to pry into; to sniff out || *intr* to smell, to smell fragrant, to smell bad; **no oler bien** (coll) to look suspicious; **oler a** to smell of, to smell like; to smack of
**olfatear** *tr* to smell, scent, sniff; (coll) (*p.ej., un buen negocio*) to scent, to sniff out
**olfato** *m* smell, sense of smell; scent; keen insight
**olíbano** *m* frankincense
**oliente** *adj* smelling, odorous
**oligarquía** *f* oligarchy
**Olimpíada** *f* Olympiad
**olímpi•co -ca** *adj* Olympian; Olympic; haughty
**oliscar §73** *tr* to smell, scent, sniff; to investigate || *intr* to smell bad
**oliva** *f* olive; olive tree; barn owl; olive branch, peace
**olivar** *m* olive grove
**olivillo** *m* mock privet
**olivo** *m* olive tree; **tomar el olivo** (taur) to duck behind the barrier; (coll) to beat it
**olmeda** *f* or **olmedo** *m* elm grove
**olmo** *m* elm tree
**olor** *m* odor; promise, hope; trace, suspicion; **olores** (Chile, Mex) spice, condiment
**oloro•so -sa** *adj* odorous, fragrant
**olote** *m* (CAm & Mex) cob, corncob
**olvidadi•zo -za** *adj* forgetful; ungrateful
**olvida•do -da** *adj* forgetful; ungrateful
**olvidar** *tr & intr* to forget; **olvidar + *inf*** to forget to + *inf* || *ref* to forget oneself; **olvidarse de** to forget; **olvidarse de + *inf*** to forget to + *inf*; **olvidársele a uno** to forget, e.g., **se me olvidó mi pasaporte** I forgot my passport; **olvidársele a uno + *inf*** to forget to + *inf*, e.g., **se me olvidó cerrar la ventana** I forgot to close the window
**olvido** *m* forgetfulness; oblivion
**olla** *f* pot, kettle; stew; eddy, whirlpool; **olla a** or **de presión** pressure cooker
**ombligo** *m* navel; (*centro, punto medio*) (fig) navel
**omino•so -sa** *adj* ominous
**omisión** *f* omission; oversight, neglect
**omi•so -sa** *adj* neglectful, remiss
**omitir** *tr* to omit; to overlook, neglect
**ómni•bus** *adj* (*tren*) accommodation || *m* (*pl* **-bus**) bus, omnibus; **ómnibus de dos pisos** double-decker
**omnímo•do -da** *adj* all-inclusive
**omnipotente** *adj* omnipotent
**omnisciente** or **omnis•cio -cia** *adj* omniscient
**omnívo•ro -ra** *adj* omnivorous
**omóplato** *m* shoulder blade
**once** *adj & pron* eleven; **las once** eleven o'clock || *m* eleven; (*en las fechas*) eleventh
**oncea•vo -va** *adj & m* eleventh
**once•no -na** *adj & m* eleventh
**onda** *f* wave; flicker; (*en el pelo*) wave; **onda portadora** (rad) carrier wave; **ondas entretenidas** (rad) continuous waves
**ondear** *tr* (*el pelo*) to wave || *intr* to wave; to ripple; to flow; to flicker; to be wavy || *ref* to wave, sway, swing
**ondo•so -sa** *adj* wavy
**ondulación** *f* undulation; wave; wave motion
**ondula•do -da** *adj* wavy, ripply; rolling; corrugated || *m* (*en el pelo*) wave
**ondular** *tr* (*el pelo*) to wave || *intr* to undulate; (*una bandera*) to wave, flutter; (*las ondas del mar*) to billow; (*una culebra*) to wriggle
**onero•so -sa** *adj* onerous, burdensome
**ónice** *m*, **ónique** *m* or **ónix** *m* onyx
**onomásti•co -ca** *adj* of proper names || *m* name day || *f* study of proper names
**ONU** *f* UN
**onza** *f* ounce; (zool) snow leopard
**onza•vo -va** *adj & m* eleventh
**opa•co -ca** *adj* opaque; sad, gloomy
**ópalo** *m* opal
**opción** *f* option, choice
**ópera** *f* opera; **ópera semiseria** light opera; **ópera seria** grand opera
**operación** *f* operation; transaction
**operar** *tr* to operate on || *intr* to operate; to work || *ref* to occur, come about; to be operated on
**opera•rio -ria** *mf* worker || *m* workman || *f* working woman
**opereta** *f* operetta
**operista** *mf* opera singer
**operísti•co -ca** *adj* operatic
**opia•to -ta** *adj, m & f* opiate
**opinable** *adj* moot
**opinar** *intr* to opine; to think; to pass judgment
**opinión** *f* opinion, view; reputation, public image
**opio** *m* opium
**opípa•ro -ra** *adj* sumptuous, lavish
**oponer §54** *tr* to oppose; (*resistencia*) to offer, put up || *ref* to oppose each other; to face each other; **oponerse a** to oppose, be opposed to; to be against, to resist; to compete for
**oporto** *m* port, port wine
**oportunidad** *f* opportunity; opportuneness; **oportunidades** *fpl* witticisms
**oportunista** *adj* opportunistic || *mf* opportunist
**oportu•no -na** *adj* opportune, timely; proper; witty

**oposición** *f* opposition; competitive examination
**oposi•tor -tora** *adj* rivaling, competing || *mf* opponent; competitor
**opresión** *f* oppression
**opresi•vo -va** *adj* oppressive
**opre•sor -sora** *adj* oppressive || *mf* oppressor
**oprimir** *tr* to oppress; to squeeze, to press
**oprobiar** *tr* to defame, to revile
**oprobio** *m* opprobrium
**oprobio•so -sa** *adj* opprobrious
**optar** *tr* to choose, to select; *intr* — **optar entre** to choose between; **optar por** to choose to
**ópti•co -ca** *adj* optical || *mf* optician || *f* optics
**óptimamente** *adv* to perfection
**optimismo** *m* optimism
**optimista** *adj* optimistic || *mf* optimist
**ópti•mo -ma** *adj* fine, excellent
**optometrista** *mf* optometrist
**opues•to -ta** *adj* opposite, contrary
**opugnar** *tr* to attack; to lay siege to; to contradict
**opulen•to -ta** *adj* opulent
**opúsculo** *m* short work, opuscule
**oquedad** *f* hollow; hollowness
**ora** *conj* — **ora . . . ora** now . . . now, now . . . then
**oración** *f* oration, speech; prayer; sentence; **oración dominical** Lord's prayer; **ponerse en oración** to get down on one's knees
**oráculo** *m* oracle
**ora•dor -dora** *mf* orator, speaker; **orador de plazuela** soapbox orator; **orador de sobremesa** after-dinner speaker
**oraje** *m* rough weather, storm
**oral** *adj* oral
**orangután** *m* orang-outang
**orar** *intr* to pray; to make a speech
**orato•rio -ria** *adj* oratorical || *m* oratorio; (*capilla privada*) oratory || *f* (*arte de la elocuencia*) oratory
**orbe** *m* orb; world
**órbita** *f* orbit
**orca** *f* killer whale
**Órcadas** *fpl* Orkney Islands
**órdago** — **de órdago** (coll) swell, real
**orden** *m & f* order; **hasta nueva orden** until further notice; **orden** *f* **de allanamiento** search warrant; **orden** *m* **de colocación** word order
**ordenancista** *adj* strict, severe || *mf* taskmaster, disciplinarian, martinet
**ordenanza** *m* errand boy; (mil) orderly || *f* ordinance; order, system; command; **ser de ordenanza** (coll) to be the rule
**ordenar** *tr* to order; to put in order; to ordain || *ref* to be ordained, to take orders
**ordeñadero** *m* milk pail
**ordeñar** *tr* to milk
**ordeño** *m* milking
**ordinal** *adj* orderly; ordinal || *m* ordinal
**ordinariez** *f* (coll) coarseness, crudeness
**ordina•rio -ria** *adj* ordinary || *m* daily household expenses; delivery man
**orear** *tr* to air || *ref* to be aired; to dry in the air; to take an airing
**orégano** *m* pot or wild marjoram, winter sweet
**oreja** *f* ear; (*del zapato*) flap; (*de martillo*) claw; lug, flange, ear; **aguzar las orejas** to prick up one's ears; **con las orejas caídas** crestfallen; **con las orejas tan largas** all ears; **descubrir** or **enseñar las orejas** (coll) to give oneself away
**oreja•no -na** *adj* (*res*) unbranded; (*animal*) (Am) skittish; (Am) shy; (Am) cautious
**orejera** *f* earflap, earmuff
**orejeta** *f* lug
**ore•jón -jona** *adj* (Am) coarse, uncouth; (Mex) skinny || *m* strip of dried peach; pull on the ear; (*de la hoja de un libro*) dog's-ear
**oreju•do -da** *adj* big-eared
**oreo** *m* breeze
**orfanato** *m* orphanage
**orfandad** *f* orphanage, orphanhood
**orfebre** *m* goldsmith; silversmith
**Orfeo** *m* Orpheus
**orfeón** *m* glee club, choral society
**organ•dí** *m* (*pl* **-díes**) organdy
**orgáni•co -ca** *adj* organic
**organillero -ra** *mf* organ-grinder
**organillo** *m* barrel organ, hand organ, hurdy-gurdy
**organismo** *m* organism; organization
**organista** *mf* organist
**organizar §60** *tr* to organize
**órgano** *m* organ; (*de una máquina*) part; (*medio, conducto*) organ; (mus) organ
**orgía** *f* orgy
**orgullo** *m* haughtiness; pride
**orgullo•so -sa** *adj* haughty; proud
**oriental** *adj* eastern; oriental
**orientar** *tr* to orient; to guide, direct; (*una vela*) to trim || *ref* to orient oneself; to find one's bearings
**oriente** *m* east; source, origin; east wind; youth || **Oriente** *m* Orient; **el Cercano Oriente** the Near East; **el Extremo Oriente** the Far East; **el Lejano Oriente** the Far East; **el Oriente Medio** the Middle East; **el Próximo Oriente** the Near East; **gran oriente** (*logia masónica central*) grand lodge
**orificar §73** *tr* to fill with gold
**orífice** *m* goldsmith
**orificio** *m* orifice, aperture, hole
**origen** *m* origin; source
**original** *adj* original; queer, odd, quaint || *m* original; character, queer duck; **de buen original** on good authority; **original de imprenta** copy
**originar** *tr & ref* to originate, to start
**orilla** *f* border, edge; margin; bank, shore; sidewalk; breeze; **orillas** (Arg, Mex) outskirts; **salir a la orilla** to manage to get through
**orillar** *tr* to put a border or edge on; to trim || *intr* to come up to the shore
**orillo** *m* selvage, list
**orín** *m* rust; **orines urine; tomarse de orines** to get rusty
**orina** *f* urine
**orinal** *m* chamber pot

**orinar** *tr* to pass, to urinate ‖ *intr & ref* to urinate
**oriun•do -da** *adj & mf* native; **ser oriundo de** to come from, to hail from
**orla** *f* border, edge; trimming, fringe
**orlar** *tr* to border, to put an edge on; to trim, to trim with a fringe
**orn.** *abbr* **orden**
**ornamentar** *tr* to ornament, adorn
**ornamento** *m* ornament, adornment
**ornar** *tr* to adorn
**ornato** *m* adornment, show
**oro** *m* gold; playing card (*representing a gold coin*) equivalent to diamond; **de oro y azul** (coll) all dressed up; **oro batido** gold leaf; **oro de ley** standard gold; **poner de oro y azul** (coll) to rake over the coals; **ponerle colores al oro** to gild the lily
**oron•do -da** *adj* big-bellied; (coll) hollow, spongy, puffed up; (coll) pompous, self-satisfied
**oropel** *m* tinsel; **gastar mucho oropel** (coll) to put up a big front
**oropéndola** *f* golden oriole
**orozuz** *m* licorice
**orquesta** *f* orchestra; **orquesta típica** regional orchestra
**orquestar** *tr* to orchestrate
**órquide** *f* or **orquídea** *f* orchid
**ortiga** *f* nettle; **ser como unas ortigas** (coll) to be a grouch
**orto** *m* rise (*of sun or star*)
**ortodo•xo -xa** *adj* orthodox
**ortografía** *f* orthography; spelling
**ortografiar** §77 *tr & intr* to spell
**oruga** *f* caterpillar
**orujo** *m* bagasse of grapes or olives
**orzuelo** *m* sty
**os** *pron pers & reflex* (used as object of verb and corresponding to **vos** and **vosotros**) you, to you; yourself, to yourself; yourselves, to yourselves; each other, to each other
**osa** *f* she-bear; **Osa mayor** Great Bear; **Osa menor** Little Bear
**osadía** *f* boldness, daring
**osa•do -da** *adj* bold, daring
**osamenta** *f* skeleton; bones
**osar** *intr* to dare
**osario** *m* ossuary, charnel house
**oscilar** *intr* to oscillate; to fluctuate; to waver, hesitate
**ósculo** *m* kiss
**oscurecer** §22 *tr, intr & ref* var of **obscurecer**
**oscuridad** *f* var of **obscuridad**
**oscu•ro -ra** *adj & m* var of **obscuro**
**osera** *f* bear's den
**osificar** §73 *tr & ref* to ossify
**oso** *m* bear; **hacer el oso** (coll) to make a fool of oneself; (coll) to make love in the open; **oso blanco** polar bear; **oso hormiguero** ant bear, anteater; **oso lavador** raccoon
**ostensorio** *m* (eccl) monstrance
**ostentar** *tr* to show; to make a show of ‖ *ref* to show off; to boast
**ostentati•vo -va** *adj* ostentatious
**ostento** *m* portent, prodigy
**ostento•so -sa** *adj* magnificent, showy
**osteópata** *mf* osteopath
**osteopatía** *f* osteopathy
**ostión** *m* large oyster
**ostra** *f* oyster; **ostras en su concha** oyster cocktail, oysters on the half shell
**ostracismo** *m* ostracism
**ostral** *m* oyster bed, oyster farm
**ostrería** *f* oysterhouse
**ostre•ro -ra** *adj* oyster ‖ *m* oysterman; oyster bed, oyster farm
**osu•do -da** *adj* bony
**osu•no -na** *adj* bearish, bearlike
**O.T.A.N., la** Nato
**O.T.A.S.E., la** Seato
**otate** *m* Mexican giant grass (*Guadua amplexifolia*); otate stick
**otero** *m* hillock, knoll
**otomán** *m* ottoman
**otoma•no -na** *adj & mf* Ottoman ‖ *f* ottoman
**otoñal** *adj* autumnal
**otoño** *m* autumn, fall
**otorgar** §44 *tr* to agree to; to grant, to confer; (law) to execute
**o•tro -tra** *adj indef* other, another ‖ *pron indef* other one, another one; **como dijo el otro** as someone said
**ovación** *f* ovation
**ovacionar** *tr* to give an ovation to
**oval** *adj* oval
**óvalo** *m* oval
**ovante** *adj* victorious, triumphant
**ovario** *m* ovary
**oveja** *f* ewe, female sheep; **oveja negra** (fig) black sheep; **oveja perdida** (fig) lost sheep
**oveje•ro -ra** *adj* sheep ‖ *mf* sheep raiser
**oveju•no -na** *adj* sheep, of sheep
**ove•ro -ra** *adj* blossom-colored; egg-colored
**Ovidio** *m* Ovid
**ovillar** *tr* to wind up; to sum up ‖ *intr* to form into a ball ‖ *ref* to curl up into a ball
**ovillo** *m* ball of yarn; ball, heap; tangled ball; **hacerse un ovillo** (coll) to cower, to recoil; (*hablando*) (coll) to get all tangled up
**oxear** *tr & intr* to shoo
**oxiacanta** *f* hawthorn
**oxidar** *tr* to oxidize ‖ *ref* to oxidize; to get rusty
**óxido** *m* oxide; **óxido de carbono** carbon monoxide; **óxido de mercurio** mercuric oxide
**oxígeno** *m* oxygen
**oxíto•no -na** *adj* oxytone
**oxte** *interj* get out!, beat it!; **sin decir oxte ni moxte** (coll) without opening one's mouth
**oyente** *mf* hearer; (*a la radio*) listener; (*en la escuela*) auditor
**ozono** *m* ozone

# P

**P, p** (pe) *f* nineteenth letter of the Spanish alphabet
**P.** *abbr* **Padre, Papa, Pregunta**
**pabellón** *m* pavilion; bell tent; flag, banner; (*de fusiles*) stack; canopy; summerhouse; (*de instrumento de viento*) bell
**pabilo** *or* **pábilo** *m* wick
**Pablo** *m* Paul
**pábulo** *m* food; support, encouragement, fuel
**pacana** *f* pecan
**paca•to -ta** *adj* mild, gentle
**pacer §22** *tr* to pasture, graze; to gnaw, eat away || *intr* to pasture, graze
**paciencia** *f* patience
**paciente** *adj* & *mf* patient
**pacienzu•do -da** *adj* long-suffering
**pacificar §73** *tr* to pacify || *intr* to sue for peace || *ref* to calm down
**pacífi•co -ca** *adj* pacific
**pacifismo** *m* pacifism
**pacifista** *adj* & *mf* pacifist
**pa•co -ca** *adj* (Chile) bay, reddish || *m* paco, alpaca; Moorish sniper; sniper || **Paco** *m* Frank
**pacotilla** *f* trash, junk; (Chile) rabble, mob; **hacer su pacotilla** (coll) to make a cleanup; **ser de pacotilla** to be shoddy, to be poorly made
**pacotille•ro -ra** *mf* (Chile, Ven) peddler
**pactar** *tr* to agree upon || *intr* to come to an agreement
**pacto** *m* pact, covenant
**pacha•cho -cha** *adj* (Chile) short-legged; (Chile) lax, lazy; (Chile) chubby
**pa•chón -chona** *adj* (CAm) shaggy, hairy, wooly || *m* (*perro*) pointer; (*hombre flemático*) (coll) sluggard
**pachorra** *f* (coll) sluggishness, indolence
**padecer §22** *tr* to suffer; to be victim of || *intr* to suffer
**padrastro** *m* stepfather; hangnail
**padre** *adj* (Am) huge; (Peru) terrific || *m* father; stallion, sire; **padres** parents; ancestors; **tener el padre alcalde** to have pull, to have a friend at court
**padrina** *f* godmother
**padrinazgo** *m* godfathership; sponsorship, patronage
**padrino** *m* godfather; sponsor; (*en un desafío*) second; **padrino de boda** best man; **padrinos** godparents
**padrón** *m* poll, census; pattern, model; memorial column; (coll) indulgent father; (Am) stallion; (Col) stock bull
**padrote** *m* (Am) stock animal; (Mex) pimp, procurer
**paella** *f* saffron-flavored stew of chicken, seafood, and rice with vegetables
**paf** *interj* bang!
**pág.** *abbr* **página**
**paga** *f* pay, payment; wages; fine
**paga-alquiler** *f* rent, rent money
**pagadero -ra** *adj* payable
**paga•do -da** *adj* pleased, cheerful; **estamos pagados** we are quits; **pagado de sí mismo** self-satisfied, conceited
**paga•dor -dora** *adj* paying || *mf* payer || *m* paymaster
**paganismo** *m* paganism
**paga•no -na** *adj* & *mf* pagan || *m* (coll) easy mark
**pagar §44** *tr* to pay; to pay for; (*una bondad, una visita*) to return || *intr* to pay || *ref* to become fond; to be flattered; to boast; to be satisfied
**pagaré** *m* promissory note, I.O.U.
**página** *f* page
**paginar** *tr* to page
**pago** *m* payment; (*de viñas u olivares*) district, region
**pagote** *m* (coll) easy mark
**paila** *f* large pan
**pairar** *intr* (naut) to lie to
**país** *m* country, land; landscape; **el país de Gales** Wales; **los Países Bajos** (*Bélgica, Holanda y Luxemburgo*) the Low Countries; (*Holanda*) The Netherlands
**paisaje** *m* landscape
**paisajista** *mf* landscape painter
**paisa•no -na** *adj* of the same country || *mf* peasant; civilian; (Mex) Spaniard || *m* fellow countryman; **de paisano** in civies
**paja** *f* straw; chaff; trash, rubbish; **no dormirse en las pajas** to not let the grass grow under one's feet; **no levantar paja del suelo** to not lift a hand, to not do a stroke of work
**pájara** *f* paper kite; paper rooster; bird; crafty female
**pajarera** *f* aviary; large bird cage
**pajarería** *f* flock of birds; bird store; pet shop
**pajare•ro -ra** *adj* (coll) bright, cheerful; (coll) bright-colored, gaudy || *m* bird dealer; bird fancier || *f* see **pajarera**
**pajarita** *f* paper kite; bow tie; wing collar, piccadilly
**pájaro** *m* bird; crafty fellow; expert; **pájaro bobo** penguin; (Am) motmot; **pájaro carpintero** woodpecker; **pájaro de cuenta** (coll) big shot; **pájaro mosca** hummingbird
**pajarota** or **pajarotada** *f* hoax, canard
**paje** *m* page; valet; dressing table; (naut) cabin boy
**pajilla** *f* cornhusk cigarette; **pajilla de madera** excelsior
**paji•zo -za** *adj* straw; straw-colored; straw-thatched
**pajuela** *f* short straw; sulfur match or fuse; (Am) toothpick; (Bol) match
**Pakistán, el** var of **Paquistán**
**pakista•ní** (*pl* **-níes**) *adj* & *mf* var of **paquistaní**
**pala** *f* shovel; (*de remo, de la azada, etc.*) blade; (*del panadero*) peel; scoop; racket; (*del calzado*) upper; (*de excavadora*) bucket; shoulder strap; (coll) cunning, craftiness
**palabra** *f* word; speech; (*de una canción*) words; (*derecho para hablar en asambleas*) floor; **palabras mayores**

words, angry words; **remojar la palabra** (coll) to wet one's whistle; **usar de la palabra** to speak, make a speech
**palabre•ro -ra** *adj* wordy, windy ‖ *mf* windbag
**palabrota** *f* vulgarity, obscenity
**palacie•go -ga** *adj* palace, court ‖ *m* courtier
**palacio** *m* palace; mansion; **palacio municipal** city hall
**palada** *f* shovelful; (*de remo*) stroke
**paladar** *m* palate; taste; gourmet
**paladear** *tr* to taste, to relish
**paladín** *m* champion, hero
**palafrén** *m* palfrey
**palanca** *f* lever; pole; crowbar; **palanca de mando** (aer) control stick; **palanca de mayúsculas** shift key
**palancada** *f* leverage
**palangana** *f* washbowl, basin
**palanganero** *m* washstand
**palangre** *m* trawl, trawl line
**palanqueta** *f* jimmy; **palanquetas** (Arg) dumbbell
**palatal** *adj* & *f* palatal
**palco** *m* (theat) box
**palear** *tr* to beat, to pound; (Am) to shovel
**palenque** *m* paling, palisade; (SAm) hitching post; (C-R) Indian ranch; (Chile) pandemonium
**paleta** *f* palette; small shovel; trowel; (*de una rueda*) paddle; blade, bucket, vane; shoulder blade; (*dulce con un palito que sirve de mango*) lollipop
**paletilla** *f* shoulder blade
**paleto** *m* fallow deer; rustic, yokel
**palia** *f* altar cloth; (eccl) pall
**paliacate** *m* (Mex) bandanna
**paliar** §77 & **regular** *tr* to palliate
**palidecer** §22 *intr* to pale, to turn pale
**palidez** *f* paleness, pallor
**páli•do -da** *adj* pale, pallid
**palillo** *m* toothpick; drumstick; bobbin; **palillos** chopsticks; castanets; (coll) rudiments; (coll) trifles
**palinodia** *f* backdown; **cantar la palinodia** to eat crow, eat humble pie
**palique** *m* (coll) chit-chat, small talk
**paliquear** *intr* (coll) to chat, to gossip
**paliza** *f* beating, thrashing
**palizada** *f* fenced-in enclosure; stockade; embankment
**palma** *f* (*de la mano*) palm; (*árbol y hoja*) palm; **batir palmas** to clap, to applaud; **llevarse la palma** to carry off the palm
**palmada** *f* slap; hand, applause, clapping; **dar palmadas** to clap hands
**palma•rio -ria** *adj* clear, evident
**palmatoria** *f* candlestick
**palmera** *f* date palm
**palmito** *m* palmetto; (coll) woman's face; (coll) slender figure
**palmo** *m* span, palm; **dejar con un palmo de narices** (coll) to disappoint
**palmotear** *tr* to pat; to clap, applaud ‖ *intr* to clap, applaud
**palo** *m* stick; pole; staff; handle; (*golpe*) whack; (*madera*) wood; (*grupo de naipes de la baraja*) suit; (naut) mast; (Am) tree; **dar palos de ciego** to lay about, to swing wildly; **de tal palo tal astilla** like father like son; **palo de escoba** broomstick; **palo en alto** (fig) big stick; **palo mayor** (naut) mainmast; **servir del palo** to follow suit
**paloma** *f* pigeon, dove; prostitute; (fig) dove, meek person; **paloma mensajera** carrier pigeon; **palomas** whitecaps
**palomar** *m* pigeon house, dovecot
**palomilla** *f* doveling; small butterfly; white horse; (*del caballo*) back; pillow block, journal bearing; **palomillas** whitecaps
**palomita** *f* doveling; (baseball) fly; **palomitas** (Am) popcorn
**palpable** *adj* palpable
**palpar** *tr* to touch, to feel; to grope through ‖ *intr* to grope
**palpitante** *adj* throbbing; thrilling; (*cuestión*) burning
**palpitar** *intr* to palpitate, to throb; (*un afecto*) to flash, break forth
**pálpito** *m* (SAm) hunch
**palta** *f* (SAm) alligator pear, avocado (*fruit*)
**palto** *m* (SAm) alligator pear, avocado (*tree*)
**palúdi•co -ca** *adj* marshy; malarial
**paludismo** *m* malaria
**palur•do -da** *adj* rustic, boorish ‖ *mf* rustic, boor
**pallador** *m* (SAm) Gaucho minstrel
**pampa** *f* pampa; **La Pampa** the Pampas
**pámpana** *f* vine leaf
**pámpano** *m* tendril; vine leaf
**pan** *m* bread; loaf; loaf of bread; wheat; food; livelihood; pie dough; (*de jabón, cera, etc.*) cake; gold foil or leaf; silver foil or leaf; **como el pan bendito** (coll) as easy as pie; **de pan llevar** arable, tillable; **llamar al pan pan y al vino vino** to call a spade a spade; **panes** grain, breadstuff; **venderse como pan bendito** to sell like hot cakes ‖ **Pan** *m* Pan
**pana** *f* corduroy; (aut) breakdown
**panacea** *f* panacea
**panadería** *f* bakery; baking business
**panade•ro -ra** *mf* baker; (Chile) flatterer
**panadizo** *m* felon; (coll) sickly person
**panal** *m* honeycomb
**pana•má** *m* (*pl* **-maes**) Panama hat
**paname•ño -ña** *adj* & *mf* Panamanian
**panamerica•no -na** *adj* Pan-American
**pancarta** *f* placard, poster
**pancista** *adj* weaseling ‖ *mf* weaseler
**páncre•as** *m* (*pl* **-as**) pancreas
**pancho** *m* (coll) paunch, belly
**pandear** *intr* & *ref* to warp, to bulge, to buckle, to sag, to bend
**pandereta** *f* tambourine
**pandilla** *f* party, faction; gang, band; picnic, excursion
**pan•do -da** *adj* bulging; slow-moving; slow, deliberate
**pandorga** *f* kite; (coll) fat, lazy woman
**panecillo** *m* roll, crescent
**panfleto** *m* pamphlet
**paniaguado** *m* servant, minion; protégé, favorite

**páni•co -ca** *adj* panic, panicky ‖ *m* panic
**panizo** *m* Italian millet; (Chile) gangue; (Chile) abundance
**panocha** *f* ear of grain; ear of corn; (Am) pancake made of corn and cheese; (Mex) panocha (*brown sugar*)
**panoja** *f* ear of grain; ear of corn
**panorama** *m* panorama
**pano•so -sa** *adj* mealy
**panqué** *m* or **panqueque** *m* pancake
**pantalán** *m* pier, wooden pier
**pantalón** *m* trousers; **calzarse los pantalones** to wear the pants; **pantalones** trousers, pants
**pantalla** *f* lamp shade; fire screen; motion-picture screen; television screen; (*persona que encubre a otra*) blind; (*cine, arte del cine*) screen; (Am) fan; **llevar a la pantalla** to put on the screen; **pantalla de plata** silver screen; **servir de pantalla a** to be a blind for
**pantano** *m* bog, marsh, swamp; dam, reservoir; trouble, obstacle
**pantano•so -sa** *adj* marshy, swampy; muddy; knotty, difficult
**panteísmo** *m* pantheism
**panteón** *m* pantheon; cemetery
**pantera** *f* panther
**pantomima** *f* pantomime
**pantoque** *m* (naut) bilge
**pantorrilla** *f* calf (*of leg*)
**pantufla** *f* or **pantuflo** *m* house slipper
**panza** *f* paunch, belly
**panzu•do -da** *adj* paunchy, big-bellied
**pañal** *m* diaper; shirttail; **pañales** swaddling clothes; infancy; early stages
**pañe•ro -ra** *adj* dry-goods, cloth ‖ *mf* dry-goods dealer, clothier
**paño** *m* cloth; rag; (*de agujas*) paper; (*ancho de la tela*) breadth; (*mancha en el rostro*) spot; (*en, p.ej., un espejo*) blur; sailcloth, canvas; **al paño** off-stage; **conocer el paño** (coll) to know one's business, to know the ropes; **paño de adorno** doily; **paño de cocina** washrag, dishcloth; **paño de lágrimas** helping hand, stand-by; **paño de mesa** tablecloth; **paño de tumba** crape; **paño mortuorio** pall; **paños menores** underclothing
**pañuelo** *m* handkerchief; shawl; **pañuelo de hierbas** bandanna
**papa** *m* pope ‖ *f* potato; (coll) fake, hoax; (coll) food, grub; (Am) snap, cinch; **ni papa** (Am) nothing
**pa•pá** *m* (*pl* **-pás**) papa, daddy
**papada** *f* double chin; (*de animal*) dewlap; (Guat) stupidity
**papado** *m* papacy
**papagayo** *m* parrot
**papalina** *f* sunbonnet; (coll) drunk
**papana•tas** *m* (*pl* **-tas**) (coll) simpleton, gawk
**paparrucha** *f* (coll) hoax; (coll) trifle
**papel** *m* paper; piece of paper; rôle, part; character, figure; **desempeñar** or **hacer un papel** to play a rôle; **papel alquitranado** tar paper; **papel cebolla** onionskin; **papel de empapelar** wallpaper; **papel de esmeril** emery paper; **papel de estaño** tin foil; **papel de excusado** toilet paper; **papel de fumar** cigarette paper; **papel de lija** sandpaper; **papel de oficio** foolscap; **papel de seda** tissue paper; **papel de segundón** (fig) second fiddle; **papel de tornasol** litmus paper; **papel filtrante** filter paper; **papel higiénico** toilet paper; **papel moneda** paper money; **papel pintado** wallpaper; **papel secante** blotting paper; **papel viejo** waste paper; **papel volante** handbill, printed leaflet
**papeleo** *m* red tape
**papelera** *f* paper case; writing desk; wastebasket; paper factory
**papelería** *f* stationery store; mess of papers, litter
**papele•ro -ra** *adj* paper; boastful, showy ‖ *mf* stationer; paper manufacturer; (Mex) paperboy ‖ *f* see **papelera**
**papeleta** *f* slip of paper; card, file card; ticket; **papeleta de empeño** pawn ticket
**papelista** *m* paper maker, paper manufacturer; stationer; paper hanger
**pape•lón -lona** *adj* (coll) bluffing, fourflushing ‖ *mf* (coll) bluffer, fourflusher ‖ *m* thin cardboard
**papelonear** *intr* (coll) to bluff, to fourflush
**papelote** *m* worthless piece of paper; (Am) paper kite
**papel-prensa** *m* newsprint
**papera** *f* goiter; mumps
**papilla** *f* pap; guile, deceit
**papiro** *m* papyrus
**papirote** *m* fillip, flick; (coll) nincompoop
**paq.** *abbr* **paquete**
**paquear** *tr* to snipe at ‖ *intr* to snipe
**paque•te -ta** *adj* (Arg) chic, dolled-up; (Am) self-important, pompous ‖ *m* package, parcel, bundle, bale; (coll) sport, dandy; **darse paquete** (Guat, Mex) to put on airs; **en paquete aparte** under separate cover, in a separate package; **paquetes postales** parcel post
**Paquistán, el** Pakistan
**paquista•ní** (*pl* **-níes**) or **paquistano -na** *adj* & *mf* Pakistani
**Paquita** *f* Fanny
**par** *adj* like, similar, equal; (math) even ‖ *m* pair, couple; peer; (elec, mech) couple; (math) even number; **a pares** in twos; **de par en par** wide-open; completely; overtly; **¿pares o nones?** odd or even? ‖ *f* par; **a la par** equally; jointly; at the same time; at par; **bajo la par** below par, under par; **sobre la par** above par
**para** *prep* to, for; towards; compared to; (*antes de*) by; **para** + *inf* in order to + *inf;* about to + *inf;* **para con** towards; **para que** in order that, so that
**parabién** *m* congratulation
**parábola** *f* parable
**parabri•sa** *m* or **parabri•sas** *m* (*pl* **-sas**) windshield
**paracaí•das** *m* (*pl* **-das**) parachute; **lanzarse en paracaídas** to parachute; **sal-**

**varse en paracaídas** to parachute to safety
**paracaidismo** *m* parachute jumping; (sport) sky diving
**paracaidista** *mf* parachutist ‖ *m* paratrooper
**parachis•pas** *m* (*pl* **-pas**) spark arrester
**paracho•ques** *m* (*pl* **-ques**) bumper
**parada** *f* stop; end; stay; shutdown; (*en el juego*) stake; dam; (*para el ganado*) stall; stud farm; (*en la esgrima*) parry; (*tiro de caballerías de reemplazo*) relay; (mil) parade, dress parade, review; **parada de taxi** taxi stand
**paradero** *m* end; whereabouts; stopping place; (Am) wayside station
**para•do -da** *adj* slow, spiritless, witless; idle, unemployed; closed; (Am) proud, stiff ‖ *f* see **parada**
**paradoja** *f* paradox
**paradóji•co -ca** *adj* paradoxical
**parador** *m* inn, wayside inn; motel
**parafina** *f* paraffin
**paragol•pes** *m* (*pl* **-pes**) buffer, bumper
**para•guas** *m* (*pl* **-guas**) umbrella
**Paraguay, el** Paraguay
**paraguaya•no -na** or **paragua•yo -ya** *adj* & *mf* Paraguayan
**paragüero** *m* umbrella man; umbrella stand
**paraíso** *m* paradise
**paraje** *m* place, spot; state, condition
**paralela** *f* parallel, parallel line; **paralelas** parallel bars
**paralelizar** §60 *tr* to parallel, compare
**parale•lo -la** *adj* parallel ‖ *m* (geog) parallel ‖ *f* see **paralela**
**parráli•sis** *f* (*pl* **-sis**) paralysis
**paralíti•co -ca** *adj* & *mf* paralytic
**paralizar** §60 *tr* to paralyze ‖ *ref* to become paralyzed
**páramo** *m* high barren plain; bleak windy spot; (Bol, Col, Ecuad) cold drizzle
**paranie•ves** *m* (*pl* **-ves**) snow fence
**paraninfo** *m* assembly hall, auditorium
**paranoi•co -ca** *adj* & *mf* paranoiac
**parapeto** *m* parapet
**parar** *tr* to stop; to check; to change; to prepare; to put up, to stake; to parry; to order; to get, acquire; (*la atención*) to fix; (*la caza*) to point; (typ) to set ‖ *intr* to stop; (*en un hotel*) to put up; **parar en** to become; to run to, to run as far as ‖ *ref* to stop; to stop work; to turn, to become; (*el perro de muestra*) to point; (*el pelo*) to stand on end; (Am) to stand; **pararse en** to pay attention to
**pararra•yo** or **pararra•yos** *m* (*pl* **-yos**) (*barra metálica que sirve para preservar los edificios del rayo*) lightning rod; (*dispositivo que sirve para preservar una instalación eléctrica de la electricidad atmosférica o de las chispas que produce*) lightning arrester
**parasíti•co -ca** *adj* parasitic
**parási•to -ta** *adj* parasitic; (elec) stray ‖ *m* parasite; **parásitos atmosféricos** atmospherics, static
**parasol** *m* parasol
**parato•pes** *m* (*pl* **-pes**) bumper
**Parcas** *fpl* Fates
**parcela** *f* particle; plot of ground
**parcelar** *tr* to parcel, to divide into lots
**parcial** *adj* partial; partisan ‖ *mf* partisan
**par•co -ca** *adj* frugal, sparing; moderate
**parchar** *tr* (Am) to mend, patch
**parche** *m* plaster, sticking plaster; patch; drum; drumhead; daub, botch, splotch; **parche poroso** porous plaster
**pardal** *m* linnet; (coll) sly fellow
**pardiez** *interj* (coll) by Jove!
**pardillo** *m* linnet
**par•do -da** *adj* brown, drab; dark; cloudy; (*voz*) dull, flat; (*cerveza*) dark; (Am) mulatto ‖ *mf* (Am) mulatto ‖ *m* brown, drab; leopard
**pardus•co -ca** *adj* dark-brown, drabbish
**parea•do -da** *adj* rhymed ‖ *m* couplet
**parear** *tr* to pair; to match ‖ *ref* to pair off
**parecer** *m* opinion; look, mien, countenance ‖ *v* §22 *intr* to appear; to show up; to look, to seem; **me parece que . . .** I think that . . . ‖ *ref* to look alike, to resemble each other; **parecerse a** to look like
**pareci•do -da** *adj* like, similar; **bien parecido** good-looking; **parecido a** like, e.g., **esta casa es parecida a la otra** this house is like the other one; **parecidos** alike, e.g., **estas casas son parecidas** these houses are alike ‖ *m* similarity, resemblance, likeness; **tener un gran parecido** to be a good likeness
**pared** *f* wall; **dejar pegado a la pared** to nonplus; **paredes** house
**pareja** *f* pair, couple; dancing partner; **correr parejas** or **a las parejas** to be abreast, arrive together; to go together, match, be equal; **correr parejas con** to keep up with, to keep abreast of; **parejas** (*de naipes*) pair
**pareje•ro -ra** *adj* even, equal; (Am) servile, fawning; (Am) forward, overfamiliar ‖ *m* (Am) race horse
**pare•jo -ja** *adj* equal, like; even, smooth ‖ *m* (CAm) dancing partner ‖ *f* see **pareja**
**parentela** *f* kinsfolk, relations
**parentesco** *m* relationship; bond, tie
**paréntes•sis** *m* (*pl* **-sis**) parenthesis; break, interval
**parhilera** *f* ridgepole
**paria** *mf* pariah, outcast
**paridad** *f* par, parity; comparison
**parien•te -ta** *adj* related ‖ *mf* relative; (coll) spouse
**parihuela** *f* handbarrow; (*camilla*) stretcher
**parir** *tr* to bear, give birth to, bring forth ‖ *intr* to give birth; to come forth, to come to light; to talk well
**parisiense** *adj* & *mf* Parisian
**parlamentar** *intr* to talk, chat; to parley
**parlamento** *m* parliament; parley; speech; (theat) speech
**parlan•chín -china** *adj* (coll) jabbering ‖ *mf* (coll) chatterbox
**parlar** *intr* to speak with facility; to

chatter, talk too much; (*el loro*) to talk
**parle•ro -ra** *adj* loquacious, garrulous; gossipy; (*ave*) singing, song; (*ojos*) expressive; (*arroyo, fuente*) babbling
**parlotear** *intr* (coll) to prattle, jabber, chin
**parloteo** *m* (coll) jabber, prattle
**parnaso** *m* (*colección de poesías*) Parnassus; **el Parnaso** Parnassus, Mount Parnassus
**paro** *m* shutdown, work stoppage; lockout; titmouse; (*de dados*) (SAm) throw; **paro forzoso** layoff
**parodia** *f* parody, travesty
**parodiar** *tr* to parody, to travesty, to burlesque
**paroxíto•no -na** *adj & m* paroxytone
**parpadear** *intr* to blink, wink; to flicker
**parpadeo** *m* blinking, winking; flicker
**párpado** *m* eyelid
**parque** *m* park; parking; parking lot; **parque de atracciones** amusement park
**parqué** *m* floor, inlaid floor
**parqueadero** *m* (Col) parking lot
**parquear** *tr* to park
**parquímetro** *m* parking meter
**parra** *f* grapevine; earthen jug
**párrafo** *m* paragraph; (coll) chat
**parral** *m* grape arbor
**parranda** *f* (coll) spree, party; (Col) large number; **andar de parranda** (coll) to go out on a spree, go out to celebrate
**parricida** *mf* patricide, parricide
**parricidio** *m* patricide, parricide
**parrilla** *f* grill, gridiron, broiler; grate, grating; grillroom, grill; **asar a la parrilla** to broil
**párroco** *m* parish priest
**parroquia** *f* parish; parish church; customers, clientele
**parroquial** *adj* parochial
**parroquia•no -na** *mf* parishioner; customer
**parte** *m* dispatch, communiqué; **parte meteorológico** weather report || *f* part; share; party; side; direction; (*papel de un actor*) role; (law) party; **de un mes a esta parte** for about a month past; **en ninguna otra parte** nowhere else; **en ninguna parte** nowhere; **ir a la parte** to go shares; **la mayor parte** most, the majority; **parte del león** lion's share; **parte de por medio** (theat) bit part, walk-on; **partes** parts, gifts, talent; faction; parts, genitals; **por otra parte** in another direction; elsewhere; on the other hand; **por todas partes** everywhere; **salva sea la parte** excuse me for not mentioning where
**partea•guas** *m* (*pl* **-guas**) divide, ridge
**partear** *tr* to deliver
**parte•luz** *m* (*pl* **-luces**) mullion, sash bar
**Partenón** *m* Parthenon
**partera** *f* midwife
**partición** *f* partition, division
**participar** *tr* to notify, to inform; to give notice of || *intr* to participate; to partake
**participio** *m* participle
**partícula** *f* particle
**particular** *adj* particular; peculiar; private, personal || *m* particular; matter, subject; individual
**particulizar** **§60** *tr* to itemize || *ref* to stand out; to specialize
**partida** *f* departure; entry, item; certificate; party, group, band; band of guerrillas; game; (*de cartas*) hand; (*de tenis*) set; lot, shipment; (coll) behavior; **mala partida** (coll) mean trick; **partida de campo** picnic; **partida doble** (com) double entry; **partida sencilla** (com) single entry
**partida•rio -ria** or **partidista** *adj & mf* partisan
**parti•do -da** *adj* generous, open-handed || *m* (pol) party; decision; profit; advantage; step, measure; deal, agreement; protection, support; (*casamiento que elegir*) match; district, county; (sport) team; (sport) game, match; **partido de desempate** play-off; **tomar partido** to take a stand, to take sides || *f* see **partida**
**partir** *tr* to divide; to distribute; to share; to split, split open; to break, crack; (coll) to upset, disconcert || *intr* to start, depart, leave, set out; **a partir de** beginning with || *ref* to become divided; to crack, to split
**partisa•no -na** *mf* (mil) partisan
**partitura** *f* (mus) score
**parto** *m* childbirth, confinement; newborn child; offspring; **estar de parto** to be in labor, to be confined; **parto del ingenio** brain child
**parva** *f* light breakfast (*on fast days*); heap of unthreshed grain; heap, pile
**parvulista** *mf* kindergarten teacher
**párvu•lo -la** *adj* small, tiny; simple, innocent; humble || *mf* child, tot; (*niño*) kindergartner
**pasa** *f* raisin; (*del pelo de los negros*) kink; **pasa de Corinto** currant
**pasada** *f* passage; passing; **de pasada** in passing, hastily; **mala pasada** (coll) mean trick
**pasade•ro -ra** *adj* passable || *f* stepping stone; walkway, catwalk
**pasadizo** *m* passage, corridor, hallway, alley; catwalk
**pasa•do -da** *adj* past; gone by; overripe, spoiled; overdone; stale; burned out; antiquated; faded || *m* past; **pasados** ancestors || *f* see **pasada**
**pasa•dor -dora** *mf* smuggler || *m* door bolt; bolt, pin; hatpin; brooch; stickpin; safety pin; strainer
**pasaje** *m* passage; fare; fares; passengers; **cobrar el pasaje** to collect fares
**pasaje•ro -ra** *adj* passing, fleeting; (*camino, calle*) common, traveled || *mf* passenger; **pasajero colgado** straphanger; **pasajero no presentado** no-show
**pasamano** *m* lace trimming; (*baranda*) handrail; (naut) gangway
**pasamonta•ña** *m* or **pasamonta•ñas** *m* (*pl* **-ñas**) ski mask, storm hood
**pasaporte** *m* passport
**pasar** *m* livelihood || *tr* to pass; to

cross; to take across; to send, transfer, transmit; (*contrabando*) to slip in; to spend; to swallow; to excel; to overlook, stand for; to undergo, suffer; (*un libro*) to go through; (*una película*) to show; to dry in the sun; to tutor; to study with or under; **pasarlo** to get along; to live; (*dícese de la salud*) to be; **pasar por alto** to disregard; to omit, leave out, skip || *intr* to pass; to go; to pass away; to pass over; to happen; to last; to spread; to get along; to yield; to come in, e.g., **pase Vd.** come in; **pasar de** to go beyond, to exceed; to go above; to be more than; **pasar por** to pass by, down, through, over, etc.; to pass as, pass for; to stop or call at; **pasar sin** to do without || *ref* to pass; to go; to excel; to pass over; to get along; to pass away; to take an examination; to leak; to go too far; to become overripe, become overcooked; to rot; to melt; to burn out; (*una llave, un tornillo*) to not fit, to be loose; to forget; **pasarse por** to stop or call at; **pasarse sin** to do without

**pasarela** *f* footbridge; catwalk, gangplank

**pasatiempo** *m* pastime

**pascua** *f* Passover; Easter; Twelfthnight; Pentecost; Christmas; **dar las pascuas** to wish a Happy New Year; **estar como una pascua** or **unas pascuas** (coll) to be bubbling over with joy; **¡Felices Pascuas!** Merry Christmas!; **Pascua de flores** Easter; **Pascua del Espíritu Santo** Pentecost; **Pascua de Navidad** Christmas; **Pascua de Resurrección** or **Pascua florida** Easter; **Pascuas navideñas** Christmas

**pase** *m* (*permiso; billete gratuito; movimiento de las manos del mesmerista, el torero*) pass; (*en la esgrima*) feint; **pase de cortesía** complimentary ticket

**paseante** *adj* strolling || *mf* stroller

**pasear** *tr* to walk; to promenade, show off || *intr* to take a walk; to go for a ride || *ref* to take a walk; to go for a ride; to wander, ramble; to take it easy

**paseíllo** *m* processional entrance of bullfighters

**paseo** *m* walk, stroll, promenade; ride; drive; avenue; **dar un paseo** to take a walk; to take a ride; **enviar a paseo** (coll) to send on his way, to dismiss without ceremony; **paseo de caballos** bridle path; **paseo de la cuadrilla** processional entrance of the bullfighters

**pasillo** *m* short step; passage, corridor; (theat) short piece, sketch

**pasión** *f* passion

**pasi•vo -va** *adj* passive; (*pensión*) retirement || *m* liabilities; debit side

**pasmar** *tr* to chill; to frostbite; to stun, benumb; to dumbfound, astound || *ref* to chill; to become frostbitten; to be astounded; to get lockjaw; (*los colores*) to become dull or flat

**pasmo** *m* cold; lockjaw, tetanus; astonishment; wonder, prodigy

**pasmo•so -sa** *adj* astounding; awesome

**paso** *m* step; pace; (*de la escalera*) step; gait; walk; passing; passage; step, measure, démarche; pass, permit; strait; footstep, footprint; incident, happening; (*de hélice, tornillo*) pitch; (elec) pitch; (rad) stage; (theat) short piece, sketch, skit; **al paso** in passing, on the way; **al paso que** at the rate that; (*a la vez que, mientras*) while, whereas; **ceder el paso** to make way; to keep clear; **de paso** in passing; at the same time; **paso a nivel** grade crossing; **paso de ganado** cattle crossing; **paso de ganso** goose step

**paspa** *f* (SAm) crack in the lips

**pasquín** *m* lampoon

**pasquinar** *tr* to lampoon

**pasta** *f* paste, dough, pie crust, soup paste; mash; (*para hacer papel*) pulp; cardboard; board binding; (*de un diente*) filling; (*dinero*) (coll) dough; **pasta dentrífica** tooth paste; **pasta española** marbled leather binding, tree calf; **pastas** noodles, macaroni, spaghetti, etc.; **pasta seca** cookie

**pastar** *tr & intr* to graze

**pastel** *m* pie; pastry roll; pastel; settlement, pacification; cheat, trick; (typ) pi; (typ) smear; (coll) plot, deal; **pastel de cumpleaños** birthday cake

**pastelería** *f* pastry; pastry shop

**pastele•ro -ra** *mf* pastry cook

**pastelillo** *m* tart, cake; (*de mantequilla*) pat

**pasterizar** §60 *tr* to pasteurize

**pastilla** *f* tablet, lozenge, drop; (*pequeña masa pastosa*) dab; (*de jabón, chocolate, etc.*) cake

**pasto** *m* pasture; grass; food, nourishment; **a pasto** to excess; in abundance; **a todo pasto** freely, without restriction; **de pasto** ordinary, everyday

**pastor** *m* shepherd; pastor

**pastora** *f* shepherdess

**pastoral** *adj & f* pastoral

**pastorear** *tr* (*a las ovejas o los fieles*) to shepherd; (Am) to lie in ambush for; (Am) to spoil, pamper; (Arg, Urug) to court

**pasto•so -sa** *adj* pasty, doughy; (*voz*) mellow; (Arg, Chile) grassy

**pastura** *f* pasture; fodder

**pasu•do -da** *adj* (Am) kinky

**pata** *f* paw, foot, leg; (*de un mueble*) leg; duck; **a cuatro patas** (coll) on all fours; **estirar la pata** (coll) to kick the bucket; **meter la pata** (coll) to butt in, to put one's foot in it; **pata de gallo** crow's-foot; (coll) blunder; (coll) piece of nonsense; **pata de palo** peg leg, wooden leg; **pata galana** (coll) game leg; (coll) lame person; **patas arriba** (coll) on one's back, upside down; (coll) topsy-turvy

**patada** *f* kick; stamp, stamping; (coll) step; (coll) footstep, track; **en dos patadas** (Am) in a jiffy

**patalear** *intr* to kick; to stamp the feet

**pataleta** *f* (coll) fit; (coll) **feigned fit** or convulsion; (dial) tantrum
**patán** *m* (coll) churl, boor, lout; (coll) peasant
**pataplún** *interj* kerplunk!
**patata** *f* potato
**patear** *tr* (coll) to kick; (coll) to trample on || *intr* (coll) to stamp one's foot; (coll) to bustle around; (Am) to kick
**patentar** *tr* to patent
**patente** *adj* patent, clear, evident || *f* grant, privilege, warrant; patent; **de patente** (Chile) excellent, first-class; **patente de circulación** owner's license; **patente de invención** patent; **patente de sanidad** bill of health
**paternal** *adj* paternal, fatherly
**paternidad** *f* paternity, fatherhood; **paternidad literaria** authorship
**pater·no -na** *adj* paternal
**pateta** *m* (coll) the devil; (coll) cripple
**patéti·co -ca** *adj* pathetic
**patetismo** *m* pathos
**patibula·rio -ria** *adj* hair-raising
**patíbulo** *m* scaffold
**patiesteva·do -da** *adj* bowlegged
**patilla** *f* small paw or foot; pocket flap; (naut) compass; (Am) watermelon; **patillas** sideburns, side whiskers
**patín** *m* small patio; skate; skid, slide, runner; (*ave marina*) petrel; **patín de cuchilla** or **de hielo** ice skate; **patín de ruedas** roller skate
**patinadero** *m* skating rink
**patina·dor -dora** *mf* skater
**patinaje** *m* skating; skidding; **patinaje artístico** figure skating; **patinaje de fantasía** fancy skating; **patinaje de figura** figure skating
**patinar** *intr* to skate; to skid; to slip
**patinazo** *m* skid; slip; (coll) slip, blunder
**patinete** *m* scooter
**patio** *m* patio, court, yard; campus; (rr) yard, switchyard; **patio de recreo** playground
**patituer·to -ta** *adj* crooked-legged; (coll) crooked, lopsided
**patizam·bo -ba** *adj* knock-kneed
**pato** *m* duck, drake; **pagar el pato** (coll) to be the goat; **pato de flojel** eider duck
**patochada** *f* (coll) blunder, stupidity
**patología** *f* pathology
**patota** *f* (Arg, Urug) teen-age gang
**patraña** *f* fake, humbug, hoax
**patria** *f* country; mother country, fatherland, native land; birthplace; (*p.ej., de las artes*) home; **patria chica** native heath
**patriarca** *m* patriarch
**patri·cio -cia** *adj & mf* patrician
**patrimonio** *m* patrimony
**pa·trio -tria** *adj* native, home; paternal || *f* see **patria**
**patriota** *mf* patriot
**patrióti·co -ca** *adj* patriotic
**patriotismo** *m* patriotism
**patrocinar** *tr* to sponsor, patronize
**patrocinio** *m* sponsorship
**patrón** *m* sponsor, protector; patron saint; patron; landlord; owner, master; boss, foreman; host; (*de un barco*) skipper; pattern; standard; **patrón oro** gold standard; **patrón picado** stencil
**patrona** *f* patroness; landlady; owner, mistress; hostess
**patronal** *adj* management, employers'
**patronato** *m* employers' association; foundation; board of trustees; patronage
**patronear** *tr* to skipper
**patro·no -na** *mf* sponsor, protector; employer || *m* patron; landlord; boss, foreman; lord of the manor; **los patronos** the management || *f* see **patrona**
**patrulla** *f* patrol; gang, band
**patrullar** *tr & intr* to patrol
**paulati·no -na** *adj* slow, gradual
**Paulo** *m* Paul
**pausa** *f* pause; slowness, delay; (mus) rest
**pausa·do -da** *adj* slow, calm, deliberate || **pausado** *adv* slowly, calmly
**pausar** *tr & intr* to slow down
**pauta** *f* ruler; guide lines; guideline, rule, guide, standard, model
**pava** *f* turkey hen; **pelar la pava** (coll) to make love at a window
**pavesa** *f* ember, cinder, spark
**pavimentar** *tr* to pave
**pavimento** *m* pavement
**pavo** *m* turkey; turkey cock; **comer pavo** (coll) to be a wallflower; **pavo real** peacock
**pavón** *m* bluing; peacock
**pavonar** *tr* to blue
**pavonear** *intr & ref* to strut, swagger
**pavor** *m* fear, terror, dread
**pavoro·so -sa** *adj* frightful, dreadful
**payador** *m* (SAm) gaucho minstrel
**payasada** *f* clownishness, clownish remark
**payaso** *m* clown; laughingstock
**paz** *f* (*pl* **paces**) peace; peacefulness; **dejar en paz** to leave alone, stop pestering; **estar en paz** to be even; to be quits; **hacer las paces con** to make peace with, to come to terms with; **salir en paz** to break even
**pazgua·to -ta** *adj* simple, doltish || *mf* simpleton, dolt
**pazpuerca** *f* (coll) slut, slattern
**P.D.** *abbr* **posdata**
**peaje** *m* toll
**peatón** *m* pedestrian; rural postman
**pebete** *m* punk, joss stick; fuse; (*cosa hedionda*) (coll) stinker
**peca** *f* freckle
**pecado** *m* sin
**peca·dor -dora** *adj* sinning, sinful || *mf* sinner
**pecamino·so -sa** *adj* sinful
**pecar** §73 *intr* to sin; **pecar de** to be too, e.g., **pecar de confiado** to be too trusting
**pecera** *f* fish globe, fish bowl
**pecino·so -sa** *adj* slimy
**pecio** *m* flotsam
**peciolo** *m* leafstalk
**pécora** *f* head of sheep; **buena pécora** or **mala pécora** (coll) schemer, scheming woman

**peco•so -sa** *adj* freckly, freckle-faced
**peculado** *m* embezzlement, peculation
**peculiar** *adj* peculiar
**pecunia•rio -ria** *adj* pecuniary
**pechada** *f* (Am) bump or push with the chest; (Am) tossing an animal (*with a bump of horse's chest*); (Am) bumping contest between two horsemen
**pechar** *tr* to pay as a tax; to fulfill; to take on; (Am) to drive one's horse against; (Am) to bump with the chest; (Am) to strike for a loan || *ref* (*dos jinetes*) (Am) to vie in a bumping contest
**pechera** *f* shirt front, shirt bosom; chest protector; (*del delantal*) bib; breast strap; (coll) bosom; **pechera postiza** dickey
**pecho** *m* chest; breast, bosom; heart, courage; **dar el pecho** to nurse, to suckle; (coll) to face it out; **de dos pechos** double-breasted; **de un solo pecho** single-breasted; **echar el pecho al agua** (coll) to put one's shoulder to the wheel; (coll) to speak out; **en pechos de camisa** (Am) in shirt sleeves; **tomar a pecho** to take to heart; **¡pecho al agua!** take heart!, put your shoulder to the wheel!
**pechuga** *f* (*del ave*) breast; (coll) breast, bosom; (coll) slope, hill; (Am) brass, cheek; (Am) treachery, perfidy
**pechu•gón -gona** *adj* (coll) big-chested; (Am) brazen || *mf* (Am) sponger || *m* slap or blow on the chest; fall on the chest
**pedagogía** *f* pedagogy
**pedal** *m* pedal, treadle
**pedalear** *intr* to pedal
**pedante** *adj* pedantic || *mf* pedant
**pedantería** *f* pedantry
**pedantes•co -ca** *adj* pedantic
**pedantismo** *m* pedantry
**pedazo** *m* piece; **hacer pedazos** (coll) to break to pieces; **hacerse pedazos** (coll) to fall to pieces; (coll) to strain, to wear oneself out; **pedazo de alcornoque, de animal** or **de bruto** (coll) dolt, imbecile, good-for-nothing; **pedazo del alma, de las entrañas** or **del corazón** (*niño*) (coll) darling, apple of one's eye; **pedazo de pan** (*pequeña cantidad*) crumb; (*precio bajo*) (coll) song
**pedernal** *m* flint; flintiness; flint-hearted person
**pedestal** *m* pedestal
**pedestre** *adj* pedestrian
**pedestrismo** *m* pedestrianism; walking; foot racing; cross-country racing
**pediatría** *f* pediatrics
**pedido** *m* request; (*encargo de mercancías*) order
**pedigüe•ño -ña** *adj* insistent, demanding, bothersome
**pedir §50** *tr* to ask, to ask for; to request; to demand, require; to need; to ask for the hand of; (*mercancías*) to order; (gram) to govern; **pedir prestado a** to borrow from || *intr* to ask; to beg; to bring suit; **a pedir de boca** opportunely; as desired
**pedorre•ro -ra** *adj* flatulent || *f* flatulence; (orn) tody; **pedorreras** tights
**pedrada** *f* stoning; hit or blow with a stone; (coll) hint, taunt
**pedregal** *m* rocky ground; pile of rocks
**pedrego•so -sa** *adj* stony, rocky; suffering from gallstones || *mf* sufferer from gallstones
**pedrejón** *m* boulder
**pedrera** *f* quarry, stone quarry
**pedrería** *f* precious stones, jewelry
**Pedro** *m* Peter
**pedrusco** *m* boulder
**pedúnculo** *m* stem, stalk
**peer §43** *intr & ref* to break wind
**pega** *f* sticking; pitch varnish; drubbing; (*en un examen*) catch question; (coll) trick, joke; (W-I) work, jobs; **de pega** (coll) fake
**pegadi•zo -za** *adj* sticky; catching, contagious; sponging; fake, imitation
**pegajo•so -sa** *adj* sticky; contagious; tempting; (coll) soft, gentle; (coll) mushy
**pegar §44** *tr* to stick, to paste; to fasten, attach, tie; (*carteles*) to post; (*fuego*) to set; (*una enfermedad*) to transmit; (*un botón*) to sew on; (*un grito*) to let out; (*un salto*) to take; (*un golpe, una bofetada*) to let go; to beat; **no pegar el ojo** to not sleep a wink || *intr* to stick, to catch; to take root, take hold; to cling; to join; to fit, to match; to be fitting; to pass, be accepted; to beat; to knock || *ref* to stick, to catch; to take root, take hold; to hang on, stick around; (*una enfermedad*) to be catching; **pegársela a uno** (coll) to make a fool of someone
**pegotear** *intr* (coll) to hang around, to sponge
**peina•do -da** *adj* groomed; effeminate || *m* hairdo, coiffure; (*manera de componer el pelo*) hairstyle; **peinado al agua** finger wave
**peina•dor -dora** *mf* hairdresser || *m* wrapper, dressing gown
**peinar** *tr* to comb || *ref* to comb oneself, comb one's hair
**peine** *m* comb; (coll) sly fellow
**peineta** *f* back comb
**pelada** *f* pelt, sheepskin
**peladilla** *f* sugar almond; small pebble
**peladillo** *m* clingstone peach
**pela•do -da** *adj* bare; bald; barren; penniless; (*decena, centena, etc.*) even || *m* raggedy fellow; (W-I) haircut || *f* see **pelada**
**pelafus•tán -tana** *mf* (coll) derelict, good-for-nothing
**pelaga•tos** *m* (*pl* **-tos**) (coll) wretch, ragamuffin
**pelaje** *m* coat, fur; (*especie, calidad*) (coll) sort, stripe
**pelar** *tr* (*pelo*) to cut; (*pelo, plumas*) to pluck, pull out; to peel, skin, husk, hull, shell; (*los dientes*) to show; (*en el juego*) (coll) to clean out; (Am) to beat, thrash || *ref* to peel off; to lose one's hair; to get a haircut; (Am) to clear out, make a getaway; **pelárselas por** (coll) to crave; (coll) to crave to

**peldaño** *m* step
**pelea** *f* fight; quarrel; struggle; **pelea de gallos** cockfight
**pelear** *intr* to fight; to quarrel; to struggle || *ref* to fight, fight each other
**pele•ón -ona** *adj* (coll) pugnacious, quarrelsome; (*vino*) (coll) cheap, ordinary || *mf* (coll) quarrelsome person || *m* (coll) cheap wine || *f* row, scuffle, fracas
**peletería** *f* furriery; fur shop; (Cuba) shoe store
**pelete•ro -ra** *mf* furrier; (Cuba) shoe dealer
**pellagu•do -da** *adj* furry, long-haired; (coll) arduous, ticklish
**película** *f* film; motion picture; **película de dibujos** animated cartoon; **película del Oeste** western; **película sonora** sound film
**pelicule•ro -ra** *adj* moving-picture || *mf* scenario writer || *m* movie actor || *f* movie actress
**peligrar** *intr* to be in danger
**peligro** *m* danger, peril, risk; **ponerse en peligro de paz** to be alerted for war
**peligro•so -sa** *adj* dangerous
**pelillo** *m* (coll) trifle; **echar pelillos a la mar** (coll) to bury the hatchet; **no pararse en pelillos** (coll) to not bother about trifles, to pay no attention to small matters; **no tener pelillos en la lengua** (coll) to speak right out
**pelirro•jo -ja** *adj* red-haired, redheaded || *mf* redhead
**pelo** *m* hair; (*en las frutas y el cuerpo humano*) down; (*del paño*) nap; (*de la madera*) grain; (*de un animal*) coat; (*en las piedras preciosas*) flaw; (*del caballo*) color; (*en el billar*) kiss; (*del reloj*) hairspring; hair trigger; fiber, filament; raw silk; **al pelo** with the hair, with the nap; (coll) perfectly, to the point; **con todos sus pelos y señales** chapter and verse; **en pelo** bareback; **escapar por un pelo** to escape by a hairbreadth, to have a narrow escape; **no tener pelos en la lengua** (coll) to be outspoken, to not mince words; **ponerle a uno los pelos de punta** to make one's hair stand on end; **tomar el pelo a** (coll) to make fun of, make a fool of; **venir a pelo** to come in handy
**pe•lón -lona** *adj* bald, hairless; (coll) dull, stupid; (coll) penniless
**Pélope** *m* Pelops
**peloponense** *adj & mf* Peloponnesian
**Peloponeso** *m* Peloponnesus
**pelo•so -sa** *adj* hairy
**pelota** *f* ball; ball game; handball; **en pelota** stripped; stark-naked; **pelota acuática** water polo; **pelota rodada** (baseball) grounder; **pelota vasca** pelota, jai alai
**pelotari** *mf* pelota player
**pelotear** *intr* to knock a ball around; to wrangle, to argue
**pelotera** *f* (coll) row, brawl
**pelotón** *m* large ball; gang, crowd; platoon; **pelotón de fusilamiento** firing squad; **pelotón de los torpes** awkward squad
**peltre** *m* pewter
**peluca** *f* wig
**pelu•do -da** *adj* hairy, furry; bushy
**peluquería** *f* hairdresser's, barbershop
**peluque•ro -ra** *mf* hairdresser, barber; wigmaker
**pelusa** *f* down; lint, fuzz; nap; (coll) jealousy, envy
**pellejo** *m* skin; pelt, rawhide; peel, rind; wineskin; (*la vida de uno*) (coll) hide, skin; (coll) sot, drunkard; **dar, dejar or perder el pellejo** (coll) to die
**pellizcar** §73 to pinch; to nip; to take a pinch of || *ref* (coll) to long, to pine
**pellizco** *m* pinch; nip; bit, pinch
**pena** *f* punishment; penalty; pain, hardship, toil; sorrow, grief; effort, trouble; **a duras penas** hardly, with great difficulty; **de pena** of a broken heart; **¡qué pena!** what a pity!; **so pena de** on pain of, under penalty of; **valer la pena** to be worth while (to)
**penacho** *m* crest; tuft, plume; arrogance; (bot) tassel
**pena•do -da** *adj* afflicted, grieved; difficult || *mf* convict
**penalidad** *f* trouble, hardship; (law) penalty
**penar** *tr* to penalize; to punish || *intr* to suffer; to linger; **penar por** to pine for, long for || *ref* to grieve
**penca** *f* pulpy leaf; cowhide; **coger una penca** (Am) to get a jag on
**penco** *m* nag, jade; (Am) boor
**pendejo** *m* pubes; (coll) coward
**pendencia** *f* dispute, quarrel, fight; pending litigation
**pendencie•ro -ra** *adj* quarrelsome || *mf* wrangler
**pender** *intr* to hang, dangle; to depend; to be pending
**pendiente** *adj* pendent, hanging, dangling; pending; under way; expecting; **estar pendiente de** (*las palabras de una persona*) to hang on; to depend on; to be in the process of || *m* earring, pendant; watch chain || *f* slope, grade; dip, pitch
**péndola** *f* feather; pendulum; clock; pen, quill; queen post
**pendolón** *m* king post
**pendón** *m* banner, standard, pennon
**péndulo** *m* pendulum; clock
**penetrar** *tr* to penetrate; to pierce; to grasp, fathom || *intr* to penetrate || *ref* to grasp, fathom; to realize; to become convinced
**penicilina** *f* penicilin
**península** *f* peninsula
**peninsular** *adj & mf* peninsular; (*ibero*) Peninsular
**penique** *m* penny
**penitencia** *f* penitence; penance; **hacer penitencia** to do penance; to eat sparingly; to take potluck
**penitente** *adj & mf* penitent
**penol** *m* (naut) yardarm
**peno•so -sa** *adj* arduous, difficult; suffering; (coll) conceited; (Am) shy

**pensa•dor -dora** *adj* thinking || *mf* thinker
**pensamiento** *m* thought; (*planta y flor*) pansy
**pensar** §2 *tr* to think; to think over; (*un naipe, un número, etc.*) to think of; to intend to; **pensar de** to think of, e.g., **¿qué piensa Vd. de este libro?** what do you think of this book? || *intr* to think; **pensar en** (*dirigir sus pensamientos a*) to think of (*to turn one's thoughts to*)
**pensati•vo -va** *adj* pensive, thoughtful
**pensión** *f* pension; annuity; allowance; boardinghouse; (*para ampliar estudios*) fellowship; **pensión completa** board and lodging
**pensionar** *tr* to pension
**pensionista** *mf* pensioner; boarder; boarding-school pupil; **medio pensionista** day boarder
**pentagrama** *m* staff, musical staff
**Pentecostés, el** Pentecost
**penúlti•mo -ma** *adj* penultimate; next to last || *f* penult
**penumbra** *f* penumbra; semidarkness, half-light
**penuria** *f* shortage
**peña** *f* rock, boulder; cliff; club, group, circle
**peñasco** *m* pinnacle; crag
**peñasco•so -sa** *adj* rocky, craggy
**peñón** *m* rock, spire; **peñón de Gibraltar** rock of Gibraltar
**peón** *m* laborer; pedestrian; foot soldier; (*en el ajedrez*) pawn; (*en las damas*) man; top, peg top; spindle, axle; (taur) attendant; (Am) farm hand; **peón de albañil** or **de mano** hod carrier
**peor** *adj & adv* worse; worst
**pepa** *f* (*de la manzana*) (Col) seed; (*del durazno*) (Arg) stone; (*canica*) (Arg) marble; (Col) lie, cheat, trick
**Pepe** *m* Joe
**pepinillo** *m* gherkin
**pepino** *m* cucumber
**pepita** *f* seed, pip; nugget; (vet) pip
**peque** *m* tot
**pequén** *m* (Chile) burrowing owl
**pequeñez** *f* (*pl* **-ñeces**) smallness; infancy; trifle
**peque•ño -ña** *adj* little, small; young; low, humble
**Pequín** *m* Peking
**pequi•nés -nesa** *adj & mf* Pekinese
**pera** *f* pear; goatee; cinch, sinecure; pear-shaped bulb; pear-shaped switch
**peral** *m* pear tree
**perca** *f* (ichth) perch
**percance** *m* mischance, misfortune; **percances** perquisites
**percatar** *ref* — **percatarse de** to be aware of; to beware of, guard against
**percebe** *m* barnacle; (coll) fool, sap
**percepción** *f* perception; collection
**percibir** *tr* to perceive; to collect
**percudir** *tr* to tarnish, to dull; to spread through
**percha** *f* perch, pole, roost; clothes tree; coat hanger; coat hook; barber pole
**perchero** *m* rack, clothes rack, clothes hanger
**perde•dor -dora** *adj* losing || *mf* loser
**perder** §51 *tr* to lose; to waste, squander; (*un tren, una ocasión*) to miss; (*una asignatura*) to flunk; to ruin; to spoil || *intr* to lose; to fade || *ref* to get lost; to miscarry; to sink; to become ruined; to spoil; to go to the dogs
**perdición** *f* perdition; loss; outrage; ruination
**pérdida** *f* loss; waste; ruination; **no tener pérdida** (coll) to be easy to find
**perdi•do -da** *adj* (*bala*) stray, wild; (*manga*) wide, loose; fruitless; (*horas*) off, spare, idle; distracted; inveterate; madly in love || *m* profligate, rake
**perdido•so -sa** *adj* unlucky; easily lost
**perdigón** *m* young partridge; (coll) profligate; (coll) heavy loser; (*alumno*) (coll) failure; **perdigones** (*granos de plomo*) shot; **perdigón zorrero** buckshot
**per•diz** *f* (*pl* **-dices**) partridge
**perdón** *m* pardon, forgiveness; **con perdón** by your leave
**perdonable** *adj* pardonable
**perdonar** *tr* to pardon, forgive, excuse; **no perdonar** to not miss, to not omit
**perdula•rio -ria** *adj* careless, sloppy; incorrigible, vicious || *mf* good-for-nothing, profligate
**perdurable** *adj* long-lasting; everlasting
**perdurar** *intr* to last, last a long time, survive
**perecede•ro -ra** *adj* perishable; mortal || *m* (coll) extreme want
**perecer** §22 *intr* to perish; to suffer; to be in great want || *ref* to pine; **perecerse por** to be dying for; (*una mujer*) to be mad about
**peregrinación** *f* peregrination; pilgrimage
**peregri•no -na** *adj* wandering, traveling; foreign; rare, strange; beautiful; mortal; (*ave*) migratory || *mf* pilgrim
**perejil** *m* parsley; (coll) frippery
**perenne** *adj* perennial
**pereza** *f* laziness; slowness
**perezo•so -sa** *adj* lazy; slow, dull, heavy || *mf* lazybones; sleepyhead || *m* (zool) sloth
**perfección** *f* perfection
**perfeccionar** *tr* to perfect, to improve
**perfec•to -ta** *adj & m* perfect
**perfidia** *f* perfidy
**pérfi•do -da** *adj* perfidious
**perfil** *m* profile; side view; cross section; thin stroke; outline, sketch; **perfil aerodinámico** streamlining; **perfiles** finishing touches; courtesies
**perfila•do -da** *adj* (*cara*) long and thin; (*nariz*) well-formed; (*facciones*) delicate; streamlined
**perfilar** *tr* to profile, outline; to perfect, polish, finish || *ref* to be outlined; to show one's profile, to stand sidewise; to stand out; (coll) to dress up
**perfora•dor -dora** *adj* perforating; drilling || *f* pneumatic drill, rock drill

**perforar** *tr* to perforate; to drill, to bore; to puncture; (*una tarjeta*) to punch
**perfumar** *tr* to perfume
**perfume** *m* perfume
**pergamino** *m* parchment
**pericia** *f* skill, expertness
**periclitar** *intr* to be in jeopardy, to be shaky
**perico** *m* (*pelo postizo*) periwig; parakeet; (slang) chamber pot; **perico entre ellas** (coll) lady's man
**periferia** *f* periphery; surroundings
**perifollos** *mpl* finery, frippery, chiffons
**perilla** *f* pear-shaped ornament; goatee; knob, doorknob; (*del arzón*) pommel; (*de la oreja*) lobe; **de perilla** (coll) apropos, to the point
**periodísti•co -ca** *adj* newspaper, journalistic
**periódi•co -ca** *adj* periodic ‖ *m* newspaper; periodical
**periodismo** *m* journalism
**periodista** *mf* journalist ‖ *m* newspaperman ‖ *f* newspaperwoman
**período** *m* period; compound sentence; (phys) cycle; **período lectivo** (*en la escuela*) term
**peripues•to -ta** *adj* (coll) dudish, all spruced up, sporty
**periquete** *m* (coll) jiffy; **en un periquete** (coll) in a jiffy
**periquito** *m* parakeet; **periquito de Australia** budgerigar
**periscopio** *m* periscope
**peri•to -ta** *adj* skilled, skillful; expert ‖ *m* expert
**perjudicar** §73 *tr* to damage, impair, hurt, prejudice
**perjudicial** *adj* harmful, injurious, detrimental, prejudicial
**perjuicio** *m* harm, injury, damage, prejudice; **en perjuicio de** to the detriment of
**perjurar** *intr* to commit perjury; to swear, be profane ‖ *ref* to commit perjury; to perjure oneself
**perjurio** *m* perjury
**perla** *f* pearl; **de perlas** perfectly
**perlesía** *f* palsy
**permanecer** §22 *intr* to stay, to remain
**permanencia** *f* permanence; stay, sojourn
**permanente** *adj* permanent ‖ *f* permanent wave
**permiso** *m* permission; permit; time off; (*en el monedaje*) tolerance; leave; **con permiso** excuse me; **permiso de circulación** owner's license; **permiso de conducir** driver's license
**permitir** *tr* to permit, to allow ‖ *ref* to be permitted; **no se permite fumar** no smoking
**permutar** *tr* to interchange; to barter; to permute
**pernear** *intr* to kick; (coll) to hustle; (coll) to fuss, fret
**pernera** *f* trouser leg
**pernicio•so -sa** *adj* pernicious
**pernil** *m* trouser leg; (*anca y muslo*) ham
**perno** *m* bolt; **perno con anillo** ringbolt; **perno roscado** screw bolt
**pernoctar** *intr* to spend the night
**pero** *conj* but, yet ‖ *m* (coll) but; (coll) fault, defect; **poner pero a** (coll) to find fault with
**perogrullada** *f* (coll) platitude, inanity
**peroración** *f* peroration; (coll) harangue
**perorar** *intr* to perorate; (coll) to orate
**peróxido** *m* peroxide; **peróxido de hidrógeno** hydrogen peroxide
**perpendicular** *adj* & *f* perpendicular
**perpetrar** *tr* to perpetrate
**perpetuar** §21 *tr* to perpetuate
**perpe•tuo -tua** *adj* perpetual; life
**perplejidad** *f* perplexity; worry, anxiety
**perple•jo -ja** *adj* perplexed; worried, anxious; baffling, perplexing
**perra** *f* bitch; tantrum; drunkenness
**perrada** *f* pack of dogs; (coll) dirty trick
**perrera** *f* kennel, doghouse; tantrum; toil, drudgery
**perro** *m* dog; **el perro del hortelano** dog in the manger; **perro caliente** (slang) hot dog; **perro cobrador** retriever; **perro de aguas** spaniel; **perro de lanas** poodle; **perro de muestra** pointer; **perro faldero** lap dog; **perro marino** dogfish, shark; **perro raposero** foxhound; **perro viejo** (coll) wise old owl
**perro-lazarillo** *m* (*pl* **perros-lazarillos**) Seeing Eye dog
**persa** *adj* & *mf* Persian
**persecución** *f* persecution; pursuit; annoyance, harassment
**perseguir** §67 *tr* to persecute; to pursue; to annoy, harass
**perseverar** *intr* to persevere
**persiana** *f* slatted shutter; flowered silk; louver; Venetian blind; **persiana del radiador** (aut) louver
**persistir** *intr* to persist
**persona** *f* person; personage; **persona desplazada** displaced person; **personas** people; **por persona** per capita
**personaje** *m* personage; (theat) character; person of importance
**personal** *adj* personal ‖ *m* personnel, staff, force
**personalidad** *f* personality
**personificar** §73 *tr* to personify
**perspectiva** *f* perspective; outlook, prospect; appearance
**perspi•caz** *adj* (*pl* **-caces**) perspicacious, discerning; keen-sighted
**persuadir** *tr* to persuade
**persuasión** *f* persuasion
**pertenecer** §22 *intr* to belong; to pertain ‖ *ref* to be independent, be free
**perteneciente** *adj* pertaining
**pértiga** *f* pole, rod, staff
**perti•naz** *adj* (*pl* **-naces**) pertinacious; (*dolor de cabeza*) persistent
**pertinente** *adj* pertinent, relevant
**pertrechos** *mpl* supplies, provisions, equipment; tools; **pertrechos de guerra** ordnance
**perturbar** *tr* to perturb; to disturb; to upset, disconcert; to confuse, interrupt
**Perú, el** Peru
**perua•no -na** *adj* & *mf* Peruvian
**perversidad** *f* perversity

**perversión** *f* perversion
**perver•so -sa** *adj* perverse; wicked, depraved || *mf* profligate
**perverti•do -da** *mf* pervert
**pervertir** §68 *tr* to pervert || *ref* to become perverted; to go to the bad
**pesa** *f* weight
**pesacar•tas** *m* (*pl* **-tas**) letter scales
**pesadez** *f* heaviness; slowness; tiresomeness; harshness; (phys) gravity
**pesadilla** *f* nightmare
**pesa•do -da** *adj* heavy; slow; tiresome; harsh; boring
**pesadumbre** *f* sorrow, grief; trouble; weight, heaviness
**pesaje** *m* weighing; (sport) weigh-in
**pésame** *m* condolence; **dar el pésame a** to extend one's sympathy to
**pesantez** *f* (phys) gravity
**pesar** *m* sorrow, regret; **a pesar de** in spite of || *tr* to weigh; to make sorry || *intr* to weigh; to be heavy; to cause regret, cause sorrow
**pesaro•so -sa** *adj* sorrowful, regretful
**pesca** *f* fishing; catch; **ir de pesca** to go fishing; **pesca de bajura** off-shore fishing; **pesca de gran altura** deep-sea fishing
**pescadería** *f* fish market; fish store; fish stand
**pescade•ro -ra** *mf* fish dealer, fishmonger
**pescado** *m* fish (*that has been caught*)
**pesca•dor -dora** *adj* fishing || *m* fisherman || *f* fisherwoman, fishwife
**pescante** *m* coach box; (*de una grúa*) jib; (aut) front seat; (naut) davit; (theat) trap door
**pescar** §73 *tr* to fish; to fish for; to fish out; (*peces*) to catch; (coll) to manage to get || *intr* to fish
**pescozón** *m* slap on the neck or head
**pescuezo** *m* neck
**pesebre** *m* crib, rack, manger; (Am) crèche
**pesimismo** *m* pessimism
**pesimista** *adj* pessimistic || *mf* pessimist
**pési•mo -ma** *adj* very bad, abominable
**peso** *m* weight; scale, balance; burden, load; judgment, good sense; (*unidad monetaria*) (Am) peso; **caerse de su peso** to be self-evident; **llevar el peso de la batalla** to bear the brunt of the battle
**pespuntar** *tr & intr* to backstitch
**pespunte** *m* backstitch
**pesquera** *f* fishery; fishing grounds; (*presa para detener los peces*) weir
**pesquería** *f* fishing; fishery
**pesque•ro -ra** *adj* fishing || *m* fishing boat || *f* see **pesquera**
**pesquis** *m* acumen, keenness
**pesquisa** *m* (Arg) detective || *f* inquiry, investigation
**pesquisar** *tr* to investigate, inquire into
**pestaña** *f* eyelash; flange; fringe, edging; index tab
**pestañear** *intr* to wink, blink; **sin pestañear** without batting an eye
**peste** *f* pest, plague; epidemic; stink, stench; (coll) abundance; (Col, Peru) head cold; (Chile) smallpox; **pestes** (coll) insults
**pesticida** *m* pesticide
**pestífe•ro -ra** *adj* pestiferous; stinking
**pestilencia** *f* pestilence
**pestillo** *m* bolt; doorlatch
**petaca** *f* cigar case; cigarette case; tobacco pouch; leather-covered hamper
**pétalo** *m* petal
**petardear** *tr* to swindle || *intr* (aut) to backfire
**petardeo** *m* swindling; (aut) backfire
**petardo** *m* petard; bomb; swindle, cheat
**petate** *m* sleeping bag; bedding; (coll) luggage; (coll) cheat; (coll) poor soul; **liar el petate** (coll) to pack up and get out; (coll) to kick the bucket
**petición** *f* petition; request; plea; (law) claim, bill; **a petición de** at the request of; **petición de mano** formal betrothal
**petimetre** *m* dude, sport, dandy
**petirrojo** *m* redbreast, robin
**Petrarca** *m* Petrarch
**petrificar** §73 *tr & ref* to petrify
**petróleo** *m* petroleum; **petróleo combustible** fuel oil
**petrole•ro -ra** *adj* oil, petroleum || *mf* oil dealer || *m* oil tanker
**petulancia** *f* flippancy, pertness
**petulante** *adj* flippant, pert
**pez** *m* (*pl* **peces**) fish; (coll) reward, just desert; **como un pez en el agua** (coll) snug as bug in a rug; **pez de plata** (ent) silverfish **salga pez o salga rana** (coll) blindly, hit or miss || *f* pitch, tar
**pezón** *m* stem; nipple, teat
**pezonera** *f* linchpin
**pezuña** *f* hoof
**piado•so -sa** *adj* merciful; pitiful; pious
**piafar** *intr* (*el caballo*) to paw, to stamp
**piano** *m* piano; **piano de cola** grand piano; **piano de media cola** baby grand
**piar** §77 *intr* to peep, to chirp
**pica** *f* pike; pikeman; picador's goad; (Col) pique, resentment
**picada** *f* peck; bite; (Bol) knock at the door; (Arg, Bol, Urug) narrow ford; (SAm) path, trail
**picadillo** *m* (*carne, verduras, ajos, etc. reducidos a pequeños trozos*) hash; (*carne picada*) mincemeat
**pica•do -da** *adj* perforated; pitted; (*tabaco*) cut; (*hielo*) cracked; (*mar*) choppy; piqued || *m* mincemeat; (aer) dive; **picado con motor** (aer) power dive || *f* see **picada**
**picador** *m* horsebreaker; (*torero de a caballo*) picador (*mounted bullfighter*); chopping block
**picadura** *f* bite, prick, sting; nick; puncture; cut tobacco; (*en un diente*) cavity
**picaflor** *m* hummingbird
**picahie•los** *m* (*pl* **-los**) ice pick
**picamade•ros** *m* (*pl* **-ros**) green woodpecker
**picante** *adj* biting, pricking, stinging; piquant, juicy, racy; (SAm) highly seasoned || *m* mordancy; piquancy
**picapedrero** *m* stonecutter
**picaplei•tos** *m* (*pl* **-tos**) (coll) troublemaker; (coll) shyster, pettifogger

**picaporte** *m* latch; latchkey; door knocker

**picar** §73 *tr* to prick, pierce, puncture; to sting; to bite; to burn; to peck; to nibble; to pit, to pock; to mince, chop up, cut up; to stick, poke; to spur; to goad; to perforate; (*hielo*) to crack; to harass, pursue; to tame; to pique, annoy ‖ *intr* to itch; (*el sol*) to burn; to nibble; to have a smattering; to be catching; (*los negocios*) to pick up; (aer) to dive; (*caer en el lazo*) (coll) to bite; **picar en** to nibble at; to dabble in; **picar muy alto** (coll) to aim high, expect too much ‖ *ref* to rot; (*la ropa*) to be moth-eaten; (*el vino*) to turn sour; (*un diente*) to be decayed; (*el mar*) to get rough; to be offended; (Am) to get drunk; **picarse de** to boast of being

**picardía** *f* roguishness, knavery; crudeness, coarseness; mischief

**picares·co -ca** *adj* roguish, rascally; picaresque; rough, coarse, crude; (coll) witty, humorous, gay

**píca·ro -ra** *adj* roguish; scheming, tricky; low, vile; mischievous ‖ *mf* rogue; schemer

**picaza** *f* magpie

**picazón** *f* itch, itching; (coll) annoyance

**pícea** *f* spruce tree

**pick-up** *m* pickup; phonograph

**pico** *m* beak, bill; (*de jarra*) spout; (*del yunque*) beak; (*del pañuelo*) corner; nib, tip; (*de la pluma de escribir*) point; peak; (*herramienta*) pick; (*de dinero*) pile, lot; talkativeness; (elec) peak; (naut) bow, prow; **callar el pico** (coll) to shut up; **darse el pico** (*las palomas*) to bill; **pico de oro** silver-tongue; **tener mucho pico** (coll) to talk too much; **y pico** odd, e.g., **trescientos y pico** three hundred odd; a little after, e.g., **a las tres y pico** a little after three o'clock

**picor** *m* (*del paladar*) smarting; itch, itching, burning

**pico·so -sa** *adj* pock-marked

**picota** *f* pillory; peak, point, spire

**picotazo** *m* peck

**picotear** *tr* to peck ‖ *intr* (*el caballo*) to toss the head; (coll) to chatter, jabber, gab; (*las mujeres*) (coll) to wrangle

**pichel** *m* pewter tankard

**pi·chón -chona** *mf* (coll) darling ‖ *m* young pigeon; **pichón de barro** clay pigeon

**pie** *m* foot; footing; foothold; base, stand; (*de copa*) stem; (*de la cama*) footboard; cause, origin, reason; (*de la página*) foot, bottom; (theat) cue; (Chile) down payment; **a cuatro pies** on all fours; **al pie de fábrica** (coll) at the factory; **al pie de la letra** literally; **al pie de la obra** (com) delivered; **a pie** on foot, walking; **buscar cinco** (or **tres**) **pies al gato** (coll) to be looking for trouble; **de pie** standing; up and about; firm, steady; firmly, steadily; **en pie de guerra** on a war footing; **ir a pie** to go on foot, to walk; **morir al pie del cañón** to die in the harness, to die with one's boots on; **nacer de pie** or **de pies** to be born with a silver spoon in one's mouth; **pie de atleta** athlete's foot; **pie de cabra** crowbar; **pie de imprenta** imprint, printer's mark; **pie derecho** upright, stanchion; **pie marino** sea legs; **pie quebrado** (*de verso*) short line; **vestirse por los pies** (coll) to be a man

**piedad** *f* (*devoción a las cosas santas*) piety; (*misericordia*) pity, mercy

**piedra** *f* stone; rock; (*pedernal*) flint; heavy hailstone; (pathol) stone; **piedra angular** cornerstone; (fig) cornerstone, keystone; **piedra arenisca** sandstone; **piedra azul** (chem) bluestone; **piedra de albardilla** copestone; **piedra de amolar** grindstone; **piedra de chispa** flint; **piedra de pipas** meerschaum; **piedra imán** loadstone; **piedra miliar** or **miliaria** milestone; **piedra movediza** rolling stone; **piedra pómez** pumice, pumice stone

**piel** *f* skin; hide, pelt; fur; leather; (*de las frutas*) peel, skin; **piel de cabra** goatskin; **piel de foca** sealskin; **piel de gallina** goose flesh; **piel roja** *m* (*pl* **pieles rojas**) (*indio norteamericano*) redskin

**pienso** *m* feed, feeding; **ni por pienso** by no means, don't think of it

**pierna** *f* leg; post, upright; **dormir a pierna suelta** or **tendida** (coll) to sleep like a log; **estirar la pierna** (coll) to lie down on the job; (coll) to kick the bucket; **estirar** or **extender las piernas** (coll) to stretch one's legs, go for a walk; **ser buena pierna** (Arg, Urug) to be a good-natured fellow

**pieza** *f* (*órgano de una máquina o artefacto; obra dramática; composición suelta de música; cañón; figura que sirve para jugar a las damas, al ajedrez, etc.; moneda*) piece; (*objeto; mueble; porción de tela*) piece or article; (*habitación, cuarto*) room; **buena pieza** hussy; sly fox; **pieza de recambio** or **de repuesto** spare part; **quedarse en una pieza** or **hecho una pieza** to be dumbfounded, to stand motionless

**pífano** *m* fife; fifer

**pifia** *f* (billiards) miscue; (coll) miscue, slip

**pifiar** *intr* to miscue

**pigmentar** *tr* & *ref* to pigment

**pigmento** *m* pigment

**pigme·o -a** *adj* & *mf* pygmy

**pijama** *f* pajamas

**pila** *f* basin; trough; sink; font; pile, heap; (elec) battery, cell; (elec & phys) pile; **pila de linterna** flashlight battery

**pilar** *m* (*de una fuente*) basin, bowl; pillar; stone post, milestone; (*persona*) (fig) pillar ‖ *tr* (*el grano*) to crush, to pound

**Pilatos** *m* Pilate

**píldora** *f* pill; (coll) bad news; **píldora para dormir** sleeping pill

**pileta** *f* sink; basin, bowl; font; swimming pool

**pilón** *m* pylon; drinking trough; loaf of sugar; counterpoise; drop hammer
**pilotar** *tr* to pilot
**pilote** *m* pile
**piloto** *m* pilot; first mate; (Chile) hail fellow well met
**pillar** *tr* to pillage, plunder; to catch
**pi•llo -lla** *adj* (coll) roguish, rascally; (coll) sly, crafty || *m* (coll) rogue, rascal; (coll) crafty fellow
**pilluelo** *m* (coll) scamp, little scamp
**pimentero** *m* pepper, black pepper; pepperbox
**pimentón** *m* cayenne pepper, red pepper; (*condimento preparado moliendo pimientos encarnados secos*) paprika
**pimienta** *f* pepper, black pepper; allspice, pimento; allspice tree
**pimiento** *m* (*planta*) pepper, black pepper; Guinea pepper
**pimpante** *adj* smart, spruce
**pimpollo** *m* sucker, shoot, sprout; rosebud; (*árbol nuevo*) sapling; (coll) handsome child; (coll) handsome young person
**pina** *f* felloe
**pinacoteca** *f* picture gallery
**pináculo** *m* pinnacle
**pincel** *m* brush; painter; painting; (*de luz*) pencil, beam
**pincelada** *f* brush stroke; touch, finish, flourish
**pincelar** *tr* to paint; to picture; (med) to pencil
**pinciano -na** *adj* Vallladolid || *mf* native or inhabitant of Valladolid
**pincha** *f* kitchenmaid
**pinchar** *tr* to prick, jab, pierce, puncture; to stir up, prod, provoke || *intr* to have a puncture; **no pinchar ni cortar** to have no say
**pinchazo** *m* prick, jab, puncture; provocation; **a prueba de pinchazos** puncture-proof
**pinche** *m* scullion, kitchen boy; helper
**pincho** *m* thorn, prick; snack; spike
**Píndaro** *m* Pindar
**pingajo** *m* (coll) rag, tatter
**pingo** *m* (coll) rag, tatter; (coll) ragamuffin; (coll) horse; **andar** or **ir de pingo** (*una mujer*) (coll) to gad about
**pingüe** *adj* oily, greasy, fat; abundant, rich; fertile; profitable
**pingüino** *m* penguin
**pinito** *m* first step, little step; **hacer pinitos** to begin to walk; (fig) to take the first steps
**pino** *m* pine tree; first step; **hacer pinos** to begin to walk; (fig) to take the first steps
**pinocha** *f* pine needle
**pinta** *m* (coll) scoundrel || *f* spot, mark, sign; dot; pint
**pintacilgo** *m* goldfinch
**pintada** *f* Guinea hen
**pinta•do -da** *adj* spotted, mottled; tipsy; accented; **el más pintado** (coll) the aptest one; (coll) the shrewdest one; (coll) the best one; **venir como pintado** to be just the thing || *m* (*acto de pintar*) painting || *f* see **pintada**
**pintar** *tr* to paint; (*una letra, un acento, etc.*) to draw; to picture, depict; to put an accent mark on; **pintarla** (coll) to put it on, to put on airs || *intr* to paint; to begin to turn red, begin to ripen; (coll) to show, to turn out || *ref* to paint, put on make-up; to begin to turn red, begin to ripen
**pintarrajear** *tr* to daub, to smear
**pin•to -ta** *adj* (Am) speckled, spotted || *f* see **pinta**
**pin•tor -tora** *mf* painter; **pintor de brocha gorda** painter, house painter; (coll) dauber
**pintores•co -ca** *adj* picturesque
**pintura** *f* (*color preparado para pintar*) paint; (*arte; obra pintada*) painting; **hacer pinturas** (coll) to prance; **no poder ver ni en pintura** to not be able to stand the sight of
**pinture•ro -ra** *adj* (coll) showy, conceited || *mf* (coll) show-off
**pinza** *f* clothespin; (*de langosta, cangrejo, etc.*) claw; **pinzas** pliers; pincers; tweezers; forceps
**pinzón** *m* pump handle; (orn) finch
**piña** *f* fir cone, pine cone; knob; plug; cluster, knot; pineapple
**piñonear** *intr* (*un arma de fuego*) to click; (coll) to reach the age of puberty; (coll) to be an old goat
**piñoneo** *m* click (*of a firearm*)
**pí•o -a** *adj* pious; merciful, compassionate; (*caballo*) pied, dappled || *m* peeping, chirping; (coll) keen desire
**piocha** *f* jeweled head adornment; artificial flower made of feathers; pick
**piojo** *m* louse
**piojo•so -sa** *adj* lousy; mean, stingy
**pione•ro -ra** *adj & mf* pioneer
**pipa** *f* (*para fumar tabaco*) pipe; (*medida para vinos*) butt; wine cask; (*simiente*) pip; (mus) pipe, reed; **pipa de espuma de mar** meerschaum pipe; **pipa de riego** watering cart; **pipa de tierra** clay pipe
**pique** *m* pique, resentment; eagerness; (*insecto*) chigger; (*naipe*) spade; **a pique** steep; **a pique de** in danger of; on the verge of; **echar a pique** to sink; to ruin; **irse a pique** to sink; to go to ruin, be ruined
**piquera** *f* bung, bunghole; (Mex) dive, joint
**piquete** *m* sharp jab; small hole; stake, picket; (*de soldados, de huelguistas*) picket; **piquete de ejecución** firing squad; **piquete de salvas** firing squad
**pira** *f* pyre
**piragua** *f* pirogue; (sport) single shell
**piragüista** *m* (sport) crewman
**pirámide** *f* pyramid
**pirata** *m* pirate
**piratear** *intr* to pirate, be a pirate
**pirca** *f* (SAm) dry stone wall
**pirco** *m* (Chile) succotash
**Pireo, el** Piraeus
**pirine•o -a** *adj* Pyrenean || **Pirineos** *mpl* Pyrenees
**pirita** *f* pyrites
**pirófa•go -ga** *adj* fire-eating || *mf* fire-eater
**piropear** *tr* (coll) to flatter, flirt with

**piropo** *m* garnet, carbuncle; (coll) flattery, compliment, flirtatious remark
**piróscafo** *m* steamship
**pirotecnia** *f* pyrotechnics
**pirotécni•co -ca** *adj* pyrotechnical || *m* powder maker, fireworks manufacturer
**pirueta** *f* pirouette; somersault; caper
**piruetear** *intr* to pirouette
**pisada** *f* tread; footstep; footprint; trampling
**pisapape•les** *m* (*pl* **-les**) paperweight
**pisar** *tr* to trample, tread on, step on; to tamp, pack down; (*p.ej., uvas*) to tread; to cover part of; to ram; (*una tecla*) to strike; (mus) to pluck; (coll) to abuse, tread all over; **pisar algo a alguien** (coll) to snitch something from someone || *intr* to be right above; to step || *ref* (Arg) to guess wrong, come out wrong
**pisaverde** *m* (coll) fop, dandy
**piscina** *f* swimming pool; fishpond
**pisco** *m* Peruvian brandy
**pisicorre** *f* (W-I) station wagon
**piso** *m* tread; floor; flooring; (*de una carretera*) surface; flat, apartment; **buscar piso** to be looking for a place to live; **piso alto** top floor; **piso bajo** street floor, ground floor; **piso principal** main floor, second floor
**pisón** *m* ram, tamper
**pisotear** *tr* to trample, to tread on, to tread under foot; (coll) to abuse, tread all over
**pisotón** *m* stamp, tread
**pista** *f* track; trace, trail; clew; race track; (*de bolera*) alley; (*de cabaret*) floor; (aer) runway; **pista de esquí** ski run; **pista de patinar** skating rink
**pisto** *m* (*para los enfermos*) chicken broth; vegetable cutlet; jumbled speech or writing; mess
**pistola** *f* pistol; sprayer; rock drill; **pistola de arzón** horse pistol; **pistola engrasadora** grease gun
**pistolera** *f* holster
**pistolerismo** *m* gangsterism
**pistolero** *m* gangster, gunman
**pistón** *m* piston
**pistonear** *intr* to knock
**pistoneo** *m* knock
**pistonu•do -da** *adj* (coll) stunning, swank
**pita** *f* century plant; hiss, hissing; glass marble
**pitar** *tr* to pay, pay off; (*a un torero*) to whistle disapproval of || *intr* to blow a whistle, to whistle; to blow the horn, to honk; (coll) to talk nonsense; **no pitar** (coll) to not be popular; **salir pitando** to run away, dash away
**pitazo** *m* blast, toot, honk
**pitillera** *f* cigarette maker; cigarette case
**pitillo** *m* cigarette
**pito** *m* whistle; horn; fife; fifer; cigarette; jackstone; (*insecto*) tick; woodpecker; (coll) continental, straw, tinker's dam
**pitón** *m* lump, sprig; tenderling; (*del cuerno*) tip; nozzle, spout; python
**pitonisa** *f* witch, siren; pythoness
**pitu•so -sa** *adj* tiny, cute || *mf* tot
**piular** *intr* to peep, to chirp
**pivotar** *intr* to pivot
**pivote** *m* pivot; **pivote de dirección** (aut) kingpin
**píxide** *f* pyx
**pizarra** *f* slate; blackboard
**pizarrero** *m* roofer, slater
**pizarrín** *m* slate pencil
**pizca** *f* (coll) mite, whit, jot
**placa** *f* plaque, tablet; badge; plate; slab, sheet; (anat, elec, electron, phot, zool) plate; (Am) scab; **placa de matrícula** license plate; **placa giratoria** (*de ferrocarril; de gramófono*) turntable
**placaminero** *m* persimmon
**placebo** *m* placebo
**pláceme** *m* congratulation
**placente•ro -ra** *adj* pleasant, agreeable
**placer** *m* pleasure; sandbank, reef; **a placer** at one's convenience || *v* §52 *tr* to please
**place•ro -ra** *adj* public || *mf* market vendor; loafer, town gossip
**pláci•do -da** *adj* placid; pleasing
**plaga** *f* plague; pest; scourge; abundance; sore; clime, region
**plagar** §44 *tr* to plague, infest; (*de minas*) to sow
**plagiar** *tr* to plagiarize
**plagio** *m* plagiarism; (Am) abduction, kidnaping
**plan** *m* plan; level, height; **plan de estudios** or **plan escolar** curriculum
**plana** *f* plain, flat country; trowel; cooper's plane; page
**plancha** *f* plate, sheet; iron, flatiron; gangplank; (coll) blunder; **a la plancha** grilled; (*huevo*) fried; **plancha de blindaje** armor plate
**planchado** *m* ironing; pressing
**planchar** *tr* (*la ropa interior blanca*) to iron; (*un traje de hombre*) to press || *intr* (Am) to be a wallflower
**planchear** *tr* to plate
**planear** *tr* to plan, to outline; (*una tabla*) to plane || *intr* to hover; (aer) to volplane, to glide
**planeta** *m* planet
**planicie** *f* plain
**planificar** §73 *tr* to plan
**planilla** *f* (Am) list, roll, schedule; (*de candidatos para un puesto público*) (Mex) panel; (Mex) ballot; (Mex) commutation ticket
**pla•no -na** *adj* plane; level, smooth, even; flat || *m* plan; map; (*superficie*) plane; (aer) plane; **de plano** clearly, plainly, flatly; flat; **levantar un plano** to make a survey; **primer plano** foreground || *f* see **plana**
**planta** *f* (*del pie*) sole; foot; plan; project; floor plan; (*del personal de una oficina*) roster; plant, factory; (bot) plant; (sport) stance; **de planta** from the ground up; **echar plantas** to swagger, to bully; **planta baja** ground floor; **planta del sortilegio** (bot) witch hazel; **tener buena planta** (coll) to make a fine appearance
**plantar** *tr* to plant; to establish, to

found; (*un golpe*) (coll) to plant; (coll) to jilt; (*en la calle, en la cárcel*) (coll) to throw || *ref* to take a stand; to gang together; (*un animal*) (coll) to balk; (coll) to land, to arrive

**plantear** *tr* to plan, to outline; to establish, execute, carry out; to state, set up, expound, pose

**plantel** *m* nursery garden; educational establishment

**plantificar** §73 *tr* to plan, to outline; (*un golpe*) (coll) to plant; (*en la calle, la cárcel*) (coll) to throw || *ref* (coll) to land, to arrive

**plantilla** *f* plantlet, young plant; insole; reinforced sole; model, pattern, template; (*de empleados*) staff; (*del personal de una oficina*) roster; plan, design; (*bizcocho*) (Am) ladyfinger

**plantío** *m* planting; garden patch; tree nursery

**plantón** *m* (*que ha de ser transplantado*) shoot; graft; guard, watchman; waiting, standing around

**plañide•ro -ra** *adj* mournful, plaintive || *f* hired mourner

**plañir** §12 *tr* to lament, grieve over || *intr* to lament, grieve, bewail

**plasmar** *tr* to mold, shape

**plasta** *f* paste, soft mass; flattened object; (coll) poor job, bungle

**plástica** *f* (*arte de plasmar*) plastic; plastic arts

**plásti•co -ca** *adj* plastic || *m* (*substancia*) plastic || *f* see **plástica**

**plata** *f* silver; (*moneda o monedas*) silver; wealth; money; **en plata** (coll) briefly, to the point; (coll) plainly; **plata de ley** sterling silver

**plataforma** *f* platform; platform car; (*del ferrocarril*) roadbed; (*programa político*) platform; (*de lanzamiento de cohete*) pad; **plataforma giratoria** (rr) turntable

**platanal** *m* or **platanar** *m* banana plantation

**plátano** *m* banana; banana tree; plane tree; **plátano de occidente** buttonwood tree

**platea** *f* (theat) orchestra, parquet

**platear** *tr* to silver, coat or plate with silver

**platero** *m* silversmith; jeweler

**plática** *f* talk, chat; talk, informal lecture; sermon

**platicar** §73 *tr* to talk over, to discuss || *intr* to talk, to chat; to discuss; to preach

**platillo** *m* plate; saucer; (*de la balanza*) pan; (mus) cymbal; **platillo volador** or **volante** flying saucer

**platino** *m* platinum

**plato** *m* dish; plate; (*de una comida*) course; daily fare; **plato fuerte** main course; **plato giratorio** (*del gramófono*) turntable

**pla•tó** *m* (*pl* **-tós**) (mov) set

**Platón** *m* Plato

**plausible** *adj* praiseworthy; acceptable

**playa** *f* beach, shore, strand; **playa infantil** sand pile

**playera** *f* fishwoman; beach shoe

**plaza** *f* plaza, square; market place; town, city; fortified town; space, room; yard; office, employment; character, reputation; seat; **sentar plaza** to enlist; **plaza de armas** parade ground; (Am) public square; **plaza de gallos** cockpit; **plaza de toros** bullring; **plaza mayor** main square

**plazo** *m* term; time; time limit; date of payment; instalment; **a plazo** on credit, on time; **en plazos** in instalments

**pleamar** *f* high tide, high water

**plebe** *f* common people

**plebe•yo -ya** *adj & mf* plebeian

**plegadi•zo -za** *adj* folding; pliable

**plegar** §66 *tr* to fold; to crease; to pleat || *ref* to yield, to give in

**plegaria** *f* prayer; noon call to prayer

**pleito** *m* litigation, lawsuit; dispute, quarrel; fight; **pleito de acreedores** bankruptcy proceedings; **pleito homenaje** (feud) homage; **pleito viciado** mistrial

**plenilunio** *m* full moon

**plenitud** *f* fullness, abundance

**ple•no -na** *adj* full; **en plena marcha** in full swing; **en pleno rostro** right in the face

**pleuresía** *f* pleurisy

**pliego** *m* (*de papel*) sheet; folder; cover, envelope; bid, specification; sealed letter; printer's proof

**pliegue** *m* fold, crease, pleat; **pliegue de tabla** box pleat

**plisar** *tr* to pleat

**plomada** *f* carpenter's lead pencil; plummet; plumb bob; sinker, sinkers; scourge tipped with lead balls

**plomar** *tr* to seal with lead

**plomazo** *m* (Guat, Mex, W-I) gunshot

**plomería** *f* lead roofing; leadwork, plumbing

**plomero** *m* lead worker; plumber

**plomi•zo -za** *adj* lead, leaden

**plomo** *m* lead; (*pedazo de plomo; bala*) lead; (elec) fuse; (coll) bore; **a plomo** plumb, perpendicularly; straight down; (coll) just right

**pluma** *f* feather; quill; plume; pen; (Am) faucet; (CAm) hoax; (Chile) crane, derrick; **pluma esferográfica** (Am) ball-point pen; **pluma estilográfica** or **pluma fuente** fountain pen

**plumaje** *m* plumage

**plúmbe•o -a** *adj* lead

**plumero** *m* (*caja o vaso para las plumas*) penholder; feather duster

**plumífe•ro -ra** *adj* (*escritor*) (coll) hack, second-rate; (poet) feathered || *m* padded or quilted jacket, ski jacket; (coll) hack writer; (coll) newshound

**plumilla** *f* small feather; (*de la pluma fuente*) point, tip

**plumón** *m* down; feather bed

**plumo•so -sa** *adj* downy, feathery

**plural** *adj & m* plural

**pluriempleo** *m* moonlighting

**plus** *m* extra, bonus

**plusmarca** *f* (sport) record

**plusmarquista** *mf* (sport) record breaker

**plusvalía** *f* appreciation (*in value*)
**Plutarco** *m* Plutarch
**plutonio** *m* plutonium
**población** *f* population; village, town, city
**poblada** *f* (SAm) riot, mob
**pobla•do -da** *adj* thick, bushy || *m* town, community || *f* see **poblada**
**poblar** §61 *tr* to people, to populate; to found, settle, colonize; (*un estanque, una colmena*) to stock; (*con árboles*) to plant || *intr* to settle, colonize; to multiply, be prolific || *ref* to become full, covered, or crowded
**pobre** *adj* poor || *mf* pauper; beggar
**pobreza** *f* poverty, want; poorness
**pocilga** *f* pigpen
**poción** *f* potion, dose
**po•co -ca** *adj* & *pron* (*comp* & *super* **menos**) little; few, e.g., **poca gente** few people; **pocos** few; **unos pocos** a few || **poco** *adv* little; **a poco** shortly afterwards; **a poco de** shortly after; **dentro de poco** shortly; **por poco** almost, nearly; **tener en poco** to hold in low esteem, to think little of; **un poco (de)** a little
**po•cho -cha** *adj* faded, discolored; overripe; rotten; (Chile) chubby
**podar** *tr* to prune, to trim
**podenco** *m* hound
**poder** *m* power; power of attorney, proxy; **el cuarto poder** the fourth estate; **obra en mi poder** I have at hand, I have in my possession; **poder adquisitivo** purchasing power || *v* §53 *intr* to be possible; to be able, to have power or strength; **a más no poder** as hard as possible; **no poder con** to not be able to stand, to not be able to manage; **no poder más** to be exhausted, to be all in; **no poder menos de** to not be able to keep from, to not be able to help || *v aux* to be able to, may, can, might, could; **no poder ver** to not be able to stand
**poderhabiente** *mf* attorney, proxy
**poderío** *m* power, might; wealth, riches; sway, dominion
**podero•so -sa** *adj* powerful, mighty; wealthy, rich
**podre** *f* pus
**podredumbre** *f* corruption, putrefaction; pus; deep grief
**poema** *m* poem
**poesía** *f* poetry; poem; **bella poesía** (fig) fairy tale
**poeta** *m* poet
**poéti•co -ca** *adj* poetic(al) || *f* poetics
**poetisa** *f* poetess
**pola•co -ca** *adj* Polish || *mf* Pole || *m* (*idioma*) Polish
**polaina** *f* legging
**polar** *adj* pole; polar || *f* polestar
**polarizar** §60 *tr* to polarize
**polea** *f* pulley
**poleame** *m* (naut) tackle
**polen** *m* pollen
**policía** *m* policeman || *f* police; policing; politeness; cleanliness, neatness; **policía urbana** street cleaning
**policía•co -ca** or **policial** *adj* police; (*novela*) detective
**polifacéti•co -ca** *adj* many-sided
**políga•mo -ma** *adj* polygamous || *mf* polygamist
**poliglo•to -ta** *adj* polyglot || *mf* polyglot, linguist
**polígono** *m* polygon
**polígrafo** *m* prolific writer; copying machine; ball-point pen; lie detector
**polilla** *f* moth
**Polimnia** *f* Polyhymnia
**polinizar** §60 *tr* to pollinate
**polinomio** *m* polynomial
**polio** *f* (path) polio
**pólipo** *m* polyp
**polisón** *m* bustle
**polista** *mf* poloist, polo player
**politeísta** *adj* polytheistic || *mf* polytheist
**política** *f* politics; policy; manners, politeness, courtesy; **política de café** parlor politics; **política del buen vecino** Good Neighbor Policy
**políti•co -ca** *adj* political; politic, tactful; polite, courteous; -in-law, e.g., **padre político** father-in-law || *mf* politician || *f* see **política**
**póliza** *f* policy, contract; draft, check; customhouse permit; **póliza de seguro** insurance policy
**polizón** *m* bum, tramp; stowaway
**polizonte** *m* (coll) cop, policeman
**polo** *m* pole; popsicle; (*juego*) polo; **polo de agua** water polo; **polo de atracción popular** drawing card
**Polonia** *f* Poland
**pol•trón -trona** *adj* idle, lazy, comfort-loving || *f* easy chair
**polvareda** *f* cloud of dust; rumpus
**polvera** *f* compact, powder case
**polvo** *m* dust; powder; pinch of snuff; **polvo dentífrico** tooth powder; **polvos** dust; powder; **polvos de la madre Celestina** (coll) hocus-pocus; **polvos de talco** talcum powder
**pólvora** *f* powder, gunpowder; fireworks; (*persona avispada*) (coll) live wire; **correr como pólvora en reguero** to spread like wildfire
**polvorear** *tr* to dust, sprinkle with dust or powder
**polvorien•to -ta** *adj* dusty; powdery
**polvorín** *m* powder magazine; powder flask; (*insecto*) (Am) tick; (Chile) spitfire
**polvoro•so -sa** *adj* dusty; **poner pies en polvorosa** (coll) to take to one's heels
**polla** *f* pullet; (*puesta en juegos de naipes*) stake, kitty; (coll) lassie
**pollera** *f* poultry woman; chicken coop; poultry yard; gocart; (Arg, Chile) skirt
**pollero** *m* poulterer; poultry yard
**polli•no -na** *mf* donkey, ass
**polli•to -ta** *mf* chick; (*persona joven*) (coll) chick, chicken
**pollo** *m* chicken; (*persona joven*) chicken
**pomada** *f* pomade
**pómez** *f* pumice stone
**pomo** *m* pome; (*de la guarnición de la espada*) pommel; (*bola aromática*) pomander; (*frasco para perfume*) flacon; **pomo de puerta** doorknob

**pompa** *f* pomp; soap bubble; swell, bulge; (*de la ropa*) billowing, ballooning; (*de las alas del pavo real*) spread; (naut) pump; **pompa fúnebre** funeral
**pompo•so -sa** *adj* pompous; high-flown, highfalutin
**pómulo** *m* cheekbone
**ponche** *m* (*bebida*) punch; **ponche de huevo** eggnog
**ponchera** *f* punch bowl
**pon•cho -cha** *adj* lazy, careless, easygoing; (Col) chubby ‖ *m* poncho; greatcoat
**ponderar** *tr* to weigh; to ponder, ponder over; to exaggerate; to praise to the skies; to balance; to weight
**ponencia** *f* paper, report
**poner** §54 *tr* to put, place, lay, set; to arrange, dispose; (*una observación*) to put in; (*una pieza dramática*) to put on; (*la mesa*) to set; to assume, suppose; (*una ley, un impuesto*) to impose; to wager, to stake; (*huevos*) to lay; (*por escrito*) to set down, put down; (*tiempo*) to take; (*p.ej., miedo*) to cause; to make, to turn; (*la luz, la radio*) to turn on; (*marcha directa*) (aut) to go in; **poner en limpio** to make a clean copy of; **poner por encima** to prefer, to put ahead ‖ *ref* to put or place oneself; to become, to get, to turn; (*el sol, los astros*) to set; (*sombrero, saco, etc.*) to put on; to dress, dress up; to get spotted; to get, reach, arrive; **ponerse a** to set out to, to begin to; **ponerse tan alto** to take offense, to become hoity-toity
**poniente** *m* west; west wind
**ponqué** *m* (Am) poundcake
**pontífice** *m* pontiff
**pontón** *m* pontoon; pontoon bridge; (*buque viejo*) hulk
**ponzoña** *f* poison
**ponzoño•so -sa** *adj* poisonous
**popa** *f* poop, stern
**popote** *m* (Mex) straw for brooms; (*para tomar refrescos*) (Mex) straw
**populache•ro -ra** *adj* popular; cheap, vulgar; rabble-rousing ‖ *mf* rabble rouser
**populacho** *m* populace, mob, rabble
**popular** *adj* popular
**popularizar** §60 *tr* to popularize
**populo•so -sa** *adj* populous
**popu•rrí** *m* (*pl* **-rríes**) medley
**poquedad** *f* paucity, scantiness; scarcity; timidity; trifle
**poqui•to -ta** *adj* very little; (Am) timid, shy, backward
**por** *prep* by; through, over; via, by way of; in, e.g., **por la mañana** in the morning; for; because of; for the sake of; on account of; in exchange for; in order to; as; about, e.g., **por Navidad** about Christmastime; out of, e.g., **por ignorancia** out of ignorance; times, e.g., **tres por cuatro** four times three; **estar por** to be on the point of, to be ready to; to be still to be, e.g., **la carta está por escribir** the letter is still to be written; **ir por** to go for, to go after; to follow; **por ciento** per cent; **por entre** among, between; **por que** because; in order that; **por qué** why; **por** + *adj* or *adv* + **que** however
**porcelana** *f* porcelain, chinaware; (*usado por los plateros*) enamel; (Mex) washbowl
**porcentaje** *m* percentage
**porción** *f* portion
**porche** *m* porch, portico
**pordiosear** *intr* to beg, to go begging
**pordiose•ro -ra** *mf* beggar
**porfía** *f* persistence, stubbornness, obstinacy; **a porfía** in emulation; insistently
**porfia•do -da** *adj* persistent, stubborn, obstinate; opinionated
**porfiar** §77 *intr* to persist; to argue stubbornly
**pórfido** *m* porphyry
**pormenor** *m* detail, particular
**pormenorizar** §60 *tr* to detail, tell in detail; to itemize
**poro** *m* pore
**poro•so -sa** *adj* porous
**poroto** *m* (SAm) bean, string bean; (Chile) little runt
**porque** *conj* because; in order that
**porqué** *m* (coll) why; (coll) quantity, share; (coll) wherewithal, money
**porquería** *f* (coll) dirt, filth; (coll) trifle; (coll) crudity; (*alimento dañoso a la salud*) (coll) junk
**porra** *f* club, bludgeon; (coll) bore, nuisance; (coll) boasting; (*pelos enredados*) (Arg, Bol) knot, tangle; (Mex) claque
**porrazo** *m* clubbing; blow, bump, thump
**porta** *f* porthole
**portaavio•nes** *m* (*pl* **-nes**) aircraft carrier, flattop
**portacandado** *m* hasp
**portada** *f* front, façade; portal; title page; (*de una revista*) cover; **falsa portada** half title
**portadis•cos** *m* (*pl* **-cos**) turntable
**porta•dor -dora** *adj* (*onda*) (rad) carrier ‖ *mf* bearer; carrier ‖ *m* waiter's tray
**portaequipaje** *m* (aut) trunk
**portaequipa•jes** *m* (*pl* **-jes**) baggage rack
**portaguan•tes** *m* (*pl* **-tes**) (aut) glove compartment
**portal** *m* vestibule, entrance hall; porch, portico; arcade; city gate; (*de un túnel*) portal *m;* (Am) crèche
**portalámpa•ras** *m* (*pl* **-ras**) (elec) socket
**portalón** *m* gate, portal; (*en el costado del buque*) gangway
**portamira** *m* (surv) rodman
**portamone•das** *m* (*pl* **-das**) pocketbook
**portanue•vas** *mf* (*pl* **-vas**) newsmonger
**portañuela** *f* (*de los pantalones*) fly; (Col, Mex) carriage door
**portapape•les** *m* (*pl* **-les**) brief case
**portaplu•mas** *m* (*pl* **-mas**) penholder
**portar** *tr* (Am) to carry, to bear; (hunt) to retrieve ‖ *ref* to behave, conduct oneself
**portase•nos** *m* (*pl* **-nos**) brassière
**portátil** *adj* portable

**portatinte•ro** *m* inkstand
**portavian•das** *m* (*pl* **-das**) dinner pail
**porta•voz** *m* (*pl* **-voces**) megaphone; mouthpiece, spokesman
**portazgo** *m* toll, road toll
**portazo** *m* bang, slam
**porte** *m* portage; carrying charge, freight; postage; behavior, conduct; dress, bearing; size, capacity; (Chile) birthday present; **porte concertado** mailing permit; **porte pagado** postage prepaid, freight prepaid
**portear** *tr* to carry, transport || *intr* to slam || *ref* (*las aves*) to migrate
**portento** *m* prodigy, wonder
**portento•so -sa** *adj* portentous, extraordinary
**porte•ño -ña** *adj* Buenos Aires; Valparaiso; pertaining to any large South American city with a port || *mf* native or inhabitant of Buenos Aires, Valparaiso or any large South American city with a port
**porte•ro -ra** *mf* doorkeeper; gatekeeper; (sport) goalkeeper || *m* porter, janitor; doorman || *f* portress, janitress
**portezuela** *f* small door; (*de un coche o automóvil*) door; pocket flap
**pórtico** *m* portico, porch; little gate
**portilla** *f* porthole; private cart road, private cattle pass
**portillo** *m* gap, opening; nick, notch; (*puerta chica en otra mayor*) wicket; gate; narrow pass; side entrance
**portorrique•ño -ña** *adj & mf* Puerto Rican
**portua•rio -ria** *adj* port, harbor, dock || *m* dock hand, dock worker
**Portugal** *m* Portugal
**portu•gués -guesa** *adj & mf* Portuguese
**porvenir** *m* future
**pos — en pos de** after, behind; in pursuit of
**posa** *f* knell, toll
**posada** *f* inn, wayside inn; lodging; boarding house; home, dwelling; camp; **posadas** (Mex) pre-Christmas celebration
**posadero -ra** *mf* innkeeper; **posaderas** buttocks
**posar** *tr* to put down || *intr* to put up, lodge; to alight, to perch; to pose || *ref* to alight, to perch; to settle; to rest
**posbéli•co -ca** *adj* postwar
**posdata** *f* postscript
**pose** *f* pose; (phot) exposure
**poseer** §43 *tr* to own, possess, hold; to have a mastery of || *ref* to control oneself
**posesión** *f* possession; **tomar posesión de** (*un cargo*) to take up
**posesionar** *tr* to give possession to || *ref* to take possession
**posfecha** *f* postdate
**posguerra** *f* postwar period
**posible** *adj* possible; **hacer todo lo posible** to do one's best || **posibles** *mpl* means, income, property
**posición** *f* position; standing
**positi•vo -va** *adj* positive || *f* (phot) print, positive
**poso** *m* sediment, dregs; grounds; rest, quiet; **poso del café** coffee grounds
**posponer** §54 *tr* to subordinate; to think less of
**posta** *f* (*de caballos*) relay; posthouse; stage; stake, wager; slice; **a posta** (coll) on purpose; **por la posta** (coll) posthaste; **postas** buckshot
**postal** *adj* postal || *f* post card; **postal ilustrada** picture post card
**poste** *m* post, pilar, pole; **poste de alumbrado** or **de farol** lamppost; **poste de telégrafo** telegraph pole; (*persona muy alta y delgada*) beanpole; **poste indicador** road sign
**postergar** §44 *tr* to delay, postpone; to pass over
**posteridad** *f* posterity; posthumous fame
**posterior** *adj* back, rear; later, subsequent
**postigo** *m* (*puerta chica en otra mayor*) wicket; (*puertecilla en una ventana*) peep window; (*puerta excusada*) postern; shutter
**posti•zo -za** *adj* false, artificial; (*cuello*) detachable || *m* switch, false hair, rat
**postóni•co -ca** *adj* posttonic
**postor** *m* bidder; **el mejor postor** the highest bidder
**postración** *f* prostration
**postrar** *tr* to prostrate; to weaken, exhaust || *ref* to collapse, be prostrated; to prostrate oneself
**postre** *adj* last, final; **a la postre** at last; afterwards || *m* dessert; **postres** dessert
**postulación** *f* postulation; nomination
**postulante** *mf* applicant, candidate
**póstu•mo -ma** *adj* posthumous
**postura** *f* posture; attitude, stand; stake, wager; agreement, pact; egg, eggs; (*de huevos*) laying; **postura del sol** sunset
**potabilizar** §60 *tr* to make drinkable
**potable** *adj* drinkable
**potaje** *m* pottage; jumble; (*bebida*) mixture; (Am) scheme; **potajes** vegetables
**potasa** *f* potash
**potasio** *m* potassium
**pote** *m* pot, jug; flowerpot; **a pote** (coll) in abundance
**potencia** *f* potency; power; **potencia de choque** striking power
**potenciación** *f* (math) involution
**potencial** *adj & m* potential
**potenciar** *tr* (*las aguas de un río; el entusiasmo de una persona*) to harness; (*elevar a una potencia*) (math) to raise
**potentado** *m* potentate
**potente** *adj* powerful; (coll) big, huge
**potestad** *f* power
**potista** *mf* (coll) toper, soak
**potosí** *m* great wealth, gold mine
**potra** *f* filly; (coll) hernia, rupture
**potranca** *f* young mare
**potro** *m* colt; pest, annoyance
**pozal** *m* bucket, pail
**pozo** *m* well; pit; whirlpool; (min) shaft; (naut) hold; (Chile, Col) pool, puddle; (Ecuad) spring, fountain;

**pozo de ciencia** fountain of knowledge; **pozo de lanzamiento** launching silo; **pozo de lobo** (mil) foxhole; **pozo negro** cesspool
**P.P.** *abbr* **porte pagado, por poder**
**p.p.do** *abbr* **próximo pasado**
**práctica** *f* practice; method; skill; **prácticas** studies, training
**prácticamente** *adv* through practice, by experience
**practicar** §73 *tr* to practice; to bring about; (*un agujero*) to make, to cut
**prácti•co -ca** *adj* practical; skillful, practiced; practicing ‖ *m* medical practitioner; (naut) pilot ‖ *f* see **práctica**
**pradera** *f* meadowland; prairie
**prado** *m* meadow, pasture; promenade
**Praga** *f* Prague
**pral.** *abbr* **principal**
**pralte.** *abbr* **principalmente**
**prángana — estar en la prángana** (Mex, W-I) to be broke; (P-R) to be naked
**preámbulo** *m* preamble; evasion; **no andarse en preámbulos** (coll) to come to the point
**prebéli•co -ca** *adj* prewar
**prebenda** *f* prebend; (coll) sinecure
**preca•rio -ria** *adj* precarious
**precaución** *f* precaution
**precaver** *tr* to stave off, head off ‖ *intr & ref* to be on one's guard; **precaverse contra** or **de** to guard against
**precavido -da** *adj* cautious
**precedente** *adj* preceding ‖ *m* precedent
**preceder** *tr & intr* to precede
**precepto** *m* precept; order, injunction; **los preceptos** the Ten Commandments
**preces** *fpl* devotions; supplications
**precia•do -da** *adj* esteemed, valued; precious, valuable; boastful, proud
**preciar** *tr* to appraise, estimate ‖ *ref* to boast
**precintar** *tr* to bind, strap; to seal
**precio** *m* price; value, worth; esteem, credit; **a precio de quemazón** (coll) at a giveaway price; **precios de cierre** closing prices; **precio tope** ceiling price
**preciosidad** *f* preciousness; beauty, gem, jewel
**precio•so -sa** *adj* precious; valuable; witty; (coll) beautiful
**precipicio** *m* precipice; destruction
**precipitación** *f* precipitation; **precipitación acuosa** rainfall; **precipitación radiactiva** fallout
**precipitar** *tr* to precipitate; to rush, hurl, throw headlong ‖ *ref* to rush, throw oneself headlong
**precipito•so -sa** *adj* precipitous, rash, reckless; risky, dangerous
**precisar** *tr* to state precisely, to specify; to fix; to need; to oblige, to force ‖ *intr* to be necessary; to be important; to be urgent; **precisar de** to need
**precisión** *f* precision; necessity, obligation; (Chile) haste; **precisiones** data
**preci•so -sa** *adj* necessary; precise; (Ven) haughty
**precita•do -da** *adj* above-mentioned
**precla•ro -ra** *adj* illustrious, famous
**preconizar** §60 *tr* to proclaim, commend publicly
**pre•coz** *adj* (*pl* **-coces**) precocious
**predato•rio -ria** *adj* predatory
**predecir** §24 *tr* to predict, foretell
**prédica** *f* protestant sermon; harangue
**predicar** §73 *tr* to preach; to praise to the skies; to scold, preach to
**predicción** *f* prediction; **predicción del tiempo** weather forecasting
**predilec•to -ta** *adj* favorite, preferred
**predio** *m* property, estate
**predisponer** §54 *tr* to predispose
**predominante** *adj* predominant
**preeminente** *adj* preëminent
**preestreno** *m* (mov) preview
**prefabricar** §73 *tr* to prefabricate
**prefacio** *m* preface
**preferencia** *f* preference; **de preferencia** preferably
**preferente** *adj* preferable; favored; (*acciones*) preferred
**preferible** *adj* preferable
**preferir** §68 *tr* to prefer
**prefigurar** *tr* to foreshadow
**prefijar** *tr* to prefix; to prearrange
**prefijo** *m* prefix
**pregón** *m* proclamation, public announcement (*by town crier*)
**pregonar** *tr* to proclaim, announce publicly; to hawk; to reveal; to outlaw; to praise openly
**pregonero** *m* auctioneer; town crier
**preguerra** *f* prewar period
**pregunta** *f* question; **hacer una pregunta** to ask a question
**preguntar** *tr* to ask; to question ‖ *intr* to ask, to inquire; **preguntar por** to ask after or for ‖ *ref* to ask oneself; to wonder
**pregun•tón -tona** *adj* (coll) inquisitive ‖ *mf* (coll) inquisitive person
**prejudicio** or **prejuicio** *m* prejudgment; prejudice
**prelado** *m* prelate
**preliminar** *adj & m* preliminary; **preliminares** (*de un libro*) front matter
**preludio** *m* prelude
**premeditar** *tr* to premeditate
**premiar** *tr* to reward; to give an award to
**premio** *m* reward, prize; premium; **a premio** at a premium; **premio de enganche** (mil) bounty; **premio gordo** first prize
**premio•so -sa** *adj* tight, close; bothersome; strict, rigid; slow, dull
**premisa** *f* premise; mark, token, clue
**premura** *f* pressure, haste, urgency
**premuro•so -sa** *adj* pressing, urgent
**prenda** *f* pledge; security; pawn; jewel, household article; garment, article of clothing; gift, talent; darling, loved one; **en prenda** in pawn; **en prenda de** as a pledge of; **prenda perdida** forfeit; **prendas** (*juego*) forfeits
**prendar** *tr* to pawn; to pledge; to charm, captivate ‖ *ref* — **prendarse de** to take a liking for, fall in love with
**prendedero** *m* fillet, brooch; stickpin
**prender** *tr* to seize, grasp; to catch; to imprison; to dress up; to pin; to

fasten || *intr* to catch; to catch fire; to take root; to turn out well || *ref* to dress up; to be fastened; to catch hold
**prendería** *f* second-hand shop
**prende•ro -ra** *mf* second-hand dealer
**prensa** *f* press; printing press; vise; press, newspapers; press, frame; **entrar en prensa** to go to press; **meter en prensa** (coll) to put the squeeze on; **prensa taladradora** drill press
**prensado** *m* pressing; (*lustre de los tejidos prensados*) sheen
**prensar** *tr* to press; to squeeze
**preña•do -da** *adj* pregnant; sagging, bulging; full, charged
**preñez** *f* pregnancy; fullness; impending danger; inherent confusion
**preocupación** *f* (*posesión anticipada; cuidado, desvelo*) preoccupation; (*posesión anticipada*) preoccupancy; bias, prejudice
**preocupar** *tr* to preoccupy, to worry || *ref* to become preoccupied, to be worried
**preparación** *f* preparation
**prepara•do -da** *adj* ready, prepared || *m* (pharm) preparation
**preparar** *tr* to prepare || *ref* to prepare, to get ready
**preparati•vo -va** *adj* preparatory || *m* preparation, readiness
**preponderante** *adj* preponderant
**preposición** *f* preposition
**prepóste•ro -ra** *adj* reversed, upset, out of order, inopportune
**prerrogativa** *f* prerogative
**presa** *f* capture, seizure; catch, prey; booty, spoils; dam; trench, ditch, flume; bit, morsel; fang, tusk, claw; fishweir; (sport) hold; **hacer presa** to seize; **ser presa de** to be a victim of; to be prey to
**presagiar** *tr* to presage, forebode
**presagio** *m* presage, omen, token
**présbita** or **présbite** *adj* far-sighted || *mf* presbyte
**presbiteria•no -na** *adj* & *mf* Presbyterian
**prescindir** *intr* — **prescindir de** to leave aside, leave out, disregard; to do without, dispense with; to avoid
**prescribir** §83 *tr* & *intr* to prescribe
**presencia** *f* presence; show, display; **presencia de ánimo** presence of mind
**presenciar** *tr* to witness, be present at
**presentación** *f* presentation; (*de una persona en el trato de otra u otras*) introduction; (*de un nuevo automóvil, libro, etc.*) appearance
**presentar** *tr* to present; to introduce || *ref* to present oneself; to appear, show up; to introduce oneself
**presente** *adj* present; **hacer presente** to notify of, to remind of; **tener presente** to bear or keep in mind || *interj* here!, present! || *m* present, gift; person present
**presentimiento** *m* presentiment, premonition
**presentir** §68 *tr* to have a presentiment of
**preservar** *tr* to preserve, protect
**preservati•vo -va** *adj* & *m* preventive; preservative
**presidencia** *f* presidency; chairmanship
**presidente** *m* president; chairman; presiding judge
**presidiario** *m* convict
**presidio** *m* garrison; fortress; citadel; penitentiary; imprisonment; hard labor; aid, help
**presidir** *tr* to preside over; to dominate || *intr* to preside
**presilla** *f* loop, fastener; clip; shoulder strap
**presión** *f* pressure; (*cerveza*) **a presión** on draught; **presión de inflado** tire pressure
**presionar** *tr* to press; to put pressure on || *intr* to press; **presionar sobre** to put pressure on
**pre•so -sa** *adj* seized; imprisoned || *mf* prisoner; convict; *f* see **presa**
**presta•do -da** *adj* lent, loaned; **dar prestado** to lend; **pedir** or **tomar prestado** to borrow
**prestamista** *mf* moneylender; pawnbroker
**préstamo** *m* loan; **préstamo lingüístico** loan word, borrowing
**prestar** *tr* to lend, to loan; (*oído; ayuda; noticias*) to give; (*atención*) to pay; (*un favor*) to do; (*un servicio*) to render; (*juramento*) to take; (*silencio*) to keep; (*paciencia*) to show || *intr* (*un paño, la ropa*) to give, to yield; to be useful || *ref* to lend oneself, to lend itself
**prestatar•rio -ria** *mf* borrower
**presteza** *f* speed, promptness, readiness
**prestidigitación** *f* sleight of hand
**prestidigita•dor -dora** *adj* captivating || *mf* magician; faker, impostor
**prestigio** *m* prestige; good standing; spell; illusion
**prestigio•so -sa** *adj* captivating, spellbinding; famous, renowned; illusory
**pres•to -ta** *adj* quick, prompt, ready; nimble || **presto** *adv* right away
**presumi•do -da** *adj* conceited, vain || *mf* would-be
**presumir** *tr* to presume || *intr* to boast, be conceited
**presunción** *f* presumption; conceit
**presuntuo•so -sa** *adj* conceited, vain
**presuponer** §54 *tr* to presuppose; to budget
**presupuestar** *tr* to budget; (*el coste de una obra*) to estimate
**presupuesto** *m* budget; reason, motive; supposition; estimate
**presuro•so -sa** *adj* speedy, quick, hasty; zealous, persistent
**pretencio•so -sa** *adj* pretentious, showy; conceited, vain
**pretender** *tr* to claim, to pretend to; to try for, to try to do; to be a suitor for || *intr* to insist; **pretender** + *inf* to try to + *inf*
**pretendiente** *mf* pretender, claimant; office seeker || *m* suitor
**pretensión** *f* pretension; claim; pretense; presumption; effort, pursuit
**pretéri•to -ta** *adj* & *m* past

**pretil** *m* parapet, railing; walk along a parapet
**pretina** *f* girdle, belt; waistband
**pretóni•co -ca** *adj* pretonic
**prevalecer** §22 *intr* to prevail; to take root; to thrive
**prevaler** §76 *ref* — **prevalerse de** to avail oneself of, take advantage of
**prevaricar** §73 *intr* to collude, connive; to play false; to transgress; (coll) to rave, be delirious
**prevención** *f* preparation; prevention; foresight; warning; prejudice; stock, supply; jail, lockup; guardhouse; **a** or **de prevención** spare, emergency
**preveni•do -da** *adj* prepared, ready; foresighted, forewarned; stocked, full
**prevenir** §79 *tr* to prepare, make ready; to forestall, prevent, anticipate; to overcome; to warn; to prejudice ‖ *intr* (*una tempestad*) to come up ‖ *ref* to get ready; to come to mind
**prever** §80 *tr* to foresee
**pre•vio -via** *adj* previous; preliminary; after, with previous, subject to, e.g., **previo acuerdo** subject to agreement
**previsión** *f* prevision, foresight; foresightedness; forecast; **previsión del tiempo** weather forecasting
**prie•to -ta** *adj* dark, blackish; stingy, mean; tight, compact; (Am) dark-complexioned ‖ *mf* (W-I) darling
**prima** *f* early morning; bonus, bounty; (ins) premium; (mil) first quarter of the night; (*cuerda*) (mus) treble
**pri•mal -mala** *adj* & *mf* yearling
**prima•rio -ria** *adj* primary ‖ *m* (elec) primary
**primavera** *f* spring, springtime; cowslip, primrose; robin
**primer** *adj* apocopated form of **primero,** used only before masculine singular nouns and adjectives
**prime•ro -ra** *adj* first; former; early; primary; prime; (*materia*) raw ‖ *m* first; **a primeros de** around the beginning of ‖ **primero** *adv* first
**primicia** *f* first fruits
**primige•nio -nia** *adj* original, primitive
**primiti•vo -va** *adj* primitive
**pri•mo -ma** *adj* first; prime, excellent; skillful; (*materia*) raw ‖ *mf* cousin; (coll) sucker, dupe; **primo carnal** or **primo hermano** first cousin, cousin-german ‖ *f* see **prima** ‖ **primo** *adv* in the first place
**primogéni•to -ta** *adj* & *mf* first-born
**primor** *m* care, skill, elegance; beauty
**primoro•so -sa** *adj* careful, skillful, elegant; fine, exquisite
**princesa** *f* princess; **princesa viuda** dowager princess
**principal** *adj* principal, main, chief; first, foremost; essential, important; famous, illustrious; (*piso*) second ‖ *m* principal, head, chief
**príncipe** *m* prince; **portarse como un príncipe** to live like a prince; **príncipe de Asturias** heir apparent of the King of Spain; **príncipe de Gales** prince of Wales; **príncipes** prince and princess
**principiante** *adj* beginning ‖ *mf* beginner, apprentice, novice
**principiar** *tr, intr* & *ref* to begin
**principio** *m* start, beginning; principle; origin, source; (culin) entree; **a principios de** around the beginning of; **en un principio** at the beginning; **principio de admiración** inverted exclamation point; **principio de interrogación** inverted question mark
**pringar** §44 *tr* to dip or soak in grease or fat; to spot or stain with grease; (coll) to make bleed; (coll) to slander, run down; (Am) to splash ‖ *intr* (coll) to meddle; (CAm, Mex) to drizzle ‖ *ref* to peculate
**pringo•so -sa** *adj* greasy, fatty
**prioridad** *f* priority; **de máxima prioridad** of the highest priority
**prisa** *f* hurry, haste; urgency; crush, crowd; **darse prisa** to hurry, make haste; **estar de prisa** or **tener prisa** to be in a hurry
**prisión** *f* seizure, capture; imprisonment; prison; **prisión celular** cell house; **prisiones** shackles, fetters
**prisione•ro -ra** *mf* prisoner; (*cautivo de una pasión o afecto*) captive ‖ *m* setscrew; studbolt
**prisma** *m* prism
**prismáticos** *mpl* binoculars
**priva•do -da** *adj* private ‖ *m* (*de un alto personaje*) favorite ‖ *f* cesspool
**privar** *tr* to deprive; to forbid, prohibit ‖ *intr* to be in vogue; to prevail; to be in favor ‖ *ref* to deprive oneself; **privarse de** to give up
**privilegiar** *tr* to grant a privilege to
**privilegio** *m* privilege
**pro** *m* & *f* profit, advantage; **¡buena pro!** good appetite!; **de pro** of note, of worth; **el pro y el contra** the pros and the cons; **en pro de** on behalf of
**proa** *f* (aer) nose; (naut) prow
**probable** *adj* probable, likely
**probar** §61 *tr* to prove; to test; to try; (*clothing*) to try on; to try out; to sample; to fit; to suit; (*vino*) to touch ‖ *intr* to taste; **probar de** to take a taste of ‖ *ref* to try on
**probidad** *f* probity, integrity, honesty
**problema** *m* problem
**pro•caz** *adj* (*pl* **-caces**) impudent, insolent, bold
**procedencia** *f* origin, source; point of departure
**procedente** *adj* coming, originating; proper
**proceder** *m* conduct, behavior ‖ *intr* to proceed; to originate; to behave; to be proper
**procedimiento** *m* procedure; proceeding; process
**procelo•so -sa** *adj* tempestuous, stormy
**prócer** *adj* high, lofty ‖ *m* hero, leader
**procesar** *tr* to sue, prosecute; to indict; to try
**procesión** *f* procession; origin, emergence
**proceso** *m* process; progress; suit, lawsuit; **proceso verbal** (Am) minutes
**proclama** *f* proclamation; marriage banns

**proclamar** *tr* to proclaim; to acclaim
**proclíti•co -ca** *adj & m* proclitic
**procurador** *m* attorney, solicitor; proxy
**procurar** *tr* to strive for; to manage as attorney; to yield, produce; to try to
**prodigar** §44 *tr* to lavish; to squander; to waste || *ref* to be a show-off
**prodigio** *m* prodigy
**prodigio•so -sa** *adj* prodigious, marvelous; fine, excellent
**pródigo -ga** *adj* prodigal; lavish || *mf* prodigal
**producción** *f* production; crop, yield, produce; **producción en masa** or **en serie** mass production
**producir** §19 *tr* to produce; to yield, to bear; to cause, bring about || *ref* to explain oneself; to come about; to take place
**producto** *m* product; produce; proceeds
**proeza** *f* prowess; feat, stunt
**prof.** *abbr* **profeta**
**profanar** *tr* to profane
**profa•no -na** *adj* profane; indecent, immodest; worldly; lay || *mf* profane; worldly person; layman
**profecía** *f* prophecy || **las Profecías** (Bib) the Prophets
**proferir** §68 *tr* to utter
**profesar** *tr & intr* to profess
**profesión** *f* profession; **profesión de fe** confession of faith
**profe•sor -sora** *mf* teacher; professor
**profeta** *m* prophet
**profetisa** *f* prophetess
**profetizar** §60 *tr* to prophesy
**profilácti•co -ca** *adj & m* prophylactic; preventive || *f* hygiene
**prófu•go -ga** *adj & mf* fugitive || *m* slacker, draft dodger
**profundidad** *f* profundity; depth
**profundizar** §60 *tr* to deepen; to fathom, get to the bottom of
**profun•do -da** *adj* profound; deep
**progenie** *f* descent, lineage, parentage
**progno•sis** *f* (*pl* **-sis**) prognosis; (*del tiempo*) forecast
**programa** *m* program; **programa continuo** (mov) continuous showing; **programa de estudios** curriculum
**programar** *tr* to program
**progresar** *intr* to progress
**progresista** *adj & mf* (pol) progressive
**progreso** *m* progress; **hacer progresos** to make progress
**prohibir** *tr* to prohibit, forbid || *ref* **se prohibe fijar carteles** post no bills
**prohijar** *tr* to adopt
**prohombre** *m* (*en los gremios de los artesanos*) master; leader, head; (coll) big shot
**prójimo** *m* fellow man, fellow creature, neighbor; (coll) fellow
**pról.** *abbr* **prólogo**
**prole** *f* progeny, offspring
**proletariado** *m* proletariat
**proleta•rio -ria** *adj & m* proletarian
**proliferar** *intr* to proliferate
**prolífi•co -ca** *adj* prolific
**proli•jo -ja** *adj* tedious, too long; fussy, fastidious; long-winded; tiresome
**prologar** §44 *tr* to preface, write a preface for
**prólogo** *m* prologue; preface
**prolongar** §44 *tr* to prolong, extend; (geom) to produce
**promediar** *tr* to divide into two equal parts; to average || *intr* to mediate; to be half over
**promedio** *m* average, mean; middle
**promesa** *f* promise
**promete•dor -dora** *adj* promising
**prometer** *tr & intr* to promise || *ref* to become engaged
**prometi•do -da** *adj* engaged, betrothed || *m* promise; fiancé || *f* fiancée
**prominente** *adj* prominent
**promiso•rio -ria** *adj* promissory
**promoción** *f* promotion; advancement; (*conjunto de individuos que obtienen un grado en un mismo año*) class, year, crop
**promontorio** *m* promontory, headland; unwieldy thing
**promover** §47 *tr* to promote; to advance, to further
**promulgar** §44 *tr* to promulgate
**pronombre** *m* pronoun
**pronosticar** §73 *tr* to prognosticate, to foretell
**pronóstico** *m* prognostic, forecast; almanac; (med) prognosis
**pron•to -ta** *adj* quick, speedy; prompt; ready || *m* jerk; (coll) sudden impulse, fit of anger || **pronto** *adv* right away, soon; early; promptly; **lo más pronto posible** as soon as possible; **tan pronto como** as soon as
**pronunciación** *f* pronunciation
**pronuncia•do -da** *adj* marked; (*curva*) sharp; (*pendiente*) steep; bulky
**pronunciamiento** *m* insurrection, uprising; (*golpe de estado militar*) pronunciamento; (law) decree
**pronunciar** *tr* to pronounce; to utter; (*un discurso*) to make, to deliver; to decide on || *ref* to rebel; to declare oneself
**propaganda** *f* propaganda; advertising
**propagar** §44 *tr* to propagate; to spread; to broadcast
**propalar** *tr* to divulge, to spread
**proparoxíto•no -na** *adj & m* proparoxytone
**propasar** *ref* to go too far, to take undue liberty
**propender** *intr* to tend, to incline, to be inclined
**propensión** *f* propensity; predisposition
**propen•so -sa** *adj* inclined, disposed, prone
**propiciar** *tr* to propitiate; (Am) to support, favor, sponsor
**propi•cio -cia** *adj* propitious, favorable
**propiedad** *f* property; ownership; naturalness, likeness; **es propiedad** copyrighted; **propiedad horizontal** one-floor ownership in an apartment house; **propiedad literaria** copyright
**propieta•rio -ria** *mf* owner || *m* proprietor || *f* proprietress
**propina** *f* tip, fee, gratuity
**propinar** *tr* (*algo a beber*) to offer; (*medicamentos*) to prescribe or ad-

minister; (*palos, golpes, etc.*) (coll) to give || *ref* (*una bebida*) to treat oneself to
**propin•cuo -cua** *adj* near, close at hand
**pro•pio -pia** *adj* proper, suitable; peculiar, characteristic; natural; same; himself, herself, etc.; own || *m* messenger; native; **propios** public lands
**proponer** §54 *tr* to propose; to propound; (*a una persona para un empleo*) to name, to present || *ref* to plan; to propose
**proporción** *f* proportion; opportunity
**proporciona•do -da** *adj* proportionate; fit, suitable
**proporcionar** *tr* to furnish, provide, supply, give; to proportion; to adapt, adjust
**proposición** *f* proposition; **proposición dominante** main clause
**propósito** *m* aim, purpose, intention; subject matter; **a propósito** by the way; apropos, fitting; in place; **a propósito de** apropos of; **de propósito** on purpose; **fuera de propósito** irrelevant, beside the point
**propuesta** *f* proposal, proposition
**propulsar** *tr* to propel, to drive
**propulsión** *f* propulsion; **propulsión a chorro** jet propulsion; **propulsión a cohete** rocket propulsion
**pror.** *abbr* **procurador**
**prorratear** *tr* to prorate
**prórroga** *f* extension, renewal
**prorrogar** §44 *tr* to defer, postpone, extend
**prorrumpir** *intr* to spurt, shoot forth; to break forth, burst out
**prosa** *f* prose; (coll) chatter, idle talk
**prosai•co -ca** *adj* prose; prosaic, dull
**proscribir** §83 *tr* to outlaw, to proscribe
**proscrip•to -ta** *mf* exile, outlaw
**prosecución** *f* continuation, prosecution; pursuit
**proseguir** §67 *tr* to continue, carry on || *intr* to continue
**prosélito** *m* proselyte
**prosista** *mf* prose writer; (coll) chatterbox
**prosódi•co -ca** *adj* (*acento*) stress
**prospectar** *tr & intr* to prospect
**prosperar** *tr* to make prosper || *intr* to prosper, to thrive
**prosperidad** prosperity
**próspe•ro -ra** *adj* prosperous, thriving, successful
**prosternar** *ref* to prostrate oneself
**prostituir** §20 *tr* to prostitute || *ref* to prostitute oneself; to become a prostitute
**prostituta** *f* prostitute
**prosu•do -da** *adj* (Chile, Ecuad, Peru) pompous, solemn
**protagonista** *mf* protagonist
**protagonizar** §60 *tr* to play the leading rôle of
**protección** *f* protection; **protección aduanera** protective tariff; **protección a la infancia** child welfare
**proteger** §17 *tr* to protect
**protegida** *f* protégée
**protegido** *m* protégé
**proteína** *f* protein
**proter•vo -va** *adj* perverse
**protesta** *f* protest; pledge, promise
**protestante** *adj & mf* protestant; Protestant
**protestar** *tr* to protest, asseverate; (*la fe*) to profess || *intr* to protest; **protestar de** (*aseverar con ahinco*) to protest (*to state positively*); **protestar contra** (*negar la validez de*) to protest (*to deny forcibly*)
**protocolo** *m* protocol
**protoplasma** *m* protoplasm
**prototipo** *m* prototype
**protozoario** or **protozoo** *m* protozoön
**provec•to -ta** *adj* old, ripe
**provecho** *m* advantage, benefit; profit, gain; advance, progress; **¡buen provecho!** good luck!; good appetite!; **de provecho** useful; **provechos** perquisites
**provecho•so -sa** *adj* advantageous, beneficial; profitable; useful
**proveedor -dora** *mf* supplier, provider, purveyor; steward
**proveer** §43 & §83 *tr* to provide, furnish; to supply; to resolve, settle || *intr* to provide; **proveer a** to provide for || *ref* to supply oneself; to have a movement of the bowels
**provenir** §79 *intr* to come, arise
**Provenza, la** Provence
**provenzal** *adj & mf* Provençal
**proverbio** *m* proverb
**providencia** *f* providence, foresight; step, measure
**providencial** *adj* providential
**provincia** *f* province
**provisión** *f* provision; supply, stock; **provisiones de boca** foodstuffs
**proviso•rio -ria** *adj* provisory, provisional
**provocar** §73 *tr* to provoke; to promote, bring about; to incite, to tempt, to move || *intr* to provoke; (coll) to vomit
**proxeneta** *mf* go-between
**proximidad** *f* proximity; **proximidades** neighborhood
**próxi•mo -ma** *adj* next; near; neighboring, close; early; **próximo pasado** last
**proyección** *f* projection; influence
**proyectar** *tr* to project; to cast; to design || *ref* to project, stick out; (*una sombra*) to be projected, to fall
**proyectil** *m* projectile; **proyectil buscador del blanco** homing missile; **proyectil dirigido** or **teleguiado** guided missile
**proyecto** *m* project; **proyecto de ley** bill
**proyector** *m* projector, searchlight; projection machine
**prudencia** *f* prudence
**prudente** *adj* prudent
**prueba** *f* proof; trial, test; examination; (*de un traje*) fitting; (*de un alimento o una bebida*) sample, sampling; evidence; (sport) event; (Am) acrobatics; (Am) sleight of hand; **a prueba** on approval, on trial; **a prueba de** proof against, -proof, e.g., **a prueba de escaladores** burglarproof;

pruebas de planas page proof; pruebas de primeras first proof (*for proofreader*); pruebas de segundas galley proof (*for author*)
**pruebista** *mf* (Am) acrobat
**prurito** *m* itching; eagerness, itch
**psicoanálisis** *m* psychoanalysis
**psicoanalizar** §60 *tr* to psychoanalyze
**psicología** *f* psychology
**psicológi·co -ca** *adj* psychologic(al)
**psicólo·go -ga** *mf* psychologist
**psicópata** *mf* psychopath
**psico·sis** *f* (*pl* **-sis**) psychosis; **psicosis de guerra** war psychosis, war scare
**psicóti·co -ca** *adj & mf* psychotic
**psique** *f* cheval glass ‖ **Psique** *f* Psyche
**psiquiatra** *mf* psychiatrist
**psiquiatría** *f* psychiatry
**psíqui·co -ca** *adj* psychic
**P.S.M.** *abbr* **por su mandato**
**pte.** *abbr* **parte, presente**
**púa** *f* point; prick, barb; tine, prong; (*del fonógrafo*) needle; (*del peine*) tooth; thorn; (*del puerco espín*) spine, quill; sting; graft; plectrum; (coll) tricky person
**pubertad** *f* puberty
**publicación** *f* publication
**publicar** §73 *tr* to publish; to publicize
**publicidad** *f* publicity; advertising; **publicidad de lanzamiento** advance publicity
**publicita·rio -ria** *adj* publicity; advertising
**públi·co -ca** *adj & m* public
**pucha** *f* (W-I) small bouquet; (Mex) crescent roll
**puchero** *m* pot, kettle; stew; (coll) daily bread; (coll) pouting; **hacer pucheros** to pout, screw up one's face
**pucho** *m* (Am) fag end, remnant; (*de cigarro*) (Am) stump; (Am) trifle, trinket; (*el hijo menor*) (Am) baby
**puden·do -da** *adj* ugly, shameful; obscene; (*partes*) private
**pudiente** *adj* powerful; well-off, well-to-do
**pudín** *m* pudding
**pudor** *m* modesty, shyness; chastity
**pudoro·so -sa** *adj* modest, shy; chaste
**pudrición** *f* rot, rotting
**pudrir** §83 *tr* to rot; to worry ‖ *intr* to be dead and buried ‖ *ref* to rot; to be worried; (*en la cárcel*) to languish
**pueblo** *m* people; common people; town, village; **pueblo de Dios** or **de Israel** children of Israel
**puente** *m* bridge; (dent, mus) bridge; (aut) axle, rear axle; **hacer puente** to take the intervening day off; **puente aéreo** airlift, air bridge; **puente colgante** suspension bridge; **puente de engrase** grease lift; **puente levadizo** drawbridge, lift bridge
**puer·co -ca** *adj* piggish, hoggish; dirty, filthy; slovenly; coarse, mean; lewd ‖ *m* hog; **puerco espín** or **espino** porcupine ‖ *f* sow; slattern, slut
**puericia** *f* childhood
**pueril** *adj* puerile, childish
**puerilidad** *f* puerility, childishness
**puerro** *m* leek
**puerta** *f* door, doorway; gate, gateway; **a puerta cerrada** or **a puertas cerradas** behind closed doors
**puerto** *m* harbor, port; haven; mountain pass; **puerto aéreo** airport; **puerto brigantino** Corunna; **puerto de arribada** port of call; **puerto de mar** seaport; **puerto franco** free port; **puerto marítimo** dock, port; **puerto seco** frontier customhouse
**puertorrique·ño -ña** *adj & mf* Puerto Rican
**pues** *adv* then, well; yes, certainly; why; anyhow; **pues bien** well then; **pues que** since ‖ *conj* for, since, because, inasmuch as ‖ *interj* well!, then!
**puesta** *f* setting; laying; putting; (*dinero apostado*) stake; **a puesta del sol** or **a puestas del sol** at sunset; **puesta a punto** adjustment; carrying out, completion; **puesta a tierra** (elec) grounding; **puesta de largo** coming out, social debut
**pues·to -ta** *adj* dressed; **puesto que** since, inasmuch as ‖ *m* place; booth, stand; office; station; barracks; (*para cazadores*) blind; **puesto de socorros** first-aid station ‖ *f* see **puesta**
**púgil** *m* pugilist
**pugilato** *m* boxing; fist fight
**pugilismo** *m* pugilism
**pugna** *f* fight, battle; struggle, conflict; **en pugna** at issue; **en pugna con** at odds with
**pugnar** *intr* to fight; to struggle; to strive, persist
**pug·naz** *adj* (*pl* **-naces**) pugnacious
**pujante** *adj* powerful, mighty, vigorous
**pujar** *tr* (*un proyecto*) to push; (*un precio*) to raise, bid up ‖ *intr* to struggle, strain; to falter; (*por decir una cosa*) to grope; (coll) to snivel; **pujar para adentro** (CAm, W-I) to keep silent, say nothing
**pul·cro -cra** *adj* neat, tidy, trim; circumspect
**pulga** *f* flea; **de malas pulgas** peppery, hot-tempered; **hacer de una pulga un camello** or **un elefante** (coll) to make a mountain out of a molehill; **no aguantar pulgas** (coll) to stand for no nonsense
**pulgada** *f* inch
**pulgar** *m* thumb
**puli·do -da** *adj* pretty; neat; polished; clean, spotless
**pulimentar** *tr* to polish
**pulimento** *m* polish
**pulir** *tr* to polish; to finish; to give a polish to
**pulmón** *m* lung; **pulmón de acero** or **de hierro** iron lung
**pulmonía** *f* pneumonia
**púlpito** *m* pulpit
**pulpo** *m* octopus
**pulsación** *f* pulsation, throb, beat; strike, striking; (*del pianista, el mecanógrafo*) touch
**pulsar** *tr* (*un botón*) to push; (*un piano, arpa, guitarra*) to play; (*una tecla*) to strike; to feel or take the pulse

of; to sound out, examine || *intr* to pulsate, throb, beat
**pulsear** *intr* to hand-wrestle
**pulsera** *f* bracelet; wristlet, watch strap; **pulsera de pedida** engagement bracelet
**pulso** *m* pulse; steadiness, steady hand; tact, care, caution; (Am) bracelet; (Am) wrist watch; **a pulso** with hand and wrist; by main strength; (*dibujo*) freehand; **sacar a pulso** (coll) to carry out against odds; **tomar el pulso a** to feel or take the pulse of
**pulular** *intr* to swarm; to bud, to sprout
**pulverizar** §60 *tr* to pulverize; to atomize; to spray
**pulla** *f* dig, cutting remark; filthy remark; witticism
**pum** *interj* bang!
**puma** *m* cougar
**puna** *f* (SAm) bleak tableland in the Andes; (SAm) mountain sickness
**pundonor** *m* point of honor; face
**pundonoro·so -sa** *adj* punctilious, scrupulous; haughty, dignified
**pungir** §27 *tr* to prick; to sting
**punta** *f* (*extremo agudo*) point; tip, end; (*del cigarro*) butt; nail; point, cape, headland; (*del toro*) horn; (*del asta del ciervo*) tine, prong; style, graver; touch, tinge, trace; (*del vino*) souring; (elec) point; **de punta** on end; on tiptoe; **de punta en blanco** in full armor; (coll) in full regalia; **estar de punta (con)** to be at odds (with); **punta de combate** (*del torpedo*) warhead; **punta de lanza** spearhead; **punta de París** wire nail; **sacar punta a** to put a point on, to sharpen; **tener en la punta de la lengua** (coll) to have on the tip of one's tongue
**puntada** *f* hint; (sew) stitch; (*dolor agudo*) (Am) stitch, sharp pain
**puntal** *m* prop, support; stay, stanchion; (naut) depth of hold; backing, support; (Am) bite, snack
**puntapié** *m* kick; **echar a puntapiés** (coll) to kick out
**puntear** *tr* to dot, mark with dots; (*guitarra*) to pluck; to stipple; to stitch || *intr* (naut) to tack
**puntera** *f* toe, toe patch; leather tip; (coll) kick
**puntería** *f* aim, aiming; marksmanship
**puntero** *m* pointer; (*del reloj*) hand; stonecutter's chisel; punch; (Am) leading animal
**puntiagu·do -da** *adj* sharp-pointed
**puntilla** *f* brad; narrow lace edging; (*de la pluma fuente*) point; (carp) tracing point; dagger; **de puntillas** on tiptoe; **puntilla francesa** finishing nail
**puntillero** *m* bullfighter who delivers coup de grace with dagger
**puntillo·so -sa** *adj* punctilious
**punto** *m* (*señal de dimensiones poco perceptibles*) point, dot; stitch, loop; mesh; (*rotura en un tejido de punto*) break; jot; cabstand, hackstand; (gram) period; (math, typ, sport, fig) point; **a buen punto** opportunely; **al punto** at once; **a punto de** on the point of; **a punto fijo** for certain; **de punto** knitted; **dos puntos** (gram) colon; **en punto** sharp, on the dot; **poner punto final a** to wind up, to bring to an end; **punto de admiración** exclamation mark or point; **punto de aguja** knitting; **punto de Hungría** herringbone; **punto de media** knitwork; **punto de mira** aim; center of attraction; **¡punto en boca!** mum's the word!; **punto interrogante** question mark; **punto menos** almost; **puntos y rayas** dots and dashes; **punto y coma** *msg* semicolon
**puntuación** *f* punctuation; mark, grade; scoring
**puntual** *adj* punctual; certain, sure; exact, accurate
**puntualizar** §60 *tr* to fix in the memory; to give a detailed account of; to finish; to draw up
**puntuar** §21 *tr & intr* to punctuate; to score
**puntura** *f* puncture, prick
**punzada** *f* prick; shooting pain; (*del remordimiento*) pang
**punzante** *adj* sharp, pricking; barbed, biting, caustic
**punzar** §60 *tr* to prick, puncture, punch; to sting; to grieve || *intr* to sting
**punzón** *m* punch; pick; burin, graver; budding horn, tenderling; **punzón de marcar** center punch
**puñada** *f* punch
**puñado** *m* handful, bunch
**puñal** *m* dagger, poniard
**puñalada** *f* stab; blow, sudden sorrow; **puñalada de misericordia** coup de grâce; **puñalada trapera** stab in the back
**puñetazo** *m* punch; bang with the fist
**puño** *m* fist; cuff; wristband; grasp; fistful, handful; hilt; (*p.ej., del paraguas*) handle; (*del bastón*) head; punch; **como un puño** (coll) whopping big; (coll) tiny, microscopic; (coll) close-fisted; **de su propio puño** or **de su puño y letra** in his own hand, in his own writing
**pupa** *f* pimple; fever blister
**pupila** *f* (*del ojo*) pupil
**pupi·lo -la** *mf* boarder; orphan, ward; pupil || *f* see **pupila**
**pupitre** *m* writing desk
**puquio** *m* (SAm) spring or pool of fresh, clear water
**puré** *m* purée; **puré de patatas** mashed potatoes; **puré de tomates** stewed tomatoes
**pureza** *f* purity
**purga** *f* purge; purgative; drain valve
**purgante** *adj & m* purgative
**purgar** §44 *tr* to purge; to physic; to drain; to purify, refine; to expiate; (*pasiones*) to control, to check; (*sospechas*) to clear away || *ref* to take a physic; to unburden oneself
**puridad** *f* purity
**purificar** §73 *tr* to purify

**purita·no -na** *adj & mf* puritan; Puritan
**pu·ro -ra** *adj* pure; sheer; (*cielo*) clear; out-and-out, outright; **de puro** completely, totally; because of being || *m* cigar
**púrpura** *f* purple
**purpura·do -da** *adj* purple || *m* (eccl) cardinal
**purpúre·o -a** *adj* purple
**pusilánime** *adj* pusillanimous
**pústula** *f* pustule
**puta** *f* whore
**putañear** or **putear** *intr* (coll) to whore around, to chase after lewd women
**putati·vo -va** *adj* spurious
**putrefac·to -ta** *adj* rotten, putrid
**pútri·do -da** *adj* putrid, rotten
**puya** *f* steel point; (*del gallo*) spur

## Q

**Q, q** (cu) *f* twentieth letter of the Spanish alphabet
**q.b.s.m.** *abbr* **que besa su mano**
**q.b.s.p.** *abbr* **que besa sus pies**
**q.e.p.d.** *abbr* **que en paz descanse**
**q.e.s.m.** *abbr* **que estrecha su mano**
**quántum** *m* (*pl* **quanta**) quantum
**que** *pron rel* that, which; who, whom; **el que** he who; which, the one which; who, the one who || *adv* than || *conj* that; for, because; let, e.g., **que entre** let him come in; **a que** (coll) I'll bet that
**qué** *adj & pron interr* what, which; **¿qué tal?** how?; hello, how's everything? || *interj* what!; what a!; how!
**quebrada** *f* gorge, ravine, gap; failure, bankruptcy; (Am) brook
**quebradi·zo -za** *adj* brittle, fragile; frail
**quebra·do -da** *adj* weakened; bankrupt; ruptured; rough; winding; fractional || *m* (math) fraction; (Am) tobacco leaf full of holes || *f* see **quebrada**
**quebrantable** *adj* breakable
**quebrantar** *tr* to break; to break open; to break out of; to grind, crush; to soften, mollify; (*un contrato; la ley; un hábito; un testamento; el corazón de una persona*) to break || *ref* to break; to become broken
**quebrantaterro·nes** *m* (*pl* **-nes**) (coll) clodhopper
**quebranto** *m* break, breaking; heavy loss; great sorrow; discouragement
**quebrar §2** *tr* to break; to bend, twist; to crush; to overcome; to temper, soften || *intr* to break; to fail; to weaken, give in || *ref* to break; to weaken; to become ruptured
**queda** *f* curfew
**quedar** *intr* to remain; to stay; to be left; to be left over; to stop, leave off; to turn out; to be; to be found, be located; **quedar en** to agree on; to agree to; **quedar por** + *inf* or **sin** + *inf* to remain to be + *pp* || *ref* to remain; to stay; to stop; to be; to be left; to put up; **quedarse con** to keep, to take; **quedarse tan fresco** (coll) to show no offense
**que·do -da** *adj* quiet, still; gentle || *f* see **queda** || **quedo** *adv* softly, in a low voice; gropingly
**quehacer** *m* work, task, chore
**queja** *f* complaint, lament; whine, moan
**quejar** *ref* to complain, lament; to whine, moan
**quejido** *m* complaint, whine, moan
**quejumbre** *f* complaining, whine, moan
**quejumbro·so -sa** *adj* complaining; whining, whiny
**quema** *f* fire; burning; **a quema ropa** point-blank; **de quema** distilled; **hacer quema** (Arg, Bol) to hit the mark
**quemada** *f* burnt brush; (Mex) fire
**quemadero** *m* incinerator; (*poste destinado para quemar a los condenados a la pena de fuego*) stake
**quema·do -da** *adj* burned; burnt out; (Am) angry || *m* burnt brush; **oler a quemado** (coll) to smell of fire; **saber a quemado** (coll) to taste burned || *f* see **quemada**
**quema·dor -dora** *adj* burning; incendiary || *m* burner
**quemadura** *f* burn; (agr) smut
**quemar** *tr* to burn; to scald; to set on fire; to scorch; to frostbite; to sell too cheap || *intr* to burn, be hot || *ref* to burn; to be burning up; (coll) to fret; (*estar cercano a lo que se busca*) (coll) to be warm, to be hot; **quemarse las cejas** (coll) to burn the midnight oil
**quemarropa** — **a quemarropa** point-blank
**quemazón** *f* burn; burning; intense heat; (*de un fusible*) blowout; (coll) itch; (coll) cutting remark; (coll) pique, anger; (hum) bargain sale; (Arg, Bol, Chile) mirage on the pampas
**que·pis** *m* (*pl* **-pis**) kepi
**querella** *f* complaint; dispute, quarrel
**querellar** *ref* to complain; to whine
**querencia** *f* liking, affection; attraction; love of home; (*de animales*) haunt; favorite spot
**querencio·so -sa** *adj* homing; (*sitio*) favorite
**querer** *m* love, affection; liking, fondness || *v* **§55** *tr* to wish, want, desire; to like; to love; **como quiera** anyhow; anyway; **como quiera que** whereas; inasmuch as; no matter how; **cuando quiera** any time; **donde quiera** anywhere; **querer bien** to love; **sin querer** unwillingly; unintentionally || *v aux* to wish to, to want to, to desire to; will; to be about to, to be trying to,

e.g., **quiere llover** it is trying to rain; **querer decir** to mean; **querer más** to prefer to, would rather
**queri•do -da** *adj* dear || *mf* lover; paramour; (coll) dearie || *f* mistress
**quermés** *f* or **quermese** *f* bazaar; village or country fair
**queroseno** *m* var of **keroseno**
**querubín** *m* cherub
**quesadilla** *f* cheesecake; sweet pastry
**quese•ro -ra** *adj* cheesy || *mf* cheesemonger; cheesemaker || *f* cheese board; cheese mold; cheese dish
**queso** *m* cheese; **queso de cerdo** headcheese; **queso helado** brick ice cream
**quevedos** *mpl* nose glasses
**quiá** *interj* oh, no!
**quicio** *m* pivot hole (*of hinge*); **fuera de quicio** out of order; **sacar de quicio** to put out of order; to unhinge
**quiebra** *f* crack; damage, loss; bankruptcy
**quien** *pron rel* who, whom; he who, she who; someone who, anyone who
**quién** *pron interr* who, whom
**quienquiera** *pron indef* anyone, anybody; **quienquiera que** whoever; **a quienquiera que** whomever
**quie•to -ta** *adj* quiet, calm; virtuous
**quietud** *f* quiet, calm, stillness
**quijada** *f* jaw, jawbone
**quijotes•co -ca** *adj* quixotic
**quilate** *m* carat
**quilo** *m* kilogram; **sudar el quilo** (coll) to slave, be a drudge
**quilla** *f* keel; (*de ave*) breastbone; **dar de quilla** (naut) to keel over
**quimera** *f* chimera; dispute, quarrel
**química** *f* chemistry
**quími•co -ca** *adj* chemical || *mf* chemist || *f* see **química**
**quimicultura** *f* tank farming
**quimono** *m* kimono
**quina** *f* cinchona, Peruvian bark
**quincalla** *f* hardware
**quincallería** *f* hardware store; hardware business; hardware factory
**quincalle•ro -ra** *mf* hardware merchant
**quince** *adj & pron* fifteen || *m* fifteen; (*en las fechas*) fifteenth
**quincea•vo -va** *adj & m* fifteenth
**quince•no -na** *adj & m* fifteenth || *f* fortnight, two weeks; two weeks' pay
**quincuagési•mo -ma** *adj & m* fiftieth
**quiniela** *f* pelota game of five; soccer lottery; daily double; (Arg, Urug) numbers game
**quinien•tos -tas** *adj & pron* five hundred || **quinientos** *m* five hundred
**quinina** *f* quinine
**quinqué** *m* student lamp, oil lamp
**quinquenal** *adj* five-year
**quinta** *f* villa, country house; draft, induction; **ir a quintas** to be drafted; **redimirse de las quintas** to be exempted from the draft
**quintacolumnista** *mf* fifth columnist
**quintal** *m* quintal, hundredweight
**quintar** *tr* to draft
**quinteto** *m* quintet
**quintilla** *f* five-line stanza of eight syllables and two rhymes; any five-line stanza with two rhymes
**quintilli•zo -za** *mf* quint, quintuplet
**Quintín — armar la de San Quintín** to raise a rumpus, raise a row
**quin•to -ta** *adj* fifth || *m* fifth; lot; pasture; draftee || *f* see **quinta**
**quinza•vo -va** *adj & m* fifteenth
**quiosco** *m* kiosk, summerhouse; stand; **quiosco de música** bandstand; **quiosco de necesidad** comfort station; **quiosco de periódicos** newsstand
**quiquiri•quí** *m* (*pl* **-quíes**) cock-a-doodle-doo; (coll) cock of the walk
**quirófano** *m* operating room
**quiromancia** or **quiromancía** *f* palmistry
**quiropodista** *mf* chiropodist
**quiropráctí•co -ca** *adj* chiropractic || *mf* chiropractor
**quirúrgi•co -ca** *adj* surgical
**quirurgo** *m* surgeon
**quiscal** *m* grackle
**quisicosa** *f* puzzler
**quisqui•do -da** *adj* (Arg) constipated
**quisquilla** *f* trifle, triviality; **pararse en quisquillas** to bicker, to make a fuss over trifles; **quisquillas** hairsplitting, quibbling
**quisquillo•so -sa** *adj* trifling; touchy; fastidious; hairsplitting
**quiste** *m* cyst
**quis•to -ta** *adj* — **bien quisto** well-liked, welcome; **mal quisto** disliked, unwelcome
**quitaesmalte** *m* nail-polish remover
**quitaman•chas** (*pl* **-chas**) *mf* (*persona*) clothes cleaner, spot remover || *m* (*substancia*) clothes cleaner, spot remover
**quitamo•tas** *mf* (*pl* **-tas**) (coll) bootlicker, apple polisher
**quitanie•ve** *m* or **quitanie•ves** *m* (*pl* **-ves**) snowplow
**quitapie•dras** *m* (*pl* **-dras**) cowcatcher
**quitapintura** *m* paint remover
**quitapón** *m* pompon for draft mules; **de quitapón** detachable, removable
**quitar** *tr* to remove; to take away; (*la mesa*) to clear; (*esfuerzo, trabajo*) to save; (*tiempo*) to take; to free; to parry; **quitar algo a algo** to take something off something, to remove something from something; **quitar algo a uno** to remove something from someone; to take something away from someone || *intr* — **de quita y pon** detachable, removable || *ref* (*el sombrero, una prenda de vestir*) to take off; (*el sombrero en señal de cortesía*) to tip; (*una mancha*) to come out, to come off; (*un vicio*) to give up; to withdraw
**quitasol** *m* parasol
**quite** *m* removal; hindrance; dodge; (*en la esgrima*) parry; (taur) passes made with the cape to draw the bull away from the man in danger
**quizá** or **quizás** *adv* maybe, perhaps
**quó•rum** *m* (*pl* **-rum**) quorum

# R

**R, r** (ere) *f* twenty-first letter of the Spanish alphabet
**R.** *abbr* **respuesta, Reverencia, Reverendo**
**rabada** *f* hind quarter, rump
**rabadilla** *f* base of the spine
**rábano** *m* radish; **rábano picante** or **rusticano** horseradish; **tomar el rábano por las hojas** (coll) to be on the wrong track
**ra·bí** *m* (*pl* **-bíes**) rabbi
**rabia** *f* anger, rage; (*hidrofobia*) rabies; **tener rabia a** (coll) to have a grudge against
**rabiar** *intr* to rage, to rave; to get mad; to go mad, to have rabies; **que rabia** like the deuce; **rabiar por** to be dying for; to be dying to
**rabieta** *f* (coll) tantrum
**rabillo** *m* leafstalk; flower stalk; (*en los cereales*) mildew spot; (*del ojo*) corner
**rabio·so -sa** *adj* mad, rabid
**rabo** *m* tail; (*del ojo*) corner; (fig) tail, train; **rabo verde** (CAm) old rake
**ra·bón -bona** *adj* bobtail; (Chile) bare, naked; (Mex) mean, wretched ‖ *f* (Am) camp follower; **hacer rabona** (coll) to play hooky
**rabotada** *f* swish of the tail; (coll) coarse remark
**rabu·do -da** *adj* long-tailed
**racial** *adj* racial
**racimar** *ref* to cluster, to gather together
**racimo** *m* bunch; cluster; (*de perlas*) string
**raciocinio** *m* reasoning
**ración** *f* ration; allowance; **ración de hambre** starvation wages
**racional** *adj* rational
**racionar** *tr* to ration
**racha** *f* split, crack; chip; squall, gust of wind; streak of luck
**rada** *f* (naut) road, roadstead
**radar** *m* radar
**radiación** *f* radiation
**radiacti·vo -va** *adj* radioactive
**radia·dor -dora** *adj* radiating ‖ *m* radiator
**radiante** *adj* radiant; (*alegre, sonriente*) radiant
**radiar** *tr* to radiate; to radio; to broadcast; to cross out, erase ‖ *intr* to radiate
**radicación** *f* taking root; (math) evolution
**radical** *adj* & *m* radical
**radicar** §73 *intr* to take root; to be located ‖ *ref* to take root; to settle; (*un negocio*) to be based
**radio** *m* edge, outskirts; (*de una rueda*) spoke, rung; (*de acción*) radius; (chem) radium; (math) radius ‖ *m* & *f* radio
**radioaficiona·do -da** *mf* radio amateur, radio fan
**radiodifundir** *tr* & *intr* to broadcast
**radiodifusión** *f* broadcasting
**radioemisora** *f* broadcasting station
**radioescucha** *mf* radio listener; radio monitor
**radiofrecuencia** *f* radio frequency
**radiografiar** §77 *tr* to X-ray; to radio, to wireless
**radiograma** *m* X ray (*photograph*)
**radioperturbación** *f* jamming
**radioyente** *mf* radio listener
**raer** §56 *tr* to scrape, scrape off; to smooth, to level; to wipe ‖ *ref* to become frayed, to wear away
**ráfaga** *f* gust, puff; gust of wind; flash of light; (*de ametralladora*) burst
**raí·do -da** *adj* threadbare; barefaced
**ra·íz** *f* (*pl* **-íces**) root; **a raíz de** close to the root of; even with; right after, hard upon; **de raíz** by the root; completely; **echar raíces** to take root
**raja** *f* crack, split; splinter, chip; slice
**rajar** *tr* to crack, to split; to splinter, chip; to slice ‖ *intr* (coll) to boast; (coll) to chatter ‖ *ref* to crack, to split; to splinter, chip; (Mex, CAm, W-I) to back down, to break one's promise
**rajatabla** — **a rajatabla** (coll) desperately, ruthlessly
**ralea** *f* kind, quality; breed, ilk
**ralear** *intr* to thin out; to be true to form
**ra·lo -la** *adj* sparse, thin
**rallador** *m* grater
**rallar** *tr* to grate; (coll) to grate on, annoy
**rallo** *m* grater; scraper; rasp; (*de la regadera*) spout, nozzle; unglazed porous jug (*for cooling water by evaporation*)
**rama** *f* branch, bough; **andarse por las ramas** (coll) to beat about the bush; **en rama** raw; unbound, in sheets; in the grain
**ramaje** *m* branches, foliage
**ramal** *m* (*de una cuerda*) strand; halter; branch; (rr) branch line
**ramalazo** *m* lash; (*señal en el cutis por un golpe o enfermedad*) spot, pock; sharp pain; blow, sudden sorrow
**rambla** *f* dry ravine; avenue, boulevard
**ramera** *f* whore, harlot
**ramificar** §73 *tr* & *ref* to ramify
**ramillete** *m* bouquet; centerpiece, epergne; (bot) cluster
**ramo** *m* branch, limb; bouquet, cluster; (*de géneros, negocios, etc.*) line; (*p.ej., de una ciencia*) branch; (*de una enfermedad*) touch, slight attack
**ramojo** *m* brushwood, dead wood
**ramonear** *intr* to trim twigs; to browse
**rampa** *f* ramp; cramp; (aer) apron; (Bol) litter, stretcher
**ram·plón -plona** *adj* (*zapato*) heavy, coarse; common, vulgar
**ramplonería** *f* coarseness, vulgarity
**rana** *f* frog; **no ser rana** (coll) to be a past master; **rana toro** bullfrog
**ran·cio -cia** *adj* rank, rancid, stale;

(*vino*) old; old, ancient; old, old-fashioned
**ranchar** *ref* (Col, Ven) to balk
**ranchear** *tr* (Am) to sack, pillage || *intr & ref* to build huts, form a settlement
**ranchero** *m* messman; (Am) rancher, ranchman
**rancho** *m* mess; meeting, gathering; camp; thatched hut; (naut) stock of provisions; (Am) ranch; (Arg) straw hat; **hacer rancho** (coll) to make room; **hacer rancho aparte** (coll) to be a lone wolf, to go one's own way
**randa** *m* (coll) pickpocket || *f* lace trimming
**rango** *m* rank; class, nature; (Am) pomp, splendor; (*elevada condición social*) (Am) status, standing
**ranura** *f* groove; slot
**rapagón** *m* stripling
**rapar** *tr* to shave; to crop; to scrape; (coll) to snatch, filch || *ref* to shave; (*una vida regalada*) to lead
**ra·paz** (*pl* **-paces**) *adj* thievish; rapacious || *m* young boy, lad
**rapaza** *f* young girl, lass
**rapé** *m* snuff
**rápi·do -da** *adj* rapid || *m* (rr) express; **rápidos** (*de un río*) rapids
**raposa** *f* fox; female fox; (*persona*) (coll) fox
**raposo** *m* male fox; (coll) foxy fellow; (coll) slipshod fellow
**raptar** *tr* to abduct; to kidnap
**rapto** *m* abduction; kidnaping; rapture; faint, swoon
**raque** *m* beachcombing; **andar al raque** to go beachcombing
**raquear** *intr* to beachcomb
**raquero** *m* pirate; beachcomber
**raqueta** *f* racket; battledore; badminton; snowshoe; **raqueta y volante** battledore and shuttlecock
**raquíti·co -ca** *adj* (*que padece raquitis*) rickety; flimsy, weak, miserable
**raquitis** *f* rickets
**raramente** *adv* rarely, seldom; oddly
**rareza** *f* rareness; rarity; oddness, strangeness; peculiarity
**ra·ro -ra** *adj* rare; odd, strange; thin, sparse
**ras** *m* evenness; **a ras** close, even, flush; **a ras de** even with, flush with; **ras con ras** flush, at the same level; grazing
**rasar** *tr* to graze, to skim || *ref* to clear up
**rascacie·los** *m* (*pl* **-los**) skyscraper
**rascamoño** *m* fancy hairpin; (bot) zinnia
**rascar** §73 *tr* to scrape; to scuff; to scratch; to scrape clean || *ref* (*una cicatriz, un grano*) to pick; (Am) to get drunk
**rasete** *m* satinet
**rasga·do -da** *adj* (*boca; ventana*) wide-open; (*ojos*) large; (Am) outspoken; (Col) generous || *m* tear, rip, rent
**rasgar** §44 *tr* to tear, to rip || *ref* to become torn
**rasgo** *m* (*de una pluma de escribir*) flourish, stroke; trait, characteristic; feat, deed; flash of wit, bright remark; **a grandes rasgos** in bold strokes; **rasgos** (*de la cara*) features
**rasguear** *tr* to thrum on || *intr* to make a flourish
**rasgón** *m* tear, rip, rent
**rasguñar** *tr* to scratch; to sketch, outline
**rasguño** *m* scratch; sketch, outline
**ra·so -sa** *adj* smooth, flat, level, even; common, plain; clear, cloudless; (coll) brazen, shameless || *m* flat country; satin; **al raso** in the open
**raspa** *f* stalk, stem; (*de mazorca de maíz*) beard; (*de pez*) spine, backbone; shell, rind
**raspadura** *f* scraping; erasure; (Am) pan sugar
**raspar** *tr* to scrape, scrape off; to scratch, scratch out; to graze; (*el vino*) to bite; to take, to steal; (W-I) to dismiss, fire; (W-I) to scold || *intr* (Ven) to go away; (Ven) to die
**raspear** *tr* (SAm) to scold || *intr* (*una pluma*) to scratch
**rastra** *f* rake; harrow; drag; track, trail; (*p.ej., de cebollas*) string; (naut) drag; **pescar a la rastra** to trawl
**rastracuero** *m* (Am) show-off; (Am) upstart; (Am) sharper, adventurer
**rastreador** *m* dredge; (nav) mine sweeper
**rastrear** *tr* to trail, track, trace; to drag; to dredge; to check into || *intr* to rake; to skim the ground, fly low
**rastre·ro -ra** *adj* dragging, trailing; creeping; low-flying; groveling, cringing; low, vile
**rastrillar** *tr* to rake; (*cáñamo, lino*) to hatchel, to comb; (Arg, Col) to shoot, to fire; (*un fósforo*) (Arg, Col) to strike (*a match*)
**rastrillo** *m* rake; hackle, hatchel, flax comb; (*de cerradura o llave*) ward; grating, iron grate; (rr) cowcatcher
**rastro** *m* rake; harrow; track, trail; scent; trace, vestige; slaughterhouse; wholesale meat market; rag fair; **rastro de condensación** (aer) contrail
**rastrojo** *m* stubble
**rasura** *f* shaving; scraping
**rasurar** *tr & ref* to shave
**rata** *f* rat; female rat; **rata del trigo** hamster
**ratear** *tr* to apportion; to snitch
**ratería** *f* baseness, meanness, vileness; petty thievery; petty theft
**rate·ro -ra** *adj* thievish; trailing, dragging; base, vile || *mf* sneak thief
**ratificar** §73 *tr* to ratify
**rato** *m* time, while, little while; **a ratos** from time to time; **a ratos perdidos** in spare time, in one's leisure hours; **buen rato** pleasant time; (coll) large amount; **pasar el rato** (coll) to waste one's time; **un rato** awhile
**ratón** *m* mouse; (Ven) hangover; **ratón de biblioteca** (coll) bookworm
**ratonera** *f* (*trampa*) mousetrap; (*agujero*) mousehole; nest of mice; (Am) hut, shop
**raudal** *m* stream, torrent; abundance
**rau·do -da** *adj* rapid, swift, impetuous

**raya** *f* stripe; (*línea fina; pez*) ray; (*en la imprenta, la escritura y la telegrafía*) dash; (*de los pantalones*) crease; (*en los cabellos*) part; boundary line, limit; (*para impedir la comunicación del incendio en los campos*) firebreak; (*del espectro*) (phys) line; (Mex) pay, wages; **a rayas** striped; **hacerse la raya** to part one's hair; **pasar de la raya** to go too far; **tener a raya** to keep within bounds

**raya•no -na** *adj* bordering; borderline

**rayar** *tr* (*papel*) to rule, to line; to stripe; to scratch, score, mark; to cross out; to underscore || *intr* to border; to stand out; (*el alba, el día, la luz, el sol*) to begin, arise, come forth; **rayar en** to verge on, to border on || *ref* (Col) to get rich

**rayo** *m* (*de luz*) ray; (*de rueda*) spoke; lightning, flash of lightning, stroke of lightning, thunderbolt; (*persona*) (fig) live wire; **echar rayos** (coll) to blow up, hit the ceiling; **rayo mortífero** death ray; **rayos X** X rays

**rayón** *m* rayon

**raza** *f* race; breed, stock; crack, slit; quality; ray of light (*coming through a crack*)

**razón** *f* reason; right, justice; account, story; (*cantidad o grado medidos por otra cosa tomada como unidad*) rate; (math) ratio; **a razón de** at the rate of; **con razón o sin ella** right or wrong; **hacer la razón** to return a toast; to join at table; **meterse en razón** to listen to reason; **no tener razón** to be wrong; **razón social** firm name, trade name; **tener razón** to be right; to be in the right

**razonable** *adj* reasonable

**razonar** *tr* to reason, reason out; to itemize || *intr* to reason

**reabrir** §83 *tr* & *ref* to reopen

**reacción** *f* reaction; **reacción en cadena** chain reaction

**reaccionar** *intr* to react

**reacciona•rio -ria** *adj* & *mf* reactionary

**rea•cio -cia** *adj* stubborn, obstinate

**reactivo** *m* reagent

**real** *adj* real; royal; fine, splendid || *m* army camp; fairground; real (*old Spanish coin; Spanish money of account equal to a quarter of a peseta*)

**realce** *m* embossment, raised work; enhancement, lustre; emphasis; **bordar de realce** to embroider in relief; (fig) to embroider, to exaggerate

**realeza** *f* royalty

**realidad** *f* reality; truth; **hecho realidad** come true, e.g., **un sueño hecho realidad** a dream come true

**realismo** *m* realism

**realista** *mf* (*persona que tiende a ver las cosas como son*) realist; (*partidario de la monarquía*) royalist

**realización** *f* realization, fulfillment; achievement; sale; **realización de beneficios** profit taking

**realizar** §60 *tr* to fulfill; to carry out; to turn into cash || *ref* to become fulfilled; to be carried out

**realquilar** *tr* to sublet

**realzar** §60 *tr* to raise, elevate; to emboss; to enhance, set off; to emphasize

**reanimar** *tr* to revive, restore; to cheer, encourage || *ref* to revive, recover one's spirits

**reanudar** *tr* to renew, to resume

**reaparecer** §22 *intr* to reappear

**reata** *f* rope to keep animals in single file; single file; **de reata** in single file; (coll) in blind submission; (coll) next, following

**rebaba** *f* burr, fin

**rebaja** *f* rebate; diminution

**rebajar** *tr* to lower; to diminish, reduce; to rebate; (*precios*) to mark down; (*a una persona*) to deflate; (carp) to rabbet || *ref* to stoop; to humble oneself

**rebajo** *m* rabbet, groove; offset, recess

**rebalsar** *tr* to dam || *ref* to become dammed up; to be checked; to pile up, accumulate

**rebanada** *f* slice

**rebanar** *tr* to slice; to cut through

**rebañadera** *f* grapnel

**rebaño** *m* flock

**rebarbati•vo -va** *adj* crabbed, surly

**rebasar** *tr* to exceed; to overflow; to sail past

**rebatiña** *f* grabbing, scramble; **andar a la rebatiña** (coll) to scramble

**rebatir** *tr* to repel, drive back; to check; to resist; to strengthen; to rebut, refute; to deduct, rebate; to beat hard

**rebato** *m* alarm, call to arms; alarm, excitement; (mil) surprise attack

**rebeca** *f* cardigan

**rebelar** *ref* to revolt, rebel; to resist; to break away

**rebelde** *adj* rebellious; stubborn || *mf* rebel

**rebeldía** *f* rebelliousness; defiance, stubbornness

**rebelión** *f* rebellion, revolt

**rebe•lón -lona** *adj* balky, restive

**reborde** *m* flange, rim, collar

**rebosar** *tr* to cause to overflow || *intr* to overflow, run over; to be in abundance; **rebosar de** or **en** to overflow with, to burst with; to be rich in; to have an abundance of || *ref* to overflow, run over

**rebotar** *tr* to bend back; to repel; (coll) to annoy, worry || *intr* to bounce; to bounce back, rebound || *ref* (coll) to become annoyed, become worried

**rebote** *m* bounce; rebound

**rebozar** §60 *tr* (*la cara*) to muffle up; to cover with batter || *ref* to muffle up, to muffle oneself up

**rebozo** *m* muffling; muffler; shawl; **de rebozo** secretly; **sin rebozo** frankly, openly

**rebulta•do -da** *adj* bulky, massive

**rebullicio** *m* hubbub, loud uproar

**rebullir** §13 *intr* to stir, begin to move; to give signs of life || *ref* to stir, begin to move

**rebusca** *f* seeking, searching; gleaning; leavings, refuse

**rebusca•do -da** *adj* affected, unnatural, recherché
**rebuscar** §73 *tr* to seek after; to search into; to glean
**rebuznar** *intr* to bray; (coll) to talk nonsense
**rebuzno** *m* braying; (coll) nonsense
**recade•ro -ra** *mf* messenger || *m* errand boy
**recado** *m* errand; message; gift, present; daily marketing; compliments, regards; safety, security; equipment, outfit; **mandar recado** to send word; **recado de escribir** writing materials
**recaer** §15 *intr* to fall again; to fall back; to relapse; to backslide; **recaer en** to fall to; **recaer sobre** to fall upon, devolve upon
**recaída** *f* relapse; backsliding
**recalar** *tr* to soak, saturate || *intr* to sight land
**recalcar** §73 *tr* to press, squeeze; to cram, pack, stuff; (*sus palabras*) to stress || *intr* (naut) to list, to heel; **recalcar en** to lay stress on || *ref* (coll) to harp on the same string; (coll) to sprawl; (*p.ej., la muñeca*) (coll) to sprain
**recalentar** §2 *tr* to overheat; (*la comida*) to warm over
**recalmón** *m* (naut) lull
**recamado** *m* embroidery
**recamar** *tr* to embroider
**recámara** *f* dressing room; (*de un arma de fuego*) breech, chamber; (coll) reserve, caution; (Mex) bedroom
**recamarera** *f* (Mex) chambermaid
**recambio** *m* spare part; (*parte, rueda, etc.*) **de recambio** spare
**recapacitar** *tr* to run over in one's mind || *intr* to refresh one's memory; to reflect
**recargar** §44 *tr* to reload; to overload; to recharge; to overcharge; to overadorn; (*una cuota de impuesto*) to increase; (elec) to recharge || *ref* to become more feverish
**recargo** *m* new burden; extra charge; new charge; (*que paga el contribuyente moroso*) penalty; (pathol) rise in temperature; **recargo de tarifa** extra fare
**recata•do -da** *adj* cautious, circumspect; modest; shy
**recatar** *tr* to hide, conceal || *ref* to hide; to be afraid to take a stand
**recato** *m* caution, reserve; modesty
**recauchutaje** *m* recapping, retreading
**recauchutar** *tr* to recap, to retread
**recaudar** *tr* (*impuestos, tributos*) to gather, collect; to guard, watch over
**recaudo** *m* tax collecting; care, precaution; bail, surety; **a buen recaudo** under guard, in safety
**recelar** *tr* to fear, distrust || *intr & ref* to fear, be afraid
**recelo** *m* fear, distrust
**recelo•so -sa** *adj* fearful, distrustful
**recensión** *f* review, book review
**recepción** *f* reception; reception desk
**recepcionista** *m* room clerk || *f* receptionist
**receptáculo** *m* receptacle; shelter, refuge
**receptar** *tr* to receive, welcome; (*delincuentes*) to hide, conceal; (*cosas robadas*) to receive
**recepti•vo -va** *adj* receptive; susceptible
**receptor** *m* receiver; **receptor de cabeza** headpiece; **receptor telefónico** receiver
**receta** *f* recipe; (pharm) prescription
**recetar** *tr* (*un medicamento*) to prescribe; (coll) to request
**recibí** *m* receipt; received payment
**recibi•dor -dora** *mf* receiver; receiving teller; ticket collector || *m* reception room
**recibimiento** *m* reception; welcome; reception room; (*visita en que una persona recibe a sus amistades*) at-home
**recibir** *tr* to receive; (*visitas*) to entertain || *intr* to receive; to entertain || *ref* to be received, be admitted; **recibirse de** to be admitted to practice as; to be graduated as
**recibo** *m* reception; receipt; hall; parlor; at-home; **acusar recibo de** to acknowledge receipt of; **estar de recibo** to be at home; **ser de recibo** to be acceptable
**recién** *adv* (used before past participles) recently, just, newly, e.g., **recién llegado** newly arrived; (Am) just now, recently
**reciente** *adv* recently
**recinto** *m* area, inclosure, place
**re•cio -cia** *adj* strong; thick, coarse, heavy; harsh; hard, bitter, arduous; (*tiempo*) severe; swift, impetuous || **recio** *adv* strongly; swiftly; hard; loud
**reciprocidad** *f* reciprocity
**recípro•co -ca** *adj* reciprocal
**recital** *m* (*de música o poesía*) recital
**recitar** *tr* to recite; (*un discurso*) to deliver
**reclamación** *f* claim, demand; objection; protest, complaint
**reclamar** *tr* to claim, demand; (*un ave*) to decoy, lure || *intr* to cry out, protest, complain
**reclamo** *m* bird call; decoy bird; (*para aves*) lure; allurement, attraction; advertisement; blurb, puff; reference; (typ) catchword
**reclinar** *tr* (*p.ej., la cabeza*) to lean, to bend || *ref* to recline
**reclinatorio** *m* prie-dieu; couch, lounge
**recluir** §20 *tr* to seclude, shut in; to imprison || *ref* to go into seclusion
**reclusión** *f* seclusion; imprisonment
**reclu•so -sa** *adj* secluded; imprisoned || *mf* prisoner; inmate
**recluta** *m* recruit || *f* recruiting; (*del ganado disperso*) (Arg) roundup
**reclutar** *tr* to recruit; (Arg) to round up
**recobrar** *tr* to recover || *ref* to recover; to come to
**recobro** *m* recovery; (*de un motor*) pickup
**recodar** *intr* to lean; to bend, twist, turn, wind
**recodo** *m* bend, twist, turn
**recoger** §17 *tr* to pick up; to gather,

collect; to harvest; to shorten, draw in; to keep; to welcome; to lock up || *ref* to take shelter, take refuge; to withdraw; (*echarse en la cama*) to retire; to go home; to cut down expenses

**recogida** *f* collection; withdrawal; suspension

**recogimiento** *m* gathering, collecting; harvesting; seclusion, retreat; concentration; self-communion

**recolectar** *tr* to gather, gather in; (*el algodón*) to pick

**recomendable** *adj* commendable

**recomendar** §2 *tr* to recommend; to commend

**recompensa** *f* recompense, reward

**recompensar** *tr* to recompense, reward

**recomprar** *tr* to buy back, to repurchase

**reconcentrar** *tr* to bring together; (*un sentimiento o afecto*) to conceal, disguise || *ref* to come together; to be absorbed in thought

**reconciliar** *tr* to reconcile || *ref* to become reconciled

**recóndi·to -ta** *adj* hidden, concealed

**reconfortar** *tr* to comfort, to cheer

**reconocer** §22 *tr* to recognize; to admit, to acknowledge; to examine; (mil) to reconnoiter || *intr* (mil) to reconnoiter || *ref* to be clear

**reconoci·do -da** *adj* grateful

**reconocimiento** *m* recognition; admission, acknowledgment; gratitude; reconnaissance; **reconocimiento médico** inquest

**reconquista** *f* reconquest

**reconsiderar** *tr* to reconsider

**reconstruir** §20 *tr* to reconstruct, to rebuild, to recast

**recontar** §61 *tr* (*volver a contar; narrar*) to recount (*to count again; to narrate*)

**reconvenir** §79 *tr* to expostulate with, to remonstrate with

**reconversión** *f* reconversion

**recopilar** *tr* to compile

**re·cord** *m* (*pl* **-cords**) (sport) record; **batir un record** to break a record; **establecer un record** to make a record

**recordar** §61 *tr* to remember; to remind || *intr* to remember; to get awake; to come to; **si mal no recuerdo** (coll) if I remember correctly

**recordati·vo -va** *adj* reminding, reminiscent || *m* reminder

**recordatorio** *m* reminder; memento

**record·man** (*pl* **-men**) record holder

**recorrer** *tr* to go over, to go through; to look over, look through; (*un libro*) to run through; to overhaul

**recorrido** *m* trip, run, route; (*del émbolo*) stroke; repair

**recortado** *m* cutout

**recortar** *tr* to trim, to cut off; (*figuras en una tela, en un papel*) to cut out; to outline || *ref* to stand out

**recorte** *m* cutting; (*de un periódico*) clipping; dodge, duck; **recortes** cuttings, trimmings

**recostar** §61 *tr* to lean || *ref* to lean, lean back, sit back

**recova** *f* poultry business; poultry stand; (Arg) portico; (SAm) food market

**recoveco** *m* bend, turn, twist; subterfuge, trick

**recreación** *f* recreation

**recreo** *m* recreation; place of amusement

**recrudecer** §22 *intr & ref* to flare up, get worse

**rectángu·lo -la** *adj* right-angled || *m* rectangle

**rectificar** §73 *tr* to rectify; (*un cilindro de motor*) to rebore

**rec·to -ta** *adj* straight; (*ángulo*) right; right, just, righteous || *m* rectum

**rec·tor -tora** *adj* governing, managing || *mf* principal, superior || *m* rector; (*de una universidad*) rector, president

**recua** *f* drove; (*de personas o cosas*) (coll) string, line

**recuadro** *m* panel, square; (*sección de un impreso encerrada dentro de un marco*) box

**recubrir** §83 *tr* to cover, cap, coat

**recuento** *m* count; recount; inventory

**recuerdo** *m* memory, remembrance; keepsake, souvenir

**recuero** *m* muleteer

**recular** *intr* to back up; (*un arma de fuego*) to recoil; (coll) to back down

**reculón** *m* (Am) backing; **a reculones** (coll) backing away, recoiling

**recuperar** *tr & ref* to recuperate, to recover

**recurrir** *intr* to resort, have recourse; to revert

**recurso** *m* recourse; resource; resort; appeal, petition

**recusar** *tr* to refuse, reject; (law) to challenge

**rechazar** §60 *tr* to refuse, to reject; to repel, drive back

**rechazo** *m* rejection; rebound, recoil

**rechifla** *f* catcall

**rechiflar** *tr & intr* to catcall, to hiss || *ref* to make fun

**rechinar** *intr* to creak, grate, squeak; to act with bad grace

**rechon·cho -cha** *adj* (coll) chubby, tubby, plump

**rechupete** — **de rechupete** (coll) fine, wonderful

**red** *f* net; netting; network, system; baggage netting; (fig) net, snare, trap; **a red barredera** with a clean sweep; **red barredera** dragnet

**redacción** *f* writing; editing; editorial staff; newspaper office, city room

**redactar** *tr* to write up; to edit

**redac·tor -tora** *mf* writer; editor, newspaper editor; **redactor publicitario** copy writer

**redada** *f* (*de peces*) catch, netful; (*p.ej., de criminales*) (coll) haul, roundup

**redecilla** *f* hair net

**rededor** *m* surroundings; **al rededor (de)** around

**redención** *f* redemption; help, recourse

**reden·tor -tora** *mf* redeemer

**redición** *f* constant repetition

**redi·cho -cha** *adj* (coll) overprecise

**redil** *m* sheepfold

**redimir** *tr* to redeem; to ransom; to buy back
**rédito** *m* income, revenue, yield
**reditnar** §21 *tr* to yield, produce
**redobla·do -da** *adj* stocky, heavy-built; heavy, strong; (mil) double-quick
**redoblar** *tr* to double; to clinch; to repeat || *intr* (*un tambor*) to roll
**redoble** *m* doubling; clinching; repeating; roll of a drum
**redoma** *f* phial, flask
**redoma·do -da** *adj* sly, crafty
**redonda** *f* district, neighborhood; (mus) semibreve; **a la redonda** around, roundabout
**redondear** *tr* to round, make round; to round off; to round out || *ref* to be well-off; to be out of debt
**redondel** *m* circle; round cloak; (*espacio destinado a la lidia*) (taur) ring
**redondilla** *f* eight-syllable quatrain with rhyme abba or abab
**redon·do -da** *adj* round; straightforward; (*terreno*) pasture; (Am) honest; (Am) stupid || *m* ring, circle; (coll) cash || *f* see **redonda**
**redopelo** *m* (coll) row, scuffle; **al redopelo** against the grain, the wrong way; (coll) roughly, violently
**reducir** §19 *tr & ref* to reduce; **reducirse a** to come to, to amount to; to be obliged to
**reducto** *m* (fort) redoubt
**redundante** *adj* redundant
**redundar** *intr* to redound; to overflow; **redundar en** to redound to
**reelección** *f* reëlection
**reembarcar** §73 *tr, intr & ref* to reship, to reëmbark
**reembarco** *m* reshipment (*of persons*), reëmbarkation
**reembarque** *m* reshipment (*of goods*)
**reembolsar** *tr* to reimburse; to refund || *ref* to collect a debt, to be reimbursed
**reembolso** *m* reimbursement; refund; **contra reembolso** collect on delivery; cash on delivery
**reemplazar** §60 *tr* to replace
**reemplazo** *m* replacement; (mil) replacements; (*hombre que sirve en lugar de otro*) (mil) replacement
**reencuadernar** *tr* (bb) to rebind
**reencuentro** *m* collision; (*de tropas*) clash
**reenganchar** *tr & ref* to reënlist
**reentrada** *f* reëntry
**reestrenar** *tr* (theat) to revive
**reestreno** *m* (theat) revival
**reexamen** *m* or **reexaminación** *f* reëxamination
**reexpedición** *f* forwarding, reshipment
**reexpedir** §50 *tr* to forward, reship
**refacción** *f* refreshment; allowance; repair, repairs; (coll) extra, bonus; (Am) spare part
**refajo** *m* underskirt, slip
**referencia** *f* reference; account, report
**referi·do -da** *adj* above-mentioned
**referir** §68 *tr* to refer; to tell, report || *ref* to refer
**refinamiento** *m* refinement
**refinar** *tr* to refine; to polish, perfect
**refinería** *f* refinery
**reflejar** *tr* to reflect; to reflect on; to show, reveal || *intr* to reflect
**reflejo** *m* glare; reflection; reflex; **reflejo patelar** or **rotuliano** knee jerk
**reflexión** *f* reflection
**reflexionar** *tr* to reflect on or upon || *intr* to reflect
**reflujo** *m* ebb
**refocilar** *tr* to cheer; to strengthen || *intr* (Arg, Urug) to lighten || *ref* to be cheered; to take it easy
**reforma** *f* reform; reformation; alteration, renovation || **la Reforma** the Reformation
**reformación** *f* reformation
**reformar** *tr* to reform; to mend, repair; to alter, renovate; to revise; to reorganize || *ref* to reform; to hold oneself in check
**reforzar** §35 *tr* to reinforce; to strengthen; to encourage
**refracción** *f* refraction
**refracta·rio -ria** *adj* rebellious, unruly, stubborn
**refrán** *m* proverb, saying
**refregar** §66 *tr* to rub; (coll) to upbraid
**refrenar** *tr* to curb, to rein; to check, restrain
**refrendar** *tr* to countersign; to authenticate; to visé; (coll) to repeat
**refrescar** §73 *tr* to refresh; to cool, to refrigerate || *intr & ref* to refresh; to refresh oneself; to cool off; to go out for fresh air; (*el viento*) (naut) to blow up
**refresco** *m* refreshment; cold drink, soft drink
**refriega** *f* fray, scuffle
**refrigerador** *m* refrigerator; ice bucket
**refrigerio** *m* coolness; relief; pick-me-up, light lunch
**refuerzo** *m* reinforcement
**refugia·do -da** *mf* refugee
**refugiar** *tr* to shelter || *ref* to take refuge
**refugio** *m* refuge; hospice; shelter; haunt; (*para peatones en medio de la calle*) safety zone; **refugio antiaéreo** air-raid shelter; **refugio antiatómico** fallout shelter
**refundición** *f* recast; revision; (*de una pieza dramática*) adaptation
**refundir** *tr* to recast; to revise; (*una pieza dramática*) to adapt || *intr* to redound
**refunfuñar** *intr* to grumble, to growl
**refutar** *tr* to refute
**regadera** *f* watering can; street sprinkler
**regadí·o -a** or **regadi·zo -za** *adj* irrigable || *m* irrigated land
**regala** *f* gunwale
**regala·do -da** *adj* dainty, delicate; pleasing, pleasant; (*vida*) of ease
**regalar** *tr* to give; to regale, entertain; to treat; to caress, fondle; to indulge
**regalía** *f* privilege, perquisite; bonus; (Arg, Chile) muff; (Am) royalty
**regaliz** *m* licorice
**regalo** *m* gift, present; treat; joy, pleasure; **regalos de fiesta** favors
**rega·lón -lona** *adj* (coll) comfort-loving, pampered; (*vida*) (coll) soft, easy
**regañar** *tr* (coll) to scold || *intr* to

growl, snarl; to grumble; to quarrel; (coll) to scold
**regaño** *m* (coll) scolding; growl, snarl; grumble
**regar** **§66** *tr* to water, sprinkle; to irrigate; to spread, sprinkle, strew
**regate** *m* dodge, duck; (fig) dodge, subterfuge
**regatear** *tr* to haggle over; to sell at retail; (coll) to avoid, to shun || *intr* to haggle, to bargain; (naut) to race; (coll) to duck, to dodge
**regazo** *m* lap
**regenerar** *tr & ref* to regenerate
**regente** *m* director, manager; registered pharmacist; (typ) foreman
**regicida** *mf* regicide
**regicidio** *m* regicide
**regi•dor -dora** *adj* ruling, governing || *m* alderman, councilman
**régimen** *m* (*pl* **regímenes**) regime; diet; rate; management; (gram) government; **régimen de hambre** starvation diet; **régimen de justicia** rule of law
**regimental** *adj* regimental
**regimentar** **§2** *tr* to regiment
**regimiento** *m* regiment; rule, government; city council
**re•gio -gia** *adj* regal, royal; magnificent
**región** *f* region
**regir** **§57** *tr* to rule, govern; to control, manage; to guide, steer; (gram) to govern || *intr* to prevail, be in force
**registra•dor -dora** *adj* registering; recording || *m* registrar, recorder; inspector || *f* cash register
**registrar** *tr* to register; to record; to examine, inspect || *ref* to register; to be recorded; to take place
**registro** *m* registration, registry; recording; examination, inspection; entry, record; bookmark; manhole; (*de chimenea*) damper; (*de reloj*) regulator; (*de órgano*) (mus) stop; (*de piano*) (mus) pedal
**regla** *f* rule; (*para trazar líneas*) ruler; measure, moderation; order; menstruation; **regla de cálculo** slide rule; **reglas** monthlies, menses
**reglamenta•rio -ria** *adj* prescribed, statutory
**reglamento** *m* rules, regulations
**reglar** *tr* to regulate; (*papel*) to rule || *ref* to guide oneself, be guided
**regleta** *f* (typ) lead
**regletear** *tr* (typ) to lead, to space
**regocijar** *tr* to cheer, delight || *ref* to rejoice
**regocijo** *m* cheer, delight, rejoicing
**regoldar** **§3** *intr* to belch
**regolfar** *intr & ref* to surge back, flow back, back up
**regorde•te -ta** *adj* dumpy, plump
**regresar** *intr* to return
**regreso** *m* return; **estar de regreso** to be back
**regüeldo** *m* belch, belching
**reguero** *m* drip, trickle; (*señal que deja una cosa que se va vertiendo*) track; irrigating ditch; **ser un reguero de pólvora** to spread like wildfire
**regulador** *m* regulator; (*de locomotora*) throttle; (mach) governor
**regular** *adj* regular; fair, moderate, medium; **por lo regular** as a rule || *tr* to regulate; to put in order; to throttle
**rehacer** **§39** *tr* to remake, make over, do over; to mend, repair, renovate || *ref* to recover, to rally
**rehén** *m* hostage; **llevarse en rehenes** to carry off as a hostage
**rehilandera** *f* pinwheel
**rehilar** *intr* to quiver; to whiz by
**rehilete** *m* shuttlecock; (*que se lanza por diversión*) dart; dig, cutting remark; (taur) banderilla
**rehuir** **§20** *tr* to avoid, shun; to shrink from; to refuse; to dislike || *intr & ref* to flee
**rehusar** *tr* to refuse, turn down
**reimpresión** *f* reprint
**reimprimir** **§83** *tr* to reprint
**reina** *f* queen; **reina Margarita** aster, China aster; **reina viuda** queen dowager
**reinado** *m* reign
**reinar** *intr* to reign; to prevail
**reincidir** *intr* to backslide; to repeat an offense
**reingreso** *m* reëntry
**reino** *m* kingdom; **Reino Unido** United Kingdom
**reinstalar** *tr* to reinstate, reinstall
**reintegrar** *tr* to refund, pay back
**reintegro** *m* refund, payment
**reír** **§58** *tr* to laugh at || *intr & ref* to laugh; **reír de** or **reírse de** to laugh at
**reja** *f* grate, grating, grille; plowshare, colter; **entre rejas** behind bars
**rejilla** *f* screen; grating; lattice, latticework; cane, cane upholstery; foot brasier; fire grate; (electron) grid; (*de acumulador*) (elec) grid; (rr) baggage rack
**rejón** *m* spear; dagger; (taur) lance
**rejonear** *tr* (*el jinete al toro*) (taur) to jab with a lance made to break off in the bull's neck
**rejuvenecimiento** *m* rejuvenation
**relación** *f* relation; account; list; (*en un drama*) speech; **relación de ciego** blind man's ballad; **relaciones** betrothal, engagement
**relacionar** *tr* to relate || *ref* to be related
**relai** *m* or **relais** *m* (elec) relay
**relajación** *f* or **relajamiento** *m* relaxation; slackening; laxity; rupture, hernia
**relajar** *tr* to relax; to slacken; to debauch || *intr* to relax || *ref* to relax, become relaxed; to become debauched; to be ruptured
**relamer** *ref* to lick one's lips; to gloat; to relish; to boast; to slick oneself up
**relami•do -da** *adj* prim, overnice
**relámpago** *m* flash of lightning; flash of wit; **relámpago fotogénico** flash bulb, flashlight; **relámpagos** lightning
**relampaguear** *intr* to lighten; to flash
**relatar** *tr* to relate, report
**relati•vo -va** *adj* relative
**relato** *m* story; statement, report
**relé** *m* (elec) relay
**releer** **§43** *tr* to reread

**relegar** §44 *tr* to relegate; to banish, exile; to shelve, lay aside
**relente** *m* night dew, light drizzle
**relevador** *m* (elec) relay
**relevante** *adj* outstanding
**relevar** *tr* to emboss; to make stand out; to relieve; to release; to absolve; to replace || *intr* to stand out in relief
**relevo** *m* (elec) relay; (mil) relief; **relevos** (sport) relay race
**relicario** *m* shrine; (*medallón*) (Am) locket
**relieve** *m* relief; merit, distinction; **en relieve** in relief; **poner de relieve** to point out; to make stand out; **relieves** scraps, leftovers
**religión** *f* religion
**religio•so -sa** *adj* religious
**relinchar** *intr* to neigh
**relincho** *m* neigh, neighing; cry of joy
**reliquia** *f* relic; trace, vestige; **reliquia de familia** heirloom
**reloj** *m* watch; clock; meter; **como un reloj** like clockwork; **conocer el reloj** to know how to tell time; **reloj de caja** grandfather's clock; **reloj de carillón** chime clock; **reloj de cuclillo** cuckoo clock; **reloj de ocho días cuerda** eight-day clock; **reloj de pulsera** wrist watch; **reloj de sol** sundial; **reloj despertador** alarm clock; **reloj registrador** time clock; **reloj registrador de tarjetas** punch clock
**relojera** *f* watch case; watch pocket
**relojería** *f* watchmaking, clockmaking; watchmaker's shop
**reloje•ro -ra** *mf* watchmaker, clockmaker || *f* see **relojera**
**reluciente** *adj* shining, brilliant, flashing
**relucir** §45 *intr* to shine
**relumbrar** *intr* to shine, dazzle, glare
**relumbre** *m* beam, sparkle; flash; dazzle, glare
**relumbrón** *m* flash, glare; tinsel; **de relumbrón** showy, tawdry
**rellano** *m* (*en la pendiente de un terreno*) level stretch; (*de escalera*) landing
**rellenar** *tr* to refill; to fill up; to stuff; to pad; to fill out; (coll) to cram, to stuff || *ref* to fill up; (coll) to cram, stuff oneself
**relle•no -na** *adj* full, packed; stuffed || *m* refill; filling, stuffing; padding, wadding; (*en un escrito*) filler
**remachar** *tr* (*un clavo ya clavado*) to clinch; (*un roblón*) to rivet; to stress, emphasize || *ref* (Col) to maintain strict silence
**remache** *m* clinching; riveting; rivet
**remanso** *m* dead water, backwater
**remar** *intr* to row; to toil, struggle
**remata•do -da** *adj* hopeless; **loco rematado** (coll) raving mad
**rematar** *tr* to finish, put an end to; to finish off, kill off; (*en una subasta*) to knock down || *intr* to end || *ref* to come to ruin
**remate** *m* end; crest, top, finial; closing; highest bid; (*en una subasta*) sale; **de remate** hopelessly
**remecer** §46 *tr* & *ref* to shake, swing, rock
**remedar** *tr* to copy, imitate; to ape, mimic; to mock
**remediar** *tr* to remedy; to help; to prevent; (*del peligro*) to free, to save
**remediava•gos** *m* (*pl* **-gos**) short cut
**remedio** *m* remedy; help; recourse; **no hay remedio** or **no hay más remedio** it can't be helped; **no tener remedio** to be unavoidable
**remedión** *m* (theat) substitute performance
**remedo** *m* copy, imitation; poor imitation
**remendar** §2 *tr* to patch, mend, repair; to darn; to emend, correct; to touch up
**remen•dón -dona** *mf* mender, repairer; shoe mender; tailor (*who does mending*)
**reme•ro -ra** *mf* rower || *m* oarsman
**remesa** *f* remittance; shipment
**remesar** *tr* to remit; to ship
**remezón** *m* (Am) hard shake; (Am) tremor
**remiendo** *m* patch; mending, repair; retouching; emendation, correction; job printing, job work; **a remiendos** (coll) piecemeal
**remilga•do -da** *adj* prim and finicky; affected, smirking
**remilgar** §44 *intr* to be prim and finicky, to smirk
**remilgo** *m* primness, affectation
**remira•do -da** *adj* circumspect, discreet
**remisión** *f* remission; reference
**remitente** *mf* sender, shipper
**remitido** *m* (*noticia de un particular a un periódico*) personal; letter to the editor
**remitir** *tr* to remit; to forward, send, ship; to refer; to defer, postpone; to pardon, forgive || *intr* to remit, let up; to refer || *ref* to remit, let up; to defer, yield
**remo** *m* oar; leg, arm, wing; toil, labor; (sport) rowing; **aguantar los remos** to lie or rest on one's oars
**remoción** *f* discharge, dismissal; removal
**remojar** *tr* to soak, to steep, to dip; to celebrate with a drink; **remojar la palabra** (coll) to wet one's whistle
**remojo** *m* soaking, steeping; **poner en remojo** (coll) to put off to a more suitable time
**remolacha** *f* beet; **remolacha azucarera** sugar beet
**remolcador** *m* tug, tugboat; towboat; tow car
**remolcar** §73 *tr* to tow; to take in tow
**remoler** §47 *tr* to grind up; (coll) to bore
**remolinear** *tr*, *intr* & *ref* to eddy, whirl about
**remolino** *m* eddy, whirlpool; swirl, whirl; disturbance, commotion; throng, crowd; cowlick
**remo•lón -lona** *adj* lazy, indolent || *mf* shirker, quitter
**remolonear** *intr* to refuse to budge
**remolque** *m* tow; towing; trailer; **a remolque** in tow
**remontar** *tr* to mend, repair; to frighten

away; to elevate, raise up; (*p.ej., un río*) to go up || *intr* (*en el tiempo*) to go back || *ref* to rise, rise up; to soar; (*en el tiempo*) to go back

**remontuar** *m* stem-winder

**remoquete** *m* punch; nickname; sarcasm; (coll) flirting

**rémora** *f* hindrance, obstacle

**remordimiento** *m* remorse

**remo·to -ta** *adj* remote; unlikely; **estar remoto** to be rusty

**remover** §47 *tr* to remove; to shake; to stir; to disturb, upset; to dismiss, to discharge || *ref* to move away

**remozar** §60 *tr* to rejuvenate || *ref* to become rejuvenated

**rempujar** *tr* (coll) to push, jostle

**rempujón** *m* (coll) push, jostle

**remuda** *f* change, replacement; change of clothes

**remudar** *tr* to change, replace; to move around

**remuneración** *f* remuneration; **remuneración por rendimiento** piece wage

**renacer** §22 *intr* to be reborn, to be born again; to recover

**renacimiento** *m* rebirth; renaissance

**renacuajo** *m* tadpole; (coll) shrimp, little squirt

**Renania** *f* Rhineland

**ren·co -ca** *adj* lame

**rencor** *m* rancor; **guardar rencor** to bear malice

**rendición** *f* surrender; submission; fatigue, exhaustion; yield

**rendi·do -da** *adj* tired, worn-out; submissive

**rendija** *f* crack, split, slit

**rendimiento** *m* submission; exhaustion; yield; output; (mech) efficiency

**rendir** §50 *tr* to conquer; to subdue; to surrender; to exhaust, wear out; to return, give back; to yield, produce; (*gracias, obsequios, homenaje*) to render || *intr* to yield || *ref* to surrender; to yield, give in; to be exhausted, to be worn out

**renegar** §66 *tr* to deny vigorously; to abhor, detest || *intr* to curse; (coll) to be insulting; **renegar de** to deny; to curse; to abhor, detest

**renegociación** *f* renegotiation

**Renfe, la** acronym for **la Red Nacional de los Ferrocarriles Españoles** the Spanish National Railroad System

**renglón** *m* line; **a renglón seguido** right below; **leer entre renglones** to read between the lines

**reniego** *m* curse

**reno** *m* reindeer

**renombra·do -da** *adj* renowned, famous

**renombre** *m* renown, fame

**renovar** §61 *tr* to renew; to renovate; to transform, restore; to remodel

**renquear** *intr* to limp

**renta** *f* income; private income; annuity; public debt; rent; **renta nacional** gross national product

**rentar** *tr* to produce, yield

**rentista** *mf* bondholder; financier; person of independent means

**renuente** *adj* reluctant, unwilling

**renuevo** *m* sprout, shoot; renewal

**renuncia** *f* renunciation; resignation; (law) waiver

**renunciar** *tr* to renounce; to resign || *intr* to renounce; (*no servir al palo que se juega*) to renege; **renunciar a** to give up, to renounce, to waive

**renuncio** *m* slip, mistake; (*en juegos de naipes*) renege; (coll) lie

**reñi·do -da** *adj* on bad terms; bitter, hard-fought

**reñir** §72 *tr* (*regañar*) to scold; (*una batalla, un desafío*) to fight || *intr* to fight; to be at odds, to fall out

**re·o -a** *adj* guilty, criminal || **reo** *mf* offender, criminal; (law) defendant

**reojo** — **de reojo** askance, out of the corner of one's eye; hostilely

**reorganizar** §60 *tr & ref* to reorganize

**reóstato** *m* rheostat

**repanchigar** or **repantigar** §44 *ref* to sprawl, to loll

**reparar** *tr* to repair, to mend; to make amends for; to notice, observe; (*un golpe*) to parry || *intr* to stop; **reparar en** to notice, pay attention to || *ref* to stop; to refrain

**reparo** *m* repairing, repairs; notice, observation; doubt, objection; shelter; bashfulness

**repa·rón -rona** *adj* (coll) faultfinding || *mf* (coll) faultfinder

**repartir** *tr* to distribute; (*naipes*) to deal

**reparto** *m* distribution; (*de naipes*) deal; (theat) cast; **reparto de acciones gratis** stock dividend

**repasar** *tr* to repass; to retrace; to review; to revise; (*la ropa*) to mend

**repasata** *f* (coll) scolding, reprimand

**repaso** *m* revision; (*de una lección*) review; mending; (coll) reprimand

**repatriar** §77 *tr* to repatriate; to send home || *intr & ref* to be repatriated; to go or come home

**repeler** *tr* to repel, to repulse

**repente** *m* start, sudden movement; **de repente** suddenly

**repenti·no -na** *adj* sudden, unexpected

**repentista** *mf* (mus) improviser; (mus) sight reader

**repentizar** §60 *intr* to improvise; (mus) to sight-read, perform at sight

**repercutir** *intr* to rebound; to reëcho, reverberate

**repertorio** *m* repertory

**repetición** *f* repetition; (mus) repeat

**repetir** §50 *tr & intr* to repeat

**repicar** §73 *tr* to mince, to chop up; to ring, to sound; to sting again || *intr* to peal, ring out, resound || *ref* to boast, be conceited

**repique** *m* chopping, mincing; peal, ringing; (coll) squabble, quarrel

**repiqueteo** *m* pealing, ringing; beating, rapping

**repisa** *f* shelf, ledge; bracket; **repisa de chimenea** mantelpiece; **repisa de ventana** window sill

**replantear** *tr* to lay out again; to reaffirm, to reimplement

**replegar** §66 *tr* to fold over and over || *ref* to fold, fold up; (mil) to fall back

**reple·to -ta** *adj* replete, full, loaded; fat, chubby

**réplica** *f* answer, retort; replica
**replicar** §73 *tr* to argue against || *intr* to answer back, retort
**repli·cón -cona** *adj* (coll) saucy, flip
**repliegue** *m* fold, crease; (mil) falling back
**repollo** *m* cabbage; (*p.ej., de lechuga, col*) head
**reponer** §54 *tr* to replace, put back; to restore; (*una pieza dramática*) to revive; **repuso** he replied || *ref* to recover; to calm down
**reportaje** *m* reporting; news coverage; report
**reportar** *tr* to check, restrain; to get, obtain; to bring, carry; to report || *ref* to restrain or control oneself
**reporte** *m* report, news report; gossip
**repórter** *m* reporter
**reporte·ro -ra** *mf* reporter
**reposar** *intr & ref* to rest, repose; to take a nap; (*en la sepultura*) to lie, be at rest; (*poso, sedimento*) to settle
**reposición** *f* replacement; (*de la salud*) recovery; (theat) revival
**reposo** *m* rest, repose
**repostar** *tr, intr & ref* to stock up; to refuel
**repostería** *f* pastry shop, confectionery; pantry
**reposte·ro -ra** *mf* pastry cook, confectioner
**repregunta** *f* (law) cross-examination
**repreguntar** *tr* (law) to cross-examine
**reprender** *tr* to reprehend, to scold
**represa** *f* dam; damming; repression, check; (*de un buque*) recapture
**represalia** *f* reprisal; retaliation
**represar** *tr* to dam; to repress, to check; (*un buque*) to recapture
**representación** *f* representation; dignity, standing; performance; **en representación de** representing
**representante** *adj* representing || *mf* representative; actor, player; (com) agent, representative
**representar** *tr* to represent; to show, express; to state, declare; to act, perform, play; (*determinada edad*) to appear to be || *ref* to imagine
**representati·vo -va** *adj* representative
**reprimenda** *f* reprimand
**reprimir** *tr* to repress
**reprobación** *f* reproof; flunk, failure
**reprobar** §61 *tr* to reprove; to flunk, to fail
**reprochar** *tr* to reproach
**reproche** *m* reproach
**reproducción** *f* reproduction; breeding
**reproducir** §19 *tr & ref* to reproduce
**repro·pio -pia** *adj* balky
**reptar** *intr* to crawl; to cringe
**reptil** *m* reptile
**república** *f* republic
**republica·no -na** *adj & mf* republican || *m* patriot
**repudiar** *tr* to repudiate, to disown, to disavow
**repues·to -ta** *adj* secluded; spare, extra || *m* stock, supply; serving table; pantry; **de repuesto** spare, extra
**repugnante** *adj* repugnant, disgusting
**repugnar** *tr* to conflict with; to contradict; to object to, to avoid; to revolt, be repugnant to || *intr* to be repugnant
**repujar** *tr* to emboss
**repulgar** §44 *tr* to hem, to border
**repulgo** *m* hem, border
**repuli·do -da** *adj* highly polished; all dolled up
**repulsar** *tr* to reject, refuse
**repulsi·vo -va** *adj* repulsive
**repuntar** *tr* (*animales dispersos*) (Arg, Chile, Urug) to round up || *intr* to begin to appear; (naut) to begin to rise; (naut) to begin to ebb || *ref* to begin to turn sour; (coll) to fall out
**repuso** see **reponer**
**reputación** *f* reputation, repute
**reputar** *tr* to repute; to esteem
**requebra·dor -dora** *adj* flirtatious || *mf* flirt
**requebrar** §2 *tr* to break into smaller pieces; to flatter, to flirt with
**requemar** *tr* to burn again; to parch; to overcook; to inflame; to bite, sting || *ref* to become tanned or sunburned; to smolder, burn within
**requerir** §68 *tr* to notify; to summon; to request; to urge; to check, examine; to require; to seek, look for; to reach for; to court, make love to
**requesón** *m* cottage cheese
**requiebro** *m* fine crushing; flattery, flattering remarks, flirtation
**requisi·to -ta** *adj* requisite || *m* requisite, requirement; accomplishment; **requisito previo** prerequisite
**res** *f* head of cattle; beast; **reses** cattle
**resabio** *m* unpleasant aftertaste; bad habit, vice
**resabio·so -sa** *adj* (Am) sly, crafty; (*caballo*) (Am) vicious
**resaca** *f* surge, surf; undertow; (com) redraft; (slang) hangover
**resalir** §65 *intr* to jut out, project
**resaltar** *tr* to emphasize || *intr* to bounce, rebound; to jut out, project; to stand out
**resanar** *tr* to retouch, patch, repair
**resarcir** §36 *tr* to indemnify, to make amends to; (*un daño, un agravio*) to repay; (*una pérdida*) to make good; to mend, repair || *ref* — **resarcirse de** to make up for
**resbaladi·zo -za** *adj* slippery; skiddy; risky; (*memoria*) shaky
**resbalar** *intr* to slide; to skid; to slip || *ref* to slide; to slip; (fig) to slip, to misstep
**rescatar** *tr* to ransom, redeem; to rescue; (*el tiempo perdido*) to make up for; to relieve; to atone for
**rescate** *m* ransom, redemption; rescue; salvage; ransom money
**rescindir** *tr* to rescind
**rescoldera** *f* heartburn
**rescoldo** *m* embers; smoldering; doubt, scruple; **arder en rescoldo** to smolder
**resenti·do -da** *adj* resentful
**resentimiento** *m* resentment; sorrow, disappointment
**resentir** §68 *ref* to be resentful; **resentirse de** to feel the bad effects of; to resent; to suffer from

**reseña** *f* outline; book review; newspaper account; (mil) review
**reseñar** *tr* to outline; (*un libro*) to review; (mil) to review
**reserva** *f* reserve; reservation; **con** or **bajo la mayor reserva** in strictest confidence; **reserva de caza** game preserve
**reservar** *tr* to reserve; to put aside; to postpone; to exempt; to keep secret || *ref* to save oneself, to bide one's time; to beware, be distrustful
**resfriado** *m* cold
**resfriar** §77 *tr* to cool, chill || *intr* to turn cold || *ref* to catch cold; to cool off, grow cold
**resguardar** *tr* to defend; to protect, shield || *ref* to take shelter; to protect oneself
**resguardo** *m* defense; protection; check, voucher; collateral; (naut) wide berth, sea room
**residencia** *f* residence; impeachment
**residenciar** *tr* to call to account; to impeach
**residir** *intr* to reside
**residuo** *m* residue, remains; remainder
**resignación** *f* resignation
**resignar** *tr* to resign || *ref* to resign, become resigned; **resignarse con** (*p.ej., su suerte*) to be resigned to
**resina** *f* resin
**resistencia** *f* resistance; strength; **resistencia de rejilla** (electron) grid leak
**resistente** *adj* resistant; strong; (hort) hardy
**resistir** *tr* to bear, to stand; (*la tentación*) to resist || *intr* to resist; to hold out; **resistir a** (*la violencia; la risa*) to resist; to refuse to || *ref* to resist; to struggle; **resistirse a** to refuse to
**resma** *f* ream
**resobrina** *f* grandniece, greatniece
**resobrino** *m* grandnephew, greatnephew
**resolución** *f* resolution; **en resolución** in brief, in a word
**resolver** §47 & §83 *tr* to resolve; to solve; to decide on; to dissolve; || *ref* to resolve; to make up one's mind
**resollar** §61 *intr* to breathe; to breathe hard, pant; to stop for a rest
**resonar** §61 *intr* to resound, to echo
**resoplar** *intr* to puff; to snort
**resoplido** *m* puffing; snort
**resorte** *m* spring; springiness; means; province, scope; (Am) rubber band; **resorte espiral** coil spring; **tocar resortes** to pull wires, to pull strings
**respailar** *intr* — **ir respailando** (coll) to scurry along
**respaldar** *m* back || *tr* to back; to indorse || *ref* to lean back; to sprawl
**respaldo** *m* back; backing; indorsement
**respectar** *tr* (with personal **a**) to concern; **por lo que respecta a . . .** as far as . . . is concerned
**respecti•vo -va** *adj* respective
**respecto** *m* respect, reference, relation; **al respecto** in the matter; **respecto a** or **de** with respect to, in or with regard to
**respetable** *adj* respectable
**respetar** *tr* to respect
**respeto** *m* respect; consideration; **campar por sus respetos** (coll) to be inconsiderate, to go one's (his, her, etc.) own way; **de respeto** spare, extra
**respetuo•so -sa** *adj* respectful; awesome, impressive; humble, obedient
**respigón** *m* hangnail
**respingar** §44 *intr* to balk, to shy; (*elevarse el borde, p.ej., de la falda*) to curl up; (coll) to give in unwillingly
**respin•gón -gona** *adj* (*nariz*) snubby, upturned; (Am) surly, churlish
**respirar** *tr* to breathe || *intr* to breathe; to breath freely; to breathe a sigh of relief; to catch one's breath, to stop for a rest; **no respirar** (coll) to not breathe a word; **sin respirar** without respite, without letup
**respiro** *m* breathing; respite, breather, breathing spell; (*para el pago de una deuda*) extension of time
**resplandecer** §22 *intr* to shine; to flash, glitter
**resplandeciente** *adj* brilliant; resplendent
**resplandor** *m* brilliance, radiance; resplendence; glare
**responder** *tr* to answer || *intr* to answer, respond; to correspond; to answer back; **responder de** (*una cosa*) to answer for; **responder por** (*una persona*) to answer for
**respon•dón -dona** *adj* (coll) saucy
**responsable** *adj* responsible; **responsable de** responsible for
**respuesta** *f* answer, response
**resquebrajar** *tr* & *ref* to crack, to split
**resquemar** *tr* & *intr* to bite, to sting || *ref* to be parched; (*resentirse sin manifestarlo*) to smolder
**resquemo** *m* bite, sting
**resquicio** *m* crack, chink; chance, opportunity
**restablecer** §22 *tr* to reëstablish, to restore || *ref* to recover
**restañar** *tr* to retin; (*sangre*) to stanch, stop the flow of
**restar** *tr* to deduct; to reduce; to take away; (*una pelota*) to return; to subtract || *intr* to remain, be left
**restaurante** *m* restaurant; **restaurante automático** automat
**restaurar** *tr* to restore; to recover
**restitución** *f* restitution, return
**restituir** §20 *tr* to return, give back; to restore || *ref* to return, come back
**resto** *m* rest, remainder, residue; (*en juegos de naipes*) stakes; (*de una pelota*) return; **a resto abierto** (coll) without limit; **echar el resto** to stake all, to shoot the works; **restos** remains, mortal remains; **restos de serie** remnants
**restregar** §66 *tr* to rub hard; to scrub hard
**restringir** §27 *tr* to restrict; to constrict, to contract
**resucitar** *tr* & *intr* to resuscitate; to resurrect; (coll) to revive
**resuel•to -ta** *adj* resolute, resolved, determined; prompt, quick

**resuello** *m* breathing; hard breathing, panting
**resulta** *f* result; outcome; vacancy; **de resultas de** as a result of
**resultado** *m* result
**resultar** *intr* to result; to prove to be, to turn out to be; to be, to become
**resumen** *m* summary, résumé; **en resumen** in brief, in a word
**resumir** *tr* to summarize, to sum up ‖ *ref* to be reduced, be transformed
**resurrección** *f* resurrection
**retaguardia** *f* rearguard
**retal** *m* piece, remnant
**retama** *f* Spanish broom; **retama de escoba** furze
**retar** *tr* to challenge, to dare; (coll) to blame, find fault with
**retardar** *tr* to retard, slow down
**retardo** *m* retard, delay
**retazo** *m* piece, remnant; scrap, fragment
**retén** *m* store, stock, reserve; catch, pawl; (mil) reserve
**retener** §71 *tr* to retain, keep, withhold; to detain, arrest; (*el pago de un haber*) to stop
**reticente** *adj* deceptive, misleading; noncommittal
**retintín** *m* jingle, tinkling; (*en el oído*) ringing; (coll) tone of reproach, sarcasm, mockery
**retiñir** §12 *intr* to jingle, to tinkle; (*los oídos*) to ring
**retirada** *f* retirement, withdrawal; place of refuge; (mil) retreat, retirement; (*toque*) (mil) retreat; **batirse en retirada** to beat a retreat
**retirar** *tr* to retire, to withdraw; to take away; to pull back ‖ *ref* to retire, to withdraw; (mil) to retire
**reto** *m* challenge, dare; threat
**retocar** §73 *tr* to retouch; to touch up; (*un disco de fonógrafo*) to play back
**retoño** *m* sprout, shoot, sucker
**retorcer** §74 *tr* to twist; to twist together; (*las manos*) to wring; (fig) to twist, misconstrue ‖ *ref* to twist; to writhe
**retóri·co -ca** *adj* rhetorical ‖ *f* rhetoric
**retornar** *tr* to return, give back; to back, back up ‖ *intr & ref* to return, go back
**retorno** *m* return; barter, exchange; reward, requital; **retorno terrestre** (elec) ground
**retorta** *f* (chem) retort
**retozar** §60 *intr* to frolic, gambol, romp
**retozo** *m* frolic, gambol, romping; **retozo de la risa** giggle, titter
**reto·zón -zona** *adj* frolicsome, frisky
**retractar** *tr & ref* to retract
**retraer** §75 *tr* to bring again, to bring back; to dissuade ‖ *ref* to withdraw, retire; to take refuge
**retraí·do -da** *adj* solitary; reserved, shy
**retransmisión** *f* rebroadcasting
**retransmitir** *tr* to rebroadcast
**retrasar** *tr* to delay, retard; to put off; (*un reloj*) to set or turn back ‖ *intr* to be too slow; (*en los estudios*) to be or fall behind ‖ *ref* to delay, be late, be slow, be behind time; (*un reloj*) to go or be slow
**retraso** *m* delay; **tener retraso** to be late
**retratar** *tr* to portray; to photograph; to imitate ‖ *ref* to sit for a portrait; to have one's picture taken
**retrato** *m* portrait; photograph; copy, imitation; description; **el vivo retrato de** the living image of
**retrepar** *ref* to lean back, to lean back in the chair
**retreta** *f* (mil) retreat, tattoo; (Am) outdoor band concert
**retrete** *m* toilet, lavatory
**retribuir** §20 *tr* to repay, to pay back
**retroacti·vo -va** *adj* retroactive
**retroceder** *intr* to retrogress; to back away; to back down, back out
**retroceso** *m* retrogression; (*de un arma de fuego*) recoil; (*de una enfermedad*) flare-up
**retrocohete** *m* retrorocket
**retrodisparo** *m* retrofiring
**retropropulsión** *f* (aer) jet propulsion
**retrospecti·vo -va** *adj* retrospective ‖ *f* (mov) flashback
**retrovisor** *m* rear-view mirror
**retrucar** §73 *intr* to answer, reply; (billiards) to kiss
**retruco** *m* (billiards) kiss
**retruécano** *m* pun
**retumbar** *intr* to resound, to rumble
**retumbo** *m* resounding, rumble, echo
**reumáti·co -ca** *adj & mf* rheumatic
**reumatismo** *m* rheumatism
**reunificación** *f* reunification
**reunión** *f* reunion, gathering, meeting; assemblage
**reunir** §59 *tr* to join, unite; to assemble, gather together, bring together; to reunite; (*dinero*) to raise ‖ *ref* to unite; to assemble, gather together, come together, meet; to reunite
**reválida** *f* final examination (*for a higher degree*)
**revejecer** §22 *intr & ref* to grow old before one's time
**revelación** *f* revelation
**revelado** *m* (phot) development
**revelador** *m* (phot) developer
**revelar** *tr* to reveal; (phot) to develop
**revender** *tr* to resell; to retail
**reventa** *f* resale
**reventar** §2 *tr* to smash, crush; to burst, blow out, explode; to ruin; to annoy, bore; (*a una persona*) to work to death; (*a un caballo*) to run to death ‖ *intr* to burst, blow out, explode; (*las olas*) to break; (*morir*) (coll) to croak; (*de ira*) (coll) to blow up, hit the ceiling; **reventar por** to be dying to ‖ *ref* to burst, blow out, explode; to be worked to death; (*un caballo*) to be run to death
**reventón** *m* burst; (aut) blowout
**rever** §80 *tr* to revise, to review; (*un caso legal*) to retry
**reverberar** *intr* to reverberate
**reverbero** *m* reflector; street lamp; (Am) chafing dish
**reverencia** *f* reverence; bow, curtsy
**reverenciar** *tr* to revere, to reverence ‖ *intr* to bow, to curtsy

**reveren•do -da** *adj & m* reverend
**reverso** *m* back; wrong side; reverse
**revertir** §68 *intr* to revert
**revés** *m* back, reverse; wrong side; backhand; (*desgracia, contratiempo*) reverse, setback; **al revés** wrong side out; inside out; upside down; backwards
**revestir** §50 *tr* to put on, to don; to cover, coat, face, line, surface; to assume, take on; to disguise; (*un cuento*) to adorn; to invest || *ref* to put on vestments; to be haughty; to gird oneself
**revirar** *tr* to turn, twist; to turn over
**revisar** *tr* to revise, review, check; to audit
**revisión** *f* revision, review, check
**revisionismo** *m* revisionism
**revisionista** *adj & mf* revisionist
**revisor** *m* inspector, examiner; (rr) conductor, ticket collector
**revista** *f* review; (mil) review; (theat) review, revue; (law) new trial
**revistar** *tr* (mil) to review
**revivir** *tr & intr* to revive
**revocar** §73 *tr* to revoke; to dissuade; to drive back, drive away; to plaster, to stucco
**revolar** §61 *intr & ref* to flutter, to flutter around
**revolcar** §81 *tr* to knock down; (*a un adversario*) (coll) to floor; (*a un alumno en un examen*) (coll) to flunk, to fail || *ref* to wallow, roll around; to be stubborn
**revolotear** *tr* to fling up || *intr* to flutter, flutter around, flit
**revoltijo** or **revoltillo** *m* mess, jumble; (Am) stew
**revolto•so -sa** *adj* rebellious, riotous; (*niño*) unruly, mischievous; complicated; winding || *mf* troublemaker, rioter
**revolución** *f* revolution
**revoluciona•rio -ria** *adj & mf* revolutionary
**revolver** §47 & §83 *tr* to shake; to stir; to turn around; to turn upside down; to wrap up; to mess up; to disturb; (*sus pasos*) to retrace; to alienate, estrange || *intr* to retrace one's steps || *ref* to retrace one's steps; to turn around; to toss and turn; (*un astro en su órbita*) to revolve; (*el mar*) to get rough
**revólver** *m* revolver
**revuelco** *m* upset, tumble; wallowing
**revuelo** *m* whirl, flying around; stir, commotion
**revuelta** *f* revolution, revolt; disturbance; turning point; fight, row
**rey** *m* king; (coll) swineherd; **los Reyes Católicos** Ferdinand and Isabella; **los Reyes Magos** the Three Wise Men; **ni rey ni roque** (coll) nobody; **rey de zarza** wren; **reyes** king and queen; **Reyes** Twelfth-night
**reyerta** *f* quarrel, wrangle
**reyezuelo** *m* (orn) kinglet; **reyezuelo moñudo** goldcrest
**rezaga•do -da** *mf* straggler, laggard
**rezagar** §44 *tr* to outstrip, leave behind; to postpone || *ref* to fall behind
**rezar** §60 *tr* (*una oración*) to pray; (*una oración; la misa*) to say; (coll) to say, to read; (*anunciar*) (coll) to call for || *intr* to pray; (coll) to grumble; (coll) to say, to read; **rezar con** (coll) to concern
**rezo** *m* prayer; devotions
**rezón** *m* grapnel
**rezongar** §44 *tr* (CAm) to scold || *intr* to grumble, growl
**rezumar** *intr* to ooze, seep || *ref* to ooze, seep; to leak; (*una especie*) (coll) to leak out
**ría** *f* estuary, fiord
**riachuelo** *m* rivulet, streamlet
**riada** *f* flood, freshet
**ribazo** *m* slope, embarkment
**ribera** *f* bank, shore; riverside
**ribere•ño -ña** *adj* riverside
**ribero** *m* levee, dike
**ribete** *m* edge, trimming, border; (*a un cuento*) embellishment
**ribetear** *tr* to edge, trim, border, bind
**ri•co -ca** *adj* rich; dear, darling
**ridiculizar** §60 *tr* to ridicule
**ridícu•lo -la** *adj* ridiculous; touchy || *m* ridiculous situation; **poner en ridículo** to ridicule, to expose to ridicule
**riego** *m* irrigation; watering
**riel** *m* ingot; curtain rod; rail
**rielar** *intr* to shimmer, gleam; (poet) to twinkle
**rienda** *f* rein; **a rienda suelta** swiftly, violently; with free rein
**riente** *adj* laughing; bright, cheerful
**riesgo** *m* risk, danger; **correr riesgo** to run or take a risk
**rifa** *f* raffle; fight, quarrel
**rifar** *tr* to raffle, to raffle off || *intr* to raffle; to fight, quarrel
**rígi•do -da** *adj* rigid, stiff; strict, severe
**riguro•so -sa** *adj* rigorous; severe
**rima** *f* rhyme; **rimas** poems, poetry
**rimar** *tr & intr* to rhyme
**rimbombante** *adj* resounding; flashy
**rimero** *m* heap, pile
**Rin** *m* Rhine
**rincón** *m* corner; nook; piece of land; (coll) home
**rinconera** *f* corner piece of furniture; corner table; corner cupboard
**ringla** *f*, **ringle** *m* or **ringlera** *f* row, tier
**ringorrango** *m* (coll) curlicue; (coll) frill, frippery
**rinoceronte** *m* rhinoceros
**riña** *f* fight, scuffle
**riñón** *m* kidney; (fig) heart, center, interior; **tener bien cubierto el riñón** (coll) to be well-heeled
**río** *m* river; **pescar en río revuelto** to fish in troubled waters
**riostra** *f* brace, stay; guy wire
**riostrar** *tr* to brace, stay
**ripia** *f* shingle
**ripio** *m* debris; rubble; (*palabras inútiles empleadas para completar el verso*) padding; **no perder ripio** (coll) to not miss a trick
**riqueza** *f* riches, wealth; richness
**risa** *f* laugh, laughter
**risco** *m* cliff, crag; honey fritter

**risible** *adj* laughable
**risotada** *f* guffaw, horse laugh
**ristra** *f* string of onions, string of garlic; (coll) string, row, file
**ristre** *m* lance rest
**risue•ño -ña** *adj* smiling
**rítmi•co -ca** *adj* rhythmic(al)
**ritmo** *m* rhythm; **a gran ritmo** at great speed
**rito** *m* rite
**rival** *mf* rival
**rivalidad** *f* rivalry; enmity
**rivalizar** §60 *intr* to vie, compete; **rivalizar con** to rival
**riza•do -da** *adj* curly; ripply || *m* curl, curling; rippling
**rizador** *m* curling iron, hair curler
**rizar** §60 *tr & ref* to curl; (*la superficie del agua*) to ripple
**ri•zo -za** *adj* curly || *m* curl, ringlet; ripple; (aer) loop; **rizar el rizo** (aer) to loop the loop
**ro** *interj* — **¡ro ro!** hushaby!, bye-bye!
**roba•dor -dora** *mf* robber, thief
**róbalo** or **robalo** *m* (*Labrax lupus*) bass; (*Centropomus undecimalis*) snook
**robar** *tr* to rob, steal; (*un naipe o ficha de dominó*) to draw || *intr & ref* to steal
**robinete** *m* faucet, spigot, cock
**roblar** *tr* to clinch, to rivet
**roble** *m* oak; (*Quercus robur*) British oak tree; (coll) husky fellow
**roblón** *m* rivet
**robo** *m* robbery, theft; (*naipe tomado del monte*) draw; **robo con escalamiento** burglary
**ro•bot** *m* (*pl* **-bots**) robot
**robus•to -ta** *adj* robust
**roca** *f* rock
**rocalla** *f* pebbles; stone chips; large glass bead
**rocallo•so -sa** *adj* stony, pebbly
**roce** *m* rubbing; close contact
**rociada** *f* sprinkling; dew; (*de balas, piedras, etc.*) shower; (*de invectivas*) volley
**rociadera** *f* sprinkling can
**rociar** §77 *tr* to sprinkle; to spray; to bedew; to scatter || *intr* to drizzle; **rocía** there is dew
**rocín** *m* hack, nag; work horse, draft horse; (coll) rough fellow; (Am) riding horse
**rocío** *m* dew; drizzle; sprinkling
**roco•so -sa** *adj* rocky
**rodada** *f* rut, track
**roda•do -da** *adj* (*fácil, flúido*) rounded, fluent; (*tránsito*) vehicular || *f* see **rodada**
**rodadura** *f* rolling; rut; (*de neumático*) tread
**rodaja** *f* disk, caster; round slice
**rodaje** *m* wheels; (*de una película cinematográfica*) shooting, filming; **en rodaje** (aut) being run in; (mov) being filmed
**rodamiento** *m* bearing; (*de un neumático*) tread; **rodamientos** running gear
**Ródano** *m* Rhone
**rodante** *adj* rolling; on wheels; (Chile) wandering
**rodapié** *m* baseboard, washboard
**rodar** §61 *tr* to roll; (*una película cinematográfica*) to shoot, to film, to take; to screen, to project; to drag along; (*una llave*) to turn; (*la escalera*) to roll down; (*un nuevo coche*) to run in; (*válvulas de un motor*) to grind || *intr* to roll, roll along; to roll down; to rotate, revolve; to tumble; to roam, wander about; (*por medio de ruedas*) to run; to prowl
**Rodas** *f* Rhodes
**rodear** *tr* to surround; (Am) to round up || *intr* to go around; to go by a roundabout way; to beat about the bush || *ref* to turn, twist, toss about
**rodela** *f* buckler, target; padded ring
**rodeo** *m* detour, roundabout way; dodge, duck; rodeo, roundup; **andar con rodeos** to beat about the bush; **dar un rodeo** to go a roundabout way
**rodilla** *f* knee; floor rag, mop; padded ring; **de rodillas** kneeling, on one's knees
**rodillera** *f* kneepad; baggy knee; (*de prenda de vestir*) knee; (*del órgano*) (mus) knee swell
**rodillo** *m* roller; rolling pin; road roller; inking roller; (*de la máquina de escribir*) platen
**rodrigar** §44 *tr* to prop, prop up, stake
**rodrigón** *m* prop, stake
**roer** §62 *tr* to gnaw, to gnaw away at; (*un hueso*) to pick; to wear down
**rogar** §63 *tr & intr* to beg; to pray; **hacerse de rogar** to like to be coaxed
**roí•do -da** *adj* (coll) miserly, stingy
**ro•jo -ja** *adj* red; ruddy; red-haired; Red || *mf* (*comunista*) Red || *m* red; **al rojo** to a red heat
**rollar** *tr* to roll, roll up
**rolli•zo -za** *adj* round, cylindrical; plump, stocky || *m* round log
**rollo** *m* roll, coil; roller, rolling pin; round log; yoke pad; rôle; (*de tela*) bolt
**romadizo** *m* cold in the head
**romance** *adj* (*neolatino*) Romance || *m* Romance language; Spanish language; romance of chivalry; octosyllabic verse with alternate lines in assonance; narrative poem in octosyllabic verse; ballad; **romance heroico** hendecasyllabic verse with alternate lines in assonance
**romancero** *m* collection of Old Spanish romances
**romancillo** *m* verse of less than eight syllables with alternate lines in assonance
**románi•co -ca** *adj* (*neolatino*) Romance, Romanic; (*arquitectura*) Romanesque || *m* Romanesque
**roma•no -na** *adj & mf* Roman
**romanticismo** *m* romanticism
**románti•co -ca** *adj* romantic
**romanza** *f* (mus) romance, romanza
**romería** *f* pilgrimage; crowd, gathering
**rome•ro -ra** *mf* pilgrim || *m* rosemary
**ro•mo -ma** *adj* blunt, dull; flat-nosed
**rompeáto•mos** *m* (*pl* **-mos**) atom smasher
**rompecabe•zas** *m* (*pl* **-zas**) riddle, puz-

zle; (*figura que ha sido cortada en trozos menudos y que hay que recomponer*) jigsaw puzzle
**rompehie·los** *m* (*pl* **-los**) iceboat, icebreaker
**rompehuel·gas** *m* (*pl* **-gas**) strikebreaker
**rompeo·las** *m* (*pl* **-las**) mole, breakwater
**romper** §83 *tr* to break; to break through; to break up; to tear || *intr* to break; (*las flores*) to break open, to burst open; to break down; **romper a** to start to, to burst out
**rompiente** *m* reef, shoal; (*oleaje que choca contra las rocas*) breaker
**rompope** *m* (Am) eggnog
**ron** *m* rum; **ron de laurel** or **de malagueta** bay rum
**ronca** *f* (*época del celo*) rut; cry of buck in rutting season; (coll) bullying
**roncar** §73 *intr* to snore; (*el viento, el mar*) to roar; to cry in rutting season; (coll) to bully
**ronce·ro -ra** *adj* slow, poky; grouchy
**ron·co -ca** *adj* hoarse; harsh || *f* see **ronca**
**roncha** *f* weal, welt; black-and-blue mark
**ronchar** *tr* to crunch
**ronda** *f* (*de un policía; de visitas; de cigarros o bebidas*) round; (*juego del corro*) (Chile) ring-around-a-rosy
**rondar** *tr* to go around; to fly around; to patrol; (coll) to hang around; (coll) to court || *intr* to patrol by night; to gad about at nighttime; to go serenading; to prowl; (mil) to make the rounds
**ronquedad** *f* hoarseness; harshness
**ronquera** *f* hoarseness
**ronquido** *m* snore; rasping sound
**ronronear** *intr* to purr
**ronroneo** *m* purr, purring
**ronzal** *m* halter
**ronzar** §60 *tr* to crunch, to munch
**roña** *f* scab, mange; sticky dirt; pine bark; stinginess; (Col) malingering; (Am) spite, ill will; **jugar a roña** (Peru) to play for fun
**roño·so -sa** *adj* scabby, mangy; dirty, filthy; stingy; (Am) spiteful
**ropa** *f* clothing, clothes; dry goods; **a quema ropa** point-blank; **ropa blanca** linen; **ropa de cama** bed linen; bedclothes; **ropa dominguera** Sunday best; **ropa hecha** ready-made clothes; **ropa interior** underwear; **ropa sucia** laundry
**ropaje** *m* clothes, clothing; gown, robe; drapery
**ropaveje·ro -ra** *mf* old-clothes dealer
**rope·ro -ra** *mf* ready-made clothier; wardrobe keeper || *m* wardrobe, clothes closet
**roque** *m* rook, castle
**roque·ño -ña** *adj* rocky; hard, flinty
**rorro** *m* baby; (Mex) doll
**rosa** *f* rose; **rosa de los vientos** or **rosa náutica** (naut) compass card; **rosas** popcorn; **verlo todo de color de rosa** to see everything through rose-colored glasses
**rosa·do -da** *adj* rose-colored, rosy; pink; flushed || *f* frost
**rosaleda** or **rosalera** *f* rose garden
**rosario** *m* rosary; (*de sucesos*) string; chain pump
**ros·bif** *m* (*pl* **-bifs**) roast beef
**rosca** *f* coil, spiral; (*de una espiral*) turn; twisted roll; (*de un tornillo*) thread; (Chile) padded ring
**roscar** §73 *tr* to thread
**roseta** *f* sprinkling spout or nozzle; red spot on cheek; **rosetas** popcorn
**rosetón** *m* rose window
**rosita** *f* little rose; (Chile) earring; **rositas** popcorn
**rosquilla** *f* coffeecake, doughnut, cruller
**rostro** *m* face; snout; beak; (*retrato*) **de rostro entero** full-faced
**rostropáli·do -da** *mf* paleface
**rota** *f* rout, defeat; (naut) route, course
**rotograbado** *m* rotogravure
**rótula** *f* lozenge; kneecap; knuckle
**rotular** *tr* to label, title, letter
**rótulo** *m* label, title; poster, show bill
**rotun·do -da** *adj* round; rotund, sonorous, full; peremptory
**rotura** *f* break, breaking; breach, opening; tear, tearing
**roya** *f* (agr) blight, rust
**rozamiento** *m* rubbing; friction; (*desavenencia*) (fig) friction
**rozar** §60 *tr* to graze; to scrape; to border on; to grub, to stub; (*las tierras*) to clear; (*la hierba*) to nibble; (*leña menuda*) to cut and gather || *intr* to graze by || *ref* to be on close terms, to rub elbows, to hobnob; to falter, stammer; to be alike
**roznar** *tr* to crunch || *intr* to bray
**roznido** *m* crunch, crunching noise; bray, braying
**Rte.** *abbr* **Remite**
**ru·bí** *m* (*pl* **-bíes**) ruby; (*de un reloj*) ruby, jewel
**rubia** *f* blonde; station wagon; (coll) peseta; **rubia oxigenada** peroxide blonde; **rubia platino** platinum blonde
**rubia·les** *mf* (*pl* **-les**) (coll) goldilocks
**ru·bio -bia** *adj* blond, fair; golden || *m* blond || *f* see **rubia**
**rubor** *m* bright red; blush, flush; bashfulness
**ruborizar** §60 *tr* to make blush || *ref* to blush
**rúbrica** *f* title, heading; (*rasgo después de la firma de uno*) flourish
**ru·bro -bra** *adj* red || *m* (Am) title, heading; (Chile) (com) entry
**rudimento** *m* rudiment
**ru·do -da** *adj* coarse, rough; rude, crude; dull, stupid; hard, severe
**rueca** *f* distaff
**rueda** *f* wheel; caster, roller; (*de gente*) ring, circle; round slice; pinwheel; (*de la cola del pavo*) spread; sunfish; **hacer la rueda** (*el pavo*) to spread its tail; **hacer la rueda a** (coll) to play up to; **rueda de andar** treadmill; **rueda de cadena** sprocket, sprocket wheel; **rueda de escape** escapement wheel; **rueda de fuego** pinwheel; **rueda dentada** gearwheel; **rueda de paletas** paddle wheel; **rueda de pro-**

sos line-up; **rueda de recambio** spare wheel; **rueda de tornillo sin fin** worm wheel; **rueda motriz** drive wheel
**ruedo** *m* turn, rotation; round mat; selvage; hemline; (taur) ring; **a todo ruedo** at all events
**ruego** *m* request, entreaty; prayer
**ru•fián -fiana** *mf* bawd, go-between ‖ *m* cur, cad
**ru•fo -fa** *adj* sandy, sandy-haired; curly-haired
**rugido** *m* roar; (*de las tripas*) rumble
**rugir** §27 *intr* to roar; to rumble
**rugo•so -sa** *adj* rugged, wrinkled
**ruibarbo** *m* rhubarb
**ruido** *m* noise; rumor; row, rumpus
**ruido•so -sa** *adj* noisy; loud; sensational
**ruin** *adj* base, mean, vile; stingy; (*animal*) vicious
**ruina** *f* ruin
**ruindad** *f* baseness, meanness, vileness; stinginess; viciousness
**ruino•so -sa** *adj* tottery, run-down
**ruiseñor** *m* nightingale
**ruleta** *f* roulette; (CAm, Arg) tape measure
**ruletero** *m* (Mex) cruising taxi driver (*in search of fares*)
**ruma•no -na** *adj* & *mf* Rumanian
**rumbo** *m* bearing, course, direction; (coll) pomp, show; (coll) generosity; **por aquellos rumbos** in those parts; **rumbo a** bound for
**rumbo•so -sa** *adj* pompous, magnificent; (coll) generous
**rumiar** *tr* & *intr* to ruminate
**rumor** *m* rumor; (*de voces*) murmur, buzz; rumble
**rumorear** *tr* to rumor, to circulate by a rumor ‖ *intr* to murmur, buzz, rumble ‖ *ref* to be rumored; **se rumorea que** it is rumored that
**rumoro•so -sa** *adj* noisy, loud, rumbling
**runfla** or **runflada** *f* (coll) string, row; (*en los naipes*) (coll) sequence
**ruptor** *m* (elec) contact breaker
**ruptura** *f* rupture, break; crack, split; (*cesación de relaciones*) rupture
**Rusia** *f* Russia; **la Rusia Soviética** Soviet Russia
**ru•so -sa** *adj* & *mf* Russian
**rúst.** *abbr* **rústica**
**rústi•co -ca** *adj* rustic; coarse, crude, clumsy; (*latín*) Vulgar; **en rústica** paper-bound ‖ *m* rustic, peasant
**ruta** *f* route; **ruta aérea** air lane
**rutilante** *adj* shining, sparkling
**rutina** *f* routine
**rutina•rio -ria** *adj* routine

## S

**S, s** (ese) *f* twenty-second letter of the Spanish alphabet
**S.** *abbr* **San, Santo, sobresaliente, sur**
**sábado** *m* (*de los cristianos*) Saturday; (*de los judíos*) Sabbath
**sábalo** *m* shad
**sabana** *f* (Am) savanna, pampa; **ponerse en la sabana** (Ven) to get rich overnight
**sábana** *f* sheet; altar cloth
**sabandija** *f* insect, bug, worm; (*persona*) vermin; **sabandijas** (*animales o personas*) vermin
**sabanilla** *f* kerchief; altar cloth
**sabañón** *m* chilblain
**sabe•dor -dora** *adj* aware, informed
**sabelotodo** *m* (*pl* **sabelotodo**) know-it-all, wise guy
**saber** *m* knowledge, learning ‖ *v* §64 *tr* & *intr* to know; to find out; to taste; **a saber** namely, to wit; **no saber dónde meterse** to not know which way to turn; **que yo sepa** as far as I know; **saber a** to taste of; to smack of; **saber a poco** to be just a taste, to taste like more; **saber de** to be aware of; to hear from ‖ *ref* to know; to be or become known
**sabidi•llo -lla** *adj* & *mf* (coll) know-it-all
**sabi•do -da** *adj* well-informed; learned; **de sabido** certainly, surely
**sabiduría** *f* wisdom; knowledge, learning
**sabiendas — a sabiendas** knowingly, consciously; **a sabiendas de que** knowing that, aware that
**sabihon•do -da** *adj* & *mf* (coll) know-it-all
**sa•bio -bia** *adj* wise; learned; (*animal*) trained ‖ *mf* wise person, scholar, scientist ‖ *m* wise man, sage
**sablazo** *m* stroke with a saber, wound made by a saber; (coll) sponging; **dar un sablazo a** (coll) to hit for a loan
**sable** *m* saber, cutlass; (coll) sponging
**sablear** *tr* (coll) to hit for a loan, to sponge on ‖ *intr* (coll) to go around sponging
**sablista** *mf* (coll) sponger
**sabor** *m* taste, flavor
**saborcillo** *m* slight taste, touch
**saborear** *tr* to flavor; to taste; to savor; to entice ‖ *ref* to smack one's lips; **saborearse de** to taste; to savor
**sabotaje** *m* sabotage
**sabotear** *tr* & *intr* to sabotage
**sabro•so -sa** *adj* tasty, savory, delicious
**sabueso** *m* bloodhound; sleuth
**saburro•so -sa** *adj* (*boca*) foul; (*lengua*) coated
**sacaboca•do** or **sacaboca•dos** *m* (*pl* **-dos**) ticket punch; (coll) sure thing
**sacabotas** *m* (*pl* **-tas**) bootjack
**sacacor•chos** *m* (*pl* **-chos**) corkscrew
**sacaman•chas** *mf* (*pl* **-chas**) clothes cleaner, spot remover; dry cleaner; dyer

**sacamue•las** *mf* (*pl* **-las**) (coll) tooth puller; (coll) quack, cheat
**sacamuer•tos** *m* (*pl* **-tos**) stagehand
**sacapintura** *m* paint remover
**sacapun•tas** *m* (*pl* **-tas**) pencil sharpener
**sacar** §73 *tr* (*un clavo, una espada, agua, una conclusión*) to draw; to pull out; to pull up; to take out; to extract, remove; to show; to bring out, publish; to find out, to solve; (*un secreto*) to elicit, draw out; to copy; (*una fotografía*) to take; to except, exclude; to get, obtain; to produce, invent, imitate; (*un premio*) to win; (*una pelota*) to serve; (*el pecho*) to stick out; **sacar a bailar** (coll) to drag in; **sacar a relucir** (coll) to bring up unexpectedly; **sacar en claro** or **en limpio** to recopy clearly; to deduce, to clear up
**sacarina** *f* saccharin
**sacasi•llas** *m* (*pl* **-llas**) stagehand
**sacerdocio** *m* priesthood
**sacerdote** *m* priest
**saciar** *tr* to satiate
**saco** *m* bag, sack; coat, jacket; sack, plunder, pillage; (*de mentiras*) pack; **saco de dormir** sleeping bag; **saco de noche** overnight bag
**sacramento** *m* sacrament
**sacrificar** §73 *tr* to sacrifice; to slaughter || *intr* to sacrifice || *ref* to sacrifice; to sacrifice onself
**sacrificio** *m* sacrifice; **sacrificio del altar** Sacrifice of the Mass
**sacrilegio** *m* sacrilege
**sacríle•go -ga** *adj* sacrilegious
**sacristán** *m* sacristan; sexton; **sacristán de amén** yes man
**sacristía** *f* sacristy, vestry
**sa•cro -cra** *adj* sacred
**sacudida** *f* shake, jar, jolt, jerk, bump; (elec) shock
**sacudi•do -da** *adj* intractable; determined || *f* see **sacudida**
**sacudir** *tr* to shake; to beat; to jar, jolt; to rock; to shake off || *ref* to shake, to shake oneself; to rock; **sacudirse bien** (coll) to wangle one's way out
**sádi•co -ca** *adj* sadistic || *mf* sadist
**saeta** *f* arrow, dart; (*del reloj*) hand; magnetic needle
**saetilla** *f* small arrow; (*del reloj*) hand; magnetic needle; (bot) arrowhead
**saetín** *m* flume, millrace
**sa•gaz** *adj* (*pl* **-gaces**) sagacious; keen-scented
**sagra•do -da** *adj* sacred || *m* asylum, haven, sanctuary; **acogerse a sagrado** to take sanctuary
**sagrario** *m* sanctuary, shrine; ciborium
**sahariana** *f* tight-fitting military jacket
**sahornar** *ref* to skin oneself
**sahumar** *tr* to perfume with smoke or incense; (Chile) to gold-plate, to silver-plate
**sainete** *m* one-act farce; flavor, relish, spice, zest; sauce, seasoning; tidbit
**sa•jón -jona** *adj* & *mf* Saxon
**sal** *f* salt; grace, charm; wit; (CAm) misfortune; **sal de sosa** washing soda; **sales aromáticas** smelling salts; **sal gema** rock salt
**sala** *f* hall; drawing room, living room, sitting room; **sala de batalla** sorting room; **sala de calderas** boiler room; **sala de enfermos** infirmary; **sala de espera** waiting room; **sala de estar** living room, sitting room; **sala de fiestas** night club; **sala del cine** moving-picture house; **sala de máquinas** engine room
**saladillo** *m* salted peanut
**Salamina** *f* Salamis
**salar** *tr* to salt; (Am) to spoil, ruin; (Am) to bring bad luck to
**salario** *m* wages, pay; **salario de hambre** starvation wages
**salcochar** *tr* to boil in salt water
**salcocho** *m* (Am) food boiled in salt water
**salchicha** *f* sausage
**salchiche•ro -ra** *mf* pork butcher
**saldar** *tr* to settle, liquidate; to sell out
**saldo** *m* settlement; balance; remnant; bargain; **saldo de mercancías** job lot; **saldo deudor** debit balance
**salero** *m* saltshaker, saltcellar; salt lick; (coll) grace, charm, wit
**salero•so -sa** *adj* (coll) charming, winsome, lively; (coll) salty, witty
**salgar** §44 *tr* (*el ganado*) to salt
**salida** *f* start; departure; exit; outcome, result; subterfuge; pretext; outlay, expenditure; projection; outlying fields; (elec) output; (sport) start; (mil) sally, sortie; (coll) witticism, sally; **salida de baño** bathrobe; **salida del sol** sunrise; **salida de teatro** evening wrap; **salida de teatros** after-theater party; **salida de tono** (coll) irrelevancy, impropriety; **salida lanzada** (sport) running start; **tener salida** to sell well; (*una muchacha*) to be popular with the boys
**saliente** *adj* projecting; (*p.ej., tren*) outbound; (*sol*) rising || *m* east || *f* projection; (*de la carretera*) shoulder
**salir** §65 *intr* to go out, come out; to leave, go away, depart; to sail; to run out, come to an end; to appear, show up; (*una mancha*) to come out, come off; (*p.ej., el sol*) to rise; to shoot, spring, come up; to project, stick out; to make the first move; to result, turn out; to be elected; **salga lo que saliere** (coll) come what may; **salir a** to amount to; to open into; to resemble, look like; **salir al encuentro a** to go to meet; to take a stand against; to get ahead of; **salir bien en un examen** to pass an examination; **salir con bien** to be successful; **salir de** to depart from; to cease being; to get rid of; (*p.ej., su juicio, sentido*) to lose; **salir disparado** to start like a shot; **salir pitando** (coll) to start off on a mad run; (coll) to blow up, hit the ceiling; **salir reprobado** (*en un examen*) to fail || *ref* to slip out, escape; to slip off, run off; to leak; to boil over; **salirse con la suya** to have one's own way; to carry one's point
**salitre** *m* saltpeter

**saliva** *f* saliva; **gastar saliva** (coll) to rattle along; (coll) to waste one's breath
**salmo** *m* psalm
**salmón** *m* salmon
**salmuera** *f* brine, pickle; salty food or drink
**salobre** *adj* brackish, saltish
**salón** *m* salon, drawing room; (*de un buque*) saloon; meeting room; **salón de actos** auditorium; **salón de baile** ballroom; **salón de belleza** beauty parlor; **salón del automóvil** automobile show; **salón de refrescos** ice-cream parlor; **salón de tertulia** or **salón social** lounge
**saloncillo** *m* (*p.ej., de un teatro*) rest room
**salpicar** §73 *tr* to splash; to sprinkle
**salpimentar** §2 *tr* to salt and pepper, season with salt and pepper; (fig) to sweeten
**salpullido** *m* rash, eruption
**salpullir** §13 *tr* to cause a rash in; to splotch || *ref* to break out
**salsa** *f* sauce, dressing, gravy; **salsa de ají** chili sauce; **salsa de tomate** catsup, ketchup; **salsa inglesa** Worcestershire sauce
**salsera** *f* gravy dish; small saucer (*to mix paints*)
**saltaban•co** or **saltaban•cos** *m* (*pl* **-cos**) quack, mountebank; prestidigitator; (coll) nuisance
**saltamon•tes** *m* (*pl* **-tes**) grasshopper
**saltar** *tr* to jump, jump over; to skip, skip over || *intr* to jump, leap, hop, skip; to bounce; to shoot up, spurt; to come loose, come off; to crack, break, burst; to chip; to project, stick out; **saltar a la vista** or **los ojos** to be self-evident; **saltar por** to jump over, to jump out of || *ref* to skip; to come off
**saltatum•bas** *m* (*pl* **-bas**) (coll) burying parson
**salteador** *m* highwayman, holdup man
**saltear** *tr* to attack, hold up, waylay; to take by surprise
**saltimbanco** *m* var of **saltabanco**
**salto** *m* jump, leap, bound; skip; dive; fall, waterfall; leapfrog; **salto de altura** high jump; **salto de ángel** swan dive; **salto de cama** morning wrap, dressing gown; **salto de carpa** jackknife; **salto de esquí** ski jump; **salto de viento** (naut) sudden shift in the wind; **salto mortal** somersault; **salto ornamental** fancy dive
**salubre** *adj* healthful, salubrious
**salud** *f* health; welfare; salvation; greeting; **gastar, vender** or **verter salud** (coll) to radiate health || *interj* greetings!; **¡salud y pesetas!** health and wealth!
**saludar** *tr* to greet, salute, hail, bow to; to give regards to || *intr* to salute; to bow
**saludo** *m* greeting, salute, bow; salutation; **saludo final** conclusion
**salutación** *f* salutation, greeting, bow
**salva** *f* greeting, welcome; salvo; oath; tray; (*de aplausos; de una batería de artillería*) round
**salvado** *m* bran
**salva•dor -dora** *mf* savior, saver, rescuer || **el Salvador** the Saviour; (*país de la América Central*) El Salvador
**salvadore•ño -ña** *adj* & *mf* Salvadoran
**salvaguardar** *tr* to safeguard
**salvaguardia** *m* bodyguard, escort || *f* safeguard, safe-conduct; protection, shelter
**salvaje** *adj* wild, uncultivated; savage; stupid || *mf* savage; dolt
**salvaji•no -na** *adj* wild; (*de la carne de los animales monteses*) gamy || *f* wild animal; wild animals
**salvamante•les** *m* (*pl* **-les**) coaster
**salvamento** *m* salvation; lifesaving; rescue; salvage; place of safety
**salvar** *tr* to save, rescue; to salvage; (*una dificultad*) to avoid, overcome; (*un obstáculo*) to clear, get around; (*una distancia*) to cover, get over; to rise above; to jump over; to make an exception of; **salvar apariencias** to save face || *ref* to save onself, escape danger; to be saved; **sálvese el que pueda** every man for himself
**salvavi•das** *m* (*pl* **-das**) life preserver; lifeboat; (*empleado de una estación de salvamento*) lifeguard
**salvedad** *f* reservation, exception
**salvia** *f* (bot) sage
**sal•vo -va** *adj* safe; omitted; **a salvo** safe, out of danger; **a salvo de** safe from || **salvo** *prep* save, except for; **salvo error u omisión** barring error or omission; **salvo que** unless || *f* see **salva**
**salvoconducto** *m* safe-conduct
**sámara** *f* (bot) key, key fruit
**san** *adj* apocopated and unstressed form of **santo**
**sanaloto•do** *m* (*pl* **-do**) cure-all
**sanar** *tr* to cure, heal || *intr* to heal; to recover
**sanción** *f* (*aprobación*) sanction; (*castigo, pena*) penalty
**sancionar** *tr* (*aprobar*) to sanction; (*imponer pena a*) to penalize
**sancochar** *tr* to parboil
**sandalia** *f* sandal
**sándalo** *m* (yellow) sandalwood
**san•dez** *f* (*pl* **-deces**) folly, nonsense; piece of folly
**sandía** *f* watermelon
**san•dio -dia** *adj* foolish, nonsensical
**saneamiento** *m* sanitation, drainage; guarantee
**sanear** *tr* to guarantee; to indemnify; to make sanitary, to drain, dry up
**sangrar** *tr* to bleed; to drain; to tap; (typ) to indent; (coll) to rob || *intr* to bleed; **estar sangrando** to be new or recent; to be plain or obvious || *ref* to have oneself bled; (*los colores*) to run
**sangre** *f* blood; **a sangre** by horsepower; **a sangre fría** in cold blood; **pura sangre** *m* thoroughbred; **sangre torera** bullfighting in the blood
**sangría** *f* bleeding; outlet, draining;

ditch, trench; (*bebida*) sangaree; tap; tapping; (typ) indentation
**sangrien•to -ta** *adj* bloody; bleeding; cruel, sanguinary
**sangüesa** *f* raspberry
**sangüeso** *m* raspberry bush
**sanguijuela** *f* leech
**sanguina•rio -ria** *adj* sanguinary, bloodthirsty
**sanidad** *f* healthiness; healthfulness; health; sanitation; **sanidad pública** health department
**sanita•rio -ria** *adj* sanitary
**sa•no -na** *adj* hale, healthy; healthful; sound; sane; earnest, sincere; safe, sure; (coll) whole, untouched, unharmed; **sano y salvo** safe and sound
**santiague•ro -ra** *adj* Santiago de Cuba || *mf* native or inhabitant of Santiago de Cuba
**santia•gués -guesa** *adj* Santiago de Compostela || *mf* native or inhabitant of Santiago de Compostela
**santiagui•no -na** *adj* Santiago de Chile || *mf* native or inhabitant of Santiago de Chile
**santiamén** *m* (coll) jiffy; **en un santiamén** (coll) in the twinkling of an eye
**santidad** *f* holiness, sanctity, saintliness; **su Santidad** his Holiness
**santificar** §73 *tr* to sanctify, to hallow, to consecrate; (*las fiestas*) to keep; (coll) to excuse, justify
**santiguar** §10 *tr* to bless, make the sign of the cross over; (coll) to punish, slap, abuse || *ref* to cross oneself, make the sign of the cross
**san•to -ta** *adj* holy, saintly, blessed; (*día*) live-long; (coll) artless, simple; **santo y bueno** well and good || *mf* saint || *m* name day; image of a saint; **a santo de** because of; **desnudar a un santo para vestir a otro** to rob Peter to pay Paul; **írsele a uno el santo al cielo** (coll) to forget what one was up to; **santo y seña** password, watchword
**Santo Domingo** Hispaniola
**santuario** *m* sanctuary, shrine; (Col) buried treasure; (Col, Ven) Indian idol
**santu•rrón -rrona** *adj* sanctimonious || *mf* sanctimonious person
**saña** *f* fury, rage; cruelty
**sañu•do -da** *adj* furious, enraged; cruel
**sapiente** *adj* wise, intelligent
**sapo** *m* toad; (coll) stuffed shirt; (Chile) little runt
**saque** *m* (*en el tenis*) serve, service; server; service line; (Col) distillery; **tener buen saque** (coll) to be a heavy eater and drinker
**saquear** *tr* to sack, plunder, pillage, loot
**sarampión** *m* measles
**sarao** *m* soirée, evening party
**sarape** *m* (Guat, Mex) bright-colored woolen poncho
**sarcásti•co -ca** *adj* sarcastic
**sardina** *f* sardine; **como sardinas en banasta** or **en lata** (coll) packed in like sardines
**sar•do -da** *adj & mf* Sardinian
**sarga** *f* serge
**sargento** *m* sergeant
**sarmiento** *m* vine shoot, running stem
**sarna** *f* itch, mange
**sarno•so -sa** *adj* itchy, mangy
**sarrace•no -na** *adj & mf* Saracen
**sarracina** *f* scuffle, free fight; bloody brawl
**sarro** *m* crust; (*p.ej., en la lengua*) fur; (*en los dientes*) tartar
**sarta** *f* string; line, file, series
**sartén** *f* frying pan; **saltar de la sartén y dar en las brasas** (coll) to jump from the frying pan into the fire
**sastre** *m* tailor
**satélite** *m* satellite
**satelizar** §60 *tr* to put into orbit; (pol) to make a satellite of || *ref* to go into orbit
**satén** *m* sateen
**satíri•co -ca** *adj* satiric(al) || *mf* satirist
**satirizar** §60 *tr & intr* to satirize
**satisfacción** *f* satisfaction
**satisfacer** §39 *tr & intr* to satisfy || *ref* to satisfy oneself, be satisfied, take satisfaction
**satisfacto•rio -ria** *adj* satisfactory
**saturar** *tr* to saturate; to satiate
**sauce** *m* willow tree; **sauce de Babilonia** or **sauce llorón** weeping willow
**saúco** *m* elder, elderberry
**savia** *f* sap
**saxofón** *m* or **saxófono** *m* saxophone
**saya** *f* skirt; petticoat
**sayo** *m* smock frock, tunic; (coll) garment
**sazón** *f* ripeness; season; time, occasion; taste, seasoning; **a la sazón** at that time; **en sazón** in season, ripe; on time, opportunely
**sazonar** *tr* to ripen; to season || *ref* to ripen, mature
**s/c** *abbr* **su cuenta**
**S.E.** *abbr* **Su Excelencia**
**se** *pron reflex* himself, to himself; herself, to herself; itself, to itself; themselves, to themselves; yourself, to yourself; yourselves, to yourselves; oneself, to oneself; each other, to each other || *pron pers* (used before the pronouns **lo, la, le,** etc.) to him, to her, to it, to them, to you
**sebo** *m* tallow; fat, suet
**seca** *f* drought; dry season
**secador** *m* drier, hair drier
**secadora** *f* clothes dryer
**secafir•mas** *m* (*pl* **-mas**) blotter
**secano** *m* dry land, unwatered land
**secansa** *f* sequence
**secante** *m* blotting paper
**secar** §73 *tr* to dry, wipe dry; to annoy, bore || *ref* to dry, get dry; to dry oneself; to wither; to be dry, be thirsty; (*un pozo*) to run dry
**secarropa** *f* clothes dryer; **secarropa de travesaños** clotheshorse
**sección** *f* section; cross section; **sección de fondo** editorial section
**secesión** *f* secession
**se•co -ca** *adj* dry; dried up, withered; lank, lean; harsh, sharp; (*bebida*) straight; indifferent; plain, unadorned || *f* see **seca**

**secreta•rio -ria** *adj* confidential, trusted || *mf* secretary
**secreter** *m* secretary (*writing desk*)
**secre•to -ta** *adj* secret || *m* secret; secrecy; hiding place, secret drawer; (*mecanismo oculto para abrir una cerradura*) key; **en el secreto de las cosas** on the inside
**secta** *f* sect
**secta•rio -ria** *adj & mf* sectarian
**sector** *m* sector; **sector de distribución** house current, power line
**se•cuaz** (*pl* **-cuaces**) *adj* partisan || *mf* partisan, follower
**secuela** *f* sequel, result
**secuencia** *f* sequence
**secuestrar** *tr* to kidnap; (law) to sequester
**secular** *adj* secular
**secundar** *tr* to second, to back
**secunda•rio -ria** *adj* secondary || *m* (elec) secondary
**sed** *f* thirst; drought; **tener sed** to be thirsty
**seda** *f* silk; **como una seda** smooth as silk; easy as pie; sweet-natured; **seda encerada** dental floss
**sedal** *m* fish line
**sedán** *m* sedan; **sedán de reparto** delivery truck
**sede** *f* (*p.ej., del gobierno*) seat; (eccl) see; **Santa Sede** Holy See
**sedenta•rio -ria** *adj* sedentary
**sede•ño -ña** *adj* silk, silken
**sedición** *f* sedition
**sedicio•so -sa** *adj* seditious
**sedien•to -ta** *adj* thirsty; (*terreno*) dry; anxious, eager
**sedimento** *m* sediment
**sedo•so -sa** *adj* silky
**seducción** *f* seduction; charm, captivation
**seducir** §19 *tr* to seduce; to tempt, lead astray; to charm, captivate
**seducti•vo -va** *adj* seductive; tempting; charming, captivating
**seduc•tor -tora** *adj* seductive; tempting; charming || *mf* seducer; tempter; charmer
**sefar•dí** (*pl* **-díes**) *adj* Sephardic || *mf* Sephardi
**sega•dor -dora** *adj* harvesting || *m* harvestman || *f* harvester; mowing machine; **segadora de césped** lawn mower; **segadora trilladora** combine
**segar** §66 *tr* to reap, harvest, mow; to mow down || *intr* to reap, harvest, mow
**segazón** *f* harvest; harvest time
**seglar** *adj* secular, lay || *m* layman || *f* laywoman
**segmento** *m* segment; **segmento de émbolo** piston ring
**segregacionista** *mf* segregationist
**segregar** §44 *tr* to segregate
**seguida** *f* series, succession; **de seguida** without interruption, continuously; at once; in a row; **en seguida** at once, immediately
**seguidilla** *f* Spanish stanza made up of a quatrain and a tercet; **seguidillas** seguidilla (*Spanish dance and music*)
**segui•do -da** *adj* continued, successive; straight, direct; running, in a row; **todo seguido** straight ahead || *f* see **seguida**
**seguimiento** *m* chase, hunt, pursuit; continuation; (*de vehículos espaciales*) tracking
**seguir** §67 *tr* to follow; to pursue; to continue; to dog, to hound || *intr* to go on, to continue; to still be, to be now; to keep + *ger* || *ref* to follow, ensue; to issue, to spring
**según** *prep* according to, as per; **según que** according as || *conj* as, according as
**segunda** *f* double meaning; (aut & mus) second
**segundero** *m* second hand; **segundero central** sweep-second, center-second
**segun•do -da** *adj* second || *m* second; **ser sin segundo** to be second to none || *f* see **segunda**
**segur** *f* axe; sickle
**segurador** *s* security, bondsman
**seguridad** *f* security; safety; surety; certainty; assurance; confidence
**segu•ro -ra** *adj* sure, certain; secure, safe; reliable; constant; steady, unfailing || *m* assurance, certainty; safety; confidence; insurance; **a buen seguro** surely, truly; **seguro contra accidentes** accident insurance; **seguro de desempleo** or **desocupación** unemployment insurance; **seguro de enfermedad** health insurance; **seguro de incendios** fire insurance; **seguro sobre la vida** life insurance; **sobre seguro** without risk || **seguro** *adv* surely
**seis** *adj & pron* six; **las seis** six o'clock || *m* six; (*en las fechas*) sixth
**seiscien•tos -tas** *adj & pron* six hundred || **seiscientos** *m* six hundred
**selección** *f* selection
**seleccionar** *tr* to select, to choose
**selec•to -ta** *adj* select, choice
**selva** *f* forest, woods; jungle
**selváti•co -ca** *adj* woodsy; rustic, wild
**sellar** *tr* to seal; to stamp; to close; to finish up
**sello** *m* seal; stamp; signet; wafer; **sello aéreo** air-mail stamp; **sello de correo** postage stamp; **sello de urgencia** special-delivery stamp; **sello fiscal** revenue stamp
**semáforo** *m* semaphore; traffic light
**semana** *f* week; week's pay; **semana inglesa** working week of five and a half days
**semanal** *adj* weekly
**semanalmente** *adv* weekly
**semana•rio -ria** *adj & m* weekly
**semánti•co -ca** *adj* semantic || *f* semantics
**semblante** *m* face, mien, countenance; appearance, expression, look
**semblanza** *f* biographical sketch, portrait
**sembrado** *m* sown ground, grain field
**sembrar** §2 *tr* to seed, to sow; to scatter, to spread; to sprinkle
**semejante** *adj* like, similar; such; **semejante a** like; **semejantes** alike, e.g., **estas sillas son semejantes** these

chairs are alike || *m* resemblance, likeness; fellow, fellow man
**semejanza** *f* similarity, resemblance; simile; **a semejanza de** like
**semejar** *tr* to resemble, to be like || *intr & ref* to be alike; **semejar a** or **semejarse a** to resemble, to be like
**semen** *m* semen
**semental** *adj* (*animal*) stud, breeding || *m* sire; stallion; stock bull
**semestral** *adj* semester
**semestre** *m* semester
**semibola** *f* little slam
**semibreve** *f* (mus) whole note
**semiconductor** *m* semiconductor
**semiconsciente** *adj* semiconscious
**semicul·to -ta** *adj* semilearned
**semidifun·to -ta** *adj* half-dead
**semidormi·do -da** *adj* half-asleep
**semifinal** *adj & f* (sport) semifinal
**semilla** *f* seed; **semilla de césped** grass seed
**semillero** *m* seedbed
**seminario** *m* seminary; seminar; nursery
**semi-remolque** *m* semitrailer
**semita** *mf* Semite || *m* (*idioma*) Semitic
**semíti·co -ca** *adj* Semitic
**semivi·vo -va** *adj* half-alive
**semovientes** *mpl* stock, livestock
**sempiter·no -na** *adj* everlasting
**Sena** *m* Seine
**senado** *m* senate
**senador** *m* senator
**senaduría** *f* senatorship
**sencillez** *f* simplicity, plainness, candor
**senci·llo -lla** *adj* simple, plain, candid; single || *m* change, loose change
**senda** *f* path, footpath
**sendero** *m* path, footpath, byway
**sen·dos -das** *adj pl* one each, one to each, e.g., **les dio sendos libros** he gave one book to each of them, he gave each of them a book
**senectud** *f* age, old age
**senil** *adj* senile
**senilidad** *f* senility
**senilismo** *m* (pathol) senility
**seno** *m* bosom, breast; lap; heart; womb; bay, gulf; cavity, hollow, recess; asylum, refuge
**sensación** *f* sensation
**sensatez** *f* good sense
**sensa·to -ta** *adj* sensible
**sensibilizar §60** *tr* to sensitize
**sensible** *adj* appreciable, perceptible, noticeable, sensible; considerable; sensitive; deplorable, regrettable
**sensiblería** *f* mawkishness
**sensible·ro -ra** *adj* mawkish
**sensiti·vo -va** *adj* (*de los sentidos*) sense, sensitive; sentient; stimulating
**senso·rio -ria** *adj* sensory
**sensual** *adj* sensual, sensuous
**sentada** *f* sitting; **de una sentada** at one sitting
**senta·do -da** *adj* seated; settled; stable, permanent; sedate; **dar por sentado** to take for granted || *f* see **sentada**
**sentar §2** *tr* to seat; to settle; to fit, to suit; to agree with || *ref* to sit, to sit down; to settle, settle down
**sentencia** *f* maxim; (law) sentence
**sentenciar** *tr* to sentence; (*una cuestión*) to decide; (*p.ej., un libro a la hoguera*) (coll) to consign
**senti·do -da** *adj* felt; deep-felt; sensitive; eloquent; **darse por sentido** to take offense || *m* sense, meaning; direction; consciousness; **sentido común** common sense
**sentimiento** *m* sentiment; feeling; sorrow, regret
**sentir** *m* feeling; opinion; judgment || **§68** *tr* to feel; to hear; to be or feel sorry for; to sense || *intr* to feel; to be sorry, to feel sorry || *ref* to feel; to feel oneself to be; to be resentful; to crack, be cracked; **sentirse de** to feel; to have a pain in; to resent
**seña** *f* sign, mark, token; password, watchword; **por las señas** (coll) to all appearances; **por más señas** or **por señas** (coll) as a greater proof; **señas** address; description
**señal** *f* sign, mark, token; landmark; bookmark; trace, vestige; scar; signal; traffic light; representation; reminder; pledge; brand; down payment; **señal de ocupado** (telp) busy signal; **señal de tramo** (rr) block signal; **señal de vídeo** video signal; **señal digital** fingerprint; **señal para marcar** (telp) dial tone
**señala** *f* (Chile) earmark (*on livestock*)
**señala·do -da** *adj* noted, distinguished
**señalar** *tr* to mark; to show, indicate; to point at, point out; to signal; to brand; to determine, fix; to appoint; to sign and seal; to scar; to threaten || *ref* to distinguish oneself, to excel
**señalizar §60** *tr* to signal
**señor** *m* sir, mister; lord, master, owner; **muy señor mío** Dear Sir; **señores** Mr. and Mrs.; ladies and gentlemen
**señora** *f* madam, missus; mistress, owner; wife; **muy señora mía** Dear Madam; **Nuestra Señora** our Lady; **señora de compañía** chaperon
**señorear** *tr* to dominate, to rule; to master, to control; to seize, take control of; to tower over; to excel || *intr* to strut, to swagger || *ref* to strut, to swagger; to control oneself; **señorearse de** to seize, take control of
**señoría** *f* lordship; ladyship; rule, sway
**señoril** *adj* lordly; haughty; majestic
**señorío** *m* dominion, sway, rule; mastery; arrogance, lordliness, majesty; gentry, nobility
**señorita** *f* young lady; miss
**señorito** *m* master; young gentleman; (coll) playboy
**señuelo** *m* decoy, lure; bait; enticement
**separa·do -da** *adj* separate; separated; apart; **por separado** separately; under separate cover
**separar** *tr* to separate; to dismiss, discharge || *ref* to separate; to resign
**separata** *f* reprint, offprint
**sept.e** *abbr* **septiembre**
**septeto** *m* septet
**sépti·co -ca** *adj* septic
**septiembre** *m* September
**sépti·mo -ma** *adj & m* seventh

**sepulcro** *m* sepulcher, tomb, grave; **santo sepulcro** Holy Sepulcher
**sepultar** *tr* to bury; to hide away
**sepultura** *f* burial; grave; **estar con un pie en la sepultura** to have one foot in the grave
**sepulturero** *m* gravedigger
**sequedad** *f* dryness, drought; gruffness, surliness
**sequía** *f* drought
**séquito** *m* retinue, suite; following, popularity
**ser** *m* being; essence; life || *v* §69 *v aux* (to form passive voice) to be, e.g., **el discurso fue aplaudido por todos** the speech was applauded by everybody || *intr* to be; **a no ser por** if it were not for; **a no ser que** unless; **érase que se era** (coll) once upon a time there was; **es decir** that is to say; **sea lo que fuere** be that as it may; **ser de** to belong to; to become of; to be, e.g., **el reloj es de oro** the watch is gold; **ser de ver** to be worth seeing; **soy yo** it is I
**serafín** *m* seraph; great beauty (*person*)
**serena** *f* night love song; (coll) night dew, night air
**serenar** *tr* to calm; to pacify; to cool; to settle
**serenata** *f* serenade
**serenidad** *f* serenity; **serenidad del espíritu** peace of mind
**sere·no -na** *adj* serene, calm; clear, cloudless || *m* night watchman; night dew, night air || *f* see **serena**
**serial** *adj* serial || *m* (rad) serial; **serial lacrimógeno** soap opera; **serial radiado** (rad) serial
**serie** *f* series; **de serie** stock, e.g., **coche de serie** stock car; **en serie** mass; **fuera de serie** custom-built, special; outsize
**seriedad** *f* seriousness; reliability; sternness, severity; solemnity
**se·rio -ria** *adj* serious; reliable; stern; solemn
**sermón** *m* sermon
**sermonear** *tr & intr* to sermonize
**serpear** or **serpentear** *intr* to wind, meander; to wriggle, squirm
**serpentín** *m* coil
**serpiente** *f* serpent, snake; **serpiente de cascabel** rattlesnake
**serranía** *f* range of mountains, mountainous country
**serra·no -na** *adj* highland, mountain || *mf* highlander, mountaineer
**serrar** §2 *tr* to saw
**serrería** *f* sawmill
**serrín** *m* sawdust
**serrucho** *m* handsaw
**Servia** *f* Serbia
**servicial** *adj* accommodating, obliging
**servicio** *m* service; (tennis) service, serve; (Am) toilet; **libre servicio** self-service; **servicio de grúa** (aut) towing service
**servi·dor -dora** *mf* servant; humble servant; (tennis) server; **servidor de Vd.** your servant, at your service || *m* waiter; suitor || *f* waitress
**servidumbre** *f* servitude; servants, help; compulsion; (law) easement; **servidumbre de la gleba** serfdom; **servidumbre de paso** (law) right of way; **servidumbre de vía** (rr) right of way
**servil** *adj* servile
**servilleta** *f* napkin
**servilletero** *m* napkin ring
**ser·vio -via** *adj & mf* Serbian || *f* see **Servia**
**servir** §50 *tr* to serve; to help, wait on; (*un pedido*) to fill; (tennis) to serve; **para servir a Vd.** at your service || *intr* to serve; (*en los naipes*) to follow suit; **servir de** to serve as; to be used as; **servir para** to be good for, to be used for || *ref* to help oneself, to serve oneself; to have the kindness to, to deign to; **servirse de** to use, to make use of; **sírvase** please
**serv.º** *abbr* **servicio**
**servocroata** *adj & mf* Serbo-Croatian
**servodirección** *f* (aut) power steering
**servoembrague** *m* (aut) automatic clutch
**sésamo** *m* sesame; **sésamo ábrete** open sesame
**sesenta** *adj, pron & m* sixty
**sesenta·vo -va** *adj & m* sixtieth
**sesgar** §44 *tr* (*el paño*) to cut on the bias; to bevel, slant, slope
**ses·go -ga** *adj* beveled, slanting, sloped; oblique; stern; calm || *m* bevel; bias; slant, slope; turn; compromise; **al sesgo** obliquely; on the bias
**sesión** *f* session; sitting; meeting; (*cada representación de un drama o película*) show; **sesión continua** (mov) continuous showing; **sesión de espiritistas** séance, spiritualistic séance
**sesionar** *intr* to be in session
**seso** *m* brain; brains, intelligence; **calentarse** or **devanarse los sesos** to rack one's brain
**sestear** *intr* to take a siesta; (*el ganado*) to rest in the shade
**sesu·do -da** *adj* brainy; (Chile) stubborn
**seta** *f* bristle; toadstool
**setecien·tos -tas** *adj & pron* **seven hundred** || **setecientos** *m* **seven hundred**
**setenta** *adj, pron & m* **seventy**
**setenta·vo -va** *adj & m* **seventieth**
**seto** *m* fence; **seto vivo** hedge, quickset
**seudónimo** *m* pseudonym, pen name
**s.e.u.o.** *abbr* **salvo error u omisión**
**seve·ro -ra** *adj* severe; stern; strict
**sevicia** *f* ferocity, cruelty
**sexo** *m* sex; **el bello sexo** the fair sex; **el sexo feo** the sterner sex
**sextante** *m* sextant
**sex·to -ta** *adj & m* sixth
**sexual** *adj* sexual, sex
**si** *conj* if; whether; I wonder if; **por si acaso** just in case; **si acaso** if by chance; **si no** otherwise
**sí** *adv* yes; indeed; (gives emphasis to verb and is often equivalent to English auxiliary verb) **él sí habla español** he does speak Spanish || *pron reflex* himself, herself, itself, themselves; yourself, yourselves; oneself; each other || *m* (*pl* **síes**) yes; **dar el sí** to say yes

**sia•més -mesa** *adj & mf* Siamese
**siberia•no -na** *adj & mf* Siberian
**sibila** *f* sibyl
**sicalipsis** *f* spiciness, suggestiveness
**sicalípti•co -ca** *adj* spicy, suggestive, sexy
**Sicilia** *f* Sicily
**sicilia•no -na** *adj & mf* Sicilian
**sicoanálisis** *m* var of **psicoanálisis**
**sicoanalizar** §60 *tr* var of **psicoanalizar**
**sicología** *f* var of **psicología**
**sicológi•co -ca** *adj* var of **psicológico**
**sicólo•go -ga** *mf* var of **psicólogo**
**sicópata** *mf* var of **psicópata**
**sico•sis** *f* (*pl* **-sis**) psychosis; (*afección de la piel*) sycosis
**sicóti•co -ca** *adj* var of **psicótico**
**sideral** or **sidére•o -a** *adj* sidereal
**siderurgia** *f* iron and steel industry
**sidra** *f* cider; **sidra achampañada** hard cider
**siega** *f* reaping, mowing; harvest; crop
**siembra** *f* sowing; seeding; seedtime; sown field
**siempre** *adv* always; **de siempre** usual; **para siempre** or **por siempre** forever; **por siempre jamás** forever and ever; **siempre que** whenever; provided
**siempreviva** *f* everlasting flower
**sien** *f* temple
**sierpe** *f* serpent, snake
**sierra** *f* saw; sierra, mountain range; **sierra circular** buzz saw; **sierra continua** band saw; **sierra de armero** hacksaw; **sierra de bastidor** bucksaw; **sierra de hilar** ripsaw; **sierra de vaivén** jig saw; **sierra sin fin** band saw
**sier•vo -va** *mf* slave; servant; **siervo de la gleba** serf
**siesta** *f* siesta; hot time of day; **siesta del carnero** nap before lunch
**siete** *adj & pron* seven; **las siete** seven o'clock || *m* seven; (*en las fechas*) seventh; (coll) V-shaped tear or rip
**sífilis** *f* syphilis
**sifón** *m* siphon; siphon bottle; (*tubo doblemente acodado*) trap
**sig.^e^** *abbr* **siguiente**
**sigilar** *tr* to seal, to stamp; to conceal, keep silent
**sigilo** *m* seal; concealment, reserve; **sigilo sacramental** inviolable secrecy of the confessional
**sigilo•so -sa** *adj* tight-lipped; reserved
**sigla** *f* initial; abbreviation, symbol
**siglo** *m* (*cien años*) century; (*comercio de los hombres*) world; (*largo tiempo*) age; **siglo de la ilustración** or **de las luces** Age of Enlightenment
**signar** *tr* to mark; to sign; to make the sign of the cross over
**signatura** *f* library number; (mus & typ) signature
**significado** *m* meaning
**significar** §73 *tr* to signify, to mean; to point out, make known || *intr* to be important
**signo** *m* sign; mark; sign of the cross; fate, destiny; **signo de admiración** exclamation mark; **signo de interrogación** question mark
**siguiente** *adj* following; next
**sílaba** *f* syllable; **última sílaba** ultima
**silbar** *tr* (*p.ej., una canción*) to whistle; (*un silbato*) to blow; (*a un actor*) to hiss || *intr* to whistle; (*ir zumbando por el aire*) to whiz, to whiz by
**silbato** *m* whistle
**silbido** *m* whistle, whistling, hiss; (rad) howling, squealing; **silbido de oídos** ringing in the ears
**silbo** *m* whistle, hiss
**silenciador** *m* silencer; (aut) muffler
**silencio** *m* silence; (*toque que manda que cada cual se acueste*) (mil) taps; (mus) rest
**silencio•so -sa** *adj* silent, noiseless; quiet, still || *m* (aut) muffler
**sílfide** *f* sylph
**silo** *m* silo; cave, dark place
**silogismo** *m* syllogism
**silueta** *f* silhouette
**siluetear** *tr* to silhouette
**silva** *f* (*materias escritas sin orden*) miscellany; verse of iambic hendecasyllables intermingled with sevensyllable lines
**silvestre** *adj* wild; rustic, uncultivated
**silvicultura** *f* forestry
**silla** *f* chair; **silla alta** high chair; **silla de balanza** (Am) rocking chair; **silla de cubierta** deck chair; **silla de junco** rush-bottomed chair; **silla de manos** sedan chair; **silla de montar** saddle, riding saddle; **silla de ruedas** wheel chair; **silla de tijera** folding chair; **silla giratoria** swivel chair; **silla hamaca** (Arg) rocking chair; **silla plegadiza** folding chair; **silla poltrona** armchair, easy chair
**sillar** *m* ashlar
**silleta** *f* bedpan
**sillico** *m* chamber pot, commode
**sillín** *m* saddle (*of bicycle*)
**sillón** *m* armchair, easy chair; **sillón de orejas** wing chair
**sima** *f* chasm, abyss
**simbóli•co -ca** *adj* symbolic(al)
**simbolizar** §60 *tr* to symbolize
**símbolo** *m* symbol; **Símbolo de la fe** or **de los Apóstoles** Apostles' Creed
**simetría** *f* symmetry
**simétri•co -ca** *adj* symmetric(al)
**simiente** *f* seed
**símil** *adj* like, similar || *m* similarity; (rhet) simile
**similar** *adj* similar
**similigrabado** *m* (typ) half-tone
**similor** *m* ormolu, similor; **de similor** fake, sham
**simón** *m* cab, hack (*in old Madrid*); hackman
**simpatía** *f* affection, attachment, fondness, liking; friendliness; congeniality; **tomar simpatía a** to take a liking for
**simpáti•co -ca** *adj* agreeable, pleasant, likeable, congenial
**simpatizar** §60 *intr* to be congenial, to get on well together; **simpatizar con** to get on well with
**simple** *adj* simple; single || *mf* simpleton || *m* (*planta medicinal*) simple
**simpleza** *f* simpleness; stupidity
**simulacro** *m* phantom, vision; idol,

image; semblance, show; pretense; sham battle; **simulacro de ataque aéreo** air-raid drill; **simulacro de combate** sham battle
**simula•do -da** *adj* fake; (com) pro forma
**simular** *tr* to simulate, feign, fake ‖ *intr* to malinger; to pretend
**simultáne•o -a** *adj* simultaneous
**simún** *m* simoon
**sin** *prep* without; **sin embargo** nevertheless, however; **sin que** + *subj* without + *ger*
**sinagoga** *f* synagogue
**sinapismo** *m* mustard plaster; (coll) bore, nuisance
**sincerar** *tr* to vindicate, justify
**sinceridad** *f* sincerity
**since•ro -ra** *adj* sincere
**síncopa** *f* (phonet) syncope
**síncope** *m* fainting spell
**sincróni•co -ca** *adj* synchronous
**sincronizar** §60 *tr* & *intr* to synchronize
**sindicar** §73 *tr* & *ref* to syndicate
**sindicato** *m* syndicate; labor union
**síndico** *m* trustee; (*en una quiebra*) receiver
**sin•diós** (*pl* **-diós**) *adj* godless ‖ *mf* atheist
**sinecura** *f* sinecure
**sinfín** *m* endless amount, number
**sinfonía** *f* symphony
**sinfóni•co -ca** *adj* symphonic
**singladura** *f* (naut) day's run; (*de mediodía a mediodía*) (naut) day
**singular** *adj* singular; special; single ‖ *m* singular; **en singular** in particular
**singularizar** §60 *tr* to distinguish, to single out ‖ *ref* to distinguish oneself, to stand out
**sinhueso** *f* (coll) tongue
**sinies•tro -tra** *adj* evil, perverse; calamitous, disastrous ‖ *m* calamity, disaster ‖ *f* left hand, left-hand side
**sinnúmero** *m* great amount, great number
**sino** *conj* but, except; **no . . . sino** only; **no . . . sino que** only; **no solo . . . sino que** not only . . . but also ‖ *m* fate, destiny
**sinóni•mo -ma** *adj* synonymous ‖ *m* synonym
**sinop•sis** *f* (*pl* **-sis**) synopsis
**sinrazón** *f* wrong, injustice
**sinsabor** *m* displeasure; anxiety, trouble, worry
**sinsonte** *m* mockingbird
**sintaxis** *f* syntax
**sínte•sis** *f* (*pl* **-sis**) synthesis
**sintéti•co -ca** *adj* synthetic(al)
**sintetizar** §60 *tr* to synthesize
**síntoma** *m* symptom
**sintonía** *f* (rad) tuning; (rad) theme song
**sintonizar** §60 *tr* (*el aparato receptor*) to tune; (*la estación emisora*) to tune in
**sinuo•so -sa** *adj* sinuous, winding; wavy; evasive
**sinvergüenza** *adj* (coll) brazen, shameless ‖ *mf* (coll) scoundrel, rascal
**sionismo** *m* Zionism
**siquiatra** *mf* var of **psiquiatra**
**siquiatría** *f* var of **psiquiatría**
**síqui•co -ca** *adj* var of **psíquico**
**siquiera** *adv* even; at least ‖ *conj* although, even though
**sirena** *f* siren; mermaid; **sirena de la playa** bathing beauty; **sirena de niebla** foghorn
**sirga** *f* towrope, towline
**sirgar** §44 *tr* to tow
**Siria** *f* Syria
**si•rio -ria** *adj* & *mf* Syrian ‖ **Sirio** *m* (astr) Sirius ‖ *f* see **Siria**
**sirvienta** *f* maid, servant girl
**sirviente** *m* servant; waiter
**sisa** *f* petty theft; (*para fijar los panes de oro*) sizing
**sisar** *tr* to filch, to snitch; (*lo que se ha de dorar*) to size
**sisear** *tr* to hiss ‖ *intr* to hiss; to sizzle
**siseo** *m* hiss, hissing; sizzle, sizzling
**Sísifo** *m* Sisyphus
**sismógrafo** *m* seismograph
**sismología** *f* seismology
**sistema** *m* system
**sistematizar** §60 *tr* to systematize
**sístole** *f* systole
**sitiar** *tr* to surround, hem in; to siege, besiege
**sitio** *m* place, spot, room; location, site; country place; seat; (mil) siege; (Am) cattle ranch; (Am) taxi stand
**si•to -ta** *adj* situated, located
**situación** *f* situation, position; **pedir situación** (aer) to ask for bearings
**situar** §21 *tr* to situate, locate, place; (*dinero*) to place, invest; (*un pedido*) to place ‖ *ref* to take a position; to settle; (aer) to get one's bearings
**s.l.** *abbr* **sin lugar**
**S.M.** *abbr* **Su majestad**
**smo•king** *m* (*pl* **-kings**) tuxedo, dinner coat
**so** *prep* under, e.g., **so pena de** under penalty of ‖ *interj* whoa!; (coll) you . . . !, e.g., **¡so animal!** you beast!
**sobaco** *m* armpit
**sobajar** *tr* to crush, to rumple; (Am) to humiliate
**sobaquera** *f* (*en el vestido*) armhole; (*para resguardar del sudor la parte del vestido correspondiente al sobaco*) shield
**sobar** *tr* to knead; to massage; to beat, slap; to paw, pet, feel; to annoy, be fresh to; (Am) to flatter; (*un hueso dislocado*) (CAm) to set; (*la cabalgadura*) (Arg) to tire out; (Col) to flay, to skin; (P-R) to bribe
**sobarba** *f* noseband
**soberanía** *f* sovereignty
**sobera•no -na** *adj* sovereign; superb ‖ *mf* sovereign ‖ *m* (*moneda*) sovereign
**sober•bio -bia** *adj* proud, haughty; arrogant; magnificent, superb ‖ *f* pride, haughtiness; arrogance; magnificence
**so•bón -bona** *adj* (coll) malingering; (coll) fresh, mushy, spoony
**sobornar** *tr* to bribe
**soborno** *m* bribery; (SAm) extra load; **de soborno** (Bol) in addition; **soborno de testigo** (law) subornation of perjury

**sobra** *f* extra, surplus; **sobras** leftovers, leavings; trash
**sobradillo** *m* penthouse
**sobra•do -da** *adj* excessive, superfluous; bold, daring; rich, wealthy || *m* attic, garret || **sobrado** *adv* too
**sobrante** *adj* remaining, leftover, surplus || *m* leftover, surplus
**sobrar** *tr* to exceed, surpass || *intr* to be more than enough; to be in the way; to be left, to remain
**sobre** *prep* on, upon; over; above; about; near; after; in addition to; out of, e.g., **en nueve casos sobre diez** in nine out of ten cases || *m* envelope; **sobre de ventanilla** window envelope
**sobrealimentar** *tr* to overfeed; to supercharge
**sobrecama** *f* bedspread
**sobrecarga** *f* overload, extra load; overcharge; surcharge
**sobrecargar** **§44** *tr* to overload, to overburden; to overcharge; to surcharge
**sobrecargo** *m* (naut) supercargo; (Am) purser || *f* (Am) air hostess, stewardess
**sobrecejo** *m* frown
**sobreceño** *m* frown
**sobrecoger** **§17** *tr* to surprise, catch; to scare, terrify || *ref* to be surprised; to be scared; **sobrecogerse de** to be seized with
**sobrecubierta** *f* extra cover; (*de un libro*) jacket, dust jacket
**sobredi•cho -cha** *adj* above-mentioned
**sobreexcitar** *tr* to overexcite || *ref* to become overexcited
**sobreexponer** **§54** *tr* to overexpose
**sobreexposición** *f* overexposure
**sobregirar** *tr & intr* to overdraw
**sobregiro** *m* overdraft
**sobrehombre** *m* superman
**sobrehuma•no -na** *adj* superhuman
**sobrellevar** *tr* to bear, carry; (*la carga de otra persona*) to ease; (*los trabajos o molestias de la vida*) to share; (*molestias*) to suffer with patience
**sobremanera** *adv* exceedingly, beyond measure
**sobremesa** *f* tablecloth, table cover; **de sobremesa** desk, e.g., **reloj de sobremesa** desk clock; after-dinner, e.g., **discurso de sobremesa** after-dinner speech
**sobremodo** *adv* var of **sobremanera**
**sobrenadar** *intr* to float
**sobrenatural** *adj* supernatural
**sobrenombrar** *tr* to surname; to nickname
**sobrenombre** *m* surname; nickname
**sobrentender** **§51** *tr* to understand || *ref* to be understood, be implied
**sobrepasar** *tr* to excel, surpass, outdo; to exceed; to overtake || *ref* to outdo each other; to go too far
**sobrepe•lliz** *f* (*pl* **-llices**) surplice
**sobreponer** **§54** *tr* to superpose, put on top; to superimpose || *ref* to control oneself; to triumph over adversity; **sobreponerse a** to overcome
**sobreprecio** *m* extra charge, surcharge
**sobreproducción** *f* overproduction
**sobrepujar** *tr* to excel, surpass
**sobresaliente** *adj* projecting; conspicuous, outstanding; (*en un examen*) distinguished || *mf* substitute; understudy
**sobresalir** **§65** *intr* to project, jut out; to stand out, excel
**sobresaltar** *tr* to assail, to rush upon; to startle, frighten || *intr* to stand out clearly || *ref* to be startled, be frightened; to start, to wince
**sobresalto** *m* fright, scare; start, shock, wince; **de sobresalto** suddenly, unexpectedly
**sobrescribir** **§83** *tr* to address
**sobrescrito** *m* address
**sobrestante** *m* boss, foreman
**sobresueldo** *m* extra wages, extra pay
**sobretiro** *m* offprint
**sobretodo** *adv* especially || *m* overcoat, topcoat
**sobrevenir** **§79** *intr* to happen, take place; to supervene, to set in; **sobrevenir a** to overtake
**sobrevidriera** *f* window screen; window grill; storm window
**sobrevivencia** *f* (Ecuad) survival
**sobreviviente** *adj* surviving || *mf* survivor
**sobrevivir** *intr* to survive; **sobrevivir a** to survive, to outlive
**sobrevolar** **§61** *tr* to overfly
**sobriedad** *f* sobriety, moderation
**sobrina** *f* niece
**sobrino** *m* nephew
**so•brio -bria** *adj* sober, moderate, temperate
**socaire** *m* (naut) lee; **al socaire de** (naut) under the lee of; (coll) under the shelter of; **estar al socaire** (coll) to shirk
**socapa** *f* subterfuge; **a socapa** clandestinely
**socarrén** *m* eaves
**socarrar** *tr* to singe, scorch
**soca•rrón -rrona** *adj* crafty, cunning, sly; sneering; roguish
**socavar** *tr* to undermine, to dig under
**socavón** *m* cave-in; cave; (min) gallery
**sociable** *adj* sociable
**social** *adj* social; company, e.g., **edificio social** company building
**socialismo** *m* socialism
**socialista** *mf* socialist
**sociedad** *f* society; company, firm; **buena sociedad** (*mundo elegante*) society; **sociedad anónima** stock company; **sociedad de control** holding company; **Sociedad de las Naciones** League of Nations
**so•cio -cia** *mf* partner; companion; member || *m* fellow; (scornful) fellow, guy
**sociología** *f* sociology
**socorrer** *tr* to aid, help, succor
**socorri•do -da** *adj* ready; handy, useful; hackneyed, trite, worn; well stocked
**socorro** *m* aid, help, succor
**socoyote** *m* (Mex) baby, youngest son
**soda** *f* soda; soda water
**sodio** *m* sodium
**so•ez** *adj* (*pl* **-eces**) base, mean, vile
**so•fá** *m* (*pl* **-fás**) sofa; **sofá cama** day bed

**soflama** *f* glow, flicker; blush; deceit, cheating
**soflamar** *tr* to flimflam; to make blush || *ref* to become scorched
**sofocar** §73 *tr* to choke, suffocate, stifle, smother; to quench, extinguish; to make blush; (coll) to bother, harass || *ref* to choke, suffocate; to blush; to get excited; to get out of breath
**sofoco** *m* blush, embarrassment
**sofrenar** *tr* (*un caballo*) to check suddenly; (*una pasión*) to control; to chide, reprimand
**soga** *m* sly fellow || *f* rope, cord; **dar soga a** (coll) to make fun of; **hacer soga** (coll) to lag behind
**soja** *f* soy, soy bean
**sojuzgar** §44 *tr* to subjugate, subdue
**sol** *m* sun; sunlight; sunny side; **de sol a sol** from sunrise to sunset; **hacer sol** to be sunny; **soles** (poet) eyes
**solamente** *adv* only
**solana** *f* sunny spot; sun porch
**solapa** *f* lapel; pretext, pretense; flap
**solapa•do -da** *adj* overlapping; cunning, underhanded, sneaky
**solapar** *tr* to put lapels on; to overlap; to conceal, cover up || *intr* to overlap
**solapo** *m* lapel; flap; (coll) chuck under chin
**solar** *adj* solar; ancestral || *m* ground, plot; manor house, ancestral mansion; noble lineage; (Cuba) tenement || *v* §61 *tr* to pave, to floor; (*zapatos*) to sole
**solarie•go -ga** *adj* ancestral; manorial
**so•laz** *m* (*pl* **-laces**) solace, consolation; recreation; **a solaz** with pleasure
**soldada** *f* wages, pay
**soldadera** *f* (Mex) camp follower
**soldadesca** *f* soldiery; undisciplined troops
**soldado** *m* soldier; **soldado de a pie** foot soldier; **soldado de juguete** toy soldier; **soldado de marina** marine; **soldado de plomo** tin soldier; **soldado de primera** private first class; **soldado raso** buck private
**soldadura** *f* solder; soldering; weld; welding; **soldadura al arco** arc welding; **soldadura autógena** welding; **soldadura a tope** butt welding; **soldadura por puntos** spot welding
**soldar** §61 *tr* to solder; (*sin materia extraña*) to weld || *ref* (*los huesos*) to knit
**solear** *tr* to sun || *ref* to sun, sun oneself
**soledad** *f* solitude, loneliness; longing, grieving; lonely spot
**soledo•so -sa** *adj* solitary, lonely; longing, grieving
**solemne** *adj* solemn; (*error, mentira, etc.*) (coll) downright
**soler** §47 *intr* to be accustomed to
**solera** *f* crossbeam; lumber, timber; mother liquor, mother of the wine; blend of sherry; old vintage sherry; tradition, standing; (Chile) curb; (Mex) brick, tile, stone; **de solera** or **de rancia solera** of the good old school, of the good old times
**solevantar** *tr* to raise up; to rouse, stir up, incite || *ref* to rise up; to revolt
**solevar** *tr* to raise up; to incite to rebellion || *ref* to rise up; to revolt
**solicitante** *mf* petitioner; applicant
**solicitar** *tr* to solicit, ask for; to apply for; to woo, to court; to drive, to pull; (*la atención*) to attract; (phys) to attract
**solíci•to -ta** *adj* solicitous; careful, diligent; obliging; (coll) fond, affectionate
**solicitud** *f* solicitude; petition, request; application
**solidar** *tr* to harden; to establish, to prove
**solida•rio -ria** *adj* jointly liable; jointly binding; **solidario con** or **de** integral with
**solidez** *f* solidity; strength, soundness; constancy
**sóli•do -da** *adj* solid; strong, sound || *m* solid
**soliloquio** *m* soliloquy
**solista** *adj* (*p.ej., instrumento*) (mus) solo || *mf* (mus) soloist
**solita•rio -ria** *adj* solitary; lonely || *mf* hermit, recluse, solitary || *m* (*juego y diamante*) solitaire || *f* tapeworm
**sóli•to -ta** *adj* accustomed, customary
**soliviantar** *tr* to rouse, stir up, incite
**soliviar** *tr* to lift, lift up
**so•lo -la** *adj* only, sole; alone; lonely; (*p.ej., whisky*) straight; (*café*) black; **a mis solas** alone, all by myself; **a solas** alone, unaided || *pron* only one || *m* (mus) solo
**sólo** *adv* only, solely
**solomillo** *m* sirloin
**solomo** *m* sirloin; loin of pork
**solsticio** *m* solstice
**soltador** *m* release; **soltador del margen** margin release
**soltar** §61 *tr* to untie, unfasten, loosen; to let go; to let go of; (*una observación*) to drop, to let slip; (*el agua*) to turn on || *ref* to get loose or free; to come loose, come off; to loosen up; to burst out; to thaw out, let oneself go
**solte•ro -ra** *adj* single, unmarried || *m* bachelor || *f* spinster, maiden lady
**solterona** *f* (coll) old maid
**soltura** *f* looseness; agility, ease, freedom; fluency; dissoluteness; release
**solución** *f* solution
**solucionar** *tr* to solve, to resolve
**solventar** *tr* (*lo que uno debe*) to settle, to pay up; (*una dificultad*) to solve
**solvente** *adj* & *m* solvent
**sollastre** *m* scullion
**sollozar** §60 *intr* to sob
**sollozo** *m* sob
**sombra** *f* (*falta de luz brillante*) shade; (*imagen obscura que proyecta un cuerpo opaco*) shadow; shady side; darkness; parasol; ignorance; ghost, spirit; grace, charm, wit; favor, protection; (coll) luck; **a la sombra** in the shade; (coll) in jail; **a sombra de tejado** (coll) stealthily, sneakingly; **ni por sombra** by no means; without any notice; **no ser su sombra** to be but a shadow of one's former self; **tener buena sombra** (coll) to be likeable; (coll) to bring good luck

**sombrear** *tr* to shade; (*un dibujo*) to hatch
**sombrerera** *f* bandbox, hatbox
**sombrerería** *f* hat store, hat factory; millinery shop
**sombrere·ro -ra** *mf* hatter, hat maker || *f* see **sombrerera**
**sombrero** *m* hat; **sombrero de copa** high hat, top hat; **sombrero de muelles** opera hat; **sombrero de paja** straw hat; **sombrero de pelo** (Am) high hat; **sombrero de tres picos** three-cornered hat; **sombrero gacho** slouch hat; **sombrero hongo** derby; **sombrero jarano** (Am) sombrero
**sombrilla** *f* parasol, sunshade; **sombrilla de playa** beach umbrella; **sombrilla protectora** (mil) umbrella
**sombrí·o -a** *adj* shady; somber; gloomy
**sombro·so -sa** *adj* shadowy, full of shadows; shady
**some·ro -ra** *adj* brief, summary; slight; superficial, shallow
**someter** *tr* to subdue, to subject; (*razones, reflexiones; un negocio*) to submit || *ref* to yield, submit, surrender
**someti·do -da** *adj* humble, submissive
**sometimiento** *m* subjection
**somier** *m* bedspring, spring mattress
**somorgujar** *tr* to plunge, to submerge || *intr* to dive || *ref* to plunge
**son** *m* sound; news, rumor; pretext, motive; manner, mode; **en son de** in the manner of, by way of; as
**sona·do -da** *adj* talked-about; famous, noted
**sonaja** *f* jingle
**sonajero** *m* rattle, child's rattle
**sonámbu·lo -la** *mf* sleepwalker, somnambulist
**sonar** §61 *tr* to sound, to ring; (*un instrumento de viento, un silbato*) to blow; (*un instrumento de viento*) to play || *intr* to sound, to ring; (*un reloj*) to strike; to seem; (coll) to sound familiar; **sonar a** to sound like, have the appearance of || *ref* to be rumored; (*las narices*) to blow
**sonda** *f* sounding; plummet, lead; drill; (surg) probe, sound
**sondar** or **sondear** *tr & intr* to sound, to probe
**sonetizar** §60 *intr* to sonneteer
**soneto** *m* sonnet
**sóni·co -ca** *adj* sonic
**sonido** *m* sound; report, rumor
**sonoridad** *f* sonority
**sonorizar** §60 *tr* (*una película cinematográfica*) to record sound effects on; (*una consonante sorda*) to voice || *ref* to voice
**sono·ro -ra** *adj* sound; clear, loud, resounding
**sonreír** §58 *intr & ref* to smile
**sonriente** *adj* smiling
**sonrisa** *f* smile
**sonrojar** or **sonrojear** *tr* to make blush || *ref* to blush
**sonrojo** *m* blush; word that causes blushing
**sonrosar** or **sonrosear** *tr* to rose-color; to make blush || *ref* to become rose-colored; to blush
**sonsacar** §73 *tr* to pilfer; to entice away; to elicit, draw out
**sonsonete** *m* rhythmical tapping; singsong
**soña·dor -dora** *adj* dreamy || *mf* dreamer
**soñar** §61 *tr* to dream; **ni soñarlo** (coll) not even in a dream, by no means || *intr* to dream; **soñar con** to dream of; **soñar despierto** to daydream
**soñolien·to -ta** *adj* sleepy, dozy, drowsy, somnolent; lazy
**sopa** *f* (*pan u otra cosa empapada en un líquido*) sop; soup; **hecho una sopa** (coll) soaked to the skin, sopping wet; **sopa de pastas** noodle soup
**sopapo** *m* chuck under the chin; (coll) blow, slap
**sopetear** *tr* to dip, to dunk; to abuse
**sopetón** *m* slap, box; **de sopetón** suddenly
**sopista** *mf* beggar
**soplar** *tr* to blow; to blow away; to blow up, inflate; to snitch, swipe; to inspire; to prompt; to tip off; (*la dama a un rival*) to cut out; (coll) to squeal on || *intr* to blow; (coll) to squeal || *ref* to be puffed up, be conceited; (coll) to swill, gulp, gobble
**soplete** *m* blowpipe
**soplillo** *m* blower, fan; chiffon, silk gauze; light sponge cake
**soplo** *m* blowing, blast; breath; gust of wind; instant, moment; (*informe dado en secreto*) tip; (coll) squealing; (coll) squealer
**so·plón -plona** *adj* (coll) tattletale || *mf* (coll) tattletale, squealer
**sopor** *m* sleepiness, drowsiness; stupor
**soportal** *m* porch, portico, arcade
**soportar** *tr* to support, hold up, bear; to endure, suffer
**soporte** *m* support, bearing, rest, standard; base, stand
**soprano** *mf* (*persona*) soprano || *m* (*voz*) soprano
**sor** *f* (used before names of nuns) Sister
**sorber** *tr* to sip; to absorb, soak up
**sorbete** *m* sherbet, water ice
**sorbetera** *f* ice-cream freezer; (coll) high hat
**sorbo** *m* sip; gulp
**sordera** *f* deafness
**sórdi·do -da** *adj* sordid
**sordina** *f* silencer; (mus) mute; (mus) damper; **a la sordina** silently, on the quiet
**sor·do -da** *adj* deaf; silent, mute; muffled, dull; (*dolor, ruido*) dull || *mf* deaf person; **hacerse el sordo** to pretend to be deaf; to turn a deaf ear
**sordomu·do -da** *adj* deaf and dumb || *mf* deaf-mute
**sorgo** *m* sorghum, broomcorn
**sorna** *f* slowness; sluggishness; cunning
**sorochar** *ref* (SAm) to become mountain-sick; (Am) to blush
**soroche** *m* (SAm) mountain sickness; (Am) flush, blush; (Bol, Chile) silver-bearing galena
**sorprendente** *adj* surprising
**sorprender** *tr* to surprise; to catch; (*un secreto*) to discover

**sorpresa** *f* surprise; surprise package
**sortear** *tr* to draw or cast lots for; to choose by lot; to dodge; to duck through || *intr* to draw or cast lots
**sorteo** *m* drawing, casting of lots; choosing by lot; dodging; (taur) workout, performance
**sortija** *f* ring; curl; hoop; **sortija de sello** signet ring
**sortilegio** *m* sorcery, witchery
**sortíle•go -ga** *mf* fortuneteller || *m* sorcerer || *f* sorceress
**sosa** *f* soda
**sosega•do -da** *adj* calm, quiet, peaceful
**sosegar** §66 *tr* to calm, quiet, allay || *intr* to become calm, to rest || *ref* to calm down, to quiet down
**sosiega** *f* nightcap
**sosiego** *m* calm, quiet, serenity
**sosla•yo -ya** *adj* slanting, oblique; **al soslayo** or **de soslayo** slantingly; askance
**so•so -sa** *adj* insipid; tasteless; dull, inane || *f* see **sosa**
**sospecha** *f* suspicion
**sospechar** *tr* to suspect
**sospecho•so -sa** *adj* suspicious; suspect || *m* suspect
**sostén** *m* support; (*de un buque*) steadiness; brassière
**sostener** §71 *tr* to support, hold up; to sustain; to maintain; to bear, to stand || *ref* to remain
**sosteni•do -da** *adj & m* (mus) sharp
**sota** *m* (Chile) boss, foreman || *f* (*en los naipes*) jack; jade, hussy
**sotana** *f* soutane, cassock
**sótano** *m* basement, cellar
**sotavento** *m* (naut) leeward
**soterrar** §2 *tr* to bury; to hide away
**soto** *m* grove; brush, thicket, copse
**so•viet** *m* (*pl* **-viets**) soviet
**soviéti•co -ca** *adj* soviet, sovietic
**sovietizar** §60 *tr* to sovietize
**sovoz — a sovoz** sotto voce, in a low tone
**Sr.** *abbr* **Señor**
**Sra.** *abbr* **Señora**
**Srta.** *abbr* **Señorita**
**S.S.S.** *abbr* **su seguro servidor**
**ss. ss.** *abbr* **seguros servidores**
**su** *adj poss* his, her, its, their, your, one's
**suave** *adj* suave, smooth, soft; gentle, mild, meek
**suavizador** *m* razor strop
**suavizar** §60 *tr* to smooth, ease, sweeten, soften, mollify; (*una navaja de afeitar*) to strop
**subalter•no -na** *adj & mf* subaltern, subordinate
**subasta** *f* auction, auction sale; **sacar a pública subasta** to sell at auction
**subastar** *tr* to auction, sell at auction
**subcampe•ón -ona** *mf* (sport) runner-up
**subcentral** *f* (elec) substation
**subconsciencia** *f* subconscious, subconsciousness
**subconsciente** *adj* subconscious
**subdesarrolla•do -da** *adj* underdeveloped
**súbdi•to -ta** *adj & mf* subject
**subentender** §51 *tr* to understand || *ref* to be understood, be implied
**subestimar** *tr* to underestimate
**subfusil** *m* submachine gun
**subi•do -da** *adj* high, fine, superior; strong, intense; (*color*) bright; high, high-priced || *f* rise; ascent; (*p.ej., al trono*) accession
**subir** *tr* to raise; to lift; to carry up; (*p.ej., una escalera*) to go up; (mus) to raise the pitch of || *intr* to go up, to come up; to rise; to get worse; to spread; **subir a** to climb; to climb on; to get in or into; to get on, to mount || *ref* to rise
**súbi•to -ta** *adj* sudden, unexpected; hurried; hasty, impetuous || **súbito** *adv* suddenly
**subjeti•vo -va** *adj* subjective
**subjunti•vo -va** *adj & m* subjunctive
**sublevación** *f* uprising, revolt
**sublevado** *m* rebel, insurrectionist
**sublevar** *tr* to incite to rebellion || *ref* to revolt
**submarinista** *mf* (sport) skin diver || *m* (nav) submariner
**submari•no -na** *adj & m* submarine
**suboficial** *m* sergeant major; noncommissioned officer
**subordina•do -da** *adj & mf* subordinate
**subordinar** *tr* to subordinate
**subproducto** *m* by-product
**subrayar** *tr* to underline; to emphasize
**subrepti•cio -cia** *adj* surreptitious
**subsanar** *tr* to excuse, overlook; to correct, repair
**subscribir** §83 *tr* to subscribe; to subscribe to, to endorse; to subscribe to or for; to sign; to sign up || *ref* to subscribe
**subseguir** §67 *intr & ref* to follow next
**subsidiar** *tr* to subsidize
**subsidio** *m* subsidy; aid, help
**subsiguiente** *adj* subsequent
**subsistencia** *f* subsistence, sustenance
**subsistir** *intr* to subsist
**substancia** *f* substance
**substanciar** *tr* to abstract, to abridge
**substanti•vo -va** *adj & m* substantive
**substitución** *f* replacement; (chem, law, math) substitution
**substitui•dor -dora** *adj & mf* substitute
**substituir** §20 *tr* to replace; to substitute for, take the place of || *intr* to take someone's place || *ref* to be replaced; to relieve each other
**substituti•vo -va** *adj & m* substitute
**substitu•to -ta** *mf* substitute
**substraer** §75 *tr* to remove; to deduct; to rob, steal; to subtract || *ref* to withdraw; **substraerse a** to evade, avoid, slip away from
**subte** *m* (Arg, Urug) subway
**subteniente** *m* second lieutenant
**subterráne•o -a** *adj* subterranean, underground || *m* subterranean; (Arg) subway
**subtitular** *tr* to subtitle
**subtítulo** *m* subtitle, subheading
**suburbio** *m* suburb; outlying slum
**subvención** *f* subvention, subsidy
**subvencionar** *tr* to subvention, to subsidize

**subvenir** §79 *intr* to provide; **subvenir a** to provide for; (*gastos*) to defray
**subvertir** §68 *tr* to subvert
**subyugar** §44 *tr* to subjugate, to subdue
**sucedáne•o -a** *adj & m* substitute
**suceder** *tr* to succeed, follow || *intr* to happen; **suceder a** (*p.ej., el trono*) to succeed to || *ref* to follow one another
**sucesi•vo -va** *adj* successive; **en lo sucesivo** in the future
**suceso** *m* event, happening; issue, outcome; **sucesos de actualidad** current events
**suciedad** *f* dirt, filth; dirtiness, filthiness
**su•cio -cia** *adj* dirty, filthy; base, low; tainted; blurred; (sport) foul || **sucio** *adv* (sport) foully, unfairly
**sucumbir** *intr* to succumb
**sucursal** *f* branch, branch office
**Sudamérica** *f* South America
**sudamerica•no -na** *adj & mf* South American
**sudar** *tr* to sweat; (coll) to cough up || *intr* to sweat; (*trabajar mucho*) (coll) to sweat
**sudario** *m* shroud, winding sheet
**sudcorea•no -na** *adj & mf* South Korean
**sudor** *m* sweat; (fig) sweat, toil; **chorrear de sudor** to swelter
**sudoro•so -sa** *adj* sweaty
**Suecia** *f* Sweden
**sue•co -ca** *adj* Swedish || *mf* Swede || *m* (*idioma*) Swedish
**suegra** *f* mother-in-law
**suegro** *m* father-in-law
**suela** *f* sole; sole leather; (*fish*) sole
**sueldacostilla** *f* grape hyacinth
**sueldo** *m* salary, pay
**suelo** *m* ground, soil, land; floor, flooring; pavement; (*p.ej., de una botella*) bottom; **no pisar en el suelo** to walk on air; **suelo franco** loam; **suelo natal** home country
**suel•to -ta** *adj* loose; free; easy; swift, agile, nimble; fluent; bold, daring; (*ejemplar*) single; (*verso*) blank; odd, separate; spare; bulk; **suelto de lengua** loose-tongued || *m* small change; news item
**sueñecillo** *m* nap; **descabezar un sueñecillo** to take a nap
**sueño** *m* sleep; dream; (*cosa de gran belleza*) (fig) dream; **conciliar el sueño** to manage to go to sleep; **ni por sueños** by no means; **no dormir sueño** to not sleep a wink; **tener sueño** to be sleepy; **último sueño** (*muerte*) last sleep; **sueño hecho realidad** dream come true; **sueños dorados** daydreams
**suero** *m* serum
**suerte** *f* fortune, luck; piece of luck; fate, lot; kind, sort; way, manner; feat, trick; (taur) play, suerte; (Peru) lottery ticket; **de esta suerte** in this way; **de suerte que** so that, with the result that; **la suerte está echada** the die is cast; **suerte de capa** (taur) capework
**suerte•ro -ra** *adj* (Am) fortunate, lucky
**sué•ter** *m* (*pl* **-ters**) sweater
**suficiente** *adj* sufficient; adequate; fit, competent
**sufijo** *m* suffix
**sufragar** §44 *tr* to help, support, favor; to defray || *intr* (SAm) to vote
**sufragio** *m* help, succor; benefit; (*voto*) suffrage
**sufragismo** *m* woman suffrage
**sufragista** *mf* woman-suffragist || *f* suffragette
**sufri•do -da** *adj* long-suffering; (*color*) serviceable; (*marido*) complaisant
**sufrir** *tr* to suffer; to undergo, experience; to support, hold up; to tolerate; (*un examen*) to take || *intr* to suffer
**sugerencia** *f* suggestion
**sugerir** §68 *tr* to suggest
**sugestión** *f* suggestion
**sugestionar** *tr* to influence by suggestion
**sugesti•vo -va** *adj* suggestive; stimulating, striking, conspicuous
**suicida** *adj* suicidal || *mf* suicide
**suicidar** *ref* to commit suicide
**suicidio** *m* suicide
**Suiza** *f* Switzerland
**sui•zo -za** *adj & mf* Swiss || *f* see **Suiza**
**sujeción** *f* subjection; surrender; fastening; fastener
**sujetahilo** *m* (elec) binding post
**sujetapape•les** *m* (*pl* **-les**) paper clip
**sujetar** *tr* to subject; to subdue; to fasten, tighten || *ref* to subject oneself, to submit; to stick, adhere
**suje•to -ta** *adj* subject, liable; (Am) able, capable || *m* subject; fellow, individual; **buen sujeto** good egg
**sulfato** *m* sulfate
**sulfito** *m* sulfite
**sulfúri•co -ca** *adj* sulfuric
**sulfuro** *m* sulfide; **sulfuro de hidrógeno** hydrogen sulfide
**sulfuro•so -sa** *adj* sulfurous
**sultán** *m* sultan; (*galanteador*) (coll) sheik
**suma** *f* sum, addition; summary; sum and substance; **en suma** in short, in a word
**sumadora** *f* adding machine
**sumamente** *adv* extremely, exceedingly
**sumar** *tr* to add; to sum up; to amount to || *intr* to add; to amount; **suma y sigue** add and carry || *ref* to add up; to adhere
**suma•rio -ria** *adj & m* summary
**sumergir** §27 *tr* to submerge || *ref* to submerge; (*un submarino*) to dive
**sumersión** *f* submersion; (*de un submarino*) dive
**sumidad** *f* top, apex, summit
**sumidero** *m* drain, sewer; sink
**suministrar** *tr* to provide, to supply
**suministro** *m* provision, supply; **suministros** supplies
**sumir** *tr* to sink; to press down; to overwhelm || *ref* to sink; (*p.ej., los carrillos, el pecho*) to be sunken; (Am) to shrink, to shrivel; (Am) to cower; (*p.ej., el sombrero*) (Am) to pull down
**sumisión** *f* submission; (*sometimiento*) subjection
**sumi•so -sa** *adj* submissive
**su•mo -ma** *adj* high, great, extreme;

supreme; **a lo sumo** at most, at the most || *f* see **suma**
**suncho** *m* hoop
**suntuo•so -sa** *adj* sumptuous
**supeditar** *tr* to hold down, oppress
**superar** *tr* to surpass, excel; to conquer
**superávit** *m* (com) surplus
**supercarburante** *m* high-test fuel
**superchería** *f* fraud, deceit
**superficial** *adj* superficial; surface
**superficie** *f* surface; exterior, outside; area; **superficie de sustentación** (aer) airfoil
**super•fluo -flua** *adj* superfluous
**superhombre** *m* superman
**superintendente** *mf* superintendent, supervisor; **superintendente de patio** (rr) yardmaster
**superior** *adj* superior; upper; higher; **superior a** superior to; higher than; more than; larger than || *m* superior
**superiora** *f* mother superior
**superioridad** *f* superiority; authorities
**superlati•vo -va** *adj & m* superlative
**supermercado** *m* supermarket
**super•no -na** *adj* highest, supreme
**superpoblar** §61 *tr* to overpopulate
**superponer** §54 *tr* to superpose
**superproducción** *f* overproduction
**supersóni•co -ca** *adj* supersonic || *f* supersonics
**superstición** *f* superstition
**supersticio•so -sa** *adj* superstitious
**supervisar** *tr* to supervise
**supervivencia** *f* survival; (law) survivorship
**súpi•to -ta** *adj* sudden; (coll) impatient; (Col) dumbfounded
**suplantar** *tr* to supplant by treachery; (*un documento*) to alter fraudulently
**suplefal•tas** *mf* (*pl* **-tas**) substitute, fill-in
**suplemento** *m* supplement; excess fare
**súplica** *f* entreaty, supplication; request
**suplicante** *adj & mf* suppliant
**suplicar** §73 *tr & intr* to entreat, implore; (law) to petition
**suplicio** *m* torture; punishment, execution; anguish
**suplir** *tr* to supplement, make up for; to replace, take the place of; (*un defecto de otra persona*) to cover up; (gram) to understand
**suponer** §54 *tr* to suppose; to presuppose, imply; to entail || *intr* to have weight, have authority
**suposición** *f* supposition; distinction; falsehood, imposture
**supositorio** *m* suppository
**supradi•cho -cha** *adj* above-mentioned
**supre•mo -ma** *adj* supreme
**supresión** *f* suppression, elimination, omission; cancellation; deletion
**suprimir** *tr* to suppress, eliminate, do away with; to cancel; to delete
**supues•to -ta** *adj* supposed, assumed, hypothetical; **supuesto que** since, inasmuch as || *m* assumption, hypothesis; **dar por supuesto** to take for granted; **por supuesto** of course, naturally
**supurar** *intr* suppurate, discharge pus
**sur** *m* south; south wind
**Suramérica** *f* South America
**surcar** §73 *tr* to furrow; to plough; to cut through; to streak through
**surco** *m* furrow; wrinkle, rut, cut; (*del disco gramofónico*) groove; **echarse en el surco** (coll) to lie down on the job
**surcorea•no -na** *adj & mf* South Korean
**sure•ño -ña** *adj* (Am) southern || *mf* (Am) southerner
**surestada** *f* (Arg) southeaster
**surgir** §27 *intr* to spout, spurt; to come forth, spring up; to arise, appear
**suripanta** *f* (hum) chorine; (scornful) slut, jade
**surti•do -da** *adj* assorted || *m* assortment; supply, stock
**surtidor** *m* jet, spout, fountain; **surtidor de gasolina** gasoline pump
**surtir** *tr* to furnish, provide, supply || *intr* to spout, spurt, shoot up
**susceptible** *adj* susceptible; touchy
**suscitar** *tr* to stir up, provoke; (*dudas, una cuestión*) to raise
**susodi•cho -cha** *adj* above-mentioned
**suspender** *tr* to hang; to suspend; to astonish; to postpone; to fail, to flunk || *ref* to be suspended
**suspensión** *f* suspension; astonishment; **suspensión de fuegos** cease fire
**suspen•so -sa** *adj* suspended, hanging; baffled, bewildered; (theat) closed || *m* flunk, condition
**suspensores** *mpl* (Am) suspenders
**suspensorio** *m* jockstrap, supporter
**suspi•caz** *adj* (*pl* **-caces**) suspicious, distrustful
**suspirar** *intr* to sigh
**suspiro** *m* sigh; ladyfinger; (mus) quarter rest
**sustentación** *f* support, prop; (aer) lift
**sustentar** *tr* to sustain, support, feed; to maintain; (*una tesis*) to defend
**sustento** *m* sustenance, support, food; maintenance
**susto** *m* scare, fright
**susurrar** *tr* to whisper || *intr* to whisper; to murmur, rustle, purl, hum; to be bruited about || *ref* to be bruited about
**susurro** *m* whisper; murmur, rustle, purling, hum
**susu•rrón -rrona** *adj* (coll) whispering || *mf* (coll) whisperer
**sutil** *adj* subtle; keen, observant; thin, delicate
**su•yo -ya** *adj poss* of his, of hers, of yours, of theirs, e.g., **un amigo suyo** a friend of his; *pron poss* his, hers, yours, theirs, its, one's; **hacer de las suyas** (coll) to be up to one's old tricks; **salirse con la suya** to have one's way; to carry one's point

# T

**T, t** (te) *f* twenty-third letter of the Spanish alphabet
**t.** *abbr* **tarde**
**taba** *f* anklebone; (*del carnero*) knucklebone; (*juego*) knucklebones
**tabaco** *m* tobacco; cigar; snuff; (Cuba, CAm, Mex) punch; **tabaco en rama** leaf tobacco
**tabalada** *f* (coll) bump, thump, heavy fall; (coll) slap
**tabalear** *tr* to rock, to sway || *intr* to drum with the fingers
**tabanazo** *m* (coll) slap; (coll) slap in the face
**tabanco** *m* stand, stall, booth
**tábano** *m* horsefly, gadfly
**tabanque** *m* treadle wheel
**tabaola** *f* noise, hubbub
**tabaquera** *f* snuffbox; (*de la pipa de fumar*) bowl; (Arg, Chile) tobacco pouch
**tabaquería** *f* tobacco store, cigar store
**tabaque·ro -ra** *adj* tobacco || *mf* tobacconist; cigar maker || *m* (Bol) pocket handkerchief || *f* see **tabaquera**
**tabardete** *m* or **tabardillo** *m* (coll) sunstroke; (coll) harum-scarum
**tabarra** *f* (coll) bore, tiresome talk
**taberna** *f* tavern, saloon, barroom, pub
**tabernáculo** *m* tabernacle
**tabernera** *f* barmaid
**tabernero** *m* tavern keeper; bartender
**tabica** *f* (*para cubrir un hueco*) board; (*del frente de un escalón*) riser
**tabicar** §73 *tr* to close up, to shut up; to wall up
**tabique** *m* thin wall; partition wall, partition
**tabla** *f* (*de madera*) board; (*de metal*) sheet; (*de piedra*) slab; (*de tierra*) strip; (*cuadro pintado en una tabla*) panel; (*lista, catálogo; índice de materias*) table; **escapar** or **salvarse en una tabla** to have a narrow escape; **tabla de lavar** washboard; **tabla de planchar** ironing board; **tabla de salvación** lifesaver, helping hand; **tablas** draw, tie; (*escenario del teatro*) stage; (*de la plaza de toros*) barrier; **tener tablas** to have stage presence
**tablado** *m* flooring; scaffold; (*escenario del teatro*) stage
**tablear** *tr* to cut into boards; to divide into plots or patches; to level, to grade
**tablero** *m* boarding; timber; table top; gambling table; cutting board; checkerboard, chessboard; counter; blackboard; **poner al tablero** to risk; **tablero de instrumentos** (aer) control panel; (aut) dashboard
**tableta** *f* small board; (*taco de papel; comprimido, pastilla*) tablet
**tabletear** *intr* to rattle
**tablilla** *f* tablet; splint; bulletin board
**tablón** *m* plank; beam
**tabloncillo** *m* (taur) seat in last row
**ta·bú** *m* (*pl* **-búes**) taboo
**tabuco** *m* hovel
**tabulador** *m* tabulator
**tabular** *tr* to tabulate
**taburete** *m* stool
**tac** *m* tick
**tacada** *f* stroke (*of a billiard cue*)
**taca·ño -ña** *adj* stingy
**táci·to -ta** *adj* tacit; silent
**tacitur·no -na** *adj* taciturn; melancholy
**taco** *m* bung, plug; wad, wadding; billiard cue; pad, tablet; drumstick; (coll) snack, bite; (coll) drink; (coll) oath, curse; (Am) heel; (Am) muddle, mess
**tacón** *m* heel
**taconear** *tr* (Chile) to fill, to stuff || *intr* to click the heels; to strut
**taconeo** *m* click, clicking (*of heels*)
**tácti·co -ca** *adj* tactical || *m* tactician || *f* tactics
**tacto** *m* (sense of) touch; (*del dactilógrafo, el pianista, el instrumento*) touch; skill; tact
**tacha** *f* defect, fault, flaw
**tachar** *tr* to erase; to strike out; to blame, find fault with
**tacho** *m* (Arg) garbage can; (Arg) watch; (Arg, Chile) boiler; (Cuba) sugar pan; (Am) tin sheet
**tachón** *m* scratch, erasure; ornamental tack or nail; trimming
**tachonar** *tr* to adorn with ornamental tacks; to trim with ribbon; to spangle, to stud
**tachuela** *f* tack; hobnail; (Chile, Mex) runt, half pint; (SAm) drinking cup
**Tadeo** *m* Thaddeus
**tafetán** *m* taffeta; **tafetanes** flags, colors; (coll) finery; **tafetán inglés** court plaster
**tafilete** *m* morocco leather; (Am) sweatband
**tagarote** *m* sparrow hawk; scrivener; (coll) lout; (coll) gentleman sponger
**tagua** *f* (Chile) mud hen; (*arbusto*) (SAm) ivory palm; (*fruto*) (SAm) ivory nut
**taha·lí** *m* (*pl* **-líes**) baldric
**tahona** *f* horse-driven flour mill; bakery
**ta·hur -hura** *adj* gambling; cheating || *mf* gambler; cheat; cardsharp
**tailan·dés -desa** *adj & mf* Thai
**Tailandia** *f* Thailand
**taima·do -da** *adj* sly, crafty; (Arg, Ecuad) lazy; (Chile) gruff, sullen
**tajada** *f* cut; slice; (coll) hoarseness; (coll) drunk
**tajadero** *m* chopping block
**tajalá·piz** *m* (*pl* **-pices**) pencil sharpener
**tajamar** *m* cutwater; (Am) dike, dam
**tajar** *tr* to cut; to slice; (*un lápiz*) to sharpen
**tajo** *m* cut; cutting edge; chopping block; execution block; steep cliff || **Tajo** *m* Tagus
**tal** *adj indef* such; such a || *pron indef* so-and-so; such a thing; someone || *adv* so; in such a way; **con tal (de) que** provided (that); **¿qué tal?** how?; hello!, how's everything?

**talabarte** *m* sword belt
**talabartero** *m* saddler, harness maker
**talache** *m* or **talacho** *m* (Mex) mattock
**taladrar** *tr* to bore, drill, pierce, perforate; (*un billete*) to punch; (*un problema*) to get to the bottom of
**taladro** *m* drill; auger; drill hole; drill press
**tálamo** *m* bridal bed
**talán** *m* ding-dong
**talante** *m* countenance, mien; desire, will, pleasure; way, manner
**talar** *adj* (*traje, vestidura*) long || *tr* (*árboles*) to fell; to destroy, lay waste
**talco** *m* tinsel; talc; **talco en polvo** talcum powder
**talega** *f* bag, sack; **talegas** (coll) money, wealth
**talego** *m* big bag, sack; (coll) slob; **tener talego** (coll) to have money tucked away
**taleguilla** *f* small bag; bullfighter's breeches
**talento** *m* talent
**talento·so -sa** *adj* talented
**Tales** *m* Thales
**Talía** *f* Thalia
**talismán** *m* talisman
**talón** *m* heel; (aut) lug, flange; check, voucher, coupon; (*de un cheque*) stub
**talona·rio -ria** *adj* stub || *m* stub book, checkbook
**talonear** *intr* (coll) to dash along
**talud** *m* slope
**talla** *f* cut; carving; height, stature; size; ransom; reward; (Arg) chatting, prattle; (CAm) fraud, lie; (Col) beating, thrashing
**tallar** *tr* to carve; (*una piedra preciosa*) to cut; (*naipes*) to deal; to appraise; to engrave; to grind; to size up; (Col) to beat, to thrash || *intr* (Arg) to chat, converse; (Chile) to make love
**tallarín** *m* noodle
**talle** *m* shape, figure, stature; waist; fit; appearance, outline; (Am) bodice
**taller** *m* shop, workshop; factory, mill; atelier, studio; laboratory; **taller agremiado** closed shop; **taller franco** open shop; **taller penitenciario** workhouse
**tallo** *m* stem, stalk; shoot, sprout; (Col) cabbage
**tamal** *m* (CAm, Mex) tamale; (Am) intrigue; (Chile) bundle
**tamañi·to -ta** *adj* so small; very small; confused, disconcerted
**tama·ño -ña** *adj* so big; such a big; very big, very large; so small; **abrir tamaños ojos** to open one's eyes wide || *m* size
**tambaleante** *adj* staggering
**tambalear** *intr & ref* to stagger, reel, totter
**también** *adv* also, too
**tambo** *m* (Arg, Chile) brothel; (SAm) roadside inn; (Arg, Urug) dairy
**tambor** *m* drum; (*persona que toca el tambor*) drummer; sieve, screen; eardrum; coffee roaster; **a tambor batiente** with drums beating; in triumph; **tambor mayor** drum major
**tamborilear** *tr* to praise to the skies || *intr* to drum
**Támesis** *m* Thames
**ta·miz** *m* (*pl* **-mices**) sieve
**tamizar** §60 *tr* to sift, to sieve
**tamo** *m* fuzz, fluff
**tampoco** *adv* neither, not either; **ni yo tampoco** nor I either
**tampón** *m* stamp pad
**tan** *adv* so; **tan . . . como** or **cuan** as . . . as; **tan siquiera** at least; **un tan** + *adj* such a + *adj* || *m* boom (*of a drum*)
**tanda** *f* turn; shift, relay; task; coat, layer; game, match; flock, lot, pack; (Am) show; (Am) habit, bad habit
**tangente** *adj & f* tangent; **escaparse, irse** or **salir por la tangente** (coll) to evade the issue
**Tánger** *f* Tangier
**tanguista** *f* hostess (*in a night club*)
**ta·no -na** *adj & mf* (Arg) Neapolitan, Italian
**tanque** *m* tank; (dial) dipper, drinking cup
**tantán** *m* tom-tom; clanging; boom
**tantear** *tr* to compare; to size up; to probe, test, feel out; to sketch, outline; to keep the score of || *intr* to keep score; (Am) to grope; **¡tantee Vd.!** (Am) just imagine!, fancy that!
**tanteo** *m* comparison; careful consideration; test, probe, trial; trial and error; score
**tan·to -ta** *adj & pron indef* so much; as much; **tanto . . . como** as much . . . as; both . . . and; **tan·tos -tas** so many; as many; **tantos . . . como** as many . . . as; **y tantos** odd, or more, e.g., **veinte y tantos** twenty odd, twenty or more || *m* copy; counter, chip; point; (Am) portion, part; **apuntar los tantos** to keep score; **entre tanto** in the meantime; **estar al tanto de** to be aware of, to be or keep informed about; **poner al tanto de** to make aware of, to keep informed of; **por lo tanto** or **por tanto** therefore || **tanto** *adv* so much; so hard; so often; so long; as much
**tañer** §70 *tr* (*un instrumento músico*) to play; (*una campana*) to ring || *intr* to drum with the fingers
**tañido** *m* sound, tone; twang; ring, tang
**tapa** *f* lid, cover, top, cap; (*de un cilindro, un barril*) head; (*de una compuerta*) gate; (*de un libro*) board cover; shirt front; (aut) valve cap; **levantarse** or **saltarse la tapa de los sesos** to blow one's brains out; **tapas** appetizer, free lunch
**tapabalazo** *m* (Am) fly (*of trousers*)
**tapabarro** *m* (Chile) mudguard
**tapaboca** *f* slap in the mouth; muffler; (coll) squelch, squelcher
**tapacu·bo** or **tapacu·bos** *m* (*pl* **-bos**) (aut) hubcap
**tapadera** *f* lid, cover, cap
**tapagote·ras** *m* (*pl* **-ras**) (Arg) roofing cement; (Col) roofer
**tapaguje·ros** *m* (*pl* **-ros**) (coll) bungling mason; (coll) substitute, replacement
**tapar** *tr* to cover; to cover up, to hide;

to plug, stop, stop up; to conceal; to obstruct; to wrap up; (*un diente*) (Chile) to fill
**tapara** *f* (Ven) gourd; **vaciarse como una tapara** (Ven) to spill all one knows
**taparrabo** *m* loincloth; bathing trunks
**tapera** *f* (SAm) ruins; (SAm) shack
**tapete** *m* rug; runner; table scarf; **estar sobre el tapete** to be on the carpet, be under discussion; **tapete verde** card table, gambling table
**tapia** *f* mud wall, adobe wall
**tapiar** *tr* to wall up, wall in; to close up
**tapicería** *f* tapestries; upholstery; tapestry shop; upholstery shop
**tapicero** *m* tapestry maker; upholsterer; carpet maker; carpet layer
**ta·piz** *m* (*pl* **-pices**) tapestry
**tapizar** **§60** *tr* to tapestry; to upholster; to carpet; to cover
**tapón** *m* stopper, cork; cap; bottle cap; bung, plug; (elec) fuse; (surg) tampon; **tapón de algodón** (surg) swab; **tapón de cubo** (aut) hubcap; **tapón de desagüe** drain plug; **tapón de tráfico** traffic jam; **tapón de vaciado** (aut) drain plug
**taponar** *tr* to plug, stop up; (surg) to tampon
**taponazo** *m* pop
**taque** *m* click; knock, rap
**taqué** *m* (aut) tappet
**taquigrafía** *f* shorthand, stenography
**taquigrafiar** **§77** *tr* to take down in shorthand ‖ *intr* to take shorthand
**taquígra·fo -fa** *mf* stenographer
**taquilla** *f* ticket rack; ticket window; ticket office; box office; gate, take; file; (C-R) inn, tavern
**taquille·ro -ra** *adj* box-office ‖ *mf* ticket agent
**taquimeca** *mf* (coll) shorthand-typist
**taquimecanógra·fo -fa** *mf* shorthand-typist
**tarabilla** *f* millclapper; catch; turnbuckle; (*de la hebilla de la correa*) tongue; (coll) chatterbox; (coll) jabber; **soltar la tarabilla** (coll) to talk a blue streak
**tarabita** *f* (*clavillo de la hebilla*) tongue; (SAm) rope of rope bridge
**taracea** *f* marquetry, inlaid work
**tarambana** *adj & mf* (coll) crackpot
**tararear** *tr & intr* to hum
**tarasca** *f* dragon (*in Corpus Christi procession*); (*mujer fea*) (coll) hag
**tarascada** *f* bite; (coll) tart reply
**tardanza** *f* slowness, delay, tardiness
**tardar** *intr* to be long, to be slow; to be late; **a más tardar** at the latest; **tardar en** + *inf* to be late in + *ger* ‖ *ref* to be long, to be slow; to be late
**tarde** *adv* late; too late; **hacerse tarde** to grow late; **tarde o temprano** sooner or later ‖ *f* afternoon; evening; **de la tarde a la mañana** overnight; suddenly, in no time; unexpectedly
**tardecer** **§22** *intr* to grow dark, to grow late
**tardí·o -a** *adj* late, delayed; dilatory, tardy; slow
**tar·do -da** *adj* slow; late; slow, dull, dense
**tar·dón -dona** *mf* (coll) poke, slow poke
**tarea** *f* task, job; care, worry
**tarifa** *f* tariff; price list; rate; fare; (telp) toll; **tarifa recargada** extra fare
**tarima** *f* platform; stand; stool; low bench; (*entablado para dormir*) bunk
**tarjeta** *f* card; **tarjeta de buen deseo** or **de felicitación** greeting card; **tarjeta de visita** calling card, visiting card; **tarjeta navideña** Christmas card; **tarjeta perforada** punch card; **tarjeta postal** post card, postal card
**tarjetero** *m* card case; card index
**tarquín** *m* mire, slime, mud
**tarro** *m* jar; milk pail; (Am) horn; (SAm) top hat
**tarta** *f* tart, cake; pan
**tartajear** *intr* to stutter
**tartalear** *intr* (coll) to stagger, to sway; (coll) to be speechless
**tartamudear** *intr* to stutter, to stammer
**tartamudeo** *m* stuttering, stammering
**tartamu·do -da** *mf* stutterer, stammerer
**tartán** *m* Scotch plaid
**tartana** *f* tartana (*two-wheeled round-top carriage of Valencia*)
**tarugo** *m* wooden plug; wooden paving block; (Guat, Mex) dolt, blockhead
**tasa** *f* appraisal; measure, standard; rate; ceiling price
**tasación** *f* appraisal; regulation
**tasajo** *m* jerked beef
**tasar** *tr* to appraise; to regulate; to hold down, keep within bounds; to grudge
**tasca** *f* dive, joint; tavern; (Peru) surf, breakers
**tata** *m* (coll) daddy ‖ *f* (coll) nursemaid; (Am) little sister
**tato** *m* (Am) little brother
**tatuaje** *m* tattoo, tattooing
**tatuar** **§21** *tr & ref* to tattoo
**tauri·no -na** *adj* bullfighting
**taurófi·lo -la** *mf* bullfight fan
**tauromaquia** *f* bullfighting
**taxear** *intr* (aer) to taxi
**taxi** *m* taxi, taxicab ‖ *f* taxi dancer
**taxista** *mf* taxi driver
**taza** *f* cup; (*de la fuente*) basin; (*del inodoro*) bowl
**te** *pron pers & reflex* thee, to thee; you, to you; thyself, to thyself; yourself, to yourself
**té** *m* tea; **té bailable** tea dance
**tea** *f* torch, firebrand
**teatral** *adj* theatrical
**teatre·ro -ra** *mf* (Am) theater-goer
**teatro** *m* theater; **dar teatro a** to ballyhoo; **teatro de estreno** first-run house; **teatro de repertorio** stock company
**teatrólo·go -ga** *mf* theater critic ‖ *m* actor ‖ *f* actress
**Tebas** *f* Thebes
**tebe·o -a** *adj & mf* Theban ‖ *m* comic book, funny paper
**teca** *f* teak
**tecla** *f* (*de piano, máquina de escribir, etc.*) key; touchy subject; **dar en la tecla** (coll) to get the knack of it; **tecla de cambio** shift key; **tecla de escape** margin release; **tecla de espa-**

**clos** space bar; **tecla de retroceso** backspacer
**teclado** *m* keyboard; **teclado manual** (mus) manual
**teclear** *tr* (coll) to feel out || *intr* to run over the keys; to drum, to thrum; (Chile) to be at death's door; (*un jugador*) (Chile) to be losing one's last cent
**tecleo** *m* fingering; touch; (*de la máquina de escribir*) click
**técni•co -ca** *adj* technical || *m* technician; expert || *f* technique; technics
**tecolote** *m* eagle owl (*of Central America*); (Mex) night policeman
**techado** *m* roof; **bajo techado** indoors
**techar** *tr* to roof
**techo** *m* ceiling; roof; (*sombrero*) (coll) hat; **techo de paja** thatched roof
**techumbre** *f* ceiling; roof
**tedio** *m* ennui, boredom
**tedio•so -sa** *adj* tedious, boresome
**teja** *f* roofing tile; shovel hat; yew tree; linden tree; **a toca teja** (coll) for cash; **teja de madera** shingle
**tejadillo** *m* cover, top; (*de coche*) roof
**tejado** *m* tile roof; roof; **tejado de vidrio** (fig) glass house
**tejama•ní** *m* (*pl* **-níes**) (Am) shake (*long shingle*)
**tejar** *m* tile works || *tr* to tile, roof with tiles
**teja•roz** *m* (*pl* **-roces**) eaves
**teje•dor -dora** *adj* weaving; (coll) scheming || *mf* weaver; (coll) schemer
**tejer** *tr & intr* to weave
**tejido** *m* weave, texture; web; fabric, textile; tissue; (biol & fig) tissue; **tejido adhesivo** friction tape; **tejido de saco** (Mex) burlap; **tejido de punto** knitted fabric, jersey
**tejo** *m* disk; quoit; yew tree
**tejón** *m* badger
**tela** *f* cloth, fabric; (*de cebolla*) skin; (*del insecto*) web; film; (bb) cloth; (paint) canvas; (*dinero*) (slang) dough; **poner en tela de juicio** to question, to doubt; **tela de alambre** wire screen; **tela de araña** spider web, cobweb; **tela emplástica** court plaster; **tela metálica** chicken wire; wire screen
**telar** *m* loom; frame; embroidery frame; (bb) sewing press
**telaraña** *f* spider web, cobweb
**telecontrol** *m* remote control
**teledifundir** *tr & intr* to telecast
**teledifusión** *f* telecasting; telecast
**telefonar** *tr & intr* (Am) to telephone
**telefonazo** *m* (coll) telephone call
**telefonear** *tr & intr* to telephone
**telefonema** *m* telephone message
**telefonista** *mf* telephone operator
**teléfono** *m* telephone; **teléfono automático** dial telephone; **teléfono público** pay station
**teleg.** *abbr* **telégrafo, telegrama**
**telegrafiar** §77 *tr & intr* to telegraph
**telegrafista** *mf* telegrapher
**telégrafo** *m* telegraph; **telégrafo de banderas** wigwagging; **telégrafo de máquinas** (naut) engine-room telegraph; **telégrafo sin hilos** wireless telegraph
**telegrama** *m* telegram
**teleimpresor** *m* teletype, teleprinter
**Telémaco** *m* Telemachus
**telemando** *m* remote control
**telemetrar** *tr* to telemeter
**telemetría** *f* telemetry
**telémetro** *m* telemeter; (mil) range finder
**telen•do -da** *adj* sprightly, lively
**telerreceptor** *m* television set
**telescopar** *tr & ref* to telescope
**telescopio** *m* telescope
**telesilla** *f* chair lift
**telespecta•dor -dora** *mf* viewer, televiewer
**telesquí** *m* ski lift, ski tow
**teleta** *f* blotter, blotting paper
**teletipo** *m* teletype
**teletubo** *m* (telv) picture tube
**televidente** *mf* viewer, televiewer
**televisar** *tr* to televise
**televisión** *f* television; **televisión en circuito cerrado** closed-circuit television; **televisión en colores** color television
**televi•sor -sora** *adj* televising; television || *m* television set || *f* television transmitter
**telón** *m* drop curtain; **telón de acero** (fig) iron curtain; **telón de boca** (theat) front curtain; **telón de fondo** or **foro** (theat) backdrop
**tema** *m* theme, subject; exercise; (gram) stem; (mus) theme || *f* fixed idea; persistence; grudge; **a tema** in emulation
**temario** *m* agenda
**temblar** §2 *intr* to tremble, shake, quiver, shiver; **estar temblando** to teeter
**tem•blón -blona** *adj* (coll) shaking, tremulous || *m* aspen tree
**temblor** *m* tremor, shaking, trembling; **temblor de tierra** earthquake
**tembloro•so -sa** *adj* trembling, shaking, tremulous
**tem•bo -ba** *adj* (Col) silly, stupid
**temer** *tr & intr* to fear
**temera•rio -ria** *adj* rash, reckless, foolhardy
**temeridad** *f* rashness, recklessness, foolhardiness, temerity
**temero•so -sa** *adj* frightful, dread; timid; fearful
**temible** *adj* dreadful, terrible, fearful
**temor** *m* fear, dread
**témpano** *m* small drum; drumhead; (*de barril*) head; (*de tocino*) flitch; (*de hielo*) iceberg, floe; (archit) tympan; (mus) kettledrum
**temperamental** *adj* temperamental
**temperamento** *m* temperament; conciliation, compromise; weather
**temperar** *tr* to temper, soften, moderate, calm; to tune || *intr* (Am) to go to a warmer climate
**temperatura** *f* temperature; weather
**temperie** *f* weather, state of the weather
**tempestad** *f* storm, tempest; **tempestad de arena** sandstorm; **tempestades de risas** gales of laughter

**tempesti•vo -va** *adj* opportune, timely
**tempestuo•so -sa** *adj* stormy, tempestuous
**templa•do -da** *adj* temperate; moderate; lukewarm, medium; (coll) brave, courageous; (SAm) in love; (Am) drunk, tipsy; (CAm, Mex) clever
**templanza** *f* temperance; mildness
**templar** *tr* to temper; to soften; to ease; to dilute; (*colores*) to blend; (*velas*) to trim || *intr* (*el tiempo*) to warm up || *ref* to temper; to moderate; (Am) to fall in love; (Am) to die
**temple** *m* weather, state of the weather; temper, disposition; humor; average; dash, boldness; (*del acero, el vidrio, etc.*) temper
**templo** *m* temple
**témpora** *f* Ember days
**temporada** *f* season; period; (*p.ej., de buen tiempo*) spell; **de temporada** temporarily; vacationing
**temporal** *adj* temporal; temporary || *m* weather; storm, tempest; spell of rainy weather
**temporáne•o -a** or **tempora•rio -ria** *adj* temporary
**temporizar §60** *intr* to temporize; to putter around
**temprane•ro -ra** *adj* early
**tempra•no -na** *adj* early || **temprano** *adv* early
**tenacidad** *f* tenacity; persistence
**tenacillas** *fpl* sugar tongs; hair curler; tweezers; snuffers
**te•naz** *adj* (*pl* **-naces**) tenacious; persistent
**tenazas** *fpl* pincers, pliers; tongs
**tenazón** — **a** or **de tenazón** without taking aim; offhand
**tenazuelas** *fpl* tweezers
**tendedera** *f* (Am) clothesline; (Am) litter
**tendedero** *m* drier, frame for drying clothes; drying ground
**tendencia** *f* tendency
**tender §51** *tr* to spread; to stretch out; to extend; to reach out; to offer, to tender; (*la ropa*) to hang out; (*con una capa de cal o yeso*) to coat; (*un puente*) to throw, build; (*una trampa*) to set; (*conductores eléctricos, vías de ferrocarril, cañerías*) to lay; (*la cama*) (Am) to make; (*un cadáver*) (Am) to lay out || *intr* to tend || *ref* to stretch out; to throw one's cards on the table; to run at full gallop
**ténder** *m* tender
**tenderete** *m* stand, booth
**tende•ro -ra** *mf* shopkeeper, storekeeper || *m* tent maker
**tendido** *m* (*p.ej., de un cable*) laying; (*de una cortina de humo*) spreading; (*de alambres*) hanging, stretching; wires; (*trecho de ferrocarril*) stretch; (*ropa que tiende la lavandera*) wash; (*de cal o yeso*) coat; (*del tejado*) slope; (*de panes*) batch; (taur) uncovered stand; (Col) bedclothes
**tendón** *m* tendon
**tenducha** *f* or **tenducho** *m* miserable old store
**tenebro•so -sa** *adj* dark, gloomy; (*negocio*) dark, shady; (*estilo*) obscure
**tenedor** *m* holder, bearer; fork, table fork; **tenedor de acciones** stockholder; **tenedor de bonos** bondholder; **tenedor de libros** bookkeeper
**teneduría** *f* bookkeeping
**tenencia** *f* tenure, tenancy; (mil & nav) lieutenancy
**tener §71** *tr* to have; to hold; to keep; to own, possess; to consider; (*recibir*) to get; to esteem; to stop; **no tenerlas todas consigo** (coll) to be alarmed, dismayed; **no tener nada que ver con** to have nothing to do with; **no tener sobre qué caerse muerto** (coll) to not have a cent to one's name; **tener que** to have to; for expressions like **tener hambre** to be hungry, see the noun || *ref* to stop; to catch oneself, to keep from falling; to consider oneself; to fit, to go
**tenería** *f* tannery
**tenida** *f* (Am) meeting, session
**teniente** *adj* holding, owning; unripe; mean, miserly; (coll) hard of hearing || *m* lieutenant; **teniente coronel** lieutenant colonel; **teniente de navío** (nav) lieutenant
**tenis** *m* tennis
**tenista** *mf* tennis player
**tenor** *m* tenor, character, import, drift; (mus) tenor; **a tenor de** in accordance with
**tenorio** *m* lady-killer
**tensión** *f* tension, stress; (elec) tension, voltage; (mech) stress; **tensión arterial** or **sanguínea** blood pressure
**ten•so -sa** *adj* tense, tight, taut
**tentación** *f* temptation
**tentáculo** *m* tentacle, feeler
**tenta•dor -dora** *adj* tempting || *m* tempter
**tentar §2** *tr* to touch; (*el camino*) to feel; to try, to attempt; to examine; to try out, to test; to tempt; to probe
**tentati•vo -va** *adj* tentative || *f* attempt; trial, feeler
**tentempié** *m* (coll) snack, bite, pick-me-up; (*juguete*) (coll) tumbler
**tenue** *adj* tenuous; light, soft; faint, subdued; (*estilo*) simple
**teñir §72** *tr* to dye; to stain; to tinge, shade, color
**teología** *f* theology; **no meterse en teologías** (coll) to keep out of deep water
**teorema** *m* theorem
**teoría** *f* theory
**tepe** *m* turf, sod
**tequila** *m* (Mex) tequila (*distilled liquor*)
**terapéuti•co -ca** *adj* therapeutic(al) || *f* therapeutics
**terapia** *f* therapy
**tercena** *f* government tobacco warehouse; (Ecuad) butcher shop
**terce•ro -ra** *adj* third || *mf* third; mediator; go-between || *m* procurer, bawd; referee, umpire
**terceto** *m* tercet; trio
**terciar** *tr* to place diagonally; to divide into three parts; (*p.ej., la capa, el*

*fusil*) to swing over one's shoulder; (*licor*) (Am) to water || *intr* to intercede, mediate || *ref* to happen; to be opportune

**tercia•rio -ria** *adj* tertiary

**ter•cio -cia** *adj* third || *m* third; (mil) corps; **hacer buen tercio a** to do a good turn

**terciopelo** *m* velvet

**ter•co -ca** *adj* stubborn; hard, resistant

**Teresa** *f* Theresa

**tergiversar** *tr* to slant, to twist, to distort

**terliz** *m* ticking

**termal** *adj* thermal; steam

**termas** *fpl* hot baths

**térmi•co -ca** *adj* temperature; steam; steam-generated

**terminación** *f* termination

**terminal** *adj* terminal || *m* (elec) terminal

**terminante** *adj* final, definitive, peremptory

**terminar** *tr* to end, terminate; to finish || *intr* to end, terminate

**término** *m* end, limit; boundary; bearing, manner; term; **medio término** subterfuge, evasion; compromise; **primer término** foreground; (mov) close-up; **segundo término** middle distance; **término medio** average; **último término** background

**termistor** *m* (elec) thermistor

**termite** *m* termite

**termodinámi•co -ca** *adj* thermodynamic || *f* thermodynamics

**termómetro** *m* thermometer; **termómetro clínico** clinical thermometer

**termonuclear** *adj* thermonuclear

**termopar** *m* (elec) thermocouple

**Termópilas, las** Thermopylae

**ter•mos** *m* (*pl* **-mos**) thermos bottle; hot-water heater; **termos de acumulación** (elec) off-peak heater

**termosifón** *m* hot-water boiler

**termóstato** *m* thermostat

**terna** *f* trio

**terne•jo -ja** *adj* (Ecuad, Peru) peppy, energetic

**ternera** *f* calf; (*carne*) veal

**terneza** *f* tenderness; fondness, love; **ternezas** flirting, flirtation

**ternilla** *f* gristle

**terno** *m* suit of clothes; oath, curse; trio; (coll) piece of luck; (Col) cup and saucer; (W-I) set of jewelry

**ternura** *f* tenderness; fondness, love

**terquedad** *f* stubbornness; hardness, resistance

**terraja** *f* diestock

**terral** *adj* (*viento*) land || *m* land breeze

**Terranova** *m* (*perro*) Newfoundland (*dog*) || *f* (*isla y provincia*) Newfoundland (*island and province*)

**terraplén** *m* fill; embankment; terrace, platform; earthwork, rampart

**terrateniente** *mf* landholder, landowner

**terraza** *f* terrace; veranda; flat roof; (*de jardín*) border, edge; sidewalk cafe; glazed jar with two handles

**terremoto** *m* earthquake

**terrenal** *adj* earthly, mundane, worldly

**terre•no -na** *adj* terrestrial; mundane, worldly || *m* land, ground, terrain; lot, plot; (sport) field; (fig) field, sphere; **sobre el terreno** on the spot; with data in hand; **terreno echadizo** refuse dump

**terre•ro -ra** *adj* earthly; of earth; humble || *m* pile, heap; mark, target; terrace; public square; (min) dump

**terrestre** *adj* terrestrial; ground, land

**terrible** *adj* terrible; gruff, surly, ill-tempered

**territorio** *m* territory

**terromontero** *m* hill, butte

**terrón** *m* clod; lump, cake

**terror** *m* terror

**terrorismo** *m* terrorism, frightfulness

**terro•so -sa** *adj* earthly; dirty

**terruño** *m* piece of ground; soil; country, native soil

**ter•so -sa** *adj* smooth, glossy, polished; smooth, limpid, flowing

**tertulia** *f* party, social gathering; literary gathering; game room; **estar de tertulia** to sit around and talk

**tertulia•no -na** *mf* party-goer; regular member

**Tesalia, la** Thessaly

**te•sis** *f* (*pl* **-sis**) thesis

**te•so -sa** *adj* taut, tight, tense || *m* top of hill; (*en superficie lisa*) rough spot

**tesón** *m* grit, pluck, tenacity

**tesone•ro -ra** *adj* (Am) obstinate, stubborn, tenacious

**tesorería** *f* treasury

**tesore•ro -ra** *mf* treasurer

**tesoro** *m* treasure; treasury; treasure house; thesaurus

**Tespis** *m* Thespis

**testa** *f* head; front; (coll) head, brains; **testa coronada** crowned head

**testaferro** *m* (coll) dummy, figurehead, straw man

**testamento** *m* testament, will; **Antiguo Testamento** Old Testament; **Nuevo Testamento** New Testament; **Viejo Testamento** Old Testament

**testar** *tr* (Ecuad) to cross out || *intr* to make a will

**testaru•do -da** *adj* stubborn, pig-headed

**testera** *f* front; (*de animal*) forehead; (*de coche*) back seat

**testículo** *m* testicle

**testificar** §73 *tr & intr* to testify

**testigo** *mf* witness; **testigo de vista, testigo ocular,** or **testigo presencial** eyewitness || *m* (*evidencia*) witness; (*en un experimento*) control

**testimoniar** *tr* to attest, to testify to, to bear witness to

**testimonio** *m* testimony; affidavit; false witness

**tes•tuz** *m* (*pl* **-tuces**) (*p.ej., de caballo*) face; nape

**teta** *f* teat; breast

**tetera** *f* teapot, teakettle

**tetilla** *f* nipple

**tétri•co -ca** *adj* dark, gloomy; sad, sullen, gloomy

**textil** *adj & m* textile

**texto** *m* text; **fuera de texto** tipped-in

**textura** *f* texture

**tez** *f* complexion

**ti** *pron pers* thee; you

**tía** *f* aunt; old lady, old woman; (coll) bawd; **no hay tu tía** (coll) there's no chance; **tía abuela** grandaunt
**tiara** *f* tiara
**tibante** *adj* (Col) haughty, proud
**tibia** *f* shinbone; pipe, flute
**ti•bio -bia** *adj* tepid, lukewarm; (SAm) angry || *f* see **tibia**
**tibor** *m* large porcelain vase; (Am) chamber pot
**tiburón** *m* shark
**Ticiano, El** Titian
**tictac** *m* tick-tock
**tiemblo** *m* aspen tree
**tiempo** *m* time; weather; (gram) tense; (*de un motor de combustión interna*) cycle; (*de una sinfonía*) (mus) movement; (mus) tempo; **darse buen tiempo** to have a good time; **de cuatro tiempos** (mach) four-cycle; **de dos tiempos** (mach) two-cycle; **de un tiempo a esta parte** for some time now; **el Tiempo** Father Time; **fuera de tiempo** untimely, at the wrong time; **hacer buen tiempo** to be clear; **mucho tiempo** a long time; **tomarse tiempo** to bide one's time
**tienda** *f* store, shop; tent; **ir de tiendas** to go shopping; **tienda de campaña** army tent; camping tent; **tienda de modas** ladies' dress shop; **tienda de objetos de regalo** gift shop; **tienda de raya** (Mex) company store
**tienta** *f* cleverness; probe; (taur) testing the mettle of a young bull; **andar a tientas** to grope in the dark; to feel one's way
**tiento** *m* touch; blind man's stick; ropewalker's pole; steady hand; care, caution; mahlstick; (coll) blow, hit; (coll) swig; **andarse con tiento** to watch one's step; **perder el tiento** to lose one's touch
**tier•no -na** *adj* tender; loving; tearful; soft
**tierra** *f* earth; ground; land; dirt; (elec) ground; **dar en tierra con** to upset, overthrow, ruin; **echar tierra a** to hush up; **en tierra, mar y aire** on land, on sea, and in the air; **irse a tierra** to topple, to collapse; **la tierra de nadie** (mil) no man's land; **tierra adentro** inland; **tierra de pan llevar** wheat land, cereal-growing land; **tierra firme** mainland; land, terra firma; **Tierra Firme** Spanish Main; **Tierra Santa** Holy Land; **tomar tierra** to land; to find one's way around; **venir** or **venirse a tierra** to topple, to collapse; **ver tierras** to see the world, to go traveling
**tierral** *m* (Am) cloud of dust
**tie•so -sa** *adj* stiff; tight, taut, tense; stubborn; bold, enterprising; strong, well; stiff, stuck-up; **tenérselas tiesas a** or **con** to stand up to || **tieso** *adv* hard
**ties•to -ta** *adj* stiff; tight, taut, tense; stubborn || *m* flowerpot; (*pedazo roto*) potsherd || **tiesto** *adv* hard
**tiesura** *f* stiffness
**ti•fo -fa** *adj* (coll) full, satiated || *m* typhus; **tifo de América** yellow fever; **tifo de Oriente** bubonic plague
**tifón** *m* waterspout; typhoon
**tigra** *f* tigress; (Am) female jaguar
**tigre** *m* tiger; (Am) jaguar
**tijera** *f* scissors, shears; sawbuck; **buena tijera** (coll) good cutter; (coll) good eater; (coll) gossip; **tijeras** scissors, shears
**tijeretear** *tr* to snip, clip, cut; (coll) to meddle with || *intr* (Am) to gossip
**tila** *f* linden tree; linden-blossom tea
**tildar** *tr* to put a tilde or dash over; to erase, strike out; **tildar de** to brand as
**tilde** *m* & *f* tilde; accent mark; superior dash; blemish, flaw; censure || *f* jot, tittle
**tiliche** *m* (CAm, Mex) trinket
**tiliche•ro -ra** *mf* (CAm) peddler
**tilín** *m* ting-a-ling
**tilo** *m* linden tree; (Am) linden-blossom tea
**tilo•so -sa** *adj* (CAm) dirty, filthy
**timar** *tr* to snitch; to swindle || *ref* (coll) to make eyes at each other
**timba** *f* (coll) game of chance; (coll) gambling den; (CAm, Mex) belly
**timbal** *m* kettledrum; (*pastel relleno*) casserole
**timbrar** *tr* to stamp
**timbre** *m* stamp, seal; tax stamp; stamp tax; deed of glory; (phonet & phys) timbre; **timbre nasal** twang; **timbres** glockenspiel
**tími•do -da** *adj* timid, bashful
**timo** *m* (coll) theft, swindle; (coll) lie; (coll) catch phrase
**timón** *m* (*del arado*) beam; rudder; (fig) helm; **timón de dirección** (aer) vertical rudder; **timón de profundidad** (aer) elevator
**timonel** *m* helmsman, steersman
**timonera** *f* (naut) pilot house, wheelhouse
**timora•to -ta** *adj* God-fearing; chickenhearted
**tímpano** *m* eardrum; kettledrum
**tina** *f* large earthen jar; wooden vat; bathtub
**tinaja** *f* large earthen jar
**tincazo** *m* (Arg, Ecuad) fillip
**tinglado** *m* shed; intrigue, trick; (zool) leatherback
**tinieblas** *fpl* darkness
**tino** *m* feel (*for things*); good aim; knack; insight, wisdom; **coger el tino** to get the knack of it
**tinta** *f* ink; tint, hue; dyeing; **de buena tinta** (coll) on good authority; **tinta china** India ink; **tinta simpática** invisible ink
**tinte** *m* dye; dyeing; dyer's shop; (fig) coloring, false appearance
**tinterillo** *m* (coll) clerk, lawyer's clerk; (Am) pettifogger
**tintero** *m* inkstand, inkwell
**tintín** *m* clink; jingle
**tintinear** *intr* to clink; to jingle
**tin•to -ta** *adj* red || *m* red table wine || *f* see **tinta**
**tintorería** *f* dyeing; dyeing establishment; dry-cleaning establishment
**tintore•ro -ra** *mf* dyer; dry cleaner

**tintura** *f* dye; dyeing; rouge; tincture; (fig) smattering; **tintura de tornasol** litmus, litmus solution; **tintura de yodo** iodine
**tiña** *f* ringworm; (coll) stinginess
**tiño·so -sa** *adj* scabby, mangy; (coll) stingy
**tío** *m* uncle; old man; (coll) guy, fellow; **tío abuelo** granduncle; **tíos** uncle and aunt
**tiovivo** *m* merry-go-round, carrousel
**tipiadora** *f* (*máquina*) typewriter; (*mujer*) typist
**tipiar** *tr & intr* to type, to typewrite
**tipicista** *adj* regional, local
**típi·co -ca** *adj* typical; regional; quaint
**tipismo** *m* quaintness
**tipista** *mf* typist, typewriter
**tiple** *mf* soprano (*person*); treble-guitar player || *m* soprano (*voice*); treble guitar
**tipo** *m* type; (*de descuento, de interés, de cambio*) rate; shape, figure, build; (coll) fellow, guy, specimen; **tener buen tipo** to have a good figure; **tipo de ensayo** or **prueba** eye-test chart; **tipo de impuesto** tax rate; **tipo de letra** typeface; **tipo menudo** small print
**tipografía** *f* typography
**típula** *f* (ent) daddy-longlegs
**tira** *m* (Arg, Chile, Col) detective || *f* strip; **hecho tiras** (Chile) in rags; **tira emplástica** (Arg) court plaster; **tira proyectable** film strip; **tiras cómicas** comics, funnies
**tirabala** *f* popgun
**tirabuzón** *m* corkscrew; corkscrew curl
**tirada** *f* throw; distance, stretch; time, period; printing; edition, issue; shooting party, hunting party; tirade; **de** or **en una tirada** at one stroke; **tirada aparte** reprint
**tira·do -da** *adj* dirt-cheap; (*letra*) cursive || *f* see **tirada**
**tira·dor -dora** *mf* shot, good shot || *m* knob; doorknob; pull chain; **tirador certero** sharpshooter; **tirador emboscado** sniper
**tirafondo** *m* wood screw
**tiraje** *m* draft; printing, edition
**tiramira** *f* long, narrow mountain range; (*de personas o cosas*) string; distance, stretch
**tiranía** *f* tyranny
**tiráni·co -ca** *adj* tyrannic(al)
**tira·no -na** *adj* tyrannous || *mf* tyrant
**tirante** *adj* tense, taut, tight; (fig) tense, strained || *m* (*de los arreos de una caballería*) trace; **tirantes** suspenders
**tirantez** *f* tenseness, tautness, tightness; strain
**tirar** *tr* to throw, cast, fling; to throw away; to shoot, fire; (*alambre*) to draw, pull, stretch; (*una línea*) to draw; (*una coz, un pellizco*) to give; to print; to attract; to tear down, knock down; (phot) to print || *intr* to pull; to last; to appeal, have an appeal; (*una chimenea*) to draw; (*a la derecha, a la izquierda*) to bear, to turn; **ir tirando** (coll) to get along; **tirar a** to shoot at; (*la espada*) to handle; to shade into; to tend to; to aspire to; **tirar de** to pull, pull on; (*una espada*) to draw; to attract; to boast of being; **tira y afloja** (coll) give and take; (coll) hot and cold || *ref* to rush, throw oneself; to give oneself over; to lie down
**tirilla** *f* neckband; **tirilla de bota** bootstrap; **tirilla de camisa** collarband
**tiritar** *intr* to shiver
**tiro** *m* throw; shot; charge, load; (*estampido*) report; rifle range; (*p.ej., de chimenea*) draft; (*de caballos*) team; (*de escalera*) flight; (*de las guarniciones*) trace; (*de un paño*) length; pull cord, pull chain; reach; hurt, damage; trick; theft; (min) shaft; (sport) drive, shot; (*alusión desfavorable*) shot; (fig) shot, marksman; **a tiro de fusil** within gunshot; **a tiro de piedra** within a stone's throw; **matar a tiros** to shoot to death; **ni a tiros** not for love nor money; **poner el tiro muy alto** to hitch one's wagon to a star; **tiro al blanco** target practice; **tiro al vuelo** trapshooting; **tiro de la pesa** (sport) shot-put
**tirón** *m* tyro, novice; jerk; tug, pull; **de un tirón** all at once; at a stretch
**tirotear** *tr* to snipe at, to blaze away at || *ref* to fire at each other; to bicker
**tirria** *f* (coll) dislike, grudge; **tener tirria a** (coll) to have it in for
**tisana** *f* tea, infusion
**tisis** *f* consumption, tuberculosis
**titanio** *m* titanium
**tít.** *abbr* **título**
**títere** *m* marionette, puppet; fixed idea; (coll) whipper-snapper, nincompoop; **no dejar títere con cabeza** or **cara** (coll) to upset the applecart; **títeres** puppet show
**titilar** *tr* to titillate || *intr* to flutter, quiver; to twinkle
**titubear** *intr* to stagger, totter; to stammer, stutter; to waver, hesitate
**titular** *m* bearer, holder; incumbent; headline || *f* capital letter || *tr* to title, entitle || *intr* to receive a title || *ref* to be called; to call oneself
**titulillo** *m* running head
**título** *m* title; titled person; regulation; bond; certificate; degree; diploma; headline; **a título de** as a, by way of, on the score of; **títulos** credentials
**tiza** *f* chalk
**tiznar** *tr* to soil with soot; to spot, stain; to defame || *ref* to become soiled; to get spotted or stained; (Arg, Chile, CAm) to get drunk
**tizne** *m & f* soot || *m* firebrand
**tiznón** *m* smudge, spot of soot
**tizón** *m* brand, firebrand; wheat smut; brand, dishonor
**tizonear** *intr* to stir up the fire
**tlapalería** *f* (Mex) paint store
**toalla** *f* towel; **toalla rusa** Turkish towel; **toalla sin fin** roller towel
**toallero** *m* towel rack
**toar** *tr* (naut) to tow
**tobar** *tr* (Col) to tow
**tobillera** *f* anklet; (sport) ankle support; (coll) subdeb; (coll) flapper

**tobillo** *m* ankle
**tobo** *m* (Ven) bucket
**tobogán** *m* toboggan; chute, slide
**toca** *f* toque; headdress
**tocadis•cos** *m* (*pl* **-cos**) record player; **tocadiscos automático** record changer
**toca•do -da** *adj* (*echado a perder; medio loco*) touched; **tocado de la cabeza** (coll) touched in the head ‖ *m* hairdo, coiffure; headdress
**toca•dor -dora** *mf* performer, player ‖ *m* boudoir; dressing table; dressing case, toilet case
**tocante** *adj* touching; **tocante a** concerning, with reference to
**tocar** §73 *tr* to touch; to touch on; to feel; to ring; to toll; to strike; to come to know, to suffer, to feel; (*el cabello*) to do; (*un tambor*) to beat; (mus) to play; (paint) to touch up ‖ *intr* to touch; **tocar a** to knock at; to pertain to, to concern; to fall to the lot of; to be the turn of; (*el fin*) to approach; **tocar en** (*un puerto*) to touch at; (*tierra*) to touch; to touch on; to approach, border on ‖ *ref* to put one's hat on, to cover one's head; to touch each other; to be related; to make one's toilet; to become mentally unbalanced; (*el sombrero*) to tip; **tocárselas** (coll) to beat it
**toca•yo -ya** *mf* namesake
**tocino** *m* bacon; salt pork
**tocón** *m* stump
**tocuyo** *m* (SAm) coarse cotton cloth
**tochimbo** *m* (Peru) smelting furnace
**to•cho -cha** *adj* rough, coarse, crude
**todavía** *adv* still, yet; **todavía no** not yet
**to•do -da** *adj* all, whole, every; any ‖ *m* whole; everything; **con todo** still, however; **del todo** wholly, entirely; **jugar el todo por el todo** to stake everything, to shoot the works; **sobre todo** above all, especially; **todo el que** everybody who; **todo lo que** all that; **todos** all, everybody; **todos cuantos** all those who
**todopodero•so -sa** *adj* all-powerful, almighty
**toga** *f* (academic) gown
**toldilla** *f* poop, poop deck
**toldería** *f* (SAm) Indian camp, Indian village
**toldo** *m* awning; pride, haughtiness; (SAm) Indian hut
**tole** *m* hubbub, uproar; **tole tole** gossip, talk; **tomar el tole** (coll) to run away
**tolerancia** *f* tolerance; **por tolerancia** on sufferance
**tolerar** *tr* to tolerate
**tolete** *m* (Am) club, cudgel; (Am) raft; (Cuba) dunce
**toletole** *m* (Col) persistence, obstinacy; (Ven) merry life of a wanderer
**tolon•dro -dra** *adj* scatterbrained ‖ *mf* scatterbrain ‖ *m* bump, lump
**tolva** *f* hopper; chute
**tolvanera** *f* dust storm
**tolla** *f* quagmire; (Cuba) watering trough
**tom.** *abbr* **tomo**
**toma** *f* taking; seizure, capture; tap; intake, inlet; (elec) tap, outlet; (elec) plug; (elec) terminal; (*de rapé*) pinch; **toma de posesión** installation, induction; inauguration; **toma de tierra** (aer) landing; (rad) ground connection; **toma directa** high gear
**toma-corrien•te** *m* or **toma-corrien•tes** *m* (*pl* **-tes**) (elec) current collector; (elec) tap, outlet; (elec) plug
**tomadero** *m* handle; intake, inlet
**toma•dor -dora** *mf* (com) drawee; (coll) thief; (Am) drinker, toper
**tomar** *tr* to take; to get; to seize; to take on; (*un resfriado*) to catch; (*p.ej., el desayuno*) to have, to eat; (*el café, un trago*) to take, to drink; **tomar a bien** to take in the right spirit; **tomar a mal** to take offense at; **tomarla con** to pick a quarrel with; to have a grudge against; **tomar prestado** to borrow; **tomar sobre sí** to take upon oneself ‖ *intr* to take, to turn ‖ *ref* to take; (*p.ej., el desayuno*) to have, to eat; (*el café*) to take, to drink; to get rusty
**tomate** *m* tomato; (*en medias, calcetines, etc.*) (coll) tear, run
**tomavis•tas** *m* (*pl* **-tas**) motion-picture camera; cameraman
**tómbola** *f* raffle, charity raffle
**tomillo** *m* thyme
**tomo** *m* volume; bulk; importance, consequence; **de tomo y lomo** of consequence; (coll) bulky and heavy
**ton.** *abbr* **tonelada**
**ton** *m* — **sin ton ni son** without rhyme or reason
**tonada** *f* air, melody, song; (Cuba) hoax; (*pronunciación particular*) (Arg, Chile) accent; (Am) singsong
**tonel** *m* cask, barrel
**tonelada** *f* (*unidad de peso; unidad de volumen; unidad de desplazamiento*) ton; (*medida de capacidad para el vino*) tun
**tonelaje** *m* tonnage
**tonele•ro -ra** *mf* barrelmaker, cooper
**tonga** *f* coat, layer; (Arg, Col) task; (Col) sleep; (Cuba) heap, pile
**tongonear** *ref* (Am) to strut, swagger
**tóni•co -ca** *adj* & *m* tonic ‖ *f* (mus) keynote
**tonillo** *m* singsong; (*pronunciación particular*) accent
**tono** *m* tone; tune; (mus) pitch; (mus) key; (*de un instrumento de bronce*) (mus) slide; **dar el tono** to set the standard; **darse tono** (coll) to put on airs; **de buen tono** stylish, elegant; **estar a tono** (coll) to be in style; **poner a tono** (*un motor de automóvil*) to tune up; **tono mayor** (mus) major key; **tono menor** (mus) minor key
**tonsila** *f* tonsil
**tonsilitis** *f* tonsilitis
**tonsurar** *tr* to shear, to clip
**tontear** *intr* to talk nonsense, to act foolishly
**tontería** *f* foolishness, nonsense
**ton•to -ta** *adj* foolish, stupid, silly; **a tontas y a locas** wildly, recklessly; in disorder, haphazardly ‖ *mf* fool,

dolt; **tonto de capirote** (coll) blatant fool
**tonu·do -da** *adj* (Arg) magnificent, showy, conceited
**topacio** *m* topaz
**topar** *tr* to butt; to bump; to run into, encounter || *intr* to butt; to succeed; to lie, be found; **topar con** or **en** to run into, encounter
**tope** *adj* (*precio*) top; (*fecha*) last || *m* butt; bumper; bump, collision; rub, difficulty; scuffle; masthead; **al tope** or **a tope** end to end; flush; **estar hasta el tope** or **los topes** to be loaded to the gunwales; (coll) to be fed up; **tope de puerta** doorstop
**topera** *f* molehill
**topetada** *f* butt
**topetar** *tr* to butt || *intr* to butt; **topetar con** (coll) to bump, bump into; (coll) to run across
**topetón** *m* butt; bump, collision
**tópi·co -ca** *adj* local || *m* topic; (med) external application
**topinera** *f* molehill; **beber como una topinera** to drink like a fish
**topo** *m* mole; (coll) blunderer; (coll) stumbler, awkward person
**topografía** *f* topography
**toque** *m* touch; (*de una campana*) ringing; (*del tambor*) beat; sound; knock; stroke; check, test; (*punto esencial*) gist; (paint) touch; (coll) blow; **dar un toque a** (coll) to put to the test; (coll) to feel out, to sound out; **toque a muerto** knell, toll; **toque de diana** reveille; **toque de queda** curfew; **toque de retreta** (mil) tattoo; **toque de tambor** drumbeat
**torada** *f* drove of bulls
**tó·rax** *m* (*pl* **-rax**) thorax
**torbellino** *m* whirlwind; (*persona bulliciosa*) (coll) harum-scarum
**torcecuello** *m* (orn) wryneck
**torcedura** *f* twist; sprain; dislocation
**torcer** **§74** *tr* to twist; to bend; to turn; to sprain; (*la cara*) to screw up; (*el tobillo*) to wrench; to turn; (*interpretar mal*) to distort, to misconstrue || *intr* to turn || *ref* to twist; to bend; to sprain, dislocate; to turn sour; to go crooked; to fail
**torci·do -da** *adj* twisted; crooked; bent; (*ojos*) cross; (*persona o conducta*) crooked; (Guat) unlucky || *f* wick, lampwick; curlpaper
**tor·do -da** *adj* dapple-gray || *mf* dapple-gray horse || *m* thrush; (Am) starling
**torear** *tr* (*toros*) to fight; to banter, tease, string along || *intr* to fight bulls, be a bullfighter
**toreo** *m* bullfighting; (taur) performance
**tore·ro -ra** *adj* (coll) bullfighting || *mf* bullfighter
**toril** *m* (taur) bull pen
**tormenta** *f* storm; adversity, misfortune
**tormento** *m* torment, torture; anguish
**tormento·so -sa** *adj* stormy; (*barco*) storm-ridden
**torna** *f* return; dam; tap; **se han vuelto las tornas** the luck has changed; **volver las tornas** to give tit for tat
**tornar** *tr* to return, give back; to turn, to make || *intr* to return; to turn; **tornar a** + *inf* verb + again, e.g., **tornó a abrir la puerta** he opened the door again || *ref* to turn, to become
**tornasol** *m* sunflower; litmus; iridescence
**tornasola·do -da** *adj* changeable, iridescent
**tornavía** *m* (rr) turntable
**torna·voz** *m* (*pl* **-voces**) sounding board; **hacer tornavoz** to cup one's hands to one's mouth
**tornear** *tr* to turn, turn up || *intr* to go around; to tourney; to muse, meditate
**torneo** *m* tourney; match, tournament; **torneo radiofónico** quiz program
**tornillo** *m* (*cilindro que entra en la tuerca*) screw; (*clavo con resalto helicoidal*) bolt; (*instrumento con dos mandíbulas*) vise; (mil) desertion; (CAm, Ven) screw tree; **apretar los tornillos a** (coll) to put the screws on; **tener flojos los tornillos** (coll) to have a screw loose; **tornillo de mariposa** or **de orejas** thumbscrew; **tornillo de presión** setscrew; **tornillo para metales** machine screw
**torniquete** *m* (*para contener hemorragias*) tourniquet; (*torno para cerrar un paso*) turnstile; **dar torniquete a** to twist the meaning of
**torno** *m* turn, revolution; (*máquina simple que consiste en un cilindro que gira sobre su eje*) winch, windlass; (*de alfarero*) potter's wheel; (*instrumento con dos mandíbulas*) vise; (*máquina herramienta que sirve para labrar metal o madera*) lathe; (*de coche*) brake; (*de un río*) bend, turn; revolving server; **en torno a** or **de** around; **torno de alfarero** potter's wheel; **torno de banco** bench vise; **torno de hilar** spinning wheel
**toro** *m* bull; **toro corrido** (coll) smart fellow; **toros** bullfight
**torón** *m* strand
**toronja** *f* grapefruit
**toronjo** *m* grapefruit (*tree*)
**torpe** *adj* slow, heavy; clumsy, awkward; stupid; lewd; crude, ugly
**torpedear** *tr* to torpedo
**torpedo** *m* torpedo; touring car
**torpeza** *f* torpidity, slowness; clumsiness, awkwardness; stupidity; lewdness; turpitude; crudeness, ugliness
**torrar** *tr* to toast
**torre** *f* tower; watchtower; (*en el ajedrez*) castle, rook; **torre del homenaje** donjon, keep; **torre de lanzamiento** launching tower; **torre de marfil** (fig) ivory tower; **torre de vigía** (naut) crow's-nest; **torre maestra** donjon, keep; **torre reloj** clock tower
**torreja** *f* (dial, Am) French toast
**torrentada** *f* flash flood
**torrente** *m* torrent
**torreón** *m* (archit) turret
**torreta** *f* (nav) turret
**tórri·do -da** *adj* torrid
**torrija** *f* French toast
**torta** *f* cake; (typ) font; (coll) slap; **ser tortas y pan pintado** (coll) to be a

cinch; **torta a la plancha** hot cake, griddle cake
**torticolis** *m* or **tortícolis** *m* wryneck, stiff neck
**tortilla** *f* omelet; (CAm, Mex) tortilla (*corn-meal cake*); **tortilla a la española** potato omelet; **tortilla a la francesa** plain omelet; **tortilla de tomate** Spanish omelet
**tórtola** *f* turtledove
**tortuga** *f* tortoise, turtle
**tortuo•so -sa** *adj* winding; (fig) devious
**tortura** *f* torture
**torturar** *tr* to torture
**tor•vo -va** *adj* grim, stern
**tos** *f* cough; **tos ferina** whooping cough
**tosca•no -na** *adj* Tuscan || **la Toscana** Tuscany
**tos•co -ca** *adj* coarse, rough; uncouth
**toser** *intr* to cough
**tósigo** *m* poison; sorrow
**tosiguero** *m* poison ivy
**tosquedad** *f* coarseness, roughness; uncouthness
**tostada** *f* piece of toast; toast; **dar** or **pegar la tostada** or **una tostada a** (coll) to cheat, to trick; **tostadas** toast
**tosta•do -da** *adj* brown; tan, sunburned || *m* toasting; roasting || *f* see **tostada**
**tostador** *m* toaster, roaster
**tostar §61** *tr & ref* to toast; to roast; to tan, to burn
**tostón** *m* roasted chickpea; toast dipped in olive oil; roast pig; scorched food
**total** *adj & m* total || *adv* (coll) in a word
**totalidad** *f* totality; entirety; **en su totalidad** in its entirety
**tóxi•co -ca** *adj & m* toxic
**toxicomanía** *f* drug addiction
**toxicóma•no -na** *adj* drug-addicted || *mf* drug addict
**tozu•do -da** *adj* stubborn
**tpo.** *abbr* **tiempo**
**traba** *f* bond, tie; clasp, lock; hobble, clog; obstacle, hindrance
**traba•do -da** *adj* tied, fastened; joined, connected; robust, sinewy; (*sílaba*) checked; (Am) tongue-tied; (*ojos*) (Col) cross
**trabaja•do -da** *adj* overworked, worn-out; strained, forced, labored; busy
**trabaja•dor -dora** *adj* working; industrious, hard-working || *mf* worker, toiler || *m* workman, workingman || *f* workingwoman
**trabajar** *tr* to work; to till; to bother, disturb; (*a una persona*) to work, to drive || *intr* to work; to strain; to warp; **trabajar en** or **por** to strive to || *ref* to strive, to exert oneself
**trabajo** *m* work; trouble; (*en contraposición de capital*) labor; **costar trabajo + inf** to be hard to + *inf;* **trabajo a destajo** piecework; **trabajo a domicilio** homework; **trabajo a jornal** timework; **trabajo de menores** child labor; **trabajo de oficina** clerical work; **trabajo de taller** shopwork; **trabajos** hardships, tribulations; **trabajos forzados** or **forzosos** hard labor, penal labor
**trabajo•so -sa** *adj* arduous, laborious; (*maganto*) wan, languid; (*falto de espontaneidad*) labored; (Am) unpleasant, annoying
**trabalen•guas** *m* (*pl* **-guas**) tongue twister, jawbreaker
**trabar** *tr* to join, unite; to catch, seize; to fasten; to fetter; to lock; to begin; (*una batalla*) to join; (*una conversación, amistad*) to strike up || *intr* to take hold || *ref* to become entangled; to jam; to foul; **trabársele a uno la lengua** to become tongue-tied
**trabe** *f* beam
**trabilla** *f* gaiter strap; belt loop; **end** stitch, loose stitch
**trabuco** *m* blunderbuss; popgun
**trac** *m* stage fright
**tracale•ro -ra** *adj* (CAm, Mex, W-I) cheating, tricky || *mf* (CAm, Mex, W-I) cheat, trickster
**tracción** *f* traction; **tracción delantera** front drive; **tracción trasera** rear drive
**tractor** *m* tractor; **tractor de oruga** caterpillar tractor
**tradición** *f* tradition
**tradicionista** *mf* folklorist
**traducción** *f* translation; **traducción automática** machine translation
**traducir §19** *tr* to translate; to change
**traduc•tor -tora** *mf* translator
**traer §75** *tr* to bring; to bring on; to draw, pull; to make, keep; to wear; to have, carry; **traer a mal traer** (coll) to abuse, mistreat || *intr* — **traer y llevar** to gossip || *ref* to dress; to behave; **traérselas** (coll) to get worse and worse, to cause a lot of trouble
**tráfago** *m* traffic, trade; toil, drudgery
**trafa•gón -gona** *adj* (coll) hustling, lively; (coll) slick, tricky || *mf* hustler, live wire
**traficante** *mf* dealer, merchant
**traficar §73** *intr* to deal, trade, traffic; to travel about
**tráfico** *m* trade; traffic
**tragaderas** *fpl* (coll) gullibility; (coll) tolerance; **tener buenas tragaderas** (coll) to be too gullible
**tragalda•bas** *mf* (*pl* **-bas**) (coll) glutton; (coll) easy mark
**tragale•guas** *mf* (*pl* **-guas**) (coll) great walker
**traga•luz** *m* (*pl* **-luces**) skylight, bull's-eye; cellar window
**tragamone•das** *m* (*pl* **-das**) or **tragape•rras** *m* (*pl* **-rras**) (coll) slot machine
**tragar §44** *tr* to swallow; to swallow up; to gulp down; (*creer fácilmente*) to swallow; to overlook; **no poder tragar** (coll) to not be able to stomach || *intr & ref* to swallow
**tragasable** *m* sword swallower
**tragavenado** *m* (SAm) anaconda
**tragaviro•tes** *m* (*pl* **-tes**) (coll) stuffed shirt
**tragedia** *f* tragedy
**trági•co -ca** *adj* tragic(al) || *m* tragedian
**trago** *m* swallow; swig; (coll) misfortune; **a tragos** (coll) slowly
**tra•gón -gona** *adj* (coll) gluttonous || *mf* (coll) glutton

**traición** *f* treachery, betrayal; (*delito contra la patria*) treason; treacherous act; **alta traición** high treason; **a traición** treacherously; **hacer traición a** to betray
**traicionar** *tr* to betray
**traicione•ro -ra** *adj* treacherous; treasonable || *mf* traitor
**traída** *f* conveyance, transfer; (Guat) sweetheart; **traída de aguas** water supply
**traí•do -da** *adj* worn, threadbare || *f* see **traída**
**trai•dor -dora** *adj* treacherous; treasonable || *mf* traitor; betrayer || *m* villain || *f* traitress
**traílla** *f* leash; road scraper
**traje** *m* suit; clothes; dress; gown; **cortar un traje a** (coll) to gossip about; **traje a la medida** suit made to order; **traje de baño** bathing suit; **traje de calle** street clothes; **traje de ceremonia** or **de etiqueta** dress suit; full dress; evening clothes; **traje de faena** (mil) fatigue clothes; **traje de luces** bullfighter's costume; **traje de malla** tights; **traje de montar** riding habit; **traje de paisano** civilian clothes; **traje hecho** ready-made suit; **traje sastre** lady's tailor-made suit; **traje serio** formal dress; **vestir su primer traje largo** to come out, to make one's debut
**trajear** *tr* to dress, clothe
**trajín** *m* carrying, transfer, conveyance; going and coming; bustle, commotion
**trajinar** *tr* to carry, convey; (Arg, Chile) to poke into; (Arg, Chile) to deceive; (Pan) to annoy || *intr* to bustle around
**tralla** *f* lash, whiplash, whipcord
**trama** *f* weft, woof; plot, scheme, machination; (*de un drama o novela*) plot
**tramar** *tr* to weave; to plot, to scheme; (*un enredo*) to hatch (*a plot*)
**trambucar** §73 *intr* (Col, Ven) to be shipwrecked; (Col, Ven) to go out of one's mind
**tramitación** *f* transaction, negotiation; procedure, steps; **tramitación automática de datos** data processing
**tramitar** *tr* to transact, to negotiate
**trámite** *m* step, procedure; proceeding; transaction
**tramo** *m* tract; stretch; (*de una escalera*) flight; (*de un puente*) span; (*de un canal entre dos esclusas*) level
**tramontana** *f* north; north wind; pride, haughtiness
**tramoya** *f* stage machinery; scheme
**tramoyista** *adj* scheming, tricky || *mf* schemer, impostor || *m* stagehand
**trampa** *f* trap; trap door; (*de un mostrador*) flap; (*de los pantalones*) fly; **armar una trampa a** (coll) to lay a trap for; **trampa explosiva** (mil) booby trap
**trampear** *tr* (coll) to trick, to swindle || *intr* (coll) to cheat; (coll) to manage to get along
**trampilla** *f* peephole in the floor; (*de los pantalones*) fly; (*de un secreter*) top, lid; (*de una mesa*) leaf, hinged leaf
**trampolín** *m* diving board; springboard; ski jump
**trampo•so -sa** *adj* tricky, crooked || *mf* cheat, swindler
**tranca** *f* beam, pole; crossbar; (Arg, Chile) drunk, spree; (P-R) dollar; **a trancas y barrancas** (coll) through fire and water
**trancar** §73 *tr* to bar || *intr* (coll) to stride along
**trance** *m* crisis; peril; trance; **a todo trance** at any cost; **último trance** (*de la vida*) last stage, end
**tranco** *m* long stride; threshold
**tranquera** *f* palisade, fence
**tranquilidad** *f* tranquillity
**tranquilizante** *m* tranquilizer
**tranquilizar** §60 *tr*, *intr* & *ref* to tranquilize, to calm down
**tranqui•lo -la** *adj* tranquil, calm
**tranquilla** *f* feeler
**tranquillo** *m* knack
**transacción** *f* settlement, compromise; transaction
**transaéreo** *m* air liner
**transar** *tr* (Am) to settle || *intr* (Am) to yield, give in, compromise
**transatlánti•co -ca** *adj* & *m* transatlantic
**transbordador** *m* ferry
**transbordar** *tr* to transship; to transfer || *intr* to transfer, to change trains
**transbordo** *m* transshipment; transfer
**transcribir** §83 *tr* to transcribe
**transcripción** *f* transcription
**transcurrir** *intr* to pass, elapse
**transcurso** *m* course (*of time*)
**transepto** *m* transept
**transeúnte** *adj* transient || *mf* transient; passer-by
**transferencia** *f* transfer
**transferir** §68 *tr* to transfer; to postpone
**transformador** *m* transformer
**transformar** *tr* to transform || *ref* to transform, be transformed
**tránsfuga** *mf* turncoat; fugitive
**transfusión** *f* transfusion; **transfusión de sangre** transfusion, blood transfusion
**transgredir** §1 *tr* to transgress
**transgresión** *f* transgression
**transi•do -da** *adj* overcome, paralyzed; mean, cheap, stingy
**transigencia** *f* compromise; compromising
**transigente** *adj* compromising
**transigir** §27 *tr* to settle, to compromise || *intr* to settle, to compromise; to agree
**transistor** *m* transistor
**transitable** *adj* passable, practicable
**transitar** *intr* to go, walk; to travel
**transiti•vo -va** *adj* transitive
**tránsito** *m* transit; traffic; stop; passage; transfer
**transito•rio -ria** *adj* transitory
**translúci•do -da** *adj* translucent
**transmisión** *f* transmission; **transmisión del pensamiento** thought transference
**transmisor** *m* transmitter; **transmisor de órdenes** (naut) engine-room telegraph
**transmitir** *tr* & *intr* to transmit
**transmudar** *tr* to transfer; to persuade, convince
**transmutar** *tr*, *intr* & *ref* to transmute

**transparecer** §22 *intr* to show through
**transparencia** *f* transparency; slide
**transparentar** *ref* to show through
**transparente** *adj* transparent ‖ *m* curtain, window curtain; **transparente de resorte** window blind or shade
**transpirar** *intr* to transpire; (*dejarse conocer una cosa secreta*) to transpire
**transplantar** *tr* to transplant
**transponer** §54 *tr* to transpose; to disappear behind ‖ *ref* (*ocultarse detrás del horizonte*) to set; to get sleepy
**transportar** *tr* to transport; (mus) to transpose
**transporte** *m* transport; transportation; (aer & naut) transport
**transportista** *mf* transport worker
**tranvía** *m* trolley, trolley car, streetcar; **tranvía de sangre** horsecar
**tranzar** §60 *tr* to cut off, rip off; to plait, braid
**trapacear** *tr* to cheat, swindle
**trapacería** *f* cheating, swindling
**trapace•ro -ra** *adj* cheating, swindling ‖ *mf* cheat, swindler
**trapajo** *m* rag, tatter
**trápala** *adj* (coll) chattering; (coll) cheating ‖ *mf* (coll) chatterbox; (coll) cheat ‖ *m* loquacity ‖ *f* noise, uproar; (*del trote de un caballo*) clatter; (coll) cheating
**trapear** *tr* (Am) to mop
**trapecio** *m* (geom) trapezoid; (sport) trapeze
**trapecista** *mf* trapeze performer
**trape•ro -ra** *mf* ragpicker; junk dealer
**trapiche** *m* sugar mill; olive press; ore crusher
**trapien•to -ta** *adj* raggedy, in rags
**trapío** *m* (coll) flipness, pertness; (*del toro de lidia*) spirit
**trapisonda** *f* (coll) brawl, row; (coll) scheming
**trapisondista** *mf* (coll) schemer
**trapo** *m* rag; (naut) canvas, sails; bullfighter's bright-colored cape; (*de la muleta*) cloth; **a todo trapo** full sail; **poner como un trapo** (coll) to rake over the coals; **sacar los trapos a la colada, a relucir** or **al sol** (coll) to wash one's dirty linen in public; **soltar el trapo** (coll) to burst out crying, to burst out laughing; **trapos** (coll) rags, duds; **trapos de cristianar** (coll) Sunday best
**trapo•so -sa** *adj* (Am) raggedy, in rags
**tráquea** *f* trachea, windpipe
**traquea•do -da** *adj* (*sendero*) (Arg) beaten
**traquear** *tr* to shake, to rattle; (coll) to fool with ‖ *intr* to crackle; to rattle, to chatter
**traqueo** *m* shake, rattle, chatter
**traquetear** *tr & intr* to rattle; to jerk
**tras** *prep* after; behind; **tras de** behind; in addition to
**trasatlánti•co -ca** *adj & m* var of **transatlántico**
**trasbordador** *m* var of **transbordador**
**trasbordar** *tr & intr* var of **trasbordar**
**trasbordo** *m* var of **transbordo**
**trascendencia** *f* penetration, keenness; importance
**trascendente** *adj* penetrating; important
**trascender** §51 *tr* to go into, dig up ‖ *intr* to smell; to come to be known, to leak out
**trascendi•do -da** *adj* keen, perspicacious
**trascocina** *f* scullery
**trascorral** *m* back yard; (coll) backside
**trascribir** §83 *tr* var of **transcribir**
**trascripción** *f* var of **transcripción**
**trascuarto** *m* back room
**trascurrir** *intr* var of **transcurrir**
**trascurso** *m* var of **transcurso**
**trasegar** §66 *tr* to upset, turn topsy-turvy; to decant, to draw off
**trase•ro -ra** *adj* back, rear ‖ *m* buttock, rump
**trasferir** §68 *tr* var of **transferir**
**trasformador** *m* var of **transformador**
**trasformar** *tr & intr* var of **transformar**
**trásfuga** *mf* var of **tránsfuga**
**trasfusión** *f* var of **transfusión**
**trasgo** *m* goblin, hobgoblin; imp
**trashojar** *tr* to leaf through
**trasiego** *m* upset, disorder; decantation
**trasladar** *tr* to transfer; to postpone; to copy, transcribe; to transmit; to move ‖ *intr* to go; to move
**traslado** *m* transfer; copy, transcript; moving
**traslapar** *tr, intr & ref* to overlap
**traslapo** *m* lap, overlap
**traslúci•do -da** *adj* var of **translúcido**
**traslucir** §45 *tr* to guess ‖ *intr* to leak out ‖ *ref* to be translucent; to leak out
**traslumbrar** *tr* to dazzle ‖ *ref* to be dazzled; to vanish
**trasluz** *m* diffused light; glint, gleam; **al trasluz** against the light
**trasmisión** *f* var of **transmisión**
**trasmisor** *m* var of **transmisor**
**trasmitir** *tr & intr* var of **transmitir**
**trasmóvil** *m* (Col) mobile unit, radio pickup
**trasmudar** *tr* var of **transmudar**
**trasmundo** *m* afterlife, future life
**trasmutar** *tr, intr & ref* var of **transmutar**
**trasnocha•do -da** *adj* stale; haggard, run-down; hackneyed ‖ *f* last night; sleepless night; (mil) night attack
**trasnocha•dor -dora** *mf* night owl
**trasnochar** *tr* (*un problema*) to sleep over ‖ *intr* to spend the night; to spend a sleepless night; to stay up late
**trasoír** §48 *tr* to hear wrong
**traspapelar** *tr* to mislay ‖ *ref* to become mislaid
**trasparecer** §22 *intr* var of **transparecer**
**trasparencia** *f* var of **transparencia**
**trasparente** *adj & m* var of **transparente**
**traspasar** *tr* to cross, cross over; to send; to transfer; to move; to pierce, to transfix; to pain, grieve ‖ *ref* to go too far
**traspié** *m* slip, stumble; trip
**traspirar** *intr* var of **transpirar**
**trasplantar** *tr* var of **transplantar**
**trasponer** §54 *tr & ref* var of **transponer**
**trasportar** *tr* var of **transportar**
**trasporte** *m* var of **transporte**
**trasportista** *mf* var of **transportista**

**traspunte** *m* (theat) callboy
**traspuntín** *m* flap seat, folding seat, jump seat
**trasquilar** *tr* to crop, to lop; (*las ovejas*) to shear; (coll) to curtail
**trastazo** *m* (coll) whack, blow
**traste** *m* fret; **dar al traste con** to throw away, ruin, spoil
**trastera** *f* attic, junk room
**trastienda** *f* back room
**trasto** *m* piece of furniture; piece of junk; (coll) good-for-nothing; **trastos** tools, implements, utensils; arms, weapons; junk; muleta and sword
**trastornar** *tr* to upset, overturn; to disturb; to perplex; to daze, to make dizzy; to persuade
**trastorno** *m* upset; disturbance
**trastrocar** §81 *tr* to turn around, to reverse, to change
**trasudor** *m* cold sweat
**trasueño** *m* blurred dream, vague recollection
**trasuntar** *tr* to copy; to abstract, to sum up
**trasunto** *m* copy; record; likeness
**trasverter** §51 *intr* to run over, to overflow
**trasvolar** §61 *tr* to fly over
**trata** *f* traffic, trade, slave trade; **trata de blancas** white slavery; **trata de esclavos** slave trade
**tratado** *m* (*escrito, libro*) treatise; (*convenio entre gobiernos*) treaty; agreement
**tratamiento** *m* treatment; title; **apear el tratamiento** to leave off the title
**tratante** *mf* dealer, retailer
**tratar** *tr* to handle; to deal with; to treat; **tratar a uno de** to address someone as; to charge someone with being || *intr* to deal; to treat; to try; **tratar de** to deal with; to treat of; to come in contact with; to try to || *ref* to deal; to behave; (*bien o mal*) to live; **tratarse de** to deal with; to be a question of
**trate•ro -ra** *mf* (Chile) pieceworker
**trato** *m* treatment; deal, agreement; manner; business; title; friendly relations; **tener buen trato** to be very nice, to be very pleasant; **trato colectivo** collective bargaining; **trato doble** double-dealing; **¡trato hecho!** it's a deal!
**través** *m* bend, bias, turn; reverse, misfortune; (naut) beam; **al** or **a través de** through, across; **dar al través con** to do away with; **mirar de través** to squint; to look at out of the corner of one's eye
**travesaño** *m* crosspiece; (*de cama*) bolster; (*p.ej., de una silla*) rung
**travesear** *intr* to romp, carry on; to sparkle, be witty; to lead a wild life
**travesía** *f* crossing, voyage; crossroad; distance, passage; cross wind; (Arg, Bol) wasteland; (Chile) west wind
**travesura** *f* prank, antic, caper; mischief; sparkle, wit; slick trick
**traviesa** *f* crossing, voyage; rafter; side bet; (rr) tie
**travie•so -sa** *adj* cross; keen, shrewd; restless, fidgety; naughty, mischievous; debauched || *f* see **traviesa**
**trayecto** *m* journey, passage, course; stretch, run
**trayectoria** *f* trajectory; path
**traza** *f* plan, design; scheme; means; appearance; mark, trace; footprint; streak, trait; **tener trazas de** to show signs of; to look like
**trazar** §60 *tr* to plan, design; to outline; to trace; (*una línea*) to draw; to lay out, to plot
**trazo** *m* line, stroke; trace; outline
**trebejo** *m* implement; chessman
**trébol** *m* clover; (*naipe que corresponde al basto*) club
**trece** *adj & pron* thirteen || *m* thirteen; (*en las fechas*) thirteenth; **estarse, mantenerse** or **seguir en sus trece** (coll) to stand firm
**trecea•vo -va** *adj & m* thirteenth
**trecho** *m* stretch; while; **a trechos** at intervals
**tregua** *f* truce; respite, letup
**treinta** *adj & pron* thirty || *m* thirty; (*en las fechas*) thirtieth
**treinta•vo -va** *adj & m* thirtieth
**tremar** *intr* to tremble, to shake
**tremen•do -da** *adj* frightful, terrible, tremendous; (*muy grande*) (coll) tremendous
**trementina** *f* turpentine
**tremer** *intr* to tremble, shake
**tremolar** *tr & intr* to wave
**tren** *m* (*de coches o vagones; de ondas*) train; outfit, equipment; following, retinue; show, pomp; (*de la vida*) way; **tren aerodinámico de lujo** (rr) streamliner; **tren ascendente** (rr) up train; **tren correo** (rr) mail train; **tren de aterrizaje** (aer) landing gear; **tren de laminadores** rolling mill; **tren de lavado** (Am) laundry; **tren de mercancías** freight train; **tren de mudadas** (Am) moving company; **tren descendente** (rr) down train; **tren de viajeros** passenger train; **tren ómnibus** (rr) accommodation train; **tren rápido** (rr) flyer
**treno** *m* dirge
**trenza** *f* braid, plait; tress; (*p.ej., de ajos*) (Am) string; **en trenzas** with her hair down
**trenzar** §60 *tr* to braid, plait || *intr* to caper; to prance
**trepa•dor -dora** *adj* climbing || *mf* climber || *f* (bot) climber
**trepar** *tr* to climb; to drill, bore || *intr* to climb; **trepar por** to climb up || *ref* to lean back
**trepidar** *intr* to shake, vibrate; (Chile) to hesitate, waver
**tres** *adj & pron* three; **las tres** three o'clock || *m* three; (*en las fechas*) third
**trescien•tos -tas** *adj & pron* three hundred || **trescientos** *m* three hundred
**tresillo** *m* ombre; three-piece living-room suit; (mus) triplet
**tresnal** *m* (agr) shock
**treta** *f* trick, scheme; (*del esgrimidor*) feint
**treza•vo -va** *adj & m* thirteenth

**triángulo** *m* triangle
**triar** §77 *tr* to sort
**tribu** *f* tribe
**tribuna** *f* tribune, rostrum, platform; grandstand; (*en la iglesia*) gallery; **tribuna de la prensa** press box; **tribuna del órgano** (mus) organ loft; **tribuna de los acusados** (law) dock
**tribunal** *m* tribunal, court; **tribunal tutelar de menores** juvenile court
**tributar** *tr* (*contribuciones, impuestos, etc.*) to pay; (*admiración, gratitud, etc.*) to render
**tributa•rio -ria** *adj* tributary; tax; **ser tributario de** to be indebted to ‖ *m* tributary
**tributo** *m* tribute; tax
**tricornio** *m* tricorn, three-cornered hat
**trifocal** *adj* trifocal
**trifulca** *f* (coll) wrangle, squabble
**trigési•mo -ma** *adj & m* thirtieth
**trigo** *m* wheat; (slang) dough, money; **trigo sarraceno** buckwheat
**trigonometría** *f* trigonometry
**trigue•ño -ña** *adj* swarthy, olive-skinned
**trilogía** *f* trilogy
**trilla** *f* threshing
**trilla•do -da** *adj* (*sendero*) beaten; trite, commonplace
**trilladora** *f* threshing machine
**trillar** *tr* to thresh; to mistreat; (coll) to frequent
**trilli•zo -za** *mf* triplet
**trillón** *m* British trillion; quintillion (*in U.S.A.*)
**trimestral** *adj* quarterly
**trimestre** *m* quarter
**trinado** *m* trill, warble
**trinar** *intr* to trill, warble, quaver; (coll) to get angry
**trinca** *f* trinity
**trincar** §73 *tr* to bind, to lash, to tie fast; to crush; (slang) to kill ‖ *intr* to take a drink
**trinchar** *tr* to carve, to slice
**trinchera** *f* cut; trench; trench coat
**trineo** *m* sleigh, sled
**Trinidad** *f* Trinity
**trino** *m* trill
**trinquete** *m* pawl, ratchet; (naut) foresail
**trin•quis** *m* (*pl* **-quis**) drink, swig
**trío** *m* sorting; trio; (mus) trio
**tripa** *f* gut, intestine; belly; (*del cigarro*) filler; **hacer de tripas corazón** (coll) to pluck up courage
**triple** *adj & m* triple
**triplica•do -da** *adj & m* triplicate; **por triplicado** in triplicate
**triplicar** §73 *tr* to triplicate ‖ *intr* to treble
**trípode** *m* tripod
**tríptico** *m* triptych
**tripu•do -da** *adj* big-bellied, potbellied
**tripulación** *f* crew
**tripulante** *m* crew member
**tripular** *tr* to man; to fit out, equip
**trique** *m* crack, swish; **a cada trique** (coll) at every turn; **triques** (Mex) tools, implements
**triquiñuela** *f* (coll) chicanery, subterfuge
**triquitraque** *m* clatter; firecracker
**tris** *m* crackle; (coll) shave, inch; (coll) trice
**trisar** *tr* (Chile) to crack, to chip ‖ *intr* to chirp
**triscar** §73 *tr* to mix; (*una sierra*) to set ‖ *intr* to stamp the feet; to romp, frisk around; (Col) to gossip
**trismo** *m* lockjaw
**triste** *adj* sad; dismal, gloomy; (*despreciable, ridículo*) sorry
**tristeza** *f* sadness; gloominess
**tris•tón -tona** *adj* wistful, melancholy
**tritón** *m* eft, newt, triton; (*hombre experto en la natación*) merman
**trituradora** *f* crushing machine
**triturar** *tr* to grind, crush; to abuse
**triunfal** *adj* triumphal
**triunfante** *adj* triumphant
**triunfar** *intr* to triumph; to trump; **triunfar de** to triumph over; to trump
**triunfo** *m* triumph; trump; **sin triunfo** no trump
**trivial** *adj* trivial; trite, commonplace; (*sendero*) beaten
**trivialidad** *f* triviality; triteness
**triza** *f* shred; **hacer trizas** to tear to pieces
**trizar** §60 *tr* to tear to pieces
**trocar** §81 *tr* to exchange, to swap; to barter; to confuse, to twist, to distort ‖ *intr* to swap ‖ *ref* to change; to change seats
**trocha** *f* trail, narrow path; (Am) gauge
**trofeo** *m* trophy; victory
**troj** *f* or **troje** *f* granary; olive bin
**trole** *m* trolley pole
**trolebús** *m* trolley bus, trackless trolley
**tromba** *f* (*de polvo, agua, etc.*) whirl, column; **tromba marina** waterspout; **tromba terrestre** tornado
**trombón** *m* trombone
**trompa** *f* (*del elefante*) trunk; waterspout; top; nozzle; (anat) duct, tube; (mus) horn; (Col, Chile) cowcatcher; **trompa de armonía** French horn; **trompa de Eustaquio** Eustachian tube
**trompada** *f* (coll) bump, collision; (coll) punch
**trompar** *intr* to spin a top
**trompeta** *f* trumpet; bugle, clarion; (coll) good-for-nothing; (Am) drunkenness
**trompetear** *intr* (coll) to trumpet, to sound the trumpet
**trompetilla** *f* ear trumpet; (Am) Bronx cheer
**trompicar** §44 *tr* to trip, make stumble ‖ *intr* to stumble
**trompicón** *m* stumble
**trompiza** *f* (Am) fist fight
**trompo** *m* (*juguete*) top; (*en el ajedrez*) man; (*buque malo y pesado*) tub
**tronada** *f* thunderstorm
**tronar** §61 *tr* (Mex) to shoot ‖ *intr* to thunder; (coll) to fail, collapse; **por lo que pueda tronar** (coll) just in case
**troncar** §44 *tr* to cut off the head of; (*un escrito*) to cut, shorten
**tronco** *m* (*del cuerpo, del árbol, de una familia, del ferrocarril*) trunk; (*leño*) log; (*de caballerías*) team; (coll) sap, fathead; **estar hecho un tronco** (coll)

to be knocked out; (coll) to be sound asleep
**troncha** *f* (Am) slice; (Am) cinch
**tronchar** *tr* to smash, split; to chop off
**tronera** *m* madcap, roisterer ‖ *f* embrasure, loophole; louver; (*de la mesa de billar*) pocket
**tronido** *m* thunderclap
**trono** *m* throne
**tronquista** *m* driver, teamster
**tronzar** §60 *tr* to shatter, break to pieces; to pleat; to wear out
**tropa** *f* troop; (Am) herd, drove; **en tropa** straggling, without formation; **tropas de asalto** shock troops, storm troops
**tropel** *m* crowd, throng; rush, hurry; jumble; **de** or **en tropel** in a mad rush
**tropelía** *f* mad rush; outrage
**tropero** *m* (Arg) cowboy
**tropezar** §18 *tr* to strike ‖ *intr* to stumble; to slip, to blunder; **tropezar con** or **en** to stumble over, to trip over; to run into; to come upon
**trope·zón -zona** *adj* stumbly ‖ *m* stumble; stumbling place; **a tropezones** by fits and starts; falteringly; **dar un tropezón** to stumble, to trip
**tropical** *adj* tropic(al)
**trópico** *m* tropic
**tropiezo** *m* stumble; stumbling block; slip, blunder, fault; obstacle; quarrel
**tropilla** *f* (Arg, Urug) drove of horses following a leading mare
**troposfera** *f* troposphere
**troquel** *m* die
**trotaconven·tos** *f* (*pl* **-tos**) (coll) procuress, bawd
**trotamun·dos** *m* (*pl* **-dos**) globetrotter
**trotar** *intr* to trot; (coll) to hustle
**trote** *m* trot; (coll) chore; **al trote** (coll) right away; **para todo trote** (coll) for everyday wear; **trote de perro** jog trot
**trotona** *f* chaperone
**trovador** *m* troubadour
**trovadores·co -ca** *adj* troubadour
**trovero** *m* trouvère
**Troya** *f* Troy; **ahí fué Troya** (coll) it's a shambles; **¡arda Troya!** (coll) come what may!
**troya·no -na** *adj* & *mf* Trojan
**troza** *f* log
**trozar** §60 *tr* to break to pieces; (*un tronco*) to cut into logs
**trozo** *m* piece, fragment; block; excerpt, selection
**truco** *m* contrivance, device; trick; pocketing of ball; **truco de naipes** card trick; **trucos** pool
**truculen·to -ta** *adj* truculent
**trucha** *f* trout
**trueno** *m* thunder, thunderclap; shot, report; (coll) rake, roué; **trueno gordo** finale (*of fireworks*); big scandal; **truenos** (Ven) heavy shoes
**trueque** *m* barter; exchange, swap; trade-in; **a trueque de** in exchange for; **trueques** (Col) change
**trufa** *f* truffle; fib, lie
**tru·hán -hana** *adj* crooked; clownish ‖ *mf* crook; clown
**trujal** *m* wine press; oil press
**trulla** *f* noise, bustle; crowd; trowel
**truncar** §73 *tr* to cut off the head of; (*palabras o frases*) to cut, slash; to cut off, interrupt
**trusas** *fpl* trunk hose; (Am) trunks
**tu** *adj poss* thy, your
**tú** *pron pers* thou, you
**tubérculo** *m* (*rizoma engrosado, p.ej., de la patata*) tuber; (*protuberancia*) tubercle
**tuberculosis** *f* tuberculosis
**tubería** *f* tubing; piping
**tubo** *m* tube; pipe; **tubo de desagüe** drainpipe; **tubo de ensayo** test tube; **tubo de humo** flue; **tubo de imagen** picture tube; **tubo de vacío** vacuum tube; **tubo digestivo** alimentary canal; **tubo sonoro** chime
**tuerca** *f* nut; **tuerca de aletas** wing nut
**tuer·to -ta** *adj* crooked, bent; one-eyed; **a tuertas** upside down; crosswise; **a tuertas o a derechas** rightly or wrongly; thoughtlessly ‖ *mf* one-eyed person ‖ *m* wrong, harm, injustice; **tuertos** afterpains
**tuétano** *m* marrow; pith; **hasta los tuétanos** (coll) through and through; (coll) head over heels
**tufi·llas** *mf* (*pl* **-llas**) (coll) touchy person
**tufillo** *m* whiff, smell
**tufo** *m* fume, vapor; sidelock; foul odor, foul breath; **tufos** (coll) airs, conceit
**tugurio** *m* shepherd's hut; hovel
**tuición** *f* protection, custody
**tulipán** *m* tulip
**tullecer** §22 *tr* to abuse, mistreat ‖ *intr* to be crippled
**tulli·do -da** *adj* paralyzed, crippled ‖ *mf* paralytic, cripple
**tullir** §13 *tr* to cripple, to paralyze; to abuse, mistreat ‖ *ref* to become crippled or paralyzed
**tumba** *f* grave, tomb; tombstone; arched top; (Am) felling of trees
**tumbacuarti·llos** *mf* (*pl* **-llos**) (coll) old toper, rounder
**tumbar** *tr* to knock down; to catch, to trick; (coll) to stun ‖ *intr* to tumble; to capsize ‖ *ref* (coll) to lie down
**tumbo** *m* fall, tumble; boom, rumble; crisis; rise and fall of sea; rough surf
**tumbona** *f* hammock
**tumor** *m* tumor
**túmulo** *m* catafalque
**tumulto** *m* tumult
**tuna** *f* loafing, bumming
**tunante** *adj* bumming, loafing; crooked, tricky ‖ *mf* bum, loafer; crook
**tundidora** *f* lawn mower
**tuneci·no -na** *adj* & *mf* Tunisian
**túnel** *m* tunnel
**tunes** *mpl* (Col) little steps, first steps
**Túnez** (*ciudad*) Tunis; (*país*) Tunisia
**tungsteno** *m* tungsten
**túnica** *f* tunic
**tu·no -na** *adj* crooked, tricky ‖ *mf* crook ‖ *f* see **tuna**
**tupé** *m* toupee; (coll) nerve, cheek, brass
**tupi·do -da** *adj* thick, dense, compact; dull, stupid; (Am) clogged up

**tupir** *tr* to pack tight || *ref* to stuff, stuff oneself
**turba** *f* crowd, mob; peat
**turbamulta** *f* (coll) mob, rabble
**turbar** *tr* to disturb, trouble; to stir up || *ref* to be confused
**turbiedad** *f* muddiness; confusion
**turbina** *f* turbine
**tur•bio -bia** *adj* turbid, muddy, cloudy; confused; obscure
**turbión** *m* squall, thunderstorm; (*p.ej., de balas*) (fig) hail
**turbopropulsor** *m* turboprop (*engine*)
**turborreactor** *m* turbojet (*engine*)
**turbulen•to -ta** *adj* turbulent
**tur•co -ca** *adj* Turkish || *mf* **Turk** || *m* (*idioma*) Turkish
**turfista** *adj* horsy || *m* turfman
**turismo** *m* touring; touring car
**turista** *mf* tourist
**turísti•co -ca** *adj* tourist; touring
**turnar** *intr* to alternate, take turns
**tur•nio -nia** *adj* (*ojos*) cross; cross-eyed; (*que mira con ceño*) cross-looking
**turno** *m* turn, shift; **aguardar turno** to wait one's turn; **por turno** in turn; **turno diurno** day shift
**turón** *m* polecat
**turquesa** *s* turquoise
**Turquía** *s* Turkey
**turrón** *m* nougat; (coll) plum
**tusa** *f* (Am) corncob; (Am) corn silk; (Chile) mane; (Col) pockmark; (CAm, W-I) trollop
**tusar** *tr* to shear, clip, cut
**tutear** *tr* to thou, to address familiarly || *ref* to thou each other, to address each other familiarly
**tutela** *f* guardianship; protection
**tutelar** *adj* guardian; protecting || *tr* to protect, shelter, guide
**tu•tor -tora** or **-triz** (*pl* **-trices**) *mf* guardian, tutor
**tu•yo -ya** *adj poss* of thee || *pron poss* thine, yours
**tuza** *f* gopher

## U

**U, u** (u) *f* twenty-fourth letter of the Spanish alphabet
**u** *conj* (used before words beginning with *o* or *ho*) or
**U.** *abbr* **usted**
**ubicar** §73 *tr* (Am) to locate, place || *intr & ref* to be situated
**ubi•cuo -cua** *adj* ubiquitous
**ubre** *f* udder
**Ucrania** *f* Ukraine
**ucrania•no -na** *adj & mf* Ukrainian
**ucra•nio -nia** *adj & mf* Ukrainian || *f* see **Ucrania**
**Ud.** *abbr* **usted**
**Uds.** *abbr* **ustedes**
**ufanar** *ref* — **ufanarse con** or **de** to boast of, be proud of
**ufanía** *f* pride, conceit; cheer, satisfaction; ease, smoothness
**ufa•no -na** *adj* proud, conceited; cheerful, satisfied; easy, smooth
**ujier** *m* doorman, usher
**úlcera** *f* ulcer, fester, sore; **úlcera de decúbito** bedsore
**ulcerar** *tr & ref* to ulcerate, to fester
**ulterior** *adj* ulterior; subsequent
**ulteriormente** *adv* subsequently, later
**últimamente** *adv* finally; lately, recently
**ultimar** *tr* to finish, end, conclude, wind up; (Am) to kill, finish off
**ultimátum** *m* (*pl* **-tums**) ultimatum; (coll) definite decision
**últi•mo -ma** *adj* last, latest; final; excellent, superior; (*precio*) lowest, final; most remote; (*piso*) top; (*hora*) late; **a la última** in the latest fashion; **a última hora** at the eleventh hour; **a últimos de** toward the end of, in the latter part of; **de última hora** last-minute; **estar a lo último** or **en las últimas** to be up to date, to be well-informed; to be on one's last legs; **por último** at last, finally; **último suplicio** capital punishment
**ultraatmosféri•co -ca** *adj* outer (*space*)
**ultraeleva•do -da** *adj* (rad) ultrahigh
**ultrajar** *tr* to outrage, to offend
**ultraje** *m* outrage, offense
**ultrajo•so -sa** *adj* outrageous, offensive
**ultramar** *m* country overseas
**ultramari•no -na** *adj* overseas || **ultramarinos** *mpl* groceries, delicatessen
**ultranza** — **a ultranza** to the death; unflinchingly
**ultrarro•jo -ja** *adj & m* infrared
**ultratumba** *adv* beyond the grave
**ultraviola•do -da** or **ultravioleta** *adj & m* ultraviolet
**ululación** *f* howl; whoop; (*del buho*) hoot; (*del disco del fonógrafo*) wow
**ulular** *intr* to howl; to whoop; (*el buho*) to hoot
**ululato** *m* howl; (*del buho*) hoot
**umbilical** *adj* umbilical
**umbral** *m* threshold, doorsill; (*madero que sostiene el muro encima de un vano*) lintel; (physiol, psychol & fig) threshold; **atravesar** or **pisar los umbrales** to cross the threshold; **estar en los umbrales de** to be on the threshold of
**umbralada** *f* (Col) threshold
**umbrí•o -a** *adj* shady || *f* shady side
**umbro•so -sa** *adj* shady
**un, una** (the apocopated form **un** is used before masculine singular nouns and adjectives and before feminine singular nouns beginning with stressed *a* or *ha*) *art indef* a || *adj* one
**unánime** *adj* unanimous
**unanimidad** *f* unanimity
**unción** *f* unction

**uncir** §36 *tr* (*bueyes*) to yoke, to hitch
**undéci•mo -ma** *adj & m* eleventh
**undo•so -sa** *adj* wavy
**ungir** §27 *tr* to smear with ointment or with oil; to anoint
**ungüento** *m* unguent, ointment, salve
**únicamente** *adv* only, solely
**úni•co -ca** *adj* only, sole; (*sin otro de su especie*) unique; one, e.g., **precio único** one price
**unicornio** *m* unicorn
**unidad** *f* (*concepto de una sola cosa o persona; cantidad que se toma como medida común de todas las demás de su clase; el número entero más pequeño*) unit; (*indivisión; armonía de conjunto; el número uno*) unity
**uni•do -da** *adj* united; smooth, even; close-knit
**unificar** §73 *tr* to unify
**uniformar** *tr* to make uniform; to provide with a uniform
**uniforme** *adj* uniform || *m* uniform; **uniforme de gala** (mil) full dress
**uniformidad** *f* uniformity
**unilateral** *adj* unilateral
**unión** *f* union; double ring
**unir** *tr & ref* to unite
**unisonancia** *f* (mus) unison; (*de un orador*) monotony
**unísono** — **al unísono** in unison; unanimously; **al unísono de** in unison with
**unita•rio -ria** *adj* unit
**universal** *adj* universal; (*teclado de máquina de escribir*) standard
**universidad** *f* university
**universita•rio -ria** *adj* university || *mf* (Am) university student, college student || *m* university professor
**universo** *m* universe
**u•no -na** *pron* one, someone; **a una** of one accord; **la una** one o'clock; **somos uno** we are one; **uno a otro, unos a otros** each other, one another; **uno que otro** one or more, a few; **u•nos -nas** some; a pair of, e.g., **unas gafas** a pair of glasses; **unas tijeras** a pair of scissors; **unos cuantos** some; **uno y otro** both || *pron indef* one, e.g., **uno no sabe qué hacer aquí** one does not know what to do here || *m* (*unidad y signo que la representa*) one
**untar** *tr* to smear, to grease; to anoint; (coll) to bribe || *ref* to get smeared; to grease oneself; (coll) to peculate
**unto** *m* grease; (*gordura del cuerpo del animal*) fat; (Chile) shoe polish; **unto de Méjico** or **de rana** (coll) bribe money
**untuo•so -sa** *adj* unctuous, greasy, sticky
**uña** *f* nail, fingernail, toenail; (*pezuña*) hoof; (*del ancla*) fluke, bill; (mach) claw, gripper; **enseñar** or **mostrar las uñas** to show one's teeth; **ser largo de uñas** to have long fingers; **ser uña y carne** (coll) to be hand in glove; **tener en la uña** to have on the tip of one's fingers
**uñada** *f* scratch, nail scratch; (*impulso dado con la uña*) flip
**uñero** *m* ingrowing nail; (*inflamación del dedo en la raíz de la uña*) whitlow
**ural** *adj* Ural || **Urales** *mpl* Urals
**uranio** *m* uranium
**urbanidad** *f* urbanity
**urbanismo** *m* city planning
**urbanista** *mf* city planner
**urbanísti•co -ca** *adj* city-planning || *f* city planning
**urbanizar** §60 *tr* (*convertir en poblado*) to urbanize; to refine, polish
**urba•no -na** *adj* urban, city; (*atento, cortés*) urbane || *m* policeman
**urbe** *f* metropolis
**urdema•las** *mf* (*pl* **-las**) (coll) schemer
**urdimbre** *f* warp; scheme, scheming; **estar en la urdimbre** (Chile) to be thin, be emaciated
**urdir** *tr* (*los hilos*) to beam; (*una conspiración*) to hatch
**urente** *adj* burning, smarting
**uretra** *f* urethra
**urgencia** *f* urgency; **de urgencia** special-delivery
**urgente** *adj* urgent; (*correo*) special-delivery
**urgir** §27 *intr* to be urgent
**urina•rio -ria** *adj* urinary || *m* urinal
**urna** *f* glass case; ballot box; (*para guardar las cenizas de los cadáveres*) urn; **acudir** or **ir a las urnas** to go to the polls
**urología** *f* urology
**urraca** *f* magpie
**U.R.S.S.** *abbr* **Unión de Repúblicas Socialistas Soviéticas**
**urticaria** *f* hives
**Uruguay, el** Uruguay
**urugua•yo -ya** *adj & mf* Uruguayan
**usa•do -da** *adj* (*empleado; gastado por el uso; acostumbrado*) used; skilled, experienced; (*vocablo*) **poco usado** rare
**usanza** *f* use, usage, custom
**usar** *tr* to use, make use of; (*un cargo, un oficio*) to follow || *intr* — **usar** + *inf* to be accustomed to + *inf;* **usar de** to use, to have recourse to; **usar de la palabra** to speak, make a speech || *ref* to be the custom
**usina** *f* (Am) factory, plant; (Am) powerhouse; (*estación de tranvía*) (Arg) carbarn
**uso** *m* use; custom, usage; wear, wear and tear; habit, practice; **al uso** according to custom; **en buen uso** (coll) in good condition; **hacer uso de la palabra** to speak, make a speech
**usted** *pron pers* you
**usual** *adj* (*de uso común*) usual; (*que se usa con facilidad*) usable; sociable
**usualmente** *adv* usually
**usua•rio -ria** *mf* user
**usufructo** *m* use, enjoyment
**usufructuar** §21 *tr* to enjoy the use of
**usura** *f* usury; profit; **pagar con usura** to pay back a thousandfold
**usurero** *m* loan shark; profiteer
**usurpar** *tr* to usurp
**utensilio** *m* utensil
**útero** *m* uterus, womb
**útil** *adj* useful || **útiles** *mpl* **utensils,** tools, equipment

**utilería** *f* (Arg) properties, stage equipment
**utilero** *m* (Arg) property man
**utilidad** *f* utility, usefulness; profit, earnings
**utilita•rio -ra** *adj* utilitarian
**utilizable** *adj* usable
**utilizar** §60 *tr* to utilize, to use || *ref* — **utilizarse con, de** or **en** to make use of; **utilizarse para** to be good for
**utopía** *f* utopia
**utopista** *adj & mf* utopian
**UU.** *abbr* **ustedes**
**uva** *f* grape; wart on eyelid; (*baya*) berry; **estar hecho una uva** (coll) to have a load on; **uva crespa** gooseberry; **uva de Corinto** currant; **uva de raposa** nightshade; **uva espín** or **espina** gooseberry; **uva pasa** raisin; **uvas verdes** (*de la fábula de Esopo*) sour grapes
**uve** *f* (*letra del alfabeto*) V
**uxoricida** *m* uxoricide (*husband*)
**uxoricidio** *m* uxoricide (*act*)
**uxo•rio -ria** *adj* uxorious

## V

**V, v** (ve *or* uve) *f* twenty-fifth letter of the Spanish alphabet
**V.** *abbr* **usted, véase, venerable**
**V.A.** *abbr* **Vuestra Alteza**
**vaca** *f* cow; (*cuero*) cowhide; (*carne de vaca o de buey*) beef; gambling pool; **hacer vaca** (Peru) to play truant; **vaca de la boda** (coll) goat, laughingstock; (coll) friend in need; **vaca de leche** milch cow; **vaca de San Antón** (ent) ladybird
**vacación** *f* (*cargo que está sin proveer*) vacancy; **de vacaciones** on vacation; **vacaciones** vacation; **vacaciones retribuídas** vacation with pay
**vacacionista** *mf* vacationist
**vacancia** *f* vacancy
**vacante** *adj* vacant || *f* vacancy
**vacar** §73 *intr* (*un empleo, un cargo*) to be vacant, be unfilled; to take off, take a vacation; **vacar a** to attend to; **vacar de** to lack, be devoid of
**vacia•do -da** *adj* hollow-ground || *m* cast, casting; plaster cast
**vaciante** *f* ebb tide
**vaciar** §77 & **regular** *tr* to empty, to drain; to cast, to mold; (*formar un hueco en*) to hollow out; to sharpen on a grindstone; to copy, transcribe; to explain in detail || *intr* to empty; to flow; (*el agua en el río*) to fall, go down || *ref* (coll) to blab
**vacilación** *f* vacillation; flickering; hesitancy, hesitation
**vacilada** *f* (Mex) spree, high time; (Mex) drunk
**vacilante** *adj* vacillating; (*luz*) flickering; (*irresoluto*) hesitant
**vacilar** *intr* to vacillate; (*la luz*) to flicker; to shake, wobble; (*estar irresoluto*) to hesitate, to waver
**vací•o -a** *adj* empty; (*hueco*) hollow; idle; useless, unsuccessful; (*vaca*) barren; presumptuous || *m* emptiness; (*laguna, abertura; vacante*) vacancy; (*espacio que no contiene ninguna materia*) void; (*espacio de que se ha extraído el aire*) vacuum; (*ijada*) side, flank; **de vacío** light, unloaded; **hacer el vacío a** to isolate
**vacuidad** *f* vacuity, emptiness
**vacuna** *f* (*enfermedad de las vacas*) cowpox; (*virus cuya inoculación preserva de una enfermedad determinada*) vaccine
**vacunación** *f* vaccination
**vacunar** *tr* to vaccinate
**vacu•no -na** *adj* bovine; cowhide || *f* see **vacuna**
**va•cuo -cua** *adj* vacant || *m* cavity, hollow
**vadear** *tr* (*un río*) to ford; to wade through; to overcome; to sound out || *ref* to behave; to manage
**vado** *m* ford; expedient, resource; **al vado o a la puente** (coll) one way or another; **no hallar vado** to see no way out; **tentar el vado** to feel one's way
**vagabundaje** *m* vagrancy
**vagabundear** *intr* to wander, to roam; to loaf around
**vagabun•do -da** *adj* vagabond || *mf* vagabond, tramp; wanderer
**vagancia** *f* loafing, vagrancy
**vagar** *m* leisure; **con vagar** slowly; **estar de vagar** to have nothing to do || §44 *intr* to wander, to roam; to be idle; to have plenty of leisure; (*una cosa*) to lie around; (*p.ej., una sonrisa por los labios*) to play
**vagido** *m* cry of a newborn baby
**vagneria•no -na** *adj & mf* Wagnerian
**va•go -ga** *adj* wandering, roaming; idle, loafing; lax, loose; hesitating, wavering; (*indefinido, indeciso*) vague; (*mirada*) blank || *m* vagabond; idler, loafer; **en vago** shakily; in vain; in the air; **poner en vago** to tilt
**vagón** *m* car, railroad car; **vagón cama** sleeping car; **vagón carbonero** coal car; **vagón cerrado** boxcar; **vagón cisterna** tank car; **vagón de carga** freight car; **vagón de cola** caboose; **vagón de mercancías** freight car; **vagón de plataforma** flatcar; **vagón frigorífico** refrigerator car; **vagón salón** chair car; **vagón tolva** hopper-bottom car; **vagón volquete** dump car
**vagoneta** *f* tip car; station wagon
**vaguear** *intr* to wander around
**vaguedad** *f* vagueness; vague remark
**vaguido** *m* faintness, fainting spell
**vaharada** *f* breath, exhalation

**vahear** *intr* to emit odors, to give forth an aroma
**vahido** *f* faintness, fainting spell
**vaho** *m* odor, aroma, vapor, fume
**vaina** *f* sheath; scabbard; knife case; (*de ciertas semillas*) pod, husk; (Am) annoyance, bother; (Col) luck, stroke of luck
**vainica** *f* hemstitch
**vainilla** *f* vanilla
**vainita** *f* (Ven) string bean
**vaivén** *m* swing, seesaw, backward and forward motion; unsteadiness, inconstancy; risk, chance
**vajilla** *f* dishes, set of dishes; **lavar la vajilla** to wash the dishes; **vajilla de oro** gold plate; **vajilla de plata** silver plate, silverware; **vajilla de porcelana** chinaware
**vale** *m* promissory note; voucher; farewell; (Ven) chum, pal; **vale respuesta** reply coupon
**valede•ro -ra** *adj* valid, effective
**vale•dor -dora** *mf* defender, protector; (Mex) friend, companion
**valedura** *f* (Mex) favor, protection
**valencia** *f* (chem) valence
**valentía** *f* bravery, valor; feat, exploit; dash, boldness; boast; **pisar de valentía** to strut, swagger
**valen•tón -tona** *adj* arrogant, boastful ‖ *mf* braggart, boaster ‖ *f* bragging
**valer** *m* worth, merit, value ‖ **§76** *tr* to defend, protect; to favor, patronize; to avail; to yield; to be worth, be valued at; to be equal to; to suit; **valer la pena** to be worth while (to); **valerle a uno** + *inf* to help someone to + *inf*, to get someone to + *inf;* **valer lo que pesa** (coll) to be worth its (his, her, etc.) weight in gold; **valga lo que valiere** come what may; **¡válgame Dios!** bless my soul!, so help me God! ‖ *intr* to have worth; to be worthy; to be valuable; to be valid; to prevail; to hold, to count; to have influence; **hacer valer** (*sus derechos*) to assert; to make felt; to make good; to turn to account; **más vale** it is better (to); **vale** O.K.; **valer para** to be useful for; **valer por** to be equal to ‖ *ref* to help oneself, to defend oneself; **valerse de** to make use of, to avail oneself of
**valero•so -sa** *adj* valorous, brave; strong, active, effective
**va•let** *m* (*pl* **-lets**) (cards) jack
**valía** *f* value, worth; favor, influence; **mayor valía** or **plus valía** appreciation, increased value; unearned increment
**validación** *f* validation
**validar** *tr* to validate
**validez** *f* validity; strength, vigor
**vali•do -da** *adj* highly esteemed, influential ‖ *m* court favorite; prime minister
**váli•do -da** *adj* valid; strong, robust
**valiente** *adj* valiant; strong, robust; fine, excellent; (*grande y excesivo*) terrific ‖ *m* brave fellow; bully
**valija** *f* satchel, brief case; mailbag, mailpouch; mail; **valija diplomática** diplomatic pouch
**valimiento** *m* favor, protection; favor at court, favoritism
**valio•so -sa** *adj* valuable; influential; wealthy
**va•lón -lona** *adj & mf* Walloon
**valor** *m* value, worth; valor, courage; meaning, import; efficacy; equivalence; (*rédito*) income, return; effrontery; (*persona, cosa o cualidad dignas de ser poseídas*) (fig) asset; **¿cómo va ese valor?** (coll) how are you?; **valor de rescate** (ins) surrender value; **valores** securities
**valoración** *f* valuation, appraisal
**valorar** or **valorear** *tr* (*poner precio a*) to value, to appraise; to enhance the value of
**valorizar** **§60** *tr* to value; to enhance the value of; (Am) to sell off (*for quick realization*)
**vals** *m* waltz
**valsar** *intr* to waltz
**valuación** *f* valuation, appraisal
**valuar** **§21** *tr* to estimate
**válvula** *f* valve; **válvula corrediza** slide valve; **válvula de admisión** intake valve; **válvula de escape** exhaust valve; **válvula de escape libre** cutout; **válvula de seguridad** safety valve; **válvula en cabeza** valve in the head, overhead valve
**valla** *f* fence, railing; barricade; hindrance, obstacle; (sport) hurdle; (W-I) cockpit; **valla paranieves** snow fence
**vallado** *m* barricade, stockade
**valle** *m* valley; river bed; valley dwellings; **valle de lágrimas** vale of tears
**vampiresa** *f* vampire
**vampíri•co -ca** *adj* vampire; ghoulish
**vampiro** *m* vampire; (*persona que se deleita con cosas horribles*) ghoul
**vanadio** *m* vanadium
**vanagloriar** **§77 & regular** *ref* to boast
**vanaglorio•so -sa** *adj* vainglorious, conceited, boastful
**vanamente** *adv* vainly
**vandalismo** *m* vandalism
**vánda•lo -la** *adj & mf* Vandal; (fig) vandal
**vanguardia** *f* (mil & fig) vanguard, van; **a vanguardia** in the vanguard
**vanguardismo** *m* avant-garde
**vanguardista** *adj* avant-garde ‖ *mf* avant-gardist
**vanidad** *f* vanity; (*fausto*) pomp, show; **ajar la vanidad de** (coll) to take down a peg; **hacer vanidad de** to boast of
**vanido•so -sa** *adj* vain, conceited
**va•no -na** *adj* vain; hollow, empty; **en vano** in vain ‖ *m* opening in a wall
**vapor** *m* steam; (*el visible: exhalación, vaho, niebla, etc.*) vapor; steamer, steamboat; **al vapor** at full speed; **vapores** gas (*belched*); blues; **vapor volandero** tramp steamer
**vaporar** *tr & ref* to evaporate
**vaporizador** *m* atomizer, sprayer
**vaporizar** **§60** *tr* to vaporize; to spray ‖ *ref* to vaporize
**vaporo•so -sa** *adj* vaporous

**vapular** or **vapulear** *tr* whip, to flog
**vaquería** *f* drove of cattle; dairy; (Mex) party
**vaqueri•zo -za** *adj* cattle || *f* winter stable for cattle
**vaque•ro -ra** *adj* cattle || *mf* cattle tender; (Peru) truant || *m* cow hand; cowboy
**vaqueta** *f* leather; (P-R) strop; **zurrarle a uno la vaqueta** (Am) to tan someone's hide
**vaquillona** *f* (Arg, Chile) heifer
**vara** *f* pole, rod, staff; (*de carruaje*) shaft; (*bastón de mando*) wand; measuring stick; (taur) thrust with goad; **tener vara alta** to have the upper hand; **vara alcándara** shaft; **vara alta** upper hand; **vara buscadora** divining rod (*ostensibly to discover water or metals*); **vara de adivinar** divining rod; **vara de oro** goldenrod; **vara de pescar** fishing rod; **vara de San José** goldenrod
**vara-alta** *m* (coll) boss
**varada** *f* beaching; running aground
**varadero** *m* repair dock
**varapalo** *m* long pole; (coll) setback, disappointment, reverse
**varar** *tr* (*una embarcación*) to beach || *intr* to run aground; (*un negocio*) to come to a standstill
**varear** *tr* (*los frutos de los árboles*) to beat down, knock down; to beat, strike; (taur) to goad; (*los caballos de carreras*) (SAm) to exercise, to train || *ref* to lose weight, get thin
**varec** *m* (bot) wrack
**varenga** *f* (naut) floor, floor timber
**vareta** *f* twig, stick; lime twig for catching birds; colored stripe; (coll) cutting remark; (coll) hint; **irse de vareta** (coll) to have diarrhea
**variable** *adj & f* variable
**variación** *f* variation
**varia•do -da** *adj* varied; variegated
**variante** *adj & f* variant
**variar** §77 to vary, to change || *intr* to vary, to change; to be different; **variar de** or **en opinión** to change one's mind
**varice** *f* or **várice** *f* varicose veins
**varicela** *f* chicken pox
**varico•so -sa** *adj* varicose
**variedad** *f* variety; **variedades** variety show, vaudeville
**varilla** *f* rod, stem, twig; (*bastón de mando*) wand; (*de paraguas, abanico, etc.*) rib; (*del corsé*) stay; (*de rueda*) wire spoke; (coll) jawbone; (Mex) peddler's wares; **varilla de nivel** dipstick; **varilla de virtudes** wand, magician's wand
**varillaje** *m* ribs, ribbing; (*de máquina de escribir*) type bars
**varille•ro -ra** *adj* (*caballo*) (Ven) race || *m* (Mex) peddler
**va•rio -ria** *adj* (*de diversos colores; que tiene variedad*) various, varied; fickle, inconstant; **varios** various; several
**varón** *adj* male, e.g., **hijo varón** male child || *m* man, male; grown man, adult male; man of standing; **santo varón** (coll) plain artless fellow
**varonía** *f* male issue
**varonil** *adj* manly, virile; courageous
**Varsovia** *f* Warsaw
**vasa•llo -lla** *adj & mf* vassal
**vas•co -ca** *adj & mf* Basque (*of Spain and France*) || *m* Basque (*language*)
**vas•cón -cona** *adj & mf* Basque (*of old Spain*)
**vasconga•do -da** *adj & mf* Basque (*of Spain*) || *m* Basque (*language*) || **las Vascongadas** the Basque Provinces
**vascuence** *adj & m* Basque (*language*) || *m* (coll) gibberish
**vaselina** *f* vaseline
**vasera** *f* kitchen shelf; bottle rack, tumbler rack
**vasija** *f* container, vessel
**vaso** *m* tumbler, glass; vase, flower jar; (anat) duct, vessel; **vaso de engrase** (mach) grease cup; **vaso de noche** pot, chamber pot; **vaso graduado** measuring glass; **vaso sanguíneo** blood vessel
**vástago** *m* shoot, sapling; scion, offspring; rod, stem; **vástago de émbolo** piston rod; **vástago de válvula** valve stem
**vastedad** *f* vastness
**vas•to -ta** *adj* vast
**vate** *m* bard, seer, poet
**váter** *m* (coll) toilet, water closet
**vatiaje** *m* wattage
**vaticinar** *tr* to prophesy, predict
**vaticinio** *m* prophecy, prediction
**vatídi•co -ca** *adj* prophetical || *mf* prophet
**vatímetro** *m* wattmeter
**vatio** *m* watt
**vatio-hora** *m* (*pl* **vatios-hora**) watt-hour
**vaya** *f* jest, jeer
**Vd.** *abbr* **usted**
**Vds.** *abbr* **ustedes**
**V.E.** *abbr* **Vuestra Excelencia**
**vece•ro -ra** *adj* alternating; yielding in alternate years || *mf* person waiting his turn
**vecinamente** *adv* nearby
**vecindad** *f* neighborhood, vicinity; residency; residents; **hacer mala vecindad** to be a bad neighbor
**vecindario** *m* neighborhood, community; people, population
**veci•no -na** *adj* neighboring; like, similar || *mf* neighbor; resident, citizen
**veda** *f* prohibition; (*de la caza y la pesca*) closed season
**vedado** *m* game preserve
**vedar** *tr* to forbid, prohibit; to hinder, stop; to veto
**vedija** *f* fleece, tuft of wool; mat of hair; matted hair
**vee•dor -dora** *adj* curious, spying || *mf* busybody || *m* supervisor, overseer
**vega** *f* fertile plain; (Cuba) tobacco plantation
**vegetación** *f* vegetation; **vegetaciones adenoideas** adenoids
**vegetal** *adj & m* vegetable
**vegetaria•no -na** *adj & mf* vegetarian
**vego•so -sa** *adj* (Chile) damp, wet
**vehemencia** *f* vehemence
**vehemente** *adj* vehement

**vehículo** *m* vehicle; **vehículo espacial** space vehicle
**veinta•vo -va** *adj & m* twentieth
**veinte** *adj & pron* twenty; **a las veinte** (coll) late, untimely ‖ *m* twenty; (*en las fechas*) twentieth
**veintena** *f* score, twenty
**veintiún** *adj* this apocopated form of **veintiuno** is used before masculine singular nouns and adjectives
**veintiu•no -na** *adj & pron* twenty-one ‖ *m* twenty-one; (*en las fechas*) twenty-first ‖ *f* (*juego de naipes*) twenty-one
**vejación** *f* vexation, annoyance
**vejamen** *m* vexation, annoyance; bantering, taunting
**vejar** *tr* to vex, annoy; to taunt
**vejestorio** *m* (coll) old dodo
**vejete** *m* (coll) little old fellow
**vejez** *f* old age; oldness; dotage; platitude, old story; **a la vejez, viruelas** there's no fool like an old fool
**vejiga** *f* (*órgano que recibe la orina de los riñones*) bladder; (*ampolla*) blister; (*saco hecho de piel, goma, etc.*) bag, pouch, bladder; **vejiga de la bilis** or **de la hiel** gall bladder
**vela** *f* wakefulness; pilgrimage; evening; work in the evening; sail; sailboat; (*cilindro con una torcida que sirve para alumbrar*) candle; vigil (*before Eucharist*); awning; (Mex) scolding; **a toda vela** full sail; **a vela** under sail; **a vela llena** under full sail; **en vela** awake; **estar entre dos velas** to be half-seas over, to have a sheet in the wind; **hacerse a la vela** to set sail; **vela latina** lateen sail; **vela mayor** mainsail; **vela romana** Roman candle
**velada** *f* evening party, soirée; vigil, watch
**vela•do -da** *adj* veiled, hidden; (phot) light-struck ‖ *f* see **velada**
**velador** *m* pedestal table, gueridon; wooden candlestick; watchman; (SAm) night table; (Mex) lamp globe
**velaje** *m* or **velamen** *m* (naut) canvas, sails
**velar** *adj & f* velar ‖ *tr* to watch over; to guard; (*la guardia*) to keep; to hold a wake over; (*cubrir con un velo*) to veil; (phot) to fog; (fig) to veil, hide, conceal ‖ *intr* to stay awake; to stay awake working; to keep vigil; (*el viento*) to keep up all night; (*un escollo, un peñasco*) to stick up out of the water; **velar por** or **sobre** to watch over ‖ *ref* (phot) to fog, to be light-struck
**velatorio** *m* wake
**veleidad** *f* whim, caprice; fickleness, flightiness
**veleido•so -sa** *adj* whimsical, capricious; fickle, flighty
**vele•ro -ra** *adj* swift-sailing ‖ *m* sailboat
**veleta** *mf* (*persona inconstante*) (coll) weathercock ‖ *f* vane, weathervane, weathercock; (*de un molino*) rudder vane; (*de la caña de pescar*) bob; streamer, pennant; **veleta de manga** (aer) air sleeve, air sock
**velís** *m* (Mex) valise
**velita** *f* little candle
**velo** *m* veil; taking the veil; confusion, perplexity; (*disfraz*) veil; (*de lágrimas*) mist; (phot) fog; **correr el velo** to pull aside the curtain, to dispel the mystery; **tomar el velo** to take the veil; **velo del paladar** soft palate
**velocidad** *f* (*rapidez*) speed, velocity; (mech) velocity; **en gran velocidad** (rr) by express; **en pequeña velocidad** (rr) by freight; **primera velocidad** (aut) low gear; **segunda velocidad** (aut) second; **tercera velocidad** (aut) high gear; **velocidad con respecto al suelo** (aer) ground speed; **velocidad permitida** speed limit
**velocímetro** *m* speedometer
**velón** *m* brass olive-oil lamp
**velorio** *m* evening party or bee; wake; wake for a dead child; (Am) dull party; (Am) come-on
**ve•loz** *adj* (*pl* **-loces**) swift, speedy; agile, quick
**vello** *m* down, fuzz
**vellocino** *m* fleece; **vellocino de oro** Golden Fleece
**vellón** *m* fleece; unsheared sheepskin; lock of wool; copper coin; copper-silver alloy
**vello•so -sa** *adj* downy, hairy, fuzzy
**velludillo** *m* velveteen
**vellu•do -da** *adj* shaggy, hairy, fuzzy ‖ *m* (*felpa*) plush; (*terciopelo*) velvet
**vena** *f* vein; (*en piedras*) grain; (fig) poetical inspiration; **estar en vena** (coll) to be all set, to be inspired; (coll) to sparkle with wit; **vena de loco** fickle disposition
**venablo** *m* dart, javelin; **echar venablos** to burst forth in anger
**venado** *m* deer, stag; **pintar el venado** (Mex) to play hooky
**venáti•co -ca** *adj* (coll) fickle, unsteady; (coll) daffy, nutty
**vence•dor -dora** *adj* conquering, victorious ‖ *mf* conqueror, victor
**vencejo** *m* band, string; (orn) European swift, black martin
**vencer** §78 *tr* to vanquish, conquer; to excel, outdo; to overcome, to surmount ‖ *intr* to conquer, be victorious; (*un plazo*) to be up; (*un contrato*) to expire; (*una letra*) to mature, fall due ‖ *ref* to control oneself; (*un camino*) to bend, turn; (Chile) to wear out, become useless
**vencetósigo** *m* milkweed, tame poison
**venci•do -da** *adj* conquered; (com) due, mature, payable
**vencimiento** *m* (*acción de vencer*) victory; (*hecho de ser vencido*) defeat; (com) expiration, maturity
**venda** *f* (*para ligar un miembro herido*) bandage; (*para tapar los ojos*) blindfold
**vendaje** *m* bandage, dressing; **vendaje enyesado** plaster cast
**vendar** *tr* (*un miembro, una herida*) to bandage; (*los ojos*) to blindfold; (*cegar*) (fig) to blind; (*engañar*) (fig) to hoodwink
**vendaval** *m* strong southeasterly wind from the sea; strong wind, gale
**vendedera** *f* saleswoman, saleslady

**vende•dor -dora** *adj* selling || *m* salesman || *f* saleslady, sales girl
**vendehu•mos** *mf* (*pl* **-mos**) (coll) influence peddler
**vendeja** *f* public sale
**vender** *tr* to sell; to betray, sell out; **vender salud** to be the picture of health || *intr* to sell; **¡vendo, vendo, vendí!** going, going, gone! || *ref* to sell oneself; to sell, be for sale; to betray oneself, to give oneself away; **venderse caro** to be hard to see; to be quite a stranger; **venderse en** (*p.ej., cien pesetas*) to sell for; **venderse por** to pass oneself off as
**ven•dí** *m* (*pl* **-díes**) certificate of sale
**vendible** *adj* salable, marketable
**vendimia** *f* vintage; (fig) big profit
**vendimia•dor -dora** *mf* vintager
**vendimiar** *tr* (*la uva*) to gather, to harvest; (*las viñas*) to gather the grapes of; to make off with; (coll) to kill
**venduta** *f* (Am) public sale; (W-I) greengrocery
**Venecia** *f* (*ciudad*) Venice; (*provincia*) Venetia
**venecia•no -na** *adj & mf* Venetian
**veneno** *m* poison, venom
**veneno•so -sa** *adj* poisonous, venomous
**venera** *f* scallop shell; (*manantial de agua*) spring; **empeñar la venera** (coll) to go all out, spare no expense
**venerable** *adj* venerable
**venerar** *tr* to venerate, revere; to worship
**venére•o -a** *adj* venereal || *m* venereal disease
**venero** *m* (*de agua*) spring; (*filón de mineral*) lode, vein; (fig) source
**venezola•no -na** *adj & mf* Venezuelan
**Venezuela** *f* Venezuela
**venga•dor -dora** *adj* avenging || *mf* avenger
**venganza** *f* vengeance, revenge
**vengar** §44 *tr* to avenge || *ref* to take revenge; **vengarse de** to take revenge on
**vengati•vo -va** *adj* vengeful, vindictive
**venia** *f* forgiveness, pardon; leave, permission; bow, greeting
**venida** *f* coming; return; flood, freshet
**venide•ro -ra** *adj* coming, future || **venideros** *mpl* successors, posterity
**venir** §79 *intr* to come; **que viene** coming, next; **venga lo que viniere** come what may; **venir** + *ger* to be + *ger;* **venir a** + *inf* to come to + *inf;* to amount to + *ger;* to happen to + *inf;* to finally + *inf,* e.g., **después de una larga enfermedad, vino a morir** after a long illness he finally died; **venir a ser** to turn out to be || *ref* to ferment; **venirse abajo** to collapse
**veno•so -sa** *adj* venous
**venta** *f* sale; roadside inn; (Chile) refreshment stand; (S-D) grocery store; **de venta** or **en venta** on sale, for sale; **ser una venta** (coll) to be an expensive place; **venta al descubierto** short sale
**ventaja** *f* advantage; (*en juegos o apuestas*) odds; extra pay
**ventajo•so -sa** *adj* advantageous
**ventalla** *f* valve
**ventana** *f* window; (*de la nariz*) nostril; **echar la casa por la ventana** (coll) to go to a lot of expense; **ventana batiente** casement; **ventana de guillotina** sash window; **ventana salediza** bay window
**ventanal** *m* church window; picture window
**ventanear** *intr* (coll) to be at the window all the time
**ventanilla** *f* (*de coche, de banco, de sobre*) window; ticket window; (*de la nariz*) nostril
**ventanillo** *m* (*postigo de puerta o ventana*) wicket; (*mirilla*) peephole
**ventar** §2 *tr* to sniff || *impers* — **vienta** it is windy
**ventarrón** *m* gale, windstorm
**ventear** *tr* to sniff; to dry in the wind; to snoop into || *intr* to snoop, pry around || *impers* — **ventea** it is windy || *ref* (*henderse*) to split; (coll) to break wind; (Am) to spend a lot of time in the open
**vente•ro -ra** *mf* innkeeper
**ventilador** *m* ventilator; fan; (naut) funnel; **ventilador aspirador** exhaust fan
**ventilar** *tr* to ventilate; (fig) to air, ventilate
**ventisca** *f* drift, snowdrift; (*borrasca*) blizzard
**ventiscar** §73 *intr* to snow and blow; (*la nieve*) to drift
**ventisquero** *m* snowdrift; blizzard; snow-capped mountain; glacier
**ventolera** *f* blast of wind; (*molinete*) pinwheel; vanity, pride; (coll) wild idea; (Mex) wind
**ventosa** *f* vent, air hole; **pegar una ventosa a** (coll) to swindle
**ventosear** *intr* to break wind
**vento•so -sa** *adj* windy || *f* see **ventosa**
**ventregada** *f* brood, litter; outpouring, abundance
**ventrículo** *m* ventricle
**ventrílo•cuo -cua** *mf* ventriloquist
**ventriloquia** *f* or **ventriloquismo** *m* ventriloquism
**ventura** *f* happiness; luck, chance; danger, risk; **a la ventura** at random; at a risk; **por ventura** perhaps, perchance; **probar ventura** to try one's luck
**venture•ro -ra** *adj* adventurous; fortunate, lucky || *mf* adventurer
**ventu•ro -ra** *adj* future, coming || *f* see **ventura**
**venturón** *m* stroke of luck
**venturo•so -sa** *adj* fortunate, lucky
**Venus** *m* (astr) Venus || *f* (myth) Venus; (*mujer de gran belleza*) Venus
**venus•to -ta** *adj* beautiful, graceful
**venza** *f* goldbeater's skin
**ver** *m* (*vista*) sight; (*apariencia*) appearance; opinion; **a mi ver** in my opinion || §80 *tr* to see; to look at; (law) to hear, to try; **no poder ver** to not be able to bear; **no tener nada que ver con** to have nothing to do with; **ver** + *inf* to see + *inf,* e.g., **ví entrar a mi hermano** I saw my

brother come in; to see + *ger*, e.g., **ví bailar a la muchacha** I saw the girl dancing; to see + *pp*, e.g., **ví ahorcar al criminal** I saw the criminal hanged; **ver venir a uno** to see what someone is up to || *intr* to see; **a más ver** so long; **a ver** let's see; **hasta más ver** good-bye, so long; **ver de** to try to; **ver y creer** seeing is believing || *ref* to be seen; to be obvious; to see oneself; to see each other; to meet; (*encontrarse*) to be, to find oneself; **verse con** to see, have a talk with; **ya se ve** of course, certainly
**vera** *f* edge, border; **a la vera de** near, beside; **de veras** in truth; **jugar de veras** to play for keeps; **veras** truth, reality; earnestness
**veracidad** *f* veracity, truthfulness
**veranda** *f* verandah; bay window, closed porch
**veraneante** *mf* summer vacationist, summer resident
**veranear** *intr* to summer
**veranie•go -ga** *adj* summer; unimportant, insignificant
**veranillo** *m* Indian summer; **veranillo de San Martín** Indian summer
**ve•raz** *adj* (*pl* **-races**) veracious, truthful
**verbena** *f* fair, country fair, night festival; (bot) verbena
**verbigracia** *adv* for example
**verbo** *m* verb || **Verbo** *m* (theol) Word
**verbo•so -sa** *adj* verbose, wordy
**verdacho** *m* green earth
**verdad** *f* truth; **a la verdad** in truth, as a matter of fact; **de verdad** really; **la verdad desnuda** the plain truth; **¿no es verdad?** or **¿verdad?** isn't that so? La traducción al inglés de esta pregunta depende generalmente de la aseveración que la precede. Si la aseveración es afirmativa, la pregunta es negativa, p.ej., **Vd. vivió aquí. ¿No es verdad?** You lived here. Did you not?; Si la aseveración es negativa, la pregunta es afirmativa, p.ej., **Vd. no vivió aquí. ¿No es verdad?** You did not live here? Did you? Si el sujeto de la aseveración es un nombre sustantivo, va representado en la pregunta con un pronombre personal, p.ej., **Juan no estuvo aquí anoche. ¿No es verdad?** John was not here last evening. Was he?; **ser verdad** to be true; **verdad trillada** truism
**verdade•ro -ra** *adj* true; real; (*que dice siempre la verdad*) truthful
**verde** *adj* green; young, youthful; (*viuda*) merry; (*viejo*) gay; (*cuento*) shady, off-color; **están verdes** (coll) they're hard to reach || *m* green; foliage, verdure
**verdear** *intr* to turn green, to look green
**verdecer** §22 *intr* to turn green, to grow green again
**verdecillo** *m* (orn) greenfinch
**verdemar** *m* sea green
**verdete** *m* verdigris
**verdín** *m* fresh green; (*capa verde de aguas estancadas*) mold, pond scum; (*cardenillo*) verdigris
**verdise•co -ca** *adj* half-dry
**verdor** *m* verdure; youth
**verdo•so -sa** *adj* greenish
**verdugado** *m* hoop skirt
**verdugo** *m* shoot, sucker; (*estoque*) rapier; (*azote*) scourge; (*roncha*) welt; executioner, hangman; torment; butcher bird, shrike
**verdugón** *m* wale, weal
**verdulería** *f* greengrocery
**verdule•ro -ra** *mf* greengrocer || *f* fishwife
**verdura** *f* greenness; (*color verde de las plantas*) verdure; (*obscenidad*) smuttiness; **verduras** vegetables, greens
**verecundia** *f* bashfulness, shyness
**verecun•do -da** *adj* bashful, shy
**vereda** *f* path, lane; (Am) sidewalk
**veredicto** *m* verdict
**verga** *f* (naut) yard
**vergel** *m* flower and fruit garden
**vergonzo•so -sa** *adj* (*que causa vergüenza*) shameful; (*que tiene vergüenza*) ashamed; (*que se avergüenza con facilidad*) bashful, shy; (*que causa humillación*) embarrassing; shabby, wretched || *mf* bashful person || *m* armadillo
**vergüenza** *f* (*arrepentimiento*) shame; (*oprobio*) shamefulness; (*pudor, timidez*) bashfulness, shyness; (*desconcierto, humillación*) embarrassment; (*pundonor*) dignity, face; public punishment; **¡qué vergüenza!** shame on you!; **tener vergüenza** to be ashamed; **vergüenzas** privates, genitals
**vericueto** *m* rough, rocky ground
**verídi•co -ca** *adj* truthful
**verificación** *f* verification; checking, testing, inspection
**verifica•dor -dora** *adj* verifying || *m* meter inspector
**verificar** §73 *tr* to verify, to check; (*llevar a cabo*) to carry out; (*los contadores de agua, gas y electricidad*) to inspect || *ref* to prove true; to take place
**verja** *f* iron gate, iron fence, grating
**ver•mú** *m* (*pl* **-mús**) vermouth; (Am) matinée
**vernácu•lo -la** *adj* vernacular
**verónica** *f* (bot) veronica; (taur) veronica (*graceful pass in which the bullfighter waits for the bull with open cape*)
**veroniquear** *intr* (taur) to perform veronicas
**verosímil** *adj* likely, probable
**verraco** *m* male hog, boar
**verraquear** *intr* (coll) to grunt, grumble; (coll) to cry hard
**verruga** *f* wart; (coll) bore, nuisance
**verrugo** *m* (coll) miser
**versal** *adj* & *f* capital
**versalilla** or **versalita** *f* small capital
**Versalles** Versailles
**versar** *intr* — **versar acerca de** or **sobre** to deal with, to treat of || *ref* — **versarse en** to be or become versed in
**versátil** *adj* fickle

**versículo** *m* verse (*in the Bible*)
**versificación** *f* versification
**versificar** §73 *tr & intr* to versify
**versión** *f* version; translation
**verso** *m* verse; (typ) verso; **versos pareados** rhymed couplet
**vertebra•do -da** *adj & m* vertebrate
**vertedero** *m* dump; weir, spillway
**verter** §51 *tr* (*un líquido, un polvo*) to pour; (*un recipiente*) to empty; (*lágrimas; luz; sangre*) to shed; (*descargar*) to dump; to translate ‖ *intr* to flow ‖ *ref* to run, to empty
**vertical** *adj & f* vertical
**vértice** *m* vertex
**vertiente** *m & f* (*declive*) slope; (*colina por donde corre el agua*) shed ‖ *f* (Arg, Col, Chile) spring, fountain
**vertigino•so -sa** *adj* dizzy
**vértigo** *m* vertigo, dizziness; fit of insanity
**vesícula** *f* vesicle; **vesícula biliar** gall bladder
**veso** *m* polecat
**Véspero** *m* Vesper
**vesperti•no -na** *adj* evening ‖ *m* evening sermon
**vestíbulo** *m* vestibule; (theat) foyer, lobby
**vestido** *m* clothing, dress; (*de mujer*) gown, dress; (*de hombre*) suit; costume; **vestido de ceremonia** dress suit; **vestido de etiqueta** evening clothes; **vestido de etiqueta de mujer** or **vestido de noche** evening gown; **vestido de gala** (mil) full dress; **vestido de serio** evening clothes; **vestido de tarde-noche** cocktail dress
**vestidura** *f* clothing; (*del sacerdote*) vestment
**vestigio** *m* vestige, trace; track, footprint
**vestir** §50 *tr* to dress, to clothe; to adorn; to cover up; to disguise; (*tal o cual vestido*) to wear; to put on; **vestir el cargo** to look the part ‖ *intr* to dress; (*una prenda o la materia*) to be dressy; **vestir de** (*p.ej., blanco*) to dress in; **vestir de etiqueta** to dress in evening clothes; **vestir de paisano** to dress in civilian clothes ‖ *ref* to dress, to get dressed; to dress oneself; (*de una enfermedad*) to be up, to be about; **vestirse de** (*nubes, flores, hierba, etc.*) to be covered with; (*importancia, humildad, etc.*) to assume
**vestuario** *m* (*las prendas de uno*) wardrobe; dressing room; bathhouse; checkroom, cloakroom; (mil) uniform; (theat) dressing room
**Vesubio, el** Vesuvius
**veta** *f* vein; streak, stripe; **descubrir la veta de** (coll) to be on to
**vetar** *tr* to veto
**vetea•do -da** *adj* veined, striped ‖ *m* graining ‖ *f* (Ecuad) whipping
**vetear** *tr* to grain, to stripe; (Ecuad) to whip, to flog
**veteranía** *f* experience, know-how
**vetera•no -na** *adj & mf* veteran
**veterina•rio -ria** *adj* veterinary ‖ *mf* veterinarian ‖ *f* veterinary medicine
**vetus•to -ta** *adj* old, ancient
**vez** *f* (*pl* **veces**) time; (*tiempo de hacer una cosa por turno*) turn; **a la vez** at the same time; **a la vez que** while; **alguna vez** sometimes; ever; **a su vez** in turn; on his part; **a veces** at times, sometimes; **cada vez** every time; **cada vez más** more and more; **cuántas veces** how often; **de una vez** at one time; once and for all; **de vez en cuando** once in a while; **dos veces** twice; **en vez de** instead of; **esperar vez** to wait one's turn; **hacer las veces de** to take the place of; **las más veces** most of the time; **muchas veces** often; **otra vez** again; **raras veces** or **rara vez** seldom, rarely; **repetidas veces** over and over again; **tal vez** perhaps; **tomar la vez a** (coll) to get ahead of; **una que otra vez** once in a while; **una vez** once
**veza** *f* vetch, spring vetch
**v.g.** or **v.gr.** *abbr* **verbigracia**
**vía** *f* road, route, way; (*par de rieles y el suelo en que se asientan*) (rr) track; (*el mismo carril*) (rr) rail, track; (anat) passage, tract; (fig) way; **por la vía de** via; **por vía aérea** by air; **por vía bucal** by mouth; **vía aérea** airway; **vía ancha** (rr) broad gauge; **vía de agua** waterway; (naut) leak; **vía estrecha** (rr) narrow gauge; **vía férrea** railway; **vía fluvial** waterway; **Vía Láctea** Milky Way; **vía muerta** (rr) siding; **vía normal** (rr) standard gauge; **vía pública** thoroughfare; **vías de hecho** (law) assault and battery ‖ *prep* via
**viable** *adj* feasible
**viaducto** *m* viaduct
**viajante** *adj* traveling ‖ *mf* traveler ‖ *m* drummer, traveling salesman
**viajar** *tr* to sell on the road; (*ciertas comarcas*) to cover as salesman ‖ *intr* to travel, to journey
**viaje** *m* trip, journey; travel book; water supply; **¡buen viaje!** bon voyage!; **viaje de ida y vuelta** or **viaje redondo** round trip
**viaje•ro -ra** *adj* traveling ‖ *mf* traveler; passenger
**vial** *adj* road, highway ‖ *m* tree-lined road
**vianda** *f* food, viand; meal
**viandante** *mf* traveler; itinerant
**viático** *m* travel allowance; (eccl) viaticum
**víbora** *f* viper
**vibración** *f* vibration
**vibrar** *tr* to vibrate; (*la voz; la r*) to roll; (*una lanza*) to hurl ‖ *intr* to vibrate ‖ *ref* to be thrilled
**vicaría** *f* vicarage
**vicario** *m* vicar
**vicealmirante** *m* vice-admiral
**vicepresiden•te -ta** *mf* vice-president
**viceversa** *adv* vice versa
**viciar** *tr* to vitiate; (*una proposición*) to slant ‖ *ref* to become vitiated; to give oneself up to vice; to become addicted; (*una tabla*) to warp
**vicio** *m* vice; pampering, spoiling; luxuriance, overgrowth; **hablar de**

**vicio** (coll) to talk all the time, to talk too much; **quejarse de vicio** (coll) to be a chronic complainer
**vicio·so -sa** *adj* vicious; faulty, defective; strong, robust; luxuriant, overgrown; dissolute; (*niño*) (coll) spoiled
**víctima** *f* victim, **víctima propiciatoria** scapegoat
**victimar** *tr* (Am) to kill, murder
**victoria** *f* victory
**victorio·so -sa** *adj* victorious
**vid** *f* vine, grapevine
**vida** *f* life; living, livelihood; **darse buena vida** to live high; to live in comfort; **de por vida** for life; **en mi vida** never; **escapar con vida** to have a narrow escape; **ganar** or **ganarse la vida** to earn one's livelihood, to make a living; **hacer por la vida** (coll) to get a bite to eat; **mudar de vida** to mend one's ways; **¡por vida mía!** upon my soul!; **vida airada** licentious living; **vida ancha** loose living; **vida de familia** or **de hogar** home life; **vida mía** my darling
**vidalita** *f* (Arg, Chile, Urug) mournful love song
**vidente** *mf* clairvoyant || *m* prophet, seer || *f* seeress
**videograbación** *f* video-tape recording
**videoseñal** *f* picture signal
**vidria·do -da** *adj* glazed; brittle || *m* glaze, glazing; glazed pottery; dishes
**vidriar** §77 & **regular** *tr* to glaze || *ref* (*los ojos*) to become glassy
**vidriera** *f* glass window, glass door; (Am) shopwindow, store window; **vidriera de colores** or **vidriera pintada** stained-glass window
**vidriería** *f* glassworks; glass store
**vidriero** *m* glass blower, glassworker; glazier; glass dealer
**vidrio** *m* glass; piece of glass; windowpane; **pagar los vidrios rotos** (coll) to take the blame, to be the goat; **vidrio cilindrado** plate glass; **vidrio de aumento** magnifying glass; **vidrio de color** stained glass; **vidrio deslustrado** ground glass; **vidrio tallado** cut glass
**vidrio·so -sa** *adj* glassy, vitreous; (*quebradizo*) brittle; (*resbaladizo*) slippery; (*que se resiente fácilmente*) (coll) touchy; (*mirada, ojos*) (fig) glassy
**vie·jo -ja** *adj* old || *m* old man; **viejo verde** old goat, old rake || *f* old woman
**vie·nés -nesa** *adj & mf* Viennese
**viento** *m* wind; course, direction; (*cuerda que mantiene una cosa derecha*) guy; (*gases intestinales*) (coll) wind; **ceñir el viento** (naut) to sail close to the wind; **viento de cola** (aer) tail wind; **viento en popa** (naut) tail wind; **vientos alisios** trade winds
**vientre** *m* belly; (*parte de la ondulación entre dos nodos*) (phys) loop; **evacuar** or **exonerar el vientre** to have a bowel movement; **vientre flojo** loose bowels
**vier·nes** *m* (*pl* **-nes**) Friday; **Viernes santo** Good Friday
**viertea·guas** *m* (*pl* **-guas**) *m* flashing
**vietna·més -mesa** *adj & mf* Vietnamese
**viga** *f* beam, girder, rafter; **estar contando las vigas** (coll) to gaze blankly at the ceiling; **viga de celosía** lattice girder
**vigencia** *f* force, operation; (*de una póliza de seguro*) life; **en vigencia** in force, in effect
**vigente** *adj* effective, in force
**vigési·mo -ma** *adj & m* twentieth
**vigía** *m* lookout, watch; **vigía de incendios** firewarden || *f* watch; watchtower; (naut) rock, reef
**vigiar** §77 *tr* to watch over
**vigilancia** *f* vigilance, watchfulness; **bajo vigilancia médica** under the care of a physician
**vigilante** *adj* vigilant, watchful || *m* guard, watchman; **vigilante nocturno** night watchman
**vigilar** *tr* to watch over; to look out for || *intr* to watch, keep guard
**vigilia** *f* vigil; wakefulness; night work, night study; (*víspera*) eve; (mil) guard, watch; **comer de vigilia** to fast, to abstain from meat
**vigor** *m* vigor; **en vigor** in force; into effect
**vigoriza·dor -dora** *adj* invigorating || *m* tonic; **vigorizador del cabello** hair tonic
**vigorizante** *adj* invigorating
**vigorizar** §60 *tr* to invigorate; to encourage
**vigoro·so -sa** *adj* vigorous
**vigueta** *f* small beam, small girder
**vihuela** *f* Spanish lute
**vil** *adj* vile, base, mean || *mf* scoundrel
**vilano** *m* bur, down
**vileza** *f* vileness, baseness
**vilipendiar** *tr* to scorn, despise
**vilipendio·so -sa** *adj* contemptible
**vilo** — **en vilo** in the air; (fig) up in the air
**vilorta** *f* reed hoop; (*arandela*) washer
**villa** *f* town; (*casa de recreo en el campo*) villa; **la Villa** the city (*Madrid*)
**villancico** *m* carol, Christmas carol
**villanes·co -ca** *adj* boorish, crude, rustic
**villanía** *f* humbleness, humble birth; vileness, meanness; foul remark
**villa·no -na** *adj* base, vile; rude, impolite || *mf* peasant; knave, scoundrel
**villorrio** *m* small country town
**vinagre** *m* vinegar; (*persona de genio áspero*) (coll) grouch
**vinagrera** *f* vinaigrette; (bot) sorrel; (SAm) heartburn; **vinagreras** cruet stand
**vinagreta** *f* French dressing, vinaigrette sauce
**vinagro·so -sa** *adj* vinegary
**vinariego** *m* vineyardist
**vinatería** *f* wine business; wine shop
**vinate·ro -ra** *adj* wine || *m* wine dealer, vintner
**vincular** *tr* to bind, to tie, to unite; to continue, to perpetuate; (*esperanzas*) to found, to base; (law) entail
**vínculo** *m* bond, tie; (law) entail
**vindicar** §73 *tr* (*vengar*) to avenge; (*exculpar*) to vindicate
**vindicta** *f* revenge

**vinicul·tor -tora** *mf* winegrower
**vinicultura** *f* winegrowing
**vinilo** *m* vinyl
**vino** *m* wine; sherry reception, wine party; **tener mal vino** to be a quarrelsome drunk; **vino cubierto** dark-red wine; **vino de Jerez** sherry; **vino del terruño** local wine; **vino de mesa** table wine; **vino de Oporto** port wine; **vino de pasto** table wine; **vino de postre** after-dinner wine; **vino de segunda** second-run wine; **vino de solera** solera sherry; **vino tinto** red table wine
**vinolen·to -ta** *adj* too fond of wine
**viña** *f* vineyard; **ser una viña** (coll) to be a mine; **tener una viña** (coll) to have a sinecure
**viña·dor -dora** *mf* vineyardist, vinedresser || *m* guard of a vineyard
**viñedo** *m* vineyard
**viñeta** *f* vignette, headpiece
**viola·do -da** *adj & m* violet (*color*)
**violar** *m* bed of violets || *tr* to violate; to ravish, rape; to profane, desecrate; to tamper with
**violencia** *f* violence
**violentar** *tr* to do violence to; (*p.ej., una casa*) to break into || *ref* to force oneself
**violen·to -ta** *adj* violent
**violeta** *m* (*color; colorante*) violet || *f* (bot) violet
**violín** *m* violin; (billiards) bridge, cue rest; **embolsar el violín** (Arg, Ven) to cower, to slink away
**violinista** *mf* violinist
**violón** *m* (mus) bass viol; **tocar el violón** (coll) to talk nonsense
**violoncelista** *mf* cellist, violoncellist
**violoncelo** *m* (mus) cello, violoncello
**violonchelista** *mf* cellist, violoncellist
**violonchelo** *m* (mus) cello, violoncello
**vira** *f* welt; (*saetilla*) dart
**virada** *f* turn, change of direction; (naut) tack
**virago** *f* mannish woman
**viraje** *m* turn, swerve; (phot) toning
**virar** *tr* (naut) to wind; (naut) to tack, to veer; (phot) to tone || *intr* to turn, to swerve; (naut) to tack, to veer
**virgen** *adj* virgin || *f* virgin, maiden
**virginidad** *f* virginity
**vírgula** *f* rod; thin line, light dash
**virgulilla** *f* fine line; diacritic mark
**virilidad** *f* virility
**virin·go -ga** *adj* (Col) naked
**virolen·to -ta** *adj* pock-marked; having smallpox
**virología** *f* virology
**virote** *m* (*saeta*) bolt; (coll) sporty young fellow; (coll) stuffed shirt
**virrey** *m* viceroy
**virtual** *adj* virtual
**virtud** *f* virtue
**virtuosismo** *m* virtuosity
**virtuo·so -sa** *adj* virtuous || *m* virtuoso
**viruela** *f* smallpox; pock mark; **viruelas locas** chicken pox
**virulencia** *f* virulence
**virulen·to -ta** *adj* virulent
**vi·rus** *m* (*pl* **-rus**) virus
**viruta** *f* shaving
**virutilla** *f* thin shaving; **virutillas de acero** steel wool
**visado** *m* visa
**visaje** *m* face, grimace
**visar** *tr* to visa; to O.K.; (arti & surv) to sight
**vísceras** *fpl* viscera
**visco** *m* birdlime
**viscosa** *f* viscose
**viscosilla** *f* rayon thread
**visco·so -sa** *adj* viscous || *f* see **viscosa**
**visera** *f* (*del yelmo, de las gorras, del parabrisas del automóvil, etc.*) visor; (*pequeña pantalla que se pone en la frente para resguardar la vista*) eyeshade; (W-I) blinder, blinker
**visible** *adj* visible; (*manifiesto*) evident; (*que llama la atención*) conspicuous
**visigo·do -da** *adj* Visigothic || *mf* Visigoth
**visillo** *m* window curtain, window shade
**visión** *f* vision; view; (*persona fea y ridícula*) (coll) sight, scarecrow; **ver visiones** (coll) to be seeing things; **visión negra** (*del aviador*) blackout
**visionar** *tr* to contemplate, to look at
**visiona·rio -ria** *adj & mf* visionary
**visir** *m* vizier; **gran visir** grand vizier
**visita** *f* visit; visitor, caller; inspection; **ir de visitas** to go calling; **pagar la visita a** to return the call of; **tener visita** to have callers; **visita de cumplido** formal call; **visita de médico** (coll) short call
**visita·dor -dora** *mf* frequent caller || *m* inspector || *f* (Hond, Ven) enema
**visitante** *adj* visiting || *mf* visitor
**visitar** *tr* to visit; to inspect
**visite·ro -ra** *adj* (coll) visiting; (*médico*) (coll) fond of making calls || *mf* (coll) visitor
**vislumbrar** *tr* to descry, to glimpse; to surmise, suspect || *ref* (*verse confusamente por la distancia*) to glimmer; (*aparecer en la distancia*) to loom
**vislumbre** *f* glimpse, glimmer; **vislumbres** inkling, notion
**viso** *m* sheen, gleam; (*de ciertas telas*) luster; streak, strain; appearance, thin veneer; elevation, height; colored material worn under transparent outer garment; **a dos visos** with a double purpose; **de viso** conspicuous; **hacer visos** to be iridescent
**visón** *m* mink
**visor** *m* (aer) bombsight; (phot) finder
**víspera** *f* eve, day before; **en vísperas de** on the eve of; **víspera de año nuevo** New Year's Eve; **víspera de Navidad** Christmas Eve; **vísperas** (eccl) vespers, evensong
**vista** *m* custom-house inspector || *f* (*sentido del ver*) vision, sight; (*paisaje que se ve desde un punto; estampa que representa un lugar*) view; (*panorama, perspectiva*) vista; comparison; purpose, design; (*ojeada*) glance, look; interview; eye; eyes; (law) hearing, trial; **a la vista** (com) at sight; **a vista de** in view of; compared with; **con vistas a** with a view to; **de vista** by sight; **doble vista** second sight; **hacer la vista gorda**

**ante** to shut one's eyes to; **hasta la vista** good-bye, so long; **medir con la vista** to size up; **saltar a la vista** to be self-evident; **tener a la vista** to keep one's eyes on; (*p.ej., una carta*) to have at hand; **torcer la vista** to squint; **vista a ojo de pájaro** bird's-eye view; **vistas** (*aberturas de un edificio*) lights, openings; view, outlook; visible parts, parts that show
**vistazo** *m* look, glance
**vistillas** *fpl* eminence, height; **irse a las vistillas** (coll) to try to get a look at one's opponent's cards
**vis•to -ta** *adj* evident, obvious; in view of; **bien visto** looked upon with approval; **mal visto** looked upon with disapproval; **no visto** or **nunca visto** unheard-of; **por lo visto** apparently, judging from the facts; **visto bueno** approved, O.K.; **visto que** whereas, inasmuch as || *m* whereas || *f* see **vista**
**isto•so -sa** *adj* showy, flashy, loud
**isual** *adj* visual || *f* line of sight
**ital** *adj* vital
**itali•cio -cia** *adj* life, lifetime || *m* life-insurance policy; life annuity
**italidad** *f* vitality
**italizar** §60 *tr* to vitalize
**itamina** *f* vitamin
**itan•do -da** *adj* hateful, odious; to be shunned
**itela** *f* vellum
**iticul•tor -tora** *mf* grape grower, vineyardist
**iticultura** *f* grape growing
**itola** *f* cigar size; mien, appearance; (Cuba) cigar band
**ítor** *interj* hurray! || *m* panegyric tablet; triumphal pageant
**itorear** *tr* to cheer, to acclaim
**itral** *m* stained-glass window
**ítre•o -a** *adj* vitreous, glassy
**itrina** *f* showcase, glass cabinet; (Am) shopwindow
**itrióli•co -ca** *adj* (chem) vitriolic
**ituallas** *fpl* victuals
**ituperable** *adj* vituperable
**ituperar** *tr* to vituperate
**iuda** *f* widow; **viuda de marido vivo** or **viuda de paja** grass widow
**iudedad** *f* widowhood; dower, widow's pension
**iudez** *f* (*estado de viuda*) widowhood; (*estado de viudo*) widowerhood
**iu•do -da** *adj* left a widow; left a widower || *m* widower || *f* see **viuda**
**iva** *interj* viva!, long live! || *m* viva
**ivacidad** *f* longevity; vivacity, liveliness; brightness, brilliance
**ivande•ro -ra** *mf* (mil) sutler, camp follower
**ivaque** *m* bivouac; guardhouse; (Am) police headquarters; **estar al vivaque** to bivouac
**ivaquear** *intr* to bivouac
**ivar** *m* warren, burrow; aquarium || *tr* (Am) to cheer, acclaim
**ivara•cho -cha** *adj* (coll) vivacious, lively
**i•vaz** *adj* (*pl* **-vaces**) long-lived; vivacious, lively; keen, perceptive; (bot) perennial
**víveres** *mpl* food, provisions, victuals
**vivero** *m* tree nursery; fishpond; (*origen de cosas perjudiciales*) (fig) hotbed
**viveza** *f* agility, briskness; ardor, vehemence; sharpness, keenness; perception; brightness, brilliance; witticism; (*de los ojos*) sparkle; (*acción o palabra poco consideradas*) thoughtlessness
**vivide•ro -ra** *adj* livable
**víví•do -da** *adj* quick, perceptive; lively
**vivienda** *f* dwelling; life, way of life
**viviente** *adj* living, alive
**vivificar** §73 *tr* to vivify, to enliven
**vivir** *m* life, living || *tr* (*una experiencia o ventura*) to live; (*toda la vida; la vejez*) to live out; (*habitar*) to live in || *intr* to live; **¿quién vive?** (mil) who goes there?; **vivir de** (*p.ej., carne*) to live on; **vivir para ver** to live and learn; **vivir y dejar vivir** to live and let live
**vivisección** *f* vivisection
**vi•vo -va** *adj* living, alive, live; (*lleno de vida; intenso*) live; (*sutil, agudo*) sharp, keen; (*dolor*) acute; (*carne*) raw; active, effective; (*luz*) bright, intense; (*pronto y ágil*) quick; (*idioma*) living, modern; **de viva voz** viva voce, by word of mouth; **herir en lo vivo** to cut or to sting to the quick || *mf* living person; **los vivos y los muertos** the quick and the dead || *m* edging, border; (vet) mange
**Vizcaya** *f* Biscay; **llevar hierro a Vizcaya** to carry coals to Newcastle
**vizconde** *m* viscount
**vizcondesa** *f* viscountess
**V.M.** *abbr* **Vuestra Majestad**
**V.°B.°** *abbr* **visto bueno**
**vocablista** *mf* punster
**vocablo** *m* word; **jugar del vocablo** to pun
**vocabulario** *m* vocabulary
**vocación** *f* vocation, calling
**vocal** *adj* vocal || *mf* director || *f* vowel
**vocalista** *mf* singer, vocalist
**vocativo** *m* vocative
**voceador** *m* town crier; (Col, Ecuad) paper boy
**vocear** *tr* to cry, shout; to cheer, acclaim; to call, to page; (coll) to boast about publicly || *intr* to shout
**vocería** *f* shouting, outcry; spokesmanship
**vocerío** *m* shouting, outcry
**vocero** *m* spokesman, mouthpiece
**vociferar** *tr* (*injurias*) to shout; to boast loudly about || *intr* to vociferate, to shout
**vocingle•ro -ra** *adj* loudmouthed; loud, talkative
**vo•dú** *m* (*pl* **-dúes**) voodoo
**voduísta** *adj & mf* voodoo
**vol.** *abbr* **volumen, voluntad**
**volada** *f* short flight; (*del jugador de billar*) (Arg) stroke; (Col, Ecuad) trick; (*noticia inventada*) (Mex) hoax
**voladi•zo -za** *adj* projecting || *m* projection

**vola·do -da** *adj* (typ) superior || *f* see volada
**vola·dor -dora** *adj* flying; hanging, dangling; swift, fast || *m* rocket; flying fish
**voladura** *f* blast, explosion
**volandas** — **en volandas** in the air; fast
**volante** *adj* flying; unsettled || *m* shuttlecock; battledore and shuttlecock; (*rueda que regula el movimiento de una máquina*) flywheel; (*rueda de mano para la dirección del automóvil*) steering wheel; (*pieza del reloj movida por la espiral*) balance wheel; flunkey, lackey; (*criado que iba a pie delante del coche o caballo*) outrunner; (*de papel*) slip, leaflet; (sew) flounce, ruffle; **un buen volante** a good driver
**volan·tín -tina** *adj* unsettled || *m* fish line; (Am) kite
**volantista** *m* (coll) driver, man at the wheel
**volan·tón -tona** *mf* fledgling || *f* (Ven) loose woman
**volapié** *m* (taur) stroke in which the matador moves in for the kill; **a volapié** half running, half flying; half walking, half swimming
**volar §61** *tr* (*llevar en un aparato de aviación*) to fly; to blow up, to explode; to irritate; (*una letra, tipo o signo*) (typ) to raise || *intr* to fly; to fly away; to disappear; to jut out, project; (*una especie*) to spread rapidly; (*p.ej., una torre*) to rise in the air; **volar sin motor** (aer) to glide || *ref* to fly away; (Am) to fly off the handle
**volatería** *f* fowling with decoys; **de volatería** offhand
**volátil** *adj* volatile
**volatilizar** *tr & ref* to volatilize
**volatín** *m* ropewalker, acrobat, tumbler
**volatine·ro -ra** *mf* ropewalker, acrobat, tumbler
**volcán** *m* volcano
**volcar §81** *tr* to upset, overturn, dump; to tip, to tilt; (*a una persona un olor fuerte*) to make dizzy; to change the mind of; to irritate, tease || *intr* to upset || *ref* to turn upside down
**volear** *tr* (tennis) to volley
**voleo** *m* (tennis) volley; reeling punch; **del primer voleo** or **de un voleo** (coll) with a smash, all at once; **sembrar al voleo** to sow broadcast
**volframio** *m* wolfram
**volibol** *m* volleyball
**volquete** *m* dumpcart, dump truck
**voltai·co -ca** *adj* voltaic
**voltaje** *m* voltage
**volta·rio -ria** *adj* fickle, inconstant; (Chile) willful; (Chile) sporty
**voltea·do -da** *mf* (Col) turncoat, deserter
**voltear** *tr* to upset, turn over; to turn around; to move, to transform || *intr* to roll over, to tumble
**volteo** *m* upset, overturning; tumbling; (P-R) scolding
**voltereta** *f* tumble; turning up card to determine trump
**voltímetro** *m* voltmeter
**voltio** *m* volt
**volti·zo -za** *adj* curled, twisted; fickle
**voluble** *adj* easily turned; fickle, inconstant
**volumen** *m* volume; **volumen sonoro** volume; (geom) volume
**volumino·so -sa** *adj* voluminous
**voluntad** *f* will; (*amor, cariño*) fondness, love; **a voluntad** at will; **buena voluntad** willingness; **de buena voluntad** willingly; **de mala voluntad** unwillingly; **de su propia voluntad** of one's own volition; **última voluntad** last will and testament; last wish; **voluntad de hierro** iron will
**voluntariedad** *f* willfulness
**volunta·rio -ria** *adj* (*que se hace por espontánea voluntad*) voluntary; (*que tiene voluntad obstinada*) willful; (*que se presta voluntariamente a hacer algo*) volunteer || *mf* volunteer
**voluntario·so -sa** *adj* willful
**voluptuo·so -sa** *adj* (*que inspira complacencia en los placeres sensuales*) voluptuous; (*dado a los placeres sensuales*) voluptuary || *mf* voluptuary
**voluta** *f* (archit) scroll, volute; (*p.ej., de humo*) ring
**volvedor** *m* screwdriver; (Col) extra, something thrown in; **volvedor de machos** tap wrench
**volver §47 & §83** *tr* to turn; to turn upside down; to turn inside out; to return, send back, give back; (*una puerta*) to push to, to pull to; to translate; to vomit || *intr* to turn; to return, come back; **volver a** + *inf* verb + again, e.g., **volvió a abrir la puerta** he opened the door again; **volver en sí** to come to; **volver por** to defend, to stand up for || *ref* to become; to turn around; to return, come back; to change one's mind; to turn, turn sour; **volverse atrás** to back out; **volverse contra** to turn on
**vomitar** *tr* to vomit, throw up; (*fuego los cañones*) to belch forth; (*maldiciones*) to utter; (*un secreto*) to let out; (*lo que uno retiene indebidamente*) (coll) to cough up || *intr* to vomit, throw up; (coll) to come across, disgorge
**vómito** *m* vomit, vomiting; **provocar a vómito** (coll) to nauseate; **vómitos del embarazo** morning sickness
**voracidad** *f* voracity
**vorágine** *f* whirlpool, vortex
**vo·raz** *adj* (*pl* **-races**) voracious
**vormela** *f* polecat
**vórtice** *m* vortex
**vos** *pron pers* (subject of verb and object of preposition; takes plural form of verb but is singular in meaning; used in addressing the Deity, the Virgin, etc., and distinguished persons; in Spanish America is much used instead of **tú**) you
**voso·tros -tras** *pron pers* (plural of **tú**) you
**votación** *f* vote, voting
**votante** *adj* voting || *mf* voter

**votar** *tr* to vote for; (*sí, no*) to vote; (*p.ej., un cirio a la Virgen*) to vow || *intr* to vote; to vow; to swear, curse
**voti•vo -va** *adj* votive
**voto** *m* (*sufragio; derecho de votar; persona que da su voto*) vote; (*promesa solemne*) vow; (*exvoto*) votive offering; (*blasfemia*) oath, curse; wish, desire; **echar votos** to swear, to curse; **regular los votos** to tally the votes; **voto de amén** (coll) vote of a yes man; (coll) yes man; **voto de calidad** casting vote; **voto informativo** straw vote; **votos** good wishes; **¡voto va!** come now!
**voz** *f* (*pl* **voces**) voice; (*vocablo*) word; **aclarar la voz** to clear one's throat; **a una voz** with one voice; **a voces** shouting; **a voz en cuello** or **en grito** at the top of one's voice; **correr la voz que** to be rumored that; **dar voces** to shout, to cry out; **de viva voz** viva voce, by word of mouth; **en alta voz** aloud, in a loud voice; **en voz baja** in a low voice; **llevar la voz cantante** (coll) to have the say, to be the boss; **voces** outcry
**vro.** *abbr* **vuestro**
**V.S.** *abbr* **Vueseñoría**
**vuelco** *m* upset, overturn; **darle a uno un vuelco el corazón** (coll) to have a presentiment
**vuelo** *m* flight; flying; (*de una falda*) flare, fullness; projection; lace cuff trimming; **al vuelo** at once; on the wing; scattered at random; (chess) en passant; **alzar el vuelo** to take flight; (coll) to dash away; **echar a vuelo las campanas** to ring a full peal; **tirar al vuelo** to shoot on the wing; **tocar a vuelo las campanas** to ring a full peal; **vuelo a ciegas** (aer) blind flying; **vuelo de distancia** (aer) long-distance flight; **vuelo de ensayo** or **de prueba** (aer) test flight; **vuelo espacial tripulado** manned space flight; **vuelo planeado** (aer) volplane; **vuelo rasante** (aer) hedgehopping; **vuelo sin escala** (aer) nonstop flight; **vuelo sin motor** (aer) glide, gliding
**vuelta** *f* turn; (*regreso; devolución*) return; (*dinero sobrante de un pago*) change; (*de un camino*) bend, turn; (*del pantalón*) cuff; cuff trimming; (*paseo corto*) stroll; (*revés*) other side; (*paliza*) beating, whipping; (*en un cabo*) loop; (*en la media*) clock; (*mudanza*) change; **a la vuelta** on returning; please turn the page; **a la vuelta de** at the end of; at the turn of; (*la esquina*) around; **a vuelta de** about; **a vuelta de correo** by return mail; **dar cien vueltas a** to run rings around, be away ahead of; **dar la vuelta de campana** to turn somersault; **darse una vuelta a la redonda** (coll) to tend to one's own business; **dar una vuelta** to take a stroll, take a walk; to take a look; to change one's ways; **dar vuelta** to turn around; (*el vino*) to turn sour; **dar vuelta a** to reverse, to turn around; **estar de vuelta** to be back; **quedarse con la vuelta** to keep the change; **vuelta de campana** somersault; **vuelta del mundo** trip around the world
**vuelto** *m* (Am) change
**vues•tro -tra** (corresponds to **vos** and **vosotros**) *adj poss* your || *pron poss* yours
**vulcanizar** §60 *tr* to vulcanize
**vulgacho** *m* (coll) populace, mob
**vulgar** *adj* vulgar, popular, common, vernacular
**vulgarismo** *m* popular expression; (philol) popular word, popular form
**vulgarizar** §60 *tr* to popularize; to translate into the vernacular || *ref* to associate with the people
**Vulgata** *f* Vulgate
**vulgo** *adv* commonly || *m* common people; (*personas que en una materia sólo conocen la parte superficial*) laity
**vulnerable** *adj* vulnerable
**vulnerar** *tr* to hurt, injure; (*la reputación de una persona*) to damage; (*una ley, un precepto*) to break
**vulpeja** *f* she-fox, vixen
**V.V.** or **VV** *abbr* **ustedes**

## X

**X, x** (equis) *f* twenty-sixth letter of the Spanish alphabet
**xenia** *f* xenia
**xenofobia** *f* xenophobia
**xenófo•bo -ba** *mf* xenophobe
**xenón** *m* xenon
**xilófono** *m* (mus) xylophone
**xilografía** *f* (*arte*) xylography; (*grabado*) xylograph
**xpiano** *abbr* **cristiano**
**Xpo** *abbr* **Cristo**
**xptiano** *abbr* **cristiano**
**Xpto** *abbr* **Cristo**
**xunde** *m* (Mex) reed basket, palm basket

## Y

**Y, y** (ye) *f* twenty-seventh letter of the Spanish alphabet
**y** *conj* and
**ya** *adv* already; right away; now; **no ya** not only; **ya no** no longer; **ya que** since, inasmuch as
**yac** *m* (*bandera de proa*) (naut) jack; (*bóvido del Tibet*) yak

**yacer** §82 *intr* to lie
**yacija** *f* bed, couch; (*sepultura*) grave
**yacimiento** *m* bed, field, deposit
**yámbi•co -ca** *adj* iambic
**yambo** *m* iamb, iambus
**yanqui** *adj & mf* Yankee
**Yanquilandia** *f* Yankeedom
**yapa** *f* (Am) bonus, extra, allowance; **de yapa** (Am) in the bargain, extra
**yarda** *f* yard; yardstick
**yate** *m* yacht
**yedra** *f* ivy
**yegua** *f* mare; (CAm) cigar butt
**yeguada** *f* stud
**yelmo** *m* helmet
**yema** *f* (*de huevo*) yolk; candied yolk; (*del invierno*) dead; (*renuevo*) bud; (fig) cream; **dar en la yema** (coll) to put one's finger on the spot; **yema del dedo** finger tip; **yema mejida** eggnog
**yente** — **yentes y vinientes** *mpl* habitués, frequenters
**yerba** *f* var of **hierba**
**yer•mo -ma** *adj* deserted, uninhabited; (*suelo*) unsown; (*mujer*) not pregnant || *m* desert, wilderness
**yerno** *m* son-in-law
**yerro** *m* error, mistake; **yerro de cuenta** miscalculation; **yerro de imprenta** printer's error
**yer•to -ta** *adj* stiff, rigid
**yesca** *f* punk, tinder; (*cosa que excita una pasión*) fuel; **echar una yesca** to strike a light
**yeso** *m* gypsum; plaster cast
**yo** *pron pers* I; **soy yo** it is I
**yodhídri•co -ca** *adj* hydriodic
**yodo** *m* iodine
**yoduro** *m* iodide
**yola** *f* (sport) shell
**yugo** *m* yoke; **sacudir el yugo** to throw off the yoke
**Yugoeslavia** *f* Yugoslavia
**yugoesla•vo -va** *adj & mf* Yugoslav
**yugular** *adj & f* jugular || *tr* to cut off, to nip in the bud
**yunque** *m* anvil; (fig) drudge, work horse
**yunta** *f* yoke, team
**yute** *m* jute
**yuxtaponer** §54 *tr* to juxtapose
**yuyo** *m* (Arg, Chile) weed; **yuyos** (Col, Ecuad, Peru) greens

## Z

**Z, z** (zeda or zeta) *f* twenty-eighth letter of the Spanish alphabet
**zabordar** *intr* (naut) to run aground
**zabullir** §13 *tr* (*p.ej., a un perro*) to duck, give a ducking to; (coll) to throw, to hurl || *ref* (*meterse debajo del agua con ímpetu*) to dive; (*esconderse rápidamente*) to duck
**zacapela** or **zacapella** *f* row, rumpus
**zacate** *m* (CAm, Mex) hay, fodder; **zacate de empaque** (Am) excelsior
**zacateca** *m* (Cuba) undertaker, gravedigger
**zacatín** *m* old-clothes market
**zacear** *tr* (*al perro*) to chase away || *intr* to lisp
**zafaduría** *f* (Arg) brazenness, effrontery
**zafar** *tr* to adorn, bedeck; to loosen, untie; to clear, to free; (*un buque*) to lighten || *ref* to slip away; to slip off, come off; **zafarse de** to get out of
**zafarrancho** *m* (naut) clearing the decks; (coll) havoc, ravage; (coll) scuffle, row; **zafarrancho de combate** (naut) clearing the deck for action
**za•fio -fia** *adj* rough, uncouth, boorish
**zafiro** *m* sapphire
**za•fo -fa** *adj* unhurt, intact; (naut) free, clear || **zafo** *prep* (Col) except
**zafra** *f* olive-oil can; drip jar; sugar crop; sugar making; sugar-making season; (min) rubbish, muck
**zaga** *f* rear; load carried in the rear; (mil) rearguard; **a la zaga, a zaga** or **en zaga** behind, in the rear; **no ir en zaga a** (coll) to not be behind, to be as good as
**zagal** *m* young fellow; strapping young fellow; shepherd boy; footboy
**zagala** *f* lass, maiden; young shepherdess
**zaguán** *m* vestibule, hall, entry
**zague•ro -ra** *adj* back, rear || *m* (sport) back, backstop
**zaherir** §68 *tr* to upbraid, reproach; to scold shamefully
**zahones** *mpl* chaps, hunting breeches
**zaho•rí** *m* (*pl* **-ríes**) keen observer; seer, clairvoyant
**zahurda** *f* pigpen
**zai•no -na** *adj* treacherous, false; (*caballo*) vicious; (*caballo*) dark-chestnut; **mirar a lo zaino** or **de zaino** to look askance at
**za•lá** *f* (*pl* **-laes**) Mohammedan prayer; **hacer la zalá a** (coll) to fawn on
**zalagarda** *f* ambush; skirmish; (*trampa para cazar animales*) trap; (coll) trick; (coll) row, rumpus; (coll) mock fight
**zalamería** *f* flattery, cajolery
**zalame•ro -ra** *adj* flattering, fawning || *mf* flatterer, fawner
**zalea** *f* unsheared sheepskin
**zalear** *tr* to drag around, to shake; (*al perro*) to chase away
**zalema** *f* salaam
**zamacuco** *m* (coll) blockhead; (coll) sullen fellow; (coll) drunkenness
**zamacueca** *f* cueca (*Chilean courtship dance*)
**zamarra** *f* undressed sheepskin; sheepskin jacket
**zam•bo -ba** *adj* knock-kneed
**zambra** *f* merrymaking, celebration; Moorish boat
**zambucar** §73 *tr* (coll) to slip away, hide away

**zambullida** *f* dive, plunge; (fencing) thrust to the breast
**zambulli•dor -dora** *adj* diving, plunging || *mf* diver, plunger || *m* (orn) diver, loon
**zambullir** §13 *tr* (*p.ej., a un perro*) to duck, to give a ducking to; (coll) to throw, to hurl || *ref* (*meterse debajo del agua con ímpetu*) to dive; (*esconderse rápidamente*) to duck
**zampa** *f* pile, bearing pile
**zampacuarti•llos** *mf* (*pl* **-llos**) (coll) toper, soak
**zampalimos•nas** *mf* (*pl* **-nas**) (coll) bum, ordinary bum
**zampar** *tr* to slip away, hide away; to gobble down || *ref* to slip away, hide away
**zampator•tas** *mf* (*pl* **-tas**) (coll) glutton; (coll) boor
**zampear** *tr* (*el terreno*) to strengthen with piles and rubble
**zampoña** *f* shepherd's pipe, rustic flute; (coll) nonsense, folly
**zampuzar** §60 *tr* to duck, give a ducking to; (coll) to slip away, hide away
**zanahoria** *f* carrot
**zanca** *f* long leg; (*de la escalera*) horse
**zancada** *f* long stride; **en dos zancadas** (coll) in a flash, in a jiffy
**zancadilla** *f* (coll) booby trap; **echar la zancadilla a** to stick out one's foot and trip
**zancajo** *m* heel; **no llegar a los zancajos a** (coll) to not come up to, to not be equal to
**zancajo•so -sa** *adj* duck-toed; down-at-the-heel
**zancarrón** *m* (coll) dirty old fellow
**zanco** *m* stilt; **en zancos** (coll) from a vantage point
**zancu•do -da** *adj* long-legged; (orn) wading || *m* mosquito || *f* wading bird
**zanfonía** *f* hurdy-gurdy
**zangala** *f* buckram
**zangamanga** *f* (coll) trick
**zanganada** *f* (coll) impertinence, impudence
**zanganear** *intr* (coll) to loaf around
**zángano** *m* (ent) drone; (fig) drone, loafer; (CAm) scoundrel
**zangarrear** *intr* (coll) to thrum a guitar
**zangolotear** *tr* (coll) to jiggle || *intr* (coll) to fuss around || *ref* (coll) to jiggle, to flop around, to rattle
**zangoloteo** *m* (coll) jiggle, jiggling, rattle; (coll) fuss, bother
**zanguanga** *f* (coll) malingering; (coll) flattery; **hacer la zanguanga** (coll) to malinger
**zanguan•go -ga** *adj* (coll) slow, lazy || *mf* (coll) loafer || *f* see **zanguanga**
**zanja** *f* ditch, trench; (SAm) gully; **abrir las zanjas** to lay the foundations
**zanquear** *intr* to waddle; to rush around
**zanquilar•go -ga** *adj* leggy, long-legged
**zanquituer•to -ta** *adj* bandy-legged
**zapa** *f* spade; sharkskin, shagreen; (mil) sap
**zapapico** *m* mattock, pickax
**zapar** *tr* (mil) to sap, mine, excavate
**zaparrastrar** *intr* — **ir zaparrastrando** (coll) to go along trailing one's clothes on the ground
**zapateado** *m* clog dance, tap dance
**zapatear** *tr* to hit with the shoe; to tap with the feet; (coll) to abuse, ill-treat || *intr* to tap-dance; (*las velas*) to flap || *ref* — **zapatearse con** to hold out against
**zapatería** *f* shoemaking; shoemaker's shop; (*tienda*) shoe store
**zapate•ro -ra** *adj* poorly cooked || *mf* shoemaker; shoe dealer; **quedarse zapatero** (coll) to not take a trick; **¡zapatero, a tus zapatos!** stick to your last!; **zapatero de viejo** or **zapatero remendón** cobbler, shoemaker
**zapatilla** *f* slipper; (*escarpín*) pump; (*del grifo*) washer; (*del florete*) leather tip or button; cloven hoof
**zapato** *m* shoe, low shoe; **andar con zapatos de fieltro** to gumshoe; **como tres en un zapato** (coll) hard up; (coll) like sardines; **zapato de goma** overshoe; **zapato inglés** low shoe
**zapatón** *m* (Guat, SAm) overshoe
**zapear** *tr* (*al gato*) to scare away, chase away
**zaque** *m* wineskin; (coll) tippler, drunk
**zaquiza•mí** *m* (*pl* **-míes**) attic, garret; hovel, pigpen
**zar** *m* czar
**zarabanda** *f* (mus) saraband; (coll) noise, confusion, uproar; (Mex) beating, thrashing
**zaragata** *f* (coll) scuffle, row; **zaragatas** (W-I) flattery
**Zaragoza** *f* Saragossa
**zaranda** *f* sieve, screen; colander; (Ven) horn; (Ven) top
**zarandajas** *fpl* (coll) odds and ends, trinkets
**zarandar** *tr* to sift, to screen; to winnow, pick out, select; (coll) to jiggle || *ref* (coll) to jiggle; (Am) to swagger, strut
**zaraza** *f* chintz, printed cotton
**zarcillo** *m* eardrop; (bot) tendril
**zarigüeya** *f* opossum
**zarina** *f* czarina
**zarpa** *f* claw, paw; (naut) weighing anchor
**zarpar** *tr* (*el ancla*) (naut) to weigh (*anchor*) || *intr* (naut) to weigh anchor, to set sail
**zarpo•so -sa** *adj* mud-splashed
**zarracatería** *f* (coll) cajolery, insincere flattery
**zarracatín** *m* (coll) sharp trader
**zarramplín** *m* (coll) botcher, bungler
**zarrien•to -ta** *adj* mud-splashed
**zarza** *f* blackberry, bramble (*bush*)
**zarzamora** *f* blackberry (*fruit*)
**zarzaparrilla** *f* sarsaparilla
**zarzo** *m* hurdle, wattle
**zarzo•so -sa** *adj* brambly
**zarzuela** *f* small bramble; (theat) zarzuela (*Spanish musical comedy*); **zarzuela grande** three-act zarzuela
**zas** *interj* bang!; **¡zas, zas!** bing, bang!
**zascandilear** *intr* (coll) to meddle, to scheme
**zepelín** *m* zeppelin
**Zeus** *m* Zeus

**zigzag** *m* zigzag
**zigzaguear** *intr* to zigzag
**zinc** *m* (*pl* **zinces**) zinc
**zipizape** *m* (coll) scuffle, row, rumpus
**ziszás** *m* zigzag
**zoca** *f* public square
**zócalo** *m* (archit) socle; (*de una pared*) dado; (rad) socket; (Mex) public square, center square
**zoca•to -ta** *adj* (*fruto*) corky, pithy; (coll) left; (coll) left-handed || *mf* (coll) left-handed person
**zoclo** *m* clog, wooden shoe
**zo•co -ca** *adj* (coll) left; (coll) left-handed || *mf* (coll) left-handed person || *m* clog, wooden shoe; Moroccan market place; (archit) socle; **andar de zocos en colodros** (coll) to jump from the frying pan into the fire || *f* see **zoca**
**zodíaco** *m* zodiac
**zofra** *f* Moorish carpet, Moorish rug
**zolo•cho -cha** *adj* (coll) stupid, simple || *mf* (coll) simpleton
**zollipar** *intr* (coll) to sob
**zollipo** *m* (coll) sob
**zona** *m* (pathol) shingles || *f* zone; (*banda, faja*) belt, girdle; **zona a batir** target area
**zon•zo -za** *adj* tasteless, insipid; dull, inane || *mf* dolt, dimwit
**zoófito** *m* zoöphyte
**zoología** *f* zoölogy
**zoológi•co -ca** *adj* zoölogic(al)
**zoólo•go -ga** *mf* zoölogist
**zopen•co -ca** *adj* (coll) dull, stupid || *mf* (coll) dullard, blockhead
**zopilote** *m* (Mex, CAm) turkey buzzard, turkey vulture
**zo•po -pa** *adj* crippled; awkward, gauche || *mf* cripple
**zoquete** *m* (*de madera*) block, chunk, end; (*de pan*) bit, crust; (coll) chump, lout
**zoquetu•do -da** *adj* coarse, crude
**zorra** *f* fox; female fox; (coll) foxy person; (coll) prostitute; (coll) drunkenness; dray, truck; **pillar una zorra** (coll) to get drunk
**zorrera** *f* (*cueva de zorros*) foxhole; smoke-filled room; (coll) worry, confusion
**zorrería** *f* (coll) foxiness
**zorre•ro -ra** *adj* (coll) sly, foxy; (coll) slow, heavy, tardy || *f* see **zorrera**
**zorrillo** *m* (Am) skunk
**zorro** *m* male fox; (*piel*) fox; (*hombre taimado*) (coll) fox; **estar hecho un zorro** (coll) to be overwhelmed with sleep; (coll) to be dull and sullen; **zorros** duster
**zorzal** *m* (orn) fieldfare; sly fellow; (Chile) simpleton
**zozobra** *f* capsizing, sinking; anxiety
**zozobrar** *tr* (*un buque*) to sink; (*un negocio*) to wreck || *intr* to capsize, sink; (*la embarcación en la tempestad*) to wallow; (*un negocio*) to be in great danger; to be greatly worried || *ref* to capsize, sink
**zueco** *m* clog, wooden shoe, sabot
**zulacar** §73 *tr* to waterproof
**zulaque** *m* waterproofing
**zulú** (*pl* **-lús** o **-lúes**) *adj* & *mf* Zulu
**zullar** *ref* (coll) to have a movement of the bowels; (coll) to break wind
**zullen•co -ca** *adj* (coll) windy, flatulent
**zumaque** *m* sumach; (coll) wine
**zumaya** *f* (*autillo*) tawny owl; (*chotacabras*) goatsucker
**zumba** *f* bell worn by leading mule; (Mex) drunkenness; **hacer zumba a** to make fun of; **sin zumba** (Mex) in a rush, in a hurry
**zumbador** *m* buzzer; (Mex) pauraque; (Mex, CAm, W-I) hummingbird
**zumbar** *tr* to make fun of; (*un golpe, una bofetada*) to let have || *intr* to buzz; to zoom; (*los oídos*) to ring; **zumbar a** (*frisar con*) to be close to, to border on || *ref* (Cuba) to go too far, to forget oneself; (P-R) to rush ahead; **zumbarse de** to make fun of
**zumbido** *m* buzz; zoom; (coll) blow, smack; **zumbido de ocupación** (telp) busy signal; **zumbido de oídos** ringing in the ears
**zum•bón -bona** *adj* waggish, playful || *mf* wag, jester
**zumien•to -ta** *adj* juicy
**zumo** *m* juice; advantage, profit; **zumo de cepas** or **de parras** (coll) fruit of the vine
**zumo•so -sa** *adj* juicy
**zunchar** *tr* to band, to hoop
**zuncho** *m* band, hoop
**zupia** *f* (*del vino*) dregs; slop, wine full of dregs; (fig) junk, trash
**zurcido** *m* darning; darn; invisible mending
**zurcir** §36 *tr* to darn; (*una mentira*) (coll) to hatch, concoct; (*unas mentiras*) (coll) to weave (*a tissue of lies*)
**zurdazo** *m* (box) left, blow with the left
**zur•do -da** *adj* left; left-handed; **a zurdas** with the left hand; the wrong way || *mf* left-handed person
**zurear** *intr* to coo
**zuro** *m* stripped corncob
**zurra** *f* dressing, currying; scuffle, quarrel; drubbing, thrashing; (*trabajo o estudio continuados*) grind
**zurrapa** *f* thread, filament; (coll) trash, rubbish; **con zurrapas** (coll) in a sloppy manner
**zurrar** *tr* (*el cuero*) to dress, to curry; to get the best of; (*censurar con dureza*) to dress down; (*castigar con azotes*) to drub, to thrash || *ref* (*hacer sus necesidades involuntariamente*) to have an accident; (coll) to be scared to death; (Arg) to break wind noiselessly
**zurriagar** §44 *tr* to whip, to horsewhip
**zurriago** *m* whip, lash
**zurribanda** *f* (coll) rain of blows; (coll) rumpus, scuffle
**zurrir** *intr* to buzz, to grate
**zurrón** *m* shepherd's leather bag; leather bag; (*cáscara*) husk
**zurrona** *f* (coll) loose, evil woman
**zurullo** *m* (coll) soft roll; (coll) turd
**zurupeto** *m* (coll) unregistered broker; (coll) shyster notary
**zuta•no -na** *mf* (coll) so-and-so

# MODEL VERBS

## ORDER OF TENSES

(a) gerund
(b) past participle
(c) imperative
(d) present indicative
(e) present subjunctive
(f) imperfect indicative
(g) future indicative
(h) preterit indicative

All simple tenses are shown in these tables if they contain one irregular form or more, except the conditional (which can always be derived from the stem of the future indicative) and the imperfect and future subjunctive (which can always be derived from the third plural preterit indicative minus the last syllable **-ron**). The tenses are identified with the letters (a) to (h) as shown above.

---

§1 **abolir:** defective verb used only in forms whose endings contain the vowel **i**

§2 **acertar**
(c) **acierta,** acertad
(d) **acierto, aciertas, acierta,** acertamos, acertáis, **aciertan**
(e) **acierte, aciertes, acierte,** acertemos, acertéis, **acierten**

§3 **agorar:** like **§61** but with diaeresis on the **u** of **ue**
(c) **agüera,** agorad
(d) **agüero, agüeras, agüera,** agoramos, agoráis, **agüeran**
(e) **agüere, agüeres, agüere,** agoremos, agoréis, **agüeren**

§4 **airar**
(c) **aíra,** airad
(d) **aíro, aíras, aíra,** airamos, airáis, **aíran**
(e) **aíre, aíres, aíre,** airemos, airéis, **aíren**

§5 **andar**
(h) **anduve, anduviste, anduvo, anduvimos, anduvisteis, anduvieron**

§6 **argüir:** like **§20** but with diaeresis on **u** in forms with accented **i** in the ending
(a) **arguyendo**
(b) **argüído**
(c) **arguye,** argüid
(d) **arguyo, arguyes, arguye,** argüimos, argüís, **arguyen**
(e) **arguya, arguyas, arguya, arguyamos, arguyáis, arguyan**
(h) argüí, argüiste, **arguyó,** argüimos, argüisteis, **arguyeron**

§7 **asir**
(d) **asgo,** ases, ase, asimos, asís, asen
(e) **asga, asgas, asga, asgamos, asgáis, asgan**

§8 **aunar**
(c) **aúna,** aunad
(d) **aúno, aúnas, aúna,** aunamos, aunáis, **aúnan**
(e) **aúne, aúnes, aúne,** aunemos, aunéis, **aúnen**

§9 **avergonzar:** combination of **§3** and **§60**
(c) **avergüenza,** avergonzad

(d) **avergüenzo, avergüenzas, avergüenza,** avergonzamos, avergonzáis, **avergüenzan**
(e) **avergüence, avergüences, avergüence, avergoncemos, avergoncéis, avergüencen**
(h) **avergoncé,** avergonzaste, avergonzó, avergonzamos, avergonzasteis, avergonzaron

§10 **averiguar**
(e) **averigüe, averigües, averigüe, averigüemos, averigüéis, averigüen**
(h) **averigüé,** averiguaste, averiguó, averiguamos, averiguasteis, averiguaron

§11 **bendecir**
(a) **bendiciendo**
(c) **bendice,** bendecid
(d) **bendigo, bendices, bendice,** bendecimos, bendecís, **bendicen**
(e) **bendiga, bendigas, bendiga, bendigamos, bendigáis, bendigan**
(h) **bendije, bendijiste, bendijo, bendijimos, bendijisteis, bendijeron**

§12 **bruñir**
(a) **bruñendo**
(h) bruñí, bruñiste, **bruñó,** bruñimos, bruñisteis, **bruñeron**

§13 **bullir**
(a) **bullendo**
(h) bullí, bulliste, **bulló,** bullimos, bullisteis, **bulleron**

§14 **caber**
(d) **quepo,** cabes, cabe, cabemos, cabéis, caben
(e) **quepa, quepas, quepa, quepamos, quepáis, quepan**
(g) **cabré, cabrás, cabrá, cabremos, cabréis, cabrán**
(h) **cupe, cupiste, cupo, cupimos, cupisteis, cupieron**

§15 **caer**
(a) **cayendo**
(b) **caído**
(d) **caigo,** caes, cae, caemos, caéis, caen
(e) **caiga, caigas, caiga, caigamos, caigáis, caigan**
(h) caí, **caíste, cayó, caímos, caísteis, cayeron**

§16 **cocer:** combination of **§47** and **§78**
(c) **cuece,** coced
(d) **cuezo, cueces, cuece,** cocemos, cocéis, **cuecen**
(e) **cueza, cuezas, cueza, cozamos, cozáis, cuezan**

§17 **coger**
(d) **cojo,** coges, coge, cogemos, cogéis, cogen
(e) **coja, cojas, coja, cojamos, cojáis, cojan**

§18 **comenzar:** combination of **§2** and **§60**
(c) **comienza,** comenzad
(d) **comienzo, comienzas, comienza,** comenzamos, comenzáis, **comienzan**
(e) **comience, comiences, comience, comencemos, comencéis, comiencen**
(h) **comencé,** comenzaste, comenzó, comenzamos, comenzasteis, comenzaron

**§19 conducir**

(d) **conduzco,** conduces, conduce, conducimos, conducís, conducen

(e) **conduzca, conduzcas, conduzca, conduzcamos, conduzcáis, conduzcan**

(h) **conduje, condujiste, condujo, condujimos, condujisteis, condujeron**

**§20 construir**

(a) **construyendo**

(b) **construído**

(c) **construye,** construid

(d) **construyo, construyes, construye,** construimos, construís, **construyen**

(e) **construya, construyas, construya, construyamos, construyáis, construyan**

(h) construí, construiste, **construyó,** construimos, construisteis, **construyeron**

**§21 continuar**

(c) **continúa,** continuad

(d) **continúo, continúas, continúa,** continuamos, continuáis, **continúan**

(e) **continúe, continúes, continúe,** continuemos, continuéis, **continúen**

**§22 crecer**

(d) **crezco,** creces, crece, crecemos, crecéis, crecen

(e) **crezca, crezcas, crezca, crezcamos, crezcáis, crezcan**

**§23 dar**

(d) **doy,** das, da, damos, dais, dan

(e) **dé,** des, **dé,** demos, deis, den

(h) **dí, diste, dio, dimos, disteis, dieron**

**§24 decir**

(a) **diciendo**

(b) **dicho**

(c) **di,** decid

(d) **digo, dices, dice,** decimos, decís, **dicen**

(e) **diga, digas, diga, digamos, digáis, digan**

(g) **diré, dirás, dirá, diremos, diréis, dirán**

(h) **dije, dijiste, dijo, dijimos, dijisteis, dijeron**

**§25 delinquir**

(d) **delinco,** delinques, delinque, delinquimos, delinquís, delinquen

(e) **delinca, delincas, delinca, delincamos, delincáis, delincan**

**§26 desosar:** like §61 but with **h** before **ue**

(c) **deshuesa,** desosad

(d) **deshueso, deshuesas, deshuesa,** desosamos, desosáis, **deshuesan**

(e) **deshuese, deshueses, deshuese,** desosemos, desoséis, **deshuesen**

**§27 dirigir**

(d) **dirijo,** diriges, dirige, dirigimos, dirigís, dirigen

(e) **dirija, dirijas, dirija, dirijamos, dirijáis, dirijan**

§28 **discernir**
(c) **discierne,** discernid
(d) **discierno, disciernes, discierne,** discernimos, discernís, **disciernen**
(e) **discierna, disciernas, discierna,** discernamos, discernáis, **disciernan**

§29 **distinguir**
(d) **distingo,** distingues, distingue, distinguimos, distinguís, distinguen
(e) **distinga, distingas, distinga, distingamos, distingáis, distingan**

§30 **dormir**
(a) **durmiendo**
(c) **duerme,** dormid
(d) **duermo, duermes, duerme,** dormimos, dormís, **duermen**
(e) **duerma, duermas, duerma, durmamos, durmáis, duerman**
(h) dormí, dormiste, **durmió,** dormimos, dormisteis, **durmieron**

§31 **empeller**
(a) **empellendo**
(h) empellí, empelliste, **empelló,** empellimos, empellisteis, **empelleron**

§32 **enraizar:** combination of §4 and §60
(c) **enraíza,** enraizad
(d) **enraízo, enraízas, enraíza,** enraizamos, enraizáis, **enraízan**
(e) **enraíce, enraíces, enraíce, enraicemos, enraicéis, enraícen**
(h) **enraicé,** enraizaste, enraizó, enraizamos, enraizasteis, enraizaron

§33 **erguir:** combination of §29 and §50 or §68
(a) **irguiendo**
(c) **irgue** or **yergue,** erguid
(d) **irgo, irgues, irgue,** / **yergo, yergues, yergue,** } erguimos, erguís, { **irguen** / **yerguen**
(e) **irga, irgas, irga,** / **yerga, yergas, yerga,** } **irgamos, irgáis,** { **irgan** / **yergan**
(h) erguí, erguiste, **irguió,** erguimos, erguisteis, **irguieron**

§34 **errar:** like §2 but with initial **ye** for **ie**
(c) **yerra,** errad
(d) **yerro, yerras, yerra,** erramos, erráis, **yerran**
(e) **yerre, yerres, yerre,** erremos, erréis, **yerren**

§35 **esforzar:** combination of §60 and §61
(c) **esfuerza,** esforzad
(d) **esfuerzo, esfuerzas, esfuerza,** esforzamos, esforzáis, **esfuerzan**
(e) **esfuerce, esfuerces, esfuerce, esforcemos, esforcéis, esfuercen**
(h) **esforcé,** esforzaste, esforzó, esforzamos, esforzasteis, esforzaron

§36 **esparcir**
(d) **esparzo,** esparces, esparce, esparcimos, esparcís, esparcen
(e) **esparza, esparzas, esparza, esparzamos, esparzáis, esparzan**

**§37 estar**
(c) **está**, estad
(d) **estoy, estás, está**, estamos, estáis, **están**
(e) **esté, estés, esté**, estemos, estéis, **estén**
(h) **estuve, estuviste, estuvo, estuvimos, estuvisteis, estuvieron**

**§38 haber**
(c) **hé**, habed
(d) **he, has, ha, hemos**, habéis, **han** (*v impers*) **hay**
(e) **haya, hayas, haya, hayamos, hayáis, hayan**
(g) **habré, habrás, habrá, habremos, habréis, habrán**
(h) **hube, hubiste, hubo, hubimos, hubisteis, hubieron**

**§39 hacer**
(b) **hecho**
(c) **haz**, haced
(d) **hago**, haces, hace, hacemos, hacéis, hacen
(e) **haga, hagas, haga, hagamos, hagáis, hagan**
(g) **haré, harás, hará, haremos, haréis, harán**
(h) **hice, hiciste, hizo, hicimos, hicisteis, hicieron**

**§40 inquirir**
(c) **inquiere**, inquirid
(d) **inquiero, inquieres, inquiere**, inquirimos, inquirís, **inquieren**
(e) **inquiera, inquieras, inquiera**, inquiramos, inquiráis, **inquieran**

**§41 ir**
(a) **yendo**
(c) **vé, vamos, id**
(d) **voy, vas, va, vamos, vais, van**
(e) **vaya, vayas, vaya, vayamos, vayáis, vayan**
(f) **iba, ibas, iba, íbamos, ibais, iban**
(h) **fui, fuiste, fue, fuimos, fuisteis, fueron**

**§42 jugar:** like §63 but with radical **u**
(c) **juega**, jugad
(d) **juego, juegas, juega**, jugamos, jugáis, **juegan**
(e) **juegue, juegues, juegue, juguemos, juguéis, jueguen**
(h) **jugué**, jugaste, jugó, jugamos, jugasteis, jugaron

**§43 leer**
(a) **leyendo**
(b) **leído**
(h) leí, **leíste, leyó, leímos, leísteis, leyeron**

**§44 ligar**
(e) **ligue, ligues, ligue, liguemos, liguéis, liguen**
(h) **ligué**, ligaste, ligó, ligamos, ligasteis, ligaron

**§45 lucir**
(d) **luzco**, luces, luce, lucimos, lucís, lucen
(e) **luzca, luzcas, luzca, luzcamos, luzcáis, luzcan**

**§46 mecer**
(d) **mezo**, meces, mece, mecemos, mecéis, mecen
(e) **meza, mezas, meza, mezamos, mezáis, mezan**

**§47 mover**

(c) **mueve**, moved
(d) **muevo, mueves, mueve**, movemos, movéis, **mueven**
(e) **mueva, muevas, mueva**, movamos, mováis, **muevan**

**§48 oír**

(a) **oyendo**
(b) **oído**
(c) **oye, oíd**
(d) **oigo, oyes, oye, oímos**, oís, **oyen**
(e) **oiga, oigas, oiga, oigamos, oigáis, oigan**
(h) oí, **oíste, oyó, oímos, oísteis, oyeron**

**§49 oler:** like §47 but with **h** before **ue**

(c) **huele**, oled
(d) **huelo, hueles, huele**, olemos, oléis, **huelen**
(e) **huela, huelas, huela**, olamos, oláis, **huelan**

**§50 pedir**

(a) **pidiendo**
(c) **pide**, pedid
(d) **pido, pides, pide**, pedimos, pedís, **piden**
(e) **pida, pidas, pida, pidamos, pidáis, pidan**
(h) pedí, pediste, **pidió**, pedimos, pedisteis, **pidieron**

**§51 perder**

(c) **pierde**, perded
(d) **pierdo, pierdes, pierde**, perdemos, perdéis, **pierden**
(e) **pierda, pierdas, pierda**, perdamos, perdáis, **pierdan**

**§52 placer**

(d) **plazco**, places, place, placemos, placéis, placen
(e) **plazca, plazcas, plazca, plazcamos, plazcáis, plazcan**
(h) plací, placiste, plació (or **plugo**), placimos, placisteis, placieron

**§53 poder**

(a) **pudiendo**
(c) (**puede**, poded)
(d) **puedo, puedes, puede**, podemos, podéis, **pueden**
(e) **pueda, puedas, pueda**, podamos, podáis, **puedan**
(g) **podré, podrás, podrá, podremos, podréis, podrán**
(h) **pude, pudiste, pudo, pudimos, pudisteis, pudieron**

**§54 poner**

(b) **puesto**
(c) **pon**, poned
(d) **pongo**, pones, pone, ponemos, ponéis, ponen
(e) **ponga, pongas, ponga, pongamos, pongáis, pongan**
(g) **pondré, pondrás, pondrá, pondremos, pondréis, pondrán**
(h) **puse, pusiste, puso, pusimos, pusisteis, pusieron**

**§55 querer**

(c) **quiere**, quered
(d) **quiero, quieres, quiere**, queremos, queréis, **quieren**
(e) **quiera, quieras, quiera**, queramos, queráis, **quieran**
(g) **querré, querrás, querrá, querremos, querréis, querrán**
(h) **quise, quisiste, quiso, quisimos, quisisteis, quisieron**

**§56 raer**
(a) **rayendo**
(b) **raído**
(d) **raigo** (or **rayo**), raes, rae, raemos, raéis, raen
(e) **raiga** (or **raya**), **raigas, raiga, raigamos, raigáis, raigan**
(h) raí, **raíste, rayó, raímos, raísteis, rayeron**

**§57 regir:** combination of **§27** and **§50**
(a) **rigiendo**
(c) **rige,** regid
(d) **rijo, riges, rige,** regimos, regís, **rigen**
(e) **rija, rijas, rija, rijamos, rijáis, rijan**
(h) regí, registe, **rigió,** regimos, registeis, **rigieron**

**§58 reír**
(a) **riendo**
(b) **reído**
(c) **ríe, reíd**
(d) **río, ríes, ríe, reímos,** reís, **ríen**
(e) **ría, rías, ría, riamos, riáis, rían**
(h) reí, **reíste, rió, reímos, reísteis, rieron**

**§59 reunir**
(c) **reúne,** reunid
(d) **reúno, reúnes, reúne,** reunimos, reunís, **reúnen**
(e) **reúna, reúnas, reúna,** reunamos, reunáis, **reúnan**

**§60 rezar**
(e) **rece, reces, rece, recemos, recéis, recen**
(h) **recé,** rezaste, rezó, rezamos, rezasteis, rezaron

**§61 rodar**
(c) **rueda,** rodad
(d) **ruedo, ruedas, rueda,** rodamos, rodáis, **ruedan**
(e) **ruede, ruedes, ruede,** rodemos, rodéis, **rueden**

**§62 roer**
(a) **royendo**
(b) **roído**
(d) roo (**roigo,** or **royo**), roes, roe, roemos, roéis, roen
(e) roa (**roiga,** or **roya**), roas, roa, roamos, roáis, roan
(h) roí, **roíste, royó, roímos, roísteis, royeron**

**§63 rogar:** combination of **§44** and **§61**
(c) **ruega,** rogad
(d) **ruego, ruegas, ruega,** rogamos, rogáis, **ruegan**
(e) **ruegue, ruegues, ruegue, roguemos, roguéis, rueguen**
(h) **rogué,** rogaste, rogó, rogamos, rogasteis, rogaron

**§64 saber**
(d) **sé,** sabes, sabe, sabemos, sabéis, saben
(e) **sepa, sepas, sepa, sepamos, sepáis, sepan**
(g) **sabré, sabrás, sabrá, sabremos, sabréis, sabrán**
(h) **supe, supiste, supo, supimos, supisteis, supieron**

**§65 salir**
(c) **sal,** salid
(d) **salgo,** sales, sale, salimos, salís, salen
(e) **salga, salgas, salga, salgamos, salgáis, salgan**
(g) **saldré, saldrás, saldrá, saldremos, saldréis, saldrán**

**§66 segar:** combination of §2 and §44
(c) **siega,** segad
(d) **siego, siegas, siega,** segamos, segáis, **siegan**
(e) **siegue, siegues, siegue, seguemos, seguéis, sieguen**
(h) **segué,** segaste, segó, segamos, segasteis, segaron

**§67 seguir:** combination of §29 and §50
(a) **siguiendo**
(c) **sigue,** seguid
(d) **sigo, sigues, sigue,** seguimos, seguís, **siguen**
(e) **siga, sigas, siga, sigamos, sigáis, sigan**
(h) seguí, seguiste, **siguió,** seguimos, seguisteis, **siguieron**

**§68 sentir**
(a) **sintiendo**
(c) **siente,** sentid
(d) **siento, sientes, siente,** sentimos, sentís, **sienten**
(e) **sienta, sientas, sienta, sintamos, sintáis, sientan**
(h) sentí, sentiste, **sintió,** sentimos, sentisteis, **sintieron**

**§69 ser**
(c) **sé,** sed
(d) **soy, eres, es, somos, sois, son**
(e) **sea, seas, sea, seamos, seáis, sean**
(f) **era, eras, era, éramos, erais, eran**
(h) **fui, fuiste, fue, fuimos, fuisteis, fueron**

**§70 tañer**
(a) **tañendo**
(h) tañí, tañiste, **tañó,** tañimos, tañisteis, **tañeron**

**§71 tener**
(c) **ten,** tened
(d) **tengo, tienes, tiene,** tenemos, tenéis, **tienen**
(e) **tenga, tengas, tenga, tengamos, tengáis, tengan**
(g) **tendré, tendrás, tendrá, tendremos, tendréis, tendrán**
(h) **tuve, tuviste, tuvo, tuvimos, tuvisteis, tuvieron**

**§72 teñir:** combination of §12 and §50
(a) **tiñendo**
(c) **tiñe,** teñid
(d) **tiño, tiñes, tiñe,** teñimos, teñís, **tiñen**
(e) **tiña, tiñas, tiña, tiñamos, tiñáis, tiñan**
(h) teñí, teñiste, **tiñó,** teñimos, teñisteis, **tiñeron**

**§73 tocar**
(e) **toque, toques, toque, toquemos, toquéis, toquen**
(h) **toqué,** tocaste, tocó, tocamos, tocasteis, tocaron

**§74 torcer:** combination of §47 and §78
(c) **tuerce,** torced
(d) **tuerzo, tuerces, tuerce,** torcemos, torcéis, **tuercen**
(e) **tuerza, tuerzas, tuerza, torzamos, torzáis, tuerzan**

**§75 traer**
(a) **trayendo**
(b) **traído**
(d) **traigo,** traes, trae, traemos, traéis, traen
(e) **traiga, traigas, traiga, traigamos, traigáis, traigan**
(h) **traje, trajiste, trajo, trajimos, trajisteis, trajeron**

§76 **valer**
(d) **valgo**, vales, vale, valemos, valéis, valen
(e) **valga, valgas, valga, valgamos, valgáis, valgan**
(g) **valdré, valdrás, valdrá, valdremos, valdréis, valdrán**

§77 **variar**
(c) **varía**, variad
(d) **varío, varías, varía**, variamos, variáis, **varían**
(e) **varíe, varíes, varíe**, variemos, variéis, **varíen**

§78 **vencer**
(d) **venzo**, vences, vence, vencemos, vencéis, vencen
(e) **venza, venzas, venza, venzamos, venzáis, venzan**

§79 **venir**
(a) **viniendo**
(c) **ven**, venid
(d) **vengo, vienes, viene**, venimos, venís, **vienen**
(e) **venga, vengas, venga, vengamos, vengáis, vengan**
(g) **vendré, vendrás, vendrá, vendremos, vendréis, vendrán**
(h) **vine, viniste, vino, vinimos, vinisteis, vinieron**

§80 **ver**
(b) **visto**
(d) **veo**, ves, ve, vemos, veis, ven
(e) **vea, veas, vea, veamos, veáis, vean**
(f) **veía, veías, veía, veíamos, veíais, veían**

§81 **volcar:** combination of §61 and §73
(c) **vuelca**, volcad
(d) **vuelco, vuelcas, vuelca**, volcamos, volcáis, **vuelcan**
(e) **vuelque, vuelques, vuelque, volquemos, volquéis, vuelquen**
(h) **volqué**, volcaste, volcó, volcamos, volcasteis, volcaron

§82 **yacer**
(c) **yaz** (or yace), yaced
(d) **yazco (yazgo**, or **yago)**, yaces, yace, yacemos, yacéis, yacen
(e) **yazca (yazga**, or **yaga)**, **yazcas, yazca, yazcamos, yazcáis, yazcan**

§83 The following verbs, some of which are included in the foregoing table, and their compounds have irregular past participles:

| | | | |
|---|---|---|---|
| **abrir** | **abierto** | **morir** | **muerto** |
| **cubrir** | **cubierto** | **poner** | **puesto** |
| **decir** | **dicho** | **proveer** | **provisto** |
| **escribir** | **escrito** | **pudrir** | **podrido** |
| **freír** | **frito** | **romper** | **roto** |
| **hacer** | **hecho** | **solver** | **suelto** |
| **imprimir** | **impreso** | **ver** | **visto** |
| | | **volver** | **vuelto** |

# PART TWO

# Inglés-Español

# La pronunciación del inglés

Los símbolos siguientes representan aproximadamente todos los sonidos del idioma inglés.

VOCALES

| SÍMBOLO | SONIDO | EJEMPLO |
|---|---|---|
| [æ] | Más cerrado que la **a** de **caro.** | **hat** [hæt] |
| [ɑ] | Como la **a** de **bajo.** | **father** ['fɑðər]<br>**proper** ['prɑpər] |
| [ɛ] | Como la **e** de **perro.** | **met** [mɛt] |
| [e] | Más cerrado que la **e** de **canté.** Suena como si fuese seguido de [ɪ]. | **fate** [fet]<br>**they** [ðe] |
| [ə] | Como la **e** de la palabra francesa **le.** | **heaven** ['hɛvən]<br>**pardon** ['pɑrdən] |
| [i] | Como la **i** de **nido.** | **she** [ʃi]<br>**machine** [mə'ʃin] |
| [ɪ] | Como la **i** de **tilde.** | **fit** [fɪt]<br>**beer** [bɪr] |
| [o] | Más cerrado que la **o** de **habló.** Suena como si fuese seguido de [ʊ]. | **nose** [noz]<br>**road** [rod] |
| [ɔ] | Menos cerrado que la **o** de **torre.** | **bought** [bɔt]<br>**law** [lɔ] |
| [ʌ] | Más o menos como **eu** en la palabra francesa **peur.** | **cup** [kʌp]<br>**come** [kʌm]<br>**mother** ['mʌðər] |
| [ʊ] | Menos cerrado que la **u** de **bulto.** | **pull** [pʊl]<br>**book** [bʊk]<br>**wolf** [wʊlf] |
| [u] | Como la **u** de **agudo.** | **rude** [rud]<br>**move** [muv]<br>**tomb** [tum] |

DIPTONGOS

| SÍMBOLO | SONIDO | EJEMPLO |
|---|---|---|
| [aɪ] | Como **ai** de **amáis.** | **night** [naɪt]<br>**eye** [aɪ] |
| [aʊ] | Como **au** de **causa.** | **found** [faʊnd]<br>**cow** [kaʊ] |
| [ɔɪ] | Como **oy** de **estoy.** | **voice** [vɔɪs]<br>**oil** [ɔɪl] |

CONSONANTES

| SÍMBOLO | SONIDO | EJEMPLO |
|---|---|---|
| [b] | Como la **b** de **hombre.** Sonido bilabial oclusivo sonoro. | **bed** [bɛd]<br>**robber** ['rɑbər] |
| [d] | Como la **d** de **conde.** Sonido dental oclusivo sonoro. | **dead** [dɛd]<br>**add** [æd] |
| [dʒ] | Como la **y** de **cónyuge.** Sonido palatal africado sonoro. | **gem** [dʒɛm]<br>**jail** [dʒel] |
| [ð] | Como la **d** de **nada.** Sonido interdental fricativo sonoro. | **this** [ðɪs]<br>**father** ['fɑðər] |
| [f] | Como la **f** de **fecha.** Sonido labiodental sordo. | **face** [fes]<br>**phone** [fon] |
| [g] | Como la **g** de **gato.** Sonido velar oclusivo sonoro. | **go** [go]<br>**get** [gɛt] |

| SÍMBOLO | SONIDO | EJEMPLO |
|---|---|---|
| [h] | Sonido más aspirado pero menos áspero que el sonido velar fricativo sordo de la **j** de **junto**. | **hot** [hɑt]<br>**alcohol** ['ælkə,hɔl] |
| [j] | Como la **y** de **cuyo**. Sonido palatal semiconsonantal sonoro. | **yes** [jɛs]<br>**unit** ['junɪt] |
| [k] | Como la **c** de **cama**. Sonido velar oclusivo sordo. | **cat** [kæt]<br>**chord** [kɔrd]<br>**kill** [kɪl] |
| [l] | Como la **l** de **lado**. Sonido alveolar fricativo lateral sonoro. | **late** [let]<br>**allow** [ə'laʊ] |
| [m] | Como la **m** de **madre**. Sonido bilabial nasal sonoro. | **more** [mor]<br>**command** [kə'mænd] |
| [n] | Como la **n** de **carne**. Sonido alveolar nasal sonoro. | **nest** [nɛst]<br>**manner** ['mænər] |
| [ŋ] | Como la **n** de **banco**. Sonido velar nasal sonoro. | **king** [kiŋ]<br>**conquer** ['kɑŋkər] |
| [p] | Como la **p** de **tapar**. Sonido bilabial oclusivo sordo. | **pen** [pɛn]<br>**cap** [kæp] |
| [r] | La **r** más común en muchas partes de Inglaterra y en la mayor parte de los Estados Unidos y el Canadá es un sonido semivocal que se articula con la punta de la lengua elevada más hacia el paladar duro que en la **r** fricativa española y aun doblada hacia atrás. Intervocálica y al final de sílaba, es muy débil y casi no se puede oír. | **run** [rʌn]<br>**far** [fɑr]<br>**art** [ɑrt]<br>**carry** ['kæri] |
| | La **r**, precedida de los sonidos [ʌ] o [ə], da colorido propio a estos sonidos y desaparece completamente como sonido consonantal. | **burn** [bʌrn]<br>**learn** [lʌrn]<br>**weather** ['wɛðər] |
| [s] | Como la **s** de **clase**. Sonido alveolar fricativo sordo. | **send** [send]<br>**cellar** ['sɛlər] |
| [ʃ] | Como **ch** de la palabra francesa **chose**. Sonido palatal fricativo sordo. | **shall** [ʃæl]<br>**machine** [mə'ʃin]<br>**nation** ['neʃən] |
| [t] | Como la **t** de **arte**. Sonido dental oclusivo sordo. | **ten** [tɛn]<br>**dropped** [drɑpt] |
| [tʃ] | Como la **ch** de **mucho**. Sonido palatal africado sordo. | **child** [tʃaɪld]<br>**much** [mʌtʃ]<br>**nature** ['netʃər] |
| [θ] | Como la **z** de **zapato** en la pronunciación de Castilla. Sonido interdental fricativo sordo. | **think** [θɪŋk]<br>**truth** [truθ] |
| [v] | Como la **v** de la palabra francesa **avant**. Sonido labiodental fricativo sonoro. | **vest** [vɛst]<br>**over** ['ovər]<br>**of** [ɑv] |
| [w] | Como la **u** de **hueso**. Sonido labiovelar fricativo sonoro. | **work** [wʌrk]<br>**tweed** [twid]<br>**queen** [kwin] |
| [z] | Como la **s** de **mismo**. Sonido alveolar fricativo sonoro. | **zeal** [zil]<br>**busy** ['bɪzi]<br>**his** [hɪz] |
| [ʒ] | Como la **j** de la palabra francesa **jardin**. Sonido palatal fricativo sonoro. | **azure** ['eʒər]<br>**measure** ['mɛʒər] |

# INGLÉS—ESPAÑOL

## A

**A, a** [e] primera letra del alfabeto inglés
**a** [e] *art indef* un
**aback** [ə'bæk] *adv* atrás; **to be taken aback** quedar desconcertado; **to take aback** desconcertar
**abaft** [ə'bæft] o [ə'bɑft] *adv* a popa, en popa; *prep* detrás de
**abandon** [ə'bændən] *s* abandono ‖ *tr* abandonar
**abase** [ə'bes] *tr* degradar, humillar
**abash** [ə'bæʃ] *tr* avergonzar
**abate** [ə'bet] *tr* disminuir, reducir; deducir ‖ *intr* disminuir, moderarse
**aba·tis** ['æbətɪs] *s* (*pl* **-tis**) abatida
**abattoir** ['æbə,twɑr] *s* matadero
**abba·cy** ['æbəsi] *s* (*pl* **-cies**) abadía
**abbess** ['æbɪs] *s* abadesa
**abbey** ['æbi] *s* abadía
**abbot** ['æbət] *s* abad *m*
**abbreviate** [ə'brivɪ,et] *tr* abreviar
**abbreviation** [ə,brivɪ'eʃən] *s* (*shortening*) abreviación; (*shortened form*) abreviatura
**A B C** [,e,bi'si] *s* abecé *m;* **A B C's** abecedario
**abdicate** ['æbdɪ,ket] *tr & intr* abdicar
**abdomen** ['æbdəmən] o [æb'domən] *s* abdomen *m*
**abduct** [æb'dʌkt] *tr* raptar, secuestrar
**abed** [ə'bɛd] *adv* en cama, acostado
**abet** [ə'bɛt] *v* (*pret & pp* **abetted;** *ger* **abetting**) *tr* incitar (*a una persona, esp. al mal*); fomentar (*el crimen*)
**abeyance** [ə'be·əns] *s* suspensión; **in abeyance** en suspenso
**ab·hor** [æb'hɔr] *v* (*pret & pp* **-horred;** *ger* **-horring**) *tr* aborrecer, detestar
**abhorrent** [æb'hɑrənt] o [æb'hɔrənt] *adj* aborrecible, detestable
**abide** [ə'baɪd] *v* (*pret & pp* **abode** o **abided**) *tr* esperar; tolerar ‖ *intr* permanecer; **to abide by** cumplir con; atenerse a
**abili·ty** [ə'bɪlɪti] *s* (*pl* **-ties**) habilidad, capacidad; talento
**abject** [æb'dʒɛkt] *adj* abyecto, servil
**ablative** ['æblətɪv] *s* ablativo
**ablaut** ['æblaʊt] *s* apofonía
**ablaze** [ə'blez] *adj* brillante; ardiente; encolerizado ‖ *adv* en llamas, ardiendo
**able** ['ebəl] *adj* hábil, capaz; **to be able to** poder
**able-bodied** ['ebəl'bɑdid] *adj* sano; fornido; experto
**abloom** [ə'blum] *adj* floreciente ‖ *adv* en flor
**abnormal** [æb'nɔrməl] *adj* anormal
**aboard** [ə'bord] *adv* a bordo; al bordo; **all aboard!** ¡señores viajeros al tren!; **to go aboard** ir a bordo; **to take aboard** embarcar ‖ *prep* a bordo de; (*a train*) en
**abode** [ə'bod] *s* domicilio, residencia
**abolish** [ə'bɑlɪʃ] *tr* eliminar, suprimir
**A-bomb** ['e,bɑm] *s* bomba atómica
**abomination** [ə,bɑmɪ'neʃən] *s* abominación
**aborigines** [,æbə'rɪdʒɪ,niz] *spl* aborígenes *mf*
**abort** [ə'bɔrt] *tr & intr* abortar
**abortion** [ə'bɔrʃən] *s* aborto
**abound** [ə'baʊnd] *intr* abundar
**about** [ə'baʊt] *adv* casi; aquí; **to be about to** estar a punto de, estar para ‖ *prep* acerca de; con respecto a; cerca de; hacia, a eso de; **to be about** tratar de
**above** [ə'bʌv] *adj* antedicho ‖ *adv* arriba, encima ‖ *prep* sobre, encima de, más alto que; superior a; **above all** sobre todo
**above-mentioned** [ə'bʌv'mɛnʃənd] *adj* sobredicho, antedicho, susodicho
**abrasive** [ə'bresɪv] o [ə'breziv] *adj & s* abrasivo
**abreast** [ə'brɛst] *adj & adv* de frente; **to be abreast of** correr parejas con; estar al corriente de
**abridge** [ə'brɪdʒ] *tr* abreviar; disminuir; condensar, resumir
**abroad** [ə'brɔd] *adv* al extranjero; en el extranjero; fuera de casa
**abrupt** [ə'brʌpt] *adj* brusco; repentino; áspero; abrupto, escarpado
**abscess** ['æbsɛs] *s* absceso
**abscond** [æb'skɑnd] *intr* irse a hurtadillas; **to abscond with** alzarse con
**absence** ['æbsəns] *s* ausencia
**absent** ['æbsənt] *adj* ausente ‖ [æb'sɛnt] *tr*—**to absent oneself** ausentarse
**absentee** [,æbsən'ti] *s* ausente *mf*
**absent-minded** ['æbsənt'maɪndɪd] *adj* distraído, absorto
**absinth** ['æbsɪnθ] *s* (*plant*) absintio, ajenjo; (*drink*) absenta, ajenjo
**absolute** ['æbsə,lut] *adj & s* absoluto
**absolutely** ['æbsə,lutli] *adv* absolutamente ‖ [,æbsə'lutli] *adv* (coll) positivamente
**absolve** [æb'sɑlv] *tr* absolver
**absorb** [æb'sɔrb] *tr* absorber; **to be o become absorbed** ensimismarse
**absorbent** [æb'sɔrbənt] *adj* absorbente; (*cotton*) hidrófilo
**absorbing** [æb'sɔrbɪŋ] *adj* absorbente
**abstain** [æb'sten] *intr* abstenerse
**abstemious** [æb'stimɪ·əs] *adj* abstemio, sobrio
**abstinent** ['æbstɪnənt] *adj* abstinente

**abstract** ['æbstrækt] *adj* abstracto || *s* resumen *m*, sumario, extracto || *tr* resumir, compendiar, extractar || [æb'strækt] *tr* abstraer; quitar
**abstruse** [æb'strus] *adj* abstruso
**absurd** [æb'sʌrd] o [æb'zʌrd] *adj* absurdo
**absurdi•ty** [æb'sʌrdɪti] o [æb'zʌrdɪti] *s* (*pl* **-ties**) absurdidad, absurdo
**abundant** [ə'bʌndənt] *adj* abundante
**abuse** [ə'bjus] *s* maltrato; injuria, insulto; (*bad practice; injustice*) abuso || [ə'bjuz] *tr* maltratar; injuriar, insultar; (*to misapply, take unfair advantage of*) abusar de
**abusive** [ə'bjusɪv] *adj* injurioso, insultante; abusivo
**abut** [ə'bʌt] *v* (*pret & pp* **abutted**; *ger* **abutting**) *intr*—**to abut on** confinar con, terminar en
**abutment** [ə'bʌtmənt] *s* confinamiento; estribo, contrafuerte *m*
**abyss** [ə'bɪs] *s* abismo
**academic** [,ækə'dɛmɪk] *adj* académico
**academic costume** *s* toga, traje *m* de catedrático
**academic freedom** *s* libertad de cátedra, libertad de enseñanza
**academician** [ə,kædə'mɪʃən] *s* académico
**academic subjects** *spl* materias no profesionales
**academic year** *s* año escolar
**acade•my** [ə'kædəmi] *s* (*pl* **-mies**) academia
**accede** [æk'sid] *intr* acceder; **to accede to** acceder a, condescender a; (*e.g., the throne*) ascender a, subir a
**accelerate** [æk'sɛlə,ret] *tr* acelerar || *intr* acelerarse
**accelerator** [æk'sɛlə,retər] *s* acelerador *m*
**accent** ['æksent] *s* acento || ['æksent] o [æk'sent] *tr* acentuar
**accent mark** *s* acento ortográfico
**accentuate** [æk'sɛntʃʊ,et] *tr* acentuar
**accept** [æk'sɛpt] *tr* aceptar
**acceptable** [æk'sɛptəbəl] *adj* aceptable
**acceptance** [æk'sɛptəns] *s* aceptación
**access** ['æksɛs] *s* acceso
**accessible** [æk'sɛsɪbəl] *adj* accesible
**accession** [æk'sɛʃən] *s* accesión; (*to a dignity*) ascenso; (*of books in a library*) adquisición
**accesso•ry** [æk'sɛsəri] *adj* accesorio || *s* (*pl* **-ries**) accesorio; (*to a crime*) cómplice *mf*
**accident** ['æksɪdənt] *s* accidente *m*; **by accident** por casualidad
**accidental** [,æksɪ'dɛntəl] *adj* accidental
**acclaim** [ə'klem] *s* aclamación || *tr & intr* aclamar
**acclimate** ['æklɪ,met] *tr* aclimatar || *intr* aclimatarse
**accolade** [,ækə'led] *s* acolada; elogio, premio
**accommodate** [ə'kɑmə,det] *tr* acomodar; alojar
**accommodating** [ə'kɑmə,detɪŋ] *adj* acomodadizo, servicial
**accommodation** [ə,kɑmə'deʃən] *s* acomodación; **accommodations** facilidades, comodidades; (*in a train*) localidad; (*in a hotel*) alojamiento
**accommodation train** *s* tren *m* omnibus
**accompaniment** [ə'kʌmpənɪmənt] *s* acompañamiento
**accompanist** [ə'kʌmpənɪst] *s* acompañante *m*
**accompa•ny** [ə'kʌmpəni] *v* (*pret & pp* **-nied**) *tr* acompañar
**accomplice** [ə'kɑmplɪs] *s* cómplice *mf*, codelincuente *mf*
**accomplish** [ə'kɑmplɪʃ] *tr* realizar, llevar a cabo
**accomplished** [ə'kɑmplɪʃt] *adj* realizado; culto, talentoso; (*fact*) consumado
**accomplishment** [ə'kɑmplɪʃmənt] *s* realización; **accomplishments** prendas, talentos
**accord** [ə'kɔrd] *s* acuerdo; **in accord with** de acuerdo con: **of one's own accord** de buen grado, voluntariamente; **with one accord** de común acuerdo || *tr* conceder, otorgar || *intr* concordar, avenirse
**accordance** [ə'kɔrdəns] *s* conformidad; **in accordance with** de acuerdo con
**according** [ə'kɔrdɪŋ] *adj* — **according as** según que; **according to** según
**accordingly** [ə'kɔrdɪŋli] *adv* en conformidad; por consiguiente
**accordion** [ə'kɔrdɪ•ən] *s* acordeón *m*
**accost** [ə'kɔst] o [ə'kɑst] *tr* abordar, acercarse a
**accouchement** [ə'kuʃmənt] *s* alumbramiento, parto
**account** [ə'kaunt] *s* informe *m*, relato; cuenta; estado de cuenta; importancia; **by all accounts** según el decir general; **of no account** de poca importancia; **on account of** a causa de; **to bring to account** pedir cuentas a; **to buy on account** comprar a plazos; **to turn to account** sacar provecho de, hacer valer || *intr*—**to account for** explicar; responder de
**accountable** [ə'kauntəbəl] *adj* responsable; explicable
**accountant** [ə'kauntənt] *s* contador *m*, contable *m*
**accounting** [ə'kauntɪŋ] *s* arreglo de cuentas; contabilidad
**accouterments** [ə'kutərmənts] *spl* equipo, avíos
**accredit** [ə'krɛdɪt] *tr* acreditar
**accrue** [ə'kru] *intr* acumularse; resultar
**acct.** *abbr* **account**
**accumulate** [ə'kjumjə,let] *tr* acumular || *intr* acumularse
**accuracy** ['ækjərəsi] *s* exactitud, precisión
**accurate** ['ækjərɪt] *adj* exacto
**accusation** [,ækjə'zeʃən] *s* acusación
**accusative** [ə'kjuzətɪv] *adj & s* acusativo
**accuse** [ə'kjuz] *tr* acusar
**accustom** [ə'kʌstəm] *tr* acostumbrar
**ace** [es] *s* as *m*; **to be within an ace of** estar a dos dedos de

**acetate** ['æsɪ,tet] *s* acetato
**acetic acid** [ə'sitɪk] *s* ácido acético
**aceti•fy** [ə'sɛtɪ,faɪ] *v* (*pret & pp* **-fied**) *tr* acetificar || *intr* acetificarse
**acetone** ['æsɪ,ton] *s* acetona
**acetylene** [ə'sɛtɪ,lin] *s* acetileno
**acetylene torch** *s* soplete oxiacetilénico
**ache** [ek] *s* achaque *m*, dolor *m* || *intr* doler
**achieve** [ə'tʃiv] *tr* llevar a cabo; alcanzar, ganar, lograr
**achievement** [ə'tʃivmənt] *s* realización; (*feat*) hazaña
**Achilles' heel** [ə'kɪliz] *s* talón *m* de Aquiles
**acid** ['æsɪd] *adj* ácido; agrio, mordaz || *s* ácido
**acidi•fy** [ə'sɪdɪ,faɪ] *v* (*pret & pp* **-fied**) *tr* acidificar || *intr* acidificarse
**acidi•ty** [ə'sɪdɪti] *s* (*pl* **-ties**) acidez *f*
**acid test** *s* prueba decisiva
**ack-ack** ['æk'æk] *s* (slang) artillería antiaérea; (slang) fuego antiaéreo
**acknowledge** [æk'nɑlɪdʒ] *tr* reconocer; acusar (*recibo de una carta*); agradecer (*p. ej., un favor*)
**acknowledgment** [æk'nɑlɪdʒmənt] *s* reconocimiento; (*of receipt of a letter*) acuse *m*; (*of a favor*) agradecimiento
**acme** ['ækmi] *s* auge *m*, colmo
**acolyte** ['ækə,laɪt] *s* acólito
**acorn** ['ekɔrn] o ['ekərn] *s* bellota
**acoustic** [ə'kustɪk] *adj* acústico || **acoustics** *ssg* acústica
**acquaint** [ə'kwent] *tr* informar, poner al corriente; **to be acquainted** conocerse; **to be acquainted with** conocer; estar al corriente de
**acquaintance** [ə'kwentəns] *s* conocimiento; (*person*) conocido
**acquiesce** [,ækwɪ'ɛs] *intr* consentir, condescender, asentir
**acquiescence** [,ækwɪ'ɛsəns] *s* consentimiento, condescendencia, aquiescencia
**acquire** [ə'kwaɪr] *tr* adquirir
**acquisition** [,ækwɪ'zɪʃən] *s* adquisición
**acquit** [ə'kwɪt] *v* (*pret & pp* **acquitted**; *ger* **acquitting**) *tr* absolver, exculpar; **to acquit oneself** conducirse, portarse
**acquittal** [ə'kwɪtəl] *s* absolución, exculpación
**acrid** ['ækrɪd] *adj* acre, acrimonioso
**acrobat** ['ækrə,bæt] *s* acróbata *mf*
**acrobatic** [,ækrə'bætɪk] *adj* acrobático || **acrobatics** *ssg* (*profession*) acrobatismo; *spl* (*stunts*) acrobacia
**acronym** ['ækrənɪm] *s* acrónimo
**acropolis** [ə'krɑpəlɪs] *s* acrópolis *f*
**across** [ə'krɔs] o [ə'krɑs] *prep* al través de; al otro lado de; **to come across** encontrarse con; **to go across** atravesar
**across'-the-board'** *adj* comprensivo, general
**acrostic** [ə'krɔstɪk] o [ə'krɑstɪk] *s* acróstico
**act** [ækt] *s* acto; (law) decreto; **in the act** en flagrante || *tr* representar; desempeñar (*un papel*); **to act the fool** hacer el bufón; **to act the part of** hacer o desempeñar el papel de || *intr* actuar; funcionar, obrar; conducirse; **to act as if** hacer como que; **to act for** representar; **to act up** travesear; **to act up to** hacer fiestas a
**acting** ['æktɪŋ] *adj* interino || *s* actuación
**action** ['ækʃən] *s* acción; **to take action** tomar medidas
**activate** ['æktɪ,vet] *tr* activar
**active** ['æktɪv] *adj* activo
**activi•ty** [æk'tɪvɪti] *s* (*pl* **-ties**) actividad
**act of God** *s* fuerza mayor
**actor** ['æktər] *s* actor *m*
**actress** ['æktrɪs] *s* actriz *f*
**actual** ['æktʃʊ•əl] *adj* real, efectivo
**actually** ['æktʃʊ•əli] *adv* en realidad
**actuar•y** ['æktʃʊ,ɛri] *s* (*pl* **-ies**) actuario (de seguros)
**actuate** ['æktʃʊ,et] *tr* actuar; estimular, mover
**acuity** [ə'kju•ɪti] *s* agudeza
**acumen** [ə'kjumən] *s* cacumen *m*, perspicacia
**acute** [ə'kjut] *adj* agudo
**A.D.** *abbr* **anno Domini** (**Lat**) **in the year of our Lord**
**ad** [æd] *s* (coll) anuncio
**adage** ['ædɪdʒ] *s* adagio, refrán *m*
**Adam** ['ædəm] *s* Adán *m*; **the old Adam** la inclinación al pecado
**adamant** ['ædəmənt] *adj* firme, inexorable
**Adam's apple** *s* nuez *f*
**adapt** [ə'dæpt] *tr* adaptar; refundir (*un drama*)
**adaptation** [,ædæp'teʃən] *s* adaptación; (*of a play*) refundición
**add** [æd] *tr* agregar, añadir; sumar || *intr* sumar; **to add up to** subir a; (coll) querer decir
**added line** *s* (mus) línea suplementaria
**adder** ['ædər] *s* víbora; serpiente *f*
**addict** ['ædɪkt] *s* enviciado; adicto, partidario || [ə'dɪkt] *tr* enviciar; entregar; **to addict oneself to** enviciarse con o en; entregarse a
**addiction** [ə'dɪkʃən] *s* enviciamiento; adhesividad
**adding machine** *s* sumadora, máquina de sumar
**addition** [ə'dɪʃən] *s* adición; **in addition to** además de
**additive** ['ædɪtɪv] *adj & s* aditivo
**address** [ə'drɛs] o ['ædrɛs] *s* dirección; consignación || [ə'drɛs] *s* alocución, discurso; **to deliver an address** hacer uso de la palabra || *tr* dirigirse a; dirigir (*p. ej., una alocución, una carta*); consignar
**addressee** [,ædrɛ'si] *s* destinatario; (com) consignatario
**addressing machine** *s* máquina para dirigir sobres
**adduce** [ə'djus] o [ə'dus] *tr* aducir
**adenoids** ['ædə,nɔɪdz] *spl* vegetaciones adenoides
**adept** [ə'dɛpt) *adj & s* experto, perito
**adequate** ['ædɪkwɪt] *adj* suficiente

**adhere** [æd'hɪr] *intr* adherir, adherirse; conformarse
**adherence** [æd'hɪrəns] *s* adhesión
**adherent** [æd'hɪrənt] *adj & s* adherente *m*
**adhesion** [æd'hiʒən] *s* (*sticking*) adherencia; (*support, loyalty*) adhesión; (pathol) adherencia; (phys) adherencia o adhesión
**adhesive** [æd'hisɪv] o [æd'hizɪv] *adj* adhesivo
**adhesive tape** *s* tafetán adhesivo
**adieu** [ə'dju] o [ə'du] *interj* ¡adiós! ‖ *s* (*pl* **adieus** o **adieux**) adiós *m;* **to bid adieu to** despedirse de
**adjacent** [ə'dʒesənt] *adj* adyacente
**adjective** ['ædʒɪktɪv] *adj & s* adjetivo
**adjoin** [ə'dʒɔɪn] *tr* lindar con ‖ *intr* colindar
**adjoining** [ə'dʒɔɪnɪŋ] *adj* colindante, contiguo
**adjourn** [ə'dʒʌrn] *tr* prorrogar, suspender ‖ *intr* prorrogarse, suspenderse; (coll) ir
**adjournment** [ə'dʒʌrnmənt] *s* prorrogación, suspensión
**adjust** [ə'dʒʌst] *tr* ajustar, arreglar; corregir, verificar; (ins) liquidar
**adjustable** [ə'dʒʌstəbəl] *adj* ajustable, arreglable
**adjustment** [ə'dʒʌstmənt] *s* ajuste *m,* arreglo; (ins) liquidación de la avería
**adjutant** ['ædʒətənt] *s* ayudante *m*
**ad·lib** [,æd'lɪb] *v* (*pret & pp* **-libbed;** *ger* **-libbing**) *tr & intr* improvisar
**Adm.** *abbr* **Admiral**
**administer** [æd'mɪnɪstər] *tr* administrar; **to administer an oath** tomar juramento ‖ *intr* — **to administer to** cuidar de
**administrator** [æd'mɪnɪs,tretər] *s* administrador *m*
**admiral** ['ædmɪrəl] *s* almirante *m;* buque *m* almirante
**admiral·ty** ['ædmɪrəlti] *s* (*pl.* **-ties**) almirantazgo
**admire** [æd'maɪr] *tr* admirar
**admirer** [æd'maɪrər] *s* admirador *m;* enamorado
**admissible** [æd'mɪsɪbəl] *adj* admisible
**admission** [æd'mɪʃən] *s* admisión; (*in a school*) ingreso; precio de entrada; **to gain admission** lograr entrar
**ad·mit** [æd'mɪt] *v* (*pret & pp* **-mitted;** *ger* **-mitting**) *tr* admitir ‖ *intr* dar entrada; **to admit of** admitir, permitir
**admittance** [æd'mɪtəns] *s* admisión; derecho de entrar; **no admittance** acceso prohibido, se prohibe la entrada
**admonish** [æd'mɑnɪʃ] *tr* amonestar
**ado** [ə'du] *s* bulla, excitación
**adobe** [ə'dobi] *s* adobe *m;* casa de adobe
**adolescence** [,ædə'lɛsəns] *s* adolescencia
**adolescent** [,ædə'lesənt] *adj & s* adolescente *mf*
**adopt** [ə'dɑpt] *tr* adoptar
**adoption** [ə'dɑpʃən] *s* adopción
**adorable** [ə'dorəbəl] *adj* adorable
**adore** [ə'dor] *tr* adorar
**adorn** [ə'dɔrn] *tr* adornar
**adornment** [ə'dɔrnmənt] *s* adorno
**adrenal gland** [æd'rinəl] *s* glándula suprarrenal
**Adriatic** [,edrɪ'ætɪk] o [,ædrɪ'ætɪk] *adj & s* Adriático
**adrift** [ə'drɪft] *adj & adv* al garete, a la deriva
**adroit** [ə'drɔɪt] *adj* diestro
**adult** [ə'dʌlt] o ['ædʌlt] *adj & s* adulto
**adulterate** [ə'dʌltə,ret] *tr* adulterar
**adulterer** [ə'dʌltərər] *s* adúltero
**adulteress** [ə'dʌltərɪs] *s* adúltera
**adulter·y** [ə'dʌltəri] *s* (*pl* **-ies**) adulterio
**advance** [æd'væns] o [æd'vɑns] *adj* adelantado; anticipado ‖ *s* adelanto, avance *m;* aumento, subida; **advances** propuestas; requerimiento amoroso; propuesta indecente; préstamo; **in advance** de antemano, por anticipado ‖ *tr* adelantar ‖ *intr* adelantar; adelantarse
**advanced** [æd'vænst] o [æd'vɑnst] *adj* avanzado; **advanced in years** avanzado de edad, entrado en años
**advanced standing** *s* traspaso de matrículas, traspaso de crédito académico
**advanced studies** *spl* altos estudios
**advancement** [æd'vænsmənt] o [æd'vɑnsmənt] *s* adelanto, avance *m;* subida; promoción
**advance publicity** *s* publicidad de lanzamiento
**advantage** [æd'væntɪdʒ] o [æd'vɑntɪdʒ] *s* ventaja; **to take advantage of** aprovecharse de; abusar de, engañar
**advantageous** [,ædvən'tedʒəs] *adj* ventajoso
**advent** ['ædvɛnt] *s* advenimiento ‖ **Advent** *s* (eccl) Adviento
**adventure** [æd'vɛntʃər] *s* aventura ‖ *tr* aventurar ‖ *intr* aventurarse
**adventurer** [æd'vɛntʃərər] *s* aventurero
**adventuresome** [æd'vɛntʃərsəm] *adj* aventurero
**adventuress** [æd'vɛntʃərɪs] *s* aventurera
**adventurous** [æd'vɛntʃərəs] *adj* aventurero
**adverb** ['ædvʌrb] *s* adverbio
**adversar·y** ['ædvər,sɛri] *s* (*pl* **-ies**) adversario
**adversi·ty** [æd'vʌrsɪti] *s* (*pl* **-ties**) adversidad
**advertise** ['ædvər,taiz] o [,ædvər'taɪz] *tr & intr* anunciar
**advertisement** [,ædvər'taɪzmənt] o [æd'vʌrtɪzmənt] *s* anuncio
**advertiser** ['ædvər,taɪzər] o [,ædvər'taɪzər] *s* anunciante *mf*
**advertising** ['ædvər,taɪzɪŋ] *s* propaganda, publicidad, anuncios
**advertising agency** *s* empresa anunciadora
**advertising campaign** *s* campaña de publicidad
**advertising man** *s* empresario de publicidad
**advertising manager** *s* gerente *m* de publicidad

**advice** [æd'vaɪs] *s* consejo; aviso, noticia; **a piece of advice** un consejo
**advisable** [æd'vaɪzəbəl] *adj* aconsejable
**advise** [æd'vaɪz] *tr* aconsejar, asesorar; advertir, avisar
**advisement** [æd'vaɪzmənt] *s* consideración; **to take under advisement** someter a consideración
**advisory** [æd'vaɪʒəri] *adj* consultivo
**advocate** ['ædvə,ket] *s* defensor *m;* abogado || *tr* abogar por
**Aegean Sea** [ɪ'dʒi·ən] *s* Archipiélago; (*of the ancients*) mar Egeo
**aegis** ['idʒɪs] *s* égida
**aerate** ['ɛret] o ['e·ə,ret] *tr* airear
**aerial** ['ɛrɪ·əl] *adj* aéreo || *s* antena
**aerialist** ['ɛrɪ·əlɪst] *s* volatinero
**aerodrome** ['ɛrə,drom] *s* aeródromo
**aerodynamic** [,erodaɪ'næmɪk] *adj* aerodinámico || **aerodynamics** *ssg* aerodinámica
**aeronaut** ['ɛrə,nɔt] *s* aeronauta *mf*
**aeronautic** [,ɛrə'nɔtɪk] *adj* aeronáutico || **aeronautics** *ssg* aeronáutica
**aerosol** ['ɛrə,sol] *s* aerosol *m*
**aerospace** ['ɛro,spes] *adj* aeroespacial
**aesthete** ['ɛsθit] *s* esteta *mf*
**aesthetic** [ɛs'θɛtɪk] *adj* estético || **aesthetics** *ssg* estética
**afar** [ə'fɑr] *adv* lejos
**affable** ['æfəbəl] *adj* afable
**affair** [ə'fɛr] *s* asunto, negocio; lance *m;* amorío; encuentro, combate *m;* **affairs** negocios
**affect** [ə'fɛkt] *tr* influir en; impresionar, enternecer; (*to assume; to pretend*) afectar; aficionarse a
**affectation** [,æfɛk'teʃən] *s* afectación
**affected** [ə'fɛktɪd] *adj* afectado
**affection** [ə'fɛkʃən] *s* afecto, cariño, afección; (pathol) afección
**affectionate** [ə'fɛkʃənɪt] *adj* afectuoso, cariñoso
**affidavit** [,æfɪ'devɪt] *s* declaración jurada, acta notarial
**affiliate** [ə'fɪlɪ,et] *adj* afiliado || *s* afiliado; filial *f* || *tr* afiliar || *intr* afiliarse
**affini·ty** [ə'fɪnɪti] *s* (*pl* **-ties**) afinidad
**affirm** [ə'fʌrm] *tr & intr* afirmar
**affirmative** [ə'fʌrmətɪv] *adj* afirmativo || *s* afirmativa
**affix** ['æfɪks] *s* añadidura; (gram) afijo || [ə'fɪks] *tr* añadir; atribuir (*p.ej., culpa*); poner (*una firma, sello, etc.*)
**afflict** [ə'flɪkt] *tr* afligir; **to be afflicted with** sufrir de, adolecer de
**affliction** [ə'flɪkʃən] *s* aflicción, desgracia; achaque *m*
**affluence** ['æflu·əns] *s* (*abundance*) afluencia; (*wealth*) opulencia
**afford** [ə'fɔrd] *tr* proporcionar; **to be able to afford (to)** poder darse el lujo de, poder permitirse
**affray** [ə'fre] *s* pendencia, riña
**affront** [ə'frʌnt] *s* afrenta || *tr* afrentar
**Afghan** ['æfgən] o ['æfgæn] *adj & s* afgano
**Afghanistan** [æf'gænɪ,stæn] *s* el Afganistán
**afire** [ə'faɪr] *adj & adv* ardiendo
**aflame** [ə'flem] *adj & adv* en llamas
**afloat** [ə'flot] *adj & adv* a flote; a bordo; inundado; sin rumbo; (*rumor*) en circulación
**afoot** [ə'fʊt] *adj & adv* a pie; en marcha
**afoul** [ə'faul] *adj & adv* enredado; en colisión; **to run afoul of** enredarse con
**afraid** [ə'fred] *adj* asustado; **to be afraid** tener miedo
**Africa** ['æfrɪkə] *s* África
**African** ['æfrɪkən] *adj & s* africano
**aft** [æft] o [ɑft] *adj & adv* en popa
**after** ['æftər] o ['ɑftər] *adj* siguiente || *adv* después || *prep* después de; según; **after all** al fin y al cabo || *conj* después de que
**af'ter-din'ner speaker** *s* orador *m* de sobremesa
**after-dinner speech** *s* discurso de sobremesa
**af'ter·hours'** *adv* después del trabajo
**af'ter·life'** *s* vida venidera; resto de la vida
**aftermath** ['æftər,mæθ] o ['ɑftər,mæθ] *s* segunda siega; consecuencias, consecuencias desastrosas
**af'ter·noon'** *s* tarde *f*
**af'ter·taste'** *s* dejo, gustillo, resabio
**af'ter·thought'** *s* idea tardía, expediente tardío
**afterward** ['æftərwərd] o ['ɑftərwərd] *adv* después, luego
**af'ter·while'** *adv* dentro de poco
**again** [ə'gen] *adv* otra vez, de nuevo; además; **to** + *inf* + **again** volver a + *inf,* p.ej., **he will come again** volverá a venir
**against** [ə'genst] *prep* contra; cerca de; en contraste con; por; para
**agape** [ə'gep] *adj* abierto de par en par || *adv* con la boca abierta
**age** [edʒ] *s* edad; (*old age*) vejez *f;* (*one hundred years; a long time*) siglo; edad mental; **of age** mayor de edad; **to come of age** alcanzar su mayoría de edad, llegar a mayor edad; **under age** menor de edad || *tr* envejecer || *intr* envejecer, envejecerse
**aged** [edʒd] *adj* de la edad de || ['edʒɪd] *adj* anciano, viejo
**ageless** ['edʒlɪs] *adj* eternamente joven
**agen·cy** ['edʒənsi] *s* (*pl* **-cies**) agencia; mediación
**agenda** [ə'dʒɛndə] *s* agenda, temario
**agent** ['edʒənt] *s* agente *m*
**Age of Enlightenment** *s* siglo de las luces
**agglomeration** [ə,glɑmə'reʃən] *s* aglomeración
**aggrandizement** [ə'grændɪzmənt] *s* engrandecimiento
**aggravate** ['ægrə,vet] *tr* agravar; (coll) exasperar, irritar
**aggregate** ['ægrɪ,get] *adj & s* agregado || *tr* agregar, juntar; ascender a
**aggression** [ə'grɛʃən] *s* agresión

**aggressive** [ə'gresɪv] *adj* agresivo
**aggressor** [ə'gresər] *s* agresor *m*
**aghast** [ə'gæst] o [ə'gɑst] *adj* horrorizado
**agile** ['ædʒɪl] *adj* ágil
**agitate** ['ædʒɪ,tet] *tr & intr* agitar
**aglow** [ə'glo] *adj & adv* fulgurante
**agnostic** [æg'nɑstɪk] *adj & s* agnóstico
**ago** [ə'go] *adv* hace, p.ej., **two days ago** hace dos días
**ago·ny** ['ægəni] *s* (*pl* **-nies**) angustia, congoja; (*anguish; death struggle*) agonía
**agrarian** [ə'grerɪ·ən] *adj* agrario || *s* agrariense *mf*
**agree** [ə'gri] *intr* estar de acuerdo, ponerse de acuerdo; sentar bien; (gram) concordar
**agreeable** [ə'gri·əbəl] *adj* (*to one's liking*) agradable; (*willing to consent*) acorde, conforme
**agreement** [ə'grimənt] *s* acuerdo, convenio; concordancia; **in agreement** de acuerdo
**agric.** *abbr* **agriculture**
**agriculture** ['ægrɪ,kʌltʃər] *s* agricultura
**agronomy** [ə'grɑnəmi] *s* agronomía
**aground** [ə'graʊnd] *adv* encallado, varado; **to run aground** encallar, varar
**agt.** *abbr* **agent**
**ague** ['egju] *s* escalofrío; fiebre *f* intermitente
**ahead** [ə'hed] *adj & adv* delante, al frente; **ahead of** antes de; delante de; al frente de; **to get ahead (of)** adelantarse (a)
**ahoy** [ə'hɔɪ] *interj* — **ship ahoy!** ¡ah del barco!
**aid** [ed] *s* ayuda, auxilio; (mil) ayudante *m* || *tr* ayudar, auxiliar; **to aid and abet** auxiliar e incitar, ser cómplice de || *intr* ayudar
**aide-de-camp** ['eddə'kæmp] *s* (*pl* **aides-de-camp**) ayudante *m* de campo, edecán *m*
**ail** [el] *tr* inquietar; **what ails you?** ¿qué tiene Vd.? || *intr* sufrir, estar enfermo
**aileron** ['elə,rɑn] *s* alerón *m*
**ailing** ['elɪŋ] *adj* enfermo, achacoso
**ailment** ['elmənt] *s* enfermedad, achaque *m*
**aim** [em] *s* puntería; intento; punto de mira || *tr* apuntar, encarar; dirigir (*p.ej., una observación*) || *intr* apuntar
**air** [er] *s* aire *m;* **by air** por vía aérea; **in the open air** al aire libre; **on the air** en antena, en la radio; **to let the air out of** desinflar; **to put on airs** darse aires; **to put on the air** llevar a las antenas; **to walk on air** no pisar en el suelo || *tr* airear, ventilar; radiodifundir; (fig) ventilar
**air'-a·tom'ic** *adj* aeroatómico
**air'-borne'** *adj* aerotransportado
**air brake** *s* freno de aire comprimido
**air castle** *s* castillo en el aire
**air'-condi'tion** *tr* climatizar
**air conditioner** *s* acondicionador *m* de aire
**air conditioning** *s* acondicionamiento del aire, clima *m* artificial
**air corps** *s* cuerpo de aviación
**air'craft'** *ssg* máquina de volar; *spl* máquinas de volar
**aircraft carrier** *s* portaaviones *m*
**airdrome** ['er,drom] *s* aeródromo
**air'drop'** *s* lanzamiento || *tr* lanzar
**air field** *s* campo de aviación
**air'foil'** *s* superficie *f* de sustentación
**air force** *s* fuerza aérea, ejército del aire
**air gap** *s* (phys) entrehierro
**air'-ground'** *adj* aeroterrestre
**air hostess** *s* aeromoza, azafata
**air lane** *s* ruta aérea
**air'lift'** *s* puente aéreo
**air liner** *s* transaéreo, avión *m* de travesía
**air mail** *s* correo aéreo, aeroposta
**air'-mail' letter** *s* carta aérea, carta por avión
**air-mail pilot** *s* aviador *m* postal
**air-mail stamp** *s* sello aéreo
**air·man** ['ermən] o ['er,mæn] *s* (*pl* **-men** [mən] o [,men]) aviador *m*
**air'plane'** *s* avión *m*
**airplane carrier** *s* portaaviones *m*
**air pocket** *s* bache aéreo
**air pollution** *s* contaminación atmosférica
**air'port'** *s* aeropuerto
**air raid** *s* ataque aéreo
**air'-raid' drill** *s* simulacro de ataque aéreo
**air-raid shelter** *s* abrigo antiaéreo
**air-raid warning** *s* alarma aérea
**air rifle** *s* escopeta de viento, escopeta de aire comprimido
**air'ship'** *s* aeronave *f*
**air'sick'** *adj* mareado en el aire
**air sleeve** o **sock** *s* veleta de manga
**air'strip'** *s* pista de despegue, pista de aterrizaje
**air'tight'** *adj* herméticamente cerrado, estanco al aire
**air'waves'** *spl* ondas de radio
**air'way'** *s* aerovía, vía aérea
**airway lighting** *s* balizaje *m*
**air·y** ['eri] *adj* (*comp* **-ier;** *super* **-iest**) airoso; aireado; alegre; impertinente; (coll) afectado
**aisle** [aɪl] *s* (*in theater, movie, etc.*) pasillo; (*in a store, factory, etc.*) nave *f;* (archit) nave *f* lateral; (*any of the long passageways of a church*) (archit) nave *f*
**ajar** [ə'dʒɑr] *adj* entreabierto, entornado
**akimbo** [ə'kɪmbo] *adj & adv* — **with arms akimbo** en jarras
**akin** [ə'kɪn] *adj* emparentado; semejante
**alabaster** ['ælə,bæstər] o ['ælə,bɑstər] *s* alabastro
**alarm** [ə'lɑrm] *s* alarma || *tr* alarmar
**alarm clock** *s* reloj *m* despertador
**alarmist** [ə'lɑrmɪst] *s* alarmista *mf*
**alas** [ə'læs] o [ə'lɑs] *interj* ¡ay!, ¡ay de mí!
**Albanian** [æl'benɪ·ən] *adj & s* albanés *m*

**albatross** ['ælbə,trɔs] o ['ælbə,trɑs] *s* albatros *m*
**album** ['ælbəm] *s* álbum *m*
**albumen** [æl'bjumən] *s* albumen *m;* albúmina
**alchemy** ['ælkɪmi] *s* alquimia
**alcohol** ['ælkə,hɔl] o ['ælkə,hɑl] *s* alcohol *m*
**alcoholic** [,ælkə'hɔlɪk] o [,ælkə'hɑlɪk] *adj & s* alcohólico
**alcove** ['ælkov] *s* gabinete *m,* rincón *m;* (*in a bedroom*) trasalcoba; (*in a garden*) cenador *m*
**alder** ['ɔldər] *s* aliso
**alder•man** ['ɔldərmən] *s* (*pl* **-men** [mən]) concejal *m*
**ale** [el] *s* ale *f* (*cerveza inglesa, obscura, espesa y amarga*)
**alembic** [ə'lembɪk] *s* alambique *m*
**alert** [ə'lʌrt] *adj* listo, vivo; vigilante || *s* (aer) alarma; (mil) alerta *m;* **to be on the alert** estar sobre aviso, estar alerta || *tr* alertar
**Aleutian Islands** [ə'luʃən] *spl* islas Aleutas, islas Aleutianas
**Alexandrine** [,ælɪg'zændrɪn] *adj & s* alejandrino
**alg.** *abbr* **algebra**
**algae** ['ældʒi] *spl* algas
**algebra** ['ældʒɪbrə] *s* álgebra
**algebraic** [,ældʒɪ'bre•ɪk] *adj* algebraico
**Algeria** [æl'dʒɪrɪ•ə] *s* Argelia
**Algerian** [æl'dʒɪrɪ•ən] *adj & s* argelino
**Algiers** [æl'dʒɪrz] *s* Argel *f*
**alias** ['elɪ•əs] *adv* alias || *s* alias *m,* nombre supuesto
**ali•bi** ['ælɪ,baɪ] *s* (*pl* **-bis**) coartada; (coll) excusa
**alien** ['eljən] o ['elɪ•ən] *adj & s* extranjero
**alienate** ['eljə,net] o ['elɪ•ə,net] *tr* enajenar, alienar
**alight** [ə'laɪt] *v* (*pret & pp* **alighted** o **alit** [ə'lɪt]) *intr* bajar, apearse; posarse (*un ave*)
**align** [ə'laɪn] *tr* alinear || *intr* alinearse
**alike** [ə'laɪk] *adj* semejantes; **to look alike** parecerse || *adv* igualmente
**alimentary canal** [,ælɪ'mentəri] *s* canal alimenticio, tubo digestivo
**alimony** ['ælɪ,moni] *s* alimentos
**alive** [ə'laɪv] *adj* vivo, viviente; animado; **alive to** despierto para, sensible a; **alive with** hormigueante en
**alka•li** ['ælkə,laɪ] *s* (*pl* **-lis** o **-lies**) álcali *m*
**alkaline** ['ælkə,laɪn] o ['ælkəlɪn] *adj* alcalino
**all** [ɔl] *adj indef* todo, todos; todo el, todos los || *pron indef* todo; todos, todo el mundo; **after all** sin embargo; **all of** todo el, todos los; **all that** todo lo que, todos los que; **for all I know** que yo sepa; a lo mejor; **not at all** nada; no hay de qué || *adv* enteramente; **all along** desde el principio; a lo largo de; **all at once** de golpe; **all right** bueno, corriente; **all too** excesivamente
**Allah** ['ælə] *s* Alá *m*
**allay** [ə'le] *tr* aliviar, calmar
**all-clear** ['ɔl'klɪr] *s* cese *m* de alarma
**allege** [ə'ledʒ] *tr* alegar
**allegiance** [ə'lidʒəns] *s* fidelidad, lealtad; homenaje *m;* **to swear allegiance to** jurar fidelidad a; rendir homenaje a
**allegoric(al)** [,ælɪ'gɑrɪk(əl)] o [,ælɪ'gɔrɪk(əl)] *adj* alegórico
**allego•ry** ['ælɪ,gori] *s* (*pl* **-ries**) alegoría
**aller•gy** ['ælərdʒi] *s* (*pl* **-gies**) alergia
**alleviate** [ə'livɪ,et] *tr* aliviar
**alley** ['æli] *s* callejuela; paseo arbolado, paseo de jardín; (bowling) pista; (tennis) espacio lateral
**All Fools' Day** *s* var of **April Fools' Day**
**Allhallows** [,ɔl'hæloz] *s* día *m* de todos los santos
**alliance** [ə'laɪ•əns] *s* alianza
**alligator** ['ælɪ,getər] *s* caimán *m*
**alligator pear** *s* aguacate *m*
**alligator wrench** *s* llave *f* de mandíbulas dentadas
**alliteration** [ə,lɪtə'reʃən] *s* aliteración
**all-knowing** ['ɔl'no•ɪŋ] *adj* omnisciente
**allocate** ['ælə,ket] *tr* asignar, distribuir
**allot** [ə'lɑt] *v* (*pret & pp* **allotted;** *ger* **allotting**) *tr* asignar, distribuir
**all'-out'** *adj* acérrimo
**allow** [ə'laʊ] *tr* dejar, permitir; admitir; conceder || *intr* — **to allow for** tener en cuenta; **to allow of** permitir; admitir
**allowance** [ə'laʊ•əns] *s* permiso; concesión; ración; descuento, rebaja; tolerancia; **to make allowance for** tener en cuenta
**alloy** ['ælɔɪ] o [ə'lɔɪ] *s* aleación, liga || [ə'lɔɪ] *tr* alear, ligar
**all-powerful** ['ɔl'paʊ•ərfəl] *adj* todopoderoso
**All Saints' Day** *s* día *m* de todos los santos
**All Souls' Day** *s* día *m* de los difuntos
**allspice** ['ɔl,spaɪs] *s* pimienta inglesa
**all'-star' game** *s* (sport) juego de estrellas
**allude** [ə'lud] *intr* aludir
**allure** [ə'lʊr] *s* tentación, encanto, fascinación || *tr* tentar, encantar
**alluring** [ə'lʊrɪŋ] *adj* tentador, encantador, fascinante
**allusion** [ə'luʒən] *s* alusión
**al•ly** ['ælaɪ] o [ə'laɪ] *s* (*pl* **-lies**) aliado || [ə'laɪ] *v* (*pret & pp* **-lied**) *tr* aliar || *intr* aliarse
**almanac** ['ɔlmə,næk] *s* almanaque *m*
**almighty** [ɔl'maɪti] *adj* todopoderoso, omnipotente
**almond** ['ɑmənd] o ['æmənd] *s* almendra
**almond brittle** *s* crocante *m*
**almond tree** *s* almendro
**almost** ['ɔlmost] o [ɔl'most] *adv* casi
**alms** [ɑmz] *s* limosna
**alms'house'** *s* casa de beneficencia
**aloe** ['ælo] *s* áloe *m*
**aloft** [ə'lɔft] o [ə'lɑft] *adv* arriba; (aer) en vuelo; (naut) en la arboladura
**alone** [ə'lon] *adj* solo; **let alone** sin

mencionar; y mucho menos; **to let alone** no molestar; no mezclarse en || *adv* solamente
**along** [ə'lɔŋ] o [ə'lɑŋ] *adv* conmigo, consigo, etc.; **all along** desde el principio; **along with** junto con || *prep* a lo largo de
**along'side'** *adv* a lo largo; (naut) al costado; **to bring alongside** acostar || *prep* a lo largo de; (naut) al costado de
**aloof** [ə'luf] *adj* apartado; reservado || *adv* lejos, a distancia
**aloud** [ə'laʊd] *adv* alto, en voz alta
**alphabet** ['ælfə,bɛt] *s* alfabeto
**alpine** ['ælpaɪn] *adj* alpestre, alpino
**Alps** [ælps] *spl* Alpes *mpl*
**already** [ɔl'rɛdi] *adv* ya
**Alsace** [æl'ses] o ['ælsæs] *s* Alsacia
**Alsatian** [æl'seʃən] *adj & s* alsaciano
**also** ['ɔlso] *adv* también
**alt.** *abbr* **alternate, altitude**
**altar** ['ɔltər] *s* altar *m;* **to lead to the altar** conducir al altar
**altar boy** *s* acólito, monaguillo
**altar cloth** *s* sabanilla, palia
**al'tar·piece'** *s* retablo
**altar rail** *s* comulgatorio
**alter** ['ɔltər] *tr* alterar || *intr* alterarse
**alteration** [,ɔltə'reʃən] *s* alteración; (*in a building*) reforma; (*in clothing*) arreglo
**alternate** ['ɔltərnɪt] o ['æltərnɪt] *adj* alterno || ['ɔltər,net] o ['æltər,net] *tr & intr* alternar
**alternating current** *s* corriente alterna o alternativa
**although** [ɔl'ðo] *conj* aunque
**altimetry** [æl'tɪmɪtri] *s* altimetría
**altitude** ['æltɪ,tjud] o ['æltɪ,tud] *s* altitud, altura
**al·to** ['ælto] *s* (*pl* **-tos**) contralto
**altogether** [,ɔltə'gɛðər] *adv* enteramente; en conjunto
**altruist** ['æltrʊ·ɪst] *s* altruísta *mf*
**altruistic** [,æltrʊ'ɪstɪk] *adj* altruísta
**alum** ['æləm] *s* alumbre *m*
**aluminum** [ə'lumɪnəm] *s* aluminio
**alum·na** [ə'lʌmnə] *s* (*pl* **-nae** [ni]) graduada
**alum·nus** [ə'lʌmnəs] *s* (*pl* **-ni** [naɪ]) graduado
**alveo·lus** [æl'vi·ələs] *s* (*pl* **-li** [,laɪ]) alvéolo
**always** ['ɔlwɪz] o ['ɔlwez] *adv* siempre
**A.M.** *abbr* **ante meridiem, i.e., before noon; amplitude modulation**
**Am.** *abbr* **America, American**
**amalgam** [ə'mælgəm] *s* amalgama *f*
**amalgamate** [ə'mælgə,met] *tr* amalgamar || *intr* amalgamarse
**amass** [ə'mæs] *tr* amontonar; amasar (*dinero*)
**amateur** ['æmətʃər] *adj & s* chapucero, principiante *mf;* aficionado
**amateur performance** *s* función de aficionados
**amaze** [ə'mez] *tr* asombrar, maravillar
**amazing** [ə'mezɪŋ] *adj* asombroso, maravilloso
**Amazon** ['æmə,zɑn] o ['æməzən] *s* Amazonas *m*
**ambassador** [æm'bæsədər] *s* embajador *m*
**ambassadress** [æm'bæsədrɪs] *s* embajadora
**amber** ['æmbər] *adj* ambarino || *s* ámbar *m*
**ambigui·ty** [,æmbɪ'gju·ɪti] *s* (*pl* **-ties**) ambigüidad
**ambiguous** [æm'bɪgju·əs] *adj* ambiguo
**ambition** [æm'bɪʃən] *s* ambición
**ambitious** [æm'bɪʃəs] *adj* ambicioso
**amble** ['æmbəl] *s* ambladura || *intr* amblar
**ambulance** ['æmbjələns] *s* ambulancia
**ambush** ['æmbʊʃ] *s* emboscada; **to lie in ambush** estar emboscado || *tr* (*to station in ambush*) emboscar; (*to lie in wait for and attack*) insidiar || *intr* emboscarse
**amelioration** [ə,miljə'reʃən] *s* mejoramiento
**amen** ['e'mɛn] o ['ɑ'mɛn] *interj* ¡amén! || *s* amén *m*
**amenable** [ə'minəbəl] o [ə'mɛnəbəl] *adj* dócil; responsable
**amend** [ə'mɛnd] *tr* enmendar || *intr* enmendarse || **amends** *spl* enmienda; **to make amends for** enmendar
**amendment** [ə'mɛndmənt] *s* enmienda
**ameni·ty** [ə'minɪti] o [ə'mɛnɪti] *s* (*pl* **-ties**) amenidad
**America** [ə'mɛrɪkə] *s* América
**American** [ə'mɛrɪkən] *adj & s* americano; norteamericano, estadounidense
**Americanize** [ə'mɛrɪkə,naɪz] *tr* americanizar
**amethyst** ['æmɪθɪst] *s* amatista
**amiable** ['emɪ·əbəl] *adj* amable, bonachón
**amicable** ['æmɪkəbəl] *adj* amigable
**amid** [ə'mɪd] *prep* en medio de
**amidship** [ə'mɪdʃɪp] *adv* en medio del navío
**amiss** [ə'mɪs] *adj* inoportuno; malo || *adv* inoportunamente; mal; **to take amiss** llevar a mal, tomar en mala parte
**ami·ty** ['æmɪti] *s* (*pl* **-ties**) amistad
**ammeter** ['æm,mitər] *s* anmetro, amperímetro
**ammonia** [ə'monɪ·ə] *s* amoníaco; agua amoniacal
**ammunition** [,æmjə'nɪʃən] *s* munición
**amnes·ty** ['æmnɪsti] *s* (*pl* **-ties**) amnistía || *v* (*pret & pp* **-tied**) *tr* amnistiar
**amoeba** [ə'mibə] *s* amiba
**among** [ə'mʌŋ] *prep* entre, en medio de, en el número de
**amorous** ['æmərəs] *adj* amoroso; erótico, sensual, voluptuoso
**amortize** ['æmər,taɪz] *tr* amortizar
**amount** [ə'maʊnt] *s* cantidad, importe *m* || *intr* — **to amount to** ascender a; significar
**amp.** *abbr* **ampere, amperage**
**ampere** ['æmpɪr] *s* amperio
**am'pere-hour'** *s* amp rio-hora *m*
**amphibious** [æm'fɪbɪ·əs] *adj* anfibio
**amphitheater** ['æmfɪ,θi·ətər] *s* anfiteatro
**ample** ['æmpəl] amplio; bastante, suficiente; abundante

**amplifier** ['æmplɪ,faɪ·ər] *s* amplificador *m*
**ampli·fy** ['æmplɪ,faɪ] *v* (*pret & pp* **-fied**) *tr* amplificar ‖ *intr* espaciarse
**amplitude** ['æmplɪ,tjud] o ['æmplɪ,tud] *s* amplitud
**amplitude modulation** *s* modulación de amplitud
**amputate** ['æmpjə,tet] *tr* amputar
**amt.** *abbr* **amount**
**amuck** [ə'mʌk] *adv* frenéticamente; **to run amuck** atacar a ciegas
**amulet** ['æmjəlɪt] *s* amuleto
**amuse** [ə'mjuz] *tr* divertir, entretener
**amusement** [ə'mjuzmənt] *s* diversión, entretenimiento; pasatiempo, recreación; (*in a park or circus*) atracción
**amusement park** *s* parque *m* de atracciones
**amusing** [ə'mjuzɪŋ] *adj* divertido, gracioso
**an** [æn] o [ən] *art indef* (antes de sonido vocal) un
**anachronism** [ə'nækrə,nɪzəm] *s* anacronismo
**anaemia** [ə'nimi·ə] *s* anemia
**anaemic** [ə'nimɪk] *adj* anémico
**anaesthesia** [,ænɪs'θiʒə] *s* anestesia
**anaesthetic** [,ænɪs'θɛtɪk] *adj & s* anestésico
**anaesthetize** [æ'nɛsθɪ,taɪz] *tr* anestesiar
**analogous** [ə'næləgəs] *adj* análogo
**analo·gy** [ə'nælədʒi] *s* (*pl* **-gies**) analogía
**analyse** ['ænə,laɪz] *tr* analizar
**analy·sis** [ə'nælɪsɪs] *s* (*pl* **-ses** [,siz]) análisis *m & f*
**analyst** ['ænəlɪst] *s* analista *mf*
**analytic(al)** [,ænə'lɪtɪk(əl)] *adj* analítico
**analyze** ['ænə,laɪz] *tr* analizar
**anarchist** ['ænərkɪst] *s* anarquista *mf*
**anarchy** ['ænərki] *s* anarquía
**anathema** [ə'næθɪmə] *s* anatema *m & f*
**anatomic(al)** [,ænə'tɑmɪk(əl)] *adj* anatómico
**anato·my** [ə'nætəmi] *s* (*pl* **-mies**) anatomía
**ancestor** ['ænsɛstər] *s* antecesor *m*, antepasado
**ances·try** ['ænsɛstri] *s* (*pl* **-tries**) abolengo, alcurnia
**anchor** ['æŋkər] *s* ancla, áncora; (fig) áncora; **to cast anchor** echar anclas; **to weigh anchor** levar anclas ‖ *tr* sujetar con el ancla ‖ *intr* anclar, ancorar
**ancho·vy** ['æntʃovi] *s* (*pl* **-vies**) anchoa
**ancient** ['enʃənt] *adj* antiguo
**and** [ænd] o [ənd] *conj* y; **and so forth** y así sucesivamente
**Andalusia** [,ændə'luʒə] *s* Andalucía
**Andalusian** [,ændə'luʒən] *adj & s* andaluz *m*
**Andean** [æn'di·ən] o ['ændɪ·ən] *adj & s* andino
**Andes** ['ændiz] *spl* Andes *mpl*
**andirons** ['ænd,aɪ·ərnz] *spl* morillos
**anecdote** ['ænɪk,dot] *s* anécdota
**anemia** [ə'nimɪ·ə] *s* anemia
**anemic** [ə'nimɪk] *adj* anémico
**aneroid barometer** ['ænə,rɔɪd] *s* barómetro aneroide
**anesthesia** [,ænɪs'θiʒə] *s* anestesia
**anesthetic** [,ænɪs'θɛtɪk] *adj & s* anestésico
**anesthetize** [æ'nɛsθɪ,taɪz] *tr* anestesiar
**aneurysm** ['ænjə,rɪzəm] *s* aneurisma *m*
**anew** [ə'nju] o [ə'nu] *adv* de nuevo, nuevamente
**angel** ['endʒəl] *s* ángel *m*; (*financial backer*) caballo blanco
**angelic(al)** [æn'dʒɛlɪk(əl)] *adj* angélico, angelical
**anger** ['æŋgər] *s* cólera, ira ‖ *tr* encolerizar, airar
**angina pectoris** [æn'dʒaɪnə 'pɛktərɪs] *s* angina de pecho
**angle** ['æŋgəl] *s* ángulo; punto de vista ‖ *intr* pescar con caña; intrigar
**angle iron** *s* ángulo de hierro, hierro angular
**angler** ['æŋglər] *s* pescador *m* de caña; intrigante *mf*
**Anglo-Saxon** [,æŋglo'sæksən] *adj & s* anglosajón *m*
**an·gry** ['æŋgri] *adj* (*comp* **-grier**; *super* **-griest**) encolerizado, airado; (pathol) inflamado, irritado; **to become angry at** enojarse de; **to become angry with** enojarse con o contra
**anguish** ['æŋgwɪʃ] *s* angustia, congoja
**angular** ['æŋgjələr] *adj* angular; (*features*) anguloso
**anhydrous** [æn'haɪdrəs] *adj* anhidro
**aniline dyes** ['ænɪlɪn] o ['ænɪ,laɪn] *s* colores *mpl* de anilina
**animal** ['ænɪməl] *adj & s* animal *m*
**animal spirits** *spl* ardor *m*, vigor *m*, vivacidad
**animated cartoon** ['ænɪ,metɪd] *s* película de dibujos, dibujo animado
**animation** [,ænɪ'meʃən] *s* animación
**animosi·ty** [,ænɪ'mɑsɪti] *s* (*pl* **-ties**) animosidad
**anion** ['æn,aɪ·ən] *s* anión *m*
**anise** ['ænɪs] *s* anís *m*
**aniseed** ['ænɪ,sid] *s* grano de anís
**anisette** [,ænɪ'zɛt] *s* anisete *m*
**ankle** ['æŋkəl] *s* tobillo
**an'kle·bone'** *s* hueso del tobillo
**ankle support** *s* tobillera
**anklet** ['æŋklɪt] *s* ajorca; (*sock*) tobillera
**annals** ['ænəlz] *spl* anales *mpl*
**anneal** [ə'nil] *tr* recocer
**annex** ['ænɛks] *s* anexo; (*of a building*) pabellón *m* ‖ [ə'nɛks] *tr* anexar
**annihilate** [ə'naɪ·ɪ,let] *tr* aniquilar
**anniversa·ry** [,ænɪ'vʌrsəri] *adj* aniversario ‖ *s* (*pl* **-ries**) aniversario
**annotate** ['ænə,tet] *tr* anotar
**announce** [ə'naʊns] *tr* anunciar
**announcement** [ə'naʊnsmənt] *s* anuncio
**announcer** [ə'naʊnsər] *s* anunciador *m*; (rad) locutor *m*
**annoy** [ə'nɔɪ] *tr* fastidiar, molestar
**annoyance** [ə'nɔɪ·əns] *s* fastidio, molestia
**annoying** [ə'nɔɪ·ɪŋ] *adj* fastidioso, molesto
**annual** ['ænjʊ·əl] *adj* anual ‖ *s* publicación anual; planta anual

**annui•ty** ['nju·ɪti] o [ə'nu·ɪti] *s* (*pl* **-ties**) anualidad; renta vitalicia
**an•nul** [ə'nʌl] *v* (*pret & pp* **-nulled;** *ger* **-nulling**) *tr* anular, invalidar
**anode** ['ænod] *s* ánodo
**anoint** [ə'nɔɪnt] *tr* ungir, untar
**anomalous** [ə'nɑmələs] *adj* anómalo
**anoma•ly** [ə'nɑməli] *s* (*pl* **-lies**) anomalía
**anon.** *abbr* **anonymous**
**anonymity** [,ænə'nɪmɪti] *s* anónimo; **to preserve one's anonymity** guardar o conservar el anónimo
**anonymous** [ə'nɑnɪməs] *adj* anónimo
**another** [ə'nʌðər] *adj & pron indef* otro
**ans.** *abbr* **answer**
**answer** ['ænsər] o ['ɑnsər] *s* contestación, respuesta; (*to a problem or puzzle*) solución || *tr* contestar, responder; resolver (*un problema o un enigma*) || *intr* contestar, responder; **to answer for** responder de (*una cosa*); responder por (*una persona*)
**ant** [ænt] *s* hormiga
**antagonism** [æn'tægə,nɪzəm] *s* antagonismo
**antagonize** [æn'tægə,naɪz] *tr* oponerse a; enemistar, enajenar
**antarctic** [ænt'ɑrktɪk] *adj* antártico || **the Antarctic** las Tierras Antárticas
**antecedent** [,æntɪ'sidənt] *adj* antecedente || *s* antecedente *m;* **antecedents** antecedentes *mpl;* antepasados
**antechamber** ['æntɪ,tʃembər] *s* antecámara
**antedate** ['æntɪ,det] *tr* antedatar; preceder
**antelope** ['æntɪ,lop] *s* antílope *m*
**anten•na** [æn'tenə] *s* (*pl* **-nae** [ni]) (ent) antena || *s* (*pl* **-nas**) (rad) antena
**antepenult** [,æntɪ'pinʌlt] *s* antepenúltima
**anteroom** ['æntɪ,rum] o ['æntɪ,rʊm] *s* antecámara
**anthem** ['ænθəm] *s* himno; antífona
**ant'hill'** *s* hormiguero
**antholo•gy** [æn'θɑlədʒi] *s* (*pl* **-gies**) antología
**anthracite** ['ænθrə,saɪt] *s* antracita
**anthrax** ['ænθræks] *s* ántrax *m*
**anthropology** [,ænθrə'pɑlədʒi] *s* antropología
**anti-aircraft** [,æntɪ'er,kræft] o [,æntɪ'er,krɑft] *adj* antiaéreo
**antibiotic** [,æntɪbaɪ'ɑtɪk] *adj & s* antibiótico
**antibod•y** ['æntɪ,bɑdi] *s* (*pl* **-ies**) anticuerpo
**anticipate** [æn'tɪsɪ,pet] *tr* esperar, prever; anticipar; (*to get ahead of*) anticiparse a; impedir; prometerse (*p. ej., un placer*); temerse (*algo desagradable*)
**antics** ['æntɪks] *spl* cabriolas, gracias, travesuras
**antidote** ['æntɪ,dot] *s* antídoto
**antifreeze** [,æntɪ'friz] *s* anticongelante *m*
**antiglare** [,æntɪ'gler] *adj* antideslumbrante
**antiknock** [,æntɪ'nɑk] *adj & s* antidetonante *m*
**antilabor** [,æntɪ'lebər] *adj* antiobrero
**Antilles** [æn'tɪliz] *spl* Antillas
**antimissile** [,æntɪ'mɪsɪl] *adj* antiproyectil
**antimony** ['æntɪ,moni] *s* antimonio
**antipas•to** [,ɑntɪ'pɑsto] *s* (*pl* **-tos**) aperitivo, entremés *m*
**antipa•thy** [æn'tɪpəθi] *s* (*pl* **-thies**) antipatía
**antiquar•y** ['æntɪ,kweri] *s* (*pl* **-ies**) anticuario
**antiquated** ['æntɪ,kwetɪd] *adj* anticuado
**antique** [æn'tik] *adj* antiguo || *s* antigüedad
**antique dealer** *s* anticuario
**antique store** *s* tienda de antigüedades
**antiqui•ty** [æn'tɪkwɪti] *s* (*pl* **-ties**) antigüedad
**anti-Semitic** [,æntɪsɪ'mɪtɪk] *adj* antisemítico
**antiseptic** [,æntɪ'septɪk] *adj & s* antiséptico
**antislavery** [,æntɪ'slevəri] *adj* antiesclavista
**anti-Soviet** [,æntɪ'sovɪ,et] *adj* antisoviético
**antitank** [,æntɪ'tæŋk] *adj* antitanque
**antithe•sis** [æn'tɪθɪsɪs] *s* (*pl* **-ses** [,siz]) antítesis *f*
**antitoxin** [,æntɪ'tɑksɪn] *s* antitoxina
**antitrust** [,æntɪ'trʌst] *adj* anticartel
**antiwar** [,æntɪ'wɔr] *adj* antibélico
**antler** ['æntlər] *s* cuerna
**antonym** ['æntənɪm] *s* antónimo
**Antwerp** ['æntwərp] *s* Amberes *f*
**anvil** ['ænvɪl] *s* yunque *m*
**anxie•ty** [æŋ'zaɪ·əti] *s* (*pl* **-ties**) ansiedad, inquietud; ansia, anhelo
**anxious** ['æŋkʃəs] *adj* ansioso, inquieto; anhelante; **to be anxious to** tener ganas de
**any** ['eni] *adj indef* algún, cualquier; todo; **any place** dondequiera; **any time** cuando quiera; alguna vez || *pron indef* alguno, cualquiera || *adv* algo
**an'y•bod'y** *pron indef* alguno, alguien, cualquiera, quienquiera; todo el mundo; **not anybody** nadie
**an'y•how'** *adv* de cualquier modo; de todos modos; sin embargo
**an'y•one'** *pron indef* alguno, alguien, cualquiera
**an'y•thing'** *pron indef* algo, alguna cosa; cualquier cosa; todo cuanto; **anything at all** cualquier cosa que sea; **anything else** cualquier otra cosa; **anything else?** ¿algo más?; **not anything** nada
**an'y•way'** *adv* de cualquier modo; de todos modos; sin embargo; sin esmero, sin orden ni concierto
**an'y•where'** *adv* dondequiera; adondequiera; **not anywhere** en ninguna parte
**apace** [ə'pes] *adv* aprisa
**apart** [ə'pɑrt] *adv* aparte; en pedazos; **to fall apart** caerse a pedazos; desunirse; ir al desastre; **to live apart**

vivir separados; vivir aislado; **to stand apart** mantenerse apartado; **to take apart** descomponer, desarmar, desmontar; **to tell apart** distinguir
**apartment** [ə'pɑrtmənt] *s* apartamento
**apartment house** *s* casa de pisos
**apathetic** [ˌæpə'θetɪk] *adj* apático
**apa·thy** ['æpəθi] *s* (*pl* **-ties**) apatía
**ape** [ep] *s* mono ‖ *tr* imitar, remedar
**aperture** ['æpərtʃər] *s* abertura, orificio
**apex** ['epɛks] *s* (*pl* **apexes** o **apices** ['æpɪˌsiz]) ápex *m*, ápice *m*
**aphorism** ['æfəˌrɪzəm] *s* aforismo
**aphrodisiac** [ˌæfrə'dɪzɪˌæk] *adj* & *s* afrodisíaco
**apiar·y** ['epɪˌɛri] *s* (*pl* **-ies**) abejar *m*, colmenar *m*
**apiece** [ə'pis] *adv* cada uno; por persona
**apish** ['epɪʃ] *adj* monesco; tonto
**aplomb** [ə'plɑm] *s* aplomo, sangre fría
**apogee** ['æpəˌdʒi] *s* apogeo
**apologetic** [əˌpɑlə'dʒɛtɪk] *adj* lleno de excusas
**apologize** [ə'pɑləˌdʒaɪz] *intr* excusarse, disculparse; **to apologize for** disculparse de; **to apologize to** disculparse con
**apolo·gy** [ə'pɑlədʒi] *s* (*pl* **-gies**) excusa; (*makeshift*) expediente *m*
**apoplectic** [ˌæpə'plɛktɪk] *adj* & *s* apoplético
**apoplexy** ['æpəˌplɛksi] *s* apoplejía
**apostle** [ə'pɑsəl] *s* apóstol *m*
**apostrophe** [ə'pɑstrəfi] *s* (*written sign*) apóstrofo; (*words addressed to absent person*) apóstrofe *m* & *f*
**apothecar·y** [ə'pɑθɪˌkɛri] *s* (*pl* **-ies**) boticario
**apothecary's jar** *s* bote *m* de porcelana
**apothecary's shop** *s* botica
**appall** [ə'pɔl] *tr* espantar, pasmar
**appalling** [ə'pɔlɪŋ] *adj* aterrador, espantoso, pasmoso
**appara·tus** [ˌæpə'retəs] o [ˌæpə'rætəs] *s* (*pl* **-tus** o **-tuses**) aparato
**apparel** [ə'pærəl] *s* indumentaria, vestido
**apparent** [ə'pærənt] o [ə'pɛrənt] *adj* aparente
**apparition** [ˌæpə'rɪʃən] *s* aparición
**appeal** [ə'pil] *s* súplica, instancia, solicitud; atracción, interés *m;* (law) apelación ‖ *intr* ser atrayente; **to appeal to** (*to make an entreaty to*) suplicar; (*to be attractive to*) atraer, interesar; (law) apelar a
**appear** [ə'pɪr] *intr* (*to come into sight; to be in sight; to be published*) aparecer; (*to come into sight; to be in sight; to look; to seem*) parecer; (*to come before the public*) presentarse; (*to come before a court*) comparecer
**appearance** [ə'pɪrəns] *s* (*act of appearing*) aparición; (*outward look*) apariencia, aspecto; (law) comparecencia
**appease** [ə'piz] *tr* apaciguar
**appeasement** [ə'pizmənt] *s* apaciguamiento
**appendage** [ə'pɛndɪdʒ] *s* apéndice *m*
**appendicitis** [əˌpɛndɪ'saɪtɪs] *s* apendicitis *f*
**appen·dix** [ə'pɛndɪks] *s* (*pl* **-dixes** o **-dices** [dɪˌsiz]) apéndice *m*
**appertain** [ˌæpər'ten] *intr* relacionarse
**appetite** ['æpɪˌtaɪt] *s* apetito
**appetizer** ['æpɪˌtaɪzər] *s* aperitivo, apetite *m*
**appetizing** ['æpɪˌtaɪzɪŋ] *adj* apetitoso
**applaud** [ə'plɔd] *tr* & *intr* aplaudir
**applause** [ə'plɔz] *s* aplauso, aplausos
**apple** ['æpəl] *s* manzana
**ap'ple·jack'** *s* aguardiente *m* de manzana
**apple of the eye** *s* niña del ojo
**apple pie** *s* pastel *m* de manzana
**apple polisher** *s* (slang) quitamotas *mf*
**ap'ple·sauce'** *s* compota de manzanas; (slang) música celestial
**apple tree** *s* manzano
**appliance** [ə'plaɪ·əns] *s* artificio, dispositivo, aparato; aplicación
**applicant** ['æplɪkənt] *s* aspirante *mf*, pretendiente *mf*, solicitante *mf*
**ap·ply** [ə'plaɪ] *v* (*pret* & *pp* **-plied**) *tr* aplicar ‖ *intr* aplicarse; dirigirse; **to apply for** pedir, solicitar
**appoint** [ə'pɔɪnt] *tr* designar, nombrar; señalar; amueblar
**appointment** [ə'pɔɪntmənt] *s* designación, nombramiento; empleo, puesto; cita; **appointments** instalación, accesorios, adornos; **by appointment** cita previa
**apportion** [ə'porʃən] *tr* prorratear
**appraisal** [ə'prezəl] *s* tasación, valoración, apreciación
**appraise** [ə'prez] *tr* tasar, valorar, apreciar
**appreciable** [ə'priʃɪ·əbəl] *adj* apreciable; sensible
**appreciate** [ə'priʃɪˌet] *tr* apreciar; aprobar; comprender; estar agradecido por ‖ *intr* subir de valor
**appreciation** [əˌpriʃɪ'eʃən] *s* aprecio; agradecimiento; plusvalía, aumento de valor
**appreciative** [ə'priʃɪˌetɪv] *adj* apreciador; agradecido
**apprehend** [ˌæprɪ'hɛnd] *tr* aprehender, prender; comprender; temer
**apprehension** [ˌæprɪ'hɛnʃən] *s* aprehensión; (*fear, worry*) aprensión; comprensión
**apprehensive** [ˌæprɪ'hɛnsɪv] *adj* (*fearful, worried*) aprehensivo, aprensivo
**apprentice** [ə'prɛntɪs] *s* aprendiz *m*, meritorio ‖ *tr* poner de aprendiz
**apprenticeship** [ə'prɛntɪsˌʃɪp] *s* aprendizaje *m*
**apprise** o **apprize** [ə'praɪz] *tr* informar; apreciar, tasar
**approach** [ə'protʃ] *s* acercamiento; vía de entrada; proposición; (*to a problem*) enfoque *m* ‖ *tr* abordar, acercarse a; (*to bring closer*) acercar ‖ *intr* acercarse, aproximarse
**approbation** [ˌæprə'beʃən] *s* aprobación
**appropriate** [ə'proprɪ·ɪt] *adj* apropiado, a propósito ‖ [ə'proprɪˌet] *tr*

apropiarse; asignar, destinar (*el parlamento determinada suma a un determinado fin*)
**approval** [ə'pruvəl] *s* aprobación; **on approval** a prueba
**approve** [ə'pruv] *tr & intr* aprobar
**approximate** [ə'prɑksɪmɪt] *adj* aproximado || [ə'prɑksɪ,met] *tr* aproximar || *intr* aproximarse
**apricot** ['eprɪ,kɑt] o ['æprɪ,kɑt] *s* albaricoque *m*
**apricot tree** *s* albaricoquero
**April** ['eprɪl] *s* abril *m*
**April fool** *s* — **to make an April fool of** coger por inocente
**April Fools' Day** *s* día *m* de engañabobos, primer día de abril, en que se coge por inocente a la gente
**apron** ['eprən] *s* delantal *m; (of a workman)* mandil *m;* **tied to the apron strings of** cosido a las faldas de
**apropos** [,æprə'po] *adj* oportuno || *adv* a propósito; **apropos of** a propósito de
**apse** [æps] *s* ábside *m*
**apt** [æpt] *adj* apto; a propósito; dispuesto, inclinado
**aptitude** ['æptɪ,tjud] o ['æptɪ,tud] *s* aptitud
**aquamarine** [,ækwəmə'rin] *s* aguamarina
**aquaplane** ['ækwə,plen] *s* acuaplano || *intr* correr en acuaplano
**aquari•um** [ə'kwerɪ·əm] *s* (*pl* **-ums** o **-a** [ə]) acuario
**aquatic** [ə'kwætɪk] o [ə'kwɑtɪk] *adj* acuático || **aquatics** *spl* deportes acuáticos
**aqueduct** ['ækwə,dʌkt] *s* acueducto
**aquiline nose** ['ækwɪ,laɪn] *s* nariz aguileña
**Arab** ['ærəb] *adj* árabe || *s* árabe *mf;* caballo árabe
**Arabia** [ə'rebɪ·ə] *s* la Arabia
**Arabian** [ə'rebɪ·ən] *adj* árabe; arábigo || *s* árabe *mf*
**Arabic** ['ærəbɪk] *adj* arábigo || *s* árabe *m,* arábigo
**Aragon** ['ærə,gɑn] *s* Aragón *m*
**Arago•nese** [,ærəgə'niz] *adj* aragonés || *s* (*pl* **-nese**) aragonés *m*
**arbiter** ['ɑrbɪtər] *s* árbitro
**arbitrary** ['ɑrbɪ,treri] *adj* arbitrario
**arbitrate** ['ɑrbɪ,tret] *tr & intr* arbritrar
**arbitration** [,ɑrbɪ'treʃən] *s* arbitraje *m*
**arbor** ['ɑrbər] *s* emparrado, glorieta
**arbore•tum** [,ɑrbə'ritəm] *s* (*pl* **-tums** o **-ta** [tə]) jardín botánico de árboles
**arbor vitae** ['ɑrbər 'vaɪti] *s* árbol *m* de la vida
**arbutus** [ɑr'bjutəs] *s* madroño
**arc** [ɑrk] *s* arco
**arcade** [ɑr'ked] *s* arcada, galería
**arch.** *abbr* **archaic, archaism, archipelago, architect**
**arch** [ɑrtʃ] *adj* astuto; travieso; principal || *s* arco || *tr* arquear, enarcar; atravesar
**archaeology** [,ɑrkɪ'ɑlədʒi] *s* arqueología
**archaic** [ɑr'ke·ɪk] *adj* arcaico
**archaism** ['ɑrke,ɪzəm] o ['ɑrki,ɪzəm] *s* arcaísmo
**archangel** ['ɑrk,endʒəl] *s* arcángel *m*
**archbishop** ['ɑrtʃ'bɪʃəp] *s* arzobispo
**archduke** ['ɑrtʃ'djuk] o ['ɑrtʃ'duk] *s* archiduque *m*
**archene•my** ['ɑrtʃ,ɛnɪmi] *s* (*pl* **-mies**) archienemigo
**archeology** [,ɑrkɪ'ɑlədʒi] *s* arqueología
**archer** ['ɑrtʃər] *s* arquero, flechero
**archery** ['ɑrtʃəri] *s* tiro de flechas
**archipela•go** [,ɑrkɪ'pɛləgo] *s* (*pl* **-gos** o **-goes**) archipiélago
**architect** ['ɑrkɪ,tɛkt] *s* arquitecto
**architectural** [,ɑrkɪ'tɛktʃərəl] *adj* arquitectónico, arquitectural
**architecture** ['ɑrkɪ,tɛktʃər] *s* arquitectura
**archives** ['ɑrkaɪvz] *spl* archivo
**arch'way'** *s* arcada
**arc lamp** *s* lámpara de arco
**arctic** ['ɑrktɪk] *adj* ártico || **the Arctic** las Tierras Árticas
**arc welding** *s* soldadura de arco
**ardent** ['ɑrdənt] *adj* ardiente
**ardor** ['ɑrdər] *s* ardor *m*
**arduous** ['ɑrdʒu·əs] o ['ɑrdju·əs] *adj* arduo, difícil; enérgico; (*steep*) escarpado
**area** ['ɛrɪ·ə] *s* área, superficie *f;* comarca, región; zona; patio
**ar'ea•way'** *s* entrada baja de un sótano
**Argentina** [,ɑrdʒən'tinə] *s* la Argentina
**Argentine** ['ɑrdʒən,tin] o ['ɑrdʒən,taɪn] *adj & s* argentino || **the Argentine** la Argentina
**Argentinean** [,ɑrdʒən'tɪnɪ·ən] *adj & s* argentino
**Argonaut** ['ɑrgə,nɔt] *s* argonauta *m*
**argue** ['ɑrgju] *tr* argüir; **to argue into** persuadir a + *inf;* **to argue out of** disuadir de + *inf* || *intr* argüir
**argument** ['ɑrgjəmənt] *s* argumento; disputa
**argumentative** [,ɑrgjə'mɛntətɪv] *adj* argumentador
**aria** ['ɑrɪ·ə] o ['ɛrɪ·ə] *s* (**mus**) aria
**arid** ['ærɪd] *adj* árido
**aridity** [ə'rɪdɪti] *s* aridez *f*
**aright** [ə'raɪt] *adv* acertadamente; **to set aright** rectificar
**arise** [ə'raɪz] *v* (*pret* **arose** [ə'roz]; *pp* **arisen** [ə'rɪzən]) *intr* levantarse; subir; aparecer; **to arise from** provenir de
**aristocra•cy** [,ærɪs'tɑkrəsi] *s* (*pl* **-cies**) aristocracia
**aristocrat** [ə'rɪstə,kræt] *s* aristócrata *mf*
**aristocratic** [ə,rɪstə'krætɪk] *adj* aristocrático
**Aristotelian** [,ærɪstə'tilɪ·ən] *adj & s* aristotélico
**Aristotle** ['ærɪ,tɑtəl] *s* Aristóteles *m*
**arith.** *abbr* **arithmetic**
**arithmetic** [ə'rɪθmətɪk] *s* aritmética
**arithmetical** [,ærɪθ'mɛtɪkəl] *adj* aritmético
**arithmetician** [ə,rɪθmə'tɪʃən] *s* aritmético
**ark** [ɑrk] *s* arca de Noé

**ark of the covenant** *s* arca de la alianza
**arm** [ɑrm] *s* brazo; (*weapon*) arma; **arm in arm** de bracero, asidos del brazo; **in arms** de pecho, de teta; **the three arms of the service** los tres ejércitos; **to be up in arms** estar en armas; **to keep at arm's length** mantener a distancia; mantenerse a distancia; **to lay down one's arms** rendir las armas; **to rise up in arms** alzarse en armas; **under arms** sobre las armas || *tr* armar || *intr* armarse
**armament** ['ɑrməmənt] *s* armamento
**armature** ['ɑrmə,tʃər] *s* armadura; (*of a dynamo or motor*) (elec) inducido
**arm'chair'** *adj* de gabinete || *s* butaca, sillón *m*, silla de brazos
**Armenian** [ɑr'minɪ·ən] *adj & s* armenio
**armful** ['ɑrm,fʊl] *s* brazado
**arm'hole'** *s* (*in clothing*) sobaquera
**armistice** ['ɑrmɪstɪs] *s* armisticio
**armor** ['ɑrmər] *s* armadura; coraza, blindaje *m* || *tr* acorazar, blindar
**armored car** *s* carro blindado
**armorial bearings** [ɑr'morɪ·əl] *spl* blasón *m*, escudo de armas
**armor plate** *s* plancha de blindaje
**ar'mor-plate'** *tr* acorazar, blindar
**armor·y** ['ɑrməri] *s* (*pl* **-ies**) arsenal *m*; (*arms factory*) armería
**arm'pit'** *s* sobaco, hueco de la axila
**arm'rest'** *s* apoyabrazos *m*
**ar·my** ['ɑrmi] *adj* militar, castrense || *s* (*pl* **-mies**) ejército
**army corps** *s* cuerpo de ejército
**aroma** [ə'romə] *s* aroma *m*, fragancia
**aromatic** [,ærə'mætɪk] *adj* aromático
**around** [ə'raʊnd] *adv* alrededor, a la redonda; en la dirección opuesta || *prep* alrededor de, en torno a o de; cerca de; (*the corner*) a la vuelta de
**arouse** [ə'raʊz] *tr* despertar; excitar, incitar
**arpeg·gio** [ɑr'pɛdʒo] *s* (*pl* **-gios**) arpegio
**arraign** [ə'ren] *tr* acusar; presentar al tribunal
**arrange** [ə'rendʒ] *tr* arreglar, disponer; (mus) adaptar, refundir
**array** [ə're] *s* orden *m*; orden *m* de batalla; adorno, atavío || *tr* poner en orden; poner en orden de batalla; adornar, ataviar
**arrears** [ə'rɪrz] *spl* atrasos; **in arrears** atrasado en pagos
**arrest** [ə'rɛst] *s* arresto, prisión; detención; **under arrest** bajo arresto || *tr* arrestar; detener; atraer (*la atención*)
**arresting** [ə'rɛstɪŋ] *adj* impresionante
**arrival** [ə'raɪvəl] *s* llegada; (*person*) llegado
**arrive** [ə'raɪv] *intr* llegar; tener éxito
**arrogance** ['ærəgəns] *s* arrogancia
**arrogant** ['ærəgənt] *adj* arrogante
**arrogate** ['ærə,get] *tr* — **to arrogate to oneself** arrogarse
**arrow** ['æro] *s* flecha
**ar'row·head'** *s* punta de flecha; (bot) saetilla
**arsenal** ['ɑrsənəl] *s* arsenal *m*
**arsenic** ['ɑrsɪnɪk] *s* arsénico
**arson** ['ɑrsən] *s* incendio premeditado, delito de incendio
**art** [ɑrt] *s* arte *m & f*
**arter·y** ['ɑrtəri] *s* (*pl* **-ies**) arteria
**artful** ['ɑrtfəl] *adj* astuto, mañoso; diestro, ingenioso
**arthritic** [ɑr'θrɪtɪk] *adj & s* artrítico
**arthritis** [ɑr'θraɪtɪs] *s* artritis *f*
**artichoke** ['ɑrtɪ,tʃok] *s* alcachofa
**article** ['ɑrtɪkəl] *s* artículo; **an article of clothing** una prenda de vestir
**articulate** [ɑr'tɪkjəlɪt] *adj* claro, distinto; capaz de hablar || [ɑr'tɪkjə,let] *tr* articular
**artifact** ['ɑrtɪ,fækt] *s* artefacto
**artifice** ['ɑrtɪfɪs] *s* artificio
**artificial** [,ɑrtɪ'fɪʃəl] *adj* artificial
**artillery** [ɑr'tɪləri] *s* artillería
**artillery·man** [ɑr'tɪlərimən] *s* (*pl* **-men** [mən]) artillero
**artisan** ['ɑrtɪzən] *s* artesano
**artist** ['ɑrtɪst] *s* artista *mf*
**artistic** [ɑr'tɪstɪk] *adj* artístico
**artistry** ['ɑrtɪstri] *s* habilidad artística
**artless** ['ɑrtlɪs] *adj* sencillo, natural; ingenuo, inocente; (*crude, clumsy*) chabacano
**arts and crafts** *spl* artes y oficios
**art·y** ['ɑrti] *adj* (*comp* **-ier**; *super* **-iest**) (coll) ostentosamente artístico
**Aryan** ['ɛrɪ·ən] o ['ɑrjən] *adj & s* ario
**as** [æz] o [əz] *pron rel* que; **the same as** el mismo que || *adv* tan; **as . . . as** tan . . . como; **as for** en cuanto a; **as long as** mientras que; ya que; **as many as** tantos como; **as much as** tanto como; **as regards** en cuanto a; **as soon as** tan pronto como; **as soon as possible** cuanto antes, lo más pronto posible; **as though** como si; **as to** en cuanto a; **as well** también; **as yet** hasta ahora || *conj* como; que; ya que; a medida que; **as it seems** por lo visto, según parece || *prep* por, como; **as a rule** por regla general
**asbestos** [æs'bɛstəs] *s* asbesto, amianto
**ascend** [ə'sɛnd] *tr* subir a (*p.ej., el trono*) || *intr* ascender
**ascendancy** [ə'sɛndənsi] *s* ascendiente *m*
**ascension** [ə'sɛnʃən] *s* ascensión
**Ascension Day** *s* fiesta de la Ascensión
**ascent** [ə'sɛnt] *s* ascensión, subida; ascenso, promoción
**ascertain** [,æsər'ten] *tr* averiguar
**ascertainable** [,æsər'tenəbəl] *adj* averiguable
**ascetic** [ə'sɛtɪk] *adj* ascético || *s* asceta *mf*
**ascorbic acid** [ə'skɔrbɪk] *s* ácido ascórbico
**ascribe** [ə'skraɪb] *tr* atribuir
**aseptic** [ə'sɛptɪk] o [e'sɛptɪk] *adj* aséptico
**ash** [æʃ] *s* ceniza; (*tree; wood*) fresno; **ashes** ceniza, cenizas; (*mortal remains*) cenizas
**ashamed** [ə'ʃemd] *adj* avergonzado; **to be ashamed** tener vergüenza
**ashlar** ['æʃlər] *s* sillar *m*
**ashore** [ə'ʃor] *adv* en tierra, a tierra

**ash tray** *s* cenicero
**Ash Wednesday** *s* miércoles *m* de ceniza
**Asia** [ˈeʒə] o [ˈeʃə] *s* Asia
**Asia Minor** *s* el Asia Menor
**Asian** [ˈeʒən] o [ˈeʃən] o **Asiatic** [ˌeʒɪˈætɪk] o [ˌeʃɪˈætɪk] *adj & s* asiático
**aside** [əˈsaɪd] *adv* aparte; **aside from** además de; **to step aside** hacerse a un lado ‖ *s* (theat) aparte *m*
**asinine** [ˈæsɪˌnaɪn] *adj* tonto, necio
**ask** [æsk] o [ɑsk] *tr* (*to request*) pedir; (*to inquire of*) preguntar; hacer (*una pregunta*); invitar; **to ask in** invitar a entrar ‖ *intr* — **to ask about, after,** or **for** preguntar por; **to ask for** pedir
**askance** [əˈskæns] *adv* al sesgo, de soslayo; con desdén, sospechosamente
**asleep** [əˈslip] *adj* dormido; **to fall asleep** dormirse
**asp** [æsp] *s* áspid *m*
**asparagus** [əˈspærəgəs] *s* espárrago
**aspect** [ˈæspɛkt] *s* aspecto
**aspen** [ˈæspən] *s* tiemblo, álamo temblón
**aspersion** [əˈspʌrʒən] o [əˈspʌrʃən] *s* calumnia, difamación
**asphalt** [ˈæsfɔlt] o [ˈæsfælt] *s* asfalto ‖ *tr* asfaltar
**asphyxiate** [æsˈfɪksɪˌet] *tr* asfixiar
**aspirant** [əˈspaɪrənt] o [ˈæspɪrənt] *s* pretendiente *mf*, candidato
**aspire** [əˈspaɪr] *intr* aspirar
**aspirin** [ˈæspɪrɪn] *s* aspirina
**ass** [æs] *s* asno
**assail** [əˈsel] *tr* asaltar, acometer
**assassin** [əˈsæsɪn] *s* asesino
**assassinate** [əˈsæsɪˌnet] *tr* asesinar
**assassination** [əˌsæsɪˈneʃən] *s* asesinato
**assault** [əˈsɔlt] *s* asalto ‖ *tr* asaltar
**assault and battery** *s* vías de hecho, violencias
**assay** [əˈse] o [ˈæse] *s* ensaye *m;* muestra de ensaye ‖ [əˈse] *tr* ensayar; apreciar
**assemble** [əˈsɛmbəl] *tr* reunir; (mach) armar, montar ‖ *intr* reunirse
**assem·bly** [əˈsɛmbli] *s* (*pl* **-blies**) asamblea; reunión; (mach) armadura, montaje *m*
**assembly hall** *s* aula magna, paraninfo; salón *m* de sesiones
**assembly line** *s* línea de montaje
**assembly plant** *s* fábrica de montaje
**assembly room** *s* sala de reunión; (mach) taller *m* de montaje
**assent** [əˈsɛnt] *s* asentimiento, asenso ‖ *intr* asentir
**assert** [əˈsʌrt] *tr* afirmar, aseverar, declarar; **to assert oneself** imponerse, hacer valer sus derechos
**assertion** [əˈsʌrʃən] *s* aserción, aseveración
**assess** [əˈsɛs] *tr* amillarar, gravar; fijar (*daños y perjuicios*); apreciar, estimar
**assessment** [əˈsɛsmənt] *s* amillaramiento, gravamen *m;* fijación; apreciación, estimación
**asset** [ˈæsɛt] *s* posesión, ventaja; (*person, thing, or quality worth having*) (fig) valor *m;* **assets** (com) activo
**assiduous** [əˈsɪdʒʊ·əs] o [əˈsɪdjʊ·əs] *adj* asiduo
**assign** [əˈsaɪn] *tr* asignar
**assignment** [əˈsaɪnmənt] *s* asignación, cometido; lección
**assimilate** [əˈsɪmɪˌlet] *tr* asimilarse (*los alimentos, el conocimiento*) ‖ *intr* asimilarse
**assist** [əˈsɪst] *tr* ayudar, asistir, auxiliar
**assistant** [əˈsɪstənt] *adj & s* auxiliar *mf*, ayudante *mf*
**assn.** *abbr* **association**
**associate** [əˈsoʃɪ·ɪt] o [əˈsoʃɪˌet] *adj* asociado ‖ *s* asociado, socio ‖ [əˈsoʃɪˌet] *tr* asociar ‖ *intr* asociarse
**association** [əˌsoʃɪˈeʃən] *s* asociación
**assort** [əˈsɔrt] *tr* clasificar, ordenar
**assortment** [əˈsɔrtment] *s* surtido; clase *f*, grupo
**asst.** *abbr* **assistant**
**assume** [əˈsum] o [əˈsjum] *tr* asumir (*p.ej., responsabilidades*); arrogarse; suponer, dar por sentado
**assumption** [əˈsʌmpʃən] *s* asunción; suposición
**assurance** [əˈʃʊrəns] *s* aseguramiento; seguridad, confianza; (com) seguro
**assure** [əˈʃʊr] *tr* asegurar; (com) asegurar
**Assyria** [əˈsɪrɪ·ə] *s* Asiria
**Assyrian** [əˈsɪrɪ·ən] *adj & s* asirio
**astatine** [ˈæstəˌtin] *s* ástato
**aster** [ˈæstər] *s* (bot) aster *m;* (*China aster*) reina Margarita
**asterisk** [ˈæstəˌrɪsk] *s* asterisco
**astern** [əˈstʌrn] *adv* por la popa
**asthma** [ˈæzmə] *o* [ˈæsmə] *s* asma *f*
**astonish** [əˈstɑnɪʃ] *tr* asombrar
**astonishing** [əˈstɑnɪʃɪŋ] *adj* asombroso
**astound** [əˈstaʊnd] *tr* pasmar
**astounding** [əˈstaʊndɪŋ] *adj* pasmoso
**astraddle** [əˈstrædəl] *adv* a horcajadas
**astray** [əˈstre] *adv* por mal camino; **to go astray** extraviarse; **to lead astray** extraviar
**astride** [əˈstraɪd] *adv* a horcajadas ‖ *prep* a horcajadas de
**astrology** [əˈstrɑlədʒi] *s* astrología
**astronaut** [ˈæstrəˌnɔt] *s* astronauta *m*
**astronautic** [ˌæstrəˈnɔtɪk] *adj* astronáutico ‖ **astronautics** *s* astronáutica
**astronomer** [əˈstrɔnəmər] *s* astrónomo
**astronomic(al)** [ˌæstrəˈnɑmɪk(əl)] *adj* astronómico
**astronomy** [əˈstrɑnəmi] *s* astronomía
**Asturian** [əˈstʊrɪ·ən] *adj & s* asturiano
**astute** [əˈstjut] o [əˈstut] *adj* astuto, sagaz
**asunder** [əˈsʌndər] *adv* a pedazos, en dos
**asylum** [əˈsaɪləm] *s* asilo
**asymmetry** [əˈsɪmɪtri] *s* asimetría
**at** [æt] o [ət] *prep* en, p.ej., **I saw her at the library** la ví en la biblioteca; a, p.ej., **at five o'clock** a las cinco; de, p.ej., **to be surprised at** estar sorprendido de; **to laugh at** reírse de; en casa de, p.ej., **at John's** en casa de Juan

**atheism** ['eθi,ɪzəm] *s* ateísmo
**atheist** ['eθi·ɪst] *s* ateísta *mf,* ateo
**Athenian** [ə'θinɪ·ən] *adj & s* ateniense *mf*
**Athens** ['æθɪnz] *s* Atenas *f*
**athirst** [ə'θʌrst] *adj* sediento
**athlete** ['æθlit] *s* atleta *mf*
**athlete's foot** *s* pie *m* de atleta
**athletic** [æθ'letɪk] *adj* atlético ‖ **athletics** *s* atletismo
**Atlantic** [æt'læntɪk] *adj & s* Atlántico
**atlas** ['ætləs] *s* atlas *m*
**atmosphere** ['ætməs,fɪr] *s* atmósfera
**atmospheric** [,ætməs'fɛrɪk] *adj* atmosférico ‖ **atmospherics** *spl* parásitos atmosféricos
**atom** ['ætəm] *s* átomo
**atom bomb** *s* bomba atómica
**atomic** [ə'tɑmɪk] *adj* atómico
**atomic bomb** *s* bomba atómica
**atomize** ['ætə,maɪz] *tr* atomizar
**atomizer** ['ætə,maɪzər] *s* pulverizador *m,* vaporizador *m*
**atom smasher** *s* rompeátomos *m*
**atone** [ə'ton] *intr* dar reparación; **to atone for** dar reparación por, expiar
**atonement** [ə'tonmənt] *s* reparación, expiación
**atop** [ə'tɑp] *adv* encima ‖ *prep* encima de
**atrocious** [ə'troʃəs] *adj* atroz; (coll) abominable, muy malo
**atroci·ty** [ə'trɑsɪti] *s pl* **-ties**) atrocidad
**atro·phy** ['ætrəfi] *s* atrofia ‖ *v* (*pret & pp* **-phied**) *tr* atrofiar ‖ *intr* atrofiarse
**attach** [ə'tætʃ] *tr* atar, ligar; atribuir (*p.ej., importancia*); (law) embargar; **to be attached to** aficionarse a; (*to be officially associated with*) depender de
**attaché** [,ætə'ʃe] o [ə'tæʃe] *s* agregado
**attachment** [ə'tætʃmənt] *s* atadura, enlace *m;* atribución; apego, cariño; accesorio; (law) embargo
**attack** [ə'tæk] *s* ataque *m* ‖ *tr & intr* atacar
**attain** [ə'ten] *tr* alcanzar, lograr
**attainment** [ə'tenmənt] *s* consecución, logro; **attainments** dotes *fpl,* prendas
**attempt** [ə'tɛmpt] *s* tentativa; (*assault*) atentado, conato ‖ *tr* procurar, intentar; (*e.g., the life of a person*) atentar a o contra
**attend** [ə'tɛnd] *tr* atender, asistir; asistir a (*p.ej., la escuela*); auxiliar (*a un moribundo*) ‖ *intr* atender; **to attend to** atender a
**attendance** [ə'tɛndəns] *s* asistencia, concurrencia; **to dance attendance** hacer antesala
**attendant** [ə'tɛndənt] *adj & s* asistente *mf;* concomitante *m*
**attention** [ə'tɛnʃən] *s* atención; **to attract attention** llamar la atención; **to call attention to** hacer presente; **to pay attention to** hacer caso de
**attentive** [ə'tɛntɪv] *adj* atento
**attenuate** [ə'tɛnjʊ,et] *tr* adelgazar; debilitar ‖ *intr* debilitarse; desaparecer
**attest** [ə'tɛst] *tr* atestiguar; juramentar ‖ *intr* dar fe; **to attest to** dar fe de
**attic** ['ætɪk] *s* buharda, guardilla, desván *m*
**attire** [ə'taɪr] *s* atavío, traje *m* ‖ *tr* ataviar, vestir
**attitude** ['ætɪ,tjud] o ['ætɪ,tud] *s* actitud, ademán *m*
**attorney** [ə'tʌrni] *s* abogado; procurador *m*
**attract** [ə'trækt] *tr* atraer; llamar (*la atención*)
**attraction** [ə'trækʃən] *s* atracción; (*personal charm*) atractivo
**attractive** [ə'træktɪv] *adj* atractivo; (*agreeable, interesting*) atrayente
**attribute** ['ætrɪ,bjut] *s* atributo ‖ [ə'trɪbjʊt] *tr* atribuir
**atty.** *abbr* **attorney**
**auburn** ['ɔbərn] *adj & s* castaño rojizo
**auction** ['ɔkʃən] *s* almoneda, remate *m,* subasta ‖ *tr* rematar, subastar
**auctioneer** [,ɔkʃən'ɪr] *s* subastador *m* ‖ *tr & intr* rematar, subastar
**auction house** *s* martillo
**audacious** [ɔ'deʃəs] *adj* audaz
**audaci·ty** [ɔ'dæsɪti] *s* (*pl* **-ties**) audacia
**audience** ['ɔdɪ·əns] *s* (*hearing; formal interview*) audiencia; público, auditorio
**audio frequency** ['ɔdɪ,o] *s* audiofrecuencia
**audiometer** [,ɔdɪ'ɑmɪtər] *s* audiómetro
**audit** ['ɔdɪt] *s* intervención ‖ *tr* intervenir
**audition** [ɔ'dɪʃən] *s* audición ‖ *tr* dar audición a
**auditor** ['ɔdɪtər] *s* oyente *mf;* (com) interventor *m*
**auditorium** [,ɔdɪ'torɪ·əm] *s* auditorio, anfiteatro, paraninfo
**auger** ['ɔgər] *s* barrena
**augment** [ɔg'mɛnt] *tr & intr* aumentar
**augur** ['ɔgər] *s* augur *m* ‖ *tr & intr* augurar; **to augur well** ser de buen agüero
**augu·ry** ['ɔgəri] *s* (*pl* **-ries**) augurio
**august** [ɔ'gʌst] *adj* augusto ‖ **August** ['ɔgəst] *s* agosto
**aunt** [ænt] o [ɑnt] *s* tía
**aurora** [ə'rorə] *s* aurora
**auspice** ['ɔspɪs] *s* auspicio; **under the auspices of** bajo los auspicios de
**austere** [ɔs'tɪr] *adj* austero
**Australia** [ɔ'streljə] *s* Australia
**Australian** [ɔ'streljən] *adj & s* australiano
**Austria** ['ɔstrɪ·ə] *s* Austria
**Austrian** ['ɔstrɪ·ən] *adj & s* austríaco
**authentic** [ɔ'θɛntɪk] *adj* auténtico
**authenticate** [ɔ'θɛntɪ,ket] *tr* autenticar
**author** ['ɔθər] *s* autor *m*
**authoress** ['ɔθərɪs] *s* autora
**authoritarian** [ɑ,θɑrɪ'tɛrɪ·ən] o [ɔ,θɔrɪ'tɛrɪ·ən] *adj & s* autoritario
**authoritative** [ɔ'θɑrɪ,tetɪv] o [ɔ'θɔrɪ,tetɪv] *adj* autorizado; (*dictatorial*) autoritario
**authori·ty** [ɔ'θɑrɪti] o [ɔ'θɔrɪti] *s* (*pl* **-ties**) autoridad; **on good authority** de buena tinta, de fuente fidedigna
**authorize** ['ɔθə,raɪz] *tr* autorizar

**authorship** ['ɔθər,ʃɪp] *s* paternidad literaria
**au·to** ['ɔto] *s* (*pl* **-tos**) (coll) auto, coche *m*
**autobiogra·phy** [,ɔtobaɪ'ɑgrəfi] u [,ɔtobɪ'ɑgrəfi] *s* (*pl* **-phies**) autobiografía
**autobus** ['ɔto,bʌs] *s* autobús *m*
**autocratic(al)** [,ɔtə'krætɪk(əl)] *adj* autocrático
**autograph** ['ɔtə,græf] u ['ɔtə,grɑf] *adj* & *s* autógrafo || *tr* autografiar
**autograph seeker** *s* cazaautógrafos *m*
**automat** ['ɔtə,mæt] *s* restaurante automático
**automatic** [,ɔtə'mætɪk] *adj* automático
**automatic clutch** *s* servoembrague *m*
**automation** [,ɔtə'meʃən] *s* automación, automatización
**automa·ton** [ɔ'tɑmə,tɑn] *s* (*pl* **-tons** o **-ta** [tə]) autómata
**automobile** [,ɔtəmo'bil] u [,ɔtə'mobil] *s* automóvil *m*
**automobile show** *s* salón *m* del automóvil
**autonomous** [ɔ'tɑnəməs] *adj* autónomo
**autonomy** [ɔ'tɑnəmi] *s* autonomía
**autop·sy** ['ɔtɑpsi] *s* (*pl* **-sies**) autopsia
**autumn** ['ɔtəm] *s* otoño
**autumnal** [ə'tʌmnəl] *adj* otoñal
**auxilia·ry** [ɔg'zɪljəri] *adj* auxiliar || *s* (*pl* **-ries**) auxiliar *mf*; **auxiliaries** tropas auxiliares
**av.** *abbr* **avenue, average, avoirdupois**
**avail** [ə'vel] *s* provecho, utilidad || *tr* beneficiar; **to avail oneself of** aprovecharse de, valerse de || *intr* aprovechar
**available** [ə'veləbəl] *adj* disponible; **to make available to** poner a la disposición de
**avalanche** ['ævə,lænt∫] o ['ævə,lɑnt∫] *s* alud *m*, avalancha
**avant-garde** [avɑ̃'gard] *adj* vanguardista || *s* vanguardismo
**avant-guardist** [avɑ̃'gardɪst] *s* vanguardista *mf*
**avarice** ['ævərɪs] *s* avaricia
**avaricious** [,ævə'rɪʃəs] *adj* avaricioso, avariento
**Ave.** *abbr* **Avenue**
**avenge** [ə'vɛndʒ] *tr* vengar; **to avenge oneself on** vengarse en
**avenue** ['ævə,nju] o ['ævə,nu] *s* avenida
**aver** [ə'vʌr] *v* (*pret* & *pp* **averred**; *ger* **averring**) *tr* afirmar, declarar
**average** ['ævərɪdʒ] *adj* común, mediano, ordinario || *s* promedio, término medio; (naut) avería || *tr* calcular el término medio de; prorratear; ser de un promedio de
**averse** [ə'vʌrs] *adj* renuente, contrario
**aversion** [ə'vʌrʒən] *s* aversión, antipatía; cosa aborrecida
**avert** [ə'vʌrt] *tr* apartar, desviar; impedir
**aviar·y** ['evɪ,ɛri] *s* (*pl* **-ies**) avería, pajarera
**aviation** [,evɪ'eʃən] *s* aviación
**aviation medicine** *s* aeromedicina
**aviator** ['evɪ,etər] *s* aviador *m*
**avid** ['ævɪd] *adj* ávido
**avidity** [ə'vɪdɪti] *s* avidez *f*
**avocation** [,ævə'keʃən] *s* distracción, diversión
**avoid** [ə'vɔid] *tr* evitar
**avoidable** [ə'vɔɪdəbəl] *adj* evitable
**avoidance** [ə'vɔɪdəns] *s* evitación
**avow** [ə'vaʊ] *tr* admitir, confesar
**avowal** [ə'vaʊ·əl] *s* admisión, confesión
**await** [ə'wet] *tr* aguardar, esperar
**awake** [ə'wek] *adj* despierto || *v* (*pret* & *pp* **awoke** [ə'wok] o **awaked**) *tr* & *intr* despertar
**awaken** [ə'wekən] *tr* & *intr* despertar
**awakening** [ə'wekənɪŋ] *s* despertamiento; desilusión
**award** [ə'wɔrd] *s* premio; condecoración; adjudicación || *tr* conceder; adjudicar
**aware** [ə'wɛr] *adj* enterado; **to become aware of** enterarse de, darse cuenta de
**awareness** [ə'wɛrnɪs] *s* conciencia
**away** [ə'we] *adj* ausente; distante || *adv* lejos; a lo lejos; **away from** lejos de; **to do away with** deshacerse de; **to get away** escapar; **to go away** irse; **to make away with** robar, hurtar; **to run away** fugarse; **to send away** enviar; despedir; **to take away** llevarse; quitar
**awe** [ɔ] *s* temor *m* reverencial || *tr* infundir temor reverencial a
**awesome** ['ɔsəm] *adj* imponente
**awestruck** ['ɔ,strʌk] *adj* espantado
**awful** ['ɔfəl] *adj* atroz, horrible; impresionante; (coll) muy malo, muy feo, enorme
**awfully** ['ɔfəli] *adv* atrozmente, horriblemente; (coll) muy, excesivamente
**awhile** [ə'hwaɪl] *adv* un rato, algún tiempo
**awkward** ['ɔkwərd] *adj* desmañado, torpe, lerdo; embarazoso, delicado
**awkward squad** *s* pelotón *m* de los torpes
**awl** [ɔl] *s* alesna, lezna
**awning** ['ɔnɪŋ] *s* toldo
**ax** [æks] *s* hacha
**axiom** ['æksɪ·əm] *s* axioma *m*
**axiomatic** [,æksɪ·ə'mætɪk] *adj* axiomático
**axis** ['æksɪs] *s* (*pl* **axes** ['æksiz]) *s* eje *m*
**axle** ['æksəl] *s* eje *m*, árbol *m*
**ax'le·tree'** *s* eje *m* de carretón
**ay** [aɪ] *adv* & *s* sí || [e] *adv* siempre; **for ay** por siempre || [e] *interj* ¡ay!
**aye** [aɪ] *adv* & *s* sí || [e] *adv* siempre; **for aye** por siempre
**azimuth** ['æzɪməθ] *s* acimut *m*
**Azores** [ə'zorz] o ['ezorz] *spl* Azores *fpl*
**Aztec** ['æztɛk] *adj* & *s* azteca *mf*
**azure** ['æʒər] o ['eʒər] *adj* & *s* azul *m*

## B

**B, b** [bi] segunda letra del alfabeto inglés
**b.** *abbr* **bass, bay, born, brother**
**baa** [bɑ] *s* be *m,* balido ‖ *intr* balar
**babble** [ˈbæbəl] *s* barboteo; charla; (*of a brook*) murmullo ‖ *tr* barbotar; decir indiscretamente ‖ *intr* barbotar; murmurar (*un arroyo*)
**babe** [beb] *s* rorro, criatura; (*innocent, gullible person*) niño; (slang) chica, chica hermosa
**baboon** [bæˈbun] *s* babuíno
**ba•by** [ˈbebi] *s* (*pl* **-bies**) rorro, criatura, bebé *m;* (*the youngest child*) benjamín *m* ‖ *v* (*pret & pp* **-bied**) *tr* mimar; tratar como niño
**baby carriage** *s* cochecillo para niños
**baby grand** *s* piano de media cola
**babyhood** [ˈbebi ˌhʊd] *s* primera infancia, niñez *f*
**babyish** [ˈbebi·ɪʃ] *adj* aniñado, infantil
**Babylon** [ˈbæbɪlən] o [ˈbæbɪˌlɑn] *s* Babilonia (*ciudad*)
**Babylonia** [ˌbæbɪˈlonɪ·ə] *s* Babilonia (*imperio*)
**Babylonian** [ˌbæbɪˈlonɪ·ən] *adj & s* babilonio
**baby sitter** *s* niñera tomada por horas
**baccalaureate** [ˌbækəˈlɔrɪ·ɪt] *s* bachillerato
**bachelor** [ˈbætʃələr] *s* (*unmarried man*) soltero; (*holder of bachelor's degree*) bachiller *mf;* (*apprentice knight*) doncel *m*
**bachelorhood** [ˈbætʃələrˌhʊd] *s* celibato, soltería (*del hombre*)
**bacil•lus** [bəˈsɪləs] *s* (*pl* **-li** [laɪ]) bacilo
**back** [bæk] *adj* trasero, posterior; atrasado ‖ *adv* atrás, detrás; de vuelta; (*ago*) hace; **back of** detrás de; **to go back to** remontarse a; **to send back** devolver ‖ *s* espalda; dorso; (*of a coin*) reverso; (*of a chair*) espaldar *m,* respaldo; (*of an animal, of a book*) lomo; (*of a hall, a room*) fondo; (*of a writing, a book*) final *m;* **behind one's back** a espaldas de uno; **on one's back** postrado, en cama; a cuestas ‖ *tr* mover hacia atrás; apoyar, respaldar ‖ *intr* moverse hacia atrás; **to back down** u **out** volverse atrás, echarse atrás; **to back up** retroceder; regolfar (*el agua*)
**back'ache'** *s* dolor *m* de espalda
**back'bone'** *s* espinazo; (*of a book*) nervura; firmeza, resistencia
**back'break'ing** *adj* deslomador
**back'down'** *s* palinodia, retractación
**back'drop'** *s* telón *m* de fondo o de foro
**backer** [ˈbækər] *s* sostenedor *m,* defensor *m;* (*of a business venture*) impulsador *m*
**back'fire'** *s* (aut) petardeo ‖ *intr* (aut) petardear
**back'ground'** *s* fondo; antecedentes *mpl;* conocimientos, educación; (*of a painting*) lontananza
**background music** *s* música de fondo
**backing** [ˈbækɪŋ] *s* apoyo, sostén *m;* garantía, respaldo; (bb) lomera
**back'lash'** *s* (mach) contragolpe *m;* (mach) juego; (fig) reacción violenta
**back'log'** *s* (com) reserva de pedidos pendientes; (*e.g., of work*) acumulación
**back number** *s* número atrasado; (coll) persona anticuada
**back pay** *s* sueldo retrasado
**back seat** *s* puesto secundario; **to take a back seat** perder influencia
**back'side'** *s* espalda; trasero
**back'slide'** *v* (*pret & pp* **-slid** [ˌslɪd]) *intr* reincidir
**backspacer** [ˈbækˌspesər] *s* tecla de retroceso
**back'stage'** *adv* detrás del telón; entre bastidores
**back'stairs'** *adj* indirecto, secreto
**back stairs** *spl* escalera trasera; medios indirectos
**back'stitch'** *s* pespunte *m* ‖ *tr & intr* pespuntar
**back'stop'** *s* reja o red *f* para detener la pelota
**back'swept' wing** *s* (aer) ala en flecha
**back talk** *s* respuesta insolente
**backward** [ˈbækwərd] *adj* atrasado, tardío; tímido ‖ *adv* de atrás; de espaldas; al revés; cada vez peor; para atrás, hacia atrás
**back'wa'ter** *s* remanso; (fig) atraso, yermo
**back'woods'** *spl* monte *m,* región alejada de los centros de población
**back yard** *s* patio trasero, corral trasero
**bacon** [ˈbekən] *s* tocino
**bacteria** [bækˈtɪrɪ·ə] *pl de* **bacterium**
**bacterial** [bækˈtɪrɪ·əl] *adj* bacteriano
**bacteriologist** [bækˌtɪrɪˈɑlədʒɪst] *s* bacteriólogo
**bacteriology** [bækˌtɪrɪˈɑlədʒi] *s* bacteriología
**bacteri•um** [bækˈtɪrɪ·əm] *s* (*pl* **-a** [ə]) bacteria
**bad** [bæd] *adj* (*comp* **worse** [wʌrs]; *super* **worst** [wʌrst]) malo; (*money*) falso; (*debt*) incobrable; **from bad to worse** de mal en peor; **to be in bad** (coll) caer en desgracia; **to be too bad** ser lástima; **to go to the bad** (coll) ir por mal camino; (coll) arruinarse; **to look bad** tener mala cara
**bad breath** *s* mal aliento
**badge** [bædʒ] *s* divisa, insignia
**badger** [ˈbædʒər] *s* tejón *m*
**badly** [ˈbædli] *adv* mal; con urgencia; gravemente
**badly off** *adj* malparado; muy enfermo
**badminton** [ˈbædmɪntən] *s* juego del volante
**baffle** [ˈbæfəl] *s* deflector *m;* (rad)

pantalla acústica || *tr* confundir; burlar, frustrar
**baffling** ['bæflɪŋ] *adj* perplejo, desconcertador
**bag** [bæg] *s* saco; saquito de mano; (*in clothing*) bolsa; (*purse*) bolso; (*take of game*) caza; **to be in the bag** (slang) ser cosa segura || *v* (*pret & pp* **bagged**; *ger* **bagging**) *tr* ensacar; coger, cazar || *intr* hacer bolsa (*un vestido*)
**baggage** ['bægɪdʒ] *s* equipaje *m;* (mil) bagaje *m*
**baggage car** *s* furgón *m* de equipajes
**baggage check** *s* contraseña de equipajes
**baggage rack** *s* red *f* de equipajes
**baggage room** *s* sala de equipajes
**bag'pipe'** *s* gaita, cornamusa
**bag'pi'per** *s* gaitero
**bail** [bel] *s* caución, fianza; **to go bail for** salir fiador por || *tr* caucionar, afianzar; achicar (*la embarcación; el agua*); **to bail out** salir fiador por; achicar || *intr* achicar; **to bail out** lanzarse en paracaídas
**bailiff** ['belɪf] *s* algualcil *m,* corchete *m*
**bailiwick** ['belɪwɪk] *s* alguacilazgo; **to be in the bailiwick of** ser de la pertenencia de
**bait** [bet] *s* carnada, cebo; señuelo; **to swallow the bait** tragar el anzuelo || *tr* cebar, encarnar (*el anzuelo*); tentar, seducir; (*to pester*) hostigar
**baize** [bez] *s* bayeta
**bake** [bek] *tr* cocer al horno; cocer (*loza, gres, etc.*)
**bakelite** ['bekə,laɪt] *s* baquelita
**baker** ['bekər] *s* panadero, hornero
**baker's dozen** *s* docena del fraile
**baker·y** ['bekəri] *s* (*pl* **-ies**) panadería
**baking powder** ['bekɪŋ] *s* levadura en polvo
**baking soda** *s* bicarbonato de sosa
**bal.** *abbr* **balance**
**balance** ['bæləns] *s* (*instrument for weighing*) balanza; (*state of equilibrium*) equilibrio; (*amount left over*) resto; (*amount still owed*) saldo; (*statement of debits and credits*) balance *m;* **to lose one's balance** perder el equilibrio; **to strike a balance** hacer o pasar balance || *tr* balancear; equilibrar; equilibrar, nivelar (*el presupuesto*) || *intr* equilibrarse; (*to waver*) balancear
**balance of payments** *s* balanza de pagos
**balance of power** *s* equilibrio político
**balance sheet** *s* balance *m,* avanzo
**balco·ny** ['bælkəni] *s* (*pl* **-nies**) balcón *m;* (*in a theater*) galería, paraíso
**bald** [bɔld] *adj* calvo; franco, directo
**baldness** ['bɔldnɪs] *s* calvicie *f*
**baldric** ['bɔldrɪk] *s* tahalí *m*
**bale** [bel] *s* bala || *tr* embalar
**Balearic** [,bælɪ'ærɪk] *adj* balear
**Balearic Islands** *spl* islas Baleares
**baleful** ['belfəl] *adj* funesto, maligno
**balk** [bɔk] *tr* burlar, frustrar || *intr* emperrarse, resistirse
**Balkan** ['bɔlkən] *adj* balcánico || **the Balkans** los Balcanes
**balk·y** ['bɔki] *adj* (*comp* **-ier;** *super* **-iest**) rebelón, repropio
**ball** [bɔl] *s* bola, pelota; esfera, globo; (*of wool, yarn*) ovillo; (*of finger*) yema; (*projectile*) bala; (*dance*) baile *m*
**ballad** ['bæləd] *s* balada
**ballade** [bə'lɑd] *s* (mus) balada
**ballast** ['bæləst] *s* (aer, naut) lastre *m;* (rr) balasto || *tr* lastrar; balastar
**ball bearing** *s* cojinete *m* de bolas
**ballerina** [,bælə'rinə] *s* bailarina
**ballet** ['bæle] *s* ballet *m,* baile *m*
**ballistic** [bə'lɪstɪk] *adj* balístico
**balloon** [bə'lun] *s* globo
**ballot** ['bælət] *s* balota; sufragio || *intr* balotar
**ballot box** *s* urna electoral
**ball'play'er** *s* pelotari *m;* beisbolero
**ball'-point' pen** *s* polígrafo, bolígrafo, pluma esferográfica
**ball'room'** *s* salón *m* de baile
**ballyhoo** ['bælɪ,hu] *s* alharaca, bombo || *tr* dar teatro a, dar bombo a
**balm** [bɑm] *s* bálsamo
**balm·y** ['bɑmi] *adj* (*comp* **-ier;** *super* **-iest**) bonancible, suave
**balsam** ['bɔlsəm] *s* bálsamo
**Baltic** ['bɔltɪk] *adj* báltico
**Baltimore oriole** ['bɔltɪ,mor] *s* cacique veranero
**baluster** ['bæləstər] *s* balaustre *m*
**bamboo** [bæm'bu] *s* bambú *m*
**bamboozle** [bæm'buzəl] *tr* (coll) embaucar, engañar
**bamboozler** [bæm'buzlər] *s* (coll) embaucador *m,* engañabobos *mf*
**ban** [bæn] *s* prohibición; excomunión, entredicho; (*of marriage*) amonestación || *v* (*pret & pp* **banned;** *ger* **banning**) *tr* prohibir; excomulgar
**banana** [bə'nænə] *s* banana, plátano; (*tree*) banano, bananero, plátano
**banana oil** *s* esencia de pera
**band** [bænd] *s* banda; (*of people*) cuadrilla; (*of a hat*) cintillo; (*of a cigar*) anillo; liga de goma; (mus) banda, música, charanga || *intr* abanderizarse
**bandage** ['bændɪdʒ] *s* venda || *tr* vendar
**bandanna** [bæn'dænə] *s* pañuelo de hierbas
**band'box'** *s* sombrerera
**bandit** ['bændɪt] *s* bandido
**band'mas'ter** *s* músico mayor
**bandoleer** [,bændə'lɪr] *s* bandolera
**band saw** *s* sierra continua, sierra sin fin
**band'stand'** *s* quiosco de música
**baneful** ['benfəl] *adj* nocivo, venenoso; (*e.g., influence*) funesto
**bang** [bæŋ] *adv* de golpe || *interj* ¡pum! || *s* golpazo; (*of a door*) portazo; **bangs** flequillo || *tr* golpear con ruido; cerrar (*p.ej., una puerta*) de golpe || *intr* hacer estrépito
**banish** ['bænɪʃ] *tr* desterrar; despedir (*p.ej., miedo*)
**banishment** ['bænɪʃmənt] *s* destierro
**banister** ['bænɪstər] *s* balaustre *m*
**bank** [bæŋk] *s* banco; (*in certain games*) banca; (*small container for*

*coins*) alcancía; (*of a river*) ribera, orilla; (*of earth, snow, clouds*) montón *m* || *tr* depositar o guardar (*dinero*) en un banco; amontonar; cubrir (*un fuego*) con cenizas || *intr* depositar dinero; **to bank on** (coll) contar con
**bank account** *s* cuenta de banco
**bank'book'** *s* libreta de banco
**banker** ['bæŋkər] *s* banquero
**banking** ['bæŋkɪŋ] *adj* bancario || *s* banca
**bank note** *s* billete *m* de banco
**bank roll** *s* lío de papel moneda
**bankrupt** ['bæŋkrʌpt] *adj* & *s* bancarrotero; **to go bankrupt** hacer bancarrota || *tr* hacer quebrar; arruinar
**bankrupt•cy** ['bæŋkrʌptsi] *s* (*pl* **-cies**) bancarrota
**banner** ['bænər] *s* bandera, estandarte *m*
**banner cry** *s* grito de combate
**banquet** ['bæŋkwɪt] *s* banquete *m* || *tr* & *intr* banquetear
**banter** ['bæntər] *s* burla, chanza || *intr* burlar, chancear
**baptism** ['bæptɪzəm] *s* bautizo tizo
**Baptist** ['bæptɪst] *adj* & *s* baptista *mf*, bautista *mf*
**baptister•y** ['bæptɪstəri] *s* (*pl* **-ies**) baptisterio, bautisterio
**baptize** [bæp'taɪz] o ['bæptaɪz] *tr* bautizar
**bar.** *abbr* **barometer, barrel, barrister**
**bar** [bɑr] *s* barra; (*of door or window*) tranca; (*of jail*) reja; barrera; (*legal profession*) abogacía; (*members of legal profession*) curia; (*of public opinion*) tribunal *m;* (mus) barra; (*unit between two bars*) (mus) compás *m;* **behind bars** entre rejas || *prep* salvo; **bar none** sin excepción || *v* (*pret* & *pp* **barred;** *ger* **barring**) *tr* barrear, atrancar; impedir; prohibir; excluir
**bar association** *s* colegio de abogados
**barb** [bɑrb] *s* púa, lengüeta; (*of a pen*) barbilla
**Barbados** [bɑr'bedoz] *s* la Barbada
**barbarian** [bɑr'bɛrɪ•ən] *s* bárbaro
**barbaric** [bɑr'bærɪk] *adj* bárbaro
**barbarism** ['bɑrbə,rɪzəm] *s* barbaridad *f;* (gram) barbarismo
**barbari•ty** [bɑr'bærɪti] *s* (*pl* **-ties**) barbarie *f*
**barbarous** ['bɑrbərəs] *adj* bárbaro
**Barbary ape** ['bɑrbəri] *s* mono de Gibraltar
**barbed** [bɑrbd] *adj* armado de púas; mordaz, punzante
**barbed wire** *s* alambre *m* de espino, alambre de púas
**barber** ['bɑrbər] *adj* barberil || *s* barbero, peluquero
**barber pole** *s* percha de barbero
**bar'ber•shop'** *s* barbería, peluquería
**bard** [bɑrd] *s* bardo; (*horse armor*) barda || *tr* bardar
**bare** [bɛr] *adj* desnudo; (*head*) descubierto; (*unfurnished*) desamueblado; (*wire*) sin aislar; mero, sencillo, puro || *tr* desnudar; descubrir
**bare'back'** *adj* & *adv* en pelo, sin silla
**barefaced** ['bɛr,fest] *adj* desvergonzado
**bare'foot'** *adj* descalzo || *adv* con los pies desnudos
**bareheaded** ['bɛr,hɛdɪd] *adj* descubierto || *adv* con la cabeza descubierta
**barelegged** ['bɛr,lɛgɪd] o ['bɛr,lɛgd] *adj* con las piernas desnudas
**barely** ['bɛrli] *adv* apenas
**bargain** ['bɑrgɪn] *s* (*deal*) convenio, trato; (*cheap purchase*) ganga; **in the bargain** de añadidura || *tr* — **to bargain away** vender regalado || *intr* negociar; (*to haggle*) regatear
**bargain counter** *s* baratillo
**bargain sale** *s* venta de saldos
**barge** [bɑrdʒ] *s* gabarra, lanchón *m* || *intr* moverse pesadamente; **to barge in** entrar sin pedir permiso, entrar sin llamar a la puerta
**barium** ['bɛrɪ•əm] *s* bario
**bark** [bɑrk] *s* (*of tree*) corteza; (*of dog*) ladrido; (*boat*) barca || *tr* ladrar (*p.ej., injurias*) || *intr* ladrar
**barley** ['bɑrli] *s* cebada
**barley water** *s* hordiate *m*
**bar magnet** *s* barra imantada
**bar'maid'** *s* moza de taberna
**barn** [bɑrn] *s* granero, troje *m;* caballeriza, establo; cochera
**barnacle** ['bɑrnəkəl] *s* cirrópodo
**barn owl** *s* lechuza, oliva
**barn'yard'** *s* corral *m*
**barnyard fowl** *spl* aves *fpl* de corral
**barometer** [bə'rɑmɪtər] *s* barómetro
**baron** ['bærən] *s* barón *m*
**baroness** ['bærənɪs] *s* baronesa
**baroque** [bə'rok] *adj* & *s* barroco
**barracks** ['bærəks] *spl* cuartel *m*
**barrage** [bə'rɑʒ] *s* (*dam*) presa; (mil) barrera de fuego
**barrel** ['bærəl] *s* barril *m*, tonel *m;* (*of a gun, pen, etc.*) cañón *m*
**barrel organ** *s* organillo
**barren** ['bærən] *adj* árido, estéril
**barricade** [,bærɪ'ked] *s* barrera || *tr* barrear
**barrier** ['bærɪ•ər] *s* barrera
**barrier reef** *s* barrera de arrecifes
**barrister** ['bærɪstər] *s* (Brit) abogado
**bar'room'** *s* bar *m*, cantina
**bar'tend'er** *s* cantinero, tabernero
**barter** ['bɑrtər] *s* trueque *m* || *tr* trocar
**base** [bes] *adj* bajo, humilde; infame, vil; (*metal*) bajo de ley || *s* base *f;* (*of electric light or vacuum tube; of projectile*) culote *m;* (mus) bajo || *tr* basar
**base'ball'** *s* béisbol *m;* pelota de béisbol
**base'board'** *s* rodapié *m*
**Basel** ['bɑzəl] *s* Basilea
**baseless** ['beslɪs] *adj* infundado
**basement** ['besmənt] *s* sótano
**bashful** ['bæʃfəl] *adj* encogido, tímido
**basic** ['besɪk] *adj* básico
**basic commodities** *spl* artículos de primera necesidad
**basilica** [bə'sɪlɪkə] *s* basílica
**basin** ['besɪn] *s* jofaina, palangana;

(*of a fountain*) tazón *m;* (*of a river*) cuenca; (*of a harbor*) dársena
**ba•sis** [ˈbesɪs] *s* (*pl* **-ses** [siz]) base *f;* **on the basis of** a base de
**bask** [bæsk] o [bɑsk] *intr* asolearse, calentarse
**basket** [ˈbæskɪt] o [ˈbɑskɪt] *s* cesta; (*large basket*) cesto; (*with two handles*) canasta; (*with lid*) excusabaraja; (*sport*) cesto, red *f*
**bas′ket•ball′** *s* baloncesto, basquetbol *m*
**Basle** [bɑl] *s* Basilea
**Basque** [bæsk] *adj & s* (*of Spain*) vascongado; (*of Spain and France*) vasco; (*of old Spain*) vascón *m*
**bas-relief** [ˌbɑrɪˈlif] o [ˌbærɪˈlif] *s* bajo relieve
**bass** [bes] *adj & s* (mus) bajo ‖ [bæs] *s* (ichth) róbalo; (ichth) micróptero
**bass drum** *s* bombo
**bass horn** *s* tuba
**bas•so** [ˈbæso] o [ˈbɑso] *s* (*pl* **-sos** o **-si** [si]) (mus) bajo
**bassoon** [bəˈsun] *s* bajón *m*
**bass viol** [ˈvaɪ•əl] *s* violón *m,* contrabajo
**bastard** [ˈbæstərd] *adj & s* bastardo
**bastard title** *s* anteportada
**baste** [best] *tr* (*to sew slightly*) hilvanar; (*to moisten with drippings while roasting*) enlardar; (*to thrash*) azotar; (*to scold*) regañar
**bat.** *abbr* **battalion, battery**
**bat** [bæt] *s* palo; (coll) golpe *m;* (zool) murciélago ‖ *v* (*pret & pp* **batted;** *ger* **batting**) *tr* golpear; batear (*una pelota*); **without batting an eye** sin inmutarse, sin pestañear ‖ *intr* golpear
**batch** [bætʃ] *s* (*of bread*) hornada; (*of papers*) lío
**bath** [bæθ] o [bɑθ] *s* baño
**bathe** [beð] *tr* bañar ‖ *intr* bañarse; **to go bathing** ir a bañarse
**bather** [ˈbeðər] *s* bañista *mf*
**bath′house′** *s* casa de baños; caseta de baños
**bathing beach** *s* playa de baños
**bathing beauty** *s* sirena de la playa
**bathing resort** *s* estación balnearia
**bathing suit** *s* traje *m* de baño, bañador *m*
**bathing trunks** *spl* taparrabo
**bath′robe′** *s* albornoz *m,* bata de baño; bata, peinador *m*
**bath′room′** *s* baño, cuarto de baño
**bathroom fixtures** *spl* aparatos sanitarios
**bath′tub′** *s* bañera, baño
**baton** [bæˈtɑn] o [ˈbætən] *s* bastón *m;* (mus) batuta
**battalion** [bəˈtæljən] *s* batallón *m*
**batter** [ˈbætər] *s* pasta, batido; (baseball) bateador *m* ‖ *tr* magullar, estropear
**battering ram** *s* ariete *m*
**batter•y** [ˈbætəri] *s* (*pl* **-ies**) batería; (*primary*) (elec) pila; (*secondary*) (elec) acumulador *m;* (law) violencia
**battle** [ˈbætəl] *s* batalla; **to do battle** librar batalla ‖ *tr* batallar
**battle array** *s* orden *m* de batalla
**battle cry** *s* grito de combate
**battledore** [ˈbætəlˌdor] *s* raqueta; **battledore and shuttlecock** raqueta y volante
**bat′tlefield′** *s* campo de batalla
**battle front** *s* frente *m* de combate
**battlement** [ˈbætəlmənt] *s* almenaje *m*
**battle piece** *s* (paint) batalla
**bat′tle•ship′** *s* acorazado
**battue** [bæˈtu] o [bæˈtju] *s* batida
**bauble** [ˈbɔbəl] *s* chuchería; cetro de bufón
**Bavaria** [bəˈverɪ•ə] *s* Baviera
**Bavarian** [bəˈverɪ•ən] *adj & mf* bávaro
**bawd** [bɔd] *s* alcahuete *m,* alcahueta
**bawd•y** [ˈbɔdi] *adj* (*comp* **-ier;** *super* **-iest**) indecente, obsceno
**bawd′y•house′** *s* mancebía, lupanar *m*
**bawl** [bɔl] *s* voces *fpl,* gritos ‖ *tr* **— to bawl out** (slang) regañar ‖ *intr* vocear, gritar; llorar ruidosamente
**bay** [be] *adj* bayo ‖ *s* bahía; aullido, ladrido; caballo bayo; (bot) laurel *m;* **to keep at bay** tener a raya ‖ *intr* aullar, ladrar
**Bay of Biscay** *s* golfo de Vizcaya
**bayonet** [ˈbe•ənɪt] *s* bayoneta ‖ *tr* herir o matar con bayoneta
**bay rum** *s* ron *m* de laurel, ron de malagueta
**bay window** *s* ventana salediza, mirador *m*
**bazooka** [bəˈzukə] *s* bazuca
**bbl.** *abbr* **barrel, barrels**
**B.C.** *abbr* **before Christ**
**bd.** *abbr* **board**
**be** [bi] *v* (*pres* **am** [æm], **is** [ɪz], **are** [ɑr]; *pret* **was** [wɑz] o [wʌz], **were** [wʌr]; *pp* **been** [bɪn]) *intr* estar; ser; tener, p.ej., **to be cold** tener frío; **to be wrong** no tener razón; tener la culpa; **here is** o **here are** aquí tiene Vd.; **there is** o **there are** hay ‖ *v aux* estar, p.ej., **he is studying** está estudiando; ser, p.ej., **she was hit by a car** fué atropellada por un coche; deber, p.ej., **what am I to do?** ¿qué debo hacer? ‖ *v impers* ser, p.ej., **it is necessary to get up early** es necesario levantarse temprano; haber, p.ej., **it is sunny** hay sol; hacer, p.ej., **it is cold** hace frío
**beach** [bitʃ] *s* playa
**beach′comb′** *intr* raquear; **to go beachcombing** andar al raque
**beach′comb′er** *s* raquero; vago de playa
**beach′head′** *s* cabeza de playa
**beach robe** *s* albornoz *m*
**beach shoe** *s* playera
**beach umbrella** *s* sombrilla de playa
**beach wagon** *s* rubia, coche *m* rural
**beacon** [ˈbikən] *s* señal luminosa; (*lighthouse*) faro; (*hill overlooking sea*) hacho; radiofaro; (*guide*) faro ‖ *tr* iluminar, guiar ‖ *intr* brillar
**bead** [bid] *s* cuenta; (*of glass*) abalorio; (*of sweat*) gota; (*moulding on corner of wall*) guardavivo; **to say** o **tell one's beads** rezar el rosario
**beadle** [ˈbidəl] *s* bedel *m*
**beagle** [ˈbigəl] *s* sabueso
**beak** [bik] *s* pico; cabo, promontorio

**beam** [bim] *s* (*of wood*) viga; (*of light, heat, etc.*) rayo; (naut) bao; (*direction perpendicular to the keel*) (naut) través *m;* (*of hope*) (fig) rayo; **on the beam** siguiendo el haz del radiofaro; (coll) siguiendo el buen camino ‖ *tr* emitir (*luz, ondas*) ‖ *intr* brillar; sonreír alegremente

**bean** [bin] *s* haba (*Vicia faba*); alubia, judía (*Phaseolus vulgaris*); (*of coffee, cocoa*) haba; (slang) cabeza

**bean'pole'** *s* rodrigón *m* para frijoles; (*tall, skinny person*) (coll) poste *m* de telégrafo

**bear** [bɛr] *s* oso; (*in stock market*) bajista *mf* ‖ *v* (*pret* **bore** [bor]; *pp* **borne** [born]) *tr* cargar; traer; llevar (*armas*); apoyar; aguantar; sentir, experimentar; producir, rendir (*frutos; interés*); (*to give birth to*) parir; tener (*amor, odio*); **to bear out** confirmar ‖ *intr* dirigirse, volver; **to bear on** referirse a; **to bear up** no perder la esperanza; **to bear with** ser indulgente para con

**beard** [bɪrd] *s* barba; (*of wheat*) arista

**beardless** ['bɪrdlɪs] *adj* imberbe

**bearer** ['bɛrər] *s* portador *m*

**bearing** ['bɛrɪŋ] *s* porte *m*, presencia; referencia, relación; (mach) cojinete *m;* **bearings** orientación; **to lose one's bearings** desorientarse

**bearish** ['bɛrɪʃ] *adj* bajista

**bear'skin'** *s* piel *f* de oso; (*military cap*) morrión *m*

**beast** [bist] *s* bestia

**beast·ly** ['bistli] *adj* (*comp* **-lier;** *super* **-liest**) bestial; (coll) muy malo ‖ *adv* (coll) muy mal

**beast of burden** *s* bestia de carga, acémila

**beat** [bit] *s* golpe *m;* (*of heart*) latido; (*of rhythm*) compás *m;* marca del compás; (mus) tiempo; (phys) batimiento; (rad) batido; (*of a policeman*) ronda; (*sponger*) (slang) embestidor *m* ‖ *v* (*pret* **beat;** *pp* **beat** o **beaten**) *tr* azotar, pegar; batir; sacudir (*una alfombra*); aventajar; llevar (*el compás*); tocar (*un tambor*); (*a una persona en una contienda*) ganar; **to beat it** (slang) largarse; **to beat up** batir (*p.ej., huevos*); (slang) aporrear ‖ *intr* batir; latir (*el corazón*); **to beat against** azotar

**beaten path** ['bitən] *s* camino trillado

**beater** ['bitər] *s* batidor *m;* (*mixer*) batidora

**beautician** [bju'tɪʃən] *s* embellecedora, esteta *mf*, esteticista *mf*

**beati·fy** [bɪ'ætɪ,faɪ] *v* (*pret & pp* **-fied**) *tr* beatificar

**beating** ['bitɪŋ] *s* golpeo; (*of wings*) aleteo; (*with a whip*) paliza; (*defeat*) derrota

**beau** [bo] *s* (*pl* **beaus** o **beaux** [boz]) galán *m*, cortejo; novio; elegante *m*

**beautiful** ['bjutɪfəl] *adj* bello, hermoso

**beauti·fy** ['bjutɪ,faɪ] *v* (*pret & pp* **-fied**) *tr* hermosear, embellecer

**beau·ty** ['bjuti] *s* (*pl* **-ties**) beldad *f*, belleza

**beauty contest** *s* concurso de belleza

**beauty parlor** *s* salón *m* de belleza

**beauty queen** *s* reina de la belleza

**beauty sleep** *s* primer sueño (*antes de medianoche*)

**beauty spot** *s* lunar postizo; sitio pintoresco

**beaver** ['bivər] *s* castor *m;* piel *f* de castor

**becalm** [bɪ'kɑm] *tr* calmar, serenar

**because** [bɪ'kɔz] *conj* porque; **because of** por, por causa de

**beck** [bɛk] *s* seña (*con la cabeza o la mano*); **at the beck and call of** a la disposición de

**beckon** ['bɛkən] *s* seña (*con la cabeza o la mano*) ‖ *tr* llamar por señas; atraer, tentar ‖ *intr* hacer señas

**be·come** [bɪ'kʌm] *v* (*pret* **-came;** *pp* **-come**) *tr* convenir, sentar bien ‖ *intr* hacerse; llegar a ser; ponerse, volverse; convertirse en; **to become of** ser de, p.ej., **what will become of the soldier?** ¿qué será del soldado; hacerse, p.ej., **what became of his pencil?** ¿qué se ha hecho su lápiz?

**becoming** [bɪ'kʌmɪŋ] *adj* conveniente, decente; que sienta bien

**bed** [bɛd] *s* cama; (*of a river*) cauce *m;* (*of flower garden*) macizo; **to go to bed** acostarse; **to take to bed** encamarse

**bed and board** *s* pensión completa, casa y comida

**bed'bug'** *s* chinche *f*

**bed'cham'ber** *s* alcoba, cuarto de dormir

**bed'clothes'** *spl* ropa de cama

**bed'cov'er** *s* cubrecama, cobertor *m*

**bedding** ['bɛdɪŋ] *s* ropa de cama; (*for animals*) cama

**bedev·il** [bɪ'dɛvəl] *v* (*pret & pp* **-iled** o **-illed;** *ger* **-iling** o **-illing**) *tr* atormentar, confundir

**bed'fast'** *adj* postrado en cama

**bed'fel'low** *s* compañero o compañera de cama

**bedlam** ['bɛdləm] *s* confusión, desorden *m*, tumulto

**bed linen** *s* ropa de cama

**bed'pan'** *s* silleta

**bed'post'** *s* pilar *m* de cama

**bedridden** ['bɛd,rɪdən] *adj* postrado en cama

**bed'room'** *s* alcoba, cuarto de dormir

**bed'side'** *s* cabecera

**bed'sore'** *s* úlcera de decúbito; **to get bedsores** decentarse

**bed'spread'** *s* sobrecama, cobertor *m*

**bed'spring'** *s* colchón *m* de muelles, somier *m*

**bed'stead'** *s* cuja

**bed'straw'** *s* paja de jergón

**bed'tick'** *s* cutí *m*

**bed'time'** *s* hora de acostarse

**bed warmer** *s* calientacamas *m*

**bee** [bi] *s* abeja

**beech** [bitʃ] *s* haya

**beech'nut'** *s* hayuco

**beef** [bif] *s* carne *f* de vaca; ganado vacuno de engorde; (coll) fuerza muscular; (slang) queja ‖ *tr* — **to**

**beef up** (coll) reforzar || *intr* (slang) quejarse; (slang) soplar
**beef cattle** *s* ganado vacuno de engorde
**beef'steak'** *s* biftec *m*
**bee'hive'** *s* colmena
**bee'line'** *s* — **to make a beeline for** ir en línea recta hacia, ir derecho a
**beer** [bɪr] *s* cerveza; **dark beer** cerveza parda, cerveza negra; **light beer** cerveza clara
**beeswax** ['biz,wæks] *s* cera de abejas || *tr* encerar
**beet** [bit] s remolacha
**beetle** ['bitəl] *s* escarabajo
**beetle-browed** ['bitəl,braud] *adj* cejijunto; (*sullen*) ceñudo
**beet sugar** *s* azúcar *m* de remolacha
**be•fall** [bɪ'fɔl] *v* (*pret* **-fell** ['fɛl]; *pp* **-fallen** ['fɔlən]) *tr* acontecer a || *intr* acontecer
**befitting** [bɪ'fɪtɪŋ] *adj* conveniente; decoroso
**before** [bɪ'for] *adv* antes; delante, enfrente || *prep* (*in time*) antes de; (*in place*) delante de; (*in the presence of*) ante || *conj* antes (de) que
**before'hand'** *adv* de antemano, con anticipación
**befriend** [bɪ'frend] *tr* ofrecer amistad a, amparar, proteger
**befuddle** [bɪ'fʌdəl] *tr* aturdir, confundir
**beg** [bɛg] *v* (*pret & pp* **begged**; *ger* **begging**) *tr* pedir, rogar, solicitar; mendigar || *intr* mendigar; **to beg off** excusarse
**be•get** [bɪ'gɛt] *v* (*pret* **-got** ['gɑt]; *pp* **-gotten** o **-got**; *ger* **-getting**) *tr* engendrar
**beggar** ['bɛgər] *s* mendigo; pobre *mf*; pícaro, bribón *m*; sujeto, tipo
**be•gin** [bɪ'gɪn] *v* (*pret* **-gan** ['gæn]; *pp* **-gun** ['gʌn]; *ger* **-ginning**) *tr & intr* comenzar, empezar; **beginning with** a partir de
**beginner** [bɪ'gɪnər] *s* principiante *mf*; iniciador *m*
**beginning** [bɪ'gɪnɪŋ] *s* comienzo, principio
**begrudge** [bɪ'grʌdʒ] *tr* dar de mala gana; envidiar
**beguile** [bɪ'gaɪl] *tr* engañar; divertir, entretener; engañar (*el tiempo*)
**behalf** [bɪ'hæf] o [bɪ'hɑf] *s* — **on behalf of** en nombre de; a favor de
**behave** [bɪ'hev] *intr* conducirse, comportarse; portarse bien; funcionar
**behavior** [bɪ'hevjər] *s* conducta, comportamiento; funcionamiento
**behead** [bɪ'hɛd] *tr* decapitar, descabezar
**behind** [bɪ'haɪnd] *adv* detrás; hacia atrás; con retraso; **to stay behind** quedarse atrás || *prep* detrás de; **behind the back of** a espaldas de; **behind the times** atrasado de noticias; **behind time** tarde || *s* (slang) trasero
**behold** [bɪ'hold] *v* (*pret & pp* **-held** ['hɛld]) *tr* contemplar || *interj* ¡he aquí!
**behoove** [bɪ'huv] *tr* convenir, tocar
**being** ['bi•ɪŋ] *adj* existente; **for the time being** por ahora, por el momento || *s* ser, ente *m*
**belch** [bɛltʃ] *s* eructo, regüeldo || *tr* vomitar (*p.ej., llamas, injurias*) || *intr* eructar, regoldar
**beleaguer** [bɪ'ligər] *tr* sitiar, cercar
**bel•fry** ['bɛlfri] *s* (*pl* **-fries**) campanario
**Belgian** ['bɛldʒən] *adj & s* belga *mf*
**Belgium** ['bɛldʒəm] *s* Bélgica
**be•lie** [bɪ'laɪ] *v* (*pret & pp* **-lied** ['laɪd]; *ger* **-lying** ['laɪ•ɪŋ]) *tr* desmentir
**belief** [bɪ'lif] *s* creencia
**believable** [bɪ'livəbəl] *adj* creíble
**believe** [bɪ'liv] *tr & intr* creer
**believer** [bɪ'livər] *s* creyente *mf*
**belittle** [bɪ'lɪtəl] *tr* empequeñecer, despreciar
**bell** [bɛl] *s* campana; (*electric bell*) timbre *m*, campanilla; (*ring of bell*) campanada || *intr* bramar, berrear
**bell'boy'** *s* botones *m*
**belle** [bɛl] *s* beldad *f*, belleza
**belles-lettres** [,bɛl'lɛtrə] *spl* bellas letras
**bell gable** *s* espadaña
**bell glass** *s* fanal *m*
**bell'hop'** *s* (slang) botones *m*
**bellicose** ['bɛlɪ,kos] *adj* belicoso
**belligerent** [bə'lɪdʒərənt] *adj & s* beligerante *mf*
**bellow** ['bɛlo] *s* bramido; **bellows** fuelle *m*, barquín *m* || *tr* gritar || *intr* bramar
**bell ringer** *s* campanero
**bellwether** ['bel,wɛðər] *s* manso
**bel•ly** ['bɛli] *s* (*pl* **-lies**) barriga, vientre *m*; estómago || *v* (*pret & pp* **-lied**) *intr* hacer barriga; hacer bolso (*las velas*)
**bel'ly•ache'** *s* (slang) dolor *m* de barriga || *intr* (slang) quejarse
**belly button** *s* (coll) ombligo
**belly dance** *s* (coll) danza del vientre
**bellyful** ['bɛlɪ,ful] *s* (slang) panzada
**bel'ly-land'** *intr* (aer) aterrizar de panza
**belong** [bɪ'lɔŋ] o [bɪ'lɑŋ] *intr* pertenecer; deber estar
**belongings** [bɪ'lɔŋɪŋz] o [bɪ'lɑŋɪŋz] *spl* pertenencias, efectos
**beloved** [bɪ'lʌvɪd] o [bɪ'lʌvd] *adj & s* querido, amado
**below** [bɪ'lo] *adv* abajo; (*in a text*) más abajo; bajo cero, p.ej., **ten below** diez grados bajo cero || *prep* debajo de; inferior a
**belt** [bɛlt] *s* cinturón *m*; (aer, mach) correa; (geog) faja, zona; **to tighten one's belt** ceñirse
**bemoan** [bɪ'mon] *tr* deplorar, lamentar
**bench** [bɛntʃ] *s* banco; (law) tribunal *m*
**bend** [bɛnd] *s* curva; (*in a road, river, etc.*) recodo, vuelta || *v* (*pret & pp* **bent** [bɛnt]) *tr* encorvar; doblar (*un tubo; la rodilla*); inclinar (*la cabeza*); dirigir (*sus esfuerzos*) || *intr* encorvarse; doblarse; inclinarse
**beneath** [bɪ'niθ] *adv* abajo || *prep* debajo de; inferior a

**benediction** [ˌbɛnɪˈdɪkʃən] *s* bendición *f*
**benefaction** [ˌbɛnɪˈfækʃən] *s* beneficio
**benefactor** [ˈbɛnɪˌfæktər] o [ˌbɛnɪˈfæktər] *s* bienhechor *m*
**benefactress** [ˈbɛnɪˌfæktrɪs] o [ˌbɛnɪˈfæktrɪs] *s* bienhechora
**beneficence** [bɪˈnɛfɪsəns] *s* beneficencia
**beneficent** [bɪˈnɛfɪsənt] *adj* bienhechor
**beneficial** [ˌbɛnɪˈfɪʃəl] *adj* beneficioso
**beneficiar•y** [ˌbɛnɪˈfɪʃɪˌɛri] *s* (*pl* **-ies**) beneficiario
**benefit** [ˈbɛnɪfɪt] *s* beneficio; **for the benefit of** a beneficio de || *tr* beneficiar
**benefit performance** *s* beneficio
**benevolence** [bɪˈnɛvələns] *s* benevolencia
**benevolent** [bɪˈnɛvələnt] *adj* benévolo; (*e.g., institution*) benéfico
**benign** [bɪˈnaɪn] *adj* benigno
**benigni•ty** [bɪˈnɪgnɪti] *s* (*pl* **-ties**) benignidad
**bent** [bɛnt] *adj* encorvado, doblado, torcido; **bent on** resuelto a, empeñado en; **bent over** cargado de espaldas || *s* encorvadura; inclinación *f*, propensión *f*
**benzine** [bɛnˈzin] *s* bencina
**bequeath** [bɪˈkwið] o [bɪˈkwiθ] *tr* legar
**bequest** [bɪˈkwɛst] *s* manda, legado
**berate** [bɪˈret] *tr* regañar, reñir
**be•reave** [bɪˈriv] *v* (*pret & pp* **-reaved** o **-reft** [ˈrɛft]) *tr* despojar, privar; desconsolar
**bereavement** [bɪˈrivmənt] *s* despojo, privación *f*; desconsuelo
**berkelium** [bərˈkilɪ•əm] *s* berkelio
**Berliner** [bərˈlɪnər] *s* berlinés *m*
**ber•ry** [ˈbɛri] *s* (*pl* **-ries**) baya; (*of coffee plant*) grano, haba
**berserk** [ˈbʌrsʌrk] *adj* frenético || *adv* frenéticamente
**berth** [bʌrθ] *s* (*bed*) litera; (*room*) camarote *m*; (*for a ship*) amarradero; (coll) empleo, puesto
**beryllium** [bəˈrɪlɪ•əm] *s* berilio
**be•seech** [bɪˈsitʃ] *v* (*pret & pp* **-sought** [ˈsɔt] o **-seeched**) *tr* suplicar
**be•set** [bɪˈsɛt] *v* (*pret & pp* **-set**; *ger* **-setting**) *tr* acometer, acosar; cercar, sitiar
**beside** [bɪˈsaɪd] *adv* además, también || *prep* cerca de, junto a; en comparación de; excepto; **beside oneself** fuera de sí; **beside the point** incongruente
**besiege** [bɪˈsidʒ] *tr* asediar, sitiar
**besmirch** [bɪˈsmʌrtʃ] *tr* ensuciar, manchar
**bespatter** [bɪˈspætər] *tr* salpicar
**be•speak** [bɪˈspik] *v* (*pret* **-spoke** [ˈspok]; *pp* **-spoken**) *tr* apalabrar, pedir de antemano
**best** [bɛst] *adj super* mejor; óptimo || *adv super* mejor; **had best** debería || *s* (lo) mejor; (lo) más; **at best** a lo más; **to do one's best** hacer lo mejor posible; **to get the best of** aventajar, sobresalir; **to make the best of** sacar el mejor partido de
**best girl** *s* (coll) amiga preferida, novia
**be•stir** [bɪˈstʌr] *v* (*pret & pp* **-stirred**; *ger* **-stirring**) *tr* excitar, incitar; **to bestir oneself** esforzarse, afanarse
**best man** *s* padrino de boda
**bestow** [bɪˈsto] *tr* otorgar, conferir; dedicar
**best seller** *s* éxito de venta, campeón *m* de venta; éxito de librería
**bet.** *abbr* **between**
**bet** [bɛt] *s* apuesta || *v* (*pret & pp* **bet** o **betted**; *ger* **betting**) *tr & intr* apostar; **I bet** a que, apuesto a que; **to bet on** apostar por; **you bet** (slang) ya lo creo
**be•take** [bɪˈtek] *v* (*pret* **-took** [ˈtʊk]; *pp* **-taken**) *tr* — **to betake oneself** dirigirse; darse, entregarse
**be•think** [bɪˈθɪŋk] *v* (*pret & pp* **-thought** [ˈθɔt]) *tr* — **to bethink oneself of** considerar, acordarse de
**Bethlehem** [ˈbɛθlɪ•əm] o [ˈbɛθlɪˌhɛm] *s* Belén *m*
**betide** [bɪˈtaɪd] *tr* presagiar; acontecer a || *intr* acontecer
**betoken** [bɪˈtokən] *tr* anunciar, indicar, presagiar
**betray** [bɪˈtre] *tr* traicionar; descubrir, revelar
**betrayal** [bɪˈtre•əl] *s* traición; descubrimiento, revelación
**betroth** [bɪˈtroð] o [bɪˈtrɔθ] *tr* prometer en matrimonio; **to become betrothed** desposarse
**betrothal** [bɪˈtroðəl] o [bɪˈtrɔθəl] *s* desposorios, esponsales *mpl*
**betrothed** [bɪˈtroðd] o [bɪˈtrɔθt] *s* prometido, novio
**better** [ˈbɛtər] *adj comp* mejor; **it is better to** más vale; **to grow better** mejorarse; **to make better** mejorar || *adv comp* mejor; más; **had better** debería; **to like better** preferir || *s* superior; ventaja; **to get the better of** llevar la ventaja a || *tr* aventajar; mejorar; **to better oneself** mejorar su posición
**better half** *s* (coll) cara mitad
**betterment** [ˈbɛtərmənt] *s* mejoramiento; (*in an illness*) mejoría
**between** [bɪˈtwin] *adv* en medio, entremedias || *prep* entre; **between you and me** entre Vd. y yo; acá para los dos
**be•tween'-decks'** *s* entrecubiertas, entrepuentes *mpl*
**between decks** *adv* entrecubiertas
**bev•el** [ˈbɛvəl] *adj* biselado || *s* (*instrument*) cartabón *m*; (*sloping part*) bisel *m* || *v* (*pret & pp* **-eled** o **-elled**; *ger* **-eling** o **-elling**) *tr* biselar
**beverage** [ˈbɛvərɪdʒ] *s* bebida
**bev•y** [ˈbɛvi] *s* (*pl* **-ies**) (*of birds*) bandada; (*of girls*) grupo
**bewail** [bɪˈwel] *tr & intr* lamentar
**beware** [bɪˈwɛr] *tr* guardarse de || *intr* tener cuidado; **beware of . . . !** ¡ojo con . . . !, ¡cuidado con . . . !; **to beware of** guardarse de

**bewilder** [bɪ'wɪldər] *tr* aturdir, dejar perplejo, desatinar
**bewilderment** [bɪ'wɪldərmənt] *s* aturdimiento, perplejidad
**beyond** [bɪ'jɑnd] *adv* más allá, más lejos || *prep* más allá de; además de; no capaz de; **beyond a doubt** fuera de duda; **beyond the reach of** fuera del alcance de || *s* — **the great beyond** el más allá, el otro mundo
**bg.** *abbr* **bag**
**bias** ['baɪ·əs] *s* sesgo, diagonal *f;* prejuicio; (electron) polarización de rejilla || *tr* predisponer, prevenir
**Bib.** *abbr* **Bible, Biblical**
**bib** [bɪb] *s* babero; (*of apron*) pechera
**Bible** ['baɪbəl] *s* Biblia
**Biblical** ['bɪblɪkəl] *adj* bíblico
**bibliographer** [ˌbɪblɪ'ɑgrəfər] *s* bibliógrafo
**bibliogra·phy** [ˌbɪblɪ'ɑgrəfi] *s* (*pl* **-phies**) bibliografía
**bibliophile** ['bɪblɪ·əˌfaɪl] *s* bibliófilo
**bicameral** [baɪ'kæmərəl] *adj* bicameral
**bicarbonate** [baɪ'kɑrbəˌnet] *s* bicarbonato
**bicker** ['bɪkər] *s* discusión ociosa || *intr* discutir ociosamente
**bicycle** ['baɪsɪkəl] *s* bicicleta
**bid** [bɪd] *s* oferta, postura; (*in bridge*) declaración || *v* (*pret* **bade** [bæd] o **bid**; *ger* **bidden** ['bɪdən]) *tr & intr* ofrecer, pujar, licitar; (*in bridge*) declarar
**bidder** ['bɪdər] *s* postor *m;* (*in bridge*) declarante *mf;* **the highest bidder** el mejor postor
**bidding** ['bɪdɪŋ] *s* mandato, orden *f;* postura; (*in bridge*) declaración
**bide** [baɪd] *tr* — **to bide one's time** esperar la hora propicia
**biennial** [baɪ'enɪ·əl] *adj* bienal
**bier** [bɪr] *s* féretro, andas
**bifocal** [baɪ'fokəl] *adj* bifocal || **bifocals** *spl* anteojos bifocales
**big** [bɪg] *adj* (*comp* **bigger;** *super* **biggest**) grande; (*considerable*) importante; (*grown-up*) adulto; **big with child** preñada || *adv* (coll) con jactancia; **to talk big** (coll) hablar gordo
**bigamist** ['bɪgəmɪst] *s* bígamo
**bigamous** ['bɪgəməs] *adj* bígamo
**bigamy** ['bɪgəmi] *s* bigamia
**big-bellied** ['bɪg ˌbelɪd] *adj* panzudo
**Big Dipper** *s* Carro mayor
**big game** *s* caza mayor
**big-hearted** ['bɪg ˌhɑrtɪd] *adj* magnánimo, generoso
**bigot** ['bɪgət] *s* intolerante *mf,* fanático
**bigoted** ['bɪgətɪd] *adj* intolerante, fanático
**bigot·ry** ['bɪgətri] *s* (*pl* **-ries**) intolerancia, fanatismo
**big shot** *s* (slang) pájaro de cuenta, señorón *m*
**big stick** *s* palo en alto
**big toe** *s* dedo gordo o grande (*del pie*)
**bile** [baɪl] *s* bilis *f*
**bilge** [bɪldʒ] *s* pantoque *m* || *tr* desfondar
**bilge pump** *s* bomba de sentina
**bilge water** *s* agua de pantoque
**bilge ways** *spl* anguilas
**bilingual** [baɪ'lɪŋgwəl] *adj* bilingüe
**bilious** ['bɪljəs] *adj* bilioso
**bilk** [bɪlk] *tr* estafar, trampear
**bill** [bɪl] *s* (*statement of charges for goods or service*) cuenta, factura; (*paper money*) billete *m;* (*poster*) cartel *m,* aviso; cartel de teatro; (*draft of law*) proyecto de ley; (*handbill*) hoja suelta; (*of bird*) pico; (com) giro, letra de cambio || *tr* facturar; cargar en cuenta a; anunciar por carteles || *intr* darse el pico (*las palomas*); acariciarse (*los enamorados*); **to bill and coo** acariciarse y arrullarse
**bill'board'** *s* cartelera
**billet** ['bɪlɪt] *s* (mil) boleta; (mil) alojamiento || *tr* (mil) alojar
**billet-doux** ['bɪle'du] *s* (*pl* **billets-doux** ['bɪle'duz]) esquela amorosa
**bill'fold'** *s* cartera de bolsillo, billetero
**bill'head'** *s* encabezamiento de factura
**billiards** ['bɪljərdz] *s* billar *m*
**billion** ['bɪljən] *s* (U.S.A.) mil millones; (Brit) billón *m*
**bill of exchange** *s* letra de cambio
**bill of fare** *s* lista de comidas, menú *m*
**bill of lading** *s* conocimiento de embarque
**bill of sale** *s* escritura de venta
**billow** ['bɪlo] *s* oleada, ondulación || *intr* ondular, hincharse
**bill'post'er** *s* fijacarteles *m,* fijador *m* de carteles
**bil·ly** ['bɪli] *s* (*pl* **-lies**) cachiporra
**billy goat** *s* macho cabrío
**bin** [bɪn] *s* arcón *m,* hucha
**bind** [baɪnd] *v* (*pret & pp* **bound** [baʊnd]) *tr* ligar, atar; juntar, unir; (*with a garland*) enguirlandar; ribetear (*la orilla del vestido*); agavillar (*las mieses*); vendar (*una herida*); encuadernar (*un libro*); estreñir (*el vientre*)
**binder·y** ['baɪndəri] *s* (*pl* **-ies**) taller *m* de encuadernación
**binding** ['baɪndɪŋ] *s* atadura; (*of a book*) encuadernación
**binding post** *s* borne *m,* sujetahilo
**binge** [bɪndʒ] *s* (slang) borrachera; **to go on a binge** (slang) pegarse una mona
**binnacle** ['bɪnəkəl] *s* bitácora
**binoculars** [bɪ'nɑkjələrz] o [baɪ'nɑkjələrz] *spl* gemelos, prismáticos
**biochemical** [ˌbaɪ·ə'kemɪkəl] *adj* bioquímico
**biochemist** [ˌbaɪ·ə'kemɪst] *s* bioquímico
**biochemistry** [ˌbaɪ·ə'kemɪstri] *s* bioquímica
**biog.** *abbr* **biographical, biography**
**biographer** [baɪ'ɑgrəfər] *s* biógrafo
**biographic(al)** [ˌbaɪ·ə'græfɪk(əl)] *adj* biográfico
**biogra·phy** [baɪ'ɑgrəfi] *s* (*pl* **-phies**) biografía

**biologist** [baɪ'ɑlədʒɪst] *s* biólogo
**biology** [baɪ'ɑlədʒi] *s* biología
**biophysical** [,baɪ·ə'fɪzɪkəl] *adj* biofísico
**biophysics** [,baɪ·ə'fɪzɪks] *s* biofísica
**birch** [bʌrtʃ] *s* abedul *m* || *tr* azotar, varear
**bird** [bʌrd] *s* ave *f*, pájaro
**bird cage** *s* jaula
**bird call** *s* reclamo
**bird'lime'** *s* liga
**bird of passage** *s* ave *f* de paso
**bird of prey** *s* ave *f* de rapiña
**bird'seed'** *s* alpiste *m*, cañamones *mpl*
**bird's'-eye' view** *s* vista a ojo de pájaro
**bird shot** *s* perdigones *mpl*
**birth** [bʌrθ] *s* nacimiento; (*childbirth*) parto; origen *m*
**birth certificate** *s* partida de nacimiento
**birth control** *s* limitación de la natalidad
**birth'day'** *s* cumpleaños *m*, natal *m*; (*of any event*) aniversario; **to have a birthday** cumplir años
**birthday cake** *s* pastel *m* de cumpleaños
**birthday present** *s* regalo de cumpleaños
**birth'mark'** *s* antojo, nevo materno
**birth'place'** *s* suelo natal, patria, lugar *m* de nacimiento
**birth rate** *s* natalidad
**birth'right'** *s* derechos de nacimiento; primogenitura
**Biscay** ['bɪske] *s* Vizcaya
**biscuit** ['bɪskɪt] *s* panecillo redondo; bizcocho
**bisect** [baɪ'sekt] *tr* bisecar || *intr* empalmar (*dos caminos*)
**bishop** ['bɪʃəp] *s* obispo; (*in chess*) alfil *m*
**bismuth** ['bɪzməθ] *s* bismuto
**bison** ['baɪsən] o ['baɪzən] *s* bisonte *m*
**bit** [bɪt] *s* poquito, pedacito; (*of food*) bocado; (*of time*) ratito; (*part of bridle*) bocado, freno; (*for drilling*) barrena; **a good bit** una buena cantidad
**bitch** [bɪtʃ] *s* (*dog*) perra; (*fox*) zorra; (*wolf*) loba; (vulg) mujer *f* de mal genio
**bite** [baɪt] *s* mordedura; (*of bird or insect*) picadura; (*burning sensation on tongue*) resquemo; (*of food*) bocado; (*snack*) (coll) tentempié *m*, refrigerio || *v* (*pret* **bit** [bɪt]; *pp* **bit** o **bitten** ['bɪtən]) *tr* morder; picar (*los peces, los insectos*); resquemar (*la lengua los alimentos*); comerse (*las uñas*) || *intr* morder; picar; resquemar; (*to be caught by a trick*) (slang) picar
**biting** ['baɪtɪŋ] *adj* penetrante; mordaz, picante
**bitter** ['bɪtər] *adj* amargo; (*e.g., struggle*) encarnizado; **to the bitter end** hasta el extremo; hasta la muerte
**bitter almond** *s* almendra amarga
**bitterness** ['bɪtərnɪs] *s* amargura
**bitumen** [bɪ'tjumən] o [bɪ'tumən] *s* betún *m*
**bivou·ac** ['bɪvʊ·æk] o ['bɪvwæk] *s* vivaque *m* || *v* (*pret & pp* **-acked**; *ger* **-acking**) *intr* vivaquear
**bizarre** [bɪ'zɑr] *adj* original, raro
**bk.** *abbr* **bank, block, book**
**bkg.** *abbr* **banking**
**bl.** *abbr* **barrel**
**b.l.** *abbr* **bill of lading**
**blabber** ['blæbər] *tr & intr* barbullar
**black** [blæk] *adj* negro || *s* negro; luto; **to wear black** ir de luto
**black'-and-blue'** *adj* encardenalado, amoratado
**black'-and-white'** *adj* en blanco y negro
**black'ber'ry** *s* (*pl* **-ries**) (*bush*) zarza; (*fruit*) zarzamora
**black'bird'** *s* mirlo
**black'board'** *s* encerado, pizarra
**black'damp'** *s* mofeta
**blacken** ['blækən] *tr* ennegrecer; (*to defame*) desacreditar, denigrar
**blackguard** ['blægɑrd] *s* bribón *m*, canalla *m* || *tr* injuriar, vilipendiar
**black'head'** *s* espinilla, comedón *m*
**blackish** ['blækɪʃ] *adj* negruzco
**black'jack'** *s* (*club*) cachiporra; (*flag*) bandera negra (*de pirata*) || *tr* aporrear
**black'mail'** *s* chantaje *m* || *tr* amenazar con chantaje
**blackmailer** ['blæk,melər] *s* chantajista *mf*
**Black Maria** [mə'raɪ·ə] *s* (coll) coche *m* celular
**black market** *s* estraperlo, mercado negro
**blackness** ['blæknɪs] *s* negror *m*, negrura
**black'out'** *s* (*in wartime*) apagón *m*; (*in theater*) apagamiento de luces; (*of aviators*) visión negra; pérdida de la memoria
**black sheep** *s* (fig) oveja negra, garbanzo negro
**black'smith'** *s* (*man who works with iron*) herrero; (*man who shoes horses*) herrador *m*
**black'thorn'** *s* espino negro, endrino
**black tie** corbata de smoking; smoking *m*
**bladder** ['blædər] *s* vejiga
**blade** [bled] *s* (*of a knife, sword*) hoja; (*of a propeller*) aleta; (*of a fan*) paleta; (*of an oar*) pala; (*of an electric switch*) cuchilla; (*sword*) espada; tallo de hierba; (coll) gallardo joven
**blame** [blem] *s* culpa || *tr* culpar
**blameless** ['blemlɪs] *adj* inculpable, irreprochable
**blanch** [blæntʃ] o [blɑntʃ] *tr* blanquear || *intr* palidecer
**bland** [blænd] *adj* apacible; suave; (*character; weather*) blando
**blandish** ['blændɪʃ] *tr* engatusar, lisonjear
**blank** [blæŋk] *adj* en blanco; blanco, vacío; (*stare, look*) vago || *s* blanco; papel blanco; formulario
**blank check** *s* firma en blanco; (fig) carta blanca

**blanket** ['blæŋkɪt] *adj* general, comprensivo || *s* manta, frazada; (fig) capa, manto || *tr* cubrir con manta; cubrir, obscurecer
**blasé** [blɑ'ze] *adj* hastiado
**blaspheme** [blæs'fim] *tr* blasfemar contra || *intr* blasfemar
**blasphemous** ['blæsfɪməs] *adj* blasfemo
**blasphe·my** ['blæsfɪmi] *s* (*pl* **-mies**) blasfemia
**blast** [blæst] o [blɑst] *s* (*of wind*) ráfaga; (*of air, sand, water*) chorro; (*of bellows*) soplo; (*of a horn*) toque *m;* carga de pólvora; voladura, explosión; **full blast** en plena marcha || *tr* (*to blow up*) volar; arruinar; infamar, maldecir
**blast furnace** *s* alto horno
**blast'off'** *s* lanzamiento de cohete
**blatant** ['bletənt] *adj* ruidoso; vocinglero; intruso; chillón, cursi
**blaze** [blez] *s* llamarada; (*fire*) incendio; (*bonfire*) hoguera; luz *f* brillante || *tr* encender, inflamar; **to blaze a trail** abrir una senda || *intr* encenderse; resplandecer
**bldg.** *abbr* **building**
**bleach** [blitʃ] *s* blanqueo || *tr* blanquear; colar (*la ropa*)
**bleachers** ['blitʃərz] *spl* gradas al aire libre
**bleak** [blik] *adj* desierto, yermo, frío, triste
**bleat** [blit] *s* balido || *intr* balar
**bleed** [blid] *v* (*pret & pp* **bled** [blɛd]) *tr & intr* sangrar
**blemish** ['blɛmɪʃ] *s* mancha || *tr* manchar
**blend** [blɛnd] *s* mezcla; armonía || *v* (*pret & pp* **blended** o **blent** [blɛnt]) *tr* mezclar; armonizar; fusionar || *intr* mezclarse; armonizar; fusionarse
**bless** [blɛs] *tr* bendecir; **to be blessed with** estar dotado de
**blessed** ['blɛsɪd] *adj* bendito, santo
**blessedness** ['blɛsɪdnɪs] *s* bienaventuranza
**blessing** ['blɛsɪŋ] *s* bendición
**blight** [blaɪt] *s* niebla, roya; ruina || *tr* anublar; arruinar
**blimp** [blɪmp] *s* dirigible pequeño
**blind** [blaɪnd] *adj* ciego || *s* (*window shade*) estor *m,* transparente *m* de resorte; (*Venetian blind*) persiana; pretexto, subterfugio || *tr* cegar; (*to dazzle*) deslumbrar; (*to deceive*) cegar, vendar
**blind alley** *s* callejón *m* sin salida
**blind date** *s* cita a ciegas
**blinder** ['blaɪndər] *s* anteojera
**blind flying** *s* (aer) vuelo a ciegas
**blind'fold'** *adj* vendado de ojos || *s* venda || *tr* vendar los ojos a
**blind landing** *s* aterrizaje *m* a ciegas
**blind man** *s* ciego
**blind'man's' buff** *s* gallina ciega
**blindness** ['blaɪndnɪs] *s* ceguedad
**blink** [blɪŋk] *s* guiñada, parpadeo || *tr* guiñar (*el ojo*) || *intr* guiñar, parpardear, pestañear; oscilar (*la luz*)
**blip** [blɪp] *s* bache *m*
**bliss** [blɪs] *s* bienaventuranza, felicidad
**blissful** ['blɪsfəl] *adj* bienaventurado, feliz
**blister** ['blɪstər] *s* ampolla, vejiga || *tr* ampollar || *intr* ampollarse
**blithe** [blaɪð] *adj* alegre, animado
**blitzkrieg** ['blɪts,krig] *s* guerra relámpago
**blizzard** ['blɪzərd] *s* ventisca, chubasco de nieve
**bloat** [blot] *tr* hinchar || *intr* hincharse, abotagarse
**block** [blɑk] *s* bloque *m;* (*of hatter*) horma; (*of houses*) manzana; (*for chopping meat*) tajo; estorbo, obstáculo || *tr* cerrar, obstruir; conformar (*un sombrero*)
**blockade** [blɑ'ked] *s* bloqueo || *tr* bloquear
**blockade runner** *s* forzador *m* de bloqueo
**block and tackle** *s* aparejo de poleas
**block'bust'er** *s* (coll) bomba rompedora
**block'head'** *s* tonto, zoquete *m*
**block signal** *s* (rr) señal *f* de tramo
**blond** [blɑnd] *adj* rubio, blondo || *s* rubio (*hombre rubio*)
**blonde** [blɑnd] *s* rubia (*mujer rubia*)
**blood** [blʌd] *s* sangre *f;* **in cold blood** a sangre fría
**bloodcurdling** ['blʌd,kʌrdlɪŋ] *adj* horripilante
**blood'hound'** *s* sabueso
**blood poisoning** *s* envenenamiento de la sangre
**blood pressure** *s* presión arterial
**blood pudding** *s* morcilla
**blood relation** *s* pariente consanguíneo
**blood'shed'** *s* efusión de sangre
**blood'shot'** *adj* inyectado en sangre, encarnizado
**blood test** *s* análisis *m* de sangre
**blood'thirst'y** *adj* sanguinario
**blood transfusion** *s* transfusión de sangre
**blood vessel** *s* vaso sanguíneo
**blood·y** ['blʌdi] *adj* (*comp* **-ier;** *super* **-iest**) sangriento || *v* (*pret & pp* **-ied**) *tr* ensangrentar
**bloom** [blum] *s* florecimiento; flor *f* || *intr* florecer
**blossom** ['blɑsəm] *s* brote *m,* flor *f;* **in blossom** en cierne || *intr* cerner, florecer
**blot** [blɑt] *s* borrón *m* || *v* (*pret & pp* **blotted;** *ger* **blotting**) *tr* (*to smear*) borrar; secar con papel secante; **to blot out** borrar || *intr* borrarse; echar borrones (*una pluma*)
**blotch** [blɑtʃ] *s* manchón *m;* (*in the skin*) erupción
**blotter** ['blɑtər] *s* teleta, secafirmas *m*
**blotting paper** *s* papel *m* secante
**blouse** [blaʊs] *s* blusa
**blow** [blo] *s* (*hit, stroke*) golpe; (*blast of air*) soplo, soplido; (*blast of wind*) ventarrón *m;* (*of horn*) toque *m,* trompetazo; (*sudden sorrow*) estocada, ramalazo; (*boaster*) (slang) fanfarrón *m;* **to come to blows** venir a las manos || *v* (*pret* **blew** [blu]; *pp*

blown) || *tr* soplar; sonar, tocar (*un instrumento de viento*); silbar (*un silbato*); sonarse (*las narices*); quemar (*un fusible*); (slang) malgastar (*dinero*); **to blow out** apagar soplando; quemar (*un fusible*); **to blow up** (*with air*) inflar; (*e.g., with dynamite*) volar, hacer saltar; ampliar (*una foto*) || *intr* soplar; (*to pant*) jadear, resoplar; fundirse (*un fusible*); (slang) fanfarronear; **to blow out** apagarse con el aire; quemarse, fundirse (*un fusible*); reventar (*un neumático*); **to blow up** volarse; (*to fail*) fracasar; (*with anger*) (slang) estallar, reventar

**blow'out'** *s* (aut) reventón *m;* (*of a fuse*) quemazón *f;* (slang) tertulia concurrida, festín *m*

**blowout patch** *s* parche *m* para neumático

**blow'pipe'** *s* (*torch*) soplete *m;* (*peashooter*) cerbatana

**blow'torch'** *s* antorcha a soplete, lámpara de soldar

**blubber** ['blʌbər] *s* grasa de ballena; lloro ruidoso || *intr* llorar ruidosamente

**bludgeon** ['blʌdʒən] *s* cachiporra || *tr* aporrear; intimidar

**blue** [blu] *adj* azul; abatido, triste || *s* azul *m;* **the blues** la murria, la morriña || *tr* azular; añilar (*la ropa blanca*) || *intr* azularse

**blue chip** *s* valor *m* de primera fila

**blue'ber'ry** *s* (*pl* **-ries**) mirtilo

**blue'jay'** *s* cianocita

**blue moon** *s* cosa muy rara; **once in a blue moon** cada muerte de obispo, de Pascuas a Ramos

**Blue Nile** *s* Nilo Azul

**blue'-pen'cil** *tr* marcar o corregir con lápiz azul

**blue'print'** *s* cianotipo || *tr* copiar a la cianotipia

**blue'stock'ing** *s* (coll) marisabidilla

**blue streak** *s* (coll) rayo; **to talk a blue streak** (coll) soltar la tarabilla

**bluff** [blʌf] *adj* escarpado || *s* risco, peñasco escarpado; (*deception*) farol *m;* **to call someone's bluff** cogerle la palabra a uno || *intr* farolear, papelonear

**blunder** ['blʌndər] *s* disparate *m,* desatino || *intr* disparatar, desatinar

**blunt** [blʌnt] *adj* despuntado, embotado; brusco, franco, directo || *tr* despuntar, embotar

**bluntness** ['blʌntnɪs] *s* embotadura; brusquedad, franqueza

**blur** [blʌr] *s* borrón *m,* mancha || *v* (*pret & pp* **blurred;** *ger* **blurring**) *tr* empañar; obscurecer (*la vista*) || *intr* empañarse

**blurb** [blʌrb] *s* anuncio efusivo

**blurt** [blʌrt] *tr* — **to blurt out** soltar abrupta e impulsivamente

**blush** [blʌʃ] *s* rubor *m,* sonrojo || *intr* ruborizarse, sonrojarse

**bluster** ['blʌstər] *s* tumulto, gritos; jactancia || *intr* soplar con furia (*el viento*); bravear, fanfarronear

**blustery** ['blʌstəri] *adj* tempestuoso; (*wind*) violento; (*swaggering*) fanfarrón

**blvd.** *abbr* **boulevard**

**boar** [bor] *s* (*male swine*) verraco; (*wild hog*) jabalí *m*

**board** [bord] *s* tabla; (*to post announcements*) tablillo; (*table with meal*) mesa; (*daily meals*) pensión; (*organized group*) junta, consejo; (naut) bordo; **in boards** (bb) en cartoné; **on board** en el tren; (naut) a bordo || *tr* entablar; subir a (*un tren*); embarcarse en (*un buque*) || *intr* hospedarse; estar de pupilo

**board and lodging** *s* mesa y habitación, pensión completa

**boarder** ['bordər] *s* pensionista *mf,* pupilo

**boarding house** *s* pensión, casa de huéspedes

**boarding school** *s* escuela de internos

**board of health** *s* junta de sanidad

**board of trade** *s* junta de comercio

**board of trustees** *s* consejo de administración

**board'walk'** *s* paseo entablado a la orilla del mar

**boast** [bost] *s* jactancia, baladronada || *intr* jactarse, baladronear

**boastful** ['bostfəl] *adj* jactancioso

**boat** [bot] *s* barco, buque *m,* nave *f;* (*small boat*) bote *m;* **to be in the same boat** correr el mismo riesgo

**boat hook** *s* bichero

**boat'house'** *s* casilla para botes

**boating** ['botɪŋ] *s* paseo en barco

**boat·man** ['botmən] *s* (*pl* **-men** [mən]) barquero, lanchero

**boat race** *s* regata

**boatswain** *s* ['bosən] o ['bot,swən] *s* contramaestre *m*

**boatswain's chair** *s* guindola

**boatswain's mate** *s* segundo contramaestre

**bob** [bɑb] *s* (*of pendulum of clock*) lenteja; (*of plumb line*) plomo; (*of a fishing line*) corcho; (*of a horse*) cola cortada; (*of a girl*) pelo cortado corto; (*jerky motion*) sacudida || *v* (*pret & pp* **bobbed;** *ger* **bobbing**) *tr* cortar corto || *intr* agitarse, menearse; **to bob up and down** subir y bajar con sacudidas cortas

**bobbin** ['bɑbɪn] *s* broca, canilla, bobina

**bobby pin** ['bɑbi] *s* horquillita para el pelo

**bob'by·socks'** *spl* (coll) tobilleras (*de jovencita*)

**bobbysoxer** ['bɑbɪ,sɑksər] *s* (coll) tobillera

**bobolink** ['bɑbə,lɪŋk] *s* chambergo

**bob'sled'** *s* doble trineo articulado

**bob'tail'** *s* animal *m* rabón; cola corta; cola cortada

**bob'white'** *s* colín *m* de Virginia

**bock beer** [bɑk] *s* cerveza de marzo

**bode** [bod] *tr & intr* anunciar, presagiar; **to bode ill** ser un mal presagio; **to bode well** ser un buen presagio

**bodice** ['badɪs] *s* jubón *m,* corpiño
**bodily** ['badɪli] *adj* corporal, corpóreo || *adv* en persona; en conjunto
**bodkin** ['badkɪn] *s* (*needle*) aguja roma; (*for lady's hair*) espadilla; (*to make holes in cloth*) punzón *m*
**bod•y** ['badi] *s* (*pl* **-ies**) cuerpo; (*of a carriage or auto*) caja, carrocería
**bod'y•guard'** *s* (mil) guardia de corps; guardaespaldas *m*
**Boer** [bor] o [bʊr] *s* bóer *mf*
**Boer War** *s* guerra del Transvaal
**bog** [bag] *s* pantano || *v* (*pret & pp* **bogged**; *ger* **bogging**) *intr* — **to bog down** atascarse, hundirse
**bogey** ['bogi] *s* duende *m,* coco
**bo'gey•man'** *s* (*pl* **-men** [,mɛn]) duende *m,* espantajo
**bogus** ['bogəs] *adj* (coll) fingido, falso
**bo•gy** ['bogi] *s* (*pl* **-gies**) duende *m,* demonio, coco
**Bohemian** [bo'himɪ•ən] *adj & s* bohemio
**boil** [bɔɪl] *s* hervor *m,* ebullición; (pathol) divieso, furúnculo || *tr* hacer hervir, herventar || *intr* hervir, bullir; **to boil over** salirse (*un líquido*) al hervir
**boiler** ['bɔɪlər] *s* caldera; (*for cooking*) marmita, olla
**boil'er•mak'er** *s* calderero
**boiler room** *s* sala de calderas
**boiling** ['bɔɪlɪŋ] *adj* hirviente, hirviendo || *s* hervor *m,* ebullición
**boiling point** *s* punto de ebullición
**boisterous** ['bɔɪstərəs] *adj* bullicioso, ruidoso, estrepitoso
**bold** [bold] *adj* audaz, arrojado, osado; descarado, impudente; temerario
**bold'face'** *s* negrilla
**boldness** ['boldnɪs] *s* audacia, arrojo, osadía; descaro, impudencia; temeridad
**Bolivia** [bo'lɪvɪ•ə] *s* Bolivia
**Bolivian** [bo'lɪvɪ•ən] *adj & s* boliviano
**boll weevil** [bol] *s* gorgojo del algodón
**Bologna** [bə'lonjə] *s* Bolonia
**Bolshevik** ['balʃəvɪk] o ['bolʃəvɪk] *adj & s* bolchevique *mf*
**Bolshevism** ['balʃə,vɪzəm] o ['bolʃə,vɪzəm] *s* bolchevismo
**bolster** ['bolstər] *s* (*of bed*) larguero, travesaño; refuerzo, soporte *m* || *tr* apoyar, sostener; animar, alentar
**bolt** [bolt] *s* perno; (*to fasten a door*) cerrojo, pasador *m;* (*arrow*) cuadrillo; (*of lightning*) rayo; (*of cloth or paper*) rollo || *tr* empernar; acerrojar; deglutir de una vez; cribar, tamizar; disidir de (*un partido político*) || *intr* salir de repente; disidir; desbocarse (*un caballo*)
**bolter** ['boltər] *s* disidente *mf;* (*sieve*) criba, tamiz *m*
**bolt from the blue** *s* rayo en cielo sin nubes; suceso inesperado
**bomb** [bam] *s* bomba || *tr* bombear, bombardear
**bombard** [bam'bard] *tr* bombardear; (*e.g., with questions*) asediar
**bombardment** [bam'bardmənt] *s* bombardeo
**bombast** ['bambæst] *s* ampulosidad
**bombastic** [bam'bæstɪk] *adj* ampuloso
**bomb crater** *s* (mil) embudo de bomba
**bomber** ['bamər] *s* bombardero
**bomb'proof'** *adj* a prueba de bombas
**bomb release** *s* lanzabombas *m*
**bomb'shell'** *s* bomba; **to fall like a bombshell** caer como una bomba
**bomb shelter** *s* refugio antiaéreo
**bomb'sight'** *s* mira de bombardeo, visor *m*
**bona fide** ['bonə ,faɪdə] *adj & adv* de buena fe
**bonbon** ['ban ,ban] *s* bombón *m,* confite *m*
**bond** [band] *s* (*tie, union*) enlace *m,* vínculo, lazo de unión; (*interest-bearing certificate*) bono, obligación; (*surety*) fianza; (mas) aparejo; **bonds** cadenas, grillos; **in bond** en depósito bajo fianza
**bondage** ['bandɪdʒ] *s* cautiverio, servidumbre
**bonded warehouse** *s* depósito comercial
**bond'hold'er** *s* obligacionista *mf,* tenedor *m* de bonos
**bonds•man** ['bandzmən] *s* (*pl* **-men** [mən]) fiador *m*
**bone** [bon] *s* hueso; (*of fish*) espina; **bones** esqueleto; (*mortal remains*) huesos; castañuelas; (*dice*) (coll) dados; **to have a bone to pick with** tener una queja con; **to make no bones about** no andarse con rodeos en || *tr* desosar; quitar la espina a; emballenar (*un corsé*) || *intr* — **to bone up on** (coll) empollar, estudiar con ahinco
**bone'head'** *s* (coll) mentecato, zopenco
**boneless** ['bonlɪs] *adj* mollar, desosado; (*fish*) sin espinas
**boner** ['bonər] *s* (coll) patochada, plancha, gazapo
**bonfire** ['ban ,faɪr] *s* hoguera
**bonnet** ['banɪt] *s* gorra; (*sunbonnet*) papalina; (*of auto*) cubierta, capó *m*
**bonus** ['bonəs] *s* prima, plus *m;* dividendo extraordinario
**bon•y** ['boni] *adj* (*comp* **-ier**; *super* **-iest**) osudo; descarnado; (*fish*) espinoso
**boo** [bu] *s* rechifla; **not to say boo** no decir ni chus ni mus || *tr & intr* abuchear, rechiflar
**boo•by** ['bubi] *s* (*pl* **-bies**) bobalicón *m,* zopenco; el peor jugador
**booby prize** *s* premio al peor jugador
**booby trap** *s* (*mine*) trampa explosiva; (*trick*) zancadilla
**boogie-woogie** ['bʊgi'wʊgi] *s* buguibugui *m*
**book** [bʊk] *s* libro; (*bankbook*) libreta; (*book containing records of business transactions*) libro-registro; (*of cigaret paper, stamps, etc.*) librillo; **to keep books** llevar libros || *tr* reservar (*un pasaje*); escriturar (*a un actor*)
**bookbinder** ['bʊk ,baɪndər] *s* encuadernador *m*

**book'bind'er•y** *s* (*pl* **-ies**) encuadernación (*taller*)
**book'bind'ing** *s* encuadernación (*acción, arte*)
**book'case'** *s* armario para libros, estante *m* para libros
**book end** *s* apoyalibros *m*
**bookie** ['bʊki] *s* (coll) corredor *m* de apuestas
**booking** ['bʊkɪŋ] *s* (*of passage*) reservación; (*of an actor*) escritura
**booking clerk** *s* taquillero (*que despacha pasajes o localidades*)
**bookish** ['bʊkɪʃ] *adj* libresco
**book'keep'er** *s* tenedor *m* de libros
**book'keep'ing** *s* teneduría de libros, contabilidad
**book'mak'er** *s* corredor *m* de apuestas
**book'mark'** *s* registro
**book'plate'** *s* ex libris *m*
**book review** *s* reseña
**book'sell'er** *s* librero
**book'shelf'** *s* (*pl* **-shelves** [,ʃɛlvz]) estante *m* para libros
**book'stand'** *s* (*rack*) atril *m;* mostrador *m* para libros; puesto de venta para libros
**book'store'** *s* librería
**book'worm'** *s* polilla que roe los libros; (fig) ratón *m* de biblioteca
**boom** [bum] *s* (*sudden prosperity*) auge *m;* (*noise*) estampido, trueno; (*of a crane*) aguilón *m;* (naut) botalón *m* ‖ *intr* hacer estampido, tronar; estar en auge
**boomerang** ['bumə,ræŋ] *s* bumerán *m*
**boom town** *s* pueblo en bonanza
**boon** [bun] *s* bendición, dicha
**boon companion** *s* buen compañero
**boor** [bʊr] *s* patán *m*, rústico
**boorish** ['bʊrɪʃ] *adj* rústico, zafio
**boost** [bust] *s* empujón *m* hacia arriba; (*in price*) alza; alabanza; ayuda ‖ *tr* empujar hacia arriba; alzar (*el precio*); alabar; ayudar
**booster** ['bustər] *s* cohete *m* lanzador; primera etapa de un cohete lanzador; (*enthusiastic backer*) bombista *mf;* (med) inyección secundaria
**boot** [but] *s* bota; **to boot** de añadidura, además; **to die with one's boots on** morir al pie del cañón ‖ *tr* dar un puntapié a; **to boot out** (slang) poner en la calle
**boot'black'** *s* limpiabotas *m*
**booth** [buθ] *s* casilla, quiosco; (*to telephone, to vote, etc.*) cabina; (*at a fair or market*) puesto
**boot'jack'** *s* sacabotas *m*
**boot'leg'** *adj* contrabandista; de contrabando ‖ *s* contrabando de licores ‖ *v* (*pret & pp* **-legged;** *ger* **-legging**) *tr* pasar de contrabando ‖ *intr* contrabandear en bebidas alcohólicas
**bootlegger** ['but,legər] *s* destilador *m* clandestino, contrabandista *m*
**boot'leg'ging** *s* contrabando en bebidas alcohólicas
**bootlicker** ['but,lɪkər] *s* (slang) quitamotas *mf*, lavacaras *mf*
**boot'strap'** *s* tirilla de bota
**boo•ty** ['buti] *s* (*pl* **-ties**) botín *m*, presa
**booze** [buz] *s* (coll) bebida alcohólica ‖ *intr* borrachear
**bor.** *abbr* **borough**
**borax** ['boræks] *s* bórax *m*
**Bordeaux** [bɔr'do] *s* Burdeos
**border** ['bɔrdər] *adj* frontero, fronterizo ‖ *s* borde *m*, margen *m & f;* frontera; **borders** bambalinas ‖ *tr* bordear; deslindar ‖ *intr* confinar
**border clash** *s* encuentro fronterizo
**bor'der•line'** *adj* incierto, indefinido ‖ *s* frontera
**bore** [bor] *s* (*drill hole*) barreno; (*size of hole*) calibre *m;* (*of firearm*) alma, ánima; (*of cylinder*) alesaje *m;* (*wearisome person*) latoso, machaca *mf;* fastidio ‖ *tr* aburrir, fastidiar; barrenar, hacer (*un agujero*)
**boredom** ['bordəm] *s* aburrimiento, fastidio
**boring** ['borɪŋ] *adj* aburrido, pesado
**born** [bɔrn] *adj* nacido; (*natural, by birth*) nato, innato; **to be born** nacer
**borough** ['bʌro] *s* (*town*) villa; distrito electoral de municipio
**borrow** ['bɑro] o ['bɔro] *tr* pedir o tomar prestado; apropiarse (*p.ej., una idea*); incorporar (*un elemento lingüístico extranjero*); **to borrow trouble** tomarse una molestia sin motivo alguno
**borrower** ['bɑro•ər] o ['bɔro•ər] *s* prestatario
**borrowing** ['bɑro•ɪŋ] o ['bɔro•ɪŋ] *s* préstamo; préstamo lingüístico, extranjerismo
**bosom** ['bʊzəm] *s* seno; (*of shirt*) pechera; corazón *m*, pecho
**bosom friend** *s* amigo de la mayor confianza
**Bosporus** ['bɑspərəs] *s* Bósforo
**boss** [bɔs] o [bɑs] *s* (coll) amo, capataz *m*, mandamás, *m*, jefe *m;* (*in politics*) (coll) cacique *m;* protuberancia ‖ *tr* (coll) mandar, dominar
**boss•y** ['bɔsi] o ['bɑsi] *adj* (*comp* **-ier;** *super* **-iest**) mandón
**botanical** [bə'tænɪkəl] *adj* botánico
**botanist** ['bɑtənɪst] *s* botánico
**botany** ['bɑtəni] *s* botánica
**botch** [bɑtʃ] *s* remiendo chapucero ‖ *tr* remendar chapuceramente
**both** [boθ] *adj & pron* ambos ‖ *adv* igualmente ‖ *conj* a la vez; **both . . . and** tanto . . . como, así . . . como
**bother** ['bɑðər] *s* incomodidad, molestia ‖ *tr* incomodar, molestar ‖ *intr* molestarse
**bothersome** ['bɑðərsəm] *adj* incómodo, molesto, fastidioso
**bottle** ['bɑtəl] *s* botella, frasco ‖ *tr* embotellar; **to bottle up** (nav) embotellar
**bot'tle•neck'** *s* gollete *m;* (*in traffic*) embotellado
**bottle opener** ['opənər] *s* abrebotellas *m*
**bottom** ['bɑtəm] *adj* (*price*) (el) más bajo; (*e.g., dollar*) último ‖ *s* fondo; (*of a chair*) asiento; (*of jar*) culo;

(coll) trasero; **at bottom** en el fondo; **to go to the bottom** irse a pique
**bottomless** [ˈbatəmlɪs] *adj* sin fondo, insondable
**boudoir** [buˈdwar] *s* tocador *m*
**bough** [bau] *s* rama
**bouillon** [ˈbuljan] *s* caldo
**boulder** [ˈboldər] *s* pedrejón *m*
**boulevard** [ˈbulə,vard] *s* bulevar *m*
**bounce** [bauns] *s* rebote *m* || *tr* hacer botar; (slang) despedir || *intr* botar, rebotar; saltar; **to bounce along** dar saltos al andar
**bouncer** [ˈbaunsər] *s* cosa grande; (slang) apagabroncas *m*
**bouncing** [ˈbaunsɪŋ] *adj* frescachón, vigoroso; (*baby*) gordinflón
**bound** [baund] *adj* atado, ligado; (*book*) encuadernado; dispuesto, propenso; puesto en aprendizaje; **bound for** con destino a, con rumbo a; **bound in boards** (bb) encartonado, en cartoné; **bound up in** entregado a, muy adicto a; absorto en || *s* salto; (*of a ball*) bote *m;* límite *m,* confín *m;* **bounds** región, comarca; **out of bounds** fuera de los límites; **within bounds** a raya
**bounda·ry** [ˈbaundəri] *s* (*pl* **-ries**) límite *m,* frontera
**boundary stone** *s* mojón *m*
**bounder** [ˈbaundər] *s* persona vulgar y malcriada
**boundless** [ˈbaundlɪs] *adj* ilimitado, inmenso, infinito
**bountiful** [ˈbauntɪfəl] *adj* generoso, liberal; abundante
**boun·ty** [ˈbaunti] *s* (*pl* **-ties**) generosidad, liberalidad; don *m,* favor *m;* galardón *m,* premio; (*bonus*) prima; (mil) premio de enganche
**bouquet** [buˈke] o [boˈke] *s* ramillete *m;* (*aroma of a wine*) nariz *f*
**bourgeois** [ˈburʒwa] *adj* & *s* burgués *m*
**bourgeoisie** [,burʒwaˈzi] *s* burguesía
**bout** [baut] *s* encuentro; rato; (*of an illness*) ataque *m*
**bow** [bau] *s* inclinación, reverencia; (*of a ship*) proa || *tr* inclinar (*la cabeza*) || *intr* inclinarse; **to bow and scrape** hacer reverencias obsequiosas; **to bow to** saludar, inclinarse delante || [bo] *s* (*for shooting an arrow*) arco; lazo, nudo; (mus) arco; (*stroke of bow*) (mus) arqueada || *tr* (mus) tocar con arco || *intr* arquearse
**bowdlerize** [ˈbaudlə,raɪz] *tr* expurgar
**bowel** [ˈbau·əl] *s* intestino; **bowels** intestinos; (*inner part*) entrañas
**bowel movement** *s* evacuación del vientre; **to have a bowel movement** evacuar el vientre
**bower** [ˈbau·ər] *s* emparrado, glorieta
**bower·y** [ˈbau·əri] *adj* frondoso, sombreado || *s* (*pl* **-ies**) finca, granja
**bowknot** [ˈbo,nat] *s* lazada
**bowl** [bol] *s* (*for soup or broth*) escudilla, cuenco; (*for washing hands*) jofaina, palangana; (*of toilet*) cubeta, taza; (*of fountain*) tazón *m;* (*of spoon*) paleta; (*of pipe*) hornillo; (*hollow place*) concavidad, cuenco || *tr* — **to bowl over** tumbar || *intr* jugar a los bolos; **to bowl along** rodar
**bowlegged** [ˈbo,lɛgd] o [ˈbo,lɛgɪd] *adj* patiestevado
**bowler** [ˈbolər] *s* jugador *m* de bolos; (Brit) sombrero hongo
**bowling** [ˈbolɪŋ] *s* juego de bolos, boliche *m*
**bowling alley** *s* bolera, boliche *m*
**bowling green** *s* bolera encespada
**bowshot** [ˈbo,ʃat] *s* tiro de flecha
**bowsprit** [ˈbausprɪt] o [ˈbosprɪt] *s* bauprés *m*
**bow tie** [bo] *s* corbata de mariposa, pajarita
**bowwow** [ˈbau,wau] *interj* ¡guau! || *s* guau guau *m*
**box** [baks] *s* caja; (*slap*) bofetada; (*plant*) boj *m;* (*in newspaper*) recuadro; (theat) palco || *tr* encajonar; (*to slap*) abofetear; (naut) cuartear (*la aguja*) || *intr* boxear
**box′car′** *s* vagón *m* de carga cerrado
**boxer** [ˈbaksər] *s* embalador *m;* (sport) boxeador *m*
**boxing** [ˈbaksɪŋ] *s* embalaje *m;* (sport) boxeo
**boxing gloves** *spl* guantes *mpl* de boxeo
**box office** *s* taquilla, despacho de localidades; boletería (Am)
**box′-of′fice hit** *s* éxito de taquilla
**box-office record** *s* marca de taquilla
**box-office sale** *s* venta de localidades en taquilla
**box pleat** *s* pliegue *m* de tabla
**box seat** *s* asiento de palco
**box′wood′** *s* boj *m*
**boy** [bɔɪ] *s* muchacho; (*servant*) mozo; (coll) compadre *m*
**boycott** [ˈbɔɪkat] *s* boicoteo || *tr* boicotear
**boyhood** [ˈbɔɪhud] *s* muchachez *f;* muchachería
**boyish** [ˈbɔɪ·ɪʃ] *adj* amuchachado, muchachil
**boy scout** *s* niño explorador
**Bp.** *abbr* **bishop**
**b.p.** *abbr* **bills payable, boiling point**
**br.** *abbr* **brand, brother**
**b.r.** *abbr* **bills receivable**
**bra** [bra] *s* (coll) portasenos *m,* sostén *m*
**brace** [bres] *s* riostra; berbiquí *m;* **braces** (Brit) tirantes *mpl* || *tr* arriostrar; asegurar, vigorizar; **to brace oneself** (coll) cobrar ánimo || *intr* — **to brace up** (coll) cobrar ánimo
**brace and bit** *s* berbiquí y barrena
**bracelet** [ˈbreslɪt] *s* brazalete *m,* pulsera
**bracer** [ˈbresər] *s* (coll) trago de licor
**bracing** [ˈbresɪŋ] *adj* fortificante, tónico
**bracket** [ˈbrækɪt] *s* puntal *m,* soporte *m;* ménsula, repisa; (*mark used in printing*) corchete *m;* clase *f,* categoría || *tr* acorchetar; agrupar
**brackish** [ˈbrækɪʃ] *adj* salobre
**brad** [bræd] *s* clavito, estaquilla
**brag** [bræg] *s* jactancia || *v* (*pret & pp* **bragged;** *ger* **bragging**) *intr* jactarse

**braggart** ['brægərt] *s* fanfarrón *m*
**braid** [bred] *s* (*flat strip of cotton, silk, etc.*) cinta, galón *m;* (*something braided*) trenza || *tr* encintar, galonear; trenzar
**brain** [bren] *s* cerebro; **brains** cerebro, inteligencia; **to rack one's brains** devanarse los sesos || *tr* descerebrar
**brain child** *s* parto del ingenio
**brain drain** *s* (coll) éxodo de técnicos
**brainless** ['brenlɪs] *adj* tonto, sin seso
**brain power** *s* capacidad mental
**brain'storm'** *s* acceso de locura; (coll) confusión mental; (coll) buena idea, hallazgo
**brain trust** *s* grupo de peritos
**brain'wash'ing** *s* lavado cerebral
**brain wave** *s* onda encefálica; (coll) buena idea, hallazgo
**brain'work'** *s* trabajo intelectual
**brain•y** ['breni] *adj* (*comp* **-ier;** *super* **-iest**) (coll) inteligente, sesudo
**braise** [brez] *tr* soasar y cocer (*la carne*) a fuego lento en vasija bien tapada
**brake** [brek] *s* freno; (*for dressing flax*) agramadera; (*thicket*) matorral *m;* (*fern*) helecho común || *tr* frenar; agramar (*el lino o el cáñamo*)
**brake band** *s* cinta de freno
**brake drum** *s* tambor *m* de freno
**brake lining** *s* forro o cinta de freno
**brake•man** ['brekmən] *s* (*pl* **-men** [mən]) guardafrenos *m*
**brake shoe** *s* zapata de freno
**bramble** ['bræmbəl] *s* frambueso, zarza
**bram•bly** ['bræmbli] *adj* (*comp* **-blier;** *super* **-bliest**) zarzoso
**bran** [bræn] *s* afrecho, salvado
**branch** [bræntʃ] *s* (*of tree*) rama; (*smaller branch; branch cut from tree; of a science, etc.*) ramo; (*of vine*) sarmiento; (*of road, railroad*) ramal *m;* (*of candlestick, river, etc.*) brazo; (*of a store, bank*) sucursal *f* || *intr* ramificarse; **to branch out** extender sus actividades
**branch line** *s* ramal *m,* línea de empalme
**branch office** *s* sucursal *f*
**brand** [brænd] *s* (*kind, make*) marca; (*trademark*) marca de fábrica; (*branding iron*) hierro de marcar; (*mark stamped with hot iron*) hierro; (*dishonor*) tizón *m* || *tr* poner marca de fábrica en; herrar con hierro candente; tiznar (*la reputación de una persona*); **to brand as** tildar de
**brandied** ['brændid] *adj* macerado en aguardiente
**branding iron** *s* hierro de marcar
**brandish** ['brændɪʃ] *tr* blandear
**brand'-new'** *adj* nuevecito, flamante
**bran•dy** ['brændi] *s* (*pl* **-dies**) aguardiente *m*
**brash** [bræʃ] *adj* atrevido, impetuoso; descarado, respondón || *s* acceso, ataque *m*
**brass** [bræs] o [brɑs] *s* latón *m;* (*in army and navy*) (slang) los mandamases; (coll) descaro; **brasses** (mus) cobres *mpl*
**brass band** *s* banda, charanga
**brass hat** *s* (slang) espadón *m,* mandamás *m*
**brassière** [brə'zɪr] *s* portasenos *m,* sostén *m*
**brass knuckles** *s* llave inglesa, bóxer *m*
**brass tack** *s* clavito dorado de tapicería; **to get down to brass tacks** (coll) entrar en materia
**brass winds** *spl* (mus) cobres *mpl,* instrumentos músicos de metal
**brass•y** ['bræsi] o ['brɑsi] *adj* (*comp* **-ier;** *super* **-iest**) hecho de latón; metálico; descarado
**brat** [bræt] *s* rapaz *m,* mocoso, braguillas *m*
**brava•do** [brə'vɑdo] *s* (*pl* **-does** o **-dos**) bravata
**brave** [brev] *adj* bravo, valiente || *s* valiente *m;* guerrero indio norteamericano || *tr* hacer frente a, arrostrar; desafiar, retar
**bravery** ['brevəri] *s* bravura, valor *m*
**bra•vo** ['brɑvo] *interj* ¡bravo! || *s* (*pl* **-vos**) bravo
**brawl** [brɔl] *s* pendencia, reyerta; alboroto || *intr* armar pendencia; alborotar
**brawler** ['brɔlər] *s* pendenciero; alborotador *m*
**brawn** [brɔn] *s* fuerza musculosa
**brawn•y** ['brɔni] *adj* (*comp* **-ier;** *super* **-iest**) fornido, musculoso
**bray** [bre] *s* rebuzno || *intr* rebuznar
**braze** [brez] *s* soldadura de latón || *tr* soldar con latón; cubrir de latón; adornar con latón
**brazen** ['brezən] *adj* de latón; descarado || *tr* — **to brazen through** llevar a cabo descaradamente
**brazier** [brə'zɪr] *s* brasero
**Brazil** [brə'zɪl] *s* el Brasil
**Brazilian** [brə'zɪljən] *adj* & *s* brasileño
**Brazil nut** *s* castaña de Pará
**breach** [britʃ] *s* (*opening*) abertura; (*in a wall*) brecha; abuso, violación || *tr* abrir brecha en
**breach of faith** *s* falta de fidelidad
**breach of peace** *s* perturbación del orden público
**breach of promise** *s* incumplimiento de la palabra de matrimonio
**breach of trust** *s* abuso de confianza
**bread** [brɛd] *s* pan *m* || *tr* empanar
**bread and butter** *s* pan *m* con mantequilla; (coll) pan de cada día
**bread crumbs** *spl* pan rallado
**breaded** ['brɛdɪd] *adj* empanado
**bread line** *s* cola del pan
**breadth** [brɛdθ] *s* anchura; alcance *m,* extensión; (*e.g., of judgment*) amplitud *f*
**bread'win'ner** *s* sostén *m* de la familia
**break** [brek] *s* rompimiento; interrupción; intervalo, pausa; (*split*) hendidura, grieta; (*in prices*) baja; (*in clouds*) claro; (*from jail*) evasión, huída; (*among friends*) ruptura; (*luck, good or bad*) (slang) suerte *f;* (slang) disparate *m;* **to give someone a break** abrirle a uno la puerta || *v* (*pret* **broke** [brok]; *pp* **broken**) *tr*

romper, quebrar; cambiar (*un billete*); comunicar (*una mala noticia*); suspender (*relaciones*); faltar a (*la palabra*); batir (*un récord*); cortar (*un circuito*); quebrantar (*un testamento; un hábito*); romper (*una ley*); levantar (*el campo*); (mil) degradar; **to break in** forzar (*una puerta*); **to break open** abrir por la fuerza || *intr* romperse, quebrarse; reventar; aclarar (*el tiempo*); bajar (*los precios*); quebrantarse (*la salud*); **to break down** perder la salud; prorrumpir en llanto; **to break even** salir sin ganar ni perder; **to break in** entrar por fuerza; irrumpir en; **to break loose** desprenderse; escaparse; desbocarse (*un caballo*); desencadenarse (*una tempestad*); **to break out** estallar, declararse; (*in laughter, weeping*) romper; (*on the skin*) brotar granos; **to break through** abrirse paso; abrir paso por entre; **to break up** desmenuzarse; levantarse (*una reunión*); **to break with** romper con

**breakable** [ˈbrekəbəl] *adj* rompible

**breakage** [ˈbrekɪdʒ] *s* estropicio; indemnización por objetos rotos

**break′down′** *s* mal éxito; avería, pana; (*in health*) colapso; (*in negotiations*) ruptura; análisis *m*

**breaker** [ˈbrekər] *s* cachón *m*, rompiente *m*

**breakfast** [ˈbrekfəst] *s* desayuno || *intr* desayunar

**breakfast food** *s* cereal *m* para el desayuno

**break′neck′** *adj* vertiginoso; **at breakneck speed** a mata caballo

**break of day** *s* alba, amanecer *m*

**break′through′** *s* (mil) brecha, ruptura; (fig) descubrimiento sensacional

**break′up′** *s* disolución, dispersión; desplome *m*; (*in health*) postración

**break′wa′ter** *s* rompeolas *m*, escollera

**breast** [brest] *s* pecho, seno; (*of fowl*) pechuga; (*of garment*) pechera; **to make a clean breast of it** confesarlo todo

**breast′bone′** *s* esternón *m*; (*of fowl*) quilla

**breast drill** *s* berbiquí *m* de pecho

**breast′pin′** *s* alfiler *m* de pecho

**breast stroke** *s* brazada de pecho

**breath** [breθ] *s* aliento, respiración; **out of breath** sin aliento; **short of breath** corto de resuello; **to gasp for breath** respirar anhelosamente; **under one's breath** por lo bajo, en voz baja

**breathe** [brið] *tr* respirar; **to breathe one's last** dar el último suspiro || *intr* respirar; **to breathe freely** cobrar aliento; **to breathe in** aspirar; **to breathe out** espirar

**breathing spell** *s* respiro, rato de descanso

**breathless** [ˈbreθlɪs] *adj* falto de aliento, jadeante; intenso, vivo; sin aliento

**breath′tak′ing** *adj* conmovedor, imponente

**breech** [britʃ] *s* culata, recámara; **breeches** [ˈbrɪtʃɪz] calzones *mpl;* (coll) pantalones *mpl;* **to wear the breeches** (coll) calzarse los pantalones

**breed** [brid] *s* casta, raza; clase *f*, especie *f* || *v* (*pret & pp* **bred** [bred]) *tr* criar || *intr* criar; criarse

**breeder** [ˈbridər] *s* (*of animals*) criador *m*; (*animal*) reproductor *m*

**breeding** [ˈbridɪŋ] *s* cría; crianza, modales *mpl;* **bad breeding** mala crianza; **good breeding** buena crianza

**breeze** [briz] *s* brisa

**breez•y** [ˈbrizi] *adj* (*comp* **-ier;** *super* **-iest**) airoso; animado, vivo; (coll) desenvuelto, vivaracho

**brevi•ty** [ˈbrevɪti] *s* (*pl* **-ties**) brevedad

**brew** [bru] *s* calderada de cerveza; mezcla || *tr* fabricar (*cerveza*); preparar (*té*); (fig) tramar, urdir || *intr* amenazar (*una tormenta*)

**brewer** [ˈbru•ər] *s* cervecero

**brewer's yeast** *s* levadura de cerveza

**brewer•y** [ˈbru•əri] *s* (*pl* **-ies**) cervecería, fábrica de cerveza

**bribe** [braɪb] *s* soborno || *tr* sobornar

**briber•y** [ˈbraɪbəri] *s* (*pl* **-ies**) soborno

**bric-a-brac** [ˈbrɪkə,bræk] *s* chucherías, curiosidades *fpl*

**brick** [brɪk] *s* ladrillo; (coll) buen sujeto || *tr* enladrillar

**brick′bat′** *s* pedazo de ladrillo; (coll) palabra hiriente

**brick ice cream** *s* queso helado, helado al corte

**brickkiln** [ˈbrɪk,kɪl] *s* horno de ladrillero

**bricklayer** [ˈbrɪk,le•ər] *s* ladrillador *m*

**brick′yard′** *s* ladrillal *m*

**bridal** [ˈbraɪdəl] *adj* nupcial; de novia

**bridal wreath** *s* corona nupcial

**bride** [braɪd] *s* desposada, novia

**bride′groom′** *s* desposado, novio

**bridesmaid** [ˈbraɪdz,med] *s* madrina de boda

**bridge** [brɪdʒ] *s* puente *m*; (*of nose*) caballete *m*; (*card game*) bridge *m* || *tr* tender un puente sobre; salvar (*un obstáculo*); colmar, llenar (*un vacío*)

**bridge′head′** *s* (mil) cabeza de puente

**bridle** [ˈbraɪdəl] *s* brida || *tr* embridar || *intr* engallarse, erguirse

**bridle path** *s* camino de herradura

**brief** [brif] *adj* breve, corto, conciso || *s* resumen *m*; (law) escrito; **in brief** en resumen || *tr* resumir; dar consejos anticipados a; dar informes a

**brief case** *s* cartera

**brier** [ˈbraɪ•ər] *s* zarza; brezo blanco

**brig** [brɪg] *s* (naut) bergantín *m*; prisión en buque de guerra

**brigade** [brɪˈged] *s* brigada

**brigadier** [,brɪgəˈdɪr] *s* general *m* de brigada

**brigand** [ˈbrɪgənd] *s* bandolero

**brigantine** [ˈbrɪgən,tin] o [ˈbrɪgən,taɪn] *s* (naut) bergantín *m* goleta

**bright** [braɪt] *adj* brillante; (*e.g., day*) claro; (*color*) subido; listo, inteligente, despierto; (*idea, thought*) luminoso; (*disposition*) alegre, vivo

**brighten** ['braɪtən] *tr* abrillantar; alegrar, avivar || *intr* avivarse; alegrarse; despejarse (*el cielo*)
**bright lights** *spl* luces *fpl* brillantes; (aut) faros o luces de carretera
**brilliance** ['brɪljəns] o **brilliancy** ['brɪljənsi] *s* brillantez *f*, brillo
**brilliant** ['brɪljənt] *adj* brillante
**brim** [brɪm] *s* borde *m*; (*of hat*) ala
**brim'stone'** *s* azufre *m*
**brine** [braɪn] *s* salmuera, agua salobre
**bring** [brɪŋ] *v* (*pret & pp* **brought** [brɔt]) *tr* traer; llevar; **to bring about** efectuar; **to bring back** devolver; **to bring down** abatir; **to bring forth** sacar a luz; **to bring in** traer a colación; servir (*una comida*); introducir, presentar; **to bring into play** poner en juego; **to bring on** causar, producir; **to bring out** sacar; presentar al público; **to bring suit** poner pleito; **to bring to** sacar de un desmayo; **to bring together** reunir; confrontar; reconciliar; **to bring to pass** efectuar, llevar a cabo; **to bring up** arrimar (*p.ej., una silla*); educar, criar; traer a colación; **to bring upon oneself** atraerse (*un infortunio*)
**bringing-up** ['brɪŋɪŋ'ʌp] *s* educación, crianza
**brink** [brɪŋk] *s* borde *m*, margen *m*; **on the brink of** al borde de
**brisk** [brɪsk] *adj* animado, vivo, vivaz
**bristle** ['brɪsəl] *s* cerda || *intr* erizarse, encresparse; (*to be visibly annoyed*) encresparse
**bris•tly** ['brɪsli] *adj* (*comp* **-tlier**; *super* **-tliest**) cerdoso, erizado
**Britannic** [brɪ'tænɪk] *adj* británico
**British** ['brɪtɪʃ] *adj* británico || **the British** los britanos
**Britisher** ['brɪtɪʃər] *s* britano
**Briton** ['brɪtən] *s* britano
**Brittany** ['brɪtəni] *s* Bretaña
**brittle** ['brɪtəl] *adj* quebradizo, frágil
**bro.** *abbr* **brother**
**broach** [brotʃ] *s* (*skewer*) asador *m*, espetón *m*; (*ornamental pin*) broche *m*, prendedero || *tr* sacar a colación
**broad** [brɔd] *adj* ancho; liberal, tolerante; (*day, noon, etc.*) pleno
**broad'cast'** *s* radiodifusión; audición, programa radiotelefónico || *v* (*pret & pp* **-cast**) *tr* difundir, esparcir || (*pret & pp* **-cast** o **-casted**) *tr* radiodifundir, radiar, emitir
**broadcasting station** *s* emisora, estación de radiodifusión
**broad'cloth'** *s* paño fino
**broaden** ['brɔdən] *tr* ensanchar || *intr* ensancharse
**broad'loom'** *adj* tejido en telar ancho y en color sólido
**broad-minded** ['brɔd'maɪndɪd] *adj* tolerante, de amplias miras
**broad-shouldered** ['brɔd'ʃoldərd] *adj* ancho de espaldas
**broad'side'** *s* (naut) costado; (naut) andanada; (coll) torrente *m* de injurias
**broad'sword'** *s* espada ancha
**brocade** [bro'ked] *s* brocado
**broccoli** ['brɑkəli] *s* brécol *m*, brécoles *mpl*
**brochure** [bro'ʃʊr] *s* folleto
**brogue** [brog] *s* acento irlandés
**broil** [brɔɪl] *tr* asar a la parrilla || *intr* asarse
**broiler** ['brɔɪlər] *s* parrilla; pollo para asar a la parrilla
**broken** ['brokən] *adj* roto, quebrado; agotado; amansado; (*accent*) chapurrado; suelto
**bro'ken-down'** *adj* abatido; descompuesto; destartalado
**broken-hearted** ['brokən'hɑrtɪd] *adj* abrumado por el dolor
**broker** ['brokər] *s* corredor *m*
**brokerage** ['brokərɪdʒ] *s* corretaje *m*
**bromide** ['bromaɪd] *s* bromuro; (slang) trivialidad
**bromine** ['bromin] *s* bromo
**bronchitis** [brɑŋ'kaɪtɪs] *s* bronquitis *f*
**bron•co** ['brɑŋko] *s* (*pl* **-cos**) potro cerril
**bron'co•bust'er** *s* domador *m* de potros; vaquero
**bronze** [brɑnz] *adj* bronceado || *s* bronce *m* || *tr* broncear || *intr* broncearse
**brooch** [brotʃ] o [brutʃ] *s* alfiler *m* de pecho, prendedero, pasador *m*
**brood** [brud] *s* cría; nidada; casta, raza || *tr* empollar || *intr* enclocar; **to brood on** meditar con preocupación
**brook** [brʊk] *s* arroyo || *tr* — **to brook no** no tolerar, no aguantar
**broom** [brum] o [brʊm] *s* escoba; (bot) hiniesta
**broom'corn'** *s* sorgo
**broom'stick'** *s* palo de escoba
**bros.** *abbr* **brothers**
**broth** [brɔθ] o [brɑθ] *s* caldo
**brothel** ['brɑθəl] o ['brɑðəl] *s* burdel *m*
**brother** ['brʌðər] *s* hermano
**brotherhood** ['brʌðər,hʊd] *s* hermandad
**broth'er-in-law'** *s* (*pl* **brothers-in-law**) cuñado, hermano político; (*husband of one's wife's or husband's sister*) concuñado
**brotherly** ['brʌðərli] *adj* fraternal
**brow** [braʊ] *s* (*forehead*) frente *f*; (*eyebrow*) ceja; **to knit one's brow** fruncir las cejas
**brow'beat'** *v* (*pret* **-beat**; *pp* **beaten**) *tr* intimidar con mirada ceñuda
**brown** [braʊn] *adj* pardo, castaño, moreno; (*race*) cobrizo; tostado del sol || *s* castaño, moreno || *tr* poner moreno; tostar, quemar, broncear; (culin) dorar
**brownish** ['braʊnɪʃ] *adj* que tira a moreno
**brown study** *s* absorción, pensamiento profundo, ensimismamiento
**brown sugar** *s* azúcar terciado
**browse** [braʊz] *intr* (*to nibble at twigs*) ramonear; (*to graze*) pacer; hojear un libro ociosamente; **to browse about** o **around** curiosear
**bruise** [bruz] *s* contusión, magulladura

|| *tr* contundir, magullar || *intr* contundirse, magullarse
**brunet** [bru'net] *adj* moreno || *s* moreno (*hombre moreno*)
**brunette** [bru'net] *s* morena (*mujer morena*)
**brunt** [brʌnt] *s* fuerza, choque *m*, empuje *m;* (*e.g., of a battle*) peso, (lo) más reñido
**brush** [brʌʃ] *s* brocha, cepillo, escobilla; (*stroke*) brochada; (*light touch*) roce *m;* (*brief encounter*) encuentro, escaramuza; (*growth of bushes*) maleza; (elec) escobilla || *tr* acepillar; (*to graze*) rozar; **to brush aside** echar a un lado || *intr* pasar ligeramente; **to brush up on** repasar
**brush'-off'** *s* (slang) desaire *m;* **to give the brush-off to** (slang) despedir noramala
**brush'wood'** *s* broza, ramojo
**brusque** [brʌsk] *adj* brusco, rudo
**brusqueness** ['brʌsknɪs] *s* brusquedad
**Brussels** ['brʌsəlz] *s* Bruselas
**Brussels sprouts** *spl* bretones *mpl*, col *f* de Bruselas
**brutal** ['brutəl] *adj* brutal, bestial
**brutali·ty** [bru'tælɪti] *s* (*pl* **-ties**) brutalidad, crueldad
**brute** [brut] *adj* bruto; (*force*) inconsciente, ciego || *s* bruto
**brutish** ['brutɪʃ] *adj* abrutado, estúpido
**bu.** *abbr* **bushel**
**bubble** ['bʌbəl] *s* burbuja; ampolla; ilusión, quimera || *intr* burbujear; **to bubble over** desbordar, rebosar
**buck** [bʌk] *s* (*goat*) cabrón *m;* (*deer*) gamo; (*rabbit*) conejo; (*of a horse*) corveta, encorvada; (*youth*) pisaverde *m;* (slang) dólar *m;* **to pass the buck** (coll) echar la carga a otro || *tr* hacer frente a, resistir a; (*to butt*) acornear, topetar; colar (*la ropa*); **to buck up** (coll) alentar, animar || *intr* botarse, encorvarse; **to buck against** embestir contra
**bucket** ['bʌkɪt] *s* balde *m*, cubo; (*of a well*) pozal *m;* **to kick the bucket** (slang) estirar la pata, liar el petate
**bucket seat** *s* baquet *m*
**buckle** ['bʌkəl] *s* hebilla; (*bend, bulge*) alabeo, pandeo || *tr* abrochar con hebilla || *intr* (*to bend, bulge*) alabearse, pandear; **to buckle down to** (coll) dedicarse con empeño a
**buck private** *s* (slang) soldado raso
**buckram** ['bʌkrəm] *s* zangala; (bb) bocací *m*, bucarán *m*
**buck'saw'** *s* sierra de bastidor
**buck'shot'** *s* postas
**buck'tooth'** *s* (*pl* **-teeth**) diente *m* saliente
**buck'wheat'** *s* alforfón *m*, trigo sarraceno
**bud** [bʌd] *s* botón *m*, brote *m;* **to nip in the bud** cortar de raíz || *v* (*pret & pp* **budded;** *ger* **budding**) *intr* abotonar, brotar
**bud·dy** ['bʌdi] *s* (*pl* **-dies**) (coll) camarada *m;* (coll) muchachito
**budge** [bʌdʒ] *tr* mover || *intr* moverse
**budget** ['bʌdʒɪt] *s* presupuesto || *tr* presuponer, presupuestar
**budgetary** ['bʌdʒɪ,teri] *adj* presupuestario
**buff** [bʌf] *adj* de ante || *s* (*leather*) ante *m;* color *m* de ante; chaqueta de ante; rueda pulidora; (coll) piel desnuda; aficionado || *tr* dar color de ante a; pulimentar
**buffa·lo** ['bʌfə,lo] *s* (*pl* **-loes** o **-los**) búfalo || *tr* (slang) intimidar
**buffer** ['bʌfər] *s* amortiguador *m* de choques; tope *m*, paragolpes *m;* pulidor *m*
**buffer state** *s* estado tapón
**buffet** [bʊ'fe] *s* (*piece of furniture*) aparador *m;* restaurante *m* de estación || ['bʌfɪt] *tr* abofetear, golpear, pegar
**buffet car** [bʊ'fe] *s* coche *m* bar
**buffet lunch** [bʊ'fe] *s* servicio de bufet
**buffet supper** [bʊ'fe] *s* ambigú *m*, bufet *m*
**buffoon** [bə'fun] *s* bufón *m*, payaso
**buffoner·y** [bə'funəri] *s* (*pl* **-ies**) bufonada, chocarrería
**bug** [bʌg] *s* insecto, bicho, sabandija; microbio; (*bedbug*) (Brit) chinche *f;* (coll) defecto; (slang) micrófono escondido; (slang) loco; (slang) entusiasta *mf* || *v* (*pret & pp* **bugged;** *ger* **bugging**) *tr* (slang) esconder un micrófono en
**bug'bear'** *s* espantajo; aversión
**bug·gy** ['bʌgi] *adj* (*comp* **-gier;** *super* **-giest**) infestado de bichos; (slang) loco || *s* (*pl* **-gies**) calesa
**bug'house'** *adj* (slang) loco || *s* (slang) manicomio, casa de locos
**bugle** ['bjugəl] *s* corneta
**bugle call** *s* toque *m* de corneta
**bugler** ['bjuglər] *s* corneta *m*
**build** [bɪld] *s* forma, hechura, figura; (*of human being*) talle *m* || *v* (*pret & pp* **built** [bɪlt]) *tr* construir, edificar; componer; establecer, fundar; crearse (*p.ej., una clientela*)
**builder** ['bɪldər] *s* constructor *m;* aparejador *m*, maestro de obras
**building** ['bɪldɪŋ] *s* construcción; edificio; (*one of several in a group*) pabellón *m*
**building and loan association** *s* sociedad *f* de crédito para la construcción
**building lot** *s* solar *m*
**building site** *s* terreno para construir
**building trades** *spl* oficios de edificación
**build'-up'** *s* acumulación, formación; (coll) propaganda anticipada
**built'in'** *adj* integrante, incorporado, empotrado
**built'-up'** *adj* armado, montado; (*land*) aglomerado
**bulb** [bʌlb] *s* (*of plant*) bulbo; (*of thermometer*) bola, cubeta; (*of syringe*) pera; (*of electric light*) ampolla, bombilla
**Bulgaria** [bʌl'gerɪ·ə] *s* Bulgaria
**Bulgarian** [bʌl'gerɪ·ən] *adj & s* búlgaro
**bulge** [bʌldʒ] *s* protuberancia, bulto, bombeo; **to get the bulge on** (coll)

llevar la ventaja a || *intr* hacer bulto, bombearse
**bulk** [bʌlk] *s* bulto, volumen *m;* (*main mass*) grueso; **in bulk** a granel || *intr* abultar, hacer bulto; tener importancia
**bulk'head'** *s* mamparo; tabique hermético
**bulk•y** ['bʌlki] *adj* (*comp* **-ier;** *super* **-iest**) abultado, voluminoso, grueso
**bull** [bul] *s* toro; (*in stockmarket*) alcista *m;* (*papal document*) bula; disparate *m;* **to take the bull by the horns** asir al toro por las astas || *tr* — **to bull the market** jugar al alza
**bull'dog'** *s* dogo
**bulldoze** ['bul,doz] *tr* coaccionar, intimidar con amenazas
**bulldozer** ['bul,dozər] *s* explanadora de empuje, empujatierra
**bullet** ['bulɪt] *s* bala
**bulletin** ['bulətɪn] *s* boletín *m;* comunicado; (*of a school*) anuario
**bulletin board** *s* tablilla
**bul'let•proof'** *adj* a prueba de balas, blindado
**bull'fight'** *s* corrida de toros
**bull'fight'er** *s* torero
**bull'fight'ing** *adj* torero || *s* toreo
**bull'finch'** *s* (orn) camachuelo
**bull'frog'** *s* rana toro
**bull-headed** ['bul,hedɪd] *adj* obstinado, terco
**bullion** ['buljən] *s* oro en barras, plata en barras; (*twisted fringe*) entorchado
**bullish** ['bulɪʃ] *adj* obstinado; (*market*) en alza; (*speculator*) alcista; optimista
**bullock** ['bulək] *s* buey *m*
**bull'pen'** *s* (taur) toril *m;* (*jail*) (coll) prevención
**bull'ring'** *s* plaza de toros
**bull's-eye** ['bulz,aɪ] *s* (*of a target*) diana; (archit, meteor, naut) ojo de buey; **to hit the bull's-eye** hacer diana
**bul•ly** ['buli] *adj* (coll) excelente, magnífico || *s* (*pl* **-lies**) matón *m,* valentón *m* || *v* (*pret & pp* **-lied**) *tr* intimidar, maltratar
**bulrush** ['bul,rʌʃ] *s* junco; junco de laguna; (*Typha*) anea, espadaña; (Bib) papiro
**bulwark** ['bulwərk] *s* baluarte *m* || *tr* abaluartar; defender, proteger
**bum** [bʌm] *s* (slang) holgazán *m;* (slang) vagabundo; (slang) mendigo || *v* (*pret & pp* **bummed;** *ger* **bumming**) *tr* (slang) mendigar || *intr* holgazanear; (slang) vagabundear; (slang) mendigar
**bumblebee** ['bʌmbəl,bi] *s* abejorro
**bump** [bʌmp] *s* (*collision*) topetón *m;* (*shake*) sacudida; (*on falling*) batacazo; (*of plane in rough air*) rebote *m;* (*swelling*) hinchazón *f,* chichón *m;* protuberancia || *tr* dar contra, topar; (*to bruise*) abollar || *intr* chocar; dar sacudidas; **to bump into** tropezar con; encontrarse con
**bumper** ['bʌmpər] *adj* (coll) abundante, grande || *s* tope *m,* paratopes *m;* (aut) amortiguador *m,* parachoques *m;* vaso lleno
**bumpkin** ['bʌmpkɪn] *s* patán *m,* palurdo
**bumptious** ['bʌmpʃəs] *adj* engreído, presuntuoso
**bump•y** ['bʌmpi] *adj* (*comp* **-ier;** *super* **-iest**) (*ground*) desigual, áspero; (*air*) agitado
**bun** [bʌn] *s* buñuelo, bollo; (*of hair*) castaña
**bunch** [bʌntʃ] *s* manojo, puñado; (*of grapes, bananas, etc.*) racimo; (*of flowers*) ramillete *m;* (*of people*) grupo || *tr* agrupar, juntar || *intr* agruparse; arracimarse
**bundle** ['bʌndəl] *s* atado, bulto, lío, paquete *m;* (*of papers*) legajo; (*of wood*) haz *m* || *tr* atar, liar, empaquetar, envolver; **to bundle off** despedir precipitadamente; **to bundle up** arropar || *intr* — **to bundle up** arroparse
**bung** [bʌŋ] *s* bitoque *m,* tapón *m*
**bungalow** ['bʌŋgə,lo] *s* bungalow *m,* casa de una sola planta
**bung'hole'** *s* piquera, boca de tonel
**bungle** ['bʌŋgəl] *s* chapucería || *tr & intr* chapucear
**bungler** ['bʌŋglər] *s* chapucero
**bungling** ['bʌŋglɪŋ] *adj* chapucero || *s* chapucería
**bunion** ['bʌnjən] *s* juanete *m*
**bunk** [bʌŋk] *s* tarima; (slang) palabrería vana, música celestial
**bunker** ['bʌŋkər] *s* carbonera; (mil) fortín *m*
**bun•ny** ['bʌni] *s* (*pl* **-nies**) conejito
**bunting** ['bʌntɪŋ] *s* banderas colgadas como adorno; (*of a ship*) empavesado; (orn) gorrión triguero
**buoy** [bɔɪ] o ['bu·i] *s* boya; boya salvavidas, guindola || *tr* — **to buoy up** mantener a flote; animar, alentar
**buoyancy** ['bɔɪ·ənsi] o ['bujənsi] *s* flotación; alegría, animación
**buoyant** ['bɔɪ·ənt] o ['bujənt] *adj* boyante; alegre, animado
**bur** [bʌr] *s* erizo, vilano
**burble** ['bʌrbəl] *s* burbujeo || *intr* burbujear
**burden** ['bʌrdən] *s* carga; (*of a speech*) tema *m;* (*of a poem*) estribillo || *tr* cargar; agobiar, gravar
**burden of proof** *s* peso de la prueba
**burdensome** ['bʌrdənsəm] *adj* gravoso, oneroso
**burdock** ['bʌrdɑk] *s* bardana, cadillo
**bureau** ['bjuro] *s* cómoda; despacho, oficina; departamento, negociado
**bureaucra•cy** [bju'rɑkrəsi] *s* (*pl* **-cies**) burocracia
**bureaucrat** ['bjurə,kræt] *s* burócrata *mf*
**bureaucratic** [,bjurə'krætɪk] *adj* burocrático
**burgess** ['bʌrdʒɪs] *s* burgués *m,* ciudadano; alcalde *m* de un pueblo o villa
**burglar** ['bʌrglər] *s* escalador *m*
**burglar alarm** *s* alarma de ladrones

**bur'glar·proof'** *adj* a prueba de escaladores
**burglar·y** ['bʌrgləri] *s* (*pl* **-ies**) robo con escalamiento
**Burgundian** [bər'gʌndɪ·ən] *adj* & *s* borgoñón *m*
**Burgundy** ['bʌrgəndi] *s* la Borgoña; (*wine*) borgoña *m*
**burial** ['berɪ·əl] *s* entierro
**burial ground** *s* cementerio
**burlap** ['bʌrlæp] *s* arpillera
**burlesque** [bər'lesk] *adj* burlesco, festivo || *s* parodia || *tr* parodiar
**burlesque show** *s* espectáculo de bailes y cantos groseros, music-hall *m*
**bur·ly** ['bʌrli] *adj* (*comp* **-lier**; *super* **-liest**) fornido, corpulento, membrudo
**Burma** ['bʌrmə] *s* Birmania
**Bur·mese** [bər'miz] *adj* birmano || *s* (*pl* **-mese**) birmano
**burn** [bʌrn] *s* quemadura, quemazón *f* || *v* (*pret* & *pp* **burned** o **burnt** [bʌrnt]) *tr* quemar || *intr* quemar, quemarse; estar encendido (*p.ej., un faro*); **to burn out** quemarse (*un fusible*); fundirse (*una bombilla*); **to burn within** requemarse
**burner** ['bʌrnər] *s* (*of furnace*) quemador *m;* (*of gas fixture or lamp*) mechero
**burning** ['bʌrnɪŋ] *adj* ardiente || *s* quema, incendio
**burning question** *s* cuestión palpitante
**burnish** ['bʌrnɪʃ] *s* bruñido || *tr* bruñir || *intr* bruñirse
**burnoose** [bər'nus] *s* albornoz *m*
**burnt almond** [bʌrnt] *s* almendra tostada
**burr** [bʌr] *s* (*of plant*) erizo; (*of cut in metal*) rebaba
**burrow** ['bʌro] *s* madriguera, conejera || *tr* hacer madrigueras en; socavar || *intr* amadrigarse; esconderse
**bursar** ['bʌrsər] *s* tesorero universitario
**burst** [bʌrst] *s* explosión, reventón *m*, estallido; (*of machine gun*) ráfaga; salida brusca || *v* (*pret* & *pp* **burst**) *tr* reventar || *intr* reventar, reventarse; partirse (*el corazón*); **to burst into** irrumpir en (*un cuarto*); desatarse en (*amenazas*); prorrumpir en (*lágrimas*); **to burst out crying** deshacerse en lágrimas; **to burst with laughter** reventar de risa
**bur·y** ['beri] *v* (*pret* & *pp* **-ied**) *tr* enterrar; **to be buried in thought** estar absorto en meditación; **to bury the hatchet** hacer la paz, echar pelillos a la mar
**burying ground** *s* cementerio
**bus.** *abbr* **business**
**bus** [bʌs] *s* (*pl* **busses** o **buses**) autobús *m* || *tr* llevar en un autobús
**bus boy** *s* ayudante *m* de camarero
**bus·by** ['bʌzbi] *s* (*pl* **-bies**) morrión *m* de húsar, colbac *m*
**bush** [bʊʃ] *s* arbusto; (*scrubby growth*) matorral *m*, monte *m;* **to beat about the bush** andar con rodeos
**bushel** ['bʊʃəl] *s* medida para áridos (*35,23 litros en E.U.A. y 36,35 litros en Inglaterra*)
**bushing** ['bʊʃɪŋ] *s* buje *m*, forro
**bush·y** ['bʊʃi] *adj* (*comp* **-ier**; *super* **-iest**) arbustivo; peludo, lanudo; espeso
**business** ['bɪznɪs] *adj* comercial, de negocios || *s* negocio, comercio; (*company, concern*) empresa; (*job, employment*) empleo, oficio; (*matter*) asunto, cuestión; (*duty*) obligación; (*right*) derecho; **on business** por negocios; **to have no business to** no tener derecho a; **to make it one's business to** proponerse; **to mean business** (coll) obrar en serio, hablar en serio; **to mind one's own business** no meterse en lo que no le importa a uno; **to send about one's business** mandar a paseo
**business district** *s* barrio comercial
**businesslike** ['bɪznɪs,laɪk] *adj* práctico, sistemático, serio
**business·man** ['bɪznɪs,mæn] *s* (*pl* **-men** [,men]) comerciante *m*, hombre *m* de negocios
**business suit** *s* traje *m* de calle
**bus·man** ['bʌsmən] *s* (*pl* **-men** [mən]) conductor *m* de autobús
**buss** [bʌs] *s* (coll) beso sonado || *tr* (coll) dar besos sonados a || *intr* (coll) dar besos sonados; (coll) darse besos sonados
**bust** [bʌst] *s* busto; (*of woman*) pecho; (slang) fracaso; (slang) borrachera || *tr* (slang) reventar, romper; (slang) arruinar; (slang) golpear, pegar || *intr* (slang) reventar; (slang) fracasar
**buster** ['bʌstər] *s* muchachito
**bustle** ['bʌsəl] *s* (*of woman's dress*) polisón *m;* alboroto, bullicio || *intr* ajetrearse, menearse
**bus·y** ['bɪzi] *adj* (*comp* **-ier**; *super* **-iest**) ocupado; (*e.g., street*) concurrido; (*meddling*) intruso, entremetido || *v* (*pret* & *pp* **-ied**) *tr* ocupar; **to busy oneself with** ocuparse de
**busybod·y** ['bɪzɪ,bɑdi] *s* (*pl* **-ies**) entremetido, fisgón *m*
**busy signal** *s* (telp) señal *f* de ocupado
**but** [bʌt] *adv* sólo, solamente, no . . . más que; **but for** a no ser por; **but little** muy poco || *prep* excepto, salvo; **all but** casi || *conj* pero; sino, p.ej., **nobody came but John** no vino sino Juan
**butcher** ['bʊtʃər] *s* carnicero || *tr* matar (*reses para el consumo*); dar muerte a; (*to bungle*) chapucear
**butcher knife** *s* cuchilla de carnicero
**butcher shop** *s* carnicería
**butcher·y** ['bʊtʃəri] *s* (*pl* **-ies**) (*slaughterhouse*) matadero; (*wanton slaughter*) matanza, carnicería
**butler** ['bʌtlər] *s* despensero, mayordomo
**butt** [bʌt] *s* (*of gun*) culata; (*of cigaret*) colilla, punta; (*of horned animal*) cabezada, topetada, topetón *m;* (*target*) blanco; hazmerreír *m;* (*large*

*cask*) pipa || *tr* topar, topetar; acornear || *intr* dar cabezadas; **to butt against** confinar con; **to butt in** (slang) entremeterse
**butter** [ˈbʌtər] *s* mantequilla || *tr* untar con mantequilla; **to butter up** (coll) adular, lisonjear
**but′ter•cup′** *s* botón *m* de oro
**butter dish** *s* mantequillera
**but′ter•fly′** *s* (*pl* **-flies**) mariposa
**butter knife** *s* cuchillo mantequillero
**but′ter•milk′** *s* leche *f* de manteca
**butter sauce** *s* mantequilla fundida
**but′ter•scotch′** *s* bombón *m* escocés, bombón hecho con azúcar terciado y mantequilla
**buttocks** [ˈbʌtəks] *spl* nalgas
**button** [ˈbʌtən] *s* botón *m* || *tr* abotonar, abrocharse
**but′ton•hole′** *s* ojal *m* || *tr* detener con conversación
**but′ton•hook′** *s* abotonador *m*
**but′ton•wood′ tree** *s* plátano de occidente
**buttress** [ˈbʌtrɪs] *s* contrafuerte *m*; (fig) apoyo, sostén *m* || *tr* estribar; (fig) apoyar, sostener
**butt weld** *s* soldadura a tope
**buxom** [ˈbʌksəm] *adj* rolliza, frescachona
**buy** [baɪ] *s* (coll) compra; (*bargain*) (coll) ganga || *v* (*pret & pp* **bought** [bɔt]) *tr* comprar; **to buy back** recomprar; **to buy off** comprar, sobornar; **to buy out** comprar la parte de (*un socio*); **to buy up** acaparar
**buyer** [ˈbaɪ•ər] *s* comprador *m*
**buzz** [bʌz] *s* zumbido || *intr* zumbar; **to buzz about** ajetrearse, cazcalear
**buzzard** [ˈbʌzərd] *s* alfaneque *m*
**buzz bomb** *s* bomba volante
**buzzer** [ˈbʌzər] *s* zumbador *m*
**buzz saw** *s* sierra circular
**bx.** *abbr* **box**
**by** [baɪ] *adv* cerca; a un lado; **by and by** luego || *prep* por; cerca de, al lado de; (*not later than*) para; **by far** con mucho; **by the way** de paso; a propósito
**by-and-by** [ˈbaɪ•əndˈbaɪ] *s* porvenir *m*
**bye-bye** [ˈbaɪˈbaɪ] *s* mu *f*; **to go bye-bye** ir a la mu || *interj* (coll) ¡adiosito!; (*to a child*) ¡ro ro!
**bygone** [ˈbaɪˌgɔn] o [ˈbaɪˌgɑn] *adj* pasado || *s* pasado; **let bygones be bygones** olvidemos lo pasado
**bylaw** [ˈbaɪˌlɔ] *s* reglamento, estatuto
**bypass** [ˈbaɪˌpæs] o [ˈbaɪˌpɑs] *s* desviación; tubo de paso || *tr* desviar; (*a difficulty*) eludir
**by′-prod′uct** *s* subproducto, derivado
**bystander** [ˈbaɪˌstændər] *s* asistente *mf*, circunstante *mf*
**byway** [ˈbaɪˌwe] *s* camino apartado
**byword** [ˈbaɪˌwʌrd] *s* objeto de oprobio; refrán *m*, muletilla; apodo
**Byzantine** [ˈbɪzənˌtin] o [bɪˈzæntin] *adj & s* bizantino
**Byzantium** [bɪˈzænʃɪ•əm] o [bɪˈzæntɪ•əm] *s* Bizancio

## C

**C, c** [si] tercera letra del alfabeto inglés
**c.** *abbr* **cent, center, centimeter**
**C.** *abbr* **centigrade, Congress, Court**
**cab** [kæb] *s* coche *m* de plaza o de punto; taxi *m*; (*of a truck*) casilla
**cabaret** [ˌkæbəˈre] *s* cabaret *m*
**cabbage** [ˈkæbɪdʒ] *s* col *f*, berza
**cab driver** *s* cochero de plaza; taxista *mf*
**cabin** [ˈkæbɪn] *s* (*hut, cottage*) cabaña; (aer) cabina; (naut) camarote *m*
**cabin boy** *s* mozo de cámara
**cabinet** [ˈkæbɪnɪt] *s* (*piece of furniture for displaying objects*) escaparate *m*, vitrina; (*for a radio*) caja, mueble *m*; (*closet*) armario; (*private room; ministry of a government*) gabinete *m*
**cab′inet•ma′ker** *s* ebanista *m*
**cab′inet•ma′king** *s* ebanistería
**cable** [ˈkebəl] *adj* cablegráfico || *s* cable *m*; cablegrama *m* || *tr & intr* cablegrafiar
**cable address** *s* dirección cablegráfica
**cable car** *s* tranvía *m* de tracción por cable
**cablegram** [ˈkebəlˌgræm] *s* cablegrama *m*
**caboose** [kəˈbus] *s* (rr) furgón de cola
**cab′stand′** *s* punto de coches, punto de taxis
**cache** [kæʃ] *s* escondrijo; víveres escondidos || *tr* depositar en un escondrijo; ocultar
**cachet** [kæˈʃe] *s* sello
**cackle** [ˈkækəl] *s* (*of a hen*) cacareo; (*idle talk*) charla || *intr* cacarear; charlar
**cac•tus** [ˈkæktəs] *s* (*pl* **-tuses** o **-ti** [taɪ]) cacto
**cad** [kæd] *s* sinvergüenza *mf*
**cadaver** [kəˈdævər] *s* cadáver *m*
**cadaverous** [kəˈdævərəs] *adj* cadavérico
**caddie** [ˈkædi] *s* caddie *m* (*muchacho que lleva los utensilios en el juego de golf*) || *intr* servir de caddie
**cadence** [ˈkedəns] *s* cadencia
**cadet** [kəˈdɛt] *s* hermano menor, hijo menor; (*student at military school*) cadete *m*
**cadmium** [ˈkædmɪ•əm] *s* cadmio
**cadre** [ˈkædri] *s* (mil) cuadro
**Caesar** [ˈsizər] *s* César *m*

**café** [kæ'fe] *s* bar *m*, cabaret *m;* restaurante *m*
**café society** *s* gente *f* del mundo elegante que frecuenta los cabarets de moda
**cafeteria** [ˌkæfə'tɪrɪ·ə] *s* cafetería
**cage** [kedʒ] *s* jaula ‖ *tr* enjaular
**cageling** ['kedʒlɪŋ] *s* pájaro enjaulado
**ca·gey** ['kedʒi] *adj* (*comp* **-gier;** *super* **-giest**) (coll) astuto
**cahoots** [kə'huts] *s* — **to be in cahoots** (slang) confabularse (*dos o más personas*); **to go cahoots** (slang) entrar por partes iguales
**Cain** [ken] *s* Caín *m;* **to raise Cain** (slang) armar camorra
**Cairo** ['kaɪro] *s* El Cairo
**caisson** ['kesən] *s* cajón *m* de aire comprimido, esclusa de aire
**cajole** [kə'dʒol] *tr* adular, lisonjear, halagar
**cajoler·y** [kə'dʒoləri] *s* (*pl* **-ies**) adulación, lisonja, halago
**cake** [kek] *s* pastel *m*, bollo; (*small cake*) pastelillo; (*sponge cake*) bizcocho; (*of fish*) fritada; (*of earth*) terrón *m;* (*of soap*) pan *m*, pastilla; (*of ice*) témpano; **to take the cake** (coll) ser el colmo ‖ *intr* apelmazarse, aterronarse
**calabash** ['kælə ˌbæʃ] *s* calabacera; (*fruit*) calabaza
**calamitous** [kə'læmɪtəs] *adj* calamitoso
**calami·ty** [kə'læmɪti] *s* (*pl* **-ties**) calamidad
**calci·fy** ['kælsɪ ˌfaɪ] *v* (*pret & pp* **-fied**) calcificar ‖ *intr* calcificarse
**calcium** ['kælsɪ·əm] *s* calcio
**calculate** ['kælkjə ˌlet] *tr* calcular; (*to reckon*) (coll) calcular ‖ *intr* calcular; **to calculate on** contar con
**calculating** ['kælkjə ˌletɪŋ] *adj* de calcular; astuto, intrigante
**calculating machine** *s* calculadora, máquina de calcular
**calcu·lus** ['kælkjələs] *s* (*pl* **-luses** o **-li** [ˌlaɪ]) (math, pathol) cálculo
**caldron** ['kɔldrən] *s* calderón *m*
**calendar** ['kæləndər] *s* calendario, almanaque *m*
**calf** [kæf] o [kɑf] *s* (*pl* **calves** [kævz] o [kɑvz]) ternero; (*of the leg*) pantorrilla
**calf'skin'** *s* becerro, becerrillo
**caliber** ['kælɪbər] *s* calibre *m*
**calibrate** ['kælɪ ˌbret] *tr* calibrar
**cali·co** ['kælɪ ˌko] *s* (*pl* **-coes** o **-cos**) calicó *m*, indiana
**California** [ˌkælɪ'fɔrnɪ·ə] *s* California
**calipers** ['kælɪpərz] *spl* calibrador *m*, compás *m* de calibres
**caliph** ['kelɪf] o ['kælɪf] *s* califa *m*
**caliphate** ['kælɪ ˌfet] *s* califato
**calisthenic** [ˌkælɪs'θenɪk] *adj* calisténico ‖ **calisthenics** *spl* calistenia
**calk** [kɔk] *tr* calafatear
**calking** ['kɔkɪŋ] *s* calafateo
**call** [kɔl] *s* llamada; visita; (*of a boat or airplane*) escala; vocación; **within call** al alcance de la voz ‖ *tr* llamar; convocar (*p.ej., una huelga*); **to call back** mandar volver; **to call down** (coll) reprender, regañar; **to call in** hacer entrar; (*from circulation*) retirar; **to call off** aplazar, suspender; **to call out** llamar (*a uno*) que salga; **to call together** convocar, reunir; **to call up** llamar por teléfono; evocar, recordar ‖ *intr* llamar, gritar; hacer una visita; (naut) hacer escala; **to call on** acudir a; visitar; **to call out** gritar; **to go calling** ir de visitas
**calla lily** ['kælə] *s* cala, lirio de agua
**call bell** *s* timbre *m* de llamada
**call'boy'** *s* (*in a hotel*) botones *m;* (theat) traspunte *m*
**caller** ['kɔlər] *s* visitante *mf*
**call girl** *s* chica de cita
**calling** ['kɔlɪŋ] *s* profesión, vocación
**calling card** *s* tarjeta de visita
**calliope** [kə'laɪ·əpi] o ['kælɪ·op] *s* (mus) órgano de vapor ‖ **Calliope** [kə'laɪ·əpi] *s* Calíope *f*
**call number** *s* número de teléfono; (*of a book*) número de clasificación
**callous** ['kæləs] *adj* calloso; (fig) duro, insensible
**call to arms** *s* — **to sound the call to arms** (mil) batir o tocar a llamada
**call to the colors** *s* (mil) llamada a filas
**callus** ['kæləs] *s* callo
**calm** [kɑm] *adj* tranquilo, quieto; (*sea*) bonancible ‖ *s* tranquilidad, calma ‖ *tr* tranquilizar, calmar ‖ *intr* — **to calm down** tranquilizarse, calmarse; abonanzar, calmar (*el viento, el tiempo*)
**calmness** ['kɑmnɪs] *s* tranquilidad, calma
**calorie** ['kæləri] *s* caloría
**calum·ny** ['kæləmni] *s* (*pl* **-nies**) calumnia
**calva·ry** ['kælvəri] *s* (*pl* **-ries**) (*at the entrance to a town*) humilladero ‖ **Calvary** *s* Calvario
**calyp·so** [kə'lɪpso] *s* (*pl* **-sos**) calipso ‖ **Calypso** *s* Calipso *f*
**cam** [kæm] *s* leva
**cambric** ['kembrɪk] *s* batista
**camel** ['kæməl] *s* camello
**came·o** ['kæmɪ·o] *s* (*pl* **-os**) camafeo
**camera** ['kæmərə] *s* cámara fotográfica, máquina fotográfica
**camera·man** ['kæmərə ˌmæn] *s* (*pl* **-men** [ˌmen]) camarógrafo, tomavistas *m*
**camomile** ['kæmə ˌmaɪl] *s* manzanilla
**camouflage** ['kæmə ˌflɑʒ] *s* camuflaje *m* ‖ *tr* camuflar
**camp** [kæmp] *s* campamento ‖ *intr* acampar
**campaign** [kæm'pen] *s* campaña ‖ *intr* hacer campaña
**campaigner** [kæm'penər] *s* propagandista *mf;* veterano
**camp'fire'** *s* hoguera de campamento
**camphor** ['kæmfər] *s* alcanfor *m*
**camp'stool'** *s* silla de tijera, catrecillo
**campus** ['kæmpəs] *s* terrenos, recinto (*de la universidad*)
**cam'shaft'** *s* árbol *m* de levas
**can** [kæn] *s* bote *m*, envase *m*, lata ‖ *v* (*pret & pp* **canned;** *ger* **canning**) *tr* envasar, enlatar ‖ *v* (*pret & cond*

could) *v aux* **he can come tomorrow** puede venir mañana; **can you swim?** ¿sabe Vd. nadar?
**Canada** ['kænədə] *s* el Canadá
**Canadian** [kə'nedɪ·ən] *adj & s* canadiense
**canal** [kə'næl] *s* canal *m*
**canar·y** [kə'nɛri] *s* (*pl* **-ies**) canario ‖ **Canaries** *spl* Canarias
**can·cel** ['kænsəl] (*pret & pp* **-celed** o **-celled**; *ger* **-celing** o **-celling**) *tr* cancelar, eliminar, suprimir; matasellar, obliterar (*sellos de correo*)
**canceler** ['kænsələr] *s* matasellos *m*
**cancellation** [,kænsə'leʃən] *s* cancelación, eliminación, supresión; (*of stamps*) obliteración
**cancer** ['kænsər] *s* cáncer *m*
**cancerous** ['kænsərəs] *adj* canceroso
**candela·brum** [,kændə'lebrəm] *s* (*pl* **-bra** [brə] o **-brums**) candelabro
**candid** ['kændɪd] *adj* franco, sincero; imparcial
**candida·cy** ['kændɪdəsi] *s* (*pl* **-cies**) candidatura
**candidate** ['kændɪ,det] *s* candidato; (*for a degree*) graduando
**candid camera** *s* cámara indiscreta
**candle** ['kændəl] *s* bujía, candela, vela
**can'dle·hold'er** *s* candelero
**can'dle·light'** *s* luz *f* de vela; crepúsculo
**candle power** *s* bujía
**can'dle·stick'** *s* palmatoria
**candor** ['kændər] *s* franqueza, sinceridad; imparcialidad
**can·dy** ['kændi] *s* (*pl* **-dies**) bombón *m*, confite *m*, dulce *m*; dulces *mpl* ‖ *v* (*pret & pp* **-died**) *tr* almibarar, confitar, garapiñar ‖ *intr* almibararse
**candy box** *s* bombonera, confitera
**candy store** *s* confitería, dulcería
**cane** [ken] *s* (*plant; stem*) caña; (*walking stick*) bastón *m*; (*for chair seats*) junco, mimbre *m*, rejilla
**cane seat** *s* asiento de rejilla
**cane sugar** *s* azúcar *m* de caña
**canine** ['kenaɪn] *adj* canino ‖ *s* (*tooth*) canino; perro
**canned goods** *spl* conservas alimenticias
**canner·y** ['kænəri] *s* (*pl* **-ies**) conservera, fábrica de conservas
**cannibal** ['kænɪbəl] *adj & s* caníbal *mf*
**canning** ['kænɪŋ] *adj* conservero ‖ *s* conservería
**cannon** ['kænən] *s* cañón *m*; cañones
**cannonade** [,kænə'ned] *s* cañoneo ‖ *tr* cañonear
**cannon ball** *s* bala de cañón
**cannon fodder** *s* carne *f* de cañón
**can·ny** ['kæni] *adj* (*comp* **-nier**; *super* **-niest**) cauteloso, cuerdo; astuto
**canoe** [kə'nu] *s* canoa
**canoeist** [kə'nu·ɪst] *s* canoero
**canon** ['kænən] *s* canon *m*; (*priest*) canónigo
**canonical** [kə'nɑnɪkəl] *adj* canónico; aceptado, auténtico, establecido ‖ **canonicals** *spl* vestiduras sacerdotales
**canonize** ['kænə,naɪz] *tr* canonizar
**canon law** *s* cánones *mpl*, derecho canónico
**canon·ry** ['kænənri] *s* (*pl* **-ries**) canonjía
**can opener** ['opənər] *s* abrelatas *m*
**cano·py** ['kænəpi] *s* (*pl* **-pies**) dosel *m*, pabellón *m*; (*over an entrance*) marquesina; (*for electrical fixtures*) campana
**canopy of heaven** *s* bóveda celeste
**cant** [kænt] *s* hipocresía; jerga, jerigonza
**cantaloupe** ['kæntə,lop] *s* cantalupo
**cantankerous** [kæn'tæŋkərəs] *adj* de mal genio, pendenciero
**canteen** [kæn'tin] *s* (*shop*) cantina; (*water flask*) cantimplora; (mil) centro de recreo
**canter** ['kæntər] *s* medio galope ‖ *intr* ir a medio galope
**canticle** ['kæntɪkəl] *s* cántico
**cantilever** ['kæntɪ,livər] *adj* voladizo ‖ *s* viga voladiza
**cantle** ['kæntəl] *s* arzón trasero
**canton** [kæn'tɑn] *tr* acantonar
**cantonment** [kæn'tɑnmənt] *s* acantonamiento
**cantor** ['kæntər] o ['kæntɔr] *s* chantre *m*; (*in a synagogue*) cantor *m* principal
**canvas** ['kænvəs] *s* cañamazo, lona; (naut) vela, lona; (*painting*) lienzo; **under canvas** (mil) en tiendas; (naut) con las velas izadas
**canvass** ['kænvəs] *s* pesquisa, escrutinio; (*of votes*) solicitación ‖ *tr* escrutar, solicitar; discutir detenidamente
**canyon** ['kænjən] *s* cañón *m*
**cap.** *abbr* **capital, capitalize**
**cap** [kæp] *s* gorra, gorra de visera; (*of academic costume*) birrete *m*; (*of bottle*) cápsula; (*e.g., of a fountain pen*) capuchón *m* ‖ *v* (*pret & pp* **capped**; *ger* **capping**) *tr* cubrir con gorra; capsular (*una botella*); **to cap the climax** ser el colmo
**capabili·ty** [,kepə'bɪlɪti] *s* (*pl* **-ties**) habilidad, capacidad
**capable** ['kepəbəl] *adj* hábil, capaz
**capacious** [kə'peʃəs] *adj* espacioso, capaz
**capaci·ty** [kə'pæsɪti] *s* (*pl* **-ties**) (*room, space; ability, aptitude*) capacidad; (*status, function*) calidad; **in the capacity of** en calidad de
**cap and bells** *spl* caperuza de bufón; cetro de la locura
**cap and gown** *s* birrete y toga
**caparison** [kə'pærɪsən] *s* caparazón *m* ‖ *tr* engualdrapar
**cape** [kep] *s* cabo, promontorio; (*garment*) capa, esclavina
**Cape Colony** *s* la Colonia del Cabo
**Cape Horn** *s* el Cabo de Hornos
**Cape of Good Hope** *s* Cabo de Buena Esperanza
**caper** ['kepər] *s* (*gay jump*) cabriola; (*prank*) travesura; **to cut capers** dar

cabriolas; hacer travesuras || *intr* cabriolear; retozar
**Cape'town'** o **Cape Town** *s* El Cabo, la Ciudad del Cabo
**cape'work'** *s* (taur) suerte *f* de capa, lance *m*
**capital** ['kæpɪtəl] *adj* capital || *s* (*money*) capital *m;* (*city*) capital *f;* (*top of a column*) capitel *m;* **to make capital out of** sacar beneficio de
**capitalism** ['kæpɪtə,lɪzəm] *s* capitalismo
**capitalize** ['kæpɪtə,laɪz] *tr* escribir con mayúscula; capitalizar || *intr* — **to capitalize on** aprovecharse de
**capital letter** *s* letra mayúscula
**capitol** ['kæpɪtəl] *s* capitolio
**capitulate** [kə'pɪtʃə,let] *intr* capitular
**capon** ['kepɑn] *s* capón *m*
**caprice** [kə'pris] *s* capricho, antojo; veleidad
**capricious** [kə'prɪʃəs] *adj* caprichoso, antojadizo
**Capricorn** ['kæprɪ,kɔrn] *s* Capricornio
**capsize** ['kæpsaɪz] *tr* volcar || *intr* volcar; tumbar, zozobrar (*un barco*)
**capstan** ['kæpstən] *s* cabrestante *m*
**cap'stone'** *s* coronamiento
**capsule** ['kæpsəl] *s* cápsula
**Capt.** *abbr* **Captain**
**captain** ['kæptən] *s* capitán *m* || *tr* capitanear
**captain·cy** ['kæptənsi] *s* (*pl* **-cies**) capitanía
**caption** ['kæpʃən] *s* título; (*in a movie*) subtítulo
**captivate** ['kæptɪ,vet] *tr* cautivar, encantar
**captive** ['kæptɪv] *adj* & *s* cautivo
**captivi·ty** [kæp'tɪvɪti] *s* (*pl* **-ties**) cautividad, cautiverio
**captor** ['kæptər] *s* aprenhensor *m*
**capture** ['kæptʃər] *s* apresamiento, captura; (*of a stronghold*) toma || *tr* apresar, capturar; tomar (*una plaza*); captar (*p.ej., la atención de una persona*)
**Capuchin nun** ['kæpjʊtʃɪn] o ['kæpjʊʃɪn] *s* capuchina
**car** [kɑr] *s* coche *m;* (*of an elevator*) caja, carro
**carafe** [kə'ræf] *s* garrafa
**caramel** ['kærəməl] o ['kɑrməl] *s* (*burnt sugar*) caramelo; bombón *m* de caramelo
**carat** ['kærət] *s* quilate *m*
**caravan** ['kærə,væn] *s* caravana
**caravansa·ry** [,kærə'vænsəri] *s* (*pl* **-ries**) caravanera
**caraway** ['kærə,we] *s* alcaravea
**car'barn'** *s* cochera de tranvías
**carbide** ['kɑrbaɪd] *s* carburo
**carbine** ['kɑrbaɪn] *s* carabina
**carbolic acid** [kɑr'bɑlɪk] *s* ácido carbólico
**carbon** ['kɑrbən] *s* (*chemical element*) carbono; (*pole of arc light or battery*) carbón *m;* papel *m* carbón; (*in auto cylinders*) carbonilla
**carbon copy** *s* copia al carbón
**carbon dioxide** *s* dióxido de carbono
**carbon monoxide** *s* óxido de carbono, monóxido de carbono
**carbon paper** *s* papel *m* carbón
**car'boy'** *s* bombona, garrafón *m*
**carbuncle** ['kɑrbʌŋkəl] *s* (*stone*) carbunclo, carbúnculo; (pathol) carbunclo, carbunco
**carburetor** ['kɑrbə,retər] o ['kɑrbjə,retər] *s* carburador *m*
**car caller** *s* avisacoches *m*
**carcass** ['kɑrkəs] *s* res muerta, cadáver *m*
**card** [kɑrd] *s* tarjeta; (*for playing games*) naipe *m*, carta; (*for filing*) ficha; (*person*) (coll) sujeto, tipo
**card'board'** *s* cartón *m*
**cardboard binding** *s* encuadernación en pasta
**card case** *s* tarjetero
**card catalogue** *s* catálogo de fichas
**cardiac** ['kɑrdɪ,æk] *adj* cardíaco || *s* (*medicine; sufferer*) cardíaco
**cardigan** ['kɑrdɪgən] *s* albornoz *m*, rebeca
**cardinal** ['kɑrdɪnəl] *adj* cardinal; purpurado || *s* (*prelate; bird*) cardenal *m;* número cardinal
**card index** *s* fichero, tarjetero
**card party** *s* tertulia de baraja
**card'sharp'** *s* fullero, tahur *m*
**card trick** *s* truco de naipes
**care** [ker] *s* (*worry*) inquietud, ansiedad; (*watchful attention*) esmero; (*charge*) cargo, custodia; **care of** suplicada en casa de; **to take care of oneself** cuidarse || *intr* inquietarse, preocuparse; **to care for** cuidar de; amar, querer; **to care to** tener ganas de
**careen** [kə'rin] *intr* inclinarse; mecerse precipitadamente
**career** [kə'rɪr] *adj* de carrera || *s* carrera
**care'free'** *adj* despreocupado, libre de cuidados
**careful** ['kerfəl] *adj* (*acting with care*) cuidadoso; (*done with care*) esmerado; **to be careful to** cuidarse de
**careless** ['kerlɪs] *adj* descuidado, negligente
**carelessness** ['kerlɪsnɪs] *s* descuido, negligencia
**caress** [kə'rɛs] *s* caricia || *tr* acariciar || *intr* acariciarse
**caretaker** ['ker,tekər] *s* curador *m*, guardián *m*, custodio
**care'worn'** *adj* fatigado, rendido
**car'fare'** *s* pasaje *m* de tranvía o autobús
**car·go** ['kɑrgo] *s* (*pl* **-goes** o **-gos**) carga, cargamento
**cargo boat** *s* barco de carga
**Caribbean** [,kærɪ'bi·ən] o [kə'rɪbɪ·ən] *adj* caribe || *s* mar *m* Caribe
**caricature** ['kærɪkətʃər] *s* caricatura || *tr* caricaturizar
**caricaturist** ['kærɪkətʃərɪst] *s* caricaturista *mf*
**carillon** ['kærɪ,lɑn] o [kə'rɪljən] *s* carillón *m*
**car'load'** *s* furgonada, vagonada

**carnage** ['kɑrnɪdʒ] *s* carnicería, matanza
**carnation** [kɑr'neʃən] *adj* encarnado || *s* clavel *m*, clavel reventón
**carnival** ['kɑrnɪvəl] *adj* carnavalesco || *s* (*period before Lent*) carnaval *m;* verbena, espectáculo de atracciones
**car•ol** ['kærəl] *s* canción alegre, villancico || *v* (*pret & pp* **-oled** o **-olled;** *ger* **-oling** o **-olling**); *tr* celebrar con villancicos || *intr* cantar con alegría
**carom** ['kærəm] *s* carambola || *intr* carambolear
**carousal** [kə'raʊzəl] *s* juerga, borrachera, jarana
**carouse** [kə'raʊz] *intr* emborracharse, jaranear
**carp** [kɑrp] *s* carpa || *intr* quejarse
**carpenter** ['kɑrpəntər] *s* carpintero
**carpentry** ['kɑrpəntri] *s* carpintería
**carpet** ['kɑrpɪt] *s* alfombra; **to be on the carpet** estar sobre el tapete || *tr* alfombrar
**carpet sweeper** *s* barredora de alfombras
**car'-rent'al service** *s* alquiler *m* de coches
**carriage** ['kærɪdʒ] *s* carruaje *m;* (*cost of carrying*) porte *m*, transporte *m;* (*bearing*) porte *m*, continente *m;* (mach) carro
**carrier** ['kærɪ•ər] *s* portador *m*, transportador *m;* portador de gérmenes; empresa de transportes; (*mailman*) cartero; vendedor *m* de periódicos; portaaviones *m;* (rad) onda portadora
**carrier pigeon** *s* paloma mensajera
**carrier wave** *s* (rad) onda portadora
**carrion** ['kærɪ•ən] *adj* carroño; inmundo || *s* carroña; inmundicia
**carrot** ['kærət] *s* zanahoria
**carrousel** [,kærə'zel] *s* caballitos, tiovivo
**car•ry** ['kæri] *v* (*pret & pp* **-ried**) *tr* llevar, portar, traer; transportar; sostener (*una carga*); **to carry away** llevarse; encantar, entusiasmar; **to carry into effect** llevar a cabo; **to carry one's point** salirse con la suya; **to carry out** llevar a cabo; **to carry the day** quedar victorioso, ganar la palma; **to carry weight** ser de peso || *intr* tener alcance; **to carry on** continuar, perseverar; (coll) travesear; (coll) comportarse de un modo escandaloso; (coll) hacer locuras
**cart** [kɑrt] *s* carreta, carro || *tr* carretear
**carte blanche** ['kɑrt'blɑnʃ] *s* carta blanca
**cartel** [kɑr'tel] *s* cartel *m*
**Carthage** ['kɑrθɪdʒ] *s* Cartago
**Carthaginian** [,kɑrθə'dʒɪnɪ•ən] *adj & s* cartaginés *m*
**cart horse** *s* caballo de tiro
**cartilage** ['kɑrtɪlɪdʒ] *s* cartílago
**cartoon** [kɑr'tun] *s* caricatura; (*comic strip*) tira cómica; (*film*) película de dibujos || *tr* caricaturizar
**cartoonist** [kɑr'tunɪst] *s* caricaturista *mf*
**cartridge** ['kɑrtrɪdʒ] *s* cartucho
**cartridge belt** *s* canana
**carve** [kɑrv] *tr* trinchar (*carne*); esculpir, tallar
**carving knife** ['kɑrvɪŋ] *s* cuchillo de trinchar
**car washer** *s* lavacoches *m*
**caryatid** [,kærɪ'ætɪd] *s* cariátide *f*
**cascade** [kæs'ked] *s* cascada
**case** [kes] *s* (*instance; form of a word*) caso; (*box*) caja; (*small container*) estuche *m;* (*for cigarettes*) pitillera; (*sheath*) vaina, funda; (law) causa, pleito; **in case** caso que; **in no case** de ninguna manera || *tr* encajonar, enfundar
**casement** ['kesmənt] *s* ventana batiente; bastidor *m* (*de la ventana*)
**cash** [kæʃ] *s* dinero contante; pago al contado; **cash on delivery** contra reembolso, pago contra entrega; **to pay cash** pagar al contado || *tr* cobrar (*un cheque el portador*); abonar, pagar (*un cheque el banco*) || *intr* — **to cash in on** (coll) sacar provecho de
**cash and carry** *s* pago al contado con transporte a cargo del comprador
**cash'box'** *s* caja
**cashew** ['kæʃu] *s* anacardo, marañón *m*
**cashew nut** *s* anacardo, nuez *f* de marañón
**cashier** [kæ'ʃɪr] *s* cajero || *tr* destruir; (*in the army*) degradar
**cashier's check** *s* cheque *m* de caja
**cashier's desk** *s* caja
**cashmere** ['kæʃmɪr] *s* casimir *m*, cachemir *m*
**cash on hand** *s* efectivo en caja
**cash payment** *s* pago al contado
**cash purchase** *s* compra al contado
**cash register** *s* caja registradora
**casing** ['kesɪŋ] *s* caja, cubierta, envoltura; (*of door or window*) marco, cerco; (*of tire*) cubierta; (sew) jareta
**cask** [kæsk] o [kɑsk] *s* casco, pipa, tonel *m*
**casket** ['kæskɪt] o ['kɑskɪt] *s* (*box for valuables*) cajita, joyero; (*coffin*) caja, ataúd *m*
**casserole** ['kæsə,rol] *s* cacerola; (*dish cooked in a casserole*) timbal *m*
**cassock** ['kæsək] *s* balandrán *m*, sotana
**cast** [kæst] o [kɑst] *s* echada, tiro; forma, molde *m;* aire *m*, semblante *m;* matiz *m*, tinte *m;* (*of actors*) reparto || *v* (*pret & pp* **cast**) *tr* echar, tirar; volver (*los ojos*); proyectar (*una sombra*); colar, fundir (*metales*); depositar (*votos*); echar (*suertes*); (theat) repartir (*papeles*); **to cast aside** desechar; **to cast loose** soltar; **to cast out** arrojar, echar fuera; despedir, desterrar || *intr* echar los dados; arrojar el sedal o el anzuelo; **to cast about** revolver proyectos; **to cast off** (naut) soltar las amarras

**castanet** [ˌkæstəˈnet] *s* castañuela, castañeta
**cast'a•way'** *adj & s* proscrito, réprobo; náufrago
**caste** [kæst] o [kɑst] *s* casta; **to lose caste** desprestigiarse
**caster** [ˈkæstər] o [ˈkɑstər] *s* ruedecilla de mueble; (*cruet stand*) angarillas, vinagreras; frasco
**Castile** [kæsˈtil] *s* Castilla
**Castile soap** *s* jabón *m* de Castilla
**Castilian** [kæsˈtɪljən] *adj & s* castellano
**casting** [ˈkæstɪŋ] o [ˈkɑstɪŋ] *s* fundición, pieza fundida; (theat) reparto
**casting vote** *s* voto de calidad
**cast iron** *s* hierro colado, hierro fundido
**cast'-i'ron** *adj* de hierro colado; fuerte, endurecido; duro, inflexible
**castle** [ˈkæsəl] o [ˈkɑsəl] *s* castillo; (chess) roque *m*, torre *f* || *tr & intr* (chess) enrocar
**castle in Spain, castle in the air** *s* castillo en el aire
**cast'off'** *adj* abandonado, desechado; (*clothing*) de desecho || *s* desecho
**castor oil** [ˈkæstər] o [kɑstər] *s* aceite *m* de ricino
**castrate** [ˈkæstret] *tr* capar, castrar
**casual** [ˈkæʒʊ·əl] *adj* casual, fortuito; descuidado, indiferente
**casual•ty** [ˈkæʒʊ·əlti] *s* (*pl* **-ties**) desgracia, accidente *m;* accidentado, víctima; (*in war*) baja
**casualty list** *s* lista de bajas
**cat.** *abbr* **catalogue, catechism**
**cat** [kæt] *s* gato; mujer maligna; **to bell the cat** ponerle cascabel al gato; **to let the cat out of the bag** revelar el secreto
**catacomb** [ˈkætəˌkom] *s* catacumba
**Catalan** [ˈkætəˌlæn] *adj & s* catalán *m*
**catalogue** [ˈkætəˌlɔg] o [ˈkætəˌlɑg] *s* catálogo || *tr* catalogar
**Catalonia** [ˌkætəˈlonɪ·ə] *s* Cataluña
**Catalonian** [ˌkætəˈlonɪ·ən] *adj & s* catalán *m*
**catapult** [ˈkætəˌpʌlt] *s* catapulta || *tr* catapultar
**cataract** [ˈkætəˌrækt] *s* catarata; (pathol) catarata
**catarrh** [kəˈtɑr] *s* catarro
**catastrophe** [kəˈtæstrəfi] *s* catástrofe *f*
**cat'call'** *s* rechifla || *tr & intr* rechiflar
**catch** [kætʃ] *s* (*of a ball*) cogida; (*of fish*) pesca; (*of a lock*) cerradera, pestillo; (*booty*) botín *m*, presa; (*fastener*) broche *m;* (*good match*) buen partido || *v* (*pret & pp* **caught** [kɔt]) *tr* asir, coger, atrapar; llegar a oír; coger (*un resfriado*); (*to come upon suddenly*) sorprender; comprender; capturar (*al delincuente*); **to catch fire** encenderse; **to catch hold of** agarrar, coger; apoderarse de; **to catch it** (coll) merecerse un regaño; **to catch oneself** contenerse; recobrar el equilibrio; **to catch sight of** alcanzar a ver; **to catch up** arrebatar; coger al vuelo; (*in a mistake*) cazar || *intr* pegarse (*una enfermedad*); enredarse; encenderse; **to catch at** agarrarse a, tratar de asir; **to catch on** prender en (*p.ej., un gancho*); comprender, coger el tino; **to catch up** salir del atraso; (*in one's debts*) ponerse al día; **to catch up with** emparejar con
**catcher** [ˈkætʃər] *s* (baseball) receptor, parador *m*
**catching** [ˈkætʃɪŋ] *adj* pegajoso, contagioso; atrayente, cautivador
**catch question** *s* pega
**catchup** [ˈkætʃəp] o [ˈketʃəp] *s* salsa de tomate condimentada
**catch'word'** *s* lema *m*, palabra de efecto; (*actor's cue*) pie *m;* (typ) reclamo
**catch•y** [ˈkætʃi] *adj* (*comp* **-ier;** *super* **-iest**) (*tune*) animado, vivo; (*title of a book*) impresionante, llamativo; (*question*) intrincado; (*breathing*) espasmódico
**catechism** [ˈkætɪˌkɪzəm] *s* catecismo
**catego•ry** [ˈkætɪˌgori] *s* (*pl* **-ries**) categoría
**cater** [ˈketər] *tr & intr* abastecer, proveer; **to cater to** proveer a
**cater-cornered** [ˈkætərˌkɔrnərd] *adj* diagonal || *adv* diagonalmente
**caterer** [ˈketərər] *s* abastecedor *m*, proveedor *m* de alimentos (*esp. para fiestas caseras*)
**caterpillar** [ˈkætərˌpɪlər] *s* oruga
**caterpillar tractor** *s* tractor *m* de oruga
**cat'fish'** *s* bagre *m*
**cat'gut'** *s* (mus) cuerda de tripa; (surg) catgut *m*
**Cath.** *abbr* **Catholic**
**cathartic** [kəˈθɑrtɪk] *adj & s* catártico
**cathedral** [kəˈθidrəl] *s* catedral *f*
**catheter** [ˈkæθɪtər] *s* catéter *m*
**catheterize** [ˈkæθɪtəˌraɪz] *tr* cateterizar
**cathode** [ˈkæθod] *s* cátodo
**catholic** [ˈkæθəlɪk] *adj* católico || **Catholic** *adj & s* católico
**catkin** [ˈkætkɪn] *s* candelilla, amento
**cat nap** *s* sueñecito
**catnip** [ˈkætnɪp] *s* hierba gatera, nébeda
**cat-o'-nine-tails** [ˌkætəˈnaɪnˌtelz] *s* azote *m* con nueve ramales
**cat's cradle** *s* juego de la cuna
**cat's-paw** o **catspaw** [ˈkætsˌpɔ] *s* mano *f* de gato, instrumento
**catsup** [ˈkætsəp] o [ketʃəp] *s* salsa de tomate condimentada
**cat'tail'** *s* anea, espadaña; amento
**cattle** [ˈkætəl] *s* ganado vacuno
**cattle crossing** *s* paso de ganado
**cattle•man** [ˈkætəlmən] *s* (*pl* **-men** [mən]) *s* ganadero
**cattle raising** *s* ganadería
**cattle ranch** *s* hacienda de ganado
**cat•ty** [ˈkæti] *adj* (*comp* **-tier;** *super* **-tiest**) (*like a cat*) felino, gatuno; (*spiteful*) malicioso; (*gossipy*) chismoso
**cat'walk'** *s* pasadero, pasarela

**Caucasian** [kɔ'keʒən] o [kɔ'keʃən] *adj & s* caucasiano, caucásico
**Caucasus** ['kɔkəsəs] *s* Cáucaso
**caucus** ['kɔkəs] *s* junta de políticos
**cauliflower** ['kɔlɪ,flaʊ·ər] *s* coliflor *f*
**cause** [kɔz] *s* causa; (*person*) causante *mf* || *tr* causar
**cause'way'** *s* (*highway*) calzada; calzada elevada
**caustic** ['kɔstɪk] *adj* cáustico
**cauterize** ['kɔtə,raɪz] *tr* cauterizar
**caution** ['kɔʃən] *s* (*carefulness*) cautela; (*warning*) advertencia, amonestación || *tr* advertir, amonestar
**cautious** ['kɔʃəs] *adj* cauteloso, cauto
**Cav.** *abbr* **Cavalry**
**cavalcade** [,kævəl'ked] o ['kævəl,ked] *s* cabalgata
**cavalier** [,kævə'lɪr] *adj* (*haughty*) altivo, desdeñoso; (*offhand*) alegre, desenvuelto, inceremonioso || *s* (*horseman*) caballero; (*lady's escort*) galán *m*
**caval·ry** ['kævəlri] *s* (*pl* **-ries**) caballería
**cavalry·man** ['kævəlrimən] *s* (*pl* **-men** [mən]) soldado de caballería
**cave** [kev] *s* cueva, caverna || *intr* — **to cave in** hundirse; (*to give in, yield*) (coll) ceder, rendirse
**cave'-in'** *s* hundimiento, derrumbe *m*, socavón *m*
**cave man** *s* hombre grosero
**cavern** ['kævərn] *s* caverna
**cav·il** ['kævɪl] *v* (*pret & pp* **-iled** o **-illed**; *ger* **-iling** o **-illing**) *intr* buscar quisquillas
**cavi·ty** ['kævɪti] *s* (*pl* **-ties**) cavidad; (*in a tooth*) picadura
**cavort** [kə'vɔrt] *intr* (coll) cabriolar
**caw** [kɔ] *s* graznido || *intr* graznar
**cc.** *abbr* **cubic centimeter**
**cease** [sis] *tr* parar, suspender || *intr* cesar; cesar de, dejar de + *inf*
**cease'fire'** *s* cese *m* de fuego || *intr* suspender hostilidades
**ceaseless** ['sislɪs] *adj* incesante, continuo
**cedar** ['sidər] *s* cedro
**cede** [sid] *tr* ceder, traspasar
**ceiling** ['silɪŋ] *s* techo, cielo raso; (aer) techo, cielo máximo
**ceiling price** *s* precio tope
**celebrant** ['selɪbrənt] *s* celebrante *m*
**celebrate** ['selɪ,bret] *tr* celebrar || *intr* (*to say mass*) celebrar; divertirse, festejarse
**celebrated** ['selɪ,bretɪd] *adj* célebre, renombrado
**celebration** [,selɪ'breʃən] *s* celebración; diversión, festividad
**celebri·ty** [sɪ'lebrɪti] *s* (*pl* **-ties**) (*fame; famous person*) celebridad
**celery** ['seləri] *s* apio
**celestial** [sɪ'lestʃəl] *adj* celeste, celestial
**celiba·cy** ['selɪbəsi] *s* (*pl* **-cies**) celibato
**celibate** ['seli,bet] o ['selɪbɪt] *adj & s* célibe *mf*
**cell** [sel] *s* (*of convent or jail*) celda; (*of honeycomb*) celdilla; (*of electric battery*) elemento; (*of plant or animal; of photoelectric device; of political group*) célula
**cellar** ['selər] *s* sótano; (*for wine*) bodega
**cellaret** [,selə'ret] *s* licorera
**cell house** *s* prisión celular
**cellist** o **'cellist** ['tʃelɪst] *s* violoncelista *mf*
**cel·lo** o **'cel·lo** ['tʃelo] *s* (*pl* **-los**) violoncelo
**cellophane** ['selə,fen] *s* celofán *m*
**celluloid** ['seljə,lɔɪd] *s* celuloide *m*
**Celt** [selt] o [kelt] *s* celta *mf*
**Celtic** ['seltɪk] o ['keltɪk] *adj* céltico || *s* (*language*) celta *m*
**cement** [sɪ'ment] *s* cemento || *tr* revestir con cemento; (*la amistad*) consolidar
**cemeter·y** ['semɪ,teri] *s* (*pl* **-ies**) cementerio
**cen.** *abbr* **central**
**censer** ['sensər] *s* incensario
**censor** ['sensər] *s* censor *m* || *tr* censurar
**censure** ['senʃər] *s* censura || *tr* censurar
**census** ['sensəs] *s* censo; **to take the census** levantar el censo
**cent.** *abbr* **centigrade, central, century**
**cent** [sent] *s* centavo
**centaur** ['sentɔr] *s* centauro
**centennial** [sen'tenɪ·əl] *adj & s* centenario
**center** ['sentər] *adj* centrista || *s* centro || *tr* centrar
**cen'ter·piece'** *s* centro de mesa
**center punch** *s* granete *m*, punzón *m* de marcar
**centigrade** ['sentɪ,gred] *adj* centígrado
**centimeter** ['sentɪ,mitər] *s* centímetro
**centipede** ['sentɪ,pid] *s* ciempiés *m*
**central** ['sentrəl] *adj* central || *s* (telp) central *f*, central de teléfonos; (*operator*) telefonista *mf*
**Central America** *s* Centro América, la América Central
**Central American** *adj & mf* centroamericano
**centralize** ['sentrə,laɪz] *tr* centralizar || *intr* centralizarse
**centu·ry** ['sentʃəri] *s* (*pl* **-ries**) siglo
**century plant** *s* pita, maguey *m*
**ceramic** [sɪ'ræmɪk] *adj* cerámico
**cereal** ['sɪrɪ·əl] *adj & s* cereal *m*
**ceremonious** [,serɪ'monɪ·əs] *adj* ceremonioso, etiquetero
**ceremo·ny** ['serɪ,moni] *s* (*pl* **-nies**) ceremonia; **to stand on ceremony** hacer ceremonias, ser etiquetero
**certain** ['sʌrtən] *adj* cierto; **a certain** cierto; **for certain** por cierto
**certainly** ['sertənli] *adj* ciertamente; (*gladly*) con mucho gusto
**certain·ty** ['sʌrtənti] *s* (*pl* **-ties**) certeza; **with certainty** a ciencia cierta
**certificate** [sər'tɪfɪkɪt] *s* certificación, certificado; (*of birth, death, etc.*) partida, fe *f*; (*document representing financial assets*) título || [sər'tɪfɪ,ket] *tr* certificar

**certified public accountant** ['sʌrtɪ-ˌfaɪd] *s* censor jurado de cuentas
**certi•fy** ['sʌrtɪˌfaɪ] *v* (*pret & pp* **-fied**) *tr* certificar
**cervix** ['sʌrvɪks] *s* (*pl* **cervices** [sər-'vaɪsiz]) cerviz *f*
**cessation** [sɛ'seʃən] *s* cesación
**cessation of hostilities** *s* suspensión de hostilidades
**cesspool** ['sɛsˌpul] *s* pozo negro; (fig) sitio inmundo
**Ceylon** [sɪ'lɑn] *s* Ceilán
**Ceylo•nese** [ˌsilə'niz] *adj* ceilanés || *s* (*pl* **-nese**) ceilanés *m*
**cf.** *abbr* **confer, i.e., compare**
**C.F.I., c.f.i.** *abbr* **cost, freight, and insurance**
**cg.** *abbr* **centigram**
**ch.** *abbr* **chapter, church**
**chafe** [tʃef] *s* fricción, roce *m;* desgaste *m;* irritación || *tr* (*to rub*) frotar; (*to rub and make sore*) escocer; (*to wear*) desgastar; irritar || *intr* escocerse; desgastarse; irritarse
**chaff** [tʃæf] o [tʃɑf] *s* barcia; paja menuda; broza, desperdicio
**chafing dish** ['tʃefɪŋ] *s* cocinilla, infernillo
**chagrin** [ʃə'grɪn] *s* desazón *f,* disgusto || *tr* desazonar, disgustar
**chain** [tʃen] *s* cadena || *tr* encadenar
**chain gang** *s* cadena de presidiarios, collera, cuerda de presos
**chain reaction** *s* reacción en cadena
**chain'smoke'** *intr* fumar un pitillo tras otro
**chain store** *s* empresa con una cadena de tiendas; tienda de una cadena de tiendas
**chair** [tʃɛr] *s* silla; (*de catedrático*) cátedra; presidencia; **to take the chair** presidir la reunión; abrir la sesión || *tr* presidir (*una reunión*)
**chair lift** *s* telesilla
**chair•man** ['tʃɛrmən] *s* (*pl* **-men** [mən]) presidente *m*
**chairmanship** ['tʃɛrmənˌʃɪp] *s* presidencia
**chair rail** *s* guardasilla
**chalice** ['tʃælɪs] *s* cáliz *m*
**chalk** [tʃɔk] *s* (*soft white limestone*) creta; (*piece used for writing*) tiza || *tr* marcar o escribir con tiza; **to chalk up** apuntar; marcar (*un tanto*)
**challenge** ['tʃælɪndʒ] *s* desafío; (law) recusación || *tr* desafiar; (law) recusar
**chamber** ['tʃembər] *s* cámara; (*of a gun*) recámara; dormitorio; **chambers** oficina de juez
**chamberlain** ['tʃembərlɪn] s chambelán *m*
**cham'ber•maid'** *s* camarera
**chamber pot** *s* orinal *m*
**chameleon** [kə'milɪ•ən] *s* camaleón *m*
**chamfer** ['tʃæmfər] *s* chaflán *m* || *tr* chaflanar
**cham•ois** ['ʃæmi] *s* (*pl* **-ois**) gamuza
**champ** [tʃæmp] *s* mordisco; (slang) campeón *m* || *tr & intr* mordiscar; (*el freno*) morder
**champagne** [ʃæm'pen] *s* champaña *m*
**champion** ['tʃæmpɪ•ən] *s* campeón *m* || *tr* defender
**championess** ['tʃæmpɪ•ənɪs] *s* campeona
**championship** ['tʃæmpɪ•ənˌʃɪp] *s* campeonato
**chance** [tʃæns] o [tʃɑns] *adj* casual, imprevisto || *s* oportunidad, ocasión; casualidad, suerte *f;* probabilidad; peligro, riesgo; **by chance** por casualidad; **to not stand a chance** no tener probabilidad de éxito; **to take a chance** probar fortuna; comprar un billete de lotería; **to take chances** probar fortuna; **to wait for a chance** esperar la oportunidad || *intr* acontecer; **to chance on** o **upon** tropezar con; **to chance to** acertar a
**chancel** ['tʃænsəl] o ['tʃɑnsəl] *s* entrecoro
**chanceller•y** ['tʃænsələri] o ['tʃɑnsələrɪ] *s* (*pl* **-ies**) cancillería
**chancellor** ['tʃænsələr] o ['tʃɑnsələr] *s* canciller *m*
**chandelier** [ˌʃændə'lɪr] *s* araña de luces
**change** [tʃendʒ] *s* cambio, mudanza; suelto, moneda suelta; (*surplus money returned with a purchase*) vuelta; (*of clothing*) muda; **for a change** por variedad; **to keep the change** quedarse con la vuelta; || *tr* cambiar, mudar; cambiar de, mudar de; reemplazar; **to change clothes** cambiar de ropa; **to change gears** cambiar de velocidades; **to change hands** cambiar de dueño; **to change money** cambiar moneda; **to change one's mind** cambiar de parecer; **to change trains** cambiar de tren, transbordar || *intr* cambiar, mudar; corregirse
**changeable** ['tʃendʒəbəl] *adj* cambiable; inconstante, cambiante, mudable
**change of clothing** *s* muda de ropa
**change of heart** *s* arrepentimiento, conversión
**change of life** *s* cesación natural de las reglas
**change of voice** *s* muda
**chan•nel** ['tʃænəl] *s* (*body of water joining two others*) canal *m;* (*bed of river*) álveo, cauce *m;* (*means of communication*) vía; (*passage*) conducto; (*groove*) ranura, surco; (telv) canal *m;* **the Channel** el Canal de la Mancha || *v* (*pret & pp* **-neled** o **-nelled;** *ger* **-neling** o **-nelling**) *tr* acanalar; canalizar (*esfuerzos, dinero, etc.*)
**chant** [tʃænt] o [tʃɑnt] *s* (*song*) canción; (*song sung in a monotone*) canto || *tr & intr* cantar
**chanter** ['tʃæntər] o ['tʃɑntər] *s* cantor *m;* (*priest*) chantre *m*
**chanticleer** ['tʃæntɪˌklɪr] *s* el gallo
**chaos** ['ke•ɑs] *s* caos *m*
**chaotic** [ke'ɑtɪk] *adj* caótico
**chap.** *abbr* **chaplain, chapter**
**chap** [tʃæp] *s* (*jaw*) mandíbula; (*cheek*) mejilla; (*crack in the skin*)

grieta; chico, tipo; **chaps** zahones *mpl* || *v* (*pret & pp* **chapped;** *ger* **chapping**) *tr* agrietar, rajar || *intr* agrietarse, rajarse
**chapel** [ˈtʃæpəl] *s* capilla
**chaperon** o **chaperone** [ˈʃæpəˌron] *s* carabina, señora de compañía || *tr* acompañar (*una señora a una o más señoritas*)
**chaplain** [ˈtʃæplɪn] *s* capellán *m*
**chaplet** [ˈtʃæplɪt] *s* (*wreath for head*) guirnalda; rosario
**chapter** [ˈtʃæptər] *s* capítulo; (*of the Scriptures*) capítula; (*of a cathedral*) cabildo
**chapter and verse** *adv* con todos sus pelos y señales
**char** [tʃɑr] *v* (*pret & pp* **charred;** *ger* **charring**) *tr* carbonizar; (*to scorch*) socarrar
**character** [ˈkærɪktər] *s* carácter *m;* (*conspicuous person; person in a play or novel*) personaje *m;* (*part or role in a play*) papel *m;* (*fellow*) (coll) tipo, sujeto
**characteristic** [ˌkærɪktəˈrɪstɪk] *adj* característico || *s* característica
**characterize** [ˈkærɪktəˌraɪz] *tr* caracterizar
**char'coal'** *s* carbón *m* de leña; (*for sketching*) carboncillo; (*sketch*) dibujo al carbón
**charcoal burner** *s* (*person*) carbonero; horno para hacer carbón de leña
**charge** [tʃɑrdʒ] *s* (*of an explosive, of electricity, of soldiers against the enemy; responsibility*) carga; (*accusation; amount owed; recording of amount owed*) cargo; (heral) blasón *m;* (*attack*) embestida; **in charge of** a cargo de; **to reverse the charges** (telp) cargar al número llamado; **to take charge of** hacerse cargo de || *tr* cargar; cobrar (*cierto precio*); (*to order*) encargar, mandar; cargar (*un acumulador; al enemigo*); **to charge to the account of someone** cargarle a uno en cuenta; **to charge with** cargar de || *intr* embestir
**charge account** *s* cuenta corriente
**chargé d'affaires** [ʃɑrˈʒe dəˈfɛr] *s* (*pl* **chargés d'affaires**) encargado de negocios
**charger** [ˈtʃɑrdʒər] *s* caballo de guerra; (*of a battery*) cargador *m*
**chariot** [ˈtʃærɪ·ət] *s* carro romano
**charioteer** [ˌtʃærɪ·əˈtɪr] *s* carretero, auriga *m*
**charitable** [ˈtʃærɪtəbəl] *adj* caritativo
**chari·ty** [ˈtʃærɪti] *s* (*pl* **-ties**) caridad; asociación de beneficencia, obra pía; **charity begins at home** la caridad bien ordenada empieza por uno mismo
**charity performance** *s* función benéfica
**charlatan** [ˈʃɑrlətən] *s* charlatán *m*
**charlatanism** [ˈʃɑrlətənˌɪzəm] *s* charlatanismo
**Charlemagne** [ˈʃɑrləˌmen] *s* Carlomagno
**Charles** [tʃɑrlz] *s* Carlos *m*
**charlotte** [ˈʃɑrlət] *s* carlota || **Charlotte** *s* Carlota
**charlotte russe** [ˈʃɑrlət ˈrus] *s* carlota rusa
**charm** [tʃɑrm] *s* encanto, hechizo; (*trinket*) amuleto, dije *m* || *tr* encantar, hechizar
**charming** [ˈtʃɑrmɪŋ] *adj* encantador
**charnel** [ˈtʃɑrnəl] *adj* cadavérico, horrible || *s* carnero, osario
**charnel house** *s* carnero, osario
**chart** [tʃɑrt] *s* mapa geográfico; (naut) carta de marear; cuadro, diagrama *m* || *tr* bosquejar; **to chart a course** trazar una ruta
**charter** [ˈtʃɑrtər] *s* carta (de privilegio) || *tr* alquilar (*un autobús*); fletar (*un barco*)
**charter member** *s* socio fundador
**char·woman** [ˈtʃɑrˌwʊmən] *s* (*pl* **-women** [ˌwɪmɪn]) alquilona, asistenta
**Charybdis** [kəˈrɪbdɪs] *s* Caribdis *f*
**chase** [tʃes] *s* caza, persecución || *tr* cazar, perseguir; **to chase away** ahuyentar
**chasm** [ˈkæzəm] *s* abismo
**chas·sis** [ˈtʃæsi] *s* (*pl* **-sis** [siz]) chasis *m*
**chaste** [tʃest] *adj* casto; (*style*) castizo
**chasten** [ˈtʃesən] *tr* castigar, corregir
**chastise** [tʃæsˈtaɪz] *tr* castigar
**chastity** [ˈtʃæstɪti] *s* castidad
**chasuble** [ˈtʃæzjəbəl] *s* casulla
**chat** [tʃæt] *s* charla, plática || *v* (*pret & pp* **chatted;** *ger* **chatting**) *intr* charlar, platicar
**chatelaine** [ˈʃætəˌlen] *s* castellana
**chattels** [ˈtʃætəlz] *spl* bienes *mpl* muebles, enseres *mpl*
**chatter** [ˈtʃætər] *s* (*talk*) cháchara; (*rattling*) traqueo; (*of teeth*) castañeteo; (*of birds*) chirrido || *intr* chacharear; traquear; castañetear, dentellar (*los dientes*)
**chat'ter·box'** *s* charlador *m*, tarabilla
**chauffeur** [ˈʃofər] o [ʃoˈfʌr] *s* chófer *m*
**cheap** [tʃip] *adj* barato; (*charging low prices*) no carero, baratero; (*flashy*) cursi; **to feel cheap** sentirse avergonzado || *adv* barato
**cheapen** [ˈtʃipən] *tr* abaratar
**cheapness** [ˈtʃipnɪs] *s* baratura; (*flashiness*) cursilería
**cheat** [tʃit] *s* trampa, fraude *m;* (*person*) trampista *mf*, defraudador *m* || *tr* trampear, defraudar
**check** [tʃɛk] *s* (*of bank*) cheque *m;* (*for baggage*) talón *m*, contraseña; (*in a restaurant*) cuenta; (*in theater or movie*) contraseña, billete *m* de salida; (*restraint*) freno; (*to hold a door*) amortiguador *m;* (*in chess*) jaque *m;* inspección; comprobación, verificación; (*cloth*) paño a cuadros; **in check en** jaque; **to hold in check** contener, refrenar || *interj* ¡jaque! || *tr* parar súbitamente; contener, refrenar; amortiguar; facturar (*equipajes*); inspeccionar; comprobar, verificar; marcar, señalar; (*in chess*)

jaquear, dar jaque a; **to check up** comprobar, verificar || *intr* pararse súbitamente; corresponder punto por punto; **to check in** (*at a hotel*) llegar e inscribirse; **to check out** pagar la cuenta y despedirse; (slang) morir
**check'book'** *s* talonario (de cheques)
**checker** ['tʃɛkər] *s* inspector *m;* cuadro; dibujo a cuadros; (*in game of checkers*) ficha, pieza; **checkers** damas, juego de damas || *tr* marcar con cuadros; diversificar, variar
**check'er·board'** *s* damero, tablero
**check girl** *s* moza de guardarropa
**checking account** *s* cuenta corriente
**check'mate'** *s* mate *m,* jaque *m* mate || *tr* dar mate a, dar jaque mate a; (fig) derrotar completamente
**check'out'** *s* (*from a hotel*) salida; hora de salida; (*in a self-service retail store*) revisión y pago
**checkout counter** *s* mostrador *m* de revisión
**check'point'** *s* punto de inspección
**check'rein'** *s* engallador *m*
**check'room'** *s* guardarropa *m;* (rr) consigna, depósito de equipajes
**check'up'** *s* verificación rigurosa; (*of an automobile*) revisión; (med) reconocimiento general
**cheek** [tʃik] *s* mejilla, carrillo; (coll) descaro, frescura
**cheek'bone'** *s* pómulo
**cheek by jowl** *adv* cara a cara, en estrecha intimidad
**cheek·y** ['tʃiki] *adj* (*comp* **-ier**; *super* **-iest**) (coll) descarado, fresco
**cheer** [tʃɪr] *s* alegría, regocijo; (*shout*) viva *m,* aplauso; **what cheer?** ¿qué tal? || *tr* alegrar, animar; aplaudir, vitorear; dar la bienvenida a, con vivas y aplausos || *intr* alegrarse, animarse; **cheer up!** ¡ánimo!
**cheerful** ['tʃɪrfəl] *adj* alegre
**cheerio** ['tʃɪrɪ,o] *interj* (coll) ¡hola!, ¡qué tal!; (coll) ¡adiós!, ¡hasta la vista!
**cheerless** ['tʃɪrlɪs] *adj* sombrío, triste
**cheese** [tʃiz] *s* queso
**cheese'cloth'** *s* estopilla
**chef** [ʃɛf] *s* primer cocinero, jefe *m* de cocina
**chem.** *abbr* **chemical, chemist, chemistry**
**chemical** ['kɛmɪkəl] *adj* químico || *s* producto químico, substancia química
**chemise** [ʃə'miz] *s* camisa (de mujer)
**chemist** ['kɛmɪst] *s* químico
**chemistry** ['kɛmɪstri] *s* química
**cherish** ['tʃɛrɪʃ] *tr* acariciar; (*a hope*) abrigar, acariciar
**cher·ry** ['tʃɛri] *s* (*pl* **-ries**) (*fruit; color*) cereza; (*tree*) cerezo
**cher·ub** ['tʃɛrəb] *s* (*pl* **-ubim** [əbɪm]) querubín *m* || *s* (*pl* **-ubs**) niño angelical
**chess** [tʃɛs] *s* ajedrez *m*
**chess'board'** *s* tablero de ajedrez
**chess·man** ['tʃɛs,mæn] *s* (*pl* **-men** [,mɛn]) pieza de ajedrez, trebejo
**chess player** *s* ajedrecista *mf*
**chess set** *s* ajedrez *m*
**chest** [tʃɛst] *s* (*part of body*) pecho; (*receptacle*) cajón *m,* cofre *m;* (*piece of furniture*) cómoda
**chestnut** ['tʃɛsnət] *s* (*tree, wood, color*) castaño; (*fruit*) castaña
**chest of drawers** *s* cómoda
**cheval glass** [ʃə'væl] *s* psique *f*
**chevalier** [,ʃɛvə'lɪr] *s* caballero
**chevron** ['ʃɛvrən] *s* galón *m* en forma de V invertida
**chew** [tʃu] *s* mascadura || *tr* mascar; **to chew the rag** (slang) dar la lengua || *intr* mascar
**chewing gum** *s* goma de mascar, chicle *m*
**chg.** *abbr* **charge**
**chic** [ʃik] *adj* & *s* chic *m*
**chicaner·y** [ʃɪ'kenəri] *s* (*pl* **-ies**) triquiñuela
**chick** [tʃɪk] *s* pollito; (slang) polla
**chicken** ['tʃɪkən] *s* pollo; (*young person*) pollo; (*young girl*) polla
**chicken coop** *s* pollera
**chicken feed** *s* (coll) calderilla
**chickenhearted** ['tʃɪkən,hɑrtɪd] *adj* gallina
**chicken pox** *s* viruelas locas
**chicken wire** *s* alambrada, tela metálica
**chick'pea'** *s* garbanzo
**chico·ry** ['tʃɪkəri] *s* (*pl* **-ries**) achicoria
**chide** [tʃaɪd] *v* (*pret* **chided** o **chid** [tʃɪd]; *pp* **chided, chid** o **chidden** ['tʃɪdən]) *tr* reprender, regañar
**chief** [tʃif] *adj* principal || *s* jefe *m;* (*of American Indians*) cacique *m*
**chief executive** *s* jefe *m* del gobierno
**chief justice** *s* presidente *m* de sala; presidente del tribunal supremo
**chiefly** ['tʃifli] *adv* principalmente, mayormente
**chief of staff** *s* jefe *m* de estado mayor
**chief of state** *s* jefe *m* del estado
**chieftain** ['tʃiftən] *s* (*of a clan or tribe*) jefe *m;* adalid *m,* caudillo
**chiffon** [ʃɪ'fɑn] *s* gasa, soplillo; **chiffons** atavíos, perifollos
**chiffonier** [,ʃɪfə'nɪr] *s* cómoda alta
**chignon** ['ʃinjɑn] *s* castaña, moño
**chilblain** ['tʃɪl,blen] *s* sabañón *m*
**child** [tʃaɪld] *s* (*pl* **children** ['tʃɪldrən]) *s* (*infant, youngster*) niño; (*one's offspring*) hijo; descendiente *mf;* **with child** encinta, embarazada
**child'birth'** *s* alumbramiento, parto
**childhood** ['tʃaɪldhʊd] *s* niñez *f,* puericia; **from childhood** desde niño
**childish** ['tʃaɪldɪʃ] *adj* aniñado, pueril
**childishness** ['tʃaɪldɪʃnɪs] *s* puerilidad
**child labor** *s* trabajo de menores
**childless** ['tʃaɪldlɪs] *adj* sin hijos
**child'like'** *adj* aniñado
**child's play** *s* juego de niños
**child welfare** *s* protección a la infancia
**Chile** ['tʃɪli] *s* Chile *m*
**Chilean** ['tʃɪlɪ·ən] *adj* & *s* chileno
**chili sauce** ['tʃɪli] *s* ají *m,* salsa de ají
**chill** [tʃɪl] *adj* frío || *s* frío desapaci-

ble; (*sensation of cold*) escalofrío; (*lack of cordiality*) frialdad || *tr* enfriar || *intr* calofriarse

**chill•y** [ˈtʃɪli] *adj* (*comp* **-ier;** *super* **-iest**) (*causing shivering*) frío; (*sensitive to cold*) escalofriado, friolero; (*indifferent*) (fig) frío

**chime** [tʃaɪm] *s* campaneo, repique *m;* tubo sonoro; **chimes** juego de campanas || *tr & intr* campanear, repicar

**chime clock** *s* reloj *m* de carillón

**chimera** [kaɪˈmɪrə] o [kɪˈmɪrə] *s* quimera

**chimney** [ˈtʃɪmni] *s* chimenea; (*for a lamp*) tubo

**chimney cap** *s* caperuza

**chimney flue** *s* cañón *m* de chimenea

**chimney pot** *s* mitra, guardavientos *m*

**chimney sweep** *s* limpiachimeneas *m,* deshollinador *m*

**chimpanzee** [tʃɪmˈpænzi] o [ˌtʃɪmpænˈzi] *s* chimpancé *m*

**chin** [tʃɪn] *s* barba, mentón *m;* **to keep one's chin up** (coll) no desanimarse || *v* (*pret & pp* **chinned;** *ger* **chinning**) *intr* (coll) charlar

**china** [ˈtʃaɪnə] *s* china, porcelana || **China** *s* China

**china closet** *s* chinero

**China•man** [ˈtʃaɪnəmən] *s* (*pl* **-men** [mən]) (offensive) chino

**chi'na•ware'** *s* porcelana, vajilla de porcelana

**Chi•nese** [tʃaɪˈniz] *adj* chino || *s* (*pl* **-nese**) chino

**Chinese gong** *s* batintín *m*

**Chinese lantern** *s* farolillo veneciano

**Chinese puzzle** *s* problema embrollado

**chink** [tʃɪŋk] *s* grieta, hendidura; sonido metálico

**chin strap** *s* barboquejo, carrillera

**chintz** [tʃɪnts] *s* zaraza

**chip** [tʃɪp] *s* astilla, brizna; (*in china*) desconchado; (*in poker*) ficha; **chip off the old block** hijo de su padre || *v* (*pret & pp* **chipped;** *ger* **chipping**) *tr* astillar (*la madera*); desconchar (*la porcelana*); **to chip in** contribuir con su cuota || *intr* astillarse; desconcharse

**chipmunk** [ˈtʃɪpˌmʌŋk] *s* ardilla listada

**chipper** [ˈtʃɪpər] *adj* (coll) alegre, jovial, vivo

**chiropodist** [kaɪˈrɑpədɪst] o [kɪˈrɑpədɪst] *s* quiropodista *mf*

**chiropractor** [ˈkaɪrəˌpræktər] *s* quiropráctico

**chirp** [tʃʌrp] *s* chirrido, gorjeo || *intr* chirriar, gorjear; hablar alegremente

**chis•el** [ˈtʃɪzəl] *s* (*for wood*) escoplo, formón *m;* (*for stone and metal*) cincel *m* || *v* (*pret & pp* **-eled** o **-elled;** *ger* **-eling** o **-elling**) *tr* escoplear; cincelar; (slang) estafar

**chit-chat** [ˈtʃɪtˌtʃæt] *s* charla, palique *m;* hablilla, chismes *mpl*

**chivalric** [ˈʃɪvəlrɪk] o [ʃɪˈvælrɪk] *adj* caballeresco

**chivalrous** [ˈʃɪvəlrəs] *adj* caballeroso

**chivalry** [ˈʃɪvəlri] *s* (*knighthood*) caballería; (*gallantry, gentlemanliness*) caballerosidad

**chloride** [ˈkloraɪd] *s* cloruro

**chlorine** [ˈklorin] *s* cloro

**chloroform** [ˈkloroˌfɔrm] *s* cloroformo || *tr* cloroformizar

**chlorophyll** [ˈklorəfɪl] *s* clorofila

**chock-full** [ˈtʃɑkˈfʊl] *adj* de bote en bote, colmado

**chocolate** [ˈtʃɔkəlɪt] o [ˈtʃɑkəlɪt] *s* chocolate *m*

**choice** [tʃɔɪs] *adj* escogido, selecto, superior || *s* elección, selección; lo más escogido; **to have no choice** no tener alternativa

**choir** [kwaɪr] *s* coro

**choir'boy'** *s* niño de coro, infante *m* de coro

**choir desk** *s* facistol *m*

**choir loft** *s* coro

**choir'mas'ter** *s* jefe *m* de coro, maestro de capilla

**choke** [tʃok] *s* estrangulación; (*of carburetor*) cierre *m,* obturador *m;* (elec) choque *m* || *tr* ahogar, sofocar, estrangular; obstruir, tapar; (aut) obturar; **to choke down** atragantar || *intr* sofocarse; atragantarse; **to choke on** atragantarse con

**choke coil** *s* (elec) bobina de reacción, choque *m*

**cholera** [ˈkɑlərə] *s* cólera *m*

**choleric** [ˈkɑlərɪk] *adj* colérico

**cholesterol** [kəˈlɛstəˌrol] o [kəˈlɛstəˌrɑl] *s* colesterol *m*

**choose** [tʃuz] *v* (*pret* **chose** [tʃoz]; *pp* **chosen** [ˈtʃozən]) *tr* escoger, elegir || *intr* — **to choose between** optar entre; **to choose to** optar por

**chop** [tʃɑp] *s* golpe *m* cortante; (*of meat*) chuleta; **chops** boca, labios || *v* (*pret & pp* **chopped;** *ger* **chopping**) *tr* cortar, tajar; picar (*la carne*); **to chop off** tronchar; **to chop up** desmenuzar

**chop'house'** *s* restaurante *m,* figón *m,* colmado

**chopper** [ˈtʃɑpər] *s* (*person*) tajador *m;* (*tool*) hacha; (*of butcher*) cortante *m;* (slang) helicóptero

**chopping block** *s* tajo

**chop•py** [ˈtʃɑpi] *adj* (*comp* **-pier;** *super* **-piest**) (*sea*) agitado, picado; (*wind*) variable; (*style*) cortado, inciso

**chop'sticks'** *spl* palillos

**choral** [ˈkorəl] *adj* coral

**chorale** [koˈrɑl] *s* coral *m*

**choral society** *s* orfeón *m*

**chord** [kɔrd] *s* (*harmonious combination of tones*) (mus) acorde *m;* (aer, anat, geom) cuerda

**chore** [tʃor] *s* tarea, quehacer *m*

**choreography** [ˌkorɪˈɑgrəfi] *s* coreografía

**chorine** [koˈrin] *s* (slang) corista, suripanta

**chorus** [ˈkorəs] *s* coro; (*refrain of a song*) estribillo

**chorus girl** *s* corista, conjuntista

**chorus man** *s* corista *m,* conjuntista *m*

**chowder** ['tʃaʊdər] *s* estofado de almejas o pescado
**Chr.** *abbr* **Christian**
**Christ** [kraɪst] *s* Cristo
**christen** ['krɪsən] *tr* bautizar
**Christendom** ['krɪsəndəm] *s* cristiandad
**christening** ['krɪsənɪŋ] *s* bautismo, bautizo
**Christian** ['krɪstʃən] *adj & s* cristiano
**Christianity** [,krɪstʃɪ'ænɪti] *s* cristianismo
**Christianize** ['krɪstʃə,naɪz] *tr* cristianizar
**Christian name** *s* nombre *m* de pila
**Christmas** ['krɪsməs] *adj* navideño || *s* Navidad, Pascua de Navidad
**Christmas card** *s* aleluya navideña
**Christmas carol** *s* villancico
**Christmas Eve** *s* nochebuena
**Christmas gift** *s* aguinaldo, regalo de Navidad
**Christmas tree** *s* árbol *m* de Navidad
**Christopher** ['krɪstəfər] *s* Cristóbal *m*
**chrome** [krom] *adj* cromado || *s* cromo || *tr* cromar
**chromium** ['kromɪ·ən] *s* cromo
**chro·mo** ['kromo] *s* (*pl* **-mos**) (*colored picture*) cromo; (*piece of junk*) (slang) trasto
**chromosome** ['kromə,som] *s* cromosoma *m*
**chron.** *abbr* **chronological, chronology**
**chronic** ['krɑnɪk] *adj* crónico
**chronicle** ['krɑnɪkəl] *s* crónica || *tr* narrar en una crónica; narrar, contar
**chronicler** ['krɑnɪklər] *s* cronista *mf*
**chronolo·gy** [krə'nɑlədʒi] *s* (*pl* **-gies**) cronología
**chronometer** [krə'nɑmɪtər] *s* cronómetro
**chrysanthemum** [krɪ'sænθɪməm] *s* crisantemo
**chub·by** ['tʃʌbi] *adj* (*comp* **-bier**; *super* **-biest**) rechoncho, regordete
**chuck** [tʃʌk] *s* (*throw*) echada, tirada; (*under the chin*) mamola; (*of a lathe*) mandril *m* || *tr* arrojar; **to chuck under the chin** hacer la mamola a
**chuckle** ['tʃʌkəl] *s* risa ahogada || *intr* reírse con risa ahogada
**chug** [tʃʌg] *s* ruido explosivo sordo; (*of a locomotive*) resoplido || *v* (*pret & pp* **chugged**; *ger* **chugging**) *intr* hacer ruidos explosivos sordos, moverse con ruidos explosivos sordos
**chum** [tʃʌm] *s* (coll) compinche *mf*; compañero de cuarto || *v* (*pret & pp* **chummed**; *ger* **chumming**) *intr* (coll) ser compinche, ser compinches; (coll) compartir un cuarto
**chum·my** ['tʃʌmi] *adj* (*comp* **-mier**; *super* **-miest**) muy amigable, íntimo
**chump** [tʃʌmp] *s* tarugo, zoquete *m*; (coll) estúpido, tonto
**chunk** [tʃʌŋk] *s* trozo, pedazo grueso
**church** [tʃʌrtʃ] *s* iglesia
**churchgoer** ['tʃʌrtʃ,go·ər] *s* persona que frecuenta la iglesia
**church·man** ['tʃʌrtʃmən] *s* (*pl* **-men** [mən]) sacerdote *m*, eclesiástico; feligrés *m*
**church member** *s* feligrés *m*
**Church of England** *s* Iglesia Anglicana
**church'ward'en** *s* capiller *m*
**church'yard'** *s* patio de iglesia; cementerio
**churl** [tʃʌrl] *s* palurdo, patán *m*
**churlish** ['tʃʌrlɪʃ] *adj* palurdo, insolente
**churn** [tʃʌrn] *s* mantequera || *tr* mazar (*leche*); hacer (*mantequilla*) en una mantequera; agitar, revolver || *intr* revolverse
**chute** [ʃut] *s* cascada, salto de agua; rápidos; conducto inclinado; (*e.g., into a swimming pool*) tobogán *m*; (*e.g., for grain*) tolva; paracaídas *m*
**cibori·um** [sɪ'borɪ·əm] *s* (*pl* **-a** [ə]) (*canopy*) ciborio, baldaquín *m*; (*cup*) copón *m*
**Cicero** ['sɪsə,ro] *s* Cicerón *m*
**cider** ['saɪdər] *s* sidra
**C.I.F., c.i.f.** *abbr* **cost, insurance, and freight**
**cigar** [sɪ'gɑr] *s* cigarro, puro
**cigar band** *s* anillo de cigarro
**cigar case** *s* cigarrera, petaca
**cigar cutter** *s* cortacigarros *m*
**cigaret** o **cigarette** [,sɪgə'ret] *s* cigarrillo, pitillo
**cigarette case** *s* pitillera
**cigarette holder** *s* boquilla
**cigarette lighter** *s* mechero, encendedor *m* de bolsillo
**cigarette paper** *s* papel *m* de fumar
**cigar holder** *s* boquilla
**cigar store** *s* estanco, tabaquería
**cinch** [sɪntʃ] *s* (*of saddle*) cincha; (*sure grip*) (coll) agarro; (*something easy*) (slang) breva || *tr* cinchar; (coll) agarrar
**cinder** ['sɪndər] *s* ceniza; (*coal burning without flame*) pavesa
**cinder bank** *s* escorial *m*
**Cinderella** [,sɪndə'relə] *s* la Cenicienta
**cinder track** *s* pista de cenizas
**cinema** ['sɪnəmə] *s* cine *m*
**cinematograph** [,sɪnə'mætə,græf] o [,sɪnə'mætə,grɑf] *s* cinematógrafo || *tr & intr* cinematografiar
**cinnabar** ['sɪnə,bɑr] *s* cinabrio
**cinnamon** ['sɪnəmən] *s* canela
**cipher** ['saɪfər] *s* cifra; cero; (*nonentity*) cero a la izquierda; (*key to a cipher*) clave *f* || *tr* cifrar; calcular
**circle** ['sʌrkəl] *s* círculo || *tr* circundar; dar la vuelta a; girar alrededor de
**circuit** ['sʌrkɪt] *s* circuito
**circuit breaker** *s* disyuntor *m*
**circuitous** [sər'kju·ɪtəs] *adj* indirecto, tortuoso
**circular** ['sʌrkjələr] *adj* tortuoso || *s* circular *f*, carta circular
**circularize** ['sʌrkjələ,raɪz] *tr* anunciar por circular; enviar circulares a
**circulate** ['sʌrkjə,let] *tr & intr* circular
**circumcise** ['sʌrkəm,saɪz] *tr* circuncidar

**circumference** [sər'kʌmfərəns] *s* circunferencia
**circumflex** ['sʌrkəm,flɛks] *adj* circunflejo
**circumlocution** [,sʌrkəmlo'kjuʃən] *s* circunlocución, circunloquio
**circumnavigate** [,sʌrkəm'nævɪ,get] *tr* circunnavegar
**circumnavigation** [,sʌrkəm,nævɪ'geʃən] *s* circunnavegación
**circumscribe** [,sʌrkəm'skraɪb] *tr* circunscribir
**circumspect** ['sʌrkəm,spɛkt] *adj* circunspecto
**circumstance** ['sʌrkəm,stæns] *s* circunstancia; ceremonia, ostentación; **in easy circumstances** acomodado; **under no circumstances** de ninguna manera
**circumstantial** [,sʌrkəm'stænʃəl] *adj* (*derived from circumstances*) circunstancial; (*detailed*) circunstanciado
**circumstantial evidence** *s* (law) indicios vehementes
**circumstantiate** [,sʌrkəm'stænʃɪ,et] *tr* apoyar con pruebas y detalles; (*to describe in detail*) circunstanciar
**circumvent** [,sʌrkəm'vent] *tr* (*to catch by a trick*) entrampar, embaucar; (*to outwit*) burlar; (*to keep away from, get around*) evitar
**circus** ['sʌrkəs] *s* circo
**cistern** ['sɪstərn] *s* cisterna, aljibe *m*
**citadel** ['sɪtədəl] *s* ciudadela
**citation** [saɪ'teʃən] *s* (*of a text*) cita; (*before a court of law*) citación; (*for gallantry*) mención
**cite** [saɪt] *tr* (*to quote; to summon*) citar; (*for gallantry*) mencionar
**citizen** ['sɪtɪzən] *s* ciudadano; (*civilian*) paisano
**citizen·ry** ['sɪtɪzənri] *s* (*pl* **-ries**) conjunto de ciudadanos
**citizenship** ['sɪtɪzən,ʃɪp] *s* ciudadanía
**citron** ['sɪtrən] *s* (*fruit*) cidra; (*tree*) cidro; (*candied rind*) cidrada
**citronella** [,sɪtrə'nɛlə] *s* limoncillo (*Andropogon nardus*); aceite *m* de limoncillo
**citrus fruit** ['sɪtrəs] *s* agrios, frutas cítricas
**cit·y** ['sɪti] *s* (*pl* **-ies**) ciudad
**city clerk** *s* archivero
**city council** *s* ayuntamiento
**city editor** *s* redactor de periódico encargado de noticias locales
**city fathers** *spl* concejales *mpl*
**city hall** *s* casa consistorial
**city plan** *s* plano de la ciudad
**city planner** *s* urbanista *mf*
**city planning** *s* urbanismo
**city room** *s* redacción
**cit'y-state'** *s* ciudad-estado *f*
**civic** ['sɪvɪk] *adj* cívico || **civics** *s* estudio de los deberes y derechos del ciudadano
**civies** ['sɪviz] *spl* (coll) traje *m* de paisano; **in civies** (coll) de paisano
**civil** ['sɪvɪl] *adj* civil
**civilian** [sɪ'vɪljən] *adj* civil || *s* civil *mf*, paisano
**civilian clothes** *spl* traje *m* de paisano
**civili·ty** [sɪ'vɪlɪti] *s* (*pl* **-ties**) civilidad
**civilization** [,sɪvɪlɪ'zeʃən] *s* civilización
**civilize** ['sɪvɪ,laɪz] *tr* civilizar
**civil servant** *s* funcionario del estado
**claim** [klem] *s* demanda, pretensión, reclamación || *tr* demandar, pretender, reclamar; afirmar, declarar; **to claim to** + *inf* pretender + *inf*
**claim check** *s* comprobante *m*
**clairvoyance** [klɛr'vɔɪ·əns] *s* clarividencia
**clairvoyant** [klɛr'vɔɪ·ənt] *adj* & *s* clarividente *mf*
**clam** [klæm] *s* almeja; (*tight-lipped person*) (coll) chiticalla *m* || *intr* — **to clam up** (coll) callarse la boca
**clamber** ['klæmər] *intr* — **to clamber up** subir gateando
**clamor** ['klæmər] *s* clamor *m*, clamoreo || *intr* clamorear
**clamorous** ['klæmərəs] *adj* clamoroso
**clamp** [klæmp] *s* abrazadera, grapa; (*vise-like device*) mordaza || *tr* agrapar, afianzar con abrazadera; sujetar en una mordaza || *intr* — **to clamp down on** (coll) apretar los tornillos a
**clan** [klæn] *s* clan *m*
**clandestine** [klæn'destɪn] *adj* clandestino
**clang** [klæŋ] *s* tantán *m*, sonido metálico resonante || *tr* hacer sonar fuertemente || *intr* sonar fuertemente
**clank** [klæŋk] *s* sonido metálico seco || *tr* hacer sonar secamente || *intr* sonar secamente
**clannish** ['klænɪʃ] *adj* exclusivista
**clap** [klæp] *s* golpe seco; (*of the hands*) palmada; (*of thunder*) estampido || *v* (*pret & pp* **clapped**; *ger* **clapping**) *tr* batir (*palmas*); palmotear, aplaudir; **to clap shut** cerrar de golpe || *intr* palmotear, dar palmadas
**clap of thunder** *s* estampido de trueno
**clapper** ['klæpər] *s* palmoteador *m*; (*of a bell*) badajo; (*to cause grain to slide*) tarabilla
**clap'trap'** *s* faramalla; (*of an actor*) latiguillo
**claque** [klæk] *s* (*paid clappers*) claque *f*; (*crush hat*) clac *m*
**claret** ['klærɪt] *s* clarete *m*
**clari·fy** ['klærɪ,faɪ] *v* (*pret & pp* **-fied**) *tr* clarificar; encolar (*el vino*)
**clarinet** [,klærɪ'nɛt] *s* clarinete *m*
**clarion** ['klærɪ·ən] *adj* claro, brillante || *s* clarín *m*
**clarity** ['klærɪti] *s* claridad
**clash** [klæʃ] *s* choque *m*, encontrón *m*; estruendo, ruido || *intr* chocar, entrechocarse
**clasp** [klæsp] o [klɑsp] *s* (*fastener*) abrazadera, cierre *m*; (*for, e.g., a necktie*) broche *m*; (*buckle*) hebilla; (*embrace*) abrazo; (*grip*) agarro || *tr*

abrochar; abrazar; agarrar, apretar (*la mano*); apretarse (*la mano*)
**class.** *abbr* **classical**
**class** [klæs] o [klɑs] *s* clase *f;* (slang) elegancia, buen tono || *tr* clasificar || *intr* clasificarse
**class consciousness** *s* sentimiento de clase
**classic** ['klæsɪk] *adj & s* clásico; **the classics** las obras clásicas
**classical** ['klæsɪkəl] *adj* clásico
**classical scholar** *s* erudito en las lenguas clásicas
**classicist** ['klæsɪsɪst] *s* clasicista *mf*
**classified** ['klæsɪ,faɪd] *adj* clasificado; clasificado como secreto
**classified ads** *spl* anuncios clasificados en secciones
**classi•fy** ['klæsɪ,faɪ] *v* (*pret & pp* **-fied**) *tr* clasificar
**class'mate'** *s* compañero de clase
**class'room'** *s* aula, sala de clase
**class struggle** *s* lucha de clases
**class•y** ['klæsi] *adj* (*comp* **-ier;** *super* **-iest**) (slang) elegante
**clatter** ['klætər] *s* estruendo confuso; algazara, gresca; (*of hoofs*) trápala || *intr* caer o moverse con estruendo confuso; hablar rápida y ruidosamente; **to clatter down the stairs** bajar la escalera ruidosamente
**clause** [klɔz] *s* (*article in a legal document*) cláusula; (gram) oración dependiente
**clavichord** ['klævɪ,kɔrd] *s* clavicordio
**clavicle** ['klævɪkəl] *s* clavícula
**clavier** ['klævɪ•ər] o [klə'vɪr] *s* teclado || [klə'vɪr] *s* instrumento musical con teclado
**claw** [klɔ] *s* garra, uña; (*of lobster, crab, etc.*) pinza; (*of hammer, wrench, etc.*) oreja; (coll) dedos, mano *f* || *tr* (*to clutch*) agarrar; (*to scratch*) arañar; (*to tear*) desgarrar
**clay** [kle] *adj* arcilloso || *s* arcilla
**clay pigeon** *s* pichón *m* de barro
**clay pipe** *s* pipa de tierra
**clean** [klin] *adj* limpio; distinto, neto, nítido; completo || *adv* completamente; **to come clean** (slang) confesarlo todo || *tr* limpiar; (*to tidy up*) asear; **to be cleaned out** (*of money*) (slang) quedar limpio; **to clean out** limpiar; (slang) dejar limpio || *intr* limpiarse; asearse; **to clean up** limpiarse; (coll) llevárselo todo; (*in gambling*) (slang) hacer mesa limpia; **to clean up after someone** limpiar lo que alguno ha ensuciado
**clean bill of health** *s* patente limpia de sanidad
**cleaner** ['klinər] *s* limpiador *m;* (*dry cleaner*) tintorero; (*preparation*) quitamanchas *m;* **to send to the cleaners** (slang) dejar limpio
**cleaning** ['klinɪŋ] *s* limpieza
**cleaning fluid** *s* quitamanchas *m*
**cleaning woman** *s* criada que hace la limpieza, alquilona
**cleanliness** ['klenlɪnɪs] *s* limpieza
**clean•ly** ['klenli] *adj* (*comp* **-lier;** *super* **-liest**) limpio (*que tiene el hábito del aseo*)
**cleanse** [klenz] *tr* limpiar, lavar, depurar
**clean-shaven** ['klin'ʃevən] *adj* lisamente afeitado
**clean'up'** *s* limpieza general; **to make a cleanup** (slang) hacer su pacotilla
**clear** [klɪr] *adj* claro; (*cloudless*) despejado; (*of guilt, debts, annoyances*) libre || *adv* claro, claramente; **clear through** de parte a parte || *tr* despejar (*un bosque*); clarificar (*lo que estaba turbio*); (*to make less dark*) aclarar; saltar por encima de; (*to prove the innocence of*) absolver; sacar (*una ganancia neta*); abonar, acreditar; liquidar (*una cuenta*); (*in the customhouse*) despachar; salvar (*un obstáculo*); levantar (*la mesa*); desmontar (*un terreno*); **to clear the way** abrir camino || *intr* clarificarse; aclararse; **to clear away** (coll) irse, desaparecer; **to clear up** abonanzarse (*el tiempo*); despejarse (*el cielo, el tiempo*)
**clearance** ['klɪrəns] *s* aclaración; abono, acreditación; (*between two objects*) espacio libre; (*in a cylinder*) espacio muerto; (com) compensación
**clearance sale** *s* venta de liquidación
**clearing** ['klɪrɪŋ] *s* (*in a woods*) claro; (com) compensación
**clearing house** *s* cámara de compensación
**clear-sighted** ['klɪr'saɪtɪd] *adj* clarividente, perspicaz
**clear'sto'ry** *s* (*pl* **-ries**) var of **clerestory**
**cleat** [klit] *s* abrazadera, listón *m*
**cleavage** ['klivɪdʒ] *s* división, hendidura; (fig) desunión
**cleave** [kliv] *v* (*pret & pp* **cleft** [kleft] o **cleaved**) *tr* rajar, partir; hender (*las aguas un buque, los aires una flecha*) || *intr* adherirse, pegarse; apegarse, ser fiel
**cleaver** ['klivər] *s* cortante *m*, cuchilla de carnicero
**clef** [klef] *s* (mus) clave *f*
**cleft palate** [kleft] *s* fisura del paladar
**clematis** ['klemətɪs] *s* clemátide *f*
**clemen•cy** ['klemənsi] *s* (*pl* **-cies**) clemencia; (*of the weather*) benignidad
**clement** ['klemənt] *adj* clemente; (*weather*) benigno
**clench** [klentʃ] *s* agarro || *tr* agarrar; apretar, cerrar (*el puño, los dientes*)
**clereto•ry** ['klɪr,stori] *s* (*pl* **-ries**) claraboya
**cler•gy** ['klerdʒi] *s* (*pl* **-gies**) clerecía, clero
**clergy•man** ['klerdʒimən] *s* (*pl* **-men** [mən]) clérigo, pastor *m*
**cleric** ['klerɪk] *s* clérigo
**clerical** ['klerɪkəl] *adj* (*of clergy*) clerical; (*of office work*) oficinesco || *s* clérigo, eclesiático; (*supporter of power of clergy*) clerical *m;* **clericals** (coll) hábitos clericales
**clerical error** *s* error *m* de pluma
**clerical work** *s* trabajo de oficina

**clerk** [klʌrk] *s* (*in a store*) dependiente *mf;* (*in an office*) oficinista *mf;* (*in a city hall*) archivero; (*in a church*) lego, seglar *m;* (*in law office, in court*) escribano
**clever** ['klevər] *adj* hábil, diestro, mañoso; inteligente
**cleverness** ['klevərnɪs] *s* habilidad, destreza, maña; inteligencia
**clew** [klu] *s* indicio, pista
**cliché** [kli'ʃe] *s* (*printing plate*) clisé *m;* (*trite expression*) cliché *m*
**click** [klɪk] *s* golpecito; (*of typewriter*) tecleo; (*of firearm*) piñoneo; (*of heels*) taconeo; (*of tongue*) claqueo, chasquido ‖ *tr* hacer sonar con un golpecito seco; chascar (*la lengua*); **to click the heels** taconear; cuadrarse (*un soldado*) ‖ *intr* sonar con un golpecito seco; piñonear (*el gatillo de un arma de fuego*); claquear (*la lengua*)
**client** ['klaɪ·ənt] *s* cliente *mf;* cliente de abogado
**clientele** [,klaɪ·ən'tɛl] *s* clientela
**cliff** [klɪf] *s* acantilado, escarpa, risco
**climate** ['klaɪmɪt] *s* clima *m*
**climax** ['klaɪmæks] *s* colmo; **to cap the climax** ser el colmo
**climb** [klaɪm] *s* subida, trepa ‖ *tr & intr* escalar, subir, trepar
**climber** ['klaɪmər] *s* trepador *m;* ambicioso de figurar; (bot) enredadera, trepadora
**clinch** [klɪntʃ] *s* agarro, abrazo; (*of a nail*) remache *m* ‖ *tr* afianzar, sujetar; agarrar, abrazar; apretar (*el puño*); remachar (*un clavo ya clavado*); resolver decisivamente
**cling** [klɪŋ] *v* (*pret & pp* **clung** [klʌŋ]) *intr* adherirse, pegarse; **to cling to** agarrarse a, asirse de
**cling'stone' peach** *s* albérchigo, peladillo
**clinic** ['klɪnɪk] *s* clínica
**clinical** ['klɪnɪkəl] *adj* clínico
**clinical chart** *s* hoja clínica
**clinician** [klɪ'nɪʃən] *s* clínico
**clink** [kliŋk] *s* tintín *m* ‖ *tr* hacer tintinear; chocar (*vasos, copas*) ‖ *intr* tintinear
**clinker** ['klɪŋkər] *s* escoria de hulla
**clip** [klɪp] *s* tijereteo, esquileo; grapa, pinza; (*to fasten papers*) sujetapapeles *m,* presilla de alambre; **at a good clip** a buen paso ‖ *v* (*pret & pp* **clipped;** *ger* **clipping**) *tr* tijeretear, esquilar; (*to fasten with a clip*) afianzar, sujetar; recortar (*p.ej., un cupón*) ‖ *intr* moverse con rapidez
**clipper** ['klɪpər] *s* tijera, cizalla; **clippers** maquinilla cortapelos; tijeras podadoras
**clipping** ['klɪpɪŋ] *s* tijereteo, esquileo; (*from a newspaper*) recorte *m*
**clique** [klik] *s* pandilla, corrillo ‖ *intr* — **to clique together** apandillarse
**cliquish** ['klikɪʃ] *adj* exclusivista
**clk.** *abbr* **clerk, clock**
**cloak** [klok] *s* capote *m;* (*disguise, excuse*) capa ‖ *tr* encapotar; disimular, encubrir
**cloak-and-dagger** ['klokən'dægər] *adj* de capa y espada (*dícese de duelos, espionaje, etc.*)
**cloak-and-sword** ['klokən'sord] *adj* de capa y espada (*dícese, p.ej., de las costumbres caballerescas*)
**cloak hanger** *s* cuelgacapas *m*
**cloak'room'** *s* guardarropa *m;* (Brit) excusado
**clock** [klɑk] *s* reloj *m* (de pared o de mesa); (*in a stocking*) cuadrado ‖ *tr* registrar; (sport) cronometrar
**clock'mak'er** *s* relojero
**clock tower** *s* torre *f* reloj
**clock'wise'** *adj & adv* en el sentido de las agujas del reloj
**clock'work'** *s* mecanismo de relojería; **like clockwork** como un reloj
**clod** [klɑd] *s* terrón *m*
**clod'hop'per** *s* destripaterrones *m,* quebrantaterrones *m;* **clodhoppers** zapatos fuertes de trabajo
**clog** [klɑg] *s* estorbo, obstáculo; (*wooden shoe*) zueco; (*dance*) zapateado; (*hobble on animal*) traba ‖ *v* (*pret & pp* **clogged;** *ger* **clogging**) *tr* atascar ‖ *intr* atascarse; bailar el zapateado
**clog dance** *s* zapateado
**cloister** ['klɔɪstər] *s* claustro ‖ *tr* enclaustrar
**cloistral** ['klɔɪstrəl] *adj* claustral
**close** [klos] *adj* cercano, próximo; casi igual; (*translation*) fiel, exacto; (*fabric*) compacto; (*weather, atmosphere*) pesado, sofocante; (*stingy*) tacaño; (*battle, race, election*) reñido; (*friend*) íntimo; (*shut in, enclosed*) cerrado; (*narrow*) estrecho ‖ *adv* cerca; **close to** cerca de ‖ [kloz] *s* fin *m,* terminación; (*of business, of stock market*) cierre *m;* **at the close of day** a la caída de la tarde; **to bring to a close** poner término a; **to come to a close** tocar a su fin ‖ *tr* cerrar; (*to cover*) tapar; (*to finish*) concluir; saldar (*una cuenta*); cerrar (*un trato*); **to close in** cerrar, encerrar; **to close ranks** cerrar las filas ‖ *intr* cerrar, cerrarse; **to close in on** cerrar con (*el enemigo*)
**close call** [klos] *s* (coll) escape *m* por un pelo
**closed car** [klozd] *s* coche cerrado, conducción interior
**closed chapter** *s* asunto concluído
**closed season** *s* veda
**closed shop** *s* taller agremiado
**closefisted** ['klos'fɪstɪd] *adj* cicatero, tacaño, manicorto
**close-fitting** ['klos'fɪtɪŋ] *adj* ajustado, ceñido al cuerpo
**close-lipped** ['klos'lɪpt] *adj* callado, reservado
**closely** ['klosli] *adv* de cerca; estrechamente; fielmente; atentamente
**close quarters** [klos] *spl* lugar muy estrecho, lugares estrechos
**close shave** [klos] *s* afeitado a ras; (coll) escape *m* por un pelo
**closet** ['klɑsɪt] *s* alacena; (*wardrobe*) armario; (*small private room*) apo-

sento, gabinete *m;* (*for keeping clothing*) guardarropa *m;* (*toilet*) retrete *m* || *tr* — **to be closeted with** encerrarse con
**close-up** ['klos,ʌp] *s* (*moving picture*) vista de cerca; fotografía de cerca
**closing** ['klozɪŋ] *s* cerradura, cierre *m*
**closing prices** *spl* precios de cierre
**clot** [klɑt] *s* grumo, coágulo || *v* (*pret & pp* **clotted;** *ger* **clotting**) *intr* engrumecerse, coagularse
**cloth** [klɔθ] o [klɑθ] *s* paño, tela; ropa clerical; (*canvas, sails*) lona, trapo, vela; (*for binding books*) tela; **the cloth** la clerecía
**clothe** [kloð] *v* (*pret & pp* **clothed** o **clad** [klæd]) *tr* trajear, vestir; cubrir; (*e.g., with authority*) investir
**clothes** [kloz] o [kloθz] *spl* ropa, vestidos; ropa de cama
**clothes'bas'ket** *s* cesto de la ropa, cesto de la colada
**clothes'brush'** *s* cepillo de ropa
**clothes closet** *s* ropero
**clothes dryer** *s* secadora de ropa, secarropa
**clothes hanger** *s* colgador *m,* perchero
**clothes'horse'** *s* enjugador *m,* secarropa de travesaños
**clothes'line'** *s* cordel *m* para tender la ropa, tendedera
**clothes'pin'** *s* pinza, alfiler *m* de madera
**clothes tree** *s* percha
**clothes wringer** *s* exprimidor *m* de ropa
**clothier** ['kloðjər] *s* (*person who sells ready-made clothes*) ropero; (*dealer in cloth*) pañero
**clothing** ['kloðɪŋ] *s* ropa, vestidos, ropaje *m*
**cloud** [klaʊd] *s* nube *f* || *tr* anublar || *intr* — **to cloud over** anublarse
**cloud bank** *s* mar *m* de nubes
**cloud'burst'** *s* aguacero, chaparrón *m*
**cloud-capped** ['klaʊd,kæpt] *adj* coronado de nubes
**cloudless** ['klaʊdlɪs] *adj* despejado, sin nubes
**cloud of dust** *s* polvareda, nube *f* de polvo
**cloud•y** ['klaʊdi] *adj* (*comp* **-ier;** *super* **-iest**) nuboso, nublado; (*muddy, turbid*) turbio; confuso, obscuro; melancólico, sombrío
**clove** [klov] *s* (*flower*) clavo de especia; (*spice*) clavo
**clover** ['klovər] *s* trébol *m;* **to be in clover** vivir en el lujo
**clo'ver•leaf'** *s* (*pl* **-leaves** [,livz]) *s* cruce *m* en trébol
**clove tree** *s* clavero
**clown** [klaʊn] *s* bufón *m,* payaso; (*rustic*) patán *m* || *intr* hacer el payaso
**clownish** ['klaʊnɪʃ] *adj* bufonesco; rústico
**cloy** [klɔɪ] *tr* hastiar, empalagar
**club** [klʌb] *s* porra, clava; (*playing card*) basto, trébol *m;* club *m,* casino || *v* (*pret & pp* **clubbed;** *ger* **clubbing**) *tr* aporrear || *intr* — **to club together** unirse; formar club
**club car** *s* coche *m* club, coche bar
**club'house'** *s* casino, club *m*
**club•man** ['klʌbmən] *s* (*pl* **-men** [mən]) clubista *m*
**club•woman** ['klʌb,wʊmən] *s* (*pl* **-women** [,wɪmɪn]) clubista *f*
**cluck** [klʌk] *s* cloqueo, clo clo || *intr* cloquear, hacer clo clo
**clue** [klu] *s* indicio, pista
**clump** [klʌmp] *s* (*of earth*) terrón *m;* (*of trees or shrubs*) grupo; pisada fuerte || *intr* — **to clump along** andar pesadamente
**clum•sy** ['klʌmzi] *adj* (*comp* **-sier;** *super* **-siest**) (*worker*) chapucero, desmañado, torpe; (*work*) chapucero, tosco, grosero
**cluster** ['klʌstər] *s* grupo; (*of grapes or other things growing or joined together*) racimo || *intr* arracimarse; **to cluster around** reunirse en torno a; **to cluster together** agruparse
**clutch** [klʌtʃ] *s* (*grasp, grip*) agarro, apretón *m* fuerte; (aut) embrague *m;* (aut) pedal *m* de embrague; **to fall into the clutches of** caer en las garras de; **to throw the clutch in** embragar; **to throw the clutch out** desembragar || *tr* agarrar, empuñar
**clutter** ['klʌtər] *tr* — **to clutter up** cubrir o llenar desordenadamente
**cm.** *abbr* **centimeter**
**cml.** *abbr* **commercial**
**Co.** *abbr* **Company, County**
**coach** [kotʃ] *s* coche *m,* diligencia; (aut) coche cerrado; (rr) coche de viajeros, coche ordinario *m;* (sport) entrenador *m* || *tr* aleccionar; (sport) entrenar || *intr* entrenarse
**coach house** *s* cochera
**coaching** ['kotʃɪŋ] *s* lecciones *fpl* particulares; (sport) entrenamiento
**coach•man** ['kotʃmən] *s* (*pl* **-men** [mən]) *s* cochero
**coagulate** [ko'ægjə,let] *tr* coagular || *intr* coagularse
**coal** [kol] *s* carbón *m,* hulla || *tr* proveer de carbón || *intr* proveerse de carbón
**coal'bin'** *s* carbonera
**coal bunker** *s* carbonera
**coal car** *s* vagón carbonero
**coal'deal'er** *s* carbonero
**coaling** ['kolɪŋ] *adj* carbonero || *s* toma de carbón
**coalition** [,ko•ə'lɪʃən] *s* unión; (*alliance between states or factions*) coalición
**coal mine** *s* mina de carbón
**coal oil** *s* aceite *m* mineral
**coal scuttle** *s* cubo para carbón
**coal tar** *s* alquitrán *m* de hulla
**coal'yard'** *s* carbonería
**coarse** [kors] *adj* (*of inferior quality*) basto, burdo; (*composed of large particles*) grueso; (*crude in manners*) grosero, rudo, vulgar
**coast** [kost] *s* costa; **the coast is clear** ya no hay peligro || *tr* costear || *intr*

deslizarse cuesta abajo; **to coast along** avanzar sin esfuerzo
**coastal** ['kostəl] *adj* costero
**coaster** ['kostər] *s* salvamanteles *m*
**coaster brake** *s* freno de contrapedal
**coast guard** *s* guardacostas *mpl;* guardia *m* de los guardacostas
**coast guard cutter** *s* escampavía de los guardacostas
**coasting trade** *s* cabotaje *m*
**coast'land'** *s* litoral *m*
**coast'line'** *s* línea de la costa
**coast'wise'** *adj* costanero || *adv* a lo largo de la costa
**coat** [kot] *s* (*jacket*) americana, saco; (*topcoat*) abrigo, sobretodo; (*of an animal*) lana, pelo; (*of paint*) capa, mano *f* || *tr* cubrir, revestir; dar una capa de pintura a
**coated** ['kotɪd] *adj* revestido; (*tongue*) saburroso
**coat hanger** *s* colgador *m*
**coating** ['kotɪŋ] *s* revestimiento; (*of paint*) capa; (*of plaster*) enlucido
**coat of arms** *s* escudo de armas
**coat'room'** *s* guardarropa *m*
**coat'tail'** *s* faldón *m*
**coax** [koks] *tr* engatusar
**cob** [kɑb] *s* zuro; **to eat corn on the cob** comer maíz en la mazorca
**cobalt** ['kobɔlt] *s* cobalto
**cobbler** ['kɑblər] *s* remendón *m*, zapatero de viejo
**cob'ble•stone'** *s* guijarro
**cob'web'** *s* telaraña
**cocaine** [ko'ken] *s* cocaína
**cock** [kɑk] *s* (*rooster*) gallo; (*faucet, valve*) espita, grifo; (*of firearm*) martillo; (*weathervane*) veleta; caudillo, jefe *m* || *tr* amartillar (*un arma de fuego*); ladear (*la cabeza*); enderezar, levantar
**cockade** [kɑ'ked] *s* cucarda, escarapela
**cock-a-doodle-doo** ['kɑkə,dudəl'du] *s* quiquiriquí *m*
**cock-and-bull story** ['kɑkənd'bʊl] *s* cuento absurdo, cuento increíble
**cocked hat** [kɑkt] *s* sombrero de candil, sombrero de tres picos; **to knock into a cocked hat** (slang) apabullar
**cockeyed** ['kɑk,aɪd] *adj* bisojo, bizco; (coll) encorvado, torcido; (slang) disparatado, extravagante
**cock'fight'** *s* pelea de gallos
**cockney** ['kɑkni] *s* londinense *mf* de la clase pobre que habla un dialecto característico; dialecto de la clase pobre de Londres
**cock of the walk** *s* quiquiriquí *m*, gallito del lugar
**cock'pit'** *s* gallera; (aer) carlinga
**cock'roach'** *s* cucaracha
**cockscomb** ['kɑks,kom] *s* cresta de gallo; gorro de bufón; (bot) cresta de gallo, moco de pavo
**cock'sure'** *adj* muy seguro de sí mismo
**cock'tail'** *s* coctel *m;* (*of fruit, oysters, etc.*) aperitivo
**cocktail party** *s* coctel *m*
**cocktail shaker** ['ʃekər] *s* coctelera
**cock•y** ['kɑki] *adj* (*comp* **-ier;** *super* **-iest**) (coll) arrogante, hinchado; **to be cocky** (coll) tener mucho gallo
**cocoa** ['koko] *s* cacao; (*drink*) chocolate *m*
**cocoanut** o **coconut** ['kokə,nʌt] *s* coco
**cocoanut palm** o **tree** *s* cocotero
**cocoon** [kə'kun] *s* capullo
**C.O.D., c.o.d.** *abbr* **collect on delivery;** (Brit) **cash on delivery**
**cod** [kɑd] *s* abadejo, bacalao
**coddle** ['kɑdəl] *tr* consentir, mimar
**code** [kod] *s* (*of laws; of manners; of signals*) código; (*of telegraphy*) alfabeto; (*secret system of writing*) cifra, clave *f;* (com) cifrario; **in code** en cifra || *tr* (*to put in code*) cifrar
**code word** *s* clave telegráfica
**codex** ['kodɛks] *s* (*pl* **codices** ['kodɪ,siz] o ['kɑdɪ,siz] *s* códice *m*
**cod'fish'** *s* abadejo, bacalao
**codger** ['kɑdʒər] *s* — **old codger** (coll) anciano, tío
**codicil** ['kɑdɪsɪl] *s* codicilo; apéndice *m*
**codi•fy** ['kɑdɪ,faɪ] o ['kodɪ,faɪ] *v* (*pret & pp* **-fied**) *tr* codificar
**cod'-liv'er oil** *s* aceite *m* de hígado de bacalao
**coed** o **co-ed** ['ko,ɛd] *s* alumna de una escuela coeducativa
**coeducation** [,ko,ɛdʒə'keʃən] *s* coeducación
**coefficient** [,ko•ɪ'fɪʃənt] *adj & s* coeficiente *m*
**coerce** [ko'ʌrs] *tr* forzar, coactar
**coercion** [ko'ʌrʃən] *s* compulsión, coacción
**coeval** [ko'ivəl] *adj & s* coetáneo
**coexist** [,ko•ɪg'zɪst] *intr* coexistir
**coexistence** [,ko•ɪg'zɪstəns] *s* coexistencia
**coffee** ['kɔfi] o ['kɑfi] *s* café *m;* (*plant*) cafeto; **black coffee** café solo
**coffee bean** *s* grano de café
**cof'fee•cake'** *s* rosquilla (que se come con el café)
**coffee grinder** *s* molinillo de café
**coffee grounds** *spl* poso del café
**coffee mill** *s* molinillo de café
**coffee plantation** *s* cafetal *m*
**coffee pot** *s* cafetera
**coffee tree** *s* cafeto
**coffer** ['kɔfər] o ['kɑfər] *s* arca, cofre *m;* **coffers** tesoro, fondos
**cof'fer•dam'** *s* ataguía, encajonado
**coffin** ['kɔfɪn] o ['kɑfɪn] *s* ataúd *m*
**C. of S.** *abbr* **Chief of Staff**
**cog** [kɑg] *s* diente *m* (*de rueda dentada*); rueda dentada; **to slip a cog** equivocarse
**cogency** ['kodʒənsi] *s* fuerza (*de un argumento*)
**cogent** ['kodʒənt] *adj* fuerte, convincente
**cogitate** ['kɑdʒɪ,tet] *tr & intr* cogitar, meditar
**cognac** ['konjæk] o ['kɑnjæk] *s* coñac *m*
**cognizance** ['kɑgnɪzəns] o ['kɑnɪzəns]

*s* conocimiento; **to take cognizance of** enterarse de
**cognizant** ['kɑgnɪzənt] o ['kɑnɪzənt] *adj* sabedor, enterado
**cog'wheel'** *s* rueda dentada
**cohabit** [ko'hæbɪt] *intr* cohabitar
**coheir** [ko'er] *s* coheredero
**cohere** [ko'hɪr] *intr* adherirse, pegarse; conformarse, corresponder
**coherent** [ko'hɪrənt] *adj* coherente
**cohesion** [ko'hiʒən] *s* cohesión
**coiffeur** [kwɑ'fʌr] *s* peluquero
**coiffure** [kwɑ'fjʊr] *s* peinado, tocado
**coil** [kɔɪl] *s* (*something wound in a spiral*) rollo; (*single turn of spiral*) vuelta; (*of a still*) serpentín *m;* (*of hair*) rizo; (*of a spring*) espiral *f;* (elec) carrete *m* ‖ *tr* arrollar, enrollar; (naut) adujar ‖ *intr* arrollarse, enrollarse; (*like a snake*) serpentear
**coil spring** *s* resorte *m* espiral
**coin** [kɔɪn] *s* moneda; (*wedge*) cuña; **to pay back in one's own coin** pagar en la misma moneda; **to toss a coin** echar a cara o cruz ‖ *tr* acuñar; forjar, inventar (*palabras o frases*); **to coin money** (coll) ganar mucho dinero
**coincide** [,ko·ɪn'saɪd] *intr* coincidir
**coincidence** [ko'ɪnsɪdəns] *s* coincidencia
**coition** [ko'ɪʃən] o **coitus** ['ko·ɪtəs] *s* coito
**coke** [kok] *s* coque *m*, cok *m*
**col.** *abbr* **colored, colony, column**
**colander** ['kʌləndər] o ['kɑləndər] *s* colador *m*, escurridor *m*
**cold** [kold] *adj* frío; **to be cold** (*said of a person*) tener frío; (*said of the weather*) hacer frío ‖ *s* frío; (*indisposition*) resfriado; **to catch cold** resfriarse, coger un resfriado
**cold blood** *s* — **in cold blood** a sangre fría
**cold chisel** *s* cortafrío
**cold comfort** *s* poca consolación
**cold cream** *s* colcrén *m*
**cold cuts** *spl* fiambres *mpl*
**cold feet** *spl* (coll) desánimo, miedo
**cold'heart'ed** *adj* duro, insensible
**cold meat** *s* carne *f* fiambre
**coldness** ['koldnɪs] *s* frialdad
**cold shoulder** *s* — **to turn a cold shoulder on** (coll) tratar con suma frialdad
**cold snap** *s* corto rato de frío agudo
**cold storage** *s* conservación en cámara frigorífica
**cold war** *s* guerra fría
**coleslaw** ['kol,slɔ] *s* ensalada de col
**colic** ['kɑlɪk] *adj* & *s* cólico
**coliseum** [,kɑlɪ'si·əm] *s* coliseo
**coll.** *abbr* **colleague, collection, college, colloquial**
**collaborate** [kə'læbə,ret] *intr* colaborar
**collaborationist** [kə,læbə'reʃənɪst] *s* colaboracionista *mf*
**collaborator** [kə'læbə,retər] *s* colaborador *m*
**collapse** [kə'læps] *s* desplome *m;* (*in business*) fracaso; (pathol) colapso ‖ *intr* desplomarse; fracasar; postrarse, sufrir colapso
**collapsible** [kə'læpsɪbəl] *adj* abatible, plegable, desmontable
**collar** ['kɑlər] *s* cuello; (*of dog, horse*) collar *m;* (mach) collar
**col'lar·band'** *s* tirilla de camisa
**col'lar·bone'** *s* clavícula
**collate** [kə'let] o ['kɑlet] *tr* colacionar, cotejar
**collateral** [kə'lætərəl] *adj* colateral ‖ *s* (*relative*) colateral *mf;* (com) colateral *m*
**collation** [kə'leʃən] *s* (*act of comparing; light meal*) colación
**colleague** ['kɑlig] *s* colega *mf*
**collect** ['kɑlɛkt] *s* (eccl) colecta ‖ [kə'lɛkt] *tr* acumular, reunir; colectar, recaudar (*impuestos*); coleccionar (*sellos de correo, antiguallas*); recolectar (*cosechas*); cobrar (*pasajes*); recoger (*billetes; el correo*); **to collect onself** reponerse ‖ *intr* acumularse; **collect on delivery** contra reembolso, cobro contra entrega
**collected** [kə'lɛktɪd] *adj* sosegado, dueño de sí mismo
**collection** [kə'lɛkʃən] *s* colección; (*of taxes*) recaudación; (*of mail*) recogida
**collection agency** *s* agencia de cobros de cuentas
**collective** [kə'lɛktɪv] *adj* colectivo
**collector** [kə'lɛktər] *s* (*of stamps, antiques*) coleccionista *mf;* (*of taxes*) recaudador *m;* (*of tickets*) cobrador *m*
**college** ['kɑlɪdʒ] *s* colegio universitario; (*of cardinals, electors, etc.*) colegio
**collide** [kə'laɪd] *intr* chocar; **to collide with** chocar con
**collie** ['kɑli] *s* perro pastoril escocés
**collier** ['kɑljər] *s* barco carbonero; minero de carbón
**collier·y** ['kɑljəri] *s* (*pl* **-ies**) mina de carbón
**collision** [kə'lɪʒən] *s* colisión
**colloid** ['kɑlɔɪd] *adj* & *s* coloide *m*
**colloquial** [kə'lokwɪ·əl] *adj* coloquial, familiar
**colloquialism** [kə'lokwɪ·ə,lɪzəm] *s* coloquialismo
**collo·quy** ['kɑləkwi] *s* (*pl* **-quies**) coloquio
**collusion** [kə'luʒən] *s* colusión, confabulación; **to be in collusion with** estar en inteligencia con
**cologne** [kə'lon] *s* agua de colonia, colonia ‖ **Cologne** *s* Colonia
**colon** ['kolən] *s* (anat) colon *m;* (gram) dos puntos
**colonel** ['kʌrnəl] *s* coronel *m*
**colonel·cy** ['kʌrnəlsi] *s* (*pl* **-cies**) coronelía
**colonial** [kə'lonɪ·əl] *adj* colonial ‖ *s* colono
**colonize** ['kɑlə,naɪz] *tr* & *intr* colonizar
**colonnade** [,kɑlə'ned] *s* columnata
**colo·ny** ['kɑləni] *s* (*pl* **-nies**) colonia
**colophon** ['kɑlə,fɑn] *s* colofón *m*

**color** ['kʌlər] *s* color; **the colors** los colores, la bandera; **to call to the colors** llamar a filas; **to give** o **to lend color to** dar visos de probabilidad a; **under color of** so color de, bajo pretexto de; **with flying colors** con banderas desplegadas || *tr* colorar, colorear; (*to excuse, palliate*) colorear; (*to dye*) teñir || *intr* sonrojarse, ponerse colorado, demudarse
**col'or-blind'** *adj* ciego para los colores
**colored** ['kʌlərd] *adj* de color; (*specious*) colorado
**colorful** ['kʌlərfəl] *adj* colorido; pintoresco
**coloring** ['kʌlərɪŋ] *adj* & *s* colorante *m*
**colorless** ['kʌlərlɪs] *adj* incoloro; (fig) insulso
**color photography** *s* fotografía en colores
**color salute** *s* (mil) saludo con la bandera
**color sargent** *s* sargento abanderado
**color screen** *s* (phot) pantalla de color
**color television** *s* telivisión en colores
**colossal** [kə'lɑsəl] *adj* colosal
**colossus** [kə'lɑsəs] *s* coloso
**colt** [kolt] *s* potro
**Columbus** [kə'lʌmbəs] *s* Colón *m*
**Columbus Day** *s* día *m* de la raza, fiesta de la hispanidad
**column** ['kɑləm] *s* columna
**columnist** ['kɑləmɪst] *s* columnista *mf*
**com.** *abbr* **comedy, commerce, common**
**Com.** *abbr* **Commander, Commissioner, Committee**
**coma** ['komə] *s* (pathol) coma *m*
**comb** [kom] *s* peine *m;* (*currycomb*) almohaza; (*of rooster*) cresta; cresta de ola || *tr* peinar; explorar con minuciosidad
**com•bat** ['kɑmbæt] *s* combate *m* || ['kɑmbæt] o [kəm'bæt] *v* (*pret* & *pp* **-bated** o **-batted;** *ger* **-bating** o **-batting**) *tr* & *intr* combatir
**combatant** ['kɑmkətənt] *adj* & *s* combatiente *m*
**combat duty** *s* servicio de frente
**combination** [,kɑmbɪ'neʃən] *s* combinación
**combine** ['kɑmbaɪn] *s* monopolio; segadora trilladora; (coll) combinación || [kəm'baɪn] *tr* combinar || *intr* combinarse
**combining form** *s* (gram) elemento de compuestos
**combustible** [kəm'bʌstɪbəl] *adj* combustible; (fig) ardiente, impetuoso || *s* combustible *m*
**combustion** [kəm'bʌstʃən] *s* combustión
**come** [kʌm] *v* (*pret* **came** [kem]; *pp* **come**) *intr* venir; **to come about** suceder; **to come across** encontrarse con; **to come after** venir detrás de; venir después de; venir por, venir en busca de; **to come again** volver; **to come apart** desunirse, desprenderse; **to come around** restablecerse; volver en sí; rendirse; ponerse de acuerdo; cambiar de dirección; **to come at** alcanzar; **to come back** volver; (coll) rehabilitarse; **to come before** anteponerse; **to come between** interponerse; desunir, separar; **to come by** conseguir; **to come down** bajar; (*in social position, financial status, etc.*) descender; (*from one person to another*) ser transmitido; **to come downstairs** bajar (*de un piso a otro*); **to come down with** enfermarse de; **to come for** venir por, venir en busca de; **to come forth** salir; aparecer; **to come forward** avanzar; presentarse; **to come from** venir de; provenir de; **to come in** entrar; entrar en; empezar; ponerse en uso; **to come in for** conseguir, recibir; **to come into one's own** ser reconocido; **to come off** desprenderse; acontecer; **to come out** salir; salir a luz; ponerse de largo (*una joven*); divulgarse (*una noticia*); **to come out for** anunciar su apoyo de; **to come out with** descolgarse con; **to come over** dejarse persuadir; pasar, p.ej., **what's come over him?** ¿qué le ha pasado?; **to come through** salir bien, tener éxito; ganar; **to come to** volver en sí; **to come together** juntarse, reunirse; **to come true** hacerse realidad; **to come up** subir; presentarse; **to come upstairs** subir (*de un piso a otro*); **to come up to** acercarse a; subir a; estar a la altura de; **to come up with** proponer
**come'back'** *s* (coll) rehabilitación; (slang) respuesta aguda; **to stage a comeback** (coll) rehabilitarse
**comedian** [kə'midɪ·ən] *s* cómico, comediante *m;* autor *m* de comedias
**comedienne** [kə,midɪ'en] *s* cómica, comedianta
**come'down'** *s* (coll) humillación, revés *m*
**come•dy** ['kɑmədi] *s* (*pl* **-dies**) comedia cómica; (*comicalness*) comicidad
**come•ly** ['kʌmli] *adj* (*comp* **-lier;** *super* **-liest**) (*attractive*) donairoso, gracioso; (*decorous*) conveniente, decente
**comet** ['kɑmɪt] *s* cometa *m*
**comfort** ['kʌmfərt] *s* comodidad, confort *m;* (*encouragement, consolation*) confortación; (*person*) confortador *m;* (*bed cover*) colcha, cobertor *m* || *tr* confortar
**comfortable** ['kʌmfərtəbəl] *adj* cómodo, confortable; (*fairly well off*) holgado; (*salary*) (coll) suficiente || *s* colcha, cobertor *m*
**comforter** ['kʌmfərtər] *s* confortador *m,* consolador *m;* colcha, cobertor *m;* bufanda de lana
**comforting** ['kʌmfərtɪŋ] *adj* confortante
**comfort station** *s* quiosco de necesidad
**comfrey** ['kʌmfri] *s* consuelda
**comic** ['kɑmɪk] *adj* cómico || *s* cómi-

co; (coll) periódico cómico; **comics** (coll) tiras cómicas
**comical** ['kamɪkəl] *adj* cómico
**comic book** *s* tebeo
**comic opera** *s* ópera cómica
**comic strip** *s* tira cómica
**coming** ['kʌmɪŋ] *adj* que viene, venidero; (coll) prometedor || *s* venida
**coming out** *s* (*of stocks, bonds, etc.*) emisión; (*of a young girl*) puesta de largo, entrada en sociedad
**comma** ['kamə] *s* coma
**command** [kə'mænd] o [kə'mand] *s* (*commanding*) dominio, mando; (*order, direction*) mandato, orden *f;* (*e.g., of a foreign language*) dominio; (mil) comando; **to be in command of** estar al mando de; **to take command** tomar el mando || *tr* mandar, ordenar; dominar (*un idioma extranjero*); merecer (*p.ej., respeto*); (mil) comandar || *intr* mandar
**commandant** [,kamən'dænt] o [,kamən'dant] *s* comandante *m*
**commandeer** [,kamən'dɪr] *tr* reclutar forzosamente; expropiar; (coll) apoderarse de
**commander** [kə'mændər] o [kə'mandər] *s* comandante *m;* (*of a military order*) comendador *m*
**commandment** [kə'mændmənt] o [kə'mandmənt] *s* (Bib) mandamiento
**commemorate** [kə'memə,ret] *tr* conmemorar
**commence** [kə'mens] *tr & intr* comenzar, empezar
**commencement** [kə'mensmənt] *s* comienzo, principio; día *m* de graduación; ceremonia de graduación
**commend** [kə'mend] *tr* (*to entrust*) encargar, encomendar; (*to recommend*) recomendar; (*to praise*) alabar, elogiar
**commendable** [kə'menəbəl] *adj* recomendable
**commendation** [,kamən'deʃən] *s* encargo, encomienda; recomendación; alabanza, elogio
**comment** ['kament] *s* comentario, comento || *intr* comentar; **to comment on** comentar
**commentar•y** ['kamən,teri] *s* (*pl* **-ies**) comentario
**commentator** ['kamən,tetər] *s* comentarista *mf*
**commerce** ['kamərs] *s* comercio
**commercial** [kə'mʌrʃəl] *adj* comercial || *s* anuncio publicitario radiofónico o televisivo; (rad & telv) programa publicitario
**commercial traveler** *s* agente viajero
**commiserate** [kə'mɪzə,ret] *intr* — **to commiserate with** condolerse de
**commiseration** [kə,mɪzə'reʃən] *s* conmiseración
**commissar** [,kamɪ'sar] *s* comisario (*en Rusia*)
**commissar•y** ['kamɪ,seri] *s* (*pl* **-ies**) (*deputy*) comisario; (*store*) economato
**commission** [kə'mɪʃən] *s* comisión; (mil) nombramiento; **to put in commission** poner en uso; poner (*un buque*) en servicio activo; **to put out of commission** inutilizar, descomponer; retirar (*un buque*) del servicio activo || *tr* comisionar; poner en uso; poner (*un buque*) en servicio activo; (mil) nombrar
**commissioned officer** *s* oficial *m*
**commissioner** [kə'mɪʃənər] *s* comisario; (*person authorized by a commission*) comisionado
**com•mit** [kə'mɪt] *v* (*pret & pp* **-mitted;** *ger* **-mitting**) *tr* cometer (*un crimen, una falta; un negocio a una persona*); (*to hand over*) confiar, entregar; dar, empeñar (*la palabra*); (*to bind, pledge*) comprometer; internar (*a un demente*); (*to memory*) encomendar; **to commit oneself** comprometerse, empeñarse; **to commit to writing** poner por escrito
**commitment** [kə'mɪtmənt] *s* (*act of committing*) comisión; (*to an asylum*) internación; (*written order*) auto de prisión; compromiso, cometido, empeño
**committee** [kə'mɪti] *s* comité *m,* comisión
**commode** [kə'mod] *s* (*chest of drawers*) cómoda; (*washstand*) lavabo; (*chamber pot*) sillico
**commodious** [kə'modɪ•əs] *adj* espacioso, holgado
**commodi•ty** [kə'madɪti] *s* (*pl* **-ties**) artículo de consumo, mercancía
**commodity exchange** *s* lonja, bolsa mercantil
**common** ['kamən] *adj* común || *s* campo común, ejido; **commons** estado llano; (*of a school*) refectorio; **the Commons** (Brit) los Comunes
**common carrier** *s* empresa de transportes públicos
**commoner** ['kamənər] *s* plebeyo; (Brit) miembro de la Cámara de los Comunes
**common law** *s* derecho consuetudinario
**com'mon-law' marriage** *s* matrimonio consensual
**com'mon•place'** *adj* común, trivial, ordinario || *s* lugar *m* común, trivialidad
**common sense** *s* sentido común
**com'mon-sense'** *adj* cuerdo, razonable
**common stock** *s* acción ordinaria; acciones ordinarias
**commonweal** ['kamən,wil] *s* bien público
**com'mon•wealth'** *s* estado, nación; república; (*state of U.S.A.*) estado; (*self-governing associated country*) estado libre asociado; (*association of states*) mancomunidad
**commotion** [kə'moʃən] *s* conmoción
**commune** [kə'mjun] *intr* conversar; (eccl) comulgar
**communicant** [kə'mjunɪkənt] *s* comunicante *mf;* (eccl) comulgante *mf*

**communicate** [kə'mjunɪ,ket] *tr* comunicar || *intr* comunicarse
**communicating** [kə'mjunɪ,ketɪŋ] *adj* comunicador
**communicative** [kə'mjunɪ,ketɪv] *adj* comunicativo
**communion** [kə'mjunjən] *s* comunión; **to take communion** comulgar
**communion rail** *s* comulgatorio
**communiqué** [kə,mjunɪ'ke] o [kə'mjunɪ,ke] *s* comunicado, parte *m*
**communism** ['kɑmjə,nɪzəm] *s* comunismo
**communist** ['kɑmjənɪst] *s* comunista *mf*
**communi·ty** [kə'mjunɪti] *s* (*pl* **-ties**) vecindario; (*group of people living together*) comunidad
**communize** ['kɑmjə,naɪz] *tr* comunizar
**commutation ticket** [,kɑmjə'teʃən] *s* billete *m* de abono
**commutator** ['kɑmjə,tetər] *s* (elec) colector *m*
**commute** [kə'mjut] *tr* conmutar || *intr* viajar con billete de abono
**commuter** [kə'mjutər] *s* abonado al ferrocarril
**comp.** *abbr* **compare, comparative, composer, composition, compound**
**compact** [kəm'pækt] *adj* compacto; breve, preciso || ['kɑmpækt] *s* convenio, pacto; estuche *m* de afeites
**companion** [kəm'pænjən] *s* compañero
**companionable** [kəm'pænjənəbəl] *adj* afable, sociable, simpático
**companionship** [kəm'pænjən,ʃɪp] *s* compañerismo
**companionway** [kəm'pænjən,we] *s* (naut) escalera de cámara
**compa·ny** ['kʌmpəni] *s* (*pl* **-nies**) compañía; visita, visitas, invitado, invitados; (naut) tripulación; **to be good company** ser compañero alegre; **to keep company** ir juntos (*un hombre y una mujer*); **to keep someone company** hacerle compañía a una persona; **to part company** separarse; enemistarse
**company building** *s* edificio social
**company office** *s* domicilio social
**comparative** [kəm'pærətɪv] *adj & s* comparativo
**compare** [kəm'pɛr] *s* — **beyond compare** sin comparación, sin par || *tr* comparar
**comparison** [kəm'pærɪsən] *s* comparación
**compartment** [kəm'pɑrtmənt] *s* compartimiento; (rr) departamento
**compass** ['kʌmpəs] *s* brújula, compás *m;* ámbito, recinto; alcance *m,* extensión; **compass** o **compasses** (*for drawing circles*) compás *m*
**compass card** *s* (naut) rosa náutica, rosa de los vientos
**compassion** [kəm'pæʃən] *s* compasión
**compassionate** [kəm'pæʃənɪt] *adj* compasivo
**com·pel** [kəm'pɛl] *v* (*pret & pp* **-pelled;** *ger* **-pelling**) *tr* forzar, obligar, compeler; imponer (*respeto, silencio*)
**compendious** [kəm'pɛndɪ·əs] *adj* compendioso
**compendi·um** [kəm'pɛndɪ·əm] *s* (*pl* **-ums** o **-a** [ə]) compendio
**compensate** ['kɑmpən,set] *tr & intr* compensar; **to compensate for** compensar
**compensation** [,kɑmpən'seʃən] *s* compensación
**compete** [kəm'pit] *intr* competir
**competence** ['kɑmpɪtens] o **competency** ['kɑmpɪtənsi] *s* (*aptitude; legal capacity*) competencia; (*sufficient means to live comfortably*) buen pasar *m*
**competent** ['kɑmpɪtənt] *adj* competente
**competition** [,kɑmpɪ'tɪʃən] *s* (*rivalry*) competencia; (*in a match, examination, etc.*) certamen *m,* concurso; (*in business*) concurrencia
**competitive examination** [kəm'pɛtɪtɪv] *s* oposición
**competitive prices** *spl* precios de competencia
**competitor** [kəm'pɛtɪtər] *s* competidor *m*
**compilation** [,kɑmpɪ'leʃən] *s* compilación, recopilación
**compile** [kəm'paɪl] *tr* compilar, recopilar
**complacence** [kəm'plesəns] o **complacency** [kəm'plesənsi] *s* (*quiet satisfaction*) complacencia; satisfacción de sí mismo
**complacent** [kəm'plesənt] *adj* (*willing to please*) complaciente; satisfecho de sí mismo
**complain** [kəm'plen] *intr* quejarse
**complainant** [kəm'plenənt] *s* (law) demandante *mf*
**complaint** [kəm'plent] *s* queja; (*grievance*) agravio; (*illness*) enfermedad, mal *m;* (law) demanda, querella
**complaisance** [kəm'plezəns] o ['kɑmplɪ,zæns] *s* amabilidad, cortesía
**complaisant** [kəm'plezənt] o ['kɑmplɪ,zænt] *adj* amable, cortés
**complement** ['kɑmplɪmənt] *s* complemento; (nav) dotación || ['kɑmplɪ,mɛnt] *tr* complementar
**complete** [kəm'plit] *adj* completo || *tr* completar, terminar, realizar
**completion** [kəm'pliʃən] *s* terminación, realización
**complex** [kəm'plɛks] o ['kɑmplɛks] *adj* (*not simple*) complexo; (*composite*) complejo; (*intricate*) complicado || ['kɑmplɛks] *s* complejo; (psychol) complejo; (coll) obsesión
**complexion** [kəm'plɛkʃən] *s* (*constitution*) complexión; (*texture of skin, esp. of face*) tez *f;* aspecto general, índole *f*
**compliance** [kəm'plaɪ·əns] *s* condescendencia; sumisión, rendimiento; **in compliance with** de acuerdo con, en conformidad con
**complicate** ['kɑmplɪ,ket] *tr* complicar

**complicated** ['kamplɪ,ketɪd] *adj* complicado
**complici·ty** [kəm'plɪsɪti] *s* (*pl* **-ties**) complicidad, codelincuencia
**compliment** ['kamplɪmənt] *s* (*show of courtesy*) cumplimiento; (*praise*) alabanza, halago; **compliments** saludos, recuerdos || ['kamplɪ,mɛnt] *tr* cumplimentar; alabar, halagar
**complimentary copy** [,kamplɪ'mɛntəri] *s* ejemplar *m* de cortesía
**complimentary ticket** *s* billete *m* de regalo, pase *m* de cortesía
**com·ply** [kəm'plaɪ] *v* (*pret & pp* **-plied**) *intr* conformarse; **to comply with** conformarse con, obrar de acuerdo con
**component** [kəm'ponənt] *adj* componente || *m* componente *m;* (mech) componente *f*
**compose** [kəm'poz] *tr* componer; **to be composed of** estar compuesto de
**composed** [kəm'pozd] *adj* sosegado, tranquilo
**composer** [kəm'pozər] *s* componedor *m;* (mus) compositor *m;* autor *m*
**composing stick** *s* componedor *m*
**composite** [kəm'pazɪt] *adj & s* compuesto
**composition** [,kampə'zɪʃən] *s* composición
**compositor** [kəm'pazɪtər] *s* cajista *mf,* componedor *m*
**composure** [kəm'poʒər] *s* serenidad, sosiego
**compote** ['kampot] *s* (*stewed fruit*) compota; (*dish*) compotera
**compound** ['kampaund] *adj* compuesto || *s* compuesto; (gram) vocablo compuesto || [kam'paund] *tr* componer, combinar; (*interest*) capitalizar
**comprehend** [,kamprɪ'hɛnd] *tr* comprender
**comprehensible** [,kamprɪ'hɛnsɪbəl] *adj* comprensible
**comprehension** [,kamprɪ'hɛnʃən] *s* comprensión
**comprehensive** [,kamprɪ'hɛnsɪv] *adj* comprensivo, inclusivo, completo
**compress** ['kamprɛs] *s* (med) compresa || [kəm'prɛs] *tr* comprimir
**compression** [kəm'prɛʃən] *s* compresión
**comprise o comprize** [kəm'praɪz] *tr* abarcar, comprender, incluir
**compromise** ['kamprə,maɪz] *s* (*adjustment*) componenda, transigencia, transacción; (*endangering*) comprometimiento || *tr* (*by mutual concessions*) componer, transigir; (*to endanger*) comprometer, exponer || *intr* transigir, avenirse
**comptroller** [kən'trolər] *s* contralor *m,* interventor *m*
**compulsory** [kəm'pʌlsəri] *adj* obligatorio
**compute** [kəm'pjut] *tr & intr* computar, calcular
**computer** [kəm'pjutər] *s* computador *m*
**comrade** ['kamræd] o ['kamrɪd] *s* camarada *m*
**con.** *abbr* **conclusion, consolidated, contra**
**con** [kan] *s* (*opposite opinion*) contra *m* || *v* (*pret & pp* **conned;** *ger* **conning**) *tr* leer con atención, aprender de memoria
**concave** ['kankev] o [kan'kev] *adj* cóncavo
**conceal** [kən'sil] *tr* encubrir, ocultar
**concealment** [kən'silmənt] *s* encubrimiento, ocultación; (*place*) escondite *m*
**concede** [kən'sid] *tr* conceder
**conceit** [kən'sit] *s* (*vanity*) orgullo, engreimiento; (*witty expression*) concepto, dicho ingenioso
**conceited** [kən'sitɪd] *adj* orgulloso, engreído
**conceivable** [kən'sivəbəl] *adj* concebible
**conceive** [kən'siv] *tr & intr* concebir
**concentrate** ['kansən,tret] *tr* concentrar || *intr* concentrarse; **to concentrate on o upon** reconcentrarse en
**concentric** [kən'sɛntrɪk] *adj* concéntrico
**concept** ['kansɛpt] *s* concepto
**conception** [kən'sɛpʃən] *s* concepción
**concern** [kən'sʌrn] *s* (*business establishment*) empresa, casa comercial, razón *f* social; (*worry*) inquietud, preocupación; (*relation, reference*) concernencia; (*matter*) asunto, negocio || *tr* atañer, concernir; interesar; **as concerns** respecto de; **to whom it may concern** a quien pueda interesar, a quien corresponda
**concerning** [kən'sʌrnɪŋ] *prep* respecto de, tocante a
**concert** ['kansərt] *s* concierto || [kən'sʌrt] *tr & intr* concertar
**con'cert·mas'ter** *s* concertino
**concer·to** [kən'tʃɛrto] *s* (*pl* **-tos** o **-ti** [ti]) concierto
**concession** [kən'sɛʃən] *s* concesión
**concessive** [kən'sɛsɪv] *adj* concesivo
**concierge** [,kansɪ'ʌrʒ] *s* conserje *m*
**conciliate** [kən'sɪlɪ,et] *tr* conciliar; conciliarse (*el respeto, la estima*)
**conciliatory** [kən'sɪlɪ·ə,tori] *adj* conciliador
**concise** [kən'saɪs] *adj* conciso
**conclude** [kən'klud] *tr & intr* concluir
**conclusion** [kən'kluʒən] *s* conclusión; (*of a letter*) despedida
**conclusive** [kən'klusɪv] *adj* concluyente
**concoct** [kən'kakt] *tr* confeccionar; (*a story*) forjar, inventar
**concomitant** [kən'kamɪtənt] *adj & s* concomitante *m*
**concord** ['kaŋkərd] *s* concordia; (gram, mus) concordancia
**concordance** [kən'kərdəns] *s* concordancia
**concourse** ['kaŋkors] *s* (*of people*) concurso; (*of streams*) confluencia; bulevar *m,* gran vía; (*of railroad station*) gran salón *m*

**concrete** ['kɑnkrit] o [kɑn'krit] *adj* concreto; de hormigón || *s* hormigón *m*
**concrete block** *s* bloque *m* de hormigón
**concrete mixer** *s* hormigonera, mezcladora de hormigón
**concubine** ['kɑŋkjə,baɪn] *s* concubina
**con·cur** [kən'kʌr] *v* (*pret & pp* **-curred;** *ger* **-curring**) *intr* concurrir
**concurrence** [kən'kʌrəns] *s* (*happening together*) concurrencia; (*agreement*) acuerdo
**concussion** [kən'kʌʃən] *s* concusión
**condemn** [kən'dɛm] *tr* condenar
**condemnation** [,kɑndɛm'neʃən] *s* condenación
**condense** [kən'dɛns] *tr* condensar || *intr* condensarse
**condescend** [,kɑndɪ'sɛnd] *intr* dignarse
**condescending** [,kɑndɪ'sɛndɪŋ] *adj* condescendiente con inferiores
**condescension** [,kɑndɪ'sɛnʃən] *s* dignación, aire *m* protector
**condiment** ['kɑndɪmənt] *s* condimento
**condition** [kən'dɪʃən] *s* condición; **on condition that** a condición (de) que || *tr* acondicionar
**conditional** [kən'dɪʃənəl] *adj* condicional
**condole** [kən'dol] *intr* condolerse
**condolence** [kən'doləns] *s* condolencia
**condone** [kən'don] *tr* condonar
**conduce** [kən'djus] o [kən'dus] *intr* conducir
**conducive** [kən'djusiv] o [kən'dusɪv] *adj* conducente, contribuyente
**conduct** ['kɑndʌkt] *s* conducta || [kən'dʌkt] *tr* conducir; **to conduct oneself** conducirse, comportarse
**conductor** [kən'dʌktər] *s* conductor *m*, guía *mf;* (elec & phys) conductor *m*, conductora *f;* (rr) revisor *m;* (*on trolley or bus*) cobrador *m*
**conduit** ['kɑndɪt] o ['kɑndu·ɪt] *s* canal *f* para alambres o cables
**cone** [kon] *s* cono; (*of pastry*) barquillo; (*of paper*) cucurucho
**confectioner·y** [kən'fɛkʃə,nɛri] *s* (*pl* **-ies**) (*shop*) confitería; (*sweetmeats*) dulces *mpl*, confites *mpl*, confituras
**confedera·cy** [kən'fɛdərəsi] (*pl* **-cies**) confederación; (*for unlawful purpose*) conjuración
**confederate** [kən'fɛdərɪt] *s* confederado; cómplice *mf* || [kən'fɛdə,ret] *tr* confederar || *intr* confederarse
**con·fer** [kən'fʌr] *v* (*pret & pp* **-ferred;** *ger* **-ferring**) *tr* conferir || *intr* conferenciar, consultar
**conference** ['kɑnfərəns] *s* conferencia, coloquio
**confess** [kən'fɛs] *tr* confesar || *intr* confesar, confesarse
**confession** [kən'fɛʃən] *s* confesión
**confessional** [kən'fɛʃənəl] *s* confesonario
**confession of faith** *s* profesión de fe
**confessor** [kən'fɛsər] *s* (*person who confesses*) confesante *mf;* (*Christian, esp. in spite of persecution; priest*) confesor *m*
**confide** [kən'faɪd] *tr* confiar || *intr* confiar, confiarse; **to confide in** confiarse en
**confidence** ['kɑnfɪdəns] *s* confianza; (*secret*) confidencia; **in strictest confidence** bajo la mayor reserva
**confident** ['kɑnfɪdənt] *adj* seguro || *s* confidente *m*, confidenta
**confidential** [,kɑnfɪ'dɛnʃəl] *adj* confidencial
**confine** ['kɑnfaɪn] *s* confín *m;* **the confines** los confines || [kən'faɪn] *tr* (*to keep within limits*) limitar, restringir; (*to keep shut in*) encerrar; **to be confined** estar de parto; **to be confined to bed** tener que guardar cama
**confinement** [kən'faɪnmənt] *s* limitación; encierro; parto, sobreparto
**confirm** [kən'fʌrm] *tr* confirmar
**confirmed** [kən'fʌrmd] *adj* confirmado; empedernido, inveterado
**confiscate** ['kɑnfɪs,ket] *tr* confiscar
**conflagration** [,kɑnflə'greʃən] *s* conflagración
**conflict** ['kɑnflɪkt] *s* conflicto; (*of interests, class hours, etc.*) incompatibilidad || [kən'flɪkt] *intr* chocar, desavenirse
**conflicting** [kən'flɪktɪŋ] *adj* contradictorio; (*events, appointments, class hours, etc.*) incompatible
**confluence** ['kɑnflu·əns] *s* confluencia
**conform** [kən'fɔrm] *intr* conformar, conformarse
**conformance** [kən'fɔrməns] *s* conformidad
**conformi·ty** [kən'fɔrmɪti] *s* (*pl* **-ties**) conformidad
**confound** [kɑn'faʊnd] *tr* confundir || ['kɑn'faʊnd] *tr* maldecir; **confound it!** ¡maldito sea!
**confounded** [kɑn'faʊndɪd] o ['kɑn'faʊndɪd] *adj* confundido; aborrecible; maldito
**confrere** ['kɑnfrɛr] *s* colega *m*
**confront** [kən'frʌnt] *tr* (*to face boldly*) confrontarse con, hacer frente a; (*to meet face to face*) encontrar cara a cara; (*to bring face to face; to compare*) confrontar
**confuse** [kən'fjuz] *tr* confundir
**confusion** [kən'fuʒən] *s* confusión
**confute** [kən'fjut] *tr* confutar
**Cong.** *abbr* **Congregation, Congressional**
**congeal** [kən'dʒil] *tr* congelar || *intr* congelarse
**congenial** [kən'dʒinjəl] *adj* simpático; agradable; compatible; (*having the same nature*) congenial
**congenital** [kən'dʒɛnɪtəl] *adj* congénito
**conger eel** ['kɑŋgər] *s* congrio
**congest** [kən'dʒɛst] *tr* congestionar || *intr* congestionarse
**congestion** [kən'dʒɛstʃən] *s* congestión
**congratulate** [kən'grætʃə,let] *tr* congratular, felicitar

**congratulation** [kən ˌgrætʃəˈleʃən] *s* congratulación, felicitación
**congregate** [ˈkɑŋgrɪ ˌget] *intr* congregarse
**congregation** [ˌkɑŋgrɪˈgeʃən] *s* congregación; feligresía, fieles *mf* (*de una iglesia*)
**congress** [ˈkɑŋgrɪs] *s* congreso
**congress•man** [ˈkɑŋgrɪsmən] *s* (*pl* **-men** [mən]) congresista *m*
**conical** [ˈkɑnɪkəl] *adj* cónico
**conj.** *abbr* **conjugation, conjunction**
**conjecture** [kənˈdʒɛktʃər] *s* conjetura || *tr & intr* conjeturar
**conjugal** [ˈkɑndʒəgəl] *adj* conyugal
**conjugate** [ˈkɑndʒəˌget] *tr* conjugar
**conjugation** [ˌkɑndʒəˈgeʃən] *s* conjugación
**conjunction** [kənˈdʒʌŋkʃən] *s* conjunción
**conjuration** [ˌkɑndʒəˈreʃən] *s* (*superstitious invocation*) conjuro; (*magic spell*) hechizo
**conjure** [kənˈdʒʊr] *tr* (*to appeal to solemnly*) conjurar || [ˈkʌndʒər] o [ˈkɑndʒər] *tr* (*to exorcise, drive away*) conjurar; **to conjure away** conjurar; **to conjure up** evocar; crear, suscitar (*dificultades*)
**connect** [kəˈnɛkt] *tr* conectar; asociar, relacionar || *intr* enlazarse; asociarse, relacionarse; empalmar, enlazar (*dos trenes*)
**connecting rod** *s* biela
**connection** [kəˈnɛkʃən] *s* conexión; (*relative*) pariente *mf;* (*of trains*) combinación, enlace *m*, empalme *m;* (*in subway*) correspondencia; **in connection with** con respecto a; juntamente con
**conning tower** [ˈkɑnɪŋ] *s* torreta de mando
**conniption** [kəˈnɪpʃən] *s* pataleta, berrinche *m*
**connive** [kəˈnaɪv] *intr* confabularse, estar en connivencia
**conquer** [ˈkɑŋkər] *tr* vencer; (*by force of arms*) conquistar || *intr* triunfar
**conqueror** [ˈkɑŋkərər] *s* conquistador *m*, vencedor *m*
**conquest** [ˈkɑŋkwest] *s* conquista
**conscience** [ˈkɑnʃəns] *s* conciencia; **in all conscience** en conciencia
**conscientious** [ˌkɑnʃɪˈenʃəs] *adj* concienzudo
**conscientious objector** [ɑbˈdʒɛktər] *s* objetante *m* de conciencia
**conscious** [ˈkɑnʃəs] *adj* (*aware of one's own existence*) consciente; (*deliberate*) intencional; (*self-conscious*) encogido, tímido; **to become conscious** volver en sí
**consciousness** [ˈkɑnʃəsnɪs] *s* conciencia, conocimiento
**conscript** [ˈkɑnskrɪpt] *s* conscripto || [kənˈskrɪpt] *tr* reclutar
**conscription** [kənˈskrɪpʃən] *s* conscripción
**consecrate** [ˈkɑnsɪ ˌkret] *tr* consagrar
**consecutive** [kənˈsɛkjətɪv] *adj* (*successive*) consecutivo; (*continuous*) consecuente
**consensus** [kənˈsɛnsəs] *s* consenso; **the consensus of opinion** la opinión general
**consent** [kənˈsɛnt] *s* consentimiento; **by common consent** de común acuerdo || *intr* consentir; **to consent to** consentir en
**consequence** [ˈkɑnsɪ ˌkwɛns] *s* consecuencia; aires *mpl* de importancia
**consequential** [ˌkɑnsɪˈkwɛnʃəl] *adj* consiguiente; importante; altivo, pomposo
**consequently** [ˈkɑnsɪ ˌkwɛntli] *adv* por consiguiente
**conservation** [ˌkɑnsərˈveʃən] *s* conservación
**conservatism** [kənˈsʌrvəˌtɪzəm] *s* conservadurismo
**conservative** [kənˈsʌrvətɪv] *adj* (*preservative*) conservativo; (*disposed to maintain existing views and institutions*) conservador; cauteloso, moderado || *s* preservativo; conservador *m*
**conservato•ry** [kənˈsʌrvə ˌtori] *s* (*pl* **-ries**) (*school of music*) conservatorio; (*greenhouse*) invernadero
**consider** [kənˈsɪdər] *tr* considerar
**considerable** [kənˈsɪdərəbəl] *adj* considerable
**considerate** [kənˈsɪdərɪt] *adj* considerado
**consideration** [kən ˌsɪdəˈreʃən] *s* consideración; **for a consideration** por un precio; **in consideration of** en consideración de; en cambio de; **on no consideration** bajo ningún concepto; **out of consideration for** por respeto a; **without due consideration** sin reflexión
**considering** [kənˈsɪdərɪŋ] *adv* (coll) teniendo en cuentas las circunstancias || *prep* en vista de, en razón de || *conj* en vista de que
**consign** [kənˈsaɪn] *tr* consignar
**consignee** [ˌkɑnsaɪˈni] *s* consignatario
**consignment** [kənˈsaɪnmənt] *s* consignación
**consist** [kənˈsɪst] *intr* — **to consist in** consistir en; **to consist of** consistir en, constar de
**consisten•cy** [kənˈsɪstənsi] *s* (*pl* **-cies**) (*firmness, amount of firmness*) consistencia; (*logical connection*) consecuencia
**consistent** [kənˈsɪstənt] *adj* (*holding firmly together*) consistente; (*agreeing with itself or oneself*) consecuente; **consistent with** (*in accord with*) compatible con
**consisto•ry** [kənˈsɪstəri] *s* (*pl* **-ries**) consistorio
**consolation** [ˌkɑnsəˈleʃən] *s* consolación, consuelo
**console** [ˈkɑnsol] *s* consola; mesa de consola || [kənˈsol] *tr* consolar
**consommé** [ˌkɑnsəˈme] *s* consumado, consommé *m*
**consonant** [ˈkɑnsənənt] *adj & s* consonante *f*
**consort** [ˈkɑnsɔrt] *s* consorte *mf;* embarcación que acompaña a otra ||

[kən'sɔrt] *tr* asociar || *intr* asociarse; armonizar, concordar
**consorti·um** [kən'sɔrʃɪ·əm] *s* (*pl* -a [ə]) consorcio
**conspicuous** [kən'spɪkjʊ·əs] *adj* manifiesto, claro, evidente; llamativo, vistoso, sugestivo; conspicuo, notable
**conspira·cy** [kən'spɪrəsi] *s* (*pl* -cies) conspiración, conjuración
**conspire** [kən'spaɪr] *intr* conspirar, conjurar
**constable** ['kɑnstəbəl] o ['kʌnstəbəl] *s* policía *m*, guardia *m*, alguacil *m*
**constancy** ['kɑnstənsi] *s* constancia; fidelidad
**constant** ['kɑnstənt] *adj* constante; incesante; fiel || *s* constante *f*
**constellation** [ˌkɑnstə'leʃən] *s* constelación
**constipate** ['kɑnstɪˌpet] *tr* estreñir
**constipation** [ˌkɑnstɪ'peʃən] *s* estreñimiento
**constituen·cy** [kən'stɪtʃʊ·ənsi] *s* (*pl* -cies) votantes *mpl;* clientela; comitentes *mpl;* distrito electoral
**constituent** [kən'stɪtʃʊ·ənt] *adj* constitutivo, componente; (*having power to create or revise a constitution*) constituyente || *s* constitutivo, componente *m;* (*person who appoints another to act for him*) comitente *m*
**constitute** ['kɑnstɪˌtjut] o ['kɑnstɪˌtut] *tr* constituir
**constitution** [ˌkɑnstɪ'tjuʃən] o [ˌkɑnstɪ'tuʃən] *s* constitución
**constrain** [kən'stren] *tr* constreñir; detener, encerrar; restringir
**construct** [kən'strʌkt] *tr* construir
**construction** [kən'strʌkʃən] *s* construcción; interpretación
**construe** [kən'stru] *tr* interpretar; deducir, inferir; traducir; (*to combine syntactically*) construir; (*to explain the syntax of*) analizar
**consul** ['kɑnsəl] *s* cónsul *m*
**consular** ['kɑnsələr] o ['kɑnsjələr] *adj* consular
**consulate** ['kɑnsəlɪt] o ['kɑnsjəlɪt] *s* consulado
**consulship** ['kɑnsəlˌʃɪp] *s* consulado
**consult** [kən'sʌlt] *tr & intr* consultar
**consultant** [kən'sʌltənt] *s* consultor *m*
**consultation** [ˌkɑnsəl'teʃən] *s* (*consulting*) consulta; (*meeting*) consulta, consultación
**consume** [kən'sum] o [kən'sjum] *tr* consumir; (*to absorb the interest of*) preocupar; || *intr* consumirse
**consumer** [kən'sumər] o [kən'sjumər] *s* consumidor *m;* (*of gas, electricity, etc.*) abonado
**consumer credit** *s* crédito consuntivo
**consumer goods** *spl* bienes *mpl* de consumo
**consummate** [kən'sʌmɪt] *adj* consumado || ['kɑnsəˌmet] *tr* consumar
**consumption** [kən'sʌmpʃən] *s* consunción, consumo; (pathol) consunción, tisis *f*
**consumptive** [kən'sʌmptɪv] *adj* consuntivo; (path) tísico || *s* tísico
**cont.** *abbr* contents, continental, continued
**contact** ['kɑntækt] *s* contacto; (elec) contacto; (elec) toma de corriente || *tr* (coll) ponerse en contacto con || *intr* contactar
**contact breaker** *s* (elec) ruptor *m*
**contact lens** *s* lente *m* de contacto, lente invisible
**contagion** [kən'tedʒən] *s* contagio
**contagious** [kən'tedʒəs] *adj* contagioso
**contain** [kən'ten] *tr* contener; **to contain oneself** contenerse, refrenarse
**container** [kən'tenər] *s* continente *m*, recipiente *m*, vaso, caja, envase *m*
**containment** [kən'tenmənt] *s* contención, refrenamiento
**contaminate** [kən'tæmɪˌnet] *tr* contaminar
**contamination** [kənˌtæmɪ'neʃən] *s* contaminación
**contd.** *abbr* continued
**contemplate** ['kɑntəmˌplet] *tr & intr* contemplar; pensar, proyectar
**contemplation** [ˌkɑntəm'pleʃən] *s* contemplación; intención, propósito
**contemporaneous** [kənˌtɛmpə'renɪ·əs] *adj* contemporáneo
**contemporar·y** [kən'tɛmpəˌreri] *adj* contemporáneo, coetáneo || *s* (*pl* -ies) contemporáneo, coetáneo
**contempt** [kən'tɛmpt] *s* desprecio; (law) contumacia
**contemptible** [kən'tɛmptɪbəl] *adj* despreciable
**contemptuous** [kən'tɛmptʃʊ·əs] *adj* despreciativo, desdeñoso
**contend** [kən'tɛnd] *tr* sostener, mantener || *intr* contender
**contender** [kən'tɛndər] *s* contendiente *mf*, concurrente *mf*
**content** [kən'tɛnt] *adj & s* contento || ['kɑntɛnt] *s* contenido; **contents** contenido || [kən'tɛnt] *tr* contentar
**contented** [kən'tɛntɪd] *adj* contento, satisfecho
**contentedness** [kən'tɛndɪdnɪs] *s* contentamiento, satisfacción
**contention** [kən'tɛnʃən] *s* (*strife; dispute*) contención; (*point argued for*) argumento
**contentious** [kən'tɛnʃəs] *adj* contencioso
**contentment** [kən'tɛntmənt] *s* contentamiento, contento
**contest** ['kɑntɛst] *s* (*struggle, fight*) contienda; (*competition*) competencia, concurso || [kən'tɛst] *tr* disputar; tratar de conseguir || *intr* contender
**contestant** [kən'tɛstənt] *s* contendiente *mf*
**context** ['kɑntɛkst] *s* contexto
**contiguous** [kən'tɪgjʊ·əs] *adj* contiguo
**continence** ['kɑntɪnəns] *s* continencia
**continent** ['kɑntɪnənt] *adj & s* continente *m;* **the Continent** la Europa continental
**continental** [ˌkɑntɪ'nɛntəl] *adj* continental || **Continental** *s* habitante *mf* del continente europeo

**contingen•cy** [kən'tɪndʒənsi] *s* (*pl* **-cies**) contingencia
**contingent** [kən'tɪndʒənt] *adj* & *s* contingente *m*
**continual** [kən'tɪnjʊ•əl] *adj* continuo
**continue** [kən'tɪnjʊ] *tr* & *intr* continuar; **to be continued** continuará
**continui•ty** [,kɑntɪ'nju•ɪti] o [,kɑntɪ'nu•ɪti] *s* (*pl* **-ties**) continuidad; (mov, rad, telv) guión *m;* (rad, telv) comentarios o anuncios entre las partes de un programa
**continuous** [kən'tɪnjʊ•əs] *adj* continuo
**continuous showing** *s* (mov) sesión continua
**continuous waves** *spl* (rad) ondas entretenidas
**contortion** [kən'tɔrʃən] *s* contorsión
**contour** ['kɑntʊr] *s* contorno
**contr.** *abbr* **contracted, contraction**
**contraband** ['kɑntrə,bænd] *adj* contrabandista || *s* contrabando
**contrabass** ['kɑntrə,bes] *s* contrabajo
**contraceptive** [,kɑntrə'septɪv] *adj* & *s* anticonceptivo, contraceptivo
**contract** ['kɑntrækt] *s* contrato || ['kɑntrækt] o [kən'trækt] *tr* contraer (*p.ej., matrimonio*) || *intr* (*to shrink*) contraerse; (*to enter into an agreement*) comprometerse; **to contract for** contratar
**contraction** [kən'trækʃən] *s* contracción
**contractor** [kən'træktər] *s* contratista *mf*
**contradict** [,kɑntrə'dɪkt] *tr* contradecir
**contradiction** [,kɑntrə'dɪkʃən] *s* contradicción
**contradictory** [,kɑntrə'dɪktəri] *adj* (*involving contradiction*) contradictorio; (*inclined to contradict*) contradictor
**contrail** ['kɑn,trel] *s* (aer) estela de vapor, rastro de condensación
**contral•to** [kən'trælto] *s* (*pl* **-tos**) (*person*) contralto *mf;* (*voice*) contralto *m*
**contraption** [kən'træpʃən] *s* (coll) artilugio, dispositivo
**contra•ry** ['kɑntreri] *adv* contrariamente || *adj* contrario || [kən'treri] *adj* obstinado, terco || ['kɑntreri] *s* (*pl* **-ries**) contrario; **on the contrary** al contrario
**contrast** ['kɑntræst] *s* contraste *m* || [kən'træst] *tr* comparar; poner en contraste || *intr* contrastar
**contravene** [,kɑntrə'vin] *tr* contradecir; contravenir a (*una ley*)
**contribute** [kən'trɪbjʊt] *tr* contribuir || *intr* contribuir; (*to a newspaper, conference, etc.*) colaborar
**contribution** [,kɑntrɪ'bjuʃən] *s* contribución; (*to a newspaper, conference, etc.*) colaboración
**contributor** [kən'trɪbjʊtər] *s* contribuidor *m,* contribuyente *mf;* colaborador *m*
**contrite** [kən'traɪt] *adj* contrito
**contrition** [kən'trɪʃən] *s* contrición
**contrivance** [kən'traɪvəns] *s* aparato, dispositivio; idea, plan *m,* designio
**contrive** [kən'traɪv] *tr* (*to devise*) idear, inventar; (*to scheme up*) maquinar, tramar; (*to bring about*) efectuar || *intr* maquinar; **to contrive to** + *inf* ingeniarse a + *inf*
**con•trol** [kən'trol] *s* gobierno, mando; (*of a scientific experiment*) contrarregistro, control *m;* **controls** mandos; **to get under control** conseguir dominar (*un incendio*) || *v* (*pret* & *pp* **-trolled;** *ger* **-trolling**) *tr* gobernar, mandar; comprobar, controlar; **to control oneself** dominarse
**controlling interest** *s* (el) mayor porcentaje de acciones
**control panel** *s* (aer) tablero de instrumentos
**control stick** *s* (aer) mango de escoba, palanca de mando
**controversial** [,kɑntrə'vʌrʃəl] *adj* controvertible, disputable; disputador
**controver•sy** ['kɑntrə,vʌrsi] *s* (*pl* **-sies**) controversia, polémica
**controvert** ['kɑntrə,vʌrt] o [,kɑntrə'vʌrt] *tr* (*to argue against*) contradecir; (*to argue about*) controvertir
**contumacious** [,kɑntjʊ'meʃəs] o [,kɑntʊ'meʃəs] *adj* contumaz
**contuma•cy** ['kɑntjʊməsi] o ['kɑntʊməsi] *s* (*pl* **-cies**) contumacia
**contume•ly** ['kɑntjʊmɪli] o ['kɑntʊmɪli] *s* (*pl* **-lies**) contumelia
**contusion** [kən'tjuʒən] o [kən'tuʒən] *s* contusión
**conundrum** [kə'nʌndrəm] *s* acertijo, adivinanza; problema complicado
**convalesce** [,kɑnvə'lɛs] *intr* convalecer
**convalescence** [,kɑnvə'lɛsəns] *s* convalecencia
**convalescent** [,kɑnvə'lɛsənt] *adj* & *s* convaleciente *mf*
**convalescent home** *s* clínica de reposo
**convene** [kən'vin] *tr* convocar || *intr* convenir, reunirse
**convenience** [kən'vinjəns] *s* comodidad, conveniencia; **at your earliest convenience** a la primera oportunidad que Vd. tenga
**convenient** [kən'vinjənt] *adj* cómodo, conveniente; próximo
**convent** ['kɑnvent] *s* convento; convento de religiosas
**convention** [kən'venʃən] *s* (*agreement*) convención, conveniencia; (*accepted usage*) costumbre *f,* conveniencia social, convención; (*meeting*) congreso, convención
**conventional** [kən'venʃənəl] *adj* convencional
**conventionali•ty** [kən,venʃə'nælɪti] *s* (*pl* **-ties**) precedente *m* convencional
**converge** [kən'vʌrd] *intr* convergir
**conversant** [kən'vʌrsənt] *adj* familiarizado, versado
**conversation** [,kɑnvər'seʃən] *s* conversación
**conversational** [,kɑnvər'seʃənəl] *adj* conversacional
**converse** ['kɑnvʌrs] *adj* & *s* contrario || [kən'vʌrs] *intr* conversar
**conversion** [kən'vʌrʒən] *s* conversión;

(*unlawful appropriation*) malversación
**convert** ['kɑnvʌrt] *s* convertido, converso ‖ [kən'vʌrt] *tr* convertir ‖ *intr* convertirse
**convertible** [kən'vʌrtɪbəl] *adj* convertible ‖ *s* (aut) convertible *m*, descapotable *m*
**convex** ['kɑnvɛks] o [kɑn'vɛks] *adj* convexo
**convey** [kən've] *tr* llevar, transportar; comunicar, participar (*informes*); transferir, traspasar (*bienes de una persona a otra*)
**conveyance** [kən've·əns] *s* transporte *m;* comunicación, participación; vehículo; (*transfer of property*) traspaso; escritura de traspaso
**convict** ['kɑnvɪkt] *s* reo convicto, presidiario ‖ [kən'vɪkt] *tr* probar la culpabilidad de; declarar convicto (*a un acusado*)
**conviction** [kən'vɪkʃən] *s* convencimiento; condena, fallo de culpabilidad
**convince** [kən'vɪns] *tr* convencer
**convincing** [kən'vɪnsɪŋ] *adj* convincente
**convivial** [kən'vɪvɪ·əl] *adj* jovial
**convocation** [,kɑnvə'keʃən] *s* asamblea
**convoke** [kən'vok] *tr* convocar
**convoy** ['kɑnvɔɪ] *s* convoy *m*, conserva ‖ *tr* convoyar
**convulse** [kən'vʌls] *tr* convulsionar; agitar; **to convulse with laughter** mover a risas convulsivas
**coo** [ku] *intr* arrullar
**cook** [kʊk] *s* cocinero ‖ *tr* cocer, cocinar, guisar; **to cook up** (coll) falsificar; (coll) maquinar, tramar ‖ *intr* cocer, cocinar
**cook'book'** *s* libro de cocina
**cookie** ['kʊki] *s* var de **cooky**
**cooking** ['kʊkɪŋ] *s* cocina, arte *m* de cocinar
**cook'stove'** *s* cocina económica
**cook·y** ['kʊki] *s* (*pl* **-ies**) pasta seca, pastelito dulce
**cool** [kul] *adj* fresco; frío, indiferente ‖ *s* fresco ‖ *tr* refrescar; moderar ‖ *intr* refrescarse; moderarse; **to cool off** refrescarse; serenarse
**cooler** ['kulər] *s* heladera, refrigerador *m;* refrigerante *m;* (coll) cárcel *f*
**cool'-head'ed** *adj* sereno, tranquilo, juicioso
**coolie** ['kuli] *s* culí *m*
**coolish** ['kulɪʃ] *adj* fresquito
**coolness** ['kulnɪs] *s* fresco, frescura; (fig) frialdad
**coon** [kun] *s* mapache *m*, oso lavandero
**coop** [kup] *s* gallinero; (*for fattening capons*) caponera; jaula, redil *m;* (*jail*) (slang) caponera; **to fly the coop** (slang) escabullirse ‖ *tr* encerrar en un gallinero; enjaular; **to coop up** emparedar
**coöp.** *abbr* **cooperative**
**cooper** ['kupər] *s* barrilero, tonelero
**coöperate** [ko'ɑpə,ret] *intr* cooperar
**coöperation** [ko,ɑpə'reʃən] *s* cooperación
**coöperative** [ko'ɑpə,retɪv] *adj* cooperativo
**coördinate** [ko'ɔrdɪnɪt] *adj* coordenado; (gram) coordinante ‖ *s* (math) coordenada ‖ [ko'ɔrdɪ,net] *tr & intr* coordinar
**cootie** ['kuti] *s* (slang) piojo
**cop** [kɑp] *s* (slang) polizonte *m* ‖ *v* (*pret & pp* **copped;** *ger* **copping**) *tr* (slang) hurtar
**copartner** [ko'pɑrtnər] *s* consocio, copartícipe *mf*
**cope** [kop] *intr* — **to cope with** hacer frente a, enfrentarse con
**cope'stone'** *s* piedra de albardilla
**copier** ['kɑpɪ·ər] *s* (*person who copies*) copiante *mf*, copista *mf;* imitador *m;* (*apparatus*) copiador *m*
**copilot** ['ko,paɪlət] *s* copiloto
**coping** ['kopɪŋ] *s* albardilla
**copious** ['kopɪ·əs] *adj* copioso
**copper** ['kɑpər] *adj* cobreño; (*in color*) cobrizo ‖ *s* cobre *m;* (*coin*) calderilla, vellón *m;* (slang) polizonte *m*
**cop'per·head'** *s* víbora de cabeza de cobre
**cop'per·smith'** *s* cobrero
**coppery** ['kɑpəri] *adj* cobreño; (*in color*) cobrizo
**coppice** ['kɑpɪs] o **copse** [kɑps] *s* soto, monte bajo
**copulate** ['kɑpjə,let] *intr* copularse
**cop·y** ['kɑpi] *s* (*pl* **-ies**) copia; (*of a book*) ejemplar *m;* (*of a magazine*) número; (*document to be reproduced in print*) original *m*, manuscrito ‖ *v* (*pret & pp* **-ied**) *tr* copiar
**cop'y·book'** *s* cuaderno de escritura
**copyist** ['kɑpɪ·ɪst] *s* copiante *mf*, copista *mf;* imitador *m*
**cop'y·right'** *s* (derechos de) propiedad literaria ‖ *tr* registrar en el registro de la propiedad literaria
**copy writer** *s* escritor publicitario
**co·quet** [ko'kɛt] *v* (*pret & pp* **-quetted;** *ger* **-quetting**) *intr* coquetear; burlarse
**coquet·ry** ['kokətri] o [ko'kɛtri] *s* (*pl* **-ries**) coquetería; burla
**coquette** [ko'kɛt] *s* coqueta
**coquettish** [ko'kɛtɪʃ] *adj* coqueta
**cor.** *abbr* **corner, coroner, correction, corresponding**
**coral** ['kɑrəl] o ['kɔrəl] *adj* coralino ‖ *s* coral *m*
**coral reef** *s* arrecife *m* de coral
**cord** [kɔrd] *s* cordón *m* ‖ *tr* acordonar
**cordial** ['kɔrdʒəl] *adj* cordial ‖ *s* licor tónico; (*stimulating medicine*) cordial *m*
**cordiali·ty** [kɔr'dʒælɪti] *s* (*pl* **-ties**) cordialidad
**corduroy** ['kɔrdə,rɔɪ] *s* pana; **corduroys** pantalones *mpl* de pana
**core** [kor] *s* corazón *m;* (*of an electromagnet*) núcleo
**corespondent** [,korɪs'pɑndənt] *s* cóm-

plice *mf* del demandado en juicio de divorcio
**Corinth** ['kɑrɪnθ] o ['kɔrɪnθ] *s* Corinto *f*
**cork** [kɔrk] *s* corcho; corcho, tapón *m* de corcho; tapón (*de cualquier materia*) || *tr* encorchar, tapar con corcho
**corking** ['kɔrkɪŋ] *adj* (slang) brutal, extraordinario
**cork oak** *s* alcornoque *m*
**cork'screw'** *s* sacacorchos *m*, tirabuzón *m*
**cormorant** ['kɔrmərənt] *s* cormorán *m*, cuervo marino
**corn** [kɔrn] *s* (*in U.S.A.*) maíz *m;* (*in England*) trigo; (*in Scotland*) avena; grano (*de maíz, trigo*); (*on the foot*) callo; (coll) aguardiente *m;* (slang) trivialidad
**corn bread** *s* pan *m* de maíz
**corn'cake'** *s* tortilla de maíz
**corn'cob'** *s* mazorca de maíz, carozo
**corncob pipe** *s* pipa de fumar hecha de una mazorca de maíz
**corn'crib'** *s* granero para maíz
**corn cure** *s* callicida *m*
**cornea** ['kɔrnɪ·ə] *s* córnea
**corner** ['kɔrnər] *s* ángulo; (*esp. where two streets meet*) esquina; (*inside angle formed by two or more surfaces; secluded place; region, quarter*) rincón *m;* (*of eye*) comisura, rabillo; (*of lips*) comisura; (*awkward position*) apuro, aprieto; monopolio; **around the corner** a la vuelta de la esquina; **to turn the corner** doblar la esquina; pasar el punto más peligroso || *tr* arrinconar; monopolizar
**corner cupboard** *s* rinconera
**corner room** *s* habitación de esquina
**cor'ner·stone'** *s* piedra angular; (*of a new building*) primera piedra
**cornet** [kɔr'nɛt] *s* corneta
**corn exchange** *s* bolsa de granos
**corn'field'** *s* (*in U.S.A.*) maizal *m;* (*in England*) trigal *m;* (*in Scotland*) avenal *m*
**corn flour** *s* harina de maíz
**corn'flow'er** *s* cabezuela
**corn'husk'** *s* perfolla
**cornice** ['kɔrnɪs] *s* cornisa
**Cornish** ['kɔrnɪʃ] *adj* & *s* córnico
**corn liquor** *s* chicha
**corn meal** *s* harina de maíz
**corn on the cob** *s* maíz *m* en la mazorca
**corn plaster** *s* emplasto para los callos
**corn silk** *s* cabellos, barbas del maíz
**corn'stalk'** *s* tallo de maíz
**corn'starch'** *s* almidón *m* de maíz
**cornucopia** [,kɔrnə'kopɪ·ə] *s* cornucopia
**Cornwall** ['kɔrn,wɔl] o ['kɔrnwəl] *s* Cornualles
**corn·y** ['kɔrni] *adj* (*comp* **-ier**; *super* **-iest**) de maíz; (coll) gastado, trivial, pesado
**corollar·y** ['kɑrə,lɛri] o ['kɔrə,lɛri] *s* (*pl* **-ies**) corolario
**coronation** [,kɑrə'neʃən] o [,kɔrə'neʃən] *s* coronación
**coroner** ['kɑrənər] o ['kɔrənər] *s* juez *m* de guardia
**coroner's inquest** *s* pesquisa dirigida por el juez de guardia
**coronet** ['kɑrə,nɛt] o ['kɔrə,nɛt] *s* (*worn by members of nobility*) corona; (*ornamental band of jewels worn on head*) diadema *f*
**Corp.** *abbr* **Corporation**
**corporal** ['kɔrpərəl] *adj* corporal || *s* (mil) cabo
**corporation** [,kɔrpə'reʃən] *s* (*provincial, municipal, or service entity*) corporación; sociedad anónima por acciones
**corps** [kor] *s* (*pl* **corps** [korz]) cuerpo; (mil) cuerpo
**corps de ballet** [kɔr də bæ'le] *s* cuerpo de baile
**corpse** [kɔrps] *s* cadáver *m*
**corpulent** ['kɔrpjələnt] *adj* corpulento
**corpuscle** ['kɔrpəsəl] *s* corpúsculo, partícula; (physiol) glóbulo
**corr.** *abbr* **correspondence, corresponding**
**cor·ral** [kə'ræl] *s* corral *m* || *v* (*pret* & *pp* **-ralled**; *ger* **-ralling**) *tr* acorralar
**correct** [kə'rɛkt] *adj* correcto; (*proper*) cumplido || *tr* corregir
**correction** [kə'rɛkʃən] *s* corrección
**corrective** [kə'rɛktɪv] *adj* & *s* correctivo
**correctness** [kə'rɛktnɪs] *s* corrección; cumplimiento, cumplido
**correlate** ['kɑrə,let] o ['kɔrə,let] *tr* correlacionar || *intr* correlacionarse
**correlation** [,kɑrə'leʃən] o [,kɔrə'leʃən] *s* correlación
**correlative** [kə'rɛlətɪv] *adj* & *s* correlativo
**correspond** [,kɑrɪ'spɑnd] o [,kɔrɪ'spɑnd] *intr* corresponder; (*to communicate by writing*) corresponderse
**correspondence** [,kɑrɪ'spɑndəns] o [,kɔrɪ'spɑndəns] *s* correspondencia
**correspondence school** *s* escuela por correspondencia
**correspondent** [,kɑrɪ'spɑndənt] o [,kɔrɪ'spɑndənt] *adj* correspondiente || *s* correspondiente *mf;* (*for a newspaper*) corresponsal *mf*
**corresponding** [,kɑrɪ'spɑndɪŋ] o [,kɔrɪ'spɑndɪŋ] *adj* correspondiente
**corridor** ['kɑrɪdər] o ['kɔrɪdər] *s* corredor *m*, pasillo
**corroborate** [kə'rɑbə,ret] *tr* corroborar
**corrode** [kə'rod] *tr* corroer || *intr* corroerse
**corrosion** [kə'roʒən] *s* corrosión
**corrosive** [kə'rosɪv] *adj* & *s* corrosivo
**corrugated** ['kɑrə,getɪd] o ['kɔrə,getɪd] *adj* acanalado, ondulado
**corrupt** [kə'rʌpt] *adj* corrompido || *tr* corromper || *intr* corromperse
**corruption** [kə'rʌpʃən] *s* corrupción
**corsage** [kɔr'sɑʒ] *s* (*bodice*) corpiño, jubón *m;* (*bouquet*) ramillete *m* que se lleva en el pecho o la cintura
**corsair** ['kɔr,sɛr] *s* corsario
**corset** ['kɔrsɪt] *s* corsé *m*
**corset cover** *s* cubrecorsé *m*

**Corsica** ['kɔrsɪkə] *s* Córcega
**Corsican** ['kɔrsɪkən] *adj & s* corso
**cortege** [kɔr'teʒ] *s* procesión; (*retinue*) cortejo, séquito
**cor•tex** ['kɔr,teks] *s* (*pl* **-tices** [tɪ,siz]) corteza; corteza cerebral
**cortisone** ['kɔrtɪ,son] *s* cortisona
**corvette** [kɔr'vet] *s* corbeta
**cosmetic** [kɑz'metɪk] *adj & s* cosmético
**cosmic** ['kɑzmɪk] *adj* cósmico
**cosmonaut** ['kɑzmə,nɔt] *s* cosmonauta *mf*
**cosmopolitan** [,kɑzmə'pɑlɪtən] *adj & s* cosmopolita *mf*
**cosmos** ['kɑzməs] *s* cosmos *m;* (bot) cosmos
**Cossack** ['kɑ,sæk] *adj & s* cosaco
**cost** [kɔst] o [kɑst] *s* coste *m,* costo; **at cost** a coste y costas; **at all costs** a toda costa; **costs** (law) costas || *v* (*pret & pp* **cost**) *intr* costar; **cost what it may** cueste lo que cueste
**cost accounting** *s* escandallo
**Costa Rican** ['kɑstə 'rikən] o ['kɔste 'rikən] *adj & s* costarricense *mf,* costarriqueño
**cost, insurance, and freight** costo, seguro y flete
**cost•ly** ['kɔstli] o ['kɑstli] *adj* (*comp* **-lier;** *super* **-liest**) costoso, dispendioso; (*lavish*) pródigo; (*magnificent*) suntuoso
**cost of living** *s* costo de la vida, carestía de la vida
**costume** ['kɑstjum] o ['kɑstum] *s* traje *m;* (*garb worn on stage, at balls, etc.*) disfraz *m,* traje de época
**costume ball** *s* baile *m* de trajes
**costume jewelry** *s* joyas de fantasía, bisutería
**cot** [kɑt] *s* catre *m*
**coterie** ['kotəri] *s* círculo, grupo; (*clique*) corrillo
**cottage** ['kɑtɪdʒ] *s* cabaña; casita de campo
**cottage cheese** *s* naterón *m,* requesón *m*
**cotter pin** ['kɑtər] *s* chaveta
**cotton** ['kɑtən] *s* algodón *m* || *intr* — **to cotton up to** (coll) aficionarse a
**cotton field** *s* algodonal *m*
**cotton gin** *s* desmotadera de algodón
**cotton picker** ['pɪkər] *s* recogedor *m* de algodón; máquina para recolectar el algodón
**cot'ton•seed'** *s* semilla de algodón
**cottonseed oil** *s* aceite *m* de algodón
**cotton waste** *s* hilacha de algodón, estopa de algodón
**cot'ton•wood'** *s* chopo del Canadá, chopo de Virginia
**cottony** ['kɑtəni] *adj* algodonoso
**couch** [kaʊtʃ] *s* canapé *m,* sofá *m* || *tr* expresar
**cougar** ['kugər] *s* puma *m*
**cough** [kɔf] o [kɑf] *s* tos *f* || *tr* — **to cough up** arrojar por la boca; (slang) sudar, entregar || *intr* toser; (*artificially, to attract attention*) destoserse
**cough drop** *s* pastilla para la tos
**cough syrup** *s* jarabe *m* para la tos
**could** [kʊd] *v aux* pude, podía; podría
**council** ['kaʊnsəl] *s* (*deliberative or legislative assembly*) consejo; (*of a municipality*) concejo; (eccl) concilio
**council•man** ['kaʊnsəlmən] *s* (*pl* **-men** [mən]) concejal *m*
**councilor** ['kaʊnsələr] *s* consejero
**coun•sel** ['kaʊnsəl] *s* consejo; (*advisor*) consejero; (*consultant*) consultor *m;* (*lawyer*) abogado consultor; **to keep one's own counsel** no revelar sus intenciones || *v* (*pret & pp* **-seled** o **-selled;** *ger* **-seling** o **-selling**) *tr* aconsejar || *intr* aconsejarse
**counselor** ['kaʊnsələr] *s* consejero; abogado
**count** [kaʊnt] *s* (*act of counting*) cuenta, recuento; (*result of counting*) suma, total *m;* (*nobleman*) conde *m;* (*charge*) (law) cargo; **to take the count** (box) dejarse contar diez || *tr* contar; **to count off** separar contando; **to count out** no incluir; (sport) declarar vencido || *intr* contar; (*to be worth consideration*) valer; **to count for** valer; **to count on** contar con
**countable** ['kaʊntəbəl] *adj* contable
**count'-down'** *s* cuenta a cero
**countenance** ['kaʊntɪnəns] *s* cara, rostro, semblante *m;* (*composure*) compostura, serenidad; **to keep one's countenance** contenerse; **to lose countenance** conturbarse; **to put out of countenance** avergonzar, confundir || *tr* aprobar, apoyar, favorecer
**counter** ['kaʊntər] *adj* contrario || *adv* en el sentido opuesto; **counter to** a contrapelo de || *s* contador *m;* (*piece of wood or metal for keeping score*) ficha; (*board in shop over which business is transacted*) mostrador *m;* (box) contragolpe *m* || *tr* oponerse a; contradecir || *intr* (box) dar un contragolpe; **to counter with** replicar con
**coun'ter•act'** *tr* contrarrestar, contrariar
**coun'ter•attack'** *s* contraataque *m* || **coun'ter•attack'** *tr & intr* contraatacar
**coun'ter•bal'ance** *s* contrabalanza, contrapeso || **coun'ter•bal'ance** *tr* contrabalancear, contrapesar
**coun'ter•clock'wise'** *adj & adv* en el sentido contrario al de las agujas del reloj
**coun'ter•es'pionage** *s* contraespionaje *m*
**counterfeit** ['kaʊntərfɪt] *adj* contrahecho, falsificado || *s* contrahechura, falsificación; moneda falsa || *tr* contrahacer, falsificar
**counterfeiter** ['kaʊntər,fɪtər] *s* contrahacedor *m,* falsificador *m;* monedero falso
**counterfeit money** *s* moneda falsa
**countermand** ['kaʊndər,mænd] o ['kaʊntər,mɑnd] *s* contramandato || *tr* contramandar; hacer volver

**coun'ter·march'** *s* contramarcha || *intr* contramarchar
**coun'ter·offen'sive** *s* contraofensiva
**coun'ter·pane'** *s* cubrecama
**coun'ter·part'** *s* contraparte *f;* copia, duplicado
**coun'ter·plot'** *s* contratreta || *v* (*pret & pp* **-plotted;** *ger* **-plotting**) *tr* complotar contra (*la treta de otro u otros*)
**coun'ter·point'** *s* contrapunto
**Counter Reformation** *s* Contrarreforma
**coun'ter·rev'olu'sion** *s* contrarrevolución
**coun'ter·sign'** *s* contraseña || *tr* refrendar
**coun'ter·sink'** *v* (*pret & pp* **-sunk**) *tr* avellanar
**coun'ter·spy'** *s* (*pl* **-spies**) contraespía *mf*
**coun'ter·stroke'** *s* contragolpe *m*
**coun'ter·weight'** *s* contrapeso
**countess** ['kauntɪs] *s* condesa
**countless** ['kauntlɪs] *adj* incontable, innumerable
**countrified** ['kʌntrɪ,faɪd] *adj* campesino, rústico
**coun·try** ['kʌntri] *s* (*pl* **-tries**) (*territory of a nation*) país *m;* (*land of one's birth*) patria; (*not the city*) campo
**country club** *s* club *m* campestre
**country cousin** *s* isidro
**country estate** *s* heredad, hacienda de campo
**coun'try·folk'** *s* gente *f* del campo, campesinos
**country gentleman** *s* propietario acomodado de finca rural
**country house** *s* casa de campo, quinta
**country jake** [dʒek] *s* (coll) patán *m*
**country life** *s* vida rural
**country·man** ['kʌntrimən] *s* (*pl* **-men** [mən]) compatriota *m;* campesino
**country people** *s* gente *f* del campo, gente de capa parda
**coun'try·side'** *s* campiña
**coun'try·wide'** *adj* nacional
**country·woman** ['kʌntrɪ,wumən] *s* (*pl* **-women** [,wɪmɪn]) compatriota *f;* campesina
**coun·ty** ['kaunti] *s* (*pl* **-ties**) (*small political unit*) partido; (*domain of a count*) condado
**county seat** *s* cabeza de partido
**coup** [ku] *s* golpe *m*
**coup de grâce** [ku də 'grɑs] *s* puñalada de misericordia, golpe *m* de gracia
**coup d'état** [ku de'tɑ] *s* golpe *m* de estado
**coupé** [ku'pe] *s* cupé *m*
**couple** ['kʌpəl] *s* par *m;* (*man and wife*) matrimonio; (*two people dancing together*) pareja; (elec, mech) par *m;* (*two more or less*) (coll) par *m* || *tr* acoplar, juntar, unir || *intr* juntarse, unirse
**coupler** ['kʌplər] *s* (rr) enganche *m*
**couplet** ['kʌplɪt] *s* copla, pareado
**coupon** ['ku'pɑn] o ['kju'pɑn] *s* (*of a bond*) cupón *m;* (*piece detached from larger piece*) talón *m*
**courage** ['kʌrɪdʒ] *s* valor *m,* ánimo; firmeza, resolución; **to have the courage of one's convictions** ajustarse abiertamente con su conciencia; **to pluck up courage** hacer de tripas corazón
**courageous** [kə'redʒəs] *adj* valiente, animoso
**courier** ['kʌrɪ·ər] o ['kurɪ·ər] *s* estafeta, mensajero; guía *m*
**course** [kors] *s* (*onward movement*) curso; (*of a ship*) derrota, rumbo; (*of time*) transcurso; (*of events*) marcha; (*in school*) asignatura, curso; (*of a meal*) plato; campo de golf; (mas) hilada; **in the course of** en el decurso de; **of course** por supuesto, naturalmente
**court** [kort] *s* (*of justice*) tribunal *m;* (*of a king*) corte *f;* (*open space enclosed by a building*) atrio, patio; (*for tennis*) cancha, pista; **to pay court to** hacer la corte a || *tr* cortejar; buscar, solicitar
**courteous** ['kʌrtɪ·əs] *adj* cortés
**courtesan** ['kʌrtɪzən] o ['kortɪzən] *s* cortesana
**courte·sy** ['kʌrtɪsi] *s* (*pl* **-sies**) cortesía
**court'house'** *s* palacio de justicia
**courtier** ['kortɪ·ər] *s* cortesano, palaciego
**court jester** *s* bufón *m*
**court·ly** ['kortli] *adj* (*comp* **-lier;** *super* **-liest**) cortés, cortesano; (*pertaining to the court*) cortesano
**court'-mar'tial** *s* (*pl* **courts-martial**) consejo de guerra || *v* (*pret & pp* **-tialed** o **-tialled;** *ger* **-tialing** o **-tialling**) *tr* someter a consejo de guerra
**court plaster** *s* tafetán *m* inglés
**court'room'** *s* sala de justicia, tribunal *m*
**courtship** ['kortʃɪp] *s* cortejo, galanteo; noviazgo
**court'yard'** *s* atrio, patio
**cousin** ['kʌzɪn] *s* primo
**cove** [kov] *s* cala, ensenada
**covenant** ['kʌvənənt] *s* convenio, pacto; contrato; (Bib) alianza || *tr & intr* pactar
**cover** ['kʌvər] *s* cubierta; (*of a magazine*) portada; (*place for one person at table*) cubierto; (*for a bed*) cobertor *m;* **to take cover** ocultarse; **under cover** bajo cubierto, bajo techado; oculto; disfrazado; **under cover of** (*e.g., the night*) a cubierto de; so capa de; **under separate cover** bajo cubierta separada, por separado || *tr* cubrir; (*to line, to coat*) recubrir, revestir; recorrer (*cierta distancia*); cubrirse (*la cabeza*); tapar (*una olla*) || *intr* cubrirse
**coverage** ['kʌvərɪdʒ] *s* (*amount or space covered*) alcance *m;* (*of news*) reportaje *m;* (*funds to meet liabilities*) cobertura
**coveralls** ['cʌvər,ɔlz] *s* mono

**cover charge** *s* precio del cubierto
**covered** ['kʌvərd] *adj* cubierto; (*wire*) forrado; (*bridge*) cubierto
**covered wagon** *s* carromato
**cover girl** *s* (coll) muchacha hermosa en la portada de una revista
**covering** ['kʌvərɪŋ] *s* cubierta, envoltura
**covert** ['kʌvərt] *adj* disimulado, secreto
**cov'er·up'** *s* efugio, subterfugio
**covet** ['kʌvɪt] *tr* codiciar
**covetous** ['kʌvɪtəs] *adj* codicioso
**covetousness** ['kʌvɪtəsnɪs] *s* codicia
**covey** ['kʌvi] *s* (*brood*) nidada; (*in flight*) bandada; corro, grupo
**cow** [kaʊ] *s* vaca || *tr* acobardar, intimidar
**coward** ['kaʊ·ərd] *s* cobarde *mf*
**cowardice** ['kaʊ·ərdɪs] *s* cobardía
**cowardly** ['kaʊ·ərdli] *adj* cobarde || *adv* cobardemente
**cow'bell'** *s* cencerro
**cow'boy'** *s* vaquero; gaucho (Arg)
**cowcatcher** ['kaʊ,kætʃər] *s* quitapiedras *m,* rastrillo; trompa (Col, Chile)
**cower** ['kaʊ·ər] *intr* agacharse
**cow'herd'** *s* vaquero, pastor *m* de ganado vacuno
**cow'hide'** *s* cuero; (*whip*) zurriago || *tr* zurriagar
**cowl** [kaʊl] *s* capucha, cogulla; (aer) cubierta del motor; (aut) cubretablero, bóveda
**cow'lick'** *s* mechón *m,* remolino (*pelos que se levantan sobre la frente*)
**cowpox** ['kaʊ,pɑks] *s* vacuna
**coxcomb** ['kɑks,kom] *s* petimetre *m,* mequetrefe *m*
**coxswain** ['kɑksən] o ['kɑk,swen] *s* timonel *m;* contramaestre *m*
**coy** [kɔɪ] *adj* recatado, modesto; coquetón
**co·zy** ['kozi] *adj* (*comp* **-zier;** *super* **-ziest**) cómodo || *s* (*pl* **-zies**) cubretetera
**cp.** *abbr* **compare**
**c.p.** *abbr* **candle power**
**C.P.A.** *abbr* **certified public accountant**
**cpd.** *abbr* **compound**
**cr.** *abbr* **credit, creditor**
**crab** [kræb] *s* cangrejo; (*grouch*) cascarrabias *mf*
**crab apple** *s* manzana silvestre
**crabbed** ['kræbɪd] *adj* avinagrado, ceñudo
**crab grass** *s* garranchuelo
**crab louse** *s* ladilla
**crack** [kræk] *adj* (coll) de primera clase; (*shot*) (coll) certero || *s* grieta, hendidura; (*noise*) crujido, estallido; (coll) instante *m,* momento; (*joke*) (slang) chiste *m;* **at the crack of dawn** al romper el alba || *tr* agrietar, hender; chasquear (*un látigo*); abrir (*una caja fuerte*) por la fuerza; cascar (*nueces*); descifrar (*un código*); (slang) decir (*un chiste*); (slang) descubrir (*un secreto*); **to crack a smile** (slang) sonreír; **to crack up** (coll) alabar, elogiar || *intr* agrietarse; crujir; cascarse (*la voz de una persona*); enloquecerse; ceder, someterse; **to crack up** fracasar; perder la salud; estrellarse (*un avión*)
**cracked** [krækt] *adj* agrietado; (*ice*) picado; (coll) mentecato, loco
**cracker** ['krækər] *s* galleta
**crack'le·ware'** *s* grietado
**crack'pot'** *adj & s* (slang) excéntrico, tarambana *mf*
**crack'-up'** *s* fracaso; colisión; derrota; (aer) aterrizaje violento; (coll) colapso
**cradle** ['kredəl] *s* cuna; (*of handset*) horquilla || *tr* acunar
**cra'dle·song'** *s* canción de cuna, arrullo
**craft** [kræft] o [krɑft] *s* arte *m,* arte manual; astucia, maña; nave *f* || *spl* naves
**craftiness** ['kræftɪnɪs] o ['krɑftɪnɪs] *s* astucia
**crafts·man** ['kræftsmən] o ['krɑftsmən] *s* (*pl* **-men** [mən]) artesano; artista *m*
**craftsmanship** ['kræftsmən,ʃɪp] o ['krɑftsmən,ʃɪp] *s* artesanía
**craft·y** ['kræfti] o ['krɑfti] *adj* (*comp* **-ier;** *super* **-iest**) astuto, mañoso
**crag** [kræg] *s* peñasco, despeñadero
**cram** [kræm] *v* (*pret & pp* **crammed;** *ger* **cramming**) *tr* atascar, atracar, embutir; (coll) aprender apresuradamente || *intr* atracarse; (*to study hard*) (coll) empollar
**cramp** [kræmp] *s* (*metal bar*) grapa, laña; (*clamp*) abrazadera; (*painful contraction of muscle*) calambre *m;* **cramps** retortijón *m* de tripas || *tr* engrapar, lañar; apretar; dar calambre a
**cranber·ry** ['kræn,bɛri] *s* (*pl* **-ries**) arándano agrio
**crane** [kren] *s* (*bird*) grulla; (*derrick*) grúa || *tr* estirar (*el cuello*) || *intr* estirar el cuello
**crani·um** ['krenɪ·əm] *s* (*pl* **-a** [ə]) cráneo
**crank** [kræŋk] *s* manivela, manubrio; (coll) estrafalario || *tr* hacer girar (*el motor*) con la manivela
**crank'case'** *s* caja de cigüeñal, cárter *m* del cigüeñal
**crank'shaft'** *s* cigüeñal *m*
**crank·y** ['kræŋki] *adj* (*comp* **-ier;** *super* **-iest**) malhumorado; (*queer*) estrafalario
**cran·ny** ['kræni] *s* (*pl* **-nies**) hendidura, grieta, rendija
**crape** [krep] *s* crespón *m;* crespón fúnebre, crespón negro
**crape'hang'er** *s* (slang) aguafiestas *mf*
**craps** [kræps] *s* juego de dados; **to shoot craps** jugar a los dados
**crash** [kræʃ] *s* caída, desplome *m;* colisión, choque *m;* estallido, estrépito; fracaso; crac financiero; lienzo grueso; (aer) aterrizaje violento || *tr* romper con estrépito, estrellar; **to crash a party** (slang) asistir a una fiesta sin invitación; **to crash the gate**

(slang) colarse de gorra || *intr* caer, desplomarse; romperse con estrépito, estallar; (*in business*) quebrar; aterrizar violentamente, estrellarse (*un avión*); **to crash into** chocar con
**crash dive** *s* sumersión instantánea (*de submarino*)
**crash landing** *s* aterrizaje violento
**crash program** *s* programa intensivo
**crass** [kræs] *adj* espeso, tosco; (*ignorance, mistake*) craso
**crate** [kret] *s* (*box made of slats*) jaula; (*basket*) banasta, cuévano || *tr* embalar en jaula, embalar con listones
**crater** ['kretər] *s* cráter *m*
**cravat** [krə'væt] *s* corbata
**crave** [krev] *tr* anhelar, ansiar; pedir (*indulgencia*) || *intr* — **to crave for** anhelar, ansiar; pedir con insistencia
**craven** ['krevən] *adj & s* cobarde *mf*
**craving** ['krevɪŋ] *s* anhelo, ansia, deseo ardiente
**craw** [krɔ] *s* buche *m*
**crawl** [krɔl] *s* arrastre *m;* gateado || *intr* reptar, arrastrarse, gatear; (*to have a feeling of insects on skin*) hormiguear; **to crawl along** andar paso a paso; **to crawl up** trepar
**crayon** ['kre·ən] *s* creyón *m*
**craze** [krez] *s* boga, moda; locura, manía || *tr* enloquecer
**cra·zy** ['krezi] *adj* (*comp* **-zier;** *super* **-ziest**) loco; (*rickety*) desvencijado; achacoso, débil; **crazy as a bedbug** (slang) loco de atar; **to be crazy about** (coll) estar loco por; **to drive crazy** volver loco
**crazy bone** *s* hueso de la alegría
**creak** [krik] *s* crujido, rechinamiento || *intr* crujir, rechinar
**creak·y** ['kriki] *adj* (*comp* **-ier;** *super* **-iest**) crujidero, rechinador
**cream** [krim] *s* crema; (*e.g., of society*) crema, nata y flor || *tr* desnatar (*la leche*)
**creamer·y** ['kriməri] *s* (*pl* **-ies**) mantequería, quesería, lechería
**cream puff** *s* bollo de crema
**cream separator** *s* desnatadora
**cream·y** ['krimi] *adj* (*comp* **-ier;** *super* **-iest**) cremoso
**crease** [kris] *s* arruga, pliegue *m;* (*in trousers*) raya || *tr* arrugar, plegar
**create** [kri'et] *tr* crear
**creation** [kri'eʃən] *s* creación
**creative** [kri'etɪv] *adj* creativo
**creator** [kri'etər] *s* creador *m*
**creature** ['kritʃər] *s* criatura; (*being, strange being*) ente *m;* animal *m*
**credence** ['kridəns] *s* creencia; **to give credence to** dar fe a
**credentials** [krɪ'dɛnʃəlz] *spl* credenciales *fpl*
**credible** ['krɛdɪbəl] *adj* creíble
**credit** ['krɛdɪt] *s* crédito; **to take credit for** atribuirse el mérito de || *tr* acreditar; **to credit a person with** atribuirle a una persona el mérito de
**creditable** ['krɛdɪtəbəl] *adj* honorable, estimable
**credit card** *s* tarjeta de crédito
**creditor** ['krɛdɪtər] *s* acreedor *m*
**cre·do** ['krido] o ['kredo] *s* (*pl* **-dos**) credo
**credulous** ['krɛdʒələs] *adj* crédulo
**creed** [krid] *s* credo
**creek** [krik] *s* arroyo, riachuelo
**creep** [krip] *v* (*pret & pp* **crept** [krɛpt]) *intr* arrastrarse; (*on all fours*) gatear; (*to climb*) trepar; (*with a sensation of insects*) hormiguear; **to creep up on** acercarse insensiblemente a
**creeper** ['kripər] *s* planta rastrera, planta trepadora
**creeping** ['kripɪŋ] *adj* lento, progresivo; (*plant*) rastrero || *s* arrastramiento
**cremate** ['krimet] *tr* incinerar
**cremation** [krɪ'meʃən] *s* cremación, incineración
**cremato·ry** ['krimə,tori] *adj* crematorio || *s* (*pl* **-ries**) crematorio
**crème de menthe** [krɛm də 'mɑ̃t] *s* crema de menta
**Creole** ['kri·ol] *adj & s* criollo
**crescent** ['krɛsənt] *s* (*moon in first or last quarter*) creciente *f* de la luna; (*shape of moon in either of these phases*) media luna; panecillo (*en forma de media luna*)
**cress** [krɛs] *s* mastuerzo
**crest** [krɛst] *s* cresta
**crestfallen** ['krɛst,fɔlən] *adj* cabizbajo
**Cretan** ['kritən] *adj & s* cretense *mf*
**Crete** [krit] *s* Creta
**cretonne** [krɪ'tɑn] *s* cretona
**crevice** ['krɛvɪs] *s* grieta
**crew** [kru] *s* equipo; (*of a ship*) dotación, tripulación; (*group, esp. of armed men*) banda, cuadrilla
**crew cut** *s* corte *m* de pelo a cepillo
**crib** [krɪb] *s* pesebre *m;* camita de niño; (coll) plagio; (*student's pony*) (coll) chuleta || *v* (*pret & pp* **cribbed;** *ger* **cribbing**) *tr & intr* (coll) hurtar
**cricket** ['krɪkɪt] *s* (ent) grillo; (sport) cricquet *m;* (coll) juego limpio
**crier** ['kraɪ·ər] *s* pregonero
**crime** [kraɪm] *s* crimen *m*, delito
**criminal** ['krɪmɪnəl] *adj & s* criminal *mf*
**criminal code** *s* código penal
**criminal law** *s* derecho penal
**criminal negligence** *s* imprudencia temeraria
**crimp** [krɪmp] *s* rizado, rizo; **to put a crimp in** (coll) estorbar, impedir || *tr* rizar
**crimple** ['krɪmpəl] *tr* arrugar, rizar || *intr* arrugarse, rizarse
**crimson** ['krɪmzən] *adj & s* carmesí *m* || *intr* enrojecerse
**cringe** [krɪndʒ] *intr* arrastrarse, reptar, encogerse
**crinkle** ['krɪŋkəl] *s* arruga, pliegue *m;* (*in the water*) rizo u onda || *tr* arrugar, plegar || *intr* arrugarse
**cripple** ['krɪpəl] *s* zopo, lisiado || *tr* lisiar, estropear; dañar, perjudicar
**cri·sis** ['kraɪsɪs] *s* (*pl* **-ses** [siz]) crisis *f*

**crisp** [krɪsp] *adj* frágil, quebradizo; (*air, weather*) refrescante; decisivo
**criteri•on** [kraɪˈtɪrɪ•ən] *s* (*pl* **-a** [ə]) u **-ons**) criterio
**critic** [ˈkrɪtɪk] *s* crítico; (*faultfinder*) criticón *m*
**critical** [ˈkrɪtɪkəl] *adj* crítico; (*faultfinding*) criticón
**criticism** [ˈkrɪtɪˌsɪzəm] *s* crítica
**criticize** [ˈkrɪtɪˌsaɪz] *tr & intr* criticar
**critique** [krɪˈtik] *s* (*art of criticism*) crítica; ensayo crítico
**croak** [krok] *s* (*of raven*) graznido; canto de ranas || *intr* graznar (*el cuervo*); croar (*la rana*); (*morir*) (slang) reventar
**Croat** [krot] *s* (*native or inhabitant*) croata *mf*; (*language*) croata *m*
**Croatian** [kroˈeʃən] *adj & mf* croata *mf*
**cro•chet** [kroˈʃe] *s* croché *m* || *v* (*pret & pp* **-cheted** [ˈʃed]); *ger* **-cheting** [ˈʃe•ɪŋ]) *tr* trabajar con aguja de gancho || *intr* hacer croché
**crocheting** [kroˈʃe•ɪŋ] *s* labor *f* de ganchillo
**crochet needle** *s* aguja de gancho
**crock** [krɑk] *s* cacharro, vasija de barro cocido
**crockery** [ˈkrɑkəri] *s* loza
**crocodile** [ˈkrɑkəˌdaɪl] *s* cocodrilo
**crocodile tears** *spl* lágrimas de cocodrilo
**crocus** [ˈkrokəs] *s* azafrán *m*, croco
**crone** [kron] *s* vieja acartonada, vieja arrugada
**cro•ny** [ˈkroni] *s* (*pl* **-nies**) compinche *mf*
**crook** [krʊk] *s* gancho, garfio; curva; (*of shepherd*) cayado; (coll) fullero, ladrón *m* || *tr* encorvar; (slang) empinar (*el codo*) || *intr* encorvarse
**crooked** [ˈkrʊkɪd] *adj* encorvado, torcido; (*person or his conduct*) torcido; **to go crooked** (coll) torcerse
**croon** [krun] *intr* cantar con voz suave, cantar con melancolía exagerada
**crooner** [ˈkrunər] *s* cantor de voz suave, cantor melancólico
**crop** [krɑp] *s* cosecha; (*head of hair*) cabellera; cabello corto; (*of a bird*) buche *m*; (*whip*) látigo; (*of appointments, promotions, heroes, etc.*) hornada || *v* (*pret & pp* **cropped**; *ger* **cropping**) *tr* desmochar (*un árbol*); desorejar (*a un animal*); esquilar, trasquilar || *intr* — **to crop out** o **up** aflorar; asomar, dejarse ver, manifestarse inesperadamente
**crop dusting** *s* aerofumigación, fumigación aérea
**croquet** [kroˈke] *s* crocquet *m*
**croquette** [kroˈkɛt] *s* croqueta
**crosier** [ˈkroʒər] *s* báculo pastoral, cayado
**cross** [krɔs] o [krɑs] *adj* transversal, travieso; (*breed*) cruzado; malhumorado, enfadado || *s* cruz *f*; (*of races; of two roads*) cruce *m*; **to take the cross** (*to join a crusade*) cruzarse || *tr* cruzar; (*to oppose*) contrariar, frustrar; **to cross off** u **out** borrar; **to cross oneself** hacerse la señal de la cruz; **to cross one's mind** ocurrírsele a uno; **to cross one's t's** poner travesaño a las tes, poner el palo a las tes || *intr* cruzar; cruzarse; **to cross over** atravesar de un lado a otro
**cross'bones'** *spl* huesos cruzados (*símbolo de la muerte*)
**cross'bow'** *s* ballesta
**cross'breed'** *v* (*pret & pp* **-bred** [ˌbred]) *tr* cruzar (*animales o plantas*)
**cross'coun'try** *adj* a campo traviesa; a través del país
**cross'cur'rent** *s* contracorriente *f*; (fig) tendencia encontrada
**cross'-exam'i•na'tion** *s* interrogatorio riguroso; (law) repregunta
**cross'-ex•am'ine** *tr* interrogar rigurosamente; (law) repreguntar
**cross-eyed** [ˈkrɔsˌaɪd] o [ˈkrɑsˌaɪd] *adj* bisojo, bizco, ojituerto
**crossing** [ˈkrɔsɪŋ] o [ˈkrɑsɪŋ] *s* (*of lines, streets, etc.*) cruce *m*; (*of the ocean*) travesía; (*of a river*) vado; (rr) crucero, paso a nivel
**crossing gate** *s* barrera, barrera de paso a nivel
**crossing point** *s* punto de cruce
**cross'patch'** *s* (coll) gruñón *m*
**cross'piece'** *s* travesaño
**cross reference** *s* contrarreferencia, remisión
**cross'road'** *s* vía transversal; **crossroads** encrucijada, cruce *m*; **at the crossroads** en el momento crítico
**cross section** *s* corte *m* transversal; (fig) sección representativa
**cross street** *s* calle traviesa, calle de travesía
**cross'word' puzzle** *s* crucigrama *m*
**crotch** [krɑtʃ] *s* (*forked piece*) horcajadura, bifurcación; (*between legs*) entrepierna, bragadura, horcajadura
**crotchety** [ˈkrɑtʃɪti] *adj* caprichoso, estrambótico, de mal genio
**crouch** [krautʃ] *s* posición agachada || *intr* agacharse, acuclillarse
**croup** [krup] *s* garrotillo, crup *m*; (*of horse*) anca, grupa
**croupier** [ˈkrupɪ•ər] *s* crupié *m*
**crouton** [ˈkrutɑn] *s* corteza de pan
**crow** [kro] *s* corneja, grajo, chova; (*cry of the cock*) quiquiriquí *m*; (*crowbar*) alzaprima; **as the crow flies** a vuelo de pájaro; **to eat crow** (coll) cantar la palinodia; **to have a crow to pick with** (coll) tener que habérselas con || *intr* cantar (*el gallo*); jactarse; **to crow over** jactarse de
**crow'bar'** *s* alzaprima, pie *m* de cabra
**crowd** [kraud] *s* gentío, multitud; (*flock of people*) caterva, tropel *m*; (*mob, common people*) populacho, vulgo; (*clique, set*) corrillo, grupo || *tr* apiñar, apretar, atestar; (*to push*) empujar || *intr* apiñarse, apretarse, atestarse; (*to mill around*) arremolinarse

**crowded** ['kraudɪd] *adj* atestado, concurrido
**crown** [kraun] *s* corona; (*of hat*) copa || *tr* coronar; (checkers) coronar; (slang) golpear en la cabeza
**crowned head** *s* testa coronada
**crown prince** *s* príncipe heredero
**crown princess** *s* princesa heredera
**crow's'-foot'** *s* (*pl* **-feet'**) pata de gallo
**crow's'-nest'** *s* (naut) cofa de vigía, torre *f* de vigía
**crucial** ['kruʃəl] *adj* crucial; difícil, penoso
**crucible** ['krusɪbəl] *s* crisol *m*
**crucifix** ['krusɪfɪks] *s* crucifijo
**crucifixion** [,krusɪ'fɪkʃən] *s* crucifixión
**cruci•fy** ['krusɪ,faɪ] *v* (*pret & pp* **-fied**) *tr* crucificar
**crude** [krud] *adj* (*raw, unrefined*) crudo; (*lacking culture*) grosero, tosco; (*unfinished*) basto, sin labrar
**crudi•ty** ['krudɪti] *s* (*pl* **-ties**) crudeza; grosería, tosquedad; bastedad
**cruel** ['kru•əl] *adj* cruel
**cruel•ty** ['kru•əlti] *s* (*pl* **-ties**) crueldad
**cruet** ['kru•ɪt] *s* ampolleta
**cruet stand** *s* angarillas, vinagreras
**cruise** [kruz] *s* viaje *m* por mar; (aer, naut) crucero || *tr* (naut) cruzar || *intr* cruzar; (coll) andar de un lado a otro
**cruiser** ['kruzər] *s* (nav) crucero
**cruising** ['kruzɪŋ] *adj* de crucero || *s* (aer, naut) crucero
**cruising radius** *s* autonomía
**cruller** ['krʌlər] *s* buñuelo
**crumb** [krʌm] *s* migaja; (*soft part of bread*) miga; (*given to a beggar*) mendrugo || *tr* desmigar (*el pan*); (culin) empanar, cubrir con pan rallado; limpiar (*la mesa*) de migajas || *intr* desmigarse, desmenuzarse
**crumble** ['krʌmbəl] *tr* desmenuzar || *intr* desmenuzarse; (*to fall to pieces gradually*) desmoronarse
**crum•my** ['krʌmi] *adj* (*comp* **-mier**; *super* **-miest**) (slang) desaseado, sucio; (slang) de mal gusto, de mala muerte
**crumple** ['krʌmpəl] *tr* arrugar, ajar, chafar || *intr* arrugarse, ajarse
**crunch** [krʌntʃ] *tr* ronchar, ronzar || *intr* crujir
**crusade** [kru'sed] *s* cruzada || *intr* hacer una cruzada
**crusader** [kru'sedər] *s* cruzado
**crush** [krʌʃ] *s* aplastamiento; (*of people*) aglomeración, bullaje *m*; **to have a crush on** (slang) estar perdido por || *tr* aplastar, machacar, magullar; (*to grind*) moler; bocartear (*el mineral*); (*to oppress, grieve*) abrumar
**crush hat** *s* clac *m*
**crust** [krʌst] *s* corteza; corteza de pan; (*scab*) costra
**crustacean** [krʌs'teʃən] *s* crustáceo
**crustaceous** [krʌs'teʃəs] *adj* crustáceo
**crust•y** ['krʌsti] *adj* (*comp* **-ier**; *super* **-iest**) (*scabby*) costroso; áspero, grosero, rudo

**crutch** [krʌtʃ] *s* muleta
**crux** [krʌks] *s* punto capital; enigma *m*
**cry** [kraɪ] *s* (*pl* **cries**) grito; (*weeping*) lloro; (*of peddler*) pregón *m*; (*of wolf*) aullido; (*of bull*) bramido; **in full cry** en plena persecución; **to have a good cry** desahogarse en lágrimas abundantes || *v* (*pret & pp* **cried**) *tr* decir a gritos; (*to announce publicly*) pregonar; **to cry one's eyes o heart out** llorar amargamente; **to cry out** decir a gritos; pregonar || *intr* gritar; (*to weep*) llorar; aullar (*el lobo*); bramar (*el toro*); **to cry for** clamar por; **to cry for joy** llorar de alegría; **to cry out** clamar; **to cry out against** clamar contra; **to cry out for** clamar, clamar por
**cry'ba'by** *s* (*pl* **-bies**) llorón *m*, llorona, lloraduelos *mf*
**crypt** [krɪpt] *s* cripta
**cryptic(al)** ['krɪptɪk(əl)] *adj* enigmático, misterioso
**crystal** ['krɪstəl] *s* cristal *m*
**crystal ball** *s* bola de cristal
**crystalline** ['krɪstəlɪn] o ['krɪstə,laɪn] *adj* cristalino
**crystallize** ['krɪstə,laɪz] *tr* cristalizar || *intr* cristalizarse
**C.S.** *abbr* **Christian Science, Civil Service**
**ct.** *abbr* **cent**
**cu.** *abbr* **cubic**
**cub** [kʌb] *s* cachorro
**Cuban** ['kjubən] *adj & s* cubano
**cubbyhole** ['kʌbɪ,hol] *s* chiribitil *m*
**cube** [kjub] *adj* (*root*) cúbico || *s* cubo; (*of ice*) cubito || *tr* cubicar
**cubic** ['kjubɪk] *adj* cúbico
**cub reporter** *s* (coll) reportero novato
**cuckold** ['kʌkəld] *adj & s* cornudo || *tr* encornudar
**cuckoo** ['kuku] *adj* (slang) mentecato, loco || *s* cuclillo, cuco; (*call of cuckoo*) cucú *m*
**cuckoo clock** *s* reloj *m* de cuclillo
**cucumber** ['kjukəmbər] *s* pepino
**cud** [kʌd] *s* bolo alimenticio; **to chew the cud** rumiar
**cuddle** ['kʌdəl] *s* abrazo cariñoso || *tr* abrazar con cariño || *intr* estar abrazados, arrimarse cariñosamente
**cudg•el** ['kʌdʒəl] *s* garrote *m*, porra; **to take up the cudgels for** salir a la defensa de || *v* (*pret & pp* **-eled** o **-elled**; *ger* **-eling** o **-elling**) *tr* apalear, aporrear
**cue** [kju] *s* señal *f*, indicación; (*hint*) indirecta; (*rôle*) papel *m*; (*rod used in billiards*) taco; (*of hair*) coleta; (*of people in line*) cola; (theat) apunte *m*
**cuff** [kʌf] *s* (*of shirt*) puño; (*of trousers*) doblez *f*, vuelta; (*blow*) bofetada || *tr* abofetear
**cuff links** *spl* gemelos
**cuirass** [kwɪ'ræs] *s* coraza
**cuisine** [kwɪ'zin] *s* cocina (*arte culinario*)
**culinary** ['kjulɪ,neri] *adj* culinario
**cull** [kʌl] *tr* (*to choose, pick*) entresa-

car, escoger; (*to gather, pluck*) coger, recoger
**culm** [kʌlm] *s* (*coal dust*) cisco; (*stalk of grasses*) caña, tallo
**culminate** ['kʌlmɪ,net] *intr* culminar; **to culminate in** conducir a, terminar en
**culpable** ['kʌlpəbəl] *adj* culpable
**culprit** ['kʌlprɪt] *s* acusado; reo
**cult** [kʌlt] *s* culto; secta
**cultivate** ['kʌltɪ,vet] *tr* cultivar
**cultivated** ['kʌltɪ,vetɪd] *adj* culto, cultivado
**cultivation** [,kʌltɪ'veʃən] *s* (*of the land, the arts, one's memory, etc.*) cultivo; (*refinement*) cultura
**culture** ['kʌltʃər] *s* cultura
**cultured** ['kʌltʃərd] *adj* culto
**culvert** ['kʌlvərt] *s* alcantarilla
**cumbersome** ['kʌmbərsəm] *adj* incómodo, molesto; (*clumsy*) pesado, inmanejable
**cunning** ['kʌnɪŋ] *adj* (*sly*) astuto; (*clever*) hábil; (*attractive*) gracioso, mono || *s* astucia; habilidad, destreza
**cup** [kʌp] *s* taza; (*of thermometer*) cubeta; (mach) vaso de engrase; (sport) copa; (*of sorrow*) (fig) copa; **in one's cups** borracho || *v* (*pret & pp* **cupped**; *ger* **cupping**) *tr* ahuecar dando forma de taza o copa a; poner ventosa a
**cupboard** ['kʌbərd] *s* alacena, aparador *m*, armario
**cupidity** [kjʊ'pɪdɪti] *s* codicia
**cupola** ['kjupələ] *s* cúpula
**cur** [kʌr] *s* perro mestizo, perro de mala raza; (*despicable fellow*) canalla *m*
**curate** ['kjʊrɪt] *s* cura *m*
**curative** ['kjʊrətɪv] *adj* curativo || *s* curativa
**curator** [kjʊ'retər] *s* conservador *m*
**curb** [kʌrb] *s* (*of sidewalk*) encintado; (*of well*) brocal *m*; (*of bit*) barbada; (*market*) bolsín *m*; (*check, restraint*) freno; (vet) corva || *tr* contener, refrenar
**curb'stone'** *s* piedra de encintado; brocal *m* de pozo
**curd** [kʌrd] *s* cuajada || *tr* cuajar || *intr* cuajarse
**curdle** ['kʌrdəl] *tr* cuajar; **to curdle the blood** horrorizar || *intr* cuajar
**cure** [kjʊr] *s* cura, curación || *tr* curar || *intr* curar; curarse
**cure'-all'** *s* sanalotodo
**curfew** ['kʌrfju] *s* queda, cubrefuego; toque *m* de queda
**curi•o** ['kjʊrɪ,o] *s* (*pl* **-os**) curiosidad
**curiosi•ty** [,kjʊrɪ'ɑsɪti] *s* (*pl* **-ties**) curiosidad
**curious** ['kjʊrɪ·əs] *adj* curioso
**curl** [kʌrl] *s* bucle *m*, rizo; (*spiral-shaped curl*) tirabuzón *m*; (*of smoke*) espiral *f*; (*curling*) rizado || *tr* encrespar, ensortijar, rizar; (*to coil, to roll up*) arrollar; fruncir (*los labios*) || *intr* encresparse, ensortijarse, rizarse; arrollarse; **to curl up** arrollarse; (*in bed*) encogerse; (*to break up, collapse*) (coll) desplomarse
**curlicue** ['kʌrlɪ,kju] *s* ringorrango
**curling iron** *s* rizador *m*, maquinilla de rizar
**curl'pa'per** *s* torcida, papelito para rizar el pelo
**curl•y** ['kʌrli] *adj* (*comp* **-ier**; *super* **-iest**) crespo, rizo
**curmudgeon** [kər'mʌdʒən] *s* cicatero, tacaño, erizo
**currant** ['kʌrənt] *s* pasa de Corinto; (*Ribes alpinum*) calderilla
**curren•cy** ['kʌrənsi] *s* (*pl* **-cies**) moneda corriente, dinero en circulación; uso corriente
**current** ['kʌrənt] *adj* corriente || *s* corriente *f*; (elec) corriente *f*
**current account** *s* cuenta corriente
**current events** *spl* actualidades, sucesos de actualidad
**curricu•lum** [kə'rɪkjələm] *s* (*pl* **-lums** o **-la** [lə]) plan *m* de estudios
**cur•ry** ['kʌri] *s* (*pl* **-ries**) cari *m* || *v* (*pret & pp* **-ried**) *tr* curtir (*las pieles*); almohazar (*el caballo*); **to curry favor** procurar complacer
**cur'ry•comb'** *s* almohaza || *tr* almohazar
**curse** [kʌrs] *s* maldición; (*profane oath*) reniego, voto; (*evil, misfortune*) calamidad || *tr* maldecir || *intr* jurar, echar votos
**cursed** ['kʌrsɪd] o [kʌrst] *adj* maldito; aborrecible
**cursive** ['kʌrsɪv] *adj* cursivo || *s* cursiva
**cursory** ['kʌrsəri] *adj* apresurado, rápido, superficial, de paso
**curt** [kʌrt] *adj* áspero, brusco; corto, conciso
**curtail** [kər'tel] *tr* acortar, abreviar, cercenar
**curtain** ['kʌrtən] *s* cortina; (theat) telón *m*; **to draw the curtain** correr la cortina; **to drop the curtain** (theat) bajar el telón || *tr* encortinar; separar con cortina; cubrir, ocultar
**curtain call** *s* llamada a la escena para recibir aplausos
**curtain raiser** ['rezər] *s* (theat) pieza preliminar
**curtain ring** *s* anilla
**curtain rod** *s* riel *m*
**curt•sy** ['kʌrtsi] *s* (*pl* **-sies**) cortesía, reverencia || *v* (*pret & pp* **-sied**) *intr* hacer una cortesía
**curve** [kʌrv] *s* curva || *tr* encorvar || *intr* encorvarse; volver, virar
**curved** [kʌrvd] *adj* curvo, encorvado; (*crooked*) combo
**cushion** ['kʊʃən] *s* cojín *m*, almohada; (*of billiard table*) baranda || *tr* amortiguar
**cusp** [kʌsp] *s* cúspide *f*
**cuspidor** ['kʌspɪ,dɔr] *s* escupidera
**custard** ['kʌstərd] *s* flan *m*, natillas
**custodian** [kəs'todɪ·ən] *s* custodio; (*of a house or building*) casero
**custo•dy** ['kʌstədi] *s* (*pl* **-dies**) custodia; **in custody** en prisión; **to take into custody** prender
**custom** ['kʌstəm] *s* costumbre; (*cus-*

*tomers*) parroquia, clientela; **customs** aduana; derechos de aduana
**customary** [ˈkʌstəˌmɛri] *adj* acostumbrado, de costumbre
**cus′tom-built′** *adj* hecho por encargo, fuera de serie
**customer** [ˈkʌstəmər] *s* parroquiano, cliente *mf;* (*of a café or restaurant*) consumidor *m;* (coll) individuo, sujeto, tipo
**cus′tom·house′** *adj* aduanero ‖ *s* aduana
**cus′tom-made′** *adj* hecho a la medida
**customs clearance** *s* despacho de aduana
**customs officer** *s* aduanero
**custom tailor** *s* sastre *m* a la medida
**custom work** *s* trabajo hecho a la medida
**cut** [kʌt] *s* corte *m;* (*piece cut off*) tajada; (*wound*) cuchillada; (*for a canal, highway, etc.*) desmonte *m;* (*shortest way*) atajo; (*in prices, wages, etc.*) reducción; (*of a garment*) corte *m,* hechura; (*in winnings, earnings, etc.*) parte *f;* (typ) estampa, grabado; (tennis) golpe *m* cortante; (*absence from school*) (coll) falta de asistencia; (*snub*) (coll) desaire *m;* (coll) palabra hiriente ‖ *v* (*pret & pp* **cut;** *ger* **cutting**) *tr* cortar; practicar (*un agujero*); reducir (*gastos*); capar, castrar; desleír, diluir; (coll) ausentarse de, faltar a (*la clase*); (coll) desairar; (coll) herir; **to cut down** cortar; derribar cortando; castigar (*gastos*); **to cut off** cortar; desheredar; amputar (*una pierna*); (elec) cortar (*la corriente, la ignición*); cerrar (*el carburador*); **to cut open** abrir cortando; **to cut out** cortar; sacar cortando; labrar; suprimir, omitir; (*to take the place of*) desbancar; soplar (*la dama a un rival*); (slang) dejarse de (*disparates*); **to cut short** terminar de repente; interrumpir, chafar; **to cut teeth** endentecer; **to cut up** desmenuzar, despedazar; criticar severamente; (coll) afligir ‖ *intr* cortar; cortarse; salir (*los dientes*); (coll) fumarse la clase; **to cut in** entrar de repente; interrumpir; (*in a dance*) cortar o separar la pareja; **to cut under** vender a menor precio que; **to cut up** (slang) travesear, hacer travesuras; (slang) jaranear
**cut-and-dried** [ˈkʌtənˈdraɪd] *adj* dispuesto de antemano; monótono, poco interesante
**cutaway coat** [ˈkʌtəˌwe] *s* chaqué *m*
**cut′back′** *s* reducción; discontinuación, incumplimiento; (mov) retorno a una época anterior
**cute** [kjut] *adj* (coll) mono, monono; (coll) astuto, listo
**cut glass** *s* cristal tallado
**cuticle** [ˈkjutɪkəl] *s* cutícula
**cutlass** [ˈkʌtləs] *s* alfanje *m*
**cutler** [ˈkʌtlər] *s* cuchillero
**cutlery** [ˈkʌtləri] *s* cuchillería; (*knives, forks, and spoons*) cubierto
**cutlet** [ˈkʌtlɪt] *s* chuleta; croqueta
**cut′out′** *s* (*design to be cut out*) recortado; (aut) escape *m* libre, válvula de escape libre
**cut′-rate′** *adj* de precio reducido
**cutter** [ˈkʌtər] *s* cortador *m;* (*machine*) cortadora; (naut) escampavía
**cut′throat′** *adj* asesino; implacable ‖ *s* asesino
**cutting** [ˈkʌtɪŋ] *adj* cortante; hiriente, mordaz ‖ *s* corte *m;* (*from a newspaper*) recorte *m;* (hort) esqueje *m*
**cutting edge** *s* canto de corte
**cuttlefish** [ˈkʌtəlˌfɪʃ] *s* jibia
**cut′wa′ter** *s* espolón *m,* tajamar *m*
**cwt.** *abbr* **hundredweight**
**cyanamide** [saɪˈænəˌmaɪd] *s* cianamida; cianamida de calcio
**cyanide** [ˈsaɪ·əˌnaɪd] *s* cianuro
**cycle** [ˈsaɪkəl] *s* ciclo; bicicleta; (*of an internal-combustion engine*) tiempo; (phys) período ‖ *intr* montar en bicicleta
**cyclic(al)** [ˈsaɪklɪk(əl)] o [ˈsɪklɪk(əl)] *adj* cíclico
**cyclone** [ˈsaɪklon] *s* ciclón *m*
**cyl.** *abbr* **cylinder, cylindrical**
**cylinder** [ˈsɪlɪndər] *s* cilindro
**cylinder block** *s* bloque *m* de cilindros
**cylinder bore** *s* alesaje *m*
**cylinder head** *s* (*of steam engine*) tapa del cilindro; (*of gas engine*) culata del cilindro
**cylindric(al)** [sɪˈlɪndrɪk(əl)] *adj* cilíndrico
**cymbal** [ˈsɪmbəl] *s* címbalo, platillo
**cynic** [ˈsɪnɪk] *adj & s* cínico
**cynical** [ˈsɪnɪkəl] *adj* cínico
**cynicism** [ˈsɪnɪˌsɪzəm] *s* cinismo
**cynosure** [ˈsaɪnəˌʃʊr] o [ˈsɪnəˌʃʊr] *s* blanco de las miradas; guía, norte *m*
**cypress** [ˈsaɪprəs] *s* ciprés *m*
**Cyprus** [ˈsaɪprəs] *s* Chipre *f*
**Cyrillic** [sɪˈrɪlɪk] *adj* cirílico
**Cyrus** [ˈsaɪrəs] *s* Ciro
**cyst** [sɪst] *s* quiste *m*
**czar** [zɑr] *s* zar *m;* (fig) autócrata *m*
**czarina** [zɑˈrinə] *s* zarina
**Czech** [tʃɛk] *adj & s* checo
**Czecho-Slovak** [ˈtʃɛkoˈslovæk] *adj & s* checoeslovaco o checoslovaco
**Czecho-Slovakia** [ˌtʃɛkosloˈvækɪ·ə] *s* Checoeslovaquia o Checoslovaquia

# D

**D, d** [di] cuarta letra del alfabeto inglés
**d.** *abbr* **date, day, dead, degree, delete, diameter, died, dollar, denarius (penny)**
**D.** *abbr* **December, Democrat, Duchess, Duke, Dutch**
**D.A.** *abbr* **District Attorney**
**dab** [dæb] *s* toque ligero; masa pastosa ‖ *v* (*pret & pp* **dabbed**; *ger* **dabbing**) *tr* tocar ligeramente, frotar suavemente
**dabble** [ˈdæbəl] *tr* salpicar ‖ *intr* chapotear; **to dabble in** meterse en; jugar a (*la Bolsa*); especular en (*granos*)
**dad** [dæd] *s* (coll) papá *m*
**dad·dy** [ˈdædi] *s* (*pl* **-dies**) (coll) papá *m*
**daffodil** [ˈdæfədɪl] *s* narciso trompón
**daff·y** [ˈdæfi] *adj* (*comp* **-ier**; *super* **-iest**) (coll) chiflado
**dagger** [ˈdægər] *s* daga, puñal *m;* (typ) cruz *f*, obelisco; **to look daggers at** apuñalar con la mirada
**dahlia** [ˈdæljə] *s* dalia
**dai·ly** [ˈdeli] *adj* cotidiano, diario ‖ *adv* diariamente ‖ *s* (*pl* **-lies**) diario
**dain·ty** [ˈdenti] *adj* (*comp* **-tier**; *super* **-tiest**) delicado ‖ *s* (*pl* **-ties**) golosina
**dair·y** [ˈdɛri] *s* (*pl* **-ies**) lechería, vaquería
**dais** [ˈde·ɪs] *s* estrado
**dai·sy** [ˈdezi] *s* (*pl* **-sies**) margarita
**dal·ly** [ˈdæli] *v* (*pret & pp* **-lied**) *intr* juguetear, retozar; tardar, malgastar el tiempo
**dam** [dæm] *s* represa, embalse *m;* (*female quadruped*) madre *f;* (dent) dique *m* ‖ *v* (*pret & pp* **dammed**; *ger* **damming**) *tr* represar, embalsar; cerrar, tapar, obstruir
**damage** [ˈdæmɪdʒ] *s* daño, perjuicio; (*to one's reputation*) desdoro; (com) avería; **damages** daños y perjuicios ‖ *tr* dañar, perjudicar; averiar
**damascene** [ˈdæməˌsin] o [ˌdæməˈsin] *adj* damasquino ‖ *s* ataujía, damasquinado ‖ *tr* ataujiar, damasquinar
**dame** [dem] *s* dama, señora; (coll) mujer *f*
**damn** [dæm] *s* terno; **I don't give a damn** (slang) maldito lo que me importa; **that's not worth a damn** (slang) eso no vale un pito ‖ *tr* condenar (a pena eterna); condenar; maldecir ‖ *intr* maldecir, echar ternos
**damnation** [dæmˈneʃən] *s* damnación; (theol) condenación
**damned** [dæmd] *adj* condenado (a pena eterna); abominable, detestable ‖ **the damned** los malditos, los condenados (a pena eterna)
**damp** [dæmp] *adj* húmedo, mojado ‖ *s* humedad; (*firedamp*) grisú *m* ‖ *tr* humedecer, mojar; (*to deaden, muffle*) amortecer, amortiguar; (*to discourage*) abatir, desalentar; (elec) amortiguar (*ondas electromagnéticas*)
**dampen** [ˈdæmpən] *tr* humedecer, mojar; amortecer, amortiguar; abatir, desalentar
**damper** [ˈdæmpər] *s* (*of chimney*) registro; (*of piano*) apagador *m*, sordina
**damsel** [ˈdæmzəl] *s* señorita, muchacha
**dance** [dæns] o [dɑns] *s* baile *m*, danza ‖ *tr & intr* bailar, danzar
**dance band** *s* orquesta de jazz
**dance floor** *s* pista de baile
**dance hall** *s* salón *m* de baile
**dancer** [ˈdænsər] o [ˈdɑnsər] *s* bailador *m*, danzador *m;* (*professional*) bailarín *m*
**dancing partner** *s* pareja (de baile)
**dandelion** [ˈdændɪˌlaɪ·ən] *s* diente *m* de león
**dandruff** [ˈdændrəf] *s* caspa
**dan·dy** [ˈdændi] *adj* (*comp* **-dier**; *super* **-diest**) (coll) excelente, magnífico ‖ *s* (*pl* **-dies**) currutaco, petimetre *m*
**Dane** [den] *s* danés *m*, dinamarqués *m*
**danger** [ˈdendʒər] *s* peligro
**dangerous** [ˈdendʒərəs] *adj* peligroso
**dangle** [ˈdæŋgəl] *tr & intr* colgar flojamente, colgar en el aire
**Danish** [ˈdenɪʃ] *adj & s* danés *m*, dinamarqués *m*
**dank** [dæŋk] *adj* húmedo, liento
**Danube** [ˈdænjub] *s* Danubio
**dapper** [ˈdæpər] *adj* aseado, apuesto
**dapple** [ˈdæpəl] *adj* habado, rodado ‖ *tr* motear
**dare** [dɛr] *s* desafío, reto ‖ *tr* retar; **to dare to** (*to challenge to*) desafiar a ‖ *intr* osar, atreverse; **I dare say** talvez; **to dare to** (*to have the courage to*) atreverse a
**dare'dev'il** *s* calavera *m*, temerario
**daring** [ˈdɛrɪŋ] *adj* atrevido, osado ‖ *s* atrevimiento, osadía
**dark** [dɑrk] *adj* obscuro; (*in complexion*) moreno; secreto, oculto; (*gloomy*) lóbrego; (*beer*) pardo ‖ *s* obscuridad, tinieblas; noche *f;* **in the dark** a obscuras
**Dark Ages** *spl* edad media; principios de la edad media
**dark-complexioned** [ˈdɑrkkəmˈplekʃənd] *adj* moreno
**darken** [ˈdɑrkən] *tr* obscurecer; entristecer; cegar ‖ *intr* obscurecerse
**dark horse** *s* caballo desconocido; candidato nombrado inesperadamente
**darkly** [ˈdɑrkli] *adv* obscuramente; secretamente, misteriosamente
**dark meat** *s* carne *f* del ave que no es la pechuga
**darkness** [ˈdɑrknɪs] *s* obscuridad
**dark'room'** *s* (phot) cuarto obscuro
**darling** [ˈdɑrlɪŋ] *adj & s* querido, amado; predilecto
**darn** [dɑrn] *tr & intr* zurcir; (coll) maldecir

**darnel** ['dɑrnəl] *s* cizaña
**darning** ['dɑrnɪŋ] *s* zurcido
**darning needle** *s* aguja de zurcir
**dart** [dɑrt] *s* dardo; (*small missile used in a game*) rehilete *m* || *intr* lanzarse, precipitarse; volar como dardo
**dash** [dæʃ] *s* arranque *m;* (*splash*) rociada; carrera corta; (*spirit*) brío; pequeña cantidad; (*in printing, writing, telegraphy*) raya || *tr* lanzar; estrellar, romper; frustrar (*las esperanzas de uno*); rociar, salpicar; **to dash off** escribir de prisa; **to dash to pieces** hacer añicos || *intr* estrellarse (*las olas del mar*); lanzarse, precipitarse; **to dash by** pasar corriendo; **to dash in** entrar como un rayo
**dash'board'** *s* tablero de instrumentos; (*on front or side of vehicle*) guardabarros *m*
**dashing** ['dæʃɪŋ] *adj* brioso; ostentoso, vistoso || *s* (*of waves*) embate *m*
**dastard** ['dæstərd] *adj & s* vil *mf*, miserable *mf*, cobarde *mf*
**data processing** ['detə] *s* tramitación automática de datos
**date** [det] *s* (*time*) fecha, data; (*palm*) datilera; (*fruit*) dátil *m;* (*appointment*) (coll) cita; **out of date** anticuado, fuera de moda; **to date** hasta la fecha; **under date of** con fecha de || *tr* fechar, datar; (coll) tener cita con || *intr* — **to date from** datar de
**date line** *s* línea de cambio de fecha
**date palm** *s* palmera (datilera)
**dative** ['detɪv] *adj & s* dativo
**datum** ['detəm] o ['dætəm] *s* (*pl* **data** ['detə] o ['dætə]) dato
**dau.** *abbr* **daughter**
**daub** [dɔb] *s* embadurnamiento || *tr* embadurnar
**daughter** ['dɔtər] *s* hija
**daughter-in-law** ['dɔtərɪn,lɔ] *s* (*pl* **daughters-in-law**) nuera, hija política
**daunt** [dɔnt] *tr* asustar, espantar; desanimar, acobardar
**dauntless** ['dɔntlɪs] *adj* atrevido, intrépido, impávido
**dauphin** ['dɔfɪn] *s* delfín *m*
**davenport** ['dævən,port] *s* sofá *m* cama
**davit** ['dævɪt] *s* (naut) pescante *m*, grúa de bote
**daw** [dɔ] *s* corneja
**dawdle** ['dɔdəl] *intr* malgastar el tiempo, haronear
**dawn** [dɔn] *s* amanecer *m*, alba || *intr* amanecer; despuntar (*el día, la mañana*); empezar a mostrarse; **to dawn on** empezar a hacerse patente a
**day** [de] *adj* diurno || *s* día *m;* (*of travel, work, worry, etc.*) jornada; (*from noon to noon*) (naut) singladura; **any day now** de un día para otro; **by day** de día; **the day after** el día siguiente; **the day after tomorrow** pasado mañana; **the day before** la víspera; la víspera de; **the day before yesterday** anteayer; **to call it a day** (coll) dejar de trabajar; **to win the day** ganar la jornada
**day bed** *s* sofá *m* cama
**day'break'** *s* amanecer *m*
**day coach** *s* (rr) coche *m* de viajeros
**day'dream'** *s* ensueño || *intr* soñar despierto
**day laborer** *s* jornalero
**day'light'** *s* luz *f* del día; amanecer *m;* **in broad daylight** en pleno día; **to see daylight** comprender; ver el fin de una tarea difícil
**day'light'-sav'ing time** *s* hora de verano
**day nursery** *s* guardería infantil
**day off** *s* asueto
**day of reckoning** *s* día *m* de ajustar cuentas
**day shift** *s* turno diurno
**day'time'** *adj* diurno || día *m*
**daze** [dez] *s* aturdimiento; **in a daze** aturdido || *tr* aturdir
**dazzle** ['dæzəl] *s* deslumbramiento || *tr* deslumbrar
**dazzling** ['dæzlɪŋ] *adj* deslumbrante
**deacon** ['dikən] *s* diácono
**deaconess** ['dikənɪs] *s* diaconisa
**dead** [dɛd] *adj* muerto; (coll) cansado || *adv* (coll) completamente, muy || *s* — **in the dead of night** en plena noche; **the dead** los muertos; **the dead of winter** lo más frío del invierno
**dead beat** *s* (slang) gorrón *m;* (slang) holgazán *m*
**dead bolt** *s* cerrojo dormido
**dead calm** *s* calma chicha, calmazo
**dead center** *s* punto muerto
**dead'drunk'** *adj* difunto de taberna
**deaden** ['dɛdən] *tr* amortiguar, amortecer
**dead end** *s* callejón *m* sin salida
**dead'latch'** *s* aldaba dormida
**dead'-let'ter office** *s* departamento de cartas no reclamadas
**dead'line'** *s* línea vedada; fin *m* del plazo
**dead'lock'** *s* cerradura dormida; desacuerdo insuperable || *tr* estancar
**dead·ly** ['dɛdli] *adj* (*comp* **-lier;** *super* **-liest**) mortal; (*sin*) capital; abrumador
**dead pan** *s* (slang) semblante *m* sin expresión
**dead reckoning** *s* (naut) estima
**dead ringer** ['rɪŋər] *s* segunda edición
**dead'wood'** *s* leña seca; cosa inútil, gente *f* inútil
**deaf** [dɛf] *adj* sordo; **to turn a deaf ear** hacerse el sordo, hacer oídos de mercader
**deaf and dumb** *adj* sordomudo
**deafen** ['dɛfən] *tr* asordar, ensordecer
**deafening** ['dɛfənɪŋ] *adj* ensordecedor
**deaf'-mute'** *s* sordomudo
**deafness** ['dɛfnɪs] *s* sordera
**deal** [dil] *s* negocio, trato; (*of cards*) mano *f;* turno de dar; (*share*) parte *f*, porción; (coll) convenio secreto; **a good deal (of)** o **a great deal (of)** mucho; **to make a great deal of** hacer fiestas a || *v* (*pret & pp* **dealt** [dɛlt]) *tr* asestar (*un golpe*); repartir (*la baraja*) || *intr* negociar, comerciar; intervenir; (*in card games*) ser

mano; **to deal with** entender en; tratar de; tratar con
**dealer** [ˈdilər] *s* comerciante *mf*, concesionario; (*of cards*) repartidor *m*
**dean** [din] *s* decano; (eccl) deán *m*
**deanship** [ˈdinʃɪp] *s* decanato
**dear** [dɪr] *adj* (*beloved*) caro; (*expensive*) caro; (*charging high prices*) carero; **dear me!** ¡Dios mío! ‖ *s* querido
**dearie** [ˈdɪri] *s* (coll) queridito
**dearth** [dʌrθ] *s* carestía
**death** [dɛθ] *s* muerte *f*; **to bleed to death** morir desangrado; **to bore to death** matar de aburrimiento; **to burn to death** morir quemado; **to choke to death** morir atragantado; **to die a violent death** morir vestido; **to freeze to death** morir helado; **to put to death** dar la muerte a; **to shoot to death** matar a tiros; **to stab to death** escabechar; **to starve to death** matar de hambre; morir de hambre
**death'bed'** *s* lecho de muerte
**death'blow'** *s* golpe *m* mortal
**death certificate** *s* fe *f* de óbito, partida de defunción
**death house** *s* capilla (*de los reos de muerte*)
**deathless** [ˈdɛθlɪs] *adj* inmortal, eterno
**deathly** [ˈdɛθli] *adj* mortal, de muerte ‖ *adv* mortalmente; excesivamente
**death penalty** *s* pena de muerte
**death rate** *s* mortalidad
**death rattle** *s* estertor agónico
**death ray** *s* rayo mortífero
**death warrant** *s* sentencia de muerte; fin *m* de toda esperanza
**death'watch'** *s* vela de un difunto; guardia de un reo de muerte
**debacle** [deˈbɑkəl] *s* desastre *m*, ruina, derrota; (*in a river*) deshielo
**de·bar** [dɪˈbɑr] *v* (*pret & pp* **-barred**; *ger* **-barring**) *tr* excluir; prohibir
**debark** [dɪˈbɑrk] *tr & intr* desembarcar
**debarkation** [ˌdibɑrˈkeʃən] *s* (*of passengers*) desembarco; (*of freight*) desembarque *m*
**debase** [dɪˈbes] *tr* degradar; falsificar
**debatable** [dɪˈbetəbəl] *adj* disputable
**debate** [dɪˈbet] *s* debate *m* ‖ *tr* debatir ‖ *intr* debatir; deliberar
**debauchee** [ˌdɛbɔˈʃi] o [ˌdɛbɔˈtʃi] *s* libertino, disoluto
**debaucher·y** [dɪˈbɔtʃəri] *s* (*pl* **-ies**) libertinaje *m*, crápula
**debenture** [dɪˈbɛntʃər] *s* (*bond*) obligación; (*voucher*) vale *m*
**debilitate** [dɪˈbɪlɪˌtet] *tr* debilitar
**debili·ty** [dɪˈbɪlɪti] *s* (*pl* **-ties**) debilidad
**debit** [ˈdɛbɪt] *s* debe *m*; (*entry on debit side*) cargo ‖ *tr* adeudar, cargar
**debit balance** *s* saldo deudor
**debonair** [ˌdɛbəˈnɛr] *adj* alegre; cortés
**debris** [deˈbri] *s* despojos, ruinas
**debt** [dɛt] *s* deuda; **to run into debt** endeudarse, entramparse
**debtor** [ˈdɛtər] *s* deudor *m*
**debut** [deˈbju] o [ˈdebju] *s* estreno, debut *m*; **to make one's debut** estrenarse, debutar; ponerse de largo, entrar en sociedad (*una joven*)
**debutante** [ˌdɛbjuˈtɑnt] o [ˈdɛbjəˌtænt] *s* joven *f* que se pone de largo
**dec.** *abbr* **deceased**
**decade** [ˈdɛked] *s* decenio
**decadence** [dɪˈkedəns] *s* decadencia
**decadent** [dɪˈkedənt] *adj & s* decadente *mf*
**decanter** [dɪˈkæntər] *s* garrafa
**decapitate** [dɪˈkæpɪˌtet] *tr* decapitar
**decay** [dɪˈke] *s* (*decline*) decaimiento, descaecimiento; (*rotting*) podredumbre; (*of teeth*) caries *f* ‖ *tr* pudrir ‖ *intr* pudrirse; decaer; cariarse (*los dientes*)
**decease** [dɪˈsis] *s* fallecimiento ‖ *intr* fallecer
**deceased** [dɪˈsist] *adj & s* difunto
**deceit** [dɪˈsit] *s* engaño, fraude *m*
**deceitful** [dɪˈsitfəl] *adj* engañoso, fraudulento
**deceive** [dɪˈsiv] *tr & intr* engañar
**decelerate** [dɪˈsɛləˌret] *tr* desacelerar ‖ *intr* desacelerarse
**December** [dɪˈsɛmbər] *s* diciembre *m*
**decen·cy** [ˈdisənsi] *s* (*pl* **-cies**) decencia, honestidad; (*propriety*) conveniencia
**decent** [ˈdisənt] *adj* decente, honesto; (*proper*) conveniente
**decentralize** [dɪˈsɛntrəˌlaɪz] *tr* descentralizar
**deception** [dɪˈsɛpʃən] *s* engaño
**deceptive** [dɪˈsɛptɪv] *adj* engañoso
**decide** [dɪˈsaɪd] *tr & intr* decidir
**decimal** [ˈdɛsɪməl] *adj & s* decimal *m*
**decimal point** *s* (*in Spanish the comma is used to separate the decimal fraction from the integer*) coma
**decimate** [ˈdɛsɪˌmet] *tr* diezmar
**decipher** [dɪˈsaɪfər] *tr* descifrar
**decision** [dɪˈsɪʒən] *s* decisión
**decisive** [dɪˈsaɪsɪv] *adj* decisivo; determinado, resuelto
**deck** [dɛk] *s* (*of cards*) baraja; (*of ship*) cubierta; **between decks** (naut) entre cubiertas ‖ *tr* — **to deck out** adornar, engalanar
**deck chair** *s* silla de cubierta
**deck hand** *s* marinero de cubierta
**deck'-land'** *intr* apontizar
**deck'-land'ing** *s* apontizaje *m*
**deckle edge** [ˈdɛkəl] *s* barba
**declaim** [dɪˈklem] *tr & intr* declamar
**declaration** [ˌdɛkləˈreʃən] *s* declaración
**declarative** [dɪˈklærətɪv] *adj* declarativo; (gram) enunciativo
**declare** [dɪˈklɛr] *tr & intr* declarar
**declension** [dɪˈklɛnʃən] *s* declinación
**declination** [ˌdɛklɪˈneʃən] *s* declinación
**decline** [dɪˈklaɪn] *s* bajada, declinación; (*in prices*) baja; (*in health, wealth, etc.*) bajón *m*; (*of sun*) ocaso ‖ *tr & intr* declinar; rehusar
**declivi·ty** [dɪˈklɪvɪti] *s* (*pl* **-ties**) declividad, declive *m*
**decode** [diˈkod] *tr* descifrar
**décolleté** [ˌdekɑlˈte] *adj* escotado

**decompose** [ˌdikəmˈpoz] *tr* descomponer ‖ *intr* descomponerse
**decomposition** [ˌdikɑmpəˈzɪʃən] *s* descomposición
**decompression** [ˌdikəmˈprɛʃən] *s* descompresión
**decontamination** [ˌdikəmˌtæmɪˈneʃən] *s* descontaminación
**décor** [deˈkɔr] *s* decoración; (theat) decorado
**decorate** [ˈdɛkəˌret] *tr* decorar; (*with medal, badge*) condecorar
**decoration** [ˌdɛkəˈreʃən] *s* decoración; (*medal, badge*) condecoración
**decorator** [ˈdɛkəˌretər] *s* decorador *m;* (*of interiors*) adornista *mf*
**decorous** [ˈdɛkərəs] o [dɪˈkorəs] *adj* decoroso
**decorum** [dɪˈkorəm] *s* decoro
**decoy** [dɪˈkɔɪ] o [ˈdikɔɪ] *s* añagaza, señuelo; (*person*) entruchón *m* ‖ [dɪˈkɔɪ] *tr* atraer con señuelo; entruchar
**decoy pigeon** *s* cimbel *m*
**decrease** [ˈdikris] o [dɪˈkris] *s* disminución ‖ [dɪˈkris] *tr* disminuir ‖ *intr* disminuir, disminuirse
**decree** [dɪˈkri] *s* decreto ‖ *tr* decretar
**decrepit** [dɪˈkrɛpɪt] *adj* decrépito
**de•cry** [dɪˈkraɪ] *v* (*pret & pp* **-cried**) *tr* censurar, denigrar
**dedicate** [ˈdɛdɪˌket] *tr* dedicar
**dedication** [ˌdɛdɪˈkeʃən] *s* dedicación; (*inscription in a book*) dedicatoria
**deduce** [dɪˈdjus] o [dɪˈdus] *tr* deducir (*inferir, concluir; derivar*)
**deduct** [dɪˈdʌkt] *tr* deducir (*rebajar, substraer*)
**deduction** [dɪˈdʌkʃən] *s* deducción
**deed** [did] *s* acto, hecho; (*feat, exploit*) hazaña; (law) escritura ‖ *tr* traspasar por escritura
**deem** [dim] *tr & intr* creer, juzgar
**deep** [dip] *adj* profundo; (*sound*) grave; (*color*) subido; de hondo, p.ej., **two meters deep** dos metros de hondo; **deep in debt** cargado de deudas; **deep in thought** absorto en la meditación ‖ *adv* hondo; **deep into the night** muy entrada la noche
**deepen** [ˈdipən] *tr* profundizar ‖ *intr* profundizarse
**deep-laid** [ˈdipˌled] *adj* concebido con astucia
**deep mourning** *s* luto riguroso
**deep-rooted** [ˈdipˌrutɪd] *adj* profundamente arraigado
**deep′-sea′ fishing** *s* pesca de gran altura
**deep-seated** [ˈdipˌsitɪd] *adj* profundamente arraigado
**deer** [dɪr] *s* ciervo, venado
**deer′skin′** *s* piel *f* de ciervo
**def.** *abbr* **defendant, deferred, definite**
**deface** [dɪˈfes] *tr* desfigurar
**de facto** [diˈfækto] *adv* de hecho
**defamation** [ˌdɛfəˈmeʃən] o [ˌdifəˈmeʃən] *s* difamación
**defame** [dɪˈfem] *tr* difamar
**default** [dɪˈfɔlt] *s* falta, incumplimiento; **by default** (sport) por no presentarse; **in default of** por falta de ‖ *tr* dejar de cumplir; no pagar ‖ *intr* faltar; (sport) perder por no presentarse
**defeat** [dɪˈfit] *s* derrota ‖ *tr* derrotar, vencer
**defeatism** [dɪˈfitɪzəm] *s* derrotismo
**defeatist** [dɪˈfitɪst] *adj & s* derrotista *mf*
**defecate** [ˈdɛfɪˌket] *intr* defecar
**defect** [dɪˈfɛkt] o [ˈdifɛkt] *s* defecto, imperfección ‖ [dɪˈfɛkt] *intr* desertar
**defection** [dɪˈfɛkʃən] *s* defección; (*lack, failure*) falta
**defective** [dɪˈfɛktɪv] *adj* defectivo, defectuoso
**defend** [dɪˈfɛnd] *tr* defender
**defendant** [dɪˈfɛndənt] *s* (law) demandado, acusado
**defender** [dɪˈfɛndər] *s* defensor *m*
**defense** [dɪˈfɛns] *s* defensa
**defenseless** [dɪˈfɛnslɪs] *adj* indefenso
**defensive** [dɪˈfɛnsɪv] *adj* defensivo ‖ *s* defensiva
**de•fer** [dɪˈfʌr] *v* (*pret & pp* **-ferred;** *ger* **-ferring**) *tr* aplazar, diferir ‖ *intr* deferir
**deference** [ˈdɛfərəns] *s* deferencia
**deferential** [ˌdɛfəˈrɛnʃəl] *adj* deferente
**deferment** [dɪˈfʌrmənt] *s* aplazamiento, dilación
**defiance** [dɪˈfaɪ•əns] *s* oposición; desafío, provocación; **in defiance of** sin mirar a, a despecho de
**defiant** [dɪˈfaɪ•ənt] *adj* provocante, hostil
**deficien•cy** [dɪˈfɪʃənsi] *s* (*pl* **-cies**) carencia, deficiencia; (com) descubierto
**deficient** [dɪˈfɪʃənt] *adj* deficiente, defectuoso
**deficit** [ˈdɛfɪsɪt] *adj* deficitario ‖ *s* déficit *m*
**defile** [dɪˈfaɪl] o [ˈdifaɪl] *s* desfiladero ‖ [dɪˈfaɪl] *tr* corromper, manchar ‖ *intr* desfilar
**define** [dɪˈfaɪn] *tr* definir
**definite** [ˈdɛfɪnɪt] *adj* definido
**definition** [ˌdɛfɪˈnɪʃən] *s* definición
**definitive** [dɪˈfɪnɪtɪv] *adj* definitivo
**deflate** [dɪˈflet] *tr* desinflar
**deflation** [dɪˈfleʃən] *s* desinflación; (*of prices*) deflación
**deflect** [dɪˈflɛkt] *tr* desviar ‖ *intr* desviarse
**deflower** [diˈflaʊ•ər] *tr* desflorar
**deforest** [diˈfɑrest] o [diˈfɔrest] *tr* desforestar, despoblar
**deform** [dɪˈfɔrm] *tr* deformar
**deformed** [dɪˈfɔrmd] *adj* deforme
**deformi•ty** [dɪˈfɔrmɪti] *s* (*pl* **-ties**) deformidad
**defraud** [dɪˈfrɔd] *tr* defraudar
**defray** [dɪˈfre] *tr* sufragar, subvenir a
**defrost** [diˈfrɔst] o [diˈfrɑst] *tr* descongelar, deshelar
**deft** [dɛft] *adj* diestro, hábil
**defunct** [dɪˈfʌŋkt] *adj* difunto
**de•fy** [dɪˈfaɪ] *v* (*pret & pp* **-fied**) *tr* desafiar, provocar
**deg.** *abbr* **degree**

**degeneracy** [dɪˈdʒenərəsi] *s* degeneración
**degenerate** [dɪˈdʒenərɪt] *adj* & *s* degenerado ‖ [dɪˈdʒenəˌret] *intr* degenerar
**degrade** [dɪˈgred] *tr* degradar
**degrading** [dɪˈgredɪŋ] *adj* degradante
**degree** [dɪˈgri] *s* grado; **by degrees** de grado en grado; **to take a degree** graduarse, recibir un grado o título
**dehumidifier** [ˌdihjuˈmɪdɪˌfaɪ·ər] *s* deshumedecedor *m*
**dehydrate** [diˈhaɪdret] *tr* deshidratar
**deice** [diˈaɪs] *tr* deshelar
**dei·fy** [ˈdi·ɪˌfaɪ] *v* (*pret* & *pp* **-fied**) *tr* deificar
**deign** [den] *intr* dignarse
**dei·ty** [ˈdi·ɪti] *s* (*pl* **-ties**) deidad; **the Deity** Dios *m*
**dejected** [dɪˈdʒektɪd] *adj* abatido
**dejection** [dɪˈdʒekʃən] *s* abatimiento
**del.** *abbr* **delegate, delete**
**delay** [dɪˈle] *s* retraso, tardanza ‖ *tr* retrasar ‖ *intr* demorarse
**delectable** [dɪˈlektəbəl] *adj* deleitable
**delegate** [ˈdelɪˌget] o [ˈdelɪgɪt] *s* diputado, delegado; (*to a convention*) congresista *mf* ‖ [ˈdelɪˌget] *tr* delegar
**delete** [dɪˈlit] *tr* borrar, suprimir
**deletion** [dɪˈliʃən] *s* supresión
**deliberate** [dɪˈlɪbərɪt] *adj* pensado, reflexionado; (*slow in deciding*) cauto, circunspecto; (*slow in moving*) espacioso, lento ‖ [dɪˈlɪbəˌret] *tr* & *intr* deliberar
**delica·cy** [ˈdelɪkəsi] *s* (*pl* **-cies**) delicadeza; (*choice food*) golosina
**delicatessen** [ˌdelɪkəˈtesən] *s* colmado, tienda de ultramarinos ‖ *spl* ultramarinos
**delicious** [dɪˈlɪʃəs] *adj* delicioso, sabroso
**delight** [dɪˈlaɪt] *s* deleite *m*, delicia ‖ *tr* deleitar ‖ *intr* deleitarse
**delightful** [dɪˈlaɪtfəl] *adj* deleitoso, ameno, exquisito
**delinquen·cy** [dɪˈlɪŋkwənsi] *s* (*pl* **-cies**) culpa; (*in payment of debt*) morosidad; (*debt in arrears*) atrasos
**delinquent** [dɪˈlɪŋkwənt] *adj* culpado; (*in payment*) moroso, atrasado; no pagado ‖ *s* culpado; deudor moroso
**delirious** [dɪˈlɪrɪ·əs] *adj* delirante
**deliri·um** [dɪˈlɪrɪ·əm] *s* (*pl* **-ums** o **-a** [ə]) delirio
**deliver** [dɪˈlɪvər] *tr* entregar; asestar (*un golpe*); pronunciar, recitar (*un discurso*); transmitir, rendir (*energía*); partear (*a la mujer que está de parto*)
**deliver·y** [dɪˈlɪvəri] *s* (*pl* **-ies**) entrega; (*of mail*) distribución, reparto; (*of a speech*) declamación; (*childbirth*) alumbramiento, parto
**delivery·man** [dɪˈlɪvərimən] *s* (*pl* **-men** [mən]) mozo de reparto
**delivery room** *s* sala de alumbramiento
**delivery truck** *s* sedán *m* de reparto
**dell** [del] *s* vallecito
**delouse** [diˈlaus] o [diˈlauz] *tr* despiojar
**delphinium** [delˈfɪnɪ·əm] *s* (*Delphinium ajacis*) espuela de caballero; (*Delphinium consolida*) consuelda real
**delude** [dɪˈlud] *tr* deludir, engañar
**deluge** [ˈdeljudʒ] *s* diluvio ‖ *tr* inundar
**delusion** [dɪˈluʃən] *s* engaño, decepción
**de luxe** [dɪˈluks] o [dɪˈlʌks] *adj* & *adv* de lujo
**delve** [delv] *intr* cavar; **to delve into** cavar en
**demagnetize** [diˈmægnɪˌtaɪz] *tr* desimantar
**demagogue** [ˈdeməˌgɑg] *s* demagogo
**demand** [dɪˈmænd] o [dɪˈmɑnd] *s* demanda; **to be in demand** tener demanda ‖ *tr* demandar perentoriamente
**demanding** [dɪˈmændɪŋ] o [dɪˈmɑndɪŋ] *adj* exigente
**demarcate** [dɪˈmɑrket] o [ˈdimɑrˌket] *tr* demarcar
**démarche** [deˈmɑrʃ] *s* diligencia, gestión, paso
**demeanor** [dɪˈminər] *s* conducta, porte *m*
**demented** [dɪˈmentɪd] *adj* demente
**demigod** [ˈdemɪˌgɑd] *s* semidiós *m*
**demijohn** [ˈdemɪˌdʒɑn] *s* damajuana
**demilitarize** [diˈmɪlɪtəˌraɪz] *tr* desmilitarizar
**demimonde** [ˈdemɪˌmɑnd] *s* mujeres de vida alegre
**demise** [dɪˈmaɪz] *s* fallecimiento
**demisemiquaver** [ˌdemɪˈsemɪˌkwevər] *s* (mus) fusa
**demitasse** [ˈdemɪˌtæs] o [ˈdemɪˌtɑs] *s* taza pequeña
**demobilize** [diˈmobɪˌlaɪz] *tr* desmovilizar
**democra·cy** [dɪˈmɑkrəsi] *s* (*pl* **-cies**) democracia
**democrat** [ˈdeməˌkræt] *s* demócrata *mf*
**democratic** [ˌdeməˈkrætɪk] *adj* democrático
**demodulate** [diˈmɑdjəˌlet] *tr* desmodular
**demolish** [dɪˈmɑlɪʃ] *tr* demoler
**demolition** [ˌdeməˈlɪʃən] o [ˌdiməˈlɪʃən] *s* demolición
**demon** [ˈdimən] *s* demonio
**demoniacal** [ˌdiməˈnaɪ·əkəl] *adj* demoníaco
**demonstrate** [ˈdemənˌstret] *tr* demostrar ‖ *intr* demostrar; (*to show feelings in public gatherings*) manifestar
**demonstration** [ˌdemənˈstreʃən] *s* demostración; (*public show of feeling*) manifestación
**demonstrative** [dɪˈmɑnstrətɪv] *adj* demostrativo; (*giving open exhibition of emotion*) extremoso
**demonstrator** [ˈdemənˌstretər] *s* demostrador *m*; manifestante *mf*
**demoralize** [dɪˈmɑrəˌlaɪz] o [dɪˈmɔrəˌlaɪz] *tr* desmoralizar

**demote** [dɪ'mot] *tr* degradar
**demotion** [dɪ'moʃən] *s* degradación
**de•mur** [dɪ'mʌr] *v* (*pret & pp* **-murred**; *ger* **-murring**) *intr* poner reparos
**demure** [dɪ'mjʊr] *adj* modesto, recatado; grave, serio
**demurrage** [dɪ'mʌrɪdʒ] *s* (com) estadía
**den** [dɛn] *s* (*of animals, thieves*) madriguera; (*dirty little room*) cuchitril *m;* lugar *m* de retiro; cuarto de estudio; (*of lions*) (Bib) fosa
**denaturalize** [di'nætjərə,laɪz] *tr* desnaturalizar
**denatured alcohol** [di'netʃərd] *s* alcohol desnaturalizado
**denial** [dɪ'naɪ·əl] *s* denegación; negación, desmentida
**denim** ['dɛnɪm] *s* dril *m* de algodón
**denizen** ['dɛnɪzən] *s* habitante *mf,* vecino
**Denmark** ['dɛnmɑrk] *s* Dinamarca
**denomination** [dɪ,nɑmɪ'neʃən] *s* denominación; categoría, clase *f;* secta, confesión, comunión
**denote** [dɪ'not] *tr* denotar
**dénoument** [denu'mɑ̃] *s* desenlace *m*
**denounce** [dɪ'naʊns] *tr* denunciar
**dense** [dɛns] *adj* denso; estúpido
**densi•ty** ['dɛnsɪti] *s* (*pl* **-ties**) densidad
**dent** [dɛnt] *s* abolladura, mella || *tr* abollar, mellar || *intr* abollarse, mellarse
**dental** ['dɛntəl] *adj & s* dental *f*
**dental floss** *s* hilo dental, seda encerada
**dentifrice** ['dɛntɪfrɪs] *s* dentífrico
**dentist** ['dɛntɪst] *s* dentista *mf*
**dentistry** ['dɛntɪstri] *s* odontología
**denture** ['dɛntʃər] *s* dentadura artificial
**denunciation** [dɪ,nʌnsɪ'eʃən] o [dɪ,nʌnʃɪ'eʃən] *s* denuncia
**de•ny** [dɪ'naɪ] *v* (*pret & pp* **-nied**) *tr* (*to declare not to be true*) negar; (*to refuse*) denegar; **to deny oneself to callers** negarse || *intr* negar; denegar
**deodorant** [di'odərənt] *adj & s* desodorante *m*
**deodorize** [di'odə,raɪz] *tr* desodorizar
**deoxidize** [di'ɑksɪ,daɪz] *tr* desoxidar
**dep.** *abbr* **department, departs, deputy**
**depart** [dɪ'pɑrt] *intr* partir, salir, irse; desviarse
**department** [dɪ'pɑrtmənt] *s* departamento; (*of government*) ministerio
**department store** *s* grandes almacenes *mpl*
**departure** [dɪ'pɑrtʃər] *s* partida, salida; desviación
**depend** [dɪ'pɛnd] *intr* depender; **to depend on** depender de
**dependable** [dɪ'pɛndəbəl] *adj* confiable, fidedigno
**dependence** [dɪ'pɛndəns] *s* dependencia
**dependen•cy** [dɪ'pɛndənsi] *s* (*pl* **-cies**) dependencia; (*country, territory*) posesión
**dependent** [dɪ'pɛndənt] *adj* dependiente || *s* carga de familia, familiar *m* dependiente
**depict** [dɪ'pɪkt] *tr* describir, representar, pintar
**deplete** [dɪ'plit] *tr* agotar, depauperar
**deplorable** [dɪ'plorəbəl] *adj* deplorable
**deplore** [dɪ'plor] *tr* deplorar
**deploy** [dɪ'plɔɪ] *tr* (mil) desplegar || *intr* (mil) desplegarse
**deployment** [dɪ'plɔɪmənt] *s* (mil) despliegue *m*
**depolarize** [di'polə,raɪz] *tr* despolarizar
**depopulate** [di'pɑpjə,let] *tr* despoblar
**deport** [dɪ'port] *tr* deportar; **to deport oneself** conducirse, portarse
**deportation** [,dipor'teʃən] *s* deportación
**deportee** [,dipor'ti] *s* deportado
**deportment** [dɪ'portmənt] *s* conducta, comportamiento
**depose** [dɪ'poz] *tr & intr* deponer
**deposit** [dɪ'pɑzɪt] *s* depósito; (*down payment*) señal *f,* pago anticipado; (min) yacimiento || *tr* depositar || *intr* depositarse
**deposit account** *s* cuenta corriente
**depositor** [dɪ'pɑzɪtər] *s* cuentacorrentista *mf,* imponente *mf*
**depot** ['dipo] o ['dɛpo] *s* almacén *m,* depósito; (mil) depósito; (rr) estación
**depraved** [dɪ'prevd] *adj* depravado
**depravi•ty** [dɪ'prævɪti] *s* (*pl* **-ties**) depravación
**deprecate** ['deprɪ,ket] *tr* desaprobar
**depreciate** [dɪ'priʃɪ,et] *tr* (*to lower value or price of*) depreciar; (*to disparage*) desapreciar || *intr* depreciarse
**depreciation** [dɪ,priʃɪ'eʃən] *s* (*drop in value*) depreciación; (*disparagement*) desaprecio
**depress** [dɪ'prɛs] *tr* deprimir; desanimar, desalentar; bajar (*los precios*)
**depression** [dɪ'prɛʃən] *s* depresión; desaliento; (*slump*) crisis *f*
**deprive** [dɪ'praɪv] *tr* privar
**dept.** *abbr* **department**
**depth** [dɛpθ] *s* profundidad; (*of a house, of a room*) fondo; **in the depth of night** en mitad de la noche; **in the depth of winter** en pleno invierno; **to go beyond one's depth** meterse en agua demasiado profunda; (fig) meterse en honduras
**depth of hold** *s* (naut) puntal *m*
**depu•ty** ['dɛpjəti] *s* (*pl* **-ties**) diputado
**derail** [dɪ'rel] *tr* hacer descarrilar || *intr* descarrilar
**derailment** [dɪ'relmənt] *s* descarrilamiento
**derange** [dɪ'rendʒ] *tr* desarreglar, descomponer; trastornar el juicio a
**derangement** [dɪ'rendʒmənt] *s* desarreglo, descompostura; locura
**der•by** ['dʌrbi] *s* (*pl* **-bies**) sombrero hongo
**derelict** ['dɛrɪlɪkt] *adj* abandonado; negligente || *s* pelafustán *m;* (naut) derrelicto
**deride** [dɪ'raɪd] *tr* burlarse de, ridiculizar

**derision** [dɪˈrɪʒən] *s* burla, irrisión
**derive** [dɪˈraɪv] *tr & intr* derivar
**derogatory** [dɪˈrɑgəˌtori] *adj* despreciativo
**derrick** [ˈdɛrɪk] *s* grúa
**dervish** [ˈdʌrvɪʃ] *s* derviche *m*
**desalinization** [dɪˌsɛlɪnɪˈzeʃən] *s* desalinización
**desalt** [diˈsɔlt] *tr* desalar
**descend** [dɪˈsɛnd] *tr* bajar, descender (*la escalera*) || *intr* bajar, descender; **to descend on** caer sobre, invadir
**descendant** [dɪˈsɛndənt] *adj* descendente || *s* descendiente *mf*
**descendent** [dɪˈsɛndənt] *adj* descendente
**descent** [dɪˈsɛnt] *s* (*passing from higher to lower state*) descenso; (*extraction; lineage*) descendencia; cuesta, bajada; invasión
**describe** [dɪˈskraɪb] *tr* describir
**description** [dɪˈskrɪpʃən] *s* descripción
**descriptive** [dɪˈskrɪptɪv] *adj* descriptivo
**de•scry** [dɪˈskraɪ] *v* (*pret & pp* **-scried**) *tr* avistar, divisar; descubrir
**desecrate** [ˈdɛsɪˌkret] *tr* profanar
**desegregation** [diˌsɛgrɪˈgeʃən] *s* desegregación
**desert** [ˈdɛzərt] *adj & s* desierto, yermo || [dɪˈzʌrt] *s* mérito; **he received his just deserts** llevó su merecido || *tr* desertar de || *intr* desertar
**deserter** [dɪˈzʌrtər] *s* desertor *m*
**desertion** [dɪˈzʌrʃən] *s* deserción; abandono de cónyuge
**deserve** [dɪˈzʌrv] *tr & intr* merecer
**deservedly** [dɪˈzʌrvɪdli] *adv* merecidamente
**design** [dɪˈzaɪn] *s* diseño; (*combination of details; art of designing*) dibujo; (*plan, scheme*) designio; **to have designs on** poner la mira en || *tr* diseñar, dibujar; idear, proyectar || *intr* diseñar, dibujar
**designate** [ˈdɛzɪgˌnet] *tr* designar
**designing** [dɪˈzaɪnɪŋ] *adj* intrigante, maquinador
**desirable** [dɪˈzaɪrəbəl] *adj* deseable
**desire** [dɪˈzaɪr] *s* deseo || *tr* desear
**desirous** [dɪˈzaɪrəs] *adj* deseoso
**desist** [dɪˈzɪst] *intr* desistir
**desk** [dɛsk] *s* bufete *m,* escritorio; (*lectern*) atril *m;* (*clerk's counter in a hotel*) caja
**desk clerk** *s* cajero, recepcionista *m*
**desk set** *s* juego de escritorio
**desolate** [ˈdɛsəlɪt] *adj* (*hopeless*) desolado; despoblado, yermo, desierto; solitario; (*dismal*) lúgubre || [ˈdɛsəˌlet] *tr* desconsolar; (*to lay waste*) desolar, devastar; despoblar
**desolation** [ˌdɛsəˈleʃən] *s* (*devastation; great affliction*) desolación; (*dreariness*) lobreguez *f*
**despair** [dɪˈspɛr] *s* desesperación || *intr* desesperar, desesperarse
**despairing** [dɪˈspɛrɪŋ] *adj* desesperado
**despera•do** [ˌdɛspəˈredo] o [ˌdɛspəˈrɑdo] *s* (*pl* **-does** o **-dos**) criminal dispuesto a todo
**desperate** [ˈdɛspərɪt] *adj* dispuesto a todo; (*bitter, excessive*) encarnizado; (*hopeless*) desesperado; (*remedy*) heroico
**despicable** [ˈdɛspɪkəbəl] *adj* despreciable, ruin
**despise** [dɪˈspaɪz] *tr* despreciar, desdeñar
**despite** [dɪˈspaɪt] *prep* a despecho de
**desponden•cy** [dɪˈspɑndənsi] *s* (*pl* **-cies**) abatimiento, desaliento
**despondent** [dɪˈspɑndənt] *adj* abatido, desalentado
**despot** [ˈdɛspɑt] *s* déspota *m*
**despotic** [dɛsˈpɑtɪk] *adj* despótico
**despotism** [ˈdɛspəˌtɪzəm] *s* despotismo
**dessert** [dɪˈzʌrt] *s* postre *m*
**destination** [ˌdɛstɪˈneʃən] *s* (*end of a journey or shipment*) destino; (*purpose*) destinación
**destine** [ˈdɛstɪn] *tr* destinar
**desti•ny** [ˈdɛstɪni] *s* (*pl* **-nies**) destino
**destitute** [ˈdɛstɪˌtjut] o [ˈdɛstɪˌtut] *adj* (*being in complete poverty*) indigente; (*lacking, deprived*) desprovisto
**destitution** [ˌdɛstɪˈtjuʃən] o [ˌdɛstɪˈtuʃən] *s* indigencia
**destroy** [dɪˈstrɔɪ] *tr* destruir
**destroyer** [dɪˈstrɔɪ•ər] *s* (nav) destructor *m*
**destruction** [dɪˈstrʌkʃən] *s* destrucción
**destructive** [dɪˈstrʌktɪv] *adj* destructivo
**desultory** [ˈdɛsəlˌtori] *adj* deshilvanado, descosido
**detach** [dɪˈtætʃ] *tr* desprender, separar; (mil) destacar
**detachable** [dɪˈtætʃəbəl] *adj* desprendible, separable; (*collar*) postizo
**detached** [dɪˈtætʃt] *adj* separado, suelto; imparcial, desinteresado
**detachment** [dɪˈtætʃmənt] *s* desprendimiento, separación; imparcialidad, desinterés *m;* (mil) destacamento
**detail** [dɪˈtel] o [ˈditel] *s* detalle *m,* pormenor *m;* (mil) destacamento || [dɪˈtel] *tr* detallar; (mil) destacar
**detain** [dɪˈten] *tr* detener; tener preso
**detect** [dɪˈtɛkt] *tr* detectar
**detection** [dɪˈtɛkʃən] *s* detección
**detective** [dɪˈtɛktɪv] *s* detective *m*
**detective story** *s* novela policíaca o policial
**detector** [dɪˈtɛktər] *s* detector *m*
**detention** [dɪˈtɛnʃən] *s* detención
**de•ter** [dɪˈtʌr] *v* (*pret & pp* **-terred;** *ger* **-terring**) *tr* impedir, refrenar
**detergent** [dɪˈtʌrdʒənt] *adj & s* detergente *m*
**deteriorate** [dɪˈtɪrɪ•əˌret] *tr* deteriorar || *intr* deteriorarse
**determine** [dɪˈtʌrmɪn] *tr* determinar
**deterrent** [dɪˈtʌrənt] *s* impedimento, refrenamiento
**detest** [dɪˈtɛst] *tr* detestar, aborrecer
**dethrone** [dɪˈθron] *tr* destronar
**detonate** [ˈdɛtəˌnet] o [ˈditəˌnet] *tr* hacer estallar || *intr* detonar
**detour** [ˈditʊr] o [dɪˈtʊr] *s* desvío;

rodeo, vuelta; manera indirecta || *tr* desviar (*el tráfico*) || *intr* desviarse
**detract** [dɪ'trækt] *tr* detraer || *intr* — **to detract from** disminuir, rebajar
**detriment** ['detrɪmənt] *s* perjuicio, detrimento; **to the detriment of** en perjuicio de
**detrimental** [,detrɪ'mentəl] *adj* perjudicial
**deuce** [djus] o [dus] *s* (*in cards*) dos *m;* **the deuce!** ¡demonio!
**devaluation** [di,væljʊ'eʃən] *s* desvalorización, devaluación
**devastate** ['devəs,tet] *tr* devastar
**devastation** [,devəs'teʃən] *s* devastación
**develop** [dɪ'veləp] *tr* desarrollar, desenvolver; (phot) revelar; explotar (*una mina*) || *intr* desarrollarse, desenvolverse; evolucionar, manifestarse
**developer** [dɪ'vɛləpər] *s* fomentador *m;* (phot) revelador *m*
**development** [dɪ'veləpmənt] *s* desarrollo, desenvolvimiento; (phot) revelado; (*of a mine*) explotación; acontecimiento nuevo
**deviate** ['divɪ,et] *tr* desviar || *intr* desviarse
**deviation** [,divɪ'eʃən] *s* desviación
**deviationism** [,divɪ'eʃə,nɪzəm] *s* desviacionismo
**deviationist** [,divɪ'eʃənɪst] *s* desviacionista *mf*
**device** [dɪ'vaɪs] *s* dispositivo, aparato; (*trick*) ardid *m,* treta; (*motto*) lema *m,* divisa; **to leave someone to his own devices** dejarle a uno que haga lo que se le antoje
**dev·il** ['devəl] *s* diablo; **between the devil and the deep blue sea** entre la espada y la pared; **to raise the devil** (slang) armar un alboroto || *v* (*pret & pp* **-iled** o **-illed;** *ger* **-iling** o **-illing**) *tr* condimentar con picantes; (coll) acosar, molestar
**devilish** ['devəlɪʃ] *adj* diabólico
**devilment** ['devəlmənt] *s* (*mischief*) diablura; (*evil*) maldad
**devil·try** ['devəltri] *s* (*pl* **-tries**) maldad, crueldad; (*mischief*) diablura
**devious** ['divɪ·əs] *adj* (*straying*) desviado, extraviado; (*roundabout; shifty*) tortuoso
**devise** [dɪ'vaɪz] *tr* idear, inventar; (law) legar
**devoid** [dɪ'vɔɪd] *adj* desprovisto
**devote** [dɪ'vot] *tr* dedicar
**devoted** [dɪ'votɪd] *adj* (*zealous, ardent*) devoto; dedicado
**devotee** [,devə'ti] *s* devoto
**devotion** [dɪ'voʃən] *s* devoción; (*to study, work, etc.*) dedicación; **devotions** oraciones, preces *fpl*
**devour** [dɪ'vaʊr] *tr* devorar
**devout** [dɪ'vaʊt] *adj* devoto; cordial, sincero
**dew** [dju] o [du] *s* rocío
**dew'drop'** *s* gota de rocío
**dew'lap'** *s* papada
**dew·y** ['dju·i] o ['du·i] *adj* rociado
**dexterity** [deks'terɪti] *s* destreza
**D.F.** *abbr* **Defender of the Faith**
**diabetes** [,daɪ·ə'bitɪs] o [,daɪ·ə'bitiz] *s* diabetes *f*
**diabetic** [,daɪ·ə'betɪk] o [,daɪ·ə'bitɪk] *adj & s* diabético
**diabolic(al)** [,daɪ·ə'bɑlɪk(əl)] *adj* diabólico
**diacritical** [,daɪ·ə'krɪtɪkəl] *adj* diacrítico
**diadem** ['daɪ·ə,dem] *s* diadema *f*
**diaere·sis** [daɪ'erɪsɪs] *s* (*pl* **-ses** [,siz]) diéresis *f*
**diagnose** [,daɪ·əg'nos] o [,daɪ·əg'noz] *tr* diagnosticar
**diagno·sis** [,daɪ·əg'nosɪs] *s* (*pl* **-ses** [siz]) diagnosis *f,* diagnóstico
**diagonal** [daɪ'ægənəl] *adj & s* diagonal *f*
**diagram** ['daɪ·ə,græm] *s* diagrama *m*
**dial.** *abbr* **dialect**
**dial** ['daɪ·əl] *s* (*of radio*) cuadrante *m;* (*of watch*) cuadrante *m,* esfera, muestra; (*of telephone*) disco selector || *tr* sintonizar (*el radiorreceptor*); marcar (*el número telefónico*); llamar (*a una persona*) por teléfono automático || *intr* (telp) marcar
**dialect** ['daɪ·ə,lekt] *s* dialecto
**dialing** ['daɪ·əlɪŋ] *s* (telp) marcaje *m*
**dialogue** ['daɪ·ə,lɔg] o ['daɪ·ə,lɑg] *s* diálogo
**dial telephone** *s* teléfono automático
**dial tone** *s* (telp) señal *f* para marcar
**diam.** *abbr* **diameter**
**diameter** [daɪ'æmɪtər] *s* diámetro
**diametric(al)** [,daɪ·ə'metrɪk(əl)] *adj* diamétrico
**diamond** ['daɪmənd] *s* diamante *m;* (*figure of a rhombus*) losange *m;* (*playing card*) carró *m,* diamante *m;* (baseball) losange *m*
**diaper** ['daɪ·pər] *s* pañal *m*
**diaphanous** [daɪ'æfənəs] *adj* diáfano
**diaphragm** ['daɪ·ə,fræm] *s* diafragma *m*
**diarrhea** [,daɪ·ə'ri·ə] *s* diarrea
**dia·ry** ['daɪ·əri] *s* (*pl* **-ries**) diario
**diastole** [daɪ'æstəli] *s* diástole *f*
**diathermy** ['daɪ·ə,θʌrmi] *s* diatermia
**dice** [daɪs] *spl* dados; (*small cubes*) cubitos; **to load the dice** cargar los dados || *tr* cortar en cubos
**dice'box'** *s* cubilete *m*
**dichloride** [daɪ'kloraɪd] *s* dicloruro
**dichoto·my** [daɪ'kɑtəmi] *s* (*pl* **-mies**) dicotomía
**dickey** ['dɪki] *s* camisolín *m,* pechera postiza; babero de niño
**dict.** *abbr* **dictionary**
**dictaphone** ['dɪktə,fon] *s* dictáfono
**dictate** ['dɪktet] *s* mandato || ['dɪktet] o [dɪk'tet] *tr* dictar; mandar
**dictation** [dɪk'teʃən] *s* dictado; (*orders; giving orders*) mandato; **to take dictation** escribir al dictado
**dictator** ['dɪktetər] o [dɪk'tetər] *s* dictador *m*
**dictatorship** ['dɪktetər,ʃɪp] o [dɪk'tetərʃɪp] *s* dictadura
**diction** ['dɪkʃən] *s* dicción
**dictionar·y** ['dɪkʃən,eri] *s* (*pl* **-ies**) diccionario

**dic•tum** ['dɪktəm] *s* (*pl* **-ta** [tə]) dictamen *m;* aforismo, sentencia
**didactic(al)** [daɪ'dæktɪk(əl)] o [dɪ'dæktɪk(əl)] *adj* didáctico
**die** [daɪ] *s* (*pl* **dice** [daɪs]) dado; **the die is cast** la suerte está echada ‖ *s* (*pl* **dies**) (*for stamping coins, medals, etc.*) troquel *m;* (*for cutting threads*) hembra de terraja ‖ *v* (*pret & pp* **died;** *ger* **dying**) *intr* morir; **to be dying** estar agonizando; **to die laughing** morir de risa
**die'-hard'** *adj & s* intransigente *mf*
**diesel oil** ['dizəl] *s* gas-oil *m*
**die'stock'** *s* terraja
**diet** ['daɪ•ət] *s* dieta, régimen alimenticio ‖ *intr* estar a dieta
**dietitian** [,daɪ•ə'tɪʃən] *s* dietista *mf*
**diff.** *abbr* **difference, different**
**differ** ['dɪfər] *intr* (*to be different*) diferir, diferenciarse; (*to dissent*) diferenciar; **to differ with** desavenirse con
**difference** ['dɪfərəns] *s* diferencia; **to make no difference** no importar; **to split the difference** partir la diferencia
**different** ['dɪfərənt] *adj* diferente
**differentiate** [,dɪfə'renʃɪ,et] *tr* diferenciar ‖ *intr* diferenciarse
**difficult** ['dɪfɪ,kʌlt] *adj* difícil
**difficul•ty** ['dɪfɪ,kʌlti] *s* (*pl* **-ties**) dificultad
**diffident** ['dɪfɪdənt] *adj* apocado, tímido
**diffuse** [dɪ'fjus] *adj* difuso ‖ [dɪ'fjuz] *tr* difundir ‖ *intr* difundirse
**dig** [dɪg] *s* (*poke*) empuje *m;* (*jibe*) pulla, palabra hiriente ‖ *v* (*pret & pp* **dug** [dʌg] o **digged;** *ger* **digging**) *tr* cavar, excavar; **to dig up** desenterrar ‖ *intr* cavar, excavar; **to dig in** (coll) poner manos a la obra; (mil) atrincherarse; **to dig under** socavar
**digest** ['daɪdʒest] *s* compendio, resumen *m;* (law) digesto ‖ [dɪ'dʒest] o [daɪ'dʒest] *tr & intr* digerir
**digestible** [dɪ'dʒestɪbəl] o [daɪ'dʒestɪbəl] *adj* digerible, digestible
**digestion** [dɪ'dʒestʃən] o [daɪ'dʒestʃən] *s* digestión
**digestive** [dɪ'dʒestɪv] o [daɪ'dʒestɪv] *adj & s* digestivo
**digit** ['dɪdʒɪt] *s* dígito
**dignified** ['dɪgnɪ,faɪd] *adj* digno, grave, decoroso
**digni•fy** ['dɪgnɪ,faɪ] *v* (*pret & pp* **-fied**) *tr* dignificar; engrandecer el mérito de
**dignitar•y** ['dɪgnɪ,teri] *s* (*pl* **-ies**) dignatario
**digni•ty** ['dɪgnɪti] *s* (*pl* **-ties**) dignidad; **to stand upon one's dignity** ponerse tan alto
**digress** [dɪ'gres] o [daɪ'gres] *intr* divagar
**digression** [dɪ'greʃən] o [daɪ'greʃən] *s* digresión, divagación
**dike** [daɪk] *s* dique *m;* (*bank of earth thrown up in digging*) montón *m;* (*causeway*) arrecife *m,* malecón *m*
**dilapidated** [dɪ'læpɪ,detɪd] *adj* destartalado, desvencijado
**dilate** [daɪ'let] *tr* dilatar ‖ *intr* dilatarse
**dilatory** ['dɪlə,tori] *adj* tardío
**dilemma** [dɪ'lɛmə] *s* dilema *m,* disyuntiva
**dilettan•te** [,dɪlə'tænti] *adj* diletante ‖ *s* (*pl* **-tes** o **-ti** [ti]) diletante *mf*
**diligence** ['dɪlɪdʒəns] *s* diligencia
**diligent** ['dɪlɪdʒənt] *adj* diligente
**dill** [dɪl] *s* eneldo
**dillydal•ly** ['dɪlɪ,dæli] *v* (*pret & pp* **-lied**) *intr* malgastar el tiempo, haraganear
**dilute** [dɪ'lut] o [daɪ'lut] *adj* diluído ‖ [dɪ'lut] *tr* diluir ‖ *intr* diluirse
**dilution** [dɪ'luʃən] *s* dilución
**dim.** *abbr* **diminutive**
**dim** [dɪm] *adj* (*comp* **dimmer;** *super* **dimmest**) débil, indistinto, confuso; obscuro, poco claro; (*chance*) escaso; (*not clearly understanding*) torpe, lerdo; **to take a dim view of** mirar escépticamente ‖ *v* (*pret & pp* **dimmed;** *ger* **dimming**) *tr* amortiguar (*la luz*); poner (*un faro*) a media luz; disminuir ‖ *intr* obscurecerse
**dime** [daɪm] *s* moneda de diez centavos
**dimension** [dɪ'menʃən] *s* dimensión
**diminish** [dɪ'mɪnɪʃ] *tr* disminuir ‖ *intr* disminuir, disminuirse
**diminutive** [dɪ'mɪnjətɪv] *adj* (*tiny*) diminuto; (gram) diminutivo ‖ *s* diminutivo
**dimi•ty** ['dɪmɪti] *s* (*pl* **-ties**) cotonía
**dimly** ['dɪmli] *adv* indistintamente
**dimmer** ['dɪmər] *s* amortiguador *m* de luz; (aut) lámpara de cruce, luz *f* de cruce
**dimple** ['dɪmpəl] *s* hoyuelo
**dimwit** ['dɪm,wɪt] *s* (slang) mentecato, bobo
**dim-witted** ['dɪm,wɪtɪd] *adj* (slang) mentecato, bobo
**din** [dɪn] *s* estruendo, ruido ensordecedor ‖ *v* (*pret & pp* **dinned;** *ger* **dinning**) *tr* ensordecer con mucho ruido; repetir insistentemente; impresionar con repetición ruidosa ‖ *intr* sonar estrepitosamente
**dine** [daɪn] *tr* dar de comer a; obsequiar con una cena o comida ‖ *intr* cenar, comer; **to dine out** cenar fuera de casa
**diner** ['daɪnər] *s* invitado a una cena, convidado a una comida; coche-comedor *m*
**ding-dong** ['dɪŋ,dɔŋ] o ['dɪŋ,dɑŋ] *s* dindán *m*
**din•gy** ['dɪndʒi] *adj* (*comp* **-gier;** *super* **-giest**) deslustrado, sucio
**dining car** *s* coche-comedor *m*
**dining room** *s* comedor *m*
**din'ing-room' suit** *s* juego de comedor
**dinner** ['dɪnər] *s* cena, comida; (*formal meal*) banquete *m*
**dinner coat** o **jacket** *s* smoking *m*
**dinner pail** *s* fiambrera, portaviandas *m*
**dinner set** *s* vajilla
**dinner time** *s* hora de la cena o comida

**dint** [dɪnt] *s* abolladura; **by dint of** a fuerza de || *tr* abollar
**diocese** [ˈdaɪ·ə‚sis] o [ˈdaɪ·əsɪs] *s* diócesi *f* o diócesis *f*
**diode** [ˈdaɪ·od] *s* diodo
**dioxide** [daɪˈɑksaɪd] *s* dióxido
**dip** [dɪp] *s* zambullida, inmersión; baño corto; (*in a road*) depresión; (*of magnetic needle*) inclinación || *v* (*pret & pp* **dipped**; *ger* **dipping**) *tr* sumergir; sacar con cuchara; (*bread*) sopetear; **to dip the colors** saludar con la bandera || *intr* sumergirse; inclinarse hacia abajo; desaparecer súbitamente; **to dip into** hojear (*un libro*); meterse en (*un comercio*); **to dip into one's purse** gastar dinero
**diphtheria** [dɪfˈθɪrɪ·ə] *s* difteria
**diphthong** [ˈdɪfθɔŋ] o [ˈdɪfθɑŋ] *s* diptongo
**diphthongize** [ˈdɪfθɔŋ‚gaɪz] o [ˈdɪfθɑŋ‚gaɪz] *tr* diptongar || *intr* diptongarse
**diploma** [dɪˈplomə] *s* diploma *m*
**diploma·cy** [dɪˈploməsi] *s* (*pl* **-cies**) diplomacia
**diplomat** [ˈdɪplə‚mæt] *s* diplomático
**diplomatic** [‚dɪpləˈmætɪk] *adj* diplomático
**diplomatic pouch** *s* valija diplomática
**dipper** [ˈdɪpər] *s* cazo, cucharón *m*
**dip'stick'** *s* varilla de nivel
**dire** [daɪr] *adj* horrendo, espantoso
**direct** [dɪˈrɛkt] o [daɪˈrɛkt] *adj* directo; franco, sincero || *tr* dirigir; mandar, ordenar
**direct current** *s* corriente continua
**direct discourse** *s* (gram) estilo directo
**direct hit** *s* blanco directo, impacto directo
**direction** [dɪˈrɛkʃən] o [daɪˈrɛkʃən] *s* dirección; instrucción
**direct object** *s* (gram) complemento directo
**director** [dɪˈrɛktər] o [daɪˈrɛktər] *s* director *m*, administrador *m*; (*member of a governing body*) vocal *m*
**directorship** [dɪˈrɛktər‚ʃɪp] o [daɪˈrɛktər‚ʃɪp] *s* dirección, directorio
**directo·ry** [dɪˈrɛktəri] o [daɪˈrɛktəri] *s* (*pl* **-ries**) (*list of names and addresses; board of directors*) directorio; anuario telefónico, guía telefónica
**dirge** [dʌrdʒ] *s* endecha, canto fúnebre, treno; (eccl) misa de réquiem
**dirigible** [ˈdɪrɪdʒɪbəl] *adj & s* dirigible *m*
**dirt** [dʌrt] *s* (*soil*) tierra, suelo; (*dust*) polvo; (*mud*) barro, lodo; excremento; (*accumulation of dirt*) suciedad; (*moral filth*) suciedad, porquería, obscenidad; (*gossip*) chismes *mpl*
**dirt'cheap'** *adj* tirado, muy barato
**dirt road** *s* camino de tierra
**dirt·y** [ˈdʌrti] *adj* (*comp* **-ier**; *super* **-iest**) puerco, sucio; barroso, enlodado; polvoriento; (*obscene*) hediondo; bajo, vil || *v* (*pret & pp* **-tied**) *tr* ensuciar
**dirty linen** *s* ropa sucia; **to air one's dirty linen in public** sacar los trapos sucios a relucir
**dirty trick** *s* (slang) perrada, mala partida
**disabili·ty** [‚dɪsəˈbɪlɪti] *s* (*pl* **-ties**) incapacidad, inhabilidad
**disable** [dɪsˈebəl] *tr* incapacitar, inhabilitar, lisiar; (law) descalificar
**disabuse** [‚dɪsəˈbjuz] *tr* desengañar
**disadvantage** [‚dɪsədˈvæntɪdʒ] o [‚dɪsədˈvɑntɪdʒ] *s* desventaja
**disadvantageous** [dɪs‚ædvənˈtdʒəs] *adj* desventajoso
**disagree** [‚dɪsəˈgri] *intr* desavenirse, desconvenirse; (*to quarrel*) altercar, contender; **to disagree with** no estar de acuerdo con; no sentar bien
**disagreeable** [‚dɪsəˈgri·əbəl] *adj* desagradable
**disagreement** [‚dɪsəˈgrimənt] *s* desavenencia, desacuerdo; disensión
**disappear** [‚dɪsəˈpɪr] *intr* desaparecer, desaparecerse
**disappearance** [‚dɪsəˈpɪrəns] *s* desaparecimiento, desaparición
**disappoint** [‚dɪsəˈpɔɪnt] *tr* decepcionar, desilusionar, chasquear; **to be disappointed** chasquearse, llevarse chasco
**disappointment** [‚dɪsəˈpɔɪntmənt] *s* decepción, desilusión, chasco
**disapproval** [‚dɪsəˈpruvəl] *s* desaprobación
**disapprove** [‚dɪsəˈpruv] *tr & intr* desaprobar
**disarm** [dɪsˈɑrm] *tr* desarmar || *intr* desarmar, desarmarse
**disarmament** [dɪsˈɑrməmənt] *s* desarme *m*
**disarming** [dɪsˈɑrmɪŋ] *adj* congraciador, simpático
**disarray** [‚dɪsəˈre] *s* desorden *m*; (*in apparel*) desatavío || *tr* desordenar; desataviar
**disaster** [dɪˈzæstər] o [dɪˈzɑstər] *s* desastre *m*, siniestro
**disastrous** [dɪˈzæstrəs] o [dɪˈzɑstrəs] *adj* desastroso, desastrado
**disavow** [‚dɪsəˈvaʊ] *tr* desconocer, negar, repudiar
**disband** [dɪsˈbænd] *tr* disolver (*una asamblea*); licenciar (*tropas*) || *intr* desbandarse
**dis·bar** [dɪsˈbɑr] *v* (*pret & pp* **-barred**; *ger* **-barring**) *tr* (law) expulsar del foro
**disbelief** [‚dɪsbɪˈlif] *s* incredulidad
**disbelieve** [‚dɪsbɪˈliv] *tr & intr* descreer
**disburse** [dɪsˈbʌrs] *tr* desembolsar
**disbursement** [dɪsˈbʌrsmənt] *s* desembolso
**disc.** *abbr* **discount, discoverer**
**disc** [dɪsk] *s* disco
**discard** [dɪsˈkɑrd] *s* descarte *m*; **to put into the discard** desechar || *tr* descartar; desechar
**discern** [dɪˈzʌrn] o [dɪˈsʌrn] *tr* discernir, percibir
**discerning** [dɪˈzʌrnɪŋ] o [dɪˈsʌrnɪŋ] *adj* discerniente, perspicaz
**discharge** [dɪsˈtʃɑrdʒ] *s* (*of a gun, of*

*a battery*) descarga; (*of a prisoner*) liberación; (*of a duty*) desempeño; (*of a debt, of an obligation*) descargo; (*from a job*) despedida, remoción; (mil) certificado de licencia; (pathol) derrame *m* || *tr* descargar; desempeñar (*un deber*); libertar (*a un preso*); despedir, remover (*a un empleado*); (*from the hospital*) dar de alta; (mil) licenciar || *intr* descargar (*un tubo, río, etc.*); descargarse (*un arma de fuego*)
**disciple** [dɪ'saɪpəl] *s* discípulo
**disciplinarian** [,dɪsɪplɪ'nerɪ·ən] *s* ordenancista *mf*
**discipline** ['dɪsɪplɪn] *s* disciplina; castigo || *tr* disciplinar; castigar
**disclaim** [dɪs'klem] *tr* desconocer, negar
**disclose** [dɪs'kloz] *tr* divulgar, revelar; descubrir
**disclosure** [dɪs'kloʒər] *s* divulgación, revelación; descubrimiento
**discolor** [dɪs'kʌlər] *tr* descolorar || *intr* descolorarse
**discomfiture** [dɪs'kʌmfɪtʃər] *s* desconcierto; frustración
**discomfort** [dɪs'kʌmfərt] *s* incomodidad || *tr* incomodar
**disconcert** [,dɪskən'sʌrt] *tr* desconcertar, confundir
**disconnect** [,dɪskə'nɛkt] *tr* desunir, separar; desconectar
**disconsolate** [dɪs'kɑnsəlɪt] *adj* desconsolado, desolado
**discontent** [,dɪskən'tent] *adj* & *s* descontento || *tr* descontentar
**discontented** [,dɪskən'tentɪd] *adj* descontento
**discontinue** [,dɪskən'tɪnjʊ] *tr* descontinuar
**discord** ['dɪskɔrd] *s* desacuerdo, discordia; discordancia
**discordance** [dɪs'kɔrdəns] *s* discordancia
**discotheque** [,dɪsko'tɛk] *s* discoteca
**discount** ['dɪskaʊnt] *s* descuento || ['dɪskaʊnt] o [dɪs'kaʊnt] *tr* descontar; descontar por exagerado
**discount rate** *s* tipo de descuento; tipo de redescuento
**discourage** [dɪs'kʌrɪdʒ] *tr* desalentar, desanimar; desaprobar; disuadir
**discouragement** [dɪs'kʌrɪdʒmənt] *s* desaliento; desaprobación; disuasión
**discourse** ['dɪskors] o [dɪs'kors] *s* discurso || [dɪs'kors] *intr* discurrir
**discourteous** [dɪs'kʌrtɪ·əs] *adj* descortés
**discourte·sy** [dɪs'kʌrtəsi] *s* (*pl* **-sies**) descortesía
**discover** [dɪs'kʌvər] *tr* descubrir
**discover·y** [dɪs'kʌvəri] *s* (*pl* **-ies**) descubrimiento
**discredit** [dɪs'kredɪt] *s* descrédito || *tr* desacreditar
**discreditable** [dɪs'kredɪtəbəl] *adj* deshonroso
**discreet** [dɪs'krit] *adj* discreto
**discrepan·cy** [dɪs'krepənsi] *s* (*pl* **-cies**) discrepancia
**discrete** [dɪs'krit] *adj* discreto
**discretion** [dɪs'kreʃən] *s* discreción; **at discretion** a discreción
**discriminate** [dɪs'krɪmɪ,net] *intr* discriminar; **to discriminate against** discriminar
**discrimination** [dɪs,krɪmɪ'neʃən] *s* discriminación
**discriminatory** [dɪs'krɪmɪnə,tori] *adj* discriminatorio
**discus** ['dɪskəs] *s* (sport) disco
**discuss** [dɪs'kʌs] *tr* & *intr* discutir
**discussion** [dɪs'kʌʃən] *s* discusión
**discus thrower** ['θro·ər] *s* discóbolo
**disdain** [dɪs'den] *s* desdén *m* || *tr* desdeñar
**disdainful** [dɪs'denfəl] *adj* desdeñoso
**disease** [dɪ'ziz] *s* enfermedad
**diseased** [dɪ'zizd] *adj* morboso
**disembark** [,dɪsem'bɑrk] *tr* & *intr* desembarcar
**disembarkation** [dɪs,embɑr'keʃən] *s* (*of passengers*) desembarco; (*of freight*) desembarque *m*
**disembowel** [,dɪsem'baʊ·əl] *tr* desentrañar
**disenchant** [,dɪsen'tʃænt] o [,dɪsen'tʃɑnt] *tr* desencantar
**disenchantment** [,dɪsen'tʃæntmənt] o [,dɪsen'tʃɑntmənt] *s* desencanto
**disengage** [,dɪsen'gedʒ] *tr* (*from a pledge*) desempeñar; (*to disconnect*) desenganchar; desembragar (*el motor*)
**disengagement** [,dɪsen'gedʒmənt] *s* desempeño; desenganche *m*; desembrague *m*
**disentangle** [,dɪsen'tæŋgəl] *tr* desenredar
**disentanglement** [,dɪsen'tæŋgəlmənt] *s* desenredo
**disestablish** [,dɪses'tæblɪʃ] *tr* separar (*la Iglesia*) del Estado
**disfavor** [dɪs'fevər] *s* disfavor *m*
**disfigure** [dɪs'fɪgjər] *tr* desfigurar
**disfranchise** [dɪs'fræntʃaiz] *tr* privar de los derechos de ciudadanía
**disgorge** [dɪs'gɔrdʒ] *tr* & *intr* vomitar
**disgrace** [dɪs'gres] *s* deshonra, vergüenza; disfavor *m* || *tr* deshonrar, avergonzar; despedir con ignominia
**disgraceful** [dɪs'gresfəl] *adj* deshonroso, vergonzoso
**disgruntle** [dɪs·grʌntəl] *tr* disgustar, enfadar
**disguise** [dɪs'gaɪz] *s* disfraz *m* || *tr* disfrazar
**disgust** [dɪs'gʌst] *s* asco, repugnancia || *tr* dar asco a, repugnar
**disgusting** [dɪs'gʌstɪŋ] *adj* asqueroso, repugnante
**dish** [dɪʃ] *s* (*any container used at table*) vasija; (*shallow, circular dish; its contents*) plato; **to wash the dishes** lavar la vajilla || *tr* servir en un plato; (slang) arruinar
**dish'cloth'** *s* albero
**dishearten** [dɪs'hɑrtən] *tr* descorazonar, desalentar, desanimar
**dishev·el** [dɪ'ʃevəl] *v* (*pret* & *pp* **-eled** o **-elled**; *ger* **-eling** o **-elling**) desgreñar, desmelenar

**dishonest** [dɪsˈɑnɪst] *adj* no honrado, ímprobo
**dishones·ty** [dɪsˈɑnɪsti] *s* (*pl* **-ties**) falta de honradez, improbidad
**dishonor** [dɪsˈɑnər] *s* deshonra, deshonor *m* ‖ *tr* deshonrar, deshonorar; (com) no aceptar, no pagar
**dishonorable** [dɪsˈɑnərəbəl] *adj* ignominioso, deshonroso
**dish'pan'** *s* paila de lavar la vajilla
**dish rack** *s* escurreplatos *m*
**dish'rag'** *s* albero
**dish'tow'el** *s* paño para secar platos
**dish'wash'er** *s* (*person*) fregona; (*machine*) lavaplatos *m*
**dish'wa'ter** *s* agua de lavar platos, agua sucia
**disillusion** [ˌdɪsɪˈluʒən] *s* desilusión ‖ *tr* desilusionar
**disillusionment** [ˌdɪsɪˈluʒənmənt] *s* desilusión
**disinclination** [dɪsˌɪnklɪˈneʃən] *s* aversión, desafición
**disinclined** [ˌdɪsɪnˈklaɪnd] *adj* desinclinado
**disinfect** [ˌdɪsɪnˈfɛkt] *tr* desinfectar, desinficionar
**disinfectant** [ˌdɪsɪnˈfɛktənt] *adj* & *s* desinfectante *m*
**disingenuous** [ˌdɪsɪnˈdʒenjʊ·əs] *adj* insincero, poco ingenuo
**disinherit** [ˌdɪsɪnˈherɪt] *tr* desheredar
**disintegrate** [dɪsˈɪntɪˌgret] *tr* desagregar, desintegrar ‖ *intr* desagregarse, desintegrarse
**disintegration** [dɪsˌɪntɪˈgreʃən] *s* desagregación, desintegración
**disin·ter** [ˌdɪsɪnˈtʌr] *v* (*pret* & *pp* **-terred**; *ger* **-terring**) *tr* desenterrar
**disinterested** [dɪsˈɪntəˌrɛstɪd] o [dɪsˈɪntrɪstɪd] *adj* desinteresado
**disinterestedness** [dɪsˈɪntəˌrɛstɪdnɪs] o [dɪsˈɪntrɪstɪdnɪs] *s* desinterés *m*
**disjunctive** [dɪsˈdʒʌŋktɪv] *adj* disyuntivo
**disk** [dɪsk] *s* disco
**disk jockey** *s* (rad) locutor *m* de un programa de discos
**dislike** [dɪsˈlaɪk] *s* aversión, antipatía; **to take a dislike for** cobrar aversión a ‖ *tr* desamar
**dislocate** [ˈdɪsloˌket] *tr* dislocar, dislocarse (*un hueso*)
**dislodge** [dɪsˈlɑdʒ] *tr* desalojar
**disloyal** [dɪsˈlɔɪ·əl] *adj* desleal
**disloyal·ty** [dɪsˈlɔɪ·əlti] *s* (*pl* **-ties**) deslealtad
**dismal** [ˈdɪzməl] *adj* lúgubre, tenebroso; terrible, espantoso
**dismantle** [dɪsˈmæntəl] *tr* desarmar, desmontar
**dismay** [dɪsˈme] *s* consternación ‖ *tr* consternar
**dismember** [dɪsˈmembər] *tr* desmembrar
**dismiss** [dɪsˈmɪs] *tr* despedir, destituir; desechar; alejar del pensamiento, echar en olvido
**dismissal** [dɪsˈmɪsəl] *s* despedida, destitución
**dismount** [dɪsˈmaʊnt] *tr* desmontar ‖ *intr* desmontarse

**disobedience** [ˌdɪsəˈbidɪ·əns] *s* desobediencia
**disobedient** [ˌdɪsəˈbidɪ·ənt] *adj* desobediente
**disobey** [ˌdɪsəˈbe] *tr* & *intr* desobedecer
**disorder** [dɪsˈɔrdər] *s* desorden *m* ‖ *tr* desordenar
**disorderly** [dɪsˈɔrdərli] *adj* desordenado; alborotador, revoltoso
**disorderly conduct** *s* conducta contra el orden público
**disorderly house** *s* burdel *m*, lupanar *m*
**disorganize** [dɪsˈɔrgəˌnaɪz] *tr* desorganizar
**disown** [dɪsˈon] *tr* desconocer, repudiar
**disparage** [dɪsˈpærɪdʒ] *tr* desacreditar, desdorar
**disparagement** [dɪsˈpærɪdʒmənt] *s* descrédito, desdoro
**disparate** [ˈdɪspərɪt] *adj* disparejo
**dispari·ty** [dɪsˈpærɪti] *s* (*pl* **-ties**) disparidad
**dispassionate** [dɪsˈpæʃənɪt] *adj* desapasionado
**dispatch** [dɪsˈpætʃ] *s* despacho ‖ *tr* despachar; (coll) despabilar (*una comida*)
**dis·pel** [dɪsˈpel] *v* (*pret* & *pp* **-pelled**; *ger* **-pelling**) *tr* desvanecer, disipar
**dispensa·ry** [dɪsˈpensəri] *s* (*pl* **-ries**) dispensario
**dispense** [dɪsˈpens] *tr* dispensar (*medicamentos*); administrar (*justicia*); expender (*p.ej., gasolina*); (*to exempt*) eximir ‖ *intr* — **to dispense with** deshacerse de; pasar sin, prescindir de
**disperse** [dɪsˈpʌrs] *tr* dispersar ‖ *intr* dispersarse
**displace** [dɪsˈples] *tr* remover, trasladar; despedir, deponer; reemplazar; desplazar (*un volumen de agua*)
**displaced person** *s* persona desplazada
**display** [dɪsˈple] *s* despliegue *m*; exhibición, exposición; ostentación ‖ *tr* (*to unfold; to reveal*) desplegar; (*to exhibit, show*) exhibir, exponer; (*to show ostentatiously*) ostentar
**display cabinet** *s* vitrina, escaparate *m*
**display window** *s* escaparate *m* de tienda
**displease** [dɪsˈpliz] *tr* desagradar, disgustar, desplacer
**displeasing** [dɪsˈplizɪŋ] *adj* desagradable
**displeasure** [dɪsˈpleʒər] *s* desagrado, disgusto, desplacer *m*
**disposable** [dɪsˈpozəbəl] *adj* (*available for any use*) disponible; (*made to be thrown away after serving its purpose*) desechable, descartable
**disposal** [dɪsˈpozəl] *s* disposición; donación, liquidación, venta; **at the disposal of** a la disposición de; **to have at one's disposal** disponer de
**dispose** [dɪsˈpoz] *tr* disponer; inducir, mover ‖ *intr* disponer; **to dispose of** disponer de; deshacerse de; dar, vender; acabar con

**disposition** [ˌdɪspəˈzɪʃən] *s* disposición; índole *f*, genio, natural *m;* ajuste *m*, arreglo; venta
**dispossess** [ˌdɪspəˈzɛs] *tr* desposeer; (*to evict, oust*) desahuciar
**disproof** [dɪsˈpruf] *s* confutación, refutación
**disproportionate** [ˌdɪsprəˈporʃənɪt] *adj* desproporcionado
**disprove** [dɪsˈpruv] *tr* confutar, refutar
**dispute** [dɪsˈpjut] *s* disputa; **beyond dispute** sin disputa; **in dispute** disputado ‖ *tr & intr* disputar
**disquali·fy** [dɪsˈkwalɪˌfaɪ] *v* (*pret & pp* **-fied**) *tr* descalificar, desclasificar
**disquiet** [dɪsˈkwaɪ·ət] *s* desasosiego, inquietud ‖ *tr* desasosegar, inquietar
**disregard** [ˌdɪsrɪˈgard] *s* desatención, desaire *m* ‖ *tr* desatender, desairar, pasar por alto
**disrepair** [ˌdɪsrɪˈpɛr] *s* desconcierto, descompostura
**disreputable** [dɪsˈrɛpjətəbəl] *adj* desacreditado, de mala fama; raído, usado, desaliñado
**disrepute** [ˌdɪsrɪˈpjut] *s* descrédito, mala fama; **to bring into disrepute** desacreditar, dar mala fama a
**disrespect** [ˌdɪsrɪˈspɛkt] *s* desacato ‖ *tr* desacatar
**disrespectful** [ˌdɪsrɪˈspɛktfəl] *adj* irrespetuoso
**disrobe** [dɪsˈrob] *tr* desnudar ‖ *intr* desnudarse
**disrupt** [dɪsˈrʌpt] *tr* romper; (*to throw into disorder*) desbaratar
**dissatisfaction** [ˌdɪssætɪsˈfækʃən] *s* desagrado, descontento
**dissatisfied** [dɪsˈsætɪsˌfaɪd] *adj* descontento
**dissatis·fy** [dɪsˈsætɪsˌfaɪ] *v* (*pret & pp* **-fied**) *tr* descontentar
**dissect** [dɪˈsɛkt] *tr* disecar
**dissemble** [dɪˈsɛmbəl] *tr* disimular ‖ *intr* disimular; obrar hipócritamente
**disseminate** [dɪˈsɛmɪˌnet] *tr* diseminar, difundir
**dissension** [dɪˈsɛnʃən] *s* disensión
**dissent** [dɪˈsɛnt] *s* disensión; (*nonconformity*) disidencia ‖ *intr* disentir; (*from doctrine or authority*) disidir
**dissenter** [dɪˈsɛntər] *s* disidente *mf*
**disservice** [dɪˈsʌrvɪs] *s* deservicio
**dissidence** [ˈdɪsɪdəns] *s* disidencia
**dissident** [ˈdɪsɪdənt] *adj & s* disidente *mf*
**dissimilar** [dɪˈsɪmɪlər] *adj* disímil, desemejante
**dissimilate** [dɪˈsɪmɪˌlet] *tr* disimilar ‖ *intr* disimilarse
**dissimulate** [dɪˈsɪmjəˌlet] *tr & intr* disimular
**dissipate** [ˈdɪsɪˌpet] *tr* disipar ‖ *intr* disiparse; entregarse a la disipación
**dissipated** [ˈdɪsɪˌpetɪd] *adj* disipado, disoluto
**dissipation** [ˌdɪsɪˈpeʃən] *s* disipación
**dissociate** [dɪˈsoʃɪˌet] *tr* disociar
**dissolute** [ˈdɪsəˌlut] *adj* disoluto
**dissolution** [ˌdɪsəˈluʃən] *s* disolución
**dissolve** [dɪˈzalv] *tr* disolver ‖ *intr* (*to have the power of dissolving*) disolver; (*to pass into a liquid*) disolverse
**dissonance** [ˈdɪsənəns] *s* disonancia
**dissuade** [dɪˈswed] *tr* disuadir
**dissyllabic** [ˌdɪssɪˈlæbɪk] *adj* disílabo, disilábico
**dissyllable** [dɪˈsɪləbəl] *s* disílabo
**dist.** *abbr* **distance, distinguish, district**
**distaff** [ˈdɪstæf] o [ˈdɪstaf] *s* rueca
**distaff side** *s* rama femenina de la familia
**distance** [ˈdɪstəns] *s* distancia; **at a distance** a distancia; **in the distance** a lo lejos; **to keep at a distance** no permitir familiaridades; **to keep one's distance** mantenerse a distancia
**distant** [ˈdɪstənt] *adj* distante; (*relative*) lejano; (*not familiar*) frío, indiferente
**distaste** [dɪsˈtest] *s* aversión, repugnancia
**distasteful** [dɪsˈtestfəl] *adj* desagradable, repugnante
**distemper** [dɪsˈtɛmpər] *s* enfermedad; (*of dogs*) moquillo
**distend** [dɪsˈtɛnd] *tr* ensanchar, distender ‖ *intr* ensancharse, distender
**distension** [dɪsˈtɛnʃən] *s* ensanche *m*, distensión
**distill** [dɪsˈtɪl] *tr* destilar
**distillation** [ˌdɪstɪˈleʃən] *s* destilación
**distiller·y** [dɪsˈtɪləri] *s* (*pl* **-ies**) destilería, destilatorio
**distinct** [dɪsˈtɪŋkt] *adj* distinto; cierto, indudable; (*not blurred*) nítido, bien definido
**distinction** [dɪsˈtɪŋkʃən] *s* distinción; (*distinguishing characteristic*) distintivo
**distinctive** [dɪsˈtɪŋktɪv] *adj* distintivo
**distinguish** [dɪsˈtɪŋgwɪʃ] *tr* distinguir
**distinguished** [dɪsˈtɪŋgwɪʃt] *adj* distinguido
**distort** [dɪsˈtɔrt] *tr* deformar, torcer; (*the truth*) falsear
**distortion** [dɪsˈtɔrʃən] *s* deformación, torcimiento; (*of the truth*) falseamiento; (rad) deformación, distorsión
**distract** [dɪsˈtrækt] *tr* distraer
**distraction** [dɪsˈtrækʃən] *s* distracción
**distraught** [dɪsˈtrɔt] *adj* trastornado, perplejo, aturdido
**distress** [dɪsˈtrɛs] *s* pena, aflicción, angustia; infortunio, peligro ‖ *tr* apenar, afligir, angustiar
**distressing** [dɪsˈtrɛsɪŋ] *adj* penoso, angustioso
**distress signal** *s* señal *f* de socorro
**distribute** [dɪsˈtrɪbjut] *tr* distribuir, repartir
**distribution** [ˌdɪstrɪˈbjuʃən] *s* distribución, repartimiento
**distributor** [dɪsˈtrɪbjətər] *s* distribuidor *m;* (aut) distribuidor
**district** [ˈdɪstrɪkt] *s* comarca, región; (*of a city*) barrio; (*administrative division*) distrito ‖ *tr* dividir en distritos
**district attorney** *s* fiscal *m*

**distrust** [dɪs'trʌst] *s* desconfianza ‖ *tr* desconfiar de
**distrustful** [dɪs'trʌstfəl] *adj* desconfiado
**disturb** [dɪs'tʌrb] *tr* disturbar, incomodar, molestar; desordenar, revolver; inquietar, dejar perplejo; perturbar (*el orden público*)
**disturbance** [dɪs'tʌrbəns] *s* disturbio, molestia; desorden *m;* inquietud; tumulto, trastorno
**disuse** [dɪs'jus] *s* desuso
**ditch** [dɪtʃ] *s* zanja ‖ *tr* zanjar; echar en una zanja; (slang) deshacerse de ‖ *intr* amarar forzosamente
**ditch reed** *s* carrizo
**dither** ['dɪðər] *s* agitación, temblor; **to be in a dither** (coll) estar muy agitado
**dit•to** ['dɪto] *s* (*pl* **-tos**) ídem *m;* (*ditto symbol*) íd.; copia, duplicado ‖ *tr* copiar, duplicar
**ditto mark** *s* la sigla " (*es decir:* íd.)
**dit•ty** ['dɪti] *s* (*pl* **-ties**) cancioneta
**div.** *abbr* **dividend, division**
**diva** ['divɑ] *s* (mus) diva
**divan** ['daɪvæn] o [dɪ'væn] *s* diván *m*
**dive** [daɪv] *s* zambullida; (*of a submarine*) sumersión; (aer) picado; (coll) leonera, tasca ‖ *v* (*pret & pp* **dived** o **dove** [dov]) *intr* zambullirse; (*to work as a diver*) bucear; sumergirse (*un submarino*); (aer) picar
**dive'-bomb'** *tr & intr* bombardear en picado
**dive bombing** *s* bombardeo en picado
**diver** ['daɪvər] *s* zambullidor *m;* (*person who works under water*) escafandrista *mf,* buzo; (orn) zambullidor *m*
**diverge** [dɪ'vʌrdʒ] o [daɪ'vʌrdʒ] *intr* divergir
**divers** ['daɪvərz] *adj* diversos, varios
**diverse** [dɪ'vʌrs], [daɪ'vʌrs] o ['daɪvʌrs] *adj* (*different*) diverso; (*of various kinds*) variado
**diversification** [dɪ,vʌrsɪfɪ'keʃən] o [daɪ,vʌrsɪfɪ'keʃən] *s* diversificación
**diversi•fy** [dɪ'vʌrsɪ,faɪ] o [daɪ'vʌrsɪ,faɪ] *v* (*pret & pp* **-fied**) *tr* diversificar ‖ *intr* diversificarse
**diversion** [dɪ'vʌrʒən] o [daɪ'vʌrʒən] *s* diversión
**diversi•ty** [dɪ'vʌrsɪti] o [daɪ'vʌrsɪti] *s* (*pl* **-ties**) diversidad
**divert** [dɪ'vʌrt] o [daɪ'vʌrt] *tr* apartar, divertir; (*to entertain*) divertir, entretener; (mil) divertir
**diverting** [dɪ'vʌrtɪŋ] o [daɪ'vʌrtɪŋ] *adj* divertido
**divest** [dɪ'vest] o [daɪ'vest] *tr* desnudar; despojar, desposeer; **to divest oneself of** desposeerse de
**divide** [dɪ'vaɪd] *s* (geog) divisoria ‖ *tr* dividir ‖ *intr* dividirse
**dividend** ['dɪvɪ,dend] *s* dividendo
**dividers** [dɪ'vaɪdərz] *spl* compás *m* de división
**divination** [,dɪvɪ'neʃən] *s* adivinación
**divine** [dɪ'vaɪn] *adj* divino ‖ *s* sacerdote *m,* clérigo ‖ *tr* adivinar
**diving** ['daɪvɪŋ] *s* zambullida; buceo
**diving bell** *s* campana de buzo
**diving board** *s* trampolín *m*
**diving suit** *s* escafandra
**divining rod** [dɪ'vaɪnɪŋ] *s* vara de adivinar; (*ostensibly to discover water or metals*) vara buscadora
**divini•ty** [dɪ'vɪnɪti] *s* (*pl* **-ties**) divinidad; teología; **the Divinity** Dios *m*
**division** [dɪ'vɪʒən] *s* división
**divisor** [dɪ'vaɪzər] *s* (math) divisor *m*
**divorce** [dɪ'vors] *s* divorcio; **to get a divorce** divorciarse ‖ *tr* divorciar (*los cónyuges*); divorciarse de (*la mujer o el marido*) ‖ *intr* divorciarse
**divorcee** [dɪvor'si] *s* persona divorciada; mujer divorciada
**divulge** [dɪ'vʌldʒ] *tr* divulgar, revelar
**dizziness** ['dɪzɪnɪs] *s* vértigo; confusión, perplejidad
**diz•zy** ['dɪzi] *adj* (*comp* **-zier;** *super* **-ziest**) (*suffering or causing dizziness*) vertiginoso; confuso, perplejo; aturdido, incauto; (coll) tonto
**do.** *abbr* **ditto**
**do** [du] *v* (*tercera persona* **does** [dʌz]; *pret* **did** [dɪd]; *pp* **done** [dʌn]) *tr* hacer; resolver (*un problema*); recorrer (*cierta distancia*); cumplir con (*un deber*); aprender (*una lección*); componer (*la cama*); tocar (*el cabello*); rendir (*homenaje*); **to do one's best** hacer todo lo posible; **to do over** volver a hacer; repetir; renovar; **to do right by** tratar bien; **to do someone out of something** (coll) defraudar algo a alguien; **to do to death** despachar, matar; **to do up** empaquetar; poner en orden; almidonar y planchar (*una camisa*) ‖ *intr* actuar, obrar; conducirse; servir, ser suficiente; estar, hallarse; **how do you do?** ¿cómo está Vd.?; **that will do** eso sirve, eso es bastante; no digas más; **to have done** haber terminado; **to have done with** no tener más que ver con; **to have nothing to do with** no tener nada que ver con; **to have to do with** tratar de; **to do away with** suprimir; matar; **to do for** servir para; **to do well** salir bien; **to do without** pasar sin ‖ *v aux* úsase 1) en oraciones interrogativas: **Do you speak Spanish?** ¿Habla Vd. español?; 2) en oraciones negativas: **I do not speak Spanish** No hablo español; 3) para substituir a otro verbo en oraciones elípticas: **Did you go to church this morning? Yes, I did** ¿Fué Vd. a la iglesia esta mañana? Sí, fuí; 4) para dar más energía a la oración: **I do believe what you told me** Yo sí creo lo que me dijo Vd.; 5) en inversiones después de ciertos adverbios: **Seldom does he come to see me** él rara vez viene a verme; 6) en tono suplicante con el imperativo: **Do come in** pase Vd., por favor
**docile** ['dɑsɪl] *adj* dócil
**dock** [dɑk] *s* (*wharf*) muelle *m;* (*wa-*

*terway between two piers*) dársena; (*area including piers and waterways*) puerto de mar; muñón *m* de cola; (law) tribuna de los acusados || *tr* (naut) atracar en el muelle; derrabar, descolar (*a un animal*); reducir o suprimir (*el salario*) || *intr* (naut) atracar

**dockage** ['dakɪdʒ] *s* entrada en un puerto; (*charges*) muellaje *m*

**docket** ['dakɪt] *s* actas, orden *m* del día; lista de causas pendientes; **on the docket** (coll) pendiente, entre manos

**dock hand** *s* portuario

**dock'yard'** *s* arsenal *m*, astillero

**doctor** ['daktər] *s* doctor *m*; (*physician*) médico || *tr* medicinar; (coll) componer, reparar || *intr* (coll) ejercer la medicina; (coll) tomar medicinas

**doctorate** ['daktərɪt] *s* doctorado

**doctrine** ['daktrɪn] *s* doctrina

**document** ['dakjəmənt] *s* documento || ['dakjə,ment] *tr* documentar

**documenta·ry** [,dakjə'mentəri] *adj* documental || *s* (*pl* **-ries**) documental *m*

**documentation** [,dakəmen'teʃən] *s* documentación

**doddering** ['dadərɪŋ] *adj* chocho, temblón

**dodge** [dadʒ] *s* esguince *m*, regate *m*; (fig) regate || *tr* evitar (*un golpe*); (fig) evitar mañosamente || *intr* regatear, hurtar el cuerpo; **to dodge around the corner** voltear la esquina

**do·do** ['dodo] *s* (*pl* **-dos** o **-does**) (coll) inocente *m* de ideas anticuadas

**doe** [do] *s* cierva, gama, coneja

**doeskin** ['do,skɪn] *s* ante *m*, piel *f* de ante; tejido fino de lana

**doff** [daf] o [dɔf] *tr* quitarse (*el sombrero, la ropa*)

**dog** [dɔg] o [dag] *s* perro; **to go to the dogs** darse al abandono; **to put on the dog** (coll) darse ínfulas || *v* (*pret & pp* **dogged**; *ger* **dogging**) *tr* acosar, perseguir

**dog'catch'er** *s* lacero

**dog days** *spl* canícula, caniculares *mpl*

**doge** [dodʒ] dux *m*

**dogged** ['dɔgɪd] o ['dagɪd] *adj* tenaz, terco

**doggerel** ['dɔgərəl] o ['dagərəl] *s* coplas de ciego

**dog·gy** ['dɔgi] o ['dagi] *adj* (*comp* **-gier**; *super* **-giest**) emperejilado || *s* (*pl* **-gies**) perrito

**dog'house'** *s* perrera

**dog in the manger** *s* el perro del hortelano

**dog Latin** *s* latinajo, latín *m* de cocina

**dogmatic** [dɔg'mætɪk] o [dag'mætɪk] *adj* dogmático

**dog racing** *s* carreras de galgos

**dog's-ear** ['dɔgz,ɪr] o ['dagz,ɪr] *s* orejón *m*

**dog show** *s* exposición canina

**dog's life** *s* vida miserable

**Dog Star** *s* Canícula

**dog'-tired'** *adj* cansadísimo

**dog'tooth'** *s* (*pl* **-teeth** [,tiθ]) colmillo

**dog track** *s* galgódromo

**dog'watch'** *s* (naut) guardia de cuartillo

**dog'wood'** *s* cornejo

**doi·ly** ['dɔɪli] *s* (*pl* **-lies**) pañito de adorno

**doings** ['du·ɪŋz] *spl* acciones, obras, actividad

**doldrums** ['daldrəmz] *spl* (naut) calmas ecuatoriales; desanimación, inactividad

**dole** [dol] *s* limosna; subsidio a los desocupados || *tr* — **to dole out** distribuir en pequeñas porciones

**doleful** ['dolfəl] *adj* triste, lúgubre

**doll** [dal] *s* muñeca || *intr* — **to doll up** (slang) emperejilarse

**dollar** ['dalər] *s* dólar *m*

**dollar mark** *s* signo del dólar

**dol·ly** ['dali] *s* (*pl* **-lies**) muñequita; (*low, wheeled frame for moving heavy loads*) gato rodante

**dolphin** ['dalfɪn] *s* delfín *m*

**dolt** [dolt] *s* bobalicón *m*

**doltish** ['doltɪʃ] *adj* bobalicón

**dom.** *abbr* **domestic, dominion**

**domain** [do'men] *s* dominio; heredad, propiedad; (*of learning*) campo

**dome** [dom] *s* cúpula, domo

**dome light** *s* (aut) lámpara de techo

**domestic** [də'mestɪk] *adj & s* doméstico

**domesticate** [də'mestɪ,ket] *tr* domesticar

**domicile** ['damɪsɪl] o ['damɪ,saɪl] *s* domicilio || *tr* domiciliar

**dominance** ['damɪnəns] *s* dominación

**dominant** ['damɪnənt] *adj & s* dominante *f*

**dominate** ['damɪ,net] *tr & intr* dominar

**domination** [,damɪ'neʃən] *s* dominación

**domineer** [,damɪ'nɪr] *intr* dominar

**domineering** [,damɪ'nɪrɪŋ] *adj* dominante, mandón

**Dominican** [də'mɪnɪkən] *adj & s* dominicano

**dominion** [də'mɪnjən] *s* dominio

**domi·no** ['damɪ,no] *s* (*pl* **-noes** o **-nos**) (*costume*) dominó *m*; antifaz *m*; persona que lleva dominó; ficha (*del juego de dominó*); **dominoes** *ssg* dominó (*juego*)

**don** [dan] *s* caballero, señor *m*, personaje *m* de alta categoría; (coll) preceptor *m*, socio de uno de los colegios de las Universidades de Oxford y Cambridge || *v* (*pret & pp* **donned**; *ger* **donning**) *tr* ponerse (*el sombrero, la ropa*)

**donate** ['donet] *tr* dar, donar

**donation** [do'neʃən] *s* donación

**done** [dʌn] *adj* hecho, terminado; cansado, rendido; bien asado

**done for** *adj* (coll) cansado, rendido, agotado; (coll) arruinado, destruído; (coll) fuera de combate; (coll) muerto

**donjon** ['dʌndʒən] o ['dandʒən] *s* torre *f* del homenaje

**donkey** [ˈdɑŋki] *s* asno, burro
**donnish** [ˈdɑnɪʃ] *adj* magistral, pedantesco
**donor** [ˈdonər] *s* donador *m*
**doodle** [ˈdudəl] *tr & intr* borrajear
**doom** [dum] *s* ruina, perdición, muerte *f;* condena, juicio; juicio final; hado, destino || *tr* condenar; sentenciar a muerte; predestinar a la ruina, a la muerte
**doomsday** [ˈdumzˌde] *s* día *m* del juicio final; día del juicio
**door** [dor] *s* puerta; (*of a carriage or automobile*) portezuela; (*one part of a double door*) hoja, batiente *m;* **behind closed doors** a puertas cerradas; **to see to the door** acompañar a la puerta
**door'bell'** *s* campanilla de puerta, timbre *m* de puerta
**door check** *s* amortiguador *m,* cierre *m* de puerta
**door'frame'** *s* bastidor *m* de puerta, marco de puerta
**door'head'** *s* dintel *m*
**door'jamb'** *s* jamba de puerta
**door'knob'** *s* botón *m* de puerta, pomo de puerta
**door knocker** *s* aldaba
**door latch** *s* pestillo
**door•man** [ˈdormən] *s* (*pl* **-men** [mən]) portero; (*one who helps people in and out of cars*) abrecoches *m*
**door'mat'** *s* felpudo de puerta
**door'nail'** *s* clavo de adorno para puertas; **dead as a doornail** (coll) muerto sin duda alguna
**door'post'** *s* jamba de puerta
**door scraper** *s* limpiabarros *m*
**door'sill'** *s* umbral *m*
**door'step'** *s* escalón *m* delante de la puerta; escalera exterior
**door'stop'** *s* tope *m* de puerta
**door'way'** *s* puerta, portal *m*
**dope** [dop] *s* grasa lubricante; (aer) barniz *m,* nobabia; (slang) bobo, tonto; (slang) informes *mpl;* (slang) narcótico || *tr* (slang) narcotizar, drogar; **to dope out** (slang) descifrar
**dope fiend** *s* (slang) toxicómano
**dope sheet** *s* (slang) hoja confidencial sobre los caballos de carreras
**dormant** [ˈdɔrmənt] *adj* durmiente, latente
**dormer window** [ˈdɔrmər] *s* buharda, buhardilla
**dormito•ry** [ˈdɔrmɪˌtori] *s* (*pl* **-ries**) dormitorio común
**dor•mouse** [ˈdɔrˌmaʊs] *s* (*pl* **-mice** [ˌmaɪs]) lirón *m*
**dosage** [ˈdosɪdʒ] *s* dosificación
**dose** [dos] *s* dosis *f;* (coll) mal trago || *tr* medicinar; dosificar (*un medicamento*)
**dossier** [ˈdɑsɪˌe] *s* expediente *m*
**dot** [dɑt] *s* punto; **on the dot** (coll) en punto || *v* (*pret & pp* **dotted;** *ger* **dotting**) *tr* (*to make with dots*) puntear; poner punto a; **to dot one's i's** poner los puntos sobre las íes
**dotage** [ˈdotɪdʒ] *s* chochera, chochez *f;* **to be in one's dotage** chochear
**dotard** [ˈdotərd] *s* viejo chocho
**dote** [dot] *intr* chochear; **to dote on** estar chocho por
**doting** [ˈdotɪŋ] *adj* chocho
**dots and dashes** *spl* (telg) puntos y rayas
**dotted line** [ˈdɑtɪd] *s* línea de puntos; **to sign on the dotted line** firmar ciegamente
**double** [ˈdʌbəl] *adj* doble || *adv* doble; dos juntos || *s* doble *m,* duplo; (mov, theat) doble *mf;* **doubles** (tennis) juego de dobles || *tr* doblar; ser el doble de; (bridge) doblar || *intr* doblarse; (mov, theat, bridge) doblar; **to double up** doblarse en dos; ocupar una misma habitación, dormir en una misma cama (*dos personas*)
**double-barreled** [ˈdʌbəlˈbærəld] *adj* de dos cañones; (fig) para dos fines
**double bass** [bes] *s* contrabajo
**double bassoon** *s* contrabajón *m*
**double bed** *s* cama de matrimonio
**double-breasted** [ˈdʌbəlˈbrestɪd] *adj* cruzado, de dos pechos
**double chin** *s* papada
**dou'ble-cross'** *tr* traicionar (*a un cómplice*)
**double date** *s* cita de dos parejas
**doub'le-deal'er** *s* persona doble
**double-edged** [ˈdʌbəlˈɛdʒd] *adj* de dos filos
**double entry** *s* (com) partida doble
**double feature** *s* (mov) programa *m* doble, programa de dos películas de largo metraje
**double-header** [ˈdʌbəlˈhɛdər] *s* tren *m* con dos locomotoras; (baseball) dos partidos jugados sucesivamente
**double-jointed** [ˈdʌbəlˈdʒɔɪntɪd] *adj* de articulaciones dobles
**dou'ble-park'** *tr & intr* aparcar en doble fila
**dou'ble-quick'** *adj & adv* a paso ligero || *s* paso ligero || *intr* marchar a paso ligero
**doublet** [ˈdʌblɪt] *s* (*close-fitting jacket*) jubón *m;* (*counterfeit stone; each of two words having the same origin*) doblete *m*
**double talk** *s* (coll) galimatías *m;* (coll) habla ambigua para engañar
**double time** *s* pago doble por horas extraordinarias de trabajo; (mil) paso redoblado
**doubleton** [ˈdʌbəltən] *s* doblete *m*
**double track** *s* doble vía
**doubt** [daʊt] *s* duda; **beyond doubt** sin duda; **if in doubt** en caso de duda; **no doubt** sin duda || *tr* dudar, dudar de || *intr* dudar
**doubter** [ˈdaʊtər] *s* incrédulo
**doubtful** [ˈdaʊtfəl] *adj* dudoso
**doubtless** [ˈdaʊtlɪs] *adj* indudable || *adv* sin duda; probablemente
**douche** [duʃ] *s* ducha; (*instrument*) jeringa || *tr* duchar || *intr* ducharse
**dough** [do] *s* masa, pasta; (*money*) (slang) pasta
**dough'boy'** *s* (coll) soldado norteamericano de infantería

**dough'nut'** *s* rosquilla, buñuelo
**dough•ty** ['daʊti] *adj* (*comp* **-tier;** *super* **-tiest**) (hum) fuerte, valiente
**dough•y** ['do·i] *adj* (*comp* **-ier;** *super* **-iest**) pastoso
**dour** [daʊr] o [dʊr] *adj* triste, melancólico, austero
**douse** [daʊs] *tr* empapar, mojar, salpicar; (slang) apagar (*la luz*)
**dove** [dʌv] *s* paloma
**dovecote** ['dʌv,kot] *s* palomar *m*
**dove'tail'** *s* cola de milano, cola de pato || *tr* ensamblar a cola de milano, ensamblar a cola de pato; (*to make fit*) encajar || *intr* (*to fit*) encajar; concordar, corresponder
**dowager** ['daʊ·ədʒər] *s* viuda con título o bienes que proceden del marido, p.ej., **dowager duchess** duquesa viuda; (coll) matrona, señora anciana respetable
**dow•dy** ['daʊdi] *adj* (*comp* **-dier;** *super* **-diest**) desaliñado
**dow•el** ['daʊ·əl] *s* clavija || *v* (*pret & pp* **-eled** o **-elled;** *ger* **-eling** o **-elling**) *tr* enclavijar
**dower** ['daʊ·ər] *s* (*widow's portion*) viudedad; (*marriage portion*) dote *m & f;* (*natural gift*) prenda || *tr* señalar viudedad a; dotar
**down** [daʊn] *adj* descendente; abatido, triste; enfermo, malo; acostado, echado; (*money, payment*) anticipado; (*storage battery*) agotado || *adv* abajo; hacia abajo; en tierra; al sur; por escrito; al contado; **down and out** arruinado; sin blanca; **down from** desde; **down on one's knees** de rodillas; **down to** hasta; **down under** entre los antípodas; **down with . . . !** ¡abajo . . . !; **to get down to work** aplicarse resueltamente al trabajo; **to go down** bajar; **to lie down** acostarse; **to sit down** sentarse || *prep* bajando; **down the river** río abajo; **down the street** calle abajo || *s* (*of fruit and human body*) vello; (*of birds*) plumón *m;* descenso; revés *m* de fortuna; (*sand hill*) duna || *tr* derribar; (coll) tragar
**down'cast'** *adj* cariacontecido
**down'fall'** *s* caída, ruina; chaparrón *m;* nevazo
**down'grade'** *adj* (coll) pendiente, en declive || *adv* (coll) cuesta abajo || *s* bajada, declive *m;* **to be on the downgrade** decaer, declinar || *tr* disminuir la categoría de
**downhearted** ['daʊn,hɑrtɪd] *adj* abatido, desanimado
**down'hill'** *adj* pendiente || *adv* cuesta abajo; **to go downhill** ir cabeza abajo
**down'pour'** *s* aguacero, chaparrón *m*
**down'right'** *adj* absoluto, categórico; franco; claro || *adv* absolutamente
**down'stairs'** *adj* de abajo || *adv* abajo || *s* piso inferior, pisos inferiores; (*the help*) la servidumbre
**down'stream'** *adv* aguas abajo, río abajo
**down'stroke'** *s* carrera descendente
**down'town'** *adj* céntrico || *adv* al centro de la ciudad, en el centro de la ciudad || *s* barrios céntricos, calles céntricas
**down train** *s* tren *m* descendente
**down'trend'** *s* tendencia a la baja
**downtrodden** ['daʊn,trɑdən] *adj* pisoteado, oprimido
**downward** ['daʊnwərd] *adj* descendente || *adv* hacia abajo; hacia una época posterior
**down•y** ['daʊni] *adj* (*comp* **-ier;** *super* **-iest**) plumoso, felpudo, velloso; suave, blando
**dow•ry** ['daʊri] *s* (*pl* **-ries**) dote *m & f*
**doz.** *abbr* **dozen**
**doze** [doz] *s* duermevela, sueño ligero || *intr* dormitar
**dozen** ['dʌzən] *s* docena
**dozy** ['dozi] *adj* soñoliento
**D.P.** *abbr* **displaced person**
**dpt.** *abbr* **department**
**dr.** *abbr* **debtor, drawer, dram**
**Dr.** *abbr* **debtor, Doctor**
**drab** [dræb] *adj* (*comp* **drabber;** *super* **drabbest**) gris amarillento; monótono || *s* gris amarillento; ramera; mujer desaliñada
**drach•ma** ['drækmə] *s* (*pl* **-mas** o **-mae** [mi]) dracma
**draft** [dræft] o [drɑft] *s* corriente *f* de aire; (*pulling; current of air in a chimney*) tiro; (*sketch, outline*) bosquejo; (*first form of a writing*) borrador *m;* (*drink*) bebida, trago; (com) giro, letra de cambio, libranza; aire inspirado; (naut) calado; (mil) conscripción, quinta; **drafts** damas, juego de damas; **on draft** a presión; **to be exempted from the draft** redimirse de las quintas || *tr* dibujar; bosquejar; hacer un borrador de; redactar (*un documento*); (mil) quintar; **to be drafted** (mil) ir a quintas
**draft age** *s* edad *f* de quintas
**draft beer** *s* cerveza a presión
**draft board** *s* (mil) junta de reclutamiento
**draft call** *s* llamada a quintas
**draft dodger** ['dɑdʒər] *s* emboscado
**draftee** [,dræf'ti] o [,drɑf'ti] *s* conscripto, quinto
**draft horse** *s* caballo de tiro
**drafting room** *s* sala de dibujo
**drafts•man** ['dræftsmən] o ['drɑftsmən] *s* (*pl* **-men** [mən]) dibujante *m;* (*man who draws up documents*) redactor *m;* (*in checkers*) peón *m*
**draft treaty** *s* proyecto de convenio
**draft•y** ['dræfti] o ['drɑfti] *adj* (*comp* **-ier;** *super* **-iest**) airoso, con corrientes de aire
**drag** [dræg] *s* (*sledge for conveying heavy bodies*) narria; (*on a cigarette*) chupada; fumada; (naut) rastra; (aer) resistencia al avance; (fig) estorbo, impedimento; **to have a drag** (slang) tener buenas aldabas, tener enchufe || *v* (*pret & pp* **dragged;** *ger* **dragging**) *tr* arrastrar; (naut) rastrear || *intr* arrastrarse por el suelo; avanzar muy lentamente; decaer (*el*

*interés*); **to drag on** ser interminable, prolongarse interminablemente
**drag'net'** *s* red barredera
**dragon** ['drægən] *s* dragón *m*
**drag'on·fly'** *s* (*pl* **-flies**) caballito del diablo, libélula
**dragoon** [drə'gun] *s* (*soldier*) dragón *m* || *tr* tiranizar; forzar, constreñir
**drain** [dren] *s* dren *m*, desaguadero, desagüe *m*; (surg) dren *m*; (*source of continual expense*) (fig) desaguadero || *tr* drenar, desaguar; avenar (*terrenos húmedos*); escurrir (*una vasija; un líquido*) || *intr* desaguarse; escurrirse
**drainage** ['drenɪdʒ] *s* drenaje *m*, desagüe *m*
**drain'board'** *s* escurridero
**drain cock** *s* llave *f* de purga
**drain'pipe'** *s* tubo de desagüe, escurridero
**drain plug** *s* tapón *m* de desagüe; (aut) tapón de vaciado
**drake** [drek] *s* pato
**dram** [dræm] *s* dracma; trago de aguardiente
**drama** ['drɑmə] o ['dræmə] *s* drama *m*; (*art and genre*) dramática
**dramatic** [drə'mætɪk] *adj* dramático || **dramatics** *ssg* representación de aficionados; *spl* obras representadas por aficionados
**dramatist** ['dræmətɪst] *s* dramático
**dramatize** ['dræmə,taɪz] *tr* dramatizar
**dram'shop'** *s* bar *m*, taberna
**drape** [drep] *s* cortina, colgadura; (*hang of a curtain, skirt, etc.*) caída || *tr* cubrir con colgaduras; adornar con colgaduras; disponer los pliegues de (*una colgadura, una prenda de vestir*)
**draper·y** ['drepəri] *s* (*pl* **-ies**) colgaduras, ropaje *m*
**drastic** ['dræstɪk] *adj* drástico
**draught** [dræft] o [drɑft] *s* & *tr* var de **draft**
**draught beer** *s* cerveza a presión
**draw** [drɔ] *s* (*in a game or other contest*) empate *m*; (*in chess or checkers*) tablas; (*in a lottery*) sorteo; (*card drawn from the bank*) robo; (*of a drawbridge*) compuerta; (*of a chimney*) tiro || *v* (*pret* **drew** [dru]; *pp* **drawn** [drɔn]) *tr* tirar (*una línea; alambre*); (*to attract*) tirar; (*to pull*) tirar de; derretir (*la mantequilla*); sacar (*un clavo, una espada, agua, una conclusión*); atraerse (*aplausos*); atraer (*a la gente*); aspirar (*el aire*); llamar (*la atención*); dar (*un suspiro*); correr (*una cortina*); cobrar (*un salario*); sacarse (*un premio*); empatar (*una partida*); robar (*fichas, naipes*); levantar (*un puente levadizo*); calar (*un buque cierta profundidad*); hacer (*una comparación*); consumir (*amperios*); (*to sketch in lines*) dibujar; (*to sketch in words*) redactar; (com) girar, librar; (com) devengar (*interés*); **to draw forth** hacer salir; **to draw off** sacar, extraer; trasegar (*un líquido*); **to draw on** ocasionar, provocar; ponerse (*p.ej., los zapatos*); (com) girar a cargo de; **to draw oneself up** enderezarse con dignidad; **to draw out** (*to persuade to talk*) sonsacar, tirar de la lengua a; **to draw up** redactar (*un documento*); (mil) ordenar para el combate || *intr* tirar, tirar bien (*una chimenea*); empatar; echar suertes; atraer mucha gente; dibujar; **to draw aside** apartarse; **to draw back** retroceder, retirarse; **to draw near** acercarse; acercarse a; **to draw to a close** estar para terminar; **to draw together** juntarse, unirse
**draw'back'** *s* desventaja, inconveniente *m*
**draw'bridge'** *s* puente levadizo
**drawee** [,drɔ'i] *s* girado, librado
**drawer** ['drɔ·ər] *s* dibujante *mf*; (com) girador *m*, librador *m* || [drɔr] *s* cajón *m*, gaveta; **drawers** calzoncillos
**drawing** ['drɔ·ɪŋ] *s* dibujo; (*in a lottery*) sorteo
**drawing board** *s* tablero de dibujo
**drawing card** *s* polo de atracción popular
**drawing room** *s* sala, salón *m*
**draw'knife'** *s* (*pl* **-knives** [,naɪvz]) cuchilla de dos mangos
**drawl** [drɔl] *s* habla lenta y prolongada || *tr* decir lenta y prolongadamente || *intr* hablar lenta y prolongadamente
**drawn butter** [drɔn] *s* mantequilla derretida
**drawn work** *s* calado, deshilado
**dray** [dre] *s* carro fuerte, camión *m*; (*sledge*) narria
**drayage** ['dre·ɪdʒ] *s* acarreo
**dread** [drɛd] *adj* espantoso, terrible || *s* pavor *m*, terror *m* || *tr* & *intr* temer
**dreadful** ['drɛdfəl] *adj* espantoso, terrible; (coll) feo, desagradable
**dread'naught'** *s* (nav) gran buque acorazado
**dream** [drim] *s* sueño, ensueño; (*thing of great beauty*) sueño; (*fancy, illusion*) ensueño; **dream come true** sueño hecho realidad || *v* (*pret* & *pp* **dreamed** o **dreamt** [drɛmt]) *tr* soñar; **to dream up** (coll) imaginar, inventar; || *intr* soñar; **to dream of** soñar con
**dreamer** ['drimər] *s* soñador *m*
**dream'land'** *s* reino del ensueño
**dream world** *s* tierra de la fantasía
**dream·y** ['drimi] *adj* (*comp* **-ier**; *super* **-iest**) soñador; visionario; vago
**drear·y** ['drɪri] *adj* (*comp* **-ier**; *super* **-iest**) sombrío, triste; monótono, pesado
**dredge** [drɛdʒ] *s* draga || *tr* dragar, rastrear; (culin) enharinar
**dredger** ['drɛdʒər] *s* draga (*barco*)
**dredging** ['drɛdʒɪŋ] *s* dragado
**dregs** [drɛgz] *spl* heces *fpl*; (*of society*) hez *f*
**drench** [drɛntʃ] *tr* mojar, empapar
**dress** [drɛs] *s* ropa, vestidos; vestido de mujer; (*skirt*) falda; traje *m* de

etiqueta; (*of a bird*) plumaje *m* || *tr* vestir; (*to provide with clothing*) trajear; peinar (*el pelo*); curar (*una herida*); zurrar (*el cuero*); empavesar (*un barco*); adornar, ataviar; aderezar, aliñar (*los manjares*); **to dress down** (coll) reprender; **to get dressed** vestirse || *intr* (*to put one's clothing on*) vestirse; (*to wear clothes*) vestir; (mil) alinearse; **to dress up** vestirse de etiqueta; ponerse de veinticinco alfileres; disfrazarse
**dress ball** *s* baile *m* de etiqueta
**dress coat** *s* frac *m*
**dresser** ['dresər] *s* tocador *m;* cómoda con espejo; (*sideboard*) aparador *m;* **to be a good dresser** vestir con elegancia
**dress form** *s* maniquí *m*
**dress goods** *spl* géneros para vestidos
**dressing** ['dresɪŋ] *s* adorno; (*for food*) aliño, salsa; (*stuffing for fowl*) relleno; (*fertilizer*) abono; (*for a wound*) vendaje *m*
**dress'ing-down'** *s* (coll) repasata, regaño
**dressing gown** *s* bata, peinador *m*
**dressing room** *s* cuarto de vestir; (theat) camarín *m*
**dressing station** *s* (mil) puesto de socorro
**dressing table** *s* tocador *m*
**dress'mak'er** *s* costurera, modista
**dress'mak'ing** *s* costura, modistería
**dress rehearsal** *s* ensayo general
**dress shirt** *s* camisa de pechera almidonada, camisa de pechera de encaje
**dress shop** *s* casa de modas
**dress suit** *s* traje *m* de etiqueta
**dress tie** *s* corbata de smoking, corbata de frac
**dress·y** ['dresi] *adj* (*comp* **-ier;** *super* **-iest**) (coll) elegante; (*showy*) acicalado, vistoso, peripuesto
**dribble** ['drɪbəl] *s* goteo; (coll) llovizna || *tr* (sport) driblar || *intr* gotear; (*at the mouth*) babear; (sport) driblar
**driblet** ['drɪblɪt] *s* gotita; pedacito
**dried beef** [draɪd] *s* cecina
**dried fig** *s* higo paso
**dried peach** *s* orejón *m*
**drier** ['draɪ·ər] *s* enjugador *m;* (*for hair*) secador *m;* (*for clothes*) secadora; (*rack for drying clothes*) tendedero (de ropa)
**drift** [drɪft] *s* movimiento; (*of sand, snow*) montón *m;* (*movement of snow*) ventisca; tendencia, dirección; intención, sentido; (aer, naut) deriva; (rad, telv) desviación || *intr* flotar a la deriva; amontonarse (*la nieve*); ventiscar; (aer, naut) derivar, ir a la deriva; (fig) vivir sin rumbo
**drift ice** *s* hielo flotante
**drift'wood'** *s* madera flotante; madera llevada por el agua; madera arrojada a la playa por el agua; (*people*) vagos
**drill** [drɪl] *s* taladro; instrucción; (*fabric*) dril *m;* (mil) ejercicio || *tr* taladrar; instruir; (mil) enseñar el ejercicio a || *intr* adiestrarse; (mil) hacer el ejercicio
**drill'mas'ter** *s* amaestrador *m;* (mil) instructor *m*
**drill press** *s* prensa taladradora
**drink** [drɪŋk] *s* bebida; **the drinks are on the house!** ¡convida la casa! || *v* (*pret* **drank** [dræŋk]; *pp* **drunk** [drʌŋk]) *tr* beber; beberse (*su sueldo*); **to drink down** beber de una vez; **to drink in** beber (*las palabras de una persona*); beberse (*un libro*); aspirar (*el aire*) || *intr* beber; **to drink out of** beber de o en; **to drink to the health of** beber a o por la salud de
**drinkable** ['drɪŋkəbəl] *adj* bebedizo, potable
**drinker** ['drɪŋkər] *s* bebedor *m*
**drinking** ['drɪnkɪŋ] *s* (el) beber
**drinking cup** *s* taza para beber
**drinking fountain** *s* fuente *f* para beber
**drinking song** *s* canción báquica, canción de taberna
**drinking trough** *s* abrevadero
**drinking water** *s* agua para beber
**drip** [drɪp] *s* goteo; gotas || *v* (*pret & pp* **dripped;** *ger* **dripping**) *intr* caer gota a gota, gotear
**drip coffee** *s* café *m* de maquinilla
**drip'-dry'** *adj* de lava y pon
**drip pan** *s* colector *m* de aceite
**drive** [draɪv] *s* paseo en coche; calzada; fuerza, vigor *m;* urgencia; campaña vigorosa; venta a bajo precio; (aut) tracción (*delantera o trasera*); (mach) transmisión, mando || *v* (*pret* **drove** [drov]; *ger* **driven** ['drɪvən]) *tr* conducir, guiar, manejar (*un automóvil*); clavar, hincar (*un clavo*); arrear (*a las bestias*); (*in a carriage or auto*) llevar (*a una persona*); empujar, impeler; estimular; forzar, compeler; obligar a trabajar mucho; (sport) golpear con gran fuerza; **to drive away** ahuyentar; **to drive back** rechazar; **to drive mad** volver loco || *intr* ir en coche; **to drive at** aspirar a; querer decir; **to drive hard** trabajar mucho; **to drive in** entrar en coche; entrar en (*un sitio*) en coche; **to drive on the right** circular por la derecha; **to drive out** salir en coche; **to drive up** llegar en coche
**drive-in movie theater** ['draɪv ˌɪn] *s* auto-teatro
**drive-in restaurant** *s* restaurante *m* donde los clientes no necesitan dejar sus coches
**driv·el** ['drɪvəl] *s* (*slobber*) baba; (*nonsense*) bobería || *v* (*pret* **-eled** o **-elled;** *ger* **-eling** o **-elling**) *intr* babear; (*to talk nonsense*) bobear
**driver** ['draɪvər] *s* conductor *m;* (*of a carriage*) cochero; (*of a locomotive*) maquinista *m;* (*of pack animals*) arriero
**driver's license** *s* carnet *m* de chófer, permiso de conducir
**drive shaft** *s* árbol *m* de mando, eje *m* motor

**drive'way'** *s* calzada; camino de entrada para coches
**drive wheel** *s* rueda motriz
**drive'-your·self' service** *s* alquiler *m* sin chófer
**driving school** *s* auto-escuela
**drizzle** ['drɪzəl] *s* llovizna ‖ *intr* lloviznar
**droll** [drol] *adj* chusco, gracioso
**dromedar·y** ['drɑmə,deri] *s* (*pl* **-ies**) dromedario
**drone** [dron] *s* zángano; (*buzz, hum*) zumbido; (*of bagpipe*) bordón *m*, roncón *m*; avión radiodirigido ‖ *tr* decir monótonamente ‖ *intr* hablar monótonamente; (*to live in idleness*) zanganear; (*to buzz, hum*) zumbar
**drool** [drul] *s* (*slobber*) baba; (slang) bobería ‖ *intr* babear; (slang) bobear
**droop** [drup] *s* inclinación ‖ *intr* caer, colgar; inclinarse; marchitarse; abatirse; encamarse (*el grano*)
**drooping** ['drupɪŋ] *adj* (*eyelid, shoulder*) caído
**drop** [drɑp] *s* gota; (*slope*) pendiente *f*; (*earring*) pendiente *m*; (*in temperature*) descenso; (*of supplies from an airplane*) lanzamiento; (*trap door*) escotillón *m*; (*gallows*) horca; (*lozenge*) pastilla; (*small amount*) chispa; (*slit for letters*) buzón *m*; (*curtain*) telón *m*; **a drop in the bucket** una gota en el mar ‖ *v* (*pret & pp* **dropped**; *ger* **dropping**) *tr* dejar caer; echar (*una carta*) al buzón; bajar (*una cortina*); soltar (*una indirecta*); escribir (*una esquela*); omitir, suprimir; abandonar, dejar; echar (*el ancla*); borrar de la lista (*a un alumno*); lanzar (*bombas o suministros de un avión*) ‖ *intr* caer; bajar; cesar, terminar; **to drop dead** caer muerto; **to drop in** entrar al pasar, visitar de paso; **to drop off** desaparecer; quedarse dormido; morir de repente; **to drop out** desaparecer; retirarse; darse de baja
**drop curtain** *s* telón *m*
**drop hammer** *s* martinete *m*
**drop'-leaf' table** *s* mesa de hoja plegadiza
**drop'light'** *s* lámpara colgante
**drop'out'** *s* fracasado, desertor *m* escolar; **to become a dropout** ahorcar los libros
**dropper** ['drɑpər] *s* cuentagotas *m*
**drop shutter** *s* obturador *m* de guillotina
**dropsical** ['drɑpsɪkəl] *adj* hidrópico
**dropsy** ['drɑpsi] *s* hidropesía
**drop table** *s* mesa perezosa
**dross** [drɔs] o [drɑs] *s* (*of metals*) escoria; (fig) escoria, hez *f*
**drought** [draʊt] *s* (*long period of dry weather*) sequía; (*dryness*) sequedad
**drove** [drov] *s* manada, rebaño, hato; gentío, multitud
**drover** ['drovər] *s* ganadero
**drown** [draʊn] *tr* anegar, ahogar ‖ *intr* anegarse, ahogarse
**drowse** [draʊz] *intr* adormecerse, amodorrarse
**drow·sy** ['draʊzi] *adj* (*comp* **-sier**; *super* **-siest**) soñoliento, modorro
**drub** [drʌb] *v* (*pret & pp* **drubbed**; *ger* **-drubbing**) *tr* apalear, pegar, tundir; derrotar completamente
**drudge** [drʌdʒ] *s* yunque *m*, esclavo del trabajo ‖ *intr* afanarse
**drudger·y** ['drʌdʒəri] *s* (*pl* **-ies**) trabajo penoso
**drug** [drʌg] *s* droga, medicamento; narcótico; **drug on the market** macana, artículo invendible ‖ *v* (*pret & pp* **drugged**; *ger* **drugging**) *tr* narcotizar; mezclar con drogas
**drug addict** *s* toxicómano
**drug addiction** *s* toxicomanía
**druggist** ['drʌgɪst] *s* boticario, farmacéutico; (*dealer in drugs, chemicals, dyes, etc.*) droguero
**drug habit** *s* vicio de los narcóticos
**drug store** *s* farmacia, botica, droguería
**drug traffic** *s* contrabando de narcóticos
**druid** ['dru·ɪd] *s* druida *m*
**drum** [drʌm] *s* (*cylinder; instrument of percussion*) tambor *m*; (*container for oil, gasoline, etc.*) bidón *m* ‖ *v* (*pret & pp* **drummed**; *ger* **drumming**) *tr* reunir a toque de tambor; **to drum up trade** fomentar ventas ‖ *intr* tocar el tambor; (*with the fingers*) teclear
**drum'beat'** *s* toque *m* de tambor
**drum corps** *s* banda de tambores
**drum'fire'** *s* fuego graneado, fuego nutrido
**drum'head'** *s* parche *m* de tambor
**drum major** *s* tambor *m* mayor
**drummer** ['drʌmər] *s* tambor *m*, tamborilero; agente viajero
**drum'stick'** *s* baqueta, palillo; (coll) muslo (*de ave cocida*)
**drunk** [drʌŋk] *adj* borracho; **to get drunk** emborracharse ‖ *s* (coll) borracho; (*spree*) (coll) borrachera
**drunkard** ['drʌŋkərd] *s* borrachín *m*
**drunken** ['drʌŋkən] *adj* borracho
**drunken driving** *s* — **to be arrested for drunken driving** ser arrestado por conducir en estado de embriaguez
**drunkenness** ['drʌŋkənnɪs] *s* embriaguez *f*
**dry** [draɪ] *adj* (*comp* **drier**; *super* **driest**) seco; (*thirsty*) sediento; (*dull, boring*) árido ‖ *s* (*pl* **drys**) (*prohibitionist*) (coll) seco ‖ *v* (*pret & pp* **dried**) *tr* secar; (*to wipe dry*) enjugar ‖ *intr* secarse; **to dry up** secarse completamente; (slang) callar, dejar de hablar
**dry battery** *s* pila seca; (*group of dry cells*) batería seca
**dry cell** *s* pila seca
**dry'-clean'** *tr* lavar en seco, limpiar en seco
**dry cleaner** *s* tintorero
**dry cleaning** *s* lavado a seco, limpieza en seco
**dry'-clean'ing establishment** *s* tintorería
**dry dock** *s* dique seco
**dryer** ['draɪ·ər] *s* var de **drier**

**dry'-eyed'** *adj* ojienjuto
**dry farming** *s* cultivo de secano
**dry goods** *spl* mercancías generales (*tejidos, lencería, pañería, sedería*)
**dry ice** *s* carbohielo, hielo seco
**dry law** *s* ley seca
**dry measure** *s* medida para áridos
**dryness** ['draɪnɪs] *s* sequedad; (*e.g., of a speaker*) aridez *f*
**dry nurse** *s* ama seca
**dry season** *s* estación de la seca
**dry wash** *s* ropa lavada y secada pero no planchada
**d.s.** *abbr* **days after sight, daylight saving**
**D.S.T.** *abbr* **Daylight Saving Time**
**dual** ['dju·əl] o ['du·əl] *adj & s* dual *m*
**duali·ty** [dju'ælɪti] o [du'ælɪti] *s* (*pl* **-ties**) dualidad
**dub** [dʌb] *s* (slang) jugador *m* torpe ‖ *v* (*pret & pp* **dubbed**; *ger* **dubbing**) *tr* apellidar; armar caballero; (mov) doblar
**dubbing** ['dʌbɪŋ] *s* doblado, doblaje *m*
**dubious** ['djubɪ·əs] o ['dubɪ·əs] *adj* dudoso
**ducat** ['dʌkət] *s* ducado
**duchess** ['dʌtʃɪs] *s* duquesa
**duch·y** ['dʌtʃi] *s* (*pl* **-ies**) ducado
**duck** [dʌk] *s* pato; (*female*) pata; agachada rápida; (*in the water*) zambullida; **ducks** (coll) pantalones *mpl* de dril ‖ *tr* bajar rápidamente (*la cabeza*); (*in water*) chapuzar; (coll) esquivar, evitar (*un golpe*) ‖ *intr* chapuzar; **to duck out** (coll) escabullirse
**duck'-toed'** *adj* zancajoso
**duct** [dʌkt] *s* conducto, canal *m*
**ductile** ['dʌktɪl] *adj* dúctil
**ductless gland** ['dʌktlɪs] *s* glándula cerrada
**duct'work'** *s* canalización
**dud** [dʌd] *s* (slang) bomba que no estalla; (slang) fracaso; **duds** (coll) trapos, prendas de vestir
**dude** [djud] o [dud] *s* caballerete *m*
**due** [dju] o [du] *adj* debido; aguardado, esperado; pagadero; **due to** debido a; **to fall due** vencer; **when is the train due?** ¿a qué hora debe llegar el tren? ‖ *adv* directamente, derecho ‖ *s* deuda; **dues** derechos; (*of a member*) cuota; **to get one's due** llevar su merecido; **to give the devil his due** ser justo hasta con el diablo
**duel** ['dju·əl] o ['du·əl] *s* duelo; **to fight a duel** batirse en duelo ‖ *v* (*pret & pp* **dueled** o **duelled**; *ger* **dueling** o **duelling**) *intr* batirse en duelo
**duelist** o **duellist** ['dju·əlɪst] o ['du·əlɪst] *s* duelista *m*
**dues-paying** ['djuz,pe·ɪŋ] o ['duz,pe·ɪŋ] *adj* cotizante
**duet** [dju'ɛt] o [du'ɛt] *s* dúo
**duke** [djuk] o [duk] *s* duque *m*
**dukedom** ['djukdəm] o ['dukdəm] *s* ducado
**dull** [dʌl] *adj* (*not sharp*) embotado, romo; (*color*) apagado; (*sound; pain*) sordo; (*stupid*) lerdo, torpe; (*business*) inactivo, muerto; (*boring*) aburrido, tedioso; (*flat*) deslucido, deslustrado ‖ *tr* embotar, enromar; deslucir, deslustrar; enfriar (*el entusiasmo*) ‖ *intr* embotarse, enromarse; deslucirse, deslustrarse
**dullard** ['dʌlərd] *s* estúpido
**duly** ['djuli] o ['duli] *adv* debidamente
**dumb** [dʌm] *adj* (*lacking the power to speak*) mudo; (coll) estúpido, torpe
**dumb'bell'** *s* halterio; (slang) estúpido, tonto
**dumb creature** *s* animal *m*, bruto
**dumb show** *s* pantomima
**dumb'wait'er** *s* montaplatos *m*
**dumfound** [,dʌm'faʊnd] *tr* pasmar, dejar sin habla
**dum·my** ['dʌmi] *adj* falso, fingido, simulado ‖ *s* (*pl* **-mies**) (*dress form*) maniquí *m*; cabeza para pelucas; (*in card games*) muerto; cartas del muerto; (*figurehead, straw man*) testaferro; (*skeleton copy of a book*) maqueta; imitación, copia; (slang) estúpido
**dump** [dʌmp] *s* basurero, vertedero; montón *m* de basuras; (mil) depósito de municiones; (min) terrero; **to be down in the dumps** (coll) tener murria ‖ *tr* descargar, verter; vaciar de golpe; vender en grandes cantidades y a precios inferiores a los corrientes
**dumping** ['dʌmpɪŋ] *s* descarga; venta en grandes cantidades y a precios inferiores a los corrientes
**dumpling** ['dʌmplɪŋ] *s* bola de pasta rellena de fruta o carne
**dump truck** *s* camión *m* volquete
**dump·y** ['dʌmpi] *adj* (*comp* **-ier**; *super* **-iest**) regordete, rollizo
**dun** [dʌn] *adj* bruno, pardo, castaño ‖ *s* acreedor importuno; (*demand for payment*) apremio ‖ *v* (*pret & pp* **dunned**; *ger* **dunning**) *tr* importunar para el pago, apremiar (*a un deudor*)
**dunce** [dʌns] *s* zopenco, bodoque *m*
**dunce cap** *s* capirote *m* que se le pone al alumno torpe
**dune** [djun] o [dun] *s* duna, médano
**dung** [dʌŋ] *s* estiércol *m* ‖ *tr* estercolar
**dungarees** [,dʌŋgə'riz] *spl* pantalones *mpl* de trabajo de tela basta de algodón
**dungeon** ['dʌndʒən] *s* calabozo, mazmorra; (*fortified tower of medieval castle*) torre *f* del homenaje
**dung'hill'** *s* estercolar *m*; lugar inmundo
**dunk** [dʌŋk] *tr* sopetear, ensopar
**duo** ['dju·o] o ['du·o] *s* dúo
**duode·num** [,dju·ə'dinəm] o [,du·ə'dinəm] *s* (*pl* **-na** [nə]) duodeno
**dupe** [djup] o [dup] *s* víctima, primo, inocentón *m* ‖ *tr* embaucar, engañar
**duplex house** ['djuplɛks] o ['duplɛks] *s* casa para dos familias
**duplicate** ['djuplɪkɪt] o ['duplɪkɪt] *adj & s* duplicado; **in duplicate** por

duplicado || ['djuplɪ,ket] o ['duplɪ,ket] *tr* duplicar
**dupliciˑty** [dju'plɪsɪti] o [du'plɪsɪti] *s* (*pl* **-ties**) duplicidad
**durable** ['djurəbəl] o ['durəbəl] *adj* durable, duradero
**durable goods** *spl* artículos duraderos
**duration** [dju'reʃən] o [du'reʃən] *s* duración
**during** ['djurɪŋ] o ['durɪŋ] *prep* durante
**dusk** [dʌsk] *s* crepúsculo
**dust** [dʌst] *s* polvo || *tr* (*to free of dust*) desempolvar; (*to sprinkle with dust*) polvorear; **to dust off** desempolvar
**dust bowl** *s* cuenca de polvo
**dust'cloth'** *s* trapo para quitar el polvo
**dust cloud** *s* nube *f* de polvo, polvareda
**duster** ['dʌstər] *s* paño, plumero; (*light overgarment*) guardapolvo
**dust jacket** *s* sobrecubierta
**dust'pan'** *s* pala para recoger la basura
**dust rag** *s* trapo para quitar el polvo
**dust storm** *s* tolvanera
**dustˑy** ['dʌsti] *adj* (*comp* **-ier**; *super* **-iest**) polvoriento; (*grayish*) grisáceo
**Dutch** [dʌtʃ] *adj* holandés; (slang) alemán || *s* (*language*) holandés *m;* (*language*) (slang) alemán *m;* **in Dutch** (slang) en la desgracia; (slang) en un apuro; **the Dutch** los holandeses; (slang) los alemanes; **to go Dutch** (coll) pagar a escote
**Dutchˑman** ['dʌtʃmən] *s* (*pl* **-men** [mən]) holandés *m;* (slang) alemán *m*
**Dutch treat** *s* (coll) convite *m* a escote
**dutiable** ['djutɪˑəbəl] o ['dutɪˑəbəl] *adj* sujeto a derechos de aduana
**dutiful** ['djutɪfəl] o ['dutɪfəl] *adj* obediente, sumiso, solícito
**duˑty** ['djuti] o ['duti] *s* (*pl* **-ties**) deber *m;* (*task*) faena, quehacer *m;* derechos de aduana; **off duty** libre; **on duty** de servicio, de guardia; **to do one's duty** cumplir con su deber; **to take up one's duties** entrar en funciones
**du'ty-free'** *adj* libre de derechos
**D.V.** *abbr* **Deo volente, i.e., God willing**
**dwarf** [dwɔrf] *adj* & *s* enano || *tr* achicar, empequeñecer || *intr* achicarse, empequeñecerse
**dwarfish** ['dwɔrfɪʃ] *adj* enano, diminuto
**dwell** [dwel] *v* (*pret* & *pp* **dwelled** o **dwelt** [dwɛlt]) *intr* vivir, morar; **to dwell on** o **upon** hacer hincapié en
**dwelling** ['dwelɪŋ] *s* morada, vivienda
**dwelling house** *s* casa, domicilio
**dwindle** ['dwɪndəl] *intr* disminuir; decaer, consumirse
**dwt.** *abbr* **pennyweight**
**dye** [daɪ] *s* tinte *m,* tintura, color *m* || *v* (*pret* & *pp* **dyed;** *ger* **dyeing**) *tr* teñir
**dyed-in-the-wool** ['daɪdɪnðə,wul] *adj* intransigente
**dyeing** ['daɪˑɪŋ] *s* tinte *m,* tintura
**dyer** ['daɪˑər] *s* tintorero
**dye'stuff'** *s* materia colorante
**dying** ['daɪˑɪŋ] *adj* moribundo
**dynamic** [daɪ'næmɪk] o [dɪ'næmɪk] *adj* dinámico
**dynamite** ['daɪnə,maɪt] *s* dinamita || *tr* dinamitar
**dynaˑmo** ['daɪnə,mo] *s* (*pl* **-mos**) dínamo *f*
**dynast** ['daɪnæst] *s* dinasta *m*
**dynasˑty** ['daɪnəsti] *s* (*pl* **-ties**) dinastía
**dysentery** ['dɪsən,teri] *s* disentería
**dyspepsia** [dɪs'pepsɪˑə] o [dɪs'pepʃə] *s* dispepsia
**dz.** *abbr* **dozen**

## E

**E, e** [i] quinta letra del alfabeto inglés
**ea.** *abbr* **each**
**each** [itʃ] *adj indef* cada || *pron indef* cada uno; **each other** nos, se; uno a otro, unos a otros || *adv* cada uno; por persona
**eager** ['igər] *adj* (*enthusiastic*) ardiente, celoso; **eager for** muy deseoso de; **eager to** + *inf* muy deseoso de + *inf*
**eagerness** ['igərnɪs] *s* ardor *m,* celo; deseo ardiente, empeño
**eagle** ['igəl] *s* águila
**eagle owl** *s* buho
**ear** [ɪr] *s* (*organ and sense of hearing*) oído; (*external part*) oreja; (*of corn*) mazorca; (*of wheat*) espiga; **all ears** con las orejas tan largas; **to be all ears** ser todo oídos, abrir tanto oído; **to prick up one's ears** aguzar las orejas; **to turn a deaf ear** hacer o tener oídos de mercader
**ear'ache'** *s* dolor *m* de oído
**ear'drop'** *s* arete *m*
**ear'drum'** *s* tímpano
**ear'flap'** *s* orejera
**earl** [ʌrl] *s* conde *m*
**earldom** ['ʌrldəm] *s* condado
**earˑly** ['ʌrli] (*comp* **-lier;** *super* **-liest**) *adj* (*occurring before customary time*) temprano; (*first in a series*) primero; (*far back in time*) primero, remoto, antiguo; (*occurring in near future*) cercano, próximo || *adv* temprano; al principio; en los primeros tiempos; **as early as** (*a certain time of day*) ya a; (*a certain time or date*) ya en; **as early as possible** lo más pronto posible; **early in** (*e.g., the month of December*) ya en; **early in**

**the morning** muy de mañana; **early in the year** a principios del año; **to rise early** madrugar
**early bird** *s* (coll) madrugador *m*
**early mass** *s* misa de prima
**early riser** *s* madrugador *m*
**ear'mark'** *s* señal *f*, distintivo || *tr* destinar, poner aparte (*para un fin determinado*)
**ear'muff'** *s* orejera
**earn** [ʌrn] *tr* ganar, ganarse; (*to get as one's due*) merecerse; (com) devengar (*intereses*) || *intr* ganar; rendir
**earnest** ['ʌrnɪst] *adj* serio, grave; **in earnest** en serio, de buena fe || *s* arras
**earnest money** *s* arras
**earnings** ['ʌrnɪŋz] *s* ganancia; salario
**ear'phone'** *s* audífono
**ear'piece'** *s* auricular *m*
**ear'ring'** *s* arete *m*
**ear'shot'** *s* alcance *m* del oído; **within earshot** al alcance del oído
**ear'split'ting** *adj* ensordecedor
**earth** [ʌrθ] *s* tierra; **to come back to** o **down to earth** bajar de las nubes
**earthen** ['ʌrθən] *adj* de tierra; de barro
**ear'then·ware'** *s* loza, vasijas de barro
**earthly** ['ʌrθli] *adj* terrenal; concebible, posible; **to be of no earthly use** no servir para nada
**earth'quake'** *s* terremoto, temblor *m* de tierra
**earth'work'** *s* terraplén *m*
**earth'worm'** *s* lombriz *f* de tierra
**earth·y** ['ʌrθi] *adj* (*comp* **-ier**; *super* **-iest**) terroso; (*worldly*) mundanal; (*unrefined*) grosero; franco, sincero
**ear trumpet** *s* trompetilla
**ear'wax'** *s* cera de los oídos
**ease** [iz] *s* facilidad; (*readiness, naturalness*) desenvoltura, soltura; (*comfort, wellbeing*) comodidad, bienestar *m;* **with ease** con facilidad || *tr* facilitar; aligerar (*un peso*); (*to let up on*) aflojar, soltar; aliviar, mitigar || *intr* aliviarse, mitigarse, disminuir; moderar la marcha
**easel** ['izəl] *s* caballete *m*
**easement** ['izmənt] *s* alivio; (law) servidumbre
**easily** ['izɪli] *adj* fácilmente; suavemente; sin duda; probablemente
**easiness** ['izɪnɪs] *s* facilidad; desenvoltura, soltura; (*e.g., of motion of a machine*) suavidad; indiferencia
**east** [ist] *adj* oriental, del este || *adv* al este, hacia el este || *s* este *m*
**Easter** ['istər] *s* Pascua de flores, Pascua de Resurrección, Pascua florida
**Easter egg** *s* huevo duro decorado o huevo de imitación que se da como regalo en el día de Pascua de Resurrección
**Easter Monday** *s* lunes *m* de Pascua de Resurrección
**eastern** ['istərn] *adj* oriental
**East'er·tide'** *s* aleluya *m*, tiempo de Pascua
**eastward** ['istwərd] *adv* hacia el este
**eas·y** ['izi] *adj* (*comp* **-ier**; *super* **-iest**) fácil; (*conducive to ease*) cómodo; (*not tight*) holgado; (*amenable*) manejable; (*not forced or hurried*) lento, pausado, moderado || *adv* (coll) fácilmente; (coll) despacio; **to take it easy** (coll) descansar, holgar; (coll) ir despacio
**easy chair** *s* poltrona, silla poltrona
**eas'y·go'ing** *adj* despacioso, comodón
**easy mark** *s* (coll) víctima, inocentón *m*
**easy money** *s* dinero ganado sin pena; (com) dinero abundante
**easy payments** *spl* facilidades de pago
**eat** [it] *v* (*pret* **ate** [et]; *pp* **eaten** ['itən]) *tr* comer; **to eat away** corroer; **to eat up** comerse || *intr* comer
**eatable** ['itəbəl] *adj* comestible || **eatables** *spl* comestibles *mpl*
**eaves** [ivz] *spl* alero, socarrén *m*, tejaroz *m*
**eaves'drop'** *v* (*pret & pp* **-dropped**; *ger* **-dropping**) *intr* escuchar a escondidas, estar de escucha
**ebb** [ɛb] *s* reflujo; decadencia || *intr* bajar (*la marea*); decaer
**ebb and flow** *s* flujo y reflujo
**ebb tide** *s* marea menguante
**ebon·y** ['ɛbəni] *s* (*pl* **-ies**) ébano
**ebullient** [ɪ'bʌljənt] *adj* hirviente; entusiasta
**eccentric** [ɛk'sɛntrɪk] *adj* excéntrico || *m* (*odd person*) excéntrico; (*device*) excéntrica
**eccentrici·ty** [,ɛksɛn'trɪsɪti] *s* (*pl* **-ties**) excentricidad
**ecclesiastic** [ɪ,klizɪ'æstɪk] *adj & s* eclesiástico
**echelon** ['ɛʃə,lɑn] *s* escalón *m;* (mil) escalón || *tr* (mil) escalonar
**ech·o** ['ɛko] *s* (*pl* **-oes**) eco || *tr* repetir (*un sonido*); imitar || *intr* hacer eco
**éclair** [e'klɛr] *s* bollo de crema
**eclectic** [ɛk'lɛktɪk] *adj & s* ecléctico
**eclipse** [ɪ'klɪps] *s* eclipse *m* || *tr* eclipsar
**eclogue** ['ɛklɔg] o ['ɛklɑg] *s* égloga
**economic** [,ikə'nɑmɪk] o [,ɛkə'nɑmɪk] *adj* económico (*perteneciente a la economía*)
**economical** [,ikə'nɑmɪkəl] o [,ɛkə'nɑmɪkəl] *adj* económico (*ahorrador; poco costoso*)
**economics** [,ikə'nɑmɪks] o [,ɛkə'nɑmɪks] *s* economía política
**economist** [ɪ'kɑnəmɪst] *s* economista *mf*
**economize** [ɪ'kɑnə,maɪz] *tr & intr* economizar
**econo·my** [ɪ'kɑnəmi] *s* (*pl* **-mies**) economía
**ecsta·sy** ['ɛkstəsi] *s* (*pl* **-sies**) éxtasis *m*
**ecstatic** [ɛk'stætɪk] *adj* extático
**Ecuador** ['ɛkwə,dɔr] *s* el Ecuador
**Ecuadoran** [,ɛkwə'dorən] o **Ecuadorian** [,ɛkwə'dorɪ·ən] *adj & s* ecuatoriano
**ecumenic(al)** [,ɛkjə'mɛnɪk(əl)] *adj* ecuménico
**eczema** ['ɛksɪmə] o [ɛg'zimə] *s* eczema *m & f*, eccema *m & f*
**ed.** *abbr* **edited, edition, editor**

**ed•dy** ['ɛdi] *s* (*pl* **-dies**) remolino ‖ *v* (*pret & pp* **-died**) *tr & intr* remolinear
**edelweiss** ['edəl,vaɪs] *s* estrella de los Alpes
**edge** [ɛdʒ] *s* (*of a knife, sword, etc.*) filo, corte *m;* (*of a cup, glass, piece of paper, piece of cloth, an abyss, etc.*) borde *m;* (*of a piece of cloth; of a body of water*) orilla; (*of a table*) canto; (*of a book*) corte *m;* (*of clothing*) ribete *m;* (slang) ventaja; **on edge** de canto; (fig) nervioso; **to have the edge on** (coll) llevar ventaja a; **to set the teeth on edge** dar dentera ‖ *tr* afilar, aguzar; bordear; ribetear (*un vestido*) ‖ *intr* avanzar de lado; **to edge in** lograr entrar
**edgeways** ['ɛdʒ,wez] *adv* de filo, de canto; **to not let a person get a word in edgeways** no dejarle a una persona decir ni una palabra
**edging** ['ɛdʒɪŋ] *s* orla, pestaña
**edgy** ['ɛdʒi] *adj* agudo, angular; nervioso, irritable
**edible** ['ɛdɪbəl] *adj & s* comestible *m*
**edict** ['idɪkt] *s* edicto
**edification** [,ɛdɪfɪ'keʃən] *s* edificación
**edifice** ['ɛdɪfɪs] *s* edificio
**edi•fy** ['ɛdɪ,faɪ] *v* (*pret & pp* **-fied**) *tr* edificar
**edifying** ['ɛdɪ,faɪ•ɪŋ] *adj* edificante
**edit.** *abbr* **edited, edition, editor**
**edit** ['ɛdɪt] *tr* preparar para la publicación; dirigir, redactar (*un periódico*)
**edition** [ɪ'dɪʃən] *s* edición
**editor** ['ɛdɪtər] *s* (*of a newspaper or magazine*) director *m,* redactor *m;* (*of a manuscript*) revisor *m;* (*of an editorial*) cronista *mf*
**editorial** [,ɛdɪ'torɪ•əl] *adj* editorial ‖ editorial *m,* artículo de fondo
**editorial staff** *s* redacción, cuerpo de redacción
**editor in chief** *s* jefe *m* de redacción
**educate** ['ɛdʒʊ,ket] *tr* educar, instruir
**education** [,ɛdʒʊ'keʃən] *s* educación, instrucción
**educational** [,ɛdʒʊ'keʃənəl] *adj* educativo, educacional
**educational institution** *s* centro docente
**educator** ['ɛdʒʊ,ketər] *s* educador *m*
**eel** [il] *s* anguila; **to be as slippery as an eel** escurrirse como una anguila
**ee•rie** o **ee•ry** ['ɪri] *adj* (*comp* **-rier;** *super* **-riest**) espectral, misterioso
**efface** [ɪ'fes] *tr* destruir; borrar; **to efface oneself** retirarse, no dejarse ver
**effect** [ɪ'fɛkt] *s* efecto; **in effect** vigente; en efecto, en realidad; **to feel the effects of** resentirse de; **to go into effect** o **to take effect** hacerse vigente, entrar en vigor; **to put into effect** poner en vigor ‖ *tr* efectuar
**effective** [ɪ'fɛktɪv] *adj* eficaz; (*actually in effect*) efectivo; (*striking*) impresionante; **to become effective** hacerse efectivo, entrar en vigencia
**effectual** [ɪ'fɛktʃʊ•əl] *adj* eficaz
**effectuate** [ɪ'fɛktʃʊ,et] *tr* efectuar
**effeminacy** [ɪ'fɛmɪnəsi] *s* afeminación
**effeminate** [ɪ'fɛmɪnɪt] *adj* afeminado
**effervesce** [,ɛfər'vɛs] *intr* estar en efervescencia
**effervescence** [,ɛfər'vɛsəns] *s* efervescencia
**effervescent** [,ɛfər'vɛsənt] *adj* efervescente
**effete** [ɪ'fit] *adj* estéril, infructuoso
**efficacious** [,ɛfɪ'keʃəs] *adj* eficaz
**effica•cy** ['ɛfɪkəsi] *s* (*pl* **-cies**) eficacia
**efficien•cy** [ɪ'fɪʃənsi] *s* (*pl* **-cies**) eficiencia; (mech) rendimiento, efecto útil
**efficient** [ɪ'fɪʃənt] *adj* eficiente, eficaz; (*person*) competente; (mech) de buen rendimiento
**effi•gy** ['ɛfɪdʒi] *s* (*pl* **-gies**) efigie *f*
**effort** ['ɛfərt] *s* esfuerzo, empeño
**effronter•y** [ɪ'frʌntəri] *s* (*pl* **-ies**) desfachatez *f,* descaro
**effusion** [ɪ'fjuʒən] *s* efusión
**effusive** [ɪ'fjusɪv] *adj* efusivo, expansivo
**e.g.** *abbr* **exempli gratia, i.e., for example**
**egg** [ɛg] *s* huevo; (slang) buen sujeto ‖ *tr* — **to egg on** incitar, instigar
**egg beater** *s* batidor *m* de huevos
**egg'cup'** *s* huevera
**egg'head'** *s* intelectual *mf,* erudito
**eggnog** ['ɛg,nɑg] *s* caldo de la reina, yema mejida
**egg'plant'** *s* berenjena
**egg'shell'** *s* cascarón *m,* cáscara de huevo
**egoism** ['ɛgo,ɪzəm] o ['igo,ɪzəm] *s* egoísmo
**egoist** ['ɛgo•ɪst] o ['igo•ɪst] *s* egoísta *mf*
**egotism** ['ɛgo,tɪzəm] o ['igo,tɪzəm] *s* egotismo
**egotist** ['ɛgotɪst] o ['igotɪst] *s* egotista *mf*
**egregious** [ɪ'gridʒəs] *adj* enorme, escandaloso
**egress** ['igrɛs] *s* salida
**Egypt** ['idʒɪpt] *s* Egipto
**Egyptian** [ɪ'dʒɪpʃən] *adj & s* egipcio
**eider** ['aɪdər] *s* pato de flojel
**eider down** *s* edredón *m*
**eight** [et] *adj & pron* ocho ‖ *s* ocho; **eight o'clock** las ocho
**eight'-day'** **clock** *s* reloj *m* de ocho días cuerda
**eighteen** ['et'tin] *adj, pron & s* dieciocho, diez y ocho
**eighteenth** ['et'tinθ] *adj & s* (*in a series*) decimoctavo; (*part*) dieciochavo ‖ *s* (*in dates*) dieciocho, diez y ocho
**eighth** [etθ] *adj & s* octavo, ochavo ‖ *s* (*in dates*) ocho
**eight hundred** *adj & pron* ochocientos ‖ *s* ochocientos *m*
**eightieth** ['etɪ•ɪθ] *adj & s* (*in a series*) octogésimo; (*part*) ochentavo
**eigh•ty** ['eti] *adj & pron* ochenta ‖ *s* (*pl* **-ties**) ochenta *m*
**either** ['iðər] o ['aɪðər] *adj* uno u otro, cada . . . (de los dos), cual-

quier . . . de los dos; ambos || *pron* uno u otro, cualquiera de los dos || *adv* — **not either** tampoco, no . . . tampoco || *conj* — **either . . . or** o . . . o
**ejaculate** [ɪ'dʒækjə,let] *tr & intr* exclamar; (physiol) eyacular
**eject** [ɪ'dʒɛkt] *tr* arrojar, expulsar, echar; (*to evict*) desahuciar
**ejection** [ɪ'dʒɛkʃən] *s* expulsión; (*of a tenant*) desahucio
**ejection seat** *s* (aer) asiento lanzable
**eke** [ik] *tr* — **to eke out** ganarse (*la vida*) con dificultad
**elaborate** [ɪ'læbərɪt] *adj* (*done with great care*) elaborado; (*detailed, ornate*) primoroso, recargado || [ɪ'læbə,ret] *tr* elaborar || *intr* — **to elaborate on** o **upon** explicar con más detalles
**elapse** [ɪ'læps] *intr* pasar, transcurrir
**elastic** [ɪ'læstɪk] *adj & s* elástico
**elasticity** [ɪ,læs'tɪsɪti] o [,ilæs'tɪsɪti] *s* elasticidad
**elated** [ɪ'letɪd] *adj* alborozado, regocijado
**elation** [ɪ'leʃən] *s* alborozo, regocijo
**elbow** ['ɛlbo] *s* codo; (*in a river*) recodo; (*of a chair*) brazo; **at one's elbow** a la mano; **out at the elbows** andrajoso, enseñando los codos; **to crook the elbow** empinar el codo; **to rub elbows** codearse, rozarse; **up to the elbows** hasta los codos || *tr* — **to elbow one's way** abrirse paso a codazos || *intr* codear
**elbow grease** *s* (coll) muñeca, jugo de muñeca
**elbow patch** *s* codera
**elbow rest** *s* ménsula
**el'bow·room'** *s* espacio suficiente; libertad de acción
**elder** ['ɛldər] *adj* mayor, más antiguo || *s* mayor, señor *m* mayor; (eccl) anciano; (*plant*) saúco
**el'der·ber'ry** *s* (*pl* **-ries**) saúco; baya del saúco
**elderly** ['ɛldərli] *adj* viejo, anciano
**elder statesman** *s* veterano de la política
**eldest** ['ɛldɪst] *adj* (el) mayor, (el) más antiguo
**elec.** *abbr* **electrical, electricity**
**elect** [ɪ'lɛkt] *adj* (*chosen*) escogido; (*selected but not yet installed*) electo || *s* elegido; **the elect** los elegidos || *tr* elegir
**election** [ɪ'lɛkʃən] *s* elección
**electioneer** [ɪ,lɛkʃə'nɪr] *intr* solicitar votos
**elective** [ɪ'lɛktɪv] *adj* electivo || *s* asignatura electiva
**electorate** [ɪ'lɛktərɪt] *s* electorado
**electric(al)** [ɪ'lɛktrɪk(əl)] *adj* eléctrico
**electric fan** *s* ventilador eléctrico
**electrician** [ɪ,lɛk'trɪʃən] o [,ɛlɛk'trɪʃən] *s* electricista *mf*
**electricity** [ɪ,lɛk'trɪsɪti] o [,ɛlɛk'trɪsɪti] *s* electricidad
**electric percolator** *s* cafetera eléctrica
**electric shaver** *s* electroafeitadora
**electric tape** *s* cinta aislante
**electri·fy** [ɪ'lɛktrɪ,faɪ] *v* (*pret & pp* **-fied**) *tr* (*to provide with electric power*) electrificar; (*to communicate electricity to; to thrill*) electrizar
**electrocute** [ɪ'lɛktrə,kjut] *tr* electrocutar
**electrode** [ɪ'lɛktrod] *s* electrodo
**electrolysis** [ɪ,lɛk'trɑlɪsɪs] o [,ɛlɛk'trɑlɪsɪs] *s* electrolisis *f*
**electrolyte** [ɪ'lɛktrə,laɪt] *s* electrólito
**electromagnet** [ɪ,lɛktrə'mægnɪt] *s* electro, electroimán *m*
**electromagnetic** [ɪ,lɛktrəmæg'nɛtɪk] *adj* electromagnético
**electromotive** [ɪ,lɛktrə'motɪv] *adj* electromotor
**electron** [ɪ'lɛktrɑn] *s* electrón *m*
**electronic** [ɪ,lɛk'trɑnɪk] o [,ɛlɛk'trɑnɪk] *adj* electrónico || **electronics** *s* electrónica
**electroplating** [ɪ'lɛktrə,pletɪŋ] *s* galvanoplastia
**electrostatic** [ɪ,lɛktrə'stætɪk] *adj* electrostático
**electrotype** [ɪ'lɛktrə,taɪp] *s* electrotipo || *tr* electrotipar
**eleemosynary** [,ɛlɪ'mɑsɪ,nɛri] *adj* limosnero
**elegance** ['ɛlɪgəns] *s* elegancia
**elegant** ['ɛlɪgənt] *adj* elegante
**elegiac** [,ɛlɪ'dʒaɪ·æk] o [ɪ'lidʒɪ,æk] *adj* elegíaco
**ele·gy** ['ɛlɪdʒi] *s* (*pl* **-gies**) elegía
**element** ['ɛlɪmənt] *s* elemento; **to be in one's element** estar en su elemento
**elementary** [,ɛlɪ'mɛntəri] *adj* elemental
**elephant** ['ɛlɪfənt] *s* elefante *m*
**elevate** ['ɛlɪ,vet] *tr* elevar
**elevated** ['ɛlɪ,vetɪd] *adj* elevado || *s* (coll) ferrocarril aéreo o elevado
**elevation** [,ɛlɪ'veʃən] *s* elevación
**elevator** ['ɛlɪ,vetər] *s* ascensor *m*; elevador *m* (Am); (*for freight*) montacargas *m*; (*for hoisting grain*) elevador de granos; (*warehouse for storing grain*) depósito de cereales; (aer) timón *m* de profundidad
**eleven** [ɪ'lɛvən] *adj & pron* once || *s* once *m*; **eleven o'clock** las once
**eleventh** [ɪ'lɛvənθ] *adj & s* (*in a series*) undécimo, onceno; (*part*) onzavo || *s* (*in dates*) once *m*
**eleventh hour** *s* último momento
**elf** [ɛlf] *s* (*pl* **elves** [ɛlvz]) elfo, trasgo; enano
**elicit** [ɪ'lɪsɪt] *tr* sacar, sonsacar
**elide** [ɪ'laɪd] *tr* elidir
**eligible** ['ɛlɪdʒɪbəl] *adj* elegible; deseable, aceptable
**eliminate** [ɪ'lɪmɪ,net] *tr* eliminar
**elision** [ɪ'lɪʒən] *s* elisión
**elite** [e'lit] *adj* selecto || *s* — **the elite** la élite
**elk** [ɛlk] *s* alce *m*
**ellipse** [ɪ'lɪps] *s* (geom) elipse *f*
**ellip·sis** [ɪ'lɪpsɪs] *s* (*pl* **-ses** [siz]) (gram) elipsis *f*
**elliptic(al)** [ɪ'lɪptɪk(əl)] *adj* (geom & gram) elíptico
**elm tree** [ɛlm] *s* olmo

**elope** [ɪ'lop] *intr* fugarse con un amante
**elopement** [ɪ'lopmənt] *s* fuga con un amante
**eloquence** ['ɛləkwəns] *s* elocuencia
**eloquent** ['ɛləkwənt] *adj* elocuente
**else** [ɛls] *adj* — **nobody else** ningún otro, nadie más; **nothing else** nada más; **somebody else** algún otro, otra persona; **something else** otra cosa; **what else** qué más, qué otra cosa; **who else** quién más; **whose else** de qué otra persona ‖ *adv* de otro modo; **how else** de qué otro modo; **or else** si no, o bien; **when else** en qué otro tiempo; a qué otra hora; **where else** en qué otra parte
**else'where'** *adv* en otra parte, a otra parte
**elucidate** [ɪ'lusɪ,det] *tr* elucidar
**elude** [ɪ'lud] *tr* eludir
**elusive** [ɪ'lusɪv] *adj* fugaz, efímero; evasivo; (*baffling*) deslumbrador
**emaciated** [ɪ'meʃɪ,etɪd] *adj* enflaquecido, macilento
**emancipate** [ɪ'mænsɪ,pet] *tr* emancipar
**embalm** [ɛm'bɑm] *tr* embalsamar
**embankment** [ɛm'bæŋkmənt] *s* terraplén *m*
**embar•go** [ɛm'bɑrgo] *s* (*pl* **-goes**) embargo ‖ *tr* embargar
**embark** [ɛm'bɑrk] *intr* embarcarse
**embarkation** [,ɛmbɑr'keʃən] *s* (*of passengers*) embarco; (*of freight*) embarque *m*
**embarrass** [ɛm'bærəs] *tr* (*to make feel self-conscious*) avergonzar; (*to put obstacles in the way of*) embarazar; poner en apuros de dinero
**embarrassing** [ɛm'bærəsɪŋ] *adj* desconcertante, vergonzoso; embarazoso
**embarrassment** [ɛm'bærəsmənt] *s* desconcierto, vergüenza; (*interference; perplexity*) embarazo; (*financial difficulties*) apuros
**embas•sy** ['ɛmbəsi] *s* (*pl* **-sies**) embajada
**em•bed** [ɛm'bɛd] *s* (*pret & pp* **-bedded**; *ger* **-bedding**) *tr* empotrar, encajar
**embellish** [ɛm'bɛlɪʃ] *tr* embellecer
**embellishment** [ɛm'bɛlɪʃmənt] *s* embellecimiento
**ember** ['ɛmbər] *s* ascua, pavesa; **embers** rescoldo
**Ember days** *spl* témpora
**embezzle** [ɛm'bɛzəl] *tr & intr* desfalcar, malversar
**embezzlement** [ɛm'bɛzəlmənt] *s* desfalco, malversación
**embezzler** [ɛm'bɛzlər] *s* malversador *m*
**embitter** [ɛm'bɪtər] *tr* amargar
**emblazon** [ɛm'blezən] *tr* blasonar; (fig) blasonar
**emblem** ['ɛmbləm] *s* emblema *m*
**emblematic(al)** [,ɛmblə'mætɪk(əl)] *adj* emblemático
**embodiment** [ɛm'bɑdɪmənt] *s* incorporación; personificación, encarnación
**embod•y** [ɛm'bɑdi] *v* (*pret & pp* **-ied**) *tr* incorporar; personificar, encarnar
**embolden** [ɛm'boldən] *tr* envalentonar
**embolism** ['ɛmbə,lɪzəm] *s* embolia
**emboss** [ɛm'bɔs] o [ɛm'bɑs] *tr* (*to raise in relief*) realzar; abollonar (*metal*); repujar (*cuero*)
**embrace** [ɛm'bres] *s* abrazo ‖ *tr* abrazar ‖ *intr* abrazarse
**embrasure** [ɛm'breʒər] *s* alféizar *m*
**embroider** [ɛm'brɔɪdər] *tr* bordar, recamar
**embroider•y** [ɛm'brɔɪdəri] *s* (*pl* **-ies**) bordado, recamado
**embroil** [ɛm'brɔɪl] *tr* embrollar; (*to involve in contention*) envolver
**embroilment** [ɛm'brɔɪlmənt] *s* embrollo; (*in contention*) envolvimiento
**embry•o** ['ɛmbrɪ,o] *s* (*pl* **-os**) embrión *m*
**embryology** [,ɛmbrɪ'ɑlədʒi] *s* embriología
**emend** [ɪ'mɛnd] *tr* enmendar
**emendation** [,imɛn'deʃən] *s* enmienda
**emerald** ['ɛmərəld] *s* esmeralda
**emerge** [ɪ'mʌrdʒ] *intr* emerger
**emergence** [ɪ'mʌrdʒəns] *s* emergencia (*acción de emerger*)
**emergen•cy** [ɪ'mʌrdʒənsi] *s* (*pl* **-cies**) emergencia (*caso urgente*)
**emergency exit** *s* salida de auxilio
**emergency landing** *s* aterrizaje forzoso
**emergency landing field** *s* aeródromo de urgencia
**emersion** [ɪ'mʌrʒən] o [ɪ'mʌrʃən] *s* emersión
**emery** ['ɛməri] *s* esmeril *m*
**emery cloth** *s* tela de esmeril
**emery wheel** *s* esmeriladora, rueda de esmeril, muela de esmeril
**emetic** [ɪ'mɛtɪk] *adj & s* emético
**emigrant** ['ɛmɪgrənt] *adj & s* emigrante *mf*
**emigrate** ['ɛmɪ,gret] *intr* emigrar
**émigré** [emi'gre] o ['ɛmɪ,gre] *s* emigrado
**eminence** ['ɛmɪnəns] *s* eminencia
**eminent** ['ɛmɪnənt] *adj* eminente
**emissar•y** ['ɛmɪ,sɛri] *s* (*pl* **-ies**) emisario
**emission** [ɪ'mɪʃən] *s* emisión
**emit** [ɪ'mɪt] *v* (*pret & pp* **emitted**; *ger* **emitting**) *tr* emitir
**emotion** [ɪ'moʃən] *s* emoción
**emotional** [ɪ'moʃənəl] *adj* emocional, emotivo
**emperor** ['ɛmpərər] *s* emperador *m*
**empha•sis** ['ɛmfəsɪs] *s* (*pl* **-ses** [,siz]) énfasis *m*
**emphasize** ['ɛmfə,saɪz] *tr* acentuar, hacer hincapié en
**emphatic** [ɛm'fætɪk] *adj* enfático
**emphysema** [,ɛmfɪ'simə] *s* enfisema *m*
**empire** ['ɛmpaɪr] *s* imperio
**empiric(al)** [ɛm'pɪrɪk(əl)] *adj* empírico
**empiricist** [ɛm'pɪrɪsɪst] *s* empírico
**emplacement** [ɛm'plesmənt] *s* emplazamiento
**employ** [ɛm'plɔɪ] *s* empleo ‖ *tr* emplear
**employee** [ɛm'plɔɪ•i] o [,ɛmplɔɪ'i] *s* empleado
**employer** [ɛm'plɔɪ•ər] *s* patrono

**employment** [ɛm'plɔɪmənt] *s* empleo, colocación
**employment agency** *s* agencia de colocaciones
**empower** [ɛm'paʊ·ər] *tr* autorizar, facultar; habilitar, permitir
**empress** ['ɛmprɪs] *s* emperatriz *f*
**emptiness** ['ɛmptɪnɪs] *s* vaciedad, vacuidad
**emp·ty** ['ɛmpti] *adj* (*comp* **-tier;** *super* **-tiest**) vacío; (coll) hambriento ‖ *v* (*pret & pp* **-tied**) *tr & intr* vaciar
**empty-handed** ['ɛmpti'hændɪd] *adj* manivacío
**empty-headed** ['ɛmpti'hɛdɪd] *adj* tonto, ignorante
**empye·ma** [,ɛmpɪ'imə] *s* (*pl* **-mata** [mətə]) empiema *m*
**empyrean** [,ɛmpɪ'ri·ən] *adj & s* empíreo
**emulate** ['ɛmjə,let] *tr & intr* emular
**emulator** ['ɛmjə,letər] *s* émulo
**emulous** ['ɛmjələs] *adj* émulo
**emulsi·fy** [ɪ'mʌlsɪ,faɪ] *v* (*pret & pp* **-fied**) *tr* emulsionar
**emulsion** [ɪ'mʌlʃən] *s* emulsión
**enable** [ɛn'ebəl] *tr* habilitar, facilitar
**enact** [ɛn'ækt] *tr* decretar, promulgar; hacer el papel de
**enactment** [ɛn'æktmənt] *s* ley *f;* (*of a law*) promulgación; (*of a play*) representación
**enam·el** [ɛn'æməl] *s* esmalte *m* ‖ *v* (*pret & pp* **-eled** o **-elled;** *ger* **-eling** o **-elling**) *tr* esmaltar
**enam'el·ware'** *s* utensilios de cocina de hierro esmaltado
**enamor** [ɛn'æmər] *tr* enamorar
**encamp** [ɛn'kæmp] *tr* acampar ‖ *intr* acampar, acamparse
**encampment** [ɛn'kæmpmənt] *s* acampamiento
**enchant** [ɛn'tʃænt] o [ɛn'tʃɑnt] *tr* encantar
**enchanting** [ɛn'tʃæntɪŋ] o [ɛn'tʃɑntɪŋ] *adj* encantador
**enchantment** [ɛn'tʃæntmənt] o [ɛn'tʃɑntmənt] *s* encanto
**enchantress** [ɛn'tʃæntrɪs] o [ɛn'tʃɑntrɪs] *s* encantadora
**enchase** [ɛn'tʃes] *tr* engastar
**encircle** [ɛn'sʌrkəl] *tr* encerrar, rodear; (mil) envolver
**enclitic** [ɛn'klɪtɪk] *adj & s* enclítico
**enclose** [ɛn'kloz] *tr* encerrar; (*in a letter*) adjuntar, incluir; **to enclose herewith** remitir adjunto
**enclosure** [ɛn'kloʒər] *s* recinto; cosa inclusa, carta inclusa
**encomi·um** [ɛn'komɪ·əm] *s* (*pl* **-ums** o **-a** [ə]) encomio
**encompass** [ɛn'kʌmpəs] *tr* encuadrar, abarcar
**encore** ['ɑnkor] *s* bis *m* ‖ *interj* ¡bis!, ¡que se repita! ‖ *tr* pedir la repetición de (*p.ej., de una pieza o canción*); pedir la repetición a (*un actor*)
**encounter** [ɛn'kaʊntər] *s* encuentro ‖ *tr* encontrar, encontrarse con ‖ *intr* batirse, combatirse
**encourage** [ɛn'kʌrɪdʒ] *tr* animar, alentar; (*to foster*) fomentar
**encouragement** [ɛn'kʌrɪdʒmənt] *s* ánimo, aliento; fomento
**encroach** [ɛn'krotʃ] *intr* — **to encroach on** o **upon** pasar los límites de; abusar de; invadir, entremeterse en
**encumber** [ɛn'kʌmbər] *tr* embarazar, estorbar, impedir; (*to load with debts, etc.*) gravar
**encumbrance** [ɛn'kʌmbrəns] *s* embarazo; estorbo; gravamen *m*
**ency.** o **encyc.** *abbr* **encyclopedia**
**encyclical** [ɛn'sɪklɪkəl] o [ɛn'saɪklɪkəl] *s* encíclica
**encyclopedia** [ɛn,saɪklə'pidɪ·ə] *s* enciclopedia
**encyclopedic** [ɛn,saɪklə'pidɪk] *adj* enciclopédico
**end** [ɛnd] *s* (*in time*) fin *m;* (*in space*) extremo, remate *m;* (*e.g., of the month*) fines *mpl;* (*small piece*) cabo, pieza, fragmento; (*purpose*) intento, objeto, fin, mira; **at the end of** al cabo de; a fines de; **in the end** al fin; **no end of** (coll) un sin fin de; **to make both ends meet** pasar con lo que se tiene; **to no end** sin efecto; **to stand on end** poner de punta; ponerse de punta; erizarse, encresparse (*el pelo*); **to the end that** a fin de que ‖ *tr* acabar, terminar ‖ *intr* acabar, terminar; desembocar (*p.ej., una calle*); **to end up** acabar, morir; **to end up as** acabar siendo, parar en (*p.ej., ladrón*)
**endanger** [ɛn'dendʒər] *tr* poner en peligro
**endear** [ɛn'dɪr] *tr* hacer querer; **to endear oneself to** hacerse querer por
**endeavor** [ɛn'dɛvər] *s* esfuerzo, empeño ‖ *intr* esforzarse, empeñarse
**endemic** [ɛn'demɪk] *adj* endémico ‖ *s* endemia
**ending** ['ɛndɪŋ] *s* fin *m*, terminación; (gram) desinencia, terminación
**endive** ['ɛndaɪv] *s* escarola
**endless** ['ɛndlɪs] *adj* interminable; (*chain, screw, etc.*) sin fin
**end'most'** *adj* último, extremo
**endorse** [ɛn'dɔrs] *tr* endosar; (fig) apoyar, aprobar
**endorsee** [,ɛndɔr'si] *s* endosatario
**endorsement** [ɛn'dɔrsmənt] *s* endoso; (fig) apoyo, aprobación
**endorser** [ɛn'dɔrsər] *s* endosante *mf*
**endow** [ɛn'daʊ] *tr* dotar
**endowment** [ɛn'daʊmənt] *adj* dotal ‖ *s* (*of an institution*) dotación; (*gift, talent*) dote *f*, prenda
**endurance** [ɛn'djʊrəns] o [ɛn'dʊrəns] *s* aguante *m*, paciencia; (*ability to hold out*) resistencia, fortaleza; (*lasting time*) duración
**endure** [ɛn'djʊr] o [ɛn'dʊr] *tr* aguantar, tolerar, sufrir ‖ *intr* durar; sufrir con paciencia
**enduring** [ɛn'djʊrɪŋ] o [ɛn'dʊrɪŋ] *adj* duradero, permanente, resistente
**enema** ['ɛnəmə] *s* enema, ayuda; (*liquid and apparatus*) lavativa
**ene·my** ['ɛnəmi] *adj* enemigo ‖ *s* (*pl* **-mies**) enemigo

**enemy alien** *s* extranjero enemigo
**energetic** [ˌɛnərˈdʒɛtɪk] *adj* enérgico, vigoroso
**ener•gy** [ˈɛnərdʒi] *s* (*pl* **-gies**) energía
**enervate** [ˈɛnərˌvet] *tr* enervar
**enfeeble** [ɛnˈfibəl] *tr* debilitar
**enfold** [ɛnˈfold] *tr* arrollar, envolver
**enforce** [ɛnˈfors] *tr* hacer cumplir, poner en vigor; obtener por fuerza; (*e.g., obedience*) imponer; (*an argument*) hacer valer
**enforcement** [ɛnˈforsmənt] *s* compulsión; (*e.g., of a law*) ejecución
**enfranchise** [ɛnˈfræntʃaɪz] *tr* franquear, libertar; conceder el derecho de sufragio a
**eng.** *abbr* **engineer, engraving**
**engage** [ɛnˈgedʒ] *tr* ocupar, emplear; alquilar, reservar; atraer (*p.ej., la atención de una persona*); engranar con; trabar batalla con; **to be engaged, to be engaged to be married** estar prometido, estar comprometido para casarse; **to engage someone in conversation** entablar conversación con una persona || *intr* empeñarse, comprometerse; empotrar, encajar; engranar; **to engage in** ocuparse en
**engaged** [ɛnˈgedʒd] *adj* comprometido, prometido; (*column*) embebido, entregado
**engagement** [ɛnˈgedʒmənt] *s* ajuste *m*, contrato, empeño; esponsales *mpl*, palabra de casamiento; (*duration of betrothal*) noviazgo; (*appointment*) cita; (mil) acción, batalla
**engagement ring** *s* anillo de compromiso, anillo de pedida
**engaging** [ɛnˈgedʒɪŋ] *adj* agraciado, simpático
**engender** [ɛnˈdʒɛndər] *tr* engendrar
**engine** [ˈɛndʒɪn] *s* máquina; (*of automobile*) motor *m;* (rr) máquina, locomotora
**engine driver** *s* maquinista *m*
**engineer** [ˌɛndʒəˈnɪr] *s* ingeniero; (*engine driver*) maquinista *m* || *tr* dirigir o construir como ingeniero; llevar a cabo con acierto
**engineering** [ˌɛndʒəˈnɪrɪŋ] *s* ingeniería
**engine house** *s* cuartel *m* de bomberos
**engine•man** [ˈɛndʒɪnmən] *s* (*pl* **-men** [mən]) maquinista *m*, conductor *m* de locomotora
**engine room** *s* sala de máquinas; (naut) cámara de las máquinas
**en'gine-room' telegraph** *s* (naut) transmisor *m* de órdenes, telégrafo de máquinas
**England** [ˈɪŋglənd] *s* Inglaterra
**Englander** [ˈɪŋgləndər] *s* natural *m* inglés
**English** [ˈɪŋglɪʃ] *adj* inglés || *s* inglés *m;* (*in billiards*) efecto; **the English** los ingleses
**English Channel** *s* Canal *m* de la Mancha
**English daisy** *s* margarita de los prados
**English horn** *s* (mus) corno inglés, cuerno inglés
**English•man** [ˈɪŋglɪʃmən] *s* (*pl* **-men** [mən]) inglés *m*
**Eng'lish-speak'ing** *adj* de habla inglesa
**Eng'lish•wom'an** *s* (*pl* **-wom'en**) inglesa
**engraft** [ɛnˈgræft] o [ɛnˈgrɑft] *tr* (hort & surg) injertar; (fig) implantar
**engrave** [ɛnˈgrev] *tr* grabar; (*in the memory*) grabar
**engraver** [ɛnˈgrevər] *s* grabador *m*
**engraving** [ɛnˈgrevɪŋ] *s* grabado
**engross** [ɛnˈgros] *tr* absorber; poner en limpio; copiar caligráficamente
**engrossing** [ɛnˈgrosɪŋ] *adj* acaparador, absorbente
**engulf** [ɛnˈgʌlf] *tr* hundir, inundar
**enhance** [ɛnˈhæns] o [ɛnˈhɑns] *tr* realzar
**enhancement** [ɛnˈhænsmənt] o [ɛnˈhɑnsmənt] *s* realce *m*
**enigma** [ɪˈnɪgmə] *s* enigma *m*
**enigmatic(al)** [ˌɪnɪgˈmætɪk(əl)] *adj* enigmático
**enjambment** [ɛnˈdʒæmmənt] o [ɛnˈdʒæmbmənt] *s* encabalgamiento
**enjoin** [ɛnˈdʒɔɪn] *tr* encargar, ordenar
**enjoy** [ɛnˈdʒɔɪ] *tr* gozar; **to enjoy** + *ger* gozarse en + *inf;* **to enjoy oneself** divertirse
**enjoyable** [ɛnˈdʒɔɪ·əbəl] *adj* agradable, deleitable
**enjoyment** [ɛnˈdʒɔɪmənt] *s* (*pleasure*) placer *m;* (*pleasurable use*) goce *m*
**enkindle** [ɛnˈkɪndəl] *tr* encender
**enlarge** [ɛnˈlɑrdʒ] *tr* agrandar, aumentar; (phot) ampliar || *intr* agrandarse, aumentar; (*to talk at length*) explayarse; exagerar; **to enlarge on** o **upon** tratar con más extensión; exagerar
**enlargement** [ɛnˈlɑrdʒmənt] *s* agrandamiento, aumento; (phot) ampliación
**enlighten** [ɛnˈlaɪtən] *tr* ilustrar, instruir
**enlightenment** [ɛnˈlaɪtənmənt] *s* ilustración, instrucción
**enlist** [ɛnˈlɪst] *tr* alistar; ganar (*a una persona; el favor, los servicios de una persona*) || *intr* alistarse; **to enlist in** (*a cause*) poner empeño en
**enliven** [ɛnˈlaɪvən] *tr* avivar, animar
**enmesh** [ɛnˈmɛʃ] *tr* enredar
**enmi•ty** [ˈɛnmɪti] *s* (*pl* **-ties**) enemistad
**ennoble** [ɛnˈnobəl] *tr* ennoblecer
**ennui** [ˈɑnwi] *s* aburrimiento, tedio
**enormous** [ɪˈnɔrməs] *adj* enorme
**enough** [ɪˈnʌf] *adj, adv & s* bastante *m* || *interj* ¡basta!, ¡no más!
**enounce** [ɪˈnauns] *tr* enunciar; pronunciar
**en passant** [ˌɑn pæˈsɑnt] *adv* (chess) al vuelo
**enrage** [ɛnˈredʒ] *tr* enrabiar, encolerizar
**enrapture** [ɛnˈræptʃər] *tr* embelesar, transportar, arrebatar
**enrich** [ɛnˈrɪtʃ] *tr* enriquecer
**enroll** [ɛnˈrol] *tr* alistar, inscribir; (*to wrap up*) envolver, enrollar || *intr* alistarse, inscribirse
**en route** [ɑn ˈrut] *adv* en camino; **en route to** camino de, rumbo a
**ensconce** [ɛnˈskɑns] *tr* esconder, abrigar; **to ensconce oneself** instalarse cómodamente
**ensemble** [ɑnˈsɑmbəl] *s* conjunto;

grupo de músicos que tocan o cantan juntos; traje armonioso
**ensign** ['ɛnsaɪn] *s* (*standard*) enseña, bandera; (*badge*) divisa, insignia ‖ ['ɛnsən] o ['ɛnsaɪn] *s* (nav) alférez *m* de fragata
**enslave** [ɛn'slev] *tr* esclavizar
**enslavement** [ɛn'slevmənt] *s* esclavización
**ensnare** [ɛn'snɛr] *tr* entrampar
**ensue** [ɛn'su] o [ɛn'sju] *intr* seguirse; resultar
**ensuing** [ɛn'su·ɪŋ] o [ɛn'sju·ɪŋ] *adj* siguiente; resultante
**ensure** [ɛn'ʃʊr] *tr* asegurar, garantizar
**entail** [ɛn'tel] *s* (law) vínculo ‖ *tr* acarrear, ocasionar; (law) vincular
**entangle** [ɛn'tæŋgəl] *tr* enmarañar, enredar
**entanglement** [ɛn'tæŋgəlmənt] *s* enmarañamiento, enredo
**enter** ['ɛntər] *tr* entrar en (*una habitación*); entrar por (*una puerta*); (*in the customhouse*) declarar; (*to make a record of*) registrar, asentar; matricular (*a un alumno*); matricularse en; hacer miembro a; hacerse miembro de; (*to undertake*) emprender; asentar (*un pedido*); **to enter one's head** metérsele a uno en la cabeza ‖ *intr* entrar; (theat) entrar en escena, salir; **to enter into** entrar en; celebrar (*p.ej., un contrato*); **to enter on o upon** emprender
**enterprise** ['ɛntər,praɪz] *s* (*undertaking*) empresa; (*spirit, push*) empuje *m*
**enterprising** ['ɛntər,praɪzɪŋ] *adj* emprendedor
**entertain** [,ɛntər'ten] *tr* entretener, divertir; (*to show hospitality to*) recibir; considerar, abrigar (*esperanzas, ideas, etc.*) ‖ *intr* recibir
**entertainer** [,ɛntər'tenər] *s* (*host*) anfitrión *m;* (*in public*) actor *m,* bailador *m,* músico, vocalista *mf* (*esp. en un café cantante*)
**entertaining** [,ɛntər'tenɪŋ] *adj* entretenido
**entertainment** [,ɛntər'tenmənt] *s* entretenimiento, diversión; atracción, espectáculo; buen recibimiento; (*of hopes, ideas, etc.*) consideración, abrigo
**enthrall** [ɛn'θrɔl] *tr* cautivar, encantar; esclavizar, sojuzgar
**enthrone** [ɛn'θron] *tr* entronizar
**enthuse** [ɛn'θuz] o [ɛn'θjuz] *tr* (coll) entusiasmar ‖ *intr* (coll) entusiasmarse
**enthusiasm** [ɛn'θuzɪ,æzəm] o [ɛn'θjuzɪ,æzəm] *s* entusiasmo
**enthusiast** [ɛn'θuzɪ,æst] o [ɛn'θjuzɪ,æst] *s* entusiasta *mf*
**enthusiastic** [ɛn,θuzɪ'æstɪk] o [ɛn,θjuzɪ'æstɪk] *adj* entusiástico
**entice** [ɛn'taɪs] *tr* atraer, tentar; inducir al mal, extraviar
**enticement** [ɛn'taɪsmənt] *s* atracción, tentación; extravío
**entire** [ɛn'taɪr] *adj* entero
**entirely** [ɛn'taɪrli] *adv* enteramente; (*exclusively*) solamente
**entire·ty** [ɛn'taɪrti] *s* (*pl* **-ties**) entereza; conjunto, totalidad
**entitle** [ɛn'taɪtəl] *tr* dar derecho a; (*to give a name to; to honor with a title*) intitular
**enti·ty** ['ɛntɪti] *s* (*pl* **-ties**) entidad
**entomb** [ɛn'tum] *tr* sepultar
**entombment** [ɛn'tummənt] *s* sepultura
**entomology** [,ɛntə'mɑlədʒi] *s* entomología
**entourage** [,ɑntu'rɑʒ] *s* cortejo, séquito
**entrails** ['ɛntrelz] o ['ɛntrəlz] *spl* entrañas
**entrain** [ɛn'tren] *tr* despachar en el tren ‖ *intr* embarcar, salir en el tren
**entrance** ['ɛntrəns] *s* entrada, ingreso; (theat) entrada en escena ‖ [ɛn'træns] o [ɛn'trɑns] *tr* arrebatar, encantar
**entrance examination** *s* examen *m* de ingreso; **to take entrance examinations** examinarse de ingreso
**entrancing** [ɛn'trænsɪŋ] o [ɛn'trɑnsɪŋ] *adj* arrebatador, encantador
**entrant** ['ɛntrənt] *s* entrante *mf;* (sport) concurrente *mf*
**en·trap** [ɛn'træp] *v* (*pret & pp* **-trapped;** *ger* **-trapping**) *tr* entrampar
**entreat** [ɛn'trit] *tr* rogar, suplicar
**entreat·y** [ɛn'triti] *s* (*pl* **-ies**) ruego, súplica
**entree** ['ɑntre] *s* entrada, ingreso; (culin) entrada, principio
**entrench** [ɛn'trɛntʃ] *tr* atrincherar ‖ *intr* — **to entrench on o upon** infringir, violar
**entrust** [ɛn'trʌst] *tr* confiar
**en·try** ['ɛntri] *s* (*pl* **-tries**) entrada; (*item*) partida, entrada; (*in a dictionary*) artículo; (sport) concurrente *mf*
**entwine** [ɛn'twaɪn] *tr* entretejer, entrelazar
**enumerate** [ɪ'njumə,ret] o [ɪ'numə,ret] *tr* enumerar
**enunciate** [ɪ'nʌnsɪ,et] o [ɪ'nʌnʃɪ,et] *tr* enunciar; pronunciar
**envelop** [ɛn'vɛləp] *tr* envolver
**envelope** ['ɛnvə,lop] o ['ɑnvə,lop] *s* (*for a letter*) sobre *m;* (*wrapper*) envoltura
**envenom** [ɛn'vɛnəm] *tr* envenenar
**enviable** ['ɛnvɪ·əbəl] *adj* envidiable
**envious** ['ɛnvɪ·əs] *adj* envidioso
**environment** [ɛn'vaɪrənmənt] *s* medio ambiente; (*surroundings*) inmediaciones
**environs** [ɛn'vaɪrəns] *spl* inmediaciones, alrededores *mf*
**envisage** [ɛn'vɪzɪdʒ] *tr* (*to look in the face of*) encarar; considerar, representarse
**envoi** ['ɛnvɔɪ] *s* despedida (*copla al fin de una composición poética*)
**envoy** ['ɛnvɔɪ] *s* (*diplomatic agent*) enviado; (*short concluding stanza*) despedida
**en·vy** ['ɛnvi] *s* (*pl* **-vies**) envidia ‖ *v* (*pret & pp* **-vied**) *tr* envidiar
**enzyme** ['ɛnzaɪm] o ['ɛnzɪm] *s* enzima *f*

**epaulet** o **epaulette** ['ɛpə,let] *s* charretera
**epenthe·sis** [ɛ'pɛnθɪsɪs] *s* (*pl* **-ses** [,siz]) epéntesis *f*
**epergne** [ɪ'pʌrn] o [e'pɛrn] *s* ramillete *m*, centro de mesa
**ephemeral** [ɪ'fɛmərəl] *adj* efímero
**epic** ['ɛpɪk] *adj* épico ‖ *s* epopeya
**epicure** ['ɛpɪ,kjʊr] *s* epicúreo
**epicurean** [,ɛpɪkjʊ'ri·ən] *adj* & *s* epicúreo
**epidemic** [,ɛpɪ'dɛmɪk] *adj* epidémico ‖ *s* epidemia
**epidemiology** [,ɛpɪ,dimɪ'ɑlədʒi] *s* epidemiología
**epidermis** [,ɛpɪ'dʌrmɪs] *s* epidermis *f*
**epigram** ['ɛpɪ,græm] *s* epigrama *m*
**epilepsy** ['ɛpɪ,lɛpsi] *s* epilepsia
**epileptic** [,ɛpɪ'lɛptɪk] *adj* & *s* epiléptico
**Epiphany** [ɪ'pɪfəni] *s* Epifanía
**Episcopalian** [ɪ,pɪskə'pelɪ·ən] *adj* & *s* episcopalista *mf*
**episode** ['ɛpɪ,sod] *s* episodio
**epistemology** [ɪ,pɪstɪ'mɑlədʒi] *s* epistemología
**epistle** [ɪ'pɪsəl] *s* epístola
**epitaph** ['ɛpɪ,tæf] *s* epitafio
**epithet** ['ɛpɪ,θɛt] *s* epíteto
**epitome** [ɪ'pɪtəmi] *s* epítome *m*; (fig) esencia, personificación
**epitomize** [ɪ'pɪtə,maɪz] *tr* epitomar; (fig) encarnar, personificar
**epoch** ['ɛpək] o ['ipɑk] *s* época
**epochal** ['ɛpəkəl] *adj* memorable, trascendental
**ep'och-mak'ing** *adj* que hace época
**equable** ['ɛkwəbəl] o ['ikwəbəl] *adj* constante, uniforme; sereno
**equal** ['ikwəl] *adj* igual; **equal to** a la altura de ‖ *s* igual *mf* ‖ *v* (*pret & pp* **equaled** o **equalled**; *ger* **equaling** o **equalling**) *tr* (*to be equal to*) igualarse a o con; (*to make equal*) igualar
**equali·ty** [ɪ'kwɑlɪti] *s* (*pl* **-ties**) igualdad
**equalize** ['ikwə,laɪz] *tr* igualar; (*to make uniform*) equilibrar
**equally** ['ikwəli] *adv* igualmente
**equanimity** [,ikwə'nɪmɪti] *s* ecuanimidad, igualdad de ánimo
**equate** [i'kwet] *tr* poner en ecuación; considerar equivalente(s)
**equation** [i'kweʒən] o [i'kweʃən] *s* ecuación
**equator** [i'kwetər] *s* ecuador *m*
**equer·ry** ['ɛkwəri] o [ɪ'kweri] *s* (*pl* **-ries**) caballerizo
**equestrian** [ɪ'kwɛstrɪ·ən] *adj* ecuestre ‖ *m* jinete *m*, caballista *m*
**equilateral** [,ikwɪ'lætərəl] *adj* equilátero
**equilibrium** [,ikwɪ'lɪbrɪ·əm] *s* equilibrio
**equinoctial** [,ikwɪ'nɑkʃəl] *adj* equinoccial
**equinox** ['ikwɪ,nɑks] *s* equinoccio
**equip** [ɪ'kwɪp] *v* (*pret & pp* **equipped**; *ger* **equipping**) *tr* equipar
**equipment** [ɪ'kwɪpmənt] *s* equipo, avíos, pertrechos; aptitud, capacidad
**equipoise** ['ikwɪ,pɔɪz] o ['ɛkwɪ,pɔɪz] *s* equilibrio; contrapeso ‖ *tr* equilibrar; equipesar
**equitable** ['ɛkwɪtəbəl] *adj* equitativo
**equi·ty** ['ɛkwɪti] *s* (*pl* **-ties**) (*fairness*) equidad; valor líquido
**equivalent** [ɪ'kwɪvələnt] *adj* & *s* equivalente *m*
**equivocal** [ɪ'kwɪvəkəl] *adj* equívoco
**equivocate** [ɪ'kwɪvə,ket] *intr* usar de equívocos para engañar, mentir
**equivocation** [ɪ,kwɪvə'keʃən] *s* equívoco
**era** ['ɪrə] o ['irə] *s* era
**eradicate** [ɪ'rædɪ,ket] *tr* erradicar
**erase** [ɪ'res] *tr* borrar
**eraser** [ɪ'resər] *s* goma de borrar; (*for blackboard*) cepillo
**erasure** [ɪ'reʃər] o [ɪ'reʒər] *s* borradura, tachón *m*
**ere** [ɛr] *prep* antes de ‖ *conj* antes de que; más bien que
**erect** [ɪ'rɛkt] *adj* derecho, enhiesto, erguido; (*hair*) erizado ‖ *tr* (*to set in upright position*) erguir, enhestar; erigir (*un edificio*); armar, montar (*una máquina*)
**erection** [ɪ'rɛkʃən] *s* erección
**erg** [ʌrg] *s* ergio
**ermine** ['ʌrmɪn] *s* armiño; (fig) toga, judicatura
**erode** [ɪ'rod] *tr* erosionar ‖ *intr* erosionarse
**erosion** [ɪ'roʒən] *s* erosión
**err** [ʌr] *intr* errar, equivocarse, marrar; pecar, marrar
**errand** ['ɛrənd] *s* mandado, recado, comisión; **to run an errand** hacer un mandado
**errand boy** *s* recadero, mandadero
**erratic** [ɪ'rætɪk] *adj* irregular, inconstante, variable; excéntrico
**erra·tum** [ɪ'retəm] o [ɪ'rɑtəm] *s* (*pl* **-ta** [tə]) errata
**erroneous** [ɪ'ronɪ·əs] *adj* erróneo
**error** ['ɛrər] *s* error *m*
**erudite** ['ɛrʊ,daɪt] o ['ɛrjʊ,daɪt] *adj* erudito
**erudition** [,ɛrʊ'dɪʃən] o [,ɛrjʊ'dɪʃən] *s* erudición
**erupt** [ɪ'rʌpt] *intr* hacer erupción (*la piel, los dientes de un niño*); erumpir (*un volcán*)
**eruption** [ɪ'rʌpʃən] *s* erupción
**escalate** ['ɛskə,let] *intr* escalarse
**escalation** [,ɛskə'leʃən] *s* escalada, escalación
**escalator** ['ɛskə,letər] *s* escalera mecánica, móvil o rodante
**escallop** [ɛs'kæləp] *s* concha de peregrino; (*on edge of cloth*) festón *m* ‖ *tr* hornear a la crema y con migajas de pan; cocer (*p.ej., ostras*) en su concha; festonear
**escapade** [,ɛskə'ped] *s* calaverada, aventura atolondrada; (*flight*) escapada
**escape** [ɛs'kep] *s* (*getaway*) escape *m*, escapatoria; (*from responsibilities, duties, etc.*) escapatoria ‖ *tr* evitar, eludir; **to escape someone** escapársele a uno; olvidársele a uno ‖ *intr* escapar, escaparse; **to escape from**

escaparse a (*una persona*); escaparse de (*la cárcel*)
**escapee** [,ɛskə'pi] *s* evadido
**escape literature** *s* literatura de escape o de evasión
**escapement** [ɛs'kepmənt] *s* escape *m*
**escapement wheel** *s* rueda de escape
**escarpment** [ɛs'kɑrpmənt] *s* escarpa
**eschew** [ɛs'tʃu] *tr* evitar, rehuir
**escort** ['ɛskɔrt] *s* escolta; (*man or boy who accompanies a woman or girl in public*) acompañante *m*, caballero, galán *m* ‖ [ɛs'kɔrt] *tr* escoltar
**escutcheon** [ɛs'kʌtʃən] *s* escudo de armas; (*plate in front of lock on door*) escudo, escudete *m*
**Eski•mo** ['ɛskɪ,mo] *adj* esquimal ‖ *s* (*pl* **-mos** o **-mo**) esquimal *mf*
**esopha•gus** [i'sɑfəgəs] *s* (*pl* **-gi** [,dʒaɪ]) esófago
**esp.** *abbr* **especially**
**espalier** [ɛs'pæljər] *s* espaldar *m*, espalera
**especial** [ɛs'pɛʃəl] *adj* especial
**espionage** ['ɛspɪ•ənɪdʒ] o [,ɛspɪ•ə'nɑʒ] *s* espionaje *m*
**esplanade** [,ɛsplə'ned] o [,ɛsplə'nɑd] *s* explanada
**espousal** [ɛs'paʊzəl] *s* desposorios; (*of a cause*) adhesión
**espouse** [ɛs'paʊz] *tr* casarse con; (*to advocate, adopt*) abogar por, adherirse a
**Esq.** *abbr* **Esquire**
**esquire** [ɛs'kwaɪr] o ['ɛskwaɪr] *s* escudero ‖ **Esquire** *s* título de cortesía que se escribe después del apellido y que se usa en vez de **Mr.**
**essay** ['ɛse] *s* ensayo
**essayist** ['ɛse•ɪst] *s* ensayista *mf*
**essence** ['ɛsəns] *s* esencia
**essential** [ɛ'senʃəl] *adj* & *s* esencial *m*
**est.** *abbr* **established, estate, estimated**
**establish** [ɛs'tæblɪʃ] *tr* establecer
**establishment** [ɛs'tæblɪʃmənt] *s* establecimiento
**estate** [ɛs'tet] *s* estado; situación social; (*landed property*) finca, hacienda, heredad; (*a person's possessions*) bienes *mpl*, propiedad; (*left by a decedent*) herencia, bienes relictos
**esteem** [ɛs'tim] *s* estima ‖ *tr* estimar
**esthete** ['ɛsθit] *s* esteta *mf*
**esthetic** [ɛs'θɛtɪk] *adj* estético ‖ **esthetics** *ssg* estética
**estimable** ['ɛstɪməbəl] *adj* estimable
**estimate** ['ɛstɪ,met] o ['ɛstɪmɪt] *s* (*calculation of value, judgment of worth*) estimación; (*statement of cost of work to be done*) presupuesto ‖ ['ɛstɪ,met] *tr* (*to judge, deem*) estimar; presupuestar (*el coste de una obra*)
**estimation** [,ɛstɪ'meʃən] *s* estimación
**estrangement** [ɛs'trendʒmənt] *s* extrañeza
**estuar•y** ['ɛstʃʊ,ɛri] *s* (*pl* **-ies**) estero
**etc.** *abbr* **et cetera**
**etch** [ɛtʃ] *tr* & *intr* grabar al agua fuerte
**etcher** ['ɛtʃər] *s* aguafortista *mf*
**etching** ['ɛtʃɪŋ] *s* aguafuerte *f*

**eternal** [ɪ'tʌrnəl] *adj* eterno
**eterni•ty** [ɪ'tʌrnɪti] *s* (*pl* **-ties**) eternidad
**ether** ['iθər] *s* éter *m*
**ethereal** [ɪ'θɪrɪ•əl] *adj* etéreo
**ethical** ['ɛθɪkəl] *adj* ético
**ethics** ['ɛθɪks] *ssg* ética
**Ethiopian** [,iθɪ'opɪ•ən] *adj* & *s* etíope *mf*
**Ethiopic** [,iθɪ'opɪk] *adj* & *s* etiópico
**ethnic(al)** ['ɛθnɪk(əl)] *adj* étnico
**ethnography** [ɛθ'nɑgrəfi] *s* etnografía
**ethnology** [ɛθ'nɑlədʒi] *s* etnología
**ethyl** ['ɛθɪl] *s* etilo
**ethylene** ['ɛθɪ,lin] *s* etileno
**etiquette** ['ɛtɪ,kɛt] *s* etiqueta
**et seq.** *abbr* **et sequens, et sequentes, et sequentia** (Lat) **and the following**
**étude** [e'tjud] *s* (mus) estudio
**etymology** [,ɛtɪ'mɑlədʒi] *s* etimología
**ety•mon** ['ɛtɪ,mɑn] *s* (*pl* **-mons** o **-ma** [mə]) étimo
**eucalyp•tus** [,jukə'lɪptəs] *s* (*pl* **-tuses** o **-ti** [taɪ]) eucalipto
**Eucharist** ['jukərɪst] *s* Eucaristía
**euchre** ['jukər] *s* juego de naipes ‖ *tr* (coll) ser más listo que
**eugenics** [jʊ'dʒɛnɪks] *s* eugenesia
**eulogistic** [,julə'dʒɪstɪk] *adj* elogiador
**eulogize** ['julə,dʒaɪz] *tr* elogiar
**eulo•gy** ['julədʒi] *s* (*pl* **-gies**) elogio
**eunuch** ['junək] *s* eunuco
**euphemism** ['jufɪ,mɪzəm] *s* eufemismo
**euphemistic** [,jufɪ'mɪstɪk] *adj* eufemístico
**euphonic** [ju'fɑnɪk] *adj* eufónico
**eupho•ny** ['jufəni] *s* (*pl* **-nies**) eufonía
**euphoria** [ju'forɪ•ə] *s* euforia
**euphuism** ['jufju,ɪzəm] *s* eufuísmo
**euphuistic** [,jufju'ɪstɪk] *adj* eufuístico
**Europe** ['jʊrəp] *s* Europa
**European** [,jʊrə'pi•ən] *adj* & *s* europeo
**euthanasia** [,juθə'neʒə] *s* eutanasia
**evacuate** [ɪ'vækjʊ,et] *tr* & *intr* evacuar
**evacuation** [ɪ,vækjʊ'eʃən] *s* evacuación
**evade** [ɪ'ved] *tr* evadir ‖ *intr* evadirse
**evaluate** [ɪ'væljʊ,et] *tr* evaluar
**Evangel** [ɪ'vændʒəl] *s* Evangelio
**evangelic(al)** [,ivæn'dʒelɪk(əl)] o [,ɛvən'dʒelɪk(əl)] *adj* evangélico
**Evangelist** [ɪ'vændʒəlɪst] *s* Evangelista *m*
**evaporate** [ɪ'væpə,ret] *tr* evaporar ‖ *intr* evaporarse
**evasion** [ɪ'veʒən] *s* evasión, evasiva
**evasive** [ɪ'vesɪv] *adj* evasivo
**eve** [iv] *s* víspera; **on the eve of** en vísperas de
**even** ['ivən] *adj* (*smooth*) parejo, llano, liso; (*number*) par; constante, uniforme, invariable; (*temperament*) apacible, sereno; exacto, igual; **even with** al nivel de; **to be even** estar en paz; no deber nada a nadie; **to get even** desquitarse ‖ *adv* aun, hasta; sin embargo; también; exactamente, igualmente; **even as** así como; **even if** aunque, aun cuando; **even so** aun así; **even though** aunque, aun cuando; **even when** aun cuando; **not even** ni . . . siquiera; **to break even** salir

sin ganar ni perder; (*in gambling*) salir en paz || *tr* allanar, igualar
**evening** ['ivnɪŋ] *adj* vespertino || *s* tarde *f*
**evening clothes** *spl* traje *m* de etiqueta
**evening gown** *s* vestido de noche (*de mujer*)
**evening primrose** *s* hierba del asno
**evening star** *s* estrella vespertina, lucero de la tarde
**evening wrap** *s* salida de teatro
**e'ven•song'** *s* canción de la tarde; (eccl) vísperas
**event** [ɪ'vent] *s* acontecimiento, suceso; (*outcome*) resultado; (*public function*) acto; (sport) prueba; **at all events** o **in any event** en todo caso; **in the event that** en caso que
**eventful** [ɪ'ventfəl] *adj* lleno de acontecimientos; importante, memorable
**eventual** [ɪ'ventʃʊ•əl] *adj* final
**eventuali•ty** [ɪ,ventʃʊ'ælɪti] *s* (*pl* **-ties**) eventualidad
**eventually** [ɪ'ventʃʊ•əli] *adv* finalmente, con el tiempo
**eventuate** [ɪ'ventʃʊ,et] *intr* concluir, resultar
**ever** ['evər] *adv* (*at all times*) siempre; (*at any time*) jamás, nunca, alguna vez; **as ever** como siempre; **as much as ever** tanto como antes; **ever since** (*since that time*) desde entonces; después de que; **ever so** muy; **ever so much** muchísimo; **hardly ever** o **scarcely ever** casi nunca; **not . . . ever** no . . . nunca
**ev'er•glade'** *s* tierra pantanosa cubierta de hierbas altas
**ev'er•green'** *adj* siempre verde || *s* planta siempre verde; **evergreens** ramas colgadas como adorno
**ev'er•last'ing** *adj* sempiterno; (*lasting indefinitely*) duradero; (*wearisome*) aburrido, cansado || *s* eternidad; (bot) siempreviva
**ev'er•more'** *adv* eternamente; **for evermore** para siempre jamás
**every** ['evri] *adj* todos los; (*each*) cada, todo; (*being each in a series*) cada, p.ej., **every three days** cada tres días; **every bit** (coll) todo, p.ej., **every bit a man** todo un hombre; **every now and then** de vez en cuando; **every once in a while** una que otra vez; **every other day** cada dos días, un día sí y otro no; **every which way** (coll) por todas partes; (coll) en desarreglo
**ev'ery•bod'y** *pron indef* todo el mundo
**ev'ery•day'** *adj* de todos los días; cotidiano, diario; común, ordinario
**every man Jack** o **every mother's son** *s* cada hijo de vecino
**ev'ery•one'** o **every one** *pron indef* cada uno, todos, todo el mundo
**ev'ery•thing'** *pron indef* todo
**ev'ery•where'** *adv* en o por todas partes; a todas partes
**evict** [ɪ'vɪkt] *tr* desahuciar
**eviction** [ɪ'vɪkʃən] *s* desahucio
**evidence** ['evɪdəns] *s* evidencia; (law) prueba
**evident** ['evɪdənt] *adj* evidente
**evil** ['ivəl] *adj* malo, malvado || *s* mal *m*, maldad
**e'vil•do'er** *s* malhechor *m*, malvado
**e'vil•do'ing** *s* malhecho, maldad
**evil eye** *s* mal *m* de ojo
**evil-minded** ['ivəl'maɪndɪd] *adj* mal pensado, malintencionado
**Evil One, the** el enemigo malo
**evince** [ɪ'vɪns] *tr* manifestar, mostrar
**evoke** [ɪ'vok] *tr* evocar
**evolution** [,evə'luʃən] *s* evolución; (math) extracción de raíces, radicación
**evolve** [ɪ'vɑlv] *tr* desarrollar; desprender (*olores, gases, calor*) || *intr* evolucionar
**ewe** [ju] *s* oveja
**ewer** ['ju•ər] *s* aguamanil *m*
**ex.** *abbr* **examination, example, except, exchange, executive**
**ex** [eks] *prep* sin incluir, sin participación en
**exact** [eg'zækt] *adj* exacto || *tr* exigir
**exacting** [eg'zæktɪŋ] *adj* exigente
**exaction** [eg'zækʃən] *s* exacción
**exactly** [eg'zæktli] *adv* exactamente; (*sharp, on the dot*) en punto
**exactness** [eg'zæktnɪs] *s* exactitud
**exaggerate** [eg'zædʒə,ret] *tr* exagerar
**exalt** [eg'zɔlt] *tr* exaltar, ensalzar
**exam** [eg'zæm] *s* (coll) examen *m*
**examination** [eg,zæmɪ'neʃən] *s* examen *m*; **to take an examination** sufrir un examen, examinarse
**examine** [eg'zæmɪn] *tr* examinar
**example** [eg'zæmpəl] o [eg'zɑmpəl] *s* ejemplo; (*case serving as a warning to others*) ejemplar *m*; (*of mathematics*) problema *m*; **for example** por ejemplo
**exasperate** [eg'zæspə,ret] *tr* exasperar
**excavate** ['ekskə,vet] *tr* excavar
**exceed** [ek'sid] *tr* exceder; sobrepasar (*p.ej., el límite de velocidad*)
**exceedingly** [ek'sidɪŋli] *adv* sumamente, sobremanera
**ex•cel** [ek'sel] *v* (*pret & pp* **-celled**; *ger* **-celling**) *tr* aventajar || *intr* sobresalir
**excellence** ['eksələns] *s* excelencia
**excellen•cy** ['eksələnsi] *s* (*pl* **-cies**) excelencia; **Your Excellency** Su Excelencia
**excelsior** [ek'selsɪ•ər] *s* pajilla de madera, virutas de madera
**except** [ek'sept] *prep* excepto; **except for** sin; **except that** a menos que || *tr* exceptuar
**exception** [ek'sepʃən] *s* excepción; **to take exception** poner reparos, objetar; ofenderse; **with the exception of** a excepción de
**exceptional** [ek'sepʃənəl] *adj* excepcional
**excerpt** ['eksʌrpt] o [ek'sʌrpt] *s* excerta, selección || [ek'sʌrpt] *tr* escoger
**excess** ['ekses] o [ek'ses] *adj* excedente, sobrante || [ek'ses] *s* (*amount or degree by which one thing exceeds another*) exceso, excedente *m*; (*excessive amount; immoderate indulgence, unlawful conduct*) exceso; **in excess of** más que, superior a

**excess baggage** *s* exceso de equipaje
**excess fare** *s* suplemento
**excessive** [ɛk'sɛsɪv] *adj* excesivo
**ex'cess-prof'its tax** *s* impuesto sobre beneficios extraordinarios
**excess weight** *s* exceso de peso
**exchange** [ɛks'tʃendʒ] *s* (*of greetings, compliments, blows, etc.*) cambio; (*of prisoners, merchandise, newspapers, credentials, etc.*) canje *m;* periódico de canje; (*place for buying and selling*) bolsa, lonja; estación telefónica, central *f* de teléfonos; **in exchange for** en cambio de, a trueque de ‖ *tr* cambiar; canjear (*prisioneros, mercancías, etc.*); darse, hacerse (*cortesías*); **to exchange greetings** saludarse; **to exchange shots** cambiar disparos
**exchequer** [ɛks'tʃɛkər] o ['ɛkstʃɛkər] *s* tesorería; fondos nacionales
**excise tax** [ɛk'saɪz] o ['ɛksaɪz] *m* impuesto sobre ciertas mercancías de comercio interior
**excitable** [ɛk'saɪtəbəl] *adj* excitable
**excite** [ɛk'saɪt] *tr* excitar
**excitement** [ɛk'saɪtmənt] *s* excitación
**exciting** [ɛk'saɪtɪŋ] *adj* emocionante, conmovedor; (*stimulating*) excitante
**exclaim** [ɛks'klem] *tr & intr* exclamar
**exclamation** [,ɛksklə'meʃən] *s* exclamación
**exclamation mark** o **point** *s* punto de admiración
**exclude** [ɛks'klud] *tr* excluir
**exclusion** [ɛks'kluʒən] *s* exclusión; **to the exclusion of** con exclusión de
**exclusive** [ɛks'klusɪv] *adj* exclusivo; (*clannish*) exclusivista; (*expensive*) (coll) carero; (*fashionable*) (coll) muy de moda; **exclusive of** con exclusión de
**excommunicate** [,ɛkskə'mjunɪ,ket] *tr* excomulgar
**excommunication** [,ɛkskə,mjunɪ'keʃən] *s* excomunión
**excoriate** [ɛks'korɪ,et] *tr* (fig) desollar, vituperar
**excrement** ['ɛkskrəmənt] *s* excremento
**excruciating** [ɛks'kruʃɪ,etɪŋ] *adj* atroz, agudísimo, vivísimo
**exculpate** ['ɛkskʌl,pet] o [ɛks'kʌlpet] *tr* exculpar
**excursion** [ɛks'kʌrʒən] o [ɛks'kʌrʃən] *s* excursión
**excursionist** [ɛks'kʌrʒənɪst] o [ɛks'kʌrʃənɪst] *s* excursionista *mf*
**excusable** [ɛks'kjusəbəl] *adj* excusable
**excuse** [ɛks'kjus] *s* excusa ‖ [ɛks'kjuz] *tr* excusar, disculpar; dispensar, perdonar
**execute** ['ɛksɪ,kjut] *tr* ejecutar; (law) celebrar, finalizar (*una escritura*)
**execution** [,ɛksɪ'kjuʃən] *s* ejecución
**executioner** [,ɛksɪ'kjuʃənər] *s* ejecutor *m* de la justicia, verdugo
**executive** [ɛg'zɛkjətɪv] *adj* ejecutivo ‖ *m* poder ejecutivo; (*of a school, business, etc.*) dirigente *mf*
**Executive Mansion** *s* (U.S.A.) palacio presidencial
**executor** [ɛg'zɛkjətər] *s* albacea *m,* ejecutor testamentario
**executrix** [ɛg'zɛkjətrɪks] *s* albacea *f,* ejecutora testamentaria
**exemplary** [ɛg'zɛmpləri] o ['ɛgzəm,plɛri] *adj* ejemplar
**exempli·fy** [ɛg'zɛmplɪ,faɪ] *v* (*pret & pp* **-fied**) *tr* ejemplificar
**exempt** [ɛg'zɛmpt] *adj* exento ‖ *tr* eximir, exentar
**exemption** [ɛg'zɛmpʃən] *s* exención
**exercise** ['ɛksər,saɪz] *s* ejercicio; ceremonia; **to take exercise** hacer ejercicio ‖ *tr* ejercer (*p.ej., caridad, influencia*); ejercitar (*un arte, profesión, etc.; adiestrar con el ejercicio*); inquietar, preocupar; poner (*cuidado*) ‖ *ref* ejercitarse
**exert** [ɛg'zʌrt] *tr* ejercer (*una fuerza*); **to exert oneself** esforzarse
**exertion** [ɛg'zʌrʃən] *s* esfuerzo, empeño; (*active use*) ejercicio
**exhalation** [,ɛks·hə'leʃən] *s* (*of gas, vapors, etc.*) exhalación; (*of air from lungs*) espiración
**exhale** [ɛks'hel] o [ɛg'zel] *tr* exhalar (*gases, vapores*); espirar (*el aire aspirado*) ‖ *intr* exhalarse; espirar
**exhaust** [ɛg'zɔst] *s* escape *m;* tubo de escape ‖ *tr* (*to wear out, fatigue; to use up*) agotar; hacer el vacío en; apurar (*todos los medios*)
**exhaust fan** *s* ventilador *m* aspirador
**exhaustion** [ɛg'zɔstʃən] *s* agotamiento
**exhaustive** [ɛg'zɔstɪv] *adj* exhaustivo; comprensivo
**exhaust manifold** *s* múltiple *m* de escape
**exhaust pipe** *s* tubo de escape
**exhaust valve** *s* válvula de escape
**exhibit** [ɛg'zɪbɪt] *s* exhibición; (law) documento de prueba ‖ *tr* exhibir
**exhibition** [,ɛksɪ'bɪʃən] *s* exhibición
**exhibitor** [ɛg'zɪbɪtər] *s* expositor *m*
**exhilarating** [ɛg'zɪlə,retɪŋ] *adj* alegrador, regocijador, alborozador
**exhort** [ɛg'zɔrt] *tr* exhortar
**exhume** [ɛks'hjum] o [ɛg'zjum] *tr* exhumar
**exigen·cy** ['ɛksɪdʒənsi] *s* (*pl* **-cies**) exigencia
**exigent** ['ɛksɪdʒənt] *adj* exigente
**exile** ['ɛgzaɪl] o ['ɛksaɪl] *s* destierro; (*person*) desterrado ‖ *tr* desterrar
**exist** [ɛg'zɪst] *intr* existir
**existence** [ɛg'zɪstəns] *s* existencia
**existing** [ɛg'zɪstɪŋ] *adj* existente
**exit** ['ɛgzɪt] o ['ɛksɪt] *s* salida ‖ *intr* salir
**exodus** ['ɛksədəs] *s* éxodo
**exonerate** [ɛg'zɑnə,ret] *tr* (*to free from blame*) exculpar; (*to free from an obligation*) exonerar
**exorbitant** [ɛg'zɔrbɪtənt] *adj* exorbitante
**exorcise** ['ɛksɔr,saɪz] *tr* exorcizar
**exotic** [ɛg'zɑtɪk] *adj* exótico
**exp.** *abbr* **expenses, expired, export, express**
**expand** [ɛks'pænd] *tr* dilatar (*un gas, el metal*); (*to enlarge, develop*) ampliar, ensanchar; (*to unfold, stretch out*) desplegar, extender; (math) desarrollar (*una ecuación*) ‖ *intr*

dilatarse; ampliarse, ensancharse; desplegarse, extenderse
**expanse** [ɛks'pæns] *s* extensión
**expansion** [ɛks'pænʃən] *s* expansión
**expansive** [ɛks'pænsɪv] *adj* expansivo
**expatiate** [ɛks'peʃɪ,et] *intr* espaciarse, explayarse
**expatriate** [ɛks'petrɪ·ɪt] *adj & s* expatriado
**expect** [ɛks'pɛkt] *tr* esperar; (coll) creer, suponer
**expectan·cy** [ɛks'pɛktənsi] *s* (*pl* **-cies**) expectación
**expectant mother** [ɛks'pɛktənt] *s* futura madre
**expectation** [,ɛkspɛk'teʃən] *s* expectativa
**expectorate** [ɛks'pɛktə,ret] *tr & intr* expectorar
**expedien·cy** [ɛks'pidɪ·ənsi] *s* (*pl* **-cies**) conveniencia, oportunidad; ventaja personal
**expedient** [ɛks'pidɪ·ənt] *adj* conveniente, oportuno; egoísta, ventajoso; (*acting with self-interest*) ventajista || *s* expediente *m*
**expedite** ['ɛkspɪ,daɪt] *tr* apresurar, despachar; dar curso a (*un documento*)
**expedition** [,ɛkspɪ'dɪʃən] *s* expedición
**expeditious** [,ɛkspɪ'dɪʃəs] *adj* expeditivo
**expeditiously** [,ɛkspɪ'dɪʃəsli] *adv* ejecutivamente
**ex·pel** [ɛks'pɛl] *v* (*pret & pp* **-pelled**; *ger* **-pelling**) *tr* expeler, expulsar
**expend** [ɛks'pɛnd] *tr* gastar, consumir
**expendable** [ɛks'pɛndəbəl] *adj* gastable; (*to be thrown away after use*) desechable; (*soldier*) sacrificable
**expenditure** [ɛks'pɛndɪtʃər] *s* gasto, consumo
**expense** [ɛks'pɛns] *s* gasto; **expenses** gastos, expensas; **to go to the expense of** meterse en gastos con; **to meet expenses** hacer frente a los gastos
**expense account** *s* cuenta de gastos
**expensive** [ɛks'pɛnsɪv] *adj* caro, costoso, dispendioso; (*charging high prices*) carero
**experience** [ɛks'pɪrɪ·əns] *s* experiencia || *tr* experimentar
**experienced** [ɛks'pɪrɪ·ənst] *adj* experimentado
**experiment** [ɛks'pɛrɪmənt] *s* experiencia, experimento || [ɛks'pɛrɪ,mɛnt] *intr* experimentar
**expert** ['ɛkspərt] *adj & s* experto
**expiate** ['ɛkspɪ,et] *tr* expiar
**expiation** [,ɛkspɪ'eʃən] *s* expiación
**expire** [ɛks'paɪr] *tr* expeler (*el aire de los pulmones*) || *intr* expirar (*expeler el aire de los pulmones; acabarse, p.ej., un plazo; fallecer*)
**explain** [ɛks'plen] *tr* explicar; **to explain away** descartar con explicaciones; (*to make excuse for*) explicar || *intr* explicar, explicarse
**explanation** [,ɛksplə'neʃən] *s* explicación
**explanatory** [ɛks'plænə,tori] *adj* explicativo
**explicit** [ɛks'plɪsɪt] *adj* explícito
**explode** [ɛks'plod] *tr* volar, hacer saltar; desacreditar (*una teoría*) || *intr* explotar, estallar, reventar
**exploit** [ɛks'plɔɪt] o ['ɛksplɔɪt] *s* hazaña, proeza || [ɛks'plɔɪt] *tr* explotar
**exploitation** [,ɛksplɔɪ'teʃən] *s* explotación
**exploration** [,ɛksplə'reʃən] *s* exploración
**explore** [ɛks'plor] *tr* explorar
**explorer** [ɛks'plorər] *s* explorador *m*
**explosion** [ɛks'ploʒən] *s* explosión; (*of a theory*) refutación
**explosive** [ɛks'plosɪv] *adj* explosivo || *s* explosivo; (phonet) explosiva
**exponent** [ɛks'ponənt] *s* exponente *m*, expositor *m*; (math) exponente *m*
**export** ['ɛksport] *adj* de exportación || *s* exportación; **exports** (*articles exported*) exportación || [ɛks'port] o ['ɛksport] *tr & intr* exportar
**exportation** [,ɛkspor'teʃən] *s* exportación
**exporter** ['ɛksportər] o [ɛks'portər] *s* exportador *m*
**expose** [ɛks'poz] *tr* exponer; (*to unmask*) desenmascarar; (*the Host*) manifestar, exponer; (phot) impresionar
**exposé** [,ɛkspo'ze] *s* desenmascaramiento
**exposition** [,ɛkspə'zɪʃən] *s* exposición; (rhet) exposición
**expostulate** [ɛks'pɑstʃə,let] *intr* protestar; **to expostulate with** reconvenir
**exposure** [ɛks'poʒər] *s* (*to a danger; position with respect to points of compass*) exposición; (*unmasking*) desenmascaramiento; (phot) exposición
**expound** [ɛks'paʊnd] *tr* exponer
**express** [ɛks'prɛs] *adj* expreso || *adv* (*for a special purpose*) expresamente; por expreso || *s* expreso; **by express** (rr) en gran velocidad || *tr* expresar; (*to squeeze out*) exprimir; enviar por expreso; **to express oneself** expresarse
**express company** *s* compañía de transportes rápidos
**expression** [ɛks'prɛʃən] *s* expresión
**expressive** [ɛks'prɛsɪv] *adj* expresivo
**expressly** [ɛks'prɛsli] *adv* expresamente
**express·man** [ɛks'prɛsmən] *s* (*pl* **-men** [mən]) (U.S.A.) empleado del servicio de transportes rápidos
**express train** *s* tren expreso
**express'way'** *s* carretera de vía libre
**expropriate** [ɛks'proprɪ,et] *tr* expropiar
**expulsion** [ɛks'pʌlʃən] *s* expulsión
**expunge** [ɛks'pʌndʒ] *tr* borrar, cancelar, arrasar
**expurgate** ['ɛkspər,get] *tr* expurgar
**exquisite** ['ɛkskwɪzɪt] o [ɛks'kwɪzɪt] *adj* exquisito; agudo, vivo; sensible
**ex-service·man** [,ɛks'sʌrvɪs,mæn] *s* (*pl* **-men** [,mɛn]) ex militar *m*, ex combatiente *m*

**extant** ['ɛkstənt] o [ɛks'tænt] *adj* existente
**extemporaneous** [ɛks,tempə'renɪ·əs] *adj* sin preparación; (*made for the occasion*) provisional
**extempore** [ɛks'tɛmpəri] *adj* improvisado ‖ *adv* improvisadamente
**extemporize** [ɛks'tempə,raɪz] *tr & intr* improvisar
**extend** [ɛks'tend] *tr* extender; dar, ofrecer; hacer extensivos (*p.ej., vivos deseos*); prorrogar (*un plazo*) ‖ *intr* extenderse
**extended** [ɛks'tendɪd] *adj* extenso; prolongado
**extension** [ɛks'tenʃən] *s* extensión; prolongación
**extension ladder** *s* escalera extensible
**extension table** *s* mesa de extensión
**extensive** [ɛks'tensɪv] *adj* (*having great extent*) extenso; (*characterized by extension*) extensivo
**extent** [ɛks'tent] *s* extensión; **to a certain extent** hasta cierto punto; **to a great extent** en sumo grado; **to the full extent** en toda su extensión
**extenuate** [ɛks'tenjʊ,et] *tr* (*to make seem less serious*) atenuar; (*to underrate*) menospreciar, no dar importancia a
**exterior** [ɛks'tɪrɪ·ər] *adj & s* exterior *m*
**exterminate** [ɛks'tʌrmɪ,net] *tr* exterminar
**external** [ɛks'tʌrnəl] *adj* externo ‖ **externals** *spl* exterioridad
**extinct** [ɛks'tɪŋkt] *adj* desaparecido; (*volcano*) extinto
**extinguish** [ɛks'tɪŋgwɪʃ] *tr* extinguir
**extinguisher** [ɛks'tɪŋgwɪʃər] *s* apagador *m*, extintor *m*
**extirpate** ['ɛkstər,pet] o [ɛks'tʌrpet] *tr* extirpar
**ex·tol** [ɛks'tol] o [ɛks'tɑl] *v* (*pret & pp* **-tolled**; *ger* **-tolling**) *tr* ensalzar
**extort** [ɛks'tɔrt] *tr* obtener por amenazas, fuerza o engaño
**extortion** [ɛks'tɔrʃən] *s* extorción
**extra** ['ɛkstrə] *adj* extra; (*spare*) de repuesto ‖ *adv* extraordinariamente ‖ *s* (*of a newspaper*) extra *m; pieza* de repuesto; (*something additional*) extra *m;* (theat) extra *mf*
**extract** ['ɛkstrækt] *s* selección; (pharm) extracto ‖ [ɛks'trækt] *tr* (*to pull out, remove*) extraer; seleccionar (*pasajes de un libro*); (math) extraer
**extraction** [ɛks'trækʃən] *s* extracción
**extracurricular** [,ɛkstrəkə'rɪkjələr] *adj* extracurricular
**extradition** [,ɛkstrə'dɪʃən] *s* extradición
**extra fare** *s* recargo de tarifa, tarifa recargada
**ex'tra-flat'** *adj* extraplano
**extramural** [,ɛkstrə'mjurəl] *adj* extramural
**extraneous** [ɛks'trenɪ·əs] *adj* ajeno, extraño
**extraordinary** [,ɛkstrə'ɔrdɪ,neri] o [ɛks'trɔrdɪ,neri] *adj* extraordinario
**extrapolate** [ɛks'træpə,let] *tr & intr* extrapolar
**extrasensory** [,ɛkstrə'sensəri] *adj* extrasensorio
**extravagance** [ɛks'trævəgəns] *s* derroche *m*, prodigalidad, gasto excesivo; (*wildness, folly*) extravagancia
**extravagant** [ɛks'trævəgənt] *adj* derrochador, pródigo, gastador; (*wild, foolish*) extravagante
**extreme** [ɛks'trim] *adj & s* extremo; **in the extreme** en sumo grado; **to go to extremes** excederse, propasarse
**extremely** [ɛks'trimli] *adv* extremadamente, sumamente
**extreme unction** *s* extremaunción
**extremi·ty** [ɛks'tremɪti] *s* (*pl* **-ties**) extremidad; (*great want*) extrema necesidad; **extremities** medidas extremas; (*hands and feet*) extremidades
**extricate** ['ɛkstrɪ,ket] *tr* desembarazar, desenredar
**extrinsic** [ɛks'trɪnsɪk] *adj* extrínseco
**extrovert** ['ɛkstrə,vʌrt] *s* extrovertido
**extrude** [ɛks'trud] *intr* resaltar, sobresalir
**exuberant** [ɛg'zubərənt] o [ɛg'zjubərənt] *adj* exuberante
**exude** [ɛg'zud] o [ɛk'sud] *tr & intr* exudar
**exult** [ɛg'zʌlt] *intr* exultar, gloriarse
**exultant** [ɛg'zʌltənt] *adj* exultante
**eye** [aɪ] *s* ojo; (*of hook and eye*) hembra, corcheta; **to catch one's eye** llamar la atención a uno; **to feast one's eyes on** deleitar la vista en; **to lay eyes on** alcanzar a ver; **to make eyes at** hacer guiños a; **to roll one's eyes** poner los ojos en blanco; **to see eye to eye** estar completamente de acuerdo; **to shut one's eyes to** hacer la vista gorda ante; **without batting an eye** sin pestañear, sin inmutarse ‖ *v* (*pret & pp* **eyed**; *ger* **eying** o **eyeing**) *tr* ojear; **to eye up and down** mirar de hito en hito
**eye'ball'** *s* globo del ojo
**eye'bolt'** *s* armella, cáncamo
**eye'brow'** *s* ceja; **to raise one's eyebrows** arquear las cejas
**eye'cup'** *s* ojera, lavaojos *m*
**eyeful** ['aɪfʊl] *s* (coll) buena ojeada
**eye'glass'** *s* (*of optical instrument*) ocular *m;* (*eyecup*) ojera, lavaojos *m;* **eyeglasses** gafas, anteojos
**eye'lash'** *s* pestaña
**eyelet** ['aɪlɪt] *s* ojete *m*, ojal *m;* (*hole to look through*) mirilla
**eye'lid'** *s* párpado
**eye of the morning** *s* sol *m*
**eye opener** ['opənər] *s* noticia asombrosa o inesperada; (coll) trago de licor
**eye'piece'** *s* ocular *m*
**eye'-shade'** *s* visera
**eye shadow** *s* crema para los párpados
**eye'shot'** *s* alcance *m* de la vista
**eye'sight'** *s* vista; (*range*) alcance *m* de la vista
**eye socket** *s* cuenca del ojo
**eye'sore'** *s* cosa que ofende la vista
**eye'strain'** *s* vista fatigada
**eye'-test' chart** *s* escala tipográfica oftalmométrica, tipo de ensayo, tipo de prueba

**eye'tooth'** *s* (*pl* **teeth'**) colmillo, diente canino; **to cut one's eyeteeth** (coll) tener el colmillo retorcido; **to give one's eyeteeth for** (coll) dar los ojos de la cara por
**eye'wash'** *s* colirio; (slang) halago para engañar
**eye'wit'ness** *s* testigo ocular, testigo presencial
**ey·rie** o **ey·ry** ['ɛri] *s* (*pl* **-ries**) nido de águilas, nido de aves de rapiña; (fig) altura, morada elevada

## F

**F, f** [ɛf] sexta letra del alfabeto inglés
**f.** *abbr* feminine, folio
**F.** *abbr* Fahrenheit, Friday
**fable** ['febəl] *s* fábula
**fabric** ['fæbrɪk] *s* tejido; textura; (*structure*) fábrica
**fabricate** ['fæbrɪ,ket] *tr* fabricar
**fabrication** [,fæbrɪ'keʃən] *s* fabricación; mentira
**fabulous** ['fæbjələs] *adj* fabuloso
**façade** [fə'sɑd] *s* fachada
**face** [fes] *s* cara, rostro; (*of cloth*) haz *f;* (*of earth*) faz *f;* (*grimace*) mueca; (*of watch*) esfera, muestra; (*impudence*) descaro; **in the face of** en presencia de; **to keep a straight face** contener la risa; **to lose face** desprestigiarse; **to save face** salvar las apariencias; **to show one's face** dejarse ver || *tr* volver la cara hacia; arrostrar; revestir (*un muro*); forrar (*un vestido*); **facing** cara a || *intr* — **to face about** volver la mirada; dar media vuelta; cambiar de opinión; **to face on** dar a o sobre; **to face up to** encararse con
**face card** *s* figura, naipe *m* de figura
**face lifting** *s* cirugía estética
**face powder** *s* polvos de tocador
**facet** ['fæsɪt] *s* faceta
**facial** ['feʃəl] *adj* facial || *s* masaje *m* facial
**facilitate** [fə'sɪlɪ,tet] *tr* facilitar
**facili·ty** [fə'sɪlɪti] *s* (*pl* **-ties**) facilidad
**facing** ['fesɪŋ] *s* revestimiento, paramento
**facsimile** [fæk'sɪmɪli] *s* facsímile *m*
**fact** [fækt] *s* hecho; **in fact** en realidad; **the fact is that** ello es que
**faction** ['fækʃən] *s* facción; discordia
**factional** ['fækʃənəl] *adj* faccionario
**factionalism** ['fækʃənə,lɪzəm] *s* parcialidad, partidismo
**factor** ['fæktər] *s* factor *m* || *tr* descomponer en factores
**facto·ry** ['fæktəri] *s* (*pl* **-ries**) fábrica
**factual** ['fæktʃʊ·əl] *adj* verdadero, objetivo
**facul·ty** ['fækəlti] *s* (*pl* **-ties**) facultad
**fad** [fæd] *s* afición pasajera, moda pasajera
**fade** [fed] *tr* desteñir || *intr* desteñir, desteñirse; apagarse (*un sonido*); (rad) desvanecerse
**fade'out'** *s* desaparición gradual; (rad) desvanecimiento
**fag** [fæg] *s* (*drudge*) yunque *m;* (coll) cigarrillo || *tr* — **to fag out** cansar
**fagot** ['fægət] *s* haz *m* de leña
**fail** [fel] *s* — **without fail** sin falta || *tr* faltar a; reprobar, suspender (*a un alumno*); salir mal en (*un examen*) || *intr* malograrse, fracasar; salir mal (*un alumno*); fallar (*un motor*); (com) quebrar, hacer bancarrota; **to fail to** dejar de
**failure** ['feljər] *s* malogro, fracaso, mal éxito; (*student*) perdigón *m;* (com) quiebra
**faint** [fent] *adj* débil; **to feel faint** sentirse desfallecido || *s* desmayo || *intr* desmayarse
**faint-hearted** ['fent'hɑrtɪd] *adj* cobarde, tímido, apocado
**fair** [fɛr] *adj* justo, imparcial; regular, ordinario; favorable, propicio; (*hair*) rubio; (*complexion*) blanco; (*sky*) despejado; (*weather*) bueno, bonancible || *adv* imparcialmente; **to play fair** jugar limpio || *s* (*exhibition*) feria; (*carnival*) quermese *m*, verbena
**fair'ground'** *s* real *m*, campo de una feria
**fairly** ['fɛrli] *adv* justamente; bastante
**fair-minded** ['fɛr'maɪndɪd] *adj* justo, imparcial
**fairness** ['fɛrnɪs] *s* justicia, imparcialidad; (*of weather*) serenidad; (*of complexion*) blancura
**fair play** *s* juego limpio, limpieza
**fair sex** *s* bello sexo
**fair to middling** *adj* bastante bueno, mediano
**fair'weath'er** *adj* — **a fair-weather friend** amigo del buen viento
**fair·y** ['fɛri] *adj* feérico || *s* (*pl* **-ies**) hada
**fairy godmother** *s* hada madrina
**fair'y·land'** *s* tierra de las hadas
**fairy ring** *s* corro de brujas
**fairy tale** *s* cuento de hadas; (fig) bella poesía
**faith** [feθ] *s* fe *f;* **to break faith with** faltar a la palabra dada a; **to keep faith with** cumplir la palabra dada a; **to pin one's faith on** tener puesta su esperanza en; **upon my faith!** ¡a fe mía!
**faithful** ['feθfəl] *adj* fiel, leal || **the faithful** los fieles
**faithless** ['feθlɪs] *adj* infiel, desleal
**fake** [fek] *adj* (coll) falso, fingido || *s* impostura, patraña; (*person*) farsante *mf* || *tr & intr* falsificar, fingir
**faker** ['fekər] *s* (coll) impostor *m*, patrañero; (*peddler*) (coll) buhonero
**falcon** ['fɔkən] o ['fɔlkən] *s* halcón *m*

**falconer** ['fɔkənər] o ['fɔlkənər] *s* cetrero, halconero
**falconry** ['fɔkənri] o ['fɔlkənri] *s* cetrería, halconería
**fall** [fɔl] *adj* otoñal || *s* caída; (*of water*) catarata, salto de agua; (*of prices*) baja; (*autumn*) otoño; **falls** catarata, caída de agua || *v* (*pret* **fell** [fɛl]; *pp* **fallen** ['fɔlən]) *intr* caer, caerse; **to fall apart** caerse a pedazos; **to fall back** (mil) replegarse; **to fall behind** quedarse atrás; **to fall down** caerse; **to fall due** vencer (*una letra*); **to fall flat** caer tendido; no tener éxito; **to fall for** (slang) ser engañado por; (slang) enamorarse de; **to fall in** desplomarse (*un techo*); ponerse de acuerdo; **to fall in with** trabar amistades con; ponerse de acuerdo con; **to fall off** caer de; disminuir; **to fall out** desavenirse; **to fall out of** caerse de; **to fall out with** esquinarse con; **to fall over** caerse; (coll) adular, halagar; **to fall through** fracasar, malograrse; **to fall to** recaer (*la herencia, la elección*) en; **to fall under** estar comprendido en
**fallacious** [fə'leʃəs] *adj* erróneo, engañoso
**falla·cy** ['fæləsi] *s* (*pl* **-cies**) error *m*, equivocación
**fall guy** *s* (slang) cabeza de turco
**fallible** ['fælɪbəl] *adj* falible
**falling star** *s* estrella fugaz
**fall'out'** *s* caída radiactiva, precipitación radiactiva
**fallout shelter** *s* refugio antiatómico
**fallow** ['fælo] *adj* barbechado; **to lie fallow** estar en barbecho (*tierra labrantía*); (fig) quedar sin emplear, quedar sin ejecutar (*una cosa provechosa*) || *s* barbecho || *tr* barbechar
**false** [fɔls] *adj* falso; (*hair, teeth, etc.*) postizo || *adv* falsamente; **to play false** traicionar
**false colors** *spl* pretextos falsos
**false face** *s* mascarilla; (*ugly false face*) carantamaula
**false-hearted** ['fɔls'hɑrtɪd] *adj* pérfido
**falsehood** ['fɔls·hʊd] *s* falsedad
**false pretenses** *spl* impostura, falsas apariencias
**false return** *s* declaración falsa
**falset·to** [fɔl'seto] *s* (*pl* **-tos**) (*voice*) falsete *m*; (*person*) falsetista *m*
**falsi·fy** ['fɔlsɪ‚faɪ] *v* (*pret & pp* **-fied**) *tr* falsificar; (*to disprove*) refutar || *intr* falsificar; mentir
**falsi·ty** ['fɔlsɪti] *s* (*pl* **-ties**) falsedad
**falter** ['fɔltər] *s* vacilación; (*in speech*) balbuceo || *intr* vacilar; balbucear
**fame** [fem] *s* fama
**famed** [femd] *adj* afamado
**familiar** [fə'mɪljər] *adj* familiar; conocido; común; **familiar with** familiarizado con
**familiari·ty** [fə‚mɪlɪ'ærɪti] *s* (*pl* **-ties**) familiaridad; conocimiento
**familiarize** [fə'mɪljə‚raɪz] *tr* familiarizar
**fami·ly** ['fæmɪli] *adj* familiar; **in the family way** (coll) en estado de buena esperanza || *s* (*pl* **-lies**) familia
**family man** *s* padre *m* de familia; hombre casero
**family name** *s* apellido
**family physician** *s* médico de cabecera
**family tree** *s* árbol genealógico
**famish** ['fæmɪʃ] *tr & intr* hambrear
**famished** ['fæmɪʃt] *adj* famélico
**famous** ['feməs] *adj* famoso; (*notable, excellent*) (coll) famoso
**fan** [fæn] *s* abanico; ventilador *m*; (slang) hincha *mf*, aficionado || *v* (*pret & pp* **fanned**; *ger* **fanning**) *tr* abanicar; (*to winnow*) aventar; ahuyentar con abanico; avivar (*el fuego*); excitar (*las pasiones*); (slang) azotar || *intr* abanicarse; **to fan out** salir (*un camino*) en todas direcciones
**fanatic** [fə'nætɪk] *adj & s* fanático
**fanatical** [fə'nætɪkəl] *adj* fanático
**fanaticism** [fə'nætɪ‚sɪzəm] *s* fanatismo
**fancied** ['fænsid] *adj* imaginario
**fancier** ['fænsɪ·ər] *s* aficionado; visionario; (*of animals*) criador aficionado
**fanciful** ['fænsɪfəl] *adj* fantástico, extravagante; imaginativo
**fan·cy** ['fænsi] *adj* (*comp* **-cier**; *super* **-ciest**) de fantasía, de imitación; fino, de lujo, precioso; ornamental; primoroso; fantástico, extravagante || *s* (*pl* **-cies**) fantasía; afición, gusto; **to take a fancy to** aficionarse a, prendarse de || *v* (*pret & pp* **-cied**) *tr* imaginar
**fancy ball** *s* baile *m* de trajes
**fancy dive** *s* salto ornamental
**fancy dress** *s* traje *m* de fantasía
**fancy foods** *spl* comestibles *mpl* de lujo
**fan'cy-free'** *adj* libre del poder del amor
**fancy jewelry** *s* joyas de fantasía
**fancy skating** *s* patinaje *m* de fantasía
**fan'cy·work'** *s* (sew) labor *f*
**fanfare** ['fænfer] *s* fanfarria
**fang** [fæŋ] *s* colmillo; (*of reptile*) diente *m*
**fan'light'** *s* abanico
**fantastic(al)** [fæn'tæstɪk(əl)] *adj* fantástico
**fanta·sy** ['fæntəzi] o ['fæntəsi] *s* (*pl* **-sies**) fantasía
**far** [fɑr] *adj* lejano; **on the far side of** del otro lado de || *adv* lejos; **as far as** hasta; en cuanto; **as far as I am concerned** por lo que a mí me toca; **as far as I know** que yo sepa; **by far** con mucho; **far and near** por todas partes; **far away** muy lejos; **far be it from me** no lo permita Dios; **far better** mucho mejor; **far different** muy diferente; **far from** lejos de; **far from it** ni con mucho; **far into** hasta muy adentro de; hasta muy tarde de; **far more** mucho más; **far off** a gran distancia; **how far** cuán lejos; **how far is it?** ¿cuánto hay de aquí?; **in so far as** en cuanto; **thus far** hasta ahora; **thus far this year** en lo que va del año; **to go far towards** contribuir mucho a
**faraway** ['fɑrə‚we] *adj* lejano, distante; abstraído, preocupado

**farce** [fɑrs] *s* farsa
**farcical** ['fɑrsɪkəl] *adj* ridículo
**fare** [fer] *s* pasaje *m;* pasajero; alimento; comida; **to collect fares** cobrar el pasaje ‖ *intr* pasarlo, p.ej., **how did you fare?** ¿cómo lo pasó Vd.?
**Far East** *s* Extremo Oriente, Lejano Oriente
**fare'well'** *s* despedida; **to bid farewell to** o **to take farewell of** despedirse de ‖ *interj* ¡adiós!
**far-fetched** ['fɑr'fɛtʃt] *adj* traído por los pelos
**far-flung** ['fɑr'flʌŋ] *adj* de gran alcance, vasto
**farm** [fɑrm] *adj* agrícola; agropecuario ‖ *s* granja; terreno agrícola ‖ *tr* cultivar, labrar (*la tierra*) ‖ *intr* cultivar la tierra y criar animales
**farmer** ['fɑrmər] *s* granjero; agricultor *m,* labrador *m*
**farm hand** *s* peón *m,* mozo de granja
**farm'house'** *s* alquería, cortijo
**farming** ['fɑrmɪŋ] *s* agricultura, labranza
**farm'yard'** *s* corral *m* de granja
**far'-off'** *adj* lejano, distante
**far-reaching** ['fɑr'ritʃɪŋ] *adj* de mucho alcance
**far-sighted** ['fɑr'saɪtɪd] *adj* longividente; precavido; présbita
**farther** ['fɑrðər] *adj* más lejano; adicional ‖ *adv* más lejos, más allá; además, también; **farther on** más adelante
**farthest** ['fɑrðɪst] *adj* (el) más lejano; último ‖ *adv* más lejos; más
**farthing** ['fɑrðɪŋ] *s* (Brit) cuarto de penique
**Far West** *s* (U.S.A.) Lejano Oeste
**fascinate** ['fæsɪ,net] *tr* fascinar
**fascinating** ['fæsɪ,netɪŋ] *adj* fascinante, cautivador
**fascism** ['fæsɪzəm] *s* fascismo
**fascist** ['fæsɪst] *adj* & *s* fascista *mf*
**fashion** ['fæʃən] *s* moda, boga; estilo, manera; alta sociedad; **after a fashion** en cierto modo; **in fashion** de moda; **out of fashion** fuera de moda; **to go out of fashion** pasar de moda ‖ *tr* labrar, forjar
**fashion designing** *s* alta costura
**fashion plate** *s* figurín *m;* (*person*) (coll) figurín *m,* elegante *mf;* **to be a fashion plate** (coll) ir hecho un maniquí
**fashion show** *s* desfile *m* de modas
**fast** [fæst] o [fɑst] *adj* rápido, veloz; (*clock*) adelantado; fijado; disipado; (*friend*) fiel ‖ *adv* aprisa, rápidamente; firmemente; (*asleep*) profundamente; **to hold fast** mantenerse firme; **to live fast** vivir de una manera disipada ‖ *s* ayuno; **to break one's fast** romper el ayuno ‖ *intr* ayunar
**fast day** *s* día *m* de ayuno
**fasten** ['fæsən] o ['fɑsən] *tr* fijar; atar; abrochar; cerrar con llave; (*one's belt*) ajustarse; (*blame*) aplicar ‖ *intr* fijarse
**fastener** ['fæsənər] o ['fɑsənər] *s* asilla; (*snap, clasp*) cierre *m;* (*for papers*) sujetapapeles *m*
**fastidious** [fæs'tɪdɪ·əs] *adj* esquilmoso, quisquilloso, descontentadizo
**fasting** ['fæstɪŋ] o ['fɑstɪŋ] *s* ayuno
**fat** [fæt] *adj* (*comp* **fatter;** *super* **fattest**) gordo; poderoso; opulento; (*profitable*) pingüe; (*spark*) caliente; **to get fat** engordar ‖ *s* grasa; (*suet*) gordo, sebo
**fatal** ['fetəl] *adj* fatal
**fatalism** ['fetə,lɪzəm] *s* fatalismo
**fatalist** ['fetəlɪst] *s* fatalista *mf*
**fatali·ty** [fə'tælɪti] *s* (*pl* **-ties**) fatalidad; (*in accidents, war, etc.*) muerte *f*
**fate** [fet] *s* sino, hado; **the Fates** las Parcas ‖ *tr* condenar, predestinar
**fated** ['fetɪd] *adj* hadado, predestinado
**fateful** ['fetfəl] *adj* fatídico; fatal
**fat'head'** *s* (coll) tronco, estúpido
**father** ['fɑðər] *s* padre *m;* (*an elderly man*) (coll) tío ‖ *tr* servir de padre a; engendrar; inventar
**fatherhood** ['fɑðər,hʊd] *s* paternidad
**fa'ther-in-law'** *s* (*pl* **fathers-in-law**) suegro
**fa'ther·land'** *s* patria
**fatherless** ['fɑðərlɪs] *adj* huérfano de padre, sin padre
**fatherly** ['fɑðərli] *adj* paternal
**Father's Day** *s* día *m* del padre
**Father Time** *s* el Tiempo
**fathom** ['fæðəm] *s* braza ‖ *tr* sondear; profundizar
**fathomless** ['fæðəmlɪs] *adj* insondable
**fatigue** [fə'tig] *s* fatiga; (mil) faena ‖ *tr* fatigar, cansar
**fatigue clothes** *spl* (mil) traje *m* de faena
**fatigue duty** *s* faena
**fatten** ['fætən] *tr* & *intr* engordar
**fat·ty** ['fæti] *adj* (*comp* **-tier;** *super* **-tiest**) graso; (pathol) grasoso; (*chubby*) (coll) gordiflón ‖ *s* (*pl* **-ties**) (coll) gordiflón *m*
**fatuous** ['fætʃʊ·əs] *adj* fatuo; irreal, ilusivo
**faucet** ['fɔsɪt] *s* grifo
**fault** [fɔlt] *s* (*misdeed, blame*) culpa; (*defect*) falta; (geol) falla; (sport) falta; **it's your fault** Vd. tiene la culpa; **to a fault** excesivamente; **to find fault with** culpar, echar la culpa a; hallar defecto en
**fault'find'er** *s* criticón *m,* reparón *m*
**fault'find'ing** *adj* criticón, reparón ‖ *s* manía de criticar
**faultless** ['fɔltlɪs] *adj* perfecto, impecable
**fault·y** ['fɔlti] *adj* (*comp* **-ier;** *super* **-iest**) defectuoso, imperfecto
**faun** [fɔn] *s* fauno
**fauna** ['fɔnə] *s* fauna
**favor** ['fevər] *s* favor *m;* (*letter*) atenta, grata; **do me the favor to** hágame Vd. el favor de; **by your favor** con permiso de Vd.; **favors** regalos de fiesta, objetos de cotillón; **to be in favor with** disfrutar del favor de; **to be out of favor** caer en desgracia ‖ *tr* favorecer; (coll) parecerse a

**favorable** [ˈfevərəbəl] *adj* favorable
**favorite** [ˈfevərɪt] *adj & s* favorito
**favoritism** [ˈfevərɪ,tɪzəm] *s* favoritismo
**fawn** [fɔn] *s* cervato ‖ *intr* — **to fawn on** adular servilmente; hacer fiestas a
**faze** [fez] *tr* (coll) molestar, desanimar
**FBI** [,ɛf,biˈaɪ] *s* (letterword) **Federal Bureau of Investigation**
**fear** [fɪr] *s* miedo; **for fear of** por miedo de, por temor de; **for fear that** por miedo (de) que; **no fear** no hay peligro; **to be in fear of** tener miedo de ‖ *tr & intr* temer
**fearful** [ˈfɪrfəl] *adj* medroso; (coll) enorme, muy malo
**fearless** [ˈfɪrlɪs] *adj* arrojado, intrépido
**feasible** [fisɪbəl] *adj* factible, viable
**feast** [fist] *s* fiesta; (*sumptuous meal*) festín *m*, banquete *m* ‖ *tr & intr* banquetear; **to feast on** regalarse con
**feat** [fit] *s* hazaña, proeza
**feather** [ˈfɛðər] *s* pluma; (*plume; arrogance*) penacho; clase *f*, género; **in fine feather** de buen humor; en buena salud ‖ *tr* emplumar; (carp) machihembrar; **to feather one's nest** hacer todo para enriquecerse
**feather bed** *s* colchón *m* de plumas; (*comfortable situation*) lecho de plumas
**feath'er·bed'ding** *s* empleo de más obreros de lo necesario (*exigido por los sindicatos*)
**feath'er·brain'** *s* cascabelero
**feath'er·edge'** *s* (*of board*) bisel *m;* (*of sharpened tool*) filván *m*
**feathery** [ˈfɛðəri] *adj* plumoso
**feature** [ˈfitʃər] *s* facción; característica, rasgo distintivo; película principal; artículo principal; **features** facciones ‖ *tr* delinear; ofrecer como cosa principal; (coll) destacar, hacer resaltar
**feature writer** *s* articulista *mf*
**February** [ˈfɛbru,ɛri] *s* febrero
**feces** [ˈfisiz] *spl* heces *fpl*
**feckless** [ˈfɛklɪs] *adj* abatido, sin valor; débil
**federal** [ˈfɛdərəl] *adj & s* federal *mf*
**federate** [ˈfɛdə,ret] *adj* federado ‖ *tr* federar ‖ *intr* federarse
**federation** [,fɛdəˈreʃən] *s* federación
**fedora** [fɪˈdorə] *s* sombrero de fieltro suave con ala vuelta
**fed up** [fɛd] *adj* harto
**fee** [fi] *s* honorarios; (*for admission, tuition, etc.*) cuota, precio; (*tip*) propina ‖ *tr* pagar; dar propina a
**feeble** [ˈfibəl] *adj* débil
**feeble-minded** [ˈfibəlˈmaɪndɪd] *adj* imbécil; irresoluto, vacilante
**feed** [fid] *s* alimento, comida; (mach) dispositivo de alimentación ‖ *v* (*pret & pp* **fed** [fɛd]) *tr* alimentar ‖ *intr* alimentarse
**feed'back'** *s* regeneración, realimentación
**feed bag** *s* cebadera, morral *m*
**feed pump** *s* bomba de alimentación
**feed trough** *s* comedero
**feed wire** *s* (elec) conductor *m* de alimentación
**feel** [fil] *s* sensación; (*sense of what is right*) tino ‖ *v* (*pret & pp* **felt** [fɛlt]) *tr* sentir; (*e.g., with the hands*) palpar, tentar; tomar (*el pulso*); tantear (*el camino*) ‖ *intr* (*sick, tired, etc.*) sentirse; palpar; **to feel bad** sentirse mal; condolerse; **to feel cheap** avergonzarse; **to feel comfortable** sentirse a gusto; **to feel for** buscar tentando; condolerse de; **to feel like** tener ganas de; **to feel safe** sentirse a salvo; **to feel sorry** sentir; arrepentirse; **to feel sorry for** compadecer; arrepentirse de
**feeler** [ˈfilər] *s* (*something said to draw someone out*) buscapié *m*, tranquilla; **feelers** (*of insect*) anténulas, palpos; (*of mollusk*) tentáculos
**feeling** [ˈfilɪŋ] *s* (*with senses*) sensación; (*impression, emotion*) sentimiento; presentimiento; parecer *m*
**feign** [fen] *tr* aparentar, fingir ‖ *intr* fingir; **to feign to be** fingirse
**feint** [fent] *s* (*threat*) finta; (*of fencer*) pase *m*, treta ‖ *intr* hacer una finta
**feldspar** [ˈfɛld,spɑr] *s* feldespato
**felicitate** [fəˈlɪsɪ,tet] *tr* felicitar
**felicitous** [fəˈlɪsɪtəs] *adj* (*opportune*) feliz; elocuente
**fell** [fɛl] *adj* cruel, feroz, mortal ‖ *tr* talar (*árboles*)
**felloe** [ˈfɛlo] *s* aro de la rueda; (*part of this*) pina
**fellow** [ˈfɛlo] *s* (coll) mozo, tipo, sujeto; (coll) pretendiente *m;* prójimo; (*of a society*) socio, miembro; (*holder of fellowship*) pensionista *mf*
**fellow being** *s* prójimo
**fellow citizen** *s* conciudadano
**fellow countryman** *s* compatriota *mf*
**fellow man** *s* prójimo
**fellow member** *s* consocio
**fellowship** [ˈfɛlo,ʃɪp] *s* compañerismo; (*for study*) pensión
**fellow traveler** *s* compañero de viaje
**felon** [ˈfɛlən] *s* delincuente *mf* de mayor cuantía; (pathol) panadizo
**felo·ny** [ˈfɛləni] *s* (*pl* **-nies**) delito de mayor cuantía; **to compound a felony** aceptar dinero para no procesar
**felt** [fɛlt] *s* fieltro
**female** [ˈfimel] *adj* (*sex*) femenino; (*animal, plant, piece of a device*) hembra ‖ *s* hembra
**feminine** [ˈfɛmɪnɪn] *adj & s* femenino
**feminism** [ˈfɛmɪ,nɪzəm] *s* feminismo
**fen** [fɛn] *s* pantano
**fence** [fɛns] *s* cerca, cercado; (*for stolen goods*) alcahuete *m;* (*of a saw*) guía; **on the fence** (coll) indeciso ‖ *tr* cercar ‖ *intr* esgrimir
**fencing** [ˈfɛnsɪŋ] *s* (*art*) esgrima; (*act*) esgrimidura
**fencing academy** *s* escuela de esgrima
**fend** [fɛnd] *tr* — **to fend off** apartar, resguardarse de ‖ *intr* — **to fend for oneself** (coll) tirar por su lado
**fender** [ˈfɛndər] *s* (*mudguard*) guardafango, guardabarros *m;* (*of locomotive*) quitapiedras *m;* (*of trolley car*)

salvavidas *m;* (*of fireplace*) guardafuego
**fennel** ['fɛnəl] *s* hinojo
**ferment** ['fɛrmənt] *s* fermento; fermentación ‖ [fər'mɛnt] *tr & intr* fermentar
**fern** [fʌrn] *s* helecho
**ferocious** [fə'roʃəs] *adj* feroz
**feroci•ty** [fə'rɑsɪti] *s* (*pl* **-ties**) ferocidad
**ferret** ['fɛrɪt] *s* hurón *m* ‖ *tr* — **to ferret out** huronear ‖ *intr* huronear
**Ferris wheel** ['fɛrɪs] *s* rueda de feria, noria
**fer•ry** ['fɛri] *s* (*pl* **-ries**) bote *m* de paso, ferry-boat *m* ‖ *v* (*pret & pp* **-ried**) *tr* pasar (*viajeros, mercancías*) a través del río ‖ *intr* cruzar el río en barco
**fer'ry•boat'** *s* bote *m* de paso, ferry-boat *m*
**fertile** ['fʌrtɪl] *adj* fértil
**fertilize** ['fʌrtɪ,laɪz] *tr* abonar, fertilizar; (*to impregnate*) fecundar
**fervid** ['fʌrvɪd] *adj* férvido, vehemente
**fervor** ['fʌrvər] *s* fervor *m*
**fervent** ['fʌrvənt] *adj* ferviente, fervoroso
**fester** ['fɛstər] *s* úlcera ‖ *tr* enconar ‖ *intr* enconarse (*una herida; el ánimo de uno*)
**festival** ['fɛstɪvəl] *adj* festivo ‖ *s* fiesta; (*of music*) festival *m*
**festive** ['fɛstɪv] *adj* festivo
**festivi•ty** [fɛs'tɪvɪti] *s* (*pl* **-ties**) festividad
**festoon** [fɛs'tun] *s* festón *m* ‖ *tr* festonear
**fetch** [fɛtʃ] *tr* ir por, hacer venir, traer; venderse a, venderse por
**fetching** ['fɛtʃɪŋ] *adj* (coll) encantador, atractivo
**fete** [fet] *s* fiesta ‖ *tr* festejar
**fetid** ['fɛtɪd] o ['fitɪd] *adj* fétido
**fetish** ['fitɪʃ] o ['fɛtɪʃ] *s* fetiche *m*
**fetlock** ['fɛtlɑk] *s* espolón *m;* (*tuft of hair*) cerneja
**fetter** ['fɛtər] *s* grillete *m,* grillo ‖ *tr* engrillar; impedir
**fettle** ['fɛtəl] *s* estado, condición; **in fine fettle** en buena condición
**fetus** ['fitəs] *s* feto
**feud** [fjud] *s* odio hereditario, enemistad de larga duración
**feudal** ['fjudəl] *adj* feudal
**feudalism** ['fjudə,lɪzəm] *s* feudalismo
**fever** ['fivər] *s* fiebre *f,* calentura
**fever blister** *s* escupidura, fuegos en los labios
**feverish** ['fivərɪʃ] *adj* febril, calenturiento
**few** [fju] *adj & pron* pocos, no muchos; **a few** unos pocos, unos cuantos; **quite a few** muchos
**fiancé** [,fi·ɑn'se] *s* novio, prometido
**fiancée** [,fi·ɑn'se] *s* novia, prometida
**fias•co** [fɪ'æsko] *s* (*pl* **-cos** o **-coes**) fiasco
**fib** [fɪb] *s* mentirilla ‖ *v* (*pret & pp* **fibbed;** *ger* **fibbing**) *intr* decir mentirillas
**fiber** ['faɪbər] *s* fibra; carácter *m,* índole *f*
**fibrous** ['faɪbrəs] *adj* fibroso
**fickle** ['fɪkəl] *adj* inconstante, veleidoso
**fiction** ['fɪkʃən] *s* (*invention*) ficción; (*branch of literature*) novelística; **pure fiction!** ¡puro cuento!
**fictional** ['fɪkʃənəl] *adj* novelesco
**fictionalize** ['fɪkʃənə,laɪz] *tr* novelizar
**fictitious** [fɪk'tɪʃəs] *adj* ficticio
**fiddle** ['fɪdəl] *s* violín *m* ‖ *tr* tocar (*un aire*) con el violín; **to fiddle away** (coll) malgastar ‖ *intr* tocar el violín; **to fiddle with** manosear
**fiddler** ['fɪdlər] *s* (coll) violinista *mf*
**fiddling** ['fɪdlɪŋ] *adj* (coll) despreciable, insignificante
**fideli•ty** [faɪ'dɛlɪti] o [fɪ'dɛlɪti] *s* (*pl* **-ties**) fidelidad
**fidget** ['fɪdʒɪt] *intr* agitarse, menearse; **to fidget with** manosear
**fidgety** ['fɪdʒɪti] *adj* inquieto, nervioso
**fiduciar•y** [fɪ'djuʃɪ,ɛri] o [fɪ'duʃɪ,ɛri] *adj* fiduciario ‖ *s* (*pl* **-ies**) fiduciario
**fie** [faɪ] *interj* ¡qué vergüenza!
**fief** [fif] *s* feudo
**field** [fild] *adj* (mil) de campaña ‖ *s* campo; (*sown with grain*) sembrado; (baseball) jardín *m;* (elec) campo magnético; (*of motor or dynamo*) (elec) inductor *m*
**fielder** ['fildər] *s* (baseball) jardinero
**field glasses** *spl* gemelos de campo
**field hockey** *s* hockey *m* sobre hierba
**field magnet** *s* imán *m* inductor
**field marshal** *s* (mil) mariscal *m* de campo
**field'piece'** *s* cañón *m* de campaña
**fiend** [find] *s* diablo; (*person*) fiera; **to be a fiend for** ser una fiera para
**fiendish** ['findɪʃ] *adj* diabólico
**fierce** [fɪrs] *adj* feroz, fiero; (*wind*) furioso; (coll) muy malo
**fierceness** ['fɪrsnɪs] *s* ferocidad, fiereza; furia
**fier•y** ['faɪri] o ['faɪ·əri] *adj* (*comp* **-ier;** *super* **-iest**) ardiente, caliente; brioso
**fife** [faɪf] *s* pífano
**fifteen** ['fɪf'tin] *adj, pron & s* quince *m*
**fifteenth** ['fɪf'tinθ] *adj & s* (*in a series*) decimoquinto; (*part*) quinzavo ‖ *s* (*in dates*) quince *m*
**fifth** [fɪfθ] *adj & s* quinto ‖ *s* (*in dates*) cinco
**fifth column** *s* quinta columna
**fifth columnist** *s* quintacolumnista *mf*
**fiftieth** ['fɪftɪ·ɪθ] *adj & s* (*in a series*) quincuagésimo; (*part*) cincuentavo
**fif•ty** ['fɪfti] *adj & pron* cincuenta ‖ *s* (*pl* **-ties**) cincuenta *m*
**fif'ty-fif'ty** *adv* — **to go fifty-fifty** (coll) ir a medias
**fig.** *abbr* **figure, figuratively**
**fig** *s* higo, breva; (*tree*) higuera; (*merest trifle*) bledo
**fight** [faɪt] *s* lucha, pelea; ánimo, brío; **to pick a fight with** meterse con, buscar la lengua a ‖ *v* (*pret & pp* **fought** [fɔt]) *tr* luchar con; dar (*batalla*); lidiar (*al toro*) ‖ *intr* luchar, pelear; **to fight shy of** tratar de evitar

**fighter** ['faɪtər] *s* luchador *m,* peleador *m;* (*warrior*) combatiente *m;* (*game person*) porfiador *m;* (aer) avión *m* de combate, caza *m*
**fig leaf** *s* hoja de higuera; (*on statues*) hoja de parra
**figment** ['fɪgmənt] *s* ficción, invención
**figurative** ['fɪgjərətɪv] *adj* figurado; (*representing by a likeness*) figurativo
**figure** ['fɪgjər] *s* figura; (*bodily form*) talle *m;* precio; **to be good at figures** ser listo en aritmética; **to cut a figure** hacer figura; **to have a good figure** tener buen tipo; **to keep one's figure** conservar la línea || *tr* adornar con figuras; figurarse, imaginar; suponer, calcular; **to figure out** descifrar || *intr* figurar; **to figure on** contar con
**fig'ure•head'** *s* (naut) figurón *m* de proa, mascarón *m* de proa; (*straw man*) testaferro
**figure of speech** *s* figura retórica
**figure skating** *s* patinaje artístico
**figurine** [,fɪgjə'rin] *s* figurilla, figurina
**filament** ['fɪləmənt] *s* filamento
**filch** [fɪltʃ] *tr* birlar, ratear
**file** [faɪl] *s* fila, hilera; (*tool*) lima; (*collection of papers*) archivo; (*cabinet*) archivador *m,* fichero || *tr* poner en fila; limar; archivar, clasificar; anotar || *intr* desfilar; **to file for** solicitar
**file case** *s* fichero
**file clerk** *s* fichador *m*
**filet** [fɪ'le] o ['fɪle] *s* filete *m* || *tr* cortar en filetes
**filial** ['fɪlɪ·əl] o ['fɪljəl] *adj* filial
**filiation** [,fɪlɪ'eʃən] *s* filiación
**filibuster** ['fɪlɪ,bʌstər] *s* obstrucción (*de la aprobación de una ley*); obstruccionista *mf;* (*buccaneer*) filibustero || *tr* obstruir (*la aprobación de una ley*)
**filigree** ['fɪlɪ,gri] *adj* afiligranado || *s* filigrana || *tr* afiligranar
**filing** ['faɪlɪŋ] *s* (*of documents*) clasificación; limadura; **filings** limadura, limalla
**filing cabinet** *s* archivador *m,* clasificador *m*
**filing card** *s* ficha
**Filipi•no** [,fɪlɪ'pino] *adj* filipino || *s* (*pl* **-nos**) filipino
**fill** [fɪl] *s* (*sufficiency*) hartazgo; (*place filled with earth*) terraplén *m;* **to have** o **get one's fill of** darse un hartazgo de || *tr* llenar; rellenar; despachar (*un pedido*); tapar (*un agujero*); empastar (*un diente*); inflar (*un neumático*); llenar, ocupar (*un puesto*); colmar (*lagunas*); **to fill out** llenar (*un formulario*) || *intr* llenarse; rellenarse; **to fill in** hacer de suplente; **to fill up** ahogarse de emoción
**filler** ['fɪlər] *s* relleno; (*of cigar*) tripa; (*sizing*) aparejo; (*in a writing*) relleno
**fillet** ['fɪlɪt] *s* cinta, tira; (*for hair*) prendedero; (archit, bb) filete *m* || *tr* filetear || ['fɪle] o ['fɪlɪt] *s* (*of meat or fish*) filete *m* || *tr* cortar en filetes
**filling** ['fɪlɪŋ] *s* (*of a tooth*) empaste *m;* (*e.g., of a turkey*) relleno; (*of cigar*) tripa
**filling station** *s* estación gasolinera
**fillip** ['fɪlɪp] *s* aguijón *m,* estímulo; (*with finger*) capirotazo
**fil•ly** ['fɪli] *s* (*pl* **-lies**) potra; (coll) muchacha retozona
**film** [fɪlm] *s* película; (mov) película, film *m;* (phot) película || *tr* filmar
**film star** *s* estrella de la pantalla
**film strip** *s* tira proyectable
**film•y** ['fɪlmi] *adj* (*comp* **-ier;** *super* **-iest**) delgadísimo, diáfano, sutil
**filter** ['fɪltər] *s* filtro || *tr* filtrar || *intr* filtrarse
**filtering** ['fɪltərɪŋ] *s* filtración
**filter paper** *s* papel *m* filtrante
**filter tip** *s* embocadura de filtro
**filth** [fɪlθ] *s* suciedad, porquería
**filth•y** ['fɪlθi] *adj* (*comp* **-ier;** *super* **-iest**) sucio, puerco
**filthy lucre** ['lukər] *s* (coll) el vil metal (*dinero, raíz de muchos males*)
**filtrate** ['fɪltret] *s* filtrado || *tr* filtrar || *intr* filtrarse
**fin.** *abbr* **finance**
**fin** [fɪn] *s* aleta
**final** ['faɪnəl] *adj* final; (*last in a series*) último; decisivo, terminante || *s* examen *m* final; **finals** (sport) final *f*
**finale** [fɪ'nɑli] *s* (mus) final *m*
**finalist** ['faɪnəlɪst] *s* finalista *mf*
**finally** ['faɪnəli] *adv* finalmente, por último
**finance** [fɪ'næns] o ['faɪnæns] *s* financiación; **finances** finanzas || *tr* financiar
**financial** [fɪ'nænʃəl] o [faɪ'nænʃəl] *adj* financiero
**financier** [,fɪnən'sɪr] o [,faɪnən'sɪr] *s* financiero
**financing** [fɪ'nænsɪŋ] o ['faɪnænsɪŋ] *s* financiación
**finch** [fɪntʃ] *s* pinzón *m*
**find** [faɪnd] *s* hallazgo || *v* (*pret & pp* **found** [faʊnd]) *tr* hallar, encontrar; **to find out** averiguar, darse cuenta de || *intr* (*law*) pronunciar fallo; **to find out about** informarse de
**finder** ['faɪndər] *s* (*of camera*) visor *m;* (*of microscope*) portaobjeto cuadriculado
**finding** ['faɪndɪŋ] *s* descubrimiento; (law) laudo, fallo
**fine** [faɪn] *adj* fino; (*weather*) bueno; divertido || *adv* (coll) muy bien; **to feel fine** (coll) sentirse muy bien de salud || *s* multa || *tr* multar
**fine arts** *spl* bellas artes
**fineness** *s* fineza; (*of metal*) ley *f*
**fine print** *s* letra menuda, tipo menudo
**finer•y** ['faɪnəri] *s* (*pl* **-ies**) adorno, galas, atavíos
**fine-spun** ['faɪn,spʌn] *adj* estirado en hilo finísimo; (fig) alambicado
**finesse** [fɪ'nes] *s* sutileza; (*in bridge*) impás *m* || *tr* hacer el impás con || *intr* hacer un impás
**fine-toothed comb** ['faɪn,tuθt] *s* len-

drera, peine *m* de púas finas; **to go over with a fine-toothed comb** escudriñar minuciosamente

**finger** ['fɪŋgər] *s* dedo; **to burn one's fingers** cogerse los dedos; **to put one's finger on the spot** poner el dedo en la llaga; **to slip between the fingers** irse de entre los dedos; **to snap one's fingers at** tratar con desprecio; **to twist around one's little finger** manejar a su gusto || *tr* manosear; (slang) acechar, espiar; (slang) identificar

**finger board** *s* (*of guitar*) diapasón *m;* (*of piano*) teclado

**finger bowl** *s* lavadedos *m*, lavafrutas *m*

**finger dexterity** *s* (mus) dedeo

**fingering** ['fɪŋgərɪŋ] *s* manoseo; (mus) digitación

**fin'ger•nail'** *s* uña

**fingernail polish** *s* esmalte *m* para las uñas

**fin'ger•print'** *s* huella digital, dactilograma *m* || *tr* tomar las huellas digitales de

**finger tip** *s* punta del dedo; **to have at one's finger tips** tener en la punta de los dedos, saber al dedillo

**finial** ['fɪnɪ·əl] *s* florón *m*

**finical** ['fɪnɪkəl] o **finicky** ['fɪnɪki] *adj* delicado, melindroso

**finish** ['fɪnɪʃ] *s* acabado; fin *m*, conclusión || *tr* acabar; **to be finished** estar listo || *intr* acabar; **to finish** + *ger* acabar de + *inf;* **to finish by** + *ger* acabar por + *inf*

**finishing nail** *s* puntilla francesa

**finishing school** *s* escuela particular de educación social para señoritas

**finishing touch** *s* toque *m* final, última mano

**finite** ['faɪnaɪt] *adj* finito

**finite verb** *s* forma verbal flexional

**Finland** ['fɪnlənd] *s* Finlandia

**Finlander** ['fɪnləndər] *s* finlandés *m*

**Finn** [fɪn] *s* (*member of a Finnish-speaking group of people*) finés *m;* (*native or inhabitant of Finland*) finlandés *m*

**Finnish** ['fɪnɪʃ] *adj* finlandés || *s* (*language*) finlandés *m*

**fir** [fʌr] *s* abeto

**fire** [faɪr] *s* fuego; (*destructive burning*) incendio; **through fire and water** a trancos y barrancos; **to be on fire** estar ardiendo; **to be under enemy fire** estar expuesto al fuego del enemigo; **to catch fire** encenderse; **to hang fire** estar en suspensión; **to open fire** abrir fuego, romper el fuego; **to set on fire, to set fire to** pegar fuego a; **under fire** bajo el fuego del enemigo; acusado, inculpado || *interj* (mil) ¡fuego! || *tr* encender; calentar (*el horno*); cocer (*ladrillos*); disparar (*un arma de fuego*); pegar (*un tiro*); excitar (*la imaginación*); (coll) despedir (*a un empleado*) || *intr* encenderse; **to fire on** hacer fuego sobre; **to fire up** cargar el horno; calentar el horno

**fire alarm** *s* alarma de incendios, avisador *m* de incendios; **to sound the fire alarm** tocar a fuego

**fire'arm'** *s* arma de fuego

**fire'ball'** *s* bola de fuego; (*lightning*) rayo en bola

**fire'bird'** *s* cacique veranero

**fire'boat'** *s* buque *m* con mangueras para incendios

**fire'box'** *s* caja de fuego, fogón *m*

**fire'brand'** *s* tizón *m;* (*hothead*) botafuego

**fire'break'** *s* raya

**fire'brick'** *s* ladrillo refractario

**fire brigade** *s* cuerpo de bomberos

**fire'bug'** *s* (coll) incendiario

**fire company** *s* cuerpo de bomberos; compañía de seguros

**fire'crack'er** *s* triquitraque *m*

**fire'damp'** *s* grisú *m*, mofeta

**fire department** *s* servicio de bomberos

**fire'dog'** *s* morillo

**fire drill** *s* ejercicio para caso de incendio

**fire engine** *s* coche *m* bomba, bomba de incendios, motobomba

**fire escape** *s* escalera de salvamento

**fire extinguisher** *s* extintor *m*, apagafuegos *m*

**fire'fly'** *s* (*pl* **-flies**) luciérnaga

**fire'guard'** *s* guardafuego

**fire hose** *s* manguera para incendios

**fire'house'** *s* cuartel *m* de bomberos, estación de incendios

**fire hydrant** *s* boca de incendio

**fire insurance** *s* seguro contra incendios

**fire irons** *spl* badil *m* y tenazas

**fireless cooker** ['faɪrlɪs] *s* cocinilla sin fuego

**fire•man** ['faɪrmən] *s* (*pl* **-men** [mən]) (*man who stokes fires*) fogonero; (*man who extinguishes fires*) bombero

**fire'place'** *s* chimenea, chimenea francesa

**fire plug** *s* boca de agua

**fire power** *s* (mil) potencia de fuego

**fire'proof'** *adj* incombustible || *tr* hacer incombustible

**fire sale** *s* venta de mercancías averiadas en un incendio

**fire screen** *s* pantalla de chimenea

**fire ship** *s* brulote *m*

**fire shovel** *s* badil *m*

**fire'side'** *s* hogar *m*

**fire'trap'** *s* edificio sin medios adecuados de escape en caso de incendio

**fire wall** *s* cortafuego

**fire'ward'en** *s* vigía *m* de incendios

**fire'wa'ter** *s* aguardiente *m*

**fire'wood'** *s* leña

**fire'works'** *spl* fuegos artificiales

**firing** ['faɪrɪŋ] *s* encendimiento; (*of bricks*) cocción; (*of a gun*) disparo; (*of soldiers*) tiroteo; (*of an internal-combustion engine*) encendido; (*of an employee*) (coll) despedida

**firing line** *s* línea de fuego, frente *m* de batalla

**firing order** *s* (aut) orden *m* del encendido

**firing squad** *s* (*for saluting at a burial*)

piquete *m* de salvas; (*for executing*) pelotón *m* de fusilamiento, piquete *m* de ejecución
**firm** [fʌrm] *adj* firme ‖ *s* empresa, casa comercial
**firmament** ['fʌrməmənt] *s* firmamento
**firm name** *s* razón *f* social
**firmness** ['fʌrmnɪs] *s* firmeza
**first** [fʌrst] *adj* primero ‖ *adv* primero; **first of all** ante todo ‖ *s* primero; (aut) primera (velocidad); (mus) voz *f* principal; **at first** al principio; en primer lugar; **from the first** desde el principio
**first aid** *s* cura de urgencia, primeros auxilios
**first'-aid' kit** *s* botiquín *m*, equipo de urgencia
**first-aid station** *s* puesto de socorro, puesto de primera intención
**first'-born'** *adj & s* primogénito
**first'-class'** *adj* de primera, de primera clase ‖ *adv* en primera clase
**first cousin** *s* primo hermano
**first draft** *s* borrador *m*
**first finger** *s* dedo índice, dedo mostrador
**first floor** *s* piso bajo
**first fruits** *spl* primicia
**first lieutenant** *s* teniente
**firstly** ['fʌrstli] *adv* en primer lugar
**first mate** *s* (naut) piloto
**first name** *s* nombre *m* de pila
**first night** *s* (theat) noche *f* de estreno
**first'-night'er** *s* (theat) estrenista *mf*
**first officer** *s* (naut) piloto
**first quarter** *s* cuarto creciente (*de la luna*)
**first'-rate'** *adj* de primer orden; (coll) excelente ‖ *adv* (coll) muy bien
**first'-run' house** *s* teatro de estreno
**fiscal** ['fɪskəl] *adj* (*pertaining to public treasury*) fiscal; económico ‖ *s* (*public prosecutor*) fiscal *m*
**fiscal year** *s* año económico, ejercicio
**fish** [fɪʃ] *s* pez *m;* (*that has been caught, that is ready to eat*) pescado; **to be like a fish out of water** estar como gallina en corral ajeno; **to be neither fish nor fowl** no ser carne ni pescado; **to drink like a fish** beber como una topinera, beber como una esponja ‖ *tr* pescar ‖ *intr* pescar; **to fish for compliments** buscar alabanzas; **to go fishing** ir de pesca; **to take fishing** llevar de pesca
**fish'bone'** *s* espina de pez
**fish bowl** *s* pecera
**fisher** ['fɪʃər] *s* pescador *m;* embarcación de pesca; (zool) marta del Canadá
**fisher•man** ['fɪʃərmən] *s* (*pl* **-men** [mən]) pescador *m;* barco pesquero
**fisher•y** ['fɪʃəri] *s* (*pl* **-ies**) (*activity*) pesca; (*business*) pesquería; (*grounds*) pesquera
**fish glue** *s* cola de pescado
**fish hawk** *s* halieto
**fish'hook'** *s* anzuelo
**fishing** ['fɪʃɪŋ] *adj* pesquero ‖ *s* pesca
**fishing ground** *s* pesquería, pesquera
**fishing reel** *s* carrete *m*
**fishing rod** *s* caña de pescar
**fishing tackle** *s* aparejo de pescar, avíos de pescar
**fishing torch** *s* candelero
**fish line** *s* sedal *m*
**fish market** *s* pescadería
**fish'plate'** *s* (rr) eclisa
**fish'pool'** *s* piscina
**fish spear** *s* fisga
**fish story** *s* (coll) andaluzada, patraña; **to tell fish stories** (coll) mentir por la barba
**fish'tail'** *s* (aer) coleadura ‖ *intr* (aer) colear
**fish'wife'** *s* (*pl* **-wives** [ˌwaɪvz]) pescadera; (*foul-mouthed woman*) verdulera
**fish'worm'** *s* lombriz *f* de tierra (*cebo para pescar*)
**fish•y** ['fɪʃi] *adj* (*comp* **-ier;** *super* **-iest**) que huele o sabe a pescado; (coll) dudoso, inverosímil
**fission** ['fɪʃən] *s* (biol) escisión; (phys) fisión
**fissionable** ['fɪʃənəbəl] *adj* fisionable
**fissure** ['fɪʃər] *s* hendidura, grieta; (anat, min) fisura
**fist** [fɪst] *s* puño; (typ) manecilla; **to shake one's fist at** amenazar con el puño
**fist fight** *s* pelea con los puños
**fisticuff** ['fɪstɪˌkʌf] *s* puñetazo; **fisticuffs** pelea a puñetazos
**fit** [fɪt] *adj* (*comp* **-fitter;** *super* **-fittest**) apropiado, conveniente; apto; sano; **fit to be tied** (coll) impaciente, encolerizado; **fit to eat** bueno de comer; **to feel fit** gozar de buena salud; **to see fit** juzgar conveniente ‖ *s* ajuste *m*, talle *m;* (*of one piece with another*) encaje *m;* (*of coughing*) acceso, ataque *m;* (*of anger*) arranque *m;* **by fits and starts** intermitentemente ‖ *v* (*pret & pp* **-fitted;** *ger* **fitting**) *tr* ajustar, entallar; cuadrar, sentar; encajar; cuadrar con (*p.ej., las señas de una persona*); equipar, preparar; servir para; estar de acuerdo con (*p.ej., los hechos*); **to fit out** o **up** pertrechar ‖ *intr* ajustar; encajar; sentar; **to fit in** caber en; encajar en
**fitful** ['fɪtfəl] *adj* caprichoso; intermitente, vacilante
**fitness** ['fɪtnɪs] *s* conveniencia; aptitud; tempestividad; buena salud
**fitter** ['fɪtər] *s* ajustador *m;* (*of machinery*) montador *m;* (*of clothing*) probador *m*
**fitting** ['fɪtɪŋ] *adj* apropiado, conveniente, justo ‖ *s* ajuste *m;* encaje *m;* (*of a garment*) prueba; tubo de ajuste; **fittings** accesorios, avíos; (*iron trimmings*) herraje *m*
**five** [faɪv] *adj & pron* cinco ‖ *s* cinco; **five o'clock** las cinco
**five hundred** *adj & pron* quinientos ‖ *s* quinientos *m*
**five'-year' plan** *s* plan *m* quinquenal
**fix** [fɪks] *s* — **in a tight fix** (coll) en calzas prietas; **to be in a fix** (coll) hallarse en un aprieto ‖ *tr* arreglar, componer, reparar; fijar (*una fecha;*

*los cabellos; una imagen fotográfica; los precios; la atención; una hora, una cita*); calar (*la bayoneta*); (coll) desquitarse con; (pol) muñir || *intr* fijarse; **to fix on** decidir, escoger

**fixed** [fɪkst] *adj* fijo

**fixing** ['fɪksɪŋ] *adj* fijador || *s* (*fastening*) fijación; (phot) fijado

**fixing bath** *s* fijador *m*

**fixture** ['fɪkstʃər] *s* accesorio, artefacto; (*of a lamp*) guarnición; **fixtures** (*e.g., of a store*) instalaciones

**fizz** [fɪz] *s* ruido sibilante; bebida gaseosa; (Brit) champaña || *intr* hacer un ruido sibilante

**fizzle** ['fɪzəl] *s* (coll) fracaso || *intr* chisporrotear débilmente; (coll) fracasar

**fl.** *abbr* **flourished, fluid**

**flabbergast** ['flæbərˌgæst] *tr* (coll) dejar sin habla, dejar estupefacto

**flab•by** ['flæbi] *adj* (*comp* **-bier;** *super* **-biest**) flojo, lacio

**flag** [flæg] *s* bandera || *v* (*pret & pp* **flagged;** *ger* **flagging**) *tr* hacer señal a (*una persona*) con una bandera; hacer señal de parada a (*un tren*) || *intr* aflojar, flaquear

**flag captain** *s* (nav) capitán *m* de bandera

**flageolet** [ˌflædʒə'lɛt] *s* chirimía, dulzaina

**flag•man** ['flægmən] *s* (*pl* **-men** [mən]) (rr) guardafrenos *m;* (rr) guardavía *m*

**flag of truce** *s* bandera de parlamento

**flag'pole'** *s* asta de bandera; (surv) jalón *m*

**flagrant** ['flegrənt] *adj* enorme, escandaloso

**flag'ship'** *s* (nav) capitana

**flag'staff'** *s* asta de bandera

**flag'stone'** *s* losa

**flag stop** *s* (rr) apeadero

**flail** [flel] *s* mayal *m* || *tr* golpear con mayal; golpear, azotar

**flair** [flɛr] *s* instinto, perspicacia

**flak** [flæk] *s* fuego antiaéreo

**flake** [flek] *s* (*thin piece*) hojuela; (*of snow*) copo || *intr* desprenderse en hojuelas; caer en copos pequeños

**flak•y** ['fleki] *adj* (*comp* **-ier;** *super* **-iest**) escamoso, laminoso

**flamboyant** [flæm'bɔɪ·ənt] *adj* flameante; llamativo; rimbombante; (archit) flameante, flamígero

**flame** [flem] *s* llama || *tr* (*to sterilize with a flame*) llamear || *intr* flamear

**flame thrower** ['θro·ər] *s* lanzallamas *m*

**flaming** ['flemɪŋ] *adj* llameante; flamante, resplandeciente; apasionado

**flamin•go** [flə'mɪŋgo] *s* (*pl* **-gos** o **-goes**) flamenco

**flammable** ['flæməbəl] *adj* inflamable

**Flanders** ['flændərz] *s* Flandes *f*

**flange** [flændʒ] *s* pestaña

**flank** [flæŋk] *s* flanco; *tr* flanquear

**flannel** ['flænəl] *s* franela

**flap** [flæp] *s* (*fold in clothing; of a hat*) falda; (*of a pocket*) cartera; (*of a table*) hoja plegadiza; (*of shoe*) oreja; (*of an envelope*) tapa; (*of wings*) aletazo; (*of the counter in a store*) trampa || *v* (*pret & pp* **flapped;** *ger* **flapping**) *tr* golpear con ruido seco; batir, sacudir (*las alas*) || *intr* aletear; flamear con ruido

**flare** [flɛr] *s* llamarada, destello; cohete *m* de señales; (aer) bengala; (*outward curvature*) abocinamiento; (*of a dress*) vuelo || *tr* abocinar || *intr* arder con gran llamarada, destellar; (*to spread outward*) abocinarse; **to flare up** inflamarse; recrudecer (*una enfermedad*); encolerizarse

**flare star** *s* (astr) estrella fulgurante

**flare'-up'** *s* llamarada; (*of an illness*) retroceso; (coll) llamarada, arrebato de cólera

**flash** [flæʃ] *s* (*of light*) relumbrón *m,* ráfaga; (*of lightning*) relámpago; (*of hope*) rayo; (*of joy*) acceso; (*of insight*) rasgo; mensaje *m* urgente || *tr* quemar (*pólvora*); enviar (*un mensaje*) como un rayo || *intr* destellar, centellear; relampaguear (*los ojos*); **to flash by** pasar como un rayo

**flash'back'** *s* (mov) retrospectiva

**flash bulb** *s* luz *f* de magnesio; bombilla de destello

**flash flood** *s* torrentada, avenida repentina

**flashing** ['flæʃɪŋ] *s* despidiente *m* de agua, vierteaguas *m*

**flash'light'** *s* linterna eléctrica, lámpara eléctrica de bolsillo; (*of a lighthouse*) luz *f* intermitente, fanal *m* de destellos; (*for taking photographs*) flash *m,* relámpago

**flashlight battery** *s* pila de linterna

**flashlight bulb** *s* bombilla de linterna

**flashlight photography** *s* fotografía instantánea de relámpago

**flash sign** *s* anuncio intermitente

**flash•y** ['flæʃi] *adj* (*comp* **-ier;** *super* **-iest**) chillón, llamativo

**flask** [flæsk] o [flɑsk] *s* frasco; frasco de bolsillo; (*for laboratory use*) matraz *m,* redoma

**flat** [flæt] *adj* (*comp* **flatter;** *super* **flattest**) plano; (*nose; boat*) chato; (*surface*) mate, deslustrado; (*beer*) muerto; (*tire*) desinflado; (*e.g., denial*) terminante; (mus) bemol || *adv* — **to fall flat** caer de plano; (fig) no surtir efecto, no tener éxito || *s* banco, bajío; (*apartment*) piso; (mus) bemol *m;* (coll) neumático desinflado

**flat'boat'** *s* chalana

**flat'car'** *s* vagón *m* de plataforma

**flat-footed** ['flætˌfʊtɪd] *adj* de pies planos; (coll) inflexible

**flat'head'** *s* (*of a bolt*) cabeza chata; clavo, tornillo o perno de cabeza chata; (coll) tonto, mentecato

**flat'i'ron** *s* plancha

**flatten** ['flætən] *tr* allanar, aplanar; chafar, aplastar; achatar || *intr* allanarse, aplanarse; aplastarse; achatarse; **to flatten out** ponerse horizontal, enderezarse

**flatter** ['flætər] *tr* lisonjear; (*to make more attractive than is*) favorecer || *intr* lisonjear

**flatterer** ['flætərər] *s* lisonjero
**flattering** ['flætərɪŋ] *adj* lisonjero
**flatter·y** ['flætəri] *s* (*pl* **-ies**) lisonja
**flat'top'** *s* portaaviones *m*
**flatulence** ['flætʃələns] *s* flatulencia
**flat'ware'** *s* vajilla de plata; vajilla de porcelana
**flaunt** [flɔnt] o [flɑnt] *tr* ostentar, hacer gala de
**flautist** ['flɔtɪst] *s* flautista *mf*
**flavor** ['flevər] *s* sabor *m*, gusto; condimento, sazón *f*; (*of ice cream*) clase *f* || *tr* saborear; condimentar, sazonar; aromatizar, perfumar
**flavoring** ['flevərɪŋ] *s* condimento, sainete *m*
**flaw** [flɔ] *s* defecto, imperfección; (*crack*) grieta
**flawless** ['flɔlɪs] *adj* perfecto, entero
**flax** [flæks] *s* lino
**flaxen** ['flæksən] *adj* blondo, rubio
**flax'seed'** *s* linaza
**flay** [fle] *tr* desollar
**flea** [fli] *s* pulga
**flea'bite'** *s* picadura de pulga; molestia insignificante
**fleck** [flɛk] *s* pinta, punto; partícula, pizca || *tr* puntear
**fledgling** ['flɛdʒlɪŋ] *s* pajarito, volantón *m*; (fig) novato, novel *m*
**flee** [fli] *v* (*pret & pp* **fled** [flɛd]) *tr & intr* huir
**fleece** [flis] *s* (*coat of wool*) lana; (*wool shorn at one time; tuft of wool or hair*) vellón *m* || *tr* esquilar; (*to strip of money*) desplumar
**fleec·y** ['flisi] *adj* (*comp* **-ier**; *super* **-iest**) lanudo; (*clouds*) aborregado
**fleet** [flit] *adj* veloz || *s* armada; (*of merchant vessels, airplanes, automobiles*) flota
**fleeting** ['flitɪŋ] *adj* fugaz, efímero; transitorio
**Fleming** ['flɛmɪŋ] *s* flamenco
**Flemish** ['flɛmɪʃ] *adj & s* flamenco
**flesh** [flɛʃ] *s* carne *f*; **in the flesh** en persona; **to lose flesh** perder carnes; **to put on flesh** cobrar carnes
**flesh and blood** *s* (*relatives*) carne y sangre; el cuerpo humano
**flesh-colored** ['flɛʃ,kʌlərd] *adj* encarnado, de color de carne
**fleshiness** ['flɛʃɪnɪs] *s* carnosidad
**fleshless** ['flɛʃlɪs] *adj* descarnado
**flesh'pot'** *s* olla, marmita; **fleshpots** vida regalona; suntuosos nidos de vicios
**flesh wound** *s* herida superficial
**flesh·y** ['flɛʃi] *adj* (*comp* **-ier**; *super* **-iest**) carnoso
**flex** [flɛks] *tr* doblar || *intr* doblarse
**flexible** ['flɛksɪbəl] *adj* flexible
**flexible cord** *s* (elec) flexible *m*
**flick** [flɪk] *s* (*with finger*) papirote *m*; (*with whip*) latigazo; ruido seco || *tr* golpear rápida y ligeramente
**flicker** ['flɪkər] *s* llama trémula; (*of eyelids*) parpadeo; (*of emotion*) temblor momentáneo || *intr* flamear con llama trémula; aletear
**flier** ['flaɪ·ər] *s* aviador *m*; tren rápido; (coll) negocio arriesgado; (coll) hoja volante
**flight** [flaɪt] *s* fuga, huída; (*of an airplane*) vuelo; (*of birds*) bandada; (*of stairs*) tramo; (*of fancy*) arranque *m*; **to put to flight** poner en fuga; **to take flight** darse a la fuga
**flight deck** *s* (nav) cubierta de vuelo
**flight·y** ['flaɪti] *adj* (*comp* **-ier**; *super* **-iest**) veleidoso; casquivano
**flim·flam** ['flɪm,flæm] *s* (coll) engaño, trampa; (coll) tontería || *v* (*pret & pp* **-flammed**; *ger* **-flamming**) *tr* (coll) engañar, trampear
**flim·sy** ['flɪmzi] *adj* (*comp* **-sier**; *super* **-siest**] débil, endeble, flojo
**flinch** [flɪntʃ] *intr* encogerse de miedo
**fling** [flɪŋ] *s* echada, tiro; baile escocés muy vivo; **to go on a fling** echar una cana al aire; **to have a fling at** ensayar, probar; **to have one's fling** correrla, mocear || *v* (*pret & pp* **flung** [flʌŋ]) *tr* arrojar; (*e.g., on the floor, out the window, in jail*) echar; **to fling open** abrir de golpe; **to fling shut** cerrar de golpe
**flint** [flɪnt] *s* pedernal *m*
**flint'lock'** *s* llave *f* de chispa; trabuco de chispa
**flint·y** ['flɪnti] *adj* (*comp* **-ier**; *super* **-iest**) pedernalino; (fig) empedernido
**flip** [flɪp] *adj* (*comp* **flipper**; *super* **flippest**) (coll) petulante || *s* capirotazo || *v* (*pret & pp* **flipped**; *ger* **flipping**) *tr* echar de un capirotazo, mover de un tirón; **to flip a coin** echar a cara o cruz; **to flip shut** cerrar de golpe (*p.ej., un abanico*)
**flippancy** ['flɪpənsi] *s* petulancia
**flippant** ['flɪpənt] *adj* petulante
**flirt** [flʌrt] *s* (*woman*) coqueta; (*man*) galanteador *m* || *intr* coquetear (*una mujer*); galantear (*un hombre*); **to flirt with** flirtear con; acariciar (*una idea*); jugar con (*la muerte*)
**flit** [flɪt] *v* (*pret & pp* **flitted**; *ger* **flitting**) *intr* revolotear, volar; pasar rápidamente
**flitch** [flɪtʃ] *s* hoja de tocino
**float** [flot] *s* (*raft*) balsa; (*of fishing line*) flotador *m*; (*of mason*) llana; carroza alegórica, carro alegórico || *tr* poner a flote; lanzar (*una empresa*); emitir (*acciones, bonos, etc.*) || *intr* flotar
**floating** ['flotɪŋ] *adj* flotante
**flock** [flɑk] *s* (*of birds*) bandada; (*of sheep*) grey *f*, rebaño, manada; (*of people*) muchedumbre; (*e.g., of nonsense*) hatajo; (*of faithful*) grey *f*, rebaño || *intr* congregarse, reunirse; llegar en tropel
**floe** [flo] *s* banquisa, témpano
**flog** [flɑg] *v* (*pret & pp* **flogged**; *ger* **flogging**) *tr* azotar, fustigar
**flood** [flʌd] *s* inundación; (*caused by heavy rain*) diluvio; (*sudden rise of river*) crecida; (*of tide*) pleamar *f*; (*of words, etc.*) diluvio, torrente *m* || *tr* inundar; (*to overwhelm*) abrumar || *intr* desbordar, rebosar; entrar a raudales
**flood'gate'** *s* (*of a dam*) compuerta; (*of a canal*) esclusa

**flood'light'** *s* faro de inundación || *tr* iluminar con faro de inundación
**flood tide** *s* pleamar *f*, marea montante
**floor** [flor] *s* (*inside bottom surface of room*) piso, suelo; (*story of a building*) piso, alto; (*of the sea, a swimming pool, etc.*) fondo; (*of an assembly hall*) hemiciclo; (naut) varenga; **to ask for the floor** pedir la palabra; **to have the floor** tener la palabra; **to take the floor** tomar la palabra || *tr* entarimar; derribar, echar al suelo; (coll) confundir, envolver, revolcar (*al adversario en controversia*); (coll) vencer
**floor lamp** *s* lámpara de pie
**floor mop** *s* fregasuelos *m*, estropajo
**floor plan** *s* planta
**floor show** *s* espectáculo de cabaret
**floor timber** *s* (naut) varenga
**floor'walk'er** *s* jefe *m* de sección
**floor wax** *s* cera de pisos
**flop** [flɑp] *s* (coll) fracaso, caída; **to take a flop** (coll) caerse || *v* (*pret & pp* **flopped**; *ger* **flopping**) *intr* agitarse; caerse; venirse abajo; fracasar; **to flop over** volcarse; cambiar de partido
**flora** ['florə] *s* flora
**floral** ['florəl] *adj* floral
**Florentine** ['flɑrən,tin] o ['flɔrən,tin] *adj & s* florentino
**florescence** [flo'rɛsəns] *s* florescencia
**florid** ['flɑrɪd] o ['flɔrɪd] *adj* (*complexion*) encarnado; (*showy, ornate*) florido
**Florida Keys** ['flɑrɪdə] o ['flɔrɪdə] *s* Cayos de la Florida
**florist** ['florɪst] *s* florero, florista *mf*
**floss** [flɔs] o [flɑs] *s* cadarzo; (*of corn*) cabellos
**floss silk** *s* seda floja sin torcer
**floss•y** ['flɔsi] o ['flɑsi] *adj* (*comp* **-ier**; *super* **-iest**) ligero, velloso; (slang) cursi, vistoso
**flotsam** ['flɑtsəm] *s* pecio
**flotsam and jetsam** *s* pecios, despojos; (*trifles*) baratijas; gente *f* trashumante, gente perdida
**flounce** [flauns] *s* faralá *m*, volante *m* || *tr* adornar con faralaes o volantes || *intr* moverse airadamente
**flounder** ['flaundər] *s* platija || *intr* forcejear, obrar torpemente, andar tropezando
**flour** [flaur] *adj* harinero || *s* harina
**flourish** ['flʌrɪʃ] *s* (*with the sword*) molinete *m*; (*with the pen*) plumada, rasgo; (*as part of signature*) rúbrica; (mus) floreo || *tr* blandir (*la espada*) || *intr* florecer, prosperar
**flourishing** ['flʌrɪʃɪŋ] *adj* floreciente, próspero
**flour mill** *s* molino de harina
**floury** ['flauri] *adj* harinoso
**flout** [flaut] *tr* mofarse de, burlarse de || *intr* mofarse, burlarse
**flow** [flo] *s* flujo || *intr* fluir; subir (*la marea*); ondear (*el pelo en el aire*); **to flow into** desaguar en, desembocar en; **to flow over** rebosar; **to flow with** nadar en, abundar en
**flower** ['flau·ər] *s* flor *f* || *tr* florear || *intr* florecer
**flower bed** *s* macizo, parterre *m*
**flower garden** *s* jardín *m*
**flower girl** *s* florera; (*at a wedding*) damita de honor
**flower piece** *s* ramillete *m*; (*painting*) florero
**flow'er•pot'** *s* tiesto, maceta
**flower shop** *s* floristería
**flower show** *s* exposición de flores
**flower stand** *s* florero
**flowery** ['flau·əri] *adj* florido, cubierto de flores
**flu** [flu] *s* (coll) gripe *f*, influenza
**fluctuate** ['flʌktʃu,et] *intr* fluctuar
**flue** [flu] *s* cañón *m* de chimenea; tubo de humo
**fluency** ['flu·ənsi] *s* afluencia, facundia
**fluent** ['flu·ənt] *adj* (*flowing*) fluente; afluente, facundo, flúido
**fluently** ['flu·əntli] *adv* corrientemente
**fluff** [flʌf] *s* pelusa, tamo; vello, pelusilla; (*of an actor*) gazapo || *tr* esponjar, mullir || *intr* esponjarse
**fluff•y** ['flʌfi] *adj* (*comp* **-ier**; *super* **-iest**) fofo, esponjoso, mullido; velloso
**fluid** ['flu·ɪd] *adj & s* flúido
**fluidity** [flu'ɪdɪti] *s* fluidez *f*
**fluke** [fluk] *s* (*of anchor*) uña; (*in billiards*) chiripa
**flume** [flum] *s* caz *m*, saetín *m*
**flunk** [flʌŋk] *s* (coll) reprobación || *tr* (coll) reprobar, dar calabazas a; perder (*un examen o asignatura*) || *intr* (coll) fracasar, salir mal; **to flunk out** (coll) tener que abandonar los estudios por no poder aprobar
**flunk•y** ['flʌŋki] *s* (*pl* **-ies**) lacayo; adulador *m*
**fluor** ['flu·ɔr] *s* fluorita
**fluorescence** [,flu·ə'rɛsəns] *s* fluorescencia
**fluorescent** [,flu·ə'rɛsənt] *adj* fluorescente
**fluoridate** ['flu·ərɪ,det] *tr* fluorizar
**fluoridation** [,flu·ərɪ'deʃən] *s* fluorización
**fluoride** ['flu·ə,raɪd] *s* fluoruro
**fluorine** ['flu·ə,rin] *s* flúor *m*
**fluorite** ['flu·ə,raɪt] *s* fluorita
**fluoroscope** ['flu·ərə,skop] *s* fluoroscopio
**fluor spar** *s* espato flúor
**flur•ry** ['flʌri] *s* (*pl* **-ries**) agitación; (*of wind*) racha, ráfaga; (*of rain*) chaparrón *m*; (*of snow*) nevisca || *v* (*pret & pp* **-ried**) *tr* agitar
**flush** [flʌʃ] *adj* rasante, nivelado; (*set in, in order to be flush*) embutido; abundante; robusto, vigoroso; próspero, bien provisto; coloradote; (*in printing*) justificado; **flush with** a ras de || *adv* ras con ras, al mismo nivel || *s* (*of water*) flujo repentino; (*in the cheeks*) rubor *m*; sonrojo; (*in the springtime*) floración repentina; (*of joy*) acceso; (*of youth*) vigor *m*; chorro del inodoro; (*in poker*) flux *m* || *tr* (*to cause to blush*) abochornar; limpiar con un chorro de agua; hacer saltar (*una liebre*) || *intr*

abochornarse, estar encendido (*el rostro*); (*to gush*) brotar
**Flushing** ['flʌʃɪŋ] *s* Flesinga
**flush outlet** *s* (elec) caja de enchufe embutida
**flush switch** *s* (elec) llave embutida
**flush tank** *s* depósito de limpia
**flush toilet** *s* inodoro con chorro de agua
**fluster** ['flʌstər] *s* confusión, aturdimiento || *tr* confundir, aturdir
**flute** [flut] *s* (*of a column*) estría; (mus) flauta || *tr* estriar, acanalar
**flutist** ['flutɪst] *s* flautista *mf*
**flutter** ['flʌtər] *s* aleteo, revoloteo; confusión, turbación || *intr* aletear, revolotear; flamear, ondear; agitarse; alterarse (*el pulso*); palpitar (*el corazón*)
**flux** [flʌks] *s* (*flow; flowing of tide*) flujo; (*for fusing metals*) flujo, fundente *m*
**fly** [flaɪ] *s* (*pl* **flies**) mosca; (*of trousers*) portañuela, bragueta; (*for fishing*) mosca artificial; **flies** (theat) bambalinas; **to die like flies** morir como chinches || *v* (*pret* **flew** [flu]; *pp* **flown** [flon]) *tr* hacer volar (*una cometa*); dirigir (*un avión*); (*to carry in an airship*) volar; atravesar en avión; desplegar, llevar (*una bandera*) || *intr* volar; huir; ondear (*una bandera*); **to fly off** salir volando; desprenderse; **to fly open** abrirse de repente; **to fly over** trasvolar; **to fly shut** cerrarse de repente
**fly ball** *s* (baseball) palomita
**fly'blow'** *s* cresa
**fly'-by-night'** *adj* indigno de confianza
**fly'catch'er** *s* moscareta, papamoscas *m*
**fly chaser** *s* espantamoscas *m*
**flyer** ['flaɪ·ər] *s* var de **flier**
**fly'-fish'** *tr & intr* pescar con moscas artificiales
**flying** ['flaɪ·ɪŋ] *adj* volante; rápido, veloz || *s* aviación
**flying boat** *s* hidroavión *m*
**flying buttress** *s* arbotante *m*
**flying colors** *spl* gran éxito
**flying field** *s* campo de aviación
**flying saucer** *s* platillo volante
**flying sickness** *s* mal *m* de altura
**flying time** *s* horas de vuelo
**fly in the ointment** *s* mosca muerta que malea el perfume
**fly'leaf'** *s* (*pl* **-leaves'**) guarda, hoja de guarda
**fly net** *s* (*for a bed*) mosquitero; (*for a horse*) espantamoscas *m*
**fly'pa'per** *s* papel *m* matamoscas
**fly'speck'** *s* mancha de mosca
**fly swatter** ['swɑtər] *s* matamoscas *m*
**fly'trap'** *s* atrapamoscas *m*
**fly'wheel'** *s* volante *m*
**fm.** *abbr* **fathom**
**F.M.** *abbr* **frequency modulation**
**foal** [fol] *s* potro || *intr* parir (*la yegua*)
**foam** [fom] *s* espuma || *intr* espumar
**foam extinguisher** *s* lanzaespumas *m*, extintor *m* de espuma
**foam rubber** *s* caucho esponjoso, espuma de caucho
**foam·y** ['fomi] *adj* (*comp* **-ier**; *super* **-iest**) espumoso, espumajoso
**fob** [fɑb] *s* faltriquera de reloj; (*chain*) leopoldina; (*ornament*) dije *m*
**F.O.B.** *abbr* **free on board**
**focal** ['fokəl] *adj* focal
**fo·cus** ['fokəs] *s* (*pl* **-cuses** o **-ci** [saɪ]) foco; **in focus** enfocado; **out of focus** desenfocado || *v* (*pret & pp* **-cused** o **-cussed**; *ger* **-cusing** o **-cussing**) *tr* enfocar; fijar (*la atención*) || *intr* enfocarse
**fodder** ['fɑdər] *s* forraje *m*
**foe** [fo] *s* enemigo
**fog** [fɑg] o [fɔg] *s* niebla; (phot) velo || *v* (*pret & pp* **fogged**; *ger* **fogging**) *tr* envolver en niebla; (*to blur*) empañar; (phot) velar || *intr* empañarse; (phot) velarse
**fog bank** *s* banco de nieblas
**fog bell** *s* campana de nieblas
**fog'bound'** *adj* atascado en la niebla, envuelto en la niebla
**fog·gy** ['fɑgi] o ['fɔgi] *adj* (*comp* **-gier**; *super* **-giest**) neblinoso, brumoso; confuso; (phot) velado; **it is foggy** hay neblina
**fog'horn'** *s* sirena de niebla
**foible** ['fɔɪbəl] *s* flaqueza, lado flaco
**foil** [fɔɪl] *s* (*thin sheet of metal*) hojuela, laminilla; (*of mirror*) azogado, plateado; contraste *m*, realce *m*; (*sword*) florete *m* || *tr* frustrar; azogar, platear (*un espejo*)
**foist** [fɔɪst] *tr* — **to foist something on someone** encajar una cosa a uno
**fol.** *abbr* **folio, following**
**fold** [fold] *s* pliegue *m*, doblez *m*; arruga; (*for sheep*) aprisco, redil *m*; (*of the faithful*) rebaño || *tr* plegar, doblar; cruzar (*los brazos*); **to fold up** doblar (*p.ej., un mapa*) || *intr* plegarse, doblarse
**folder** ['foldər] *s* (*covers for holding papers*) carpeta; (*pamphlet*) folleto
**folderol** ['fɑldə,rɑl] *s* tontería, necedad; bagatela
**folding** ['foldɪŋ] *adj* plegadizo, plegable; plegador
**folding camera** *s* cámara de fuelle
**folding chair** *s* silla de tijera, silla plegadiza; (*of canvas*) catrecillo
**folding cot** *s* catre m de tijera
**folding door** *s* puerta plegadiza
**folding rule** *s* metro plegadizo
**foliage** ['folɪ·ɪdʒ] *s* follaje *m*
**foli·o** ['folɪ·o] *adj* en folio || *s* (*pl* **-os**) (*sheet*) folio; infolio, libro en folio || *tr* foliar
**folk** [fok] *adj* popular, tradicional, del pueblo || *s* (*pl* **folk** o **folks**) gente *f*; **folks** (coll) gente (*familia*)
**folk'lore'** *s* folklore *m*
**folk music** *s* música folklórica
**folk song** *s* canción típica, canción tradicional
**folk·sy** ['foksi] *adj* (*comp* **-sier**; *super* **-siest**) (coll) sociable, tratable; (*like common people*) (coll) plebeyo
**folk'way'** *s* costumbre tradicional
**follicle** ['fɑlɪkəl] *s* folículo
**follow** ['fɑlo] *tr* seguir; seguir el hilo de; interesarse en (*las noticias del*

*día*) || *intr* seguir; resultar; **as follows** como sigue; **it follows** síguese
**follower** ['fɑlo·ər] *s* seguidor *m;* secuaz *mf,* partidario; imitador *m;* discípulo
**following** ['fɑlo·ɪŋ] *adj* siguiente || *s* séquito; partidarios
**fol'low-up'** *adj* consecutivo; recordativo || *s* carta recordativa, circular recordativa
**fol·ly** ['fɑli] *s* (*pl* **-lies**) desatino, locura; empresa temeraria; **follies** revista teatral
**foment** [fo'mɛnt] *tr* fomentar
**fond** [fɑnd] *adj* afectuoso, cariñoso; **to become fond of** encariñarse con, aficionarse a o de
**fondle** ['fɑndəl] *tr* acariciar, mimar
**fondness** ['fɑndnɪs] *s* afición, cariño
**font** [fɑnt] *s* (*source; source of water*) fuente *f;* (*for holy water*) pila; (*of type*) fundición
**food** [fud] *adj* alimenticio || *s* comida, alimento; **food for thought** cosa en qué pensar
**food store** *s* tienda de comestibles, colmado
**food'stuffs'** *spl* comestibles *mpl,* víveres *mpl*
**fool** [ful] *s* tonto, necio; (*jester*) bufón *m;* (*person imposed on*) inocente *mf,* víctima; **to make a fool of** poner en ridículo; **to play the fool** hacer el tonto || *tr* embaucar, engañar; **to fool away** malgastar (*tiempo, dinero*) || *intr* tontear; **to fool around** (coll) malgastar el tiempo; **to fool with** (coll) ajar, manosear
**fooler·y** ['fuləri] *s* (*pl* **-ies**) locura, tontería
**fool'har'dy** *adj* (*comp* **-dier;** *super* **-diest**) temerario
**fooling** ['fulɪŋ] *s* broma; engaño; **no fooling** hablando en serio
**foolish** ['fulɪʃ] *adj* tonto; ridículo
**fool'proof'** *adj* (coll) a prueba de mal trato; (coll) infalible
**fools'cap'** *s* gorro de bufón; papel *m* de oficio
**fool's errand** *s* caza de grillos
**fool's scepter** *s* cetro de locura
**foot** [fut] *s* (*pl* **feet** [fit]) pie *m;* **to drag one's feet** ir a paso de caracol; **to have one foot in the grave** estar con un pie en la sepultura; **to put one's best foot forward** (coll) hacer méritos; **to put one's foot in it** (coll) meter la pata; (coll) tirarse una plancha; **to stand on one's own feet** volar con sus propias alas; **to tread under foot** hollar || *tr* pagar (*la cuenta*); **to foot it** andar a pie; bailar
**footage** ['futɪdʒ] *s* distancia o largura en pies
**foot'ball'** *s* (*game*) balompié *m,* fútbol *m;* (*ball*) balón *m*
**foot'board'** *s* (*support for foot*) estribo; (*of bed*) pie *m*
**foot'bridge'** *s* pasarela, puente *m* para peatones
**foot'fall'** *s* paso
**foot'hill'** *s* colina al pie de una montaña
**foot'hold'** *s* arraigo, pie *m;* **to gain a foothold** ganar pie
**footing** ['futɪŋ] *s* pie *m,* p.ej., **he lost his footing** perdió el pie; **on a friendly footing** en relaciones amistosas; **on an equal footing** en pie de igualdad; **on a war footing** en pie de guerra
**foot'lights'** *spl* candilejas, batería; (fig) tablas, escena
**foot'loose'** *adj* libre, no comprometido
**foot·man** ['futmən] *s* (*pl* **-men** [mən]) lacayo, criado de librea
**foot'mark'** *s* huella
**foot'note'** *s* nota al pie de la página
**foot'path'** *s* senda para peatones
**foot'print'** *s* huella
**foot race** *s* carrera a pie
**foot'rest'** *s* apoyapié *m,* descansapié *m*
**foot rule** *s* regla de un pie
**foot soldier** *s* soldado de a pie
**foot'sore'** *adj* despeado
**foot'step'** *s* paso; **to follow in the footsteps of** seguir los pasos de
**foot'stone'** *s* lápida al pie de una sepultura
**foot'stool'** *s* escabel *m,* escañuelo
**foot warmer** *s* calientapiés *m*
**foot'wear'** *s* calzado
**foot'work'** *s* juego de piernas
**foot'worn'** *adj* (*road*) trillado; (*person*) despeado
**foozle** ['fuzəl] *s* chambonada; (coll) chambón *m,* torpe *m* || *tr* chafallar; errar (*un golpe*) de manera torpe || *intr* chambonear
**fop** [fɑp] *s* currutaco, petimetre *m*
**for** [fɔr] *prep* para; por; como, p.ej., **he uses his living room for an office** usa la sala como oficina; de, p.ej., **time for bed** hora de acostarse; desde hace, p.ej., **he has been here for a week** está aquí desde hace una semana; en honor de; a pesar de || *conj* pues, porque
**for.** *abbr* **foreign**
**forage** ['fɑrɪdʒ] o ['fɔrɪdʒ] *adj* forrajero || *s* forraje *m* || *tr & intr* forrajear; saquear
**foray** ['fɑre] o ['fɔre] *s* correría; saqueo || *intr* hacer correrías
**for·bear** [fɔr'bɛr] *v* (*pret* **-bore** ['bor]; *pp* **-borne** ['born]) *tr* abstenerse de || *intr* contenerse
**forbearance** [fɔr'berəns] *s* abstención; paciencia
**for·bid** [fər'bɪd] *v* (*pret* **-bade** ['bæd] o **-bad** ['bæd]; *pp* **-bidden** ['bɪdən]; *ger* **-bidding**) *tr* prohibir
**forbidding** [fər'bɪdɪŋ] *adj* repugnante, repulsivo
**force** [fors] *s* fuerza; (*staff of workers*) personal *m;* (*of soldiers, police, etc.*) cuerpo; (phys) fuerza; **by force of** a fuerza de; **by main force** con todas sus fuerzas; **in force** vigente, en vigor; en gran número; **to join forces** juntar diestra con diestra || *tr* forzar; obligar; **to force back** hacer retroceder; **to force open** abrir por

fuerza; **to force through** llevar a cabo por fuerza
**forced** [forst] *adj* forzado
**forced air** *s* aire *m* a presión
**forced landing** *s* aterrizaje forzado o forzoso
**forced march** *s* marcha forzada
**forceful** ['forsfəl] *adj* enérgico, eficaz
**for•ceps** ['fɔrsəps] *s* (*pl* **-ceps** o **-cipes** [sɪ,piz]) (dent, surg) pinzas; (obstet) fórceps *m*
**force pump** *s* bomba impelente
**forcible** ['forsɪbəl] *adj* eficaz, convincente; forzado
**ford** [ford] *s* vado || *tr* vadear
**fore** [for] *adj* anterior; (naut) de proa || *adv* antes, anteriormente; delante; (naut) avante || *interj* ¡ojo!, ¡cuidado! || *s* delantera; **to the fore** destacado; a mano; vivo
**fore and aft** *adv* de popa a proa
**fore'arm'** *s* antebrazo || **fore•arm'** *tr* armar de antemano; prevenir
**fore'bear'** *s* antepasado
**forebode** [for'bod] *tr* (*to portend*) presagiar; (*to have a presentiment of*) presentir, prever
**foreboding** [for'bodɪŋ] *s* presagio; presentimiento
**fore'cast'** *s* pronóstico || *v* (*pret & pp* **-cast** o **-casted**) *tr* pronosticar
**forecastle** ['foksəl], ['for,kæsəl] o ['for,kɑsəl] *s* castillo de proa
**fore•close'** *tr* excluir; extinguir el derecho de redimir (*una hipoteca*); privar del derecho de redimir una hipoteca
**fore•doom'** *tr* condenar de antemano, predestinar al fracaso
**fore edge** *s* canal *f*
**fore'fa'ther** *s* antepasado
**fore'fin'ger** *s* dedo índice, dedo mostrador
**fore'front'** *s* puesto delantero; sitio de actividad más intensa; **in the forefront** a vanguardia
**fore•go'** *v* (*pret* **-went'**; *pp* **-gone'**) *tr* & *intr* preceder
**foregoing** ['for,go•ɪŋ] o [for'go•ɪŋ] *adj* anterior, precedente
**fore'gone' conclusion** *s* resultado inevitable; decisión adoptada de antemano
**fore'ground'** *s* primer plano, primer término
**forehanded** ['for,hændɪd] *adj* (*thrifty*) ahorrado; hecho de antemano
**forehead** ['fɑrɪd] o ['fɔrɪd] *s* frente *f*
**foreign** ['fɑrɪn] o ['fɔrɪn] *adj* extranjero, exterior; **foreign to** (*not belonging to or connected with*) ajeno a
**foreign affairs** *spl* asuntos exteriores
**for'eign-born'** *adj* nacido en el extranjero
**foreigner** ['fɑrɪnər] o ['fɔrɪnər] *s* extranjero
**foreign exchange** *s* cambio extranjero; (*currency*) divisa
**foreign minister** *s* ministro de asuntos exteriores
**foreign office** *s* ministerio de asuntos exteriores
**foreign service** *s* servicio diplomático y consular; servicio militar extranjero
**foreign trade** *s* comercio extranjero
**fore'leg'** *s* brazo, pata delantera
**fore'lock'** *s* mechón *m* de pelo sobre la frente; (*of a horse*) copete *m*; **to take time by the forelock** asir la ocasión por la melena
**fore•man** ['formən] *s* (*pl* **-men** [mən]) capataz *m*, mayoral *m*, sobrestante *m*; (*in a machine shop*) contramaestre *m*; presidente *m* de jurado
**foremast** ['formәst], ['for,mæst] o ['for,mɑst] *s* palo de trinquete
**foremost** ['for,most] *adj* primero, principal, más eminente
**fore'noon'** *adj* matinal || *s* mañana
**fore'part'** *s* parte delantera; primera parte
**fore'paw'** *s* pata delantera
**fore'quar'ter** *s* cuarto delantero
**fore'run'ner** *s* precursor *m*; predecesor *m*; antepasado; anuncio, presagio
**fore•sail** ['forsəl] o ['for,sel] *s* trinquete *m*
**fore•see'** *v* (*pret* **-saw'**; *pp* **-seen'**) *tr* prever
**foreseeable** [for'si•əbəl] *adj* previsible
**fore•shad'ow** *tr* presagiar, prefigurar
**fore•short'en** *tr* escorzar
**fore•short'ening** *s* escorzo
**fore'sight'** *s* previsión, presciencia
**fore'sight'ed** *adj* previsor, presciente
**fore'skin'** *s* prepucio
**forest** ['fɑrɪst] o ['fɔrɪst] *adj* forestal || *s* bosque *m*
**fore•stall'** *tr* impedir, prevenir; anticipar; acaparar
**forest ranger** ['rendʒər] *s* guarda *m* forestal, montanero
**forestry** ['fɑrɪstri] o ['fɔrɪstri] *s* silvicultura, ciencia forestal
**fore'taste'** *s* goce anticipado, conocimiento anticipado
**fore•tell'** *v* (*pret & pp* **-told'**) *tr* predecir; presagiar
**fore'thought'** *s* premeditación; providencia, previsión
**forever** [fɔr'ɛvər] *adv* por siempre; siempre
**fore•warn'** *tr* prevenir, poner sobre aviso
**fore'word'** *s* advertencia, prefacio
**forfeit** ['fɔrfɪt] *adj* perdido || *s* multa, pena; prenda perdida; **forfeits** (*game*) prendas || *tr* perder el derecho a
**forfeiture** ['fɔrfɪtʃər] *s* multa, pena; prenda perdida
**forgather** [fɔr'gæðər] *intr* reunirse; encontrarse; **to forgather with** asociarse con
**forge** [fordʒ] *s* fragua; (*blacksmith shop*) herrería; || *tr* fraguar, forjar; falsificar (*la firma de otra persona*); fraguar, forjar (*mentiras*) || *intr* fraguar, forjar; **to forge ahead** avanzar despacio y con esfuerzo
**forger•y** ['fordʒəri] *s* (*pl* **-ies**) falsificación
**for•get** [fɔr'get] *v* (*pret* **-got** ['gɑt]; *pp* **-got** o **-gotten**; *ger* **-getting**) *tr* olvidar,

olvidarse de, olvidársele a uno, p.ej., **he forgot his overcoat** se le olvidó su abrigo; **forget it!** ¡no se preocupe!; **to forget oneself** no pensar en sí mismo; ser distraído; propasarse
**forgetful** [fɔr'gɛtfəl] *adj* olvidado, olvidadizo; descuidado
**forgetfulness** [fɔr'gɛtfəlnɪs] *s* olvido; descuido
**for•get'-me-not'** *s* nomeolvides *m*
**forgivable** [fɔr'gɪvəbəl] *adj* perdonable
**for•give** [fɔr'gɪv] *v* (*pret* **-gave'**; *pp* **-giv'en**) *tr* perdonar
**forgiveness** [fɔr'gɪvnɪs] *s* perdón *m;* misericordia
**forgiving** [fɔr'gɪvɪŋ] *adj* perdonador, misericordioso, clemente
**for•go** [fɔr'go] *v* (*pret* **-went'**; *pp* **-gone'**) *tr* privarse de
**fork** [fɔrk] *s* horca; (*of a gardener; of bicycle*) horquilla; (*of two rivers*) horcajo; (*of railroad*) ramal *m;* (*of a tree*) horqueta; (*for eating*) tenedor *m* || *tr* ahorquillar; cargar con horquilla; (*in chess*) amenazar (*dos piezas*); **to fork out** (slang) entregar, sudar || *intr* bifurcarse
**forked** [fɔrkt] *adj* ahorquillado
**forked lightning** *s* relámpago en zigzag
**fork'lift' truck** *s* carretilla elevadora de horquilla
**forlorn** [fɔr'lɔrn] *adj* desamparado; desesperado; miserable
**forlorn hope** *s* empresa desesperada
**form** [fɔrm] *s* forma; (*paper to be filled out*) formulario; (*construction to give shape to cement*) encofrado; (*type in a frame*) molde *m* || *tr* formar || *intr* formarse
**formal** ['fɔrməl] *adj* formal, ceremonioso; etiquetero
**formal attire** *s* vestido de etiqueta
**formal call** *s* visita de cumplido
**formali•ty** [fɔr'mælɪti] *s* (*pl* **-ties**) (*standard procedure*) formalidad; ceremonia, etiqueta
**formal party** *s* reunión de etiqueta
**formal speech** *s* discurso de aparato
**format** ['fɔrmæt] *s* formato
**formation** [fɔr'meʃən] *s* formación
**former** ['fɔrmər] *adj* (*preceding*) anterior; (*long past*) antiguo; primero (*de dos*); **the former** aquél
**formerly** ['fɔrmərli] *adv* antes, en tiempos pasados
**form'-fit'ting** *adj* ceñido al cuerpo
**formidable** ['fɔrmɪdəbəl] *adj* formidable
**formless** ['fɔrmlɪs] *adj* informe
**form letter** *s* carta general
**formu•la** ['fɔrmjələ] *s* (*pl* **-las** o **-lae** [,li]) formula
**formulate** ['fɔrmjə,let] *tr* formular
**for•sake** [fɔr'sek] *v* (*pret* **-sook** ['sʊk]; *pp* **-saken** ['sekən]) *tr* abandonar, desamparar; dejar
**fort** [fort] *s* fuerte *m,* fortaleza
**forte** [fort] *s* (*strong point*) fuerte *m,* caballo de batalla
**forth** [forθ] *adv* adelante; **and so forth** y así sucesivamente; **from this day forth** de hoy en adelante; **to go forth** salir
**forth'com'ing** *adj* próximo, venidero
**forth'right'** *adj* directo, franco, sincero || *adv* derecho; sinceramente, francamente; en seguida
**forth'with'** *adv* inmediatamente
**fortieth** ['fɔrtɪ•ɪθ] *adj* & *s* (*in a series*) cuadragésimo; (*part*) cuarentavo
**fortification** [,fɔrtɪfɪ'keʃən] *s* fortificación
**forti•fy** ['fɔrtɪ,faɪ] *v* (*pret* & *pp* **-fied**) *tr* fortificar; encabezar (*vinos*)
**fortitude** ['fɔrtɪ,tjud] o ['fɔrtɪ,tud] *s* fortaleza, firmeza
**fortnight** ['fɔrtnaɪt] o ['fɔrtnɪt] *s* quincena, dos semanas
**fortress** ['fɔrtrɪs] *s* fortaleza
**fortuitous** [fɔr'tju•ɪtəs] o [fɔr'tu•ɪtəs] *adj* fortuito
**fortunate** ['fɔrtʃənɪt] *adj* afortunado
**fortune** ['fɔrtjən] *s* fortuna; **to make a fortune** enriquecerse; **to tell someone his fortune** decirle a uno la buenaventura
**fortune hunter** *s* cazador *m* de dotes
**for'tune•tel'ler** *s* adivino, agorero
**for•ty** ['fɔrti] *adj* & *pron* cuarenta || *s* (*pl* **-ties**) cuarenta *m*
**fo•rum** ['forəm] *s* (*pl* **-rums** o **-ra** [rə]) foro; (*e.g., of public opinion*) tribunal *m*
**forward** ['fɔrwərd] *adj* delantero; precoz; atrevido, impertinente || *adv* hacia adelante; **to bring forward** pasar a cuenta nueva; **to come forward** adelantarse; **to look forward to** esperar con placer anticipado || *tr* cursar, hacer seguir, reexpedir; fomentar, patrocinar
**fossil** ['fɑsɪl] *adj* & *s* fósil *m*
**foster** ['fɑstər] o ['fɔstər] *adj* adoptivo, de leche, de crianza || *tr* fomentar
**foster home** *s* hogar *m* de adopción
**foul** [faʊl] *adj* sucio, puerco; (*air*) viciado; (*wind*) contrario; (*weather*) malo; obsceno; pérfido; (*breath*) fétido; (baseball) fuera del cuadro
**foul-mouthed** ['faʊl'maʊðd] o ['faʊl'maʊθt] *adj* deslenguado
**foul play** *s* mal encuentro; (sport) juego sucio
**foul'spo'ken** *adj* malhablado
**found** [faʊnd] *tr* fundar; (*to melt, to cast*) fundir
**foundation** [faʊn'deʃən] *s* fundación; (*endowment*) dotación; (*basis*) fundamento; (*masonry support*) cimiento
**founder** ['faʊndər] *s* fundador *m;* (*of metals*) fundidor *m* || *intr* despearse (*un caballo*); hundirse, irse a pique (*un buque*); (*to fail*) fracasar
**foundling** ['faʊndlɪŋ] *s* niño expósito
**foundling hospital** *s* casa de expósitos
**found•ry** ['faʊndri] *s* (*pl* **-ries**) fundición
**foundry•man** ['faʊndrɪmən] *s* (*pl* **-men** [mən]) fundidor *m*
**fount** [faʊnt] *s* fuente *f*
**fountain** ['faʊntən] *s* fuente *f,* manantial *m*

**foun'tain·head'** *s* nacimiento
**fountain pen** *s* pluma estilográfica, pluma fuente
**fountain syringe** *s* mangueta
**four** [for] *adj & pron* cuatro ‖ *s* cuatro; **four o'clock** las cuatro; **on all fours** a gatas
**four'-cy'cle** *adj* (mach) de cuatro tiempos
**four'-cyl'inder** *adj* (mach) de cuatro cilindros
**four'-flush'** *intr* (coll) bravear, papelonear
**fourflusher** ['for,flʌʃər] *s* (coll) bravucón *m*
**four-footed** ['for'fʊtɪd] *adj* cuadrúpedo
**four hundred** *adj & pron* cuatrocientos ‖ *s* cuatrocientos *m;* **the four hundred** la alta sociedad
**four'-in-hand'** *s* corbata de nudo corredizo; coche tirado por cuatro caballos
**four'-lane'** *adj* cuadriviario
**four'-leaf'** *adj* cuadrifoliado
**four-legged** ['for'lɛgɪd] o ['for'lɛgd] *adj* de cuatro patas; (*schooner*) de cuatro mástiles
**four'-let'ter word** *s* palabra impúdica de cuatro letras
**four'-mo'tor plane** *s* cuadrimotor *m*
**four'-o'clock'** *s* dondiego
**four'-post'er** *s* cama imperial
**four'score'** *adj* cuatro veintenas de
**foursome** ['forsəm] *s* cuatrinca; cuatro jugadores; juego de cuatro
**fourteen** ['for'tin] *adj, pron & s* catorce *m*
**fourteenth** ['for'tinθ] *adj & s* (*in a series*) decimocuarto; (*part*) catorzavo ‖ *s* (*in dates*) catorce *m*
**fourth** [forθ] *adj & s* cuarto ‖ *s* (*in dates*) cuatro
**fourth estate** *s* cuarto poder
**four'-way'** *adj* de cuatro direcciones; (elec) de cuatro terminales
**fowl** [faʊl] *s* ave *f;* aves; gallina; gallo; carne *f* de ave
**fowling piece** *s* escopeta de caza
**fox** [fɑks] *s* zorra; (*fur*) zorro; (*cunning person*) (fig) zorro ‖ *tr* (coll) engañar con astucia
**fox'glove'** *s* dedalera
**fox'hole'** *s* zorrera; (mil) pozo de lobo
**fox'hound'** *s* perro raposero, perro zorrero
**fox hunt** *s* caza de zorras
**fox terrier** *s* fox-terrier *m* (*casta de perro de talla pequeña*)
**fox trot** *s* trote corto (*de caballo*); foxtrot *m* (*baile de compás cuaternario*)
**fox·y** ['fɑksi] *adj* (*comp* **-ier;** *super* **-iest**) zorrero, astuto, taimado
**foyer** ['fɔɪ·ər] *s* (*of a private house*) vestíbulo; (theat) salón *m* de entrada, vestíbulo
**fr.** *abbr* **fragment, franc, from**
**Fr.** *abbr* **Father, French, Friday**
**Fra** [frɑ] *s* fray *m*
**fracas** ['frekəs] *s* alboroto, riña
**fraction** ['frækʃən] *s* fracción; porción muy pequeña
**fractional** ['frækʃənəl] *adj* fraccionario; insignificante
**fractious** ['frækʃəs] *adj* reacio, rebelón; quisquilloso, regañón
**fracture** ['fræktʃər] *s* fractura ‖ *tr* fracturar; (*e.g., an arm*) fracturarse; *intr* fracturarse
**fragile** ['frædʒɪl] *adj* frágil
**fragment** ['frægmənt] *s* fragmento
**fragrance** ['fregrəns] *s* fragancia
**fragrant** ['fregrənt] *adj* fragante
**frail** [frel] *adj* (*not robust*) débil; (*easily broken; morally weak*) frágil ‖ *s* cesto de junco
**frail·ty** ['frelti] *s* (*pl* **-ties**) debilidad; (*moral weakness*) fragilidad
**frame** [frem] *s* (*of a picture, mirror*) marco; (*of glasses*) montura, armadura; (*structure*) armazón *f*, esqueleto; (*for embroidering*) bastidor *m;* (*of government*) sistema *m;* (mov, telv) encuadre *m;* (naut) cuaderna ‖ *tr* (*to put in a frame*) enmarcar; formar, forjar; construir; redactar, formular; (slang) incriminar (*a un inocente*)
**frame house** *s* casa de madera
**frame of mind** *s* manera de pensar
**frame'-up'** *s* (slang) treta, trama para incriminar a un inocente
**frame'work'** *s* armazón *f*, esqueleto, entramado
**franc** [fræŋk] *s* franco
**France** [fræns] o [frɑns] *s* Francia
**Frances** ['frænsɪs] o ['frɑnsɪs] *s* Francisca
**franchise** ['fræntʃaɪz] *s* franquicia, privilegio; (*right to vote*) sufragio
**Francis** ['frænsɪs] o ['frɑnsɪs] *s* Francisco
**Franciscan** [fræn'sɪskən] *adj & s* franciscano
**frank** [fræŋk] *adj* franco, sincero ‖ *s* carta franca, envío franco; franquicia postal; sello de franquicia ‖ *tr* franquear ‖ **Frank** *s* (*member of a Frankish tribe*) franco; (*masculine name*) Paco
**frankfurter** ['fræŋkfərtər] *s* salchicha de carne de vaca y de cerdo
**frankincense** ['fræŋkɪn,sens] *s* olíbano
**Frankish** ['fræŋkɪʃ] *adj & s* franco
**frankness** ['fræŋknɪs] *s* franqueza, abertura, sinceridad
**frantic** ['fræntɪk] *adj* frenético
**frappé** [fræ'pe] *adj* helado ‖ *s* refresco helado de zumo de frutas
**frat** [fræt] *s* (slang) club *m* de estudiantes
**fraternal** [frə'tʌrnəl] *adj* fraternal
**fraterni·ty** [frə'tʌrnɪti] *s* (*pl* **-ties**) (*brotherliness*) fraternidad; cofradía; asociación secreta; (U.S.A.) club *m* de estudiantes
**fraternize** ['frætər,naɪz] *intr* fraternizar
**fraud** [frɔd] *s* fraude *m;* (*person*) (coll) impostor *m*
**fraudulent** ['frɔdjələnt] *adj* fraudulento
**fraught** [frɔt] *adj* — **fraught with** cargado de, lleno de

**fray** [fre] *s* combate *m*, riña, batalla || *intr* deshilacharse, raerse
**freak** [frik] *s* (*sudden fancy*) capricho, antojo; (*person, animal*) fenómeno
**freakish** ['frikɪʃ] *adj* caprichoso, antojadizo; raro, fantástico
**freckle** ['frɛkəl] *s* peca
**freckle-faced** ['frɛkəl,fest] *adj* pecoso
**freckly** ['frɛkli] *adj* pecoso
**Frederick** ['frɛdərɪk] *s* Federico
**free** [fri] *adj* (*comp* **freer** ['fri·ər]; *super* **freest** ['fri·ɪst]) libre; gratis, franco; liberal, generoso; **to be free with** dar abundantemente; **to set free** libertar || *adv* libremente; en libertad; de balde, gratis || *v* (*pret & pp* **freed** [frid]; *ger* **freeing** ['fri·ɪŋ]) *tr* libertar, poner en libertad; soltar; exentar, eximir
**free and easy** *adj* despreocupado
**freebooter** ['fri,butər] *s* forbante *m*, filibustero, pirata *m*
**free'born'** *adj* nacido libre; propio de un pueblo libre
**freedom** ['fridəm] *s* libertad
**freedom of speech** *s* libertad de palabra
**freedom of the press** *s* libertad de imprenta
**freedom of the seas** *s* libertad de los mares
**freedom of worship** *s* libertad de cultos
**free enterprise** *s* libertad de empresa
**free fight** *s* sarracina, riña tumultuaria
**free'-for-all'** *s* concurso abierto a todo el mundo; sarracina, riña tumultuaria
**free hand** *s* plena libertad, carta blanca
**free'hand' drawing** *s* dibujo a pulso
**freehanded** ['fri,hændɪd] *adj* dadivoso, generoso
**free'hold'** *s* (law) feudo franco
**free lance** *s* soldado mercenario; periodista *mf* sin empleo fijo; (*writer not on regular salary*) destajista *mf*
**free lunch** *s* tapas, enjutos
**free·man** ['frimən] *s* (*pl* **-men** [mən]) hombre *m* libre; ciudadano
**Free'ma'son** *s* francmasón *m*
**Free'ma'sonry** *s* francmasonería
**free of charge** *adj* gratis, de balde
**free on board** *adj* franco a bordo
**free port** *s* puerto franco
**free ride** *s* llevada gratuita
**free service** *s* servicio post-venta
**free'-spo'ken** *adj* franco, sin reserva
**free'stone'** *adj & s* abridero
**free'think'er** *s* librepensador *m*
**free thought** *s* librepensamiento
**free trade** *s* librecambio
**free'trad'er** *s* librecambista *mf*
**free'way'** *s* autopista
**free will** *s* libre albedrío
**freeze** [friz] *s* helada || *v* (*pret* **froze** [froz]; *pp* **frozen**) *tr* helar; congelar (*créditos, fondos, etc.*) || *intr* helarse; congelarse; helársele a uno la sangre (*p.ej., de miedo*)
**freezer** ['frizər] *s* heladora, sorbetera
**freight** [fret] *s* carga; (naut) flete *m*; **by freight** como carga; (rr) en pequeña velocidad || *tr* enviar por carga
**freight car** *s* vagón *m* de carga, vagón de mercancías
**freighter** ['fretər] *s* buque *m* de carga, carguero
**freight platform** *s* (rr) muelle *m*
**freight station** *s* (rr) estación de carga
**freight train** *s* mercancías *msg*, tren *m* de mercancías
**freight yard** *s* (rr) patio de carga
**French** [frɛntʃ] *adj & s* francés *m*; **the French** los franceses
**French chalk** *s* jaboncillo de sastre
**French doors** *spl* puertas vidrieras dobles
**French dressing** *s* salsa francesa, vinagreta
**French fried potatoes** *spl* patatas fritas en trocitos
**French horn** *s* (mus) trompa de armonía
**French horsepower** *s* caballo de fuerza, caballo de vapor
**French leave** *s* despedida a la francesa; **to take French leave** despedirse a la francesa
**French·man** ['frɛntʃmən] *s* (*pl* **-men** [mən]) francés *m*
**French telephone** *s* microteléfono
**French toast** *s* torrija
**French window** *s* puerta ventana
**French'wom'an** *s* (*pl* **-wom'en**) francesa
**frenzied** ['frɛnzid] *adj* frenético
**fren·zy** ['frɛnzi] *s* (*pl* **-zies**) frenesí *m*
**frequen·cy** ['frikwənsi] *s* (*pl* **-cies**) frecuencia
**frequency list** *s* lista de frecuencia
**frequency modulation** *s* modulación de frecuencia
**frequent** ['frikwənt] *adj* frecuente || [frɪ'kwɛnt] o ['frikwənt] *tr* frecuentar
**frequently** ['frikwəntli] *adv* con frecuencia, frecuentemente
**fres·co** ['frɛsko] *s* (*pl* **-coes** o **-cos**) fresco || *tr* pintar al fresco
**fresh** [frɛʃ] *adj* fresco; (*water*) dulce; (*wind*) fresquito; novicio, inexperto; (*cheeky*) (slang) fresco; (*toward women*) (slang) atrevido; **fresh paint!** ¡ojo mancha! || *adv* recientemente, recién; **fresh in** (coll) recién llegado, acabado de llegar; **fresh out** (coll) recién agotado
**freshen** ['frɛʃən] *tr* refrescar || *intr* refrescarse
**freshet** ['frɛʃɪt] *s* avenida, crecida
**fresh·man** ['frɛʃmən] *s* (*pl* **-men** [mən]) novato; estudiante *mf* de primer año
**freshness** ['frɛʃnɪs] *s* frescura; (*cheek*) (slang) frescura
**fresh'-wa'ter** *adj* de agua dulce; no acostumbrado a navegar; de poca monta
**fret** [frɛt] *s* (*interlaced design*) calado; (mus) ceja, traste *m*; queja || *v* (*pret & pp* **fretted**; *ger* **fretting**) *tr* adornar con calados || *intr* irritarse, quejarse, agitarse
**fretful** ['frɛtfəl] *adj* irritable, enojadizo, displicente
**fret'work'** *s* calado

**Freudianism** ['frɔɪdɪ·ə,nɪzəm] *s* freudismo
**friar** ['fraɪ·ər] *s* fraile *m*
**friar·y** ['fraɪ·əri] *s* (*pl* **-ies**) convento de frailes
**fricassee** [,frɪkə'si] *s* fricasé *m*
**friction** ['frɪkʃən] *s* fricción, rozamiento; (fig) desavenencia, rozamiento
**friction tape** *s* cinta aislante
**Friday** ['fraɪdi] *s* viernes *m*
**fried** [fraɪd] *adj* frito
**fried egg** *s* huevo a la plancha, huevo frito o estrellado
**friend** [frɛnd] *s* amigo; (*in answer to "Who is there?"*) gente *f* de paz; **to be friends with** ser amigo de; **to make friends** trabar amistades; **to make friends with** hacerse amigo de
**friend·ly** ['frɛndli] *adj* (*comp* **-lier;** *super* **-liest**) amigo, amistoso, amigable
**friendship** ['frɛndʃɪp] *s* amistad
**frieze** [friz] *s* (archit) friso
**frigate** ['frɪgɪt] *s* fragata
**fright** [fraɪt] *s* susto, espanto; (*grotesque or ridiculous person*) (coll) espantajo; **to take fright at** asustarse de
**frighten** ['fraɪtən] *tr* asustar, espantar; **to frighten away** espantar, ahuyentar ‖ *intr* asustarse
**frightful** ['fraɪtfəl] *adj* espantoso, horroroso; (coll) feúcho, repugnante; (coll) enorme, tremendo
**frightfulness** ['fraɪtfəlnɪs] *s* espanto, horror *m;* terrorismo
**frigid** ['frɪdʒɪd] *adj* frío; (fig) frío; (*zone*) glacial
**frigidity** [frɪ'dʒɪdɪti] *s* frialdad; (pathol) frialdad; (fig) frialdad, frigidez *f*
**frill** [frɪl] *s* lechuga; (*of birds and other animals*) collarín *m;* (*frippery*) (coll) ringorrango; (*in dress, speech, etc.*) (coll) afectación
**fringe** [frɪndʒ] *s* franja, orla; (opt) franja ‖ *tr* franjar, orlar
**fringe benefits** *spl* beneficios accesorios
**fripper·y** ['frɪpəri] *s* (*pl* **-ies**) (*flashiness*) cursilería; (*flashy clothes*) perejil *m,* perifollos
**frisk** [frɪsk] *tr* (slang) cachear; (slang) registrar y robar ‖ *intr* retozar
**frisk·y** ['frɪski] *adj* (*comp* **-ier;** *super* **-iest**) juguetón, retozón; (*horse*) fogoso
**fritter** ['frɪtər] *s* fruta de sartén; fragmento ‖ *tr* — **to fritter away** desperdiciar, malgastar poco a poco
**frivolous** ['frɪvələs] *adj* frívolo
**friz** [frɪz] *s* (*pl* **frizzes**) rizo, pelo rizado apretadamente ‖ *v* (*pret & pp* **frizzed;** *ger* **frizzing**) *tr* rizar, rizar apretadamente
**frizzle** ['frɪzəl] *s* rizo apretado; chirrido, siseo ‖ *tr* rizar apretadamente; asar o freír en parrilla ‖ *intr* chirriar, sisear
**friz·zly** ['frɪzli] *adj* (*comp* **-zlier;** *super* **-zliest**) muy ensortijado
**fro** [fro] *adv* — **to and fro** de acá para allá; **to go to and fro** ir y venir
**frock** [frɑk] *s* vestido; bata, blusa; (*of priest*) vestido talar
**frock coat** *s* levita
**frog** [frɑg] o [frɔg] *s* rana; (*button and loop on a garment*) alamar *m;* (*in throat*) ronquera, gallo
**frog'man'** *s* (*pl* **-men'**) hombre-rana *m*
**frol·ic** ['frɑlɪk] *s* juego alegre, travesura; fiesta, holgorio ‖ *v* (*pret & pp* **-icked;** *ger* **-icking**) *intr* juguetear, travesear, jaranear
**frolicsome** ['frɑlɪksəm] *adj* juguetón, travieso
**from** [frʌm], [frɑm] o [frəm] *prep* de; desde; de parte de; según; a, p.ej., **to take something away from someone** quitarle algo a alguien
**front** [frʌnt] *adj* delantero; anterior ‖ *s* frente *m & f;* (*of a shirt*) pechera; (*of a book*) principio; apariencia falsa (*p.ej., de riqueza*); ademán estudiado; (mil) frente *m;* **in front of** delante de, frente a, en frente de; **to put on a front** (coll) gastar mucho oropel; **to put up a bold front** (coll) hacer de tripas corazón ‖ *tr* (*to face*) dar a; (*to confront*) afrontar, arrostrar; (*to supply with a front*) poner frente o fachada a ‖ *intr* — **to front on** dar a; **to front towards** mirar hacia
**frontage** ['frʌntɪdʒ] *s* fachada, frontera; terreno frontero
**front door** *s* puerta de entrada
**front drive** *s* (aut) tracción delantera
**frontier** [frʌn'tɪr] *adj* fronterizo ‖ *s* frontera
**frontiers·man** [frʌn'tɪrzmən] *s* (*pl* **-men** [mən]) hombre *m* de la frontera, explorador *m*
**frontispiece** ['frʌntɪs,pis] *s* (*of book*) portada; (archit) frontispicio
**front matter** *s* preliminares *mpl* (*de un libro*)
**front page** *s* primera plana
**front porch** *s* soportal *m*
**front room** *s* cuarto que da a la calle
**front row** *s* primera fila
**front seat** *s* asiento delantero
**front steps** *spl* escalones *mpl* de acceso a la puerta de entrada
**front view** *s* vista de frente
**frost** [frɔst] o [frɑst] *s* (*freezing*) helada; (*frozen dew*) escarcha; (slang) fracaso ‖ *tr* cubrir de escarcha; escarchar (*confituras*); helar (*el frío las plantas*); deslustrar (*el vidrio*)
**frost'bit'ten** *adj* dañado por la helada; quemado por la helada o la escarcha
**frosted glass** *s* vidrio deslustrado
**frosting** ['frɔstɪŋ] o ['frɑstɪŋ] *s* garapiña; (*of glass*) deslustre *m*
**frost·y** ['frɔsti] o ['frɑsti] *adj* (*comp* **-ier;** *super* **-iest**) cubierto de escarcha; escarchado; frío, poco amistoso; canoso, gris
**froth** [frɔθ] o [frɑθ] *s* espuma; frivolidad, vanidad ‖ *intr* espumar, echar espuma; (*at the mouth*) espumajear
**froth·y** ['frɔθi] o ['frɑθi] *adj* (*comp* **-ier;** *super* **-iest**) espumoso; frívolo, vano

**froward** ['frowərd] *adj* díscolo, indócil
**frown** [fraʊn] *s* ceño, entrecejo || *intr* fruncir el entrecejo; **to frown at u on** mirar con ceño, desaprobar
**frows•y** o **frowz•y** ['fraʊzi] *adj* (*comp* **-ier**; *super* **-iest**) desaseado, desaliñado; maloliente; mal peinado
**frozen foods** ['frozən] *spl* viandas congeladas
**F.R.S.** *abbr* **Fellow of the Royal Society**
**frt.** *abbr* **freight**
**frugal** ['frugəl] *adj* (*moderate in the use of things*) parco; (*not very abundant*) frugal
**fruit** [frut] *adj* (*tree*) frutal; (*boat, dish*) frutero || *s* (*such as apple, pear, strawberry*) fruta; frutas, p.ej., **I like fruit** me gustan las frutas; (*part containing seed*) fruto; (*effect, result*) (fig) fruto
**fruit cake** *s* torta de frutas
**fruit cup** *s* compota de frutas picadas
**fruit fly** *s* mosca del vinagre; mosca de las frutas
**fruitful** ['frutfəl] *adj* fructuoso
**fruition** [fru'ɪʃən] *s* buen resultado, cumplimiento; **to come to fruition** lograrse cumplidamente
**fruit jar** *s* tarro para frutas
**fruit juice** *s* jugo de frutas
**fruitless** ['frutlɪs] *adj* infructuoso
**fruit of the vine** *s* zumo de cepas o de parras
**fruit salad** *s* ensalada de frutas, macedonia de frutas
**fruit stand** *s* puesto de frutas
**fruit store** *s* frutería
**frumpish** ['frʌmpɪʃ] *adj* basto, desgarbado, desaliñado
**frustrate** ['frʌstret] *tr* frustrar
**fry** [fraɪ] *s* (*pl* **fries**) fritada || *v* (*pret & pp* **fried**) *tr & intr* freír
**frying pan** ['fraɪ·ɪŋ] *s* sartén *f*; **to jump from the frying pan into the fire** saltar de la sartén y dar en las brasas
**ft.** *abbr* **foot, feet**
**fudge** [fʌdʒ] *s* dulce *m* de chocolate
**fuel** ['fju·əl] *s* combustible *m*; (fig) pábulo || *v* (*pret & pp* **fueled** o **fuelled**; *ger* **fueling** o **fuelling**) *tr* aprovisionar de combustible || *intr* aprovisionarse de combustible
**fuel cell** *s* cámara de combustible, célula electrógena
**fuel oil** *s* aceite *m* combustible
**fuel tank** *s* depósito de combustible
**fugitive** ['fjudʒɪtɪv] *adj & s* fugitivo
**fugue** [fjug] *s* (mus) fuga
**ful•crum** ['fʌlkrəm] *s* (*pl* **-crums** o **-cra** [krə]) fulcro
**fulfill** [fʊl'fɪl] *tr* (*to carry out*) cumplir, realizar; cumplir con (*una obligación*); llenar (*una condición*)
**fulfillment** [fʊl'fɪlmənt] *s* cumplimiento, realización
**full** [fʊl] *adj* lleno; (*dress, garment*) amplio, holgado; (*formal dress*) de etiqueta; (*voice*) sonoro, fuerte; (*of food*) harto; **full of aches and pains** lleno de goteras; **full of fun** muy divertido, muy chistoso; **full of play** muy juguetón; **full to overflowing** lleno a rebosar || *adv* completamente; **full many (a)** muchísimos; **full well** muy bien, perfectamente || *s* colmo; **in full** por completo; sin abreviar; **to the full** completamente || *tr* abatanar
**full-blooded** ['fʊl'blʌdɪd] *adj* vigoroso; completo, pletórico; de raza
**full-blown** ['fʊl'blon] *adj* (*flower, blossom*) abierto; desarrollado, maduro
**full-bodied** ['fʊl'badid] *adj* fuerte, espeso, consistente; aromático
**full dress** *s* traje *m* de etiqueta; (mil) uniforme *m* de gala
**full'-dress' coat** *s* frac *m*
**full-faced** ['fʊl'fest] *adj* carilleno; (*view*) de cuadrado; (*portrait*) de rostro entero
**full-fledged** ['fʊl'fledʒd] *adj* hecho y derecho, nada menos que
**full-grown** ['fʊl'gron] *adj* crecido, completamente desarrollado
**full house** *s* lleno, entrada llena; (poker) fulján *m*
**full'-length' mirror** *s* espejo de cuerpo entero, espejo de vestir
**full-length movie** *s* largometraje *m*, cinta de largo metraje
**full load** *s* plena carga; (aer) peso total
**full moon** *s* luna llena, plenilunio
**full name** *s* nombre *m* y apellidos
**full'-page'** *adj* a página entera
**full powers** *spl* plenos poderes, amplias facultades
**full sail** *adv* a todo trapo
**full'-scale'** *adj* de tamaño natural; total, completo; pleno
**full-sized** ['fʊl'saɪzd] *adj* de tamaño natural
**full speed** *adv* a toda velocidad
**full stop** *s* parada completa; (gram) punto
**full swing** *s* plena actividad
**full tilt** *adv* a toda velocidad
**full'-time'** *adj* a tiempo completo
**full'-view'** *adj* de vista completa
**full volume** *s* (rad) máximo de volumen
**fully** ['fʊli] o ['fʊlli] *adv* completamente; cabalmente; por lo menos
**fulsome** ['fʊlsəm] o ['fʌlsəm] *adj* bajo, craso, de mal gusto
**fumble** ['fʌmbəl] *tr* no coger (*la pelota*), dejar caer (*la pelota*) desmañadamente; manosear desmañadamente || *intr* revolver papeles; titubear; andar a tientas; (*in one's pockets*) buscar con las manos
**fume** [fjum] *s* humo, vapor *m*, gas *m*, vaho || *tr* (*to treat with fumes*) ahumar || *intr* (*to give off fumes*) humear; (*to show anger*) echar pestes; **to fume at** echar pestes contra
**fumigate** ['fjumɪ,get] *tr* fumigar
**fumigation** [,fjumɪ'geʃən] *s* fumigación
**fun** [fʌn] *s* divertimiento; broma, chacota; **to be fun** ser divertido; **to have fun** divertirse; **to make fun of** reírse de, burlarse de

**function** [ˈfʌŋkʃən] *s* función ‖ *intr* funcionar
**functional** [ˈfʌŋkʃənəl] *adj* funcional
**functionar•y** [ˈfʌŋkʃəˌnɛri] *s* (*pl* **-ies**) funcionario
**fund** [fʌnd] *s* fondo; **funds** fondos ‖ *tr* consolidar (*una deuda*)
**fundamental** [ˌfʌndəˈmɛntəl] *adj* fundamental ‖ *s* fundamento
**funeral** [ˈfjunərəl] *adj* funeral; (*march, procession*) fúnebre; (*expense*) funerario ‖ *s* funeral *m,* funerales *mpl,* pompa fúnebre (*de cuerpo presente*); **it's not my funeral** (slang) no corre a mi cuidado
**funeral director** *s* empresario de pompas fúnebres
**funeral home** o **parlor** *s* funeraria
**funeral service** *s* oficio de difuntos, misa de cuerpo presente
**funereal** [fjuˈnɪrɪ•əl] *adj* fúnebre
**fungous** [ˈfʌŋgəs] *adj* fungoso
**fungus** [ˈfʌŋgəs] *s* (*pl* **funguses** o **fungi** [ˈfʌndʒaɪ]) hongo; (pathol) fungo
**funicular** [fjuˈnɪkjələr] *adj* & *s* funicular *m*
**funk** [fʌŋk] *s* (coll) miedo, cobardía; (coll) cobarde *mf;* **in a funk** (coll) asustado
**fun•nel** [ˈfʌnəl] *s* embudo; (*smokestack*) chimenea; (*tube for ventilation*) manguera, ventilador *m* ‖ *v* (*pret* & *pp* **-neled** o **-nelled;** *ger* **-neling** o **-nelling**) *tr* verter por medio de un embudo
**funnies** [ˈfʌniz] *spl* páginas cómicas, tiras cómicas, tebeo
**fun•ny** [ˈfʌni] *adj* (*comp* **-nier;** *super* **-niest**) cómico; divertido, chistoso; (coll) extraño, raro; **to strike someone as funny** hacerle a uno gracia
**funny bone** *s* hueso de la alegría
**funny paper** *s* páginas cómicas
**fur.** *abbr* **furlong, furnished**
**fur** [fʌr] *s* piel *f;* abrigo de pieles; (*on the tongue*) sarro
**furbelow** [ˈfʌrbəˌlo] *s* (*ruffle*) faralá *m;* (*frippery*) ringorrango
**furbish** [ˈfʌrbɪʃ] *tr* acicalar, limpiar; **to furbish up** renovar
**furious** [ˈfjʊrɪ•əs] *adj* furioso
**furl** [fʌrl] *tr* enrollar; (naut) aferrar
**fur-lined** [ˈfʌrˌlaɪnd] *adj* forrado con pieles
**furlong** [ˈfʌrlɔŋ] o [ˈfʌrlɑŋ] *s* estadio
**furlough** [ˈfʌrlo] *s* licencia ‖ *tr* dar licencia a
**furnace** [ˈfʌrnɪs] *s* horno; (*to heat a house*) calorífero
**furnish** [ˈfʌrnɪʃ] *tr* amueblar; proporcionar, suministrar
**furnishings** [ˈfʌrnɪʃɪŋz] *spl* muebles *mpl;* (*things to wear*) artículos
**furniture** [ˈfʌrnɪtʃər] *s* muebles *mpl,* mobiliario; (naut) aparejo; **a piece of furniture** un mueble
**furniture dealer** *s* mueblista *mf*
**furniture store** *s* mueblería
**furrier** [ˈfʌrɪ•ər] *s* peletero
**furrier•y** [ˈfʌrɪ•əri] *s* (*pl* **-ies**) peletería
**furrow** [ˈfʌro] *s* surco ‖ *tr* surcar
**further** [ˈfʌrðər] *adj* adicional; nuevo; más lejano ‖ *adv* además; más lejos ‖ *tr* adelantar, promover, fomentar
**furtherance** [ˈfʌrðərəns] *s* adelantamiento, promoción, fomento
**furthermore** [ˈfʌrðərˌmor] *adv* además
**furthest** [ˈfʌrðɪst] *adj* (el) más lejano ‖ *adv* más lejos
**furtive** [ˈfʌrtɪv] *adj* furtivo
**fu•ry** [ˈfjʊri] *s* (*pl* **-ries**) furia
**furze** [fʌrz] *s* aulaga; retama de escoba
**fuse** [fjuz] *s* (*tube or wick filled with explosive material*) mecha; (*device for detonating an explosive charge*) espoleta; (elec) fusible *m,* cortacircuitos *m,* tapón *m;* **to burn out a fuse** quemar un fusible ‖ *tr* fundir; (*to unite*) fusionar ‖ *intr* fundirse; fusionarse
**fuse box** *s* caja de fusibles
**fuselage** [ˈfjuzəlɪdʒ] o [ˌfjuzəˈlɑʒ] *s* fuselaje *m*
**fusible** [ˈfjuzɪbəl] *adj* fundible, fusible
**fusillade** [ˌfjuzɪˈled] *s* fusilería; (*e.g., of questions*) andanada ‖ atacar o matar con una descarga de fusilería, fusilar
**fusion** [ˈfjuʒən] *s* fusión
**fuss** [fʌs] *s* alharaca, hazañería; (coll) disputa por ligero motivo; **to make a fuss** hacer alharacas; **to make a fuss over** hacer fiestas a; disputar sobre ‖ *tr* atolondrar, inquietar, confundir ‖ *intr* hacer alharacas, inquietarse por bagatelas
**fuss•y** [ˈfʌsi] *adj* (*comp* **-ier;** *super* **-iest**) alharaquiento, alborotado; descontentadizo, quisquilloso, melindroso; funcionero, hazañero; muy adornado
**fustian** [ˈfʌstʃən] *s* (*coarse cloth*) fustán *m;* (*sort of velveteen*) pana; (*bombast*) cultedad, follaje *m*
**fust•y** [ˈfʌsti] *adj* (*comp* **-ier;** *super* **-iest**) mohoso, rancio; que huele a cerrado; pasado de moda
**futile** [ˈfjutɪl] *adj* (*unproductive*) estéril; (*unimportant*) fútil
**futili•ty** [fjuˈtɪlɪti] *s* (*pl* **-ties**) esterilidad; futilidad
**future** [ˈfjutʃər] *adj* futuro ‖ *s* futuro, porvenir *m;* (gram) futuro; **futures** (com) futuros; **in the future** en el futuro; **in the near future** en un futuro próximo
**fuze** [fjuz] *s* (*tube or wick filled with explosive material*) mecha; (*device for detonating an explosive charge*) espoleta; (elec) fusible *m* ‖ *tr* poner la espoleta a
**fuzz** [fʌz] *s* (*as on a peach*) pelusa, vello; (*in pockets and corners*) borra, tamo
**fuzz•y** [ˈfʌzi] *adj* (*comp* **-ier;** *super* **-iest**) cubierto de pelusa, velloso; polvoriento; (*indistinct*) borroso

## G

**G, g** [dʒi] *s* séptima letra del alfabeto inglés
**G.** *abbr* **German, Gulf**
**g.** *abbr* **gender, genitive, gram**
**gab** [gæb] *s* (coll) cotorreo || (*pret & pp* **gabbed;** *ger* **gabbing**) *intr* (coll) cotorrear
**gabardine** ['gæbər,din] *s* gabardina
**gabble** ['gæbəl] *s* cotorreo, parloteo || *intr* cotorrear, parlotear
**gable** ['gebəl] *s* (*of roof*) aguilón *m;* (*over a door or window*) gablete *m,* frontón *m*
**gable end** *s* hastial *m*
**gable roof** *s* tejado de dos aguas
**gad** [gæd] *v* (*pret & pp* **gadded;** *ger* **gadding**) *intr* callejear, andar de acá para allá; **to gad about** pindonguear (*una mujer*)
**gad'a·bout'** *adj* callejero || *s* cirigallo; (*woman*) pindonga
**gad'fly'** *s* (*pl* **-flies**) tábano
**gadget** ['gædʒɪt] *s* adminículo, chisme *m,* artilugio
**Gael** [gel] *s* gaélico
**Gaelic** ['gelɪk] *adj & s* gaélico
**gaff** [gæf] *s* garfio, arpón *m;* **to stand the gaff** (slang) tener aguante
**gag** [gæg] *s* mordaza; (*interpolation by an actor*) morcilla; (*joke*) chiste *m,* payasada || *v* (*pret & pp* **gagged;** *ger* **gagging**) *tr* amordazar; dar bascas a || *intr* sentir bascas, arquear
**gage** [gedʒ] *s* (*pledge*) prenda; (*challenge*) desafío
**gaie·ty** ['ge·ɪti] *s* (*pl* **-ties**) alegría, algazara, diversión; (*of colors*) viveza
**gaily** ['geli] *adv* alegremente
**gain** [gen] *s* ganancia; (*increase*) aumento || *tr* ganar; (*to reach*) alcanzar || *intr* ganar terreno; mejorar (*un enfermo*); adelantarse (*un reloj*); **to gain on** ir alcanzando
**gainful** ['genfəl] *adj* ganancioso, provechoso
**gain'say'** *v* (*pret & pp* **-said** ['sed] o ['sɛd]) *tr* negar; contradecir; prohibir
**gait** [get] *s* paso, manera de andar
**gaiter** ['getər] *s* polaina corta
**gal.** *abbr* **gallon**
**gala** ['gælə] o ['gelə] *adj* de gala || *s* fiesta
**galax·y** ['gæləksi] *s* (*pl* **-ies**) galaxia
**gale** [gel] *s* ventarrón *m;* **gales of laughter** tempestades de risas; **to weather the gale** correr el temporal; (fig) ir tirando
**Galician** [gə'lɪʃən] *adj & s* gallego
**gall** [gɔl] *s* bilis *f,* hiel *f;* vejiga de la bilis; (*something bitter*) (fig) hiel *f;* rencor *m,* odio; (*gallnut*) agalla; (*audacity*) (coll) descaro || *tr* lastimar rozando; irritar || *intr* raerse; (naut) mascarse (*un cabo*)
**gallant** ['gælənt] o [gə'lænt] *adj* (*attentive to women*) galante; (*pertaining to love*) amoroso || ['gælənt] *adj* (*stately, grand*) gallardo; (*spirited, daring*) hazañoso; (*showy, gay*) vistoso, festivo || *s* hombre *m* valiente; (*man attentive to women*) galán *m*
**gallant·ry** ['gæləntri] *s* (*pl* **-ries**) galantería; gallardía
**gall bladder** *s* vejiga de la bilis, vesícula biliar
**gall duct** *s* conducto biliar
**galleon** ['gælɪ·ən] *s* (naut) galeón *m*
**galler·y** ['gæləri] *s* (*pl* **-ies**) galería; (*in church, theater, etc.*) tribuna; (*cheapest seats in theater*) gallinero; **to play to the gallery** (coll) hablar para la galería
**galley** ['gæli] *s* (naut & typ) galera; (naut) cocina
**galley proof** *s* (typ) galerada, pruebas de segundas
**galley slave** *s* galeote *m;* (*drudge*) esclavo del trabajo
**Gallic** ['gælɪk] *adj* gálico
**galling** ['gɔlɪŋ] *adj* irritante, ofensivo
**gallivant** ['gælɪ,vænt] *intr* andar a placer
**gall'nut'** *s* agalla
**gallon** ['gælən] *s* galón *m* (*medida*)
**galloon** [gə'lun] *s* galón *m* (*cinta*)
**gallop** ['gæləp] *s* galope *m;* **at a gallop** a galope || *tr* hacer galopar || *intr* galopar; **to gallop through** (fig) hacer muy aprisa
**gal·lows** ['gæloz] *s* (*pl* **-lows** o **-lowses**) horca
**gallows bird** *s* (coll) carne *f* de horca
**gall'stone'** *s* cálculo biliar
**galore** [gə'lor] *adv* en abundancia
**galosh** [gə'lɑʃ] *s* chanclo alto
**galvanize** ['gælvə,naɪz] *tr* galvanizar
**galvanized iron** *s* hierro galvanizado
**gambit** ['gæmbɪt] *s* gambito
**gamble** ['gæmbəl] *s* (coll) empresa arriesgada || *tr* aventurar en el juego; **to gamble away** perder en el juego || *intr* jugar; (*in the stock market*) especular, aventurarse
**gambler** ['gæmblər] *s* jugador *m;* especulador *m*
**gambling** ['gæmblɪŋ] *s* juego
**gambling den** *s* garito
**gambling house** *s* casa de juego, juego público
**gambling table** *s* mesa de juego
**gam·bol** ['gæmbəl] *s* cabriola, retozo, salto || *v* (*pret & pp* **-boled** o **-bolled;** *gen* **-boling** o **-bolling**) *intr* cabriolar, retozar, saltar
**gambrel** ['gæmbrəl] *s* corvejón *m*
**gambrel roof** *s* techo a la holandesa
**game** [gem] *adj* bravo, peleón; dispuesto, resuelto; (*leg*) cojo; de caza || *s* (*form of play*) juego; (*single contest*) partida; (*score*) tantos; (*in bridge*) manga; (*any sport*) deporte *m;* (*animal or bird hunted for sport or food*) caza; (*any pursuit*) actividad; (*pursuit of diplomacy*) juego;

**the game is up** estamos frescos; **to make game of** burlarse de; **to play the game** jugar limpio
**game bag** *s* morral *m*
**game bird** *s* ave *f* de caza
**game'cock'** *s* gallo de pelea
**game'keep'er** *s* guardabosque *m*
**game of chance** *s* juego de azar
**game preserve** *s* vedado
**game warden** *s* guardabosque *m*
**gamut** ['gæmət] *s* (mus & fig) gama
**gam•y** ['gemi] *adj* (*comp* **-ier**; *super* **-iest**) (*having flavor of uncooked game*) salvajino; bravo, peleón
**gander** ['gændər] *s* ganso
**gang** [gæŋ] *adj* múltiple ‖ *s* (*of workmen*) brigada, cuadrilla; (*of thugs*) pandilla ‖ *intr* — **to gang up** acuadrillarse; **to gang up against** u **on** atacar juntos; conspirar contra
**gangling** ['gæŋglɪŋ] *adj* larguirucho
**gangli•on** ['gæŋglɪ·ən] *s* (*pl* **-ons** o **-a** [ə]) ganglio
**gang'plank'** *s* plancha, pasarela
**gangrene** ['gæŋgrin] *s* gangrena ‖ *tr* gangrenar ‖ *intr* gangrenarse
**gangster** ['gæŋstər] *s* (coll) gángster *m*, pistolero
**gang'way'** *s* (*passageway*) pasillo; (*gangplank*) plancha, pasarela; (*in ship's side*) portalón *m* ‖ *interj* ¡abran paso!, ¡paso libre!
**gantlet** ['gɑntlɪt] o ['gɔntlɪt] *s* (rr) vía traslapada
**gan•try** ['gæntri] *s* (*pl* **-tries**) caballete *m*, poino; (rr) puente *m* transversal de señales
**gantry crane** *s* grúa de caballete
**gap** [gæp] *s* (*break, open space*) laguna; (*in a wall*) boquete *m*; (*between mountains*) garganta, quebrada; (*between two points of view*) sima
**gape** [gep] o [gæp] *s* abertura, brecha; (*yawn*) bostezo; mirada de asombro; **the gapes** ganas de bostezar ‖ *intr* estar abierto de par en par; bostezar; embobarse; **to gape at** mirar embobado; **to stand gaping** embobarse
**G.A.R.** *abbr* **Grand Army of the Republic**
**garage** [gə'rɑʒ] *s* garage *m*
**garb** [gɑrb] *s* vestidura ‖ *tr* vestir
**garbage** ['gɑrbɪdʒ] *s* basuras, desperdicios, bazofia
**garbage can** *s* cubo para bazofia, latón *m* de la basura
**garbage disposal** *s* evacuación de basuras
**garble** ['gɑrbəl] *tr* mutilar (*un texto*)
**garden** ['gɑrdən] *s* (*of vegetables*) huerto; (*of flowers*) jardín *m*
**gardener** ['gɑrdənər] *s* (*of vegetables*) hortelano; (*of flowers*) jardinero
**gardenia** [gɑr'dinɪ·ə] *s* gardenia, jazmín *m* de la India
**gardening** ['gɑrdənɪŋ] *s* horticultura; jardinería
**garden party** *s* fiesta que se da en un jardín o parque
**gargle** ['gɑrgəl] *s* gargarismo ‖ *intr* gargarizar
**gargoyle** ['gɑrgɔɪl] *s* gárgola
**garish** ['gɛrɪʃ] o ['gærɪʃ] *adj* charro, chillón, cursi
**garland** ['gɑrlənd] *s* guirnalda
**garlic** ['gɑrlɪk] *s* ajo
**garment** ['gɑrmənt] *s* prenda de vestir
**garner** ['gɑrnər] *tr* (*to gather, collect*) acopiar; adquirir; (*cereales*) entrojar
**garnet** ['gɑrnɪt] *adj* & *s* granate *m*
**garnish** ['gɑrnɪʃ] *s* adorno; (culin) aderezo, condimento de adorno ‖ *tr* adornar; (culin) aderezar; (law) embargar
**garret** ['gærɪt] *s* buhardilla, desván *m*
**garrison** ['gærɪsən] *s* plaza fuerte; (*troops*) guarnición ‖ *tr* guarnecer, guarnicionar (*una plaza fuerte*); guarnecer una plaza fuerte de (*tropas*)
**garrote** [gə'rɑt] o [gə'rot] *s* estrangulación para robar; (*method of execution; iron collar used for such execution*) garrote *m* ‖ *tr* estrangular; estrangular para robar; agarrotar, dar garrote a
**garrulous** ['gærələs] o ['gærjələs] *adj* gárrulo, locuaz
**garter** ['gɑrtər] *s* liga, jarretera
**garth** [gɑrθ] *s* patio de claustro
**gas** [gæs] *s* gas *m*; (coll) gasolina; (coll) palabrería ‖ *v* (*pret* & *pp* **gassed**; *ger* **gassing**) *tr* abastecer de gas; (*to attack, asphyxiate, or poison with gas*) gasear; (coll) abastecer de gasolina ‖ *intr* despedir gas; (slang) charlar
**gas'bag'** *s* (aer) cámara de gas; (slang) charlatán *m*
**gas burner** *s* mechero de gas
**Gascony** ['gæskəni] *s* Gascuña
**gas engine** *s* motor *m* a gas
**gaseous** ['gæsɪ·əs] *adj* gaseoso
**gas fitter** *s* gasista *m*
**gas generator** *s* gasógeno
**gash** [gæʃ] *s* cuchillada, chirlo ‖ *tr* acuchillar
**gas heat** *s* calefacción por gas
**gas'hold'er** *s* gasómetro
**gasi•fy** ['gæsɪ,faɪ] *v* (*pret* & *pp* **-fied**) *tr* gasificar ‖ *intr* gasificarse
**gas jet** *s* mechero de gas; llama de gas
**gasket** ['gæskɪt] *s* empaquetadura
**gas'light'** *s* luz *f* de gas
**gas main** *s* cañería de gas
**gas mask** *s* careta antigás
**gas meter** *s* contador *m* de gas
**gasoline** ['gæsə,lin] o [,gæsə'lin] *s* gasolina
**gasoline pump** *s* poste *m* distribuidor *m* de gasolina, surtidor *m* de gasolina
**gasp** [gæsp] o [gɑsp] *s* respiración entrecortada; (*of death*) boqueada ‖ *tr* decir con voz entrecortada ‖ *intr* boquear
**gas producer** *s* gasógeno
**gas range** *s* cocina a gas
**gas station** *s* estación gasolinera
**gas stove** *s* cocina a gas
**gas tank** *s* gasómetro; (aut) depósito de gasolina
**gastric** ['gæstrɪk] *adj* gástrico

**gastronomy** [gæs'trɑnəmi] *s* gastronomía
**gas'works'** *s* fábrica de gas
**gate** [get] *s* puerta; (*in fence or wall; of bird cage*) portillo; (*of sluice or lock*) compuerta; (*number of people paying admission; amount they pay*) entrada, taquilla; (rr) barrera; (fig) entrada, camino; **to crash the gate** (coll) colarse de gorra
**gate'keep'er** *s* portero; (rr) guardabarrera *mf*
**gate'post'** *s* poste *m* de una puerta de cercado
**gate'way'** *s* entrada, paso, camino
**gather** ['gæðər] *tr* recoger, reunir; recolectar (*la cosecha*); coger (*leña, flores, etc.*); cubrirse de (*polvo*); recoger (*una persona sus pensamientos*); (bb) alzar; (sew) fruncir; (*to deduce*) (fig) calcular, deducir; **to gather oneself together** componerse ‖ *intr* reunirse; amontonarse; saltar (*lágrimas*)
**gathering** ['gæðərɪŋ] *s* reunión; recolección; (bb) alzado; (sew) frunce *m*
**gaud·y** ['gɔdi] *adj* (*comp* **-ier;** *super* **-iest**) cursi, chillón, llamativo
**gauge** [gedʒ] *s* medida, norma; calibre *m;* (*of liquid in a container*) nivel *m;* (*of carpenter*) gramil *m;* (*of gasoline*) medidor *m;* (rr) ancho de vía, entrevía ‖ *tr* medir; calibrar; graduar; aforar (*la cantidad de agua de una corriente*); arquear (*una nave*)
**gauge glass** *s* tubo indicador, vidrio de nivel
**Gaul** [gɔl] *s* la Galia; (*native*) galo
**Gaulish** ['gɔlɪʃ] *adj & s* galo
**gaunt** [gɔnt] o [gɑnt] *adj* desvaído, macilento; hosco, tétrico
**gauntlet** ['gɔntlɪt] o ['gɑntlɪt] *s* guantelete *m;* guante con puño abocinado; carrera de baquetas; (rr) vía traslapada; **to run the gauntlet** correr baquetas, pasar por baquetas; **to take up the gauntlet** recoger el guante; **to throw down the gauntlet** arrojar el guante
**gauze** [gɔz] *s* gasa, cendal *m*
**gavel** ['gævəl] *s* mazo, martillo
**gavotte** [gə'vɑt] *s* gavota
**gawk** [gɔk] *s* (coll) palurdo, papanatas *m* ‖ *intr* (coll) mirar de modo impertinente; papar moscas, mirar embobado
**gawk·y** ['gɔki] *adj* (*comp* **-ier;** *super* **-iest**) desgarbado, torpe, bobo
**gay** [ge] *adj* alegre, festivo; (*brilliant*) vistoso; amigo de los placeres
**gaye·ty** ['ge·ɪti] *s* var de **gaiety**
**gaze** [gez] *s* mirada fija ‖ *intr* mirar fijamente
**gazelle** [gə'zel] *s* gacela
**gazette** [gə'zet] *s* periódico; anuncio oficial
**gazetteer** [,gæzə'tɪr] *s* diccionario geográfico
**gear** [gɪr] *s* pertrechos, utensilios; (*of transmission, steering, etc.*) mecanismo, aparato; rueda dentada; (*two or more toothed wheels meshed together*) engranaje *m;* **out of gear** desengranado; (fig) descompuesto; **to throw into gear** engranar; **to throw out of gear** desengranar; (fig) descomponer ‖ *tr & intr* engranar
**gear'box'** *s* caja de engranajes; (aut) caja de velocidades
**gear case** *s* caja de engranajes
**gear'shift'** *s* cambio de marchas, cambio de velocidades
**gearshift lever** *s* palanca de cambio de marchas
**gear'wheel'** *s* rueda dentada
**gee** [dʒi] *interj* ¡caramba!; **gee up!** (*get up!, said to a horse*) ¡arre!
**Gehenna** [gɪ'henə] *s* gehena *m*
**gel** [dʒel] *s* gel *m* ‖ *v* (*pret & pp* **gelled;** *ger* **gelling**) *intr* cuajarse en forma de gel
**gelatine** ['dʒelətɪn] *s* gelatina
**geld** [geld] *v* (*pret & pp* **gelded** o **gelt** [gelt]) *tr* castrar
**gem** [dʒem] *s* gema, piedra preciosa; (fig) joya, preciosidad
**Gemini** ['dʒemɪ,naɪ] *s* (*constellation*) Géminis *m* o Gemelos; (*sign of zodiac*) Géminis *m*
**gen.** *abbr* **gender, general, genitive, genus**
**gender** ['dʒendər] *s* (gram) género; (coll) sexo
**genealo·gy** [,dʒenɪ'ælədʒi] o [,dʒinɪ'ælədʒi] *s* (*pl* **-gies**) genealogía
**general** ['dʒenərəl] *adj & s* general *m;* **in general** en general o por lo general
**general delivery** *s* lista de correos
**generalissi·mo** [,dʒenərə'lɪsɪmo] *s* (*pl* **-mos**) generalísimo
**generali·ty** [,dʒenə'rælɪti] *s* (*pl* **-ties**) generalidad
**generalize** ['dʒenərə,laɪz] *tr & intr* generalizar
**generally** ['dʒenərəli] *adv* por lo general
**general practitioner** *s* médico general
**generalship** ['dʒenərəl,ʃɪp] *s* generalato; don *m* de mando
**general staff** *s* estado mayor general
**generate** ['dʒenə,ret] *tr* (*to beget*) engendrar; generar (*electricidad*); (geom) engendrar
**generating station** *s* central *f*
**generation** [,dʒenə'reʃən] *s* generación
**generator** ['dʒenə,retər] *s* generador *m*
**generic** [dʒɪ'nerɪk] *adj* genérico
**generous** ['dʒenərəs] *adj* generoso; abundante, grande
**gene·sis** ['dʒenɪsɪs] *s* (*pl* **-ses** [,siz]) génesis *f* ‖ **Genesis** *s* (Bib) el Génesis
**genetic** [dʒɪ'netɪk] *adj* genético ‖ **genetics** *s* genética
**Geneva** [dʒɪ'nivə] *s* Ginebra
**Genevan** [dʒɪ'nivən] *adj & s* ginebrino
**genial** ['dʒinɪ·əl] *adj* afable, complaciente
**genie** ['dʒini] *s* genio
**genital** ['dʒenɪtəl] *adj* genital ‖ **genitals** *spl* genitales *mpl*, órganos genitales
**genitive** ['dʒenɪtɪv] *adj & s* genitivo
**genius** ['dʒinjəs] o ['dʒinɪ·əs] *s* (*pl* **geniuses**) (*great inventive gift; person possessing it*) genio ‖ *s* (*pl* **genii**

['dʒinɪ,aɪ]) (*guardian spirit; pagan deity*) genio
**Genoa** ['dʒeno·ə] *s* Génova
**genocidal** [,dʒenə'saɪdəl] *adj* genocida
**genocide** ['dʒenə,saɪd] *s* (*act*) genocidio; (*person*) genocida *mf*
**Geno•ese** [,dʒeno'iz] *adj* genovés || *s* (*pl* **-ese**) genovés *m*
**genre** ['ʒɑnrə] *adj* de género
**gent.** o **Gent.** *abbr* **gentleman, gentlemen**
**genteel** [dʒen'til] *adj* gentil, elegante; cortés, urbano
**gentian** ['dʒenʃən] *s* genciana
**gentile** ['dʒentɪl] o ['dʒentaɪl] *adj* gentilicio; (gram) gentilicio || ['dʒentaɪl] *adj & s* no judío; cristiano; (*pagan*) gentil *mf*
**gentili•ty** [dʒen'tɪlɪti] *s* (*pl* **-ties**) gentileza
**gentle** ['dʒentəl] *adj* apacible, benévolo; dulce, manso, suave; cortés, fino; (*e.g., tap on the shoulder*) ligero
**gen'tle•folk'** *s* gente bien nacida
**gentle•man** ['dʒentəlmən] *s* (*pl* **-men** [mən]) *s* caballero; (*attendant to a person of high rank*) gentilhombre *m*
**gentleman in waiting** *s* gentilhombre *m* de cámara
**gentlemanly** ['dʒentəlmənli] *adj* caballeroso
**gentleman of leisure** *s* señor *m* que vive sin trabajar, caballero de vida holgada
**gentleman of the road** *s* salteador *m* de caminos
**gentleman's agreement** *s* acuerdo verbal
**gentle sex** *s* bello sexo, sexo débil
**gentry** ['dʒentri] *s* gente bien nacida
**genuine** ['dʒenjʊ·ɪn] *adj* genuino; sincero, franco
**genus** ['dʒinəs] *s* (*pl* **genera** ['dʒenərə] o **genuses**) (biol, log) género
**geog.** *abbr* **geography**
**geographer** [dʒɪ'ɑgrəfər] *s* geógrafo
**geographic(al)** [,dʒi·ə'græfɪk(əl)] *adj* geográfico
**geogra•phy** [dʒɪ'ɑgrəfi] *s* (*pl* **-phies**) geografía
**geol.** *abbr* **geology**
**geologic(al)** [,dʒi·ə'lɑdʒɪk(əl)] *adj* geológico
**geologist** [dʒɪ'ɑlədʒɪst] *s* geólogo
**geolo•gy** [dʒɪ'ɑlədʒi] *s* (*pl* **-gies**) geología
**geom.** *abbr* **geometry**
**geometric(al)** [,dʒi·ə'metrɪk(əl)] *adj* geométrico
**geometrician** [dʒɪ,ɑmɪ'trɪʃən] *s* geómetra *mf*
**geome•try** [dʒɪ'ɑmɪtri] *s* (*pl* **-tries**) geometría
**geophysics** [,dʒi·ə'fɪzɪks] *s* geofísica
**geopolitics** [,dʒi·ə'pɑlɪtɪks] *s* geopolítica
**George** [dʒɔrdʒ] *s* Jorje *m*
**geranium** [dʒɪ'renɪ·əm] *s* geranio
**geriatrical** [,dʒerɪ'ætrɪkəl] *adj* geriátrico
**geriatrician** [,dʒerɪ·ə'trɪʃən] *s* geriatra *mf*
**geriatrics** [,dʒerɪ'ætrɪks] *s* geriatría
**germ** [dʒʌrm] *s* germen *m*
**German** ['dʒʌrmən] *adj & s* alemán *m*
**germane** [dʒər'men] *adj* pertinente, relacionado
**Germanize** ['dʒʌrmə,naɪz] *tr* germanizar
**German measles** *s* rubéola
**German silver** *s* melchor *m*, alpaca
**Germany** ['dʒʌrməni] *s* Alemania
**germ carrier** *s* portador *m* de gérmenes
**germ cell** *s* célula germen
**germicidal** [,dʒʌrmɪ'saɪdəl] *adj* germicida
**germicide** ['dʒʌrmɪ,saɪd] *s* germicida *m*
**germinate** ['dʒʌrmɪ,net] *intr* germinar
**germ plasm** *s* germen *m* plasma
**germ theory** *s* teoría germinal
**germ warfare** *s* guerra bacteriana
**gerontology** [,dʒerɑn'tɑlədʒi] *s* gerontología
**gerund** ['dʒerənd] *s* gerundio
**gerundive** [dʒɪ'rʌndɪv] *s* gerundio adjetivo
**gestation** [dʒes'teʃən] *s* gestación
**gesticulate** [dʒes'tɪkjə,let] *intr* accionar, manotear
**gesticulation** [dʒes,tɪkjə'leʃən] *s* ademán *m*, manoteo
**gesture** ['dʒestʃər] *s* ademán *m*, gesto; demostración, muestra || *intr* hacer ademanes, hacer gestos
**get** [get] *v* (*pret* **got** [gɑt]; *pp* **got** o **gotten** ['gɑtən]; *ger* **getting**) *tr* conseguir, obtener; recibir; ir por, buscar; tomar (*p.ej., un billete*); alcanzar; encontrar, hallar; hacer (*p.ej., la comida*); resolver (*un problema*); aprender de memoria; captar (*una estación emisora*); **to get across** hacer aceptar; hacer comprender; **to get back** recobrar; **to get down** descolgar; (*to swallow*) tragar; **to get off** quitar (*p.ej., una mancha*); **to get someone to** + *inf* lograr que alguien + *subj;* **to get** + *pp* hacer + *inf;* **to have got** (coll) tener; **to have got to** + *inf* (coll) tener que + *inf* || *intr* (*to become*) hacerse, ponerse, volverse; (*to arrive*) llegar; **get up!** (*to an animal*) ¡arre!; **to get about** estar levantado (*un convaleciente*); **to get along** seguir andando; irse; ir tirando; tener éxito; llevarse bien; **to get along in years** ponerse viejo; **to get along with** congeniar con; **to get angry** enfadarse; **to get around** divulgarse; salir mucho, ir a todas partes; eludir; manejar (*a una persona*); **to get away** conseguir marcharse; evadirse; **to get away with** llevarse, escaparse con; (coll) hacer impunemente; **to get back** volver, regresar; **to get back at** (coll) desquitarse con; **to get behind** quedarse atrás; apoyar, abogar por; **to get by** lograr pasar; (*to manage to shift*) (coll) arreglárselas; **to get going** ponerse en marcha; **to get in** entrar; volver a casa; llegar (*un tren*); **to get in with**

llegar a ser amigo de; **to get married** casarse; **to get off** apearse; marcharse; **to get old** envejecer; **to get on** subir; llevarse bien; **to get out** salir, marcharse; divulgarse; **to get out of** bajar de (*un coche*); librarse de; perder (*la paciencia*); **to get out of the way** quitarse de en medio; **to get run over** ser atropellado; **to get through** pasar por entre; terminar; **to get to be** llegar a ser; **to get under way** ponerse en camino; **to get up** levantarse; **to not get over it** (coll) no volver de su asombro

**get'a•way'** *s* escapatoria, escape *m; (of an automobile)* arranque *m*

**get'-to•geth'er** *s* reunión, tertulia

**get'-up'** *s* (coll) disposición, presentación; (coll) atavío, traje *m*

**gewgaw** ['gjugɔ] *adj* cursi, charro, chillón || *s* fruslería, chuchería; adorno charro

**geyser** ['gaɪzər] *s* géiser *m* || ['gizər] *s* (Brit) calentador *m* de agua

**ghast•ly** ['gæstli] o ['gɑstli] *adj* (*comp* **-lier;** *super* **-liest**) cadavérico, espectral; espantoso, horrible

**Ghent** [gent] *s* Gante

**gherkin** ['gʌrkɪn] *s* pepinillo

**ghet•to** ['geto] *s* (*pl* **-tos**) ghetto

**ghost** [gost] *s* espectro, fantasma *m;* (telv) fantasma *m;* **not a ghost of a** ni sombra de; **to give up the ghost** entregar el alma, rendir el alma

**ghost•ly** ['gostli] *adj* (*comp* **-lier;** *super* **-liest**) espectral

**ghost story** *s* cuento de fantasmas

**ghost writer** *s* colaborador anónimo, escritor anónimo de obras firmadas por otra persona

**ghoul** [gul] *s* demonio que se alimenta de cadáveres; ladrón *m* de tumbas; (*person who revels in horrible things*) vampiro

**ghoulish** ['gulɪʃ] *adj* vampírico, horrible

**G.H.Q.** *abbr* **General Headquarters**

**GI** ['dʒi'aɪ] *s* (*pl* **GI's**) (coll) soldado raso (*del ejército norteamericano*)

**giant** ['dʒaɪ•ənt] *adj & s* gigante *m*

**giantess** ['dʒaɪ•əntɪs] *s* giganta

**gibberish** ['dʒɪbərɪʃ] o ['gɪbərɪʃ] *s* guirigay *m*

**gibbet** ['dʒɪbɪt] *s* horca || *tr* ahorcar; poner a la vergüenza

**gibe** [dʒaɪb] *s* remoque *m,* mofa || *intr* mofarse; **to gibe at** mofarse de

**giblets** ['dʒɪblɪts] *spl* menudillos

**giddiness** ['gɪdɪnɪs] *s* vértigo, vahido; falta de juicio

**gid•dy** ['gɪdi] *adj* (*comp* **-dier;** *super* **-diest**) vertiginoso; mareado; casquivano, ligero de cascos

**Gideon** ['gɪdɪ•ən] *s* (Bib) Gedeón *m*

**gift** [gɪft] *s* regalo; (*natural ability*) don *m,* dote *f,* prenda

**gifted** ['gɪftɪd] *adj* talentoso; muy inteligente

**gift horse** *s* — **never look a gift horse in the mouth** a caballo regalado no se le mira el diente

**gift of gab** *s* (coll) facundia, labia

**gift shop** *s* comercio de objetos de regalo, tienda de regalos

**gift'-wrap'** *v* (*pret & pp* **-wrapped;** *ger* **wrapping**) *tr* envolver en paquete regalo

**gigantic** [dʒaɪ'gæntɪk] *adj* gigantesco

**giggle** ['gɪgəl] *s* risita, risa ahogada, retozo de la risa || *intr* reírse bobamente

**gigo•lo** ['dʒɪgə,lo] *s* (*pl* **-los**) acompañante *m* profesional de mujeres; (*man supported by a woman*) mantenido

**gild** [gɪld] *v* (*pret & pp* **gilded** o **gilt** [gɪlt]) *tr* dorar

**gilding** ['gɪldɪŋ] *s* dorado

**gill** [gɪl] *s* (*of fish*) agalla; (*of cock*) barba || [dʒɪl] *s* cuarta parte de una pinta

**gillyflower** ['dʒɪlɪ,flaʊ•ər] *s* alhelí *m*

**gilt** [gɪlt] *adj & s* dorado

**gilt-edged** ['gɪlt,ɛdʒd] *adj* de toda confianza, de lo mejor que hay

**gilt'head'** *s* dorada

**gimcrack** ['dʒɪm,kræk] *adj* de oropel || *s* chuchería

**gimlet** ['gɪmlɪt] *s* barrena de mano

**gimmick** ['gɪmɪk] *s* (slang) adminículo; (slang) adminículo mágico

**gin** [dʒɪn] *s* (*alcoholic liquor*) ginebra; desmotadera de algodón; trampa; (*fish trap*) garlito; torno de izar || *v* (*pret & pp* **ginned;** *ger* **ginning**) *tr* desmotar

**gin fizz** *s* ginebra con gaseosa

**ginger** ['dʒɪndʒər] *s* jenjibre *m;* (coll) energía, viveza

**ginger ale** *s* cerveza de jengibre gaseosa

**gin'ger•bread'** *s* pan *m* de jengibre; adorno charro

**gingerly** ['dʒɪndʒərli] *adj* cauteloso, cuidadoso || *adv* cautelosamente

**gin'ger•snap'** *s* galletita de jengibre

**gingham** ['gɪŋəm] *s* guinga

**giraffe** [dʒɪ'ræf] o [dʒɪ'rɑf] *s* jirafa

**girandole** ['dʒɪrən,dol] *s* girándula

**gird** [gʌrd] *v* (*pret & pp* **girt** [gʌrt] o **girded**) *tr* ceñir; (*to equip*) dotar; (*to prepare*) aprestar; (*to surround, hem in*) rodear, encerrar

**girder** ['gʌrdər] *s* viga, trabe *f*

**girdle** ['gʌrdəl] *s* faja; corsé pequeño || *tr* ceñir; circundar, rodear

**girl** [gʌrl] *s* muchacha, niña, chica; (*servant*) moza

**girl friend** *s* (coll) amiguita

**girlhood** ['gʌrlhʊd] *s* muchachez *f;* juventud femenina

**girlish** ['gʌrlɪʃ] *adj* de muchacha; juvenil

**girl scout** *s* niña exploradora

**girth** [gʌrθ] *s* (*band*) cincha; (*waistband*) pretina; circunferencia

**gist** [dʒɪst] *s* esencia

**give** [gɪv] *s* elasticidad || *v* (*pret* **gave** [gev]; *pp* **given** ['gɪvən]) *tr* dar; ocasionar (*molestia, trabajo, etc.*); representar (*una obra dramática*); pronunciar (*un discurso*); **to give away** dar de balde; revelar; llevar (*a la novia*); (coll) traicionar; **to give back** devolver; **to give forth** despedir (*p.ej., olores*); **to give oneself up**

entregarse; **to give up** abandonar, dejar (*un empleo*); renunciar || *intr* dar; dar de sí; romperse (*p.ej., una cuerda*); **to give in** ceder, rendirse; **to give out** agotarse; no poder más; **to give up** darse por vencido

**give'-and-take'** *s* concesiones mutuas; conversación sazonada de burlas

**give'a·way'** *s* (coll) revelación involuntaria; (coll) traición; (*e.g., in checkers*) (coll) ganapierde *m & f*

**given** ['gɪvən] *adj* dado; (math) conocido; **given that** dado que, suponiendo que

**given name** *s* nombre *m* de pila

**giver** ['gɪvər] *s* dador *m*, donador *m*

**gizzard** ['gɪzərd] *s* molleja

**glacial** ['gleʃəl] *adj* glacial

**glacier** ['gleʃər] *s* glaciar *m*, helero

**glad** [glæd] *adj* (*comp* **gladder;** *super* **gladdest**) alegre, contento; **to be glad (to)** alegrarse (de)

**gladden** ['glædən] *tr* alegrar

**glade** [gled] *s* claro, claro herboso (*en un bosque*)

**glad hand** *s* (coll) acogida efusiva

**gladiola** [,glædɪ'olə] o [glə'daɪ·ələ] *s* estoque *m*

**gladly** ['glædli] *adv* alegremente; de buena gana, con mucho gusto

**gladness** ['glædnɪs] *s* alegría, regocijo

**glad rags** *spl* (slang) trapitos de cristianar; (slang) vestido de etiqueta

**glamorous** ['glæmərəs] *adj* fascinador, elegante

**glamour** ['glæmər] *s* fascinación, elegancia, hechizo

**glamour girl** *s* belleza exótica

**glance** [glæns] o [glɑns] *s* ojeada, vistazo, golpe *m* de vista; **at a glance** de un vistazo; **at first glance** a primera vista || *intr* lanzar una mirada; **to glance at** lanzar una mirada a; examinar de paso; **to glance off** desviarse de soslayo; desviarse de, al chocar; **to glance over** mirar por encima

**gland** [glænd] *s* glándula

**glanders** ['glændərz] *spl* muermo

**glare** [gler] *s* fulgor *m* deslumbrante, luz intensa; mirada feroz, mirada de indignación || *intr* relumbrar; lanzar miradas feroces; **to glare at** echar una mirada feroz a

**glaring** ['glerɪŋ] *adj* deslumbrante, relumbrante; (*look*) feroz, penetrante; manifiesto, que salta a la vista

**glass** [glæs] o [glɑs] *s* vidrio, cristal *m;* (*tumbler*) vaso, copa; (*mirror*) espejo; (*glassware*) vajilla de cristal; **glasses** anteojos

**glass blower** ['blo·ər] *s* soplador *m* de vidrio, vidriero

**glass case** *s* vitrina

**glass cutter** *s* cortavidrios *m*

**glass door** *s* puerta vidriera

**glassful** ['glæsfʊl] o ['glɑsfʊl] *s* vaso

**glass'house'** *s* invernadero; (fig) tejado de vidrio

**glassine** [glæ'sin] *s* papel *m* cristal

**glass'ware'** *s* cristalería, vajilla de vidrio

**glass wool** *s* cristal hilado

**glass'works'** *s* cristalería, vidriería

**glass'work'er** *s* vidriero

**glass·y** ['glæsi] o ['glɑsi] *adj* (*comp* **-ier;** *super* **-iest**) vidrioso

**glaze** [glez] *s* vidriado, esmalte *m;* (*of ice*) capa resbaladiza || *tr* vidriar, esmaltar; garapiñar (*golosinas*)

**glazier** ['gleʒər] *s* vidriero

**gleam** [glim] *s* destello, rayo de luz; luz *f* tenue; (*of hope*) rayo || *intr* destellar; brillar con luz tenue

**glean** [glin] *tr* espigar; (*to gather bit by bit, e.g., out of books*) espigar

**glee** [gli] *s* alegría, regocijo

**glee club** *s* orfeón *m*

**glib** [glɪb] *adj* (*comp* **glibber;** *super* **glibbest**) locuaz; (*tongue*) suelto; fácil e insincero

**glide** [glaɪd] *s* deslizamiento; (aer) vuelo sin motor, planeo; (mus) ligadura || *intr* deslizarse; (aer) volar sin motor, planear; **to glide along** pasar suavemente

**glider** ['glaɪdər] *s* (aer) planeador *m*, deslizador *m*

**glimmer** ['glɪmər] *s* luz *f* tenue; (*faint perception*) vislumbre *f* || *intr* brillar con luz tenue; (*to appear faintly*) vislumbrarse

**glimmering** ['glɪmərɪŋ] *adj* tenue, trémulo || *s* luz *f* tenue; vislumbre *f*

**glimpse** [glɪmps] *s* vislumbre *f;* **to catch a glimpse of** entrever, vislumbrar || *tr* vislumbrar

**glint** [glɪnt] *s* destello, rayo || *intr* destellar

**glisten** ['glɪsən] *s* centelleo || *intr* centellear

**glitter** ['glɪtər] *s* resplandor *m*, brillo || *intr* resplandecer, brillar

**gloaming** ['glomɪŋ] *s* crepúsculo vespertino

**gloat** [glot] *intr* relamerse; **to gloat over** mirar con satisfacción maligna

**globe** [glob] *s* globo

**globetrotter** ['glob,trɑtər] *s* trotamundos *m*

**globule** ['glɑbjʊl] *s* glóbulo

**glockenspiel** ['glɑkən,spil] *s* juego de timbres, órgano de campanas

**gloom** [glum] *s* lobreguez *f*, tinieblas, obscuridad; abatimiento, tristeza; aspecto abatido

**gloom·y** ['glumi] *adj* (*comp* **-ier;** *super* **-iest**) (*dark; sad*) lóbrego; pesimista

**glori·fy** ['glorɪ,faɪ] *v* (*pret & pp* **-fied**) *tr* glorificar; (*to enhance*) realzar

**glorious** ['glorɪ·əs] *adj* glorioso; espléndido, magnífico; (coll) alegre

**glo·ry** ['glori] *s* (*pl* **-ries**) gloria; **to go to glory** ganar la gloria; (slang) fracasar || *v* (*pret & pp* **-ried**) *intr* gloriarse

**gloss** [glɔs] o [glɑs] *s* brillo, lustre *m;* (*note, commentary*) glosa; glosario || *tr* (*to annotate*) glosar; lustrar, satinar; **to gloss over** disculpar, paliar

**glossa·ry** ['glɑsəri] *s* (*pl* **-ries**) glosario

**gloss·y** ['glɔsi] o ['glɑsi] *adj* (*comp* **-ier;** *super* **-iest**) brillante, lustroso; (*silk*) joyante

**glottal** ['glɑtəl] *adj* glótico
**glove** [glʌv] *s* guante *m*
**glove compartment** *s* portaguantes *m*
**glove stretcher** *s* ensanchador *m*, juanas
**glow** [glo] *s* (*light of incandescence*) resplandor *m;* (*e.g., of sunset*) brillo, esplendor *m;* sensación de calor; color *m* en las mejillas || *intr* brillar sin llama; estar encendido (*el rostro, el cielo*); estar muy animado
**glower** ['glaʊ·ər] *s* ceño, mirada ceñuda || *intr* mirar con ceño
**glowing** ['glo·ɪŋ] *adj* ardiente, encendido; radiante; entusiasta, elogioso
**glow'worm'** *s* gusano de luz, luciérnaga
**glucose** ['glukos] *s* glucosa
**glue** [glu] *s* cola || *tr* encolar; pegar fuertemente
**glue pot** *s* cazo de cola
**gluey** ['glu·i] *adj* (*comp* **gluier**; *super* **gluiest**) pegajoso; (*smeared with glue*) encolado
**glug** [glʌg] *s* gluglú *m* || *v* (*pret & pp* **glugged**; *ger* **glugging**) *intr* hacer gluglú (*el agua*)
**glum** [glʌm] *adj* (*comp* **glummer**; *super* **glummest**) hosco
**glut** [glʌt] *s* abundancia, gran acopio: exceso; **to be a glut on the market** abarrotarse || *v* (*pret & pp* **glutted**; *ger* **glutting**) *tr* hartar, saciar; inundar (*el mercado*); obstruir
**glutton** ['glʌtən] *adj & s* glotón *m*
**gluttonous** ['glʌtənəs] *adj* glotón
**glutton·y** ['glʌtəni] *s* (*pl* **-ies**) glotonería, gula
**glycerine** ['glɪsərɪn] *s* glicerina
**G.M.** *abbr* **general manager, Grand Master**
**G-man** ['dʒi ˌmæn] *s* (*pl* **-men** [ˌmen]) (coll) agente *m* de la policía federal
**G.M.T.** *abbr* **Greenwich mean time**
**gnarl** [nɑrl] *s* nudo || *tr* torcer || *intr* gruñir
**gnarled** [nɑrld] *adj* nudoso, retorcido
**gnash** [næʃ] *tr* hacer rechinar (*los dientes*) || *intr* hacer rechinar los dientes
**gnat** [næt] *s* jején *m*
**gnaw** [nɔ] *tr* roer; practicar (*un agujero*) royendo
**gnome** [nom] *s* gnomo
**go** [go] *s* (*pl* **goes**) ida; (coll) energía, ímpetu *m;* (coll) boga; (coll) ensayo; (*for traffic*) paso libre; **it's a go** (coll) es un trato hecho; **it's all the go** (coll) hace furor; **it's no go** (coll) es imposible; **on the go** (coll) en continuo movimiento; **to make a go of** (coll) lograr éxito en || *v* (*pret* **went** [wɛnt]; *pp* **gone** [gɔn] o [gɑn]) *tr* (coll) soportar, tolerar; **to go it alone** obrar sin ayuda || *intr* ir; (*to work, operate*) funcionar, marchar; andar (*p.ej., desnudo*); volverse (*p.ej., loco*); **going, going, gone!** ¡vendo, vendo, vendí!; **so it goes** así va el mundo; **to be going to** + *inf* ir a + *inf;* **to be gone** haber ido; haberse agotado; haber dejado de ser; **to go against** ir en contra de; **to go ahead** seguir adelante; **to go away** irse, marcharse; **to go back** volver; **to go by** pasar por; guiarse por; atenerse a; **to go down** bajar; hundirse (*un buque*); **to go fishing** ir de pesca; **to go for** ir por; **to go get** ir por, ir a buscar; **to go house hunting** ir a buscar casa; **to go hunting** ir de caza; **to go in** entrar; entrar en; (*to fit in*) caber en; **to go in for** dedicarse a, interesarse por; **to go into** entrar en; investigar; (aut) poner (*p.ej., primera*); **to go in with** asociarse con; **to go off** irse, marcharse; llevarse a cabo; estallar (*p.ej., una bomba*); dispararse (*un fusil*); **to go on** seguir adelante; ir tirando; **to go on** + *ger* seguir + *ger;* **to go on with** continuar; **to go out** salir; pasar de moda; apagarse (*un fuego, una luz*); declararse en huelga; (*for entertainment, etc.*) salir; **to go over** tener éxito; releer; examinar, revisar; pasar por encima de; **to go over to** pasarse a las filas de; **to go through** pasar por; llegar al fin de; agotar (*una fortuna*); **to go with** ir con, acompañar; salir con (*una muchacha*); hacer juego con; **to go without** andarse sin, pasarse sin
**goad** [god] *s* aguijada, aguijón *m* || *tr* aguijonear
**go'-a·head'** *adj* (coll) emprendedor || *s* (coll) señal *f* para seguir adelante, luz *f* verde
**goal** [gol] *s* meta; (*in football*) gol *m*
**goal'keep'er** *s* guardameta *m*, portero
**goal line** *s* raya de la meta
**goal post** *s* poste *m* de la meta
**goat** [got] *s* cabra; (*male goat*) macho cabrío; (coll) víctima inocente; **to be the goat** (slang) pagar el pato; **to get the goat of** (slang) tomar el pelo a; **to ride the goat** (coll) ser iniciado en una sociedad secreta
**goatee** [go'ti] *s* perilla
**goat'herd'** *s* cabrero
**goat'skin'** *s* piel *f* de cabra
**goat'suck'er** *s* chotacabras *m*
**gob** [gɑb] *s* (coll) masa informe y pequeña; (coll) marinero de guerra
**gobble** ['gɑbəl] *s* gluglú *m* || *tr* engullir; **to gobble up** engullirse ávidamente; (coll) asir de repente, apoderarse ávidamente de || *intr* engullir; gluglutear, gorgonear (*el pavo*)
**gobbledegook** ['gɑbəldɪˌgʊk] *s* (coll) lenguaje obscuro e incomprensible, galimatías *m*
**go'-be·tween'** *s* (*intermediary*) medianero; (*in promoting marriages*) casamentero; (*in shady love affairs*) alcahuete *m*, alcahueta
**goblet** ['gɑblɪt] *s* copa
**goblin** ['gɑblɪn] *s* duende *m*, trasgo
**go'-by'** *s* (coll) desaire *m;* **to give someone the go-by** (coll) negarse al trato de alguien
**go'cart'** *s* andaderas; cochecito para niños; carruaje ligero
**god** [gɑd] *s* dios *m;* **God forbid** no lo quiera Dios; **God grant** permita Dios; **God willing** Dios mediante

**god'child'** *s* (*pl* **chil'dren**) ahijado, ahijada
**god'daugh'ter** *s* ahijada
**goddess** ['gadɪs] *s* diosa
**god'fa'ther** *s* padrino
**God'-fear'ing** *adj* timorato; devoto, pío
**God'for•sak'en** *adj* dejado de la mano de Dios; (coll) desolado, desierto
**god'head'** *s* divinidad || **Godhead** *s* Dios *m*
**godless** ['gadlɪs] *adj* infiel, impío; desalmado, malvado
**god•ly** ['gadli] *adj* (*comp* **-lier;** *super* **-liest**) devoto, pío
**god'moth'er** *s* madrina
**God's acre** *s* campo santo
**god'send'** *s* cosa llovida del cielo, bendición
**god'son'** *s* ahijado
**God'speed'** *s* bienandanza, buena suerte, buen viaje *m*
**go'-get'ter** *s* (slang) buscavidas *mf*, persona emprendedora
**goggle** ['gagəl] *intr* volver los ojos; abrir los ojos desmesuradamente
**goggle-eyed** ['gagəl,aɪd] *adj* de ojos saltones
**goggles** ['gagəlz] *spl* anteojos de camino, gafas contra el polvo
**going** ['go·ɪŋ] *adj* en marcha, funcionando; **going on** casi, p.ej., **it is going on nine o'clock** son casi las nueve || *s* ida, partida
**going concern** *s* empresa que marcha
**goings on** *spl* actividades; bulla, jarana
**goiter** ['gɔɪtər] *s* bocio
**gold** [gold] *adj* áureo, de oro; dorado || *s* oro
**gold'beat'er** *s* batidor *m* de oro, batihoja *m*
**goldbeater's skin** *s* venza
**gold brick** *s* — **to sell a gold brick** (coll) vender gato por liebre
**gold'crest'** *s* reyezuelo moñudo
**gold digger** ['dɪgər] *s* (slang) extractora de oro
**golden** ['goldən] *adj* áureo, de oro; (*gilt*) dorado; (*hair*) rubio; excelente, favorable, floreciente
**golden age** *s* edad de oro, siglo de oro
**golden calf** *s* becerro de oro
**Golden Fleece** *s* vellocino de oro
**golden mean** *s* justo medio
**golden plover** *s* chorlito
**gold'en•rod'** *s* vara de oro, vara de San José
**golden rule** *s* regla de la caridad cristiana
**golden wedding** *s* bodas de oro
**gold-filled** ['gold,fɪld] *adj* empastado en oro
**gold'finch'** *s* jilguero, pintacilgo
**gold'fish'** *s* carpa dorada, pez *m* de color
**goldilocks** ['goldɪ,laks] *s* rubiales *mf*
**gold leaf** *s* pan *m* de oro
**gold mine** *s* mina de oro; **to strike a gold mine** (fig) encontrar una mina
**gold plate** *s* vajilla de oro
**gold'-plate'** *tr* dorar
**gold'smith'** *s* orfebre *m*
**gold standard** *s* patrón *m* oro
**golf** [galf] *s* golf *m* || *intr* jugar al golf
**golf club** *s* palo de golf; asociación de jugadores de golf
**golfer** ['galfər] *s* golfista *mf*
**golf links** *spl* campo de golf
**Golgotha** ['galgəθə] *s* el Gólgota
**gondola** ['gandələ] *s* góndola
**gondolier** [,gandə'lɪr] *s* gondolero
**gone** [gɔn] o [gan] *adj* agotado; arruinado; desaparecido; muerto; **gone on** (coll) enamorado de
**gong** [gɔŋ] o [gaŋ] *s* batintín *m*
**gonorrhea** [,ganə'ri·ə] *s* gonorrea
**goo** [gu] *s* (slang) substancia pegajosa
**good** [gʊd] *adj* (*comp* **better;** *super* **best**) bueno; **good and . . .** (coll) muy, p.ej., **good and cheap** muy barato; **good for** bueno para; capaz de hacer; capaz de pagar; capaz de vivir (*cierto tiempo*); **to be good at** tener talento para; **to be no good** (coll) no servir para nada; (coll) ser un perdido; **to make good** tener éxito; cumplir (*sus promesas*); pagar (*una deuda*); responder de (*los daños*) || *s* bien *m*, provecho, utilidad; **for good** para siempre; **for good and all** de una vez para siempre; **goods** efectos; géneros, mercancías; **the good** lo bueno; los buenos; **to catch with the goods** (slang) coger en flagrante; **to deliver the goods** (slang) cumplir lo prometido; **to do good** hacer el bien; dar salud o fuerzas a; **to the good** de sobra, en el haber; **what is the good of . . . ?** ¿para qué sirve . . . ?
**good afternoon** *s* buenas tardes
**good'-by'** o **good'-bye'** *s* adiós *m* || *interj* ¡adiós!
**good day** *s* buenos días
**good evening** *s* buenas noches, buenas tardes
**good fellow** *s* (coll) buen chico, buen sujeto
**good fellowship** *s* compañerismo
**good'-for-noth'ing** *adj* inútil, sin valor || *s* pelafustán *m*, perdido
**Good Friday** *s* Viernes santo
**good graces** *spl* favor *m*, estimación
**good-hearted** ['gʊd'hartɪd] *adj* de buen corazón
**good-humored** ['gʊd'hjumərd] o ['gʊd'jumərd] *adj* de buen humor; afable
**good-looking** ['gʊd'lʊkɪŋ] *adj* guapo, bien parecido
**good looks** *spl* hermosura, guapeza
**good•ly** ['gʊdli] *adj* (*comp* **-lier;** *super* **-liest**) considerable; bien parecido, hermoso; bueno, excelente
**good morning** *s* buenos días
**good-natured** ['gʊd'netʃərd] *adj* bonachón, afable
**Good Neighbor Policy** *s* política del buen vecino
**goodness** ['gʊdnɪs] *s* bondad; **for goodness' sake!** ¡por Dios!; **goodness knows!** ¡quién sabe! || *interj* ¡válgame Dios!
**good night** *s* buenas noches
**good sense** *s* buen sentido, sensatez *f*

**good-sized** ['gʊd'saɪzd] *adj* bastante grande, de buen tamaño
**good speed** *s* adiós *m* y buena suerte
**good-tempered** ['gʊd'tɛmpərd] *adj* de natural apacible
**good time** *s* rato agradable; **to have a good time** divertirse; **to make good time** ir a buen paso; llegar en poco tiempo
**good turn** *s* favor *m,* servicio
**good way** *s* buen trecho
**good will** *s* buena voluntad; (com) buen nombre *m,* clientela
**good·y** ['gʊdi] *adj* (coll) beatuco, santurrón || *s* (*pl* **-ies**) (coll) golosina || *interj* (coll) ¡qué bien!, ¡qué alegría!
**gooey** ['gu·i] *adj* (*comp* **gooier;** *super* **gooiest**) (slang) pegajoso, fangoso
**goof** [guf] *s* (slang) tonto || *tr* & *intr* (slang) chapucear
**goof·y** ['gufi] *adj* (*comp* **-ier;** *super* **-iest**) (slang) tonto, mentecato
**goon** [gun] *s* (*roughneck*) (coll) gamberro, canalla *m;* (coll) terrorista *m* de alquiler; (slang) estúpido
**goose** [gus] *s* (*pl* **geese** [gis]) *s* ánsar *m,* ganso, oca; **the goose hangs high** todo va a pedir de boca; **to cook one's goose** malbaratarle a uno los planes; **to kill the goose that lays the golden eggs** matar la gallina de los huevos de oro || *s* (*pl* **gooses**) plancha de sastre
**goose'ber'ry** *s* (*pl* **-ries**) (*plant*) grosellero silvestre; (*fruit*) grosella silvestre
**goose egg** *s* huevo de oca; (slang) cero
**goose flesh** *s* carne *f* de gallina
**goose'neck'** *s* cuello de cisne; (naut) gancho de botalones
**goose pimples** *spl* carne *f* de gallina
**goose step** *s* (mil) paso de ganso
**G.O.P.** *abbr* **Grand Old Party**
**gopher** ['gofər] *s* ardilla de tierra, ardillón *m;* (*Geomys*) tuza
**Gordian knot** ['gɔrdɪ·ən] *s* nudo gordiano; **to cut the Gordian knot** cortar el nudo gordiano
**gore** [gor] *s* sangre derramada, sangre cuajada; (*insert in a piece of cloth*) cuchillo, nesga || *tr* (*to pierce with a horn*) acornar; poner cuchillo o nesga a; nesgar
**gorge** [gɔrdʒ] *s* garganta, desfiladero; (*in a river*) atasco de hielo || *tr* atiborrar || *intr* atiborrarse
**gorgeous** ['gɔrdʒəs] *adj* primoroso, brillante, magnífico, suntuoso
**gorilla** [gə'rɪlə] *s* gorila
**gorse** [gɔrs] *s* aulaga
**gor·y** ['gori] *adj* (*comp* **-ier;** *super* **-iest**) ensangrentado, sangriento
**gosh** [gɑʃ] *interj* ¡caramba!
**goshawk** ['gɑs,hɔk] *s* azor *m*
**gospel** ['gɑspəl] *s* evangelio || **Gospel** *s* Evangelio
**gospel truth** *s* evangelio, pura verdad
**gossamer** ['gɑsəmər] *s* telaraña flotante; gasa sutilísima; tela impermeable muy delgada; impermeable *m* de tela muy delgada
**gossip** ['gɑsɪp] *s* chismes *m;* (*person*) chismoso; **piece of gossip** chisme *m* || *intr* chismear
**gossip column** *s* mentidero
**gossip columnist** *s* gacetillero, cronista *mf* social
**gossipy** ['gɑsɪpi] *adj* chismoso
**Goth** [gɑθ] *s* godo; (fig) bárbaro
**Gothic** ['gɑθɪk] *adj* & *s* gótico
**gouge** [gaʊdʒ] *s* gubia; (*cut made with a gouge*) muesca; (coll) estafa || *tr* excavar con gubia; (coll) estafar
**goulash** ['gulɑʃ] *s* puchero húngaro
**gourd** [gord] o [gʊrd] *s* calabaza
**gourmand** ['gʊrmənd] *s* gastrónomo; glotón *m,* goloso
**gourmet** ['gʊrme] *s* gastrónomo delicado
**gout** [gaʊt] *s* gota
**gout·y** ['gaʊti] *adj* (*comp* **-ier;** *super* **-iest**) gotoso
**gov.** *abbr* **governor, government**
**govern** ['gʌvərn] *tr* gobernar; (gram) regir || *intr* gobernar
**governess** ['gʌvərnɪs] *s* aya, institutriz *f*
**government** ['gʌvərnmənt] *s* gobierno; (gram) régimen *m*
**governmental** [,gʌvərn'mɛntəl] *adj* gubernamental, gubernativo
**government in exile** *s* gobierno exilado
**governor** ['gʌvərnər] *s* gobernador *m;* (*of a jail, castle, etc.*) alcaide *m;* (mach) regulador *m*
**governorship** ['gʌvərnər,ʃɪp] *s* gobierno
**govt.** *abbr* **government**
**gown** [gaʊn] *s* (*of a woman*) vestido; (*of a professor, judge, etc.*) toga; (*of a priest*) traje *m* talar; (*dressing gown*) bata, peinador *m;* (*nightgown*) camisa de dormir
**G.P.O.** *abbr* **General Post Office, Government Printing Office**
**gr.** *abbr* **gram, grams, grain, grains, gross**
**grab** [græb] *s* asimiento, presa; (coll) robo || *v* (*pret* & *pp* **grabbed;** *ger* **grabbing**) *tr* asir, agarrar; arrebatar || *intr* — **to grab at** tratar de asir
**grace** [gres] *s* (*charm; favor; pardon*) gracia; (*prayer at table*) benedícite *m;* (*extension of time*) demora; **to be in the good graces of** gozar del favor de; **to say grace** rezar el benedícite; **with good grace** de buen talante || *tr* adornar, engalanar; favorecer
**graceful** ['gresfəl] *adj* agraciado, gracioso
**grace note** *s* apoyatura, nota de adorno
**gracious** ['greʃəs] *adj* graciable, gracioso; misericordioso || *interj* ¡válgame Dios!
**grackle** ['grækəl] *s* (*myna*) estornino de los pastores; (*purple grackle*) quiscal *m*
**grad.** *abbr* **graduate**
**gradation** [gre'deʃən] *s* (*gradual change*) paso gradual; (*arrangement in grades*) graduación; (*step in a series*) paso, grado
**grade** [gred] *s* grado; (*slope*) pendiente *f;* (*mark for work in class*) calificación, nota; **to make the grade**

lograr subir la cuesta; vencer los obstáculos || *tr* graduar, calificar; dar nota a (*un alumno*); explanar, nivelar
**grade crossing** *s* (rr) paso a nivel, cruce *m* a nivel
**grade school** *s* escuela elemental
**gradient** ['gredɪ·ənt] *adj* pendiente || *s* pendiente *f;* (phys) gradiente *m*
**gradual** ['grædʒʊ·əl] *adj* paulatino
**gradually** ['grædʒʊ·əli] *adv* paulatinamente, gradualmente, poco a poco
**graduate** ['grædʒʊ·ɪt] *adj* graduado || *s* graduado; (*candidate for a degree*) graduando; vasija graduada || ['grædʒʊ,et] *tr* graduar || *intr* graduarse
**graduate school** *s* facultad de altos estudios
**graduate student** *s* estudiante graduado
**graduate work** *s* altos estudios
**graduation** [,grædʒʊ'eʃən] *s* graduación; ceremonia de graduación
**graft** [græft] o [grɑft] *s* (hort & surg) injerto; (coll) soborno político, ganancia ilegal || *tr & intr* (hort & surg) injertar; (coll) malversar
**graham bread** ['gre·əm] *s* pan *m* integral
**graham flour** *s* harina de trigo sin cerner
**grain** [gren] *s* (*small seed; tiny particle of sand, etc.; small unit of weight*) grano; (*cereal seeds*) granos; (*in stone*) vena; (*in wood*) fibra; **against the grain** a contrapelo || *tr* granear (*la pólvora; una piedra litográfica*); crispir, vetear (*la madera*); granular (*una piel*)
**grain elevator** *s* elevador *m* de granos; (*tall building where grain is stored*) depósito de cereales
**grain'field'** *s* sembrado
**graining** ['grenɪŋ] *s* veteado
**gram** [græm] *s* gramo
**grammar** ['græmər] *s* gramática
**grammarian** [grə'merɪ·ən] *s* gramático
**grammar school** *s* escuela pública elemental
**grammatical** [grə'mætɪkəl] *adj* gramático
**gramophone** ['græmə,fon] *s* (trademark) gramófono
**grana•ry** ['grænəri] *s* (*pl* **-ries**) granero
**grand** [grænd] *adj* espléndido, grandioso; importante, principal
**grand'aunt'** *s* tía abuela
**grand'child'** *s* (*pl* **-chil'dren**) nieto, nieta
**grand'daugh'ter** *s* nieta
**grand duchess** *s* gran duquesa
**grand duchy** *s* gran ducado
**grand duke** *s* gran duque *m*
**grandee** [græn'di] *s* grande *m* de España
**grandeur** ['grændʒər] o ['grændʒʊr] *s* grandeza, magnificencia
**grand'fa'ther** *s* abuelo; (*forefather*) antepasado
**grandfather's clock** *s* reloj *m* de caja
**grandiose** ['grændɪ,os] *adj* grandioso; hinchado, pomposo
**grand jury** *s* jurado de acusación
**grand larceny** *s* hurto mayor
**grand lodge** *s* gran oriente *m*
**grandma** ['grænd,mɑ], ['græm,mɑ] o ['græmə] *s* (coll) abuela, abuelita
**grand'moth'er** *s* abuela
**grand'neph'ew** *s* resobrino
**grand'niece** *s* resobrina
**grand opera** *s* ópera seria
**grandpa** ['grænd,pɑ], ['græn,pɑ] o ['græmpə] *s* (coll) abuelo, abuelito
**grand'par'ent** *s* abuelo, abuela
**grand piano** *s* piano de cola
**grand slam** *s* bola
**grand'son'** *s* nieto
**grand'stand'** *s* gradería cubierta, tribuna
**grand strategy** *s* alta estrategia
**grand total** *s* gran total *m,* suma de totales
**grand'un'cle** *s* tío abuelo
**grand vizier** *s* gran visir *m*
**grange** [grendʒ] *s* (*farm with barns, etc.*) granja; (*organization of farmers*) cámara agrícola
**granite** ['grænɪt] *s* granito
**grant** [grænt] o [grɑnt] *s* concesión; donación, subvención; traspaso de propiedad || *tr* conceder; dar (*permiso, perdón*); transferir (*bienes inmuebles*); **to take for granted** dar por sentado; tratar con indiferencia
**grantee** [græn'ti] o [grɑn'ti] *s* cesionario
**grant'-in-aid'** *s* (*pl* **grants-in-aid**) subvención concedida por el gobierno para obras de utilidad pública; pensión para estimular conocimientos científicos, literarios, artísticos
**grantor** [græn'tɔr] o [grɑn'tɔr] *s* cesionista *mf,* otorgante *mf*
**granular** ['grænjələr] *adj* granular
**granulate** ['grænjə,let] *tr* granular || *intr* granularse
**granule** ['grænjul] *s* gránulo
**grape** [grep] *s* (*fruit*) uva; (*vine*) vid *f*
**grape arbor** *s* parral *m*
**grape'fruit'** *s* (*fruit*) toronja; (*tree*) toronjo
**grape hyacinth** *s* sueldacostilla
**grape juice** *s* zumo de uva
**grape'shot'** *s* metralla
**grape'vine'** *s* vid *f,* parra; **by the grapevine** por vías secretas, por vías misteriosas
**graph** [græf] o [grɑf] *s* (*diagram*) gráfica; (gram) grafía
**graphic(al)** ['græfɪk(əl)] *adj* gráfico
**graphite** ['græfaɪt] *s* grafito
**graph paper** *s* papel cuadriculado
**grapnel** ['græpnəl] *s* rebañadera; (*anchor*) rezón *m*
**grapple** ['græpəl] *s* asimiento, presa; lucha cuerpo a cuerpo || *tr* asir, agarrar || *intr* agarrarse; luchar a brazo partido; **to grapple with** luchar a brazo partido con; tratar de resolver
**grappling iron** *s* arpeo
**grasp** [græsp] o [grɑsp] *s* asimiento; (*power, reach*) poder *m,* alcance *m;* (fig) comprensión; **to have a good grasp of** saber a fondo; **within the grasp of** al alcance de || *tr* (*with hand*) empuñar; (*to get control of*)

apoderarse de; (fig) comprender || *intr* — **to grasp at** tratar de asir; aceptar con avidez
**grasping** ['græspɪŋ] o ['grɑspɪŋ] *adj* avaro, codicioso
**grass** [græs] o [grɑs] *s* hierba; (*pasture land*) pasto; (*lawn*) césped *m;* **to go to grass** ir a pacer; disfrutar de una temporada de descanso; gastarse, arruinarse; morir; **to not let the grass grow under one's feet** no dormirse en las pajas
**grass court** *s* cancha de césped
**grass'hop'per** *s* saltamontes *m*
**grass pea** *s* almorta, guija
**grass'-roots'** *adj* (coll) de la gente común
**grass seed** *s* semilla de césped
**grass widow** *s* viuda de paja, viuda de marido vivo
**grass•y** ['græsi] o ['grɑsi] *adj* (*comp* **-ier;** *super* **-iest**) herboso
**grate** [gret] *s* (*at a window*) reja; (*for cooking*) parrilla || *tr* (*to put a grate on*) enrejar; rallar (*p.ej., queso*) || *intr* crujir, rechinar; **to grate on** (fig) rallar
**grateful** ['gretfəl] *adj* agradecido; (*pleasing*) agradable
**grater** ['gretər] *s* rallador *m*
**grati•fy** ['grætɪ,faɪ] *v* (*pret & pp* **-fied**) *tr* complacer, gratificar
**gratifying** ['grætɪ,faɪ·ɪŋ] *adj* grato, satisfactorio
**grating** ['gretɪŋ] *adj* áspero, irritante; (*sound*) chirriante || *s* enrejado
**gratis** ['getɪs] o ['grætɪs] *adj* gracioso, gratuito || *adv* gratis, de balde
**gratitude** ['grætɪ,tjud] o ['grætɪ,tud] *s* gratitud, reconocimiento
**gratuitous** [grə'tju·ɪtəs] o [grə'tu·ɪtəs] *adj* gratuito
**gratui•ty** [grə'tju·ɪti] o [grə'tu·ɪti] *s* (*pl* **-ties**) propina
**grave** [grev] *adj* (*serious, dangerous; important*) grave; solemne; (*sound; accent*) grave || *s* sepulcro, sepultura; **to have one foot in the grave** estar con un pie en la sepultura
**gravedigger** ['grev,dɪgər] *s* enterrador *m,* sepulturero
**gravel** ['grævəl] *s* grava, cascajo
**graven image** ['grevən] *s* ídolo
**grave'stone'** *s* lápida sepulcral
**grave'yard'** *s* camposanto
**gravitate** ['grævɪ,tet] *intr* gravitar; ser atraído
**gravitation** [,grævɪ'teʃən] *s* gravitación
**gravi•ty** ['grævɪti] *s* (*pl* **-ties**) gravedad
**gravure** [grə'vjʊr] o ['grevjʊr] *s* fotograbado
**gra•vy** ['grevi] *s* (*pl* **-vies**) (*juice from cooking meat*) jugo; (*sauce made with this juice*) salsa; (slang) ganga, breva
**gravy dish** *s* salsera
**gray** [gre] *adj* gris; (*gray-haired*) cano, canoso || *s* gris *m;* traje *m* gris || *intr* encanecer
**gray'beard'** *s* anciano, viejo
**gray-haired** ['gre,herd] *adj* canoso
**gray'hound'** *s* galgo
**grayish** ['gre·ɪʃ] *adj* grisáceo; (*person; hair*) entrecano
**gray matter** *s* substancia gris; (*intelligence*) (coll) materia gris
**graze** [grez] *tr* (*to touch lightly*) rozar; (*to scratch lightly in passing*) raspar; pacer (*la hierba*); apacentar (*el ganado*); (*to lead to the pasture*) pastar || *intr* pacer, pastar
**grease** [gris] *s* grasa || [gris] o [griz] *tr* engrasar; (slang) sobornar
**grease cup** [gris] *s* vaso de engrase
**grease gun** [gris] *s* engrasador *m* de pistón, jeringa de engrase
**grease lift** [gris] *s* puente *m* de engrase
**grease paint** [gris] *s* maquillaje *m*
**grease pit** [gris] *s* fosa de engrase
**grease spot** [gris] *s* lámpara, mancha de grasa
**greas•y** ['grisi] o ['grizi] *adj* (*comp* **-ier;** *super* **-iest**) grasiento, pringoso
**great** [gret] *adj* grande; (coll) excelente || **the great** los grandes
**great'-aunt'** *s* tía abuela
**Great Bear** *s* Osa Mayor
**Great Britain** ['brɪtən] *s* la Gran Bretaña
**great'coat'** *s* gabán *m* de mucho abrigo
**Great Dane** *s* mastín *m* danés
**Greater London** *s* el Gran Londres
**Greater New York** *s* el Gran Nueva York
**great'-grand'child'** *s* (*pl* **-chil'dren**) bisnieto, bisnieta
**great'-grand'daugh'ter** *s* bisnieta
**great'-grand'fa'ther** *s* bisabuelo
**great'-grand'moth'er** *s* bisabuela
**great'-grand'par'ent** *s* bisabuelo, bisabuela
**great'-grand'son'** *s* bisnieto
**greatly** ['gretli] *adj* grandemente
**great'-neph'ew** *s* resobrino
**greatness** ['gretnɪs] *s* grandeza
**great'-niece'** *s* resobrina
**great'-un'cle** *s* tío abuelo
**Great War** *s* Gran guerra
**Grecian** ['griʃən] *adj & s* griego
**Greece** [gris] *s* Grecia
**greed** [grid] *s* codicia, avaricia; (*in eating and drinking*) glotonería
**greed•y** ['gridi] *adj* (*comp* **-ier;** *super* **-iest**) codicioso, avaro; glotón
**Greek** [grik] *adj & s* griego
**green** [grin] *adj* verde; inexperto || *s* verde *m;* (*lawn*) césped *m;* **greens** verduras
**green'back'** *s* (U.S.A.) billete *m* de banco (*de dorso verde*)
**green corn** *s* maíz tierno
**green earth** *s* verdacho
**greener•y** ['grinəri] *s* (*pl* **-ies**) (*foliage*) verdura; (*hothouse*) invernáculo
**green-eyed** ['grin,aɪd] *adj* de ojos verdes; celoso
**green'gage'** *s* ciruela claudia
**green grasshopper** *s* langostón *m*
**green'gro'cer** *s* verdulero
**green'gro'cer•y** *s* (*pl* **-ies**) verdulería
**green'horn'** *s* novato; (*dupe*) primo, inocentón *m;* (coll) papanatas *m,* isidro
**green'house'** *s* invernáculo

**greenish** ['grinɪʃ] *adj* verdoso
**Greenland** ['grinlənd] *s* Groenlandia
**greenness** ['grinnɪs] *s* verdura, verdor *m;* falta de experiencia
**green'room'** *s* saloncillo; chismería de teatro
**greensward** ['grin,swɔrd] *s* césped *m*
**green thumb** *s* pulgares *mpl* verdes (*don de criar plantas*)
**green vegetables** *spl* verduras
**green'wood'** *s* bosque *m* verde, bosque frondoso
**greet** [grit] *tr* saludar; acoger, recibir; presentarse a (*los ojos u los oídos de uno*)
**greeting** ['gritɪŋ] *s* saludo; acogida, recibimiento ‖ **greetings** *interj* ¡salud!
**greeting card** *s* tarjeta de buen deseo
**gregarious** [grɪ'gerɪ·əs] *adj* (*living in the midst of others*) gregario; (*fond of the company of others*) sociable
**Gregorian** [grɪ'gorɪ·ən] *adj* gregoriano
**grenade** [grɪ'ned] *s* granada; (*to put out fires*) granada extintora
**grenadier** [,grɛnə'dɪr] *s* granadero
**grenadine** [,grɛnə'din] *s* granadina
**grey** [gre] *adj, s & intr* var de **gray**
**grid** [grɪd] *s* parrilla, rejilla; (electron) rejilla; (*of a storage battery*) (elec) rejilla
**griddle** ['grɪdəl] *s* plancha
**grid'dle·cake'** *s* tortada (de harina) a la plancha
**grid'i'ron** *s* parrilla; campo de fútbol
**grid leak** *s* (electron) resistencia de rejilla, escape *m* de rejilla
**grief** [grif] *s* aflicción, pesar *m;* (coll) desgracia, disgusto; **to come to grief** fracasar, arruinarse
**grievance** ['grivəns] *s* agravio, injusticia; despecho, disgusto; motivo de queja
**grieve** [griv] *tr* afligir, penar ‖ *intr* afligirse, apenarse; **to grieve over** añorar
**grievous** ['grivəs] *adj* doloroso, penoso; atroz, cruel; (*deplorable*) lastimoso
**griffin** ['grɪfɪn] *s* (myth) grifo
**grill** [grɪl] *s* parrilla ‖ *tr* emparrillar; someter (*a un acusado*) a un interrogatorio muy apremiante
**grille** [grɪl] *s* reja, verja; (*of an automobile*) parrilla, rejilla
**grill'room'** *s* parrilla
**grim** [grɪm] *adj* (*comp* **grimmer;** *super* **grimmest**) (*fierce*) cruel, feroz; (*repellent*) horrible, siniestro; (*unyielding*) formidable, implacable; (*stern-looking*) ceñudo
**grimace** ['grɪməs] o [grɪ'mes] *s* mueca, gesto ‖ *intr* hacer muecas, gestear
**grime** [graɪm] *s* mugre *f;* (*soot*) tizne *m & f*
**grim·y** ['graɪmi] *adj* (*comp* **-ier;** *super* **-iest**) mugriento; tiznado
**grin** [grɪn] *s* sonrisa bonachona; mueca (*mostrando los dientes*) ‖ *v* (*pret & pp* **grinned;** *ger* **grinning**) *intr* sonreírse bonachonamente; hacer una mueca (*mostrando los dientes*)
**grind** [graɪnd] *s* molienda; (*long hard work or study*) (coll) zurra; (*student*) (coll) empollón *m* ‖ *v* (*pret & pp* **ground** [graʊnd]) *tr* moler; (*to sharpen*) afilar, amolar; tallar (*lentes*); pulverizar; picar (*carne*); rodar (*las válvulas de un motor*); dar vueltas a (*un manubrio*) ‖ *intr* hacer molienda; molerse; rechinar; (coll) echar los bofes
**grinder** ['graɪndər] *s* (*to sharpen tools*) muela, esmoladera; (*to grind coffee, pepper, etc.*) molinillo; (*back tooth*) muela
**grind'stone'** *s* esmoladera, piedra de amolar; **to keep one's nose to the grindstone** trabajar con ahinco
**grin·go** ['grɪŋgo] *s* (*pl* **-gos**) (disparaging) gringo
**grip** [grɪp] *s* (*grasp*) asimiento; (*with hand*) apretón *m;* (*handle*) asidero; saco de mano; **to come to grips (with)** luchar cuerpo a cuerpo (con); arrostrarse (con) ‖ *v* (*pret & pp* **gripped;** *ger* **gripping**) *tr* asir, agarrar; tener asido; absorber (*la atención*); absorber la atención a (*una persona*)
**gripe** [graɪp] *s* (coll) queja; **gripes** retortijón *m* de tripas ‖ *intr* (coll) quejarse, refunfuñar
**grippe** [grɪp] *s* gripe *f*
**gripping** ['grɪpɪŋ] *adj* conmovedor, impresionante
**gris·ly** ['grɪzli] *adj* (*comp* **-lier;** *super* **-liest**) espantoso, espeluznante
**grist** [grɪst] *s* (*batch of grain for one grinding*) molienda; (*grain that has been ground*) harina; (coll) acopio, acervo; **to be grist to one's mill** (coll) serle a uno de mucho provecho
**gristle** ['grɪsəl] *s* cartílago, ternilla
**gris·tly** ['grɪsli] *adj* (*comp* **-tlier;** *super* **-tliest**) cartilaginoso, ternilloso
**grist'mill'** *s* molino harinero
**grit** [grɪt] *s* arena, guijo fino; (fig) ánimo, valentía; **grits** farro, sémola ‖ *v* (*pret & pp* **gritted;** *ger* **gritting**) *tr* hacer rechinar (*los dientes*); cerrar fuertemente (*los dientes*)
**grit·ty** ['grɪti] *adj* (*comp* **-tier;** *super* **-tiest**) arenoso; (fig) valiente, resuelto
**griz·zly** ['grɪzli] *adj* (*comp* **-zlier;** *super* **-zliest**) grisáceo; canoso ‖ *s* (*pl* **-zlies**) oso gris
**grizzly bear** *s* oso gris
**groan** [gron] *s* gemido, quejido ‖ *intr* gemir, quejarse; estar muy cargado, crujir por exceso de peso
**grocer** ['grosər] *s* abacero, tendero de ultramarinos
**grocer·y** ['grosəri] *s* (*pl* **-ies**) abacería, tienda de ultramarinos, colmado; **groceries** víveres *mpl,* ultramarinos
**grocery store** *s* abacería, tienda de ultramarinos, colmado
**grog** [grɑg] *s* grog *m*
**grog·gy** ['grɑgi] *adj* (*comp* **-gier;** *super* **-giest**) (coll) inseguro, vacilante;

(*shaky, e.g., from a blow*) (coll) atontado; (coll) borracho

**groin** [grɔɪn] *s* (anat) ingle *f;* (archit) arista de encuentro

**groom** [grum] *s* (*bridegroom*) novio; mozo de caballos || *tr* asear, acicalar; almohazar (*caballos*); enseñar (*a un político*) para presentarse como candidato

**grooms•man** [ˈgrumzmən] *s* (*pl* **-men** [mən]) padrino de boda

**groove** [gruv] *s* ranura; (*of a pulley*) garganta; (*of a phonograph record*) surco; (*mark left by a wheel*) rodada; (coll) rutina, hábito arraigado || *tr* ranurar, acanalar

**grope** [grop] *intr* andar a tientas; (*for words*) pujar; **to grope for** buscar a tientas, buscar tentando; **to grope through** palpar (*p.ej., la obscuridad*)

**gropingly** [ˈgropɪŋli] *adv* a tientas

**grosbeak** [ˈgros,bik] *s* pico duro

**gross** [gros] *adj* (*dense, thick*) denso, espeso; (*coarse; vulgar*) grosero; (*fat, burly*) grueso; (*with no deductions*) bruto || *s* conjunto, totalidad; (*twelve dozen*) gruesa; **in gross** en grueso || *tr* obtener un ingreso bruto de

**grossly** [ˈgrosli] *adv* aproximadamente

**gross national product** *s* renta nacional

**grotesque** [groˈtesk] *adj* (*ridiculous, extravagant*) grotesco; (f.a.) grutesco || *s* (f.a.) grutesco

**grot•to** [ˈgrɑto] *s* (*pl* **-toes** o **-tos**) gruta

**grouch** [graʊtʃ] *s* (coll) mal humor *m;* (*person*) (coll) cascarrabias *mf,* vinagre *m* || *intr* (coll) refunfuñar

**grouch•y** [ˈgraʊtʃi] *adj* (*comp* **-ier;** *super* **-iest**) (coll) gruñón, malhumorado

**ground** [graʊnd] *s* (*earth, soil, land*) tierra; (*piece of land*) terreno; (*basis, foundation*) causa, fundamento; motivo, razón *f;* (elec) tierra; (*body of automobile corresponding to ground*) (elec) masa; (elec) borne *m* de tierra; **ground for complaint** motivo de queja; **grounds** terreno; jardines *mpl;* causa, fundamento; (*of coffee*) posos; **on the ground of** con motivo de; **to break ground** empezar la excavación; **to fall to the ground** fracasar, abandonarse; **to gain ground** ganar terreno; **to give ground** ceder terreno; **to lose ground** perder terreno; **to stand one's ground** mantenerse firme; **to yield ground** ceder terreno || *tr* establecer, fundar; (elec) poner a tierra; **to be grounded** estar sin volar (*un avión*); **to be well grounded** ser muy versado || *intr* (naut) encallar, varar

**ground connection** *s* (rad) toma de tierra

**ground crew** *s* (aer) personal *m* de tierra

**grounder** [ˈgraʊndər] *s* (baseball) pelota rodada

**ground floor** *s* piso bajo

**ground glass** *s* vidrio deslustrado

**ground hog** *s* marmota de América

**ground lead** [lid] *s* (elec) conductor *m* a tierra

**groundless** [ˈgraʊndlɪs] *adj* infundado

**ground plan** *s* primer proyecto; (*of a building*) planta

**ground speed** *s* (aer) velocidad con respecto al suelo

**ground swell** *s* marejada de fondo

**ground troops** *spl* (mil) tropas terrestres

**ground wire** *s* (rad) alambre *m* de tierra; (aut) hilo de masa

**ground′work′** *s* infraestructura

**group** [grup] *adj* grupal; colectivo || *s* grupo || *tr* agrupar || *intr* agruparse

**grouse** [graʊs] *s* perdiz blanca, bonasa americana, gallo de bosque; (slang) refunfuño || *intr* (slang) refunfuñar

**grout** [graʊt] *s* lechada || *tr* enlechar

**grove** [grov] *s* arboleda, bosquecillo

**grov•el** [ˈgrʌvəl] o [ˈgrɑvəl] *v* (*pret & pp* **-eled** o **-elled;** *ger* **-eling** o **-elling**) *intr* arrastrarse servilmente; rebajarse servilmente; deleitarse en vilezas

**grow** [gro] *v* (*pret* **grew** [gru]; *pp* **grown** [gron]) *tr* cultivar (*plantas*); criar (*animales*); dejarse (*la barba*) || *intr* crecer; cultivarse; criarse; brotar, nacer; (*to become*) hacerse, ponerse, volverse; **to grow angry** enfadarse; **to grow old** envejecerse; **to grow out of** tener su origen en; perder (*p.ej., la costumbre*); **to grow together** adherirse el uno al otro; **to grow up** crecer, desarrollar

**growing child** [ˈgro·ɪŋ] *s* muchacho de creces

**growl** [graʊl] *s* gruñido; refunfuño || *intr* gruñir (*el perro*); refunfuñar

**grown′-up′** *adj* adulto; juicioso || *s* (*pl* **grown-ups**) adulto; **grown-ups** personas mayores

**growth** [groθ] *s* crecimiento; desarrollo; aumento; (*of trees, grass, etc.*) cobertura; (pathol) tumor *m*

**growth stock** *s* acción crecedera

**grub** [grʌb] *s* (*drudge*) esclavo del trabajo; (*larva*) gorgojo; (coll) comida, alimento || *v* (*pret & pp* **grubbed;** *ger* **grubbing**) *tr* arrancar (*tocones*); desmalezar (*un terreno*) || *intr* cavar; trabajar como esclavo

**grub•by** [ˈgrʌbi] *adj* (*comp* **-bier;** *super* **-biest**) gorgojoso; sucio, roñoso

**grudge** [grʌdʒ] *s* rencor *m,* inquina; **to have a grudge against** guardar rencor a, tener inquina a || *tr* dar de mala gana; envidiar

**grudgingly** [ˈgrʌdʒɪŋli] *adv* de mala gana

**gru•el** [ˈgru·əl] *s* avenate *m* || *v* (*pret & pp* **-eled** o **-elled;** *ger* **-eling** o **-elling**) *tr* agotar, castigar cruelmente

**gruesome** [ˈgrusəm] *adj* espantoso, horripilante

**gruff** [grʌf] *adj* áspero, brusco, rudo; (*voice, tone*) ronco

**grumble** [ˈgrʌmbəl] *s* gruñido, refunfuño; ruido sordo y prolongado || *intr* gruñir, refunfuñar; retumbar

**grump·y** [ˈgrʌmpi] *adj* (*comp* **-ier;** *super* **-iest**) gruñón, malhumorado
**grunt** [grʌnt] *s* gruñido || *intr* gruñir
**G-string** [ˈdʒi ˌstrɪŋ] *s* (*loincloth*) taparrabo; (*worn by women entertainers*) cubresexo
**gt.** *abbr* **great; gutta** (Lat) **drop**
**g.u.** *abbr* **genitourinary**
**Guadeloupe** [ˌgwɑdəˈlup] *s* Guadalupe *f*
**guarantee** [ˌgærənˈti] *s* garantía; (*guarantor*) garante *mf;* persona de quien otra sale fiadora || *tr* garantizar
**guarantor** [ˈgærən ˌtɔr] *s* garante *mf*
**guaran·ty** [ˈgærənti] *s* (*pl* **-ties**) garantía || *v* (*pret & pp* **-tied**) *tr* garantizar
**guard** [gɑrd] *s* (*act of guarding; part of handle of sword*) guarda; (*person who guards or takes care of something*) guarda *mf;* (*group of armed men; posture in fencing*) guardia; (*member of group of armed men*) guardia *m;* (*in front of trolley car*) salvavidas *m;* (sport) coraza; (rr) guardabarrera *mf;* (rr) guardafrenos *m;* **off guard** desprevenido; **on guard** alerta, prevenido; de centinela; **to mount guard** montar la guardia; **under guard** a buen recaudo || *tr* guardar || *intr* estar de centinela; **to guard against** guardarse de, precaverse contra o de
**guard'house'** *s* cuartel *m* de la guardia; prisión militar
**guardian** [ˈgɑrdɪ·ən] *adj* tutelar || *s* guardián *m;* (law) curador *m,* tutor *m*
**guardian angel** *s* ángel *m* custodio, ángel de la guarda
**guardianship** [ˈgɑrdɪ·ən ˌʃɪp] *s* amparo, protección; (law) curaduría, tutela
**guard'rail'** *s* baranda; (naut) barandilla; (rr) contracarril *m*
**guard'room'** *s* cuarto de guardia; cárcel *f* militar
**guards·man** [ˈgɑrdzmən] *s* (*pl* **-men** [mən]) guardia *m,* soldado de guardia
**Guatemalan** [ˌgwɑtɪˈmɑlən] *adj & s* guatemalteco
**guerrilla** [gəˈrɪlə] *s* guerrillero
**guerrilla warfare** *s* guerra de guerrillas
**guess** [gɛs] *s* conjetura, suposición; adivinación || *tr & intr* conjeturar, suponer; (*to judge correctly*) acertar, adivinar; (coll) creer, suponer; **I guess so** (coll) creo que sí, me parece que sí
**guess'work'** *s* conjetura; **by guesswork** por conjeturas
**guest** [gɛst] *s* convidado; (*lodger*) huésped *m;* (*of a boarding house*) pensionista *mf;* (*of a hotel*) cliente *mf;* (*caller*) visita
**guest book** *s* libro de oro
**guest room** *s* cuarto de reserva
**guffaw** [gəˈfɔ] *s* risotada, carcajada || *intr* risotear, reír a carcajadas
**Guiana** [gɪˈɑnə] o [gɪˈænə] *s* Guayana
**guidance** [ˈgaɪdəns] *s* guía, gobierno, dirección; **for your guidance** para su gobierno
**guide** [gaɪd] *s* (*person*) guía *mf;* (*book*) guía; (*guidance*) guía; dirección; poste *m* indicador; (mach) guía, guiadera; (mil) guía *m* || *tr* guiar
**guide'board'** *s* señal *f* de carretera
**guide'book'** *s* guía *m,* guía del viajero
**guided missile** [ˈgaɪdɪd] *s* proyectil dirigido o teleguiado
**guide dog** *s* perro-lazarillo
**guide'line'** *s* cuerda de guía; norma, pauta, directorio
**guide'post'** *s* poste *m* indicador
**guidon** [ˈgaɪdən] *s* (mil) guión *m;* (mil) portaguión *m*
**guild** [gɪld] *s* (*medieval association of craftsmen*) gremio; asociación benéfica
**guild'hall'** *s* casa consistorial
**guile** [gaɪl] *s* astucia, dolo, maña
**guileful** [ˈgaɪlfəl] *adj* astuto, doloso, mañoso
**guileless** [ˈgaɪllɪs] *adj* cándido, inocente, sencillo
**guillotine** [ˈgɪlə ˌtin] *s* guillotina || [ˌgɪləˈtin] *tr* guillotinar
**guilt** [gɪlt] *s* culpa
**guiltless** [ˈgɪltlɪs] *adj* inocente, libre de culpa
**guilt·y** [ˈgɪlti] *adj* (*comp* **-ier;** *super* **-iest**) culpable; (*charged with guilt*) culpado; (*found guilty*) reo
**guimpe** [gɪmp] o [gæmp] *s* canesú *m*
**guinea** [ˈgɪni] *s* (*monetary unit*) guinea; gallina de Guinea
**guinea fowl** *s* pintada, gallina de Guinea
**guinea hen** *s* pintada, gallina de Guinea (*hembra*)
**guinea pig** *s* conejillo de Indias
**guise** [gaɪz] *s* traje *m;* aspecto, semejanza; **under the guise of** so capa de
**guitar** [gɪˈtɑr] *s* guitarra
**guitarist** [gɪˈtɑrɪst] *s* guitarrista *mf*
**gulch** [gʌltʃ] *s* barranco, quebrada
**gulf** [gʌlf] *s* golfo
**Gulf of Mexico** *s* golfo de Méjico
**Gulf Stream** *s* Corriente *f* del Golfo
**gull** [gʌl] *s* gaviota; (coll) bobo || *tr* estafar, engañar
**gullet** [ˈgʌlɪt] *s* gaznate *m,* garguero; esófago
**gullible** [ˈgʌlɪbəl] *adj* crédulo; **to be too gullible** tener buenas tragaderas
**gul·ly** [ˈgʌli] *s* (*pl* **-lies**) barranca, arroyada; (*channel made by rain water*) badén *m*
**gulp** [gʌlp] *s* trago || *tr* — **to gulp down** engullir; reprimir (*p.ej., sollozos*) || *intr* respirar entrecortadamente
**gum** [gʌm] *s* goma; chanclo de goma; (*firm flesh around base of teeth*) encía; (*mucous on edge of eyelid*) legaña || *v* (*pret & pp* **gummed;** *ger* **gumming**) *tr* engomar || *intr* exudar goma
**gum arabic** *s* goma arábiga
**gum'boil'** *s* flemón *m*
**gum boot** *s* bota de agua

**gum'drop'** *s* frutilla
**gum·my** ['gʌmi] *adj* (*comp* **-mier**; *super* **-miest**) gomoso; (*eyelid*) legañoso
**gumption** ['gʌmpʃən] *s* (coll) ánimo, iniciativa, empuje *m*, fuerza; (coll) juicio, seso
**gum'shoe'** *s* chanclo de goma; (coll) detective *m* ‖ *v* (*pret & pp* **-shoed**; *ger* **-shoeing**) *intr* (slang) andar con zapatos de fieltro
**gun** [gʌn] *s* escopeta, fusil *m*; cañón *m*; (*for injections*) jeringa; (coll) revólver *m*; **to stick to one's guns** mantenerse en sus trece ‖ *v* (*pret & pp* **gunned**; *ger* **gunning**) *tr* hacer fuego sobre; (slang) acelerar rápidamente (*un motor, un avión*) ‖ *intr* andar a caza; disparar; **to gun for** ir en busca de; buscar para matar
**gun'boat'** *s* cañonero
**gun carriage** *s* cureña, encabalgamiento
**gun'cot'ton** *s* fulmicotón *m*, algodón *m* pólvora
**gun'fire'** *s* fuego (*de armas de fuego*); cañoneo
**gun·man** ['gʌnmən] *s* (*pl* **-men** [mən]) bandido armado, pistolero
**gun metal** *s* bronce *m* de cañón; metal pavonado
**gunnel** ['gʌnəl] *s* (naut) borda, regala
**gunner** ['gʌnər] *s* artillero; cazador *m*
**gunnery** ['gʌnəri] *s* artillería
**gunny sack** ['gʌni] *s* saco de yute
**gun'pow'der** *s* pólvora
**gun'run'ner** *s* contrabandista *m* de armas de fuego
**gun'run'ning** *s* contrabando de armas de fuego
**gun'shot'** *s* escopetazo, tiro de fusil; alcance *m* de un fusil; **within gunshot** a tiro de fusil
**gunshot wound** *s* escopetazo
**gun'smith'** *s* armero
**gun'stock'** *s* caja de fusil
**gunwale** ['gʌnəl] *s* (naut) borda, regala
**gup·py** ['gʌpi] *s* (*pl* **-pies**) lebistes *m*
**gurgle** ['gʌrgəl] *s* gorgoteo, gluglú *m*; (*of a child*) gorjeo ‖ *intr* gorgotear, hacer gluglú; gorjearse (*el niño*)
**gush** [gʌʃ] *s* borbollón *m*, chorro ‖ *intr* surgir, salir a borbollones; (coll) hacer extremos, ser extremoso
**gusher** ['gʌʃər] *s* pozo de chorro de petróleo; (coll) persona extremosa
**gushing** ['gʌʃɪŋ] *adj* surgente; (coll) extremoso ‖ *s* borbollón *m*, chorro; (coll) efusión, extremos
**gush·y** ['gʌʃi] *adj* (*comp* **-ier**; *super* **-iest**) (coll) efusivo, extremoso
**gusset** ['gʌsɪt] *s* escudete *m*
**gust** [gʌst] *s* (*of wind*) ráfaga; (*of rain*) aguacero; (*of smoke*) bocanada; (*of noise*) explosión; (*of anger or enthusiasm*) arrebato
**gusto** ['gʌsto] *s* deleite *m*, entusiasmo; **with gusto** con sumo placer
**gust·y** ['gʌsti] *adj* (*comp* **-ier**; *super* **-iest**) tempestuoso, borrascoso
**gut** [gʌt] *s* tripa; cuerda de tripa; **guts** tripas; (slang) agallas ‖ *v* (*pret & pp* **gutted**; *ger* **gutting**) *tr* destripar; destruir lo interior de
**gutta-percha** ['gʌtə'pʌrtʃə] *s* gutapercha
**gutter** ['gʌtər] *s* (*on side of road*) cuneta; (*in street*) arroyo; (*of roof*) canal *f*; (*ditch formed by rain water*) badén *m*; barrios bajos
**gut'ter·snipe'** *s* pilluelo, hijo de la miseria; gamberro
**guttural** ['gʌtərəl] *adj* gutural ‖ *s* sonido gutural
**guy** [gaɪ] *s* viento, cable *m* de retén; (coll) tipo, tío, sujeto ‖ *tr* (coll) burlarse de
**guy wire** *s* cable *m* de retén
**guzzle** ['gʌzəl] *tr & intr* beber con exceso
**guzzler** ['gʌzlər] *s* borrachín *m*
**gym** [dʒɪm] *s* (coll) gimnasio
**gymnasi·um** [dʒɪm'nezɪ·əm] *s* (*pl* **-ums** o **-a** [ə]) gimnasio
**gymnast** ['dʒɪmnæst] *s* gimnasta *mf*
**gymnastic** [dʒɪm'næstɪk] *adj* gimnástico ‖ **gymnastics** *spl* gimnasia, gimnástica
**gynecologist** [,gaɪnə'kɑlədʒɪst], [,dʒaɪnə'kɑlədʒɪst] o [,dʒɪnə'kɑlədʒɪst] *s* ginecólogo
**gynecology** [,gaɪnə'kɑlədʒi], [,dʒaɪnə'kɑlədʒi] o [,dʒɪnə'kɑlədʒi] *s* ginecología
**gyp** [dʒɪp] *s* (slang) estafa, timo; (*person*) (slang) estafador *m*, timador *m* ‖ *v* (*pret & pp* **gypped**; *ger* **gypping**) *tr* (slang) estafar, timar
**gypsum** ['dʒɪpsəm] *s* yeso, aljez *m*
**gyp·sy** ['dʒɪpsi] *adj* gitano ‖ *s* (*pl* **-sies**) gitano ‖ **Gypsy** *s* gitano (*idioma*)
**gypsyish** ['dʒɪpsɪ·ɪʃ] *adj* gitanesco
**gypsy moth** *s* lagarta
**gyrate** ['dʒaɪret] *intr* girar
**gyroscope** ['dʒaɪrə,skop] *s* giroscopio

## H

**H, h** [etʃ] octava letra del alfabeto inglés
**h.** *abbr* **harbor, high, hour, husband**
**haberdasher** ['hæbər,dæʃər] *s* camisero; (*dealer in notions*) mercero
**haberdasher·y** ['hæbər,dæʃəri] *s* (*pl* **-ies**) camisería, tienda de artículos para hombres; artículos para hombres
**habit** ['hæbɪt] *s* costumbre *f*, hábito; (*costume*) traje *m*; **to be in the habit of** acostumbrar

**habitat** ['hæbɪ,tæt] *s* habitación
**habitation** [,hæbɪ'teʃən] *s* habitación
**habit-forming** ['hæbɪt,fɔrmɪŋ] *adj* enviciador
**habitual** [hə'bɪtʃʊ·əl] *adj* habitual
**habitué** [hə,bɪtʃʊ'e] *s* habituado
**hack** [hæk] *s* (*cut*) corte *m;* (*notch*) mella; (*cough*) tos seca; coche *m* de alquiler; caballo de alquiler; caballo de silla; (*old nag*) rocín *m;* escritor *m* a sueldo || *tr* cortar, machetear
**hack•man** ['hækmən] *s* (*pl* **-men** [mən]) cochero de punto
**hackney** ['hækni] *s* caballo de silla; coche *m* de alquiler; esclavo del trabajo
**hackneyed** ['hæknid] *adj* trillado, gastado
**hack'saw'** *s* sierra de armero, sierra de cortar metales
**haddock** ['hædək] *s* eglefino
**haft** [hæft] o [hɑft] *s* mango, puño
**hag** [hæg] *s* (*ugly old woman*) tarasca; (*witch*) bruja
**haggard** ['hægərd] *adj* ojeroso, macilento, trasnochado
**haggle** ['hægəl] *intr* regatear
**Hague, The** [heg] La Haya
**hail** [hel] *s* (*frozen rain*) granizo; (*greeting*) saludo; **within hail** al alcance de la voz || *interj* ¡salud!, ¡salve! || *tr* saludar; dar vivas a, acoger con vivas; aclamar; granizar (*p.ej., golpes*) || *intr* granizar; **to hail from** venir de, ser oriundo de
**hail'-fel'low well met** *s* compañero muy afable y simpático
**Hail Mary** *s* avemaría
**hail'stone'** *s* piedra de granizo
**hail'storm'** *s* granizada
**hair** [hɛr] *s* pelo, cabellos; **to a hair** con la mayor exactitud; **to get in one's hair** (slang) enojarle a uno; **to have one's hair down** estar en melena; **to let one's hair down** (slang) hablar con mucha desenvoltura; **to make one's hair stand on end** ponerle a uno los pelos de punta; **to not turn a hair** no inmutarse; **to split hairs** pararse en quisquillas
**hair'breadth'** *s* (el) grueso de un pelo, casi nada; **to escape by a hairbreadth** escapar por un pelo
**hair'brush'** *s* cepillo de cabeza
**hair'cloth'** *s* tela de crin; (*worn as a penance*) cilicio
**hair curler** ['kʌrlər] *s* rizador *m,* tenacillas
**hair'cut'** *s* corte *m* de pelo; **to get a haircut** cortarse el pelo
**hair'do'** *s* (*pl* **-dos**) peinado, tocado
**hair'dress'er** *s* peinador *m,* peluquero
**hair dryer** *s* secador *m*
**hair dye** *s* tinte *m* para el pelo
**hairless** ['hɛrlɪs] *adj* pelón
**hair net** *s* redecilla
**hair'pin'** *s* horquilla
**hair-raising** ['hɛr,rezɪŋ] *adj* (coll) espeluznante, horripilante
**hair restorer** [rɪ'storər] *s* crecepelo
**hair ribbon** *s* cinta para el cabello
**hair set** *s* fijapeinados *m*
**hair shirt** *s* cilicio
**hairsplitting** ['hɛr,splɪtɪŋ] *adj* quisquilloso || *s* quisquillas
**hair'spring'** *s* espiral *f*
**hair'style'** *s* peinado
**hair tonic** *s* vigorizador *m* del cabello
**hair•y** ['hɛri] *adj* (*comp* **-ier;** *super* **-iest**) peludo, cabelludo
**hake** [hek] *s* merluza; (genus: *Urophycis*) fice *m*
**halberd** ['hælbərd] *s* alabarda
**halberdier** [,hælbər'dɪr] *s* alabardero
**halcyon days** ['hælsɪ·ən] *s* días tranquilos, época de paz
**hale** [hel] *adj* sano, robusto; **hale and hearty** sano y fuerte || *tr* llevar a la fuerza
**half** [hæf] o [hɑf] *adj* medio; **a half** o **half a** medio; **half the** la mitad de || *adv* medio, p.ej., **half asleep** medio dormido; a medio, p.ej., **half finished** a medio acabar; a medias, p.ej., **half owner** dueño a medias; **half past** y media, p.ej., **half past three** las tres y media; **half . . . half** medio . . . medio || *s* (*pl* **halves** [hævz] o [hɑvz]) mitad; (arith) medio; **in half** por la mitad; **to go halves** ir a medias
**half'-and-half'** *adj* mitad y mitad; indeterminado || *adv* a medias, en partes iguales || *s* mezcla de leche y crema; mezcla de dos cervezas inglesas
**half'back'** *s* (football) medio
**half-baked** ['hæf,bekt] o ['hɑf,bekt] *adj* a medio cocer; incompleto; poco juicioso, inexperto
**half binding** *s* (bb) encuadernación a la holandesa, media pasta
**half'-blood'** *s* mestizo; medio hermano
**half boot** *s* bota de media caña
**half'-bound'** *adj* (bb) a la holandesa
**half'-breed'** *s* mestizo
**half brother** *s* medio hermano
**half-cocked** ['hæf'kɑkt] o ['hɑf'kɑkt] *adv* (coll) con precipitación
**half fare** *s* medio billete
**half'-full'** *adj* mediado
**half-hearted** ['hæf,hɑrtɪd] o ['hɑf,hɑrtɪd] *adj* indiferente, frío
**half holiday** *s* mañana o tarde *f* de asueto
**half hose** *spl* calcetines *mpl*
**half'-hour'** *s* media hora; **on the half-hour** a la media en punto cada media hora
**half leather** *s* (bb) encuadernación a la holandesa, media pasta
**half'-length'** *adj* de medio cuerpo
**half'-mast'** *s* — **at half-mast** a media asta
**half moon** *s* media luna
**half mourning** *s* medio luto
**half note** *s* (mus) nota blanca
**half pay** *s* media paga; medio sueldo
**halfpen•ny** ['hepəni] o ['hepni] *s* (*pl* **-nies**) medio penique
**half pint** *s* media pinta; (*little runt*) (slang) gorgojo, mirmidón *m*
**half'-seas'** over *adj* — **to be half-seas over** (slang) estar entre dos velas, estar entre dos luces

**half shell** *s* (*either half of a bivalve*) concha; (*oysters*) **on the half shell** en su concha
**half sister** *s* media hermana
**half sole** *s* media suela
**half′-sole′** *tr* poner media suela a
**half′-staff′** *s* — **at half-staff** a media asta
**half-timbered** [ˈhæf,tɪmbərd] o [ˈhɑf-,tɪmbərd] *adj* entramado
**half title** *s* anteportada, falsa portada
**half′-tone′** *s* (phot & paint) mediatinta; (typ) similigrabado
**half′-track′** *s* media oruga, semitractor *m*
**half′truth′** *s* verdad a medias
**half′way′** *adj* a medio camino; incompleto, hecho a medias ‖ *adv* a medio camino; **halfway through** a la mitad de; **to meet halfway** partir el camino con; partir la diferencia con; hacer concesiones mutuas (*dos personas*)
**half-witted** [ˈhæf,wɪtɪd] o [ˈhɑf-,wɪtɪd] *adj* imbécil; necio, tonto
**halibut** [ˈhælɪbət] *s* halibut *m*
**halide** [ˈhælaɪd] o [ˈhelaɪd] *s* (chem) haluro
**halitosis** [,hælɪˈtosɪs] *s* halitosis *f*, aliento fétido
**hall** [hɔl] *s* (*passageway*) corredor *m;* (*entranceway*) vestíbulo, zaguán *m;* (*large meeting room*) sala, salón *m;* (*assembly room of a university*) paraninfo; (*building, e.g., of a university*) edificio
**halleluiah** o **hallelujah** [,hælɪˈlujə] *s* aleluya *m & f* ‖ *interj* ¡aleluya!
**hall′mark′** *s* marca de constraste; (*distinguishing feature*) (fig) sello
**hal•lo** [həˈlo] *s* (*pl* **-los**) grito ‖ *interj* ¡hola!; (*to incite dogs in hunting*) ¡sus! ‖ *intr* gritar
**hallow** [ˈhælo] *tr* santificar
**hallowed** [ˈhælod] *adj* santo, sagrado
**Halloween** o **Hallowe′en** [,hæloˈin] *s* víspera de Todos los Santos
**hallucination** [hə,lusɪˈneʃən] *s* alucinación
**hall′way′** *s* corredor *m;* vestíbulo, zaguán *m*
**ha•lo** [ˈhelo] *s* (*pl* **-los** o **-loes**) halo
**halogen** [ˈhælədʒən] *s* halógeno
**halt** [hɔlt] *adj* cojo, renco ‖ *s* alto, parada; **to call a halt** mandar hacer alto; **to come to a halt** pararse, detenerse, interrumpirse ‖ *tr* parar, detener ‖ *intr* hacer alto
**halter** [ˈhɔltər] *s* (*for leading or fastening horse*) cabestro, ronzal *m*, dogal *m;* (*noose*) dogal *m*, cuerda de ahorcar; muerte *f* en la horca
**halting** [ˈhɔltɪŋ] *adj* cojo, renco; vacilante
**halve** [hæv] o [hɑv] *tr* partir en dos, partir por la mitad
**halyard** [ˈhæljərd] *s* (naut) driza
**ham** [hæm] *s* (*part of leg behind knee*) corva; (*thigh and buttock*) pernil *m;* (*cured meat from hog's hind leg*) jamón *m;* (slang) comicastro; (slang) aficionado (*a la radio*); **hams** nalgas
**ham and eggs** *spl* huevos con jamón
**hamburger** [ˈhæm,bʌrgər] *s* hamburguesa
**hamlet** [ˈhæmlɪt] *s* aldehuela, caserío
**hammer** [ˈhæmər] *s* martillo; (*of piano*) macillo, martinete *m;* **to go under the hammer** venderse en pública subasta ‖ *tr* martillar; **to hammer out** formar a martillazos; sacar en limpio a fuerza de mucho esfuerzo ‖ *intr* martillar; **to hammer away** trabajar asiduamente
**hammock** [ˈhæmək] *s* hamaca
**hamper** [ˈhæmpər] *s* canasto, cesto grande con tapa ‖ *tr* estorbar, impedir
**hamster** [ˈhæmstər] *s* marmota de Alemania, rata del trigo
**ham•string** [ˈhæm,strɪŋ] *v* (*pret & pp* **-strung**) *tr* desjarretar; (fig) estropear, incapacitar
**hand** [hænd] *adj* (*done or operated with the hands*) manual ‖ *s* mano *f;* (*workman*) obrero, peón *m;* (*way of writing*) escritura, puño y letra; (*signature*) firma; (*clapping of hands*) salva de aplausos; (*of clock or watch*) mano *f*, manecilla; (*all the cards in one's hand*) juego; (*a round of play*) mano *f;* (*player*) jugador *m;* (*source, origin*) fuente *f;* (*skill*) destreza; **all hands** (naut) toda la tripulación; (coll) todos; **at first hand** de primera mano; directamente, de buena tinta; **at hand** disponible; **hand in glove** uña y carne; **hand in hand** asidos de la mano; juntos; **hands up!** ¡arriba las manos!; **hand to hand** cuerpo a cuerpo; **in hand** entre manos; **in his own hand** de su propio puño; **on hand** entre manos; disponible; **on hands and knees** (*crawling*) a gatas; (*beseeching*) de rodillas; **on the one hand** por una parte; **on the other hand** por otra parte; **out of hand** luego, en seguida; desmandado; **to be at hand** obrar en mi (nuestro) poder (*una carta*); **to change hands** mudar de manos; **to clap hands** batir palmas; **to eat out of one's hand** aceptar dócilmente la autoridad de uno; **to fall into the hands of** caer en manos de; **to have a hand in** tomar parte en; **to have one's hands full** estar ocupadísimo; **to hold hands** tomarse de las manos; **to hold up one's hands** (*as a sign of surrender*) alzar las manos; **to join hands** darse las manos; casarse; **to keep one's hands off** no tocar, no meterse en; **to lend a hand** echar una mano; **to live from hand to mouth** vivir al día, vivir de la mano a la boca; **to not lift a hand** no levantar paja del suelo; **to play into the hands of** hacer el caldo gordo a; **to raise one's hand** (*in taking an oath*) alzar el dedo; **to shake hands** estrecharse la mano; **to show one's hand** descubrir su juego; **to take in hand** hacerse cargo de; tratar, estudiar (*una cuestión*); **to throw up one's hands** darse por vencido; **to try one's hand** probar la mano; **to turn one's hand**

**to** dedicarse a, ocuparse en; **to wash one's hands of** lavarse las manos de; **under my hand** con mi firma, bajo mi firma, de mi puño y letra; **under the hand and seal of** firmado y sellado por || *tr* dar, entregar; **to hand in** entregar; **to hand on** transmitir; **to hand out** repartir

**hand'bag'** *s* saco de noche; bolso de señora

**hand baggage** *s* equipaje *m* de mano

**hand'ball'** *s* pelota; juego de pelota a mano

**hand'bill'** *s* hoja volante

**hand'book'** *s* manual *m;* guía de turistas; registro para apuestas

**hand'breadth'** *s* palmo menor

**hand'car'** *s* (rr) carrito de mano

**hand'cart'** *s* carretilla de mano

**hand control** *s* mando a mano

**hand'cuff'** *s* manilla; **handcuffs** manillas, esposas || *tr* poner esposas a

**handful** ['hænd,fʊl] *s* puñado, manojo

**hand glass** *s* espejo de mano; lupa

**hand grenade** *s* granada de mano

**handi•cap** ['hændɪ,kæp] *s* desventaja, obstáculo; (sport) handicap *m* || *v* (*pret & pp* **-capped;** *ger* **-capping**) *tr* poner trabas a; (sport) handicapar

**handicraft** ['hændɪ,kræft] o ['hændɪ,krɑft] *s* destreza manual; arte mecánica

**handiwork** ['hændɪ,wʌrk] *s* hechura, trabajo; obra manual

**handkerchief** ['hæŋkərtʃɪf] o ['hæŋkər,tʃif] *s* pañuelo

**handle** ['hændəl] *s* (*of a basket, crock, pitcher*) asa; (*of a shovel, rake, etc.*) mango; (*of an umbrella, sword*) puño; (*of a door, drawer*) tirador *m;* (*of a hand organ*) manubrio; (*of a water pump*) guimbalete *m;* (*opportunity, pretext*) asidero; **to fly off the handle** (slang) salirse de sus casillas || *tr* manosear, manipular; dirigir, manejar, gobernar; comerciar en || *intr* manejarse

**handle bar** *s* manillar *m*, guía

**handler** ['hændlər] *s* (sport) entrenador *m*

**hand'made'** *adj* hecho a mano

**hand'maid'** o **hand'maid'en** *s* criada, sirvienta

**hand'-me-down'** *s* (coll) prenda de vestir de segunda mano

**hand organ** *s* organillo

**hand'out'** *s* comida que se da de limosna; comunicado de prensa

**hand-picked** ['hænd,pɪkt] *adj* escogido a mano; escogido escrupulosamente; escogido con motivos ocultos

**hand'rail'** *s* barandilla, pasamano

**hand'saw'** *s* serrucho, sierra de mano

**hand'set'** *s* microteléfono

**hand'shake'** *s* apretón *m* de manos

**handsome** ['hænsəm] *adj* hermoso, elegante, guapo; considerable

**hand'spring'** *s* voltereta sobre las manos

**hand'-to-hand'** *adj* cuerpo a cuerpo

**hand'-to-mouth'** *adj* inseguro, precario; impróvido

**hand'work'** *s* trabajo a mano

**hand'-wres'tle** *intr* pulsear

**hand'-writ'ing** *s* escritura; (*writing by hand which characterizes a particular person*) letra

**hand•y** ['hændi] *adj* (*comp* **-ier;** *super* **-iest**) (*easy to handle*) manuable; (*within easy reach*) próximo, a la mano; (*skillful*) diestro, hábil; **to come in handy** venir a pelo

**handy man** *s* dije *m*, factótum *m*

**hang** [hæŋ] *s* (*of a dress, curtain, etc.*) caída; (*skill; insight*) tino; **I don't care a hang** (coll) no me importa un bledo; **to get the hang of it** (coll) coger el tino || *v* (*pret & pp* **hung** [hʌŋ]) *tr* colgar; tender (*la ropa mojada*); pegar (*el papel pintado*); fijar (*un cartel, un letrero*); enquiciar (*una puerta, una ventana*); bajar (*la cabeza*); **hang it!** (coll) ¡caramba!; **to hang up** colgar (*el sombrero*); impedir los progresos de || *intr* colgar, pender; estar agarrado; vacilar; **to hang around** esperar sin hacer nada; haraganear; rondar; **to hang on** colgar de; depender de; estar pendiente de (*las palabras de una persona*); estar sin acabar de morir; agarrarse; **to hang out** asomarse; (slang) recogerse, alojarse; **to hang over** (*to threaten*) cernerse sobre; **to hang together** mantenerse unidos; **to hang up** (telp) colgar || *v* (*pret* **hanged** o **hung**) *tr* ahorcar || *intr* ahorcarse

**hangar** ['hæŋər] o ['hæŋgɑr] *s* cobertizo; (aer) hangar *m*

**hang'bird'** *s* pájaro de nido colgante; (*Baltimore oriole*) cacique veranero

**hanger** ['hæŋər] *s* colgador *m*, suspensión; (*hook*) colgadero

**hang'er•on'** *s* (*pl* **hangers-on**) secuaz *mf;* parásito; (*sponger*) pegote *m*

**hanging** ['hæŋɪŋ] *adj* colgante, pendiente || *s* ahorcadura, muerte *f* en la horca; **hangings** colgaduras

**hang•man** ['hæŋmən] *s* (*pl* **-men** [mən]) verdugo

**hang'nail'** *s* padrastro, respigón *m*

**hang'out'** *s* guarida, querencia; (*place to loaf and gossip*) mentidero

**hang'o'ver** *s* (slang) resaca

**hank** [hæŋk] *s* madeja

**hanker** ['hæŋkər] *intr* sentir anhelo

**Hannibal** ['hænɪbəl] *s* Aníbal *m*

**haphazard** [,hæp'hæzərd] *adj* casual, fortuito, impensado || *adv* al acaso, a la ventura

**hapless** ['hæplɪs] *adj* desgraciado, desventurado

**happen** ['hæpən] *intr* acontecer, suceder; (*to turn out*) resultar; (*to be the case by chance*) dar la casualidad; **to happen in** entrar por casualidad; **to happen on** encontrarse con; **to happen to** hacerse de; **to happen to** + *inf* por casualidad + *ind*, p.ej., **I happened to see her at the theater** por casualidad la ví en el teatro

**happening** ['hæpənɪŋ] *s* acontecimiento, suceso

**happily** ['hæpɪli] *adv* felizmente

**happiness** ['hæpɪnɪs] *s* felicidad

**hap·py** ['hæpi] *adj* (*comp* **-pier;** *super* **-piest**) feliz; (*pleased*) contento; **to be happy to** alegrarse de, tener gusto en
**hap'py-go-luck'y** *adj* irresponsable, impróvido ‖ *adv* a la buenaventura
**happy medium** *s* justo medio
**Happy New Year** *interj* ¡Feliz Año Nuevo!
**harangue** [hə'ræŋ] *s* arenga ‖ *tr & intr* arengar
**harass** ['hærəs] o [hə'ræs] *tr* acosar, hostigar; molestar, vejar
**harbinger** ['hɑrbɪndʒər] *s* precursor *m;* anuncio, presagio ‖ *tr* anunciar, presagiar
**harbor** ['hɑrbər] *adj* portuario ‖ *s* puerto ‖ *tr* albergar; alcahuetar, encubrir (*delincuentes u objetos robados*); guardar (*sentimientos de odio*)
**harbor master** *s* capitán *m* de puerto
**hard** [hɑrd] *adj* duro; (*difficult*) difícil; (*water*) crudo, duro; (*solder*) fuerte; (*work*) asiduo; (*drinker*) empedernido; espiritoso, fuertemente alcohólico; **to be hard on** (*to treat severely*) ser muy duro con; (*to wear out fast*) gastar, echar a perder ‖ *adv* duro; fuerte; mucho; **hard upon** a raíz de; **to drink hard** beber de firme; **to rain hard** llover de firme
**hard and fast** *adj* inflexible, riguroso ‖ *adv* firmemente
**hard-bitten** ['hɑrd'bɪtən] *adj* terco, tenaz, inflexible
**hard-boiled** ['hɑrd'bɔɪld] *adj* (*egg*) duro, muy cocido; (coll) duro, inflexible
**hard candy** *s* caramelos
**hard cash** *s* dinero contante y sonante
**hard cider** *s* sidra muy fermentada
**hard coal** *s* antracita
**hard-earned** ['hɑrd'ʌrnd] *adj* ganado a pulso
**harden** ['hɑrdən] *tr* endurecer ‖ *intr* endurecerse
**hardening** ['hɑrdənɪŋ] *s* endurecimiento
**hard facts** *spl* realidades
**hard-fought** ['hɑrd'fɔt] *adj* reñido
**hard-headed** ['hɑrd'hɛdɪd] *adj* astuto, sagaz; terco, tozudo
**hard-hearted** ['hɑrd'hɑrtɪd] *adj* duro de corazón
**hardihood** ['hɑrdɪ,hʊd] *s* audacia, resolución; descaro, insolencia
**hardiness** ['hɑrdɪnɪs] *s* fuerza, robustez; audacia, resolución
**hard labor** *s* trabajos forzados
**hard luck** *s* mala suerte
**hard'-luck' story** *s* (coll) cuento de penas; **to tell a hard-luck story** (coll) contar lástimas
**hardly** ['hɑrdli] *adv* apenas; casi no; (*with great difficulty*) a duras penas; (*grievously*) penosamente; **hardly ever** casi nunca
**hardness** ['hɑrdnɪs] *s* dureza; (*of water*) crudeza
**hard of hearing** *adj* duro de oído, teniente
**hard-pressed** ['hɑrd'prɛst] *adj* acosado; (*for money*) apurado, alcanzado
**hard rubber** *s* vulcanita
**hard sauce** *s* mantequilla azucarada
**hard'-shell' clam** *s* almeja redonda
**hard-shell crab** *s* cangrejo de cáscara dura
**hardship** ['hɑrdʃɪp] *s* penalidad, infortunio, apuro
**hard'tack'** *s* galleta, sequete *m*
**hard times** *spl* período de miseria, apuros
**hard to please** *adj* difícil de contentar
**hard up** *adj* (coll) apurado, alcanzado
**hard'ware'** *s* ferretería, quincalla; (*metal trimmings*) herraje *m*
**hardware·man** ['hɑrd,wɛrmən] *s* (*pl* **-men** [mən]) ferretero, quincallero
**hardware store** *s* ferretería, quincallería
**hard-won** ['hɑrd,wʌn] *adj* ganado a pulso
**hard'wood'** *s* madera dura; árbol *m* de madera dura
**hardwood floor** *s* entarimado
**har·dy** ['hɑrdi] *adj* (*comp* **-dier;** *super* **-diest**) fuerte, robusto; audaz, resuelto; (*rash*) temerario; (hort) resistente
**hare** [hɛr] *s* liebre *f*
**harebrained** ['hɛr,brend] *adj* atolondrado
**hare'lip'** *s* labio leporino
**harelipped** ['hɛr,lɪpt] *adj* labiohendido
**harem** ['hɛrəm] *s* harén *m*
**hark** [hɑrk] *intr* escuchar; **to hark back** volver (*la jauría*) sobre la pista; **to hark back to** volver a, recordar
**harken** ['hɑrkən] *intr* escuchar, atender
**harlequin** ['hɑrləkwɪn] *s* arlequín *m*
**harlot** ['hɑrlət] *s* meretriz *f*
**harm** [hɑrm] *s* daño, perjuicio ‖ *tr* dañar, perjudicar, hacer daño a
**harmful** ['hɑrmfəl] *adj* dañoso, perjudicial; (*e.g., pests*) dañino
**harmless** ['hɑrmlɪs] *adj* innocuo, inofensivo
**harmonic** [hɑr'mɑnɪk] *adj & s* armónico
**harmonica** [hɑr'mɑnɪkə] *s* armónica
**harmonious** [hɑr'monɪ·əs] *adj* armonioso
**harmonize** ['hɑrmə,naɪz] *tr & intr* armonizar
**harmo·ny** ['hɑrməni] *s* (*pl* **-nies**) armonía
**harness** ['hɑrnɪs] *s* arreos, guarniciones; **to get back in the harness** volver a la rutina; **to die in the harness** morir al pie del cañón ‖ *tr* enjaezar, poner las guarniciones a; enganchar; captar (*las aguas de un río*)
**harness maker** *s* guarnicionero
**harness race** *s* carrera con sulky
**harp** [hɑrp] *s* arpa ‖ *intr* — **to harp on** repetir porfiadamente
**harpist** ['hɑrpɪst] *s* arpista *mf*
**harpoon** [hɑr'pun] *s* arpón *m* ‖ *tr & intr* arponear
**harpsichord** ['hɑrpsɪ,kɔrd] *s* clave *m*

**har·py** ['hɑrpi] *s* (*pl* **-pies**) arpía
**harrow** ['hæro] *s* (agr) grada ‖ *tr* (agr) gradar; atormentar
**harrowing** ['hæro·ɪŋ] *adj* horripilante, espantoso
**har·ry** ['hæri] *v* (*pret & pp* **-ried**) *tr* acosar, hostilizar, hostigar; atormentar, molestar
**harsh** [hɑrʃ] *adj* (*to touch, taste, eyes, hearing*) áspero; duro, cruel
**harshness** ['hɑrʃnɪs] *s* aspereza; dureza, crueldad
**hart** [hɑrt] *s* ciervo
**harum-scarum** ['herəm'skerəm] *adj* atolondrado ‖ *adv* atolondradamente ‖ *s* mataperros *m*
**harvest** ['hɑrvɪst] *s* cosecha ‖ *tr & intr* cosechar
**harvester** ['hɑrvɪstər] *s* cosechero; (*helper*) agostero; (*machine*) segadora
**harvest home** *s* entrada de los frutos; fiesta de segadores; canción de segadores
**harvest moon** *s* luna de la cosecha
**has-been** ['hæz,bɪn] *s* (coll) antigualla
**hash** [hæʃ] *s* picadillo ‖ *tr* picar
**hash house** *s* bodegón *m*
**hashish** ['hæʃiʃ] *s* hachich *m*
**hasp** [hæsp] o [hɑsp] *s* portacandado; (*of book covers*) broche *m*
**hassle** ['hæsəl] *s* (coll) riña, disputa
**hassock** ['hæsək] *s* cojín *m* (*para los pies o las rodillas*)
**haste** [hest] *s* prisa; **in haste** de prisa; **to make haste** darse prisa
**hasten** ['hesən] *tr* apresurar; apretar (*el paso*) ‖ *intr* apresurarse
**hast·y** ['hesti] *adj* (*comp* **-ier**; *super* **-iest**) apresurado; inconsiderado, impulsivo, colérico
**hat** [hæt] *s* sombrero; **to keep under one's hat** (coll) callar, no divulgar; **to throw one's hat in the ring** (coll) decidirse a bajar a la arena
**hat'band'** *s* cintillo; (*worn to show mourning*) gasa
**hat block** *s* horma, conformador *m*
**hat'box'** *s* sombrerera
**hatch** [hætʃ] *s* (*brood*) cría, nidada; (*trap door*) escotillón *m;* (*lower half of door*) media puerta; (*opening in ship's deck*) escotilla; (*lid for opening in ship's deck*) cuartel *m* ‖ *tr* empollar (*huevos*); sombrear (*un dibujo*); maquinar, tramar ‖ *intr* empollarse; salir del huevo
**hat'-check' girl** *s* guardarropa
**hatchet** ['hætʃɪt] *s* destral *m,* hacha pequeña; **to bury the hatchet** envainar la espada
**hatch'way'** *s* (*trap door*) escotillón *m;* (*opening in ship's deck*) escotilla
**hate** [het] *s* odio, aborrecimiento ‖ *tr & intr* odiar, aborrecer, detestar
**hateful** ['hetfəl] *adj* odioso, aborrecible
**hat'pin'** *s* aguja de sombrero, pasador *m*
**hat'rack'** *s* percha
**hatred** ['hetrɪd] *s* odio, aborrecimiento
**hatter** ['hætər] *s* sombrerero

**haughtiness** ['hɔtɪnɪs] *s* altanería, altivez *f*
**haugh·ty** ['hɔti] *adj* (*comp* **-tier;** *super* **-tiest**) altanero, altivo
**haul** [hɔl] *s* (*pull, tug*) tirón *m;* (*amount caught*) redada; (*distance transported*) trayecto, recorrido; (*roundup, e.g., of thieves*) redada ‖ *tr* acarrear, transportar; (naut) halar
**haunch** [hɔntʃ] o [hɑntʃ] *s* (*hip*) cadera; (*hind quarter of an animal*) anca; (*leg of animal used for food*) pierna
**haunt** [hɔnt] o [hɑnt] *s* guarida, nidal *m,* querencia ‖ *tr* andar por, vagar por; frecuentar; inquietar, molestar; perseguir (*las memorias a una persona*)
**haunted house** *s* casa de fantasmas
**haute couture** [ot ku'tyr] *s* alta moda
**Havana** [hə'vænə] *s* La Habana
**have** [hæv] *v* (*pret & pp* **had** [hæd]) *tr* tener; (*to get, to take*) tomar; **to have and to hold** (úsase sólo en el infinitivo) para ser poseído en propiedad; **to have got** (coll) tener, poseer; **to have got to** + *inf* (coll) tener que + *inf;* **to have it in for** (coll) tener tirria a; **to have it out with** (coll) habérselas con, emprenderla con; **to have on** llevar puesto; **to have** (*something*) **to do with** tener que ver con; **to have** + *inf* hacer, mandar + *inf,* p.ej., **I had him go out that door** le hice salir por esa puerta; **to have** + *pp* hacer, mandar + *inf,* p.ej., **I had my watch repaired** hice componer mi reloj ‖ *intr* — **to have at** atacar, embestir; **to have to** + *inf* tener que + *inf;* **to have to do with** (*to be concerned with*) tratar de; (*to have connections with*) tener relaciones con ‖ *v aux* haber, p.ej., **he has studied his lesson** ha estudiado su lección
**havelock** ['hævlɑk] *s* cogotera
**haven** ['hevən] *s* puerto; abrigo, asilo, buen puerto
**have-not** ['hæv,nɑt] *s* — **the haves and the have-nots** (coll) los ricos y los desposeídos
**haversack** ['hævər,sæk] *s* barjuleta; (*of soldier*) mochila
**havoc** ['hævək] *s* estrago, estragos; **to play havoc with** hacer grandes estragos en
**haw** [hɔ] *s* (*of hawthorn*) baya, simiente *f;* (*in speech*) vacilación ‖ *interj* ¡a la izquierda! ‖ *tr & intr* volver a la izquierda
**haw'-haw'** *s* carcajada
**hawk** [hɔk] *s* halcón *m,* gavilán *m,* cernícalo; (*mortarboard*) esparavel *m;* (*sharper*) (coll) fullero ‖ *tr* pregonar; **to hawk up** arrojar tosiendo ‖ *intr* carraspear, gargajear
**hawker** ['hɔkər] *s* buhonero
**hawksbill turtle** ['hɔks,bɪl] *s* carey *m*
**hawse** [hɔz] *s* (naut) muz *m;* (*hole*) (naut) escobén *m;* (naut) longitud de cadenas
**hawse'hole'** *s* (naut) escobén *m*

**hawser** ['hɔzər] *s* (naut) guindaleza
**haw'thorn'** *s* espino, oxiacanta
**hay** [he] *s* heno; **to hit the hay** (slang) acostarse; **to make hay while the sun shines** hacer su agosto
**hay fever** *s* fiebre *f* del heno
**hay'field'** *s* henar *m*
**hay'fork'** *s* horca; (*machine*) elevador *m* de heno
**hay'loft'** *s* henil *m*, henal *m*
**hay'mak'er** *s* (box) golpe *m* que pone fuera de combate
**haymow** ['he,maʊ] *s* henil *m;* acopio de heno
**hay'rack'** *s* pesebre *m*
**hayrick** ['he,rɪk] *s* almiar *m*
**hay ride** *s* paseo de placer en carro de heno
**hay'seed'** *s* simiente *f* de heno; (coll) patán *m*, campesino
**hay'stack'** *s* almiar *m*
**hay'wire'** *adj* (slang) descompuesto; (slang) destornillado, loco || *s* alambre *m* para embalar el heno
**hazard** ['hæzərd] *s* peligro, riesgo; (*chance*) acaso, azar *m;* (golf) obstáculo; **at all hazards** por grande que sea el riesgo || *tr* arriesgar; aventurar (*una opinión*)
**hazardous** ['hæzərdəs] *adj* peligroso, arriesgado
**haze** [hez] *s* calina, bruma; (fig) confusión, vaguedad || *tr* dar novatada a
**hazel** ['hezəl] *adj* castaño claro || *s* avellano
**ha'zel•nut'** *s* avellana
**hazing** ['hezɪŋ] *s* novatada
**ha•zy** ['hezi] *adj* (*comp* **-zier;** *super* **-ziest)** calinoso, brumoso; confuso, vago
**H-bomb** ['etʃ,bɑm] *s* bomba de hidrógeno
**H.C.** *abbr* **House of Commons**
**hd.** *abbr* **head**
**hdqrs.** *abbr* **headquarters**
**H.E.** *abbr* **His Eminence, His Excellency**
**he** [hi] *pron pers* (*pl* **they**) él || *s* (*pl* **hes**) macho, varón *m*
**head** [hɛd] *s* cabeza; (*of a bed*) cabecera; (*caption*) encabezamiento; (*of a boil*) centro; (*on a glass of beer*) espuma; (*of a drum*) parche *m;* (*of a cane*) puño; (*of a barrel, cylinder, etc.*) fondo, tapa; (*of cylinder of automobile engine*) culata; crisis *f*, punto decisivo; **at the head of** al frente de; **from head to foot** de pies a cabeza; **head over heels** en un salto mortal; hasta los tuétanos; precipitadamente; **heads** (*of a coin*) cara; **heads or tails** a cara o cruz; **over one's head** fuera del alcance de uno; (*going to a higher authority*) por encima de uno; **to be out of one's head** (coll) delirar; **to come into one's head** pasarle a uno por la cabeza; **to go to one's head** subírsele a uno a la cabeza; **to keep one's head** no perder la cabeza; **to keep one's head above water** no dejarse vencer; **to put heads together** consultarse entre sí; **to not make head or tail of** no ver pies ni cabeza a || *tr* acaudillar, dirigir, mandar; estar a la cabeza de (*p.ej., la clase*); venir primero en (*una lista*) || *intr* — **to head towards** dirigirse hacia
**head'ache'** *s* dolor *m* de cabeza
**head'band'** *s* cinta para la cabeza; (*of a book*) cabezada
**head'board'** *s* cabecera de cama
**head'cheese'** *s* queso de cerdo
**head'dress'** *s* (*style of hair*) tocado; prenda para la cabeza
**header** ['hɛdər] *s* — **to take a header** (coll) caerse de cabeza
**head'first'** *adv* de cabeza; precipitadamente
**head'gear'** *s* sombrero; (*for protection*) casco
**head'hunt'er** *s* cazador *m* de cabezas
**heading** ['hɛdɪŋ] *s* encabezamiento; (*of a letter*) membrete *m;* (*of a chapter of a book*) cabecera
**headland** ['hɛdlənd] *s* promontorio
**headless** ['hɛdlɪs] *adj* sin cabeza; sin jefe; estúpido
**head'light'** *s* (aut) faro; (naut) farol *m* de tope; (rr) farol *m*
**head'line'** *s* (*of newspaper*) cabecera; (*of a page of a book*) titulillo, título de página || *tr* poner cabecera a; (slang) destacar, dar cartel a (*un actor*)
**head'lin'er** *s* (slang) atracción principal
**head'long'** *adj* de cabeza; precipitado || *adv* de cabeza; precipitadamente
**head•man** ['hɛd,mæn] *s* (*pl* **-men** [,mɛn]) caudillo, jefe *m*
**head'mas'ter** *s* director *m* de un colegio
**head'most'** *adj* delantero, primero
**head office** *s* oficina central
**head of hair** *s* cabellera
**head'-on'** *adj & adv* de frente; **head-on collision** colisión de frente
**head'phone'** *s* auricular *m* de casco, receptor *m* de cabeza
**head'piece'** *s* (*any covering for head*) casco, yelmo, morrión *m;* (*brains, judgment*) cabeza, juicio; cabecera de cama; (*headset*) auricular *m* de casco, receptor *m* de cabeza; (typ) cabecera, viñeta
**head'quar'ters** *s* centro de dirección; (*of police*) jefatura; (mil) cuartel *m* general
**head'rest'** *s* apoyo para la cabeza
**head'set'** *s* auricular *m* de casco, receptor *m* de cabeza
**head'ship'** *s* jefatura, dirección
**head'stone'** *s* (*cornerstone*) piedra angular; (*on a grave*) lápida sepulcral
**head'stream'** *s* afluente *m* principal
**head'strong'** *adj* cabezudo, terco
**head'wait'er** *s* jefe *m* de camareros, encargado de comedor
**head'wa'ters** *spl* cabecera
**head'way'** *s* avance *m*, progreso; espacio libre; **to make headway** avanzar, progresar
**head'wear'** *s* prendas de cabeza
**head wind** *s* viento de frente, viento por la proa

**head'work'** *s* trabajo intelectual
**head·y** ['hedi] *adj* (*comp* **-ier;** *super* **-iest**) excitante, emocionante; impetuoso, violento; (*intoxicating*) cabezudo; (*clever*) sesudo
**heal** [hil] *tr* curar, sanar; cicatrizar; remediar (*un daño*) || *intr* curar, sanar; cicatrizarse; remediarse
**healer** ['hilər] *s* curador *m*, sanador *m*
**health** [helθ] *s* salud *f;* **to be in good health** estar bien de salud; **to be in poor health** estar mal de salud; **to drink to the health of** beber a la salud de; **to radiate health** verter salud; **to your health!** ¡a su salud!
**healthful** ['helθfəl] *adj* saludable; sano
**health·y** ['helθi] *adj* (*comp* **-ier;** *super* **-iest**) sano; saludable
**heap** [hip] *s* montón *m* || *tr* amontonar, apilar; (*to supply with, e.g., favors*) colmar; (*to bestow in great quantity*) dar generosamente || *intr* amontonarse, apilarse
**hear** [hɪr] *v* (*pret & pp* **heard** [hʌrd]) *tr* oír; **to hear it said** oírlo decir || *intr* oír; **hear! hear!** ¡bravo!; **to hear about** oír hablar de; **to hear from** tener noticias de; **to hear of** oír hablar de; **to hear tell of** oír hablar de; **to hear that** oír decir que
**hearer** ['hɪrər] *s* oyente *mf*
**hearing** ['hɪrɪŋ] *s* (*sense*) oído; (*act*) oída; audiencia; **in the hearing of** en presencia de; **within hearing** al alcance del oído
**hearing aid** *s* aparato auditivo
**hear'say'** *s* rumor *m;* **by hearsay de o** por oídas
**hearse** [hʌrs] *s* coche *m* fúnebre, carroza fúnebre
**heart** [hɑrt] *s* corazón *m;* (*e.g., of lettuce*) cogollo; **after one's heart** enteramente del gusto de uno; **by heart** de memoria; **heart and soul** de todo corazón; **to break the heart of** partir el corazón de; **to die of a broken heart** morir de pena; **to eat one's heart out** sufrir en silencio; **to get to the heart of** llegar al fondo de; **to have one's heart in one's work** trabajar con entusiasmo; **to have one's heart in the right place** tener buenas intenciones; **to lose heart** descorazonarse; **to open one's heart to** descubrirse con; **to take heart** cobrar aliento; **to take to heart** tomar a pecho; **to wear one's heart on one's sleeve** llevar el corazón en la mano; **with all one's heart** con toda el alma de uno; **with one's heart in one's mouth** con el credo en la boca
**heart'ache'** *s* angustia, congoja
**heart attack** *s* ataque *m* de corazón, ataque cardíaco
**heart'beat'** *s* latido del corazón
**heart'break'** *s* angustia, dolor *m* abrumador
**heart'break'er** *s* ladrón *m* de corazones
**heartbroken** ['hɑrt,brokən] *adj* transido de dolor, muerto de pena
**heart'burn'** *s* acedía, rescoldera; (*jealousy*) celos
**heart disease** *s* enfermedad del corazón
**hearten** ['hɑrtən] *tr* alentar, animar
**heart failure** *s* debilidad coronaria; (*death*) paro del corazón; (*faintness*) desfallecimiento, desmayo
**heartfelt** ['hɑrt,felt] *adj* cordial, sentido, sincero
**hearth** [hɑrθ] *s* hogar *m*
**hearth'stone'** *s* solera del hogar; (*home*) hogar *m*
**heartily** ['hɑrtɪli] *adv* cordialmente; con buen apetito; de buena gana; bien, mucho
**heartless** ['hɑrtlɪs] *adj* cruel, inhumano
**heart-rending** ['hɑrt,rendɪŋ] *adj* angustioso, que parte el corazón
**heart'seed'** *s* farolillo
**heart'sick'** *adj* afligido, desconsolado
**heart'strings'** *spl* fibras del corazón, entretelas
**heart'-to-heart'** *adj* franco, sincero
**heart trouble** *s* — **to have heart trouble** enfermar del corazón
**heart'wood'** *s* madera de corazón
**heart·y** ['hɑrti] *adj* (*comp* **-ier;** *super* **-iest**) cordial, sincero; sano, fuerte; (*meal*) abundante; (*laugh*) bueno; (*eater*) grande
**heat** [hit] *adj* térmico || *s* calor *m;* (*warming of a room, house, etc.*) calefacción; (*rut of animals*) celo; (*in horse racing*) carrera de prueba; (fig) ardor *m*, ímpetu *m;* **in heat** en celo || *tr* calentar; calefaccionar (*p.ej., una casa*); (fig) acalorar, excitar || *intr* calentarse; (fig) acalorarse, excitarse
**heated** ['hitɪd] *adj* acalorado
**heater** ['hitər] *s* calentador *m;* (*for central heating*) calorífero; (electron) calefactor *m*
**heater man** *s* calefactor *m*
**heath** [hiθ] *s* (*shrub*) brezo; (*tract of land*) brezal *m*
**hea·then** ['hiðən] *adj* gentil, pagano; irreligioso || *s* (*pl* **-then** o **-thens**) gentil *mf*, pagano
**heathendom** ['hiðəndəm] *s* gentilidad
**heather** ['heðər] *s* brezo
**heating** ['hitɪŋ] *adj* calentador || *s* calefacción
**heat lightning** *s* fucilazo, relámpago de calor
**heat shield** *s* blindaje térmico, escudo térmico
**heat'stroke'** *s* insolación
**heat wave** *s* (phys) onda calorífica; (coll) ola de calor
**heave** [hiv] *s* esfuerzo para levantar; esfuerzo para levantarse; **heaves** (vet) huélfago || *v* (*pret & pp* **heaved** o **hov** [hov]) *tr* alzar, levantar; arrojar, lanzar; exhalar (*un suspiro*) || *intr* levantarse y bajar alternativamente; palpitar (*el pecho*); elevarse; hacer esfuerzos por vomitar
**heaven** ['hevən] *s* cielo; **for heaven's sake!** o **good heavens!** ¡válgame Dios!; **heavens** (*firmament*) cielo ||

**Heaven** *s* cielo (*mansión de los bienaventurados*)
**heavenly** ['hɛvənli] *adj* (*body*) celeste; (*life, home*) celestial; (fig) celestial
**heavenly body** *s* astro, cuerpo celeste
**heav·y** ['hɛvi] *adj* (*comp* **-ier;** *super* **-iest**) (*of great weight*) pesado; (*liquid*) espeso, denso; (*cloth, paper, sea, line*) grueso; (*traffic*) denso; (*crop, harvest*) abundante, copioso; (*expense*) fuerte; (*rain*) recio; (*features*) basto; (*eyes*) agravado; (*gunfire*) fragoroso; (*heart*) abatido, triste; (*drinker*) grande; (*stock market*) postrado; (*clothing*) de mucho abrigo || *adv* pesadamente; **to hang heavy** pasar (*el tiempo*) con gran lentitud
**heav'y·du'ty** *adj* extrafuerte
**heavy-hearted** ['hɛvɪ'hartɪd] *adj* afligido, acongojado
**heav'y·set'** *adj* costilludo, espaldudo
**heav'y·weight'** *s* (box) peso pesado
**Hebrew** ['hibru] *adj* & *s* hebreo
**hecatomb** ['hɛkə,tom] o ['hɛkə,tum] *s* hecatombe *f*
**heckle** ['hɛkəl] *tr* interrumpir (*a un orador*) con preguntas impertinentes
**hectic** ['hɛktɪk] *adj* (coll) agitado, turbulento
**hedge** [hɛdʒ] *s* cercado, vallado; (*of bushes*) seto vivo; apuesta compensatoria; (*in stock market*) operación compensatoria || *tr* cercar con vallado; cercar con seto vivo; **to hedge in** encerrar, rodear || *intr* no querer comprometerse; hacer apuestas compensatorias; hacer operaciones compensatorias
**hedge'hog'** *s* erizo; (*porcupine*) puerco espín *m*
**hedge'hop'** *v* (*pret* & *pp* **-hopped;** *ger* **-hopping**) *intr* (aer) volar rasando el suelo
**hedgehopping** ['hɛdʒ,hapɪŋ] *s* (aer) vuelo rasante
**hedge'row'** *s* cercado de arbustos, seto vivo
**heed** [hid] *s* atención, cuidado; **to take heed** ir con cuidado || *tr* atender a, hacer caso de || *intr* atender, hacer caso
**heedless** ['hidlɪs] *adj* desatento, descuidado
**heehaw** ['hi,hɔ] *s* (*of donkey*) rebuzno; risotada || *intr* rebuznar; reír groseramente
**heel** [hil] *s* (*of foot*) calcañar *m*, talón *m;* (*of stocking or shoe*) talón *m;* (*raised part of shoe below heel*) tacón *m;* (slang) sinvergüenza *mf;* **down at the heel** desaliñado, mal vestido; **to cool one's heels** (coll) hacer antesala; **to kick up one's heels** (slang) mostrarse alegre; **to show a clean pair of heels** o **to take to one's heels** poner pies en polvorosa
**heeler** ['hilər] *s* (slang) muñidor *m*
**heft·y** ['hɛfti] *adj* (*comp* **-ier;** *super* **-iest**) (*heavy*) pesado; (*strong*) fuerte, fornido
**hegemo·ny** [hɪ'dʒɛməni] o ['hɛdʒɪ,moni] *s* (*pl* **-nies**) hegemonía
**hegira** [hɪ'dʒaɪrə] o ['hɛdʒɪrə] *s* fuga, huída
**heifer** ['hɛfər] *s* novilla, vaquilla
**height** [haɪt] *s* altura; (*e.g., of folly*) colmo
**heighten** ['haɪtən] *tr* hacer más alto; (*to increase the amount of*) aumentar; (*to set off, bring out*) realzar || *intr* aumentarse
**heinous** ['henəs] *adj* atroz, nefando
**heir** [ɛr] *s* heredero
**heir apparent** *s* (*pl* **heirs apparent**) heredero forzoso
**heirdom** ['ɛrdəm] *s* herencia
**heiress** ['ɛrɪs] *s* heredera
**heirloom** ['ɛr,lum] *s* joya de familia, reliquia de familia
**helicopter** ['hɛlɪ,kaptər] *s* helicóptero
**heliotrope** ['hilɪ·ə,trop] *s* heliotropo
**heliport** ['hɛlɪ,port] *s* helipuerto
**helium** ['hilɪ·əm] *s* helio
**helix** ['hilɪks] *s* (*pl* **helixes** o **helices** ['hɛlɪ,siz]) hélice *f*
**hell** [hɛl] *s* infierno
**hell-bent** ['hɛl'bɛnt] *adj* (slang) muy resuelto; **hell-bent on** (slang) empeñado en
**hell'cat'** *s* (*bad-tempered woman*) arpía, mujer perversa; (*witch*) bruja
**hellebore** ['hɛlɪ,bor] *s* eléboro
**Hellene** ['hɛlin] *s* heleno
**Hellenic** [hɛ'lɛnɪk] o [hɛ'linɪk] *adj* helénico
**hell'fire'** *s* fuego del infierno
**hellish** ['hɛlɪʃ] *adj* infernal
**hel·lo** [hɛ'lo] *s* saludo || *interj* ¡qué tal!; (*on telephone*) ¡diga!
**hello girl** *s* (coll) chica telefonista
**helm** [hɛlm] *s* barra del timón; rueda del timón; (fig) timón *m* || *tr* dirigir, gobernar
**helmet** ['hɛlmɪt] *s* casco; (*of ancient armor*) yelmo
**helms·man** ['hɛlmzmən] *s* (*pl* **-men** [mən]) timonel *m*
**help** [hɛlp] *s* ayuda, socorro; (*of food*) ración; (*relief*) remedio, p.ej., **there's no help for it** no hay remedio; criados; empleados; obreros; **to come to the help of** acudir en socorro de || *interj* ¡socorro! || *tr* ayudar, socorrer; aliviar, mitigar; (*to wait on*) servir; **it can't be helped** no hay remedio; **so help me God!** ¡así Dios me salve!; **to help down** ayudar a bajar; **to help a person with his coat** ayudarle a una persona a ponerse el abrigo; **to help oneself** valerse por sí mismo; servirse; **to help up** ayudar a subir; ayudar a levantarse; **to not be able to help** + *ger* no poder menos de + *inf*, p.ej., **he can't help laughing** no puede menos de reír || *intr* ayudar
**helper** ['hɛlpər] *s* ayudante *mf;* (*in a drug store, barbershop, etc.*) mancebo
**helpful** ['hɛlpfəl] *adj* útil, provechoso; servicial
**helping** ['hɛlpɪŋ] *s* ración (*de alimento*)
**helpless** ['hɛlplɪs] *adj* (*weak*) débil; (*powerless*) impotente; (*penniless*)

desvalido; (*confused*) perplejo; (*situation*) irremediable
**help'meet'** *s* compañero; (*wife*) compañera
**helter-skelter** ['heltər'skeltər] *adj, adv & s* cochite hervite *m*
**hem** [hɛm] *s* tos fingida; (*of a garment*) bastilla, dobladillo || *interj* ¡ejem! || *v* (*pret & pp* **hemmed**; *ger* **hemming**) *tr* bastillar, dobladillar; **to hem in** encerrar, rodear || *intr* destoserse; vacilar; **to hem and haw** vacilar al hablar; ser evasivo
**hemisphere** ['hɛmɪ,sfɪr] *s* hemisferio
**hemistich** ['hɛmɪ,stɪk] *s* hemistiquio
**hem'line'** *s* ruedo de la falda, borde *m* de la falda
**hem'lock'** *s* (*Tsuga canadensis*) abeto del Canadá; (*herb and poison*) cicuta
**hemoglobin** [,hɛmə'globɪn] o [,himə'globɪn] *s* hemoglobina
**hemophilia** [,hɛmə'fɪlɪ·ə] o [,himə'fɪlɪ·ə] *s* hemofilia
**hemorrhage** ['hɛmərɪdʒ] *s* hemorragia
**hemorrhoids** ['hɛmə,rɔɪdz] *spl* hemorroides *fpl*
**hemostat** ['hɛmə,stæt] o ['himə,stæt] *s* hemóstato
**hemp** [hɛmp] *s* cáñamo
**hemstitch** ['hɛm,stɪtʃ] *s* vainica || *tr* hacer vainica en || *intr* hacer vainica
**hen** [hɛn] *s* gallina
**hence** [hɛns] *adv* de aquí; desde ahora; por lo tanto, por consiguiente; de aquí a, p.ej., **three weeks hence** de aquí a tres semanas
**hence'forth'** *adv* de aquí en adelante
**hench·man** ['hɛntʃmən] *s* (*pl* **-men** [mən]) secuaz *m*, servidor *m*; (*political schemer*) muñidor *m*
**hen'coop'** *s* gallinero
**hen'house'** *s* gallinero
**henna** ['hɛnə] *s* alcana, alheña; (*dye*) henna *f* || *tr* alheñarse (*el pelo*)
**hen'peck'** *tr* dominar (*la mujer al marido*)
**henpecked husband** *s* calzonazos *m*, gurrumino
**hep** [hɛp] *adj* (slang) enterado; **to be hep to** (slang) estar al corriente de
**her** [hʌr] *adj poss* su; el . . . de ella || *pron pers* la; ella; **to her** le; a ella
**herald** ['hɛrəld] *s* heraldo; anunciador *m* || *tr* anunciar; ser precursor de
**heraldic** [hɛ'rældɪk] *adj* heráldico
**herald·ry** ['hɛrəldri] *s* (*pl* **-ries**) (*office or duty of herald*) heraldía; (*science of armorial bearings*) blasón *m*, heráldica; (*heraldic device; coat of arms*) blasón; pompa heráldica
**herb** [ʌrb] o [hʌrb] *s* hierba; hierba aromática; hierba medicinal
**herbaceous** [hʌr'beʃəs] *adj* herbáceo
**herbage** ['ʌrbɪdʒ] o ['hʌrbɪdʒ] *s* herbaje *m*
**herbal** ['ʌrbəl] o ['hʌrbəl] *adj & s* herbario
**herbalist** ['hʌrbəlɪst] o ['ʌrbəlɪst] *s* herbolario
**herbari·um** [hʌr'bɛrɪ·əm] *s* (*pl* **-ums** o **-a** [ə]) herbario
**herb doctor** *s* herbolario
**herculean** [hʌr'kjulɪ·ən] o [,hʌrkju'li·ən] *adj* (*hard to perform*) penoso, laborioso; (*strong, big*) hercúleo
**herd** [hʌrd] *s* manada, rebaño, hato; (*of people*) chusma, multitud || *tr* reunir en manada; reunir || *intr* reunirse en manada; reunirse, ir juntos
**herds·man** ['hʌrdzmən] *s* (*pl* **-men** [mən]) manadero; (*of sheep*) pastor *m;* (*of cattle*) vaquero
**here** [hɪr] *adj* presente || *adv* aquí; **here and there** acá y allá; **here is** o **here are** aquí tiene Vd.; **that's neither here nor there** eso no viene al caso || *s* — **the here and the hereafter** esta vida y la futura || *interj* ¡presente!
**hereabouts** ['hɪrə,baʊts] *adv* por aquí, cerca de aquí
**here·af'ter** *adv* de aquí en adelante; en lo sucesivo; en la vida futura || **the hereafter** la otra vida, el más allá
**here·by'** *adv* por esto; por la presente
**hereditary** [hɪ'rɛdɪ,tɛri] *adj* hereditario
**heredi·ty** [hɪ'rɛdɪti] *s* (*pl* **-ties**) herencia
**here·in'** *adv* aquí dentro; en este asunto
**here·of'** *adv* de esto
**here·on'** *adv* en esto, sobre esto
**here·sy** ['hɛrəsi] *s* (*pl* **-sies**) herejía
**heretic** ['hɛrətɪk] *adj* herético || *s* hereje *mf*
**heretical** [hɪ'rɛtɪkəl] *adj* herético
**heretofore** [,hɪrtu'for] *adv* antes, hasta ahora
**here'u·pon'** *adv* en esto, sobre esto; en seguida
**here·with'** *adv* adjunto, con la presente; de este modo
**heritage** ['hɛrɪtɪdʒ] *s* herencia
**hermetic(al)** [hʌr'mɛtɪk(əl)] *adj* hermético
**hermit** ['hʌrmɪt] *s* eremita *m*, ermitaño
**hermitage** ['hʌrmɪtɪdʒ] *s* ermita
**herni·a** ['hʌrnɪ·ə] *s* (*pl* **-as** o **-ae** [,i]) hernia
**he·ro** ['hɪro] *s* (*pl* **-roes**) héroe *m*
**heroic** [hɪ'ro·ɪk] *adj* heroico || **heroics** *spl* verso heroico; lenguaje rimbombante
**heroin** ['hɛro·ɪn] *s* heroína (*polvo cristalino*)
**heroine** ['hɛro·ɪn] *s* heroína (*mujer*)
**heroism** ['hɛro,ɪzəm] *s* heroísmo
**heron** ['hɛrən] *s* garza; (*Ardea cinerea*) airón *m*, garza real
**herring** ['hɛrɪŋ] *s* arenque *m*
**her'ring·bone'** *s* (*in fabrics*) espina de pescado; (*in hardwood floors*) espinapez *m*, punto de Hungría
**hers** [hʌrz] *pron poss* el suyo, el de ella; suyo
**herself** [hʌr'sɛlf] *pron pers* ella misma; sí, sí misma; se, p.ej., **she enjoyed herself** se divirtió; **with herself** consigo
**hesitan·cy** ['hɛzɪtənsi] *s* (*pl* **-cies**) vacilación
**hesitant** ['hɛzɪtənt] *adj* vacilante

**hesitate** ['hɛzɪ,tet] *intr* vacilar, titubear; (*to stutter*) titubear
**hesitation** [,hɛzɪ'teʃən] *s* vacilación
**heterodox** ['hɛtərə,dɑks] *adj* heterodoxo
**heterodyne** ['hɛtərə,daɪn] *adj* heterodino || *tr* heterodinar
**heterogenei·ty** [,hɛtərədʒɪ'ni·ɪti] *s* (*pl* **-ties**) heterogeneidad
**heterogeneous** [,hɛtərə'dʒinɪ·əs] *adj* heterogéneo
**hew** [hju] *v* (*pret* **hewed**; *pp* **hewed** o **hewn**) *tr* cortar, tajar; (*with an ax*) hachear; labrar (*madera*); picar (*piedra*); **to hew down** derribar a hachazos || *intr* — **to hew close to the line** (coll) hilar delgado
**hex** [hɛks] *s* (coll) bruja; (coll) hechizo || *tr* (coll) embrujar
**hexameter** [hɛks'æmɪtər] *s* hexámetro
**hey** [he] *interj* ¡oye!, ¡oiga!
**hey'day'** *s* época de mayor prosperidad
**hf.** *abbr* **half**
**H.H.** *abbr* **His Highness, Her Highness; His Holiness**
**hia·tus** [haɪ'etəs] *s* (*pl* **-tuses** o **-tus**) (*gap*) abertura, laguna; (*in a text; in verse*) hiato
**hibernate** ['haɪbər,net] *intr* invernar; estar inactivo
**hibiscus** [hɪ'bɪskəs] o [haɪ'bɪskəs] *s* hibisco
**hiccough** o **hiccup** ['hɪkəp] *s* hipo || *intr* hipar
**hick** [hɪk] *adj* & *s* (coll) campesino, palurdo
**hicko·ry** ['hɪkəri] *s* (*pl* **-ries**) nuez encarcelada, nuez dura (*árbol*)
**hickory nut** *s* nuez encarcelada, nuez dura (*fruto*)
**hidden** ['hɪdən] *adj* escondido, oculto; obscuro
**hide** [haɪd] *s* cuero, piel *f*; **hides** corambre *f*; **neither hide nor hair** ni un vestigio; **to tan someone's hide** (coll) zurrarle a uno la badana || *v* (*pret* **hid** [hɪd]; *pp* **hid** o **hidden** ['hɪdən]) *tr* esconder, ocultar || *intr* esconderse, ocultarse; **to hide out** (coll) recatarse
**hide'-and-seek'** *s* escondite *m*; **to play hide-and-seek** jugar al escondite
**hide'bound'** *adj* fanático, obstinado, dogmático
**hideous** ['hɪdɪ·əs] *adj* (*very ugly*) feote; (*heinous*) atroz, nefando; (*distressingly large*) brutal, enorme
**hide'-out'** *s* (coll) guarida, refugio, escondrijo
**hiding** ['haɪdɪŋ] *s* ocultación; (*place of concealment*) escondite *m*, escondrijo; **in hiding** escondido, oculto; (*in ambush*) emboscado
**hiding place** *s* escondite *m*, escondrijo
**hie** [haɪ] *v* (*pret* & *pp* **hied**; *ger* **hieing** o **hying**) *tr* — **hie thee home** apresúrate a volver a casa || *intr* apresurarse, ir volando
**hierar·chy** ['haɪ·ə,rɑrki] *s* (*pl* **-chies**) jerarquía
**hieroglyphic** [,haɪ·ərə'glɪfɪk] *adj* & *s* jeroglífico
**hi·fi** ['haɪ'faɪ] *adj* (coll) de alta fidelidad || *s* (coll) alta fidelidad
**hi-fi fan** *s* (coll) aficionado a la alta fidelidad
**higgledy-piggledy** ['hɪgəldi'pɪgəldi] *adj* confuso, revuelto || *adv* confusamente, revueltamente
**high** [haɪ] *adj* alto; (*river*) crecido; (*sound*) agudo; (*wind*) fuerte; (coll) borracho; (culin) manido; **high and dry** abandonado, desamparado; **high and mighty** (coll) muy arrogante || *adv* en sumo grado; a gran precio; **to aim high** poner el tiro muy alto; **to come high** venderse caro || *s* (aut) marcha directa; **on high** en el cielo
**high altar** *s* altar *m* mayor
**high'ball'** *s* highball *m*
**high blood pressure** *s* hipertensión arterial
**high'born'** *adj* linajudo, de ilustre cuna
**high'boy'** *s* cómoda alta con patas altas
**high'brow'** *adj* & *s* (slang) erudito
**high chair** *s* silla alta
**high command** *s* alto mando
**high cost of living** *s* carestía de la vida
**higher education** *s* enseñanza superior
**higher-up** [,haɪ·ər'ʌp] *s* (coll) superior jerárquico
**high explosive** *s* explosivo rompedor
**highfalutin** [,haɪfə'lutən] *adj* (coll) pomposo, presuntuoso
**high fidelity** *s* alta fidelidad
**high'-fre'quency** *adj* de alta frecuencia
**high gear** *s* marcha directa, toma directa
**high'-grade'** *adj* de calidad superior
**high-handed** ['haɪ'hændɪd] *adj* arbitrario
**high hat** *s* sombrero de copa
**high'-hat'** *adj* (coll) copetudo, esnob; **to be high-hat** (coll) tener mucho copete || **high'-hat'** *v* (*pret* & *pp* **-hatted**; *ger* **-hatting**) *tr* (coll) desairar
**high-heeled shoe** ['haɪ,hild] *s* zapato de tacón alto
**high horse** *s* ademán *m* arrogante
**high'jack'** *tr* var de **hijack**
**high jinks** [dʒɪŋks] *s* (slang) jarana, payasada
**high jump** *s* salto de altura
**highland** ['haɪlənd] *s* región montañosa; **highlands** montañas, tierras altas
**high life** *s* alta sociedad, gran mundo
**high'light'** *s* elemento sobresaliente || *tr* destacar
**highly** ['haɪli] *adv* altamente; en sumo grado; a gran precio; con aplauso general; **to speak highly of** decir mil bienes de
**High Mass** *s* misa cantada, misa mayor
**high-minded** ['haɪ'maɪndɪd] *adj* noble, magnánimo
**highness** ['haɪnɪs] *s* altura || **Highness** *s* Alteza
**high noon** *s* pleno mediodía
**high-pitched** ['haɪ'pɪtʃt] *adj* agudo; tenso, impresionable
**high-powered** ['haɪ'paʊ·ərd] *adj* de alta potencia
**high'-pres'sure** *adj* de alta presión;

(fig) emprendedor, enérgico || *tr* (coll) apremiar
**high-priced** [ˈhaɪˈpraɪst] *adj* de precio elevado
**high priest** *s* sumo sacerdote
**high rise** *s* edificio de muchos pisos
**high'road'** *s* camino real
**high school** *s* escuela de segunda enseñanza
**high sea** *s* mar gruesa; **high seas** alta mar
**high society** *s* alta sociedad, gran mundo
**high'-speed'** *adj* de alta velocidad
**high-spirited** [ˈhaɪˈspɪrɪtɪd] *adj* animoso; vivaz; (*horse*) fogoso
**high spirits** *spl* alegría, buen humor *m*, animación
**high-strung** [ˈhaɪˈstrʌŋ] *adj* tenso, impresionable
**high'-test' fuel** *s* supercarburante *m*
**high tide** *s* pleamar *f*, marea alta; (fig) punto culminante
**high time** *s* hora, p.ej., **it is high time for you to go** ya es hora de que Vd. se marche; (slang) jarana, parranda
**high treason** *s* alta traición
**high water** *s* aguas altas; pleamar *f*, marea alta
**high'way'** *s* carretera
**highway·man** [ˈhaɪˌwemən] *s* (*pl* **-men** [mən]) salteador *m* de caminos
**hijack** [ˈhaɪˌdʒæk] *tr* (coll) robar (*a un contrabandista de licores*); (coll) robar (*el licor a un contrabandista*)
**hike** [haɪk] *s* caminata, marcha; (*increase, rise*) aumento || *tr* elevar de un tirón; aumentar || *intr* dar una caminata
**hiker** [ˈhaɪkər] *s* caminador *m*, aficionado a las caminatas
**hilarious** [hɪˈlɛrɪ·əs] o [haɪˈlɛrɪ·əs] *adj* jubiloso, regocijado
**hill** [hɪl] *s* colina, collado || *tr* aporcar (*las hortalizas*)
**hillbil·ly** [ˈhɪlˌbɪli] *s* (*pl* **-lies**) (coll) rústico montañés (*del sur de los EE.UU.*)
**hillock** [ˈhɪlək] *s* altozano, montecillo
**hill'side'** *s* ladera
**hill'top'** *s* cumbre *f*, cima
**hill·y** [ˈhɪli] *adj* (*comp* **-ier**; *super* **-iest**) colinoso; (*steep*) empinado
**hilt** [hɪlt] *s* empuñadura, puño; **up to the hilt** completamente
**him** [hɪm] *pron pers* le, lo; **él**; **to him** le; a él
**himself** [hɪmˈself] *pron pers* él mismo; sí, sí mismo; se, p.ej., **he enjoyed himself** se divirtió; **with himself** consigo
**hind** [haɪnd] *adj* posterior, trasero || *s* cierva
**hinder** [ˈhɪndər] *tr* estorbar, impedir
**hindmost** [ˈhaɪndˌmost] *adj* postrero, último
**Hindoo** [ˈhɪndu] *adj* & *s* hindú *m*
**hind'quar'ter** *s* cuarto trasero
**hindrance** [ˈhɪndrəns] *s* estorbo, impedimento, obstáculo
**hind'sight'** *s* (*of a firearm*) mira posterior; percepción tardía, sabiduría tardía
**Hindu** [ˈhɪndu] *adj* & *s* hindú *m*
**hinge** [hɪndʒ] *s* (*of a door*) charnela, gozne *m*, bisagra; (*of a mollusk*) charnela; (bb) cartivana; punto capital || *tr* engoznar || *intr* — **to hinge on** depender de
**hin·ny** [ˈhɪni] *s* (*pl* **-nies**) burdégano, mohino
**hint** [hɪnt] *s* indirecta, insinuación; **to take the hint** darse por aludido || *tr* & *intr* insinuar; indicar; **to hint at** aludir indirectamente a
**hinterland** [ˈhɪntərˌlænd] *s* región interior
**hip** [hɪp] *s* cadera; (*of a roof*) caballete *m*, lima
**hip'bone'** *s* cía, hueso de la cadera
**hipped** [hɪpt] *adj* (*livestock*) renco; (*roof*) a cuatro aguas; **hipped on** (coll) obsesionado por
**hippety-hop** [ˈhɪpɪtɪˈhɑp] *adv* (coll) a coxcojita
**hip·po** [ˈhɪpo] *s* (*pl* **-pos**) (coll) hipopótamo
**hippodrome** [ˈhɪpəˌdrom] *s* hipódromo
**hippopota·mus** [ˌhɪpəˈpɑtəməs] *s* (*pl* **-muses** o **-mi** [ˌmaɪ]) hipopótamo
**hip roof** *s* tejado a cuatro aguas
**hire** [haɪr] *s* alquiler *m*; precio; salario; **for hire** de alquiler || *tr* alquilar (*p.ej., un coche*); ajustar (*p.ej., a un criado*) || *intr* — **to hire out** ajustarse
**hired girl** *s* criada
**hired man** *s* (coll) mozo de campo
**hireling** [ˈhaɪrlɪŋ] *adj* & *s* alquiladizo
**his** [hɪz] *adj poss* su; el . . . de él || *pron poss* el suyo, el de él; suyo
**Hispanic** [hɪsˈpænɪk] *adj* hispánico
**Hispaniola** [ˌhɪspənˈjolə] *s* Santo Domingo
**hispanist** [ˈhɪspənɪst] *s* hispanista *mf*
**hiss** [hɪs] *s* siseo, silbido || *tr* sisear, silbar (*p.ej., una escena, a un actor por malo*) || *intr* sisear, silbar
**hist.** *abbr* **historian, history**
**histology** [hɪsˈtɑlədʒi] *s* histología
**historian** [hɪsˈtorɪ·ən] *s* historiador *m*
**historic(al)** [hɪsˈtɑrɪk(əl)] o [hɪsˈtɔrɪk(əl)] *adj* histórico
**histo·ry** [ˈhɪstəri] *s* (*pl* **-ries**) historia
**histrionic** [ˌhɪstrɪˈɑnɪk] *adj* histriónico; teatral || **histrionics** *s* actitud teatral, modales *mpl* teatrales
**hit** [hɪt] *s* golpe *m*; (*of a bullet*) impacto; (*blow that hits its mark*) tiro certero; (*sarcastic remark*) censura acerba; (baseball) batazo; (coll) éxito; **to make a hit** (coll) dar golpe; **to make a hit with** caer en la gracia de (*una persona*) || *v* (*pret* & *pp* **hit**; *ger* **hitting**) *tr* golpear, pegar; dar con, dar contra, chocar con; dar en (*p.ej., el blanco*); censurar acerbamente; (*to run over in a car*) atropellar; afectar mucho (*un acontecimiento a una persona*) || *intr* chocar; **to hit against** dar contra; **to hit on** dar con (*lo que se busca*)
**hit'-and-run'** *adj* que atropella y se da a la huída
**hitch** [hɪtʃ] *s* (*jerk*) tirón *m*; dificultad; obstáculo; **without a hitch** a

pedir de boca, sin tropiezo || *tr* (*to tie*) atar, sujetar; enganchar (*un caballo*); uncir (*bueyes*); (slang) casar
**hitch'hike'** *intr* (coll) hacer autostop, viajar en autostop
**hitch'hik'er** *s* autostopista *mf*
**hitching post** *s* poste *m* para atar a las cabalgaduras
**hither** ['hɪðər] *adv* acá, hacia acá; **hither and thither** acá y allá
**hith'er•to'** *adv* hasta ahora, hasta aquí
**hit'-or-miss'** *adj* descuidado, casual
**hit parade** *s* (rad) canciones que gozan de más popularidad en la actualidad
**hit record** *s* (coll) disco de mucho éxito
**hit'-run'** *adj* que atropella y se da a la huída
**hive** [haɪv] *s* (*box for bees*) colmena; (*swarm*) enjambre *m;* **hives** urticaria || *tr* encorchar (*abejas*)
**H.M.** *abbr* **Her Majesty, His Majesty**
**H.M.S.** *abbr* **Her Majesty's Ship, His Majesty's Ship**
**hoard** [hord] *s* (*of money, provisions, etc.*) cúmulo; tesoro escondido || *tr* acumular secretamente; atesorar (*dinero*) || *intr* guardar víveres; atesorar dinero
**hoarding** ['hordɪŋ] *s* acumulación secreta; atesoramiento
**hoar'frost'** *s* helada blanca, escarcha
**hoarse** [hors] *adj* ronco
**hoarseness** ['horsnɪs] *s* ronquedad; (*from a cold*) ronquera
**hoar•y** ['hori] *adj* (*comp* **-ier;** *super* **-iest**) cano, canoso; (*old*) vetusto
**hoax** [hoks] *s* pajarota, mistificación || *tr* mistificar
**hob** [hɑb] *s* repisa interior del hogar; **to play hob with** (coll) trastornar
**hobble** ['hɑbəl] *s* (*limp*) cojera; (*rope used to tie legs of animal*) manea, traba || *tr* dejar cojo; manear, trabar; dificultar || *intr* cojear; tambalear
**hobble skirt** *s* falda de medio paso
**hob•by** ['hɑbi] *s* (*pl* **-bies**) comidilla, afición favorita, trabajo preferido; **to ride a hobby** entregarse demasiado al tema favorito
**hob'by•horse'** *s* (*stick with horse's head*) caballito; (*rocking horse*) caballo mecedor
**hob'gob'lin** *s* duende *m,* trasgo; (*bogy*) bu *m,* coco
**hob'nail'** *s* tachuela || *tr* clavetear con tachuelas; (fig) atropellar
**hob•nob** ['hɑb,nɑb] *v* (*pret & pp* **-nobbed;** *ger* **-nobbing**) *intr* codearse, rozarse; beber juntos
**ho•bo** ['hobo] *s* (*pl* **-bos** o **-boes**) vagabundo
**Hobson's choice** ['hɑbsənz] *s* alternativa entre la cosa ofrecida o ninguna
**hock** [hɑk] *s* jarrete *m,* corvejón *m* || *tr* (*to hamstring*) desjarretar; (coll) empeñar
**hockey** ['hɑki] *s* hockey *m,* chueca
**hock'shop'** *s* (slang) casa de empeños, monte *m* de piedad
**hocus-pocus** ['hokəs'pokəs] *s* (*meaningless formula*) abracadabra *m;* burla, engaño; juego de manos
**hod** [hɑd] *s* capacho, cuezo; cubo para carbón
**hod carrier** *s* peón *m* de albañil, peón de mano
**hodgepodge** ['hɑdʒ,pɑdʒ] *s* baturrillo
**hoe** [ho] *s* azada, azadón *m* || *tr & intr* azadonar
**hog** [hɑg] o [hɔg] *s* cerdo, puerco || *v* (*pret & pp* **hogged;** *ger* **hogging**) *tr* (slang) tragarse lo mejor de
**hog'back'** *s* cuchilla
**hoggish** ['hɑgɪʃ] o ['hɔgɪʃ] *adj* comilón; glotón; egoísta
**hog Latin** *s* latín *m* de cocina
**hogs'head'** *s* pipa de 63 galones o más; medida de capacidad de 63 galones
**hog'wash'** *s* bazofia
**hoist** [hɔɪst] *s* (*apparatus for lifting*) montacargas *m,* torno izador, grúa; empujón *m* hacia arriba || *tr* alzar, levantar; enarbolar (*p.ej., una bandera*); (naut) izar
**hoity-toity** ['hɔɪti'tɔɪti] *adj* frívolo, veleidoso; arrogante, altanero; **to be hoity-toity** ponerse tan alto
**hokum** ['hokəm] *s* (coll) música celestial, tonterías
**hold** [hold] *s* (*grip*) agarro; (*handle*) asa, mango; autoridad, dominio; (*in wrestling*) presa; (aer) cabina de carga; (mus) calderón *m;* (naut) bodega; **to take hold of** agarrar, coger; apoderarse de || *v* (*pret & pp* **held** [hɛld]) *tr* tener, retener; (*to hold up, support*) apoyar, sostener; (*e.g., with a pin*) sujetar; contener, tener cabida para; ocupar (*un cargo, puesto, etc.*); celebrar (*una reunión*); sostener (*una opinión*); (mus) sostener (*una nota*); **to hold back** detener; retener; contener; **to hold in** refrenar; **to hold one's own** mantenerse firme, no perder terreno; **to hold over** aplazar, diferir; **to hold up** apoyar, sostener; (*to rob*) (coll) atracar || *intr* ser valedero, seguir vigente; pegarse; **hold on!** ¡un momento!; **to hold back** refrenarse; **to hold forth** poner cátedra; **to hold off** esperar; mantenerse a distancia; **to hold on** agarrarse bien; **to hold on to** asirse de; **to hold out** no cejar; ir tirando; **to hold out for** insistir en
**holder** ['holdər] *s* tenedor *m,* posesor *m;* (*for a cigar or cigaret*) boquilla; (*to hold, e.g., a hot plate*) cojinillo; (*e.g., of a passport*) titular *m;* asa, mango
**holding** ['holdɪŋ] *s* tenencia, posesión; **holdings** valores habidos
**holding company** *s* sociedad de control, compañía tenedora
**hold'up'** *s* (*stop, delay*) detención; (coll) atraco, asalto; (coll) precio excesivo
**holdup man** *s* (coll) atracador *m,* salteador *m*
**hole** [hol] *s* agujero; (*in cheese, bread, etc.*) ojo; (*in a road*) bache *m;* (*den of animals; den of vice*) guarida; (*dirty, disorderly dwelling*) cochitril

*m;* **in the hole** adeudado, perdidoso; **to burn a hole in one's pocket** írsele a uno (*el dinero*) de entre las manos; **to pick holes in** (coll) poner reparos a ‖ *intr* — **to hole up** encovarse; buscar un rincón cómodo
**holiday** [ˈhɑlɪ,de] *s* día festivo; vacación
**holiday attire** *s* trapos de cristianar
**holiness** [ˈholɪnɪs] *s* santidad; **his Holiness** su Santidad
**Holland** [ˈhɑlənd] *s* Holanda
**Hollander** [ˈhɑləndər] *s* holandés *m*
**hollow** [ˈhɑlo] *adj* hueco; (*voice*) ahuecado, sepulcral; (*eyes, cheeks*) hundido; falso, engañoso ‖ *adv* — **to beat all hollow** (coll) derrotar completamente ‖ *s* hueco, cavidad; (*small valley*) vallecito ‖ *tr* ahuecar, excavar
**hol•ly** [ˈhɑli] *s* (*pl* **-lies**) acebo
**hol'ly•hock'** *s* malva arbórea
**holm oak** [hom] *s* encina
**holocaust** [ˈhɑlə,kɔst] *s* holocausto
**holster** [ˈholstər] *s* pistolera
**ho•ly** [ˈholi] *adj* (*comp* **-lier;** *super* **-liest**) santo; (*e.g., writing*) sagrado; (*e.g., water*) bendito
**Holy Ghost** *s* Espíritu Santo
**holy orders** *spl* órdenes sagradas; **to take holy orders** recibir las órdenes sagradas, ordenarse
**holy rood** [rud] *s* crucifijo ‖ **Holy Rood** *s* Santa Cruz
**Holy Scripture** *s* Sagrada Escritura
**Holy See** *s* Santa Sede
**Holy Sepulcher** *s* santo sepulcro
**holy water** *s* agua bendita
**Holy Writ** *s* Sagrada Escritura
**homage** [ˈhɑmɪdʒ] o [ˈɑmɪdʒ] *s* homenaje *m;* (feud) homenaje, pleito homenaje
**home** [hom] *adj* casero, doméstico; nacional ‖ *s* casa, domicilio, hogar *m;* (*native heath*) patria chica; (*of the arts, etc.*) patria; (*for the sick, poor, etc.*) asilo; (sport) meta; **at home** en casa; en su propio país; (*ready to receive callers*) de recibo; (*at ease, comfortable*) a gusto; (sport) en campo propio; **away from home** fuera de casa; **make yourself at home** está Vd. en su casa ‖ *adv* en casa; a casa; **to see home** acompañar a casa; **to strike home** dar en lo vivo
**home'bod'y** *s* (*pl* **-ies**) hogareño
**homebred** [ˈhom,bred] *adj* doméstico; sencillo, inculto, tosco
**home'-brew'** *s* cerveza o vino caseros
**home-coming** [ˈhom,kʌmɪŋ] *s* regreso al hogar
**home country** *s* suelo natal
**home delivery** *s* distribución a domicilio
**home front** *s* frente doméstico
**home'land'** *s* tierra natal, patria
**homeless** [ˈhomlɪs] *adj* sin casa, sin hogar
**home life** *s* vida de familia
**home-loving** [ˈhom,lʌvɪŋ] *adj* casero, hogareño
**home•ly** [ˈhomli] *adj* (*comp* **-lier;** *super* **-liest**) (*not attractive or good-looking*) feo; (*plain, not elegant*) sencillo, llano
**homemade** [ˈhomˈmed] *adj* casero, hecho en casa
**homemaker** [ˈhom,mekər] *s* ama de casa
**home office** *s* domicilio social, oficina central ‖ **Home Office** *s* (Brit) ministerio de la Gobernación
**homeopath** [ˈhomɪ•ə,pæθ] o [ˈhɑmɪ•ə,pæθ] *s* homeópata *mf*
**homeopathy** [,homɪˈɑpəθi] o [,hɑmɪˈɑpəθi] *s* homeopatía
**home plate** *s* (baseball) puesto meta
**home port** *s* puerto de origen
**home rule** *s* autonomía, gobierno autónomo
**home run** *s* (baseball) jonrón *m;* cuadrangular *m*
**home'sick'** *adj* nostálgico; **to be homesick (for)** sentir nostalgia (de)
**home'sick'ness** *s* nostalgia, mal *m* de la tierra
**homespun** [ˈhom,spʌn] *adj* hilado en casa; sencillo, llano
**home'stead'** *s* casa y terrenos, heredad
**home stretch** *s* esfuerzo final, último trecho
**home town** *s* ciudad natal
**homeward** [ˈhomwərd] *adj* de regreso ‖ *adv* hacia casa; hacia su país
**home'work'** *s* trabajo a domicilio; (*of a student*) deber *m*, trabajo escolar
**homey** [ˈhomi] *adj* (*comp* **homier;** *super* **homiest**) (coll) íntimo, cómodo
**homicidal** [,hɑmɪˈsaɪdəl] *adj* homicida
**homicide** [ˈhɑmɪ,saɪd] *s* (*act*) homicidio; (*person*) homicida *mf*
**homi•ly** [ˈhɑmɪli] *s* (*pl* **-lies**) homilía
**homing** [ˈhomɪŋ] *adj* (*animal*) querencioso; (*weapon*) buscador del blanco
**homing pigeon** *s* paloma mensajera
**hominy** [ˈhɑmɪni] *s* maíz molido
**homogenei•ty** [,homədʒɪˈni•ɪti] o [,hɑmədʒɪˈni•ɪti] *s* (*pl* **-ties**) homogeneidad
**homogeneous** [,homəˈdʒinɪ•əs] o [,hɑməˈdʒinɪ•əs] *adj* homogéneo
**homogenize** [həˈmɑdʒə,naɪz] *tr* homogeneizar
**homonym** [ˈhɑmənɪm] *s* homónimo
**homonymous** [həˈmɑnɪməs] *adj* homónimo
**homosexual** [,homəˈsekʃʊ•əl] *adj & s* homosexual *mf*
**hon.** *abbr* **honorary**
**Hon.** *abbr* **Honorable**
**Honduran** [hɑnˈdurən] *adj & s* hondureño
**hone** [hon] *s* piedra de afilar ‖ *tr* afilar, amolar, asentar
**honest** [ˈɑnɪst] *adj* honrado, probo, recto; (*money*) bien adquirido; sincero; genuino
**honesty** [ˈɑnɪsti] *s* honradez *f*, probidad, rectitud; (bot) hierba de la plata
**hon•ey** [ˈhʌni] *adj* meloso, dulce; (coll) querido ‖ *s* miel *f;* (coll) vida mía; **it's a honey** (slang) es una preciosidad ‖ *v* (*pret & pp* **-eyed** o **-ied**)

*tr* enmelar, endulzar con miel; adular, lisonjear
**hon'ey·bee'** *s* abeja doméstica, abeja de miel
**hon'ey·comb'** *s* panal *m* ‖ *tr* (*to riddle*) acribillar; llenar, penetrar
**hon'ey·dew' melon** *s* melón muy dulce, blanco y terso
**honeyed** ['hʌnid] *adj* dulce, enmelado; melodioso; adulador
**honey locust** *s* acacia de tres espinas
**hon'ey·moon'** *s* luna de miel; viaje *m* de bodas ‖ *intr* pasar la luna de miel
**honeysuckle** ['hʌni,sʌkəl] *s* madreselva
**honk** [hɑŋk] o [hɔŋk] *s* (*of wild goose*) graznido; (*of automobile horn*) bocinazo ‖ *tr* tocar (*la bocina*) ‖ *intr* graznar (*el ganso silvestre*); tocar la bocina
**honkytonk** ['hɑŋki,tɑŋk] o ['hɔŋki,tɔŋk] *s* (slang) sala de fiestas de mala muerte
**honor** ['ɑnər] *s* (*distinction; award for distinction; integrity*) honor *m;* (*good reputation; chastity*) honor, honra ‖ *tr* honrar; hacer honor a (*su firma*); aceptar y pagar (*una letra*)
**honorable** ['ɑnərəbəl] *adj* (*behaving with honor; performed with honor*) honrado; (*bringing honor; associated with honor*) honroso; (*worthy, of honor*) honorable
**honorary** ['ɑnə,reri] *adj* honorario
**honorific** [,ɑnə'rɪfɪk] *adj* honorífico ‖ *s* antenombre *m*
**honor system** *s* acatamiento voluntario del reglamento
**hood** [hʊd] *s* capilla; (*one with a point*) caperuza; (*one which covers the face*) capirote *m;* (*worn with academic gown*) muceta, capirote *m;* (*of a chimney*) sombrerete *m;* (aut) capó *m,* cubierta; (slang) gamberro ‖ *tr* encapirotar; ocultar
**hoodlum** ['hudləm] *s* (coll) gamberro, maleante *m*
**hoodoo** ['hudu] *s* (*body of primitive rites*) vudú *m;* (coll) mala suerte ‖ *tr* traer mala suerte a
**hood'wink'** *tr* burlar, engañar, vendar
**hooey** ['hu·i] *s* (slang) música celestial
**hoof** [huf] o [hʊf] *s* casco, pezuña; **on the hoof** (*cattle*) vivo, en pie ‖ *tr & intr* (coll) caminar; **to hoof it** (coll) caminar, ir a pie; (coll) bailar
**hoof'beat'** *s* pisada, ruido de la pisada (*de animal ungulado*)
**hook** [hʊk] *s* gancho; (*for fishing*) anzuelo; (*to join two things*) enganche *m;* (*bend, curve*) ángulo, recodo; (box) crochet *m,* golpe *m* de gancho; (*of hook and eye*) corchete *m,* macho; **by hook or by crook** por fas o por nefas; **to swallow the hook** tragar el anzuelo ‖ *tr* enganchar; (*to bend*) encorvar, doblar; coger, pescar (*un pez*); (*to wound with the horns*) acornar ‖ *intr* engancharse; encorvarse, doblarse
**hookah** ['hukə] *s* narguile *m*
**hook and eye** *s* broche *m,* corchete *m* (*macho y hembra*)
**hook and ladder** *s* carro de escaleras de incendio
**hooked rug** *s* tapete *m* de crochet
**hook'nose'** *s* nariz *f* de pico de loro
**hook'up'** *s* montaje *m*
**hook'worm'** *s* anquilostoma *m*
**hooky** ['hʊki] *s* — **to play hooky** hacer novillos
**hooligan** ['hulɪgən] *s* gamberro
**hooliganism** ['hulɪgən,ɪzəm] *s* gamberrismo
**hoop** [hup] o [hʊp] *s* aro ‖ *tr* herrar, enarcar, enzunchar
**hoop skirt** *s* miriñaque *m*
**hoot** [hut] *s* resoplido, ululato; grito ‖ *tr* reprobar a gritos; echar a gritos (*p.ej., a un cómico*) ‖ *intr* resoplar, ulular; **to hoot at** dar grita a
**hoot owl** *s* autillo, cárabo
**hop** [hɑp] *s* saltito; (coll) vuelo en avión; (coll) sarao; (coll) baile *m;* lúpulo, hombrecillo; **hops** (*dried flowers of hop vine*) lúpulo ‖ *v* (*pret & pp* **hopped;** *ger* **hopping**) *tr* cruzar de un salto; (coll) atravesar (*p.ej., el mar*) en avión; (coll) subir a (*un tren, taxi, etc.*) ‖ *intr* saltar, brincar; (*on one foot*) saltar a la pata coja
**hope** [hop] *s* esperanza ‖ *tr & intr* esperar; **to hope for** esperar
**hope chest** *s* ajuar *m* de novia
**hopeful** ['hopfəl] *adj* (*feeling hope*) esperanzado; (*giving hope*) esperanzador
**hopeless** ['hoplɪs] *adj* desesperanzado; (*situation*) desesperado
**hopper** ['hɑpər] *s* (*funnel-shaped container*) tolva; (*of blast furnace*) tragante *m*
**hopper car** *s* (rr) vagón *m* tolva
**hop'scotch'** *s* infernáculo
**horde** [hord] *s* horda
**horehound** ['hor,haʊnd] *s* marrubio; extracto de marrubio
**horizon** [hə'raɪzən] *s* horizonte *m*
**horizontal** [,hɑrɪ'zɑntəl] o [,hɔrɪ'zɑntəl] *adj & s* horizontal *f*
**hormone** ['hɔrmon] *s* hormón *m* u hormona
**horn** [hɔrn] *s* (*bony projection on head of certain animals*) cuerno; (*of bull*) asta, cuerno; (*of moon, anvil, etc.*) cuerno; (*of automobile*) bocina; (mus) cuerno; (*French horn*) (mus) trompa de armonía; **to blow one's own horn** cantar sus propias alabanzas; **to pull in one's horns** contenerse, volverse atrás ‖ *intr* — **to horn in** (slang) entrometerse (en)
**hornet** ['hɔrnɪt] *s* crabrón *m,* avispón *m*
**hornet's nest** *s* panal *m* del avispón; **to stir up a hornet's nest** (coll) armar camorra, armar cisco
**horn of plenty** *s* cuerno de la abundancia
**horn'pipe'** *s* chirimía
**horn-rimmed glasses** ['hɔrn'rɪmd] *spl* anteojos de concha
**horn·y** ['hɔrni] *adj* (*comp* **-ier;** *super*

-iest) córneo; (*callous*) calloso; (*having hornlike projections*) cornudo
**horoscope** ['hɑrə,skop] o ['hɔrə,skop] *s* horóscopo; **to cast a horoscope** sacar un horóscopo
**horrible** ['hɑrɪbəl] o ['hɔrɪbəl] *adj* horrible; (coll) muy desagradable
**horrid** ['hɑrɪd] o ['hɔrɪd] *adj* horroroso; (coll) muy desagradable
**horri•fy** ['hɑrɪ,faɪ] o ['hɔrɪ,faɪ] *v* (*pret & pp* **-fied**) *tr* horrorizar
**horror** ['hɑrər] o ['hɔrər] *s* horror *m;* **to have a horror of** tener horror a
**hors d'oeuvre** [ɔr 'dʌrv] *s* (*pl* **hors d'oeuvres** [ɔr 'dʌrvz]) *s* entremés *m*
**horse** [hɔrs] *s* caballo; (*of carpenter*) caballete *m;* **hold your horses** (coll) pare Vd. el carro; **to back the wrong horse** (coll) jugar a la carta mala; **to be a horse of another color** (coll) ser harina de otro costal
**horse'back'** *s* — **on horseback** a caballo ‖ *adv* — **to ride horseback** montar a caballo
**horse blanket** *s* manta para caballo
**horse block** *s* montadero
**horse'break'er** *s* domador *m* de caballos
**horse'car'** *s* tranvía *m* de sangre
**horse chestnut** *s* (*tree*) castaño de Indias; (*nut*) castaña de Indias
**horse collar** *s* collera
**horse dealer** *s* chalán *m*
**horse doctor** *s* veterinario
**horse'fly'** *s* (*pl* **-fies**) mosca borriquera, tábano
**horse'hair'** *s* crines *fpl* de caballo; (*fabric*) tela de crin
**horse'hide'** *s* cuero de caballo
**horse laugh** *s* risotada
**horse•man** ['hɔrsmən] *s* (*pl* **-men** [mən]) jinete *m*, caballista *m*
**horsemanship** ['hɔrsmən,ʃɪp] *s* equitación, manejo
**horse meat** *s* carne *f* de caballo
**horse opera** *s* (U.S.A.) melodrama *m* del Oeste
**horse pistol** *s* pistola de arzón
**horse'play'** *s* chanza pesada, payasada
**horse'pow'er** *s* caballo de vapor inglés
**horse race** *s* carrera de caballos
**horse'rad'ish** *s* (*plant*) rábano picante o rusticano; (*condiment*) mostaza de los alemanes
**horse sense** *s* (coll) sentido común
**horse'shoe'** *s* herradura
**horseshoe magnet** *s* imán *m* de herradura
**horseshoe nail** *s* clavo de herrar
**horse show** *s* concurso hípico
**horse'tail'** *s* cola de caballo
**horse thief** *s* abigeo, cuatrero
**horse'-trade'** *intr* chalanear
**horse trading** *s* chalanería
**horse'-trad'ing** *adj* chalanesco
**horse'whip'** *s* látigo ‖ *v* (*pret & pp* **-whipped;** *ger* **-whipping**) *tr* dar latigazos a
**horse•woman** ['hɔrs,wumən] *s* (*pl* **-women** [,wɪmɪn]) amazona, caballista *f*
**hors•y** ['hɔrsi] *adj* (*comp* **-ier;** *super* **-iest**) caballar, hípico; (*interested in horses and horse racing*) carrerista, turfista; (coll) desmañado
**horticultural** [,hɔrtɪ'kʌltʃərəl] *adj* hortícola
**horticulture** ['hɔrtɪ,kʌltʃər] *s* horticultura
**horticulturist** [,hɔrtɪ'kʌltʃərɪst] *s* horticultor *m*
**hose** [hoz] *s* (*stocking*) media; (*sock*) calcetín *m;* (*flexible tube*) manguera ‖ **hose** *spl* calzas
**hosier** ['hoʒər] *s* mediero, calcetero
**hosiery** ['hoʒəri] *s* calcetas; calcetería
**hospice** ['hɑspɪs] *s* hospicio
**hospitable** ['hɑspɪtəbəl] o [hɑs'pɪtəbəl] *adj* hospitalario
**hospital** ['hɑspɪtəl] *s* hospital *m*
**hospitali•ty** [,hɑspɪ'tælɪti] *s* (*pl* **-ties**) hospitalidad
**hospitalize** ['hɑspɪtə,laɪz] *tr* hospitalizar
**host** [host] *s* anfitrión *m;* (*at an inn*) huésped *m*, mesonero; (*army*) hueste *f;* multitud, sinnúmero ‖ **Host** *s* (eccl) hostia
**hostage** ['hɑstɪdʒ] *s* rehén *m;* **to be held a hostage** quedar en rehenes
**hostel•ry** ['hɑstəlri] *s* (*pl* **-ries**) parador *m*, hostería
**hostess** ['hostɪs] *s* anfitriona; dueña, patrona; (*in a night club*) tanguista; (aer) azafata, aeromoza; (*e.g., on a bus*) jefa de ruta
**hostile** ['hɑstɪl] *adj* hostil
**hostili•ty** [hɑs'tɪlɪti] *s* (*pl* **-ties**) hostilidad
**hostler** ['hɑslər] o ['ɑslər] *s* mozo de cuadra, mozo de paja y cebada
**hot** [hɑt] *adj* (*comp* **hotter;** *super* **hottest**) (*water, air, coffee, etc.*) caliente; (*climate, country; taste*) cálido; (*fiery, excitable*) caluroso; (*pursuit*) enérgico; (*in rut*) caliente; (coll) muy radiactivo; **to be hot** (*said of a person*) tener calor; (*said of the weather*) hacer calor; **to make it hot for** (coll) hostilizar
**hot air** *s* (slang) palabrería, música celestial
**hot'-air' furnace** *s* calorífero de aire
**hot and cold running water** *s* circulación de agua fría y caliente
**hot baths** *spl* caldas, termas
**hot'bed'** *s* (hort) almajara; (*e.g., of vice*) sementera, semillero
**hot-blooded** ['hɑt'blʌdɪd] *adj* apasionado; temerario, irreflexivo
**hot cake** *s* torta a la plancha; **to sell like hot cakes** (coll) venderse como pan bendito
**hot dog** *s* (slang) perro caliente
**hotel** [ho'tɛl] *adj* hotelero ‖ *s* hotel *m*
**ho•tel'-keep'er** *s* hotelero
**hot'head'** *s* botafuego
**hot-headed** ['hɑt'hɛdɪd] *adj* caliente de cascos
**hot'house'** *s* estufa, invernáculo
**hot plate** *s* hornillo, calientaplatos *m*
**hot springs** *spl* fuentes *fpl* termales

**hot-tempered** ['hɑt'tempərd] *adj* irascible
**hot water** *s* — **to be in hot water** (coll) estar en calzas prietas
**hot'-wa'ter boiler** *s* termosifón *m*
**hot-water bottle** *s* bolsa de agua caliente
**hot-water heater** *s* calentador *m* de acumulación
**hot-water heating** *s* calefacción por agua caliente
**hot-water tank** *s* depósito de agua caliente
**hound** [haʊnd] *s* podenco, perro de caza; **to follow the hounds** o **to ride to hounds** cazar a caballo con jauría || *tr* acosar, hostigar
**hour** [aʊr] *s* hora; **by the hour** por horas; **in an evil hour** en hora mala; **on the hour** a la hora en punto cada hora; **to keep late hours** acostarse tarde; **to work long hours** trabajar muchas horas cada día
**hour'glass'** *s* reloj *m* de arena
**hour hand** *s* horario
**hourly** ['aʊrli] *adj* de cada hora; por hora || *adv* cada hora; muy a menudo
**house** [haʊs] *s* (*pl* **houses** ['haʊzɪz]) casa; (*legislative body*) cámara; teatro; (*size of audience*) entrada, p.ej., **a good house** mucha entrada; **to keep house** tener casa puesta; hacer los quehaceres domésticos; **to put one's house in order** arreglar sus asuntos || [haʊz] *tr* domiciliar, alojar, hospedar
**house arrest** *s* arresto domiciliario
**house'boat'** *s* barco vivienda
**house'break'er** *s* escalador *m*
**housebreaking** ['haʊs,brekɪŋ] *s* escalo, allanamiento de morada
**housebroken** ['haʊs,brokən] *adj* (*perro o gato*) enseñado (*a hábitos de limpieza*)
**house cleaning** *s* limpieza de la casa
**house coat** *s* bata
**house current** *s* sector *m* de distribución, canalización de consumo
**house'fly'** *s* (*pl* **-flies**) mosca doméstica
**houseful** ['haʊs,fʊl] *s* casa llena
**house'fur'nishings** *spl* menaje *m*, enseres domésticos
**house'hold'** *adj* casero, doméstico || *s* casa, familia
**house'hold'er** *s* dueño de la casa; jefe *m* de familia
**house'-hunt'** *intr* — **to go house-hunting** ir a buscar casa
**house'keep'er** *s* ama de llaves, mujer *f* de gobierno
**house'keep'ing** *s* manejo doméstico, gobierno doméstico; **to set up housekeeping** poner casa
**housekeeping apartment** *s* apartamento con cocina
**house'maid'** *s* criada de casa
**house meter** *s* contador *m* de abonado
**house'moth'er** *s* mujer encargada de una residencia de estudiantes
**house of cards** *s* castillo de naipes
**house of ill fame** *s* lupanar *m*, casa de prostitución
**house painter** *s* pintor *m* de brocha gorda
**house physician** *s* médico residente
**house'top'** *s* tejado; **to shout from the housetops** pregonar a los cuatro vientos
**housewarming** ['haʊs,wɔrmɪŋ] *s* fiesta para celebrar el estreno de una casa; **to have a housewarming** estrenar la casa
**house'wife'** *s* (*pl* **-wives**) ama de casa, madre *f* de familia
**house'work'** *s* quehaceres domésticos
**housing** ['haʊzɪŋ] *s* (*of a horse*) gualdrapa; (aut) cárter *m;* (mach) caja, bastidor *m*
**housing shortage** *s* crisis *f* de viviendas
**hovel** ['hʌvəl] o ['hɑvəl] *s* casucha, choza; (*shed for cattle, tools, etc.*) cobertizo
**hover** ['hʌvər] o ['hɑvər] *intr* cernerse (*un ave*); (*to hesitate; to be in danger*) fluctuar; asomar (*p.ej., una sonrisa en los labios de uno*)
**how** [haʊ] *adv* cómo; (*at what price*) a cómo; **how early** cuándo, a qué hora; **how else** de qué otra manera; **how far** hasta dónde; cuánto, p.ej., **how far is it to the airport?** ¿cuánto hay de aquí al aeropuerto?; **how long** cuánto tiempo; **how many** cuántos; **how much** cuánto; lo mucho que; **how often** cuántas veces; **how old are you?** ¿cuántos años tiene Vd.?; **how soon** cuándo, a qué hora; **how** + *adj* qué + *adj*, p.ej., **how beautiful she is!** ¡qué hermosa es!; lo + *adj*, p.ej., **you know how intelligent he is** Vd. sabe lo inteligente que es; **to know how to** + *inf* saber + *inf*
**howdah** ['haʊdə] *s* castillo
**how·ev'er** *adv* no obstante, sin embargo; por muy . . . que, por mucho . . . que
**howitzer** ['haʊ·ɪtsər] *s* cañón *m* obús
**howl** [haʊl] *s* aullido; chillido; risa muy aguda; (*of wind*) bramido || *tr* decir a gritos; **to howl down** imponerse a gritos a (*una persona*) || *intr* aullar; chillar; reír a más no poder; bramar (*el viento*)
**howler** ['haʊlər] *s* aullador *m;* (coll) plancha, desacierto
**hoyden** ['hɔɪdən] *s* muchacha traviesa, tunantuela
**H.P.** *abbr* **horsepower**
**hr.** *abbr* **hour**
**H.R.H.** *abbr* **Her** (o **His**) **Royal Highness**
**ht.** *abbr* **height**
**hub** [hʌb] *s* cubo; (fig) centro, eje *m*
**hubbub** ['hʌbəb] *s* gritería, alboroto
**hub'cap'** *s* tapacubo, embellecedor *m*
**huckster** ['hʌkstər] *s* (*peddler*) buhonero; vendedor *m* ambulante de hortalizas; vil traficante *m*, sujeto ruin
**huddle** ['hʌdəl] *s* (coll) reunión secreta; **to go into a huddle** (coll) conferenciar en secreto || *intr* acurrucarse, arrimarse
**hue** [hju] *s* matiz *m;* gritería; **hue and cry** vocería de indignación

**huff** [hʌf] *s* arrebato de cólera; **in a huff** encolerizado, ofendido
**hug** [hʌg] *s* abrazo ‖ *v* (*pret & pp* **hugged**; *ger* **hugging**) *tr* abrazar, apretar con los brazos; ahogar entre los brazos; navegar muy cerca de (*la costa*); ceñirse a (*p.ej., un muro*) ‖ *intr* abrazarse
**huge** [hjudʒ] *adj* enorme, descomunal
**huh** [hʌ] *interj* ¡eh!
**hulk** [hʌlk] *s* (*body of an old ship*) casco; (*clumsy old ship*) carcamán *m*, carraca; (*old ship tied up at a wharf and used as a warehouse, prison, etc.*) pontón *m*; (*shell of an old building, piece of furniture, machine, etc.*; *heavy, unwieldy person*) armatoste *m*
**hulking** ['hʌlkɪŋ] *adj* grueso, pesado
**hull** [hʌl] *s* (*of ship or hydroplane*) casco; (*of a dirigible*) armazón *f*; (*of certain vegetables*) hollejo, vaina ‖ *tr* deshollejar, desvainar; mondar, pelar
**hullabaloo** ['hʌləbə ˌlu] o [ˌhʌləbə'lu] *s* alboroto, gritería, tumulto
**hum** [hʌm] *s* canturreo, tarareo; (*of a bee, machine, etc.*) zumbido ‖ *interj* ¡ejem! ‖ *v* (*pret & pp* **hummed**; *ger* **humming**) *tr* canturrear, tararear ‖ *intr* canturrear, tararear; (*to buzz*) zumbar; (coll) estar muy activo
**human** ['hjumən] *adj* humano (*perteneciente al hombre*)
**human being** *s* ser humano
**humane** [hju'men] *adj* humano (*compasivo*)
**humanist** ['hjumənɪst] *adj & s* humanista *mf*
**humanitarian** [hju ˌmænɪ'terɪ·ən] *adj & s* humanitario
**humani·ty** [hju'mænɪti] *s* (*pl* **-ties**) humanidad
**hu'man·kind'** *s* género humano
**humble** ['hʌmbəl] o ['ʌmbəl] *adj* humilde ‖ *tr* humillar
**humble pie** *s* — **to eat humble pie** cantar la palinodia
**hum'bug'** *s* patraña; (*person*) patrañero ‖ *v* (*pret & pp* **-bugged**; *ger* **-bugging**) *tr* embaucar, engaitar
**hum'drum'** *adj* monótono, tedioso
**humer·us** ['hjumərəs] *s* (*pl* **-i** [ˌaɪ]) húmero
**humid** ['hjumɪd] *adj* húmedo
**humidifier** [hju'mɪdɪ ˌfaɪ·ər] *s* humectador *m*
**humidi·fy** [hju'mɪdɪ ˌfaɪ] *v* (*pret & pp* **-fied**) *tr* humedecer
**humidity** [hju'mɪdɪti] *s* humedad
**humiliate** [hju'mɪlɪ ˌet] *tr* humillar
**humiliating** [hju'mɪlɪ ˌetɪŋ] *adj* humillante
**humili·ty** [hju'mɪlɪti] *s* (*pl* **-ties**) humildad
**hummingbird** ['hʌmɪŋ ˌbʌrd] *s* colibrí *m*, pájaro mosca
**humor** ['hjumər] o ['jumər] *s* humor *m*; **out of humor** de mal humor; **to be in the humor for** estar de humor para ‖ *tr* seguir el humor a; manejar con delicadeza
**humorist** ['hjumərɪst] o ['jumərɪst] *s* humorista *mf*
**humorous** ['hjumərəs] o ['jumərəs] *adj* humorístico
**hump** [hʌmp] *s* corcova, joroba; (*in the ground*) montecillo
**hump'back'** *s* corcova, joroba; (*person*) corcovado, jorobado
**humus** ['hjuməs] *s* mantillo
**hunch** [hʌntʃ] *s* corcova, joroba; (*premonition*) (coll) corazonada ‖ *tr* encorvar ‖ *intr* encorvarse
**hunch'back'** *s* corcova, joroba; (*person*) corcovado, jorobado
**hundred** ['hʌndrəd] *adj* cien ‖ *s* ciento, cien; **a hundred** u **one hundred** ciento, cien; **by the hundreds** a centenares
**hundredth** ['hʌndrədθ] *adj & s* centésimo
**hun'dred·weight'** *s* quintal *m*
**Hundred Years' War** *s* guerra de los Cien Años
**Hungarian** [hʌŋ'gerɪ·ən] *adj & s* húngaro
**Hungary** ['hʌŋgəri] *s* Hungría
**hunger** ['hʌŋgər] *s* hambre *f* ‖ *intr* hambrear; **to hunger for** tener hambre de
**hunger march** *s* marcha del hambre
**hunger strike** *s* huelga de hambre
**hun·gry** ['hʌŋgri] *adj* (*comp* **-grier**; *super* **-griest**) hambriento; **to be hungry** tener hambre; **to go hungry** pasar hambre
**hunk** [hʌŋk] *s* (coll) buen pedazo, pedazo grande
**hunt** [hʌnt] *s* (*act of hunting*) caza; (*hunting party*) cacería; (*a search*) busca; **on the hunt for** a caza de ‖ *tr* cazar; (*to seek, look for*) buscar ‖ *intr* cazar; buscar; **to go hunting** ir de caza; **to hunt for** buscar; **to take hunting** llevar de caza
**hunter** ['hʌntər] *s* cazador *m*; perro de caza
**hunting** ['hʌntiŋ] *adj* de caza ‖ *s* (*act*) caza; (*art*) cacería, montería
**hunting dog** *s* perro de caza
**hunting ground** *s* cazadero
**hunt'ing·horn'** *s* cuerno de caza
**hunting jacket** *s* cazadora
**hunting lodge** *s* casa de montería
**hunting season** *s* época de caza
**huntress** ['hʌntrɪs] *s* cazadora
**hunts·man** ['hʌntsmən] *s* (*pl* **-men** [mən]) cazador *m*, montero
**hurdle** ['hʌrdəl] *s* (*hedge over which horses must jump*) zarzo; (*wooden frame over which runners and horses must jump*) valla; (fig) obstáculo; **hurdles** carrera de vallas ‖ *tr* saltar por encima de
**hurdle race** *s* carrera de vallas
**hurdy-gur·dy** ['hʌrdi'gʌrdi] *s* (*pl* **-dies**) organillo
**hurl** [hʌrl] *s* lanzamiento ‖ *tr* lanzar
**hurrah** [hʊ'rɑ] o **hurray** [hʊ're] *s* viva *m* ‖ *interj* ¡viva!; **hurrah for . . . !** ¡viva . . . ! ‖ *tr* aplaudir, vitorear ‖ *intr* dar vivas
**hurricane** ['hʌrɪ ˌken] *s* huracán *m*

**hurried** [ˈhʌrid] *adj* apresurado; hecho de prisa
**hur•ry** [ˈhʌri] *s* (*pl* **-ries**) prisa; **to be in a hurry** tener prisa, estar de prisa || *v* (*pret & pp* **-ried**) *tr* apresurar, dar prisa a || *intr* apresurarse, darse prisa; **to hurry after** correr en pos de; **to hurry away** marcharse de prisa; **to hurry back** volver de prisa; **to hurry up** darse prisa
**hurt** [hʌrt] *adj* (*injured*) lastimado, herido; (*offended*) resentido, herido || *s* (*harm*) daño; (*injury*) herida; (*pain*) dolor *m* || *v* (*pret & pp* **hurt**) *tr* (*to harm*) dañar, perjudicar; (*to injure*) lastimar, herir; (*to offend*) ofender, herir; (*to pain*) doler || *intr* doler
**hurtle** [ˈhʌrtəl] *intr* lanzarse con violencia, pasar con gran estruendo
**husband** [ˈhʌzbənd] *s* marido, esposo || *tr* manejar con economía
**husband•man** [ˈhʌzbəndmən] *s* (*pl* **-men** [mən]) agricultor *m*, granjero
**husbandry** [ˈhʌzbəndri] *s* agricultura, labranza; buena dirección, buen gobierno (*de la hacienda de uno*)
**hush** [hʌʃ] *s* silencio || *interj* ¡chito! || *tr* callar; **to hush up** echar tierra a (*un escándalo*) || *intr* callarse
**hushaby** [ˈhʌʃə ˌbaɪ] *interj* ¡ro ro!
**hush'-hush'** *adj* muy secreto
**hush money** *s* precio del silencio
**husk** [hʌsk] *s* cáscara, hollejo, vaina; (*of corn*) perfolla || *tr* descascarar, deshollejar, desvainar; espinochar (*el maíz*)
**husk•y** [ˈhʌski] *adj* (*comp* **-ier**; *super* **-iest**) fortachón, fornido; (*voice*) ronco
**hus•sy** [ˈhʌzi] o [ˈhʌsi] *s* (*pl* **-sies**) buena pieza, moza descarada; mujer desvergonzada
**hustle** [ˈhʌsəl] *s* (coll) energía, vigor *m* || *tr* apresurar; echar a empellones || *intr* apresurarse; (coll) menearse, trabajar con gran ahinco
**hustler** [ˈhʌslər] *s* trafagón *m*, buscavidas *mf*
**hut** [hʌt] *s* casucha, choza
**hyacinth** [ˈhaɪ•əsɪnθ] *s* jacinto
**hybrid** [ˈhaɪbrɪd] *adj & s* híbrido
**hybridization** [ˌhaɪbrɪdɪˈzeʃən] *s* hibridación
**hybridize** [ˈhaɪbrɪ ˌdaɪz] *tr & intr* hibridar
**hy•dra** [ˈhaɪdrə] *s* (*pl* **-dras** o **-drae** [dri]) hidra
**hydrant** [ˈhaɪdrənt] *s* boca de agua, boca de riego; (*water faucet*) grifo
**hydrate** [ˈhaɪdret] *s* hidrato || *tr* hidratar || *intr* hidratarse
**hydraulic** [haɪˈdrɔlɪk] *adj* hidráulico || **hydraulics** *s* hidráulica
**hydraulic ram** *s* ariete hidráulico
**hydriodic** [ˌhaɪdrɪˈɑdɪk] *adj* yodhídrico
**hydrobromic** [ˌhaɪdrəˈbromɪk] *adj* bromhídrico
**hydrocarbon** [ˌhaɪdrəˈkɑrbən] *s* hidrocarburo
**hydrochloric** [ˌhaɪdrəˈklorɪk] *adj* clorhídrico
**hydroelectric** [ˌhaɪdro•ɪˈlɛktrɪk] *adj* hidroeléctrico
**hydrofluoric** [ˌhaɪdrəfluˈɑrɪk] o [ˌhaɪdrəfluˈɔrɪk] *adj* fluorhídrico
**hydrofoil** [ˈhaɪdrə ˌfɔɪl] *s* superficie hidrodinámica; (*wing designed to lift vessel*) hidroaleta; (*vessel*) hidroala *m*
**hydrogen** [ˈhaɪdrədʒən] *s* hidrógeno
**hydrogen bomb** *s* bomba de hidrógeno
**hydrogen peroxide** *s* peróxido de hidrógeno
**hydrogen sulfide** *s* sulfuro de hidrógeno
**hydrometer** [haɪˈdrɑmɪtər] *s* areómetro
**hydrophobia** [ˌhaɪdrəˈfobɪ•ə] *s* hidrofobia
**hydroplane** [ˈhaɪdrə ˌplen] *s* hidroavión *m*
**hydroxide** [haɪˈdrɑksaɪd] *s* hidróxido
**hyena** [haɪˈinə] *s* hiena
**hygiene** [ˈhaɪdʒin] o [ˈhaɪdʒɪ ˌin] *s* higiene *f*
**hygienic** [ˌhaɪdʒɪˈɛnɪk] o [haɪˈdʒinɪk] *adj* higiénico
**hymn** [hɪm] *s* himno
**hymnal** [ˈhɪmnəl] *s* himnario
**hyp.** *abbr* **hypotenuse, hypothesis**
**hyperacidity** [ˌhaɪpərəˈsɪdɪti] *s* hiperacidez *f*
**hyperbola** [haɪˈpʌrbələ] *s* (geom) hipérbola
**hyperbole** [haɪˈpʌrbəli] *s* (rhet) hipérbole *f*
**hyperbolic** [ˌhaɪpərˈbɑlɪk] *adj* (geom & rhet) hiperbólico
**hypersensitive** [ˌhaɪpərˈsɛnsɪtɪv] *adj* extremadamente sensible; (*allergic*) hipersensible
**hypertension** [ˌhaɪpərˈtɛnʃən] *s* hipertensión
**hyphen** [ˈhaɪfən] *s* guión *m*
**hyphenate** [ˈhaɪfə ˌnet] *tr* unir con guión; escribir con guión
**hypno•sis** [hɪpˈnosɪs] *s* (*pl* **-ses** [siz]) hipnosis *f*
**hypnotic** [hɪpˈnɑtɪk] *adj* hipnótico || *s* (*person; sedative*) hipnótico
**hypnotism** [ˈhɪpnə ˌtɪzəm] *s* hipnotismo
**hypnotist** [ˈhɪpnətɪst] *s* hipnotista *mf*
**hypnotize** [ˈhɪpnə ˌtaɪz] *tr* hipnotizar
**hypochondriac** [ˌhaɪpəˈkɑndrɪ ˌæk] o [ˌhɪpəˈkɑndrɪ ˌæk] *s* hipocondríaco
**hypocri•sy** [hɪˈpɑkrəsi] *s* (*pl* **-sies**) hipocresía
**hypocrite** [ˈhɪpəkrɪt] *s* hipócrita *mf*
**hypocritical** [ˌhɪpəˈkrɪtɪkəl] *adj* hipócrita
**hypodermic** [ˌhaɪpəˈdʌrmɪk] *adj* hipodérmico
**hyposulfite** [ˌhaɪpəˈsʌlfaɪt] *m* hiposulfito
**hypotenuse** [haɪˈpɑtɪ ˌnus] o [haɪˈpɑtɪ ˌnjus] *s* hipotenusa
**hypothe•sis** [haɪˈpɑθɪsɪs] *s* (*pl* **-ses** [ˌsiz]) hipótesis *f*
**hypothetic(al)** [ˌhaɪpəˈθɛtɪk(əl)] *adj* hipotético

**hyssop** ['hɪsəp] *s* (bot) hisopo
**hysteria** [hɪs'tɪrɪ·ə] *s* histerismo, histeria
**hysteric** [hɪs'terɪk] *adj* histérico ‖ **hysterics** *s* paroxismo histérico
**hysterical** [hɪs'terɪkəl] *adj* histérico

# I

**I, i** [aɪ] novena letra del alfabeto inglés
**I.** *abbr* **Island**
**I** [aɪ] *pron pers* (*pl* **we** [wi]) yo; **it is I** soy yo
**iambic** [aɪ'æmbɪk] *adj* yámbico
**iam·bus** [aɪ'æmbəs] *s* (*pl* **-bi** [baɪ]) yambo
**ib.** *abbr* **ibidem**
**Iberian** [aɪ'bɪrɪ·ən] *adj* ibérico ‖ *s* ibero
**ibex** ['aɪbeks] *s* (*pl* **ibexes** o **ibices** ['ɪbɪ,siz]) íbice *m*, cabra montés
**ibid.** *abbr* **ibidem**
**ice** [aɪs] *s* hielo; **to break the ice** (*to overcome reserve*) romper el hielo; **to cut no ice** (coll) no importar nada; **to skate on thin ice** (coll) buscar el peligro ‖ *tr* helar; enfriar con hielo; (*to cover with icing*) garapiñar ‖ *intr* helarse
**ice age** *s* época glacial
**ice bag** *s* bolsa para hielo
**iceberg** ['aɪs,bʌrg] *s* banquisa, iceberg *m*
**ice'boat'** *s* cortahielos *m*, rompehielos *m;* trineo con vela para deslizarse sobre el hielo
**ice'bound'** *adj* rodeado de hielo; detenido por el hielo
**ice'box'** *s* nevera, fresquera
**ice'break'er** *s* cortahielos *m*, rompehielos *m*
**ice'cap'** *s* bolsa para hielo; manto de hielo
**ice cream** *s* helado
**ice'-cream' cone** *s* cucurucho de helado, barquillo de helado
**ice-cream freezer** *s* heladora, garapiñera
**ice-cream parlor** *s* salón *m* de refrescos, tienda de helados
**ice-cream soda** *s* agua gaseosa con helado
**ice cube** *s* cubito de hielo
**ice hockey** *s* hockey *m* sobre patines
**Iceland** ['aɪslənd] *s* Islandia
**Icelander** ['aɪs,lændər] o ['aɪsləndər] *s* islandés *m*
**Icelandic** [aɪs'lændɪk] *adj* islandés ‖ *s* islandés *m* (*idioma*)
**ice·man** ['aɪs,mæn] *s* (*pl* **-men** [,men]) vendedor *m* de hielo, repartidor *m* de hielo
**ice pack** *s* hielo flotante; bolsa de hielo
**ice pail** *s* enfriadera
**ice pick** *s* picahielos *m*
**ice skate** *s* patín *m* de cuchilla, patín de hielo
**ice tray** *s* bandejita de hielo
**ice water** *s* agua helada
**ichthyology** [,ɪkθɪ'alədʒi] *s* ictiología
**icicle** ['aɪsɪkəl] *s* carámbano
**icing** ['aɪsɪŋ] *s* garapiña, capa de azúcar; (aer) formación de hielo
**iconoclasm** [aɪ'kanə,klæzəm] *s* iconoclasia, iconoclasmo
**iconoclast** [aɪ'kanə,klæst] *s* iconoclasta *mf*
**iconoscope** [aɪ'kanə,skop] *s* (trademark) iconoscopio
**icy** ['aɪsi] *adj* (*comp* **icier**; *super* **iciest**) cubierto de hielo; (*slippery*) resbaladizo; (fig) frío
**id.** *abbr* **idem**
**id** [ɪd] *s* (psychoanalysis) ello
**idea** [aɪ'di·ə] *s* idea
**ideal** [aɪ'di·əl] *adj* & *s* ideal *m*
**idealist** [aɪ'di·əlɪst] *adj* & *s* idealista *mf*
**idealize** [aɪ'di·ə,laɪz] *tr* idealizar
**identic(al)** [aɪ'dentɪk(əl)] *adj* idéntico
**identification** [aɪ,dentɪfɪ'keʃən] *s* identificación
**identification tag** *s* disco de identificación
**identify** [aɪ'dentɪ,faɪ] *v* (*pret* & *pp* **-fied**) *tr* identificar
**identi·ty** [aɪ'dentɪti] *s* (*pl* **-ties**) identidad
**ideolo·gy** [,aɪdɪ'alədʒi] o [,ɪdɪ'alədʒi] *s* (*pl* **-gies**) ideología
**ides** [aɪdz] *spl* idus *mpl*
**idio·cy** ['ɪdɪ·əsi] *s* (*pl* **-cies**) idiotez *f*
**idiom** ['ɪdɪ·əm] *s* (*expression that is contrary to the usual patterns of the language*) modismo; (*style of language*) idioma *m*, lenguaje *m;* (*style of an author*) estilo; (*character of a language*) índole *f*
**idiomatic** [,ɪdɪ·ə'mætɪk] *adj* idiomático
**idiosyncra·sy** [,ɪdɪ·ə'sɪnkrəsi] *s* (*pl* **-sies**) idiosincrasia
**idiot** ['ɪdɪ·ət] *s* idiota *mf*
**idiotic** [,ɪdɪ·'atɪk] *adj* idiota
**idle** ['aɪdəl] *adj* desocupado, ocioso; **at idle moments** a ratos perdidos; **to run idle** marchar en ralentí ‖ *tr* — **to idle away** gastar ociosamente (*el tiempo*) ‖ *intr* estar ocioso, holgar; marchar (*un motor*) en ralentí
**idleness** ['aɪdəlnɪs] *s* desocupación, ociosidad
**idler** ['aɪdlər] *s* haragán *m*, ocioso
**idol** ['aɪdəl] *s* ídolo
**idola·try** [aɪ'dalətri] *s* (*pl* **-tries**) idolatría
**idolize** ['aɪdə,laɪz] *tr* idolatrar
**idyll** ['aɪdəl] *s* idilio
**idyllic** [aɪ'dɪlɪk] *adj* idílico
**if** [ɪf] *conj* si; **as if** como si; **even if**

aunque; **if so** si es así; **if true** si es cierto
**ignis fatuus** ['ɪgnɪs'fætʃu·əs] *s* (*pl* **ignes fatui** ['ɪgniz'fætʃu,aɪ]) fuego fatuo
**ignite** [ɪg'naɪt] *tr* encender ‖ *intr* encenderse
**ignition** [ɪg'nɪʃən] *s* inflamación; (aut) encendido
**ignition switch** *s* (aut) interruptor *m* de encendido
**ignoble** [ɪg'nobəl] *adj* innoble
**ignominious** [,ɪgnə'mɪnɪ·əs] *adj* ignominioso
**ignoramus** [,ɪgnə'reməs] *s* ignorante *mf*
**ignorance** ['ɪgnərəns] *s* ignorancia
**ignorant** ['ɪgnərənt] *adj* ignorante
**ignore** [ɪg'nor] *tr* no hacer caso de, pasar por alto
**ilk** [ɪlk] *s* especie *f*, jaez *m*
**ill.** *abbr* **illustrated, illustration**
**ill** [ɪl] *adj* (*comp* **worse** [wʌrs]; *super* **worst** [wʌrst]) enfermo, malo ‖ *adv* mal; **to take ill** tomar a mal; caer enfermo
**ill-advised** ['ɪləd'vaɪzd] *adj* desaconsejado, malaconsejado
**ill at ease** *adj* inquieto, incómodo
**ill-bred** ['ɪl'bred] *adj* malcriado
**ill-considered** ['ɪlkən'sɪdərd] *adj* desconsiderado, mal considerado
**ill-disposed** ['ɪldɪs'pozd] *adj* malintencionado, maldispuesto
**illegal** [ɪ'ligəl] *adj* ilegal
**illegible** [ɪ'lɛdʒɪbəl] *adj* ilegible
**illegitimate** [,ɪlɪ'dʒɪtɪmɪt] *adj* ilegítimo
**ill fame** *s* mala fama, reputación de inmoral
**ill-fated** ['ɪl'fetɪd] *adj* aciago, funesto
**ill-gotten** ['ɪl'gɑtən] *adj* mal ganado
**ill health** *s* mala salud
**ill-humored** ['ɪl'hjumərd] *adj* malhumorado
**illicit** [ɪ'lɪsɪt] *adj* ilícito
**illitera·cy** [ɪ'lɪtərəsi] *s* (*pl* **-cies**) ignorancia; analfabetismo
**illiterate** [ɪ'lɪtərɪt] *adj* (*uneducated*) iliterato; (*unable to read or write*) analfabeto ‖ *s* analfabeto
**ill-mannered** ['ɪl'mænərd] *adj* de malos modales
**illness** ['ɪlnɪs] *s* enfermedad
**illogical** [ɪ'lɑdʒɪkəl] *adj* ilógico
**ill-spent** ['ɪl'spent] *adj* malgastado
**ill-starred** ['ɪl'stɑrd] *adj* malhadado
**ill-tempered** ['ɪl'tempərd] *adj* de mal genio
**ill-timed** ['ɪl'taɪmd] *adj* inoportuno, intempestivo
**ill'-treat'** *tr* maltratar
**illuminate** [ɪ'lumɪ,net] *tr* alumbrar, iluminar; miniar (*un manuscrito*)
**illuminating gas** *s* gas *m* de alumbrado
**illumination** [ɪ,lumɪ'neʃən] *s* iluminación
**illusion** [ɪ'luʒən] *s* ilusión
**illusive** [ɪ'lusɪv] *adj* ilusivo
**illusory** [ɪ'lusəri] *adj* ilusorio
**illustrate** ['ɪləs,tret] o [ɪ'lʌstret] *tr* ilustrar
**illustration** [,ɪləs'treʃən] *s* ilustración
**illustrious** [ɪ'lʌstrɪ·əs] *adj* ilustre
**ill will** *s* mala voluntad
**image** ['ɪmɪdʒ] *s* imagen *f*; **the very image of** la propia estampa de
**image·ry** ['ɪmɪdʒri] o ['ɪmɪdʒəri] *s* (*pl* **-ries**) (*formation of mental images; product of the imagination*) fantasía; (*images collectively*) imágenes *fpl*
**imaginary** [ɪ'mædʒɪ,neri] *adj* imaginario
**imagination** [ɪ,mædʒɪ'neʃən] *s* imaginación
**imagine** [ɪ'mædʒɪn] *tr* & *intr* imaginar; (*to conjecture*) imaginarse
**imbecile** ['ɪmbɪsɪl] *adj* & *s* imbécil *mf*
**imbecili·ty** [,ɪmbɪ'sɪlɪti] *s* (*pl* **-ties**) imbecilidad
**imbibe** [ɪm'baɪb] *tr* (*to drink*) beber; (*to absorb*) embeber; (*to become absorbed in*) embeberse de o en ‖ *intr* beber, empinar el codo
**imbue** [ɪm'bju] *tr* imbuir
**imitate** ['ɪmɪ,tet] *tr* imitar
**imitation** [,ɪmɪ'teʃən] *adj* (*e.g., jewelry*) imitado, imitación, de imitación ‖ *s* imitación; **in imitation of** a imitación de
**immaculate** [ɪ'mækjəlɪt] *adj* inmaculado
**immaterial** [,ɪmə'tɪrɪ·əl] *adj* inmaterial; poco importante
**immature** [,ɪmə'tjur] o [,ɪmə'tur] *adj* inmaturo
**immeasurable** [ɪ'meʒərəbəl] *adj* inmensurable
**immediacy** [ɪ'midɪ·əsi] *s* inmediación
**immediate** [ɪ'midɪ·ɪt] *adj* inmediato
**immediately** [ɪ'midɪ·ɪtli] *adv* inmediatamente
**immemorial** [,ɪmɪ'morɪ·əl] *adj* inmemorial
**immense** [ɪ'mens] *adj* inmenso; (coll) excelente
**immerge** [ɪ'mʌrdʒ] *intr* sumergirse
**immerse** [ɪ'mʌrs] *tr* sumergir, inmergir
**immersion** [ɪ'mʌrʃən] o [ɪ'mʌrʒən] *s* sumersión, inmersión
**immigrant** ['ɪmɪgrənt] *adj* & *s* inmigrante *mf*
**immigrate** ['ɪmɪ,gret] *intr* inmigrar
**immigration** [,ɪmɪ'greʃən] *s* inmigración
**imminent** ['ɪmɪnənt] *adj* inminente
**immobile** [ɪ'mobɪl] o [ɪ'mobil] *adj* inmoble, inmóvil
**immobilize** [ɪ'mobɪ,laɪz] *tr* inmovilizar
**immoderate** [ɪ'mɑdərɪt] *adj* inmoderado
**immodest** [ɪ'mɑdɪst] *adj* inmodesto
**immoral** [ɪ'mɑrəl] o [ɪ'mɔrəl] *adj* inmoral
**immortal** [ɪ'mɔrtəl] *adj* & *s* inmortal *mf*
**immortalize** [ɪ'mɔrtə,laɪz] *tr* inmortalizar
**immune** [ɪ'mjun] *adj* inmune
**immunize** ['ɪmjə,naɪz] o [ɪ'mjunaɪz] *tr* inmunizar
**imp** [ɪmp] *s* diablillo; (*child*) niño travieso

**impact** ['ɪmpækt] *s* impacto
**impair** [ɪm'pɛr] *tr* empeorar, deteriorar
**impan·el** [ɪm'pænəl] *v* (*pret & pp* **-eled** o **-elled**; *ger* **-eling** o **-elling**) *tr* inscribir en la lista de los jurados; elegir (*un jurado*)
**impart** [ɪm'pɑrt] *tr* (*to make known*) dar a conocer, hacer saber; (*to transmit, communicate*) imprimir
**impartial** [ɪm'pɑrʃəl] *adj* imparcial
**impassable** [ɪm'pæsəbəl] o [ɪm'pɑsəbəl] *adj* intransitable, impracticable
**impasse** [ɪm'pæs] o ['ɪmpæs] *s* callejón *m* sin salida
**impassible** [ɪm'pæsɪbəl] *adj* impasible
**impassioned** [ɪm'pæʃənd] *adj* ardiente, vehemente
**impassive** [ɪm'pæsɪv] *adj* impasible
**impatience** [ɪm'peʃəns] *s* impaciencia
**impatient** [ɪm'peʃənt] *adj* impaciente
**impeach** [ɪm'pitʃ] *tr* residenciar
**impeachment** [ɪm'pitʃmənt] *s* residencia
**impeccable** [ɪm'pɛkəbəl] *adj* impecable
**impecunious** [,ɪmpɪ'kjunɪ·əs] *adj* inope
**impedance** [ɪm'pidəns] *s* impedancia
**impede** [ɪm'pid] *tr* estorbar, dificultar
**impediment** [ɪm'pɛdɪmənt] *s* impedimento; (*e.g., in speech*) defecto
**im·pel** [ɪm'pɛl] *v* (*pret & pp* **-pelled**; *ger* **-pelling**) *tr* impeler, impulsar
**impending** [ɪm'pɛndɪŋ] *adj* inminente
**impenetrable** [ɪm'pɛnətrəbəl] *adj* impenetrable
**impenitent** [ɪm'pɛnɪtənt] *adj & s* impenitente *mf*
**imperative** [ɪm'pɛrɪtɪv] *adj* (*commanding*) imperativo; (*urgent, absolutely necessary*) imperioso || *s* imperativo
**imperceptible** [,ɪmpər'sɛptɪbəl] *adj* imperceptible, inapreciable
**imperfect** [ɪm'pʌrfɪkt] *adj & s* imperfecto
**imperfection** [,ɪmpər'fɛkʃən] *s* imperfección
**imperial** [ɪm'pɪrɪ·əl] *adj* imperial; majestuoso || *s* (*goatee*) perilla; (*top of coach*) imperial *f*
**imperialist** [ɪm'pɪrɪ·əlɪst] *adj & s* imperialista *mf*
**imper·il** [ɪm'pɛrɪl] *v* (*pret & pp* **-iled** o **-illed**; *ger* **-iling** o **-illing**) *tr* poner en peligro
**imperious** [ɪm'pɪrɪ·əs] *adj* imperioso
**imperishable** [ɪm'pɛrɪʃəbəl] *adj* imperecedero
**impersonal** [ɪm'pʌrsənəl] *adj* impersonal
**impersonate** [ɪm'pʌrsə,net] *tr* personificar; hacer el papel de
**impertinence** [ɪm'pʌrtɪnəns] *s* impertinencia
**impertinent** [ɪm'pʌrtɪnənt] *adj & s* impertinente *mf*
**impetuous** [ɪm'pɛtʃʊ·əs] *adj* impetuoso
**impetus** ['ɪmpɪtəs] *s* ímpetu *m*
**impie·ty** [ɪm'paɪ·əti] *s* (*pl* **-ties**) impiedad
**impinge** [ɪm'pɪndʒ] *intr* — **to impinge on** o **upon** incidir en o sobre, herir; infringir, violar
**impious** ['ɪmpɪ·əs] *adj* impío
**impish** ['ɪmpɪʃ] *adj* endiablado, travieso
**implant** [ɪm'plænt] *tr* implantar
**implement** ['ɪmplɪmənt] *s* instrumento, utensilio, herramienta || ['ɪmplɪ,mɛnt] *tr* poner por obra, llevar a cabo; (*to provide with implements*) pertrechar
**implicate** ['ɪmplɪ,ket] *tr* implicar, comprometer, enredar
**implicit** [ɪm'plɪsɪt] *adj* implícito; (*unquestioning*) absoluto, ciego
**implied** [ɪm'plaɪd] *adj* implícito, sobrentendido
**implore** [ɪm'plor] *tr* implorar, suplicar
**im·ply** [ɪm'plaɪ] *v* (*pret & pp* **-plied**) *tr* dar a entender; implicar, incluir en esencia
**impolite** [,ɪmpə'laɪt] *s* descortés
**import** ['ɪmport] *s* importación; artículo importado; importancia, significación || [ɪm'port] o ['ɪmport] *tr* importar; significar || *intr* importar
**importance** [ɪm'pɔrtəns] *s* importancia
**important** [ɪm'pɔrtənt] *adj* importante
**importation** [,ɪmpor'teʃən] *s* importación
**importer** [ɪm'portər] *s* importador *m*
**importunate** [ɪm'pɔrtʃənɪt] *adj* importuno
**importune** [,ɪmpər'tjun] o [,ɪmpər'tun] *tr* importunar
**impose** [ɪm'poz] *tr* imponer || *intr* — **to impose on** o **upon** abusar de
**imposing** [ɪm'pozɪŋ] *adj* imponente
**imposition** [,ɪmpə'zɪʃən] *s* (*of someone's will*) imposición; abuso, engaño
**impossible** [ɪm'pɑsɪbəl] *adj* imposible
**impostor** [ɪm'pɑstər] *s* impostor *m*
**imposture** [ɪm'pɑstʃər] *s* impostura
**impotence** ['ɪmpətəns] *s* impotencia
**impotent** ['ɪmpətənt] *adj* impotente
**impound** [ɪm'paʊnd] *tr* acorralar, encerrar; rebalsar (*agua*); (law) embargar, secuestrar
**impoverish** [ɪm'pɑvərɪʃ] *tr* empobrecer
**impracticable** [ɪm'præktɪkəbəl] *adj* impracticable; (*intractable*) intratable
**impractical** [ɪm'præktɪkəl] *adj* impracticable; soñador, utópico
**impregnable** [ɪm'pregnəbəl] *adj* inexpugnable
**impregnate** [ɪm'pregnet] *tr* (*to make pregnant*) empreñar; (*to soak*) empapar; (*to fill the interstices of*) impregnar; (*to infuse, infect*) imbuir
**impresari·o** [,ɪmprɪ'sɑrɪ,o] *s* (*pl* **-os**) empresario, empresario de teatro
**impress** [ɪm'pres] *tr* (*to have an effect on the mind or emotions of*) impresionar; (*to mark by using pres-*

*sure*) imprimir; (*on the memory*) grabar; (mil) enganchar
**impression** [ɪm'prɛʃən] *s* impresión
**impressionable** [ɪm'prɛʃənəbəl] *adj* impresionable
**impressive** [ɪm'presɪv] *adj* impresionante
**imprint** ['ɪmprɪnt] *s* impresión; (typ) pie *m* de imprenta || [ɪm'prɪnt] *tr* imprimir
**imprison** [ɪm'prɪzən] *tr* encarcelar
**imprisonment** [ɪm'prɪzənmənt] *s* encarcelamiento
**improbable** [ɪm'prɑbəbəl] *adj* improbable
**impromptu** [ɪm'prɑmptju] o [ɪm'prɑmptu] *adj* improvisado || *adv* de improviso || *s* improvisación; (mus) impromptu *m*
**improper** [ɪm'prɑpər] *adj* impropio; (*contrary to good taste or decency*) indecoroso
**improve** [ɪm'pruv] *tr* perfeccionar, mejorar; aprovechar (*la oportunidad*) || *intr* perfeccionarse, mejorar; **to improve on** o **upon** mejorar
**improvement** [ɪm'pruvmənt] *s* perfeccionamiento, mejoramiento; (*e.g., in health*) mejoría; (*useful employment, e.g., of time*) aprovechamiento
**improvident** [ɪm'prɑvɪdənt] *adj* imprevisor
**improvise** ['ɪmprə,vaɪz] *tr* & *intr* improvisar
**imprudent** [ɪm'prudənt] *adj* imprudente
**impudence** ['ɪmpjədəns] *s* insolencia, descaro, impertinencia
**impudent** ['ɪmpjədənt] *adj* insolente, descarado, impertinente
**impugn** [ɪm'pjun] *tr* poner en tela de juicio
**impulse** ['ɪmpʌls] *s* impulso
**impulsive** [ɪm'pʌlsɪv] *adj* impulsivo
**impunity** [ɪm'pjunɪti] *s* impunidad
**impure** [ɪm'pjʊr] *adj* impuro
**impuri·ty** [ɪm'pjʊrɪti] *s* (*pl* **-ties**) impureza, impuridad
**impute** [ɪm'pjut] *tr* imputar
**in** [ɪn] *adj* interior || *adv* dentro; en casa, en la oficina; **in here** aquí dentro; **in there** allí dentro; **to be in** estar en casa; **to be in for** estar expuesto a; **to be in with** gozar del favor de || *prep* en; (*within*) dentro de; (*over, through*) por; (*a period of the day*) en o por; **dressed in . . .** vestido de . . . ; **in so far as** en tanto que; **in that** en que, por cuanto || *s* — **ins and outs** recovecos, pormenores minuciosos
**inability** [,ɪnə'bɪlɪti] *s* inhabilidad, incapacidad
**inaccessible** [,ɪnæk'sɛsɪbəl] *adj* inaccesible
**inaccura·cy** [ɪn'ækjərəsi] *s* (*pl* **-cies**) inexactitud, incorrección
**inaccurate** [ɪn'ækjərɪt] *adj* inexacto, incorrecto
**inaction** [ɪn'ækʃən] *s* inacción
**inactive** [ɪn'æktɪv] *adj* inactivo
**inactivity** [,ɪnæk'tɪvɪti] *s* inactividad
**inadequate** [ɪn'ædɪkwɪt] *adj* insuficiente, inadecuado
**inadvertent** [,ɪnəd'vʌrtənt] *adj* inadvertido
**inadvisable** [,ɪnəd'vaɪzəbəl] *adj* poco aconsejable, imprudente
**inane** [ɪn'en] *adj* inane
**inanimate** [ɪn'ænɪmɪt] *adj* inanimado
**inappreciable** [,ɪnə'priʃɪ·əbəl] *adj* inapreciable
**inappropriate** [,ɪnə'propri·ɪt] *adj* no apropiado, no a propósito
**inarticulate** [,ɪnɑr'tɪkjəlɪt] *adj* (*sounds, words*) inarticulado; (*person*) incapaz de expresarse
**inartistic** [,ɪnɑr'tɪstɪk] *adj* antiartístico, inartístico
**inasmuch as** [,ɪnəz'mʌtʃ,æz] *conj* ya que, puesto que; en cuanto, hasta donde
**inattentive** [,ɪnə'tentɪv] *adj* desatento
**inaugural** [ɪn'ɔgjərəl] *adj* inaugural || *s* discurso inaugural
**inaugurate** [ɪn'ɔgjə,ret] *tr* inaugurar
**inauguration** [ɪn,ɔgjə'reʃən] *s* (*formal initiation or opening*) inauguración; (*investiture of a head of government*) toma de posesión
**inborn** ['ɪn,bɔrn] *adj* innato, ingénito
**inbreeding** ['ɪn,bridɪŋ] *s* intracruzamiento
**inc.** *abbr* **inclosure, included, including, incorporated, increase**
**Inca** ['ɪŋkə] *adj* incaico || *s* inca *mf*
**incandescent** [,ɪnkən'dɛsənt] *adj* incandescente
**incapable** [ɪn'kepəbəl] *adj* incapaz
**incapacitate** [,ɪnkə'pæsɪ,tet] *tr* incapacitar, inhabilitar
**incapaci·ty** [,ɪnkə'pæsɪti] *s* (*pl* **-ties**) incapacidad
**incarcerate** [ɪn'kɑrsə,ret] *tr* encarcelar
**incarnate** [ɪn'kɑrnɪt] o [ɪn'kɑrnet] *adj* encarnado || [ɪn'kɑrnet] *tr* encarnar
**incarnation** [,ɪnkɑr'neʃən] *s* encarnación
**incendiarism** [ɪn'sɛndɪ·ə,rɪzəm] *s* incendio intencionado; incitación al desorden
**incendiar·y** [ɪn'sɛndɪ,ɛri] *adj* incendiario || *s* (*pl* **-ies**) incendiario
**incense** ['ɪnsens] *s* incienso || *tr* (*to burn incense before*) incensar || [ɪn'sens] *tr* exasperar, encolerizar
**incense burner** *s* incensario
**incentive** [ɪn'sɛntɪv] *adj* & *s* incentivo
**inception** [ɪn'sɛpʃən] *s* principio, comienzo
**incertitude** [ɪn'sʌrtɪ,tjud] o [ɪn'sʌrtɪ,tud] *s* incertidumbre
**incessant** [ɪn'sɛsənt] *adj* incesante
**incest** ['ɪnsest] *s* incesto
**incestuous** [ɪn'sɛstʃʊ·əs] *adj* incestuoso
**inch** [ɪntʃ] *s* pulgada; **to be within an inch of** estar a dos dedos de || *intr* — **to inch ahead** avanzar poco a poco
**incidence** ['ɪnsɪdəns] *s* incidencia; (*range of occurrence*) extensión
**incident** ['ɪnsɪdənt] *adj* & *s* incidente *m*

**incidental** [ˌɪnsɪˈdɛntəl] *adj* incidente; (*incurred in addition to the regular amount*) obvencional ‖ *s* elemento incidental; **incidentals** gastos menudos
**incidentally** [ˌɪnsɪˈdɛntəli] *adv* incidentemente; a propósito
**incipient** [ɪnˈsɪpɪ·ənt] *adj* incipiente
**incision** [ɪnˈsɪʒən] *s* incisión
**incisive** [ɪnˈsaɪsɪv] *adj* incisivo
**incite** [ɪnˈsaɪt] *tr* incitar
**incl.** *abbr* **inclosure, inclusive**
**inclemen·cy** [ɪnˈklɛmənsi] *s* (*pl* **-cies**) inclemencia
**inclement** [ɪnˈklɛmənt] *adj* inclemente
**inclination** [ˌɪnklɪˈneʃən] *s* inclinación
**incline** [ˈɪnklaɪn] o [ɪnˈklaɪn] *s* declive *m*, pendiente *f* ‖ [ɪnˈklaɪn] *tr* inclinar ‖ *intr* inclinarse
**inclose** [ɪnˈkloz] *tr* encerrar; (*in a letter*) adjuntar, incluir; **to inclose herewith** remitir adjunto
**inclosure** [ɪnˈkloʒər] *s* recinto; cosa inclusa, carta inclusa
**include** [ɪnˈklud] *tr* incluir, comprender
**including** [ɪnˈkludɪŋ] *prep* incluso, inclusive
**inclusive** [ɪnˈklusɪv] *adj* inclusivo; **inclusive of** comprensivo de ‖ *adv* inclusive
**incogni·to** [ɪnˈkɑgnɪˌto] *adj* incógnito ‖ *adv* de incógnito ‖ *s* (*pl* **-tos**) incógnito
**incoherent** [ˌɪnkoˈhɪrənt] *adj* incoherente
**incombustible** [ˌɪnkəmˈbʌstɪbəl] *adj* incombustible
**income** [ˈɪnkʌm] *s* renta, ingreso, utilidad
**income tax** *s* impuesto sobre rentas
**in'come-tax' return** *s* declaración de impuesto sobre rentas
**in'com'ing** *adj* de entrada, entrante; (*tide*) ascendente ‖ *s* entrada
**incomparable** [ɪnˈkɑmpərəbəl] *adj* incomparable
**incompatible** [ˌɪnkəmˈpætɪbəl] *adj* incompatible
**incompetent** [ɪnˈkɑmpɪtənt] *adj* incompetente
**incomplete** [ˌɪnkəmˈplit] *adj* incompleto
**incomprehensible** [ˌɪnkɑmprɪˈhɛnsɪbəl] *adj* incomprensible
**inconceivable** [ˌɪnkənˈsivəbəl] *adj* inconcebible
**inconclusive** [ˌɪnkənˈklusɪv] *adj* inconcluyente
**incongruous** [ɪnˈkɑŋgrʊ·əs] *adj* incongruo
**inconsequential** [ɪnˌkɑnsɪˈkwɛnʃəl] *adj* (*lacking proper sequence of thought or speech*) inconsecuente; (*trivial*) de poca importancia
**inconsiderate** [ˌɪnkənˈsɪdərɪt] *adj* desconsiderado, inconsiderado
**inconsisten·cy** [ˌɪnkənˈsɪstənsi] *s* (*pl* **-cies**) (*lack of coherence*) inconsistencia; (*lack of logical connection or uniformity*) inconsecuencia
**inconsistent** [ˌɪnkənˈsɪstənt] *adj* (*lacking coherence of parts*) inconsistente; (*not agreeing with itself or oneself*) inconsecuente
**inconsolable** [ˌɪnkənˈsoləbəl] *adj* inconsolable
**inconspicuous** [ˌɪnkənˈspɪkjʊ·əs] *adj* poco impresionante, poco aparente
**inconstant** [ɪnˈkɑnstənt] *adj* inconstante
**incontinent** [ɪnˈkɑntɪnənt] *adj* incontinente
**incontrovertible** [ˌɪnkɑntrəˈvʌrtɪbəl] *adj* incontrovertible
**inconvenience** [ˌɪnkənˈvinɪ·əns] *s* incomodidad, inconveniencia, molestia ‖ *tr* incomodar, molestar
**inconvenient** [ˌɪnkənˈvinɪ·ənt] *adj* incómodo, inconveniente, molesto
**incorporate** [ɪnˈkɔrpəˌret] *tr* incorporar; constituir en sociedad anónima ‖ *intr* incorporarse; constituirse en sociedad anónima
**incorporation** [ɪnˌkɔrpəˈreʃən] *s* incorporación; constitución en sociedad anónima
**incorrect** [ˌɪnkəˈrɛkt] *adj* incorrecto
**increase** [ˈɪnkris] *s* aumento; ganancia, interés *m*; **to be on the increase** ir en aumento ‖ [ɪnˈkris] *tr* aumentar; (*by propagation*) multiplicar ‖ *intr* aumentar; multiplicarse
**increasingly** [ɪnˈkrisɪŋli] *adv* cada vez más
**incredible** [ɪnˈkrɛdɪbəl] *adj* increíble
**incredulous** [ɪnˈkrɛdʒələs] *adj* incrédulo
**increment** [ˈɪnkrɪmənt] *s* incremento
**incriminate** [ɪnˈkrɪmɪˌnet] *tr* acriminar, incriminar
**incrust** [ɪnˈkrʌst] *tr* incrustar
**incubate** [ˈɪnkjəˌbet] *tr & intr* incubar
**incubator** [ˈɪnkjəˌbetər] *s* incubadora
**inculcate** [ɪnˈkʌlket] o [ˈɪnkʌlˌket] *tr* inculcar
**incumben·cy** [ɪnˈkʌmbənsi] *s* (*pl* **-cies**) incumbencia
**incumbent** [ɪnˈkʌmbənt] *adj* — **to be incumbent on** incumbir a ‖ *s* titular *m*
**incunabula** [ˌɪnkjʊˈnæbjələ] *spl* (*beginnings*) orígenes *mpl*; (*early printed books*) incunables *mpl*
**in·cur** [ɪnˈkʌr] *v* (*pret & pp* **-curred**; *ger* **-curring**) *tr* incurrir en; (*a debt*) contraer
**incurable** [ɪnˈkjʊrəbəl] *adj & s* incurable *mf*
**incursion** [ɪnˈkʌrʒən] o [ɪnˈkʌrʃən] *s* incursión, correría
**ind.** *abbr* **independent, industrial**
**indebted** [ɪnˈdɛtɪd] *adj* adeudado; obligado
**indecen·cy** [ɪnˈdisənsi] *s* (*pl* **-cies**) indecencia, deshonestidad
**indecent** [ɪnˈdisənt] *adj* indecente, deshonesto
**indecisive** [ˌɪndɪˈsaɪsɪv] *adj* indeciso
**indeclinable** [ˌɪndɪˈklaɪnəbəl] *adj* (gram) indeclinable
**indeed** [ɪnˈdid] *adv* verdaderamente, claro ‖ *interj* ¡de veras!
**indefatigable** [ˌɪndɪˈfætɪgəbəl] *adj* incansable, infatigable

**indefensible** [ˌɪndɪˈfɛnsɪbəl] *adj* indefendible
**indefinable** [ˌɪndɪˈfaɪnəbəl] *adj* indefinible
**indefinite** [ɪnˈdɛfɪnɪt] *adj* indefinido
**indelible** [ɪnˈdɛlɪbəl] *adj* indeleble
**indelicate** [ɪnˈdɛlɪkɪt] *adj* indelicado
**indemnification** [ɪnˌdɛmnɪfɪˈkeʃən] *s* indemnización
**indemni·fy** [ɪnˈdɛmnɪˌfaɪ] *v* (*pret & pp* **-fied**) *tr* indemnizar
**indemni·ty** [ɪnˈdɛmnɪti] *s* (*pl* **-ties**) (*security against loss*) indemnidad; (*compensation*) indemnización
**indent** [ɪnˈdɛnt] *tr* dentar, mellar; (typ) sangrar
**indentation** [ˌɪndɛnˈteʃən] *s* mella, muesca; (typ) sangría
**indenture** [ɪnˈdɛntʃər] *s* escritura, contrato; contrato de aprendizaje || *tr* obligar por contrato
**independence** [ˌɪndɪˈpɛndəns] *s* independencia
**independen·cy** [ˌɪndɪˈpɛndənsi] *s* (*pl* **-cies**) independencia; país *m* independiente
**independent** [ˌɪndɪˈpɛndənt] *adj & s* independiente *mf*
**indescribable** [ˌɪndɪˈskraɪbəbəl] *adj* indescriptible
**indestructible** [ˌɪndɪˈstrʌktɪbəl] *adj* indestructible
**indeterminate** [ˌɪndɪˈtʌrmɪnɪt] *adj* indeterminado
**index** [ˈɪndɛks] *s* (*pl* **indexes** o **indices** [ˈɪndɪˌsiz]) *s* índice *m;* (typ) manecilla || *tr* poner índice a; poner en un índice || **Index** *s* Índice de los libros prohibidos
**index card** *s* ficha catalográfica
**index finger** *s* dedo índice
**index tab** *s* pestaña
**India** [ˈɪndɪ·ə] *s* la India
**India ink** *s* tinta china
**Indian** [ˈɪndɪ·ən] *adj & s* indio
**Indian club** *s* maza de gimnasia
**Indian corn** *s* maíz *m*, panizo
**Indian file** *s* fila india || *adv* en fila india
**Indian Ocean** *s* mar *m* de las Indias, océano Índico
**Indian summer** *s* veranillo de San Martín
**India paper** *s* papel *m* de China
**India rubber** *s* caucho
**indicate** [ˈɪndɪˌket] *tr* indicar
**indication** [ˌɪndɪˈkeʃən] *s* indicación
**indicative** [ɪnˈdɪkətɪv] *adj & s* indicativo
**indicator** [ˈɪndɪˌketər] *s* indicador *m*
**indict** [ɪnˈdaɪt] *tr* (law) acusar, procesar
**indictment** [ɪnˈdaɪtmənt] *s* acusación, procesamiento; auto de acusación formulado por el gran jurado
**indifferent** [ɪnˈdɪfərənt] *adj* indiferente; (*not particularly good*) pasadero, mediano
**indigenous** [ɪnˈdɪdʒɪnəs] *adj* indígena
**indigent** [ˈɪndɪdʒənt] *adj* indigente
**indigestible** [ˌɪndɪˈdʒɛstɪbəl] *adj* indigestible
**indigestion** [ˌɪndɪˈdʒɛstʃən] *s* indigestión
**indignant** [ɪnˈdɪgnənt] *adj* indignado
**indignation** [ˌɪndɪgˈneʃən] *s* indignación
**indigni·ty** [ɪnˈdɪgnɪti] *s* (*pl* **-ties**) indignidad
**indi·go** [ˈɪndɪˌgo] *adj* azul de añil || *s* (*pl* **-gos** o **-goes**) índigo
**indirect** [ˌɪndɪˈrɛkt] o [ˌɪndaɪˈrɛkt] *adj* indirecto
**indirect discourse** *s* estilo indirecto
**indiscernible** [ˌɪndɪˈzʌrnɪbəl] o [ˌɪndɪˈsʌrnɪbəl] *adj* indiscernible
**indiscreet** [ˌɪndɪsˈkrit] *adj* indiscreto
**indispensable** [ˌɪndɪsˈpɛnsəbəl] *adj* indispensable, imprescindible
**indispose** [ˌɪndɪsˈpoz] *tr* indisponer
**indisposed** [ˌɪndɪsˈpozd] *adj* (*disinclined*) maldispuesto; (*somewhat ill*) indispuesto
**indissoluble** [ˌɪndɪˈsɑljəbəl] *adj* indisoluble
**indistinct** [ˌɪndɪˈstɪŋkt] *adj* indistinto
**indite** [ɪnˈdaɪt] *tr* redactar, poner por escrito
**individual** [ˌɪndɪˈvɪdʒʊ·əl] *adj* individual || *s* individuo
**individuali·ty** [ˌɪndɪˌvɪdʒʊˈælɪti] *s* (*pl* **-ties**) individualidad; (*person of distinctive character*) personaje *m*
**Indochina** [ˈɪndoˈtʃaɪnə] *s* la Indochina
**Indo-Chi·nese** [ˈɪndotʃaɪˈniz] *adj* indochino || *s* (*pl* **-nese**) indochino
**indoctrinate** [ɪnˈdɑktrɪˌnet] *tr* adoctrinar
**Indo-European** [ˈɪndoˌjʊrəˈpi·ən] *adj & s* indoeuropeo
**indolent** [ˈɪndələnt] *adj* indolente
**Indonesia** [ˌɪndoˈniʃə] o [ˌɪndoˈniʒə] *s* la Indonesia
**Indonesian** [ˌɪndoˈniʃən] o [ˌɪndoˈniʒən] *adj & s* indonesio
**indoor** [ˈɪnˌdor] *adj* interior, de puertas adentro; (*inclined to stay in the house*) casero
**indoors** [ˈɪnˈdorz] *adv* dentro, en casa, bajo techado, bajo cubierto
**indorse** [ɪnˈdɔrs] *tr* endosar; (fig) apoyar, aprobar
**indorsee** [ˌɪndɔrˈsi] *s* endosatario
**indorsement** [ɪnˈdɔrsmənt] *s* endoso; (fig) apoyo, aprobación
**indorser** [ɪnˈdɔrsər] *s* endosante *mf*
**induce** [ɪnˈdjus] o [ɪnˈdus] *tr* inducir; causar, ocasionar
**inducement** [ɪnˈdjusmənt] o [ɪnˈdusmənt] *s* aliciente *m*, estímulo, incentivo
**induct** [ɪnˈdʌkt] *tr* instalar; introducir, iniciar; (mil) quintar
**induction** [ɪnˈdʌkʃən] *s* instalación; introducción; (elec & log) inducción; (mil) quinta
**indulge** [ɪnˈdʌldʒ] *tr* gratificar (*p.ej., los deseos de uno*); mimar (*a un niño*) || *intr* abandonar; **to indulge in** entregarse a, permitirse el placer de
**indulgence** [ɪnˈdʌldʒəns] *s* gusto, inclinación; intemperancia, desenfreno; (*leniency*) indulgencia

**indulgent** [ɪn'dʌldʒənt] *adj* indulgente
**industrial** [ɪn'dʌstrɪ·əl] *adj* industrial
**industrialist** [ɪn'dʌstrɪ·əlɪst] *s* industrial *m*
**industrialize** [ɪn'dʌstrɪ·ə,laɪz] *tr* industrializar
**industrious** [ɪn'dʌstrɪ·əs] *adj* industrioso, aplicado
**indus•try** ['ɪndəstri] *s* (*pl* **-tries**) industria
**inebriation** [ɪn,ibrɪ'eʃən] *s* embriaguez *f*
**inedible** [ɪn'ɛdɪbəl] *adj* incomible
**ineffable** [ɪn'ɛfəbəl] *adj* inefable
**ineffective** [,ɪnɪ'fɛktɪv] *adj* ineficaz; (*person*) incapaz
**ineffectual** [,ɪnɪ'fɛktʃʊ·əl] *adj* ineficaz, fútil
**inefficacy** [ɪn'ɛfɪkəsi] *s* ineficacia
**inefficient** [,ɪnɪ'fɪʃənt] *adj* de mal rendimiento
**ineligible** [ɪn'ɛlɪdʒɪbəl] *adj* inelegible
**inequali•ty** [,ɪnɪ'kwɑlɪti] *s* (*pl* **-ties**) desigualdad
**inequi•ty** [ɪn'ɛkwɪti] *s* (*pl* **-ties**) inequidad
**ineradicable** [,ɪnɪ'rædɪkəbəl] *adj* inextirpable
**inertia** [ɪn'ʌrʃə] *s* inercia
**inescapable** [,ɪnɛs'kepəbəl] *adj* ineludible
**inevitable** [ɪn'ɛvɪtəbəl] *adj* inevitable
**inexact** [,ɪnɛg'zækt] *adj* inexacto
**inexcusable** [,ɪnɛks'kjuzəbəl] *adj* indisculpable, inexcusable
**inexhaustible** [,ɪnɛg'zɔstɪbəl] *adj* inagotable
**inexorable** [ɪn'ɛksərəbəl] *adj* inexorable
**inexpedient** [,ɪnɛk'spidɪ·ənt] *adj* malaconsejado, inoportuno
**inexpensive** [,ɪnɛk'spɛnsɪv] *adj* barato, poco costoso
**inexperience** [,ɪnɛk'spɪrɪ·əns] *s* inexperiencia
**inexplicable** [ɪn'ɛksplɪkəbəl] *adj* inexplicable
**inexpressible** [,ɪnɛk'sprɛsɪbəl] *adj* inexpresable
**Inf.** *abbr* **Infantry**
**infallible** [ɪn'fælɪbəl] *adj* infalible
**infamous** ['ɪnfəməs] *adj* infame
**infa•my** ['ɪnfəmi] *s* (*pl* **-mies**) infamia
**infan•cy** ['ɪnfənsi] *s* (*pl* **-cies**) infancia
**infant** ['ɪnfənt] *adj* infantil; (*in the earliest stage*) (fig) naciente || *s* criatura, nene *m*
**infantile** ['ɪnfən,taɪl] o ['ɪnfəntɪl] *adj* infantil; (*childish*) aniñado
**infan•try** ['ɪnfəntri] *s* (*pl* **-tries**) infantería
**infantry•man** ['ɪnfəntrimən] *s* (*pl* **-men** [mən]) infante *m*, soldado de infantería
**infatuated** [ɪn'fætʃʊ,etɪd] *adj* apasionado, locamente enamorado
**infect** [ɪn'fɛkt] *tr* inficionar, infectar; influir sobre
**infection** [ɪn'fɛkʃən] *s* infección
**infectious** [ɪn'fɛkʃəs] *adj* infeccioso
**in•fer** [ɪn'fʌr] *v* (*pret & pp* **-ferred**; *ger* **-ferring**) *tr* inferir; (coll) conjeturar, suponer
**inferior** [ɪn'fɪrɪ·ər] *adj & s* inferior *m*
**inferiority** [ɪn,fɪrɪ'ɑrɪti] *s* inferioridad
**inferiority complex** *s* complejo de inferioridad
**infernal** [ɪn'fʌrnəl] *adj* infernal
**infest** [ɪn·fɛst] *tr* infestar
**infidel** ['ɪnfɪdəl] *adj & s* infiel *mf*
**infideli•ty** [,ɪnfɪ'dɛlɪti] *s* (*pl* **-ties**) infidelidad
**in'field'** *s* (baseball) cuadro interior
**infiltrate** [ɪn'fɪltret] o ['ɪnfɪl,tret] *tr* infiltrar; infiltrarse en || *intr* infiltrarse
**infinite** ['ɪnfɪnɪt] *adj & s* infinito
**infinitive** [ɪn'fɪnɪtɪv] *adj & s* infinitivo
**infini•ty** [ɪn'fɪnɪti] *s* (*pl* **-ties**) infinidad; (math) infinito
**infirm** [ɪn'fʌrm] *adj* infirme, achacoso; (*unsteady*) inestable, inseguro; poco firme, poco sólido
**infirma•ry** [ɪn'fʌrməri] *s* (*pl* **-ries**) enfermería
**infirmi•ty** [ɪn'fʌrmɪti] *s* (*pl* **-ties**) achaque *m;* inestabilidad
**in'fix** *s* (gram) infijo
**inflame** [ɪn'flem] *tr* inflamar
**inflammable** [ɪn'flæməbəl] *adj* inflamable
**inflammation** [,ɪnflə'meʃən] *s* inflamación
**inflate** [ɪn'flet] *tr* inflar || *intr* inflarse
**inflation** [ɪn'fleʃən] *s* inflación; (*of a tire*) inflado
**inflect** [ɪn'flɛkt] *tr* doblar, torcer; modular (*la voz*); (gram) modificar por inflexión
**inflection** [ɪn'flɛkʃən] *s* inflexión
**inflexible** [ɪn'flɛksɪbəl] *adj* inflexible
**inflict** [ɪn'flɪkt] *tr* infligir
**influence** ['ɪnflu·əns] *s* influencia || *tr* influir sobre, influenciar
**influential** [,ɪnflu'ɛnʃəl] *adj* influyente
**influenza** [,ɪnflu'ɛnzə] *s* influenza
**inform** [ɪn'fɔrm] *tr* informar, avisar, enterar || *intr* informar
**informal** [ɪn'fɔrməl] *adj* (*not according to established rules*) informal; (*unceremonious; colloquial*) familiar
**information** [,ɪnfər'meʃən] *s* información, informes *mpl*
**informational** [,ɪnfər'meʃənəl] *adj* informativo
**informed sources** *spl* los entendidos
**infraction** [ɪn'frækʃən] *s* infracción
**infrared** [,ɪnfrə'rɛd] *adj & s* infrarrojo
**infrequent** [ɪn'frikwənt] *adj* infrecuente
**infringe** [ɪn'frɪndʒ] *tr* infringir || *intr* — **to infringe on** o **upon** invadir, abusar de
**infringement** [ɪn'frɪndʒmənt] *s* infracción
**infuriate** [ɪn'fjʊrɪ,et] *tr* enfurecer
**infuse** [ɪn'fjuz] *tr* infundir
**infusion** [ɪn'fjuʒən] *s* infusión
**ingenious** [ɪn'dʒinjəs] *adj* ingenioso
**ingenui•ty** [,ɪndʒɪ'nju·ɪti] o [,ɪndʒɪ'nu·ɪti] *s* (*pl* **-ties**) ingeniosidad
**ingenuous** [ɪn'dʒɛnjʊ·əs] *adj* ingenuo
**ingenuousness** [ɪn'dʒɛnjʊ·əsnɪs] *s* ingenuidad
**ingest** [ɪn'dʒɛst] *tr* injerir
**in'go'ing** *adj* entrante

**ingot** [ˈɪŋgət] *s* lingote *m*
**ingraft** [ɪnˈgræft] o [ɪnˈgrɑft] *tr* (hort & surg) injertar; (fig) implantar
**ingrate** [ˈɪngret] *s* ingrato
**ingratiate** [ɪnˈgreʃɪ,et] *tr* — **to ingratiate oneself with** congraciarse con
**ingratiating** [ɪnˈgreʃɪ,etɪŋ] *adj* atrayente, obsequioso
**ingratitude** [ɪnˈgrætɪ,tjud] o [ɪnˈgrætɪ,tud] *s* ingratitud, desagradecimiento
**ingredient** [ɪnˈgridɪ·ənt] *s* ingrediente *m*
**in'grow'ing nail** *s* uñero
**ingulf** [ɪnˈgʌlf] *tr* hundir, inundar
**inhabit** [ɪnˈhæbɪt] *tr* habitar, poblar
**inhabitant** [ɪnˈhæbɪtənt] *s* habitante *mf*
**inhale** [ɪnˈhel] *tr* aspirar, inspirar ‖ *intr* aspirar, inspirar; tragar el humo
**inherent** [ɪnˈhɪrənt] *adj* inherente
**inherit** [ɪnˈhɛrɪt] *tr & intr* heredar
**inheritance** [ɪnˈhɛrɪtəns] *s* herencia
**inheritor** [ɪnˈhɛrɪtər] *s* heredero
**inhibit** [ɪnˈhɪbɪt] *tr* inhibir, prohibir
**inhospitable** [ɪnˈhɑspɪtəbəl] o [,ɪnhɑsˈpɪtəbəl] *adj* inhospitalario; (*affording no shelter or protection*) inhóspito
**inhuman** [ɪnˈhjumən] *adj* inhumano
**inhumane** [,ɪnhjuˈmen] *adj* inhumano
**inhumani·ty** [,ɪnhjuˈmænɪti] *s* (*pl* **-ties**) inhumanidad
**inimical** [ɪˈnɪmɪkəl] *adj* enemigo
**iniqui·ty** [ɪˈnɪkwɪti] *s* (*pl* **-ties**) iniquidad
**ini·tial** [ɪˈnɪʃəl] *adj & s* inicial *f* ‖ *v* (*pret* **-tialed** o **-tialled**; *ger* **-tialing** o **-tialling**) *tr* firmar con sus iniciales; marcar (*p.ej., un pañuelo*)
**initiate** [ɪˈnɪʃɪ,et] *tr* iniciar
**initiation** [ɪ,nɪʃɪˈeʃən] *s* iniciación
**initiative** [ɪˈnɪʃɪ·ətɪv] o [ɪˈnɪʃətɪv] *s* iniciativa
**inject** [ɪnˈdʒɛkt] *tr* inyectar; introducir (*una especie, una advertencia*)
**injection** [ɪnˈdʒɛkʃən] *s* inyección
**injudicious** [,ɪndʒuˈdɪʃəs] *adj* imprudente
**injunction** [ɪnˈdʒʌŋkʃən] *s* admonición, mandato; (law) entredicho
**injure** [ˈɪndʒər] *tr* (*to harm*) dañar, hacer daño a; (*to wound*) herir, lisiar, lastimar; (*to offend*) agraviar
**injurious** [ɪnˈdʒʊrɪ·əs] *adj* dañoso, perjudicial; (*offensive*) agravioso
**inju·ry** [ˈɪndʒəri] *s* (*pl* **-ries**) (*harm*) daño; (*wound*) herida, lesión; (*offense*) agravio
**injustice** [ɪnˈdʒʌstɪs] *s* injusticia
**ink** [ɪŋk] *s* tinta ‖ *tr* entintar
**inkling** [ˈɪŋklɪŋ] *s* sospecha, indicio, noción vaga, vislumbre *f*
**ink'stand'** *s* (*cuplike container*) tintero; (*stand for ink, pens, etc.*) portatintero
**ink'well'** *s* tintero
**ink·y** [ˈɪŋki] *adj* (*comp* **-ier**; *super* **-iest**) entintado; negro
**inlaid** [ˈɪn,led] o [,ɪnˈled] *adj* embutido, taraceado
**inland** [ˈɪnlənd] *adj & s* interior *m* ‖ *adv* tierra adentro
**in'-law'** *s* (coll) pariente político
**in·lay** [ˈɪn,le] *s* embutido ‖ [ɪnˈle] o [ˈɪn,le] *v* (*pret & pp* **-laid**) *tr* embutir, taracear
**in'let** *s* ensenada, cala, caleta
**in'mate'** *s* (*in a hospital or home*) asilado, recluso, acogido; (*in a jail*) presidiario, preso
**inn** [ɪn] *s* mesón *m*, posada
**innate** [ɪˈnet] o [ˈɪnet] *adj* ingénito, innato
**inner** [ˈɪnər] *adj* interior; secreto
**in'ner·spring' mattress** *s* colchón *m* de muelles interiores
**inner tube** *s* cámara (de neumático)
**inning** [ˈɪnɪŋ] *s* mano *f*, entrada, turno
**inn'keep'er** *s* mesonero, posadero
**innocence** [ˈɪnəsəns] *s* inocencia
**innocent** [ˈɪnəsənt] *adj & s* inocente *mf*
**innovate** [ˈɪnə,vet] *tr* innovar
**innovation** [,ɪnəˈveʃən] *s* innovación
**innuen·do** [,ɪnjʊˈɛndo] *s* (*pl* **-does**) indirecta, insinuación
**innumerable** [ɪˈnjumərəbəl] o [ɪˈnumərəbəl] *adj* innumerable, incontable
**inoculate** [ɪnˈɑkjə,let] *tr* inocular; (fig) imbuir
**inoculation** [ɪn,ɑkjəˈleʃən] *s* inoculación
**inoffensive** [,ɪnəˈfɛnsɪv] *adj* inofensivo
**inopportune** [ɪn,ɑpərˈtjun] o [ɪn,ɑpərˈtun] *adj* inoportuno
**inordinate** [ɪnˈɔrdɪnɪt] *adj* excesivo; (*unrestrained*) desenfrenado
**inorganic** [,ɪnɔrˈgænɪk] *adj* inorgánico
**in'put'** *s* gasto, consumo; (elec) entrada; (mech) potencia consumida
**inquest** [ˈɪnkwɛst] *s* encuesta; (*of coroner*) pesquisa judicial, levantamiento del cadáver
**inquire** [ɪnˈkwaɪr] *tr* averiguar, inquirir ‖ *intr* preguntar; **to inquire about, after** o **for** preguntar por; **to inquire into** averiguar, inquirir
**inquir·y** [ɪnˈkwaɪri] o [ˈɪnkwɪri] *s* (*pl* **-ies**) averiguación, encuesta; pregunta
**inquisition** [,ɪnkwɪˈzɪʃən] *s* inquisición
**inquisitive** [ɪnˈkwɪzɪtɪv] *adj* curioso, preguntón
**in'road'** *s* incursión
**ins.** *abbr* **insulated, insurance**
**insane** [ɪnˈsen] *adj* loco, insano
**insane asylum** *s* manicomio, casa de locos
**insani·ty** [ɪnˈsænɪti] *s* (*pl* **-ties**) demencia, locura, insania
**insatiable** [ɪnˈseʃəbəl] *adj* insaciable
**inscribe** [ɪnˈskraɪb] *tr* inscribir; dedicar (*una obra literaria*)
**inscription** [ɪnˈskrɪpʃən] *s* inscripción; (*of a book*) dedicatoria
**inscrutable** [ɪnˈskrutəbel] *adj* inescrutable
**insect** [ˈɪnsɛkt] *s* insecto
**insecticide** [ɪnˈsɛktɪ,saɪd] *adj & s* insecticida *m*
**insecure** [,ɪnsɪˈkjʊr] *adj* inseguro

**inseparable** [ɪn'sepərəbəl] *adj* inseparable
**insert** ['ɪnsʌrt] *s* inserción || [ɪn'sʌrt] *tr* insertar
**insertion** [ɪn'sʌrʃən] *s* inserción; (*strip of lace*) entredós *m*
**in•set** ['ɪn,set] *s* intercalación || [ɪn'set] o ['ɪn,set] *v* (*pret & pp* **-set**; *ger* **-setting**) *tr* intercalar, encastrar
**in'shore'** *adj* cercano a la orilla || *adv* cerca de la orilla; hacia la orilla
**in'side'** *adj* interior; interno; secreto || *adv* dentro, adentro; **inside of** dentro de; **to turn inside out** volver al revés; volverse al revés || *prep* dentro de || *s* interior *m;* **insides** (coll) entrañas; **on the inside** (coll) en el secreto de las cosas
**inside information** *s* informes *mpl* confidenciales
**insider** [,ɪn'saɪdər] *s* persona enterada
**insidious** [ɪn'sɪdɪ·əs] *adj* insidioso
**in'sight'** *s* penetración
**insigni•a** [ɪn'sɪgnɪ·ə] *s* (*pl* **-a** o **-as**) insignia
**insignificant** [,ɪnsɪg'nɪfɪkənt] *adj* insignificante
**insincere** [,ɪnsɪn'sɪr] *adj* insincero
**insinuate** [ɪn'sɪnjʊ,et] *tr* insinuar
**insipid** [ɪn'sɪpɪd] *adj* insípido
**insist** [ɪn'sɪst] *intr* insistir
**insofar as** [,ɪnso'fɑr,æz] *conj* en cuanto
**insolence** ['ɪnsələns] *s* insolencia
**insolent** ['ɪnsələnt] *adj* insolente
**insoluble** [ɪn'sɑljəbəl] *adj* insoluble
**insolven•cy** [ɪn'sɑlvənsi] *s* (*pl* **-cies**) insolvencia
**insomnia** [ɪn'sɑmnɪ·ə] *s* insomnio
**insomuch** [,ɪnso'mʌtʃ] *adv* hasta tal punto; **insomuch as** ya que, puesto que; **insomuch that** hasta el punto que
**inspect** [ɪn'spekt] *tr* inspeccionar
**inspection** [ɪn'spekʃən] *s* inspección
**inspiration** [,ɪnspɪ'reʃən] *s* inspiración
**inspire** [ɪn'spaɪr] *tr & intr* inspirar
**inspiring** [ɪn'spaɪrɪŋ] *adj* inspirante
**inst.** *abbr* **instant** (*i.e.*, **present month**)
**Inst.** *abbr* **Institute, Institution**
**install** [ɪn'stɔl] *tr* instalar
**installment** [ɪn'stɔlmənt] *s* instalación; entrega; **in installments** por entregas; a plazos
**installment buying** *s* compra a plazos
**installment plan** *s* pago a plazos, compra a plazos; **on the installment plan** con facilidades de pago
**instance** ['ɪnstəns] *s* caso, ejemplo; **for instance** por ejemplo
**instant** ['ɪnstənt] *adj* instantáneo || *s* instante *m*, momento; mes *m* corriente
**instantaneous** [,ɪnstən'tenɪ·əs] *adj* instantáneo
**instantly** ['ɪnstəntli] *adv* al instante
**instead** [ɪn'sted] *adv* preferiblemente; en su lugar; **instead of** en vez de, en lugar de
**in'step'** *s* empeine *m*
**instigate** ['ɪnstɪ,get] *tr* instigar
**in•still'** *tr* instilar
**instinct** ['ɪnstɪŋkt] *s* instinto
**instinctive** [ɪn'stɪŋktɪv] *adj* instintivo
**institute** ['ɪnstɪ,tjut] o ['ɪnstɪ,tut] *s* instituto || *tr* instituir
**institution** [,ɪnstɪ'tjuʃən] o [,ɪnstɪ'tuʃən] *s* institución
**instruct** [ɪn'strʌkt] *tr* instruir
**instruction** [ɪn'strʌkʃən] *s* instrucción
**instructive** [ɪn'strʌktɪv] *adj* instructivo
**instructor** [ɪn'strʌktər] *s* instructor *m*
**instrument** ['ɪnstrəmənt] *s* instrumento || ['ɪnstrə,ment] *tr* instrumentar
**instrumentalist** [,ɪnstrə'mentəlɪst] *s* instrumentista *mf*
**instrumentali•ty** [,ɪnstrəmən'tælɪti] *s* (*pl* **-ties**) agencia, mediación
**insubordinate** [,ɪnsə'bɔrdɪnɪt] *adj* insubordinado
**insufferable** [ɪn'sʌfərəbəl] *adj* insufrible
**insufficient** [,ɪnsə'fɪʃənt] *adj* insuficiente
**insular** ['ɪnsələr] o ['ɪnsjʊlər] *adj* insular; (fig) de miras estrechas
**insulate** ['ɪnsə,let] *tr* aislar
**insulation** [,ɪnsə'leʃən] *s* aislación
**insulator** ['ɪnsə,letər] *s* aislador *m*
**insulin** ['ɪnsəlɪn] *s* insulina
**insult** ['ɪnsʌlt] *s* insulto || [ɪn'sʌlt] *tr* insultar
**insurance** [ɪn'ʃʊrəns] *s* seguro
**insure** [ɪn'ʃʊr] *tr* asegurar
**insurer** [ɪn'ʃʊrər] *s* asegurador *m*
**insurgent** [ɪn'sʌrdʒənt] *adj & s* insurgente *mf*
**insurmountable** [,ɪnsər'maʊntəbəl] *adj* insuperable
**insurrection** [,ɪnsə'rekʃən] *s* insurrección
**insusceptible** [,ɪnsə'septɪbəl] *adj* insusceptible
**int.** *abbr* **interest, interior, internal, international**
**intact** [ɪn'tækt] *adj* intacto, ileso
**in'take'** *s* (*place of taking in*) entrada; (*act or amount*) toma; (mach) admisión
**intake manifold** *s* múltiple *m* de admisión, colector *m* de admisión
**intake valve** *s* válvula de admisión
**intangible** [ɪn'tændʒɪbəl] *adj* intangible; vago, indefinido
**integer** ['ɪntɪdʒər] *s* (arith) entero
**integral** ['ɪntɪgrəl] *adj* íntegro; **integral with** solidario de || *s* conjunto
**integration** [,ɪntɪ'greʃən] *s* integración
**integrity** [ɪn'tegrɪti] *s* integridad
**intellect** ['ɪntə,lekt] *s* intelecto; (*person*) intelectual *mf*
**intellectual** [,ɪntə'lektʃʊ·əl] *adj & s* intelectual *mf*
**intellectuali•ty** [,ɪntə,lektʃʊ'ælɪti] *s* (*pl* **-ties**) intelectualidad
**intelligence** [ɪn'telɪdʒəns] *s* inteligencia; información
**intelligence bureau** *s* departamento de inteligencia
**intelligence quotient** *s* cociente *m* intelectual
**intelligent** [ɪn'telɪdʒənt] *adj* inteligente
**intelligentsia** [ɪn,telɪ'dʒentsɪ·ə] o [ɪn,telɪ'gentsɪ·ə] *s* intelectualidad (*con-*

*junto de los intelectuales de un país o región*)
**intelligible** [ɪn'telɪdʒɪbəl] *adj* inteligible
**intemperance** [ɪn'tempərəns] *s* intemperancia
**intemperate** [ɪn'tempərɪt] *adj* intemperante; (*climate*) riguroso
**intend** [ɪn'tend] *tr* pensar, proponerse, intentar; (*to mean for a particular purpose*) destinar; (*to signify*) querer decir
**intendance** [ɪn'tendəns] *s* intendencia
**intendant** [ɪn'tendənt] *s* intendente *m*
**intended** [ɪn'tendɪd] *adj* & *s* (coll) prometido, prometida
**intense** [ɪn'tens] *adj* intenso
**intensi•fy** [ɪn'tensɪ,faɪ] *v* (*pret* & *pp* **-fied**) *tr* intensificar, intensar; (phot) reforzar || *intr* intensificarse, intensarse
**intensi•ty** [ɪn'tensɪti] *s* (*pl* **-ties**) intensidad
**intensive** [ɪn'tensɪv] *adj* intensivo
**intent** [ɪn'tent] *adj* atento; resuelto; intenso; **intent on** resuelto a || *s* (*purpose*) intento; (*meaning*) acepción, sentido; **to all intents and purposes** en realidad de verdad
**intention** [ɪn'tenʃən] *s* intención
**intentional** [ɪn'tenʃənəl] *adj* intencional, deliberado
**in•ter** [ɪn'tʌr] *v* (*pret* & *pp* **-terred**; *ger* **-terring**) *tr* enterrar
**interact** ['ɪntər,ækt] *s* (theat) entreacto || [,ɪntər'ækt] *intr* obrar recíprocamente
**interaction** [,ɪntər'ækʃən] *s* interacción
**inter-American** [,ɪntərə'merɪkən] *adj* interamericano
**inter•breed** [,ɪntər'brid] *v* (*pret* & *pp* **-bred** ['bred]) *tr* entrecruzar || *intr* entrecruzarse
**intercalate** [ɪn'tʌrkə,let] *tr* intercalar
**intercede** [,ɪntər'sid] *intr* interceder
**intercept** [,ɪntər'sept] *tr* interceptar
**interceptor** [,ɪntər'septər] *s* interceptor *m*
**interchange** ['ɪntər,tʃendʒ] *s* intercambio; (*on a highway*) correspondencia || [,ɪntər'tʃendʒ] *tr* intercambiar || *intr* intercambiarse
**intercollegiate** [,ɪntərkə'lidʒɪ·ɪt] *adj* interescolar
**intercom** ['ɪntər,kɑm] *s* interfono
**intercourse** ['ɪntər,kors] *s* comunicación, trato; (*interchange of products, ideas, etc.*) intercambio; (*copulation*) cópula, comercio; **to have intercourse** juntarse
**intercross** [,ɪntər'krɔs] o [,ɪntər'krɑs] *tr* entrecruzar || *intr* entrecruzarse
**interdict** ['ɪntər,dɪkt] *s* entredicho || [,ɪntər'dɪkt] *tr* interdecir
**interest** ['ɪntərɪst] o ['ɪntrɪst] *s* interés *m*; **the interests** las grandes empresas, el grupo influyente; **to put out at interest** poner a interés || ['ɪntərɪst], ['ɪntrɪst] o ['ɪntə,rest] *tr* interesar
**interested** ['ɪntrɪstɪd] o ['ɪntə,restɪd] *adj* interesado
**interesting** ['ɪntrɪstɪŋ] o ['ɪntə,restɪŋ] *adj* interesante
**interfere** [,ɪntər'fɪr] *intr* inmiscuirse, injerirse, interferir; (sport) parar una jugada; **to interfere with** dificultar, impedir, interferir
**interference** [,ɪntər'fɪrəns] *s* injerencia, interferencia
**interim** ['ɪntərɪm] *adj* interino || *s* intermedio, intervalo; **in the interim** entretanto
**interior** [ɪn'tɪrɪ·ər] *adj* & *s* interior *m*
**interject** [,ɪntər'dʒekt] *tr* interponer || *intr* interponerse
**interjection** [,ɪntər'dʒekʃən] *s* interposición; exclamación; (gram) interjección
**interlard** [,ɪntər'lɑrd] *tr* interpolar; mechar (*la carne*)
**interline** [,ɪntər'laɪn] *tr* interlinear; entretelar (*una prenda de vestir*)
**interlining** ['ɪntər,laɪnɪŋ] *s* (*of a garment*) entretela
**interlink** [,ɪntər'lɪŋk] *tr* eslabonar
**interlock** [,ɪntər'lɑk] *tr* trabar || *intr* trabarse
**interlope** [,ɪntər'lop] *intr* entremeterse; traficar sin derecho
**interloper** [,ɪntər'lopər] *s* intruso
**interlude** ['ɪntər,lud] *s* intervalo; (mus) interludio; (theat) intermedio
**intermarriage** [,ɪntər'mærɪdʒ] *s* casamiento entre parientes; casamiento entre personas de distintas razas, castas, etc.
**intermediar•y** [,ɪntər'midɪ,eri] *adj* intermediario || *s* (*pl* **-ies**) intermediario
**intermediate** [,ɪntər'midɪ·ɪt] *adj* intermedio
**interment** [ɪn'tʌrmənt] *s* entierro
**intermez•zo** [,ɪntər'metso] o [,ɪntər'medzo] *s* (*pl* **-zos** o **-zi** [tsi] o [dzi]) (mus) intermedio, intermezzo
**intermingle** [,ɪntər'mɪŋgəl] *tr* entremezclar || *intr* entremezclarse
**intermittent** [,ɪntər'mɪtənt] *adj* intermitente
**intermix** [,ɪntər'mɪks] *tr* entremezclar || *intr* entremezclarse
**intern** ['ɪntʌrn] *s* interno de hospital || [ɪn'tʌrn] *tr* internar, recluir
**internal** [ɪn'tʌrnəl] *adj* interno
**inter'nal-combus'tion engine** *s* motor *m* de explosión
**internal revenue** *s* rentas internas
**international** [,ɪntər'næʃənəl] *adj* internacional
**international date line** *s* línea internacional de cambio de fecha
**internationalize** [,ɪntər'næʃənə,laɪz] *tr* internacionalizar
**internecine** [,ɪntər'nisɪn] *adj* sanguinario
**internee** [,ɪntʌr'ni] *s* (mil) internado
**internist** [ɪn'tʌrnɪst] *s* internista *mf*
**internment** [ɪn'tʌrnmənt] *s* internamiento
**internship** ['ɪntʌrn,ʃɪp] *s* residencia de un médico en un hospital

**interpellate** [ˌɪntərˈpelet] o [ɪnˈtʌrpɪˌlet] *tr* interpelar
**interplay** [ˈɪntərˌple] *s* interacción
**interpolate** [ɪnˈtʌrpəˌlet] *tr* interpolar
**interpose** [ˌɪntərˈpoz] *tr* interponer
**interpret** [ɪnˈtʌrprɪt] *tr* interpretar
**interpreter** [ɪnˈtʌrprɪtər] *s* intérprete *mf*
**interrogate** [ɪnˈteraˌget] *tr & intr* interrogar
**interrogation** [ɪnˌterəˈgeʃən] *s* interrogación
**interrogation mark** o **point** *s* signo de interrogación
**interrupt** [ˌɪntəˈrʌpt] *tr* interrumpir
**interscholastic** [ˌɪntərskəˈlæstɪk] *adj* interescolar
**intersection** [ˌɪntərˈsɛkʃən] *s* (*of streets, roads, etc.*) cruce *m;* (geom) intersección
**intersperse** [ˌɪntərˈspʌrs] *tr* entremezclar, esparcir
**interstice** [ɪnˈtʌrstɪs] *s* intersticio
**intertwine** [ˌɪntərˈtwaɪn] *tr* entrelazar ‖ *intr* entrelazarse
**interval** [ˈɪntərvəl] *s* intervalo; **at intervals** (*now and then*) de vez en cuando; (*here and there*) de trecho en trecho
**intervene** [ˌɪntərˈvin] *intr* intervenir
**intervening** [ˌɪntərˈvinɪŋ] *adj* intermedio
**intervention** [ˌɪntərˈvenʃən] *s* intervención
**interview** [ˈɪntərˌvju] *s* entrevista, interview *m* ‖ *tr* entrevistarse con
**inter•weave** [ˌɪntərˈwiv] *v* (*pret* **-wove** [ˈwov] o **-weaved;** *pp* **-wove, woven** o **weaved**) *tr* entretejer
**intestate** [ɪnˈtɛstet] o [ɪnˈtestɪt] *adj & s* intestado
**intestine** [ɪnˈtɛstɪn] *s* intestino
**inthrall** [ɪnˈθrɔl] *tr* cautivar, encantar; esclavizar, sojuzgar
**inthrone** [ɪnˈθron] *tr* entronizar
**intima•cy** [ˈɪntɪməsi] *s* (*pl* **-cies**) intimidad
**intimate** [ˈɪntɪmɪt] *adj* íntimo ‖ *s* amigo íntimo ‖ [ˈɪntɪˌmet] *tr* insinuar, intimar
**intimation** [ˌɪntɪˈmeʃən] *s* insinuación
**intimidate** [ɪnˈtɪmɪˌdet] *tr* intimidar
**intitle** [ɪnˈtaɪtəl] *tr* dar derecho a; (*to give a name to; to honor with a title*) intitular
**into** [ˈɪntu] o [ˈɪntʊ] *prep* en; hacia; hacia el interior de
**intolerant** [ɪnˈtɑlərənt] *adj & s* intolerante *mf*
**intomb** [ɪnˈtum] *tr* sepultar
**intombment** [ɪnˈtummənt] *s* sepultura
**intonation** [ˌɪntoˈneʃən] *s* entonación
**intone** [ɪnˈton] *tr* entonar
**intoxicant** [ɪnˈtɑksɪkənt] *s* bebida alcohólica
**intoxicate** [ɪnˈtɑksɪˌket] *tr* embriagar, emborrachar; (*to exhilarate*) alegrar, excitar; (*to poison*) envenenar, intoxicar
**intoxication** [ɪnˌtɑksɪˈkeʃən] *s* embriaguez *f;* alegría, excitación; (*poisoning*) envenenamiento, intoxicación
**intractable** [ɪnˈtræktəbəl] *adj* intratable
**intransigent** [ɪnˈtrænsɪdʒənt] *adj & s* intransigente *mf*
**intransitive** [ɪnˈtrænsɪtɪv] *adj* intransitivo
**intrench** [ɪnˈtrentʃ] *tr* atrincherar ‖ *intr* — **to intrench on** o **upon** infringir, violar
**intrepid** [ɪnˈtrɛpɪd] *adj* intrépido
**intrepidity** [ˌɪntrɪˈpɪdɪti] *s* intrepidez *f*
**intricate** [ˈɪntrɪkɪt] *adj* intrincado
**intrigue** [ɪnˈtrig] o [ˈɪntrig] *s* intriga; intriga amorosa, enredo amoroso ‖ [ɪnˈtrig] *tr* (*to arouse the curiosity of*) intrigar ‖ *intr* intrigar; tener intrigas amorosas
**intrinsic(al)** [ɪnˈtrɪnsɪk(əl)] *adj* intrínseco
**introd.** *abbr* **introduction**
**introduce** [ˌɪntrəˈdjus] o [ˌɪntrəˈdus] *tr* introducir; (*to make acquainted*) presentar
**introduction** [ˌɪntrəˈdʌkʃən] *s* introducción; (*of one person to another or others*) presentación
**introductory offer** [ˌɪntrəˈdʌktəri] *s* ofrecimiento de presentación, oferta preliminar
**introit** [ˈɪntro·ɪt] *s* (eccl) introito
**introspective** [ˌɪntrəˈspektɪv] *adj* introspectivo
**introvert** [ˈɪntrəˌvʌrt] *s* introvertido
**intrude** [ɪnˈtrud] *intr* injerirse, entremeterse
**intruder** [ɪnˈtrudər] *s* intruso, entremetido
**intrusive** [ɪnˈtrusɪv] *adj* intruso
**intrust** [ɪnˈtrʌst] *tr* confiar
**intuition** [ˌɪntʊˈɪʃən] o [ˌɪntjʊˈɪʃən] *s* intuición
**inundate** [ˈɪnənˌdet] *tr* inundar
**inundation** [ˌɪnənˈdeʃən] *s* inundación
**inure** [ɪnˈjʊr] *tr* acostumbrar, endurecer, aguerrir ‖ *intr* ponerse en efecto; **to inure to** redundar en
**inv.** *abbr* **inventor, invoice**
**invade** [ɪnˈved] *tr* invadir
**invader** [ɪnˈvedər] *s* invasor *m*
**invalid** [ɪnˈvælɪd] *adj* inválido (*nulo, de ningún valor*) ‖ [ˈɪnvəlɪd] *adj* inválido (*por viejo o por enfermo*) ‖ [ˈɪnvəlɪd] *s* inválido
**invalidate** [ɪnˈvælɪˌdet] *tr* invalidar
**invalidity** [ˌɪnvəˈlɪdɪti] *s* invalidez *f*
**invaluable** [ɪnˈvæljʊ·əbəl] *adj* inestimable, inapreciable
**invariable** [ɪnˈverɪ·əbəl] *adj* invariable
**invasion** [ɪnˈveʒən] *s* invasión
**invective** [ɪnˈvɛktɪv] *s* invectiva
**inveigh** [ɪnˈve] *intr* — **to inveigh against** lanzar invectivas contra
**inveigle** [ɪnˈvegəl] o [ɪnˈvigəl] *tr* engatusar
**invent** [ɪnˈvent] *tr* inventar
**invention** [ɪnˈvɛnʃən] *s* invención, invento
**inventive** [ɪnˈvɛntɪv] *adj* inventivo
**inventiveness** [ɪnˈvɛntɪvnɪs] *s* inventiva

**inventor** [ɪnˈventər] *s* inventor *m*
**invento·ry** [ˈɪnvən,tori] *s* (*pl* **-ries**) inventario ‖ *v* (*pret & pp* **-ried**) *tr* inventariar
**inverse** [ɪnˈvʌrs] *adj* inverso
**inversion** [ɪnˈvʌrʒən] o [ɪnˈvʌrʃən] *s* inversión
**invert** [ˈɪnvʌrt] *s* invertido ‖ [ɪnˈvʌrt] *tr* invertir
**invertebrate** [ɪnˈvʌrtɪ,bret] o [ɪnˈvʌrtɪbrɪt] *adj & s* invertebrado
**inverted exclamation point** *s* principio de admiración
**inverted question mark** *s* principio de interrogación
**invest** [ɪnˈvest] *tr* (*to vest, to install*) investir; invertir (*dinero*); (*to besiege*) cercar, sitiar; (*to surround, envelop*) cubrir, envolver
**investigate** [ɪnˈvestɪ,get] *tr* investigar
**investigation** [ɪn,vestɪˈgeʃən] *s* investigación
**investment** [ɪnˈvestmənt] *s* (*of money*) inversión; (*with an office or dignity*) investidura; (*siege*) cerco, sitio
**investor** [ɪnˈvestər] *s* inversionista *mf*
**inveterate** [ɪnˈvetərɪt] *adj* inveterado, empedernido
**invidious** [ɪnˈvɪdɪ·əs] *adj* irritante, odioso, injusto
**invigorate** [ɪnˈvɪgə,ret] *tr* vigorizar
**invigorating** [ɪnˈvɪgə,retɪŋ] *adj* vigorizador, vigorizante
**invincible** [ɪnˈvɪnsɪbəl] *adj* invencible
**invisible** [ɪnˈvɪzɪbəl] *adj* invisible
**invisible ink** *s* tinta simpática
**invitation** [,ɪnvɪˈteʃən] *s* invitación, convite *m*
**invite** [ɪnˈvaɪt] *tr* invitar, convidar
**inviting** [ɪnˈvaɪtɪŋ] *adj* atractivo, seductor; (*e.g., food*) apetitoso
**invoice** [ˈɪnvɔɪs] *s* factura; **as per invoice** según factura ‖ *tr* facturar
**invoke** [ɪnˈvok] *tr* invocar; evocar, conjurar (*p.ej., los demonios*)
**involuntary** [ɪnˈvɑlən,teri] *adj* involuntario
**involution** [,ɪnvəˈluʃən] *s* (math) elevación a potencias, potenciación
**involve** [ɪnˈvɑlv] *tr* envolver, comprometer
**invulnerable** [ɪnˈvʌlnərəbəl] *adj* invulnerable
**inward** [ˈɪnwərd] *adj* interior ‖ *adv* interiormente, hacia dentro
**iodide** [ˈaɪ·ə,daɪd] *s* yoduro
**iodine** [ˈaɪ·ə,din] *s* yodo ‖ [ˈaɪ·ə,daɪn] *s* tintura de yodo
**ion** [ˈaɪ·ən] o [ˈaɪ·ɑn] *s* ion *m*
**ionize** [ˈaɪ·ə,naɪz] *tr* ionizar
**IOU** [ˈaɪ,oˈju] *s* (letterword) pagaré *m*
**I.Q.** [ˈaɪˈkju] *abbr & s* (letterword) **intelligence quotient**
**Iran** [ɪˈrɑn] o [aɪˈræn] *s* el Irán
**Iranian** [aɪˈrenɪ·ən] *adj & s* iranés *m* o iranio
**Iraq** [ɪˈrɑk] *s* el Irak
**Ira·qi** [ɪˈrɑki] *adj* iraqués o iraquiano ‖ *s* (*pl* **-qis**) iraqués *m* o iraquiano
**irate** [ˈaɪret] o [aɪˈret] *adj* airado
**ire** [aɪr] *s* ira, cólera
**Ireland** [ˈaɪrlənd] *s* Irlanda
**iris** [ˈaɪrɪs] *s* (*of the eye*) iris *m;* (*rainbow*) iris, arco iris; (bot) lirio
**Irish** [ˈaɪrɪʃ] *adj* irlandés ‖ *s* (*language*) irlandés *m;* whisky *m* de Irlanda; **the Irish** los irlandeses
**Irish·man** [ˈaɪrɪʃmən] *s* (*pl* **-men** [mən]) irlandés *m*
**Irish stew** *s* guisado de carne con patatas y cebollas
**I′rish·wom′an** *s* (*pl* **-wom′en**) irlandesa
**irk** [ʌrk] *tr* fastidiar, molestar
**irksome** [ˈʌrksəm] *adj* fastidioso, molesto
**iron** [ˈaɪ·ərn] *adj* férreo ‖ *s* hierro; (*implement used to press or smooth clothes*) plancha; **irons** (*fetters*) hierros, grilletes *mpl;* **strike while the iron is hot** a hierro caliente batir de repente ‖ *tr* planchar (*la ropa*); **to iron out** allanar (*una dificultad*)
**i′ron-bound′** *adj* zunchado con hierro; (*unyielding*) férreo, duro, inflexible; (*rock-bound*) escabroso, rocoso
**ironclad** [ˈaɪ·ərn,klæd] *adj* acorazado, blindado; inflexible, exigente
**iron curtain** *s* (fig) telón *m* de hierro, cortina de hierro
**iron digestion** *s* estómago de avestruz
**iron horse** *s* (coll) locomotora
**ironic(al)** [aɪˈrɑnɪk(əl)] *adj* irónico
**ironing** [ˈaɪ·ərnɪŋ] *s* planchado; planchada; ropa por planchar
**ironing board** *s* tabla de planchar
**iron lung** *s* pulmón *m* de acero o de hierro
**i′ron·ware′** *s* ferretería
**iron will** *s* voluntad de hierro
**i′ron·work′** *s* herraje *m;* **ironworks** ferrería, herrería
**i′ron·work′er** *s* herrero de grueso; (*metalworker*) cerrajero
**iro·ny** [ˈaɪrəni] *s* (*pl* **-nies**) ironía
**irradiate** [ɪˈredɪ,et] *tr* irradiar; (med) someter a radiación ‖ *intr* irradiar
**irrational** [ɪˈræʃənəl] *adj* irracional
**irrecoverable** [,ɪrɪˈkʌvərəbəl] *adj* incobrable, irrecuperable
**irredeemable** [,ɪrɪˈdiməbəl] *adj* irredimible
**irrefutable** [,ɪrɪˈfjutəbəl] o [ɪˈrɛfjutəbəl] *adj* irrebatible
**irregular** [ɪˈrɛgjələr] *adj* irregular ‖ *s* (mil) irregular *m*
**irrelevance** [ɪˈrɛləvəns] *s* impertinencia, inaplicabilidad
**irrelevant** [ɪˈrɛləvənt] *adj* impertinente, inaplicable
**irreligious** [,ɪrɪˈlɪdʒəs] *adj* irreligioso
**irremediable** [,ɪrɪˈmidɪ·əbəl] *adj* irremediable
**irremovable** [,ɪrɪˈmuvəbəl] *adj* inamovible
**irreparable** [ɪˈrɛpərəbəl] *adj* irreparable
**irreplaceable** [,ɪrɪˈplesəbəl] *adj* insubstituíble, irreemplazable
**irrepressible** [,ɪrɪˈprɛsɪbəl] *adj* irreprimible, incontenible
**irreproachable** [,ɪrɪˈprotʃəbəl] *adj* irreprochable
**irresistible** [,ɪrɪˈzɪstɪbəl] *adj* irresistible
**irrespective** [,ɪrɪˈspɛktɪv] *adj* — **irre-**

**spective of** sin hacer caso de, independiente de
**irresponsible** [ˌɪrɪˈspɑnsɪbəl] *adj* irresponsable
**irretrievable** [ˌɪrɪˈtrivəbəl] *adj* irrecuperable
**irreverent** [ɪˈrɛvərənt] *adj* irreverente
**irrevocable** [ɪˈrɛvəkəbəl] *adj* irrevocable
**irrigate** [ˈɪrɪˌget] *tr* irrigar
**irrigation** [ˌɪrɪˈgeʃən] *s* irrigación
**irritant** [ˈɪrɪtənt] *adj & s* irritante *m*
**irritate** [ˈɪrɪˌtet] *tr* irritar
**irruption** [ɪˈrʌpʃən] *s* irrupción
**is.** *abbr* **island**
**isinglass** [ˈaɪzɪŋˌglæs] o [ˈaɪzɪŋˌglɑs] *s* (*form of gelatine*) cola de pescado, colapez *f;* mica
**isl.** *abbr* **island**
**Islam** [ˈɪsləm] o [ɪsˈlɑm] *s* el Islam
**island** [ˈaɪlənd] *adj* isleño || *s* isla
**islander** [ˈaɪləndər] *s* isleño
**isle** [aɪl] *s* isleta
**isolate** [ˈaɪsəˌlet] o [ˈɪsəˌlet] *tr* aislar
**isolation** [ˌaɪsəˈleʃən] o [ˌɪsəˈleʃən] *s* aislamiento
**isolationist** [ˌaɪsəˈleʃənɪst] o [ˌɪsəˈleʃənɪst] *s* aislacionista *mf*
**isosceles** [aɪˈsɑsəˌliz] *adj* isosceles
**isotope** [ˈaɪsəˌtop] *s* isótopo
**Israe•li** [ɪzˈreli] *adj* israelí || *s* (*pl* **-lis** [liz]) israelí *mf*
**Israelite** [ˈɪzrɪ•əˌlaɪt] *adj & s* israelita *mf*
**issuance** [ˈɪʃʊ•əns] *s* emisión, expedición
**issue** [ˈɪʃʊ] *s* (*outgoing; outlet*) salida; (*result*) consecuencia, resultado; (*offspring*) descendencia, sucesión; (*of a magazine*) edición, impresión, tirada, número; (*e.g., of a bond*) emisión; (*yield, profit*) beneficios, producto; punto en disputa; (pathol) flujo; **at issue** en disputa; **to face the issue** afrontar la situación; **to force the issue** forzar la solución; **to take issue with** llevar la contraria a || *tr* publicar, dar a luz (*un nuevo libro, una revista, etc.*); emitir, expedir (*títulos, obligaciones, etc.*); distribuir (*ropa, alimento*) || *intr* salir; **to issue from** provenir de
**isthmus** [ˈɪsməs] *s* istmo
**it** [ɪt] *pron pers* (aplícase a cosas inanimadas, a niños de teta, a animales cuyo sexo no se conoce; y muchas veces no se traduce) él, ella; lo, la; **it is I** soy yo; **it is snowing** nieva; **it is three o'clock** son las tres
**ital.** *abbr* **italics**
**Ital.** *abbr* **Italian, Italy**
**Italian** [ɪˈtæljən] *adj & s* italiano
**italic** [ɪˈtælɪk] *adj* (typ) itálico || **italics** *s* (typ) itálica, bastardilla || **Italic** *adj* itálico
**italicize** [ɪˈtælɪˌsaɪz] *tr* imprimir en bastardilla; subrayar
**Italy** [ˈɪtəli] *s* Italia
**itch** [ɪtʃ] *s* comezón *f;* (pathol) sarna; (*eagerness*) (fig) comezón, prurito || *tr* dar comezón a || *intr* picar; **to itch to** tener prurito por
**itch•y** [ˈɪtʃi] *adj* (*comp* **-ier;** *super* **-iest**) picante, hormigoso; (pathol) sarnoso
**item** [ˈaɪtəm] *s* artículo; noticia, suelto; (*in an account*) partida
**itemize** [ˈaɪtəˌmaɪz] *tr* particularizar, especificar, pormenorizar
**itinerant** [aɪˈtɪnərənt] o [ɪˈtɪnərənt] *adj* ambulante, errante || *s* viandante *mf*
**itinerar•y** [aɪˈtɪnəˌrɛri] o [ɪˈtɪnəˌrɛri] *adj* itinerario || *s* (*pl* **-ies**) itinerario
**its** [ɪts] *adj poss* su || *pron poss* el suyo; suyo
**itself** [ɪtˈsɛlf] *pron pers* mismo; sí, sí mismo; se
**ivied** [ˈaɪvid] *adj* cubierto de hiedra
**ivo•ry** [ˈaɪvəri] *adj* marfileño || *s* (*pl* **-ries**) marfil *m;* **ivories** (slang) teclas del piano; (slang) bolas de billar; (*dice*) (slang) dados; (slang) dientes *mpl*
**ivory tower** *s* (fig) torre *f* de marfil
**ivy** [ˈaɪvi] *s* (*pl* **ivies**) hiedra

## J

**J, j** [dʒe] décima letra del alfabeto inglés
**J.** *abbr* **Judge, Justice**
**jab** [dʒæb] *s* hurgonazo; (*prick*) pinchazo; (*with elbow*) codazo || *v* (*pret & pp* **jabbed;** *ger* **jabbing**) *tr* hurgonear; dar un codazo a || *intr* hurgonear
**jabber** [ˈdʒæbər] *s* chapurreo || *tr & intr* chapurrear
**jabot** [dʒæˈbo] o [ˈdʒæbo] *s* chorrera
**jack** [dʒæk] *s* (*for lifting heavy objects*) gato, cric *m;* (*fellow*) mozo, sujeto; (*jackass*) asno, burro; (*in card games*) sota, valet *m;* (*small ball for bowling*) boliche *m;* (*jackstone*) cantillo; (*device for turning a spit*) torno de asador; (*figure which strikes a clock bell*) jaquemar *m;* (*to remove a boot*) sacabotas *m;* marinero; (*flag at the bow*) (naut) yac *m;* (rad & telv) jack *m;* (elec) caja de enchufe; (slang) dinero; **every man Jack** cada hijo de vecino; **jacks** cantillos, juego de los cantillos || *tr* — **to jack up** alzar con el gato; (coll) subir (*sueldos, precios, etc.*); (coll) recordar su obligación a
**jackal** [ˈdʒækəl] *s* chacal *m*
**jackanapes** [ˈdʒækəˌneps] *s* mequetrefe *m*
**jack'ass'** *s* asno, burro
**jack'daw'** *s* corneja
**jacket** [ˈdʒækɪt] *s* chaqueta; (*folded*

*paper*) cubierta, envoltura; (*paper cover of a book*) sobrecubierta; (*metal casing*) camisa
**jack'ham'mer** *s* martillo perforador
**jack'-in-the-box'** *s* caja de sorpresa, jugete-sorpresa *m*, muñeco en una caja de resorte
**jack'knife'** *s* (*pl* **-knives'**) navaja de bolsillo; (*fancy dive*) salto de carpa
**jack of all trades** *s* hombre que hace toda clase de oficios, dije *m*
**jack-o'-lantern** ['dʒækə,læntərn] *s* fuego fatuo; linterna hecha con una calabaza cortada de modo que remede una cabeza humana
**jack pot** *s* — **to hit the jack pot** (slang) ponerse las botas
**jack rabbit** *s* liebre grande norteamericana
**jack'screw'** *s* cric *m* o gato de tornillo
**jack'stone'** *s* cantillo; **jackstones** cantillos, juego de los cantillos
**jack'-tar'** *s* (coll) marinero
**jade** [dʒed] *adj* verdoso como el jade || *s* (*ornamental stone*) jade *m;* verde *m* de jade; (*worn-out horse*) jamelgo; picarona, mujerzuela || *tr* cansar, ahitar, saciar
**jaded** ['dʒedɪd] *adj* ahito, saciado
**jag** [dʒæg] *s* diente *m*, púa; **to have a jag on** (slang) estar borracho
**jagged** ['dʒægɪd] *adj* dentado, mellado; rasgado en sietes
**jaguar** ['dʒægwɑr] *s* jaguar *m*
**jail** [dʒel] *s* cárcel *f;* **to break jail** escaparse de la cárcel || *tr* encarcelar
**jail'bird'** *s* (coll) preso, encarcelado; (coll) infractor *m* habitual
**jail delivery** *s* evasión de la cárcel
**jailer** ['dʒelər] *s* carcelero
**jalop·y** [dʒə'lɑpi] *s* (*pl* **-ies**) automóvil viejo y ruinoso
**jam** [dʒæm] *s* apiñadura, apretura; (*e.g., in traffic*) embotellamiento, bloqueo; (*preserve*) compota, conserva; (*difficult situation*) (coll) aprieto, apuros || *v* (*pret & pp* **jammed;** *ger* **jamming**) *tr* apiñar, apretujar; machucarse (*p.ej., un dedo*); (rad) perturbar, sabotear; **to jam on the brakes** frenar de golpe
**Jamaican** [dʒə'mekən] *adj & s* jamaicano; jamaiquino (Am)
**jamb** [dʒæm] *s* jamba
**jamboree** [,dʒæmbə'ri] *s* (coll) francachela, holgorio; reunión de niños exploradores
**jamming** ['dʒæmɪŋ] *s* radioperturbación
**jam nut** *s* contratuerca
**jam-packed** ['dʒæm'pækt] *adj* (coll) apiñado, apretujado, atestado
**jam session** *s* reunión de músicos de jazz para tocar improvisaciones
**jangle** ['dʒæŋgəl] *s* cencerreo; altercado, riña || *tr* hacer sonar con ruido discordante || *intr* cencerrear; reñir
**janitor** ['dʒænɪtər] *s* portero, conserje *m*
**janitress** ['dʒænɪtrɪs] *s* portera
**January** ['dʒænjʊ,ɛri] *s* enero
**ja·pan** [dʒə'pæn] *s* laca japonesa; obra japonesa laqueada; aceite *m* secante japonés || *v* (*pret & pp* **-panned;** *ger* **-panning**) *tr* barnizar, charolar, laquear con laca japonesa || **Japan** *s* el Japón
**Japa·nese** [,dʒæpə'niz] *adj* japonés || *s* (*pl* **-nese**) japonés *m*
**Japanese beetle** *s* escarabajo japonés
**Japanese lantern** *s* farolillo veneciano
**Japanese persimmon** *s* caqui *m*
**jar** [dʒɑr] *s* tarro; (*e.g., of olives*) frasco; (*of a storage battery*) recipiente *m;* (*jolt*) sacudida; ruido desapacible; sorpresa desagradable; **on the jar** (*said of a door*) entreabierto, entornado || *v* (*pret & pp* **jarred;** *ger* **jarring**) *tr* sacudir; chocar; (*with a noise*) traquetear || *intr* sacudirse; traquetear; disputar; **to jar on** irritar
**jardiniere** [,dʒɑrdɪ'nɪr] *s* (*stand*) jardinera; (*pot, bowl*) florero
**jargon** ['dʒɑrgən] *s* jerga, jerigonza
**jasmine** ['dʒæsmɪn] o ['dʒæzmɪn] *s* jazmín *m*
**jasper** ['dʒæspər] *s* jaspe *m*
**jaundice** ['dʒɔndɪs] o ['dʒɑndɪs] *s* ictericia; (fig) envidia, celos, negro humor
**jaundiced** ['dʒɔndɪst] o ['dʒɑndɪst] *adj* ictericiado; (fig) avinagrado
**jaunt** [dʒɔnt] o [dʒɑnt] *s* caminata, excursión, paseo
**jaun·ty** ['dʒɔnti] o ['dʒɑnti] *adj* (*comp* **-tier;** *super* **-tiest**) airoso, gallardo, vivo; elegante, de buen gusto
**Java·nese** [,dʒævə'niz] *adj* javanés || *s* (*pl* **-nese**) javanés *m*
**javelin** ['dʒævlɪn] o ['dʒævəlɪn] *s* jabalina
**jaw** [dʒɔ] *s* mandíbula, quijada; **into the jaws of death** a las garras de la muerte; **jaws** boca, garganta || *tr* (slang) regañar || *intr* (slang) regañar; (slang) chacharear, chismear
**jaw'bone'** *s* mandíbula, quijada
**jaw'break'er** *s* (*word*) (coll) trabalenguas *m;* (*candy*) (coll) hinchabocas *m;* (mach) trituradora de quijadas
**jay** [dʒe] *s* (orn) arrendajo; (coll) tonto, necio
**jay'walk'** *intr* (coll) cruzar la calle descuidadamente
**jay'walk'er** *s* (coll) peatón descuidado
**jazz** [dʒæz] *s* (mus) jazz *m;* (coll) animación, viveza || *tr* — **to jazz up** (coll) animar, dar viveza a
**jazz band** *s* orquesta de jazz
**J.C.** *abbr* **Jesus Christ, Julius Caesar**
**jct.** *abbr* **junction**
**jealous** ['dʒɛləs] *adj* celoso; envidioso; (*watchful in keeping or guarding something*) solícito, vigilante
**jealous·y** ['dʒɛləsi] *s* (*pl* **-ies**) celosía, celos; envidia; solicitud, vigilancia
**jean** [dʒin] *s* dril *m;* **jeans** pantalones *mpl* de dril
**Jeanne d'Arc** [,ʒɑn'dɑrk] *s* Juana de Arco
**jeep** [dʒip] *s* jip *m*, pequeño automóvil de propulsión total
**jeer** [dʒɪr] *s* befa, mofa, vaya || *tr*

befar || *intr* mofarse; **to jeer at** befar, mofarse de
**jelab** [dʒəˈlɑb] *s* chilaba
**jell** [dʒɛl] *s* jalea || *intr* (*to become jellylike*) cuajarse; (*to take hold, catch on*) (fig) cuajar
**jel·ly** [ˈdʒɛli] *s* (*pl* **-lies**) jalea || *v* (*pret & pp*) *tr* convertir en jalea || *intr* convertirse en jalea
**jel'ly·fish'** *s* aguamala, medusa; (*weak person*) (coll) calzonazos *m*
**jeopardize** [ˈdʒɛpərˌdaɪz] *tr* arriesgar, exponer, poner en peligro
**jeopardy** [ˈdʒɛpərdi] *s* riesgo, peligro
**jeremiad** [ˌdʒɛrɪˈmaɪ·æd] *s* jeremiada
**Jericho** [ˈdʒɛrɪˌko] *s* Jericó
**jerk** [dʒʌrk] *s* arranque *m,* estirón *m,* tirón *m;* tic *m,* espasmo muscular; **by jerks** a sacudidas || *tr* mover de un tirón; arrojar de un tirón; atasajar (*carne*) || *intr* avanzar a tirones
**jerked beef** *s* tasajo
**jerkin** [ˈdʒʌrkɪn] *s* jubón *m,* justillo
**jerk'wa'ter train** *s* (coll) tren de ferrocarril económico
**jerk·y** [ˈdʒʌrki] *adj* (*comp* **-ier;** *super* **-iest**) (*road; style*) desigual; que va dando tumbos, que anda a tirones
**Jerome** [dʒəˈrom] *s* Jerónimo
**jersey** [ˈdʒʌrsi] *s* jersey *m,* chaqueta de punto
**Jerusalem** [dʒɪˈrusələm] *s* Jerusalén
**jest** [dʒɛst] *s* broma, chanza, chiste *m;* cosa de risa; **in jest** en broma || *intr* bromear
**jester** [ˈdʒɛstər] *s* bromista *mf,* burlón *m;* (*professional fool of medieval rulers*) bufón *m*
**Jesuit** [ˈdʒɛʒu·ɪt] o [ˈdʒɛzju·ɪt] *adj & s* jesuíta *m*
**Jesuitic(al)** [ˌdʒɛʒuˈɪtɪk(əl)] o [ˌdʒɛzjuˈɪtɪk(əl)] *adj* jesuítico
**Jesus** [ˈdʒizəs] *s* Jesús *m*
**Jesus Christ** *s* Jesucristo
**jet** [dʒɛt] *adj* de azabache; azabachado || *s* (*of a fountain*) surtidor *m;* (*of gas*) mechero; (*stream shooting forth from nozzle, etc.*) chorro; avión *m* a reacción, avión de chorro; (*hard black mineral; lustrous black*) azabache *m* || *v* (*pret & pp* **jetted;** *ger* **jetting**) *tr* arrojar en chorro || *intr* chorrear, salir en chorro; volar en avión de chorro
**jet age** *s* era de los aviones de chorro
**jet'-black'** *adj* azabachado
**jet bomber** *s* bombardero de reacción a chorro
**jet coal** *s* carbón *m* de bujía, carbón de llama larga
**jet engine** *s* motor *m* a chorro, motor de reacción
**jet fighter** *s* caza *m* de reacción, cazarreactor *m*
**jet'lin'er** *s* avión *m* de travesía con propulsión a chorro
**jet plane** *s* avión *m* de chorro
**jet propulsion** *s* propulsión a chorro, propulsión de escape
**jetsam** [ˈdʒɛtsəm] *s* (naut) echazón *f;* cosas desechadas
**jet stream** *s* escape *m* de un motor cohete; (meteor) chorros de viento (*que soplan de oeste a este a la altura de 10 kilómetros*)
**jettison** [ˈdʒɛtɪsən] *s* (naut) echazón *f* || *tr* (naut) echar al mar; desechar, rechazar
**jettison gear** *s* (aer) lanzador *m*
**jet·ty** [ˈdʒɛti] *s* (*pl* **-ties**) (*structure projecting into sea to protect harbor*) escollera, malecón *m;* (*wharf*) muelle *m,* desembarcadero
**Jew** [dʒu] *s* judío
**jewel** [ˈdʒu·əl] *s* piedra preciosa; (*valuable personal ornament*) alhaja, joya; (*of a watch*) rubí *m;* (*article of costume jewelry*) joya de imitación; (*highly prized person or thing*) alhaja, joya
**jewel case** *s* guardajoyas *m,* estuche *m,* joyero
**jeweler** o **jeweller** [ˈdʒu·ələr] *s* joyero; relojero
**jewelry** [ˈdʒu·əlri] *s* joyería, joyas
**jewelry shop** *s* joyería; relojería
**Jewess** [ˈdʒu·ɪs] *s* judía
**jew'fish'** *s* mero
**Jewish** [ˈdʒu·ɪʃ] *adj* judío
**Jew·ry** [ˈdʒu·ri] *s* (*pl* **-ries**) judería
**jews'-harp** o **jew's-harp** [ˈdjuzˌhɑrp] *s* birimbao
**jib** [dʒɪb] *s* (*of a crane*) aguilón *m,* pescante *m;* (naut) foque *m*
**jib boom** *s* (naut) botalón *m* de foque
**jibe** [dʒaɪb] *s* remoque *m,* mofa || *intr* mofarse; (coll) concordar (*dos cosas*); **to jibe at** mofarse de
**jif·fy** [ˈdʒɪfi] *s* (*pl* **-fies**) — **in a jiffy** (coll) en un santiamén
**jig** [dʒɪg] *s* (*dance and music*) giga; **the jig is up** (slang) ya se acabó todo, estamos perdidos
**jigger** [ˈdʒɪgər] *s* (*for fishing*) anzuelo de cuchara; (*for separating ore*) criba de vaivén; (*flea*) nigua; (*gadget*) cosilla, chisme *m,* dispositivo; vasito para medir el licor de un coctel (*onza y media*)
**jiggle** [ˈdʒɪgəl] *s* zangoloteo || *tr* zangolotear || *intr* zangolotearse
**jig saw** *s* sierra de vaivén
**jig'saw' puzzle** *s* rompecabezas *m* (*figura que ha sido cortada caprichosamente en trozos menudos y que hay que recomponer*)
**jilt** [dʒɪlt] *tr* dar calabazas a (*un novio*)
**jim·my** [ˈdʒɪmi] *s* (*pl* **-mies**) palanqueta || *v* (*pret & pp* **-mied**) *tr* forzar con palanqueta; **to jimmy open** abrir con palanqueta
**jingle** [ˈdʒɪŋgəl] *s* (*small bell*) cascabel *m;* (*of tambourine*) sonaja; (*sound*) cascabeleo; rima infantil; (rad) anuncio rimado y cantado || *tr* hacer sonar || *intr* cascabelear
**jin·go** [ˈdʒɪŋgo] *adj* jingoísta || *s* (*pl* **-goes**) jingoísta *mf;* **by jingo!** (coll) ¡caramba!
**jingoism** [ˈdʒɪŋgoˌɪzəm] *s* jingoísmo
**jinx** [dʒɪŋks] *s* gafe *m* || *tr* (coll) traer mala suerte a
**jitters** [ˈdʒɪtərz] *spl* (coll) inquietud, nerviosidad; **to give the jitters to**

(coll) poner nervioso; **to have the jitters** (coll) ponerse nervioso

**jittery** [ˈdʒɪtəri] *adj* (coll) nervioso

**Joan of Arc** [ˈdʒon əv ˈɑrk] *s* Juana de Arco

**job** [dʒɑb] *s* (*piece of work*) trabajo; (*task, chore*) quehacer *m*, tarea; (*work done by contract*) destajo; (*employment*) empleo, oficio; (coll) robo; **by the job** a destajo; **on the job** trabajando de aprendiz; (slang) vigilante, atento a sus obligaciones; **to be out of a job** estar desocupado, estar sin trabajo; **to lie down on the job** (slang) echarse en el surco, estirar la pierna

**job analysis** *s* análisis *m* ocupacional

**jobber** [ˈdʒɑbər] *s* comerciante medianero; (*pieceworker*) destajero; (*dishonest official*) agiotista *m*

**job'hold'er** *s* empleado; (*in the government*) burócrata *mf*

**jobless** [ˈjɑblɪs] *adj* desocupado, sin empleo

**job lot** *s* saldo de mercancías

**job printer** *s* impresor *m* de remiendos

**job printing** *s* remiendo

**jockey** [ˈdʒɑki] *s* jockey *m* ‖ *tr* montar (*un caballo*) en la pista; maniobrar; embaucar

**jockstrap** [ˈdʒɑk ˌstræp] *s* suspensorio (*para sostener el escroto*)

**jocose** [dʒoˈkos] *adj* jocoso

**jocular** [ˈdʒɑkjələr] *adj* jocoso, festivo

**jog** [dʒɑg] *s* golpecito; (*to the memory*) estímulo; trote corto ‖ *v* (*pret & pp* **jogged**; *ger* **jogging**) *tr* empujar levemente; estimular (*la memoria*) ‖ *intr* — **to jog along** avanzar al trote corto

**jog trot** *s* trote *m* de perro; (fig) rutina

**John** [dʒɑn] *s* Juan *m*

**John Bull** *s* el inglés típico, el pueblo inglés

**John Hancock** [ˈhænkɑk] *s* (coll) la firma de uno

**johnnycake** [ˈdʒɑni ˌkek] *s* pan *m* de maíz

**John'ny-come'-late'ly** *s* (coll) recién llegado

**John'ny-jump'-up'** *s* (*pansy*) pensamiento, trinitaria; violeta

**John'ny-on-the-spot'** *s* (coll) el que está siempre presente y listo

**John the Baptist** *s* San Juan Bautista

**join** [dʒɔɪn] *tr* juntar, unir, ensamblar; asociarse a, unirse a; incorporarse a, ingresar en; abrazar (*un partido*); hacerse socio de (*una asociación*); alistarse en (*el ejército*); trabar (*batalla*); desaguar en (*el océano*) ‖ *intr* juntarse, unirse; confluir (*p.ej., dos ríos*)

**joiner** [ˈdʒɔɪnər] *s* carpintero; (coll) el que tiene la manía de incorporarse a muchas asociaciones

**joint** [dʒɔɪnt] *s* (*in a pipe*) empalme *m*, juntura; (*of bones*) articulación, juntura, coyuntura; (*backbone of book*) nervura; (*hinge of book*) cartivana; (*in woodwork*) emsambladura; (*of meat*) tajada; (elec) empalme *m*; (*gambling den*) (slang) garito; (slang) restaurante *m* de mala muerte; **out of joint** desencajado, descoyuntado; (fig) en desorden, desbarajustado; **to throw out of joint** descoyuntarse (*p.ej., el brazo*)

**joint account** *s* cuenta en común

**Joint Chiefs of Staff** *spl* (U.S.A.) Estado mayor conjunto

**jointly** [ˈdʒɔɪntli] *adv* juntamente, en común

**joint owner** *s* condueño

**joint session** *s* sesión conjunta

**joint'-stock' company** *s* sociedad anónima, compañía por acciones

**joist** [dʒɔɪst] *s* viga

**joke** [dʒok] *s* broma, chiste *m*; (*trifling matter*) cosa de reír; (*person laughed at*) bufón *m*, hazmerreír *m*; **no joke** cosa seria; **to tell a joke** contar un chiste; **to play a joke on** gastar una broma a ‖ *tr* — **to joke one's way into** conseguir (*p.ej., un empleo*) burla burlando ‖ *intr* bromear, hablar en broma; **joking aside** o **no joking** burlas aparte

**joke book** *s* libro de chistes

**joker** [ˈdʒokər] *s* bromista *mf*; (*wise guy*) sábelotodo; (*playing card*) comodín *m*; (*hidden provision*) cláusula engañadora

**jol·ly** [ˈdʒɑli] *adj* (*comp* **-lier**; *super* **-liest**) alegre, festivo ‖ *adv* (coll) muy, harto ‖ *v* (*pret & pp* **-lied**) *tr* (coll) candonguear

**jolt** [dʒolt] *s* sacudida ‖ *tr* sacudir ‖ *intr* dar tumbos

**Jonah** [ˈdʒonə] *s* Jonás *m*; (fig) ave *f* de mal agüero

**jongleur** [ˈdʒɑŋglər] *s* juglar *m*, trovador *m*

**jonquil** [ˈdʒɑŋkwɪl] *s* junquillo

**Jordan** [ˈdʒɔrdən] *s* (*country*) Jordania; (*river*) Jordán *m*

**Jordan almond** *s* almendra de Málaga

**Jordanian** [dʒɔrˈdenɪ·ən] *adj & s* jordano

**josh** [dʒɑʃ] *tr* (coll) dar broma a ‖ *intr* dar broma

**jostle** [ˈdʒɑsəl] *s* empellón *m*, empujón *m* ‖ *tr* empellar, empujar ‖ *intr* chocar, encontrarse; avanzar a fuerza de empujones o codazos

**jot** [dʒɑt] *s* — **I don't care a jot for** no se me da un bledo de ‖ *v* (*pret & pp* **jotted**; *ger* **jotting**) *tr* — **to jot down** apuntar, anotar

**jounce** [dʒauns] *s* sacudida ‖ *tr* sacudir ‖ *intr* dar tumbos

**journal** [ˈdʒʌrnəl] *s* (*newspaper*) periódico; (*magazine*) revista; (*daily record*) diario; (com) libro diario; (naut) cuaderno de bitácora; (mach) gorrón *m*, muñón *m*

**journalese** [ˌdʒʌrnəˈliz] *s* lenguaje periodístico

**journalism** [ˈdʒʌrnəˌlɪzəm] *s* periodismo

**journalist** [ˈdʒʌrnəlɪst] *s* periodista *mf*

**journalistic** [ˌdʒʌrnəˈlɪstɪk] *adj* periodístico

**journey** [ˈdʒʌrni] *s* viaje *m* ‖ *intr* viajar

**journey·man** ['dʒʌrnimən] *s* (*pl* **-men** [mən]) oficial *m*
**joust** [dʒʌst] o [dʒust] o [dʒaʊst] *s* justa || *intr* justar
**jovial** ['dʒovɪ·əl] *adj* jovial
**joviality** [,dʒovɪ'ælɪti] *s* jovialidad
**jowl** [dʒaʊl] *s* (*cheek*) moflete *m;* (*jawbone*) quijada; (*of cattle*) papada; (*of fowl*) barba
**joy** [dʒɔɪ] *s* alegría, regocijo; **to leap with joy** saltar de gozo
**joyful** ['dʒɔɪfəl] *adj* alegre; **joyful over** gozoso con o de
**joyless** ['dʒɔɪlɪs] *adj* triste, sin alegría
**joyous** ['dʒɔɪ·əs] *adj* alegre
**joy ride** *s* (coll) paseo de recreo en coche; (coll) paseo alocado en coche
**J.P.** *abbr* **Justice of the Peace**
**Jr.** *abbr* **junior**
**jubilant** ['dʒubɪlənt] *adj* jubiloso
**jubilation** [,dʒubɪ'leʃən] *s* júbilo, viva alegría
**jubilee** ['dʒubɪ,li] *s* (*jubilation*) júbilo; aniversario; quincuagésimo aniversario; (eccl) jubileo
**Judaism** ['dʒude,ɪzəm] *s* judaísmo
**judge** [dʒʌdʒ] *s* juez *m;* **to be a good judge of** ser buen juez de o en || *tr & intr* juzgar; **judging by** a juzgar por
**judge advocate** *s* (*in the army*) auditor *m* de guerra; (*in the navy*) auditor de marina
**judgeship** ['dʒʌdʒʃɪp] *s* judicatura
**judgment** ['dʒʌdʒmənt] *s* juicio; (*legal decision*) sentencia, fallo
**judgment day** *s* día *m* del juicio
**judgment seat** *s* tribunal *m*
**judicature** ['dʒudɪkətʃər] *s* judicatura
**judicial** [dʒu'dɪʃəl] *adj* judicial; (*becoming a judge*) crítico, juicioso
**judiciar·y** [dʒu'dɪʃɪ,ɛri] *adj* judicial || *s* (*pl* **-ies**) (*judges of a city, country, etc.*) judicatura; (*branch of government that administers justice*) poder *m* judicial
**judicious** [dʒu'dɪʃəs] *adj* juicioso
**jug** [dʒʌg] *s* botija, jarra, cántaro; (*jail*) (slang) chirona
**juggle** ['dʒʌgəl] *s* juego de manos; (*trick, deception*) trampa || *tr* hacer suertes con (*p.ej., bolas*); alterar fraudulentamente, falsear (*cuentas, documentos, etc.*); **to juggle away** escamotear || *intr* hacer suertes; hacer trampas
**juggler** ['dʒʌglər] *s* malabarista *mf;* impostor *m*
**juggling** ['dʒʌglɪŋ] *s* juegos malabares
**Jugoslav** ['jugo'slɑv] *adj & s* yugoeslavo
**Jugoslavia** ['jugo'slɑvɪ·ə] *s* Yugoeslavia
**jugular** ['dʒʌgjələr] o ['dʒugjələr] *adj & s* yugular *f*
**juice** [dʒus] *s* jugo, zumo; (*natural fluid of an animal body*) jugo; (slang) electricidad; (slang) gasolina; **to stew in one's own juice** (coll) freír en su aceite
**juic·y** ['dʒusi] *adj* (*comp* **-ier;** *super* **-iest**) jugoso, zumoso; (*interesting, spicy*) picante
**jukebox** ['dʒuk,bɑks] *s* tocadiscos *m* tragamonedas
**julep** ['dʒulɪp] *s* julepe *m*
**julienne** [,dʒulɪ'ɛn] *s* sopa juliana
**July** [dʒu'laɪ] *s* julio
**jumble** ['dʒʌmbəl] *s* revoltijo, masa confusa || *tr* emburujar, revolver
**jum·bo** ['dʒʌmbo] *adj* (coll) enorme, colosal || *s* (*pl* **-bos**) (*large clumsy person*) (coll) elefante *m;* (coll) objeto enorme
**jump** [dʒʌmp] *s* salto; (*in a parachute*) lanzamiento; (*of prices*) alza repentina; **to be always on the jump** (coll) andar siempre de aquí para allí; **to get** o **to have the jump on** (slang) ganar la ventaja a || *tr* saltar; hacer saltar (*a un caballo*); (*in checkers*) comer; salir (*un tren*) fuera de (*el carril*) || *intr* saltar; (*in a parachute from an airplane*) lanzarse; pasar del tope (*el carro de la máquina de escribir*); **to jump at** apresurarse a aceptar (*un convite*); apresurarse a aprovechar (*la oportunidad*); **to jump on** saltar a (*un tren*); (slang) regañar, criticar; **to jump over** saltar por, pasar de un salto; saltar (*la página de un libro*); **to jump to a conclusion** sacar una conclusión precipitadamente
**jumper** ['dʒʌmpər] *s* saltador *m;* blusa de obrero; **jumpers** traje holgado de juego para niños
**jumping jack** ['dʒʌmpɪŋ] *s* títere *m*
**jump'ing-off' place** *s* fin *m* del camino
**jump seat** *s* estrapontín *m*, traspuntín *m*
**jump spark** *s* (elec) chispa de entrehierro
**jump wire** *s* (elec) alambre *m* de cierre
**jump·y** ['dʒʌmpi] *adj* (*comp* **-ier;** *super* **-iest**) saltón; asustadizo, nervioso
**junc.** *abbr* **junction**
**junction** ['dʒʌŋkʃən] *s* juntura, unión; (*of pieces of wood*) ensambladura; (*of two rivers*) confluencia; (*rail connection*) empalme *m;* (rr) estación de empalme
**juncture** ['dʒʌŋktʃər] *s* juntura, unión; (*time, occasion*) coyuntura; **at this juncture** a esta sazón, a estas alturas
**June** [dʒun] *s* junio
**jungle** ['dʒʌŋgəl] *s* jungla, selva; revoltijo, maraña
**junior** ['dʒunjər] *adj* menor, de menor edad; joven; del penúltimo año; hijo, p.ej., **John Jones, Junior** Juan Jones, hijo || *s* menor *m;* socio menor; alumno del penúltimo año
**junior college** *s* escuela de estudios universitarios de primero y segundo años
**junior high school** *s* escuela intermedia entre la primaria y la secundaria
**juniper** ['dʒunɪpər] *s* enebro; (*red cedar*) cedro de Virginia
**juniper berry** *s* enebrina
**junk** [dʒʌŋk] *s* chatarra, hierro viejo; ropa vieja; (*useless stuff*) (coll) trastos viejos, baratijas viejas; (*old cable*) jarcia trozada; (*Chinese ship*) junco; (naut) carne salada || *tr*

(slang) echar a la basura; reducir a hierro viejo
**junk dealer** *s* chatarrero, chapucero
**junket** ['dʒʌŋkɪt] *s* manjar *m* de leche, cuajo y azúcar; (*outing*) viaje *m* de recreo; (*trip paid out of public funds*) jira || *intr* hacer un viaje de recreo; ir de jira
**junk•man** ['dʒʌŋk,mæn] *s* (*pl* **-men** [,mɛn]) chatarrero, chapucero; ropavejero; tripulante *m* de junco
**junk room** *s* leonera, trastera
**junk shop** *s* tienda de trastos viejos
**junk yard** *s* chatarrería
**juridical** [dʒʊ'rɪdɪkəl] *adj* jurídico
**jurisdiction** [,dʒʊrɪs'dɪkʃən] *s* jurisdicción
**jurisprudence** [,dʒʊrɪs'prudəns] *s* jurisprudencia
**jurist** ['dʒʊrɪst] *s* jurista *mf*
**juror** ['dʒʊrər] *s* (*individual*) jurado
**ju•ry** ['dʒʊri] *s* (*pl* **-ries**) (*group*) jurado
**jury box** *s* tribuna del jurado
**jury•man** ['dʒʊrimən] *s* (*pl* **-men** [mən]) (*individual*) jurado
**Jus. P.** *abbr* **justice of the peace**
**just** [dʒʌst] *adj* justo || *adv* justamente, justo; hace poco, apenas; sólo; (coll) absolutamente; **just** + *pp* acabado de + *inf*, p.ej., **just received** acabado de recibir; recién + *pp*, p.ej., **just arrived** recién llegado; **just as** como; en el momento en que; tal como, lo mismo que; **just beyond** un poco más allá (de); **just now** hace poco; ahora mismo; **just out** acabado de aparecer, recién publicado; **to have just** + *pp* acabar de + *inf*, p.ej., **I have just arrived** acabo de llegar; **I had just arrived** acababa de llegar
**justice** ['dʒʌstɪs] *s* justicia; (*judge*) juez *m;* (*just deserts*) premio merecido; **to bring to justice** aprehender y condenar por justicia; **to do justice to** hacer justicia a; apreciar debidamente
**justice of the peace** *s* juez *m* de paz
**justifiable** ['dʒʌstɪ,faɪ•əbəl] *adj* justificable
**justi•fy** ['dʒʌstɪ,faɪ] *v* (*pret & pp* **-fied**) *tr* justificar; (typ) justificar
**justly** ['dʒʌstli] *adj* justamente, debidamente
**jut** [dʒʌt] *v* (*pret & pp* **jutted**; *ger* **jutting**) *intr* — **to jut out** resaltar, proyectarse
**jute** [dʒut] *s* yute *m* || **Jute** *m* juto
**Jutland** ['dʒʌtlənd] *s* Jutlandia
**juvenile** ['dʒuvənɪl] o ['dʒuvə,naɪl] *adj* juvenil; para jóvenes || *s* joven *mf*, mocito; libro para niños; (theat) galán *m*, galancete *m*
**juvenile court** *s* tribunal *m* tutelar de menores
**juvenile delinquency** *s* delincuencia de menores
**juvenile lead** [lid] *s* (theat) papel *m* de galancete; (theat) galancete *m*
**juvenilia** [,dʒuvə'nɪlɪ•ə] *spl* obras de juventud
**juxtapose** [,dʒʌkstə'poz] *tr* yuxtaponer

# K

**K, k** [ke] undécima letra del alfabeto inglés
**k.** *abbr* **karat, kilogram**
**K.** *abbr* **King, Knight**
**kale** [kel] *s* col *f*, berza; (slang) dinero, pasta
**kaleidoscope** [kə'laɪdə,skop] *s* calidoscopio
**kangaroo** [,kæŋgə'ru] *s* canguro
**kapok** ['kepɑk] *s* capoc *m*, lana de ceiba
**katydid** ['ketidɪd] *s* saltamontes *m* cuyo macho emite un sonido chillón
**kc.** *abbr* **kilocycle**
**kedge** [kɛdʒ] *s* (naut) anclote *m*
**keel** [kil] *s* quilla || *intr* — **to keel over** (naut) dar de quilla; volcarse; (coll) desmayarse
**keelson** ['kɛlsən] o ['kilsən] *s* (naut) sobrequilla
**keen** [kin] *adj* (*having a sharp edge*) agudo, afilado; (*sharp, cutting*) mordaz, penetrante; (*sharp-witted*) sutil, astuto, perspicaz; (*eager, much interested*) entusiasta; intenso, vivo; (slang) maravilloso; **to be keen on** ser muy aficionado a
**keep** [kip] *s* manutención, subsistencia; (*of medieval castle*) torre *f* del homenaje; **for keeps** (coll) de veras; (coll) para siempre; **to earn one's keep** (coll) ganarse la vida || *v* (*pret & pp* **kept** [kɛpt]) *tr* guardar, conservar; (*deciding to make a purchase*) quedarse con; cumplir, guardar (*su palabra, su promesa*); llevar (*cuentas*); apuntar (*los tantos*); tener (*criados, caballos, huéspedes*); cultivar (*una huerta*); dirigir (*un hotel, una escuela*); celebrar (*una fiesta*); hacer tardar (*a una persona*); **to keep away** tener alejado; **to keep back** retener; beberse (*las lágrimas*); reservar, no divulgar; **to keep down** reprimir; reducir (*los gastos*) al mínimo; **to keep** (*a person*) **from** + *ger* no dejarle (*a una persona*) + *inf;* **to keep in** no dejar salir; **to keep off** tener a distancia; no dejar penetrar (*p.ej., la lluvia*); evitar (*p.ej., el polvo*); **to keep out** no dejar entrar; no dejar penetrar; **to keep someone informed** (**about**) ponerle a uno al corriente (de); **to keep someone waiting** hacerle a uno esperar; **to keep up** mantener, conservar || *intr*

permanecer, quedarse; conservarse, no echarse a perder; **to keep** + *ger* seguir + *ger;* **to keep away** mantenerse a distancia; no dejarse ver; **to keep from** + *ger* abstenerse de + *inf;* **to keep informed (about)** ponerse al corriente (de); **to keep in with** (coll) congraciarse con, no perder el favor de; **to keep off** no acercarse a; no pisar (*el césped*); **to keep on** + *ger* seguir + *ger;* **to keep on with** continuar con; **to keep out** mantenerse fuera, no entrar; **to keep out of** no entrar en; no meterse en; evitar (*el peligro*); **to keep quiet** estarse quieto; **to keep to** seguir por, llevar (*la derecha, la izquierda*); **to keep to oneself** quedarse a solas; **to keep up** continuar; no rezagarse; **to keep up with** correr parejas con; llevar adelante, proseguir

**keeper** [ˈkipər] *s* guardián *m,* custodio; (*of a game preserve*) guardabosque *m;* (*of a magnet*) armadura, culata

**keeping** [ˈkipɪŋ] *s* custodia, cuidado; (*of a holiday*) celebración; **in keeping with** de acuerdo con, en armonía con; **in safe keeping** en lugar seguro, a buen recaudo; **out of keeping with** en desacuerdo con

**keep'sake'** *s* recuerdo

**keg** [kɛg] *s* cuñete *m,* cubeto

**ken** [kɛn] *s* alcance *m* de la vista, alcance del saber; **beyond the ken of** fuera del alcance de

**kennel** [ˈkɛnəl] *s* perrera

**kep•i** [ˈkepi] o [ˈkɛpi] *s* (*pl* **-is**) quepis *m*

**kept woman** [kɛpt] *s* entretenida, manceba

**kerchief** [ˈkʌrtʃɪf] *s* pañuelo, mantón *m*

**kerchoo** [kərˈtʃu] *interj* ¡ah-chís!

**kernel** [ˈkʌrnəl] *s* (*inner part of a nut or fruit stone*) almendra, núcleo; (*of wheat or corn*) grano; (fig) medula

**kerosene** [ˈkɛrəˌsin] o [ˌkɛrəˈsin] *s* keroseno

**kerosene lamp** *s* lámpara de petróleo

**kerplunk** [kərˈplʌŋk] *interj* ¡pataplún!

**ketchup** [ˈketʃəp] *s* salsa de tomate condimentada

**kettle** [ˈkɛtəl] *s* caldera, marmita; (*teakettle*) tetera

**ket'tle•drum'** *s* timbal *m,* tímpano

**key** [ki] *adj* clave || *s* (*of door, trunk, etc.*) llave *f;* (*of piano, typewriter, etc.*) tecla; (*wedge or cotter used to lock parts together*) clavija, cuña, chaveta; (*reef or low island*) cayo; (bot) sámara; (*tone of voice*) tono; (mus) clave *f* o llave *f;* (telg) manipulador *m;* (*to a puzzle, secret, translation, code*) (fig) clave o llave; (*place giving control to a region*) (fig) llave *f;* (fig) persona principal; **off key** desafinado; desafinadamente || *tr* acuñar, enchavetar; **to key up** alentar, excitar

**key'board'** *s* teclado

**key fruit** *s* sámara

**key'hole'** *s* ojo de la cerradura; (*of a clock*) agujero de cuerda

**key'note'** *s* (mus) tónica, nota tónica; (fig) idea fundamental

**keynote speech** *s* discurso de apertura (*en que se expone el programa de un partido político*)

**key ring** *s* llavero

**key'stone'** *s* clave *f,* espinazo; (fig) piedra angular

**Key West** *s* Cayo Hueso

**key word** *s* palabra clave

**kg.** *abbr* **kilogram**

**K.G.** *abbr* **Knight of the Garter**

**kha•ki** [ˈkɑki] o [ˈkæki] *adj* caqui || *s* (*pl* **-kis**) caqui *m*

**khedive** [kəˈdiv] *s* jedive *m*

**kibitz** [ˈkɪbɪts] *intr* (coll) dar consejos molestos a los jugadores

**kibitzer** [ˈkɪbɪtsər] *s* (coll) mirón molesto (*de una partida de juego*); (coll) entremetido

**kiblah** [ˈkɪblɑ] *s* alquibla

**kibosh** [ˈkaɪbɑʃ] o [kɪˈbɑʃ] *s* (coll) música celestial; **to put the kibosh on** (coll) desbaratar, imposibilitar

**kick** [kɪk] *s* puntapié *m;* (*of an animal*) coz *f;* (*of a gun*) coz, culatazo; (*complaint*) (slang) queja, protesta; (*of liquor*) (slang) fuerza, estímulo; (*thrill*) gusto, placer intenso; **to get a kick out of** (slang) hallar mucho placer en || *tr* acocear, dar de puntapiés a; sacudir (*los pies*); **to kick out** (coll) echar a puntapiés a la calle; (coll) echar, despedir; **to kick up a row** (slang) armar un bochinche || *intr* cocear; dar culetazos (*un arma de fuego*); (coll) quejarse; **to kick about** (coll) quejarse de; **to kick against the pricks** dar coces contra el aguijón; **to kick off** (football) dar el golpe de salida

**kick'back'** *s* (coll) contragolpe *m;* (slang) devolución a un cómplice de una parte de lo robado

**kick'off'** *s* (football) golpe *m* de salida, puntapié *m* inicial

**kid** [kɪd] *s* (*young goat*) cabrito; (*leather*) cabritilla; (coll) chiquillo, chico; **kids** guantes *mpl* o zapatos de cabritilla || *v* (*pret & pp* **kidded;** *ger* **kidding**) *tr* (slang) embromar, tomar el pelo a; **to kid oneself** (slang) forjarse ilusiones || *intr* (slang) decirlo en broma

**kidder** [ˈkɪdər] *s* (slang) bromista *mf*

**kid gloves** *spl* guantes *mpl* de cabritilla; **to handle with kid gloves** tratar con suma discreción o cautela

**kid'nap'** *s* (*pret & pp* **-naped** o **-napped;** *ger* **-naping** o **-napping**) *tr* secuestrar

**kidnaper** o **kidnapper** [ˈkɪdˌnæpər] *s* secuestrador *m,* ladrón *m* de niños

**kidney** [ˈkɪdni] *s* riñón *m;* (coll) clase *f,* especie *f;* (coll) carácter *m*

**kidney bean** *s* judía

**kidney stone** *s* cálculo renal

**kill** [kɪl] *s* matanza; (*of a wild beast, an army, a pack of hounds*) ataque *m* final; (*creek*) arroyo, riachuelo; **for the kill** para el golpe final || *tr*

matar; ahogar (*un proyecto de ley*); quitar (*el sabor*); producir una impresión irresistible en
**killer** ['kɪlər] *s* matador *m*
**killer whale** *s* orca
**killing** ['kɪlɪŋ] *adj* matador; (*exhausting*) abrumador; (coll) muy divertido, de lo más ridículo || *s* matanza; (*game killed on a hunt*) cacería, piezas; (coll) gran ganancia; **to make a killing** (coll) enriquecerse de golpe
**kill'-joy'** *s* aguafiestas *mf*
**kiln** [kɪl] o [kɪln] *s* horno
**kil•o** ['kɪlo] o ['kilo] *s* (*pl* **-os**) kilo, kilogramo; kilómetro
**kilocycle** ['kɪlə,saɪkəl] *s* kilociclo
**kilogram** ['kɪlə,græm] *s* kilogramo
**kilometer** ['kɪlə,mitər] o [kɪ'lɑmɪtər] *s* kilómetro
**kilometric** [,kɪlə'mɛtrɪk] *adj* kilométrico
**kilowatt** ['kɪlə,wɑt] *s* kilovatio
**kilowatt-hour** ['kɪlə,wɑt'aur] *s* (*pl* **kilowatt-hours**) kilovatio-hora
**kilt** [kɪlt] *s* enagüillas, falda corta
**kilter** ['kɪltər] *s* — **to be out of kilter** (coll) estar descompuesto
**kimo•no** [kɪ'monə] o [kɪ'mono] *s* (*pl* **-nos**) quimono
**kin** [kɪn] *s* (*family relationship*) parentesco; (*relatives*) deudos; **near of kin** muy allegado; **of kin** allegado; **the next of kin** el pariente más próximo, los parientes próximos
**kind** [kaɪnd] *adj* bueno, bondadoso; (*greeting*) afectuoso; **kind to** bueno para con || *s* clase *f*, especie *f*, suerte *f*, género; **a kind of** uno a modo de; **all kinds of** (coll) gran cantidad de; **in kind** en especie; en la misma moneda; **kind of** (coll) algo, más bien; **of a kind** de una misma clase; (*poor, mediocre*) de poco valor, de mala muerte; **of the kind** por el estilo
**kindergarten** ['kɪndər,gɑrtən] *s* escuela de párvulos, jardín *m* de la infancia
**kindergartner** ['kɪndər,gɑrtnər] *s* (*child*) párvulo; (*teacher*) parvulista *mf*
**kind-hearted** ['kaɪnd'hɑrtɪd] *adj* bondadoso, de buen corazón
**kindle** ['kɪndəl] *tr* encender || *intr* encenderse
**kindling** ['kɪndlɪŋ] *s* encendajas
**kindling wood** *s* leña
**kind•ly** ['kaɪndli] *adj* (*comp* **-lier**; *super* **-liest**) (*kind-hearted*) bondadoso; apacible, benigno; favorable || *adv* bondadosamente; cordialmente; con gusto; por favor; **to not take kindly to** no aceptar de buen grado
**kindness** ['kaɪndnɪs] *s* bondad; **have the kindness to** tenga Vd. la bondad de
**kindred** ['kɪndrɪd] *adj* emparentado; afín, semejante || *s* parentela; semejanza, afinidad
**kinescope** ['kɪnɪ,skop] *s* (trademark) cinescopio, kinescopio
**kinetic** [kɪ'nɛtɪk] o [kaɪ'nɛtɪk] *adj* cinético || **kinetics** *s* cinética
**kinetic energy** *s* fuerza viva, energía cinética
**king** [kɪŋ] *s* rey *m;* (cards, chess, & fig) rey; (checkers) dama
**king'bolt'** *s* pivote *m* central
**kingdom** ['kɪŋdəm] *s* reino
**king'fish'er** *s* martín *m* pescador
**king•ly** ['kɪŋli] *adj* (*comp* **-lier**; *super* **-liest**) real, regio; (*stately*) majestuoso || *adv* regiamente
**king'pin'** *s* (bowling) bolo delantero; pivote *m* central; (aut) pivote de dirección; (coll) persona principal
**king post** *s* pendolón *m*
**king's evil** *s* escrófula
**kingship** ['kɪŋʃɪp] *s* dignidad real
**king'-size'** *adj* de tamaño largo
**king's ransom** *s* riquezas de Creso
**kink** [kɪŋk] *s* (*twist, e.g., in a rope*) enroscadura, coca; (*e.g., in Negro's hair*) pasa; (*soreness in neck*) tortícolis *m;* (*flaw, difficulty*) estorbo, traba; (*mental twist*) chifladura, manía || *tr* enroscar || *intr* enroscarse
**kink•y** ['kɪŋki] *adj* (*comp* **-ier**; *super* **-iest**) encarrujado, ensortijado
**kinsfolk** ['kɪnz,fok] *s* parentela, familia, deudos
**kinship** ['kɪnʃɪp] *s* parentesco; semejanza, afinidad
**kins•man** ['kɪnzmən] *s* (*pl* **-men** [mən]) pariente *m*
**kins•woman** ['kɪnz,wumən] *s* (*pl* **-women** [,wɪmɪn]) *s* parienta
**kipper** ['kɪpər] *s* arenque acecinado, salmón acecinado || *tr* acecinar (*el arenque o el salmón*)
**kiss** [kɪs] *s* beso; (billiards) retruco; (*confection*) dulce *m*, merengue *m* || *tr* besar; **to kiss away** borrar con besos (*las penas de una persona*) || *intr* besar; besarse; (billiards) retrucar
**kit** [kɪt] *s* cartera de herramientas; (*case and its contents for various purposes*) estuche *m;* (*of a soldier*) equipo, pertrechos; (*of a traveler*) equipaje *m;* (*pail, tub*) balde *m*
**kitchen** ['kɪtʃən] *s* cocina
**kitchenette** [,kɪtʃə'nɛt] *s* cocinilla
**kitchen garden** *s* huerto
**kitch'en•maid'** *s* ayudanta de cocina, pincha
**kitchen police** *s* (mil) trabajo de cocina; soldados que están de cocina
**kitchen range** *s* cocina económica
**kitchen sink** *s* fregadero
**kitch'en•ware'** *s* utensilios de cocina
**kite** [kaɪt] *s* cometa; (orn) milano; **to fly a kite** hacer volar una cometa
**kith and kin** [kɪθ] *spl* parientes *mpl;* parientes y amigos
**kitten** ['kɪtən] *s* gatito, minino
**kittenish** ['kɪtənɪʃ] *adj* juguetón, retozón; (*coy, flirtatious*) coquetón
**kit•ty** ['kɪti] *s* (*pl* **-ties**) gatito, minino; (*in card games*) polla, puesta || *interj* ¡miz!
**kleptomaniac** [,klɛptə'menɪ,æk] *s* cleptómano
**km.** *abbr* **kilometer**
**knack** [næk] *s* tino, tranquillo, maña
**knapsack** ['næp,sæk] *s* mochila

**knave** [nev] *s* bribón *m,* pícaro; (cards) sota
**knaver•y** ['nevəri] *s* (*pl* **-ies**) bribonería, picardía
**knead** [nid] *tr* amasar, sobar
**knee** [ni] *s* rodilla; (*of animal*) codillo; (*e.g., of trousers*) rodillera; (mach) ángulo, codo; **to bring** (*someone*) **to his knees** rendir, vencer; **to go down on one's knees** hincarse de rodillas, caer de rodillas; **to go down on one's kness to** implorar de rodillas
**knee breeches** ['brɪtʃɪz] *spl* pantalones cortos
**knee'cap'** *s* rótula; (*protective covering*) rodillera
**knee'-deep'** *adj* metido hasta las rodillas
**knee'-high'** *adj* que llega hasta la rodilla
**knee'hole'** *s* hueco para acomodar las rodillas
**knee jerk** *s* reflejo rotuliano
**kneel** [nil] *v* (*pret & pp* **knelt** [nɛlt] o **kneeled**) *intr* arrodillarse; estar de rodillas
**knee'pad'** *s* rodillera
**knee'pan'** *s* rótula
**knee swell** *s* (*of organ*) (mus) rodillera
**knell** [nɛl] *s* doble *m,* toque *m* de difuntos; mal agüero; **to toll the knell of** anunciar la muerte de, anunciar el fin de || *intr* doblar, tocar a muerto; sonar tristemente
**knickers** ['nɪkərz] *spl* pantalones *mpl* de media pierna
**knickknack** ['nɪk,næk] *s* chuchería, bujería, baratija
**knife** [naɪf] *s* (*pl* **knives** [naɪvz]) cuchillo; (*of a paper cutter or other instrument*) cuchilla; **to go under the knife** (coll) hacerse operar || *tr* acuchillar; (slang) traicionar
**knife sharpener** *s* afilador *m,* afilón *m*
**knife switch** *s* (elec) interruptor *m* de cuchilla
**knight** [naɪt] *s* caballero; (chess) caballo || *tr* armar caballero
**knight-errant** ['naɪt'ɛrənt] *s* (*pl* **knights-errant**) caballero andante
**knight-errant•ry** ['naɪt'ɛrəntri] *s* (*pl* **-ries**) caballería andante; (*quixotic behavior*) quijotada
**knighthood** ['naɪt·hʊd] *s* caballería
**knightly** ['naɪtli] *adj* caballeroso, caballeresco
**Knight of the Rueful Countenance** *s* Caballero de la triste figura (*Don Quijote*)
**knit** [nɪt] *v* (*pret & pp* **knitted** o **knit**; *ger* **knitting**) *tr* tejer a punto de aguja; enlazar, unir; fruncir (*las cejas*), arrugar (*la frente*) || *intr* hacer calceta, hacer malla; trabarse, unirse; soldarse (*un hueso*)
**knit goods** *spl* géneros de punto
**knitting** ['nɪtɪŋ] *s* punto de media, trabajo de punto
**knitting machine** *s* máquina de hacer tejidos de punto
**knitting needle** *s* aguja de hacer media
**knit'wear'** *s* géneros de punto
**knob** [nɑb] *s* (*lump*) bulto, protuberancia; (*of a door*) botón *m,* tirador *m;* (*of a radio set*) botón, perilla; (*ornament on furniture*) manzana; colina o montaña redondeada
**knock** [nɑk] *s* golpe *m;* (*e.g., on a door*) toque *m,* llamada; (*with a door knocker*) aldabazo; (*of an internal-combustion engine*) pistoneo; (slang) censura, crítica || *tr* golpear; (*repeatedly*) golpetear; (slang) censurar, criticar; **to knock down** (*with a blow, punch, etc.*) derribar; (*to the highest bidder*) rematar; desarmar, desmontar (*un aparato o máquina*); **to knock off** hacer saltar con un golpe; suspender (*el trabajo*); poner fin a; (slang) matar; **to knock out** agotar; (box) poner fuera de combate || *intr* tocar, llamar; golpear, pistonear (*el motor de combustión interna*); (slang) censurar, criticar; **to knock about** andar vagando; **to knock against** dar contra, tropezar con; **to knock at** tocar a, llamar a (*la puerta*); **to knock off** dejar de trabajar
**knocker** ['nɑkər] *s* (*on a door*) aldaba; (coll) criticón *m*
**knock-kneed** ['nɑk,nid] *adj* patizambo, zambo
**knock'out'** *s* golpe decisivo, puñetazo decisivo; (box) (el) fuera de combate; (elec) destapadero; (coll) real moza
**knockout drops** *spl* (slang) gotas narcóticas
**knoll** [nol] *s* loma, otero
**knot** [nɑt] *s* nudo; (*worn as ornament*) lazo; corrillo, grupo; (*difficult matter; bond or tie*) nudo; nudo o lazo de matrimonio; (*protuberance in a fabric*) envoltorio; (naut) nudo; **to tie the knot** (coll) casarse || *v* (*pret & pp* **knotted**; *ger* **knotting**) *tr* anudar; fruncir (*las cejas*) || *intr* anudarse
**knot'hole'** *s* agujero en la madera (*que deja un nudo al desprenderse*)
**knot•ty** ['nɑti] *adj* (*comp* **-tier**; *super* **-tiest**) nudoso; (fig) espinoso, difícil
**know** [no] *s* — **to be in the know** estar enterado, tener informes secretos || *v* (*pret* **knew** [nju] o [nu]; *pp* **known**) *tr & intr* (*by reasoning or learning*) saber; (*by the senses or by perception; through acquaintance or recognition*) conocer; **as far as I know** que yo sepa; **to know about** saber de; **to know best** ser el mejor juez, saber lo que más conviene; **to know how to** + *inf* saber + *inf;* **to know it all** (coll) sabérselo todo; **to know what one is doing** obrar con conocimiento de causa; **to know what's what** (coll) saber cuántas son cinco; **you ought to know better** deberías tener vergüenza
**knowable** ['no·əbəl] *adj* conocible
**know'-how'** *s* conocimiento, destreza, habilidad
**knowingly** ['no·ɪŋli] *adv* a sabiendas,

con conocimiento de causa; (*on purpose*) adrede
**know'-it-all'** *adj & s* (coll) sabidillo
**knowledge** ['nɑlɪdʒ] *s* (*faculty*) ciencia, conocimientos, el saber; (*awareness, acquaintance, familiarity*) conocimiento; **to have a thorough knowledge of** conocer a fondo; **to my knowledge** que yo sepa; **to the best of my knowledge** según mi leal saber y entender; **with full knowledge** con conocimiento de causa; **without my knowledge** sin saberlo yo
**knowledgeable** ['nɑlɪdʒəbəl] *adj* (coll) conocedor, inteligente
**know'-noth'ing** *s* ignorante *mf*
**knuckle** ['nʌkəl] *s* nudillo; (*of a quadruped*) jarrete *m;* (mach) junta de charnela; **knuckles** bóxer *m* || *intr* — **to knuckle down** someterse, darse por vencido; aplicarse con empeño al trabajo
**knurl** [nʌrl] *s* moleteado || *tr* moletear, cerrillar (*p.ej., las piezas de moneda*)
**k.o.** *abbr* **knockout**
**Koran** [ko'rɑn] o [ko'ræn] *s* Corán *m*
**Korea** [ko'ri·ə] *s* Corea
**Korean** [ko'ri·ən] *adj & s* coreano
**kosher** ['koʃər] *adj* autorizado por la ley judía; (coll) genuino
**kowtow** ['kaʊ'taʊ] o ['ko'taʊ] *intr* arrodillarse y tocar el suelo con la frente; doblegarse servilmente, mostrarse servilmente obsequioso
**Kt.** *abbr* **Knight**
**kudos** ['kjudɑs] o ['kudɑs] *s* (coll) gloria, renombre *m,* fama
**kw.** *abbr* **kilowatt**
**K.W.H.** *abbr* **kilowatt-hour**

# L

**L, l** [ɛl] duodécima letra del alfabeto inglés
**l.** *abbr* **liter, line, league, length**
**L.** *abbr* **Latin, Low**
**la·bel** ['lebəl] *s* etiqueta, marbete *m,* rótulo; (*descriptive word*) calificación || *v* (*pret & pp* **-beled** o **-belled;** *ger* **-beling** o **-belling**) *tr* poner etiqueta o marbete a, rotular; calificar
**labial** ['lebɪ·əl] *adj & s* labial *f*
**labor** ['lebər] *adj* obrero || *s* trabajo, labor *f;* (*job, task*) tarea, faena; (*manual work involved in an undertaking; the wages for such work*) mano *f* de obra; (*wage-earning workers as contrasted with capital and management*) los obreros; (*childbirth*) parto; **labors** esfuerzos; **to be in labor** estar de parto || *intr* trabajar; (*to exert oneself*) forcejar; estar de parto; moverse penosamente; cabecear y balancear (*un buque*); **to labor under** ser víctima de
**labor and management** *spl* los obreros y los patronos
**laborato·ry** ['læbərə,tori] *s* (*pl* **-ries**) laboratorio
**labored** ['lebərd] *adj* penoso, dificultoso; artificial, forzado
**laborer** ['lebərər] *s* trabajador *m,* obrero; (*unskilled worker*) bracero, jornalero, peón *m*
**laborious** [lə'borɪ·əs] *adj* laborioso
**la'bor-man'agement** *adj* obrero-patronal
**labor union** *s* gremio obrero, sindicato
**Labourite** ['lebə,raɪt] *s* laborista *mf*
**Labrador** ['læbrə,dɔr] *s* el Labrador
**labyrinth** ['læbɪrɪnθ] *s* laberinto
**lace** [les] *s* encaje *m;* (*string to tie shoe, corset, etc.*) cordón *m,* lazo; (*braid*) galón *m* de oro o plata || *tr* adornar con encaje; atar (*los zapatos, el corsé*); (coll) dar una paliza a
**lace trimming** *s* randa
**lace'work'** *s* encaje *m,* obra de encaje
**lachrymose** ['lækrɪ,mos] *adj* lacrimoso
**lacing** ['lesɪŋ] *s* cordón *m;* lazo; galón *m;* (coll) paliza
**lack** [læk] *s* carencia, falta; (*complete lack*) defecto || *tr* carecer de, necesitar || *intr* (*to be lacking*) faltar
**lackadaisical** [,lækə'dezɪkəl] *adj* desaprovechado, indiferente
**lackey** ['læki] *s* lacayo; secuaz *m* servil
**lacking** ['lækɪŋ] *prep* sin, carente de
**lack'lus'ter** *adj* deslustrado, deslucido
**laconic** [lə'kɑnɪk] *adj* lacónico
**lacquer** ['lækər] *s* laca || *tr* laquear
**lacquer ware** *s* lacas, objetos de laca
**lacu·na** [lə'kjunə] *s* (*pl* **-nas** o **-nae** [ni]) laguna
**lac·y** ['lesi] *adj* (*comp* **-ier;** *super* **-iest**) de encaje; (fig) diáfano
**lad** [læd] *s* muchacho, chico
**ladder** ['lædər] *s* escalera; (*stepladder*) escala, escalera de mano; (*two ladders fastened together at the top with hinges*) escalera de tijera; (*stepping stone*) (fig) escalón *m*
**ladder truck** *s* carro de escaleras de incendio
**ladies' room** *s* cuarto tocador
**ladle** ['ledəl] *s* cazo; (*for soup*) cucharón *m;* (*of tinsmith*) cucharilla || *tr* servir con cucharón; sacar con cucharón
**la·dy** ['ledi] *s* (*pl* **-dies**) señora, dama
**la'dy·bird'** o **la'dy·bug'** *s* mariquita, vaca de San Antón
**la'dy·fin'ger** *s* melindre *m*
**lady in waiting** *s* camarera de la reina
**la'dy-kil'ler** *s* ladrón *m* de corazones
**la'dy·like'** *adj* elegante; **to be ladylike** ser muy dama

**la'dy·love'** *s* amada, amiga querida
**lady of the house** *s* ama de casa
**ladyship** ['ledi,ʃɪp] *s* señoría
**lady's maid** *s* doncella
**lady's man** *s* perico entre ellas
**lag** [læg] *s* retraso ‖ *v* (*pret & pp* **lagged;** *ger* **lagging**) *intr* retrasarse; **to lag behind** quedarse atrás, rezagarse
**lager beer** ['lɑgər] *s* cerveza reposada
**laggard** ['lægərd] *s* perezoso, rezagado
**lagoon** [lə'gun] *s* laguna
**laid paper** [led] *s* papel vergueteado
**laid up** *adj* almacenado, ahorrado; (naut) inactivo; (coll) encamado por estar enfermo
**lair** [lɛr] *s* cubil *m*
**lai·ty** ['le·ɪti] *s* legos
**lake** [lek] *adj* lacustre ‖ *s* lago
**lamb** [læm] *s* cordero; carne *f* de cordero; piel *f* de cordero; (*meek person*) (fig) cordero
**lambaste** [læm'best] *tr* (*to thrash*) (coll) dar una paliza a; (*to reprimand harshly*) (coll) dar una jabonadura a
**lamb chop** *s* chuleta de cordero
**lambkin** ['læmkɪn] *s* corderito; (fig) nenito
**lamb'skin'** *s* piel *f* de cordero, corderina; (*dressed with its wool*) corderillo
**lame** [lem] *adj* cojo; (*sore*) dolorido; (*e.g., excuse*) débil, pobre ‖ *tr* encojar
**lament** [lə'ment] *s* lamento; (*dirge*) elegía ‖ *tr* lamentar ‖ *intr* lamentarse
**lamentable** ['læməntəbəl] *adj* lamentable
**lamentation** [,læmən'teʃən] *s* lamentación
**laminate** ['læmɪ,net] *tr* laminar
**lamp** [læmp] *s* lámpara
**lamp'black'** *s* negro de humo
**lamp chimney** *s* tubo de lámpara
**lamp'light'** *s* luz *f* de lámpara
**lamp'light'er** *s* farolero
**lampoon** [læm'pun] *s* pasquín *m*, libelo ‖ *tr* pasquinar
**lamp'post'** *s* poste *m* de farol
**lamp shade** *s* pantalla de lámpara
**lamp'wick'** *s* mecha de lámpara, torcida
**lance** [læns] o [lɑns] *s* lanza; (surg) lanceta ‖ *tr* alancear; (surg) abrir con lanceta
**lance rest** *s* ristre *m*
**lancet** ['lænsɪt] o ['lɑnsɪt] *s* (surg) lanceta
**land** [lænd] *adj* terrestre; (*wind*) terral ‖ *s* tierra; **on land, on sea, and in the air** en tierra, mar y aire; **to make land** atracar a tierra; **to see how the land lies** medir el terreno, ver el cariz que van tomando las cosas ‖ *tr* desembarcar; conducir (*un avión*) a tierra; coger (*un pez*); (coll) conseguir ‖ *intr* desembarcar; (*to reach land*) arribar, aterrar; aterrizar (*un avión*); (*to arrive or come to rest*) ir a dar, ir a parar; **to land on one's feet** caer de pies; **to land on one's head** caer de cabeza
**landau** ['lændɔ] o ['lændaʊ] *s* landó *m*
**land breeze** *s* terral *m*
**landed** ['lændɪd] *adj* (*owning land*) hacendado; (*real-estate*) inmobiliario; **landed property** bienes *mpl* raíces
**land'fall'** *s* (*sighting land*) aterrada; (*landing of ship or plane*) aterraje *m;* tierra vista desde el mar; (*landslide*) derrumbe *m*
**land grant** *s* donación de tierras
**land'hold'er** *s* terrateniente *mf*, hacendado
**landing** ['lændɪŋ] *s* (*of ship or plane*) aterraje *m;* (*of passengers*) desembarco; (*place where passengers and goods are landed*) desembarcadero; (*of stairway*) desembarco, descanso
**landing beacon** *s* (aer) radiofaro de aterrizaje
**landing craft** *s* (nav) lancha de desembarco
**landing field** *s* (aer) pista de aterrizaje
**landing force** *s* (nav) compañía de desembarco
**landing gear** *s* (aer) tren *m* de aterrizaje
**landing stage** *s* embarcadero flotante
**landing strip** *s* (aer) faja de aterrizaje
**land'la'dy** *s* (*pl* **-dies**) (*e.g., of an apartment*) casera, dueña; (*of a lodging house*) ama, patrona; (*of an inn*) mesonera, posadera
**landlocked** ['lænd,lɑkt] *adj* rodeado de tierra
**land'lord'** *s* (*e.g., of an apartment*) casero, dueño; (*of a lodging house*) amo, patrón *m;* (*of an inn*) mesonero, posadero
**land'lub'ber** *s* (*person unacquainted with the sea*) marinero de agua dulce; (*awkward and unskilled seaman*) marinero matalote
**land'mark'** *s* (*boundary stone*) mojón *m;* (*feature of landscape that marks a location*) guía; suceso que hace época; (naut) marca de reconocimiento
**land office** *s* oficina del catastro
**land'-of'fice business** *s* (coll) negocio de mucho movimiento
**land'own'er** *s* terrateniente *mf*, hacendado
**landscape** ['lænd,skep] *s* paisaje *m* ‖ *tr* ajardinar
**landscape architect** *s* arquitecto paisajista
**landscape gardener** *s* jardinero adornista, jardinista *mf*
**landscape painter** *s* paisajista *mf*
**landscapist** ['lænd,skepɪst] *s* paisajista *mf*
**land'slide'** *s* derrumbe *m*, derrumbamiento de tierra, corrimiento; (fig) mayoría de votos abrumadora; (fig) victoria arrolladora
**landward** ['lændwərd] *adv* hacia tierra, hacia la costa
**land wind** *s* terral *m*
**lane** [len] *s* (*narrow street or passage*) callejuela; (*path*) carril *m;* (*of an*

*automobile highway*) faja; (*of an air or ocean route*) derrotero, vía

**langsyne** ['læŋ'saɪn] *adv* (Scotch) hace mucho tiempo || *s* (Scotch) tiempo de antaño

**language** ['læŋgwɪdʒ] *s* idioma *m*, lengua; (*way of speaking or writing, style; figurative or poetic expression; communication of meaning said to be employed by flowers, birds, art, etc.*) lenguaje *m*; (*of a special group of people*) jerga

**languid** ['læŋgwɪd] *adj* lánguido

**languish** ['læŋgwɪʃ] *intr* languidecer; afectar languidez

**languor** ['læŋgər] *s* languidez *f*

**languorous** ['læŋgərəs] *adj* lánguido; (*causing languor*) enervante

**lank** [læŋk] *adj* descarnado, larguirucho; (*hair*) lacio

**lank•y** ['læŋki] *adj* (*comp* **-ier**; *super* **-iest**) descarnado, larguirucho

**lantern** ['læntərn] *s* linterna

**lantern slide** *s* diapositiva, tira de vidrio

**lanyard** ['lænjərd] *s* (naut) acollador *m*

**lap** [læp] *s* (*of human body or clothing*) regazo; (*loose fold*) caída, doblez *f*; (*overlap of garment*) traslapo; (*with the tongue*) lametada; (*of the waves*) chapaleteo; (*in a race*) (sport) etapa, vuelta; **to live in the lap of luxury** llevar una vida regalada || *v* (*pret & pp* **lapped**; *ger* **lapping**) *tr* beber con la lengua; lamer (*las olas la playa*); (*to overlap*) traslapar; juntar a traslapo; **to lap up** tragar a lengüetadas; (coll) aceptar con entusiasmo || *intr* traslapar; traslaparse (*dos o más cosas*); **to lap against** lamer (*las olas la playa*); **to lap over** salir fuera, rebosar

**lap'board'** *s* tabla faldera

**lap dog** *s* perro de falda

**lapel** [lə'pɛl] *s* solapa

**Lap'land'** *s* Laponia

**Laplander** ['læp,lændər] *s* lapón *m* (*habitante*)

**Lapp** [læp] *s* lapón *m* (*habitante; idioma*)

**lap robe** *s* manta de coche

**lapse** [læps] *s* (*passing of time; slipping into guilt or error*) lapso; (*fall, decline*) caída; caída en desuso; (*e.g., of an insurance policy*) invalidación || *intr* caer en culpa o error; decaer, pasar (*p.ej., el entusiasmo*); caducar (*p.ej., una póliza de seguro*)

**lap'wing'** *s* ave fría

**larce•ny** ['lɑrsəni] *s* (*pl* **-nies**) hurto, robo

**larch** [lɑrtʃ] *s* alerce *m*, lárice *m*

**lard** [lɑrd] *s* cochevira, manteca de puerco || *tr* (culin) mechar

**larder** ['lɑrdər] *s* despensa

**large** ['lɑrdʒ] *adj* grande; **at large** en libertad

**large intestine** *s* intestino grueso

**largely** ['lɑrdʒli] *adj* por la mayor parte

**largeness** ['lɑrdʒnɪs] *s* grandeza

**large'-scale'** *adj* en grande escala, grande escala

**lariat** ['lærɪ•ət] *s* (*for catching animals*) lazo; (*for tying grazing animals*) cuerda, soga

**lark** [lɑrk] *s* alondra; (coll) parranda; **to go on a lark** (coll) andar de parranda, echar una cana al aire

**lark'spur'** *s* (*rocket larkspur*) espuela de caballero; (*field larkspur*) consuelda real

**lar•va** ['lɑrvə] *s* (*pl* **-vae** [vi]) larva

**laryngeal** [lə'rɪndʒɪ•əl] o [,lærɪn'dʒi•əl] *adj* laríngeo

**laryngitis** [,lærɪn'dʒaɪtɪs] *s* laringitis *f*

**laryngoscope** [lə'rɪŋgə,skop] *s* laringoscopio

**larynx** ['lærɪŋks] *s* (*pl* **larynxes** o **larynges** [lə'rɪndʒiz]) laringe *f*

**lascivious** [lə'sɪvɪ•əs] *adj* lascivo

**lasciviousness** [lə'sɪvɪ•əsnɪs] *s* lascivia

**lash** [læʃ] *s* (*cord on end of whip*) tralla; (*blow with whip; scolding*) latigazo; (*e.g., of animal's tail*) coletazo; (*of waves*) embate *m*; (*eyelash*) pestaña || *tr* (*to beat, whip*) azotar; (*to bind, tie*) atar; (*to shake, to switch*) agitar, sacudir; (*to attack with words*) increpar, reñir || *intr* lanzarse, pasar rápidamente; **to lash out at** azotar; embestir; vituperar

**lashing** ['læʃɪŋ] *s* atadura; paliza, zurra; (*severe scolding*) latigazo

**lass** [læs] *s* muchacha, chica; amada

**las•so** ['læso] o [læ'su] *s* (*pl* **-sos** o **-soes**) lazo || *tr* lazar

**last** [læst] o [lɑst] *adj* (*after all others; the only remaining; utmost, extreme*) último; (*most recent*) pasado; **before last** antepasado; **every last one** todos sin excepción; **last but one** penúltimo || *adv* después de todos; por último; por última vez || *s* última persona; última cosa; fin *m*; (*for holding shoe*) horma; **at last** por fin; **at long last** al fin y al cabo; **stick to your last!** ¡zapatero, a tus zapatos!; **the last of the month** a fines del mes; **to breathe one's last** dar el último suspiro; **to see the last of** no volver a ver; **to the last** hasta el fin || *intr* durar; resistir; dar buen resultado (*p.ej., una prenda de vestir*); seguir así

**lasting** ['læstɪŋ] o ['lɑstɪŋ] *adj* perdurable, duradero

**lastly** ['læstli] o ['lɑstli] *adv* finalmente, por último

**last'-min'ute news** *s* noticias de última hora

**last name** *s* apellido

**last night** *adv* anoche

**last quarter** *s* cuarto menguante

**last sleep** *s* último sueño

**last straw** *s* acabóse *m*, colmo

**Last Supper, the** la Cena

**last will and testament** *s* última disposición, última voluntad

**last word** *s* última palabra; (*latest style*) (coll) última palabra

**lat.** *abbr* **latitude**

**Lat.** *abbr* **Latin**

**latch** [lætʃ] *s* picaporte *m* || *tr* cerrar con picaporte
**latch'key'** *s* llavín *m*
**latch'string'** *s* cordón *m* de aldaba; **the latchstring is out** ya sabe Vd. que ésta es su casa
**late** [let] *adj* (*happening after the usual time*) tardío; (*person*) atrasado; (*hour of the night*) avanzado; (*news*) de última hora; (*party, meeting, etc.*) que termina tarde; (*coming toward the end of a period of time*) de fines de; (*incumbent of an office*) anterior; (*deceased*) difunto, fallecido; **of late** recientemente, últimamente; **to be late** ser tarde; tardar (*p.ej., el tren*); **to be late in** + *ger* tardar en + *inf;* **to grow late** hacerse tarde || *adv* tarde; **late in** (*the week, the month, etc.*) a fines de, hacia fines de; **late in life** a una edad avanzada
**late-comer** ['let ˌkʌmər] *s* recién llegado; (*one who arrives late*) rezagado
**lateen sail** [læ'tin] *s* vela latina
**lateen yard** *s* entena
**lately** ['letli] *adv* recientemente, últimamente
**latent** ['letənt] *adj* latente
**lateral** ['lætərəl] *adj* lateral
**lath** [læθ] o [lɑθ] *s* lata, listón; enlistonado || *tr* enlistonar
**lathe** [leð] *s* torno (*máquina que sirve para labrar madera, hierro, etc. con un movimiento circular*)
**lather** ['læðər] *s* espuma de jabón; espuma de sudor || *tr* enjabonar; (coll) tundir, zurrar || *intr* espumar
**lathery** ['læðəri] *adj* espumoso, jabonoso
**lathing** ['læθɪŋ] o ['lɑθɪŋ] *s* enlistonado
**Latin** ['lætɪn] o ['lætən] *adj* latino || *s* (*language*) latín *m;* (*person*) latino
**Latin America** *s* Latinoamérica, la América Latina
**Latin American** *s* latinoamericano
**Lat'in-Amer'ican** *adj* latinoamericano
**latitude** ['lætɪˌtjud] o ['lætɪˌtud] *s* latitud
**latrine** [lə'trin] *s* letrina
**latter** ['lætər] *adj* (*more recent*) posterior; segundo (*de dos*); **the latter** éste; **the latter part of** fines *mpl* de (*p.ej., el siglo*)
**lattice** ['lætɪs] *s* enrejado || *tr* enrejar
**lattice girder** *s* viga de celosía
**lat'tice•work'** *s* enrejado
**Latvia** ['lætvɪ·ə] *s* Letonia, Latvia
**laudable** ['lɔdəbəl] *adj* laudable
**laudanum** ['lɔdənəm] o ['lɔdnəm] *s* láudano
**laudatory** ['lɔdəˌtori] *adj* laudatorio
**laugh** [læf] o [lɑf] *s* risa || *tr* — **to laugh away** ahogar en risas; **to laugh off** tomar a risa || *intr* reír, reírse
**laughable** ['læfəbəl] o ['lɑfəbəl] *adj* risible
**laughing** ['læfɪŋ] o ['lɑfɪŋ] *adj* reidor; **to be no laughing matter** no ser cosa de risa || *s* risa, (el) reír
**laughing gas** *s* gas *m* hilarante
**laugh'ing•stock'** *s* hazmerreír *m*
**laughter** ['læftər] o ['lɑftər] *s* risa, risas
**launch** [lɔntʃ] o [lɑntʃ] *s* (*of a ship*) botadura; (*of a rocket*) lanzamiento; (*open motorboat*) lancha automóvil; (nav) lancha || *tr* botar, lanzar (*un buque*); (*to throw; to start, set going, send forth*) lanzar || *intr* lanzarse
**launching** ['lɔntʃɪŋ] o ['lɑntʃɪŋ] *s* lanzamiento
**launching pad** *s* plataforma de lanzamiento
**launder** ['lɔndər] o ['lɑndər] *tr* lavar y planchar || *intr* resistir el lavado
**launderer** ['lɔndərər] o ['lɑndərər] *s* lavandero
**laundress** ['lɔndrɪs] o ['lɑndrɪs] *s* lavandera
**laun•dry** ['lɔndri] o ['lɑndri] *s* (*pl* **-dries**) lavadero; lavado de la ropa; ropa lavada o para lavar
**laundry•man** ['lɔndrimən] o ['lɑndrimən] *s* (*pl* **-men** [mən]) lavandero
**laun'dry•wom'an** *s* (*pl* **-wom'en**) lavandera
**laureate** ['lɔrɪ·ɪt] *adj* laureado || *s* laureado; poeta laureado
**lau•rel** ['lɔrəl] o ['lɑrəl] *s* laurel *m;* **laurels** laurel (*de la victoria*); **to rest o sleep on one's laurels** dormirse sobre sus laureles || *v* (*pret & pp* **-reled** o **-relled;** *ger* **-reling** o **-relling**) *tr* laurear, coronar de laurel
**lava** ['lɑvə] o ['lævə] *s* lava
**lavato•ry** ['lævəˌtori] *s* (*pl* **-ries**) (*room equipped for washing hands and face*) lavabo; (*bowl with running water*) lavamanos *m;* (*toilet*) excusado
**lavender** ['lævəndər] *s* alhucema, espliego, lavanda
**lavender water** *s* agua de alhucema, agua de lavanda
**lavish** ['lævɪʃ] *adj* pródigo || *tr* prodigar
**law** [lɔ] *s* (*of man, of nature, of science*) ley *f;* (*branch of knowledge concerned with law; body of laws; study of law, profession of law*) derecho; **to enter the law** hacerse abogado; **to go to law** recurrir a la ley; **to lay down the law** dar órdenes terminantes; **to maintain law and order** mantener la paz; **to practice law** ejercer la profesión de abogado; **to read law** estudiar derecho
**law-abiding** ['lɔ·əˌbaɪdɪŋ] *adj* observante de la ley
**law'break'er** *s* infractor *m* de la ley
**law court** *s* tribunal *m* de justicia
**lawful** ['lɔfəl] *adj* legal, legítimo
**lawless** ['lɔlɪs] *adj* ilegal; (*unbridled*) desenfrenado, licencioso
**law'mak'er** *s* legislador *m*
**lawn** [lɔn] *s* césped *m;* (*fabric*) linón *m*
**lawn mower** *s* cortacésped *m,* tundidora de césped
**law office** *s* bufete *m,* despacho de abogado
**law of nations** *s* derecho de gentes
**law of the jungle** *s* ley *f* de la selva
**law student** *s* estudiante *mf* de derecho

**law'suit'** *s* pleito, proceso, litigio
**lawyer** ['lɔjər] *s* abogado
**lax** [læks] *adj* (*in morals, discipline, etc.*) laxo, relajado; vago, indeterminado; (*loose, not tense*) laxo, flojo, suelto
**laxative** ['læksətɪv] *adj & s* laxante *m*
**lay** [le] *adj* (*not belonging to clergy*) lego, seglar; (*not having special training*) lego, profano || *s* situación, orientación || *v* (*pret & pp* **laid** [led]) *tr* poner, colocar; dejar en el suelo; tender (*un cable*); echar (*los cimientos; la culpa*); situar (*la acción de un drama*); asentar (*el polvo*); poner (*huevos la gallina; la mesa una criada*); formar (*planes*); hacer (*una apuesta*); **to be laid in** ser (*la escena*) en; **to lay aside** echar a un lado; ahorrar; **to lay down** afirmar, declarar; dar (*la vida*); deponer (*las armas*); **to lay low** abatir, derribar; obligar a guardar cama; matar; **to lay off** despedir (*a obreros*); (*to mark off the boundaries of*) marcar, trazar; **to lay open** descubrir, revelar; (*to a risk or danger*) exponer; **to lay out** extender, tender; marcar (*una tarea, un trabajo*); gastar (*dinero*); amortajar (*a un difunto*); **to lay up** obligar a guardar cama; ahorrar; (naut) desarmar || *intr* poner (*las gallinas*); **to lay about** dar palos de ciego; **to lay for** acechar; **to lay off** (coll) dejar de trabajar; (coll) dejar de molestar; **to lay over** detenerse durante un viaje; **to lay to** (naut) capear
**lay brother** *s* donado, lego
**lay day** *s* (naut) día *m* de estadía
**layer** ['le·ər] *s* (*e.g., of paint*) capa; (*e.g., of bricks*) camada; (*e.g., of coal, rocks*) estrato, capa; (hort) codadura || *tr* (hort) acodar
**layer cake** *s* bizcocho de varias camadas
**layette** [le'ɛt] *s* canastilla
**lay figure** *s* maniquí *m*
**laying** ['le·ɪŋ] *s* colocación; (*of eggs*) postura; (*of a cable*) tendido
**lay·man** ['lemən] *s* (*pl* **-men** [mən]) (*person who is not a clergyman*) lego, seglar *m;* (*person who has no special training*) lego, profano
**lay'off'** *s* (*dismissal of workmen*) despido; (*period of unemployment*) paro forzoso
**lay of the land** *s* cariz *m* que van tomando las cosas
**lay'out'** *s* plan *m;* (*of tools*) equipo; disposición, organización; (coll) banquete *m,* festín *m*
**lay'o'ver** *s* parada en un viaje
**lay sister** *s* donada
**laziness** ['lezɪnɪs] *s* pereza
**la·zy** ['lezi] *adj* (*comp* **-zier;** *super* **-ziest**) perezoso
**la'zy·bones'** *s* (coll) perezoso
**lb.** *abbr* **pound**
**l.c.** *abbr* **lower case; loco citato** (Lat) **in the place cited**
**Ld.** *abbr* **Lord**
**lea** [li] *s* prado
**lead** [lɛd] *adj* plomizo || *s* plomo; (*of lead pencil*) mina; (*for sounding depth*) (naut) escandallo; (typ) interlínea, regleta || [lɛd] *v* (*pret & pp* **leaded;** *ger* **leading**) *tr* emplomar; (typ) interlinear, regletear || *s* [lid] *s* (*foremost place*) primacía; (*guidance*) conducta, guía, dirección; indicación; ejemplo; (cards) salida; (*leash*) traílla; (*of a newspaper article*) primer párrafo; (elec) conductor *m;* (elec & mach) avance *m;* (min) filón *m;* (rad) alambre *m* de entrada; (theat) papel *m* principal; (theat) galán *m;* (theat) dama; **to take the lead** tomar la delantera || [lid] *v* (*pret & pp* **led** [lɛd]) *tr* conducir, llevar; (*to command*) acaudillar, mandar; estar a la cabeza de; dirigir (*p.ej., una orquesta*); llevar (*buena o mala vida*); salir con (*cierto naipe*); (elec & mach) avanzar; **to lead someone to** + *inf* llevar a alguien a + *inf* || *intr* ir delante, enseñar el camino; ser el primero; tener el mando; (cards) salir, ser mano; (mus) llevar la batuta; **to lead up to** conducir a, llevar a; llevar la conversación a
**leaden** ['lɛdən] *adj* (*of lead; like lead*) plomizo; (*heavy as lead*) plúmbeo; (*sluggish*) tardo, indolente; (*with sleep*) cargado; triste, lóbrego
**leader** ['lidər] *s* caudillo, jefe *m,* líder *m;* (*ringleader*) cabecilla *m;* (*of an orchestra*) director *m;* (*in a dance; among animals*) guión *m;* (*horse*) guía; (*in a newspaper*) artículo de fondo
**leader dog** *s* perro-lazarillo
**leadership** ['lidər,ʃɪp] *s* caudillaje *m,* jefatura; dotes *fpl* de mando
**leading** ['lidɪŋ] *adj* primero, principal; preeminente; delantero
**leading article** *s* artículo de fondo
**leading edge** *s* (aer) borde *m* de ataque
**leading lady** *s* primera actriz, dama
**leading man** *s* primer actor *m,* primer galán *m*
**leading question** *s* pregunta tendenciosa
**leading strings** *spl* andadores *mpl*
**lead-in wire** ['lid,ɪn] *s* (rad) bajada de antena, alambre *m* de entrada
**lead pencil** [lɛd] *s* lápiz *m*
**leaf** [lif] *s* (*pl* **leaves** [livz]) hoja; (*of vine*) pámpano; (*hinged leaf of table*) trampilla; **to shake like a leaf** temblar como un azogado; **to turn over a new leaf** hacer libro nuevo || *intr* echar hojas; **to leaf through** hojear, trashojar
**leafless** ['liflɪs] *adj* deshojado
**leaflet** ['liflɪt] *s* hoja suelta, hoja volante; (*blade of compound leaf*) hojuela
**leaf'stalk'** *s* pecíolo
**leaf·y** ['lifi] *adj* (*comp* **-ier;** *super* **-iest**) hojoso, frondoso
**league** [lig] *s* (*unit of distance*) legua; (*association, alliance*) liga || *tr* asociar || *intr* asociarse, ligarse

**League of Nations** *s* Sociedad de las Naciones
**leak** [lik] *s* (*in a roof*) gotera; (*in a ship*) agua, vía de agua; (*of water, gas, electricity, steam*) escape *m*, fuga, salida; agujero, grieta, raja (*por donde se escapa el agua, etc.*); (*of money, news, etc.*) filtración; **to spring a leak** tener un escape; (naut) empezar a hacer agua || *tr* dejar escapar, dejar salir (*el agua, gas, etc.*); dejar filtrar (*una noticia*) || *intr* rezumarse (*un barril*); escaparse, salirse (*el agua, gas, etc.*); (naut) hacer agua; **to leak away** filtrarse (*el dinero*); **to leak out** rezumarse (*una especie*); trascender (*un hecho que estaba oculto*)
**leakage** ['likɪdʒ] *s* escape *m*, fuga, salida; (com) merma
**leak•y** ['liki] *adj* (*comp* **-ier**; *super* **-iest**) agujereado, roto; (*roof*) llovedizo; (naut) que hace agua; (coll) indiscreto
**lean** [lin] *adj* magro, mollar; (*thin*) flaco; (*gasoline mixture*) pobre; **lean years** años de carestía || *v* (*pret & pp* **leaned** o **leant** [lɛnt]) *tr* inclinar, ladear, arrimar || *intr* inclinarse, ladearse, arrimarse; (fig) inclinarse, tender; **to lean against** arrimarse a, estar arrimado a; **to lean back** retreparse, recostarse; **to lean on** apoyarse en; (*with the elbows*) acodarse sobre; **to lean out (of)** asomarse (a); **to lean over backwards** (coll) extremar la imparcialidad; **to lean toward** (fig) inclinarse a, ladearse a
**leaning** ['linɪŋ] *adj* inclinado || *s* inclinación; (fig) inclinación, tendencia
**lean'-to'** *s* (*pl* **-tos**) colgadizo
**leap** [lip] *s* salto; **by leaps and bounds** a pasos agigantados; **leap in the dark** salto a ciegas, salto en vago || *v* (*pret & pp* **leaped** o **leapt** [lɛpt]) *tr* saltar || *intr* saltar; dar un salto (*el corazón de uno*)
**leap day** *s* día *m* intercalar
**leap'frog'** *s* fil derecho, juego del salto; **to play leapfrog** jugar a la una la mula
**leap year** *s* año bisiesto
**learn** [lʌrn] *v* (*pret & pp* **learned** o **learnt** [lʌrnt]) *tr* aprender; oír decir; saber (*una noticia*) || *intr* aprender
**learned** ['lʌrnɪd] *adj* docto, erudito; (*e.g., word*) culto
**learned journal** *s* revista científica
**learned society** *s* sociedad de eruditos
**learned word** *s* cultismo, voz culta
**learned world** *s* mundo de la erudición
**learner** ['lʌrnər] *s* principiante *mf*, aprendiz *m*, estudiante *mf*
**learning** ['lʌrnɪŋ] *s* (*act and time devoted*) aprendizaje *m;* (*scholarship*) erudición
**lease** [lis] *s* arrendamiento, locación; **to give a new lease on life to** renovar completamente; volver a hacer feliz || *tr* arrendar || *intr* arrendarse
**lease'hold'** *adj* arrendado || *s* arrendamiento; bienes raíces arrendados
**leash** [liʃ] *s* traílla; **to strain at the leash** sufrir la sujeción con impaciencia || *tr* atraillar
**least** [list] *adj* (el) menor, mínimo, más pequeño || *adv* menos || *s* (el) menor; (lo) menos; **at least** o **at the least** al menos, a lo menos, por lo menos; **not in the least** de ninguna manera
**leather** ['lɛðər] *s* cuero
**leath'er•back' turtle** *s* laúd *m*
**leath'er•neck'** *s* (slang) soldado de infantería de marina de los EE.UU.
**leathery** ['lɛðəri] *adj* correoso, coriáceo
**leave** [liv] *s* (*permission*) permiso; (*permission to be absent*) licencia; (*farewell*) despedida; **on leave** con licencia; **to give leave to** dar licencia a; **to take leave (of)** despedirse (de) || *v* (*pret & pp* **left** [lɛft]) *tr* (*to let stay; to stop, give up; to disregard*) dejar; (*to go away from*) salir de; (*to bequeath*) legar; **leave it to me!** ¡déjemelo a mí!; **to be left** quedar p.ej., **the letter was left unanswered** la carta quedó sin contestar; **to leave alone** dejar en paz, dejar tranquilo; **to leave no stone unturned** no dejar piedra por mover; **to leave off** dejar; no ponerse (*una prenda de vestir*); **to leave out** omitir; **to leave things as they are** dejarlo como está || *intr* irse, marcharse; salir (*un avión, un tren, un vapor*)
**leaven** ['lɛvən] *s* levadura; (fig) influencia || *tr* leudar; (fig) transformar
**leavening** ['lɛvənɪŋ] *s* levadura
**leave of absence** *s* licencia
**leave'-tak'ing** *s* despedida
**leavings** ['livɪŋz] *spl* desperdicios, sobras
**Leba•nese** [,lɛbə'niz] *adj* libanés || *s* (*pl* **-nese**) libanés *m*
**Lebanon** ['lɛbənən] *s* el Líbano
**Lebanon Mountains** *spl* cordillera del Líbano
**lecher** ['lɛtʃər] *s* libertino, lujurioso
**lecherous** ['lɛtʃərəs] *adj* lascivo, lujurioso
**lechery** ['lɛtʃəri] *s* lascivia, lujuria
**lectern** ['lɛktərn] *s* atril *m*
**lecture** ['lɛktʃər] *s* conferencia; (*tedious reprimand*) sermoneo || *tr* instruir por medio de una conferencia; sermonear || *intr* dar una conferencia, dar conferencias
**lecturer** ['lɛktʃərər] *s* conferenciante *mf*
**ledge** [lɛdʒ] *s* (*projection in a wall*) retallo; cama de roca; arrecife *m*
**ledger** ['lɛdʒər] *s* (com) libro mayor
**ledger line** *s* (mus) línea suplementaria
**lee** [li] *s* (*shelter*) (naut) socaire *m;* (*quarter sheltered from the wind*) sotavento; **lees** heces *fpl*
**leech** [litʃ] *s* sanguijuela; **to stick like a leech** pegarse como ladilla
**leek** [lik] *s* puerro
**leer** [lɪr] *s* mirada de soslayo, mirada lujuriosa || *intr* — **to leer at** mirar de soslayo, mirar lujuriosamente

**leery** ['lɪri] *adj* (coll) receloso, suspicaz
**leeward** ['liwərd] o ['lu·ərd] *adj* (naut) de sotavento || *adv* (naut) a sotavento || *s* (naut) sotavento
**Leeward Islands** ['liwərd] *spl* islas de Sotavento
**lee'way'** *s* (aer & naut) deriva; (coll) tiempo de sobra, espacio de sobra, dinero de sobra; (coll) libertad de acción
**left** [lɛft] *adj* izquierdo || *adv* hacia la izquierda || *s* (*left hand*) izquierda; (box) zurdazo; (pol) izquierda; **on the left** a la izquierda
**left field** *s* (baseball) jardín izquierdo
**left'-hand' drive** *s* conducción o dirección a la izquierda
**left-handed** ['lɛft'hændɪd] *adj* (*individual*) zurdo; (*clumsy*) desmañado, torpe; insincero; contrario a las agujas del reloj
**leftish** ['lɛftɪʃ] *adj* izquierdizante
**leftist** ['lɛftɪst] *adj & s* izquierdista *mf*
**left'o'ver** *adj & s* sobrante *m;* **leftovers** *spl* sobras
**left'-wing'** *adj* izquierdista
**left-winger** ['lɛft'wɪŋər] *s* (coll) izquierdista *mf*
**leg.** *abbr* **legal, legislature**
**leg** [lɛg] *s* (*of man or animal*) pierna; (*of animal, table, chair, etc.*) pata; (*of boot or stocking*) caña; (*of trousers*) pernera; (*of a cooked fowl*) muslo; (*of a journey*) etapa, trecho; **to be on one's last legs** estar sin recursos; estar en las últimas; **to not have a leg to stand on** (coll) no tener justificación alguna, no tener disculpa alguna; **to pull the leg of** (coll) tomar el pelo a; **to shake a leg** (coll) darse prisa; (*to dance*) (coll) bailar; **to stretch one's legs** estirar las piernas, dar un paseíto
**lega·cy** ['lɛgəsi] *s* (*pl* **-cies**) legado
**legal** ['ligəl] *adj* legal
**legali·ty** [lɪ'gælɪti] *s* (*pl* **-ties**) legalidad
**legalize** ['ligə,laɪz] *tr* legalizar
**legal tender** *s* curso legal
**legate** ['lɛgɪt] *s* legado
**legatee** [,lɛgə'ti] *s* legatario
**legation** [lɪ'geʃən] *s* legación
**legend** ['lɛdʒənd] *s* leyenda
**legendary** ['lɛdʒən,dɛri] *adj* legendario
**legerdemain** [,lɛdʒərdɪ'men] *s* juego de manos, prestidigitación; (*cheating, trickery*) trapacería
**legging** ['lɛgɪŋ] *s* polaina
**leg·gy** ['lɛgi] *adj* (*comp* **-gier;** *super* **-giest**) zanquilargo; de piernas largas y elegantes
**leg'horn'** *s* sombrero de paja de Italia || **Leghorn** *s* Liorna
**legible** ['lɛdʒɪbəl] *adj* legible
**legion** ['lidʒən] *s* legión
**legislate** ['lɛdʒɪs,let] *tr* imponer mediante legislación || *intr* legislar
**legislation** [,lɛdʒɪs'leʃən] *s* legislación
**legislative** ['lɛdʒɪs,letɪv] *adj* legislativo
**legislator** ['lɛdʒɪs,letər] *s* legislador *m*
**legislature** ['lɛdʒɪs,letʃər] *s* asamblea legislativa, cuerpo legislativo
**legitimacy** [lɪ'dʒɪtɪməsi] *s* legitimidad
**legitimate** [lɪ'dʒɪtɪmɪt] *adj* legítimo || [lɪ'dʒɪtɪ,met] *tr* legitimar
**legitimate drama** *s* drama serio (*a distinción del cine o el melodrama*)
**legitimize** [lɪ'dʒɪtɪ,maɪz] *tr* legitimar
**leg'work'** *s* (coll) el mucho caminar
**leisure** ['liʒər] o ['lɛʒər] *s* desocupación, ocio; **at leisure** desocupado, libre; **at one's leisure** a la comodidad de uno, cuando uno pueda
**leisure class** *s* gente acomodada
**leisure hours** *spl* horas de ocio, ratos perdidos
**leisurely** ['liʒərli] o ['lɛʒərli] *adj* lento, pausado || *adv* lentamente, despacio, sin prisa
**lemon** ['lɛmən] *s* limón *m*
**lemonade** [,lɛmə'ned] *s* limonada
**lemon squeezer** *s* exprimidera de limón
**lemon verbena** *s* luisa
**lend** [lɛnd] *s* (*pret & pp* **lent** [lɛnt]) *tr* prestar
**lending library** *s* biblioteca de préstamo
**length** [lɛŋθ] *s* largura, largo; (*of time*) extensión; (naut) eslora; **at length** por fin; largamente; **to go to any length** hacer cuanto esté de su parte; **to keep at arm's length** mantener a distancia; mantenerse a distancia
**lengthen** ['lɛŋθən] *tr* alargar || *intr* alargarse
**length'wise'** *adj* longitudinal || *adv* longitudinalmente
**length·y** ['lɛŋθi] *adj* (*comp* **-ier;** *super* **-iest**) muy largo, prolongado
**leniency** ['linɪ·ənsi] *s* clemencia, indulgencia, lenidad
**lenient** ['linɪ·ənt] *adj* clemente, indulgente
**lens** [lɛnz] *s* lente *m & f;* (*of the eye*) cristalino
**Lent** [lɛnt] *s* cuaresma *f*
**Lenten** ['lɛntən] *adj* cuaresmal
**lentil** ['lɛntəl] *s* lenteja
**leopard** ['lɛpərd] *s* leopardo
**leotard** ['li·ə,tɑrd] *s* leotardo
**leper** ['lɛpər] *s* leproso
**leper house** *s* leprosería
**leprosy** ['lɛprəsi] *s* lepra
**leprous** ['lɛprəs] *adj* leproso; (*covered with scales*) escamoso
**Lesbian** ['lɛzbɪ·ən] *adj* lesbio || *s* lesbio; (*female homosexual*) lesbia
**lesbianism** ['lɛzbɪ·ə,nɪzəm] *s* lesbianismo
**lese majesty** ['liz'mædʒɪsti] *s* delito de lesa majestad
**lesion** ['liʒən] *s* lesión
**less** [lɛs] *adj* menor || *adv* menos; **less and less** cada vez menos; **less than** menos que; (*followed by numeral*) menos de; (*followed by verb*) menos de lo que || *s* menos *m*
**lessee** [lɛs'i] *s* arrendatario
**lessen** ['lɛsən] *tr* disminuir, reducir a menos; quitar importancia a || *intr*

disminuirse, reducirse; amainar (*el viento*)
**lesser** ['lɛsər] *adj* menor, más pequeño
**lesson** ['lɛsən] *s* lección
**lessor** ['lɛsər] *s* arrendador *m*
**lest** [lɛst] *conj* no sea que, de miedo que
**let** [lɛt] *v* (*pret & pp* **let**; *ger* **letting**) *tr* dejar, permitir; alquilar, arrendar; **let** + *inf* que + *subj*, p.ej., **let him come in** que entre; **let alone** y mucho menos; **let good enough alone** bueno está lo bueno; **let us** + *inf* vamos a + *inf*, p.ej., **let us eat** vamos a comer, comamos; **to let** se alquila; **to let alone** dejar en paz, dejar tranquilo; **to let be** no tocar; dejar en paz; **to let by** dejar pasar; **to let down** dejar bajar; desilusionar, traicionar; dejar plantado; **to let fly** disparar; (fig) disparar, soltar (*palabras injuriosas*); **to let go** soltar, desasirse de; vender; **to let in** dejar entrar, dejar entrar en; **to let it go at that** no hacer o decir nada más; **to let know** hacer saber; **to let loose** soltar; **to let on** (coll) dar a entender; **to let out** dejar salir; revelar, publicar; dar, soltar (*p.ej., más cuerda*); dar (*un grito*); ensanchar (*un vestido que aprieta*); dar en arrendamiento; (coll) despedir; **to let through** dejar pasar, dejar pasar por; **to let up** dejar subir; dejar levantarse || *intr* alquilarse, arrendarse; **to let down** (coll) ir más despacio; **to let go** desasirse; **to let go of** desasirse de; **to let on** (coll) fingir; **to let out** (coll) despedirse, cerrarse (*p.ej., la escuela*); **to let up** (coll) desistir; (coll) aflojar, amainar
**let'down'** *s* disminución; aflojamiento; desilusión, decepción; humillación
**lethal** ['liθəl] *adj* letal
**lethargic** [lɪ'θɑrdʒɪk] *adj* (*affected with lethargy*) letárgico; (*producing lethargy*) letargoso
**lethar·gy** ['lɛθərdʒi] *s* (*pl* **-gies**) letargo
**Lett** [lɛt] *s* letón *m*
**letter** ['lɛtər] *s* (*written message*) carta; (*of the alphabet*) letra; (*literal meaning*) (fig) letra; **letters** (*literature*) letras; **to the letter** al pie de la letra || *tr* estampar o marcar con letras
**letter box** *s* buzón *m* (*caja*)
**letter carrier** *s* cartero
**letter drop** *s* buzón *m* (*agujero*)
**letter file** *s* guardacartas *m*
**let'ter·head'** *s* membrete *m*; (*paper with printed heading*) memorándum *m*
**lettering** ['lɛtərɪŋ] *s* inscripción; letras
**letter of credit** *s* carta de crédito
**letter opener** ['opənər] *s* abrecartas *m*
**letter paper** *s* papel *m* de cartas
**let'ter·per'fect** *adj* que tiene bien aprendido su papel; correcto, exacto
**let'ter·press'** *s* impresión tipográfica; texto (*a distinción de los grabados*)
**letter scales** *spl* pesacartas *m*
**Lettish** ['lɛtɪʃ] *adj* letón || *s* letón *m*
**lettuce** ['lɛtɪs] *s* lechuga
**let'up'** *s* (coll) calma, interrupción; **without letup** (coll) sin cesar
**leucorrhea** [,lukə'ri·ə] *s* leucorrea
**leukemia** [lu'kimɪ·ə] *s* leucemia
**Levant** [lɪ'vænt] *s* Levante *m* (*países de la parte oriental del Mediterráneo*)
**Levantine** ['lɛvən,tin] o [lɪ'væntin] *adj & s* levantino
**levee** ['lɛvi] *s* (*embankment to hold back water*) ribero; (*reception at court*) besamanos *m*
**lev·el** ['lɛvəl] *adj* raso, llano; nivelado; (coll) sensato, juicioso; **level with** al nivel de, a flor de, a ras de || *s* (*device for determining horizontal position; degree of elevation*) nivel *m*; (*flat and even area of land*) terreno llano, llanura; (*part of a canal between two locks*) tramo; **to be on the level** obrar sin engaño, decir la pura verdad; **to find one's level** hallar su propio nivel || *v* (*pret & pp* **-eled** o **-elled**; *ger* **-eling** o **-elling**) *tr* nivelar; (*to smooth, flatten out*) arrasar, allanar; (*to bring down*) derribar, echar por tierra; apuntar (*un arma de fuego*); (fig) allanar (*dificultades*) || *intr* — **to level off** (aer) enderezarse para aterrizar
**level-headed** ['lɛvəl'hɛdɪd] *adj* sensato, juicioso
**leveling rod** *s* (surv) jalón *m* de mira
**lever** ['livər] o ['lɛvər] *s* palanca || *tr* apalancar
**leverage** ['livərɪdʒ] o ['lɛvərɪdʒ] *s* palancada; poder *m* de una palanca; (fig) influencia, poder *m*
**leviathan** [lɪ'vaɪ·əθən] *s* (Bib & fig) leviatán *m*; buque *m* muy grande
**levitation** [,lɛvɪ'teʃən] *s* levitación
**levi·ty** ['lɛvɪti] *s* (*pl* **-ties**) frivolidad; (*fickleness*) ligereza
**lev·y** ['lɛvi] *s* (*pl* **-ies**) (*of taxes*) exacción, recaudación; dinero recaudado; (mil) leva, enganche *m*, recluta || *v* (*pret & pp* **-ied**) *tr* exigir, recaudar (*impuestos*); (mil) enganchar, reclutar; hacer (*la guerra*)
**lewd** [lud] *adj* lascivo, lujurioso; obsceno
**lewdness** ['ludnɪs] *s* lascivia, lujuria; obscenidad
**lexical** ['lɛksɪkəl] *adj* léxico
**lexicographer** [,lɛksɪ'kɑgrəfər] *s* lexicógrafo
**lexicographic(al)** [,lɛksɪkə'græfɪk(əl)] lexicográfico
**lexicography** [,lɛksɪ'kɑgrəfi] *s* lexicografía
**lexicology** [,lɛksɪ'kɑlədʒi] *s* lexicología
**lexicon** ['lɛksɪkən] *s* léxico, lexicón *m*
**liabili·ty** [,laɪ·ə'bɪlɪti] *s* (*pl* **-ties**) (*e.g., to disease*) propensión; responsabilidad, obligación; desventaja; **liabilities** deudas; (*as detailed in balance sheet*) pasivo
**liability insurance** *s* seguro de responsabilidad civil
**liable** ['laɪ·əbəl] *adj* (*e.g., to disease*) propenso, expuesto; responsable; **to**

be liable to + *inf* (coll) amenazar + *inf*
**liaison** ['li·ə,zɑn] o [li'ezən] *s* enlace *m*, unión; (*illicit relationship between a man and woman*) amancebamiento, enredo, lío; (mil, nav & phonet) enlace *m*
**liaison officer** *s* (mil) oficial *m* de enlace
**liar** ['laɪ·ər] *s* mentiroso
**lb.** *abbr* **librarian, library**
**libation** [laɪ'beʃən] *s* libación; (*drink*) libación
**li·bel** ['laɪbəl] *s* calumnia, difamación; (*defamatory writing*) libelo || *v* (*pret & pp* **-beled** o **-belled;** *ger* **-beling** o **-belling**) *tr* calumniar, difamar
**libelous** ['laɪbələs] *adj* calumniador
**liberal** ['lɪbərəl] *adj* (*generous; done or given generously*) liberal; (*open-minded*) tolerante, de amplias miras; (*translation*) libre; (pol) liberal || *s* liberal *mf*
**liberali·ty** [,lɪbə'rælɪti] *s* (*pl* **-ties**) liberalidad
**liberal-minded** ['lɪbərəl'maɪndɪd] *adj* tolerante, de amplias miras
**liberate** ['lɪbə,ret] *tr* libertar; (*to disengage from a combination*) (chem) desprender
**liberation** [,lɪbə'reʃən] *s* liberación; (chem) desprendimiento
**liberator** ['lɪbə,retər] *s* libertador *m*
**libertine** ['lɪbər,tin] *adj & s* libertino
**liber·ty** ['lɪbərti] *s* (*pl* **-ties**) libertad; **to take the liberty to** tomarse la libertad de
**liberty-loving** ['lɪbərti'lʌvɪŋ] *adj* amante de la libertad
**libidinous** [lɪ'bɪdɪnəs] *adj* libidinoso
**libido** [lɪ'bido] o [lɪ'baɪdo] *s* libídine *f*, libido *f*
**librarian** [laɪ'brerɪ·ən] *s* bibliotecario
**librar·y** ['laɪ,breri] o ['laɪbrəri] *s* (*pl* **-ies**) biblioteca
**library number** *s* signatura
**library school** *s* escuela de bibliotecarios
**library science** *s* bibliotecnia
**libret·to** [lɪ'brɛto] *s* (*pl* **-tos**) (mus) libreto
**license** ['laɪsəns] *s* licencia ||*tr* licenciar
**license number** *s* número de matrícula
**license plate** o **tag** *s* chapa de circulación, placa de matrícula
**licentious** [laɪ'sɛnʃəs] *adj* licencioso, disoluto
**lichen** ['laɪkən] *s* liquen *m*
**lick** [lɪk] *s* lamedura; (*place where animals go to lick*) lamedero; (*blow*) (coll) bofetón *m;* (*speed*) (coll) velocidad; (*beating*) (coll) zurra; (*quick cleaning*) (coll) limpión *m;* **to give a lick and a promise to** (coll) hacer rápida y superficialmente || *tr* lamer; lamerse (*p.ej., los dedos*); lamer (*las llamas un tejado*); (*to beat, thrash*) (coll) zurrar; (*to conquer*) (coll) vencer
**licorice** ['lɪkərɪs] *s* regaliz *m*, orozuz *m;* dulce *m* de regaliz
**lid** [lɪd] *s* (*of a box, trunk, chest, etc.*) tapa, tapadera; (*of a dish, pot, etc.*) cobertera; (*eyelid*) párpado; (*hat*) (slang) techo
**lie** [laɪ] *s* mentira; **to catch in a lie** coger en una mentira; **to give the lie to** dar un mentís a || *v* (*pret & pp* **lied;** *ger* **lying**) *tr* — **to lie oneself out of** o **to lie one's way out of** librarse de un aprieto mintiendo || *intr* mentir || *v* (*pret* **lay** [le]; *pp* **lain** [len]; *ger* **lying**) *intr* estar echado; hallarse, estar situado; (*e.g., in the grave*) yacer, estar enterrado; **to lie down** echarse, acostarse
**lie detector** *s* detector *m* de mentiras
**lien** [lin] o ['li·ən] *s* gravamen *m*, derecho de retención
**lieu** [lu] *s* — **in lieu of** en lugar de, en vez de
**lieutenant** [lu'tɛnənt] *s* lugarteniente *m;* (mil) teniente *m;* (nav) teniente de navío
**lieutenant colonel** *s* (mil) teniente coronel *m*
**lieutenant commander** *s* (nav) capitán *m* de corbeta
**lieutenant governor** *s* (U.S.A.) vicegobernador *m* (*de un Estado*)
**lieutenant junior grade** *s* (nav) alférez *m* de navío
**life** [laɪf] *adj* (*animate*) vital; (*lifelong*) perpetuo; (*annuity, income*) vitalicio; (*working from nature*) (fa) del natural || *s* (*pl* **lives** [laɪvz]) vida; (*of an insurance policy*) vigencia; **for life** de por vida; **for the life of me** así me maten; **the life and soul of** (*e.g., a party*) la alegría de; **to come to life** volver a la vida; **to depart this life** partir de esta vida; **to run for one's life** salvarse por los pies
**life annuity** *s* renta vitalicia
**life belt** *s* cinturón *m* salvavidas
**life'boat'** *s* bote *m* de salvamento, bote salvavidas; (*for shore-based rescue services*) lancha de auxilio
**life buoy** *s* boya salvavidas, guindola
**life float** *s* balsa salvavidas
**life'guard'** *s* salvavidas *m*, guardavida *m*
**life imprisonment** *s* cadena perpetua
**life insurance** *s* seguro sobre la vida
**life jacket** *s* chaleco salvavidas
**lifeless** ['laɪflɪs] *adj* muerto, sin vida; (*in a faint*) desmayado, exánime; (*dull, colorless*) deslucido
**life'like'** *adj* natural, vivo
**life line** *s* cuerda salvavidas; cuerda de buzo
**life'long'** *adj* perpetuo, de toda la vida
**life of leisure** *s* vida de ocio
**life of Riley** ['raɪli] *s* (slang) vida regalada
**life of the party** *s* (coll) alegría de la fiesta, alma de la fiesta
**life preserver** [prɪ'zʌrvər] *s* chaleco salvavidas
**lifer** ['laɪfər] *s* (slang) presidiario de por vida
**life'sav'er** *s* salvador *m* (*de vidas*); (*something that saves a person from*

*a predicament*) (coll) tabla de salvación

**lifesaving** [ˈlaɪf,sevɪŋ] *adj* de salvamento ‖ *s* salvamento (*de vidas*)

**life sentence** *s* condena a cadena perpetua

**life′-size′** *adj* de tamaño natural

**life′time′** *adj* vitalicio ‖ *s* vida, curso de la vida, jornada

**life′work′** *s* obra principal de la vida de uno

**lift** [lɪft] *s* elevación, levantamiento; ayuda (*para levantar una carga*); (aer) sustentación; **to give a lift to** invitar (*a un peatón*) a subir a un coche; llevar en un coche; (fig) reanimar ‖ *tr* elevar, levantar; quitarse (*el sombrero*); (naut) izar (*velas, vergas, etc.*); (fig) reanimar, exaltar; (coll) robar; (coll) plagiar ‖ *intr* elevarse, levantarse; disiparse (*las nubes, las nieblas, la obscuridad, etc.*)

**lift bridge** *s* puente levadizo

**lift′-off′** *s* despegue *m* vertical

**lift truck** *s* carretilla elevadora

**ligament** [ˈlɪgəmənt] *s* ligamento

**ligature** [ˈlɪgətʃər] *s* (mus & surg) ligadura; (mus & typ) ligado

**light** [laɪt] *adj* (*in weight*) ligero, leve, liviano; (*having illumination; whitish*) claro; (*hair*) blondo, rubio; (*complexion*) blanco; (*oil*) flúido; (*beer*) claro; (*reading*) poco serio; (*heart*) alegre, despreocupado; (*carrying a small cargo or none at all*) (naut) boyante; **light in the head** (*dizzy*) aturdido, mareado; (*simple, silly*) tonto, necio; **to make light of** no dar importancia a, no tomar en serio ‖ *adv* sin carga; sin equipaje ‖ *s* luz *f;* (*to light a cigarette*) lumbre *f*, fuego; (*to control traffic*) luz, señal *f;* (*window or other opening in a wall*) luz, claro, hueco; (*example, shining figure*) lumbrera; **according to one's lights** según Dios le da a uno a entender; **against the light** al trasluz; **in this light** desde este punto de vista; **lights** noticias; (*of sheep, etc.*) bofes *mpl;* **to come to light** salir a luz, descubrirse; **to shed** o **throw light on** echar luz sobre; **to strike a light** echar una yesca; encender un fósforo ‖ *v* (*pret & pp* **lighted** o **lit** [lɪt]) *tr* (*to furnish with illumination*) alumbrar, iluminar; (*to set afire, ignite*) encender; **to light up** iluminar ‖ *intr* alumbrarse; encenderse; posar (*un ave*); (*from an auto*) bajar; **to light into** (*to attack*) (slang) arremeter contra; (*to scold, berate*) (slang) poner de oro y azul; **to light out** (slang) poner pies en polvorosa; **to light upon** tropezar con, hallar por casualidad

**light bulb** *s* (elec) bombilla

**light complexion** *s* tez blanca

**lighten** [ˈlaɪtən] *tr* (*to make lighter in weight*) aligerar; iluminar; (*to cheer up*) alegrar, regocijar ‖ *intr* (*to become less dark*) iluminarse; (*to give off flashes of lightning*) relampaguear; (fig) iluminarse (*los ojos, la cara de una persona*)

**lighter** [ˈlaɪtər] *s* (*to light a cigarette*) encendedor *m;* (*flat-bottomed barge*) alijador *m*

**light-fingered** [ˈlaɪtˈfɪŋgərd] *adj* largo de uñas, listo de manos

**light-footed** [ˈlaɪtˈfʊtɪd] *adj* ligero de pies

**light-headed** [ˈlaɪtˈhedɪd] *adj* (*dizzy*) aturdido, mareado; (*simple, silly*) tonto, necio, ligero de cascos

**light-hearted** [ˈlaɪtˈhɑrtɪd] *adj* alegre, libre de cuidados

**light′house′** *s* faro

**lighting** [ˈlaɪtɪŋ] *s* alumbrado, iluminación

**lighting fixtures** *spl* artefactos de alumbrado

**lightly** [ˈlaɪtli] *adj* ligeramente

**light meter** *s* exposímetro

**lightness** [ˈlaɪtnɪs] *s* (*in weight*) ligereza; (*in illumination*) claridad

**lightning** [ˈlaɪtnɪŋ] *s* relámpagos, relampagueo ‖ *intr* relampaguear

**lightning arrester** [əˈrestər] *s* pararrayos *m*

**lightning bug** *s* luciérnaga

**lightning rod** *s* pararrayos *m*

**light opera** *s* opereta

**light′ship′** *s* buque *m* fanal, buque faro

**light-struck** [ˈlaɪt,strʌk] *adj* velado

**light′weight′** *adj* ligero; de entretiempo, p.ej., **lightweight coat** abrigo de entretiempo

**light′-year′** *s* año luz

**lignite** [ˈlɪgnaɪt] *s* lignito

**lignum vitae** [ˈlɪgnəmˈvaɪti] *s* guayaco, palo santo

**likable** [ˈlaɪkəbəl] *adj* simpático

**like** [laɪk] *adj* parecido, semejante; parecido a, semejante a, p.ej., **this hat is like mine** este sombrero es parecido al mío; (elec) del mismo nombre; **like father like son** de tal palo tal astilla; **to feel like** + *ger* tener ganas de + *inf;* **to look like** parecerse a; parecer que, p.ej., **it looks like rain** parece que va a llover ‖ *adv* como; **like enough** (coll) probablemente; **nothing like** ni con mucho ‖ *prep* a semejanza de ‖ *conj* (coll) del mismo modo que; (coll) que, p.ej., **it seems like he is right** parece que tiene razón ‖ *s* (*liking*) gusto, preferencia; (*fellow, fellow man*) prójimo, semejante *m;* **and the like** y cosas por el estilo; **to give like for like** pagar en la misma moneda ‖ *tr* gustar de, p.ej., **I like music** gusto de la música; gustar, p.ej., **Mary likes peaches** a María le gustan los melocotones; **to like best** o **better** preferir; **to like it in** encontrarse a gusto en (*p.ej., el campo*); **to like to** + *inf* gustarle a uno + *inf*, p.ej., **I like to travel** me gusta viajar; gustarle a uno que + *subj*, p.ej., **I should like him to come to see me** me gustaría que él viniese a verme ‖

*intr* querer, p.ej., **as you like** como Vd. quiera; **if you like** si Vd. quiere

**likelihood** ['laɪklɪ,hʊd] *s* probabilidad

**like·ly** ['laɪkli] *adj* (*comp* **-lier;** *super* **-liest**) probable; a propósito; prometedor; **to be likely to** + *inf* ser probable que + *ind*, p.ej., **Mary is likely to come to see us tomorrow** es probable que María vendrá a vernos mañana || *adv* probablemente

**like-minded** ['laɪk'maɪndɪd] *adj* del mismo parecer; de natural semejante

**liken** ['laɪkən] *tr* asemejar, comparar

**likeness** ['laɪknɪs] *s* (*picture or image*) retrato; (*similarity*) semejanza, parecido; forma, aspecto, apariencia

**like'wise'** *adv* igualmente, asimismo; **to do likewise** hacer lo mismo

**liking** ['laɪkɪŋ] *s* gusto, afición, simpatía; **to be to the liking of** ser del gusto de; **to have a liking for** aficionarse a

**lilac** ['laɪlək] *adj* de color lila || *s* lilac *m*, lila

**Lilliputian** [,lɪlɪ'pjuʃən] *adj & s* liliputiense *mf*

**lilt** [lɪlt] *s* paso airoso, movimiento airoso; canción cadenciosa, música alegre

**lil·y** ['lɪli] *s* (*pl* **-ies**) (*Lilium candidum*) azucena, lirio blanco; cala, lirio de agua; (*fleur-de-lis, the royal arms of France*) flor *f* de lis; **to gild the lily** ponerle colores al oro

**lily of the valley** *s* lirio de los valles, muguete *m*

**lily pad** *s* hoja de nenúfar

**Lima bean** ['laɪmə] *s* judía de la peladilla, frijol *m* de media luna

**limb** [lɪm] *s* (*arm or leg*) miembro; (*of a tree*) rama; (*of a cross; of the sea*) brazo; **to be out on a limb** (coll) estar en un aprieto

**limber** ['lɪmbər] *adj* ágil; flexible || *intr* — **to limber up** agilitarse

**lim·bo** ['lɪmbo] *s* (*pl* **-bos**) lugar *m* de olvido; (theol) limbo

**lime** [laɪm] *s* (*calcium oxide*) cal *f*; (*Citrus aurantifolia*) limero agrio; (*its fruit*) lima agria; (*linden tree*) tila o tilo

**lime'kiln'** *s* calera, horno de cal

**lime'light'** *s* — **to be in the limelight** estar a la vista del público

**limerick** ['lɪmərɪk] *s* quintilla jocosa

**lime'stone'** *adj* calizo || *s* caliza, piedra caliza

**limit** ['lɪmɪt] *s* límite *m*; **to be the limit** (slang) ser el colmo; **to go the limit** no dejar piedra por mover || *tr* limitar

**lim'ited-ac'cess high'way** *s* carretera de vía libre

**limited monarchy** *s* monarquía constitucional

**limitless** ['lɪmɪtlɪs] *adj* ilimitado

**limousine** ['lɪmə,zin] o [,lɪmə'zin] *s* (aut) limusina

**limp** [lɪmp] *adj* flojo, débil, flexible || *s* cojera || *intr* cojear

**limpid** ['lɪmpɪd] *adj* diáfano, cristalino

**linage** ['laɪnɪdʒ] *s* (typ) número de líneas

**linchpin** ['lɪntʃ,pɪn] *s* pezonera

**linden** ['lɪndən] *s* tila, tilo

**line** [laɪn] *s* línea; (*of people, houses, etc.*) hilera; (*rope, string*) cuerda, cordel *m*; (*wrinkle*) arruga; (*for fishing*) sedal *m*; (*written or printed line; line of goods*) renglón *m*; manera (*de pensar*); (*of the spectrum*) (phys) raya; **all along the line** por todas partes; desde cualquier punto de vista; **in line** alineado; dispuesto, preparado; **in line with** de acuerdo con; **out of line** desalineado; en desacuerdo; **to bring into line** poner de acuerdo; **to draw the line at** no ir más allá de; **to fall in line** conformarse; formar cola; alinearse; **to have a line on** (coll) estar enterado de; **to read between the lines** leer entre líneas; **to stand in line** hacer cola; **to toe the line** obrar como se debe; **to wait in line** hacer cola, esperar vez || *tr* alinear, rayar; arrugar (*p.ej., la cara*); formar hilera a lo largo de (*la acera, la calle*); forrar (*un vestido*); guarnecer (*un freno*) || *intr* — **to line up** ponerse en fila; hacer cola

**lineage** ['lɪnɪ·ɪdʒ] *s* linaje *m*

**lineaments** ['lɪnɪ·əmənts] *spl* lineamentos

**linear** ['lɪnɪ·ər] *adj* lineal

**line·man** ['laɪnmən] *s* (*pl* **-men** [mən]) (elec) celador *m*, recorredor *m* de la línea; (rr) guardavía *m*; (surv) cadenero

**linen** ['lɪnən] *adj* de lino || *s* (*fabric*) lienzo, lino; (*yarn*) hilo de lino; ropa blanca, ropa de cama

**linen closet** *s* armario para la ropa blanca

**line of battle** *s* línea de batalla

**line of fire** *s* (mil) línea de tiro

**line of least resistance** *s* ley *f* del menor esfuerzo; **to follow the line of least resistance** seguir la corriente, no oponer resistencia

**line of sight** *s* visual *f*; (*of firearm*) línea de mira

**liner** ['laɪnər] *s* vapor *m* de travesía; (baseball) pelota rasa, lineazo

**line'-up'** *s* agrupación, formación; (*of prisoners*) rueda

**linger** ['lɪŋgər] *intr* estarse, quedarse; (*to be tardy*) demorar, tardar; tardar en marcharse; tardar en morirse; pasearse con paso lento; **to linger over** contemplar, reflexionar

**lingerie** [,lænʒə'ri] *s* ropa interior de mujer

**lingering** ['lɪŋgərɪŋ] *adj* prolongado

**lingual** ['lɪŋgwəl] *adj & s* lingual *f*

**linguist** ['lɪŋgwɪst] *s* (*person skilled in several languages*) poligloto; (*specialist in linguistics*) lingüista *mf*

**linguistic** [lɪŋ'gwɪstɪk] *adj* lingüístico || **linguistics** *s* lingüística

**liniment** ['lɪnɪmənt] *s* linimento

**lining** ['laɪnɪŋ] *s* (*of a coat*) forro; (*of auto brake*) guarnición; (*of a fur-*

*nace*) camisa; (*of a wall*) revestimiento
**link** [lɪŋk] *s* eslabón *m;* **links** campo de golf || *tr* eslabonar || *intr* eslabonarse
**linnet** ['lɪnɪt] *s* pardillo
**linoleum** [lɪ'nolɪ·əm] *s* linóleo
**linotype** ['laɪnə,taɪp] (trademark) *adj* linotípico || *s* (*machine*) linotipia; (*matter produced by machine*) linotipo || *tr* componer con linotipia
**linotype operator** *s* linotipista *mf*
**linseed** ['lɪn,sid] *s* linaza
**linseed oil** *s* aceite *m* de linaza
**lint** [lɪnt] *s* borra, pelusa, hilaza; (*used to dress wounds*) hilas
**lintel** ['lɪntəl] *s* dintel *m,* umbral *m*
**lion** ['laɪ·ən] *s* león *m;* (*man of strength and courage*) (fig) león; (fig) celebridad muy solicitada; **to beard the lion in his den** ir a desafiar la cólera de un jefe; **to put one's head in the lion's mouth** meterse en la boca del lobo
**lioness** ['laɪ·ənɪs] *s* leona
**lion-hearted** ['laɪ·ən,hɑrtɪd] *adj* valiente
**lionize** ['laɪ·ə,naɪz] *tr* agasajar
**lions' den** *s* (Bib) fosa de los leones
**lion's share** *s* (la) parte *f* del león
**lip** [lɪp] *s* labio; (slang) lenguaje *m* insolente; **to hang on the lips of** estar pendiente de las palabras de; **to smack one's lips** chuparse los labios
**lip'-read'** *v* (*pret & pp* **-read** [,rɛd]) *tr & intr* leer en los labios
**lip reading** *s* labiolectura
**lip service** *s* homenaje *m* de boca, jarabe *m* de pico
**lip'stick'** *s* lápiz *m* de labios, lápiz labial
**liq.** *abbr* **liquid, liquor**
**lique·fy** ['lɪkwɪ,faɪ] *v* (*pret & pp* **-fied**) *tr* liquidar || *intr* liquidarse
**liqueur** [lɪ'kʌr] *s* licor *m*
**liquid** ['lɪkwɪd] *adj* líquido || *s* líquido; (phonet) líquida
**liquidate** ['lɪkwɪ,det] *tr & intr* liquidar
**liquidity** [lɪ'kwɪdɪti] *s* liquidez *f*
**liquid measure** *s* medida para líquidos
**liquor** ['lɪkər] *s* licor *m*
**Lisbon** ['lɪzbən] *s* Lisboa
**lisle** [laɪl] *s* hilo fino de algodón, muy retorcido, sedalina
**lisp** [lɪsp] *s* ceceo || *intr* cecear
**lissome** ['lɪsəm] *adj* flexible, elástico; ágil, ligero
**list** [lɪst] *s* lista; (*strip*) lista, tira; (*border*) orilla; (*selvage*) orillo; (naut) ladeo; **lists** liza; **to enter the lists** entrar en liza; **to have a list** (naut) irse a la banda || *tr* alistar, listar; registrar || *intr* (naut) irse a la banda
**listen** ['lɪsən] *intr* escuchar; obedecer; **to listen in** escuchar a hurtadillas; escuchar por radio; **to listen to** escuchar; obedecer; **to listen to reason** meterse en razón
**listener** ['lɪsənər] *s* oyente *mf;* radioescucha *mf,* radioyente *mf*
**listening post** ['lɪsənɪŋ] *s* puesto de escucha
**listless** ['lɪstlɪs] *adj* distraído, desatento, indiferente
**list price** *s* precio de catálogo, precio de tarifa
**lit.** *abbr* **liter, literal, literature**
**lita·ny** ['lɪtəni] *s* (*pl* **-nies**) letanía; (*repeated series*) (fig) letanía
**liter** ['litər] *s* litro
**literacy** ['lɪtərəsi] *s* capacidad de leer y escribir; instrucción
**literal** ['lɪtərəl] *adj* literal
**literary** ['lɪtə,rɛri] *adj* literario; (*individual*) literato
**literate** ['lɪtərɪt] *adj* que sabe leer y escribir; (*well-read*) literato, muy leído; (*educated*) instruído || *s* persona que sabe leer y escribir; literato, erudito
**literati** [,lɪtə'rɑti] *spl* literatos
**literature** ['lɪtərətʃər] *s* literatura; impresos, escritos de publicidad
**lithe** [laiθ] *adj* flexible, cimbreño
**lithia** ['lɪθɪ·ə] *s* (chem) litina
**lithium** ['lɪθɪ·əm] *s* (chem) litio
**lithograph** ['lɪθə,græf] o ['lɪθə,grɑf] *s* litografía || *tr* litografiar
**lithographer** [lɪ'θɑgrəfər] *s* litógrafo
**lithography** [lɪ'θɑgrəfi] *s* litografía
**litigant** ['lɪtɪgənt] *adj & s* litigante *mf*
**litigate** ['lɪtɪ,get] *tr & intr* litigar
**litigation** [,lɪtɪ'geʃən] *s* litigación; (*lawsuit*) litigio
**litigious** [lɪ'tɪdʒəs] *adj* litigioso
**litmus** ['lɪtməs] *s* tornasol *m*
**litmus paper** *s* papel *m* de tornasol
**litter** ['lɪtər] *s* desorden *m;* (*scattered rubbish*) basura, papelería; (*young brought forth at one birth*) camada, ventregada; (*bedding for animals*) cama, paja; (*vehicle carried by men or animals*) litera; (*stretcher*) camilla, parihuela || *tr* esparcir papeles por; esparcir (*desechos, papeles, etc.*); cubrir (*el suelo*) con paja || *intr* parir
**lit'ter·bug'** *s* persona que ensucia las calles tirando papeles rotos
**littering** ['lɪtərɪŋ] *s* — **no littering** se prohibe tirar papeles rotos
**little** ['lɪtəl] *adj* (*in size*) pequeño; (*in amount*) poco, p.ej., **little money** poco dinero; **a little** un poco de, p.ej., **a little money** un poco de dinero || *adv* poco; **little by little** poco a poco || *s* poco; **a little** un poco; (*somewhat*) algo; **to make little of** no dar importancia a, no tomar en serio; **to think little of** tener en poco; no vacilar en
**Little Bear** *s* Osa menor
**Little Dipper** *s* Carro menor
**little finger** *s* dedo auricular, dedo meñique; **to twist around one's little finger** manejar con suma facilidad
**lit'tle·neck'** *s* almeja redonda (*Venus mercenaria*)
**little owl** *s* mochuelo (*Athene noctua*)
**little people** *spl* hadas; gente menuda
**Little Red Ridinghood** ['raɪdɪŋ,hud] *s* Caperucita Roja
**little slam** *s* (bridge) semibola

**liturgic(al)** [lɪˈtʌrdʒɪk(əl)] *adj* litúrgico
**litur•gy** [ˈlɪtərdʒi] *s* (*pl* **-gies**) liturgia
**livable** [ˈlɪvəbəl] *adj* habitable, vividero; llevadero, tolerable
**live** [laɪv] *adj* (*living; full of life; intense*) vivo; (*coals; flame*) ardiente; de actualidad; (elec) cargado || [lɪv] *tr* llevar (*tal o cual vida*); vivir (*una experiencia, una aventura; un actor sus personajes*); **to live down** borrar (*una falta*); **to live out** vivir (*toda la vida*); salir con vida de (*un desastre, una guerra*) || *intr* vivir; **to live and learn** vivir para ver; **to live and let live** vivir y dejar vivir; **to live high** darse buena vida; **to live on** seguir viviendo; vivir de (*p.ej., carne*); vivir a expensas de; **to live up to** cumplir (*lo prometido*); gastar (*todas sus rentas*)
**live coal** *s* ascua
**livelihood** [ˈlaɪvlɪˌhʊd] *s* vida; **to earn one's livelihood** ganarse la vida
**livelong** [ˈlɪvˌlɔŋ] o [ˈlɪvˌlɑŋ] *adj* — **all the livelong day** todo el santo día
**live•ly** [ˈlaɪvli] *adj* (*comp* **-lier**; *super* **-liest**) animado, vivaz; alegre, festivo; (*active, keen*) vivo; (*resilient*) elástico
**liven** [ˈlaɪvən] *tr* animar, regocijar || *intr* animarse, regocijarse
**liver** [ˈlɪvər] *s* vividor *m;* habitante *mf;* (anat) hígado
**liver•y** [ˈlɪvəri] *s* (*pl* **-ies**) librea
**livery•man** [ˈlɪvərimən] *s* (*pl* **-men** [mən]) dueño de una cochera; mozo de cuadra
**livery stable** *s* cochera de carruajes de alquiler
**live'stock'** *adj* ganadero || *s* ganadería
**live wire** *s* (elec) alambre cargado; (slang) trafagón *m*
**livid** [ˈlɪvɪd] *adj* lívido, amoratado; encolerizado; pálido
**living** [ˈlɪvɪŋ] *adj* vivo, viviente || *s* vida; **to earn** o **to make a living** ganarse la vida
**living quarters** *spl* aposentos, habitaciones
**living room** *s* sala, sala de estar
**living wage** *s* jornal *m* suficiente para vivir
**lizard** [ˈlɪzərd] *s* lagarto; (slang) holgón *m*
**load** [lod] *s* carga; **loads** (coll) muchísimo; **loads of** (coll) gran cantidad de; **to get a load of** (slang) escuchar, oír; (slang) mirar; **to have a load on** (slang) estar borracho || *tr* cargar || *intr* cargar; cargarse
**loaded** [ˈlodɪd] *adj* cargado; (slang) muy borracho; (slang) muy rico
**loaded dice** *spl* dados cargados
**load'stone'** *s* piedra imán; (fig) imán *m*
**loaf** [lof] *s* (*pl* **loaves** [lovz]) pan *m;* (*of sugar*) pilón *m* || *intr* haraganear
**loafer** [ˈlofər] *s* haragán *m*
**loam** [lom] *s* suelo franco; (*mixture used in making molds*) tierra de moldeo
**loamy** [ˈlomi] *adj* franco
**loan** [lon] *s* (*among individuals*) préstamo; (*between companies or governments*) empréstito; **to hit for a loan** (coll) dar un sablazo a || *tr* prestar
**loan shark** *s* (coll) usurero
**loan word** *s* préstamo lingüístico
**loath** [loθ] *adj* poco dispuesto; **nothing loath** de buena gana
**loathe** [loð] *tr* abominar, detestar
**loathing** [ˈloðɪŋ] *s* abominación, detestación
**loathsome** [ˈloðsəm] *adj* abominable, asqueroso
**lob** [lɑb] *v* (*pret & pp* **lobbed**; *ger* **lobbing**) *tr* (tennis) volear desde muy alto
**lob•by** [ˈlɑbi] *s* (*pl* **-bies**) salón *m* de entrada, vestíbulo; cabilderos || *v* (*pret & pp* **-bied**) *intr* cabildear
**lobbying** [ˈlɑbɪ•ɪŋ] *s* cabildeo
**lobbyist** [ˈlɑbɪ•ɪst] *s* cabildero
**lobster** [ˈlɑbstər] *s* (*spiny lobster*) langosta; (*Homarus*) bogavante *m*
**lobster pot** *s* langostera
**local** [ˈlokəl] *adj* local || *s* tren suburbano; (*branch of a union*) junta local; noticia de interés local
**locale** [loˈkæl] *s* localidad
**locali•ty** [loˈkælɪti] *s* (*pl* **-ties**) localidad
**localize** [ˈlokəˌlaɪz] *tr* localizar
**local option** *s* derecho local de legislar sobre la venta de bebidas alcohólicas
**locate** [loˈket] o [ˈloket] *tr* (*to discover the location of*) localizar; (*to place, to settle*) colocar, establecer; (*to ascribe a particular location to*) situar || *intr* establecerse
**location** [loˈkeʃən] *s* (*place, position*) localidad; (*act of placing*) colocación; (*act of finding*) localización; **on location** (mov) en exteriores
**loc. cit.** *abbr* **loco citato (Lat) in the place cited**
**lock** [lɑk] *s* cerradura; (*of a canal*) esclusa; (*of hair*) bucle *m;* (*of a firearm*) llave *f;* **lock, stock, and barrel** (coll) del todo, por completo; **under lock and key** bajo llave || *tr* echar la llave a, cerrar con llave; (*to key*) acuñar; hacer pasar (*un buque*) por la esclusa; abrazar, enlazar; **to lock in** encerrar, poner debajo de llave; **to lock out** cerrar la puerta a, dejar en la calle; dejar sin trabajo (*a los obreros*); **to lock up** encerrar, poner debajo de llave; encarcelar
**locker** [ˈlɑkər] *s* armario cerrado con llave
**locket** [ˈlɑkɪt] *s* guardapelo, medallón *m*
**lock'jaw'** *s* trismo, oclusión forzosa de la boca
**lock nut** *s* contratuerca
**lock'out'** *s* huelga patronal
**lock'smith'** *s* cerrajero
**lock step** *s* marcha en fila apretada
**lock stitch** *s* punto encadenado
**lock tender** *s* esclusero
**lock'up'** *s* cárcel *f*
**lock washer** *s* arandela de seguridad

**locomotive** [ˌlokəˈmotɪv] *s* locomotora
**lo•cus** [ˈlokəs] *s* (*pl* **-ci** [saɪ]) sitio, lugar *m;* lugar (geométrico)
**locust** [ˈlokəst] *s* (ent) langosta (*Pachytylus*); (ent) cigarra (*Cicada*); (bot) acacia falsa
**lode** [lod] *s* filón *m,* venero, veta
**lode'star'** *s* (astr) estrella polar; estrella de guía; (*guide, direction*) guía, norte *m*
**lodge** [lɑdʒ] *s* casa de guarda; casa de campo; (*e.g., of Masons*) logia || *tr* alojar, hospedar; depositar, colocar; presentar (*una queja*) || alojarse, hospedarse; quedar colgado, ir a parar
**lodger** [ˈlɑdʒər] *s* inquilino (*en parte de una casa*)
**lodging** [ˈlɑdʒɪŋ] *s* alojamiento, hospedaje *m;* (*without meals*) cobijo
**loft** [lɔft] o [lɑft] *s* (*attic*) desván *m,* sobrado; (*hayloft*) henal *m,* pajar *m;* (*in theater or church*) galería; (*in a store or office building*) piso alto
**loft•y** [ˈlɔfti] o [ˈlɑfti] *adj* (*comp* **-ier;** *super* **-iest**) (*towering; sublime*) encumbrado; (*haughty*) altivo, orgulloso
**log.** *abbr* **logarithm**
**log** [lɔg] o [lɑg] *s* leño, tronco; (*log chip*) (naut) barquilla; (*chip and line*) (naut) corredera; (aer) diario de vuelo; **to sleep like a log** dormir como un leño || *v* (*pret & pp* **logged;** *ger* **logging**) *tr* registrar; recorrer (*cierta distancia*)
**logarithm** [ˈlɔgəˌrɪðəm] o [ˈlɑgəˌrɪðəm] *s* logaritmo
**log'book'** *s* (aer) libro de vuelo; (naut) cuaderno de bitácora
**log cabin** *s* cabaña de troncos
**log chip** *s* (naut) barquilla
**log driver** *s* ganchero, maderero
**log driving** *s* flotaje *m*
**logger** [ˈlɔgər] o [ˈlɑgər] *s* leñador *m,* maderero; grúa de troncos; tractor *m*
**log'ger•head'** *s* mentecato; **at loggerheads** reñidos
**loggia** [ˈlodʒə] *s* (archit) logia
**logic** [ˈlɑdʒɪk] *s* lógica
**logical** [ˈlɑdʒɪkəl] *adj* lógico
**logician** [loˈdʒɪʃən] *s* lógico
**logistic(al)** [loˈdʒɪstɪk(əl)] *adj* logístico
**logistics** [loˈdʒɪstɪks] *s* logística
**log'jam'** *s* atasco de rollizos; (fig) estancación
**log line** *s* (naut) corredera
**log'roll'** *intr* trocar favores políticos
**log'wood'** *s* campeche *m*
**loin** [lɔɪn] *s* lomo; **to gird up one's loins** apercibirse para la acción
**loin'cloth'** *s* taparrabo
**loiter** [ˈlɔɪtər] *tr* — **to loiter away** malgastar (*el tiempo*) || *intr* holgazanear, rezagarse
**loiterer** [ˈlɔɪtərər] *s* holgazán *m,* rezagado
**loll** [lɑl] *intr* colgar flojamente; arrellanarse, repantigarse
**lollipop** [ˈlɑliˌpɑp] *s* paleta (*dulce en el extremo de un palito*)
**Lombard** [ˈlɑmbɑrd] o [ˈlɑmbərd] *adj & s* lombardo
**Lombardy** [ˈlɑmbərdi] *s* Lombardía
**Lombardy poplar** *s* álamo de Italia, chopo lombardo
**lon.** *abbr* **longitude**
**London** [ˈlʌndən] *adj* londinense || *s* Londres *m*
**Londoner** [ˈlʌndənər] *s* londinense *mf*
**lone** [lon] *adj* solo, solitario; (*sole, single*) único
**loneliness** [ˈlonlinɪs] *s* soledad
**lone•ly** [ˈlonli] *adj* (*comp* **-lier;** *super* **-liest**) soledoso
**lonesome** [ˈlonsəm] *adj* soledoso; (*spot, atmosphere*) solitario
**lone wolf** *s* (fig) lobo solitario
**long.** *abbr* **longitude**
**long** [lɔŋ] o [lɑŋ] (*comp* **longer** [ˈlɔŋgər] o [ˈlɑŋgər]; *super* **longest** [ˈlɔŋgɪst] o [ˈlɑŋgɪst]) *adj* largo; de largo, p.ej., **two meters long** dos metros de largo || *adv* mucho tiempo, largo tiempo; **as long as** mientras; (*provided*) con tal de que; (*inasmuch as*) puesto que; **before long** dentro de poco; **how long** cuánto tiempo; **long ago** hace mucho tiempo; **long before** mucho antes; **longer** más tiempo; **long since** desde hace mucho tiempo; **no longer** ya no; **so long!** (coll) ¡hasta luego!; **so long as** con tal de que || *intr* anhelar, suspirar; **to long for** anhelar por, ansiar
**long'boat'** *s* (naut) lancha
**long'-dis'tance call** *s* (telp) llamada a larga distancia
**long-distance flight** *s* (aer) vuelo a distancia
**long'-drawn'-out'** *adj* prolongado, pesado
**longeron** [ˈlɑndʒərən] *s* larguero
**longevity** [lɑnˈdʒɛvɪti] *s* longevidad
**long face** *s* (coll) cara triste
**long'hair'** *adj & s* intelectual *mf;* aficionado a la música clásica
**long'hand'** *s* escritura a mano
**longing** [ˈlɔŋɪŋ] o [ˈlɑŋɪŋ] *adj* anhelante || *s* anhelo, ansia
**longitude** [ˈlɑndʒɪˌtjud] o [ˈlɑndʒɪˌtud] *s* longitud
**long-lived** [ˈlɔŋˈlaɪvd], [ˈlɔŋˈlɪvd], [ˈlɑŋˈlaɪvd] o [ˈlɑŋˈlɪvd] *adj* longevo, de larga vida
**long-playing record** [ˈlɔŋˈple•ɪŋ] o [ˈlɑŋˈple•ɪŋ] *s* disco de larga duración
**long primer** [ˈprɪmər] *s* (typ) entredós *m*
**long'-range'** *adj* de largo alcance
**longshore•man** [ˈlɔŋˌʃormən] o [ˈlɑŋˌʃormən] *s* (*pl* **-men** [mən]) *s* estibador *m,* portuario
**long'-stand'ing** *adj* que existe desde hace mucho tiempo
**long'-suf'fering** *adj* longánimo, sufrido
**long suit** *s* (cards) palo fuerte; (fig) fuerte *m*
**long'-term'** *adj* a largo plazo
**long'-wind'ed** *adj* difuso, palabrero
**look** [lʊk] *s* (*appearance*) aspecto, apariencia; (*glance*) mirada; (*search*) búsqueda; **looks** aspecto, aparien-

cia; **to take a look at** echar una mirada a || *tr* expresar con la mirada; representar (*la edad que uno tiene*); **to look daggers at** apuñalar con la mirada; **to look the part** vestir el cargo; **to look up** (*e.g., in a dictionary*) buscar; ir a visitar, venir a ver || *intr* mirar; buscar; parecer; **look out!** ¡cuidado!, ¡ojo!; **to look after** mirar por; ocuparse en; **to look at** mirar; **to look back** mirar hacia atrás; (fig) mirar el pasado; **to look down on** mirar por encima del hombro; **to look for** buscar; creer, p.ej., **I look for rain** creo que va a llover; **to look forward to** esperar con placer anticipado; **to look ill** tener mala cara; **to look in on** pasar por la casa o la oficina de; **to look into** averiguar, estudiar; **to look like** parecerse a; amenazar, p.ej., **it looks like rain** amenaza lluvia, parece que va a llover; **to look oneself** parecer el mismo; tener buena cara; **to look out** tener cuidado; mirar por (*p.ej., la ventana*); **to look out for** mirar por, cuidar de; guardarse de; **to look out on** dar a; **to look through** mirar por; hojear (*un libro*); **to look toward** dar a; **to look up to** admirar, mirar con respeto; **to look well** tener buena cara

**looker-on** [ˌlʊkər'ɑn] o [ˌlʊkər'ɔn] *s* (*pl* **lookers-on**) mirón *m*, espectador *m*

**looking glass** ['lʊkɪŋ] *s* espejo

**look'out'** *s* vigilancia; (*tower*) atalaya; (*person keeping watch*) vigilante *mf;* (*man watching from lookout tower*) atalaya *m;* (*care, concern*) (coll) cuidado; **to be on the lookout for** estar a la mira de

**loom** [lum] *s* telar *m* || *intr* (*to appear indistinctly*) vislumbrarse; amenazar, parecer inevitable

**loon** [lun] *s* tonto, bobo; (orn) zambullidor *m*

**loon•y** ['luni] *adj* (*comp* **-ier;** *super* **-iest**) (slang) loco || *s* (*pl* **-ies**) (slang) loco

**loop** [lup] *s* lazo; (*in a cable or rope*) vuelta; (*of a river*) meandro; (*of a road*) recoveco; (*for fastening a button*) presilla; (aer) rizo; (elec) circuito cerrado; (*part of vibrating body between two nodes*) vientre *m;* **to loop the loop** (aer) rizar el rizo || *tr* hacer lazos en; enlazar || *intr* formar lazo; (aer) hacer el rizo

**loop'hole'** *s* (*narrow opening in wall*) lucerna; (*means of evasion*) efugio, escapatoria

**loose** [lus] *adj* (*dress, tooth, screw, bowels*) flojo; (*fitting, thread, wire, rivet, tongue, bowels*) suelto; (*sleeve*) perdido; (*earth, soil*) desmenuzado; (*unpackaged*) a granel, sin envase; (*unbound papers*) sin encuadernar; (*pulley*) loco; (*translation*) libre; (*life, morals*) relajado; (*woman*) fácil, frágil; **to become loose** desatarse, aflojarse; **to break loose** ponerse en libertad; **to turn loose** soltar || *s* — **to be on the loose** (coll) ser libre, estar sin trabas; (coll) estar de juerga || *tr* soltar; desatar, desencadenar

**loose end** *s* cabo suelto; **at loose ends** desarreglado, indeciso

**loose'-leaf' notebook** *s* cuaderno de hojas cambiables, cuaderno de hojas sueltas

**loosen** ['lusən] *tr* desatar, aflojar, desapretar; aflojar, laxar (*el vientre*) || *intr* desatarse, aflojarse, desapretarse

**looseness** ['lusnɪs] *s* flojedad, soltura; (*in morals*) relajamiento

**loose'strife'** *s* lisimaquia; salicaria

**loose-tongued** ['lus'tʌŋd] *adj* largo de lengua, ligero de lengua

**loot** [lut] *s* botín *m*, presa || *tr* saquear, pillar

**lop** [lɑp] *v* (*pret & pp* **lopped;** *ger* **lopping**) *tr* dejar caer (*p.ej., los brazos*); **to lop off** cortar; podar (*un árbol, una vid*) || *intr* colgar

**lopsided** ['lɑp'saɪdɪd] *adj* ladeado, sesgado; desproporcionado, asimétrico, patituerto

**loquacious** [lo'kweʃəs] *adj* locuaz

**lord** [lɔrd] *s* señor *m;* (Brit) lord *m;* (hum & poet) marido || *tr* — **to lord it over** dominar despóticamente, imponerse a

**lord•ly** ['lɔrdli] *adj* (*comp* **-lier;** *super* **-liest**) señoril; magnífico; despótico, imperioso; altivo, arrogante

**Lord's Day, the** el domingo

**lordship** ['lɔrdʃɪp] *s* señoría, excelencia

**Lord's Prayer** *s* oración dominical, padrenuestro

**Lord's Supper** *s* sagrada comunión; Cena del Señor

**lore** [lor] *s* ciencia, saber *m;* ciencia popular, saber *m* popular

**lorgnette** [lɔrn'jɛt] *s* (*eyeglasses*) impertinentes *mpl;* (*opera glasses*) gemelos de teatro con manija

**lor•ry** ['lɑri] o ['lɔri] *s* (*pl* **-ries**) carro de plataforma; (Brit) autocamión *m;* (Brit) vagoneta

**lose** [luz] *v* (*pret & pp* **lost** [lɔst] o [lɑst]) *tr* perder; no lograr salvar (*el médico al enfermo*); **to lose heart** desalentarse; **to lose oneself** perderse, errar el camino; ensimismarse || *intr* perder; quedar vencido; retrasarse (*el reloj*)

**loser** ['luzər] *s* perdedor *m*

**losing** ['luzɪŋ] *adj* perdedor || **losings** *spl* pérdidas, dinero perdido

**loss** [lɔs] o [lɑs] *s* pérdida; **to be at a loss** estar perplejo, no saber qué hacer; **to be at a loss to** + *inf* no saber como + *inf;* **to sell at a loss** vender con pérdida

**loss of face** *s* pérdida de prestigio, desprestigio

**lost** [lɔst] o [lɑst] *adj* perdido; **lost in thought** ensimismado, abismado; **lost to** perdido para; insensible a

**lost'-and-found' department** *s* oficina de objetos perdidos

**lost sheep** *s* oveja perdida

**lot** [lɑt] *s* (*for building*) solar *m*, parcela; (*fate, destiny*) suerte *f*; (*portion, parcel*) lote *m*; (*of people*) grupo; (coll) gran cantidad, gran número; (coll) sujeto, tipo; **a lot (of)** o **lots of** (coll) mucho, muchos; **to cast** o **to throw in one's lot with** compartir la suerte de; **to draw** o **to cast lots** echar suertes
**lotion** [ˈloʃən] *s* loción
**lotter·y** [ˈlɑtəri] *s* (*pl* **-ies**) lotería
**lotto** [ˈlɑto] *s* lotería
**lotus** [ˈlotəs] *s* loto
**loud** [laʊd] *adj* alto; (*noisy*) ruidoso; (*voice*) fuerte; (*garish*) chillón, llamativo; (*conspicuously vulgar*) charro, cursi; (*foul-smelling*) apestoso, maloliente || *adv* alto, en voz alta; ruidosamente
**loudmouthed** [ˈlaʊd ˌmaʊθt] o [ˈlaʊd ˌmaʊðd] *adj* vocinglero
**loud'speak'er** *s* altavoz *m*
**lounge** [laʊndʒ] *s* diván *m*, sofá *m* cama; salón *m* de descanso, salón social || *intr* repantigarse a su sabor, recostarse cómodamente; **to lounge around** estar arrimado a la pared, pasearse perezosamente
**lounge lizard** *s* (slang) holgón *m*
**louse** [laʊs] *s* (*pl* **lice** [laɪs]) piojo
**lous·y** [ˈlaʊzi] *adj* (*comp* **-ier**; *super* **-iest**) piojoso; (*mean*) (coll) vil, ruin; (*filthy*) (coll) asqueroso, sucio; (*bungling*) (coll) chapucero; **lousy with** (slang) colmado de (*p.ej.*, *dinero*)
**lout** [laʊt] *s* patán *m*
**louver** [ˈluvər] *s* (*opening to let in air and light*) lumbrera; tablilla de persiana; (aut) persiana del radiador
**lovable** [ˈlʌvəbəl] *adj* amable
**love** [lʌv] *s* amor *m*; (*tennis*) cero, nada; **not for love nor money** ni a tiros; **to be in love (with)** estar enamorado (de); **to fall in love (with)** enamorarse (de); **to make love to** cortejar, galantear || *tr* amar, querer; gustar de, tener afición a
**love affair** *s* amores *mpl*, amorío
**love'bird'** *s* inseparable *m*; **lovebirds** recién casados muy enamorados
**love child** *s* hijo del amor
**love feast** *s* ágape *m*
**loveless** [ˈlʌvlɪs] *adj* abandonado, sin amor; (*feeling no love*) desamado
**lovelorn** [ˈlʌv ˌlɔrn] *adj* abandonado por su amor, herido de amor
**love·ly** [ˈlʌvli] *adj* (*comp* **-lier**; *super* **-liest**) bello, hermoso; adorable, precioso; (coll) encantador, gracioso
**love match** *s* matrimonio de amor
**love potion** *s* filtro, filtro de amor
**lover** [ˈlʌvər] *s* amante *mf*; (*e.g.*, *of hunting, sports*) aficionado; (*e.g.*, *of work*) amigo
**love seat** *s* confidente *m*
**love'sick'** *adj* enfermo de amor
**love'sick'ness** *s* mal *m* de amor
**love song** *s* canción de amor
**loving** [ˈlʌvɪŋ] *adj* amoroso, afectuoso
**lov'ing-kind'ness** *s* bondad infinita, misericordia
**low** [lo] *adj* bajo; (*diet; visibility; opinion*) malo; (*dress, waist*) escotado; (*depressed*) abatido; gravemente enfermo; (*fire*) lento; **to lay low** dejar tendido, derribar; matar; **to lie low** no dejarse ver || *adv* bajo || *s* punto bajo; precio más bajo, precio mínimo; (*moo of cow*) mugido; (aut) primera marcha, primera velocidad; (meteor) depresión || *intr* mugir (*la vaca*)
**low'born'** *adj* de humilde cuna
**low'boy'** *s* cómoda baja con patas cortas
**low'brow'** *adj* & *s* (slang) ignorante *mf*
**low'-cost' housing** *s* casas baratas
**Low Countries, the** los Países Bajos
**low'-down'** *adj* (coll) bajo, vil, ruin || **low'-down'** *s* (slang) informes *mf* confidenciales, hechos verdaderos
**lower** [ˈlo·ər] *adj* bajo, inferior || *tr* & *intr* bajar || [ˈlaʊ·ər] *intr* poner mala cara, fruncir el entrecejo; encapotarse (*el cielo*)
**lower berth** [ˈlo·ər] *s* litera baja, cama baja
**Lower California** [ˈlo·ər] *s* la Baja California
**lower case** [ˈlo·ər] *s* (typ) caja baja
**lower middle class** [ˈlo·ər] *s* pequeña burguesía
**lowermost** [ˈlo·ər ˌmost] *adj* (el) más bajo
**low'-fre'quency** *adj* de baja frecuencia
**low gear** *s* primera marcha, primera velocidad
**lowland** [ˈlolənd] *s* tierra baja || **Lowlands** *spl* Tierra Baja (*de Escocia*)
**low·ly** [ˈloli] *adj* (*comp* **-lier**; *super* **-liest**) humilde; (*in growth or position*) bajo
**Low Mass** *s* misa rezada
**low-minded** [ˈloˈmaɪndɪd] *adj* vil, ruin
**low neck** *s* escote *m*, escotado
**low-necked** [ˈloˈnɛkt] *adj* escotado
**low-pitched** [ˈloˈpɪtʃt] *adj* (*sound*) grave; (*roof*) de poco declive
**low'-pres'sure** *adj* de baja presión
**low-priced** [ˈloˈpraɪst] *adj* barato, de precio bajo
**low shoe** *s* zapato inglés
**low'-speed'** *adj* de baja velocidad
**low-spirited** [ˈloˈspɪrɪtɪd] *adj* abatido
**low spirits** *spl* abatimiento
**low tide** *s* bajamar *f*, marea baja; (fig) punto más bajo
**low visibility** *s* (aer) poca visibilidad
**low water** *s* (*of a river*) nivel mínimo; (*because of drought*) estiaje *m*; bajamar *f*, marea baja
**loyal** [ˈlɔɪ·əl] *adj* leal
**loyalist** [ˈlɔɪ·əlɪst] *s* leal *m*
**loyal·ty** [ˈlɔɪ·əlti] *s* (*pl* **-ties**) lealtad
**lozenge** [ˈlɑzɪndʒ] *s* losange *m*; (*candy cough drop*) pastilla, tableta
**LP** [ˈɛlˈpi] *s* (letterword) (trademark) disco de larga duración
**Ltd.** *abbr* **limited**
**lubricant** [ˈlubrɪkənt] *adj* & *s* lubricante *m*
**lubricate** [ˈlubrɪ ˌket] *tr* lubricar
**lubricous** [ˈlubrɪkəs] *adj* (*slippery; lewd*) lúbrico (*resbaladizo; lascivo*); incierto, inconstante

**lucerne** [lu'sʌrn] *s* mielga

**lucid** ['lusɪd] *adj* claro, inteligible; (*rational, sane*) lúcido; (*bright, shining*) luciente; (*clear, transparent*) cristalino

**Lucifer** ['lusɪfər] *s* Lucifer *m*

**luck** [lʌk] *s* (*good or bad*) suerte *f;* (*good*) suerte, buena suerte; **down on one's luck** de mala suerte, de malas; **in luck** de buena suerte, de buenas; **out of luck** de mala suerte, de malas; **to bring luck** traer buena suerte; **to try one's luck** probar fortuna; **worse luck** desgraciadamente

**luckily** ['lʌkɪli] *adv* afortunadamente

**luckless** ['lʌklɪs] *adj* desgraciado

**luck·y** ['lʌki] *adj* (*comp* **-ier;** *super* **-iest**) afortunado; (*supposed to bring luck*) de buen agüero; **to be lucky** tener suerte

**lucky hit** *s* (coll) golpe *m* de fortuna

**lucrative** ['lukrətɪv] *adj* lucrativo

**ludicrous** ['ludɪkrəs] *adj* absurdo, ridículo

**lug** [lʌg] *s* orejeta; (*pull, tug*) estirón *m,* esfuerzo || *v* (*pret & pp* **lugged;** *ger* **lugging**) *tr* tirar con fuerza de; (*to bring up irrelevantly*) (coll) traer a colación

**luggage** ['lʌgɪdʒ] *s* equipaje *m*

**lugubrious** [lu'gubrɪ·əs] o [lu'gjubrɪ·əs] *adj* lúgubre

**lukewarm** ['luk,wɔrm] *adj* tibio, templado

**lull** [lʌl] *s* momento de calma, momento de silencio; (naut) recalmón *m* || *tr* adormecer; calmar, aquietar; apaciguar

**lulla·by** ['lʌlə,baɪ] *s* (*pl* **-bies**) arrullo, canción de cuna

**lumbago** [lʌm'bego] *s* lumbago

**lumber** ['lʌmbər] *s* madera aserrada, madera aserradiza, madera de sierra; trastos viejos || *intr* andar pesadamente

**lum'ber·jack'** *s* leñador *m,* hachero

**lumber·man** ['lʌmbərmən] *s* (*pl* **-men** [mən]) (*dealer*) maderero; (*man who cuts down lumber*) leñador *m,* hachero

**lumber room** *s* leonera, trastera

**lum'ber·yard'** *s* maderería, depósito de maderas

**luminar·y** ['lumɪ,neri] *s* (*pl* **-ies**) luminar *m,* lumbrera

**luminescent** [,lumɪ'nesənt] *adj* luminiscente

**luminous** ['lumɪnəs] *adj* luminoso

**lummox** ['lʌməks] *s* (coll) jergón *m*

**lump** [lʌmp] *s* terrón *m;* (*swelling*) chichón *m,* bulto, hinchazón *m;* (*stupid person*) (coll) bodoque *m;* **in the lump** en grueso, por junto; **to get a lump in one's throat** hacérsele a (*uno*) un nudo en la garganta || *tr* juntar, mezclar; (*to make into lumps*) aterronar; (coll) aguantar, tragar (*cosa repulsiva*)

**lumpish** ['lʌmpɪʃ] *adj* hobachón, torpe, pesado

**lump sum** *s* suma global, suma total

**lump·y** ['lʌmpi] *adj* (*comp* **-ier;** *super* **-iest**) aterronado, borujoso; torpe, pesado; (*sea*) agitado

**luna·cy** ['lunəsi] *s* (*pl* **-cies**) demencia, locura

**lunar** ['lunər] *adj* lunar

**lunar landing** *s* alunizaje *m*

**lunatic** ['lunətɪk] *adj & s* lunático, loco

**lunatic asylum** *s* manicomio

**lunatic fringe** *s* minoría fanática

**lunch** [lʌntʃ] *s* (*regular midday meal*) almuerzo; (*light meal*) colación, merienda || *intr* almorzar; merendar, tomar una colación

**lunch basket** *s* fiambrera

**lunch cloth** *s* mantelito

**luncheon** ['lʌntʃən] *s* almuerzo; almuerzo de ceremonia

**lunch'room'** *s* cantina, merendero

**lung** [lʌŋ] *s* pulmón *m*

**lunge** [lʌndʒ] *s* arremetida, embestida; (*with a sword*) estocada || *intr* arremeter, lanzarse; **to lunge at** arremeter contra

**lurch** [lʌrtʃ] *s* sacudida, tumbo; (naut) bandazo; **to leave in the lurch** dejar en la estacada, dejar colgado || *intr* dar una sacudida, dar un tumbo; (naut) dar un bandazo

**lure** [lur] *s* (*decoy*) cebo, señuelo; (fig) aliciente *m,* señuelo || *tr* atraer con cebo, atraer con señuelo; (fig) atraer, tentar, seducir; **to lure away** llevarse con señuelo; (*from one's obligations*) desviar

**lurid** ['lurɪd] *adj* sensacional; (*gruesome*) espeluznante; (*fiery*) ardiente, encendido

**lurk** [lʌrk] *intr* acechar, andar furtivamente

**luscious** ['lʌʃəs] *adj* delicioso; lujoso; voluptuoso

**lush** [lʌʃ] *adj* jugoso, lozano; lujuriante; lujoso

**Lusitanian** [,lusɪ'tenɪ·ən] *adj & s* lusitano

**lust** [lʌst] *s* deseo vehemente; (*greed*) codicia; (*strong sexual appetite*) lujuria; entusiasmo || *intr* lujuriar; **to lust after** o **for** codiciar; desear con lujuria

**luster** ['lʌstər] *s* (*gloss*) lustre *m;* (*of certain fabrics*) viso; (*fame, glory*) (fig) lustre

**lus'ter·ware'** *s* loza con visos metálicos

**lustful** ['lʌstfəl] *adj* lujurioso

**lustrous** ['lʌstrəs] *adj* lustroso

**lust·y** ['lʌsti] *adj* (*comp* **-ier;** *super* **-iest**) fuerte, robusto, lozano

**lute** [lut] *s* (mus) laúd *m;* (*substance used to close or seal a joint*) (chem) lodo

**Lutheran** ['luθərən] *adj & s* luterano

**luxuriance** [lʌg'ʒurɪ·əns] *s* lozanía

**luxuriant** [lʌg'ʒurɪ·ənt] *adj* lozano, lujuriante; (*overornamented*) recargado

**luxuriate** [lʌg'ʒurɪ,et] o [lʌk'ʃurɪ,et] *intr* crecer con lozanía; entregarse al lujo; (*to find keen pleasure*) lozanearse

**luxurious** [lʌg'ʒurɪ·əs] o [lʌk'ʃurɪ·əs] *adj* lujoso

**luxu·ry** ['lʌkʃəri] o ['lʌgʒəri] *s* (*pl* **-ries**) lujo
**lye** [laɪ] *s* lejía
**lying** ['laɪ·ɪŋ] *adj* mentiroso ‖ *s* el mentir
**ly'ing-in' hospital** *s* casa de maternidad, clínica de parturientas
**lymph** [lɪmf] *s* linfa
**lymphatic** [lɪm'fætɪk] *adj* linfático
**lynch** [lɪntʃ] *tr* linchar
**lynching** ['lɪntʃɪŋ] *s* linchamiento
**lynch law** *s* justicia de la soga
**lynx** [lɪŋks] *s* lince *m*
**lynx-eyed** ['lɪŋks,aɪd] *adj* de ojos linces
**lyonnaise** [,laɪ·ə'nez] *adj* (culin) a la lionesa
**lyre** [laɪr] *s* (mus) lira
**lyric** ['lɪrɪk] *adj* lírico ‖ *s* poema lírico; (*words of a song*) (coll) letra
**lyrical** ['lɪrɪkəl] *adj* lírico
**lyricism** ['lɪrɪ,sɪzəm] *s* lirismo
**lyricist** ['lɪrɪsɪst] *s* (*writer of words for songs*) letrista *mf*; (*poet*) poeta lírico

## M

**M, m** [ɛm] decimotercera letra del alfabeto inglés
**m.** *abbr* **married, masculine, meter, midnight, mile, minute, month**
**ma'am** [mæm] o [mɑm] *s* (coll) señora
**macadam** [mə'kædəm] *s* macadán *m*
**macadamize** [mə'kædə,maɪz] *tr* macadamizar
**macaro·ni** [,mækə'roni] *s* (*pl* **-nis** o **-nies**) macarrones *mpl*
**macaroon** [,mækə'run] *s* mostachón *m*, almendrado
**macaw** [mə'kɔ] *s* aracanga, guacamayo
**mace** [mes] *s* maza; (*spice*) macis *m*
**mace'bear'er** *s* macero
**machination** [,mækɪ'neʃən] *s* maquinación
**machine** [mə'ʃin] *s* máquina; automóvil *m*, coche *m*; (*of a political party*) camarilla ‖ *tr* trabajar a máquina
**machine gun** *s* ametralladora
**ma·chine'-gun'** *tr* ametrallar
**ma·chine'-made'** *adj* hecho a máquina
**machiner·y** [mə'ʃinəri] *s* (*pl* **-ies**) maquinaria
**machine screw** *s* tornillo para metales
**machine shop** *s* taller mecánico
**machine tool** *s* máquina-herramienta
**machine translation** *s* traducción automática
**machinist** [mə'ʃinɪst] *s* (*person who makes machines*) maquinista *mf*; (*person who operates machines*) mecánico; (naut) segundo maquinista; (theat) maquinista *mf*, tramoyista *mf*
**mackerel** ['mækərəl] *s* caballa, escombro
**mackerel sky** *s* cielo aborregado
**mackintosh** ['mækɪn,tɑʃ] *s* impermeable *m*
**mad** [mæd] *adj* (*comp* **madder**; *super* **maddest**) (*angry*) enojado, furioso; (*crazy*) loco; (*foolish*) tonto, necio; (*rabid*) rabioso; **to be mad about** (coll) estar loco por; **to drive mad** volver loco; **to go mad** volverse loco; rabiar (*un perro*)
**madam** ['mædəm] *s* señora
**mad'cap'** *s* alocado, tarambana *mf*
**madden** ['mædən] *tr* (*to make angry*) enojar, enfurecer; (*to make insane*) enloquecer
**made-to-order** ['medtə'ɔrdər] *adj* hecho de encargo; (*clothing*) hecho a la medida
**made'-up'** *adj* inventado, ficticio; (*artificial*) postizo; (*face*) pintado
**mad'house'** *s* casa de locos, manicomio
**madman** ['mæd,mæn] *s* (*pl* **-men** [,mɛn]) loco
**madness** ['mædnɪs] *s* furia, rabia; locura; (*of a dog*) rabia
**Madonna lily** [mə'dɑnə] *s* azucena
**maelstrom** ['melstrəm] *s* remolino
**mag.** *abbr* **magazine**
**magazine** ['mægə,zin] o [,mægə'zin] *s* (*periodical*) revista, magazine *m*; (*warehouse*) almacén *m*; (*for cartridges*) cámara; (*for powder*) polvorín *m*; (naut) santabárbara; (phot) almacén *m*
**Magellan** [mə'dʒɛlən] *s* Magallanes *m*
**maggot** ['mægət] *s* cresa
**Magi** ['medʒaɪ] *spl* magos de Oriente, Reyes Magos
**magic** ['mædʒɪk] *adj* mágico ‖ *s* magia; ilusionismo, prestidigitación; **as if by magic** como por encanto
**magician** [mə'dʒɪʃən] *s* (*entertainer with sleight of hand*) ilusionista *mf*, prestidigitador *m*; (*sorcerer*) mágico
**magistrate** ['mædʒɪs,tret] *s* magistrado
**magnanimous** [mæg'nænɪməs] *adj* magnánimo
**magnesium** [mæg'niʃɪ·əm] o [mæg'niʒɪ·əm] *s* magnesio
**magnet** ['mægnɪt] *s* imán *m*
**magnetic** [mæg'nɛtɪk] *adj* magnético; (fig) atrayente, cautivador
**magnetic curves** *spl* fantasma magnético
**magnetism** ['mægnɪ,tɪzəm] *s* magnetismo
**magnetize** ['mægnɪ,taɪz] *tr* magnetizar, imanar
**magne·to** [mæg'nito] *s* (*pl* **-tos**) magneto *m & f*
**magnificent** [mæg'nɪfɪsənt] *adj* magnífico
**magni·fy** ['mægnɪ,faɪ] *v* (*pret & pp* **-fied**) *tr* magnificar; exagerar
**magnifying glass** *s* lupa, vidrio de aumento
**magnitude** ['mægnɪ,tjud] o ['mægnɪ,tud] *s* magnitud
**magpie** ['mæg,paɪ] *s* picaza, urraca

**Magyar** ['mægjɑr] *adj & s* magiar *mf*
**mahlstick** ['mɑl,stɪk] o ['mɔl,stɪk] *s* tiento
**mahoga•ny** [mə'hɑgəni] *s* (*pl* **-nies**) caoba
**Mahomet** [mə'hɑmɪt] *s* Mahoma *m*
**mahout** [mə'haut] *s* naire *m*, cornaca *m*
**maid** [med] *s* (*female servant*) criada, moza; (*young girl; housemaid*) doncella; (*spinster*) soltera
**maiden** ['medən] *s* doncella
**maid'en•hair'** *s* (bot) cabello de Venus
**maid'en•head'** *s* himen *m*
**maidenhood** ['medən,hud] *s* doncellez *f*
**maiden lady** *s* soltera
**maiden name** *s* apellido de soltera
**maiden voyage** *s* primera travesía
**maid'-in-wait'ing** *s* (*pl* **maids-in-waiting**) dama
**maid of honor** *s* (*at a wedding*) primera madrina de boda; (*attendant on a princess*) doncella de honor; (*attendant on a queen*) dama de honor
**maid'serv'ant** *s* criada, doméstica
**mail** [mel] *s* correspondencia, correo; (*of armor*) malla; **by return mail** a vuelta de correo ‖ *tr* echar al correo
**mail'bag'** *s* valija
**mail'boat'** *s* vapor *m* correo
**mail'box'** *s* buzón *m*
**mail car** *s* carro correo, coche-correo, ambulancia de correos
**mail carrier** *s* cartero
**mailing list** *s* lista de envío
**mailing permit** *s* porte concertado
**mail•man** ['mel,mæn] *s* (*pl* **-men** [,men]) cartero
**mail order** *s* pedido postal
**mail'-or'der house** *s* casa de ventas por correo
**mail'plane'** *s* avión-correo
**mail train** *s* tren *m* correo
**maim** [mem] *tr* estropear, mutilar
**main** [men] *adj* principal, primero, maestro, mayor ‖ *s* cañería maestra; **in the main** mayormente
**main clause** *s* proposición dominante
**main course** *s* plato principal, plato fuerte
**main deck** *s* cubierta principal
**mainland** ['men,lænd] o ['menlənd] *s* continente *m*, tierra firme
**main line** *s* (rr) tronco, línea principal
**mainly** ['menli] *adv* principalmente, en su mayor parte
**mainmast** ['menməst], ['men,mæst] o ['men,mɑst] *s* palo mayor
**mainsail** ['mensəl] o ['men,sel] *s* vela mayor
**main'spring'** *s* (*of watch*) muelle *m* real; (fig) móvil *m*, origen *m*
**main'stay'** *s* (naut) estay *m* mayor; (fig) soporte *m* principal
**main street** *s* calle *f* mayor
**maintain** [men'ten] *tr* mantener; (*to support*) (law) manutener
**maintenance** ['mentɪnəns] *s* mantenimiento; (*upkeep*) conservación; gastos de conservación
**maître d'hôtel** [,metər do'tɛl] *s* (*butler*) mayordomo; (*headwaiter*) jefe *m* de comedor
**maize** [mez] *s* maíz *m*
**majestic** [mə'dʒɛstɪk] *adj* majestuoso
**majes•ty** ['mædʒɪsti] *s* (*pl* **-ties**) majestad
**major** ['medʒər] *adj* (*greater*) mayor; (*elder*) mayor de edad; (mus) mayor ‖ *s* (educ) especialización; (mil) comandante *m* ‖ *intr* (educ) especializarse
**Majorca** [mə'dʒɔrkə] *s* Mallorca
**Majorcan** [mə'dʒɔrkən] *adj & s* mallorquín *m*
**major•do•mo** [,medʒər'domo] *s* (*pl* **-mos**) mayordomo
**major general** *s* general *m* de división
**majori•ty** [mə'dʒɑrɪti] o [mə'dʒɔrɪti] *adj* mayoritario ‖ *s* (*pl* **-ties**) (*being of full age; larger number or part*) mayoría; (*full age*) mayoridad; (mil) comandancia
**make** [mek] *s* (*brand*) marca; (*form, build*) hechura; carácter *m*, natural *m*; **on the make** (slang) buscando provecho ‖ *v* (*pret & pp* **made** [med]) *tr* hacer; cometer (*un error*); efectuar (*un pago*); ganar (*dinero; una baza*); coger (*un tren*); dar (*dinero una empresa*); pronunciar (*un discurso*); cerrar (*un circuito*); poner (*a uno, p.ej., nervioso*); ser, p.ej., **she will make a good wife** será una buena esposa; **to make** + *inf* hacer + *inf*, p.ej., **she made him study** le hizo estudiar; **to make into** convertir en; **to make known** declarar; dar a conocer; **to make of** pensar de; **to make oneself known** darse a conocer; **to make out** distinguir, vislumbrar; descifrar; escribir (*una receta*); llenar (*un cheque*); **to make over** convertir; rehacer (*un traje*); (com) transferir; **to make up** preparar, confeccionar; inventar (*un cuento*); recobrar (*el tiempo perdido*); (theat) maquillar ‖ *intr* estar (*p.ej., seguro*); **to make away with** llevarse; deshacerse de; matar; **to make believe** fingir, p.ej., **he made believe he knew me** fingió conocerme; **to make for** ir hacia; embestir contra; contribuir a (*p.ej., mejores relaciones*); **to make much of** (coll) hacer fiestas a, mostrar cariño a; **to make off** largarse; **to make off with** llevarse, hacerse con; **to make out** arreglárselas; **to make toward** encaminarse a; **to make up** maquillarse, pintarse; componerse, hacer las paces; **to make up for** suplir; compensar por (*una pérdida*); **to make up to** (coll) tratar de congraciarse con
**make'-be•lieve'** *adj* simulado ‖ *s* pretexto, simulación, fantasía
**maker** ['mekər] *s* constructor *m*, fabricante *mf*
**make'shift'** *adj* de fortuna, provisional ‖ *s* expediente *m*; (*person*) tapagujeros *m*
**make'-up'** *s* composición, constitución;

afeite *m*, maquillaje *m;* (typ) imposición
**make-up man** *s* (theat) maquillador *m*
**make'weight'** *s* contrapeso; suplente *mf*
**making** ['mekɪŋ] *s* fabricación; material necesario; causa del éxito; **makings** elementos, materiales *mpl;* (*personal qualities necessary for some purpose*) madera
**malachite** ['mælə,kaɪt] *s* malaquita
**maladjustment** [,mælə'dʒʌstmənt] *s* desadaptación
**mala·dy** ['mælədi] *s* (*pl* **-dies**) dolencia, enfermedad
**malaise** [mæ'lez] *s* indisposición, malestar *m*
**malapropos** [,mælæprə'po] *adj* impropio || *adv* fuera de propósito
**malaria** [mə'lɛrɪ·ə] *s* malaria, paludismo
**Malay** ['mele] o [mə'le] *adj & s* malayo
**malcontent** ['mælkən,tent] *adj & s* malcontento
**male** [mel] *adj* (*sex*) masculino; (*animal, plant, piece of a device*) macho; (*human being*) varón, p.ej., **male child** hijo varón || *s* macho; varón *m*
**malediction** [,mælɪ'dɪkʃən] *s* maldición
**malefactor** ['mælɪ,fæktər] *s* malhechor *m*
**male nurse** *s* enfermero
**malevolent** [mə'lɛvələnt] *adj* malévolo
**malice** ['mælɪs] *s* malicia, malevolencia; **to bear malice** guardar rencor; **with malice prepense** [prɪ'pɛns] (law) con malicia y premeditación
**malicious** [mə'lɪʃəs] *adj* malicioso, malévolo
**malign** [mə'laɪn] *adj* maligno || *tr* calumniar
**malignant** [mə'lɪgnənt] *adj* maligno
**maligni·ty** [mə'lɪgnɪti] *s* (*pl* **-ties**) malignidad
**malinger** [mə'lɪŋgər] *intr* hacer la zanguanga, fingirse enfermo
**mall** [mɔl] o [mæl] *s* alameda, paseo de árboles
**mallet** ['mælɪt] *s* (*wooden hammer*) mazo; (*for croquet and polo*) mallete *m*
**mallow** ['mælo] *s* malva
**malnutrition** [,mælnju'trɪʃən] o [,mælnu'trɪʃən] *s* desnutrición
**malodorous** [mæl'odərəs] *adj* maloliente
**malt** [mɔlt] *s* malta *m;* (coll) cerveza
**maltreat** [mæl'trit] *tr* maltratar
**mamma** ['mɑmə] o [mə'mɑ] *s* mama o mamá *f*
**mammal** ['mæməl] *s* mamífero
**mammalian** [mæ'melɪ·ən] *adj & s* mamífero
**mammoth** ['mæməθ] *adj* gigantesco, enorme || *s* mamut *m*
**man** [mæn] *s* (*pl* **men** [mɛn]) *s* hombre *m;* (*in chess*) pieza; (*in checkers*) pieza, peón *m;* **a man** uno, p.ej., **a man can't get work in this town** uno no puede obtener empleo en este pueblo; **as one man** unánimemente; **man alive!** ¡hombre!; **man and wife** marido y mujer; **to be one's own man** no depender de nadie || *v* (*pret & pp* **manned;** *ger* **manning**) *tr* dotar, tripular (*un buque*); guarnecer (*una fortaleza*); servir (*los cañones*)
**man about town** *s* bulevardero, hombre *m* de mucho mundo
**manacle** ['mænəkəl] *s* manilla; **manacles** esposas || *tr* poner esposas a
**manage** ['mænɪdʒ] *tr* manejar || *intr* arreglárselas; **to manage to** ingeniarse a o para; **to manage to get along** ingeniarse para ir viviendo
**manageable** ['mænɪdʒəbəl] *adj* manejable
**management** ['mænɪdʒmənt] *s* manejo, dirección, gerencia; (*group who manage a business*) la empresa, la parte patronal, los patronos
**manager** ['mænədʒər] *s* director *m*, administrador *m*, gerente *mf;* empresario; (sport) manager *m*
**managerial** [,mænə'dʒɪrɪ·əl] *adj* empresarial
**mandate** ['mændet] *s* mandato || *tr* asignar por mandato
**mandolin** ['mændəlɪn] *s* mandolina
**mandrake** ['mændrek] *s* mandrágora
**mane** [men] *s* (*of horse*) crines *fpl;* (*of lion; of person*) melena
**maneuver** [mə'nuvər] *s* maniobra || *tr* hacer maniobrar || *intr* maniobrar
**manful** ['mænfəl] *adj* varonil, resuelto
**manganese** ['mæŋgə,nis] o ['mæŋgə,niz] *s* manganeso
**mange** [mendʒ] *s* sarna
**manger** ['mendʒər] *s* pesebre *m*
**mangle** ['mæŋgəl] *tr* lacerar, aplastar
**man·gy** ['mendʒi] *adj* (*comp* **-gier;** *super* **-giest**) sarnoso; (*dirty, squalid*) roñoso
**man'han'dle** *tr* maltratar
**man'hole'** *s* caja de registro, pozo de inspección
**manhood** ['mænhʊd] *s* virilidad; hombres *mpl*
**man hunt** *s* caza al hombre
**mania** ['menɪ·ə] *s* manía
**maniac** ['menɪ,æk] *adj & s* maníaco
**manicure** ['mænɪ,kjʊr] *s* (*care of hands*) manicura; (*person*) manicuro, manicura || *tr* hacer la manicura a (*una persona*); hacer (*las manos y las uñas*)
**manicurist** ['mænɪ,kjʊrɪst] *s* manicuro, manicura
**manifest** ['mænɪ,fɛst] *adj* manifiesto || *s* (naut) manifiesto || *tr* manifestar
**manifes·to** [,mænɪ'fɛsto] *s* (*pl* **-toes**) manifiesto
**manifold** ['mænɪ,fold] *adj* múltiple, vario || *s* copia, ejemplar *m;* (*pipe with outlets or inlets*) colector *m*, múltiple *m*
**manikin** ['mænɪkɪn] *s* maniquí *m;* (*dwarf*) enano
**man in the moon** *s* cara o cuerpo de hombre imaginarios en la luna llena
**manipulate** [mə'nɪpjə,let] *tr* manipular

**man'kind'** *s* el género humano || **man'kind'** *s* el sexo masculino, los hombres
**manliness** ['mænlɪnɪs] *s* masculinidad, virilidad
**man·ly** ['mænli] *adj* (*comp* **-lier;** *super* **-liest**) masculino, varonil
**manned spaceship** [mænd] *s* astronave tripulada
**mannequin** ['mænɪkɪn] *s* maniquí *m;* (*young woman employed to exhibit clothing*) maniquí *f*
**manner** ['mænər] *s* manera; **by all manner of means** de todos modos; **in a manner of speaking** como si dijéramos; **in the manner of** a la manera de; **manners** modales *mpl,* crianza; **to the manner born** avezado desde la cuna
**mannish** ['mænɪʃ] *adj* hombruno
**man of letters** *s* hombre *m* de letras
**man of means** *s* hombre *m* de dinero
**man of parts** *s* hombre *m* de buenas prendas
**man of straw** *s* hombre *m* de suposición
**man of the world** *s* hombre *m* de mundo
**man-of-war** [ˌmænəv'wɔr] *s* (*pl* **men-of-war** [ˌmɛnəv'wɔr]) *s* buque *m* de guerra
**manor** ['mænər] *s* señorío
**manor house** *s* casa solariega
**man overboard** *interj* ¡hombre al agua!
**man'pow'er** *s* número de hombres; personal *m* competente; (mil) fuerzas nacionales
**mansard** ['mænsɑrd] *s* mansarda; piso de mansarda
**man'serv'ant** *s* (*pl* **men'serv'ants**) criado
**mansion** ['mænʃən] *s* hotel *m,* palacio; (*manor house*) casa solariega
**man'slaugh'ter** *s* (law) homicidio sin premeditación
**mantel** ['mæntəl] *s* manto (*de chimenea*); (*shelf above it*) mesilla, repisa de chimenea
**man'tel·piece'** *s* mesilla, repisa de chimenea
**mantle** ['mæntəl] *s* capa, manto || *tr* vestir con manto; cubrir, tapar; ocultar || *intr* encenderse (*el rostro*)
**manual** ['mænju·əl] *adj* manual || *s* (*book*) manual *m;* (mil) ejercicio; (mus) teclado manual
**manual training** *s* enseñanza de los artes y oficios
**manufacture** [ˌmænjə'fæktjər] *s* fabricación; (*thing manufactured*) manufactura || *tr* fabricar, manufacturar
**manufacturer** [ˌmænjə'fæktjərər] *s* fabricante *mf*
**manure** [mə'njur] o [mə'nur] *s* estiércol *m* || *tr* estercolar
**manuscript** ['mænjəˌskrɪpt] *adj* & *s* manuscrito
**many** ['mɛni] *adj* & *pron* muchos; **a good many** o **a great many** un buen número; **as many as** tantos como; hasta, p.ej., **as many as twenty** hasta veinte; **how many** cuántos; **many a** muchos, p.ej., **many a person** muchas personas; **many another** muchos otros; **many more** muchos más; **so many** tantos; **too many** demasiados; **twice as many as** dos veces más que
**many-sided** ['mɛniˌsaɪdɪd] *adj* multilátero; (*having many interests or capabilities*) polifacético
**map** [mæp] *s* mapa *m;* (*of a city*) plano || *v* (*pret* & *pp* **mapped;** *ger* **mapping**) *tr* trazar el mapa de; indicar en el mapa; **to map out** trazar el plan de
**maple** ['mepəl] *s* arce *m*
**maquette** [mɑ'kɛt] *s* maqueta
**Mar.** *abbr* **March**
**mar** [mɑr] *v* (*pret* & *pp* **marred;** *ger* **marring**) *tr* desfigurar, estropear; frustrar
**maraud** [mə'rɔd] *tr* saquear || *intr* merodear
**marauder** [mə'rɔdər] *s* merodeador *m*
**marble** ['mɑrbəl] *adj* marmóreo || *s* mármol *m;* (*little ball of glass, etc.*) canica; **marbles** (*game*) canica || *tr* crispir, jaspear
**march** [mɑrtʃ] *s* marcha; (*frontier, territory*) marca; **to steal a march on someone** ganarle a uno por la mano || *tr* hacer marchar || *intr* marchar || **March** *s* marzo
**marchioness** ['mɑrʃənɪs] *s* marquesa
**mare** [mɛr] *s* (*female horse*) yegua; (*female donkey*) asna
**margarine** ['mɑrdʒərɪn] *s* margarina
**margin** ['mɑrdʒɪn] *s* margen *m* & *f;* (*collateral deposited with a broker*) doble *m*
**marginal** ['mɑrdʒɪnəl] *adj* marginal
**margin release** *s* tecla de escape
**margin stop** *s* fijamárgenes *m,* cierrarrenglón *m,* cortarrenglón *m*
**marigold** ['mærɪˌgold] *s* clavelón *m;* (*Calendula*) maravilla, flamenquilla
**marihuana** o **marijuana** [ˌmɑrɪ'hwɑnə] *s* mariguana
**marinate** ['mærɪˌnet] *tr* escabechar, marinar
**marine** [mə'rin] *adj* marino, marítimo || *s* marina; soldado de infantería de marina; **marines** infantería de marina; **tell that to the marines** (coll) cuénteselo a su abuela, a otro perro con ese hueso
**mariner** ['mærɪnər] *s* marino
**marionette** [ˌmærɪ·ə'nɛt] *s* marioneta, títere *m*
**marital status** ['mærɪtəl] *s* estado civil
**maritime** ['mærɪˌtaɪm] *adj* marítimo
**marjoram** ['mɑrdʒərəm] *s* orégano; mejorana
**mark** [mɑrk] *s* marca, señal *f;* (*label*) marbete *m;* (*of punctuation*) punto; (*in an examination*) calificación, nota; (*used instead of signature by an illiterate person*) cruz *f,* signo; (*spot, stain*) mancha; (*coin*) marco; (*starting point in a race*) raya; (*target to shoot at*) blanco; **to be beside the mark** no venir al caso; **to hit the mark** dar en el blanco; **to leave one's mark** dejar memoria de sí; **to make one's mark** llegar a ser célebre; **to miss the mark** errar el tiro; **to toe**

the mark ponerse en la raya; obedecer rigurosamente || *tr* marcar, señalar; dar nota a (*un alumno*); calificar (*un examen*); advertir, notar; **to mark down** poner por escrito; rebajar el precio de
**mark'down'** *s* reducción de precio
**market** ['mɑrkɪt] *s* mercado; **to bear the market** jugar a la baja; **to bull the market** jugar al alza; **to play the market** jugar a la bolsa; **to put on the market** lanzar al mercado || *tr* llevar al mercado; vender
**marketable** ['mɑrkɪtəbəl] *adj* comerciable, vendible
**market basket** *s* cesta para compras
**marketing** ['mɑrkɪtɪŋ] *s* mercología, mercadotecnia
**market place** *s* plaza del mercado
**market price** *s* precio corriente
**marking gauge** ['mɑrkɪŋ] *s* gramil *m*
**marks·man** ['mɑrksmən] *s* (*pl* **-men** [mən]) tirador *m*; **a good marksman** un buen tiro
**marksmanship** ['mɑrksmən,ʃɪp] *s* puntería
**mark'up'** *s* aumento de precio
**marl** [mɑrl] *s* marga || *tr* margar
**marmalade** ['mɑrmə,led] *s* mermelada
**marmot** ['mɑrmət] *s* marmota
**maroon** [mə'run] *adj & s* marrón *m*, castaño obscuro || *tr* dejar abandonado (*en una isla desierta*)
**marquee** [mɑr'ki] *s* marquesina
**marquess** ['mɑrkwɪs] *s* marqués *m*
**marque·try** ['mɑrkətri] *s* (*pl* **-tries**) marquetería (*taracea*)
**marquis** ['mɑrkwɪs] *s* marqués *m*
**marquise** [mɑr'kiz] *s* marquesa; (*over the entrance to a hotel*) marquesina
**marriage** ['mærɪdʒ] *s* casamiento, matrimonio; (*married life; intimate union*) maridaje *m*
**marriageable** ['mærɪdʒəbəl] *adj* casadero
**marriage portion** *s* dote *m & f*
**marriage rate** *s* nupcialidad
**married life** ['mærid] *s* vida conyugal
**marrow** ['mæro] *s* médula, tuétano
**mar·ry** ['mæri] *v* (*pret & pp* **-ried**) *tr* casar (*el sacerdote o el juez a un hombre y una mujer*); (*to take in marriage*) casar con, casarse con; (*to unite intimately*) maridar; **to get married to** casar con, casarse con || *intr* casar, casarse; **to marry into** emparentar con (*p.ej., una familia rica*); **to marry the second time** casarse en segundas nupcias
**Mars** [mɑrz] *s* Marte *m*
**Marseille** [mɑr'se:j] *s* Marsella
**marsh** [mɑrʃ] *s* ciénaga, pantano
**mar·shal** ['mɑrʃəl] *s* cursor *m* de procesiones, maestro de ceremonias; (mil) mariscal *m*; (U.S.A.) oficial *m* de justicia || *v* (*pret & pp* **-shaled** o **-shalled**; *ger* **-shaling** o **-shalling**) *tr* conducir con ceremonia; ordenar, reunir (*los hechos de una argumentación*)
**marsh mallow** *s* (bot) malvavisco
**marsh'mal'low** *s* bombón *m* de merengue y gelatina; bombón de malvavisco
**marsh·y** ['mɑrʃi] *adj* (*comp* **-ier**; *super* **-iest**) pantanoso, palúdico
**marten** ['mɑrtən] *s* (*pine marten*) marta; (*beech marten*) garduña
**martial** ['mɑrʃəl] *adj* marcial
**martial law** *s* ley *f* marcial; **to be under martial law** estar en estado de guerra
**martin** ['mɑrtɪn] *s* (orn) avión *m*
**martinet** [,mɑrtɪ'net] o ['mɑrtɪ,net] *s* ordenancista *mf*
**martyr** ['mɑrtər] *s* mártir *mf*
**martyrdom** ['mɑrtərdəm] *s* martirio
**mar·vel** ['mɑrvəl] *s* maravilla || *v* (*pret & pp* **-veled** o **-velled**; *ger* **-veling** o **-velling**) *intr* maravillarse; **to marvel at** maravillarse con o de
**marvelous** ['mɑrvələs] *adj* maravilloso
**Marxist** ['mɑrksɪst] *adj & s* marxista *mf*
**masc.** *abbr* **masculine**
**mascara** [mæs'kærə] *s* tinte *m* para las pestañas
**mascot** ['mæskɑt] *s* mascota
**masculine** ['mæskjəlɪn] *adj & s* masculino
**mash** [mæʃ] *s* (*crushed mass*) masa; (*to form wort*) masa de cebada || *tr* machacar, majar
**mashed potatoes** [mæʃt] *spl* puré *m* de patatas
**masher** ['mæʃər] *s* (*device*) mano *f*; (slang) galanteador atrevido
**mask** [mæsk] o [mɑsk] *s* máscara; (*of beekeeper*) carilla; (*made from a corpse*) mascarilla; (*person*) máscara *mf*; (phot) desvanecedor *m* || *tr* enmascarar; (phot) desvanecer || *intr* enmascararse
**masked ball** [mæskt] *s* baile *m* de máscaras
**mason** ['mesən] *s* albañil *m* || **Mason** *s* masón *m*
**mason·ry** ['mesənri] *s* (*pl* **-ries**) albañilería || **Masonry** *s* masonería
**masquerade** [,mæskə'red] o [,mɑskə'red] *s* mascarada; (*costume, disguise*) máscara; (*false show*) farsa || *intr* enmascararse; **to masquerade as** disfrazarse de
**masquerade ball** *s* baile *m* de máscaras
**mass** [mæs] *s* masa; gran cantidad; (*bulk, heap*) mole *f*; (*something glimpsed, e.g., in the fog*) bulto informe; (*big splotch in a painting*) gran mancha; (*celebration of the Eucharist*) misa; **the masses** las masas || *tr* juntar, reunir; enmasar (*tropas*) || *intr* juntarse, reunirse
**massacre** ['mæsəkər] *s* carnicería, matanza || *tr* degollar, matar
**massage** [mə'sɑʒ] *s* masaje *m* || *tr* masar, masajear
**masseur** [mæ'sœr] *s* masajista *m*
**masseuse** [mæ'sœz] *s* masajista *f*
**massive** ['mæsɪv] *adj* macizo; sólido, imponente
**mass meeting** *s* mitin *m* popular
**mass production** *s* fabricación en serie
**mast** [mæst] o [mɑst] *s* (*for a flag*) palo; (*of a ship*) palo, mástil *m*;

(*food for swine*) bellotas, hayucos; **before the mast** como simple marinero
**master** ['mæstər] o ['mɑstər] *s* (*employer*) dueño, patrón *m;* (*male head of household*) amo; (*man who possesses some special skill; teacher*) maestro; (*commander of merchant vessel*) capitán *m;* (*title of respect for a boy*) señorito || *tr* dominar
**master bedroom** *s* alcoba de respeto
**master blade** *s* hoja maestra (*de una ballesta*)
**master builder** *s* maestro de obras
**masterful** ['mæstərfəl] o ['mɑstərfəl] *adj* hábil, experto; dominante, imperioso
**master key** *s* llave maestra
**masterly** ['mæstərli] o ['mɑstərli] *adj* magistral || *adv* magistralmente
**master mechanic** *s* maestro mecánico
**mas'ter•mind'** *s* mente directora || *tr* dirigir con gran acierto
**master of ceremonies** *s* maestro de ceremonias; (*in a night club, radio, etc.*) animador *m*
**mas'ter•piece'** *s* obra maestra
**master stroke** *s* golpe maestro
**mas'ter•work'** *s* obra maestra
**master•y** ['mæstəri] o ['mɑstəri] *s* (*pl* **-ies**) (*command, as of a subject*) dominio; ventaja, superioridad; (*skill*) maestría
**mast'head'** *s* (*of a newspaper*) cabecera editorial; (naut) tope *m*
**masticate** ['mæstɪ,ket] *tr* masticar
**mastiff** ['mæstɪf] o ['mɑstɪf] *s* mastín *m*
**masturbate** ['mæstər,bet] *intr* masturbarse
**mat** [mæt] *s* (*for floor*) estera; (*for a cup, vase, etc.*) esterilla, ruedo; (*before a door*) felpudo; (*around a picture*) borde *m* de cartón || *v* (*pret & pp* **matted;** *ger* **matting**) *tr* (*to cover with matting*) esterar; enmarañar || *intr* enmarañarse
**match** [mætʃ] *s* fósforo; (*wick*) mecha; (*counterpart*) compañero; (*suitable partner in marriage*) partido; (*suitably associated pair*) pareja; (*game, contest*) match *m,* partido; **to be a match for** poder con, poder vencer; **to meet one's match** hallar la horma de su zapato || *tr* igualar; aparear, emparejar; hacer juego con; **to match someone for the drinks** jugarle a uno las bebidas || *intr* hacer juego, correr parejas; **to match** a juego, p.ej., **a chair to match** una silla a juego
**match'box'** *s* fosforera; (*of wax matches*) cerillera
**matchless** ['mætʃlɪs] *adj* incomparable, sin par
**matchmaker** ['mætʃ,mekər] *s* casamentero
**mate** [met] *s* compañero; (*e.g., of a shoe*) compañero, hermano; (*husband or wife*) cónyuge *mf;* (*to a female*) macho; (*to a male*) hembra; (*in chess*) mate *m;* (naut) piloto || *tr* aparear, casar; (*in chess*) dar jaque mate a; **to be well mated** hacer una buena pareja || *intr* aparearse, casarse
**material** [mə'tɪrɪ·əl] *adj* material; importante || *s* material *m;* (*what a thing is made of*) materia; (*cloth, fabric*) tela, género
**materialism** [mə'tɪrɪ·ə,lɪzəm] *s* materialismo
**materialize** [mə'tɪrɪ·ə,laɪz] *intr* realizarse
**matériel** [mə,tɪrɪ'ɛl] *s* material *m;* material de guerra
**maternal** [mə'tʌrnəl] *adj* materno; (*motherly*) maternal
**maternity** [mə'tʌrnɪti] *s* maternidad
**maternity hospital** *s* casa de maternidad
**math.** *abbr* **mathematics**
**mathematical** [,mæθɪ'mætɪkəl] *adj* matemático
**mathematician** [,mæθɪmə'tɪʃən] *s* matemático
**mathematics** [,mæθɪ'mætɪks] *s* matemática, matemáticas
**matinée** [,mætɪ'ne] *s* matinée *f,* función de tarde
**mating season** *s* época de celo
**matins** ['mætɪnz] *spl* maitines *mpl*
**matriarch** ['metrɪ,ɑrk] *s* matriarca
**matricidal** [,metrɪ'saɪdəl] o [,mætrɪ'saɪdəl] *adj* matricida
**matricide** ['metrɪ,saɪd] o ['mætrɪ,saɪd] *s* (*act*) matricidio; (*person*) matricida *mf*
**matriculate** [mə'trɪkjə,let] *tr* matricular || *intr* matricularse
**matrimo•ny** ['mætrɪ,moni] *s* (*pl* **-nies**) matrimonio
**matron** ['metrən] *s* matrona
**matronly** ['metrənli] *adj* matronal
**matter** ['mætər] *s* (*physical substance; pus*) materia; (*subject talked or written about*) asunto; (*reason, ground*) motivo; (*copy for printer*) material *m;* (*printed material*) impresos; **a matter of** cosa de, obra de; **for that matter** en cuanto a eso; **in the matter** al respecto; **no matter** no importa; **no matter when** cuando quiera; **no matter where** dondequiera; **what is the matter?** ¿qué hay?; **what is the matter with you?** ¿qué tiene Vd.? || *intr* importar
**matter of course** *s* cosa de cajón; **as a matter of course** por rutina
**matter of fact** *s* — **as a matter of fact** en realidad, en honor a la verdad
**matter-of-fact** ['mætərəv,fækt] *adj* prosaico, práctico, de poca imaginación
**mattock** ['mætək] *s* zapapico
**mattress** ['mætrɪs] *s* colchón *m*
**mature** [mə'tʃʊr] o [mə'tʊr] *adj* maduro; (*due*) pagadero, vencido || *tr* madurar || *intr* madurar; (*to become due*) (com) vencer
**maturity** [mə'tʃʊrɪti] o [mə'tʊrɪti] *s* madurez *f;* (com) vencimiento
**maudlin** ['mɔdlɪn] *adj* lacrimoso, sensiblero; chispo y lloroso
**maul** [mɔl] *tr* aporrear, maltratar
**maulstick** ['mɔl,stɪk] *s* tiento

**maundy** [ˈmɔndi] *s* lavatorio
**Maundy Thursday** *s* Jueves Santo
**mausole·um** [ˌmɔsəˈli·əm] *s* (*pl* **-ums** o **-a** [ə]) mausoleo
**maw** [mɔ] *s* (*of fowl*) buche *m;* (*of fish*) vejiga de aire
**mawkish** [ˈmɔkɪʃ] *adj* (*sickening*) empalagoso; (*sentimental*) sensiblero
**max.** *abbr* **maximum**
**maxim** [ˈmæksɪm] *s* máxima
**maximum** [ˈmæksɪməm] *adj* & *s* máximo
**may** *v aux* **it may be** puede ser; **may I come in?** ¿puedo entrar? **may you be happy!** ¡que seas feliz! || **May** *s* mayo
**maybe** [ˈmebi] o [ˈmebɪ] *adv* acaso, quizá, tal vez
**May Day** *s* primero de mayo; fiesta del primero de mayo
**mayhem** [ˈmehɛm] o [ˈme·əm] *s* (law) mutilación criminal
**mayonnaise** [ˌme·əˈnez] *s* mayonesa
**mayor** [ˈme·ər] o [mɛr] *s* alcalde *m*
**mayoress** [ˈme·ərɪs] o [ˈmɛrɪs] *s* alcaldesa
**May'pole'** *s* mayo
**Maypole dance** *s* danza de cintas
**May queen** *s* maya
**maze** [mez] *s* laberinto
**M.C.** *abbr* **Master of Ceremonies, Member of Congress**
**mdse.** *abbr* **merchandise**
**me** [mi] *pron pers* me; mí; **to me** me; a mí; **with me** conmigo
**meadow** [ˈmɛdo] *s* prado, vega
**mead'ow·land'** *s* pradera
**meager** [ˈmigər] *adj* escaso, pobre; flaco, magro
**meal** [mil] *s* (*regular repast*) comida; (*edible grain coarsely ground*) harina
**meal'time'** *s* hora de comer
**mean** [min] *adj* (*intermediate*) medio; (*low in station or rank*) humilde, obscuro; (*shabby*) andrajoso, raído; (*stingy*) mezquino, tacaño; (*of poor quality*) inferior, pobre; (*small-minded*) vil, ruin, innoble; insignificante; (*vicious, as a horse*) arisco, mal intencionado; (coll) indispuesto; (coll) avergonzado; (coll) de mal genio; **no mean** famoso, excelente || *s* promedio, término medio; **by all means** sí, por cierto, sin falta; **by means of** por medio de; **by no means** de ningún modo, en ningún caso; **means** bienes *mpl* de fortuna; (*agency*) medio, medios; **means to an end** paso para lograr un fin; **to live on one's means** vivir de sus rentas || *v* (*pret & pp* **meant** [mɛnt]) *tr* significar, querer decir; **to mean to** pensar || *intr* — **to mean well** tener buenas intenciones
**meander** [mɪˈændər] *s* meandro || *intr* serpentear; vagar
**meaning** [ˈminɪŋ] *s* sentido, significado
**meaningful** [ˈminɪŋfəl] *adj* significativo
**meaningless** [ˈminɪŋlɪs] *adj* sin sentido
**meanness** [ˈminnɪs] *s* bajeza, vileza, ruindad; (*stinginess*) mezquindad; (*lowliness*) humildad, pobreza
**mean'time'** *adv* entretanto, mientras tanto || *s* medio tiempo; **in the meantime** entretanto, mientras tanto
**mean'while'** *adv* & *s* var de **meantime**
**measles** [ˈmizəlz] *s* sarampión *m;* (*German measles*) rubéola
**mea·sly** [ˈmizli] *adj* (*comp* **-slier;** *super* **-sliest**) sarampioso; (slang) despreciable, mezquino
**measurable** [ˈmɛʒərəbəl] *adj* medible
**measure** [ˈmɛʒər] *s* medida; (*step, procedure*) paso, gestión; (*legislative bill*) proyecto de ley; (*of verse*) pie *m;* (mus) compás *m;* **beyond measure** con exceso; **in a measure** hasta cierto punto; **in great measure** en gran parte; (*suit*) **to measure** hecho a la medida; **to take measures** tomar las medidas necesarias; **to take someone's measure** tomarle a uno las medidas || *tr* medir; recorrer (*cierta distancia*); **to measure out** medir; distribuir || *intr* medir
**measurement** [ˈmɛʒərmənt] *s* (*act of measuring*) medición; (*measuring; dimension*) medida
**measuring glass** *s* vaso graduado
**meat** [mit] *s* carne *f;* (*food in general*) manjar *m*, vianda; (*substance, gist*) meollo
**meat ball** *s* albóndiga
**meat'hook'** *s* garabato de carnicero
**meat market** *s* carnicería
**meat·y** [ˈmiti] *adj* (*comp* **-ier;** *super* **-iest**) carnoso; (fig) jugoso, substancioso
**Mecca** [ˈmɛkə] *s* La Meca
**mechanic** [mɪˈkænɪk] *s* mecánico
**mechanical** [mɪˈkænɪkəl] *adj* mecánico, maquinal; (*machinelike*) (fig) maquinal
**mechanical toy** *s* juguete *m* de movimiento
**mechanics** [mɪˈkænɪks] *ssg* mecánica
**mechanism** [ˈmɛkəˌnɪzəm] *s* mecanismo
**mechanize** [ˈmɛkəˌnaɪz] *tr* mecanizar
**med.** *abbr* **medicine, medieval**
**medal** [ˈmɛdəl] *s* medalla
**medallion** [mɪˈdæljən] *s* medallón *m*
**meddle** [ˈmɛdəl] *intr* meterse, entremeterse
**meddler** [ˈmɛdlər] *s* entremetido
**meddlesome** [ˈmɛdəlsəm] *adj* entremetido
**median** [ˈmidɪ·ən] *adj* intermedio, medio || *s* punto medio, número medio
**median strip** *s* faja central o divisoria
**mediate** [ˈmidɪˌet] *tr* dirimir (*una controversia*); reconciliar || *intr* (*to be in the middle*) mediar; (*to intervene to settle a dispute*) intervenir
**mediation** [ˌmidɪˈeʃən] *s* mediación
**mediator** [ˈmidɪˌetər] *s* mediador *m*
**medical** [ˈmɛdɪkəl] *adj* médico
**medical student** *s* estudiante *mf* de medicina
**medicine** [ˈmɛdɪsɪn] *s* (*science and art*) medicina; (*remedy, treatment*) medicina, medicamento
**medicine cabinet** *s* armario botiquín
**medicine kit** *s* botiquín *m*

**medicine man** *s* curandero, hechicero (*entre los pieles rojas*)
**medieval** [ˌmidɪˈivəl] o [ˌmɛdɪˈivəl] *adj* medieval
**medievalist** [ˌmidɪˈivəlɪst] o [ˌmɛdɪˈivəlɪst] *s* medievalista *mf*
**mediocre** [ˈmidɪˌokər] o [ˌmidɪˈokər] *adj* mediocre
**mediocri·ty** [ˌmidɪˈɑkrɪti] *s* (*pl* **-ties**) mediocridad
**meditate** [ˈmɛdɪˌtet] *tr & intr* meditar
**Mediterranean** [ˌmɛdɪtəˈrenɪ·ən] *adj & s* Mediterráneo
**medi·um** [ˈmidɪ·əm] *adj* intermedio; a medio asar ‖ *s* (*pl* **-ums** o **-a** [ə]) medio; (*in spiritualism*) medio, médium *m;* (*publication*) órgano; **through the medium of** por medio de
**me'dium-range'** *adj* de alcance medio
**medlar** [ˈmɛdlər] *s* (*tree and fruit*) níspero; (*fruit*) níspola
**medley** [ˈmɛdli] *s* mescolanza; (mus) popurrí *m*
**medul·la** [mɪˈdʌlə] *s* (*pl* **-lae** [li]) médula
**meek** [mik] *adj* dócil, manso
**meekness** [ˈmiknɪs] *s* docilidad, mansedumbre
**meerschaum** [ˈmɪrʃəm] s [ˈmɪrʃɔm] *s* espuma de mar; pipa de espuma de mar
**meet** [mit] *adj* conveniente, a propósito ‖ *s* concurso deportivo ‖ *v* (*pret & pp* **met** [mɛt]) *tr* encontrar, encontrarse con; (*to make the acquaintance of*) conocer; empalmar con (*otro tren o autobús*); ir a esperar; honrar, pagar (*una letra*); hacer frente a (*gastos*); cumplir (*sus obligaciones*); batirse con; hallar (*la muerte*); tener (*mala suerte*); aparecer a (*la vista*) ‖ *intr* encontrarse; reunirse; conocerse; **till we meet again** hasta la vista; **to meet with** encontrarse con; reunirse con; empalmar (*un tren*) con (*otro tren*); tener (*un accidente*)
**meeting** [ˈmitɪŋ] *s* junta, sesión; reunión; encuentro; (*of two rivers or roads*) confluencia; desafío, duelo
**meeting of the minds** *s* concierto de voluntades
**meeting place** *s* lugar *m* de reunión
**megacycle** [ˈmɛgəˌsaɪkəl] *s* megaciclo
**megaphone** [ˈmɛgəˌfon] *s* megáfono
**megohm** [ˈmɛgˌom] *s* megohmio
**melancholia** [ˌmɛlənˈkolɪ·ə] *s* melancolía
**melanchol·y** [ˈmɛlənˌkɑli] *adj* melancólico ‖ *s* (*pl* **-ies**) melancolía
**melee** [ˈmele] o [ˈmɛle] *s* refriega, reyerta
**mellow** [ˈmɛlo] *adj* maduro, jugoso; suave, meloso; melodioso ‖ *tr* suavizar ‖ *intr* suavizarse
**melodious** [mɪˈlodɪ·əs] *adj* melodioso
**melodramatic** [ˌmɛlədrəˈmætɪk] *adj* melodramático
**melo·dy** [ˈmɛlədi] *s* (*pl* **-dies**) melodía
**melon** [ˈmɛlən] *s* melón *m*
**melt** [mɛlt] *tr* derretir; fundir (*metales*); ablandar, aplacar ‖ *intr* derretirse; fundirse; ablandarse, aplacarse; **to melt away** desvanecerse; **to melt into** convertirse gradualmente en; deshacerse en (*lágrimas*)
**melting pot** *s* crisol *m;* (fig) caldero de razas
**member** [ˈmɛmbər] *s* miembro
**membership** [ˈmɛmbərˌʃɪp] *s* asociación; (*e.g., of a club*) personal *m;* número de miembros
**membrane** [ˈmɛmbren] *s* membrana
**memen·to** [mɪˈmɛnto] *s* (*pl* **-tos** o **-toes**) recordatorio, prenda de recuerdo
**mem·o** [ˈmɛmo] *s* (*pl* **-os**) (coll) apunte *m,* membrete *m*
**memoir** [ˈmɛmwɑr] *s* memoria; biografía; **memoirs** memorias
**memoran·dum** [ˌmɛməˈrændəm] *s* (*pl* **-dums** o **-da** [də]) apunte *m,* membrete *m*
**memorial** [mɪˈmorɪ·əl] *adj* conmemorativo ‖ *s* monumento conmemorativo; (*petition*) memorial *m*
**memorial arch** *s* arco triunfal
**Memorial Day** *s* día *m* de los caídos
**memorialize** [mɪˈmorɪ·əˌlaɪz] *tr* conmemorar
**memorize** [ˈmɛməˌraɪz] *tr* aprender de memoria
**memo·ry** [ˈmɛməri] *s* (*pl* **-ries**) memoria; **to commit to memory** encomendar a la memoria
**menace** [ˈmɛnɪs] *s* amenaza ‖ *tr & intr* amenazar
**ménage** [meˈnɑʒ] *s* casa, hogar *m;* economía doméstica
**menagerie** [məˈnæʒəri] o [məˈnædʒəri] *s* casa de fieras; colección de fieras
**mend** [mɛnd] *s* remiendo; **to be on the mend** ir mejorando ‖ *tr* (*to repair*) componer, reparar; (*to patch*) remendar; (*to improve*) reformar, mejorar ‖ *intr* mejorar
**mendacious** [mɛnˈdeʃəs] *adj* mendaz
**mendicant** [ˈmɛndɪkənt] *adj & s* mendicante *mf*
**mending** [ˈmɛndɪŋ] *s* remiendo, zurcido
**menfolk** [ˈmɛnˌfok] *spl* hombres *mpl*
**menial** [ˈminɪ·əl] *adj* bajo, servil ‖ *s* criado, doméstico
**menses** [ˈmɛnsiz] *spl* menstruo
**men's furnishings** *spl* artículos para caballeros
**men's room** *s* lavabo para caballeros
**menstruate** [ˈmɛnstruˌet] *intr* menstruar
**mental illness** [ˈmɛntəl] *s* enfermedad mental
**mental reservation** *s* reserva mental
**mental test** *s* prueba de inteligencia
**mention** [ˈmɛnʃən] *s* mención ‖ *tr* mencionar; **don't mention it** no hay de qué; **not to mention** sin contar
**menu** [ˈmɛnju] o [ˈmenju] *s* menú *m,* lista de comidas; comida
**meow** [mɪˈaʊ] *s* maullido ‖ *intr* maullar
**Mephistophelian** [ˌmɛfɪstəˈfilɪ·ən] *adj* mefistofélico
**mercantile** [ˈmʌrkənˌtil] o [ˈmʌrkənˌtaɪl] *adj* mercantil

**mercenar•y** ['mʌrsə,nɛri] *adj* mercenario || *s* (*pl* **-ies**) mercenario
**merchandise** ['mʌrtʃən,daɪz] *s* mercancías, mercaderías
**merchant** ['mʌrtʃənt] *adj* mercante || *s* mercante *m*, mercader *m*
**merchant•man** ['mʌrtʃəntmən] *s* (*pl* **-men** [mən]) buque *m* mercante
**merchant marine** *s* marina mercante
**merchant vessel** *s* buque *m* mercante
**merciful** ['mʌrsɪfəl] *adj* misericordioso
**merciless** ['mʌrsɪlɪs] *adj* despiadado, cruel, implacable
**mercu•ry** ['mʌrkjəri] *s* (*pl* **-ries**) mercurio, azogue *m;* columna de mercurio
**mer•cy** ['mʌrsi] *s* (*pl* **-cies**) misericordia; (*discretionary power*) merced *f;* **at the mercy of** a merced de
**mere** [mɪr] *adj* mero, puro; nada más que
**meretricious** [,mɛrɪ'trɪʃəs] *adj* postizo, de oropel; cursi, llamativo
**merge** [mʌrdʒ] *tr* enchufar, fusionar || *intr* enchufarse, fusionarse; convergir (*p.ej., dos caminos*); **to merge into** convertirse gradualmente en
**merger** ['mʌrdʒər] *s* fusión de empresas
**meridian** [mə'rɪdɪ•ən] *adj* meridiano; (el) más elevado || *s* meridiano; (fig) auge *m*, apogeo
**meringue** [mə'ræŋ] *s* merengue *m*
**meri•no** [mə'rino] *adj* merino || *s* (*pl* **-nos**) merino
**merit** ['mɛrɪt] *s* mérito || *tr* merecer
**merlon** ['mʌrlən] *s* almena, merlón *m*
**mermaid** ['mʌr,med] *s* sirena; (*girl who swims well*) ninfa marina
**mer•man** ['mʌr,mæn] *s* (*pl* **-men** [,mɛn]) tritón *m;* (*good swimmer*) tritón
**merriment** ['mɛrɪmənt] *s* alegría, regocijo
**mer•ry** ['mɛri] *adj* (*comp* **-rier;** *super* **-riest**) alegre, regocijado; **to make merry** divertirse
**Merry Christmas** *interj* ¡Felices Pascuas!, ¡Felices Navidades!
**mer'ry-go-round'** *s* tiovivo, caballito; serie ininterrumpida (de fiestas, tertulias, etc.)
**mer'ry•mak'er** *s* fiestero, jaranero
**mesh** [mɛʃ] *s* (*net, network*) red *f;* (*each open space of net*) malla; (*engagement of gears*) engrane *m;* **meshes** celada, red *f* || *tr* enredar; (mach) engranar || *intr* enredarse; (mach) engranar
**mess** [mɛs] *s* (*dirty condition*) cochinería; fregado, lío, embrollo; (*meal for a group of people; such a group*) rancho; (*refuse*) bazofia; **to get into a mess** meterse en un lío; **to make a mess of** ensuciar, echar a perder || *tr* ensuciar; desarreglar; estropear, echar a perder || *intr* comer; **to mess around** (coll) ocuparse en fruslerías
**message** ['mɛsɪdʒ] *s* mensaje *m;* recado
**messenger** ['mɛsəndʒər] *s* mensajero; (*one who goes on errands*) mandadero; precursor *m*
**mess hall** *s* sala de rancho; comedor *m* de militares
**Messiah** [mə'saɪ•ə] *s* Mesías *m*
**mess kit** *s* utensilios de rancho
**mess'mate'** *s* comensal *mf*, compañero de rancho
**mess of pottage** ['pɑtɪdʒ] *s* (Bib) plato de lentejas; cosa de ningún valor
**Messrs.** ['mɛsərz] *pl* de **Mr.**
**mess•y** ['mɛsi] *adj* (*comp* **-ier;** *super* **-iest**) desaliñado, desarreglado; sucio
**met.** *abbr* **metropolitan**
**metal** ['mɛtəl] *adj* metálico || *s* metal *m;* (fig) brío, ánimo
**metallic** [mɪ'tælɪk] *adj* metálico
**metallurgy** ['mɛtə,lʌrdʒi] *s* metalurgia
**metal polish** *s* limpiametales *m*
**met'al•work'** *s* metalistería
**metamorpho•sis** [,mɛtə'mɔrfəsɪs] *s* (*pl* **-ses** [,siz]) metamorfosis *f*
**metaphore** ['mɛtəfər] o ['mɛtə,fɔr] *s* metáfora
**metaphorical** [,mɛtə'fɑrɪkəl] o [,mɛtə'fɔrɪkəl] *adj* metafórico
**metathe•sis** [mɪ'tæθɪsɪs] *s* (*pl* **-ses** [,siz]) metátesis *f*
**mete** [mit] *tr* — **to mete out** repartir
**meteor** ['mitɪ•ər] *s* estrella fugaz; (*atmospheric phenomenon*) meteoro
**meteorology** [,mitɪ•ə'rɑlədʒi] *s* meteorología
**meter** ['mitər] *s* (*unit of measurement; verse*) metro; (*instrument for measuring gas, electricity, water*) contador *m;* (mus) compás *m*, tiempo || *tr* medir (con contador)
**metering** ['mitərɪŋ] *s* medición
**meter reader** *s* lector *m* (del contador)
**methane** ['mɛθen] *s* metano
**method** ['mɛθəd] *s* método
**methodic(al)** [mɪ'θɑdɪk(əl)] *adj* metódico
**Methodist** ['mɛθədɪst] *adj & s* metodista *mf*
**Methuselah** [mɪ'θuzələ] *s* Matusalén *m;* **to be as old as Methuselah** vivir más años que Matusalén
**meticulous** [mɪ'tɪkjələs] *adj* meticuloso, minucioso
**metric(al)** ['mɛtrɪk(əl)] *adj* métrico
**metronome** ['mɛtrə,nom] *s* metrónomo
**metropolis** [mɪ'trɑpəlɪs] *s* metrópoli *f*
**metropolitan** [,mɛtrə'pɑlɪtən] *adj* metropolitano || *s* (eccl) metropolitano
**mettle** ['mɛtəl] *s* ánimo, brío; **on one's mettle** dispuesto a hacer todo el esfuerzo posible
**mettlesome** ['mɛtəlsəm] *adj* animoso, brioso
**mew** [mju] *s* maullido; (orn) gaviota; **mews** (Brit) caballerizas alrededor de un corral
**Mexican** ['mɛksɪkən] *adj & s* mejicano
**Mexico** ['mɛksɪ,ko] *s* Méjico
**mezzanine** ['mɛzə,nin] *s* entresuelo
**mfr.** *abbr* **manufacturer**
**mi.** *abbr* **mile**
**mica** ['maɪkə] *s* mica
**microbe** ['maɪkrob] *s* microbio
**microbiology** [,maɪkrəbaɪ'ɑlədʒi] *s* microbiología
**microcard** ['maɪkrə,kɑrd] *s* microficha

**microfarad** [ˌmaɪkrəˈfæræd] *s* microfaradio
**microfilm** [ˈmaɪkrəˌfɪlm] *s* microfilm *m,* micropelícula || *tr* microfilmar
**microgroove** [ˈmaɪkrəˌgruv] *adj* microsurco || *s* microsurco; disco microsurco
**microphone** [ˈmaɪkrəˌfon] *s* micrófono
**microscope** [ˈmaɪkrəˌskop] *s* microscopio
**microscopic** [ˌmaɪkrəˈskɑpɪk] *adj* microscópico
**microwave** [ˈmaɪkrəˌwev] *s* microonda
**mid** [mɪd] *adj* medio, p.ej., **in mid course** a medio camino
**mid'day'** *adj* del mediodía || *s* mediodía *m*
**middle** [ˈmɪdəl] *adj* medio || *s* centro, medio; (*of the human body*) cintura; **about the middle of** a mediados de; **in the middle of** en medio de
**middle age** *s* mediana edad || **Middle Ages** *spl* Edad Media
**middle class** *s* burguesía, clase media
**Middle East** *s* Oriente Medio
**Middle English** *s* el inglés medio
**middle finger** *s* dedo cordial, de en medio o del corazón
**mid'dle•man'** *s* (*pl* **-men** [ˌmɛn]) intermediario
**middling** [ˈmɪdlɪŋ] *adj* mediano, regular, pasadero || *adv* (coll) medianamente; **fairly middling** (coll) así, así || *s* (*coarsely ground wheat*) cabezuela; **middlings** artículos de calidad o precio medianos
**mid•dy** [ˈmɪdi] *s* (*pl* **-dies**) (coll) aspirante *m* de marina; (*child's blouse*) marinera
**middy blouse** *s* marinera
**midget** [ˈmɪdʒɪt] *s* enano, liliputiense *mf*
**midland** [ˈmɪdlənd] *adj* de tierra adentro || *s* región central
**mid'night'** *adj* de medianoche; **to burn the midnight oil** quemarse las cejas || *s* medianoche *f*
**midriff** [ˈmɪdrɪf] *s* (anat) diafragma *m;* talle *m*
**midship•man** [ˈmɪdˌʃɪpmən] *s* (*pl* **-men** [mən]) guardia marina *m,* aspirante *m* de marina
**midst** [mɪdst] *s* centro; **in the midst of** en medio de; en lo más recio de
**mid'stream'** *s* — **in midstream** en pleno río
**mid'sum'mer** *s* pleno verano
**mid'way'** *adj* situado a mitad del camino || *adv* a mitad del camino || *s* mitad del camino; (*of a fair or exposition*) avenida central
**mid'week'** *s* mediados de la semana
**mid'wife'** *s* (*pl* **-wives**) partera, comadrona
**mid'win'ter** *s* pleno invierno
**mid'year'** *adj* de mediados del año || *s* mediados del año; **midyears** (coll) examen *m* de mediados del año escolar
**mien** [min] *s* aspecto, semblante *m,* porte *m*
**miff** [mɪf] *s* (coll) desavenencia || *tr* (coll) ofender
**might** [maɪt] *s* fuerza, poder *m;* **with might and main** con todas sus fuerzas, a más no poder || *v aux* se emplea para formar el modo potencial, p.ej., **she might not come** es posible que no venga
**might•y** [ˈmaɪti] *adj* (*comp* **-ier;** *super* **-iest**) potente, poderoso; (*of great size*) grandísimo || *adv* (coll) muy
**migrate** [ˈmaɪgret] *intr* emigrar
**migratory** [ˈmaɪgrəˌtori] *adj* migratorio
**mil.** *abbr* **military, militia**
**milch** [mɪltʃ] *adj* lechero
**mild** [maɪld] *adj* blando, suave; dócil, manso; leve, ligero; (*climate*) templado
**mildew** [ˈmɪlˌdju] o [ˈmɪlˌdu] *s* (*mold*) moho; (*plant disease*) mildeu *m*
**mile** [maɪl] *s* milla inglesa
**mileage** [ˈmaɪlɪdʒ] *s* recorrido en millas
**mileage ticket** *s* billete contado por millas, semejante al billete kilométrico
**mile'post'** *s* poste miliario
**mile'stone'** *s* piedra miliaria; **to be a milestone** hacer época
**milieu** [mɪlˈjʊ] *s* ambiente *m,* medio
**militancy** [ˈmɪlɪtənsi] *s* belicosidad
**militant** [ˈmɪlɪtənt] *adj* militante, belicoso
**militarism** [ˈmɪlɪtəˌrɪzəm] *s* militarismo
**militarist** [ˈmɪlɪtərɪst] *adj & s* militarista *mf*
**militarize** [ˈmɪlɪtəˌraɪz] *tr* militarizar
**military** [ˈmɪlɪˌteri] *adj* militar || *s* (los) militares
**Military Academy** *s* (U.S.A.) Academia General Militar
**military police** *s* policía militar
**militate** [ˈmɪlɪˌtet] *intr* militar
**militia** [mɪˈlɪʃə] *s* milicia
**militia•man** [mɪˈlɪʃəmən] *s* (*pl* **-men** [mən]) miliciano
**milk** [mɪlk] *adj* lechero, de leche || *s* leche *f* || *tr* ordeñar; chupar (*los bienes de uno*); abusar de, explotar || *intr* dar leche
**milk can** *s* lechera
**milk diet** *s* régimen lácteo
**milking** [ˈmɪlkɪŋ] *s* ordeño
**milk'maid'** *s* lechera
**milk•man** [ˈmɪlkˌmæn] *s* (*pl* **-men** [ˌmɛn]) lechero
**milk of human kindness** *s* compasión, humanidad
**milk pail** *s* ordeñadero
**milk shake** *s* batido de leche
**milk'sop'** *s* calzonazos *m,* marica *m*
**milk'weed'** *s* algodoncillo, vencetósigo
**milk•y** [ˈmɪlki] *adj* (*comp* **-ier;** *super* **-iest**) lechoso, lácteo
**Milky Way** *s* Vía Láctea
**mill** [mɪl] *s* (*for grinding grain*) molino; (*for making fabrics*) hilandería; (*for cutting wood*) aserradero; (*for refining sugar*) ingenio; (*for produc-*

*ing steel*) fábrica; (*to grind coffee*) molinillo; (*part of a dollar*) milésima; **to put through the mill** (coll) poner a prueba, someter a un entrenamiento riguroso || *tr* moler (*granos*); acordonar, cerrillar (*monedas*); laminar (*el acero*); triturar (*mena*); (*with a milling cutter*) fresar; batir (*chocolate*) || *intr* — **to mill about** o **around** arremolinarse

**mill end** *s* retal *m* de hilandería

**millennial** [mɪ'lɛnɪ·əl] *adj* milenario

**millenni·um** [mɪ'lɛnɪ·əm] *s* (*pl* **-ums** o **-a** [ə]) milenario, milenio

**miller** ['mɪlər] *s* molinero; (ent) polilla blanca

**millet** ['mɪlɪt] *s* mijo, millo

**milliampere** [,mɪlɪ'æmpɪr] *s* miliamperio

**milligram** ['mɪlɪ,græm] *s* miligramo

**millimeter** ['mɪlɪ,mitər] *s* milímetro

**milliner** ['mɪlɪnər] *s* modista *mf* de sombreros

**millinery** ['mɪlɪ,neri] o ['mɪlɪnəri] *s* artículos para sombreros de señora; confección de sombreros de señora; venta de sombreros de señora

**millinery shop** *s* sombrerería

**milling** ['mɪlɪŋ] *s* (*of grain*) molienda; (*of coins*) acordonamiento, cordoncillo; fresado

**milling machine** *s* fresadora

**million** ['mɪljən] *adj* millón de, millones de || *s* millón *m*

**millionaire** [,mɪljən'ɛr] *s* millonario

**millionth** ['mɪljənθ] *adj & s* millonésimo

**millivolt** ['mɪlɪ,volt] *s* milivoltio

**mill'pond'** *s* represa de molino

**mill'race'** *s* caz *m*

**mill'stone'** *s* muela de molino; (fig) carga pesada

**mill wheel** *s* rueda de molino

**mill'work'** *s* carpintería de taller

**mime** [maɪm] *s* mimo || *tr* remedar

**mimeograph** ['mɪmɪ·ə,græf] o ['mɪmɪ·ə,grɑf] *s* (trademark) mimeógrafo || *tr* mimeografiar

**mim·ic** ['mɪmɪk] *s* imitador *m*, remedador *m* || *v* (*pret & pp* **-icked**; *ger* **-icking**) *tr* imitar, remedar

**mimic·ry** ['mɪmɪkri] *s* (*pl* **-ries**) mímica, remedo

**min.** *abbr* **minimum, minute**

**minaret** [,mɪnə'rɛt] o ['mɪnə,rɛt] *s* alminar *m*, minarete *m*

**mince** [mɪns] *tr* desmenuzar; picar (*carne*) || *intr* andar remilgadamente; hablar remilgadamente

**mince'meat'** *s* cuajado, picadillo

**mince pie** *s* pastel relleno de carne picada con frutas

**mind** [maɪnd] *s* mente *f*, espíritu *m*; **to bear in mind** tener presente; **to be not in one's right mind** no estar en sus cabales; **to be of one mind** estar de acuerdo; **to be out of one's mind** estar fuera de juicio; **to change one's mind** mudar de parecer; **to go out of one's mind** volverse loco; **to have a mind to** tener ganas de; **to have in mind to** pensar en; **to have on one's mind** preocuparse con; **to lose one's mind** perder el juicio; **to make up one's mind** resolverse; **to my mind** a mi parecer; **to say whatever comes into one's mind** decir lo que se le viene a la boca; **to set one's mind on** resolverse a; **to slip one's mind** escaparse de la memoria; **to speak one's mind** decir su parecer; **with one mind** unánimamente || *tr* (*to take care of*) cuidar, estar al cuidado de; obedecer; fijarse en; sentir molestia por; **do you mind the smoke?** ¿le molesta el humo?; **mind your own business** no se meta Vd. en lo que no le toca || *intr* tener inconveniente; tener cuidado; **never mind** no se preocupe, no se moleste

**mindful** ['maɪndfəl] *adj* atento; **mindful of** atento a, cuidadoso de

**mind reader** *s* adivinador *m* del pensamiento ajeno, lector *m* mental

**mind reading** *s* adivinación del pensamiento ajeno, lectura de la mente

**mine** [maɪn] *pron poss* el mío; mío || *s* mina; **to work a mine** beneficiar una mina || *tr* minar; beneficiar (*un terreno*); extraer (*mineral, carbón, etc.*) || *intr* minar; abrir minas

**mine field** *s* campo de minas

**mine layer** *s* buque *m* portaminas, lanzaminas *m*

**miner** ['maɪnər] *s* minero; (mil, nav) minador *m*

**mineral** ['mɪnərəl] *adj & s* mineral *m*

**mineralogy** [,mɪnə'rælədʒi] *s* mineralogía

**mineral wool** *s* lana de escorias

**mine sweeper** *s* dragaminas *m*

**mingle** ['mɪŋgəl] *tr* mezclar, confundir || *intr* mezclarse, confundirse; asociarse

**miniature** ['mɪnɪ·ətʃər] o ['mɪnɪtʃər] *s* miniatura; **to paint in miniature** miniar, pintar de miniatura

**miniaturization** [,mɪnɪ·ətʃərɪ'zeʃən] o [,mɪnɪtʃərɪ'zeʃən] *s* miniaturización

**minimal** ['mɪnɪməl] *adj* mínimo

**minimize** ['mɪnɪ,maɪz] *tr* empequeñecer

**minimum** ['mɪnɪməm] *adj & s* mínimo

**minimum wage** *s* jornal mínimo

**mining** ['maɪnɪŋ] *adj* minero || *s* mineraje *m*, minería; (nav) minado

**minion** ['mɪnjən] *s* paniaguado

**minion of the law** *s* esbirro, polizonte *m*

**minister** ['mɪnɪstər] *s* ministro; pastor *m* prostestante || *tr & intr* ministrar

**ministerial** [,mɪnɪs'tɪrɪ·əl] *adj* ministerial

**minis·try** ['mɪnɪstri] *s* (*pl* **-tries**) ministerio

**mink** [mɪŋk] *s* visón *m*

**minnow** ['mɪno] *s* pececillo; (ichth) foxino

**minor** ['maɪnər] *adj* (*smaller*) menor; de menor importancia; (*younger*) menor de edad; (mus) menor || *s* menor *m* de edad; (educ) asignatura secundaria

**Minorca** [mɪ'nɔrkə] *s* Menorca
**Minorcan** [mɪ'nɔrkən] *adj & s* menorquín *m*
**minori·ty** [mɪ'nɑrɪti] o [mɪ'nɔrɪti] *adj* minoritario || *s* (*pl* **-ties**) (*being under age; smaller number or part*) minoría; (*less than full age*) minoridad
**minstrel** ['mɪnstrəl] *s* (*retainer who sang and played for his lord*) ministril *m;* (*medieval musician and poet*) juglar *m,* trovador *m;* (U.S.A.) cantor cómico disfrazado de negro
**minstrel·sy** ['mɪnstrəlsi] *s* (*pl* **-sies**) juglaría; compañía de juglares; poesía trovadoresca
**mint** [mɪnt] *s* casa de moneda; (*plant*) menta, hierbabuena; montón *m* de dinero; fuente *f* inagotable || *tr* acuñar; (fig) inventar
**minuet** [,mɪnjʊ'ɛt] *s* minué *m,* minuete *m*
**minus** ['maɪnəs] *adj* menos || *prep* menos; falto de, sin || *s* menos *m*
**minute** [maɪ'njut] o [maɪ'nut] *adj* diminuto, menudo || ['mɪnɪt] *s* minuto; (*short space of time*) momento; **minutes** acta; **to write up the minutes** levantar acta; **up to the minute** al corriente; de última hora
**minute hand** ['mɪnɪt] *s* minutero
**minutiae** [mɪ'njuʃɪ,i] o [mɪ'nuʃɪ,i] *spl* minucias
**minx** [mɪŋks] *s* moza descarada
**miracle** ['mɪrəkəl] *s* milagro
**miracle play** *s* auto
**miraculous** [mɪ'rækjələs] *adj* milagroso
**mirage** [mɪ'rɑʒ] *s* espejismo
**mire** [maɪr] *s* fango, lodo
**mirror** ['mɪrər] *s* espejo; (aut) retrovisor *m* || *tr* reflejar
**mirth** [mʌrθ] *s* alegría, regocijo
**mir·y** ['maɪri] *adj* (*comp* **-ier;** *super* **-iest**) fangoso, lodoso; sucio
**misadventure** [,mɪsəd'vɛntʃər] *s* desgracia, contratiempo
**misanthrope** ['mɪsən,θrop] *s* misántropo
**misanthropy** [mɪs'ænθrəpi] *s* misantropía
**misapprehension** [,mɪsæprɪ'hɛnʃən] *s* malentendido
**misappropriation** [,mɪsə,proprɪ'eʃən] *s* malversación
**misbehave** [,mɪsbɪ'hev] *intr* conducirse mal, portarse mal
**misbehavior** [,mɪsbɪ'hevɪ·ər] *s* mala conducta, mal comportamiento
**misc.** *abbr* **miscellaneous, miscellany**
**miscalculation** [,mɪskælkjə'leʃən] *s* mal cálculo
**miscarriage** [mɪs'kærɪdʒ] *s* aborto, malparto; fracaso, malogro; (*of a letter*) extravío
**miscar·ry** [mɪs'kæri] *v* (*pret & pp* **-ried**) *intr* abortar, malparir; malograrse; extraviarse (*una carta*)
**miscellaneous** [,mɪsə'lenɪ·əs] *adj* misceláneo
**miscella·ny** ['mɪsə,leni] *s* (*pl* **-nies**) miscelánea
**mischief** ['mɪstʃɪf] *s* (*harm*) daño, mal *m;* (*disposition to annoy*) malicia; (*prankishness*) travesura
**mis'chief-mak'er** *s* malsín *m,* cizañero
**mischievous** ['mɪstʃɪvəs] *adj* dañoso, malo; malicioso; travieso
**misconception** [,mɪskən'sɛpʃən] *s* concepto erróneo, mala interpretación
**misconduct** [mɪs'kɑndəkt] *s* mala conducta
**misconstrue** [,mɪskən'stru] o [mɪs'kɑnstru] *tr* interpretar mal
**miscount** [mɪs'kaʊnt] *s* cuenta errónea || *tr & intr* contar mal
**miscue** [mɪs'kju] *s* (*in billiards*) pifia; (*slip*) pifia || *intr* pifiar; (theat) equivocarse de apunte
**mis·deal** ['mɪs,dil] *s* repartición errónea || [mɪs'dil] *v* (*pret & pp* **-dealt** ['dɛlt]) *tr & intr* repartir mal
**misdeed** [mɪs'did] o ['mɪs,did] *s* malhecho, fechoría
**misdemeanor** [,mɪsdɪ'minər] *s* mala conducta; (law) delito de menor cuantía
**misdirect** [,mɪsdɪ'rɛkt] o [,mɪsdaɪ'rɛkt] *tr* dirigir erradamente; hacer perder el camino
**misdoing** [mɪs'du·ɪŋ] *s* mala acción
**miser** ['maɪzər] *s* avaro, verrugo
**miserable** ['mɪzərəbəl] *adj* miserable; (coll) achacoso, indispuesto
**miserly** ['maɪzərli] *adj* avariento, mezquino
**miser·y** ['mɪzəri] *s* (*pl* **-ies**) miseria
**misfeasance** [mɪs'fizəns] *s* (law) fraude *m*
**misfire** [mɪs'faɪr] *s* falla de tiro; (*of internal-combustion engine*) falla de encendido || *intr* fallar (*un arma de fuego, el encendido de un motor*)
**mis·fit** ['mɪs,fɪt] *s* vestido mal cortado; cosa que no encaja bien; persona mal adaptada a su ambiente || [mɪs'fɪt] *v* (*pret & pp* **-fitted;** *ger* **-fitting**) *tr & intr* encajar mal, sentar mal
**misfortune** [mɪs'fɔrtʃən] *s* desgracia
**misgiving** [mɪs'gɪvɪŋ] *s* mal presentimiento, rescoldo
**misgovern** [mɪs'gʌvərn] *tr* desgobernar
**misguidance** [mɪs'gaɪdəns] *s* error *m,* extravío
**misguided** [mɪs'gaɪdɪd] *adj* descarriado, malaconsejado
**mishap** ['mɪshæp] o [mɪs'hæp] *s* accidente *m,* percance *m*
**misinform** [,mɪsɪn'fɔrm] *tr* dar informes erróneos a
**misinterpret** [,mɪsɪn'tɛrprɪt] *tr* interpretar mal
**misjudge** [mɪs'dʒʌdʒ] *tr & intr* juzgar mal
**mis·lay** [mɪs'le] *v* (*pret & pp* **-laid** [,led]) *tr* extraviar, perder; (*among one's papers*) traspapelar
**mis·lead** [mɪs'lid] *v* (*pret & pp* **-led** [,lɛd]) *tr* (*to lead astray*) extraviar, descaminar; (*to lead into wrongdoing*) seducir, inducir al mal; (*to deceive*) engañar
**misleading** [mɪs'lidɪŋ] *adj* engañoso
**mismanagement** [mɪs'mænɪdʒmənt] *s* mala administración, desgobierno

**misnomer** [mɪsˈnomər] *s* nombre impropio, mal nombre
**misplace** [mɪsˈples] *tr* colocar fuera de su lugar; colocar mal; (*to mislay*) (coll) extraviar, perder
**misprint** [ˈmɪsˌprɪnt] *s* errata de imprenta || [mɪsˈprɪnt] *tr* imprimir con erratas
**mispronounce** [ˌmɪsprəˈnaʊns] *tr* pronunciar mal
**mispronunciation** [ˌmɪsprəˌnʌnsɪˈeʃən] o [ˌmɪsprəˌnʌnʃɪˈeʃən] *s* pronunciación incorrecta
**misquote** [mɪsˈkwot] *tr* citar equivocadamente
**misrepresent** [ˌmɪsreprɪˈzent] *tr* tergiversar
**miss** [mɪs] *s* falta, error *m;* fracaso, malogro; tiro errado; jovencita, muchacha || *tr* echar de menos; perder (*el tren, la función, la oportunidad*); errar (*el blanco; la vocación*); no entender, no comprender; omitir; no ver; no dar con, no encontrar; librarse de (*p.ej., la muerte*); escapársele a uno, p.ej., **I missed what you said** se me escapó lo que dijo Vd.; por poco, p.ej., **the car missed hitting me** el coche por poco me atropella || *intr* fallar; errar el blanco; malograrse || **Miss** *s* señorita
**missal** [ˈmɪsəl] *s* misal *m*
**misshapen** [mɪsˈʃepən] *adj* deforme, contrahecho
**missile** [ˈmɪsɪl] *adj* arrojadizo || *s* arma arrojadiza; proyectil *m;* proyectil dirigido
**missing** [ˈmɪsɪŋ] *adj* extraviado, perdido; desaparecido; ausente; **to be missing** hacer falta; haber desaparecido
**missing link** *s* hombre *m* mono
**missing persons** *spl* desaparecidos
**mission** [ˈmɪʃən] *s* misión; casa de misión
**missionar·y** [ˈmɪʃənˌeri] *adj* misional || *s* (*pl* **-ies**) (*one sent to work to propagate his faith*) misionario, misionero; (*on a political or diplomatic mission*) misionario
**missive** [ˈmɪsɪv] *adj* misivo || *s* misiva
**mis·spell** [mɪsˈspel] *v* (*pret & pp* **-spelled** o **-spelt** [ˈspelt]) *tr & intr* deletrear mal, escribir mal
**misspelling** [mɪsˈspelɪŋ] *s* falta de ortografía
**misspent** [mɪsˈspent] *adj* malgastado
**misstatement** [mɪsˈstetmənt] *s* relación equivocada, relación falsa
**misstep** [mɪsˈstep] *s* paso falso; (*slip in conduct*) resbalón *m*
**miss·y** [ˈmɪsi] *s* (*pl* **-ies**) (coll) señorita
**mist** [mɪst] *s* neblina; (*of tears*) velo; (*fine spray*) vapor *m*
**mis·take** [mɪsˈtek] *s* error *m,* equivocación; **and no mistake** sin duda alguna; **by mistake** por descuido; **to make a mistake** equivocarse || *v* (*pret* **-took** [ˈtʊk]; *pp* **-taken**) *tr* tomar (*por otro; por lo que no es*); entender mal; **to be mistaken for** equivocarse con
**mistaken** [mɪsˈtekən] *adj* (*person*) equivocado; (*idea*) erróneo; (*act*) desacertado
**mistakenly** [mɪsˈtekənli] *adv* equivocadamente, por error
**mistletoe** [ˈmɪsəlˌto] *s* (*Viscum album*) muérdago; (*Phoradendron flavescens, used in Christmas decorations in the U.S.A.*) cabellera
**mistreat** [mɪsˈtrit] *tr* maltratar
**mistreatment** [mɪsˈtritmənt] *s* maltratamiento
**mistress** [ˈmɪstrɪs] *s* (*of a household*) ama, dueña; moza, querida, manceba; (Brit) maestra de escuela
**mistrial** [mɪsˈtraɪ·əl] *s* pleito viciado de nulidad
**mistrust** [mɪsˈtrʌst] *s* desconfianza || *tr* desconfiar de || *intr* desconfiar
**mistrustful** [mɪsˈtrʌstfəl] *adj* desconfiado
**mist·y** [ˈmɪsti] *adj* (*comp* **-ier;** *super* **-iest**) brumoso, neblinoso; indistinto
**misunder·stand** [ˌmɪsʌndərˈstænd] *v* (*pret & pp* **-stood** [ˈstʊd]) *tr* no comprender, entender mal
**misunderstanding** [ˌmɪsʌndərˈstændɪŋ] *s* malentendido; (*disagreement*) desavenencia
**misuse** [mɪsˈjus] *s* abuso, mal uso; (*of funds*) malversación || [mɪsˈjuz] *tr* abusar de, emplear mal; malversar (*fondos*)
**misword** [mɪsˈwʌrd] *tr* redactar mal
**mite** [maɪt] *s* (*small contribution*) óbolo; (*small amount*) pizca; (ent) ácaro
**miter** [ˈmaɪtər] *s* mitra; (carp) inglete *m* || *tr* cortar ingletes en; juntar con junta a inglete
**miter box** *s* caja de ingletes
**mitigate** [ˈmɪtɪˌget] *tr* mitigar, atenuar, paliar
**mitten** [ˈmɪtən] *s* confortante *m,* mitón *m*
**mix** [mɪks] *tr* mezclar; amasar (*una torta*); aderezar (*ensalada*); **to mix up** equivocar, confundir || *intr* mezclarse; asociarse
**mixed** [mɪkst] *adj* mixto, mezclado; (*e.g., candy*) variados; (coll) confundido
**mixed company** *s* reunión de personas de ambos sexos
**mixed drink** *s* bebida mezclada
**mixed feeling** *s* concepto vacilante
**mixer** [ˈmɪksər] *s* (*of concrete*) mezcladora, hormigonera; **to be a good mixer** (coll) tener don de gentes
**mixture** [ˈmɪkstʃər] *s* mezcla, mixtura
**mix′-up′** *s* confusión; enredo, lío; (*of people*) equivocación
**mizzen** [ˈmɪzən] *s* mesana
**mo.** *abbr* **month**
**M.O.** *abbr* **money order**
**moan** [mon] *s* gemido || *intr* gemir
**moat** [mot] *s* foso
**mob** [mɑb] *s* chusma, populacho; (*crowd bent on violence*) muchedumbre airada || *v* (*pret & pp* **mobbed;** *ger* **mobbing**) *tr* asaltar, atropellar
**mobile** [ˈmobɪl] o [ˈmobil] *adj* móvil
**mobility** [moˈbɪlɪti] *s* movilidad

**mobilization** [ˌmobɪlɪˈzeʃən] *s* movilización
**mobilize** [ˈmobɪˌlaɪz] *tr* movilizar ‖ *intr* movilizar, movilizarse
**mob rule** *s* gobierno del populacho
**mobster** [ˈmɑbstər] *s* (slang) gamberro, pandillero
**moccasin** [ˈmɑkəsɪn] *s* mocasín *m*
**Mocha coffee** [ˈmokə] *s* moca *m*, café *m* de moca
**mock** [mɑk] *adj* simulado, fingido ‖ *s* burla, mofa ‖ *tr* burlarse de, mofarse de; despreciar; engañar ‖ *intr* mofarse; **to mock at** mofarse de
**mocker•y** [ˈmɑkəri] *s* (*pl* **-ies**) burla, mofa, escarnio; (*subject of derision*) hazmerreír *m*; (*poor imitation*) mal remedo; (*e.g.*, *of justice*) negación
**mock'ing•bird'** *s* burlón *m*, sinsonte *m*
**mock orange** *s* jeringuilla, celinda
**mock privet** *s* olivillo
**mock turtle soup** *s* sopa de cabeza de ternera
**mock'-up'** *s* maqueta
**mode** [mod] *s* modo, manera; (*fashion*) moda; (gram) modo
**mod•el** [ˈmɑdəl] *adj* modelo, p.ej., **model city** ciudad modelo ‖ *s* modelo ‖ *v* (*pret & pp* **-eled** o **-elled**; *ger* **-eling** o **-elling**) *tr* (*to fashion in clay, wax, etc.*) modelar ‖ *intr* modelarse; servir de modelo
**model airplane** *s* aeromodelo
**mod'el-air'plane builder** *s* aeromodelista *mf*
**model-airplane building** *s* aeromodelismo
**model sailing** *s* navegación de modelos a vela
**moderate** [ˈmɑdərɪt] *adj* moderado; (*tiempo*) templado; (*precio*) módico ‖ [ˈmɑdəˌret] *tr* moderar; presidir (*una asamblea*) ‖ *intr* moderarse
**moderator** [ˈmɑdəˌretər] *s* (*over an assembly*) presidente *m*; (*mediator*) árbitro; (*for slowing down neutrons*) moderador *m*
**modern** [ˈmɑdərn] *adj* moderno
**modernize** [ˈmɑdərˌnaɪz] *tr* modernizar
**modest** [ˈmɑdɪst] *adj* modesto
**modes•ty** [ˈmɑdɪsti] *s* (*pl* **-ties**) modestia
**modicum** [ˈmɑdɪkəm] *s* pequeña cantidad
**modifier** [ˈmɑdɪˌfaɪ•ər] *s* (gram) modificante *m*
**modi•fy** [ˈmɑdɪˌfaɪ] *v* (*pret & pp* **-fied**) *tr* modificar
**modish** [ˈmodɪʃ] *adj* de moda, elegante
**modulate** [ˈmɑdʒəˌlet] *tr & intr* modular
**modulation** [ˌmɑdʒəˈleʃən] *s* modulación
**mohair** [ˈmoˌhɛr] *s* mohair *m* (*pelo de cabra de Angora*)
**Mohammedan** [moˈhæmɪdən] *adj & s* mahometano
**Mohammedanism** [moˈhæmɪdəˌnɪzəm] *s* mahometismo
**moist** [mɔɪst] *adj* húmedo, mojado; (*weather*) lluvioso; (*eyes*) lagrimoso
**moisten** [ˈmɔɪsən] *tr* humedecer ‖ *intr* humedecerse
**moisture** [ˈmɔɪstʃər] *s* humedad
**molar** [ˈmolər] *s* diente *m* molar
**molasses** [məˈlæsɪz] *s* melaza
**molasses candy** *s* melcocha
**mold** [mold] *s* molde *m*; cosa moldeada; (*shape*) forma; (*fungus*) moho; (*humus*) mantillo; (fig) carácter *m*, índole *f* ‖ *tr* amoldar, moldear; (*to make moldy*) enmohecer ‖ *intr* enmohecerse
**molder** [ˈmoldər] *s* moldeador *m* ‖ *intr* convertirse en polvo, consumirse
**molding** [ˈmoldɪŋ] *s* moldeado; (*cornice, shaped strip of wood, etc.*) moldura
**mold•y** [ˈmoldi] *adj* (*comp* **-ier**; *super* **-iest**) (*overgrown with mold*) mohoso; (*stale*) rancio, pasado
**mole** [mol] *s* (*breakwater*) rompeolas *m*; (*inner harbor*) dársena; (*spot on skin*) lunar *m*; (*small mammal*) topo
**molecule** [ˈmɑlɪˌkjul] *s* molécula
**mole'hill'** *s* topinera
**mole'skin'** *s* piel *f* de topo, molesquina
**molest** [məˈlest] *tr* molestar; faltar al respeto a (*una mujer*)
**moll** [mɑl] *s* (slang) mujer *f* del hampa; (slang) ramera
**molli•fy** [ˈmɑlɪˌfaɪ] *v* (*pret & pp* **-fied**) *tr* apaciguar, aplacar
**mollusk** [ˈmɑləsk] *s* molusco
**mollycoddle** [ˈmɑlɪˌkɑdəl] *s* mantecón *m*, marica *m* ‖ *tr* consentir, mimar
**molt** [molt] *s* muda ‖ *intr* hacer la muda
**molten** [ˈmoltən] *adj* fundido, derretido; fundido, vaciado
**molybdenum** [məˈlɪbdɪnəm] o [ˌmɑlɪbˈdinəm] *s* molibdeno
**moment** [ˈmomənt] *s* momento; **at any moment** de un momento a otro
**momentary** [ˈmomənˌteri] *adj* momentáneo
**momentous** [moˈmentəs] *adj* importante, grave
**momen•tum** [moˈmentəm] *s* (*pl* **-tums** o **-ta** [tə]) ímpetu *m*; (mech) cantidad de movimiento
**monarch** [ˈmɑnərk] *s* monarca *m*
**monarchic(al)** [məˈnɑrkɪk(əl)] *adj* monárquico
**monarchist** [ˈmɑnərkɪst] *adj & s* monárquico, monarquista *mf*
**monar•chy** [ˈmɑnərki] *s* (*pl* **-chies**) monarquía
**monaster•y** [ˈmɑnəsˌteri] *s* (*pl* **-ies**) monasterio
**monastic** [məˈnæstɪk] *adj* monástico
**monasticism** [məˈnæstɪˌsɪzəm] *s* monaquismo
**Monday** [ˈmʌndi] *s* lunes *m*
**monetary** [ˈmɑnɪˌteri] *adj* monetario; pecuniario
**money** [ˈmʌni] *s* dinero; **to make money** ganar dinero; dar dinero (*una empresa*)
**mon'ey•bag'** *s* monedero, talega; **moneybags** (*wealth*) (coll) talegas; (*wealthy person*) (coll) ricacho

**moneychanger** ['mʌni ˌtʃendʒər] *s* cambista *mf*
**moneyed** ['mʌnid] *adj* adinerado
**moneylender** ['mʌni ˌlendər] *s* prestamista *mf*
**mon'ey·mak'er** *s* acaudalador *m;* (fig) manantial *m* de beneficios
**money order** *s* giro postal
**Mongol** ['maŋgəl] o ['maŋgal] *adj & s* mogol *mf*
**Mongolian** [maŋ'golɪ·ən] *adj & s* mogol *mf*
**mon·goose** ['maŋgus] *s* (*pl* **-gooses**) mangosta
**mongrel** ['mʌŋgrəl] o ['maŋgrəl] *adj & s* mestizo
**monitor** ['manɪtər] *s* monitor *m* || *tr* controlar (*la señal*); escuchar (*radiotransmisiones*); superentender
**monk** [maŋk] *s* monje *m*
**monkey** ['mʌŋki] *s* mono; **to make a monkey of** tomar el pelo a || *intr* — **to monkey around** haraganear; **to monkey with** ajar, manosear
**mon'key·shine'** *s* (slang) monería, monada, payasada
**monkey wrench** *s* llave inglesa
**monkhood** ['maŋkhud] *s* monacato; los monjes
**monkshood** ['maŋks·hud] *s* cogulla de fraile
**monocle** ['manəkəl] *s* monóculo
**monogamy** [mə'nagəmi] *s* monogamia
**monogram** ['manəˌgræm] *s* monograma *m*
**monograph** ['manəˌgræf] o ['manəˌgraf] *s* monografía
**monolithic** [ˌmanə'lɪθɪk] *adj* monolítico
**monologue** ['manəˌlɔg] o ['manəˌlag] *s* monólogo
**monomania** [ˌmanə'menɪ·ə] *s* monomanía
**monomial** [mə'nomɪ·əl] *s* monomio
**monopolize** [mə'napəˌlaɪz] *tr* monopolizar; acaparar (*p.ej., la conversación*)
**monopo·ly** [mə'napəli] *s* (*pl* **-lies**) monopolio
**monorail** ['manəˌrel] *s* monorriel *m*
**monosyllable** ['manəˌsɪləbəl] *s* monosílabo
**monotheist** ['manəˌθi·ɪst] *adj & s* monoteísta *mf*
**monotonous** [mə'natənəs] *adj* monótono
**monotony** [mə'natəni] *s* monotonía
**monotype** ['manəˌtaɪp] *s* (*machine; method*) monotipia; (*machine*) monotipo
**monotype operator** *s* monotipista *mf*
**monoxide** [mə'naksaɪd] *s* monóxido
**monseigneur** [ˌmansen'jœr] *s* monseñor *m*
**monsignor** [man'sinjər] *s* (*pl* **monsignors** o **monsignori** [ˌmonsi'njori]) (eccl) monseñor *m*
**monsoon** [man'sun] *s* monsón *m*
**monster** ['manstər] *adj* monstruoso || *s* monstruo
**monstrance** ['manstrəns] *s* custodia, ostensorio
**monstrosi·ty** [man'strasɪti] *s* (*pl* **-ties**) monstruosidad
**monstrous** ['manstrəs] *adj* monstruoso
**month** [mʌnθ] *s* mes *m*
**month·ly** ['mʌnθli] *adj* mensual || *adv* mensualmente || *s* (*pl* **-lies**) revista mensual; **monthlies** (coll) reglas
**monument** ['manjəmənt] *s* monumento
**moo** [mu] *s* mugido || *intr* mugir
**mood** [mud] *s* humor *m,* genio; (gram) modo; **moods** accesos de mal humor
**mood·y** ['mudi] *adj* (*comp* **-ier;** *super* **-iest**) triste, hosco, melancólico; caprichoso, veleidoso
**moon** [mun] *s* luna
**moon'beam'** *s* rayo lunar
**moon'light'** *s* claror *m* de luna, luz *f* de la luna
**moon'light'ing** *s* multiempleo, pluriempleo
**moon'sail'** *s* (naut) monterilla
**moon'shine'** *s* luz *f* de la luna; (*idle talk*) cháchara, música celestial; (coll) whisky destilado ilegalmente
**moon shot** *s* lanzamiento a la Luna
**moor** [mur] *s* brezal *m,* páramo || *tr* (naut) amarrar || *intr* (naut) echar las amarras || **Moor** *s* moro
**Moorish** ['murɪʃ] *adj* moro
**moor'land'** *s* brezal *m*
**moose** [mus] *s* (*pl* **moose**) alce *m* de América
**moot** [mut] *adj* discutible, dudoso
**mop** [map] *s* aljofifa, fregasuelos *m,* estropajo; (*of hair*) espesura || *v* (*pret & pp* **mopped;** *ger* **mopping**) *tr* aljofifar; enjugarse (*la frente con un pañuelo*); **to mop up** limpiar de enemigos
**mope** [mop] *intr* andar abatido, entregarse a la melancolía
**mopish** ['mopɪʃ] *adj* abatido, melancólico
**moral** ['marəl] o ['mɔrəl] *adj* moral || *s* (*of a fable*) moraleja, moral *f;* **morals** (*ethics; conduct*) moral *f*
**moral certainty** *s* evidencia moral
**morale** [mə'ræl] o [mə'ral] *s* moral *f* (*estado de ánimo, confianza en sí mismo*)
**morali·ty** [mə'rælɪti] *s* (*pl* **-ties**) moralidad
**morals charge** *s* acusación por delito sexual
**morass** [mə'ræs] *s* pantano
**moratori·um** [ˌmɔrə'torɪ·əm] o [ˌmarə'torɪ·əm] *s* (*pl* **-ums** o **-a** [ə]) *s* moratoria
**morbid** ['mɔrbɪd] *adj* (*feelings, curiosity*) malsano; (*gruesome*) horripilante; (*pertaining to disease; pathologic*) morboso
**mordacious** [mɔr'deʃəs] *adj* mordaz
**mordant** ['mɔrdənt] *adj* mordaz || *s* mordiente *m*
**more** [mor] *adj & adv* más; **more and more** cada vez más; **more than** más que; (*followed by numeral*) más de; (*followed by verb*) más de lo que || *s* más *m*
**more·o'ver** *adv* además, por otra parte

**Moresque** [mo'rɛsk] *adj* moro; (archit) árabe || *s* estilo árabe
**morgue** [mɔrg] *s* depósito de cadáveres
**moribund** ['mɔrɪ,bʌnd] o ['mɑrɪ,bʌnd] *adj* moribundo
**Moris•co** [mə'rɪsko] *adj* morisco, moro || *s* (*pl* **-cos** o **-coes**) moro; moro de España; (*offspring of mulatto and Spaniard, in Mexico*) morisco
**morning** ['mɔrnɪŋ] *adj* matinal || *s* mañana; (*time between midnight and dawn*) madrugada; **in the morning** de mañana, por la mañana
**morning coat** *s* chaqué *m*
**morn'ing-glo'ry** *s* (*pl* **-ries**) dondiego de día
**morning sickness** *s* vómitos del embarazo
**morning star** *s* lucero del alba
**Moroccan** [mə'rɑkən] *adj* & *s* marroquí *mf* o marroquín *m*
**morocco** [mə'rɑko] *s* (*leather*) marroquí *m* o marroquín *m* || **Morocco** *s* Marruecos *m*
**moron** ['morɑn] *s* (*person of arrested intelligence*) morón *m*; (coll) imbécil *mf*
**morose** [mə'ros] *adj* adusto, hosco, malhumorado
**morphine** ['mɔrfin] *s* morfina
**morphology** [mɔr'fɑlədʒi] *s* morfología
**Morris chair** ['mɑrɪs] o ['mɔrɪs] *s* poltrona extensible
**morrow** ['mɑro] o ['mɔro] *s* (*future time*) mañana *m*; (*time following some event*) día *m* siguiente; **on the morrow** en el día de mañana; el día siguiente
**morsel** ['mɔrsəl] *s* bocadito; pedacito
**mortal** ['mɔrtəl] *adj* & *s* mortal *m*
**mortality** [mɔr'tælɪti] *s* mortalidad; (*death or destruction on a large scale*) mortandad
**mortar** ['mɔrtər] *s* (*bowl used for crushing; mixture of lime, etc.*) mortero; (arti) mortero
**mor'tar•board'** *s* esparavel *m*; gorro académico cuadrado
**mortgage** ['mɔrgɪdʒ] *s* hipoteca || *tr* hipotecar
**mortgagee** [,mɔrgɪ'dʒi] *s* acreedor hipotecario
**mortgagor** ['mɔrgɪdʒər] *s* deudor hipotecario
**mortician** [mɔr'tɪʃən] *s* empresario de pompas fúnebres
**morti•fy** ['mɔrtɪ,faɪ] *v* (*pret & pp* **-fied**) *tr* humillar; mortificar (*el cuerpo, las pasiones*); **to be mortified** avergonzarse
**mortise** ['mɔrtɪs] *s* mortaja, muesca || *tr* amortajar, enmuescar
**mortise lock** *s* cerradura embutida
**mortuar•y** ['mɔrtʃʊ,eri] *adj* mortuorio || *s* (*pl* **-ies**) depósito de cadáveres; funeraria
**mosaic** [mo'ze•ɪk] *m* mosaico
**Moscow** ['mɑskaʊ] o ['mɑsko] *s* Moscú
**Moses** ['mozɪz] o ['mozɪs] *s* Moisés *m*
**Mos•lem** ['mɑzləm] o ['mɑsləm] *adj* muslime, musulmán || *s* (*pl* **-lems** o **-lem**) muslime *mf*, musulmán *m*
**mosque** [mɑsk] *s* mezquita
**mosqui•to** [məs'kito] *s* (*pl* **-toes** o **-tos**) mosquito
**mosquito net** *s* mosquitero
**moss** [mɔs] o [mɑs] *s* musgo
**moss'back'** *s* (coll) reaccionario; (*old-fashioned person*) (coll) fósil *m*
**moss•y** ['mɔsi] o ['mɑsi] *adj* (*comp* **-ier**; *super* **-iest**) musgoso
**most** [most] *adj* más; la mayor parte de, los más de || *adv* más; muy, sumamente; (coll) casi || *s* la mayor parte, el mayor número, los más; **most of** la mayor parte de, el mayor número de; **to make the most of** sacar el mejor partido de
**mostly** ['mostli] *adv* por la mayor parte, mayormente; casi
**moth** [mɔθ] o [mɑθ] *s* mariposa nocturna; (*clothes moth*) polilla
**moth ball** *s* bola de alcanfor, bola de naftalina
**moth'-ball' fleet** *s* (nav) flota en conserva
**moth'-eat'en** *adj* apolillado; (fig) anticuado
**mother** ['mʌðər] *adj* (*love*) maternal; (*tongue*) materno; (*country*) madre; (*church*) metropolitano || *s* madre *f*; (*an elderly woman*) (coll) tía || *tr* servir de madre a
**mother country** *s* madre patria
**Mother Goose** *s* supuesta autora o narradora de una colección de cuentos infantiles (in Spain: *Cuentos de Calleja*)
**motherhood** ['mʌðər,hʊd] *s* maternidad
**moth'er-in-law'** *s* (*pl* **mothers-in-law**) suegra
**moth'er•land'** *s* patria
**motherless** ['mʌðərlɪs] *adj* huérfano de madre, sin madre
**motherly** ['mʌðərli] *adj* maternal
**mother-of-pearl** ['mʌðərəv'pʌrl] *adj* nacarado || *s* nácar *m*
**Mother's Day** *s* día *m* de la madre
**mother superior** *s* superiora
**mother tongue** *s* (*language naturally acquired by reason of nationality*) lengua materna; (*language from which another language is derived*) lengua madre, lengua matriz
**mother wit** *s* gracia natural, chispa
**moth hole** *s* apolilladura
**moth•y** ['mɔθi] o ['mɑθi] *adj* (*comp* **-ier**; *super* **-iest**) apolillado
**motif** [mo'tif] *s* motivo
**motion** ['moʃən] *s* movimiento; (*signal, gesture*) seña, indicación; (*in a deliberating assembly*) moción || *intr* hacer señas con la mano o la cabeza
**motionless** ['moʃənlɪs] *adj* inmoble
**motion picture** *s* película cinematográfica
**mo'tion-pic'ture** *adj* cinematográfico
**motivate** ['motɪ,vet] *tr* animar, incitar, mover
**motive** ['motɪv] *adj* (*promoting action*) motivo; (*producing motion*) motor || *s* motivo
**motive power** *s* fuerza motriz, potencia

motora o motriz; (rr) conjunto de locomotoras de un ferrocarril
**motley** ['mɑtli] *adj* abigarrado; mezclado, variado
**motor** ['motər] *adj* motor ‖ *s* motor *m;* motor eléctrico; automóvil *m* ‖ *intr* viajar en automóvil
**mo'tor•boat'** *s* gasolinera, canoa automóvil
**mo'tor•bus'** *s* autobús *m*
**motorcade** ['motər‚ked] *s* caravana de automóviles
**mo'tor•car'** *s* automóvil *m*
**mo'tor•cy'cle** *s* motocicleta
**motorist** ['motərɪst] *s* motorista *mf,* automovilista *mf*
**motorize** ['motə‚raɪz] *tr* motorizar
**motor launch** *s* lancha automóvil
**motor•man** ['motərmən] *s* (*pl* **-men** [mən]) conductor *m* de tranvía, conductor de locomotora eléctrica
**motor sailer** ['selər] *s* motovelero
**motor scooter** *s* motoneta
**motor ship** *s* motonave *f*
**motor truck** *s* autocamión *m*
**motor vehicle** *s* vehículo motor, autovehículo
**mottle** ['mɑtəl] *tr* abigarrar, jaspear, motear
**mot•to** ['mɑto] *s* (*pl* **-toes** o **-tos**) lema *m,* divisa
**mould** [mold] *s, tr, & intr* var de **mold**
**moulder** ['moldər] *s & intr* var de **molder**
**moulding** ['moldɪn] *s* var de **molding**
**mouldy** ['moldi] *adj* var de **moldy**
**mound** [maʊnd] *s* montón *m* de tierra; montecillo
**mount** [maʊnt] *s* (*hill, mountain*) monte *m;* (*horse for riding*) montura; (*setting for a jewel*) montadura; soporte *m;* cartón *m,* tela (*en que está pegada una fotografía*); (mach) montaje *m* ‖ *tr* subir (*una escalera, una cuesta*); subir a (*una plataforma*); escalar (*una muralla*); montar (*un servicio; una piedra preciosa*); poner a caballo; pegar (*vistas, pruebas*); (mil) montar (*la guardia*) ‖ *intr* montar, montarse; aumentar, subir (*los precios*)
**mountain** ['maʊntən] *s* montaña; **to make a mountain out of a molehill** hacer de una pulga un camello
**mountain climbing** *s* alpinismo, montañismo
**mountaineer** [‚maʊntə'nɪr] *s* montañés *m*
**mountainous** ['maʊntənəs] *adj* montañoso
**mountain railroad** *s* ferrocarril *m* de cremallera
**mountain range** *s* cordillera, sierra
**mountain sickness** *s* mal *m* de las montañas
**mountebank** ['maʊntɪ‚bæŋk] *s* saltabanco
**mounting** ['maʊntɪŋ] *s* (*of a precious stone, of an astronomical instrument*) montura; papel *m* de soporte; papel o tela (*en que está pegada una fotografía*); (mach) montaje *m*
**mourn** [morn] *tr* llorar (*p.ej., la muerte de una persona*); lamentar (*una desgracia*) ‖ *intr* lamentarse; vestir de luto
**mourner** ['mornər] *s* doliente *mf;* (*person who makes a public profession of penitence*) penitente *mf;* (*person hired to attend a funeral*) plañidera; **mourners** duelo
**mourners' bench** *s* banco de los penitentes
**mournful** ['mornfəl] *adj* (*sorrowful*) doloroso; (*gloomy*) lúgubre
**mourning** ['mornɪŋ] *s* luto; **to be in mourning** estar de luto
**mourning band** *s* crespón *m* fúnebre, brazal *m* de luto
**mouse** [maʊs] *s* (*pl* **mice** [maɪs]) ratón *m*
**mouse'hole'** *s* ratonera
**mouser** ['maʊzər] *s* desmurador *m*
**mouse'trap'** *s* ratonera
**moustache** [məs'tæʃ] o [məs'tɑʃ] *s* bigote *m,* mostacho
**mouth** [maʊθ] *s* (*pl* **mouths** [maʊðz]) boca; (*of a river*) desembocadura, embocadura; **by mouth** por vía bucal; **to be born with a silver spoon in one's mouth** nacer de pie; **to make one's mouth water** hacérsele a uno la boca agua; **to not open one's mouth** no decir esta boca es mía
**mouthful** ['maʊθ‚fʊl] s bocado
**mouth organ** *s* armónica de boca
**mouth'piece'** *s* (*of wind instrument*) boquilla; (*of bridle*) embocadura; (*spokesman*) portavoz *m*
**mouth'wash'** *s* enjuague *m,* enjuagadientes *m*
**movable** ['muvəbəl] *adj* movible, móvil
**move** [muv] *s* movimiento; (*démarche*) acción, gestión, paso; (*from one house to another*) mudanza; **on the move** en marcha, en movimiento; **to get a move on** (slang) menearse, darse prisa; **to make a move** dar un paso; hacer una jugada ‖ *tr* mover; evacuar (*el vientre*); (*to stir, excite the feelings of*) conmover, enternecer; **to move up** adelantar (*una fecha*) ‖ *intr* moverse; desplazarse (*un viajante; un planeta*); mudarse, mudar de casa; (*e.g., to another store, to another city*) trasladarse; hacer una jugada; hacer una moción; venderse, tener salida (*una mercancía*); evacuarse, moverse (*el vientre*); **to move away** apartarse; marcharse; mudarse de casa; **to move in** instalarse; alternar con, frecuentar (*la buena sociedad*); **to move off** alejarse
**movement** ['muvmənt] *s* movimiento; aparato de relojería; (*of the bowels*) evacuación; (*e.g., of a symphony*) tiempo
**movie** ['muvi] *s* (coll) película, cinta
**movie•goer** ['movi‚go•ər] *s* (**coll**) aficionado al cine
**movie house** *s* (coll) cineteatro
**mov'ie•land'** *s* (coll) cinelandia
**moving** ['muvɪŋ] *adj* conmovedor, impresionante ‖ *s* movimiento; (*from one house to another*) mudanza

**moving picture** *s* película cinematográfica
**moving spirit** *s* alma (*de una empresa*)
**moving stairway** *s* escalera mecánica, móvil o rodante
**mow** [mo] *v* (*pret* **mowed;** *pp* **mowed** o **mown**) *tr* segar; **to mow down** matar (*soldados*) con fuego graneado || *intr* segar
**mower** [ˈmo·ər] *s* segador *m;* segadora mecánica
**mowing machine** *s* segadora mecánica
**Mozarab** [moˈzærəb] *s* mozárabe *mf*
**Mozarabic** [moˈzærəbɪk] *adj* mozárabe
**M.P.** *abbr* **Member of Parliament, Military Police**
**m.p.h.** *abbr* **miles per hour**
**Mr.** [ˈmɪstər] *s* (*pl* **Messrs.** [ˈmɛsərz]) señor *m* (*tratamiento*)
**Mrs.** [ˈmɪsɪz] *s* señora (*tratamiento*)
**MS.** o **ms.** *abbr* **manuscript**
**Mt.** *abbr* **Mount**
**much** [mʌtʃ] *adj & pron* mucho; **too much** demasiado || *adv* mucho; **however much** por mucho que; **how much** cuánto; **too much** demasiado; **very much** muchísimo
**mucilage** [ˈmjusɪlɪdʒ] *s* goma para pegar; (*gummy secretion in plants*) mucílago
**muck** [mʌk] *s* estiércol húmedo; suciedad, porquería; (min) zafra
**muck'rake'** *intr* (coll) exponer ruindades
**mucous** [ˈmjukəs] *adj* mucoso
**mucus** [ˈmjukəs] *s* moco
**mud** [mʌd] *s* barro, fango, lodo; **to sling mud at** llenar de fango
**muddle** [ˈmʌdəl] *s* confusión, embrollo || *tr* confundir, embrollar; atontar, aturdir || *intr* obrar torpemente; **to muddle through** salir del paso a pesar suyo
**mud'dle·head'** *s* farraguista *mf,* cajón *m* de sastre
**mud·dy** [ˈmʌdi] *adj* (*comp* **-dier;** *super* **-diest**) barroso, fangoso, lodoso; (*obscure*) turbio || *v* (*pret & pp* **-died**) *tr* embarrar, enturbiar
**mud'guard'** *s* guardabarros *m*
**mud'hole'** *s* atolladero, ciénaga
**mudslinger** [ˈmʌd,slɪŋər] *s* (fig) lanzador *m* de lodo
**muezzin** [mjuˈezɪn] *s* almuecín *m,* almuédano
**muff** [mʌf] *s* manguito || *tr & intr* chapucear
**muffin** [ˈmʌfɪn] *s* mollete *m*
**muffle** [ˈmʌfəl] *tr* arropar; (*about the face*) embozar; amortiguar (*un ruido*); enfundar (*un tambor*)
**muffler** [ˈmʌflər] *s* bufanda, tapaboca; (aut) silenciador *m,* silencioso
**mufti** [ˈmʌfti] *s* traje *m* de paisano
**mug** [mʌg] *s* pichel *m;* (slang) jeta, hocico || *v* (*pret & pp* **mugged;** *ger* **mugging**) *tr* (slang) fotografiar; (slang) atacar || *intr* (slang) hacer muecas
**mug·gy** [ˈmʌgi] *adj* (*comp* **-gier;** *super* **-giest**) bochornoso, sofocante
**mulat·to** [mjuˈlæto] o [məˈlæto] *s* (*pl* **-toes**) mulato
**mulber·ry** [ˈmʌl,bɛri] *s* (*pl* **-ries**) (*tree*) moral *m;* (*fruit*) mora
**mulct** [mʌlkt] *tr* defraudar
**mule** [mjul] *s* mulo, macho; (*slipper*) babucha
**mule chair** *s* artolas, jamugas
**muleteer** [,mjuləˈtɪr] *s* mulatero
**mulish** [ˈmjulɪʃ] *adj* terco, obstinado
**mull** [mʌl] *tr* calentar (*vino*) con especias || *intr* — **to mull over** reflexionar sobre
**mullion** [ˈmʌljən] *s* parteluz *m*
**multigraph** [ˈmʌltɪ,græf] o [ˈmʌltɪ,grɑf] *s* (trademark) multígrafo || *tr* multigrafiar
**multilateral** [,mʌltɪˈlætərəl] *adj* (*having many sides*) multilátero; (*participated in by more than two nations*) multilateral
**multiple** [ˈmʌltɪpəl] *adj* múltiple, múltiplo || *s* (math) múltiplo
**multiplici·ty** [,mʌltɪˈplɪsɪti] *s* (*pl* **-ties**) multiplicidad
**multi·ply** [ˈmʌltɪ,plaɪ] *v* (*pret & pp* **-plied**) *tr* multiplicar || *intr* multiplicar, multiplicarse
**multitude** [ˈmʌltɪ,tjud] o [ˈmʌltɪ,tud] *s* multitud
**mum** [mʌm] *adj* callado; **mum's the word!** ¡punto en boca!; **to keep mum about** callar || *interj* ¡chitón!
**mumble** [ˈmʌmbəl] *tr & intr* mascullar, mascujar
**mummer·y** [ˈmʌməri] *s* (*pl* **-ies**) mojiganga
**mum·my** [ˈmʌmi] *s* (*pl* **-mies**) momia
**mumps** [mʌmps] *s* papera
**munch** [mʌntʃ] *tr* ronzar
**mundane** [ˈmʌnden] *adj* mundano
**municipal** [mjuˈnɪsɪpəl] *adj* municipal
**municipali·ty** [mju,nɪsɪˈpælɪti] *s* (*pl* **-ties**) municipio
**munificent** [mjuˈnɪfɪsənt] *adj* munífico
**munition** [mjuˈnɪʃən] *s* munición || *tr* municionar
**munition dump** *s* depósito de municiones
**mural** [ˈmjurəl] *adj* mural || *s* pintura mural; decoración mural
**murder** [ˈmʌrdər] *s* asesinato, homicidio || *tr* asesinar; (*to spoil, mar*) (coll) estropear
**murderer** [ˈmʌrdərər] *s* asesino
**murderess** [ˈmʌrdərɪs] *s* asesina
**murderous** [ˈmʌrdərəs] *adj* asesino; cruel, sanguinario
**murk·y** [ˈmʌrki] *adj* (*comp* **-ier;** *super* **-iest**) (*hazy*) calinoso; (*gloomy*) lóbrego
**murmur** [ˈmʌrmər] *s* murmullo || *tr & intr* murmurar
**mus.** *abbr* **museum, music**
**muscle** [ˈmʌsəl] *s* músculo; (fig) fuerza muscular
**muscular** [ˈmʌskjələr] *adj* musculoso
**muse** [mjuz] *s* musa; **the Muses** las Musas || *intr* meditar, reflexionar; **to muse on** contemplar
**museum** [mjuˈzi·əm] *s* museo
**mush** [mʌʃ] *s* gachas; (coll) sentimentalismo exagerado, sensiblería
**mush'room'** *s* hongo, seta || *intr* aparecer de la noche a la mañana; **to**

**mushroom into** convertirse rápidamente en
**mushroom cloud** *s* nube-hongo *f*
**mush•y** ['mʌʃi] *adj* (*comp* **-ier;** *super* **-iest**) mollar, pulposo; (coll) sensiblero, sobón; (*with women*) (coll) baboso; **to be mushy** (coll) hacerse unas gachas
**music** ['mjuzɪk] *s* música; **to face the music** (coll) afrontar las consecuencias; **to set to music** poner en música
**musical** ['mjuzɪkəl] *adj* musical, músico
**musical comedy** *s* comedia musical
**musicale** [,mjuzɪ'kæl] *s* velada musical, concierto casero
**music box** *s* caja de música
**music cabinet** *s* musiquero
**music hall** *s* salón *m* de conciertos; (Brit) teatro de variedades
**musician** [mju'zɪʃən] *s* músico
**musicianship** [mju'zɪʃən,ʃɪp] *s* musicalidad
**musicologist** [,mjuzɪ'kɑlədʒɪst] *s* musicólogo
**musicology** [,mjuzɪ'kɑlədʒi] *s* musicología
**music rack** o **music stand** *s* atril *m*
**musk** [mʌsk] *s* almizcle *m;* olor *m* de almizcle
**musk deer** *s* almizclero
**musket** ['mʌskɪt] *s* mosquete *m*
**musketeer** [,mʌskɪ'tɪr] *s* mosquetero
**musk'mel'on** *s* melón *m*
**musk'rat'** *s* almizclera
**muslin** ['mʌzlɪn] *s* muselina
**muss** [mʌs] *tr* (*the hair*) (coll) descabellar, desarreglar; (*clothing*) (coll) chafar, arrugar
**Mussulman** ['mʌsəlmən] *adj* & *s* musulmán *m*
**muss•y** ['mʌsi] *adj* (*comp* **-ier;** *super* **-iest**) desaliñado, desgreñado
**must** [mʌst] *s* mosto; (*mold*) moho; cosa que debe hacerse || *v aux* **I must study my lesson** debo estudiar mi lección; **he must work tomorrow** tiene que trabajar mañana; **she must be ill** estará enferma
**mustache** [məs'tæʃ], [məs'tɑʃ] o ['mʌstæʃ] *s* bigote *m,* mostacho
**mustard** ['mʌstərd] *s* mostaza
**mustard plaster** *s* sinapismo, cataplasma *f*
**muster** ['mʌstər] *s* asamblea; matrícula de revista; **to pass muster** pasar revista; ser aceptable || *tr* llamar a asamblea; reunir para pasar revista; reunir, acumular; **to muster in** alistar; **to muster out** dar de baja a; **to muster up courage** cobrar ánimo
**muster roll** *s* lista de revista
**mus•ty** ['mʌsti] *adj* (*comp* **-tier;** *super* **-tiest**) (*moldy*) mohoso; (*stale*) trasnochado; anticuado, pasado de moda
**mutation** [mju'teʃən] *s* mutación
**mute** [mjut] *adj* & *s* mudo || *tr* poner sordina a
**mutilate** ['mjutɪ,let] *tr* mutilar
**mutineer** [,mjutɪ'nɪr] *s* amotinado
**mutinous** ['mjutɪnəs] *adj* amotinado
**muti•ny** ['mjutɪni] *s* (*pl* **-nies**) motín *m* || *v* (*pret* & *pp* **-nied**) *intr* amotinarse
**mutt** [mʌt] *s* (slang) perro cruzado; (slang) bobo, tonto
**mutter** ['mʌtər] *tr* & *intr* murmurar
**mutton** ['mʌtən] *s* carnero, carne *f* de carnero
**mutton chop** *s* chuleta de carnero
**mutual** ['mutʃu·əl] *adj* mutual, mutuo
**mutual aid** *s* apoyo mutuo
**mutual benefit association** *s* mutualidad
**muzzle** ['mʌzəl] *s* (*projecting part of head of animal*) hocico; (*device to keep animal from biting*) bozal *m;* (*of firearm*) boca || *tr* abozalar; (*to keep from speaking*) amordazar
**my** [maɪ] *adj poss* mi
**myriad** ['mɪrɪ·əd] *s* miríada
**myrrh** [mʌr] *s* mirra
**myrtle** ['mʌrtəl] *s* arrayán *m,* mirto
**myself** [maɪ'self] *pron pers* yo mismo; mí, mí mismo; me, p.ej., **I enjoyed myself** me divertí; **with myself** conmigo
**mysterious** [mɪs'tɪrɪ·əs] *adj* misterioso
**myster•y** ['mɪstəri] *s* (*pl* **-ies**) misterio
**mystic** ['mɪstɪk] *adj* & *s* místico
**mystical** ['mɪstɪkəl] *adj* místico
**mysticism** ['mɪstɪ,sɪzəm] *s* misticismo
**mystification** [,mɪstɪfɪ'keʃən] *s* confusión, mistificación
**mysti•fy** ['mɪstɪ,faɪ] *v* (*pret* & *pp* **-fied**) *tr* rodear de misterio; (*to hoax*) confundir, mistificar
**myth** [mɪθ] *s* mito
**mythical** ['mɪθɪkəl] *adj* mítico
**mythological** [,mɪθə'lɑdʒɪkəl] *adj* mitológico
**mytholo•gy** [mɪ'θɑlədʒi] *s* (*pl* **-gies**) mitología

## N

**N, n** [ɛn] decimocuarta letra del alfabeto inglés
**n.** *abbr* **neuter, nominative, noon, north, noun, number**
**N.** *abbr* **Nationalist, Navy, Noon, North, November**
**N.A.** *abbr* **National Academy, National Army, North America**
**nab** [næb] *v* (*pret* & *pp* **nabbed;** *ger* **nabbing**) *tr* (slang) agarrar, coger; (slang) poner preso, prender
**nag** [næg] *s* caballejo, jaco; pequeño caballo de silla || *v* (*pret* & *pp* **nagged;** *ger* **nagging**) *tr* importunar regañando || *intr* regañar
**naiad** ['ne·æd] o ['naɪ·æd] *s* náyade *f;* (fig) nadadora
**nail** [nel] *s* (*of finger*) uña; (*to fasten*

*wood, etc.*) clavo; **to hit the nail on the head** dar en el clavo || *tr* clavar
**nail brush** *s* cepillo de uñas
**nail file** *s* lima para las uñas
**nail polish** *s* esmalte *m* para las uñas, laca de uñas
**nailset** [ˈnel ˌsɛt] *s* contrapunzón *m*
**naïve** [nɑˈiv] *adj* cándido, ingenuo
**naked** [ˈnekɪd] *adj* desnudo; **to go naked** ir desnudo, andar a la cordobana; **to strip naked** desnudar; desnudarse; **with the naked eye** a simple vista
**name** [nem] *s* nombre *m*; (*first name*) nombre de pila; (*last name*) apellido; fama, reputación, renombre *m*; linaje, *m*, raza; **to call someone names** maltratar a uno de palabra; **to go by the name of** ser conocido por el nombre de; **to make a name for oneself** darse a conocer, hacerse un nombre; **what is your name?** ¿cómo se llama Vd.? || *tr* nombrar; fijar (*un precio*)
**name day** *s* santo
**nameless** [ˈnemlɪs] *adj* sin nombre, anónimo
**namely** [ˈnemli] *adv* a saber, es decir
**namesake** [ˈnem ˌsek] *s* homónimo, tocayo
**nanny goat** [ˈnæni] *s* (coll) cabra
**nap** [næp] *s* lanilla, flojel *m*; sueñecillo; **to take a nap** descabezar un sueñecillo || *v* (*pret & pp* **napped**; *ger* **napping**) *intr* echar un sueñecillo; estar desprevenido; **to catch napping** coger desprevenido
**napalm** [ˈnepɑm] *s* (mil) gelatina incendiaria
**nape** [nep] *s* cogote *m*, nuca
**naphtha** [ˈnæfθə] *s* nafta
**napkin** [ˈnæpkɪn] *s* servilleta; (*of a baby*) (Brit) pañal *m*
**napkin ring** *s* servilletero
**Naples** [ˈnepəlz] *s* Nápoles
**Napoleonic** [nəˌpolɪˈɑnɪk] *adj* napoleónico
**narcissus** [nɑrˈsɪsəs] *s* (bot) narciso || **Narcissus** *s* Narciso
**narcotic** [nɑrˈkɑtɪk] *adj & s* narcótico
**narrate** [næˈret] *tr* narrar
**narration** [næˈreʃən] *s* narración
**narrative** [ˈnærətɪv] *adj* narrativo || *s* (*story, tale; art of telling stories*) narrativa
**narrator** [næˈretər] *s* narrador *m*
**narrow** [ˈnæro] *adj* angosto, estrecho; intolerante; minucioso; (*sense of a word*) estricto || **narrows** *spl* angostura, paso estrecho || *tr* enangostar, estrechar; reducir, limitar || *intr* enangostarse, estrecharse; reducirse, limitarse
**narrow escape** *s* trance *m* difícil; **to have a narrow escape** escapar por un pelo, salvarse en una tabla
**narrow gauge** *s* trocha angosta, vía estrecha
**narrow-minded** [ˈnæroˈmaɪndɪd] *adj* intolerante, de miras estrechas, poco liberal
**nasal** [ˈnezəl] *adj & s* nasal *f*
**nasalize** [ˈnezəˌlaɪz] *tr* nasalizar || *intr* ganguear
**nasturtium** [nəˈstʌrʃəm] *s* capuchina, espuela de galán
**nas·ty** [ˈnæsti] o [ˈnɑsti] *adj* (*comp* **-tier**; *super* **-tiest**) asqueroso, sucio; desagradable; desvergonzado; amenazador; horrible
**natatorium** [ˌnetəˈtorɪ·əm] *s* piscina de natación
**nation** [ˈneʃən] *s* nación
**national** [ˈnæʃənəl] *adj & s* nacional *mf*
**national anthem** *s* himno nacional
**national hero** *s* benemérito de la patria
**national holiday** *s* fiesta nacional
**nationalism** [ˈnæʃənəˌlɪzəm] *s* nacionalismo
**nationalist** [ˈnæʃənəlɪst] *adj & s* nacionalista *mf*
**nationali·ty** [ˌnæʃənˈælɪti] *s* (*pl* **-ties**) nacionalidad, naturalidad
**nationalize** [ˈnæʃənəˌlaɪz] *tr* nacionalizar
**na'tion-wide'** *adj* de toda la nación
**native** [ˈnetɪv] *adj* nativo, natural; indígena; (*language*) materno; **to go native** vivir como los indígenas || *s* natural *mf*; indígena *mf*
**native land** *s* patria
**nativi·ty** [nəˈtɪvɪti] *s* (*pl* **-ties**) nacimiento || **Nativity** *s* (*day; festival; painting*) natividad
**Nato** [ˈneto] *s* (acronym) la O.T.A.N.
**nat·ty** [ˈnæti] *adj* (*comp* **-tier**; *super* **-tiest**) elegante, garboso
**natural** [ˈnætʃərəl] *adj* natural; (mus) natural || *s* imbécil *mf*; (mus) tono natural, nota natural; (*sign*) (mus) becuadro; (mus) tecla blanca; (coll) cosa de éxito certero
**naturalism** [ˈnætʃərəˌlɪzəm] *s* naturalismo
**naturalist** [ˈnætʃərəlɪst] *s* naturalista *mf*
**naturalization** [ˌnætʃərəlɪˈzeʃən] *s* naturalización
**naturalization papers** *spl* carta de naturaleza
**naturalize** [ˈnætʃərəˌlaɪz] *tr* naturalizar
**naturally** [ˈnætʃərəli] *adv* naturalmente; claro, desde luego, por supuesto
**nature** [ˈnetʃər] *s* naturaleza; **from nature** del natural
**naught** [nɔt] *s* nada; cero; **to bring to naught** anular, invalidar, destruir; **to come to naught** reducirse a nada, frustrarse
**naugh·ty** [ˈnɔti] *adj* (*comp* **-tier**; *super* **-tiest**) desobediente, pícaro; desvergonzado; (*story, tale*) verde
**nausea** [ˈnɔʃɪ·ə] o [ˈnɔsɪ·ə] *s* náusea
**nauseate** [ˈnɔʃɪ ˌet] o [ˈnɔsɪ ˌet] *tr* dar náuseas a || *intr* nausear, marearse
**nauseating** [ˈnɔʃɪ ˌetɪŋ] o [ˈnɔsɪ ˌetɪŋ] *adj* nauseabundo, asqueroso
**nauseous** [ˈnɔʃɪ·əs] o [ˈnɔsɪ·əs] *adj* nauseabundo
**nautical** [ˈnɔtɪkəl] *adj* náutico, marino, naval
**nav.** *abbr* **naval, navigation**
**naval** [ˈnevəl] *adj* naval, naval militar

**Naval Academy** *s* (U.S.A.) Escuela Naval Militar
**naval officer** *s* oficial *m* de marina
**naval station** *s* apostadero
**nave** [nev] *s* (*of a church*) nave *f* central, nave principal; (*of a wheel*) cubo
**navel** [ˈnevəl] *s* ombligo; (*center point, middle*) (fig) ombligo
**navel orange** *s* navel *f*, naranja de ombligo
**navigability** [ˌnævɪgəˈbɪlɪti] *s* (*of a river*) navegabilidad; (*of a ship*) buen gobierno
**navigable** [ˈnævɪgəbəl] *adj* (*river, canal, etc.*) navegable; (*ship*) marinero, de buen gobierno
**navigate** [ˈnævɪˌget] *tr & intr* navegar
**navigation** [ˌnævɪˈgeʃən] *s* navegación
**navigator** [ˈnævɪˌgetər] *s* navegador *m*, navegante *m*; (*he who is in charge of course of ship or plane*) oficial *m* de derrota; (Brit) peón *m*
**nav•vy** [ˈnævi] *s* (*pl* **-vies**) (Brit) bracero, peón *m*
**na•vy** [ˈnevi] *adj* azul oscuro ‖ *s* (*pl* **-vies**) marina de guerra; (*personnel*) marina; azul oscuro
**navy bean** *s* frijol blanco común
**navy blue** *s* azul marino, azul oscuro
**navy yard** *s* arsenal *m* de puerto
**Nazarene** [ˌnæzəˈrin] *adj & s* nazareno
**Nazi** [ˈnɑtsi] o [ˈnætsi] *adj & s* nazi *mf*, nacista *mf*
**n.b.** *abbr* **nota bene** (Lat) **note well**
**N-bomb** [ˈenˌbɑm] *s* bomba de neutrones
**Neapolitan** [ˌni·əˈpɑlɪtən] *adj & s* napolitano
**neap tide** [nip] *s* marea muerta
**near** [nɪr] *adj* cercano, próximo; íntimo; imitado ‖ *adv* cerca; íntimamente ‖ *prep* cerca de; hacia, por ‖ *tr* acercarse **a** ‖ *intr* acercarse
**nearby** [ˈnɪrˌbaɪ] *adj* cercano, próximo ‖ *adv* cerca
**Near East** *s* Cercano Oriente, Próximo Oriente
**nearly** [ˈnɪrli] *adv* casi; de cerca; íntimamente; por poco, p.ej., **he nearly fell** por poco se cae
**near-sighted** [ˈnɪrˈsaɪtɪd] *adj* miope
**near-sightedness** *s* miopía
**neat** [nit] *adj* aseado, pulcro; pulido; diestro, primoroso; puro, sin mezcla ‖ *ssg* res vacuna ‖ *spl* ganado vacuno
**neat's'-foot' oil** *s* aceite *m* de pie de buey
**Nebuchadnezzar** [ˌnebjəkədˈnezər] *s* Nabucodonosor *m*
**nebu•la** [ˈnebjələ] *s* (*pl* **-lae** [ˌli] o **-las**) nebulosa
**nebular** [ˈnebjələr] *adj* nebular
**nebulous** [ˈnebjələs] *adj* nebuloso
**necessary** [ˈnesɪˌseri] *adj* necesario
**necessitate** [nɪˈsesɪˌtet] *tr* necesitar, exigir
**necessitous** [nɪˈsesɪtəs] *adj* necesitado
**necessi•ty** [nɪˈsesɪti] *s* (*pl* **-ties**) necesidad
**neck** [nek] *s* cuello; (*of a bottle*) gollete *m*; (*of violin or guitar*) mástil *m*; istmo, península; estrecho; **neck and neck** parejos; **to break one's neck** (coll) matarse trabajando; **to stick one's neck out** (coll) descubrir el cuerpo ‖ *intr* (slang) acariciarse (*dos enamorados*)
**neck'band'** *s* tirilla de camisa
**necklace** [ˈneklɪs] *s* gargantilla, collar *m*
**necktie** [ˈnekˌtaɪ] *s* corbata
**necktie pin** *s* alfiler *m* de corbata
**necrology** [neˈkrɑlədʒi] *s* necrología
**necromancy** [ˈnekrəˌmænsi] *s* necromancia, nigromancia
**nectarine** [ˌnektəˈrin] *s* griñón *m*
**née** o **nee** [ne] *adj* nacida o de soltera, p.ej., **Mary Wilson, née Miller** María Wilson, nacida Miller o María Wilson, de soltera Miller
**need** [nid] *s* necesidad; pobreza; **in need** necesitado ‖ *tr* necesitar ‖ *intr* estar necesitado; ser necesario ‖ *v aux* — **if need be** si fuere necesario; **to need** + *inf* deber, tener que + *inf*
**needful** [ˈnidfəl] *adj* necesario ‖ **the needful** lo necesario; (slang) el dinero
**needle** [ˈnidəl] *s* aguja; **to look for a needle in a haystack** buscar una aguja en un pajar ‖ *tr* coser con aguja; (coll) aguijonear, incitar; (coll) añadir alcohol a (*la cerveza o el vino*)
**needle bath** *s* ducha en alfileres
**needle'case'** *s* alfiletero
**needle point** *s* bordado al pasado; encaje *m* de mano
**needless** [ˈnidlɪs] *adj* innecesario, inútil
**needle'work'** *s* costura, labor *f*
**needs** [nidz] *adv* necesariamente, forzosamente
**need•y** [ˈnidi] *adj* (*comp* **-ier**; *super* **-iest**) necesitado, indigente ‖ **the needy** los necesitados
**ne'er-do-well** [ˈnerduˌwel] *adj & s* holgazán, perdido
**negation** [nɪˈgeʃən] *s* negación
**negative** [ˈnegətɪv] *adj* negativo ‖ *s* negativa; electricidad negativa, borne negativo; (gram) negación; (math) término negativo; (phot) prueba negativa ‖ *tr* desaprobar; anular
**neglect** [nɪˈglekt] *s* negligencia, descuido ‖ *tr* descuidar; **to neglect to** dejar de, olvidarse de
**neglectful** [nɪˈglektfəl] *adj* negligente, descuidado
**négligée** o **negligee** [ˌneglɪˈʒe] *s* bata de mujer, traje *m* de casa
**negligence** [ˈneglɪdʒəns] *s* negligencia, descuido
**negligent** [ˈneglɪdʒənt] *adj* negligente, descuidado
**negligible** [ˈneglɪdʒɪbəl] *adj* insignificante, imperceptible
**negotiable** [nɪˈgoʃɪ·əbəl] *adj* negociable; transitable
**negotiate** [nɪˈgoʃɪˌet] *tr* negociar; (coll) salvar, vencer ‖ *intr* negociar
**negotiation** [nɪˌgoʃɪˈeʃən] *s* negociación; trámite *m*

**Ne•gro** ['nigro] *adj* negro || *s* (*pl* **-groes**) negro
**neigh** [ne] *s* relincho || *intr* relinchar
**neighbor** ['nebər] *adj* vecino || *s* vecino; (*fellow man*) prójimo || *tr* ser vecino de; ser amigo de || *intr* estar cercano; tener relaciones amistosas
**neighborhood** ['nebər,hʊd] *s* vecindad, vecindario, cercanías; **in the neighborhood of** en las inmediaciones de; (coll) cerca de, aproximadamente
**neighboring** ['nebərɪŋ] *adj* vecino, colindante
**neighborly** ['nebərli] *adj* buen vecino, amable, sociable
**neither** ['niðər] o ['naɪðər] *adj indef* ninguno . . . (de los dos); **neither one** ninguno de los dos || *pron indef* ninguno (de los dos); ni uno ni otro, ni lo uno ni lo otro || *conj* ni; tampoco, ni . . . tampoco, p.ej., **neither do I** yo tampoco, ni yo tampoco; **neither . . . nor** ni . . . ni
**neme•sis** ['nɛmɪsɪs] *s* (*pl* **-ses** [,siz]) (*someone or something that punishes*) némesis *f* || **Nemesis** *s* Némesis *f*
**neologism** [ni'ɑlə,dʒɪzəm] *s* neologismo
**neomycin** [,ni·ə'maɪsɪn] *s* neomicina
**neon** ['ni·ɑn] *s* neo, neón *m*
**neophyte** ['ni·ə,faɪt] *s* neófito
**Nepal** [nɪ'pɔl] *s* el Nepal
**Nepa•lese** [,nɛpə'liz] *adj* nepalés || *s* (*pl* **-lese**) nepalés *m*
**nepenthe** [nɪ'pɛnθi] *s* nepente *m*
**nephew** ['nɛfju] o ['nɛvju] *s* sobrino
**Nepos** ['nipɑs] o ['nɛpɑs] *s* Nepote *m*
**Neptune** ['nɛptʃun] o ['nɛptjun] *s* Neptuno
**neptunium** [nɛp'tʃunɪ·əm] o [nɛp'tjunɪ·əm] *s* neptunio
**Nereid** ['nɪrɪ·ɪd] *s* nereida
**Nero** ['nɪro] *s* Nerón *m*
**nerve** [nʌrv] *adj* (*center; system; tonic; disease; prostration; breakdown*) nervioso || *s* nervio; ánimo, valor *m;* audacia; (coll) descaro; **nerves** excitabilidad nerviosa; **to get on one's nerves** irritar los nervios a uno; **to strain every nerve** esforzarse al máximo
**nerve-racking** ['nʌrv,rækɪŋ] *adj* irritante, exasperante
**nervous** ['nʌrvəs] *adj* nervioso
**nervous breakdown** *s* colapso nervioso
**nervousness** ['nʌrvəsnɪs] *s* nerviosidad
**nervous shudder** *s* muerte chiquita
**nerv•y** ['nʌrvi] *adj* (*comp* **-ier;** *super* **-iest**) (*strong, vigorous*) nervioso; atrevido, audaz; (coll) descarado
**nest** [nɛst] *s* nido; (*where hen lays eggs*) nidal *m;* (*birds in a nest*) nidada; (*set of things fitting within each other*) juego; (*of, e.g., thieves*) nido; **to feather one's nest** hacer todo para enriquecerse || *tr* colocar en un nido || *intr* anidar
**nest egg** *s* (*eggs left in a nest to induce hen to lay more*) nidal *m;* ahorros, hucha
**nestle** ['nɛsəl] *tr* poner en un nido; arrimar afectuosamente || *intr* anidar; arrimarse cómodamente; **to nestle up to** arrimarse a
**net** [nɛt] *adj* neto, líquido || *s* red *f;* precio neto, peso neto, ganancia líquida || *v* (*pret & pp* **netted;** *super* **netting**) *tr* enredar, tejer; coger con red; producir (*cierta ganancia líquida*)
**nether** ['nɛðər] *adj* inferior, más bajo
**Netherlander** ['nɛðər,lændər] o ['nɛðərləndər] *s* neerlandés *m*
**Netherlandish** ['nɛðər,lændɪʃ] o ['nɛðərləndɪʃ] *adj* neerlandés || *s* neerlandés *m*
**Netherlands, The** ['nɛðərləndz] los Países Bajos (*Holanda*)
**netting** ['nɛtɪŋ] *s* red *f*
**nettle** ['nɛtəl] *s* ortiga || *tr* irritar, provocar
**net'work'** *s* red *f;* (rad & telv) cadena
**neuralgia** [njʊ'rældʒə] o [nʊ'rældʒə] *s* neuralgia
**neurology** [njʊ'rɑlədʒi] o [nʊ'rɑlədʒi] *s* neurología
**neuro•sis** [njʊ'rosɪs] o [nʊ'rosɪs] *s* (*pl* **-ses** [siz]) neurosis *f*
**neurotic** [njʊ'rɑtɪk] o [nʊ'rɑtɪk] *adj & s* neurótico
**neut.** *abbr* **neuter**
**neuter** ['njutər] o ['nutər] *adj* neutro || *s* género neutro
**neutral** ['njutrəl] o ['nutrəl] *adj* (*on neither side in a quarrel or war*) neutral; (*having little or no color*) neutro; (bot, chem, elec, phonet, zool) neutro || *s* neutral *mf;* (aut) punto neutral, punto muerto
**neutralism** ['njutrə,lɪzəm] o ['nutrə,lɪzəm] *s* neutralismo
**neutralist** ['njutrəlɪst] o ['nutrəlɪst] *adj & s* neutralista *mf*
**neutrality** [nju'trælɪti] o [nu'trælɪti] *s* neutralidad
**neutralize** ['njutrə,laɪz] o ['nutrə,laɪz] *tr* neutralizar
**neutron** ['njutrɑn] o ['nutrɑn] *s* neutrón *m*
**neutron bomb** *s* bomba de neutrones, bomba neutrónica
**never** ['nɛvər] *adv* nunca; en mi vida; de ningún modo; **never fear** no hay cuidado; **never mind** no importa
**nev'er•more'** *adv* nunca más
**nevertheless** [,nɛvərðə'lɛs] *adv* no obstante, sin embargo
**new** [nju] o [nu] *adj* nuevo; **what's new?** ¿qué hay de nuevo?
**new arrival** *s* recién llegado; recién nacido
**new'born'** *adj* recién nacido; renacido
**New Castile** *s* Castilla la Nueva
**New'cas'tle** *s* — **to carry coals to Newcastle** echar agua al mar, llevar hierro a Vizcaya, llevar leña al monte
**newcomer** ['nju,kʌmər] o ['nu,kʌmər] *s* recién llegado, recién venido
**New England** *s* la Nueva Inglaterra
**newfangled** ['nju,fæŋgəld] o ['nu,fæŋgəld] *adj* de última moda, recién inventado
**Newfoundland** ['njufənd,lænd] o

[ˈnufənd ˌlænd] *s* (*island and province*) Terranova || [njuˈfaundlənd] o [nuˈfaundlənd] *s* (*dog*) Terranova *m*
**newly** [ˈnjuli] o [ˈnuli] *adv* nuevamente; **newly** + *pp* recién + *pp*
**new'ly·wed'** *s* recién casado
**New Mexican** *adj & s* neomejicano, nuevomejicano
**New Mexico** *s* Nuevo Méjico
**new moon** *s* luna nueva, novilunio
**news** [njuz] o [nuz] *s* noticias; periódico; **a news item** una noticia; **a piece of news** una noticia
**news agency** *s* agencia de noticias
**news beat** *s* exclusiva, anticipación de una noticia por un periódico
**news'boy'** *s* vendedor *m* de periódicos
**news'cast'** *s* noticiario radiofónico || *tr* radiodifundir (*noticias*) || *intr* radiodifundir noticias
**news'cast'er** *s* cronista *mf* de radio
**news conference** *s* var de **press conference**
**news coverage** *s* reportaje *m*
**news·man** [ˈnjuzmən] o [ˈnuzmən] *s* (*pl* **-men** [mən]) noticiero
**New South Wales** *s* la Nueva Gales del Sur
**news'pa'per** *adj* periodístico || *s* periódico
**newspaper·man** [ˈnjuz ˌpepər ˌmæn] o [ˈnuz ˌpepər ˌmæn] *s* (*pl* **-men** [ˌmɛn]) periodista *m*
**news'print'** *s* papel-prensa *m*
**news'reel'** *s* actualidades, noticiario cinematográfico
**news'stand'** *s* quiosco de periódicos, puesto de periódicos
**news'week'ly** *s* (*pl* **-lies**) semanario de noticias
**news'wor'thy** *adj* de gran actualidad, de interés periodístico
**news·y** [ˈnjuzi] o [ˈnuzi] *adj* (*comp* **-ier;** *super* **-iest**) (coll) informativo
**new'-world'** *adj* del Nuevo Mundo
**New Year's card** *s* tarjeta de felicitación de Año Nuevo
**New Year's Day** *s* el Día de Año Nuevo
**New Year's Eve** *s* la noche vieja, la víspera de año nuevo
**New York** [jɔrk] *adj* neoyorkino || *s* Nueva York
**New Yorker** [ˈjɔrkər] *s* neoyorkino
**New Zealand** [ˈzilənd] *adj* neocelandés || *s* Nueva Zelanda
**New Zealander** [ˈziləndər] *s* neocelandés *m*
**next** [nɛkst] *adj* próximo, siguiente; de al lado; venidero, que viene || *adv* luego, después; la próxima vez; **next to** junto a; después de; **next to nothing** casi nada; **the next best** lo mejor después de eso; **to come next** venir después, ser el que sigue
**next door** *s* la casa de al lado; **next door to** en la casa siguiente de; (coll) casi
**next'door'** *adj* siguiente, de al lado
**next of kin** *s* (*pl* **next of kin**) pariente más cercano
**niacin** [ˈnaɪ·əsɪn] *s* niacina
**Niagara Falls** [naɪˈægərə] *spl* las Cataratas del Niágara
**nibble** [ˈnɪbəl] *s* mordisco || *tr & intr* mordiscar; picar (*un pez*); **to nibble at** picar de o en
**Nicaraguan** [ˌnɪkəˈrɑgwən] *adj & s* nicaragüense, nicaragüeño
**nice** [naɪs] *adj* delicado, fino, sutil; primoroso, pulido, refinado; dengoso, melindroso; atento, cortés, culto; escrupuloso, esmerado; agradable, simpático; decoroso, conveniente; complaciente; preciso; satisfactorio; (*weather*) bueno; (*attractive*) bonito; **nice and . . .** (coll) muy, mucho; **not nice** (coll) feo
**nice-looking** [ˈnaɪsˈlʊkɪŋ] *adj* hermoso, guapo, bien parecido
**nicely** [ˈnaɪsli] *adv* con precisión; escrupulosamente; satisfactoriamente; (coll) muy bien
**nice·ty** [ˈnaɪsəti] *s* (*pl* **-ties**) precisión; sutileza; finura; **to a nicety** con la mayor precisión
**niche** [nɪtʃ] *s* hornacina, nicho; colocación conveniente
**Nicholas** [ˈnɪkələs] *s* Nicolás *m*
**nick** [nɪk] *s* mella, muesca; **in the nick of time** en el momento crítico || *tr* mellar; hacer muescas en; cortar
**nickel** [ˈnɪkəl] *s* níquel *m;* (U.S.A.) moneda de cinco centavos || *tr* niquelar
**nick'el-plate'** *tr* niquelar
**nicknack** [ˈnɪk ˌnæk] *s* chuchería, friolera
**nick'name'** *s* apodo, mote *m* || *tr* apodar
**nicotine** [ˈnɪkə ˌtin] *s* nicotina
**niece** [nis] *s* sobrina
**nif·ty** [ˈnɪfti] *adj* (*comp* **-tier;** *super* **-tiest**) (slang) elegante; (slang) excelente
**niggard** [ˈnɪgərd] *adj & s* tacaño
**night** [naɪt] *adj* nocturno || *s* noche *f;* **at** o **by night** de noche o por la noche; **night before last** anteanoche; **to make a night of it** (coll) divertirse hasta muy entrada la noche
**night'cap'** *s* gorro de dormir; trago antes de acostarse, sosiega
**night club** *s* cabaret *m*, café *m* cantante, sala de fiestas
**night driving** *s* conducción de noche
**night'fall'** *s* anochecer *m*, caída de la noche
**night'gown'** *s* camisa de dormir
**nightingale** [ˈnaɪtən ˌgel] *s* ruiseñor *m*
**night latch** *s* cerradura de resorte
**night letter** *s* carta telegráfica nocturna
**night'long'** *adj* de toda la noche || *adv* durante toda la noche
**nightly** [ˈnaɪtli] *adj* nocturno; de cada noche || *adv* de noche, por la noche; cada noche
**night'mare'** *s* pesadilla
**nightmarish** [ˈnaɪt ˌmɛrɪʃ] *adj* espeluznante, horroroso
**night owl** *s* buho nocturno; (coll) anochecedor *m*, trasnochador *m*
**night'shirt'** *s* camisa de dormir
**night'time'** *adj* nocturno || *s* noche *f*

**night'walk'er** *s* vagabundo nocturno; ladrón nocturno; ramera callejera nocturna; sonámbulo
**night watch** *s* guardia de noche, ronda de noche; sereno; (mil) vigilia
**night watchman** *s* vigilante nocturno
**nihilism** [ˈnaɪ·ɪ ˌlɪzəm] *s* nihilismo
**nihilist** [ˈnaɪ·ɪlɪst] *s* nihilista *mf*
**nil** [nɪl] *s* nada
**Nile** [naɪl] *s* Nilo
**nimble** [ˈnɪmbəl] *adj* ágil, ligero; listo, vivo
**nim•bus** [ˈnɪmbəs] *s* (*pl* **-buses** o **-bi** [baɪ]) nimbo
**Nimrod** [ˈnɪmrɑd] *s* Nemrod *m*
**nincompoop** [ˈnɪnkəm ˌpup] *s* badulaque *m*, papirote *m*
**nine** [naɪn] *adj & pron* nueve ‖ *s* nueve *m*; equipo de béisbol; **nine o'clock** las nueve; **the Nine** las nueve musas
**nine hundred** *adj & pron* novecientos ‖ *s* novecientos *m*
**nineteen** [ˈnaɪnˈtin] *adj, pron & s* diecinueve *m*, diez y nueve *m*
**nineteenth** [ˈnaɪnˈtinθ] *adj & s* (*in a series*) decimonono; (*part*) diecinueveavo ‖ *s* (*in dates*) diecinueve *m*
**ninetieth** [ˈnaɪntɪ·ɪθ] *adj & s* (*in a series*) nonagésimo; (*part*) noventavo
**nine•ty** [ˈnaɪnti] *adj & pron* noventa ‖ *s* (*pl* **-ties**) noventa *m*
**ninth** [naɪnθ] *adj & s* nono, noveno ‖ *s* (*in dates*) nueve *m*
**nip** [nɪp] *s* mordisco, pellizco; helada, escarcha; traguito; **nip and tuck** a quién ganará ‖ *v* (*pret & pp* **nipped**; *ger* **nipping**) *tr* mordiscar, pellizcar; helar, escarchar; (slang) asir, coger; **to nip in the bud** atajar en el principio ‖ *intr* beborrotear
**nipple** [ˈnɪpəl] *s* (*of female*) pezón *m*; (*of male; of nursing bottle*) tetilla; (mach) tubo roscado de unión, enterrosca
**Nippon** [nɪˈpɑn] o [ˈnɪpɑn] *s* el Japón
**Nippon•ese** [ˌnɪpəˈniz] *adj* nipón ‖ *s* (*pl* **-ese**) nipón *m*
**nip•py** [ˈnɪpi] *adj* (*comp* **-pier**; *super* **-piest**) mordaz, picante; frío, helado; (Brit) ágil, ligero
**nirvana** [nɪrˈvɑnə] *s* el nirvana
**nit** [nɪt] *s* piojito; (*egg of insect*) liendre *f*
**niter** [ˈnaɪtər] *s* nitro; (agr) nitro de Chile
**nitrate** [ˈnaɪtret] *s* nitrato; (agr) nitrato de potasio, nitrato de sodio
**nitric acid** [ˈnaɪtrɪk] *s* ácido nítrico
**nitride** [ˈnaɪtraɪd] *s* nitruro
**nitrogen** [ˈnaɪtrədʒən] *s* nitrógeno
**nitroglycerin** [ˌnaɪtrəˈglɪsərɪn] *s* nitroglicerina
**nitrous oxide** [ˈnaɪtrəs] *s* óxido nitroso
**nitwit** [ˈnɪt ˌwɪt] *s* (slang) bobalicón *m*
**no** [no] *adj indef* ninguno; **no admittance** no se permite la entrada; **no matter** no importa; **no parking** se prohibe estacionarse; **no smoking** se prohibe fumar; **no thoroughfare** prohibido el paso; **no use** inútil; **with no sin** ‖ *adv* no; **no good** de ningún valor; ruin, vil; **no longer** ya no; **no sooner** no bien
**Noah** [ˈno·ə] *s* Noé *m*
**nob•by** [ˈnɑbi] *adj* (*comp* **-bier**; *super* **-biest**) (slang) elegante; (slang) excelente
**nobili•ty** [noˈbɪlɪti] *s* (*pl* **-ties**) nobleza; (*of sentiments, character, etc.*) nobleza, ennoblecimiento
**noble** [ˈnobəl] *adj & s* noble *m*
**noble•man** [ˈnobəlmən] *s* (*pl* **-men** [mən]) noble *m*, hidalgo
**nobod•y** [ˈno ˌbɑdi] o [ˈnobədi] *pron indef* nadie, ninguno; **nobody but** nadie más que; **nobody else** nadie más, ningún otro ‖ *s* (*pl* **-ies**) nadie *m*, don nadie
**nocturnal** [nɑkˈtʌrnəl] *adj* nocturno
**nod** [nɑd] *s* inclinación de cabeza; seña con la cabeza; (*of a person going to sleep*) cabezada ‖ *v* (*pret & pp* **nodded**; *ger* **nodding**) *tr* inclinar (*la cabeza*); indicar con una inclinación de cabeza ‖ *intr* inclinar la cabeza; (*in going to sleep*) cabecear
**node** [nod] *s* bulto, protuberancia; nudo, enredo; (astr, med & phys) nodo; (bot) nudo
**nohow** [ˈno ˌhaʊ] *adv* (coll) de ninguna manera
**noise** [nɔɪz] *s* ruido ‖ *tr* divulgar
**noiseless** [ˈnɔɪzlɪs] *adj* silencioso, sin ruido
**nois•y** [ˈnɔɪzi] *adj* (*comp* **-ier**; *super* **-iest**) ruidoso; (*boisterous*) estrepitoso
**nom.** *abbr* **nominative**
**nomad** [ˈnomæd] *adj & s* nómada *mf*
**nomadic** [noˈmædɪk] *adj* nomádico
**no man's land** *s* terreno sin reclamar; (mil) la tierra de nadie
**nominal** [ˈnɑmɪnəl] *adj* nominal; (*price*) módico
**nominate** [ˈnɑmɪ ˌnet] *tr* postular como candidato; (*to appoint*) nombrar, designar
**nomination** [ˌnɑmɪˈneʃən] *s* postulación
**nominative** [ˈnɑmɪnətɪv] *adj & s* nominativo
**nominee** [ˌnɑmɪˈni] *s* propuesto, candidato
**nonbelligerent** [ˌnɑnbəˈlɪdʒərənt] *adj & s* no beligerante *m*
**nonbreakable** [nɑnˈbrekəbəl] *adj* irrompible
**nonchalance** [ˈnɑnʃələns] o [ˌnɑnʃəˈlɑns] *s* indiferencia, desenvoltura
**nonchalant** [ˈnɑnʃələnt] o [ˌnɑnʃəˈlɑnt] *adj* indiferente, desenvuelto
**noncom** [ˈnɑn ˌkɑm] *s* (coll) clase, suboficial *m*
**noncombatant** [nɑnˈkɑmbətənt] *adj & s* no combatiente *m*
**noncommissioned officer** [ˌnɑnkəˈmɪʃənd] *s* clase, suboficial *m*
**noncommittal** [ˌnɑnkəˈmɪtəl] *adj* evasivo, reticente
**noncommitted** [ˌnɑnkəˈmɪtɪd] *adj* no empeñado

**non compos mentis** ['nɑn'kɑmpəs-'mɛntɪs] *adj* falto de juicio, loco
**nonconformist** [ˌnɑnkən'fɔrmɪst] *s* disidente *mf*
**nondelivery** [ˌnɑndɪ'lɪvəri] *s* falta de entrega
**nondescript** ['nɑndɪˌskrɪpt] *adj* inclasificable, indefinido
**none** [nʌn] *pron indef* nadie, ninguno, ningunos; **none of** ninguno de; nada de; **none other** ningún otro || *adv* nada, de ninguna manera; **none the less** sin embargo, no obstante
**nonenti·ty** [nɑn'ɛntɪti] *s* (*pl* **-ties**) cosa inexistente; (*person*) nulidad
**nonfiction** [nɑn'fɪkʃən] *s* literatura no novelesca
**nonfulfillment** [ˌnɑnfʊl'fɪlmənt] *s* incumplimiento
**nonintervention** [ˌnɑnɪntər'venʃən] *s* no intervención
**nonmetal** ['nɑnˌmɛtəl] *s* metaloide *m*
**nonpayment** [nɑn'pemənt] *s* falta de pago
**non·plus** ['nɑnplʌs] o [nɑn'plʌs] *s* estupefacción || *v* (*pret & pp* **-plused** o **-plussed**; *ger* **-plusing** o **-plussing**) *tr* dejar estupefacto, dejar pegado a la pared
**nonprofit** [nɑn'prɑfɪt] *adj* sin fin lucrativo
**nonrefillable** [ˌnɑnrɪ'fɪləbəl] *adj* irrellenable
**nonresident** [nɑn'rɛzɪdənt] *s* transeúnte *mf*
**nonresidential** [nɑnˌrɛzɪ'denʃəl] *adj* comercial
**nonscientific** [nɑnˌsaɪ·ən'tɪfɪk] *adj* anticientífico
**nonsectarian** [ˌnɑnsek'terɪ·ən] *adj* no sectario
**nonsense** ['nɑnsens] *s* disparate *m*, tontería
**nonsensical** [nɑn'sɛnsɪkəl] *adj* disparatado, tonto
**nonskid** ['nɑn'skɪd] *adj* antideslizante
**nonstop** ['nɑn'stɑp] *adj & adv* sin parar, sin escala
**nonsupport** [ˌnɑnsə'port] *s* falta de manutención
**noodle** ['nudəl] *s* tallarín *m;* (slang) mentecato, tonto; (slang) cabeza
**noodle soup** *s* sopa de pastas, sopa de fideos
**nook** [nʊk] *s* rinconcito
**noon** [nun] *s* mediodía *m;* **at high noon** en pleno mediodía
**no one** o **no-one** ['no ˌwʌn] *pron indef* nadie, ninguno; **no one else** nadie más, ningún otro
**noontime** ['nun ˌtaɪm] *s* mediodía *m*
**noose** [nus] *s* lazo corredizo; (*to hang a criminal*) dogal *m;* trampa || *tr* lazar; hacer un lazo corredizo en
**nor** [nɔr] *conj* ni
**Nordic** ['nɔrdɪk] *adj & s* nórdico
**norm** [nɔrm] *s* norma
**normal** ['nɔrməl] *adj* normal
**Norman** ['nɔrmən] *adj & s* normando
**Normandy** ['nɔrməndi] *s* Normandía
**Norse** [nɔrs] *adj* nórdico; noruego || *s* (*ancient Scandanavian language*) nórdico; (*language of Norway*) noruego; **the Norse** los nórdicos; los noruegos
**Norse·man** ['nɔrsmən] *s* (*pl* **-men** [mən]) normando
**north** [nɔrθ] *adj* septentrional, del norte || *adv* al norte, hacia el norte || *s* norte *m*
**North America** *s* Norteamérica, la América del Norte
**North American** *adj & s* norteamericano
**north'east'er** *s* (*wind*) nordestada, nordeste *m* (*viento*)
**northern** ['nɔrðərn] *adj* septentrional; (*Hemisphere*) boreal
**North Korea** *s* la Corea del Norte
**North Korean** *adj & s* norcoreano
**northward** ['nɔrθwərd] *adv* hacia el norte
**north wind** *s* norte *m*, aquilón *m*
**Norway** ['nɔrwe] *s* Noruega
**Norwegian** [nɔr'widʒən] *adj & s* noruego
**nos.** *abbr* **numbers**
**nose** [noz] *s* nariz *f;* (aer) proa; **to blow one's nose** sonarse las narices; **to count noses** averiguar cuántas personas hay; **to follow one's nose** seguir todo derecho; avanzar guiándose por el instinto; **to hold one's nose** tabicarse las narices; **to lead by the nose** llevar por la barba, tener agarrado por las narices; **to look down one's nose at** mirar por encima del hombro; **to pay through the nose** pagar un precio escandaloso; **to pick one's nose** hurgarse las narices; **to poke one's nose into** meter las narices en; **to speak through the nose** ganguear; **to thumb one's nose at** señalar (*a una persona*) poniendo el pulgar sobre la nariz en son de burla; tratar con sumo desprecio; **to turn up one's nose at** mirar con desprecio; **under the nose of** en las narices de, en las barbas de || *tr* olfatear || *intr* ventear; **to nose about** curiosear; **to nose over** capotar (*un avión*); **to nose up** encabritarse (*un buque, un avión*)
**nose bag** *s* cebadera, morral *m*
**nose'band'** *s* muserola, sobarba
**nose'bleed'** *s* hemorragia nasal
**nose cone** *s* cono de proa
**nose dive** *s* (aer) descenso de picado; (fig) descenso precipitado
**nose'-dive'** *intr* (aer) picar; (fig) descender precipidamente
**nosegay** ['noz ˌge] *s* ramillete *m*
**nose ring** *s* nariguera
**no'-show'** *s* pasajero no presentado
**nostalgia** [nɑ'stældʒə] *s* nostalgia
**nostril** ['nɑstrɪl] *s* nariz *f*, ventana
**nos·y** ['nozi] *adj* (*comp* **-ier;** *super* **-iest**) (coll) curioso, husmeador
**not** [nɑt] *adv* no; **not at all** nada, de ningún modo; **not yet** todavía no; **to think not** creer que no; **why not?** ¿cómo no?
**notable** ['notəbəl] *adj & s* notable *m*
**notarize** ['notəˌraɪz] *tr* abonar con fe notarial
**nota·ry** ['notəri] *s* (*pl* **-ries**) notario

**notch** [nɑtʃ] *s* muesca, mella, corte *m;* (U.S.A.) desfiladero, paso; (coll) grado || *tr* hacer muescas en, mellar
**note** [not] *s* nota; apunte *m;* esquela, cartita; marca, señal *f;* (com) pagaré *m,* vale *m;* canto, melodía; acento, voz *f;* (mus) nota || *tr* notar, apuntar; marcar, señalar
**note'book'** *s* cuaderno, libro de apuntes
**noted** ['notɪd] *adj* afamado, conocido
**note paper** *s* papel *m* de cartas
**note'wor'thy** *adj* notable, digno de notarse
**nothing** ['nʌθɪŋ] *pron indef* nada; **for nothing** inútilmente; de balde, gratis; **nothing doing** (slang) ni por pienso; **nothing else** nada más; **that's nothing to me** eso nada me importa; **to make nothing of** no hacer caso de; no aprovecharse de; no entender; despreciar; **to think nothing of** no hacer caso de; tener por fácil; despreciar || *adv* nada, de ninguna manera; **nothing daunted** sin temor alguno || *s* nada; nadería, friolera
**notice** ['notɪs] *s* atención, reparo, advertencia; aviso, noticia; letrero; mención, reseña; llamada; notificación; **on short notice** con poco tiempo de aviso; **to escape one's notice** pasarle inadvertido a uno; **to serve notice** dar noticia, hacer saber || *tr* notar, observar, reparar, reparar en; mencionar
**noticeable** ['notɪsəbəl] *adj* sensible, perceptible; notable
**noti·fy** ['notɪ,faɪ] *v* (*pret & pp* **-fied**) *tr* notificar, avisar, hacer saber
**notion** ['noʃən] *s* noción; capricho; **notions** mercería, artículos menudos; **to have a notion to** + *inf* pensar + *inf,* tener ganas de + *inf*
**notorie·ty** [,notə'raɪ·ɪti] *s* (*pl* **-ties**) mala reputación; (*condition of being well known*) notoriedad; (*person*) notable *mf*
**notorious** [no'torɪ·əs] *adj* reputado, mal reputado; bien conocido
**no'-trump'** *adj & s* sin triunfo; **a no-trump hand** un sin triunfo
**notwithstanding** [,nɑtwɪð'stændɪŋ] o [,nɑtwɪθ'stændɪŋ] *adv* no obstante || *prep* a pesar de || *conj* a pesar de que
**nougat** ['nugət] *s* turrón *m*
**noun** [naun] *s* nombre, nombre sustantivo
**nourish** ['nʌrɪʃ] *tr* alimentar, nutrir; abrigar (*p.ej., esperanzas*)
**nourishing** ['nʌrɪʃɪŋ] *adj* alimenticio, nutritivo
**nourishment** ['nʌrɪʃmənt] *s* alimento, nutrimento
**Nov.** *abbr* **November**
**Nova Scotia** ['novə'skoʃə] *s* la Nueva Escocia
**Nova Scotian** ['novə'skoʃən] *adj & s* neoescocés *m*
**novel** ['nɑvəl] *adj* nuevo; insólito, extraño, original || *s* novela
**novelist** ['nɑvəlɪst] *s* novelista *mf*
**novel·ty** ['nɑvəlti] *s* (*pl* **-ties**) novedad, innovación; **novelties** bisutería, baratijas
**November** [no'vɛmbər] *s* noviembre *m*
**novice** ['nɑvɪs] *s* novicio
**novocaine** ['novə,ken] *s* novocaína
**now** [nau] *adv* ahora; ya; entonces; **from now on** de ahora en adelante; **how now?** ¿cómo?; **just now** hace un momento; **now and again** o **now and then** de vez en cuando; **now . . . now** ora . . . ora, ya . . . ya; **now that** ya que; **now then** ahora bien || *interj* ¡vamos! || *s* actualidad
**nowadays** ['nau·ə,dez] *adv* hoy en día, hoy día
**no'way'** o **no'ways'** *adv* de ningún modo
**no'where'** *adv* en ninguna parte, a ninguna parte; **nowhere else** en ninguna otra parte
**noxious** ['nɑkʃəs] *adj* nocivo
**nozzle** ['nɑzəl] *s* (*of hose*) lanza; (*of sprinkling can*) rallo, roseta; (*of candlestick*) cubo; (slang) nariz *f*
**N.T.** *abbr* **New Testament**
**nth** [ɛnθ] *adj* $n^{mo}$ (***enésimo***); **to the nth degree** elevado a la potencia **n;** a más no poder
**nuance** [nju'ɑns] o ['nju·ɑns] *s* matiz *m*
**nub** [nʌb] *s* protuberancia; pedazo; (coll) meollo
**nuclear** ['njuklɪ·ər] o ['nuklɪ·ər] *adj* nuclear
**nuclear test ban** *s* proscripción de las pruebas nucleares
**nucle·us** ['njuklɪ·əs] o ['nuklɪ·əs] *s* (*pl* **-i** [,aɪ] o **-uses**) núcleo
**nude** [njud] o [nud] *adj* desnudo || *s* — **in the nude** desnudo; **the nude** el desnudo
**nudge** [nʌdʒ] *s* codazo suave || *tr* dar un codazo suave a, empujar suavemente
**nugget** ['nʌgɪt] *s* pedazo; (*of, e.g., gold*) pepita; preciosidad
**nuisance** ['njusəns] o ['nusəns] *s* molestia, estorbo; persona o cosa fastidiosas
**null** [nʌl] *adj* nulo; **null and void** nulo, írrito, nulo y sin valor
**nulli·fy** ['nʌlɪ,faɪ] *v* (*pret & pp* **-fied**) *tr* anular, invalidar
**nulli·ty** ['nʌlɪti] *s* (*pl* **-ties**) nulidad
**numb** [nʌm] *adj* entumecido || *tr* entumecer
**number** ['nʌmbər] *s* número; **a number of** varios || *tr* numerar; ascender a (*cierto número*); **his days are numbered** tiene sus días contados o sus horas contadas; **to be numbered among** hallarse entre; **to number among** contar entre
**numberless** ['nʌmbərlɪs] *adj* innumerable
**numeral** ['njumərəl] o ['numərəl] *adj* numeral || *s* número
**numerical** [nju'merɪkəl] o [nu'merɪkəl] *adj* numérico
**numerous** ['njumərəs] o ['numərəs] *adj* numeroso
**numskull** ['nʌm,skʌl] *s* (coll) bodoque *m,* mentecato

**nun** [nʌn] *s* monja, religiosa
**nuptial** [ˈnʌpʃəl] *adj* nupcial ‖ **nuptials** *spl* nupcias, bodas
**nurse** [nʌrs] *s* enfermera; (*to suckle a child*) ama de cría, nodriza; (*to take care of a child*) niñera ‖ *tr* cuidar (*a una persona enferma*); amamantar; alimentar; criar; tratar de curarse de (*p.ej., un resfriado*); abrigar (*p.ej., odio*) ‖ *intr* ser enfermera
**nurser•y** [ˈnʌrsəri] *s* (*pl* **-ies**) cuarto de los niños; (*of plants*) criadero, plantel *m*, semillero; (fig) semillero
**nursery•man** [ˈnʌrsərɪmən] *s* (*pl* **-men** [mən]) cultivador *m* de semillero
**nursery rhymes** *spl* versos para niños
**nursery tales** *spl* cuentos para niños
**nursing bottle** *s* biberón *m*
**nursing home** *s* clínica de reposo
**nurture** [ˈnʌrtʃər] *s* alimentación, nutrimento; crianza, educación ‖ *tr* alimentar, nutrir; criar, educar; acariciar (*p.ej., una esperanza*)
**nut** [nʌt] *s* nuez *f*; (*to screw on a bolt*) tuerca; (slang) estrafalario; **a hard nut to crack** (coll) hueso duro de roer
**nut'crack'er** *s* cascanueces *m*
**nutmeg** [ˈnʌtˌmeg] *s* nuez moscada; (*tree*) mirística
**nutriment** [ˈnjutrɪmənt] o [ˈnutrɪmənt] *s* nutrimento
**nutrition** [njuˈtrɪʃən] o [nuˈtrɪʃən] *s* nutrición
**nutritious** [njuˈtrɪʃəs] o [nuˈtrɪʃəs] *adj* nutricioso, nutritivo
**nut'shell'** *s* cáscara de nuez; **in a nutshell** en pocas palabras
**nut•ty** [ˈnʌti] *adj* (*comp* **-tier**; *super* **-tiest**) abundante en nueces; que sabe a nueces; (slang) chiflado, loco; **nutty about** (slang) loco por
**nuzzle** [ˈnʌzəl] *tr* hocicar, hozar ‖ *intr* hocicar; arrimarse cómodamente; arroparse bien
**nylon** [ˈnaɪlɑn] *s* **nilón** *m*; **nylons** medias de nilón
**nymph** [nɪmf] *s* ninfa

## O

**O, o** [o] decimoquinta letra del alfabeto inglés
**O** *interj* ¡oh!; ¡ay!, p.ej., **O, how pretty she is!** ¡Ay qué linda!; **O that . . . !** ¡Ojalá que . . . !
**oaf** [of] *s* zoquete *m*, zamacuco; niño contrahecho
**oak** [ok] *s* roble *m*
**oaken** [ˈokən] *adj* hecho de roble
**oakum** [ˈokəm] *s* estopa, estopa de calafatear
**oar** [or] *s* remo; **to lie o rest on one's oars** aguantar los remos; aflojar en el trabajo ‖ *tr* conducir a remo ‖ *intr* remar, bogar
**oars•man** [ˈorzmən] *s* (*pl* **-men** [mən]) remero
**OAS** [ˈoˈeˈes] *s* (letterword) OEA *f*
**oa•sis** [oˈesɪs] *s* (*pl* **-ses** [siz]) oasis *m*
**oat** [ot] *s* avena; **oats** (*edible grain*) avena; **to feel one's oats** (slang) estar fogoso y brioso; (slang) estar muy pagado de sí mismo; **to sow one's wild oats** correrla, pasar las mocedades
**oath** [oθ] *s* juramento; **on oath** bajo juramento; **to take an oath** prestar juramento
**oat'meal'** *s* harina de avena; gachas de avena
**ob.** *abbr* **obiit** (Lat) **died**
**obbligato** [ˌɑblɪˈgɑto] *adj & s* obligado
**obduracy** [ˈɑbdjərəsi] *s* obduración
**obdurate** [ˈɑbdjərɪt] *adj* obstinado, terco; empedernido
**obedience** [oˈbidɪ·əns] *s* obediencia
**obedient** [oˈbidɪ·ənt] *adj* obediente
**obeisance** [oˈbesəns] u [oˈbisəns] *s* saludo respetuoso; homenaje *m*, respeto
**obelisk** [ˈɑbəlɪsk] *s* obelisco
**obese** [oˈbis] *adj* obeso
**obesity** [oˈbisɪti] *s* obesidad
**obey** [oˈbe] *tr & intr* obedecer
**obfuscate** [ɑbˈfʌsket] o [ˈɑbfəsˌket] *tr* ofuscar
**obituar•y** [oˈbɪtʃuˌeri] *adj* necrológico ‖ *s* (*pl* **-ies**) necrología
**obj.** *abbr* **object, objection, objective**
**object** [ˈɑbdʒɪkt] *s* objeto ‖ [ɑbˈdʒekt] *tr* objetar ‖ *intr* hacer objeciones
**objection** [ɑbˈdʒekʃən] *s* reparo, objeción; **to have no objections to make** no tener nada que objetar
**objectionable** [ɑbˈdʒekʃənəbəl] *adj* desagradable, reprensible; (*causing disapproval*) objetable
**objective** [ɑbˈdʒektɪv] *adj & s* objetivo
**obl.** *abbr* **oblique, oblong**
**obligate** [ˈɑblɪˌget] *tr* obligar
**obligation** [ˌɑblɪˈgeʃən] *s* obligación
**oblige** [əˈblaɪdʒ] *tr* obligar; complacer; **much obliged** muchas gracias
**obliging** [əˈblaɪdʒɪŋ] *adj* complaciente, condescendiente, servicial
**oblique** [əˈblik] *adj* oblicuo; indirecto, evasivo
**obliterate** [əˈblɪtəˌret] *tr* borrar; arrasar, destruir
**oblivion** [əˈblɪvɪ·ən] *s* olvido
**oblivious** [əˈblɪvɪ·əs] *adj* olvidadizo
**oblong** [ˈɑblɔŋ] o [ˈɑblɑŋ] *adj* oblongo
**obnoxious** [əbˈnɑkʃəs] *adj* detestable, ofensivo
**oboe** [ˈobo] *s* oboe *m*
**oboist** [ˈobo·ɪst] *s* oboísta *mf*
**obs.** *abbr* **obsolete**
**obscene** [ɑbˈsin] *adj* obsceno

**obsceni•ty** [ɑb'senɪti] o [ɑb'sinɪti] *s* (*pl* **-ties**) obscenidad
**obscure** [əb'skjʊr] *adj* obscuro; (*vowel*) relajado, neutro
**obscuri•ty** [əb'skjʊrɪti] *s* (*pl* **-ties**) obscuridad
**obsequies** ['ɑbsɪkwiz] *spl* exequias
**obsequious** [əb'sikwɪ•əs] *adj* obsequioso, servil, rastrero
**observance** [əb'zʌrvəns] *s* observancia; ceremonia, rito
**observant** [əb'zʌrvənt] *adj* observador
**observation** [,ɑbzər'veʃən] *s* observación; observancia
**observato•ry** [əb'zʌrvə,tori] *s* (*pl* **-ries**) observatorio
**observe** [əb'zʌrv] *tr* observar; (*a holiday; silence*) guardar
**observer** [əb'zʌrvər] *s* observador *m*
**obsess** [əb'sɛs] *tr* obsesionar
**obsession** [əb'sɛʃən] *s* obsesión
**obsolescent** [,ɑbsə'lesənt] *adj* arcaizante
**obsolete** ['ɑbsə,lit] *adj* desusado, caído en desuso
**obstacle** ['ɑbstəkəl] *s* obstáculo
**obstetrical** [ɑb'stetrɪkəl] *adj* obstétrico
**obstetrics** [ɑb'stetrɪks] *ssg* obstetricia
**obstina•cy** ['ɑbstɪnəsi] *s* (*pl* **-cies**) obstinación
**obstinate** ['ɑbstɪnɪt] *adj* obstinado
**obstruct** [əb'strʌkt] *tr* obstruir
**obstruction** [əb'strʌkʃən] *s* obstrucción
**obtain** [əb'ten] *tr* obtener || *intr* existir, prevalecer
**obtrusive** [əb'trusɪv] *adj* entremetido, intruso
**obtuse** [əb'tjus] o [əb'tus] *adj* obtuso
**obviate** ['ɑbvɪ,et] *tr* obviar
**obvious** ['ɑbvɪ•əs] *adj* obvio
**occasion** [ə'keʒən] *s* ocasión; **to improve the occasion** aprovechar la ocasión
**occasional** [ə'keʒənəl] *adj* raro, poco frecuente; alguno que otro; de circunstancia
**occasionally** [ə'keʒənəli] *adv* ocasionalmente, de vez en cuando
**occident** ['ɑksɪdənt] *s* occidente *m*
**occidental** [,ɑksɪ'dentəl] *adj* occidental
**occlusive** [ə'klusɪv] *adj* oclusivo || *s* oclusiva
**occult** [ə'kʌlt] o ['ɑkʌlt] *adj* oculto
**occupancy** ['ɑkjəpənsi] *s* ocupación
**occupant** ['ɑkjəpənt] *s* ocupante *mf;* inquilino
**occupation** [,ɑkjə'peʃən] *s* ocupación
**occu•py** ['ɑkjə,paɪ] *v* (*pret & pp* **-pied**) *tr* ocupar; habitar
**oc•cur** [ə'kʌr] *v* (*pret & pp* **-curred;** *ger* **-curring**) *intr* ocurrir, acontecer, suceder; encontrarse; (*to come to mind*) ocurrir
**occurrence** [ə'kʌrəns] *s* acontecimiento; caso, aparición
**ocean** ['oʃən] *s* océano
**oceanic** [,oʃɪ'ænɪk] *adj* oceánico
**ocean liner** *s* buque transoceánico
**o'clock** [ə'klɑk] *adv* por el reloj; **it is one o'clock** es la una; **it is two o'clock** son las dos; **what o'clock is it?** ¿qué hora es?
**Oct.** *abbr* **October**
**octave** ['ɑktɪv] o ['ɑktev] *s* octava
**October** [ɑk'tobər] *s* octubre *m*
**octo•pus** ['ɑktəpəs] *s* (*pl* **-puses** o **-pi** [,paɪ]) pulpo
**octoroon** [,ɑktə'run] *s* octavo
**ocular** ['ɑkjələr] *adj & s* ocular *m*
**oculist** ['ɑkjəlɪst] *s* oculista *mf*
**O.D.** *abbr* **officer of the day, olive drab**
**odd** [ɑd] *adj* suelto; (*number*) impar; (*that doesn't match*) dispar; libre, de ocio; sobrante; extraño, raro, singular; y pico, y tantos, p.ej., **two hundred odd** doscientos y pico || **odds** *ssg* o *spl* (*in betting*) ventaja; apuesta desigual; puntos de ventaja; **at odds** de monos, riñendo; **by all odds** muy probablemente, sin duda alguna; **it makes no odds** lo mismo da; **the odds are** lo probable es; la ventaja es de; **to be at odds** estar de punta, estar encontrados; **to set at odds** enemistar, malquistar
**oddi•ty** ['ɑdɪti] *s* (*pl* **-ties**) rareza, cosa rara
**odd jobs** *spl* pequeñas tareas
**odd lot** *s* lote *m* inferior al centenar
**odds and ends** *spl* pedacitos varios, cajón *m* de sastre
**ode** [od] *s* oda
**odious** ['odɪ•əs] *adj* odioso, abominable
**odor** ['odər] *s* olor *m;* **to be in bad odor** tener mala fama
**odorless** ['odərlɪs] *adj* inodoro
**odorous** ['odərəs] *adj* oloroso
**Odysseus** [o'dɪsjus] u [o'dɪsɪ•əs] *s* Odiseo
**Odyssey** ['ɑdɪsi] *s* Odisea
**Oedipus** ['edɪpəs] o ['idɪpəs] *s* Edipo
**of** [ɑv] o [əv] *prep* de, p.ej., **the top of the mountain** la cima de la montaña; a: **to smell of** oler a; con: **to dream of** soñar con; en: **to think of** pensar en; menos: **a quarter of two** las dos menos un cuarto
**off.** *abbr* **office, officer, official**
**off** [ɔf] o [ɑf] *adj* malo, p.ej., **off day** día malo; (*account, sum*) errado; más distante; libre; sin trabajo; quitado; apagado; (*electric current*) cortado; de descuento, de rebaja; de la parte del mar; (*season*) muerto || *adv* fuera, a distancia, lejos; allá; **off of** (coll) de; (coll) a expensas de; **to be off** ponerse en marcha || *prep* de, desde; al lado de, a nivel de; fuera de; libre de; (naut) a la altura de
**offal** ['ɑfəl] u ['ɔfəl] *s* (*of butchered meat*) carniza; basura, desperdicios
**off and on** *adv* unas veces sí y otras no
**off'beat'** *adj* (slang) insólito, chocante, original
**off'chance'** *s* posibilidad poco probable
**off'-col'or** *adj* descolorido; indispuesto; (*indecent, risqué*) colorado, subido de color
**offend** [ə'fend] *tr & intr* ofender
**offender** [ə'fendər] *s* ofensor *m*

**offense** [ə'fɛns] *s* ofensa; **to take offense (at)** ofenderse (de)
**offensive** [ə'fɛnsɪv] *adj* ofensivo ‖ *f* ofensiva
**offer** ['ɔfər] o ['ɑfər] *s* ofrecimiento, oferta ‖ *tr* ofrecer; rezar (*oraciones*); oponer (*resistencia*)
**offering** ['ɔfərɪŋ] o ['ɑfərɪŋ] *s* ofrecimiento; (*gift, present*) oferta; (*presentation in worship*) ofrenda
**off'hand'** *adj* hecho de improviso; brusco, desenvuelto ‖ *adv* de improviso, súbitamente; bruscamente
**office** ['ɔfɪs] o ['ɑfɪs] *s* oficina, despacho; función, oficio; cargo, ministerio; (*of a lawyer*) bufete *m;* (*of a doctor*) consultorio
**office boy** *s* mandadero
**office desk** *s* escritorio ministro
**of'fice•hold'er** *s* funcionario, burócrata *m*
**office hours** *spl* horas de oficina; (*of a doctor*) horas de consultorio
**officer** ['ɔfɪsər] o ['ɑfɪsər] *s* jefe *m,* director *m;* (*of army, an order, a society, etc.*) oficial *m;* agente *m* de policía
**office seeker** ['sikər] *s* aspirante *m,* pretendiente *m*
**office supplies** *spl* suministros para oficinas
**official** [ə'fɪʃəl] *adj* oficial ‖ *s* jefe *m,* director *m;* (*of a society*) dignatario
**officiate** [ə'fɪʃɪ,et] *intr* oficiar
**officious** [ə'fɪʃəs] *adj* oficioso
**off'-peak' heater** *s* (elec) termos *m* de acumulación
**off-peak load** *s* (elec) carga de las horas de valle
**off'print'** *s* sobretiro
**off'set'** *s* compensación; (typ) offset *m* ‖ **off'set'** *v* (*pret & pp* **-set;** *ger* **-setting**) *tr* compensar; imprimir por offset
**off'shoot'** *s* (*of plant*) retoño, renuevo; (*of a family or race*) descendiente *mf;* (*branch*) ramal *m;* consecuencia
**off'shore'** *adj* (*wind*) terral; (*fishing*) de bajura; (*said of islands*) costero ‖ *adv* a lo largo
**off'spring'** *s* descendencia, sucesión; hijo, hijos
**off'-stage'** *adj* de entre bastidores
**off'-the-rec'ord** *adj* extraoficial, confidencial
**often** ['ɔfən] o ['ɑfən] *adv* a menudo, muchas veces; **how often?** ¿cuántas veces?; **not often** pocas veces
**ogive** ['odʒaɪv] u [o'dʒaɪv] *s* ojiva
**ogle** ['ogəl] *tr & intr* ojear; mirar amorosamente
**ogre** ['ogər] *s* ogro
**ohm** [om] *s* ohmio
**oil** [ɔɪl] *adj* (*burner; field; well*) de petróleo; (*pump; stove*) de aceite; (*company; tanker*) petrolero; (*land*) petrolífero ‖ *s* aceite *m;* (*consecrated oil; painting*) óleo; **to burn the midnight oil** quemarse las cejas; **to pour oil on troubled waters** mojar la pólvora; **to strike oil** encontrar una capa de petróleo; (fig) enriquecerse de súbito ‖ *tr* aceitar; lubricar; lisonjear; (*to bribe*) untar ‖ *intr* proveerse de petróleo (*un buque*)
**oil'can'** *s* aceitera
**oil'cloth'** *s* encerado, hule *m*
**oil gauge** indicador *m* del nivel de aceite
**oil pan** *s* colector *m* de aceite
**oil tanker** *s* petrolero
**oil•y** ['ɔɪli] *adj* (*comp* **-ier;** *super* **-iest**) aceitoso; liso, resbaladizo; zalamero
**ointment** ['ɔɪntmənt] *s* ungüento
**O.K.** ['o'ke] *adj* (coll) aprobado, conforme ‖ *adv* (coll) muy bien, está bien ‖ *s* (coll) aprobación ‖ *v* (*pret & pp* **O.K.'d;** *ger* **O.K.'ing**) *tr* (coll) aprobar
**okra** ['okrə] *s* quingombó *m*
**old** [old] *adj* viejo; antiguo; (*wine*) añejo; **how old is . . . ?** ¿cuántos años tiene . . . ?; **of old** de antaño, antiguamente; **to be . . . years old** tener . . . años
**old age** *s* ancianidad, vejez *f;* **to die of old age** morir de viejo
**old boy** *s* viejo; graduado; **the Old Boy** (slang) el diablo
**Old Castile** *s* Castilla la Vieja
**old-clothes•man** ['old'kloðz,mæn] *s* (*pl* **-men** [,mɛn]) ropavejero
**old country** *s* madre patria
**old-fashioned** ['old'fæʃənd] *adj* chapado a la antigua; anticuado, fuera de moda
**old fo•gey** u **old fo•gy** ['fogi] *s* (*pl* **-gies**) persona un poco ridícula por sus ideas o costumbres atrasadas
**Old Glory** *s* la bandera de los Estados Unidos
**Old Guard** *s* (U.S.A.) bando conservador del partido republicano
**old hand** *s* practicón *m,* veterano
**old maid** *s* solterona
**old master** *s* (paint) gran maestro; obra de un gran maestro
**old moon** *s* luna menguante
**old salt** *s* lobo de mar
**old school** *s* gente chapada a la antigua
**old'-time'** *adj* del tiempo viejo
**old-timer** ['old'taɪmər] *s* (coll) antiguo residente, veterano; (coll) persona chapada a la antigua
**old wives' tale** *s* cuento de viejas
**old'-world'** *adj* del Viejo Mundo
**oleander** [,olɪ'ændər] *s* adelfa
**oligar•chy** ['ɑlɪ,gɑrki] *s* (*pl* **-chies**) oligarquía
**olive** ['ɑlɪv] *adj* aceitunado ‖ *s* aceituna
**olive branch** *s* ramo de olivo; (*peace*) oliva; hijo, vástago
**olive grove** *s* olivar *m*
**olive oil** *s* aceite *m,* aceite de oliva
**olive tree** *s* aceituno, olivo
**Olympiad** [o'lɪmpɪ,æd] *s* Olimpíada
**Olympian** [o'lɪmpɪ·ən] *adj* olímpico ‖ *s* dios griego
**Olympic** [o'lɪmpɪk] *adj* olímpico
**omelet** u **omelette** ['ɑmələt] o ['ɑmlɪt] *s* tortilla (de huevos)
**omen** ['omən] *s* agüero
**ominous** ['ɑmɪnəs] *adj* ominoso
**omission** [o'mɪʃən] *s* omisión

**omit** [o'mɪt] *v* (*pret & pp* **omitted;** *ger* **omitting**) *tr* omitir
**omnibus** ['ɑmnɪ,bʌs] o ['ɑmnɪbəs] *adj* general; (*volume*) colecticio || *s* ómnibus *m*
**omnipotent** [ɑm'nɪpətənt] *adj* omnipotente
**omniscient** [ɑm'nɪʃənt] *adj* omnisciente
**omnivorous** [ɑm'nɪvərəs] *adj* omnívoro
**on** [ɑn] u [ɔn] *adj* puesto, p.ej., **with his hat on** con el sombrero puesto; principiando; en funcionamiento; encendido; conectado; **the deal is on** ya está concertado el trato; **the game is on** ya están jugando; **the race is on** allá van los corredores; **what is on at the theater this evening?** ¿qué representan esta noche? || *adv* adelante; encima; **and so on** y así sucesivamente; **come on!** ¡anda, anda!; **farther on** más allá, más adelante; **later on** más tarde, después; **to be on to a person** (coll) conocerle a uno el juego; **to have on** tener puesto; **to . . . on** seguir + *ger*, **he played on** siguió tocando || *prep* en, sobre, encima de; a, p.ej., **on foot** a pie; **on my arrival** a mi llegada; bajo, p.ej., **on my responsibility** bajo mi responsabilidad; contra, p.ej., **an attack on liberty** un ataque contra la libertad; de, p.ej., **on good authority** de buena tinta; **on a journey** de viaje; hacia, p.ej., **to march on the capital** marchar hacia la capital; por, p.ej., **on all sides** por todos lados; tras, p.ej., **defeat on defeat** derrota tras derrota; **on** + *ger* al + *inf*, p.ej., **on arriving** al llegar
**on and on** *adv* continuamente, sin cesar, sin parar
**once** [wʌns] *adv* una vez; antes, p.ej., **once so happy** antes tan feliz; alguna vez, p.ej., **if this once becomes known** si esto llega a saberse alguna vez; **all at once** de súbito, de repente; **at once** en seguida; a la vez, en el mismo momento; **for once** una vez por lo menos; **once and again** repetidas veces; **once in a blue moon** cada muerte de obispo; **once in a while** de vez en cuando; **once more** otra vez; una vez más; **once upon a time there was** érase una vez, érase que se era || *conj* una vez que || *s* una vez; vez, p.ej., **this once** esta vez
**once'-o'ver** *s* (slang) examen rápido; **to give a thing the once-over** (coll) examinar una cosa superficialmente
**one** [wʌn] *adj* un, uno; un tal, p.ej., **one Smith** un tal Smith; único, p.ej., **one price** precio único || *pron* uno, p.ej., **one does not know what to do here** uno no sabe qué hacer aquí; se, p.ej., **how does one go to the station?** ¿cómo se va a la estación?; **I for one** yo por lo menos; **it's all one and the same to me** me es igual; **my little one** mi chiquito; **of one another** el uno del otro, los unos de los otros, p.ej., **we took leave of one another** nos despedimos el uno del otro; **one and all** todos; **one another** se, p.ej., **they greeted one another** se saludaron; uno a otro, unos a otros, p.ej., **they looked at one another** se miraron uno a otro; **one by one** uno a uno; **one o'clock** la una; **one or two** unos pocos; **one's** su, el . . . de uno; **the blue book and the red one** el libro azul y el rojo; **the one and only** el único; **the one that** el que, la que; **this one** éste; **that one** ése, aquél; **to make one** unir; casar || *s* uno
**one'-horse'** *adj* de un solo caballo, tirado por un solo caballo; (coll) insignificante, de poca monta
**onerous** ['ɑnərəs] *adj* oneroso
**one'self'** *pron* uno mismo; sí, sí mismo; se; **to be oneself** tener dominio de sí mismo; conducirse con naturalidad
**one-sided** ['wʌn'saɪdɪd] *adj* de un solo lado; injusto, parcial; desigual; unilateral
**one'-track'** *adj* de carril único; (coll) con un solo interés
**one'-way'** *adj* de una sola dirección, de dirección única; (*ticket*) sencillo, de ida
**onion** ['ʌnjən] *s* cebolla
**on'ion•skin'** *s* papel *m* de seda, papel cebolla
**on'look'er** *s* mirón *m*, espectador *m*
**only** ['onlɪ] *adj* solo, único || *adv* solamente, sólo, únicamente; no . . . más que; **not only . . . but also** no sólo . . . sino también || *conj* sólo que, pero
**on'set'** *s* arremetida, embestida; (*of an illness*) principio
**onward** ['ɑnwərd] u **onwards** ['ɑnwərdz] *adv* adelante, hacia adelante
**onyx** ['ɑnɪks] *s* ónice *m* u ónix *m*
**ooze** [uz] *s* chorro suave; cieno, limo, lama || *tr* rezumar || *intr* rezumar, rezumarse; manar suavemente (*p.ej., la sangre de una herida*); agotarse poco a poco
**op.** *abbr* **opera, operation, opus, opposite**
**opal** ['opəl] *s* ópalo
**opaque** [o'pek] *adj* opaco; (*writer's style*) obscuro; estúpido
**open** ['opən] *adj* abierto; descubierto, destapado; sin tejado; vacante; (*hour*) libre; discutible, pendiente; (*hand*) liberal; (*hunting season*) legal; **to break** o **to crack open** abrir con violencia, abrir por la fuerza; **to throw open** abrir de par en par || *s* abertura; (*in the woods*) claro; **in the open** al aire libre; a campo raso; en alta mar; abiertamente || *tr* abrir; desbullar (*una ostra*) || *intr* abrir; abrirse; estrenarse (*un drama*); **to open into** desembocar en; **to open on** dar a; **to open up** descubrirse; descubrir el pecho
**o'pen-air'** *adj* al aire libre, a cielo abierto
**open-eyed** ['opən,aɪd] *adj* alerta, vigi-

lante; con ojos asombrados; hecho con los ojos abiertos
**open-handed** ['opən'hændɪd] *adj* maniabierto, liberal
**open-hearted** ['opən'hɑrtɪd] *adj* franco, sincero
**open house** *s* coliche *m;* **to keep open house** recibir a todos, gustar de tener siempre convidados en casa
**opening** ['opənɪŋ] *s* abertura; (*of, e.g., school*) apertura; (*in the woods*) claro; (*vacancy*) hueco, vacante *f;* (*chance to say something*) ocasión
**opening night** *s* noche *f* de estreno
**opening number** *s* primer número
**opening price** *s* primer curso, precio de apertura
**open-minded** ['opən'maɪndɪd] *adj* receptivo, razonable, imparcial
**open secret** *s* secreto a voces
**open shop** *s* taller franco
**o'pen•work'** *s* calado
**opera** ['ɑpərə] *s* ópera
**opera glasses** *spl* gemelos de teatro
**opera hat** *s* clac *m,* sombrero de muelles
**opera house** *s* teatro de la ópera
**operate** ['ɑpə,ret] *tr* hacer funcionar; dirigir, manejar; explotar || *intr* funcionar; operar; **to operate on** operar (*p.ej., una hernia; a un niño*)
**operatic** [,ɑpə'rætɪk] *adj* operístico
**operating expenses** *spl* gastos de explotación
**operating room** *s* quirófano
**operating table** *s* mesa operatoria
**operation** [,ɑpə'reʃən] *s* operación; funcionamiento; explotación
**operator** ['ɑpə,retər] *s* operador *m,* maquinista *m;* (com) empresario; (coll) corredor *m* de bolsa; (surg, telp) operador *m*
**operetta** [,ɑpə'rɛtə] *s* opereta
**opiate** ['opɪ•ɪt] u ['opɪ,et] *adj & s* opiato
**opinion** [ə'pɪnjən] *s* opinión; **in my opinion** a mi parecer; **to have a high opinion of** tener buen concepto de
**opinionated** [ə'pɪnjə,netɪd] *adj* porfiado en su parecer, dogmático
**opium** ['opɪ•əm] *s* opio
**opium den** *s* fumadero de opio
**opossum** [ə'pɑsəm] *s* zarigüeya
**opponent** [ə'ponənt] *s* contrario
**opportune** [,ɑpər'tjun] o [,ɑpər'tun] *adj* oportuno
**opportunist** [,ɑpər'tjunɪst] o [,ɑpər'tunɪst] *s* oportunista *mf*
**opportuni•ty** [,ɑpər'tjunɪti] o [,ɑper'tunɪti] *s* (*pl* **-ties**) oportunidad, ocasión
**oppose** [ə'poz] *tr* oponerse a
**opposite** ['ɑpəsɪt] *adj* opuesto; de enfrente, p.ej., **the house opposite** la casa de enfrente || *prep* enfrente de || *s* contrario
**opposite number** *s* igual *mf,* doble *mf*
**opposition** [,ɑpə'zɪʃən] *s* oposición
**oppress** [ə'prɛs] *tr* oprimir
**oppression** [ə'prɛʃən] *s* opresión
**oppressive** [ə'prɛsɪv] *adj* opresivo; sofocante, bochornoso
**opprobrious** [ə'probrɪ•əs] *adj* oprobioso
**opprobrium** [ə'probrɪ•əm] *s* oprobio
**optic** ['ɑptɪk] *adj* óptico || *s* (coll) ojo; **optics** *ssg* óptica
**optical** ['ɑptɪkəl] *adj* óptico
**optician** [ɑp'tɪʃən] *s* óptico
**optimism** ['ɑptɪ,mɪzəm] *s* optimismo
**optimist** ['ɑptɪmɪst] *s* optimista *mf*
**optimistic** [,ɑptɪ'mɪstɪk] *adj* optimístico
**option** ['ɑpʃən] *s* opción
**optional** ['ɑpʃənəl] *adj* facultativo, potestativo
**optometrist** [ɑp'tɑmɪtrɪst] *s* optometrista *mf*
**opulent** ['ɑpjələnt] *adj* opulento
**or** [ɔr] *conj* o, u
**oracle** ['ɑrəkəl] u ['ɔrəkəl] *s* oráculo
**oracular** [o'rækjələr] *adj* sentencioso; ambiguo, misterioso; fatídico; sabio
**oral** ['orəl] *adj* oral
**orange** ['ɑrɪndʒ] u ['ɔrɪndʒ] *adj* anaranjado || *s* naranja
**orangeade** [,ɑrɪndʒ'ed] u [,ɔrɪndʒ'ed] *s* naranjada
**orange blossom** *s* azahar *m*
**orange grove** *s* naranjal *m*
**orange juice** *s* zumo de naranja
**orange squeezer** *s* exprimidera de naranjas
**orange tree** *s* naranjo
**orang-outang** [o'ræŋu,tæŋ] *s* orangután *m*
**oration** [o'reʃən] *s* oración, discurso
**orator** ['ɑrətər] u ['ɔrətər] *s* orador *m*
**oratorical** [,ɑrə'tɑrɪkəl] u [,ɔrə'tɔrɪkəl] *adj* oratorio
**oratori•o** [,ɑrə'torɪ,o] u [,ɔrə'torɪ,o] *s* (*pl* **-os**) oratorio
**orato•ry** ['ɑrə,tori] u ['ɔrə,tori] *s* (*pl* **-ries**) (*art of public speaking*) oratoria; (*small chapel*) oratorio
**orb** [ɔrb] *s* orbe *m*
**orbit** ['ɔrbɪt] *s* órbita; **to go into orbit** entrar en órbita || *tr* poner en órbita; moverse en órbita alrededor de || *intr* moverse en órbita
**orchard** ['ɔrtʃərd] *s* huerto
**orchestra** ['ɔrkɪstrə] *s* orquesta; (*parquet*) platea
**orchestrate** ['ɔrkɪs,tret] *tr* orquestar
**orchid** ['ɔrkɪd] *s* orquídea
**ordain** [ɔr'den] *tr* (eccl) ordenar; destinar; mandar
**ordeal** [ɔr'dil] u [ɔr'di•əl] *s* prueba rigurosa o penosa; (hist) juicio de Dios
**order** ['ɔrdər] *s* (*way one thing follows another; formal or methodical arrangement; peace, quiet; class, category*) orden *m;* (*command; honor society; monastic brotherhood; fraternal organization*) orden *f;* tarea, p.ej., **a big order** una tarea peliaguda; (com) pedido; (com) giro, libranza; (*formation*) (mil) orden *m;* (*command*) (mil) orden *f;* **in order that** para que, a fin de que; **in order to** + *inf* para + *inf,* a fin de + *inf;* **to get out of order** descomponerse; **to give an order** dar una orden; (com) hacer un pedido || *tr* ordenar;

mandar; encargar, pedir; mandar hacer; **to order around** ser muy mandón con; **to order someone away** mandar a uno que se marche
**order blank** *s* hoja de pedidos
**order•ly** [ˈɔrdərli] *adj* ordenado, gobernoso; tranquilo, obediente ‖ *s* (*pl* **-lies**) asistente *m* en un hospital; (mil) ordenanza *m*
**ordinal** [ˈɔrdɪnəl] *adj & s* ordinal *m*
**ordinance** [ˈɔrdɪnəns] *s* ordenanza
**ordinary** [ˈɔrdɪˌneri] *adj* ordinario
**ordnance** [ˈɔrdnəns] *s* artillería, cañones *mpl;* pertrechos de guerra
**ore** [or] *s* mena, mineral metalífero
**organ** [ˈɔrgən] *s* órgano
**organ•dy** [ˈɔrgəndi] *s* (*pl* **-dies**) organdí *m*
**or′gan-grind′er** *s* organillero
**organic** [ɔrˈgænɪk] *adj* orgánico
**organism** [ˈɔrgəˌnɪzəm] *s* organismo
**organist** [ˈɔrgənɪst] *s* organista *mf*
**organize** [ˈɔrgəˌnaɪz] *tr* organizar
**organ loft** *s* tribuna del órgano
**or•gy** [ˈɔrdʒi] *s* (*pl* **-gies**) orgía
**orient** [ˈorɪ·ənt] *s* oriente *m* ‖ **Orient** *s* oriente ‖ **orient** [ˈorɪˌɛnt] *tr* orientar
**oriental** [ˌorɪˈɛntəl] *adj* oriental
**orifice** [ˈɑrɪfɪs] u [ˈɔrɪfɪs] *s* orificio
**origin** [ˈɑrɪdʒɪn] u [ˈɔrɪdʒɪn] *s* origen *m*
**original** [əˈrɪdʒɪnəl] *adj & s* original *m*
**originate** [əˈrɪdʒɪˌnet] *tr* originar ‖ *intr* originarse
**oriole** [ˈorɪˌol] *s* oropéndola
**Orkney Islands** [ˈɔrkni] *spl* Órcadas
**ormolu** [ˈɔrməˌlu] *s* (*gold powder used in gilding*) oro molido; (*alloy of zinc and copper*) similor m; bronce dorado
**ornament** [ˈɔrnəmənt] *s* ornamento ‖ [ˈɔrnəˌmɛnt] *tr* ornamentar
**ornate** [ɔrˈnet] u [ˈɔrnet] *adj* muy ornado; (*style*) florido
**orphan** [ˈɔrfən] *adj & s* huérfano ‖ *tr* dejar huérfano
**orphanage** [ˈɔrfənɪdʒ] *s* (*institution*) orfanato; (*state, condition*) orfandad
**orphan asylum** *s* asilo de huérfanos
**Orpheus** [ˈɔrfjus] u [ˈɔrfɪ·əs] *s* Orfeo
**orthodox** [ˈɔrθəˌdɑks] *adj* ortodoxo
**orthogra•phy** [ɔrˈθɑgrəfi] *s* (*pl* **-phies**) ortografía
**oscillate** [ˈɑsɪˌlet] *intr* oscilar
**osier** [ˈoʒər] *s* mimbre *m & f;* sauce mimbrero
**ossi•fy** [ˈɑsɪˌfaɪ] *v* (*pret & pp* **-fied**) *tr* osificar ‖ *intr* osificarse
**ostensible** [ɑsˈtɛnsɪbəl] *adj* aparente, pretendido, supuesto
**ostentatious** [ˌɑstɛnˈteʃəs] *adj* (*pretentious*) ostentativo; (*showy*) ostentoso
**osteopath** [ˈɑstɪ·əˌpæθ] *s* osteópata *mf*
**osteopathy** [ˌɑstɪˈɑpəθi] *s* osteopatía
**ostracism** [ˈɑstrəˌsɪzəm] *s* ostracismo
**ostrich** [ˈɑstrɪtʃ] *s* avestruz *m*
**O.T.** *abbr* **Old Testament**
**other** [ˈʌðər] *adj & pron indef* otro ‖ *adv* — **other than** de otra manera que
**otherwise** [ˈʌðərˌwaɪz] *adv* otramente, de otra manera; en otras circunstancias; fuera de eso; si no, de otro modo
**otter** [ˈɑtər] *s* nutria
**ottoman** [ˈɑtəmən] *s* (*corded fabric*) otomán *m;* (*sofa*) otomana; escañuelo con cojín ‖ **Ottoman** *adj & s* otomano
**ouch** [aʊtʃ] *interj* ¡ax!
**ought** [ɔt] *s* alguna cosa; cero; **for ought I know** por lo que yo sepa ‖ *v aux* se emplea para formar el modo potencial, p.ej., **he ought to go at once** debiera salir en seguida
**ounce** [aʊns] *s* onza
**our** [aʊr] *adj poss* nuestro
**ours** [aʊrz] *pron poss* el nuestro; nuestro
**ourselves** [aʊrˈsɛlvz] *pron pers* nosotros mismos; nos, p.ej., **we enjoyed ourselves** nos divertimos
**oust** [aʊst] *tr* echar fuera, desposeer; desahuciar (*al inquilino*)
**out** [aʊt] *adj* ausente; apagado; exterior; divulgado; publicado; (*size*) poco común ‖ *adv* afuera, fuera; al aire libre; hasta el fin; **out for** buscando; **out of** de; entre; de entre; fuera de; más allá de; (*kindness, fear, etc.*) por; (*money*) sin; (*a suit of cards*) fallo a; sobre, p.ej., **in nine out of ten cases** en nueve casos sobre diez; **out to** + *inf* esforzándose por + *inf* ‖ *prep* por; allá en ‖ *interj* ¡fuera de aquí! ‖ *s* cesante *mf;* **to be at outs** u **on the outs** estar de monos
**out and away** *adv* con mucho
**out′-and-out′** *adj* perfecto, verdadero, rematado ‖ *adv* completamente
**out′-and-out′er** *s* intransigente *mf;* extremista *mf*
**out•bid′** *v* (*pret* **-bid;** *pp* **-bid** o **-bidden;** *ger* **-bidding**) *tr* pujar más que (*otra persona*); (bridge) sobrepasar
**out′board′ motor** *s* motor *m* fuera de borda
**out′break′** *s* tumulto, motín *m;* (*of anger*) arranque *m;* (*of war*) estallido; (*of an epidemic*) brote *m*
**out′build′ing** *s* dependencia, edificio accesorio
**out′burst′** *s* explosión, arranque *m;* **outburst of laughter** carcajada
**out′cast′** *s* proscripto, paria *mf;* vagabundo
**out′come′** *s* resultado
**out′cry′** *s* (*pl* **-cries**) grito; gritería, clamoreo
**out•dat′ed** *adj* fuera de moda, anticuado
**out•do′** *v* (*pret* **-did;** *pp* **-done**) *tr* exceder; **to outdo oneself** excederse a sí mismo
**out′door′** *adj* al aire libre
**out′doors′** *adv* al aire libre, fuera de casa ‖ *s* aire *m* libre, campo raso
**outer space** [ˈaʊtər] *s* espacio exterior
**out′field′** *s* (baseball) jardín *m*
**out′field′er** *s* (baseball) jardinero
**out′fit** *s* equipo; traje *m;* juego de herramientas; (*of soldiers*) cuerpo; (*of a bride*) ajuar *m;* (com) compañía ‖

*v* (*pret & pp* **-fitted;** *ger* **-fitting**) *tr* equipar
**out'go'ing** *adj* de salida; cesante; (*tide*) descendente; (*nature, character*) exteriorista || *s* salida
**out·grow'** *v* (*pret* **-grew;** *pp* **-grown**) *tr* crecer más que; ser ya grande para; ser ya viejo para; ser ya más apto que; dejar (*las cosas de los niños; a los amigos de la niñez, etc.*) || *intr* extenderse
**out'growth'** *s* excrecencia, bulto; (*of leaves in springtime*) nacimiento; consecuencia, resultado
**outing** ['autɪŋ] *s* jira, excursión al campo
**outlandish** [aut'lændɪʃ] *adj* estrafalario; de aspecto extranjero; de acento extranjero
**out·last'** *tr* durar más que; sobrevivir a
**out'law'** *s* forajido, bandido; prófugo, proscrito || *tr* proscribir; declarar ilegal
**out'lay'** *s* desembolso || **out·lay'** *v* (*pret & pp* **-laid**) *tr* desembolsar
**out'let** *s* salida; desaguadero; orificio de salida; (elec) caja de enchufe; (*tap*) (elec) toma-corriente *m*
**out'line'** *s* contorno; trazado; esquema *m;* esbozo, bosquejo; compendio || *tr* contornar; trazar; trazar el esquema de; esbozar, bosquejar; compendiar
**out·live'** *tr* sobrevivir a; durar más que
**out'look'** *s* perspectiva; expectativa; concepto de la vida, punto de vista; atalaya
**out'ly'ing** *adj* remoto, circundante, de las afueras
**out·mod'ed** *adj* fuera de moda
**out·num'ber** *tr* exceder en número, ser más numeroso que
**out'-of-date'** *adj* fuera de moda, anticuado
**out'-of-door'** *adj* al aire libre
**out'-of-doors'** *adj* al aire libre || *adv* al aire libre, fuera de casa || *s* aire *m* libre, campo raso
**out'-of-print'** *adj* agotado
**out'-of-the-way'** *adj* apartado, remoto; poco usual, poco común
**out of tune** *adj* desafinado || *adv* desafinadamente
**out of work** *adj* desempleado, sin trabajo
**out'pa'tient** *s* paciente *mf* de consulta externa
**out'post'** *s* avanzada
**out'put'** *s* rendimiento; (elec) salida; (mech) rendimiento de trabajo, efecto útil
**out'rage** *s* atrocidad; ultraje *m* || *tr* maltratar; ultrajar; escandalizar
**outrageous** [aut'redʒəs] *adj* (*grossly offensive*) ultrajoso; (*shocking, fierce*) atroz; (*extreme*) extravagante
**out·rank'** *tr* exceder en rango o grado
**out'rid'er** *s* carrerista *m;* (Brit) viajante *m* de comercio
**out'right'** *adj* cabal, completo; franco, sincero || *adv* enteramente; de una vez; sin rodeos; en seguida
**out'run'ner** *s* volante *m* (*criado*)
**out'set'** *s* principio
**out'side'** *adj* exterior; superficial; ajeno; (*price*) (el) máximo || *adv* fuera, afuera; **outside of** fuera de || *prep* fuera de; más allá de; (coll) a excepción de || *s* exterior *m;* superficie *f;* apariencia
**outsider** [,aut'saɪdər] *s* forastero; intruso
**out'skirts'** *spl* afueras
**out'spo'ken** *adj* boquifresco, franco
**out·stand'ing** *adj* sobresaliente; prominente; sin pagar, sin cobrar
**outward** ['autwərd] *adj* exterior; superficial || *adv* exteriormente, hacia fuera
**out·weigh'** *tr* pesar más que; contrapesar, compensar
**out·wit'** *v* (*pret & pp* **-witted;** *ger* **-witting**) *tr* burlar, ser más listo que; despistar (*al perseguidor*)
**oval** ['ovəl] *adj* oval || *s* óvalo
**ova·ry** ['ovəri] *s* (*pl* **-ries**) ovario
**ovation** [o'veʃən] *s* ovación
**oven** ['ʌvən] *s* horno
**over** ['ovər] *adj* acabado, concluído; superior; adicional; excesivo || *adv* encima; al otro lado, a la otra orilla; hacia abajo; al revés; patas arriba; otra vez, de nuevo; de añadidura; (*at the bottom of a page*) a la vuelta; acá, p.ej., **hand over the money** déme acá el dinero; **over again** una vez más; **over against** enfrente de; a distinción de; en contraste con; **over and over** repetidas veces; **over here** acá; **over in** allá en; **over there** allá || *prep* sobre, encima de, por encima de; por; de un extremo a otro de; al otro lado de; más allá de; desde; (*a certain number*) más de; acerca de; por causa de; durante; **over and above** además de, en exceso de
**o'ver·all'** *adj* cabal, completo; extremo, total || **overalls** *spl* pantalones *mf* de trabajo
**o'ver·bear'ing** *adj* altanero, imperioso
**o'ver·board'** *adv* al agua; **man overboard!** ¡hombre al agua!; **to throw overboard** arrojar, echar o tirar por la borda
**o'ver·cast'** *adj* encapotado, nublado || *s* cielo encapotado || *v* (*pret & pp* **-cast**) *tr* nublar
**o'ver·charge'** *s* cargo excesivo; recargo de precio; sobrecarga; (elec) carga excesiva || **o'ver·charge'** *tr* hacer pagar más del valor, cobrar demasiado a; cargar (*p.ej., 50 pesetas*) de más; (elec) poner una carga excesiva a
**o'ver·coat'** *s* abrigo, gabán *m,* sobretodo
**o'ver·come'** *v* (*pret* **-came;** *pp* **-come**) *tr* vencer; rendir; superar (*dificultades*)
**o'ver·crowd'** *tr* atestar, apiñar; poblar con exceso
**o'ver·do'** *v* (*pret* **-did;** *pp* **-done**) *tr* exagerar; agobiar; asurar, requemar || *intr* cansarse mucho, excederse en el trabajo
**o'ver·dose'** *s* dosis excesiva

**o'ver·draft'** *s* sobregiro, giro en descubierto
**o'ver·draw'** *v* (*pret* **-drew;** *pp* **-drawn**) *tr & intr* sobregirar
**o'ver·due'** *adj* atrasado; vencido y no pagado
**o'ver·eat'** *v* (*pret* **-ate;** *pp* **-eaten**) *tr & intr* comer con exceso
**o'ver·exer'tion** *s* esfuerzo excesivo
**o'ver·expose'** *tr* sobreexponer
**o'ver·expo'sure** *s* sobreexposición
**o'ver·flow'** *s* desbordamiento, rebosamiento, derrame *m;* caño de reboso ‖ **o'ver·flow'** *intr* desbordar, rebosar
**o'ver·fly'** *v* (*pret* **-flew;** *pp* **-flown**) *tr* sobrevolar
**o'ver·grown'** *adj* demasiado grande para su edad; denso, frondoso
**o'ver·hang'** *v* (*pret & pp* **-hung**) *tr* sobresalir por encima de, estar pendiente o colgando sobre, salir fuera del nivel de; amenazar ‖ *intr* estar pendiente, estar colgando
**o'ver·haul'** *tr* examinar, registrar, revisar; ir alcanzando, alcanzar; componer, rehabilitar, reacondicionar
**o'ver·head'** *adj* de arriba; aéreo, elevado; general, de conjunto ‖ **o'ver·head'** *adv* por encima de la cabeza; arriba, en lo alto ‖ **o'ver·head'** *s* gastos generales
**o'ver·hear'** *v* (*pret & pp* **-heard**) *tr* oír por casualidad; acertar a oír, alcanzar a oír
**o'ver·heat'** *tr* recalentar ‖ *intr* recalentarse
**overjoyed** [ˌovərˈdʒɔɪd] *adj* lleno de alegría; **to be overjoyed** no caber de contento
**overland** [ˈovərˌlænd] u [ˈovərlənd] *adj & adv* por tierra, por vía terrestre
**o'ver·lap'** *v* (*pret & pp* **-lapped;** *ger* **-lapping**) *tr* solapar, traslapar ‖ *intr* solapar, traslapar; traslaparse (*dos o más cosas*); suceder (*dos hechos*) en parte al mismo tiempo
**o'ver·load'** *s* sobrecarga ‖ **o'ver·load'** *tr* sobrecargar
**o'ver·look'** *tr* dominar con la vista; pasar por alto, no hacer caso de; perdonar, tolerar; espiar, vigilar; cuidar de, dirigir; dar a, p.ej., **the window overlooks the garden** la ventana da al jardín
**o'ver·lord'** *s* jefe supremo ‖ **o'ver·lord'** *tr* dominar despóticamente, imponerse a
**overly** [ˈovərli] *adv* (coll) excesivamente, demasiado
**o'ver·night'** *adv* toda la noche; de la tarde a la mañana; **to stay overnight** pasar la noche
**overnight bag** *s* saco de noche
**o'ver·pass'** *s* viaducto
**o'ver·pop'u·late'** *tr* superpoblar
**o'verpow'er** *tr* dominar, supeditar, subyugar; colmar, dejar estupefacto
**overpowering** *adj* abrumador, arrollador, irresistible
**o'ver·produc'tion** *s* superproducción, sobreproducción
**o'ver·rate'** *tr* exagerar el valor de
**o'ver·run'** *v* (*pret* **-ran;** *pp* **-run;** *ger* **-running**) *tr* cubrir enteramente; infestar; exceder; **to overrun one's time** quedarse más de lo justo; hablar más de lo justo
**o'ver·sea'** u **o'ver·seas'** *adj* de ultramar ‖ **o'ver·sea'** u **o'ver·seas'** *adv* allende los mares, en ultramar
**o'ver·seer'** *s* director *m,* superintendente *mf*
**o'ver·shad'ow** *tr* sombrear; (fig) eclipsar
**o'ver·shoe'** *s* chanclo, zapato de goma
**o'ver·shoot'** *v* (*pret & pp* **-shot**) *tr* tirar por encima de o más allá de; **to overshoot oneself** pasarse de listo, excederse
**o'ver·sight'** *s* inadvertencia, descuido
**o'ver·sleep'** *v* (*pret & pp* **-slept**) *intr* dormir demasiado tarde
**o'ver·step'** *v* (*pret & pp* **-stepped;** *ger* **-stepping**) *tr* exceder, traspasar
**o'ver·stock'** *tr* abarrotar
**o'ver·sup·ply'** *s* (*pl* **-plies**) provisión excesiva ‖ **o'ver·sup·ply'** *v* (*pret* **-plied**) *tr* proveer en exceso
**overt** [ˈovərt] u [oˈvʌrt] *adj* abierto, manifiesto; premeditado
**o'ver·take'** *v* (*pret* **-took;** *pp* **-taken**) *tr* alcanzar; sobrepasar; sorprender; sobrevenir a
**o'ver-the-count'er** *adj* vendido directamente al comprador; vendido en tienda al por mayor
**o'ver·throw'** *s* derrocamiento; trastorno ‖ **o'ver·throw'** *v* (*pret* **-threw;** *pp* **-thrown**) *tr* derrocar; trastornar
**o'ver·time'** *adj & adv* en exceso de las horas regulares ‖ *s* horas extraordinarias de trabajo
**o'ver·trump'** *s* contrafallo ‖ **o'ver·trump'** *tr & intr* contrafallar
**overture** [ˈovərtʃər] *s* insinuación, proposición; (mus) obertura
**o'ver·turn'** *s* vuelco; movimiento de mercancías ‖ **o'ver·turn'** *tr* volcar; trastornar; derrocar ‖ *intr* volcar; trastornarse
**overweening** [ˌovərˈwinɪŋ] *adj* arrogante, presuntuoso
**o'ver·weight'** *adj* excesivamente gordo o grueso ‖ *s* sobrepeso; exceso de peso; peso de añadidura
**overwhelm** [ˌovərˈhwɛlm] *tr* abrumar; inundar; anonadar; (*with favors, gifts, etc.*) colmar
**o'ver·work'** *s* trabajo excesivo, exceso de trabajo; trabajo fuera de las horas regulares ‖ **o'ver·work'** *tr* hacer trabajar demasiado; oprimir con el trabajo ‖ *intr* trabajar demasiado
**Ovid** [ˈɑvɪd] *s* Ovidio
**ow** [aʊ] *interj* ¡ax!
**owe** [o] *tr* deber, adeudar ‖ *intr* tener deudas
**owing** [ˈo·ɪŋ] *adj* adeudado; debido, pagadero; **owing to** debido a, por causa de
**owl** [aʊl] *s* buho, lechuza, mochuelo
**own** [on] *adj* propio, p.ej., **my own brother** mi propio hermano ‖ *s* suyo, lo suyo; **on one's own** (coll) por su propia cuenta; (*without tak-*

*ing advice from anyone*) por su cabeza; (*without help from anyone*) de su cabeza; **to come into one's own** entrar en posesión de lo suyo; tener el éxito merecido, recibir el honor merecido; **to hold one's own** no aflojar, no cejar, mantenerse firme || *tr* poseer; reconocer || *intr* confesar; **to own up to** (coll) confesar de plano (*una culpa, un delito, etc.*)
**owner** ['onər] *s* amo, dueño, poseedor *m*, propietario
**ownership** ['onər,ʃɪp] *s* posesión, propiedad
**owner's license** *s* permiso de circulación, patente *f* de circulación
**ox** [ɑks] *s* (*pl* **oxen** ['ɑksən]) buey *m*
**ox'cart'** *s* carreta de bueyes
**oxide** ['ɑksaɪd] *s* óxido
**oxidize** ['ɑksɪ,daɪz] *tr* oxidar || *intr* oxidarse
**oxygen** ['ɑksɪdʒən] *s* oxígeno
**oxygen tent** *s* cámara o tienda de oxígeno
**oxytone** ['ɑksɪ,ton] *adj & s* oxítono
**oyster** ['ɔɪstər] *adj* ostrero || *s* ostra
**oyster bed** *s* ostrero
**oyster cocktail** *s* ostras en su concha
**oyster fork** *s* desbullador *m*
**oys'ter·house'** *s* ostrería
**oys'ter·knife'** *s* abreostras *m*
**oyster·man** ['ɔɪstərmən] *s* (*pl* **-men** [mən]) ostrero
**oyster opener** ['opənər] *s* desbullador *m*
**oyster shell** *s* desbulla, concha de ostra
**oyster stew** *s* sopa de ostras
**oz.** *abbr* **ounce, ounces**
**ozone** ['ozon] *s* ozono; (coll) aire fresco
**ozs.** *abbr* **ounces**

# P

**P, p** [pi] decimosexta letra del alfabeto inglés
**p.** *abbr* **page, participle**
**P.A.** *abbr* **Passenger Agent, power of attorney, Purchasing Agent**
**pace** [pes] *s* paso; **to keep pace with** ir, andar o avanzar al mismo paso que; **to put through one's paces** poner (*a uno*) a prueba; dar a (*uno*) ocasión de lucirse; **to set the pace** establecer el paso; dar el ejemplo || *tr* establecer el paso para; medir a pasos; recorrer a pasos; **to pace the floor** pasearse desesperadamente por la habitación || *intr* andar a pasos regulares
**pace'mak'er** *s* (med) marcapaso
**pacific** [pə'sɪfɪk] *adj* pacífico || **Pacific** *adj & s* Pacífico
**pacifier** ['pæsɪ,faɪ·ər] *s* pacificador *m*; (*teething ring*) chupador *m*
**pacifism** ['pæsɪ,fɪzəm] *s* pacifismo
**pacifist** ['pæsɪfɪst] *adj & s* pacifista *mf*
**paci·fy** ['pæsɪ,faɪ] *v* (*pret & pp* **-fied**) *tr* pacificar
**pack** [pæk] *s* lío, fardo; paquete *m*; (*of hounds*) jauría; (*of cattle*) manada; (*of evildoers*) pandilla; (*of lies*) sarta, montón *m*; (*of playing cards*) baraja; (*of cigarettes*) cajetilla; (*of floating ice*) témpano; (med) compresa || *tr* empaquetar; embaular; encajonar; hacer (*el baúl, la maleta*); conservar en latas; apretar, atestar; cargar (*una acémila*); escoger de modo fraudulento (*un jurado*); **to be packed in** (coll) estar como sardinas en banasta || *intr* empaquetarse; hacer el baúl, hacer la maleta; consolidarse, formar masa compacta
**package** ['pækɪdʒ] *s* paquete *m* || *tr* empaquetar
**pack animal** *s* acémila, animal *m* de carga
**packing box** o **case** *s* caja de embalaje
**packing house** *s* frigorífico
**packing slip** *s* hoja de embalaje
**pack'sad'dle** *s* albarda
**pack'thread'** *s* bramante *m*
**pack train** *s* recua
**pact** [pækt] *s* pacto
**pad** [pæd] *s* cojincillo, almohadilla; (*of writing paper*) bloc *m*; (*for inking*) tampón *m*; (*of an aquatic plant*) hoja; (*for launching a rocket*) plataforma *f*; (*sound of footsteps*) pisada || *v* (*pret & pp* **padded**; *ger* **padding**) *tr* acolchar, rellenar; meter mucho ripio en (*un escrito*) || *intr* andar, caminar; caminar despacio y pesadamente
**paddle** ['pædəl] *s* (*of a canoe*) canalete *m*; (*of a wheel*) pala, paleta; (*for spanking*) palo || *tr* impulsar con canalete; (*to spank*) apalear || *intr* remar con canalete; remar suavemente; (*to splash*) chapotear
**paddle wheel** *s* rueda de paletas
**paddock** ['pædək] *s* dehesa; (*at racecourse*) paddock *m*
**pad'lock'** *s* candado || *tr* cerrar con candado; (*to lock up officially*) condenar (*una habitación, un teatro*)
**pagan** ['pegən] *adj & s* pagano
**paganism** ['pegə,nɪzəm] *s* paganismo
**page** [pedʒ] *s* (*of a book*) página; (*boy attendant*) paje *m*; (*in a hotel or club*) botones *m* || *tr* paginar; buscar llamando
**pageant** ['pædʒənt] *s* espectáculo público
**pageant·ry** ['pædʒəntri] *s* (*pl* **-ries**) pompa, fausto; (*empty display*) bambolla
**pail** [pel] *s* balde *m*, cubo
**pain** [pen] *s* dolor *m*; **on pain of** so pena de; **pains** esmero, trabajo; dolores de parto; **to take pains** esmerarse || *tr & intr* doler

**painful** ['penfəl] *adj* doloroso; penoso
**pain'kill'er** *s* (coll) remedio contra el dolor
**painless** ['penlɪs] *adj* sin dolor, indoloro; fácil, sin trabajo
**pains'tak'ing** *adj* esmerado
**paint** [pent] *s* pintura; (*rouge*) afeite *m*, colorete *m* ‖ *tr* pintar ‖ *intr* pintar; pintarse, repintarse
**paint'box'** *s* caja de colores
**paint'brush'** *s* brocha, pincel *m*
**painter** ['pentər] *s* pintor *m*
**painting** ['pentɪŋ] *s* pintura
**paint remover** [rɪ'muvər] *s* sacapintura *m*, quitapintura *m*
**pair** [per] *s* par *m*; (*of people*) pareja; (*of cards*) parejas ‖ *tr* aparear ‖ *intr* aparearse
**pair of scissors** *s* tijeras
**pair of trousers** *s* pantalones *mpl*
**pajamas** [pə'dʒɑməz] o [pə'dʒæməz] *spl* pijama
**Pakistan** [,pɑkɪ'stɑn] *s* el Paquistán
**Pakistani** [,pɑkɪ'stɑni] *adj* & *s* paquistano, paquistaní *mf*
**pal** [pæl] *s* (coll) compañero ‖ *v* (*pret* & *pp* **palled**; *ger* **palling**) *intr* (coll) ser compañeros
**palace** ['pælɪs] *s* palacio
**palatable** ['pælətəbəl] *adj* sabroso, apetitoso
**palatal** ['pælətəl] *adj* & *s* palatal *f*
**palate** ['pælɪt] *s* paladar *m*
**pale** [pel] *adj* pálido; (*color*) claro ‖ *s* estaca; palizada; límite *m*, término ‖ *intr* palidecer
**pale'face'** *s* rostropálido
**palette** ['pælɪt] *s* paleta
**palfrey** ['pælfri] *s* palafrén *m*
**palisade** [,pælɪ'sed] *s* estaca; estacada; (*line of cliffs*) acantilado
**pall** [pɔl] *s* paño de ataúd, paño mortuorio; (eccl) palia ‖ *tr* hartar, saciar; quitar el sabor a ‖ *intr* perder el sabor; **to pall on** hartar, saciar
**pall'bear'er** *s* acompañante *m* de un cadáver; portador *m* del féretro
**palliate** ['pælɪ,et] *tr* paliar
**pallid** ['pælɪd] *adj* pálido
**pallor** ['pælər] *s* palidez *f*, palor *m*
**palm** [pɑm] *s* (*of the hand*) palma; (*measure*) palmo; (*tree and leaf*) palma; **to carry off the palm** llevarse la palma; **to grease the palm of** (slang) untar la mano a; **to yield the palm to** reconocer por vencedor ‖ *tr* esconder en la mano; escamotear (*una carta*); **to palm off something on someone** encajarle una cosa a uno
**palmet·to** [pæl'meto] *s* (*pl* **-tos** o **-toes**) palmito
**palmist** ['pɑmɪst] *s* quiromántico
**palmistry** ['pɑmɪstri] *s* quiromancia
**palm leaf** *s* palma, hoja de la palmera
**palm oil** *s* aceite *m* de palma; (slang) propina; (slang) soborno
**Palm Sunday** *s* domingo de ramos
**palpable** ['pælpəbəl] *adj* palpable
**palpitate** ['pælpɪ,tet] *intr* palpitar
**pal·sy** ['pɔlzi] *s* (*pl* **-sies**) perlesía ‖ *v* (*pret* & *pp* **-sied**) *tr* paralizar
**pal·try** ['pɔltri] *adj* (*comp* **-trier**; *super* **-triest**) vil, ruin, mezquino
**pamper** ['pæmpər] *tr* mimar, consentir
**pamphlet** ['pæmflɪt] *s* folleto, panfleto
**pan** [pæn] *s* cacerola, cazuela, sartén *f*; caldera, perol *m* ‖ *v* (*pret* & *pp* **panned**; *ger* **panning**) *tr* cocer, freír; separar (*el oro*) en la gamella; (coll) criticar ásperamente ‖ *intr* separar el oro en la gamella; dar oro; **to pan out well** (coll) tener éxito, dar buen resultado ‖ **Pan** *s* Pan
**panacea** [,pænə'si·ə] *s* panacea
**Panama Canal** ['pænə,mɑ] *s* canal *m* de Panamá
**Panama Canal Zone** *s* Zona del Canal
**Panama hat** *s* panamá *m*
**Panamanian** [,pænə'menɪ·ən] o [,pænə'mɑnɪ·ən] *adj* & *s* panameño
**Pan-American** [,pænə'merɪkən] *adj* panamericano
**pan'cake'** *s* hojuela, panqueque *m* ‖ *intr* (aer) desplomarse
**pancake landing** *s* aterrizaje aplastado, aterrizaje en desplome
**pancreas** ['pænkrɪ·əs] *s* páncreas *m*
**pander** ['pændər] *s* alcahuete *m* ‖ *intr* alcahuetear; **to pander to** gratificar
**pane** [pen] *s* cristal *m*, vidrio, hoja de vidrio
**pan·el** ['pænəl] *s* panel *m*, entrepaño, cuarterón *m*; grupo de personas en discusión cara al público; (aut, elec) tablero, panel *m*; (law) lista de personas que pueden servir como jurados ‖ *v* (*pret* & *pp* **-eled** o **-elled**; *ger* **-eling** o **-elling**) *tr* adornar con cuarterones, labrar en cuarterones; artesonar (*un techo o bóveda*)
**panel discussion** *s* coloquio cara al público
**panelist** ['pænəlɪst] *s* coloquiante *mf* cara al público
**panel lights** *spl* luces *fpl* del tablero
**pang** [pæŋ] *s* dolor agudo; (*of remorse*) punzada; (*of death*) agonía
**pan'han'dle** *s* mango de sartén ‖ *intr* (slang) mendigar, pedir limosna
**pan·ic** ['pænɪk] *adj* & *s* pánico ‖ *v* (*pret* & *pp* **-icked**; *ger* **-icking**) *tr* sobrecoger de pánico ‖ *intr* sobrecogerse de pánico
**pan'ic-strick'en** *adj* muerto de miedo, sobrecogido de terror
**pano·ply** ['pænəpli] *s* (*pl* **-plies**) panoplia; traje *m* ceremonial
**panorama** [,pænə'ræmə] o [,pænə'rɑmə] *s* panorama *m*
**pan·sy** ['pænzi] *s* (*pl* **-sies**) pensamiento
**pant** [pænt] *s* jadeo; palpitación; **pants** pantalones *mpl*; **to wear the pants** (coll) calzarse los pantalones ‖ *intr* jadear; palpitar
**pantheism** ['pænθɪ,ɪzəm] *s* panteísmo
**pantheon** ['pænθɪ,ɑn] o ['pænθɪ·ən] *s* panteón *m*
**panther** ['pænθər] *s* pantera; puma
**panties** ['pæntiz] *spl* pantaloncillos de mujer
**pantomime** ['pæntə,maɪm] *s* pantomima

**pan•try** ['pæntri] *s* (*pl* **-tries**) despensa
**pap** [pæp] *s* papilla, papas
**papa•cy** ['pepəsi] *s* (*pl* **-cies**) papado
**paper** ['pepər] *s* papel *m;* (*newspaper*) periódico; (*of needles*) paño || *tr* empapelar
**pa'per•back'** *s* libro en rústica
**pa'per•boy'** *s* vendedor *m* de periódicos
**paper clip** *s* sujetapapeles *m*
**paper cone** *s* cucurucho
**paper cutter** *s* cortapapeles *m*, guillotina
**paper doll** *s* muñeca de papel
**paper hanger** *s* empapelador *m*, papelista *mf*
**paper knife** *s* cortapapeles *m*
**paper mill** *s* fábrica de papel
**paper money** *s* papel *m* moneda
**paper profits** *spl* ganancias no realizadas sobre valores no vendidos
**paper tape** *s* cinta perforada
**pa'per•weight'** *s* pisapapeles *m*
**paper work** *s* preparación o comprobación de escritos
**paprika** [pæ'prikə] o ['pæprɪkə] *s* pimentón *m*
**papy•rus** [pə'paɪrəs] *s* (*pl* **-ri** [raɪ]) papiro
**par.** *abbr* **paragraph, parallel, parenthesis, parish**
**par** [pɑr] *adj* a la par; nominal; normal || *s* paridad; valor *m* nominal; **above par** sobre la par; con beneficio, con premio; **below par** o **under par** bajo la par; con pérdida; (coll) indispuesto; **to be on a par with** correr parejas con
**parable** ['pærəbəl] *s* parábola
**parachute** ['pærə,ʃut] *s* paracaídas *m* || *intr* lanzarse en paracaídas; **to parachute to safety** salvarse en paracaídas
**parachute jump** *s* salto en paracaídas
**parachutist** ['pærə,ʃutɪst] *s* paracaidista *mf*
**parade** [pə'red] *s* desfile *m;* paseo; ostentación || *tr* ostentar, pasear || *intr* desfilar, pasar por las calles; (mil) formar en parada
**paradise** ['pærə,daɪs] *s* paraíso
**paradox** ['pærə,dɑks] *s* paradoja; persona o cosa incomprensibles
**paradoxical** [,pærə'dɑksɪkəl] *adj* paradójico
**paraffin** ['pærəfɪn] *s* parafina
**paragon** ['pærə,gɑn] *s* dechado
**paragraph** ['pærə,græf] o ['pærə,grɑf] *s* párrafo
**Paraguay** ['pærə,gwe] o ['pærə,gwaɪ] *s* el Paraguay
**Paraguayan** [,pærə'gwe•ən] o [,pærə'gwaɪ•ən] *adj* & *s* paraguayano, paraguayo
**parakeet** ['pærə,kit] *s* perico, periquito
**paral•lel** ['pærə,lel] *adj* paralelo || *s* (línea) paralela; (plano) paralelo; (geog) paralelo; **parallels** (typ) doble raya vertical || *v* (*pret* & *pp* **-leled** o **-lelled;** *ger* **-leling** o **-lelling**) *tr* ser paralelo a; poner en dirección paralela; correr parejas con; (*to compare*) paralelizar
**parallel bars** *spl* paralelas, barras paralelas
**paraly•sis** [pə'rælɪsɪs] *s* (*pl* **-ses** [,siz]) parálisis *f*
**paralytic** [,pærə'lɪtɪk] *adj* & *s* paralítico
**paralyze** ['pærə,laɪz] *tr* paralizar
**paramount** ['pærə,maunt] *adj* capital, supremo, principalísimo
**paranoiac** [,pærə'nɔɪ•æk] *adj* & *s* paranoico
**parapet** ['pærə,pet] *s* parapeto
**paraphernalia** [,pærəfər'nelɪ•ə] *spl* trastos, atavíos
**parasite** ['pærə,saɪt] *s* parásito
**parasitic(al)** [,pærə'sɪtɪk(əl)] *adj* parasítico, parasitario
**parasol** ['pærə,sɔl] o ['pærə,sɑl] *s* quitasol *m*, parasol *m*
**pa'ra•troop'er** *s* paracaidista *m*
**pa'ra•troops'** *spl* tropas paracaidistas
**parboil** ['pɑr,bɔɪl] *tr* sancochar; calentar con exceso
**par•cel** ['pɑrsəl] *s* paquete *m*, atado, bulto || *v* (*pret* & *pp* **-celed** o **-celled;** *ger* **-celing** o **-celling**) *tr* empaquetar; parcelar (*el terreno*); **to parcel out** repartir
**parcel post** *s* paquetes *mpl* postales
**parch** [pɑrtʃ] *tr* abrasar, tostar; **to be parched** tener mucha sed
**parchment** ['pɑrtʃmənt] *s* pergamino
**pardon** ['pɑrdən] *s* perdón *m;* (*remission of penalty by the state*) indulto; **I beg your pardon** dispense Vd. || *tr* perdonar, dispensar; indultar
**pardonable** ['pɑrdənəbəl] *adj* perdonable
**pardon board** *s* junta de perdones
**pare** [per] *tr* mondar (*fruta*); pelar (*patatas*); cortar (*callos, uñas*); despalmar (*la palma córnea de los animales*); adelgazar; reducir (*gastos*)
**parent** ['perənt] *adj* madre, matriz, principal || *s* padre o madre; autor *m*, fuente *f*, origen *m;* **parents** padres *mpl*
**parentage** ['perəntɪdʒ] *s* paternidad o maternidad; abolengo, linaje *m*
**parenthe•sis** [pə'renθɪsɪs] *s* (*pl* **-ses** [,siz]) paréntesis *m*
**parenthood** ['perənt,hud] *s* paternidad o maternidad
**pariah** [pə'raɪ•ə] o ['pɑrɪ•ə] *s* paria *mf*
**paring knife** ['perɪŋ] *s* cuchillo para mondar
**parish** ['pærɪʃ] *s* parroquia, feligresía
**parishioner** [pə'rɪʃənər] *s* parroquiano, feligrés *m*
**Parisian** [pə'rɪʒən] *adj* & *s* parisiense *mf*
**parity** ['pærɪti] *s* paridad
**park** [pɑrk] *s* parque *m* || *tr* estacionar, parquear; (coll) colocar, dejar || *intr* estacionar, parquear
**parking** ['pɑrkɪŋ] *s* aparcamiento, estacionamiento; **no parking** se prohibe estacionarse
**parking lights** *spl* (aut) faros de situación
**parking lot** *s* parque *m* de estacionamiento

**parking meter** *s* reloj *m* de estacionamiento, parquímetro
**parking ticket** *s* aviso de multa
**park'way'** *s* gran vía adornada con árboles
**parley** ['pɑrli] *s* parlamento ‖ *intr* parlamentar
**parliament** ['pɑrlɪmənt] *s* parlamento
**parlor** ['pɑrlər] *s* sala; parlatorio, locutorio
**parlor car** *s* coche-salón *m*
**parlor politics** *spl* política de café
**Parnassus** [pɑr'næsəs] *s* (*collection of poems*) parnaso; el Parnaso; **to try to climb Parnassus** hacer pinos en poesía
**parochial** [pə'rokɪ·əl] *adj* parroquial; estrecho, limitado
**paro·dy** ['pærədi] *s* (*pl* **-dies**) parodia ‖ *v* (*pret & pp* **-died**) *tr* parodiar
**parole** [pə'rol] *s* palabra de honor; libertad bajo palabra ‖ *tr* dejar libre bajo palabra
**paroxytone** [pær'ɑksɪ,ton] *adj & s* paroxítono
**par·quet** [pɑr'ke] *s* entarimado; (theat) platea ‖ *v* (*pret & pp* **-queted** ['ked]; *ger* **-queting** ['ke·ɪŋ]) *tr* entarimar
**parricide** ['pærɪ,saɪd] *s* (*act*) parricidio; (*person*) parricida *mf*
**parrot** ['pærət] *s* papagayo, loro; (fig) papagayo ‖ *tr* repetir o imitar como loro
**par·ry** ['pæri] *s* (*pl* **-ries**) parada, quite *m* ‖ *v* (*pret & pp* **-ried**) *tr* parar; defenderse de
**parse** [pɑrs] *tr* analizar (*una oración*) gramaticalmente; describir (*una palabra*) gramaticalmente
**parsley** ['pɑrsli] *s* perejil *m*
**parsnip** ['pɑrsnɪp] *s* chirivía
**parson** ['pɑrsən] *s* cura *m*, párroco; clérigo; pastor *m* protestante
**part** [pɑrt] *s* parte *f*; (*of a machine*) pieza; (*of the hair*) raya; (theat) parte *f*, papel *m*; **part and parcel** parte esencial, parte inseparable, elemento esencial; **parts** partes *fpl*; prendas, dotes *fpl*; **to do one's part** cumplir con su obligación; **to look the part** vestir el cargo; **to take the part of** tomar el partido de, defender; desempeñar el papel de ‖ *tr* dividir, partir, separar; **to part the hair** hacerse la raya ‖ *intr* separarse; **to part with** deshacerse de, abandonar; despedirse de
**par·take** [pɑr'tek] *v* (*pret* **-took** ['tʊk]; *pp* **-taken**) *tr* compartir; comer; beber ‖ *intr* participar
**Parthenon** ['pɑrθɪ,nɑn] *s* Partenón *m*
**partial** ['pɑrʃəl] *adj* parcial; aficionado
**participate** [pɑr'tɪsɪ,pet] *intr* participar
**participle** ['pɑrtɪ,sɪpəl] *s* participio
**particle** ['pɑrtɪkəl] *s* partícula, corpúsculo
**particular** [pər'tɪkjələr] *adj* particular; difícil, exigente, quisquilloso; esmerado; minucioso; **a particular . . .** cierto . . . ‖ *s* particular *m*
**partisan** ['pɑrtɪzən] *adj & s* partidario, partidista *mf*; (mil) partisano
**partition** [pɑr'tɪʃən] *s* partición, distribución; división; porción; tabique *m* ‖ *tr* repartir; dividir en cuartos, aposentos; tabicar
**partner** ['pɑrtnər] *s* compañero; (*wife or husband*) cónyuge *mf*; (*in a dance*) pareja *f*; (*in business*) socio
**partnership** ['pɑrtnər,ʃɪp] *s* asociación; consorcio, vida en común; (com) sociedad, asociación comercial
**partridge** ['pɑrtrɪdʒ] *s* perdiz *f*
**part'-time'** *adj* por horas, parcial
**par·ty** ['pɑrti] *adj* de partido; de gala ‖ *s* (*pl* **-ties**) convite *m*, reunión, fiesta, tertulia, recepción; (*for fishing, hunting, etc.*; *of armed men*) partida; cómplice *mf*, interesado; (pol) partido; (coll) persona, individuo
**party girl** *s* chica de vida alegre
**party-goer** ['pɑrti,go·ər] *s* tertuliano; fiestero
**party line** *s* (*between two properties*) linde *m*, lindero; (*of communist party*) línea del partido; (telp) línea compartida
**party politics** *s* política de partido
**pass.** *abbr* **passenger, passive**
**pass** [pæs] o [pɑs] *s* paso; (*permit; free ticket; movement of hands of mesmerist, of bullfighter*) pase *m*; (*in an examination*) aprobación; nota de aprobación ‖ *tr* pasar; pasar de largo (*una luz roja*); aprobar (*un proyecto de ley; un examen; a un alumno*); ser aprobado en (*un examen*); dejar atrás; cruzarse con; expresar (*una opinión*); pronunciar (*una sentencia*); dar (*la palabra*); dejar sin protestar; no pagar (*un dividendo*); **to pass off** colar, pasar, hacer aceptar (*una moneda falsa*); disimular (*p.ej., una ofensa con una risa*); **to pass over** omitir, pasar por alto; excusar; desdeñar; dejar sin protestar; postergar (*a un empleado*) ‖ *intr* pasar; pasarse (*introducirse*); aprobar; **to bring to pass** llevar a cabo; **to come to pass** suceder; **to pass as** pasar por; **to pass away** pasar, pasar a mejor vida; **to pass off** pasar (*una enfermedad, una tempestad, etc.*); tener lugar; **to pass out** salir; (slang) desmayarse; **to pass over to** pasarse a (*p.ej., el enemigo*)
**passable** ['pæsəbəl] o ['pɑsəbəl] *adj* pasadero; (*law*) promulgable
**passage** ['pæsɪdʒ] *s* pasaje *m*; paso; pasillo; (*of time*) transcurso; (*of bowels*) evacuación
**pass'book'** *s* cartilla, libreta de banco
**passenger** ['pæsəndʒər] *adj* de viajeros ‖ *s* pasajero, viajero
**passer-by** ['pæsər'baɪ] o ['pɑsər'baɪ] *s* (*pl* **passers-by**) transeúnte *mf*
**passing** ['pæsɪŋ] o ['pɑsɪŋ] *adj* pasajero; corriente; de aprobado ‖ *s* (*act of passing; death*) paso; (*in an examination*) aprobación
**passion** ['pæʃən] *s* pasión
**passionate** ['pæʃənɪt] *adj* apasionado

**passive** [ˈpæsɪv] *adj* pasivo ‖ *s* voz pasiva, verbo pasivo
**pass'key'** *s* llave *f* de paso
**Pass'o'ver** *s* pascua (*de los hebreos*)
**pass'port'** *s* pasaporte *m*
**pass'word'** *s* santo y seña
**past** [pæst] o [pɑst] *adj* pasado; último; que fué, p.ej., **past president** presidente que fué; acabado, concluído ‖ *adv* más allá; por delante ‖ *prep* más allá de; más de; por delante de; fuera de; después de, p.ej., **past two o'clock** después de las dos; **past belief** increíble; **past cure** incurable; **past hope** sin esperanza ‖ *s* pasado
**paste** [pest] *s* (*dough; spaghetti, etc.*) pasta; (*for sticking things together*) engrudo ‖ *tr* engrudar, pegar con engrudo
**paste'board'** *s* cartón *m*
**pasteurize** [ˈpæstəˌraɪz] *tr* pasterizar
**pastime** [ˈpæsˌtaɪm] o [ˈpɑsˌtaɪm] *s* pasatiempo
**pastor** [ˈpæstər] o [ˈpɑstər] *s* pastor *m*, clérigo, cura *m*
**pastoral** [ˈpæstərəl] o [ˈpɑstərəl] *adj* & *s* pastoral *f*
**pas·try** [ˈpestri] *s* (*pl* **-tries**) pastelería
**pastry cook** *s* pastelero, repostero
**pastry shop** *s* pastelería, repostería
**pasture** [ˈpæstʃər] o [ˈpɑstʃər] *s* pasto, pastura, dehesa ‖ *tr* apacentar, pacer ‖ *intr* apacentarse, pacer
**past·y** [ˈpesti] *adj* (*comp* **-ier**; *super* **-iest**) pastoso; flojo, fofo, pálido
**pat** [pæt] *s* golpecito, palmadita; ruido de pasos ligeros; (*of butter*) pastelillo ‖ *v* (*pret* & *pp* **patted**; *ger* **patting**) *tr* dar golpecitos a, golpear ligeramente; palmotear, acariciar con la mano; **to pat on the back** elogiar, cumplimentar
**patch** [pætʃ] *s* remiendo, parche *m*; terreno, pedazo de terreno; mancha; lunar postizo ‖ *tr* remendar; **to patch up** componer (*una desavenencia*); componer lo mejor posible (*una cosa descompuesta*); hacer aprisa y mal
**patent** [ˈpetənt] *adj* patente; abierto ‖ [ˈpætənt] *adj* de patentes ‖ *s* patente *f*, patente de invención; propiedad industrial; **patent applied for** se ha solicitado patente ‖ *tr* patentar
**patent leather** [ˈpætənt] *s* charol *m*
**patent medicine** [ˈpætənt] *s* medicamento de patente
**patent rights** [ˈpætənt] *spl* derechos de patente
**paternal** [pəˈtʌrnəl] *adj* paterno; (*affection*) paternal
**paternity** [pəˈtʌrnɪti] *s* paternidad
**path** [pæθ] o [pɑθ] *s* senda, sendero; trayectoria
**pathetic** [pəˈθɛtɪk] *adj* patético
**path'find'er** *s* baquiano; explorador *m*
**patholo·gy** [pəˈθɑlədʒi] *s* patología
**pathos** [ˈpeθɑs] *s* patetismo
**path'way'** *s* senda, sendero
**patience** [ˈpeʃəns] *s* paciencia
**patient** [ˈpeʃənt] *adj* paciente ‖ *s* paciente *mf*, enfermo
**patriarch** [ˈpetrɪˌɑrk] *s* patriarca *m*
**patrician** [pəˈtrɪʃən] *adj* & *s* patricio
**patricide** [ˈpætrɪˌsaɪd] *s* (*act*) parricidio; (*person*) parricida *mf*
**Patrick** [ˈpætrɪk] *s* Patricio
**patrimo·ny** [ˈpætrɪˌmoni] *s* (*pl* **-nies**) patrimonio
**patriot** [ˈpetrɪ·ət] o [ˈpætrɪ·ət] *s* patriota *mf*
**patriotic** [ˌpetrɪˈɑtɪk] o [ˌpætrɪˈɑtɪk] *adj* patriótico
**patriotism** [ˈpetrɪ·əˌtɪzəm] o [ˈpætrɪ·əˌtɪzəm] *s* patriotismo
**pa·trol** [pəˈtrol] *s* patrulla ‖ *v* (*pret* & *pp* **-troled** o **-trolled**; *ger* **-troling** o **-trolling**) *tr* & *intr* patrullar
**patrol·man** [pəˈtrolmən] *s* (*pl* **-men** [mən]) guardia *m* municipal, vigilante *m* de policía
**patrol wagon** *s* camión *m* de policía
**patron** [ˈpetrən] o [ˈpætrən] *adj* tutelar ‖ *s* parroquiano; patrocinador *m*
**patronize** [ˈpetrəˌnaɪz] o [ˈpætrəˌnaɪz] *tr* ser parroquiano de (*un tendero*); comprar de costumbre en; patrocinar; tratar con aire protector
**patron saint** *s* patrón *m*, santo titular
**patter** [ˈpætər] *s* golpeteo; (*of rain*) chapaleteo; charla, parloteo ‖ *intr* golpetear; charlar, parlotear
**pattern** [ˈpætərn] *s* patrón *m*; modelo
**P.A.U.** *abbr* **Pan American Union**
**paucity** [ˈpɔsɪti] *s* corto número; falta, escasez *f*, insuficiencia
**Paul** [pɔl] *s* Pablo; (*name of popes*) Paulo
**paunch** [pɔntʃ] *s* panza
**paunchy** [ˈpɔntʃi] *adj* panzudo
**pauper** [ˈpɔpər] *s* pobre *mf*, indigente *mf*
**pause** [pɔz] *s* pausa; (mus) calderón *m*; **to give pause (to)** dar que pensar (a) ‖ *intr* hacer pausa, detenerse brevemente; vacilar
**pave** [pev] *tr* pavimentar; (*with flagstones*) enlosar; (*with bricks*) enladrillar; (*with pebbles*) enchinar; **to pave the way (for)** preparar el terreno (para), abrir el camino (a)
**pavement** [ˈpevmənt] *s* pavimento; (*of brick*) enladrillado; (*of flagstone*) enlosado; (*sidewalk*) acera
**pavilion** [pəˈvɪljən] *s* pabellón *m*
**paw** [pɔ] *s* pata; garra, zarpa; (coll) mano *f* ‖ *tr* dar zarpazos a, restregar con las uñas; golpear, patear (*el suelo los caballos*); (coll) manosear; (*to handle overfamiliarly*) (coll) sobar ‖ *intr* piafar (*el caballo*)
**pawn** [pɔn] *s* (*in chess*) peón *m*; (*security, pledge*) prenda; (*tool of another person*) instrumento; víctima ‖ *tr* empeñar, dar en prenda
**pawn'bro'ker** *s* prestamista *mf*
**pawn'shop'** *s* casa de empeños, monte *m* de piedad
**pawn ticket** *s* papeleta de empeño
**pay** [pe] *s* paga; recompensa; castigo merecido ‖ *v* (*pret* & *pp* **paid** [ped]) *tr* pagar; prestar o poner (*atención*);

dar (*cumplidos*); dar (*dinero una actividad comercial*); dar dinero a, ser provechoso a; pagar en la misma moneda; pagar con creces; sufrir (*el castigo de una ofensa*); hacer (*una visita*); cubrir (*los gastos*); **to pay back** devolver; pagar en la misma moneda; **to pay off** pagar y despedir (*a un empleado*); pagar todo lo adeudado a; vengarse de; redimir (*una hipoteca*) || *intr* pagar; ser provechoso, valer la pena; **pay as you enter** pague a la entrada; **pay as you go** pagar el impuesto de utilidades con descuentos anticipados; **pay as you leave** pague a la salida

**payable** [ˈpe·əbəl] *adj* pagadero

**pay boost** *s* aumento de salario

**pay′check′** *s* cheque *m* en pago del sueldo; sueldo

**pay′day′** *s* día *m* de pago

**payee** [peˈi] *s* portador *m* o tenedor *m* (*de un giro*)

**pay envelope** *s* sobre *m* con el jornal; jornal *m*, salario

**payer** [ˈpe·ər] *s* pagador *m*

**pay load** *s* carga útil

**pay′mas′ter** *s* pagador *m*

**payment** [ˈpemənt] *s* pago; castigo

**pay roll** *s* nómina, hoja de paga

**pay station** *s* teléfono público

**pd.** *abbr* **paid**

**p.d.** *abbr* **per diem, potential difference**

**pea** [pi] *s* guisante *m*, chícharo

**peace** [pis] *s* paz *f*; **to make peace with** hacer las paces con

**peaceable** [ˈpisəbəl] *adj* pacífico

**peaceful** [ˈpisfəl] *adj* tranquilo, pacífico, sosegado

**peace′mak′er** *s* iris *m* de paz

**peace of mind** *s* serenidad del espíritu

**peace pipe** *s* pipa ceremonial (*de los pieles rojas*)

**peach** [pitʃ] *s* melocotón *m*; (slang) persona o cosa admirables

**peach tree** *s* melocotonero

**peach·y** [ˈpitʃi] *adj* (*comp* **-ier**; *super* **-iest**) (slang) estupendo, magnífico

**pea′cock′** *s* pavo real, pavón *m*; (fig) pinturero

**peak** [pik] *s* pico, cima, cumbre *f*; punta, extremo; máximo; (*of a cap*) visera; (*of a curve*) cresta; (elec) pico

**peak hour** *s* hora punta

**peak load** *s* (elec) carga de punta

**peal** [pil] *s* fragor *m*; estruendo; (*of bells*) repique *m*; juego de campanas || *intr* repicar; resonar

**peal of laughter** *s* carcajada

**peal of thunder** *s* trueno

**pea′nut′** *s* cacahuete *m*, aráquida

**pear** [pɛr] *s* pera

**pearl** [pʌrl] *s* margarita, perla; (*of running water*) murmullo || *tr* aljofarar

**pearl oyster** *s* madreperla

**pear tree** *s* peral *m*

**peasant** [ˈpɛzənt] *adj* & *s* campesino, rústico

**pea′shoot′er** *s* cerbatana, bodoquera

**pea soup** *s* sopa de guisantes; (coll) neblina espesa y amarillenta

**peat** [pit] *s* turba

**pebble** [ˈpɛbəl] *s* china, guija || *tr* agranelar (*el cuero*)

**peck** [pɛk] *s* medida de áridos (*nueve litros*); montón *m*; picotazo; beso dado de mala gana || *tr* picotear || *intr* picotear; (coll) comer melindrosamente; **to peck at** querer picar; regañar constantemente; (coll) comer melindrosamente

**peculate** [ˈpɛkjəˌlet] *tr* & *intr* malversar

**peculiar** [pɪˈkjuljər] *adj* peculiar; singular, raro; excéntrico

**pedagogue** [ˈpɛdəˌgɑg] *s* pedagogo; dómine *m*, pedante *m*

**pedagogy** [ˈpɛdəˌgodʒi] o [ˈpɛdəˌgɑdʒi] *s* pedagogía

**ped·al** [ˈpɛdəl] *s* pedal *m* || *v* (*pret & pp* **-aled** o **-alled**; *ger* **-aling** o **-alling**) *tr* impulsar pedaleando || *intr* pedalear

**pedant** [ˈpɛdənt] *s* pedante *mf*

**pedantic** [pɪˈdæntɪk] *adj* pedantesco

**pedant·ry** [ˈpɛdəntri] *s* (*pl* **-ries**) pedantería

**peddle** [ˈpɛdəl] *tr* ir vendiendo de puerta en puerta; traer y llevar (*chismes*); vender (*favores*) || *intr* ser buhonero

**peddler** [ˈpɛdlər] *s* buhonero

**pedestal** [ˈpɛdɪstəl] *s* pedestal *m*

**pedestrian** [pɪˈdɛstrɪ·ən] *adj* pedestre || *s* peatón *m*

**pediatrics** [ˌpidɪˈætrɪks] o [ˌpɛdɪˈætrɪks] *ssg* pediatría

**pedigree** [ˈpɛdɪˌgri] *s* árbol genealógico; ascendencia; fuente *f*, origen *m*

**pediment** [ˈpɛdɪmənt] *s* frontón *m*

**peek** [pik] *s* mirada rápida y furtiva || *intr* mirar a hurtadillas

**peel** [pil] *s* cáscara, pellejo || *tr* pelar || *intr* pelarse

**peep** [pip] *s* mirada a hurtadillas; (*of chickens*) pío || *intr* mirar a hurtadillas; piar (*los pollos*)

**peep′hole′** *s* atisbadero; (*in a door*) mirilla, ventanillo

**peep show** *s* mundonuevo; (slang) vistas sicalípticas

**peer** [pɪr] *s* par *m* || *intr* mirar fijando la vista de cerca; **to peer at** mirar con ojos de miope; **to peer into** mirar hacia lo interior de, escudriñar

**peerless** [ˈpɪrlɪs] *adj* sin par

**peeve** [piv] *s* (coll) cojijo || *tr* (coll) enojar, irritar

**peevish** [ˈpivɪʃ] *adj* cojijoso, displicente

**peg** [pɛg] *s* clavija, claveta, estaquilla; **to take down a peg** (coll) bajar los humos a || *v* (*pret & pp* **pegged**; *ger* **pegging**) *tr* enclavijar; señalar con clavijas; fijar (*precios*) || *intr* trabajar con ahinco; **to peg away at** afanarse en

**peg leg** *s* pata de palo

**peg top** *s* peonza; **peg tops** pantalones anchos de caderas y perniles ajustados

**Peking** [ˈpiˈkɪŋ] *s* Pequín

**Peking•ese** [ˌpikɪˈniz] *adj* pequinés || *s* (*pl* -ese) pequinés *m*
**pelf** [pɛlf] *s* dinero mal ganado
**pell-mell** [ˈpɛlˈmɛl] *adj* tumultuoso || *adv* atropelladamente
**Peloponnesian** [ˌpɛləpəˈniʃən] *adj & s* peloponense *mf*
**Peloponnesus** [ˌpɛləpəˈnisəs] *s* Peloponeso
**Pelops** [ˈpilɑps] *s* Pélope *m*
**pelota** [peˈlotə] *s* pelota vasca
**pelt** [pɛlt] *s* pellejo; golpe violento; (*of a person*) (hum) pellejo || *tr* golpear violentamente; apedrear || *intr* golpear violentamente; caer con fuerza (*el granizo, la lluvia, etc.*); apresurarse
**pen.** *abbr* **peninsula**
**pen** [pɛn] *s* pluma; corral *m*, redil *m*; **the pen and the sword** las letras y las armas || *v* (*pret & pp* **penned**; *ger* **penning**) *tr* escribir (*con pluma*); redactar || *v* (*pret & pp* **penned** o **pent** [pɛnt]) *tr* acorralar, encerrar
**penalize** [ˈpinəˌlaɪz] *tr* penar; (sport) sancionar
**penal•ty** [ˈpɛnəlti] *s* (*pl* **-ties**) pena; (*for late payment*) recargo; (sport) sanción; **under penalty of** so pena de
**penance** [ˈpɛnəns] *s* penitencia; **to do penance** hacer penitencia
**penchant** [ˈpɛnʃənt] *s* afición, inclinación, tendencia
**pen•cil** [ˈpɛnsəl] *s* lápiz *m*; (*of light*) pincel *m*, haz *m* || *v* (*pret & pp* **-ciled** o **-cilled**; *ger* **-ciling** o **-cilling**) *tr* marcar con lápiz; (med) pincelar
**pencil sharpener** *s* afilalápices *m*, cortalápices *m*
**pendent** [ˈpɛndənt] *adj* pendiente; sobresaliente || *s* medallón *m*; (*earring*) pendiente *m*
**pending** [ˈpɛndɪŋ] *adj* pendiente || *prep* hasta; durante
**pendulum** [ˈpɛndʒələm] *s* péndulo; (*of a clock*) péndola
**pendulum bob** *s* lenteja
**penetrate** [ˈpɛnɪˌtret] *tr & intr* penetrar
**penguin** [ˈpɛŋgwɪn] *s* pingüino, pájaro bobo
**pen'hold'er** *s* (*handle*) portaplumas *m*; (*box*) plumero
**penicillin** [ˌpɛnɪˈsɪlɪn] *s* penicilina
**peninsula** [pəˈnɪnsələ] *s* península
**peninsular** [pəˈnɪnsələr] *adj & s* peninsular *mf* || **Peninsular** *adj & s* (*Iberian*) peninsular *mf*
**penitence** [ˈpɛnɪtəns] *s* penitencia
**penitent** [ˈpɛnɪtənt] *adj & s* penitente *mf*
**pen'knife'** *s* (*pl* **-knives**) navaja, cortaplumas *m*
**penmanship** [ˈpɛnmənˌʃɪp] *s* caligrafía; (*hand of a person*) letra
**pen name** *s* seudónimo
**pennant** [ˈpɛnənt] *s* gallardete *m*
**penniless** [ˈpɛnɪlɪs] *adj* pelón, sin dinero
**pennon** [ˈpɛnən] *s* pendón *m*
**pen•ny** [ˈpɛni] *s* (*pl* **-nies**) (U.S.A.) centavo || *s* (*pl* **pence** [pɛns]) (Brit) penique *m*
**pen'ny•weight'** *s* peso de 24 granos
**pen pal** *s* (coll) amigo por correspondencia
**pen point** *s* punta de la pluma; puntilla de la pluma fuente
**pension** [ˈpɛnʃən] *s* pensión, jubilación || *tr* pensionar, jubilar
**pensioner** [ˈpɛnʃənər] *s* pensionista *mf*; **pensioners** clases pasivas
**pensive** [ˈpɛnsɪv] *adj* pensativo; melancólico
**Pentecost** [ˈpɛntɪˌkɔst] o [ˈpɛntɪˌkɑst] *s* el Pentecostés
**penthouse** [ˈpɛntˌhaʊs] *s* alpende *m*, colgadizo; casa de azotea
**pent-up** [ˈpɛntˌʌp] *adj* contenido, reprimido
**penult** [ˈpinʌlt] *s* penúltima
**penum•bra** [pɪˈnʌmbrə] *s* (*pl* **-brae** [bri] o **-bras**) penumbra
**penurious** [pɪˈnʊrɪ•əs] *adj* (*stingy*) tacaño, mezquino; (*poor*) pobre, indigente
**penury** [ˈpɛnjəri] *s* tacañería, mezquindad; pobreza, miseria
**pen'wip'er** *s* limpiaplumas *m*
**people** [ˈpipəl] *spl* gente *f*; personas; gente del pueblo; se, p.ej., **people say** se dice || *ssg* (*pl* **peoples**) pueblo, nación || *tr* poblar
**pep** [pɛp] *s* (slang) ánimo, brío, vigor *m* || *v* (*pret & pp* **pepped**; *ger* **pepping**) *tr* — **to pep up** (slang) animar, dar vigor a
**pepper** [ˈpɛpər] *s* (*spice*) pimienta; (*plant and fruit*) pimiento || *tr* sazonar con pimienta; (*with bullets*) acribillar; salpicar
**pep'per•box'** *s* pimentero
**pep'per•mint'** *s* (*plant*) menta piperita; esencia de menta; pastilla de menta
**per** [pʌr] *prep* por; **as per** según
**perambulator** [pərˈæmbjəˌletər] *s* cochecillo de niño
**per capita** [pər ˈkæpɪtə] por cabeza, por persona
**perceive** [pərˈsiv] *tr* percibir
**per cent** o **percent** [pərˈsɛnt] por ciento
**percentage** [pərˈsɛntɪdʒ] *s* porcentaje *m*; (slang) provecho, ventaja
**perception** [pərˈsɛpʃən] *s* percepción; comprensión, penetración
**perch** [pʌrtʃ] *s* percha, rama, varilla; sitio o posición elevada; (*fish*) perca || *tr* colocar en un sitio algo elevado || *intr* sentarse en un sitio algo elevado; posar (*un ave*)
**percolator** [ˈpʌrkəˌletər] *s* cafetera filtradora
**per diem** [pər ˈdaɪ•əm] por día
**perdition** [pərˈdɪʃən] *s* perdición
**perennial** [pəˈrɛnɪ•əl] *adj* perenne; (bot) vivaz || *s* planta vivaz
**perfect** [ˈpʌrfɪkt] *adj & s* perfecto || [pərˈfɛkt] *tr* perfeccionar
**perfidious** [pərˈfɪdɪ•əs] *adj* pérfido
**perfi•dy** [ˈpʌrfɪdi] *s* (*pl* **-dies**) perfidia
**perforate** [ˈpʌrfəˌret] *tr* perforar
**perforce** [pərˈfors] *adv* por fuerza, necesariamente

**perform** [pər'fɔrm] *tr* ejecutar; (theat) representar || *intr* ejecutar; funcionar (*p.ej., una máquina*)
**performance** [pər'fɔrməns] *s* ejecución; representación; funcionamiento; (theat) función
**performer** [pər'fɔrmər] *s* ejecutante *mf;* actor *m;* acróbata *mf*
**perfume** ['pʌrfjum] *s* perfume *m* || [pər'fjum] *tr* perfumar
**perfunctory** [pər'fʌŋktəri] *adj* hecho sin cuidado, hecho a la ligera; indiferente, negligente
**perhaps** [pər'hæps] *adv* acaso, tal vez, quizá
**per•il** ['perəl] *s* peligro || *v* (*pret & pp* **-iled** o **-illed;** *ger* **-iling** o **-illing**) *tr* poner en peligro
**perilous** ['perɪləs] *adj* peligroso
**period** ['pɪrɪ·əd] *s* período; (*in school*) hora; (gram) punto; (sport) división
**period costume** *s* traje *m* de época
**periodic** [ˌpɪrɪ'ɑdɪk] *adj* periódico
**periodical** [ˌpɪrɪ'ɑdɪkəl] *adj* periódico || *s* periódico, revista periódica
**peripher•y** [pə'rɪfəri] *s* (*pl* **-ies**) periferia
**periscope** ['perɪˌskop] *s* periscopio
**perish** ['perɪʃ] *intr* perecer
**perishable** ['perɪʃəbəl] *adj* perecedero; (*merchandise*) corruptible
**periwig** ['perɪˌwɪg] *s* perico
**perjure** ['pʌrdʒər] *tr* hacer (*a una persona*) quebrantar el juramento; **to perjure oneself** perjurarse
**perju•ry** ['pʌrdʒəri] *s* (*pl* **-ries**) perjurio
**perk** [pʌrk] *tr* alzar (*la cabeza*); aguzar (*las orejas*) || *intr* pavonearse; engalanarse; **to perk up** reanimarse, sentirse mejor
**permanence** ['pʌrmənəns] *s* permanencia
**permanen•cy** ['pʌrmənənsi] *s* (*pl* **-cies**) permanencia; persona, cosa o posición permanentes
**permanent** ['pʌrmənənt] *adj* permanente || *s* permanente *f*, ondulación permanente
**permanent tenure** *s* inamovilidad
**permanent way** *s* (rr) material fijo
**permeate** ['pʌrmɪˌet] *tr & intr* penetrar
**permission** [pər'mɪʃən] *s* permisión
**per•mit** ['pʌrmɪt] *s* permiso; cédula de aduana || [pər'mɪt] *v* (*pret & pp* **-mitted;** *ger* **-mitting**) *tr* permitir
**permute** [pər'mjut] *tr* permutar
**pernicious** [pər'nɪʃəs] *adj* pernicioso
**pernickety** [pər'nɪkɪti] *adj* (coll) descontentadizo, quisquilloso
**perorate** ['perəˌret] *intr* perorar
**peroration** [ˌperə'reʃən] *s* peroración
**peroxide** [pər'ɑksaɪd] *s* peróxido; peróxido de hidrógeno
**peroxide blonde** *s* rubia oxigenada
**perpendicular** [ˌpʌrpən'dɪkjələr] *adj & s* perpendicular *f*
**perpetrate** ['pʌrpɪˌtret] *tr* perpetrar
**perpetual** [pər'petʃʊ·əl] *adj* perpetuo
**perpetuate** [pər'petʃʊˌet] *tr* perpetuar
**perplex** [pər'pleks] *tr* dejar perplejo
**perplexed** [pər'plekst] *adj* perplejo
**perplexi•ty** [pər'pleksɪti] *s* (*pl* **-ties**) perplejidad; problema *m*
**per se** [pər 'si] por sí mismo, en sí mismo, esencialmente
**persecute** ['pʌrsɪˌkjut] *tr* perseguir
**persecution** [ˌpʌrsɪ'kjuʃən] *s* persecución
**persevere** [ˌpʌrsɪ'vɪr] *intr* perseverar
**Persian** ['pʌrʒən] *adj & s* persa *mf*
**persimmon** [pər'sɪmən] *s* placaminero
**persist** [pər'sɪst] o [pər'zɪst] *intr* persistir
**persistent** [pər'sɪstənt] o [pər'zɪstənt] *adj* persistente; (*insistent*) porfiado; (*e.g., headache*) pertinaz
**person** ['pʌrsən] *s* persona; **no person** nadie
**personage** ['pʌrsənɪdʒ] *s* personaje *m;* persona
**personal** ['pʌrsənəl] *adj* personal; de uso personal || *s* nota de sociedad; (*in a newspaper*) remitido
**personali•ty** [ˌpʌrsə'nælɪti] *s* (*pl* **-ties**) personalidad
**personality cult** *s* culto a la personalidad
**personal property** *s* bienes *mpl* muebles
**personi•fy** [pər'sɑnɪˌfaɪ] *v* (*pret & pp* **-fied**) *tr* personificar
**personnel** [ˌpʌrsə'nel] *s* personal *m*
**perspective** [pər'spektɪv] *s* perspectiva
**perspicacious** [ˌpʌrspɪ'keʃəs] *adj* perspicaz
**perspire** [pər'spaɪr] *intr* sudar, transpirar
**persuade** [pər'swed] *tr* persuadir
**persuasion** [pər'sweʒən] *s* persuasión; creencia religiosa; creencia fuerte
**pert** [pʌrt] *adj* atrevido, descarado; (coll) animado, vivo
**pertain** [pər'ten] *intr* pertenecer; **pertaining to** perteneciente a
**pertinacious** [ˌpʌrtɪ'neʃəs] *adj* pertinaz
**pertinent** ['pʌrtɪnənt] *adj* pertinente
**perturb** [pər'tʌrb] *tr* perturbar
**Peru** [pə'ru] *s* el Perú
**perusal** [pə'ruzəl] *s* lectura cuidadosa
**peruse** [pə'ruz] *tr* leer con atención
**Peruvian** [pə'ruvɪ·ən] *adj & s* peruano
**pervade** [pər'ved] *tr* penetrar, esparcirse por, extenderse por
**perverse** [pər'vʌrs] *adj* perverso; avieso, díscolo; contumaz
**perversion** [pər'vʌrʒən] *s* perversión
**perversi•ty** [pər'vʌrsɪti] *s* (*pl* **-ties**) perversidad; indocilidad; contumacia
**pervert** ['pʌrvərt] *s* renegado, apóstata; pervertido || [pər'vʌrt] *tr* pervertir; emplear mal (*p.ej., los talentos que uno tiene*)
**pes•ky** ['peski] *adj* (*comp* **-kier;** *super* **-kiest**) (coll) cargante, molesto
**pessimism** ['pesɪˌmɪzəm] *s* pesimismo
**pessimist** ['pesɪmɪst] *s* pesimista *mf*
**pessimistic** [ˌpesɪ'mɪstɪk] *adj* pesimista
**pest** [pest] *s* peste *f;* insecto nocivo; (*misfortune*) plaga; (*annoying person, bore*) machaca *mf*
**pester** ['pestər] *tr* molestar, importunar

**pest'house'** *s* lazareto, hospital *m* de contagiosos
**pesticide** ['pɛstɪ,saɪd] *s* pesticida *m*
**pestiferous** [pɛs'tɪfərəs] *adj* pestífero; (coll) engorroso, molesto
**pestilence** ['pɛstɪləns] *s* pestilencia
**pestle** ['pɛsəl] *s* mano *f* de almirez
**pet** [pɛt] *s* animal mimado, animal casero; niño mimado; favorito; enojo pasajero || *v* (*pret & pp* **petted**; *ger* **petting**) *tr* acariciar, mimar || *intr* (slang) besuquearse
**petal** ['pɛtəl] *s* pétalo
**petard** [pɪ'tɑrd] *s* petardo
**pet'cock'** *s* llave *f* de desagüe, llave de purga
**Peter** ['pitər] *s* Pedro; **to rob Peter to pay Paul** desnudar a un santo para vestir a otro
**petition** [pɪ'tɪʃən] *s* petición; (*formal request signed by a number of people*) memorial *m*, instancia, solicitud || *tr* suplicar; dirigir una instancia a, solicitar
**pet name** *s* nombre *m* de cariño
**Petrarch** ['pitrɑrk] *s* Petrarca *m*
**petri·fy** ['pɛtrɪ,faɪ] *v* (*pret & pp* **-fied**) *tr* petrificar || *intr* petrificarse
**petrol** ['pɛtrəl] *s* (Brit) gasolina
**petroleum** [pɪ'trolɪ·əm] *s* petróleo
**pet shop** *s* pajarería
**petticoat** ['pɛtɪ,kot] *s* enaguas; (*woman, girl*) (slang) falda
**pet·ty** ['pɛti] *adj* (*comp* **-tier**; *super* **-tiest**) insignificante, pequeño; mezquino; intolerante
**petty cash** *s* caja de menores, efectivo para gastos menores
**petty larceny** *s* ratería, hurto
**petty officer** *s* (naut) suboficial *m*
**petulant** ['pɛtjələnt] *adj* malhumorado, enojadizo
**pew** [pju] *s* banco de iglesia
**pewter** ['pjutər] *s* peltre *m;* vajilla de peltre
**pfd.** *abbr* **preferred**
**Phaëthon** ['fe·ɪθən] *s* Faetón *m*
**phalanx** ['felæŋks] o ['fælæŋks] *s* falange *f*
**phantasm** ['fæntæzəm] *s* fantasma *m*
**phantom** ['fæntəm] *s* fantasma *m*
**Pharaoh** ['fɛro] *s* Faraón *m*
**pharisee** ['færɪ,si] *s* fariseo || **Pharisee** *s* fariseo
**pharmaceutical** [,fɑrmə'sutɪkəl] *adj* farmacéutico
**pharmacist** ['fɑrməsɪst] *s* farmacéutico
**pharma·cy** ['fɑrməsi] *s* (*pl* **-cies**) farmacia
**pharynx** ['færɪŋks] *s* faringe *f*
**phase** [fez] *s* fase *f* || *tr* poner en fase; llevar a cabo a etapas uniformes; (coll) inquietar, molestar; **to phase out** deshacer paulatinamente
**pheasant** ['fɛzənt] *s* faisán *m*
**phenobarbital** [,fino'bɑrbɪ,tæl] *s* fenobarbital *m*
**phenomenal** [fɪ'nɑmɪnəl] *adj* fenomenal
**phenome·non** [fɪ'nɑmɪ,nɑn] *s* (*pl* **-na** [nə]) fenómeno
**phial** ['faɪ·əl] *s* frasco pequeño
**Phidias** ['fɪdɪ·əs] *s* Fidias *m*
**philanderer** [fɪ'lændərər] *s* galanteador *m*, tenorio
**philanthropist** [fɪ'lænθrəpɪst] *s* filántropo
**philanthro·py** [fɪ'lænθrəpi] *s* (*pl* **-pies**) filantropía
**philatelist** [fɪ'lætəlɪst] *s* filatelista *mf*
**philately** [fɪ'lætəli] *s* filatelia
**Philip** ['fɪlɪp] *s* Felipe *m;* (*of Macedon*) Filipo
**Philippine** ['fɪlɪ,pin] *adj* filipino || **Philippines** *spl* Islas Filipinas
**Philistine** [fɪ'lɪstin], ['fɪlɪ,stin] o ['fɪlɪ,staɪn] *adj & s* filisteo
**philologist** [fɪ'lɑlədʒɪst] *s* filólogo
**philology** [fɪ'lɑlədʒi] *s* filología
**philosopher** [fɪ'lɑsəfər] *s* filósofo
**philosophic(al)** [,fɪlə'sɑfɪk(əl)] *adj* filosófico
**philoso·phy** [fɪ'lɑsəfi] *s* (*pl* **-phies**) filosofía
**philter** ['fɪltər] *s* filtro
**phlebitis** [flɪ'baɪtɪs] *s* flebitis *f*
**phlegm** [flɛm] *s* flema *f*, gargajo; **to cough up phlegm** gargajear
**phlegmatic(al)** [flɛg'mætɪk(əl)] *adj* flemático
**Phoebe** ['fibi] *s* Febe *f*
**Phoebus** ['fibəs] *s* Febo
**Phoenicia** [fɪ'nɪʃə] o [fɪ'niʃə] *s* Fenicia
**Phoenician** [fɪ'nɪʃən] o [fɪ'niʃən] *adj & s* fenicio
**phoenix** ['finɪks] *s* fénix *m*
**phone** [fon] *s* (coll) teléfono; **to come** o **to go to the phone** acudir al teléfono, ponerse al aparato || *tr & intr* (coll) telefonear
**phone call** *s* llamada telefónica
**phonetic** [fo'nɛtɪk] *adj* fonético
**phonograph** ['fonə,græf] o ['fonə,grɑf] *s* fonógrafo
**phonology** [fə'nɑlədʒi] *s* fonología
**pho·ny** ['foni] *adj* (*comp* **-nier**; *super* **-niest**) falso, contrahecho || *s* (*pl* **-nies**) (slang) farsa; (coll) farsante *mf*
**phosphate** ['fɑsfet] *s* fosfato
**phosphorescent** [,fɑsfə'rɛsənt] *adj* fosforescente
**phospho·rus** ['fɑsfərəs] *s* (*pl* **-ri** [,raɪ]) fósforo
**pho·to** ['foto] *s* (*pl* **-tos**) foto *f*
**photoengraving** [,foto·ɛn'grevɪŋ] *s* fotograbado
**photo finish** *s* (sport) llegada a la meta, determinada mediante el fotofija
**pho'to-fin'ish camera** *s* fotofija *m*
**photogenic** [,foto'dʒɛnɪk] *adj* fotogénico
**photograph** ['fotə,græf] o ['fotə,grɑf] *s* fotografía || *tr & intr* fotografiar
**photographer** [fə'tɑgrəfər] *s* fotógrafo
**photography** [fə'tɑgrəfi] *s* fotografía
**photojournalism** [,fotə'dʒʌrnə,lɪzəm] *s* fotoperiodismo
**pho'to·play'** *s* fotodrama *m*
**photostat** ['fotə,stæt] *s* (trademark) fotóstato || *tr & intr* fotostatar
**phototube** ['fotə,tjub] o ['fotə,tub] *s* fototubo
**phrase** [frez] *s* frase *f* || *tr* frasear
**phrenology** [frɪ'nɑlədʒi] *s* frenología

**Phyllis** [ˈfɪlɪs] *s* Filis *f*
**phys.** *abbr* **physical, physician, physics, physiology**
**phys•ic** [ˈfɪzɪk] *s* medicamento; purgante *m* || *v* (*pret & pp* **-icked;** *ger* **-icking**) *tr* curar; purgar
**physical** [ˈfɪzɪkəl] *adj* físico
**physician** [fɪˈzɪʃən] *s* médico
**physicist** [ˈfɪzɪsɪst] *s* físico
**physics** [ˈfɪzɪks] *s* física
**physiognomy** [ˌfɪzɪˈɑgnəmi] o [ˌfɪzɪˈɑnəmi] *s* fisonomía
**physiological** [ˌfɪzɪ•əˈlɑdʒɪkəl] *adj* fisiológico
**physiology** [ˌfɪzɪˈɑlədʒi] *s* fisiología
**physique** [fɪˈzɪk] *s* físico, talle *m,* exterior *m*
**pi** [paɪ] *s* (math) pi *f;* (typ) pastel *m* || *v* (*pret & pp* **pied;** *ger* **piing**) *tr* (typ) empastelar
**pian•o** [pɪˈæno] *s* (*pl* **-os**) piano
**picaresque** [ˌpɪkəˈrɛsk] *adj* picaresco
**picayune** [ˌpɪkəˈjun] *adj* de poca monta, mezquino
**piccadil•ly** [ˌpɪkəˈdɪli] *s* (*pl* **-lies**) cuello de pajarita
**picco•lo** [ˈpɪkəˌlo] *s* (*pl* **-los**) flautín *m*
**pick** [pɪk] *s* (*tool*) pico; (*choice*) selección; (*choicest*) flor *f* || *tr* escoger; recoger (*p.ej., flores*); recolectar (*p.ej., algodón*); romper (*el hielo*) con un picahielos; escarbarse (*los dientes*); descañonar, desplumar (*un ave*); hurgarse (*la nariz*); rascarse (*una cicatriz, un grano*); roer (*un hueso*); mondar (*las frutas*); falsear, forzar (*una cerradura*); armar (*una pendencia*); herir (*las cuerdas de un instrumento*); buscar (*defectos*); hurtar de (*los bolsillos*); **to pick out** entresacar; **to pick someone to pieces** (coll) no dejarle a uno un hueso sano; **to pick up** recoger; recobrar (*ánimo; velocidad*); descolgar (*el receptor*); hallar por casualidad; aprender con la práctica; aprender de oídas; invitar a subir a un coche; entablar conservación con (*sin presentación previa*); captar (*una señal de radio*) || *intr* comer melindrosamente; escoger esmeradamente; **to pick at** comer melindrosamente; tomarla con, regañar; **to pick on** escoger; (coll) regañar; (coll) molestar; **to pick over** ir revolviendo y examinando; **to pick up** (coll) ir mejor, sentirse mejor; recobrar velocidad
**pick'ax'** *s* zapapico
**picket** [ˈpɪkɪt] *s* (*stake, pale*) piquete *m;* (*of strikers; of soldiers*) piquete *m* || *tr* poner un cordón de piquetes a || *intr* servir de piquete
**picket fence** *s* cerca de estacas
**picket line** *s* línea de piquetes
**pickle** [ˈpɪkəl] *s* encurtido; escabeche *m,* salmuera; (coll) apuro, aprieto || *tr* encurtir; escabechar
**pick-me-up** [ˈpɪkmiˌʌp] *s* (coll) tentempié *m;* (coll) trago fortificante
**pick'pock'et** *s* carterista *m,* ratero
**pick'up'** *s* recolección; (*of a motor*) recobro; (*of an automobile*) aceleración; (elec) pick-up, fonocaptor *m*
**pic•nic** [ˈpɪknɪk] *s* jira, partida de campo || *v* (*pret & pp* **-nicked;** *ger* **-nicking**) *intr* hacer una jira al campo, merendar en el campo
**pictorial** [pɪkˈtorɪ•əl] *adj* gráfico; ilustrado || *s* revista ilustrada
**picture** [ˈpɪktʃər] *s* cuadro; retrato; imagen *f;* lámina, grabado; fotografía; película; pintura || *tr* dibujar; pintar; describir; **to picture to oneself** representarse
**picture gallery** *s* galería de pinturas
**picture post card** *s* postal ilustrada
**picture show** *s* exhibición de pinturas; cine *m*
**picture signal** *s* videoseñal *f*
**picturesque** [ˌpɪktjəˈrɛsk] *adj* pintoresco
**picture tube** *s* tubo de imagen, tubo de televisión
**picture window** *s* ventana panorámica
**piddling** [ˈpɪdlɪŋ] *adj* de poca monta, insignificante
**pie** [paɪ] *s* pastel *m;* (*bird*) picaza; (typ) pastel *m* || *v* (*pret & pp* **pied;** *ger* **pieing**) *tr* (typ) empastelar
**piece** [pis] *s* (*fragment; section of cloth*) pedazo; (*part of a machine; drama; single composition of music; coin; figure or block used in checkers, chess, etc.*) pieza; (*of land*) lote *m,* parcela; **a piece of advice** un consejo; **a piece of baggage** un bulto; **a piece of furniture** un mueble; **to break to pieces** despedazar, hacer pedazos; despedazarse; **to fall to pieces** desbaratarse, caer en ruina; **to give someone a piece of one's mind** decirle a uno su parecer con toda franqueza; **to go to pieces** desvencijarse; darse a la desesperación; ir al desastre (*un negocio*); sufrir un ataque de nervios; perder por completo la salud; **to pick someone to pieces** (coll) no dejarle a uno un hueso sano || *tr* formar juntando piezas; remendar || *intr* (coll) comer a deshora
**piece'work'** *s* destajo, trabajo a destajo
**piece'work'er** *s* destajero, destajista *mf*
**pier** [pɪr] *s* muelle *m;* (*of a bridge*) estribo, sostén *m;* (*of a harbor*) rompeolas *m;* (*wall between two openings*) (archit) entrepaño
**pierce** [pɪrs] *tr* agujerear, horadar, taladrar; atravesar, traspasar; picar, pinchar, punzar; (fig) traspasar (*de dolor*) || *intr* penetrar, entrar a la fuerza
**piercing** [ˈpɪrsɪŋ] *adj* agudo, penetrante, desgarrador; (*pain*) lancinante
**pier glass** *s* espejo de cuerpo entero
**pie•ty** [ˈpaɪ•əti] *s* (*pl* **-ties**) piedad, devoción
**piffle** [ˈpɪfəl] *s* (coll) disparates *mpl,* música celestial
**pig** [pɪg] *s* cerdo; (*young hog*) lechón *m;* (*domestic hog*) puerco, cochino; carne *f* de puerco; (metal) lingote *m;* (*person who acts like a pig*) (coll) marrano, cochino
**pigeon** [ˈpɪdʒən] *s* paloma

**pi'geon·hole'** *s* hornilla, casilla de paloma; casilla || *tr* encasillar
**pigeon house** *s* palomar *m*
**piggish** ['pɪgɪʃ] *adj* glotón, voraz
**pig'gy·back'** *adv* a cuestas, en hombros
**pig'-head'ed** *adj* terco, cabezudo
**pig iron** *s* arrabio, hierro en lingotes
**pigment** ['pɪgmənt] *s* pigmento || *tr* pigmentar || *intr* pigmentarse
**pig'pen'** *s* pocilga; (fig) pocilga, corral *m* de vacas
**pig'skin'** *s* piel *f* de cerdo; (coll) balón *m* (*con que se juega al fútbol*)
**pig'sty'** *s* (*pl* **-sties**) pocilga
**pig'tail'** *s* coleta, trenza; (*of tobacco*) andullo
**pike** [paɪk] *s* pica; (*of an arrow*) punta; carretera; camino de barrera; (*fish*) lucio
**piker** ['paɪkər] *s* (slang) persona de poco fuste
**Pilate** ['paɪlət] *s* Pilatos *m*
**pile** [paɪl] *s* pila, montón *m;* (*stake*) pilote *m;* lanilla, pelusa; pira; (elec, phys) pila; (coll) caudal *m;* **piles** almorranas || *tr* apilar, amontonar || *intr* apilarse, amontonarse; **to pile in** o **into** entrar atropelladamente en; entrar todos en; subir todos a (*p.ej., un coche*)
**pile driver** *s* martinete *m*
**pilfer** ['pɪlfər] *tr & intr* ratear
**pilgrim** ['pɪlgrɪm] *s* peregrino, romero
**pilgrimage** ['pɪlgrɪmɪdʒ] *s* peregrinación, romería
**pill** [pɪl] *s* píldora; mal trago, sinsabor *m;* (coll) persona molesta
**pillage** ['pɪlɪdʒ] *s* pillaje *m*, saqueo || *tr & intr* pillar, saquear
**pillar** ['pɪlər] *s* pilar *m;* **from pillar to post** de acá para allá sin objeto determinado
**pillo·ry** ['pɪləri] *s* (*pl* **-ries**) picota || *v* (*pret & pp* **-ried**) *tr* empicotar; (fig) motejar, poner en ridículo
**pillow** ['pɪlo] *s* almohada
**pil'low·case'** o **pil'low·slip'** *s* funda de almohada
**pilot** ['paɪlət] *s* piloto; (*of a harbor*) práctico; (*of a gas range*) mechero encendedor; (rr) trompa, delantera || *tr* pilotar; conducir
**pimp** [pɪmp] *s* alcahuete *m*
**pimple** ['pɪmpəl] *s* barro, grano
**pim·ply** ['pɪmpli] *adj* (*comp* **-plier;** *super* **-pliest**) granujoso
**pin** [pɪn] *s* alfiler *m;* (*e.g., for a necktie*) prendedero; (*peg*) clavija; (*e.g., to hold scissors together*) clavillo, clavito; (bowling) bolo; **to be on pins and needles** estar en espinas || *v* (*pret & pp* **pinned;** *ger* **pinning**) *tr* alfilerar; clavar, fijar, sujetar; **to pin something on someone** (coll) acusarle a uno de una cosa; **to pin up** recoger y apuntar con alfileres; fijar en la pared con alfileres
**pinafore** ['pɪnə,for] *s* delantal *m* de niño
**pin'ball'** *s* billar romano, bagatela
**pince-nez** ['pæns,ne] *s* lentes *mpl* de nariz, lentes de pinzas
**pincers** ['pɪnsərz] *ssg* o *spl* pinzas
**pinch** [pɪntʃ] *s* pellizco; (*of hunger*) tormento; (slang) arresto; (slang) hurto, robo; **in a pinch** en un aprieto; en caso necesario || *tr* pellizcar; cogerse (*los dedos, p.ej., en una puerta*); apretar (*p.ej., el zapato a una persona*); contraer (*el frío la cara de uno*); limitar los gastos de; (slang) arrestar, prender; (slang) hurtar, robar || *intr* apretar; economizar, privarse de lo necesario
**pinchers** ['pɪntʃərz] *ssg* o *spl* var of **pincers**
**pin'cush'ion** *s* acerico
**Pindar** ['pɪndər] *s* Píndaro
**pine** [paɪn] *s* pino || *intr* languidecer; **to pine away** consumirse; **to pine for** penar por
**pine'ap'ple** *s* ananás *m*, piña
**pine cone** *s* piña
**pine needle** *s* pinocha
**ping** [pɪŋ] *s* silbido de bala || *intr* silbar (*una bala*); silbar como una bala
**pin'head'** *s* cabecilla de alfiler; cosa muy pequeña o insignificante; (coll) bobalicón *m*
**pink** [pɪŋk] *adj* rosado, sonrosado || *s* estado perfecto; comunistoide *mf;* (bot) clavel *m*, clavellina
**pin money** *s* alfileres *mpl*
**pinnacle** ['pɪnəkəl] *s* pináculo
**pin'point'** *adj* exacto, preciso || *s* punta de alfiler || *tr & intr* señalar con precisión
**pin'prick'** *s* alfilerazo
**pinup girl** ['pɪn,ʌp] *s* guapa
**pin'wheel'** *s* rueda de fuego, rueda giratoria de fuegos artificiales; (*child's toy*) rehilandera, ventolera
**pioneer** [,paɪ·ə'nɪr] *s* pionero; (mil) zapador *m* || *intr* abrir nuevos caminos, explorar
**pious** ['paɪ·əs] *adj* pío, piadoso; mojigato; respetuoso
**pip** [pɪp] *s* (*seed*) pepita; (*on a card, dice, etc.*) punto; (vet) pepita
**pipe** [paɪp] *s* caño, conducto, tubo; (*to smoke tobacco*) pipa; (mus) pipa, caramillo, zampoña; (*of an organ*) cañón *m* || *tr* conducir por medio de tubos o cañerías; proveer de tuberías o cañerías || *intr* tocar el caramillo; **to pipe down** (slang) callarse
**pipe cleaner** *s* limpiapipas *m*
**pipe dream** *s* esperanza imposible, castillo en el aire
**pipe line** *s* cañería, tubería; oleoducto; fuente *f* de informes confidenciales
**pipe organ** *s* (mus) órgano
**piper** ['paɪpər] *s* flautista *m;* gaitero; **to pay the piper** pagar los vidrios rotos
**pipe wrench** *s* llave *f* para tubos
**pippin** ['pɪpɪn] *s* (*apple*) camuesa; (*tree*) camueso; (slang) real moza
**piquancy** ['pikənsi] *s* picante *m*
**piquant** ['pikənt] *adj* picante
**pique** [pik] *s* pique *m*, resentimiento || *tr* picar, enojar; despertar, excitar
**Piraeus** [paɪ'ri·əs] *s* el Pireo
**pirate** ['paɪrɪt] *s* pirata *m* || *tr* pillar,

robar; publicar fraudulentamente || *intr* piratear
**pirouette** [ˌpɪruˈet] *s* pirueta || *intr* piruetear
**pistol** [ˈpɪstəl] *s* pistola
**piston** [ˈpɪstən] *s* (mach) émbolo, pistón *m;* (mus) pistón *m*
**piston displacement** *s* cilindrada
**piston ring** *s* anillo de émbolo, aro de émbolo, segmento de émbolo
**piston rod** *s* vástago de émbolo
**piston stroke** *s* carrera de émbolo
**pit** [pɪt] *s* hoyo; (*in the skin*) cacaraña; (*of certain fruit*) hueso; (*for cockfights, etc.*) cancha, reñidero; (*of the stomach*) boca; abismo, infierno; (min) pozo; (theat) foso || *v* (*pret & pp* **pitted;** *ger* **pitting**) *tr* marcar con hoyos; dejar hoyoso (*el rostro*); deshuesar (*p.ej., una ciruela*)
**pitch** [pɪtʃ] *s* (*black sticky substance*) pez *f;* echada, lanzamiento; cosa lanzada; pelota lanzada; (*of a boat*) arfada, cabezada; (*of a roof*) pendiente *f;* (*of, e.g., a screw*) paso; (*of a winding*) (elec) paso; (mus) tono, altura; (fig) grado, extremo; (coll) bombo, elogio || *tr* echar, lanzar; elevar (*el heno*) con la horquilla; armar o plantar (*una tienda de campaña*); embrear; (mus) graduar el tono de || *intr* caerse, caer de cabeza; bajar en declive, inclinarse; arfar, cabecear (*un buque*); **to pitch in** (coll) poner manos a la obra; (coll) comenzar a comer
**pitch accent** *s* acento de altura
**pitcher** [ˈpɪtʃər] *s* jarro; (*in baseball*) lanzador *m*
**pitch'fork'** *s* horca, horquilla; **to rain pitchforks** (coll) llover a cántaros
**pitch pipe** *s* (mus) diapasón *m*
**pit'fall'** *s* callejo, trampa; (*danger for the unwary*) escollo, atascadero
**pith** [pɪθ] *s* médula; (*essential part*) (fig) médula; (fig) fuerza, vigor *m*
**pith•y** [ˈpɪθi] *adj* (*comp* **-ier;** *super* **-iest**) medular; enérgico, expresivo
**pitiful** [ˈpɪtɪfəl] *adj* lastimoso; compasivo; despreciable
**pitiless** [ˈpɪtɪlɪs] *adj* despiadado, empedernido, incompasivo
**pit•y** [ˈpɪti] *s* (*pl* **-ies**) piedad, compasión, lástima; **for pity's sake!** ¡por piedad!; **to have** o **to take pity on** tener piedad de, apiadarse de; **what a pity!** ¡qué lástima!, ¡qué pena! || *v* (*pret & pp* **-ied**) *tr* apiadarse de, compadecer
**pivot** [ˈpɪvət] *s* pivote *m,* gorrón *m,* eje *m* de rotación; (fig) eje *m* || *intr* pivotar; **to pivot on** girar sobre; depender de
**placard** [ˈplækɑrd] *s* cartel *m* || *tr* fijar carteles en; fijar (*un anuncio*) en sitio público; publicar por medio de carteles
**place** [ples] *s* sitio, lugar *m;* (*of business*) local *m;* (*job*) puesto; grado, rango; **in no place** en ninguna parte; **in place of** en lugar de; **out of place** fuera de su lugar; fuera de propósito; **to be looking for a place to live** buscar piso; **to take place** tener lugar || *tr* poner, colocar; acordarse bien de; dar empleo a; prestar (*dinero*) a interés || *intr* colocarse (*un caballo en las carreras*)
**place•bo** [pləˈsibo] *s* (*pl* **-bos** o **-boes**) placebo
**place card** *s* tarjetita con el nombre (*que indica la colocación de uno en la mesa*)
**placement** [ˈplesmənt] *s* colocación
**place name** *s* nombre *m* de lugar, topónimo
**placid** [ˈplæsɪd] *adj* plácido, tranquilo
**plagiarism** [ˈpledʒəˌrɪzəm] *s* plagio
**plagiarize** [ˈpledʒəˌraɪz] *tr* plagiar
**plague** [pleg] *s* peste *f,* plaga; (*great public calamity*) plaga || *tr* apestar, plagar; atormentar, molestar
**plaid** [plæd] *s* (*cloth*) tartán *m;* cuadros a la escocesa
**plain** [plen] *adj* llano, claro, evidente; abierto, franco; ordinario; feo; humilde; solo, natural; **in plain English** sin rodeos; **in plain sight** o **view** en plena vista || *s* llano, llanura
**plain clothes** *spl* traje *m* de calle, traje de paisano
**plainclothesman** [ˈplenˈkloðzˌmæn] *s* (*pl* **-men** [ˌmɛn]) policía *m* que lleva traje de paisano
**plain omelet** *s* tortilla a la francesa
**plains•man** [ˈplenzmən] *s* (*pl* **-men** [mən]) llanero
**plaintiff** [ˈplentɪf] *s* (law) demandante *mf*
**plaintive** [ˈplentɪv] *adj* quejumbroso
**plan** [plæn] *s* plan *m,* intento, proyecto; (*drawing, diagram*) plan *m,* plano; **to change one's plans** cambiar de proyecto || *v* (*pret & pp* **planned;** *ger* **planning**) *tr* planear, planificar; **to plan to** proponerse || *intr* hacer proyectos
**plane** [plen] *adj* plano || *s* (*surface*) plano; aeroplano, avión *m;* (*of an airplane*) plano; (carp) cepillo; (*tree*) plátano || *tr* cepillar || *intr* viajar en aeroplano
**plane sickness** *s* mareo del aire, mal *m* de vuelo
**planet** [ˈplænɪt] *s* planeta *m*
**plane tree** *s* plátano
**planing mill** [ˈplenɪŋ] *s* taller *m* de cepillado
**plank** [plæŋk] *s* tabla gruesa, tablón *m;* artículo de un programa político || *tr* entablar, entarimar
**plant** [plænt] o [plɑnt] *s* fábrica, taller *m;* (*of an automobile*) grupo motor; (*educational establishment*) plantel *m;* (bot) planta || *tr* plantar; sembrar (*semillas*); inculcar (*doctrinas*); (slang) ocultar (*géneros robados*)
**plantation** [plænˈteʃən] *s* plantación, campo de plantas; (*estate cultivated by workers living on it*) hacienda
**planter** [ˈplæntər] *s* plantador *m,* cultivador *m*
**plaster** [ˈplæstər] o [ˈplɑstər] *s* (*gypsum*) yeso; (*mixture of lime, sand,*

*water, etc.*) argamasa; (*coating*) enlucido; (*poultice*) emplasto || *tr* enyesar; argamasar; enlucir; emplastar; embadurnar; pegar (*anuncios*)
**plas'ter·board'** *s* cartón *m* de yeso y fieltro
**plaster cast** *s* (surg) vendaje enyesado; (sculp) yeso
**plaster of Paris** *s* estuco de París
**plastic** ['plæstɪk] *adj* plástico || *s* (*substance*) plástico; (*art of modeling*) plástica
**plate** [plet] *s* (*dish*) plato; (*sheet of metal, etc.*), chapa, placa; vajilla de oro, vajilla de plata; dentadura postiza, base *f* de la dentadura postiza; (baseball) puesto meta, puesto del batter; (anat, elec, electron, phot, zool) placa; (typ) clisé *m* || *tr* chapear, planchear; blindar; platear, dorar, niquelar (*por la galvanoplastia*); (typ) clisar
**plateau** [plæ'to] *s* meseta
**plate glass** *s* vidrio o cristal cilindrado
**platen** ['plætən] *s* rodillo
**platform** ['plæt,fɔrm] *s* plataforma *f;* (*of passenger station*) andén *m;* (*of freight station*) cargadero; (*of a speaker*) tribuna; (*political program*) plataforma
**platform car** *s* plataforma *f*
**platinum** ['plætɪnəm] *s* platino
**platinum blonde** *s* rubia platino
**platitude** ['plætɪ,tjud] o ['plætɪ,tud] *s* perogrullada, trivialidad
**Plato** ['pleto] *s* Platón *m*
**platoon** [plə'tun] *s* pelotón *m*
**platter** ['plætər] *s* fuente *f;* (slang) disco de fonógrafo
**plausible** ['plɔzɪbəl] *adj* aparente, especioso; bien hablado; (coll) creíble
**play** [ple] *s* juego; (*act or move in a game*) jugada; (*drama*) pieza; (*of water, colors, lights*) juego; (mach) huelgo, juego; **to give full play to** dar rienda suelta a || *tr* jugar (*p.ej., un naipe, una partida de juego*); jugar a (*p.ej., los naipes*); jugar con (*un contrario*); dar (*un chasco*); gastar (*una broma*); hacer (*una mala jugada*); dirigir (*agua, una manguera*); desempeñar (*un papel*); desempeñar el papel de; representar (*una obra dramática, un film*); apostar por (*un caballo*); tocar (*un instrumento, una pieza, un disco de fonógrafo*) || *intr* jugar; desempeñar un papel, representar; correr (*una fuente*); rielar (*la luz en la superficie del agua*); vagar (*p.ej., una sonrisa por los labios*); **to play out** rendirse; agotarse; acabarse; **to play safe** tomar sus precauciones; **to play sick** hacerse el enfermo; **to play up to** hacer la rueda a
**play'back'** *s* lectura; aparato de lectura
**play'bill'** *s* (*poster*) cartel *m;* (*of a play*) programa *m*
**player piano** ['ple·ər] *s* autopiano
**playful** ['plefəl] *adj* juguetón, retozón; dicho en broma
**playgoer** ['ple,go·ər] *s* aficionado al teatro
**play'ground'** *s* campo de juego; patio de recreo
**play'house'** *s* casita de muñecas; teatro
**playing card** ['ple·ɪŋ] *s* naipe *m*
**playing field** *s* campo de deportes
**play'mate'** *s* compañero de juego
**play'-off'** *s* partido de desempate
**play'pen'** *s* parque *m*, corral *m* (*para bebés*)
**play'thing'** *s* juguete *m*
**play'time'** *s* hora de recreo, hora de juego
**playwright** ['ple,raɪt] *s* dramaturgo, autor dramático
**play'writ'ing** *s* dramaturgia, dramática
**plea** [pli] *s* ruego, súplica; disculpa, excusa; (law) contestación a la demanda
**plead** [plid] *v* (*pret & pp* **pleaded** o **pled** [plɛd]) *tr* defender (*una causa*) || *intr* suplicar; abogar; **to plead guilty** confesarse culpable; **to plead not guilty** negar la acusación, declararse inocente
**pleasant** ['plɛzənt] *adj* agradable; simpático
**pleasant·ry** ['plɛzəntri] *s* (*pl* **-ries**) broma, chiste *m*, dicho gracioso
**please** [pliz] *tr & intr* gustar; **as you please** como Vd. quiera; **if you please** si me hace el favor; **please** + *inf* hágame Vd. el favor de + *inf;* **to be pleased to** alegrarse de, complacerse en; **to be pleased with** estar satisfecho de o con
**pleasing** ['plizɪŋ] *adj* agradable, grato
**pleasure** ['plɛʒər] *s* placer *m*, gusto; **what is your pleasure?** ¿en qué puedo servirle?, ¿qué es lo que Vd. desea?; **with pleasure** con mucho gusto
**pleasure seeker** ['sikər] *s* amigo de los placeres
**pleat** [plit] *s* pliegue *m*, plisado || *tr* plegar, plisar
**plebeian** [plɪ'bi·ən] *adj & s* plebeyo
**pledge** [plɛdʒ] *s* empeño, prenda; (*vow*) voto, promesa; (*toast*) brindis *m;* **as a pledge of** en prenda de; **to take the pledge** comprometerse a no tomar bebidas alcohólicas || *tr* empeñar, prendar; dar (*la palabra*); brindar por
**plentiful** ['plɛntɪfəl] *adj* abundante, copioso
**plenty** ['plɛnti] *adv* (coll) completamente || *s* abundancia, copia; suficiencia
**pleurisy** ['plʊrɪsi] *s* pleuresía
**pliable** ['plaɪ·əbəl] *adj* flexible, plegable; dócil
**pliers** ['plaɪ·ərz] *ssg* o *spl* alicates *mpl*
**plight** [plaɪt] *s* estado, situación; apuro, aprieto; compromiso solemne || *tr* dar o empeñar (*su palabra*); **to plight one's troth** prometer fidelidad; dar palabra de casamiento
**plod** [plɑd] *v* (*pret & pp* **plodded;** *ger* **plodding**) *tr* recorrer (*un camino*) pausada y pesadamente || *intr* caminar pausada y pesadamente; trabajar laboriosamente
**plot** [plɑt] *s* complot *m*, conspiración; (*of a play or novel*) argumento,

trama; parcela, solar *m;* cuadro de flores; cuadro de hortalizas; plano, mapa *m* || *v* (*pret & pp* **plotted;** *ger* **plotting**) *tr* fraguar, tramar, urdir, maquinar; dividir en parcelas o solares; trazar el plano de; trazar, tirar (*líneas*) || *intr* conspirar

**plough** [plaʊ] *s, tr & intr* var de **plow**

**plover** [ˈplʌvər] o [ˈplovər] *s* chorlito

**plow** [plaʊ] *s* arado; quitanieve *m* || *tr* arar; surcar; quitar o barrer (*la nieve*); **to plow back** reinvertir (*ganancias*) || *intr* arar; avanzar como un arado

**plow•man** [ˈplaʊmən] *s* (*pl* **-men** [mən]) arador *m,* yuguero

**plow'share'** *s* reja de arado

**pluck** [plʌk] *s* ánimo, coraje *m,* valor *m;* tirón *m* || *tr* arrancar; coger (*flores*); desplumar (*un ave*); puntear (*p.ej., una guitarra*) || *intr* dar un tirón; **to pluck up** recobrar ánimo

**pluck•y** [ˈplʌki] *adj* (*comp* **-ier;** *super* **-iest**) animoso, valiente

**plug** [plʌg] *s* taco, tarugo; boca de agua; tableta de tabaco; (*hat*) (slang) chistera; (elec) clavija, toma, ficha; (aut) bujía; (coll) rocín; (slang) elogio incidental || *v* (*pret & pp* **plugged;** *ger* **plugging**) *tr* atarugar; calar (*un melón*); **to plug in** (elec) enchufar || *intr* (coll) trabajar con ahinco

**plum** [plʌm] *s* (*tree*) ciruelo; (*fruit*) ciruela; (slang) turrón *m,* pingüe destino

**plumage** [ˈplumɪdʒ] *s* plumaje *m*

**plumb** [plʌm] *adj* vertical; (coll) completo || *adv* a plomo; (coll) verticalmente; (coll) directamente || *tr* aplomar; sondear

**plumb bob** *s* plomada

**plumber** [ˈplʌmər] *s* fontanero; (*worker in lead*) plomero

**plumbing** [ˈplʌmɪŋ] *s* instalación sanitaria; conjunto de cañerías; (*working in lead*) plomería; sondeo

**plumbing fixtures** *spl* artefactos sanitarios

**plumb line** *s* cuerda de plomada

**plum cake** *s* pastel aderezado con pasas de Corinto y ron

**plume** [plum] *s* (*of a bird*) pluma; (*tuft of feathers worn as ornament*) penacho || *tr* emplumar; componerse (*las plumas*); **to plume oneself on** enorgullecerse de

**plummet** [ˈplʌmɪt] *s* plomada || *intr* caer a plomo, precipitarse

**plump** [plʌmp] *adj* rechoncho, regordete; brusco, franco || *adv* de golpe; francamente || *s* (coll) caída pesada; (coll) ruido sordo || *intr* caer a plomo

**plum pudding** *s* pudín *m* inglés con pasas de Corinto, corteza de limón, huevos y ron

**plum tree** *s* ciruelo

**plunder** [ˈplʌndər] *s* pillaje *m;* botín *m* || *tr* pillar, saquear

**plunge** [plʌndʒ] *s* zambullida; caída a plomo; sacudida violenta; salto; baño de agua fría; (*of a boat*) cabeceo || *tr* zambullir; sumergir; hundir (*p.ej., un puñal*) || *intr* zambullirse; sumergirse; hundirse (*p.ej., en la tristeza*); caer a plomo; arrojarse, precipitarse; cabecear (*un buque*); (slang) entregarse al juego, entregarse a las especulaciones

**plunger** [ˈplʌndʒər] *s* zambullidor *m;* émbolo buzo; (*of a tire valve*) obús *m;* (slang) jugador o especulador desenfrenado

**plunk** [plʌŋk] *adv* (coll) con un golpe seco, con un ruido de golpe seco || *tr* (coll) arrojar, empujar o dejar caer pesadamente || *intr* sonar o caer con un ruido de golpe seco

**plural** [ˈplurəl] *adj & s* plural *m*

**plus** [plʌs] *adj* más; y pico; **to be plus** (coll) tener por añadidura || *prep* más || *s* (*sign*) más *m;* añadidura

**plush** [plʌʃ] *adj* afelpado; (coll) lujoso, suntuoso || *s* felpa

**Plutarch** [ˈplutɑrk] *s* Plutarco

**plutonium** [pluˈtonɪ•əm] *s* plutonio

**ply** [plaɪ] *s* (*pl* **plies**) (*e.g., of a cloth*) capa, doblez *m;* (*of a cable*) cordón *m* || *v* (*pret & pp* **plied**) *tr* manejar (*la aguja, etc.*); ejercer (*un oficio*); batir (*el agua con los remos*); importunar; navegar por (*p.ej., un río*) || *intr* avanzar; **to ply between** hacer (*un barco*) el servicio entre

**ply'wood'** *s* chapeado, madera laminada

**P.M.** *abbr* **Postmaster, post meridiem** (Lat) **afternoon**

**pneumatic** [njuˈmætɪk] o [nuˈmætɪk] *adj* neumático

**pneumatic drill** *s* perforadora de aire comprimido

**pneumonia** [njuˈmonɪ•ə] o [nuˈmonɪ•ə] *s* neumonía o pulmonía

**P.O.** *abbr* **post office**

**poach** [potʃ] *tr* escalfar (*huevos*) || *intr* cazar o pescar en vedado

**poacher** [ˈpotʃər] *s* cazador furtivo, pescador furtivo

**pock** [pɑk] *s* cacaraña, hoyuelo

**pocket** [ˈpɑkɪt] *s* bolsillo, faltriquera; (*in billiards*) tronera; (aer) bolsa de aire; (mil) bolsón *m* || *tr* embolsar; entronerar (*una bola de billar*); tragarse (*injurias*)

**pock'et•book'** *s* portamonedas *m;* (*of a woman*) bolsa

**pocket handkerchief** *s* pañuelo de bolsillo o de mano

**pock'et•knife'** *s* (*pl* **-knives**) navaja, cortaplumas *m*

**pocket money** *s* alfileres *mpl,* dinero de bolsillo

**pock'mark'** *s* cacaraña, hoyuelo

**pod** [pɑd] *s* vaina

**poem** [ˈpo•ɪm] *s* poema *m,* poesía

**poet** [ˈpo•ɪt] *s* poeta *m*

**poetess** [ˈpo•ɪtɪs] *s* poetisa

**poetic** [poˈetɪk] *adj* poético || **poetics** *ssg* poética

**poetry** [ˈpo•ɪtri] *s* poesía

**pogrom** [ˈpogrəm] *s* levantamiento contra los judíos

**poignancy** [ˈpɔɪnənsi] *s* picante *m,* viveza, intensidad

**poignant** [ˈpɔɪnənt] *adj* picante, vivo, intenso

**point** [pɔɪnt] *s* (*of a sword, pencil; of land*) punta; (*of pen*) pico; (*of fountain pen*) puntilla; (*mark of imperceptible dimensions*) punto; (*of a joke*) gracia; (elec) punta; (math, typ, sport, fig) punto; (coll) indirecta, insinuación; **beside the point** fuera de propósito; **on the point of** a punto de; **to carry one's point** salirse con la suya; **to come to the point** venir al caso o al grano; **to get the point** caer en la cuenta ‖ *tr* aguzar, sacar punta a; apuntar (*p.ej., un arma de fuego*); resanar (*una pared*); **to point one's finger at** señalar con el dedo; **to point out** señalar, indicar, hacer notar ‖ *intr* apuntar; pararse (*el perro de muestra*); **to point at** señalar con el dedo

**point′blank′** *adj & adv* a quemarropa

**pointed** [ˈpɔɪntɪd] *adj* puntiagudo; picante; acentuado, directo

**pointer** [ˈpɔɪntər] *s* puntero; indicador *m;* (*of a clock*) manecilla; perro de muestra; (mas) fijador *m;* (coll) indicación, dirección

**poise** [pɔɪz] *s* aplomo, equilibrio ‖ *tr* equilibrar; considerar ‖ *intr* equilibrarse; estar suspendido

**poison** [ˈpɔɪzən] *s* veneno, ponzoña ‖ *tr* envenenar

**poison ivy** *s* tosiguero

**poisonous** [ˈpɔɪzənəs] *adj* venenoso

**poke** [pok] *s* (*push*) empuje *m,* empujón *m;* (*thrust*) hurgonazo; (*with elbow*) codazo; (*slow person*) tardón *m* ‖ *tr* empujar; hacer (*un agujero*) a empujones; abrirse (*paso*) a empujones; atizar, hurgar (*el fuego*); **to poke fun at** burlarse de; **to poke one's nose into** entremeterse en ‖ *intr* fisgar, husmear; andar perezosamente

**poker** [ˈpokər] *s* hurgón *m;* (*card game*) póker *m,* pócar *m*

**poker face** *s* (coll) cara de jugador de póker; **to keep a poker face** (coll) disfrazar la expresión del rostro, mantener una expresión imperturbable

**pok·y** [ˈpoki] *adj* (*comp* **-ier;** *super* **-iest**) (coll) tardo, roncero

**Poland** [ˈpolənd] *s* Polonia

**polar bear** [ˈpolər] *s* oso blanco

**polarize** [ˈpoləˌraɪz] *tr* polarizar

**pole** [pol] *s* (*long rod or staff*) pértiga; (*of a flag*) asta; (*upright support*) poste *m;* (*to push a boat*) botador *m;* (astr, biol, elec, geog, math) polo ‖ *tr* impeler (*un barco*) con botador ‖ **Pole** *s* polaco

**pole′cat′** *s* turón *m,* veso

**pole′star′** *s* estrella polar; (*guide*) norte *m;* (*center of interest*) miradero

**pole vault** *s* salto con garrocha o con pértiga

**police** [pəˈlis] *s* policía ‖ *tr* poner o mantener servicio de policía en; (mil) limpiar

**police·man** [pəˈlismən] *s* (*pl* **-men** [mən]) policía *m,* guardia urbano

**police state** *s* estado-policía *m*

**police station** *s* cuartel *m* o estación de policía

**poli·cy** [ˈpɑlɪsi] *s* (*pl* **-cies**) política; (ins) póliza

**polio** [ˈpolɪˌo] *s* (coll) polio *f*

**polish** [ˈpɑlɪʃ] *s* pulimento; cera de lustrar; (*for shoes*) bola, betún *m,* lustre *m;* elegancia; cultura, urbanidad ‖ *tr* pulimentar, pulir; embolar, dar betún a (*los zapatos*); **to polish off** (coll) terminar de prisa; (slang) engullir (*la comida, un trago*) ‖ **Polish** [ˈpolɪʃ] *adj & s* polaco

**polisher** [ˈpɑlɪʃər] *s* pulidor *m;* (*machine*) pulidora; (*for floors, tables, etc.*) enceradora

**polite** [pəˈlaɪt] *adj* cortés, fino, urbano; culto

**politeness** [pəˈlaɪtnɪs] *s* cortesía, fineza, urbanidad; cultura

**politic** [ˈpɑlɪtɪk] *adj* prudente, sagaz; astuto; juicioso

**political** [pəˈlɪtɪkəl] *adj* político

**politician** [ˌpɑlɪˈtɪʃən] *s* político; (*politician seeking personal or partisan gain*) politiquero

**politics** [ˈpɑlɪtɪks] *ssg* o *spl* política

**poll** [pol] *s* (*questionnaire to determine opinion*) encuesta; votación; lista electoral; cabeza; **polls** urnas electorales; **to go to the polls** acudir a las urnas; **to take a poll** hacer una encuesta ‖ *tr* dar (*un voto*); recibir (*votos*)

**pollen** [ˈpɑlən] *s* polen *m*

**pollinate** [ˈpɑlɪˌnet] *tr* polinizar

**polling booth** [ˈpolɪŋ] *s* cabina o caseta de votar

**polliwog** [ˈpɑlɪˌwɑg] *s* renacuajo; (slang) persona que atraviesa el ecuador en un barco por primera vez

**poll tax** *s* capitación, impuesto por cabeza

**pollute** [pəˈlut] *tr* contaminar, corromper, ensuciar

**pollution** [pəˈluʃən] *s* contaminación

**polo** [ˈpolo] *s* polo

**polo player** *s* polista *mf,* jugador *m* de polo

**polygamist** [pəˈlɪgəmɪst] *s* polígamo

**polygamous** [pəˈlɪgəməs] *adj* polígamo

**polyglot** [ˈpɑlɪˌglɑt] *adj & s* poligloto

**polygon** [ˈpɑlɪˌgɑn] *s* polígono

**Polyhymnia** [ˌpɑlɪˈhɪmnɪ·ə] *s* Polimnia

**polynomial** [ˌpɑlɪˈnomɪ·əl] *s* polinomio

**polyp** [ˈpɑlɪp] *s* pólipo

**polytheist** [ˈpɑlɪˌθi·ɪst] *s* politeísta *mf*

**polytheistic** [ˌpɑlɪθiˈɪstɪk] *adj* politeísta

**pomade** [pəˈmed] o [pəˈmɑd] *s* pomada

**pomegranate** [ˈpɑmˌgrænɪt] *s* (*shrub*) granado; (*fruit*) granada

**pom·mel** [ˈpʌməl] o [ˈpɑməl] *s* (*on hilt of sword*) pomo; (*on saddle*) perilla ‖ *v* (*pret & pp* **-meled** o

**-melled;** *ger* **-meling** o **-melling)** *tr* apuñear, aporrear
**pomp** [pamp] *s* pompa, fausto
**pompadour** ['pampə,dor] o ['pampə,dur] *s* copete *m*
**pompous** ['pampəs] *adj* pomposo, faustoso
**pon•cho** ['pantʃo] *s* (*pl* **-chos**) capote *m* de monte, poncho
**pond** [pand] *s* estanque *m*, charca
**ponder** ['pandər] *tr* ponderar ‖ *intr* meditar; **to ponder over** ponderar, considerar con cuidado
**ponderous** ['pandərəs] *adj* pesado, inmanejable; tedioso, fastidioso
**pond scum** *s* lama, verdín *m*
**poniard** ['panjərd] *s* puñal *m*
**pontiff** ['pantɪf] *s* pontífice *m*
**pontoon** [pan'tun] *s* pontón *m*
**po•ny** ['poni] *s* (*pl* **-nies**) jaca, caballito; (*for drinking liquor*) (coll) pequeño vaso; (*translation used dishonestly in school*) (coll) chuleta
**poodle** ['pudəl] *s* perro de lanas
**pool** [pul] *s* (*small puddle*) charco; (*for swimming*) piscina; (*game*) trucos; (*in certain games*) polla, puesta; combinación de intereses; caudales unidos para un fin ‖ *tr* mancomunar
**pool'room'** *s* sala de trucos
**pool table** *s* mesa de trucos
**poop** [pup] *s* popa; (*deck*) toldilla
**poor** [pur] *adj* (*having few possessions; arousing pity*) pobre; (*not good, inferior*) malo
**poor box** *s* cepillo, caja de limosnas
**poor'house'** *s* asilo de pobres, casa de caridad
**poorly** ['purli] *adv* mal
**poor white** *s* pobre *mf* de la raza blanca (*en el sur de los EE.UU.*)
**pop.** *abbr* **popular, population**
**pop** [pap] *s* estallido, taponazo; bebida gaseosa ‖ *v* (*pret & pp* **popped;** *ger* **popping)** *tr* hacer estallar; **to pop the question** (coll) hacer una declaración de amor ‖ *intr* estallar
**pop'corn'** *s* rosetas, palomitas (de maíz)
**pope** [pop] *s* papa *m*
**popeyed** ['pap,aɪd] *adj* de ojos saltones; (*with fear, surprise, etc.*) desorbitado
**pop'gun'** *s* tirabala
**poplar** ['paplər] *s* álamo, chopo
**pop•py** ['papi] *s* (*pl* **-pies**) amapola
**pop'py•cock'** *s* (coll) necedad, tontería
**popsicle** ['papsɪkəl] *s* polo
**populace** ['papjəlɪs] *s* populacho
**popular** ['papjələr] *adj* popular
**popularize** ['papjələ,raɪz] *tr* popularizar, vulgarizar
**populous** ['papjələs] *adj* populoso
**porcelain** ['pɔrsəlɪn] o ['pɔrslɪn] *s* porcelana
**porch** [portʃ] *s* porche *m*, pórtico
**porcupine** ['pɔrkjə,paɪn] *s* puerco espín
**pore** [por] *s* poro ‖ *intr* — **to pore over** estudiar larga y detenidamente
**pork** [pork] *s* carne *f* de cerdo
**pork chop** *s* chuleta de cerdo
**porous** ['porəs] *adj* poroso
**porous plaster** *s* parche poroso
**porphy•ry** ['pɔrfɪri] *s* (*pl* **-ries**) pórfido
**porpoise** ['pɔrpəs] *s* marsopa, puerco de mar; (*dolphin*) delfín *m*
**porridge** ['parɪdʒ] o ['pɔrɪdʒ] *s* gachas
**port** [port] *adj* portuario ‖ *s* puerto; (*opening in ship's side*) portilla; (*left side of ship or airplane*) babor *m;* oporto, vino de Oporto; (mach) lumbrera
**portable** ['portəbəl] *adj* portátil
**portal** ['portəl] *s* portal *m*
**portend** [por'tend] *tr* anunciar de antemano, presagiar
**portent** ['portent] *s* augurio, presagio
**portentous** [por'tentəs] *adj* portentoso, extraordinario; amenazante, ominoso
**porter** ['portər] *s* (*doorkeeper*) portero, conserje *m;* (*in hotels and trains*) mozo de servicio; pórter *m* (*cerveza de Inglaterra de color obscuro*)
**portfoli•o** [port'folɪ,o] *s* (*pl* **-os**) cartera
**port'hole'** *s* porta, portilla
**porti•co** ['portɪ,ko] *s* (*pl* **-coes** o **-cos**) pórtico
**portion** ['porʃən] *s* porción; (*dowry*) dote *m & f*
**port•ly** ['portli] *adj* (*comp* **-lier;** *super* **-liest**) corpulento; grave, majestuoso
**port of call** *s* escala
**portrait** ['portret] o ['portrɪt] *s* retrato; **to sit for a portrait** retratarse
**portray** [por'tre] *tr* retratar
**portrayal** [por'tre•əl] *s* representación gráfica; retrato, descripción acertada
**Portugal** ['portʃəgəl] *s* Portugal *m*
**Portu•guese** ['portʃə,giz] *adj* portugués ‖ *s* (*pl* **-guese**) portugués *m*
**port wine** *s* vino de Oporto
**pose** [poz] *s* pose *f* ‖ *tr* plantear (*una pregunta, cuestión, etc.*) ‖ *intr* posar (*para retratarse; como modelo*); tomar una postura afectada; **to pose as** hacerse pasar por
**posh** [paʃ] *adj* (slang) elegante; (slang) lujoso, suntuoso
**position** [pə'zɪʃən] *s* posición; empleo, puesto; opinión; **to be in a position to** estar en condiciones de
**positive** ['pazɪtɪv] *adj* positivo ‖ *s* positiva
**possess** [pə'zes] *tr* poseer
**possession** [pə'zeʃən] *s* posesión
**possible** ['pasɪbəl] *adj* posible
**possum** ['pasəm] *s* zarigüeya; **to play possum** hacer la mortecina
**post** [post] *s* (*piece of wood, metal, etc. set upright*) poste *m;* (*position*) puesto; (*job*) puesto, cargo; casa de correos ‖ *tr* fijar (*carteles*); echar al correo; apostar, situar; tener al corriente; **post no bills** se prohibe fijar carteles
**postage** ['postɪdʒ] *s* porte *m*, franqueo; **postage will be paid by addressee** a franquear en destino
**postage meter** *s* franqueadora
**postage stamp** *s* sello de correo; estampilla, timbre *m* (Am)

**postal** ['postəl] *adj* postal || *s* postal *f*
**postal card** *s* tarjeta postal
**postal permit** *s* franqueo concertado
**postal savings bank** *s* caja postal de ahorros
**post card** *s* tarjeta postal
**post'date'** *s* posfecha || **post'date'** *tr* posfechar
**poster** ['postər] *s* cartel *m*, cartelón *m*, letrero
**posterity** [pɑs'terɪti] *s* posteridad
**postern** ['postərn] *s* postigo, portillo
**post'haste'** *adv* por la posta, a toda prisa
**posthumous** ['pɑstʃuməs] *adj* póstumo
**post•man** ['postmən] *s* (*pl* **-men** [mən]) cartero
**post'mark'** *s* matasellos *m*, timbre *m* de correos || *tr* matasellar, timbrar
**post'mas'ter** *s* administrador *m* de correos
**post-mortem** [,post'mɔrtəm] *adj* posterior a la muerte || *s* examen *m* de un cadáver
**post office** *s* casa de correos
**post'-of'fice box** *s* apartado de correos, casilla postal
**postpaid** ['post,ped] *adj* con porte pagado, franco de porte
**postpone** [post'pon] *tr* aplazar
**postscript** ['post,skrɪpt] *s* posdata
**posttonic** [post'tɑnɪk] *adj* postónico
**posture** ['pɑstʃər] *s* postura || *intr* adoptar una postura
**post'war'** *adj* de la posguerra
**po•sy** ['pozi] *s* (*pl* **-sies**) flor *f*, ramillete *m*
**pot** [pɑt] *s* pote *m*; (*for flowers*) tiesto; (*for the kitchen*) caldera, olla, puchero; vaso de noche, orinal *m*; (*in gambling*) puesta; (slang) mariguana
**potash** ['pɑt,æʃ] *s* potasa
**potassium** [pə'tæsɪ•əm] *s* potasio
**pota•to** [pə'teto] *s* (*pl* **-toes**) patata, papa; (*sweet potato*) batata, buniato
**potato omelet** *s* tortilla a la española
**potbellied** ['pɑt,bɛlid] *adj* barrigón, panzudo
**poten•cy** ['potənsi] *s* (*pl* **-cies**) potencia
**potent** ['potənt] *adj* potente
**potentate** ['potən,tet] *s* potentado
**potential** [pə'tenʃəl] *adj* & *s* potencial *m*
**pot'hang'er** *s* llares *fpl*
**pot'hook'** *s* garabato
**potion** ['poʃən] *s* poción
**pot'luck'** *s* lo que hay de comer; **to take potluck** hacer penitencia
**pot shot** *s* tiro a corta distancia
**potter** ['pɑtər] *s* alfarero || *intr* ocuparse en fruslerías
**potter's clay** *s* arcilla figulina
**potter's field** *s* cementerio de los pobres, hoyanca
**potter's wheel** *s* torno de alfarero
**potter•y** ['pɑtəri] *s* (*pl* **-ies**) alfarería; cacharros (de alfarería)
**pouch** [pautʃ] *s* bolsa, saquillo; (*of kangaroo*) bolsa; (*for tobacco*) petaca; valija
**poulterer** ['poltərər] *s* pollero
**poultice** ['poltɪs] *s* cataplasma *f*
**poultry** ['poltri] *s* aves *fpl* de corral
**pounce** [pauns] *intr* — **to pounce on** saltar sobre, precipitarse sobre
**pound** [paund] *s* (*weight*) libra; (*for stray animals*) corral *m* de concejo || *tr* golpear; machacar, moler; encerrar en el corral de concejo; bombardear incesantemente; (*to keep walking over*) desempedrar || *intr* golpear
**pound'cake'** *s* pastel *m* en que entra una libra de cada ingrediente; ponqué *m* (Am)
**pound sterling** *s* libra esterlina
**pour** [por] *tr* vaciar, verter, derramar; echar, servir (*p.ej.*, *té*); escanciar (*vino*) || *intr* fluir rápidamente; llover a torrentes; **to pour out of** salir a montones de (*p.ej.*, *el teatro*)
**pout** [paut] *s* mala cara, puchero || *intr* poner mala cara, hacer pucheros
**poverty** ['pɑvərti] *s* pobreza
**POW** *abbr* **prisoner of war**
**powder** ['paudər] *s* polvo; (*for face*) polvos; (*explosive*) pólvora || *tr* pulverizar; (*to sprinkle with powder*) empolvar, polvorear
**powder puff** *s* borla para empolvarse
**powder room** *s* cuarto tocador, cuarto de aseo
**powdery** ['paudəri] *adj* (*like powder*) polvoriento; (*sprinkled with powder*) empolvado; (*crumbly*) quebradizo
**power** ['pau•ər] *s* (*ability to act or do something; possession*) poder *m*; (*control, influence; wealth*) poderío; (*influential nation; energy, force, strength*) potencia; **the powers that be** las autoridades, los que mandan || *tr* accionar, impulsar
**power dive** *s* (aer) picado con motor
**powerful** ['pau•ərfəl] *adj* poderoso
**pow'er•house'** *s* central eléctrica
**powerless** ['pau•ərlɪs] *adj* impotente
**power line** *s* (elec) sector *m* de distribución
**power mower** *s* motosegadora
**power of attorney** *s* poder *m*
**power plant** *s* (aer) grupo motopropulsor; (aut) grupo motor; (elec) central eléctrica, estación generadora
**power steering** *s* (aut) servodirección
**power tool** *s* herramienta motriz
**pp.** *abbr* **pages**
**p.p.** *abbr* **parcel post, postpaid**
**pr.** *abbr* **pair, present, price**
**practical** ['præktɪkəl] *adj* práctico
**practically** ['præktɪkəli] *adv* poco más o menos
**practice** ['præktɪs] *s* práctica; uso, costumbre; ensayo; (*of a profession*) ejercicio; (*of a doctor*) clientela || *tr* practicar; ejercitar (*p.ej.*, *la caridad*); ejercer (*una profesión*); estudiar (*p.ej.*, *el piano*); tener por costumbre || *intr* ejercitarse; practicar la medicina; ensayarse; entrenarse, adiestrarse; **to practice as** ejercer de (*p.ej.*, *abogado*)
**practitioner** [præk'tɪʃənər] *s* (*medical doctor*) práctico
**Prague** [prɑg] o [preg] *s* Praga

**prairie** ['prɛri] *s* pradera, llanura, pampa
**prairie dog** *s* ardilla ladradora
**prairie wolf** *s* coyote *m*
**praise** [prez] *s* alabanza, elogio || *tr* alabar, elogiar
**praise'wor'thy** *adj* laudable, plausible
**pram** [præm] *s* cochecillo de niño
**prance** [præns] o [prɑns] *s* cabriola, trenzado || *intr* cabriolar, trenzar
**prank** [præŋk] *s* travesura
**prate** [pret] *intr* charlar, parlotear
**prattle** ['prætəl] *s* charla, parloteo || *intr* charlar, parlotear; balbucear (*un niño*)
**pray** [pre] *tr* implorar, rogar, suplicar; rezar (*una oración*) || *intr* orar, rezar; **pray tell me** sírvase decirme
**prayer** [prɛr] *s* ruego, súplica; oración, rezo
**prayer book** *s* devocionario
**preach** [pritʃ] *tr* predicar; aconsejar (*p.ej., la paciencia*) || *intr* predicar
**preacher** ['pritʃər] *s* predicador *m*
**preamble** ['pri,æmbəl] *s* preámbulo
**prebend** ['prɛbənd] *s* prebenda
**precarious** [prɪ'kɛrɪ·əs] *adj* precario
**precaution** [prɪ'kɔʃən] *s* precaución
**precede** [prɪ'sid] *tr & intr* preceder
**precedent** ['prɛsɪdənt] *s* precedente *m*
**precept** ['prisɛpt] *s* precepto
**precinct** ['prisɪŋkt] *s* barriada; distrito electoral
**precious** ['prɛʃəs] *adj* precioso; caro, amado; (coll) considerable || *adv* (coll) muy, p.ej., **precious little** muy poco
**precipice** ['prɛsɪpɪs] *s* precipicio
**precipitate** [prɪ'sɪpɪ,tet] *adj & s* precipitado || *tr* precipitar || *intr* precipitarse
**precipitous** [prɪ'sɪpɪtəs] *adj* empinado, escarpado; (*hurried, reckless*) precipitoso
**precise** [prɪ'saɪs] *adj* preciso; meticuloso
**precision** [prɪ'sɪʒən] *s* precisión
**preclude** [prɪ'klud] *tr* excluir, imposibilitar
**precocious** [prɪ'koʃəs] *adj* precoz
**predatory** ['prɛdə,tori] *adj* predatorio
**predicament** [prɪ'dɪkəmənt] *s* apuro, situación difícil
**predict** [prɪ'dɪkt] *tr* predecir
**prediction** [prɪ'dɪkʃən] *s* predicción
**predispose** [,pridɪs'poz] *tr* predisponer
**predominant** [prɪ'dɑmɪnənt] *adj* predominante
**preëminent** [prɪ'ɛmɪnənt] *adj* preeminente
**preëmpt** [prɪ'ɛmpt] *tr* apropiarse o apropiarse de
**preen** [prin] *tr* arreglarse (*las plumas*) con el pico; **to preen oneself** componerse, vestirse cuidadosamente
**pref.** *abbr* **preface, preferred, prefix**
**prefabricate** [pri'fæbrɪ,ket] *tr* prefabricar
**preface** ['prɛfɪs] *s* prefacio, advertencia || *tr* introducir, empezar
**pre·fer** [prɪ'fʌr] *v* (*pret & pp* **-ferred;** *ger* **-ferring**) *tr* preferir; presentar; promover
**preferable** ['prɛfərəbəl] *adj* preferible
**preference** ['prɛfərəns] *s* preferencia
**prefix** ['prifɪks] *s* prefijo || *tr* prefijar
**pregnan·cy** ['prɛgnənsi] *s* (*pl* **-cies**) preñez *f*, embarazo
**pregnant** ['prɛgnənt] *adj* preñado
**prejudice** ['prɛdʒədɪs] *s* prejuicio; (*detriment*) perjuicio; **to the prejudice of** con perjuicio de; **without prejudice** (law) sin detrimento de sus propios derechos || *tr* predisponer, prevenir; (*to harm*) perjudicar
**prejudicial** [,prɛdʒə'dɪʃəl] *adj* perjudicial
**prelate** ['prɛlɪt] *s* prelado
**pre-Lenten** [pri'lɛntən] *adj* carnavalesco
**preliminar·y** [prɪ'lɪmɪ,nɛri] *adj* preliminar || *s* (*pl* **-ies**) preliminar *m*
**prelude** ['prɛljud] o ['prilud] *s* preludio || *tr* preludiar
**premeditate** [pri'mɛdɪ,tet] *tr* premeditar
**premier** [prɪ'mɪr] o ['primɪ·ər] *s* primer ministro, presidente *m* del consejo
**première** [prə'mjɛr] o [prɪ'mɪr] *s* estreno; actriz *f* principal
**premise** ['prɛmɪs] *s* premisa; **on the premises** en el local mismo; **premises** predio, local *m*
**premium** ['primɪ·əm] *s* premio; (ins) prima
**premonition** [,primə'nɪʃən] *s* presagio; presentimiento
**preoccupancy** [pri'ɑkjəpənsi] *s* preocupación
**preoccupation** [pri,ɑkjə'peʃən] *s* preocupación
**preoccu·py** [pri'ɑkjə,paɪ] *v* (*pret & pp* **-pied**) *tr* preocupar
**prepaid** [pri'ped] *adj* pagado por adelantado; con porte pagado
**preparation** [,prɛpə'reʃən] *s* preparación; (*e.g., for a trip*) preparativo; (pharm) preparado
**preparatory** [prɪ'pærə,tori] *adj* preparativo, preparatorio
**prepare** [prɪ'pɛr] *tr* preparar || *intr* prepararse
**preparedness** [prɪ'pɛrɪdnɪs] o [prɪ'pɛrdnɪs] *s* preparación; preparación militar
**pre·pay** [pri'pe] *v* (*pret & pp* **-paid**) *tr* pagar por adelantado
**preponderant** [prɪ'pɑndərənt] *adj* preponderante
**preposition** [,prɛpə'zɪʃən] *s* preposición
**prepossessing** [,pripə'zɛsɪŋ] *adj* atractivo, simpático
**preposterous** [prɪ'pɑstərəs] *adj* absurdo, ridículo
**prep school** [prɛp] *s* (coll) escuela preparatoria
**prerecorded** [,prirɪ'kɔrdɪd] *adj* (rad & telv) grabado de antemano
**prerequisite** [pri'rɛkwɪzɪt] *s* requisito previo
**prerogative** [prɪ'rɑgətɪv] *s* prerrogativa
**Pres.** *abbr* **Presbyterian, President**

**presage** ['prɛsɪdʒ] *s* presagio ‖ [prɪ'sedʒ] *tr* presagiar
**Presbyterian** [,prɛzbɪ'tɪrɪ·ən] *adj & s* presbiteriano
**prescribe** [prɪ'skraɪb] *tr & intr* prescribir
**prescription** [prɪ'skrɪpʃən] *s* prescripción; (pharm) receta
**presence** ['prɛzəns] *s* presencia
**present** ['prɛzənt] *adj* presente ‖ *s* presente *m*, regalo ‖ [prɪ'zɛnt] *tr* presentar, obsequiar
**presentable** [prɪ'zɛntəbəl] *adj* bien apersonado
**presentation** [,prɛzən'teʃən] o [,prizən'teʃən] *s* presentación
**presentation copy** *s* ejemplar *m* de cortesía con dedicatoria del autor
**presentiment** [prɪ'zɛntɪmənt] *s* presentimiento
**presently** ['prɛzəntli] *adv* luego, dentro de poco
**preserve** [prɪ'zʌrv] *s* conserva, compota; (*for game*) vedado ‖ *tr* conservar; preservar, proteger
**preserved fruit** *s* dulce *m* de almíbar
**preside** [prɪ'zaɪd] *intr* presidir; **to preside over** presidir
**presiden·cy** ['prɛzɪdənsi] *s* (*pl* **-cies**) presidencia
**president** ['prɛzɪdənt] *s* presidente *m;* (*of a university*) rector *m*
**press** [prɛs] *s* apretón *m*, empujón *m;* (*e.g., of business*) urgencia; muchedumbre; (*machine for printing, for making wine; newspapers and newspapermen*) prensa; (*printing*) imprenta; (*closet*) armario; **to go to press** entrar en prensa ‖ *tr* apretar (*p.ej., un botón*); (*in a press*) prensar; planchar (*la ropa*); imprimir (*discos de fonógrafo*); oprimir (*una tecla*); apresurar; abrumar; apremiar, instar; insistir en
**press agent** *s* agente *m* de publicidad
**press conference** *s* conferencia de prensa
**pressing** ['prɛsɪŋ] *adj* apremiante, urgente ‖ *s* planchado
**press release** *s* comunicado de prensa
**pressure** ['prɛʃər] *s* presión; premura, urgencia
**pressure cooker** ['kʊkər] *s* olla de presión, cocina de presión
**prestige** [prɛs'tiʒ] o ['prɛstɪdʒ] *s* prestigio
**presumably** [prɪ'zuməbli] o [prɪ'zjuməbli] *adv* probablemente, verosímilmente
**presume** [prɪ'zum] o [prɪ'zjum] *tr* presumir; suponer; **to presume to** tomar la libertad de ‖ *intr* suponer; **to presume on** o **upon** abusar de
**presumption** [prɪ'zʌmpʃən] *s* presunción; pretensión
**presumptuous** [prɪ'zʌmptʃʊ·əs] *adj* confianzudo, desenvuelto
**presuppose** [,prisə'poz] *tr* presuponer
**pretend** [prɪ'tɛnd] *tr* aparentar, fingir ‖ *intr* fingir; **to pretend to** pretender (*p.ej., el trono*)
**pretender** [prɪ'tɛndər] *s* pretendiente *mf*
**pretense** [prɪ'tɛns] o ['pritɛns] *s* pretensión; fingimiento; **under false pretenses** con apariencias fingidas; **under pretense of** so pretexto de
**pretentious** [prɪ'tɛnʃəs] *adj* pretencioso, aparatoso; ambicioso, vasto
**pretonic** [prɪ'tɑnɪk] *adj* pretónico
**pret·ty** ['prɪti] *adj* (*comp* **-tier;** *super* **-tiest**) bonito, lindo; (coll) bastante, considerable ‖ *adv* algo; bastante; muy
**prevail** [prɪ'vel] *intr* prevalecer, reinar; **to prevail on** o **upon** persuadir
**prevailing** [prɪ'velɪŋ] *adj* prevaleciente, reinante; común, corriente
**prevalent** ['prɛvələnt] *adj* común, corriente, en boga
**prevaricate** [prɪ'værɪ,ket] *intr* mentir
**prevent** [prɪ'vɛnt] *tr* impedir ‖ *intr* obstar
**prevention** [prɪ'vɛnʃən] *s* (el) impedir; medidas de precaución
**preventive** [prɪ'vɛntɪv] *adj & s* preservativo
**preview** ['pri,vju] *s* vista anticipada; (*private showing*) (mov) preestreno; (*showing of brief scenes for advertising*) (mov) avance *m*
**previous** ['privɪ·əs] *adj* previo, anterior ‖ *adv* previamente; **previous to** con anterioridad a, antes de
**prewar** ['pri,wɔr] *adj* prebélico, de preguerra
**prey** [pre] *s* presa; víctima; **to be prey to** ser presa de ‖ *intr* cazar; **to prey on** o **upon** apresar y devorar; pillar, robar; tener preocupado
**price** [praɪs] *s* precio ‖ *tr* apreciar, estimar; fijar el precio de, poner precio a; pedir el precio de
**price control** *s* intervención de precios
**price cutting** *s* reducción de precios
**price fixing** *s* fijación de precios
**price freezing** *s* congelación de precios
**priceless** ['praɪslɪs] *adj* inapreciable, sin precio; (coll) absurdo, divertido
**price war** *s* guerra de precios
**prick** [prɪk] *s* (*pointed weapon or instrument*) espiche *m;* (*sharp point*) púa; (*small hole made with sharp point*) agujerillo; (*spur*) aguijón *m;* (*jab; sharp pain*) pinchazo, punzada; **to kick against the pricks** dar coces contra el aguijón ‖ *tr* pinchar; marcar con agujerillos; dar una punzada a; (*to sting*) punzar; **to prick up** aguzar (*las orejas*)
**prick·ly** ['prɪkli] *adj* (*comp* **-lier;** *super* **-liest**) espinoso, puado, punzante
**prickly heat** *s* salpullido causado por el calor
**prickly pear** *s* (*plant*) chumbera; (*fruit*) higo chumbo
**pride** [praɪd] *s* orgullo; arrogancia; **the pride of** la flor y nata de ‖ *tr* — **to pride oneself on** o **upon** enorgullecerse de
**priest** [prist] *s* sacerdote *m*
**priesthood** ['prist·hʊd] *s* sacerdocio
**priest·ly** ['pristli] *adj* (*comp* **-lier;** *super* **-liest**) sacerdotal
**prig** [prɪg] *s* gazmoño, pedante *mf*
**prim** [prɪm] *adj* (*comp* **primmer;** *super* **primmest**) estirado, relamido

**prima·ry** [ˈpraɪˌmɛri] o [ˈpraɪməri] *adj* primario ‖ *s* (*pl* **-ries**) elección preliminar; (elec) primario
**prime** [praɪm] *adj* primero, principal; (*of the best quality*) primo ‖ *s* flor *f*, juventud, primavera; alba, aurora; (la) flor y nata; (*of a degree*) (phys) minuto; (typ) virgulilla; **prime of life** edad viril, flor *f* de edad ‖ *tr* informar de antemano; cebar (*un arma de fuego, una bomba, un carburador*); (*for painting*) imprimar; poner la primera capa o la primera mano a; poner virgulilla a
**prime minister** *s* primer ministro
**primer** [ˈprɪmər] *s* cartilla ‖ [ˈpraɪmər] *s* (*for paint*) aprestado *m;* (mach) cebador *m*
**primitive** [ˈprɪmɪtɪv] *adj* primitivo
**primp** [prɪmp] *tr* acicalar, engalanar ‖ *intr* acicalarse, engalanarse
**prim'rose'** *s* primavera
**primrose path** *s* vida dada a los placeres de los sentidos
**prin.** *abbr* **principal**
**prince** [prɪns] *s* príncipe *m;* **to live like a prince** portarse como un príncipe
**Prince of Wales** *s* príncipe *m* de Gales
**princess** [ˈprɪnsɪs] *s* princesa
**principal** [ˈprɪnsɪpəl] *adj* principal ‖ *s* principal *m*, jefe *m;* (*of a school*) director *m;* criminal *mf;* (*main sum, not interest*) capital *m*
**principle** [ˈprɪnsɪpəl] *s* principio
**print** [prɪnt] *s* marca, impresión; (*printed cloth*) estampado; (*design in printed cloth*) diseño; grabado, lámina; letras de molde; (*act of printing*) impresión; edición, tirada; (phot) impresión; **in print** impreso, publicado; **out of print** agotado ‖ *tr* imprimir; estampar; hacer imprimir; publicar; escribir en caracteres de imprenta; (phot) tirar, imprimir; (fig) imprimir o grabar (*en la memoria*)
**printed matter** *s* impresos
**printer** [ˈprɪntər] *s* impresor *m*
**printer's devil** *s* aprendiz *m* de imprenta
**printer's ink** *s* tinta de imprenta
**printer's mark** *s* pie *m* de imprenta
**printing** [ˈprɪntɪŋ] *s* impresión; caracteres impresos; edición, tirada; letras de mano imitación de las impresas; (phot) tiraje *m*
**prior** [ˈpraɪ·ər] *adj* anterior ‖ *adv* anteriormente; **prior to** antes de
**priori·ty** [praɪˈarɪti] o [praɪˈɔrɪti] *s* (*pl* **-ties**) prioridad; **of the highest priority** de máxima prioridad
**prism** [ˈprɪzəm] *s* prisma *m*
**prison** [ˈprɪzən] *s* cárcel *f*, prisión ‖ *tr* encarcelar
**prisoner** [ˈprɪzənər] o [ˈprɪznər] *s* preso; (mil) prisionero
**prison van** *s* coche *m* celular
**pris·sy** [ˈprɪsi] *adj* (*comp* **-sier;** *super* **-siest**) (coll) remilgado, melindroso
**priva·cy** [ˈpraɪvəsi] *s* (*pl* **-cies**) aislamiento, retiro; secreto, reserva
**private** [ˈpraɪvɪt] *adj* particular, privado; confidencial; ‖ *s* soldado raso; **in private** privadamente; en secreto; **privates** partes pudendas
**private first class** *s* soldado de primera, aspirante *m* a cabo
**private hospital** *s* clínica, casa de salud
**private property** *s* bienes *mpl* particulares
**private view** *s* día *m* de inauguración
**privet** [ˈprɪvɪt] *s* aligustre *m*
**privilege** [ˈprɪvɪlɪdʒ] *s* privilegio
**priv·y** [ˈprɪvi] *adj* privado; **privy to** enterado secretamente de ‖ *s* (*pl* **-ies**) letrina
**prize** [praɪz] *s* premio; (*something captured*) presa ‖ *tr* apreciar, estimar
**prize fight** *s* partido de boxeo profesional
**prize fighter** *s* boxeador *m* profesional
**prize ring** *s* cuadrilátero de boxeo
**pro** [pro] *prep* en pro de ‖ *s* (*pl* **pros**) voto afirmativo; (coll) deportista *mf* profesional; **the pros and the cons** el pro y el contra
**probabili·ty** [ˌprabəˈbɪlɪti] *s* (*pl* **-ties**) probabilidad; acontecimiento probable; tiempo probable
**probable** [ˈprabəbəl] *adj* probable
**probation** [proˈbeʃən] *s* libertad vigilada; período de prueba
**probe** [prob] *s* encuesta, indagación; (*instrument*) sonda ‖ *tr* indagar; sondar
**problem** [ˈprabləm] *s* problema *m*
**procedure** [proˈsidʒər] *s* procedimiento
**proceed** [proˈsid] *intr* proceder ‖ **proceeds** [ˈprosidz] *spl* producto, ganancia
**proceeding** [proˈsidɪŋ] *s* procedimiento; **proceedings** actas; diligencias
**process** [ˈprasɛs] *s* procedimiento; proceso, progreso; **in the process of time** con el tiempo ‖ *tr* elaborar
**process server** [ˈsʌrvər] *s* entregador *m* de la citación
**proclaim** [proˈklem] *tr* proclamar
**proclitic** [proˈklɪtɪk] *adj & s* proclítico
**procommunist** [proˈkamjənɪst] *adj & s* filocomunista *mf*
**procrastinate** [proˈkræstɪˌnet] *tr* diferir de un día para otro ‖ *intr* tardar, no decidirse
**procure** [proˈkjur] *tr* conseguir, obtener ‖ *intr* alcahuetear
**prod** [prad] *s* aguijada; empuje *m* ‖ *v* (*pret & pp* **prodded;** *ger* **prodding**) *tr* aguijar, pinchar; aguijonear, estimular
**prodigal** [ˈpradɪgəl] *adj & s* pródigo
**prodigious** [proˈdɪdʒəs] *adj* prodigioso, maravilloso; enorme, inmenso
**prodi·gy** [ˈpradɪdʒi] *s* (*pl* **-gies**) prodigio
**produce** [ˈprodjus] o [ˈprodus] *s* producto; productos agrícolas ‖ [proˈdjus] o [proˈdus] *tr* producir; presentar (*p.ej., un drama*) al público; (geom) prolongar
**product** [ˈpradəkt] *s* producto
**production** [proˈdʌkʃən] *s* producción
**profane** [proˈfen] *adj* profano; (*lan-*

*guage*) injurioso, blasfemo || *s* profano || *tr* profanar
**profani·ty** [pro'fænɪti] *s* (*pl* **-ties**) blasfemia
**profess** [pro'fɛs] *tr* & *intr* profesar
**profession** [pro'fɛʃən] *s* profesión
**professor** [pro'fɛsər] *s* profesor *m*, catedrático; (coll) profesor, maestro
**proffer** ['prɑfər] *s* oferta, propuesta || *tr* ofrecer, proponer
**proficient** [pro'fɪʃənt] *adj* perito, diestro, hábil
**profile** ['profaɪl] *s* perfil *m* || *tr* perfilar
**profit** ['prɑfɪt] *s* provecho, beneficio, utilidad, ganancia; **at a profit** con ganancia || *tr* servir, ser de utilidad a || *intr* sacar provecho, ganar; adelantar, mejorar; **to profit by** aprovechar, sacar provecho de
**profitable** ['prɑfɪtəbəl] *adj* provechoso
**profit and loss** *s* ganancias y pérdidas
**profiteer** [,prɑfɪ'tɪr] *s* logrero, explotador *m* || *intr* logrear, explotar
**profit taking** *s* realización de beneficios
**profligate** ['prɑflɪgɪt] *adj* & *s* libertino; pródigo
**pro forma invoice** [pro 'fɔrmə] *s* factura simulada
**profound** [pro'faʊnd] *adj* profundo
**profuse** [prə'fjus] *adj* (*extravagant*) pródigo; (*abundant*) profuso
**proge·ny** ['prɑdʒəni] *s* (*pl* **-nies**) prole *f*
**progno·sis** [prɑg'nosɪs] *s* (*pl* **-ses** [siz]) pronóstico
**prognostic** [prɑg'nɑstɪk] *s* pronóstico
**program** ['progræm] *s* programa *m* || *tr* programar
**progress** ['prɑgrɛs] *s* progreso; progresos; **to make progress** hacer progresos || [prə'grɛs] *intr* progresar
**progressive** [prə'grɛsɪv] *adj* progresivo; (pol) progresista || *s* (pol) progresista *mf*
**prohibit** [pro'hɪbɪt] *tr* prohibir
**project** ['prɑdʒɛkt] *s* proyecto || [prə'dʒɛkt] *tr* proyectar || *intr* proyectarse
**projectile** [prə'dʒɛktɪl] *s* proyectil *m*
**projection** [prə'dʒɛkʃən] *s* proyección
**projector** [prə'dʒɛktər] *s* proyector *m*
**proletarian** [,prolɪ'tɛrɪ·ən] *adj* & *s* proletario
**proletariat** [,prolɪ'tɛrɪ·ət] *s* proletariado
**proliferate** [prə'lɪfə,ret] *intr* proliferar
**prolific** [prə'lɪfɪk] *adj* prolífico
**prolix** ['prolɪks] o [pro'lɪks] *adj* difuso, verboso
**prologue** ['prolɔg] o ['prolɑg] *s* prólogo
**prolong** [pro'lɔŋ] o [pro'lɑŋ] *tr* prolongar
**promenade** [,prɑmɪ'ned] o [,prɑmɪ'nɑd] *s* paseo; baile *m* de gala || *intr* pasear o pasearse
**promenade deck** *s* (naut) cubierta de paseo
**prominent** ['prɑmɪnənt] *adj* prominente
**promise** ['prɑmɪs] *s* promesa || *tr* & *intr* prometer
**promising young man** *s* joven *m* de esperanzas
**promissory** ['prɑmɪ,sori] *adj* promisorio
**promissory note** *s* pagaré *m*
**promonto·ry** ['prɑmən,tori] *s* (*pl* **-ries**) promontorio
**promote** [prə'mot] *tr* promover; fomentar
**promotion** [prə'moʃən] *s* promoción; fomento
**prompt** [prɑmpt] *adj* pronto, puntual; listo, dispuesto || *tr* incitar, mover; inspirar, sugerir; (theat) apuntar
**prompter** ['prɑmptər] *s* (theat) apuntador *m*
**prompter's box** *s* (theat) concha
**promulgate** ['prɑməl,get] o [pro'mʌlget] *tr* promulgar
**prone** [pron] *adj* postrado boca abajo; extendido sobre el suelo; dispuesto, propenso
**prong** [prɔŋ] o [prɑŋ] *s* punta (*de un tenedor, horquilla, etc.*)
**pronoun** ['pronaʊn] *s* pronombre *m*
**pronounce** [prə'naʊns] *tr* pronunciar
**pronouncement** [prə'naʊnsmənt] *s* declaración; decisión, opinión
**pronunciamen·to** [prə,nʌnsɪ·ə'mɛnto] *s* (*pl* **-tos**) pronunciamiento
**pronunciation** [prə,nʌnsɪ'eʃən] o [prə,nʌnʃɪ'eʃən] *s* pronunciación
**proof** [pruf] *adj* de prueba; **proof against** a prueba de || *s* prueba
**proof'read'er** *s* corrector *m* de pruebas
**prop** [prɑp] *s* apoyo, puntal *m*; (*to hold up a plant*) rodrigón *m*; **props** (theat) accesorios || *v* (*pret* & *pp* **propped**; *ger* **propping**) *tr* apoyar, apuntalar; poner un rodrigón a
**propaganda** [,prɑpə'gændə] *s* propaganda
**propagate** ['prɑpə,get] *tr* propagar
**proparoxytone** [,propær'ɑksɪ,ton] *adj* & *s* proparoxítono
**pro·pel** [prə'pɛl] *v* (*pret* & *pp* **-pelled**; *ger* **-pelling**) *tr* propulsar, impeler
**propeller** [prə'pɛlər] *s* hélice *f*
**propensi·ty** [prə'pɛnsɪti] *s* (*pl* **-ties**) propensión
**proper** ['prɑpər] *adj* propio, conveniente; decente, decoroso; exacto, justo
**proper·ty** ['prɑpərti] *s* (*pl* **-ties**) propiedad; **properties** (theat) accesorios
**property owner** *s* propietario de bienes raíces
**prophe·cy** ['prɑfɪsi] *s* (*pl* **-cies**) profecía
**prophe·sy** ['prɑfɪ,saɪ] *v* (*pret* & *pp* **-sied**) *tr* profetizar
**prophet** ['prɑfɪt] *s* profeta *m*
**prophetess** ['prɑfɪtɪs] *s* profetisa
**prophylactic** [,profɪ'læktɪk] *adj* & *s* profiláctico
**propitiate** [prə'pɪʃɪ,et] *tr* propiciar
**propitious** [prə'pɪʃəs] *adj* propicio
**prop'jet'** *s* turbohélice *m*
**proportion** [prə'porʃən] *s* proporción; **in proportion as** a medida que; **out of proportion** desproporcionado || *tr* proporcionar

**proportionate** [prəˈporʃənɪt] *adj* proporcionado
**proposal** [prəˈpozəl] *s* propuesta; oferta de matrimonio
**propose** [prəˈpoz] *tr* proponer ‖ *intr* proponer matrimonio; **to propose to** pedir la mano a; proponerse a + *inf*
**proposition** [ˌprɑpəˈzɪʃən] *s* proposición, propuesta
**propound** [prəˈpaʊnd] *tr* proponer
**proprietor** [prəˈpraɪ·ətər] *s* propietario
**proprietress** [prəˈpraɪ·ətrɪs] *s* propietaria
**proprie·ty** [prəˈpraɪ·əti] *s* (*pl* **-ties**) corrección, conducta decorosa, conveniencia; **proprieties** cánones *mpl* sociales, convenciones
**propulsion** [prəˈpʌlʃən] *s* propulsión
**prorate** [proˈret] *tr* prorratear
**prosaic** [proˈze·ɪk] *adj* prosaico
**proscribe** [proˈskraɪb] *tr* proscribir
**prose** [proz] *adj* prosaico ‖ *s* prosa
**prosecute** [ˈprɑsɪˌkjut] *tr* llevar a cabo; (law) procesar
**prosecutor** [ˈprɑsɪˌkjutər] *s* acusador *m*, demandante *mf*; (*lawyer*) fiscal *m*
**proselyte** [ˈprɑsɪˌlaɪt] *s* prosélito
**prose writer** *s* prosista *mf*
**prosody** [ˈprɑsədi] *s* métrica
**prospect** [ˈprɑspɛkt] *s* vista; esperanza; probabilidad de éxito; cliente *mf* o comprador *m* probable ‖ *tr & intr* prospectar; **to prospect for** buscar (*p.ej., oro, petróleo*)
**prosper** [ˈprɑspər] *tr & intr* prosperar
**prosperi·ty** [prɑsˈperɪti] *s* (*pl* **-ties**) prosperidad
**prosperous** [ˈprɑspərəs] *adj* próspero
**prostitute** [ˈprɑstɪˌtjut] o [ˈprɑstɪˌtut] *s* prostituta ‖ *tr* prostituir
**prostrate** [ˈprɑstret] *adj* postrado, prosternado ‖ *tr* postrar
**prostration** [prɑsˈtreʃən] *s* postración
**Prot.** *abbr* **Protestant**
**protagonist** [proˈtægənɪst] *s* protagonista *mf*
**protect** [prəˈtɛkt] *tr* proteger
**protection** [prəˈtɛkʃən] *s* protección
**protégé** [ˈprotəˌʒe] *s* protegido
**protégée** [ˈprotəˌʒe] *s* protegida
**protein** [ˈproti·ɪn] o [ˈprotin] *s* proteína
**pro-tempore** [proˈtɛmpəri] *adj* interino
**protest** [ˈprotɛst] *s* protesta ‖ [proˈtɛst] *tr & intr* protestar
**protestant** [ˈprɑtɪstənt] *adj & s* protestante *mf* ‖ **Protestant** *adj & s* protestante *mf*
**prothonotar·y** [proˈθɑnəˌteri] *s* (*pl* **-ies**) escribano principal (*de un tribunal*)
**protocol** [ˈprotəˌkɑl] *s* protocolo
**protoplasm** [ˈprotəˌplæzəm] *s* protoplasma *m*
**prototype** [ˈprotəˌtaɪp] *s* prototipo
**protozoön** [ˌprotəˈzo·ɑn] *s* protozoo
**protract** [proˈtrækt] *tr* prolongar
**protrude** [proˈtrud] *intr* resaltar
**proud** [praʊd] *adj* orgulloso; soberbio; glorioso
**proud flesh** *s* carnosidad, bezo
**prov.** *abbr* **provincialism**
**prove** [pruv] *v* (*pret* **proved**; *pp* **proved** o **proven**) *tr* probar ‖ *intr* resultar; **to prove to be** venir a ser, resultar
**proverb** [ˈprɑvərb] *s* proverbio
**provide** [prəˈvaɪd] *tr* proporcionar, suministrar ‖ *intr* — **to provide for** proveer a; asegurarse (*el porvenir*)
**provided** [prəˈvaɪdɪd] *conj* a condición (de) que, con tal (de) que
**providence** [ˈprɑvɪdəns] *s* providencia
**providential** [ˌprɑvɪˈdɛnʃəl] *adj* providencial
**providing** [prəˈvaɪdɪŋ] *conj* var de **provided**
**province** [ˈprɑvɪns] *s* provincia; (*sphere of activity or knowledge*) competencia
**provision** [prəˈvɪʃən] *s* provisión; condición, estipulación
**provi·so** [prəˈvaɪzo] *s* (*pl* **-sos** o **-soes**) condición, estipulación, salvedad
**provoke** [prəˈvok] *tr* provocar
**provoking** [prəˈvokɪŋ] *adj* provocador, irritante
**prow** [praʊ] *s* proa
**prowess** [ˈpraʊ·ɪs] *s* proeza; destreza
**prowl** [praʊl] *intr* cazar al acecho, rodar, vagabundear
**prowler** [ˈpraʊlər] *s* rondador *m*; ladrón *m*
**proximity** [prɑkˈsɪmɪti] *s* proximidad
**prox·y** [ˈprɑksi] *s* (*pl* **-ies**) poder *m*, poderhabiente *mf*
**prude** [prud] *s* mojigato, gazmoño
**prudence** [ˈprudəns] *s* prudencia
**prudent** [ˈprudənt] *adj* prudente
**pruder·y** [ˈprudəri] *s* (*pl* **-ies**) mojigatería, gazmoñería
**prudish** [ˈprudɪʃ] *adj* mojigato, gazmoño
**prune** [prun] *s* ciruela pasa ‖ *tr* podar, escamondar
**pry** [praɪ] *v* (*pret & pp* **pried**) *tr* — **to pry open** forzar con la alzaprima o palanca; **to pry out of** arrancar (*p.ej., un secreto*) a (*una persona*) ‖ *intr* entremeterse; **to pry into** entremeterse en
**P.S.** *abbr* **postscript, Privy Seal**
**psalm** [sɑm] *s* salmo
**Psalter** [ˈsɔltər] *s* Salterio
**pseudo** [ˈsudo] o [ˈsjudo] *adj* supuesto, falso, fingido
**pseudonym** [ˈsudənɪm] o [ˈsjudənɪm] *s* seudónimo
**Psyche** [ˈsaɪki] *s* Psique *f*
**psychiatrist** [saɪˈkaɪ·ətrɪst] *s* psiquiatra *mf*
**psychiatry** [saɪˈkaɪ·ətri] *s* psiquiatría
**psychic** [ˈsaɪkɪk] *adj* psíquico; mediúmnico ‖ *s* médium *mf*
**psychoanalysis** [ˌsaɪko·əˈnælɪsɪs] *s* psicoanálisis *m*
**psychoanalyze** [ˌsaɪkoˈænəˌlaɪz] *tr* psicoanalizar
**psychologic(al)** [ˌsaɪkoˈlɑdʒɪk(əl)] *adj* psicológico
**psychologist** [saɪˈkɑlədʒɪst] *s* psicólogo
**psychology** [saɪˈkɑlədʒi] *s* psicología
**psychopath** [ˈsaɪkəˌpæθ] *s* psicópata *mf*

**psycho·sis** [saɪ'kosɪs] *s* (*pl* **-ses** [siz]) psicosis *f*; estado mental
**psychotic** [saɪ'kɑtɪk] *adj* & *s* psicótico
**pt.** *abbr* **part, pint, point**
**pub** [pʌb] *s* (Brit) taberna
**puberty** ['pjubərti] *s* pubertad
**public** ['pʌblɪk] *adj* & *s* público
**publication** [,pʌblɪ'keʃən] *s* publicación
**public conveyance** *s* vehículo de servicio público
**publicity** [pʌb'lɪsɪti] *s* publicidad
**publicize** ['pʌblɪ,saɪz] *tr* publicar
**public library** *s* biblioteca municipal
**public school** *s* (U.S.A.) escuela pública; (Brit) internado privado con dote
**public speaking** *s* elocución, oratoria
**public spirit** *s* celo patriótico del buen ciudadano
**public toilet** *s* quiosco de necesidad
**public utility** *s* empresa de servicio público; **public utilities** acciones emitidas por empresas de servicio público
**publish** ['pʌblɪʃ] *tr* publicar
**publisher** ['pʌblɪʃər] *s* editor *m*
**publishing house** *s* casa editorial
**pucker** ['pʌkər] *s* (*small fold*) frunce *m;* pliego mal hecho || *tr* fruncir (*una tela; la frente*); plegar mal || *intr* plegarse mal
**pudding** ['pʊdɪŋ] *s* budín *m,* pudín *m*
**puddle** ['pʌdəl] *s* aguazal *m*, charco
**pudg·y** ['pʌdʒi] *adj* (*comp* **-ier;** *super* **-iest**) gordinflón, rechoncho
**puerile** ['pju·ərɪl] *adj* pueril
**puerili·ty** [,pju·ə'rɪlɪti] *s* (*pl* **-ties**) puerilidad
**Puerto Rican** ['pwerto 'rikən] *adj* & *s* puertorriqueño
**puff** [pʌf] *s* soplo vivo; (*of smoke*) bocanada; (*in clothing*) bullón *m;* borla de polvos; pastelillo de crema o jalea; alabanza exagerada; ráfaga, ventolera || *tr* soplar; hinchar; alabar exageradamente || *intr* soplar; hincharse; enorgullecerse exageradamente
**puff paste** *s* hojaldre *m* & *f*
**pugilism** ['pjudʒɪ,lɪzəm] *s* pugilismo
**pugilist** ['pjudʒɪlɪst] *s* pugilista *m*
**pug-nosed** ['pʌg,nozd] *adj* braco
**puke** [pjuk] *s* (slang) vómito || *tr* & *intr* (slang) vomitar
**pull** [pʊl] *s* estirón *m,* tirón *m;* (*on a cigar*) chupada; (*of a door*) tirador *m;* (slang) enchufe *m,* buenas aldabas || *tr* tirar de; torcer (*un ligamento*); (typ) sacar (*una impresión o prueba*); **to pull down** demoler, derribar; bajar (*p.ej., la cortinilla*); abatir, degradar; **to pull oneself together** componerse, recobrar la calma || *intr* tirar; moverse despacio, moverse con esfuerzo; **to pull at** tirar de (*p.ej., la corbata*); chupar (*p.ej., un cigarro*); **to pull for** (slang) abogar por, ayudar; **to pull for oneself** tirar por su lado; **to pull in** llegar (*un tren*) a la estación; **to pull out** partir (*un tren*) de la estación; **to pull through** salir a flote; recobrar la salud
**pullet** ['pʊlɪt] *s* polla
**pulley** ['pʊli] *s* polea
**pulp** [pʌlp] *s* pulpa; (*to make paper*) pasta; (*of tooth*) bulbo
**pulpit** ['pʊlpɪt] *s* púlpito
**pulsate** ['pʌlset] *intr* pulsar; vibrar
**pulsation** [pʌl'seʃən] *s* pulsación; vibración
**pulse** [pʌls] *s* pulso; **to feel** o **take the pulse of** tomar el pulso a
**pulverize** ['pʌlvə,raɪz] *tr* pulverizar
**pumice stone** ['pʌmɪs] *s* pómez *f*, piedra pómez
**pum·mel** ['pʌməl] *v* (*pret* & *pp* **-meled** o **-melled;** *ger* **-meling** o **-melling**)· *tr* apuñear, aporrear
**pump** [pʌmp] *s* bomba; (*slipperlike shoe*) escarpín *m*, zapatilla || *tr* elevar o sacar (*agua*) por medio de una bomba; (coll) tirar de la lengua a (*una persona*); **to pump up** hinchar, inflar (*un neumático*)
**pump handle** *s* guimbalete *m*
**pumpkin** ['pʌmpkɪn] o ['pʌŋkɪn] *s* calabaza común; **some pumpkins** (coll) persona de muchas campanillas
**pump-priming** ['pʌmp,praɪmɪŋ] *s* inyección económica (*por parte del gobierno*)
**pun** [pʌn] *s* equívoco, retruécano || *v* (*pret* & *pp* **punned;** *ger* **punning**) *intr* decir equívocos, jugar del vocablo
**punch** [pʌntʃ] *s* puñetazo; (*tool*) punzón *m;* (*for tickets*) sacabocado; (*drink*) ponche *m* || *tr* dar un puñetazo a; taladrar, perforar (*un billete, una tarjeta*)
**punch bowl** *s* ponchera
**punch card** *s* tarjeta perforada
**punch clock** *s* reloj *m* registrador de tarjetas
**punch'-drunk'** *adj* atontado (*p.ej., por una tunda de golpes*); completamente aturdido
**punched tape** *s* cinta perforada
**punching bag** *s* punching *m,* boxibalón *m*
**punch line** *s* broche *m* de oro, colofón *m* del artículo
**punctilious** [pʌŋk'tɪlɪ·əs] *adj* puntilloso, pundonoroso
**punctual** ['pʌŋktʃʊ·əl] *adj* puntual
**punctuate** ['pʌŋktʃʊ,et] *tr* puntuar; acentuar, destacar; interrumpir || *intr* puntuar
**punctuation** [,pʌŋktʃʊ'eʃən] *s* puntuación
**punctuation mark** *s* signo de puntuación
**puncture** ['pʌŋktʃər] *s* puntura; (*of a tire*) picadura, pinchazo || *tr* pinchar, picar, perforar
**punc'ture-proof'** *adj* a prueba de pinchazos
**pundit** ['pʌndɪt] *s* erudito, sabio
**pungent** ['pʌndʒənt] *adj* picante; estimulante
**punish** ['pʌnɪʃ] *tr* castigar; (coll) maltratar
**punishment** ['pʌnɪʃmənt] *s* castigo; (coll) maltrato

**punk** [pʌŋk] *adj* (slang) malo, de mala calidad || *s* yesca, pebete *m;* (*decayed wood*) hupe *m;* (slang) pillo, gamberro
**punster** [ˈpʌnstər] *s* equivoquista *mf,* vocablista *mf*
**pu•ny** [ˈpjuni] *adj* (*comp* **-nier;** *super* **-niest**) encanijado, débil; insignificante, mezquino
**pup** [pʌp] *s* cachorro
**pupil** [ˈpjupəl] *s* alumno; (*of the eye*) pupila
**puppet** [ˈpʌpɪt] *s* títere *m;* (*doll*) muñeca; (*person controlled by another*) maniquí *m*
**puppet government** *s* gobierno de monigotes
**puppet show** *s* función de títeres
**puppy love** [ˈpʌpi] *s* (coll) primeros amores
**purchase** [ˈpʌrtʃəs] *s* compra; agarre *m* firme || *tr* comprar
**purchasing power** *s* poder adquisitivo
**pure** [pjʊr] *adj* puro
**purgative** [ˈpʌrgətɪv] *adj* & *s* purgante *m*
**purge** [pʌrdʒ] *s* purga || *tr* purgar
**puri•fy** [ˈpjʊrɪ ˌfaɪ] *v* (*pret* & *pp* **-fied**) *tr* purificar
**puritan** [ˈpjʊrɪtən] *adj* & *s* puritano || **Puritan** *adj* & *s* puritano
**purity** [ˈpjʊrɪti] *s* pureza
**purloin** [pərˈlɔɪn] *tr* & *intr* robar, hurtar
**purple** [ˈpʌrpəl] *adj* purpurado, rojo morado || *m* púrpura, rojo morado
**purport** [ˈpʌrport] *s* significado, idea principal || [pərˈport] *tr* significar, querer decir
**purpose** [ˈpʌrpəs] *s* intención, propósito; fin *m,* objeto; **for the purpose** al efecto; **for what purpose?** ¿con qué fin?; **on purpose** adrede, de propósito; **to good purpose** con buenos resultados; **to no purpose** sin resultado; **to serve one's purpose** servir para el caso
**purposely** [ˈpʌrpəsli] *adv* adrede, de propósito
**purr** [pʌr] *s* ronroneo || *intr* ronronear
**purse** [pʌrs] *s* bolsa; (*money collected for charity*) colecta || *tr* fruncir
**purser** [ˈpʌrsər] *s* contador *m* de navío, comisario de a bordo
**purse snatcher** [ˈsnætʃər] *s* carterista *mf*
**purse strings** *spl* cordones *mpl* de la bolsa; **to hold the purse strings** tener las llaves de la caja
**pursue** [pərˈsu] o [pərˈsju] *tr* perseguir (*al que huye*); proseguir (*lo empezado*); seguir (*una carrera*); dedicarse a
**pursuit** [pərˈsut] o [pərˈsjut] *s* persecución; prosecución; (*e.g., of happiness*) busca o búsqueda; empleo
**pursuit plane** *s* caza *m,* avión *m* de caza
**purvey** [pərˈve] *tr* proveer, suministrar
**pus** [pʌs] *s* pus *m*
**push** [pʊʃ] *s* empuje *m,* empujón *m* || *tr* empujar; pulsar (*un botón*); extender (*p.ej., conquistas*); **to push around** (coll) tratar a empujones; **to push aside** hacer a un lado; **to push through** forzar (*p.ej., una resolución*) || *intr* empujar; **to push off** (coll) irse, salir; (naut) desatracarse
**push button** *s* botón *m* de llamada, botón interruptor
**push'-but'ton control** *s* mando por botón
**push'cart'** *s* carretilla de mano
**pushing** [ˈpʊʃɪŋ] *adj* emprendedor; entremetido, agresivo
**pusillanimous** [ˌpjusɪˈlænɪməs] *adj* pusilánime
**puss** [pʊs] *interj* ¡miz! || *s* micho; chica, muchacha; (slang) cara, boca
**puss in the corner** *s* las cuatro esquinas
**puss•y** [ˈpʊsi] *s* (*pl* **-ies**) michito
**pussy willow** *s* sauce norteamericano de amentos muy sedosos
**pustule** [ˈpʌstʃʊl] *s* pústula
**put** [pʊt] *v* (*pret* & *pp* **put;** *ger* **putting**) *tr* poner, colocar; arrojar, echar, lanzar; hacer (*una pregunta*); **to put across** llevar a cabo; hacer aceptar; **to put aside** poner aparte; rechazar; ahorrar (*dinero*); **to put down** anotar, apuntar; sofocar (*una insurrección*); rebajar (*los precios*); **to put off** posponer; deshacerse de; **to put on** ponerse (*la ropa*); poner en escena; llevar (*p.ej., un drama a la pantalla*); accionar (*un freno*); cargar (*impuestos*); fingir; atribuir; **to put oneself out** incomodarse, molestarse; afanarse, desvivirse; **to put out** extender (*la mano*); apagar (*el fuego, la luz*); poner en la calle; dar a luz, publicar; decepcionar; (sport) sacar fuera de la partida; **to put over** o **through** (coll) llevar a cabo; **to put up** construir, edificar; abrir (*un paraguas*); conservar (*fruta, legumbres*); (coll) incitar || *intr* dirigirse; **to put on** fingir; **to put up** parar, hospedarse; **to put up with** aguantar, tolerar
**put'-out'** *adj* contrariado, enojado
**putrid** [ˈpjutrɪd] *adj* pútrido; corrompido, perverso
**Putsch** [pʊtʃ] *s* intentona de sublevación; sublevación
**putter** [ˈpʌtər] *intr* trabajar sin orden ni sistema; **to putter around** ocuparse en fruslerías, temporizar
**put•ty** [ˈpʌti] *s* (*pl* **-ties**) masilla || *v* (*pret* & *pp* **-tied**) *tr* enmasillar
**putty knife** *s* cuchillo de vidriero, espátula
**put'-up'** *adj* (coll) premeditado con malicia
**puzzle** [ˈpʌzəl] *s* enigma *m;* acertijo, rompecabezas *m* || *tr* confundir, poner perplejo; **to puzzle out** descifrar || *intr* estar perplejo; **to puzzle over** tratar de descifrar
**puzzler** [ˈpʌzlər] *s* quisicosa
**PW** *abbr* **prisoner of war**
**pyg•my** [ˈpɪgmi] *adj* pigmeo || *s* (*pl* **-mies**) pigmeo
**pylon** [ˈpaɪlɑn] *s* pilón *m*
**pyramid** [ˈpɪrəmɪd] *s* pirámide *f* || *tr* aumentar (*su dinero*) comprando o

vendiendo al crédito y empleando las ganancias para comprar o vender más
**pyre** [paɪr] *s* pira
**Pyrenean** [ˌpɪrɪˈni·ən] *adj* pirineo
**Pyrenees** [ˈpɪrɪˌniz] *spl* Pirineos
**pyrites** [paɪˈraɪtiz] o [ˈpaɪraɪts] *s* pirita
**pyrotechnical** [ˌpaɪrəˈtɛknɪkəl] *adj* pirotécnico
**pyrotechnics** [ˌpaɪrəˈtɛknɪks] *spl* pirotecnia
**python** [ˈpaɪθɑn] o [ˈpaɪθən] *s* pitón *m*
**pythoness** [ˈpaɪθənɪs] *s* pitonisa
**pyx** [pɪks] *s* píxide *f*, copón *m*

## Q

**Q, q** [kju] decimoséptima letra del alfabeto inglés
**Q.** *abbr* **quarto, queen, question, quire**
**Q.M.** *abbr* **quartermaster**
**qr.** *abbr* **quarter, quire**
**qt.** *abbr* **quantity, quart**
**qu.** *abbr* **quart, quarter, quarterly, queen, query, question**
**quack** [kwæk] *adj* falso || *s* graznido del pato; charlatán *m;* medicastro, curandero || *intr* parpar (*el pato*)
**quacker·y** [ˈkwækəri] *s* (*pl* **-ies**) charlatanismo
**quadrangle** [ˈkwɑdˌræŋgəl] *s* cuadrángulo; patio cuadrangular
**quadrant** [ˈkwɑdrənt] *s* cuadrante *m*
**quadroon** [kwɑdˈrun] *s* cuarterón *m*
**quadruped** [ˈkwɑdruˌpɛd] *adj* & *s* cuadrúpedo
**quadruple** [ˈkwɑdrupəl] o [kwɑdˈrupəl] *adj* & *s* cuádruple *m* || *tr* cuadruplicar || *intr* cuadruplicarse
**quadruplet** [ˈkwɑdruˌplɛt] o [kwɑdˈruplɛt] *s* cuatrillizo
**quaff** [kwɑf] o [kwæf] *s* trago grande || *tr* & *intr* beber en gran cantidad
**quail** [kwel] *s* codorniz *f* || *intr* acobardarse
**quaint** [kwent] *adj* curioso, raro; afectado, rebuscado; fantástico, singular
**quake** [kwek] *s* temblor *m*, terremoto || *intr* temblar
**Quaker** [ˈkwekər] *adj* & *s* cuáquero
**Quaker meeting** *s* reunión de cuáqueros; reunión en que hay poca conversación
**quali·fy** [ˈkwɑlɪˌfaɪ] *v* (*pret* & *pp* **-fied**) *tr* calificar; capacitar, habilitar || *intr* capacitarse, habilitarse
**quali·ty** [ˈkwɑlɪti] *s* (*pl* **-ties**) (*characteristic; virtue*) calidad; (*property, attribute*) cualidad; (*of a sound*) timbre *m*
**qualm** [kwɑm] *s* escrúpulo de conciencia; duda, inquietud; (*nausea*) basca
**quanda·ry** [ˈkwɑndəri] *s* (*pl* **-ries**) incertidumbre, perplejidad
**quanti·ty** [ˈkwɑntɪti] *s* (*pl* **-ties**) cantidad
**quan·tum** [ˈkwɑntəm] *adj* cuántico || *s* (*pl* **-ta** [tə]) cuanto, quántum *m*
**quantum theory** *s* teoría cuántica
**quarantine** [ˈkwɑrənˌtin] o [ˈkwɔrənˌtin] *s* cuarentena; estación de cuarentena || *tr* poner en cuarentena
**quar·rel** [ˈkwɑrəl] o [ˈkwɔrəl] *s* disputa, riña, pelea; **to have no quarrel with** no estar en desacuerdo con; **to pick a quarrel with** tomarse con || *v* (*pret* & *pp* **-reled** o **-relled;** *ger* **-reling** o **-relling**) *intr* disputar, reñir, pelear
**quarrelsome** [ˈkwɑrəlsəm] o [ˈkwɔrəlsəm] *adj* pendenciero
**quar·ry** [ˈkwɑri] o [ˈkwɔri] *s* (*pl* **-ries**) cantera, pedrera; caza, presa || *v* (*pret* & *pp* **-ried**) *tr* sacar de una cantera; extraer, sacar
**quart** [kwɔrt] *s* cuarto de galón
**quarter** [ˈkwɔrtər] *adj* cuarto || *s* cuarto, cuarta parte; (*three months*) trimestre *m;* moneda de 25 centavos; cuarto de luna; barrio; región, lugar *m;* (*clemency*) (mil) cuartel *m;* **quarters** morada, vivienda; local *m;* (mil) cuarteles *mpl;* **to take up quarters** alojarse || *tr* descuartizar
**quar'ter·deck'** *s* alcázar *m*
**quar'ter-hour'** *s* cuarto de hora; **on the quarter-hour** al cuarto en punto cada cuarto de hora
**quarter·ly** [ˈkwɔrtərli] *adj* trimestral || *adv* trimestralmente || *s* (*pl* **-lies**) publicación o revista trimestral
**quar'ter·mas'ter** *s* (mil) comisario; (nav) cabo de brigadas
**quartet** [kwɔrˈtɛt] *s* cuarteto
**quartz** [kwɔrts] *s* cuarzo
**quasar** [ˈkwesɑr] *s* (astr) objeto del espacio, fuente *f* cuasiestelar de radio
**quash** [kwɑʃ] *tr* sofocar, reprimir; anular, invalidar
**quaver** [ˈkwevər] *s* temblor *m*, estremecimiento; (mus) trémolo || *intr* temblar, estremecerse
**quay** [ki] *s* muelle *m*, desembarcadero
**queen** [kwin] *s* reina; (*in chess*) dama o reina; (*in cards*) dama (*que corresponde al caballo*); abeja reina
**queen bee** *s* abeja reina, abeja maestra; (slang) marimandona, la que lleva la voz cantante
**queen dowager** *s* reina viuda
**queen·ly** [ˈkwinli] *adj* (*comp* **-lier;** *super* **-liest**) de reina; como reina; regio
**queen mother** *s* reina madre
**queen olive** *s* aceituna de la reina, aceituna gordal
**queen post** *s* péndola
**queen's English** *s* inglés castizo
**queer** [kwɪr] *adj* curioso, raro; estrambótico, estrafalario; aturdido, indispuesto; (coll) sospechoso, misterioso || *tr* (slang) echar a perder; (slang) comprometer
**quell** [kwel] *tr* sofocar, reprimir; mitigar (*una pena o dolor*)

**quench** [kwentʃ] *tr* apagar (*el fuego; la sed*); sofocar, reprimir; (electron) amortiguar
**que·ry** ['kwɪri] *s* (*pl* **-ries**) pregunta; signo de interrogación; duda ‖ *v* (*pret & pp* **-ried**) *tr* interrogar; marcar con signo de interrogación; dudar
**ques.** *abbr* **question**
**quest** [kwest] *s* búsqueda; (*of the Holy Grail*) demanda; **in quest of** en busca de
**question** ['kwestʃən] *s* pregunta; (*problem for discussion*) cuestión; asunto, proposición; **beside the question** que no viene al caso; **beyond question** fuera de duda; **out of the question** imposible, indiscutible; **to ask a question** hacer una pregunta; **to be a question of** tratarse de, ser cuestión de; **to call in question** poner en duda; **without question** sin duda ‖ *tr* interrogar; cuestionar (*poner en tela de juicio*)
**questionable** ['kwestʃənəbəl] *adj* cuestionable
**question mark** *s* punto interrogante, signo de interrogación
**questionnaire** [,kwestʃən'er] *s* cuestionario
**queue** [kju] *s* (*of hair*) coleta; (*of people*) cola ‖ *intr* hacer cola
**quibble** [kwɪbəl] *intr* sutilizar
**quick** [kwɪk] *adj* rápido, veloz; ágil, vivo; despierto, listo; **the quick and the dead** los vivos y los muertos; **to cut** o **to sting to the quick** herir en lo vivo, tocar en la herida
**quicken** ['kwɪkən] *tr* acelerar, avivar; animar ‖ *intr* acelerarse; animarse
**quick'lime'** *s* cal viva
**quick lunch** *s* servicio de la barra, servicio rápido
**quick'sand'** *s* arena movediza
**quick'sil'ver** *s* azogue *m*
**quiet** ['kwaɪ·ət] *adj* (*still*) quieto; silencioso; (*market*) (com) encalmado; **to keep quiet** callarse ‖ *s* quietud; silencio; **on the quiet** a las calladas ‖ *tr* aquietar; acallar ‖ *intr* aquietarse; callarse; **to quiet down** calmarse
**quill** [kwɪl] *s* pluma de ave; cañón *m* de pluma; (*of hedgehog, porcupine*) púa
**quilt** [kwɪlt] *s* edredón *m*, colcha ‖ *tr* acolchar
**quince** [kwɪns] *s* membrillo
**quinine** ['kwaɪnaɪn] *s* quinina
**quinsy** ['kwɪnzi] *s* cinanquia, esquinencia
**quintessence** [kwɪn'tesəns] *s* quintaesencia
**quintet** [kwɪn'tet] *s* quinteto
**quintuplet** [kwɪn'tjuplet] o [kwɪn'tuplet] *s* quintillizo
**quip** [kwɪp] *s* chufleta, pulla ‖ *v* (*pret & pp* **quipped**; *ger* **quipping**) *tr* decir en son de burla ‖ *intr* echar pullas
**quire** [kwaɪr] *s* mano *f* de papel; (bb) alzado
**quirk** [kwʌrk] *s* excentricidad, rareza; sutileza; vuelta repentina
**quit** [kwɪt] *adj* libre, descargado; **to be quits** estar desquitados; **to cry quits** pedir treguas ‖ *v* (*pret & pp* **quit** o **quitted**; *ger* **quitting**) *tr* dejar ‖ *intr* irse; (coll) dejar de trabajar
**quite** [kwaɪt] *adv* enteramente; verdaderamente; (coll) bastante, muy
**quitter** ['kwɪtər] *s* remolón *m*; (*of a cause*) desertor *m*
**quiver** ['kwɪvər] *s* temblor *m*; (*to hold arrows*) aljaba, carcaj *m* ‖ *intr* temblar
**quixotic** [kwɪks'ɑtɪk] *adj* quijotesco
**quiz** [kwɪz] *s* (*pl* **quizzes**) examen *m*; interrogatorio ‖ *v* (*pret & pp* **quizzed**; *ger* **quizzing**) *tr* examinar; interrogar
**quiz game** *s* torneo de preguntas y respuestas
**quiz program** *s* programa *m* de preguntas y respuestas, torneo radiofónico
**quiz section** *s* grupo de práctica
**quizzical** ['kwɪzɪkəl] *adj* curioso; cómico; burlón
**quoin** [kɔɪn] o [kwɔɪn] *s* esquina; piedra angular; (*wedge*) cuña ‖ *tr* (typ) acuñar
**quoit** [kwɔɪt] o [kɔɪt] *s* herrón *m*, tejo; **quoits** *ssg* hito
**quondam** ['kwɑndæm] *adj* antiguo, de otro tiempo
**quorum** ['kworəm] *s* quórum *m*
**quota** ['kwotə] *s* cuota
**quotation** [kwo'teʃən] *s* (*from a book*) cita; (*of prices*) cotización
**quotation marks** *spl* comillas
**quote** [kwot] *s* (coll) cita; (coll) cotización; **close quote** fin de la cita; **quotes** (coll) comillas ‖ *tr & intr* citar; cotizar; **quote** cito
**quotient** ['kwoʃənt] *s* cociente *m*
**q.v.** *abbr* **quod vide** (Lat) **which see**

# R

**R, r** [ɑr] decimoctava letra del alfabeto inglés
**r.** *abbr* **railroad, railway, road, rod, ruble, rupee**
**R.** *abbr* **railroad, railway, Regina** (Lat) **Queen; Republican, response, Rex** (Lat) **King; River, Royal**
**rabbet** ['ræbɪt] *s* barbilla, rebajo ‖ *tr* embarbillar, rebajar
**rab·bi** ['ræbaɪ] *s* (*pl* **-bis** o **-bies**) rabino
**rabbit** ['ræbɪt] *s* conejo
**rabble** ['ræbəl] *s* canalla, gentuza
**rabble rouser** ['rauzər] *s* populachero, alborotapueblos *mf*
**rabies** ['rebiz] o ['rebɪ,iz] *s* rabia
**raccoon** [ræ'kun] *s* mapache *m*, oso lavador

**race** [res] *s* (*people of same stock*) raza; (*contest in speed, etc.*) carrera; (*channel to lead water*) caz *m* || *tr* competir con, en una carrera; hacer correr de prisa; hacer funcionar (*un motor*) a velocidad excesiva || *intr* correr de prisa; correr en una carrera; competir en una carrera; embalarse (*un motor*); (naut) regatear
**race horse** *s* caballo de carreras
**race riot** *s* disturbio racista
**race track** *s* pista de carreras
**racial** [ˈreʃəl] *adj* racial
**racing car** *s* coche *m* de carreras
**rack** [ræk] *s* (*sort of shelf*) estante *m;* (*to hang clothes*) percha; (*for fodder for cattle*) pesebre *m;* (*for baggage*) red *f* de equipaje; (*for guns*) armero; (*bar made to gear with a pinion*) cremallera; **to go to rack and ruin** desvencijarse; ir al desastre || *tr* estirar, forzar; atormentar; despedazar; oprimir, agobiar; **to rack off** trasegar (*el vino*); **to rack one's brains** calentarse la cabeza, devanarse los sesos
**racket** [ˈrækɪt] *s* raqueta; (*noise*) baraúnda, alboroto; (slang) trapisonda, trapacería; **to raise a racket** armar un alboroto
**racketeer** [ˌrækɪˈtɪr] *s* trapisondista *mf*, trapacista *mf* || *intr* trapacear
**rack railway** *s* ferrocarril *m* de cremallera
**rac•y** [ˈresi] *adj* (*comp* **-ier;** *super* **-iest**) espiritoso, chispeante; perfumado; (*somewhat indecent*) picante
**radar** [ˈredɑr] *s* radar *m*
**radiant** [ˈredɪ•ənt] *adj* radiante, resplandeciente; (*cheerful, smiling*) radiante
**radiate** [ˈredɪˌet] *tr* radiar; difundir (*p.ej., felicidad*) || *intr* radiar, irradiar
**radiation** [ˌredɪˈeʃən] *s* radiación
**radiation sickness** *s* enfermedad de radiación, mal *m* de rayos
**radiator** [ˈredɪˌetər] *s* radiador *m*
**radiator cap** *s* tapón *m* de radiador
**radical** [ˈrædɪkəl] *adj* & *s* radical *m*
**radi•o** [ˈredɪˌo] *s* (*pl* **-os**) radio *f;* radiograma *m* || *tr* radiodifundir
**radioactive** [ˌredɪ•oˈæktɪv] *adj* radiactivo
**radio amateur** *s* radioaficionado
**radio announcer** *s* locutor *m* de radio
**ra'dio•broad'cast'ing** *s* radiodifusión
**radio frequency** *s* radiofrecuencia
**radio listener** *s* radioescucha *mf*, radioyente *mf*
**radiology** [ˌredɪˈɑlədʒi] *s* radiología
**radio network** *s* red *f* de emisoras
**radio newscaster** *s* cronista *mf* de radio
**radio receiver** *s* radiorreceptor *m*
**radio set** *s* aparato de radio
**radish** [ˈrædɪʃ] *s* rábano
**radium** [ˈredɪ•əm] *s* radio
**radi•us** [ˈredɪ•əs] *s* (*pl* **-i** [ˌaɪ] o **-uses**) radio; (*range of operation*) radio; **within a radius of** en . . . a la redonda
**raffle** [ˈræfəl] *s* rifa || *tr* & *intr* rifar
**raft** [ræft] o [rɑft] *s* armadía, balsa; (coll) gran número
**rafter** [ˈræftər] o [ˈrɑftər] *s* cabrio, contrapar *m*, traviesa
**rag** [ræg] *s* trapo; **to chew the rag** (slang) dar la lengua
**ragamuffin** [ˈrægəˌmʌfɪn] *s* pelagatos *m;* golfo, chiquillo haraposo
**rag baby** o **rag doll** *s* muñeca de trapo
**rage** [redʒ] *s* rabia; **to be all the rage** estar en boga, hacer furor; **to fly into a rage** montar en cólera
**ragged** [ˈrægɪd] *adj* andrajoso; (*edge*) cortado en dientes
**ragpicker** [ˈrægˌpɪkər] *s* andrajero, trapero
**rag'weed'** *s* ambrosía
**raid** [red] *s* incursión, invasión; ataque de sorpresa; ataque aéreo || *tr* invadir; atacar inesperadamente; capturar (*p.ej., la policía un garito*)
**rail** [rel] *s* carril *m*, riel *m;* (*railing*) barandilla; (*of a bridge*) guardalado; (*at a bar*) apoyo para los pies; palo; **by rail** por ferrocarril; **rails** títulos o valores de ferrocarril || *tr* poner barandilla a || *intr* quejarse amargamente; **to rail at** injuriar, ultrajar
**rail fence** *s* cerca hecha de palos horizontales
**rail'head'** *s* (rr) cabeza de línea
**railing** [ˈrelɪŋ] *s* barandilla, pasamano
**rail'road'** *adj* ferroviario || *s* ferrocarril *m* || *tr* (coll) llevar a cabo con demasiada precipitación; (slang) encarcelar falsamente || *intr* trabajar en el ferrocarril
**railroad crossing** *s* paso a nivel
**rail'way'** *adj* ferroviario || *s* ferrocarril *m*
**raiment** [ˈremənt] *s* prendas de vestir, indumentaria
**rain** [ren] *s* lluvia; **rain or shine** llueva o no, con buen o mal tiempo || *tr* & *intr* llover
**rain'bow'** *s* arco iris
**rain'coat'** *s* impermeable *m*
**rain'fall'** *s* lluvia repentina; precipitación acuosa
**rain•y** [ˈreni] *adj* (*comp* **-ier;** *super* **-iest**) lluvioso
**rainy day** *s* día lluvioso; tiempo futuro de posible necesidad
**raise** [rez] *s* aumento || *tr* levantar; aumentar; criar (*a niños, animales*); cultivar (*plantas*); reunir (*dinero*); suscitar (*una duda*); resucitar (*a los muertos*); dejarse (*barba, bigote*); poner (*una objeción*); plantear (*una pregunta*); levantar (*tropas; un sitio*); (math) elevar; (*to come in sight of*) (naut) avistar
**raisin** [ˈrezən] *s* pasa, uva seca
**rake** [rek] *s* rastro, rastrillo; (*person*) calavera *m*, libertino || *tr* rastrillar; **to rake together** acumular (*dinero*)
**rake'-off'** *s* (slang) dinero obtenido ilícitamente
**rakish** [ˈrekɪʃ] *adj* airoso, gallardo; listo, vivo; libertino
**ral•ly** [ˈræli] *s* (*pl* **-lies**) reunión popular, reunión política; recuperación, recobro || *v* (*pret* & *pp* **-lied**) *tr* reu-

nir; reanimar; recobrar (*la fuerza, la salud, el ánimo*) || *intr* reunirse; recobrarse (*p.ej., los precios en la Bolsa*); recobrar la fuerza, la salud, el ánimo; **to rally to the side of** acudir a, ir en socorro de

**ram** [ræm] *s* (*male sheep*) morueco, carnero padre; (*device for battering, crushing, etc.*) pisón *m* || *v* (*pret & pp* **rammed;** *ger* **ramming**) *tr* dar contra, chocar en; atestar, rellenar || *intr* chocar; **to ram into** chocar en

**ramble** [ˈræmbəl] *s* paseo || *intr* pasear; serpentear (*p.ej., un río*); extenderse serpenteando (*las enredaderas*); (*to wander aimlessly; to talk in an aimless way*) divagar

**rami•fy** [ˈræmɪ,faɪ] *v* (*pret & pp* **-fied**) *tr* ramificar || *intr* ramificarse

**ramp** [ræmp] *s* rampa

**rampage** [ˈræmpedʒ] *s* alboroto; **to go on a rampage** alborotar, comportarse como un loco

**rampart** [ˈræmpɑrt] *s* muralla, terraplén *m;* amparo, defensa

**ram'rod'** *s* atacador *m,* baqueta

**ram'shack'le** *adj* desvencijado, destartalado

**ranch** [ræntʃ] *s* granja, hacienda

**rancid** [ˈrænsɪd] *adj* rancio

**rancor** [ˈræŋkər] *s* rencor *m*

**random** [ˈrændəm] *adj* casual, fortuito; **at random** al azar, a la ventura

**range** [rendʒ] *s* (*row, line*) fila, hilera; (*scope, reach*) alcance *m;* (*of speeds, prices, etc.*) escala; campo de tiro; terreno de pasto; (*of a boat or airplane*) autonomía; (*of the voice*) extensión; (*of colors*) gama, serie *f;* (*stove*) cocina económica; **within range of** al alcance de || *tr* alinear; recorrer (*un terreno*); ir a lo largo de (*la costa*); arreglar, ordenar || *intr* fluctuar, variar (*entre ciertos límites*); extenderse; divagar, errar; **to range over** recorrer

**range finder** *s* telémetro

**rank** [ræŋk] *adj* exuberante, lozano; denso, espeso; grosero; maloliente; excesivo; incorregible, rematado; indecente, vulgar || *s* categoría, rango; condición, posición; distinción; (*line of soldiers standing abreast*) fila; (mil) empleo, grado || *tr* alinear; ordenar; tener grado o posición más alta que || *intr* ocupar el último grado; **to rank high** ocupar alta posición; ser tenido en alta estima; sobresalir; **to rank low** ocupar baja posición; **to rank with** estar al nivel de; tener el mismo grado que

**rank and file** *s* soldados de fila; pueblo, gente *f* común

**rankle** [ˈræŋkəl] *tr* enconar, irritar || *intr* enconarse

**ransack** [ˈrænsæk] *tr* registrar, escudriñar; robar, saquear

**ransom** [ˈrænsəm] *s* rescate *m* || *tr* rescatar

**rant** [rænt] *intr* desvariar, despotricar

**rap** [ræp] *s* golpe corto y seco; (*noise*) taque *m;* (coll) ardite *m,* bledo; (slang) crítica mordaz; **to take the rap** (slang) pagar la multa; sufrir las consecuencias || *v* (*pret & pp* **rapped;** *ger* **rapping**) *tr* golpear con golpe corto y seco; decir vivamente; (slang) criticar mordazmente || *intr* golpear con golpe corto y seco; **to rap at the door** tocar a la puerta

**rapacious** [rəˈpeʃəs] *adj* rapaz

**rape** [rep] *s* rapto; (*of a woman*) estupro, violación || *tr* raptar; estuprar, violar

**rapid** [ˈræpɪd] *adj* rápido || **rapids** *spl* (*of a river*) rápidos

**rap'id-fire'** *adj* de tiro rápido; hecho vivamente

**rapier** [ˈrepɪ•ər] *s* estoque *m,* espadín *m*

**rapt** [ræpt] *adj* arrebatado, extático, transportado; absorto

**rapture** [ˈræptʃər] *s* embeleso, éxtasis *f,* rapto

**rare** [rɛr] *adj* raro; (*word*) poco usado; (*meat*) poco asado; (*gem*) precioso

**rare bird** *s* mirlo blanco

**rare•fy** [ˈrɛrɪ,faɪ] *v* (*pret & pp* **-fied**) *tr* enrarecer || *intr* enrarecerse

**rarely** [ˈrɛrli] *adv* rara vez

**rascal** [ˈræskəl] *s* bellaco, bribón *m,* pícaro

**rash** [ræʃ] *adj* temerario || *s* brote *m,* salpullido, erupción

**rasp** [ræsp] o [rɑsp] *s* escofina; (*sound of a rasp*) sonido áspero || *tr* escofinar; irritar, molestar; decir con voz ronca || *intr* hacer sonido áspero

**raspber•ry** [ˈræz,beri] o [ˈrɑz,beri] *s* (*pl* **-ries**) frambuesa, sangüesa

**raspberry bush** *s* frambueso, sangüeso

**rat** [ræt] *s* rata; (*false hair*) (coll) postizo; **to smell a rat** (coll) olerse una trama, sospechar una intriga

**ratchet** [ˈrætʃɪt] *s* trinquete *m*

**rate** [ret] *s* (*amount or degree measured in proportion to something else*) razón *f;* (*of interest*) tipo; velocidad; precio; **at any rate** de todos modos; **at the rate of** a razón de || *tr* valuar; estimar, juzgar; clasificar || *intr* ser considerado, ser tenido; estar clasificado

**rate of exchange** *s* tipo de cambio

**rather** [ˈræðər] o [ˈrɑðər] *adv* algo, un poco; bastante; antes, más bien; mejor dicho; por el contrario; muy, mucho; **rather than** antes que, más bien que || *interj* ¡ya lo creo!

**rati•fy** [ˈrætɪ,faɪ] *v* (*pret & pp* **-fied**) *tr* ratificar

**ra•tio** [ˈreʃo] o [ˈreʃɪ,o] *s* (*pl* **-tios**) (math) razón *f;* (math) cociente *m*

**ration** [ˈreʃən] o [ˈræʃən] *s* ración || *tr* racionar

**ration book** *s* cartilla de racionamiento

**rational** [ˈræʃənəl] *adj* racional

**rat poison** *s* matarratas *m*

**rattle** [ˈrætəl] *s* (*number of short, sharp sounds*) traqueteo; (*noise-making device*) carraca, matraca; (*child's toy*) sonajero; baraúnda; (*in the throat*) estertor *m* || *tr* tabletear, traquetear; (*to confuse*) (coll) atortolar, desconcertar; **to rattle off**

decir rápidamente || *intr* tabletear, traquetear
**rat'tle·snake'** *s* serpiente *f* de cascabel
**rat'trap'** *s* ratonera; trance apurado, atolladero
**raucous** ['rɔkəs] *adj* ronco
**ravage** ['rævɪdʒ] *s* destrucción, estrago, ruina || *tr* destruir, estragar, arruinar
**rave** [rev] *intr* desvariar, delirar; bramar, enfurecerse; **to rave about** hacerse lenguas de, deshacerse en elogios de
**raven** ['revən] *s* cuervo
**ravenous** ['rævənəs] *adj* famélico, hambriento, voraz; rapaz
**ravine** [rə'vin] *s* cañón *m*, hondonada
**ravish** ['rævɪʃ] *tr* encantar, entusiasmar; raptar; violar (*a una mujer*)
**ravishing** ['rævɪʃɪŋ] *adj* encantador
**raw** [rɔ] *adj* crudo; (*cotton, silk*) en rama; inexperto, principiante; ulceroso; (*weather, day*) crudo
**raw deal** *s* (slang) mala pasada
**raw'hide'** *s* cuero en verde; látigo hecho de cuero en verde
**raw material** *s* primera materia, materia prima
**ray** [re] *s* (*of light*) rayo; (*fine line; fish*) raya
**rayon** ['re·ɑn] *s* rayón *m*
**raze** [rez] *tr* arrasar, asolar
**razor** ['rezər] *s* navaja de afeitar
**razor blade** *s* hoja u hojita de afeitar
**razor strop** *s* asentador *m*, suavizador *m*
**razz** [ræz] *s* (slang) irrisión || *tr* (slang) mofarse de
**R.C.** *abbr* **Red Cross, Reserve Corps, Roman Catholic**
**R.D.** *abbr* **Rural Delivery**
**reach** [ritʃ] *s* alcance *m;* extensión; **out of reach (of)** fuera del alcance (de); **within reach of** al alcance de || *tr* alcanzar; extender; entregar con la mano; llegar a; ponerse en contacto con; influenciar; cumplir (*cierto número de años*) || *intr* alcanzar; extender la mano o el brazo; **to reach after** o **for** esforzarse por coger
**react** [rɪ'ækt] *intr* reaccionar
**reaction** [rɪ'ækʃən] *s* reacción
**reactionar·y** [rɪ'ækʃən,ɛri] *adj* reaccionario || *s* (*pl* **-ies**) reaccionario
**read** [rid] *v* (*pret & pp* **read** [rɛd]) *tr* leer; recitar (*poesía*); estudiar (*derecho*); leer en, adivinar (*el pensamiento ajeno*); **to read over** recorrer, repasar || *intr* leer; rezar, p.ej., **this page reads thus** esta página reza así; leerse, p.ej., **this book reads easily** este libro se lee con facilidad; **to read on** seguir leyendo
**reader** ['ridər] *s* lector *m;* libro de lectura
**readily** ['rɛdɪli] *adv* de buena gana; fácilmente
**reading** ['ridɪŋ] *s* lectura; recitación
**reading desk** *s* atril *m*
**reading glass** *s* lente *f* para leer, vidrio de aumento; **reading glasses** anteojos para la lectura
**reading lamp** *s* lámpara de sobremesa
**reading room** *s* gabinete *m* de lectura; sala de lectura
**read·y** ['rɛdi] *adj* (*comp* **-ier;** *super* **-iest**) listo, preparado, pronto; ágil, diestro; vivo; disponible; **to make ready** preparar; prepararse || *v* (*pret & pp* **-ied**) *tr* preparar || *intr* prepararse
**ready cash** *s* dinero a la mano, dinero contante y sonante
**read'y-made' clothing** *s* ropa hecha
**ready-made suit** *s* traje hecho
**reagent** [rɪ'edʒənt] *s* reactivo
**real** ['ri·əl] *adj* real, verdadero
**real estate** *s* bienes *mpl* raíces, bienes inmuebles
**re'al-es·tate'** *adj* inmobiliario
**realism** ['ri·ə,lɪzəm] *s* realismo
**realist** ['ri·əlɪst] *s* realista *mf*
**reali·ty** [rɪ'ælɪti] *s* (*pl* **-ties**) realidad
**realize** ['ri·ə,laɪz] *tr* darse cuenta de; realizar, llevar a cabo; adquirir (*ganancias*); reportar (*ganancias*) || *intr* (*to sell property for ready money*) realizar
**realm** [rɛlm] *s* reino
**realtor** ['ri·əl,tɔr] o ['ri·əltər] *s* corredor *m* de bienes raíces
**realty** ['ri·əlti] *s* bienes *mpl* raíces, bienes inmuebles
**ream** [rim] *s* resma; **reams** (coll) montones *mpl* || *tr* escariar
**reap** [rip] *tr & intr* (*to cut*) segar; (*to gather*) cosechar
**reaper** ['ripər] *s* (*person*) segador *m;* máquina segadora
**reappear** [,ri·ə'pɪr] *intr* reaparecer
**reapportionment** [,ri·ə'porʃənmənt] *s* nuevo prorrateo
**rear** [rɪr] *adj* posterior, trasero; de atrás || *s* espalda; (*of a room*) fondo; (*of a row; of an automobile*) cola; retaguardia; (slang) culo, trasero || *tr* levantar; edificar; criar, educar || *intr* encabritarse (*un caballo*)
**rear admiral** *s* contraalmirante *m*
**rear drive** *s* tracción trasera
**rearmament** [ri'ɑrməmənt] *s* rearme *m*
**rear'-view' mirror** *s* retrovisor *m*, espejo de retrovisión
**rear window** *s* (aut) luneta, luneta posterior
**reason** ['rizən] *s* razón *f;* **by reason of** con motivo de, a causa de; **to listen to reason** meterse en razón; **to stand to reason** ser razonable || *tr & intr* razonar
**reasonable** ['rizənəbəl] *adj* razonable
**reassessment** [,ri·ə'sɛsmənt] *s* nuevo amillaramiento; nueva estimación
**reassure** [,ri·ə'ʃʊr] *tr* volver a asegurar; tranquilizar
**reawaken** [,ri·ə'wekən] *tr* volver a despertar || *intr* volver a despertarse
**rebate** ['ribet] o [rɪ'bet] *s* rebaja || *tr* rebajar
**rebel** ['rɛbəl] *adj & s* rebelde *mf* ||
**re·bel** [rɪ'bɛl] *v* (*pret & pp* **-belled;** *ger* **-belling**) *intr* rebelarse
**rebellion** [rɪ'bɛljən] *s* rebelión
**rebellious** [rɪ'bɛljəs] *adj* rebelde
**re·bind** [ri'baɪnd] *v* (*pret & pp* **-bound**

['baund]) *tr* reatar; (*to edge, to border*) ribetear; (bb) reencuadernar
**rebirth** ['ribʌrθ] o [ri'bʌrθ] *s* renacimiento
**rebore** [ri'bor] *tr* rectificar
**rebound** ['ri,baund] o [ri'baund] *s* rebote *m* || [ri'baund] *intr* rebotar
**rebroad•cast** [ri'brɔd,kæst] o [ri'brɔd,kɑst] *s* retransmisión || *v* (*pret & pp* **-cast** o **-casted**) *tr* retransmitir
**rebuff** [rɪ'bʌf] *s* desaire *m*, rechazo || *tr* desairar, rechazar
**re•build** [ri'bɪld] *v* (*pret & pp* **-built** ['bɪlt]) *tr* reconstruir, reedificar
**rebuke** [rɪ'bjuk] *s* reprensión || *tr* reprender
**re•but** [rɪ'bʌt] *v* (*pret & pp* **-butted**; *ger* **-butting**) *tr* rebatir, refutar
**rebuttal** [rɪ'bʌtəl] *s* rebatimiento, refutación
**rec.** *abbr* **receipt, recipe, record, recorder**
**recall** [rɪ'kɔl] o ['rikɔl] *s* llamada; recordación; revocación; (*of a diplomat*) retirada || [rɪ'kɔl] *tr* hacer volver, mandar volver; recordar; revocar; retirar (*a un diplomático*)
**recant** [rɪ'kænt] *tr* retractar || *intr* retractarse
**re•cap** ['ri,kæp] o [ri'kæp] *v* (*pret & pp* **-capped**; *ger* **-capping**) *tr* recauchutar
**recapitalization** [ri,kæpɪtəlɪ'zeʃən] *s* recapitalización
**recapitulation** [,rikə,pɪtʃə'leʃən] *s* recapitulación
**re•cast** ['ri,kæst] o ['ri,kɑst] *s* refundición; (*of a sentence*) reconstrucción || [ri'kæst] o [ri'kɑst] *v* (*pret & pp* **-cast**) *tr* refundir; reconstruir (*p.ej., una frase*)
**recd.** o **rec'd.** *abbr* **received**
**recede** [rɪ'sid] *intr* (*to move back*) retroceder; (*to move away*) alejarse, retirarse; deprimirse (*p.ej., la frente de una persona*)
**receipt** [rɪ'sit] *s* recepción; (*acknowledgment*) recibo; (*acknowledgment of payment*) recibí *m*; (*recipe*) receta; **receipt in full** finiquito; **receipts** entradas, ingresos || *tr* poner el recibí a
**receive** [rɪ'siv] *tr* recibir; receptar (*cosas que son materia de delito*); **received payment** recibí || *intr* recibir
**receiver** [rɪ'sivər] *s* receptor *m*; (*in bankruptcy*) contador *m*, síndico; receptor telefónico
**receiving set** *s* aparato receptor
**receiving teller** *s* recibidor *m* (*de un banco*)
**recent** ['risənt] *adj* reciente
**recently** ['risəntli] *adv* recientemente; recién, p.ej., **recently arrived** recién llegado
**receptacle** [rɪ'septəkəl] *s* receptáculo
**reception** [rɪ'sepʃən] *s* recepción; (*welcome*) recibimiento
**reception desk** *s* recepción
**receptionist** [rɪ'sepʃənɪst] *s* recepcionista *f*
**receptive** [rɪ'septɪv] *adj* receptivo
**recess** [rɪ'ses] o ['rises] *s* intermisión; descanso; hora de recreo; (*in a surface*) depresión; (*in a wall*) hueco, nicho; escondrijo || [rɪ'ses] *tr* ahuecar; empotrar; deprimir || *intr* prorrogarse, suspenderse
**recession** [rɪ'sɛʃən] *s* retroceso, retirada; (*e.g., in a wall*) depresión; procesión de vuelta; contracción económica
**recipe** ['resɪ,pi] *s* receta (de cocina)
**reciprocal** [rɪ'sɪprəkəl] *adj* recíproco
**reciprocity** [,resɪ'prɑsɪti] *s* reciprocidad
**recital** [rɪ'saɪtəl] *s* narración; (*of music or poetry*) recital *m*
**recite** [rɪ'saɪt] *tr* narrar; (*formally*) recitar
**reckless** ['rɛklɪs] *adj* atolondrado, temerario
**reckon** ['rɛkən] *tr* calcular; considerar; (coll) calcular, conjeturar || *intr* calcular; **to reckon on** contar con; **to reckon with** tener en cuenta
**reclaim** [rɪ'klem] *tr* hacer utilizable; hacer labrantío (*un terreno*); ganar (*terreno*) a la mar; recuperar (*materiales usados*); conducir, guiar (*a los que hacen mala vida*)
**recline** [rɪ'klaɪn] *intr* reclinarse
**recluse** [rɪ'klus] o ['rɛklus] *s* solitario, ermitaño
**recognize** ['rɛkəg,naɪz] *tr* reconocer
**recoil** [rɪ'kɔɪl] *s* reculada; (*of a firearm*) reculada, culetazo || *intr* recular, apartarse; recular (*un arma de fuego*)
**recollect** [,rɛkə'lɛkt] *tr & intr* recordar
**recommend** [,rɛkə'mɛnd] *tr* recomendar
**recompense** ['rɛkəm,pɛns] *s* recompensa || *tr* recompensar
**reconcile** ['rɛkən,saɪl] *tr* reconciliar; **to reconcile oneself** resignarse
**reconnaissance** [rɪ'kɑnɪsəns] *s* reconocimiento
**reconnoiter** [,rɛkə'nɔɪtər] o [,rikə'nɔɪtər] *tr & intr* reconocer
**reconquest** [ri'kɑŋkwest] *s* reconquista
**reconsider** [,rikən'sɪdər] *tr* reconsiderar
**reconstruct** [,rikən'strʌkt] *tr* reconstruir
**reconversion** [,rikən'vʌrʒən] o [,rikən'vʌrʃən] *s* reconversión
**record** ['rɛkərd] *s* anotación; ficha, historial *m*, historia personal; (*of a notary*) protocolo; (*of a phonograph*) disco; (educ) expediente académico; (sport) record *m*, plusmarca; **off the record** confidencialmente; **records** anales *mpl*, memorias; archivo; **to break a record** batir un record; **to make a record** establecer un record; grabar un disco || [rɪ'kɔrd] *tr* asentar; registrar; inscribir; grabar (*un sonido, una canción, un disco fonográfico, etc.*)
**record breaker** *s* plusmarquista *mf*
**record changer** ['tʃendʒər] *s* cambiadiscos *m*, tocadiscos automático
**record holder** *s* (sport) recordman *m*
**recording** [rɪ'kɔrdɪŋ] *adj* registrador;

(*wire or tape*) magnetofónico || *s* registro; (*of phonograph records*) grabación o grabado
**recording secretary** *s* secretario escribiente, secretario de actas
**record player** *s* tocadiscos *m*
**recount** [ˈri ˌkaʊnt] *s* recuento || [riˈkaʊnt] *tr* (*to count again*) recontar || [rɪˈkaʊnt] *tr* (*to narrate*) recontar
**recourse** [rɪˈkors] o [ˈrikors] *s* recurso; (*helping hand*) paño de lágrimas; **to have recourse to** recurrir a
**recover** [rɪˈkʌvər] *tr* recobrar; rescatar; **to recover consciousness** recobrar el conocimiento, volver en sí || *intr* recobrarse; recobrar la salud; ganar un pleito
**recover•y** [rɪˈkʌvəri] *s* (*pl* **-ies**) recobro, recuperación; **past recovery** sin remedio
**recreant** [ˈrɛkrɪ·ənt] *adj & s* cobarde *mf*, traidor *m*
**recreation** [ˌrɛkrɪˈeʃən] *s* recreación
**recruit** [rɪˈkrut] *s* recluta *m* || *tr* reclutar || *intr* alistar reclutas; ganar reclutas; restablecerse, reponerse
**rect.** *abbr* **receipt, rector, rectory**
**rectangle** [ˈrɛk ˌtæŋgəl] *s* rectángulo
**recti•fy** [ˈrɛktɪˌfaɪ] *v* (*pret & pp* **-fied**) *tr* rectificar
**rec•tum** [ˈrɛktəm] *s* (*pl* **-ta** [tə]) recto
**recumbent** [rɪˈkʌmbənt] *adj* reclinado, recostado
**recuperate** [rɪˈkjupəˌret] *tr* recuperar; restablecer, reponer || *intr* recuperarse, recobrarse
**re•cur** [rɪˈkʌr] *v* (*pret & pp* **-curred**; *ger* **-curring**) *intr* volver a ocurrir; volver a presentarse (*a la memoria*); volver (*a un asunto*)
**recurrent** [rɪˈkʌrənt] *adj* repetido; periódico; (*illness*) recurrente
**red** [rɛd] *adj* (*comp* **redder**; *super* **reddest**) rojo, colorado; (*wine*) tinto; enrojecido, inflamado || *s* rojo; **in the red** (coll) endeudado; **to see red** (coll) enfurecerse || **Red** *adj & s* (*communist*) rojo
**red′bait′** *tr* motejar (*a uno*) de rojo o comunista
**red′bird′** *s* cardenal *m;* piranga
**red-blooded** [ˈrɛd ˌblʌdɪd] *adj* fuerte, valiente, vigoroso
**red′breast′** *s* petirrojo
**red′bud′** *s* ciclamor *m* del Canadá
**red′cap′** *s* (Brit) policía militar; (U.S.A.) mozo de estación
**red cell** *s* glóbulo rojo, hematíe *m*
**red′coat′** *s* (hist) soldado inglés
**redden** [ˈrɛdən] *tr* enrojecer || *intr* enrojecerse
**redeem** [rɪˈdim] *tr* redimir; cumplir (*una promesa*)
**redeemer** [rɪˈdimər] *s* redentor *m*
**redemption** [rɪˈdɛmpʃən] *s* redención
**red-haired** [ˈrɛd ˌhɛrd] *adj* pelirrojo
**red′head′** *s* pelirrojo
**red herring** *s* artificio para distraer la atención del asunto de que se trata
**red′-hot′** *adj* candente, calentado al rojo; ardiente, entusiasta; fresco, nuevo
**rediscount rate** [riˈdɪskaʊnt] *s* tipo de redescuento
**rediscover** [ˌridɪsˈkʌvər] *tr* redescubrir
**red′-let′ter day** *s* día *m* memorable
**red′-light′ district** *s* barrio de los lupanares, barrio de mala vida
**red man** *s* piel roja *m*
**re•do** [ˈriˈdu] *v* (*pret* **-did** [ˈdɪd]; *pp* **-done** [ˈdʌn]) *tr* rehacer, repetir; refundir; reformar
**redolent** [ˈrɛdələnt] *adj* fragante, perfumado; **redolent of** que huele a
**redoubt** [rɪˈdaʊt] *s* (fort) reducto
**redound** [rɪˈdaʊnd] *intr* redundar; **to redound to** redundar en
**red pepper** *s* pimentón *m*
**redress** [rɪˈdrɛs] o [ˈridrɛs] *s* reparación; remedio || [rɪˈdrɛs] *tr* reparar; remediar
**Red Ridinghood** [ˈraɪdɪŋ ˌhʊd] *s* Caperucita Roja
**red′skin′** *s* piel roja *m*
**red tape** *s* expedienteo, papeleo
**reduce** [rɪˈdjus] o [rɪˈdus] *tr* reducir; (mil) degradar || *intr* redúcirse; reducir peso
**reducing exercises** *spl* ejercicios físicos para reducir peso
**redundant** [rɪˈdʌndənt] *adj* redundante
**red′wood′** *s* secoya
**reed** [rid] *adj* (*organ, musical instrument*) de lengüeta || *s* (*stalk*) caña; (*plant*) carrizo, caña; (mus) instrumento de lengüeta; (*of instrument*) lengüeta
**reëdit** [riˈɛdɪt] *tr* refundir
**reef** [rif] *s* arrecife *m*, escollo; (min) filón *m*, veta || *tr* (naut) arrizar
**reefer** [ˈrifər] *s* chaquetón *m;* (slang) pitillo de mariguana
**reek** [rik] *intr* vahear, humear; estar bañado en sudor; estar mojado con sangre; **to reek of** o **with** oler a
**reel** [ril] *s* (*spool*) carrete *m;* (*of a shuttle*) broca; (*of motion pictures*) cinta; (*sway, staggering*) tambaleo; **off the reel** (coll) fácil y prestamente || *tr* aspar, devanar; **to reel off** (coll) narrar fácil y prestamente || *intr* tambalear; cejar (*p.ej., el enemigo*)
**reëlection** [ˌri·ɪˈlɛkʃən] *s* reelección
**reënlist** [ˌri·ɛnˈlɪst] *tr* reenganchar || *intr* reengancharse
**reën•try** [rɪˈɛntri] *s* (*pl* **-tries**) reingreso, nueva entrada; (*return to earth's atmosphere*) reentrada
**reëxamination** [ˌri·ɛgˌzæmɪˈneʃən] *s* reexaminación
**ref.** *abbr* **referee, reference, reformation**
**re•fer** [rɪˈfʌr] *v* (*pret & pp* **-ferred**; *ger* **-ferring**) *tr* referir || *intr* referirse
**referee** [ˌrɛfəˈri] *s* árbitro || *tr & intr* arbitrar
**reference** [ˈrɛfərəns] *adj* (*library, book, work*) de consulta || *s* referencia
**referen•dum** [ˌrɛfəˈrɛndəm] *s* (*pl* **-da** [də]) *s* referéndum *m*
**refill** [ˈrifɪl] *s* relleno || [riˈfɪl] *tr* rellenar
**refine** [rɪˈfaɪn] *tr* refinar

**refinement** [rɪˈfaɪnmənt] *s* refinamiento; buena crianza, cultura
**refiner·y** [rɪˈfaɪnəri] *s* (*pl* **-ies**) refinería
**reflect** [rɪˈflɛkt] *tr* reflejar ‖ *intr* reflejar; (*to meditate*) reflexionar; **to reflect on** o **upon** reflexionar en o sobre; perjudicar
**reflection** [rɪˈflɛkʃən] *s* (*thinking*) reflexión; (*reflected light; image*) reflejo
**reforestation** [ˌrifɑrɪsˈteʃən] o [ˌrifɔrɪsˈteʃən] *s* reforestación
**reform** [rɪˈfɔrm] *s* reforma ‖ *tr* reformar ‖ *intr* reformarse
**reformation** [ˌrɛfərˈmeʃən] *s* reformación ‖ **the Reformation** la Reforma
**reformato·ry** [rɪˈfɔrməˌtori] *s* (*pl* **-ries**) reformatorio
**reform school** *s* casa de corrección
**refraction** [rɪˈfrækʃən] *s* refracción
**refrain** [rɪˈfren] *s* estribillo ‖ *intr* abstenerse
**refresh** [rɪˈfrɛʃ] *tr* refrescar ‖ *intr* refrescarse
**refreshing** [rɪˈfrɛʃɪŋ] *adj* confortante, restaurante
**refreshment** [rɪˈfrɛʃmənt] *s* refresco
**refrigerator** [rɪˈfrɪdʒəˌretər] *s* heladera, nevera, refrigerador *m*
**refrigerator car** *s* carro o vagón frigorífico
**refuel** [riˈfjul] *tr & intr* repostar
**refuge** [ˈrɛfjudʒ] *s* refugio; expediente *m*, subterfugio; **to take refuge (in)** refugiarse (en)
**refugee** [ˌrɛfjuˈdʒi] *s* refugiado
**refund** [ˈrifʌnd] *s* reembolso ‖ [rɪˈfʌnd] *tr* reembolsar ‖ [riˈfʌnd] *tr* consolidar
**refurnish** [riˈfʌrnɪʃ] *tr* amueblar de nuevo
**refusal** [rɪˈfjuzəl] *s* negativa
**refuse** [ˈrɛfjus] *s* basura, desecho, desperdicios ‖ [rɪˈfjuz] *tr* rehusar; rechazar, no querer aceptar; **to refuse to** negarse a
**refute** [rɪˈfjut] *tr* refutar
**reg.** *abbr* **register, registrar, registry, regular**
**regain** [rɪˈgen] *tr* recobrar, recuperar; volver a alcanzar; **to regain consciousness** recobrar el conocimiento, volver en sí
**regal** [ˈrigəl] *adj* regio
**regale** [rɪˈgel] *tr* regalar, agasajar
**regalia** [rɪˈgelɪ·ə] *spl* (*of an office or order*) distintivos; galas, trajes *mpl* de lujo
**regard** [rɪˈgɑrd] *s* consideración, miramiento; (*esteem*) respeto; (*particular matter*) respecto; (*look*) mirada; **in regard to** respecto a o de; **regards** recuerdos; **without regard to** sin hacer caso de; **with regard to** respecto a o de ‖ *tr* considerar; mirar; tocar a, referirse a; **as regards** en cuanto a
**regarding** [rɪˈgɑrdɪŋ] *prep* tocante a, respecto a o de
**regardless** [rɪˈgɑrdlɪs] *adj* desatento, indiferente ‖ *adv* (coll) pese a quien pese, cueste lo que cueste; **regardless of** sin hacer caso de; a pesar de
**regenerate** [rɪˈdʒɛnəˌret] *tr* regenerar ‖ *intr* regenerarse
**regent** [ˈridʒənt] *s* regente *mf*
**regicide** [ˈrɛdʒɪˌsaɪd] *s* (*act*) regicidio; (*person*) regicida *mf*
**regime** o **régime** [reˈʒim] *s* régimen *m*
**regiment** [ˈrɛdʒɪmənt] *s* regimiento ‖ [ˈrɛdʒɪˌmɛnt] *tr* regimentar
**regimental** [ˌrɛdʒɪˈmɛntəl] *adj* regimental ‖ **regimentals** *spl* uniforme *m* militar
**region** [ˈridʒən] *s* región, comarca
**register** [ˈrɛdʒɪstər] *s* (*record; book for keeping such a record*) registro; reja regulable de calefacción; (*of the voice or an instrument*) extensión ‖ *tr* (*to indicate by a record; to show, as on a scale*) registrar; empadronar (*los vecinos en el padrón*); manifestar, dar a conocer; certificar (*envíos por correo*); inscribir ‖ *intr* registrarse; empadronarse; inscribirse
**registered letter** *s* carta certificada
**registrar** [ˈrɛdʒɪsˌtrɑr] *s* registrador *m*, archivero
**registration fee** [ˌrɛdʒɪsˈtreʃən] *s* derechos de matrícula
**re·gret** [rɪˈgrɛt] *s* pesar *m*, sentimiento; pesadumbre, remordimiento; **regrets** excusas ‖ *v* (*pret & pp* **-gretted**; *ger* **-gretting**) *tr* sentir, lamentar; lamentar la pérdida de; arrepentirse de; **to regret to** sentir
**regrettable** [rɪˈgrɛtəbəl] *adj* lamentable
**regular** [ˈrɛgjələr] *adj* regular; (coll) cabal, completo, verdadero ‖ *s* obrero permanente; parroquiano regular; **regulars** tropas regulares
**regulate** [ˈrɛgjəˌlet] *tr* regular
**rehabilitate** [ˌrihəˈbɪlɪˌtet] *tr* rehabilitar
**rehearsal** [rɪˈhʌrsəl] *s* ensayo
**rehearse** [rɪˈhʌrs] *tr* ensayar ‖ *intr* ensayarse
**reign** [ren] *s* reinado ‖ *intr* reinar
**reimburse** [ˌri·ɪmˈbʌrs] *tr* reembolsar
**rein** [ren] *s* rienda; **to give free rein to** dar rienda suelta a ‖ *tr* dirigir por medio de riendas; contener, refrenar, gobernar
**reincarnation** [ˌri·ɪnkɑrˈneʃən] *s* reencarnación
**reindeer** [ˈrenˌdɪr] *s* reno
**reinforce** [ˌri·ɪnˈfors] *tr* reforzar; armar (*el hormigón*)
**reinforcement** [ˌri·ɪnˈforsmənt] *s* refuerzo
**reinstate** [ˌri·ɪnˈstet] *tr* reinstalar
**reiterate** [riˈɪtəˌret] *tr* reiterar
**reject** [rɪˈdʒɛkt] *tr* rechazar
**rejection** [rɪˈdʒɛkʃən] *s* rechazamiento
**rejoice** [rɪˈdʒɔɪs] *intr* regocijarse
**rejoinder** [rɪˈdʒɔɪndər] *s* contestación; (law) contrarréplica
**rejuvenation** [rɪˌdʒuvɪˈneʃən] *s* rejuvenecimiento
**rel.** *abbr* **relating, relative, religion, religious**
**relapse** [rɪˈlæps] *s* recaída ‖ *intr* recaer
**relate** [rɪˈlet] *tr* (*to establish relationship between*) relacionar; (*to narrate*) contar, relatar

**relation** [rɪˈleʃən] *s* (*connection; narration*) relación; (*narration*) relato; (*relative*) pariente *mf;* (*kinship*) parentesco; **in relation to** o **with** tocante a, respecto a o de
**relationship** [rɪˈleʃən,ʃɪp] *s* (*connection*) relación; (*kinship*) parentesco
**relative** [ˈrɛlətɪv] *adj* relativo || *s* deudo, pariente *mf*
**relax** [rɪˈlæks] *tr & intr* relajar
**relaxation** [,rilæksˈeʃən] *s* relajación; despreocupación
**relaxation of tension** *s* disminución de tensión; disminución de la tirantez internacional
**relaxing** [rɪˈlæksɪŋ] *adj* relajador; despreocupante, tranquilizador
**relay** [ˈrile] o [rɪˈle] *s* (elec) relais *m*, relevador *m*, relevo; (mil & sport) relevo; (sport) carrera de relevos || *v* (*pret & pp* **-layed**) *tr* transmitir relevándose; transmitir con un relais; retransmitir (*una emisión*); reexpedir (*un radiotelegrama*) || [rɪˈle] *v* (*pret & pp* **-laid**) *tr* volver a colocar, volver a tender
**relay race** *s* carrera de relevos
**release** [rɪˈlis] *s* liberación; (*from jail*) excarcelación; alivio; permiso de publicación, venta, etc.; obra o pieza lista para la publicación, venta, etc.; (aer) lanzamiento; (mach) escape *m*, disparador *m* || *tr* soltar; libertar; excarcelar (*a un preso*); permitir la publicación, venta, etc. de; (aer.) lanzar (*una bomba*)
**relent** [rɪˈlɛnt] *intr* ablandarse, aplacarse
**relentless** [rɪˈlɛntlɪs] *adj* implacable
**relevant** [ˈrɛlɪvənt] *adj* pertinente
**reliable** [rɪˈlaɪ·əbəl] *adj* confiable, fidedigno
**reliance** [rɪˈlaɪ·əns] *s* confianza
**relic** [ˈrɛlɪk] *s* reliquia
**relief** [rɪˈlif] *s* alivio; caridad; (*projection of figures; elevation*) relieve *m;* (mil) relevo; **in relief** en relieve; **on relief** viviendo de socorro, recibiendo auxilio social
**relieve** [rɪˈliv] *tr* (*to release from a post*) relevar; aliviar; auxiliar (*a los necesitados*); (mil) relevar
**religion** [rɪˈlɪdʒən] *s* religión
**religious** [rɪˈlɪdʒəs] *adj* religioso
**relinquish** [rɪˈlɪŋkwɪʃ] *tr* abandonar, dejar
**relish** [ˈrɛlɪʃ] *s* buen sabor, gusto; condimento, sazón *f;* entremés *m;* buen apetito || *tr* gustar de; comer o beber con placer
**reluctance** [rɪˈlʌktəns] *s* renuencia, aversión
**reluctant** [rɪˈlʌktənt] *adj* renuente, maldispuesto
**re•ly** [rɪˈlaɪ] *v* (*pret & pp* **-lied**) *intr* depender, confiar; **to rely on** depender de, confiar en
**remain** [rɪˈmen] *intr* permanecer, quedarse || **remains** *spl* desechos, restos; restos mortales; obra póstuma
**remainder** [rɪˈmendər] *s* resto, residuo; libro casi invendible || *tr* saldar (*libros que ya no se venden*)
**re•make** [riˈmek] *v* (*pret & pp* **-made** [ˈmed]) *tr* rehacer
**remark** [rɪˈmɑrk] *s* observación || *tr & intr* observar; **to remark on** aludir a, comentar
**remarkable** [rɪˈmɑrkəbəl] *adj* notable, extraordinario
**remar•ry** [riˈmæri] *v* (*pret & pp* **-ried**) *intr* volver a casarse
**reme•dy** [ˈrɛmɪdi] *s* (*pl* **-dies**) remedio || *v* (*pret & pp* **-died**) *tr* remediar
**remember** [rɪˈmɛmbər] *tr* acordarse de, recordar; dar recuerdos de parte de, p.ej., **remember me to your brother** déle Vd. a su hermano recuerdos de mi parte || *intr* acordarse, recordar; **if I remember correctly** si mal no me acuerdo
**remembrance** [rɪˈmɛmbrəns] *s* recuerdo
**remind** [rɪˈmaɪnd] *tr* recordar
**reminder** [rɪˈmaɪndər] *s* recordatorio, recordativo
**reminisce** [,rɛmɪˈnɪs] *intr* entregarse a los recuerdos, contar sus recuerdos
**remiss** [rɪˈmɪs] *adj* descuidado, negligente
**re•mit** [rɪˈmɪt] *v* (*pret & pp* **-mitted;** *ger* **-mitting**) *tr* (*to send, to ship; to pardon*) remitir
**remittance** [rɪˈmɪtəns] *s* remesa
**remnant** [ˈrɛmnənt] *s* (*something left over*) remanente *m;* (*of cloth*) retal *m*, retazo; (*piece of cloth to be sold at reduced price*) saldo; vestigio
**remod•el** [riˈmɑdəl] *v* (*pret & pp* **-eled** o **-elled;** *ger* **-eling** o **-elling**) *tr* modelar de nuevo; rehacer, reconstruir; convertir, transformar
**remonstrate** [rɪˈmɑnstret] *intr* protestar; **to remonstrate with** reconvenir
**remorse** [rɪˈmɔrs] *s* remordimiento
**remorseful** [rɪˈmɔrsfəl] *adj* compungido, arrepentido
**remote** [rɪˈmot] *adj* remoto
**remote control** *s* comando a distancia, telecontrol *m*
**removable** [rɪˈmuvəbəl] *adj* amovible
**removal** [rɪˈmuvəl] *s* remoción; mudanza, traslado; (*dismissal*) deposición
**remove** [rɪˈmuv] *tr* remover; quitar de en medio, apartar matando || *intr* removerse
**remuneration** [rɪ,mjunəˈreʃən] *s* remuneración
**renaissance** [,rɛnəˈsɑns] o [rɪˈnesəns] *s* renacimiento
**rend** [rɛnd] *v* (*pret & pp* **rent** [rɛnt]) *tr* (*to tear*) desgarrar; (*to split*) hender, rajar; estremecer (*un ruido el aire*)
**render** [ˈrɛndər] *tr* rendir (*gracias, obsequios, homenaje*); prestar, suministrar (*ayuda*); pagar (*tributo*); desempeñar (*un papel*); traducir (*sentimientos*); (*from one language to another*) verter; hacer (*justicia*); ejecutar (*una pieza de música*); derretir (*cera, manteca*); extraer la grasa o el sebo de; poner, volver
**rendezvous** [ˈrɑndə,vu] *s* (*pl* **-vous** [,vuz]) cita; (*in space*) encuentro,

reunión || *v* (*pret & pp* **-voused** [ˌvud]; *ger* **-vousing** [ˌvu·ɪŋ]) *intr* reunirse en una cita
**rendition** [rɛnˈdɪʃən] *s* rendición; traducción; (mus) ejecución
**renege** [rɪˈnɪg] *s* renuncio || *intr* renunciar; (coll) volverse atrás
**renegotiation** [ˌrinɪˌgoʃɪˈeʃən] *s* renegociación
**renew** [rɪˈnju] o [rɪˈnu] *tr* renovar || *intr* renovarse
**renewable** [rɪˈnju·əbəl] o [rɪˈnu·əbəl] *adj* renovable
**renewal** [rɪˈnju·əl] o [rɪˈnu·əl] *s* renovación
**renounce** [rɪˈnaʊns] *tr* renunciar; renunciar a (*p.ej., el mundo*) || *intr* renunciar
**renovate** [ˈrɛnəˌvet] *tr* renovar; reformar (*p.ej., una tienda, una casa*)
**renown** [rɪˈnaʊn] *s* renombre *m*
**renowned** [rɪˈnaʊnd] *adj* renombrado
**rent** [rɛnt] *adj* desgarrado || *s* alquiler *m*, arriendo; (*tear, slit*) desgarro || *tr* alquilar, arrendar || *intr* alquilarse, arrendarse
**rental** [ˈrɛntəl] *s* alquiler *m*, arriendo
**renunciation** [rɪˌnʌnsɪˈeʃən] o [rɪˌnʌnʃɪˈeʃən] *s* renunciación
**reopen** [riˈopən] *tr* reabrir || *intr* reabrirse
**reorganize** [riˈɔrgəˌnaɪz] *tr* reorganizar || *intr* reorganizarse
**rep.** *abbr* **report, reporter, representative, republic**
**repair** [rɪˈper] *s* reparación; **in repair** en buen estado || *tr* reparar || *intr* dirigirse; volver
**repaper** [riˈpepər] *tr* empapelar de nuevo
**reparation** [ˌrɛpəˈreʃən] *s* reparación
**repartee** [ˌrɛpɑrˈti] *s* respuesta viva; agudeza y gracia en responder
**repast** [rɪˈpæst] o [rɪˈpɑst] *s* comida, comilona
**repatriate** [riˈpetrɪˌet] *tr* repatriar
**re·pay** [rɪˈpe] *v* (*pret & pp* **-paid** [ˈped]) *tr* reembolsar; resarcir (*un daño, una injuria*); compensar
**repayment** [rɪˈpemənt] *s* reembolso; resarcimiento; compensación
**repeal** [rɪˈpil] *s* abrogación, revocación || *tr* abrogar, revocar
**repeat** [rɪˈpit] *s* repetición || *tr & intr* repetir
**re·pel** [rɪˈpel] *v* (*pret & pp* **-pelled**; *ger* **-pelling**) *tr* rechazar, repeler; repugnar
**repent** [rɪˈpent] *tr* arrepentirse de || *intr* arrepentirse
**repentance** [rɪˈpentəns] *s* arrepentimiento
**repentant** [rɪˈpɛntənt] *adj* arrepentido
**repertory theater** [ˈrɛpərˌtori] *s* teatro de repertorio
**repetition** [ˌrɛpɪˈtɪʃən] *s* repetición
**repine** [rɪˈpaɪn] *intr* afligirse, quejarse
**replace** [rɪˈples] *tr* (*to put back*) reponer; (*to take the place of*) reemplazar
**replacement** [rɪˈplesmənt] *s* reposición; reemplazo; pieza de repuesto; soldado reemplazante
**replenish** [rɪˈplenɪʃ] *tr* rellenar; reaprovisionar
**replete** [rɪˈplit] *adj* repleto
**replica** [ˈrɛplɪkə] *s* réplica
**re·ply** [rɪˈplaɪ] *s* (*pl* **-plies**) contestación, respuesta || *v* (*pret & pp* **-plied**) *tr & intr* contestar, responder
**reply coupon** *s* vale *m* respuesta
**report** [rɪˈport] *s* relato, informe *m*; voz *f*, rumor *m*; (*e.g., of a firearm*) detonación, tiro; denuncia || *tr* relatar, informar acerca de; denunciar || *intr* hacer un relato; redactar un informe; ser repórter; presentarse; **to report on** dar cuenta de, notificar
**report card** *s* certificado escolar
**reportedly** [rɪˈportɪdli] *adv* según se informa
**reporter** [rɪˈportər] *s* repórter *m*
**reporting** [rɪˈportɪŋ] *s* reportaje *m*
**repose** [rɪˈpoz] *s* descanso || *tr* descansar; poner (*confianza*) || *intr* descansar
**reprehend** [ˌrɛprɪˈhend] *tr* reprender
**represent** [ˌrɛprɪˈzent] *tr* representar
**representative** [ˌrɛprɪˈzentətɪv] *adj* representativo || *s* representante *mf*
**repress** [rɪˈpres] *tr* reprimir
**reprieve** [rɪˈpriv] *s* suspensión temporal de un castigo, suspensión temporal de la pena de muerte; respiro, alivio temporal || *tr* suspender temporalmente el castigo de o la pena de muerte de; aliviar temporalmente
**reprimand** [ˈrɛprɪˌmænd] o [ˈrɛprɪˌmɑnd] *s* reprimenda || *tr* reconvenir, reprender
**reprint** [ˈriˌprɪnt] *s* reimpresión; tirada aparte || [riˈprɪnt] *tr* reimprimir
**reprisal** [rɪˈpraɪzəl] *s* represalia
**reproach** [rɪˈprotʃ] *s* reproche *m*; oprobio || *tr* reprochar; oprobiar
**reproduce** [ˌriprəˈdjus] o [ˌriprəˈdus] *tr* reproducir || *intr* reproducirse
**reproduction** [ˌriprəˈdʌkʃən] *s* reproducción
**reproof** [rɪˈpruf] *s* reprobación
**reprove** [rɪˈpruv] *tr* reprobar
**reptile** [ˈrɛptɪl] *s* reptil *m*
**republic** [rɪˈpʌblɪk] *s* república
**republican** [rɪˈpʌblɪkən] *adj & s* republicano
**repudiate** [rɪˈpjudɪˌet] *tr* repudiar; no reconocer (*p.ej., una deuda*)
**repugnant** [rɪˈpʌgnənt] *adj* repugnante
**repulse** [rɪˈpʌls] *s* repulsión, rechazo || *tr* repeler, rechazar
**repulsive** [rɪˈpʌlsɪv] *adj* repulsivo
**reputation** [ˌrɛpjəˈteʃən] *s* reputación; buena reputación
**repute** [rɪˈpjut] *s* reputación; buena reputación || *tr* reputar
**reputedly** [rɪˈpjutɪdli] *adv* según la opinión común
**request** [rɪˈkwɛst] *s* petición, solicitud; **at the request of** a petición de || *tr* pedir
**require** [rɪˈkwaɪr] *tr* exigir, requerir
**requirement** [rɪˈkwaɪrmənt] *s* requisito; necesidad
**requisite** [ˈrɛkwɪzɪt] *adj & s* requisito
**requital** [rɪˈkwaɪtəl] *s* compensación, retorno

**requite** [rɪˈkwaɪt] *tr* corresponder a (*los beneficios, el amor, etc.*); corresponder con (*el bienhechor*)
**re•read** [riˈrid] *v* (*pret & pp* **-read** [ˈrɛd]) *tr* releer
**resale** [ˈri,sel] o [riˈsel] *s* reventa
**rescind** [rɪˈsɪnd] *tr* rescindir
**rescue** [ˈrɛskju] *s* salvación, rescate *m*, liberación; **to go to the rescue of** acudir al socorro de ‖ *tr* salvar, rescatar, libertar
**rescue party** *s* pelotón *m* de salvamento
**research** [rɪˈsʌrtʃ] o [ˈrisʌrtʃ] *s* investigación ‖ *intr* investigar
**re•sell** [riˈsɛl] *v* (*pret & pp* **-sold** [ˈsold]) *tr* revender
**resemblance** [rɪˈzɛmbləns] *s* parecido, semejanza
**resemble** [rɪˈzɛmbəl] *tr* parecerse a, asemejarse a
**resent** [rɪˈzɛnt] *tr* resentirse de o por
**resentful** [rɪˈzɛntfəl] *adj* resentido
**resentment** [rɪˈzɛntmənt] *s* resentimiento
**reservation** [,rɛzərˈveʃən] *s* reserva
**reserve** [rɪˈzʌrv] *s* reserva ‖ *tr* reservar
**reservoir** [ˈrɛzər,vwɑr] *s* depósito; (*where water is dammed back*) embalse *m*, pantano; (*of wisdom*) fondo
**re•ship** [riˈʃɪp] *v* (*pret & pp* **-shipped**; *ger* **-shipping**) *tr* reenviar, reexpedir; (*on a ship*) reembarcar ‖ *intr* reembarcarse
**reshipment** [riˈʃɪpmənt] *s* reenvío, reexpedición; (*of persons*) reembarco; (*of goods*) reembarque *m*
**reside** [rɪˈzaɪd] *intr* residir
**residence** [ˈrɛzɪdəns] *s* residencia
**resident** [ˈrɛzɪdənt] *adj & s* residente *mf*, vecino
**residue** [ˈrɛzɪ,dju] o [ˈrɛzɪ,du] *s* residuo
**resign** [rɪˈzaɪn] *tr* dimitir, resignar, renunciar ‖ *intr* dimitir; (*to yield, submit*) resignarse; **to resign to** resignarse con (*p.ej., su suerte*)
**resignation** [,rɛzɪgˈneʃən] *s* (*from a job, etc.*) dimisión; (*state of being submissive*) resignación
**resin** [ˈrɛzɪn] *s* resina
**resist** [rɪˈzɪst] *tr* resistir (*la tentación*); resistir a (*la violencia; la risa*) ‖ *intr* resistirse
**resistance** [rɪˈzɪstəns] *s* resistencia
**resole** [riˈsol] *tr* sobresolar
**resolute** [ˈrɛzə,lut] *adj* resuelto
**resolution** [,rɛzəˈluʃən] *s* resolución; **good resolutions** buenos propósitos
**resolve** [rɪˈzɔlv] *s* resolución ‖ *tr* resolver ‖ *intr* resolverse
**resort** [rɪˈzɔrt] *s* lugar muy frecuentado; (*e.g., for vacations*) estación; (*for help or support*) recurso; **as a last resort** como último recurso ‖ *intr* recurrir
**resound** [rɪˈzaʊnd] *intr* resonar
**resource** [rɪˈsors] o [ˈrisors] *s* recurso
**resourceful** [rɪˈsorsfəl] *adj* ingenioso
**respect** [rɪˈspɛkt] *s* (*deference, esteem*) respeto; (*reference, relation; detail*) respecto; **respects** recuerdos, saludos; **to pay one's respects (to)** ofrecer sus respetos (a); **with respect to** respecto a o de ‖ *tr* respetar
**respectable** [rɪˈspɛktəbəl] *adj* respetable; decente, presentable
**respectful** [rɪˈspɛktfəl] *adj* respetuoso
**respectfully** [rɪˈspɛktfəli] *adj* respetuosamente; **respectfully yours** de Vd. atento y seguro servidor
**respecting** [rɪˈspɛktɪŋ] *prep* con respecto a, respecto de
**respective** [rɪˈspɛktɪv] *adj* respectivo
**respire** [rɪˈspaɪr] *tr & intr* respirar
**respite** [ˈrɛspɪt] *s* (*temporary relief*) respiro; (*postponement, especially of death sentence*) suspensión; **without respite** sin respirar
**resplendent** [rɪˈsplɛndənt] *adj* resplandeciente
**respond** [rɪˈspɑnd] *intr* responder
**response** [rɪˈspɑns] *s* respuesta
**responsible** [rɪˈspɑnsɪbəl] *adj* responsable; (*job, position*) de confianza; **responsible for** responsable de
**rest** [rɛst] *s* (*after exertion or work; sleep*) descanso; (*lack of motion*) reposo; (*of the dead*) paz *f*; (*what remains*) resto; (mus) pausa; **at rest** (*not moving*) en reposo; tranquilo; dormido; (*dead*) muerto; **the rest** lo demás; los demás; **to come to rest** venir a parar; **to lay to rest** enterrar ‖ *tr* descansar; parar; poner (*p.ej., confianza*) ‖ *intr* descansar; estar, hallarse; **to rest assured (that)** estar seguro, tener la seguridad (de que); **to rest on** descansar en o sobre, estribar en
**restaurant** [ˈrɛstərənt] o [ˈrɛstə,rɑnt] *s* restaurante *m*
**rest cure** *s* cura de reposo
**restful** [ˈrɛstfəl] *adj* descansado, tranquilo, reposado
**resting place** *s* lugar *m* de descanso; (*of a staircase*) descansadero; (*of the dead*) última morada
**restitution** [,rɛstɪˈtjuʃən] o [,rɛstɪˈtuʃən] *s* restitución
**restless** [ˈrɛstlɪs] *adj* intranquilo; (*sleepless*) insomne
**restock** [riˈstɑk] *tr* reaprovisionar; repoblar (*p.ej., un acuario*)
**restore** [rɪˈstor] *tr* restaurar; (*to give back*) devolver
**restrain** [rɪˈstren] *tr* contener, refrenar; aprisionar
**restraint** [rɪˈstrent] *s* restricción; comedimiento, moderación
**restrict** [rɪˈstrɪkt] *tr* restringir
**rest room** *s* sala de descanso; excusado, retrete *m*; (*of a theater*) saloncillo
**result** [rɪˈzʌlt] *s* resultado; **as a result of** de resultas de ‖ *intr* resultar; **to result in** dar por resultado, parar en
**resume** [rɪˈzum] o [rɪˈzjum] *tr* reasumir; reanudar (*el viaje, el vuelo, etc.*); volver a tomar (*su asiento*) ‖ *intr* continuar; recomenzar; reanudar el hilo del discurso
**résumé** [,rɛzʊˈme] o [,rɛzjʊˈme] *s* resumen *m*
**resurface** [riˈsʌrfɪs] *tr* dar nueva superficie a ‖ *intr* volver a emerger (*un submarino*)

**resurrect** [ˌrɛzəˈrɛkt] *tr & intr* resucitar
**resurrection** [ˌrɛzəˈrɛkʃən] *s* resurrección
**resuscitate** [rɪˈsʌsɪˌtet] *tr & intr* resucitar
**retail** [ˈritel] *adj & adv* al por menor ‖ *s* venta al por menor ‖ *tr* detallar, vender al por menor ‖ *intr* vender al por menor; venderse al por menor
**retailer** [ˈritelər] *s* detallista *mf,* comerciante *mf* al por menor
**retain** [rɪˈten] *tr* retener; contratar (*a un abogado*)
**retaliate** [rɪˈtælɪˌet] *intr* desquitarse, vengarse
**retaliation** [rɪˌtælɪˈeʃən] *s* desquite *m,* venganza
**retard** [rɪˈtɑrd] *s* retardo ‖ *tr* retardar
**retch** [retʃ] *tr* vomitar ‖ *intr* arquear, esforzarse por vomitar
**retching** [ˈretʃɪŋ] *s* arcadas
**ret'd.** *abbr* **returned**
**reticence** [ˈretɪsəns] *s* reserva, circunspección, sigilo
**reticent** [ˈretɪsənt] *adj* reservado, circunspecto
**retinue** [ˈrɛtɪˌnju] o [ˈretɪˌnu] *s* comitiva, séquito
**retire** [rɪˈtaɪr] *tr* retirar; jubilar (*a un empleado*) ‖ *intr* retirarse; jubilarse; (*to go to bed*) recogerse; (mil) retirarse
**retirement** [rɪˈtaɪrmənt] *s* retiro; (*of an employee with pension*) jubilación; (mil) retirada
**retirement annuity** *s* jubilación
**retort** [rɪˈtɔrt] *s* respuesta pronta y aguda, réplica; (chem) retorta ‖ *intr* replicar
**retouch** [riˈtʌtʃ] *tr* retocar
**retrace** [rɪˈtres] *tr* repasar; **to retrace one's steps** volver sobre sus pasos
**retract** [rɪˈtrækt] *tr* retractarse de, desdecirse de (*lo que se ha dicho*) ‖ *intr* retractarse, desdecirse
**re•tread** [ˈriˌtrɛd] *s* neumático recauchutado; neumático ranurado ‖ [riˈtrɛd] *v* (*pret & pp* **-treaded**) *tr* recauchutar; volver a ranurar ‖ *v* (*pret* **-trod** [ˈtrɑd]; *pp* **-trod** o **-trodden**) *tr* desandar ‖ *intr* volverse atrás
**retreat** [rɪˈtrit] *s* (*act of withdrawing; place of seclusion*) retiro; (eccl) retiro; (mil) retreta, retirada; (*signal*) (mil) retreta; **to beat a retreat** retirarse; (mil) batirse en retirada ‖ *intr* retirarse
**retrench** [rɪˈtrentʃ] *tr* cercenar ‖ *intr* recogerse
**retribution** [ˌretrɪˈbjuʃən] *s* justo castigo; (theol) juicio final
**retrieve** [rɪˈtriv] *tr* cobrar; reparar (*p.ej., un daño*); desquitarse de (*una pérdida, una derrota*); (hunt) cobrar, portar ‖ *intr* (hunt) cobrar, portar
**retriever** [rɪˈtrivər] *s* perro cobrador, perro traedor
**retroactive** [ˌretroˈæktɪv] *adj* retroactivo
**retrofiring** [ˌretroˈfaɪrɪŋ] *s* retrodisparo
**retrogress** [ˈretrəˌgres] *intr* retroceder; empeorar
**retrorocket** [ˌrɛtroˈrɑkɪt] *s* retrocohete *m*
**retrospect** [ˈretrəˌspɛkt] *s* retrospección; **in retrospect** retrospectivamente
**retrospective** [ˌrɛtrəˈspɛktɪv] *adj* retrospectivo
**re•try** [riˈtraɪ] *v* (*pret & pp* **-tried**) *tr* reensayar; rever (*un caso legal*); procesar de nuevo (*a una persona*)
**return** [rɪˈtʌrn] *adj* repetido; de vuelta; **by return mail** a vuelta de correo ‖ *s* vuelta; devolución; recompensa; respuesta; informe *m,* noticia; ganancia, beneficio, rédito; (*of an election*) resultado; (*of income tax*) declaración; **in return (for)** en cambio (de); **many happy returns of the day!** ¡que cumpla muchos más! ‖ *tr* devolver; dar en cambio; corresponder a (*un favor*); dar (*una respuesta, las gracias*) ‖ *intr* volver; responder
**return address** *s* dirección del remitente
**return bout** o **engagement** *s* (box) combate *m* revancha
**return game** *s* desquite *m*
**return ticket** *s* billete *m* de vuelta; billete de ida y vuelta
**return trip** *s* viaje *m* de vuelta
**reunification** [riˌjunɪfɪˈkeʃən] *s* reunificación
**reunion** [riˈjunjən] *s* reunión
**reunite** [ˌrijuˈnaɪt] *tr* reunir ‖ *intr* reunirse
**rev.** *abbr* **revenue, reverse, review, revised, revision, revolution**
**Rev.** *abbr.* **Revelation, Reverend**
**rev** [rɛv] *s* revolución ‖ *v* (*pret & pp* **revved;** *ger* **revving**) *tr* cambiar la velocidad de; **to rev up** acelerar ‖ *intr* acelerarse
**revamp** [riˈvæmp] *tr* componer, renovar, remendar
**reveal** [rɪˈvil] *tr* revelar
**reveille** [ˈrɛvəli] *s* diana, toque *m* de diana
**rev•el** [ˈrɛvəl] *s* jarana, regocijo tumultuoso ‖ *v* (*pret & pp* **-eled** o **-elled;** *ger* **-eling** o **-elling**) *intr* jaranear; deleitarse
**revelation** [ˌrɛvəˈleʃən] *s* revelación
**revel•ry** [ˈrɛvəlri] *s* (*pl* **-ries**) jarana, diversión tumultuosa
**revenge** [rɪˈvendʒ] *s* venganza ‖ *tr* vengar
**revengeful** [rɪˈvendʒfəl] *adj* vengativo
**revenue** [ˈrɛvəˌnju] o [ˈrɛvəˌnu] *s* renta, rédito; rentas públicas
**revenue cutter** *s* escampavía
**revenue stamp** *s* sello fiscal, timbre *m* del estado
**reverberate** [rɪˈvʌrbəˌret] *intr* reverberar
**revere** [rɪˈvɪr] *tr* reverenciar, venerar
**reverence** [ˈrevərəns] *s* reverencia ‖ *tr* reverenciar
**reverend** [ˈrɛvərənd] *adj & s* reverendo
**reverie** [ˈrɛvəri] *s* ensueño
**reversal** [rɪˈvʌrsəl] *s* inversión; (*e.g., of opinion*) cambio
**reverse** [rɪˈvʌrs] *adj* invertido; con-

trario; de marcha atrás || *s* (*opposite or rear*) revés *m;* contrario; contramarcha, marcha atrás; (*check, defeat*) revés *m,* contratiempo || *tr* invertir; dar vuelta a; poner en marcha atrás; **to reverse oneself** cambiar de opinión; **to reverse the charges** cobrar al destinatario; (telp) cobrar al número llamado || *intr* invertirse

**reverse lever** *s* palanca de marcha atrás

**revert** [rɪ'vʌrt] *intr* revertir; saltar atrás; **to revert to one's old tricks** volver a las andadas

**review** [rɪ'vju] *s* (*reëxamination; survey; magazine; musical show*) revista; (*of a book*) reseña, revista; (*of a lesson*) repaso; (mil) reseña, revista || *tr* rever, revisar; reseñar (*un libro*); repasar (*una lección*); (mil) revistar

**revile** [rɪ'vaɪl] *tr* ultrajar, vilipendiar

**revise** [rɪ'vaɪz] *s* revisión; refundición; (typ) segunda prueba || *tr* rever, revisar; refundir (*un libro*); enmendar

**revision** [rɪ'vɪʒən] *s* revisión; (*of a book*) refundición; enmienda

**revisionism** [rɪ'vɪʒə,nɪzəm] *s* revisionismo

**revisionist** [rɪ'vɪʒənɪst] *adj & s* revisionista

**revival** [rɪ'vaɪvəl] *s* resucitación; reanimación; (*e.g., of learning*) renacimiento; despertamiento religioso; (theat) reestreno, reposición

**revive** [rɪ'vaɪv] *tr* revivir; (theat) reestrenar, reponer || *intr* revivir; volver en sí, recordar

**revoke** [rɪ'vok] *tr* revocar

**revolt** [rɪ'volt] *s* rebelión, sublevación || *tr* dar asco a, repugnar || *intr* rebelarse, sublevarse

**revolting** [rɪ'voltɪŋ] *adj* asqueroso, repugnante; rebelde

**revolution** [,rɛvə'luʃən] *s* revolución

**revolutionar•y** [,rɛvə'luʃə,nɛri] *adj* revolucionario || *s* (*pl* **-ies**) revolucionario

**revolve** [rɪ'vɑlv] *tr* hacer girar; (*in one's mind*) revolver || *intr* girar; revolverse (*un astro en su órbita*)

**revolver** [rɪ'vɑlvər] *s* revólver *m*

**revolving bookcase** *s* giratoria

**revolving door** *s* puerta giratoria

**revolving fund** *s* fondo rotativo

**revue** [rɪ'vju] *s* (theat) revista

**revulsion** [rɪ'vʌlʃən] *s* aversión, repugnancia; reacción fuerte

**reward** [rɪ'wɔrd] *s* premio, recompensa; (*money used to recapture or recover*) rescate *m;* hallazgo, p.ej., **five dollars reward** cinco dólares de hallazgo || *tr* premiar, recompensar

**rewarding** [rɪ'wɔrdɪŋ] *adj* remunerador, provechoso, agradecido

**re•write** [ri'raɪt] *v* (*pret* **-wrote** ['rot]; *pp* **-written** ['rɪtən]) *tr* escribir de nuevo; refundir (*un escrito*); redactar (*un escrito de otra persona*)

**R.F.** *abbr* **radio frequency**

**R.F.D.** *abbr* **Rural Free Delivery**

**R.H.** *abbr* **Royal Highness**

**rhapso•dy** ['ræpsədi] *s* (*pl* **-dies**) rapsodia

**rheostat** ['ri·ə,stæt] *s* reóstato

**rhesus** ['risəs] *s* macaco de la India

**rhetoric** ['rɛtərɪk] *s* retórica

**rhetorical** [rɪ'tɑrɪkəl] o [rɪ'tɔrɪkəl] *adj* retórico

**rheumatic** [ru'mætɪk] *adj & s* reumático

**rheumatism** ['rumə,tɪzəm] *s* reumatismo

**Rhine** [raɪn] *s* Rin *m*

**Rhineland** ['raɪn,lænd] *s* Renania

**rhine'stone'** *s* diamante de imitación hecho de vidrio

**rhinoceros** [raɪ'nɑsərəs] *s* rinoceronte *m*

**Rhodes** [rodz] *s* Rodas *f*

**Rhone** [ron] *s* Ródano

**rhubarb** ['rubɑrb] *s* ruibarbo

**rhyme** [raɪm] *s* rima; **without rhyme or reason** sin ton ni son || *tr & intr* rimar

**rhythm** ['rɪðəm] *s* ritmo

**rhythmic(al)** ['rɪðmɪk(əl)] *adj* rítmico

**rial•to** [rɪ'ælto] *s* (*pl* **-tos**) mercado || **the Rialto** el puente del Rialto; el centro teatral de Nueva York

**rib** [rɪb] *s* costilla; (*of a fan or umbrella*) varilla; (*of a tire*) cuerda; (*in cloth*) canilla; (*of the wing of an insect*) nervio || *v* (*pret & pp* **ribbed;** *ger* **ribbing**) *tr* proveer de costillas; hacer canillas en; (slang) tomar el pelo a

**ribald** ['rɪbəld] *adj* grosero y obsceno

**ribbon** ['rɪbən] *s* cinta

**rice** [raɪs] *s* arroz *m*

**rich** [rɪtʃ] *adj* rico; (*color*) vivo; (*voice*) sonoro; (*wine*) generoso; azucarado, condimentado; (coll) divertido; (coll) ridículo; **to strike it rich** descubrir un buen filón || **riches** *spl* riquezas; **the rich** los ricos

**rickets** ['rɪkɪts] *s* raquitis *f*

**rickety** ['rɪkiti] *adj* (*object*) destartalado, desvencijado; (*person*) tambaleante, vacilante; (*suffering from rickets*) raquítico

**rid** [rɪd] *v* (*pret & pp* **rid;** *ger* **ridding**) *tr* desembarazar; **to get rid of** desembarazarse de, deshacerse de; matar

**riddance** ['rɪdəns] *s* supresión, libramiento; **good riddance!** ¡adiós, gracias!, ¡de buena me he librado!

**riddle** ['rɪdəl] *s* acertijo, adivinanza; (*person or thing hard to understand*) enigma *m;* criba gruesa || *tr* acribillar; destruir (*un argumento; la reputación de una persona*); **to riddle with bullets** acribillar a balazos; **to riddle with questions** acribillar a preguntas

**ride** [raɪd] *s* paseo || *v* (*pret* **rode** [rod]; *pp* **ridden** ['rɪdən]) *tr* montar (*un caballo*); montar sobre (*los hombros de una persona*); recorrer a caballo; flotar sobre (*las olas*); dominar, tiranizar; (coll) burlarse de; **to ride down** atropellar; vencer; **to ride out** luchar felizmente con (*una tempestad*); aguantar con buen éxito (*una desgracia*) || *intr* montar; pasear en coche o carruaje; **to let ride** (slang) dejar correr; **to take riding** llevar de paseo

**rider** [ˈraɪdər] *s* jinete *m;* pasajero

**ridge** [rɪdʒ] *s* (*of a roof; of earth between two furrows*) caballete *m;* (*of a fabric*) cordoncillo; (*of mountains*) cordillera; (*of two plane surfaces*) arista

**ridge'pole'** *s* parhilera

**ridicule** [ˈrɪdɪ,kjul] *s* irrisión; **to expose to ridicule** poner en ridículo ‖ *tr* ridiculizar

**ridiculous** [rɪˈdɪkjələs] *adj* ridículo

**riding academy** *s* escuela de equitación

**riding boot** *s* bota de montar

**riding habit** *s* amazona, traje *m* de montar

**rife** [raɪf] *adj* común, corriente, general; abundante, lleno; **rife with** abundante en, lleno de

**riffraff** [ˈrɪf,ræf] *s* bahorrina, canalla

**rifle** [ˈraɪfəl] *s* rifle *m,* fusil *m* ‖ *tr* hurtar, robar; escudriñar y robar; desnudar, despojar

**rift** [rɪft] *s* abertura, raja; desacuerdo, desavenencia

**rig** [rɪg] *s* equipaje *m;* carruaje *m* con caballo o caballos; traje extraño; (naut) aparejo ‖ *v* (*pret & pp* **rigged;** *ger* **rigging**) *tr* equipar; aprestar, disponer; improvisar; vestir de una manera extraña; arreglar de una manera fraudulenta; (naut) aparejar

**rigging** [ˈrɪgɪŋ] *s* avíos, instrumentos, equipo; (naut) aparejo, cordaje *m*

**right** [raɪt] *adj* derecho; verdadero; exacto; conveniente; favorable; sano, normal; bien; correcto; señalado; correspondiente; que se busca, p.ej., **this is the right house** ésta es la casa que se busca; que se necesita, p.ej., **this is the right train** éste es el tren que se necesita; que debe, p.ej., **he is going the right way** sigue el camino que debe; **right or wrong** con razón o sin ella, bueno o malo; **to be all right** estar bien; estar bien de salud; **to be right** tener razón ‖ *adv* derechamente; directamente; correctamente; exactamente; favorablemente; en orden, en buen estado; hacia la derecha; completamente; (coll) muy; mismo, p.ej., **right here** aquí mismo; **all right** muy bien ‖ *interj* ¡bien! ‖ *s* (*justice, reason*) derecho; (*right hand*) derecha; (box) derechazo; (com) derecho; (pol) derecha; **by right** según derecho; **on the right** a la derecha; **to be in the right** tener razón ‖ *tr* enderezar; corregir, rectificar; hacer justicia a, deshacer (*un entuerto*) ‖ *intr* enderezarse

**righteous** [ˈraɪtʃəs] *adj* recto, justo; virtuoso

**right field** *s* (baseball) jardín derecho

**rightful** [ˈraɪtfəl] *adj* justo; legítimo

**right'-hand' drive** *s* conducción o dirección a la derecha

**right-hand man** *s* mano derecha, brazo derecho

**rightist** [ˈraɪtɪst] *adj & s* derechista *mf*

**rightly** [ˈraɪtli] *adv* derechamente; correctamente; con razón; convenientemente; **rightly or wrongly** con razón o sin ella; **rightly so** a justo título

**right mind** *s* entero juicio

**right of way** *s* derecho de tránsito o de paso; (law) servidumbre de paso; (rr) servidumbre de vía; **to yield the right of way** ceder el paso

**rights of man** *spl* derechos del hombre

**right'-wing'** *adj* derechista

**right-winger** [ˈraɪtˈwɪŋər] *s* (coll) derechista *mf*

**rigid** [ˈrɪdʒɪd] *adj* rígido

**rigmarole** [ˈrɪgmə,rol] *s* galimatías *m*

**rigorous** [ˈrɪgərəs] *adj* riguroso

**rile** [raɪl] *tr* (coll) exasperar

**rill** [rɪl] *s* arroyuelo

**rim** [rɪm] *s* canto, borde *m;* (*of a wheel*) llanta; (*of a tire*) aro

**rime** [raɪm] *s* (*in verse*) rima; (*frost*) escarcha; **without rime or reason** sin ton ni son ‖ *tr & intr* rimar

**rind** [raɪnd] *s* cáscara, corteza

**ring** [rɪŋ] *s* (*circular band, line, or mark*) anillo; (*for the finger*) sortija; (*for curtains; for gymnastics*) anilla; (*for nose of animal*) argolla; (*for fruit jars*) círculo de goma; (*for some sport or exhibition*) circo; (*for boxing*) cuadrilátero, ruedo; (*for bullfight*) redondel *m,* ruedo; boxeo; (*of a group of people*) corro; (*of evildoers*) pandilla; (*under the eyes*) ojera; (*of the anchor*) arganeo; (*sound of a bell, of a clock*) campanada; (*of a small bell; of the glass of glassware*) tintineo; (*to summon a person*) llamada; (*character, nature, spirit*) tono; **to be in the ring (for)** ser candidato (a); **to run rings around** dar cien vueltas a ‖ *v* (*pret & pp* **ringed**) *tr* cercar, rodear; (*to put a ring on*) anillar ‖ *intr* formar círculo o corro ‖ *v* (*pret* **rang** [ræŋ]; *pp* **rung** [rʌŋ]) *tr* tañer, tocar; (*to peal, ring out*) repicar; llamar al timbre; dar (*las horas la campana del reloj*); llamar por teléfono; **to ring up** llamar por teléfono; marcar (*una compra*) con el timbre ‖ *intr* sonar (*una campana, un timbre, el teléfono*); tintinear (*el choque de copas, una campanilla*); resonar, retumbar; llamar; zumbar (*los oídos*); **to ring for** llamar, llamar al timbre; **to ring off** terminar una llamada por teléfono; **to ring up** llamar por teléfono

**ring-around-a-rosy** [ˈrɪŋə,raundəˈrozi] *s* juego del corro

**ringing** [ˈrɪŋɪŋ] *adj* resonante, retumbante ‖ *s* anillamiento; campaneo, repique *m;* (*of the glass of glassware*) tintineo; (*in the ears*) retintín *m,* silbido

**ring'lead'er** *s* cabecilla *m*

**ring'mas'ter** *s* hombre encargado de los ejercicios ecuestres y acrobáticos de un circo

**ring'side'** *s* lugar junto al cuadrilátero; lugar desde el cual se puede ver de cerca

**ring'worm'** *s* tiña
**rink** [rɪŋk] *s* patinadero
**rinse** [rɪns] *s* aclaración, enjuague *m* ‖ *tr* aclarar, enjuagar
**riot** ['raɪ·ət] *s* alboroto, tumulto; regocijos ruidosos; (*of colors*) exhibición brillante; **to run riot** desenfrenarse; crecer lozanamente (*las plantas*) ‖ *intr* alborotarse, amotinarse
**rioter** ['raɪ·ətər] *s* alborotador *m*, amotinado
**rip** [rɪp] *s* rasgón *m*, siete *m;* (*open seam*) descosido ‖ *v* (*pret & pp* **ripped;** *ger* **ripping**) *tr* desgarrar, rasgar; descoser (*lo que estaba cosido*) ‖ *intr* desgarrarse, rasgarse; (coll) adelantar o moverse de prisa o con violencia; **to rip out with** (coll) decir con violencia
**ripe** [raɪp] *adj* maduro; acabado, hecho; dispuesto, preparado; (*boil, tumor*) madurado; (*olive*) negro
**ripen** ['raɪpən] *tr & intr* madurar
**ripple** ['rɪpəl] *s* temblor *m*, rizo; (*sound*) murmullo, susurro ‖ *tr* rizar ‖ *intr* rizarse; murmurar, susurrar
**rise** [raɪz] *s* (*of temperature, prices, a road*) subida; (*of ground, of the voice*) elevación; (*of a heavenly body*) salida; (*of a step*) altura; (*in one's employment*) ascenso; (*of water*) crecida; (*of a source of water*) nacimiento; (*of a valve*) levantamiento; **to get a rise out of** (slang) sacar una réplica mordaz a; **to give rise to** dar origen a ‖ *v* (*pret* **rose** [roz]; *pp* **risen** ['rɪzən]) *intr* subir; levantarse; salir (*un astro*); asomar (*un peligro*); brotar (*un manantial, una planta*); (*in someone's esteem*) ganar; resucitar; **to rise above** alzarse por encima de; mostrarse superior a; **to rise early** madrugar; **to rise to** ponerse a la altura de
**riser** ['raɪzər] *s* contraescalón *m*, contrahuella; **early riser** madrugador *m;* **late riser** dormilón *m*
**risk** [rɪsk] *s* riesgo; **to run** o **take a risk** correr riesgo, correr peligro ‖ *tr* arriesgar; arriesgarse en (*una empresa dudosa*)
**risk·y** ['rɪski] *adj* (*comp* **-ier;** *super* **-iest**) arriesgado; escabroso
**risqué** [rɪs'ke] *adj* escabroso
**rite** [raɪt] *s* rito; **last rites** honras fúnebres
**ritual** ['rɪtʃʊ·əl] *adj & s* ritual *m*
**riv.** *abbr* **river**
**ri·val** ['raɪvəl] *s* rival *mf* ‖ *v* (*pret & pp* **-valed** o **-valled;** *ger* **-valing** o **-valling**) *tr* rivalizar con
**rival·ry** ['raɪvəlri] *s* (*pl* **-ries**) rivalidad
**river** ['rɪvər] *s* río; **down the river** río abajo; **up the river** río arriba
**river basin** *s* cuenca de río
**river bed** *s* cauce *m*
**river front** *s* orilla del río
**riv'er·side'** *adj* ribereño ‖ *s* ribera
**rivet** ['rɪvɪt] *s* roblón *m*, remache *m;* (*e.g., to hold scissors together*) clavillo ‖ *tr* remachar; clavar (*p.ej., los ojos en una persona*)
**rm.** *abbr* **ream, room**
**R.N.** *abbr* **registered nurse, Royal Navy**
**roach** [rotʃ] *s* cucaracha
**road** [rod] *adj* itinerario, caminero ‖ *s* camino; (naut) rada; **to be in the road** estorbar el paso; incomodar; **to get out of the road** quitarse de en medio
**road'bed'** *s* (*of a highway*) firme *m;* (rr) infraestructura
**road'block'** *s* (mil) barricada; (fig) obstáculo
**road'house'** *s* posada en el camino
**road laborer** *s* peón caminero
**road map** *s* mapa itinerario
**road service** *s* auxilio en carretera
**road'side'** *s* borde *m* del camino, borde de la carretera
**roadside inn** *s* posada en el camino
**road sign** *s* señal *f* de carretera, poste *m* indicador
**road'stead'** *s* rada
**road'way'** *s* camino, vía
**roam** [rom] *s* vagabundeo ‖ *tr* vagar por, recorrer a la ventura ‖ *intr* vagar, andar errante
**roar** [ror] *s* bramido, rugido ‖ *intr* bramar, rugir; reírse a carcajadas
**roast** [rost] *s* asado; café tostado ‖ *tr* asar; tostar (*café*); (coll) despellejar ‖ *intr* asarse; tostarse
**roast beef** *s* rosbif *m*
**roast of beef** *s* carne de vaca asada o para asar
**roast pork** *s* carne de cerdo asada
**rob** [rɑb] *v* (*pret & pp* **robbed;** *ger* **robbing**) *tr & intr* robar
**robber** ['rɑbər] *s* robador *m*, ladrón *m*
**robber·y** ['rɑbəri] *s* (*pl* **-ies**) robo
**robe** [rob] *s* manto; abrigo; (*of a woman*) traje *m*, vestido; (*of a professor, judge, etc.*) toga, túnica; (*of a priest*) traje *m* talar; (*dressing gown*) bata; (*for lap in a carriage*) manta ‖ *tr* vestir ‖ *intr* vestirse
**robin** ['rɑbɪn] *s* (*in Europe*) petirrojo; (*in North America*) primavera
**robot** ['robɑt] *s* robot *m*
**robust** [ro'bʌst] *adj* robusto; vigoroso
**rock** [rɑk] *s* roca; (*sticking out of water*) escollo; (*one that is thrown*) piedra; (slang) diamante *m*, piedra preciosa; **on the rocks** arruinado, en pobreza extrema; (*said of hard liquor*) (coll) sobre hielo ‖ *tr* acunar, mecer; (*to sleep*) arrullar; sacudir; **to rock to sleep** adormecer meciendo ‖ *intr* mecerse; sacudirse
**rock'-bot'tom** *adj* (el) mínimo, (el) más bajo
**rock candy** *s* azúcar *m* cande
**rock crystal** *s* cristal *m* de roca
**rocker** ['rɑkər] *s* (*chair*) mecedora; (*curved piece at bottom of rocking chair or cradle*) arco; (mach) balancín *m;* (mach) eje *m* de balancín
**rocket** ['rɑkɪt] *s* cohete *m* ‖ *intr* subir como un cohete
**rocket bomb** *s* bomba cohete
**rocket launcher** ['lɔntʃər] o ['lɑntʃər] *s* lanzacohetes *m*
**rocket ship** *s* aeronave *f* cohete
**rock garden** *s* jardín *m* entre rocas

**rocking chair** *s* mecedora, sillón *m* de hamaca
**rocking horse** *s* caballo mecedor
**Rock of Gibraltar** [dʒɪˈbrɔltər] *s* peñón *m* de Gibraltar
**rock salt** *s* sal *f* de compás, sal gema
**rock wool** *s* lana mineral
**rock•y** [ˈrɑki] *adj* (*comp* **-ier;** *super* **-iest**) rocoso, roqueño; (slang) débil, poco firme
**rod** [rɑd] *s* vara; varilla; barra; (*authority*) vara alta; opresión, tiranía; (*of the retina*) bastoncillo; (*elongated microörganism*) bastoncito; (mach) vástago; (surv) jalón *m;* (Bib) linaje *m,* raza, vástago; (slang) revólver *m,* pistola; **to spare the rod** excusar la vara
**rodent** [ˈrodənt] *adj* & *s* roedor *m*
**rod•man** [ˈrɑdmən] *s* (*pl* **-men** [mən]) jalonero, portamira *m*
**roe** [ro] *s* (*deer*) corzo; (*of fish*) hueva
**rogue** [rog] *s* bribón *m,* pícaro
**rogues' gallery** *s* colección de retratos de malhechores para uso de la policía
**roguish** [ˈrogɪʃ] *adj* bribón, pícaro; travieso, retozón
**rôle** o **role** [rol] *s* papel *m;* **to play a rôle** desempeñar un papel
**roll** [rol] *s* (*of cloth, film, paper, fat, etc.*) rollo; (*roller*) rodillo; (*cake of bread*) panecillo; (*of dice*) echada; (*of a boat*) balance *m;* (*of a drum*) redoble *m;* (*of thunder*) retumbo; bamboleo; ondulación; rol *m;* lista; (*of paper money*) fajo; **to call the roll** pasar lista ‖ *tr* hacer rodar; empujar hacia adelante; cilindrar, laminar; (*to wrap up with rolling motion*) arrollar; alisar con rodillo; liar (*un cigarrillo*); mover de un lado a otro; poner (*los ojos*) en blanco; tocar redobles con (*el tambor*); vibrar (*la voz; la r*); **to roll one's own** liárselos; **to roll up** arremangar (*p.ej., las mangas*); amontonar (*p.ej., una fortuna*) ‖ *intr* rodar; bambolear; balancear (*un barco*); girar; retumbar (*el trueno*); redoblar (*un tambor*); **to roll around** revolcarse
**roll call** *s* lista, (el) pasar lista
**roller** [ˈrolər] *s* rodillo; (*of a piece of furniture*) ruedecilla; (*of a skate*) rueda; ola larga y creciente
**roller bearing** *s* cojinete *m* de rodillos
**roller coaster** *s* montaña rusa
**roller skate** *s* patín *m* de ruedas
**roller towel** *s* toalla sin fin
**rolling mill** [ˈrolɪŋ] *s* taller *m* de laminación; tren *m* de laminadores
**rolling pin** *s* rodillo, hataca
**rolling stock** *s* (rr) material *m* móvil, material rodante
**rolling stone** *s* piedra movediza
**roll'-top' desk** *s* escritorio norteamericano, escritorio de cortina corrediza
**roly-poly** [ˈroliˈpoli] *adj* regordete, rechoncho
**Rom.** *abbr* **Roman, Romance**
**roman** [ˈromən] *adj* (typ) redondo ‖ *s* (typ) letra redonda ‖ **Roman** *adj* & *s* romano
**Roman candle** *s* vela romana
**Roman Catholic** *adj* & *s* católico romano
**romance** [roˈmæns] o [ˈromæns] *s* (*tale of chivalry*) romance *m;* cuento de aventuras; cuento de amor; intriga amorosa; novela sentimental; (mus) romanza ‖ [roˈmæns] *intr* contar o escribir romances, cuentos de aventuras o cuentos de amor; pensar o hablar de un modo romántico; exagerar, mentir ‖ **Romance** [ˈromæns] o [roˈmæns] *adj* (*Neo-Latin*) romance o románico
**romance of chivalry** *s* libro de caballerías
**Roman Empire** *s* Imperio romano
**Romanesque** [ˌromənˈɛsk] *adj* & *s* románico
**Roman nose** *s* nariz aguileña
**romantic** [roˈmæntɪk] *adj* romántico; (*spot, place*) encantador
**romanticism** [roˈmæntɪˌsɪzəm] *s* romanticismo
**romp** [rɑmp] *intr* corretear, triscar
**rompers** [ˈrɑmpərz] *spl* traje holgado de juego
**roof** [ruf] o [rʊf] *s* (*top outer covering of a house*) tejado; (*of a car or bus*) imperial *f,* tejadillo; (*of the mouth*) paladar *m;* (*of heaven*) bóveda; (*home, dwelling*) (fig) techo; **to raise the roof** (slang) poner el grito en el cielo ‖ *tr* techar
**roofer** [ˈrufər] o [ˈrʊfər] *s* techador *m,* pizarrero
**roof garden** *s* (*garden on the roof*) pérgola; azotea de baile y diversión
**rook** [rʊk] *s* (*bird*) grajo; (*in chess*) roque *m* ‖ *tr* trampear
**rookie** [ˈrʊki] *s* (slang) bisoño, novato
**room** [rum] o [rʊm] *s* aposento, cuarto, habitación, pieza; espacio, sitio, lugar *m;* ocasión; **to make room** abrir paso, hacer lugar ‖ *intr* alojarse
**room and board** *s* pensión completa
**room clerk** *s* empleado en la recepción, encargado de las reservas
**roomer** [ˈrumər] o [ˈrʊmər] *s* inquilino
**rooming house** *s* casa donde se alquilan cuartos
**room'mate'** *s* compañero de cuarto
**room•y** [ˈrumi] o [ˈrʊmi] *adj* (*comp* **-ier;** *super* **-iest**) amplio, espacioso
**roost** [rust] *s* percha de gallinero; gallinero; lugar *m* de descanso; **to rule the roost** ser el amo del cotarro, tener el mando y el palo ‖ *intr* descansar (*las aves*) en la percha; estar alojado; pasar la noche
**rooster** [ˈrustər] *s* gallo
**root** [rut] o [rʊt] *s* raíz *f;* **to get to the root of** profundizar; **to take root** echar raíces ‖ *tr* hocicar, hozar ‖ *intr* arraigar; **to root for** (slang) gritar alentando
**rooter** [ˈrutər] o [ˈrʊtər] *s* (slang) hincha *mf*
**rope** [rop] *s* cuerda; (*of a hangman*)

dogal *m;* (*to catch an animal*) lazo; **to jump rope** saltar a la comba; **to know the ropes** (slang) saber todas las tretas || *tr* atar con una cuerda; coger con lazo; **to rope in** (slang) embaucar, engañar

**rope'walk'er** *s* funámbulo, volatinero

**rosa•ry** ['rozəri] *s* (*pl* **-ries**) rosario

**rose** [roz] *adj* de color de rosa || *s* rosa

**rose'bud'** *s* pimpollo, capullo de rosa

**rose'bush'** *s* rosal *m*

**rose'-col'ored** *adj* rosado; **to see everything through rose-colored glasses** verlo todo de color de rosa

**rose garden** *s* rosaleda, rosalera

**rosemar•y** ['roz,mɛri] *s* (*pl* **-ies**) romero

**rose of Sharon** ['ʃɛrən] *s* granado blanco, rosa de Siria

**rose window** *s* rosetón *m*

**rose'wood'** *s* palisandro

**rosin** ['rɑzɪn] *s* colofonia, brea seca

**roster** ['rɑstər] *s* catálogo, lista; horario escolar, horas de clase

**rostrum** ['rɑstrəm] *s* tribuna

**ros•y** ['rozi] *adj* (*comp* **-ier;** *super* **-iest**) rosado, sonrosado; alegre

**rot** [rɑt] *s* podredumbre; (slang) tontería || *v* (*pret & pp* **rotted;** *ger* **rotting**) *tr* pudrir || *intr* pudrirse

**rotate** ['rotet] o [ro'tet] *tr* hacer girar; alternar || *intr* girar; alternar

**rote** [rot] *s* rutina, repetición maquinal; **by rote** de memoria, maquinalmente

**rot'gut'** *s* (slang) matarratas *m*

**rotogravure** [,rotəgrə'vjʊr] o [,rotə'grevjʊr] *s* rotograbado

**rotten** ['rɑtən] *adj* putrefacto, pútrido; corrompido

**rotund** [ro'tʌnd] *adj* redondo de cuerpo; (*language*) redondo

**rouge** [ruʒ] *s* arrebol *m,* colorete *m* || *tr* arrebolar, pintar || *intr* arrebolarse, pintarse

**rough** [rʌf] *adj* áspero; (*sea*) agitado, picado; (*crude, unwrought*) tosco, grosero; aproximado || *tr* — **to rough it** vivir sin comodidades, hacer vida campestre

**rough'cast'** *s* modelo tosco; mezcla gruesa || *v* (*pret & pp* **-cast**) *tr* (*to prepare in rough form*) bosquejar; dar a (*la pared*) una capa de mezcla gruesa

**rough copy** *s* borrador *m*

**roughly** ['rʌfli] *adv* asperamente; brutalmente; aproximadamente

**roulette** [ru'lɛt] *s* ruleta

**round** [raʊnd] *adj* redondo || *adv* redondamente; alrededor; de boca en boca; por todas partes || *prep* alrededor de; (*e.g., the corner*) a la vuelta de; cerca de; acá y allá en || *s* camino, circuito; (*of a policeman; of visits; of drinks or cigars*) ronda; (*of applause; discharge of guns*) salva; (*discharge of a single gun*) disparo, tiro; (*of people*) corro, círculo; (*of golf*) partido; rutina, serie *f,* sucesión; redondez *f;* revolución; (box) asalto; **to go the rounds** ir de boca en boca; ir de mano en mano || *tr* (*to make round*) redondear; cercar, rodear; doblar (*una esquina, un promontorio*); **to round off** u **out** redondear; acabar, completar, perfeccionar; **to round up** juntar, recoger; rodear (*el ganado*)

**roundabout** ['raʊndə,baʊt] *adj* indirecto || *s* curso indirecto; (Brit) tío vivo; (Brit) glorieta de tráfico

**rounder** ['raʊndər] *s* (coll) pródigo; (coll) catavinos *m,* borrachín habitual

**round'house'** *s* cocherón *m,* casa de máquinas, depósito de locomotoras

**round-shouldered** ['raʊnd'ʃoldərd] *adj* cargado de espaldas

**Round Table** *s* Tabla Redonda

**round'-trip' ticket** *s* billete *m* de ida y vuelta

**round'up'** *s* (*of cattle*) rodeo; (*of criminals*) redada; (*of old friends*) reunión

**rouse** [raʊz] *tr* despertar; excitar, provocar; levantar (*la caza*) || *intr* despertarse, despabilarse

**rout** [raʊt] *s* derrota; fuga desordenada || *tr* derrotar; poner en fuga desordenada; arrancar hozando || *intr* hozar

**route** [rut] o [raʊt] *s* ruta; itinerario || *tr* encaminar

**routine** [ru'tin] *adj* rutinario || *s* rutina

**rove** [rov] *intr* andar errante, vagar

**row** [raʊ] *s* (coll) camorra, pendencia, riña; (coll) alboroto, bullicio; **to raise a row** (coll) armar camorra || [ro] *s* fila, hilera; (*of houses*) crujía; **in a row** seguidos, p.ej., **five hours in a row** cinco horas seguidas || *intr* remar

**rowboat** ['ro,bot] *s* bote *m,* bote de remos

**row•dy** ['raʊdi] *adj* (*comp* **-dier;** *super* **-diest**) gamberro || *s* (*pl* **-dies**) gamberro

**rower** ['ro•ər] *s* remero

**royal** ['rɔɪ•əl] *adj* real; (*magnificent, splendid*) regio

**royalist** ['rɔɪ•əlɪst] *s* realista *mf*

**royal•ty** ['rɔɪ•əlti] *s* (*pl* **-ties**) realeza; personaje *m* real, personajes reales; derechos de autor; derechos de inventor

**r.p.m.** *abbr* **revolutions per minute**

**R.R.** *abbr* **railroad, Right Reverend**

**rub** [rʌb] *s* frotación, roce *m;* **there's the rub** ahí está el busilis || *v* (*pret & pp* **rubbed;** *ger* **rubbing**) *tr* frotar; **to rub elbows with** rozarse mucho con; **to rub out** borrar; (slang) asesinar || *intr* frotar; **to rub off** quitarse frotando; borrarse

**rubber** ['rʌbər] *s* caucho, goma; goma de borrar; chanclo, zapato de goma; (*in bridge*) robre *m* || *intr* (slang) estirar el cuello o volver la cabeza para ver

**rubber band** *s* liga de goma

**rubber plant** *s* árbol *m* del caucho

**rubber plantation** *s* cauchal *m*

**rubber stamp** *s* cajetín *m,* sello de goma; (*with a person's signature*)

estampilla; (coll) persona que aprueba sin reflexionar
**rub'ber-stamp'** *tr* estampar con un sello de goma; (*with a person's signature*) estampillar; (coll) aprobar sin reflexionar
**rubbish** ['rʌbɪʃ] *s* basura, desecho, desperdicios; (coll) disparate *m*, tontería
**rubble** ['rʌbəl] *s* (*broken stone*) ripio; (*masonry*) mampostería
**rub'down'** *s* masaje *m*, fricción
**rube** [rub] *s* (slang) isidro, rústico
**ru•by** ['rubi] *s* (*pl* **-bies**) rubí *m*
**rudder** ['rʌdər] *s* timón *m*, gobernalle *m*
**rud•dy** ['rʌdi] *adj* (*comp* **-dier;** *super* **-diest**) coloradote, rubicundo
**rude** [rud] *adj* rudo
**rudiment** ['rudɪmənt] *s* rudimento
**rue** [ru] *tr* lamentar, arrepentirse de
**rueful** ['rufəl] *adj* lamentable; triste
**ruffian** ['rʌfɪ•ən] *s* hombre grosero y brutal
**ruffle** ['rʌfəl] *s* arruga; (*of drum*) redoble *m;* (sew) volante *m* ‖ *tr* arrugar; agitar, descomponer; enojar, molestar; confundir; redoblar (*el tambor*); (sew) fruncir un volante en, adornar o guarnecer con volante
**rug** [rʌg] *s* alfombra; alfombrilla; (*lap robe*) manta
**rugged** ['rʌgɪd] *adj* áspero, rugoso; recio, vigoroso; tempestuoso
**ruin** ['ru•ɪn] *s* ruina ‖ *tr* arruinar; estropear; echar a perder
**rule** [rul] *s* regla; autoridad, mando; regla de imprenta; (*reign*) reinado; (*of a court of law*) decisión, fallo; **as a rule** por regla general; **to be the rule** ser lo que se hace ‖ *tr* gobernar, regir; dirigir, guiar; contener, reprimir; (*to mark with lines*) reglar; (law) decidir, determinar; **to rule out** excluir, rechazar ‖ *intr* gobernar, regir; prevalecer; **to rule over** gobernar, regir
**rule of law** *s* régimen *m* de justicia
**ruler** ['rulər] *s* gobernante *mf;* soberano; (*for ruling lines*) regla
**ruling** ['rulɪŋ] *adj* gobernante, dirigente, imperante ‖ *s* (*of a court or judge*) decisión, fallo; (*of paper*) rayado
**rum** [rʌm] *s* ron *m;* (*any alcoholic drink*) (U.S.A.) aguardiente *m*
**Rumanian** [ru'menɪ•ən] *adj* & *s* rumano
**rumble** ['rʌmbəl] *s* retumbo; (*of the intestines*) rugido; (slang) riña entre pandillas ‖ *intr* retumbar; avanzar retumbando
**ruminate** ['rumɪ‚net] *tr* & *intr* rumiar
**rummage** ['rʌmɪdʒ] *tr* & *intr* buscar revolviéndolo todo
**rummage sale** *s* venta de prendas usadas
**rumor** ['rumər] *s* rumor *m* ‖ *tr* rumorear; **it is rumored that** se rumorea que
**rump** [rʌmp] *s* anca, nalga; (*cut of beef*) cuarto trasero
**rumple** ['rʌmpəl] *s* arruga ‖ *tr* arrugar, ajar, chafar ‖ *intr* arrugarse
**rumpus** ['rʌmpəs] *s* (coll) batahola, alboroto; **to raise a rumpus** (coll) armar la de San Quintín
**run** [rʌn] *s* carrera; clase *f*, tipo; arroyo; (*e.g., in a stocking*) carrera; (*on a bank by depositors*) asedio; (*of consecutive performances of a play*) serie *f;* (baseball & mus) carrera; **in the long run** a la larga; **on the run** a escape; en fuga desordenada; **the common run of people** el común de las gentes; **the general run of** la generalidad de; **to have a long run** permanecer en cartel durante mucho tiempo; **to have the run of** hallar el secreto de; tener libertad de ir y venir por ‖ *v* (*pret* **ran** [ræn]; *pp* **run;** *ger* **running**) *tr* hacer funcionar; dirigir, manejar; trazar, tirar (*una línea*); exhibir (*un cine*); hacer (*mandados*); tener como candidato; burlar, violar (*un bloqueo*); tener (*calentura*); correr (*un caballo; un riesgo*); **to run down** cazar y matar; derribar; atropellar (*a un peatón*); (coll) denigrar, desacreditar; **to run in** rodar (*un nuevo coche*); **to run off** tocar (*una pieza de música*); tirar, imprimir; **to run up** (coll) aumentar (*gastos*) ‖ *intr* correr; (*on wheels*) rodar; darse prisa; trepar (*la vid*); ir y venir (*un vapor*); supurar (*una llaga*); colar (*un líquido*); correrse (*un color o tinte*); presentar su candidatura; andar, funcionar, marchar; deshilarse (*las medias*); migrar (*los peces*); estar en fuerza; (*to be worded or written*) rezar; **to run across** dar con, tropezar con; **to run away** correr, huir; desbocarse (*un caballo*); **to run down** escurrir, gotear (*un líquido*); descargarse (*un acumulador*); distenderse (*el muelle de un reloj*); acabarse la cuerda, p.ej., **the watch ran down** se acabó la cuerda; **to run for** presentar su candidatura a; **to run in the family** venir de familia; **to run into** tropezar con; chocar con, topar con; **to run off the track** descarrilar (*un tren*); **to run out** salir; expirar, terminar; acabarse; agotarse; **to run out of** acabársele a uno, e.g., **I have run out of money** se me ha acabado el dinero; **to run over** atropellar (*a un peatón*); registrar a la ligera; pasar por encima; leer rápidamente; rebosar (*un líquido*); **to run through** disipar rápidamente (*una fortuna*); registrar a la ligera; estar difundido en
**run'a•way'** *adj* fugitivo; (*horse*) desbocado ‖ *s* fugitivo; caballo desbocado; fuga
**run'-down'** *adj* desmedrado; desmantelado; inculto; (*clock spring*) sin cuerda, distendido; (*storage battery*) descargado
**rung** [rʌŋ] *s* (*of ladder or chair*) travesaño; (*of wheel*) radio, rayo
**runner** ['rʌnər] *s* corredor *m;* caballo

de carreras; mensajero; (*of an ice skate*) cuchilla; (*of a sleigh*) patín *m;* (*long narrow rug*) pasacaminos *m;* (*strip of cloth for table top*) tapete *m;* (*in stockings*) carrera
**run'ner-up'** *s* (*pl* **runners-up**) subcampeón *m*
**running** ['rʌnɪŋ] *adj* corredor; (*expenses; water*) corriente; (*knot*) corredizo; (*sore*) supurante; (*writing*) cursivo; continuo; consecutivo; en marcha; (*start*) (sport) lanzado || *s* carrera, corrida; administración, dirección; marcha, funcionamiento; **to be in the running** tener esperanzas o posibilidades de ganar
**running board** *s* estribo
**running head** *s* titulillo
**running start** *s* (sport) salida lanzada
**run-of-mine coal** ['rʌnəv'maɪn] *s* carbón *m* tal como sale
**run'proof'** *adj* indesmallable
**runt** [rʌnt] *s* enano, hombrecillo; (*little child*) redrojo; animal achaparrado
**run'way'** *s* (*of a stream*) cauce *m;* senda trillada; (aer) pista de aterrizaje
**rupture** ['rʌptʃər] *s* ruptura; (pathol) quebradura; (*break in relations*) ruptura || *tr* romper; causar una hernia en || *intr* romperse; padecer hernia
**rural free delivery** ['rurəl] *s* distribución gratuita del correo en el campo
**rural police** *s* guardia civil
**rural policeman** *s* guardiacivil *m*
**ruse** [ruz] *s* astucia, artimaña
**rush** [rʌʃ] *adj* urgente || *s* prisa grande, precipitación; agolpamiento de gente; (bot) junco; **in a rush** de prisa || *tr* empujar con violencia o prisa; despachar con prontitud; (slang) cortejar insistentemente (*a una mujer*); **to rush through** ejecutar de prisa, despachar rápidamente || *intr* lanzarse, precipitarse; venir de prisa, ir de prisa; actuar con prontitud; **to rush through** lanzarse a través de, lanzarse por entre
**rush-bottomed chair** ['rʌʃ'bɑtəmd] *s* silla de junco
**rush hour** *s* hora de aglomeración, horas de punta
**rush'light'** *s* mariposa, lamparilla
**rush order** *s* pedido urgente
**russet** ['rʌsɪt] *adj* canelo
**Russia** ['rʌʃə] *s* Rusia
**Russian** ['rʌʃən] *adj & s* ruso
**rust** [rʌst] *s* orín *m,* moho, herrumbre; (agr) roña, roya; color rojizo o anaranjado || *tr* aherrumbrar || *intr* aherrumbrarse
**rustic** ['rʌstɪk] *adj* rústico; sencillo, sin artificio || *s* rústico
**rustle** ['rʌsəl] *s* susurro, crujido || *tr* hacer susurrar, hacer crujir; hurtar (*ganado*) || *intr* susurrar, crujir; (slang) trabajar con ahinco
**rust•y** ['rʌsti] *adj* (*comp* **-ier;** *super* **-iest**) herrumbroso, mohoso; rojizo; (*out of practice*) empolvado, desusado, remoto
**rut** [rʌt] *s* (*track, groove in road*) rodada, bache *m;* hábito arraigado; (*sexual excitement in animals*) celo; (*period of this excitement*) brama
**ruthless** ['ruθlɪs] *adj* despiadado, cruel
**Ry.** *abbr* **railway**
**rye** [raɪ] *s* centeno; whisky de centeno

## S

**S, s** [ɛs] decimonona letra del alfabeto inglés
**s** *abbr* **second, shilling, singular**
**Sabbath** ['sæbəθ] *s* (*of Jews*) sábado; (*of Christians*) domínica; **to keep the Sabbath** observar el descanso dominical, guardar el domingo
**saber** ['sebər] *s* sable *m*
**sable** ['sebəl] *adj* negro || *s* marta cebellina; **sables** vestidos de luto
**sabotage** ['sæbə,tɑʒ] *s* sabotaje *m* || *tr & intr* sabotear
**saccharin** ['sækərɪn] *s* sacarina
**sachet** ['sæʃe] o [sæ'ʃe] *s* polvo oloroso; saquito de perfumes
**sack** [sæk] *s* saco; vino blanco generoso; (mil) saqueo, saco; (*of an employee*) (slang) despedida || *tr* ensacar; saquear, pillar; (slang) despedir (*a un empleado*)
**sack'cloth'** *s* harpillera; (*worn for penitence*) cilicio
**sacrament** ['sækrəmənt] *s* sacramento
**sacred** ['sekrəd] *adj* sagrado
**sacrifice** ['sækrɪ,faɪs] *s* sacrificio; **at a sacrifice** con pérdida || *tr* sacrificar; (*to sell at a loss*) malvender || *intr* sacrificar; sacrificarse
**Sacrifice of the Mass** *s* sacrificio del altar
**sacrilege** ['sækrɪlɪdʒ] *s* sacrilegio
**sacrilegious** [,sækrɪ'lɪdʒəs] o [,sækrɪ'lidʒəs] *adj* sacrílego
**sacristan** ['sækrɪstən] *s* sacristán *m*
**sacris•ty** ['sækrɪsti] *s* (*pl* **-ties**) sacristía
**sad** [sæd] *adj* (*comp* **sadder;** *super* **saddest**) triste; (slang) malo
**sadden** ['sædən] *tr* entristecer || *intr* entristecerse
**saddle** ['sædəl] *s* silla de montar; (*of a bicycle*) sillín *m* || *tr* ensillar; **to saddle with** echar a cuestas a
**sad'dle•bags'** *spl* alforjas
**sad'dle•bow'** [,bo] *s* arzón delantero
**sad'dle•tree'** *s* arzón *m*
**sadist** ['sædɪst] o ['sedɪst] *s* sádico
**sadistic** [sæ'dɪstɪk] o [se'dɪstɪk] *adj* sádico
**sadness** ['sædnɪs] *s* tristeza
**safe** [sef] *adj* seguro, ileso, salvo;

cierto, digno de confianza; sin peligro, a salvo; **safe and sound** sano y salvo; **safe from** a salvo de || *s* caja fuerte, caja de caudales
**safe'-con'duct** *s* salvoconducto
**safe'-depos'it box** *s* caja de seguridad
**safe'guard'** *s* salvaguardia, medida de seguridad || *tr* salvaguardar
**safe·ty** ['sefti] *adj* de seguridad || *s* (*pl* **-ties**) seguridad; **to parachute to safety** lanzarse en paracaídas; **to reach safety** ponerse a salvo, llegar a lugar seguro
**safety belt** *s* (aer, aut) correa de seguridad; (naut) cinturón *m* salvavidas
**safety match** *s* fósforo de seguridad
**safety pin** *s* imperdible *m*, alfiler *m* de seguridad
**safety rail** *s* guardarriel *m*
**safety razor** *s* maquinilla de seguridad
**safety valve** *s* válvula de seguridad
**saffron** ['sæfrən] *adj* azafranado || *s* azafrán *m* || *tr* azafranar
**sag** [sæg] *s* comba, combadura; (*e.g., of a cable*) flecha || *v* (*pret & pp* **sagged**; *ger* **sagging**) *intr* combarse; (*to slacken, yield*) aflojar, ceder, doblegarse; bajar (*los precios*)
**sagacious** [sə'geʃəs] *adj* sagaz
**sage** [sedʒ] *adj* sabio, cuerdo || *s* sabio; (bot) salvia; (bot) artemisa
**sage'brush'** *s* (bot) artemisa
**sail** [sel] *s* vela; barco de vela; paseo en barco de vela; **to set sail** hacerse a la vela; **under full sail** a vela llena || *tr* gobernar (*un barco de vela*); navegar (*un mar, río, etc.*) || *intr* navegar, navegar a la vela; salir, salir de viaje; deslizarse, flotar, volar; **to sail into** (slang) atacar, regañar, reñir
**sail'boat'** *s* barco de vela, buque *m* de vela, velero
**sail'cloth'** *s* lona, paño
**sailing** ['selɪŋ] *adj* de salida || *s* paseo en barco de vela; navegación; salida
**sailing vessel** *s* buque velero
**sailor** ['selər] *s* (*one who makes a living sailing*) marinero; (*an enlisted man in the navy*) marino
**saint** [sent] *adj & s* santo || *tr* (coll) canonizar
**saintliness** ['sentlɪnɪs] *s* santidad
**Saint Vitus's dance** ['vaɪtəsəs] *s* (pathol) baile *m* de San Vito
**sake** [sek] *s* respeto, bien, amor *m*; **for his sake** por su bien; **for the sake of** por, por motivo de, por amor a; **for your own sake** por su propio bien
**salaam** [sə'lɑm] *s* zalema || *tr* saludar con zalemas, hacer zalemas a
**salable** ['seləbəl] *adj* vendible
**salad** ['sæləd] *s* ensalada
**salad bowl** *s* ensaladera
**salad oil** *s* aceite *m* de comer
**Salamis** ['sæləmɪs] *s* Salamina
**sala·ry** ['sæləri] *s* (*pl* **-ries**) sueldo
**sale** [sel] *s* venta; (*auction*) almoneda, subasta; **for sale** de venta; se vende(n)
**sales'clerk'** *s* dependiente *mf* de tienda
**sales'la'dy** *s* (*pl* **-dies**) vendedora
**sales·man** ['selzmən] *s* (*pl* **-men** [mən]) vendedor *m*, dependiente *m* de tienda
**sales manager** *s* gerente *m* de ventas
**sales'man·ship'** *s* arte de vender
**sales'room'** *s* salón *m* de ventas; salón de exhibición
**sales talk** *s* argumento para inducir a comprar
**sales tax** *s* impuesto sobre ventas
**saliva** [sə'laɪvə] *s* saliva
**sallow** ['sælo] *adj* cetrino
**sal·ly** ['sæli] *s* (*pl* **-lies**) paseo, viaje *m*; ímpetu *m*, arranque *m*; salida, ocurrencia; (mil) salida, surtida || *v* (*pret & pp* **-lied**) *intr* salir, hacer una salida; ir de paseo; **to sally forth** salir, avanzar con denuedo
**salmon** ['sæmən] *s* salmón *m*
**salon** [sæ'lɑn] *s* salón *m*
**saloon** [sə'lun] *s* cantina, taberna; (*on a steamer*) salón *m*
**saloon'keep'er** *s* tabernero
**salt** [sɔlt] *s* sal *f*; **to be not worth one's salt** no valer (*uno*) el pan que come || *tr* salar; (*to preserve with salt*) salpresar; marinar (*el pescado*); salgar (*al ganado*); **to salt away** (slang) ahorrar, guardar para uso futuro
**salt'cel'lar** *s* salero
**salted peanuts** *spl* saladillos
**saltine** [sɔl'tin] *s* galletita salada
**saltish** ['sɔltɪʃ] *adj* salobre
**salt lick** *s* salero, lamedero
**salt of the earth, the** lo mejor del mundo
**salt'pe'ter** *s* (*potassium nitrate*) salitre *m*; (*sodium nitrate*) nitro de Chile
**salt'sha'ker** *s* salero
**salt·y** ['sɔlti] *adj* (*comp* **-ier**; *super* **-iest**) salado
**salubrious** [sə'lubrɪ·əs] *adj* salubre
**salutation** [,sæljə'teʃən] *s* salutación
**salute** [sə'lut] *s* saludo || *tr* saludar
**Salvadoran** [,sælvə'dorən] o **Salvadorian** [,sælvə'dorɪ·ən] *adj & s* salvadoreño
**salvage** ['sælvɪdʒ] *s* salvamento || *tr* salvar; recobrar
**Salvation Army** [sæl'veʃən] *s* ejército de Salvación
**salve** [sæv] o [sɑv] *s* ungüento || *tr* curar con ungüento; preservar; aliviar
**sal·vo** ['sælvo] *s* (*pl* **-vos** o **-voes**) salva
**Samaritan** [sə'mærɪtən] *adj & s* samaritano
**same** [sem] *adj & pron indef* mismo; **it's all the same to me** lo mismo me da; **just the same** lo mismo, sin embargo; **same . . . as** mismo . . . que
**samite** ['sæmaɪt] o ['semaɪt] *s* jamete *m*
**sample** ['sæmpəl] *s* muestra || *tr* catar, probar
**sample copy** *s* ejemplar *m* muestra
**sancti·fy** ['sæŋktɪ,faɪ] *v* (*pret & pp* **-fied**) *tr* santificar
**sanctimonious** [,sæŋktɪ'monɪ·əs] *adj* santurrón
**sanction** ['sæŋkʃən] *s* sanción || *tr* sancionar
**sanctuar·y** ['sæŋktʃu,eri] *s* (*pl* **-ies**)

santuario; asilo, refugio; **to take sanctuary** acogerse a sagrado
**sand** [sænd] *s* arena ‖ *tr* enarenar; lijar con papel de lija
**sandal** ['sændəl] *s* sandalia
**san'dal•wood'** *s* (bot) sándalo
**sand'bag'** *s* saco de arena
**sand'bank'** *s* banco de arena
**sand bar** *s* barra de arena
**sand'blast'** *s* chorro de arena ‖ *tr* limpiar con chorro de arena
**sand'box'** *s* (rr) arenero
**sand dune** *s* duna, médano
**sand'glass'** *s* reloj *m* de arena, ampolleta
**sand'pa'per** *s* papel *m* de lija ‖ *tr* lijar
**sand'stone'** *s* piedra arenisca
**sand'storm'** *s* tempestad de arena
**sandwich** ['sændwɪtʃ] *s* emparedado, sandwich *m* ‖ *tr* intercalar
**sandwich man** *s* hombre-anuncio
**sand•y** ['sændi] *adj* (*comp* **-ier;** *super* **-iest**) arenoso; (*hair*) rufo; cambiante, movible
**sane** [sen] *adj* cuerdo, sensato; (*principles*) sano
**sanguinary** ['sæŋgwɪn,eri] *adj* sanguinario
**sanguine** ['sæŋgwɪn] *adj* confiado, esperanzado; (*countenance*) coloradote
**sanitary** ['sænɪ,teri] *adj* sanitario
**sanitary napkin** *s* compresa higiénica
**sanitation** [,sænɪ'teʃən] *s* (*sanitary measures*) sanidad; (*drainage*) saneamiento
**sanity** ['sænɪti] *s* cordura, sensatez *f*
**Santa Claus** ['sæntə,klɔz] *s* el Papá Noel, San Nicolás
**sap** [sæp] *s* savia; (mil) zapa; (coll) necio, tonto ‖ *v* (*pret & pp* **sapped;** *ger* **sapping**) *tr* agotar, debilitar; zapar, socavar
**sap'head'** *s* (coll) cabeza de chorlito
**sapling** ['sæplɪŋ] *s* árbol *m* muy joven, pimpollo; jovenzuelo, mozuelo
**sapphire** ['sæfaɪr] *s* zafiro
**saraband** ['særə,bænd] *s* zarabanda
**Saracen** ['særəsən] *adj & s* sarraceno
**Saragossa** [,særə'gɑsə] *s* Zaragoza
**sardine** [sɑr'din] *s* sardina; **packed in like sardines** como sardinas en banasta o en lata
**Sardinia** [sɑr'dɪnɪ•ə] *s* Cerdeña
**Sardinian** [sɑr'dɪnɪ•ən] *adj & s* sardo
**sarsaparilla** [,sɑrsəpə'rɪlə] *s* zarzaparrilla
**sash** [sæʃ] *s* banda, faja; (*of a window*) marco
**sash window** *s* ventana de guillotina
**satchel** ['sætʃəl] *s* maletín *m;* (*of a schoolboy*) cartapacio
**sateen** [sæ'tin] *s* satén *m*
**satellite** ['sætə,laɪt] *s* satélite *m*
**satellite country** *s* país *m* satélite
**satiate** ['seʃɪ,et] *adj* ahito, harto ‖ *tr* saciar
**satin** ['sætən] *s* raso
**satinet** [,sætɪ'net] *s* rasete *m*
**satiric(al)** [sə'tɪrɪk(əl)] *adj* satírico
**satirist** ['sætɪrɪst] *s* satírico
**satirize** ['sætɪ,raɪz] *tr & intr* satirizar
**satisfaction** [,sætɪs'fækʃən] *s* satisfacción
**satisfactory** [,sætɪs'fæktəri] *adj* satisfactorio
**satis•fy** ['sætɪs,faɪ] *v* (*pret & pp* **-fied**) *tr & intr* satisfacer
**saturate** ['sætʃə,ret] *tr* saturar
**Saturday** ['sætərdi] *s* sábado
**sauce** [sɔs] *s* salsa; (*of fruit*) compota; (*of chocolate*) crema; gracia, viveza; (coll) insolencia, lenguaje descomedido ‖ *tr* condimentar ‖ [sɔs] o [sæs] *tr* (coll) ser respondón con
**sauce'pan'** *s* cacerola
**saucer** ['sɔsər] *s* platillo
**sau•cy** ['sɔsi] *adj* (*comp* **-cier;** *super* **-ciest**) descarado, insolente; gracioso, vivo
**sauerkraut** ['saʊr,kraʊt] *s* chucruta
**saunter** ['sɔntər] *s* paseo tranquilo y alegre ‖ *intr* dar un paseo tranquilo y alegre; pasear tranquila y alegremente
**sausage** ['sɔsɪdʒ] *s* salchicha, embutido
**savage** ['sævɪdʒ] *adj & s* salvaje *mf*
**savant** ['sævənt] *s* sabio, erudito
**save** [sev] *prep* salvo, excepto, menos ‖ *tr* salvar (*p.ej., una vida, un alma*); ahorrar (*dinero*); conservar, guardar; proteger, amparar; **God save the Queen!** ¡Dios guarde a la Reina!; **to save face** salvar las apariencias
**saving** ['sevɪŋ] *prep* salvo, excepto; con el debido respeto a ‖ *adj* económico ‖ **savings** *spl* ahorros, economías
**savings account** *s* cuenta de ahorros
**savings bank** *s* banco de ahorros, caja de ahorros
**savior** ['sevjər] *s* salvador *m*
**Saviour** ['sevjər] *s* Salvador *m*
**savor** ['sevər] *s* sabor *m* ‖ *tr* saborear ‖ *intr* oler; **to savor of** oler a, saber a
**savor•y** ['sevəri] *adj* (*comp* **-ier;** *super* **-iest**) sabroso; picante; fragante ‖ *s* (*pl* **-ies**) (bot) ajedrea
**saw** [sɔ] *s* (*tool*) sierra; proverbio, refrán *m* ‖ *tr* aserrar, serrar
**saw'buck'** *s* cabrilla, caballete *m*
**saw'dust'** *s* aserrín *m*, serrín *m*
**saw'horse'** *s* cabrilla, caballete *m*
**saw'mill'** *s* aserradero, serrería
**Saxon** ['sæksən] *adj & s* sajón *m*
**saxophone** ['sæksə,fon] *s* saxofón *m*
**say** [se] *s* decir *m;* **to have one's say** decir su parecer ‖ *v* (*pret & pp* **said** [sɛd]) *tr* decir; **I should say so!** ¡ya lo creo!; **it is said** se dice; **no sooner said than done** dicho y hecho; **that is to say** es decir, esto es; **to go without saying** caerse de su peso
**saying** ['se•ɪŋ] *s* dicho; proverbio, refrán *m*
**sc.** *abbr* **scene, science, scruple, scilicet** (Lat) **namely**
**scab** [skæb] *s* costra; (*strikebreaker*) esquirol *m;* (slang) bribón *m*, golfo
**scabbard** ['skæbərd] *s* funda, vaina
**scab•by** ['skæbi] *adj* (*comp* **-bier;** *super* **-biest**) costroso; (coll) ruin, vil
**scabrous** ['skæbrəs] *adj* escabroso
**scads** [skædz] *spl* (slang) montones *mpl*

**scaffold** ['skæfəld] *s* andamio; (*to execute a criminal*) cadalso, patíbulo
**scaffolding** ['skæfəldɪŋ] *s* andamiaje *m*
**scald** [skɔld] *tr* escaldar
**scale** [skel] *s* escama; balanza; platillo de balanza; (*e.g., of a map*) escala; (mus) escala; **on a scale of** en escala de; **on a large scale** en grande escala; **scales** balanza; **to tip the scales** inclinar la balanza ‖ *tr* escamar; descortezar, descostrar; escalar, subir, trepar; graduar ‖ *intr* descamarse; descortezarse, descostrarse; subir, trepar
**scallop** ['skɑləp] o ['skæləp] *s* concha de peregrino; (*shell or dish for serving fish*) concha; (*thin slice of meat*) escalope *m;* (*on edge of cloth*) festón *m* ‖ *tr* cocer (*p.ej., ostras*) en su concha; festonear
**scalp** [skælp] *s* cuero cabelludo ‖ *tr* escalpar; comprar y revender (*billetes de teatro*) a precios extraoficiales
**scalpel** ['skælpəl] *s* escalpelo
**scal•y** ['skeli] *adj* (*comp* **-ier**; *super* **-iest**) escamoso
**scamp** [skæmp] *s* bribón *m*, golfo
**scamper** ['skæmpər] *intr* escaparse precipitadamente; **to scamper away** escaparse precipitadamente
**scan** [skæn] *v* (*pret & pp* **scanned**; *ger* **scanning**) *tr* escudriñar; escandir (*versos*); (telv) explorar; (coll) dar un vistazo a
**scandal** ['skændəl] *s* escándalo
**scandalize** ['skændə,laɪz] *tr* escandalizar
**scandalous** ['skændələs] *adj* escandaloso
**Scandinavian** [,skændɪ'nevɪ•ən] *adj & s* escandinavo
**scanning** ['skænɪŋ] *s* (telv) escansión, exploración
**scansion** ['skænʃən] *s* escansión
**scant** [skænt] *adj* escaso, insuficiente; solo, apenas suficiente ‖ *tr* escatimar
**scant•y** ['skænti] *adj* (*comp* **-ier**; *super* **-iest**) escaso, insuficiente, poco suficiente; (*clothing*) ligero
**scape'goat'** *s* cabeza de turco, víctima propiciatoria
**scar** [skɑr] *s* cicatriz *f*, señal *f* ‖ *v* (*pret & pp* **scarred**; *ger* **scarring**) *tr* señalar, marcar ‖ *intr* cicatrizarse
**scarce** [skers] *adj* escaso, raro; **to make oneself scarce** (coll) no dejarse ver
**scarcely** ['skersli] *adv* apenas; probablemente no; ciertamente no; **scarcely ever** raramente
**scarci•ty** ['skersɪti] *s* (*pl* **-ties**) escasez *f*, carestía
**scare** [sker] *s* susto, alarma ‖ *tr* asustar, espantar; **to scare away** espantar, ahuyentar; **to scare up** (coll) juntar, recoger (*dinero*)
**scare'crow'** *s* espantajo, espantapájaros *m*
**scarf** [skɑrf] *s* (*pl* **scarfs** o **scarves** [skɑrvz]) bufanda; pañuelo para el cuello; (*cover for a table, bureau, etc.*) tapete *m;* corbata
**scarf'pin'** *s* alfiler *m* de corbata
**scarlet** ['skɑrlɪt] *adj* escarlata
**scarlet fever** *s* escarlata
**scar•y** ['skeri] *adj* (*comp* **-ier**; *super* **-iest**) (*easily frightened*) (coll) asustadizo, espantadizo; (*causing fright*) (coll) espantoso
**scathing** ['skeðɪŋ] *adj* acerbo, duro
**scatter** ['skætər] *tr* esparcir, dispersar ‖ *intr* esparcirse, dispersarse
**scatterbrained** ['skætər,brend] *adj* (coll) alegre de cascos, casquivano
**scattered showers** *spl* lluvias aisladas
**scenari•o** [sɪ'nerɪ,o] o [sɪ'nɑrɪ,o] *s* (*pl* **-os**) guión *m*, escenario
**scenarist** [sɪ'nerɪst] o [sɪ'nɑrɪst] *s* guionista *mf*, escenarista *mf*
**scene** [sin] *s* (*view*) paisaje *m;* (*in literature, art, the theater, the movie*) escena; escándalo, demostración de pasión; **behind the scenes** entre bastidores; **to make a scene** causar escándalo
**scener•y** ['sinəri] *s* (*pl* **-ies**) paisaje *m;* (theat) decoraciones
**scene shifter** ['ʃɪftər] *s* tramoyista *m*
**scenic** ['sinɪk] o ['senɪk] *adj* pintoresco; (*representing an action graphically*) gráfico; (*pertaining to the stage*) escénico
**scent** [sent] *s* olor *m;* perfume *m;* (*sense of smell*) olfato; (*trail*) rastro, pista ‖ *tr* oler; perfumar; olfatear, ventear; sospechar
**scepter** ['septər] *s* cetro
**sceptic** ['skeptɪk] *adj & s* escéptico
**sceptical** ['skeptɪkəl] *adj* escéptico
**schedule** ['skedjʊl] *s* catálogo, cuadro, lista; plan *m*, programa *m;* (*of trains, planes, etc.*) horario ‖ *tr* catalogar; proyectar; fijar la hora de
**scheme** [skim] *s* esquema *m;* plan *m*, proyecto; (*trick*) ardid *m*, treta; (*plot*) intriga, trama ‖ *tr & intr* proyectar; tramar
**schemer** ['skimər] *s* proyectista *mf;* intrigante *mf*
**scheming** ['skimɪŋ] *adj* astuto, mañoso, intrigante ‖ *s* intriga
**schism** ['sɪzəm] *s* cisma *m;* facción cismática
**schist** [ʃɪst] *s* esquisto
**scholar** ['skɑlər] *s* (*pupil*) alumno; (*scholarship holder*) becario; (*learned person*) sabio, erudito
**scholarly** ['skɑlərli] *adj* sabio, erudito
**scholarship** ['skɑlər,ʃɪp] *s* erudición; (*grant to study*) beca
**school** [skul] *s* escuela; (*of a university*) facultad; (*of fish*) banco, cardume *m* ‖ *tr* enseñar, instruir, disciplinar
**school age** *s* edad escolar
**school attendance** *s* escolaridad
**school board** *s* junta de instrucción pública
**school'boy'** *s* alumno de escuela
**school day** *s* día lectivo
**school'girl'** *s* alumna de escuela
**school'house'** *s* escuela
**schooling** ['skulɪŋ] *s* instrucción, enseñanza; experiencia
**school'mate'** *s* compañero de escuela
**school'room'** *s* aula, sala de clase

**school'teach'er** *s* maestro de escuela
**school year** *s* año lectivo
**schooner** ['skunər] *s* goleta
**sci.** *abbr* **science, scientific**
**science** ['saɪ·əns] *s* ciencia
**scientific** [,saɪ·ən'tɪfɪk] *adj* científico
**scientist** ['saɪ·əntɪst] *s* científico, sabio, hombre *m* de ciencia
**scil.** *abbr* **scilicet** (Lat) **namely**
**scimitar** ['sɪmɪtər] *s* cimitarra
**scintillate** ['sɪntɪ,let] *intr* chispear, centellear
**scion** ['saɪ·ən] *s* vástago
**Scipio** ['sɪpɪ,o] *s* Escipión *m*
**scissors** ['sɪzərz] *ssg* o *spl* tijeras
**scoff** [skɔf] o [skɑf] *s* burla, mofa ‖ *intr* burlarse, mofarse; **to scoff at** burlarse de, mofarse de
**scold** [skold] *s* regañón *m*, regañona ‖ *tr & intr* regañar
**scoop** [skup] *s* (*instrument like a spoon*) cuchara, cucharón *m;* (*tool like a shovel*) pala; (*kitchen utensil*) paleta; (*for water*) achicador *m;* cucharada, palada, paletada; (*hollow made by a scoop*) hueco; (*big haul*) (coll) buena ganancia ‖ *tr* sacar con cuchara, pala, paleta; achicar (*agua*); **to scoop out** ahuecar, vaciar
**scoot** [skut] *s* (coll) carrera precipitada ‖ *intr* (coll) correr precipitadamente
**scooter** ['skutər] *s* monopatín *m*, patinete *m*
**scope** [skop] *s* alcance *m*, extensión; campo, espacio; **to give free scope to** dar campo libre a
**scorch** [skɔrtʃ] *s* chamusco ‖ *tr* chamuscar; (*to dry, wither*) abrasar; criticar acerbamente ‖ *intr* chamuscarse; abrasarse
**scorching** ['skɔrtʃɪŋ] *adj* abrasador; acerbo, duro, mordaz
**score** [skor] *s* (*in a game*) cuenta, tantos; (*in an examination*) nota; entalladura, muesca; línea, raya; (*twenty*) veintena; (mus) partitura; **on the score of** a título de; **to keep score** apuntar los tantos ‖ *tr* anotar (*los tantos*); ganar, tantear (*tantos*); rayar, señalar; regañar acerbamente; (mus) instrumentar ‖ *intr* ganar tantos; marcar los tantos
**score board** *s* marcador *m*, cuadro indicador
**scorn** [skɔrn] *s* desdén *m*, desprecio ‖ *tr & intr* desdeñar, despreciar; **to scorn to** no dignarse
**scornful** ['skɔrnfəl] *adj* desdeñoso
**scorpion** ['skɔrpɪ·ən] *s* alacrán *m*, escorpión *m*
**Scot** [skɑt] *s* escocés *m*
**Scotch** [skɑtʃ] *adj* escocés ‖ *s* (*dialect*) escocés *m;* whisky *m* escocés; **the Scotch** los escoceses
**Scotch·man** ['skɑtʃmən] *s* (*pl* **-men** [mən]) escocés *m*
**Scotland** ['skɑtlənd] *s* Escocia
**Scottish** ['skɑtɪʃ] *adj* escocés ‖ *s* (*dialect*) escocés *m;* **the Scottish** los escoceses
**scoundrel** ['skaʊndrəl] *s* bribón *m*, pícaro
**scour** [skaʊr] *tr* fregar, estregar; recorrer, explorar detenidamente
**scourge** [skʌrdʒ] *s* azote *m* ‖ *tr* azotar
**scout** [skaʊt] *s* (mil) escucha, explorador *m;* niño explorador, niña exploradora; exploración, reconocimiento; (slang) individuo, sujeto, tipo ‖ *tr* explorar, reconocer (*un territorio*); observar (*al enemigo*); negarse a creer
**scout'mas'ter** *s* jefe *m* de tropa de niños exploradores
**scowl** [skaʊl] *s* ceño, semblante ceñudo ‖ *intr* mirar con ceño, poner mal gesto, poner mala cara
**scramble** ['skræmbəl] *s* arrebatiña ‖ *tr* arrebatar; recoger de prisa; revolver; hacer un revoltillo de (*huevos*); trepar ‖ *intr* luchar; trepar
**scrambled eggs** *spl* revoltillo, huevos revueltos
**scrap** [skræp] *s* fragmento, pedacito; desecho; chatarra; (slang) riña, contienda; **scraps** desperdicios, desechos; (*from the table*) sobras ‖ *v* (*pret & pp* **scrapped;** *ger* **scrapping**) *tr* desechar, descartar, echar a la basura; reducir a hierro viejo ‖ *intr* (slang) reñir, pelear
**scrap'book'** *s* álbum *m* de recortes, libro de recuerdos
**scrape** [skrep] *s* raspadura; (*place scratched*) raspazo; aprieto, enredo; ‖ *tr* raspar; (*to gather together with much difficulty*) arañar ‖ *intr* raspar; **to scrape along** ir tirando; **to scrape through** aprobar justo
**scrap heap** *s* montón *m* de cachivaches
**scrap iron** *s* chatarra, desecho de hierro
**scrap paper** *s* papel *m* para apuntes; papel de desecho
**scratch** [skrætʃ] *s* arañazo, rasguño; marca, raya, garrapato; (billiards) chiripa; (sport) línea de partida; **to start from scratch** empezar desde el principio; **up to scratch** en buena condición ‖ *tr* arañar, rasguñar; borrar, rasgar (*lo escrito*); garrapatear; (sport) borrar (*a un corredor o caballo*) ‖ *intr* arañar, rasguñar; garrapatear; raspear (*una pluma*)
**scratch pad** *s* cuadernillo de apuntes
**scratch paper** *s* papel *m* para apuntes
**scrawl** [skrɔl] *s* garrapatos ‖ *tr & intr* garrapatear
**scraw·ny** ['skrɔni] *adj* (*comp* **-nier;** *super* **-niest**) huesudo, flaco
**scream** [skrim] *s* chillido, grito ‖ *tr* vociferar ‖ *intr* chillar, gritar; reírse a gritos
**screech** [skritʃ] *s* chillido ‖ *intr* chillar
**screech owl** *s* buharro; (*barn owl*) lechuza
**screen** [skrin] *s* mampara, biombo; (*in front of chimney*) pantalla; (*to keep flies out*) alambrera; (*to sift sand*) tamiz *m;* (mov, phys, telv) pantalla; **to put on the screen** llevar a la pantalla, llevar al celuloide ‖ *tr* defender, proteger; cubrir, ocultar; cinematografiar; rodar, proyectar (*una película*); adaptar para el cine; tamizar (*p.ej., arena*)

**screen grid** *s* (electron) rejilla blindada
**screen'play'** *s* cinedrama *m*
**screw** [skru] *s* tornillo; (*internal or female screw*) rosca, tuerca; (*of a boat*) hélice *f*; **to have a screw loose** (slang) tener flojos los tornillos; **to put the screws on** apretar los tornillos a ‖ *tr* atornillar; (*to twist, twist in*) enroscar; **to screw up** torcer (*el rostro*); ‖ *intr* atornillarse
**screw'ball'** *s* (slang) estrafalario, excéntrico
**screw'driv'er** *s* destornillador *m*
**screw eye** *s* armella
**screw jack** *s* gato de tornillo
**screw propeller** *s* hélice *f*
**scribal error** ['skraɪbəl] *s* error *m* de escribiente
**scribble** ['skrɪbəl] *s* garrapatos ‖ *tr & intr* garrapatear
**scribe** [skraɪb] *s* (*teacher of Jewish law*) escriba *m*; escribiente *mf*; copista *mf*; autor *m*, escritor *m* ‖ *tr* arañar, rayar; trazar con punzón
**scrimp** [skrɪmp] *tr & intr* escatimar
**script** [skrɪpt] *s* escritura, letra cursiva; manuscrito, texto; (*of a play, movie, etc.*) palabras; (rad, telv) guión *m*; (typ) plumilla inglesa
**scripture** ['skrɪptʃər] *s* escrito sagrado ‖ **Scripture** *s* Escritura
**script'writ'er** *s* guionista *mf*, cinematurgo
**scrofula** ['skrɑfjələ] *s* escrófula
**scroll** [skrol] *s* rollo de papel, rollo de pergamino; (archit) voluta
**scroll'work'** *s* obra de volutas, adornos de voluta
**scrub** [skrʌb] *s* chaparral *m*, monte bajo; animal achaparrado; persona de poca monta; (*act of scrubbing*) fregado; (sport) jugador *m* no oficial ‖ *v* (*pret & pp* **scrubbed**; *ger* **scrubbing**) *tr* fregar, restregar
**scrub oak** *s* chaparro
**scrub woman** *s* fregona
**scruff** [skrʌf] *s* nuca; piel *f* que cubre la nuca; capa, superficie *f*; espuma
**scruple** ['skrupəl] *s* escrúpulo
**scrupulous** ['skrupjələs] *adj* escrupuloso
**scrutinize** ['skrutɪ,naɪz] *tr* escudriñar, escrutar
**scruti•ny** ['skrutɪni] *s* (*pl* **-nies**) escudriñamiento, escrutinio
**scuff** [skʌf] *s* rascadura, desgaste *m* ‖ *tr* rascar, desgastar
**scuffle** ['skʌfəl] *s* lucha, sarracina ‖ *intr* forcejear, luchar
**scull** [skʌl] *s* espadilla ‖ *tr* impulsar con espadilla ‖ *intr* remar con espadilla
**sculler•y** ['skʌləri] *s* (*pl* **-ies**) trascocina
**scullery maid** *s* fregona
**scullion** ['skʌljən] *s* pinche *m*
**sculptor** ['skʌlptər] *s* escultor *m*
**sculptress** ['skʌlptrɪs] *s* escultora
**sculpture** ['skʌlptʃər] *s* escultura ‖ *tr & intr* esculpir
**scum** [skʌm] *s* espuma, nata; (*on metals*) escoria; (fig) escoria, canalla, gente baja ‖ *v* (*pret & pp* **scummed**; *ger* **scumming**) *tr & intr* espumar
**scum•my** ['skʌmi] *adj* (*comp* **-mier**; *super* **-miest**) espumoso; (fig) vil, ruin
**scurf** [skʌrf] *s* (*shed by the skin*) caspa; (*shed by any surface*) costra
**scurrilous** ['skʌrɪləs] *adj* chocarrero, grosero, insolente, difamatorio
**scur•ry** ['skʌri] *v* (*pret & pp* **-ried**) *intr* echar a correr, escabullirse; **to scurry around** menearse; **to scurry away** ir respailando
**scur•vy** ['skʌrvi] *adj* (*comp* **-vier**; *super* **-viest**) despreciable, ruin, vil ‖ *s* escorbuto
**scuttle** ['skʌtəl] *s* (*bucket for coal*) cubo, balde *m*; (*trap door*) escotillón *m*; fuga, paso acelerado; (naut) escotilla ‖ *tr* barrenar, dar barreno a ‖ *intr* echar a correr
**Scylla** ['sɪlə] *s* Escila; **between Scylla and Charybdis** entre Escila y Caribdis
**scythe** [saɪð] *s* dalle *m*, guadaña
**sea** [si] *s* mar *m & f*; **at sea** en el mar; confuso, perplejo; **by the sea** a la orilla del mar; **to follow the sea** correr los mares, ser marinero; **to put to sea** hacerse a la mar
**sea'board'** *adj* costanero, costero ‖ *s* costa del mar, litoral *m*
**sea breeze** *s* brisa de mar
**sea'coast'** *s* costa marítima, litoral *m*
**sea dog** *s* (*seal*) foca; (coll) marinero viejo, lobo de mar
**seafarer** ['si,ferər] *s* marinero; viajero por mar
**sea'food'** *s* mariscos
**seagoing** ['si,go•ɪŋ] *adj* de alta mar
**sea gull** *s* gaviota
**seal** [sil] *s* (*raised design; stamp; mark*) sello; (*sea animal*) foca ‖ *tr* sellar; cerrar herméticamente; decidir irrevocablemente; (*with sealing wax*) lacrar
**sea legs** *spl* pie marino
**sea level** *s* nivel *m* del mar
**sealing wax** *s* lacre *m*
**seal'skin'** *s* piel *f* de foca
**seam** [sim] *s* costura; (*edges left after making a seam*) metido; (*mark, line*) arruga; (*scar*) costurón *m*; grieta, juntura; (min) filón *m*, veta
**sea•man** ['simən] *s* (*pl* **-men** [mən]) marinero; (nav) marino
**sea mile** *s* milla náutica
**seamless** ['simlɪs] *adj* inconsútil, sin costura
**seamstress** ['simstrɪs] *s* costurera; (*dressmaker's helper*) modistilla
**seam•y** ['simi] *adj* (*comp* **-ier**; *super* **-iest**) lleno de costuras; tosco, burdo; vil, soez; miserable
**séance** ['se•ɑns] *s* sesión de espiritistas
**sea'plane'** *s* hidroavión *m*, hidroplano
**sea'port'** *s* puerto de mar
**sea power** *s* potencia naval
**sear** [sɪr] *adj* seco, marchito; gastado, raído ‖ *s* chamusco, socarra ‖ *tr* chamuscar, socarrar; quemar; marchitar; cauterizar
**search** [sʌrtʃ] *s* busca; pesquisa, in-

dagación; (*frisking a person*) cacheo; **in search of** en busca de || *tr* averiguar, explorar; registrar || *intr* buscar; **to search for** buscar; **to search into** indagar, investigar
**search'light'** *s* reflector *m*, proyector *m*
**search warrant** *s* auto de registro domiciliario, orden *f* de allanamiento
**sea'scape'** *s* vista del mar; (*painting*) marina
**sea shell** *s* concha marina
**sea'shore'** *s* costa, playa, ribera del mar
**sea'sick'** *adj* mareado
**sea'sick'ness** *s* mareo
**sea'side'** *s* orilla del mar, ribera del mar, playa
**season** ['sizən] *s* (*one of four parts of year*) estación; (*period of the year; period marked by certain activities*) temporada; (*opportune time; time of maturity, of ripening*) sazón *f*; **in season** en sazón; **in season and out of season** en tiempo y a destiempo; **out of season** fuera de sazón || *tr* condimentar, sazonar; curar (*la madera*); moderar, templar
**seasonal** ['sizənəl] *adj* estacional
**seasoning** ['sizənɪŋ] *s* aderezo, aliño, condimento; (*of wood*) cura; (fig) sal *f*, chiste *m*
**season ticket** *s* billete *m* de abono
**seat** [sit] *s* asiento; (*of trousers*) fondillos; morada; sitio, lugar *m*; (*e.g., of government*) sede *f*; (*in parliament*) escaño; (*e.g., of a war*) teatro; (*e.g., of learning*) centro; (*of a saddle*) batalla; (*of human body*) nalgas; (theat) localidad || *tr* sentar; tener asientos para; poner asiento a (*una silla*); echar fondillos a (*pantalones*); arraigar, establecer; **to be seated** estar sentado; **to seat oneself** sentarse
**seat belt** *s* cinturón *m* de asiento
**seat cover** *s* funda de asiento, cubreasiento
**SEATO** ['sito] *s* (acronym) la O.T.A.S.E.
**sea wall** *s* dique marítimo
**sea'way'** *s* ruta marítima; avance *m* de un buque por mar; vía de agua interior para buques de alta mar; mar gruesa
**sea'weed'** *s* alga marina; plantas marinas
**sea wind** *s* viento que sopla del mar
**sea'wor'thy** *adj* marinero, en condiciones de navegar
**sec.** *abbr* **secant, second, secondary, secretary, section, sector**
**secede** [sɪ'sid] *intr* separarse, retirarse
**secession** [sɪ'sɛʃən] *s* secesión
**seclude** [sɪ'klud] *tr* recluir
**secluded** [sɪ'kludɪd] *adj* aislado, apartado, solitario
**seclusion** [sɪ'kluʒən] *s* reclusión, soledad
**second** ['sɛkənd] *adj* segundo; **to be second to none** ser tan bueno como el que más, no tener segundo || *adv* en segundo lugar || *s* segundo; artículo de segunda calidad; (*in dates*) dos *m*; (*in a challenge*) padrino; (aut) segunda (velocidad); (mus) segunda || *tr* secundar; apoyar (*una moción*)
**secondar•y** ['sɛkən,deri] *adj* secundario || *s* (*pl* **-ies**) (elec) secundario
**sec'ond-best'** *adj* (el) mejor después del primero
**sec'ond-class'** *adj* de segunda clase
**second hand** *s* segundero
**sec'ond-hand'** *adj* de segunda mano, de ocasión
**second-hand bookshop** *s* librería de viejo
**second lieutenant** *s* alférez *m*, subteniente *m*
**sec'ond-rate'** *adj* de segundo orden; de calidad inferior
**second sight** *s* doble vista
**second wind** *s* nuevo aliento
**secre•cy** ['sikrəsi] *s* (*pl* **-cies**) secreto; **in secrecy** en secreto
**secret** ['sikrɪt] *adj* & *s* secreto; **in secret** en secreto
**secretar•y** ['sɛkrɪ,teri] *s* (*pl* **-ies**) secretario; (*desk*) secreter *m*, escritorio
**secrete** [sɪ'krit] *tr* encubrir, esconder; (physiol) secretar
**secretive** [sɪ'kritɪv] *adj* callado, reservado
**sect** [sɛkt] *s* secta, comunión
**sectarian** [sɛk'terɪ•ən] *adj* & *s* sectario
**section** ['sɛkʃən] *s* sección; (*of a country*) región; (*of a city*) barrio; (*of a law*) artículo; (*department, bureau*) negociado; (rr) tramo
**secular** ['sɛkjələr] *adj* secular, seglar || *s* clérigo secular
**secularism** ['sɛkjələ,rɪzəm] *s* laicismo
**secure** [sɪ'kjʊr] *adj* seguro || *tr* asegurar; conseguir, obtener
**securi•ty** [sɪ'kjʊrɪti] *s* (*pl* **-ties**) seguridad; (*person*) segurador *m*; **securities** valores *mpl*, obligaciones, títulos
**secy.** o **sec'y.** *abbr* **secretary**
**sedan** [sɪ'dæn] *s* silla de manos; (aut) sedán *m*
**sedate** [sɪ'det] *adj* sentado, sosegado
**sedative** ['sɛdətɪv] *adj* & *s* sedativo
**sedentary** ['sɛdən,teri] *adj* sedentario
**sedge** [sɛdʒ] *s* juncia
**sediment** ['sɛdɪmənt] *s* sedimento
**sedition** [sɪ'dɪʃən] *s* sedición
**seditious** [sɪ'dɪʃəs] *adj* sedicioso
**seduce** [sɪ'djus] o [sɪ'dus] *tr* seducir
**seducer** [sɪ'djusər] o [sɪ'dusər] *s* seductor *m*
**seduction** [sɪ'dʌkʃən] *s* seducción
**seductive** [sɪ'dʌktɪv] *adj* seductivo
**sedulous** ['sɛdjələs] *adj* cuidadoso, diligente
**see** [si] *s* (eccl) sede *f* || *v* (*pret* **saw** [sɔ]; *pp* **seen** [sin]) *tr* ver; **to see off** ir a despedir; **to see through** llevar a cabo; ayudar en un trance difícil || *intr* ver; **see here!** ¡mire Vd.!; **to see into** o **to see through** conocer el juego de
**seed** [sid] *s* semilla, simiente *f*; **to go to seed** dar semilla; echarse a perder || *tr* sembrar; (*to remove the seeds from*) despepitar || *intr* sembrar; dejar caer semillas
**seed'bed'** *s* semillero

**seedling** ['sidlɪŋ] *s* planta de semilla; árbol *m* de pie
**seed•y** ['sidi] *adj* (*comp* **-ier;** *super* **-iest**) lleno de granos; (coll) andrajoso, raído
**seeing** ['si•ɪŋ] *adj* vidente || *s* vista, visión || *conj* visto que
**Seeing Eye dog** *s* perro-lazarillo
**seek** [sik] *v* (*pret & pp* **sought** [sɔt]) *tr* buscar; recorrer buscando; dirigirse a || *intr* buscar; **to seek after** tratar de obtener; **to seek to** esforzarse por
**seem** [sim] *intr* parecer
**seemingly** ['simɪŋli] *adv* aparentemente, al parecer
**seem•ly** ['simli] *adj* (*comp* **-lier;** *super* **-liest**) decente, decoroso, correcto; bien parecido
**seep** [sip] *intr* escurrirse, rezumarse
**seer** [sɪr] *s* profeta *m*, vidente *m*
**see'saw'** *s* balancín *m*, columpio de tabla; (*motion*) vaivén *m* || *intr* columpiarse; alternar; vacilar
**seethe** [sið] *intr* hervir
**segment** ['sɛgmənt] *s* segmento
**segregate** ['sɛgrɪ,get] *tr* segregar
**segregationist** [,sɛgrɪ'geʃənɪst] *s* segregacionista *mf*
**Seine** [sen] *s* Sena *m*
**seismograph** ['saɪzmə,græf] o ['saɪzme,grɑf] *s* sismógrafo
**seismology** [saɪz'mɑlədʒi] *s* sismología
**seize** [siz] *tr* agarrar, asir, coger; atar, prender, sujetar; apoderarse de; comprender; (law) embargar, secuestrar; aprovecharse de (*una oportunidad*)
**seizure** ['siʒər] *s* prendimiento, prisión; captura, toma; (*of an illness*) ataque *m;* (law) embargo, secuestro
**seldom** ['sɛldəm] *adv* raramente, rara vez
**select** [sɪ'lɛkt] *adj* escogido, selecto || *tr* seleccionar
**selectee** [sɪ,lɛk'ti] *s* (mil) quinto
**selection** [sɪ'lɛkʃən] *s* selección; trozo escogido; (*of goods for sale*) surtido
**self** [sɛlf] *adj* mismo || *pron* sí mismo || *s* (*pl* **selves** [sɛlvz]) uno mismo; ser *m;* yo; **all by one's self** sin ayuda de nadie
**self'-abuse'** *s* abuso de sí mismo; masturbación
**self'-addressed' envelope** *s* sobre *m* con el nombre y dirección del remitente
**self'-cen'tered** *adj* egocéntrico
**self'-con'scious** *adj* cohibido, apocado, tímido
**self'-con•trol'** *s* dominio de sí mismo
**self'-de•fense'** *s* autodefensa; **in self-defense** en defensa propia
**self'-de•ni'al** *s* abnegación
**self'-de•ter'mi•na'tion** *s* autodeterminación
**self'-dis'cipline** *s* autodisciplina
**self'-ed'u•cat'ed** *adj* autodidacto
**self'-em•ployed'** *adj* que trabaja por su propia cuenta
**self'-ev'i•dent** *adj* patente, manifiesto
**self'-ex•plan'a•tor'y** *adj* que se explica por sí mismo
**self'-gov'ernment** *s* autogobierno, autonomía; dominio sobre sí mismo
**self'-im•por'tant** *adj* altivo, arrogante
**self'-in•dul'gence** *s* intemperancia, desenfreno
**self'-in'terest** *s* egoísmo, interés *m* personal
**selfish** ['sɛlfɪʃ] *adj* egoísta
**selfishness** ['sɛlfɪʃnɪs] *s* egoísmo
**selfless** ['sɛlflɪs] *adj* desinteresado
**self'-liq'ui•dat'ing** *adj* autoamortizable
**self'-love'** *s* amor propio, egoísmo
**self'-made' man** *s* hijo de sus propias obras
**self'-por'trait** *s* autorretrato
**self'-pos•sessed'** *adj* dueño de sí mismo
**self'-pres'er•va'tion** *s* propia conservación
**self'-re•li'ant** *adj* confiado en sí mismo
**self'-re•spect'ing** *adj* lleno de dignidad, decoroso
**self'-right'eous** *adj* santurrón
**self'-sac'ri•fice'** *s* sacrificio de sí mismo
**self'same'** *adj* mismísimo
**self'-sat'is•fied'** *adj* pagado de sí mismo
**self'-seek'ing** *adj* egoísta || *s* egoísmo
**self'-ser'vice restaurant** *s* restaurante *m* de libre servicio, restaurante de autoservicio
**self'-start'er** *s* arranque automático
**self'sup•port'** *s* mantenimiento económico propio
**self'-taught'** *adj* autodidacto
**self'-willed'** *adj* obstinado, terco
**self'-wind'ing clock** *s* reloj *m* de cuerda automática, reloj de autocuerda
**sell** [sɛl] *v* (*pret & pp* **sold** [sold]) *tr* vender; **to sell out** realizar, saldar; (*to betray*) vender || *intr* venderse, estar de venta; **to sell for** venderse a o en (*p.ej., cien pesetas*); **to sell off** bajar (*el mercado de valores*); **to sell out** venderlo todo, realizar
**seller** ['sɛlər] *s* vendedor *m*
**sell'out'** *s* (slang) realización, saldo; (slang) traición
**Seltzer water** ['sɛltsər] *s* agua de seltz
**selvage** ['sɛlvɪdʒ] *s* orillo, vendo
**semantic** [sɪ'mæntɪk] *adj* semántico || **semantics** *s* semántica
**semaphore** ['sɛmə,for] *s* semáforo; (rr) disco de señales
**semblance** ['sɛmbləns] *s* apariencia, imagen *f*, simulacro
**semen** ['simen] *s* semen *m*
**semester** [sɪ'mɛstər] *adj* semestral || *s* semestre *m*
**semester hour** *s* hora semestral
**sem'ico'lon** *s* punto y coma
**sem'iconduc'tor** *s* semiconductor *m*
**sem'icon'scious** *adj* semiconsciente
**sem'ifi'nal** *adj & s* (sport) semifinal *f*
**sem'ilearn'ed** *adj* semiculto
**sem'imonth'ly** *adj* quincenal || *s* (*pl* **-lies**) periódico quincenal
**seminar** ['sɛmɪ,nɑr] o [,sɛmɪ'nɑr] *s* seminario
**seminar•y** ['sɛmɪ,neri] *s* (*pl* **-ies**) seminario
**sem'ipre'cious** *adj* semiprecioso, fino
**Semite** ['sɛmaɪt] o ['simaɪt] *s* semita *mf*

**Semitic** [sɪ'mɪtɪk] *adj* semítico ‖ *s* semita *mf;* (*language*) semita *m*
**sem'itrail'er** *s* semi-remolque *m*
**sem'iweek'ly** *adj* bisemanal ‖ *s* (*pl* **-lies**) periódico bisemanal
**sem'iyear'ly** *adj* semestral
**Sen.** o **sen.** *abbr* **Senate, Senator, Senior**
**senate** ['sɛnɪt] *s* senado
**senator** ['sɛnətər] *s* senador *m*
**senatorship** ['sɛnətər,ʃɪp] *s* senaduría
**send** [sɛnd] *v* (*pret & pp* **sent** [sɛnt]) *tr* enviar, mandar; expedir, remitir; lanzar (*una bola, flecha, etc.*); **to send back** devolver, reenviar; **to send packing** despedir con cajas destempladas ‖ *intr* (rad) transmitir; **to send for** enviar por, enviar a buscar
**sender** ['sɛndər] *s* remitente *mf;* (telg) transmisor *m*
**send'-off'** *s* (coll) despedida afectuosa
**senile** ['sinaɪl] o ['sinɪl] *adj* senil
**senility** [sɪ'nɪlɪti] *s* senilidad; (pathol) senilismo
**senior** ['sinjər] *adj* mayor, de mayor edad; viejo; del último año; padre, p.ej., **John Jones, Senior** Juan Jones, padre ‖ *s* mayor *m;* socio más antiguo; alumno del último año
**senior citizens** *spl* gente *f* de edad
**seniority** [sin'jɑrɪti] o [sin'jɔrɪti] *s* antigüedad; precedencia, prioridad
**sensation** [sɛn'seʃən] *s* sensación
**sense** [sɛns] *s* sentido; **to make sense out of** comprender, explicarse ‖ *tr* intuir, sentir, sospechar; (coll) comprender
**senseless** ['sɛnslɪs] *adj* falto de sentido; desmayado; insensato, necio
**sense of guilt** *s* cargo de conciencia
**sense organ** *s* órgano sensorio
**sensibili•ty** [,sɛnsɪ'bɪlɪti] *s* (*pl* **-ties**) sensibilidad; **sensibilities** sentimientos delicados
**sensible** ['sɛnsɪbəl] *adj* cuerdo, sensato; perceptible, sensible
**sensitive** ['sɛnsɪtɪv] *adj* sensible; (*of the senses*) sensorio, sensitivo
**sensitize** ['sɛnsɪ,taɪz] *tr* sensibilizar
**sensory** ['sɛnsəri] *adj* sensorio
**sensual** ['sɛnʃʊ•əl] *adj* sensual, voluptuoso
**sensuous** ['sɛnʃʊ•əs] *adj* sensual
**sentence** ['sɛntəns] *s* (gram) frase *f,* oración; (law) sentencia ‖ *tr* sentenciar, condenar
**sentiment** ['sɛntɪmənt] *s* sentimiento
**sentimentali•ty** [,sɛntɪmen'tælɪti] *s* (*pl* **-ties**) sentimentalismo
**sentinel** ['sɛntɪnəl] *s* centinela *m* or *f;* **to stand sentinel** estar de centinela, hacer centinela
**sen•try** ['sɛntri] *s* (*pl* **-tries**) centinela *m* or *f*
**sentry box** *s* garita de centinela
**separate** ['sɛpərɪt] *adj* separado; suelto ‖ ['sɛpə,ret] *tr* separar ‖ *intr* separarse
**Sephardic** [sɪ'fɑrdɪk] *adj* sefardí, sefardita
**Sephardim** [sɪ'fɑrdɪm] *spl* sefardíes *mpl*
**September** [sɛp•tɛmbər] *s* septiembre *m*
**septet** [sɛp'tɛt] *s* septeto
**septic** ['sɛptɪk] *adj* séptico
**sepulcher** ['sɛpəlkər] *s* sepulcro
**seq.** *abbr* **sequentia** (Lat) **the following**
**sequel** ['sikwəl] *s* resultado, secuela; continuación
**sequence** ['sikwəns] *s* serie *f,* sucesión; (cards) secansa, escalera, runfla; (gram, mov & mus) secuencia
**sequester** [sɪ'kwɛstər] *tr* apartar, separar; (law) secuestrar
**sequin** ['sikwɪn] *s* lentejuela
**ser•aph** ['sɛrəf] *s* (*pl* **-aphs** o **-aphim** [əfɪm]) serafín *m*
**Serb** [sʌrb] *adj & s* servio
**Serbia** ['sʌrbɪ•ə] *s* Servia
**Serbian** ['sʌrbɪ•ən] *adj & s* servio
**Serbo-Croatian** [,sʌrbokro'eʃən] *adj & s* servocroata *mf*
**sere** [sɪr] *adj* seco, marchito
**serenade** [,sɛrə'ned] *s* serenata ‖ *tr* dar serenata a ‖ *intr* dar serenatas
**serene** [sɪ'rin] *adj* sereno
**serenity** [sɪ'rɛnɪti] *s* serenidad
**serf** [sʌrf] *s* siervo de la gleba
**serfdom** ['sʌrfdəm] *s* servidumbre de la gleba
**serge** [sʌrdʒ] *s* sarga
**sergeant** ['sɑrdʒənt] *s* sargento
**ser'geant-at-arms'** *s* (*pl* **sergeants-at-arms**) oficial *m* de orden
**sergeant major** *s* (*pl* **sergeant majors**) sargento mayor
**serial** ['sɪrɪ•əl] *adj* serial; publicado por entregas ‖ *s* cuento o novela por entregas; (rad) serial *m,* serial radiado, emisión seriada
**serially** ['sɪrɪ•əli] *adv* en serie, por series; por entregas
**serial number** *s* número de serie
**se•ries** ['sɪriz] *s* (*pl* **-ries**) serie *f*
**serious** ['sɪrɪ•əs] *adj* (*e.g., person, face, matter*) serio; (*e.g., condition, illness*) grave
**sermon** ['sʌrmən] *s* sermón *m*
**sermonize** ['sʌrmə,naɪz] *tr & intr* sermonear
**serpent** ['sʌrpənt] *s* serpiente *f*
**se•rum** ['sɪrəm] *s* (*pl* **-rums** o **-ra** [rə]) suero
**servant** ['sʌrvənt] *s* criado, sirviente *m*
**servant girl** *s* criada, sirvienta
**servant problem** *s* crisis *f* del servicio doméstico
**serve** [sʌrv] *s* (*in tennis*) saque *m,* servicio ‖ *tr* servir; (*to supply*) abastecer, proporcionar; cumplir (*una condena*); (*in tennis*) servir; **it serves me right** bien me lo merezco ‖ *intr* servir; **to serve as** servir de
**service** ['sʌrvɪs] *s* servicio; **at your service** para servir a Vd.; **the services** las fuerzas armadas ‖ *tr* instalar; mantener, reparar
**serviceable** ['sʌrvɪsəbəl] *adj* útil; duradero; cómodo
**service•man** ['sʌrvɪs,mæn] *s* (*pl* **-men** [,mɛn]) reparador *m,* mecánico; militar *m*
**service record** *s* hoja de servicios

**service station** *s* estación de servicio, taller *m* de reparaciones
**service stripe** *s* galón *m* de servicio
**servile** ['sʌrvɪl] *adj* servil
**servitude** ['sʌrvɪ,tjud] o ['sʌrvɪ,tud] *s* servidumbre; trabajos forzados
**sesame** ['sesəmi] *s* sésamo; **open sesame** sésamo ábrete
**session** ['sɛʃən] *s* sesión; **to be in session** sesionar
**set** [set] *adj* determinado, resuelto; inflexible, obstinado; fijo, firme; estudiado, meditado ‖ *s* (*of books, chairs, etc.*) juego; (*of gears*) tren *m;* (*of horses*) pareja; (*of diamonds*) aderezo; (*of tennis*) partida; (*of dishes*) servicio; (*of kitchen utensils*) batería; clase *f*, grupo; equipo; porte *m*, postura; (*of a garment*) caída, ajuste *m;* (*of glue*) endurecimiento; (*of cement*) fraguado; (*of artificial teeth*) caja; (mov) plató *m;* (rad) aparato; (theat) decoración ‖ *v* (*pret & pp* **set**; *ger* **setting**) *tr* asentar; colocar, poner; establecer, instalar; arreglar, preparar; adornar; apostar; poner (*un reloj*) en hora; (*in bridge*) reenvidar; poner, meter, pegar (*fuego*); fijar (*el precio*); engastar, montar (*una piedra preciosa*); encasar (*un hueso dislocado*); disponer (*los tipos*); triscar (*una sierra*); armar, colocar (*una trampa*); fijar (*el peinado*); poner (*la mesa*); dar (*un ejemplo*); **to set back** parar; poner obstáculos a; hacer retroceder; atrasar, retrasar (*el reloj*); **to set forth** exponer, dar a conocer; **to set one's heart on** tener la esperanza puesta en; **to set store by** dar mucha importancia a; **to set up shop** poner tienda; **to set up the drinks** (coll) convidar a beber ‖ *intr* ponerse (*el Sol, la Luna, etc.*); cuajarse (*un líquido*); endurecerse (*la cola*); fraguar (*el cemento, el yeso*); empollar (*una gallina*); caer, sentar (*una prenda de vestir*); **to set about** ponerse a; **to set out** ponerse en camino; emprender un negocio; **to set out to** ponerse a; **to set to work** poner manos a la obra; **to set upon** acometer, atacar
**set'back'** *s* revés *m*, contrariedad
**set'screw'** *s* tornillo de presión
**settee** [sɛ'ti] *s* sofá *m*, canapé *m*
**setting** ['setɪŋ] *s* (*environment*) ambiente *m;* (*of a gem*) engaste *m*, montadura; (*of cement*) fraguado; (*e.g., of the sun*) puesta, ocaso; (theat) escena; (theat) puesta en escena, decoración
**set'ting-up' exercises** *spl* ejercicios sin aparatos, gimnasia sueca
**settle** ['setəl] *tr* asentar, colocar; asegurar, fijar; componer, conciliar; calmar, moderar; matar (*el polvo*); casar; poblar, colonizar; ajustar, arreglar (*cuentas*) ‖ *intr* asentarse (*un líquido, un edificio*); establecerse; componerse; calmarse, moderarse; solidificarse; **to settle down to work** ponerse seriamente a trabajar; **to settle on** escoger; fijar (*p.ej., una fecha*)
**settlement** ['setəlmənt] *s* establecimiento; colonia, caserío; decisión; (*of accounts*) arreglo, ajuste *m;* traspaso; casa de beneficencia
**settler** ['setlər] *s* fundador *m;* poblador *m;* colono; árbitro, conciliador *m*
**set'up'** *s* porte *m*, postura; (*e.g., of the parts of a machine*) disposición; (coll) organización; (slang) invitación a beber
**seven** ['sɛvən] *adj & pron* siete ‖ *s* siete *m;* **seven o'clock** las siete
**seven hundred** *adj & pron* setecientos ‖ *s* setecientos *m*
**seventeen** ['sɛvən'tin] *adj, pron & s* diecisiete *m*, diez y siete
**seventeenth** ['sɛvən'tinθ] *adj & s* (*in a series*) decimoséptimo; (*part*) diecisieteavo ‖ *s* (*in dates*) diecisiete *m*
**seventh** ['sevənθ] *adj & s* séptimo ‖ *s* (*in dates*) siete *m*
**seventieth** ['sevəntɪ·ɪθ] *adj & s* (*in a series*) septuagésimo; (*part*) setentavo
**seven·ty** ['sevənti] *adj & pron* setenta ‖ *s* (*pl* **-ties**) setenta *m*
**sever** ['sevər] *tr* desunir, separar; romper (*relaciones*) ‖ *intr* desunirse, separarse
**several** ['sevərəl] *adj* diversos, varios; distintos, respectivos ‖ *spl* varios; algunos
**severance pay** ['sevərəns] *s* indemnización por despido
**severe** [sɪ'vɪr] *adj* severo; (*weather*) riguroso; recio, violento; (*look*) adusto; (*pain*) agudo; (*illness*) grave
**sew** [so] *v* (*pret* **sewed**; *pp* **sewed** o **sewn**) *tr & intr* coser
**sewage** ['su·ɪdʒ] o ['sju·ɪdʒ] *s* agua de albañal, aguas cloacales
**sewer** ['su·ər] o ['sju·ər] *s* albañal *m*, cloaca, alcantarilla ‖ *tr* alcantarillar
**sewerage** ['su·ərɪdʒ] o ['sju·ərɪdʒ] *s* desagüe *m;* (*system*) alcantarillado; aguas de albañal
**sewing basket** ['so·ɪŋ] *s* cesta de costura
**sewing machine** *s* máquina de coser
**sex** [seks] *s* sexo; **the fair sex** el bello sexo; **the sterner sex** el sexo feo
**sex appeal** *s* atracción sexual; encanto femenino
**sextant** ['sekstənt] *s* sextante *m*
**sextet** [seks'tet] *s* sexteto
**sexton** ['sekstən] *s* sacristán *m*
**sexual** ['sɛkʃʊ·əl] *adj* sexual
**sex·y** ['seksi] *adj* (*comp* **-ier**; *super* **-iest**) (slang) sicalíptico, erótico
**shab·by** ['ʃæbi] *adj* (*comp* **-bier**; *super* **-biest**) gastado, raído, usado; andrajoso, desaseado; ruin, vil
**shack** [ʃæk] *s* casucha, choza
**shackle** ['ʃækəl] *s* grillete *m;* (*to tie an animal*) maniota; (fig) impedimento, traba; **shackles** cadenas, esposas, grillos ‖ *tr* poner grilletes a, poner esposas a; encadenar; (fig) trabar
**shad** [ʃæd] *s* sábalo, alosa
**shade** [ʃed] *s* sombra; (*of a lamp*)

pantalla; (*of a window*) cortina, estor *m*, visillo, cortina de resorte; (*for the eyes*) visera; (*hue; slight difference*) matiz *m*; **the shades** las tinieblas; (*of the dead*) las sombras || *tr* sombrear; obscurecer; rebajar ligeramente (*el precio*)

**shadow** [ˈʃædo] *s* sombra || *tr* sombrear; simbolizar; acechar, espiar (*a una persona*); **to shadow forth** representar vagamente, representar de un modo profético

**shadowy** [ˈʃædo·i] *adj* sombroso; ligero, vago; imaginario; simbólico

**shad·y** [ˈʃedi] *adj* (*comp* **-ier**; *super* **-iest**) sombrío, umbroso; (coll) sospechoso; (coll) de mala fama; (*story*) (coll) verde; **to keep shady** (slang) no dejarse ver

**shaft** [ʃæft] o [ʃɑft] *s* dardo, flecha, saeta; (*of an arrow; of a feather*) astil *m*; (*of light*) rayo; (*of a wagon*) vara alcándara, limonera; (*of a mine; of an elevator*) pozo; (*of a column*) fuste *m*, caña; (*of a flag*) asta; (*of a motor*) árbol *m*; (*to make fun of someone*) dardo

**shag·gy** [ˈʃægi] *adj* (*comp* **-gier**; *super* **-giest**) hirsuto, peludo, veludo; lanudo; áspero

**shake** [ʃek] *s* sacudida; (coll) apretón *m* de manos; (slang) instante *m*, momento || *v* (*pret* **shook** [ʃʊk]; *pp* **shaken**) *tr* sacudir; agitar; apretar, estrechar (*la mano a uno*); inquietar, perturbar; (*to get rid of*) (slang) dar esquinazo a, zafarse de || *intr* sacudirse; agitarse; temblar; inquietarse, perturbarse; (*from cold*) tiritar; **shake!** (coll) ¡choque Vd. esos cinco!, ¡vengan esos cinco!

**shake′down′** *s* (slang) exacción, concusión

**shake′-up′** *s* profunda conmoción; cambio de personal, reorganización completa

**shak·y** [ˈʃeki] *adj* (*comp* **-ier**; *super* **-iest**) trémulo, vacilante, movedizo; indigno de confianza

**shall** [ʃæl] *v* (*cond* **should** [ʃʊd]) *v aux* empléase para formar (1) el fut de ind, p.ej., **I shall do it** lo haré; (2) el fut perf de ind, p.ej., **I shall have done it** lo habré hecho; (3) el modo potencial, p.ej., **what shall I do?** ¿qué he de hacer?, ¿qué debo hacer?

**shallow** [ˈʃælo] *adj* bajo, poco profundo; (fig) frívolo, superficial

**sham** [ʃæm] *adj* falso, fingido; postizo || *s* fingimiento, falsificación, engaño; (*person*) (coll) farsante *mf* || *v* (*pret & pp* **shammed**; *ger* **shamming**) *tr & intr* fingir

**sham battle** *s* simulacro de combate

**shambles** [ˈʃæmbəlz] *s* destrucción, ruina; (*confusion, mess*) lío, revoltijo

**shame** [ʃem] *s* vergüenza; deshonra; **shame on you!** ¡qué vergüenza!; **what a shame!** ¡qué lástima! || *tr* avergonzar; deshonrar

**shameful** [ˈʃemfəl] *adj* vergonzoso

**shameless** [ˈʃemlɪs] *adj* descarado, desvergonzado

**shampoo** [ʃæmˈpu] *s* champú *m* || *tr* lavar (*la cabeza*); lavar la cabeza a

**shamrock** [ˈʃæmrɑk] *s* trébol *m* irlandés

**shanghai** [ˈʃæŋhaɪ] o [ʃæŋˈhaɪ] *tr* embarcar emborrachando, embarcar narcotizando; llevarse con violencia, llevarse con engaño

**shank** [ʃæŋk] *s* (*of the leg*) caña, canilla; (*of an animal*) pierna; (*of a bird*) zanca; (*of an anchor*) caña; (*of the sole of a shoe*) enfranque *m*; astil *m*, caña, fuste *m*; extremidad, remate *m*; **to go** o **to ride on shank's mare** caminar en coche de San Francisco

**shan·ty** [ˈʃænti] *s* (*pl* **-ties**) chabola, choza

**shape** [ʃep] *s* forma; **in bad shape** (coll) arruinado; (coll) muy enfermo; **out of shape** deformado; descompuesto || *tr* formar, dar forma a; amoldar || *intr* formarse; **to shape up** tomar forma; desarrollarse bien

**shapeless** [ˈʃeplɪs] *adj* informe

**shape·ly** [ˈʃepli] *adj* (*comp* **-lier**; *super* **-liest**) bien formado, esbelto

**share** [ʃer] *s* parte *f*, porción; (*of stock in a company*) acción; **to go shares** ir a la parte || *tr* (*to enjoy jointly*) compartir; (*to apportion*) repartir || *intr* participar, tener parte

**share′hold′er** *s* accionista *mf*

**shark** [ʃɑrk] *s* tiburón *m*; (*swindler*) estafador *m*; (slang) experto, perito

**sharp** [ʃɑrp] *adj* afilado, agudo; anguloso; (*curve, slope, etc.*) fuerte, pronunciado; (*photograph*) nítido; (*hearing*) fino; (*step, gait*) rápido; atento, despierto; picante, mordaz; listo, vivo; (mus) sostenido; (slang) elegante; **sharp features** facciones bien marcadas || *adv* agudamente; en punto, p.ej., **at four o'clock sharp** a las cuatro en punto || *s* (mus) sostenido

**sharpen** [ˈʃɑrpən] *tr* aguzar; sacar punta a (*un lápiz*) || *intr* afilarse

**sharper** [ˈʃɑrpər] *s* fullero, jugador *m* de ventaja

**sharp′shoot′er** *s* tirador certero; (mil) tirador distinguido

**shatter** [ˈʃætər] *tr* hacer astillas, romper de un golpe; quebrantar (*la salud*); destruir, destrozar; agitar, perturbar || *intr* hacerse pedazos, romperse

**shat′ter·proof′** *adj* inastillable

**shave** [ʃev] *s* afeitado; rebanada delgada; **to have a close shave** (coll) escapar en una tabla || *tr* afeitar (*la cara*); raer, raspar; (*to graze; to cut close*) rozar; (*to slice thin*) rebanar; (carp) cepillar || *intr* afeitarse

**shaving** [ˈʃevɪŋ] *adj* de afeitar, para afeitar, p.ej., **shaving soap** jabón *m* de o para afeitar || *s* afeitado; **shavings** acepilladuras, virutas

**shawl** [ʃɔl] *s* chal *m*, mantón *m*

**she** [ʃi] *pron pers* (*pl* **they**) ella || *s* (*pl* **shes**) hembra

**sheaf** [ʃif] *s* (*pl* **sheaves** [ʃivz]) gavilla; (*of paper*) atado

**shear** [ʃɪr] *s* hoja de la tijera; **shears** tijeras grandes; (*to cut metal*) cizallas ‖ *v* (*pret* **sheared;** *pp* **sheared** o **shorn** [ʃorn]) *tr* esquilar, trasquilar (*las ovejas*); cizallar; quitar cortando; tundir (*paño*)
**sheath** [ʃiθ] *s* (**sheaths** [ʃiðz]) envoltura, estuche *m*, funda; (*for a sword*) funda, vaina
**sheathe** [ʃið] *tr* enfundar, envainar
**shed** [ʃɛd] *s* cobertizo; (*line from which water flows in two directions*) vertiente *m & f* ‖ *v* (*pret & pp* **shed;** *ger* **shedding**) *tr* derramar, verter (*p.ej., sangre*); dar, echar, esparcir (*luz*); mudar (*la pluma, el pellejo*)
**sheen** [ʃin] *s* brillo, lustre *m;* (*of pressed cloth*) prensado
**sheep** [ʃip] *s* (*pl* **sheep**) carnero; (*female*) oveja; tonto; **to make sheep's eyes (at)** mirar con ojos de carnero degollado
**sheep dog** *s* perro ovejero, perro de pastor
**sheep'fold'** *s* aprisco, redil *m*
**sheepish** ['ʃipɪʃ] *adj* avergonzado, corrido; tímido, tonto
**sheep'skin'** *s* (*undressed*) zalea; (*dressed*) badana; (coll) diploma *m*
**sheer** [ʃɪr] *adj* delgado, fino, ligero; casi transparente; escarpado; puro, sin mezcla; completo ‖ *intr* desviarse
**sheet** [ʃit] *s* (*e.g., for the bed*) sábana; (*of paper*) hoja; (*of metal*) hoja, lámina; (*of water*) extensión; hoja impresa; periódico; (naut) escota
**sheet lightning** *s* fucilazo
**sheet metal** *s* metal laminado
**sheet music** *s* música en hojas sueltas
**sheik** [ʃik] *s* jeque *m;* (*great lover*) (slang) sultán *m*
**shelf** [ʃɛlf] *s* (*pl* **shelves** [ʃɛlvz]) estante *m*, anaquel *m;* bajío, banco de arena; **on the shelf** arrinconado, desechado, olvidado
**shell** [ʃɛl] *s* (*of an egg, nut, etc.*) cáscara; (*of a crustacean*) caparazón *m*, concha; (*of a vegetable*) vaina; (*of a cartridge*) cápsula; (*of a boiler*) cuerpo; armazón *f*, esqueleto; bomba, proyectil *m;* (*long, narrow racing boat*) (sport) yola ‖ *tr* descascarar; desgranar, desvainar (*legumbres*); bombardear, cañonear; **to shell out** (coll) entregar (*dinero*)
**shel·lac** [ʃə'læk] *s* laca, goma laca ‖ *v* (*pret & pp* **-lacked;** *ger* **-lacking**) *tr* barnizar con goma laca; (slang) azotar, zurrar; (slang) derrotar
**shell'fish'** *s* marisco, mariscos
**shell hole** *s* (mil) embudo
**shell shock** *s* neurosis *f* de guerra
**shelter** ['ʃɛltər] *s* abrigo, asilo, amparo, refugio; **to take shelter** abrigarse, refugiarse ‖ *tr* abrigar, amparar, proteger
**shelve** [ʃɛlv] *tr* poner sobre un estante; proveer de estantes; arrinconar, dejar a un lado; diferir indefinidamente
**shepherd** ['ʃɛpərd] *s* pastor *m* ‖ *tr* pastorear (*a las ovejas o los fieles*)
**shepherd dog** *s* perro ovejero, perro de pastor
**shepherdess** ['ʃɛpərdɪs] *s* pastora
**sherbet** ['ʃʌrbət] *s* sorbete *m*
**shereef** [ʃɛ'rif] *s* jerife *m*
**sheriff** ['ʃɛrɪf] *s* alguacil *m* mayor
**sher·ry** ['ʃɛri] *s* (*pl* **-ries**) jerez *m*, vino de Jerez
**shield** [ʃild] *s* escudo; (*for armpit*) sobaquera; (elec) blindaje *m* ‖ *tr* amparar, defender, escudar; (elec) blindar
**shift** [ʃɪft] *s* cambio; (*order of work or other activity*) turno; (*group of workmen*) tanda; maña, subterfugio ‖ *tr* cambiar; deshacerse de; echar (*la culpa*); (aut) cambiar de (*marcha*) ‖ *intr* cambiar, cambiar de puesto; mañear; (naut) correrse (*el lastre*); (rr) maniobrar; **to shift for oneself** ayudarse, ingeniarse
**shift key** *s* tecla de cambio, palanca de mayúsculas
**shiftless** ['ʃɪftlɪs] *adj* desidioso, perezoso
**shift·y** ['ʃɪfti] *adj* (*comp* **-ier;** *super* **-iest**) ingenioso, mañoso; evasivo, tramoyista; (*glance*) huyente
**shilling** ['ʃɪlɪŋ] *s* chelín *m*
**shimmer** ['ʃɪmər] *s* lúz trémula ‖ *intr* rielar
**shin** [ʃɪn] *s* espinilla ‖ *v* (*pret & pp* **shinned;** *ger* **shinning**) *tr & intr* trepar
**shin'bone'** *s* espinilla
**shine** [ʃaɪn] *s* brillo, luz *f;* bruñido, lustre *m;* buen tiempo; (*on shoes*) (coll) lustre *m;* **to take a shine to** (slang) tomar simpatía a ‖ *v* (*pret & pp* **shined**) *tr* pulir, lustrar; (coll) embolar, limpiar (*el calzado*) ‖ *v* (*pret & pp* **shone** [ʃon]) *intr* brillar, lucir, resplandecer; hacer sol, hacer buen tiempo; (*to be distinguished, to stand out*) (fig) brillar, lucir
**shingle** ['ʃɪŋgəl] *s* ripia, teja de madera; tejamaní *m* (Am); pelo a la garçonne; (coll) letrero de oficina; **shingles** (pathol) zona; **to hang out one's shingle** (coll) abrir una oficina; (coll) abrir un consultorio médico ‖ *tr* cubrir con ripias; cortar (*el pelo*) a la garçonne
**shining** ['ʃaɪnɪŋ] *adj* brillante, luciente
**shin·y** ['ʃaɪni] *adj* (*comp* **-ier;** *super* **-iest**) brillante, lustroso; (*paper*) glaseado; (*from much wear*) brilloso
**ship** [ʃɪp] *s* nave *f*, buque *m*, barco, navío; (*steamer*) vapor *m;* aeronave *f* ‖ *v* (*pret & pp* **shipped;** *ger* **shipping**) *tr* embarcar; enviar, remitir, remesar; armar (*los remos*); embarcar (*agua*) ‖ *intr* embarcarse
**ship'board'** *s* bordo; **on shipboard** a bordo
**ship'build'er** *s* arquitecto naval, constructor *m* de buques
**ship'build'ing** *s* arquitectura naval, construcción de buques
**ship'mate'** *s* camarada *m* de a bordo
**shipment** ['ʃɪpmənt] *s* embarque *m* (*por agua*); envío, expedición, remesa

**shipper** ['ʃɪpər] *s* embarcador *m;* expedidor *m,* remitente *mf*
**shipping memo** ['ʃɪpɪŋ] *s* nota de remisión
**ship'shape'** *adj & adv* en buen orden
**ship'side'** *adj & adv* al costado del buque ‖ *s* zona de embarque y desembarque; muelle *m*
**ship's papers** *spl* documentación del buque
**ship's time** *s* hora local del buque
**ship'wreck'** *s* naufragio; barco náufrago ‖ *tr* hacer naufragar ‖ *intr* naufragar
**ship'yard'** *s* astillero, varadero
**shirk** [ʃʌrk] *tr* evitar (*el trabajo*); faltar a (*un deber*) ‖ *intr* escurrir el hombro
**shirred eggs** [ʃʌrd] *spl* huevos al plato
**shirt** [ʃʌrt] *s* camisa; **to keep one's shirt on** (slang) quedarse sereno; **to lose one's shirt** (slang) perder hasta la camisa
**shirt'band'** *s* cuello de camisa
**shirt front** *s* pechera de camisa, camisolín *m*
**shirt sleeve** *s* manga de camisa; **in shirt sleeves** en mangas de camisa
**shirt'tail'** *s* faldón *m,* pañal *m*
**shirt'waist'** *s* blusa (*de mujer*)
**shiver** ['ʃɪvər] *s* estremecimiento, tiritón *m* ‖ *intr* estremecerse, tiritar
**shoal** [ʃol] *s* bajío, banco de arena
**shock** [ʃɑk] *s* (*sudden and violent blow or encounter*) choque *m;* (*sudden agitation of mind or emotions*) sobresalto; temblor *m* de tierra; (*of hair*) greña; (agr) tresnal *m;* (elec) sacudida; (med) choque *m;* (*profound depression*) (pathol) choque *m;* (coll) parálisis *f* ‖ *tr* chocar; sobresaltar; dar una sacudida eléctrica a; chocar, escandalizar
**shock absorber** [æb'sɔrbər] *s* amortiguador *m*
**shocking** ['ʃɑkɪŋ] *adj* chocante, escandalizador
**shock troops** *spl* tropas de asalto
**shod·dy** ['ʃɑdi] *adj* (*comp* **-dier;** *super* **-diest**) falso, de imitación
**shoe** [ʃu] *s* (*which goes above the ankle*) bota, botina; (*which does not go above the ankle*) zapato; (*of a tire*) cubierta; **to put on one's shoes** calzarse ‖ *v* (*pret & pp* **shod** [ʃɑd]) *tr* calzar; herrar (*un caballo*)
**shoe'black'** *s* limpiabotas *m*
**shoe'horn'** *s* calzador *m*
**shoe'lace'** *s* cordón *m* de zapato, lazo de zapato
**shoe'mak'er** *s* zapatero; zapatero remendón
**shoe mender** ['mendər] *s* zapatero remendón
**shoe polish** *s* betún *m,* bola
**shoe'shine'** *s* brillo, lustre *m;* limpiabotas *m*
**shoe store** *s* zapatería
**shoe'string'** *s* cordón *m* de zapato, lazo de zapato; **on a shoestring** con muy poco dinero
**shoe tree** *s* horma
**shoo** [ʃu] *tr & intr* oxear
**shoot** [ʃut] *s* (*sprout, twig*) renuevo, vástago; conducto inclinado; (*for grain, sand, etc.*) tolva; tiro al blanco, certamen *m* de tiradores; (*hunting party*) partida de caza ‖ *v* (*pret & pp* **shot** [ʃɑt]) *tr* tirar, disparar (*un arma*); herir o matar con arma; (*to execute with a discharge of rifles*) fusilar; fotografiar; (*to take a moving picture of*) rodar; echar (*los dados*); medir la altura de (*p.ej., el Sol*); **to shoot down** derribar (*un avión*); **to shoot up** (slang) destrozar echando balas a diestra y siniestra ‖ *intr* tirar; nacer, brotar; lanzarse, precipitarse, moverse rápidamente; punzar (*un dolor, una llaga*); **to shoot at** tirar a; (*to strive for*) (coll) poner el tiro en
**shooting gallery** *s* galería de tiro al blanco
**shooting match** *s* certamen *m* de tiro al blanco; (slang) conjunto, totalidad
**shooting star** *s* estrella fugaz, estrella filante
**shop** [ʃɑp] *s* (*store*) tienda; (*workshop*) taller *m;* **to talk shop** hablar de su oficio, hablar del propio trabajo (*fuera de tiempo*) ‖ *v* (*pret & pp* **shopped;** *ger* **shopping**) *intr* ir de compras, ir de tiendas; **to go shopping** ir de compras, ir de tiendas; **to send shopping** mandar a la compra; **to shop around** ir de tienda en tienda buscando gangas
**shop'girl'** *s* muchacha de tienda
**shop'keep'er** *s* tendero
**shoplifter** ['ʃɑp ˌlɪftər] *s* mechera, ratero de tiendas
**shopper** ['ʃɑpər] *s* comprador *m*
**shopping center** *s* centro comercial (*grupo de establecimientos minoristas, con aparcamiento*)
**shopping district** *s* barrio comercial
**shop'win'dow** *s* escaparate *m*
**shop'work'** *s* trabajo de taller
**shop'worn'** *adj* desgastado con el trajín de la tienda
**shore** [ʃor] *s* orilla, ribera; costa, playa; **shores** (poet) clima *m,* región ‖ *tr* acodalar, apuntalar
**shore dinner** *s* comida de pescado y mariscos
**shore leave** *s* (nav) permiso para ir a tierra
**shore line** *s* línea de la playa; línea de buques costeros
**shore patrol** *s* (nav) patrulla en tierra
**short** [ʃɔrt] *adj* (*in space, time, and quantity*) corto; (*in time*) breve; (*in stature*) bajo; (fig) corto, sucinto; (fig) brusco, seco; **in a short time** dentro de poco; **in short** en fin; **on short notice** con poco tiempo de aviso; **to be short of** estar escaso de; **short of breath** corto de resuello ‖ *adv* brevemente; bruscamente; (*without possessing the stock sold*) al descubierto, p.ej., **to sell short** vender al descubierto; **to run short of** acabársele a uno, p.ej., **I am running short of gasoline** se me acaba la

gasolina; **to stop short** parar de repente || *s* (elec) cortocircuito; (mov) cortometraje *m;* **shorts** calzones cortos, calzoncillos || *tr* (elec) poner en cortocircuito || *intr* (elec) ponerse en cortocircuito

**shortage** [ˈʃɔrtɪdʒ] *s* carestía, escasez *f,* falta; déficit *m;* (*from pilfering*) substracción

**short′cake′** *s* torta de frutas; torta quebradiza

**short′change′** *tr* (coll) no devolver la vuelta debida a

**short circuit** *s* (elec) cortocircuito

**short′cir′cuit** *tr* (elec) cortocircuitar || *intr* (elec) cortocircuitarse

**short′com′ing** *s* falta, defecto, desperfecto

**short cut** *s* atajo; (*method*) remediavagos *m*

**shorten** [ˈʃɔrtən] *tr* acortar, abreviar || *intr* acortarse, abreviarse

**short′hand′** *adj* taquigráfico || *s* taquigrafía; **to take shorthand** taquigrafiar

**short-lived** [ˈʃɔrtˈlaɪvd] o [ˈʃɔrtˈlɪvd] *adj* de breve vida, de breve duración

**shortly** [ˈʃɔrtli] *adv* en breve, luego; descortésmente; **shortly after** poco tiempo después (de)

**short′-range′** *adj* de poco alcance

**short sale** *s* (coll) venta al descubierto

**short-sighted** [ˈʃɔrtˈsaɪtɪd] *adj* miope; (fig) falto de perspicacia

**short′stop′** *s* (baseball) medio; guardabosque *m,* torpedero (Am)

**short story** *s* cuento

**short-tempered** [ˈʃɔrtˈtɛmpərd] *adj* de mal genio

**short′-term′** *adj* a corto plazo

**shot** [ʃɑt] *s* tiro, disparo; (*hit or wound made with a bullet*) balazo; (*distance*) alcance *m;* (*in certain games*) jugada, tirada, golpe *m;* (*of a rocket into space*) lanzamiento; conjetura, tentativa; fotografía, instantánea; (*small pellets of lead*) perdigones *mpl;* munición; (*marksman*) tiro; (*heavy metal ball*) (sport) pesa; (*hypodermic injection*) (slang) jeringazo; (*drink of liquor*) (slang) trago; **not by a long shot** ni con mucho, ni por pienso; **to start like a shot** salir disparado

**shot′gun′** *s* escopeta

**shot′-put′** *s* (sport) tiro de la pesa

**should** [ʃʊd] *v aux* empléase para formar (1) el pres de cond, p.ej., **if I should wait for him, I should miss the train** si yo le esperase, perdería el tren; (2) el perf de cond, p.ej., **if I had waited for him, I should have missed the train** si yo le hubiese esperado, habría perdido el tren; y (3) el modo potencial, p.ej., **he should go at once** debiera salir en seguida; **he should have gone at once** debiera haber salido en seguida

**shoulder** [ˈʃoldər] *s* hombro; (*of slaughtered animal*) brazuelo; (*of a garment*) hombrera; **across the shoulder** en bandolera; **to put one's shoulders to the wheel** arrimar el hombro, echar el pecho al agua; **to turn a cold shoulder to** volver las espaldas a || *tr* cargar sobre las espaldas; tomar sobre sí, hacerse responsable de; empujar con el hombro para abrirse paso

**shoulder blade** *s* escápula, omóplato

**shoulder strap** *s* (*of underwear*) presilla; (mil) charretera

**shout** [ʃaʊt] *s* grito, voz *f* || *tr* gritar, vocear; **to shout down** hacer callar a gritos || *intr* gritar, dar voces

**shove** [ʃʌv] *s* empujón *m* || *tr* empujar || *intr* dar empujones, avanzar a empujones; **to shove off** alejarse de la costa; (slang) ponerse en marcha, salir

**shov•el** [ˈʃʌvəl] *s* pala || *v* (*pret & pp* **-eled** o **-elled;** *ger* **-eling** o **-elling**) *tr* traspalar; espalar (*p.ej., la nieve*) || *intr* trabajar con pala

**show** [ʃo] *s* exhibición, exposición, muestra; espectáculo; (*in the theater*) función; (*each performance of a play or movie*) sesión; demostración, prueba; indicación, señal *f,* signo; apariencia; (*e.g., of confidence*) alarde *m;* (coll) ocasión, oportunidad; ostentación; espectáculo ridículo, hazmerreír *m;* **to make a show of** hacer gala de; **to steal the show from** robar la obra a (*otro actor*) || *tr* mostrar, enseñar; demostrar, probar; poner, proyectar (*un film*); (*e.g., to the door*) acompañar; **to show up** (coll) desenmascarar || *intr* mostrarse, aparecer, asomar; salir (*p.ej., las enaguas*); **to show off** fachendear; **to show through** clarearse, transparentarse; **to show up** (coll) presentarse, dejarse ver

**show bill** *s* cartel *m*

**show business** *s* comercio de los espectáculos

**show′case′** *s* vitrina (de exposición)

**show′down′** *s* cartas boca arriba; (coll) revelación forzosa, arreglo terminante

**shower** [ˈʃau·ər] *s* (*sudden fall of rain*) aguacero, chaparrón *m;* (*shower bath*) ducha; (*e.g., of bullets*) rociada; despedida de soltera || *tr* regar; **to shower with** colmar de || *intr* llover

**shower bath** *s* ducha, baño de ducha

**show girl** *s* (theat) corista *f,* conjuntista *f*

**show•man** [ˈʃomən] *s* (*pl* **-men** [mən]) empresario de teatro, empresario de circo

**show′-off′** *s* (coll) pinturero

**show′piece′** *s* objeto de arte sobresaliente

**show′place′** *s* sitio o edificio que se exhibe por su belleza o lujo

**show′room′** *s* sala de muestras, sala de exhibición

**show window** *s* escaparate *m* de tienda

**show•y** [ˈʃo·i] *adj* (*comp* **-ier;** *super* **-iest**) aparatoso, cursi, ostentoso

**shrapnel** [ˈʃræpnəl] *s* granada de metralla

**shred** [ʃrɛd] *s* jirón *m,* tira, triza; frag-

mento, pizca; **to tear to shreds** hacer trizas || *v* (*pret & pp* **shredded** o **shred**; *ger* **shredding**) *tr* desmenuzar, hacer trizas; deshilar (*carne*)
**shrew** [ʃru] *s* (*nagging woman*) arpía, fierecilla; (*animal*) musaraña
**shrewd** [ʃrud] *adj* astuto; despierto; listo
**shriek** [ʃrik] *s* chillido, grito agudo; risotada chillona || *intr* chillar
**shrill** [ʃrɪl] *adj* agudo, chillón
**shrimp** [ʃrɪmp] *s* camarón *m*; (*little insignificant person*) renacuajo
**shrine** [ʃraɪn] *s* relicario; sepulcro de santo; lugar sagrado
**shrink** [ʃrɪŋk] *v* (*pret* **shrank** [ʃræŋk] o **shrunk** [ʃrʌŋk]; *pp* **shrunk** o **shrunken**) *tr* contraer, encoger || *intr* contraerse, encogerse; moverse hacia atrás; rehuirse, retirarse
**shrinkage** [ˈʃrɪŋkɪdʒ] *s* contracción, encogimiento; disminución, reducción; merma, pérdida
**shriv•el** [ˈʃrɪvəl] *v* (*pret & pp* **-eled** o **-elled**; *ger* **-eling** o **-elling**) *tr* arrugar, marchitar, fruncir || *intr* arrugarse, marchitarse, fruncirse; **to shrivel up** avellanarse
**shroud** [ʃraʊd] *s* mortaja, sudario; cubierta, velo || *tr* amortajar; cubrir, velar
**Shrove Tuesday** [ʃrov] *s* martes *m* de carnaval
**shrub** [ʃrʌb] *s* arbusto
**shrubber•y** [ˈʃrʌbəri] *s* (*pl* **-ies**) arbustos; plantío de arbustos
**shrug** [ʃrʌg] *s* encogimiento de hombros || *v* (*pret & pp* **shrugged**; *ger* **shrugging**) *tr* contraer; **to shrug one's shoulders** encogerse de hombros || *intr* encogerse de hombros
**shudder** [ˈʃʌdər] *s* estremecimiento || *intr* estremecerse
**shuffle** [ˈʃʌfəl] *s* (*of cards*) barajadura; turno de barajar; (*of feet*) arrastramiento; evasiva; recomposición || *tr* barajar (*naipes*); arrastrar (*los pies*); mezclar, revolver || *intr* barajar; caminar arrastrando los pies; bailar arrastrando los pies; moverse rápidamente de un lado a otro; **to shuffle along** ir arrastrando los pies; ir tirando; **to shuffle off** irse arrastrando los pies
**shuf'fle•board'** *s* juego de tejo
**shun** [ʃʌn] *v* (*pret & pp* **shunned**; *ger* **shunning**) *tr* esquivar, evitar, rehuir
**shunt** [ʃʌnt] *tr* apartar, desviar; (elec) poner en derivación; (rr) desviar
**shut** [ʃʌt] *adj* cerrado || *v* (*pret & pp* **shut**; *ger* **shutting**) *tr* cerrar; **to shut in** encerrar; **to shut off** cortar (*electricidad, gas, etc.*); **to shut up** cerrar bien; aprisionar; (coll) hacer callar || *intr* cerrarse; **to shut up** (coll) callarse la boca
**shut'down'** *s* cierre *m*, paro
**shutter** [ˈʃʌtər] *s* celosía, persiana; (*outside a window*) contraventana; (*outside a show window*) cierre metálico; (phot) obturador *m*
**shuttle** [ˈʃʌtəl] *s* (*used in sewing*) lanzadera || *intr* hacer viajes cortos de ida y vuelta
**shuttle train** *s* tren *m* lanzadera
**shy** [ʃaɪ] *adj* (*comp* **shyer** o **shier**; *super* **shyest** o **shiest**) arisco, recatado, tímido. (*fearful*) asustadizo; escaso, pobre; **I am shy a dollar** me falta un dólar || *v* (*pret & pp* **shied**) *intr* esquivarse, hacerse a un lado; espantarse, respingar; **to shy away** alejarse asustado
**shyster** [ˈʃaɪstər] *s* (coll) abogado trampista
**Sia•mese** [ˌsaɪ-əˈmiz] *adj* siamés || *s* (*pl* **-mese**) siamés *m*
**Siamese twins** *spl* hermanos siameses
**Siberian** [saɪˈbɪrɪ•ən] *adj & s* siberiano
**sibilant** [ˈsɪbɪlənt] *adj & s* sibilante *f*
**sibyl** [ˈsɪbɪl] *s* sibila
**Sicilian** [sɪˈsɪljən] *adj & s* siciliano
**Sicily** [ˈsɪsɪli] *s* Sicilia
**sick** [sɪk] *adj* enfermo, malo; nauseado; **sick and tired of** (coll) harto y cansado de, **sick at heart** afligido de corazón; **to be sick at one's stomach** tener náuseas; **to take sick** caer enfermo || *tr* azuzar (*a un perro*)
**sick'bed'** *s* lecho de enfermo
**sicken** [ˈsɪkən] *tr & intr* enfermar
**sickening** [ˈsɪkənɪŋ] *adj* repelente, repugnante, nauseabundo
**sick headache** *s* jaqueca con náuseas
**sickle** [ˈsɪkəl] *s* hoz *f*
**sick leave** *s* licencia por enfermedad
**sick•ly** [ˈsɪkli] *adj* (*comp* **-lier**; *super* **-liest**) enfermizo
**sickness** [ˈsɪknɪs] *s* enfermedad; náusea
**side** [saɪd] *adj* lateral || *s* lado; (*of a solid; of a phonograph record*) cara; (*of a hill*) falda; (*of human body, of a ship*) costado; facción, partido || *intr* tomar partido; **to side with** tomar el partido de
**side arms** *spl* armas de cinto
**side'board'** *s* aparador *m*
**side'burns'** *spl* patillas
**side dish** *s* plato de entrada
**side door** *s* puerta lateral; puerta excusada
**side effect** *s* efecto secundario perjudicial (*de ciertos medicamentos*)
**side glance** *s* mirada de soslayo
**side issue** *s* cuestión secundaria
**side line** *s* negocio accesorio; **on the side lines** sin tomar parte
**sidereal** [saɪˈdɪrɪ•əl] *adj* sidéreo
**side'sad'dle** *adv* a asentadillas, a mujeriegas
**side show** *s* función secundaria, espectáculo de atracciones
**side'split'ting** *adj* desternillante
**side'track'** *s* apartadero, desviadero, vía muerta || *tr* desviar (*un tren*); echar a un lado
**side view** *s* perfil *m*, vista de lado
**side'walk'** *s* acera; banqueta (Guat, Mex); vereda (Arg, Cuba, Peru)
**sidewalk café** *s* terraza, café *m* en la acera
**sideward** [ˈsaɪdwərd] *adj* oblicuo, sesgado || *adv* de lado, hacia un lado

**side'ways'** *adj* oblicuo, sesgado || *adv* de lado, hacia un lado; al través
**side whiskers** *spl* patillas
**side'wise'** *adj* oblicuo, sesgado || *adv* de lado, hacia un lado; al través
**siding** ['saɪdɪŋ] *s* (rr) apartadero, desviadero, vía muerta
**sidle** ['saɪdəl] *intr* ir de lado; **to sidle up to** acercarse de lado a (*una persona*) para no ser visto
**siege** [sidʒ] *s* sitio, cerco; **to lay siege to** poner sitio o cerco a; (fig) asediar (*p.ej., el corazón de una mujer*)
**sieve** [sɪv] *s* cedazo, tamiz *m* || *tr* cerner, tamizar
**sift** [sɪft] *tr* cerner, cribar; escudriñar, examinar; (*to screen, separate*) entresacar; (*to scatter with or as with a sieve*) empolvar
**sigh** [saɪ] *s* suspiro; **to breathe a sigh of relief** respirar || *tr* decir con suspiros || *intr* suspirar; **to sigh for** suspirar por
**sight** [saɪt] *s* vista; cosa digna de verse; (*of a firearm, telescope, etc.*) mira; (coll) gran cantidad, montón *m;* (coll) horror *m,* atrocidad; **at first sight** a primera vista; **at sight** a primera vista; (*translation*) a libro abierto; (com) a la vista; **out of sight** fuera del alcance de la vista; (*prices*) por las nubes; **to catch sight of** alcanzar a ver; **to know by sight** conocer de vista; **to not be able to stand the sight of** no poder ver ni en pintura; **to see the sights** visitar los puntos de interés || *tr* avistar, alcanzar con la vista || *intr* apuntar con una mira; (arti & surv) visar
**sight draft** *s* (com) giro a la vista, letra a la vista
**sight'-read'** *v* (*pret & pp* **-read** [,rɛd]) *tr* leer a libro abierto; (mus) ejecutar a la primera lectura || *intr* leer a libro abierto; (mus) repentizar
**sight reader** *s* lector *m* a libro abierto; (mus) repentista *mf*
**sight'see'ing** *s* turismo, visita de puntos de interés; **to go sightseeing** ir a ver los puntos de interés
**sightseer** ['saɪt,si·ər] *s* turista *mf,* excursionista *mf*
**sign** [saɪn] *s* signo; señal *f,* marca; huella, vestigio; letrero, muestra; **to show signs of** dar muestras de, tener trazas de; **to make the sign of the cross** hacerse la señal de la cruz || *tr* firmar; contratar; ceder, traspasar || *intr* firmar; **to sign off** (rad) terminar la transmisión; **to sign up** (coll) firmar el contrato
**sig·nal** ['sɪgnəl] *adj* señalado, notable || *s* señal *f* || *v* (*pret & pp* **-naled** o **-nalled;** *ger* **-naling** o **-nalling**) *tr* señalar || *intr* hacer señales
**signal tower** *s* (rr) garita de señales
**signato·ry** ['sɪgnɪ,tori] *s* (*pl* **-ries**) firmante *mf*
**signature** ['sɪgnətʃər] *s* firma; (mus & typ) signatura
**sign'board'** *s* cartelón *m,* letrero
**signer** ['saɪnər] *s* firmante *mf*
**signet ring** ['sɪgnɪt] *s* anillo sigilar, sortija de sello
**signi·fy** ['sɪgnɪ,faɪ] *v* (*pret & pp* **-fied**) *tr* significar
**sign'post'** *s* hito, poste *m* de guía
**silence** ['saɪləns] *s* silencio || *tr* acallar; (mil) apagar el fuego de; (mil) apagar (*el fuego del enemigo*)
**silent** ['saɪlənt] *adj* silencioso
**silent movie** *s* cine mudo
**silhouette** [,sɪlu'ɛt] *s* silueta || *tr* siluetear
**silk** [sɪlk] *adj* sedeño || *s* seda; **to hit the silk** (slang) lanzarse en paracaídas
**silken** ['sɪlkən] *adj* sedeño
**silk hat** *s* sombrero de copa
**silk'-stock'ing** *adj* aristocrático || *s* aristócrata *mf*
**silk'worm'** *s* gusano de seda
**silk·y** ['sɪlki] *adj* (*comp* **-ier;** *super* **-iest**) sedoso, asedado
**sill** [sɪl] *s* travesaño; (*of a door*) umbral *m;* (*of a window*) antepecho
**sil·ly** ['sɪli] *adj* (*comp* **-lier;** *super* **-liest**) necio, tonto
**si·lo** ['saɪlo] *s* (*pl* **-los**) silo || *tr* asilar
**silt** [sɪlt] *s* cieno, sedimento
**silver** ['sɪlvər] *adj* de plata; (*voice*) argentino; elocuente || *s* plata || *tr* platear; azogar (*un espejo*)
**sil'ver·fish'** *s* (ent) pez *m* de plata
**silver foil** *s* hoja de plata
**silver lining** *s* aspecto agradable de una condición desgraciada o triste
**silver plate** *s* vajilla de plata
**silver screen** *s* pantalla de plata
**sil'ver·smith'** *s* platero, orfebre *m*
**silver spoon** *s* riqueza heredada; **to be born with a silver spoon in one's mouth** nacer de pie
**sil'ver-tongue'** *s* (coll) pico de oro
**sil'ver·ware'** *s* plata, vajilla de plata
**similar** ['sɪmɪlər] *adj* similar, semejante, análogo
**simile** ['sɪmɪli] *s* (rhet) símil *m*
**simmer** ['sɪmər] *tr* cocer a fuego lento || *intr* cocer a fuego lento; (coll) estar a punto de estallar; **to simmer down** (coll) tranquilizarse lentamente
**simoon** [sɪ'mun] *s* simún *m*
**simper** ['sɪmpər] *s* sonrisa boba || *intr* sonreír bobamente
**simple** ['sɪmpəl] *adj* simple, sencillo || *s* (*medicinal plant*) simple *m*
**simple-minded** ['sɪmpəl'maɪndɪd] *adj* candoroso, ingenuo; idiota, mentecato; estúpido, ignorante
**simple substance** *s* (chem) cuerpo simple
**simpleton** ['sɪmpəltən] *s* simple *mf,* bobo, mentecato
**simulate** ['sɪmjə,let] *tr* simular
**simultaneous** [,saɪməl'tenɪ·əs] o [,sɪməl'tenɪ·əs] *adj* simultáneo
**sin** [sɪn] *s* pecado || *v* (*pret & pp* **sinned;** *ger* **sinning**) *intr* pecar
**since** [sɪns] *adv* desde entonces, después || *prep* desde; después de || *conj* desde que; después (de) que; ya que, puesto que
**sincere** [sɪn'sɪr] *adj* sincero
**sincerity** [sɪn'sɛrɪti] *s* sinceridad

**sinecure** ['saɪnɪ,kjʊr] o ['sɪnɪ,kjʊr] *s* sinecura
**sinew** ['sɪnju] *s* tendón *m;* (fig) fibra, nervio, vigor *m*
**sinful** ['sɪnfəl] *adj* (*person*) pecador; (*act, intention, etc.*) pecaminoso
**sing** [sɪŋ] *v* (*pret* **sang** [sæŋ] o **sung** [sʌŋ]; *pp* **sung**) *tr* cantar; **to sing to sleep** arrullar || *intr* cantar
**singe** [sɪndʒ] *v* (*ger* **singeing**) *tr* chamuscar, socarrar
**singer** ['sɪŋər] *s* cantante *mf;* (*in a night club*) vocalista *mf*
**single** ['sɪŋgəl] *adj* solo, único; simple, sencillo; particular; (*e.g., room in a hotel*) individual; (*copy*) suelto; (*unmarried*) soltero; solteril, de soltero || *tr* escoger, elegir; **to single out** singularizar
**single blessedness** *s* el bendito celibato
**single-breasted** ['sɪŋgəl'brestɪd] *adj* sin cruzar, de un solo pecho
**single entry** *s* (com) partida simple
**single file** *s* fila india; **in single file** de reata
**single-handed** ['sɪŋgəl'hændɪd] *adj* solo, sin ayuda
**single life** *s* vida de soltero
**sin'gle-track'** *adj* de vía única; (coll) de cortos alcances
**sing'song'** *adj* monótono || *s* sonsonete *m*
**singular** ['sɪŋgjələr] *adj* & *s* singular *m*
**sinister** ['sɪnɪstər] *adj* amenazante, ominoso, funesto
**sink** [sɪŋk] *s* fregadero, pila || *v* (*pret* **sank** [sæŋk] o **sunk** [sʌŋk]; *pp* **sunk**) *tr* hundir, sumergir; echar a pique; abrir, cavar (*un pozo*); hincar (*los dientes*); invertir (*mucho dinero*) perdiéndolo todo || *intr* hundirse; irse a pique; hundirse (*p.ej., el Sol en el horizonte*); descender, desaparecer; decaer (*un enfermo; una llama*); (*e.g., in a chair*) dejarse caer
**sinking fund** *s* fondo de amortización
**sinless** ['sɪnlɪs] *adj* impecable
**sinner** ['sɪnər] *s* pecador *m*
**sinuous** ['sɪnjʊ·əs] *adj* sinuoso
**sinus** ['saɪnəs] *s* seno
**sip** [sɪp] *s* sorbo, trago || *v* (*pret* & *pp* **sipped**; *ger* **sipping**) *tr* sorber, beber a tragos
**siphon** ['saɪfən] *s* sifón *m* || *tr* sacar con sifón, trasegar con sifón
**siphon bottle** *s* sifón *m*
**sir** [sʌr] *s* señor *m;* (*British title*) sir *m;* **Dear Sir** Muy señor mío, Estimado señor
**sire** [saɪr] *s* padre *m,* semental *m;* caballo padre || *tr* engendrar
**siren** ['saɪrən] *s* sirena
**Sirius** ['sɪrɪ·əs] *s* (astr) Sirio
**sirloin** ['sʌrlɔɪn] *s* solomillo
**sirup** ['sɪrəp] o ['sʌrəp] *s* var de **syrup**
**sissi·fy** ['sɪsɪ,faɪ] *v* (*pret* & *pp* **-fied**) *tr* (coll) afeminar
**sis·sy** ['sɪsi] *s* (*pl* **-sies**) (coll) hermanita; (coll) maricón *m,* santito
**sister** ['sɪstər] *adj* (*ship*) gemelo; (*language*) hermano || *s* hermana
**sis'ter-in-law'** *s* (*pl* **sisters-in-law**) cuñada, hermana política; (*wife of one's husband's or wife's brother*) concuñada
**Sisyphus** ['sɪsɪfəs] *s* Sísifo
**sit** [sɪt] *v* (*pret* & *pp* **sat** [sæt]; *ger* **sitting**) *intr* estar sentado; sentarse; echarse (*un ave sobre los huevos*); reunirse, celebrar junta; descansar; **to sit down** sentarse; **to sit still** estarse quieto; **to sit up** incorporarse (*el que estaba echado*)
**sit'-down' strike** *s* huelga de sentados, huelga de brazos caídos
**site** [saɪt] *s* sitio, paraje *m*
**sitting** ['sɪtɪŋ] *s* (*period one remains seated*) sentada; (*before a painter*) estadía; (*of a court or legislature*) sesión; **at one sitting** de una sentada
**sitting duck** *s* pato sentado en el agua (*fácil de matar a tiro de escopeta*); (coll) blanco de fácil alcance
**sitting room** *s* sala de estar
**situate** ['sɪtʃʊ,et] *tr* situar
**situation** [,sɪtʃʊ'eʃən] *s* situación; colocación, puesto
**sitz bath** [sɪts] *s* baño de asiento
**six** [sɪks] *adj* & *pron* seis || *s* seis *m;* **at sixes and sevens** en confusión, en desacuerdo; **six o'clock** las seis
**six hundred** *adj* & *pron* seiscientos || *s* seiscientos *m*
**sixteen** ['sɪks'tin] *adj, pron* & *s* dieciséis *m,* diez y seis
**sixteenth** ['sɪks'tinθ] *adj* & *s* (*in a series*) decimosexto; (*part*) dieciseisavo || *s* (*in dates*) dieciséis *m*
**sixth** [sɪksθ] *adj* & *s* sexto || *s* (*in dates*) seis *m*
**sixtieth** ['sɪkstɪ·ɪθ] *adj* & *s* (*in a series*) sexagésimo; (*part*) sesentavo
**six·ty** ['sɪksti] *adj* & *pron* sesenta || *s* (*pl* **-ties**) sesenta *m*
**sizable** ['saɪzəbəl] *adj* considerable, bastante grande
**size** [saɪz] *s* tamaño; (*of a person or garment*) talla; (*of a pipe, a wire*) diámetro; (*for gilding*) sisa, cola de retazo; (coll) verdadera situación || *tr* clasificar según tamaño; sisar, encolar; **to size up** enfocar (*un problema*); medir con la vista
**sizzle** ['sɪzəl] *s* siseo || *intr* sisear
**S.J.** *abbr* **Society of Jesus**
**skate** [sket] *s* patín *m;* (slang) adefesio, tipo || *intr* patinar; **to skate on thin ice** buscar el peligro
**skating rink** *s* patinadero, pista de patinar
**skein** [sken] *s* madeja; enredo, maraña
**skeleton** ['skelɪtən] *adj* esquelético || *s* esqueleto
**skeleton key** *s* llave maestra
**skeptic** ['skeptɪk] *adj* & *s* escéptico
**skeptical** ['skeptɪkəl] *adj* escéptico
**sketch** [sketʃ] *s* boceto, dibujo; bosquejo, esbozo; drama corto, pieza corta || *tr* dibujar; bosquejar, esbozar
**sketch'book'** *s* libro de bocetos; libro de esbozos literarios
**skewer** ['skju·ər] *s* broqueta || *tr* espetar; traspasar con aguja

**ski** [ski] *s* (*pl* **skis** o **ski**) esquí *m* || *intr* esquiar
**skid** [skɪd] *s* (*of an auto*) resbalón *m;* (*of a wheel*) patinaje *m,* patinazo; calzo || *v* (*pret & pp* **skidded;** *ger* **skidding**) *tr* calzar || *intr* resbalar (*un coche*); patinar (*una rueda*)
**skier** ['ski·ər] *s* esquiador *m*
**skiff** [skɪf] *s* esquife *m*
**skiing** ['ski·ɪŋ] *s* esquiismo
**ski jacket** *s* plumífero
**skijoring** [ski'dʒorɪŋ] *s* esquí remolcado
**ski jump** *s* salto de esquí; cancha de esquiar; trampolín *m*
**ski lift** *s* telesquí *m*
**skill** [skɪl] *s* destreza, habilidad, pericia
**skilled** [skɪld] *adj* hábil, experimentado, experto
**skillet** ['skɪlɪt] *s* cacerola de mango largo; sartén *f*
**skillful** ['skɪlfəl] *adj* diestro, hábil
**skim** [skɪm] *v* (*pret & pp* **skimmed;** *ger* **skimming**) *tr* desnatar (*la leche*); espumar (*el caldo, el almíbar*); (*to graze*) rasar, rozar; examinar ligeramente || *intr* rozar; **to skim over** pasar rozando; examinar a la ligera
**ski mask** *s* pasamontaña *m*
**skimmer** ['skɪmər] *s* (*utensil*) espumadera; (*straw hat*) canotié *m*
**skim milk** *s* leche desnatada
**skimp** [skɪmp] *tr* escatimar; chapucear || *intr* economizar, apretarse; chapucear
**skimp·y** ['skɪmpi] *adj* (*comp* **-ier;** *super* **-iest**) escaso; tacaño, mezquino
**skin** [skɪn] *s* piel *f;* (*of an animal, of fruit*) pellejo; **to be nothing but skin and bones** estar hecho un costal de huesos, estar en los huesos; **to get soaked to the skin** calarse hasta los huesos; **to save one's skin** salvar el pellejo || *v* (*pret & pp* **skinned;** *ger* **skinning**) *tr* pelar, desollar; escoriarse (*p.ej., el codo*); (coll) timar; **to skin alive** (coll) desollar vivo; (coll) vencer completamente
**skin'-deep'** *adj* superficial
**skin diver** *s* submarinista *mf*
**skin'flint'** *s* escasero, avaro
**skin game** *s* (slang) fullería
**skin·ny** ['skɪni] *adj* (*comp* **-nier;** *super* **-niest**) flaco, enjuto, magro, seco
**skip** [skɪp] *s* salto || *v* (*pret & pp* **skipped;** *ger* **skipping**) *tr* saltar || *intr* saltar; saltar espacios (*la máquina de escribir*); moverse saltando; irse precipitadamente
**skip bombing** *s* (aer) bombardeo de rebote
**ski pole** *s* bastón *m* de esquiar
**skipper** ['skɪpər] *s* caudillo, jefe *m;* (*of a boat*) patrón *m;* gusano del queso || *tr* patronear
**skirmish** ['skʌrmɪʃ] *s* escaramuza || *intr* escaramuzar
**skirt** [skʌrt] *s* falda; borde *m,* orilla; (*woman*) (slang) falda || *tr* seguir el borde de; moverse a lo largo de
**ski run** *s* pista de esquí
**ski stick** *s* bastón *m* de esquiar
**skit** [skɪt] *s* boceto burlesco, paso cómico
**skittish** ['skɪtɪʃ] *adj* caprichoso; asustadizo; tímido; (*bull*) abanto
**skulduggery** [skʌl'dʌgəri] *s* (coll) trampa, embuste *m*
**skull** [skʌl] *s* cráneo, calavera
**skull'cap'** *s* casquete *m*
**skunk** [skʌŋk] *s* mofeta; (*person*) (coll) canalla *m*
**sky** [skaɪ] *s* (*pl* **skies**) cielo; **to praise to the skies** poner por las nubes, poner en el cielo
**sky'lark'** *s* alondra || *intr* jaranear
**sky'light'** *s* tragaluz *m,* claraboya
**sky'line'** *s* línea del horizonte, línea de los edificios contra el cielo
**sky'rock'et** *s* cohete *m* || *intr* subir como un cohete
**sky'scrap'er** *s* rascacielos *m*
**sky'writ'ing** *s* escritura aérea
**slab** [slæb] *s* losa; plancha, tabla
**slack** [slæk] *adj* flojo; perezoso; negligente; inactivo || *s* flojedad; inactividad; estación muerta, temporada inactiva; **slacks** pantalones flojos || *tr* aflojar; apagar (*la cal*) || *intr* atrasarse; descuidarse; **to slack up** aflojar el paso
**slacker** ['slækər] *s* perezoso; (mil) prófugo
**slag** [slæg] *s* escoria
**slake** [slek] *tr* aplacar, calmar; apagar (*la cal*)
**slalom** ['slɑləm] *s* eslálom *m*
**slam** [slæm] *s* golpe *m;* (*of a door*) portazo; (coll) crítica acerba || *v* (*pret & pp* **slammed;** *ger* **slamming**) *tr* cerrar de golpe; golpear o empujar estrepitosamente; (coll) criticar acerbamente || *intr* cerrarse de golpe
**slam'-bang'** *adv* (coll) de golpe y porrazo
**slander** ['slændər] *s* calumnia, difamación || *tr* calumniar, difamar
**slanderous** ['slændərəs] *adj* calumnioso, difamatorio
**slang** [slæŋ] *s* caló *m,* jerigonza
**slant** [slænt] *s* inclinación; parecer *m,* punto de vista || *tr* inclinar, sesgar; deformar, tergiversar (*un informe*) || *intr* inclinarse, sesgarse
**slap** [slæp] *s* manazo, palmada; (*in the face*) bofetada; (*in the back*) espaldarazo; desaire *m,* insulto || *v* (*pret & pp* **slapped;** *ger* **slapping**) *tr* dar una palmada a; abofetear
**slash** [slæʃ] *s* cuchillada || *tr* acuchillar; hacer fuerte rebaja de (*precios, sueldos, etc.*)
**slat** [slæt] *s* lámina, tablilla
**slate** [slet] *s* pizarra; candidatura, lista de candidatos || *tr* empizarrar; designar, destinar; poner en la lista de candidatos
**slate pencil** *s* pizarrín *m*
**slate roof** *s* empizarrado
**slattern** ['slætərn] *s* mujer desaliñada, pazpuerca
**slaughter** ['slɔtər] *s* carnicería, matanza || *tr* matar
**slaughter house** *s* matadero
**Slav** [slɑv] o [slæv] *adj & s* eslavo

**slave** [slev] *adj & s* esclavo || *intr* trabajar como esclavo
**slave driver** *s* negrero; (fig) negrero
**slave'hold'er** *s* dueño de esclavos
**slavery** ['slevəri] *s* esclavitud
**slave trade** *s* trata de esclavos
**slave trader** *s* negrero
**Slavic** ['slɑvɪk] o ['slævɪk] *adj & s* eslavo
**slay** [sle] *v* (*pret* **slew** [slu]; *pp* **slain** [slen]) *tr* matar
**slayer** ['sle·ər] *s* matador *m*
**sled** [slɛd] *s* luge *m* || *v* (*pret & pp* **sledded**; *ger* **sledding**) *intr* deslizarse en luge o trineo
**sledge hammer** [slɛdʒ] *s* acotillo
**sleek** [slik] *adj* liso y brillante || *tr* alisar y pulir; suavizar
**sleep** [slip] *s* sueño; **to be overcome with sleep** caerse de sueño; **to go to sleep** dormirse; dormirse, morirse (*un miembro*); **to put to sleep** adormecer; matar por anestesia || *v* (*pret & pp* **slept** [slɛpt]) *tr* pasar durmiendo; **to sleep it off** dormir la mona; **to sleep it over** consultar con la almohada; **to sleep off** dormir (*p.ej., una borrachera*) || *intr* dormir
**sleeper** ['slipər] *s* (*person*) durmiente *mf*; (*girder*) durmiente *m*
**sleeping bag** *s* saco de dormir
**sleeping car** *s* coche-cama *m*
**sleeping pill** *s* píldora para dormir
**sleepless** ['sliplɪs] *adj* insomne, desvelado; pasado en vela
**sleep'walk'er** *s* sonámbulo
**sleep·y** ['slipi] *adj* (*comp* **-ier**; *super* **-iest**) soñoliento; **to be sleepy** tener sueño
**sleep'y·head'** *s* dormilón *m*
**sleet** [slit] *s* cellisca || *intr* cellisquear
**sleeve** [sliv] *s* manga; (mach) manguito; **to laugh in** o **up one's sleeve** reírse para sí
**sleigh** [sle] *s* trineo || *intr* pasearse en trineo
**sleigh bell** *s* cascabel *m*
**sleigh ride** *s* paseo en trineo
**sleight of hand** [slaɪt] *s* juego de manos, prestidigitación
**slender** ['slɛndər] *adj* esbelto, flaco, delgado; escaso, insuficiente
**sleuth** [sluθ] *s* sabueso
**slew** [slu] *s* (coll) montón *m*
**slice** [slaɪs] *s* rebanada, tajada; (*of an orange*) gajo || *tr* rebanar, tajar; dividir; cortar
**slick** [slɪk] *adj* liso y brillante; meloso, suave; (coll) astuto, mañoso || *s* lugar aceitoso y lustroso (*en el agua*)
**slicker** ['slɪkər] *s* impermeable *m* de hule; (coll) embaucador *m*
**slide** [slaɪd] *s* resbalón *m*; (*slippery place*) resbaladero; (*slippery surface*) desliz *m*; derrumbamiento de tierra; (*image for projection*) diapositiva, transparencia; (*of a microscope*) plaquilla de vidrio; (*piece of a device that slides*) cursor *m*; (*of a trombone*) corredera (tubular) || *v* (*pret & pp* **slid** [slɪd]) *tr* deslizar || *intr* deslizar, resbalar; **to let slide** dejar pasar, no hacer caso de
**slide fastener** *s* cierre *m* cremallera, cierre relámpago
**slide rule** *s* regla de cálculo
**slide valve** *s* corredera, válvula corrediza
**sliding contact** *s* cursor *m*
**sliding door** *s* puerta de corredera
**sliding scale** *s* regla de cálculo; (*of salaries*) escala móvil
**slight** [slaɪt] *adj* delgado; leve; pequeño; escaso || *s* desatención, descuido; desaire *m*, menosprecio || *tr* desatender, descuidar; desairar
**slim** [slɪm] *adj* (*comp* **slimmer**; *super* **slimmest**) delgado, esbelto; débil, leve, pequeño, escaso
**slime** [slaɪm] *s* légamo; (*of snakes, fish, etc.*) baba
**slim·y** ['slaɪmi] *adj* (*comp* **-ier**; *super* **-iest**) legamoso; baboso, viscoso; puerco, sucio
**sling** [slɪŋ] *s* (*to shoot stones*) honda; (*to hold up a broken arm*) cabestrillo || *v* (*pret & pp* **slung** [slʌŋ]) *tr* lanzar con una honda; lanzar, tirar; poner en cabestrillo; colgar flojamente
**sling'shot'** *s* honda
**slink** [slɪŋk] *v* (*pret & pp* **slunk** [slʌŋk]) *intr* andar furtivamente; **to slink away** escabullirse, salir con el rabo entre piernas
**slip** [slɪp] *s* resbalón *m*, desliz *m*; falta, error *m*, desliz *m*; lapso; embarcadero; (*cover for a pillow, for furniture*) funda; (*piece of paper*) papeleta; (*cutting from a plant*) sarmiento; (*piece of underclothing*) combinación; (*of a dog*) traílla; huída, evasión; mozuelo, mozuela; **to give the slip to** burlar la vigilancia de || *v* (*pret & pp* **slipped**; *ger* **slipping**) *tr* poner rápidamente; quitar rápidamente; pasar por alto; eludir, evadir; **to slip off** (coll) quitarse de prisa; **to slip on** (coll) ponerse de prisa; **to slip one's mind** olvidársele a uno || *intr* deslizarse; patinar (*el embrague*); errar, equivocarse; (coll) declinar, deteriorarse; **to let slip** dejar pasar; decir inadvertidamente; **to slip away** escurrirse; **to slip by** pasar inadvertido; pasar rápidamente (*el tiempo*); **to slip out of one's hands** escurrirse de entre las manos; **to slip up** (coll) errar, equivocarse
**slip cover** *s* funda
**slip of the pen** *s* error *m* de pluma
**slip of the tongue** *s* error *m* de lengua
**slipper** ['slɪpər] *s* zapatilla, babucha
**slippery** ['slɪpəri] *adj* deslizadizo, resbaladizo; astuto, zorro, evasivo
**slip'-up'** *s* (coll) error *m*, equivocación
**slit** [slɪt] *s* hendidura, raja; cortada, incisión || *v* (*pret & pp* **slit**; *ger* **slitting**) *tr* hender, rajar; cortar
**slob** [slɑb] *s* (slang) sujeto desaseado, puerco
**slobber** ['slɑbər] *s* baba; sensiblería || *intr* babear; hablar con sensiblería
**sloe** [slo] *s* (*shrub*) endrino; (*fruit*) endrina

**slogan** ['slogən] *s* lema *m*, mote *m*; grito de combate; (*striking phrase used in advertising*) eslogan *m*
**sloop** [slup] *s* balandra
**slop** [slɑp] *s* gacha, zupia, agua sucia || *v* (*pret & pp* **slopped**; *ger* **slopping**) *tr* salpicar, ensuciar || *intr* derramarse; chapotear
**slope** [slop] *s* cuesta, pendiente *f*; (*of a continent or a roof*) vertiente *m* & *f* || *tr* inclinar || *intr* inclinarse
**slop·py** ['slɑpi] *adj* (*comp* **-pier**; *super* **-piest**) mojado y sucio; (*in one's dress*) desgalichado; (*in one's work*) chapucero
**slot** [slɑt] *s* ranura; (*for letters*) buzón *m*
**sloth** [sloθ] o [slɔθ] *s* pereza; (zool) perezoso
**slot machine** *s* tragamonedas *m*, máquina sacaperras
**slot meter** *s* contador automático
**slouch** [slaʊtʃ] *s* postura relajada; persona torpe de movimientos || *intr* agacharse, andar caído de hombros; **to slouch in a chair** repanchigarse
**slouch hat** *s* sombrero gacho
**slough** [slaʊ] *s* cenagal *m*, fangal *m*; estado de abandono moral || [slʌf] *s* (*of a snake*) camisa; (pathol) escara || *tr* mudar, echar de sí || *intr* caerse, desprenderse
**Slovak** ['slovæk] o [slo'væk] *adj* & *s* eslovaco
**sloven·ly** ['slʌvənli] *adj* (*comp* **-lier**; *super* **-liest**) desaseado, desaliñado
**slow** [slo] *adj* lento; (*sluggish*) cachazudo, despacioso; (*clock, watch*) atrasado; (*in understanding*) lerdo, tardo, torpe || *adv* despacio || *tr* retrasar; atrasar (*un reloj*) || *intr* retardarse, ir más despacio; atrasarse (*un reloj*)
**slow'down'** *s* huelga de brazos caídos
**slow'-mo'tion** *adj* a cámara lenta
**slow'poke'** *s* tardón *m*
**slug** [slʌg] *s* (*heavy piece of metal*) lingote *m*; (*metal disk used as a coin*) ficha; (zool) limaza, babosa; (coll) porrazo, puñetazo || *v* (*pret & pp* **slugged**; *ger* **slugging**) *tr* (coll) aporrear, apuñear
**sluggard** ['slʌgərd] *s* pachón *m*, perezoso
**sluggish** ['slʌgɪʃ] *adj* inactivo, indolente, tardo; pachorrudo, perezoso
**sluice** [slus] *s* canal *m*; (*floodgate*) compuerta; (*dam; flume*) presa
**sluice gate** *s* compuerta de presa
**slum** [slʌm] *s* barrio bajo || *v* (*pret & pp* **slummed**; *ger* **slumming**) *intr* visitar los barrios bajos
**slumber** ['slʌmbər] *s* sueño ligero, sueño tranquilo || *intr* dormir; dormitar
**slump** [slʌmp] *s* depresión, crisis económica; (*in prices, stocks, etc.*) baja repentina || *intr* hundirse, desplomarse; bajar repentinamente (*los precios, valores, etc.*)
**slur** [slʌr] *s* pronunciación indistinta; reparo crítico; (mus) ligado || *v* (*pret & pp* **slurred**; *ger* **slurring**) *tr* comerse (*sonidos, sílabas*); despreciar, insultar; (mus) ligar
**slush** [slʌʃ] *s* fango muy blando, agua nieve fangosa, nieve *f* a medio derretir; sentimentalismo tonto
**slut** [slʌt] *s* perra; (*slovenly woman*) pazpuerca; ramera, mala mujer
**sly** [slaɪ] *adj* (*comp* **slyer** o **slier**; *super* **slyest** o **sliest**) furtivo, secreto; astuto, socarrón; travieso; **on the sly** a hurtadillas
**smack** [smæk] *adv* (coll) de golpe, de sopetón || *s* dejo, gustillo; palmada, manotada; golpe *m*; beso sonado; (*of a whip*) chasquido || *tr* dar una manotada a; golpear; hacer chasquidos con (*un látigo*); besar sonoramente; **to smack one's lips** chuparse los labios || *intr* — **to smack of** saber a, oler a
**small** [smɔl] *adj* pequeño, chico; (*short in stature*) bajo; pobre, obscuro, humilde; (typ) minúsculo
**small arms** *spl* armas ligeras
**small beer** *s* cerveza floja; bagatela; persona de poca monta
**small business** *s* pequeña empresa
**small capital** *s* versalilla o versalita
**small change** *s* suelto, dinero menudo
**small fry** *s* gente menuda; gente de poca monta
**small'-fry'** *adj* de niños, para niños; de poca monta
**small hours** *spl* primeras horas (*de la mañana*)
**small intestine** *s* intestino delgado
**small-minded** ['smɔl'maɪndɪd] *adj* tacaño, mezquino; intolerante
**smallpox** ['smɔl,pɑks] *s* viruela
**small print** *s* tipo menudo
**small talk** *s* palique *m*, charlas frívolas
**small'-time'** *adj* de poca monta
**small'-town'** *adj* lugareño, apegado a cosas lugareñas
**smart** [smɑrt] *adj* listo, vivo, inteligente; agudo, penetrante; astuto; elegante, majo; picante, punzante; (coll) grande, considerable || *s* escozor *m*; dolor vivo || *intr* escocer, picar; padecer, sufrir
**smart aleck** ['ælɪk] *s* (coll) fatuo, sabihondo
**smart set** *s* gente *f* chic, gente de buen tono
**smash** [smæʃ] *s* rotura violenta; fracaso, ruina; quiebra, bancarrota; (coll) choque violento, tope violento || *tr* romper con fuerza; arruinar, destrozar; aplastar || *intr* romperse con fuerza; arruinarse, destrozarse; aplastarse; **to smash into** chocar con, topar con
**smash hit** *s* (coll) éxito rotundo
**smash'-up'** *s* colisión violenta; ruina, desastre *m*; quiebra, bancarrota
**smattering** ['smætərɪŋ] *s* barniz *m*, tintura, migaja
**smear** [smɪr] *s* embarradura; calumnia; (bact) frotis *m* || *tr* embarrar; calumniar || *intr* embarrarse
**smear campaign** *s* campaña de calumnias
**smell** [smɛl] *s* olor *m*; (*sense*) olfato;

fragancia, perfume *m* || *v* (*pret & pp* **smelled** o **smelt** [smɛlt]) *tr* oler, olfatear || *intr* oler; heder, oler mal; **to smell of** oler a

**smelling salts** *spl* sales aromáticas

**smell·y** [ˈsmɛli] *adj* (*comp* **-ier**; *super* **-iest**) hediondo, maloliente

**smelt** [smɛlt] *s* (*fish*) eperlano, esperinque *m* || *tr & intr* fundir

**smile** [smaɪl] *s* sonrisa || *intr* sonreír, sonreírse

**smiling** [ˈsmaɪlɪŋ] *adj* risueño

**smirk** [smʌrk] *s* sonrisa fatua y afectada || *intr* sonreír fatua y afectadamente

**smite** [smaɪt] *v* (*pret* **smote** [smot]; *pp* **smitten** [ˈsmɪtən] o **smit** [smɪt]) *tr* golpear o herir súbitamente y con fuerza; caer con fuerza sobre; apenar, afligir; castigar

**smith** [smɪθ] *s* forjador *m*, herrero

**smith·y** [ˈsmɪθi] *s* (*pl* **-ies**) herrería

**smitten** [ˈsmɪtən] *adj* afligido; (coll) muy enamorado

**smock** [smɑk] *s* bata

**smock frock** *s* blusa de obrero

**smog** [smɑg] *s* (coll) mezcla de humo y niebla

**smoke** [smok] *s* humo; **to go up in smoke** irse todo en humo || *tr* (*to cure or treat with smoke*) ahumar; fumar (*tabaco*); **to smoke out** ahuyentar con humo, dar humazo a; descubrir || *intr* humear; fumar; hacer humo (*una chimenea dentro de la habitación*)

**smoked glasses** *spl* gafas ahumadas

**smokeless powder** [ˈsmoklɪs] *s* pólvora sin humo

**smoker** [ˈsmokər] *s* fumador *m*; (*room*) fumadero; (rr) coche-fumador *m*; reunión de fumadores

**smoke rings** *spl* anillos de humo; **to blow smoke rings** sacar humo formando anillos

**smoke screen** *s* cortina de humo

**smoke'stack'** *s* chimenea

**smoking** [ˈsmokɪŋ] *s* el fumar; **no smoking** se prohibe fumar

**smoking car** *s* coche-fumador *m*, vagón *m* de fumar

**smoking jacket** *s* batín *m*

**smoking room** *s* fumadero, saloncito para fumadores

**smok·y** [ˈsmoki] *adj* (*comp* **-ier**; *super* **-iest**) humoso; (*emitting smoke*) humeante

**smolder** [ˈsmoldər] *s* fuego lento sin llama y con mucho humo || *intr* arder en rescoldo, arder sin llamas; (fig) estar latente; (*to burn within*) (fig) requemarse; (fig) expresar (*p.ej., los ojos*) una ira latente

**smooth** [smuð] *adj* liso, terso, suave; plano, llano; igual; acaramelado, afable, blando, meloso; (*water*) tranquilo; (*style*) flúido; **smooth as butter** como manteca || *tr* alisar, suavizar; allanar; facilitar; **to smooth away** quitar (*p.ej., obstáculos*) suavemente; **to smooth down** ablandar, calmar

**smooth-faced** [ˈsmuð,fest] *adj* barbilampiño

**smooth-spoken** [ˈsmuθ,spokən] *adj* meloso, lisonjero

**smooth·y** [ˈsmuði] *s* (*pl* **-ies**) (coll) galante *m*; (coll) elegante *m*; (coll) adulador *m*

**smother** [ˈsmʌðər] *tr* ahogar, sofocar; suprimir; reprimir

**smudge** [smʌdʒ] *s* tiznón *m*; mancha || *tr* tiznar; manchar; ahumar, fumigar (*una huerta*)

**smug** [smʌg] *adj* (*comp* **smugger**; *super* **smuggest**) pagado de sí mismo; compuesto, pulcro; relamido

**smuggle** [ˈsmʌgəl] *tr* meter de contrabando || *intr* contrabandear

**smuggler** [ˈsmʌglər] *s* contrabandista *mf*

**smuggling** [ˈsmʌglɪŋ] *s* contrabando

**smut** [smʌt] *s* tiznón *m*; obscenidad; (agr) carbón *m*, tizón *m*

**smut·ty** [ˈsmʌti] *adj* (*comp* **-tier**; *super* **-tiest**) tiznado, manchado; obsceno; (agr) atizonado

**snack** [snæk] *s* parte *f*, porción; bocadillo, tentempié *m*

**snag** [snæg] *s* (*of a tree*) tocón *m*; (*of a tooth*) raigón *m*; obstáculo, tropiezo; **to strike** o **to hit a snag** tropezar con un obstáculo

**snail** [snel] *s* caracol *m*; (*slow person*) pachón *m*; **at a snail's pace** a paso de caracol, a paso de tortuga

**snake** [snek] *s* culebra, serpiente *f*

**snake in the grass** *s* traidor *m*, amigo pérfido

**snap** [snæp] *s* (*crackling sound*) chasquido, estallido; (*of the fingers*) castañetazo; (*bite*) mordisco; (*cracker*) galletita; (*of cold weather*) corto período; (*catch or fastener*) broche *m* de presión; (phot) instantánea; (coll) brío, vigor *m*; (slang) breva, cosa fácil || *v* (*pret & pp* **snapped**; *ger* **snapping**) *tr* asir, cerrar, etc. de golpe; castañetear (*los dedos*); chasquear (*el látigo*); fotografiar instantáneamente; tomar (*una instantánea*); **to snap one's fingers at** tratar con desprecio; **to snap up** aceptar con avidez, comprar con avidez; cortar la palabra a || *intr* chasquear, estallar; (*to crack*) saltar; (*from fatigue*) estallar; **to snap at** querer morder; asir (*una oportunidad*); **to snap out of it** (slang) cambiarse repentinamente; **to snap shut** cerrarse de golpe

**snap'drag'on** *s* (bot) boca de dragón

**snap fastener** *s* corchete *m* de presión

**snap judgment** *s* decisión atolondrada

**snap·py** [ˈsnæpi] *adj* (*comp* **-pier**; *super* **-piest**) mordaz; (coll) elegante, garboso; (coll) enérgico, vivo; (*food*) acre, picante

**snap'shot'** *s* instantánea

**snap switch** *s* (elec) interruptor *m* de resorte

**snare** [snɛr] *s* lazo, trampa; (*of a drum*) bordón *m*, tirante *m*

**snare drum** *s* caja clara

**snarl** [snɑrl] *s* gruñido; regaño; maraña, enredo || *tr* decir con un gru-

ñido; enmarañar, enredar || *intr* gruñir; regañar; enmarañarse, enredarse
**snatch** [snætʃ] *s* arrebatamiento; pedacito, trocito; ratito || *tr & intr* arrebatar; **to snatch at** tratar de asir o agarrar; **to snatch from** arrebatar a
**sneak** [snik] *adj* furtivo || *s* sujeto solapado || *tr* mover a hurtadillas || *intr* andar furtivamente, moverse a hurtadillas
**sneaker** ['snikər] *s* sujeto solapado; (coll) zapato blando, zapato de lona
**sneak thief** *s* ratero, descuidero
**sneak·y** ['sniki] *adj* (*comp* **-ier**; *super* **-iest**) solapado, furtivo
**sneer** [snɪr] *s* expresión de desprecio || *intr* hablar con desprecio, echar una mirada de desprecio; **to sneer at** mofarse de
**sneeze** [sniz] *s* estornudo || *intr* estornudar; **not to be sneezed at** (coll) no ser despreciable
**snicker** ['snɪkər] *s* risa tonta || *intr* reírse tontamente
**sniff** [snɪf] *s* husmeo, venteo; sorbo por las narices || *tr* husmear, ventear; sorber por las narices; (fig) husmear, averiguar; (fig) sospechar || *intr* ventear; **to sniff at** husmear; menospreciar
**sniffle** ['snɪfəl] *s* resuello fuerte y repetido; **the sniffles** ataque *m* de resoplidos || *intr* resollar fuerte y repetidamente
**snip** [snɪp] *s* tijeretada; recorte *m*, pedacito; (coll) persona pequeña e insignificante || *v* (*pret & pp* **snipped**; *ger* **snipping**) *tr* tijeretear
**snipe** [snaɪp] *s* agachadiza, becacín *m* || *intr* paquear, tirar desde un escondite
**sniper** ['snaɪpər] *s* paco, tirador emboscado
**snippet** ['snɪpɪt] *s* recorte *m*; (coll) persona pequeña e insignificante
**snip·py** ['snɪpi] *adj* (*comp* **-pier**; *super* **-piest**) (coll) arrogante, desdeñoso; (coll) acre, brusco
**snitch** [snɪtʃ] *tr & intr* (slang) escamotear, ratear
**sniv·el** ['snɪvəl] *s* gimoteo, lloriqueo; moqueo || *v* (*pret & pp* **-eled** o **-elled**; *ger* **-eling** o **-elling**) *intr* gimotear, lloriquear; (*to have a runny nose*) moquear
**snob** [snɑb] *s* esnob *mf*
**snobbery** ['snɑbəri] *s* esnobismo
**snobbish** ['snɑbɪʃ] *adj* esnob, esnobista
**snoop** [snup] *s* (coll) buscavidas *mf*, curioso || *intr* (coll) curiosear, ventear
**snoopy** ['snupi] *adj* (coll) curioso, entremetido
**snoot** [snut] *s* (slang) cara, narices *fpl*
**snoot·y** ['snuti] *adj* (*comp* **-ier**; *super* **-iest**) (slang) esnob
**snooze** [snuz] *s* (coll) sueñecito || *intr* echar un sueñecito
**snore** [snor] *s* ronquido || *intr* roncar
**snort** [snɔrt] *s* bufido || *intr* bufar
**snot** [snɑt] *s* (slang) mocarro
**snot·ty** ['snɑti] *adj* (*comp* **-tier**; *super* **-tiest**) (coll) mocoso; (coll) asqueroso, sucio; (slang) engreído
**snout** [snaʊt] *s* hocico; (*something shaped like the snout of an animal*) morro; (*of a person*) (coll) hocico
**snow** [sno] *s* nieve *f* || *intr* nevar
**snow'ball'** *s* bola de nieve || *tr* lanzar bolas de nieve a || *intr* aumentar rápidamente
**snow'-blind'** *adj* cegado por reflejos de la nieve
**snow-capped** ['sno ,kæpt] *adj* coronado de nieve
**snow'drift'** *s* ventisquero, masa de nieve
**snow'fall'** *s* nevada
**snow fence** *s* valla paranieves
**snow'flake'** *s* copo de nieve, ampo
**snow flurry** *s* nevisca
**snow line** o **limit** *s* límite *m* de las nieves perpetuas
**snow man** *s* figura de nieve
**snow'plow'** *s* expulsanieves *m*, quitanieves *m*
**snow'shoe'** *s* raqueta de nieve
**snow'storm'** *s* nevasca, fuerte nevada
**snow'-white'** *adj* blanco como la nieve
**snow·y** ['sno·i] *adj* (*comp* **-ier**; *super* **-iest**) nevoso
**snowy owl** *s* lechuza blanca
**snub** [snʌb] *s* desaire *m* || *v* (*pret & pp* **snubbed**; *ger* **snubbing**) *tr* desairar
**snub·by** ['snʌbi] *adj* (*comp* **-bier**; *super* **-biest**) (*nose*) respingona
**snuff** [snʌf] *s* rapé; (*of a candlewick*) moco; **up to snuff** (slang) en buena condición; (slang) difícil de engañar || *tr* husmear, olfatear; sorber por la nariz; despabilar (*una candela*); **to snuff out** apagar, extinguir
**snuff'box'** *s* tabaquera
**snuffers** ['snʌfərz] *spl* despabiladeras
**snug** [snʌg] *adj* (*comp* **snugger**; *super* **snuggest**) cómodo; (*garment*) ajustado, ceñido; (*well-off*) acomodado; (*in hiding*) escondido
**snuggle** ['snʌgəl] *intr* apretarse, arrimarse; dormir bien abrigado; **to snuggle up to** arrimarse a
**so** [so] *adv* así; tan + *adj* o *adv*; por tanto; también; **and so** así pues; también, lo mismo; **and so on** y así sucesivamente; **or so** más o menos; **to think so** creer que sí; **so as to** + *inf* para + *inf*; **so far** hasta aquí; hasta ahora; **so long** hasta la vista; **so many** tantos; **so much** tanto; **so so** tal cual, así así; **so that** de modo que, de suerte que, así que; para que; con tal de que; **so to speak** por decirlo así || *conj* así que || *interj* ¡bien!; ¡verdad!
**soak** [sok] *s* mojada; (*toper*) (coll) potista *mf* || *tr* empapar, remojar; embeber; (slang) aporrear; (slang) hacer pagar un precio exorbitante; **to soak up** absorber, embeber; (fig) entender; **soaked to the skin** calado hasta los huesos || *intr* empaparse, remojarse
**so'-and-so'** *s* (*pl* **-sos**) fulano, fulano de tal; tal cosa
**soap** [sop] *s* jabón *m* || *tr* jabonar

**soap'box'** *s* caja de jabón; tribuna callejera
**soapbox orator** *s* orador *m* de plazuela
**soap bubble** *s* burbuja de jabón, pompa de jabón
**soap dish** *s* jabonera
**soap flakes** *spl* copos de jabón
**soap'mak'er** *s* jabonero
**soap opera** *s* (coll) serial lacrimógeno
**soap powder** *s* jabón *m* en polvo, polvo de jabón
**soap'stone'** *s* jaboncillo de sastre
**soap'suds'** *spl* jabonaduras
**soap·y** ['sopi] *adj* (*comp* **-ier;** *super* **-iest**) jabonoso
**soar** [sor] *intr* encumbrarse, subir muy alto, volar a gran altura; aspirar, pretender; (aer) planear
**sob** [sɑb] *s* sollozo ‖ *v* (*pret & pp* **sobbed;** *ger* **sobbing**) *tr* decir o expresar sollozando ‖ *intr* sollozar
**sober** ['sobər] *adj* sobrio; no embriagado; grave, serio; cuerdo, sensato; sereno, tranquilo; (*color*) apagado ‖ *tr* poner sobrio; desemborrachar ‖ *intr* volverse sobrio; desemborracharse; **to sober down** calmarse, sosegarse; **to sober up** desemborracharse
**sobriety** [so'braɪ·əti] *s* sobriedad, moderación; gravedad, seriedad; cordura, sensatez; serenidad
**sobriquet** ['sobrɪ,ke] *s* apodo
**sob sister** *s* (slang) periodista llorona
**sob story** *s* (slang) historia de lagrimitas
**soc.** o **Soc.** *abbr* **society**
**so'-called'** *adj* llamado, así llamado; supuesto
**soccer** ['sɑkər] *s* fútbol *m* asociación
**sociable** ['soʃəbəl] *adj* sociable
**social** ['soʃəl] *adj* social ‖ *s* reunión social
**social climber** ['klaɪmər] *s* ambicioso de figurar
**socialism** ['soʃə,lɪzəm] *s* socialismo
**socialist** ['soʃəlɪst] *s* socialista *mf*
**socialite** ['soʃə,laɪt] *s* (coll) personaje *m* de la buena sociedad
**social register** *s* guía *m* social, registro de la buena sociedad
**socie·ty** [sə'saɪ·əti] *s* (*pl* **-ties**) sociedad; (*companionship or company*) compañía; buena sociedad, mundo elegante
**society editor** *s* cronista *mf* de la vida social
**sociology** [,sosɪ'ɑlədʒi] o [,soʃɪ'ɑlədʒi] *s* sociología
**sock** [sɑk] *s* calcetín *m;* (slang) golpe *m* fuerte ‖ *tr* (slang) golpear con fuerza
**socket** ['sɑkɪt] *s* (*of the eyes*) cuenca; (*of a tooth*) alvéolo; (*of a candlestick*) cañón *m;* (*of a socket wrench*) cubo; (elec) portalámparas; (rad) zócalo
**socket wrench** *s* llave *f* de caja, llave de cubo
**sod** [sɑd] *s* césped *m;* terrón *m* de césped ‖ *v* (*pret & pp* **sodded;** *ger* **sodding**) *tr* encespedar
**soda** ['sodə] *s* soda, sosa; (*drink*) soda
**soda fountain** *s* fuente *f* de sodas
**soda water** *s* agua gaseosa
**sodium** ['sodɪ·əm] *adj* sódico, de sodio ‖ *s* sodio
**sofa** ['sofə] *s* sofá *m*
**soft** [sɔft] o [sɑft] *adj* blando, muelle; (*skin*) suave; (*iron*) dulce; (*hat*) flexible; (*solder*) tierno; (coll) fácil
**soft-boiled egg** ['sɔft'bɔɪld] o ['sɑft'bɔɪld] *s* huevo pasado por agua
**soft coal** *s* hulla grasa
**soft drink** *s* bebida no alcohólica, refresco
**soften** ['sɔfən] o ['sɑfən] *tr* ablandar; **to soften up** (*by bombardment*) ablandar ‖ *intr* ablandarse
**soft'-ped'al** *tr* (mus) disminuir la intensidad de, por medio del pedal suave; (slang) moderar
**soft soap** *s* jabón blando o graso; (coll) adulación
**soft'-soap'** *tr* (coll) enjabonar, dar jabón a
**sog·gy** ['sɑgi] *adj* (*comp* **-gier;** *super* **-giest**) remojado, ensopado
**soil** [sɔɪl] *s* suelo; país *m*, región; (*spot, stain*) mancha; (fig) mancha, deshonra ‖ *tr* manchar, ensuciar; manchar, deshonrar; viciar, corromper ‖ *intr* mancharse, ensuciarse
**soil pipe** *s* tubo de desagüe sanitario
**soiree** o **soirée** [swɑ're] *s* sarao, velada
**sojourn** ['sodʒʌrn] *s* estancia, permanencia ‖ ['sodʒʌrn] o [so'dʒʌrn] *intr* estarse, permanecer
**sol.** *abbr* **soluble, solution**
**solace** ['sɑlɪs] *s* solaz *m*, consuelo ‖ *tr* solazar, consolar
**solar** ['solər] *adj* solar
**solar battery** *s* fotopila
**solder** ['sɑdər] *s* soldadura ‖ *tr* soldar
**soldering iron** *s* cautín *m*, soldador *m*
**soldier** ['soldʒər] *s* (*enlisted man as distinguished from an officer*) soldado; (*man in military service*) militar *m* ‖ *intr* servir como soldado
**soldier of fortune** *s* aventurero militar
**soldier·y** ['soldʒəri] *s* (*pl* **-ies**) soldadesca
**sold out** [sold] *adj* agotado; **the theater is sold out** todas las localidades están vendidas; **we are sold out of those neckties** se nos han agotado esas corbatas
**sole** [sol] *adj* solo, único; exclusivo ‖ *s* (*of foot*) planta; (*of shoe*) suela; (*fish*) lenguado ‖ *tr* solar
**solely** ['solli] *adv* solamente, únicamente
**solemn** ['sɑləm] *adj* solemne
**solicit** [sə'lɪsɪt] *tr* solicitar; intentar seducir
**solicitor** [sə'lɪsɪtər] *s* solicitador *m*, agente *m;* (law) procurador *m*
**solicitous** [sə'lɪsɪtəs] *adj* solícito
**solicitude** [sə'lɪsɪ,tjud] o [sə'lɪsɪ,tud] *s* solicitud
**solid** ['sɑlɪd] *adj* sólido; unánime; (*sound, good*) sólido, macizo; (*e.g., clouds*) denso; (*without pause or interruption*) entero; (*e.g., gold*) puro ‖ *s* sólido
**solid geometry** *s* geometría del espacio
**solidity** [sə'lɪdɪti] *s* (*pl* **-ties**) solidez *f*

**solid tire** *s* (aut) macizo
**solilo·quy** [sə'lɪləkwi] *s* (*pl* **-quies**) soliloquio
**solitaire** ['sɑlɪ,tɛr] *s* (*game and diamond*) solitario; sortija solitario
**solitar·y** ['sɑlɪ,teri] *adj* solitario ‖ *s* (*pl* **-ies**) solitario
**solitary confinement** *s* incomunicación, aislamiento penal
**solitude** ['sɑlɪ,tjud] o ['sɑlɪ,tud] *s* soledad
**so·lo** ['solo] *adj* (*instrument*) solista; a solas, hecho a solas ‖ *s* (*pl* **-los**) (mus) solo
**soloist** ['solo·ɪst] *s* solista *mf*
**solstice** ['sɑlstɪs] *s* solsticio
**solution** [sə'luʃən] *s* solución
**solve** [sɑlv] *tr* resolver, solucionar; adivinar (*un enigma*)
**solvent** ['sɑlvənt] *adj* & *s* solvente *m*
**somber** ['sɑmbər] *adj* sombrío
**some** [sʌm] *adj indef* algún; un poco de; unos; (coll) grande, bueno, famoso ‖ *pron indef pl* algunos, unos
**some'bod'y** *pron indef* alguien; **somebody else** algún otro, otra persona ‖ *s* (*pl* **-ies**) (coll) personaje *m*
**some'day'** *adv* algún día
**some'how'** *adv* de algún modo, de alguna manera; **somehow or other** de un modo u otro
**some'one'** *pron indef* alguien; **someone else** algún otro, otra persona
**somersault** ['sʌmər,sɔlt] *s* salto mortal ‖ *intr* dar un salto mortal
**something** ['sʌmθɪŋ] *adv* algo, un poco; (coll) muy, excesivamente ‖ *pron indef* alguna cosa, algo; **something else** otra cosa
**some'time'** *adj* antiguo, de otro tiempo ‖ *adv* alguna vez; antiguamente
**some'times'** *adv* a veces, algunas veces
**some'way'** *adv* de algún modo
**some'what'** *adv* algo, un poco ‖ *s* alguna cosa, algo
**some'where'** *adv* en alguna parte, a alguna parte; en algún tiempo; **somewhere else** en otra parte, a otra parte
**somnambulist** [sɑm'næmbjəlɪst] *s* sonámbulo
**somnolent** ['sɑmnələnt] *adj* soñoliento
**son** [sʌn] *s* hijo
**song** [sɔŋ] o [sɑŋ] *s* canción, canto; **for a song** muy barato; **to sing the same old song** volver a la misma canción
**song'bird'** *s* ave canora
**Song of Songs** *s* Cantar *m* de los Cantares
**sonic** ['sɑnɪk] *adj* sónico
**sonic boom** *s* (aer) estampido sónico
**son'-in-law'** *s* (*pl* **sons-in-law**) yerno, hijo político
**sonnet** ['sɑnɪt] *s* soneto
**sonneteer** [,sɑnɪ'tɪr] *s* sonetista *mf;* poetastro ‖ *intr* sonetizar
**son·ny** ['sʌni] *s* (*pl* **-nies**) hijito
**sonori·ty** [sə'nɑrɪti] o [sə'nɔrɪti] *s* (*pl* **-ties**) sonoridad
**soon** [sun] *adv* pronto, en breve; temprano; de buena gana; **as soon as** así que, en cuanto, luego que, tan pronto como; **as soon as possible** cuanto antes, lo más pronto posible; **had sooner** preferiría; **how soon?** ¿cuándo?; **soon after** poco después, poco después de; **sooner or later** tarde o temprano
**soot** [sʊt] o [sut] *s* hollín *m*
**soothe** [suð] *tr* aliviar, calmar, sosegar
**soothsayer** ['suθ,se·ər] *s* adivino
**soot·y** ['sʊti] o ['suti] *adj* (*comp* **-ier;** *super* **-iest**) holliniento, tiznado
**sop** [sɑp] *s* (*food soaked in milk, etc.*) sopa; regalo (*para acallar, apaciguar o sobornar*) ‖ *v* (*pret & pp* **sopped;** *ger* **sopping**) *tr* empapar, ensopar; **to sop up** absorber
**sophisticated** [sə'fɪstɪ,ketɪd] *adj* mundano, falto de simplicidad, corrido
**sophomore** ['sɑfə,mor] *s* estudiante *mf* de segundo año
**sopping** ['sɑpɪŋ] *adj* empapado; **sopping wet** hecho una sopa
**sopran·o** [sə'præno] o [sə'prɑno] *adj* de soprano; para soprano ‖ *s* (*pl* **-os**) soprano *mf*
**sorcerer** ['sɔrsərər] *s* brujo, hechicero
**sorceress** ['sɔrsərɪs] *s* bruja, hechicera
**sorcer·y** ['sɔrsəri] *s* (*pl* **-ies**) brujería, hechicería, sortilegio
**sordid** ['sɔrdɪd] *adj* sórdido
**sore** [sor] *adj* enrojecido, inflamado; (coll) resentido, picado; **to be sore at** (coll) estar enojado con ‖ *s* llaga, úlcera; pena, dolor *m*, aflicción; **to open an old sore** renovar la herida
**sorely** ['sorli] *adv* penosamente; con urgencia
**sore throat** *s* dolor *m* de garganta
**sorori·ty** [sə'rɑrɪti] o [sə'rɔrɪti] *s* (*pl* **-ties**) hermandad de estudiantas
**sorrel** ['sɑrəl] o ['sɔrəl] *adj* alazán
**sorrow** ['sɑro] o ['sɔro] *s* dolor *m*, pena, pesar *m;* arrepentimiento ‖ *intr* dolerse, apenarse, sentir pena; arrepentirse; **to sorrow for** añorar
**sorrowful** ['sɑrəfəl] o ['sɔrəfəl] *adj* doloroso, pesaroso, acongojado
**sor·ry** ['sɑri] o ['sɔri] *adj* (*comp* **-rier;** *super* **-riest**) afligido, apenado, pesaroso; arrepentido; malo, pésimo; despreciable, ridículo; **to be o feel sorry** sentir; arrepentirse; **to be o feel sorry for** compadecer; arrepentirse de
**sort** [sɔrt] *s* clase *f*, especie *f;* modo, manera; **a sort of** uno a modo de; **out of sorts** de mal humor; **sort of** (coll) algo, en cierta medida ‖ *tr* clasificar, separar; escoger, entresacar
**so'-so'** *adj* mediano, regular, talcualillo ‖ *adv* así así, tal cual
**sot** [sɑt] *s* borracho
**sotto voce** ['sɑto 'votʃe] *adv* a sovoz, en voz baja
**soubrette** [su'bret] *s* (theat) confidenta de comedia; (theat) doncella coqueta
**soul** [sol] *s* alma; **upon my soul!** ¡por vida mía!
**sound** [saund] *adj* sano; sólido, firme; solvente; sonoro; (*sleep*) profundo;

prudente; legal, válido || *adv* profundamente || *s* sonido; ruido; (*passage of water*) estrecho, brazo de mar; (surg) sonda, tienta; **within sound of** al alcance de || *tr* sonar; tocar (*p.ej., campanas*); tantear, sondear; auscultar (*p.ej., los pulmones*); entonar (*p.ej., alabanzas*) || *intr* sonar, resonar; sondar; parecer; **to sound like** sonar a, sonar como
**sound film** *s* película sonora
**soundly** ['saʊndli] *adv* sanamente; profundamente; a fondo, completamente
**sound'proof'** *adj* antisonoro || *tr* insonorizar
**soup** [sup] *s* sopa
**soup kitchen** *s* comedor *m* de beneficencia, dispensario de alimentos
**soup spoon** *s* cuchara de sopa
**sour** [saʊr] *adj* agrio || *tr* agriar || *intr* agriarse
**source** [sors] *s* fuente *f*, manantial *m*
**source material** *s* fuentes *fpl* originales
**sour cherry** *s* (*tree*) guindo; (*fruit*) guinda
**sour grapes** *interj* ¡están verdes las uvas!
**south** [saʊθ] *adj* meridional, del sur || *adv* al sur, hacia el sur || *s* sur *m*, mediodía *m*
**South America** *s* Sudamérica, la América del Sur
**South American** *adj* & *s* sudamericano
**southern** ['sʌðərn] *adj* meridional
**Southern Cross** *s* Cruz *f* del Sur
**southerner** ['sʌðərnər] *s* meridional *mf;* sureño (Am)
**South Korea** *s* la Corea del Sur
**South Korean** *adj* & *s* surcoreano
**south'paw'** *adj* & *s* (slang in sport) zurdo
**southward** ['saʊθwərd] *adv* hacia el sur
**south wind** *s* austro, noto
**souvenir** [,suvə'nɪr] o ['suvə,nɪr] *s* recuerdo, memoria
**sovereign** ['sɑvrɪn] o ['sʌvrɪn] *adj* soberano || *s* (*king; coin*) soberano; (*queen*) soberana
**sovereign·ty** ['sɑvrɪnti] o ['sʌvrɪnti] *s* (*pl* **-ties**) soberanía
**soviet** ['sovɪ,et] o [,sovɪ'et] *adj* soviético || *s* soviet *m*
**sovietize** ['sovɪ·e,taɪz] *tr* sovietizar
**Soviet Russia** *s* la Rusia Soviética
**Soviet Union** *s* Unión Soviética
**sow** [saʊ] *s* puerca || [so] *v* (*pret* **sowed;** *pp* **sown** o **sowed**) *tr* sembrar; (*with mines*) plagar
**soybean** ['sɔɪ,bin] *s* soja; semilla de soja
**sp.** *abbr* **special, species, specific, specimen, spelling**
**spa** [spɑ] *s* caldas, balneario
**space** [spes] *adj* espacial, del espacio || *s* espacio; **in the space of** por espacio de || *tr* espaciar
**space bar** *s* espaciador *m*, tecla de espacios
**space'craft'** *s* astronave *f*
**space flight** *s* vuelo espacial
**space key** *s* llave *f* espacial
**space·man** ['spes,mæn] *s* (*pl* **-men** [,men]) navegador *m* del espacio; visitante *m* a la Tierra del espacio exterior
**space'ship'** *s* nave *f* del espacio
**space suit** *s* escafandra espacial
**space vehicle** *s* vehículo espacial
**spacious** ['speʃəs] *adj* espacioso
**spade** [sped] *s* laya; (*playing card*) pique *m;* **to call a spade a spade** llamar al pan pan y al vino vino
**spade'work'** *s* trabajo preliminar
**Spain** [spen] *s* España
**span** [spæn] *s* palmo, cuarta, llave *f* de la mano; espacio, lapso, trecho; (*of horses*) pareja; (*of a bridge*) ojo; (aer) envergadura || *v* (*pret* & *pp* **spanned;** *ger* **spanning**) *tr* medir a palmos; atravesar, extenderse sobre
**spangle** ['spæŋgəl] *s* lentejuela || *tr* adornar con lentejuelas; (*to stud with bright objects*) estrellar || *intr* brillar
**Spaniard** ['spænjərd] *s* español *m*
**spaniel** ['spænjəl] *s* perro de aguas
**Spanish** ['spænɪʃ] *adj* & *s* español *m;* **the Spanish** los españoles
**Spanish America** *s* la América Española, Hispanoamérica
**Spanish broom** *s* retama
**Spanish fly** *s* abadejo, cantárida
**Spanish Main** *s* Costa Firme, Tierra Firme; mar *m* Caribe
**Spanish moss** *s* barba española
**Spanish omelet** *s* tortilla de tomate
**Span'ish-speak'ing** *adj* de habla española, hispanohablante
**spank** [spæŋk] *tr* azotar, zurrar
**spanking** ['spæŋkɪŋ] *adj* rápido; fuerte; (coll) muy grande, muy hermoso, extraordinario || *s* azote *m*
**spar** *s* (mineral) espato; (naut) mástil *m*, palo, verga || *v* (*pret* & *pp* **sparred;** *ger* **sparring**) *intr* pelear, reñir; boxear
**spare** [sper] *adj* sobrante; libre, disponible; de repuesto; delgado, enjuto, flaco; parco, sobrio || *tr* pasar sin; perdonar; guardar, salvar; ahorrar; **to have . . . to spare** tener de sobra; **to spare oneself** ahorrarse esfuerzos
**spare bed** *s* cama de sobra
**spare parts** *spl* piezas de repuesto o de recambio
**spare room** *s* cuarto de reserva
**sparing** ['sperɪŋ] *adj* económico; (*scanty*) escaso
**spark** [spɑrk] *s* chispa; (*e.g., of truth*) centellita || *tr* (coll) cortejar, galantear (*a una mujer*) || *intr* chispear
**spark coil** *s* bobina de chispas, bobina de encendido
**spark gap** *s* (*of induction coil*) entrehierro; (*of spark plug*) espacio de chispa
**sparkle** ['spɑrkəl] *s* chispita, destello; (*wit*) travesura; alegría, viveza || *intr* chispear; ser alegre; espumar, ser efervescente
**sparkling** ['spɑrklɪŋ] *adj* centelleante, chispeante; (*wine*) espumante, espumoso; (*water*) gaseoso

**spark plug** *s* bujía
**sparrow** ['spæro] *s* gorrión *m*
**sparse** [spɑrs] *adj* (*population*) poco denso; (*hair*) ralo
**Spartan** ['spɑrtən] *adj & s* espartano
**spasm** ['spæzəm] *s* espasmo; esfuerzo súbito y de breve duración
**spasmodic** [spæz'mɑdɪk] *adj* espasmódico; intermitente; caprichoso
**spastic** ['spæstɪk] *adj* espástico
**spat** [spæt] *s* disputa, riña; botín *m*, polaina corta
**spatial** ['speʃəl] *adj* espacial
**spatter** ['spætər] *tr* salpicar; manchar ‖ *intr* chorrear; chapotear
**spatula** ['spætʃələ] *s* espátula
**spavin** ['spævɪn] *s* esparaván *m*
**spawn** [spɔn] *s* freza; prole *f;* producto, resultado ‖ *tr* engendrar ‖ *intr* desovar, frezar (*los peces*)
**speak** [spik] *v* (*pret* **spoke** [spok]; *pp* **spoken**) *tr* hablar (*un idioma*); decir (*la verdad*) ‖ *intr* hablar; **so to speak** por decirlo así; **speaking!** ¡al habla!; **to speak out** o **up** osar hablar, elevar la voz
**speak'-eas'y** *s* (*pl* **-ies**) (slang) taberna clandestina
**speaker** ['spikər] *s* hablante *mf;* orador *m;* (*of a legislative assembly*) presidente *m;* (rad) altavoz *m*
**speaking** ['spikɪŋ] *adj* hablante; **to be on speaking terms** hablarse ‖ *s* habla; elocuencia
**speaking tube** *s* tubo acústico
**spear** [spɪr] *s* lanza; (*for fishing*) arpón *m;* (*of grass*) hoja ‖ *tr* alancear, herir con lanza
**spear'head'** *s* punta de lanza ‖ *tr* dirigir, conducir; encabezar; dar impulso a
**spear'mint'** *s* menta verde, menta romana
**spec.** *abbr* **special**
**special** ['speʃəl] *adj* especial ‖ *s* tren *m* especial
**spe'cial-deliv'ery** *adj* urgente, de urgencia
**specialist** ['speʃəlɪst] *s* especialista *mf*
**speciali•ty** [,speʃɪ'ælɪti] *s* (*pl* **-ties**) especialidad
**specialize** ['speʃə,laɪz] *tr* especializar ‖ *intr* especializar o especializarse
**special•ty** ['speʃəlti] *s* (*pl* **-ties**) especialidad
**spe•cies** ['spisiz] *s* (*pl* **-cies**) especie *f*
**specific** [spɪ'sɪfɪk] *adj & s* específico
**speci•fy** ['spesɪ,faɪ] *v* (*pret & pp* **-fied**) *tr* especificar
**specimen** ['spesɪmən] *s* espécimen *m;* (coll) tipo, sujeto
**specious** ['spiʃəs] *adj* especioso, engañoso
**speck** [spek] *s* mota, manchita ‖ *tr* motear, manchar, salpicar de manchas
**speckle** ['spekəl] *s* mota, punto ‖ *tr* motear, puntear
**spectacle** ['spektəkəl] *s* espectáculo; **spectacles** anteojos, gafas
**spectator** ['spektetər] o [spek'tetər] *s* espectador *m*
**specter** ['spektər] *s* espectro
**spec•trum** ['spektrəm] *s* (*pl* **-tra** [trə] o **-trums**) espectro
**speculate** ['spekjə,let] *intr* especular
**speech** [spitʃ] *s* habla; (*of an actor*) parlamento; (*talk before an audience*) conferencia, discurso
**speech clinic** *s* clínica de la palabra
**speech correction** *s* rehabilitación del habla
**speechless** ['spitʃlɪs] *adj* sin habla; estupefacto
**speed** [spid] *s* velocidad; (aut) marcha, velocidad ‖ *v* (*pret & pp* **sped** [sped]) *tr* apresurar; despedir; ayudar ‖ *intr* apresurarse; adelantar, progresar; ir con exceso de velocidad
**speeding** ['spidɪŋ] *s* exceso de velocidad
**speed king** *s* as *m* del volante
**speed limit** *s* velocidad permitida
**speedometer** [spi'dɑmɪtər] *s* (*to indicate speed*) velocímetro; velocímetro y cuentakilómetros unidos
**speed record** *s* marca de velocidad
**speed•y** ['spidi] *adj* (*comp* **-ier**; *super* **-iest**) rápido, veloz
**spell** [spel] *s* encanto, hechizo; tanda, turno; rato, poco tiempo; (*e.g., of good weather*) temporada; **to cast a spell on** encantar, hechizar ‖ *v* (*pret & pp* **spelled** o **spelt** [spelt]) *tr* deletrear; indicar, significar; **to spell out** (coll) explicar detalladamente ‖ *intr* deletrear ‖ *v* (*pret & pp* **spelled**) *tr* reemplazar, relevar
**spell'bind'er** *s* (coll) orador *m* fascinante, orador persuasivo
**spelling** ['spelɪŋ] *adj* ortográfico ‖ *s* (*act*) deletreo; (*subject or study*) ortografía; (*way a word is spelled*) grafía
**spelunker** [spɪ'lʌŋkər] *s* espeleólogo de afición
**spend** [spend] *v* (*pret & pp* **spent** [spent]) *tr* gastar; pasar (*una hora, un día, etc.*)
**spender** ['spendər] *s* gastador *m*
**spending money** *s* dinero para gastos menudos
**spend'thrift'** *s* derrochador *m*, pródigo
**sperm** [spʌrm] *s* esperma *f*
**sperm whale** *s* cachalote *m*
**spew** [spju] *tr & intr* vomitar
**sp. gr.** *abbr* **specific gravity**
**sphere** [sfɪr] *s* esfera; astro, cuerpo celeste
**spherical** ['sferɪkəl] *adj* esférico
**sphinx** [sfɪŋks] *s* (*pl* **sphinxes** o **sphinges** ['sfɪndʒiz]) esfinge *f*
**spice** [spaɪs] *s* especia; (*zest, piquancy*) sainete *m;* fragancia ‖ *tr* especiar; dar gusto o picante a
**spice box** *s* especiero
**spick-and-span** ['spɪkənd'spæn] *adj* flamante; limpio, pulcro
**spic•y** ['spaɪsi] *adj* (*comp* **-ier**; *super* **-iest**) especiado; picante; aromático; sicalíptico
**spider** ['spaɪdər] *s* araña
**spider web** *s* tela de araña, telaraña

**spiff·y** [ˈspɪfi] *adj* (*comp* **-ier;** *super* **-iest**) (slang) guapo, elegante
**spigot** [ˈspɪgət] *s* grifo; (*plug to stop a vent*) espiche *m*
**spike** [spaɪk] *s* (*long, heavy nail*) estaca, escarpia; (*sharp projection or part*) punta, pico, púa; (bot) espiga || *tr* empernar; acabar, poner fin a
**spill** [spɪl] *s* derrame *m;* líquido derramado; (coll) caída, vuelco || *v* (*pret & pp* **spilled** o **spilt** [spɪlt]) *tr* derramar, verter; (coll) hacer caer, volcar || *intr* derramarse, verterse; (coll) caer, volcarse
**spill'way'** *s* bocacaz *m,* canal *m* de desagüe
**spin** [spɪn] *s* vuelta, giro muy rápido; (coll) paseo en coche, etc.; **to go into a spin** (aer) entrar en barrena || *v* (*pret & pp* **spun** [spʌn]; *ger* **spinning**) *tr* hacer girar; hilar (*p.ej., lino*); bailar (*un trompo*); **to spin out** extender, prolongar; **to spin yarns** contar cuentos increíbles || *intr* dar vueltas, girar; hilar; bailar (*un trompo*); (aer) entrar en barrena
**spinach** [ˈspɪnɪtʃ] o [ˈspɪnɪdʒ] *s* espinaca; (*leaves used as food*) espinacas
**spinal** [ˈspaɪnəl] *adj* espinal
**spinal column** *s* espina dorsal, columna vertebral
**spinal cord** *s* médula espinal
**spindle** [ˈspɪndəl] *s* (*rounded rod tapering toward each end*) huso; (*small shaft, axle*) eje *m;* (*turned ornament in a baluster*) mazorca
**spine** [spaɪn] *s* espina, púa; (*rib, ridge*) cordoncillo; loma, cerro; (anat) espina; (bb) lomo; (fig) ánimo, valor *m*
**spineless** [ˈspaɪnlɪs] *adj* sin espinas, sin espinazo; sin firmeza de carácter
**spinet** [ˈspɪnɪt] *s* espineta
**spinner** [ˈspɪnər] *s* hilandero; máquina de hilar
**spinning** [ˈspɪnɪŋ] *adj* hilador || *s* (*act*) hila; (*art*) hilandería
**spinning wheel** *s* torno de hilar
**spinster** [ˈspɪnstər] *s* solterona
**spi·ral** [ˈspaɪrəl] *adj & s* espiral *f* || *v* (*pret & pp* **-raled** o **-ralled;** *ger* **-raling** o **-ralling**) *intr* dar vueltas como una espiral; (aer) volar en espiral
**spiral staircase** *s* escalera de caracol
**spire** [spaɪr] *s* cima, ápice *m;* (*of a steeple*) aguja, chapitel *m;* (*e.g., of grass*) tallo
**spirit** [ˈspɪrɪt] *s* espíritu *m;* humor *m,* temple *m;* personaje *m;* licor *m* || *tr* — **to spirit away** llevarse misteriosamente
**spirited** [ˈspɪrɪtɪd] *adj* fogoso, espiritoso
**spirit lamp** *s* lámpara de alcohol
**spiritless** [ˈspɪrɪtlɪs] *adj* apocado, tímido, sin ánimo
**spirit level** *s* nivel *m* de burbuja
**spiritual** [ˈspɪrɪtʃu·əl] *adj* espiritual
**spiritualism** [ˈspɪrɪtʃuəˌlɪzəm] *s* espiritismo; (*belief that all reality is spiritual*) espiritualismo
**spirituous liquors** [ˈspɪrɪtʃu·əs] *spl* licores espirituosos
**spit** [spɪt] *s* esputo, saliva; (*for roasting*) asador *m,* espetón *m;* punta o lengua de tierra; **the spit and image of** la segunda edición de, el retrato de || *v* (*pret & pp* **spat** [spæt] o **spit;** *ger* **spitting**) *tr* escupir || *intr* escupir; lloviznar; neviscar; fufar (*el gato*)
**spite** [spaɪt] *s* despecho, rencor *m,* inquina; **in spite of** a pesar de, a despecho de; **out of spite** por despecho || *tr* despechar, molestar, picar
**spiteful** [ˈspaɪtfəl] *adj* despechado, rencoroso
**spit'fire'** *s* fierabrás *m;* mujer *f* de mal genio
**spittoon** [spɪˈtun] *s* escupidera
**splash** [splæʃ] *s* rociada, salpicadura; (*e.g., with the hands*) chapaleo, chapoteo; **to make a splash** (coll) hacer impresión, llamar la atención || *tr & intr* salpicar; chapotear
**splash'down'** *s* acuatizaje *m*
**spleen** [splin] *s* mal humor *m;* (anat) bazo; **to vent one's spleen** descargar la bilis
**splendid** [ˈsplendɪd] *adj* espléndido; (coll) magnífico, maravilloso
**splendor** [ˈsplendər] *s* esplendor *m*
**splice** [splaɪs] *s* empalme *m,* junta || *tr* empalmar, juntar
**splint** [splɪnt] *s* (*splinter*) astilla, tablilla; (surg) tablilla || *tr* entablillar (*un hueso roto*)
**splinter** [ˈsplɪntər] *s* astilla; (*of stone, glass, bone*) esquirla || *tr* astillar || *intr* astillarse, hacerse astillas
**splinter group** *s* grupo disidente
**split** [splɪt] *adj* hendido, partido; dividido || *s* división, fractura; (slang) porción || *v* (*pret & pp* **split;** *ger* **splitting**) *tr* dividir, partir; **to split one's sides with laughter** desternillarse de risa || *intr* dividirse a lo largo; **to split away (from)** separarse (de)
**split fee** *s* dicotomía (*entre médicos*)
**split personality** *s* personalidad desdoblada
**splitting** [ˈsplɪtɪŋ] *adj* partidor; fuerte, violento; (*headache*) enloquecedor
**splotch** [splɑtʃ] *s* borrón *m,* mancha grande || *tr* salpicar, manchar
**splurge** [splʌrdʒ] *s* (coll) fachenda, ostentación || *intr* (coll) fachendear
**splutter** [ˈsplʌtər] *s* chisporroteo; (*manner of speaking*) farfulla || *tr* farfullar || *intr* chisporrotear; farfullar
**spoil** [spɔɪl] *s* botín *m,* presa; **spoils** (*taken from an enemy*) botín, despojos; (*of political victory*) enchufes *mpl* || *v* (*pret & pp* **spoiled** o **spoilt** [spɔɪlt]) *tr* echar a perder, estropear; mimar (*a un niño*); amargar (*una tertulia*) || *intr* echarse a perder
**spoiled** [spɔɪld] *adj* (*child*) consentido, mimado; (*food*) pasado, podrido
**spoils·man** [ˈspɔɪlzmən] *s* (*pl* **-men** [mən]) enchufista *m*
**spoils system** *s* enchufismo
**spoke** [spok] *s* (*of a wheel*) radio, rayo; (*of a ladder*) escalón *m*

**spokes·man** ['spoksmən] *s* (*pl* **-men** [mən]) portavoz *m*, vocero
**sponge** [spʌndʒ] *s* esponja; **to throw in** (o **up**) **the sponge** (coll) tirar la esponja ‖ *tr* limpiar con esponja; borrar; absorber ‖ *intr* ser absorbente; **to sponge on** (coll) vivir a costa de
**sponge cake** *s* bizcocho muy ligero
**sponger** ['spʌndʒər] *s* esponja (*gorrón, parásito*)
**sponge rubber** *s* caucho esponjoso
**spon·gy** ['spʌndʒi] *adj* (*comp* **-gier**; *super* **-giest**) esponjoso
**sponsor** ['spɑnsər] *s* patrocinador *m*; (*godfather*) padrino; (*godmother*) madrina ‖ *tr* patrocinar
**sponsorship** ['spɑnsər,ʃɪp] *s* patrocinio
**spontaneous** [spɑn'tenɪ·əs] *adj* espontáneo
**spoof** [spuf] *s* (slang) mistificación, engaño; (slang) broma ‖ *tr* (slang) mistificar, engañar ‖ *intr* (slang) bromear, burlar; (slang) parodiar
**spook** [spuk] *s* (coll) aparecido, espectro
**spook·y** ['spuki] *adj* (*comp* **-ier**; *super* **-iest**) (coll) espectral, espeluznante; (*horse*) (coll) asustadizo
**spool** [spul] *s* carrete *m*, bobina
**spoon** [spun] *s* cuchara ‖ *tr* cucharear ‖ *intr* (slang) besuquearse (*los enamorados*)
**spoonful** ['spun,fʊl] *s* cucharada
**spoon·y** ['spuni] *adj* (*comp* **-ier**; *super* **-iest**) (coll) baboso, sobón
**sporadic(al)** [spə'rædɪk(əl)] *adj* esporádico
**spore** [spor] *s* espora
**sport** [sport] *adj* deportivo, de deporte ‖ *s* deporte *m*; deportista *mf*; (*person or thing controlled by some power or passion*) juguete *m*; (*laughingstock*) hazmerreír *m*; (*gambler*) (coll) tahur *m*, jugador *m*; (*in gambling or playing games*) (coll) buen perdedor; (*flashy fellow*) (coll) guapo, majo; (biol) mutación; **to make sport of** burlarse de, reírse de ‖ *tr* (coll) lucir (*p.ej., un traje nuevo*) ‖ *intr* divertirse; estar de burla; juguetear
**sport clothes** *spl* trajes *mpl* de sport
**sport fan** *s* (slang) aficionado al deporte, deportista *mf*
**sporting chance** *s* (coll) riesgo de buen perdedor
**sporting goods** *spl* artículos de deporte
**sporting house** *s* (coll) casa de juego; (coll) casa de rameras
**sports'cast'er** *s* locutor deportivo
**sports·man** ['sportsmən] *s* (*pl* **-men** [mən]) deportista *m*; jugador honrado
**sports news** *s* noticiario deportivo
**sports'wear'** *s* trajes deportivos
**sports writer** *s* cronista deportivo
**sport·y** ['sporti] *adj* (*comp* **-ier**; *super* **-iest**) (coll) elegante, guapo; (coll) alegre, brillante; (coll) magnánimo; (coll) disipado, libertino
**spot** [spɑt] *s* mancha; sitio, lugar *m*; (coll) poquito; **on the spot** allí mismo; al punto; (slang) en dificultad; (slang) en peligro de muerte; **to hit the spot** tener razón; (coll) dar completa satisfacción ‖ *v* (*pret & pp* **spotted**; *ger* **spotting**) *tr* manchar; (coll) descubrir, reconocer ‖ *intr* mancharse, tener manchas
**spot cash** *s* dinero contante
**spotless** ['spɑtlɪs] *adj* inmaculado, sin manchas
**spot'light'** *s* proyector *m* orientable; luz concentrada; (aut) faro piloto, faro giratorio; (fig) atención del público
**spot remover** [rɪ'muvər] *s* (*person*) quitamanchas *mf*; (*material*) quitamanchas *m*
**spot welding** *s* soldadura por puntos
**spouse** [spauz] o [spaus] *s* cónyuge *mf*, consorte *mf*
**spout** [spaut] *s* (*to carry off water from roof*) canalón *m*; (*of a jar, pitcher, etc.*) pico; (*of a sprinkling can*) rallo, roseta; (*jet*) chorro; **up the spout** (slang) acabado, arruinado ‖ *tr* echar en chorro; (coll) declamar ‖ *intr* chorrear; (coll) declamar
**sprain** [spren] *s* torcedura, esguince *m* ‖ *tr* torcer, torcerse
**sprawl** [sprɔl] *intr* arrellanarse
**spray** [spre] *s* rociada; (*of the sea*) espuma; (*device*) pulverizador *m*; (*twig*) ramita ‖ *tr & intr* rociar
**sprayer** ['spre·ər] *s* rociador *m*, pulverizador *m*, vaporizador *m*
**spread** [sprɛd] *s* extensión; amplitud, anchura; difusión; diferencia; cubrecama, sobrecama; mantel *m*, tapete *m*; (*of the wings of a bird; of the wings of an airplane*) envergadura; (coll) festín *m*, comilona ‖ *v* (*pret & pp* **spread**) *tr* extender; difundir, propagar; esparcir; escalonar; abrir, separar; poner (*la mesa*) ‖ *intr* extenderse; difundirse; esparcirse; abrirse, separarse
**spree** [spri] *s* juerga, parranda; borrachera; **to go on a spree** ir de juerga; pillar una mona
**sprig** [sprɪg] *s* ramita
**spright·ly** ['spraɪtli] *adj* (*comp* **-lier**; *super* **-liest**) alegre, animado, vivo
**spring** [sprɪŋ] *adj* primaveral; de manantial; de muelle, de resorte ‖ *s* (*season of the year*) primavera; (*issue of water from earth*) fuente *f*, manantial *m*; (*elastic device*) muelle *m*, resorte *m*; (*of an automobile or wagon*) ballesta; (*leap, jump*) brinco, salto; abertura, grieta; tensión, tirantez *f* ‖ *v* (*pret* **sprang** [spræŋ] o **sprung** [sprʌŋ]; *pp* **sprung**) *tr* soltar (*un muelle o resorte*); torcer, combar, encorvar; hacer saltar (*una trampa, una mina*) ‖ *intr* saltar; saltar de golpe; brotar, nacer, proceder; torcerse, combarse, encorvarse; **to spring at** abalanzarse sobre; **to spring forth** precipitarse; brotar; **to spring up** levantarse de un salto; brotar, nacer; presentarse a la vista
**spring'board'** *s* trampolín *m*

**spring chicken** *s* polluelo; (*young person*) (coll) pollita
**spring fever** *s* (hum) ataque *m* primaveral, galbana
**spring mattress** *s* colchón *m* de muelles, somier *m*
**spring'time'** *s* primavera
**sprinkle** ['sprɪŋkəl] *s* rociada; llovizna; pizca || *tr* regar, rociar; salpicar, sembrar; espolvorear (*p.ej., azucar*) || *intr* rociar; lloviznar, gotear
**sprinkling can** *s* regadera, rociadera
**sprint** [sprɪnt] *s* (sport) embalaje *m* || *intr* (sport) embalarse, lanzarse
**sprite** [spraɪt] *s* duende *m*, trasgo
**sprocket** ['sprɑkɪt] *s* diente *m* de rueda de cadena; rueda de cadena
**sprout** [spraʊt] *s* brote *m*, renuevo, retoño || *intr* brotar, germinar, echar renuevos; crecer rápidamente
**spruce** [sprus] *adj* apuesto, elegante, garboso || *s* abeto del Norte, abeto falso, pícea || *tr* ataviar, componer || *intr* ataviarse, componerse; **to spruce up** emperifollarse
**spry** [spraɪ] *adj* (*comp* **spryer** o **sprier**; *super* **spryest** o **spriest**) activo, ágil
**spud** [spʌd] *s* (*chisel*) escoplo; (agr) escoda; (coll) patata
**spun glass** [spʌn] *s* vidrio hilado, cristal hilado
**spunk** [spʌŋk] *s* (coll) ánimo, coraje *m*, corazón *m*, valor *m*
**spun silk** *s* seda cardada o hilada
**spur** [spʌr] *s* espuela; (*central point of an auger*) gusanillo; (*of a cock, mountain, warship*) espolón *m;* (rr) ramal corto; (*goad, stimulus*) (fig) espuela; **on the spur of the moment** impulsivamente, sin la reflexión debida || *v* (*pret & pp* **spurred;** *ger* **spurring**) *tr* espolear; **to spur on** espolear, aguijonear
**spurious** ['spjʊrɪ·əs] *adj* espurio
**spurn** [spʌrn] desdén *m*, menosprecio || *tr* desdeñar, menospreciar; rechazar con desdén
**spurt** [spʌrt] *s* chorro repentino; esfuerzo repentino; arranque *m* || *intr* salir en chorro, salir a borbotones
**sputter** ['spʌtər] *s* (*manner of speaking*) farfulla; (*sizzling*) chisporroteo || *tr* farfullar || *intr* farfullar; chisporrotear
**spy** [spaɪ] *s* (*pl* **spies**) espía *mf* || *v* (*pret & pp* **spied**) *tr* columbrar, divisar || *intr* espiar; **to spy on** espiar
**spy'glass'** *s* catalejo, anteojo
**sq.** *abbr* **square**
**squabble** ['skwɑbəl] *s* reyerta, riña || *intr* reñir, disputar
**squad** [skwɑd] *s* escuadra
**squadron** ['skwɑdrən] *s* (aer) escuadrilla; (*of cavalry*) (mil) escuadrón *m;* (nav) escuadra
**squalid** ['skwɑlɪd] *adj* escuálido
**squall** [skwɔl] *s* grupada, turbión *m;* (*quarrel*) (coll) riña; (*upset, commotion*) (coll) chubasco
**squalor** ['skwɑlər] *s* escualidez *f*
**squander** ['skwɑndər] *tr* despilfarrar, malgastar
**square** [skwer] *adj* cuadrado, p.ej., **eight square inches** ocho pulgadas cuadradas; en cuadro, de lado, p.ej., **eight inches square** ocho pulgadas en cuadro, ocho pulgadas de lado; rectangular; justo, recto; honrado, leal; saldado; fuerte, sólido; (coll) abundante, completo; **to get square with** (coll) hacérselas pagar a || *adv* en cuadro; en ángulo recto; honradamente, lealmente || *s* cuadrado; (*of checkerboard or chessboard*) casilla, escaque *m;* (*city block*) manzana; (*open area in town or city*) plaza; (*carpenter's tool*) escuadra; **to be on the square** (coll) obrar de buena fe || *tr* cuadrar; dividir en cuadros; ajustar, nivelar, conformar; saldar (*una cuenta*); (carp) escuadrar || *intr* cuadrarse; **to square off** (coll) colocarse en posición de defensa
**square dance** *s* danza de figuras
**square deal** *s* (coll) trato equitativo
**square meal** *s* (coll) comida abundante
**square shooter** ['ʃutər] *s* (coll) persona leal y honrada
**squash** [skwɑʃ] *s* aplastamiento; (bot) calabaza; (sport) frontón *m* con raqueta; || *tr* aplastar, despachurrar; confutar (*un argumento*); acallar con un argumento, respuesta, etc. || *intr* aplastarse
**squash·y** ['skwɑʃi] *adj* (*comp* **-ier;** *super* **-iest**) mojado y blando; (*muddy*) lodoso; (*fruit*) modorro
**squat** [skwɑt] *adj* en cuclillas; rechoncho || *v* (*pret & pp* **squatted;** *ger* **squatting**) *intr* acuclillarse, agacharse; sentarse en el suelo; establecerse en terreno ajeno sin derecho; establecerse en terreno público para crear un derecho
**squatter** ['skwɑtər] *s* advenedizo, intruso, colono usurpador
**squaw** [skwɔ] *s* india norteamericana; mujer, esposa, muchacha
**squawk** [skwɔk] *s* graznido; (slang) queja chillona || *intr* graznar; (slang) quejarse chillando
**squaw man** *s* blanco casado con india
**squeak** [skwik] *s* chillido; chirrido || *intr* dar chillidos; chirriar
**squeal** [skwil] *s* chillido || *intr* dar chillidos; (slang) delatar, soplar; **to squeal on** (slang) delatar, soplar (*a una persona*)
**squealer** ['skwilər] *s* (coll) soplón *m*
**squeamish** ['skwimɪʃ] *adj* escrupuloso, remilgado; excesivamente modesto; (*easily nauseated*) asqueroso
**squeeze** [skwiz] *s* apretón *m;* **to put the squeeze on someone** (coll) hacer a uno la forzosa, meter en prensa a uno || *tr* apretar; agobiar, oprimir; exprimir || *intr* apretar; **to squeeze through** abrirse paso a estrujones por entre; salir de un aprieto a duras penas
**squeezer** ['skwizər] *s* exprimidera
**squelch** [skwɛltʃ] *s* (coll) tapaboca || *tr* apabullar, despachurrar
**squid** [skwɪd] *s* calamar *m*

**squint** [skwɪnt] *s* mirada bizca; mirada furtiva; (*strabismus*) bizquera || *tr* achicar, entornar (*los ojos*) || *intr* bizquear; torcer la vista; tener los ojos medio cerrados
**squint-eyed** [ˈskwɪnt,aɪd] *adj* bisojo, bizco; malévolo, sospechoso
**squire** [skwaɪr] *s* acompañante *m* (*de una señora*); (Brit) terrateniente *m* de antigua heredad; (U.S.A.) juez *m* de paz, juez local || *tr* acompañar (*a una señora*)
**squirm** [skwʌrm] *s* retorcimiento || *intr* retorcerse; **to squirm out of** escaparse de (*p.ej., un aprieto*) haciendo mucho esfuerzo
**squirrel** [ˈskwʌrəl] *s* ardilla
**squirt** [skwʌrt] *s* chorro; jeringazo; (coll) mono, presuntuoso || *tr* arrojar a chorros || *intr* salir a chorros
**Sr.** *abbr* **senior, Sir**
**S.S.** *abbr* **Secretary of State, steamship, Sunday school**
**St.** *abbr* **Saint, Strait, Street**
**stab** [stæb] *s* puñalada; (coll) tentativa; **to make a stab at** (slang) esforzarse por hacer || *v* (*pret & pp* **stabbed**; *ger* **stabbing**) *tr* apuñalar; traspasar || *intr* apuñalar
**stab in the back** *s* puñalada trapera
**stable** [ˈstebəl] *adj* estable || *s* establo, cuadra, caballeriza
**stack** [stæk] *s* montón *m*, pila; (*of rifles*) pabellón *m;* (*of books in a library*) estantería, depósito; (*of a chimney*) cañón *m;* (*of straw*) niara; (*of firewood*) hacina; (coll) montón *m*, gran número || *tr* amontonar, apilar; florear (*el naipe*); hacinar (*leña*)
**stadi·um** [ˈstedɪ·əm] *s* (*pl* **-ums** o **-a** [ə]) estadio
**staff** [stæf] o [stɑf] *s* bastón *m*, apoyo, sostén *m;* personal *m;* (mil) estado mayor; (mus) pentagrama *m* || *tr* dotar, proveer de personal, nombrar personal para
**stag** [stæg] *adj* exclusivo para hombres, de hombres solos || *s* (*male deer*) ciervo; varón *m;* varón solo (*no acompañado de mujeres*)
**stage** [stedʒ] *s* escena; etapa, jornada; (*coach*) diligencia; (*scene of an event*) teatro; (*of a microscope*) portaobjeto; (rad) etapa; **by easy stages** a pequeñas etapas; lentamente; **to go on the stage** hacerse actor || *tr* poner en escena, representar; preparar, organizar
**stage'coach'** *s* diligencia
**stage'craft'** *s* arte *f* teatral
**stage door** *s* (theat) entrada de los artistas
**stage fright** *s* trac *m*, miedo al público
**stage'hand'** *s* tramoyista *m*, metemuertos *m*, metesillas *m*
**stage manager** *s* director *m* de escena
**stage'-struck'** *adj* loco por el teatro
**stage whisper** *s* susurro en voz alta
**stagger** [ˈstægər] *tr* sorprender; asustar; escalonar (*las horas de trabajo*) || *intr* tambalear, hacer eses al andar
**staggering** *adj* tambaleante; sorprendente
**stagnant** [ˈstægnənt] *adj* estancado; (fig) estancado, inactivo, paralizado
**staid** [sted] *adj* grave, serio, formal
**stain** [sten] *s* mancha; tinte *m*, tintura; materia colorante || *tr* manchar; teñir; colorar || *intr* mancharse; hacer manchas
**stained glass** *s* vidrio de color
**stained'glass' window** *s* vidriera de colores, vidriera pintada, vitral *m*
**stainless** [ˈstenlɪs] *adj* inmanchable; (*steel*) inoxidable; inmaculado
**stair** [ster] *s* escalera; (*step of a series*) escalón *m;* **stairs** escalera
**stair'case'** *s* escalera
**stair'way'** *s* escalera
**stair well** *s* hueco de escalera
**stake** [stek] *s* estaca; (*of a cart or truck*) telero; (*to hold up a plant*) rodrigón *m;* (*in gambling*) puesta; premio del vencedor; **at stake** en juego; en gran peligro; **to die at the stake** morir en la hoguera; **to pull up stakes** (coll) irse; (coll) mudarse de casa || *tr* estacar; atar a una estaca; rodrigar (*plantas*); apostar; arriesgar, aventurar; **to stake all** jugarse el todo por el todo; **to stake off** o **to stake out** estacar, señalar con estacas
**stale** [stel] *adj* añejo, rancio, viejo; (*air*) viciado; (*joke*) mohoso; anticuado
**stale'mate'** *s* mate ahogado; **to reach a stalemate** llegar a un punto muerto || *tr* dar mate ahogado a; estancar, paralizar
**stalk** [stɔk] *s* tallo || *tr* cazar al acecho; acechar, espiar || *intr* cazar al acecho; andar con paso majestuoso; andar con paso altivo; **to stalk out** salir con paso airado
**stall** [stɔl] *s* cuadra, establo; pesebre *m;* (*booth in a market*) puesto; (*at a fair*) caseta; (Brit) butaca; (slang) pretexto || *tr* encerrar en un establo; poner trabas a; parar (*un motor*); **to stall off** (coll) eludir, evitar || *intr* atascarse, atollarse; pararse (*un motor*); (slang) eludir para engañar o demorar; **to stall for time** (slang) tardar para ganar tiempo
**stallion** [ˈstæljən] *s* caballo padre, caballo semental
**stalwart** [ˈstɔlwərt] *adj* fornido, forzudo; valiente; leal, constante || *s* persona fornida; partidario leal
**stamen** [ˈstemən] *s* estambre *m*
**stamina** [ˈstæmɪnə] *s* fuerza, nervio, vigor *m*, resistencia
**stammer** [ˈstæmər] *s* balbuceo, tartamudeo || *tr* balbucear (*p.ej., excusas*) || *intr* balbucear, tartamudear
**stamp** [stæmp] *s* (*device used for making an impression; mark made with it; piece of paper or mark used to show payment of postage*) sello; (*tool used for crushing or marking*) pisón *m;* (*tool for stamping coins and medals*) cuño, troquel *m;* marca, impresión; clase *f*, tipo || *tr* sellar; troquelar; estampar, imprimir; hollar,

pisotear; indicar, señalar; poner el sello a; bocartear (*el mineral*); **to stamp out** apagar pateando; extinguir por la fuerza; suprimir; **to stamp the feet** dar patadas || *intr* patalear

**stampede** [stæm'pid] *s* fuga precipitada; estampida (Am) || *tr* hacer huir en desorden; provocar a pánico || *intr* huir en tropel; obrar por común impulso

**stamping grounds** *spl* (slang) guarida (*sitio frecuentado por una persona*)

**stamp pad** *s* tampón *m*

**stamp'-vend'ing machine** *s* máquina expendedora de sellos

**stance** [stæns] *s* (sport) postura, planta

**stanch** [stɑntʃ] *adj* firme, fuerte; constante, leal; (*watertight*) estanco || *tr* estancar; restañar (*la sangre de una herida*)

**stand** [stænd] *s* parada; alto para defenderse; postura, posición; resistencia; estrado, tribuna; sostén *m*, soporte *m*, pie *m;* puesto, quiosco || *v* (*pret & pp* **stood** [stʊd]) *tr* poner, colocar; poner derecho; soportar, tolerar, resistir; (coll) aguantar (*a una persona*); (coll) sufragar (*un gasto*); **to stand off** tener a raya; **to stand one's ground** mantenerse firme || *intr* estar, estar situado; estar parado; estacionarse; estar de pie, estar derecho; ponerse de pie, levantarse; resultar; persistir; mantenerse; **to stand aloof, apart** o **aside** mantenerse apartado; **to stand back of** respaldar; **to stand for** significar, representar; apoyar, defender; apadrinar; mantener (*p.ej., una opinión*); presentarse como candidato de; navegar hacia; (coll) tolerar; **to stand in line** hacer cola; **to stand out** sobresalir; destacarse, resaltar; **to stand up** ponerse de pie, levantarse; durar; **to stand up to** hacer resueltamente frente a

**standard** ['stændərd] *adj* normal; (*typewriter keyboard*) universal; corriente, regular; legal; clásico || *s* patrón *m;* norma, regla establecida; bandera, estandarte *m;* emblema *m*, símbolo; soporte *m*, pilar *m*

**standardize** ['stændər,daɪz] *tr* normalizar, estandardizar

**standard of living** *s* nivel *m* de vida

**standard time** *s* hora legal, hora oficial

**standee** [stæn'di] *s* (coll) espectador *m* que asiste de pie; (coll) pasajero de pie

**stand'-in'** *s* (theat & mov) doble *mf;* (coll) buenas aldabas

**standing** ['stændɪŋ] *adj* derecho, en pie; de pie; parado, inmóvil; (*water*) encharcado, estancado; (*army; committee*) permanente; vigente || *s* condición, posición; reputación; parada; **in good standing** en posición acreditada; **of long standing** de mucho tiempo, de antigua fecha

**standing army** *s* ejército permanente

**standing room** *s* sitio para estar de pie

**stand'point'** *s* punto de vista

**stand'still'** *s* detención, parada; alto; descanso, inactividad; **to come to a standstill** cesar, pararse

**stanza** ['stænzə] *s* estancia, estrofa

**staple** ['stepəl] *adj* primero, principal; corriente, establecido || *s* (*to fasten papers*) grapa; artículo o producto de primera necesidad; materia prima; fibra textil || *tr* sujetar con grapas

**stapler** ['steplər] *s* engrapador *m*, cosepapeles *m*

**star** [stɑr] *s* (*heavenly body*) astro; (*heavenly body except sun and moon; figure that represents a star*) estrella; (mov & theat) estrella; (*of football*) as *m;* (typ) estrella o asterisco; (*fate, destiny*) (fig) estrella; **to see stars** (coll) ver las estrellas; **to thank one's lucky stars** estar agradecido por su buena suerte || *v* (*pret & pp* **starred;** *ger* **starring**) *tr* estrellar, adornar o señalar con estrellas; marcar con asterisco; presentar como estrella (*a un actor*) || *intr* ser la estrella; lucirse; sobresalir

**starboard** ['stɑrbərd] o ['stɑr,bord] *adj* de estribor || *adv* a estribor || *s* estribor *m*

**starch** [stɑrtʃ] *s* almidón *m*, fécula; arrogancia, entono; (slang) fuerza, vigor *m* || *tr* almidonar

**stare** [stɛr] *s* mirada fija || *intr* mirar fijamente; **to stare at** clavar la vista en, mirar con fijeza

**star'fish'** *s* estrella de mar, estrellamar *m*

**star'gaze'** *intr* mirar las estrellas; ser distraído, soñar despierto

**stark** [stɑrk] *adj* cabal, completo, puro; rígido, tieso; duro, severo || *adv* completamente, enteramente; rígidamente, severamente

**stark'-na'ked** *adj* en pelota, en cueros

**star'light'** *s* luz *f* de las estrellas

**starling** ['stɑrlɪŋ] *s* estornino

**Star'-Span'gled Banner** *s* bandera estrellada (*bandera de los EE.UU.*)

**start** [stɑrt] *s* comienzo, principio; salida, partida; lugar *m* de partida; (*scare*) sobresalto; (*sudden start*) arranque *m;* (*advantage*) ventaja || *tr* empezar, principiar; poner en marcha; hacer arrancar; dar la señal de partida a; entablar (*una conversación*); levantar (*la caza*) || *intr* empezar, principiar; ponerse en marcha; arrancar; (*to be startled*) sobresaltar; nacer, provenir; **starting from** o **with** a partir de; **to start after** salir en busca de

**starter** ['stɑrtər] *s* iniciador *m;* (*of a series*) primero; (aut) arranque *m*, motor *m* de arranque; (sport) juez *m* de salida

**starting** ['stɑrtɪŋ] *adj* de salida; de arranque || *s* puesta en marcha

**starting crank** *s* manivela de arranque

**starting point** *s* punto de partida, arrancadero

**startle** ['stɑrtəl] *tr* asustar, sorprender, sobrecoger || *intr* asustarse, sorprenderse, sobrecogerse

**startling** ['stɑrtlɪŋ] *adj* alarmante, asombroso

**starvation** [stɑrˈveʃən] *s* hambre *f,* inanición
**starvation diet** *s* régimen *m* de hambre, cura de hambre
**starvation wages** *spl* salario de hambre
**starve** [stɑrv] *tr* hambrear; hacer morir de hambre; **to starve out** hacer rendirse por hambre ‖ *intr* hambrear; morir de hambre; (coll) tener hambre
**starving** [ˈstɑrvɪŋ] *adj* hambriento, famélico
**stat.** *abbr* **statuary, statute, statue**
**state** [stet] *adj* de estado; del estado; estatal; público; de gala, de lujo ‖ *s* estado; fausto, ceremonia, pompa; **to lie in state** estar expuesto en capilla ardiente, estar de cuerpo presente; **to live in state** gastar mucho lujo; **to ride in state** pasear en carruaje de lujo ‖ *tr* afirmar, declarar; exponer, manifestar; plantear (*un problema*)
**state·ly** [ˈstetli] *adj* (*comp* **-lier;** *super* **-liest**) imponente, majestuoso
**statement** [ˈstetmənt] *s* declaración; exposición, informe *m,* relación; (com) estado de cuentas
**state of mind** *s* estado de ánimo
**state'room'** *s* camarote *m;* (rr) compartimiento particular
**states·man** [ˈstetsmən] *s* (*pl* **-men** [mən]) estadista *m,* hombre *m* de estado
**static** [ˈstætɪk] *adj* estático; (rad) atmosférico ‖ *s* (rad) parásitos atmosféricos
**station** [ˈsteʃən] *s* estación; condición, situación ‖ *tr* estacionar, apostar
**station agent** *s* jefe *m* de estación
**stationary** [ˈsteʃən,eri] *adj* estacionario
**station break** *s* (rad) descanso, intermedio
**stationer** [ˈsteʃənər] *s* papelero
**stationery** [ˈsteʃən,eri] *s* efectos de escritorio; papel *m* para cartas
**stationery store** *s* papelería
**station house** *s* cuartelillo de policía
**station identification** *s* (rad & telv) indicativo de la emisora
**sta'tion·mas'ter** *s* jefe *m* de estación
**station wagon** *s* rubia, coche *m* rural, vagoneta
**statistical** [stəˈtɪstɪkəl] *adj* estadístico
**statistician** [,stætɪsˈtɪʃən] *s* estadístico
**statistics** [stəˈtɪstɪks] *ssg* (*science*) estadística; *spl* (*data*) estadística o estadísticas
**statue** [ˈstætʃʊ] *s* estatua
**statuesque** [,stætʃʊˈesk] *adj* escultural
**stature** [ˈstætʃər] *s* estatura, talla; carácter *m,* habilidad
**status** [ˈstetəs] *s* condición, estado; situación social, legal o profesional; (*prestige or superior rank*) categoría
**status seeking** *s* esfuerzo por adquirir categoría
**status symbol** *s* símbolo de categoría social
**statute** [ˈstætʃʊt] *s* estatuto, ley *f*
**statutory** [ˈstætʃʊ,tori] *adj* estatutario, legal
**staunch** [stɔntʃ] o [stɑntʃ] *adj & tr* var de **stanch**
**stave** [stev] *s* (*of a barrel*) duela; (*of a ladder*) peldaño; (mus) pentagrama *m* ‖ *v* (*pret & pp* **staved** o **stove** [stov]) *tr* romper, destrozar; (*to break a hole in*) desfondar; **to stave off** mantener a distancia; evitar, impedir, diferir
**stay** [ste] *s* morada, permanencia, estancia; suspensión; (*of a corset*) ballena, varilla; apoyo, sostén *m;* (law) espera; (naut) estay *m* ‖ *tr* aplazar, detener; poner freno a ‖ *intr* quedar, quedarse, permanecer; parar, hospedarse; habitar; **to stay up** no acostarse, velar
**stay'-at-home'** *adj & s* hogareño
**stead** [stɛd] *s* lugar *m;* **in his stead** en su lugar, en lugar de él; **to stand in good stead** ser de provecho, ser ventajoso
**stead'fast'** *adj* fijo; resuelto; constante
**stead·y** [ˈstedi] *adj* (*comp* **-ier;** *super* **-iest**) constante, fijo, firme, seguro; regular, uniforme; resuelto; asentado, serio ‖ *v* (*pret & pp* **-ied**) *tr* estabilizar, reforzar; calmar (*los nervios*) ‖ *intr* estabilizarse; calmarse
**steak** [stek] *s* lonja, tajada; biftec *m*
**steal** [stil] *s* (coll) hurto, robo ‖ *v* (*pret* **stole** [stol]; *pp* **stolen**) *tr* hurtar, robar; atraer, cautivar ‖ *intr* hurtar, robar; **to steal away** escabullirse; **to steal into** meterse a hurtadillas en; **to steal upon** aproximarse sin ruido a
**stealth** [stɛlθ] *s* cautela, recato; **by stealth** a hurtadillas
**steam** [stim] *adj* de vapor ‖ *s* vapor *m;* vaho, humo; **to get up steam** dar presión; **to let off steam** descargar vapor; (fig) desahogarse ‖ *tr* cocer al vapor; saturar de vapor; empañar (*p.ej., las ventanas*) ‖ *intr* echar vapor, emitir vapor; evaporarse; funcionar o marchar a vapor; **to steam ahead** avanzar por medio del vapor; (fig) hacer grandes progresos
**steam'boat'** *s* buque *m* de vapor
**steamer** [ˈstimər] *s* vapor *m*
**steamer rug** *s* manta de viaje
**steamer trunk** *s* baúl *m* de camarote
**steam heat** *s* calefacción por vapor
**steam roller** *s* apisonadora movida a vapor; (coll) fuerza arrolladora
**steam'ship'** *s* vapor *m,* buque *m* de vapor
**steam shovel** *s* pala mecánica de vapor
**steam table** *s* plancha caliente
**steed** [stid] *s* caballo; (*high-spirited horse*) corcel *m*
**steel** [stil] *adj* acerado; (*business, industry*) siderúrgico; (fig) duro, frío ‖ *s* acero; (*for striking fire from flint; for sharpening knives*) eslabón *m* ‖ *tr* acerar; **to steel oneself** acerarse
**steel wool** *s* virutillas de acero, estopa de acero
**steelyard** [ˈstil,jɑrd] o [ˈstiljərd] *s* romana
**steep** [stip] *adj* escarpado, empinado;

(*price*) alto, excesivo || *tr* empapar, remojar; **steeped in** absorbido en
**steeple** ['stipəl] *s* aguja, campanario
**stee'ple•chase'** *s* carrera de campanario, carrera de obstáculos
**stee'ple•jack'** *s* escalatorres *m*
**steer** [stɪr] *s* buey *m* || *tr* conducir, gobernar, guiar || *intr* conducirse; **to steer clear of** (coll) evitar, eludir
**steerage** ['stɪrɪdʒ] *s* dirección; (naut) proa, entrepuente *m*
**steerage passenger** *s* (naut) pasajero de entrepuente
**steering wheel** *s* (aut) volante *m;* (naut) rueda del timón
**stem** [stɛm] *s* (*of a goblet*) pie *m;* (*of a pipe, of a feather*) cañón *m;* (*of a column*) fuste *m;* (*of a watch*) botón *m;* (*of a key*) espiga, tija; (*of a word*) tema *m;* (bot) tallo, vástago; **from stem to stern** de proa a popa || *v* (*pret & pp* **stemmed;** *ger* **stemming**) *tr* (*to remove the stem from*) desgranar; (*to check*) detener, refrenar; (*to plug*) estancar; hacer frente a; rendir (*la marea*) || *intr* nacer, provenir; **to stem from** originarse en, provenir de
**stem'-wind'er** *s* remontuar *m*
**stench** [stɛntʃ] *s* hedor *m*, hediondez *f*
**sten•cil** ['stɛnsəl] *s* cartón picado; (*work produced by it*) estarcido || *v* (*pret & pp* **-ciled** o **-cilled;** *ger* **-ciling** o **-cilling**) *tr* estarcir
**stenographer** [stə'nɑgrəfər] *s* estenógrafo
**stenography** [stə'nɑgrəfi] *s* estenografía
**step** [stɛp] *s* paso; (*of staircase*) grada, peldaño; (*footprint*) huella, pisada; (*of carriage*) estribo; (*measure, démarche*) gestión, medida; (mus) intervalo; **step by step** paso a paso; **to watch one's step** proceder con cautela, andarse con tiento || *v* (*pret & pp* **stepped;** *ger* **stepping**) *tr* escalonar; **to step off** medir a pasos || *intr* dar un paso, dar pasos; caminar, ir; (coll) andar de prisa; **to step on it** (coll) acelerar la marcha, darse prisa; **to step on the starter** pisar el arranque
**step'broth'er** *s* medio hermano, hermanastro
**step'child'** *s* (*pl* **-children** [,tʃɪldrən]) hijastro
**step'daugh'ter** *s* hijastra
**step'fa'ther** *s* padrastro
**step'lad'der** *s* escala, escalera de tijera
**step'moth'er** *s* madrastra
**steppe** [stɛp] *s* estepa
**stepping stone** *s* estriberón *m*, pasadera; (fig) escalón *m*, escabel *m*
**step'sis'ter** *s* media hermana, hermanastra
**step'son'** *s* hijastro
**stere•o** ['stɛrɪ,o] o ['stɪrɪ,o] *adj* (coll) estereofónico; (coll) estereoscópico || *s* (*pl* **-os**) (coll) música estereofónica, disco estereofónico; (coll) radiodifusión estereofónica; (coll) fotografía estereoscópica
**stereotyped** ['stɛrɪ·ə,taɪpt] o ['stɪrɪ·ə,taɪpt] *adj* estereotipado
**sterile** ['stɛrɪl] *adj* estéril
**sterilize** ['stɛrɪ,laɪz] *tr* esterilizar
**sterling** ['stʌrlɪŋ] *adj* fino, de ley; verdadero, genuino, puro, excelente || *s* libras esterlinas; plata de ley; vajilla de plata
**stern** [stʌrn] *adj* austero, severo; decidido, firme || *s* popa
**stethoscope** ['stɛθə,skop] *s* estetoscopio
**stevedore** ['stivə,dor] *s* estibador *m*
**stew** [stju] o [stu] *s* guisado, estofado || *tr* guisar, estofar || *intr* abrasarse; (coll) estar apurado
**steward** ['stju·ərd] o ['stu·ərd] *s* mayordomo; administrador *m;* (*of ship or plane*) camarero
**stewardess** ['stju·ərdɪs] o ['stu·ərdɪs] *s* mayordoma; (*of ship or plane*) camarera; (*of plane*) azafata, aeromoza
**stewed fruit** *s* compota de frutas
**stewed tomatoes** *spl* puré *m* de tomates
**stick** [stɪk] *s* palo, palillo; bastón *m*, vara; (*of dynamite*) barra; (naut) mástil *m*, verga; (typ) componedor *m* || *v* (*pret & pp* **stuck** [stʌk]) *tr* picar, punzar; apuñalar; clavar, hincar; pegar; (coll) confundir; **to stick out** asomar (*la cabeza*); sacar (*la lengua*); **to stick up** (*in order to rob*) (slang) asaltar, atracar || *intr* estar prendido, estar hincado; pegarse; agarrarse (*la pintura*); encastillarse (*p.ej., una ventana*); resaltar, sobresalir; continuar, persistir; permanecer; atascarse; **to stick out** salir (*p.ej., el pañuelo del bolsillo*); sobresalir, proyectarse; velar (*un escollo*); resultar evidente; **to stick together** (coll) quedarse unidos, no abandonarse; **to stick up** destacarse; estar de punta (*el pelo*); **to stick up for** (coll) defender
**sticker** ['stɪkər] *s* etiqueta engomada, marbete engomado; punta, espina; (coll) problema arduo
**sticking plaster** *s* esparadrapo
**stick'pin'** *s* alfiler *m* de corbata
**stick'-up'** *s* (slang) asalto, atraco
**stick•y** ['stɪki] *adj* (*comp* **-ier;** *super* **-iest**) pegajoso; (coll) húmedo, mojado; (*weather*) bochornoso
**stiff** [stɪf] *adj* tieso; entorpecido, entumecido; arduo, difícil; (*price*) (coll) excesivo || *s* (slang) cadáver *m*
**stiff collar** *s* cuello almidonado
**stiffen** ['stɪfən] *tr* atiesar; endurecer; espesar || *intr* atiesarse; endurecerse; espesarse; obstinarse
**stiff neck** *s* torticolis *m;* obstinación
**stiff-necked** ['stɪf,nɛkt] *adj* terco, obstinado
**stiff shirt** *s* camisola
**stifle** ['staɪfəl] *tr* ahogar, sofocar; apagar, suprimir
**stig•ma** ['stɪgmə] *s* (*pl* **-mas** o **-mata** [mətə]) estigma *m*
**stigmatize** ['stɪgmə,taɪz] *tr* estigmatizar
**stilet•to** [stɪ'lɛto] *s* (*pl* **-tos**) estilete *m*, puñal *m*
**still** [stɪl] *adj* inmóvil, quieto, tran-

quilo; callado, silencioso; (*wine*) no espumoso || *adv* tranquilamente; silenciosamente; aún, todavía || *conj* con todo, sin embargo || *s* alambique *m*, destiladera; destilería; fotografía de lo inmóvil; (poet) silencio || *tr* acallar; amortiguar; calmar || *intr* callar; calmarse

**still'birth'** *s* parto muerto

**still'born'** *adj* nacido muerto

**still life** *s* (*pl* **still lifes** o **still lives**) bodegón *m*, naturaleza muerta

**stilt** [stɪlt] *s* zanco; (*in the water*) pilote *m*

**stilted** ['stɪltɪd] *adj* elevado; hinchado, pomposo, tieso

**stimulant** ['stɪmjələnt] *adj* & *s* estimulante *m*, excitante *m*

**stimulate** ['stɪmjə,let] *tr* estimular

**stimu•lus** ['stɪmjələs] *s* (*pl* **-li** [,laɪ]) estímulo

**sting** [stɪŋ] *s* picadura; aguijón *m* || *v* (*pret* & *pp* **stung** [stʌŋ]) *tr* picar; aguijonear || *intr* picar

**stin•gy** ['stɪndʒi] *adj* (*comp* **-gier**; *super* **-giest**) mezquino, tacaño

**stink** [stiŋk] *s* hedor *m*, mal olor *m* || *v* (*pret* **stank** [stæŋk] o **stunk** [stʌŋk]; *pp* **stunk**) *tr* dar mal olor a || *intr* heder, oler muy mal; **to stink of** heder a; (slang) poseer (*p.ej.*, *dinero*) en un grado que da asco

**stint** [stɪnt] *s* faena, tarea || *tr* limitar, restringir || *intr* ser económico, ahorrar con mezquindad

**stipend** ['staɪpənd] *s* estipendio

**stipulate** ['stɪpjə,let] *tr* estipular

**stir** [stʌr] *s* agitación, meneo; alboroto, tumulto; **to create a stir** meter ruido || *v* (*pret* & *pp* **stirred**; *ger* **stirring**) *tr* agitar, mover; revolver; conmover, excitar; atizar, avivar (*el fuego*); remover (*un líquido*); **to stir up** revolver; despertar; conmover; fomentar (*discordias*) || *intr* bullirse, moverse

**stirring** ['stʌrɪŋ] *adj* conmovedor, emocionante

**stirrup** ['stʌrəp] o ['stɪrəp] *s* estribo

**stitch** [stɪtʃ] *s* puntada, punto; pedazo de tela; punzada, dolor *m* punzante; (coll) poquito; **to be in stitches** (coll) desternillarse de risa || *tr* coser, bastear, hilvanar || *intr* coser

**stock** [stɑk] *adj* común, regular; banal, vulgar; bursátil; ganadero, del ganado; (theat) de repertorio || *s* surtido; capital *f* comercial; acciones, valores *mpl*; (*of meat*) caldo; (*of a tree*) tronco; (*of an anvil*) cepo; (*of a rifle*) caja, culata; (*of a tree; of a family*) cepa; mango, manija; palo, madero; leño; (*livestock*) ganado; (theat) programa *m*, repertorio; **in stock** en existencia; **out of stock** agotado; **to take stock** hacer el inventario; **to take stock in** (coll) dar importancia a, confiar en || *tr* abastecer, surtir; tener existencias de; acopiar, acumular; poblar (*un estanque, una colmena, etc.*)

**stockade** [stɑ'ked] *s* estacada, empalizada || *tr* empalizar

**stock'breed'er** *s* criador *m* de ganado

**stock'bro'ker** *s* bolsista *mf*, corredor *m* de bolsa

**stock car** *s* (aut) coche *m* de serie; (rr) vagón *m* para el ganado

**stock company** *s* (com) sociedad anónima; (theat) teatro de repertorio

**stock dividend** *s* acción liberada

**stock exchange** *s* bolsa

**stock'hold'er** *s* accionista *mf*, tenedor *m* de acciones

**stockholder of record** *s* accionista *mf* que como tal figura en el libro-registro de la compañía

**Stockholm** ['stɑkhom] *s* Estocolmo

**stocking** ['stɑkɪŋ] *s* media

**stock market** *s* bolsa, mercado de valores; **to play the stock market** jugar a la bolsa

**stock'pile'** *s* reserva de materias primas || *tr* acumular (*materias primas*) || *intr* acumular materias primas

**stock raising** *s* ganadería

**stock'room'** *s* almacén *m*; sala de exposición

**stock split** *s* reparto de acciones gratis

**stock•y** ['stɑki] *adj* (*comp* **-ier**; *super* **-iest**) bajo, grueso y fornido

**stock'yard'** *s* corral *m* de concentración de ganado

**stoic** ['sto•ɪk] *adj* & *s* estoico

**stoke** [stok] *tr* atizar, avivar (*el fuego*); alimentar, cebar (*el horno*)

**stoker** ['stokər] *s* fogonero

**stolid** ['stɑlɪd] *adj* impasible, insensible

**stomach** ['stʌmək] *s* estómago; apetito; deseo, inclinación || *tr* tragar; **to not be able to stomach** (coll) no poder tragar

**stone** [ston] *s* piedra; (*of fruit*) hueso; (pathol) mal *m* de piedra || *tr* lapidar, apedrear; deshuesar (*la fruta*)

**stone'-broke'** *adj* arrancado, sin blanca

**stone'-deaf'** *adj* sordo como una tapia

**stone'ma'son** *s* albañil *m*

**stone quarry** *s* cantera, pedrera

**stone's throw** *s* tiro de piedra; **within a stone's throw** a tiro de piedra

**ston•y** ['stoni] *adj* (*comp* **-ier**; *super* **-iest**) pedregoso; duro, empedernido

**stool** [stul] *s* escabel *m*, taburete *m*; sillico, retrete *m*; (*bowel movement*) cámara, evacuación

**stoop** [stup] *s* encorvada, inclinación; escalinata de entrada || *intr* doblarse, inclinarse, encorvarse; andar encorvado; humillarse, rebajarse

**stoop-shouldered** ['stup'ʃoldərd] *adj* cargado de espaldas

**stop** [stɑp] *s* parada, alto; estada, estancia; cesación, fin *m*, suspensión; cerradura, tapadura; impedimento, obstáculo; freno; tope *m*, retén *m*; (*in writing; in telegrams*) punto; (*of a guitar*) llave *f*, traste *m*; **to put a stop to** poner fin a || *v* (*pret* & *pp* **stopped**; *ger* **stopping**) *tr* parar, detener; acabar, terminar; estorbar, obstruir; interceptar; suspender; cerrar, tapar; rechazar (*un golpe*); retener (*un sueldo o parte de él*); **to stop up** cegar, obstruir, tapar || *intr* parar, pararse, detenerse; quedarse, permanecer; alojarse, hospedarse; acabarse, terminarse; **to stop** + *ger* cesar de + *inf*, dejar de + *inf*

**stop'cock'** *s* llave *f* de cierre, llave de paso

**stop'gap'** *adj* provisional || *s* substituto provisional

**stop light** *s* luz *f* de parada

**stop'o'ver** *s* parada intermedia, escala; billete *m* de parada intermedia

**stoppage** ['stɑpɪdʒ] *s* parada, detención; (*of work*) paro; interrupción; suspensión; obstáculo; (*of wages*) retención; (pathol) obstrucción

**stopper** ['stɑpər] *s* tapón *m;* taco, tarugo

**stop sign** o **stop signal** *s* señal *f* de alto, señal de parada

**stop watch** *s* reloj *m* de segundos muertos, cronómetro

**storage** ['storɪdʒ] *s* almacenaje *m;* (*costs*) derechos de almacenaje

**storage battery** *s* (elec) acumulador *m*

**store** [stor] *s* tienda, almacén *m;* **I know what is in store for you** sé lo que le espera; **to set store by** dar mucha importancia a || *tr* abastecer; tener guardado, almacenar; **to store away** acumular

**store'house'** *s* almacén *m*, depósito; (*e.g., of wisdom*) (fig) mina

**store'keep'er** *s* tendero, almacenista *mf*

**store'room'** *s* cuarto de almacenar; (*for furniture*) guardamuebles *m;* (naut) despensa

**stork** [stɔrk] *s* cigüeña; **to have a visit from the stork** recibir a la cigüeña

**storm** [stɔrm] *s* borrasca, tempestad, tormenta; (mil) asalto; (naut) borrasca; (fig) tempestad, tumulto; **to take by storm** tomar por asalto || *tr* asaltar || *intr* tempestear; precipitarse

**storm cloud** *s* nubarrón *m*

**storm door** *s* contrapuerta, guardapuerta

**storm sash** *s* contravidriera

**storm troops** *spl* tropas de asalto

**storm window** *s* guardaventana, sobrevidriera

**storm•y** ['stɔrmi] *adj* (*comp* **-ier;** *super* **-iest**) borrascoso, tempestuoso; (*session, meeting, etc.*) tumultuoso

**sto•ry** ['stori] *s* (*pl* **-ries**) historia, cuento, anécdota; enredo, trama; (coll) mentira; piso, alto || *v* (*pret & pp* **-ried**) *tr* historiar

**sto'ry•tel'ler** *s* narrador *m;* (coll) mentiroso

**stout** [staʊt] *adj* corpulento, gordo, robusto; animoso; leal; terco || *s* cerveza obscura fuerte

**stove** [stov] *s* (*for heating a house or room*) estufa; (*for cooking*) hornillo, cocina de gas, cocina eléctrica

**stove'pipe'** *s* tubo de estufa, tubo de hornillo; (*hat*) (coll) chistera, chimenea

**stow** [sto] *tr* guardar, meter, esconder; (naut) arrumar, estibar || *intr* — **to stow away** embarcarse clandestinamente, esconderse en un barco o avión

**stowage** ['sto·ɪdʒ] *s* arrumaje *m*, estiba

**stow'a•way'** *s* llovido, polizón *m*

**str.** *abbr* **strait, steamer**

**straddle** ['strædəl] *s* esparrancamiento || *tr* montar a horcajadas; (coll) tratar de favorecer a ambas partes en (*p.ej., un pleito*) || *intr* ponerse a horcajadas; (coll) tratar de favorecer a ambas partes

**strafe** [strɑf] o [stref] *s* (slang) bombardeo violento || *tr* (slang) bombardear violentamente

**straggle** ['strægəl] *intr* errar, vagar; andar perdido, extraviarse; separarse; estar esparcido

**straight** [stret] *adj* derecho; recto; erguido; (*hair*) lacio; continuo, seguido; honrado, sincero; correcto; decidido, intransigente; (*e.g., whiskey*) solo; **to set a person straight** mostrar el camino a una persona; dar consejo a una persona; mostrar a una persona el modo de proceder || *adv* derecho; sin interrupción; sinceramente; exactamente; en seguida; **straight ahead** todo seguido, derecho; **to go straight** (coll) enmendarse

**straighten** ['stretən] *tr* enderezar; poner en orden || *intr* enderezarse

**straight face** *s* cara seria

**straight'for'ward** *adj* franco, sincero; honrado

**straight off** *adv* luego, en seguida

**straight razor** *s* navaja barbera

**straight'way'** *adv* luego, en seguida

**strain** [stren] *s* tensión, tirantez *f;* esfuerzo muy grande; fatiga excesiva, agotamiento; (*of a muscle*) torcedura; aire *m*, melodía; (*of a family or lineage*) cepa; linaje *m*, raza; rasgo racial; genio, vena; huella, rastro || *tr* estirar; torcer o torcerse (*p.ej., la muñeca*); forzar (*p.ej., los nervios, la vista*); apretar; deformar; colar, tamizar || *intr* esforzarse; deformarse; colarse, tamizarse; filtrarse; exprimirse (*un jugo*); resistirse; **to strain at** hacer grandes esfuerzos por

**strained** [strend] *adj* (*smile*) forzado; (*friendship*) tirante

**strainer** ['strenər] *s* colador *m*

**strait** [stret] *s* estrecho; **straits** estrecho; **to be in dire straits** estar en el mayor apuro, hallarse en gran estrechez

**strait jacket** *s* camisa de fuerza

**strait-laced** ['stret,lest] *adj* gazmoño

**strand** [strænd] *s* playa; filamento; (*of rope or cable*) torón *m*, ramal *m;* (*of pearls*) hilo; pelo || *tr* deshebrar; retorcer, trenzar (*cuerda, cable, etc.*); dejar extraviado; (naut) varar

**stranded** ['strændɪd] *adj* desprovisto, desamparado; (*ship*) encallado; (*rope or cable*) trenzado, retorcido

**strange** [strendʒ] *adj* extraño, singular; nuevo, desconocido; novel, no acostumbrado

**stranger** ['strendʒər] *s* forastero; visi-

tador *m;* intruso; desconocido; principiante *mf*
**strangle** ['stræŋgəl] *tr* estrangular; reprimir, suprimir || *intr* estrangularse
**strap** [stræp] *s* (*of leather*) correa; (*of cloth, metal, etc.*) banda, tira; (*to sharpen a razor*) asentador *m* || *v* (*pret & pp* **strapped;** *ger* **strapping**) *tr* atar o liar con correa, banda o tira; azotar con una correa; fajar, vendar; asentar (*una navaja*)
**strap'hang'er** *s* (coll) pasajero colgado
**stratagem** ['strætədʒəm] *s* estratagema *f*
**strategic(al)** [strə'tidʒɪk(əl)] *adj* estratégico
**strategist** ['strætɪdʒɪst] *s* estratega *m*
**strate•gy** ['strætɪdʒi] *s* (*pl* **-gies**) estrategia
**strati•fy** ['strætɪ,faɪ] *v* (*pret & pp* **-fied**) *tr* estratificar || *intr* estratificarse
**stratosphere** ['strætə,sfɪr] o ['stretə,sfɪr] *s* estratosfera
**stra•tum** ['stretəm] o ['strætəm] *s* (*pl* **-ta** [tə] o **-tums**) estrato; (*e.g., of society*) clase *f*
**straw** [strɔ] *adj* pajizo; baladí, de poca importancia; falso; ficticio || *s* paja; (*for drinking*) pajita; **I don't care a straw** no se me da un bledo; **to be the last straw** ser el colmo, no faltar más
**straw'ber'ry** *s* (*pl* **-ries**) fresa
**straw hat** *s* sombrero de paja; (*with low flat crown*) canotié *m*
**straw man** *s* figura de paja; (*figurehead*) testaferro; testigo falso
**straw vote** *s* voto informativo
**stray** [stre] *adj* extraviado, perdido; aislado, suelto || *s* animal extraviado o perdido || *intr* extraviarse, perderse
**streak** [strik] *s* lista, raya; vena, veta; rasgo, traza; (*of light*) rayo; (*of good luck*) racha; (coll) tiempo muy breve; **like a streak** (coll) como un rayo || *tr* listar, rayar; abigarrar || *intr* rayarse; (coll) andar o pasar como un rayo
**stream** [strim] *s* (*current*) corriente *f;* arroyo, río; chorro, flujo; (*of people*) torrente *m;* (*e.g., of automobiles*) desfile *m* || *intr* correr, manar (*un líquido*); chorrear; flotar, ondear; salir a torrentes
**streamer** ['strimər] *s* flámula, banderola; cinta ondeante; rayo de luz
**streamlined** ['strim,laɪnd] *adj* aerodinámico, perfilado
**stream'lin'er** *s* tren aerodinámico de lujo
**street** [strit] *adj* callejero || *s* calle *f*
**street'car'** *s* tranvía *m*
**street cleaner** *s* basurero; (*device*) barredera
**street clothes** *spl* traje *m* de calle
**street floor** *s* piso bajo
**street lamp** *s* farol *m* (de la calle)
**street sprinkler** ['sprɪŋklər] *s* carricuba, carro de riego, regadera
**street'walk'er** *s* cantonera, carrerista
**strength** [streŋθ] *s* fuerza; intensidad; (*of spirituous liquors*) graduación; (com) tendencia a la subida; (mil) número; **on the strength of** fundándose en, confiando en
**strengthen** ['streŋθən] *tr* fortificar, reforzar; confirmar || *intr* fortificarse, reforzarse
**strenuous** ['strenjʊ•əs] *adj* estrenuo, enérgico, vigoroso; arduo, difícil
**stress** [stres] *s* tensión, fuerza; compulsión; acento; (mech) tensión; **to lay stress on** hacer hincapié en || *tr* someter a esfuerzo; hacer hincapié en; acentuar
**stress accent** *s* acento prosódico
**stretch** [stretʃ] *s* estiramiento, estirón *m;* (*distance in time or space*) trecho; (*section of road*) tramo; extensión; (*of the imagination*) esfuerzo; (*confinement in jail*) (slang) condena; **at a stretch** de un tirón || *tr* estirar; extender; tender; forzar, violentar; (fig) estirar (*el dinero*); **to stretch a point** hacer una concesión; **to stretch oneself** desperezarse || *intr* estirarse; extenderse; tenderse; desperezarse; **to stretch out** (coll) echarse
**stretcher** ['stretʃər] *s* (*for gloves*) ensanchador *m;* (*for a painting*) bastidor *m;* (*to carry sick or wounded*) camilla
**stretch'er-bear'er** *s* camillero
**strew** [stru] *v* (*pret* **strewed;** *pp* **strewed** o **strewn**) *tr* derramar, esparcir; sembrar, salpicar; polvorear
**stricken** ['strɪkən] *adj* afligido; inhabilitado; herido; **stricken in years** debilitado por los años
**strict** [strɪkt] *adj* estricto, riguroso; (*exacting*) severo
**stricture** ['strɪktʃər] *s* crítica severa; (pathol) estrictura
**stride** [straɪd] *s* zancada, tranco; **to hit one's stride** alcanzar la actividad o velocidad acostumbrada; **to make great** (o **rapid**) **strides** avanzar a grandes pasos; **to take in one's stride** hacer sin esfuerzo || *v* (*pret* **strode** [strod]; *pp* **stridden** ['strɪdən]) *tr* cruzar de un tranco; montar a horcajadas || *intr* dar zancadas, caminar a paso largo, andar a trancos
**strident** ['straɪdənt] *adj* estridente
**strife** [straɪf] *s* contienda; rivalidad
**strike** [straɪk] *s* (*blow*) golpe *m;* (*stopping of work*) huelga; (*discovery of ore, oil, etc.*) descubrimiento repentino; golpe *m* de fortuna; **to go on strike** ir a la huelga || *v* (*pret & pp* **struck** [strʌk]) *tr* golpear; pulsar (*una tecla*); herir, percutir; topar, dar con; acuñar (*monedas*); echar (*raíces*); frotar, rayar, encender (*un fósforo*); descubrir repentinamente (*mineral, aceite, etc.*); cerrar (*un trato*); arriar (*las velas*); dar (*la hora*); asumir, tomar (*una postura*); borrar, cancelar; impresionar; atraer (*la atención*); **to strike it rich** descubrir un buen filón, tener un golpe de fortuna || *intr* dar, sonar (*una campana, un reloj*); declararse en huelga;

(mil) dar el asalto; **to strike out** ponerse en marcha, echar camino adelante

**strike'break'er** *s* rompehuelgas *m,* esquirol *m*

**striker** ['straɪkər] *s* golpeador *m;* huelguista *mf*

**striking** ['straɪkɪŋ] *adj* impresionante, llamativo, sorprendente; en huelga

**striking power** *s* potencia de choque

**string** [strɪŋ] *s* cuerdecilla; (*of pearls; of lies*) sarta; (*of beans*) hebra; (*of onions or garlic*) ristra; (*row*) hilera; (mus) cuerda; (*limitation, proviso*) (coll) condición; **strings** instrumentos de cuerda; **to pull strings** tocar resortes || *v* (*pret & pp* **strung** [strʌŋ]) *tr* enhebrar, ensartar; atar con cuerdas; proveer de cuerdas; colgar de una cuerda; tender (*un cable, un alambre*); encordar (*un violín, una raqueta*); colocar en fila; (slang) engañar, burlar; **to string along** (slang) traer al retortero; **to string up** (coll) ahorcar

**string bean** *s* habichuela verde, judía verde

**stringed instrument** [strɪŋd] *s* instrumento de cuerda

**stringent** ['strɪndʒənt] *adj* riguroso, severo, estricto; convincente

**string quartet** *s* cuarteto de cuerdas

**strip** [strɪp] *s* tira; (*of metal*) lámina; (*of land*) faja || *v* (*pret & pp* **stripped;** *ger* **stripping**) *tr* desnudar; despojar; desforrar; deshacer (*la cama*); estropear (*el engranaje, un tornillo*); desvenar (*tabaco*); descortezar; **to strip of** despojar de || *intr* desnudarse; despojarse; descortezarse

**stripe** [straɪp] *s* banda, lista, raya; gaya; cinta, franja; (mil & nav) galón *m;* índole *f,* tipo; **to win one's stripes** ganar los entorchados || *tr* listar, rayar; gayar

**strip mining** *s* mineraje *m* a tajo abierto

**strive** [straɪv] *v* (*pret* **strove** [strov]; *pp* **striven** ['strɪvən]) *intr* esforzarse; luchar

**stroke** [strok] *s* golpe *m;* (*of bell or clock*) campanada; (*of pen*) plumada; (*of brush*) pincelada, brochada; (*of arms in swimming*) brazada; (*in a game*) jugada; (*caress with hand*) caricia; (*with a racket*) raquetazo; (*of a piston*) carrera, embolada; (*of a paddle*) palada; (*of an oar*) remada; (*of lightning*) rayo; (*line, mark*) raya; (*of good luck*) golpe *m;* (*of wit*) agudeza, chiste *m;* (*of genius*) rasgo; ataque *m* de parálisis; **at the stroke of** (*e.g., five*) al dar las (*p.ej., cinco*); **to not do a stroke of work** no dar golpe, no levantar paja del suelo || *tr* frotar suavemente, acariciar con la mano

**stroll** [strol] *s* paseo; **to take a stroll** dar un paseo || *intr* pasear, pasearse; callejear, errar, vagar

**stroller** ['strolər] *s* paseante *mf;* cochecito para niños

**strong** [strɔŋ] o [strɑŋ] *adj* fuerte, resistente; recio, robusto; intenso; (*stock market*) firme; enérgico; marcado; picante; rancio

**strong'box'** *s* cofre *m* fuerte, caja de caudales

**strong drink** *s* bebida alcohólica, bebida fuerte

**strong'hold'** *s* plaza fuerte

**strong man** *s* (*e.g., in a circus*) hércules *m;* (*leader, good planner*) alma, promotor *m;* (*dictator*) hombre *m* fuerte

**strong-minded** ['strɔŋ,maɪndɪd] o [strɑŋ,maɪndɪd] *adj* independiente; de inteligencia vigorosa; (*e.g., woman*) hombruna

**strontium** ['strɑnʃɪ·əm] *s* estroncio

**strop** [strɑp] *s* suavizador *m* || *v* (*pret & pp* **stropped;** *ger* **stropping**) *tr* suavizar, afilar

**strophe** ['strofi] *s* estrofa

**structure** ['strʌktʃər] *s* estructura; edificio

**struggle** ['strʌgəl] *s* lucha; esfuerzo, forcejeo || *intr* luchar; esforzarse, forcejear

**strum** [strʌm] *v* (*pret & pp* **strummed;** *ger* **strumming**) *tr* arañar (*un instrumento músico*) sin arte || *intr* cencerrear; **to strum on** rasguear

**strumpet** ['strʌmpɪt] *s* ramera

**strut** [strʌt] *s* (*brace, prop*) riostra, tornapunta; contoneo, pavoneo || *v* (*pret & pp* **strutted;** *ger* **strutting**) *intr* contonearse, pavonearse

**strychnine** ['strɪknaɪn] o ['strɪknin] *s* estricnina

**stub** [stʌb] *s* fragmento, trozo; (*of a cigar*) colilla; (*of a tree*) tocón *m;* (*of a pencil*) cabo; (*of a check*) talón *m* || *v* (*pret & pp* **stubbed;** *ger* **stubbing**) *tr* — **to stub one's toe** dar un tropezón

**stubble** ['stʌbəl] *s* rastrojo; (*of beard*) cañón *m*

**stubborn** ['stʌbərn] *adj* terco, testarudo, obstinado; porfiado; intratable

**stuc·co** ['stʌko] *s* (*pl* **-coes** o **-cos**) estuco || *tr* estucar

**stuck'-up'** *adj* (coll) estirado, orgulloso

**stud** [stʌd] *s* tachón *m;* botón *m* de camisa; montante *m,* pie derecho; clavo de adorno; (*bolt*) espárrago; caballeriza; (*of mares*) yeguada || *v* (*pret & pp* **studded;** *ger* **studding**) *tr* tachonar

**stud bolt** *s* espárrago

**stud'book'** *s* registro genealógico de caballos

**student** ['stjudənt] o ['studənt] *adj* estudiantil || *s* estudiante *mf;* (*person who investigates*) estudioso

**student body** *s* estudiantado, alumnado

**stud'horse'** *s* caballo padre, caballo semental

**studied** ['stʌdid] *adj* premeditado, hecho adrede; (*affected*) estudiado

**studi·o** ['stjudɪ,o] o ['studɪ,o] *s* (*pl* **-os**) estudio, taller *m;* (mov & rad) estudio

**studious** ['stjudɪ·əs] o ['studɪ·əs] *adj* estudioso; asiduo, solícito

**stud·y** ['stʌdi] *s* (*pl* **-ies**) estudio; solicitud; meditación profunda; (*e.g.,* *of a professor*) gabinete *m*, estudio || *v* (*pret & pp* **-ied**) *tr & intr* estudiar

**stuff** [stʌf] *s* materia; género, paño, tela; muebles *mpl*, baratijas; medicina; fruslerías; cosa, cosas || *tr* rellenar; henchir, llenar; atascar, cerrar, tapar; embutir; (*with food*) atracar; meter sin orden, llenar sin orden; disecar (*un animal muerto*) || *intr* atracarse, hartarse

**stuffed shirt** *s* (slang) tragavirotes *m*

**stuffing** [ˈstʌfɪŋ] *s* relleno

**stuff·y** [ˈstʌfi] *adj* (*comp* **-ier**; *super* **-iest**) sofocante, mal ventilado; aburrido, sin interés; (*prim*) (coll) relamido

**stumble** [ˈstʌmbəl] *intr* tropezar, dar un traspié; moverse a tropezones; hablar a tropezones; **to stumble on** o **upon** tropezar con

**stumbling block** *s* escollo, tropezadero

**stump** [stʌmp] *s* (*of a tree, arm, etc.*) tocón *m*; (*of an arm*) muñón *m*; (*of a tooth*) raigón *m*; (*of a cigar*) colilla; (*of a tail*) rabo; paso pesado; fragmento, resto; tribuna pública; (*for shading drawings*) esfumino || *tr* recorrer (*el país*) pronunciando discursos políticos; (coll) confundir, dejar sin habla; esfumar

**stump speaker** *s* orador callejero

**stump speech** *s* arenga electoral

**stun** [stʌn] *v* (*pret & pp* **stunned**; *ger* **stunning**) *tr* atolondrar, aturdir

**stunning** [ˈstʌnɪŋ] *adj* (coll) pasmoso, estupendo, pistonudo, elegante

**stunt** [stʌnt] *s* atrofia; (*underdeveloped creature*) engendro; (coll) suerte acrobática; (coll) faena, hazaña, proeza || *tr* atrofiar || *intr* (coll) hacer suertes acrobáticas

**stunt flying** *s* vuelo acrobático

**stunt man** *s* (mov) doble *m* que hace suertes peligrosas

**stupe·fy** [ˈstjupɪ,faɪ] o [ˈstupɪ,faɪ] *v* (*pret & pp* **-fied**) *tr* dejar estupefacto, pasmar; causar estupor a

**stupendous** [stjuˈpɛndəs] o [stuˈpɛndəs] *adj* estupendo; enorme

**stupid** [ˈstjupɪd] o [ˈstupɪd] *adj* estúpido

**stupor** [ˈstjupər] o [ˈstupər] *s* estupor *m*, modorra

**stur·dy** [ˈstʌrdi] *adj* (*comp* **-dier**; *super* **-diest**) fuerte, robusto, fornido; firme, tenaz

**sturgeon** [ˈstʌrdʒən] *s* esturión *m*

**stutter** [ˈstʌtər] *s* tartamudeo || *tr* decir tartamudeando || *intr* tartamudear

**sty** [staɪ] *s* (*pl* **sties**) pocilga, zahurda; (pathol) orzuelo

**style** [staɪl] *s* estilo; moda; elegancia; **to live in great style** vivir en gran lujo || *tr* intitular, nombrar

**stylish** [ˈstaɪlɪʃ] *adj* de moda, elegante

**styptic pencil** [ˈstɪptɪk] *s* lápiz estíptico

**Styx** [stɪks] *s* Estigia

**suave** [swɑv] o [swev] *adj* suave; afable, fino, zalamero, pulido

**sub.** *abbr* **subscription, substitute, suburban**

**subaltern** [səbˈɔltərn] *adj & s* subalterno

**subconscious** [səbˈkɑnʃəs] *adj* subconsciente || *s* subconsciencia

**subconsciousness** [səbˈkɑnʃəsnɪs] *s* subconsciencia

**subdeb** [ˈsʌb,dɛb] *s* tobillera

**subdivide** [ˈsʌbdɪ,vaɪd] o [,sʌbdɪˈvaɪd] *tr* subdividir || *intr* subdividirse

**subdue** [səbˈdju] o [səbˈdu] *tr* sojuzgar, subyugar; amansar, dominar; suavizar

**subdued** [səbˈdjud] o [səbˈdud] *adj* sojuzgado; sumiso; (*e.g., light*) suave

**subheading** [ˈsʌb,hɛdɪŋ] *s* subtítulo

**subject** [ˈsʌbdʒɪkt] *adj* sujeto; súbdito || *s* asunto, materia, tema *m*; (*person in his relationship to a ruler or government*) súbdito; (gram, med, philos) sujeto || [səbˈdʒɛkt] *tr* sujetar, someter, sojuzgar

**subject index** *s* índice *m* de materias

**subjection** [səbˈdʒɛkʃən] *s* sumisión, sometimiento

**subjective** [səbˈdʒɛktɪv] *adj* subjetivo

**subject matter** *s* asunto, materia

**subjugate** [ˈsʌbdʒə,get] *tr* subyugar

**subjunctive** [səbˈdʒʌŋktɪv] *adj & s* subjuntivo

**sub·let** [sʌbˈlɛt] o [ˈsʌb,lɛt] *v* (*pret & pp* **-let**; *ger* **-letting**) *tr* realquilar, subarrendar

**submachine gun** [,sʌbməˈʃin] *s* subfusil *m* ametrallador

**submarine** [ˈsʌbmə,rin] *adj & s* submarino || *tr* (coll) atacar o hundir con un submarino

**submarine chaser** [ˈtʃesər] *s* cazasubmarinos *m*

**submerge** [səbˈmʌrdʒ] *tr* sumergir || *intr* sumergirse

**submersion** [səbˈmʌrʒən] o [səbˈmʌrʃən] *s* sumersión

**submission** [səbˈmɪʃən] *s* sumisión

**submissive** [səbˈmɪsɪv] *adj* sumiso

**sub·mit** [səbˈmɪt] *v* (*pret & pp* **-mitted**; *ger* **-mitting**) *tr* someter; proponer, permitirse decir || *intr* someterse

**subordinate** [səbˈɔrdɪnɪt] *adj & s* subordinado || [səbˈɔrdɪ,net] *tr* subordinar

**subornation of perjury** [,sʌbɔrˈneʃən] *s* (law) soborno de testigo

**subplot** [ˈsʌb,plɑt] *s* trama secundaria

**subpoena** o **subpena** [sʌbˈpinə] o [səˈpinə] *s* comparendo || *tr* mandar comparecer

**sub rosa** [sʌbˈrozə] *adv* en secreto, en confianza

**subscribe** [səbˈskraɪb] *tr* subscribir || *intr* subscribir; subscribirse, abonarse; **to subscribe to** subscribirse a, abonarse a (*una publicación periódica*); subscribir (*una opinión*)

**subscriber** [səbˈskraɪbər] *s* abonado

**subsequent** [ˈsʌbsɪkwənt] *adj* subsiguiente, posterior

**subservient** [səbˈsʌrvɪ·ənt] *adj* servil; subordinado; útil

**subside** [səbˈsaɪd] *intr* calmarse; acabarse, cesar; bajar (*el nivel del agua*); amainar (*el viento*)

**subsidize** ['sʌbsɪ,daɪz] *tr* subsidiar, subvencionar; (*to bribe*) sobornar
**subsi·dy** ['sʌbsɪdi] *s* (*pl* **-dies**) subsidio, subvención
**subsist** [səb'sɪst] *intr* subsistir
**subsistence** [səb'sɪstəns] *s* subsistencia
**substance** ['sʌbstəns] *s* substancia
**substandard** [sʌb'stændərd] *adj* inferior al nivel normal
**substantial** [səb'stænʃəl] *adj* considerable, importante; fuerte, sólido; acomodado, rico; esencial; (*food*) substancial
**substantiate** [səb'stænʃɪ,et] *tr* comprobar, establecer, verificar
**substantive** ['sʌbstəntɪv] *adj & s* substantivo
**substation** ['sʌb,steʃən] *s* (elec) subcentral *f*
**substitute** ['sʌbstɪ,tjut] o ['sʌbstɪ,tut] *adj* substitutivo ‖ *s* (*person*) substituto; (*thing, substance*) substitutivo; (mil) reemplazo ‖ *tr* poner (*a una persona o cosa*) en lugar de otra ‖ *intr* actuar de substituto; **to substitute for** substituir (with personal a)
**substitution** [,sʌbstɪ'tjuʃən] o [,sʌbstɪ'tuʃən] *s* empleo o uso (de una persona o cosa en lugar de otra); (chem, law, math) substitución; (coll) imitación fraudulenta
**subterranean** [,sʌbtə'renɪ·ən] *adj & s* subterráneo
**subtitle** ['sʌb,taɪtəl] *s* subtítulo ‖ *tr* subtitular
**subtle** ['sʌtəl] *adj* sutil; astuto; insidioso
**subtle·ty** ['sʌtəlti] *s* (*pl* **-ties**) sutileza; agudeza; distinción sutil
**subtract** [səb'trækt] *tr* substraer; (math) substraer, restar
**suburb** ['sʌbʌrb] *s* suburbio, arrabal *m;* **the suburbs** las afueras, los barrios externos
**subvention** [səb'venʃən] *s* subvención ‖ *tr* subvencionar
**subversive** [səb'vʌrsɪv] *adj* subversivo ‖ *s* subversor *m*
**subvert** [səb'vʌrt] *tr* subvertir
**subway** ['sʌb,we] *s* galería subterránea; metro, ferrocarril subterráneo
**succeed** [sək'sid] *tr* suceder (*a una persona o cosa*) ‖ *intr* tener buen éxito
**success** [sək'ses] *s* buen éxito
**successful** [sək'sesfəl] *adj* feliz, próspero; acertado; logrado
**succession** [sək'seʃən] *s* sucesión; **in succession** seguidos, uno tras otro
**successive** [sək'sesɪv] *adj* sucesivo
**succor** ['sʌkər] *s* socorro ‖ *tr* socorrer
**succotash** ['sʌkə,tæʃ] *s* guiso de maíz tierno y habas
**succumb** [sə'kʌm] *intr* sucumbir
**such** [sʌtʃ] *adj & pron indef* tal, semejante; **such a** tal, semejante; **such a** + *adj* un tan + *adj;* **such as** quienes, los que
**suck** [sʌk] *s* chupada; mamada ‖ *tr* chupar; mamar; aspirar (*el aire*)
**sucker** ['sʌkər] *s* chupador *m;* mamón *m;* (bot & mach) chupón *m;* (coll) bobo, primo
**suckle** ['sʌkəl] *tr* lactar; criar, educar
**suckling pig** ['sʌklɪŋ] *s* lechón *m,* cerdo de leche
**suction** ['sʌkʃən] *adj* aspirante ‖ *s* succión
**sudden** ['sʌdən] *adj* súbito, repentino; **all of a sudden** de repente
**suds** [sʌdz] *spl* jabonadura; (coll) espuma, cerveza
**sue** [su] o [sju] *tr* demandar; pedir; (law) procesar ‖ *intr* (law) poner pleito, entablar juicio; **to sue for damages** demandar por daños y perjuicios; **to sue for peace** pedir la paz
**suede** [swed] *s* gamuza, ante *m*
**suet** ['su·ɪt] o ['sju·ɪt] *s* sebo
**suffer** ['sʌfər] *tr & intr* sufrir, padecer
**sufferance** ['sʌfərəns] *s* tolerancia; paciencia; **on sufferance** por tolerancia
**suffering** ['sʌfərɪŋ] *adj* doliente ‖ *s* dolencia, sufrimiento
**suffice** [sə'faɪs] *intr* bastar, ser suficiente
**sufficient** [sə'fɪʃənt] *adj* suficiente
**suffix** ['sʌfɪks] *s* sufijo
**suffocate** ['sʌfə,ket] *tr* sofocar ‖ *intr* sofocarse
**suffrage** ['sʌfrɪdʒ] *s* sufragio; aprobación, voto favorable
**suffragette** [,sʌfrə'dʒet] *s* sufragista (*mujer*)
**suffuse** [sə'fjuz] *tr* saturar, bañar
**sugar** ['ʃʊgər] *adj* azucarero ‖ *s* azúcar *m* ‖ *tr* azucarar
**sugar beet** *s* remolacha azucarera
**sugar bowl** *s* azucarero
**sugar cane** *s* caña de azúcar
**sug'ar-coat'** *tr* azucarar; (fig) endulzar, dorar
**suggest** [səg'dʒest] *tr* sugerir
**suggestion** [səg'dʒetʃən] *s* sugestión, sugerencia; sombra, traza ligera
**suggestive** [səg'dʒestɪv] *adj* sugestivo; sicalíptico
**suicidal** [,su·ɪ'saɪdəl] o [,sju·ɪ'saɪdəl] *adj* suicida
**suicide** ['su·ɪ,saɪd] o ['sju·ɪ,saɪd] *s* (*act*) suicidio; (*person*) suicida *mf;* **to commit suicide** suicidarse
**suit** [sut] o [sjut] *s* traje *m,* terno; (*of a lady*) traje *m* sastre; (*group forming a set*) juego; (*of cards*) palo; petición, súplica; cortejo, galanteo; (law) pleito, proceso; **to follow suit** servir del palo; seguir la corriente ‖ *tr* adaptar, ajustar; adaptarse a; sentar, ir o venir bien a; favorecer, satisfacer; **to suit oneself** hacer (*uno*) lo que le guste ‖ *intr* convenir, ser a propósito
**suitable** ['sutəbəl] o ['sjutəbəl] *adj* apropiado, conveniente, adecuado
**suit'case'** *s* maleta, valija
**suite** [swit] *s* comitiva, séquito; (*group forming a set*) juego; serie *f;* (*of rooms*) crujía; habitación salón; (mus) suite *f*
**suiting** ['sutɪŋ] o ['sjutɪŋ] *s* corte *m* de traje
**suit of clothes** *s* traje completo (*de hombre*)

**suitor** ['sutər] o ['sjutər] *s* pretendiente *m;* (law) demandante *mf*
**sulfa drugs** ['sʌlfə] *spl* medicamentos sulfas
**sulfate** ['sʌlfet] *s* sulfato
**sulfide** ['sʌlfaɪd] *s* sulfuro
**sulfite** ['sʌlfaɪt] *s* sulfito
**sulfur** ['sʌlfər] *s* (chem) azufre *m;* véase **sulphur**
**sulfuric** [sʌl'fjurɪk] *adj* sulfúrico
**sulfur mine** *s* azufrera
**sulfurous** ['sʌlfərəs] *adj* sulfuroso ‖ ['sʌlfərəs] o [sʌl'fjurəs] *adj* (chem) sulfuroso
**sulk** [sʌlk] *s* murria ‖ *intr* amorrarse, enfurruñarse
**sulk•y** ['sʌlki] *adj* (*comp* **-ier;** *super* **-iest**) enfurruñado, murrio, resentido
**sullen** ['sʌlən] *adj* hosco, malhumorado, taciturno, triste
**sul•ly** ['sʌli] *v* (*pret & pp* **-lied**) *tr* empañar, manchar
**sulphur** ['sʌlfər] *adj* azufrado ‖ *s* azufre *m;* color de azufre ‖ *tr* azufrar
**sultan** ['sʌltən] *s* sultán *m*
**sul•try** ['sʌltri] *adj* (*comp* **-trier;** *super* **-triest**) bochornoso, sofocante
**sum** [sʌm] *s* suma; (coll) problema *m* de aritmética ‖ *v* (*pret & pp* **summed;** *ger* **summing**) *tr* sumar; **to sum up** sumar, resumir
**sumac** o **sumach** ['ʃumæk] o ['sumæk] *s* zumaque *m*
**summarize** ['sʌmə,raɪz] *tr* resumir
**summa•ry** ['sʌməri] *adj* sumario ‖ *s* (*pl* **-ries**) sumario, resumen *m*
**summer** ['sʌmər] *adj* estival, veraniego ‖ *s* verano, estío ‖ *intr* veranear
**summer resort** *s* lugar *m* de veraneo
**summersault** ['sʌmər,sɔlt] *s* salto mortal ‖ *intr* dar un salto mortal
**summer school** *s* escuela de verano
**summery** ['sʌməri] *adj* estival, veraniego
**summit** ['sʌmɪt] *s* cima, cumbre *f*
**summit conference** *s* conferencia en la cumbre
**summon** ['sʌmən] *tr* convocar, llamar; evocar; (law) citar, emplazar
**summons** ['sʌmənz] *s* orden *f,* señal *f;* (law) citación, emplazamiento ‖ *tr* (coll) citar, emplazar
**sumptuous** ['sʌmptʃu•əs] *adj* suntuoso
**sun** [sʌn] *s* sol *m;* **to have a place in the sun** ocupar su puesto en el mundo ‖ *v* (*pret & pp* **sunned;** *ger* **sunning**) *tr* asolear ‖ *intr* asolearse
**sun bath** *s* baño de sol
**sun'beam'** *s* rayo de sol
**sun'bon'net** *s* papalina
**sun'burn'** *s* quemadura de sol ‖ *v* (*pret & pp* **-burned** o **burnt**) *tr* quemar al sol ‖ *intr* quemarse al sol
**sundae** ['sʌndi] *s* helado con frutas, jarabes o nueces
**Sunday** ['sʌndi] *adj* dominical; (*used or worn on Sunday*) dominguero ‖ *s* domingo
**Sunday best** *s* (coll) trapos de cristianar, ropa dominguera
**Sunday's child** *s* niño nacido de pies, niño mimado de la fortuna
**Sunday school** *s* escuela dominical, doctrina dominical
**sunder** ['sʌndər] *tr* separar; romper
**sun'di'al** *s* reloj *m* de sol, cuadrante *m* solar
**sun'down'** *s* puesta del sol
**sundries** ['sʌndriz] *spl* artículos diversos
**sundry** ['sʌndri] *adj* diversos, varios
**sun'flow'er** *s* girasol *m,* tornasol *m*
**sun'glass'es** *spl* gafas de sol, gafas para el sol
**sunken** ['sʌŋkən] *adj* hundido, sumido
**sun lamp** *s* lámpara de rayos ultravioletas
**sun'light'** *s* luz *f* del sol
**sun'lit'** *adj* iluminado por el sol
**sun•ny** ['sʌni] *adj* (*comp* **-nier;** *super* **-niest**) de sol; asoleado; brillante, resplandeciente; alegre, risueño; **to be sunny** hacer sol
**sunny side** *s* sol *m;* (fig) lado bueno, lado favorable
**sun porch** *s* solana
**sun'rise'** *s* salida del sol; **from sunrise to sunset** de sol a sol
**sun'set'** *s* puesta del sol
**sun'shade'** *s* quitasol *m,* sombrilla; toldo; visera contra el sol
**sun'shine'** *s* claridad del sol; alegría; **in the sunshine** al sol
**sun'spot'** *s* mancha solar
**sun'stroke'** *s* insolación
**sup.** *abbr* **superior, supplement**
**sup** [sʌp] *v* (*pret & pp* **supped;** *ger* **supping**) *intr* cenar
**superannuated** [,supər'ænju,etɪd] *adj* jubilado, inhabilitado por ancianidad o enfermedad; fuera de moda
**superb** [su'pʌrb] o [sə'pʌrb] *adj* soberbio, estupendo, magnífico
**supercar•go** ['supər,kɑrgo] *s* (*pl* **-goes** o **-gos**) (naut) sobrecargo
**supercharge** [,supər'tʃɑrdʒ] *tr* sobrealimentar
**supercilious** [,supər'sɪlɪ•əs] *adj* arrogante, altanero, desdeñoso
**superficial** [,supər'fɪʃəl] *adj* superficial
**superfluous** [su'pʌrflu•əs] *adj* superfluo
**superhuman** [,supər'hjumən] *adj* sobrehumano
**superimpose** [,supərɪm'poz] *tr* sobreponer
**superintendent** [,supərɪn'tendənt] *s* superintendente *mf*
**superior** [sə'pɪrɪ•ər] o [su'pɪrɪ•ər] *adj* superior; indiferente, sereno; arrogante; (typ) volado ‖ *s* superior *m*
**superiority** [sə,pɪrɪ'ɑrɪti] o [su,pɪrɪ'ɑrɪti] *s* superioridad; indiferencia, serenidad; arrogancia
**superlative** [sə'pʌrlətɪv] o [su'pʌrlətɪv] *adj & s* superlativo
**super•man** ['supər,mæn] *s* (*pl* **-men** [,mɛn]) sobrehombre *m,* superhombre *m*
**supermarket** ['supər,mɑrkɪt] *s* supermercado
**supernatural** [,supər'nætʃərəl] *adj* sobrenatural
**superpose** [,supər'poz] *tr* sobreponer, superponer

**supersede** [ˌsupərˈsid] *tr* reemplazar; desalojar
**supersonic** [ˌsupərˈsɑnɪk] *adj* supersónico ‖ **supersonics** *ssg* supersónica
**superstitious** [ˌsupərˈstɪʃəs] *adj* supersticioso
**supervene** [ˌsupərˈvin] *intr* sobrevenir
**supervise** [ˈsupərˌvaɪz] *tr* superintender, supervisar, dirigir
**supervisor** [ˈsupərˌvaɪzər] *s* superintendente *mf*, supervisor *m*, dirigente *mf*
**supp.** *abbr* **supplement**
**supper** [ˈsʌpər] *s* cena
**supplant** [səˈplænt] *tr* reemplazar
**supple** [ˈsʌpəl] *adj* flexible; dócil
**supplement** [ˈsʌplɪmənt] *s* suplemento ‖ [ˈsʌplɪˌmɛnt] *tr* suplir, completar
**suppliant** [ˈsʌplɪ·ənt] *adj* & *s* suplicante *mf*
**supplication** [ˌsʌplɪˈkeʃən] *s* súplica
**sup·ply** [səˈplaɪ] *s* (*pl* **-plies**) suministro, provisión; surtido, repuesto; oferta, existencia; **supplies** pertrechos, provisiones, víveres *mf;* artículos, efectos ‖ *v* (*pret* & *pp* **-plied**) *tr* suministrar, aprovisionar; reemplazar
**supply and demand** *spl* oferta y demanda
**support** [səˈport] *s* apoyo, soporte *m*, sostén *m;* sustento ‖ *tr* apoyar, soportar, sostener; sustentar; aguantar
**supporter** [səˈportər] *s* partidario; (*jockstrap*) suspensorio; faja abdominal, faja medical
**suppose** [səˈpoz] *tr* suponer; creer; **to be supposed to** deber; **to suppose so** creer que sí
**supposed** [səˈpozd] *adj* supuesto
**supposition** [ˌsʌpəˈzɪʃən] *s* suposición
**supposito·ry** [səˈpɑzɪˌtori] *s* (*pl* **-ries**) supositorio
**suppress** [səˈprɛs] *tr* suprimir
**suppression** [səˈprɛʃən] *s* supresión
**suppurate** [ˈsʌpjəˌret] *intr* supurar
**supreme** [səˈprim] o [sʊˈprim] *adj* supremo
**supt.** *abbr* **superintendent**
**surcharge** [ˈsʌrˌtʃɑrdʒ] *s* sobrecarga ‖ [ˌsʌrˈtʃɑrdʒ] o [ˈsʌrˌtʃɑrʒ] *tr* sobrecargar
**sure** [ʃʊr] *adj* seguro; **to be sure** seguramente, sin duda ‖ *adv* (coll) seguramente, claro; **sure enough** efectivamente
**sure thing** *adv* (slang) seguramente ‖ *interj* ¡claro!, ¡seguro! ‖ *s* (slang) sacabocados *m*
**sure·ty** [ˈʃʊrti] o [ˈʃʊrɪti] *s* (*pl* **-ties**) seguridad, garantía, fianza
**surf** [sʌrf] *s* cachones *mpl*, olas que rompen en la playa
**surface** [ˈsʌrfɪs] *adj* superficial ‖ *s* superficie *f* ‖ *tr* alisar, allanar; recubrir ‖ *intr* emerger (*p.ej., un submarino*)
**surface mail** *s* correo por vía ordinaria
**surf'board'** *s* patín *m* de mar
**surfeit** [ˈsʌrfɪt] *s* exceso; hartura, hastío; empacho, indigestión ‖ *tr* atracar, hastiar; encebadar (*las bestias*) ‖ *intr* atracarse, hastiarse; encebadarse
**surf'-rid'ing** *s* patinaje *m* sobre las olas
**surge** [sʌrdʒ] *s* oleada; (elec) sobretensión ‖ *intr* agitarse, ondular
**surgeon** [ˈsʌrdʒən] *s* cirujano
**surger·y** [ˈsʌrdʒəri] *s* (*pl* **-ies**) cirugía; sala de operaciones
**surgical** [ˈsʌrdʒɪkəl] *adj* quirúrgico
**sur·ly** [ˈsʌrli] *adj* (*comp* **-lier;** *super* **-liest**) áspero, rudo, hosco, insolente
**surmise** [sərˈmaɪz] o [ˈsʌrmaɪz] *s* conjetura, suposición ‖ [sərˈmaɪz] *tr* & *intr* conjeturar, suponer
**surmount** [sərˈmaʊnt] *tr* levantarse sobre; aventajar, sobrepujar; superar; coronar
**surname** [ˈsʌrˌnem] *s* apellido; (*added name*) sobrenombre *m* ‖ *tr* apellidar; sobrenombrar
**surpass** [sərˈpæs] o [sərˈpɑs] *tr* aventajar, sobrepasar
**surplice** [ˈsʌrplɪs] *s* sobrepelliz *f*
**surplus** [ˈsʌrplʌs] *adj* sobrante, excedente ‖ *s* sobrante *m*, exceso; (com) superávit *m*
**surprise** [sərˈpraɪz] *adj* inesperado, improviso ‖ *s* sorpresa; **to take by surprise** coger por sorpresa ‖ *tr* sorprender
**surprise package** *s* sorpresa
**surprise party** *s* reunión improvisada para felicitar por sorpresa a una persona
**surprising** [sərˈpraɪzɪŋ] *adj* sorprendente
**surrender** [səˈrɛndər] *s* rendición ‖ *tr* rendir ‖ *intr* rendirse
**surrender value** *s* (ins) valor *m* de rescate
**surreptitious** [ˌsʌrɛpˈtɪʃəs] *adj* subrepticio
**surround** [səˈraʊnd] *tr* cercar, rodear, circundar; (mil) sitiar
**surrounding** [səˈraʊndɪŋ] *adj* circundante, circunstante ‖ **surroundings** *spl* alrededores *mpl*, contornos; ambiente *m*, medio
**surtax** [ˈsʌrˌtæks] *s* impuesto complementario
**surveillance** [sərˈveləns] o [sərˈveljəns] *s* vigilancia
**survey** [ˈsʌrve] *s* estudio, examen *m*, inspección, reconocimiento; agrimensura, medición, plano; levantamiento de planos; (*of opinion*) encuesta; (*of literature*) bosquejo ‖ [sʌrˈve] o [ˈsʌrve] *tr* estudiar, examinar, inspeccionar, reconocer; medir; levantar el plano de ‖ *intr* levantar el plano
**surveyor** [sərˈve·ər] *s* inspector *m;* agrimensor *m*
**survival** [sərˈvaɪvəl] *s* supervivencia
**survive** [sərˈvaɪv] *tr* sobrevivir a (*otra persona; algún acontecimiento*) ‖ *intr* sobrevivir
**surviving** [sərˈvaɪvɪŋ] *adj* sobreviviente
**survivor** [sərˈvaɪvər] *s* sobreviviente *mf*
**survivorship** [sərˈvaɪvərˌʃɪp] *s* (law) sobrevivencia
**susceptible** [səˈsɛptɪbəl] *adj* susceptible; (*to love*) enamoradizo
**suspect** [ˈsʌspɛkt] o [səsˈpɛkt] *adj* &

*s* sospechoso || [səsˈpɛkt] *tr* sospechar
**suspend** [səsˈpɛnd] *tr* suspender || *intr* dejar de obrar; suspender pagos
**suspenders** [səsˈpɛndərz] *spl* tirantes *mpl*
**suspense** [səsˈpɛns] *s* suspenso, suspensión; duda, incertidumbre; indecisión, irresolución; ansiedad
**suspension bridge** [səsˈpɛnʃən] *s* puente *m* colgante
**suspicion** [səsˈpɪʃən] *s* sospecha, suspicacia; sombra, traza ligera
**suspicious** [səsˈpɪʃəs] *adj* (*inclined to suspect*) suspicaz; (*subject to suspicion*) sospechoso
**sustain** [səsˈten] *tr* sostener, sustentar; apoyar, defender; confirmar, probar; sufrir (*p.ej., un daño, una pérdida*)
**sustenance** [ˈsʌstɪnəns] *s* sustento, alimentos; sostenimiento
**sutler** [ˈsʌtlər] *s* (mil) vivandero
**swab** [swɑb] *s* escobón *m*, estropajo; (naut) lampazo; (surg) tapón *m* de algodón || *v* (*pret & pp* **swabbed**; *ger* **swabbing**) *tr* fregar, limpiar; (naut) lampacear; (surg) limpiar con algodón
**swaddle** [ˈswɑdəl] *tr* empañar, fajar
**swaddling clothes** *spl* pañales *mpl*
**swagger** [ˈswægər] *adj* (coll) muy elegante || *s* fanfarronada; contoneo, paso jactancioso || *intr* fanfarronear; contonear
**swain** [swen] *s* (*lad*) zagal; galán *m*, amante *m*
**swallow** [ˈswɑlo] *s* trago; (orn) golondrina || *tr* tragar, deglutir; (fig) tragar, tragarse || *intr* tragar, deglutir
**swallow-tailed coat** [ˈswɑlo ˌteld] *s* frac *m*
**swal′low·wort′** *s* vencetósigo
**swamp** [swɑmp] *s* pantano, marisma || *tr* encharcar, inundar; (*e.g., with work*) abrumar
**swamp·y** [ˈswɑmpi] *adj* (*comp* **-ier**; *super* **-iest**) pantanoso
**swan** [swɑn] *s* cisne *m*
**swan dive** *s* salto de ángel
**swank** [swæŋk] *adj* (slang) elegante, vistoso || *s* (slang) elegancia vistosa
**swan knight** *s* caballero del cisne
**swan's-down** [ˈswɑnzˌdaʊn] *s* plumón *m* de cisne; moletón *m*, paño de vicuña
**swan song** *s* canto del cisne
**swap** [swɑp] *s* (coll) trueque *m*, cambalache *m* || *v* (*pret & pp* **swapped**; *ger* **swapping**) *tr & intr* trocar, cambalachear
**swarm** [swɔrm] *s* enjambre *m* || *intr* enjambrar; volar en enjambres; hormiguear (*una multitud de gente o animales*)
**swarth·y** [ˈswɔrði] o [ˈswɔrθi] *adj* (*comp* **-ier**; *super* **-iest**) atezado, carinegro, moreno
**swashbuckler** [ˈswɑʃˌbʌklər] *s* espadachín *m*, matasiete *m*, valentón *m*
**swat** [swɑt] *s* (coll) golpe violento || *v* (*pret & pp* **swatted**; *ger* **swatting**) *tr* (coll) golpear con fuerza; (coll) aporrear, aplastar (*una mosca*)
**sway** [swe] *s* oscilación, vaivén *m*; dominio, imperio || *tr* hacer oscilar; conmover; disuadir; gobernar, dominar || *intr* oscilar; desviarse; tambalear, flaquear
**swear** [swɛr] *v* (*pret* **swore** [swor]; *pp* **sworn** [sworn]) *tr* jurar; juramentar; prestar (*juramento*); **to swear in** tomar juramento a; **to swear off** jurar renunciar a; **to swear out** obtener mediante juramento || *intr* jurar; **to swear at** maldecir; **to swear by** jurar por; poner toda su confianza en; **to swear to** prestar juramento a; declarar bajo juramento; jurar + *inf*
**sweat** [swɛt] *s* sudor *m* || *v* (*pret & pp* **sweat** o **sweated**) *tr* sudar (*agua por los poros; la ropa*); (slang) hacer sudar; **to sweat it out** (slang) aguantarlo hasta el fin || *intr* sudar
**sweater** [ˈswɛtər] *s* suéter *m*
**sweat·y** [ˈswɛti] *adj* (*comp* **-ier**; *super* **-iest**) sudoroso
**Swede** [swid] *s* sueco
**Sweden** [ˈswidən] *s* Suecia
**Swedish** [ˈswidɪʃ] *adj & s* sueco
**sweep** [swip] *s* barrido; alcance *m*, extensión; (*of wind*) soplo; (*of a well*) cigoñal *m* || *v* (*pret & pp* **swept** [swɛpt]) *tr* barrer; arrastrar; rozar, tocar; recorrer con la mirada, los dedos, etc. || *intr* barrer; pasar rápidamente; extenderse; precipitarse; andar con paso majestuoso
**sweeper** [ˈswipər] *s* (*person*) barrendero; (*machine for sweeping streets*) barredera; barredera de alfombra; (nav) dragaminas *m*
**sweeping** [ˈswipɪŋ] *adj* arrebatador; comprensivo, extenso, vasto || **sweepings** *spl* barreduras
**sweep′-sec′ond** *s* segundero central
**sweep′stakes′** *ssg* o *spl* lotería en la cual una persona gana todas las apuestas; carrera que decide todas las apuestas; premio en las carreras de caballos
**sweet** [swit] *adj* dulce; oloroso; melodioso, grato al oído; fresco; bonito, lindo; amable; querido; **to be sweet on** (coll) estar enamorado de || *adv* dulcemente; **to smell sweet** tener buen olor || **sweets** *spl* dulces *mpl*, golosinas
**sweet′bread′** *s* lechecillas, mollejas
**sweet′bri′er** *s* eglantina
**sweeten** [ˈswitən] *tr* azucarar, endulzar; suavizar; purificar || *intr* azucararse, endulzarse; suavizarse
**sweet′heart′** *s* enamorado o enamorada; amiga querida; galán *m*, cortejo
**sweet marjoram** *s* mejorana
**sweet′meats′** *spl* dulces *mpl*, confites *mpl*, confitura
**sweet pea** *s* guisante *m* de olor
**sweet potato** *s* batata, camote *m*
**sweet-scented** [ˈswit ˌsɛntɪd] *adj* oloroso, perfumado
**sweet tooth** *s* gusto por los dulces
**sweet-toothed** [ˈswit ˌtuθt] *adj* dulcero, goloso

**sweet william** *s* clavel *m* de ramillete, minutisa

**swell** [swɛl] *adj* (coll) muy elegante; (slang) de órdago, magnífico ‖ *s* hinchazón *f;* bulto; marejada; oleaje *m;* (*of a crowd of people*) oleada; (coll) petimetre *m,* pisaverde *m* ‖ *v* (*pret* **swelled;** *pp* **swelled** o **swollen** [ˈswolən]) *tr* hinchar, inflar; abultar, aumentar; elevar, levantar; (fig) hinchar, engreír ‖ *intr* hincharse; abultarse, aumentar, crecer; elevarse, levantarse; embravecerse (*el mar*); (fig) hincharse, engreírse

**swelled head** *s* entono; **to have a swelled head** estar muy pagado de sí mismo, creerse gran cosa

**swelter** [ˈsweltər] *intr* sofocarse de sudor

**swept'back' wing** *s* (aer) ala en flecha

**swerve** [swʌrv] *s* viraje *m,* desvío brusco ‖ *tr* desviar ‖ *intr* desviarse, torcer

**swift** [swɪft] *adj* rápido, veloz; pronto; repentino ‖ *adv* rápidamente, velozmente ‖ *s* vencejo

**swig** [swɪg] *s* (coll) chisguete, tragantada ‖ *v* (*pret & pp* **swigged;** *ger* **swigging**) *tr & intr* (coll) beber a grandes tragos

**swill** [swɪl] *s* basura, inmundicia; tragantada ‖ *tr* beber a grandes tragos; emborrachar ‖ *intr* beber a grandes tragos; emborracharse

**swim** [swɪm] *s* natación; **the swim** (*in affairs, society, etc.*) (coll) la corriente ‖ *v* (*pret* **swam** [swæm]; *pp* **swum** [swʌm]; *ger* **swimming**) *tr* pasar a nado ‖ *intr* nadar; deslizarse, escurrirse; padecer vahidos; dar vueltas (*la cabeza*); **to swim across** atravesar a nado

**swimmer** [ˈswɪmər] *s* nadador *m*

**swimming pool** *s* piscina

**swimming suit** *s* traje *m* de baño

**swindle** [ˈswɪndəl] *s* estafa, timo ‖ *tr & intr* estafar, timar

**swine** [swaɪn] *s* cerdo, puerco; *spl* ganado porcino

**swing** [swɪŋ] *s* balance *m,* oscilación, vaivén *m;* (*device used for recreation*) columpio; hamaca; turno, período; fuerza, ímpetu *m;* (*trip*) jira; (box) golpe *m* de lado; (mus) ritmo constantemente repetido; **in full swing** en plena marcha ‖ *v* (*pret & pp* **swung** [swʌŋ]) *tr* blandir (*p.ej., un arma*); menear (*los brazos*); hacer oscilar; columpiar; manejar con éxito ‖ *intr* oscilar; balancearse; columpiar; estar colgado; dar una vuelta; **to swing open** abrirse de pronto (*una puerta*)

**swinging door** [ˈswɪŋɪŋ] *s* batiente *m* oscilante, puerta de vaivén

**swinish** [ˈswaɪnɪʃ] *adj* porcuno; (fig) cochino, puerco

**swipe** [swaɪp] *s* (coll) golpe *m* fuerte ‖ *tr* (coll) dar un golpe fuerte a; (slang) hurtar, robar

**swirl** [swʌrl] *s* remolino, torbellino ‖ *tr* hacer girar ‖ *intr* arremolinarse, remolinar; girar

**swish** [swɪʃ] *s* (*e.g., of a whip*) chasquido; (*of a dress*) crujido ‖ *tr* chasquear (*el látigo*) ‖ *intr* chasquear; crujir (*un vestido*)

**Swiss** [swɪs] *adj & s* suizo

**Swiss chard** [tʃɑrd] *s* acelga

**Swiss cheese** *s* Gruyère *m,* queso suizo

**Swiss Guards** *spl* guardia suiza

**switch** [swɪtʃ] *s* bastoncillo, latiguillo; latigazo; coletazo; (*false hair*) trenza postiza, moño postizo; (elec) llave *f,* interruptor *m,* conmutador *m;* (rr) agujas ‖ *tr* azotar, fustigar; (elec) conmutar; (rr) desviar; **to switch off** (elec) cortar, desconectar; **to switch on** (elec) cerrar (*el circuito*); (elec) encender, poner (*la luz, la radio, etc.*) ‖ *intr* cambiarse, moverse; desviarse

**switch'back'** *s* vía en zigzag

**switch'board'** *s* cuadro de distribución

**switching engine** *s* locomotora de maniobras

**switch•man** [ˈswɪtʃmən] *s* (*pl* **-men** [mən]) agujetero, guardagujas *m*

**switch'yard'** *s* patio de maniobras

**Switzerland** [ˈswɪtsərlənd] *s* Suiza

**swiv•el** [ˈswɪvəl] *s* eslabón giratorio ‖ *v* (*pret & pp* **-eled** o **-elled;** *ger* **-eling** o **-elling**) *intr* girar sobre un eje

**swivel chair** *s* silla giratoria

**swoon** [swun] *s* desmayo ‖ *intr* desmayarse

**swoop** [swup] *s* descenso súbito; (*of a bird of prey*) calada ‖ *intr* bajar rápidamente, precipitarse; abatirse (*p.ej., el ave de rapiña*)

**sword** [sord] *s* espada; **at swords' points** enemistados a sangre y fuego; **to put to the sword** pasar al filo de la espada, pasar a cuchillo

**sword belt** *s* cinturón *m*

**sword'fish'** *s* pez *m* espada

**sword handler** *s* (taur) mozo de estoques

**sword rattling** *s* fanfarronería

**swords•man** [ˈsordzmən] *s* (*pl* **-men** [mən]) espada *m;* esgrimidor *m*

**sword swallower** [ˈswɑlo•ər] *s* tragasable *m*

**sword thrust** *s* estocada, golpe *m* de espada

**sworn** [sworn] *adj* (*enemy*) jurado

**sycophant** [ˈsɪkəfənt] *s* adulador *m;* parásito

**sycosis** [saɪˈkosɪs] *s* (pathol) sicosis *f*

**syll.** *abbr* **syllable**

**syllable** [ˈsɪləbəl] *s* sílaba

**syllogism** [ˈsɪləˌdʒɪzəm] *s* silogismo

**sylph** [sɪlf] *s* sílfide *f*

**sym.** *abbr* **symbol, symmetrical, symphony, symptom**

**symbol** [ˈsɪmbəl] *s* símbolo

**symbolic(al)** [sɪmˈbɑlɪk(əl)] *adj* simbólico

**symbolize** [ˈsɪmbəˌlaɪz] *tr* simbolizar

**symmetric(al)** [sɪˈmɛtrɪk(əl)] *adj* simétrico

**symme•try** [ˈsɪmɪtri] *s* (*pl* **-tries**) simetría

**sympathetic** [ˌsɪmpəˈθɛtɪk] *adj* compasivo; favorablemente dispuesto

**sympathize** [ˈsɪmpəˌθaɪz] *intr* compa-

decerse; **to sympathize with** compadecerse de; comprender
**sympa•thy** ['sɪmpəθi] *s* (*pl* **-thies**) compasión, conmiseración; **to be in sympathy with** estar de acuerdo con, ser partidario de; **to extend one's sympathy to** dar el pésame a
**symphonic** [sɪm'fɑnɪk] *adj* sinfónico
**sympho•ny** ['sɪmfəni] *s* (*pl* **-nies**) sinfonía
**symposi•um** [sɪm'pozɪ•əm] *s* (*pl* **-a** [ə]) coloquio
**symptom** ['sɪmptəm] *s* síntoma *m*
**syn.** *abbr* **synonym, synonymous**
**synagogue** ['sɪnə,gɔg] o ['sɪnə,gɑg] *s* sinagoga
**synchronize** ['sɪŋkrə,naɪz] *tr & intr* sincronizar
**synchronous** ['sɪŋkrənəs] *adj* sincrónico
**syncope** ['sɪŋkə,pi] *s* (phonet) síncopa
**syndicate** ['sɪndɪkɪt] *s* sindicato || ['sɪndɪ,ket] *tr* sindicar || *intr* sindicarse
**synonym** ['sɪnənɪm] *s* sinónimo
**synonymous** [sɪ'nɑnɪməs] *adj* sinónimo
**synop•sis** [sɪ'nɑpsɪs] *s* (*pl* **-ses** [siz]) sinopsis *f*
**syntax** ['sɪntæks] *s* sintaxis *f*
**synthe•sis** ['sɪnθɪsɪs] *s* (*pl* **-ses** [,siz]) síntesis *f*
**synthesize** ['sɪnθɪ,saɪz] *tr* sintetizar
**synthetic(al)** [sɪn'θɛtɪk(əl)] *adj* sintético
**syphilis** ['sɪfɪlɪs] *s* sífilis *f*
**Syria** ['sɪrɪ•ə] *s* Siria
**Syrian** ['sɪrɪ•ən] *adj & s* sirio
**syringe** [sɪ'rɪndʒ] o ['sɪrɪndʒ] *s* jeringa; (*fountain syringe*) mangueta; (*syringe fitted with needle for hypodermic injections*) jeringuilla || *tr* jeringar
**syrup** ['sɪrəp] o ['sʌrəp] *s* almíbar *m;* (*with fruit juices or medicinal substances*) jarabe *m*
**system** ['sɪstəm] *s* sistema *m*
**systematic(al)** [,sɪstə'mætɪk(əl)] *adj* sistemático
**systematize** ['sɪstəmə,taɪz] *tr* sistematizar
**systole** ['sɪstəli] *s* sístole *f*

## T

**T, t** [ti] vigésima letra del alfabeto inglés
**t.** *abbr* **teaspoon, temperature, tenor, tense, territory, town**
**T.** *abbr* **Territory, Testament**
**tab** [tæb] *s* apéndice *m,* proyección; marbete *m;* **to keep tab on** (coll) tener a la vista; **to pick up the tab** (coll) pagar la cuenta
**tab•by** ['tæbi] *s* (*pl* **-bies**) gato atigrado; gata; solterona; chismosa
**tabernacle** ['tæbər,nækəl] *s* tabernáculo
**table** ['tebəl] *s* mesa; (*list, catalogue; index of a book*) tabla; **to set the table** poner la mesa; **to turn the tables** volver las tornas; **under the table** completamente emborrachado || *tr* aplazar la discusión de
**tab•leau** ['tæblo] *s* (*pl* **-leaus** o **-leaux** [loz]) cuadro vivo
**ta'ble•cloth'** *s* mantel *m*
**table d'hôte** ['tɑbəl'dot] *s* mesa redonda; comida a precio fijo
**ta'ble•land'** *s* meseta
**table linen** *s* mantelería
**table manners** *spl* modales *mpl* que uno tiene en la mesa
**table of contents** *s* índice *m* de materias, tabla de materias
**ta'ble•spoon'** *s* cuchara de sopa
**tablespoonful** ['tebəl,spun,fʊl] *s* cucharada
**tablet** ['tæblɪt] *s* (*writing pad*) bloc *m;* (*slab*) lápida, placa; (*lozenge, pastille*) comprimido, tableta
**table talk** *s* conversación de sobremesa
**table tennis** *s* tenis de mesa
**ta'ble•ware'** *s* servicio de mesa, artículos para la mesa
**tabloid** ['tæblɔɪd] *s* periódico sensacional
**taboo** [tə'bu] *adj* prohibido || *s* tabú *m* || *tr* prohibir
**tabulate** ['tæbjə,let] *tr* tabular
**tabulator** ['tæbjə,letər] *s* tabulador *m*
**tacit** ['tæsɪt] *adj* tácito
**taciturn** ['tæsɪ,tʌrn] *adj* taciturno
**tack** [tæk] *s* tachuela; nuevo plan de acción; (naut) virada; (sew) hilván *m* || *tr* clavar con tachuelas; añadir; unir; (naut) virar; (sew) hilvanar || *intr* cambiar de plan; (naut) virar
**tackle** ['tækəl] *s* avíos, enseres *mpl;* (naut) poleame *m* || *tr* atacar, embestir; emprender
**tack•y** ['tæki] *adj* (*comp* **-ier;** *super* **-iest**) pegajoso; (coll) desaliñado
**tact** [tækt] *s* tacto, juicio, tino
**tactful** ['tæktfəl] *adj* discreto, político
**tactical** ['tæktɪkəl] *adj* táctico
**tactician** [tæk'tɪʃən] *s* táctico
**tactics** ['tæktɪks] *ssg* (mil) táctica || *spl* táctica
**tactless** ['tæklɪs] *adj* indiscreto
**tad'pole'** *s* renacuajo
**taffeta** ['tæfɪtə] *s* tafetán *m*
**taffy** ['tæfi] *s* arropía, melcocha; (coll) lisonja, zalamería
**tag** [tæg] *s* etiqueta, marbete *m;* herrete *m;* pingajo; mechón *m;* vedija; (*curlicue in writing*) ringorrango; **to play tag** jugar al tócame tú || *v* (*pret & pp* **tagged;** *ger* **tagging**) *tr* pegar un marbete a; marcar con marbete || *intr* (coll) seguir de cerca
**tag end** *s* cabo flojo; retal *m,* retazo
**Tagus** ['tegəs] *s* Tajo
**tail** [tel] *adj* de cola || *s* cola; **tails** (*of a coin*) cruz *f;* (coll) frac *m;* **to turn**

**tail** mostrar los talones || *tr* atar, juntar || *intr* formar cola; **to tail after** pisar los talones a
**tail assembly** *s* (aer) empenaje *m*, planos de cola
**tail end** *s* cola, extremo; conclusión; **at the tail end** al final
**tail'light'** *s* faro trasero; (rr) disco de cola
**tailor** ['telər] *s* sastre *m* || *tr* entallar (*un traje*) || *intr* ser sastre
**tailoring** ['telərɪŋ] *s* sastrería, costura
**tai'lor-made' suit** *s* traje *m* de sastre, traje hecho a la medida
**tail'piece'** *s* apéndice *m*, cabo; (*of stringed instrument*) (mus) cordal *m;* (typ) florón *m*
**tail'race'** *s* cauce *m* de salida; (min) canal *m* de desechos
**tail spin** *s* (aer) barrena picada
**tail wind** *s* (aer) viento de cola; (naut) viento en popa
**taint** [tent] *s* mancha; corrupción, infección || *tr* manchar; corromper, inficionar
**take** [tek] *s* toma; presa, redada; (mov) toma; (slang) entradas, ingresos || *v* (*pret* **took** [tʊk]; *pp* **taken**) *tr* tomar; (*to carry off with one*) llevarse; (*to remove*) quitar; quedarse con (*p.ej., una compra en una tienda*); comer (*una pieza, en el juego de ajedrez y en el de damas*); dar (*un paso, un salto, un paseo*); hacer (*un viaje; ejercicio*); seguir (*un consejo; una asignatura*); sacar (*una fotografía*); calzar, usar (*cierto tamaño de zapatos o guantes*); estudiar (*p.ej., historia, francés, matemáticas*); echar (*una siesta*); tomar (*un tren, autobús, tranvía*); aguantar, tolerar; soportar; **to take amiss** llevar a mal; **to take apart** descomponer, desarmar, desmontar; **to take down** bajar; descolgar; poner por escrito, tomar nota de; desmontar; (*to humble*) quitar los humos a; **to take for** tomar por, p.ej., **I took you for someone else** le tomé por otra persona; **to take from** quitar a; **to take in** acoger, admitir; (*to welcome into one's home, one's company*) recibir; (*to encompass*) abarcar, comprender; ganar (*dinero*); visitar (*los puntos de interés*); (*to win over by flattery or deceit*) cazar; meter (*p.ej., las costuras de una prenda de vestir*); **to take it that** suponer que; **to take off** quitarse (*p.ej., el sombrero*); descontar; (coll) imitar, parodiar; **to take on** tomar, contratar; empezar; cargar con, tomar sobre sí; desafiar; **to take out** sacar; pasear (*p.ej., a un niño, un caballo*); omitir; extraer, separar; **to take place** tener lugar; **to take up** subir; levantar; apretar; coger; recoger; emprender, comenzar; tomar posesión de (*un cargo, un puesto*); tomar, estudiar; ocupar, llenar (*un espacio*) || *intr* arraigar, prender; cuajar; actuar, obrar; salir, resultar; adherirse; pegar; (coll) tener éxito; **to take after** parecerse a; **to take off** levantarse; salir; (aer) despegar; **to take up with** (coll) estrechar amistad con; (coll) vivir con; **to take well** (coll) sacar buen retrato
**take'-off'** *s* (aer) despegue *m;* (coll) imitación burlesca, parodia
**talcum powder** ['tælkəm] *s* polvos de talco; talco en polvo
**tale** [tel] *s* cuento, relato; embuste *m*, mentira
**tale'bear'er** *s* chismoso, cuentista *mf*
**talent** ['tælənt] *s* talento; gente *f* de talento
**talented** ['tæləntɪd] *adj* talentoso
**talent scout** *s* buscador *m* de nuevas figuras
**talk** [tɔk] *s* charla, plática; (*gossip*) fábula, comidilla; (*lecture*) conferencia; **to cause talk** dar que hablar || *tr* hablar; convencer hablando; **to talk up** ensalzar || *intr* hablar; parlar (*el loro*); **to talk on** discutir (*un asunto*); hablar sin parar; continuar hablando; **to talk up** elevar la voz, osar hablar
**talkative** ['tɔkətɪv] *adj* hablador, locuaz
**talker** ['tɔkər] *s* hablador *m;* orador *m;* charlatán *m*, parlón *m*
**talkie** ['tɔki] *s* (coll) cine hablado
**talking doll** ['tɔkɪŋ] *s* muñeca parlante
**talking film** *s* película hablada
**talking machine** *s* máquina parlante
**talking picture** *s* cine hablado, cine parlante
**tall** [tɔl] *adj* alto; (coll) exagerado
**tallow** ['tælo] *s* sebo
**tal·ly** ['tæli] *s* (*pl* **-lies**) cuenta || *v* (*pret & pp* **-lied**) *tr* echar la cuenta de || *intr* echar la cuenta; concordar, corresponder, conformarse
**tally sheet** *s* hoja en que se anota una cuenta
**talon** ['tælən] *s* garra
**tambourine** [ˌtæmbə'rin] *s* pandereta
**tame** [tem] *adj* manso, domesticado; dócil, sumiso; insípido || *tr* amansar, domesticar; domar (*a un animal salvaje*); someter; captar (*una caída de agua*)
**tamp** [tæmp] *tr* atacar (*un barreno*); apisonar
**tamper** ['tæmpər] *s* (*person*) apisonador *m;* (*ram*) pisón *m* || *intr* entremeterse; **to tamper with** manosear, tocar ajando; tratar de forzar (*una cerradura*); falsificar (*un documento*); corromper (*p.ej., a un testigo*)
**tampon** ['tæmpɑn] *s* (surg) tapón *m* || *tr* (surg) taponar
**tan** [tæn] *adj* requemado, tostado; de color de canela; marrón; café (Am) || *v* (*pret & pp* **tanned;** *ger* **tanning**) *tr* adobar, curtir, zurrar; quemar, tostar; (coll) zurrar, dar una paliza a
**tang** [tæŋ] *s* sabor *m* u olor *m* fuerte y picante; dejo, gustillo; (*ringing sound*) tañido
**tangent** ['tændʒənt] *adj* tangente || *s* tangente *f;* **to fly off at a tangent** tomar súbitamente nuevo rumbo, cambiar de repente

**tangerine** [ˌtændʒəˈrin] *s* mandarina
**tangible** [ˈtændʒɪbəl] *adj* palpable, tangible
**Tangier** [tænˈdʒɪr] *s* Tánger *f*
**tangle** [ˈtæŋgəl] *s* enredo, maraña, lío || *tr* enredar, enmarañar || *intr* enredarse, enmarañarse
**tank** [tæŋk] *s* tanque *m,* depósito; (mil) tanque, carro de combate; (rr) ténder *m;* (*heavy drinker*) (slang) bodega
**tank car** *s* (rr) carro cuba, vagón *m* tanque
**tanker** [ˈtæŋkər] *s* barco tanque, buque *m* cisterna; avión-nodriza *m*
**tank farming** *s* quimicultura, cultivo hidropónico
**tank truck** *s* camión *m* tanque
**tanner** [ˈtænər] *s* curtidor *m*
**tanner•y** [ˈtænəri] *s* (*pl* **-ies**) curtiduría, tenería
**tantalize** [ˈtæntəˌlaɪz] *tr* atormentar con falsas promesas
**tantamount** [ˈtæntəˌmaʊnt] *adj* equivalente
**tantrum** [ˈtæntrəm] *s* berrinche *m,* rabieta
**tap** [tæp] *s* golpecito, palmadita; canilla, espita; grifo; (elec) toma; (mach) macho de terraja; **on tap** sacado del barril, servido al grifo; listo, a mano; **taps** (*signal to put out lights*) (mil) silencio || *v* (*pret & pp* **tapped;** *ger* **tapping**) *tr* dar golpecitos o un golpecito a o en; espitar, poner la espita a; sacar o tomar (*quitando la espita*); sangrar (*un árbol*); intervenir (*un teléfono*); derivar (*electricidad*); aterrajar (*tuercas*) || *intr* dar golpecitos
**tap dance** *s* zapateado
**tap′-dance′** *intr* zapatear
**tape** [tep] *s* cinta || *tr* proveer de cinta; medir con cinta; (coll) grabar en cinta magnetofónica
**tape measure** *s* cinta de medir
**taper** [ˈtepər] *s* cerilla, velita larga y delgada || *tr* ahusar || *intr* ahusarse; ir disminuyendo
**tape′-re•cord′** *tr* grabar sobre cinta
**tape recorder** [rɪˈkɔrdər] *s* magnetófono, grabadora de cinta
**tapes•try** [ˈtæpɪstri] *s* (*pl* **-tries**) tapiz *m* || *v* (*pret & pp* **-tried**) *tr* tapizar
**tape′worm′** *s* solitaria, lombriz solitaria
**tappet** [ˈtæpɪt] *s* (aut) alzaválvulas *m,* taqué *m*
**tap′room′** *s* bodegón *m,* taberna
**tap water** *s* agua de grifo
**tap wrench** *s* volvedor *m* de machos
**tar** [tɑr] *s* alquitrán *m;* (coll) marinero || *v* (*pret & pp* **tarred;** *ger* **tarring**) *tr* alquitranar; **to tar and feather** embrear y emplumar
**tar•dy** [ˈtɑrdi] *adj* (*comp* **-dier;** *super* **-diest**) tardío
**target** [ˈtɑrgɪt] *s* blanco
**target area** *s* zona a batir
**target practice** *s* tiro al blanco
**tariff** [ˈtærɪf] *adj* arancelario || *s* (*duties*) arancel *m;* (*rates in general*) tarifa
**tarnish** [ˈtɑrnɪʃ] *s* deslustre *m* || *tr* deslustrar || *intr* deslustrarse
**tar paper** *s* papel alquitranado
**tarpaulin** [tɑrˈpɔlɪn] *s* alquitranado, encerado, empegado
**tar•ry** [ˈtɑri] *adj* alquitranado, embreado || [ˈtæri] *v* (*pret & pp* **-ried**) *intr* detenerse, quedarse; tardar
**tart** [tɑrt] *adj* acre, agrio; (fig) áspero, mordaz || *s* tarta; (coll) puta
**task** [tæsk] o [tɑsk] *s* tarea; **to bring o take to task** llamar a capítulo
**task′mas′ter** *s* amo, superintendente *mf;* ordenancista *mf,* tirano
**tassel** [ˈtæsəl] *s* borla; (bot) penacho
**taste** [test] *s* gusto, sabor *m;* sorbo, trago; muestra; gusto, buen gusto; **in bad taste** de mal gusto; **in good taste** de buen gusto; **to acquire a taste for** tomar gusto a || *tr* gustar; (*to sample*) probar || *intr* saber; **to taste of** saber a
**tasteless** [ˈtestlɪs] *adj* desabrido, insípido; de mal gusto
**tast•y** [ˈtesti] *adj* (*comp* **-ier;** *super* **-iest**) (coll) sabroso; (coll) de buen gusto
**tatter** [ˈtætər] *s* andrajo, harapo, guiñapo || *tr* hacer andrajos
**tattered** [ˈtætərd] *adj* andrajoso, haraposo
**tattle** [ˈtætəl] *s* charla; habladuría || *intr* charlar; chismear, murmurar
**tat′tle•tale′** *adj* revelador || *s* cuentista *mf,* chismoso
**tattoo** [tæˈtu] *s* tatuaje *m;* (mil) retreta || *tr* tatuar o tatuarse
**taunt** [tɔnt] o [tɑnt] *s* mofa, pulla || *tr* provocar con insultos
**taut** [tɔt] *adj* tieso, tirante
**tavern** [ˈtævərn] *s* taberna; mesón *m,* posada
**taw•dry** [ˈtɔdri] *adj* (*comp* **-drier;** *super* **-driest**) cursi, charro, vistoso
**taw•ny** [ˈtɔni] *adj* (*comp* **-nier;** *super* **-niest**) leonado
**tax** [tæks] *s* contribución, impuesto || *tr* poner impuestos a (*una persona*); poner impuestos sobre (*la propiedad*); abrumar, cargar; agotar (*la paciencia de uno*)
**taxable** [ˈtæksəbəl] *adj* imponible
**taxation** [tækˈseʃən] *s* imposición de contribuciones; contribuciones, impuestos
**tax collector** *s* recaudador *m* de impuestos
**tax cut** *s* reducción de impuestos
**tax evader** [ɪˈvedər] *s* burlador *m* de impuestos
**tax′-ex•empt′** *adj* exento de impuesto
**tax•i** [ˈtæksi] *s* (*pl* **-is**) taxi *m* || *v* (*pret & pp* **-ied;** *ger* **-iing** o **-ying**) *tr* (aer) carretear || *intr* ir en taxi; (aer) carretear, taxear
**tax′i•cab′** *s* taxi *m*
**taxi dancer** *s* taxi *f*
**taxi driver** *s* taxista *mf*
**tax′i•plane′** *s* avioneta de alquiler
**taxi stand** *s* parada de taxis
**tax′pay′er** *s* contribuyente *mf*
**tax rate** *s* tipo impositivo
**t.b.** *abbr* **tuberculosis**

**tbs.** o **tbsp.** *abbr* **tablespoon, tablespoons**
**tea** [ti] *s* té *m;* (*medicinal infusion*) tisana; caldo de carne
**tea bag** *s* muñeca
**tea ball** *s* huevo del té
**tea'cart'** *s* mesita de té (*con ruedas*)
**teach** [titʃ] *v* (*pret & pp* **taught** [tɔt]) *tr & intr* enseñar
**teacher** ['titʃər] *s* maestro, instructor *m;* (*such as adversity*) (fig) maestra
**teacher's pet** *s* alumno mimado
**teaching** ['titʃɪŋ] *adj* docente ‖ *s* enseñanza; doctrina
**teaching aids** *spl* material *m* auxiliar de instrucción
**teaching staff** *s* personal *m* docente
**tea'cup'** *s* taza para té
**tea dance** *s* té *m* bailable
**teak** [tik] *s* teca
**tea'ket'tle** *s* tetera
**team** [tim] *s* (*e.g., of horses*) tiro, tronco; (*of oxen*) yunta; (sport) equipo ‖ *tr* enganchar, uncir, enyugar ‖ *intr* — **to team up** asociarse, unirse; formar un equipo
**team'mate'** *s* compañero de equipo, equipier *m*
**teamster** ['timstər] *s* (*of horses*) tronquista *m;* (*of a truck*) camionista *m*
**team'work'** *s* espíritu de equipo; trabajo de equipo
**tea'pot'** *s* tetera
**tear** [tɪr] *s* lágrima; **to burst into tears** romper a llorar; **to fill with tears** arrasarse (*los ojos*) de o en lágrimas; **to hold back one's tears** beberse las lágrimas; **to laugh away one's tears** convertir las lágrimas en risas ‖ [tɛr] *s* desgarro, rasgón *m* ‖ [tɛr] *v* (*pret* **tore** [tor]; *pp* **torn** [torn]) *tr* desgarrar, rasgar; acongojar, afligir; mesarse (*los cabellos*); **to tear apart** romper en dos; **to tear down** derribar (*un edificio*); desarmar (*una máquina*); **to tear off** desgajar; **to tear up** romper (*p.ej., un papel*) ‖ *intr* desgarrarse, rasgarse; **to tear along** correr a toda velocidad
**tear bomb** [tɪr] *s* bomba lacrimógena
**tearful** ['tɪrfəl] *adj* lacrimoso
**tear gas** [tɪr] *s* gas lacrimógeno
**tear-jerker** ['tɪr,dʒʌrkər] *s* (slang) drama *m* o cine *m* que arrancan lágrimas
**tear-off** ['tɛr,ɔf] o ['tɛr,ɑf] *adj* exfoliador
**tea'room'** *s* salón *m* de té
**tear sheet** [tɛr] *s* hoja del anunciante
**tease** [tiz] *tr* embromar, azuzar
**tea'spoon'** *s* cucharilla, cucharita
**teaspoonful** ['ti,spun,fʊl] *s* cucharadita
**teat** [tit] *s* teta, pezón *m*
**tea time** *s* hora del té
**technical** ['tɛknɪkəl] *adj* técnico
**technicali•ty** [,tɛknɪ'kælɪti] *s* (*pl* **-ties**) detalle técnico
**technician** [tɛk'nɪʃən] *s* técnico
**technics** ['tɛknɪks] *ssg* técnica
**technique** [tɛk'nik] *s* técnica
**Teddy bear** ['tɛdi] *s* oso de juguete, oso de trapo
**tedious** ['tidɪ·əs] o ['tidʒəs] *adj* tedioso, enfadoso
**teem** [tim] *intr* hormiguear; llover a cántaros; **to teem with** hervir de
**teeming** ['timɪŋ] *adj* hormigueante; (*rain*) torrencial
**teen age** [tin] *s* edad de 13 a 19 años
**teen-ager** ['tin,edʒər] *s* joven *mf* de 13 a 19 años de edad
**teens** [tinz] *spl* números ingleses que terminan en **-teen** (de 13 a 19); edad de 13 a 19 años; **to be in one's teens** tener de 13 a 19 años
**tee•ny** ['tini] *adj* (*comp* **-nier;** *super* **-niest**) (coll) diminuto, pequeñito
**teeter** ['titər] *s* vaivén *m,* balanceo ‖ *intr* balancear, oscilar
**teethe** [tið] *intr* endentecer
**teething** ['tiðɪŋ] *s* dentición
**teething ring** *s* chupador *m*
**teetotaler** [ti'totələr] *s* teetotalista *mf,* nefalista *mf,* abstemio
**tel.** *abbr* **telegram, telegraph, telephone**
**tele•cast** ['tɛlɪ,kæst] o ['tɛlɪ,kɑst] *s* teledifusión ‖ *v* (*pret & pp* **-cast** o **-casted**) *tr & intr* teledifundir
**telegram** ['tɛlɪ,græm] *s* telegrama *m*
**telegraph** ['tɛlɪ,græf] o ['tɛlɪ,grɑf] *s* telégrafo ‖ *tr & intr* telegrafiar
**telegrapher** [tɪ'lɛgrəfər] *s* telegrafista *mf*
**telegraph pole** *s* poste *m* de telégrafo
**Telemachus** [tɪ'lɛməkəs] *s* Telémaco
**telemeter** [tɪ'lɛmɪtər] *s* telémetro ‖ *tr* telemetrar
**telemetry** [tɪ'lɛmɪtri] *s* telemetría
**telephone** ['tɛlɪ,fon] *s* teléfono ‖ *tr & intr* telefonear
**telephone booth** *s* locutorio, cabina telefónica
**telephone call** *s* llamada telefónica
**telephone directory** *s* anuario telefónico, guía telefónica
**telephone exchange** *s* estación telefónica, central *f* de teléfonos
**telephone operator** *s* telefonista *mf*
**telephone receiver** *s* receptor telefónico
**telephone table** *s* mesita portateléfono
**teleprinter** ['tɛlɪ,prɪntər] *s* teleimpresor *m*
**telescope** ['tɛlɪ,skop] *s* telescopio ‖ *tr* telescopar ‖ *intr* telescoparse
**teletype** ['tɛlɪ,taɪp] *s* teletipo ‖ *tr & intr* transmitir por teletipo
**televiewv** ['tɛlɪ,vju] *tr & intr* ver por televisión
**televiewer** ['tɛlɪ,vju·ər] *s* televidente *mf,* telespectador *m*
**televise** ['tɛlɪ,vaɪz] *tr* televisar
**television** ['tɛlɪ,vɪʒən] *adj* televisor ‖ *s* televisión
**television screen** *s* pantalla televisora
**television set** *s* televisor *m,* telerreceptor *m*
**tell** [tɛl] *v* (*pret & pp* **told** [told]) *tr* decir; (*to narrate; to count*) contar; determinar; conocer, distinguir; **I told you so!** ¡por algo te lo dije!; **to tell someone to** + *inf* decirle a uno que + *subj* ‖ *intr* hablar; surtir efecto; **to tell on** dejarse ver en (*p.ej., la salud de uno*); (coll) denunciar

**teller** ['tɛlər] *s* narrador *m;* (*of a bank*) cajero; (*of votes*) escrutador *m*
**temper** ['tɛmpər] *s* temple *m,* natural *m,* genio; cólera, mal genio; (*of steel, glass, etc.*) temple *m;* **to keep one's temper** dominar su mal genio; **to lose one's temper** encolerizarse, perder la paciencia ‖ *tr* templar ‖ *intr* templarse
**temperament** ['tɛmpərəmənt] *s* disposición; temperamento sensible o excitable
**temperamental** [,tɛmpərə'mɛntəl] *adj* temperamental
**temperance** ['tɛmpərəns] *s* templanza
**temperate** ['tɛmpərɪt] *adj* templado
**temperature** ['tɛmpərətʃər] *s* temperatura
**tempest** ['tɛmpɪst] *s* tempestad
**tempestuous** [tɛm'pɛstʃu·əs] *adj* tempestuoso
**temple** ['tɛmpəl] *s* (*place of worship*) templo; (*side of forehead*) sien *f;* (*sidepiece of spectacles*) gafa
**tem•po** ['tɛmpo] *s* (*pl* **-pos** o **-pi** [pi]) (mus) tiempo; (fig) ritmo (*p.ej., de la vida*)
**temporal** ['tɛmpərəl] *adj* temporal
**temporary** ['tɛmpə,rɛri] *adj* temporáneo, temporario, provisional, interino
**temporize** ['tɛmpə,raɪz] *intr* contemporizar, temporizar
**tempt** [tɛmpt] *tr* tentar
**temptation** [tɛmp'teʃən] *s* tentación
**tempter** ['tɛmptər] *s* tentador *m*
**tempting** ['tɛmptɪŋ] *adj* tentador
**ten** [tɛn] *adj & pron* diez ‖ *s* diez *m;* **ten o'clock** las diez
**tenable** ['tɛnəbəl] *adj* defendible
**tenacious** [tɪ'neʃəs] *adj* tenaz
**tenacity** [tɪ'næsɪti] *s* tenacidad
**tenant** ['tɛnənt] *s* arrendatario, inquilino; morador *m,* residente *mf*
**tend** [tɛnd] *tr* cuidar, vigilar; servir ‖ *intr* tender, dirigirse; **to tend to** atender a; **to tend to** + *inf* tender a + *inf*
**tenden•cy** ['tɛndənsi] *s* (*pl* **-cies**) tendencia
**tender** ['tɛndər] *adj* tierno; (*painfully sensitive*) dolorido ‖ *n* oferta; (naut) alijador *m,* falúa; (rr) ténder *m* ‖ *tr* ofrecer, tender
**tender-hearted** ['tɛndər,hɑrtɪd] *adj* compasivo, tierno de corazón
**ten'der•loin'** *s* filete *m* ‖ **Tenderloin** *s* barrio de mala vida
**tenderness** ['tɛndərnɪs] *s* ternura, terneza; sensibilidad
**tendon** ['tɛndən] *s* tendón *m*
**tendril** ['tɛndrɪl] *s* zarcillo
**tenement** ['tɛnɪmənt] *s* habitación, vivienda; casa de vecindad
**tenement house** *s* casa de vecindad
**tenet** ['tɛnɪt] *s* dogma *m,* credo, principio
**tennis** ['tɛnɪs] *s* tenis *m*
**tennis court** *s* campo de tenis
**tennis player** *s* tenista *mf*
**tenor** ['tɛnər] *s* tenor *m,* carácter *m,* curso, tendencia; (mus) tenor
**tense** [tɛns] *adj* tenso, tieso; (*person; situation*) (fig) tenso; (*relations*) tirante ‖ *s* (gram) tiempo
**tension** ['tɛnʃən] *s* tensión; ansia, congoja, esfuerzo mental; (*in personal or diplomatic relations*) tirantez *f*
**tent** [tɛnt] *s* tienda; tienda de campaña
**tentacle** ['tɛntəkəl] *s* tentáculo
**tentative** ['tɛntətɪv] *adj* tentativo
**tenth** [tɛnθ] *adj & s* décimo ‖ *s* (*in dates*) diez *m*
**tenuous** ['tɛnju·əs] *adj* tenue; (*thin in consistency*) raro
**tenure** ['tɛnjər] *s* (*of property*) tenencia; (*of an office*) ejercicio; (*protection from dismissal*) inamovilidad
**tepid** ['tɛpɪd] *adj* tibio
**tercet** ['tʌrsɪt] *s* terceto
**term** [tʌrm] *s* término; (*of imprisonment*) condena; semestre *m,* período escolar; (*of the presidency of the U.S.A.*) mandato, período; **terms** condiciones ‖ *tr* llamar, nombrar
**termagant** ['tʌrməgənt] *s* mujer regañona, mujer de mal genio
**terminal** ['tʌrmɪnəl] *adj* terminal ‖ *s* término, fin *m;* (elec) terminal *m;* (rr) estación de fin de línea
**terminate** ['tʌrmɪ,net] *tr & intr* terminar
**termination** [,tʌrmɪ'neʃən] *s* terminación
**terminus** ['tʌrmɪnəs] *s* término; (rr) estación de cabeza, estación extrema
**termite** ['tʌrmaɪt] *s* termite *m,* comején *m*
**terrace** ['tɛrəs] *s* terraza; (*flat roof of a house*) azotea
**terra firma** ['tɛrə 'fʌrmə] *s* tierra firme; **on terra firma** sobre suelo firme
**terrain** [tɛ'ren] *s* terreno
**terrestrial** [tə'rɛstrɪ·əl] *adj* terrestre
**terrible** ['tɛrɪbəl] *adj* terrible; muy desagradable
**terrific** [tə'rɪfɪk] *adj* terrífico; (coll) enorme, intenso, brutal
**terri•fy** ['tɛrɪ,faɪ] *v* (*pret & pp* **-fied**) *tr* aterrorizar, atemorizar
**territo•ry** ['tɛrɪ,tori] *s* (*pl* **-ries**) territorio
**terror** ['tɛrər] *s* terror *m*
**terrorize** ['tɛrə,raɪz] *tr* aterrorizar; imponerse a, mediante el terror
**terry cloth** ['tɛri] *s* albornoz *m*
**terse** [tʌrs] *adj* breve, sucinto
**tertiary** ['tʌrʃɪ,ɛri] o ['tʌrʃəri] *adj* terciario
**Test.** *abbr* **Testament**
**test** [tɛst] *s* prueba, ensayo; examen *m* ‖ *tr* probar, poner a prueba; examinar
**testament** ['tɛstəmənt] *s* testamento
**test flight** *s* vuelo de ensayo
**testicle** ['tɛstɪkəl] *s* testículo
**testi•fy** ['tɛstɪ,faɪ] *v* (*pret & pp* **-fied**) *tr & intr* testificar
**testimonial** [,tɛstɪ'monɪ·əl] *s* recomendación, certificado; (*expression of esteem, gratitude, etc.*) homenaje *m*
**testimo•ny** ['tɛstɪ,moni] *s* (*pl* **-nies**) testimonio
**test pilot** *s* (aer) piloto de pruebas
**test tube** *s* probeta, tubo de ensayo

**tether** ['tɛðər] *s* atadura, traba; **at the end of one's tether** al límite de las posibilidades o la paciencia de uno || *tr* apersogar
**tetter** ['tɛtər] *s* empeine *m*
**text** [tɛkst] *s* texto; tema *m*, lema *m*
**text'book'** *s* libro de texto
**textile** ['tɛkstɪl] o ['tɛkstaɪl] *adj & s* textil *m*
**texture** ['tɛkstʃər] *s* textura
**Thai** ['tɑ·i] o ['taɪ] *adj & s* tailandés *m*
**Thailand** ['taɪlənd] *s* Tailandia
**Thales** ['θeliz] *s* Tales *m*
**Thalia** [θə'laɪ·ə] *s* Talía
**Thames** [tɛmz] *s* Támesis *m*
**than** [ðæn] *conj* que, p.ej., **he is richer than I** es más rico que yo; (*before a numeral*) de, p.ej., **more than twenty** más de veinte; (*before a verb*) de lo que, p.ej., **the crop is larger than was expected** la cosecha es mayor de lo que se esperaba; (*before a verb with direct object understood*) del (de la, de los, de las) que, p.ej., **they sent us more coffee than we ordered** nos enviaron más café del que pedimos
**thank** [θæŋk] *tr* agradecer, dar las gracias a; **to thank someone for something** agradecerle a uno una cosa || **thanks** *spl* gracias; **thanks to** gracias a, merced a || **thanks** *interj* ¡gracias!
**thankful** ['θæŋkfəl] *adj* agradecido
**thankless** ['θæŋklɪs] *adj* ingrato
**thanksgiving** [,θæŋks'gɪvɪŋ] *s* acción de gracias
**Thanksgiving Day** *s* (U.S.A.) día *m* de acción de gracias
**that** [ðæt] *adj dem* (*pl* **those**) ese; aquel; **that one** ése; aquél || *pron dem* (*pl* **those**) ése; aquél; eso; aquello || *pron rel* que, quien, el cual, el que || *adv* tan; **that far** tan lejos; hasta allí; **that many** tantos; **that much** tanto || *conj* que; para que
**thatch** [θætʃ] *s* barda, paja; techo de paja || *tr* cubrir de paja, techar con paja, bardar
**thaw** [θɔ] *s* deshielo, derretimiento || *tr* deshelar, derretir || *intr* deshelarse, derretirse
**the** [ðə], [ðɪ] o [ði] *art def* el || *adv* cuanto, p.ej., **the more the merrier** cuanto más mejor; **the more . . . the more** cuanto más . . . tanto más
**theater** ['θi·ətər] *s* teatro
**the'ater-go'er** *s* teatrero
**theater news** *s* actualidad escénica
**theater page** *s* noticiario teatral
**theatrical** [θɪ'ætrɪkəl] *adj* teatral
**Thebes** [θibz] *s* Tebas *f*
**thee** [ði] *pron pers* (archaic, poet, Bib) te; ti; **with thee** contigo
**theft** [θɛft] *s* hurto, robo
**their** [ðɛr] *adj poss* su; el . . . de ellos
**theirs** [ðɛrz] *pron poss* el suyo, el de ellos
**them** [ðɛm] *pron pers* los; ellos; **to them** les; a ellos
**theme** [θim] *s* tema *m;* (mus) tema *m*
**theme song** *s* (mus) tema *m* central; (rad) sintonía
**them·selves'** *pron pers* ellos mismos; sí, sí mismos; se, p.ej., **they enjoyed themselves** se divirtieron; **with themselves** consigo
**then** [ðɛn] *adv* entonces; después, luego, en seguida; además, también; **by then** para entonces; **from then on** desde entonces, de allí en adelante; **then and there** ahí mismo
**thence** [ðɛns] *adv* desde allí; desde entonces; por eso
**thence'forth'** *adv* de allí en adelante; desde entonces
**theolo·gy** [θi'ɑlədʒi] *s* (*pl* **-gies**) teología
**theorem** ['θi·ərəm] *s* teorema *m*
**theo·ry** ['θi·əri] *s* (*pl* **-ries**) teoría
**therapeutic** [,θɛrə'pjutɪk] *adj* terapéutico || **therapeutics** *ssg* terapéutica
**thera·py** ['θɛrəpi] *s* (*pl* **-pies**) terapia
**there** [ðɛr] *adv* allí, allá; **there is** o **there are** hay; aquí tiene Vd.
**there'a·bouts'** *adv* por allí; cerca, aproximadamente
**there·af'ter** *adv* de allí en adelante, después de eso
**there·by'** *adv* con eso; así, de tal modo; por allí cerca
**therefore** ['ðɛrfor] *adv* por lo tanto, por consiguiente
**there·in'** *adv* en esto, en eso; en ese respecto
**there·of'** *adv* de ello, de eso
**Theresa** [tə'risə] o [tə'rɛsə] *s* Teresa
**there'u·pon'** *adv* sobre eso, encima de eso; por consiguiente; en seguida
**thermistor** [θər'mɪstər] *s* (elec) termistor *m*
**thermocouple** ['θʌrmo,kʌpəl] *s* (elec) termopar *m*
**thermodynamic** [,θʌrmodaɪ'næmɪk] *adj* termodinámico || **thermodynamics** *ssg* termodinámica
**thermometer** [θər'mɑmɪtər] *s* termómetro
**thermonuclear** [,θʌrmo'njuklɪ·ər] o [,θʌrmo'nuklɪ·ər] *adj* termonuclear
**Thermopylae** [θər'mɑpɪ,li] *s* las Termópilas
**thermos bottle** ['θʌrməs] *s* termos *m*, botella termos
**thermostat** ['θʌrmə,stæt] *s* termóstato
**thesau·rus** [θɪ'sɔrəs] *s* (*pl* **-ri** [raɪ]) tesoro; (*dictionary or the like*) tesauro, tesoro
**these** [ðiz] *pl de* **this**
**the·sis** ['θisɪs] *s* (*pl* **-ses** [siz]) tesis *f*
**Thespis** ['θɛspɪs] *s* Tespis *m*
**Thessaly** ['θɛsəli] *s* la Tesalia
**they** [ðe] *pron pers* ellos, ellas
**thick** [θɪk] *adj* espeso; grueso; denso; (coll) estúpido; (coll) íntimo || *s* espesor *m;* **the thick of** (*e.g., a crowd*) lo más denso de; (*e.g., a battle*) lo más reñido de; **through thick and thin** contra viento y marea
**thicken** ['θɪkən] *tr* espesar || *intr* espesarse; complicarse (*el enredo*)
**thicket** ['θɪkɪt] *s* espesura, matorral *m*, soto
**thick-headed** ['θɪk'hɛdɪd] *adj* (coll) torpe, estúpido
**thick'-set'** *adj* grueso, rechoncho

**thief** [θif] *s* (*pl* **thieves** [θivz]) ladrón *m*
**thieve** [θiv] *intr* hurtar, robar
**thiever•y** [ˈθivəri] *s* (*pl* **-ies**) latrocinio, hurto, robo
**thigh** [θaɪ] *s* muslo
**thigh′bone′** *s* hueso del muslo, fémur *m*
**thimble** [ˈθɪmbəl] *s* dedal *m*
**thin** [θɪn] *adj* (*comp* **thinner;** *super* **thinnest**) delgado, flaco, tenue; (*cloth, paper, sole of shoe, etc.*) fino; (*hair*) ralo; (*broth*) aguado; (*excuse*) débil; claro, ligero, escaso || *v* (*pret & pp* **thinned;** *ger* **thinning**) *tr* adelgazar, enflaquecer; enrarecer; aclarar; aguar; desleír (*los colores*) || *intr* adelgazarse, enflaquecerse; enrarecerse; **to thin out** ralear (*el pelo*)
**thine** [ðaɪn] *adj poss* (archaic & poet) tu || *pron poss* (archaic & poet) tuyo; el tuyo
**thing** [θɪŋ] *s* cosa; **of all things!** ¡qué sorpresa!; **to be the thing** ser la última moda; **to be the thing to do** ser lo que debe hacerse; **to see things** ver visiones, padecer alucinaciones
**think** [θɪŋk] *v* (*pret & pp* **thought** [θɔt]) *tr* pensar; **to think it over** pensarlo; **to think nothing of** tener en poco; creer fácil; no dar importancia a; **to think of** pensar de, p.ej., **what do you think of this book?** ¿qué piensa Vd. de este libro?; **to think up** imaginar; inventar (*p.ej., una excusa*) || *intr* pensar; **to think not** creer que no; **to think of** (*to turn one's thoughts to*) pensar en; pensar (*un número, un naipe, etc.*); **to think so** creer que sí; **to think well of** tener buena opinión de
**thinker** [ˈθɪŋkər] *s* pensador *m*
**third** [θʌrd] *adj* tercero || *s* (*in a series*) tercero; (*one of three equal parts*) tercio; (*in dates*) tres *m*
**third degree** *s* (coll) interrogatorio bajo tortura
**third rail** *s* (rr) tercer carril *m*, carril de toma
**thirst** [θʌrst] *s* sed *f* || *intr* tener sed; **to thirst for** tener sed de
**thirst•y** [ˈθʌrsti] *adj* (*comp* **-ier;** *super* **-iest**) sediento; **to be thirsty** tener sed
**thirteen** [ˈθʌrˈtin] *adj, pron & s* trece *m*
**thirteenth** [ˈθʌrˈtinθ] *adj & s* (*in a series*) decimotercero; (*part*) trezavo || *s* (*in dates*) trece *m*
**thirtieth** [ˈθʌrtɪ•ɪθ] *adj & s* (*in a series*) trigésimo; (*part*) treintavo || *s* (*in dates*) treinta *m*
**thir•ty** [ˈθʌrti] *adj & pron* treinta || *s* (*pl* **-ties**) treinta *m*
**this** [ðɪs] *adj dem* (*pl* **these**) este; **this one** éste || *pron dem* (*pl* **these**) éste; esto || *adv* tan
**thistle** [ˈθɪsəl] *s* cardo
**thither** [ˈθɪðər] o [ˈðɪðər] *adv* allá, hacia allá
**Thomas** [ˈtɑməs] *s* Tomás *m*
**thong** [θɔŋ] o [θɑŋ] *s* correa
**tho•rax** [ˈθoræks] *s* (*pl* **-raxes** o **-races** [rəˌsiz]) tórax *m*
**thorn** [θɔrn] *s* espina
**thorn•y** [ˈθɔrni] *adj* (*comp* **-ier;** *super* **-iest**) espinoso; (*difficult*) (fig) espinoso
**thorough** [ˈθʌro] *adj* cabal, completo; concienzudo, cuidadoso
**thor′ough•bred′** *adj* de pura sangre; bien nacido || *s* pura sangre *m;* persona bien nacida
**thor′ough•fare′** *s* vía pública; **no thoroughfare** se prohibe el paso
**thor′ough•go′ing** *adj* cabal, completo, esmerado, perfecto
**thoroughly** [ˈθʌroli] *adv* a fondo
**those** [ðoz] *pl de* **that**
**thou** [ðaʊ] *pron pers* (archaic, poet & Bib) tú || *tr & intr* tutear
**though** [ðo] *adv* sin embargo || *conj* aunque, bien que; **as though** como si
**thought** [θɔt] *s* pensamiento
**thoughtful** [ˈθɔtfəl] *adj* pensativo; atento, considerado
**thoughtless** [ˈθɔtlɪs] *adj* irreflexivo; descuidado; inconsiderado
**thought transference** *s* transmisión del pensamiento
**thousand** [ˈθaʊzənd] *adj & s* mil *m;* **a thousand** u **one thousand** mil *m*
**thousandth** [ˈθaʊzəndθ] *adj & s* milésimo
**thralldom** [ˈθrɔldəm] *s* esclavitud, servidumbre
**thrash** [θræʃ] *tr* (agr) trillar; azotar, zurrar; **to thrash out** decidir después de una discusión cabal || *intr* trillar; agitarse, menearse
**thread** [θrɛd] *s* hilo; (mach) filete *m*, rosca; (*of a speech, of life*) hilo; **to lose the thread of** perder el hilo de || *tr* enhebrar, enhilar; ensartar (*p.ej., cuentas*); (mach) aterrajar, filetear
**thread′bare′** *adj* raído; gastado, usado, viejo
**threat** [θrɛt] *s* amenaza
**threaten** [ˈθrɛtən] *tr & intr* amenazar
**threatening** [ˈθrɛtənɪŋ] *adj* amenazante
**three** [θri] *adj & pron* tres || *s* tres *m;* **three o'clock** las tres
**three′-cor′nered** *adj* triangular; (*hat*) de tres picos
**three hundred** *adj & pron* trescientos || *s* trescientos *m*
**threepence** [ˈθrɛpəns] o [ˈθrɪpəns] *s* suma de tres peniques; moneda de tres peniques
**three′-ply′** *adj* de tres capas
**three R's** [ɑrz] *spl* lectura, escritura y aritmética, primeras letras
**three′score′** *adj* tres veintenas de
**threno•dy** [ˈθrɛnədi] *s* (*pl* **-dies**) treno
**thresh** [θrɛʃ] *tr* (agr) trillar; **to thresh out** decidir después de una discusión cabal || *intr* trillar; agitarse, menearse
**threshing machine** *s* máquina trilladora
**threshold** [ˈθrɛʃold] *s* umbral *m;* (physiol, psychol & fig) umbral, limen *m;* **to be on the threshold of** estar en los umbrales de; **to cross the threshold** atravesar o pisar los umbrales
**thrice** [θraɪs] *adv* tres veces; repetidamente, sumamente

**thrift** [θrɪft] *s* economía, parquedad
**thrift•y** [ˈθrɪfti] *adj* (*comp* **-ier;** *super* **-iest**) económico, parco; próspero
**thrill** [θrɪl] *s* emoción viva || *tr* emocionar, conmover || *intr* emocionarse, conmoverse
**thriller** [ˈθrɪllər] *s* cuento o pieza de teatro espeluznante
**thrilling** [ˈθrɪlɪŋ] *adj* emocionante; espeluznante
**thrive** [θraɪv] *v* (*pret* **thrived** o **throve** [θrov]; *pp* **thrived** o **thriven** [ˈθrɪvən]) *intr* medrar, prosperar
**throat** [θrot] *s* garganta; **to clear one's throat** aclarar la voz
**throb** [θrɑb] *s* latido, palpitación, pulsación || *v* (*pret & pp* **throbbed;** *ger* **throbbing**) *intr* latir, palpitar, pulsar
**throe** [θro] *s* congoja, dolor *m;* **throes** angustia, agonía; esfuerzo penoso
**throne** [θron] *s* trono
**throng** [θrɔŋ] o [θrɑŋ] *s* gentío, tropel *m,* muchedumbre || *intr* agolparse, apiñarse
**throttle** [ˈθrɑtəl] *s* válvula reguladora; (*of a locomotive*) regulador *m;* (*of an automobile*) acelerador *m* || *tr* ahogar, sofocar; impedir, suprimir; (mach) regular; **to throttle down** reducir la velocidad de
**through** [θru] *adj* directo, sin paradas; acabado, terminado; **to be through with** haber terminado; no querer ocuparse más de || *adv* a través, de un lado a otro; completamente || *prep* por, a través de; por medio de; a causa de; todo lo largo de
**through•out'** *adv* por todas partes; en todos respectos; desde el principio hasta el fin || *prep* por todo . . .; durante todo . . .; a lo largo de
**through'way'** *s* carretera de peaje de acceso limitado
**throw** [θro] *s* echada, tirada, lance *m;* cobertor ligero || *v* (*pret* **threw** [θru]; *pp* **thrown**) *tr* arrojar, echar, lanzar; tirar (*los dados*); lanzar (*una mirada*); desarzonar (*a un jinete*); proyectar (*una sombra*); tender (*un puente*); perder con premeditación (*un juego, una carrera*); **to throw away** tirar; malgastar; perder, no aprovechar; **to throw in** añadir, dar de más; **to throw out** arrojar, botar, desechar; echar a la calle; **to throw over** abandonar, dejar || *intr* arrojar, echar, lanzar; **to throw up** vomitar
**thrum** [θrʌm] *v* (*pret & pp* **thrummed;** *ger* **thrumming**) *intr* teclear; zangarrear; **to thrum on** rasguear
**thrush** [θrʌʃ] *s* tordo
**thrust** [θrʌst] *s* empuje *m;* acometida; (*with horns*) cornada; (*with dagger*) puñalada; (*with sword*) estocada; (*with knife*) cuchillada || *v* (*pret & pp* **thrust**) *tr* empujar; acometer; clavar, hincar; atravesar, traspasar
**thud** [θʌd] *s* baque *m,* ruido sordo || *v* (*pret & pp* **thudded;** *ger* **thudding**) *tr & intr* golpear con ruido sordo
**thug** [θʌg] *s* ladrón *m,* asesino
**thumb** [θʌm] *s* pulgar *m,* dedo gordo; **all thumbs** (coll) desmañado, chapucero, torpe; **to twiddle one's thumbs** menear ociosamente los pulgares; no hacer nada; **under the thumb of** bajo la férula de || *tr* manosear sin cuidado; ensuciar con los dedos; hojear (*un libro*) con el pulgar; **to thumb a ride** pedir ser llevado en automóvil indicando la dirección con el pulgar; **to thumb one's nose at** (coll) señalar (*a una persona*) poniendo el pulgar sobre la nariz en son de burla; (coll) tratar con sumo desprecio
**thumb index** *s* escalerilla, índice *m* con pestañas
**thumb'print'** *s* impresión del pulgar || *tr* marcar con impresión del pulgar
**thumb'screw'** *s* tornillo de mariposa, tornillo de orejas
**thumb'tack'** *s* chinche *m*
**thump** [θʌmp] *s* golpazo, porrazo || *tr* golpear, aporrear || *intr* caer con golpe pesado; andar con pasos pesados; latir (*el corazón*) con golpes pesados
**thumping** [ˈθʌmpɪŋ] *adj* (coll) enorme, pesado
**thunder** [ˈθʌndər] *s* trueno; (*of applause*) estruendo; amenaza || *tr* fulminar (*p.ej., censuras, amenazas*) || *intr* tronar; **to thunder at** tronar contra
**thun'der•bolt'** *s* rayo
**thun'der•clap'** *s* tronido
**thunderous** [ˈθʌndərəs] *adj* atronador, tronitoso
**thun'der•show'er** *s* chubasco con truenos
**thun'der•storm'** *s* tronada
**thun'der•struck'** *adj* atónito, estupefacto, pasmado
**Thursday** [ˈθʌrsdi] *s* jueves *m*
**thus** [ðʌs] *adv* así; **thus far** hasta aquí, hasta ahora
**thwack** [θwæk] *s* golpe *m,* porrazo || *tr* golpear, pegar
**thwart** [θwɔrt] *adj* transversal, oblicuo || *adv* de través || *tr* desbaratar, impedir, frustrar
**thy** [ðaɪ] *adj poss* (archaic & poet) tu
**thyme** [taɪm] *s* tomillo
**thyroid gland** [ˈθaɪrɔɪd] *s* glándula tiroides
**thyself** [ðaɪˈself] *pron* (archaic & poet) tú mismo; ti mismo; te; ti
**tiara** [taɪˈɑrə] o [taɪˈɛrə] *s* (*papal miter*) tiara; (*female adornment*) diadema *f*
**tick** [tɪk] *s* tictac *m;* funda (*de almohada o colchón*); (coll) crédito; (ent) garrapata; **on tick** (coll) al fiado || *intr* hacer tictac; latir (*el corazón*)
**ticker** [ˈtɪkər] *s* teleimpresor *m* de cinta; (slang) reloj *m;* (slang) corazón *m*
**ticker tape** *s* cinta de teleimpresor
**ticket** [ˈtɪkɪt] *s* billete *m;* boleto (Am); (theat) entrada, localidad; (*for wrong parking*) (coll) aviso de multa; (*of a political party*) (U.S.A.) lista de candidatos; **that's the ticket** (coll) eso es, eso es lo que se necesita

**ticket agent** *s* taquillero
**ticket collector** *s* revisor *m*
**ticket office** *s* taquilla, despacho de billetes
**ticket scalper** ['skælpər] *s* revendedor *m* de billetes de teatro
**ticket window** *s* taquilla, ventanilla
**ticking** ['tɪkɪŋ] *s* cutí *m*, terliz *m*
**tickle** ['tɪkəl] *s* cosquillas || *tr* cosquillear; gustar, satisfacer; divertir || *intr* cosquillear
**ticklish** ['tɪklɪʃ] *adj* cosquilloso; difícil, delicado; inseguro
**tick-tock** ['tɪk ,tɑk] *s* tictac *m*
**tidal wave** ['taɪdəl] *s* aguaje *m*, ola de marea; (*e.g., of popular indignation*) ola
**tidbit** ['tɪd,bɪt] *s* buen bocado, bocadito
**tiddlywinks** ['tɪdli,wɪŋks] *s* juego de la pulga
**tide** [taɪd] *s* marea; temporada; **to go against the tide** ir contra la corriente; **to stem the tide** rendir la marea || *tr* llevar, hacer flotar; **to tide over** ayudar un poco; superar (*una dificultad*)
**tide'wa'ter** *adj* costanero || *s* agua de marea; orilla del mar
**tidings** ['taɪdɪŋz] *spl* noticias, informes *mpl*
**ti•dy** ['taɪdi] *adj* (*comp* **-dier**; *super* **-diest**) aseado, limpio, pulcro, ordenado || *s* (*pl* **-dies**) pañito bordado, cubierta de respaldar || *v* (*pret & pp* **-died**) *tr* asear, limpiar, arreglar, poner en orden || *intr* asearse
**tie** [taɪ] *s* atadura; lazo, nudo; (*worn on neck*) corbata; (*in games and elections*) empate *m*; (mus) ligado; (rr) traviesa || *v* (*pret & pp* **tied**; *ger* **tying**) *tr* atar, liar; enlazar; hacer (*la corbata*); confinar, limitar; empatar (*p.ej., una elección*); empatársela a (*una persona*); **to be tied up** estar ocupado; **to tie down** confinar, limitar; **to tie up** atar; envolver; obstruir (*el tráfico*) || *intr* atar; empatar o empatarse (*dos candidatos, dos equipos*)
**tie'pin'** *s* alfiler *m* de corbata
**tier** [tɪr] *s* fila, ringlera; (theat) fila de palcos
**tiger** ['taɪgər] *s* tigre *m*
**tiger lily** *s* azucena atigrada
**tight** [taɪt] *adj* apretado, estrecho, ajustado; bien cerrado, hermético; compacto, denso; fijo, firme, sólido; (com) escaso; (sport) casi igual; (coll) agarrado, tacaño; (slang) borracho || *adv* firmemente; **to hold tight** mantener fijo; agarrarse bien || **tights** *spl* traje *m* de malla
**tighten** ['taɪtən] *tr* apretar; atiesar, estirar || *intr* apretarse; atiesarse, estirarse
**tight-fisted** ['taɪt'fɪstɪd] *adj* agarrado, tacaño
**tight'-fit'ting** *adj* ceñido, muy ajustado
**tight'rope'** *s* cuerda tirante
**tight squeeze** *s* (coll) brete *m*, aprieto
**tigress** ['taɪgrɪs] *s* tigresa
**tile** [taɪl] *s* azulejo; (*for floors*) baldosa; (*for roofs*) teja || *tr* azulejar; embaldosar; tejar
**tile roof** *s* tejado (de tejas)
**till** [tɪl] *prep* hasta || *conj* hasta que || *s* cajón *m* o gaveta del dinero || *tr* labrar, cultivar
**tilt** [tɪlt] *s* inclinación; justa, torneo; **full tilt** a toda velocidad || *tr* inclinar; asestar (*una lanza*) || *intr* inclinarse; justar, tornear; luchar; **to tilt at** luchar con, arremeter contra; protestar contra
**timber** ['tɪmbər] *s* madera de construcción; madero, viga; bosque *m*, árboles *mpl* de monte
**tim'ber•land'** *s* bosque *m* maderable
**timber line** *s* límite *m* de la vegetación, límite del bosque maderable
**timbre** ['tɪmbər] *s* (phonet & phys) timbre *m*
**time** [taɪm] *s* tiempo; hora, p.ej., **time to eat** hora de comer; vez, p.ej., **five times** cinco veces; rato, p.ej., **a nice time** un buen rato; (*period for payment*) plazo; horas de trabajo; sueldo; tiempo de parir, término del embarazo; última hora; (phot) tiempo de exposición; **for the time being** por ahora, por el momento; **on time** a tiempo, a la hora debida; (*in installments*) a plazos; **to bide one's time** esperar la hora propicia; **to do time** (coll) cumplir una condena; **to have a good time** darse buen tiempo; **to have no time for** no poder tolerar; **to lose time** atrasarse (*el reloj*); **to make time** avanzar con rapidez; **to pass the time of day** saludarse (*dos personas*); **to take one's time** no darse prisa, ir despacio; **what time is it?** ¿qué hora es? || *tr* calcular el tiempo de; medir el tiempo de; (sport) cronometrar
**time bomb** *s* bomba-reloj *f*
**time'card'** *s* hoja de presencia, tarjeta registradora
**time clock** *s* reloj *m* registrador
**time exposure** *s* exposición de tiempo
**time fuse** *s* espoleta de tiempos
**time'keep'er** *s* alistador *m* de tiempo; reloj *m*; (sport) cronometrador *m*, juez *m* de tiempo
**time•ly** ['taɪmli] *adj* (*comp* **-lier**; *super* **-liest**) oportuno
**time'piece'** *s* reloj *m*
**time signal** *s* señal horaria
**time'ta'ble** *s* horario, itinerario
**time'work'** *s* trabajo a jornal
**time'worn'** *adj* gastado por el tiempo
**time zone** *s* huso horario
**timid** ['tɪmɪd] *adj* tímido
**timing gears** ['taɪmɪŋ] *spl* engranaje *m* de distribución, mando de las válvulas
**timorous** ['tɪmərəs] *adj* tímido, miedoso
**tin** [tɪn] *s* (*element*) estaño; (*tin plate*) hojalata; (*cup, box, etc.*) lata || *v* (*pret & pp* **tinned**; *ger* **tinning**) *tr* estañar; (*to pack in cans*) enlatar; recubrir de hojalata
**tin can** *s* lata, envase *m* de hojalata
**tincture** ['tɪŋktʃər] *s* tintura

**tin cup** *s* taza de hojalata
**tinder** ['tɪndər] *s* yesca
**tin'der•box'** *s* lumbres *fpl*, yesquero; persona muy excitable; semillero de violencia
**tin foil** *s* hojuela de estaño, papel *m* de estaño
**ting-a-ling** ['tɪŋə,lɪŋ] *s* tilín *m*
**tinge** [tɪndʒ] *s* matiz *m*, tinte *m*; dejo, gustillo ‖ *v* (*ger* **tingeing** o **tinging**) *tr* matizar, teñir; dar gusto o sabor a
**tingle** ['tɪŋgəl] *s* comezón *f*, picazón *f* ‖ *intr* sentir comezón; zumbar (*los oídos*); (*e.g., with enthusiasm*) estremecerse
**tin hat** *s* (coll) yelmo de acero
**tinker** ['tɪŋkər] *s* calderero remendón; chapucero ‖ *intr* ocuparse vanamente
**tinkle** ['tɪŋkəl] *s* retintín *m* ‖ *tr* hacer retiñir ‖ *intr* retiñir
**tin plate** *s* hojalata
**tin roof** *s* tejado de hojalata
**tinsel** ['tɪnsəl] *s* oropel *m*; (*e.g., for a Christmas tree*) lentejuelas de hojas de estaño
**tin'smith'** *s* hojalatero
**tin soldier** *s* soldadito de plomo
**tint** [tɪnt] *s* tinte *m*, matiz *m* ‖ *tr* teñir, matizar, colorar ligeramente
**tin'type'** *s* ferrotipo
**tin'ware'** *s* objetos de hojalata
**ti•ny** ['taɪni] *adj* (*comp* **-nier**; *super* **-niest**) diminuto, menudo, pequeñito
**tip** [tɪp] *s* extremo, extremidad; (*of shoestring*) herrete *m*; (*of arrow*) casquillo; (*of umbrella*) regatón *m*; (*of tongue*) punta; (*of shoe*) puntera; (*of cigarette*) embocadura; inclinación; golpecito; soplo, aviso confidencial; (*fee*) propina ‖ *v* (*pret & pp* **tipped**; *ger* **tipping**) *tr* herretear; inclinar, ladear; volcar; golpear ligeramente; dar propina a; informar por debajo de cuerda; tocarse (*el sombrero*) con los dedos; quitarse (*el sombrero en señal de cortesía*); **to tip in** (typ) encañonar (*un pliego*) ‖ *intr* dar una propina o propinas; inclinarse, ladearse; volcarse
**tip'cart'** *s* volquete *m*
**tip'-off'** *s* (coll) informe dado por debajo de cuerda
**tipped'-in'** *adj* (bb) fuera de texto
**tipple** ['tɪpəl] *intr* beborrotear
**tip'staff'** *s* vara de justicia; alguacil *m* de vara
**tip•sy** ['tɪpsi] *adj* (*comp* **-sier**; *super* **-siest**) achispado
**tip'toe'** *s* punta del pie; **on tiptoe** de puntillas; alerta; furtivamente ‖ *v* (*pret & pp* **-toed**; *ger* **-toeing**) *intr* andar de puntillas
**tirade** ['taɪred] *s* diatriba, invectiva
**tire** [taɪr] *s* neumático, llanta de goma; (*of metal*) calce *m*, llanta ‖ *tr* cansar; aburrir, fastidiar ‖ *intr* (*to be tiresome*) cansar; (*to get tired*) cansarse; aburrirse, fastidiarse
**tire chain** *s* cadena de llanta, cadena antirresbaladiza
**tired** [taɪrd] *adj* cansado, rendido
**tire gauge** *s* indicador *m* de presión de inflado
**tireless** ['taɪrlɪs] *adj* incansable, infatigable
**tire pressure** *s* presión de inflado
**tire pump** *s* bomba para inflar neumáticos
**tiresome** ['taɪrsəm] *adj* cansado, aburrido, pesado
**tissue** ['tɪsjʊ] *s* tejido fino; papel *m* de seda; (biol & fig) tejido
**tissue paper** *s* papel *m* de seda
**titanium** [tai'tenɪ·əm] o [tɪ'tenɪ·əm] *s* titanio
**tithe** [taɪð] *s* décimo, décima parte; (*tax paid to church*) diezmo ‖ *tr* diezmar
**Titian** ['tɪʃən] *adj* castaño rojizo ‖ *s* el Ticiano
**title** ['taɪtəl] *s* título; (sport) campeonato ‖ *tr* titular
**title deed** *s* título de propiedad
**ti'tle•hold'er** *s* titulado; (sport) campeón *m*
**title page** *s* portada, frontispicio
**title rôle** *s* (theat) papel *m* principal (*el que corresponde al título de la obra*)
**titter** ['tɪtər] *s* risita ahogada, risita disimulada ‖ *intr* reír a medias, reír con disimulo
**titular** ['tɪtʃələr] *adj* titular; nominal
**tn.** *abbr* **ton**
**to** [tu], [tʊ] o [tə] *adv* hacia adelante; **to and fro** de una parte a otra, de aquí para allá; **to come to** volver en sí ‖ *prep* a, p.ej., **he is going to Madrid** va a Madrid; **they gave something to the beggar** dieron algo al pobre; **we are learning to dance** aprendemos a bailar; para, p.ej., **he is reading to himself** lee para sí; por, p.ej., **work to do** trabajo por hacer; hasta, p.ej., **to a certain extent** hasta cierto punto; en, p.ej., **from door to door** de puerta en puerta; con, p.ej., **kind to her** amable con ella; segun, p.ej., **to my way of thinking** según mi modo de pensar; menos, p.ej., **five minutes to ten** las diez menos cinco
**toad** [tod] *s* sapo
**toad'stool'** *s* agárico, seta; seta venenosa
**to-and-fro** ['tu·ənd'fro] *adj* alternativo, de vaivén
**toast** [tost] *s* tostadas; (*drink*) brindis *m*; **a piece of toast** una tostada ‖ *tr* tostar; brindar a o por ‖ *intr* tostarse; brindar
**toaster** ['tostər] *s* (*of bread*) tostador *m*; brindador *m*
**toast'mas'ter** *s* el que presenta a los oradores en un banquete, maestro de ceremonias
**tobac•co** [tə'bæko] *s* (*pl* **-cos**) tabaco
**tobacco pouch** *s* petaca
**toboggan** [tə'bɑgən] *s* tobogán *m* ‖ *intr* deslizarse en tobogán
**tocsin** ['tɑksɪn] *s* campana de alarma; campanada de alarma
**today** [tʊ'de] *adv & s* hoy
**toddle** ['tɑdəl] *s* pasitos vacilantes ‖ *intr* andar con pasitos vacilantes; hacer pinitos (*un niño o un enfermo*)

**tod·dy** ['tɑdi] *s* (*pl* **-dies**) ponche *m*
**to-do** [tə'du] *s* (coll) alharaca, alboroto
**toe** [to] *s* dedo del pie; (*of stocking*) punta ‖ *v* (*pret & pp* **toed;** *ger* **toeing**) *tr* — **to toe the line** o **the mark** ponerse a la raya; obrar como se debe
**toe'nail'** *s* uña del dedo del pie
**tog** [tɑg] *s* (coll) prenda de vestir
**together** [tʊ'gɛðər] *adv* juntamente; juntos; al mismo tiempo; sin interrupción; de acuerdo; **to bring together** reunir; confrontar; reconciliar; **to call together** convocar; **to go together** ir juntos; ser novios; hacer juego; **to stick together** (coll) quedarse unidos, no abandonarse
**toil** [tɔɪl] *s* afán *m,* fatiga; faena, obra laboriosa; **toils** red *f,* lazo ‖ *intr* atrafagar; moverse con fatiga
**toilet** ['tɔɪlɪt] *s* tocado, atavío; (*dressing table*) tocador *m;* retrete *m,* inodoro, excusado; **to make one's toilet** asearse, acicalarse
**toilet articles** *spl* artículos de tocador
**toilet paper** *s* papel higiénico
**toilet powder** *s* polvos de tocador
**toilet soap** *s* jabón *m* de olor, jabón de tocador
**toilet water** *s* agua de tocador
**token** ['tokən] *s* señal *f,* prueba; prenda, recuerdo; (*used as money*) ficha, tanto; **by the same token** por el mismo motivo; **in token of** en señal de
**tolerance** ['tɑlərəns] *s* tolerancia
**tolerate** ['tɑlə,ret] *tr* tolerar
**toll** [tol] *s* (*of bells*) doble *m;* (*to pass along a road or over a bridge*) peaje *m;* (*to use a canal*) derechos de paso; (*to use a telephone*) tarifa; (*number of victims*) baja, mortalidad ‖ *tr* tocar a muerto (*una campana*); llamar con toque de difuntos ‖ *intr* doblar
**toll bridge** *s* puente *m* de peaje
**toll call** *s* (telp) llamada a larga distancia
**toll'gate'** *s* barrera de peaje
**toma·to** [tə'meto] o [tə'mɑto] *s* (*pl* **-toes**) (*plant*) tomatera o tomate *m;* (*fruit*) tomate
**tomb** [tum] *s* tumba, sepulcro
**tomboy** ['tɑm,bɔɪ] *s* moza retozona, muchacha traviesa
**tomb'stone'** *s* piedra o lápida sepulcral
**tomcat** ['tɑm,kæt] *s* gato macho
**tome** [tom] *s* tomo; libro grueso
**tomorrow** [tʊ'mɑro] o [tʊ'mɔro] *adv* mañana ‖ *s* mañana *m;* **the day after tomorrow** pasado mañana
**tom-tom** ['tɑm,tɑm] *s* tantán *m*
**ton** [tʌn] *s* tonelada; **tons** (coll) montones *mpl*
**tone** [ton] *s* tono ‖ *tr* entonar ‖ *intr* armonizar; **to tone down** moderarse; **to tone up** reforzarse
**tone poem** *s* poema sinfónico
**tongs** [tɔŋz] o [tɑŋz] *spl* tenazas; (*e.g., for sugar*) tenacillas
**tongue** [tʌŋ] *s* (anat) lengua; (*of a wagon*) vara, lanza; (*of a belt buckle*) tarabilla; (*of shoe*) lengua, lengüeta; (*language*) lengua, idioma *m;* **to hold one's tongue** morderse la lengua
**tongue twister** ['twɪstər] *s* trabalenguas *m*
**tonic** ['tɑnɪk] *adj & s* tónico
**tonic accent** *s* acento prosódico
**tonight** [tʊ'naɪt] *adv & s* esta noche
**tonnage** ['tʌnɪdʒ] *s* tonelaje *m*
**tonsil** ['tɑnsəl] *s* tonsila, amígdala
**tonsillitis** [,tɑnsɪ'laɪtɪs] *s* tonsilitis *f,* amigdalitis *f*
**ton·y** ['toni] *adj* (*comp* **-ier;** *super* **-iest**) (slang) elegante, aristocrático
**too** [tu] *adv* (*also*) también; (*more than enough*) demasiado; **too bad!** ¡qué lástima!; **too many** demasiados; **too much** demasiado
**tool** [tul] *s* herramienta; (*person used for one's own ends*) instrumento ‖ *tr* trabajar con herramienta; (bb) filetear, estampar
**tool bag** *s* bolsa de herramientas
**tool'mak'er** *s* tallador *m* de herramientas, herrero de herramientas
**toot** [tut] *s* (*of horn*) toque *m;* (*of klaxon*) bocinazo; (*of locomotive*) pitazo; (coll) parranda ‖ *tr* sonar; **to toot one's own horn** cantar sus propias alabanzas ‖ *intr* sonar
**tooth** [tuθ] *s* (*pl* **teeth** [tiθ]) diente *m*
**tooth'ache'** *s* dolor *m* de muelas
**tooth'brush'** *s* cepillo de dientes
**toothless** ['tuθlɪs] *adj* desdentado
**tooth paste** *s* pasta dentífrica
**tooth'pick'** *s* limpiadientes *m,* mondadientes *m,* palillo
**tooth powder** *s* polvo dentífrico
**top** [tɑp] *s* (*of a mountain, tree, etc.*) cima; (*of a mountain; high point*) cumbre *f;* (*of a tree*) copa; (*of a barrel, box, etc.*) tapa; (*of a page*) principio; (*of a table*) tablero; (*of a wall*) coronamiento; (*of a bathing suit*) camiseta; (*of a carriage or auto*) capota; (*toy*) peón *m,* peonza; (naut) cofa; **at the top of** en lo alto de; (*e.g., one's class*) a la cabeza de; **at the top of one's voice** a voz en grito; **from top to bottom** de arriba abajo; de alto a bajo; completamente; **on top of** en lo alto de; encima de; **the tops** (slang) la flor de la canela; **to sleep like a top** dormir como un leño ‖ *v* (*pret & pp* **topped;** *ger* **topping**) *tr* coronar, rematar; cubrir; aventajar, superar; descopar (*p.ej., un árbol*)
**topaz** ['topæz] *s* topacio
**top billing** *s* cabecera de cartel
**top'coat'** *s* sobretodo; abrigo de entretiempo
**toper** ['topər] *s* borrachín *m*
**top hat** *s* chistera, sombrero de copa
**top'-heav'y** *adj* más pesado arriba que abajo
**topic** ['tɑpɪk] *s* asunto, materia, tema *m*
**top'knot'** *s* moño
**top'mast'** *s* (naut) mastelero
**top'most** *adj* (el) más alto
**topogra·phy** [tə'pɑgrəfi] *s* (*pl* **-phies**) topografía
**topple** ['tɑpəl] *tr* derribar, volcar ‖

*intr* derribarse, volcarse; caerse, venirse abajo

**top priority** *s* máxima prioridad

**topsail** ['tɑpsəl] o ['tɑp,sel] *s* (naut) gavia

**top'soil'** *s* capa superficial del suelo

**topsy-turvy** ['tɑpsi'tʌrvi] *adj* desbarajustado ‖ *adv* en cuadro, patas arriba ‖ *s* desbarajuste *m*

**torch** [tɔrtʃ] *s* antorcha; lámpara de bolsillo; **to carry the torch for** (slang) amar desesperadamente

**torch'bear'er** *s* hachero; (fig) adicto, partidario

**torch'light'** *s* luz *f* de antorcha

**torch song** *s* canción lenta y melancólica de amor no correspondido

**torment** ['tɔrmɛnt] *s* tormento ‖ [tɔr'mɛnt] *tr* atormentar

**torna•do** [tɔr'nedo] *s* (*pl* **-does** o **-dos**) tornado, tromba terrestre

**torpe•do** [tɔr'pido] *s* (*pl* **-does**) torpedo ‖ *tr* torpedear

**torrent** ['tɑrənt] o ['tɔrənt] *s* torrente *m*

**torrid** ['tɑrɪd] o ['tɔrɪd] *adj* tórrido

**tor•so** ['tɔrso] *s* (*pl* **-sos**) torso

**tortoise** ['tɔrtəs] *s* tortuga

**tortoise shell** *s* carey *m*

**torture** ['tɔrtʃər] *s* tortura ‖ *tr* torturar, atormentar

**toss** [tɔs] o [tɑs] *s* echada; alcance *m* de una echada ‖ *tr* arrojar, echar; lanzar al aire; agitar, menear; levantar airosamente (*la cabeza*); lanzar (*p.ej., un comentario*); echar a cara o cruz; **to toss off** hacer muy rápidamente; tragar de un golpe ‖ *intr* agitarse, menearse; **to toss and turn** (*in bed*) revolverse, dar vueltas

**toss'-up'** *s* cara o cruz; probabilidad igual

**tot** [tɑt] *s* párvulo, peque *m*, chiquitín *m*

**to•tal** ['totəl] *adj* total; (*e.g., loss*) completo ‖ *s* total *m* ‖ *v* (*pret & pp* **-taled** o **-talled**; *ger* **-taling** o **-talling**) *tr* ascender a, sumar

**totter** ['tɑtər] *s* tambaleo ‖ *intr* tambalear; estar para desplomarse

**touch** [tʌtʃ] *s* (*act*) toque *m*; (*sense*) tacto, tiento; (*of piano, pianist, typewriter, typist*) tacto; (*of an illness*) ramo, ataque ligero; pizca, poquito; **to get in touch with** ponerse en comunicación o contacto con; **to lose one's touch** perder el tiento ‖ *tr* tocar; conmover, enternecer; probar (*vino, licor*); (*for a loan*) (slang) pedir prestado a, dar un sablazo a; **to touch up** retocar ‖ *intr* tocar; **to touch at** tocar en (*un puerto*)

**touching** ['tʌtʃɪŋ] *adj* conmovedor, enternecedor ‖ *prep* tocante a

**touch typewriting** *s* escritura al tacto

**touch•y** ['tʌtʃi] *adj* (*comp* **-ier**; *super* **-iest**) quisquilloso, enojadizo

**tough** [tʌf] *adj* correoso; tenaz; difícil; gamberro; (*e.g., luck*) malo ‖ *s* gamberro, guapetón *m*

**toughen** ['tʌfən] *tr* hacer correoso; hacer tenaz; dificultar ‖ *intr* ponerse correoso; hacerse tenaz; hacerse difícil

**tour** [tʊr] *s* jira, paseo, vuelta; viaje largo; **on tour** de jira, de viaje ‖ *tr* viajar por, recorrer ‖ *intr* viajar por distracción o diversión

**touring car** ['tʊrɪŋ] *s* coche *m* de turismo

**tourist** ['tʊrɪst] *adj* turístico ‖ *s* turista *mf*

**tournament** ['tʊrnəmənt] o ['tʌrnəmənt] *s* torneo

**tourney** ['tʊrni] o ['tʌrni] *s* torneo ‖ *intr* tornear

**tourniquet** ['tʊrnɪ,kɛt] o ['tʌrnɪ,ke] *s* torniquete *m*

**tousle** ['tauzəl] *tr* despeinar, enmarañar

**tow** [to] *s* remolque *m*; (*e.g., of hemp*) estopa; **to take in tow** dar remolque a; (fig) encargarse de ‖ *tr* remolcar

**towage** ['to•ɪdʒ] *s* remolque *m*; derechos de remolque

**toward(s)** [tord(z)] o [tə'wɔrd(z)] *prep* (*in the direction of*) hacia; (*with regard to*) para con; (*a certain hour*) cerca de, a eso de

**tow'boat'** *s* remolcador *m*

**tow•el** ['tau•əl] *s* toalla ‖ *v* (*pret & pp* **-eled** o **-elled**; *ger* **-eling** o **-elling**) *tr* secar con toalla

**towel rack** *s* toallero

**tower** ['tau•ər] *s* torre *f* ‖ *intr* encumbrarse, empinarse

**towering** ['tau•ərɪŋ] *adj* encumbrado; sobresaliente; excesivo

**towing service** ['to•ɪŋ] *s* servicio de grúa

**tow'line'** *s* cable *m* de remolque, sirga

**town** [taun] *s* población, pueblo, villa; **in town** a la ciudad, en la ciudad

**town clerk** *s* escribano municipal

**town council** *s* concejo municipal

**town crier** *s* pregonero público

**town hall** *s* ayuntamiento, casa de ayuntamiento

**towns'folk'** *spl* vecinos del pueblo

**township** ['taunʃɪp] *s* sexmo; terreno público de seis millas en cuadro

**towns•man** ['taunzmən] *s* (*pl* **-men** [mən]) ciudadano, vecino; conciudadano, paisano

**towns'peo'ple** *spl* vecinos del pueblo

**town talk** *s* comidilla o hablillas del pueblo

**tow'path'** *s* camino de sirga

**tow plane** *s* avión *m* de remolque

**tow'rope'** *s* cuerda de remolque

**tow truck** *s* camión-grúa *m*

**toxic** ['tɑksɪk] *adj & s* tóxico

**toy** [tɔɪ] *adj* de juguete ‖ *s* juguete *m*; (*trifle*) bagatela; (*trinket*) dije *m*, bujería ‖ *intr* jugar; divertirse; **to toy with** jugar con (*los sentimientos de una persona*); acariciar (*una idea*)

**toy bank** *s* alcancía, hucha

**toy soldier** *s* soldado de juguete

**trace** [tres] *s* huella, rastro; indicio, vestigio; (*of harness*) tirante *m*; pizca ‖ *tr* rastrear; trazar (*p.ej., una curva; los rasgos de una persona o cosa*); averiguar el paradero de; remontar al origen de

**trache·a** ['trekɪ·ə] *s* (*pl* **-ae** [ˌi]) tráquea
**track** [træk] *s* (*of foot*) huella; (*of a wheel*) rodada, carril *m;* (*of a boat*) estela; (*of railroad*) vía; (*of an airplane, a hurricane*) trayectoria; (*of a tractor*) llanta de oruga; camino, senda; (*course followed by a boat*) derrota; (*of ideas, events, etc.*) sucesión; (sport) pista; **to keep track of** no perder de vista; no olvidar; **to lose track of** perder de vista; olvidar; **to make tracks** dejar pisadas; irse muy de prisa ‖ *tr* rastrear; seguir la huella o la pista de; dejar pisadas en, manchar pisando; **to track down** seguir y capturar; averiguar el origen de
**tracking** ['trækɪŋ] *s* seguimiento (*de vehículos espaciales*)
**tracking station** *s* estación de seguimiento
**trackless trolley** ['træklɪs] *s* filobús *m*, trolebús *m*
**track meet** *s* concurso de carreras y saltos
**track'walk'er** *s* guardavía *m*
**tract** [trækt] *s* espacio, tracto; folleto; (anat) canal *m*, sistema *m*
**traction** ['trækʃən] *s* tracción
**traction company** *s* empresa de tranvías
**tractor** ['træktər] *s* tractor *m*
**trade** [tred] *s* comercio; negocio, trato; trueque *m*, canje *m;* (*calling, job*) oficio; clientela, parroquia; (*e.g., in slaves*) trata ‖ *tr* cambiar, trocar; **to trade in** dar como parte del pago; **to trade off** cambalachear; ‖ *intr* comerciar; comprar; **to trade in** comerciar en; **to trade on** aprovecharse de
**trade'mark'** *s* marca de fábrica, marca registrada
**trade name** *s* nombre *m* comercial, razón *f* social; nombre de fábrica
**trader** ['tredər] *s* traficante *mf*
**trade school** *s* escuela de artes y oficios
**trades·man** ['tredzmən] *s* (*pl* **-men** [mən]) tendero; comerciante *m;* (Brit) artesano
**trades union** o **trade union** *s* sindicato, gremio de obreros
**trade unionist** *s* sindicalista *mf*
**trade winds** *spl* vientos alisios
**trading post** ['tredɪŋ] *s* factoría; (*in stock exchange*) puesto de compraventa
**trading stamp** *s* sello de premio, sello de descuento
**tradition** [trə'dɪʃən] *s* tradición
**traduce** [trə'djus] o [trə'dus] *tr* calumniar
**traf·fic** ['træfɪk] *s* tráfico, comercio; tráfico, circulación; (*e.g., in slaves*) trata ‖ *v* (*pret & pp* **-ficked;** *ger* **-ficking**) *intr* traficar
**traffic circle** *s* glorieta de tráfico
**traffic court** *s* juzgado de tráfico
**traffic jam** *s* embotellamiento, tapón *m* de tráfico
**traffic light** *s* luz *f* de tráfico, semáforo
**traffic sign** o **signal** *s* señal *f* de tráfico
**traffic ticket** *s* aviso de multa
**tragedian** [trə'dʒidɪ·ən] *s* trágico
**trage·dy** ['trædʒɪdi] *s* (*pl* **-dies**) tragedia
**tragic** ['trædʒɪk] *adj* trágico
**trail** [trel] *s* rastro, huella, pista; (*path through rough country*) trocha, senda, vereda; (*of a gown*) cola; (*of smoke, a rocket, etc.*) estela ‖ *tr* arrastrar; seguir la pista de; andar detrás de; llevar (*p.ej., barro*) con los pies ‖ *intr* arrastrar; rezagarse; arrastrarse, trepar (*una planta*); **to trail off** desaparecer poco a poco
**trailer** ['trelər] *s* remolque *m*, coche-habitación *m*, casa rodante; planta rastrera
**trailing arbutus** ['trelɪŋ] *s* epigea rastrera
**train** [tren] *s* (*of railway cars; of waves*) tren *m;* (*of thought*) hilo ‖ *tr* adiestrar; guiar (*las plantas*); (sport) entrenar ‖ *intr* adiestrarse; (sport) entrenarse
**trained nurse** *s* enfermera graduada
**trainer** ['trenər] *s* (sport) entrenador *m*
**training** ['trenɪŋ] *s* adiestramiento; instrucción; (sport) entrenamiento
**training school** *s* escuela práctica; reformatorio
**training ship** *s* buque *m* escuela
**trait** [tret] *s* característica, rasgo
**traitor** ['tretər] *s* traidor *m*
**traitress** ['tretrɪs] *s* traidora
**trajecto·ry** [trə'dʒɛktəri] *s* (*pl* **-ries**) trayectoria
**tramp** [træmp] *s* vagabundo; marcha pesada, ruido de pisadas ‖ *tr* pisar con fuerza; recorrer a pie ‖ *intr* andar a pie; vagabundear
**trample** ['træmpəl] *tr* pisotear ‖ *intr* — **to trample on** o **upon** pisotear
**tramp steamer** *s* vapor volandero
**trance** [træns] o [trɑns] *s* arrobamiento, rapto; estado hipnótico
**tranquil** ['træŋkwɪl] *adj* tranquilo
**tranquilize** ['træŋkwɪˌlaɪz] *tr & intr* tranquilizar
**tranquilizer** ['træŋkwɪˌlaɪzər] *s* tranquilizante *m*
**tranquillity** [træŋ'kwɪlɪti] *s* tranquilidad
**transact** [træn'zækt] o [træns'ækt] *tr* tramitar; llevar a cabo
**transaction** [træn'zækʃən] o [træns'ækʃən] *s* tramitación, transacción
**transatlantic** [ˌtrænsət'læntɪk] *adj & s* transatlántico
**transcend** [træn'sɛnd] *tr* exceder, superar ‖ *intr* sobresalir
**transcribe** [træn'skraɪb] *tr* transcribir
**transcript** ['trænskrɪpt] *s* trasunto, traslado; (educ) hoja de estudios, certificado de estudios
**transcription** [træn'skrɪpʃən] *s* transcripción
**transept** ['trænsɛpt] *s* crucero, transepto
**trans·fer** ['trænsfər] *s* traslado; transbordo; contraseña o billete *m* de transferencia ‖ [træns'fʌr] o ['trænsfər] *v* (*pret & pp* **-ferred;** *ger*

**-ferring)** *tr* trasladar, transferir; transbordar || *intr* cambiar de tren, tranvía, etc.

**transfix** [træns'fɪks] *tr* espetar, traspasar; dejar atónito

**transform** [træns'fɔrm] *tr* transformar || *intr* transformarse

**transformer** [træns'fɔrmər] *s* transformador *m*

**transfusion** [træns'fjuʃən] *s* transfusión; (med) transfusión de la sangre

**transgress** [træns'grɛs] *tr* transgredir, violar; exceder, traspasar (*p.ej., los límites de la prudencia*) || *intr* pecar, prevaricar

**transgression** [træns'grɛʃən] *s* transgresión; pecado, prevaricación

**transient** ['trænʃənt] *adj* pasajero, transitorio; de tránsito || *s* transeúnte *mf*

**transistor** [træn'zɪstər] *s* transistor *m*

**transit** ['trænsɪt] o ['trænzɪt] *s* tránsito

**transitive** ['trænsɪtɪv] *adj* transitivo || *s* verbo transitivo

**transitory** ['trænsɪ,tori] *adj* transitorio

**translate** [træns'let] o ['trænslet] *tr* (*from one language to another*) traducir; (*from one place to another*) trasladar || *intr* traducirse

**translation** [træns'leʃən] *s* traducción; traslación

**translator** [træns'letər] *s* traductor *m*

**transliterate** [træns'lɪtə,ret] *tr* transcribir

**translucent** [træns'lusənt] *adj* translúcido

**transmission** [træns'mɪʃən] *s* transmisión; (aut) cambio de marchas, cambio de velocidades

**transmis'sion-gear' box** *s* caja de cambio de marchas, caja de velocidades

**trans•mit** [træns'mɪt] *v* (*pret & pp* **-mitted;** *ger* **-mitting)** *tr & intr* transmitir

**transmitter** [træns'mɪtər] *s* transmisor *m*

**transmitting set** *s* aparato transmisor

**transmitting station** *s* estacion transmisora, emisora

**transmute** [træns'mjut] *tr & intr* transmutar

**transom** [trænsəm] *s* (*crosspiece*) travesaño; (*window over door*) montante *m;* (*of ship*) yugo de popa

**transparen•cy** [træns'pɛrənsi] *s* (*pl* **-cies)** transparencia

**transparent** [træns'pɛrənt] *adj* transparente

**transpire** [træns'paɪr] *intr* transpirar; (*to become known, leak out*) transpirar; (coll) acontecer, tener lugar

**transplant** [træns'plænt] o [træns'plɑnt] *tr* transplantar || *intr* transplantarse

**transport** ['trænsport] *s* transporte *m;* (aer & naut) transporte *m;* rapto, éxtasis *m,* transporte *m* || [træns'port] *tr* transportar

**transportation** [,trænspor'teʃən] *s* transporte *m;* (U.S.A.) pasaje *m,* billete *m* de viaje

**transport worker** *s* transportista *mf*

**transpose** [træns'poz] *tr* transponer; (mus) transportar

**trans•ship** [træns'ʃɪp] *v* (*pret & pp* **-shipped;** *ger* **-shipping)** *tr* transbordar

**transshipment** [træns'ʃɪpmənt] *s* transbordo

**trap** [træp] *s* trampa; (*double-curved pipe*) sifón *m;* coche ligero de dos ruedas; (sport) lanzaplatos *m* || *v* (*pret & pp* **trapped;** *ger* **trapping)** *tr* entrampar; atrapar (*a un ladrón*)

**trap door** *s* escotillón *m,* trampa; (theat) escotillón *m,* pescante *m*

**trapeze** [trə'piz] *s* trapecio

**trapezoid** ['træpɪ,zɔɪd] *s* trapecio

**trapper** ['træpər] *s* cazador *m* de alforja

**trappings** ['træpɪŋz] *spl* (*adornments*) adornos, atavíos; (*of a horse's harness*) jaeces *mpl*

**trap'shoot'ing** *s* tiro al vuelo

**trash** [træʃ] *s* broza, basura, desecho; (*junk*) cachivaches *mpl;* (*nonsense*) disparates *mpl;* (*worthless people*) gentuza

**trash can** *s* basurero

**travail** ['trævel] o [trə'vel] *s* afán *m,* labor *f,* pena; dolores *mpl* del parto

**trav•el** ['trævəl] *s* viaje *m;* el viajar; (mach) recorrido || *v* (*pret & pp* **-eled** o **-elled;** *ger* **-eling** o **-elling)** *tr* viajar por; recorrer || *intr* viajar; andar, recorrer

**travel bureau** *s* oficina de turismo

**traveler** ['trævələr] *s* viajero; (*salesman*) viajante *m*

**traveler's check** *s* cheque *m* de viajeros

**traveling expenses** *spl* gastos de viaje

**traveling salesman** *s* viajante *m,* agente viajero

**traverse** ['trævərs] o [trə'vʌrs] *tr* atravesar; recorrer, pasar por

**traves•ty** ['trævɪsti] *s* (*pl* **-ties)** parodia || *v* (*pret & pp* **-tied)** *tr* parodiar

**trawl** [trɔl] *s* red barredera, espinel *m,* palangre *m* || *tr & intr* pescar a la rastra

**tray** [tre] *s* bandeja; (chem & phot) cubeta

**treacherous** ['trɛtʃərəs] *adj* traicionero, traidor; incierto, poco seguro

**treacher•y** ['trɛtʃəri] *s* (*pl* **-ies)** traición, alevosía

**tread** [trɛd] *s* (*stepping*) pisada; (*of stairs*) grada, huella, peldaño; (*of stilts*) horquilla; (*of a tire*) banda de rodamiento; (*of shoe*) suela; (*of an egg*) meaje, galladura || *v* (*pret* **trod** [trɑd]; *pp* **trodden** ['trɑdən] o **trod)** *tr* pisar, pisotear; abrumar, agobiar || *intr* andar, caminar

**treadle** ['trɛdəl] *s* pedal *m*

**tread'mill'** *s* rueda de andar; (*futile drudgery*) noria

**treas.** *abbr* **treasurer, treasury**

**treason** ['trizən] *s* traición

**treasonable** ['trizənəbəl] *adj* traicionero, traidor

**treasure** ['trɛʒər] *s* tesoro || *tr* atesorar

**treasurer** ['trɛʒərər] *s* tesorero

**treasur•y** ['trɛʒəri] *s* (*pl* **-ies)** tesorería; tesoro

**treat** [trit] *s* convite *m;* (*to a drink*) convidada; (*something providing particular enjoyment*) regalo, deleite *m* || *tr* tratar; convidar, regalar; curar (*a un enfermo*) || *intr* tratar; convidar, regalar; **to treat of** tratar de
**treatise** ['tritɪs] *s* tratado
**treatment** ['tritmənt] *s* tratamiento
**trea•ty** ['triti] *s* (*pl* **-ties**) tratado
**treble** ['trɛbəl] *adj* (*threefold*) tresdoble, triple; sobreagudo; (mus) atiplado; (mus) de tiple || *s* (*person*) tiple *mf;* (*voice*) tiple *m* || *tr* triplicar || *intr* triplicarse
**tree** [tri] *s* árbol *m*
**tree farm** *s* monte *m* tallar
**treeless** ['trilɪs] *adj* pelado, sin árboles
**tree'top'** *s* copa, cima de árbol
**trellis** ['trɛlɪs] *s* enrejado, espaldera; emparrado
**tremble** ['trɛmbəl] *s* temblor *m*, estremecimiento || *intr* temblar, estremecerse
**tremendous** [trɪ'mɛndəs] *adj* tremendo
**tremor** ['trɛmər] o ['trimər] *s* temblor *m*
**trench** [trɛntʃ] *s* foso, zanja; (*for irrigation*) acequia; (mil) trinchera
**trenchant** ['trɛntʃənt] *adj* mordaz, punzante; enérgico, bien definido
**trench coat** *s* trinchera
**trench mortar** *s* (mil) lanzabombas *m*
**trench'-plow'** *tr* (agr) desfondar
**trend** [trɛnd] *s* curso, dirección, tendencia || *intr* dirigirse, tender
**trespass** ['trɛspəs] *s* entrada sin derecho; infracción, violación; culpa, pecado || *intr* entrar sin derecho; pecar; **no trespassing** prohibida la entrada; **to trespass against** pecar contra; **to trespass on** entrar sin derecho en; infringir, violar; abusar de (*p.ej., la paciencia de uno*)
**tress** [trɛs] *s* (*braid of hair*) trenza; (*curl*) bucle *m*, rizo
**trestle** ['trɛsəl] *s* caballete *m;* puente *m* o viaducto de caballetes
**trial** ['traɪ•əl] *s* ensayo, prueba; aflicción, desgracia; (law) juicio, proceso, vista; **on trial** a prueba; (law) en juicio; **to bring to trial** encausar
**trial and error** *s* método de tanteos
**trial balloon** *s* globo sonda; **to send up a trial balloon** (fig) lanzar un globo sonda
**trial by jury** *s* juicio por jurado
**trial jury** *s* jurado procesal
**trial order** *s* (com) pedido de ensayo
**triangle** ['traɪ,æŋgəl] *s* triángulo
**tribe** [traɪb] *s* tribu *f*
**tribunal** [trɪ'bjunəl] o [traɪ'bjunəl] *s* tribunal *m*
**tribune** ['trɪbjun] *s* tribuna
**tributar•y** ['trɪbjə,tɛri] *adj* tributario || *s* (*pl* **-ies**) tributario
**tribute** ['trɪbjut] *s* tributo
**trice** [traɪs] *s* momento, instante *m;* **in a trice** en un periquete
**trick** [trɪk] *s* ardid *m*, artimaña; (*knack*) maña; (*feat*) suerte *f;* (*prank*) travesura, burla, chasco; tanda, turno; ilusión; (*feat with cards*) truco; (*cards in one round*) baza; (coll) chiquita; **to be up to one's old tricks** hacer de las suyas; **to play a dirty trick on** hacer una mala jugada a || *tr* trampear; burlar, engañar; ataviar
**tricker•y** ['trɪkəri] *s* (*pl* **-ies**) trampería, malas mañas
**trickle** ['trɪkəl] *s* chorro delgado, goteo || *intr* escurrir, gotear; pasar gradual e irregularmente
**trickster** ['trɪkstər] *s* tramposo, embustero
**trick•y** ['trɪki] *adj* (*comp* **-ier;** *super* **-iest**) tramposo, engañoso; difícil; (*animal*) vicioso; (*ticklish to deal with*) delicado
**tricorn** ['traɪkɔrn] *adj & s* tricornio
**tried** [traɪd] *adj* fiel, probado, seguro
**trifle** ['traɪfəl] *s* bagatela, friolera, fruslería; (*trinket*) bagatela, baratija || *tr* — **to trifle away** malgastar || *intr* estar ocioso, holgar; **to trifle with** manosear; jugar con, burlarse de
**trifling** ['traɪflɪŋ] *adj* frívolo, fútil, ligero; insignificante, trivial
**trifocal** [traɪ'fokəl] *adj* trifocal || *s* lente *f* trifocal; **trifocals** anteojos trifocales
**trig.** *abbr* **trigonometric, trigonometry**
**trigger** ['trɪgər] *s* (*e.g., of a gun*) disparador *m*, gatillo; (*of any device*) disparador || *tr* poner en movimiento, provocar
**trigonometry** [,trɪgə'nɑmɪtri] *s* trigonometría
**trill** [trɪl] *s* trinado, trino; (*made with voice, esp. of birds*) gorjeo; (phonet) vibración || *tr* decir o cantar gorjeando; pronunciar con vibración || *intr* trinar; gorjear
**trillion** ['trɪljən] *s* (U.S.A.) billón *m;* (Brit) trillón *m*
**trilo•gy** ['trɪlədʒi] *s* (*pl* **-gies**) trilogía
**trim** [trɪm] *adj* (*comp* **trimmer;** *super* **trimmest**) acicalado, compuesto, elegante || *s* condición, estado; buena condición; adorno, atavío; traje *m*, vestido; (*of sails*) orientación || *v* (*pret & pp* **trimmed;** *ger* **trimming**) *tr* ajustar, adaptar; arreglar, componer; adornar, decorar; decorar, enguirnaldar (*el árbol de Navidad*); recortar; cortar ligeramente (*el pelo*); despabilar (*una lámpara o vela*); mondar, podar (*árboles, plantas*); acepillar, desbastar; (naut) orientar (*las velas*); (coll) derrotar, vencer; (coll) regañar
**trimming** ['trɪmɪŋ] *s* adorno, guarnición; franja, orla; (coll) paliza, zurra; (coll) derrota; **trimmings** accesorios, arrequives *mpl;* recortes *mpl*
**trini•ty** ['trɪnɪti] *s* (*pl* **-ties**) (*group of three*) trinca || **Trinity** *s* Trinidad
**trinket** ['trɪŋkɪt] *s* (*small ornament*) dije *m;* (*trivial object*) baratija, bujería, chuchería
**tri•o** ['tri•o] *s* (*pl* **-os**) (*group of three*) terna, trío; (mus) trío
**trip** [trɪp] *s* viaje *m;* jira, recorrido;

(*stumble*) tropiezo; (*act of causing a person to stumble*) traspié *m*, zancadilla; (*blunder*) desliz *m* || *v* (*pret & pp* **tripped;** *ger* **tripping**) *tr* trompicar, echar la zancadilla a; detener, estorbar; inclinar; coger en falta; coger en una mentira || *intr* ir con paso rápido y ligero; brincar, saltar, correr; tropezar; **to trip over** tropezar con, contra o en

**tripe** [traɪp] *s* callos, mondongo; (slang) disparate *m*, barbaridad

**trip'ham'mer** *s* martillo pilón

**triphthong** ['trɪfθɔŋ] o ['trɪfθɑŋ] *s* triptongo

**triple** ['trɪpəl] *adj & s* triple *m* || *tr* triplicar || *intr* triplicarse

**triplet** ['trɪplɪt] *s* (*offspring*) trillizo; (*stanza of three lines*) terceto; (mus) terceto, tresillo

**triplicate** ['trɪplɪkɪt] *adj & s* triplicado; **in triplicate** por triplicado || ['trɪplɪ,ket] *tr* triplicar

**tripod** ['traɪpɑd] *m* trípode *m*

**triptych** ['trɪptɪk] *s* tríptico

**trite** [traɪt] *adj* gastado, trillado, trivial

**triumph** ['traɪ·əmf] *s* triunfo || *intr* triunfar; **to triumph over** triunfar de

**triumphal arch** [traɪ'ʌmfəl] *s* arco triunfal

**triumphant** [traɪ'ʌmfənt] *adj* triunfante

**trivia** ['trɪvɪ·ə] *spl* bagatelas, trivialidades

**trivial** ['trɪvɪ·əl] *adj* trivial, insignificante

**triviali·ty** [,trɪvɪ'ælɪti] *s* (*pl* **-ties**) trivialidad

**Trojan** ['trodʒən] *adj & s* troyano

**Trojan horse** *s* caballo de Troya

**Trojan War** *s* guerra de Troya

**troll** [trol] *tr & intr* pescar a la cacea

**trolley** ['trɑli] *s* polea o arco de trole; tranvía *m*

**trolley bus** *s* trolebús *m*

**trolley car** *s* coche *m* de tranvía

**trolley pole** *s* trole *m*

**trolling** ['trolɪŋ] *s* cacea, pesca a la cacea

**trollop** ['trɑləp] *s* (*slovenly woman*) cochina; mujer *f* de mala vida

**trombone** ['trɑmbon] *s* trombón *m*

**troop** [trup] *s* tropa; (*of actors*) compañía; (*of cavalry*) escuadrón *m* || *intr* agruparse; marcharse en tropel

**trooper** ['trupər] *s* soldado de caballería; corcel *m* de guerra; policía *m* de a caballo; (*ship*) transporte *m;* **to swear like a trooper** jurar como un carretero

**tro·phy** ['trofi] *s* (*pl* **-phies**) trofeo; (*any memento*) recuerdo

**tropic** ['trɑpɪk] *adj* tropical || *s* trópico

**tropical** ['trɑpɪkəl] *adj* tropical

**tropics** o **Tropics** ['trɑpɪks] *spl* zona tropical

**troposphere** ['trɑpə,sfɪr] *s* troposfera

**trot** [trɑt] *s* trote *m* || *v* (*pret & pp* **trotted;** *ger* **trotting**) *tr* hacer trotar; **to trot out** (slang) sacar para mostrar || *intr* trotar

**troth** [trɔθ] o [troθ] *s* fe *f;* verdad; esponsales *mpl;* **in troth** en verdad; **to plight one's troth** prometer fidelidad; dar palabra de casamiento

**troubadour** ['trubə,dor] o ['trubə,dʊr] *adj* trovadoresco || *s* trovador *m*

**trouble** ['trʌbəl] *s* apuro, dificultad; confusión, estorbo; conflicto; inquietud, preocupación; pena, molestia; mal *m*, enfermedad; (*of a mechanical nature*) avería, falla, pana; **not to be worth the trouble** no valer la pena; **that's the trouble** ahí está el busilis; **the trouble is that . . .** lo malo es que . . .; **to be in trouble** estar en un aprieto; **to be looking for trouble** buscar tres pies al gato; **to get into trouble** enredarse, meterse en líos; **to take the trouble to** tomarse la molestia de || *tr* apurar; confundir, estorbar; inquietar, preocupar; apenar, afligir; incomodar, molestar; dar que hacer a; **to be troubled with** padecer de; **to trouble oneself** molestarse || *intr* apurarse; inquietarse, preocuparse; molestarse, darse molestia; **to trouble to** molestarse en

**trouble lamp** *s* lámpara de socorro

**trou'ble·mak'er** *s* perturbador *m*, alborotador *m*

**troubleshooter** ['trʌbəl,ʃutər] *s* localizador *m* de averías; (*in disputes*) componedor *m*

**troubleshooting** ['trʌbəl,ʃutɪŋ] *s* localización de averías; (*of disputes*) composición, arbitraje *m*

**troublesome** ['trʌbəlsəm] *adj* molesto, pesado, gravoso; impertinente; perturbador

**trouble spot** *s* lugar *m* de conflicto

**trough** [trɔf] o [trɑf] *s* (*e.g., to knead bread*) artesa; (*for water for animals*) abrevadero; (*for feeding animals*) comedero; (*under eaves*) canal *f;* (*between two waves*) seno

**troupe** [trup] *s* compañía de actores o de circo

**trousers** ['traʊzərz] *spl* pantalones *mpl*

**trous·seau** [tru'so] o ['truso] *s* (*pl* **-seaux** o **-seaus**) ajuar *m* de novia, equipo de novia

**trout** [traʊt] *s* trucha

**trouvère** [tru'vɛr] *s* trovero

**trowel** ['traʊ·əl] *s* paleta, llana

**Troy** [trɔɪ] *s* Troya

**truant** ['tru·ənt] *s* novillero; **to play truant** hacer novillos

**truce** [trus] *s* tregua

**truck** [trʌk] *s* carro; vagoneta; camión *m;* autocamión *m;* (*to be moved by hand*) carretilla; (*of locomotive or car*) carretón *m;* hortalizas para el mercado; (coll) desperdicios; (coll) negocio, relaciones || *tr* acarrear

**truck driver** *s* camionista *mf*

**truck garden** *s* huerto de hortalizas (*para el mercado*)

**truculent** ['trʌkjələnt] o ['trukjələnt] *adj* truculento

**trudge** [trʌdʒ] *intr* caminar, ir a pie; **to trudge along** marchar con pena y trabajo

**true** [tru] *adj* verdadero; exacto; constante, uniforme; fiel, leal; alineado; a plomo, a nivel; **to come true** hacerse realidad; **true to life** conforme a la realidad
**true copy** *s* copia fiel
**true-hearted** ['tru ,hɑrtɪd] *adj* fiel, leal, sincero
**true'love'** *s* fiel amante *mf;* (bot) hierba de París
**truelove knot** *s* lazo de amor
**truffle** ['trʌfəl] o ['trufəl] *s* trufa
**truism** ['tru·ɪzəm] *s* perogrullada, verdad trillada
**truly** ['truli] *adv* verdaderamente; efectivamente; fielmente; **truly yours** de Vd. atto. y S.S., su seguro servidor
**trump** [trʌmp] *s* triunfo; (coll) buen chico, buena chica; **no trump** sin triunfo || *tr* matar con un triunfo; aventajar, sobrepujar; **to trump up** forjar, inventar (*para engañar*) || *intr* triunfar
**trumpet** ['trʌmpɪt] *s* trompeta; trompeta acústica; **to blow one's own trumpet** cantar sus propias alabanzas || *tr* pregonar a son de trompeta || *intr* trompetear
**truncheon** ['trʌntʃən] *s* cachiporra; bastón *m* de mando
**trunk** [trʌŋk] *s* (*of living body, tree, family, railroad*) tronco; (*chest for clothes, etc.*) baúl *m;* (*of an automobile*) portaequipaje *m;* (*of elephant*) trompa; **trunks** taparrabo
**trunk hose** *spl* trusas
**truss** [trʌs] *s* (*framework*) armadura; haz *m,* paquete *m,* lío; (*for holding back a hernia*) braguero || *tr* armar; empaquetar; espetar; apretar (*barriles*)
**trust** [trʌst] *s* confianza; esperanza; cargo, custodia; depósito; crédito; obligación; (econ) trust *m,* cartel *m;* (law) fideicomiso; **in trust** en confianza; en depósito; **on trust** a crédito, al fiado || *tr* confiar; confiar en; vender a crédito a || *intr* confiar; fiar; **to trust in** fiarse a o de
**trust company** *s* banco fideicomisario, banco de depósitos
**trustee** [trʌs'ti] *s* administrador *m,* comisario; regente (universitario); (*of an estate*) fideicomisario
**trusteeship** [trʌs'tiʃɪp] *s* cargo de administrador, fideicomisario; (*of the UN*) fideicomiso
**trustful** ['trʌstfəl] *adj* confiado
**trust'wor'thy** *adj* confiable, fidedigno
**trust·y** ['trʌsti] *adj* (*comp* **-ier;** *super* **-iest**) honrado, fidedigno || *s* (*pl* **-ies**) presidiario fidedigno (*que se ha merecido ciertos privilegios*)
**truth** [truθ] *s* verdad; **in truth** a la verdad, en verdad
**truthful** ['truθfəl] *adj* verídico, veraz
**try** [traɪ] *s* (*pl* **tries**) ensayo, intento, prueba || *v* (*pret & pp* **tried**) *tr* ensayar, intentar, probar; comprobar, verificar; cansar; exasperar, irritar; (law) procesar (*a una persona*); (law) ver (*un pleito*); **to try on** probarse (*una prenda de vestir*) || *intr* ensayar, probar; esforzarse; **to try to** tratar de, intentar
**trying** ['traɪ·ɪŋ] *adj* cansado, molesto, irritante; penoso
**tryst** [trɪst] o [traɪst] *s* cita; lugar *m* de cita
**tub** [tʌb] *s* cuba, tina; (coll) baño; (*clumsy boat*) (coll) carcamán *m,* trompo; (*fat person*) (coll) cuba
**tube** [tjub] o [tub] *s* tubo; túnel *m;* (*of a tire*) cámara; (coll) ferrocarril subterráneo
**tuber** ['tjubər] o ['tubər] *s* tubérculo
**tubercle** ['tjubərkəl] o ['tubərkəl] *s* tubérculo
**tuberculosis** [tju,bʌrkjə'losɪs] o [tu,bʌrkjə'losɪs] *s* tuberculosis *f*
**tuck** [tʌk] *s* alforza || *tr* alforzar; **to tuck away** encubrir, ocultar; **to tuck in** arropar, enmantar; remeter (*p.ej., la ropa de cama*); **to tuck up** arremangar (*un vestido*); guarnecer (*la cama*)
**tucker** ['tʌkər] *s* escote *m* || *tr* — **to tucker out** (coll) agotar, cansar
**Tuesday** ['tjuzdi] o ['tuzdi] *s* martes *m*
**tuft** [tʌft] *s* (*of feathers, hair, etc.*) penacho, copete *m;* manojo, racimo, ramillete *m;* borla || *tr* empenachar || *intr* crecer formando mechones
**tug** [tʌg] *s* estirón *m,* tirón *m;* (*boat*) remolcador *m* || *v* (*pret & pp* **tugged;** *ger* **tugging**) *tr* arrastrar, tirar con fuerza de; remolcar (*un barco*) || *intr* tirar con fuerza; esforzarse, luchar
**tug'boat'** *s* remolcador *m*
**tug of war** *s* lucha de la cuerda
**tuition** [tju'ɪʃən] o [tu'ɪʃən] *s* enseñanza; precio de la enseñanza
**tulip** ['tjulɪp] o ['tulɪp] *s* tulipán *m*
**tumble** ['tʌmbəl] *s* caída, tumbo; (*somersault*) voltereta, tumba; confusión, desorden *m* || *intr* caerse, rodar; voltear; derribarse, volcarse; brincar, dar saltos; (*into bed*) echarse; (*to catch on*) (slang) caer, comprender; **to tumble down** desplomarse, hundirse, venirse abajo
**tum'ble-down'** *adj* destartalado, desvencijado
**tumbler** ['tʌmblər] *s* (*for drinking*) vaso; (*person who performs bodily feats*) volatinero; (*self-righting toy*) dominguillo, tentemozo
**tumor** ['tjumər] o ['tumər] *s* tumor *m*
**tumult** ['tjumʌlt] o ['tumʌlt] *s* tumulto
**tun** [tʌn] *s* barril *m,* tonel *m;* (*measure of capacity for wine*) tonelada
**tuna** ['tunə] *s* atún *m*
**tune** [tjun] o [tun] *s* tonada, aire *m;* (*manner of acting or speaking*) tono; **in tune** afinado; afinadamente; **out of tune** desafinado; desafinadamente; **to change one's tune** mudar de tono || *tr* acordar, afinar; (rad) sintonizar; **to tune in** (rad) sintonizar; **to tune out** (rad) desintonizar; **to tune up** poner a punto; poner a tono (*un motor de automóvil*)
**tungsten** ['tʌŋstən] *s* tungsteno
**tunic** ['tjunɪk] o ['tunɪk] *s* túnica
**tuning coil** *s* (rad) bobina de sintonía

**tuning fork** *s* diapasón *m*
**Tunis** ['tjunɪs] o ['tunɪs] *s* Túnez (*ciudad*)
**Tunisia** [tju'niʒə] o [tu'niʒə] *s* Túnez (*país*)
**Tunisian** [tju'niʒən] o [tu'niʒən] *adj & s* tunecino
**tun•nel** ['tʌnəl] *s* túnel *m;* (min) galería ‖ *v* (*pret & pp* **-neled** o **-nelled;** *ger* **-neling** o **-nelling**) *tr* construir un túnel a través de o debajo de
**turban** ['tʌrbən] *s* turbante *m*
**turbid** ['tʌrbɪd] *adj* turbio
**turbine** ['tʌrbɪn] o ['tʌrbaɪn] *s* turbina
**turbojet** ['tʌrbo,dʒɛt] *s* turborreactor *m;* avión *m* de turborreacción
**turboprop** ['tʌrbo,prɑp] *s* turbopropulsor *m;* avión *m* de turbopropulsión
**turbulent** ['tʌrbjələnt] *adj* turbulento
**tureen** [tʊ'rin] o [tjʊ'rin] *s* sopera
**turf** [tʌrf] *s* (*surface layer of grassland*) césped *m;* terrón *m* de césped; (*peat*) turba; **the turf** el hipódromo; las carreras de caballos
**turf•man** ['tʌrfmən] *s* (*pl* **-men** [mən]) turfista *m*
**Turk** [tʌrk] *s* turco
**turkey** ['tʌrki] *s* pavo ‖ **Turkey** *s* Turquía
**turkey vulture** *s* aura
**Turkish** ['tʌrkɪʃ] *adj & s* turco
**Turkish towel** *s* toalla rusa
**turmoil** ['tʌrmɔɪl] *s* alboroto, disturbio, tumulto
**turn** [tʌrn] *s* vuelta; (*time of action*) turno; (*change of direction*) virada; (*bend*) recodo; (*walk*) paseo corto; (*of a spiral, roll of wire, etc.*) espira; aspecto; inclinación; vahido, vértigo; giro, expresión; servicio; (coll) sacudida, susto; **at every turn** a cada paso; **in turn** por turno; **to be one's turn** tocarle a uno, p.ej., **it's your turn** le toca a Vd.; **to take turns** alternar, turnar; **to wait one's turn** aguardar turno, esperar vez ‖ *tr* volver; dar vuelta a (*p.ej., una llave*); torcer (*p.ej., el tobillo*); doblar (*la esquina*); dirigir (*p.ej., los ojos*); (*to make sour*) agriar; (*on a lathe*) tornear; tener (*p.ej., veinte años cumplidos*); **to turn against** predisponer en contra de; **to turn around** volver; voltear; torcer (*las palabras de una persona*); **to turn aside** desviar; **to turn away** desviar; despedir; **to turn back** devolver; hacer retroceder; retrasar (*el reloj*); **to turn down** doblar hacia abajo; invertir; rechazar, rehusar; bajar (*p.ej., el gas*); **to turn in** doblar hacia adentro; entregar; **to turn off** apagar (*la luz, la radio*); cortar (*el agua, gas, etc.*); cerrar (*la llave del agua, gas, etc.; la radio, la televisión*); interrumpir (*la corriente eléctrica*); **to turn on** encender (*la luz*); poner (*la luz, la radio, etc.*); abrir (*la llave del agua, gas, etc.*); establecer (*la corriente eléctrica*); **to turn out** despedir; echar al campo (*a los animales*); volver al revés; apagar (*la luz*); hacer, fabricar; **to turn up** doblar hacia arriba; levantar; arremangar (*p.ej., las mangas*); volver (*un naipe*); poner más alto o más fuerte (*la radio*); abrir la llave de (*p.ej., el gas*) ‖ *intr* volver, p.ej., **the road turns to the right** el camino vuelve a la derecha; virar (*un automóvil, un avión, etc.*); (*to revolve*) girar; volverse (*p.ej., la conversación; la opinión; ciertos licores*); **to turn against** cobrar aversión a; rebelarse contra; **to turn around** dar vuelta; **to turn aside** o **away** desviarse; alejarse; **to turn back** volver, regresar; retroceder; **to turn down** doblarse hacia abajo; invertirse; **to turn in** doblarse hacia adentro; replegarse; recogerse, volver a casa; (coll) recogerse, acostarse; **to turn into** entrar en; convertirse en; **to turn on** volverse contra; depender de; versar sobre; ocuparse de; **to turn out badly** salir mal; **to turn out right** acabar bien; **to turn out to be** venir a ser; resultar, salir; **to turn over** volcar, derribarse (*un vehículo*); **to turn up** doblarse hacia arriba; levantarse; acontecer; aparecer
**turn'coat'** *s* tránsfuga *mf*, apóstata *mf*, renegado; **to become a turncoat** volver la casaca, cambiarse la camisa
**turn'down'** *adj* (*collar*) caído ‖ *s* rechazamiento
**turning point** *s* punto de transición, punto decisivo
**turnip** ['tʌrnɪp] *s* nabo; (*cheap watch*) (slang) calentador *m;* (slang) tipo
**turn'key'** *s* carcelero, llavero de cárcel
**turn of life** *s* menopausia
**turn of mind** *s* natural *m*, inclinación
**turn'out'** *s* (*gathering of people*) concurrencia; (*number attending a show, etc.*) entrada; (*side track or passage*) apartadero; (*amount produced*) producción; (*array, outfit*) equipaje *m;* carruaje *m* de lujo
**turn'o'ver** *s* (*spill, upset*) vuelco; cambio de personal; movimiento de mercancías; ciclo de compra y venta
**turn'pike'** *s* carretera de peaje
**turnstile** ['tʌrn,staɪl] *s* torniquete *m*
**turn'ta'ble** *s* (*of phonograph*) placa giratoria, plato giratorio; (rr) placa giratoria, plataforma giratoria
**turpentine** ['tʌrpən,taɪn] *s* trementina
**turpitude** ['tʌrpɪ,tjud] o ['tʌrpɪ,tud] *s* torpeza, infamia, vileza
**turquoise** ['tʌrkɔɪz] o ['tʌrkwɔɪz] *s* turquesa
**turret** ['tʌrɪt] *s* torrecilla; (archit) torreón *m;* (nav) torreta
**turtle** ['tʌrtəl] *s* tortuga; **to turn turtle** derribarse patas arriba
**tur'tle•dove'** *s* tórtola
**Tuscan** ['tʌskən] *adj & s* toscano
**Tuscany** ['tʌskəni] *s* la Toscana
**tusk** [tʌsk] *s* colmillo
**tussle** ['tʌsəl] *s* agarrada ‖ *intr* agarrarse, asirse, reñir
**tutor** ['tjutər] o ['tutər] *s* maestro particular; (*guardian*) tutor *m* ‖ *tr* dar enseñanza particular a ‖ *intr*

dar enseñanza particular; (coll) tomar lecciones particulares
**tuxe·do** [tʌk'sido] *s* (*pl* **-dos**) esmoquin *m*, smoking *m*
**TV** *abbr* **television**
**twaddle** ['twɑdəl] *s* charla, tonterías, música celestial ‖ *intr* charlar, decir tonterías
**twang** [twæŋ] *s* (*of musical instrument*) tañido; (*of voice*) timbre *m* nasal ‖ *tr* tocar con un tañido; decir con timbre nasal ‖ *intr* hablar por la nariz
**twang·y** [twæŋi] *adj* (*comp* **-ier**; *super* **-iest**) (*device*) tañente; (*person, voice*) gangoso
**tweed** [twid] *s* mezcla de lana; traje *m* de mezcla de lana; **tweeds** ropa de mezcla de lana
**tweet** [twit] *s* pío ‖ *intr* piar
**tweeter** ['twitər] *s* altavoz *m* para audiofrecuencias elevadas
**tweezers** ['twizərz] *spl* bruselas, pinzas, tenacillas
**twelfth** [twɛlfθ] *adj* & *s* (*in a series*) duodécimo; (*part*) dozavo ‖ *s* (*in dates*) doce *m*
**Twelfth'-night'** *s* la víspera del día de Reyes; la noche del día de Reyes
**twelve** [twɛlv] *adj* & *pron* doce ‖ *s* doce *m*; **twelve o'clock** las doce
**twentieth** ['twɛntɪ·ɪθ] *adj* & *s* (*in a series*) vigésimo; (*part*) veintavo ‖ *s* (*in dates*) veinte *m*
**twen·ty** ['twɛnti] *adj* & *pron* veinte ‖ *s* (*pl* **-ties**) veinte *m*
**twice** [twaɪs] *adv* dos veces
**twice'-told'** *adj* dicho dos veces; trillado, sabido
**twiddle** ['twɪdəl] *tr* menear o revolver ociosamente
**twig** [twɪg] *s* ramito; **twigs** leña menuda
**twilight** ['twaɪ,laɪt] *adj* crepuscular ‖ *s* crepúsculo
**twill** [twɪl] *s* tela cruzada; (*pattern of weave*) cruzado ‖ *tr* cruzar
**twin** [twɪn] *adj* & *s* gemelo
**twine** [twaɪn] *s* guita, cuerda, bramante *m* ‖ *tr* enroscar, retorcer ‖ *intr* enroscarse, retorcerse
**twinge** [twɪndʒ] *s* punzada, dolor agudo
**twin'jet' plane** *s* avión *m* birreactor
**twinkle** ['twɪŋkəl] *s* centelleo; (*of eye*) pestañeo; instante *m* ‖ *intr* centellear; pestañear; moverse rápidamente
**twin'-screw'** *adj* (naut) de doble hélice
**twirl** [twʌrl] *s* vuelta, giro ‖ *tr* hacer girar; (baseball) lanzar (*la pelota*) ‖ *intr* dar vueltas, girar; piruetear
**twist** [twɪst] *s* torcedura; enroscadura; curva, recodo; giro, vuelta; propensión, prejuicio; (*of mind or disposition*) sesgo ‖ *tr* torcer; retorcer; enroscar; hacer girar; entrelazar; desviar; (*to give a different meaning to*) torcer ‖ *intr* torcerse; retorcerse; enroscarse; dar vueltas; entrelazarse; desviarse; serpentear; **to twist and turn** (*in bed*) dar vueltas
**twit** [twɪt] *v* (*pret* & *pp* **twitted**; *ger* **twitting**) *tr* reprender (*a uno*) recordando algo desagradable o poniéndole en ridículo
**twitch** [twɪtʃ] *s* crispatura; ligero temblor ‖ *intr* crisparse; temblar (*p.ej., los párpados*)
**twitter** ['twɪtər] *s* gorjeo; risita sofocada; inquietud ‖ *intr* gorjear; reír sofocadamente; temblar de inquietud
**two** [tu] *adj* & *pron* dos ‖ *s* dos *m*; **to put two and two together** atar cabos, sacar la conclusión evidente; **two o'clock** las dos
**two'-cy'cle** *adj* (mach) de dos tiempos
**two'-cyl'inder** *adj* (mach) de dos cilindros
**two-edged** ['tu,ɛdʒd] *adj* de dos filos
**two hundred** *adj* & *pron* doscientos ‖ *s* doscientos *m*
**twosome** ['tusəm] *s* pareja; pareja de jugadores; juego de dos
**two'-time'** *tr* (slang) engañar en amor, ser infiel a (*una persona del otro sexo*)
**tycoon** [taɪ'kun] *s* (coll) magnate *m*
**type** [taɪp] *s* tipo; (*piece*) (typ) tipo, letra; (*pieces collectively*) (typ) letra; letras impresas, letras escritas a máquina ‖ *tr* escribir a máquina, tipiar; representar, simbolizar ‖ *intr* escribir a máquina
**type'face'** *s* tipo de letra
**type'script'** *s* material escrito a máquina
**typesetter** ['taɪp,sɛtər] *s* (typ) cajista *mf*; (typ) máquina de componer
**type'write'** *v* (*pret* **-wrote** [,rot]; *pp* **-written** [,rɪtən]) *tr* & *intr* escribir a máquina, tipiar
**type'writ'er** *s* máquina de escribir; tipista *mf*
**typewriter ribbon** *s* cinta para máquinas de escribir
**type'writ'ing** *s* mecanografía; trabajo hecho con máquina de escribir
**typhoid fever** ['taɪfɔɪd] *s* fiebre tifoidea
**typhoon** [taɪ'fun] *s* tifón *m*
**typical** ['tɪpɪkəl] *adj* típico
**typi·fy** ['tɪpɪ,faɪ] *v* (*pret* & *pp* **-fied**) *tr* simbolizar; ser ejemplo o modelo de
**typist** ['taɪpɪst] *s* mecanógrafo, tipista *mf*
**typographic(al)** [,taɪpə'græfɪk(əl)] *adj* tipográfico
**typographical error** *s* error *m* de imprenta
**typography** [taɪ'pɑgrəfi] *s* tipografía
**tyrannic(al)** [tɪ'rænɪk(əl)] o [taɪ'rænɪk(əl)] *adj* tiránico
**tyrannous** ['tɪrənəs] *adj* tirano
**tyran·ny** ['tɪrəni] *s* (*pl* **-nies**) tiranía
**tyrant** ['taɪrənt] *s* tirano
**ty·ro** ['taɪro] *s* (*pl* **-ros**) tirón *m*, novicio

# U

**U, u** [ju] vigésima primera letra del alfabeto inglés
**U.** *abbr* **University**
**ubiquitous** [ju'bɪkwɪtəs] *adj* ubicuo
**udder** ['ʌdər] *s* ubre *f*
**ugliness** ['ʌglɪnɪs] *s* fealdad; (coll) malhumor *m*
**ug•ly** ['ʌgli] *adj* (*comp* **-lier;** *super* **-liest**) feo; (coll) malhumorado
**ugly mug** *s* (slang) carantamaula
**Ukraine** ['jukren] o [ju'kren] *s* Ucrania
**Ukrainian** [ju'krenɪ·ən] *adj & s* ucraniano, ucranio
**ulcer** ['ʌlsər] *s* llaga, úlcera; (*corrupting influence*) (fig) llaga
**ulcerate** ['ʌlsə,ret] *tr* ulcerar ‖ *intr* ulcerarse
**ulterior** [ʌl'tɪrɪ·ər] *adj* ulterior; (*concealed*) escondido, oculto
**ultimate** ['ʌltɪmɪt] *adj* último
**ultima•tum** [,ʌltɪ'metəm] *s* (*pl* **-tums** o **-ta** [tə]) ultimátum *m*
**ultimo** ['ʌltɪ,mo] *adv* de o en el mes próximo pasado
**ultrahigh** [,ʌltrə'haɪ] *adj* (electron) ultraelevado
**ultraviolet** [,ʌltrə'vaɪ·əlɪt] *adj & s* ultravioleta, ultraviolado
**umbilical cord** [ʌm'bɪlɪkəl] *s* cordón *m* umbilical
**umbrage** ['ʌmbrɪdʒ] *s* — **to take umbrage at** resentirse de o por
**umbrella** [ʌm'brɛlə] *s* paraguas *m;* (mil) sombrilla protectora
**umbrella man** *s* paragüero
**umbrella stand** *s* paragüero
**umlaut** ['ʊmlaʊt] *s* inflexión vocálica, metafonía; (*mark*) diéresis *f* ‖ *tr* inflexionar; escribir con diéresis
**umpire** ['ʌmpaɪr] *s* árbitro ‖ *tr & intr* arbitrar
**UN** ['ju'ɛn] *s* (letterword) ONU *f*
**unable** [ʌn'ebəl] *adj* incapaz, imposibilitado; **to be unable to** no poder
**unabridged** [,ʌnə'brɪdʒd] *adj* sin abreviar, íntegro
**unaccented** [ʌn'æksɛntɪd] o [,ʌnæk'sɛntɪd] *adj* inacentuado
**unaccountable** [,ʌnə'kaʊntəbəl] *adj* inexplicable; irresponsable
**unaccounted-for** [,ʌnə'kaʊntɪd,fɔr] *adj* inexplicado; no hallado
**unaccustomed** [,ʌnə'kʌstəmd] *adj* (*unusual*) desacostumbrado; inhabituado
**unafraid** [,ʌnə'fred] *adj* sin miedo
**unaligned** [,ʌnə'laɪnd] *adj* no empeñado
**unanimity** [,junə'nɪmɪti] *s* unanimidad
**unanimous** [jʊ'nænɪməs] *adj* unánime
**unanswerable** [ʌn'ænsərəbəl] *adj* incontestable; (*argument*) incontrastable
**unappreciative** [,ʌnə'priʃɪ,etɪv] *adj* ingrato, desagradecido
**unapproachable** [,ʌnə'protʃəbəl] *adj* inabordable; incomparable, único
**unarmed** [ʌn'ɑrmd] *adj* desarmado, inerme
**unascertainable** [ʌn,æsər'tenəbəl] *adj* inaveriguable
**unasked** [ʌn'æskt] o [ʌn'ɑskt] *adj* no solicitado; no convidado
**unassembled** [,ʌnə'sɛmbəld] *adj* desmontado, desarmado
**unassuming** [,ʌnə'sumɪŋ] o [,ʌnə'sjumɪŋ] *adj* modesto, sencillo
**unattached** [,ʌnə'tætʃt] *adj* independiente; (*loose*) suelto; (*not engaged to be married*) no prometido; (law) no embargado; (mil & nav) de reemplazo
**unattainable** [,ʌnə'tenəbəl] *adj* inasequible, inalcanzable
**unattractive** [,ʌnə'træktɪv] *adj* poco atrayente, desairado
**unavailable** [,ʌnə'veləbəl] *adj* indisponible
**unavailing** [,ʌnə'velɪŋ] *adj* ineficaz, inútil, vano
**unavoidable** [,ʌnə'vɔɪdəbəl] *adj* inevitable, ineluctable
**unaware** [,ʌnə'wɛr] *adj* — **to be unaware of** no estar al corriente de ‖ *adv* de improviso; sin saberlo
**unawares** [,ʌnə'wɛrz] *adv* (*unexpectedly*) de improviso; (*unknowingly*) sin saberlo
**unbalanced** [ʌn'bælənst] *adj* desequilibrado
**unbandage** [ʌn'bændɪdʒ] *tr* desvendar
**un•bar** [ʌn'bɑr] *v* (*pret & pp* **-barred;** *ger* **-barring**) *tr* desatrancar
**unbearable** [ʌn'bɛrəbəl] *adj* inaguantable
**unbeatable** [ʌn'bitəbəl] *adj* imbatible
**unbecoming** [,ʌnbɪ'kʌmɪŋ] *adj* inconveniente, indecente; que sienta mal
**unbelievable** [,ʌnbɪ'livəbəl] *adj* increíble
**unbending** [ʌn'bɛndɪŋ] *adj* inflexible
**unbiased** o **unbiassed** [ʌn'baɪ·əst] *adj* imparcial
**un•bind** [ʌn'baɪnd] *v* (*pret & pp* **-bound** ['baʊnd]) *tr* desatar
**unbleached** [ʌn'blitʃt] *adj* sin blanquear
**unbolt** [ʌn'bolt] *tr* desatrancar (*p.ej., una puerta*); (*to remove the bolts from*) desempernar
**unborn** [ʌn'bɔrn] *adj* no nacido, por nacer, futuro
**unbosom** [ʌn'bʊzəm] *tr* confesar, descubrir (*sus pensamientos, sus secretos*); **to unbosom oneself** abrir su pecho, desahogarse
**unbound** [ʌn'baʊnd] *adj* (*book*) sin encuadernar
**unbreakable** [ʌn'brekəbəl] *adj* irrompible
**unbuckle** [ʌn'bʌkəl] *tr* deshebillar
**unburden** [ʌn'bʌrdən] *tr* descargar; **to unburden oneself of** desahogarse de
**unburied** [ʌn'bɛrid] *adj* insepulto
**unbutton** [ʌn'bʌtən] *tr* desabotonar
**uncalled-for** [ʌn'kɔld,fɔr] *adj* inne-

cesario, no justificado; insolente
**uncanny** [ʌn'kæni] *adj* espectral, misterioso; extraordinario, maravilloso
**uncared-for** [ʌn'kerd,fɔr] *adj* desamparado, descuidado, abandonado
**unceasing** [ʌn'sisɪŋ] *adj* incesante
**unceremonious** [,ʌnserɪ'monɪ·əs] *adj* inceremonioso
**uncertain** [ʌn'sʌrtən] *adj* incierto
**uncertain•ty** [ʌn'sʌrtənti] *s* (*pl* **-ties**) incertidumbre
**unchain** [ʌn'tʃen] *tr* desencadenar
**unchangeable** [ʌn'tʃendʒəbəl] *adj* incambiable, inmutable
**uncharted** [ʌn'tʃartɪd] *adj* inexplorado
**unchecked** [ʌn'tʃɛkt] *adj* no verificado; no refrenado; desenfrenado
**uncivilized** [ʌn'sɪvɪ,laɪzd] *adj* incivilizado
**unclad** [ʌn'klæd] *adj* desvestido
**unclaimed** [ʌn'klemd] *adj* sin reclamar; (*mail*) rechazado, sobrante
**unclasp** [ʌn'klæsp] o [ʌn'klɑsp] *tr* desabrochar
**unclassified** [ʌn'klæsɪ,faɪd] *adj* no clasificado; no clasificado como secreto
**uncle** ['ʌŋkəl] *s* tío
**unclean** [ʌn'klin] *adj* desaseado, sucio
**un•clog** [ʌn'klɑg] *v* (*pret & pp* **-clogged;** *ger* **-clogging**) *tr* desatrancar
**unclouded** [ʌn'klaʊdɪd] *adj* despejado
**uncollectible** [,ʌnkə'lɛktɪbəl] *adj* incobrable
**uncomfortable** [ʌn'kʌmfərtəbəl] *adj* incómodo
**uncommitted** [,ʌnkə'mɪtɪd] *adj* no empeñado, no comprometido
**uncommon** [ʌn'kɑmən] *adj* raro, poco común
**uncompromising** [ʌn'kɑmprə,maɪzɪŋ] *adj* intransigente
**unconcerned** [,ʌnkən'sʌrnd] *adj* despreocupado, indiferente
**unconditional** [,ʌnkən'dɪʃənəl] *adj* incondicional
**uncongenial** [,ʌnkən'dʒinɪ·əl] *adj* antipático; incompatible; desagradable
**unconquerable** [ʌn'kɑŋkərəbəl] *adj* inconquistable
**unconquered** [ʌn'kɑŋkərd] *adj* invicto
**unconscionable** [ʌn'kɑnʃənəbəl] *adj* inescrupuloso; desrazonable, excesivo
**unconscious** [ʌn'kɑnʃəs] *adj* inconsciente; (*temporarily deprived of consciousness*) desmayado; (*unintentional*) involuntario
**unconsciousness** [ʌn'kɑnʃəsnɪs] *s* inconsciencia; desmayo
**unconstitutional** [,ʌnkɑnstɪ'tjuʃənəl] o [,ʌnkɑnstɪ'tuʃənəl] *adj* inconstitucional
**uncontrollable** [,ʌnkən'troləbəl] *adj* ingobernable; (*laughter*) inextinguible
**unconventional** [,ʌnkən'venʃənəl] *adj* no convencional
**uncork** [ʌn'kɔrk] *tr* destapar, descorchar
**uncouth** [ʌn'kuθ] *adj* desgarbado, torpe, rústico
**uncover** [ʌn'kʌvər] *tr* descubrir
**unction** ['ʌŋkʃən] *s* (*anointing*) unción; suavidad hipócrita
**unctuous** ['ʌŋktʃʊ·əs] *adj* untuoso; zalamero
**uncultivated** [ʌn'kʌltɪ,vetɪd] *adj* inculto (*que no está cultivado; rústico, grosero*)
**uncultured** [ʌn'kʌltʃərd] *adj* inculto, rústico, grosero
**uncut** [ʌn'kʌt] *adj* sin cortar; (*book or magazine*) intonso
**undamaged** [ʌn'dæmɪdʒd] *adj* indemne, ileso
**undaunted** [ʌn'dɔntɪd] *adj* impávido, denodado
**undecided** [,ʌndɪ'saɪdɪd] *adj* indeciso
**undefeated** [,ʌndɪ'fitɪd] *adj* invicto
**undefended** [,ʌndɪ'fɛndɪd] *adj* indefenso
**undefiled** [,ʌndɪ'faɪld] *adj* inmaculado, impoluto
**undeniable** [,ʌndɪ'naɪ·əbəl] *adj* innegable
**under** ['ʌndər] *adj* inferior; (*clothing*) interior ‖ *adv* debajo; más abajo; **to go under** hundirse; (*to fail*) fracasar ‖ *prep* bajo, debajo de; inferior a; **under full sail** a vela llena; **under lock and key** bajo llave; **under oath** bajo juramento; **under penalty of death** so pena de muerte; **under sail** a vela; **under separate cover** por separado, bajo cubierta separada; **under steam** bajo presión; **under the hand and seal of** firmado y sellado por; **under the nose of** (coll) en las barbas de; **under the weather** (coll) algo indispuesto; **under way** en camino
**un'der•age'** *adj* menor de edad
**un'der•bid'** *v* (*pret & pp* **-bid;** *ger* **-bidding**) *tr* ofrecer menos que
**un'der•brush'** *s* maleza
**un'der•car'riage** *s* carro inferior; (aer) tren *m* de aterrizaje
**un'der•clothes'** *s* ropa interior
**un'der•con•sump'tion** *s* infraconsumo
**un'der•cov'er** *adj* secreto
**underdeveloped** [,ʌndərdɪ'vɛləpt] *adj* subdesarrollado
**un'der•dog'** *s* víctima, perdidoso; **the underdogs** los de abajo
**underdone** ['ʌndər,dʌn] *adj* a medio asar, soasado
**un'der•es'ti•mate'** *tr* subestimar
**un'der•gar'ment** *s* prenda de vestir interior
**un'der•go'** *v* (*pret* **-went;** *pp* **-gone**) *tr* experimentar; sufrir, padecer
**un'der•grad'uate** *adj* no graduado; (*course*) para el bachillerato ‖ *s* alumno no graduado de universidad
**un'der•ground'** *adj* subterráneo; clandestino ‖ *adv* bajo tierra; ocultamente ‖ *s* ferrocarril subterráneo; movimiento de resistencia
**un'der•growth'** *s* maleza
**underhanded** ['ʌndər'hændɪd] *adj* clandestino, taimado, disimulado
**un'der•line'** o **un'der•line'** *tr* subrayar
**underling** ['ʌndərlɪŋ] *s* subordinado, secuaz *m* servil
**un'der•mine'** *tr* socavar, minar

**underneath** [ˌʌndərˈniθ] *adj* inferior, más bajo ‖ *adv* debajo ‖ *prep* debajo de ‖ *s* parte baja, superficie *f* inferior
**undernourished** [ˌʌndərˈnʌrɪʃt] *adj* desnutrido
**un'der•nour'ish•ment** *s* desnutrición
**un'der•pass'** *s* paso inferior
**un'der•pay'** *s* pago insuficiente ‖ *v* (*pret & pp* **-paid**) *tr & intr* pagar insuficientemente
**un'der•pin'** *v* (*pret & pp* **-pinned;** *ger* **-pinning**) *tr* apuntalar, socalzar
**underprivileged** [ˌʌndərˈprɪvɪlɪdʒd] *adj* desheredado, desamparado
**un'der•rate'** *tr* menospreciar
**un'der•score'** *tr* subrayar
**un'der•sea'** *adj* submarino ‖ **un'der•sea'** *adv* debajo de la superficie del mar
**un'der•sec're•tar'y** *s* (*pl* **-ies**) subsecretario
**un'der•sell'** *v* (*pret & pp* **-sold**) *tr* vender a menor precio que; (*for less than the actual value*) malbaratar
**un'der•shirt'** *s* camiseta
**undersigned** [ˈʌndərˌsaɪnd] *adj* infrascrito, subscrito
**un'der•skirt'** *s* enaguas, refajo
**un'der•stand'** *v* (*pret & pp* **-stood**) *tr* entender, comprender; sobrentender, subentender (*una cosa que no está expresa*) ‖ *intr* entender, comprender
**understandable** [ˌʌndərˈstændəbəl] *adj* comprensible
**understanding** [ˌʌndərˈstændɪŋ] *adj* entendedor; (*tolerant, sympathetic*) comprensivo ‖ *s* comprensión; (*intellectual faculty, mind*) entendimiento; (*agreement*) acuerdo; **to come to an understanding** llegar a un acuerdo
**un'der•stud'y** *s* (*pl* **-ies**) sobresaliente *mf*
**un'der•take'** *v* (*pret* **-took;** *pp* **-taken**) *tr* emprender; (*to agree to perform*) comprometerse a
**undertaker** [ˌʌndərˈtekər] o [ˈʌndərˌtekər] *s* empresario ‖ [ˈʌndərˌtekər] *s* empresario de pompas fúnebres, director *m* de funeraria
**undertaking** [ˌʌndərˈtekɪŋ] *s* (*task*) empresa; (*pledge*) empeño ‖ [ˈʌndərˌtekɪŋ] *s* (*business of funeral director*) funeraria
**un'der•tak'ing establishment** *s* funeraria, empresa de pompas fúnebres
**un'der•tone'** *s* voz baja; (*background sound*) fondo; color apagado
**un'der•tow'** *s* (*countercurrent below surface*) contracorriente *f;* (*on the beach*) resaca
**un'der•wear'** *s* ropa interior
**un'der•world'** *s* (*criminal world*) inframundo, bajos fondos sociales; (*the earth*) mundo terrenal; (*pagan world of the dead*) averno, infierno; (*world under the water*) mundo submarino; (*opposite side of earth*) antípodas
**un'der•write'** o **un'der•write'** *v* (*pret* **-wrote;** *pp* **-written**) *tr* subscribir; (*to insure*) asegurar
**un'der•writ'er** *s* subscritor *m;* asegurador *m;* compañía aseguradora
**undeserved** [ˌʌndɪˈzʌrvd] *adj* inmerecido
**undesirable** [ˌʌndɪˈzaɪrəbəl] *adj & s* indeseable *mf*
**undetachable** [ˌʌndɪˈtætʃəbəl] *adj* inamovible
**undignified** [ʌnˈdɪgnɪˌfaɪd] *adj* poco digno, poco grave, indecoroso
**undiscernible** [ˌʌndɪˈzʌrnɪbəl] o [ˌʌndɪˈsʌrnəbəl] *adj* imperceptible, invisible
**un•do'** *v* (*pret* **-did;** *pp* **-done**) *tr* deshacer; anular, borrar; arruinar
**undoing** [ʌnˈdu·ɪŋ] *s* destrucción, pérdida, ruina
**undone** [ʌnˈdʌn] *adj* sin hacer, por hacer; **to come undone** deshacerse, desatarse; **to leave nothing undone** no dejar nada por hacer
**undoubtedly** [ʌnˈdaʊtɪdli] *adv* indudablemente, sin duda
**undramatic** [ˌʌndrəˈmætɪk] *adj* poco dramático
**undress** [ˈʌnˌdres] o [ʌnˈdres] *s* traje *m* de casa; vestido de calle; (*mil*) traje de cuartel ‖ [ʌnˈdrɛs] *tr* desnudar; desvendar (*una herida*) ‖ desnudarse
**undrinkable** [ʌnˈdrɪŋkəbəl] *adj* impotable
**undue** [ʌnˈdju] o [ʌnˈdu] *adj* indebido
**undulate** [ˈʌndjəˌlet] *intr* ondular
**unduly** [ʌnˈdjuli] o [ʌnˈduli] *adv* indebidamente
**undying** [ʌnˈdaɪ·ɪŋ] *adj* imperecedero
**unearned increment** [ʌnˈʌrnd] *s* plusvalía
**unearth** [ʌnˈʌrθ] *tr* desenterrar
**unearthly** [ʌnˈʌrθli] *adj* sobrenatural; fantástico, espectral; extraordinario
**uneasy** [ʌnˈizi] *adj* (*worried*) inquieto; (*constrained*) encogido, embarazado
**uneatable** [ʌnˈitəbəl] *adj* incomible
**uneconomic(al)** [ˌʌnikəˈnɑmɪk(əl)] o [ˌʌnɛkəˈnɑmɪk(əl)] *adj* antieconómico
**uneducated** [ʌnˈɛdjəˌketɪd] *adj* ineducado, sin instrucción
**unemployed** [ˌʌnɛmˈplɔɪd] *adj* desocupado, desempleado; improductivo
**unemployment** [ˌʌnemˈplɔɪmənt] *s* desocupación, desempleo
**unemployment insurance** *s* seguro de desempleo o desocupación, seguro contra el paro obrero
**unending** [ʌnˈɛndɪŋ] *adj* interminable
**unequal** [ʌnˈikwəl] *adj* desigual; **to be unequal to** (*a task*) no estar a la altura de
**unequaled** o **unequalled** [ʌnˈikwəld] *adj* inigualado
**unerring** [ʌnˈʌrɪŋ] o [ʌnˈɛrɪŋ] *adj* infalible, seguro
**unessential** [ˌʌnɛˈsenʃəl] *adj* no esencial
**uneven** [ʌnˈivən] *adj* desigual; (*number*) impar
**unexceptionable** [ˌʌnɛkˈsɛpʃənəbəl] *adj* intachable, irreprensible
**unexpected** [ˌʌnɛkˈspɛktɪd] *adj* inesperado
**unexplained** [ˌʌnɛkˈsplend] *adj* inexplicado

**unexplored** [ˌʌnɛkˈsplord] *adj* inexplorado
**unexposed** [ˌʌnɛkˈspozd] *adj* (phot) inexpuesto
**unfading** [ʌnˈfedɪŋ] *adj* inmarcesible
**unfailing** [ʌnˈfelɪŋ] *adj* indefectible; (*inexhaustible*) inagotable
**unfair** [ʌnˈfɛr] *adj* injusto; desleal, doble, falso; (sport) sucio
**unfaithful** [ʌnˈfeθfəl] *adj* infiel
**unfamiliar** [ˌʌnfəˈmɪljər] *adj* poco familiar; poco familiarizado
**unfasten** [ʌnˈfæsən] o [ʌnˈfɑsən] *tr* desatacar, desatar, soltar
**unfathomable** [ʌnˈfæðəməbəl] *adj* insondable
**unfavorable** [ʌnˈfevərəbəl] *adj* desfavorable
**unfeathered** [ʌnˈfɛðərd] *adj* implume
**unfeeling** [ʌnˈfilɪŋ] *adj* insensible
**unfetter** [ʌnˈfɛtər] *tr* desencadenar
**unfilled** [ʌnˈfɪld] *adj* no lleno; por cumplir, pendiente
**unfinished** [ʌnˈfɪnɪʃt] *adj* sin acabar; imperfecto, mal acabado; (*business*) pendiente
**unfit** [ʌnˈfɪt] *adj* impropio, incapaz, inhábil; inservible, inútil
**unfold** [ʌnˈfold] *tr* desplegar || *intr* desplegarse
**unforeseeable** [ˌʌnforˈsi·əbəl] *adj* imprevisible
**unforeseen** [ˌʌnforˈsin] *adj* imprevisto
**unforgettable** [ˌʌnfərˈgɛtəbəl] *adj* inolvidable
**unforgivable** [ˌʌnfərˈgɪvəbəl] *adj* imperdonable
**unfortunate** [ʌnˈfɔrtjənɪt] *adj & s* desgraciado
**unfounded** [ʌnˈfaʊndɪd] *adj* infundado
**unfreeze** [ʌnˈfriz] *tr* deshelar; desbloquear (*el crédito*)
**unfriendly** [ʌnˈfrɛndli] *adj* inamistoso; desfavorable
**unfruitful** [ʌnˈfrutfəl] *adj* infructuoso
**unfulfilled** [ˌʌnfəlˈfɪld] *adj* incumplido
**unfurl** [ʌnˈfʌrl] *tr* desplegar, extender
**unfurnished** [ʌnˈfʌrnɪʃt] *adj* desamueblado
**ungainly** [ʌnˈgenli] *adj* desgarbado, desmañado
**ungentlemanly** [ʌnˈdʒɛntəlmənli] *adj* poco caballeroso, descortés
**ungird** [ʌnˈgʌrd] *tr* desceñir
**ungodly** [ʌnˈgɑdli] *adj* impío, irreligioso; (*dreadful*) (coll) atroz
**ungracious** [ʌnˈgreʃəs] *adj* descortés; desagradable
**ungrammatical** [ˌʌngrəˈmætɪkəl] *adj* ingramatical
**ungrateful** [ʌnˈgretfəl] *adj* ingrato, desagradecido
**ungrudgingly** [ʌnˈgrʌdʒɪŋli] *adj* de buena gana, sin quejarse
**unguarded** [ʌnˈgɑrdɪd] *adj* indefenso; descuidado; (*moment*) de inadvertencia
**unguent** [ˈʌŋgwənt] *s* ungüento
**unhandy** [ʌnˈhændi] *adj* inmanejable; (*awkward*) desmañado
**unhappiness** [ʌnˈhæpɪnɪs] *s* infelicidad
**unhap·py** [ʌnˈhæpi] *adj* (*comp* **-pier;** *super* **-piest**) infeliz; (*unlucky*) desgraciado; (*fateful*) aciago
**unharmed** [ʌnˈhɑrmd] *adj* indemne
**unharmonious** [ˌʌnhɑrˈmonɪ·əs] *adj* inarmónico
**unharness** [ʌnˈhɑrnɪs] *tr* desenjaezar, desguarnecer; desenganchar
**unhealthy** [ʌnˈhɛlθi] *adj* malsano
**unheard-of** [ʌnˈhʌrd ˌɑv] *adj* inaudito
**unhinge** [ʌnˈhɪndʒ] *tr* desgonzar; (fig) desequilibrar, trastornar
**unhitch** [ʌnˈhɪtʃ] *tr* desenganchar
**unho·ly** [ʌnˈholi] *adj* (*comp* **-lier;** *super* **-liest**) impío, malo, profano
**unhook** [ʌnˈhʊk] *tr* desabrochar; desenganchar; (*to take down from a hook*) descolgar
**unhoped-for** [ʌnˈhopt ˌfɔr] *adj* inesperado, no esperado
**unhorse** [ʌnˈhɔrs] *tr* desarzonar
**unhurt** [ʌnˈhʌrt] *adj* incólume, ileso
**unicorn** [ˈjunɪ ˌkɔrn] *s* unicornio
**unification** [ˌjunɪfɪˈkeʃən] *s* unificación
**uniform** [ˈjunɪ ˌfɔrm] *adj & s* uniforme *m* || *tr* uniformar
**uniformi·ty** [ˌjunɪˈfɔrmɪti] *s* (*pl* **-ties**) uniformidad
**uni·fy** [ˈjunɪ ˌfaɪ] *v* (*pret & pp* **-fied**) *tr* unificar
**unilateral** [ˌjunɪˈlætərəl] *adj* unilateral
**unimpeachable** [ˌʌnɪmˈpitʃəbəl] *adj* irrecusable, intachable
**unimportant** [ˌʌnɪmˈpɔrtənt] *adj* poco importante
**uninhabited** [ˌʌnɪnˈhæbɪtɪd] *adj* inhabitado
**uninspired** [ˌʌnɪnˈspaɪrd] *adj* sin inspiración; aburrido, fastidioso
**unintelligent** [ˌʌnɪnˈtɛlɪdʒənt] *adj* ininteligente
**unintelligible** [ˌʌnɪnˈtɛlɪdʒɪbəl] *adj* ininteligible
**uninterested** [ʌnˈɪntrɪstɪd] o [ʌnˈɪntəˌrɛstɪd] *adj* desinteresado
**uninteresting** [ʌnˈɪntrɪstɪŋ] o [ʌnˈɪntəˌrɛstɪŋ] *adj* poco interesante
**uninterrupted** [ˌʌnɪntəˈrʌptɪd] *adj* ininterrumpido
**union** [ˈjunjən] *s* unión; (*organization of workmen*) gremio obrero, sindicato; unión matrimonial
**unionize** [ˈjunjə ˌnaɪz] *tr* agremiar || *intr* agremiarse
**union shop** *s* taller *m* de obreros agremiados
**union suit** *s* traje *m* interior de una sola pieza
**unique** [jʊˈnik] *adj* único
**unison** [ˈjunɪsən] o [ˈjunɪzən] *s* unisonancia; **in unison (with)** al unísono (de)
**unit** [ˈjunɪt] *adj* unitario || *s* unidad; (mach & elec) grupo
**unite** [jʊˈnaɪt] *tr* unir || *intr* unirse
**united** [jʊˈnaɪtɪd] *adj* unido
**United Kingdom** *s* Reino Unido
**United Nations** *spl* Naciones Unidas
**United States** *adj* estadounidense || **the United States** *s* los Estados Unidos *mpl;* Estados Unidos *msg*
**uni·ty** [ˈjunɪti] *s* (*pl* **-ties**) unidad
**univ.** *abbr* **universal, university**

**universal** [ˌjunɪˈvʌrsəl] *adj* universal
**universal joint** *s* cardán *m*, junta universal
**universe** [ˈjunɪˌvʌrs] *s* universo
**universi·ty** [ˌjunɪˈvʌrsɪti] *adj* universitario || *s* (*pl* **-ties**) universidad
**unjust** [ʌnˈdʒʌst] *adj* injusto
**unjustified** [ʌnˈdʒʌstɪˌfaɪd] *adj* injustificado
**unkempt** [ʌnˈkɛmpt] *adj* despeinado
**unkind** [ʌnˈkaɪnd] *adj* poco amable; duro, despiadado
**unknowable** [ʌnˈno·əbəl] *adj* inconocible, insabible
**unknowingly** [ʌnˈno·ɪŋli] *adv* desconocidamente, sin saberlo
**unknown** [ʌnˈnon] *adj* desconocido, ignoto, incógnito || *s* desconocido; (math) incógnita
**unknown quantity** *s* (math & fig) incógnita
**unknown soldier** *s* soldado desconocido
**unlace** [ʌnˈles] *tr* desenlazar; desatar (*los cordones del zapato*)
**unlatch** [ʌnˈlætʃ] *tr* abrir levantando el picaporte
**unlawful** [ʌnˈlɔfəl] *adj* ilegal
**unleash** [ʌnˈliʃ] *tr* destraillar; soltar, desencadenar
**unleavened** [ʌnˈlɛvənd] *adj* ázimo
**unless** [ʌnˈlɛs] *conj* a menos que, a no ser que
**unlettered** [ʌnˈlɛtərd] *adj* iletrado, indocto; sin rotular; (*illiterate*) analfabeto
**unlike** [ʌnˈlaɪk] *adj* desemejante; desemejante de; (*poles of a magnet*) (elec) de nombres contrarios; (elec) de signo contrario || *prep* a diferencia de
**unlikely** [ʌnˈlaɪkli] *adj* improbable
**unlimber** [ʌnˈlɪmbər] *tr* preparar para la acción || *intr* prepararse para la acción
**unlined** [ʌnˈlaɪnd] *adj* (*coat*) sin forro; (*paper*) sin rayar; (*face*) sin arrugas
**unload** [ʌnˈlod] *tr* descargar; (coll) deshacerse de || *intr* descargar
**unloading** [ʌnˈlodɪŋ] *s* descarga, descargue *m*
**unlock** [ʌnˈlɑk] *tr* abrir (*p.ej., una puerta*); (typ) desapretar
**unloose** [ʌnˈlus] *tr* aflojar, soltar, desatar
**unloved** [ʌnˈlʌvd] *adj* desamado
**unlovely** [ʌnˈlʌvli] *adj* desgraciado
**unluck·y** [ʌnˈlʌki] *adj* (*comp* **-ier**; *super* **-iest**) desgraciado, desdichado; aciago, nefasto; de mala suerte
**un·make** [ʌnˈmek] *v* (*pret & pp* **-made** [ˈmed]) *tr* deshacer; destruir
**unmanageable** [ʌnˈmænɪdʒəbəl] *adj* inmanejable
**unmanly** [ʌnˈmænli] *adj* afeminado; bajo, cobarde
**unmannerly** [ʌnˈmænərli] *adj* descortés, malcriado
**unmarketable** [ʌnˈmɑrkɪtəbəl] *adj* incomerciable
**unmarriageable** [ʌnˈmærɪdʒəbəl] *adj* incasable
**unmarried** [ʌnˈmærid] *adj* soltero
**unmask** [ʌnˈmæsk] o [ʌnˈmɑsk] *tr* desenmascarar || *intr* desenmascararse
**unmatchable** [ʌnˈmætʃəbəl] *adj* incomparable, sin igual; (*price*) incompetible
**unmerciful** [ʌnˈmʌrsɪfəl] *adj* despiadado, inclemente
**unmesh** [ʌnˈmɛʃ] *tr* desengranar || *intr* desengranarse
**unmindful** [ʌnˈmaɪndfəl] *adj* desatento, descuidado; **to be unmindful of** olvidar, no pensar en
**unmistakable** [ˌʌnmɪsˈtekəbəl] *adj* inequívoco, inconfundible
**unmixed** [ʌnˈmɪkst] *adj* puro, sin mezcla
**unmoor** [ʌnˈmʊr] *tr* desamarrar (*un buque*); desaferrar (*las áncoras*)
**unmoved** [ʌnˈmuvd] *adj* fijo, inmoto; impasible
**unmuzzle** [ʌnˈmʌzəl] *tr* desbozalar
**unnatural** [ʌnˈnætʃərəl] *adj* innatural; (*artificial, forced*) afectado; anormal; inhumano
**unnecessary** [ʌnˈnesəˌseri] *adj* innecesario
**unnerve** [ʌnˈnʌrv] *tr* acobardar, trastornar
**unnoticeable** [ʌnˈnotɪsəbəl] *adj* imperceptible
**unnoticed** [ʌnˈnotɪst] *adj* inadvertido
**unobliging** [ˌʌnəˈblaɪdʒɪŋ] *adj* poco servicial, poco amable
**unobserved** [ˌʌnəbˈzʌrvd] *adj* inadvertido, sin ser visto
**unobtainable** [ˌʌnəbˈtenəbəl] *adj* inencontrable, inasequible
**unobtrusive** [ˌʌnəbˈtrusɪv] *adj* discreto, reservado
**unoccupied** [ʌnˈɑkjəˌpaɪd] *adj* libre, vacante; (*not busy*) desocupado
**unofficial** [ˌʌnəˈfɪʃəl] *adj* extraoficial, oficioso
**unopened** [ʌnˈopənd] *adj* sin abrir; (*book*) no cortado
**unorthodox** [ʌnˈɔrθəˌdɑks] *adj* inortodoxo
**unpack** [ʌnˈpæk] *tr* desembalar, desempaquetar
**unpalatable** [ʌnˈpælətəbəl] *adj* desabrido, ingustable
**unparalleled** [ʌnˈpærəˌlɛld] *adj* incomparable, sin par, sin igual
**unpardonable** [ʌnˈpɑrdənəbəl] *adj* imperdonable
**unpatriotic** [ˌʌnpetrɪˈɑtɪk] o [ˌʌnpætrɪˈɑtɪk] *adj* antipatriótico
**unperceived** [ˌʌnpərˈsivd] *adj* inadvertido
**unperturbable** [ˌʌnpərˈtʌrbəbəl] *adj* infracto, imperturbable
**unpleasant** [ʌnˈplɛzənt] *adj* antipático, desagradable
**unpopular** [ʌnˈpɑpjələr] *adj* impopular
**unpopularity** [ʌnˌpɑpjəˈlærɪti] *s* impopularidad
**unprecedented** [ʌnˈpresɪˌdɛntɪd] *adj* sin precedente, inaudito
**unprejudiced** [ʌnˈprɛdʒədɪst] *adj* sin prejuicios, imparcial
**unpremeditated** [ˌʌnprɪˈmɛdɪˌtetɪd] *adj* impremeditado

**unprepared** [ˌʌnprɪˈperd] *adj* desprevenido; falto de preparación
**unprepossessing** [ˌʌnpripəˈzesɪŋ] *adj* poco atrayente
**unpresentable** [ˌʌnprɪˈzentəbəl] *adj* impresentable
**unpretentious** [ˌʌnprɪˈtenʃəs] *adj* modesto, sencillo
**unprincipled** [ʌnˈprɪnsɪpəld] *adj* sin principios, sin conciencia
**unproductive** [ˌʌnprəˈdʌktɪv] *adj* improductivo
**unprofitable** [ʌnˈprɑfɪtəbəl] *adj* no provechoso, inútil
**unpronounceable** [ˌʌnprəˈnaʊnsəbəl] *adj* impronunciable
**unpropitious** [ˌʌnprəˈpɪʃəs] *adj* impropicio
**unpublished** [ʌnˈpʌblɪʃt] *adj* inédito
**unpunished** [ʌnˈpʌnɪʃt] *adj* impune
**unpurchasable** [ʌnˈpʌrtʃəsəbəl] *adj* incomprable
**unquenchable** [ʌnˈkwentʃəbəl] *adj* inextinguible
**unquestionable** [ʌnˈkwestʃənəbəl] *adj* incuestionable
**unrav•el** [ʌnˈrævəl] *v* (*pret & pp* **-eled** o **-elled**; *ger* **-eling** o **-elling**) *tr* deshebrar; desenredar, desenmarañar || *intr* desenredarse, desenmarañarse
**unreachable** [ʌnˈritʃəbəl] *adj* inalcanzable
**unreal** [ʌnˈri•əl] *adj* irreal
**unreali•ty** [ˌʌnrɪˈælɪti] *s* (*pl* **-ties**) irrealidad
**unreasonable** [ʌnˈrizənəbəl] *adj* irrazonable, desrazonable
**unrecognizable** [ʌnˈrekəgˌnaɪzəbəl] *adj* irreconocible
**unreel** [ʌnˈril] *tr* desenrollar || *intr* desenrollarse
**unrefined** [ˌʌnrɪˈfaɪnd] *adj* no refinado, impuro; grosero, rudo, tosco
**unrelenting** [ˌʌnrɪˈlentɪŋ] *adj* inexorable, inflexible, implacable
**unreliable** [ˌʌnrɪˈlaɪ•əbəl] *adj* indigno de confianza, informal
**unremitting** [ˌʌnrɪˈmɪtɪŋ] *adj* constante, incesante; infatigable
**unrenewable** [ˌʌnrɪˈnju•əbəl] o [ˌʌnrɪˈnu•əbəl] *adj* irrenovable; (com) improrrogable
**unrented** [ʌnˈrentɪd] *adj* desalquilado
**unrepentant** [ˌʌnrɪˈpentənt] *adj* impenitente
**unrequited love** [ˌʌnrɪˈkwaɪtɪd] *s* amor no correspondido
**unresponsive** [ˌʌnrɪˈspɑnsɪv] *adj* insensible, frío, desinteresado
**unrest** [ʌnˈrest] *s* intranquilidad, inquietud; alboroto, desorden *m*
**un•rig** [ʌnˈrɪg] *v* (*pret & pp* **-rigged**; *ger* **-rigging**) *tr* (naut) desaparejar
**unrighteous** [ʌnˈraɪtʃəs] *adj* injusto, malvado, vicioso
**unripe** [ʌnˈraɪp] *adj* inmaturo, verde; prematuro, precoz
**unrivaled** o **unrivalled** [ʌnˈraɪvəld] *adj* sin rival, sin par
**unroll** [ʌnˈrol] *tr* desenrollar, desplegar
**unromantic** [ˌʌnroˈmæntɪk] *adj* poco romántico
**unruffled** [ʌnˈrʌfəld] *adj* tranquilo, sereno
**unruly** [ʌnˈruli] *adj* ingobernable, indómito, revoltoso
**unsaddle** [ʌnˈsædəl] *tr* desensillar (*un caballo*); desarzonar (*al jinete*)
**unsafe** [ʌnˈsef] *adj* inseguro, peligroso
**unsaid** [ʌnˈsed] *adj* callado, no dicho
**unsalable** [ʌnˈseləbəl] *adj* invendible
**unsanitary** [ʌnˈsænɪˌteri] *adj* antihigiénico, insalubre
**unsatisfactory** [ʌnˌsætɪsˈfæktəri] *adj* insatisfactorio, poco satisfactorio
**unsatisfied** [ʌnˈsætɪsˌfaɪd] *adj* insatisfecho
**unsavory** [ʌnˈsevəri] *adj* desabrido; (fig) infame, deshonroso
**unscathed** [ʌnˈskeðd] *adj* ileso, sano y salvo
**unscientific** [ˌʌnsaɪ•ənˈtɪfɪk] *adj* anticientífico
**unscrew** [ʌnˈskru] *tr* destornillar || *intr* destornillarse
**unscrupulous** [ʌnˈskrupjələs] *adj* inescrupuloso
**unseal** [ʌnˈsil] *tr* desellar; (fig) abrir
**unseasonable** [ʌnˈsizənəbəl] *adj* intempestivo, inoportuno
**unseaworthy** [ʌnˈsiˌwʌrði] *adj* innavegable
**unseemly** [ʌnˈsimli] *adj* impropio, indecoroso, indigno
**unseen** [ʌnˈsin] *adj* invisible, oculto
**unselfish** [ʌnˈselfɪʃ] *adj* desinteresado, generoso, altruísta
**unsettled** [ʌnˈsetəld] *adj* inhabitado, despoblado; sin residencia fija; indeciso; descompuesto; (*bills*) por pagar
**unshackle** [ʌnˈʃækəl] *tr* desherrar, desencadenar
**unshaken** [ʌnˈʃekən] *adj* imperturbado
**unshapely** [ʌnˈʃepli] *adj* desproporcionado, mal formado
**unshatterable** [ʌnˈʃætərəbəl] *adj* inastillable
**unshaven** [ʌnˈʃevən] *adj* sin afeitar
**unsheathe** [ʌnˈʃið] *tr* desenvainar
**unshod** [ʌnˈʃɑd] *adj* descalzo; (*horse*) desherrado
**unshrinkable** [ʌnˈʃrɪŋkəbəl] *adj* inencogible
**unsightly** [ʌnˈsaɪtli] *adj* feo, de aspecto malo, repugnante
**unsinkable** [ʌnˈsɪŋkəbəl] *adj* insumergible
**unskilled** [ʌnˈskɪld] *adj* inexperto
**unskilled laborer** *s* bracero, peón *m*
**unskillful** [ʌnˈskɪlfəl] *adj* desmañado
**unsnarl** [ʌnˈsnɑrl] *tr* desenredar
**unsociable** [ʌnˈsoʃəbəl] *adj* insociable, huraño
**unsold** [ʌnˈsold] *adj* invendido
**unsolder** [ʌnˈsɑdər] *tr* desoldar; (fig) desunir, separar
**unsophisticated** [ˌʌnsəˈfɪstɪˌketɪd] *adj* ingenuo, natural, sencillo
**unsound** [ʌnˈsaʊnd] *adj* poco firme; falso, erróneo; (*decayed*) podrido; (*sleep*) ligero
**unsown** [ʌnˈson] *adj* yermo, no sembrado
**unspeakable** [ʌnˈspikəbəl] *adj* indeci-

ble, inefable; (*atrocious, infamous*) incalificable

**unsportsmanlike** [ʌn'sportsmən,laɪk] *adj* antideportivo

**unstable** [ʌn'stebəl] *adj* inestable

**unsteady** [ʌn'stɛdi] *adj* inseguro, inestable; irresoluto, inconstante; poco juicioso

**unstinted** [ʌn'stɪntɪd] *adj* no escatimado, generoso, liberal

**unstitch** [ʌn'stɪtʃ] *tr* descoser

**un•stop** [ʌn'stɑp] *v* (*pret & pp* **-stopped**; *ger* **-stopping**) *tr* destaponar

**unstressed** [ʌn'strest] *adj* sin énfasis; (*syllable*) inacentuado

**unstrung** [ʌn'strʌŋ] *adj* nervioso, trastornado

**unsuccessful** [,ʌnsək'sɛsfəl] *adj* (*person*) desairado; (*undertaking*) impróspero; **to be unsuccessful** no tener éxito

**unsuitable** [ʌn'sutəbəl] o [ʌn'sjutəbəl] *adj* inadecuado, inconveniente

**unsurpassable** [,ʌnsər'pæsəbəl] o [,ʌnsər'pɑsəbəl] *adj* insuperable

**unsuspected** [,ʌnsəs'pɛktɪd] *adj* insospechado

**unswerving** [ʌn'swʌrvɪŋ] *adj* firme, inmutable, resoluto

**unsymmetrical** [,ʌnsɪ'metrɪkəl] *adj* asimétrico, disimétrico

**unsympathetic** [,ʌnsɪmpə'θɛtɪk] *adj* incompasivo, indiferente

**unsystematic(al)** [,ʌnsɪstə'mætɪk(əl)] *adj* poco sistemático, sin sistema

**untactful** [ʌn'tæktfəl] *adj* indiscreto, falto de tacto

**untamed** [ʌn'temd] *adj* indomado, bravío

**untangle** [ʌn'tæŋgəl] *tr* desenredar, desenmarañar

**unteachable** [ʌn'titʃəbəl] *adj* indócil

**untenable** [ʌn'tɛnəbəl] *adj* insostenible

**unthankful** [ʌn'θæŋkfəl] *adj* ingrato, desagradecido

**unthinkable** [ʌn'θɪŋkəbəl] *adj* impensable

**unthinking** [ʌn'θɪŋkɪŋ] *adj* irreflexivo, desatento; irracional, instintivo

**untidy** [ʌn'taɪdi] *adj* desaseado, desaliñado

**un•tie** [ʌn'taɪ] *v* (*pret & pp* **-tied**; *ger* **-tying**) *tr* desatar; deshacer (*un nudo, una cuerda*); (*to free from restraint*) soltar; resolver || *intr* desatarse

**until** [ʌn'tɪl] *prep* hasta || *conj* hasta que; **to wait until** aguardar a que, esperar a que

**untillable** [ʌn'tɪləbəl] *adj* incultivable

**untimely** [ʌn'taɪmli] *adj* intempestivo

**untiring** [ʌn'taɪrɪŋ] *adj* incansable

**untold** [ʌn'told] *adj* nunca dicho; (*uncounted*) innumerable, incalculable

**untouchable** [ʌn'tʌtʃəbəl] *adj* intangible || *s* intocable *mf*

**untouched** [ʌn'tʌtʃt] *adj* intacto; íntegro; impasible; no mencionado

**untoward** [ʌn'tord] *adj* desfavorable; indecoroso

**untrammeled** o **untrammelled** [ʌn'træməld] *adj* libre, sin trabas

**untried** [ʌn'traɪd] *adj* no probado, no ensayado

**untroubled** [ʌn'trʌbləd] *adj* tranquilo, sosegado

**untrue** [ʌn'tru] *adj* falso; infiel

**untrustworthy** [ʌn'trʌst,wʌrði] *adj* indigno de confianza

**untruth** [ʌn'truθ] *s* falsedad, mentira

**untruthful** [ʌn'truθfəl] *adj* falso, mentiroso

**untwist** [ʌn'twɪst] *tr* destorcer || *intr* destorcerse

**unused** [ʌn'juzd] *adj* inutilizado, no usado; nuevo; **unused to** [ʌn'juzdtʊ] o [ʌn'justʊ] *adj* no acostumbrado a

**unusual** [ʌn'juʒʊ·əl] *adj* inusual, insólito

**unutterable** [ʌn'ʌtərəbəl] *adj* indecible, inexpresable

**unvanquished** [ʌn'væŋkwɪʃt] *adj* invicto

**unvarnished** [ʌn'vɑrnɪʃt] *adj* sin barnizar; (fig) sencillo, sin adornos

**unveil** [ʌn'vel] *tr* quitar el velo a; descubrir, develar, inaugurar (*una estatua*) || *intr* quitarse el velo

**unveiling** [ʌn'velɪŋ] *s* develación, inauguración

**unventilated** [ʌn'ventɪ,letɪd] *adj* sin ventilar

**unvoice** [ʌn'vɔɪs] *tr* afonizar, ensordecer || *intr* afonizarse, ensordecerse

**unwanted** [ʌn'wɑntɪd] *adj* indeseado

**unwarranted** [ʌn'wɑrəntɪd] *adj* injustificado; no autorizado; sin garantía

**unwary** [ʌn'weri] *adj* incauto, imprudente

**unwavering** [ʌn'wevərɪŋ] *adj* firme, determinado, resuelto

**unwelcome** [ʌn'wɛlkəm] *adj* mal acogido; importuno, molesto

**unwell** [ʌn'wel] *adj* indispuesto, enfermo; (coll) menstruante

**unwholesome** [ʌn'holsəm] *adj* insalubre

**unwieldy** [ʌn'wildi] *adj* inmanejable, abultado, pesado

**unwilling** [ʌn'wɪlɪŋ] *adj* desinclinado, maldispuesto, renuente

**unwillingly** [ʌn'wɪlɪŋli] *adv* de mala gana

**un•wind** [ʌn'waɪnd] *v* (*pret & pp* **-wound** ['waʊnd]) *tr* desenvolver || *intr* desenvolverse; distenderse (*el muelle del reloj*)

**unwise** [ʌn'waɪz] *adj* indiscreto, malaconsejado

**unwished-for** [ʌn'wɪʃt,fɔr] *adj* indeseado

**unwitting** [ʌn'wɪtɪŋ] *adj* inadvertido, inconsciente

**unwonted** [ʌn'wʌntɪd] *adj* poco común, raro, insólito

**unworldly** [ʌn'wʌrldli] *adj* no terrenal, no mundano, espiritual

**unworthy** [ʌn'wʌrði] *adj* indigno, desmerecedor

**un•wrap** [ʌn'ræp] *v* (*pret & pp* **-wrapped**; *ger* **-wrapping**) *tr* desenvolver, desempapelar

**unwrinkle** [ʌn'rɪŋkəl] *tr* desarrugar || *intr* desarrugarse

**unwritten** [ʌn'rɪtən] *adj* no escrito; (*blank*) en blanco; oral
**unyielding** [ʌn'jildɪŋ] *adj* firme, inflexible; terco, reacio
**unyoke** [ʌn'jok] *tr* desuncir
**up** [ʌp] *adj* ascendente; alto, elevado; derecho, en pie; terminado; cumplido; levantado de la cama; **to be up and about** estar levantado (*el que estaba enfermo*) || *s* subida; **ups and downs** altibajos, vicisitudes || *adv* arriba; en el aire; hacia arriba; al norte; **to be up** estar levantado; vencer (*un plazo*); **to be up in arms** estar sobre las armas; protestar vehementemente; **to be up to a person** tocarle a una persona; **to get up** levantarse; **to go up** subir; **to keep up** mantener; continuar; mantenerse firme; **to keep up with** correr parejas con; **up above** allá arriba; **up against it** (slang) en apuros; **up to** hasta; (*capable of*) a la altura de; (*informed of*) al corriente de; (*scheming*) armando, tramando; **what is up?** ¿qué pasa? || *prep* subiendo; **up the river** río arriba; **up the street** calle arriba
**up-and-coming** ['ʌpən'kʌmɪŋ] *adj* (coll) prometedor
**up-and-doing** ['ʌpən'du·ɪŋ] *adj* (coll) emprendedor
**up-and-up** ['ʌpən'ʌp] *s* — **on the up-and-up** (coll) mejorándose; (coll) abiertamente, sin dolo
**up•braid'** *tr* regañar, reprender
**upbringing** ['ʌp,brɪŋɪŋ] *s* educación, crianza
**up'coun'try** *adv* (coll) hacia el interior, tierra adentro || *s* (coll) interior *m* del país
**up•date'** *tr* poner al día
**upheaval** [ʌp'hivəl] *s* trastorno, cataclismo
**up'hill'** *adj* ascendente; arduo, difícil, penoso || **up'hill'** *adv* cuesta arriba
**up•hold'** *v* (*pret & pp* **-held**) *tr* levantar; apoyar, sostener; defender
**upholster** [ʌp'holstər] *tr* tapizar
**upholsterer** [ʌp'holstərər] *s* tapicero
**upholster•y** [ʌp'holstəri] *s* (*pl* **-ies**) tapicería
**up'keep'** *s* conservación, manutención; gastos de conservación, gastos de entretenimiento
**upland** ['ʌplənd] o ['ʌplænd] *adj* alto, elevado || *s* tierra alta, terreno elevado
**up'lift'** *s* (*lifting*) elevación, levantamiento; mejora social; (*moral or spiritual improvement*) edificación || **up•lift'** *tr* elevar, levantar; edificar
**upon** [ə'pɑn] *prep* en, sobre, encima de; **upon** + *ger* al + *inf*, p.ej., **upon arriving** al llegar; **upon my word!** ¡por mi palabra!
**upper** ['ʌpər] *adj* alto, superior; (*country*) interior; (*clothing*) exterior || *s* (*of shoe*) pala; **on one's uppers** con las suelas gastadas; (coll) andrajoso, pobre, sin blanca
**upper berth** *s* litera alta, cama alta
**upper case** *s* (typ) caja alta
**upper classes** *spl* altas clases
**upper hand** *s* dominio, ventaja; **to have the upper hand** tener vara alta
**upper middle class** *s* alta burguesía
**up'per•most'** *adj* (el) más alto; (el) principal || *adv* en lo más alto; primero, en primer lugar
**uppish** ['ʌpɪʃ] *adj* (coll) copetudo, arrogante
**up•raise'** *tr* levantar
**up'right'** *adj* derecho, vertical; probo, recto || *adv* verticalmente || *s* montante *m*
**uprising** [ʌp'raɪzɪŋ] o ['ʌp,raɪzɪŋ] *s* insurrección, levantamiento
**up'roar'** *s* alboroto, conmoción, tumulto
**uproarious** [ʌp'rorɪ·əs] *adj* tumultuoso; (*noisy*) ruidoso; (*funny*) muy cómico
**up•root'** *tr* desarraigar
**up•set'** o **up'set'** *adj* (*overturned*) volcado; trastornado; indispuesto || **up'set'** *s* (*overturn*) vuelco; (*unexpected defeat*) contratiempo; (*disturbance*) trastorno; (*illness*) indisposición, enfermedad || **up•set'** *v* (*pret & pp* **-set**; *ger* **-setting**) *tr* volcar; trastornar; indisponer || *intr* volcar
**upset price** *s* precio mínimo fijado en una subasta
**upsetting** [ʌp'setɪŋ] *adj* desconcertante
**up'shot'** *s* conclusión, resultado; esencia, quid *m*
**up'side'** *s* parte *f* superior, lado superior; **on the upside** (*said of prices*) subiendo
**upside down** *adv* al revés, lo de arriba abajo, patas arriba; en confusión, revuelto; **to turn upside down** volcar; trastornar; volcarse; trastornarse
**up'stage'** *adj* situado al fondo de la escena; (coll) altanero, arrogante || *adv* al fondo de la escena || **up'stage'** *tr* (coll) mirar por encima del hombro, desairar
**up'stairs'** *adj* de arriba || *adv* arriba || *s* piso superior, pisos superiores
**upstanding** [ʌp'stændɪŋ] *adj* derecho; gallardo; probo, recto
**up'start'** *adj & s* advenedizo
**up'stream'** *adv* aguas arriba, río arriba
**up'stroke'** *s* carrera ascendente
**up'swing'** *s* movimiento hacia arriba; mejora notable; **on the upswing** mejorando notablemente
**up'-to-date'** *adj* corriente; reciente, moderno; de última hora, de última moda
**up'-to-the-min'ute** *adj* al día, de actualidad
**up'town'** *adj* de la parte alta de la ciudad || *adv* en la parte alta de la ciudad
**up train** *s* tren *m* ascendente
**up'trend'** *s* tendencia al alza
**up'turn'** *s* alza, subida, mejora
**upturned** [ʌp'tʌrnd] *adj* revuelto; (*part of clothing*) arremangado; (*nose*) respingada
**upward** ['ʌpwərd] *adj* ascendente || *adv* hacia arriba; **upward of** más de

**Ural** [ˈjʊrəl] *adj* ural ‖ **Urals** *spl* Urales *mpl*
**uranium** [jʊˈrenɪ·əm] *s* uranio
**urban** [ˈʌrbən] *adj* urbano (*perteneciente a la ciudad*)
**urbane** [ʌrˈben] *adj* urbano (*atento, cortés*)
**urbanite** [ˈʌrbəˌnaɪt] *s* ciudadano
**urbanity** [ʌrˈbænɪti] *s* urbanidad
**urbanize** [ˈʌrbəˌnaɪz] *tr* urbanizar
**urchin** [ˈʌrtʃɪn] *s* pilluelo, galopín *m*
**ure•thra** [jʊˈriθrə] *s* (*pl* **-thras** o **-thrae** [θri]) uretra
**urge** [ʌrdʒ] *s* impulso, estímulo ‖ *tr* apremiar, impeler, estimular; pedir instantemente; (*to try to persuade*) instar ‖ *intr* instar
**urgen•cy** [ˈʌrdʒənsi] *s* (*pl* **-cies**) urgencia; instancia, apremio
**urgent** [ˈʌrdʒənt] *adj* urgente; apremiante
**urinal** [ˈjʊrɪnəl] *s* (*receptacle*) orinal *m;* (*place*) urinario
**urinary** [ˈjʊrɪˌneri] *adj* urinario
**urinate** [ˈjʊrɪˌnet] *tr* orinar (*p.ej., sangre*) ‖ *intr* orinar, orinarse
**urine** [ˈjʊrɪn] *s* orina, orines *mpl*
**urn** [ʌrn] *s* (*decorative vase*) jarrón *m;* cafetera o tetera con grifo; (*to hold ashes of the dead after cremation*) urna
**urology** [jʊˈrɑlədʒi] *s* urología
**Uruguay** [ˈjʊrəˌgwe] o [ˈjʊrəˌgwaɪ] *s* el Uruguay
**Uruguayan** [ˌjʊrəˈgwe·ən] o [ˌjʊrəˈgwaɪ·ən] *adj & s* uruguayo
**us** [ʌs] *pron pers* nos; nosotros; **to us** nos; a nosotros
**U.S.A.** *abbr* **United States of America, United States Army, Union of South Africa**
**usable** [ˈjuzəbəl] *adj* aprovechable, utilizable
**usage** [ˈjusɪdʒ] o [ˈjuzɪdʒ] *s* usanza; (*e.g., of a language*) uso
**use** [jus] *s* uso, empleo; utilidad; **in use** en uso; **out of use** desusado; **to be of no use** no servir para nada; **to have no use for** no necesitar; no servirse de; (coll) tener en poco; **to make use of** servirse de ‖ [juz] *tr* usar, emplear, servirse de; **to use badly** maltratar; **to use up** agotar, consumir ‖ *intr* (empléase sólo en el pretérito y se traduce al español con el pretérito imperfecto o el verbo **soler**), p.ej., **I used to go out for a walk every evening** salía de paseo todas las tardes o solía salir de paseo todas las tardes
**used** [juzd] *adj* (*customarily employed; worn, partly worn-out; accustomed*) usado; **used to** [ˈjuzdtʊ] o [ˈjustʊ] acostumbrado a
**useful** [ˈjusfəl] *adj* útil
**usefulness** [ˈjusfəlnɪs] *s* utilidad
**useless** [ˈjuslɪs] *adj* inservible, inútil
**user** [ˈjuzər] *s* usuario
**usher** [ˈʌʃər] *s* (*in a theater*) acomodador *m;* (*doorkeeper*) ujier *m,* portero ‖ *tr* acomodar; **to usher in** anunciar, introducir
**U.S.S.R.** *abbr* **Union of Soviet Socialist Republics**
**usual** [ˈjuʒʊ·əl] *adj* usual, acostumbrado; **as usual** como de costumbre
**usually** [ˈjuʒʊ·əli] *adj* usualmente, de ordinario
**usurp** [jʊˈzʌrp] *tr* usurpar
**usu•ry** [ˈjuʒəri] *s* (*pl* **-ries**) usura
**utensil** [jʊˈtɛnsɪl] *s* utensilio
**uter•us** [ˈjutərəs] *s* (*pl* **-i** [ˌaɪ]) útero
**utilitarian** [ˌjutɪlɪˈterɪ·ən] *adj* utilitario
**utili•ty** [juˈtɪlɪti] *s* (*pl* **-ties**) utilidad; empresa de servicio público
**utilize** [ˈjutɪˌlaɪz] *tr* utilizar
**utmost** [ˈʌtˌmost] *adj* sumo, extremo, último; más grande, mayor posible; más lejano ‖ *s* — **the utmost** lo sumo, lo mayor, lo más; **to the utmost** a lo sumo, a más no poder; **to do one's utmost** hacer todo lo posible
**utopia** [juˈtopɪ·ə] *s* utopía
**utopian** [juˈtopɪ·ən] *adj* utópico, utopista ‖ *s* utopista *mf*
**utter** [ˈʌtər] *adj* total, absoluto ‖ *tr* proferir, pronunciar; dar (*un suspiro*)
**utterance** [ˈʌtərəns] *s* expresión, pronunciación; declaración
**utterly** [ˈʌtərli] *adj* completamente, totalmente, absolutamente
**uxoricide** [ʌkˈsorɪˌsaɪd] *s* (*husband*) uxoricida *m;* (*act*) uxoricidio
**uxorious** [ʌkˈsorɪ·əs] *adj* uxorio

## V

**V, v** [vi] vigésima segunda letra del alfabeto inglés
**v.** *abbr* **verb, verse, versus, vide** (Lat) **see, voice, volt, volume**
**V.** *abbr* **Venerable, Vice, Viscount, Volunteer**
**vacan•cy** [ˈvekənsi] *s* (*pl* **-cies**) (*emptiness; gap, opening*) vacío; (*unfilled position or job*) vacancia, vacante *f,* vacío; piso vacante; cargo vacante
**vacant** [ˈvekənt] *adj* (*empty*) vacío; (*having no occupant; untenanted*) vacante; (*expression, look*) vago; distraído
**vacate** [ˈveket] *tr* dejar vacante; anular, invalidar, revocar ‖ *intr* (*to move out*) desalojar; (coll) irse, marcharse
**vacation** [veˈkeʃən] *s* vacaciones; **on vacation** de vacaciones ‖ *intr* tomar vacaciones
**vacationist** [veˈkeʃənɪst] *s* vacacionista *mf*
**vacation with pay** *s* vacaciones retribuídas

**vaccinate** ['væksɪ,net] *tr* vacunar
**vaccination** [,væksɪ'neʃən] *s* vacunación
**vaccine** [væk'sin] *s* vacuna
**vacillate** ['væsɪ,let] *intr* vacilar
**vacillating** ['væsɪ,letɪŋ] *adj* vacilante
**vacui·ty** [væ'kju·ɪti] *s* (*pl* **-ties**) vacuidad
**vacu·um** ['vækju·əm] *s* (*pl* **-ums** o **-a** [ə]) vacío || *tr* (coll) limpiar
**vacuum cleaner** *s* aspirador *m* de polvo
**vacuum tank** *s* (aut) aspirador *m* de gasolina, nodriza
**vacuum tube** *s* tubo de vacío
**vagabond** ['vægə,bɑnd] *adj* & *s* vagabundo
**vagar·y** [və'geri] *s* (*pl* **-ies**) capricho
**vagran·cy** ['vegrənsi] *s* (*pl* **-cies**) vagabundaje *m*
**vagrant** ['vegrənt] *adj* & *s* vagabundo
**vague** [veg] *adj* vago
**vain** [ven] *adj* vano; (*conceited*) vanidoso; **in vain** en vano
**vainglorious** [ven'glorɪ·əs] *adj* vanaglorioso
**valance** ['væləns] *s* (*across the top of a window*) guardamalleta; (*drapery*) doselera
**vale** [vel] *s* valle *m*
**valedictorian** [,vælɪdɪk'torɪ·ən] *s* alumno que pronuncia el discurso de despedida al fin del curso
**valedicto·ry** [,vælɪ'dɪktəri] *adj* de despedida || *s* (*pl* **-ries**) discurso de despedida
**valence** ['veləns] *s* (chem) valencia
**valentine** ['vælən,taɪn] *s* tarjeta amorosa o jocosa del día de San Valentín
**Valentine Day** *s* día *m* de los corazones, día de los enamorados (*14 de febrero*)
**vale of tears** *s* valle *m* de lágrimas
**valet** ['vælɪt] o ['væle] *s* ayuda *m*, paje *m*
**valiant** ['væljənt] *adj* valiente, valeroso
**valid** ['vælɪd] *adj* válido, valedero
**validate** ['vælɪ,det] *tr* validar; (sport) homologar
**validation** [,vælɪ'deʃən] *s* validación; (sport) homologación
**validi·ty** [və'lɪdɪti] *s* (*pl* **-ties**) validez *f*
**valise** [və'lis] *s* maleta
**valley** ['væli] *s* valle *m*; (*of roof*) lima hoya
**valor** ['vælər] *s* valor *m*, ánimo
**valorous** ['vælərəs] *adj* valeroso
**valuable** ['vælju·əbəl] o ['væljəbəl] *adj* (*having monetary value*) valioso; (*highly thought of*) estimable || **valuables** *spl* alhajas, objetos de valor
**value** ['vælju] *s* valor *m*; (*return for one's money in a purchase*) (coll) adquisición, inversión, p.ej., **an excellent value** una adquisición excelente || *tr* (*to think highly of*) estimar; (*to set a price for*) valorar, valuar
**valueless** ['væljulɪs] *adj* sin valor
**valve** [vælv] *s* válvula; (*of mollusk*) valva; (mus) llave *f*
**valve cap** *s* capuchón *m*
**valve gears** *spl* distribución
**valve'-in-head' engine** *s* motor *m* con válvulas en cabeza
**valve lifter** ['lɪftər] *s* levantaválvulas *m*
**valve seat** *s* asiento de válvula
**valve spring** *s* muelle *m* de válvula
**valve stem** *s* vástago de válvula
**vamp** [væmp] *s* (*of shoe*) empella; (*patchwork*) remiendo; (*woman who preys on men*) (slang) mujer *f* fatal, vampiresa || *tr* poner empella a (*un zapato*); remendar; (*to concoct*) componer, enmendar; (jazz) improvisar (*un acompañamiento*); (slang) seducir (*una mujer mundana a un hombre*)
**vampire** ['væmpaɪr] *s* vampiro; (*woman who preys on men*) mujer *f* fatal, vampiresa
**van** [væn] *s* carro de carga, camión *m* de mudanzas; (mil & fig) vanguardia; (Brit) furgón *m* de equipajes
**vanadium** [və'nedɪ·əm] *s* vanadio
**vandal** ['vændəl] *adj* & *s* vándalo || **Vandal** *adj* & *s* vándalo
**vandalism** ['vændə,lɪzəm] *s* vandalismo
**vane** [ven] *s* (*weathervane*) veleta; (*of windmill*) aspa; (*of propeller or turbine*) paleta; (*of feather*) barba
**vanguard** ['væn,gɑrd] *s* (mil & fig) vanguardia; **in the vanguard** a vanguardia
**vanilla** [və'nɪlə] *s* vainilla
**vanish** ['vænɪʃ] *intr* desvanecerse
**vanishing cream** ['vænɪʃɪŋ] *s* crema desvanecedora
**vani·ty** ['vænɪti] *s* (*pl* **-ties**) vanidad; (*dressing table*) tocador *m*; (*vanity case*) estuche *m* de afeites
**vanity case** *s* estuche *m* de afeites, neceser *m* de belleza
**vanquish** ['væŋkwɪʃ] *tr* vencer, rendir
**vantage ground** ['væntɪdʒ] *s* posición ventajosa
**vapid** ['væpɪd] *adj* insípido
**vapor** ['vepər] *s* vapor *m* (*el visible; exhalación, vaho, niebla, etc.*)
**vaporize** ['vepə,raɪz] *tr* vaporizar || *intr* vaporizarse
**vaporous** ['vepərəs] *adj* vaporoso
**vapor trail** *s* (aer) estela de vapor, rastro de condensación
**var.** *abbr* **variant**
**variable** ['verɪ·əbəl] *adj* & *s* variable *f*
**variance** ['verɪ·əns] *s* diferencia, variación; **at variance with** en desacuerdo con
**variant** ['verɪ·ənt] *adj* & *s* variante *f*
**variation** [,verɪ'eʃən] *s* variación
**varicose** ['værɪ,kos] *adj* varicoso
**varicose vein** *s* (pathol) varice *f*
**varied** ['verid] *adj* variado, vario
**variegated** ['verɪ·ə,getɪd] o ['verɪ,getɪd] *adj* abigarrado, variado
**varie·ty** [və'raɪ·ɪti] *s* (*pl* **-ties**) variedad
**variety show** *s* variedades
**variola** [və'raɪ·ələ] *s* (pathol) viruela
**various** ['verɪ·əs] *adj* (*several; of different kinds*) varios; (*many-sided; many-colored*) vario
**varnish** ['vɑrnɪʃ] *s* barniz *m*; (fig) capa, apariencia || *tr* barnizar; (fig) dar apariencia falsa a
**varsi·ty** ['vɑrsɪti] *adj* (sport) universi-

tario || *s* (*pl* **-ties**) (sport) equipo principal de la universidad
**var·y** ['veri] *v* (*pret & pp* **-ied**) *tr & intr* variar
**vase** [ves] o [vez] *s* florero, jarrón *m*
**vaseline** ['væsə,lin] *s* (trademark) vaselina
**vassal** ['væsəl] *adj & s* vasallo
**vast** [væst] o [vɑst] *adj* vasto
**vastly** ['væstli] o ['vɑstli] *adv* enormemente
**vastness** ['væstnɪs] o ['vɑstnɪs] *s* vastedad
**vat** [væt] *s* cuba, tina
**vaudeville** ['vodvɪl] o ['vɔdəvɪl] *s* variedades; (*light theatrical piece interspersed with songs*) zarzuela
**vault** [vɔlt] *s* (*underground chamber*) bodega; (*of a bank*) cámara acorazada; (*burial chamber*) sepultura, tumba; (*firmament*) bóveda celeste; (*leap*) salto; (archit) bóveda || *tr* abovedar; saltar || *intr* saltar
**vaunt** [vɔnt] o [vɑnt] *s* jactancia || *tr* jactarse de || *intr* jactarse
**veal** [vil] *s* ternera, carne *f* de ternera
**veal chop** *s* chuleta de ternera
**vedette** [vɪ'det] *s* buque *m* escucha; centinela *m* de avanzada
**veer** [vɪr] *s* viraje *m* || *tr* virar || *intr* virar; (naut) llamar (*el viento*)
**vegetable** ['vedʒɪtəbəl] *adj* vegetal || *s* (*plant*) vegetal *m;* (*edible part of plant*) hortaliza, legumbre *f*
**vegetable garden** *s* huerto de hortalizas, huerto de verduras
**vegetable soup** *s* menestra, sopa de hortalizas
**vegetarian** [,vedʒɪ'terɪ·ən] *adj & s* vegetariano
**vehemence** ['vi·ɪməns] *s* vehemencia
**vehement** ['vi·ɪmənt] *adj* vehemente
**vehicle** ['vi·ɪkəl] *s* vehículo
**vehicular traffic** [vɪ'hɪkjələr] *s* circulación rodada
**veil** [vel] *s* velo; **to take the veil** tomar el velo || *tr* velar (*cubrir con un velo; cubrir, disimular*)
**vein** [ven] *s* vena; (*streak*) veta; (*distinctive quality*) rasgo || *tr* vetear
**velar** ['vilər] *adj & s* velar *f*
**vellum** ['veləm] *s* vitela; papel *m* vitela
**veloci·ty** [vɪ'lɑsɪti] *s* (*pl* **-ties**) velocidad
**velvet** ['velvɪt] *adj* de terciopelo || *s* terciopelo; (slang) ganancia limpia
**velveteen** [,velvɪ'tin] *s* velludillo
**velvety** ['velvɪti] *adj* aterciopelado
**Ven.** *abbr* **Venerable**
**vend** [vend] *tr* vender como buhonero
**vending machine** *s* distribuidor automático
**vendor** ['vendər] *s* vendedor *m,* buhonero
**veneer** [və'nɪr] *s* chapa, enchapado; (fig) apariencia || *tr* enchapar
**venerable** ['venərəbəl] *adj* venerable
**venerate** ['venə,ret] *tr* venerar
**venereal** [vɪ'nɪrɪ·əl] *adj* venéreo
**Venetia** [vɪ'niʃɪ·ə] o [vɪ'niʃə] *s* Venecia (*provincia*)
**Venetian** [vɪ'niʃən] *adj & s* veneciano
**Venetian blind** *s* persiana
**Venezuela** [,venɪ'zwilə] *s* Venezuela
**Venezuelan** [,venɪ'zwilən] *adj & s* venezolano
**vengeance** ['vendʒəns] *s* venganza; **with a vengeance** con furia, con violencia; excesivamente, con creces
**vengeful** ['vendʒfəl] *adj* vengativo
**Venice** ['venɪs] *s* Venecia (*ciudad*)
**venire** [vɪ'naɪri] *s* (law) auto de convocación del jurado
**venison** ['venɪsən] o ['venɪzən] *s* carne *f* de venado
**venom** ['venəm] *s* veneno
**venomous** ['venəməs] *adj* venenoso
**vent** [vent] *s* agujero, orificio; (*outlet*) salida; **to give vent to** dar libre curso a || *tr* proveer de abertura; desahogar, expresar; **to vent one's spleen** descargar la bilis
**vent'hole'** *s* respiradero
**ventilate** ['ventɪ,let] *tr* ventilar
**ventilator** ['ventɪ,letər] *s* ventilador *m*
**ventricle** ['ventrɪkəl] *s* ventrículo
**ventriloquism** [ven'trɪlə,kwɪzəm] *s* ventriloquia
**ventriloquist** [ven'trɪləkwɪst] *s* ventrílocuo
**venture** ['ventʃər] *s* empresa arriesgada; **at a venture** a la buena ventura || *tr* aventurar || *intr* aventurarse; **to venture on** arriesgarse en
**venturesome** ['ventʃərsəm] *adj* (*bold, daring*) aventurero; (*hazardous*) aventurado
**venturous** ['ventʃərəs] *adj* (*bold, daring*) aventurero; (*hazardous*) aventurado, arriesgado
**venue** ['venju] *s* (law) lugar *m* del crimen; (law) lugar donde se reúne el jurado; **change of venue** (law) traslado de jurisdicción
**Venus** ['vinəs] *s* (astr) Venus *m;* (myth) Venus *f;* (*very beautiful woman*) Venus *f*
**veracious** [vɪ'reʃəs] *adj* veraz
**veraci·ty** [vɪ'ræsɪti] *s* (*pl* **-ties**) veracidad
**veranda** o **verandah** [və'rændə] *s* terraza, veranda, galería
**verb** [vʌrb] *adj* verbal || *s* verbo
**verbatim** [vər'betɪm] *adj* textual || *adv* palabra por palabra, al pie de la letra
**verbena** [vər'binə] *s* (bot) verbena
**verbiage** ['vʌrbɪ·ɪdʒ] *s* palabrería, verbosidad
**verbose** [vər'bos] *adj* verboso
**verdant** ['vʌrdənt] *adj* verde; cándido, sencillo
**verdict** ['vʌrdɪkt] *s* veredicto, fallo
**verdigris** ['vʌrdɪ,gris] *s* verdete *m*
**verdure** ['vʌrdʒər] *s* verdor *m*
**verge** [vʌrdʒ] *s* borde *m,* límite *m;* (*of a column*) fuste *m;* báculo; (eccl) cetro; **on the verge of** al borde de; a punto de; **within the verge of** al alcance de || *intr* — **to verge on** o **upon** llegar casi hasta, rayar en
**verification** [,verɪfɪ'keʃən] *s* verificación
**veri·fy** ['verɪ,faɪ] *v* (*pret & pp* **-fied**) *tr* verificar, comprobar; (law) afirmar bajo juramento

**verily** ['verɪli] *adv* verdaderamente, en verdad
**veritable** ['vɛrɪtəbəl] *adj* verdadero
**vermicelli** [ˌvʌrmɪ'sɛli] *s* fideos
**vermilion** [vər'mɪljən] *adj* bermejo || *s* bermellón *m*
**vermin** ['vʌrmɪn] *ssg* (*objectionable person*) sabandija || *spl* (*objectionable animals or persons*) sabandijas
**vermouth** [vər'muθ] o ['vʌrmuθ] *s* vermú *m*
**vernacular** [vər'nækjələr] *adj* vernáculo || *s* lenguaje vernáculo; idioma *m* corriente; (*language peculiar to a class or profession*) jerga
**veronica** [və'rɑnɪkə] *s* (bot & taur) verónica; lienzo de la Verónica
**Versailles** [vɛr'saɪ] *s* Versalles
**versatile** ['vʌrsətɪl] *adj* (*person*) de muchas habilidades; (*informed on many subjects*) polifacético, universal; (*device or tool*) útil para muchas cosas
**verse** [vʌrs] *s* verso; (*in the Bible*) versículo
**versed** [vʌrst] *adj* versado; **to become versed in** versarse en
**versification** [ˌvʌrsɪfɪ'keʃən] *s* versificación
**versi•fy** ['vʌrsɪˌfaɪ] *v* (*pret & pp* **-fied**) *tr & intr* versificar
**version** ['vʌrʒən] *s* versión
**ver•so** ['vʌrso] *s* (*pl* **-sos**) (*e.g., of a coin*) reverso; (typ) verso
**versus** ['vʌrsəs] *prep* contra
**verte•bra** ['vʌrtɪbrə] *s* (*pl* **-brae** [ˌbri] o **-bras**) vértebra
**vertebrate** ['vʌrtɪˌbret] *adj & s* vertebrado
**ver•tex** ['vʌrtɛks] *s* (*pl* **-texes** o **-tices** [tɪˌsiz]) (*top, summit*) ápice *m*; (geom) vértice *m*
**vertical** ['vʌrtɪkəl] *adj & s* vertical *f*
**vertical hold** *s* (telv) bloqueo vertical
**vertical rudder** *s* (aer) timón *m* de dirección
**verti•go** ['vʌrtɪˌgo] *s* (*pl* **-gos** o **-goes**) vértigo
**verve** [vʌrv] *s* brío, ánimo, vigor *m*
**very** ['veri] *adj* mismísimo; (*sheer, utter*) mero, puro; (*actual*) verdadero || *adv* muy; mucho, p.ej., **to be very hungry** tener mucha hambre
**vesicle** ['vɛsɪkəl] *s* vesícula
**vesper** ['vɛspər] *s* tarde *f*, caída de la tarde; oración de la tarde; canción de la tarde; **vespers** (eccl) vísperas || **Vesper** *s* Véspero
**vesper bell** *s* campana que llama a vísperas
**vessel** ['vɛsəl] *s* vasija, recipiente *m*; (*ship*) bajel *m*, embarcación, buque *m*; (anat) vaso
**vest** [vɛst] *s* (*of man's suit*) chaleco; (*jabot*) chorrera; (*undershirt*) camiseta || *tr* vestir; **to vest in** conceder (*p.ej., poder*) a; **to vest with** investir de || *intr* vestirse; **to vest in** pasar a
**vested interests** *spl* intereses creados
**vestibule** ['vɛstɪˌbjul] *s* vestíbulo, zaguán *m*
**vestige** ['vɛstɪdʒ] *s* vestigio
**vestment** ['vɛstmənt] *s* vestidura
**vest'-pock'et** *adj* de bolsillo, en miniatura; diminuto
**ves•try** ['vɛstri] *s* (*pl* **-tries**) sacristía; (*chapel*) capilla; junta parroquial; reunión de la junta parroquial
**vestry•man** ['vɛstrimən] *s* (*pl* **-men** [mən]) miembro de la junta parroquial
**Vesuvius** [vɪ'suvɪ·əs] o [vɪ'sjuvɪ·əs] *s* el Vesubio
**vet.** *abbr* **veteran, veterinary**
**vetch** [vɛtʃ] *s* arveja, veza; (*grass pea*) almorta
**veteran** ['vɛtərən] *adj & s* veterano
**veterinarian** [ˌvɛtərɪ'nɛrɪ·ən] *s* veterinario
**veterinar•y** ['vɛtərɪˌnɛri] *adj* veterinario || *s* (*pl* **-ies**) veterinario
**veterinary medicine** *s* veterinaria, medicina veterinaria
**ve•to** ['vito] *s* (*pl* **-toes**) veto || *tr* vetar
**vex** [vɛks] *tr* vejar, molestar
**vexation** [vɛk'seʃən] *s* vejación, molestia
**v.g.** *abbr* **verbi gratia** (Lat) **for example**
**via** ['vaɪ·ə] *prep* vía, p.ej., **via Lisbon** vía Lisboa
**viaduct** ['vaɪ·əˌdʌkt] *s* viaducto
**vial** ['vaɪ·əl] *s* redoma, frasco pequeño
**viati•cum** [vaɪ'ætɪkəm] *s* (*pl* **-cums** o **-ca** [kə]) (eccl) viático
**viand** ['vaɪ·ənd] *s* vianda, manjar *m*
**vibrate** ['vaɪbret] *tr & intr* vibrar
**vibration** [vaɪ'breʃən] *s* vibración
**vicar** ['vɪkər] *s* vicario
**vicarage** ['vɪkərɪdʒ] *s* casa del vicario; (*duties of vicar*) vicaría
**vicarious** [vaɪ'kɛrɪ·əs] o [vɪ'kɛrɪ·əs] *adj* substituto; (*punishment*) sufrido por otro; (*power, authority*) delegado; (*enjoyment*) reflejado
**vice** [vaɪs] *s* vicio
**vice'-ad'miral** *s* vicealmirante *m*
**vice'-pres'ident** *s* vicepresidente *m*
**viceroy** ['vaɪsrɔɪ] *s* virrey *m*
**vice versa** ['vaɪsi 'vʌrsə] o ['vaɪs 'vʌrsə] *adv* viceversa
**vicini•ty** [vɪ'sɪnɪti] *s* (*pl* **-ties**) vecindad
**vicious** ['vɪʃəs] *adj* vicioso; (*dog*) bravo; (*horse*) arisco
**victim** ['vɪktɪm] *s* víctima
**victimize** ['vɪktɪˌmaɪz] *tr* hacer víctima; engañar, estafar
**victor** ['vɪktər] *s* vencedor *m*
**victorious** [vɪk'torɪ·əs] *adj* victorioso
**victo•ry** ['vɪktəri] *s* (*pl* **-ries**) victoria
**victuals** ['vɪtəlz] *spl* vituallas, provisiones de boca
**vid.** *abbr* **vide** (Lat) **see**
**video signal** ['vɪdɪˌo] *s* señal *f* de vídeo
**video tape** *s* cinta grabada de televisión
**vid'eo-tape' recording** *s* videograbación
**vie** [vaɪ] *v* (*pret & pp* **vied**; *ger* **vying**) *intr* competir, emular, rivalizar
**Vien•nese** [ˌvi·ə'niz] *adj* vienés || *s* (*pl* **-nese**) vienés *m*
**Vietnam•ese** [vɪˌɛtnə'miz] *adj* vietnamés || *s* (*pl* **-ese**) vietnamés *m*
**view** [vju] *s* vista; (*purpose*) intento, propósito, vista; **to be on view** estar expuesto (*p.ej., un cadáver*); **to keep in view** no perder de vista; no olvi-

dar, tener presente; **to take a dim view of** no entusiasmarse por, mirar escépticamente; **with a view to** con vistas a || *tr* ver, mirar; considerar, contemplar; examinar, inspeccionar
**viewer** ['vju·ər] *s* espectador *m;* telespectador *m,* televidente *mf;* proyector *m* de transparencias; mirador *m* de transparencias
**view finder** *s* (phot) visor *m*
**view′point′** *s* punto de vista
**vigil** ['vɪdʒɪl] *s* vigilia; **to keep vigil** velar
**vigilance** ['vɪdʒɪləns] *s* vigilancia
**vigilant** ['vɪdʒɪlənt] *adj* vigilante
**vignette** [vɪn'jɛt] *s* viñeta
**vigor** ['vɪgər] *s* vigor *m*
**vigorous** ['vɪgərəs] *adj* vigoroso
**vile** [vaɪl] *adj* vil; (*disgusting*) asqueroso, repugnante; (*weather*) muy malo
**vili·fy** ['vɪlɪ,faɪ] *v* (*pret & pp* **-fied**) *tr* difamar, denigrar
**villa** ['vɪlə] *s* villa, quinta
**village** ['vɪlɪdʒ] *s* aldea
**villager** ['vɪlɪdʒər] *s* aldeano
**villain** ['vɪlən] *s* malvado; (*of a play*) malo, traidor *m*
**villainous** ['vɪlənəs] *adj* malvado
**villain·y** ['vɪləni] *s* (*pl* **-ies**) maldad, perfidia
**vim** [vɪm] *s* fuerza, brío, vigor *m*
**vinaigrette** [,vɪnə'grɛt] *s* vinagrera
**vinaigrette sauce** *s* vinagreta
**vindicate** ['vɪndɪ,ket] *tr* vindicar, exculpar
**vindictive** [vɪn'dɪktɪv] *adj* vengativo
**vine** [vaɪn] *s* (*creeping or climbing plant*) enredadera; (*grape plant*) vid *f,* parra
**vine′dress′er** *s* viñador *m,* viticultor *m*
**vinegar** ['vɪnɪgər] *s* vinagre *m*
**vinegarish** ['vɪnɪgərɪʃ] *adj* avinagrado
**vinegary** ['vɪnɪgəri] *adj* vinagroso
**vineyard** ['vɪnjərd] *s* viña, viñedo
**vineyardist** ['vɪnjərdɪst] *s* viñador *m,* viticultor *m*
**vintage** ['vɪntɪdʒ] *s* vendimia; vino de buena cosecha; (coll) categoría, clase *f*
**vintager** ['vɪntɪdʒər] *s* vendimiador *m*
**vintage wine** *s* vino de buena cosecha
**vintage year** *s* año de buen vino
**vintner** ['vɪntnər] *s* vinatero
**vinyl** ['vaɪnɪl] o ['vɪnɪl] *s* vinilo
**violate** ['vaɪ·ə,let] *tr* violar
**violence** ['vaɪ·ələns] *s* violencia
**violent** ['vaɪ·ələnt] *adj* violento
**violet** ['vaɪ·əlɪt] *adj* violado || *s* (*color*) violeta *m,* violado; (*dye*) violeta *m;* (bot) violeta *f*
**violin** [,vaɪ·ə'lɪn] *s* violín *m*
**violinist** [,vaɪ·ə'lɪnɪst] *s* violinista *mf*
**violoncellist** [,vaɪ·ələn'tʃɛlɪst] o [,viələn'tʃɛlɪst] *s* violoncelista *mf*
**violoncel·lo** [,vaɪ·ələn'tʃɛlo] o [,vi·ələn'tʃɛlo] *s* (*pl* **-los**) violoncelo
**viper** ['vaɪpər] *s* víbora
**vira·go** [vɪ'rego] *s* (*pl* **-goes** o **-gos**) mujer de mal genio
**virgin** ['vʌrdʒɪn] *adj & s* virgen *f*
**virgin birth** *s* parto virginal de María Santísima; (zool) partenogénesis *f*
**Virginia creeper** [vər'dʒɪnɪ·ə] *s* (bot) guau *m*
**virginity** [vər'dʒɪnɪti] *s* virginidad
**virility** [vɪ'rɪlɪti] *s* virilidad
**virology** [vaɪ'rɑlədʒi] *s* virología
**virtual** ['vʌrtʃʊ·əl] *adj* virtual
**virtue** ['vʌrtʃʊ] *s* virtud
**virtuosi·ty** [,vʌrtʃʊ'ɑsɪti] *s* (*pl* **-ties**) virtuosismo
**virtuo·so** [,vʌrtʃʊ'oso] *s* (*pl* **-sos** o **-si** [si]) virtuoso
**virtuous** ['vʌrtʃʊ·əs] *adj* virtuoso
**virulence** ['vɪrjələns] *s* virulencia
**virulent** ['vɪrjələnt] *adj* virulento
**virus** ['vaɪrəs] *s* virus *m*
**Vis.** *abbr* **Viscount**
**visa** ['vizə] *s* visa || *tr* visar
**visage** ['vɪzɪdʒ] *s* cara, semblante *m;* aspecto, apariencia
**vis-à-vis** [,vizə'vi] *adj* enfrentados || *adv* frente a frente || *prep* enfrente de; respecto de
**viscera** ['vɪsərə] *spl* vísceras
**viscount** ['vaɪkaunt] *s* vizconde *m*
**viscountess** ['vaɪkauntɪs] *s* vizcondesa
**viscous** ['vɪskəs] *adj* viscoso
**vise** [vaɪs] *s* tornillo, torno
**visé** ['vize] o [vi'ze] *s & tr* var de **visa**
**visible** ['vɪzɪbəl] *adj* visible
**Visigoth** ['vɪzɪ,gɑθ] *s* visigodo
**vision** ['vɪʒən] *s* visión; (*sense of sight*) vista
**visionar·y** ['vɪʒə,nɛri] *adj* visionario || *s* (*pl* **-ies**) visionario
**visit** ['vɪzɪt] *s* visita || *tr* visitar; afligir, acometer; enviar (*p.ej., castigo, venganza*) || *intr* hacer visitas; visitarse (*dos o más personas*)
**visitation** [,vɪzɪ'teʃən] *s* visitación; gracia del cielo, castigo del cielo
**visiting card** *s* tarjeta de visita
**visiting hours** *spl* horas de visita
**visiting nurse** *s* enfermera ambulante
**visitor** ['vɪsɪtər] *s* visitante *mf*
**visor** ['vaɪzər] *s* visera; (*disguise*) máscara
**vista** ['vɪstə] *s* vista, panorama *m*
**visual** ['vɪʒʊ·əl] *adj* visual
**visual acuity** *s* agudeza visual
**visualize** ['vɪʒʊ·ə,laɪz] *tr* representarse en la mente; hacer visible
**vital** ['vaɪtəl] *adj* vital; (*deadly*) mortal || **vitals** *spl* partes *fpl* vitales, órganos vitales
**vitality** [vaɪ'tælɪti] *s* vitalidad
**vitalize** ['vaɪtə,laɪz] *tr* vitalizar
**vitamin** ['vaɪtəmɪn] *s* vitamina
**vitiate** ['vɪʃɪ,et] *tr* viciar
**vitreous** ['vɪtrɪ·əs] *adj* vítreo
**vitriolic** [,vɪtrɪ'ɑlɪk] *adj* (chem) vitriólico; (fig) cáustico, mordaz
**vituperable** [vaɪ'tupərəbəl] o [vaɪ'tjupərəbəl] *adj* vituperable
**vituperate** [vaɪ'tupə,ret] o [vaɪ'tjupə,ret] *tr* vituperar
**viva** ['vivə] *interj* ¡viva! || *s* viva *m*
**vivacious** [vɪ'veʃəs] o [vaɪ'veʃəs] *adj* vivaz, vivaracho
**vivaci·ty** [vɪ'væsɪti] o [vaɪ'væsɪti] *s* (*pl* **-ties**) vivacidad, animación
**viva voce** ['vaɪvə 'vosi] *adv* de viva voz

**vivid** ['vɪvɪd] *adj* vivo (*intenso; brillante; expresivo*)
**vivi•fy** ['vɪvɪ,faɪ] *v* (*pret & pp* **-fied**) *tr* vivificar
**vivisection** [,vɪvɪ'sɛkʃən] *s* vivisección
**vixen** [vɪksən] *s* vulpeja; mujer regañona y colérica
**viz.** *abbr* **videlicet** (Lat) **namely, to wit**
**vizier** [vɪ'zɪr] o ['vɪzjər] *s* visir *m*
**vocabular•y** [vo'kæbjə,lɛri] *s* (*pl* **-ies**) vocabulario
**vocal** ['vokəl] *adj* vocal; (*inclined to express oneself freely*) expresivo
**vocalist** ['vokəlɪst] *s* vocalista *mf*
**vocation** [vo'keʃən] *s* vocación; empleo, ocupación
**vocative** ['vɑkətɪv] *s* vocativo
**vociferate** [vo'sɪfə,ret] *intr* vociferar
**vociferous** [vo'sɪfərəs] *adj* clamoroso, vocinglero
**vogue** [vog] *s* boga, moda; **in vogue** en boga, de moda
**voice** [vɔɪs] *s* voz *f;* **in a loud voice** en alta voz; **in a low voice** en voz baja; **with one voice** a una voz || *tr* expresar; sonorizar (*una consonante sorda*) || *intr* sonorizarse
**voiceless** ['vɔɪslɪs] *adj* sin voz; mudo; silencioso; (phonet) sordo
**void** [vɔɪd] *adj* (*empty*) vacío; (*useless*) vano; (law) inválido, nulo; **void of** desprovisto de || *s* vacío; (*gap*) hueco || *tr* vaciar; evacuar (*el vientre*); anular || *intr* excretar
**voile** [vɔɪl] *s* espumilla
**vol.** *abbr* **volume**
**volatile** ['vɑlətɪl] *adj* volátil
**volatilize** ['vɑlətɪ,laɪz] *tr* volatilizar || *intr* volatilizarse
**volcanic** [vɑl'kænɪk] *adj* volcánico
**volca•no** [vɑl'keno] *s* (*pl* **-noes** o **-nos**) volcán *m*
**volition** [və'lɪʃən] *s* voluntad; **of one's own volition** por su propia voluntad
**volley** ['vɑli] *s* (*of stones, bullets, etc.*) descarga, lluvia; (mil) descarga; (tennis) voleo || *tr & intr* volear
**vol'ley•ball'** *s* volibol *m*
**volplane** ['vɑl,plen] *s* vuelo planeado || *intr* planear
**volt** [volt] *s* voltio
**voltage** ['voltɪdʒ] *s* voltaje *m*
**voltage divider** *s* (rad) divisor *m* de voltaje
**voltaic** [vɑl'te•ɪk] *adj* voltaico
**volte-face** [vɔlt'fɑs] *s* cambio de dirección; cambio de opinión
**volt'me'ter** *s* voltímetro
**voluble** ['vɑljəbəl] *adj* locuaz, hablador
**volume** ['vɑljəm] *s* (*book; bulk; mass, e.g., of water*) volumen *m;* (*each book in a set*) tomo; (*degree of loudness*) volumen sonoro; (geom) volumen *m;* **to speak volumes** ser muy significativo; ser muy expresivo
**voluminous** [və'lumɪnəs] *adj* voluminoso
**voluntar•y** ['vɑlən,teri] *adj* voluntario || *s* (*pl* **-ies**) (eccl) solo de órgano
**volunteer** [,vɑlən'tɪr] *adj & s* voluntario || *tr* ofrecer (*sus servicios*) || *intr* ofrecerse; servir como voluntario; **to volunteer to** + *inf* ofrecerse a + *inf*
**voluptuar•y** [və'lʌptʃu,ɛri] *adj* voluptuoso || *s* (*pl* **-ies**) voluptuoso, sibarita *mf*
**voluptuous** [və'lʌptʃu•əs] *adj* voluptuoso
**volute** [və'lut] *s* voluta
**vomit** ['vɑmɪt] *s* vómito; (*emetic*) vomitivo || *tr & intr* vomitar
**voodoo** ['vudu] *adj* voduísta || *s* (*practice*) vodú *m;* (*person*) voduísta *mf*
**voracious** [və'reʃəs] *adj* voraz
**voracity** [və'ræsɪti] *s* voracidad
**vor•tex** ['vɔrtɛks] *s* (*pl* **-texes** o **-tices** [tɪ,siz]) vórtice *m*
**vota•ry** ['votəri] *s* (*pl* **-ries**) persona ligada por votos solemnes; aficionado, partidario
**vote** [vot] *s* (*formal expression of choice; right to vote; person who votes*) voto; (*act of voting; votes considered together*) votación; **to put to the vote** poner a votación; **to tally the votes** regular los votos || *tr* votar (*sí, no*); **to vote down** derrotar por votación; **to vote in** elegir por votación || *intr* votar
**vote getter** ['getər] *s* acaparador *m* de votos; (*slogan*) consigna que gana votos
**voter** ['votər] *s* votante *mf*
**voting machine** ['votɪŋ] *s* máquina registradora de votos
**votive** ['votɪv] *adj* votivo
**votive offering** *s* voto, exvoto
**vouch** [vaʊtʃ] *tr* garantizar || *intr* — **to vouch for** responder de (*una cosa*); responder por (*una persona*)
**voucher** ['vaʊtʃər] *s* garante *mf;* (*certificate*) comprobante *m*
**vouch•safe'** *tr* conceder, otorgar; permitir || *intr* — **to vouchsafe to** + *inf* dignarse + *inf*
**voussoir** [vu'swɑr] *s* dovela
**vow** [vaʊ] *s* voto; **to take vows** tomar el hábito religioso || *tr* votar (*p.ej., un cirio a la Virgen*); jurar (*venganza*) || *intr* votar; **to vow to** hacer votos de
**vowel** ['vaʊ•əl] *s* vocal *f*
**voyage** ['vɔɪ•ɪdʒ] *s* travesía, trayecto; (*any journey*) viaje *m* || *tr* atravesar (*p.ej., el mar*) || *intr* viajar
**voyager** ['vɔɪ•ɪdʒər] *s* pasajero, navegante *mf,* viajero
**V.P.** *abbr* **Vice-President**
**vs.** *abbr* **versus**
**Vul.** *abbr* **Vulgate**
**vulcanize** ['vʌlkə,naɪz] *tr* vulcanizar
**vulg.** *abbr* **vulgar**
**Vulg.** *abbr* **Vulgate**
**vulgar** ['vʌlgər] *adj* grosero; (*popular, common; vernacular*) vulgar
**vulgari•ty** [vʌl'gærɪti] *s* (*pl* **-ties**) grosería
**Vulgar Latin** *s* latín vulgar, latín rústico
**Vulgate** ['vʌlget] *s* Vulgata
**vulnerable** ['vʌlnərəbəl] *adj* vulnerable
**vulture** ['vʌltʃər] *s* buitre *m;* (*American vulture*) catartes *m,* aura (*buitre americano*)

# W

**W, w** [ˈdʌbəl ˌju] vigésima tercera letra del alfabeto inglés
**w** *abbr* **watt**
**w.** *abbr* **week, west, wide, wife**
**W.** *abbr* **Wednesday, west**
**wad** [wɑd] *s* (*of cotton*) bolita, tapón *m;* (*of papers*) fajo, lío; (*in a gun*) taco ‖ *v* (*pret & pp* **wadded;** *ger* **wadding**) *tr* emborrar, rellenar; atacar (*una escopeta*)
**waddle** [ˈwɑdəl] *s* anadeo ‖ *intr* anadear
**wade** [wed] *intr* andar sobre terreno cubierto de agua; andar descalzo por la orilla; chapotear (*los niños*) con los pies desnudos; **to wade into** (coll) embestir con violencia; (coll) meter el hombro a; **to wade through** (coll) avanzar con dificultad por; (coll) leer con dificultad
**wading bird** [ˈwedɪŋ] *s* ave zancuda
**wafer** [ˈwefər] *s* (*for sealing letters; pill*) oblea; (*thin, crisp cake*) hostia; (eccl) hostia
**waffle** [ˈwɑfəl] *s* barquillo
**waffle iron** *s* barquillero
**waft** [wæft] o [wɑft] *tr* llevar por el aire; llevar por encima del agua ‖ *intr* flotar
**wag** [wæg] *s* (*of head*) meneo; (*of tail*) coleada; (*jester*) bromista *mf* ‖ *v* (*pret & pp* **wagged;** *ger* **wagging**) *tr* menear (*la cabeza, la cola*) ‖ *intr* menearse
**wage** [wedʒ] *s* salario; **wages** galardón *m*, premio ‖ *tr* hacer (*la guerra*)
**wage earner** [ˈʌrnər] *s* asalariado
**wager** [ˈwedʒər] *s* apuesta; **to lay a wager** hacer una apuesta ‖ *tr & intr* apostar
**wage′work′er** *s* asalariado
**waggish** [ˈwægɪʃ] *adj* divertido, gracioso; (*person*) bromista
**Wagnerian** [vɑgˈnɪrɪ·ən] *adj & s* vagneriano
**wagon** [ˈwægən] *s* carro, furgón *m*, carretón *m;* **on the wagon** (slang) sin tomar bebidas alcohólicas; **to hitch one's wagon to a star** poner el tiro muy alto
**wag′tail′** *s* aguanieves *m*, aguzanieves *m*
**waif** [wef] *s* (*foundling*) expósito; animal extraviado o abandonado; (*stray child*) granuja *m*
**wail** [wel] *s* gemido, lamento ‖ *intr* gemir, lamentar
**wain·scot** [ˈwenskət] o [ˈwenskɑt] *s* arrimadillo, friso de madera ‖ *v* (*pret & pp* **-scoted** o **-scotted;** *ger* **-scoting** o **-scotting**) *tr* poner arrimadillo o friso de madera a
**waist** [west] *s* (*of human body; corresponding part of garment*) talle *m*, cintura; (*garment*) corpiño, jubón *m*, blusa
**waist′band′** *s* pretina
**waist′cloth′** *s* taparrabo
**waistcoat** [ˈwestˌkot] o [ˈwɛskət] *s* chaleco
**waist′line′** *s* cintura
**wait** [wet] *s* espera; **to have a good wait** (coll) esperar sentado; **to lie in wait for** acechar emboscado ‖ *tr* — **to wait one's turn** esperar vez ‖ *intr* esperar, aguardar; **to wait for** esperar, aguardar; **to wait on** atender, despachar (*a los parroquianos en una tienda*); servir (*a una persona a la mesa*); **to wait until** esperar a que
**waiter** [ˈwetər] *s* camarero, mozo de restaurante; (*tray*) bandeja
**waiting list** *s* lista de espera
**waiting room** *s* (*of station*) sala de espera; (*of doctor's office*) antesala
**waitress** [ˈwetrɪs] *s* camarera, moza de restaurante
**waive** [wev] *tr* renunciar a (*un derecho*); diferir, poner a un lado
**waiver** [ˈwevər] *s* renuncia
**wake** [wek] *s* (*watch by the body of a dead person*) velatorio; (*of a boat or other moving object*) estela; **in the wake of** siguiendo inmediatamente; de resultas de ‖ *v* (*pret* **waked** o **woke** [wok]; *pp* **waked**) *tr* despertar ‖ *intr* — **to wake to** darse cuenta de; **to wake up** despertar
**wakeful** [ˈwekfəl] *adj* desvelado
**wakefulness** [ˈwekfəlnɪs] *s* desvelo
**waken** [ˈwekən] *tr & intr* despertar
**wale** [wel] *s* verdugón *m*
**Wales** [welz] *s* Gales, el país de Gales
**walk** [wɔk] *s* (*act*) paseo; (*distance*) caminata; (*way of walking, bearing*) andar *m*, paso; (*of a horse*) andadura; (*place to walk animals*) cercado; empleo, cargo, carrera; **at a walk** al paso de una persona; **to go for a walk** salir a pasear; **to take a walk** dar un paseo ‖ *tr* pasear (*a un niño, un caballo*); caminar (*recorrer caminando*); hacer ir al paso (*un caballo*); **to walk off** quitarse (*p.ej., un dolor de cabeza*) caminando ‖ *intr* andar, caminar, ir a pie; (*to stroll*) pasear; **to walk away from** alejarse caminando de; **to walk off with** cargar con, llevarse; **to walk out** salir repentinamente; declararse en huelga; **to walk out on** (coll) dejar airadamente
**walkaway** [ˈwɔkəˌwe] *s* (coll) triunfo fácil
**walker** [ˈwɔkər] *s* caminante *mf;* (*pedestrian*) peatón *m;* (*gocart*) andaderas
**walkie-talkie** [ˈwɔkiˈtɔki] *s* (rad) transmisor-receptor *m* portátil
**walking papers** *spl* (coll) despedida de un empleo
**walking stick** *s* bastón *m*
**walk′-on′** *s* (theat) parte *f* de por medio
**walk′out′** *s* (coll) huelga
**walk′o′ver** *s* (coll) triunfo fácil
**wall** [wɔl] *s* muro; (*between rooms; of a pipe, boiler, etc.*) pared *f;* (*of a*

*fortification*) muralla; **to drive to the wall** poner entre la espada y la pared; **to go to the wall** rendirse; fracasar || *tr* murar, amurallar (*una ciudad, un castillo*); emparedar (*a un criminal*); **to wall up** cerrar con muro

**wall'board'** *s* cartón *m* tabla

**wallet** ['walɪt] *s* cartera de bolsillo

**wall'flow'er** *s* alhelí *m;* **to be a wallflower** (coll) comer pavo, planchar el asiento

**Walloon** [wa'lun] *adj & s* valón *m*

**wallop** ['waləp] *s* (coll) golpazo, puñetazo || *tr* (coll) golpear fuertemente; (coll) vencer cabalmente

**wallow** ['walo] *s* revuelco; (*place*) revolcadero || *intr* revolcarse; (*e.g., in wealth*) nadar

**wall'pa'per** *s* papel *m* de empapelar, papel pintado || *tr* empapelar

**walnut** ['wɔlnət] *s* (*tree and wood*) nogal *m;* nuez *f* de nogal

**walrus** ['wɔlrəs] o ['walrəs] *s* morsa

**Walter** ['wɔltər] *s* Gualterio

**waltz** [wɔlts] *s* vals *m* || *tr* hacer valsar; (coll) conducir directamente || *intr* valsar

**wan** [wan] *adj* (*comp* **wanner;** *super* **wannest**) pálido, macilento; débil

**wand** [wand] *s* vara; (*of deviner or magician*) varilla de virtudes

**wander** ['wandər] *tr* recorrer a la ventura || *intr* errar, vagar; extraviarse, perderse; **to wander around** errar de una parte a otra

**wanderer** ['wandərər] *s* vagabundo; peregrino

**wan'der·lust'** *s* ansia de viajar

**wane** [wen] *s* decadencia, declinación; menguante *f* de la luna; **on the wane** decayendo, declinando; menguando (*la luna*) || *intr* decaer, declinar; menguar (*la luna*)

**wangle** ['wæŋgəl] *tr* (*to obtain by scheming*) (coll) mamar o mamarse; (coll) adulterar, falsear (*cuentas*); **to wangle one's way out of** (coll) salir con maña de || *intr* (*to get along by scheming*) (coll) sacudirse

**want** [want] o [wɔnt] *s* deseo; necesidad; carencia; **for want of** a falta de; **to be in want** pasar necesidad || *tr* desear; necesitar; carecer de || *intr* desear; **to want for** necesitar; carecer de

**want ad** *s* anuncio clasificado

**wanton** ['wantən] *adj* inconsiderado, desconsiderado; insensible, perverso; disoluto, licencioso; lascivo; cabezudo

**war** [wɔr] *s* guerra; **to go to war** declarar la guerra; (*as a soldier*) ir a la guerra; **to wage war** hacer la guerra || *v* (*pret & pp* **warred;** *ger* **warring**) *intr* guerrear; **to war on** guerrear con, hacer la guerra a

**warble** ['wɔrbəl] *s* gorjeo, trino || *intr* gorjear, trinar

**warbler** ['wɔrblər] *s* pájaro cantor; curruca de cabeza negra

**war cloud** *s* amenaza de guerra

**ward** [wɔrd] *s* (*person, usually a minor, under protection of another*) pupilo; (*guardianship*) custodia, tutela; (*of a city*) barrio, distrito; (*of a hospital*) cuadra, crujía; (*of a lock*) guarda || *tr* — **to ward off** parar, desviar

**warden** ['wɔrdən] *s* guardián *m;* (*of a jail*) alcaide *m,* carcelero; (*of a church*) capiller *m;* (*in charge of fire prevention*) vigía *m*

**ward heeler** *s* muñidor *m*

**ward'robe'** *s* (*closet or cabinet for holding clothes*) guardarropa *m;* (*stock of clothing for a person*) vestuario; (theat) guardarropía

**wardrobe trunk** *s* baúl ropero

**ward'room'** *s* (nav) cámara de oficiales

**ware** [wɛr] *s* loza; **wares** efectos, artículos de comercio, mercancías

**war effort** *s* esfuerzo bélico

**ware'house'** *s* almacén *m;* (*for furniture*) guardamuebles *m*

**warehouse·man** ['wɛr,hausmən] *s* (*pl* **-men** [mən]) almacenista *m;* guardaalmacén *m*

**war'fare'** *s* guerra

**war'head'** *s* punta de combate

**war horse** *s* corcel *m* de guerra; (coll) veterano

**warily** ['wɛrɪli] *adv* cautelosamente

**wariness** ['wɛrɪnɪs] *s* cautela

**war'like'** *adj* guerrero

**war loan** *s* empréstito de guerra

**war lord** *s* jefe *m* militar

**warm** [wɔrm] *adj* (*being moderately hot*) caliente; (*neither hot nor cold*) templado; (*clothing*) abrigador; (*climate, region*) caluroso; (*color*) cálido; (fig) caluroso, cordial; **to be warm** (*said of a person*) tener calor; (*said of the weather*) hacer calor || *tr* calentar, acalorar; (fig) animar, acalorar; **to warm up** recalentar (*p.ej., la comida*); hacer más amistoso || *intr* calentarse; **to warm up** templar (*el tiempo*); (*with work or exercise*) acalorarse; **to warm up to** cobrar afecto a

**warm-blooded** ['wɔrm'blʌdɪd] *adj* apasionado, ardiente; (*animals*) de sangre caliente

**war memorial** *s* monumento a los caídos

**warmer** ['wɔrmər] *s* calentador *m*

**warm-hearted** ['wɔrm'hartɪd] *adj* afectuoso, de buen corazón

**warming pan** *s* mundillo

**warmonger** ['wɔr,mʌŋgər] *s* belicista *mf*

**war mother** *s* madrina de guerra

**warmth** [wɔrmθ] *s* calor *m;* ardor *m,* entusiasmo; cordialidad

**warm'-up'** *s* calentón *m*

**warn** [wɔrn] *tr* advertir, avisar; (*to exhort*) amonestar; (*to advise*) aconsejar

**warning** *adj* de aviso || *s* advertencia, aviso

**War of the Roses** *s* guerra de las dos Rosas

**warp** [wɔrp] *s* (*of a fabric*) urdimbre *f;* (*of a board*) comba, alabeo; aberración mental; (naut) espía || *tr* combar, alabear; pervertir (*el juicio* *de una persona*); (naut) mover con espía ‖ *intr* combarse, alabearse; (naut) espiar

**war'path'** *s* — **to be on the warpath** prepararse para la guerra; estar buscando pendencia

**war'plane'** *s* avión *m* de guerra

**warrant** ['wɑrənt] o ['wɔrənt] *s* garantía, promesa; (*for arrest*) orden *f* de prisión; (*before a judge*) citación; cédula, certificado ‖ *tr* garantizar, prometer; autorizar; justificar

**warrantable** ['wɑrəntəbəl] o ['wɔrəntəbəl] *adj* garantizable; justificable

**warrant officer** *s* suboficial *m* de las clases

**warren** ['wɑrən] o ['wɔrən] *s* (*where rabbits breed*) conejera; barrio densamente poblado

**warrior** ['wɔrjər] o ['wɑrjər] *s* guerrero

**Warsaw** ['wɔrsɔ] *s* Varsovia

**war'ship'** *s* buque *m* de guerra

**wart** [wɔrt] *s* verruga

**war'time'** *s* tiempo de guerra

**war'-torn'** *adj* devastado por la guerra

**war to the death** *s* guerra a muerte

**war•y** ['wɛri] *adj* (*comp* **-ier;** *super* **-iest**) cauteloso

**wash** [wɑʃ] o [wɔʃ] *s* lavado; (*clothes washed or to be washed*) jabonado; (*dirty water*) lavazas; loción; (*place where surf breaks*) batiente *m;* (aer) estela turbulenta ‖ *tr* lavar; fregar (*los platos*); bañar, mojar; **to wash away** quitar lavando; derrubiar (*las aguas corrientes la tierra de las riberas*) ‖ *intr* lavarse; lavar la ropa; batir (*el agua*); derrubiarse

**washable** ['wɑʃəbəl] o ['wɔʃəbəl] *adj* lavable

**wash and wear** *adj* de lava y pon

**wash'ba'sin** *s* jofaina, palangana

**wash'bas'ket** *s* cesto de la colada

**wash'board'** *s* lavadero, tabla de lavar; (*baseboard*) rodapié *m*

**wash'bowl'** *s* jofaina, palangana

**wash'cloth'** *s* paño para lavarse

**wash'day'** *s* día *m* de la colada

**washed-out** ['wɑʃt‚aʊt] o ['wɔʃt‚aʊt] *adj* desteñido; (coll) debilitado, rendido

**washed-up** ['wɑʃt‚ʌp] o ['wɔʃt‚ʌp] *adj* (coll) agotado, deslomado

**washer** ['wɑʃər] o ['wɔʃər] *s* lavador *m;* (*machine*) lavadora; (*ring of metal placed under head of bolt*) arandela; (*ring of rubber, etc. to keep a spigot from leaking*) zapatilla; (phot) lavador

**wash'er•wom'an** *s* (*pl* **-wom'en**) lavandera

**wash goods** *spl* tejidos lavables

**washing** ['wɑʃɪŋ] o ['wɔʃɪŋ] *s* (*act of washing; washed clothes or clothes to be washed*) lavado; **washings** (*dirty water; abraded material*) lavadura

**washing machine** *s* lejiadora, lavadora mecánica

**washing soda** *s* sal *f* de sosa

**wash'out'** *s* derrubio; derrumbe *m;* (coll) desilusión, fracaso

**wash'rag'** *s* paño para lavarse; paño de cocina

**wash'room'** *s* gabinete *m* de aseo, lavabo

**wash'stand'** *s* lavamanos *m*

**wash'tub'** *s* cuba de colada, tina de lavar

**wash water** *s* lavazas

**wasp** [wɑsp] *s* avispa

**waste** [west] *s* derroche *m,* desgaste *m;* (*garbage*) basura, despojo; (*wild region*) despoblado, yermo; (*of time*) pérdida; (*useless by-products*) desperdicios; excremento; (*for wiping machinery*) hilacha de algodón; **to lay waste** devastar, poner a fuego y sangre ‖ *tr* malgastar, perder ‖ *intr* — **to waste away** consumirse

**waste'bas'ket** *s* papelera

**wasteful** ['westfəl] *adj* derrochador, manirroto; devastador, destructivo

**waste paper** *s* papeles usados, papel de desecho, papel viejo

**waste pipe** *s* tubo de desagüe

**waste products** *spl* desperdicios; materia excretada

**wastrel** ['westrəl] *s* derrochador *m,* malgastador *m;* pródigo, perdido

**watch** [wɑtʃ] *s* reloj *m* (*de bolsillo o de pulsera*); (*lookout*) vigía *m;* (mil) vigilia; (naut) guardia; **to be on the watch for** estar a la mira de; **to keep watch over** velar ‖ *tr* (*to look at*) mirar; (*to oversee*) velar, vigilar; guardar; tener cuidado con ‖ *intr* mirar; (*to keep awake*) velar; **to watch for** acechar; **to watch out** tener cuidado; **to watch out for** estar a la mira de; tener cuidado con; guardarse de; **to watch over** velar, vigilar

**watch'case'** *s* caja de reloj

**watch charm** *s* dije *m*

**watch crystal** *s* cristal *m* de reloj

**watch'dog'** *s* perro de guarda, perro guardián; (fig) guardián *m* fiel

**watchful** ['wɑtʃfəl] *adj* desvelado, vigilante

**watchfulness** ['wɑtʃfəlnɪs] *s* desvelo, vigilancia

**watch'mak'er** *s* relojero

**watch•man** ['wɑtʃmən] *s* (*pl* **-men** [mən]) vigilante *m,* velador *m*

**watch night** *s* noche vieja; oficio de noche vieja

**watch pocket** *s* relojera

**watch strap** *s* pulsera

**watch'tow'er** *s* atalaya, vigía

**watch'word'** *s* santo y seña; (*slogan*) lema *m*

**water** ['wɔtər] o ['wɑtər] *s* agua; **of the first water** de lo mejor; **to back water** ciar; **to carry water on both shoulders** nadar entre dos aguas; **to fish in troubled waters** pescar en río revuelto; **to hold water** (coll) ser bien fundado; **to make water** (*to urinate*) hacer aguas; (naut) hacer agua; **to pour** o **throw cold water on** echar un jarro de agua (fría) a ‖ *tr* regar, rociar; abrevar (*el ganado*); aguar (*el vino*); proveer de agua ‖ *intr*

abrevarse (*el ganado*); tomar agua (*una locomotora*); llorar (*los ojos*)
**water carrier** *s* aguador *m*
**water closet** *s* excusado, retrete *m*, váter *m*
**water color** *s* acuarela
**wa'ter•course'** *s* corriente *f* de agua; lecho de corriente
**water cress** *s* berzo
**water cure** *s* cura de aguas
**wa'ter•fall'** *s* cascada, caída de agua
**water front** *s* terreno ribereño
**water gap** *s* garganta, hondonada
**water hammer** *s* golpe *m* de ariete
**water heater** *s* calentador *m* de agua
**water ice** *s* sorbete *m*
**watering can** *s* regadera
**watering place** *s* aguadero; balneario
**watering pot** *s* regadera
**watering trough** *s* abrevadero
**water jacket** *s* camisa de agua
**water lily** *s* ninfea, nenúfar *m*
**water line** *s* línea de agua, línea de flotación; nivel *m* de agua
**water main** *s* cañería de agua
**wa'ter•mark'** *s* (*in paper*) filigrana; marca de nivel de agua
**wa'ter•mel'on** *s* sandía
**water meter** *s* contador *m* de agua
**water pipe** *s* cañería de agua
**water polo** *s* polo de agua
**water power** *s* fuerza de agua, hulla blanca
**wa'ter•proof'** *adj* & *s* impermeable *m*
**wa'ter•shed'** *s* divisoria de aguas; (*drainage area*) cuenca
**water ski** *s* esquí acuático
**wa'ter•spout'** *s* (*to carry water from roof*) canalón *m*; (*funnel of wet air extending from cloud to surface of water*) manga de agua, tromba marina
**wa'ter-sup•ply' system** *s* fontanería
**wa'ter•tight'** *adj* estanco, hermético; (fig) seguro
**water tower** *s* arca de agua
**water wagon** *s* (mil) carro de agua; **on the water wagon** (slang) sin tomar bebidas alcohólicas
**wa'ter•way'** *s* vía de agua, vía fluvial; (naut) canalizo
**water wheel** *s* rueda de agua; turbina de agua; (*of steamboat*) rueda de paletas
**water wings** *spl* nadaderas
**wa'ter•works'** *s* estación de bombas
**watery** ['wɔtəri] o ['wɑtəri] *adj* acuoso; (*said of the eyes*) lagrimoso, lloroso; insípido; húmedo, mojado
**watt** [wɑt] *s* vatio
**wattage** ['wɑtɪdʒ] *s* vatiaje *m*
**watt'-hour'** *s* (*pl* **watt-hours**) vatiohora
**wattle** ['wɑtəl] *s* (*of bird*) barba; (*of fish*) barbilla
**watt'me'ter** *s* vatímetro
**wave** [wev] *s* onda; (*of hair*) onda, ondulación; (*e.g., of heat or cold*) ola; (*e.g., of strikes*) oleaje *m*; señal hecha con la mano ‖ *tr* blandir (*la espada*); ondear, ondular (*el cabello*); hacer señal con (*la mano*); decir (*adiós*) con la mano; **to wave aside** rechazar ‖ *intr* ondear u ondearse; hacer señal con la mano
**wave motion** *s* movimiento ondulatorio
**waver** ['wevər] *intr* oscilar; (*to hesitate*) vacilar, titubear; (*to totter*) tambalear
**wav•y** ['wevi] *adj* (*comp* **-ier**; *super* **-iest**) undoso, ondoso; (*water*) ondulado; (*hair*) ondeado
**wax** [wæks] *s* cera; **to be wax in one's hands** ser como una cera ‖ *tr* encerar; cerotear (*el hilo*) ‖ *intr* hacerse, volverse; crecer (*la luna*)
**wax paper** *s* papel encerado, papel parafinado
**wax taper** *s* cerilla
**wax'works'** *s* museo de cera
**way** [we] *s* vía, camino; dirección, sentido; manera, modo; costumbre, hábito; **across the way** enfrente; **a good way** un buen trecho; **all the way** hasta el fin del camino; **any way** de cualquier modo; **by the way** a propósito; **in a way** hasta cierto punto; **in every way** en todos respectos; **in this way** de este modo; **on the way to** camino de, rumbo a; **on the way out** saliendo; desapareciendo; **out of the way** hecho, despachado; inconveniente, impropio; a un lado, apartado; fuera de lo común; **that way** por allí; de ese modo; **this way** por aquí; de este modo; **to be in the way** estorbar; **to feel one's way** tantear el camino; proceder con tiento; **to force one's way** abrirse paso por fuerza; **to get out of the way** quitarse de en medio; (*to finish*) quitarse de encima; **to give way** ceder, retroceder; romperse (*una cuerda*); fracasar; **to give way to** entregarse a; **to go out of one's way** dar un rodeo; dar un rodeo innecesario; darse molestia; **to have one's way** salirse con la suya; **to keep out of the way** no obstruir el paso; **to know one's way around** saber entendérselas; **to know one's way to** conocer el camino a, saber ir a; **to lead the way** enseñar el camino; ir o entrar primero; **to lose one's way** perder el camino, extraviarse; **to make one's way** avanzar; hacer carrera, acreditarse; **to make way for** dar paso a, hacer lugar para; **to mend one's ways** mudar de vida; **to not know which way to turn** no saber dónde meterse; **to put out of the way** alejar, apartar; quitar de en medio; **to see one's way to** ver el modo de; **to take one's way** irse, marcharse; **to wend one's way** seguir camino; **to wind one's way through** serpentear por; **to wing one's way** ir volando; **under way** en marcha, en camino; **way in** entrada; **way out** salida; **ways** maneras, modales *mpl*; (*for launching a ship*) anguilas; **which way?** ¿por dónde?; ¿cómo?
**way'bill'** *s* hoja de ruta
**wayfarer** ['we ˌfɛrər] *s* caminante *mf*
**way'lay'** *v* (*pret & pp* **-laid'**) *tr* detener de improviso; (*to attack from ambush*) insidiar, asaltar

**way′side′** *s* borde *m* del camino; **to fall by the wayside** (*to disappear*) caer en el camino; fracasar
**way station** *s* apeadero
**way train** *s* tren *m* ómnibus
**wayward** ['wewərd] *adj* díscolo, voluntarioso; voltario, caprichoso
**w.c.** *abbr* **water closet, without charge**
**we** [wi] *pron pers* nosotros
**weak** [wik] *adj* débil, flaco; (*vowel; verb*) débil
**weaken** ['wikən] *tr* debilitar, enflaquecer || *intr* debilitarse, enflaquecerse
**weakling** ['wiklɪŋ] *s* alfeñique *m,* canijo
**weak-minded** ['wik'maɪndɪd] *adj* irresoluto; simple, mentecato
**weakness** ['wiknɪs] *s* debilidad, flaqueza; lado débil; afición, gusto
**weal** [wil] *s* verdugón *m*
**wealth** [wɛlθ] *s* riqueza
**wealth•y** ['wɛlθi] *adj* (*comp* **-ier;** *super* **-iest**) rico
**wean** [win] *tr* destetar; **to wean away from** apartar gradualmente de
**weanling** ['winlɪŋ] *adj & s* destetado
**weapon** ['wɛpən] *s* arma
**wear** [wɛr] *s* (*act of wearing*) uso; (*clothing*) ropa; estilo, moda; (*wasting away from use*) desgaste *m,* deterioro; (*lasting quality*) durabilidad; **for all kinds of wear** a todo llevar; **for everyday wear** para todo trote || *v* (*pret* **wore** [wor]; *pp* **worn** [worn]) *tr* llevar, traer, llevar puesto; calzar (*cierto tamaño de zapato o guante*); (*to waste away by use*) desgastar, deteriorar; (*to tire*) agotar, cansar; **to wear out** consumir, gastar; agotar, cansar; abusar de (*la hospitalidad de una persona*) || *intr* desgastarse, deteriorarse; **to wear off** pasar, desaparecer; **to wear out** gastarse, usarse; **to wear well** durar, ser duradero
**wear and tear** *s* uso y desgaste
**weariness** ['wɪrɪnɪs] *s* cansancio; aburrimiento
**wearing apparel** ['wɛrɪŋ] *s* ropaje *m,* prendas de vestir
**wearisome** ['wɪrɪsəm] *adj* aburrido, cansado, fastidioso
**wea•ry** ['wɪri] *adj* (*comp* **-rier;** *super* **-riest**) cansado || *v* (*pret & pp* **-ried**) *tr* cansar || *intr* cansarse
**weasel** ['wizəl] *s* comadreja
**weaseler** ['wizələr] *s* pancista *mf*
**weasel words** *spl* palabras ambiguas
**weather** ['wɛðər] *s* tiempo; mal tiempo; **to be under the weather** (coll) no estar muy católico; (coll) estar borracho || *tr* aguantar (*el temporal, la adversidad*)
**weather-beaten** ['wɛðər ˌbitən] *adj* curtido por la intemperie
**weather bureau** *s* meteo *f,* servicio meteorológico
**weath′er•cock′** *s* veleta; (*fickle person*) (fig) veleta
**weather forecasting** *s* pronóstico del tiempo, previsión del tiempo
**weather•man** ['wɛðər ˌmæn] *s* (*pl* **-men** [ˌmɛn]) meteorologista *m,* pronosticador *m* del tiempo
**weather report** *s* parte meteorológico
**weather stripping** ['strɪpɪŋ] *s* burlete *m,* cierre hermético
**weather vane** *s* veleta
**weave** [wiv] *s* tejido || *v* (*pret* **wove** [wov] o **weaved;** *pp* **wove** o **woven** ['wovən]) *tr* tejer; **to weave one's way** avanzar zigzagueando || *intr* tejer; zigzaguear
**weaver** ['wivər] *s* tejedor *m*
**web** [wɛb] *s* tejido, tela; (*of spider*) tela; (*between toes of birds and other animals*) membrana; (*of an iron rail*) alma; (fig) tejido, tela, enredo
**web-footed** ['wɛb ˌfutɪd] *adj* palmípedo, de pie palmeado
**wed** [wɛd] *v* (*pret & pp* **wed** o **wedded;** *ger* **wedding**) *tr* (*to join in marriage*) casar; casarse con || *intr* casarse
**wedding** ['wɛdɪŋ] *adj* nupcial || *s* bodas, nupcias, matrimonio
**wedding cake** *s* pastel *m* de boda
**wedding day** *s* día *m* de bodas
**wedding march** *s* marcha nupcial
**wedding night** *s* noche *f* de bodas
**wedding ring** *s* anillo nupcial
**wedge** [wɛdʒ] *s* cuña || *tr* acuñar, apretar con cuña
**wed′lock′** *s* matrimonio
**Wednesday** ['wɛnzdi] *s* miércoles *m*
**wee** [wi] *adj* pequeñito, diminuto
**weed** [wid] *s* mala hierba; (coll) tabaco; **weeds** ropa de luto (*especialmente, de una viuda*) || *tr* desherbar, escardar
**weeding hoe** *s* escardillo
**weed killer** *s* matamalezas *m,* herbicida *m*
**week** [wik] *s* semana; **week in week out** semana tras semana
**week′day′** *s* día *m* laborable
**week′end′** *s* fin *m* de semana || *intr* pasar el fin de semana
**week•ly** ['wikli] *adj* semanal || *adv* cada semana || *s* (*pl* **-lies**) revista semanal, semanario
**weep** [wip] *v* (*pret & pp* **wept** [wɛpt]) *tr* llorar (*p.ej., la muerte de una persona*); derramar (*lágrimas*) || *intr* llorar
**weeper** ['wipər] *s* llorón *m;* (*hired mourner*) llorona, plañidera
**weeping willow** *s* sauce *m* llorón
**weep•y** ['wipi] *adj* (*comp* **-ier;** *super* **-iest**) (coll) lloroso
**weevil** ['wivəl] *s* gorgojo
**weft** [wɛft] *s* (*yarns running across warp*) trama; (*fabric*) tejido
**weigh** [we] *tr* pesar; (naut) levantar (*el ancla*) || *intr* pesar; **to weigh in** pesarse (*un jockey*)
**weight** [wet] *s* peso; (*of scales, clock, gymnasium, etc.*) pesa; **to lose weight** rebajar de peso; **to put on weight** ponerse gordo; **to throw one's weight around** (coll) hacer valer su poder || *tr* cargar, gravar; (*statistically*) ponderar
**weightless** ['wetlɪs] *adj* ingrávido
**weightlessness** ['wetlɪsnɪs] *s* ingravidez *f.*
**weight•y** ['weti] *adj* (*comp* **-ier;** *super*

-iest) (*heavy*) pesado; (*troublesome*) gravoso; importante, influyente
**weir** [wɪr] *s* presa, vertedero; (*for catching fish*) pescadera
**weird** [wɪrd] *adj* misterioso, sobrenatural, espectral; extraño, raro
**welcome** ['wɛlkəm] *adj* bienvenido; grato, agradable; **you are welcome** (*i.e., gladly received*) sea Vd. bienvenido; (*in answer to thanks*) no hay de qué; **you are welcome to it** está a la disposición de Vd.; **you are welcome to your opinion** piense Vd. lo que quiera || *interj* ¡bienvenido! || *s* bienvenida, buena acogida || *tr* dar la bienvenida a; acoger con gusto, recibir con amabilidad
**weld** [wɛld] *s* autógena; (bot) gualda || *tr* soldar con autógena; (fig) unir || *intr* soldarse
**welder** ['wɛldər] *s* soldador *m;* (*machine*) soldadora
**welding** ['wɛldɪŋ] *s* autógena, soldadura autógena
**wel'fare'** *s* bienestar *m;* (*effort to improve living conditions of the underprivileged*) asistencia, beneficencia; **to be on welfare** vivir de la asistencia pública
**welfare state** *s* gobierno socializante, estado de beneficencia
**well** [wɛl] *adj* bien; bien de salud || *adv* bien; pues; pues bien; **as well** también; **as well as** así como; además de || *interj* ¡vaya! || *s* pozo; (*natural source of water*) fuente *f,* manantial *m* || *intr* — **to well up** salir a borbotones
**well-appointed** ['wɛlə'pɔɪntɪd] *adj* bien amueblado, bien equipado
**well-attended** ['wɛlə'tɛndɪd] *adj* muy concurrido
**well-behaved** ['wɛlbɪ'hevd] *adj* de buena conducta
**well'-be'ing** *s* bienestar *m*
**well'born'** *adj* bien nacido
**well-bred** ['wɛl'brɛd] *adj* cortés, bien criado
**well-disposed** ['wɛldɪs'pozd] *adj* bien dispuesto
**well-done** ['wɛl'dʌn] *adj* bien hecho; (*meat*) bien asado
**well-fixed** ['wɛl'fɪkst] *adj* (coll) acaudalado
**well-formed** ['wɛl'fɔrmd] *adj* bien formado; (*nose*) perfilado
**well-founded** ['wɛl'faʊndɪd] *adj* bien fundado
**well-groomed** ['wɛl'grumd] *adj* de mucho aseo, atildado
**well-heeled** ['wɛl'hild] *adj* (coll) acomodado; **to be well-heeled** (coll) tener bien cubierto el riñón
**well-informed** ['wɛlɪn'fɔrmd] *adj* versado, bien enterado
**well-intentioned** ['wɛlɪn'tɛnʃənd] *adj* bien intencionado
**well-kept** ['wɛl'kɛpt] *adj* bien cuidado, bien atendido; (*secret*) bien guardado
**well-known** ['wɛl'non] *adj* bien conocido; familiar
**well-meaning** ['wɛl'minɪŋ] *adj* bien intencionado
**well-nigh** ['wɛl'naɪ] *adv* casi
**well'-off'** *adj* adinerado, acaudalado
**well-preserved** ['wɛlprɪ'zʌrvd] *adj* bien conservado
**well-read** ['wɛl'rɛd] *adj* leído, muy leído
**well-spent** ['wɛl'spɛnt] *adj* (*money, youth, life*) bien empleado
**well-spoken** ['wɛl'spokən] *adj* (*person*) bienhablado; (*word*) bien dicho
**well'spring'** *s* fuente *f,* manantial *m;* fuente inagotable
**well sweep** *s* cigoñal *m*
**well-tempered** ['wɛl'tɛmpərd] *adj* bien templado
**well-thought-of** ['wɛl'θɔt,ɑv] *adj* bien mirado
**well-timed** ['wɛl'taɪmd] *adj* oportuno
**well-to-do** ['wɛltə'du] *adj* adinerado, acaudalado
**well-wisher** ['wɛl'wɪʃər] *s* amigo, favorecedor *m*
**well-worn** ['wɛl'worn] *adj* trillado, vulgar
**welsh** [wɛlʃ] *intr* (slang) dejar de cumplir; **to welsh on** (slang) dejar de cumplir con || **Welsh** *adj* galés || *s* (*language*) galés *m;* **the Welsh** los galeses
**Welsh·man** ['wɛlʃmən] *s* (*pl* **-men** [mən]) galés *m*
**Welsh rabbit** o **rarebit** ['rɛrbɪt] *s* tostada cubierta de queso derretido en cerveza
**welt** [wɛlt] *s* (*finish along a seam*) ribete *m;* (*of a shoe*) vira; (*wale from a blow*) verdugón *m*
**welter** ['wɛltər] *s* confusión, conmoción; (*a tumbling about*) revuelco || *intr* revolcar
**wel'ter·weight'** *s* (box) peso mediano ligero
**wen** [wɛn] *s* lobanillo
**wench** [wɛntʃ] *s* muchacha, jovencita; moza, criada
**wend** [wɛnd] *tr* — **to wend one's way** dirigir sus pasos, seguir su camino
**west** [wɛst] *adj* occidental, del oeste || *adv* al oeste, hacia el oeste || *s* oeste *m*
**western** ['wɛstərn] *adj* occidental || *s* película del Oeste
**West Indies** ['ɪndiz] *spl* Indias Occidentales
**westward** ['wɛstwərd] *adv* hacia el oeste
**wet** [wɛt] *adj* (*comp* **wetter;** *super* **wettest**) mojado; (*damp*) húmedo; (*paint*) fresco; (*weather*) lluvioso; (coll) antiprohibicionista || *s* (coll) antiprohibicionista *mf* || *v* (*pret & pp* **wet** o **wetted;** *ger* **wetting**) *tr* mojar || *intr* mojarse
**wet'back'** *s* mojado
**wet battery** *s* pila húmeda
**wet blanket** *s* aguafiestas *mf*
**wet goods** *spl* caldos
**wet nurse** *s* ama de cría o de leche
**w.f.** *abbr* **wrong font**
**w.g.** *abbr* **wire gauge**
**whack** [hwæk] *s* (coll) golpe ruidoso;

(coll) prueba, tentativa || *tr* (coll) golpear ruidosamente

**whale** [hwel] *s* ballena; (*sperm whale*) cachalote *m;* **a whale at** (coll) un as de; **a whale for** (coll) un genio para; **a whale of a difference** (coll) una enorme diferencia; **a whale of a meal** (coll) una comida brutal || *tr* (coll) azotar || *intr* pescar ballenas

**whale'bone'** *s* ballena

**wharf** [hwɔrf] *s* (*pl* **wharves** [hwɔrvz] o **wharfs**) muelle *m,* embarcadero

**what** [hwɑt] *pron interr* qué; cuál; **what else?** ¿qué más?; **what if . . .?** ¿y si . . .?, ¿qué le parece si?; **what of it?** ¿qué importa? || *pron rel* lo que; **what's what** lo que hay, toda la verdad || *adj interr* qué || *adj rel* el . . . que, la . . . que, etc. || *interj* qué; **what a . . .!** qué . . . más o tan, p.ej., **what a beautiful day!** ¡qué día más (o tan) hermoso!

**what·ev'er** *pron* cualquiera; todo lo que || *adj* cualquier; cualquier . . . que

**what'not'** *s* juguetero

**what's-his-name** ['hwɑtsɪz,nem] *s* (coll) el señor fulano

**wheal** [hwil] *s* roncha

**wheat** [hwit] *s* trigo

**wheedle** ['hwidəl] *tr* engatusar; conseguir por medio de halagos

**wheel** [hwil] *s* rueda; (coll) bicicleta; **at the wheel** en el volante || *tr* pasear (*a un niño*) en un cochecito; conducir (*a un enfermo*) en una silla de ruedas || *intr* (coll) ir en bicicleta; **to wheel about** o **around** dar una vuelta; cambiar de opinión

**wheelbarrow** ['hwil,bæro] *s* carretilla

**wheel base** *s* batalla, paso, distancia entre ejes

**wheel chair** *s* silla de ruedas, cochecillo para inválidos

**wheeler-dealer** ['hwilər'dilər] *s* (slang) negociante *m* de gran influencia e independencia

**wheel horse** *s* caballo de varas; (fig) esclavo (*el que trabaja mucho y cumple con sus obligaciones*)

**wheelwright** ['hwil,raɪt] *s* carpintero de carretas

**wheeze** [hwiz] *s* resuello ruidoso || *intr* resollar produciendo un silbido

**whelp** [hwɛlp] *s* cachorro || *intr* parir

**when** [hwɛn] *adv* cuándo || *conj* cuando

**whence** [hwɛns] *adv* de dónde; por lo tanto || *conj* de donde

**when·ev'er** *conj* siempre que, cada vez que

**where** [hwɛr] *adv* dónde; adónde || *conj* donde; adonde

**whereabouts** ['hwɛrə,baʊts] *s* paradero

**whereas** [hwɛr'æz] *conj* mientras que, al paso que; considerando || *s* considerando

**where·by'** *adv* por medio del cual

**wherefore** ['hwɛrfor] *adv* por qué, para qué; por eso, por tanto || *conj* por lo cual || *s* motivo, razón *f*

**where·from'** *adv* de donde

**where·in'** *adv* dónde, en qué || *conj* donde; en el que; en lo cual

**where·of'** *adv* de qué || *conj* de que; de lo cual

**where'up·on'** *adv* con lo cual, después de lo cual

**wherever** [hwɛr'ɛvər] *conj* dondequiera que

**wherewithal** ['hwɛrwɪð,ɔl] *s* cumquibus *m,* medios

**whet** [hwɛt] *v* (*pret & pp* **whetted;** *ger* **whetting**) *tr* afilar, aguzar; despertar, estimular; abrir (*el apetito*)

**whether** ['wɛðər] *conj* si; **whether or no** en todo caso, de todas maneras; **whether or not** si . . . o no, ya sea que . . . o no

**whet'stone'** *s* piedra de afilar

**whey** [hwe] *s* suero de la leche

**which** [hwɪtʃ] *pron interr* cuál; **which is which** cuál es el uno y cuál el otro || *pron rel* que, el (la, etc.) que || *adj interr* qué; cuál, cuál de los (las) || *adj rel* el (la, etc.) . . . que

**which·ev'er** *pron rel* cualquiera || *adj rel* cualquier; **whichever ones** cualesquiera

**whiff** [hwɪf] *s* soplo; fumada; olorcillo; acceso, arranque *m;* **to get a whiff of** percibir un olor fugaz de || *intr* soplar (*el viento*); echar bocanadas (*el que fuma*)

**while** [hwaɪl] *conj* mientras, mientras que || *s* rato; **a long while** largo rato; **a while ago** hace un rato; **between whiles** de vez en cuando || *tr* — **to while away** entretener (*el tiempo*); pasar (*p.ej., la tarde*) de un modo entretenido

**whim** [hwɪm] *s* capricho, antojo

**whimper** ['hwɪmpər] *s* lloriqueo || *tr* decir lloriqueando || *intr* lloriquear

**whimsical** ['hwɪmzɪkəl] *adj* caprichoso, extravagante, fantástico

**whine** [hwaɪn] *s* gimoteo, quejido || *intr* gimotear, quejarse

**whin·ny** ['hwɪni] *s* (*pl* **-nies**) relincho || *v* (*pret & pp* **-nied**) *intr* relinchar

**whip** [hwɪp] *s* látigo, zurriago; huevos batidos con nata || *v* (*pret & pp* **whipped** o **whipt;** *ger* **whipping**) *tr* azotar, zurriagar, fustigar; batir (*huevos y nata*); (coll) derrotar, vencer; **to whip off** (coll) escribir de prisa; **to whip out** sacar de repente; **to whip up** (coll) preparar de prisa; (coll) avivar, excitar

**whip'cord'** *s* tralla; tejido fuerte con costurones diagonales

**whip hand** *s* mano *f* del látigo; (*upper hand*) vara alta

**whip'lash'** *s* tralla

**whipped cream** *s* nata, crema batida

**whipper-snapper** ['hwɪpər,snæpər] *s* arrapiezo, mequetrefe *m*

**whippet** ['hwɪpɪt] *s* perro lebrel

**whipping boy** ['hwɪpɪŋ] *s* cabeza de turco, víctima inocente

**whipping post** *s* poste *m* de flagelación

**whippoorwill** [,hwɪpər'wɪl] *s* chotacabras norteamericano (*Caprimulgus vociferus*)

**whir** [hwʌr] *s* zumbido || *v* (*pret & pp*

**whirred;** *ger* **whirring)** *intr* girar zumbando
**whirl** [hwʌrl] *s* vuelta, giro; remolino; (*of events, parties, etc.*) serie *f* interminable || *tr & intr* remolinear; **my head whirls** siento vértigo
**whirligig** [ˈhwʌrlɪ,gɪg] *s* (ent) escribano del agua; tíovivo; (*pinwheel*) rehilandera, molinete *m;* peonza
**whirl'pool'** *s* remolino, vorágine *f*
**whirl'wind'** *s* torbellino, manga de viento
**whirlybird** [ˈhwʌrli,bʌrd] *s* (coll) helicóptero
**whish** [hwɪʃ] *s* zumbido suave || *intr* zumbar suavemente
**whisk** [hwɪsk] *s* escobilla; toque ligero || *tr* barrer, cepillar; **to whisk out of sight** escamotear || *intr* moverse rápidamente
**whisk broom** *s* escobilla
**whiskers** [ˈhwɪskərz] *spl* barbas; (*on side of face*) patillas; (*of cat*) bigotes *mpl*
**whiskey** [ˈhwɪski] *adj* (*voice*) (coll) aguardentoso || *s* whisky *m*
**whisper** [ˈhwɪspər] *s* cuchicheo; (*of leaves*) susurro; **in a whisper** en voz baja || *tr* susurrar, decir al oído || *intr* cuchichear, hablar al oído; susurrar (*p.ej., las hojas*); (*to gossip*) susurrar, murmurar
**whisperer** [ˈhwɪspərər] *s* susurrón *m*
**whispering** [ˈhwɪspərɪŋ] *adj & s* (*gossiping*) susurrón *m*
**whist** [hwɪst] *s* whist *m* (*juego de naipes*)
**whistle** [ˈhwɪsəl] *s* (*sound*) silbido, silbo; (*device*) silbato, pito; **to wet one's whistle** (coll) remojar la palabra || *tr* silbar (*p.ej., una canción*) || *intr* silbar; **to whistle for** llamar con un silbido; (coll) tener que componérselas sin
**whistle stop** *s* apeadero, pueblecito
**whit** [hwɪt] *s* — **not a whit** ni pizca; **to not care a whit** no importarle a (*uno*) un bledo
**white** [hwaɪt] *adj* blanco || *s* blanco; (*of an egg*) clara; **whites** (pathol) pérdidas blancas, flujo blanco
**white'caps'** *spl* cabrillas, palomas
**white coal** *s* hulla blanca
**white'-col'lar** *adj* oficinesco
**white feather** *s* — **to show the white feather** mostrarse cobarde
**white goods** *spl* tejidos de algodón; ropa blanca; aparatos electrodomésticos
**white-haired** [ˈhwaɪt,herd] *adj* de pelo blanco; (*gray-haired*) cano; (coll) favorito, predilecto
**white heat** *s* blanco, calor blanco; (fig) viva agitación
**white lead** [led] *s* albayalde *m*
**white lie** *s* mentirilla, mentira inocente u oficiosa
**white meat** *s* pechuga, carne *f* de la pechuga del ave
**whiten** [ˈhwaɪtən] *tr* blanquear, emblanquecer || *intr* blanquear, emblanquecerse; palidecer
**whiteness** [ˈhwaɪtnɪs] *s* blancura
**white plague** *s* peste blanca (*tuberculosis*)
**white slavery** *s* trata de blancas
**white tie** *s* corbatín blanco; traje *m* de etiqueta
**white'wash'** *s* jalbegue *m,* lechada; (*e.g., of a scandal*) encubrimiento || *tr* jalbegar, enjalbegar, encalar; absolver sin justicia; encubrir (*un escándalo*)
**whither** [ˈhwɪðər] *adv* adónde || *conj* adonde
**whitish** [ˈhwaɪtɪʃ] *adj* blanquecino, blancuzco
**whitlow** [ˈhwɪtlo] *s* panadizo, uñero
**Whitsuntide** [ˈhwɪtsən,taɪd] *s* semana de Pentecostés
**whittle** [ˈhwɪtəl] *tr* sacar pedazos a (*un trozo de madera*); **to whittle away o down** reducir poco a poco
**whiz** o **whizz** [hwɪz] *s* silbido, zumbido; (slang) perito, fenómeno || *v* (*pret & pp* **whizzed;** *ger* **whizzing)** *intr* — **to whiz by** rehilar, silbar; pasar como una flecha
**who** [hu] *pron interr* quién; **who else?** ¿quién más?; **who goes there?** (mil) ¿quién vive?; **who's who** quién es el uno y quién el otro; quiénes son gente de importancia || *pron rel* que, quien; el (la, etc.) que
**whoa** [hwo] o [wo] *interj* ¡so!
**who•ev'er** *pron rel* quienquiera que, cualquiera que
**whole** [hol] *adj* todo, entero; (*intact*) ileso; (*not scattered or dispersed*) único, p.ej., **the whole interest for him was the child he was raising** el único interés para él era el niño que educaba; **made out of the whole cloth** enteramente falso o imaginario || *s* conjunto, todo; **as a whole** en conjunto; **on the whole** en general; por la mayor parte
**wholehearted** [ˈhol,hɑrtɪd] *adj* sincero, cordial
**whole note** *s* (mus) semibreve *f*
**whole'sale'** *adj & adv* al por mayor || *s* venta al por mayor || *tr* vender al por mayor || *intr* vender al por mayor; venderse al por mayor
**wholesaler** [ˈhol,selər] *s* comerciante *mf* al por mayor
**wholesome** [ˈholsəm] *adj* (*conducive to good health*) saludable; (*in good health*) fresco, rollizo
**wholly** [ˈholi] *adv* enteramente, completamente
**whom** [hum] *pron interr* a quién || *pron rel* que, a quien; al (a la, etc.) que
**whom•ev'er** *pron rel* a quienquiera que
**whoop** [hup] o [hwup] *s* ululato || *tr* — **to whoop it up** (slang) armar una gritería || *intr* ulular
**whooping cough** [ˈhupɪŋ] o [ˈhupɪŋ] *s* tos ferina, tos convulsiva
**whopper** [ˈhwɑpər] *s* (coll) enormidad; (coll) mentirón *m*
**whopping** [ˈhwɑpɪŋ] *adj* (coll) enorme, grandísimo
**whore** [hor] *s* puta || *intr* — **to whore around** putañear, putear

**whortleber•ry** ['hwʌrtəl,beri] *s* (*pl* **-ries**) arándano
**whose** [huz] *pron interr* de quién || *pron rel* de quien, cuyo
**why** [hwaɪ] *adv* por qué; **why not?** ¿cómo no? || *s* (*pl* **whys**) porqué *m* || *interj* ¡toma!; **why, certainly!** ¡desde luego!, ¡por supuesto!; **why, yes!** ¡claro!, ¡pues sí!
**wick** [wɪk] *s* mecha, pabilo
**wicked** ['wɪkɪd] *adj* malo; (*mischievous*) travieso, revoltoso; (*vicious*) arisco; ofensivo
**wicker** ['wɪkər] *adj* mimbroso || *s* mimbre *m & f*
**wicket** ['wɪkɪt] *s* (*small door in a larger one*) portillo, postigo; (*small opening in a door*) ventanillo; (*ticket window*) taquilla; (*gate to regulate flow of water*) compuerta; (cricket) meta; (croquet) aro
**wide** [waɪd] *adj* ancho; de ancho; (*sense of a word*) amplio, lato || *adv* de par en par; enteramente; lejos; **wide of the mark** lejos del blanco; fuera de propósito
**wide'-an'gle** *adj* granangular
**wide'-a•wake'** *adj* despabilado
**widen** ['waɪdən] *tr* ensanchar || *intr* ensancharse
**wide'-o'pen** *adj* abierto de par en par; **to be wide-open** estar (*p.ej., una ciudad*) abierta a los jugadores
**wide'spread'** *adj* (*arms, wings*) extendido; difundido, extenso
**widow** ['wɪdo] *s* viuda; (cards) baceta || *tr* dejar viuda
**widower** ['wɪdo•ər] *s* viudo
**widowhood** ['wɪdo,hʊd] *s* viudez *f*
**widow's mite** *s* limosna que da un pobre
**widow's pension** *s* viudedad
**widow's weeds** *spl* luto de viuda
**width** [wɪdθ] *s* anchura
**wield** [wild] *tr* esgrimir, manejar (*la espada*); ejercer (*el poder*)
**wife** [waɪf] *s* (*pl* **wives** [waɪvz]) esposa, mujer *f*
**wig** [wɪg] *s* peluca
**wiggle** ['wɪgəl] *s* meneo rápido || *tr* menear rápidamente || *intr* menearse rápidamente
**wig'wag'** *s* comunicación con banderas || *v* (*pret & pp* **-wagged**; *ger* **-wagging**) *tr* menear; mandar (*informes*) moviendo banderas || *intr* menearse; señalar con banderas
**wigwam** ['wɪgwɑm] *s* choza cónica (*de los pieles rojas*)
**wild** [waɪld] *adj* (*not domesticated; growing without cultivation; uncivilized*) salvaje; (*unrestrained*) descabellado; (*frantic, mad*) frenético; (*riotous*) desenfrenado, revoltoso; extravagante; (*bullet, shot*) perdido; **wild about** loco por || *adv* disparatadamente; **to run wild** crecer locamente; estar sin gobierno || *s* desierto, yermo; **wilds** monte *m*, despoblado
**wild boar** *s* jabalí *m*
**wild card** *s* comodín *m*
**wild'cat'** *s* gato montés; lince *m*; empresa arriesgada
**wildcat strike** *s* huelga no autorizada por el sindicato
**wilderness** ['wɪldərnɪs] *s* desierto, yermo
**wild'fire'** *s* fuego fatuo; fucilazo; **to spread like wildfire** ser un reguero de pólvora, correr como pólvora en reguero
**wild flower** *s* flor *f* del campo
**wild goose** *s* ganso bravo
**wild'-goose' chase** *s* caza de grillos
**wild'life'** *s* animales *mf* salvajes
**wild oats** *spl* excesos de la juventud, mocedad; **to sow one's wild oats** llevar (*los mozos*) una vida de excesos
**wild olive** *s* acebuche *m*
**wile** [waɪl] *s* ardid *m*, engaño; (*cunning*) astucia || *tr* engatusar; **to wile away** entretener (*el tiempo*); pasar (*p.ej., la tarde*)
**will** [wɪl] *s* voluntad; (law) testamento; **at will** a voluntad || *tr* querer; (*to bequeath*) legar || *intr* querer; **do as you will** haga Vd. lo que quiera || *v* (*pret & cond* **would**) *v aux* **he will arrive at six o'clock** llegará a las seis; **he will go for days without smoking** pasa días enteros sin fumar
**willful** ['wɪlfəl] *adj* voluntarioso
**willfulness** ['wɪlfəlnɪs] *s* voluntariedad
**William** ['wɪljəm] *s* Guillermo
**willing** ['wɪlɪŋ] *adj* dispuesto; gustoso, pronto; espontáneo; **willing or unwilling** que quiera, que no quiera
**willingly** ['wɪlɪŋli] *adv* de buena gana, de buena voluntad
**willingness** ['wɪlɪŋnɪs] *s* buena gana, buena voluntad
**will-o'-the-wisp** ['wɪləðə'wɪsp] *s* fuego fatuo; ilusión, quimera
**willow** ['wɪlo] *s* sauce *m*
**willowy** ['wɪlo•i] *adj* (*pliant*) juncal, mimbreño; (*slender, graceful*) juncal, cimbreño, esbelto; lleno de sauces
**will power** *s* fuerza de voluntad
**willy-nilly** ['wɪli'nɪli] *adv* de grado o por fuerza
**wilt** [wɪlt] *tr* marchitar || *intr* marchitarse
**wil•y** ['waɪli] *adj* (*comp* **-ier**; *super* **-iest**) artero, engañoso; astuto
**wimple** ['wɪmpəl] *s* griñón *m*, impla
**win** [wɪn] *s* (coll) éxito, triunfo || *v* (*pret & pp* **won** [wʌn]; *ger* **winning**) *tr* ganar; **to win over** ganar, conquistar || *intr* ganar; **to win out** ganar; (coll) tener éxito
**wince** [wɪns] *s* sobresalto || *intr* sobresaltarse
**winch** [wɪntʃ] *s* maquinilla, torno; (*handle, crank*) manubrio
**wind** [wɪnd] *s* viento; (*gas in intestines*) (coll) viento; (*breath*) respiración, resuello; **to break wind** ventosear; **to get wind of** saber de, tener noticia de; **to sail close to the wind** (naut) ceñir el viento; **to take the wind out of one's sails** apagarle a uno los fuegos || *tr* dejar sin aliento || [waɪnd] *v* (*pret & pp* **wound**

[waʊnd]) *tr* (*to coil; to wrap up*) arrollar, envolver; devanar (*alambre*); ovillar (*hilo*); torcer (*hebras*); hacer girar (*un manubrio*); dar cuerda a (*un reloj*); **to wind one's way through** serpentear por; **to wind up** arrollar, envolver; (coll) poner punto final a || *intr* serpentear (*un camino*)
**windbag** ['wɪnd,bæg] *s* (*of bagpipe*) odre *m;* (coll) charlatán *m,* palabrero
**windbreak** ['wɪnd,brek] *s* guardavientos *m*
**wind cone** [wɪnd] *s* (aer) cono de viento
**winded** ['wɪndɪd] *adj* falto de respiración, sin resuello
**windfall** ['wɪnd,fɔl] *s* fruta caída del árbol; fortunón *m,* cosa llovida del cielo
**winding sheet** ['waɪndɪŋ] *s* sudario, mortaja
**winding stairs** *spl* escalera de caracol
**wind instrument** [wɪnd] *s* (mus) instrumento de viento
**windlass** ['wɪndləs] *s* maquinilla, torno
**windmill** ['wɪnd,mɪl] *s* (*mill operated by wind*) molino de viento; (*modern wind-driven source of power*) aeromotor *m;* (*pinwheel*) molinete *m;* **to tilt at windmills** luchar con los molinos de viento
**window** ['wɪndo] *s* ventana; (*of ticket office; of envelope*) ventanilla; (*of coach, automobile*) ventanilla, portezuela
**window dresser** *s* escaparatista *mf*
**window dressing** *s* adorno de escaparates
**window frame** *s* marco de ventana
**win'dow•pane'** *s* cristal *m* o vidrio de ventana
**window screen** *s* alambrera, sobrevidriera
**window shade** *s* visillo, transparente *m* de resorte
**win'dow-shop'** *v* (*pret & pp* **-shopped;** *ger* **-shopping**) *intr* mirar los escaparates sin comprar
**window shutter** *s* contraventana
**window sill** *s* repisa de ventana
**windpipe** ['wɪnd,paɪp] *s* tráquea
**windshield** ['wɪnd,ʃild] *s* parabrisa *m*
**windshield washer** *s* lavaparabrisas *m*
**windshield wiper** *s* limpiaparabrisas *m*
**wind sock** *s* (aer) cono de viento
**windstorm** ['wɪnd,stɔrm] *s* ventarrón *m*
**wind-up** ['waɪnd,ʌp] *s* conclusión; (sport) final *f* de partido
**windward** ['wɪndwərd] *s* barlovento; **to turn to windward** barloventear
**Windward Islands** *spl* islas de Barlovento
**Windward Passage** *s* paso de los Vientos
**wind•y** ['wɪndi] *adj* (*comp* **-ier;** *super* **-iest**) ventoso; (*unsubstantial*) vacío; palabrero, ampuloso; **it is windy** hace viento
**wine** [waɪn] *s* vino || *tr* obsequiar con vino || *intr* beber vino
**wine cellar** *s* bodega
**wine'glass'** *s* copa para vino
**winegrower** ['waɪn,gro•ər] *s* vinicultor *m*
**winegrowing** ['waɪn,gro•ɪŋ] *s* vinicultura
**wine press** *s* lagar *m*
**winer•y** ['waɪnəri] *s* (*pl* **-ies**) lagar *m*
**wine'skin'** *s* odre *m*
**winetaster** ['waɪn,testər] *s* catavinos *m*
**wing** [wɪŋ] *s* ala; facción, bando; (theat) bastidor *m;* **to take wing** alzar el vuelo || *tr* herir en el ala; **to wing one's way** avanzar volando
**wing chair** s sillón *m* de orejas
**wing collar** *s* cuello de pajarita
**wing nut** *s* tuerca de aletas
**wing'spread'** *s* envergadura
**wink** [wɪŋk] *s* guiño; **to not sleep a wink** no pegar los ojos; **to take forty winks** (coll) descabezar el sueño || *tr* guiñar (*el ojo*) || *intr* guiñar; (*to blink*) parpadear, pestañear; **to wink at** guiñar el ojo a; fingir no ver
**winner** ['wɪnər] *s* ganador *m,* vencedor *m;* premiado
**winning** ['wɪnɪŋ] *adj* triunfante, victorioso; atrayente, simpático || **winnings** *spl* ganancias
**winnow** ['wɪno] *tr* aventar; entresacar || *intr* aletear
**winsome** ['wɪnsəm] *adj* atrayente, simpático, engañador; alegre
**winter** ['wɪntər] *adj* invernal || *s* invierno || *intr* invernar
**win'ter•green'** *s* gaulteria, té *m* del Canadá; esencia de gaulteria
**win•try** ['wɪntri] *adj* (*comp* **-trier;** *super* **-triest**) invernal, invernizo; helado, frío
**wipe** [waɪp] *tr* frotar para limpiar; enjugar (*la cara, el sudor, las manos*); **to wipe away** enjugar (*lágrimas*); **to wipe off** quitar frotando; **to wipe out** (coll) borrar, cancelar; (coll) aniquilar, destruir; (coll) enjugar (*deudas, un déficit*)
**wiper** ['waɪpər] *s* paño, trapo; (elec) contacto deslizante
**wire** [waɪr] *s* (*thread of metal*) alambre *m;* telégrafo; telegrama *m;* teléfono; **to pull wires** (coll) tocar resortes || *tr* alambrar; telegrafiar || *intr* telegrafiar
**wire cutter** *s* cortaalambres *m*
**wire entanglement** *s* (mil) alambrado
**wire gauge** *s* calibrador *m* de alambre
**wire-haired** ['waɪr,herd] *adj* de pelo áspero
**wireless** ['waɪrlɪs] *adj* inalámbrico, sin hilos
**wire nail** *s* punta de París, clavo de alambre
**wire pulling** ['pʊlɪŋ] *s* (coll) empleo de resortes
**wire recorder** *s* grabadora de alambre
**wire screen** *s* alambrera, tela de alambre
**wire'tap'** *v* (*pret & pp* **-tapped;** *ger* **-tapping**) *tr* intervenir (*una conversación telefónica*)
**wiring** ['waɪrɪŋ] *s* (elec) alambraje *m*
**wir•y** ['waɪri] *adj* (*comp* **-ier;** *super*

-iest) alambrino; cimbreante; nervudo; vibrante

**wisdom** ['wɪzdəm] *s* sabiduría, cordura

**wisdom tooth** *s* muela cordal, muela del juicio

**wise** [waɪz] *adj* sabio, cuerdo; (*step, decision*) acertado, juicioso; **to be wise to** (slang) conocer el juego de; **to get wise** (coll) caer en el chiste ‖ *s* modo, manera; **in no wise** de ningún modo

**wiseacre** ['waɪz,ekər] *s* sabihondo

**wise'crack'** *s* (slang) cuchufleta ‖ *intr* (slang) cuchufletear

**wise guy** *s* (slang) sabelotodo

**wish** [wɪʃ] *s* deseo; **to make a wish** pensar algo que se desea ‖ *tr* desear; dar (*los buenos días*) ‖ *intr* desear; **to wish for** desear, anhelar

**wish'bone'** *s* espoleta, hueso de la suerte

**wishful** ['wɪʃfəl] *adj* deseoso

**wishful thinking** *s* optimismo a ultranza; **to indulge in wishful thinking** forjarse ilusiones

**wistful** ['wɪstfəl] *adj* melancólico, tristón, pensativo

**wit** [wɪt] *s* agudeza; (*person*) chistoso; (*keen mental power*) juicio; **to be at one's wits' end** no saber qué hacer; **to have the wit to** tener el tino de; **to live by one's wits** vivir del cuento

**witch** [wɪtʃ] *s* bruja, hechicera; (*old hag*) bruja

**witch'craft'** *s* brujería

**witches' Sabbath** *s* aquelarre *m*

**witch hazel** *s* (*shrub*) nogal *m* de la brujería, planta del sortilegio; (*liquid*) hamamelina, hazelina

**with** [wɪð] o [wɪθ] *prep* con; de

**with•draw'** *v* (*pret* **-drew;** *pp* **-drawn)** *tr* retirar ‖ *intr* retirarse

**withdrawal** [wɪð'drɔ•əl] o [wɪθ'drɔ•əl] *s* retirada

**wither** ['wɪðər] *tr* marchitar; (fig) aplastar, confundir ‖ *intr* marchitarse; confundirse

**with•hold'** *v* (*pret & pp* **-held)** *tr* retener; suspender (*pago*); negar (*un permiso*)

**withholding tax** *s* impuesto deducido del sueldo

**with•in'** *adv* dentro ‖ *prep* dentro de; al alcance de; poco menos de; con un margen de

**with•out'** *adv* fuera ‖ *prep* fuera de; (*lacking, not with*) sin; **to do without** pasar sin; **without** + *ger* sin + *inf,* p.ej., **he left without saying goodbye** salió sin despedirse; sin que + *subj,* p.ej., **he came in without anyone seeing him** entró sin que nadie le viese

**with•stand'** *v* (*pret & pp* **-stood)** *tr* aguantar, resistir

**witness** ['wɪtnɪs] *s* testigo *mf;* **in witness whereof** en fe de lo cual; **to bear witness** dar testimonio ‖ *tr* (*to be present at*) presenciar; (*to attest*) atestiguar, testimoniar; firmar como testigo

**witness stand** *s* banquillo o estrado de los testigos

**witticism** ['wɪtɪ,sɪzəm] *s* agudeza, dicho agudo, ocurrencia

**wittingly** ['wɪtɪŋli] *adv* a sabiendas

**wit•ty** ['wɪti] *adj* (*comp* **-tier;** *super* **-tiest)** agudo, ingenioso; (*person*) ocurrente, chistoso

**wizard** ['wɪzərd] *s* brujo, hechicero; (coll) as *m,* experto

**wizardry** ['wɪzərdri] *s* hechicería, magia

**wizened** ['wɪzənd] *adj* acartonado, arrugado

**wk.** *abbr* **week**

**w.l.** *abbr* **wave length**

**woad** [wod] *s* hierba pastel

**wobble** ['wɑbəl] *s* bamboleo, tambaleo ‖ *intr* bambolear, tambalear; bailar (*una silla*); (fig) vacilar, ser inconstante

**wob•bly** ['wɑbli] *adj* (*comp* **-blier;** *super* **-bliest)** bamboleante, inseguro; vacilante

**woe** [wo] *s* aflicción, miseria, infortunio ‖ *interj* — **woe is me!** ¡ay de mí!

**woebegone** ['wobɪ,gɔn] o ['wobɪ,gɑn] *adj* cariacontecido, triste

**woeful** ['wofəl] *adj* triste, miserable; (*of poor quality*) malo, pésimo

**wolf** [wulf] *s* (*pl* **wolves** [wulvz]) lobo; persona cruel, persona mañosa; (coll) tenorio; **to cry wolf** dar falsa alarma; **to keep the wolf from the door** ponerse a cubierto del hambre ‖ *tr & intr* comer vorazmente, engullir

**wolf'hound'** *s* galgo lobero

**wolfram** ['wulfrəm] *s* (*element*) volframio; (*mineral*) volframita

**wolf's-bane** o **wolfsbane** ['wulfs,ben] *s* matalobos *m*

**woman** ['wumən] *s* (*pl* **women** ['wɪmɪn]) mujer *f*

**womanhood** ['wumən,hud] *s* el sexo femenino; las mujeres

**womanish** ['wumənɪʃ] *adj* mujeril; (*effeminate*) afeminado

**wom'an•kind'** *s* el sexo femenino

**womanly** ['wumənli] *adj* (*comp* **-lier;** *super* **-liest)** femenil, mujeriego

**woman suffrage** *s* sufragismo

**woman-suffragist** ['wumən'sʌfrədʒɪst] *s* sufragista *mf*

**womb** [wum] *s* útero; (fig) seno

**womenfolk** ['wɪmɪn,fok] *spl* las mujeres

**wonder** ['wʌndər] *s* (*something strange or surprising*) maravilla; (*feeling of surprise*) admiración; (*something strange, miracle*) milagro; **for a wonder** cosa extraña; **no wonder that . . .** no es mucho que . . .; **to work wonders** hacer milagros ‖ *tr* preguntarse ‖ *intr* admirarse, maravillarse; **to wonder at** admirarse de, maravillarse con o de

**wonder drugs** *spl* drogas milagrosas

**wonderful** ['wʌndərfəl] *adj* maravilloso

**won'der•land'** *s* tierra de las maravillas; reino de las hadas

**wonderment** ['wʌndərmənt] *s* asombro, sorpresa

**wont** [wʌnt] o [wont] *adj* acostumbrado; **to be wont to** acostumbrar || *s* costumbre, hábito

**wonted** [ˈwʌntɪd] o [ˈwɔntɪd] *adj* acostumbrado, habitual

**woo** [wu] *tr* cortejar (*a una mujer*); tratar de conquistar; tratar de persuadir

**wood** [wʊd] *s* madera; (*for making a fire*) leña; barril *m* de madera; **out of the woods** (coll) fuera de peligro; (coll) libre de dificultades; **to take to the woods** andar a monte; **woods** bosque *m*

**woodbine** [ˈwʊdˌbaɪn] *s* (*honeysuckle*) madreselva; (*Virginia creeper*) guau *m*

**wood carving** *s* labrado de madera

**wood'chuck'** *s* marmota de América

**wood'cock'** *s* becada, coalla, chocha

**wood'cut'** *s* (typ) grabado en madera

**wood'cut'ter** *s* leñador *m*

**wooded** [ˈwʊdɪd] *adj* arbolado, enselvado

**wooden** [ˈwʊdən] *adj* de madera, hecho de madera; torpe, estúpido; sin ánimo

**wood engraving** *s* (typ) grabado en madera

**wooden-headed** [ˈwʊdənˌhɛdɪd] *adj* (coll) torpe, estúpido

**wooden leg** *s* pata de palo

**wooden shoe** *s* zueco

**wood grouse** *s* gallo de bosque

**woodland** [ˈwʊdlənd] *adj* selvático || *s* bosque *m*, monte *m*

**woodland scene** *s* (paint) boscaje *m*

**wood•man** [ˈwʊdmən] *s* (*pl* **-men** [mən]) leñador *m*

**woodpecker** [ˈwʊdˌpɛkər] *s* carpintero, pájaro carpintero; (*green woodpecker*) picamaderos *m*

**wood'pile'** *s* montón *m* de leña

**wood screw** *s* tirafondo

**wood'shed'** *s* leñero

**woods•man** [ˈwʊdzmən] *s* (*pl* **-men** [mən]) leñador *m*

**wood'wind'** *s* (mus) instrumento de viento de madera

**wood'work'** *s* (*working in wood*) ebanistería, obra de carpintería; (*things made of wood*) maderaje *m*

**wood'work'er** *s* ebanista *mf*, carpintero

**wood'worm'** *s* carcoma

**wood•y** [ˈwʊdi] *adj* (*comp* **-ier**; *super* **-iest**) arbolado, enselvado; (*like wood*) leñoso

**wooer** [ˈwu·ər] *s* pretendiente *m*, galán *m*

**woof** [wuf] *s* (*yarns running across warp*) trama; (*fabric*) tejido

**woofer** [ˈwʊfər] *s* altavoz *m* para audiofrecuencias bajas

**wool** [wʊl] *s* lana

**woolen** [ˈwʊlən] *adj* de lana, hecho de lana || *s* tejido de lana; **woolens** lanerías

**woolgrower** [ˈwʊlˌgro·ər] *s* criador *m* de ganado lanar

**wool•ly** [ˈwʊli] *adj* (*comp* **-lier**; *super* **-liest**) lanoso, lanudo; borroso, confuso

**word** [wʌrd] *s* palabra; **to be as good as one's word** cumplir lo prometido; **to have a word with** hablar cuatro palabras con; **to have word from** recibir noticias de; **to keep one's word** cumplir su palabra; **to leave word** dejar dicho; **to send word that** mandar decir que; **words** (*a quarrel*) palabras mayores; (*text of a song*) letra || *tr* redactar, formular || **Word** *s* (theol) Verbo

**word count** *s* recuento de vocabulario

**word formation** *s* (gram) formación de palabras

**wording** [ˈwʌrdɪŋ] *s* fraseología, estilo

**word order** *s* (gram) orden *m* de colocación

**word'stock'** *s* vocabulario, léxico

**word•y** [ˈwʌrdi] *adj* (*comp* **-ier**; *super* **-iest**) verboso

**work** [wʌrk] *s* (*exertion; labor, toil*) trabajo; (*result of exertion; human output; engineering structure*) obra; (sew) labor *f*; **at work** trabajando; (*not at home*) en la oficina, en el taller, en la tienda; **out of work** sin trabajo, desempleado; **to shoot the works** (slang) echar el resto; **works** fábrica; mecanismo; (*of clock*) movimiento || *tr* hacer trabajar; trabajar, obrar (*la madera, el hierro*); obrar (*un milagro*); explotar (*una mina*); **to work up** preparar; estimular, excitar || *intr* trabajar; funcionar, marchar (*un aparato, un motor*); obrar (*p.ej., un remedio*); **to work loose** aflojarse; **to work out** resolverse

**workable** [ˈwʌrkəbəl] *adj* (*feasible*) practicable; (*that can be worked*) laborable

**work'bench'** *s* banco de trabajo, banco de taller

**work'book'** *s* (*manual of instructions*) libro de reglas; libro de ejercicios

**work'box'** *s* caja de herramientas; (*for needlework*) caja de labor

**work'day'** *adj* de cada día; ordinario, vulgar || *s* día *m* de trabajo; (*number of hours of work*) jornada

**worked-up** [ˈwʌrktˈʌp] *adj* muy conmovido, sobreexcitado, exaltado

**worker** [ˈwʌrkər] *s* trabajador *m*, obrero

**work force** *s* mano *f* de obra, personal obrero

**work'horse'** *s* caballo de carga; (*tireless worker*) yunque *m*

**work'house'** *s* taller penitenciario; (Brit) asilo de pobres

**working class** *s* clase obrera

**work'ing•girl'** *s* trabajadora joven

**working hours** *spl* horas de trabajo

**working•man** [ˈwʌrkɪŋˌmæn] *s* (*pl* **-men** [ˌmɛn]) *s* obrero, trabajador *m*

**working•woman** [ˈwʌrkɪŋˌwʊmən] *s* (*pl* **-women** [ˌwɪmɪn]) obrera, trabajadora

**work•man** [ˈwʌrkmən] *s* (*pl* **-men** [mən]) obrero, trabajador *m*; (*skilled worker*) artífice *m*

**workmanship** [ˈwʌrkmənˌʃɪp] *s* destreza en el trabajo; (*work executed*) hechura, obra

**work of art** *s* obra de arte

**work'out'** *s* ensayo, prueba; (*physical exercise*) ejercicio
**work'room'** *s* (*for manual work*) obrador *m,* taller *m;* (*study*) gabinete *m* de trabajo
**work'shop'** *s* obrador *m,* taller *m*
**work stoppage** *s* paro
**world** [wʌrld] *adj* mundial || *s* mundo; **a world of** la mar de; **half the world** (*a lot of people*) medio mundo; **since the world began** desde que el mundo es mundo; **the other world** el otro mundo; **to bring into the world** echar al mundo; **to see the world** ver mundo; **to think the world of** tener un alto concepto de
**world affairs** *spl* asuntos internacionales
**world·ly** ['wʌrldli] *adj* (*comp* **-lier;** *super* **-liest**) mundano
**world'ly-wise'** *adj* que tiene mucho mundo
**world's fair** *s* exposición mundial
**World War** *s* Guerra Mundial
**world'-wide'** *adj* global, mundial
**worm** [wʌrm] *s* gusano; **worms** (pathol) lombrices *fpl* || *tr* limpiar de lombrices; **to worm a secret out of a person** arrancar mañosamente un secreto a una persona; **to worm one's way into** insinuarse en
**worm-eaten** ['wʌrm ,itən] *adj* carcomido; (fig) decaído, desgastado
**worm gear** *s* engranaje *m* de tornillo sin fin
**worm'wood'** *s* (*Artemisia*) ajenjo; (*Artemisia absinthium*) ajenjo del campo o ajenjo mayor; (*something bitter or grievous*) (fig) ajenjo
**worm·y** ['wʌrmi] *adj* (*comp* **-ier;** *super* **-iest**) gusaniento, gusanoso; (*worm-eaten*) carcomido; (*groveling*) rastrero, servil
**worn** [worn] *adj* roto, raído, gastado
**worn'-out'** *adj* muy gastado, inservible; (*by toil, illness*) consumido, rendido
**worrisome** ['wʌrisəm] *adj* inquietante; (*inclined to worry*) aprensivo, inquieto
**wor·ry** ['wʌri] *s* (*pl* **-ries**) inquietud, preocupación; (*cause of anxiety*) molestia || *v* (*pret & pp* **-ried**) *tr* inquietar, preocupar; (*to harass, pester*) acosar, molestar; **to be worried** estar inquieto || *intr* inquietarse, preocuparse; **don't worry** pierda Vd. cuidado
**worse** [wʌrs] *adj & adv comp* peor; **worse and worse** de mal en peor
**worsen** ['wʌrsən] *tr & intr* empeorar
**wor·ship** ['wʌrʃɪp] *s* adoración, culto; **your worship** vuestra merced || *v* (*pret & pp* **-shiped** o **-shipped;** *ger* **-shiping** o **-shipping**) *tr & intr* adorar, venerar
**worshiper** o **worshipper** ['wʌrʃɪpər] *s* adorador *m,* devoto
**worst** [wʌrst] *adj & adv super* peor || *s* (lo) peor; **at worst** en las peores circunstancias; **if worst comes to worst** si pasa lo peor; **to get the worst of** llevar la peor parte, salir perdiendo
**worsted** ['wʊstɪd] *adj* de estambre || *s* estambre *m;* tela de estambre
**wort** [wʌrt] *s* (bot) hierba, planta; mosto de cerveza
**worth** [wʌrθ] *adj* del valor de; digno de; **to be worth** valer; tener una fortuna de; **to be worth** + *ger* valer la pena de + *inf;* **to be worth while** valer la pena; ser de mérito || *s* valor *m;* mérito; **a dollar's worth of** un dólar de
**worthless** ['wʌrθlɪs] *adj* sin valor, inútil, inservible; (*person*) despreciable
**worth'while'** *adj* de mérito, digno de atención
**wor·thy** ['wʌrði] *adj* (*comp* **-thier;** *super* **-thiest**) digno; benemérito, meritorio || *s* (*pl* **-thies**) benemérito; (*hum & iron*) personaje *m*
**would** [wʊd] *v aux* **she said she would do it** dijo que lo haría; **he would come if he could** vendría si pudiese; **he would go for days without smoking** pasaba días enteros sin fumar; **would that . . .!** ¡ojalá que . . .!
**would'-be'** *adj* llamado; supuesto || *s* presumido
**wound** [wund] *s* herida || *tr* herir
**wounded** ['wundɪd] *adj* herido || **the wounded** los heridos
**wow** [waʊ] *s* (*of phonograph record*) ululación; (slang) éxito rotundo || *tr* (slang) entusiasmar
**wrack** [ræk] *s* naufragio; vestigio; (*fucaceous seaweed*) varec *m;* **to go to wrack and ruin** desvencijarse; ir al desastre
**wraith** [reθ] *s* fantasma *m,* espectro
**wrangle** ['ræŋgəl] *s* pendencia, riña || *intr* pelotear, reñir
**wrap** [ræp] *s* abrigo, manto || *v* (*pret & pp* **wrapped;** *ger* **wrapping**) *tr* envolver; **to be wrapped up in** (fig) estar prendado de; **to wrap up** envolver; (*in clothing*) arropar; (coll) concluir || *intr* — **to wrap up** arroparse
**wrapper** ['ræpər] *s* bata, peinador *m;* (*of newspaper or magazine*) faja; (*of tobacco*) capa
**wrapping paper** ['ræpɪŋ] *s* papel *m* de envolver, papel de embalar
**wrath** [ræθ] o [rɑθ] *s* cólera, ira; venganza
**wrathful** ['ræθfəl] o ['rɑθfəl] *adj* colérico, iracundo
**wreak** [rik] *tr* descargar (*la cólera*); infligir (*venganza*)
**wreath** [riθ] *s* (*pl* **wreaths** [riðz]) guirnalda; corona funeraria; (*worn as a mark of honor or victory*) corona de laurel; (*of smoke*) espiral *f*
**wreathe** [rið] *tr* enguirnaldar; ceñir, envolver; tejer (*una guirnalda*) || *intr* elevarse en espirales (*el humo*)
**wreck** [rek] *s* destrucción, ruina; naufragio; catástrofe *f,* desastre *m;* despojos, restos; (*of one's hopes*) naufragio; **to be a wreck** estar hecho un cascajo, estar hecho una ruina || *tr* destruir, arruinar; hacer

naufragar; hacer chocar, descarrilar (*un tren*)
**wrecking ball** *s* bola rompedora
**wrecking car** *s* (aut) camión *m* de auxilio; (rr) carro de grúa
**wrecking crane** *s* grúa de auxilio
**wren** [rɛn] *s* buscareta, coletero, rey *m* de zarza
**wrench** [rɛntʃ] *s* llave *f;* (*pull*) arranque *m,* tirón *m;* (*twist of a joint*) esguince *m* || *tr* torcerse (*p.ej., la muñeca*); (fig) torcer (*el sentido de una oración*)
**wrest** [rɛst] *tr* arrebatar, arrancar violentamente
**wrestle** ['rɛsəl] *s* lucha; partido de lucha || *intr* luchar
**wrestling match** ['rɛslɪŋ] *s* partido de lucha
**wretch** [rɛtʃ] *s* miserable *mf*
**wretched** ['rɛtʃɪd] *adj* miserable; (*poor, worthless*) malísimo, pésimo
**wriggle** ['rɪgəl] *s* culebreo, meneo serpentino || *tr* menear rápidamente || *intr* culebrear, ondular; **to wriggle out of** escabullirse de
**wrig•gly** ['rɪgli] *adj* (*comp* **-glier;** *super* **-gliest**) retorciéndose; (fig) evasivo, tramoyista
**wring** [rɪŋ] *v* (*pret & pp* **wrung** [rʌŋ]) *tr* torcer; retorcer (*las manos*); exprimir (*el zumo, la ropa, etc.*); sacar por fuerza (*la verdad*); arrancar (*dinero*); **to wring out** exprimir (*la ropa*)
**wringer** ['rɪŋər] *s* exprimidor *m*
**wrinkle** ['rɪŋkəl] *s* arruga; (*clever trick or idea*) (coll) ardid *m,* truco || *tr* arrugar || *intr* arrugarse
**wrin•kly** ['rɪŋkli] *adj* (*comp* **-klier;** *super* **-kliest**) arrugado
**wrist** [rɪst] *s* muñeca
**wrist'band'** *s* bocamanga, puño
**wrist watch** *s* reloj *m* de pulsera
**writ** [rɪt] *s* escrito, escritura; (law) mandato, orden *f*
**write** [raɪt] *v* (*pret* **wrote** [rot]; *pp* **written** ['rɪtən]) *tr* escribir; **to write down** poner por escrito; bajar el precio de; **to write off** cancelar (*una deuda*); **to write up** describir extensamente por escrito; (*to ballyhoo*) dar bombo a || *intr* escribir; **to write back** contestar por carta
**writer** ['raɪtər] *s* escritor *m*
**writer's cramp** *s* grafospasmo
**write'-up'** *s* (*favorable report*) bombo; (com) valoración excesiva
**writhe** [raɪð] *intr* contorcerse, retorcerse
**writing** ['raɪtɪŋ] *s* el escribir; (*something written*) escrito; profesión de escritor; **at this writing** al escribir ésta; **in one's own writing** de su puño y letra; **to put in writing** poner por escrito
**writing desk** *s* escritorio
**writing materials** *spl* recado de escribir
**writing paper** *s* papel *m* de escribir, papel de cartas
**written accent** ['rɪtən] *s* acento ortográfico
**wrong** [rɔŋ] o [rɑŋ] *adj* injusto; malo; erróneo, equivocado; impropio; no . . . que se busca, p.ej., **this is the wrong house** ésta no es la casa que se busca; no . . . que se necesita, p.ej., **this is the wrong train** éste no es el tren que se necesita; no . . . que debe, p.ej., **he is going the wrong way** no sigue el camino que debe; **in the wrong place** mal colocado; **to be wrong** no tener razón; tener la culpa; **to be wrong with** pasar algo a, p.ej., **something is wrong with the motor** algo le pasa al motor || *adv* mal; sin razón; al revés; **to go wrong** ir por mal camino; darse a la mala vida || *s* daño, perjuicio; agravio, injusticia; error *m;* **to be in the wrong** no tener razón; tener la culpa; **to do wrong** obrar mal || *tr* agraviar, hacer daño a, ofender, ser injusto con
**wrongdoer** ['rɔŋ,du•ər] o ['rɑŋ,du•ər] *s* malhechor *m*
**wrongdoing** ['rɔŋ,du•ɪŋ] o ['rɑŋ,du•ɪŋ] *s* malhecho, maldad
**wrong number** *s* (telp) número equivocado
**wrong side** *s* contrahaz *f,* revés *m;* (*of the street*) lado contrario; **to get out of bed on the wrong side** levantarse del lado izquierdo; **wrong side out** al revés
**wrought iron** [rɔt] *s* hierro dulce
**wrought'-up'** *adj* muy conmovido, sobreexcitado, exaltado
**wry** [raɪ] *adj* (*comp* **wrier;** *super* **wriest**) torcido; desviado, pervertido; irónico, burlón
**wry'neck'** *s* (orn) torcecuello; (pathol) torticolis *m*
**wt.** *abbr* **weight**

## X

**X, x** [ɛks] vigésima cuarta letra del alfabeto inglés
**Xanthippe** [zæn'tɪpi] *s* Jantipa
**Xavier** ['zævɪ•ər] o ['zevɪ•ər] *s* Javier *m*
**xebec** ['zibɛk] *s* (naut) jabeque *m*
**xenia** ['zinɪ•ə] *s* xenia
**xenon** ['zinɑn] o ['zɛnɑn] *s* xenón *m*
**xenophobe** ['zɛnə,fob] *s* xenófobo
**xenophobia** [,zɛnə'fobɪ•ə] *s* xenofobia
**Xenophon** ['zɛnəfən] *s* Jenofonte *m*
**Xerxes** ['zʌrksiz] *s* Jerjes *m*
**Xmas** ['krɪsməs] *s* Navidad

**X ray** *s* rayo X; (*photograph*) radiograma *m*
**X-ray** [ˈɛks ˌre] *adj* radiográfico ‖ [ˈɛksˈre] *tr* radiografiar; tratar por medio de los rayos X
**xylograph** [ˈzaɪləˌgræf] o [ˈzaɪləˌgrɑf] *s* xilografía
**xylography** [zaɪˈlɑgrəfi] *s* xilografía
**xylophone** [ˈzaɪləˌfon] *s* (mus) xilófono

# Y

**Y, y** [waɪ] vigésima quinta letra del alfabeto inglés
**y.** *abbr* **yard, year**
**yacht** [jɑt] *s* yate *m*
**yacht club** *s* club náutico
**yak** [jæk] *s* (zool) yac *m*
**yam** [jæm] *s* ñame *m;* (*sweet potato*) boniato, camote *m*
**yank** [jæŋk] *s* (coll) tirón *m* ‖ *tr* (coll) sacar de un tirón ‖ *intr* (coll) dar un tirón
**Yankee** [ˈjæŋki] *adj & s* yanqui *mf*
**Yankeedom** [ˈjæŋkidəm] *s* Yanquilandia; los yanquis
**yap** [jæp] *s* ladrido corto; (slang) charla necia y ruidosa ‖ *v* (*pret & pp* **yapped;** *ger* **yapping**) *intr* ladrar con ladrido corto; (slang) charlar necia y ruidosamente
**yard** [jɑrd] *s* cercado, patio; (*measure*) yarda; (naut) verga; (rr) patio
**yard'arm'** *s* (naut) penol *m*
**yard goods** *spl* géneros de pieza
**yard'mas'ter** *s* (rr) superintendente *m* de patio
**yard'stick'** *s* yarda, vara de medir; (fig) criterio, norma
**yarn** [jɑrn] *s* hilado, hilaza; (coll) cuento increíble, burlería
**yarrow** [ˈjæro] *s* milenrama
**yaw** [jɔ] *s* (naut) guiñada; **yaws** (pathol) frambesia ‖ *intr* (naut) guiñar
**yawl** [jɔl] *s* (naut) bote *m;* (naut) queche *m*
**yawn** [jɔn] *s* bostezo ‖ *intr* bostezar; abrirse desmesuradamente
**yd.** *abbr* **yard**
**yea** [je] *adv & s* sí *m*
**yean** [jin] *intr* parir (*la oveja, la cabra, etc.*)
**year** [jɪr] *s* año; **to be . . . years old** cumplir . . . años; **year in, year out** año tras año
**year'book'** *s* anuario
**yearling** [ˈjɪrlɪŋ] *adj & s* primal *m*
**yearly** [ˈjɪrli] *adj* anual ‖ *adv* anualmente
**yearn** [jʌrn] *intr* suspirar; **to yearn for** suspirar por, anhelar por
**yearning** [ˈjʌrnɪŋ] *s* anhelo, deseo ardiente
**yeast** [jist] *s* levadura
**yeast cake** *s* levadura comprimida, pastilla de levadura
**yell** [jɛl] *s* grito, voz *f* ‖ *tr* decir a gritos ‖ *intr* gritar, dar voces
**yellow** [ˈjɛlo] *adj* amarillo; (*cowardly*) (coll) blanco; (*journalism*) sensacional ‖ *s* amarillo; yema de huevo ‖ *intr* amarillecer
**yellowish** [ˈjɛlo·ɪʃ] *adj* amarillento
**yellow jacket** *s* avispón *m*
**yellowness** [ˈjɛlonɪs] *s* amarillez *f*
**yellow streak** *s* vena de cobarde
**yelp** [jɛlp] *s* gañido ‖ *intr* gañir
**yeo•man** [ˈjomən] *s* (*pl* **-men** [mən]) (naut) pañolero; (naut) oficinista *m* de a bordo; (Brit) labrador acomodado
**yeoman of the guard** *s* (Brit) alabardero de palacio, continuo
**yeoman's service** *s* ayuda leal
**yes** [jɛs] *adv* sí ‖ *s* sí *m;* **to say yes** dar el sí ‖ *v* (*pret & pp* **yessed;** *ger* **yessing**) *tr* decir sí a ‖ *intr* decir sí
**yes man** *s* (coll) sacristán *m* de amén
**yesterday** [ˈjɛstərdi] o [ˈjɛstərˌde] *adj & s* ayer *m*
**yet** [jɛt] *adv* todavía, aún; **as yet** hasta ahora; **not yet** todavía no ‖ *conj* sin embargo
**yew tree** [ju] *s* tejo
**yield** [jild] *s* producción, rendimiento; (*crop*) cosecha; (*income produced*) rédito ‖ *tr* producir, rendir, redituar ‖ *intr* entregarse, rendirse, someterse; acceder, ceder, consentir; producir
**yodeling** o **yodelling** [ˈjodəlɪŋ] *s* tirolesa
**yoke** [jok] *s* (*pair of draft animals*) yunta; (*device to join a pair of draft animals*) yugo; (fig) yugo; (*of a shirt*) hombrillo; (elec) culata; **to throw off the yoke** sacudir el yugo ‖ *tr* uncir
**yokel** [ˈjokəl] *s* patán *m*
**yolk** [jok] *s* yema
**yonder** [ˈjɑndər] *adj* aquel, de más allá ‖ *adv* allá, más allá
**yore** [jor] *s* — **of yore** antaño, antiguamente
**you** [ju] *pron pers* usted, ustedes; le, la, les; **with you** consigo ‖ *pron indef se,* p.ej., **you go in this way** se entra por aquí
**young** [jʌŋ] *adj* (*comp* **younger** [ˈjʌŋgər]; *super* **youngest** [ˈjʌŋgɪst]) joven ‖ **the young** los jóvenes, la gente joven
**young hopeful** *s* joven *m* de esperanzas
**young people** *spl* jóvenes *mpl,* gente *f* joven
**youngster** [ˈjʌŋstər] *s* jovencito; (*child*) chico, chiquillo
**your** [jʊr] *adj poss* **su, el (o su) de** Vd. o de Vds.
**yours** [jʊrz] *pron poss* suyo; de Vd., de Vds.; el suyo; el de Vd., el de Vds.; **of yours** suyo; de Vd., de

Vds.; **yours truly** su seguro servidor; (coll) este cura (*yo*)
**your•self** [jʊr'sɛlf] *pron pers* (*pl* **-selves** ['sɛlvz]) usted mismo; sí, sí mismo; se, p.ej., **you enjoyed yourself** se divirtió Vd.
**youth** [juθ] *s* (*pl* **youths** [juθs] o [juðz]) juventud; (*person*) jovenzuelo; jovenzuelos, jóvenes *mpl*
**youthful** ['juθfəl] *adj* juvenil, mocil
**yowl** [jaʊl] *s* aullido, alarido ‖ *intr* aullar, dar alaridos
**yr.** *abbr* **year**
**Yugoslav** ['jugo'slɑv] *adj & s* yugoeslavo
**Yugoslavia** ['jugo'slɑvɪ•ə] *s* Yugoeslavia
**Yule** [jul] *s* la Navidad; la pascua de Navidad
**Yule log** *s* nochebueno, leño de nochebuena
**Yuletide** ['jul,taɪd] *s* la pascua de Navidad

## Z

**Z, z** [zi] vigésima sexta letra del alfabeto inglés
**za•ny** ['zeni] *adj* (*comp* **-nier;** *super* **-niest**) cómico, gracioso, chiflado ‖ *s* (*pl* **-nies**) bufón *m*, payaso; mentecato
**zeal** [zil] *s* celo, entusiasmo
**zealot** ['zɛlət] *s* fanático, entusiasta *mf*
**zealotry** ['zɛlətri] *s* fanatismo
**zealous** ['zɛləs] *adj* celoso, entusiasta
**zebra** ['zibrə] *s* cebra
**zebu** ['zibju] *s* cebú *m*
**zenith** ['zinɪθ] *s* cenit *m*
**zephyr** ['zɛfər] *s* céfiro
**zeppelin** ['zɛpəlɪn] *s* zepelín *m*
**ze•ro** ['zɪro] *s* (*pl* **-ros** o **-roes**) cero
**zero gravity** *s* gravedad nula
**zest** [zest] *s* entusiasmo; (*agreeable and piquant flavor*) gusto, sabor *m*
**Zeus** [zus] *s* Zeus *m*
**zig•zag** ['zɪg,zæg] *adj & adv* en zigzag ‖ *s* zigzag *m*, ziszas *m* ‖ *v* (*pret & pp* **-zagged;** *ger* **-zagging**) *intr* zigzaguear
**zinc** [zɪŋk] *s* cinc *m*
**zinc etching** *s* cincograbado
**zinnia** ['zɪnɪ•ə] *s* rascamoño
**Zionism** ['zaɪ•ə,nɪzəm] *s* sionismo
**zip** [zɪp] *s* (coll) silbido, zumbido; (coll) energía, brío ‖ *v* (*pret & pp* **zipped;** *ger* **zipping**) *tr* cerrar con cierre relámpago, abrir con cierre relámpago; (coll) llevar con rapidez; **to zip up** dar gusto a ‖ *intr* silbar, zumbar; (coll) moverse con energía; **to zip by** (coll) pasar rápidamente
**zipper** ['zɪpər] *s* cierre *m* relámpago, cierre cremallera; chanclo con cierre relámpago
**zircon** ['zʌrkɑn] *s* circón *m*
**zirconium** [zər'konɪ•əm] *s* circonio
**zither** ['zɪθər] *s* (mus) cítara
**zodiac** ['zodɪ,æk] *s* zodíaco
**zone** [zon] *s* zona; distrito postal ‖ *tr* dividir en zonas
**zoölogic(al)** [,zo•ə'lɑdʒɪk(əl)] *adj* zoológico
**zoölogist** [zo'ɑlədʒɪst] *s* zoólogo
**zoölogy** [zo'ɑlədʒi] *s* zoología
**zoom** [zum] *s* zumbido; (aer) empinada ‖ *tr* (aer) empinar ‖ *intr* zumbar; (aer) empinarse
**zoöphyte** ['zo•ə,faɪt] *s* zoófito
**Zu•lu** ['zulu] *adj* zulú ‖ *s* (*pl* **-lus**) zulú *mf*